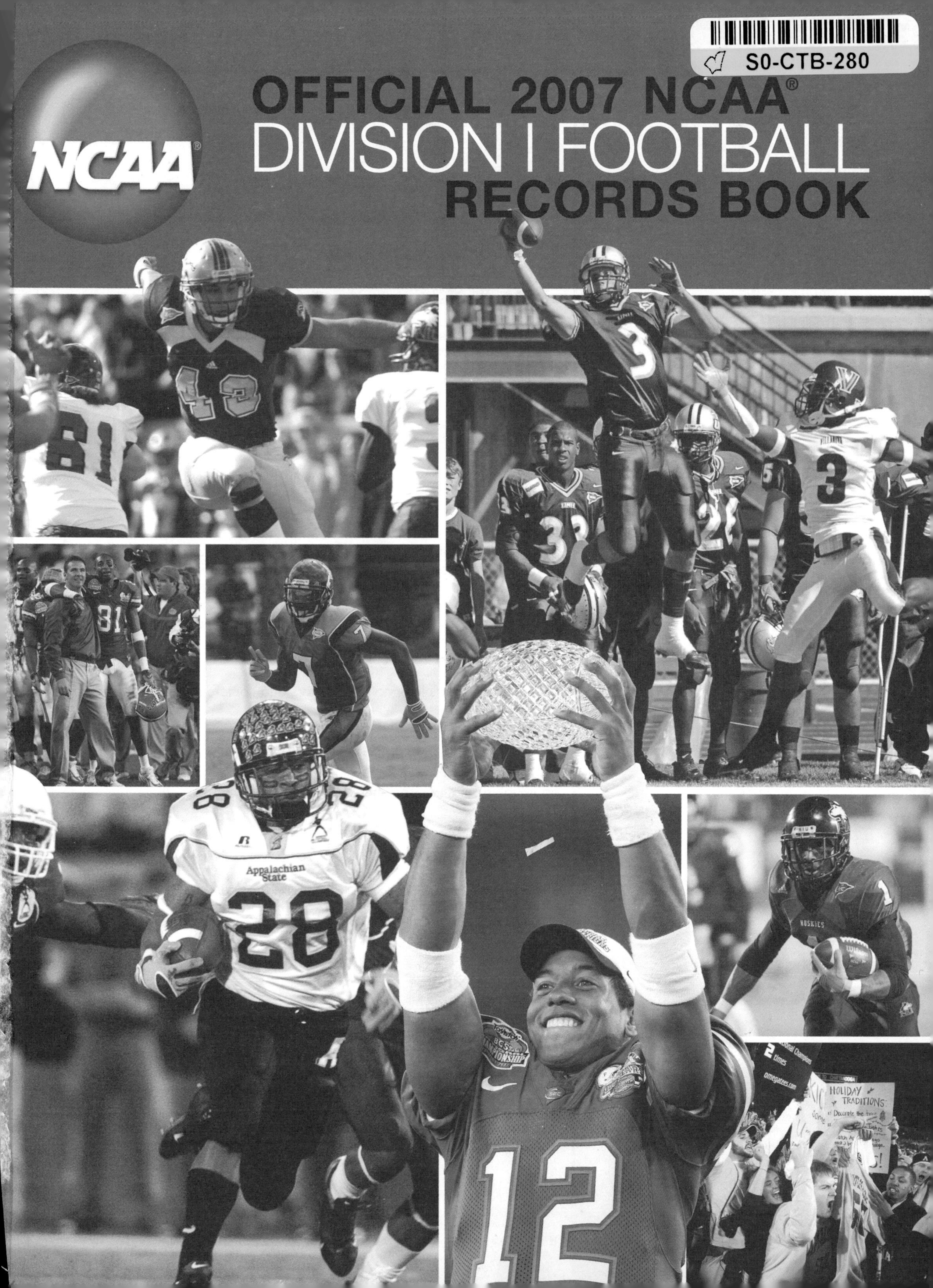
S0-CTB-280
NCAA®
OFFICIAL 2007 NCAA®
DIVISION I FOOTBALL
RECORDS BOOK
Appalachian State
HUSKIES

THE NATIONAL COLLEGIATE ATHLETIC ASSOCIATION
P.O. Box 6222, Indianapolis, Indiana
46206-6222
NCAA.org

August 2007

Compiled By:

Richard M. Campbell, *Former Assistant Director of Statistics.*
Gary K. Johnson, *Associate Director of Statistics.*
Sean W. Straziscar, *Associate Director of Statistics.*
J.D. Hamilton, *Assistant Director of Statistics.*
David Worlock, *Former Assistant Director of Statistics.*
Jim Wright, *Director of Statistics.*
Jackie Paquette, *2007 Summer Statistics Intern.*

Distributed to sports information directors and conference publicity directors.

ISSN 0735-5475

Front Cover Photos
(clockwise from top left)

Ameer Ismail, Western Michigan *(Photo courtesy of GS Photo)*; David Ball, New Hampshire *(Photo courtesy of New Hampshire Sports Information Office)*; Garrett Wolfe, Northern Illinois *(Photo courtesy of Northern Illinois Sports Information Office)*; Appalachian State fans *(Photo courtesy of NCAA Photos)*; Chris Leak, Florida *(Photo courtesy of NCAA Photos)*; Kevin Richardson, Appalachian State *(Photo courtesy of NCAA Photos)*; Quinton Teal, Coastal Carolina *(Photo courtesy of Coastal Carolina Sports Information Office)*; Urban Meyer, Florida *(Photo courtesy of NCAA Photos)*.

Contents

School Name-Change/Abbreviation Key

Various schools have changed their name. The current school name is listed along with other names by which the schools have been referred. (Note: Not all schools in this list currently sponsor or have sponsored football.)

SCHOOL name changes

Current school name/tabular style:	Changed from:
Akron	Buchtel
Albertson	Col. of Idaho
Alcorn St.	Alcorn A&M
Alliant Int'l	U.S. Int'l; Cal Western
Arcadia	Beaver
Arizona St.	Tempe St.
Ark.-Pine Bluff	Arkansas AM&N
Armstrong Atlantic	Armstrong St.
Auburn	Alabama Poly
Augusta St.	Augusta
Benedictine (Ill.)	Ill. Benedictine
Bradley	Bradley Tech
UC Davis	California Aggies
Cal St. East Bay	Cal St. Hayward
Cal St. Fullerton	Orange County State College; Orange St.
Cal St. L.A.	Los Angeles St.
Cal St. Northridge	San Fernando Valley St.
Carnegie Mellon	Carnegie Tech
Case Reserve	Case Institute of Technology
Castleton	Castleton St.
Central Ark.	Conway St.
Central Conn. St.	New Haven St.
Central Mich.	Mt. Pleasant
Central Mo.	Central Mo. St.
Central Okla.	Central St. (Okla.)
Charleston So.	Baptist (S.C.)
Charleston (W.V.)	Morris Harvey
Charlotte	UNC Charlotte
Chattanooga	Tenn.-Chatt.
Cleveland St.	Fenn
Colorado St.	Colorado A&M
Colorado St.-Pueblo	Southern Colo.
Columbus St.	Columbus
Concordia (Calif.)	Christ College-Irvine
Connecticut	Connecticut Aggies
Crown (Minn.)	St. Paul Bible
Dayton	St. Mary's Institute
Delaware Valley	National Aggies
DeSales	Allentown
Detroit	Detroit Mercy; Detroit Tech
Dist. Columbia	Federal City
Dominican (Ill.)	Rosary
Drexel	Drexel Tech
Dubuque	Columbia Col.
Duke	Trinity (N.C.)
Eastern Conn. St.	Willimantic St.
Eastern Mich.	Michigan Normal
Eckerd	Fla. Presbyterian
Emporia St.	Kansas St. Normal
FDU-Florham	FDU-Madison
Farmingdale St.	Farmingdale
Me.-Farmington	Western State Normal School
Fort Hays St.	Kansas St. Normal-Western
Fresno St.	Fresno Pacific
Idaho St.	Academy of Idaho; Idaho Tech. Inst.; Idaho-Southern
Ill.-Chicago	Ill.-Chicago Circle
Illinois St.	Illinois St. Normal; Illinois Normal
Indiana (Pa.)	Indiana St. (Pa.)
Indianapolis	Indiana Central
Iowa	State University of Iowa
Iowa St.	Ames
James Madison	Madison

Current school name/tabular style:	Changed from:
Johnson C. Smith	Johnson Smith
Kansas St.	Kansas Aggies
Kean	Newark St.
Kent St.	Kent
La Sierra	Loma Linda
Lamar	Lamar Tech
Liberty	Lynchburg Baptist; Liberty Baptist
La.-Lafayette	Southwestern La.
La.-Monroe	Northeast La.
Loyola Marymount	St. Vincent; Loyola U. of L.A.
Lycoming	Williamsport Dickinson Seminary
Lynn	College of Boca Raton
Lyon	Arkansas Col.
Maritime (N.Y.)	N.Y. Maritime
Marycrest Int'l	Teikyo Marycrest
Md.-East. Shore	Maryland St.
Massachusetts	Massachusetts St.; Massachusetts Agriculture Col.
Mass.-Dartmouth	Southeastern Mass.
Mass.-Lowell	Lowell; Lowell St.; Lowell Tech
McDaniel	Western Md.
Memphis	Memphis St.; West Tenn. St. Normal
Michigan Tech	Michigan Mines and Tech
Millersville	Millersville St.
Millikin	James Millikin
Minn. St. Mankato	Mankato St.
Minn. St. Moorhead	Moorhead St.
Mississippi Col.	Mississippi A&M
Mississippi Val.	Mississippi Vocational
Missouri St.	Southwest Mo. St.
Mo.-Rolla	Missouri School of Mines
Mont. St.-Billings	Eastern Montana
Montana St.-Northern	Northern Montana
Neb.-Kearney	Kearney St.
Neb.-Omaha	Omaha
New England U.	St. Francis (Me.)
New Jersey City	Jersey City St.
New Mexico St.	New Mexico A&M
New Orleans	Louisiana St. (N.O.)
North Ala.	Florence St.
N.C. Central	North Caro. College
UNC Pembroke	Pembroke St.
North Central Texas	Cooke County
North Texas	North Tex. St.
Northeastern St.	Northeastern Okla. St.
Northern Ariz.	Arizona St.-Flagstaff
Northern Colo.	Colorado St. Col.; State Teachers
Okla. Panhandle	Panhandle A&M; Panhandle St.
Oklahoma St.	Oklahoma A&M
Old Dominion	William & Mary (Norfolk)
Penn St.-Berks	Penn St. Berks-Lehigh Val.; Berks & Lehigh
Penn St.-Harrisburg	Penn St.-Capitol
Pepperdine	George Pepperdine
Phila. Sciences	Phila. Pharmacy
Philadelphia U.	Phila. Textile
Pittsburgh	Western Pennsylvania
Plymouth St.	Plymouth Normal; Plymouth Teachers
Polytechnic (N.Y.)	New York Poly; Brooklyn Poly
Portland St.	Vanport
Post	Teikyo Post
Randolph	Randolph-Macon Woman's
Rhodes	Southwestern (Tenn.)
Rice	Rice Institute
Richard Stockton	Stockton St.
Rochester Inst.	Mechanics Institute
Rose-Hulman	Rose Polytechnic Institute
Rowan	Glassboro St.
Salem Int'l	Salem-Teikyo; Salem
Samford	Howard Col.
S.C. Upstate	S.C.-Spartanburg
Southern Ark.	Magnolia A&M
Southern Conn. St.	New Britain St.
Southern Ind.	Indiana St.-Evansville
Southern Me.	Maine Portland-Gorham; Gorham St. (Me.)
Southern Miss.	Mississippi Southern Col.; Mississippi Normal
Southern N.H.	New Hamp. Col.
Southern U.	Southern B.R.
Southwest Minn. St.	Southwest St.
Stevens Institute	Stevens Tech
Taylor-Ft. Wayne	Summit Christian
Tex. A&M-Commerce	East Texas St.
Tex. A&M-Kingsville	Texas A&I

Current school name/tabular style:	Changed from:
Tex.-Pan American	Pan American
Texas St.	Southwest Tex. St.
Towson	Towson St.
Troy	Troy St.
Truman	Northeast Mo. St.; Truman St.
Tulsa	Henry Kendall
Washburn	Lincoln Col.
Washington-St. Louis	Washington (Mo.)
Washington St.	Washington Agricultural Col.
West Ala.	Livingston
West Tex. A&M	West Texas St.
Western N.M.	New Mexico Western
Western Ore.	Monmouth Normal; Oregon Tech; Oregon College of Education
Western St.	Colo. Western; Colorado Normal
Westmar	Western Union Col.; Teikyo Westmar
Wichita St.	Fairmount
Widener	Pennsylvania Military Col.
Wm. Paterson	Paterson St.
Wis.-Superior	Superior Normal
Xavier	St. Xavier

In the early days of colleges and universities, many schools used the designation of Teachers College. Due to the high numbers of such schools, they are not listed here.

SCHOOLS also known as

Current school name/tabular style:	Changed from:
A&M-Corpus Christi	Tex. A&M-Corp. Chris.
Air Force	U.S. Air Force Academy
Apprentice School	Newport News
Army	U.S. Military Academy; West Point
Baruch	Bernard M. Baruch
BYU	Brigham Young
Case Reserve	Case Western Reserve
CCNY	City College of New York
Coast Guard	U.S. Coast Guard Academy
GCSU	Georgia College & State
Hawthorne	Nathaniel Hawthorne
IPFW	Indiana/Purdue-Ft. Wayne
IUPUI	Indiana/Purdue-Indianapolis
Lehman	Herbert H. Lehman
Lipscomb	David Lipscomb
Long Island	LIU-Brooklyn
LSU	Louisiana St.
Mass. Liberal Arts	Massachusetts College (was North Adams St.)
Merchant Marine	King's Point; U.S. Merchant Marine Academy
MIT	Massachusetts Institute of Technology
Navy	U.S. Naval Academy
City Tech	New York City Tech (was NYCCT)
NJIT	Newark Engineering (was N.J. Inst. of Tech.)
NYIT	New York Institute of Technology; New York Tech
Rensselaer	RPI, Rensselaer Poly Inst.
Rochester Inst.	RIT
Sewanee	University of the South
SMU	Southern Methodist
Southampton	LIU-Southampton
SUNYIT	Utica/Rome
TCNJ	The College of New Jersey (was Trenton St.)
TCU	Texas Christian (was AddRan Christian)
UAB	Ala.-Birmingham
UCF	Central Fla. (was Florida Tech)
UCLA	University of California, Los Angeles
UMBC	Md.-Balt. County
UMKC	Mo.-Kansas City
UNI	Northern Iowa (was Iowa Normal; State Col. of Iowa)
UNLV	Nevada-Las Vegas (was Nevada Southern)
UTEP	Texas-El Paso (was Texas Western)
UTSA	Texas-San Antonio
VCU	Va. Commonwealth
VMI	Va. Military
WPI	Worcester Poly Inst.; Worcester Tech

SCHOOL MERGERS

Current school name:	Two Schools Merged & Year:
Case Reserve	Case Tech & Western Reserve; 1971-72
Martin Luther	Northwestern (Wis.) & Dr. Martin Luther, 1995-96
Mass.-Lowell	Lowell St. & Lowell Tech; 1975-76

New To this Book

Football Bowl Subdivision

Award Winners

Football Bowl Subdivision Records

Individual Records

Under a three-division reorganization plan adopted by the special NCAA Convention of August 1973, teams classified major-college in football on August 1, 1973, were placed in Division I. College-division teams were divided into Division II and Division III. At the NCAA Convention of January 1978, Division I was divided into Division I-A and Division I-AA for football only.

Before 2002, postseason games were not included in NCAA final football statistics or records. Beginning with the 2002 season, all postseason games were included in NCAA final football statistics and records.

From 1937, when official national statistics rankings began, through 1969, individual rankings were by totals. Beginning in 1970, most season individual rankings were by per-game averages. In total offense, rushing and scoring, it is yards or points per game; in receiving, catches per game and yards per game; in interceptions, catches per game; and in punt and kickoff returns, yards per return. Punting always has been by average, and all team rankings have been per game. Beginning in 1979, passers were rated in all divisions on "pass efficiency rating points," which are derived from a formula that compares passers to the national averages for 14 seasons of two-platoon Division I football starting with the 1965 season. One hundred points equals the 14-year averages for all players in Division I. Those averages break down to 6.29 yards per attempt, 47.14 percent completions, 3.97 percent touchdown passes and 6.54 percent interceptions. The formula assumes that touchdowns are as good as interceptions are bad; therefore, these two figures offset each other for the average player. To determine efficiency rating points, multiply a passer's yards per attempt by 8.4, add his completion percentage, add his touchdown percentage times 3.3, then subtract his interception percentage times two.

Passers must have a minimum of 15 attempts per game to determine rating points because fewer attempts could allow a player to win the championship with fewer than 100 attempts in a season. A passer must play in at least 75 percent of his team's games to qualify for the rankings (e.g., a player on a team with a nine-game season could qualify by playing in seven games); thus, a passer with 105 attempts could qualify for the national rankings.

A pass efficiency rating comparison for each year since 1979 has been added to the passing section of all-time leaders to compare that season's passers with the average rating for all passers during that year.

Individual and team records and rankings included only regular-season games through the 2001 season. Beginning in 2002, all individual and team records included postseason games. Career records of players include only those years in which they competed in Division I-A.

Statistics in some team categories were not tabulated until the advent of the computerized statistics program in 1966. The records listed in those categories begin with the 1966 season and are so indicated.

In 1954, the regular-season schedule was limited to a maximum of 10 games, and in 1970, to a limit of 11 games, excluding postseason competition.

A player whose career includes statistics from five seasons (or an active player who will play in five seasons) because he was granted an additional season of competition for reasons of hardship or a freshman redshirt is denoted by "$."

COLLEGIATE RECORDS

Individual and team collegiate records are determined by comparing the best records in all four divisions (I-A, I-AA, II and III) in comparable categories. Included are career records of players who played parts of their careers in different divisions (such as Dennis Shaw of San Diego State, Howard Stevens of Randolph-Macon and Louisville, and Doug Williams of Grambling). For individual collegiate career leaders and team records, see page 198.

NCAA DEFENSIVE FOOTBALL STATISTICS

COMPILATION POLICIES

All individual defensive statistics reported to the NCAA must be compiled by the press box statistics crew during the game. Defensive numbers compiled by the coaching staff or other university/college personnel using game film will not be considered "official" NCAA statistics.

This policy does not preclude a conference or institution from making after-the-game changes to press box numbers. This is consistent with existing NCAA policies involving corrections to any offensive statistics after a contest. Any changes to press box numbers must be obvious errors, such as misidentified players, and this should not be interpreted as a way for press box statistics to be later "updated" by the coaching films. Changes should be made within one week after the game is played. Statisticians also are reminded that NCAA policy does not permit changes to away-game statistics unless approved by the home sports information director.

It is important to note that this policy applies ONLY to official NCAA statistics and national rankings, and does not mean a coaching staff cannot compile separate defensive statistics for institutional use. Those compilations also could appear in the institution's press releases and/or Web site, as long as they are identified as coaching film numbers rather than official statistics as used by the NCAA.

The NCAA statistics staff reserves the right to review any statistics provided to the national office and may withhold publishing/posting those numbers until the accuracy of those statistics can be substantiated.

Total Offense

(Rushing Plus Passing)

MOST PLAYS

Quarter
41—Jason Davis, UNLV vs. Idaho, Sept. 17, 1994 (4th; 41 passes)

Half
57—Rusty LaRue, Wake Forest vs. Duke, Oct. 28, 1995 (2nd; 56 passes, 1 rush)

Game
94—Matt Vogler, TCU vs. Houston, Nov. 3, 1990 (696 yards)

Season
814—Kliff Kingsbury, Texas Tech, 2002 (4,903 yards)

2 Yrs
1,409—Kliff Kingsbury, Texas Tech, 2001-02 (8,357 yards)

3 Yrs
2,072—Kliff Kingsbury, Texas Tech, 2000-02 (11,794 yards)

Career
(4 yrs.) 2,587—Timmy Chang, Hawaii, $2000-04 (16,910 yards)

$See page 10 for explanation.

MOST PLAYS PER GAME

Season
64.0—David Klingler, Houston, 1990 (704 in 11)

2 Yrs
61.6—David Klingler, Houston, 1990-91 (1,293 in 21)

Career
50.1—Kliff Kingsbury, Texas Tech, 1999-02 (2,156 in 43)

MOST PLAYS BY A FRESHMAN

Game
80—Luke McCown, Louisiana Tech vs. Miami (Fla.), Oct. 28, 2000 (444 yards); Tim Hiller, Western Mich. vs. Ball St., Oct. 8, 2005 (308 yards)

Season
635—Jared Lorenzen, Kentucky, 2000 (3,827 yards)
Also holds per-game record with 57.7 (635 in 11)

MOST YARDS GAINED

Quarter
347—Jason Davis, UNLV vs. Idaho, Sept. 17, 1994 (4th)

Half
510—Andre Ware, Houston vs. SMU, Oct. 21, 1989 (1st)

Game
732—David Klingler, Houston vs. Arizona St., Dec. 2, 1990 (16 rushing, 716 passing)

Season
5,976—B.J. Symons, Texas Tech, 2003 (143 rushing, 5,833 passing)

2 Yrs
10,370—Colt Brennan, Hawaii, 2005-06 (520 rushing, 9,850 passing)

3 Yrs
13,456—Ty Detmer, BYU, 1989-91 (-323 rushing, 13,779 passing)

Career
(4 yrs.) 16,910—Timmy Chang, Hawaii, $2000-04 (-162 rushing, 17,072 passing)

$See page 10 for explanation.

MOST YARDS GAINED PER GAME

Season
474.6—David Klingler, Houston, 1990 (5,221 in 11)

2 Yrs
402.2—David Klingler, Houston, 1990-91 (8,447 in 21)

Career
382.4—Tim Rattay, Louisiana Tech, 1997-99 (12,618 in 33)

MOST YARDS GAINED, FIRST TWO SEASONS
8,808—Tim Rattay, Louisiana Tech, 1997-98
Also holds per-game record with 383.0 (8,808 in 23)

MOST SEASONS GAINING 4,000 YARDS OR MORE

3—Ty Detmer, BYU, 1989-91; Timmy Chang, Hawaii, 2002-04

MOST SEASONS GAINING 3,000 YARDS OR MORE

3—Ty Detmer, BYU, 1989-91; Chad Pennington, Marshall, 1997-99; Tim Rattay, Louisiana Tech, 1997-99; Kliff Kingsbury, Texas Tech, 2000-02; Timmy Chang, Hawaii, 2002-04; Brad Smith, Missouri, 2002-03, 05; Matt Leinart, Southern California, 2003-05; Kevin Kolb, Houston, 2003, 2005-06

MOST SEASONS GAINING 2,500 YARDS OR MORE

4—Antwaan Randle El, Indiana, 1998-01; Timmy Chang, Hawaii, 2000, 2002-04; Kevin Kolb, Houston, 2003-06

3—John Elway, Stanford, 1980-82; Doug Flutie, Boston College, 1982-84; Randall Cunningham, UNLV, 1982-84; Brian McClure, Bowling Green, 1983-85; Erik Wilhelm, Oregon St., 1986-88; Shawn Moore, Virginia, 1988-90; Ty Detmer, BYU, 1989-91; Shane Matthews, Florida, 1990-92; Stoney Case, New Mexico, 1992-94; Peyton Manning, Tennessee, 1995-97; Daunte Culpepper, UCF, 1996-98; Chris Redman, Louisville, 1997-99; Drew Brees, Purdue, 1998-00; Kliff Kingsbury, Texas Tech, 2000-02; Jose Fuentes, Utah St., 2000-02; Ben Roethlisberger, Miami (Ohio), 2001-03; Brad Smith, Missouri, 2002-03, 05; Andrew Walter, Arizona St., 2002-04; Matt Leinart, Southern California, 2003-05; John Beck, BYU, 2004-06; Jordan Palmer, UTEP, 2004-06; Brady Quinn, Notre Dame, 2004-06; Drew Tate, Iowa, 2004-06

MOST YARDS GAINED BY A FRESHMAN

Game

582—David Neill, Nevada vs. New Mexico St., Oct. 10, 1998 (61 plays)

Season

3,827—Jared Lorenzen, Kentucky, 2000 (635 plays)

Per-game record—372.3, David Neill, Nevada, 1998

MOST YARDS GAINED BY A SOPHOMORE

Game

657—Brian Lindgren, Idaho vs. Middle Tenn., Oct. 6, 2001 (20 rushing, 637 passing)

Season

4,541—Chase Holbrook, New Mexico St. (12 games, 647 plays)

Per-game record—390.8, Scott Mitchell, Utah, 1988

MOST YARDS GAINED IN FIRST GAME OF CAREER

483—Billy Stevens, UTEP vs. North Texas, Sept. 18, 1965

MOST YARDS GAINED IN TWO, THREE AND FOUR CONSECUTIVE GAMES

2 Games

1,310—David Klingler, Houston, 1990 (578 vs. Eastern Wash., Nov. 17; 732 vs. Arizona St., Dec. 2)

3 Games

1,799—B.J. Symons, Texas Tech, 2003 (618 vs. North Carolina St., Sept. 20; 681 vs. Mississippi, Sept. 27; 500 vs. Texas A&M, Oct. 4)

4 Games

2,328—B.J. Symons, Texas Tech, 2003 (618 vs. North Carolina St., Sept. 20; 681 vs. Mississippi, Sept. 27; 500 vs. Texas A&M, Oct. 4; 529 vs. Iowa St., Oct. 11)

MOST GAMES GAINING 300 YARDS OR MORE

Season

14—Colt Brennan, Hawaii, 2006

Career

33—Ty Detmer, BYU, 1988-91

MOST CONSECUTIVE GAMES GAINING 300 YARDS OR MORE

Season

14—Colt Brennan, Hawaii, 2006

Career

21*—Colt Brennan, Hawaii, 2005-06

* *Active streak.*

MOST GAMES GAINING 400 YARDS OR MORE

Season

11—B.J. Symons, Texas Tech, 2003

Career

14—*Colt Brennan, Hawaii, 2005-06

**Active player.*

MOST CONSECUTIVE GAMES GAINING 400 YARDS OR MORE

Season

9—B.J. Symons, Texas Tech, 2003

Also holds career record with 9

MOST YARDS GAINED AGAINST ONE OPPONENT

Career—5 Years

1,719—Timmy Chang, Hawaii vs. Rice, $2000-04

Career—4 Years

1,485—Brady Quinn, Notre Dame vs. Purdue, 2003-06

$See page 10 for explanation.

MOST YARDS GAINED PER GAME AGAINST ONE OPPONENT

Career

(Min. 3 games) 427.7—Byron Leftwich, Marshall vs. Buffalo, 2000-02 (1,283 yards)

(Min. 4 games) 370.8—Ty Detmer, BYU vs. San Diego St., 1988-91 (1,483 yards)

MOST YARDS GAINED BY TWO OPPOSING PLAYERS

Game

1,321—Matt Vogler, TCU (696) & David Klingler, Houston (625), Nov. 3, 1990

GAINING 1,000 YARDS RUSHING AND 1,000 YARDS PASSING

Season

Johnny Bright (HB), Drake, 1950 (1,232 rushing, 1,168 passing); Reggie Collier (QB), Southern Miss., 1981 (1,005 rushing, 1,004 passing); Bart Weiss (QB), Air Force, 1985 (1,032 rushing, 1,449 passing); Darian Hagan (QB), Colorado, 1989 (1,004 rushing, 1,002 passing); Dee Dowis (QB), Air Force, 1989 (1,286 rushing, 1,285 passing); Brian Mitchell (QB), La.-Lafayette, 1989 (1,311 rushing, 1,966 passing); Michael Carter (QB), Hawaii, 1991 (1,092 rushing, 1,172 passing); Beau Morgan (QB), Air Force, 1995 (1,285 rushing, 1,165 passing); Beau Morgan (QB), Air Force, 1996 (1,494 rushing, 1,210 passing); Chris McCoy (QB), Navy, 1997 (1,370 rushing, 1,203 passing); Scott Frost (QB), Nebraska, 1997 (1,095 rushing, 1,237 passing); Antwaan Randle El (QB), Indiana, 2000 (1,270 rushing, 1,783 passing); Keith Boyea, Air Force, 2001 (1,216 rushing, 1,253 passing); Woodrow Dantzler (QB), Clemson, 2001 (1,004 rushing, 2,360 passing); Joshua Cribbs (QB), Kent St., 2001 (1,019 rushing, 1,516 passing) (one of only two freshmen to accomplish the feat); Eric Crouch, Nebraska, 2001 (1,115 rushing, 1,510 passing); Brad Smith, Missouri, 2002 (1,029 rushing, 2,333 passing) (one of only two freshmen to accomplish the feat); Joshua Cribbs, Kent St., 2002 (1,057 rushing, 1,014 passing); Jammal Lord, Nebraska, 2002 (1,412 rushing, 1,362 passing); Chance Harridge, Air Force, 2002 (1,229 rushing, 1,062 passing); Ell Roberson, Kansas St., 2002 (1,032 rushing, 1,580 passing); Craig Candeto, Navy, 2003 (1,112 rushing, 1,140 passing); Brad Smith, Missouri, 2003 (1,406 rushing, 1,977 passing); Vince Young, Texas, 2004 (1,079 rushing, 1,849 passing); Brad Smith, Missouri, 2005 (1,301 rushing, 2,304 passing); Vince Young, Texas, 2005 (1,050 rushing, 3,036 passing); Patrick White, West Virginia, 2006 (1,219 rushing, 1,655 passing)

A QUARTERBACK GAINING 2,000 YARDS PASSING AND 1,000 YARDS RUSHING

Season

Woodrow Dantzler, Clemson, 2001 (2,360 passing, 1,004 rushing); Brad Smith, Missouri, 2002 (2,333 passing, 1,029 rushing) (only freshman to accomplish the feat); Vince Young, Texas, 2005 (3,036 passing, 1,050 rushing); Brad Smith, Missouri, 2005 (2,304 passing, 1,301 rushing)

A QUARTERBACK GAINING 3,000 YARDS PASSING AND 1,000 YARDS RUSHING

Season

Vince Young, Texas, 2005 (3,036 passing, 1,050 rushing)

A QUARTERBACK GAINING 2,000 YARDS RUSHING AND 4,000 YARDS PASSING

Career

Prince McJunkins, Wichita St., 1979-82 (2,047 rushing, 4,544 passing); John Bond, Mississippi St., 1980-83 (2,280 rushing, 4,621 passing); Rickey Foggie, Minnesota, 1984-87 (2,038 rushing, 4,903 passing); Brian Mitchell, La.-Lafayette, 1986-89 (3,335 rushing, 5,447 passing); Major Harris, West Virginia, 1987-89 (2,030 rushing, 4,834 passing); Antwaan Randle El, Indiana, 1998-01 (3,895 rushing, 7,469 passing); Woodrow Dantzler, Clemson, 1998-01 (2,615 rushing, 5,634 passing); Joshua Cribbs, Kent St., 2001-04 (3,670 rushing, 7,169 passing); Vince Young, Texas, 2003-05 (3,127 rushing, 6,040 passing); Brad Smith, Missouri, 2002-05 (4,289 rushing, 8,799 passing)

A QUARTERBACK GAINING 3,000 YARDS RUSHING AND 3,000 YARDS PASSING

Career

Brian Mitchell, La.-Lafayette, 1986-89 (3,335 rushing, 5,447 passing); Beau Morgan, Air Force, 1994-96 (3,379 rushing, 3,248 passing); Antwaan Randle El, Indiana, 1998-01 (3,895 rushing, 7,469 passing); Joshua Cribbs, Kent St., 2001-04 (3,670 rushing, 7,169 passing); Vince Young, Texas, 2003-05 (3,127 rushing, 6,040 passing); Brad Smith, Missouri, 2002-05 (4,289 rushing, 8,799 passing)

A QUARTERBACK GAINING 3,500 YARDS RUSHING AND 7,000 YARDS PASSING

Career

Antwaan Randle El, Indiana, 1998-01 (3,895 rushing, 7,469 passing); Joshua Cribbs, Kent St., 2001-04 (3,670 rushing, 7,169 passing); Brad Smith, Missouri, 2002-05 (4,289 rushing, 8,799 passing)

A QUARTERBACK GAINING 4,000 YARDS RUSHING AND 8,000 YARDS PASSING

Career

Brad Smith, Missouri, 2002-05 (4,289 rushing, 8,799 passing)

A QUARTERBACK GAINING 300 YARDS PASSING AND 100 YARDS RUSHING

Game

Archie Manning, Mississippi vs. Alabama, Oct. 4, 1969 (104 rushing, 436 passing); Steve Young, BYU vs. Baylor, Sept. 10, 1983 (113 rushing, 351 passing); Ned James, New Mexico vs. Wyoming, Nov. 1, 1986 (118 rushing, 406 passing); Randy Welniak, Wyoming vs. Air Force, Sept. 24, 1988 (108 rushing, 359 passing); Donald Douglas, Houston vs. SMU, Oct. 19, 1991 (103 rushing, 319 passing); Shaun King, Tulane vs. Army, Nov. 14, 1998 (133 rushing, 332 passing); Michael Bishop, Kansas St. vs. Nebraska, Nov. 14, 1998 (140 rushing, 306 passing); Michael Bishop, Kansas St. vs. Texas A&M, Dec. 5, 1998 (101 rushing, 341 passing); Marques Tuiasosopo, Washington vs. Stanford, Oct. 30, 1999 (207 rushing, 302 passing); Brian Broadwater, Navy vs. Tulane, Nov. 11, 2000 (115 rushing, 302 passing); Woodrow Dantzler, Clemson vs. North Carolina St., Oct. 13, 2001 (184 rushing, 333 passing); Shaun Hill, Maryland vs. Duke, Oct. 20, 2001 (105 rushing, 323 passing); Zak Kustok, Northwestern vs. Bowling Green, Nov. 17, 2001 (111 rushing, 421 passing); Kevin Kolb, Houston vs. TCU, Oct. 25, 2003 (144 rushing, 434 passing); Cory Randolph, Wake Forest vs. East Caro., Sept. 11, 2004 (117 rushing, 334 passing); Drew Stanton, Michigan St. vs. Minnesota, Oct. 16, 2004 (102 rushing, 308 passing); Kent Smith, Central Mich. vs. Miami (Ohio), Sept. 10, 2005 (122 rushing, 356 passing); Reggie McNeal, Texas A&M vs. SMU, Sept. 17, 2005 (100 rushing, 349 passing)

A QUARTERBACK GAINING 400 YARDS PASSING AND 100 YARDS RUSHING

Game

Archie Manning, Mississippi vs. Alabama, Oct. 4,

1969 (104 rushing, 436 passing); Ned James, New Mexico vs. Wyoming, Nov. 1, 1986 (118 rushing, 406 passing); Zak Kustok, Northwestern vs. Bowling Green, Nov. 17, 2001 (111 rushing, 421 passing); Kevin Kolb, Houston vs. TCU, Oct. 25, 2003 (144 rushing, 434 passing)

A QUARTERBACK GAINING 300 YARDS PASSING AND 200 YARDS RUSHING

Game

Marques Tuiasosopo, Washington vs. Stanford, Oct. 30, 1999 (207 rushing, 302 passing)

A QUARTERBACK GAINING 200 YARDS RUSHING AND 200 YARDS PASSING

Game

Reds Bagnell, Pennsylvania vs. Dartmouth, Oct. 14, 1950 (214 rushing, 276 passing); Steve Gage, Tulsa vs. New Mexico, Nov. 8, 1986 (212 rushing, 209 passing); Brian Mitchell, La.-Lafayette vs. Colorado St., Nov. 21, 1987 (271 rushing, 205 passing); Marques Tuiasosopo, Washington vs. Stanford, Oct. 30, 1999 (207 rushing, 302 passing); Antwaan Randle El, Indiana vs. Minnesota, Oct. 21, 2000 (210 rushing, 263 passing); Brad Smith, Missouri vs. Nebraska, Oct. 22, 2005 (246 rushing, 234 passing); Vince Young, Texas vs. Oklahoma St., Oct. 29, 2005 (267 rushing, 239 passing); Patrick White, West Virginia vs. Pittsburgh, Nov. 16, 2006 (220 rushing, 204 passing)

TEAM HAVING A 200-YARD RUSHER AND A 200-YARD RECEIVER IN THE SAME GAME

San Diego St., George Jones (208 rushing) and Will Blackwell (210 receiving) vs. New Mexico, Nov. 4, 1995 (San Diego St. won, 38-29); Pittsburgh, Kevan Barlow (209 rushing) and Antonio Bryant (222 receiving) vs. Boston College, Oct. 21, 2000 (Pittsburgh won, 42-26); Wisconsin, Anthony Davis (247 rushing) and Lee Evans (214 receiving) vs. Akron, Sept. 6, 2003 (Wisconsin won, 48-31); Wisconsin, Dwayne Smith (207 rushing) and Lee Evans (258 receiving) vs. Michigan St., Nov. 15, 2003 (Wisconsin won, 56-21)

TEAMS HAVING A 3,000-YARD PASSER, 1,000-YARD RUSHER AND 1,000-YARD RECEIVER IN THE SAME YEAR

32 teams. Most recent: California, 2006 (Nate Longshore [3,021 passer], Marshawn Lynch [1,356 rusher] and DeSean Jackson [1,060 receiver]); Notre Dame, 2006 (Brady Quinn [3,426 passer], Darius Walker [1,267 rusher] and Jeff Samardzija [1,017 receiver]); Akron, 2005 (Luke Getsy [3,455 passer], Brett Biggs [1,339 rusher] and Domenik Hixon [1,210 receiver]); Miami (Ohio), 2005 (Josh Betts [3,178 passer], Brandon Murphy [1,070 rusher] and Ryne Robinson [1,119 receiver]); Southern California, 2005 (Matt Leinart [3,815 passer], Reggie Bush [1,740 rusher], LenDale White [1,302 rusher] and Dwayne Jarrett [1,274 receiver]); Boise St., 2003 (Ryan Dinwiddie [4,356 passer], David Mikell [1,142 rusher] and Tim Gilligan [1,192 receiver]); Houston, 2003 (Kevin Kolb [3,131 passer], Anthony Evans [1,149 rusher] and Brandon Middleton [1,250 receiver]); Miami (Ohio), 2003 (Ben Roethlisberger [4,486 passer], Cal Murphy Jr. [1,030 rusher] and Martin Nance [1,498 receiver]); Oregon St., 2003 (Derek Anderson [4,058 passer], Steven Jackson [1,545 rusher], James Newson [1,306 receiver] and Mike Hass [1,013 receiver]); UCF, 2002 (Ryan Schneider [3,770 passer], Alex Haynes [1,038 rusher], Doug Gabriel [1,237 receiver] and Jimmy Fryzel [1,125 receiver]); BYU, 2001 (Brandon Doman [3,542 passer], Luke Staley [1,582 rusher] and Reno Mahe [1,211 receiver]); Fresno St., 2001 (David Carr [4,308 passer]. Paris Gaines [1,018 rusher], Rodney Wright [1,331 receiver] and Bernard Berrian [1,270 receiver]); Utah St., 2001 (Jose Fuentes [3,100 passer], Emmett White [1,361 rusher] and Kevin Curtis [1,531 receiver]); Louisville, 1999 (Chris Redman [3,647 passer], Frank Moreau [1,298 rusher] and Arnold Jackson [1,209 receiver]; Nevada, 1999 (David Neill [3,402 passer], Chris Lemon [1,170 rusher], and Trevor Insley [2,060 receiver]); Western Mich., 1999 (Tim Lester [3,639 passer], Robert Stanford [1,092 rusher] and Steve Neal [1,113 receiver]; Louisville, 1998 (Chris Redman [4,042 passer], Leroy Collins [1,134 rusher] and Arnold Jackson [1,165 receiver]); Western Mich., 1998 (Tim Lester [3,311 passer], Darnell Fields [1,016 rusher] and Steve Neal [1,121 receiver]); Nevada, 1998 (David Neill [3,249 passer], Chris Lemon [1,154 rusher], Geoff Noisy [1,405 receiver] and Trevor Insley [1,220 receiver]; Nevada, 1997 (John Dutton [3,526 passer], Chris Lemon [1,055 rusher], Geoff Noisy [1,184 receiver] and Trevor Insley [1,151 receiver]; Tennessee, 1997 (Peyton Manning [3,819 passer], Jamal Lewis [1,364 rusher] and Marcus Nash [1,170 receiver]); Nevada, 1995 (Mike Maxwell [3,611 passer], Kim Minor [1,052 rusher] and Alex Van Dyke [1,854 receiver]); New Mexico St., 1995 (Cody Ledbetter [3,501 passer], Denvis Manns [1,120 rusher] and Lucious Davis [1,018 receiver]); Ohio St., 1995 (Bobby Hoying [3,023 passer], Eddie George [1,826 rusher] and Terry Glenn [1,316 receiver]); San Diego St., 1995 (Billy Blanton [3,300 passer], George Jones [1,842 rusher], Will Blackwell [1,207 receiver] and Az Hakim [1,022 receiver])

(Note: Southern California in 2005 is the only team to have two 1,000-yard rushers in the same year with a 3,000-yard passer and 1,000-yard receiver.)

(Note: UCF in 2002, Fresno St. in 2001, Nevada in 1997 and 1998, and San Diego St. in 1995, are the only teams to have two 1,000-yard receivers.)

TEAMS HAVING A 2,000-YARD RUSHER AND 2,000-YARD PASSER IN THE SAME YEAR

4—Oklahoma St., 1988 (Barry Sanders [2,628 rusher] and Mike Gundy [2,163 passer]); Colorado, 1994 (Rashaan Salaam [2,055 rusher] and Kordell Stewart [2,071 passer]); Texas, 1998 (Ricky Williams [2,124 rusher] and Major Applewhite [2,453 passer]); Penn St., 2002 (Larry Johnson [2,087 rusher] and Zach Mills [2,417 passer])

TEAMS HAVING A 2,000-YARD RUSHER, 2,000-YARD PASSER AND 1,000-YARD RECEIVER IN THE SAME YEAR

2—Oklahoma St., 1988 (Barry Sanders [2,628 rusher], Mike Gundy [2,163 passer] and Hart Lee Dykes [1,278 receiver]); Texas, 1998 (Ricky Williams [2,124 rusher], Major Applewhite [2,453 passer] and Wane McGarity [1,087 receiver])

TEAMS HAVING A 4,000-YARD PASSER AND 1,000-YARD RUSHER IN THE SAME YEAR

7—Houston, 1990 (David Klingler [5,140 passer] and Chuck Weatherspoon [1,097 rusher]); Louisville, 1998 (Chris Redman [4,042 passer] and Leroy Collins [1,134 rusher]); Houston, 1989 (Andre Ware [4,699 passer] and Chuck Weatherspoon [1,146 rusher]); Fresno St., 2001 (David Carr [4,308 passer] and Paris Gaines [1,018 rusher]); Boise St., 2003 (Ryan Dinwiddie [4,356 passer] and David Mikell [1,142 rusher]); Miami (Ohio), 2003 (Ben Roethlisberger [4,486 passer] and Cal Murphy Jr. [1,030 rusher]); Bowling Green, 2004 (Omar Jacobs [4,002 passer] and P.J. Pope [1,098 rusher])

HIGHEST AVERAGE GAIN PER PLAY

Game

(Min. 37-62 plays) 14.3—Jason Martin, Louisiana Tech vs. Toledo, Oct. 19, 1996 (37 for 529)

(Min. 63 plays) 9.9—David Klingler, Houston vs. TCU, Nov. 3, 1990 (63 for 625)

Season

(Min. 3,000 yards) 9.2—Colt Brennan, Hawaii, 2006 (645 for 5,915)

Career

(Min. 7,500 yards) 8.35—Ryan Dinwiddie, Boise St., 2000-03 (1,189 for 9,924)

MOST TOUCHDOWNS RESPONSIBLE FOR (TDS SCORED AND PASSED FOR)

Game

11—David Klingler, Houston vs. Eastern Wash., Nov. 17, 1990 (passed for 11)

Season

63—Colt Brennan, Hawaii, 2006 (scored 5, passed for 58)

2 Yrs

100—Colt Brennan, Hawaii, 2005-06 (scored 7, passed for 93)

3 Yrs

122—Ty Detmer, BYU, 1989-91 (scored 14, passed for 108)

Career

(4 yrs.) 135—Ty Detmer, BYU, 1988-91 (scored 14, passed for 121)

MOST TOUCHDOWNS RESPONSIBLE FOR PER GAME

Season

5.0—David Klingler, Houston, 1990 (55 in 11)

2 Yrs

4.0—David Klingler, Houston, 1990-91 (85 in 21)

3 Yrs

3.5—Tim Rattay, Louisiana Tech, 1997-99 (117 in 33)

Career

(4 yrs.) 2.9—Ty Detmer, BYU, 1988-91 (135 in 46)

Collegiate record—3.6, Dennis Shaw, San Diego St., 1968-69 (72 in 20)

MOST POINTS RESPONSIBLE FOR (Points Scored and Passed For)

Game

66—David Klingler, Houston vs. Eastern Wash., Nov. 17, 1990 (passed for 11 TDs)

Season

384—Colt Brennan, Hawaii, 2006 (scored 5 TDs, passed for 58 TDs, accounted for 3 two-point conversions)

2 Yrs

610—Colt Brennan, Hawaii, 2005-06 (scored 7 TDs, passed for 93 TDs, accounted for 5 two-point conversions)

3 Yrs

702—Tim Rattay, Louisiana Tech, 1997-99 (scored 2 TDs, passed for 115 TDs)

Career

820—Ty Detmer, BYU, 1988-91 (scored 14 TDs, passed for 121 TDs, accounted for 5 two-point conversions)

MOST POINTS RESPONSIBLE FOR PER GAME

Season

30.4—David Klingler, Houston, 1990 (334 in 11)

2 Yrs

23.5—Colt Brennan, Hawaii, 2005-06 (610 in 26)

3 Yrs

21.3—Tim Rattay, Louisiana Tech, 1997-99 (702 in 33)

Career

(4 yrs.) 17.8—Ty Detmer, BYU, 1988-91 (820 in 46)

Collegiate record—21.6, Dennis Shaw, San Diego St., 1968-69 (432 in 20)

SCORING 200 POINTS AND PASSING FOR 200 POINTS

Career

Rick Leach, Michigan, 1975-78 (scored 204, passed for 270); Antwaan Randle El, Indiana, 1998-01 (scored 264, passed for 258); Brad Smith, Missouri, 2002-05 (scored 270, passed for 336)

RUSHED FOR 40 TOUCHDOWNS AND PASSED FOR 40 TOUCHDOWNS

Career

Antwaan Randle El, Indiana, 1998-01 (44 rushing, 42 passing); Josh Harris, Bowling Green, 2000-03 (43 rushing, 55 passing); Brad Smith, Missouri, 2002-05 (45 rushing, 56 passing)

MOST CAREER STARTS AT QUARTERBACK

51—Philip Rivers, North Carolina St., 2000-03

Rushing

MOST RUSHES

Quarter

22—Alex Smith, Indiana vs. Michigan St., Nov. 11, 1995 (1st, 114 yards)

Half

34—Tony Sands, Kansas vs. Missouri, Nov. 23, 1991 (2nd, 240 yards)

Game

58—Tony Sands, Kansas vs. Missouri, Nov. 23, 1991 (396 yards)

Season

403—Marcus Allen, Southern California, 1981 (2,342 yards)

2 Yrs
757—Marcus Allen, Southern California, 1980-81 (3,905 yards)
Career
(3 yrs.) 994—Herschel Walker, Georgia, 1980-82 (5,259 yards)
(4 yrs.) 1,215—Steve Bartalo, Colorado St., 1983-86 (4,813 yards)

MOST RUSHES PER GAME
Season
39.6—Ed Marinaro, Cornell, 1971 (356 in 9)
2 Yrs
36.0—Marcus Allen, Southern California, 1980-81 (757 in 21)
Career
34.0—Ed Marinaro, Cornell, 1969-71 (918 in 27)

MOST RUSHES BY A FRESHMAN
Game
52—Michael Turner, Northern Ill. vs. Central Mich., Nov. 18, 2000 (281 yards)
Season
339—Adrian Peterson, Oklahoma, 2004 (1,925 yards)

MOST RUSHES PER GAME BY A FRESHMAN
Season
29.2—Steve Bartalo, Colorado St., 1983 (292 in 10)

MOST CONSECUTIVE RUSHES BY SAME PLAYER
Game
16—William Howard, Tennessee vs. Mississippi, Nov. 15, 1986 (during two possessions)

MOST RUSHES IN TWO CONSECUTIVE GAMES
Season
102—Lorenzo White, Michigan St., 1985 (53 vs. Purdue, Oct. 26; 49 vs. Minnesota, Nov. 2)

MOST CONSECUTIVE RUSHES WITHOUT LOSING A FUMBLE
Season
365—Travis Prentice, Miami (Ohio), 1998
Career
862—Travis Prentice, Miami (Ohio), 1997-99

MOST YARDS GAINED
Quarter
222—Corey Dillon, Washington vs. San Jose St., Nov. 16, 1996 (1st, 16 rushes)
Half
287—Stacey Robinson, Northern Ill. vs. Fresno St., Oct. 6, 1990 (1st; 114 in first quarter, 173 in second quarter; 20 rushes); LaDainian Tomlinson, TCU vs. UTEP, Nov. 20, 1999 (2nd; 121 in third quarter, 166 in fourth quarter; 28 rushes)
Game
406—LaDainian Tomlinson, TCU vs. UTEP, Nov. 20, 1999 (43 rushes) (59 yards in first quarter, 60 in second quarter, 121 in third quarter, 166 in fourth quarter)
Season
2,628—Barry Sanders, Oklahoma St., 1988 (344 rushes, 11 games)
2 Yrs
4,195—Troy Davis, Iowa St., 1995-96 (747 rushes)
Career
(3 yrs.) 5,259—Herschel Walker, Georgia, 1980-82 (994 rushes)
(4 yrs.) 6,397—Ron Dayne, Wisconsin, 1996-99 (1,115 rushes)

MOST YARDS GAINED PER GAME
Season
238.9—Barry Sanders, Oklahoma St., 1988 (2,628 in 11)
2 Yrs
190.7—Troy Davis, Iowa St., 1995-96 (4,195 in 22)
Career
174.6—Ed Marinaro, Cornell, 1969-71 (4,715 in 27)

MOST YARDS GAINED BY A FRESHMAN
Game
386—Marshall Faulk, San Diego St. vs. Pacific, Sept. 14, 1991 (37 rushes)
Season
1,925—Adrian Peterson, Oklahoma, 2004 (339 rushes)
Per-game record—180.1, Jamario Thomas, North Texas, 2004 (1,801 in 10)

MOST YARDS GAINED BY A SOPHOMORE
Game
351—Scott Harley, East Caro. vs. North Carolina St., Nov. 30, 1996 (42 rushes)
Season
2,010—Troy Davis, Iowa St., 1995 (345 rushes)
Also holds per-game record with 182.7 (2,010 in 11)

FRESHMEN GAINING 1,000 YARDS OR MORE
Season
By 77 players (see chart after Annual Rushing Champions, pages 34 and 35)

TWO FRESHMEN, SAME TEAM, GAINING 1,000 YARDS OR MORE
Season
Mike Smith (1,062) & Gwain Durden (1,049), Chattanooga, 1977

FIRST PLAYER TO GAIN 1,000 YARDS OR MORE
Season
Byron "Whizzer" White, Colorado, 1937 (1,121)
(Note: Before NCAA records began in 1937, Morley Drury of Southern California gained 1,163 yards in 1927.)

EARLIEST GAME REACHING 1,000 YARDS
Season
5th—Ed Marinaro, Cornell, 1971 (1,026); Ricky Bell, Southern California, 1976 (1,008); Marcus Allen, Southern California, 1981 (1,136); Ernest Anderson, Oklahoma St., 1982 (1,042); Barry Sanders, Oklahoma St., 1988 (1,002); Troy Davis, Iowa St., 1995 (1,001); Troy Davis, Iowa St., 1996 (1,047); Byron Hanspard, Texas Tech, 1996 (1,112); Ricky Williams, Texas, 1998 (1,086)

EARLIEST GAME BY A FRESHMAN REACHING 1,000 YARDS
Season
7th—Emmitt Smith, Florida, 1987 (1,011 vs. Temple, Oct. 17); Marshall Faulk, San Diego St., 1991 (1,157 vs. Colorado St., Nov. 9); Adrian Peterson, Oklahoma, 2004 (1,023 vs. Kansas, Oct. 23); Jamario Thomas, North Texas, 2004 (1,216 vs. La.-Monroe, Oct. 30); P.J. Hill, Wisconsin, 2006 (1,011 vs. Minnesota, Oct. 14)

MOST YARDS GAINED BY A QUARTERBACK
Game
308—Stacey Robinson, Northern Ill. vs. Fresno St., Oct. 6, 1990 (22 rushes)
Season
1,494—Beau Morgan, Air Force, 1996 (225 rushes)
Also holds per-game record with 135.8 (1,494 in 11)
Career
4,289—Brad Smith, Missouri, 2002-05 (795 rushes)
Per-game record—109.1, Stacey Robinson, Northern Ill., 1988-90 (2,727 in 25)

MOST YARDS GAINED BY A FRESHMAN QUARTERBACK
Season
1,029—Brad Smith, Missouri, 2002 (193 rushes)

LONGEST GAIN BY A QUARTERBACK
Game
98—Mark Malone, Arizona St. vs. Utah St., Oct. 27, 1979 (TD)

MOST GAMES GAINING 100 YARDS OR MORE
Season
12—Quentin Griffin, Oklahoma, 2002
Career
34—DeAngelo Williams, Memphis, 2002-05 (44 games)

MOST GAMES GAINING 100 YARDS OR MORE BY A FRESHMAN
Season
11—Adrian Peterson, Oklahoma, 2004

MOST CONSECUTIVE GAMES GAINING 100 YARDS OR MORE
Career
31—Archie Griffin, Ohio St., began Sept. 15, 1973 (vs. Minnesota), ended Nov. 22, 1975 (vs. Michigan)

MOST CONSECUTIVE GAMES GAINING 100 YARDS OR MORE BY A FRESHMAN
Season
9—Adrian Peterson, Oklahoma, 2004

MOST CONSECUTIVE GAMES GAINING 100 YARDS OR MORE BY A QUARTERBACK
Season
5—Beau Morgan, Air Force, 1995; Brian Madden, Navy, 1999

MOST GAMES GAINING 200 YARDS OR MORE
Season
8—Marcus Allen, Southern California, 1981
Career
11—Marcus Allen, Southern California, 1978-81 (in 21 games during 1980-81); Ricky Williams, Texas, 1995-98; Ron Dayne, Wisconsin, 1996-99

MOST GAMES GAINING 200 YARDS OR MORE BY A FRESHMAN
Season
6—Jamario Thomas, North Texas, 2004

MOST CONSECUTIVE GAMES GAINING 200 YARDS OR MORE
Season
5—Marcus Allen, Southern California, 1981 (210 vs. Tennessee, Sept. 12; 274 vs. Indiana, Sept. 19; 208 vs. Oklahoma, Sept. 26; 233 vs. Oregon St., Oct. 3; 211 vs. Arizona, Oct. 10); Barry Sanders, Oklahoma St., 1988 (320 vs. Kansas St., Oct. 29; 215 vs. Oklahoma, Nov. 5; 312 vs. Kansas, Nov. 12; 293 vs. Iowa St., Nov. 19; 332 vs. Texas Tech, Dec. 3); Jamario Thomas, North Texas, 2004 (256 vs. Utah St., Oct. 9; 258 vs. New Mexico St., Oct. 23; 218 vs. La.-Monroe, Oct. 30; 203 vs. La.-Lafayette, Nov. 5; 291 vs. Idaho, Nov. 13)

MOST GAMES GAINING 300 YARDS OR MORE
Season
4—Barry Sanders, Oklahoma St., 1988
Also holds career record with 4

MOST CONSECUTIVE GAMES GAINING 300 YARDS OR MORE
Season
2—Ricky Williams, Texas, 1998 (318 vs. Rice, Sept. 26; 350 vs. Iowa St., Oct. 3)

MOST YARDS GAINED IN TWO, THREE, FOUR AND FIVE CONSECUTIVE GAMES
2 Games
668—Ricky Williams, Texas, 1998 (318 vs. Rice, Sept. 26; 350 vs. Iowa St., Oct. 3)
3 Games
937—Barry Sanders, Oklahoma St., 1988 (312 vs. Kansas, Nov. 12; 293 vs. Iowa St., Nov. 19; 332 vs. Texas Tech, Dec. 3)
4 Games
1,152—Barry Sanders, Oklahoma St., 1988 (215 vs. Oklahoma, Nov. 5; 312 vs. Kansas, Nov. 12; 293 vs. Iowa St., Nov. 19; 332 vs. Texas Tech, Dec. 3)
5 Games
1,472—Barry Sanders, Oklahoma St., 1988 (320 vs. Kansas St., Oct. 29; 215 vs. Oklahoma, Nov. 5; 312 vs. Kansas, Nov. 12; 293 vs. Iowa St., Nov. 19; 332 vs. Texas Tech, Dec. 3)

MOST SEASONS GAINING 1,500 YARDS OR MORE
Career
3—Tony Dorsett, Pittsburgh, 1973, 1975-76; Herschel Walker, Georgia, 1980-82; Travis Prentice, Miami (Ohio), 1997-99; Garrett Wolfe, Northern Ill., 2004-06

MOST SEASONS GAINING 1,000 YARDS OR MORE
Career
4—Tony Dorsett, Pittsburgh, 1973-76; Amos Lawrence, North Carolina, 1977-80; Denvis Manns, New Mexico St., 1995-98; Ron Dayne, Wisconsin, 1996-99; Cedric Benson, Texas, 2002-05
Collegiate record tied by Howard Stevens, Randolph-Macon, 1968-69; Louisville, 1971-72

MOST PLAYERS REACHING 2,000 CAREER RUSHING YARDS IN THE SAME SEASON
3—Nebraska, 2000 (Cornell Buckhalter, 2,522; Dan Alexander, 2,456; Eric Crouch, 2,319)

TWO PLAYERS, SAME TEAM, EACH GAINING 1,000 YARDS OR MORE
Season
39 times. Most recent: Arkansas, 2006—Darren McFadden (1,647) & Felix Jones (1,168); West Virginia, 2006—Steve Slaton (1,744) & Patrick White (1,219); Minnesota, 2005—Laurence Maroney (1,355) & Gary Russell (1,045); Southern California, 2005—Reggie Bush (1,740) & LenDale White (1,302); Minnesota, 2004—Laurence Maroney (1,348) & Marion Barber III (1,269);

Tennessee, 2004—Gerald Riggs Jr. (1,107) & Cedric Houston (1,005); Texas, 2004—Cedric Benson (1,834) & Vince Young (1,079); Minnesota, 2003—Marion Barber III (1,196) & Laurence Maroney (1,121); Missouri, 2003—Brad Smith (1,406) & Zack Abrow (1,155); Navy, 2003—Kyle Eckel (1,249) & Craig Candeto (1,112); Kansas St., 2002—Darren Sproles (1,465) & Ell Roberson (1,032); Nebraska, 2001—Dahrran Diedrick (1,299) & Eric Crouch (1,115); Nebraska, 1997—Ahman Green (1,877) & Scott Frost (1,016); Colorado St., 1996—Calvin Branch (1,279) & Damon Washington (1,075); Ohio, 1996—Steve Hookfin (1,125) & Kareem Wilson (1,072)

TWO PLAYERS, SAME TEAM, EACH GAINING 200 YARDS OR MORE

Game

Gordon Brown, 214 (23 rushes) & Steve Gage (QB), 206 (26 rushes), Tulsa vs. Wichita St., Nov. 2, 1985; Sedrick Irvin, 238 (28 rushes) & Marc Renaud, 203 (21 rushes), Michigan St. vs. Penn St., Nov. 29, 1997

TWO OPPOSING FBS PLAYERS EACH GAINING 200 YARDS OR MORE

Game

George Swarn, Miami (Ohio) (239) & Otis Cheathem, Western Mich. (219), Sept. 8, 1984; Barry Sanders, Oklahoma St. (215) & Mike Gaddis, Oklahoma (213), Nov. 5, 1988; Ricky Williams, Texas (249) & Michael Perry, Rice (211), Sept. 27, 1997; De'Mond Parker, Oklahoma (291) & Ricky Williams, Texas (223), Oct. 11, 1997; Chris Barclay, Wake Forest (243) & Bruce Perry, Maryland (237), Nov. 29, 2003; Garrett Wolfe, Northern Ill. (245) & Tyrell Sutton, Northwestern (214), Sept. 10, 2005

MOST YARDS GAINED BY TWO OPPOSING PLAYERS

Game

553—Marshall Faulk, San Diego St. (386) & Ryan Benjamin, Pacific (167), Sept. 14, 1991

MOST YARDS GAINED BY TWO PLAYERS, SAME TEAM

Game

476—Tony Sands (396) & Chip Hilleary (80), Kansas vs. Missouri, Nov. 23, 1991

Season

3,042—Reggie Bush (1,740) & LenDale White (1,302), Southern California, 2005 (13 games)

Per-game record—272.5, Barry Sanders (2,628) & Gerald Hudson (369), Oklahoma St., 1988 (2,997 in 11)

Career

8,193—Eric Dickerson (4,450) & Craig James (3,743), SMU, 1979-82 (alternated at the same position during the last 36 games)

MOST YARDS GAINED IN FIRST GAME OF CAREER

273—Chris McCoy (Soph.), Navy vs. SMU, Sept. 9, 1995

MOST YARDS GAINED BY A FRESHMAN IN FIRST GAME OF CAREER

212—Greg Hill, Texas A&M vs. LSU, Sept. 14, 1991 (30 carries)

LONGEST RUSH BY A FRESHMAN IN FIRST GAME OF CAREER

98—Jerald Sowell, Tulane vs. Alabama, Sept. 4, 1993

MOST YARDS GAINED IN OPENING GAME OF SEASON

343—Tony Jeffery, TCU vs. Tulane, Sept. 13, 1986 (16 rushes)

MOST YARDS GAINED AGAINST ONE OPPONENT

Career

788—LaDainian Tomlinson, TCU vs. UTEP, 1997, 1999-00 (95 rushes)

MOST YARDS GAINED PER GAME AGAINST ONE OPPONENT

Career

(Min. 2 games) 292.0—Anthony Thompson, Indiana vs. Wisconsin, 1986, 89 (584 yards, 91 rushes)

(Min. 3 games) 262.7—LaDainian Tomlinson, TCU vs. UTEP, 1997, 1999-00 (788 yards, 95 rushes)

MOST YARDS GAINED BY TWO BROTHERS

Season

3,690—Barry Sanders, Oklahoma St. (2,628) & Byron Sanders, Northwestern (1,062), 1988

RUSHING FOR AT LEAST 1,500 YARDS WITH AT LEAST 500 RECEIVING YARDS

Season

Ryan Benjamin, Pacific, 1991 (1,581 rushing and 612 receiving); Brian Calhoun, Wisconsin, 2005 (1,636 yards rushing and 571 receiving)

HIGHEST AVERAGE GAIN PER RUSH

Game

(Min. 8-14 rushes) 30.2—Kevin Lowe, Wyoming vs. South Dakota St., Nov. 10, 1984 (10 for 302)

(Min. 15-25 rushes) 21.4—Tony Jeffery, TCU vs. Tulane, Sept. 13, 1986 (16 for 343)

(Min. 26 rushes) 13.7—Eddie Lee Ivery, Georgia Tech vs. Air Force, Nov. 11, 1978 (26 for 356)

Season

(Min. 75-100 rushes) 11.5—Glenn Davis, Army, 1945 (82 for 944)

(Min. 101-213 rushes) 9.6—Chuck Weatherspoon, Houston, 1989 (119 for 1,146)

(Min. 214-281 rushes) 7.8—Mike Rozier, Nebraska, 1983 (275 for 2,148)

(Min. 282 rushes) 7.6—Barry Sanders, Oklahoma St., 1988 (344 for 2,628)

Career

(Min. 300-413 rushes) 8.3—Glenn Davis, Army, 1943-46 (358 for 2,957)

(Min. 414-780 rushes) 7.3—Reggie Bush, Southern California, 2003-05 (433 for 3,169)

(Min. 781 rushes) 6.22—DeAngelo Williams, Memphis, 2002-05 (969 for 6,026)

MOST TOUCHDOWNS SCORED BY RUSHING

Quarter

4—Dick Felt, BYU vs. San Jose St., Nov. 8, 1952 (4th); Howard Griffith, Illinois vs. Southern Ill., Sept. 22, 1990 (3rd); Frank Moreau, Louisville vs. East Caro., Nov. 1, 1997 (2nd)

Game

8—Howard Griffith, Illinois vs. Southern Ill., Sept. 22, 1990 (5, 51, 7, 41, 5, 18, 5, 3 yards; Griffith scored three touchdowns [51, 7, 41] on consecutive carries and scored four touchdowns in the third quarter)

Season

37—Barry Sanders, Oklahoma St., 1988 (11 games)

Also holds per-game record at 3.4 (37 in 11)

Career

73—Travis Prentice, Miami (Ohio), 1996-99

MOST GAMES SCORING TWO OR MORE TOUCHDOWNS BY RUSHING

Season

11—Barry Sanders, Oklahoma St., 1988

MOST CONSECUTIVE GAMES SCORING TWO OR MORE TOUCHDOWNS BY RUSHING

Career

12—Barry Sanders, Oklahoma St. (last game of 1987, all 11 in 1988)

MOST TOUCHDOWNS SCORED BY RUSHING BY A FRESHMAN

Game

7—Marshall Faulk, San Diego St. vs. Pacific, Sept. 14, 1991

Season

21—Marshall Faulk, San Diego St., 1991

Also holds per-game record with 2.3 (21 in 9)

MOST RUSHING TOUCHDOWNS SCORED BY A QUARTERBACK

Game

6—Dee Dowis, Air Force vs. San Diego St., Sept. 1, 1989 (55, 28, 12, 16, 60, 17 yards; 249 yards rushing on 13 carries); Craig Candeto, Navy vs. Army, Dec. 7, 2002 (1, 1, 42, 7, 3, 1 yards; 103 yards rushing on 18 carries)

Season

22—Chance Harridge, Air Force, 2002 (13 games)

Career

59—Eric Crouch, Nebraska, 1998-01 (43 games)

MOST CONSECUTIVE RUSHES FOR A TOUCHDOWN IN A GAME

3—Howard Griffith, Illinois vs. Southern Ill., Sept. 22, 1990 (TDs of 51, 7 and 41 yards); Tiki Barber, Virginia vs. Texas, Sept. 28, 1996 (TDs of 16, 26 and 12 yards); Chris McCoy, Navy vs. Rutgers, Sept. 13, 1997 (TDs of 2, 9 and 2 yards); Aaron Greving, Iowa vs. Kent St., Sept. 1, 2001 (TDs of 14, 1 and 26 yards); Michael Robinson, Penn St. vs. Louisiana Tech, Sept. 21, 2002 (TDs of 8, 5 and 6 yards); Joe Ayoob, California vs. New Mexico St., Sept. 23, 2005 (TDs of 1, 5 and 7 yards)

MOST RUSHING TOUCHDOWNS SCORED BY A QUARTERBACK IN TWO CONSECUTIVE SEASONS

38—Stacey Robinson, Northern Ill., 1989-90 (19 and 19); Eric Crouch, Nebraska, 2000-01 (20 and 18)

PLAYER RUSHING FOR AT LEAST 200 YARDS AND RECEIVING FOR AT LEAST 100 YARDS

Game

Steve Slaton, West Virginia vs. Pittsburgh, November 16, 2006 (215 rushing, 130 receiving)

Passing

HIGHEST PASSING EFFICIENCY RATING POINTS

Game

(Min. 12-24 atts.) 403.4—Tim Clifford, Indiana vs. Colorado, Sept. 26, 1980 (14 attempts, 11 completions, 0 interceptions, 345 yards, 5 TD passes)

(Min. 25-49 atts.) 317.4—Bruce Gradkowski, Toledo vs. Buffalo, Nov. 1, 2003 (25 attempts, 23 completions, 0 interceptions, 435 yards, 6 TD passes)

(Min. 50 atts.) 199.2—Chris Redman, Louisville vs. East Caro., Nov. 14, 1998 (56 attempts, 44 completions, 1 interception, 592 yards, 6 TD passes)

Season

(Min. 15 atts. per game) 186.0—Colt Brennan, Hawaii, 2006 (559 attempts, 406 completions, 12 interceptions, 5,549 yards, 58 TD passes)

Career

(Min. 325 comps.) 168.9—Ryan Dinwiddie, Boise St., 2000-03 (992 attempts, 622 completions, 21 interceptions, 9,819 yards, 82 TD passes)

HIGHEST PASSING EFFICIENCY RATING POINTS BY A FRESHMAN

Season

(Min. 15 atts. per game) 180.4—Michael Vick, Virginia Tech, 1999 (152 attempts, 90 completions, 5 interceptions, 1,840 yards, 12 TD passes)

MOST PASSES ATTEMPTED

Quarter

41—Jason Davis, UNLV vs. Idaho, Sept. 17, 1994 (4th, completed 28)

Half

56—Rusty LaRue, Wake Forest vs. Duke, Oct. 28, 1995 (2nd, completed 41)

Game

83—Drew Brees, Purdue vs. Wisconsin, Oct. 10, 1998 (completed 55)

Season

719—B.J. Symons, Texas Tech, 2003 (13 games, completed 470)

2 Yrs

1,241—Kliff Kingsbury, Texas Tech, 2001-02 (completed 844)

3 Yrs

1,826—Kliff Kingsbury, Texas Tech, 2000-02 (completed 1,206)

Career

(4 yrs.) 2,436—Timmy Chang, Hawaii, $2000-04 (completed 1,388)

$See page 10 for explanation.

MOST PASSES ATTEMPTED PER GAME

Season

58.5—David Klingler, Houston, 1990 (643 in 11)

Career

47.0—Tim Rattay, Louisiana Tech, 1997-99 (1,552 in 33)

MOST PASSES ATTEMPTED BY A FRESHMAN

Game

72—Luke McCown, Louisiana Tech vs. Miami (Fla.), Oct. 28, 2000 (completed 42)

Season

559—Jared Lorenzen, Kentucky, 2000 (completed 321)

MOST PASSES COMPLETED

Quarter

28—Jason Davis, UNLV vs. Idaho, Sept. 17, 1994 (4th, attempted 41)

Half
41—Rusty LaRue, Wake Forest vs. Duke, Oct. 28, 1995 (2nd, attempted 56)
Game
55—Rusty LaRue, Wake Forest vs. Duke, Oct. 28, 1995 (attempted 78); Drew Brees, Purdue vs. Wisconsin, Oct. 10, 1998 (attempted 83)
Season
479—Kliff Kingsbury, Texas Tech, 2002 (14 games, attempted 712)
2 Yrs
844—Kliff Kingsbury, Texas Tech, 2001-02 (attempted 1,241)
Per-game record—34.7, Tim Couch, Kentucky, 1997-98 (763 in 22)
3 Yrs
1,206—Kliff Kingsbury, Texas Tech, 2000-02 (attempted 1,826)
Also holds per-game record with 32.6 (1,206 in 37)
Career
(4 yrs.) 1,388—Timmy Chang, Hawaii, $2000-04 (attempted 2,436)
$See page 10 for explanation.

MOST PASSES COMPLETED PER GAME
Season
36.4—Tim Couch, Kentucky, 1998 (400 in 11)
Career
30.8—Tim Rattay, Louisiana Tech, 1997-99 (1,015 in 33)

MOST PASSES COMPLETED BY A FRESHMAN
Game
47—Luke McCown, Louisiana Tech vs. Auburn, Oct. 21, 2000 (attempted 65)
Season
321—Jared Lorenzen, Kentucky, 2000 (attempted 559)
Also holds per-game record with 29.2 (321 in 11)

MOST CONSECUTIVE PASSES COMPLETED
Game
23—Tee Martin, Tennessee vs. South Carolina, Oct. 31, 1998; Aaron Rodgers, California vs. Southern California, Oct. 9, 2004
Season
24—Tee Martin, Tennessee, 1998 (completed last attempt vs. Alabama, Oct. 24 and first 23 vs. South Carolina, Oct. 31)

MOST PASSES COMPLETED IN TWO, THREE AND FOUR CONSECUTIVE GAMES
2 Games
96—Rusty LaRue, Wake Forest, 1995 (55 vs. Duke, Oct. 28; 41 vs. Georgia Tech, Nov. 4)
3 Games
146—Rusty LaRue, Wake Forest, 1995 (55 vs. Duke, Oct. 28; 41 vs. Georgia Tech, Nov. 4; 50 vs. North Carolina St., Nov. 18)
4 Games
176—Kliff Kingsbury, Texas Tech, 2002 (41 vs. New Mexico, Sept. 27; 49 vs. Texas A&M, Oct. 5; 37 vs. Iowa, Oct. 12; 49 vs. Missouri, Oct. 19)

HIGHEST PERCENTAGE OF PASSES COMPLETED
Game
(Min. 20-29 comps.) 95.8%—Tee Martin, Tennessee vs. South Carolina, Oct. 31, 1998 (23 of 24)
(Min. 30-39 comps.) 91.2%—Steve Sarkisian, BYU vs. Fresno St., Nov. 25, 1995 (31 of 34)
(Min. 40 comps.) 83.1%—Kliff Kingsbury, Texas Tech vs. Texas A&M, Oct. 5, 2002 (49 of 59)
Season
(Min. 150 atts.) 73.6%—Daunte Culpepper, UCF, 1998 (296 of 402)
Career
(Min. 875-999 atts.) 66.2%—Scott Milanovich, Maryland, 1992-95 (650 of 982)
(Min. 1,000 atts.) 68.2%—Bruce Gradkowski, Toledo, 2002-05 (766 of 1,123)

HIGHEST PERCENTAGE OF PASSES COMPLETED BY A FRESHMAN
Season
(Min. 200 atts.) 68.4%—Rudy Carpenter, Arizona St., 2005 (156 of 228)

MOST PASSES HAD INTERCEPTED
Game
9—John Reaves, Florida vs. Auburn, Nov. 1, 1969 (attempted 66)
Season
34—John Eckman, Wichita St., 1966 (attempted 458)
Also holds per-game record with 3.4 (34 in 10)
Career
(3 yrs.) 68—Zeke Bratkowski, Georgia, 1951-53 (attempted 734)
(4 yrs.) 80—Timmy Chang, Hawaii, $2000-04 (attempted 2,436)
Per-game record—2.3, Steve Ramsey, North Texas, 1967-69 (67 in 29)
$See page 10 for explanation.

LOWEST PERCENTAGE OF PASSES HAD INTERCEPTED
Season
(Min. 150-349 atts.) 0.0%—Matt Blundin, Virginia, 1991 (0 of 224)
(Min. 350 atts.) 0.74%—Marquel Blackwell, South Fla., 2002 (3 of 403)
Career
(Min. 600-1,049 atts.) 1.3%—Billy Volek, Fresno St., 1997-99 (12 of 934)
(Min. 1,050 atts.) 1.85%—Matt Leinart, Southern California, 2002-05 (23 of 1,245)

MOST PASSES ATTEMPTED WITHOUT AN INTERCEPTION
Game
70—Timmy Chang, Hawaii vs. Rice, Sept. 27, 2003 (completed 42)
Entire Season
224—Matt Blundin, Virginia, 1991 (completed 135)

MOST CONSECUTIVE PASSES ATTEMPTED WITHOUT AN INTERCEPTION
Season
271—Trent Dilfer, Fresno St., 1993
Also holds career record with 271

MOST CONSECUTIVE PASSES ATTEMPTED WITH JUST ONE INTERCEPTION
Career
329—Damon Allen, Cal St. Fullerton, 1983-84 (during 16 games; began Oct. 8, 1983, vs. Nevada, ended Nov. 3, 1984, vs. Fresno St. Interception occurred vs. Idaho, Sept. 15, 1984)

MOST CONSECUTIVE PASSES ATTEMPTED WITHOUT AN INTERCEPTION AT THE START OF A CAREER BY A FRESHMAN
138—Mike Gundy, Oklahoma St., 1986 (during 8 games)

MOST CONSECUTIVE PASSES ATTEMPTED WITHOUT AN INTERCEPTION AT THE START OF AN FBS CAREER
202—Brad Otton, Southern California, 1994-95 (played 1993 at FCS Weber St.)

MOST YARDS GAINED
Quarter
347—Jason Davis, UNLV vs. Idaho, Sept. 17, 1994 (4th)
Half
517—Andre Ware, Houston vs. SMU, Oct. 21, 1989 (1st, completed 25 of 41)
Game
716—David Klingler, Houston vs. Arizona St., Dec. 2, 1990 (completed 41 of 70)
Season
(11 games) 5,140—David Klingler, Houston, 1990 (completed 374 of 643)
(12 games) 5,336—B.J. Symons, Texas Tech, 2003 (completed 429 of 666)
(13 games) 5,833—B.J. Symons, Texas Tech, 2003 (completed 470 of 719)
2 Yrs
9,850—Colt Brennan, Hawaii, 2005-06 (completed 756 of 1,074)
3 Yrs
13,779—Ty Detmer, BYU, 1989-91 (completed 875 of 1,377)
Career
(4 yrs.) 17,072—Timmy Chang, Hawaii, $2000-04 (completed 1,388 of 2,436)
$See page 10 for explanation.

MOST YARDS GAINED PER GAME
Season
467.3—David Klingler, Houston, 1990 (5,140 in 11)
2 Yrs
406.2—Ty Detmer, BYU, 1989-90 (9,748 in 24)
Career
(3 yrs.) 386.2—Tim Rattay, Louisiana Tech, 1997-99 (12,746 in 33)
(4 yrs.) 326.8—Ty Detmer, BYU, 1988-91 (15,031 in 46)

MOST YARDS GAINED BY A FRESHMAN
Game
611—David Neill, Nevada vs. New Mexico St., Oct. 10, 1998
Season
3,687—Jared Lorenzen, Kentucky, 2000
Per-game record—361.0, David Neill, Nevada, 1998 (3,249 in 9)

MOST YARDS GAINED BY A SOPHOMORE
Game
631—Scott Mitchell, Utah vs. Air Force, Oct. 15, 1988
Season
4,619—Chase Holbrook, New Mexico St., 2006
Per-game record—392.9, Scott Mitchell, Utah, 1988 (4,322 in 11)

MOST SEASONS GAINING 2,000 YARDS OR MORE
Career
4—Kevin Sweeney, Fresno St., 1983-86 (2,359—3,259—2,604—2,363); Todd Santos, San Diego St., 1984-87 (2,063—2,877—2,553—3,932); Tom Hodson, LSU, 1986-89 (2,261—2,125—2,074—2,655); T.J. Rubley, Tulsa, 1987-89, 1991 (2,058—2,497—2,292—2,054); Alex Van Pelt, Pittsburgh, 1989-92 (2,527—2,427—2,796—3,163); Glenn Foley, Boston College, 1990-93 (2,189—2,225—2,231—3,397); Tim Lester, Western Mich., 1996-99 (2,189—2,160—3,311—3,639); David Garrard, East Caro., 1998-01 (2,091—2,359—2,332—2,247); Jared Lorenzen, Kentucky, 2000-03 (3,678—2,179—2,267—2,227); Luke McCown, Louisiana Tech, 2000-03 (2,544—3,337—3,539—3,246); Philip Rivers, North Carolina St., 2000-03 (3,054—2,586—3,353—4,491); Timmy Chang, Hawaii, 2000, 2002-04 (3,041—4,474—4,199—4,258); Charlie Frye, Akron, 2001-04 (2,053—2,824—3,549—2,623); Kevin Kolb, Houston, 2003-06 (3,131—2,766—3,258—3,809)

MOST YARDS GAINED IN TWO, THREE AND FOUR CONSECUTIVE GAMES
2 Games
1,288—David Klingler, Houston, 1990 (572 vs. Eastern Wash., Nov. 17; 716 vs. Arizona St., Dec. 2)
3 Games
1,798—David Klingler, Houston, 1990-91 (572 vs. Eastern Wash., Nov. 17, 1990; 716 vs. Arizona St., Dec. 2, 1990; 510 vs. Louisiana Tech, Aug. 31, 1991)
4 Games
2,239—B.J. Symons, Texas Tech, 2003 (586 vs. North Carolina St., Sept. 20; 661 vs. Mississippi, Sept. 27; 505 vs. Texas A&M, Oct. 4; 487 vs. Iowa St., Oct. 11)

MOST GAMES GAINING 200 YARDS OR MORE
Season
14—Ben Roethlisberger, Miami (Ohio), 2003; Colt Brennan, Hawaii, 2006
Career
47—Timmy Chang, Hawaii, $2000-04
$See page 10 for explanation.

MOST CONSECUTIVE GAMES GAINING 200 YARDS OR MORE
Season
14—Ben Roethlisberger, Miami (Ohio), 2003; Colt Brennan, Hawaii, 2006
Career
28—Kliff Kingsbury, Texas Tech (from Oct. 10, 2000, to Nov. 16, 2002)

MOST GAMES GAINING 300 YARDS OR MORE
Season
13—Colt Brennan, Hawaii, 2006 (14 games)
Career
36—Timmy Chang, Hawaii, $2000-04
$See page 10 for explanation.

MOST CONSECUTIVE GAMES GAINING 300 YARDS OR MORE
Season
13—Ty Detmer, BYU, 1990, 1989
Career
24—Ty Detmer, BYU (from Sept. 2, 1989, to Dec. 1, 1990)

MOST GAMES GAINING 400 YARDS OR MORE
Season
9—David Klingler, Houston, 1990; B.J. Symons, Texas Tech, 2003; Colt Brennan, Hawaii, 2006

Career
14—*Colt Brennan, Hawaii, 2005-06
**Active player.*

MOST YARDS GAINED BY TWO OPPOSING PLAYERS
Game
1,253—Matt Vogler, TCU (690) & David Klingler, Houston (563), Nov. 3, 1990

TWO PLAYERS, SAME TEAM, EACH PASSING FOR 250 YARDS OR MORE
Game
Steve Cottrell (311) & John Elway (270), Stanford vs. Arizona St., Oct. 24, 1981; Andre Ware (517) & David Klingler (254), Houston vs. SMU, Oct. 21, 1989; Jason Davis (381) & Jared Brown (254), UNLV vs. Idaho, Sept. 17, 1994

MOST YARDS GAINED IN OPENING GAME OF SEASON
590—Tim Rattay, Louisiana Tech vs. Nebraska, Aug. 29, 1998

MOST YARDS GAINED AGAINST ONE OPPONENT
Career
1,718—Timmy Chang, Hawaii vs. Rice, $2000-04
$See page 10 for explanation.

MOST YARDS GAINED PER GAME AGAINST ONE OPPONENT
Career
(Min. 3 games) 426.7—Byron Leftwich, Marshall vs. Buffalo, 2000-02 (1,280 yards)
(Min. 4 games) 373.8—Ty Detmer, BYU vs. New Mexico, 1988-91 (1,495 yards)

MOST YARDS GAINED PER ATTEMPT
Game
(Min. 25-39 atts.) 18.5—David Neill, Nevada vs. Idaho, Oct. 24, 1998 (26 for 480)
(Min. 40-59 atts.) 14.1—John Walsh, BYU vs. Utah St., Oct. 30, 1993 (44 for 619)
(Min. 60 atts.) 10.5—Scott Mitchell, Utah vs. Air Force, Oct. 15, 1988 (60 for 631)
Season
(Min. 412 atts.) 11.1—Ty Detmer, BYU, 1989 (412 for 4,560)
Career
(Min. 900 atts.) 9.90—Ryan Dinwiddie, Boise St., 2000-03 (992 for 9,819)

MOST YARDS GAINED PER COMPLETION
Game
(Min. 22-41 comps.) 22.9—John Walsh, BYU vs. Utah St., Oct. 30, 1993 (27 for 619)
(Min. 42 comps.) 15.7—Matt Vogler, TCU vs. Houston, Nov. 3, 1990 (44 for 690)
Season
(Min. 109-204 comps.) 18.2—Doug Williams, Grambling, 1977 (181 for 3,286)
(Min. 205 comps.) 17.5—Danny Wuerffel, Florida, 1996 (207 for 3,625)
Career
(Min. 275-399 comps.) 17.3—J.J. Joe, Baylor, 1990-93 (347 for 5,995)
(Min. 400 comps.) 15.8—Ryan Dinwiddie, Boise St., 2000-03 (662 for 9,819)

MOST TOUCHDOWN PASSES
Quarter
6—David Klingler, Houston vs. Louisiana Tech, Aug. 31, 1991 (2nd)
Half
7—Dennis Shaw, San Diego St. vs. New Mexico St., Nov. 15, 1969 (1st); Terry Dean, Florida vs. New Mexico St., Sept. 3, 1994 (1st); Doug Johnson, Florida vs. Central Mich., Sept. 6, 1997 (1st)
Game
11—David Klingler, Houston vs. Eastern Wash., Nov. 17, 1990
Season
58—Colt Brennan, Hawaii, 2006 (14 games)
2 Yrs
93—Colt Brennan, Hawaii, 2005-06
Per-game record—4.0, David Klingler, Houston, 1990-91 (83 in 21)
3 Yrs
115—Tim Rattay, Louisiana Tech, 1997-99
Career
(3 yrs.) 115—Tim Rattay, Louisiana Tech, 1997-99
(4 yrs.) 121—Ty Detmer, BYU, 1988-91

MOST TOUCHDOWN PASSES PER GAME
Season
4.9—David Klingler, Houston, 1990 (54 in 11)
Career
3.5—Tim Rattay, Louisiana Tech, 1997-99 (115 in 33)

HIGHEST PERCENTAGE OF PASSES FOR TOUCHDOWNS
Season
(Min. 175-374 atts.) 11.6%—Dennis Shaw, San Diego St., 1969 (39 of 335)
(Min. 375 atts.) 10.6%—Jim McMahon, BYU, 1980 (47 of 445)
Career
(Min. 400-499 atts.) 9.7%—Rick Leach, Michigan, 1975-78 (45 of 462)
(Min. 500 atts.) 9.7%—Danny Wuerffel, Florida, 1993-96 (114 of 1,170)

MOST CONSECUTIVE GAMES THROWING A TOUCHDOWN PASS
Career
35—Ty Detmer, BYU (from Sept. 7, 1989, to Nov. 23, 1991)

MOST CONSECUTIVE PASSES COMPLETED FOR TOUCHDOWNS
Game
6—Brooks Dawson, UTEP vs. New Mexico, Oct. 28, 1967 (first six completions of the game)

MOST TOUCHDOWN PASSES THROWN ON CONSECUTIVE PLAYS
Game
3—Jay Stuckey, UTEP vs. New Mexico St., Sept. 25, 1999 (9, 80 and 33 yards in 1:53 of playing time in second quarter); Tim Hiller, Western Mich. vs. Central Mich., Nov. 12, 2005 (76, 7 and 40 yards in 1:59 of playing time overlapping first and second quarters)

MOST TOUCHDOWN PASSES IN FIRST GAME OF CAREER
5—John Reaves, Florida vs. Houston, Sept. 20, 1969

TOUCHDOWN PASS THROWN ON FIRST PASS OF CAREER
Matt Leinart, Southern California vs. Auburn, Aug. 30, 2003 (5 yards); Jeff Ballard, TCU vs. SMU, Sept. 11, 2004 (9 yards); Taylor Bennett, Georgia Tech vs. Connecticut, Sept. 17, 2005 (42 yards); Michael McDonald, Southern California vs. Arkansas, Sept. 17, 2005 (4 yards)

TOUCHDOWN PASS THROWN ON FIRST AND SECOND PASS OF A CAREER
Michael McDonald, Southern California vs. Arkansas, Sept. 17, 2005 (4 yards); vs. Washington, Oct. 7, 2006 (20 yards)

MOST TOUCHDOWN PASSES BY A FRESHMAN
Game
6—Bob Hoernschemeyer, Indiana vs. Nebraska, Oct. 9, 1943; Luke McCown, Louisiana Tech vs. La.-Lafayette, Oct. 14, 2000
Season
29—David Neill, Nevada, 1998

MOST TOUCHDOWN PASSES IN FRESHMAN AND SOPHOMORE SEASONS
55—Rex Grossman, Florida, 2000 (21) & 2001 (34)

MOST TOUCHDOWN PASSES BY A SOPHOMORE
39—Chad Pennington, Marshall, 1997

MOST TOUCHDOWN PASSES AT CONCLUSION OF JUNIOR SEASON
93—Colt Brennan, Hawaii, 2005 (35) & 2006 (58)
Note: Brennan used one season of eligibility before enrolling at Hawaii.

MOST TOUCHDOWN PASSES, SAME PASSER AND RECEIVER
Season
26—Tim Rattay to Troy Edwards, Louisiana Tech, 1998
Career
39—Tim Rattay to Troy Edwards, Louisiana Tech, 1997-98

MOST PASSES ATTEMPTED WITHOUT A TOUCHDOWN PASS
Season
266—Stu Rayburn, Kent St., 1984 (completed 125)

FEWEST TIMES SACKED ATTEMPTING TO PASS
Season
(Min. 300 atts.) 4—Steve Walsh, Miami (Fla.), 1988, in 390 attempts. Last 4 games of the season: Tulsa, 1 for -8 yards; LSU, 1 for -2; Arkansas, 1 for -12; BYU, 1 for -9.

Receiving

MOST PASSES CAUGHT
Game
23—Randy Gatewood, UNLV vs. Idaho, Sept. 17, 1994 (363 yards)
Season
142—Manny Hazard, Houston, 1989 (1,689 yards)
Career
(2 yrs.) 227—Alex Van Dyke, Nevada, 1994-95 (3,100 yards)
(3 yrs.) 261—Howard Twilley, Tulsa, 1963-65 (3,343 yards)
(4 yrs.) 316—Taylor Stubblefield, Purdue, 2001-04 (3,433 yards)

MOST PASSES CAUGHT PER GAME
Season
13.4—Howard Twilley, Tulsa, 1965 (134 in 10)
Career
10.5—Manny Hazard, Houston, 1989-90 (220 in 21)

MOST PASSES CAUGHT BY TWO PLAYERS, SAME TEAM
Season
236—J.R. Tolver (128) & Kassim Osgood (108), San Diego St., 2002 (3,337 yards, 21 TDs)
Career
453—Mark Templeton (262) & Charles Lockett (191), Long Beach St., 1983-86 (4,871 yards, 30 TDs)

MOST PASSES CAUGHT IN CONSECUTIVE GAMES
38—Manny Hazard, Houston, 1989 (19 vs. TCU, Nov. 4; 19 vs. Texas, Nov. 11)

MOST CONSECUTIVE GAMES CATCHING A PASS
Career
51—Taurean Henderson, Texas Tech, 2002-05

MOST PASSES CAUGHT BY A TIGHT END
Game
17—Emilio Vallez, New Mexico vs. UTEP, Oct. 27, 1967 (257 yards); Jon Harvey, Northwestern vs. Michigan, Oct. 23, 1982 (208 yards)
Season
90—James Whalen, Kentucky, 1999 (1,019 yards)
Career
217—Ibn Green, Louisville, 1996-99 (2,830 yards)

MOST PASSES CAUGHT PER GAME BY A TIGHT END
Season
8.2—James Whalen, Kentucky, 1999 (90 in 11)
Career
5.4—Gordon Hudson, BYU, 1980-83 (178 in 33)

MOST PASSES CAUGHT BY A RUNNING BACK
Game
18—Mark Templeton, Long Beach St. vs. Utah St., Nov. 1, 1986 (173 yards)
Season
99—Mark Templeton, Long Beach St., 1986 (688 yards)
Career
303—Taurean Henderson, Texas Tech, 2002-05 (2,058 yards)

MOST PASSES CAUGHT BY A FRESHMAN
Game
18—Richard Woodley (WR), TCU vs. Texas Tech, Nov. 10, 1990 (180 yards)
Season
98—Taurean Henderson, Texas Tech, 2002 (RB) (633 yards)
Per-game record—7.2, Earl Bennett, Vanderbilt, 2005 (79 in 11)

CATCHING AT LEAST 50 PASSES AND GAINING AT LEAST 1,000 YARDS RUSHING
Season
By 14 players. Most recent: Curtis Young, BYU, 2006 (62 catches and 1,010 yards rushing)
Darrin Nelson, Stanford, holds record for most seasons at 3 (1977-78, 1981)

CATCHING AT LEAST 60 PASSES AND GAINING AT LEAST 1,000 YARDS RUSHING
Darrin Nelson, Stanford, 1981 (67 catches and 1,014 yards rushing); Brad Muster, Stanford, 1986 (61 catches and 1,053 yards rushing); Johnny Johnson, San Jose St., 1988 (61 catches and 1,219 yards rushing); Brett Biggs, Akron, 2005 (65 catches and 1,230 yards rushing); Curtis Young, BYU, 2006 (62 catches and 1,010 yards rushing)

MOST YARDS GAINED
Game
405—Troy Edwards, Louisiana Tech vs. Nebraska, Aug. 29, 1998 (caught 21)
Season
2,060—Trevor Insley, Nevada, 1999 (caught 134)
Career
5,005—Trevor Insley, Nevada, 1996-99 (caught 298)

MOST YARDS GAINED PER GAME
Season
187.3—Trevor Insley, Nevada, 1999 (2,060 in 11)
Career
140.9—Alex Van Dyke, Nevada, 1994-95 (3,100 in 22)

MOST YARDS GAINED BY A TIGHT END
Game
259—Gordon Hudson, BYU vs. Utah, Nov. 21, 1981 (caught 13)
Season
1,156—Chris Smith, BYU, 1990 (caught 68)
Career
2,830—Ibn Green, Louisville, 1996-99 (caught 217)

MOST YARDS GAINED PER GAME BY A TIGHT END
Season
102.0—Mike Moore, Grambling, 1977 (1,122 in 11)
Career
75.3—Gordon Hudson, BYU, 1980-83 (2,484 in 33)

MOST YARDS GAINED BY A FRESHMAN
Game
263—Corey Alston, Western Mich. vs. Eastern Mich., Nov. 1, 1997 (caught 9)
Season
1,265—Mike Williams, Southern California, 2002 (caught 81, 13 games)
Per-game record—101.9, Brandon Stokley, La.-Lafayette, 1995 (1,121 in 11)

MOST YARDS GAINED BY A SOPHOMORE
Season
1,672—Larry Fitzgerald, Pittsburgh, 2003

MOST GAMES GAINING 100 YARDS OR MORE
Season
11—Aaron Turner, Pacific, 1991
Also holds consecutive record with 11
Career
26—Trevor Insley, Nevada, 1996-99
Consecutive record: 11, Aaron Turner, Pacific, 1991 (all one season) and Keyshawn Johnson, Southern California, 1994-95 (over two seasons)

MOST GAMES GAINING 200 YARDS OR MORE
Season
6—Trevor Insley, Nevada, 1999
Consecutive record: 3, Howard Twilley, Tulsa, 1965 & Trevor Insley, Nevada, 1999

MOST YARDS GAINED BY TWO PLAYERS, SAME TEAM
Game
640—Rick Eber (322) & Harry Wood (318), Tulsa vs. Idaho St., Oct. 7, 1967 (caught 33, 6 TDs)
Season
3,337—J.R. Tolver (1,785) & Kassim Osgood (1,552), San Diego St., 2002 (13 games)

TWO OR MORE PLAYERS, SAME TEAM, EACH GAINING 1,000 YARDS
Season
23 times. Jason Phillips (1,444; 108 catches) & James Dixon (1,103; 102 catches), Houston, 1988; Patrick Rowe (1,392; 71 catches) & Dennis Arey (1,118; 68 catches), San Diego St., 1990; Andy Boyce (1,241; 79 catches) & Chris Smith (1,156; 68 catches), BYU, 1990; Charles Johnson (1,149; 57 catches) & Michael Westbrook (1,060; 76 catches), Colorado, 1992; Bryan Reeves (1,362; 91 catches) & Michael Stephens (1,062; 80 catches), Nevada, 1993; Will Blackwell (1,207; 86 catches) & Az Hakim (1,022; 57 catches), San Diego St., 1995; E.G. Green (1,007; 60 catches) & Andre Cooper (1,002; 71 catches), Florida St., 1995; Chris Doering (1,045; 70 catches) & Ike Hilliard (1,008; 57 catches), Florida, 1995; Geoff Noisy (1,435; 98 catches) & Damond Wilkins (1,121; 114 catches), Nevada, 1996; Geoff Noisy (1,184; 86 catches) & Trevor Insley (1,151; 59 catches), Nevada, 1997; Geoff Noisy (1,405; 94 catches) & Trevor Insley (1,220; 69 catches), Nevada, 1998; Jajuan Dawson (1,051; 96 catches) & Adrian Burnette (1,095; 79 catches), Tulane, 1999; Rodney Wright (1,331; 91 catches) & Bernard Berrian (1,270; 76 catches), Fresno St., 2001; J.R. Tolver (1,785; 128 catches) & Kassim Osgood (1,552; 108 catches), San Diego St., 2002; Doug Gabriel (1,237; 75 catches) & Jimmy Fryzel (1,126; 58 catches), UCF, 2002; Mike Williams (1,265; 81 catches) & Keary Colbert (1,029; 71 catches), Southern California, 2002; Mike Williams (1,314; 95 catches) & Keary Colbert (1,013; 69 catches), Southern California, 2003; Carlos Francis (1,177; 75 catches), Wes Welker (1,099; 97 catches) & Nehemiah Glover (1,081; 77 catches), Texas Tech, 2003 (only team with three players over 1,000 yards in the same season) (see record below); Jarrett Hicks (1,177; 76 catches) & Trey Haverty (1,019; 77 catches), Texas Tech, 2004; Ryan Grice-Mullen (1,228; 85 catches) & Davone Bess (1,124; 89 catches), Hawaii, 2005; Ryne Robinson (1,119; 75 catches) & Martin Nance (1,107; 81 catches), Miami (Ohio), 2005; Davone Moss (1,220; 96 catches) & Jason Rivers (1,178; 72 catches), Hawaii, 2006; Steve Smith (1,083; 71 catches) and Dwayne Jarrett (1,015; 70 catches), Southern California, 2006

(Note: Hawaii in 2005 is the only team on which both 1,000-yard receivers were freshmen.)

THREE PLAYERS, SAME TEAM, EACH GAINING 1,000 YARDS
Season
Carlos Francis (1,177; 75 catches), Wes Welker (1,099; 97 catches) & Nehemiah Glover (1,081; 77 catches), Texas Tech, 2003

TWO PLAYERS, SAME TEAM, RANKED NO. 1 & NO. 2 IN FINAL RECEIVING RANKINGS
Season
Jason Phillips (No. 1, 9.8 catches per game) & James Dixon (No. 2, 9.3 catches per game), Houston, 1988

THREE OR MORE PLAYERS, SAME TEAM, EACH CATCHING 60 PASSES OR MORE
Season
Patrick Rowe (71), Dennis Arey (68) & Jimmy Raye (62), San Diego St., 1990; James Jordan (81), John Simon (79), Delwyn Daigre (77) & Sean Cangelosi (62), Louisiana Tech, 1999; Arnold Jackson (101), Ibn Green (60) & Lavell Boyd (60), Louisville, 1999; Wes Welker (97), Mickey Peters (78), Taurean Henderson (78), Nehemiah Glover (77) & Carlos Francis (75), Texas Tech, 2003 (only team with five players with at least 60 catches in a season (see record below); Robert Johnson (67), Taurean Henderson (67), Joel Filani (65) & Jarrett Hicks (65), Texas Tech, 2005; Davone Moss (96), Jason Rivers (72) and Nate Ilaoa (67), Hawaii, 2006; Joel Filani (91), Robert Johnson (89) and Shannon Woods (75), Texas Tech, 2006

FOUR OR MORE PLAYERS, SAME TEAM, EACH CATCHING 60 PASSES OR MORE
Season
James Jordan (81), John Simon (79), Delwyn Daigre (77) & Sean Cangelosi (62), Louisiana Tech, 1999; Wes Welker (97), Mickey Peters (78), Taurean Henderson (78), Nehemiah Glover (77) & Carlos Francis (75), Texas Tech, 2003 (only team with five players with at least 60 catches in a season (see record below); Robert Johnson (67), Taurean Henderson (67), Joel Filani (65) & Jarrett Hicks (65), Texas Tech, 2005

FIVE PLAYERS, SAME TEAM, EACH CATCHING 60 PASSES OR MORE
Season
Wes Welker (97), Mickey Peters (78), Taurean Henderson (78), Nehemiah Glover (77) & Carlos Francis (75), Texas Tech, 2003

MOST 1,000-YARD RECEIVING SEASONS
3—Marc Zeno, Tulane, 1985-87 (1,137 in 1985; 1,033 in 1986; 1,206 in 1987); Clarkston Hines, Duke, 1987-89 (1,084 in 1987; 1,067 in 1988; 1,149 in 1989); 1,206 in 1987); Aaron Turner, Pacific, 1990-92 (1,264 in 1990; 1,604 in 1991; 1,171 in 1992); Ryan Yarborough, Wyoming, 1991-93 (1,081 in 1991; 1,351 in 1992; 1,512 in 1993); Marcus Harris, Wyoming, 1993-96 (1,431 in 1994; 1,423 in 1995; 1,650 in 1996); Brandon Stokley, La.-Lafayette, 1995-96, 98 (1,121 in 1995; 1,160 in 1996; 1,175 in 1998); Geoff Noisy, Nevada, 1996-98 (1,435 in 1996; 1,184 in 1997; 1,405 in 1998); Trevor Insley, Nevada, 1997-99 (1,151 in 1997; 1,220 in 1998; 2,060 in 1999); Braylon Edwards, Michigan, 2002-04 (1,035 in 2002; 1,138 in 2003; 1,330 in 2004); Derek Hagan, Arizona St., 2003-05 (1,076 in 2003; 1,248 in 2004; 1,210 in 2005); Greg Jennings, Western Mich., 2003-05 (1,050 in 2003; 1,092 in 2004; 1,259 in 2005)

MOST SEASONS WITH AT LEAST 1,400 YARDS
3—Marcus Harris, Wyoming, 1993-96 (1,431 in 1994; 1,423 in 1995; 1,650 in 1996)

HIGHEST AVERAGE GAIN PER RECEPTION
Game
(Min. 3-4 receps.) 72.7—Terry Gallaher, East Caro. vs. Appalachian St., Sept. 13, 1975 (3 for 218; 82, 77, 59 yards)
(Min. 5-9 receps.) 52.6—Alexander Wright, Auburn vs. Pacific, Sept. 9, 1989 (5 for 263; 78, 60, 41, 73, 11 yards)
(Min. 10 receps.) 34.9—Chuck Hughes, UTEP vs. North Texas, Sept. 18, 1965 (10 for 349)
Season
(Min. 30-49 receps.) 27.9—Elmo Wright, Houston, 1968 (43 for 1,198)
(Min. 50 receps.) 24.4—Henry Ellard, Fresno St., 1982 (62 for 1,510)
Career
(Min. 75-104 receps.) 25.7—Wesley Walker, California, 1973-76 (86 for 2,206)
(Min. 105 receps.) 22.0—Herman Moore, Virginia, 1988-90 (114 for 2,504)

HIGHEST AVERAGE GAIN PER RECEPTION BY A TIGHT END
Season
(Min. 30 receps.) 22.6—Jay Novacek, Wyoming, 1984 (33 for 745)
Career
(Min. 75 receps.) 19.2—Clay Brown, BYU, 1978-80 (88 for 1,691)

MOST TOUCHDOWN PASSES CAUGHT
Half
5—Rashaun Woods, Oklahoma St. vs. SMU, Sept. 20, 2003 (TD catches of 2, 10, 34, 32 and 25 yards) (finished with 7 TD receptions)
Game
7—Rashaun Woods, Oklahoma St. vs. SMU, Sept. 20, 2003 (12 receptions for 232 yards; TD catches of 2, 10, 34, 32, 25, 5 and 11 yards)
Season
27—Troy Edwards, Louisiana Tech, 1998 (140 receptions)
Per-game record—2.3, Tom Reynolds, San Diego St., 1969 (18 in 8); Troy Edwards, Louisiana Tech, 1998 (27 in 12)
Career
50—Troy Edwards, Louisiana Tech, 1996-98 (280 receptions)

MOST GAMES CATCHING A TOUCHDOWN PASS
Season
13—Jarett Dillard, TCU, 2006
Career
27—Ryan Yarborough, Wyoming, 1990-93 (caught a total of 42 in 46 games)

MOST CONSECUTIVE GAMES CATCHING A TOUCHDOWN PASS
Season
13—Jarett Dillard, TCU, 2006
Career
18—Larry Fitzgerald, Pittsburgh, 2002-03 (last six games of 2002 and first 12 games of 2003)

MOST TOUCHDOWN PASSES CAUGHT BY A TIGHT END
Season
18—Dennis Smith, Utah, 1989 (73 receptions)
Career
33—Ibn Green, Louisville, 1996-99 (217 receptions)

HIGHEST PERCENTAGE OF PASSES CAUGHT FOR TOUCHDOWNS
Season
(Min. 10 TDs) 58.8%—Kevin Williams, Southern California, 1978 (10 of 17)
Career
(Min. 20 TDs) 35.3%—Kevin Williams, Southern California, 1977-80 (24 of 68)

HIGHEST AVERAGE YARDS PER TOUCHDOWN PASSES CAUGHT
Season
(Min. 10 TDs) 56.1—Elmo Wright, Houston, 1968 (11 for 617 yards; 87, 50, 75, 2, 80, 79, 13, 67, 61, 43, 60 yards)
Career
(Min. 15 TDs) 46.5—Charles Johnson, Colorado, 1990-93 (15 for 697 yards)

MOST TOUCHDOWN PASSES CAUGHT, 50 YARDS OR MORE
Season
8—Elmo Wright, Houston, 1968 (87, 50, 75, 80, 79, 67, 61, 60 yards); Henry Ellard, Fresno St., 1982 (68, 51, 80, 61, 67, 72, 80, 72 yards)

MOST CONSECUTIVE PASSES CAUGHT FOR TOUCHDOWNS
6—Carlos Carson, LSU, 1977 (5 vs. Rice, Sept. 24; 1 vs. Florida, Oct. 1; first receptions of his career); Gerald Armstrong, Nebraska, 1992 (1 vs. Utah, Sept. 5; 1 vs. Arizona St., Sept. 26; 1 vs. Oklahoma St., Oct. 10; 1 vs. Colorado, Oct. 31; 2 vs. Kansas, Nov. 7)

MOST TOUCHDOWN PASSES CAUGHT BY A FRESHMAN
Season
14—Jabar Gaffney, Florida, 2000; Mike Williams, Southern California, 2002; Davone Bess, Hawaii, 2005

MOST TOUCHDOWN PASSES CAUGHT IN FRESHMAN AND SOPHOMORE SEASONS
34—Larry Fitzgerald, Pittsburgh, 2002 (12) & 2003 (22)

MOST YARDS GAINED IN A GAME WITHOUT SCORING A TOUCHDOWN
326—Nate Burleson, Nevada vs. San Jose St., Nov. 10, 2001 (12 receptions)

Punting

MOST PUNTS
Game
36—Charlie Calhoun, Texas Tech vs. Centenary (La.), Nov. 11, 1939 (1,318 yards; 20 were returned, 8 went out of bounds, 6 were downed, 1 was blocked [blocked kicks counted against the punter until 1955] and 1 went into the end zone for a touchback. Thirty-three of the punts occurred on first down during a heavy downpour in the game played at Shreveport, Louisiana)
Season
101—Jim Bailey, VMI, 1969 (3,507 yards)
Career
(3 yrs.) 276—Jim Bailey, VMI, 1969-71 (10,127 yards)
(4 yrs.) 322—Nick Harris, California, 1997-00 (13,621 yards)

HIGHEST AVERAGE PER PUNT
Game
(Min. 5-9 punts) 60.4—Lee Johnson, BYU vs. Wyoming, Oct. 8, 1983 (5 for 302; 53, 44, 63, 62, 80 yards)
(Min. 10 punts) 53.6—Jim Benien, Oklahoma St. vs. Colorado, Nov. 13, 1971 (10 for 536)
Season
(Min. 36-39 punts) 50.3—Chad Kessler, LSU, 1997 (39 for 1,961)
(Min. 40-49 punts) 49.8—Reggie Roby, Iowa, 1981 (44 for 2,193)
(Min. 50-74 punts) 48.4—Todd Sauerbrun, West Virginia, 1994 (72 for 3,486)
(Min. 75 punts) 46.6—Bill Marinangel, Vanderbilt, 1996 (77 for 3,586)
Career
(Min. 150-199 punts) 46.3—Todd Sauerbrun, West Virginia, 1991-94 (167 for 7,733)
(Min. 200-249 punts) 45.3—Ryan Plackemeier, Wake Forest, 2002-05 (220 for 9,957)
(Min. 250 punts) 45.2—Daniel Sepulveda, Baylor, 2003-06 (277 for 12,531)

HIGHEST AVERAGE PER PUNT BY A FRESHMAN
Season
(Min. 40 punts) 47.0—Tom Tupa, Ohio St., 1984 (41 for 1,927)

MOST YARDS ON PUNTS
Game
1,318—Charlie Calhoun, Texas Tech vs. Centenary (La.), Nov. 11, 1939 (36 punts)
Season
4,138—Johnny Pingel, Michigan St., 1938 (99 punts)
Career
13,621—Nick Harris, California, 1997-00 (322 punts)

MOST GAMES WITH A 40-YARD AVERAGE OR MORE
Career
(Min. 4 punts) 37—Shane Lechler, Texas A&M, 1996-99 (punted in 48 games); Ryan Plackemeier, Wake Forest, 2002-05 (punted in 42 games)

MOST PUNTS, 50 YARDS OR MORE
Game
7—Mark Mariscal, Colorado vs. Southern California, Sept. 14, 2002 (8 punts)
Season
32—Todd Sauerbrun, West Virginia, 1994 (72 punts)
Career
(2 yrs.) 51—Marv Bateman, Utah, 1970-71 (133 punts)
(3 yrs.) 61—Russ Henderson, Virginia, 1976-78 (226 punts)
(4 yrs.) 88—Bill Smith, Mississippi, 1983-86 (254 punts)

MOST CONSECUTIVE GAMES WITH AT LEAST ONE PUNT OF 50 YARDS OR MORE
Career
32—Bill Smith, Mississippi, 1983-86

MOST PUNTS, 60 YARDS OR MORE
Season
13—Ryan Plackemeier, Wake Forest, 2005 (67 punts)

MOST PUNTS IN A CAREER WITHOUT HAVING ONE BLOCKED
300—Tony DeLeone, Kent St., 1981-84
Also holds consecutive record with 300

LONGEST PUNT
99—Pat Brady, Nevada vs. Loyola Marymount, Oct. 28, 1950

RANKING IN TOP 12 IN BOTH PUNTING AND FIELD GOALS
Steve Little, Arkansas, 1977 (No. 4 in punting, 44.3-yard average and No. 2 in field goals, 1.73 per game); Rob Keen, California, 1988 (No. 11 in punting, 42.6-yard average and No. 3 in field goals, 1.91 per game); Chris Gardocki, Clemson, 1990 (No. 4 in punting, 44.3-yard average and No. 4 in field goals, 1.73 per game), 1989 (No. 10 in punting, 42.7-yard average and No. 6 in field goals, 1.82 per game); Dan Eichloff, Kansas, 1991 (No. 12 in punting, 42.3-yard average and No. 3 in field goals, 1.64 per game); Daron Alcorn, Akron, 1992 (No. 11 in punting, 43.6-yard average and tied for No. 9 in field goals, 1.64 per game)

Interceptions

MOST PASSES INTERCEPTED
Game
5—Lee Cook, Oklahoma St. vs. Detroit, Nov. 28, 1942 (15 yards); Walt Pastuszak, Brown vs. Rhode Island, Oct. 8, 1949 (47 yards); Byron Beaver, Houston vs. Baylor, Sept. 22, 1962 (18 yards); Dan Rebsch, Miami (Ohio) vs. Western Mich., Nov. 4, 1972 (88 yards). Special note: Before NCAA College Division records, Dick Miller of Akron intercepted six passes vs. Baldwin-Wallace on Oct. 23, 1937.
Season
14—Al Worley, Washington, 1968 (130 yards)
Career
29—Al Brosky, Illinois, 1950-52 (356 yards)

MOST PASSES INTERCEPTED PER GAME
Season
1.4—Al Worley, Washington, 1968 (14 in 10)
Career
1.1—Al Brosky, Illinois, 1950-52 (29 in 27)

MOST PASSES INTERCEPTED BY A LINEBACKER
Game
3—Nate Kvamme, Colorado St. vs. San Jose St., Oct. 11, 1997; Aaron Humphrey, Texas vs. Rutgers, Sept. 6, 1997; Joseph Phipps, TCU vs. Oklahoma, Sept. 12, 1998; Lorenzo Ferguson, Virginia Tech vs. Clemson, Sept. 12, 1998; Dan Dawson, Rice vs. Hawaii, Oct. 21, 2000; Will Derting, Washington St. vs. Nevada, Aug. 31, 2002; Grant Steen, Iowa vs. Indiana, Oct. 19, 2002; Korey Hall, Boise St. vs. Oregon St., Sept. 10, 2004; Michael LeDet, Tulsa vs. UTEP, Nov. 27, 2004
Season
9—Bill Sibley, Texas A&M, 1941 (57 yards)

MOST PASSES INTERCEPTED BY A FRESHMAN
Game
4—Mario Edwards, Florida St. vs. Wake Forest, Nov. 14, 1998 (60 yards)
Season
13—George Shaw, Oregon, 1951 (136 yards)
Also holds per-game record with 1.3 (13 in 10)

MOST YARDS ON INTERCEPTION RETURNS
Game
182—Ashley Lee, Virginia Tech vs. Vanderbilt, Nov. 12, 1983 (2 interceptions)
Season
302—Charles Phillips, Southern California, 1974 (7 interceptions)
Career
501—Terrell Buckley, Florida St., 1989-91 (21 interceptions)

MOST TOUCHDOWNS SCORED ON INTERCEPTION RETURNS
Game
3—Johnny Jackson, Houston vs. Texas, Nov. 7, 1987 (31, 53, 97 yards)
Season
4—Deltha O'Neal, California, 1999 (9 interceptions)
Career
5—Jackie Walker, Tennessee, 1969-71 (11 interceptions); Ken Thomas, San Jose St., 1979-82 (14 interceptions); Deltha O'Neal, California, 1996-99 (11 interceptions); Darrent Williams, Oklahoma St., 2001-04 (11 interceptions)

MOST TOUCHDOWNS SCORED ON INTERCEPTION RETURNS BY A LINEBACKER
Game
2—Tom Fisher, New Mexico St. vs. Lamar, Nov. 14, 1970 (52 & 28 yards in one quarter); Randy Neal, Virginia vs. Virginia Tech, Nov. 21, 1992 (37 & 30 yards); Patrick Brown, Kansas vs. UAB, Aug. 28, 1997 (51 & 23 yards); Nate Kvamme, Colorado St. vs. San Jose St., Oct. 11, 1997 (15 & 57 yards)
Season
3—Malcolm Postell, Pittsburgh, 2004
Career
4—Randy Neal, Virginia, 1991-94; Dustin Cohen, Miami (Ohio), 1996-99

HIGHEST AVERAGE GAIN PER INTERCEPTION
Game
(Min. 2 ints.) 91.0—Ashley Lee, Virginia Tech vs. Vanderbilt, Nov. 12, 1983 (2 for 182)
Season
(Min. 5 ints.) 51.8—Norm Thompson, Utah, 1969 (5 for 259)
Career
(Min. 15 ints.) 26.5—Tom Pridemore, West Virginia, 1975-77 (15 for 398)

MOST CONSECUTIVE GAMES INTERCEPTING A PASS
15—Al Brosky, Illinois, began Nov. 11, 1950 (vs. Iowa), ended Oct. 18, 1952 (vs. Minnesota)

Punt Returns

MOST PUNT RETURNS
Game
20—Milton Hill, Texas Tech vs. Centenary (La.), Nov. 11, 1939 (110 yards)

Season

57—Wes Welker, Texas Tech, 2002 (752 yards, 14 games)

Per-game record—5.5, Dick Adams, Miami (Ohio), 1970 (55 in 10)

Career

153—Vai Sikahema, BYU, 1980-81, 1984-85 (1,312 yards)

MOST YARDS ON PUNT RETURNS

Game

277—Antonio Perkins, Oklahoma vs. UCLA, Sept. 20, 2003 (7 returns)

Season

791—Lee Nalley, Vanderbilt, 1948 (43 returns)

Also holds per-game record with 79.1 (791 in 10)

Career

1,761—Wes Welker, Texas Tech, 2000-03 (152 returns)

HIGHEST AVERAGE GAIN PER RETURN

Game

(Min. 3-4 rets.) 59.7—Chip Hough, Air Force vs. SMU, Oct. 9, 1971 (3 for 179)

(Min. 5 rets.) 43.8—Golden Richards, BYU vs. North Texas, Sept. 10, 1971 (5 for 219)

Season

(Min. 1.2 rets. per game) 28.5—Maurice Drew, UCLA, 2005 (15 for 427)

(Min. 1.5 rets. per game) 25.0—George Sims, Baylor, 1948 (15 for 375)

Career

(Min. 1.2 rets. per game) 23.6—Jack Mitchell, Oklahoma, 1946-48 (39 for 922)

(Min. 1.5 rets. per game) 20.5—Gene Gibson, Cincinnati, 1949-50 (37 for 760)

MOST TOUCHDOWNS SCORED ON PUNT RETURNS

Game

3—Antonio Perkins, Oklahoma vs. UCLA, Sept. 20, 2003 (74, 84 & 55 yards)

Season

5—Chad Owens, Hawaii, 2004

Career

8—Wes Welker, Texas Tech, 2000-03 (2 in 2000, 1 in 2001, 3 in 2002, 2 in 2003); Antonio Perkins, Oklahoma, 2001-04 (3 in 2002, 4 in 2003, 1 in 2004)

CONSECUTIVE GAMES WITH PUNT RETURN FOR A TOUCHDOWN

3—David Allen, Kansas St., 1998 (63 yards vs. Indiana St., Sept. 5; 69 yards vs. Northern Ill., Sept. 12; 93 yards vs. Texas, Sept. 19)

(Allen also returned punts for touchdowns in consecutive games in 1999 [94 yards vs. Iowa St., Sept. 25 & 74 yards vs. Texas, Oct. 2])

Kickoff Returns

MOST KICKOFF RETURNS

Game

11—Trevor Cobb, Rice vs. Houston, Dec. 2, 1989 (166 yards)

Season

55—William White, Army, 2002 (1,239 yards, 11 games)

Career

123—Jeff Liggon, Tulane, 1993-96 (2,922 yards)

MOST RETURNS PER GAME

Season

5.0—William White, Army, 2002 (55 in 11)

Career

3.0—Steve Odom, Utah, 1971-73 (99 in 33)

MOST YARDS ON KICKOFF RETURNS

Game

282—Justin Miller, Clemson vs. Florida St., Sept. 25, 2004 (6 returns)

Season

1,248—Scott Wesley, Army, 2004 (54 returns, 11 games)

Career

2,922—Jeff Liggon, Tulane, 1993-96 (123 returns)

MOST YARDS RETURNED PER GAME

Season

113.5—Scott Wesley, Army, 2004 (1,248 in 11)

Career

78.2—Steve Odom, Utah, 1971-73 (2,582 in 33)

HIGHEST AVERAGE GAIN PER RETURN

Game

(Min. 3 rets.) 72.7—Anthony Davis, Southern California vs. Notre Dame, Dec. 2, 1972 (3 for 218)

Season

(Min. 1.2 rets. per game) 40.1—Paul Allen, BYU, 1961 (12 for 481)

(Min. 1.5 rets. per game) 38.2—Forrest Hall, San Francisco, 1946 (15 for 573)

Career

(Min. 1.2 rets. per game) 36.2—Forrest Hall, San Francisco, 1946-47 (22 for 796)

(Min. 1.5 rets. per game) 31.0—Overton Curtis, Utah St., 1957-58 (32 for 991)

MOST TOUCHDOWNS SCORED ON KICKOFF RETURNS

Game

2—Paul Copoulos, Marquette vs. Iowa Pre-Flight, Nov. 6, 1943 (85 & 82 yards); Ron Horwath, Detroit vs. Hillsdale, Sept. 22, 1950 (96 & 96 yards); Ollie Matson, San Francisco vs. Fordham, Oct. 20, 1951 (94 & 90 yards); Anthony Davis, Southern California vs. Notre Dame, Dec. 2, 1972 (97 & 96 yards); Raghib Ismail, Notre Dame vs. Rice, Nov. 5, 1988 (87 & 83 yards); *Raghib Ismail, Notre Dame vs. Michigan, Sept. 16, 1989 (88 & 92 yards); Stacey Corley, BYU vs. Air Force, Nov. 11, 1989 (99 & 85 yards); Leeland McElroy, Texas A&M vs. Rice, Oct. 23, 1993 (93 & 88 yards); Tutu Atwell, Minnesota vs. Iowa St., Sept. 13, 1997 (89 & 93 yards); Tony Lukins, New Mexico St. vs. Tulsa, Oct. 6, 2001 (83 & 100 yards); Justin Miller, Clemson vs. Florida St., Sept. 25, 2004 (97 & 86 yards); Brandon Breazell, UCLA vs. Northwestern, Dec. 30, 2005 (42 & 45 yards, both onside kicks)

Season

5—Ashlan Davis, Tulsa, 2004

Career

6—Anthony Davis, Southern California, 1972-74

*Ismail is the only player in history to score twice in two games.

CONSECUTIVE GAMES WITH KICKOFF RETURN FOR A TOUCHDOWN

4—Ashlan Davis, Tulsa, 2004 (100 yards vs. Boise St., Oct. 16; 94 yards vs. Nevada, Oct. 23; 83 yards vs. Rice, Oct. 30; 96 yards vs. SMU, Nov. 6)

SCORING A TOUCHDOWN ON TEAM'S OPENING KICKOFF OF TWO SEASONS

Season

Barry Sanders, Oklahoma St., 1988 [100 yards vs. Miami (Ohio), Sept. 10] & 1987 (100 yards vs. Tulsa, Sept. 5)

Total Kick Returns

(Combined Punt and Kickoff Returns)

MOST KICK RETURNS

Game

20—Milton Hill, Texas Tech vs. Centenary (La.), Nov. 11, 1939 (20 punts, 110 yards)

Season

78—Steve Suter, Maryland, 2002 (56 punts, 22 kickoffs, 1,317 yards)

Career

203—Deltha O'Neal, California, 1996-99 (110 punts, 93 kickoffs, 3,455 yards)

MOST YARDS ON KICK RETURNS

Game

342—Chad Owens, Hawaii vs. BYU, Dec. 8, 2001 (93 punt returns, 249 kickoff returns)

Season

1,348—Derek Abney, Kentucky, 2002 (544 punt returns, 804 kickoff returns)

Per-game record—116.2, Dion Johnson, East Caro., 1990 (1,046 yards, with 167 on punt returns and 879 on kickoff returns in 9 games)

Career

3,455—Deltha O'Neal, California, 1996-99 (1,169 on punts & 2,286 on kickoffs)

GAINING 1,000 YARDS ON PUNT RETURNS AND 1,000 YARDS ON KICKOFF RETURNS

Career

Troy Slade, Duke, 1973-75 (1,021 & 1,757); Devon Ford, Appalachian St., 1973-76 (1,197 & 1,761); Anthony Carter, Michigan, 1979-82 (1,095 & 1,504); Willie Drewrey, West Virginia, 1981-84 (1,072 & 1,302); Tony James, Mississippi St., 1989-92 (1,332 & 1,862); Thomas Bailey, Auburn, 1991-94 (1,170 & 1,520); Tim Dwight, Iowa, 1994-97 (1,051 & 1,133); Deltha O'Neal, California, 1996-99 (1,169 & 2,286); Nick Davis, Wisconsin, 1998-01 (1,001 & 1,697); Derek Abney, Kentucky, 2000-03 (1,042 & 2,315)

HIGHEST AVERAGE PER KICK RETURN (Min. 1.2 Punt Returns and 1.2 Kickoff Returns Per Game)

Season

27.2—Erroll Tucker, Utah, 1985 (40 for 1,087; 16 for 389 on punt returns, 24 for 698 on kickoff returns)

Career

22.0—Erroll Tucker, Utah, 1984-85 (79 for 1,741; 38 for 650 on punt returns, 41 for 1,091 on kickoff returns)

AVERAGING 20 YARDS EACH ON PUNT RETURNS AND KICKOFF RETURNS (Min. 1.2 Returns Per Game Each)

Season

By 7 players. Most recent: Lee Gissendaner, Northwestern, 1992 (21.8 on punt returns, 15 for 327; 22.4 on kickoff returns, 17 for 381)

MOST TOUCHDOWNS SCORED ON KICK RETURNS (Must Have at Least One Punt Return and One Kickoff Return)

Game

2—By eight players. Most recent: Derek Abney, Kentucky vs. Florida, Sept. 28, 2002 (Other players: Chad Owens, Hawaii vs. BYU, Dec. 8, 2001; Kahlil Hill, Iowa vs. Western Mich., Sept. 5, 1998; Joe Rowe, Virginia vs. Central Michigan, Sept. 7, 1996; Eric Blount, North Carolina vs. William & Mary, Oct. 5, 1991; Dion Johnson, East Caro. vs. Temple, Oct. 27, 1990; Charlie Justice, North Carolina vs. Florida, Oct. 26, 1946; Ernie Steele, Washington vs. Washington St., Nov. 30, 1940)

Season

6—Derek Abney, Kentucky, 2002 (4 punts, 2 kickoffs); Ashlan Davis, Tulsa, 2004 (5 kickoffs, 1 punt)

Career

8—Cliff Branch, Colorado, 1970-71 (6 punts, 2 kickoffs); Johnny Rodgers, Nebraska, 1970-72 (7 punts, 1 kickoff); Derek Abney, Kentucky, 2000-03 (6 punts, 2 kickoffs); Chad Owens, Hawaii, 2001-04 (6 punts, 2 kickoffs)

WINNING BOTH PUNT RETURN AND KICKOFF RETURN CHAMPIONSHIPS

Season

Erroll Tucker, Utah, 1985

Career

Ira Matthews, Wisconsin, kickoff returns (1976) and punt returns (1978); Erroll Tucker, Utah, 1985

All Runbacks

(Combined Interception Returns, Blocked Kick Returns, Fumble Returns, Punt Returns and Kickoff Returns)

SCORING MORE THAN ONE TOUCHDOWN IN AT LEAST THREE CATEGORIES

Season

Erroll Tucker, Utah, 1985 (3 interceptions, 2 punt returns, 2 kickoff returns)

SCORING AT LEAST ONE TOUCHDOWN IN AT LEAST THREE CATEGORIES

Season

Dick Harris, South Carolina, 1970; Mark Haynes, Arizona St., 1974; Scott Thomas, Air Force, 1985; Joe Crocker, Virginia, 1994; Joe Walker, Nebraska, 1998; Deltha O'Neal, California, 1999

HIGHEST AVERAGE PER RUNBACK

Season

(Min. 40 rets.) 28.3—Erroll Tucker, Utah, 1985 (46 for 1,303; 6 for 216 on interceptions, 16 for 389 on punt returns, 24 for 698 on kickoff returns)

HIGHEST AVERAGE PER RUNBACK
(At Least 7 Interceptions and Min. 1.3 Punt Returns and 1.3 Kickoff Returns Per Game)
Career
22.6—Erroll Tucker, Utah, 1984-85 (87 for 1,965; 8 for 224 on interceptions, 38 for 650 on punt returns, 41 for 1,091 on kickoff returns)

MOST TOUCHDOWNS SCORED ON RUNBACKS
Game
3—Johnny Jackson, Houston vs. Texas, Nov. 7, 1987 (3 interceptions)

MOST TOUCHDOWNS SCORED ON RUNBACKS
(Must Have at Least One Touchdown in At Least Three Categories)
Season
7—Erroll Tucker, Utah, 1985 (3 interceptions, 2 punt returns, 2 kickoff returns)
Career
9—Allen Rossum, Notre Dame, 1994-97 (3 interceptions, 3 punt returns, 3 kickoff returns)

Blocked Kicks

MOST PUNTS BLOCKED BY
Game
4—Ken Irvin, Memphis vs. Arkansas, Sept. 26, 1992; James King, Central Mich. vs. Michigan St., Sept. 8, 2001
Season
7—James King, Central Mich., 2001. Special Note: Before NCAA records, Joe Stydahar of West Virginia blocked seven punts in 1934.
Career
10—James King, Central Mich., 2001-04

MOST BLOCKED FIELD GOALS
Quarter
2—Jerald Henry, Southern California vs. California, Oct. 22, 1994 (1st, returned first one 60 yards for touchdown); Pat Larson, Wyoming vs. Fresno St., Nov. 18, 1995 (2nd)
Game
2—Mike Washington, Alabama vs. Mississippi St., Nov. 3, 1973; Louis Meadows, North Carolina St. vs. Maryland, Oct. 10, 1981; Matt Harding, Hawaii vs. San Diego St., Oct. 9, 1993; Jerald Henry, Southern California vs. California, Oct. 22, 1994; Pat Larson, Wyoming vs. Fresno St., Nov. 18, 1995; Kyle Vanden Bosch, Nebraska vs. Texas A&M, Nov. 6, 1999; Antwan Peek, Cincinnati vs. Miami (Ohio), Oct. 28, 2000; Justin Pendry, Air Force vs. Tennessee Tech, Sept. 8, 2001; Alton Moore, Auburn vs. Georgia, Nov. 10, 2001; Chris Barry, Nevada vs. Washington, Oct. 11, 2003; Daniel Bazuin, Central Mich. vs. Kent St., Oct. 2, 2004
Season
6—Lonnell Dewalt, Kentucky, 2004
Career
8—James Ferebee, New Mexico St., 1978-81; Terrence Holt, North Carolina St., 1999-02

MOST BLOCKED EXTRA POINTS
Game
2—Corey Nelson, Air Force vs. Colorado St., Nov. 11, 2000; Josh Buhl, Kansas St. vs. Syracuse, Dec, 29, 2001; Kareem Bland, Middle Tenn. vs. North Texas, Nov. 23, 2002
Season
5—Ray Farmer, Duke, 1993
Career
8—Ray Farmer, Duke, 1992-95

MOST COMBINED BLOCKED KICKS
(Includes Punts, PAT Attempts, FG Attempts)
Game
4—Ken Irvin, Memphis vs. Arkansas, Sept. 26, 1992 (4 punts); James King, Central Mich. vs. Michigan St., Sept. 8, 2001 (4 punts)
Season
8—Jimmy Lisko, Arkansas St., 1975 (4 PATs, 3 punts, 1 FG); James Francis, Baylor, 1989 (4 PATs, 3 punts, 1 FG); James King, Central Mich., 2001 (7 punts, 1 FG)
Career
19—James Ferebee, New Mexico St., 1978-81 (5 punts, 6 PATs, 8 FGs)

MOST TOUCHDOWNS SCORED ON BLOCKED PUNTS
Game
2—David Langner, Auburn vs. Alabama, Dec. 2, 1972 (2nd half); Frank Staine-Pyne, Air Force vs. Hawaii, Nov. 1, 1997 (1st half)
Season
3—Joe Wessel, Florida St., 1984

All-Purpose Yards

(Yardage Gained From Rushing, Receiving and All Runbacks)

MOST PLAYS
Game
58—Tony Sands, Kansas vs. Missouri, Nov. 23, 1991 (58 rushes)
Season
432—Marcus Allen, Southern California, 1981 (403 rushes, 29 receptions)
Career
(3 yrs.) 1,034—Herschel Walker, Georgia, 1980-82 (994 rushes, 26 receptions, 14 kickoff returns)
(4 yrs.) 1,347—Steve Bartalo, Colorado St., 1983-86 (1,215 rushes, 132 receptions)

MOST YARDS GAINED
Quarter
305—Corey Dillon, Washington vs. San Jose St., Nov. 16, 1996 (1st, 222 rushing, 83 receiving)
Game
578—Emmett White, Utah St. vs. New Mexico St., Nov. 4, 2000 (322 rushing, 134 receiving, 2 punt returns, 120 kickoff returns)
Season
3,250—Barry Sanders, Oklahoma St., 1988 (2,628 rushing, 106 receiving, 95 punt returns, 421 kickoff returns; 11 games)
Career
(3 yrs.) 6,551—Reggie Bush, Southern California, 2003-05 (3,169 rushing, 1,301 receiving, 559 punt returns, 1,522 kickoff returns; 639 plays)
(4 yrs.) 7,573—DeAngelo Williams, Memphis, 2002-05 (6,026 rushing, 723 receiving, 824 kickoff returns; 1,076 plays)

MOST YARDS GAINED PER GAME
Season
295.5—Barry Sanders, Oklahoma St., 1988 (3,250 in 11 games; 2,628 rushing, 106 receiving, 95 punt returns, 421 kickoff returns)
Career
237.8—Ryan Benjamin, Pacific, 1990-92 (5,706 in 24 games; 3,119 rushing, 1,063 receiving, 100 punt returns, 1,424 kickoff returns)

MOST YARDS GAINED BY A FRESHMAN
Game
422—Marshall Faulk, San Diego St. vs. Pacific, Sept. 14, 1991 (386 rushing, 11 receiving, 25 kickoff returns)
Season
2,026—Terrell Willis, Rutgers, 1993 (1,261 rushing, 61 receiving, 704 kickoff returns; 234 plays)
Per-game record—184.8, Marshall Faulk, San Diego St., 1991 (1,663 in 9)

MOST SEASONS WITH 2,000 OR MORE YARDS
3—DeAngelo Williams, Memphis, 2003 (2,113), 2004 (2,230) & 2005 (2,075)

GAINED 1,000 YARDS RUSHING AND 1,000 YARDS RECEIVING
Career
By many players. Most recent: Taurean Henderson, Texas Tech, 2002-05 (3,241 rushing & 2,058 receiving); Reggie Bush, Southern California, 2003-05 (3,169 rushing & 1,301 receiving); Levron Williams, Indiana, 1998-01 (3,095 rushing & 1,052 receiving); Emmett White, Utah St., 1998-01 (2,791 rushing & 1,044 receiving)

GAINED 2,000 YARDS RECEIVING, 1,000 YARDS ON PUNT RETURNS AND 2,000 YARDS ON KICKOFF RETURNS
Career
Derek Abney, Kentucky, 2000-03 (2,639 receiving, 1,042 punt returns & 2,315 kickoff returns)

HIGHEST AVERAGE GAIN PER PLAY
Game
(Min. 300 yards, 25 plays) 16.8—Randy Gatewood, UNLV vs. Idaho, Sept. 17, 1994 (419 on 25)
Season
(Min. 1,500 yards, 100-124 plays) 18.5—Henry Bailey, UNLV, 1992 (1,883 on 102)
(Min. 1,500 yards, 125 plays) 17.5—Bernard Berrian, Fresno St., 2001 (2,591 on 148)
Career
(Min. 5,000 yards, 275-374 plays) 17.4—Anthony Carter, Michigan, 1979-82 (5,197 on 298)
(Min. 5,000 yards, 375 plays) 14.8—Derek Abney, Kentucky, 2000-03 (5,856 on 395)

TEAM HAVING A 200-YARD RUSHER AND 200-YARD RECEIVER IN SAME GAME
San Diego St., George Jones (208 rushing) and Will Blackwell (210 receiving) vs. New Mexico, Nov. 4, 1995 (San Diego St. won, 38-29); Pittsburgh, Kevan Barlow (209 rushing) and Antonio Bryant (222 receiving) vs. Boston College, Oct. 21, 2000 (Pittsburgh won, 42-26); Wisconsin, Anthony Davis (247 rushing) and Lee Evans (214 receiving) vs. Akron, Sept. 6, 2003 (Wisconsin won, 48-31); Wisconsin, Dwayne Smith (207 rushing) and Lee Evans (258 receiving) vs. Michigan St., Nov. 15, 2003 (Wisconsin won, 56-21)

MOST YARDS GAINED BY TWO PLAYERS, SAME TEAM
Career
10,253—Marshall Faulk (5,595) & Darnay Scott (4,658), San Diego St., 1991-93

Scoring

MOST POINTS SCORED
(By Non-Kickers)
Game
48—Howard Griffith, Illinois vs. Southern Ill., Sept. 22, 1990 (8 TDs on runs of 5, 51, 7, 41, 5, 18, 5, 3 yards)
Game vs. Major-College Opponent
44—Marshall Faulk, San Diego St. vs. Pacific, Sept. 14, 1991 (7 TDs, 1 two-point conversion)
Season
234—Barry Sanders, Oklahoma St., 1988 (39 TDs in 11 games)
2 Yrs
320—Ricky Williams, Texas, 1997-98 (53 TDs, 1 two-point conversion in 22 games)
3 Yrs
404—Ricky Williams, Texas, 1996-98 (67 TDs, 1 two-point conversion in 34 games)
Career
(4 yrs.) 468—Travis Prentice, Miami (Ohio), 1996-99 (78 TDs)

MOST POINTS SCORED PER GAME
Season
21.3—Barry Sanders, Oklahoma St., 1988 (234 in 11)
2 Yrs
14.5—Ricky Williams, Texas 1997-98 (320 in 22)
Career
12.1—Marshall Faulk, San Diego St., 1991-93 (376 in 31)

MOST POINTS SCORED BY A FRESHMAN
Game
44—Marshall Faulk, San Diego St. vs. Pacific, Sept. 14, 1991 (7 TDs, 1 two-point conversion)
Season
140—Marshall Faulk, San Diego St., 1991 (23 TDs, 1 two-point conversion)
Also holds per-game record with 15.6 (140 in 9)

MOST TOUCHDOWNS SCORED
Quarter
4—Dick Felt, BYU vs. San Jose St., Nov. 8, 1952 (all rushing, 4th); Howard Griffith, Illinois vs. Southern Ill., Sept. 22, 1990 (all rushing, 3rd); Eric Bieniemy, Colorado vs. Nebraska, Nov. 2, 1990 (all rushing, 4th); Corey Dillon, Washington vs. San Jose St., Nov. 16, 1996 (3 rushing, 1 receiving, 1st); Frank Moreau, Louisville vs. East Caro., Nov. 1, 1997 (all rushing, 2nd); Corey Thomas, Duke vs. Georgia Tech, Nov. 15, 1997 (all receiving, 4th); Terry Caulley, Connecticut vs. Kent St., Nov. 9, 2002 (3 rushing, 1 receiving, 2nd)
Game
8—Howard Griffith, Illinois vs. Southern Ill., Sept. 22, 1990 (all 8 by rushing on runs of 5, 51, 7, 41, 5, 18, 5, 3 yards)

Game vs. Major-College Opponent
7—Arnold "Showboat" Boykin, Mississippi vs. Mississippi St., Dec. 1, 1951; Marshall Faulk, San Diego St. vs. Pacific, Sept. 14, 1991; Rashaun Woods, Oklahoma St. vs. SMU, Sept. 20, 2003
Season
39—Barry Sanders, Oklahoma St., 1988 (11 games)
Also holds per-game record with 3.5 (39 in 11)
2 Yrs
53—Ricky Williams, Texas 1997-98 (22 games)
Also holds per-game record with 2.4 (53 in 22)
3 Yrs
67—Ricky Williams, Texas, 1996-98 (34 games)
Career
(4 yrs.) 78—Travis Prentice, Miami (Ohio), 1996-99 (73 rushing, 5 pass receptions)

MOST TOUCHDOWNS SCORED IN TWO AND THREE CONSECUTIVE GAMES
2 Games
11—Kelvin Bryant, North Carolina, 1981 (6 vs. East Caro., Sept. 12; 5 vs. Miami [Ohio], Sept. 19); Ricky Williams, Texas, 1998 (6 vs. Rice, Sept. 26; 5 vs. Iowa St., Oct. 3)
3 Games
15—Kelvin Bryant, North Carolina, 1981 (6 vs. East Caro., Sept. 12; 5 vs. Miami [Ohio], Sept. 19; 4 vs. Boston College, Sept. 26)

MOST TOUCHDOWNS SCORED BY PLAYERS ON THE SAME TEAM IN CONSECUTIVE GAMES
5—Tielor Robinson, Army vs. Cincinnati, Oct. 9, 2004 (3 rushing, 2 receiving) and Carlton Jones, Army vs. South Fla., Oct. 16, 2004 (5 rushing)

MOST TOUCHDOWNS SCORED BY A FRESHMAN
Game
7—Marshall Faulk, San Diego St. vs. Pacific, Sept. 14, 1991 (all by rushing)
Season
23—Marshall Faulk, San Diego St., 1991 (21 rushing, 2 pass receptions)
Also holds per-game record with 2.6 (23 in 9)

MOST GAMES SCORING A TOUCHDOWN
Season
14—Lee Suggs, Virginia Tech, 2002 (14 games)
Career
37—Cedric Benson, Texas, 2001-04

MOST CONSECUTIVE GAMES SCORING A TOUCHDOWN
Career
27—Lee Suggs, Virginia Tech (from Sept. 2, 2000 through Dec. 31, 2002; 57 touchdowns)

MOST GAMES SCORING TWO OR MORE TOUCHDOWNS
Season
11—Barry Sanders, Oklahoma St., 1988
Career
25—Travis Prentice, Miami (Ohio), 1996-99

MOST CONSECUTIVE GAMES SCORING TWO OR MORE TOUCHDOWNS
Season
11—Barry Sanders, Oklahoma St., 1988
Career
13—Barry Sanders, Oklahoma St. (from Nov. 14, 1987, through 1988)

MOST GAMES SCORING THREE OR MORE TOUCHDOWNS
Season
9—Barry Sanders, Oklahoma St., 1988

MOST CONSECUTIVE GAMES SCORING THREE OR MORE TOUCHDOWNS
Season
5—Paul Hewitt, San Diego St., 1987 (from Oct. 10 through Nov. 7); Barry Sanders, Oklahoma St., 1988 (from Sept. 10 through Oct. 15)

MOST TOUCHDOWNS AND POINTS SCORED BY TWO PLAYERS, SAME TEAM
Season
54 and 324—Barry Sanders (39-234) & Hart Lee Dykes (15-90), Oklahoma St., 1988
Career
99 and 594—LenDale White (57-342) & Reggie Bush (42-252), Southern California, 2003-05
97 and 585—Glenn Davis (59-354) & Doc Blanchard (38-231), Army, 1943-46

PASSING FOR A TOUCHDOWN AND SCORING TOUCHDOWNS BY RUSHING AND RECEIVING
Game
By many players. Most recent: Shane Boyd, Kentucky vs. Ohio, Oct. 18, 2003; Josh Harris, Bowling Green vs. Northwestern, Nov. 17, 2001; Joey Harrington, Oregon vs. Texas, Dec. 31, 2000; Craig Ochs, Colorado vs. Oklahoma St., Oct. 28, 2000; Eric Crouch, Nebraska vs. California, Sept. 11, 1999 (all in 2nd quarter); Antwaan Randle El, Indiana vs. Cincinnati, Sept. 26, 1998; Jacquez Green, Florida vs. Auburn, Oct. 18, 1997

SCORING TOUCHDOWNS BY RUSHING, RECEIVING AND RETURNING A FUMBLE
Game
Marco Nelson, Navy vs. Stanford, Sept. 10, 2005

PASSING FOR A TOUCHDOWN AND SCORING ON A PASS RECEPTION AND PUNT RETURN
Game
By many players. Most recent: Tim Dwight, Iowa vs. Indiana, Oct. 25, 1997

PLAYER RETURNING A BLOCKED PUNT, FUMBLE RECOVERY AND INTERCEPTION RETURN FOR A TOUCHDOWN
Season
By many players. Most recent: Tim Curry, Air Force, 1997

MOST EXTRA POINTS ATTEMPTED BY KICKING
Game
14—Terry Leiweke, Houston vs. Tulsa, Nov. 23, 1968 (13 made)
Season
86—Mario Danelo, Southern California, 2005 (83 made)
Career
233—Shaun Suisham, Bowling Green, 2001-04 (226 made)

MOST EXTRA POINTS MADE BY KICKING
Game
13—Terry Leiweke, Houston vs. Tulsa, Nov. 23, 1968 (14 attempts); Derek Mahoney, Fresno St. vs. New Mexico, Oct. 5, 1991 (13 attempts)
Season
83—Mario Danelo, Southern California, 2005 (86 attempts)
Per-game record—6.42, Arthur Carmody, Louisville, 2004 (77 in 12)
Career
226—Shaun Suisham, Bowling Green, 2001-04 (233 attempts)
Per-game record—5.3, Bart Edmiston, Florida, 1993-96 (137 in 26)

BEST PERFECT RECORD OF EXTRA POINTS MADE
Season
77 of 77—Arthur Carmody, Louisville, 2004

HIGHEST PERCENTAGE OF EXTRA POINTS MADE
Career
(Min. 100 atts.) 100%—Van Tiffin, Alabama, 1983-86 (135 of 135); Pete Stoyanovich, Indiana, 1985-88 (101 of 101); David Browndyke, LSU, 1986-89 (109 of 109); John Becksvoort, Tennessee, 1991-94 (161 of 161); Luke Manget, Georgia Tech, 1999-02 (160 of 160); Damon Duval, Auburn, 1999-02 (125 of 125)

MOST CONSECUTIVE EXTRA POINTS MADE
Game
13—Derek Mahoney, Fresno St. vs. New Mexico, Oct. 5, 1991 (13 attempts)
Season
77—Arthur Carmody, Louisville, 2004 (77 attempts)
Career
161—John Becksvoort, Tennessee, 1991-94

MOST POINTS SCORED BY KICKING
Game
24—Mike Prindle, Western Mich. vs. Marshall, Sept. 29, 1984 (7 FGs, 3 PATs)
Season
141—Tyler Jones, Boise St., 2004 (24 FGs, 69 PATs)
Per-game record—11.9, Roman Anderson, Houston, 1989 (131 in 11)
Career
423—Roman Anderson, Houston, 1988-91 (70 FGs, 213 PATs)
Also holds per-game record with 9.6 (423 in 44)

HIGHEST PERCENTAGE OF EXTRA POINTS AND FIELD GOALS MADE
Season
(Min. 20 PATs and 12 FGs made) 100.0%—Marc Primanti, North Carolina St., 1996 (24 of 24 PATs, 20 of 20 FGs); Ryan White, Memphis, 1998 (22 of 22 PATs, 16 of 16 FGs)
(Min. 30 PATs and 15 FGs made) 98.3%—Chuck Nelson, Washington, 1982 (34 of 34 PATs, 25 of 26 FGs)
(Min. 40 PATs and 20 FGs made) 97.3%—Chris Jacke, UTEP, 1988 (48 of 48 PATs, 25 of 27 FGs)
Career
(Min. 100 PATs and 50 FGs made) 93.3%—John Lee, UCLA, 1982-85 (116 of 117 PATs, 79 of 92 FGs)

MOST TWO-POINT ATTEMPTS MADE
Game
6—Jim Pilot, New Mexico St. vs. Hardin-Simmons, Nov. 25, 1961 (all by running, attempted 7)
Season
6—Pat McCarthy, Holy Cross, 1960 (all by running); Jim Pilot, New Mexico St., 1961 (all by running); Howard Twilley, Tulsa, 1964 (all on pass receptions)
Career
13—Pat McCarthy, Holy Cross, 1960-62 (all by running)

MOST SUCCESSFUL TWO-POINT PASSES
Season
12—John Hangartner, Arizona St., 1958 (attempted 21)
Career
19—Pat McCarthy, Holy Cross, 1960-62 (attempted 33)

Defensive Extra Points

MOST DEFENSIVE EXTRA POINTS RETURNED
Game
2—Corey Ivy, Oklahoma vs. California, Sept. 20, 1997; Tony Holmes, Texas vs. Iowa St., Oct. 3, 1998

MOST DEFENSIVE EXTRA POINTS SCORED
Game
2—Tony Holmes, Texas vs. Iowa St., Oct. 3, 1998
Season
2—Tony Holmes, Texas, 1998

MOST DEFENSIVE EXTRA POINTS SCORED BY BOTH TEAMS (Must Have One Scored by Each Team)
Game
2—Eric Kelly (fumbled snap return), Kentucky, and Mark Roman (blocked kick return), LSU, Oct. 17, 1998

LONGEST RETURN OF A DEFENSIVE EXTRA-POINT ATTEMPT
Game
100—Lee Ozmint (SS), Alabama vs. LSU, Nov. 11, 1989 (intercepted pass at Alabama goal line); Quintin Parker (DB), Illinois vs. Wisconsin, Oct. 28, 1989 (returned kick from Illinois goal line); Curt Newton (LB), Washington St. vs. Oregon St., Oct. 20, 1990 (intercepted pass from Washington St. goal line); William Price (CB), Kansas St. vs. Indiana St., Sept. 7, 1991 (intercepted pass three yards deep in Indiana St. end zone); Joe Crocker (CB), Virginia vs. North Carolina St., Nov. 25, 1994 (intercepted pass five yards deep in North Carolina St. end zone); Laymar Grant, Duke vs. Maryland, Oct. 26, 1996 (returned conversion pass attempt); Tony Holmes, Texas vs. Iowa St., Oct. 3, 1998 (intercepted pass); Brandon Ratcliff, New Mexico vs. UNLV, Oct. 12, 2002 (intercepted pass three yards deep in UNLV end zone)

FIRST DEFENSIVE EXTRA-POINT ATTEMPT
Thomas King (S), La.-Lafayette vs. Cal St. Fullerton, Sept. 3, 1988 (returned blocked kick 6 yards)

MOST DEFENSIVE EXTRA-POINT KICKS BLOCKED
Game
2—Nigel Codrington (DB), Rice vs. Notre Dame, Nov. 5, 1988 (1 resulted in a score)
Also holds season record with 2

Defensive Records

(Since 2000)

TOTAL TACKLES

Game

26—Brian Leigeb, Central Mich. vs. Northern Ill., Nov. 17, 2000; Doug Szymul, Northwestern vs. Navy, Sept. 21, 2002

Season

193—Lawrence Flugence, Texas Tech, 2002 (14 games)

Per-game record—15.6, Rick Sherrod, West Virginia, 2001 (156 in 10)

Career

545—Tim McGarigle, Northwestern, 2002-05 (48 games)

Per-game record—12.4, E.J. Henderson, Maryland, 2000-02 (434 in 35)

SOLO TACKLES

Game

20—Tyrell Johnson, Arkansas St. vs. North Texas, Nov. 26, 2005

Season

135—E.J. Henderson, Maryland, 2002 (14 games)

Per-game record—10.2, Rick Sherrod, West Virginia, 2001 (102 in 10)

Career

360—Rod Davis, Southern Miss., 2000-03 (47 games)

Per-game record—8.8, E.J. Henderson, Maryland, 2000-02 (308 in 35)

ASSISTED TACKLES

Game

19—Brad White, Wake Forest vs. Navy, Nov. 23, 2002

Season

88—David Lusky, Eastern Mich., 2002 (12 games); John Leake, Clemson, 2002 (13 games)

Per-game record—7.6, Kevin Harrison, Eastern Mich., 2004 (84 in 11)

Career

241—Justin Bariault, Ball St., 2001-04 (46 games)

Also holds per-game record with 5.24 (241 in 46)

TACKLES FOR LOSS

Game

7.0—Chris Johnson, Kansas St. vs. Kansas, Oct. 7, 2000; Richard Seigler, Oregon St. vs. Arizona St., Oct. 20, 2001; Larry Foote, Michigan vs. Iowa, Oct. 27, 2001; Elvis Dumervil, Louisville vs. Kentucky, Sept. 4, 2005

Season

32.0—Jason Babin, Western Mich., 2003 (31 solo, 2 assisted in 12 games)

Per-game record—2.8, Kenny Philpot, Eastern Mich., 2001 (30.5 in 11)

Career

75.0—Jason Babin, Western Mich., 2000-03 (75 solo in 47 games)

Per-game record—1.87, Julius Peppers, North Carolina, 2000-01 (43 in 23)

PASS SACKS

Game

6.0—Elvis Dumervil, Louisville vs. Kentucky, Sept. 4, 2005; Ameer Ismail, Western Mich. vs. Ball St., Oct. 21, 2006

Season

24.0—Terrell Suggs, Arizona St., 2002 (23 solo, 2 assisted in 14 games)

Also holds per-game record with 1.71 (24.0 in 14)

Career

44.0—Terrell Suggs, Arizona St., 2000-02 (44 in 36 games)

Per-game record—1.61, Dwight Freeney, Syracuse, 2000-01 (30.5 in 19)

PASSES DEFENDED

Game

8—Joselio Hanson, Texas Tech vs. Oklahoma St., Nov. 9, 2002

Season

32—Jason Goss, TCU, 2002 (24 pass breakups, 8 pass interceptions in 12 games); Nathan Vasher, Texas, 2003 (26 pass breakups, 6 pass interceptions in 13 games); Corey Webster, LSU, 2003 (25 pass breakups, 7 pass interceptions in 14 games)

Per-game record—2.8, Aqib Talib, Kansas, 2006 [28 (22 pass breakups, 6 pass interceptions) in 10]

Career

78—Nathan Vasher, Texas, 2000-03 (61 pass breakups, 17 pass interceptions in 46 games)

Per-game record—2.15, Eugene Wilson, Illinois, 2000-02 [71 (60 pass breakups, 11 pass interceptions) in 33]

FORCED FUMBLES

Game

3—DeLawrence Grant, Oregon St. vs. San Diego St., Sept. 23, 2000; Antwan Peek, Cincinnati vs. La.-Monroe, Dec. 1, 2001; Mason Unck, Arizona St. vs. Stanford, Sept. 28, 2002; Quintin Mikell, Boise St. vs. Hawaii, Oct. 5, 2002; Grant Wiley, West Virginia vs. Cincinnati, Sept. 13, 2003; Derrick Johnson, Texas vs. North Texas, Sept. 4, 2004

Season

10—Elvis Dumervil, Louisville, 2005

Also holds per-game record with 0.83 (10 in 12)

Career

14—Terrell Suggs, Arizona St., 2000-02; Antwan Peek, Cincinnati, 2000-02; Kenechi Udeze, Southern California, 2001-03

Peek holds per-game record with 0.41 (14 in 34)

TOUCHDOWNS SCORED BY FUMBLE RETURN AND INTERCEPTION RETURN IN SAME GAME

2—Paul McClendon, Texas Tech vs. North Texas, Sept. 22, 2001 (six-yard fumble return and 50-yard interception return); Shawn Hackett, West Virginia vs. Rutgers, Nov. 3, 2001 (50-yard interception return and 10-yard fumble return)

Fumble Returns

(Since 1992)

LONGEST FUMBLE RETURN FOR A TOUCHDOWN

100—Paul Rivers, Rutgers vs. Pittsburgh, Oct. 28, 1995; Dan Dawson, Rice vs. UNLV, Nov. 14, 1998; Kevin Thomas, UNLV vs. Baylor, Sept. 11, 1999

MOST FUMBLE RETURNS

Game

2—By many players

MOST FUMBLE RETURNS RETURNED FOR TOUCHDOWNS

Game

2—Tyrone Carter, Minnesota vs. Syracuse, Sept. 21, 1996 (63 & 20 yards); Tony Driver, Notre Dame vs. Navy, Oct. 14, 2000 (24 & 22 yards); Alvin Nnabuife, SMU vs. Nevada, Nov. 13, 2004 (17 & 95 yards)

Field Goals

MOST FIELD GOALS ATTEMPTED

Game

9—Mike Prindle, Western Mich. vs. Marshall, Sept. 29, 1984 (7 made); Denis Hopovac, North Texas vs. Florida Int'l, Oct. 7, 2006 (5 made)

Season

38—Jerry DePoyster, Wyoming, 1966 (13 made in 10 games); Billy Bennett, Georgia, 2003 (31 made in 14 games)

DePoyster holds per-game record with 3.8 (38 in 10)

Career

(3 yrs.) 93—Jerry DePoyster, Wyoming, 1965-67 (36 made)

Also holds per-game record with 3.1 (93 in 30)

(4 yrs.) 110—Billy Bennett, Georgia, 2000-03 (87 made)

Per-game record—2.4, Philip Doyle, Alabama, 1987-90 (105 in 43)

MOST FIELD GOALS MADE

Quarter

4—By 5 players. Most recent: Jose Cortez, Oregon St. vs. California, Oct. 31, 1998 (2nd)

Half

5—Dale Klein, Nebraska vs. Missouri, Oct. 19, 1985 (1st); Dat Ly, New Mexico St. vs. Kansas, Oct. 1, 1988 (1st)

Game

7—Mike Prindle, Western Mich. vs. Marshall, Sept. 29, 1984 (32, 44, 42, 23, 48, 41, 27 yards), 9 attempts; Dale Klein, Nebraska vs. Missouri, Oct. 19, 1985 (32, 22, 43, 44, 29, 43, 43 yards), 7 attempts

Season

31—Billy Bennett, Georgia, 2003 (38 attempts in 14 games)

2 Yrs

57—Billy Bennett, Georgia, 2002-03 (71 attempts)

Career

87—Billy Bennett, Georgia, 2000-03 (110 attempts)

MOST FIELD GOALS MADE PER GAME

Season

2.6—John Lee, UCLA, 1984 (29 in 11)

Career

1.84—John Lee, UCLA, 1982-85 (79 in 43)

BEST PERFECT RECORD OF FIELD GOALS MADE

Game

7 of 7—Dale Klein, Nebraska vs. Missouri, Oct. 19, 1985

Season

20 of 20—Marc Primanti, North Carolina St., 1996

MOST FIELD GOALS MADE BY A FRESHMAN

Game

6—*Mickey Thomas, Virginia Tech vs. Vanderbilt, Nov. 4, 1989 (6 attempts)

Season

23—Collin Mackie, South Carolina, 1987 (30 attempts)

**Conventional-style kicker.*

HIGHEST PERCENTAGE OF FIELD GOALS MADE

Season

(Min. 15 atts.) 100.0%—John Lee, UCLA, 1984 (16 of 16); Marc Primanti, North Carolina St., 1996 (20 of 20); Ryan White, Memphis, 1998 (16 of 16)

Career

(Min. 45-54 atts.) 87.8%—Bobby Raymond, Florida, 1983-84 (43 of 49)

(Min. 55 atts.) 85.9%—John Lee, UCLA, 1982-85 (79 of 92)

MOST CONSECUTIVE FIELD GOALS MADE

Season

25—Chuck Nelson, Washington, 1982 (first 25, missed last attempt of season vs. Washington St., Nov. 20)

Career

30—Chuck Nelson, Washington, 1981-82 (last 5 in 1981, from vs. Southern California, Nov. 14, and first 25 in 1982, ending with last attempt vs. Washington St., Nov. 20)

MOST GAMES KICKING A FIELD GOAL

Career

40—Gary Gussman, Miami (Ohio), 1984-87 (in 44 games played)

MOST CONSECUTIVE GAMES KICKING A FIELD GOAL

24—Billy Bennett, Georgia, 2002-03

MOST FIELD GOALS MADE, 60 YARDS OR MORE

Game

2—Tony Franklin, Texas A&M vs. Baylor, Oct. 16, 1976 (65 & 64 yards)

Season

3—Russell Erxleben, Texas, 1977 (67 vs. Rice, Oct. 1; 64 vs. Baylor, Oct. 16; 60 vs. Texas Tech, Oct. 29) (4 attempts)

Career

3—Russell Erxleben, Texas, 1975-78 (see Season Record above)

MOST FIELD GOALS ATTEMPTED, 60 YARDS OR MORE

Season

5—Tony Franklin, Texas A&M, 1976 (2 made)

Career

11—Tony Franklin, Texas A&M, 1975-78 (2 made)

MOST FIELD GOALS MADE, 50 YARDS OR MORE

Game

3—Jerry DePoyster, Wyoming vs. Utah, Oct. 8, 1966 (54, 54, 52 yards); Sergio Lopez-Chavero, Wichita St. vs. Drake, Oct. 27, 1984 (54, 54, 51 yards); Tim Douglas, Iowa vs. Illinois, Sept. 26, 1998 (51, 58, 51 yards); Dan Orner, North Carolina vs. Syracuse, Sept. 7, 2002 (52, 51, 51 yards)

Season
8—Fuad Reveiz, Tennessee, 1982 (10 attempts)
Career
20—Jason Hanson, Washington St., 1988-91 (35 attempts)

MOST FIELD GOALS ATTEMPTED, 50 YARDS OR MORE
Season
17—Jerry DePoyster, Wyoming, 1966 (5 made)
Career
38—Tony Franklin, Texas A&M, 1975-78 (16 made)

HIGHEST PERCENTAGE OF FIELD GOALS MADE, 50 YARDS OR MORE
Season
(Min. 10 atts.) 80.0%—Fuad Reveiz, Tennessee, 1982 (8 of 10)
Career
(Min. 15 atts.) 60.9%—Max Zendejas, Arizona, 1982-85 (14 of 23)

MOST FIELD GOALS MADE, 40 YARDS OR MORE
Game
5—Alan Smith, Texas A&M vs. Arkansas St., Sept. 17, 1983 (44, 45, 42, 59, 57 yards)
Season
14—Chris Jacke, UTEP, 1988 (16 attempts)
Career
39—Jason Hanson, Washington St., 1988-91 (66 attempts) (19 of 31, 40-49 yards; 20 of 35, 50 or more yards)

MOST FIELD GOALS ATTEMPTED, 40 YARDS OR MORE
Season
25—Jerry DePoyster, Wyoming, 1966 (6 made)
Career
66—Jason Hanson, Washington St., 1988-91 (39 made)

HIGHEST PERCENTAGE OF FIELD GOALS MADE, 40 YARDS OR MORE
Season
(Min. 10 made) 93.3%—Matt Payne, BYU, 2004 (14 of 15)
Career
(Min. 20 made) 72.1%—Billy Bennett, Georgia, 2000-03 (31 of 43)

HIGHEST PERCENTAGE OF FIELD GOALS MADE, 40-49 YARDS
Season
(Min. 10 made) 100%—John Carney, Notre Dame, 1984 (10 of 10)
Career
(Min. 15 made) 82.6%—Jeff Jaeger, Washington, 1983-86 (19 of 23)

MOST CONSECUTIVE FIELD GOALS MADE, 40-49 YARDS
Career
14—Matt Payne, BYU, 2003-04

HIGHEST PERCENTAGE OF FIELD GOALS MADE, UNDER 40 YARDS
Season
(Min. 16 made) 100%—Paul Woodside, West Virginia, 1982 (23 of 23); Randy Pratt, California, 1983 (16 of 16); John Lee, UCLA, 1984 (16 of 16); Bobby Raymond, Florida, 1984 (18 of 18); Scott Slater, Texas A&M, 1986 (16 of 16); Philip Doyle, Alabama, 1989 (19 of 19)
Career
(Min. 30-39 made) 97.0%—Bobby Raymond, Florida, 1983-84 (32 of 33)
(Min. 40 made) 96.4%—John Lee, UCLA, 1982-85 (54 of 56)

LONGEST AVERAGE DISTANCE FIELD GOALS MADE
Game
(Min. 4 made) 49.5—Jeff Heath, East Caro. vs. Texas-Arlington, Nov. 6, 1982 (58, 53, 42, 45 yards)
Season
(Min. 10 made) 50.9—Jason Hanson, Washington St., 1991 (10 made)
Career
(Min. 25 made) 42.4—Russell Erxleben, Texas, 1975-78 (49 made)

LONGEST AVERAGE DISTANCE FIELD GOALS ATTEMPTED
Season
(Min. 20 atts.) 51.2—Jason Hanson, Washington St., 1991 (22 attempts)
Career
(Min. 40 atts.) 44.7—Russell Erxleben, Texas, 1975-78 (78 attempts)

MOST TIMES KICKING TWO OR MORE FIELD GOALS IN A GAME
Season
10—Paul Woodside, West Virginia, 1982
Career
27—Kevin Butler, Georgia, 1981-84; Billy Bennett, Georgia, 2000-03

MOST TIMES KICKING THREE OR MORE FIELD GOALS IN A GAME
Season
6—Luis Zendejas, Arizona St., 1983; Joe Allison, Memphis, 1992
Career
13—Luis Zendejas, Arizona St., 1981-84

MOST TIMES KICKING FOUR FIELD GOALS IN A GAME
Season
4—Matt Bahr, Penn St., 1978
Career
6—John Lee, UCLA, 1982-85

LONGEST FIELD GOAL MADE
67—Russell Erxleben, Texas vs. Rice, Oct. 1, 1977; Steve Little, Arkansas vs. Texas, Oct. 15, 1977; Joe Williams, Wichita St. vs. Southern Ill., Oct. 21, 1978

LONGEST INDOOR FIELD GOAL MADE
62—Chip Lohmiller, Minnesota vs. Iowa, Nov. 22, 1986 (in Minnesota's Metrodome)

LONGEST FIELD GOAL MADE WITHOUT USE OF A KICKING TEE
65—Martin Gramatica, Kansas St., vs. Northern Ill., Sept. 12, 1998

LONGEST FIELD GOAL MADE BY A FRESHMAN
61—Kyle Bryant, Texas A&M vs. Southern Miss., Sept. 24, 1994

LONGEST FIELD GOAL MADE ON FIRST ATTEMPT OF CAREER
61—Ralf Mojsiejenko, Michigan St. vs. Illinois, Sept. 11, 1982

MOST FIELD GOALS MADE IN FIRST GAME OF CAREER
5—Joe Liljenquist, BYU vs. Colorado St., Sept. 20, 1969 (6 attempts); Nathan Ritter, North Carolina St. vs. East Caro., Sept. 9, 1978 (6 attempts); Jose Oceguera, Long Beach St. vs. Kansas St., Sept. 3, 1983 (5 attempts)

MOST GAMES IN WHICH FIELD GOAL(S) PROVIDED THE WINNING MARGIN
Season
6—Henrik Mike-Mayer, Drake, 1981
Career
10—Dan Miller, Miami (Fla.), 1978-81; John Lee, UCLA, 1982-85; Jeff Ward, Texas, 1983-86

Team Records

SINGLE GAME—Offense

Total Offense

MOST PLAYS
112—Montana vs. Montana St., Nov. 1, 1952 (475 yards)

MOST PLAYS VS. A MAJOR-COLLEGE TEAM
111—Texas Tech vs. Iowa St., Oct. 11, 2003 (775 yards)

MOST PLAYS, BOTH TEAMS
196—San Diego St. (99) & North Texas (97), Dec. 4, 1971 (851 yards)

MOST PLAYS, BOTH TEAMS (OVERTIME)
202—Kentucky (103) vs. Arkansas (99), Nov. 1, 2003, 7 ot (1,111 yards)

FEWEST PLAYS
12—Texas Tech vs. Centenary (La.), Nov. 11, 1939 (10 rushes, 2 passes, -1 yard)

FEWEST PLAYS, BOTH TEAMS
33—Texas Tech (12) & Centenary (La.) (21), Nov. 11, 1939 (28 rushes, 5 passes, 30 yards)

MOST YARDS GAINED
1,021—Houston vs. SMU, Oct. 21, 1989 (250 rushing, 771 passing, 86 plays)

MOST YARDS GAINED, BOTH TEAMS
1,640—San Jose St. (849) & Nevada (791), Nov. 10, 2001 (168 plays)

FEWEST YARDS GAINED
Minus 47—Syracuse vs. Penn St., Oct. 18, 1947 (-107 rushing, gained 60 passing, 49 plays)

FEWEST YARDS GAINED, BOTH TEAMS
30—Texas Tech (-1) & Centenary (La.) (31), Nov. 11, 1939 (33 plays)

MOST YARDS GAINED BY A LOSING TEAM
791—Nevada vs. San Jose St., Nov. 10, 2001 (lost 64-45)

BOTH TEAMS GAINING 600 YARDS OR MORE
In 27 games. Most recent: San Diego St. (632) & Hawaii (610), Dec. 7, 2002 (157 plays); Hawaii (646) & BYU (612), Dec. 8, 2001 (178 plays); Northwestern (624) & Bowling Green (618), Nov. 17, 2001 (183 plays); Nevada (791) & San Jose St. (849), Nov. 10, 2001 (168 plays); Idaho (760) & Middle Tenn. (685), Oct. 6, 2001 (166 plays); Nevada (653) & New Mexico St. (614), Oct. 10, 1998 (172 plays); Miami (Fla.) (689) & UCLA (670), Dec. 5, 1998 (152 plays); Tennessee (695) & Kentucky (634), Nov. 22, 1997; Kent St. (615) & UCF (612), Oct. 4, 1997 (154 plays); San Diego St. (670) & UNLV (627), Nov. 16, 1996 (166 plays); Nevada (727) & Louisiana Tech (607), Oct. 21, 1995 (180 plays); Idaho (707) & UNLV (614), Sept. 17, 1994 (181 plays); Maryland (649) & Virginia Tech (641), Sept. 25, 1993 (166 plays); Nevada (616) & Weber St. (615), Oct. 23, 1993 (180 plays)

FEWEST YARDS GAINED BY A WINNING TEAM
10—North Carolina St. vs. Virginia, Sept. 30, 1944 (won 13-0)

HIGHEST AVERAGE GAIN PER PLAY (Min. 75 Plays)
11.9—Houston vs. SMU, Oct. 21, 1989 (86 for 1,021)

MOST TOUCHDOWNS SCORED BY RUSHING AND PASSING
15—Wyoming vs. Northern Colo., Nov. 5, 1949 (9 rushing, 6 passing)

MOST TOUCHDOWNS SCORED BY RUSHING AND PASSING (OVERTIME)
16—Arkansas vs. Mississippi, Nov. 3, 2001, 7 ot (9 rushing, 7 passing)

LONGEST DRIVE IN A GAME
26 plays, 14:26 elapsed time—Navy vs. New Mexico, Dec. 30, 2004 (Emerald Bowl).
Navy started at its one-yard line with 1:41 left in the third quarter and drove 94 yards to the New Mexico five-yard line. The drive ended with a 22-yard field goal with 2:15 remaining in the game. Navy won, 34-19.

Rushing

MOST RUSHES
99—Missouri vs. Colorado, Oct. 12, 1968 (421 yards)

MOST RUSHES, BOTH TEAMS
141—Colgate (82) & Bucknell (59), Nov. 6, 1971 (440 yards)

FEWEST RUSHES
5—Houston vs. Texas Tech, Nov. 25, 1989 (36 yards)

FEWEST RUSHES, BOTH TEAMS
28—Texas Tech (10) & Centenary (La.) (18), Nov. 11, 1939 (23 yards)

MOST YARDS GAINED
768—Oklahoma vs. Kansas St., Oct. 15, 1988 (72 rushes)

MOST YARDS GAINED, BOTH TEAMS
1,039—Lenoir-Rhyne (837) & Davidson (202), Oct. 11, 1975 (111 rushes)

MOST YARDS GAINED, BOTH TEAMS, MAJOR-COLLEGE OPPONENTS
956—Oklahoma (711) & Kansas St. (245), Oct. 23, 1971 (111 rushes)

FEWEST YARDS GAINED
Minus 109—Northern Ill. vs. Toledo, Nov. 11, 1967 (33 rushes)

FEWEST YARDS GAINED, BOTH TEAMS
Minus 24—San Jose St. (-102) & UTEP (78), Oct. 22, 1966 (75 rushes)

MOST YARDS GAINED WITHOUT LOSS
677—Nebraska vs. New Mexico St., Sept. 18, 1982 (78 rushes)

MOST YARDS GAINED BY A LOSING TEAM
545—Air Force vs. Hawaii, Nov. 24, 2001 (78 rushes, lost 50-32)

HIGHEST AVERAGE GAIN PER RUSH (Min. 50 Rushes)
11.9—Alabama vs. Virginia Tech, Oct. 27, 1973 (63 for 748)

MOST PLAYERS ON ONE TEAM EACH GAINING 100 YARDS OR MORE
4—Arizona St. vs. Arizona, Nov. 10, 1951 (Bob Tarwater 140, Harley Cooper 123, Duane Morrison 118, Buzz Walker 113); Texas vs. SMU, Nov. 1, 1969 (Jim Bertelsen 137, Steve Worster 137, James Street 121, Ted Koy 111); Alabama vs. Virginia Tech, Oct. 27, 1973 (Jimmy Taylor 142, Wilbur Jackson 138, Calvin Culliver 127, Richard Todd 102); Army vs. Montana, Nov. 17, 1984 (Doug Black 183, Nate Sassaman 155, Clarence Jones 130, Jarvis Hollingsworth 124); Nebraska vs. Baylor, Oct. 13, 2001 (Thunder Collins 165, Dahrran Diedrick 137, Eric Crouch 132, Judd Davies 119)

MOST TOUCHDOWNS SCORED BY RUSHING
12—UTEP vs. New Mexico St., Nov. 25, 1948

Passing

MOST PASSES ATTEMPTED
83—Purdue vs. Wisconsin, Oct. 10, 1998 (completed 55)

MOST PASSES ATTEMPTED, BOTH TEAMS
135—TCU (79) & Houston (56), Nov. 3, 1990 (completed 81)

FEWEST PASSES ATTEMPTED
0—By many teams. Most recent: Ohio vs. Akron, Oct. 25, 1997 (61 rushes; won 21-17)

FEWEST PASSES ATTEMPTED, BOTH TEAMS
1—Michigan St. (0) & Maryland (1), Oct. 20, 1944 (not completed)

MOST PASSES ATTEMPTED WITHOUT COMPLETION
18—West Virginia vs. Temple, Oct. 18, 1946

MOST PASSES ATTEMPTED WITHOUT INTERCEPTION
72—Houston vs. TCU, Nov. 4, 1989 (completed 47)

MOST PASSES ATTEMPTED WITHOUT INTERCEPTION, BOTH TEAMS
114—Illinois (67) & Purdue (47), Oct. 12, 1985 (completed 67)

MOST CONSECUTIVE PASSES ATTEMPTED WITHOUT A RUSHING PLAY
32—North Carolina St. vs. Duke, Nov. 11, 1989 (3rd & 4th quarters, completed 16)

MOST PASSES COMPLETED
55—Wake Forest vs. Duke, Oct. 28, 1995 (attempted 78); Purdue vs. Wisconsin, Oct. 10, 1998 (attempted 83)

MOST PASSES COMPLETED, BOTH TEAMS
81—TCU (44) & Houston (37), Nov. 3, 1990 (attempted 135)

BEST PERFECT GAME (100 PCT.)
12 of 12—Iowa vs. Northwestern, Nov. 9, 2002

HIGHEST PERCENTAGE OF PASSES COMPLETED
(Min. 15-24 comps.) 96.0%—Tennessee vs. South Carolina, Oct. 31, 1998 (24 of 25)
(Min. 25-34 comps.) 92.6%—UCLA vs. Washington, Oct. 29, 1983 (25 of 27)
(Min. 35 comps.) 87.0%—South Carolina vs. Mississippi St., Oct. 14, 1995 (40 of 46)

HIGHEST PERCENTAGE OF PASSES COMPLETED, BOTH TEAMS (Min. 40 Completions)
84.6%—UCLA & Washington, Oct. 29, 1983 (44 of 52)

MOST PASSES HAD INTERCEPTED
10—Detroit vs. Oklahoma St., Nov. 28, 1942; California vs. UCLA, Oct. 21, 1978 (52 attempts)

MOST YARDS GAINED
771—Houston vs. SMU, Oct. 21, 1989 (completed 40 of 61)

MOST YARDS GAINED, BOTH TEAMS
1,253—TCU (690) & Houston (563), Nov. 3, 1990 (135 attempts)

FEWEST YARDS GAINED, BOTH TEAMS
Minus 13—North Carolina (-7 on 1 of 3 attempts) & Pennsylvania (-6 on 2 of 12 attempts), Nov. 13, 1943

MOST YARDS GAINED PER ATTEMPT
(Min. 30-39 atts.) 17.0—Nevada vs. Idaho, Oct. 24, 1998 (35 for 596)
(Min. 40 atts.) 15.9—UTEP vs. North Texas, Sept. 18, 1965 (40 for 634)

MOST YARDS GAINED PER COMPLETION
(Min. 15-24 comps.) 31.9—UTEP vs. New Mexico, Oct. 28, 1967 (16 for 510)
(Min. 25 comps.) 25.4—UTEP vs. North Texas, Sept. 18, 1965 (25 for 634)

MOST TOUCHDOWN PASSES
11—Houston vs. Eastern Wash., Nov. 17, 1990

MOST TOUCHDOWN PASSES, MAJOR-COLLEGE OPPONENTS
10—San Diego St. vs. New Mexico St., Nov. 15, 1969; Houston vs. SMU, Oct. 21, 1989

MOST TOUCHDOWN PASSES, BOTH TEAMS
14—Houston (11) & Eastern Wash. (3), Nov. 17, 1990

MOST TOUCHDOWN PASSES, BOTH TEAMS, MAJOR-COLLEGE OPPONENTS
13—San Diego St. (10) & New Mexico St. (3), Nov. 15, 1969; Hawaii (8) & BYU (5), Dec. 8, 2001

Punting

MOST PUNTS
39—Texas Tech vs. Centenary (La.), Nov. 11, 1939 (1,377 yards)
38—Centenary (La.) vs. Texas Tech, Nov. 11, 1939 (1,248 yards)

MOST PUNTS, BOTH TEAMS
77—Texas Tech (39) & Centenary (La.) (38), Nov. 11, 1939 (2,625 yards) (The game was played in a heavy downpour in Shreveport, Louisiana. Forty-two punts were returned, 19 went out of bounds, 10 were downed, 1 went into the end zone for a touchback, 4 were blocked and 1 was fair caught. Sixty-seven punts [34 by Texas Tech and 33 by Centenary] occurred on first-down plays, including 22 consecutively in the third and fourth quarters. The game was a scoreless tie.)

FEWEST PUNTS
0—By many teams. Most recent: Navy vs. Eastern Mich., November 11, 2006 (won 49-21)

FEWEST PUNTS BY A LOSING TEAM
0—By many teams. Most recent: Kentucky vs. Georgia, Oct. 25, 1997 (lost 23-13)

HIGHEST AVERAGE PER PUNT
(Min. 5-9 punts) 60.4—BYU vs. Wyoming, Oct. 8, 1983 (5 for 302)
(Min. 10 punts) 53.6—Oklahoma St. vs. Colorado, Nov. 13, 1971 (10 for 536)

HIGHEST AVERAGE PER PUNT, BOTH TEAMS (Min. 10 Punts)
55.3—BYU & Wyoming, Oct. 8, 1983 (11 for 608)

Punt Returns

MOST PUNT RETURNS
22—Texas Tech vs. Centenary (La.), Nov. 11, 1939 (112 yards)

MOST PUNT RETURNS, BOTH TEAMS
42—Texas Tech (22) & Centenary (La.) (20), Nov. 11, 1939 (233 yards)

MOST YARDS ON PUNT RETURNS
319—Texas A&M vs. North Texas, Sept. 21, 1946 (10 returns)

HIGHEST AVERAGE GAIN PER RETURN (Min. 5 Returns)
44.2—Denver vs. Colorado Col., Sept. 17, 1956 (6 for 265)

MOST TOUCHDOWNS SCORED ON PUNT RETURNS
3—Wisconsin vs. Iowa, Nov. 8, 1947; Wichita St. vs. Northern St., Oct. 22, 1949; LSU vs. Mississippi, Dec. 5, 1970; Holy Cross vs. Brown, Sept. 21, 1974; Arizona St. vs. Pacific, Nov. 15, 1975; Notre Dame vs. Pittsburgh, Nov. 16, 1996

Kickoff Returns

MOST KICKOFF RETURNS
14—Arizona St. vs. Nevada, Oct. 12, 1946 (290 yards)

MOST YARDS ON KICKOFF RETURNS
295—Cincinnati vs. Memphis, Oct. 30, 1971 (8 returns)

HIGHEST AVERAGE GAIN PER RETURN (Min. 6 Returns)
46.2—Southern California vs. Washington St., Nov. 7, 1970 (6 for 277)

MOST TOUCHDOWNS SCORED ON KICKOFF RETURNS
2—By many teams. Most recent: UCLA vs. Northwestern, Dec. 30, 2005 (Sun Bowl; consecutive returns, both onside kicks); New Mexico St. vs. Tulsa, Oct. 6, 2001; Minnesota vs. Iowa St., Sept. 13, 1997; Texas A&M vs. Rice, Oct. 23, 1993; BYU vs. Air Force, Nov. 11, 1989; Notre Dame vs. Michigan, Sept. 16, 1989; New Mexico St. vs. Drake, Oct. 15, 1983 (consecutive returns)

TOUCHDOWNS SCORED ON BACK-TO-BACK KICKOFF RETURNS, BOTH TEAMS
2—By many teams. Most recent: Ohio & Ball St., Oct. 22, 2005

Total Kick Returns

(Combined Punt and Kickoff Returns)

MOST YARDS ON KICK RETURNS
376—Florida St. vs. Virginia Tech, Nov. 16, 1974 (9 returns)

HIGHEST AVERAGE GAIN PER RETURN (Min. 7 Returns)
41.8—Florida St. vs. Virginia Tech, Nov. 16, 1974 (9 for 376)

Scoring

MOST POINTS SCORED
103—Wyoming vs. Northern Colo. (0), Nov. 5, 1949 (15 TDs, 13 PATs)

MOST POINTS SCORED AGAINST A MAJOR-COLLEGE OPPONENT
100—Houston vs. Tulsa (6), Nov. 23, 1968 (14 TDs, 13 PATs, 1 FG)

MOST POINTS SCORED, BOTH TEAMS (REGULATION)
133—San Jose St. (70) & Rice (63), Oct. 2, 2004

MOST POINTS SCORED BY A LOSING TEAM (REGULATION)
63—Rice vs. San Jose St. (70), Oct. 2, 2004

MOST POINTS SCORED BY A LOSING TEAM (OVERTIME)
63—Kentucky vs. Arkansas (71), Nov. 1, 2003 (7 ot)

MOST POINTS, BOTH TEAMS IN A TIE GAME
104—BYU (52) & San Diego St. (52), Nov. 16, 1991

MOST POINTS, BOTH TEAMS, AT THE END OF REGULATION, OVERTIME GAME
104—Akron (52) & Eastern Mich. (52), Nov. 24, 2001 (Akron won in three overtime periods, 65-62)

MOST POINTS, BOTH TEAMS, OVERTIME GAME
134—Arkansas (71) vs. Kentucky (63), Nov. 1, 2003 (7 ot)

MOST POINTS SCORED IN ONE QUARTER
49—Houston vs. Tulsa, Nov. 23, 1968 (4th); Davidson vs. Furman, Sept. 27, 1969 (2nd); Fresno St. vs. New Mexico, Oct. 5, 1991 (2nd)

MOST POINTS SCORED IN ONE QUARTER, BOTH TEAMS
61—San Jose St. (34) vs. Hawaii (27), Nov. 6, 1999 (4th; Hawaii won, 62-41)

MOST POINTS SCORED IN ONE HALF
76—Houston vs. Tulsa, Nov. 23, 1968 (2nd)

MOST TOUCHDOWNS SCORED
15—Wyoming vs. Northern Colo., Nov. 5, 1949 (9 rushing, 6 passing)

MOST TOUCHDOWNS SCORED, BOTH TEAMS
19—San Jose St. (10) & Rice (9), Oct. 2, 2004 (San Jose St. won, 70-63) (San Jose St. had 6 passing TDs, 2 rushing TDs, 1 punt return TD, 1 interception return TD; Rice had 8 rushing TDs, 1 interception return TD)

MOST EXTRA POINTS MADE BY KICKING
13—Wyoming vs. Northern Colo., Nov. 5, 1949 (attempted 15); Houston vs. Tulsa, Nov. 23, 1968 (attempted 14); Fresno St. vs. New Mexico, Oct. 5, 1991 (attempted 13)

MOST TWO-POINT ATTEMPTS SCORED
7—Pacific vs. San Diego St., Nov. 22, 1958 (attempted 9)

MOST DEFENSIVE EXTRA-POINT ATTEMPTS
2—Rice vs. Notre Dame, Nov. 5, 1988 (2 kick returns; 1 scored); Northern Ill. vs. Akron, Nov. 3, 1990 (2 interception returns); Oklahoma vs. California, Sept. 20, 1997 (2 kick returns; 1 scored); Texas vs. Iowa St., Oct. 3, 1998 (2 kick returns; 2 scored)

MOST DEFENSIVE EXTRA POINTS SCORED
2—Texas vs. Iowa St., Oct. 3, 1998 (2 kick returns)

MOST FIELD GOALS MADE
7—Western Mich. vs. Marshall, Sept. 29, 1984 (attempted 9); Nebraska vs. Missouri, Oct. 19, 1985 (attempted 7)

MOST FIELD GOALS MADE, BOTH TEAMS
9—La.-Lafayette (5) & Central Mich. (4), Sept. 9, 1989 (attempted 11)

MOST FIELD GOALS ATTEMPTED
9—Western Mich. vs. Marshall, Sept. 29, 1984 (made 7); North Texas vs. Florida Int'l, Oct. 7, 2006 (made 5)

MOST FIELD GOALS ATTEMPTED, BOTH TEAMS
16—North Texas (9) & Florida Int'l (7), Oct. 7, 2006 (made 8)

MOST FIELD GOALS MISSED
7—LSU vs. Florida, Nov. 25, 1972 (attempted 8)

First Downs

MOST FIRST DOWNS
45—Texas Tech vs. Iowa St., Oct. 11, 2003 (16 rush, 28 pass, 1 penalty)

MOST FIRST DOWNS, BOTH TEAMS
72—New Mexico (37) & San Diego St. (35), Sept. 27, 1986

FEWEST FIRST DOWNS BY A WINNING TEAM
0—North Carolina St. vs. Virginia, Sept. 30, 1944 (won 13-0); Michigan vs. Ohio St., Nov. 25, 1950 (won 9-3)

MOST FIRST DOWNS BY RUSHING
36—Nebraska vs. New Mexico St., Sept. 18, 1982

MOST FIRST DOWNS BY PASSING
33—Idaho vs. Middle Tenn., Oct. 6, 2001

Fumbles

MOST FUMBLES
17—Wichita St. vs. Florida St., Sept. 20, 1969 (lost 10)

MOST FUMBLES, BOTH TEAMS
27—Wichita St. (17) & Florida St. (10), Sept. 20, 1969 (lost 17)

MOST FUMBLES LOST
10—Wichita St. vs. Florida St., Sept. 20, 1969 (17 fumbles)

MOST FUMBLES LOST, BOTH TEAMS
17—Wichita St. (10) & Florida St. (7), Sept. 20, 1969 (27 fumbles)

MOST FUMBLES LOST IN A QUARTER
5—East Caro. vs. La.-Lafayette, Sept. 13, 1980 (3rd quarter on 5 consecutive possessions); San Diego St. vs. California, Sept. 18, 1982 (1st)

Penalties

MOST PENALTIES AGAINST
24—San Jose St. vs. Fresno St., Oct. 4, 1986 (199 yards)

MOST PENALTIES, BOTH TEAMS
36—San Jose St. (24) & Fresno St. (12), Oct. 4, 1986 (317 yards)

FEWEST PENALTIES, BOTH TEAMS
0—By many teams. Most recent: Army & Navy, Dec. 6, 1986

MOST YARDS PENALIZED
238—Arizona St. vs. UTEP, Nov. 11, 1961 (13 penalties)

MOST YARDS PENALIZED, BOTH TEAMS
421—Grambling (16 for 216 yards) & Texas Southern (17 for 205 yards), Oct. 29, 1977

Turnovers

(Number of Times Losing the Ball on Fumbles and Interceptions)

MOST TURNOVERS LOST
13—Georgia vs. Georgia Tech, Dec. 1, 1951 (5 fumbles, 8 interceptions)

MOST TURNOVERS, BOTH TEAMS
20—Wichita St. (12) & Florida St. (8), Sept. 20, 1969 (17 fumbles, 3 interceptions)

MOST TOTAL PLAYS WITHOUT A TURNOVER (Rushes, Passes, All Runbacks)
110—California vs. San Jose St., Oct. 5, 1968 (also did not fumble); Baylor vs. Rice, Nov. 13, 1976

MOST TOTAL PLAYS WITHOUT A TURNOVER, BOTH TEAMS
184—Arkansas (93) & Texas A&M (91), Nov. 2, 1968

MOST TOTAL PLAYS WITHOUT A TURNOVER OR A FUMBLE, BOTH TEAMS
158—Stanford (88) & Oregon (70), Nov. 2, 1957

MOST TURNOVERS BY A WINNING TEAM
11—Purdue vs. Illinois, Oct. 2, 1943 (9 fumbles, 2 interceptions; won 40-21)

MOST PASSES HAD INTERCEPTED BY A WINNING TEAM
7—Pittsburgh vs. Army, Nov. 15, 1980 (54 attempts; won 45-7); Florida vs. Kentucky, Sept. 11, 1993 (52 attempts; won 24-20)

MOST FUMBLES LOST BY A WINNING TEAM
9—Purdue vs. Illinois, Oct. 2, 1943 (10 fumbles; won 40-21); Arizona St. vs. Utah, Oct. 14, 1972 (10 fumbles; won 59-48)

Overtimes

MOST OVERTIME PERIODS
7—Arkansas (58) vs. Mississippi (56), Nov. 3, 2001; Arkansas (71) vs. Kentucky (63), Nov. 1, 2003; North Texas (25) vs. Florida Int'l (22), Oct. 7, 2006

MOST PLAYS IN OVERTIME GAME
103—Kentucky vs. Arkansas, Nov. 1, 2003 (7 overtime periods)

MOST PLAYS IN OVERTIME GAME, BOTH TEAMS
202—Kentucky (103) vs. Arkansas (99), Nov. 1, 2003 (7 overtime periods)

MOST POINTS SCORED IN OVERTIME PERIODS
47—Arkansas (71) vs. Kentucky (63), Nov. 1, 2003 (7 overtime periods)

MOST POINTS SCORED IN OVERTIME PERIODS, BOTH TEAMS
86—Arkansas (47) vs. Kentucky (39), Nov. 1, 2003 (7 overtime periods; Arkansas won, 71-63)

LARGEST WINNING MARGIN IN OVERTIME
13—Arizona St. (48) vs. Southern California (35), Oct. 19, 1996 (2 overtime periods); Central Mich. (36) vs. Eastern Mich. (23), Oct. 10, 1998 (one overtime period)

CONSECUTIVE OVERTIME GAMES (SEASON)
2—Southern California (41) vs. UCLA (48), Nov. 23, 1996 & Southern California (27) vs. Notre Dame (20), Nov. 30, 1996; Oklahoma St. (50) vs. Missouri (51), Oct. 25, 1997 & Oklahoma St. (25) vs. Texas A&M (28), Nov. 1, 1997; Cincinnati (38) vs. Houston (41), Oct. 18, 1997 & Cincinnati (34) vs. Miami (Ohio) (31), Oct. 25, 1997; San Diego St. (36) vs. New Mexico (33), Oct. 17, 1998 & San Diego St. (21) vs. Utah (20), Oct. 24, 1998; Mississippi (34) vs. Vanderbilt (37), Sept. 18, 1999 & Mississippi (24) vs. Auburn (17), Sept. 25, 1999; Wisconsin (28) vs. Cincinnati (25), Sept. 16, 2000 & Wisconsin (44) vs. Northwestern (47), Sept. 23, 2000; Oregon (56) vs. Arizona St. (55), Oct. 28, 2000 & Oregon (27) vs. Washington St. (24), Nov. 4, 2000; Rice (33) vs. Nevada (30), Oct. 20, 2001; & Rice (38) vs. Louisiana Tech (41), Oct. 27, 2001; New Mexico (44) vs. Utah St. (45), Oct. 19, 2002 & New Mexico (42) vs. Utah (35), Oct. 26, 2002; Utah St. (45) vs. New Mexico (42), Oct. 19, 2002 & Utah St. (48) vs. La.-Monroe (51), Oct. 26, 2002; Missouri (38) vs. Colorado (45), Nov. 9, 2002 & Missouri (33) vs. Texas A&M (27), Nov. 16, 2002; Northwestern (33) vs. Ohio St. (27), Oct. 2, 2004 & Northwestern (31) vs. Indiana (24), Oct. 9, 2004; Texas A&M (29) vs. Colorado (26), Oct. 23, 2004 & Baylor (35) vs. Texas A&M (34), Oct. 30, 2004; Central Mich. (24) vs. Western Mich. (21), Oct. 30, 2004 & Eastern Mich. (61) vs. Central Mich. (58), Nov. 6, 2004; TCU (23) vs. Utah (20), Sept. 15, 2005 & TCU (51) vs. BYU (50), Sept. 24, 2005; Miami (Fla.) (36) vs. Clemson (30), Sept. 17, 2005 & Boston College (16) vs. Clemson (13), Sept. 24, 2005

OVERTIME GAMES WITH SAME OPPONENT IN CONSECUTIVE YEARS
2—Cincinnati (34) vs. Miami (Ohio) (31), Oct. 25, 1997 & Cincinnati (30) vs. Miami (Ohio) (23), Sept. 28, 1996; Oregon (43) vs. Fresno St. (40), Sept. 20, 1997 & Oregon (30) vs. Fresno St. (27), Aug. 31, 1996; Missouri (51) vs. Oklahoma St. (50), Oct. 25, 1997 & Missouri (35) vs. Oklahoma St. (28), Oct. 26, 1996; Arizona (41) vs. California (38), Nov. 15, 1997 & Arizona (55) vs. California (56), Nov. 2, 1996; Eastern Mich. (61) vs. Central Mich. (58), Nov. 6, 2004 & Eastern Mich. (23) vs. Central Mich. (20), Sept. 24, 2005; Boston College (16) vs. Clemson (13), Sept. 24, 2005 & Boston College (34) vs. Clemson (33), Sept. 9, 2006

SINGLE GAME—Defense

Total Defense

FEWEST PLAYS ALLOWED
12—Centenary (La.) vs. Texas Tech, Nov. 11, 1939 (10 rushes, 2 passes; -1 yard)

FEWEST YARDS ALLOWED
Minus 47—Penn St. vs. Syracuse, Oct. 18, 1947 (-107 rushing, 60 passing; 49 plays)

MOST YARDS ALLOWED
1,021—SMU vs. Houston, Oct. 21, 1989 (250 rushing, 771 passing)

Rushing Defense

FEWEST RUSHES ALLOWED
5—Texas Tech vs. Houston, Nov. 25, 1989 (36 yards)

FEWEST RUSHING YARDS ALLOWED
Minus 109—Toledo vs. Northern Ill., Nov. 11, 1967 (33 rushes)

Pass Defense

FEWEST ATTEMPTS ALLOWED
0—By many teams. Most recent: Colorado vs. Oklahoma, Nov. 15, 1986

FEWEST COMPLETIONS ALLOWED
0—By many teams. Most recent: BYU vs. Rice, Nov. 9, 1996 (5 attempts)

LOWEST COMPLETION PERCENTAGE ALLOWED (Min. 10 Attempts)
0.0%—North Carolina vs. Penn St., Oct. 2, 1943 (0 of 12 attempts); Temple vs. West Virginia, Oct. 18, 1946 (0 of 18 attempts); San Jose St. vs. Cal St. Fullerton, Oct. 10, 1992 (0 of 11 attempts)

FEWEST YARDS ALLOWED
Minus 16—VMI vs. Richmond, Oct. 5, 1957 (2 completions)

MOST PASSES INTERCEPTED BY
11—Brown vs. Rhode Island, Oct. 8, 1949 (136 yards)

MOST PASSES INTERCEPTED BY AGAINST A MAJOR-COLLEGE OPPONENT
10—Oklahoma St. vs. Detroit, Nov. 28, 1942; UCLA vs. California, Oct. 21, 1978

MOST PASSES INTERCEPTED BY A LOSING TEAM
7—Army vs. Pittsburgh, Nov. 15, 1980 (54 attempts); Kentucky vs. Florida, Sept. 11, 1993 (52 attempts)

MOST YARDS ON INTERCEPTION RETURNS
240—Kentucky vs. Mississippi, Oct. 1, 1949 (6 returns)

MOST TOUCHDOWNS ON INTERCEPTION RETURNS
4—Houston vs. Texas, Nov. 7, 1987 (198 yards; 3 TDs in the 4th quarter)

Defensive Records

(Since 2000)

TACKLES FOR LOSS
23—North Carolina St. vs. Florida St., Nov. 11, 2004

PASS SACKS
15—TCU vs. Nevada, Sept. 9, 2000

PASSES DEFENDED (Pass Interceptions and Pass Breakups)
19—South Carolina vs. Alabama, Oct. 2, 2000

FORCED FUMBLES
7—Miami (Ohio) vs. North Carolina, Aug. 31, 2002; Virginia vs. South Carolina, Sept. 7, 2002; West Virginia vs. Cincinnati, Sept. 13, 2003; Miami (Ohio) vs. Buffalo, Nov. 5, 2005

First Downs

FEWEST FIRST DOWNS ALLOWED
0—By many teams. Most recent: North Carolina St. vs. Western Caro., Sept. 1, 1990

Opponent's Kicks Blocked

MOST OPPONENT'S PUNTS BLOCKED
4—SMU vs. Texas-Arlington, Sept. 30, 1944; Michigan vs. Ohio St., Nov. 25, 1950; Memphis vs. Arkansas, Sept. 26, 1992 (10 attempts); Central Mich. vs. Michigan St., Sept. 8, 2001 (6 attempts)

MOST OPPONENT'S PUNTS BLOCKED, ONE QUARTER
3—Purdue vs. Northwestern, Nov. 11, 1989 (4 attempts)

BLOCKED OPPONENT'S FIELD GOAL, PUNT AND EXTRA-POINT KICK
Oregon St. blocked each type of kick against Southern California, Sept. 14, 1996

MOST OPPONENT'S FIELD GOALS BLOCKED, ONE QUARTER
2—Southern California vs. California, Oct. 22, 1994; Wyoming vs. Fresno St., Nov. 18, 1995; Central Mich. vs. Kent St., Oct. 2, 2004

Turnovers Gained

(Number of Times Gaining the Ball on Fumbles and Interceptions)

MOST TURNOVERS GAINED
13—Georgia Tech vs. Georgia, Dec. 1, 1951 (5 fumbles, 8 interceptions)

MOST CONSECUTIVE OPPONENT'S SERIES RESULTING IN TURNOVERS
7—Florida vs. Florida St., Oct. 7, 1972 (4 fumbles lost, 3 interceptions; first seven series of the game)

Fumble Returns

(Since 1992)

MOST TOUCHDOWNS ON FUMBLE RETURNS
2—Toledo vs. Arkansas St., Sept. 5, 1992; Arizona vs. Illinois, Sept. 18, 1993; Duke vs. Wake Forest, Oct. 22, 1994 (both occurred in 1st quarter); Iowa vs. Minnesota, Nov. 19, 1994; Minnesota vs. Syracuse, Sept. 21, 1996; Florida vs. La.-Lafayette, Aug. 31, 1996; Arizona St. vs. Washington St., Nov. 1, 1997; Mississippi St. vs. BYU, Sept. 14, 2000; Notre Dame vs. Navy, Oct. 14, 2000; Southern California vs. UCLA, Nov. 22, 2003

LONGEST RETURN OF A FUMBLE
100—Rutgers vs. Pittsburgh, Oct. 28, 1995; Rice vs. UNLV, Nov. 14, 1998; UNLV vs. Baylor, Sept. 11, 1999

Defensive Extra Points

MOST DEFENSIVE EXTRA POINTS SCORED AGAINST
2—Iowa St. vs. Texas, Oct. 3, 1998 (2 kick returns)

MOST DEFENSIVE EXTRA-POINT ATTEMPTS AGAINST
2—Notre Dame vs. Rice, Nov. 5, 1988 (2 blocked kick returns, 1 scored); Akron vs. Northern Ill., Nov. 3, 1990 (2 interception returns); California vs. Oklahoma, Sept. 20, 1997 (2 kick returns; 1 scored); Iowa St. vs. Texas, Oct. 3, 1998 (2 kick returns; 2 scored)

MOST DEFENSIVE EXTRA POINTS SCORED BY BOTH TEAMS (Must Have One Scored by Each Team)
2—Kentucky (fumbled snap return) and LSU (blocked kick return), Oct. 17, 1998

Safeties

MOST SAFETIES
3—Penn St. vs. Maryland, Sept. 17, 1966; Arizona St. vs. Nebraska, Sept. 21, 1996; North Texas vs. La.-Lafayette, Sept. 27, 2003; Bowling Green vs. Miami (Ohio), Nov. 15, 2005

SEASON—Offense

Total Offense

MOST YARDS GAINED PER GAME
624.9—Houston, 1989 (6,874 in 11)

MOST YARDS GAINED
7,829—Hawaii, 2006 (14 games)

HIGHEST AVERAGE GAIN PER PLAY
8.6—Hawaii, 2006 (913 for 7,829)

GAINING 300 YARDS OR MORE PER GAME RUSHING AND 200 YARDS OR MORE PER GAME PASSING
Houston, 1968 (361.7 rushing, 200.3 passing); Arizona St., 1973 (310.2 rushing, 255.3 passing)

MOST PLAYS PER GAME
92.4—Notre Dame, 1970 (924 in 10)

MOST TOUCHDOWNS RUSHING AND PASSING
84—Nebraska, 1983; Hawaii, 2006
Nebraska holds per-game record at 7.0 (84 in 12)

Rushing

MOST YARDS GAINED PER GAME
472.4—Oklahoma, 1971 (5,196 in 11)

HIGHEST AVERAGE GAIN PER RUSH
7.6—Army, 1945 (424 for 3,238)

HIGHEST AVERAGE GAIN PER RUSH (Min. 500 Rushes)
7.0—Nebraska, 1995 (627 for 4,398)

MOST RUSHES PER GAME
73.9—Oklahoma, 1974 (813 in 11)

MOST TOUCHDOWNS RUSHING PER GAME
5.5—Nebraska, 1997 (66 in 12)

Passing

MOST YARDS GAINED PER GAME
511.3—Houston, 1989 (5,624 in 11)

MOST YARDS GAINED
6,179—Texas Tech, 2003 (13 games)

HIGHEST AVERAGE GAIN PER ATTEMPT (Min. 350 Attempts)
10.9—BYU, 1989 (433 for 4,732)

HIGHEST AVERAGE GAIN PER COMPLETION
(Min. 100-174 comps.) 19.1—Houston, 1968 (105 for 2,003)
(Min. 175-224 comps.) 18.0—Grambling, 1977 (187 for 3,360)
(Min. 225 comps.) 17.1—Florida, 1996 (234 for 4,007)

MOST PASSES ATTEMPTED PER GAME
63.1—Houston, 1989 (694 in 11)

MOST PASSES COMPLETED PER GAME
39.4—Houston, 1989 (434 in 11)

HIGHEST PERCENTAGE COMPLETED (Min. 150 Attempts)
73.5%—UCF, 1998 (302 of 411)

LOWEST PERCENTAGE HAD INTERCEPTED
(Min. 300-399 atts.) 0.84%—Fresno St., 1999 (3 of 359)
(Min. 400 atts.) 0.85%—Bowling Green, 2004 (4 of 472)

MOST TOUCHDOWN PASSES PER GAME
5.0—Houston, 1989 (55 in 11)

MOST TOUCHDOWN PASSES
62—Hawaii, 2006 (14 games)

FEWEST TOUCHDOWN PASSES
0—By 6 teams since 1975. Most recent: Vanderbilt, 1993 (11 games, 157 attempts)

HIGHEST PASSING EFFICIENCY RATING POINTS (Min. 150 Attempts)
185.9—Hawaii, 2006 (615 attempts, 444 completions, 12 interceptions, 6,178 yards, 62 TD passes)

A TEAM WITH THE NO. 1 & NO. 2 RECEIVERS
Houston, 1988 (Jason Phillips, No. 1, 9.82 catches per game & James Dixon, No. 2, 9.27 catches per game)

MOST 100-YARD RECEIVING GAMES IN A SEASON, ONE TEAM
20—Hawaii, 2006 (Davone Bass 6, Jason Rivers 5, Ryan Grice-Mullen 4, Ross Dickerson 2, Ian Sample 2 & Nate Ilaoa 1)

Punting

MOST PUNTS PER GAME
13.9—Tennessee, 1937 (139 in 10)

FEWEST PUNTS PER GAME
1.2—Hawaii, 2006 (17 in 14)

HIGHEST PUNTING AVERAGE
50.6—BYU, 1983 (24 for 1,215 yards)

HIGHEST PUNTING AVERAGE (Min. 40 Punts)
47.7—North Carolina, 1999 (81 for 3,863)

HIGHEST NET PUNTING AVERAGE
45.0—BYU, 1983 (24 for 1,215 yards, 134 yards in punts returned)

HIGHEST NET PUNTING AVERAGE (Min. 40 Punts)
44.9—San Diego St., 1996 (48 for 2,234 yards, 77 yards in punts returned)

Punt Returns

MOST PUNT RETURNS PER GAME
6.9—Texas A&M, 1943 (69 in 10)

FEWEST PUNT RETURNS PER GAME
0.5—Iowa St., 1996 (5 in 11)

MOST PUNT-RETURN YARDS PER GAME
114.5—Colgate, 1941 (916 in 8)

HIGHEST AVERAGE GAIN PER RETURN
(Min. 15-29 rets.) 25.2—Arizona St., 1952 (18 for 454)
(Min. 30 rets.) 22.4—Oklahoma, 1948 (43 for 963)

MOST TOUCHDOWNS SCORED ON PUNT RETURNS (Since 1966)
7—Southern Miss., 1987 (on 46 returns); Miami (Fla.), 2004 (on 42 returns)

Kickoff Returns

MOST KICKOFF RETURNS PER GAME
7.3—Cal St. Fullerton, 1990 (80 in 11)

FEWEST KICKOFF RETURNS PER GAME
0.7—Boston College, 1939 (7 in 10)

MOST KICKOFF-RETURN YARDS
1,588—Pittsburgh, 1996 (66 returns)

MOST KICKOFF-RETURN YARDS PER GAME
144.4—Pittsburgh, 1996 (1,588 in 11)

HIGHEST AVERAGE GAIN PER RETURN
(Min. 25-34 rets.) 30.3—Florida St., 1992 (27 for 819)
(Min. 35 rets.) 27.5—Rice, 1973 (39 for 1,074)

MOST TOUCHDOWNS SCORED ON KICKOFF RETURNS (Since 1966)
5—Tulsa, 2004 (on 52 returns)

Scoring

MOST POINTS PER GAME
56.0—Army, 1944 (504 in 9)

MOST POINTS SCORED
(13 games) 652—Texas, 2005
(14 games) 656—Hawaii, 2006

HIGHEST SCORING MARGIN
52.1—Army, 1944 (scored 504 points for 56.0 average and allowed 35 points for 3.9 average in 9 games)

MOST POINTS SCORED, TWO CONSECUTIVE GAMES
177—Houston, 1968 (77-3 vs. Idaho, Nov. 16, and 100-6 vs. Tulsa, Nov. 23)

MOST TOUCHDOWNS PER GAME
8.2—Army, 1944 (74 in 9)

MOST TOUCHDOWNS
89—Nebraska, 1983 (12 games)

MOST EXTRA POINTS MADE BY KICKING
83—Southern California, 2005 (13 games)
Nebraska, 1983, & Louisville, 2004 hold per-game record at 6.42 (77 in 12)

MOST CONSECUTIVE EXTRA POINTS MADE BY KICKING
77—Louisville, 2004 (Entire Season)

MOST TWO-POINT ATTEMPTS MADE PER GAME
2.2—Rutgers, 1958 (20 in 9, attempted 31)

MOST DEFENSIVE EXTRA-POINT ATTEMPTS
3—Rice, 1988 (1 vs. La.-Lafayette, Sept. 24, blocked kick return; 2 vs. Notre Dame, Nov. 5, 2 blocked kick returns, 1 scored)

MOST DEFENSIVE EXTRA POINTS SCORED
2—Texas, 1998 (2 vs. Iowa St., Oct. 3, 2 blocked kick returns)

MOST FIELD GOALS PER GAME
2.6—UCLA, 1984 (29 in 11); Cincinnati, 2000 (29 in 11)

First Downs

MOST FIRST DOWNS PER GAME
32.2—Texas Tech, 2003 (418 in 13)

MOST RUSHING FIRST DOWNS PER GAME
21.4—Oklahoma, 1974 (235 in 11)

MOST PASSING FIRST DOWNS PER GAME
23.5—Texas Tech, 2003 (305 in 13)

Fumbles

MOST FUMBLES
73—Cal St. Fullerton, 1992 (lost 41)

MOST FUMBLES LOST
41—Cal St. Fullerton, 1992 (73 fumbles)

FEWEST OWN FUMBLES LOST
1—Bowling Green, 1996; Miami (Ohio), 1998; Northern Ill., 2004

FEWEST OWN FUMBLES LOST IN TWO CONSECUTIVE SEASONS
3—Miami (Ohio), 1998-99 (1 in 1998; 2 in 1999)

MOST CONSECUTIVE FUMBLES LOST
14—Oklahoma, 1983 (during 5 games, Oct. 8-Nov. 5)

Penalties

MOST PENALTIES PER GAME
12.9—Grambling, 1977 (142 in 11, 1,476 yards)

MOST YARDS PENALIZED PER GAME
134.2—Grambling, 1977 (1,476 in 11, 142 penalties)

Turnovers (Giveaways)

(Fumbles Lost and Passes Had Intercepted)

FEWEST TURNOVERS
8—Clemson, 1940 (2 fumbles lost, 6 interceptions); Miami (Ohio), 1966 (4 fumbles lost, 4 interceptions); Notre Dame, 2000 (4 fumbles lost, 4 interceptions)

FEWEST TURNOVERS PER GAME
0.73—Notre Dame, 2000 (8 in 11 games)

MOST TURNOVERS
61—North Texas, 1971 (28 fumbles lost, 33 interceptions); Tulsa, 1976 (37 fumbles lost, 24 interceptions)

MOST TURNOVERS PER GAME
6.1—Mississippi St., 1949 (55 in 9 games; 30 fumbles lost, 25 interceptions)

SEASON—Defense

Total Defense

FEWEST YARDS ALLOWED PER GAME
69.9—Santa Clara, 1937 (559 in 8)

FEWEST RUSHING AND PASSING TOUCHDOWNS ALLOWED PER GAME
0.0—Duke, 1938; Tennessee, 1939

LOWEST AVERAGE YARDS ALLOWED PER PLAY
(Min. 400-599 plays) 1.7—Texas A&M, 1939 (447 for 763)
(Min. 600-699 plays) 2.5—Nebraska, 1967 (627 for 1,576)
(Min. 700 plays) 2.7—Toledo, 1971 (734 for 1,795)

MOST YARDS ALLOWED PER GAME
553.0—Maryland, 1993 (6,083 in 11)

Rushing Defense

FEWEST YARDS ALLOWED PER GAME
17.0—Penn St., 1947 (153 in 9)

MOST YARDS LOST BY OPPONENTS PER GAME
70.1—Wyoming, 1968 (701 in 10, 458 rushes)

LOWEST AVERAGE YARDS ALLOWED PER RUSH
(Min. 240-399 rushes) 0.6—Penn St., 1947 (240 for 153)
(Min. 400-499 rushes) 1.3—North Texas, 1966 (408 for 513)
(Min. 500 rushes) 2.1—Nebraska, 1971 (500 for 1,031)

Pass Defense

FEWEST YARDS ALLOWED PER GAME
13.1—Penn St., 1938 (105 in 8)

FEWEST YARDS ALLOWED PER ATTEMPT
(Min. 200-299 atts.) 3.4—Toledo, 1970 (251 for 856)
(Min. 300 atts.) 3.8—Notre Dame, 1967 (306 for 1,158)

FEWEST YARDS ALLOWED PER COMPLETION
(Min. 100-149 comps.) 8.8—Michigan, 1997 (145 for 1,275)
(Min. 150 comps.) 9.5—Notre Dame, 1993 (263 for 2,502)

LOWEST COMPLETION PERCENTAGE ALLOWED
(Min. 150-199 atts.) 31.1%—Virginia, 1952 (50 of 161)
(Min. 200 atts.) 33.3%—Notre Dame, 1967 (102 of 306)

FEWEST TOUCHDOWNS ALLOWED BY PASSING
0—By many teams. Most recent: LSU, 1959; North Texas, 1959

LOWEST PASS EFFICIENCY DEFENSIVE RATING (Since 1990)
65.7—Kansas St., 1999 (315 attempts, 118 completions, 21 interceptions, 1,364 yards, 5 TDs)

MOST PASSES INTERCEPTED BY PER GAME
4.1—Penn, 1940 (33 in 8)

HIGHEST PERCENTAGE INTERCEPTED BY (Min. 200 Attempts)
17.9%—Army, 1944 (36 of 201)

MOST YARDS GAINED ON INTERCEPTION RETURNS
782—Tennessee, 1971 (25 interceptions)

MOST INTERCEPTION YARDS PER GAME
72.5—Texas, 1943 (580 in 8)

HIGHEST AVERAGE PER INTERCEPTION RETURN
(Min. 10-14 ints.) 36.3—Oregon St., 1959 (12 for 436)
(Min. 15 ints.) 31.3—Tennessee, 1971 (25 for 782)

MOST TOUCHDOWNS ON INTERCEPTION RETURNS
7—Tennessee, 1971 (25 interceptions; 287 pass attempts against)

Punting

MOST OPPONENTS' PUNTS BLOCKED BY
11—Arkansas St., 1975 (11 games, 95 punts against)

Punt Returns

FEWEST RETURNS ALLOWED
5—Notre Dame, 1968 (52 yards); Nebraska, 1995 (12 yards)

FEWEST YARDS ALLOWED
2—Miami (Fla.), 1989 (12 returns)

LOWEST AVERAGE YARDS ALLOWED PER PUNT RETURN
0.2—Miami (Fla.), 1989 (12 for 2 yards)

Kickoff Returns

LOWEST AVERAGE YARDS ALLOWED PER KICKOFF RETURN
8.3—Richmond, 1951 (23 for 192 yards)

Opponents' Kicks Blocked

MOST PUNTS BLOCKED
Season
7—Central Mich., 2001

MOST FIELD GOALS BLOCKED
Season
6—Kentucky, 2004

MOST PAT KICKS BLOCKED
Season
6—Duke, 1993

Scoring

FEWEST POINTS ALLOWED PER GAME
0.0—Western Mich., 1922 (6 games); Duke, 1938 (9 games); Tennessee, 1939 (10 games)

MOST POINTS ALLOWED
566—Eastern Mich., 2002 (12 games)

MOST POINTS ALLOWED PER GAME
50.3—La.-Lafayette, 1997 (553 in 11)

Fumbles

MOST OPPONENTS' FUMBLES RECOVERED
36—North Texas, 1972; BYU, 1977

MOST TOUCHDOWNS SCORED ON FUMBLE RETURNS
7—Georgia Tech, 1998

Turnovers (Takeaways)

(Opponents' Fumbles Recovered and Passes Intercepted)

MOST OPPONENTS' TURNOVERS
57—Tennessee, 1970 (21 fumbles recovered, 36 interceptions)

MOST OPPONENTS' TURNOVERS PER GAME
5.4—Wyoming, 1950 (49 in 9); Penn, 1950 (49 in 9), UCLA; 1952 (49 in 9); UCLA, 1954 (49 in 9)

HIGHEST MARGIN OF TURNOVERS PER GAME OVER OPPONENTS
4.0—UCLA, 1952 (36 in 9; 13 giveaways vs. 49 takeaways)
Also holds total-margin record with 36

HIGHEST MARGIN OF TURNOVERS PER GAME BY OPPONENTS
3.1—Southern Miss., 1969 (31 in 10; 45 giveaways vs. 14 takeaways)

Defensive Extra Points

MOST DEFENSIVE EXTRA-POINT ATTEMPTS AGAINST
2—La.-Lafayette, 1988 (2 kick returns, none scored); Notre Dame, 1988 (2 kick returns, 1 scored); Akron, 1990 (2 interception returns, none scored); Oklahoma, 1992 (2 kick returns, 2 scored); Oklahoma, 1997 (2 kick returns, 1 scored); Texas, 1998 (2 kick returns, 2 scored)

MOST DEFENSIVE EXTRA POINTS SCORED AGAINST
2—Oklahoma, 1992 (vs. Texas Tech, Sept. 3, and vs. Oklahoma St., Nov. 14); Texas, 1998 (vs. Iowa St., Oct. 3)

Safeties

MOST SAFETIES
5—Wake Forest, 2001

Consecutive Records

MOST CONSECUTIVE VICTORIES
47—Oklahoma, 1953-57

MOST CONSECUTIVE GAMES WITHOUT DEFEAT (Includes pre-1937 teams)
63—Washington, 1907-17 (4 ties)

MOST CONSECUTIVE GAMES WITHOUT DEFEAT (Modern Era, 1937-present)
48—Oklahoma, 1953-57 (1 tie)

MOST CONSECUTIVE LOSSES
34—Northwestern, from Sept. 22, 1979, vs. Syracuse through Sept. 18, 1982, vs. Miami (Ohio) (ended with 31-6 victory over Northern Ill., Sept. 25, 1982)

MOST CONSECUTIVE GAMES WITHOUT A VICTORY ON THE ROAD
46—Northwestern (including one tie), from Nov. 23, 1974, through Oct. 30, 1982

MOST CONSECUTIVE GAMES WITHOUT A TIE (Includes Bowl Games)
345—Miami (Fla.), from Nov. 11, 1968, through 1995 season (after 1995, tiebreaker used in FBS)

MOST CONSECUTIVE GAMES WITHOUT BEING SHUT OUT
361—BYU, Oct. 3, 1975 through Nov. 15, 2003 (ended with 3-0 loss to Utah, Nov. 22, 2003)

MOST CONSECUTIVE SHUTOUTS (Regular Season)
17—Tennessee, from Nov. 5, 1938, through Oct. 12, 1940

MOST CONSECUTIVE QUARTERS OPPONENTS HELD SCORELESS (Regular Season)
71—Tennessee, from 2nd quarter vs. LSU, Oct. 29, 1938, to 2nd quarter vs. Alabama, Oct. 19, 1940

MOST CONSECUTIVE VICTORIES AT HOME
58—Miami (Fla.) (Orange Bowl), from Oct. 12, 1985, to Sept. 24, 1994 (lost to Washington, 38-20)

MOST CONSECUTIVE VICTORIES OVER ASSOCIATED PRESS TOP 25 TEAMS
21—Southern California, 2002-06

MOST CONSECUTIVE WINNING SEASONS (All-Time)
42—Notre Dame, 1889-32 (no teams in 1890 & 1891)

MOST CONSECUTIVE WINNING SEASONS (After 1932)
40—Nebraska, 1962-01

MOST CONSECUTIVE NON-LOSING SEASONS
49—Penn St., 1939-87 (includes two .500 seasons)

MOST CONSECUTIVE LOSING SEASONS
28—Oregon St., 1971-98

MOST CONSECUTIVE NON-WINNING SEASONS
28—Rice, 1964-91 (includes two .500 seasons)

MOST CONSECUTIVE SEASONS WINNING NINE OR MORE GAMES
33—Nebraska, 1969-01

MOST CONSECUTIVE SEASONS PLAYING IN A BOWL GAME
35—Nebraska, 1969-03

MOST CONSECUTIVE GAMES SCORING ON A PASS
62—Florida, from Oct. 1, 1992, to Oct. 4, 1997

MOST CONSECUTIVE GAMES PASSING FOR 200 YARDS OR MORE
64—BYU, from Sept. 13, 1980, through Oct. 19, 1985

MOST CONSECUTIVE GAMES INTERCEPTING A PASS (Includes Bowl Games)
39—Virginia, from Nov. 6, 1993, through Nov. 29, 1996

MOST CONSECUTIVE GAMES WITHOUT POSTING A SHUTOUT
283—New Mexico St., from Sept. 21, 1974, to Sept. 29, 2001 (31-0 over La.-Monroe)

MOST CONSECUTIVE EXTRA POINTS MADE
262—Syracuse, from Nov. 18, 1978, to Sept. 9, 1989 (By the following kickers: Dave Jacobs, last PAT of 1978; Gary Anderson, 72 from 1979 through 1981; Russ Carpentieri, 17 in 1982; Don McAulay, 62 from 1983 through 1985; Tim Vesling, 71 in 1986 and 1987; Kevin Greene, 37 in 1988; John Biskup, 2 in 1989.)

MOST CONSECUTIVE STADIUM SELLOUTS
282—Nebraska (current), from 1962

Additional Records

HIGHEST-SCORING TIE GAME
52-52—BYU & San Diego St., Nov. 16, 1991

MOST TIE GAMES IN A SEASON
4—Temple, 1937 (9 games); UCLA, 1939 (10 games); Central Mich., 1991 (11 games)

MOST SCORELESS TIE GAMES IN A SEASON
4—Temple, 1937 (9 games)

MOST CONSECUTIVE SCORELESS TIE GAMES
2—Georgia Tech, 1938, vs. Florida, Nov. 19 & vs. Georgia, Nov. 26; Alabama, 1954, vs. Georgia, Oct. 30 & vs. Tulane, Nov. 6

LAST TIE GAME
Nov. 25, 1995—Wisconsin 3, Illinois 3

LAST SCORELESS TIE GAME
Nov. 19, 1983—Oregon & Oregon St.

LONGEST DRIVE IN A GAME
26 plays, 14:26 elapsed time—Navy vs. New Mexico, Dec. 30, 2004 (Emerald Bowl).
Navy started at its one-yard line with 1:41 left in the third quarter and drove 94 yards to the New Mexico five-yard line. The drive ended with a 22-yard field goal with 2:15 remaining in the game. Navy won, 34-19.

MOST POINTS OVERCOME TO WIN A GAME (Between FBS Teams)
35—Michigan St. (41) vs. Northwestern (38), Oct. 21, 2006 (trailed 38-3 with 9:54 remaining in 3rd quarter)
31—Maryland (42) vs. Miami (Fla.) (40), Nov. 10, 1984 (trailed 31-0 with 12:35 remaining in 3rd quarter); Ohio St. (41) vs. Minnesota (37), Oct. 28, 1989 (trailed 31-0 with 4:29 remaining in 2nd quarter)
30—California (42) vs. Oregon (41), Oct. 2, 1993 (trailed 30-0 in 2nd quarter)

MOST POINTS OVERCOME IN SECOND HALF TO WIN A GAME
35—Michigan St. (41) vs. Northwestern (38), Oct. 21, 2006 (trailed 38-3 with 9:54 remaining in 3rd quarter)

MOST POINTS SCORED IN FOURTH QUARTER TO WIN OR TIE A GAME
36—BYU (50) vs. Washington St. (36), Sept. 15, 1990 (trailed 29-14 at start of 4th quarter)
34—Northern Ill. (48) vs. Miami (Ohio) (41), Oct. 12, 2002 (trailed 27-14 at start of 4th quarter)
29—Bowling Green (43) vs. Northwestern (42), Nov. 17, 2001 (trailed 28-14 at start of 4th quarter)
28—Utah (28) vs. Arizona (27), Nov. 4, 1972 (trailed 27-0 beginning 4th quarter); Washington St. (49) vs. Stanford (42), Oct. 20, 1984 (trailed 42-14 with 5:38 remaining in 3rd quarter and scored 35 consecutive points); Florida St. (31) vs. Florida (31), Nov. 26, 1994 (trailed 31-3 beginning 4th quarter); Middle Tenn. (39) vs. New Mexico St. (35), Oct. 27, 2001 (trailed 35-11 beginning 4th quarter)

MOST POINTS SCORED IN A BRIEF PERIOD OF TIME BY ONE TEAM
49 in 6:25 of possession time—Fresno St. (70) vs. Utah St. (21), Dec. 1, 2001 (7 TDs, 7 PATs. The longest drive lasted 1:42 during the first and second quarters)
41 in 2:55 of possession time during six drives—Nebraska (69) vs. Colorado (19), Oct. 22, 1983 (6 TDs, 5 PATs in 3rd quarter. Drives occurred during 9:10 of total playing time in the period)
41 in 4:30 of possession time during six drives—Northern Ill. (48) vs. Miami (Ohio) (41), Oct. 12, 2002 (6 TDs, 5 PATs in final two periods)
28 in 1:32 of possession time during four drives—Southern California (70) vs. Arkansas (17), Sept. 17, 2005 (4 TDs, 4 PATs in 1st quarter. Drives occurred during 7:42 of total playing time in the period)
21 in 1:00 of total playing time—Miami (Ohio) (51) vs. Akron (23), Oct. 15, 2005 (3 TDs, 3 PATs in 4th quarter; rush TD at 6:46, pass TD at 6:07 and rush TD at 5:46)
21 in 1:04 of total playing time—Kent St. (32) vs. Akron (17), Oct. 5, 1996 (3 TDs, 3 PATs in 4th quarter; rush TD at 2:01, rush TD at 1:33 and interception return TD at 0:57)
21 in 1:24 of total playing time—San Jose St. (42) vs. Fresno St. (7), Nov. 17, 1990 (3 TDs, 3 PATs in 2nd quarter; 1:17 of possession time on two drives and one intercepted pass returned for a TD)
20 in 0:55 of total playing time—Colorado St. (55) vs. San Jose St. (20), Oct. 11, 1997 (3 TDs, 2 PATs in 4th quarter; pass TD at 10:39, interception return TD at 10:16 and interception return TD at 9:45)
15 in :10 of total playing time—Utah (22) vs. Air Force (21), Oct. 21, 1995 (2 TDs, 2-point conversion, 1 PAT. Drives occurred during :41 of 4th quarter)

MOST POINTS SCORED IN A BRIEF PERIOD OF TIME BY BOTH TEAMS
29 in 1:34 of posession time during four drives (4th quarter)—Hawaii (62) vs. San Jose St. (41), Nov. 6, 1999 (4 TDs, 1 PAT, two 2-point conversions). San Jose St. scores TDs on a blocked punt and pass reception (adds two 2-point conversions); Hawaii scores TDs on rush and interception return (adds PAT)
20 in 0:28 of possession time during third and fourth quarters—Southern California (47) vs. UCLA (22), Nov. 22, 2003 (3 TDs, 2 PATs)
16 in 0:29 of possession time during fourth quarter—Northwestern (27) vs. Michigan St. (26), Sept. 29, 2001 (2 TDs, 1 PAT, 1 FG)

MOST POSSESSION TIME IN A QUARTER
15:00—Auburn vs. South Carolina (third quarter, 30 plays for 136 yards), Sept. 28, 2006

MOST CONSECUTIVE GAMES SCORING 20 POINTS
63—Southern California, 2002-06

MOST IMPROVED WON-LOST RECORD
8½ games—Hawaii, 1999 (9-4-0, including a bowl win) from 1998 (0-12-0)

MOST IMPROVED WON-LOST RECORD AFTER WINLESS SEASON
8½ games—Hawaii, 1999 (9-4-0, including a bowl win) from 1998 (0-12-0)

MOST GAMES PLAYED IN A SEASON (Modern Era, 1937-present)
15—BYU, 1996; Kansas St., 2003 (See Most Games Played List following Annual Team Champions, page 65)

MOST VICTORIES IN A SEASON (Modern Era, 1937-present)
14—BYU, 1996; Ohio St., 2002 (See Most Victories in a Season List following Annual Team Champions, page 65)

MOST LOSSES IN A SEASON (Modern Era, 1937-present)
13—Army, 2003 (0-13 record) (See Most Losses in a Season List following Annual Team Champions, page 65)

Annual Champions, All-Time Leaders

Total Offense

CAREER YARDS PER GAME

(Minimum 5,500 yards; Player must have concluded his career)

Player, Team	Years	G	Plays	Yards	TDR‡	Yd. PG
Tim Rattay, Louisiana Tech	1997-99	33	1,705	12,618	117	382.4
Chris Vargas, Nevada	1992-93	20	872	6,417	48	320.9
Timmy Chang, Hawaii	$2000-04	53	*2,587	*16,910	123	319.1
Ty Detmer, BYU	1988-91	46	1,795	14,665	*135	318.8
Daunte Culpepper, UCF	1996-98	33	1,468	10,344	91	313.5
Mike Perez, San Jose St.	1986-87	20	875	6,182	37	309.1
Josh Wallwork, Wyoming	1995-96	22	845	6,753	60	307.0
Doug Gaynor, Long Beach St.	1984-85	22	1,067	6,710	45	305.0
Josh Heupel, Oklahoma	1999-00	23	923	6,898	62	299.9
Tony Eason, Illinois	1981-82	22	1,016	6,589	43	299.5
Chad Pennington, Marshall	1997-99	36	1,433	10,758	104	298.9
Luke McCown, Louisiana Tech	2000-03	43	2,050	12,731	97	296.1
Omar Jacobs, Bowling Green	2003-05	25	964	7,388	78	295.5
Drew Brees, Purdue	1997-00	40	1,754	11,815	97	295.4
David Klingler, Houston	1988-91	32	1,439	9,363	93	292.6
David Neill, Nevada	1998-01	40	1,376	11,664	87	291.6
Ben Roethlisberger, Miami (Ohio)	2001-03	38	1,573	11,075	91	291.4
Steve Sarkisian, BYU	1995-96	25	953	7,253	56	290.1
Chris Redman, Louisville	1996-99	42	1,846	12,129	87	288.8
Kliff Kingsbury, Texas Tech	1999-02	43	2,156	12,263	99	285.2
Steve Young, BYU	1981-83	31	1,177	8,817	74	284.4
Tim Couch, Kentucky	1996-98	29	1,338	8,160	78	281.4
Byron Leftwich, Marshall	$1998-02	43	1,621	12,084	96	281.0
Philip Rivers, North Carolina St.	2000-03	49	1,963	13,582	113	277.2
Ryan Schneider, UCF	2000-03	39	1,472	10,703	90	274.4
Kevin Kolb, Houston	2003-06	50	2,037	13,715	106	274.3

**Record. ‡Touchdowns-responsible-for are player's TDs scored and passed for. $See page 10 for explanation.*

SEASON YARDS PER GAME

Player, Team	Year	G	Plays	Yards	TDR‡	Yd. PG
David Klingler, Houston	†1990	11	704	5,221	55	474.6
B.J. Symons, Texas Tech	†2003	13	798	*5,976	52	459.7
Andre Ware, Houston	†1989	11	628	4,661	49	423.7
Colt Brennan, Hawaii	†2006	14	645	5,915	*63	422.5
Ty Detmer, BYU	1990	12	635	5,022	45	418.5
Tim Rattay, Louisiana Tech	†1998	12	602	4,840	47	403.3
Mike Maxwell, Nevada	†1995	9	443	3,623	34	402.6
Chris Redman, Louisville	1998	10	513	4,009	31	400.9
Steve Young, BYU	†1983	11	531	4,346	41	395.1
Chris Vargas, Nevada	†1993	11	535	4,332	35	393.8
Scott Mitchell, Utah	†1988	11	589	4,299	29	390.8
Sonny Cumbie, Texas Tech	†2004	12	694	4,575	34	381.3
Tim Rattay, Louisiana Tech	†1999	10	562	3,810	35	381.0
Chase Holbrook, New Mexico St.	2006	12	647	4,541	38	378.4
Daunte Culpepper, UCF	1998	11	543	4,153	40	377.5
Tim Couch, Kentucky	1998	11	617	4,151	37	377.4
David Neill, Nevada	1998	9	409	3,351	31	372.3
Colt Brennan, Hawaii	†2005	12	614	4,455	37	371.3
Ty Detmer, BYU	1989	12	497	4,433	38	369.4
Cody Hodges, Texas Tech	2005	12	640	4,429	34	369.1
Troy Kopp, Pacific	1990	9	485	3,276	32	364.0
Tim Rattay, Louisiana Tech	†1997	11	541	3,968	35	360.7
Omar Jacobs, Bowling Green	2004	12	557	4,302	45	358.5
Drew Brees, Purdue	†2000	11	564	3,939	29	358.1
Byron Leftwich, Marshall	†2002	12	528	4,267	33	355.6
Rex Grossman, Florida	†2001	11	429	3,904	39	354.9
Philip Rivers, North Carolina St.	2003	13	561	4,600	34	353.8

**Record. †National champion. ‡Touchdowns-responsible-for are player's TDs scored and passed for.*

CAREER YARDS

Player, Team	Years	Plays	Yards Rush	Yards Pass	Yards Total	Avg.
Timmy Chang, Hawaii	$2000-04	*2,587	-162	*17,072	16,910	6.54
Ty Detmer, BYU	1988-91	1,795	-366	15,031	14,665	8.17
Kevin Kolb, Houston	2003-06	2,037	751	12,964	13,715	6.73
Philip Rivers, North Carolina St.	2000-03	1,422	98	13,484	13,582	#9.15
Brad Smith, Missouri	2002-05	2,283	4,289	8,799	13,088	5.73
Luke McCown, Louisiana Tech	2000-03	2,049	65	12,666	12,731	6.21
Tim Rattay, Louisiana Tech	1997-99	1,705	-128	12,746	12,618	7.40
Kliff Kingsbury, Texas Tech	1999-02	2,156	-166	12,429	12,263	5.69
Chris Redman, Louisville	1996-99	1,846	-412	12,541	12,129	6.57
Byron Leftwich, Marshall	$1998-02	1,621	181	11,903	12,084	7.45
Brady Quinn, Notre Dame	2003-06	1,856	182	11,762	11,944	6.44
Drew Brees, Purdue	1997-00	1,754	906	10,909	11,815	6.74
David Neill, Nevada	1998-01	1,727	761	10,903	11,664	6.75
Gino Guidugli, Cincinnati	2001-04	1,791	208	11,453	11,661	6.51
Brett Basanez, Northwestern	2002-05	1,975	996	10,580	11,576	5.86

Player, Team	Years	Plays	Yards Rush	Pass	Total	Avg.
Charlie Frye, Akron	2001-04	1,811	429	11,049	11,478	6.34
Antwaan Randle El, Indiana	1998-01	1,917	3,895	7,469	11,364	5.93
Chris Leak, Florida	2003-06	1,769	137	11,213	11,350	6.42
Doug Flutie, Boston College	1981-84	1,558	738	10,579	11,317	7.26
David Greene, Georgia	2001-04	1,644	-258	11,528	11,270	6.86
Carson Palmer, Southern California	$1998-02	1,758	-295	11,388	11,093	6.31
Tim Lester, Western Mich.	1996-99	1,747	-218	11,299	11,081	6.34
John Beck, BYU	2003-06	1,685	25	11,021	11,046	6.56
Jordan Palmer, UTEP	$2002-06	1,643	-43	11,084	11,041	6.72
Ben Roethlisberger, Miami (Ohio)	2001-03	1,573	246	10,829	11,075	7.04
Peyton Manning, Tennessee	1994-97	1,534	-181	11,201	11,020	7.18

**Record. $See page 10 for explanation. #Record for minimum of 7,500 yards.*

CAREER YARDS RECORD PROGRESSION
(Record Yards—Player, Team, Seasons Played)

3,481—Davey O'Brien, TCU, 1936-38; **3,882**—Paul Christman, Missouri, 1938-40; **4,602**—Frank Sinkwich, Georgia, 1940-42; **4,627**—Bob Fenimore, Oklahoma St., 1943-46; **4,871**—Charlie Justice, North Carolina, 1946-49; **5,903**—Johnny Bright, Drake, 1949-51; **6,354**—Virgil Carter, BYU, 1964-66; **6,568**—Steve Ramsey, North Texas, 1967-69; **7,887**—Jim Plunkett, Stanford, 1968-70; **8,074**—Gene Swick, Toledo, 1972-75; **8,444**—Mark Herrmann, Purdue, 1977-80; **9,723**—Jim McMahon, BYU, 1977-78, 1980-81; **11,317**—Doug Flutie, Boston College, 1981-84; **14,665**—Ty Detmer, BYU, 1988-91; **16,910**—Timmy Chang, Hawaii, $2000-04.

$See page 10 for explanation.

SEASON YARDS

Player, Team	Year	G	Plays	Yards Rush	Pass	Total	Avg.
B.J. Symons, Texas Tech	†2003	13	798	143	*5,833	5,976	7.49
Colt Brennan, Hawaii	†2006	14	645	366	5,549	5,915	*9.17
David Klingler, Houston	†1990	11	704	81	5,140	5,221	7.42
Ty Detmer, BYU	1990	12	635	-106	5,188	5,022	7.91
Kliff Kingsbury, Texas Tech	2002	14	*814	-114	5,017	4,903	6.02
Tim Rattay, Louisiana Tech	†1998	12	602	-103	4,943	4,840	8.04
Andre Ware, Houston	†1989	11	628	-38	4,699	4,661	7.42
Josh Harris, Bowling Green	2003	14	709	830	3,813	4,643	6.55
Jim McMahon, BYU	†1980	12	540	56	4,571	4,627	8.57
Philip Rivers, North Carolina St.	2003	13	561	109	4,491	4,600	8.20
Ben Roethlisberger, Miami (Ohio)	2003	14	562	111	4,486	4,597	8.18
Sonny Cumbie, Texas Tech	†2004	12	694	-167	4,742	4,575	6.59
Chase Holbrook, New Mexico St.	2006	12	647	-78	4,619	4,541	7.02
Graham Harrell, Texas Tech	2006	13	649	-78	4,555	4,477	6.90
Timmy Chang, Hawaii	2002	14	663	-17	4,474	4,457	6.72
Colt Brennan, Hawaii	†2005	12	614	154	4,301	4,455	7.26
Ty Detmer, BYU	1989	12	497	-127	4,560	4,433	8.92
Cody Hodges, Texas Tech	2005	12	640	191	4,238	4,429	6.92
Ryan Dinwiddie, Boise St.	2003	14	527	43	4,356	4,399	8.35
David Carr, Fresno St.	2001	13	564	97	4,299	4,396	7.79
Steve Young, BYU	†1983	11	531	444	3,902	4,346	8.18
Chris Vargas, Nevada	†1993	11	535	67	4,265	4,332	8.10
Omar Jacobs, Bowling Green	2004	12	557	300	4,002	4,302	7.72
Scott Mitchell, Utah	†1988	11	589	-23	4,322	4,299	7.30
Cody Pickett, Washington	2002	13	698	-185	4,458	4,273	6.12
Timmy Chang, Hawaii	2004	13	639	15	4,258	4,273	6.69
Byron Leftwich, Marshall	†2002	12	528	-1	4,268	4,267	8.08
Byron Leftwich, Marshall	2001	12	534	92	4,132	4,224	7.91
Josh Wallwork, Wyoming	†1996	12	525	119	4,090	4,209	8.02
Daunte Culpepper, UCF	1998	11	543	463	3,690	4,153	7.65
Tim Couch, Kentucky	1998	11	617	-124	4,275	4,151	6.73
Robbie Bosco, BYU	1985	13	578	-132	4,273	4,141	7.16
Timmy Chang, Hawaii	2003	13	644	-60	4,199	4,139	6.43
Vince Young, Texas	2005	13	480	1,050	3,036	4,086	8.51
Chris Weinke, Florida St.	2000	12	461	-97	4,167	4,070	8.83
Brett Basanez, Northwestern	2005	12	610	423	3,622	4,045	6.63
Chris Redman, Louisville	1998	10	513	-33	4,042	4,009	7.81
Brady Quinn, Notre Dame	2005	12	520	90	3,919	4,009	7.71
Ty Detmer, BYU	†1991	12	478	-30	4,031	4,001	8.37

**Record. †National champion.*

SINGLE-GAME YARDS

Yds.	Rush	Pass	Player, Team (Opponent)	Date
732	16	716	David Klingler, Houston (Arizona St.)	Dec. 2, 1990
696	6	690	Matt Vogler, TCU (Houston)	Nov. 3, 1990
681	20	661	B.J. Symons, Texas Tech (Mississippi)	Sept. 27, 2003
657	20	637	Brian Lindgren, Idaho (Middle Tenn.)	Oct. 6, 2001
625	-6	631	Scott Mitchell, Utah (Air Force)	Oct. 15, 1988
625	62	563	David Klingler, Houston (TCU)	Nov. 3, 1990
618	32	586	B.J. Symons, Texas Tech (North Carolina St.)	Sept. 20, 2003
612	-1	613	Jimmy Klingler, Houston (Rice)	Nov. 28, 1992
604	-39	643	Cody Hodges, Texas Tech (Kansas St.)	Oct. 15, 2005
603	4	599	Ty Detmer, BYU (San Diego St.)	Nov. 16, 1991
601	37	564	Troy Kopp, Pacific (New Mexico St.)	Oct. 20, 1990
599	86	513	Virgil Carter, BYU (UTEP)	Nov. 5, 1966
597	-22	619	John Walsh, BYU (Utah St.)	Oct. 30, 1993
594	-28	622	Jeremy Leach, New Mexico (Utah)	Nov. 11, 1989
585	-36	621	Dave Wilson, Illinois (Ohio St.)	Nov. 8, 1980

Yds.	Rush	Pass	Player, Team (Opponent)	Date
582	11	571	Marc Wilson, BYU (Utah)	Nov. 5, 1977
582	-29	611	David Neill, Nevada (New Mexico St.)	Oct. 10, 1998
578	6	572	David Klingler, Houston (Eastern Wash.)	Nov. 17, 1990
578	-14	592	Chris Redman, Louisville (East Caro.)	Nov. 14, 1998
578	144	434	Kevin Kolb, Houston (TCU)	Oct. 25, 2003
574	15	559	Colt Brennan, Hawaii (Arizona St.)	Dec. 24, 2006
568	11	557	John Dutton, Nevada (Boise St.)	Nov. 8, 1997
568	-22	590	Tim Rattay, Louisiana Tech (Nebraska)	Aug. 29, 1998
562	25	537	Ty Detmer, BYU (Washington St.)	Sept. 7, 1989
561	46	515	Colt Brennan, Hawaii (New Mexico St.)	Oct. 15, 2005
559	13	546	Cody Ledbetter, New Mexico St. (UNLV)	Nov. 18, 1995
558	15	543	Nick Rolovich, Hawaii (BYU)	Dec. 8, 2001
554	9	545	Rusty LaRue, Wake Forest (North Carolina St.)	Nov. 18, 1995
552	-13	565	Jim McMahon, BYU (Utah)	Nov. 21, 1981

ANNUAL CHAMPIONS

Year	Player, Team	Class	Plays	Yards Rush	Pass	Total
1937	Byron "Whizzer" White, Colorado	Sr.	224	1,121	475	1,596
1938	Davey O'Brien, TCU	Sr.	291	390	1,457	1,847
1939	Kenny Washington, UCLA	Sr.	259	811	559	1,370
1940	Johnny Knolla, Creighton	Sr.	298	813	607	1,420
1941	Bud Schwenk, Washington-St. Louis	Sr.	354	471	1,457	1,928
1942	Frank Sinkwich, Georgia	Sr.	341	795	1,392	2,187
1943	Bob Hoernschemeyer, Indiana	Fr.	355	515	1,133	1,648
1944	Bob Fenimore, Oklahoma St.	So.	241	897	861	1,758
1945	Bob Fenimore, Oklahoma St.	Jr.	203	1,048	593	1,641
1946	Travis Tidwell, Auburn	Fr.	339	772	943	1,715
1947	Fred Enke, Arizona	So.	329	535	1,406	1,941
1948	Stan Heath, Nevada	Sr.	233	-13	2,005	1,992
1949	Johnny Bright, Drake	So.	275	975	975	1,950
1950	Johnny Bright, Drake	Jr.	320	1,232	1,168	2,400
1951	Dick Kazmaier, Princeton	Sr.	272	861	966	1,827
1952	Ted Marchibroda, Detroit	Sr.	305	176	1,637	1,813
1953	Paul Larson, California	Jr.	262	141	1,431	1,572
1954	George Shaw, Oregon	Sr.	276	178	1,358	1,536
1955	George Welsh, Navy	Sr.	203	29	1,319	1,348
1956	John Brodie, Stanford	Sr.	295	9	1,633	1,642
1957	Bob Newman, Washington St.	Jr.	263	53	1,391	1,444
1958	Dick Bass, Pacific	Jr.	218	1,361	79	1,440
1959	Dick Norman, Stanford	Jr.	319	55	1,963	2,018
1960	Bill Kilmer, UCLA	Sr.	292	803	1,086	1,889
1961	Dave Hoppmann, Iowa St.	Jr.	320	920	718	1,638
1962	Terry Baker, Oregon St.	Sr.	318	538	1,738	2,276
1963	George Mira, Miami (Fla.)	Sr.	394	163	2,155	2,318
1964	Jerry Rhome, Tulsa	Sr.	470	258	2,870	3,128
1965	Bill Anderson, Tulsa	Sr.	580	-121	3,464	3,343
1966	Virgil Carter, BYU	Sr.	388	363	2,182	2,545
1967	Sal Olivas, New Mexico St.	Sr.	368	-41	2,225	2,184
1968	Greg Cook, Cincinnati	Sr.	507	-62	3,272	3,210
1969	Dennis Shaw, San Diego St.	Sr.	388	12	3,185	3,197

Beginning in 1970, ranked on per-game (instead of total) yards		Class	G	Plays	Rush	Pass	Total	Avg.
1970	Pat Sullivan, Auburn	Jr.	10	333	270	2,586	2,856	285.6
1971	Gary Huff, Florida St.	Jr.	11	386	-83	2,736	2,653	241.2
1972	Don Strock, Virginia Tech	Sr.	11	480	-73	3,243	3,170	288.2
1973	Jesse Freitas, San Diego St.	Sr.	11	410	-92	2,993	2,901	263.7
1974	Steve Joachim, Temple	Sr.	10	331	277	1,950	2,227	222.7
1975	Gene Swick, Toledo	Sr.	11	490	219	2,487	2,706	246.0
1976	Tommy Kramer, Rice	Sr.	11	562	-45	3,317	3,272	297.5
1977	Doug Williams, Grambling	Sr.	11	377	-57	3,286	3,229	293.5
1978	Mike Ford, SMU	So.	11	459	-50	3,007	2,957	268.8
1979	Marc Wilson, BYU	Sr.	11	488	-140	3,720	3,580	325.5
1980	Jim McMahon, BYU	Jr.	12	540	56	4,571	4,627	385.6
1981	Jim McMahon, BYU	Sr.	10	487	-97	3,555	3,458	345.8
1982	Todd Dillon, Long Beach St.	Jr.	11	585	70	3,517	3,587	326.1
1983	Steve Young, BYU	Sr.	11	531	444	3,902	4,346	395.1
1984	Robbie Bosco, BYU	Jr.	12	543	57	3,875	3,932	327.7
1985	Jim Everett, Purdue	Sr.	11	518	-62	3,651	3,589	326.3
1986	Mike Perez, San Jose St.	Jr.	9	425	35	2,934	2,969	329.9
1987	Todd Santos, San Diego St.	Sr.	12	562	-244	3,932	3,688	307.3
1988	Scott Mitchell, Utah	So.	11	589	-23	4,322	4,299	390.8
1989	Andre Ware, Houston	Jr.	11	628	-38	4,699	4,661	423.7
1990	David Klingler, Houston	Jr.	11	704	81	5,140	5,221	*474.6
1991	Ty Detmer, BYU	Sr.	12	478	-30	4,031	4,001	333.4
1992	Jimmy Klingler, Houston	So.	11	544	-50	3,818	3,768	342.5
1993	Chris Vargas, Nevada	Sr.	11	535	67	4,265	4,332	393.8
1994	Mike Maxwell, Nevada	Jr.	11	477	-39	3,537	3,498	318.0
1995	Mike Maxwell, Nevada	Sr.	9	443	12	3,611	3,623	402.6
1996	Josh Wallwork, Wyoming	Sr.	12	525	119	4,090	4,209	350.8
1997	Tim Rattay, Louisiana Tech	So.	11	541	87	3,881	3,968	360.7
1998	Tim Rattay, Louisiana Tech	Jr.	12	602	-103	4,943	4,840	403.3
1999	Tim Rattay, Louisiana Tech	Sr.	10	562	-112	3,922	3,810	381.0
2000	Drew Brees, Purdue	Sr.	11	564	546	3,393	3,939	358.1
2001	Rex Grossman, Florida	So.	11	429	8	3,896	3,904	354.9
2002	Byron Leftwich, Marshall	Sr.	12	528	-1	4,268	4,267	355.6

		Class	G	Plays	Rush	Pass	Total	Avg.
2003	B.J. Symons, Texas Tech	Sr.	13	798	143	*5,833	*5,976	459.7
2004	Sonny Cumbie, Texas Tech	Sr.	12	694	-167	4,742	4,575	381.3
2005	Colt Brennan, Hawaii	So.	12	614	154	4,301	4,455	371.3
2006	Colt Brennan, Hawaii	Jr.	14	645	366	5,549	5,915	422.5

**Record.*

Rushing

CAREER YARDS PER GAME

(Minimum 2,500 yards; Player must have concluded his career)

Player, Team	Years	G	Carries	Yards	TD	Yd. PG
Ed Marinaro, Cornell	1969-71	27	918	4,715	50	174.6
O.J. Simpson, Southern California	1967-68	19	621	3,124	33	164.4
Herschel Walker, Georgia	1980-82	33	994	5,259	49	159.4
Garrett Wolfe, Northern Ill.	2004-06	33	807	5,164	52	156.5
LeShon Johnson, Northern Ill.	1992-93	22	592	3,314	18	150.6
Ron Dayne, Wisconsin	1996-99	43	1,115	*6,397	63	148.8
Marshall Faulk, San Diego St.	1991-93	31	766	4,589	57	148.0
George Jones, San Diego St.	1995-96	19	486	2,810	34	147.9
Tony Dorsett, Pittsburgh	1973-76	43	1,074	6,082	55	141.4
Troy Davis, Iowa St.	1994-96	31	782	4,382	36	141.4
DeAngelo Williams, Memphis	2002-05	44	969	6,026	55	137.0
Mike Rozier, Nebraska	1981-83	35	668	4,780	50	136.6
Ricky Williams, Texas	1995-98	46	1,011	6,279	72	136.5
Howard Stevens, Louisville	1971-72	20	509	2,723	25	136.2
Jerome Persell, Western Mich.	1976-78	31	842	4,190	39	135.2
Rudy Mobley, Hardin-Simmons	1942,46	19	414	2,543	32	133.8
Adrian Peterson, Oklahoma	2004-06	31	747	4,045	41	130.5
Alex Smith, Indiana	1994-96	27	723	3,492	21	129.3
Vaughn Dunbar, Indiana	1990-91	22	565	2,842	24	129.2
Steve Owens, Oklahoma	1967-69	30	905	3,867	56	128.9
Byron Hanspard, Texas Tech	1994-96	33	760	4,219	29	127.8
Jerome Harrison, Washington St.	2004-05	22	482	2,800	25	127.3
Charles White, Southern California	1976-79	44	1,023	5,598	46	127.2
Travis Prentice, Miami (Ohio)	1996-99	44	1,138	5,596	*73	127.2
Emmitt Smith, Florida	1987-89	31	700	3,928	36	126.7
Johnny Bright, Drake	1949-51	25	513	3,134	39	125.4
Woody Green, Arizona St.	1971-73	30	601	3,754	33	125.1
Archie Griffin, Ohio St.	1972-75	42	845	5,177	25	123.3
Anthony Thompson, Indiana	1986-89	41	1,089	4,965	64	121.1
Mark Kellar, Northern Ill.	1971-73	31	743	3,745	32	120.8
Paul Gipson, Houston	1966-68	23	447	2,769	25	120.4
John Cappelletti, Penn St.	‡1972-73	22	519	2,639	29	120.0

**Record. ‡Defensive back in 1971.*

SEASON YARDS PER GAME

Player, Team	Year	G	Carries	Yards	TD	Yd. PG
Barry Sanders, Oklahoma St.	†1988	11	344	*2,628	*37	238.9
Marcus Allen, Southern California	†1981	11	*403	2,342	22	212.9
Ed Marinaro, Cornell	†1971	9	356	1,881	24	209.0
Troy Davis, Iowa St.	†1996	11	402	2,185	21	198.6
LaDainian Tomlinson, TCU	†2000	11	369	2,158	22	196.2
Ricky Williams, Texas	†1998	11	361	2,124	27	193.1
Byron Hanspard, Texas Tech	1996	11	339	2,084	13	189.5
Rashaan Salaam, Colorado	†1994	11	298	2,055	24	186.8
Troy Davis, Iowa St.	†1995	11	345	2,010	15	182.7
Charles White, Southern California	†1979	10	293	1,803	18	180.3
Jamario Thomas, North Texas	†2004	10	285	1,801	17	180.1
LeShon Johnson, Northern Ill.	†1993	11	327	1,976	12	179.6
Mike Rozier, Nebraska	†1983	12	275	2,148	29	179.0
DeAngelo Williams, Memphis	†2005	11	310	1,964	18	178.5
Tony Dorsett, Pittsburgh	†1976	11	338	1,948	21	177.1
Garrett Wolfe, Northern Ill.	2005	9	242	1,580	16	175.6
Ollie Matson, San Francisco	†1951	9	245	1,566	20	174.0
Damien Anderson, Northwestern	2000	11	293	1,914	22	174.0
Lorenzo White, Michigan St.	†1985	11	386	1,908	17	173.5
Wasean Tait, Toledo	1995	11	357	1,905	20	173.2
Jerome Harrison, Washington St.	2005	11	308	1,900	16	172.7
Ricky Williams, Texas	†1997	11	279	1,893	25	172.1
Herschel Walker, Georgia	1981	11	385	1,891	18	171.9
Brian Pruitt, Central Mich.	1994	11	292	1,890	20	171.8
O.J. Simpson, Southern California	†1968	10	355	1,709	22	170.9
Ernest Anderson, Oklahoma St.	†1982	11	353	1,877	8	170.6
Ricky Bell, Southern California	†1975	11	357	1,875	13	170.5

**Record. †National champion.*

CAREER YARDS

Player, Team	Years	Carries	Yards	Avg.	Long
Ron Dayne, Wisconsin	1996-99	1,115	6,397	5.74	80
Ricky Williams, Texas	1995-98	1,011	6,279	6.21	87
Tony Dorsett, Pittsburgh	1973-76	1,074	6,082	5.66	73
DeAngelo Williams, Memphis	2002-05	969	6,026	††6.22	86
Charles White, Southern California	1976-79	1,023	5,598	5.47	79
Travis Prentice, Miami (Ohio)	1996-99	1,138	5,596	4.92	55
Cedric Benson, Texas	2001-04	1,112	5,540	4.98	64
LaDainian Tomlinson, TCU	1997-00	907	5,263	5.80	89
Herschel Walker, Georgia	1980-82	994	5,259	5.29	76
Archie Griffin, Ohio St.	1972-75	845	5,177	6.13	75
Garrett Wolfe, Northern Ill.	2004-06	807	5,164	6.40	84
Darren Lewis, Texas A&M	1987-90	909	5,012	5.51	84
Darren Sproles, Kansas St.	2001-04	815	4,979	6.11	45
DonTrell Moore, New Mexico	2002-05	1,028	4,973	4.84	61
Anthony Thompson, Indiana	1986-89	1,089	4,965	4.56	52
George Rogers, South Carolina	1977-80	902	4,958	5.50	80
Trevor Cobb, Rice	1989-92	1,091	4,948	4.54	79
Michael Turner, Northern Ill.	2000-03	940	4,941	5.26	82
Paul Palmer, Temple	1983-86	948	4,895	5.16	78
Steve Bartalo, Colorado St.	1983-86	*1,215	4,813	3.96	39
Ken Simonton, Oregon St.	1998-01	1,005	4,802	4.78	64
Mike Rozier, Nebraska	1981-83	668	4,780	#7.16	93
Ed Marinaro, Cornell	1969-71	918	4,715	5.14	79
Denvis Manns, New Mexico St.	1995-98	889	4,692	5.28	73
Marcus Allen, Southern California	1978-81	893	4,682	5.24	45
Anthony Davis, Wisconsin	2001-04	908	4,676	5.15	42
Chester Taylor, Toledo	1998-01	803	4,659	5.80	73
Ted Brown, North Carolina St.	1975-78	860	4,602	5.35	95
Thurman Thomas, Oklahoma St.	1984-87	898	4,595	5.12	66
Marshall Faulk, San Diego St.	1991-93	766	4,589	5.99	71
Terry Miller, Oklahoma St.	1974-77	847	4,582	5.41	81
Kevin Faulk, LSU	1995-98	856	4,557	5.32	81
Darrell Thompson, Minnesota	1986-89	911	4,518	4.96	98
Lorenzo White, Michigan St.	1984-87	991	4,513	4.55	73

**Record. ††Record for minimum 781 carries. #Record for minimum 414 carries.*

CAREER YARDS RECORD PROGRESSION

(Record Yards—Player, Team, Seasons Played)

1,961—Marshall Goldberg, Pittsburgh, 1936-38; **2,105**—Tom Harmon, Michigan, 1938-40; **2,271**—Frank Sinkwich, Georgia, 1940-42; **2,301**—Bill Daley, Minnesota, 1940-42, Michigan, 1943; **2,957**—Glenn Davis, Army, 1943-46; **3,095**—Eddie Price, Tulane, 1946-49; **3,238**—John Papit, Virginia, 1947-50; **3,381**—Art Luppino, Arizona, 1953-56; **3,388**—Eugene "Mercury" Morris, West Tex. A&M, 1966-68; **3,867**—Steve Owens, Oklahoma, 1967-69; **4,715**—Ed Marinaro, Cornell, 1969-71; **5,177**—Archie Griffin, Ohio St., 1972-75; **6,082**—Tony Dorsett, Pittsburgh, 1973-76; **6,279**—Ricky Williams, Texas, 1995-98; **6,397**—Ron Dayne, Wisconsin, 1996-99.

CAREER RUSHING TOUCHDOWNS

Player, Team	Years	G	TD
Travis Prentice, Miami (Ohio)	1996-99	44	73
Ricky Williams, Texas	1995-98	46	72
Anthony Thompson, Indiana	1986-89	41	64
Cedric Benson, Texas	2001-04	49	64
Ron Dayne, Wisconsin	1996-99	43	63
Eric Crouch, Nebraska (QB)	1998-01	43	59
Marshall Faulk, San Diego St.	1991-93	31	57
Steve Owens, Oklahoma	1967-69	30	56
Ken Simonton, Oregon St.	1998-01	44	56
Tony Dorsett, Pittsburgh	1973-76	43	55
Chester Taylor, Toledo	1998-01	42	55
DeAngelo Williams, Memphis	2002-05	44	55
LaDainian Tomlinson, TCU	1997-00	44	54
Dwone Hicks, Middle Tenn.	1999-02	44	53
Chris Lemon, Nevada	1996-99	44	52
LenDale White, Southern California	2003-05	39	52
Garrett Wolfe, Northern Ill.	2004-06	33	52
Pete Johnson, Ohio St.	1973-76	41	51
DonTrell Moore, New Mexico	2002-05	48	51
Ed Marinaro, Cornell	1969-71	27	50
Billy Sims, Oklahoma	1975, 77-79	42	50
Mike Rozier, Nebraska	1982-83	35	50
Brock Forsey, Boise St.	1999-02	47	50
Taurean Henderson, Texas Tech	2002-05	51	50

(Note: Howard Stevens of Louisville played two years at college division Randolph-Macon, 1968-69, with 33 touchdowns and two years at Louisville, 1971-72, with 25 touchdowns, scoring a total of 58 touchdowns in four years.)

SEASON YARDS

Player, Team	Year	G	Carries	Yards	Avg.
Barry Sanders, Oklahoma St.	†1988	11	344	2,628	‡7.64
Marcus Allen, Southern California	†1981	11	*403	2,342	5.81
Troy Davis, Iowa St.	†1996	11	402	2,185	5.44
LaDainian Tomlinson, TCU	†2000	11	369	2,158	5.85
Mike Rozier, Nebraska	†1983	12	275	2,148	#7.81
Ricky Williams, Texas	†1998	11	361	2,124	5.88
Larry Johnson, Penn St.	†2002	13	271	2,087	7.70
Byron Hanspard, Texas Tech	1996	11	339	2,084	6.15
Rashaan Salaam, Colorado	†1994	11	298	2,055	6.90
J.J. Arrington, California	2004	12	289	2,018	6.98
Troy Davis, Iowa St.	†1995	11	345	2,010	5.83
LeShon Johnson, Northern Ill.	†1993	11	327	1,976	6.04
DeAngelo Williams, Memphis	†2005	11	310	1,964	6.34
Tony Dorsett, Pittsburgh	†1976	11	338	1,948	5.76
DeAngelo Williams, Memphis	2004	12	313	1,948	6.22
Garrett Wolfe, Northern Ill.	†2006	13	309	1,928	6.24
Adrian Peterson, Oklahoma	2004	13	339	1,925	5.68
Michael Turner, Northern Ill.	2002	12	338	1,915	5.67
Damien Anderson, Northwestern	2000	11	293	1,914	6.53
Lorenzo White, Michigan St.	†1985	11	386	1,908	4.94
Wasean Tait, Toledo	1995	11	357	1,905	5.34
Jerome Harrison, Washington St.	2005	11	308	1,900	6.17
Ricky Williams, Texas	†1997	11	279	1,893	6.78
Herschel Walker, Georgia	1981	11	385	1,891	4.91
Brian Pruitt, Central Mich.	1994	11	292	1,890	6.47
Quentin Griffin, Oklahoma	2002	14	287	1,884	6.56
Ed Marinaro, Cornell	†1971	9	356	1,881	5.28
Ernest Anderson, Oklahoma St.	†1982	11	353	1,877	5.32
Ahman Green, Nebraska	1997	12	278	1,877	6.75
Ricky Bell, Southern California	†1975	11	357	1,875	5.25
Paul Palmer, Temple	†1986	11	346	1,866	5.39
Ron Dayne, Wisconsin	1996	12	295	1,863	6.32
LaDainian Tomlinson, TCU	†1999	11	268	1,850	6.90

**Record. †National champion. ‡Record for minimum 282 carries. #Record for minimum 214 carries.*

SINGLE-GAME YARDS

Yds.	Player, Team (Opponent)	Date
406	LaDainian Tomlinson, TCU (UTEP)	Nov. 20, 1999
396	Tony Sands, Kansas (Missouri)	Nov. 23, 1991
386	Marshall Faulk, San Diego St. (Pacific)	Sept. 14, 1991
378	Troy Davis, Iowa St. (Missouri)	Sept. 28, 1996
377	Anthony Thompson, Indiana (Wisconsin)	Nov. 11, 1989
377	Robbie Mixon, Central Mich. (Eastern Mich.)	Nov. 2, 2002
376	Travis Prentice, Miami (Ohio) (Akron)	Nov. 6, 1999
373	Astron Whatley, Kent St. (Eastern Mich.)	Sept. 20, 1997
357	Rueben Mayes, Washington St. (Oregon)	Oct. 27, 1984
357	Mike Pringle, Cal St. Fullerton (New Mexico St.)	Nov. 4, 1989
356	Eddie Lee Ivery, Georgia Tech (Air Force)	Nov. 11, 1978
356	Brian Pruitt, Central Mich. (Toledo)	Nov. 5, 1994
353	Garrett Wolfe, Northern Ill. (Ball St.)	Sept. 30, 2006
351	Scott Harley, East Caro. (North Carolina St.)	Nov. 30, 1996
350	Eric Allen, Michigan St. (Purdue)	Oct. 30, 1971
350	Ricky Williams, Texas (Iowa St.)	Oct. 3, 1998

Note: There have been 79 300-yard rushing games in FBS history.

ANNUAL CHAMPIONS

Year	Player, Team	Class	Carries	Yards
1937	Byron "Whizzer" White, Colorado	Sr.	181	1,121
1938	Len Eshmont, Fordham	So.	132	831
1939	John Polanski, Wake Forest	So.	137	882
1940	Al Ghesquiere, Detroit	Sr.	146	957
1941	Frank Sinkwich, Georgia	Jr.	209	1,103
1942	Rudy Mobley, Hardin-Simmons	So.	187	1,281
1943	Creighton Miller, Notre Dame	Sr.	151	911
1944	Wayne "Red" Williams, Minnesota	Jr.	136	911
1945	Bob Fenimore, Oklahoma St.	Jr.	142	1,048
1946	Rudy Mobley, Hardin-Simmons	Sr.	227	1,262
1947	Wilton Davis, Hardin-Simmons	So.	193	1,173
1948	Fred Wendt, UTEP	Sr.	184	1,570
1949	John Dottley, Mississippi	Jr.	208	1,312
1950	Wilford White, Arizona St.	Sr.	199	1,502
1951	Ollie Matson, San Francisco	Sr.	245	1,566
1952	Howie Waugh, Tulsa	Sr.	164	1,372
1953	J.C. Caroline, Illinois	So.	194	1,256
1954	Art Luppino, Arizona	So.	179	1,359
1955	Art Luppino, Arizona	Jr.	209	1,313
1956	Jim Crawford, Wyoming	Sr.	200	1,104
1957	Leon Burton, Arizona St.	Sr.	117	1,126
1958	Dick Bass, Pacific	Jr.	205	1,361
1959	Pervis Atkins, New Mexico St.	Jr.	130	971
1960	Bob Gaiters, New Mexico St.	Sr.	197	1,338
1961	Jim Pilot, New Mexico St.	So.	191	1,278
1962	Jim Pilot, New Mexico St.	Jr.	208	1,247
1963	Dave Casinelli, Memphis	Sr.	219	1,016
1964	Brian Piccolo, Wake Forest	Sr.	252	1,044
1965	Mike Garrett, Southern California	Sr.	267	1,440
1966	Ray McDonald, Idaho	Sr.	259	1,329
1967	O.J. Simpson, Southern California	Jr.	266	1,415
1968	O.J. Simpson, Southern California	Sr.	355	1,709
1969	Steve Owens, Oklahoma	Sr.	358	1,523

Beginning in 1970, ranked on per-game (instead of total) yards

Year	Player, Team	Class	G	Carries	Yards	Avg.
1970	Ed Marinaro, Cornell	Jr.	9	285	1,425	158.3
1971	Ed Marinaro, Cornell	Sr.	9	356	1,881	209.0
1972	Pete VanValkenburg, BYU	Sr.	10	232	1,386	138.6
1973	Mark Kellar, Northern Ill.	Sr.	11	291	1,719	156.3
1974	Louie Giammona, Utah St.	Jr.	10	329	1,534	153.4
1975	Ricky Bell, Southern California	Jr.	11	357	1,875	170.5
1976	Tony Dorsett, Pittsburgh	Sr.	11	338	1,948	177.1
1977	Earl Campbell, Texas	Sr.	11	267	1,744	158.5
1978	Billy Sims, Oklahoma	Jr.	11	231	1,762	160.2
1979	Charles White, Southern California	Sr.	10	293	1,803	180.3
1980	George Rogers, South Carolina	Sr.	11	297	1,781	161.9
1981	Marcus Allen, Southern California	Sr.	11	*403	2,342	212.9
1982	Ernest Anderson, Oklahoma St.	Jr.	11	353	1,877	170.6
1983	Mike Rozier, Nebraska	Sr.	12	275	2,148	179.0
1984	Keith Byars, Ohio St.	Jr.	11	313	1,655	150.5
1985	Lorenzo White, Michigan St.	So.	11	386	1,908	173.5
1986	Paul Palmer, Temple	Sr.	11	346	1,866	169.6
1987	Elbert "Ickey" Woods, UNLV	Sr.	11	259	1,658	150.7
1988	Barry Sanders, Oklahoma St.	Jr.	11	344	*2,628	*238.9
1989	Anthony Thompson, Indiana	Sr.	11	358	1,793	163.0
1990	Gerald Hudson, Oklahoma St.	Sr.	11	279	1,642	149.3
1991	Marshall Faulk, San Diego St.	Fr.	9	201	1,429	158.8
1992	Marshall Faulk, San Diego St.	So.	10	265	1,630	163.0
1993	LeShon Johnson, Northern Ill.	Sr.	11	327	1,976	179.6
1994	Rashaan Salaam, Colorado	Jr.	11	298	2,055	186.8
1995	Troy Davis, Iowa St.	So.	11	345	2,010	182.7
1996	Troy Davis, Iowa St.	Jr.	11	402	2,185	198.6
1997	Ricky Williams, Texas	Jr.	11	279	1,893	172.1
1998	Ricky Williams, Texas	Sr.	11	361	2,124	193.1
1999	LaDainian Tomlinson, TCU	Jr.	11	268	1,850	168.2
2000	LaDainian Tomlinson, TCU	Sr.	11	369	2,158	196.2
2001	Chance Kretschmer, Nevada	Fr.	11	302	1,732	157.5
2002	Larry Johnson, Penn St.	Sr.	13	271	2,087	160.5
2003	Patrick Cobbs, North Texas	Jr.	11	307	1,680	152.7
2004	Jamario Thomas, North Texas	Fr.	10	285	1,801	180.1
2005	DeAngelo Williams, Memphis	Sr.	11	310	1,964	178.5
2006	Garrett Wolfe, Northern Ill.	Sr.	13	309	1,928	148.3

**Record.*

FRESHMAN 1,000-YARD RUSHERS

(Listed Chronologically)

Player, Team	Year	Yards
Ron "Po" James, New Mexico St.	1968	1,291
Tony Dorsett, Pittsburgh	1973	1,586
James McDougald, Wake Forest	1976	1,018
Mike Harkrader, Indiana	1976	1,003
Amos Lawrence, North Carolina	1977	1,211
Darrin Nelson, Stanford	1977	1,069
Mike Smith, Chattanooga	1977	1,062
Gwain Durden, Chattanooga	1977	1,049
Allen Ross, Northern Ill.	1977	1,043
Allen Harvin, Cincinnati	1978	1,238
Joe Morris, Syracuse	1978	1,001
Ron Lear, Marshall	1979	1,162
Herschel Walker, Georgia	1980	1,616
Kerwin Bell, Kansas	1980	1,114
Joe McIntosh, North Carolina St.	1981	1,190
Steve Bartalo, Colorado St.	1983	1,113
Spencer Tillman, Oklahoma	1983	1,047
D.J. Dozier, Penn St.	1983	1,002
Eddie Johnson, Utah	1984	1,021
Darrell Thompson, Minnesota	1986	1,240
Emmitt Smith, Florida	1987	1,341
Reggie Cobb, Tennessee	1987	1,197
Bernie Parmalee, Ball St.	1987	1,064
Curvin Richards, Pittsburgh	1988	1,228
Chuck Webb, Tennessee	1989	1,236
Robert Smith, Ohio St.	1990	1,064
Marshall Faulk, San Diego St.	1991	1,429
Greg Hill, Texas A&M	1991	1,216
David Small, Cincinnati	1991	1,004
Winslow Oliver, New Mexico	1992	1,063
Deland McCullough, Miami (Ohio)	1992	1,026

Player, Team	Year	Yards
Terrell Willis, Rutgers	1993	1,261
June Henley, Kansas	1993	1,127
Marquis Williams, Arkansas St.	1993	1,060
Leon Johnson, North Carolina	1993	1,012
Alex Smith, Indiana	1994	1,475
Astron Whatley, Kent St.	1994	1,003
Denvis Manns, New Mexico St.	1995	1,120
Silas Massey, Central Mich.	1995	1,089
Ahman Green, Nebraska	1995	1,086
Ron Dayne, Wisconsin	1996	1,863
Demond Parker, Oklahoma	1996	1,184
Sedrick Irvin, Michigan St.	1996	1,036
Jamal Lewis, Tennessee	1997	1,364
Robert Sanford, Western Mich.	1997	1,033
Derrick Nix, Southern Miss.	1998	1,180
Ken Simonton, Oregon St.	1998	1,028
Avon Cobourne, West Virginia	1999	1,139
Chance Kretschmer, Nevada	2001	1,732
Anthony Davis, Wisconsin	2001	1,466
Cedric Benson, Texas	2001	1,053
Joshua Cribbs, Kent St. (QB)	2001	1,019
Terry Caulley, Connecticut	2002	1,247
Maurice Clarett, Ohio St.	2002	1,237
DonTrell Moore, New Mexico	2002	1,134
Matt Milton, Nevada	2002	1,108
T.A. McLendon, North Carolina St.	2002	1,101
Lonta Hobbs, TCU	2002	1,029
Brad Smith, Missouri (QB)	2002	1,029
Laurence Maroney, Minnesota	2003	1,121
Jerry Seymour, Central Mich.	2003	1,117
Robert Merrill, TCU	2003	1,107
Lynell Hamilton, San Diego St.	2003	1,087
Courtney Lewis, Texas A&M	2003	1,024
Justin Vincent, LSU	2003	1,001
Adrian Peterson, Oklahoma	2004	*1,925
Jamario Thomas, North Texas	2004	1,801
Michael Hart, Michigan	2004	1,455
Tyrell Sutton, Northwestern	2005	1,474
Kevin Smith, UCF	2005	1,178
Steve Slaton, West Virginia	2005	1,128
Ray Rice, Rutgers	2005	1,120
Darren McFadden, Arkansas	2005	1,113
Ontario Sneed, Central Mich.	2005	1,065
P.J. Hill, Wisconsin	2006	1,569
Damion Fletcher, Southern Miss.	2006	1,388
Reggie Arnold, Arkansas St.	2006	1,076

*Record for freshman.

Quarterback Rushing

SEASON YARDS

Player, Team	Year	G	Carries	Yards	TD	Avg.
Beau Morgan, Air Force	1996	11	225	1,494	18	6.64
Stacey Robinson, Northern Ill.	1989	11	223	1,443	19	6.47
Jammal Lord, Nebraska	2002	14	251	1,412	8	5.63
Brad Smith, Missouri	2003	13	212	1,406	18	6.63
Chris McCoy, Navy	1997	11	246	1,370	20	5.57
Dee Dowis, Air Force	1987	12	194	1,315	10	6.78
Brian Mitchell, La.-Lafayette	1989	11	237	1,311	19	5.53
Brad Smith, Missouri	2005	12	229	1,301	16	5.68
Fred Solomon, Tampa	1974	11	193	1,300	19	6.74
Dee Dowis, Air Force	1989	12	172	1,286	18	#7.48
Beau Morgan, Air Force	1995	12	229	1,285	19	5.61
Antwaan Randle El, Indiana	2000	11	218	1,270	13	5.83
Stacey Robinson, Northern Ill.	1990	11	193	1,238	19	6.41
Chance Harridge, Air Force	2002	13	252	1,229	*22	4.88
Chris McCoy, Navy	1996	11	268	1,228	16	4.58
Patrick White, West Virginia	2006	12	165	1,219	18	7.39
Keith Boyea, Air Force	2001	12	230	1,216	18	5.29
Rob Perez, Air Force	1991	12	233	1,157	10	4.97
Jack Mildren, Oklahoma	1971	11	193	1,140	17	5.91
Nolan Cromwell, Kansas	1975	11	218	1,124	9	5.16
Eric Crouch, Nebraska	2001	12	203	1,115	18	5.49
Craig Candeto, Navy	2003	13	271	1,112	16	4.10
Scott Frost, Nebraska	1997	12	176	1,095	19	6.22
Michael Carter, Hawaii	1991	12	221	1,092	16	4.94
Vince Young, Texas	2004	12	167	1,079	14	6.46
Tory Crawford, Army	1986	11	244	1,075	15	4.41
Kareem Wilson, Ohio	1996	12	*275	1,072	14	3.90
Joshua Cribbs, Kent St.	2002	10	137	1,057	10	*7.72
Vince Young, Texas	2005	13	155	1,050	12	6.77

*Record. #Record for a minimum of 150 carries.

CAREER YARDS

Player, Team	Years	G	Carries	Yards	TD	Avg.
Brad Smith, Missouri	2002-05	48	799	4,289	45	89.4
Antwaan Randle El, Indiana	1998-01	44	857	3,895	44	88.5
Joshua Cribbs, Kent St.	2001-04	43	632	3,670	38	85.3
Dee Dowis, Air Force	1986-89	47	543	3,612	41	76.9
Kareem Wilson, Ohio	1995-98	45	*885	3,597	49	79.9
Eric Crouch, Nebraska	1998-01	43	648	3,434	*59	79.9
Chris McCoy, Navy	1995-97	32	682	3,401	43	106.3
Beau Morgan, Air Force	1994-96	35	594	3,379	42	96.5
Brian Mitchell, La.-Lafayette	1986-89	43	678	3,335	47	77.6
Fred Solomon, Tampa	1971-74	43	557	3,299	39	76.7
Vince Young, Texas	2003-05	37	457	3,127	37	84.5
Ell Roberson, Kansas St.	2000-03	47	604	2,818	40	60.0
Stacey Robinson, Northern Ill.	1988-90	25	429	2,727	38	*109.1
Jamelle Holieway, Oklahoma	1985-88	38	505	2,699	30	71.0
Woodrow Dantzler, Clemson	1998-01	36	549	2,615	27	72.6
Jammal Lord, Nebraska	2000-03	39	516	2,573	24	66.0
Bill Hurley, Syracuse	1975-79	46	685	2,551	19	55.5
Matt Jones, Arkansas	2001-04	46	382	2,535	24	55.1
Michael Carter, Hawaii	1990-93	46	574	2,534	39	55.1
Corby Jones, Missouri	1995-98	39	559	2,533	38	64.9

*Record.

Passing

SAMPLE COMPILATION OF NCAA PASSING EFFICIENCY RATING

Player	G	Att.	Cmp.	Yds.	TD	Int.
Ryan Dinwiddie, Boise St.	45	992	622	9,819	82	21

Completion Percentage:	62.70
Yards Per Attempted Pass:	9.90
Percent of Passes for TDs:	8.27
Percent of Passes Intercepted:	2.12

ADD the first three factors:

		Rating Points
Completion Percentage:	62.70	62.70
Yards Per Attempted Pass:	9.898 times 8.4	83.14
Percent of Passes for TDs:	8.27 times 3.3	27.29
		173.13

SUBTRACT the last factor:

Percent of Passes Intercepted:	2.12 times 2	-4.24
	Round off to:	**168.9**

FBS PASSING EFFICIENCY RATING COMPARISON

1979-06

Passing statistics in the FBS have increased dramatically since 1979, the first year that the NCAA official national statistics used the passing efficiency formula to rank passers in all divisions. Because passers have become more proficient every year, the average passing efficiency rating (based on final regular-season trends) also has risen at a similar rate. For historical purposes, the average passing efficiency rating for the division by year is presented below to show how any individual or team might rank in a particular season.

Year	Pass Effic. Rating	Year	Pass Effic. Rating
1979	104.49	1993	122.43
1980	106.63	1994	120.59
1981	107.00	1995	120.17
1982	110.77	1996	120.24
1983	113.56	1997	122.86
1984	113.02	1998	122.97
1985	114.58	1999	120.50
1986	115.00	2000	119.66
1987	112.67	2001	123.80
1988	114.32	2002	123.00
1989	118.35	2003	125.89
1990	117.39	2004	125.36
1991	117.94	2005	126.13
1992	114.50	2006	127.54

CAREER PASSING EFFICIENCY

(Minimum 500 Completions; Player must have concluded his career)

Player, Team	Years	Att.	Cmp.	Int.	Pct.	Yds.	TD	Pts.
Ryan Dinwiddie, Boise St.	2000-03	992	622	21	.627	9,819	82	168.9
Danny Wuerffel, Florida	1993-96	1,170	708	42	.605	10,875	114	163.6
Omar Jacobs, Bowling Green	2003-05	811	523	11	.645	6,937	71	163.5
Ty Detmer, BYU	1988-91	1,530	958	65	.626	15,031	*121	162.7
Steve Sarkisian, BYU	1995-96	789	528	26	.669	7,464	53	162.0
Matt Leinart, Southern California	2002-05	1,245	807	23	.648	10,693	99	159.5
Bruce Gradkowski, Toledo	2002-05	1,123	766	27	‡.682	9,225	85	157.4
Billy Blanton, San Diego St.	1993-96	920	588	25	.639	8,165	67	157.1
Jim McMahon, BYU	1977-78, 80-81	1,060	653	34	.616	9,536	84	156.9
Chad Pennington, Marshall	1997-99	1,265	807	30	.638	10,698	100	156.2
Donovan McNabb, Syracuse	1995-98	938	548	26	.584	8,389	77	155.1
Tim Rattay, Louisiana Tech	1997-99	1,552	1,015	35	.654	12,746	115	154.3
Daunte Culpepper, UCF	1996-98	1,097	721	32	.657	9,341	72	153.1
David Carr, Fresno St.	1997-98, 00-01	877	551	21	.628	7,309	66	152.9
Jason White, Oklahoma	$1999-04	990	627	24	.633	7,922	81	152.7
Ben Roethlisberger, Miami (Ohio)	2001-03	1,304	854	34	.655	10,829	84	151.3
Chris Weinke, Florida St.	1997-00	1,107	650	32	.587	9,839	79	151.1
Byron Leftwich, Marshall	$1998-02	1,442	939	28	.651	11,903	89	150.9

(400-499 Completions)

Player, Team	Years	Att.	Cmp.	Int.	Pct.	Yds.	TD	Pts.
Troy Smith, Ohio St.	2002-06	670	420	13	.627	5,720	54	157.1
Vinny Testaverde, Miami (Fla.)	1982, 84-86	674	413	25	.613	6,058	48	152.9
Josh Wallwork, Wyoming	1995-96	729	449	28	.616	6,453	54	152.7
Trent Dilfer, Fresno St.	1991-93	774	461	21	.596	6,944	51	151.2
Aaron Rodgers, California	2002-04	665	424	13	.638	5,469	43	150.3
Troy Aikman, Oklahoma/UCLA	1984-85, 87-88	637	401	18	.630	5,436	40	149.7
Chuck Hartlieb, Iowa	1985-88	716	461	17	.643	6,269	34	148.9
Elvis Grbac, Michigan	1989-92	754	477	29	.633	5,859	64	148.9
JaMarcus Russell, LSU	2003-06	796	492	21	.618	6,619	52	147.9
Bobby Hoying, Ohio St.	1992-95	782	463	33	.592	6,751	54	146.1
Gifford Nielsen, BYU	1975-77	708	415	29	.586	5,833	55	145.3
Tom Ramsey, UCLA	1979-82	691	411	33	.595	5,844	48	143.9

Player, Team	Years	Att.	Cmp.	Int.	Pct.	Yds.	TD	Pts.
Shawn Moore, Virginia	1987-90	762	421	32	.552	6,629	55	143.8
George Godsey, Georgia Tech	1998-01	765	484	18	.633	6,137	41	143.6
Moses Moreno, Colorado St.	1994-97	787	457	28	.581	6,689	49	142.9
Jerry Rhome, SMU/Tulsa	1961, 63-64	713	448	23	.628	5,472	47	142.6
Thad Busby, Florida St.	1994-97	715	420	27	.587	5,916	46	141.9
Charlie Ward, Florida St.	1989, 91-93	759	474	21	.625	5,747	49	141.8
Ryan Leaf, Washington St.	1995-97	845	456	23	.540	7,102	58	141.8
Justin Holland, Colorado St.	2002-05	681	426	32	.626	5,668	32	140.5
Keith Smith, Arizona	1996-99	726	434	27	.598	5,972	42	140.5

(325-399 Completions)

Player, Team	Years	Att.	Cmp.	Int.	Pct.	Yds.	TD	Pts.
Alex Smith, Utah	2002-04	587	389	8	.663	5,203	47	164.4
Joe Germaine, Ohio St.	1996-98	660	399	18	.605	5,844	52	155.4
Jim Harbaugh, Michigan	1983-86	582	368	19	.632	5,215	31	149.6
Danny White, Arizona St.	1971-73	649	345	36	.532	5,932	59	148.9
Koy Detmer, Colorado	1992, 94-96	594	350	25	.589	5,390	40	148.9
Cody Hodges, Texas Tech	2002-05	543	360	13	.662	4,308	33	148.2
Tim Gutierrez, San Diego St.	1992-94	580	357	19	.616	4,740	36	144.1
Scott McBrien, Maryland	2002-03	598	335	16	.560	5,169	34	142.0
Jim Karsatos, Ohio St.	1983-86	573	330	19	.576	4,698	36	140.6
Jerry Tagge, Nebraska	1969-71	581	348	19	.599	4,704	33	140.1
Mike Fouts, Utah	1995-96	625	356	19	.570	5,107	39	140.1
Garrett Gabriel, Hawaii	1987-90	661	356	31	.539	5,631	47	139.5
Rick Mirer, Notre Dame	1989-92	698	377	23	.540	5,996	41	139.0
Gary Sheide, BYU	1973-74	594	358	31	.603	4,524	45	138.8
Joey Lynch, Ball St.	2003-06	613	391	12	.638	4,292	37	138.6
Jeff Ballard, TCU	$2002-06	540	330	12	.611	4,204	27	138.5
Dan Speltz, Cal St. Fullerton	1988-89	583	350	19	.600	4,595	33	138.4
Mike Moschetti, Colorado	1998-99	607	366	19	.603	4,797	33	138.4
Don McPherson, Syracuse	$1983-87	687	367	29	.534	5,812	46	138.1
Joe Youngblood, Central Mich.	1990-93	572	331	28	.579	4,718	35	137.6

**Record. $See page 10 for explanation. ‡Record for minimum 1,000 attempts.*

SEASON PASSING EFFICIENCY

(Minimum 15 Attempts Per Game)

Player, Team	Year	G	Att.	Cmp.	Int.	Pct.	Yds.	TD	Pts.
Colt Brennan, Hawaii	#†2006	14	559	406	12	.726	5,549	*58	186.0
Shaun King, Tulane	†1998	11	328	223	6	.680	3,232	36	183.3
Stefan Lefors, Louisville	†2004	12	257	189	3	.735	2,596	20	181.7
Michael Vick, Virginia Tech	†1999	10	152	90	5	.592	1,840	12	180.4
Danny Wuerffel, Florida	†1995	11	325	210	10	.646	3,266	35	178.4
Jim McMahon, BYU	#†1980	12	445	284	18	.638	4,571	47	176.9
Alex Smith, Utah	2004	12	317	214	4	.675	2,952	32	176.5
Ty Detmer, BYU	†1989	12	412	265	15	.643	4,560	32	175.6
Rudy Carpenter, Arizona St.	†2005	9	228	156	2	.684	2,273	17	175.0
Joe Hamilton, Georgia Tech	1999	11	305	203	11	.666	3,060	29	175.0
Steve Sarkisian, BYU	†1996	14	404	278	12	.688	4,027	33	173.6
Trent Dilfer, Fresno St.	†1993	11	333	217	4	.652	3,276	28	173.1
Jason Campbell, Auburn	2004	13	270	188	7	.696	2,700	20	172.9
Kerry Collins, Penn St.	†1994	11	264	176	7	.667	2,679	21	172.9
Jerry Rhome, Tulsa	#†1964	10	326	224	4	.687	2,870	32	172.6
Chad Pennington, Marshall	1999	12	405	275	11	.679	3,799	37	171.4
Rex Grossman, Florida	†2001	11	395	259	12	.656	3,896	34	170.8
Bart Hendricks, Boise St.	†2000	11	347	210	8	.605	3,364	35	170.6
Danny Wuerffel, Florida	1996	12	360	207	13	.575	3,625	39	170.6
Philip Rivers, North Carolina St.	†2003	13	483	348	7	.721	4,491	34	170.5
Akili Smith, Oregon	1998	11	325	191	7	.588	3,307	30	170.4
Bobby Hoying, Ohio St.	1995	12	303	192	11	.634	3,023	28	170.4
Daunte Culpepper, UCF	1998	11	402	296	7	*.736	3,690	28	170.2

**Record. †National pass-efficiency champion. #National total-offense champion.*

ANNUAL PASSING EFFICIENCY LEADERS

(% Minimum 11 Attempts Per Game)

1946—Bill Mackrides, Nevada, 176.9; **1947**—Bobby Layne, Texas, 138.9; **1948**—Stan Heath, Nevada, 157.2 (#); **1949**—Bob Williams, Notre Dame, 159.1; **1950**—Claude Arnold, Oklahoma, 157.3; **1951**—Dick Kazmaier, Princeton, 155.3 (#); **1952**—Ron Morris, Tulsa, 177.4; **1953**—Bob Garrett, Stanford, 142.2; **1954**—Pete Vann, Army, 166.5; **1955**—George Welsh, Navy, 146.1 (#); **1956**—Tom Flores, Pacific, 147.5; **1957**—Lee Grosscup, Utah, 175.5; **1958**—John Hangartner, Arizona St., 150.1; **1959**—Charley Johnson, New Mexico St., 135.7; **1960**—Eddie Wilson, Arizona, 140.8; **1961**—Ron DiGravio, Purdue, 140.1; **1962**—John Jacobs, Arizona St., 153.9; **1963**—Bob Berry, Oregon, 164.0; **1964**—Jerry Rhome, Tulsa, 172.6 (#).

(Minimum 15 Attempts Per Game)

1946—Ben Raimondi, Indiana, 117.0; **1947**—Charley Conerly, Mississippi, 125.8; **1948**—Stan Heath, Nevada, 157.2 (#); **1949**—Dick Doheny, Fordham, 153.3; **1950**—Dick Doheny, Fordham, 149.5; **1951**—Babe Parilli, Kentucky, 130.8; **1952**—Gene Rossi, Cincinnati, 149.7; **1953**—Bob Garrett, Stanford, 142.2; **1954**—Len Dawson, Purdue, 145.8; **1955**—George Welsh, Navy, 146.1 (#); **1956**—Bob Reinhart, San Jose St., 121.3; **1957**—Bob Newman, Washington St., 126.5 (#); **1958**—Randy Duncan, Iowa, 135.1; **1959**—Charley Johnson, New Mexico St., 135.7; **1960**—Charley Johnson, New Mexico St., 134.1; **1961**—Eddie Wilson, Arizona, 134.2; **1962**—Terry Baker, Oregon St., 146.5 (#); **1963**—Bob Berry, Oregon, 164.0; **1964**—Jerry Rhome, Tulsa, 172.6 (#).

(Minimum 15 Attempts Per Game)

Year	Player, Team	G	Att.	Cmp.	Int.	Pct.	Yds.	TD	Pts.
1965	Steve Sloan, Alabama	10	160	97	3	.606	1,453	10	153.8
1966	Dewey Warren, Tennessee	10	229	136	7	.594	1,716	18	142.2

Year	Player, Team	G	Att.	Cmp.	Int.	Pct.	Yds.	TD	Pts.
1967	Bill Andrejko, Villanova	10	187	114	6	.610	1,405	13	140.6
1968	Brian Dowling, Yale	9	160	92	10	.575	1,554	19	165.8
1969	#Dennis Shaw, San Diego St.	10	335	199	26	.594	3,185	39	162.2
1970	Jerry Tagge, Nebraska	11	165	104	7	.630	1,383	12	149.0
1971	Jerry Tagge, Nebraska	12	239	143	4	.598	2,019	17	150.9
1972	John Hufnagel, Penn St.	11	216	115	8	.532	2,039	15	148.0
1973	Danny White, Arizona St.	11	265	146	12	.551	2,609	23	157.4
1974	#Steve Joachim, Temple	10	221	128	13	.579	1,950	20	150.1
1975	James Kubacki, Harvard	8	137	77	9	.562	1,273	11	147.6
1976	Steve Haynes, Louisiana Tech	10	216	120	11	.556	1,981	16	146.9
1977	Dave Wilson, Ball St.	11	177	115	7	.650	1,589	17	164.2
1978	Paul McDonald, Southern California	11	194	111	7	.572	1,667	18	152.8

(See page 42 for annual leaders beginning in 1979)

#National total-offense champion. % In many seasons during 1946-64, only a few passers threw as many as 15 passes per game; thus, a lower minimum was used.

CAREER YARDS

Player, Team	Years	Att.	Cmp.	Int.	Pct.	Yds.	TD	Long
Timmy Chang, Hawaii	$2000-04	*2,436	*1,388	*80	.570	17,072	117	75
Ty Detmer, BYU	1988-91	1,530	958	65	.626	15,031	*121	76
Philip Rivers, North Carolina St.	2000-03	1,710	1,147	34	.671	13,484	95	88
Kevin Kolb, Houston	2003-06	1,565	964	31	.616	12,964	85	83
Tim Rattay, Louisiana Tech	1997-99	1,552	1,015	35	.654	12,746	115	94
Luke McCown, Louisiana Tech	2000-03	1,775	1,063	62	.599	12,666	87	80
Chris Redman, Louisville	1996-99	1,679	1,031	51	.614	12,541	84	86
Kliff Kingsbury, Texas Tech	1999-02	1,883	1,231	40	.654	12,429	95	75
Byron Leftwich, Marshall	$1998-02	1,442	939	28	.651	11,903	89	86
Brady Quinn, Notre Dame	2003-06	1,602	929	39	.580	11,762	95	85
David Greene, Georgia	2001-04	1,440	849	32	.590	11,528	72	93
Gino Guidugli, Cincinnati	2001-04	1,556	880	48	.566	11,453	78	80
Todd Santos, San Diego St.	1984-87	1,484	910	57	.613	11,425	70	84
Carson Palmer, Southern California	$1998-02	1,515	895	49	.591	11,388	71	93
Tim Lester, Western Mich.	1996-99	1,507	875	49	.581	11,299	87	82
Derek Anderson, Oregon St.	2001-04	1,515	768	57	.507	11,249	79	90
Chris Leak, Florida	2003-06	1,458	895	42	.614	11,213	88	81
Peyton Manning, Tennessee	1994-97	1,381	863	33	.625	11,201	89	80
Eric Zeier, Georgia	1991-94	1,402	838	37	.598	11,153	67	80
Jordan Palmer, UTEP	$2002-06	1,427	851	64	.596	11,084	88	91
Charlie Frye, Akron	2001-04	1,436	913	32	.636	11,049	64	74
John Beck, BYU	2003-06	1,418	885	34	.624	11,021	79	82
Ryan Schneider, UCF	2000-03	1,354	840	51	.620	10,976	82	83
Alex Van Pelt, Pittsburgh	1989-92	1,463	845	59	.578	10,913	64	91
Drew Brees, Purdue	1997-00	1,525	942	41	.618	10,909	81	99
David Neill, Nevada	1998-01	1,376	763	33	.555	10,903	73	91
Danny Wuerffel, Florida	1993-96	1,170	708	42	.605	10,875	114	85
Ben Roethlisberger, Miami (Ohio)	2001-03	1,304	854	34	.655	10,829	84	81
Chad Pennington, Marshall	1997-99	1,265	807	30	.638	10,698	100	92
Matt Leinart, Southern California	2002-05	1,245	807	23	.648	10,693	99	73
Kevin Sweeney, Fresno St.	$1982-86	1,336	731	48	.547	10,623	66	95
Andrew Walter, Arizona St.	2001-04	1,416	777	36	.549	10,617	85	85
Brett Basanez, Northwestern	2002-05	1,584	913	36	.576	10,580	44	77
Doug Flutie, Boston College	1981-84	1,270	677	54	.533	10,579	67	80
Steve Stenstrom, Stanford	1991-94	1,320	833	36	.631	10,531	72	92
Jared Lorenzen, Kentucky	2000-03	1,514	862	41	.569	10,354	78	89
Brian McClure, Bowling Green	1982-85	1,427	900	58	.631	10,280	63	90
Troy Kopp, Pacific	1989-92	1,374	798	47	.581	10,258	87	80
Danny Wimprine, Memphis	2001-04	1,469	808	49	.550	10,215	81	92
Eli Manning, Mississippi	2000-03	1,363	829	35	.608	10,119	81	79
Glenn Foley, Boston College	1990-93	1,275	703	60	.551	10,042	72	78
Cade McNown, UCLA	1995-98	1,153	646	39	.560	10,008	61	88

**Record. $See page 10 for explanation.*

CAREER YARDS RECORD PROGRESSION
(Record Yards—Player, Team, Seasons Played)

3,075—Billy Patterson, Baylor, 1936-38; **3,777**—Bud Schwenk, Washington-St. Louis, 1939-41; **4,004**—Johnny Rauch, Georgia, 1945-48; **4,736**—John Ford, Hardin-Simmons, 1947-50; **4,863**—Zeke Bratkowski, Georgia, 1951-53; **5,472**—Jerry Rhome, SMU, 1961, Tulsa, 1963-64; **6,495**—Billy Stevens, UTEP, 1965-67; **7,076**—Steve Ramsey, North Texas, 1967-69; **7,544**—Jim Plunkett, Stanford, 1968-70; **7,549**—John Reaves, Florida, 1969-71; **7,818**—Jack Thompson, Washington St., 1975-78; **9,188**—Mark Herrmann, Purdue, 1977-80; **9,536**—Jim McMahon, BYU, 1977-78, 1980-81; **9,614**—Ben Bennett, Duke, 1980-83; **10,579**—Doug Flutie, Boston College, 1981-84; **10,623**—Kevin Sweeney, Fresno St., $1982-86; **11,425**—Todd Santos, San Diego St., 1984-87; **15,031**—Ty Detmer, BYU, 1988-91; **17,072**—Timmy Chang, Hawaii, $2000-04.

$See page 10 for explanation.

CAREER YARDS PER GAME
(Minimum 5,000 yards; Player must have concluded his career)

Player, Team	Years	G	Att.	Cmp.	Int.	Pct.	Yds.	TD	Yd.PG
Tim Rattay, Louisiana Tech	1997-99	33	1,552	1,015	35	.654	12,746	115	386.2
Ty Detmer, BYU	1988-91	46	1,530	958	65	.626	15,031	*121	326.8
Timmy Chang, Hawaii	$2000-04	53	*2,436	*1,388	*80	.570	*17,072	117	322.1
Chris Vargas, Nevada	1992-93	20	806	502	34	.623	6,359	47	318.0
Mike Perez, San Jose St.	1986-87	20	792	471	30	.595	6,194	36	309.7
Doug Gaynor, Long Beach St.	1984-85	22	837	569	35	.680	6,793	35	308.8
Tony Eason, Illinois	1981-82	22	856	526	29	.614	6,608	37	300.4

Player, Team	Years	G	Att.	Cmp.	Int.	Pct.	Yds.	TD	Yd.PG
Steve Sarkisian, BYU	1995-96	25	789	528	26	.669	7,464	53	298.6
Chris Redman, Louisville	1996-99	42	1,679	1,031	51	.614	12,541	84	298.6
Josh Heupel, Oklahoma	1999-00	23	933	590	29	.632	6,852	50	297.9
Chad Pennington, Marshall	1997-99	36	1,265	807	30	.638	10,698	100	297.2
David Klingler, Houston	1988-91	32	1,268	732	38	.577	9,466	91	295.8
Luke McCown, Louisiana Tech	2000-03	43	1,775	1,063	62	.599	12,666	87	294.6
Josh Wallwork, Wyoming	1995-96	22	729	449	28	.616	6,453	54	293.3
Tim Couch, Kentucky	1996-98	29	1,184	795	35	.671	8,435	74	290.9
Kliff Kingsbury, Texas Tech	1999-02	43	1,883	1,231	40	.654	12,429	95	289.0
Ben Roethlisberger, Miami (Ohio)	2001-03	38	1,304	854	34	.655	10,829	84	285.0
Daunte Culpepper, UCF	1996-98	33	1,097	721	32	.657	9,341	72	283.1
Ryan Schneider, UCF	2000-03	39	1,354	840	51	.620	10,976	82	281.4
Brent Snyder, Utah St.	1987-88	22	875	472	36	.539	6,105	39	277.5
Omar Jacobs, Bowling Green	2003-05	25	811	523	11	.645	6,937	71	277.5
Byron Leftwich, Marshall	$1998-02	43	1,442	939	28	.651	11,903	89	276.8
Philip Rivers, North Carolina St.	2000-03	49	1,710	1,147	34	.671	13,484	95	275.2
Chris Weinke, Florida St.	1997-00	36	1,107	650	32	.587	9,839	79	273.3
Drew Brees, Purdue	1997-00	40	1,525	942	41	.618	10,909	81	272.7
David Neill, Nevada	1998-01	40	1,376	763	33	.555	10,903	73	272.6

**Record.* *$See page 10 for explanation.*

CAREER TOUCHDOWN PASSES

Player, Team	Years	G	TD Passes
Ty Detmer, BYU	1988-91	46	121
Timmy Chang, Hawaii	$2000-04	53	117
Tim Rattay, Louisiana Tech	1997-99	33	115
Danny Wuerffel, Florida	1993-96	46	114
Chad Pennington, Marshall	1997-99	39	100
Matt Leinart, Southern California	2002-05	41	99
Kliff Kingsbury, Texas Tech	1999-02	43	95
Philip Rivers, North Carolina St.	2000-03	49	95
Brady Quinn, Notre Dame	2003-06	49	95
*Colt Brennan, Hawaii	2005-06	26	93
David Klingler, Houston	1988-91	32	91
Peyton Manning, Tennessee	1994-97	44	89
Byron Leftwich, Marshall	$1998-02	43	89
Chris Leak, Florida	2003-06	51	88
Jordan Palmer, UTEP	$2002-06	53	88
Troy Kopp, Pacific	1989-92	40	87
Tim Lester, Western Mich.	1996-99	44	87
Luke McCown, Louisiana Tech	2000-03	43	87
Ken Dorsey, Miami (Fla.)	1999-02	41	86
Andrew Walter, Arizona St.	2001-04	48	85
Bruce Gradkowski, Toledo	2002-05	50	85
Kevin Kolb, Houston	2003-06	50	85
Jim McMahon, BYU	1977-78, 80-81	44	84
Chris Redman, Louisville	1996-99	42	84
Ben Roethlisberger, Miami (Ohio)	2001-03	38	84
Paul Pinegar, Fresno St.	2002-05	48	84
Ryan Schneider, UCF	2000-03	39	82
Ryan Dinwiddie, Boise St.	2000-03	45	82
Joe Adams, Tennessee St.	1977-80	41	81
Drew Brees, Purdue	1997-00	40	81
Eli Manning, Mississippi	2000-03	43	81
Jason White, Oklahoma	$1999-04	38	81
Danny Wimprine, Memphis	2001-04	46	81

*$See page 10 for explanation. *Active player.*

SEASON YARDS

Player, Team	Year	G	Att.	Cmp.	Int.	Pct.	Yards	TD	Yds. Per Att.
B.J. Symons, Texas Tech	2003	13	*719	470	22	.654	5,833	52	8.11
Colt Brennan, Hawaii	†2006	14	559	406	12	.726	5,549	*58	9.93
Ty Detmer, BYU	1990	12	562	361	28	.642	5,188	41	9.23
David Klingler, Houston	1990	11	643	374	20	.582	5,140	54	7.99
Kliff Kingsbury, Texas Tech	2002	14	712	*479	13	.673	5,017	45	7.05
Tim Rattay, Louisiana Tech	1998	12	559	380	13	.680	4,943	46	8.84
Sonny Cumbie, Texas Tech	2004	12	642	421	18	.656	4,742	32	7.39
Andre Ware, Houston	1989	11	578	365	15	.631	4,699	46	8.13
Chase Holbrook, New Mexico St.	2006	12	567	397	9	.700	4,619	34	8.15
Jim McMahon, BYU	†1980	12	445	284	18	.638	4,571	47	10.27
Ty Detmer, BYU	†1989	12	412	265	15	.643	4,560	32	11.07
Graham Harrell, Texas Tech	2006	13	616	412	11	.669	4,555	38	7.39
Philip Rivers, North Carolina St.	†2003	13	483	348	7	.721	4,491	34	9.30
Ben Roethlisberger, Miami (Ohio)	2003	14	495	342	10	.691	4,486	37	9.06
Timmy Chang, Hawaii	2002	14	624	349	22	.559	4,474	25	7.17
Cody Pickett, Washington	2002	13	612	365	14	.596	4,458	28	7.28
Ryan Dinwiddie, Boise St.	2003	14	446	276	7	.619	4,356	31	9.77
Scott Mitchell, Utah	1988	11	533	323	15	.606	4,322	29	8.11
Colt Brennan, Hawaii	2005	12	515	350	13	.680	4,301	35	8.35
David Carr, Fresno St.	2001	13	476	308	7	.647	4,299	42	9.03
Tim Couch, Kentucky	1998	11	553	400	15	.723	4,275	36	7.73
Robbie Bosco, BYU	1985	13	511	338	24	.661	4,273	30	8.36

Player, Team	Year	G	Att.	Cmp.	Int.	Pct.	Yards	TD	Yds. Per Att.
Byron Leftwich, Marshall	2002	12	491	331	10	.674	4,268	30	8.69
Chris Vargas, Nevada	1993	11	490	331	18	.676	4,265	34	8.70
Timmy Chang, Hawaii	2004	13	602	358	13	.595	4,258	38	7.07
Cody Hodges, Texas Tech	2005	12	531	353	12	.665	4,238	31	7.98
Timmy Chang, Hawaii	2003	13	601	353	20	.587	4,199	29	6.99
Chris Weinke, Florida St.	2000	12	431	266	11	.617	4,167	33	9.67
Byron Leftwich, Marshall	2001	12	470	315	7	.670	4,132	38	8.79
Josh Wallwork, Wyoming	1996	12	458	286	15	.625	4,090	33	8.93
Derek Anderson, Oregon St.	2003	13	510	261	24	.512	4,058	24	7.96
Chris Redman, Louisville	1998	10	473	309	15	.653	4,042	29	8.55
Ty Detmer, BYU	1991	12	403	249	12	.618	4,031	35	10.00
Steve Sarkisian, BYU	†1996	14	404	278	12	.688	4,027	33	9.97
Omar Jacobs, Bowling Green	2004	12	462	309	4	.669	4,002	41	8.66

**Record. †National pass-efficiency champion.*

SEASON YARDS PER GAME

Player, Team	Year	G	Att.	Cmp.	Int.	Pct.	Yards	TD	Yd.PG
David Klingler, Houston	1990	11	643	374	20	.582	5,140	54	467.3
B.J. Symons, Texas Tech	2003	13	*719	470	22	.654	*5,833	52	448.7
Ty Detmer, BYU	1990	12	562	361	28	.642	5,188	41	432.3
Andre Ware, Houston	1989	11	578	365	15	.631	4,699	46	427.2
Tim Rattay, Louisiana Tech	1998	12	559	380	13	.680	4,943	46	411.9
Chris Redman, Louisville	1998	10	473	309	15	.653	4,042	29	404.2
Mike Maxwell, Nevada	1995	9	409	277	17	.677	3,611	33	401.2
Colt Brennan, Hawaii	†2006	14	559	406	12	.726	5,549	*58	396.4
Sonny Cumbie, Texas Tech	2004	12	642	421	18	.656	4,742	32	395.2
Scott Mitchell, Utah	1988	11	533	323	15	.606	4,322	29	392.9
Tim Rattay, Louisiana Tech	1999	10	516	342	12	.663	3,922	35	392.2
Tim Couch, Kentucky	1998	11	553	400	15	.723	4,275	36	388.6
Chris Vargas, Nevada	1993	11	490	331	18	.676	4,265	34	387.7
Chase Holbrook, New Mexico St.	2006	12	567	397	9	.700	4,619	34	384.9
Jim McMahon, BYU	†1980	12	445	284	18	.638	4,571	47	380.9
Ty Detmer, BYU	†1989	12	412	265	15	.643	4,560	32	380.0
Troy Kopp, Pacific	1990	9	428	243	14	.568	3,311	31	367.9
David Neill, Nevada	1998	9	344	199	9	.578	3,249	29	361.0
Colt Brennan, Hawaii	2005	12	515	350	13	.680	4,301	35	358.4
Kliff Kingsbury, Texas Tech	2002	14	712	*479	13	.673	5,017	45	358.4
Byron Leftwich, Marshall	2002	12	491	331	10	.674	4,268	30	355.7
Jim McMahon, BYU	†1981	10	423	272	7	.643	3,555	30	355.5
Steve Young, BYU	†1983	11	429	306	10	.713	3,902	33	354.7
Rex Grossman, Florida	†2001	11	395	259	12	.656	3,896	34	354.2
Cody Hodges, Texas Tech	2005	12	531	353	12	.665	4,238	31	353.2
Tim Couch, Kentucky	1997	11	547	363	19	.664	3,884	37	353.1
Tim Rattay, Louisiana Tech	†1997	11	477	293	10	.614	3,881	34	352.8
Graham Harrell, Texas Tech	2006	13	616	412	11	.669	4,555	38	350.3

**Record. †National pass-efficiency champion.*

SEASON TOUCHDOWN PASSES

Player, Team	Year	G	TD Passes
Colt Brennan, Hawaii	2006	14	58
David Klingler, Houston	1990	11	54
B.J. Symons, Texas Tech	2003	13	52
Jim McMahon, BYU	1980	12	47
Andre Ware, Houston	1989	11	46
Tim Rattay, Louisiana Tech	1998	12	46
Kliff Kingsbury, Texas Tech	2002	14	45
David Carr, Fresno St.	2001	13	42
Ty Detmer, BYU	1990	12	41
Omar Jacobs, Bowling Green	2004	12	41
Jason White, Oklahoma	2003	14	40
Dennis Shaw, San Diego St.	1969	10	39
Danny Wuerffel, Florida	1996	12	39
Chad Pennington, Marshall	1997	12	39
Doug Williams, Grambling	1977	11	38
Byron Leftwich, Marshall	2001	12	38
Matt Leinart, Southern California	2003	13	38
Timmy Chang, Hawaii	2004	13	38
Graham Harrell, Texas Tech	2006	13	38
Troy Kopp, Pacific	1991	12	37
Tim Couch, Kentucky	1997	11	37
Chad Pennington, Marshall	1999	12	37
Ben Roethlisberger, Miami (Ohio)	2003	14	37
Rod Rutherford, Pittsburgh	2003	13	37
Brady Quinn, Notre Dame	2006	13	37
Peyton Manning, Tennessee	1997	12	36
Shaun King, Tulane	1998	11	36
Tim Couch, Kentucky	1998	11	36
Drew Brees, Purdue	1998	12	36

CAREER YARDS PER ATTEMPT

(Minimum 900 Attempts; Player must have concluded his career)

Player, Team	Years	Att.	Cmp.	Pct.	Yards	Yards Per Cmp.	Yards Per Att.
Ryan Dinwiddie, Boise St.	2000-03	992	622	.627	9,819	*15.79	9.90
Ty Detmer, BYU	1988-91	1,530	958	.626	15,031	15.69	9.82
Danny Wuerffel, Florida	1993-96	1,170	708	.605	10,875	15.36	9.29
Jim McMahon, BYU	1977-78, 80-81	1,060	653	.616	9,536	14.60	9.00
Marvin Graves, Syracuse	1990-93	943	563	.597	8,466	15.04	8.98
Donovan McNabb, Syracuse	1995-98	938	548	.584	8,389	15.31	8.94
Chris Weinke, Florida St.	1997-00	1,107	650	.587	9,839	15.14	8.89
Billy Blanton, San Diego St.	1993-96	920	588	.639	8,165	13.89	8.88
Joe Hamilton, Georgia Tech	1996-99	1,020	629	.617	8,882	14.12	8.71
Cade McNown, UCLA	1995-98	1,153	646	.560	10,008	15.49	8.68
John Walsh, BYU	1991-94	973	587	.603	8,375	14.27	8.61
Chuck Long, Iowa	$1981-85	1,072	692	.646	9,210	13.31	8.59
Matt Leinart, Southern California	2002-05	1,245	807	.648	10,693	13.30	8.59
Steve Young, BYU	1981-83	908	592	.652	7,733	13.06	8.52
Daunte Culpepper, UCF	1996-98	1,097	721	.657	9,341	12.96	8.52
Chad Pennington, Marshall	1997-99	1,265	807	.638	10,698	13.26	8.45
Robbie Bosco, BYU	1983-85	997	638	.640	8,400	13.17	8.43
Dan McGwire, Iowa/San Diego St.	1986-87, 89-90	973	575	.591	8,164	14.20	8.39
Doug Flutie, Boston College	1981-84	1,270	677	.533	10,579	15.63	8.33
Ben Roethlisberger, Miami (Ohio)	2001-03	1,304	854	.655	10,829	12.68	8.30
Ken Dorsey, Miami (Fla.)	1999-02	1,153	668	.579	9,565	14.32	8.30
Kevin Kolb, Houston	2003-06	1,565	964	.616	12,964	13.45	8.28
Byron Leftwich, Marshall	$1998-02	1,442	939	.651	11,903	12.68	8.25
Bruce Gradkowski, Toledo	2002-05	1,123	766	#.682	9,225	12.04	8.21
Tim Rattay, Louisiana Tech	1997-99	1,552	1,015	.654	12,746	12.56	8.21
Marc Wilson, BYU	1977-79	937	535	.571	7,637	14.27	8.15
Peyton Manning, Tennessee	1994-97	1,381	863	.625	11,201	12.98	8.11
Ryan Schneider, UCF	2000-03	1,354	840	.620	10,976	13.07	8.11
Rob Johnson, Southern California	1991-94	963	623	.647	7,743	12.43	8.04
Kevin Feterik, BYU	1996-99	1,004	609	.607	8,065	13.24	8.03
David Greene, Georgia	2001-04	1,440	849	.590	11,528	13.58	8.01

**Record. $See page 10 for explanation. #Record for minimum 1,000 attempts.*

SINGLE-GAME YARDS

Yds.	Player, Team (Opponent)	Date
716	David Klingler, Houston (Arizona St.)	Dec. 2, 1990
690	Matt Vogler, TCU (Houston)	Nov. 3, 1990
661	B.J. Symons, Texas Tech (Mississippi)	Sept. 27, 2003
643	Cody Hodges, Texas Tech (Kansas St.)	Oct. 15, 2005
637	Brian Lindgren, Idaho (Middle Tenn.)	Oct. 6, 2001
631	Scott Mitchell, Utah (Air Force)	Oct. 15, 1988
622	Jeremy Leach, New Mexico (Utah)	Nov. 11, 1989
621	Dave Wilson, Illinois (Ohio St.)	Nov. 8, 1980
619	John Walsh, BYU (Utah St.)	Oct. 30, 1993
613	Jimmy Klingler, Houston (Rice)	Nov. 28, 1992
611	David Neill, Nevada (New Mexico St.)	Oct. 10, 1998
599	Ty Detmer, BYU (San Diego St.)	Nov. 16, 1991
592	Chris Redman, Louisville (East Caro.)	Nov. 14, 1998
590	Tim Rattay, Louisiana Tech (Nebraska)	Aug. 29, 1998
586	B.J. Symons, Texas Tech (North Carolina St.)	Sept. 20, 2003
585	Robbie Bosco, BYU (New Mexico)	Oct. 19, 1985
572	David Klingler, Houston (Eastern Wash.)	Nov. 17, 1990
571	Marc Wilson, BYU (Utah)	Nov. 5, 1977
568	David Lowery, San Diego St. (BYU)	Nov. 16, 1991
565	Jim McMahon, BYU (Utah)	Nov. 21, 1981

SINGLE-GAME ATTEMPTS

No.	Player, Team (Opponent)	Date
83	Drew Brees, Purdue (Wisconsin)	Oct. 10, 1998
79	Matt Vogler, TCU (Houston)	Nov. 3, 1990
78	Rusty LaRue, Wake Forest (Duke)	Oct. 28, 1995
76	David Klingler, Houston (SMU)	Oct. 20, 1990
75	Chris Vargas, Nevada (McNeese St.)	Sept. 19, 1992
73	Shane Montgomery, North Carolina St. (Duke)	Nov. 11, 1989
73	Troy Kopp, Pacific (Hawaii)	Oct. 27, 1990
73	Jeff Handy, Missouri (Oklahoma St.)	Oct. 17, 1992
73	Chase Holbrook, New Mexico St. (UTEP)	Sept. 30, 2006
72	Matt Vogler, TCU (Texas Tech)	Nov. 10, 1990
72	Luke McCown, Louisiana Tech [Miami (Fla.)]	Oct. 28, 2000
71	Sandy Schwab, Northwestern (Michigan)	Oct. 23, 1982
71	Jimmy Klingler, Houston (Rice)	Nov. 28, 1992
71	Brian Lindgren, Idaho (Middle Tenn.)	Oct. 6, 2001
70	Dave Telford, Fresno St. (Utah St.)	Nov. 14, 1987
70	David Klingler, Houston (Arizona St.)	Dec. 2, 1990
70	David Klingler, Houston (Texas Tech)	Nov. 30, 1991
70	Kliff Kingsbury, Texas Tech (Missouri)	Oct. 19, 2002
70	Timmy Chang, Hawaii (Rice)	Sept. 27, 2003
70	Kent Smith, Central Mich. (Western Mich.)	Nov. 12, 2005
70	Brett Basanez, Northwestern (UCLA)	Dec. 30, 2005

SINGLE-GAME COMPLETIONS

No.	Player, Team (Opponent)	Date
55	Rusty LaRue, Wake Forest (Duke)	Oct. 28, 1995
55	Drew Brees, Purdue (Wisconsin)	Oct. 10, 1998
50	Rusty LaRue, Wake Forest (North Carolina St.)	Nov. 18, 1995
49	Brian Lindgren, Idaho (Middle Tenn.)	Oct. 6, 2001
49	Kliff Kingsbury, Texas Tech (Texas A&M)	Oct. 5, 2002
49	Kliff Kingsbury, Texas Tech (Missouri)	Oct. 19, 2002
49	Bruce Gradkowski, Toledo (Pittsburgh)	Sept. 20, 2003
49	Chase Holbrook, New Mexico St. (Boise St.)	Oct. 15, 2006
48	David Klingler, Houston (SMU)	Oct. 20, 1990
48	Chase Holbrook, New Mexico St. (UTEP)	Sept. 30, 2006
47	Tim Couch, Kentucky (Arkansas)	Oct. 3, 1998
47	Luke McCown, Louisiana Tech (Auburn)	Oct. 21, 2000
46	Jimmy Klingler, Houston (Rice)	Nov. 28, 1992
46	Scott Milanovich, Maryland (Florida St.)	Nov. 18, 1995
46	Tim Rattay, Louisiana Tech (Nebraska)	Aug. 29, 1998
46	Tim Rattay, Louisiana Tech (UCF)	Oct. 23, 1999
46	Kent Smith, Central Mich. (Western Mich.)	Nov. 12, 2005
45	Sandy Schwab, Northwestern (Michigan)	Oct. 23, 1982
45	Tim Rattay, Louisiana Tech (Texas A&M)	Sept. 4, 1999
45	B.J. Symons, Texas Tech (Iowa St.)	Oct. 11, 2003

ANNUAL CHAMPIONS

Year	Player, Team	Class	Att.	Cmp.	Int.	Pct.	Yds.	TD
1937	Davey O'Brien, TCU	Jr.	234	94	18	.402	969	—
1938	Davey O'Brien, TCU	Sr.	167	93	4	.557	1,457	—
1939	Kay Eakin, Arkansas	Sr.	193	78	18	.404	962	—
1940	Billy Sewell, Washington St.	Sr.	174	86	17	.494	1,023	—
1941	Bud Schwenk, Washington-St. Louis	Sr.	234	114	19	.487	1,457	—
1942	Ray Evans, Kansas	Jr.	200	101	9	.505	1,117	—
1943	Johnny Cook, Georgia	Fr.	157	73	20	.465	1,007	—
1944	Paul Rickards, Pittsburgh	So.	178	84	20	.472	997	—
1945	Al Dekdebrun, Cornell	Sr.	194	90	15	.464	1,227	—
1946	Travis Tidwell, Auburn	Fr.	158	79	10	.500	943	5
1947	Charlie Conerly, Mississippi	Sr.	233	133	7	.571	1,367	18
1948	Stan Heath, Nevada	Sr.	222	126	9	.568	2,005	22
1949	Adrian Burk, Baylor	Sr.	191	110	6	.576	1,428	14
1950	Don Heinrich, Washington	Jr.	221	134	9	.606	1,846	14
1951	Don Klosterman, Loyola Marymount	Sr.	315	159	21	.505	1,843	9
1952	Don Heinrich, Washington	Sr.	270	137	17	.507	1,647	13
1953	Bob Garrett, Stanford	Sr.	205	118	10	.576	1,637	17
1954	Paul Larson, California	Sr.	195	125	8	.641	1,537	10
1955	George Welsh, Navy	Sr.	150	94	6	.627	1,319	8
1956	John Brodie, Stanford	Sr.	240	139	14	.579	1,633	12
1957	Ken Ford, Hardin-Simmons	Sr.	205	115	11	.561	1,254	14
1958	Buddy Humphrey, Baylor	Sr.	195	112	8	.574	1,316	7
1959	Dick Norman, Stanford	Jr.	263	152	12	.578	1,963	11
1960	Harold Stephens, Hardin-Simmons	Sr.	256	145	14	.566	1,254	3
1961	Chon Gallegos, San Jose St.	Sr.	197	117	13	.594	1,480	14
1962	Don Trull, Baylor	Jr.	229	125	12	.546	1,627	11
1963	Don Trull, Baylor	Sr.	308	174	12	.565	2,157	12
1964	Jerry Rhome, Tulsa	Sr.	326	224	4	.687	2,870	32
1965	Bill Anderson, Tulsa	Sr.	509	296	14	.582	3,464	30
1966	John Eckman, Wichita St.	Jr.	458	195	*34	.426	2,339	7
1967	Terry Stone, New Mexico	Jr.	336	160	19	.476	1,946	9
1968	Chuck Hixson, SMU	So.	468	265	23	.566	3,103	21
1969	John Reaves, Florida	So.	396	222	19	.561	2,896	24

Beginning in 1970, ranked on per-game (instead of total) completions

Year	Player, Team	Class	G	Att.	Cmp.	Avg.	Int.	Pct.	Yds.	TD
1970	Sonny Sixkiller, Washington	So.	10	362	186	18.6	22	.514	2,303	15
1971	Brian Sipe, San Diego St.	Sr.	11	369	196	17.8	21	.531	2,532	17
1972	Don Strock, Virginia Tech	Sr.	11	427	228	20.7	27	.534	3,243	16
1973	Jesse Freitas, San Diego St.	Sr.	11	347	227	20.6	17	.654	2,993	21
1974	Steve Bartkowski, California	Sr.	11	325	182	16.5	7	.560	2,580	12
1975	Craig Penrose, San Diego St.	Sr.	11	349	198	18.0	24	.567	2,660	15
1976	Tommy Kramer, Rice	Sr.	11	501	269	24.5	19	.537	3,317	21
1977	Guy Benjamin, Stanford	Sr.	10	330	208	20.8	15	.630	2,521	19
1978	Steve Dils, Stanford	Sr.	11	391	247	22.5	15	.632	2,943	22

Beginning in 1979, ranked on passing efficiency rating points (instead of per-game completions)

Year	Player, Team	Class	G	Att.	Cmp.	Int.	Pct.	Yds.	TD	Pts.
1979	Turk Schonert, Stanford	Sr.	11	221	148	6	.670	1,922	19	163.0
1980	Jim McMahon, BYU	Jr.	12	445	284	18	.638	4,571	47	176.9
1981	Jim McMahon, BYU	Sr.	10	423	272	7	.643	3,555	30	155.0
1982	Tom Ramsey, UCLA	Sr.	11	311	191	10	.614	2,824	21	153.5
1983	Steve Young, BYU	Sr.	11	429	306	10	.713	3,902	33	168.5
1984	Doug Flutie, Boston College	Sr.	11	386	233	11	.604	3,454	27	152.9
1985	Jim Harbaugh, Michigan	Jr.	11	212	139	6	.656	1,913	18	163.7
1986	Vinny Testaverde, Miami (Fla.)	Sr.	10	276	175	9	.634	2,557	26	165.8
1987	Don McPherson, Syracuse	Sr.	11	229	129	11	.563	2,341	22	164.3
1988	Timm Rosenbach, Washington St.	Jr.	11	302	199	10	.659	2,791	23	162.0
1989	Ty Detmer, BYU	So.	12	412	265	15	.643	4,560	32	175.6
1990	Shawn Moore, Virginia	Sr.	10	241	144	8	.598	2,262	21	160.7

Year	Player, Team	Class	G	Att.	Cmp.	Int.	Pct.	Yds.	TD	Pts.
1991	Elvis Grbac, Michigan	Jr.	11	228	152	5	.667	1,955	24	169.0
1992	Elvis Grbac, Michigan	Sr.	9	169	112	12	.663	1,465	15	154.2
1993	Trent Dilfer, Fresno St.	Jr.	11	333	217	4	.652	3,276	28	173.1
1994	Kerry Collins, Penn St.	Sr.	11	264	176	7	.667	2,679	21	172.9
1995	Danny Wuerffel, Florida	Jr.	11	325	210	10	.646	3,266	35	178.4
1996	Steve Sarkisian, BYU	Sr.	14	404	278	12	.688	4,027	33	173.6
1997	Cade McNown, UCLA	Jr.	11	283	173	5	.611	2,877	22	168.6
1998	Shaun King, Tulane	Sr.	11	328	223	6	.680	3,232	36	183.3
1999	Michael Vick, Virginia Tech	So.	10	152	90	5	.592	1,840	12	180.4
2000	Bart Hendricks, Boise St.	Sr.	11	347	210	8	.605	3,364	35	170.6
2001	Rex Grossman, Florida	So.	11	395	259	12	.656	3,896	34	170.8
2002	Brad Banks, Iowa	Sr.	13	294	170	5	.578	2,573	26	157.1
2003	Philip Rivers, North Carolina St.	Sr.	13	483	348	7	.721	4,491	34	170.5
2004	Stefan Lefors, Louisville	Sr.	12	257	189	3	.735	2,596	20	181.7
2005	Rudy Carpenter, Arizona St.	Fr.	9	228	156	2	.684	2,273	17	175.0
2006	Colt Brennan, Hawaii	Jr.	14	559	406	12	.726	5,549	*58	186.0

**Record.*

Receiving

CAREER RECEPTIONS PER GAME

(Minimum 125 Receptions; Player must have concluded his career)

Player, Team	Years	G	Rec.	Yards	TD	Rec.PG
Manny Hazard, Houston	1989-90	21	220	2,635	31	10.5
Alex Van Dyke, Nevada	1994-95	22	227	3,100	26	10.3
Howard Twilley, Tulsa	1963-65	26	261	3,343	32	10.0
Jason Phillips, Houston	1987-88	22	207	2,319	18	9.4
Troy Edwards, Louisiana Tech	1996-98	34	280	4,352	*50	8.2
Bryan Reeves, Nevada	1992-93	21	172	2,476	27	8.2
Kevin Curtis, Utah St.	2001-02	22	174	2,789	19	7.9
Nate Burleson, Nevada	2000-02	32	248	3,293	22	7.8
Siaha Burley, UCF	1997-98	22	165	2,248	15	7.5
David Williams, Illinois	1983-85	33	245	3,195	22	7.4
Geoff Noisy, Nevada	1995-98	40	295	4,249	21	7.4
James Dixon, Houston	1987-88	22	161	1,762	14	7.3
John Love, North Texas	1965-66	20	144	2,124	17	7.2
Fred Gilbert, UCLA/Houston	1989, 91-92	22	158	1,672	14	7.2
Ron Sellers, Florida St.	1966-68	30	212	3,598	23	7.1
Keyshawn Johnson, Southern California	1994-95	21	148	2,358	12	7.1
Nakia Jenkins, Utah St.	1996-97	22	155	2,483	14	7.0
Barry Moore, North Texas	1968-69	20	140	2,183	12	7.0
Taylor Stubblefield, Purdue	2001-04	45	*316	3,433	19	6.9
Arnold Jackson, Louisville	1997-00	44	300	3,670	31	6.8
Dante Ridgeway, Ball St.	2002-04	35	238	3,030	22	6.8
Mike Kelly, Davidson	1967-69	23	156	2,114	17	6.8
Paris Warren, Utah	2002-04	23	156	1,885	16	6.8
Guy Liggins, San Jose St.	1986-87	22	149	2,191	16	6.8
Trevor Insley, Nevada	1996-99	44	298	*5,005	35	6.8

**Record.*

SEASON RECEPTIONS PER GAME

Player, Team	Year	G	Rec.	Yards	TD	Rec.PG
Howard Twilley, Tulsa	†1965	10	134	1,779	16	13.4
Manny Hazard, Houston	†1989	11	*142	1,689	22	12.9
Trevor Insley, Nevada	†1999	11	134	*2,060	13	12.2
Alex Van Dyke, Nevada	†1995	11	129	1,854	16	11.7
Troy Edwards, Louisiana Tech	†1998	12	140	1,996	*27	11.7
Nate Burleson, Nevada	†2002	12	138	1,629	12	11.5
Damond Wilkins, Nevada	†1996	11	114	1,121	4	10.4
Chris Daniels, Purdue	1999	11	109	1,133	5	9.9
J.R. Tolver, San Diego St.	2002	13	128	1,785	13	9.9
Jason Phillips, Houston	†1988	11	108	1,444	15	9.8
Fred Gilbert, Houston	†1991	11	106	957	7	9.6
Jajuan Dawson, Tulane	1999	10	96	1,051	8	9.6
Dante Ridgeway, Ball St.	†2004	11	105	1,399	8	9.6
Howard Twilley, Tulsa	†1964	10	95	1,178	13	9.5
Jerry Hendren, Idaho	†1969	10	95	1,452	12	9.5
Chris Penn, Tulsa	†1993	11	105	1,578	12	9.5
Sherman Smith, Houston	†1992	11	103	923	6	9.4
Eugene Baker, Kent St.	†1997	11	103	1,549	18	9.4
James Dixon, Houston	1988	11	102	1,103	11	9.3
Troy Edwards, Louisiana Tech	1997	11	102	1,707	13	9.3
David Williams, Illinois	†1984	11	101	1,278	8	9.2
Arnold Jackson, Louisville	1999	11	101	1,209	9	9.2

**Record. †National champion.*

CAREER RECEPTIONS

Player, Team	Years	Rec.	Yards	Avg.	TD
Taylor Stubblefield, Purdue	2001-04	316	3,433	10.9	19
Josh Davis, Marshall	2001-04	306	3,889	12.7	23
Taurean Henderson, Texas Tech	2002-05	303	2,058	6.8	19
Arnold Jackson, Louisville	1997-00	300	3,670	12.2	31
Trevor Insley, Nevada	1996-99	298	*5,005	16.8	35
Geoff Noisy, Nevada	1995-98	295	4,249	14.4	21
Rashaun Woods, Oklahoma St.	2000-03	293	4,414	15.1	42
Troy Edwards, Louisiana Tech	1996-98	280	4,352	15.5	*50
Darius Watts, Marshall	2000-03	272	4,031	14.8	47
Vincent Marshall, Houston	2003-06	272	3,770	13.9	26
Aaron Turner, Pacific	1989-92	266	4,345	16.3	43
Chad Mackey, Louisiana Tech	1993-96	264	3,789	14.4	22
Terance Mathis, New Mexico	1985-87, 89	263	4,254	16.2	36
Mark Templeton, Long Beach St. (RB)	1983-86	262	1,969	7.5	11
J.R. Tolver, San Diego St.	1999-02	262	3,572	13.6	18
Howard Twilley, Tulsa	1963-65	261	3,343	12.8	32
Marcus Harris, Wyoming	1993-96	259	4,518	17.4	38
Wes Welker, Texas Tech	2000-03	259	3,069	11.8	21
Derek Hagan, Arizona St.	2002-05	258	3,939	15.3	27
Ryne Robinson, Miami (Ohio)	2003-06	258	3,697	14.3	22
Braylon Edwards, Michigan	2001-04	252	3,541	14.1	39
Jovon Bouknight, Wyoming	2002-05	250	3,626	14.5	29
John Standeford, Purdue	2000-03	249	3,618	14.5	27
Nate Burleson, Nevada	2000-02	248	3,219	13.3	22
Eric Deslauriers, Eastern Mich.	$2002-06	248	3,250	13.1	27
James Jordan, Louisiana Tech	1998-00	246	2,489	10.1	19
David Williams, Illinois	1983-85	245	3,195	13.0	22
Troy Walters, Stanford	1996-99	244	3,986	16.3	26
Brandon Stokley, La.-Lafayette	1995-98	241	3,702	15.4	25
Roy Williams, Texas	2000-03	241	3,866	16.0	36

**Record. $See page 10 for explanation.*

SEASON RECEPTIONS

Player, Team	Year	G	Rec.	Yards	TD
Manny Hazard, Houston	†1989	11	142	1,689	22
Troy Edwards, Louisiana Tech	†1998	12	140	1,996	*27
Nate Burleson, Nevada	†2002	12	138	1,629	12
Howard Twilley, Tulsa	†1965	10	134	1,779	16
Trevor Insley, Nevada	†1999	11	134	*2,060	13
Alex Van Dyke, Nevada	†1995	11	129	1,854	16
J.R. Tolver, San Diego St.	2002	13	128	1,785	13
Damond Wilkins, Nevada	†1996	11	114	1,121	4
Marcus Harris, Wyoming	1996	12	109	1,650	13
Chris Daniels, Purdue	1999	11	109	1,133	5
James Jordan, Louisiana Tech	†2000	12	109	1,003	4
Jason Phillips, Houston	†1988	11	108	1,444	15
Kassim Osgood, San Diego St.	2002	13	108	1,552	8
Rashaun Woods, Oklahoma St.	2002	13	107	1,695	17
Fred Gilbert, Houston	†1991	11	106	957	7
Chris Penn, Tulsa	†1993	11	105	1,578	12
Dante Ridgeway, Ball St.	†2004	11	105	1,399	8
Sherman Smith, Houston	†1992	11	103	923	6
Eugene Baker, Kent St.	†1997	11	103	1,549	18
Lance Moore, Toledo	†2003	12	103	1,194	9
James Dixon, Houston	1988	11	102	1,103	11
Troy Edwards, Louisiana Tech	1997	11	102	1,707	13
Chad Owens, Hawaii	2004	13	102	1,290	17
David Williams, Illinois	†1984	11	101	1,278	8
Arnold Jackson, Louisville	1999	11	101	1,209	9

Player, Team	Year	G	Rec.	Yards	TD
Jay Miller, BYU	†1973	11	100	1,181	8
Dameane Douglas, California	1998	11	100	1,150	4
Kwame Cavil, Texas	1999	13	100	1,188	6
Kevin Curtis, Utah St.	†2001	11	100	1,531	10

**Record. †National champion.*

SINGLE-GAME RECEPTIONS

Rec.	Player, Team (Opponent)	Date
23	Randy Gatewood, UNLV (Idaho)	Sept. 17, 1994
22	Jay Miller, BYU (New Mexico)	Nov. 3, 1973
21	Troy Edwards, Louisiana Tech (Nebraska)	Aug. 29, 1998
21	Chris Daniels, Purdue (Michigan St.)	Oct. 16, 1999
20	Rick Eber, Tulsa (Idaho St.)	Oct. 7, 1967
20	Kenny Christian, Eastern Mich. (Temple)	Sept. 23, 2000
19	Howard Twilley, Tulsa (Colorado St.)	Nov. 27, 1965
19	Ron Fair, Arizona St. (Washington St.)	Oct. 28, 1989
19	Manny Hazard, Houston (TCU)	Nov. 4, 1989
19	Manny Hazard, Houston (Texas)	Nov. 11, 1989
19	Josh Reed, LSU (Alabama)	Nov. 3, 2001
19	Nate Burleson, Nevada (UTEP)	Nov. 9, 2002
18	Howard Twilley, Tulsa (Southern Ill.)	Oct. 30, 1965
18	Mark Templeton (RB), Long Beach St. (Utah St.)	Nov. 1, 1986
18	Richard Woodley, TCU (Texas Tech)	Nov. 10, 1990
18	Alex Van Dyke, Nevada (Toledo)	Sept. 23, 1995
18	Alex Van Dyke, Nevada (UNLV)	Oct. 28, 1995
18	Albert Connell, Texas A&M (Colorado)	Sept. 28, 1996
18	Geoff Noisy, Nevada (Arkansas St.)	Nov. 16, 1996
18	Geoff Noisy, Nevada (Oregon)	Sept. 13, 1997
18	Randall Lane, Purdue (Wisconsin)	Oct. 10, 1998
18	J.R. Tolver, San Diego St. (Hawaii)	Dec. 7, 2002

CAREER TOUCHDOWN RECEPTIONS

Player, Team	Years	G	TD
Troy Edwards, Louisiana Tech	1996-98	34	50
Darius Watts, Marshall	2000-03	48	47
Aaron Turner, Pacific	1989-92	44	43
Ryan Yarborough, Wyoming	1990-93	46	42
Rashaun Woods, Oklahoma St.	2000-03	48	42
Dwayne Jarrett, Southern California	2004-06	38	41
Braylon Edwards, Michigan	2001-04	44	39
Greg Jennings, Western Mich.	2002-05	42	39
Clarkston Hines, Duke	1986-89	44	38
Marcus Harris, Wyoming	1993-96	46	38
Terance Mathis, New Mexico	1985-87, 89	44	36
Roy Williams, Texas	2000-03	48	36
Eugene Baker, Kent St.	1995-98	39	35
Trevor Insley, Nevada	1996-99	44	35
Roydell Williams, Tulane	2001-04	48	35
Elmo Wright, Houston	1968-70	30	34
Larry Fitzgerald, Pittsburgh	2002-03	26	34
Charles Sharon, Bowling Green	2002-05	48	34
Ibn Green, Louisville (TE)	1996-99	43	33
Howard Twilley, Tulsa	1963-65	30	32
Steve Largent, Tulsa	1973-75	30	32
David Boston, Ohio St.	1996-98	34	32
Peter Warrick, Florida St.	1996-99	43	32
Michael Larkin, Miami (Ohio)	2001-04	51	32
Jason Hill, Washington St.	2003-06	43	32
Johnnie Lee Higgins Jr., UTEP	$2002-06	57	32

$See page 10 for explanation.

SEASON TOUCHDOWN RECEPTIONS

Player, Team	Year	G	TD
Troy Edwards, Louisiana Tech	1998	12	27
Randy Moss, Marshall	1997	12	25
Manny Hazard, Houston	1989	11	22
Larry Fitzgerald, Pittsburgh	2003	13	22
Jarett Dillard, Rice	2006	13	21
Desmond Howard, Michigan	1991	11	19
Ashley Lelie, Hawaii	2001	12	19
Tom Reynolds, San Diego St.	1971	10	18
Dennis Smith, Utah	1989	12	18
Aaron Turner, Pacific	1991	11	18
Reidel Anthony, Florida	1996	12	18
Eugene Baker, Kent St.	1997	11	18
Darius Watts, Marshall	2001	12	18
Clarkston Hines, Duke	1989	11	17
Mario Bailey, Washington	1991	11	17
Bryan Reeves, Nevada	1993	10	17
J.J. Stokes, UCLA	1993	11	17
Terry Glenn, Ohio St.	1995	11	17
Chris Doering, Florida	1995	12	17
Rashaun Woods, Oklahoma St.	2002	13	17
Chad Owens, Hawaii	2004	13	17

CAREER YARDS PER GAME

(Minimum 2,200 Yards; Player must have concluded his career)

Player, Team	Years	G	Yards	Yd.PG
Alex Van Dyke, Nevada	1994-95	22	3,100	140.9
Troy Edwards, Louisiana Tech	1996-98	34	4,352	128.0
Kevin Curtis, Utah St.	2001-02	22	2,789	126.8
Manny Hazard, Houston	1989-90	21	2,635	125.5
Ron Sellers, Florida St.	1966-68	30	3,598	119.9
Bryan Reeves, Nevada	1992-93	21	2,476	117.9
Trevor Insley, Nevada	1996-99	44	*5,005	113.8
Nakia Jenkins, Utah St.	1996-97	22	2,483	112.9
Keyshawn Johnson, Southern California	1994-95	21	2,358	112.3
Elmo Wright, Houston	1968-70	30	3,347	111.6
Howard Twilley, Tulsa	1963-65	30	3,343	111.4
Chris Penn, Tulsa	1991, 93	22	2,370	107.7
Geoff Noisy, Nevada	1995-98	40	4,249	106.2
Jason Phillips, Houston	1987-88	22	2,319	105.4
Larry Fitzgerald, Pittsburgh	2002-03	26	2,677	103.0
Nate Burleson, Nevada	2000-02	32	3,293	102.9
Siaha Burley, UCF	1997-98	22	2,248	102.2
Brandon Stokley, La.-Lafayette	1995-98	37	3,702	100.1
James Newson, Oregon St.	2001-03	36	3,558	98.8
Aaron Turner, Pacific	1989-92	44	4,345	98.8
Reggie Williams, Washington	2001-03	36	3,536	98.2
Marcus Harris, Wyoming	1993-96	46	4,518	98.2
Rick Beasley, Appalachian St.	†1977-80	32	3,124	97.6
David Williams, Illinois	1982-85	33	3,195	96.8
Terance Mathis, New Mexico	1985-87, 89	44	4,254	96.7

**Record. †Played defensive back in 1977.*

CAREER YARDS

Player, Team	Years	Rec.	Yards	Avg.	TD
Trevor Insley, Nevada	1996-99	298	5,005	16.8	35
Marcus Harris, Wyoming	1993-96	259	4,518	17.4	38
Rashaun Woods, Oklahoma St.	2000-03	293	4,414	15.1	42
Ryan Yarborough, Wyoming	1990-93	229	4,357	#19.0	42
Troy Edwards, Louisiana Tech	1996-98	280	4,352	15.5	*50
Aaron Turner, Pacific	1989-92	266	4,345	16.3	43
Terance Mathis, New Mexico	1985-87, 89	263	4,254	16.2	36
Geoff Noisy, Nevada	1995-98	295	4,249	14.4	21
Darius Watts, Marshall	2000-03	272	4,031	14.8	47
Troy Walters, Stanford	1996-99	244	3,986	16.3	26
Derek Hagan, Arizona St.	2002-05	258	3,939	15.3	27
Mike Hass, Oregon St.	2002-05	220	3,924	17.8	20
Josh Davis, Marshall	2001-04	306	3,889	12.7	23
Roy Williams, Texas	2000-03	241	3,866	16.0	36
Chad Mackey, Louisiana Tech	1993-96	264	3,789	14.4	22
Vincent Marshall, Houston	2003-06	272	3,770	13.9	26
Marc Zeno, Tulane	1984-87	236	3,725	15.8	25
Brandon Stokley, La.-Lafayette	1995-98	241	3,702	15.4	25
Ryne Robinson, Miami (Ohio)	2003-06	258	3,697	14.3	22
Arnold Jackson, Louisville	1997-00	300	3,670	12.2	31
David Anderson, Colorado St.	2002-05	223	3,634	16.3	20
Jovon Bouknight, Wyoming	2002-05	250	3,626	14.5	29
John Standeford, Purdue	2000-03	249	3,618	14.5	27
Steve Neal, Western Mich.	1997-00	235	3,599	15.3	27
Ron Sellers, Florida St.	1966-68	212	3,598	17.0	23
J.R. Tolver, San Diego St.	1999-02	262	3,572	13.6	18
James Newson, Oregon St.	2001-03	212	3,558	16.8	20
Braylon Edwards, Michigan	2001-04	252	3,541	14.1	39
Greg Jennings, Western Mich.	2002-05	238	3,539	14.9	39
Reggie Williams, Washington	2001-03	238	3,536	14.9	22
Peter Warrick, Florida St.	1996-99	207	3,517	17.0	32
Eugene Baker, Kent St.	1995-98	229	3,513	15.3	35

**Record. #Record for minimum 200 catches.*

SEASON YARDS

Player, Team	Year	Rec.	Yards	Avg.	TD
Trevor Insley, Nevada	†1999	134	2,060	15.4	13
Troy Edwards, Louisiana Tech	†1998	140	1,996	14.3	*27
Alex Van Dyke, Nevada	†1995	129	1,854	14.4	16
J.R. Tolver, San Diego St.	†2002	128	1,785	14.0	13
Howard Twilley, Tulsa	1965	134	1,779	13.3	16
Josh Reed, LSU	†2001	94	1,740	18.5	7
Ashley Lelie, Hawaii	2001	84	1,713	20.4	19
Troy Edwards, Louisiana Tech	†1997	102	1,707	16.7	13
Rashaun Woods, Oklahoma St.	2002	107	1,695	15.8	17
Manny Hazard, Houston	1989	*142	1,689	11.9	22
Larry Fitzgerald, Pittsburgh	†2003	92	1,672	18.2	22
Marcus Harris, Wyoming	†1996	109	1,650	15.1	13
Randy Moss, Marshall	1997	90	1,647	18.3	25
Nate Burleson, Nevada	2002	138	1,629	11.8	12
Aaron Turner, Pacific	†1991	92	1,604	17.4	18

Player, Team	Year	Rec.	Yards	Avg.	TD
Torry Holt, North Carolina St.	1998	88	1,604	18.2	11
Chris Penn, Tulsa	†1993	105	1,578	15.0	12
Kassim Osgood, San Diego St.	2002	108	1,552	8.3	8
Eugene Baker, Kent St.	1997	103	1,549	15.0	18
Lee Evans, Wisconsin	2001	75	1,545	20.6	9
Mike Hass, Oregon St.	2005	90	1,532	17.0	6
Kevin Curtis, Utah St.	2001	100	1,531	15.3	10
Chuck Hughes, UTEP	1965	80	1,519	19.0	12
Ryan Yarborough, Wyoming	1993	67	1,512	22.6	16
Henry Ellard, Fresno St.	1982	62	1,510	††24.4	15
Geoff McArthur, California	2003	85	1,504	17.7	10
Edell Shepherd, San Jose St.	2001	83	1,500	18.1	14

**Record. †National champion. ††Record for minimum 50 catches.*

SINGLE-GAME YARDS

Yds.	Player, Team (Opponent)	Date
405	Troy Edwards, Louisiana Tech (Nebraska)	Aug. 29, 1998
363	Randy Gatewood, UNLV (Idaho)	Sept. 17, 1994
349	Chuck Hughes, UTEP (North Texas)	Sept. 18, 1965
326	Nate Burleson, Nevada (San Jose St.)	Nov. 10, 2001
322	Rick Eber, Tulsa (Idaho St.)	Oct. 7, 1967
318	Harry Wood, Tulsa (Idaho St.)	Oct. 7, 1967
316	Jeff Evans, New Mexico St. (Southern Ill.)	Sept. 30, 1978
314	Alex Van Dyke, Nevada (San Jose St.)	Nov. 18, 1995
310	Chad Mackey, Louisiana Tech (Toledo)	Oct. 19, 1996
308	Jason Rivers, Hawaii (Arizona St.)	Dec. 24, 2006
301	Chris Daniels, Purdue (Michigan St.)	Oct. 16, 1999
300	Adarius Bowman, Oklahoma St. (Kansas)	Oct. 14, 2006
297	Brian Oliver, Ball St. (Toledo)	Oct. 9, 1993
297	Aaron Jones, Utah St. (Boise St.)	Nov. 11, 2000
296	Geoffery Noisy, Nevada (Utah St.)	Nov. 9, 1996
296	J.R. Tolver, San Diego St. (Arizona St.)	Sept. 14, 2002
293	Josh Reed, LSU (Alabama)	Nov. 23, 2001
293	Mike Hass, Oregon St. (Boise St.)	Sept. 10, 2004
290	Tom Reynolds, San Diego St. (Utah St.)	Oct. 22, 1971
289	Wesley Walker, California (San Jose St.)	Oct. 2, 1976
288	Mike Siani, Villanova [Xavier (Ohio)]	Oct. 30, 1971
285	Thomas Lewis, Indiana (Penn St.)	Nov. 6, 1993
285	Ashley Lelie, Hawaii (Air Force)	Nov. 24, 2001

ANNUAL CHAMPIONS

Year	Player, Team	Class	Rec.	Yards	TD
1937	Jim Benton, Arkansas	Sr.	48	814	7
1938	Sam Boyd, Baylor	Sr.	32	537	—
1939	Ken Kavanaugh, LSU	Sr.	30	467	—
1940	Eddie Bryant, Virginia	So.	30	222	2
1941	Hank Stanton, Arizona	Sr.	50	820	—
1942	Bill Rogers, Texas A&M	Sr.	39	432	—
1943	Neil Armstrong, Oklahoma St.	Fr.	39	317	—
1944	Reid Moseley, Georgia	So.	32	506	—
1945	Reid Moseley, Georgia	Jr.	31	662	—
1946	Neil Armstrong, Oklahoma St.	Sr.	32	479	1
1947	Barney Poole, Mississippi	Jr.	52	513	8
1948	Johnny "Red" O'Quinn, Wake Forest	Jr.	39	605	7
1949	Art Weiner, North Carolina	Sr.	52	762	7
1950	Gordon Cooper, Denver	Jr.	46	569	8
1951	Dewey McConnell, Wyoming	Sr.	47	725	9
1952	Ed Brown, Fordham	Sr.	57	774	6
1953	John Carson, Georgia	Sr.	45	663	4
1954	Jim Hanifan, California	Sr.	44	569	7
1955	Hank Burnine, Missouri	Sr.	44	594	2
1956	Art Powell, San Jose St.	So.	40	583	5
1957	Stuart Vaughan, Utah	Sr.	53	756	5
1958	Dave Hibbert, Arizona	Jr.	61	606	4
1959	Chris Burford, Stanford	Sr.	61	756	6
1960	Hugh Campbell, Washington St.	So.	66	881	10
1961	Hugh Campbell, Washington St.	Jr.	53	723	5
1962	Vern Burke, Oregon St.	Jr.	69	1,007	10
1963	Lawrence Elkins, Baylor	Jr.	70	873	8
1964	Howard Twilley, Tulsa	Jr.	95	1,178	13
1965	Howard Twilley, Tulsa	Sr.	134	1,779	16
1966	Glenn Meltzer, Wichita St.	So.	91	1,115	4
1967	Bob Goodridge, Vanderbilt	Sr.	79	1,114	6
1968	Ron Sellers, Florida St.	Sr.	86	1,496	12
1969	Jerry Hendren, Idaho	Sr.	95	1,452	12

Beginning in 1970, ranked on per-game (instead of total) catches

Year	Player, Team	Class	G	Rec.	Avg.	Yards	TD
1970	Mike Mikolayunas, Davidson	Sr.	10	87	8.7	1,128	8
1971	Tom Reynolds, San Diego St.	Sr.	10	67	6.7	1,070	7
1972	Tom Forzani, Utah St.	Sr.	11	85	7.7	1,169	8
1973	Jay Miller, BYU	So.	11	100	9.1	1,181	8
1974	Dwight McDonald, San Diego St.	Sr.	11	86	7.8	1,157	7
1975	Bob Farnham, Brown	Jr.	9	56	6.2	701	2
1976	Billy Ryckman, Louisiana Tech	Sr.	11	77	7.0	1,382	10
1977	Wayne Tolleson, Western Caro.	Sr.	11	73	6.6	1,101	7
1978	Dave Petzke, Northern Ill.	Sr.	11	91	8.3	1,217	11
1979	Rick Beasley, Appalachian St.	Jr.	11	74	6.7	1,205	12
1980	Dave Young, Purdue	Sr.	11	67	6.1	917	8
1981	Pete Harvey, North Texas	Sr.	9	57	6.3	743	3
1982	Vincent White, Stanford	Sr.	10	68	6.8	677	8
1983	Keith Edwards, Vanderbilt	Jr.	11	97	8.8	909	8
1984	David Williams, Illinois	Jr.	11	101	9.2	1,278	8
1985	Rodney Carter, Purdue	Sr.	11	98	8.9	1,099	4
1986	Mark Templeton, Long Beach St. (RB)	Sr.	11	99	9.0	688	2
1987	Jason Phillips, Houston	Jr.	11	99	9.0	875	3
1988	Jason Phillips, Houston	Sr.	11	108	9.8	1,444	15
1989	Manny Hazard, Houston	Jr.	11	*142	12.9	1,689	22

Beginning in 1990, ranked on both per-game catches and yards per game

PER-GAME CATCHES

Year	Player, Team	Class	G	Rec.	Avg.	Yards	TD
1990	Manny Hazard, Houston	Sr.	10	78	7.8	946	9
1991	Fred Gilbert, Houston	Jr.	11	106	9.6	957	7
1992	Sherman Smith, Houston	Jr.	11	103	9.4	923	6
1993	Chris Penn, Tulsa	Sr.	11	105	9.6	1,578	12
1994	Alex Van Dyke, Nevada	Jr.	11	98	8.9	1,246	10
1995	Alex Van Dyke, Nevada	Sr.	11	129	11.7	1,854	16
1996	Damond Wilkins, Nevada	Sr.	11	114	10.4	1,121	4
1997	Eugene Baker, Kent St.	Jr.	11	103	9.4	1,549	18
1998	Troy Edwards, Louisiana Tech	Sr.	12	140	11.7	1,996	*27
1999	Trevor Insley, Nevada	Sr.	11	134	12.2	*2,060	13
2000	James Jordan, Louisiana Tech	Jr.	12	109	9.1	1,003	4
2001	Kevin Curtis, Utah St.	Jr.	11	100	9.1	1,531	10
2002	Nate Burleson, Nevada	Sr.	12	138	11.5	1,629	12
2003	Lance Moore, Toledo	Jr.	12	103	8.6	1,194	9
2004	Dante Ridgeway, Ball St.	Jr.	11	105	9.6	1,399	8
2005	Greg Jennings, Western Mich.	Sr.	11	98	8.9	1,259	14
2006	Chris Williams, New Mexico St.	So.	12	92	7.7	1,415	12

YARDS PER GAME

Year	Player, Team	Class	G	Rec.	Yards	Avg.	TD
1990	Patrick Rowe, San Diego St.	Jr.	11	71	1,392	126.6	8
1991	Aaron Turner, Pacific	Jr.	11	92	1,604	145.8	18
1992	Lloyd Hill, Texas Tech	Jr.	11	76	1,261	114.6	12
1993	Chris Penn, Tulsa	Sr.	11	105	1,578	143.5	12
1994	Marcus Harris, Wyoming	So.	12	71	1,431	119.3	11
1995	Alex Van Dyke, Nevada	Sr.	11	129	1,854	168.6	16
1996	Marcus Harris, Wyoming	Sr.	12	109	1,650	137.5	13
1997	Troy Edwards, Louisiana Tech	Jr.	11	102	1,707	155.2	13
1998	Troy Edwards, Louisiana Tech	Sr.	12	140	1,996	166.3	*27
1999	Trevor Insley, Nevada	Sr.	11	134	*2,060	*187.3	13
2000	Antonio Bryant, Pittsburgh	So.	10	68	1,302	130.2	11
2001	Josh Reed, LSU	Jr.	12	94	1,740	145.0	7
2002	J.R. Tolver, San Diego St.	Sr.	13	128	1,785	137.3	13
2003	Larry Fitzgerald, Pittsburgh	So.	13	92	1,672	128.6	22
2004	Dante Ridgeway, Ball St.	Jr.	11	105	1,399	127.2	8
2005	Mike Hass, Oregon St.	Sr.	11	90	1,532	139.3	6
2006	Chris Williams, New Mexico St.	So.	12	92	1,415	117.9	12

**Record.*

Scoring

CAREER POINTS PER GAME

(Minimum 225 Points; Player must have concluded his career)

Player, Team	Years	G	TD	Extra Pts. Scored	FG	Pts.	Pt.PG
Marshall Faulk, San Diego St.	1991-93	31	‡62	4	0	‡376	12.1
Ed Marinaro, Cornell	1969-71	27	52	6	0	318	11.8
Bill Burnett, Arkansas	1968-70	26	49	0	0	294	11.3
Steve Owens, Oklahoma	1967-69	30	56	0	0	336	11.2
Eddie Talboom, Wyoming	1948-50	28	34	99	0	303	10.8
Travis Prentice, Miami (Ohio)	1996-99	44	*78	0	0	*468	10.6
Garrett Wolfe, Northern Ill.	2004-06	33	57	2	0	344	10.4
Troy Edwards, Louisiana Tech	1996-98	34	57	0	0	342	10.1
Howard Twilley, Tulsa	1963-65	26	32	67	0	259	10.0
Tom Harmon, Michigan	1938-40	24	33	33	2	237	9.9
Ricky Williams, Texas	1995-98	46	75	2	0	452	9.8
Lee Suggs, Virginia Tech	1999-02	35	56	0	0	336	9.6
Glenn Davis, Army	1943-46	37	59	0	0	354	9.6
Johnny Bright, Drake	1949-51	25	40	0	0	240	9.6
Anthony Thompson, Indiana	1986-89	41	65	4	0	394	9.6
Roman Anderson, Houston	1988-91	44	0	213	70	423	9.6
Stacey Robinson, Northern Ill. (QB)	1988-90	25	38	6	0	234	9.4
Floyd Little, Syracuse	1964-66	30	46	2	0	278	9.3
Anthony Davis, Southern California	1972-74	33	50	2	0	302	9.2
Felix "Doc" Blanchard, Army	1944-46	25	38	3	0	231	9.2

**Record. ‡Three-year totals record.*

SEASON POINTS PER GAME

Player, Team	Years	G	TD	Extra Pts. Scored	FG	Pts.	Pt.PG
Barry Sanders, Oklahoma St.	†1988	11	*39	0	0	*234	21.3
Bobby Reynolds, Nebraska	†1950	9	22	25	0	157	17.4
Art Luppino, Arizona	†1954	10	24	22	0	166	16.6
Ed Marinaro, Cornell	†1971	9	24	4	0	148	16.4
Lydell Mitchell, Penn St.	1971	11	29	0	0	174	15.8
Marshall Faulk, San Diego St.	†1991	9	23	2	0	140	15.6
Troy Edwards, Louisiana Tech	†1998	12	31	0	0	186	15.5
Luke Staley, BYU	†2001	11	28	2	0	170	15.5
Ricky Williams, Texas	1998	11	28	0	0	168	15.3
Lee Suggs, Virginia Tech	†2000	11	28	0	0	168	15.3
Byron "Whizzer" White, Colorado	†1937	8	16	23	1	122	15.3

**Record. †National champion.*

CAREER POINTS
(Non-Kickers)

Player, Team	Years	TD	Extra Pts. Scored	FG	Pts.
Travis Prentice, Miami (Ohio)	1996-99	*78	0	0	468
Ricky Williams, Texas	1995-98	75	2	0	452
Taurean Henderson, Texas Tech	2002-05	69	0	0	414
Brock Forsey, Boise St.	1999-02	68	0	0	408
Cedric Benson, Texas	2001-04	67	2	0	404
Anthony Thompson, Indiana	1986-89	65	4	0	394
Ron Dayne, Wisconsin	1996-99	63	0	0	378
Marshall Faulk, San Diego St.	1991-93	‡62	4	0	‡376
Eric Crouch, Nebraska (QB)	1998-01	59	20	0	374
DeAngelo Williams, Memphis	2002-05	60	2	0	362
Dwone Hicks, Middle Tenn.	1999-02	59	4	0	358
Tony Dorsett, Pittsburgh	1973-76	59	2	0	356
DonTrell Moore, New Mexico	2002-05	59	2	0	356
Glenn Davis, Army	1943-46	59	0	0	354
Ken Simonton, Oregon St.	1998-01	57	4	0	346
Garrett Wolfe, Northern Ill.	2004-06	57	0	2	344
Troy Edwards, Louisiana Tech	1995-98	57	0	0	342
LenDale White, Southern California	2002-05	57	0	0	342
Art Luppino, Arizona	1953-56	48	49	0	337
Steve Owens, Oklahoma	1967-69	56	0	0	336
Chris Lemon, Nevada	1996-99	56	0	0	336
Lee Suggs, Virginia Tech	1999-02	56	0	0	336
Wilford White, Arizona St.	1947-50	48	27	4	327
Barry Sanders, Oklahoma St.	1986-88	54	0	0	324
Skip Hicks, UCLA	$1993-97	54	0	0	324
LaDainian Tomlinson, TCU	1997-00	54	0	0	324
Allen Pinkett, Notre Dame	1982-85	53	2	0	320

**Record. $See page 10 for explanation. ‡Three-year totals record.*

CAREER POINTS
(Kickers)

Player, Team	Years	PAT	PAT Att.	FG	FG Att.	Pts.
Roman Anderson, Houston	1988-91	213	217	70	101	423
Billy Bennett, Georgia	2000-03	148	151	*87	*110	409
Carlos Huerta, Miami (Fla.)	1988-91	178	181	73	91	397
Jason Elam, Hawaii	$1988-92	158	161	79	100	395
Derek Schmidt, Florida St.	1984-87	174	178	73	102	393
Nick Novak, Maryland	2001-04	153	159	80	107	393
Kris Brown, Nebraska	1995-98	217	222	57	77	388
Xavier Beitia, Florida St.	2001-04	174	179	67	92	375
Jeff Hall, Tennessee	1995-98	188	202	61	89	371
Shayne Graham, Virginia Tech	1996-99	167	169	68	93	371
Steve Azar, Northern Ill.	2000-03	151	158	73	92	370
Justin Ayat, Hawaii	2001-04	193	211	59	89	370
Stephen Gostkowski, Memphis	2002-05	159	165	70	92	369
Luis Zendejas, Arizona St.	1981-84	134	135	78	105	368
Jeff Chandler, Florida	$1997-01	167	180	67	80	368
Shaun Suisham, Bowling Green	2001-04	*226	*233	45	66	361
Nate Kaeding, Iowa	2000-03	165	168	63	78	^360
Jeff Jaeger, Washington	1983-86	118	123	80	99	358
Dusty Mangum, Texas	2001-04	208	211	50	73	358
Justin Medlock, UCLA	$2002-06	147	148	70	88	357
Garrett Rivas, Michigan	2003-06	162	171	64	82	354
Kevin Butler, Georgia	1981-84	122	125	77	98	353
John Lee, UCLA	1982-85	116	117	79	92	353
Max Zendejas, Arizona	1982-85	122	124	77	104	353
Derek Mahoney, Fresno St.	1990-93	216	222	45	63	351
Martin Gramatica, Kansas St.	1994-95, 97-98	187	192	54	70	349
Nick Calaycay, Boise St.	1999-02	213	222	45	56	348

**Record. $See page 10 for explanation. ^Includes one TD rushing.*

SEASON POINTS

Player, Team	Year	TD	Extra Pts. Scored	FG	Pts.
Barry Sanders, Oklahoma St.	†1988	*39	0	0	234
Brock Forsey, Boise St.	†2002	32	0	0	192
Troy Edwards, Louisiana Tech	†1998	31	0	0	186
Lydell Mitchell, Penn St.	1971	29	0	0	174
Mike Rozier, Nebraska	†1983	29	0	0	174
Luke Staley, BYU	†2001	28	2	0	170
Ricky Williams, Texas	1998	28	0	0	168
Lee Suggs, Virginia Tech	†2000	28	0	0	168
Willis McGahee, Miami (Fla.)	2002	28	0	0	168
Art Luppino, Arizona	†1954	24	22	0	166
Bobby Reynolds, Nebraska	†1950	22	25	0	157
LenDale White, Southern California	2005	26	0	0	156
Anthony Thompson, Indiana	†1989	25	4	0	154
Fred Wendt, UTEP	†1948	20	32	0	152
Randy Moss, Marshall	1997	25	2	0	152
Ricky Williams, Texas	†1997	25	2	0	152
Ian Johnson, Boise St.	†2006	25	2	0	152
Pete Johnson, Ohio St.	†1975	25	0	0	150
Skip Hicks, UCLA	1997	25	0	0	150
Travis Prentice, Miami (Ohio)	1997	25	0	0	150

**Record. †National champion.*

SINGLE-GAME POINTS

No.	Player, Team (Opponent)	Date
48	Howard Griffith, Illinois (Southern Ill.)	Sept. 22, 1990
44	Marshall Faulk, San Diego St. (Pacific)	Sept. 14, 1991
43	Jim Brown, Syracuse (Colgate)	Nov. 17, 1956
42	Fred Wendt, UTEP (New Mexico St.)	Nov. 25, 1948
42	Arnold "Showboat" Boykin, Mississippi (Mississippi St.)	Dec. 1, 1951
42	Rashaun Woods, Oklahoma St. (SMU)	Sept. 20, 2003
38	Dick Bass, Pacific (San Diego St.)	Nov. 22, 1958
37	Jimmy Nutter, Wichita St. (Northern St.)	Oct. 22, 1949
36	Tom Powers, Duke (Richmond)	Oct. 21, 1950
36	Pete Pedro, West Tex. A&M (UTEP)	Sept. 30, 1961
36	Howard Twilley, Tulsa (Louisville)	Nov. 6, 1965
36	Tom Francisco, Virginia Tech (VMI)	Nov. 24, 1966
36	Tim Delaney, San Diego St. (New Mexico St.)	Nov. 15, 1969
36	Anthony Davis, Southern California (Notre Dame)	Dec. 2, 1972
36	Andre Herrera, Southern Ill. (Northern Ill.)	Oct. 23, 1976
36	Kelvin Bryant, North Carolina (East Caro.)	Sept. 12, 1981
36	Dee Dowis, Air Force (San Diego St.)	Sept. 2, 1989
36	Blake Ezor, Michigan St. (Northwestern)	Nov. 18, 1989
36	Calvin Jones, Nebraska (Kansas)	Nov. 9, 1991
36	Madre Hill, Arkansas (South Carolina)	Sept. 9, 1995
36	Antowain Smith, Houston (Southern Miss.)	Nov. 9, 1996
36	Scott Harley, East Caro. (Ohio)	Nov. 16, 1996
36	Ricky Williams, Texas (New Mexico St.)	Sept. 5, 1998
36	Ricky Williams, Texas (Rice)	Sept. 26, 1998
36	LaDainian Tomlinson, TCU (UTEP)	Nov. 20, 1999
36	Dwone Hicks, Middle Tenn. (Louisiana Tech)	Oct. 7, 2000
36	Quentin Griffin, Oklahoma (Texas)	Oct. 7, 2000
36	Levron Williams, Indiana (Michigan St.)	Nov. 10, 2001
36	Chris Brown, Colorado (Nebraska)	Nov. 23, 2001
36	Chance Kretschmer, Nevada (UTEP)	Nov. 24, 2001
36	Jonathan Golden, Baylor (Samford)	Sept. 7, 2002
36	Craig Candeto, Navy (Army)	Dec. 7, 2002
36	Willis McGahee, Miami (Fla.) (Virginia Tech)	Dec. 7, 2002
36	Carnell Williams, Auburn (Mississippi St.)	Oct. 18, 2003
36	Steve Slaton, West Virginia (Louisville)	Oct. 15, 2005

ANNUAL CHAMPIONS

Year	Player, Team	Class	TD	Extra Pts. Scored	FG	Pts.
1937	Byron "Whizzer" White, Colorado	Sr.	16	23	1	122
1938	Parker Hall, Mississippi	Sr.	11	7	0	73
1939	Tom Harmon, Michigan	Jr.	14	15	1	102
1940	Tom Harmon, Michigan	Sr.	16	18	1	117
1941	Bill Dudley, Virginia	Sr.	18	23	1	134
1942	Bob Steuber, Missouri	Sr.	18	13	0	121
1943	Steve Van Buren, LSU	Sr.	14	14	0	98
1944	Glenn Davis, Army	So.	20	0	0	120
1945	Felix "Doc" Blanchard, Army	Jr.	19	1	0	115
1946	Gene Roberts, Chattanooga	Sr.	18	9	0	117
1947	Lou Gambino, Maryland	Jr.	16	0	0	96
1948	Fred Wendt, UTEP	Sr.	20	32	0	152
1949	George Thomas, Oklahoma	Sr.	19	3	0	117
1950	Bobby Reynolds, Nebraska	So.	22	25	0	157
1951	Ollie Matson, San Francisco	Sr.	21	0	0	126
1952	Jackie Parker, Mississippi St.	Jr.	16	24	0	120
1953	Earl Lindley, Utah St.	Sr.	13	3	0	81
1954	Art Luppino, Arizona	So.	24	22	0	166

Year	Player, Team	Class	TD	Extra Pts. Scored	FG	Pts.
1955	Jim Swink, TCU	Jr.	20	5	0	125
1956	Clendon Thomas, Oklahoma	Jr.	18	0	0	108
1957	Leon Burton, Arizona St.	Jr.	16	0	0	96
1958	Dick Bass, Pacific	Jr.	18	8	0	116
1959	Pervis Atkins, New Mexico St.	Jr.	17	5	0	107
1960	Bob Gaiters, New Mexico St.	Sr.	23	7	0	145
1961	Jim Pilot, New Mexico St.	So.	21	12	0	138
1962	Jerry Logan, West Tex. A&M	Sr.	13	32	0	110
1963	Cosmo Iacavazzi, Princeton	Jr.	14	0	0	84
	Dave Casinelli, Memphis	Sr.	14	0	0	84
1964	Brian Piccolo, Wake Forest	Sr.	17	9	0	111
1965	Howard Twilley, Tulsa	Sr.	16	31	0	127
1966	Ken Hebert, Houston	Jr.	11	41	2	113
1967	Leroy Keyes, Purdue	Jr.	19	0	0	114
1968	Jim O'Brien, Cincinnati	Jr.	12	31	13	142
1969	Steve Owens, Oklahoma	Sr.	23	0	0	138

Beginning in 1970, ranked on per-game (instead of total) points

Year	Player, Team	Class	G	TD	Extra Pts. Scored	FG	Pts.	Avg.
1970	Brian Bream, Air Force	Jr.	10	20	0	0	120	12.0
	Gary Kosins, Dayton	Jr.	9	18	0	0	108	12.0
1971	Ed Marinaro, Cornell	Sr.	9	24	4	0	148	16.4
1972	Harold Henson, Ohio St.	So.	10	20	0	0	120	12.0
1973	Jim Jennings, Rutgers	Sr.	11	21	2	0	128	11.6
1974	Bill Marek, Wisconsin	Jr.	9	19	0	0	114	12.7
1975	Pete Johnson, Ohio St.	Jr.	11	25	0	0	150	13.6
1976	Tony Dorsett, Pittsburgh	Sr.	11	22	2	0	134	12.2
1977	Earl Campbell, Texas	Sr.	11	19	0	0	114	10.4
1978	Billy Sims, Oklahoma	Jr.	11	20	0	0	120	10.9
1979	Billy Sims, Oklahoma	Sr.	11	22	0	0	132	12.0
1980	Sammy Winder, Southern Miss.	Jr.	11	20	0	0	120	10.9
1981	Marcus Allen, Southern California	Sr.	11	23	0	0	138	12.5
1982	Greg Allen, Florida St.	So.	11	21	0	0	126	11.5
1983	Mike Rozier, Nebraska	Sr.	12	29	0	0	174	14.5
1984	Keith Byars, Ohio St.	Jr.	11	24	0	0	144	13.1
1985	Bernard White, Bowling Green	Sr.	11	19	0	0	114	10.4
1986	Steve Bartalo, Colorado St.	Sr.	11	19	0	0	114	10.4
1987	Paul Hewitt, San Diego St.	Jr.	12	24	0	0	144	12.0
1988	Barry Sanders, Oklahoma St.	Jr.	11	*39	0	0	*234	*21.3
1989	Anthony Thompson, Indiana	Sr.	11	25	4	0	154	14.0
1990	Stacey Robinson, Northern Ill. (QB)	Sr.	11	19	6	0	120	10.9
1991	Marshall Faulk, San Diego St.	Fr.	9	23	2	0	140	15.6
1992	Garrison Hearst, Georgia	Jr.	11	21	0	0	126	11.5
1993	Byron Morris, Texas Tech	Jr.	11	22	2	0	134	12.2
1994	Rashaan Salaam, Colorado	Jr.	11	24	0	0	144	13.1
1995	Eddie George, Ohio St.	Sr.	12	24	0	0	144	12.0
1996	Corey Dillon, Washington	Jr.	11	23	0	0	138	12.6
1997	Ricky Williams, Texas	Jr.	11	25	2	0	152	13.8
1998	Troy Edwards, Louisiana Tech	Sr.	12	31	0	0	186	15.5
1999	Shaun Alexander, Alabama	Sr.	11	24	0	0	144	13.1
2000	Lee Suggs, Virginia Tech	So.	11	28	0	0	168	15.3
2001	Luke Staley, BYU	Jr.	11	28	2	0	170	15.5
2002	Brock Forsey, Boise St.	Sr.	13	32	0	0	192	14.8
2003	Patrick Cobbs, North Texas	Jr.	11	21	0	0	126	11.5
2004	Tyler Jones, Boise St.	Sr.	12	0	69	24	141	11.8
2005	Michael Bush, Louisville	Jr.	10	24	0	0	144	14.4
2006	Ian Johnson, Boise St.	So.	12	25	2	0	152	12.7

*Record.

Interceptions

CAREER INTERCEPTIONS

Player, Team	Years	No.	Yards	Avg.
Al Brosky, Illinois	1950-52	29	356	12.3
John Provost, Holy Cross	1972-74	27	470	17.4
Martin Bayless, Bowling Green	1980-83	27	266	9.9
Tom Curtis, Michigan	1967-69	25	440	17.6
Tony Thurman, Boston College	1981-84	25	221	8.8
Tracy Saul, Texas Tech	1989-92	25	425	17.0
Jeff Nixon, Richmond	1975-78	23	377	16.4
Jim Bolding, East Caro.	1973-76	22	143	6.5
Bennie Blades, Miami (Fla.)	1984-87	22	355	16.1
Mike Sensibaugh, Ohio St.	1968-70	21	226	10.8
Barry Hill, Iowa St.	1972-74	21	202	9.6
Chuck Cecil, Arizona	1984-87	21	241	11.5
Terrell Buckley, Florida St.	1989-91	21	*501	23.9
Jamar Fletcher, Wisconsin	1998-00	21	459	21.9
Jim Leonhard, Wisconsin	2001-04	21	251	12.0
Lynn Chandnois, Michigan St.	1946-49	20	410	20.5
Bobby Wilson, Mississippi	1946-49	20	369	18.5
Tom Wilson, Colgate	1964-66	20	215	10.8
Jackie Wallace, Arizona	1970-72	20	250	12.5
Dave Atkinson, BYU	1971-73	20	222	11.1
Artimus Parker, Southern California	1971-73	20	268	13.4
Charles Jefferson, McNeese St.	1975-78	20	95	4.8
Chris Williams, LSU	1977-80	20	91	4.6
Anthony Young, Temple	1981-84	20	230	11.5
Mark Collins, Cal St. Fullerton	1982-85	20	193	9.7
Kevin Smith, Texas A&M	1988-91	20	289	14.5
Mitch Meeuwsen, Oregon St.	2001-04	20	149	7.5

*Record.

SEASON INTERCEPTIONS

Player, Team	Year	No.	Yards
Al Worley, Washington	†1968	14	130
George Shaw, Oregon	†1951	13	136
Hank Rich, Arizona St.	†1950	12	135
Bill Albrecht, Washington	1951	12	140
Frank Polito, Villanova	†1971	12	261
Terry Hoage, Georgia	†1982	12	51
Tony Thurman, Boston College	†1984	12	99
Bob Navarro, Eastern Mich.	†1989	12	73
Cornelius Price, Houston	†1989	12	187
Terrell Buckley, Florida St.	†1991	12	238

†National champion.

ANNUAL CHAMPIONS

Year	Player, Team	Class	No.	Yards
1938	Elmer Tarbox, Texas Tech	Sr.	11	89
1939	Harold Van Every, Minnesota	Sr.	8	59
1940	Dick Morgan, Tulsa	Jr.	7	210
1941	Bobby Robertson, Southern California	Sr.	9	126
1942	Ray Evans, Kansas	Jr.	10	76
1943	Jay Stoves, Washington	Sr.	7	139
1944	Jim Hardy, Southern California	Sr.	8	73
1945	Jake Leicht, Oregon	So.	9	195
1946	Larry Hatch, Washington	So.	8	114
1947	John Bruce, William & Mary	Jr.	9	78
1948	Jay Van Noy, Utah St.	Jr.	8	228
1949	Bobby Wilson, Mississippi	Sr.	10	70
1950	Hank Rich, Arizona St.	Sr.	12	135
1951	George Shaw, Oregon	Fr.	13	136
1952	Cecil Ingram, Alabama	Jr.	10	163
1953	Bob Garrett, Stanford	Sr.	9	80
1954	Gary Glick, Colorado St.	Jr.	8	168
1955	Sam Wesley, Oregon St.	Jr.	7	61
1956	Jack Hill, Utah St.	Sr.	7	132
1957	Ray Toole, North Texas	Sr.	7	133
1958	Jim Norton, Idaho	Jr.	9	222
1959	Bud Whitehead, Florida St.	Jr.	6	111
1960	Bob O'Billovich, Montana	Jr.	7	71
1961	Joe Zuger, Arizona St.	Sr.	10	121
1962	Byron Beaver, Houston	Sr.	10	56
1963	Dick Kern, William & Mary	Sr.	8	116
1964	Tony Carey, Notre Dame	Jr.	8	121
1965	Bob Sullivan, Maryland	Sr.	10	61
1966	Henry King, Utah St.	Sr.	11	180
1967	Steve Haterius, West Tex. A&M	Sr.	11	90
1968	Al Worley, Washington	Sr.	*14	130
1969	Seth Miller, Arizona St.	Sr.	11	63

Beginning in 1970, ranked on per-game (instead of total) number

Year	Player, Team	Class	G	No.	Avg.	Yards
1970	Mike Sensibaugh, Ohio St.	Sr.	8	8	1.00	40
1971	Frank Polito, Villanova	So.	10	12	1.20	261
1972	Mike Townsend, Notre Dame	Jr.	10	10	1.00	39
1973	Mike Gow, Illinois	Jr.	11	10	0.91	142
1974	Mike Haynes, Arizona St.	Jr.	12	11	0.92	115
1975	Jim Bolding, East Caro.	Jr.	10	10	1.00	51
1976	Anthony Francis, Houston	Jr.	11	10	0.91	118
1977	Paul Lawler, Colgate	Sr.	9	7	0.78	53
1978	Pete Harris, Penn St.	Jr.	11	10	0.91	155
1979	Joe Callan, Ohio	Sr.	9	9	1.00	110
1980	Ronnie Lott, Southern California	Sr.	11	8	0.73	166
	Steve McNamee, William & Mary	Sr.	11	8	0.73	125
	Greg Benton, Drake	Sr.	11	8	0.73	119
	Jeff Hipp, Georgia	Sr.	11	8	0.73	104
	Mike Richardson, Arizona St.	So.	11	8	0.73	89
	Vann McElroy, Baylor	Jr.	11	8	0.73	73
1981	Sam Shaffer, Temple	Sr.	10	9	0.90	76
1982	Terry Hoage, Georgia	Jr.	10	12	1.20	51
1983	Martin Bayless, Bowling Green	Sr.	11	10	0.91	64
1984	Tony Thurman, Boston College	Sr.	11	12	1.09	99
1985	Chris White, Tennessee	Sr.	11	9	0.82	168

Year	Player, Team	Class	G	No.	Avg.	Yards
	Kevin Walker, East Caro.	Sr.	11	9	0.82	155
1986	Bennie Blades, Miami (Fla.)	Jr.	11	10	0.91	128
1987	Keith McMeans, Virginia	Fr.	10	9	0.90	35
1988	Kurt Larson, Michigan St. (LB)	Sr.	11	8	0.73	78
	Andy Logan, Kent St.	Sr.	11	8	0.73	54
1989	Cornelius Price, Houston	Jr.	11	12	1.09	187
	Bob Navarro, Eastern Mich.	Jr.	11	12	1.09	73
1990	Jerry Parks, Houston	Jr.	11	8	0.73	124
1991	Terrell Buckley, Florida St.	Jr.	12	12	1.00	238
1992	Carlton McDonald, Air Force	Sr.	11	8	0.73	109
1993	Orlanda Thomas, La.-Lafayette	Jr.	11	9	0.82	84
1994	Aaron Beasley, West Virginia	Jr.	12	10	0.83	133
1995	Willie Smith, Louisiana Tech	Jr.	10	8	0.80	65
1996	Dre' Bly, North Carolina	Fr.	11	11	1.00	141
1997	Brian Lee, Wyoming	Sr.	11	8	0.73	103
1998	Jamar Fletcher, Wisconsin	Fr.	9	6	0.67	99
1999	Deltha O'Neal, California	Sr.	11	9	0.82	280
	Deon Grant, Tennessee	Jr.	11	9	0.82	167
	Rodregis Brooks, UAB	Jr.	11	9	0.82	152
2000	Dwight Smith, Akron	Sr.	11	10	0.91	208
	Anthony Floyd, Louisville	So.	11	10	0.91	152
2001	Edward Reed, Miami (Fla.)	Sr.	11	9	0.82	206
2002	Jim Leonhard, Wisconsin	So.	14	11	0.79	115
2003	Sean Taylor, Miami (Fla.)	Jr.	12	10	0.83	184
2004	Chris Harris, La.-Monroe	Sr.	11	7	0.64	11
	Charles Gordon, Kansas	So.	11	7	0.64	52
2005	Aaron Gibson, Oregon	Sr.	12	7	0.64	117
2006	Stanley Franks, Idaho	Jr.	12	9	0.75	220

*Record.

DEFENSIVE RECORDS

(Since 2000)

Total Tackles

CAREER TOTAL TACKLES PER GAME

(Min. 300 Total Tackles; Player must have concluded his career)

Player, Team	Years	G	Solo	Ast.	Total	Avg.
E.J. Henderson, Maryland	2000-02	35	308	126	434	12.40
Hanik Milligan, Houston	2000-02	34	235	170	405	11.91
Tim McGarigle, Northwestern	2002-05	48	319	226	*545	11.35
Rod Davis, Southern Miss.	2000-03	47	*360	166	526	11.21
Justin Beriault, Ball St.	2001-04	46	267	241	508	11.04
Ryan Fowler, Duke	2000-03	46	286	209	495	10.76
Dantonio Burnette, North Carolina St.	2000-02	34	185	178	363	10.68
Grant Wiley, West Virginia	2000-03	47	298	194	492	10.47
Josh Smith, Navy	2002-04	34	164	190	354	10.41
Jerry Schumacher, Illinois	2000-02	35	236	115	351	10.03
Dexter Reid, North Carolina	2000-03	47	304	162	466	9.91
Alfred Fincher, Connecticut	2002-04	36	181	166	347	9.64
Matt Pusateri, Miami (Ohio)	2001-04	51	313	172	485	9.51
Adam Seward, UNLV	2001-04	46	215	218	433	9.41
Derrick Johnson, Texas	2001-04	49	281	177	458	9.35
James King, Central Mich.	2001-04	45	268	141	409	9.09
Abdul Hodge, Iowa	2002-05	50	289	164	453	9.06
John Leake, Clemson	2000-03	49	244	199	443	9.04
Terrell Jones, Miami (Ohio)	2000-03	47	258	166	424	9.02
Nick Duffy, Northern Ill.	2000-03	39	236	103	339	8.69
Barrett Ruud, Nebraska	2001-04	50	218	214	432	8.64
Akil Grant, Northern Ill.	2000-03	42	246	115	361	8.60

*Record.

SEASON TOTAL TACKLES PER GAME

Player, Team	Year	G	Solo	Ast.	Total	Avg.
Rick Sherrod, West Virginia	†2001	10	102	54	156	15.6
Jimmy Cottrell, New Mexico St.	†2005	12	90	89	179	14.9
Hanik Milligan, Houston	2001	10	82	67	149	14.9
Levar Fisher, North Carolina St.	†2000	11	93	70	163	14.8
Kyle Kayden, West Virginia	2001	11	88	71	159	14.5
Jack Brewer, Minnesota	2001	11	89	66	155	14.1
Hunter Hillenmeyer, Vanderbilt	†2002	12	116	52	168	14.0
Nick Greisen, Wisconsin	2001	12	101	66	167	13.9
Pernell Griffin, East Caro.	2001	11	72	81	153	13.9
Dexter Reid, North Carolina	2002	12	107	59	166	13.8
Lawrence Flugence, Texas Tech	2002	14	124	69	*193	13.8

*Record. †National champion.

CAREER TOTAL TACKLES

Player, Team	Years	G	Solo	Ast.	Total
Tim McGarigle, Northwestern	2002-05	48	319	226	545
Rod Davis, Southern Miss.	2000-03	47	*360	166	526
Justin Beriault, Ball St.	2001-04	46	267	241	508
Ryan Fowler, Duke	2000-03	46	286	209	495
Grant Wiley, West Virginia	2000-03	47	298	194	492
Matt Pusateri, Miami (Ohio)	2001-04	51	313	172	485
Dexter Reid, North Carolina	2000-03	47	304	162	466
Derrick Johnson, Texas	2001-04	49	281	177	458
Abdul Hodge, Iowa	2002-05	50	289	164	453
John Leake, Clemson	2000-03	49	244	199	443
E.J. Henderson, Maryland	2000-02	35	308	126	434
Adam Seward, UNLV	2001-04	46	215	218	433
Barrett Ruud, Nebraska	2001-04	50	218	214	432
Terrell Jones, Miami (Ohio)	2000-03	47	258	166	424
Chad Greenway, Iowa	2002-05	50	252	164	416
James King, Central Mich.	2001-04	45	268	141	409
Hanik Milligan, Houston	2000-02	34	235	170	405
Kirk Morrison, San Diego St.	$2000-04	47	241	125	366
Dantonio Burnette, North Carolina St.	2000-02	34	185	178	363
Akil Grant, Northern Ill.	2000-03	42	246	115	361
Stuart Schweigert, Purdue	2000-03	49	226	134	360
Josh Smith, Navy	2002-04	34	164	190	354
Jerry Schumacher, Illinois	2000-02	35	236	115	351
Bob Sanders, Iowa	2000-03	46	235	113	348
Alfred Fincher, Connecticut	2002-04	36	181	166	347

*Record. $See page 10 for explanation.

SEASON TOTAL TACKLES

Player, Team	Year	G	Solo	Ast	Total
Lawrence Flugence, Texas Tech	2002	14	124	69	193
Josh Buhl, Kansas St.	2003	15	109	75	184
Tom Ward, Toledo	2002	14	107	73	180
Jimmy Cottrell, New Mexico St.	†2005	12	90	89	179
E.J. Henderson, Maryland	2002	14	*135	40	175
John Leake, Clemson	2002	13	81	88	169
Hunter Hillenmeyer, Vanderbilt	†2002	12	116	52	168
Byron Hardmon, Florida	2002	13	104	64	168
Nick Greisen, Wisconsin	2001	12	101	66	167
Rodney Thomas, Clemson	2002	13	82	85	167
Rod Davis, Southern Miss.	2002	13	121	46	167
Grant Wiley, West Virginia	2003	13	99	68	167
Dexter Reid, North Carolina	2002	12	107	59	166
Matthew Castelo, San Jose St.	2006	13	81	84	165
Rod Davis, Southern Miss.	†2003	12	111	53	164
Levar Fisher, North Carolina St.	†2000	11	93	70	163
Kyle Kayden, West Virginia	2001	11	88	71	159
Max Yates, Marshall	2001	12	92	67	159

*Record. †National champion.

SINGLE-GAME TOTAL TACKLES

(Since 2000)

Tackles	Player, Team (Opponent)	Date
26	Brian Leigeb, Central Mich. (Northern Ill.)	Nov. 17, 2000
26	Doug Szymul, Northwestern (Navy)	Sept. 21, 2002
25	Bob Sanders, Iowa (Indiana)	Oct. 20, 2001
25	DeMeco Ryans, Alabama (Arkansas)	Sept. 27, 2003
25	Tim McGarigle, Northwestern (Wisconsin)	Oct. 8, 2005
24	Pernell Griffin, East Caro. (Wake Forest)	Sept. 1, 2001
24	Dantonio Burnette, North Carolina St. (Clemson)	Oct. 13, 2001
24	Brad White, Wake Forest (Navy)	Nov. 23, 2002
24	Chris Moore, East Caro. (Cincinnati)	Sept. 1, 2003
24	Rich Constantine, Ohio (Marshall)	Nov. 28, 2003

ANNUAL CHAMPIONS

Year	Player, Team	Class	G	Solo	Ast.	Total	Avg.
2000	Levar Fisher, North Carolina St.	Jr.	11	93	70	163	14.8
2001	Rick Sherrod, West Virginia	Sr.	10	102	54	156	*15.6
2002	Hunter Hillenmeyer, Vanderbilt	Sr.	12	116	52	168	14.0
2003	Rod Davis, Southern Miss.	Sr.	12	111	53	164	13.7
2004	Greg Washington, Army	Sr.	11	73	76	149	13.6
2005	Jimmy Cottrell, New Mexico St.	Sr.	12	90	89	179	14.9
2006	Alvin Bowen, Iowa St.	Jr.	12	95	60	155	12.9

*Record.

Solo Tackles

CAREER SOLO TACKLES PER GAME

(Min. 225 Solo Tackles; Player must have concluded his career)

Player, Team	Years	G	Solo	Avg.
E.J. Henderson, Maryland	2000-02	35	308	8.80
Rod Davis, Southern Miss.	2000-03	47	*360	7.66
Hanik Milligan, Houston	2000-02	34	235	6.91
Jerry Schumacher, Illinois	2000-02	35	236	6.74
Tim McGarigle, Northwestern	2002-05	48	319	6.65
Dexter Reid, North Carolina	2000-03	47	304	6.47
Grant Wiley, West Virginia	2000-03	47	298	6.34
Ryan Fowler, Duke	2000-03	46	286	6.22
Matt Pusateri, Miami (Ohio)	2001-04	51	313	6.14
Nick Duffy, Northern Ill.	2000-03	39	236	6.05
James King, Central Mich.	2001-04	45	268	5.96
Akil Grant, Northern Ill.	2000-03	42	246	5.86
Justin Beriault, Ball St.	2001-04	46	267	5.80
Abdul Hodge, Iowa	2002-05	50	289	5.78
Derrick Johnson, Texas	2001-04	49	281	5.73
Terrell Jones, Miami (Ohio)	2000-03	47	258	5.49
Kirk Morrison, San Diego St.	$2000-04	47	241	5.13
Bob Sanders, Iowa	2000-03	46	235	5.11
Chad Greenway, Iowa	2002-05	50	252	5.04
John Leake, Clemson	2000-03	49	244	4.98

**Record. $See page 10 for explanation.*

SEASON SOLO TACKLES PER GAME

Player, Team	Year	G	Solo	Avg.
Rick Sherrod, West Virginia	†2001	10	102	10.2
Hunter Hillenmeyer, Vanderbilt	†2002	12	116	9.7
E.J. Henderson, Maryland	2002	14	*135	9.6
E.J. Henderson, Maryland	2001	11	104	9.5
Rod Davis, Southern Miss.	2002	13	121	9.3
Rod Davis, Southern Miss.	†2003	12	111	9.3
Tito Rodriquez, UCF	2001	11	100	9.1
Chris Moore, East Caro.	2003	11	100	9.1
Patrick Willis, Mississippi	†2005	10	90	9.0
Dexter Reid, North Carolina	2002	12	107	8.9
Tito Rodriquez, UCF	2001	9	80	8.9
Lawrence Flugence, Texas Tech	2002	14	124	8.9

**Record. †National champion.*

CAREER SOLO TACKLES

Player, Team	Years	G	Solo
Rod Davis, Southern Miss.	2000-03	47	360
Tim McGarigle, Northwestern	2002-05	48	319
Matt Pusateri, Miami (Ohio)	2001-04	51	313
E.J. Henderson, Maryland	2000-02	35	308
Dexter Reid, North Carolina	2000-03	47	304
Grant Wiley, West Virginia	2000-03	47	298
Abdul Hodge, Iowa	2002-05	50	289
Ryan Fowler, Duke	2000-03	46	286
Derrick Johnson, Texas	2001-04	49	281
James King, Central Mich.	2001-04	45	268
Justin Beriault, Ball St.	2001-04	46	267
Terrell Jones, Miami (Ohio)	2000-03	47	258
Chad Greenway, Iowa	2002-05	50	252
Akil Grant, Northern Ill.	2000-03	42	246
John Leake, Clemson	2000-03	49	244
Kirk Morrison, San Diego St.	$2000-04	47	241
Jerry Schumacher, Illinois	2000-02	35	236
Nick Duffy, Northern Ill.	2000-03	39	236
Hanik Milligan, Houston	2000-02	34	235

$See page 10 for explanation.

SEASON SOLO TACKLES

Player, Team	Year	G	Solo
E.J. Henderson, Maryland	2002	14	135
Lawrence Flugence, Texas Tech	2002	14	124
Rod Davis, Southern Miss.	2002	13	121
Hunter Hillenmeyer, Vanderbilt	†2002	12	116
Andre Maddox, North Carolina St.	2003	13	113
Rod Davis, Southern Miss.	†2003	12	111
Leroy Hill, Clemson	2003	13	110
Josh Buhl, Kansas St.	2003	15	109
Dexter Reid, North Carolina	2002	12	107
Tom Ward, Toledo	2002	14	107

†National champion.

SINGLE-GAME SOLO TACKLES

(Since 2000)

Solo	Player, Team (Opponent)	Date
20	Tyrell Johnson, Arkansas St. (North Texas)	Nov. 26, 2005
19	Doug Szymul, Northwestern (Navy)	Sept. 21, 2002
18	Brian Leigeb, Central Mich. (Northern Ill.)	Nov. 17, 2000
18	Nick Duffy, Northern Ill. (Ball St.)	Nov. 17, 2001
17	Tom Ward, Toledo (UNLV)	Sept. 21, 2002
17	Matt McCoy, San Diego St. (Michigan)	Sept. 18, 2004
17	A.J. Nicholson, Florida St. (Boston College)	Sept. 17, 2005
17	Nelson Coleman, Tulsa (Rice)	Oct. 15, 2005
16	Quincy Monk, North Carolina (Wake Forest)	Nov. 10, 2001
16	Dexter Reid, North Carolina (Clemson)	Nov. 9, 2002
16	E.J. Henderson, Maryland (Wake Forest)	Nov. 30, 2002
16	Lewis Moore, Pittsburgh (Toledo)	Sept. 20, 2003
16	Rod Davis, Southern Miss. (TCU)	Nov. 20, 2003
16	Barrett Ruud, Nebraska (Kansas St.)	Oct. 23, 2004

ANNUAL CHAMPIONS

Year	Player, Team	Class	G	Solo	Avg.
2001	Rick Sherrod, West Virginia	Sr.	10	102	*10.2
2002	Hunter Hillenmeyer, Vanderbilt	Sr.	12	116	9.7
2003	Rod Davis, Southern Miss.	Sr.	12	111	9.3
2004	Tim McGarigle, Northwestern	Jr.	12	102	8.5
2005	Patrick Willis, Mississippi	Jr.	10	90	9.0
2006	Alvin Bowen, Iowa St.	Jr.	12	95	7.9

**Record.*

Tackles for Loss

CAREER TACKLES FOR LOSS PER GAME

(Min. 25 Tackles For Loss; Player must have concluded his career)

Player, Team	Years	G	Solo	Ast.	Total	Avg.
Julius Peppers, North Carolina	2000-01	23	43	0	43.0	1.87
Terrell Suggs, Arizona St.	2000-02	36	61	9	65.5	1.82
E.J. Henderson, Maryland	2000-02	35	59	4	61.0	1.74
Antwan Peek, Cincinnati	2000-02	34	56	0	56.0	1.65
Dan Klecko, Temple	2000-02	30	49	0	49.0	1.63
Jason Babin, Western Mich.	2000-03	47	73	4	*75.0	1.60
Calvin Pace, Wake Forest	2000-02	34	52	0	52.0	1.53
Tully Banta-Cain, California	2000-02	34	49	5	51.5	1.51
Greg Gathers, Georgia Tech	2000-02	26	39	0	39.0	1.50
Travis LaBoy, Hawaii	2001-03	34	50	0	50.0	1.47
Farouk Adelekan, Houston	2002-03	17	24	2	25.0	1.47
Kenechi Udeze, Southern California	2001-03	37	50	6	53.0	1.43
Eric Henderson, Georgia Tech	2002-05	42	57	5	59.5	1.42
Bo Schobel, TCU	2000-03	37	51	0	51.0	1.38

**Record.*

SEASON TACKLES FOR LOSS PER GAME

Player, Team	Year	G	Solo	Ast.	Total	Avg.
Kenny Philpot, Eastern Mich.	†2001	11	26	9	30.5	2.8
Jason Babin, Western Mich.	†2003	12	31	2	*32.0	2.7
E.J. Henderson, Maryland	2001	11	26	4	28.0	2.6
Wayne Rogers, Houston	†2000	11	27	0	27.0	2.5
Dan Bazuin, Central Mich.	†2005	11	24	5	26.5	2.4
Jonathan Goddard, Marshall	†2004	12	23	11	28.5	2.4
Bryan Knight, Pittsburgh	2000	11	26	0	26.0	2.4
Larry Foote, Michigan	2001	10	21	5	23.5	2.4
Terrell Suggs, Arizona St.	†2002	14	27	9	31.5	2.3
LeMarcus McDonald, TCU	2001	11	23	3	24.5	2.2
Robert Thomas, UCLA	2001	11	23	3	24.5	2.2
Julius Peppers, North Carolina	2000	11	24	0	24.0	2.2
Jason Babin, Western Mich.	2002	12	25	2	26.0	2.2

**Record. †National champion.*

CAREER TACKLES FOR LOSS

Player, Team	Years	G	Solo	Ast.	Total
Jason Babin, Western Mich.	2000-03	47	73	4	75.0
Terrell Suggs, Arizona St.	2000-02	36	61	9	65.5
Jonathan Goddard, Marshall	2001-04	48	60	11	65.5
Derrick Johnson, Texas	2001-04	49	65	0	65.0
E.J. Henderson, Maryland	2000-02	35	59	4	61.0
Rod Davis, Southern Miss.	2000-03	47	60	1	60.5
Shaun Phillips, Purdue	2000-03	47	53	13	59.5
Eric Henderson, Georgia Tech	2002-05	42	57	5	59.5
David Pollack, Georgia	2001-04	50	58	0	58.0
Antwan Peek, Cincinnati	2000-02	34	56	0	56.0
Kenechi Udeze, Southern California	2001-03	37	50	6	53.0
Calvin Pace, Wake Forest	2000-02	34	52	0	52.0
Tully Banta-Cain, California	2000-02	34	49	5	51.5

Player, Team	Years	G	Solo	Ast.	Total
Bo Schobel, TCU	2000-03	37	51	0	51.0
Travis LaBoy, Hawaii	2001-03	34	50	0	50.0
Barrett Ruud, Nebraska	2001-04	50	50	0	50.0

SEASON TACKLES FOR LOSS

Player, Team	Year	G	Solo	Ast.	Total
Jason Babin, Western Mich.	†2003	12	31	2	32.0
Terrell Suggs, Arizona St.	†2002	14	27	9	31.5
Kenny Philpot, Eastern Mich.	†2001	11	26	9	30.5
Jonathan Goddard, Marshall	†2004	12	23	11	28.5
E.J. Henderson, Maryland	2001	11	26	4	28.0
Wayne Rogers, Houston	†2000	11	27	0	27.0
Leroy Hill, Clemson	2003	13	27	0	27.0
Dan Bazuin, Central Mich.	†2005	11	24	5	26.5
Anthony Spencer, Purdue	2006	14	25	3	26.5
Bryan Knight, Pittsburgh	2000	11	26	0	26.0
Jason Babin, Western Mich.	2002	12	25	2	26.0
Kenechi Udeze, Southern California	2003	13	23	6	26.0
Dwight Freeney, Syracuse	2001	12	24	3	25.5
Ameer Ismail, Western Mich.	†2006	13	23	5	25.5
Chris Johnson, Kansas St.	2000	12	25	0	25.0
LaMarcus McDonald, TCU	2002	12	20	10	25.0
Jonathan Babineaux, Iowa	2004	12	24	2	25.0

†National champion.

SINGLE-GAME TACKLES FOR LOSS

(Since 2000)

TFL	Player, Team (Opponent)	Date
7.0	Chris Johnson, Kansas St. (Kansas)	Oct. 7, 2000
7.0	Richard Seigler, Oregon St. (Arizona St.)	Oct. 20, 2001
7.0	Larry Foote, Michigan (Iowa)	Oct. 27, 2001
7.0	Elvis Dumervil, Louisville (Kentucky)	Sept. 4, 2005
6.5	Terrell Suggs, Arizona St. (Washington)	Oct. 26, 2002
6.5	Alex Lewis, Wisconsin (Purdue)	Oct. 18, 2003
6.5	Ameer Ismail, Western Mich. (Ball St.)	Oct. 21, 2006
6.0	Julius Peppers, North Carolina (Virginia)	Oct. 28, 2000
6.0	James Davis, West Virginia (East Caro.)	Nov. 18, 2000
6.0	Akin Ayodele, Purdue (Cincinnati)	Sept. 2, 2001
6.0	Nate Bolling, Wake Forest (Maryland)	Sept. 22, 2001
6.0	Wendell Bryant, Wisconsin (Penn St.)	Sept. 22, 2001
6.0	Andy Stark, Ball St. (Central Mich.)	Nov. 20, 2004

ANNUAL CHAMPIONS

Year	Player, Team	G	Solo	Ast.	Total	Avg.
2000	Wayne Rogers, Houston	11	27	0	27.0	2.5
2001	Kenny Philpot, Eastern Mich.	11	26	9	30.5	*2.8
2002	Terrell Suggs, Arizona St.	14	27	9	31.5	2.3
2003	Jason Babin, Western Mich.	12	31	2	*32.0	2.7
2004	Jonathan Goddard, Marshall	12	23	11	28.5	2.4
2005	Dan Bazuin, Central Mich.	11	24	5	26.5	2.4
2006	Ameer Ismail, Western Mich.	13	23	5	25.5	2.0

**Record.*

Pass Sacks

CAREER PASS SACKS PER GAME

(Min. 20 Pass Sacks; Player must have concluded his career)

Player, Team	Years	G	Solo	Ast.	Total	Avg.
Dwight Freeney, Syracuse	2000-01	19	30	1	30.5	1.61
Terrell Suggs, Arizona St.	2000-02	36	43	2	*44.0	1.22
Julius Peppers, North Carolina	2000-01	23	24	1	24.5	1.07
Greg Gathers, Georgia Tech	2000-02	26	24	0	24.0	0.92
Dan Klecko, Temple	2000-02	30	26	0	26.0	0.87
Ameer Ismail, Western Mich.	2004-06	29	24	2	25.0	0.86
Jason Babin, Western Mich.	2000-03	47	37	2	38.0	0.81
Calvin Pace, Wake Forest	2000-02	34	27	0	27.0	0.79
Antwan Peek, Cincinnati	2000-02	34	26	2	27.0	0.79
Tully Banta-Cain, California	2000-02	34	25	3	26.5	0.78
Bo Schobel, TCU	2000-03	37	27	4	29.0	0.78
Kenechi Udeze, Southern California	2001-03	37	27	2	28.0	0.76
Elvis Dumervil, Louisville	2002-05	44	31	2	32.0	0.73
David Pollack, Georgia	2001-04	50	35	2	36.0	0.72
Shaun Phillips, Purdue	2000-03	47	31	5	33.5	0.71
Travis LaBoy, Hawaii	2001-03	34	24	0	24.0	0.71

**Record.*

SEASON PASS SACKS PER GAME

Player, Team	Year	G	Solo	Ast.	Total	Avg.
Terrell Suggs, Arizona St.	†2002	14	23	2	*24.0	1.71
Elvis Dumervil, Louisville	†2005	12	19	2	20.0	1.67
Dwight Freeney, Syracuse	†2001	12	17	1	17.5	1.5
Dan Bazuin, Central Mich.	2005	11	15	2	16.0	1.5
Michael Josiah, Louisville	†2000	9	12	1	12.5	1.4
Julius Peppers, North Carolina	2000	11	15	0	15.0	1.4
Dewayne White, Louisville	2001	11	15	0	15.0	1.4
Willie Evans, Mississippi St.	2005	11	12	6	15.0	1.4
Jonathan Goddard, Marshall	†2004	12	15	2	16.0	1.3
Osi Umenyiora, Troy	2002	12	16	0	16.0	1.3
Tom Canada, California	2002	9	12	0	12.0	1.3
Ameer Ismail, Western Mich.	†2006	13	16	2	17.0	1.3
Bryan Thomas, UAB	2001	11	14	0	14.0	1.3
Justin Parrish, Kent St.	2004	11	13	2	14.0	1.3
Dave Ball, UCLA	†2003	13	16	1	16.5	1.3
Kenechi Udeze, Southern California	†2003	13	16	1	16.5	1.3
D.D. Acholonu, Washington St.	†2003	13	16	1	16.5	1.3
Jason Babin, Western Mich.	2003	12	15	0	15.0	1.3
Antwan Peek, Cincinnati	2001	10	12	1	12.5	1.3

**Record. †National champion.*

CAREER PASS SACKS

Player, Team	Years	G	Solo	Ast.	Total
Terrell Suggs, Arizona St.	2000-02	36	43	2	44.0
Jason Babin, Western Mich.	2000-03	47	37	2	38.0
David Pollack, Georgia	2001-04	50	35	2	36.0
Shaun Phillips, Purdue	2000-03	47	31	5	33.5
Elvis Dumervil, Louisville	2002-05	44	31	2	32.0
Dwight Freeney, Syracuse	2000-01	19	30	1	30.5
Dave Ball, UCLA	2000-03	49	30	1	30.5
Matt Roth, Iowa	2001-04	50	30	0	30.0
Jorge Cordova, Nevada	2000-03	42	28	2	29.0
Bo Schobel, TCU	2000-03	37	27	4	29.0
Kenechi Udeze, Southern California	2001-03	37	27	2	28.0
Jonathan Goddard, Marshall	2001-04	48	26	3	27.5
Calvin Pace, Wake Forest	2000-02	34	27	0	27.0
Antwan Peek, Cincinnati	2000-02	34	26	2	27.0
Tully Banta-Cain, California	2000-02	34	25	3	26.5

SEASON PASS SACKS

Player, Team	Year	G	Solo	Ast.	Total
Terrell Suggs, Arizona St.	†2002	14	23	2	24.0
Elvis Dumervil, Louisville	†2005	12	19	2	20.0
Dwight Freeney, Syracuse	†2001	12	17	1	17.5
Ameer Ismail, Western Mich.	†2006	13	16	2	17.0
Dave Ball, UCLA	†2003	13	16	1	16.5
Kenechi Udeze, Southern California	†2003	13	16	1	16.5
D.D. Acholonu, Washington St.	†2003	13	16	1	16.5
Osi Umenyiora, Troy	2002	12	16	0	16.0
Jonathan Goddard, Marshall	†2004	12	15	2	16.0
Dan Bazuin, Central Mich.	2005	11	15	2	16.0
Julius Peppers, North Carolina	2000	11	15	0	15.0
Dewayne White, Louisville	2001	11	15	0	15.0
Michael Haynes, Penn St.	2002	13	14	2	15.0
Jason Babin, Western Mich.	2003	12	15	0	15.0
Bo Schobel, TCU	2003	13	13	4	15.0
Willie Evans, Mississippi St.	2005	11	12	6	15.0

†National champion.

SINGLE-GAME PASS SACKS

(Since 2000)

PS	Player, Team (Opponent)	Date
6.0	Elvis Dumervil, Louisville (Kentucky)	Sept. 4, 2005
6.0	Ameer Ismail, Western Mich. (Ball St.)	Oct. 21, 2006
5.0	Wendell Bryant, Wisconsin (Penn St.)	Sept. 22, 2001
5.0	James Harrison, Kent St. [Miami (Ohio)]	Nov. 24, 2001
5.0	Alex Lewis, Wisconsin (Purdue)	Oct. 18, 2003
5.0	Mkristo Bruce, Washington St. (Stanford)	Sept. 23, 2006
4.5	Dwight Freeney, Syracuse (Virginia Tech)	Oct. 21, 2000
4.5	Tully Banta-Cain, California (New Mexico St.)	Sept. 7, 2002
4.5	Terrell Suggs, Arizona St. (Washington)	Oct. 26, 2002
4.5	Jorge Cordova, Nevada (Washington)	Oct. 11, 2003
4.5	Brandon Perkins, Kansas (Louisiana Tech)	Sept. 17, 2005
4.5	Larry English, Northern Ill. (Temple)	Oct. 21, 2006

ANNUAL CHAMPIONS

Year	Player, Team	G	Solo	Ast.	Total	Avg.
2000	Michael Josiah, Louisville	9	12	1	12.5	1.4
2001	Dwight Freeney, Syracuse	12	17	1	17.5	1.5
2002	Terrell Suggs, Arizona St.	14	23	2	*24.0	*1.71
2003	Dave Ball, UCLA	13	16	1	16.5	1.3
	Kenechi Udeze, Southern California	13	16	1	16.5	1.3

Year	Player, Team	G	Solo	Ast.	Total	Avg.
	D.D. Acholonu, Washington St.	13	16	1	16.5	1.3
2004	Jonathan Goddard, Marshall	12	15	2	16.0	1.3
2005	Elvis Dumervil, Louisville	12	19	2	20.0	1.67
2006	Ameer Ismail, Western Mich.	13	16	2	17.0	1.3

*Record.

Passes Defended

CAREER PASSES DEFENDED PER GAME

(Min. 30 Passes Defended; Player must have concluded his career)

Player, Team	Years	G	PBU	Int.	Total	Avg.
Eugene Wilson, Illinois	2000-02	33	60	11	71	2.15
Rayshun Reed, Troy	2000-03	31	43	10	53	1.71
Nathan Vasher, Texas	2000-03	46	61	17	*78	1.70
Michael Jolivette, Arizona	2000-03	36	44	12	56	1.56
Christian Morton, Illinois	2000-03	33	41	5	46	1.39
Brian King, West Virginia	2000-03	46	54	10	64	1.39
Greg Brooks, Southern Miss.	2000-03	43	47	9	56	1.30
Blue Adams, Cincinnati	2000-02	35	30	12	42	1.20
Randee Drew, Northern Ill.	2000-03	44	38	14	52	1.18
Jameel Powell, California	2000-02	28	23	10	33	1.18
Ricky Sharpe, San Diego St.	2000-02	35	34	6	40	1.14
Michael Lehan, Minnesota	2000-02	33	33	4	37	1.12
Dustin Fox, Ohio St.	2001-03	38	34	7	41	1.08
Scott Starks, Wisconsin	2001-04	51	46	6	52	1.02
Jim Leonhard, Wisconsin	2001-04	51	29	21	50	0.98

*Record.

SEASON PASSES DEFENDED PER GAME

Player, Team	Year	G	PBU	Int.	Total	Avg.
Aqib Talib, Kansas	†2006	10	22	6	28	2.8
Jason Goss, TCU	†2002	12	24	8	*32	2.7
Eugene Wilson, Illinois	†2001	11	23	6	29	2.6
Nathan Vasher, Texas	†2003	13	26	6	*32	2.5
Justin Perkins, Connecticut	2003	11	21	6	27	2.5
Lynaris Elpheage, Tulane	2002	13	23	8	31	2.4
Christian Morton, Illinois	2001	11	22	4	26	2.4
Corey Webster, LSU	2003	14	25	7	*32	2.3
Ken Lucas, Mississippi	†2000	11	20	5	25	2.3
Fred Smoot, Mississippi St.	2000	11	19	5	24	2.2
Steve Smith, Oregon	2001	11	18	6	24	2.2
Jason Goss, TCU	2001	11	21	3	24	2.2
Daniel Wilturner, Baylor	2000	11	21	2	23	2.1
Edward Reed, Miami (Fla.)	2000	11	15	8	23	2.1
Quentin Jammer, Texas	2000	11	20	3	23	2.1
Lawrence Richardson, Arkansas	2001	11	20	3	23	2.1
Darrent Williams, Oklahoma St.	2003	11	17	6	23	2.1

*Record. †National champion.

CAREER PASSES DEFENDED

Player, Team	Years	G	PBU	Int.	Total
Nathan Vasher, Texas	2000-03	46	61	17	78
Eugene Wilson, Illinois	2000-02	33	60	11	71
Brian King, West Virginia	2000-03	46	54	10	64
Michael Jolivette, Arizona	2000-03	36	44	12	56
Greg Brooks, Southern Miss.	2000-03	43	47	6	56
Rayshun Reed, Troy	2000-03	31	43	10	53
Randee Drew, Northern Ill.	2000-03	44	38	14	52
Scott Starks, Wisconsin	2001-04	51	46	6	52
Jim Leonhard, Wisconsin	2001-04	51	29	21	50
Christian Morton, Illinois	2000-03	33	41	5	46
Vince Thompson, Northern Ill.	2000-03	30	28	15	43
Blue Adams, Cincinnati	2000-02	35	30	12	42
Abraham Elimimiam, Hawaii	2001-04	49	30	12	42
Dustin Fox, Ohio St.	2001-03	38	34	7	41
Ricky Sharpe, San Diego St.	2000-02	35	34	6	40
Zach Norton, Cincinnati	2000-03	43	31	9	40

SEASON PASSES DEFENDED

Player, Team	Year	G	PBU	Int.	Total
Jason Goss, TCU	†2002	12	24	8	32
Nathan Vasher, Texas	†2003	13	26	6	32
Corey Webster, LSU	2003	14	25	7	32
Lynaris Elpheage, Tulane	2002	13	23	8	31
Eugene Wilson, Illinois	†2001	11	23	6	29
Travis Daniels, LSU	2003	14	26	2	28
Aqib Talib, Kansas	†2006	10	22	6	28
Justin Perkins, Connecticut	2003	11	21	6	27
Christian Morton, Illinois	2001	11	22	4	26
Joselio Hanson, Texas Tech	2002	14	23	3	26
Will Poole, Southern California	2003	13	19	7	26
Ken Lucas, Mississippi	†2000	11	20	5	25
Jim Leonhard, Wisconsin	2002	14	14	11	25
Brian King, West Virginia	2003	13	19	6	25

†National champion.

SINGLE-GAME PASSES DEFENDED

(Since 2000)

PD	Player, Team (Opponent)	Date
8	Joselio Hanson, Texas Tech (Oklahoma St.)	Nov. 9, 2002
7	Demerist Whitfield, Northern Ill. (Illinois St.)	Sept. 9, 2000
7	Nashville Dyer, Kent St. (Bucknell)	Sept. 8, 2001
7	Korey Banks, Mississippi St. (Memphis)	Oct. 19, 2002
7	Jason Goss, TCU (Tulane)	Nov. 9, 2002
7	Fabian Washington, Nebraska (Kansas)	Oct. 2, 2004
6	Bobby Jackson, Illinois (Northern Ill.)	Sept. 8, 2001
6	Terence Newman, Kansas St. (Oklahoma)	Sept. 29, 2001
6	Marlin Jackson, Michigan (Washington)	Aug. 31, 2002
6	Keiwan Ratliff, Florida (Arkansas)	Oct. 18, 2003
6	Wes Nurse, Boise St. (BYU)	Oct. 30, 2003
6	Chris Carr, Boise St. (Nevada)	Nov. 29, 2003
6	Willie Gaston, Houston (UTEP)	Sept. 16, 2005
6	Aaron Ross, Texas (Iowa St.)	Sept. 23, 2006
6	Mark Parson, Ohio (Akron)	Nov. 16, 2006

ANNUAL CHAMPIONS

Year	Player, Team	G	PBU	Int.	Total	Avg.
2000	Ken Lucas, Mississippi	11	20	5	25	2.3
2001	Eugene Wilson, Illinois	11	23	6	29	2.6
2002	Jason Goss, TCU	12	24	8	*32	2.7
2003	Nathan Vasher, Texas	13	26	6	*32	2.5
2004	Brandon Payne, New Mexico	12	17	6	23	1.9
2005	Tramon Williams, Louisiana Tech	11	16	3	19	1.7
2006	Aqib Talib, Kansas	10	22	6	28	*2.8

*Record.

Forced Fumbles

CAREER FORCED FUMBLES PER GAME

(Min. 20 Games Played; Player must have concluded his career)

Player, Team	Years	G	FF	Avg.
Antwan Peek, Cincinnati	2000-02	34	*14	0.41
Tom Canada, California	2001-02	20	8	0.40
Terrell Suggs, Arizona St.	2000-02	36	*14	0.39
Kenechi Udeze, Southern California	2001-03	37	*14	0.38
Nate Jackson, Hawaii	2000-01	23	6	0.26
Heath Farwell, San Diego St.	2001-03	36	9	0.25
Guss Scott, Florida	2000-03	49	11	0.22
Derrick Johnson, Texas	2001-04	49	11	0.22
Ryan Claridge, UNLV	2000-01, 03-04	46	10	0.22
Johnathan Goddard, Marshall	2001-04	48	10	0.21
Josh Smith, Navy	2002-04	34	7	0.21
Osi Umenyiora, Troy	2000-02	35	7	0.20
Shaun Phillips, Purdue	2000-03	47	9	0.19
Lionel Hickenbottom, Northern Ill.	2001-03	21	4	0.19
Erasmus James, Wisconsin	2001-04	37	7	0.19
Pisa Tinoisamoa, Hawaii	2000-02	35	6	0.17
Clint Session, Pittsburgh	2003-06	42	7	0.17
Matt Roth, Iowa	2001-04	50	8	0.16
Chris Brown, Hawaii	2000-02	38	6	0.16
Gilbert Gardner, Purdue	2000-02	45	7	0.16
Jeramie Johnson, Mississippi St.	2003-06	46	7	0.15
Anthony Spencer, Purdue	2003-06	53	8	0.15
Rod Davis, Southern Miss.	2000-03	47	7	0.15

*Record.

SEASON FORCED FUMBLES PER GAME

Player, Team	Year	G	FF	Avg.
Elvis Dumervil, Louisville	†2005	12	*10	0.83
Tom Canada, California	†2002	9	6	0.67
Dwight Freeney, Syracuse	†2001	12	8	0.67
Dwayne Slay, Texas Tech	2005	12	8	0.67
Quintin Mikell, Boise St.	2002	13	8	0.62
Bob Sanders, Iowa	†2003	10	6	0.60
Derrick Johnson, Texas	†2004	12	7	0.58
Robert Thomas, UCLA	2000	11	6	0.55
Brian Lape, Western Mich.	2001	11	6	0.55
Cory Smith, North Carolina St.	2001	11	6	0.55
Ryan Claridge, UNLV	2001	11	6	0.55
Oshiomogho Atogwe, Stanford	2003	11	6	0.55
Byron Santiago, Louisiana Tech	2005	11	6	0.55

*Record. †National champion.

CAREER FORCED FUMBLES

Player, Team	Years	G	FF
Terrell Suggs, Arizona St.	2000-02	36	14
Antwan Peek, Cincinnati	2000-02	34	14
Kenechi Udeze, Southern California	2001-03	37	14
Guss Scott, Florida	2000-03	49	11
Derrick Johnson, Texas	2001-04	49	11
Elvis Dumervil, Louisville	2002-05	44	11
Ryan Claridge, UNLV	2000-01; 03-04	46	10
Johnathan Goddard, Marshall	2001-04	48	10
Heath Farwell, San Diego St.	2001-03	36	9
Shaun Phillips, Purdue	2000-03	47	9
Tom Canada, California	2001-02	20	8
Matt Roth, Iowa	2001-04	50	8
Anthony Spencer, Purdue	2003-06	53	8
Osi Umenyiora, Troy	2000-02	35	7
Gilbert Gardner, Purdue	2000-02	45	7
Kirk Morrison, San Diego St.	2001-03	36	7
Rod Davis, Southern Miss.	2000-03	47	7
Dave Ball, UCLA	2000-03	49	7
Josh Smith, Navy	2002-04	34	7
Erasmus James, Wisconsin	2001-04	37	7
Jeramie Johnson, Mississippi St.	2003-06	46	7
Clint Session, Pittsburgh	2003-06	42	7

SEASON FORCED FUMBLES

Player, Team	Year	G	FF
Elvis Dumervil, Louisville	†2005	12	10
Dwight Freeney, Syracuse	†2001	12	8
Quintin Mikell, Boise St.	2002	13	8
Dwayne Slay, Texas Tech	2005	12	8
Claude Harriott, Pittsburgh	2002	13	7
Michael Haynes, Penn St.	2002	13	7
Phillip Perry, San Jose St.	2002	13	7
Antwan Peek, Cincinnati	2002	14	7
Grant Wiley, West Virginia	2003	13	7
Derrick Johnson, Texas	†2004	12	7

†National champion.

SINGLE-GAME FORCED FUMBLES
(Since 2000)

FF	Player, Team (Opponent)	Date
3	DeLawrence Grant, Oregon St. (San Diego St.)	Sept. 23, 2000
3	Antwan Peek, Cincinnati (La.-Monroe)	Dec. 1, 2001
3	Mason Unck, Arizona St. (Stanford)	Sept. 28, 2002
3	Quintin Mikell, Boise St. (Hawaii)	Oct. 5, 2002
3	Grant Wiley, West Virginia (Cincinnati)	Sept. 13, 2003
3	Derrick Johnson, Texas (North Texas)	Sept. 4, 2004
3	Ramel Meekins, Rutgers (Navy)	Oct. 14, 2006

ANNUAL CHAMPIONS

Year	Player, Team	G	FF	Avg.
2000	Marques Anderson, UCLA	10	‡7	0.70
	Tony Hardman, UCF	10	‡7	0.70

‡In 2000, the total was forced fumbles plus fumbles recovered. Beginning in 2001, FF was forced fumbles only.

Year	Player, Team	G	FF	Avg.
2001	Dwight Freeney, Syracuse	12	8	0.67
2002	Tom Canada, California	9	6	0.67
2003	Bob Sanders, Iowa	10	6	0.60
2004	Derrick Johnson, Texas	12	7	0.58
2005	Elvis Dumervil, Louisville	12	*10	*0.83
2006	Jeramie Johnson, Mississippi St.	12	5	0.42
	Clint Session, Pittsburgh	12	5	0.42
	Jack Williams, Kent St.	12	5	0.42

**Record.*

BLOCKED KICKS RECORDS

Special Note About Blocked-Kick Records:
The blocked-kick records include players from 1937. Even though the other defensive statistics and records began in 2000, blocked-kick records are compiled by most institutions and those records are more reliable than tackles, assists, tackles for loss, pass sacks, passes defended and forced fumbles. The statistics service has been compiling national statistics and records since 1937.

Blocked Punts

CAREER BLOCKED PUNTS

Player, Team	Years	BP
James King, Central Mich.	2001-04	10
Barron Miles, Nebraska	1992-94	7
Tim Curry, Air Force	1996-98	7
Woody Jones, North Carolina St.	1939-41	6
Max McGeary, Baylor	1977-80	6
Bracey Walker, North Carolina	1990-93	6
Matt Harding, Hawaii	1992-95	6
Jermaine Mays, Minnesota	1998-00, 02	6
James Ferebee, New Mexico St.	1978-81	5
Merton Hanks, Iowa	1987-90	5

SEASON BLOCKED PUNTS

Player, Team	Year	BP
James King, Central Mich.	2001	7
Jermaine Mays, Minnesota	2002	5
Ken Irvin, Memphis	1992	4
Bracey Walker, North Carolina	1993	4
Tim Curry, Air Force	1997	4
Terrol Dillon, Texas	1999	4
Chris James, Alabama	2003	4
Rashad Washington, Kansas St.	2003	4
Mark Capuano, North Carolina St.	1967	3
Jimmy Lisko, Arkansas St.	1975	3
Richard Johnson, Wisconsin	1984	3
James Francis, Baylor	1989	3
Barron Miles, Nebraska	1994	3
Kendrell Bell, Georgia	1999	3
Manny Lawson, North Carolina St.	2002	3

Note: Before NCAA records, Joe Stydahar of West Virginia blocked seven punts in 1934.

SINGLE-GAME BLOCKED PUNTS

BP	Player, Team (Opponent)	Date
4	Ken Irvin, Memphis (Arkansas)	Sept. 26, 1992
4	James King, Central Mich. (Michigan St.)	Sept. 8, 2001
2	Mark Capuano, North Carolina St. (Georgia)	Sept. 14, 1967
2	Richard Johnson, Wisconsin (Missouri)	Sept. 15, 1984
2	Carlton McDonald, Air Force (Colorado St.)	Sept. 1, 1990
2	Mike Reid, North Carolina St. (Kent St.)	Sept. 14, 1991
2	Brian McCray, Air Force (Colorado St.)	Sept. 11, 1993
2	Barron Miles, Nebraska (Pacific)	Sept. 24, 1994
2	Bill Chopp, Western Mich. (Michigan St.)	Sept. 6, 1997
2	Tim Curry, Air Force (Fresno St.)	Oct. 18, 1997
2	Terrence Holt, North Carolina St. (Texas)	Aug. 28, 1999
2	Chris Crocker, Marshall (Michigan St.)	Sept. 9, 2000
2	Robert Grant, Hawaii (SMU)	Oct. 6, 2001
2	Terrence Holt, North Carolina St. (Navy)	Sept. 7, 2002
2	Lannie Hopkins, Nebraska (Kansas)	Nov. 9, 2002
2	Sean Considine, Iowa (Iowa St.)	Sept. 13, 2003
2	Fashad Washington, Kansas St. (Colorado)	Oct. 18, 2003
2	Tyrone Henderson, Colorado (Washington St.)	Sept. 11, 2004
2	Ivan Clark, Marshall (Buffalo)	Oct. 23, 2004

Blocked Field Goals

CAREER BLOCKED FIELD GOALS

Player, Team	Years	BFG
James Ferebee, New Mexico St.	1978-81	8
Terrence Holt, North Carolina St.	1999-02	8
Max McGeary, Baylor	1977-80	6
Greg Thomas, Colorado	1988-91	6
Lonnell Dewalt, Kentucky	2004	6
Matt Harding, Hawaii	1992-95	5
Rosevelt Colvin, Purdue	1995-98	5
Bobby Iwuchukwu, Purdue	2002-05	5
Mike Akiu, Hawaii	1980-82	4

SEASON BLOCKED FIELD GOALS

Player, Team	Year	BFG
Lonnell Dewalt, Kentucky	2004	6
Mike Akiu, Hawaii	1982	4
Greg Thomas, Colorado	1991	4
Matt Harding, Hawaii	1992	4
Rosevelt Colvin, Purdue	1998	4
Kyle Vanden Bosch, Nebraska	1999	3
Terrence Holt, North Carolina St.	2000	3
Boss Bailey, Georgia	2002	3
Sean Jones, Georgia	2003	3
Brian Robison, Texas	2003	3
Daniel Bazuin, Central Mich.	2004	3

SINGLE-GAME BLOCKED FIELD GOALS

BFG	Player, Team (Opponent)	Date
2	Mike Washington, Alabama (Mississippi St.)	Nov. 3, 1973
2	Louie Meadows, North Carolina St. (Maryland)	Oct. 10, 1981

BFG	Player, Team (Opponent)	Date
2	Matt Harding, Hawaii (San Diego St.)	Oct. 9, 1993
2	Jerald Henry, Southern California (California)	Oct. 22, 1994
2	Pat Larson, Wyoming (Fresno St.)	Nov. 18, 1995
2	Kyle Vanden Bosch, Nebraska (Texas A&M)	Nov. 6, 1999
2	Antwan Peek, Cincinnati [Miami (Ohio)]	Oct. 28, 2000
2	Justin Pendry, Air Force (Tennessee Tech)	Sept. 8, 2001
2	Alton Moore, Auburn (Georgia)	Nov. 10, 2001
2	Chris Barry, Nevada (Washington)	Oct. 11, 2003
2	Daniel Bazuin, Central Mich. (Kent St.)	Oct. 2, 2004

Blocked Extra Points

CAREER BLOCKED EXTRA POINTS

Player, Team	Years	BEP
Ray Farmer, Duke	1992-95	8
James Ferebee, New Mexico St.	1978-81	6
Jimmy Lisko, Arkansas St.	1972-75	4
Max McGeary, Baylor	1977-80	4
James Francis, Baylor	1986-89	4
Chad Patton, SMU	1990-93	4
Bernard Williams, Georgia	1990-93	4
Doug Mills, Purdue	1970-72	3
Corey Nelson, Air Force	1998-00	3
Kareem Bland, Middle Tenn.	1999-02	3

SEASON BLOCKED EXTRA POINTS

Player, Team	Year	BEP
Ray Farmer, Duke	1993	5
Jimmy Lisko, Arkansas St.	1975	4
James Francis, Baylor	1989	4
Bernard Williams, Georgia	1990	3
Corey Nelson, Air Force	2000	3
Doug Mills, Purdue	1972	2
Falaniko Noga, Hawaii	1983	2
Chad Patton, SMU	1992	2
Josh Buhl, Kansas St.	2001	2
Sean Butts, Hawaii	2001	2
Kareem Bland, Middle Tenn.	2002	2
James King, Central Mich.	2004	2

SINGLE-GAME BLOCKED EXTRA POINTS

BEP	Player, Team (Opponent)	Date
2	Corey Nelson, Air Force (Colorado St.)	Nov. 11, 2000
2	Josh Buhl, Kansas St. (Syracuse)	Dec. 29, 2001
2	Kareem Bland, Middle Tenn. (North Texas)	Nov. 23, 2002

Combined Blocked Kicks

CAREER COMBINED BLOCKED KICKS

Player, Team	Years	BK (#Breakdown)
James Ferebee, New Mexico St.	1978-81	19 (8 FGs; 6 PATs; 5 Punts)
Max McGeary, Baylor	1977-80	16 (6 FGs; 6 Punts; 4 PATs)
James King, Central Mich.	2001-04	13 (10 Punts; 2 PATs; 1 FG)
Matt Harding, Hawaii	1992-95	12 (6 Punts; 5 FGs; 1 PAT)
Terrence Holt, North Carolina St.	1999-02	12 (8 FGs; 4 Punts)
Richard Johnson, Wisconsin	1982-84	9 (4 Punts; 3 FGs; 2 PATs)
Tim Curry, Air Force	1996-98	9 (7 Punts; 2 FGs)
Corey Nelson, Air Force	1998-00	9 (4 Punts; 3 PAT; 2 FGs)
Jimmy Lisko, Arkansas St.	1972-75	8 (4 PATs; 3 Punts; 1 FG)
James Francis, Baylor	1986-89	8 (4 PATs; 3 Punts; 1 FG)
Carlton McDonald, Air Force	1989-92	8 (4 Punts; 2 FGs; 2 PAT)
Chad Patton, SMU	1990-93	8 (4 PATs; 2 Punts; 2 FGs)
Merton Hanks, Iowa	1987-90	7 (5 Punts; 2 FGs)
Barron Miles, Nebraska	1992-94	7 (7 Punts)
Lonnell Dewalt, Kentucky	2004	7 (6 FGs; 1 PAT)
Woody Jones, North Carolina St.	1939-41	6 (6 Punts)
Bill Hornbacher, Nebraska	1965-67	6 (No Breakdown)
Mike Akiu, Hawaii	1980-82	6 (4 FGs; 1 PAT; 1 Punt)
Greg Thomas, Colorado	1988-91	6 (6 FGs)
Bernard Williams, Georgia	1990-93	6 (4 PATs; 2 FGs)
Bracey Walker, North Carolina	1990-93	6 (6 Punts)
Jermaine Mays, Minnesota	1998-00, 02	6 (6 Punts)
Bobby Iwuchukwu, Purdue	2002-05	6 (5 FGs; 1 PAT)

SEASON COMBINED BLOCKED KICKS

Player, Team	Year	BK (#Breakdown)
Jimmy Lisko, Arkansas St.	1975	8 (4 PATs; 3 Punts; 1 FG)
James Francis, Baylor	1989	8 (4 PATs; 3 Punts; 1 FG)
James King, Central Mich.	2001	8 (7 Punts; 1 FG)
Lonnell Dewalt, Kentucky	2004	7 (6 FGs; 1 PAT)
Bill Hornbacher, Nebraska	1967	6 (No Breakdown)
Mike Akiu, Hawaii	1982	6 (4 FGs; 1 PAT; 1 Punt)
Richard Johnson, Wisconsin	1984	6 (3 Punts; 2 FGs; 1 PAT)
Tim Curry, Air Force	1997	5 (4 Punts; 1 FG)
Kendrell Bell, Georgia	1999	5 (3 Punts; 2 FGs)
Jermaine Mays, Minnesota	2002	5 (5 Punts)

SINGLE-GAME COMBINED BLOCKED KICKS

BK	Player, Team (Opponent)	Date	BK (#Breakdown)
4	Ken Irvin, Memphis (Arkansas)	Sept. 26, 1992	4 Punts
4	James King, Central Mich. (Michigan St.)	Sept. 8, 2001	4 Punts
3	Richard Johnson, Wisconsin (Missouri)	Sept. 15, 1984	2 Punts; 1 PAT
3	Carlton McDonald, Air Force (Colorado St.)	Sept. 1, 1990	2 Punts; 1 PAT

#Breakdown=No. of Punts, No. of FGs and No. of Extra Points Blocked.

Punting

CAREER AVERAGE

(Minimum 250 Punts; Player must have concluded his career)

Player, Team	Years	No.	Yards	Avg.	Long
Daniel Sepulveda, Baylor	2003-06	277	12,531	45.2	78
Shane Lechler, Texas A&M	1996-99	268	11,977	44.7	76
Bill Smith, Mississippi	1983-86	254	11,260	44.3	92
Jim Arnold, Vanderbilt	1979-82	277	12,171	43.9	79
Ralf Mojsiejenko, Michigan St.	1981-84	275	11,997	43.6	72
Jim Miller, Mississippi	1976-79	266	11,549	43.4	82
Russ Henderson, Virginia	1975-78	276	11,957	43.3	74
Maury Buford, Texas Tech	1978-81	293	12,670	43.2	75
Nate Cochran, Pittsburgh	1993-96	252	10,851	43.1	80
Chris Becker, TCU	1985-88	265	11,407	43.0	77
James Gargus, TCU	1981-84	255	10,862	42.6	74
Ron Keller, New Mexico	1983-86	252	10,737	42.6	77
Brendan Carney, Syracuse	$2002-06	270	11,490	42.6	71
Brian Morton, Duke	1997-00	282	12,000	42.6	80

(150-249 Punts)

Player, Team	Years	No.	Yards	Avg.	Long
Todd Sauerbrun, West Virginia	1991-94	167	7,733	46.3	90
Reggie Roby, Iowa	1979-82	172	7,849	45.6	69
Greg Montgomery, Michigan St.	1985-87	170	7,721	45.4	86
Ryan Plackemeier, Wake Forest	2002-05	220	9,957	45.3	82
Tom Tupa, Ohio St.	1984-87	196	8,854	45.2	75
Brandon Fields, Michigan St.	2003-06	209	9,405	45.0	79
Barry Helton, Colorado	1984-87	153	6,873	44.9	68
Aron Langley, Wyoming	1996-98	171	7,649	44.7	72
Ray Guy, Southern Miss.	1970-72	200	8,934	44.7	93
Dave Zastudil, Ohio	1998-01	207	9,225	44.6	75
Bucky Scribner, Kansas	1980-82	217	9,670	44.6	70
Terry Daniel, Auburn	1992-94	169	7,522	44.5	71
Greg Horne, Arkansas	1983-86	180	8,002	44.5	72

$See page 10 for explanation.

SEASON AVERAGE

(Qualifiers for Championship)

Player, Team	Year	No.	Yards	Avg.
Chad Kessler, LSU	†1997	39	1,961	50.3
Reggie Roby, Iowa	†1981	44	2,193	49.8
Kirk Wilson, UCLA	†1956	30	1,479	49.3
Todd Sauerbrun, West Virginia	†1994	72	3,486	‡48.4
Travis Dorsch, Purdue	†2001	49	2,370	48.4
Zack Jordan, Colorado	†1950	38	1,830	48.2
Ricky Anderson, Vanderbilt	†1984	58	2,793	48.2
Marv Bateman, Utah	†1971	68	3,269	48.1
Reggie Roby, Iowa	†1982	52	2,501	48.1
Andrew Bayes, East Caro.	†1999	47	2,259	48.1
Owen Price, UTEP	†1940	30	1,440	48.0
Matt Prater, UCF	†2003	58	2,781	48.0

†National champion. ‡Record for minimum 50 punts.

ANNUAL CHAMPIONS

Year	Player, Team	Class	No.	Yards	Avg.
1937	Johnny Pingel, Michigan St.	Jr.	49	2,101	42.9
1938	Jerry Dowd, St. Mary's (Cal.)	Sr.	62	2,711	43.7
1939	Harry Dunkle, North Carolina	So.	37	1,725	46.6
1940	Owen Price, UTEP	Jr.	30	1,440	48.0
1941	Owen Price, UTEP	Sr.	40	1,813	45.3
1942	Bobby Cifers, Tennessee	Jr.	37	1,586	42.9
1943	Harold Cox, Arkansas	Fr.	37	1,518	41.0
1944	Bob Waterfield, UCLA	Sr.	60	2,575	42.9
1945	Howard Maley, SMU	Sr.	59	2,458	41.7
1946	Johnny Galvin, Purdue	Sr.	30	1,286	42.9

Year	Player, Team	Class	No.	Yards	Avg.
1947	Leslie Palmer, North Carolina St.	Sr.	65	2,816	43.3
1948	Charlie Justice, North Carolina	Jr.	62	2,728	44.0
1949	Paul Stombaugh, Furman	Sr.	57	2,550	44.7
1950	Zack Jordan, Colorado	So.	38	1,830	48.2
1951	Chuck Spaulding, Wyoming	Jr.	37	1,610	43.5
1952	Des Koch, Southern California	Jr.	47	2,043	43.5
1953	Zeke Bratkowski, Georgia (QB)	Sr.	50	2,132	42.6
1954	A.L. Terpening, New Mexico	Sr.	41	1,869	45.6
1955	Don Chandler, Florida	Sr.	22	975	44.3
1956	Kirk Wilson, UCLA	So.	30	1,479	49.3
1957	Dave Sherer, SMU	Jr.	36	1,620	45.0
1958	Bobby Walden, Georgia	So.	44	1,991	45.3
1959	John Hadl, Kansas	So.	43	1,960	45.6
1960	Dick Fitzsimmons, Denver	So.	25	1,106	44.2
1961	Joe Zuger, Arizona St.	Sr.	31	1,305	42.1
1962	Joe Don Looney, Oklahoma	Jr.	34	1,474	43.4
1963	Danny Thomas, SMU	Jr.	48	2,110	44.0
1964	Frank Lambert, Mississippi	Sr.	50	2,205	44.1
1965	Dave Lewis, Stanford	Jr.	29	1,302	44.9
1966	Ron Widby, Tennessee	Sr.	48	2,104	43.8
1967	Zenon Andrusyshyn, UCLA	So.	34	1,502	44.2
1968	Dany Pitcock, Wichita St.	Sr.	71	3,068	43.2
1969	Ed Marsh, Baylor	Jr.	68	2,965	43.6
1970	Marv Bateman, Utah	Jr.	65	2,968	45.7
1971	Marv Bateman, Utah	Sr.	68	3,269	48.1
1972	Ray Guy, Southern Miss.	Sr.	58	2,680	46.2
1973	Chuck Ramsey, Wake Forest	Sr.	87	3,896	44.8
1974	Joe Parker, Appalachian St.	So.	63	2,788	44.3
1975	Tom Skladany, Ohio St.	Jr.	36	1,682	46.7
1976	Russell Erxleben, Texas	So.	61	2,842	46.6
1977	Jim Miller, Mississippi	So.	66	3,029	45.9
1978	Maury Buford, Texas Tech	Fr.	71	3,131	44.1
1979	Clay Brown, BYU	Jr.	43	1,950	45.3

Beginning in 1980, ranked on minimum 3.6 punts per game

Year	Player, Team	Class	No.	Yards	Long	Avg.
1980	Steve Cox, Arkansas	Sr.	47	2,186	86	46.5
1981	Reggie Roby, Iowa	Jr.	44	2,193	68	49.8
1982	Reggie Roby, Iowa	Sr.	52	2,501	66	48.1
1983	Jack Weil, Wyoming	Sr.	52	2,369	86	45.6
1984	Ricky Anderson, Vanderbilt	Sr.	58	2,793	82	48.2
1985	Mark Simon, Air Force	Jr.	53	2,506	71	47.3
1986	Greg Horne, Arkansas	Sr.	49	2,313	65	47.2
1987	Tom Tupa, Ohio St. (QB)	Sr.	63	2,963	72	47.0
1988	Keith English, Colorado	Sr.	51	2,297	77	45.0
1989	Tom Rouen, Colorado	So.	36	1,651	63	45.8
1990	Cris Shale, Bowling Green	Sr.	66	3,087	81	46.8
1991	Mark Bounds, Texas Tech	Sr.	53	2,481	78	46.8
1992	Ed Bunn, UTEP	Sr.	41	1,955	73	47.7
1993	Chris MacInnis, Air Force	Sr.	49	2,303	74	47.0
1994	Todd Sauerbrun, West Virginia	Sr.	72	3,486	90	‡48.4
1995	Brad Maynard, Ball St.	Jr.	66	3,071	67	46.5
1996	Bill Marinangel, Vanderbilt	Sr.	77	3,586	79	46.6
1997	Chad Kessler, LSU	Sr.	39	1,961	66	*50.3
1998	Joe Kristosik, UNLV	Sr.	76	3,509	69	46.2
1999	Andrew Bayes, East Caro.	Sr.	47	2,259	78	48.1
2000	Preston Gruening, Minnesota	So.	46	2,080	65	45.2
2001	Travis Dorsch, Purdue	Sr.	49	2,370	79	48.4
2002	Matt Payne, BYU	So.	51	2,427	76	47.6
2003	Matt Prater, UCF	So.	58	2,781	74	48.0
2004	Brandon Fields, Michigan St.	Jr.	50	2,394	65	47.9
2005	Ryan Plackemeier, Wake Forest	Sr.	67	3,165	82	47.2
2006	Daniel Sepulveda, Baylor	Sr.	66	3,068	78	46.5

**Record. ‡Record for minimum of 50 punts.*

Punt Returns

CAREER AVERAGE

(Minimum 1.2 Returns Per Game; Minimum 30 Returns; Player must have concluded his career)

Player, Team	Years	No.	Yards	TD	Long	Avg.
Jack Mitchell, Oklahoma	1946-48	39	922	7	70	23.6
Gene Gibson, Cincinnati	1949-50	37	760	4	75	‡20.5
Eddie Macon, Pacific	1949-51	48	907	4	*100	18.9
Jackie Robinson, UCLA	1939-40	37	694	2	89	18.8
Dan Shelton, Northern Ill.	2001-04	57	1,021	4	90	17.9
Bobby Dillon, Texas	1949-51	47	830	1	84	17.7
Mike Fuller, Auburn	1972-74	50	883	3	63	17.7
Bobby Newcombe, Nebraska	1997-00	48	829	3	94	17.3
James Dye, BYU/Utah St.	1992-93, 95-96	61	1,046	5	90	17.2
George Hoey, Michigan	1966-68	31	529	1	60	17.1
Erroll Tucker, Utah	1984-85	38	650	3	89	17.1
Jack Christiansen, Colorado St.	1948-50	37	626	2	89	16.9
Henry Pryor, Rutgers	1948-49	37	625	1	85	16.9
Adolph Bellizeare, Penn	1972-74	33	557	3	73	16.9
Ken Hatfield, Arkansas	1962-64	70	1,135	5	95	16.2
Gene Rossides, Columbia	1945-48	53	851	3	70	16.1
Bill Hillenbrand, Indiana	1941-42	65	1,042	2	88	16.0

**Record tied. ‡Record for minimum 1.5 returns per game.*

SEASON AVERAGE

(Minimum 1.2 Returns Per Game)

Player, Team	Year	No.	Yards	Avg.
Maurice Drew, UCLA	†2005	15	427	28.5
Bill Blackstock, Tennessee	1951	12	311	25.9
Ted Ginn Jr., Ohio St.	†2004	15	384	25.6
George Sims, Baylor	1948	15	375	‡25.0
Gene Derricotte, Michigan	1947	14	347	24.8
George Hoey, Michigan	1967	12	291	24.3
Erroll Tucker, Utah	†1985	16	389	24.3
Floyd Little, Syracuse	1965	18	423	23.5

†National champion. ‡Record for minimum 1.5 returns per game.

ANNUAL CHAMPIONS

(Ranked on Total Yards Until 1970)

Year	Player, Team	Class	No.	Yards	Avg.
1939	Bosh Pritchard, VMI	So.	42	583	13.9
1940	Junie Hovious, Mississippi	Sr.	33	498	15.1
1941	Bill Geyer, Colgate	Sr.	33	616	18.7
1942	Bill Hillenbrand, Indiana	Jr.	23	481	20.9
1943	Marion Flanagan, Texas A&M	Jr.	49	475	9.7
1944	Joe Stuart, California	Jr.	39	372	9.5
1945	Jake Leicht, Oregon	So.	28	395	14.1
1946	Harry Gilmer, Alabama	Jr.	37	436	11.8
1947	Lindy Berry, TCU	So.	42	493	11.7
1948	Lee Nalley, Vanderbilt	Jr.	43	791	18.4
1949	Lee Nalley, Vanderbilt	Sr.	35	498	14.2
1950	Dave Waters, Wash. & Lee	Jr.	30	445	14.8
1951	Tom Murphy, Holy Cross	So.	25	533	21.3
1952	Horton Nesrsta, Rice	Jr.	44	536	12.2
1953	Paul Giel, Minnesota	Sr.	17	288	16.9
1954	Dicky Maegle, Rice	Sr.	15	293	19.5
1955	Mike Sommer, George Washington	So.	24	330	13.8
1956	Bill Stacy, Mississippi St.	Jr.	24	290	12.1
1957	Bobby Mulgado, Arizona St.	Sr.	14	267	19.1
1958	Howard Cook, Colorado	Sr.	24	242	10.1
1959	Pervis Atkins, New Mexico St.	Jr.	16	241	15.1
1960	Lance Alworth, Arkansas	Jr.	18	307	17.1
1961	Lance Alworth, Arkansas	Sr.	28	336	12.0
1962	Darrell Roberts, Utah St.	Sr.	16	333	20.8
1963	Ken Hatfield, Arkansas	Jr.	21	350	16.7
1964	Ken Hatfield, Arkansas	Sr.	31	518	16.7
1965	Nick Rassas, Notre Dame	Sr.	24	459	19.1
1966	Vic Washington, Wyoming	Jr.	34	443	13.0
1967	Mike Battle, Southern California	Jr.	47	570	12.1
1968	Roger Wehrli, Missouri	Sr.	41	478	11.7
1969	Chris Farasopoulous, BYU	Jr.	35	527	15.1

Beginning in 1970, ranked on average per return (instead of total yards)‡

Year	Player, Team	Class	No.	Yards	TD	Long	Avg.
1970	Steve Holden, Arizona St.	So.	17	327	2	94	19.2
1971	Golden Richards, BYU	Jr.	33	624	4	87	18.9
1972	Randy Rhino, Georgia Tech	So.	25	441	1	96	17.6
1973	Gary Hayman, Penn St.	Sr.	23	442	1	83	19.2
1974	John Provost, Holy Cross	Sr.	13	238	2	85	18.3
1975	Donnie Ross, New Mexico St.	Sr.	21	338	1	#81	16.1
1976	Henry Jenkins, Rutgers	Sr.	30	449	0	#40	15.0
1977	Robert Woods, Grambling	Sr.	††11	279	3	72	25.4
1978	Ira Matthews, Wisconsin	Sr.	16	270	3	78	16.9
1979	Jeffrey Shockley, Tennessee St.	Sr.	27	456	1	79	16.9
1980	Scott Woerner, Georgia	Sr.	31	488	1	67	15.7
1981	Glen Young, Mississippi St.	Jr.	19	307	2	87	16.2
1982	Lionel James, Auburn	Jr.	25	394	0	#63	15.8
1983	Jim Sandusky, San Diego St.	Sr.	20	381	1	90	19.0
1984	Ricky Nattiel, Florida	So.	22	346	1	67	15.7
1985	Erroll Tucker, Utah	Sr.	16	389	2	89	24.3
1986	Rod Smith, Nebraska	Jr.	‡‡12	227	1	63	18.9
1987	Alan Grant, Stanford	Jr.	27	446	2	77	16.5
1988	Deion Sanders, Florida St.	Sr.	33	503	1	76	15.2
1989	Larry Hargrove, Ohio	Sr.	17	309	2	83	18.2
1990	Dave McCloughan, Colorado	Sr.	32	524	2	90	16.4
1991	Bo Campbell, Virginia Tech	Jr.	15	273	0	45	18.2
1992	Lee Gissendaner, Northwestern	Jr.	15	327	1	72	21.8
1993	Aaron Glenn, Texas A&M	Sr.	17	339	2	76	19.9
1994	Steve Clay, Eastern Mich.	Jr.	14	278	1	65	19.9

Year	Player, Team	Class	No.	Yards	TD	Long	Avg.
1995	James Dye, BYU	Jr.	20	438	2	90	21.9
1996	Allen Rossum, Notre Dame	Jr.	15	344	3	83	22.9
1997	Tim Dwight, Iowa	Sr.	19	367	3	—	19.3
1998	David Allen, Kansas St.	So.	33	730	4	93	22.1
1999	Dennis Northcutt, Arizona	Sr.	23	436	2	81	19.0
2000	Aaron Lockett, Kansas St.	Jr.	22	501	3	83	22.8
2001	Roman Hollowell, Colorado	Sr.	29	522	2	77	18.0
2002	Dan Sheldon, Northern Ill.	So.	21	477	3	90	22.7
2003	Skyler Green, LSU	So.	25	462	2	80	18.5
2004	Ted Ginn Jr., Ohio St.	Fr.	15	384	4	82	25.6
2005	Maurice Drew, UCLA	Jr.	15	427	3	81	*28.5
2006	DeSean Jackson, California	So.	25	455	4	95	18.2

**Record. #Did not score. ‡Ranked on minimum 1.5 returns per game, 1970-73; 1.2 from 1974. ††Declared champion; with three more returns (making 1.3 per game) for zero yards still would have highest average. ‡‡Declared champion; with two more returns (making 1.2 per game) for zero yards still would have highest average.*

ANNUAL PUNT RETURN LEADERS (1939-69) BASED ON AVERAGE PER RETURN

(Minimum 1.2 Returns Per Game)

1939—Jackie Robinson, UCLA, 20.0; **1940**—Jackie Robinson, UCLA, 21.0; **1941**—Walt Slater, Tennessee, 20.4; **1942**—Billy Hillenbrand, Indiana, 20.9; **1943**—Otto Graham, Northwestern, 19.7; **1944**—Glenn Davis, Army, 18.4; **1945**—Jake Leicht, Oregon, 14.8; **1946**—Harold Griffin, Florida, 20.1; **1947**—Gene Derricotte, Michigan, 24.8; **1948**—George Sims, Baylor, ‡25.0; **1949**—Gene Evans, Wisconsin, 21.8; **1950**—Lindy Hanson, Boston U., 22.5; **1951**—Bill Blackstock, Tennessee, 25.9; **1952**—Gil Reich, Kansas, 17.2; **1953**—Bobby Lee, New Mexico, 19.4; **1954**—Dicky Maegle, Rice, 19.5; **1955**—Ron Lind, Drake, 21.1; **1956**—Ron Lind, Drake, 19.1; **1957**—Bobby Mulgado, Arizona St., 19.1; **1958**—Herb Hallas, Yale, 23.4; **1959**—Jacque MacKinnon, Colgate, 17.5; **1960**—Pat Fischer, Nebraska, 21.2; **1961**—Tom Larscheid, Utah St., 23.4; **1962**—Darrell Roberts, Utah St., 20.8; **1963**—Rickie Harris, Arizona, 17.4; **1964**—Ken Hatfield, Arkansas, 16.7; **1965**—Floyd Little, Syracuse, 23.5; **1966**—Don Bean, Houston, 20.2; **1967**—George Hoey, Michigan, 24.3; **1968**—Rob Bordley, Princeton, 20.5; **1969**—George Hannen, Davidson, 22.4.

‡Record for minimum 1.5 returns per game.

Kickoff Returns

CAREER AVERAGE

(Minimum 1.2 Returns Per Game; Minimum 30 Returns; Player must have concluded his career)

Player, Team	Years	No.	Yards	Avg.
Anthony Davis, Southern California	1972-74	37	1,299	35.1
Eric Booth, Southern Miss.	1994-97	35	1,135	32.4
Overton Curtis, Utah St.	1957-58	32	991	‡31.0
Fred Montgomery, New Mexico St.	1991-92	39	1,191	30.5
Altie Taylor, Utah St.	1966-68	40	1,170	29.3
Stan Brown, Purdue	1968-70	49	1,412	28.8
Henry White, Colgate	1974-77	41	1,180	28.8
Kevin Johnson, Syracuse	1995-98	50	1,437	28.7
Pat Johnson, Oregon	1994-97	36	1,023	28.4
Ben Kelly, Colorado	1997-99	64	1,798	28.1
Paul Loughran, Temple	1970-72	40	1,123	28.1
Jim Krieg, Washington	1970-71	31	860	27.7

‡Record for minimum 1.5 returns per game.

SEASON AVERAGE

(Minimum 1.2 Returns Per Game)

Player, Team	Year	No.	Yards	Avg.
Paul Allen, BYU	1961	12	481	40.1
Tremain Mack, Miami (Fla.)	†1996	13	514	39.5
Leeland McElroy, Texas A&M	†1993	15	590	39.3
Forrest Hall, San Francisco	†1946	15	573	‡38.2
Tony Ball, Chattanooga	†1977	13	473	36.4
George Marinkov, North Carolina St.	1954	13	465	35.8
Bob Baker, Cornell	1964	11	386	35.1

†National champion. ‡Record for minimum 1.5 returns per game.

ANNUAL CHAMPIONS

(Ranked on Total Yards Until 1970)

Year	Player, Team	Class	No.	Yards	Avg.
1939	Nile Kinnick, Iowa	Sr.	15	377	25.1
1940	Jack Emigh, Montana	Sr.	18	395	21.9
1941	Earl Ray, Wyoming	So.	23	496	21.6
1942	Frank Porto, California	Sr.	17	483	28.4
1943	Paul Copoulos, Marquette	So.	11	384	34.9
1944	Paul Copoulos, Marquette	Jr.	14	337	24.1
1945	Al Dekdebrun, Cornell	Sr.	14	321	22.9
1946	Forrest Hall, San Francisco	Jr.	15	573	**38.2
1947	Doak Walker, SMU	So.	10	387	38.7
1948	Bill Gregus, Wake Forest	Jr.	19	503	26.5
1949	Johnny Subda, Nevada	Sr.	18	444	24.7
1950	Chuck Hill, New Mexico	Jr.	27	729	27.0
1951	Chuck Hill, New Mexico	Sr.	17	504	29.6
1952	Curly Powell, VMI	Sr.	27	517	19.1
1953	Max McGee, Tulane	Sr.	17	371	21.8
1954	Art Luppino, Arizona	So.	20	632	31.6
1955	Sam Woolwine, VMI	Jr.	22	471	21.4
1956	Sam Woolwine, VMI	Sr.	18	503	27.9
1957	Overton Curtis, Utah St.	Jr.	23	695	30.2
1958	Sonny Randle, Virginia	Sr.	21	506	24.1
1959	Don Perkins, New Mexico	Sr.	15	520	34.7
1960	Bruce Samples, BYU	Sr.	23	577	25.1
1961	Dick Mooney, Idaho	Sr.	23	494	21.5
1962	Donnie Frederick, Wake Forest	Sr.	29	660	22.8
1963	Gary Wood, Cornell	Sr.	19	618	32.5
1964	Dan Bland, Mississippi St.	Jr.	20	558	27.9
1965	Eric Crabtree, Pittsburgh	Sr.	25	636	25.4
1966	Marcus Rhoden, Mississippi St.	Sr.	26	572	22.0
1967	Joe Casas, New Mexico	Sr.	23	602	26.2
1968	Mike Adamle, Northwestern	So.	34	732	21.5
1969	Stan Brown, Purdue	Jr.	26	698	26.8

Beginning in 1970, ranked on average per return (instead of total yards)‡

Year	Player, Team	Class	No.	Yards	Avg.
1970	Stan Brown, Purdue	Sr.	19	638	33.6
1971	Paul Loughran, Temple	Jr.	15	502	33.5
1972	Larry Williams, Texas Tech	So.	16	493	30.8
1973	Steve Odom, Utah	Sr.	21	618	29.4
1974	Anthony Davis, Southern California	Sr.	††11	467	42.5
1975	John Schultz, Maryland	Sr.	13	403	31.0
1976	Ira Matthews, Wisconsin	So.	14	415	29.6
1977	Tony Ball, Chattanooga	Fr.	13	473	36.4
1978	Drew Hill, Georgia Tech	Sr.	19	570	30.0
1979	Stevie Nelson, Ball St.	Fr.	18	565	31.4
1980	Mike Fox, San Diego St.	So.	†11	361	32.8
1981	Frank Minnifield, Louisville	Jr.	11	334	30.4
1982	Carl Monroe, Utah	Sr.	14	421	30.1
1983	Henry Williams, East Caro.	Jr.	19	591	31.1
1984	Keith Henderson, Texas Tech	Fr.	13	376	28.9
1985	Erroll Tucker, Utah	Sr.	24	698	29.1
1986	Terrance Roulhac, Clemson	Sr.	17	561	33.0
1987	Barry Sanders, Oklahoma St.	So.	14	442	31.6
1988	Raghib Ismail, Notre Dame	Fr.	#12	433	36.1
1989	Tony Smith, Southern Miss.	So.	14	455	32.5
1990	Dale Carter, Tennessee	Jr.	17	507	29.8
1991	Fred Montgomery, New Mexico St.	Jr.	25	734	29.4
1992	Fred Montgomery, New Mexico St.	Sr.	14	457	32.6
1993	Leeland McElroy, Texas A&M	Fr.	15	590	39.3
1994	Eric Moulds, Mississippi St.	Jr.	†13	426	32.8
1995	Robert Tate, Cincinnati	Jr.	15	515	34.3
1996	Tremain Mack, Miami (Fla.)	Jr.	13	514	39.5
1997	Eric Booth, Southern Miss.	Sr.	22	766	34.8
1998	Broderick McGrew, North Texas	Jr.	18	587	32.6
1999	James Williams, Marshall	Sr.	15	493	32.9
2000	LaTarence Dunbar, TCU	So.	15	506	33.7
2001	Chris Massey, Oklahoma St.	Jr.	15	522	34.8
2002	Charles Pauley, San Jose St.	Sr.	31	978	31.6
2003	Michael Waddell, North Carolina	Sr.	15	475	31.7
	J.R. Reed, South Fla.	Sr.	18	570	31.7
2004	Justin Miller, Clemson	Jr.	20	661	33.1
2005	Jonathan Stewart, Oregon	Fr.	12	404	33.7
2006	Marcus Thigpen, Indiana	So.	24	723	30.1

***Record for minimum 1.5 returns per game. #Declared champion; with two more returns (making 1.3 per game) for zero yards still would have highest average. †Declared champion; with one more return (making 1.2 per game) for zero yards still would have highest average. ††Declared champion; with three more returns (making 1.3 per game) for zero yards still would have highest average. ‡Ranked on minimum 1.5 returns per game, 1970-73; 1.2 from 1974.*

ANNUAL KICKOFF RETURN LEADERS (1939-69) BASED ON AVERAGE PER RETURN

(Minimum 1.2 Returns Per Game)

1939—Nile Kinnick, Iowa, 25.1; **1940**—Bill Geyer, Colgate, 27.0; **1941**—Vern Lockard, Colorado, 24.4; **1942-45**—Not compiled; **1946**—Forrest Hall, San Francisco, ‡38.2; **1947**—Skippy Minisi, Penn, 28.8; **1948**—Jerry Williams, Washington St., 29.9; **1949**—Billy Conn, Georgetown, 31.1; **1950**—Johnny Turco, Holy Cross, 27.4; **1951**—Bob Mischak, Army, 31.3; **1952**—Carroll Hardy, Colorado, 32.2; **1953**—Carl Bolt, Wash. & Lee, 27.1; **1954**—George Marinkov, North Carolina St., 35.8; **1955**—Jim Brown, Syracuse, 32.0; **1956**—Paul Hornung, Notre Dame, 31.0; **1957**—Overton Curtis, Utah St., 30.2; **1958**—Marshall Starks, Illinois, 26.3; **1959**—Don Perkins, New Mexico, 34.7; **1960**—Tom Hennessey, Holy Cross, 33.4; **1961**—Paul Allen, BYU, *40.1; **1962**—Larry Coyer, Marshall, 30.2; **1963**—Gary

Wood, Cornell, 32.5; **1964**—Bob Baker, Cornell, 35.1; **1965**—Tom Barrington, Ohio St., 34.3; **1966**—Frank Moore, Louisville, 27.9; **1967**—Altie Taylor, Utah St., 31.9; **1968**—Kerry Reardon, Iowa, 32.1; **1969**—Chris Farasopoulous, BYU, 32.2.

**Record. ‡Record for minimum 1.5 returns per game.*

All-Purpose Yards

CAREER YARDS PER GAME

(Minimum 3,500 Yards; Player must have concluded his career)

Player, Team	Years	G	Rush	Rcv.	Int.	PR	KOR	Yds.	Yd.PG
Ryan Benjamin, Pacific	1990-92	24	3,119	1,063	0	100	1,424	5,706	237.8
Sheldon Canley, San Jose St.	1988-90	25	2,513	828	0	5	1,800	5,146	205.8
Howard Stevens, Louisville	1971-72	20	2,723	389	0	401	360	3,873	193.7
O.J. Simpson, Southern California	1967-68	19	3,124	235	0	0	307	3,666	192.9
Alex Van Dyke, Nevada	1994-95	22	7	3,100	0	5	1,034	4,146	188.5
Ed Marinaro, Cornell	1969-71	27	4,715	225	0	0	0	4,940	183.0
Garrett Wolfe, Northern Ill.	2004-06	33	5,164	588	0	0	231	5,983	181.3
Marshall Faulk, San Diego St.	1991-93	31	4,589	973	0	0	33	5,595	180.5
Troy Edwards, Louisiana Tech	1996-98	34	447	4,352	0	241	991	6,031	177.4
Herschel Walker, Georgia	1980-82	33	5,259	243	0	0	247	5,749	174.2
Louie Giammona, Utah St.	1973-75	30	3,499	171	0	188	1,345	5,203	173.4

SEASON YARDS PER GAME

Player, Team	Years	Rush	Rcv.	Int.	PR	KOR	Yds.	Yd.PG
Barry Sanders, Oklahoma St.	†1988	*2,628	106	0	95	421	*3,250	295.5
Ryan Benjamin, Pacific	†1991	1,581	612	0	4	798	2,995	249.6
Byron "Whizzer" White, Colorado	†1937	1,121	0	103	587	159	1,970	246.3
Mike Pringle, Cal St. Fullerton	†1989	1,727	249	0	0	714	2,690	244.6
Paul Palmer, Temple	†1986	1,866	110	0	0	657	2,633	239.4
Emmett White, Utah St.	†2000	1,322	592	0	183	531	2,628	238.9
Ryan Benjamin, Pacific	†1992	1,441	434	0	96	626	2,597	236.1
Marcus Allen, Southern California	†1981	2,342	217	0	0	0	2,559	232.6
Troy Edwards, Louisiana Tech	†1998	227	*1,996	0	235	326	2,784	232.0
Sheldon Canley, San Jose St.	1989	1,201	353	0	0	959	2,513	228.5
Ollie Matson, San Francisco	†1951	1,566	58	18	115	280	2,037	226.3
Troy Davis, Iowa St.	†1995	2,010	159	0	0	297	2,466	224.2
Reggie Bush, Southern California	†2005	1,740	478	0	179	493	2,890	222.3
Alex Van Dyke, Nevada	1995	6	1,854	0	0	583	2,443	222.1
Art Luppino, Arizona	†1954	1,359	50	84	68	632	2,193	219.3
Chuck Weatherspoon, Houston	1989	1,146	735	0	715	95	2,391	217.4
Anthony Thompson, Indiana	1989	1,793	201	0	0	394	2,388	217.1
Ricky Williams, Texas	1998	2,124	262	0	0	0	2,386	216.9
Napoleon McCallum, Navy	†1983	1,587	166	0	272	360	2,385	216.8
Troy Davis, Iowa St.	†1996	2,185	61	0	0	118	2,364	214.9
Ed Marinaro, Cornell	†1971	1,881	51	0	0	0	1,932	214.7
Rashaan Salaam, Colorado	†1994	2,055	294	0	0	0	2,349	213.6
Howard Stevens, Louisville	†1972	1,294	221	0	337	240	2,132	213.2
Napoleon McCallum, Navy	†1985	1,327	358	0	157	488	2,330	211.8
Brian Pruitt, Central Mich.	1994	1,890	69	0	0	330	2,289	208.1

**Record. †National champion.*

CAREER YARDS

Player, Team	Years	Rush	Rcv.	Int.	PR	KOR	Yds.	Yd.PP
DeAngelo Williams, Memphis	2002-05	6,026	723	0	0	824	7,573	7.0
Ricky Williams, Texas	1995-98	6,279	927	0	0	0	7,206	6.6
Napoleon McCallum, Navy	$1981-85	4,179	796	0	858	1,339	7,172	6.3
Darrin Nelson, Stanford	1977-78, 80-81	4,033	2,368	0	471	13	6,885	7.1
Kevin Faulk, LSU	1995-98	4,557	600	0	857	819	6,833	6.8
Darren Sproles, Kansas St.	2001-04	4,979	609	0	378	846	6,812	7.1
Ron Dayne, Wisconsin	1996-99	*6,397	304	0	0	0	6,701	5.8
Terance Mathis, New Mexico	1985-87, 89	329	4,254	0	115	1,993	6,691	14.6
Tony Dorsett, Pittsburgh	1973-76	6,082	406	0	0	127	6,615	5.9
Paul Palmer, Temple	1983-86	4,895	705	0	12	997	6,609	6.1
Reggie Bush, Southern California	2003-05	3,169	1,301	0	559	1,522	‡6,551	10.2
Charles White, Southern California	1976-79	5,598	507	0	0	440	6,545	6.0
Trevor Cobb, Rice	1989-92	4,948	892	0	21	651	6,512	5.3
Mewelde Moore, Tulane	2000-03	4,364	2,059	0	0	82	6,505	5.9
LaDainian Tomlinson, TCU	1997-00	5,263	236	0	0	838	6,337	6.4
Glyn Milburn, Oklahoma/Stanford	1988, 90-92	2,302	1,495	0	1,145	1,246	6,188	8.1
Cedric Benson, Texas	2001-04	5,540	621	0	0	0	6,161	5.2
Howard Jackson, UTEP	2001-04	3,466	726	0	14	1,947	6,153	7.5
Travis Prentice, Miami (Ohio)	1996-99	5,596	527	0	0	0	6,123	5.1
Anthony Thompson, Indiana	1986-89	4,965	713	0	0	412	6,090	5.1
Michael Turner, Northern Ill.	2000-03	4,941	451	0	0	646	6,038	6.0
Troy Edwards, Louisiana Tech	1996-98	447	4,352	0	241	991	‡6,031	15.8
Archie Griffin, Ohio St.	1972-75	5,177	286	0	0	540	6,003	6.7

**Record. $See page 10 for explanation. ‡Three-year totals.*

SEASON YARDS

Player, Team	Year	Rush	Rcv.	Int.	PR	KOR	Yds.	Yd.PP
Barry Sanders, Oklahoma St.	†1988	*2,628	106	0	95	421	3,250	8.3
Ryan Benjamin, Pacific	†1991	1,581	612	0	4	798	2,995	9.6

Player, Team	Year	Rush	Rcv.	Int.	PR	KOR	Yds.	Yd.PP
Reggie Bush, Southern California	†2005	1,740	478	0	179	493	2,890	10.2
Troy Edwards, Louisiana Tech	†1998	227	1,996	0	235	326	2,784	14.7
Darren Sproles, Kansas St.	2003	1,986	287	0	190	272	2,735	7.6
Mike Pringle, Cal St. Fullerton	†1989	1,727	249	0	0	714	2,690	7.6
Larry Johnson, Penn St.	†2002	2,087	349	0	0	219	2,655	8.2
Paul Palmer, Temple	†1986	1,866	110	0	0	657	2,633	6.8
Emmett White, Utah St.	†2000	1,322	592	0	183	531	2,628	7.9
Ryan Benjamin, Pacific	†1992	1,441	434	0	96	626	2,597	8.1
Bernard Berrian, Fresno St.	2001	101	1,270	0	552	668	2,591	‡17.5
Marcus Allen, Southern California	†1981	2,342	217	0	0	0	2,559	5.9
Sheldon Canley, San Jose St.	1989	1,201	353	0	0	959	2,513	7.4

**Record. †National champion. ‡Record for minimum 125 plays.*

ALL-PURPOSE SINGLE-GAME HIGHS

Yds.	Player, Team (Opponent)	Date
578	Emmett White, Utah St. (New Mexico St.)	Nov. 4, 2000
513	Reggie Bush, Southern California (Fresno St.)	Nov. 19, 2005
435	Brian Pruitt, Central Mich. (Toledo)	Nov. 5, 1994
429	Moe Williams, Kentucky (South Carolina)	Sept. 23, 1995
426	LaDainian Tomlinson, TCU (UTEP)	Nov. 20, 1999
424	Troy Edwards, Louisiana Tech (Nebraska)	Aug. 29, 1998
422	Marshall Faulk, San Diego St. (Pacific)	Sept. 14, 1991
419	Randy Gatewood, UNLV (Idaho)	Sept. 17, 1994
417	Greg Allen, Florida St. (Western Caro.)	Oct. 31, 1981
417	Paul Palmer, Temple (East Caro.)	Nov. 10, 1986
416	Anthony Thompson, Indiana (Wisconsin)	Nov. 11, 1989
411	John Leach, Wake Forest (Maryland)	Nov. 20, 1993
411	Travis Prentice, Miami (Ohio) (Akron)	Nov. 6, 1999
402	Ryan Benjamin, Pacific (Utah St.)	Nov. 21, 1992
401	Chuck Hughes, UTEP (North Texas)	Sept. 18, 1965

ANNUAL CHAMPIONS

Year	Player, Team	Class	Rush	Rcv.	Int.	PR	KOR	Yds.	Yd.PG
1937	Byron "Whizzer" White, Colorado	Sr.	1,121	0	103	587	159	1,970	246.3
1938	Parker Hall, Mississippi	Sr.	698	0	128	0	594	1,420	129.1
1939	Tom Harmon, Michigan	Jr.	868	110	98	0	132	1,208	151.0
1940	Tom Harmon, Michigan	Sr.	844	0	20	244	204	1,312	164.0
1941	Bill Dudley, Virginia	Sr.	968	60	76	481	89	1,674	186.0
1942	records not available	—	—	—	—	—	—	—	—
1943	Stan Koslowski, Holy Cross	Fr.	784	63	50	438	76	1,411	176.4
1944	Red Williams, Minnesota	Jr.	911	0	0	242	314	1,467	163.0
1945	Bob Fenimore, Oklahoma St.	Jr.	1,048	12	129	157	231	1,577	197.1
1946	Rudy Mobley, Hardin-Simmons	Sr.	1,262	13	79	273	138	1,765	176.5
1947	Wilton Davis, Hardin-Simmons	So.	1,173	79	0	295	251	1,798	179.8
1948	Lou Kusserow, Columbia	Sr.	766	463	19	130	359	1,737	193.0
1949	Johnny Papit, Virginia	Jr.	1,214	0	0	0	397	1,611	179.0
1950	Wilford White, Arizona St.	Sr.	1,502	225	0	64	274	2,065	206.5
1951	Ollie Matson, San Francisco	Sr.	1,566	58	18	115	280	2,037	226.3
1952	Billy Vessels, Oklahoma	Sr.	1,072	165	10	120	145	1,512	151.2
1953	J.C. Caroline, Illinois	So.	1,256	52	0	129	33	1,470	163.3
1954	Art Luppino, Arizona	So.	1,359	50	84	68	632	2,193	219.3
1955	Jim Swink, TCU	Jr.	1,283	111	46	64	198	1,702	170.2
	Art Luppino, Arizona	Jr.	1,313	74	0	62	253	1,702	170.2
1956	Jack Hill, Utah St.	Sr.	920	215	132	21	403	1,691	169.1
1957	Overton Curtis, Utah St.	Jr.	616	193	60	44	695	1,608	160.8
1958	Dick Bass, Pacific	Jr.	1,361	121	5	164	227	1,878	187.8
1959	Pervis Atkins, New Mexico St.	Jr.	971	301	23	241	264	1,800	180.0
1960	Pervis Atkins, New Mexico St.	Sr.	611	468	23	218	293	1,613	161.3
1961	Jim Pilot, New Mexico St.	So.	1,278	20	0	161	147	1,606	160.6
1962	Gary Wood, Cornell	Jr.	889	7	0	69	430	1,395	155.0
1963	Gary Wood, Cornell	Sr.	818	15	0	57	618	1,508	167.6
1964	Donny Anderson, Texas Tech	Jr.	966	396	0	28	320	1,710	171.0
1965	Floyd Little, Syracuse	Jr.	1,065	248	0	423	254	1,990	199.0
1966	Frank Quayle, Virginia	So.	727	420	0	30	439	1,616	161.6
1967	O.J. Simpson, Southern California	Jr.	1,415	109	0	0	176	1,700	188.9
1968	O.J. Simpson, Southern California	Sr.	1,709	126	0	0	131	1,966	196.6
1969	Lynn Moore, Army	Sr.	983	44	0	223	545	1,795	179.5
1970	Don McCauley, North Carolina	Sr.	1,720	235	0	0	66	2,021	183.7
1971	Ed Marinaro, Cornell	Sr.	1,881	51	0	0	0	1,932	214.7
1972	Howard Stevens, Louisville	Sr.	1,294	221	0	377	240	2,132	213.2
1973	Willard Harrell, Pacific	Jr.	1,319	18	0	88	352	1,777	177.7
1974	Louie Giammona, Utah St.	Jr.	1,534	79	0	16	355	1,984	198.4
1975	Louie Giammona, Utah St.	Sr.	1,454	33	0	124	434	2,045	185.9
1976	Tony Dorsett, Pittsburgh	Sr.	1,948	73	0	0	0	2,021	183.7
1977	Earl Campbell, Texas	Sr.	1,744	111	0	0	0	1,855	168.6
1978	Charles White, Southern California	Jr.	1,760	191	0	0	145	2,096	174.7
1979	Charles White, Southern California	Sr.	1,803	138	0	0	0	1,941	194.1
1980	Marcus Allen, Southern California	Jr.	1,563	231	0	0	0	1,794	179.4
1981	Marcus Allen, Southern California	Sr.	2,342	217	0	0	0	2,559	232.6
1982	Carl Monroe, Utah	Sr.	1,507	108	0	0	421	2,036	185.1
1983	Napoleon McCallum, Navy	Jr.	1,587	166	0	272	360	2,385	216.8
1984	Keith Byars, Ohio St.	Jr.	1,655	453	0	0	176	2,284	207.6
1985	Napoleon McCallum, Navy	Sr.	1,327	358	0	157	488	2,330	211.8

Year	Player, Team	Class	Rush	Rcv.	Int.	PR	KOR	Yds.	Yd.PG
1986	Paul Palmer, Temple	Sr.	1,866	110	0	0	657	2,633	239.4
1987	Eric Wilkerson, Kent St.	Jr.	1,221	269	0	0	584	2,074	188.6
1988	Barry Sanders, Oklahoma St.	Jr.	*2,628	106	0	95	421	*3,250	*295.5
1989	Mike Pringle, Cal St. Fullerton	Sr.	1,727	249	0	0	714	2,690	244.6
1990	Glyn Milburn, Stanford	So.	729	632	0	267	594	2,222	202.0
1991	Ryan Benjamin, Pacific	Jr.	1,581	612	0	4	798	2,995	249.6
1992	Ryan Benjamin, Pacific	Sr.	1,441	434	0	96	626	2,597	236.1
1993	LeShon Johnson, Northern Ill.	Sr.	1,976	106	0	0	0	2,082	189.3
1994	Rashaan Salaam, Colorado	Jr.	2,055	294	0	0	0	2,349	213.6
1995	Troy Davis, Iowa St.	So.	2,010	159	0	0	297	2,466	224.2
1996	Troy Davis, Iowa St.	Jr.	2,185	61	0	0	118	2,364	214.9
1997	Troy Edwards, Louisiana Tech	Jr.	190	1,707	0	6	241	2,144	194.9
1998	Troy Edwards, Louisiana Tech	Sr.	227	1,996	0	235	326	2,784	232.0
1999	Trevor Insley, Nevada	Sr.	5	*2,060	0	111	0	2,176	197.8
2000	Emmett White, Utah St.	Jr.	1,322	592	0	183	531	2,628	238.9
2001	Levron Williams, Indiana	Sr.	1,401	289	0	0	511	2,201	200.1
2002	Larry Johnson, Penn St.	Sr.	2,087	349	0	0	219	2,655	204.2
2003	DeAngelo Williams, Memphis	So.	1,430	384	0	0	299	2,113	192.1
2004	Darren Sproles, Kansas St.	Sr.	1,318	223	0	34	492	2,067	187.9
2005	Reggie Bush, Southern California	Jr.	1,740	478	0	179	493	2,890	222.3
2006	Garrett Wolfe, Northern Ill.	Sr.	1,928	249	0	0	0	2,177	167.5

**Record.*

Field Goals

CAREER FIELD GOALS

(One-inch tees were permitted in 1949, two-inch tees were permitted in 1965, and use of tees was eliminated in 1989. The goal posts were widened from 18 feet, 6 inches to 23 feet, 4 inches in 1959 and were narrowed back to 18 feet, 6 inches in 1991. In 1993, the hash marks were moved 6 feet, 8 inches closer to the center of the field, to 60 feet from each sideline.)

Player, Team	Years	Total	Pct.	Under 40 Yds.	40 Plus	Long	‡Won
Billy Bennett, Georgia (S)	2000-03	87-*110	.791	56-67	31-43	55	3
Jeff Jaeger, Washington (S)	1983-86	80-99	.808	59-68	21-31	52	5
Nick Novak, Maryland (S)	2001-04	80-107	.748	49-59	31-48	54	3
John Lee, UCLA (S)	1982-85	79-92	@.859	54-56	25-36	52	**10
Jason Elam, Hawaii (S)	$1988-92	79-100	.790	50-55	29-45	56	3
Luis Zendejas, Arizona St. (S)	1981-84	78-105	.743	53-59	25-46	55	1
Philip Doyle, Alabama (S)	1987-90	78-105	.743	57-61	21-44	53	6
Kevin Butler, Georgia (S)	1981-84	77-98	.786	50-56	27-42	60	7
Max Zendejas, Arizona (S)	1982-85	77-104	.740	47-53	30-51	57	7
Derek Schmidt, Florida St. (S)	1984-87	73-104	.702	44-55	29-49	54	1
Carlos Huerta, Miami (Fla.) (S)	1988-91	73-91	.802	56-60	17-31	52	3
Steve Azar, Northern Ill. (S)	2000-03	73-92	.793	57-63	16-29	52	2
Fuad Reveiz, Tennessee (S)	1981-84	71-95	.747	45-53	26-42	60	7
Mason Crosby, Colorado (S)	2003-06	71-95	.747	39-45	32-50	60	2
Barry Belli, Fresno St. (S)	1984-87	70-99	.707	47-53	23-46	55	5
Roman Anderson, Houston (S)	1988-91	70-101	.693	*61-*72	9-29	53	3
Nelson Welch, Clemson (S)	1991-94	70-100	.700	49-64	21-36	53	7
Stephen Gostkowski, Memphis (S)	2002-05	70-92	.761	47-59	23-33	53	0
Collin Mackie, South Carolina (S)	1987-90	69-95	.726	48-57	21-38	52	5
Andrew Wellock, Eastern Mich. (S)	2003-06	69-87	.793	50-55	19-32	52	0
Darren McCaleb, Southern Miss. (S)	2003-06	69-88	.784	49-54	20-34	50	2
Larry Roach, Oklahoma St. (S)	1981-84	68-101	.673	46-54	22-47	56	5
Gary Gussman, Miami (Ohio) (S)	1984-87	68-94	.723	50-57	18-37	53	2
Rusty Hanna, Toledo (S)	1989-92	68-99	.687	51-58	17-41	51	3
Shayne Graham, Virginia Tech (S)	1996-99	68-93	.731	48-57	20-36	53	5
Jeff Chandler, Florida (S)	$1997-01	67-80	.838	46-48	21-32	54	0
Xavier Beitia, Florida St. (S)	2001-04	67-92	.728	47-55	20-37	52	3
Sebastian Janikowski, Florida St. (S)	1997-99	66-83	.795	46-51	20-32	56	4
Owen Pochman, BYU (S)	1997-00	66-91	.725	32-38	34-53	56	3
Josh Scobee, Louisiana Tech (S)	2000-03	66-92	.717	51-60	15-32	53	0
Connor Hughes, Virginia (S)	2002-05	66-79	.835	50-55	16-24	53	3

**Record. $See page 10 for explanation. **Record tied. @Record for minimum 55 attempts. ‡Number of games in which his field goal(s) provided the winning margin. (S) Soccer-style kicker.*

SEASON FIELD GOALS

Player, Team	Years	Total	Pct.	Under 40 Yds.	40 Plus	Long	‡Won
Billy Bennett, Georgia (S)	†2003	31-*38	.816	20-23	11-15	52	1
John Lee, UCLA (S)	†1984	29-33	.879	16-16	13-17	51	5
Paul Woodside, West Virginia (S)	†1982	28-31	.903	23-23	5-8	45	2
Luis Zendejas, Arizona St. (S)	†1983	28-37	.757	19-22	9-15	52	1
Nick Browne, TCU (S)	2003	28-33	.848	20-22	8-11	50	1
Justin Medlock, UCLA (S)	†2006	28-32	.875	21-22	7-10	51	1
Fuad Reveiz, Tennessee (S)	1982	27-31	.871	14-14	13-17	60	2
Sebastian Janikowski, Florida St. (S)	†1998	27-32	.844	17-19	10-13	53	1
Drew Dunning, Washington St. (S)	2003	27-31	.871	19-20	8-11	49	0
Jonathan Ruffin, Cincinnati (S)	†2000	26-29	.897	24-26	2-3	42	4
Billy Bennett, Georgia (S)	2002	26-33	.788	15-18	11-15	47	2
Chuck Nelson, Washington (S)	1982	25-26	*.962	22-23	3-3	49	1
John Diettrich, Ball St. (S)	†1985	25-29	.862	16-17	9-12	54	2

Player, Team	Years	Total	Pct.	Under 40 Yds.	40 Plus	Long	‡Won
Chris Jacke, UTEP (S)	1988	25-27	.926	11-11	*14-16	52	2
Mike Nugent, Ohio St. (S)	2002	25-28	.893	15-16	10-12	51	0
Jonathan Nichols, Mississippi (S)	2003	25-29	.862	20-21	5-8	54	1
Ben Jones, Purdue (S)	2003	25-30	.833	15-19	10-11	50	1

**Record. †National champion. ‡Number of games in which his field goal(s) provided the winning margin. (S) Soccer-style kicker.*

SINGLE-GAME FIELD GOALS

No.	Player, Team (Opponent)	Date
7	Mike Prindle, Western Mich. (Marshall)	Sept. 29, 1984
7	Dale Klein, Nebraska (Missouri)	Oct. 19, 1985
6	By 15 players	

ANNUAL CHAMPIONS

(From 1959-90, goal uprights were 23 feet, 4 inches apart; and from 1991 to the present, have been 18 feet, 6 inches apart)

Year	Player, Team	Total	PG	Pct.	Under 40 Yds.	40 Plus	Long	‡Won
1959	Karl Holzwarth, Wisconsin (C)	7-8	0.8	.875	7-8	0-0	29	4
1960	Ed Dyas, Auburn (C)	13-18	1.3	.722	13-17	0-1	37	2
1961	Greg Mather, Navy (C)	11-15	1.1	.733	9-12	2-3	45	1
1962	Bob Jencks, Miami (Ohio) (C)	8-11	0.8	.727	7-9	1-2	52	3
	Al Woodall, Auburn (C)	8-20	0.8	.400	8-13	0-7	35	0
1963	Billy Lothridge, Georgia Tech (C)	12-16	1.2	.750	10-14	2-2	41	3
1964	Doug Moreau, LSU (C)	13-20	1.3	.650	13-20	0-0	36	0
1965	Charley Gogolak, Princeton (S)	16-23	1.8	.696	7-10	9-13	54	0
1966	Jerry DePoyster, Wyoming (C)	13-*38	1.3	.342	7-13	6-*25	54	1
1967	Gerald Warren, North Carolina St. (C)	17-22	1.7	.773	13-14	4-8	47	1
1968	Bob Jacobs, Wyoming (C)	14-29	1.4	.483	10-15	4-14	51	2
1969	Bob Jacobs, Wyoming (C)	18-27	1.8	.667	13-16	5-11	43	2

Beginning in 1970, ranked on per-game (instead of total) made

Year	Player, Team	Total	PG	Pct.	Under 40 Yds.	40 Plus	Long	‡Won
1970	Kim Braswell, Georgia (C)	13-17	1.3	.765	11-14	2-3	43	0
1971	Nick Mike-Mayer, Temple (S)	12-17	1.3	.706	8-10	4-7	48	1
1972	Nick Mike-Mayer, Temple (S)	13-20	1.4	.650	10-11	3-9	44	3
1973	Rod Garcia, Stanford (S)	18-29	1.6	.621	10-14	8-15	59	2
1974	Dave Lawson, Air Force (C)	19-31	1.7	.613	13-14	6-17	60	1
1975	Don Bitterlich, Temple (S)	21-31	1.9	.677	13-14	8-17	56	0
1976	Tony Franklin, Texas A&M (S)	17-26	1.6	.654	9-12	8-14	65	0
1977	Paul Marchese, Kent St. (S)	18-27	1.8	.667	13-15	5-12	51	2
1978	Matt Bahr, Penn St. (S)	22-27	2.0	.815	19-20	3-7	50	3
1979	Ish Ordonez, Arkansas (S)	18-22	1.6	.818	12-14	6-8	50	2
1980	Obed Ariri, Clemson (S)	23-30	2.1	.767	18-19	5-11	52	3
1981	Bruce Lahay, Arkansas (S)	19-24	1.7	.792	12-15	7-9	49	4
	Kevin Butler, Georgia (S)	19-26	1.7	.731	11-14	8-12	52	0
	Larry Roach, Oklahoma St. (S)	19-28	1.7	.679	12-14	7-14	56	3
1982	Paul Woodside, West Virginia (S)	28-31	2.6	.903	23-23	5-8	45	2
1983	Luis Zendejas, Arizona St. (S)	28-37	2.6	.757	19-22	9-15	52	1
1984	John Lee, UCLA (S)	29-33	*2.6	.879	16-16	13-17	51	5
1985	John Diettrich, Ball St. (S)	25-29	2.3	.862	16-17	9-12	54	2
1986	Chris Kinzer, Virginia Tech (C)	22-27	2.0	.815	14-17	8-10	50	5
1987	Collin Mackie, South Carolina (S)	23-30	2.1	.767	17-21	6-9	49	0
	Derek Schmidt, Florida St. (S)	23-31	2.1	.742	16-21	7-10	53	0
1988	Kendall Trainor, Arkansas (S)	24-27	2.2	.889	14-15	10-12	58	4
1989	Philip Doyle, Alabama (S)	22-25	2.0	.880	19-19	3-6	44	2
	Gregg McCallum, Oregon (S)	22-29	2.0	.759	15-15	7-14	47	2
	Roman Anderson, Houston (S)	22-34	2.0	.647	17-20	5-14	51	0
1990	Philip Doyle, Alabama (S)	24-29	2.2	.828	16-17	8-12	47	2
1991	Doug Brien, California (S)	19-28	1.7	.679	15-20	4-8	50	2
1992	Joe Allison, Memphis (S)	23-25	2.1	.920	13-14	10-11	51	1
1993	Michael Proctor, Alabama (S)	22-29	1.8	.759	15-20	7-9	53	0
1994	Remy Hamilton, Michigan (S)	24-29	2.2	.828	23-27	1-2	42	2
1995	Michael Reeder, TCU (S)	23-25	2.1	.920	19-19	4-6	47	3
1996	Rafael Garcia, Virginia (S)	21-27	1.9	.778	16-17	5-10	46	1
1997	Brad Palazzo, Tulane (S)	23-28	2.1	.821	15-15	8-15	52	0
1998	Sebastian Janikowski, Florida St. (S)	27-32	2.3	.844	17-19	10-13	53	1
1999	Sebastian Janikowski, Florida St. (S)	23-30	2.1	.767	15-18	8-12	54	0
2000	Jonathan Ruffin, Cincinnati (S)	26-29	2.4	.897	24-26	2-3	42	4
2001	Todd Sievers, Miami (Fla.) (S)	21-26	1.9	.808	14-17	7-9	48	1
2002	Nick Browne, TCU (S)	23-30	1.9	.767	18-20	5-10	50	0
2003	Billy Bennett, Georgia (S)	*31-*38	2.2	.816	20-23	11-15	52	1
2004	Mike Nugent, Ohio St. (S)	24-27	2.0	.889	12-12	12-15	55	2
	Tyler Jones, Boise St. (S)	24-27	2.0	.889	19-20	5-7	48	2
2005	Paul Martinez, Oregon (S)	19-24	2.1	.792	11-15	8-9	51	1
2006	Justin Medlock, UCLA (S)	28-32	2.2	.875	21-22	7-10	51	1

**Record. ‡Number of games in which his field goal(s) provided the winning margin. (C) Conventional kicker. (S) Soccer-style kicker.*

All-Time Longest Plays

Since 1941, official maximum length of all plays fixed at 100 yards.

RUSHING

Yds.	Player, Team (Opponent)	Year
99	Terry Caulley, Connecticut (Army)	2006
99	Eric Vann, Kansas (Oklahoma)	1997
99	Kelsey Finch, Tennessee (Florida)	1977
99	Ralph Thompson, West Tex. A&M (Wichita St.)	1970
99	Max Anderson, Arizona St. (Wyoming)	1967
99	Gale Sayers, Kansas (Nebraska)	1963
98	Jerald Sowell, Tulane (Alabama)	1993
98	Darrell Thompson, Minnesota (Michigan)	1987
98	George Swarn, Miami (Ohio) (Western Mich.)	1984
98	Mark Malone, Arizona St. (Utah St.)	1979
98	Stanley Howell, Mississippi St. (Southern Miss.)	1979
98	Steve Atkins, Maryland (Clemson)	1978
98	Granville Amos, VMI (William & Mary)	1964
98	Jim Thacker, Davidson (George Washington)	1952
98	Bill Powell, California (Oregon St.)	1951
98	Al Yannelli, Bucknell (Delaware)	1946
98	Meredith Warner, Iowa St. (Iowa Pre-Flight)	1943

PASSING

Yds.	Passer-Receiver, Team (Opponent)	Year
99	Dondrial Pinkins-Troy Williamson, South Carolina (Virginia)	2003
99	Jim Sorgi-Lee Evans, Wisconsin (Akron)	2003
99	Jason Johnson-Brandon Marshall, Arizona (Idaho)	2001
99	Dan Urban-Justin McCariens, Northern Ill. (Ball State)	2000
99	Drew Brees-Vinny Sutherland, Purdue (Northwestern)	1999
99	Troy DeGar-Wes Caswell, Tulsa (Oklahoma)	1996
99	John Paci-Thomas Lewis, Indiana (Penn St.)	1993
99	Gino Torretta-Horace Copeland, Miami (Fla.) (Arkansas)	1991
99	Scott Ankrom-James Maness, TCU (Rice)	1984
99	Cris Collinsworth-Derrick Gaffney, Florida (Rice)	1977
99	Terry Peel-Robert Ford, Houston (San Diego St.)	1972
99	Terry Peel-Robert Ford, Houston (Syracuse)	1970
99	Colin Clapton-Eddie Jenkins, Holy Cross (Boston U.)	1970
99	Bo Burris-Warren McVea, Houston (Washington St.)	1966
99	Fred Owens-Jack Ford, Portland [St. Mary's (Cal.)]	1947
98	Paul Pinegar-Paul Williams, Fresno St. (Boise St.)	2005
98	Dondrial Pinkins-Matthew Thomas, South Carolina (Mississippi)	2003
98	Brandon Hassell-Reggie Harrell, TCU (Arizona)	2003
98	Ryan Dinwiddie-Lawrence Bady, Boise St. (SMU)	2003
98	Derrick Vickers-Rob Turner, Central Mich. (Northern Ill.)	2001
98	Chris Weinke-Marvin Minnis, Florida St. (Clemson)	2000
98	Joe Borchard-Troy Walters, Stanford (UCLA)	2000
98	Jose Davis-Eugene Baker, Kent St. (UCF)	1997
98	Mike Neu-Brian Oliver, Ball St. (Toledo)	1993
98	Tom Dubs-Richard Hill, Ohio (Kent St.)	1991
98	Paul Oates-Sean Foster, Long Beach St. (San Diego St.)	1989
98	Barry Garrison-Al Owens, New Mexico (BYU)	1987
98	Kelly Donohoe-Willie Vaughn, Kansas (Colorado)	1987
98	Jeff Martin-Mark Flaker, Drake (New Mexico St.)	1976
98	Pete Woods-Joe Stewart, Missouri (Nebraska)	1976
98	Dan Hagemann-Jack Steptoe, Utah (New Mexico)	1976
98	Bruce Shaw-Pat Kenney, North Carolina St. (Penn St.)	1972
98	Jerry Rhome-Jeff Jordan, Tulsa (Wichita St.)	1963
98	Bob Dean-Norman Dawson, Cornell (Navy)	1947

INTERCEPTION RETURNS

Since 1941, 75 players have returned interceptions 100 yards. The most recent:

Yds.	Player, Team (Opponent)	Year
100	Josh Gordy, Central Mich. (Akron)	2006
100	R.J. Oliver, Arizona St. (Northern Ariz.)	2003
100	Matt Nixon, California (Baylor)	2002
100	Nathan Ray, Fresno St. (SMU)	2002
100	Emmanuel Franklin, Arizona St. (San Diego St.)	2001
100	Marcus Hudson, North Carolina St. (Duke)	2001
100	Deltha O'Neal, California (Oregon)	1999
100	Pat Dennis, La.-Monroe (Nicholls St.)	1998
100	Steve Rosga, Colorado (Oklahoma St.)	1996
100	Michael Hicks, UTEP (BYU)	1996
100	Mario Smith, Kansas St. (Missouri)	1996
100	Keion Carpenter, Virginia Tech [Miami (Fla.)]	1996
100	Reggie Love, North Carolina (Tulane)	1994
100	Harold Lusk, Utah (Colorado St.)	1994
100	Marlon Kerner, Ohio St. (Purdue)	1993
100	Ray Jackson, Colorado St. (UTEP)	1993
100	John Hardy, California (Wisconsin)	1990
100	Ed Givens, Army (Lafayette)	1990

PUNT RETURNS

Yds.	Player, Team (Opponent)	Year
100	Courtney Davis, Bowling Green (Kent St.)	1996
100	Eddie Kennison, LSU (Mississippi St.)	1994
100‡	Richie Luzzi, Clemson (Georgia)	1968
100‡	Don Guest, California (Washington St.)	1966
100	Jimmy Campagna, Georgia (Vanderbilt)	1952
100	Hugh McElhenny, Washington (Southern California)	1951
100	Frank Brady, Navy (Maryland)	1951
100	Bert Rechichar, Tennessee (Wash. & Lee)	1950
100	Eddie Macon, Pacific (Boston U.)	1950

‡Return of field goal attempt.

KICKOFF RETURNS

Since 1941, 251 players have returned kickoffs 100 yards. The most recent:

Yds.	Player, Team (Opponent)	Year
100	Gerald Lawson, Oregon St. (Hawaii)	2006
100	Patric Jackson, Louisiana Tech (Fresno St.)	2006
100	JaJua Spillman, Louisville (Rutgers)	2006
100	Ross Dickerson, Hawaii (Idaho)	2006
100	Felix Jones, Arkansas (Mississippi)	2006
100	Josh Wilson, Maryland (Georgia Tech)	2006
100	Terry Richardson, Arizona St. (Oregon)	2006
100	Marcus Thigpen, Indiana (Ball St.)	2006
100	Keenan Burton, Kentucky (Louisville)	2006

PUNTS

Yds.	Player, Team (Opponent)	Year
99	Pat Brady, Nevada (Loyola Marymount)	1950
96	George O'Brien, Wisconsin (Iowa)	1952
94	John Hadl, Kansas (Oklahoma)	1959
94	Carl Knox, TCU (Oklahoma St.)	1947
94	Preston Johnson, SMU (Pittsburgh)	1940

FUMBLE RETURNS

(Since 1992)

Yds.	Player, Team (Opponent)	Year
100	Kevin Thomas, UNLV (Baylor)	1999
100	Dan Dawson, Rice (UNLV)	1998
100	Paul Rivers, Rutgers (Pittsburgh)	1995
99	David Williams, Houston (East Caro.)	1998
99	Dennis Gibbs, Idaho (Boise St.)	1997
99	Izell McGill, Mississippi St. (Memphis)	1996
98	Cornelius Pearson, Eastern Mich. (Western Mich.)	1996
97	Josh Morgan, Mississippi St. (BYU)	2000
97	Chris Martin, Northwestern (Air Force)	1994
97	Mike Collins, West Virginia (Missouri)	1993
97	Ernie Lewis, East Caro. (West Virginia)	1992
96	Ben Kelly, Colorado (Kansas)	1999
96	Jeff Arneson, Illinois (Ohio St.)	1992
95	Ben Hanks, Florida (Arkansas)	1995
94	Dorian Boose, Washington St. (Colorado)	1996

FIELD GOALS

Yds.	Player, Team (Opponent)	Year
67	Joe Williams, Wichita St. (Southern Ill.)	1978
67	Steve Little, Arkansas (Texas)	1977
67	Russell Erxleben, Texas (Rice)	1977
65†	Martin Gramatica, Kansas St. (Northern Ill.)	1998
65	Tony Franklin, Texas A&M (Baylor)	1976
64	Russell Erxleben, Texas (Oklahoma)	1977
64	Tony Franklin, Texas A&M (Baylor)	1976
63	Morten Andersen, Michigan St. (Ohio St.)	1981
63	Clark Kemble, Colorado St. (Arizona)	1975
62	Terance Kitchens, Texas A&M (Southern Miss.)	1999
62	Jason Hanson, Washington St. (UNLV)	1991
62	John Diettrich, Ball St. (Ohio)	1986
62#	Chip Lohmiller, Minnesota (Iowa)	1986
62	Tom Whelihan, Missouri (Colorado)	1986
62	Dan Christopulos, Wyoming (Colorado St.)	1977
62	Iseed Khoury, North Texas (Richmond)	1977
62	Dave Lawson, Air Force (Iowa St.)	1975
61	Garret Courtney, North Texas (Idaho)	1998
61$	Kyle Bryant, Texas A&M (Southern Miss.)	1994
61	Dan Eichloff, Kansas (Ball St.)	1992
61	Mark Porter, Kansas St. (Nebraska)	1988
61	Ralf Mojsiejenko, Michigan St. (Illinois)	1982
61	Steve Little, Arkansas (Tulsa)	1976
61	Wayne Latimer, Virginia Tech (Florida St.)	1975
61	Ray Guy, Southern Miss. (Utah St.)	1972

†Longest collegiate field goal without use of a kicking tee; all kicks after 1988 season were without the use of a tee. Also longest field goal with narrower (18'6") goal posts. $Longest field goal made by a freshman. #Longest field goal made indoors.

HISTORY OF COLLEGE FOOTBALL UNDERCLASSMEN IN THE NATIONAL FOOTBALL LEAGUE DRAFT

(Underclassmen have been part of the NFL draft since 1989. Listed below is the number of players who were at least three years beyond their high-school graduation, but not yet seniors, and how they fared.)

Year	Declared	Drafted	Top-10 Pick
2007	40	29	5(1)
2006	48	35	6(1)
2005	49	37	4
2004	43	34	5
2003	54	32	5
2002	43	26	5
2001	54	31	5(1)
2000	31	20	4
1999	42	27	5(1)
1998	41	20	3
1997	44	27	7(1)
1996	46	21	4
1995	42	22	2(1)
1994	43	26	6(1)
1993	46	24	5(1)
1992	48	25	5(1)
1991	33	22	2
1990	38	18	5(1)
1989	25	12	3
Totals	**810**	**488**	**86**

Percentage of Declared that were Drafted=60.2%
Percentage of Drafted that were Top-10 Picks=17.6%
Percentage of Declared that were Top-10 Picks=10.6%

Note: (1) indicates that an underclassman was drafted overall No. 1 in entire draft. They were: 1990 (Jeff George); 1992 (Steve Emtman); 1993 (Drew Bledsoe); 1994 (Dan Wilkinson); 1995 (Ki-Jana Carter); 1997 (Orlando Pace); 1999 (Tim Couch); 2001 (Michael Vick); 2005 (Alex Smith); 2006 (Marco Williams); 2007 (JaMarcus Russell).

Team Champions

Annual Offense Champions

TOTAL OFFENSE

Year	Team	Avg.
1937	Colorado	375.4
1938	Fordham	341.6
1939	Ohio St.	309.3
1940	Lafayette	368.2
1941	Duke	372.2
1942	Georgia	429.5
1943	Notre Dame	418.0
1944	Tulsa	434.7
1945	Army	462.7
1946	Notre Dame	441.3
1947	Michigan	412.7
1948	Nevada	487.0
1949	Notre Dame	434.8
1950	Arizona St.	470.4
1951	Tulsa	480.1
1952	Tulsa	466.6
1953	Cincinnati	409.5
1954	Army	448.7
1955	Oklahoma	410.7
1956	Oklahoma	481.7
1957	Arizona St.	444.9
1958	Iowa	405.9
1959	Syracuse	451.5
1960	New Mexico St.	419.6
1961	Mississippi	418.7
1962	Arizona St.	384.4
1963	Utah St.	395.3
1964	Tulsa	461.8
1965	Tulsa	427.8
1966	Houston	437.2
1967	Houston	427.9
1968	Houston	562.0
1969	San Diego St.	532.2
1970	Arizona St.	514.5
1971	Oklahoma	566.5
1972	Arizona St.	516.5
1973	Arizona St.	565.5
1974	Oklahoma	507.7
1975	California	458.5
1976	Michigan	448.1
1977	Colgate	486.1
1978	Nebraska	501.4
1979	BYU	521.4
1980	BYU	535.0
1981	Arizona St.	498.7
1982	Nebraska	518.6
1983	BYU	584.2
1984	BYU	486.5
1985	BYU	500.2
1986	San Jose St.	481.4
1987	Oklahoma	499.7
1988	Utah	526.8
1989	Houston	*624.9
1990	Houston	586.8
1991	Fresno St.	541.9
1992	Houston	519.5
1993	Nevada	569.1
1994	Penn St.	520.2
1995	Nevada	569.4
1996	Nevada	527.3
1997	Nebraska	513.7
1998	Louisville	559.6
1999	Georgia Tech	509.0
2000	Florida St.	549.0
2001	BYU	542.9
2002	Boise St.	501.5
2003	Texas Tech	582.8
2004	Louisville	539.0
2005	Southern California	579.7
2006	Hawaii	559.2

**Record.*

RUSHING OFFENSE

Year	Team	Avg.
1937	Colorado	310.0
1938	Fordham	297.1
1939	Wake Forest	290.3
1940	Lafayette	306.4
1941	Missouri	307.7
1942	Hardin-Simmons	307.4
1943	Notre Dame	313.7
1944	Army	298.6
1945	Army	359.8
1946	Notre Dame	340.1
1947	Detroit	319.7
1948	UTEP	378.3
1949	UTEP	333.2
1950	Arizona St.	347.0
1951	Arizona St.	334.8
1952	Tulsa	321.5
1953	Oklahoma	306.9
1954	Army	322.0
1955	Oklahoma	328.9
1956	Oklahoma	391.0
1957	Colorado	322.4
1958	Pacific	259.6
1959	Syracuse	313.6
1960	Utah St.	312.0
1961	New Mexico St.	299.1
1962	Ohio St.	278.9
1963	Nebraska	262.6
1964	Syracuse	251.0
1965	Nebraska	290.0
1966	Harvard	269.0
1967	Houston	270.9
1968	Houston	361.7
1969	Texas	363.0
1970	Texas	374.5
1971	Oklahoma	*472.4
1972	Oklahoma	368.8
1973	UCLA	400.3
1974	Oklahoma	438.8
1975	Arkansas St.	340.5
1976	Michigan	362.6
1977	Oklahoma	328.9
1978	Oklahoma	427.5
1979	East Caro.	368.5
1980	Nebraska	378.3
1981	Oklahoma	334.3
1982	Nebraska	394.3
1983	Nebraska	401.7
1984	Army	345.3
1985	Nebraska	374.3
1986	Oklahoma	404.7
1987	Oklahoma	428.8
1988	Nebraska	382.3
1989	Nebraska	375.3
1990	Northern Ill.	344.6
1991	Nebraska	353.2
1992	Nebraska	328.2
1993	Army	298.5
1994	Nebraska	340.0
1995	Nebraska	399.8
1996	Army	346.5
1997	Nebraska	392.6
1998	Army	293.8

Year	Team	Avg.
1999	Navy	292.2
2000	Nebraska	349.3
2001	Nebraska	314.7
2002	Air Force	307.8
2003	Navy	323.2
2004	Rice	306.6
2005	Navy	318.7
2006	Navy	327.0

**Record.*

PASSING OFFENSE

Year	Team	Avg.
1937	Arkansas	185.0
1938	TCU	164.1
1939	TCU	148.5
1940	Cornell	186.3
1941	Arizona	177.7
1942	Tulsa	233.9
1943	Brown	133.1
1944	Tulsa	206.3
1945	St. Mary's (Cal.)	161.3
1946	Nevada	198.1
1947	Michigan	173.9
1948	Nevada	255.0
1949	Fordham	183.4
1950	SMU	214.6
1951	Loyola Marymount	210.6
1952	Fordham	225.8
1953	Stanford	179.5
1954	Purdue	177.3
1955	Navy	185.1
1956	Washington St.	206.8
1957	Utah	195.2
1958	Army	172.2
1959	Stanford	227.8
1960	Washington St.	185.5
1961	Wisconsin	188.4
1962	Tulsa	199.3
1963	Tulsa	244.8
1964	Tulsa	317.9
1965	Tulsa	346.4
1966	Tulsa	272.0
1967	UTEP	301.1
1968	Cincinnati	335.8
1969	San Diego St.	374.2
1970	Auburn	288.5
1971	San Diego St.	251.4
1972	Virginia Tech	304.4
1973	San Diego St.	305.0
1974	Colorado St.	261.8
1975	San Diego St.	291.3
1976	BYU	307.8
1977	BYU	341.6
1978	SMU	276.2
1979	BYU	368.3
1980	BYU	409.8
1981	BYU	356.9
1982	Long Beach St.	326.8
1983	BYU	381.2
1984	BYU	346.2
1985	BYU	354.5
1986	San Jose St.	312.5
1987	San Jose St.	338.1
1988	Utah	395.9
1989	Houston	*511.3
1990	Houston	473.9
1991	Houston	372.8
1992	Houston	407.1
1993	Nevada	397.5
1994	Georgia	338.3
1995	Nevada	416.3
1996	Wyoming	359.2
1997	Nevada	370.2
1998	Louisiana Tech	432.1
1999	Louisiana Tech	403.1
2000	Florida St.	384.0
2001	Florida	405.2
2002	Texas Tech	388.9
2003	Texas Tech	475.3
2004	Texas Tech	399.7
2005	Texas Tech	388.8
2006	Hawaii	441.3

**Record.*

SCORING OFFENSE

Year	Team	Avg.
1937	Colorado	31.0
1938	Dartmouth	28.2
1939	Utah	28.4
1940	Boston College	32.0
1941	Texas	33.8
1942	Tulsa	42.7
1943	Duke	37.2
1944	Army	*56.0
1945	Army	45.8
1946	Georgia	37.2
1947	Michigan	38.3
1948	Nevada	44.4
1949	Army	39.3
1950	Princeton	38.8
1951	Maryland	39.2
1952	Oklahoma	40.7
1953	Texas Tech	38.9
1954	UCLA	40.8
1955	Oklahoma	36.5
1956	Oklahoma	46.6
1957	Arizona St.	39.7
1958	Rutgers	33.4
1959	Syracuse	39.0
1960	New Mexico St.	37.4
1961	Utah St.	38.7
1962	Wisconsin	31.7
1963	Utah St.	31.7
1964	Tulsa	38.4
1965	Arkansas	32.4
1966	Notre Dame	36.2
1967	UTEP	35.9
1968	Houston	42.5
1969	San Diego St.	46.4
1970	Texas	41.2
1971	Oklahoma	44.9
1972	Arizona St.	46.6
1973	Arizona St.	44.6
1974	Oklahoma	43.0
1975	Ohio St.	34.0
1976	Michigan	38.7
1977	Grambling	42.0
1978	Oklahoma	40.0
1979	BYU	40.6
1980	BYU	46.7
1981	BYU	38.7
1982	Nebraska	41.1
1983	Nebraska	52.0
1984	Boston College	36.7
1985	Fresno St.	39.1
1986	Oklahoma	42.4
1987	Oklahoma	43.5
1988	Oklahoma St.	47.5
1989	Houston	53.5
1990	Houston	46.5
1991	Fresno St.	44.2
1992	Fresno St.	40.5
1993	Florida St.	43.2
1994	Penn St.	47.8
1995	Nebraska	52.4
1996	Florida	46.6
1997	Nebraska	47.1
1998	Kansas St.	48.0
1999	Virginia Tech	41.4
2000	Boise St.	44.9
2001	BYU	46.8
2002	Boise St.	45.6
2003	Boise St.	43.0
	Miami (Ohio)	43.0
2004	Louisville	49.8
2005	Texas	50.2
2006	Hawaii	46.7

**Record.*

Annual Defense Champions

TOTAL DEFENSE

Year	Team	Avg.
1937	Santa Clara	*69.9
1938	Alabama	77.9
1939	San Jose St.	71.3
1940	Navy	96.0
1941	Duquesne	110.6
1942	Texas	117.3
1943	Duke	121.7
1944	Virginia	96.8
1945	Alabama	109.9
1946	Notre Dame	141.7
1947	Penn St.	76.8
1948	Georgia Tech	151.3
1949	Kentucky	153.8
1950	Wake Forest	163.2
1951	Wisconsin	154.8
1952	Tennessee	166.7
1953	Cincinnati	184.3
1954	Mississippi	172.3
1955	Army	160.7
1956	Miami (Fla.)	189.4
1957	Auburn	133.0
1958	Auburn	157.5
1959	Syracuse	96.2
1960	Wyoming	149.6
1961	Alabama	132.6
1962	Mississippi	142.2
1963	Southern Miss.	131.2
1964	Auburn	164.7
1965	Southern Miss.	161.1
1966	Southern Miss.	163.7
1967	Nebraska	157.6
1968	Wyoming	206.8
1969	Toledo	209.1
1970	Toledo	185.8
1971	Toledo	179.5
1972	Louisville	202.5
1973	Miami (Ohio)	177.4
1974	Notre Dame	195.2
1975	Texas A&M	183.8
1976	Rutgers	179.2
1977	Jackson St.	207.0
1978	Penn St.	203.9
1979	Yale	175.4
1980	Pittsburgh	205.5
1981	Pittsburgh	224.8
1982	Arizona St.	228.9
1983	Texas	212.0
1984	Nebraska	203.3
1985	Oklahoma	193.5
1986	Oklahoma	169.6
1987	Oklahoma	208.1
1988	Auburn	218.1
1989	Miami (Fla.)	216.5
1990	Clemson	216.9
1991	Texas A&M	222.4
1992	Alabama	194.2
1993	Mississippi	234.5
1994	Miami (Fla.)	220.9
1995	Kansas St.	250.8
1996	West Virginia	217.5
1997	Michigan	206.9
1998	Florida St.	214.8
1999	Mississippi St.	222.5
2000	TCU	245.0
2001	Texas	236.2
2002	TCU	240.3
2003	LSU	252.0
2004	North Carolina St.	221.4
2005	Virginia Tech	247.6
2006	Virginia Tech	219.5

**Record.*

RUSHING DEFENSE

Year	Team	Avg.
1937	Santa Clara	25.3
1938	Oklahoma	43.3
1939	San Jose St.	34.2
1940	Texas A&M	44.3
1941	Duquesne	56.0
1942	Boston College	48.9
1943	Duke	39.4
1944	Navy	53.8
1945	Alabama	33.9
1946	Oklahoma	58.0
1947	Penn St.	*17.0
1948	Georgia Tech	74.9

FBS

Year	Team	Avg.
1949	Oklahoma	55.6
1950	Ohio St.	64.0
1951	San Francisco	51.6
1952	Michigan St.	83.9
1953	Maryland	83.9
1954	UCLA	73.2
1955	Maryland	75.9
1956	Miami (Fla.)	106.9
1957	Auburn	67.4
1958	Auburn	79.6
1959	Syracuse	19.3
1960	Wyoming	82.4
1961	Utah St.	50.8
1962	Minnesota	52.2
1963	Mississippi	77.3
1964	Washington	61.3
1965	Michigan St.	45.6
1966	Wyoming	38.5
1967	Wyoming	42.3
1968	Arizona St.	57.0
1969	LSU	38.9
1970	LSU	52.2
1971	Michigan	63.3
1972	Louisville	82.1
1973	Miami (Ohio)	77.0
1974	Notre Dame	102.8
1975	Texas A&M	80.3
1976	Rutgers	83.9
1977	Jackson St.	67.8
1978	Penn St.	54.5
1979	Yale	75.0
1980	Pittsburgh	65.3
1981	Pittsburgh	62.4
1982	Virginia Tech	49.5
1983	Virginia Tech	69.4
1984	Oklahoma	68.8
1985	UCLA	70.3
1986	Oklahoma	60.7
1987	Michigan St.	61.5
1988	Auburn	63.2
1989	Southern California	61.5
1990	Washington	66.8
1991	Clemson	53.4
1992	Alabama	55.0
1993	Arizona	30.1
1994	Virginia	63.6
1995	Virginia Tech	77.4
1996	Florida St.	59.0
1997	Florida St.	51.9
1998	Ohio St.	67.4
1999	Mississippi St.	66.9
2000	Memphis	72.7
2001	UAB	57.3
2002	TCU	64.8
2003	Southern California	60.2
2004	Southern California	79.4
2005	Ohio St.	73.4
2006	Michigan	43.4

**Record.*

PASSING DEFENSE

Year	Team	$Avg.
1937	Harvard	31.0
1938	Penn St.	*13.1
1939	Kansas	34.1
1940	Harvard	33.3
1941	Purdue	27.1
1942	Harvard	45.4
1943	North Carolina	36.5
1944	Michigan St.	26.7
1945	Holy Cross	37.7
1946	Holy Cross	53.7
1947	North Carolina St.	39.3
1948	Northwestern	54.1
1949	Miami (Fla.)	54.7
1950	Tennessee	67.5
1951	Wash. & Lee	67.9
1952	Virginia	50.3
1953	Richmond	40.3
1954	Alabama	45.8
1955	Florida	42.0
1956	Villanova	43.8
1957	Georgia Tech	33.4
1958	Iowa St.	39.0
1959	Alabama	45.7
1960	Iowa St.	30.2
1961	Penn	56.9
1962	New Mexico	56.8
1963	UTEP	43.8
1964	Kent St.	53.6
1965	Toledo	69.8
1966	Toledo	70.4
1967	Nebraska	90.1
1968	Kent St.	107.6
1969	Dayton	90.0
1970	Toledo	77.8
1971	Texas Tech	60.1
1972	Vanderbilt	80.3
1973	Nebraska	39.9
1974	Iowa	65.7
1975	VMI	51.1
1976	Western Mich.	78.5
1977	Tennessee St.	67.9
1978	Boston College	65.1
1979	Western Caro.	77.5
1980	Kansas St.	91.4
1981	Nebraska	100.1
1982	Missouri	123.5
1983	Ohio	115.3
1984	Texas Tech	114.8
1985	Oklahoma	103.6
1986	Oklahoma	108.9
1987	Oklahoma	102.4
1988	Baylor	117.8
1989	Kansas St.	129.3
1990	$Alabama	82.5
1991	Texas	77.4
1992	Western Mich.	83.2
1993	Texas A&M	75.0
1994	Miami (Fla.)	81.3
1995	Miami (Ohio)	85.5
1996	Ohio St.	81.3
1997	Michigan	75.8
1998	Florida St.	79.9
1999	Kansas St.	65.7
2000	Texas	88.0
2001	Miami (Fla.)	75.6
2002	Miami (Fla.)	83.9
2003	Nebraska	88.7
2004	North Carolina St.	91.8
2005	Miami (Fla.)	89.5
2006	Wisconsin	84.2

**Record. $Beginning in 1990, ranked on passing-efficiency defense rating points instead of per-game yardage allowed.*

SCORING DEFENSE

Year	Team	Avg.
1937	Santa Clara	1.1
1938	Duke	**0.0
1939	Tennessee	**0.0
1940	Tennessee	2.6
1941	Duquesne	2.9
1942	Tulsa	3.2
1943	Duke	3.8
1944	Army	3.9
1945	St. Mary's (Cal.)	4.0
1946	Notre Dame	2.7
1947	Penn St.	3.0
1948	Michigan	4.9
1949	Kentucky	4.8
1950	Army	4.4
1951	Wisconsin	5.9
1952	Southern California	4.7
1953	Maryland	3.1
1954	UCLA	4.4
1955	Georgia Tech	4.6
1956	Georgia Tech	3.3
1957	Auburn	2.8
1958	Oklahoma	4.9
1959	Mississippi	2.1
1960	LSU	5.0
1961	Alabama	2.2
1962	LSU	3.4
1963	Mississippi	3.7
1964	Arkansas	5.7
1965	Michigan St.	6.2
1966	Alabama	3.7
1967	Oklahoma	6.8
1968	Georgia	9.8
1969	Arkansas	7.6
1970	Dartmouth	4.7
1971	Michigan	6.4
1972	Michigan	5.2
1973	Ohio St.	4.3
1974	Michigan	6.8
1975	Alabama	6.0
1976	Michigan	7.4
	Rutgers	7.4
1977	North Carolina	7.4
1978	Ball St.	7.5
1979	Alabama	5.3
1980	Florida St.	7.7
1981	Southern Miss.	8.1
1982	Arkansas	10.5
1983	Virginia Tech	8.3
1984	Nebraska	9.5
1985	Michigan	6.8
1986	Oklahoma	6.6
1987	Oklahoma	7.5
1988	Auburn	7.2
1989	Miami (Fla.)	9.3
1990	Central Mich.	8.9
1991	Miami (Fla.)	9.1
1992	Arizona	8.9
1993	Florida St.	9.4
1994	Miami (Fla.)	10.8
1995	Northwestern	12.7
1996	North Carolina	10.0
1997	Michigan	8.9
1998	Wisconsin	10.2
1999	Virginia Tech	10.5
2000	TCU	9.6
2001	Miami (Fla.)	9.4
2002	Kansas St.	11.8
2003	LSU	11.0
2004	Auburn	11.3
2005	Alabama	10.7
2006	Virginia Tech	11.0

***Record tied.*

Other Annual Team Champions

NET PUNTING#

Year	Team	#Avg.
1937	Iowa	43.0
1938	Arkansas	41.6
1939	Auburn	43.3
1940	Auburn	42.3
1941	Clemson	42.3
1942	Tulsa	41.3
1943	Michigan	39.2
1944	UCLA	43.0
1945	Miami (Fla.)	39.9
1946	UTEP	41.2
1947	Duke	41.9
1948	North Carolina	44.0
1949	Furman	44.7
1950	Colorado	45.1
1951	Alabama	41.8
1952	Colorado	43.3
1953	Georgia	41.2
1954	New Mexico	42.6
1955	Michigan St.	41.2
1956	Colorado St.	42.2
1957	Utah St.	40.1
1958	Georgia	41.9
1959	BYU	43.2
1960	Georgia	43.7
1961	Arizona St.	42.1
1962	Wyoming	42.6
1963	SMU	41.4
1964	Mississippi	44.1
1965	Arizona St.	44.0
1966	Tennessee	43.4
1967	Houston	44.4
1968	Wichita St.	43.2
1969	Georgia	43.5
1970	Utah	45.0

Year	Team	#Avg.
1971	Utah	46.7
1972	Southern Miss.	45.1
1973	Wake Forest	44.1
1974	Ohio St.	44.9
1975	Ohio St.	44.1
1976	Colorado St.	44.4
1977	Mississippi	43.4
1978	Texas	41.7
1979	Mississippi	42.4
1980	Florida St.	42.6
1981	Michigan	43.1
1982	Vanderbilt	42.1
1983	BYU	*45.0
1984	Ohio St.	44.0
1985	Colorado	43.6
1986	Michigan	43.1
1987	Ohio St.	40.7
1988	BYU	42.9
1989	Colorado	43.8
1990	Pittsburgh	41.2
1991	Texas Tech	40.6
1992	Nebraska	41.7
1993	New Mexico	41.8
1994	Ball St.	42.2
1995	Ball St.	41.3
1996	San Diego St.	**44.9
1997	LSU	43.3
1998	UNLV	41.4
1999	Texas A&M	42.7
2000	Wisconsin	42.9
2001	Ohio	42.7
2002	BYU	42.7
2003	Southern California	43.7
2004	Colorado	42.7
2005	Wake Forest	41.4
2006	Utah	41.6

*#Beginning in 1975, ranked on net punting average. *Record for net punting average. **Record for net punting average, minimum 40 punts.*

PUNT RETURNS

Year	Team	Avg.
1937	—	—
1938	—	—
1939	UCLA	16.3
1940	UCLA	16.2
1941	Colgate	18.7
1942	—	—
1943	Columbia	20.9
1944	New York U.	22.0
1945	—	—
1946	Columbia	16.8
1947	Florida	19.7
1948	Oklahoma	*22.4
1949	Wichita St.	18.3
1950	Texas A&M	17.6
1951	Holy Cross	18.1
1952	Arizona St.	**25.2
1953	Kansas St.	23.8
1954	Miami (Fla.)	19.7
1955	North Carolina	22.5
1956	Cincinnati	17.7
1957	North Texas	17.5
1958	Notre Dame	17.6
1959	Wyoming	16.6
1960	Arizona	17.7
1961	Memphis	17.4
1962	West Tex. A&M	18.4
1963	Army	18.1
1964	UTEP	16.9
1965	Georgia Tech	23.0
1966	Brown	21.0
1967	Memphis	16.3
1968	Army	17.4
1969	Davidson	21.3
1970	Wichita St.	28.5
1971	Mississippi St.	20.8
1972	Georgia Tech	17.3
1973	Utah	23.4
1974	Auburn	16.6
1975	New Mexico St.	15.3
1976	Wichita St.	15.0
1977	Grambling	16.9
1978	McNeese St.	15.7
1979	Tennessee St.	16.9
1980	Georgia	16.5
1981	North Carolina St.	13.4
1982	Auburn	15.8
1983	San Diego St.	17.0
1984	Florida	13.8
1985	Utah	20.7
1986	Arizona St.	17.9
1987	Stanford	15.4
1988	Florida St.	15.5
1989	Ohio	18.2
1990	Michigan	15.6
1991	Alabama	16.9
1992	Northwestern	21.8
1993	Texas A&M	17.9
1994	Ball St.	19.9
1995	Eastern Mich.	20.8
1996	Kansas	19.5
1997	Iowa	18.2
1998	Kansas St.	21.3
1999	UAB	19.1
2000	Virginia Tech	18.2
2001	Colorado	17.4
2002	Northern Ill.	20.2
2003	Miami (Ohio)	16.3
2004	Utah St.	18.3
2005	UCLA	25.0
2006	Kentucky	20.4

**Record for minimum 30 punt returns. **Record for minimum 15 punt returns.*

KICKOFF RETURNS

Year	Team	Avg.
1937	—	—
1938	—	—
1939	Wake Forest	32.9
1940	Minnesota	36.4
1941	Tulane	32.1
1942	—	—
1943	Navy	28.8
1944	—	—
1945	—	—
1946	William & Mary	31.7
1947	SMU	31.4
1948	Wyoming	27.4
1949	Army	34.1
1950	Wyoming	29.3
1951	Marquette	25.0
1952	Wake Forest	25.1
1953	Texas Tech	23.8
1954	Arizona	26.1
1955	Southern California	25.8
1956	Georgia Tech	24.6
1957	Notre Dame	27.6
1958	Tulsa	25.8
1959	Auburn	25.8
1960	Yale	26.7
1961	Harvard	25.9
1962	Alabama	28.9
1963	Memphis	27.7
1964	Cornell	27.1
1965	Dartmouth	28.7
1966	Notre Dame	29.6
1967	Air Force	25.3
1968	Louisville	25.7
1969	BYU	28.7
1970	South Carolina	26.5
1971	Miami (Fla.)	24.1
1972	Michigan	26.9
1973	Rice	*27.5
1974	Southern California	25.7
1975	Maryland	29.5
1976	South Carolina	27.0
1977	Miami (Ohio)	24.6
1978	Utah St.	26.7
1979	BYU	26.3
1980	Oklahoma	33.2
1981	Iowa	29.1
1982	Utah	25.5
1983	Tennessee	28.8
1984	Texas Tech	25.2
1985	Air Force	27.0
1986	Clemson	26.1
1987	Oklahoma St.	23.7
1988	Notre Dame	24.2
1989	Colorado	26.1
1990	Nebraska	27.8
1991	New Mexico St.	25.2
1992	Florida St.	**30.3
1993	Texas A&M	31.2
1994	Texas A&M	27.8
1995	New Mexico	27.1
1996	Miami (Fla.)	28.9
1997	Southern Miss.	28.2
1998	Utah	27.1
1999	TCU	27.5
2000	TCU	28.8
2001	Hawaii	30.3
2002	Iowa	25.1
2003	Utah	28.2
2004	Indiana	28.1
2005	Arkansas	29.2
2006	Kansas St.	27.1

**Record for minimum 35 kickoff returns. **Record for minimum 25 kickoff returns.*

TURNOVER MARGIN

Year	Team	Avg.
1992	Nebraska	1.64
1993	UCLA	1.73
1994	Clemson	1.55
1995	Toledo	2.00
1996	North Carolina	2.00
1997	Colorado St.	2.08
1998	Wisconsin	2.00
1999	Kansas St.	1.55
2000	Toledo	2.00
2001	Miami (Fla.)	*2.36
2002	South Fla.	1.91
2003	Nebraska	1.77
2004	Southern California	1.46
2005	TCU	1.75
2006	Minnesota	1.38

**Record.*

Defensive Single-Game Records

(Since 2000)

TACKLES FOR LOSS

TFL	Team (Opponent)	Date
23	North Carolina St. (Florida St.)	Nov. 11, 2004
21	TCU (Tulane)	Nov. 9, 2002
20	TCU (Nevada)	Sept. 9, 2000
19	Kansas St. (Kansas)	Oct. 7, 2000
18	Air Force (Navy)	Oct. 6, 2000
18	Colorado (Missouri)	Nov. 4, 2000
18	Kansas (Missouri St.)	Sept. 1, 2001
18	Washington (Idaho)	Sept. 22, 2002
18	North Carolina St. (Georgia Tech)	Oct. 4, 2003
17	Toledo (Penn St.)	Sept. 2, 2000
17	Oregon St. (San Diego St.)	Sept. 23, 2000
17	Kansas St. (Oklahoma)	Oct. 14, 2000
17	Texas (Missouri)	Oct. 21, 2000
17	Toledo (Navy)	Oct. 28, 2000
17	Arizona St. (Washington)	Oct. 26, 2002
17	Houston (Army)	Nov. 15, 2003

PASS SACKS

Sacks	Team (Opponent)	Date
15	TCU (Nevada)	Sept. 9, 2000
14	Colorado (Missouri)	Nov. 4, 2000
13	Toledo (Penn St.)	Sept. 2, 2000
11	TCU (Louisville)	Nov. 23, 2001
10	North Carolina (Wake Forest)	Sept. 9, 2000
10	Maryland (Duke)	Oct. 28, 2000
10	Northern Ill. (Wisconsin)	Sept. 14, 2002
10	North Carolina St. (Virginia Tech)	Sept. 25, 2004
10	Hawaii (Idaho)	Nov. 20, 2004
9	Texas (Houston)	Sept. 23, 2000
9	UCF (Eastern Ky.)	Oct. 14, 2000
9	Arizona St. (Arizona)	Nov. 24, 2000
9	New Mexico (UTEP)	Sept. 1, 2001
9	Kansas St. (Baylor)	Oct. 26, 2002
9	New Mexico (Wyoming)	Nov. 30, 2002

Sacks	Team (Opponent)	Date
9	Fresno St. (SMU)	Nov. 1, 2003
9^	Southern California (Michigan)	Jan. 1, 2004
9	Arizona St. (Northern Ariz.)	Aug. 31, 2006
9	Virgina (Duke)	Sept. 30, 2006
9	Western Mich. (Ball St.)	Oct. 21, 2006

^2004 Rose Bowl.

PASSES DEFENDED

(Pass Interceptions and Pass Break-ups)

PD	Team (Opponent)	Date
19	South Carolina (Alabama)	Oct. 2, 2000
17	Nebraska (Iowa St.)	Oct. 7, 2000
17	Northern Ill. (Ball St.)	Oct. 5, 2002
17	Mississippi St. (Troy)	Oct. 12, 2002
17	Nebraska (Kansas)	Oct. 2, 2004
16	West Virginia (Rutgers)	Oct. 12, 2002
16	TCU (Tulane)	Nov. 9, 2002
16	Nebraska (Pittsburgh)	Sept. 18, 2004
15	Wisconsin (Indiana)	Nov. 11, 2000
15	Toledo (Eastern Mich.)	Sept. 7, 2002
15	Kansas St. (Oklahoma St.)	Oct. 12, 2002
14	Iowa (Penn St.)	Nov. 4, 2000
14	Auburn (LSU)	Dec. 1, 2001
14	Oregon St. (California)	Oct. 26, 2002
14	Florida (Arkansas)	Oct. 18, 2003
14	San Diego St. (Nevada)	Sept. 25, 2004

FORCED FUMBLES

FF	Team (Opponent)	Date
7	Miami (Ohio) (North Carolina)	Aug. 31, 2002
7	Virginia (South Carolina)	Sept. 7, 2002
7	West Virginia (Cincinnati)	Sept. 13, 2003
7	Miami (Ohio) (Buffalo)	Nov. 5, 2005
6	Washington (Idaho)	Sept. 2, 2002
6	Washington (Arizona St.)	Oct. 14, 2002
6	Boston College (Navy)	Oct. 19, 2002
6	North Carolina St. (Georgia Tech)	Oct. 4, 2003
6	Troy (La.-Monroe)	Nov. 22, 2003
5	Georgia (New Mexico St.)	Sept. 23, 2000
5	Fresno St. (Colorado)	Aug. 26, 2001
5	Clemson (UCF)	Sept. 1, 2001
5	Arizona St. (San Jose St.)	Sept. 29, 2001
5	Cincinnati (La.-Monroe)	Dec. 1, 2001
5	Iowa (Minnesota)	Nov. 16, 2002
5	Cincinnati (West Virginia)	Sept. 13, 2003
5	Hawaii (Idaho)	Nov. 20, 2004

Team Single-Season Highs

MOST GAMES PLAYED

(Counts Postseason Games)

Team, Year	No.
BYU, 1996	15
Kansas St., 2003	15
Since 1999, 45 teams have played 14. Most recent:	
Arkansas, 2006	14
Central Mich., 2006	14
Florida, 2006	14
Georgia Tech, 2006	14
Hawaii, 2006	14
Houston, 2006	14
Nebraska, 2006	14
Ohio, 2006	14
Oklahoma, 2006	14
Oregon St., 2006	14
Purdue, 2006	14
Southern Miss., 2006	14
Wake Forest, 2006	14
Before 1937 (Pre-NCAA Records):	
Yale, 1889	16
Penn, 1892	16
Yale, 1894	16
Penn, 1896	15
Penn, 1897	15
Minnesota, 1903	15
Yale, 1890	14
Harvard, 1891	14
Penn, 1895	14
Yale, 1896	14

MOST VICTORIES

(Counts Postseason Games)

Team, Year	No.
BYU, 1996	14
Ohio St., 2002	14
Nebraska, 1971	13
BYU, 1984	13
Alabama, 1992	13
Nebraska, 1994	13
Nebraska, 1997	13
Tennessee, 1998	13
Marshall, 1999	13
Oklahoma, 2000	13
Georgia, 2002	13
Boise St., 2003	13
LSU, 2003	13
Miami (Ohio), 2003	13
Auburn, 2004	13
Southern California, 2004	13
Texas, 2005	13
Boise St., 2006	13
Florida, 2006	13
Georgia Tech, 1952	12
Southern California, 1972	12
Western Mich., 1974	12
Pittsburgh, 1976	12
Southern California, 1978	12
Georgia, 1980	12
Clemson, 1981	12
Florida, 1995	12
Michigan, 1997	12
Marshall, 1998	12
Southern California, 2003	12
Oklahoma, 2003	12
Oklahoma, 2004	12
Utah, 2004	12
Southern California, 2005	12
Louisville, 2006	12
Ohio St., 2006	12
Wisconsin, 2006	12
Before 1937 (Pre-NCAA Records):	
Yale, 1894	16
Yale, 1889	15
Penn, 1892	15
Penn, 1897	15
Penn, 1895	14
Penn, 1896	14
Yale, 1888	13
Yale, 1890	13
Harvard, 1891	13
Yale, 1891	13
Yale, 1892	13
Yale, 1895	13
Yale, 1896	13
Minnesota, 1903	13
Minnesota, 1904	13

MOST LOSSES

Team, Year	No.
Army, 2003	13
Colorado St., 1981	12
Hawaii, 1998	12
SMU, 2003	12
New Mexico St., 2005	12
Duke, 2006	12
Florida Int'l, 2006	12
Mississippi St., 1976 (NCAA Sanctions)	11
Mississippi St., 1977 (NCAA Sanctions)	11
Rice, 1982	11
New Mexico, 1987	11
Rice, 1988	11
Kent St., 1993	11
Ohio, 1994	11
Duke, 1996	11
Illinois, 1997	11
Northern Ill., 1997	11
Rutgers, 1997	11
UNLV, 1998	11
Kent St., 1998	11
Ball St., 1999	11
South Carolina, 1999	11
Duke, 2000	11
Duke, 2001	11
Houston, 2001	11
Buffalo, 2002	11
Buffalo, 2003	11
East Caro., 2003	11
Illinois, 2003	11
La.-Monroe, 2003	11
Temple, 2003	11
UTEP, 2003	11
UCF, 2004	11
Temple, 2005	11
Eastern Mich., 2006	11
Stanford, 2006	11
Temple, 2006	11
Utah St., 2006	11

Toughest-Schedule Annual Leaders

The NCAA's toughest-schedule program (which began in 1977) is based on what all Division I-A opponents did against other Division I-A teams when not playing the team in question. Games against non-I-A teams are deleted, and nine intradivision games are required to qualify. (Bowl games are not included.) The leaders:

Year	Team (†Record)	¢Opponents' Record W	L	T	Pct.
1977	Miami (Fla.) (3-8-0)	66	42	2	.609
	Penn St. (10-1-0)	61	39	2	.608
1978	Notre Dame (8-3-0)	77	31	2	.709
	Southern California (11-1-0)	79	40	1	.663
1979	UCLA (5-6-0)	71	37	2	.655
	South Carolina (8-3-0)	69	38	2	.642
1980	Florida St. (10-1-0)	70	34	0	.673
	Miami (Fla.) (8-3-0)	64	33	1	.658
1981	Penn St. (9-2-0)	71	33	2	.679
	Temple (5-5-0)	71	33	2	.669
1982	Penn St. (10-1-0)	63	34	2	.646
	Kentucky (0-10-1)	63	34	5	.642
1983	Auburn (10-1-0)	70	31	3	.688
	UCLA (6-4-1)	68	37	5	.641
1984	Penn St. (6-5-0)	58	36	3	.613
	Georgia (7-4-0)	60	39	4	.602
1985	Notre Dame (5-6-0)	72	29	3	.707
	Alabama (8-2-1)	65	32	5	.662
1986	Florida (6-5-0)	64	29	3	.682
	LSU (9-2-0)	67	36	2	.648
1987	Notre Dame (8-3-0)	71	34	2	.673
	Florida St. (10-1-0)	60	29	4	.667

Year	Team (†Record)	¢Opponents' Record W	L	T	Pct.
1988	Virginia Tech (3-8-0)	74	36	0	.673
	Arizona (7-4-0)	70	37	3	.650
1989	Notre Dame (11-1-0)	74	38	4	.655
	LSU (4-7-0)	67	41	1	.619
1990	Colorado (10-1-1)	72	42	3	.628
	Stanford (5-6-0)	67	39	4	.627
1991	South Carolina (3-6-2)	57	31	2	.644
	Florida (10-2-0)	66	37	1	.639
1992	Southern California (6-5-1)	68	38	4	.636
	Stanford (10-3-0)	73	43	4	.625
1993	LSU (5-6-0)	67	38	5	.632
	Purdue (1-10-0)	66	38	3	.631
1994	Michigan (8-4-0)	67	38	6	.631
	Oklahoma (6-6-0)	66	39	4	.624
1995	Notre Dame (9-3-0)	67	37	5	.638
	Illinois (5-5-1)	69	40	2	.631
1996	Florida (12-1)	70	41	0	.631
	UCLA (5-6)	66	41	0	.617
1997	Colorado (5-6)	76	37	0	.673
	Auburn (10-3)	80	39	0	.672
1998	Auburn (3-8)	74	34	0	.685
	Missouri (7-4)	66	36	0	.647
1999	Alabama (10-3)	80	38	0	.678
	Auburn (5-6)	62	36	0	.633
2000	Florida (10-2)	79	42	0	.653
	Florida St. (11-1)	78	44	0	.639
2001	California (1-10)	73	39	0	.652
	Colorado (10-3)	79	45	0	.637

†Not including bowl games. ¢When not playing the team listed.

Top 10 Toughest-Schedule Leaders for 2002-06

2002

	Team	$Opp. Record	Pct.
1.	Southern California	107-58	.649
2.	Iowa St.	107-62	.633
3.	Texas Tech	108-66	.621
4.	Arkansas	104-64	.619
5.	Florida	97-60	.618
6.	Stanford	87-54	.617
7.	Florida St.	112-70	.615
8.	Miami (Fla.)	91-57	.615
9.	Wisconsin	108-68	.614
10.	Alabama	98-62	.613

2003

	Team	$Opp. Record	Pct.
1.	Alabama	98-50	.662
2.	Florida	89-48	.650
3.	Notre Dame	89-49	.645
4.	Texas A&M	82-53	.607
5.	Arizona	84-55	.604
6.	Iowa St.	76-50	.603
7.	Bowling Green	77-51	.602
8.	Kansas St.	86-59	.593
9.	Ohio St.	87-60	.592
10.	South Carolina	80-56	.588

2004

	Team	$Opp. Record	Pct.
1.	Texas A&M	86-42	.672
2.	North Carolina	74-39	.655
3.	Arizona	69-39	.639
4.	Arizona St.	79-48	.622
5.	Auburn	76-47	.618
6.	Baylor	66-41	.617
7.	Notre Dame	78-49	.614
8.	Arkansas	68-43	.613
9.	Georgia	71-45	.612
10.	Iowa	76-49	.608

2005

	Team	$Opp. Record	Pct.
1.	Oklahoma	84-38	.689
2.	Stanford	66-37	.641
3.	Michigan	80-46	.635
4.	Ohio St.	80-47	.630
5.	North Carolina	74-45	.622
6.	Northwestern	78-49	.614
7.	Texas	81-51	.614
8.	Arkansas	63-40	.612
9.	Southern California	81-52	.609
10.	Texas Tech	60-39	.606

2006

	Team	$Opp. Record	Pct.
1.	Florida	100-49	.671
2.	Michigan	91-53	.632
3.	Cincinnati	83-50	.624
4.	Kentucky	83-52	.615
	South Carolina	83-52	.615
6.	Connecticut	73-47	.608
7.	Southern California	90-58	.608
8.	Arizona	76-50	.603
9.	Arkansas	86-59	.593
10.	Tennessee	85-59	.590

$When not playing the team listed.

Annual Most-Improved Teams

Year	Team	$Games Improved	From		To		Coach
1937	California	4½	1936	6-5-0	1937	*10-0-1	Stub Allison
	Syracuse	4½	1936	1-7-0	1937	5-2-1	#Ossie Solem
1938	TCU	5½	1937	4-4-2	1938	*11-0-0	Dutch Meyer
1939	Texas A&M	5½	1938	4-4-1	1939	*11-0-0	Homer Norton
1940	Stanford	8	1939	1-7-1	1940	*10-0-0	#Clark Shaughnessy
1941	Vanderbilt	4½	1940	3-6-1	1941	8-2-0	Red Sanders
1942	Utah St.	5½	1941	0-8-0	1942	6-3-1	Dick Romney
1943	Purdue	8	1942	1-8-0	1943	9-0-0	Elmer Burnham
1944	Ohio St.	6	1943	3-6-0	1944	9-0-0	#Carroll Widdoes
1945	Miami (Fla.)	7	1944	1-7-1	1945	*9-1-1	Jack Harding
1946	Illinois	5	1945	2-6-1	1946	*8-2-0	Ray Eliot
	Kentucky	5	1945	2-8-0	1946	7-3-0	#Paul "Bear" Bryant
1947	California	6½	1946	2-7-0	1947	9-1-0	#Lynn "Pappy" Waldorf
1948	Clemson	6	1947	4-5-0	1948	*11-0-0	Frank Howard
1949	Tulsa	5	1948	0-9-1	1949	5-4-1	J. O. Brothers
1950	BYU	5	1949	0-11-0	1950	4-5-1	Chick Atkinson
	Texas A&M	5	1949	1-8-1	1950	*7-4-0	Harry Stiteler
1951	Georgia Tech	6	1950	5-6-0	1951	*11-0-1	Bobby Dodd
1952	Alabama	4½	1951	5-6-0	1952	*10-2-0	Harold "Red" Drew
1953	Texas Tech	7	1952	3-7-1	1953	*11-1-0	DeWitt Weaver
1954	Denver	5	1953	3-5-2	1954	9-1-0	Bob Blackman
1955	Texas A&M	6½	1954	1-9-0	1955	7-2-1	Paul "Bear" Bryant
1956	Iowa	5	1955	3-5-1	1956	*9-1-0	Forest Evashevski
1957	Notre Dame	5	1956	2-8-0	1957	7-3-0	Terry Brennan
	Texas	5	1956	1-9-0	1957	†6-4-1	#Darrell Royal
1958	Air Force	6	1957	3-6-1	1958	‡9-0-1	#Ben Martin
1959	Washington	6½	1958	3-7-0	1959	*10-1-0	Jim Owens
1960	Minnesota	5½	1959	2-7-0	1960	†8-2-0	Murray Warmath
	North Carolina St.	5½	1959	1-9-0	1960	6-3-1	Earle Edwards
1961	Villanova	6	1960	2-8-0	1961	*8-2-0	Alex Bell
1962	Southern California	6	1961	4-5-1	1962	*11-0-0	John McKay
1963	Illinois	6	1962	2-7-0	1963	*8-1-1	Pete Elliott
1964	Notre Dame	6½	1963	2-7-0	1964	9-1-0	#Ara Parseghian
1965	UTEP	6½	1964	0-8-2	1965	*8-3-0	#Bobby Dobbs
1966	Dayton	6½	1965	1-8-1	1966	8-2-0	John McVay
1967	Indiana	7	1966	1-8-1	1967	†9-2-0	John Pont
1968	Arkansas	5	1967	4-5-1	1968	*10-1-0	Frank Broyles
1969	UCLA	5½	1968	3-7-0	1969	8-1-1	Tommy Prothro
1970	Tulsa	5	1969	1-9-0	1970	6-4-0	#Claude Gibson
1971	Army	5	1970	1-9-1	1971	6-4-0	Tom Cahill

Year	Team	$Games Improved	From		To		Coach
	Georgia	5	1970	5-5-0	1971	*11-1-0	Vince Dooley
1972	Pacific	5	1971	3-8-0	1972	8-3-0	Chester Caddas
	Southern California	5	1971	6-4-1	1972	*12-0-0	John McKay
	UCLA	5	1971	2-7-1	1972	8-3-0	Pepper Rodgers
1973	Pittsburgh	5	1972	1-10-0	1973	†6-5-1	#Johnny Majors
1974	Baylor	5½	1973	2-9-0	1974	†8-4-0	Grant Teaff
1975	Arizona St.	5	1974	7-5-0	1975	*12-0-0	Frank Kush
1976	Houston	7	1975	2-8-0	1976	*10-2-0	Bill Yeoman
1977	Miami (Ohio)	7	1976	3-8-0	1977	10-1-0	Dick Crum
1978	Tulsa	6	1977	3-8-0	1978	9-2-0	John Cooper
1979	Wake Forest	6½	1978	1-10-0	1979	†8-4-0	John Mackovic
1980	Florida	7	1979	0-10-1	1980	*8-4-0	Charley Pell
1981	Clemson	5½	1980	6-5-0	1981	*12-0-0	Danny Ford
1982	La.-Lafayette	6	1981	1-9-1	1982	7-3-1	Sam Robertson
	New Mexico	6	1981	4-7-1	1982	10-1-0	Joe Morrison
1983	Kentucky	5½	1982	0-10-1	1983	†6-5-1	Jerry Claiborne
	Memphis	5½	1982	1-10-0	1983	6-4-1	Rex Dockery
1984	Army	6	1983	2-9-0	1984	*8-3-1	Jim Young
1985	Colorado	5½	1984	1-10-0	1985	†7-5-0	Bill McCartney
	Fresno St.	5½	1984	6-6-0	1985	*11-0-1	Jim Sweeney
1986	San Jose St.	7	1985	2-8-1	1986	*10-2-0	Claude Gilbert
1987	Syracuse	6	1986	5-6-0	1987	‡11-0-1	Dick MacPherson
1988	Washington St.	5	1987	3-7-1	1988	*9-3-0	Dennis Erickson
	West Virginia	5	1987	6-6-0	1988	†11-1-0	Don Nehlen
1989	Tennessee	5½	1988	5-6-0	1989	*11-1-0	Johnny Majors
1990	Temple	6	1989	1-10-0	1990	7-4-0	Jerry Berndt
1991	Tulsa	6½	1990	3-8-0	1991	*10-2-0	Dave Rader
1992	Hawaii	6	1991	4-7-1	1992	*11-2-0	Bob Wagner
1993	La.-Lafayette	6	1992	2-9-0	1993	8-3-0	Nelson Stokley
	Virginia Tech	6	1992	2-8-1	1993	*9-3-0	Frank Beamer
1994	Colorado St.	4½	1993	5-6-0	1994	†10-2-0	Sonny Lubick
	Duke	4½	1993	3-8-0	1994	†8-4-0	#Fred Goldsmith
	East Caro.	4½	1993	2-9-0	1994	†7-5-0	Steve Logan
1995	Northwestern	6	1994	3-7-1	1995	†10-2-0	Gary Barnett
1996	BYU	5	1995	7-4-0	1996	*14-1-0	LaVell Edwards
1997	Western Mich.	6	1996	2-9-0	1997	8-3-0	Gary Darnell
1998	Louisville	5½	1997	1-10-0	1998	7-5-0	#John L. Smith
	TCU	5½	1997	1-10-0	1998	7-5-0	#Dennis Franchione
1999	Hawaii	8½	1998	0-12-0	1999	*9-4-0	#June Jones
2000	South Carolina	7½	1999	0-11-0	2000	*8-4-0	Lou Holtz
2001	Bowling Green	6	2000	2-9-0	2001	8-3-0	#Urban Meyer
	Colorado	6	2000	3-8-0	2001	†10-3-0	Gary Barnett
	Hawaii	6	2000	3-9-0	2001	9-3-0	June Jones
2002	Ohio St.	6	2001	7-5-0	2002	*14-0-0	Jim Tressel
2003	Tulsa	6½	2002	1-11-0	2003	8-5-0	#Steve Kragthorpe
2004	UTEP	6½	2003	2-11-0	2004	†8-4-0	#Mike Price
2005	UCF	7	2004	0-11-0	2005	†8-5-0	#George O'Leary
2006	Wake Forest	5½	2005	4-7-0	2006	†11-3-0	Jim Grobe

$To determine games improved, add the difference in victories between the two seasons to the difference in losses, then divide by two; ties not counted. Bowl victory (*), loss (†), tie (‡) included in record. #First year as head coach at that college.

All-Time Most-Improved Teams

Games	Team (Year)
8½	Hawaii (1999)
8	Stanford (1940)
7½	South Carolina (2000)
7	Miami (Fla.) (1945)
7	Texas Tech (1953)
7	Indiana (1967)
7	Houston (1976)
7	Miami (Ohio) (1977)
7	Florida (1980)
7	San Jose St. (1986)
7	UCF (2005)
6½	California (1947)
6½	Texas A&M (1955)
6½	Washington (1959)
6½	Notre Dame (1964)
6½	UTEP (1965)
6½	Dayton (1966)
6½	Toledo (1967)
6½	Wake Forest (1979)
6½	Tulsa (1991)
6½	Tulsa (2003)
6½	UTEP (2004)
6½	Penn St. (2005)

2006 Most-Improved Teams

Team (Coach)	2005	2006	$Games Improved
Wake Forest (Jim Grobe)	4-7	11-3	5½
Hawaii (June Jones)	5-7	11-3	5
Rice (Todd Graham)	1-10	7-6	5
San Jose St. (Dick Tomey)	3-8	9-4	5
Arkansas (Houston Nutt)	4-7	10-4	4½
BYU (Bronco Mendenhall)	6-6	11-2	4½
Kent St. (Doug Martin)	1-10	6-6	4½
Boise St. (Chris Petersen)	9-4	13-0	4
Kentucky (Rich Brooks)	3-8	8-5	4
New Mexico St. (Hal Mumme)	0-12	4-8	4

$To determine games improved, add the difference in victories between the two seasons to the difference in losses, then divide by two. Includes bowl games.

All-Time Team Won-Lost Records

Includes records as senior college only. Bowl and playoff games are included, and each tie game is computed as half won and half lost. Teams listed with years in parentheses indicates reclassification to the FBS. The year in parentheses is the first year of FBS active membership. Note: Tiebreaker rule began with 1996 season.

BY PERCENTAGE

Team	Yrs.	Won	Lost	Tied	Pct.	Total Games
Michigan	127	860	282	36	.745	1,178
Notre Dame	118	821	269	42	.744	1,132
Texas	114	810	313	33	.715	1,156
Oklahoma	112	768	292	53	.714	1,113
Ohio St.	117	786	301	53	.713	1,140
Alabama	112	780	308	43	.709	1,131
Nebraska	117	803	326	40	.704	1,169
Southern California	114	743	300	54	.702	1,097
Tennessee	110	761	316	53	.697	1,130
Boise St. (1996)	39	317	140	2	.693	459
Penn St.	120	780	343	41	.688	1,164
Florida St.	60	443	211	17	.673	671
Georgia	113	702	379	54	.642	1,135
Miami (Fla.)	80	532	297	19	.639	848
LSU	113	680	376	47	.638	1,103
Miami (Ohio)	118	641	362	44	.633	1,047
Auburn	114	667	384	47	.629	1,098
Washington	117	646	379	50	.624	1,075
Florida	100	619	368	40	.622	1,027
South Fla. (2000)	10	70	43	0	.619	113
Arizona St.	94	530	324	24	.617	878
Colorado	117	652	412	36	.609	1,100
Central Mich.	106	542	342	36	.609	920
Texas A&M	112	648	419	48	.603	1,115
UCLA	88	528	344	37	.601	909
Virginia Tech	113	636	418	46	.599	1,100
Southern Miss.	90	515	345	26	.596	886
Bowling Green	88	469	311	52	.595	832
Arkansas	113	638	430	40	.594	1,108
Fresno St.	85	521	352	29	.594	902
West Virginia	114	653	440	45	.594	1,138
Georgia Tech	114	646	436	43	.593	1,125
Syracuse	117	669	452	49	.593	1,170
Army	117	631	431	51	.590	1,113
Clemson	111	616	422	45	.590	1,083
Michigan St.	110	594	408	44	.589	1,046
Minnesota	123	629	439	43	.586	1,111
Boston College	108	589	415	36	.584	1,040
Middle Tenn. (1999)	90	499	352	28	.584	879
Utah	113	572	413	31	.578	1,016
Pittsburgh	117	639	464	42	.576	1,145
Arizona	102	531	392	33	.573	956
Louisiana Tech (1989)	103	526	393	37	.570	956
North Carolina	116	627	470	54	.568	1,151
Mississippi	112	594	451	35	.566	1,080
Stanford	100	543	412	49	.565	1,004
Hawaii	91	490	374	26	.565	890
Troy	76	417	320	15	.564	752
San Diego St.	84	465	359	32	.562	856
Wisconsin	117	587	452	53	.562	1,092
BYU	82	473	367	26	.561	866
Western Mich.	101	490	381	24	.561	895
California#	111	598	463	51	.561	1,112
Tulsa	102	529	416	27	.558	972
Texas Tech	82	482	383	32	.555	897
Toledo	86	451	369	24	.549	844
Navy	126	616	506	57	.547	1,179
Oregon	111	539	457	46	.539	1,042
Purdue	119	558	474	48	.539	1,080
Air Force	51	303	260	13	.537	576
Nevada (1992)	96	467	406	32	.534	905
Maryland	114	585	509	42	.533	1,136
Virginia	117	597	522	48	.532	1,167
Missouri	116	577	506	52	.531	1,135
North Texas (1995)	91	462	411	33	.528	906
Northern Ill.	105	486	434	51	.527	971
Iowa	118	552	500	39	.524	1,091
Ball St.	82	381	347	32	.522	760
Illinois	116	549	502	50	.521	1,101
Houston	61	339	312	15	.520	666
TCU	110	537	503	56	.516	1,096
Louisville	88	426	404	17	.513	847
Marshall (1997)	103	502	476	44	.513	1,022
Akron	106	473	449	36	.513	958
San Jose St.	88	432	412	38	.511	882
East Caro.	71	359	344	12	.510	715
UAB (1996)	16	89	86	3	.508	178
Washington St.	110	482	469	45	.507	996
North Carolina St.	115	517	505	55	.506	1,077
Baylor	104	514	503	43	.505	1,060
Vanderbilt	117	542	534	50	.504	1,126
Kentucky	116	545	539	44	.503	1,128
Kansas	117	542	537	58	.502	1,137
Duke	94	443	439	31	.502	913
Utah St.	109	466	462	31	.502	959
South Carolina	113	516	514	44	.501	1,074
Rutgers	137	580	580	42	.500	1,202
UCF (1996)	28	153	154	1	.498	308
SMU	90	437	454	54	.491	945
Memphis	91	417	434	32	.490	883
Ohio	111	478	498	48	.490	1,024
Cincinnati	119	513	536	51	.490	1,100
Wyoming	110	468	489	28	.489	985
Oklahoma St.	105	482	506	48	.488	1,036
La.-Lafayette	99	455	483	32	.486	970
Arkansas St. (1992)	92	397	422	37	.485	856
Colorado St.	108	457	493	33	.482	983
Connecticut (2002)	108	447	483	38	.481	968
Mississippi St.	107	473	514	39	.480	1,026
UNLV	39	207	227	4	.477	438
Oregon St.	110	468	518	50	.476	1,036
Fla. Atlantic (2006)	6	33	37	0	.471	70
Tulane	113	479	546	38	.468	1,063
New Mexico	108	437	499	31	.468	967
Eastern Mich.	114	413	480	46	.464	939
Iowa St.	115	477	555	46	.464	1,078
Idaho (1996)	109	422	514	25	.452	961
Rice	95	413	526	32	.442	971
Temple	108	394	510	52	.439	956
New Mexico St.	111	409	530	32	.438	971
Kansas St.	111	442	583	42	.434	1,067
La.-Monroe (1994)	56	251	334	8	.430	593
Northwestern	119	451	605	44	.430	1,100
Indiana	119	429	587	44	.425	1,060
Buffalo (1999)	93	316	444	29	.419	789
UTEP	89	345	496	30	.413	871
Wake Forest	105	390	577	33	.407	1,000
Kent St.	84	294	467	28	.390	789
Florida Int'l (2006)	5	15	41	0	.268	56

BY VICTORIES

Team	Yrs.	Won	Lost	Tied	Pct.	Total Games
Michigan	127	860	282	36	.745	1,178
Notre Dame	118	821	269	42	.744	1,132
Texas	114	810	313	33	.715	1,156
Nebraska	117	803	326	40	.704	1,169
Ohio St.	117	786	301	53	.713	1,140
Alabama	112	780	308	43	.709	1,131
Penn St.	120	780	343	41	.688	1,164
Oklahoma	112	768	292	53	.714	1,113
Tennessee	110	761	316	53	.697	1,130
Southern California	114	743	300	54	.702	1,097
Georgia	113	702	379	54	.642	1,135
LSU	113	680	376	47	.638	1,103
Syracuse	117	669	452	49	.593	1,170
Auburn	114	667	384	47	.629	1,098
West Virginia	114	653	440	45	.594	1,138
Colorado	117	652	412	36	.609	1,100
Texas A&M	112	648	419	48	.603	1,115
Washington	117	646	379	50	.624	1,075
Georgia Tech	114	646	436	43	.593	1,125
Miami (Ohio)	118	641	362	44	.633	1,047
Pittsburgh	117	639	464	42	.576	1,145
Arkansas	113	638	430	40	.594	1,108
Virginia Tech	113	636	418	46	.599	1,100
Army	117	631	431	51	.590	1,113
Minnesota	123	629	439	43	.586	1,111
North Carolina	116	627	470	54	.568	1,151
Florida	100	619	368	40	.622	1,027
Clemson	111	616	422	45	.590	1,083
Navy	126	616	506	57	.547	1,179

Team	Yrs.	Won	Lost	Tied	Pct.	Total Games
California#	111	598	463	51	.561	1,112
Virginia	117	597	522	48	.532	1,167
Michigan St.	110	594	408	44	.589	1,046
Mississippi	112	594	451	35	.566	1,080
Boston College	108	589	415	36	.584	1,040
Wisconsin	117	587	452	53	.562	1,092
Maryland	114	585	509	42	.533	1,136
Rutgers	137	580	580	42	.500	1,202
Missouri	116	577	506	52	.531	1,135
Utah	113	572	413	31	.578	1,016
Purdue	119	558	474	48	.539	1,080
Iowa	118	552	500	39	.524	1,091
Illinois	116	549	502	50	.521	1,101
Kentucky	116	545	539	44	.503	1,128
Stanford	100	543	412	49	.565	1,004
Central Mich.	106	542	342	36	.609	920
Vanderbilt	117	542	534	50	.504	1,126
Kansas	117	542	537	58	.502	1,137
Oregon	111	539	457	46	.539	1,042
TCU	110	537	503	56	.516	1,096
Miami (Fla.)	80	532	297	19	.639	848
Arizona	102	531	392	33	.573	956
Arizona St.	94	530	324	24	.617	878
Tulsa	102	529	416	27	.558	972
UCLA	88	528	344	37	.601	909
Louisiana Tech (1989)	103	526	393	37	.570	956
Fresno St.	85	521	352	29	.594	902
North Carolina St.	115	517	505	55	.506	1,077
South Carolina	113	516	514	44	.501	1,074
Southern Miss.	90	515	345	26	.596	886
Baylor	104	514	503	43	.505	1,060
Cincinnati	119	513	536	51	.490	1,100
Marshall (1997)	103	502	476	44	.513	1,022
Middle Tenn. (1999)	90	499	352	28	.584	879
Hawaii	91	490	374	26	.565	890
Western Mich.	101	490	381	24	.561	895
Northern Ill.	105	486	434	51	.527	971
Texas Tech	82	482	383	32	.555	897
Washington St.	110	482	469	45	.507	996
Oklahoma St.	105	482	506	48	.488	1,036
Tulane	113	479	546	38	.468	1,063
Ohio	111	478	498	48	.490	1,024
Iowa St.	115	477	555	46	.464	1,078
BYU	82	473	367	26	.561	866
Akron	106	473	449	36	.513	958
Mississippi St.	107	473	514	39	.480	1,026
Bowling Green	88	469	311	52	.595	832
Wyoming	110	468	489	28	.489	985
Oregon St.	110	468	518	50	.476	1,036
Nevada (1992)	96	467	406	32	.534	905
Utah St.	109	466	462	31	.502	959
San Diego St.	84	465	359	32	.562	856
North Texas (1995)	91	462	411	33	.528	906
Colorado St.	108	457	493	33	.482	983
La.-Lafayette	99	455	483	32	.486	970
Toledo	86	451	369	24	.549	844
Northwestern	119	451	605	44	.430	1,100
Connecticut (2002)	108	447	483	38	.481	968
Florida St.	60	443	211	17	.673	671
Duke	94	443	439	31	.502	913
Kansas St.	111	442	583	42	.434	1,067
SMU	90	437	454	54	.491	945
New Mexico	108	437	499	31	.468	967
San Jose St.	88	432	412	38	.511	882
Indiana	119	429	587	44	.425	1,060
Louisville	88	426	404	17	.513	847
Idaho (1996)	109	422	514	25	.452	961
Troy	76	417	320	15	.564	752
Memphis	91	417	434	32	.490	883
Eastern Mich.	114	413	480	46	.464	939
Rice	95	413	526	32	.442	971
New Mexico St.	111	409	530	32	.438	971
Arkansas St. (1992)	92	397	422	37	.485	856
Temple	108	394	510	52	.439	956
Wake Forest	105	390	577	33	.407	1,000
Ball St.	82	381	347	32	.522	760
East Caro.	71	359	344	12	.510	715
UTEP	89	345	496	30	.413	871
Houston	61	339	312	15	.520	666
Boise St. (1996)	39	317	140	2	.693	459
Buffalo (1999)	93	316	444	29	.419	789
Air Force	51	303	260	13	.537	576
Kent St.	84	294	467	28	.390	789
La.-Monroe (1994)	56	251	334	8	.430	593
UNLV	39	207	227	4	.477	438
UCF (1996)	28	153	154	1	.498	308
UAB (1996)	16	89	86	3	.508	178
South Fla. (2000)	10	70	43	0	.619	113
Fla. Atlantic (2006)	6	33	37	0	.471	70
Florida Int'l (2006)	5	15	41	0	.268	56

ALPHABETICAL LISTING

Team	Yrs.	Won	Lost	Tied	Pct.	Total Games
Air Force	51	303	260	13	.537	576
Akron	106	473	449	36	.513	958
Alabama	112	780	308	43	.709	1,131
UAB (1996)	16	89	86	3	.508	178
Arizona	102	531	392	33	.573	956
Arizona St.	94	530	324	24	.617	878
Arkansas	113	638	430	40	.594	1,108
Arkansas St. (1992)	92	397	422	37	.485	856
Army	117	631	431	51	.590	1,113
Auburn	114	667	384	47	.629	1,098
Ball St.	82	381	347	32	.522	760
Baylor	104	514	503	43	.505	1,060
Boise St. (1996)	39	317	140	2	.693	459
Boston College	108	589	415	36	.584	1,040
Bowling Green	88	469	311	52	.595	832
BYU	82	473	367	26	.561	866
Buffalo (1999)	93	316	444	29	.419	789
California#	111	598	463	51	.561	1,112
UCF (1996)	28	153	154	1	.498	308
Central Mich.	106	542	342	36	.609	920
Cincinnati	119	513	536	51	.490	1,100
Clemson	111	616	422	45	.590	1,083
Colorado	117	652	412	36	.609	1,100
Colorado St.	108	457	493	33	.482	983
Connecticut (2002)	108	447	483	38	.481	968
Duke	94	443	439	31	.502	913
East Caro.	71	359	344	12	.510	715
Eastern Mich.	114	413	480	46	.464	939
Florida	100	619	368	40	.622	1,027
Fla. Atlantic (2006)	6	33	37	0	.471	70
Florida Int'l (2006)	5	15	41	0	.268	56
Florida St.	60	443	211	17	.673	671
Fresno St.	85	521	352	29	.594	902
Georgia	113	702	379	54	.642	1,135
Georgia Tech	114	646	436	43	.593	1,125
Hawaii	91	490	374	26	.565	890
Houston	61	339	312	15	.520	666
Idaho (1996)	109	422	514	25	.452	961
Illinois	116	549	502	50	.521	1,101
Indiana	119	429	587	44	.425	1,060
Iowa	118	552	500	39	.524	1,091
Iowa St.	115	477	555	46	.464	1,078
Kansas	117	542	537	58	.502	1,137
Kansas St.	111	442	583	42	.434	1,067
Kent St.	84	294	467	28	.390	789
Kentucky	116	545	539	44	.503	1,128
La.-Lafayette	99	455	483	32	.486	970
La.-Monroe (1994)	56	251	334	8	.430	593
LSU	113	680	376	47	.638	1,103
Louisiana Tech (1989)	103	526	393	37	.570	956
Louisville	88	426	404	17	.513	847
Marshall (1997)	103	502	476	44	.513	1,022
Maryland	114	585	509	42	.533	1,136
Memphis	91	417	434	32	.490	883
Miami (Fla.)	80	532	297	19	.639	848
Miami (Ohio)	118	641	362	44	.633	1,047
Michigan	127	860	282	36	.745	1,178
Michigan St.	110	594	408	44	.589	1,046
Middle Tenn. (1999)	90	499	352	28	.584	879
Minnesota	123	629	439	43	.586	1,111
Mississippi	112	594	451	35	.566	1,080
Mississippi St.	107	473	514	39	.480	1,026
Missouri	116	577	506	52	.531	1,135
Navy	126	616	506	57	.547	1,179
Nebraska	117	803	326	40	.704	1,169
Nevada (1992)	96	467	406	32	.534	905
UNLV	39	207	227	4	.477	438
New Mexico	108	437	499	31	.468	967
New Mexico St.	111	409	530	32	.438	971
North Carolina	116	627	470	54	.568	1,151
North Carolina St.	115	517	505	55	.506	1,077
North Texas (1995)	91	462	411	33	.528	906

Team	Yrs.	Won	Lost	Tied	Pct.	Total Games
Northern Ill.	105	486	434	51	.527	971
Northwestern	119	451	605	44	.430	1,100
Notre Dame	118	821	269	42	.744	1,132
Ohio	111	478	498	48	.490	1,024
Ohio St.	117	786	301	53	.713	1,140
Oklahoma	112	768	292	53	.714	1,113
Oklahoma St.	105	482	506	48	.488	1,036
Oregon	111	539	457	46	.539	1,042
Oregon St.	110	468	518	50	.476	1,036
Penn St.	120	780	343	41	.688	1,164
Pittsburgh	117	639	464	42	.576	1,145
Purdue	119	558	474	48	.539	1,080
Rice	95	413	526	32	.442	971
Rutgers	137	580	580	42	.500	1,202
San Diego St.	84	465	359	32	.562	856
San Jose St.	88	432	412	38	.511	882
South Carolina	113	516	514	44	.501	1,074
South Fla. (2000)	10	70	43	0	.619	113
Southern California	114	743	300	54	.702	1,097
SMU	90	437	454	54	.491	945
Southern Miss.	90	515	345	26	.596	886
Stanford	100	543	412	49	.565	1,004
Syracuse	117	669	452	49	.593	1,170
Temple	108	394	510	52	.439	956
Tennessee	110	761	316	53	.697	1,130

Team	Yrs.	Won	Lost	Tied	Pct.	Total Games
Texas	114	810	313	33	.715	1,156
UTEP	89	345	496	30	.413	871
Texas A&M	112	648	419	48	.603	1,115
TCU	110	537	503	56	.516	1,096
Texas Tech	82	482	383	32	.555	897
Toledo	86	451	369	24	.549	844
Troy	76	417	320	15	.564	752
Tulane	113	479	546	38	.468	1,063
Tulsa	102	529	416	27	.558	972
UCLA	88	528	344	37	.601	909
Utah	113	572	413	31	.578	1,016
Utah St.	109	466	462	31	.502	959
Vanderbilt	117	542	534	50	.504	1,126
Virginia	117	597	522	48	.532	1,167
Virginia Tech	113	636	418	46	.599	1,100
Wake Forest	105	390	577	33	.407	1,000
Washington	117	646	379	50	.624	1,075
Washington St.	110	482	469	45	.507	996
West Virginia	114	653	440	45	.594	1,138
Western Mich.	101	490	381	24	.561	895
Wisconsin	117	587	452	53	.562	1,092
Wyoming	110	468	489	28	.489	985

#1999 record was vacated by action of the NCAA Committee on Infractions.

Records in the 2000s

(2000-01-02-03-04-05-06, Including Bowls; Year in Parentheses is First Year of FBS Active Membership)

BY PERCENTAGE

Team	2000 W	2000 L	2001 W	2001 L	2002 W	2002 L	2003 W	2003 L	2004 W	2004 L	2005 W	2005 L	2006 W	2006 L	Total W	Total L	Total Pct.
Boise St.	10	2	8	4	12	1	13	1	11	1	9	4	13	0	76	13	.854
Oklahoma	13	0	11	2	12	2	12	2	12	1	8	4	11	3	79	14	.850
Texas	9	3	11	2	11	2	10	3	11	1	13	0	10	3	75	14	.843
Miami (Fla.)	11	1	12	0	12	1	11	2	9	3	9	3	7	6	71	16	.816
Ohio St.	8	4	7	5	14	0	11	2	8	4	10	2	12	1	70	18	.795
Southern California	5	7	6	6	11	2	12	1	13	0	12	1	11	2	70	19	.787
LSU	8	4	10	3	8	5	13	1	9	3	11	2	11	2	70	20	.778
Louisville	9	3	11	2	7	6	9	4	11	1	9	3	12	1	68	20	.773
Georgia	8	4	8	4	13	1	11	3	10	2	10	3	9	4	69	21	.767
Virginia Tech	11	1	8	3	10	4	8	5	10	3	11	2	10	3	68	21	.764
TCU	10	2	6	6	10	2	11	2	5	6	11	1	11	2	64	21	.753
Auburn	9	4	7	5	9	4	8	5	13	0	9	3	11	2	66	23	.742
Michigan	9	3	8	4	10	3	10	3	9	3	7	5	11	2	64	23	.736
Florida	10	3	10	2	8	5	8	5	7	5	9	3	13	1	65	24	.730
Toledo	10	1	10	2	9	5	8	4	9	4	9	3	5	7	60	26	.698
Tennessee	8	4	11	2	8	5	10	3	10	3	5	6	9	4	61	27	.693
Boston College	7	5	8	4	9	4	8	5	9	3	9	3	10	3	60	27	.690
Florida St.	11	2	8	4	9	5	10	3	9	3	8	5	7	6	62	28	.689
Oregon	10	2	11	1	7	6	8	5	5	6	10	2	7	6	58	28	.674
Nebraska	10	2	11	2	7	7	10	3	5	6	8	4	9	5	60	29	.674
Wisconsin	9	4	5	7	8	6	7	6	9	3	10	3	12	1	60	30	.667
West Virginia	7	5	3	8	9	4	8	5	8	4	11	1	11	2	57	29	.663
Utah	4	7	8	4	5	6	10	2	12	0	7	5	8	5	54	29	.651
Maryland	5	6	10	2	11	3	10	3	5	6	5	6	9	4	55	30	.647
Northern Ill.	6	5	6	5	8	4	10	2	9	3	7	5	7	6	53	30	.639
Notre Dame	9	3	5	6	10	3	5	7	6	6	9	3	10	3	54	31	.635
Texas Tech	7	6	7	5	9	5	8	5	8	4	9	3	8	5	56	33	.629
Clemson	9	3	7	5	7	6	9	4	6	5	8	4	8	5	54	32	.628
Oregon St.	11	1	5	6	8	5	8	5	7	5	5	6	10	4	54	32	.628
Fresno St.	7	5	11	3	9	5	9	5	9	3	8	5	4	8	57	34	.626
South Fla.	7	4	8	3	9	2	7	4	4	7	6	6	9	4	50	30	.625
Iowa	3	9	7	5	11	2	10	3	10	2	7	5	6	7	54	33	.621
Kansas St.	11	3	6	6	11	2	11	4	4	7	5	6	7	6	55	34	.618
Marshall	8	5	11	2	11	2	8	4	6	6	4	7	5	7	53	33	.616
Southern Miss.	8	4	6	5	7	6	9	4	7	5	7	5	9	5	53	34	.609
Georgia Tech	9	3	8	5	7	6	7	6	7	5	7	5	9	5	54	35	.607
Hawaii	3	9	9	3	10	4	9	5	8	5	5	7	11	3	55	36	.604
Bowling Green	2	9	8	3	9	3	11	3	9	3	6	5	4	8	49	34	.590
Washington St.	4	7	10	2	10	3	10	3	5	6	4	7	6	6	49	34	.590
Miami (Ohio)	6	5	7	5	7	5	13	1	8	5	7	4	2	10	50	35	.588
Pittsburgh	7	5	7	5	9	4	8	5	8	4	5	6	6	6	50	35	.588
UCLA	6	6	7	4	8	5	6	7	6	6	10	2	7	6	50	36	.581
Arkansas	6	6	7	5	9	5	9	4	5	6	4	7	10	4	50	37	.575
Purdue	8	4	6	6	7	6	9	4	7	5	5	6	8	6	50	37	.575
South Carolina	8	4	9	3	5	7	5	7	6	5	7	5	8	5	48	36	.571

	2000		2001		2002		2003		2004		2005		2006		Total		
Team	**W**	**L**	**W**	**L**	**W**	**L**	**W**	**L**	**W**	**L**	**W**	**L**	**W**	**L**	**W**	**L**	**Pct.**
BYU	6	6	12	2	5	7	4	8	5	6	6	6	11	2	49	37	.570
North Carolina St.	8	4	7	5	11	3	8	5	5	6	7	5	3	9	49	37	.570
Colorado St.	10	2	7	5	10	4	7	6	4	7	6	6	4	8	48	38	.558
Minnesota	6	6	4	7	8	5	10	3	7	5	7	5	6	7	48	38	.558
California	3	8	1	10	7	5	8	6	10	2	8	4	10	3	47	38	.553
Virginia	6	6	5	7	9	5	8	5	8	4	7	5	5	7	48	39	.552
Penn St.	5	7	5	6	9	4	3	9	4	7	11	1	9	4	46	38	.548
Texas A&M	7	5	8	4	6	6	4	8	7	5	5	6	9	4	46	38	.548
Troy	9	3	7	4	4	8	6	6	7	5	4	7	8	5	45	38	.542
Alabama	3	8	7	5	10	3	4	9	6	6	10	2	6	7	46	40	.535
Arizona St.	6	6	4	7	8	6	5	7	9	3	7	5	7	6	46	40	.535
Cincinnati	7	5	7	5	7	7	5	7	7	5	4	7	8	5	45	41	.523
New Mexico	5	7	6	5	7	7	8	5	7	5	6	5	6	7	45	41	.523
Air Force	9	3	6	6	8	5	7	5	5	6	4	7	4	8	43	40	.518
Mississippi	7	5	7	4	7	6	10	3	4	7	3	8	4	8	42	41	.506
Colorado	3	8	10	3	9	5	5	7	8	5	7	6	2	10	44	44	.500
Iowa St.	9	3	7	5	7	7	2	10	7	5	7	5	4	8	43	43	.500
Oklahoma St.	3	8	4	7	8	5	9	4	7	5	4	7	7	6	42	42	.500
Missouri	3	8	4	7	5	7	8	5	5	6	7	5	8	5	40	43	.482
Washington	11	1	8	4	7	6	6	6	1	10	2	9	5	7	40	43	.482
Akron	6	5	4	7	4	8	7	5	6	5	7	6	5	7	39	43	.476
Western Mich.	9	3	5	6	4	8	5	7	1	10	7	4	8	5	39	43	.476
Fla. Atlantic	–	–	4	6	2	9	11	3	9	3	2	9	5	7	33	37	.471
Wake Forest	2	9	6	5	7	6	5	7	4	7	4	7	11	3	39	44	.470
Middle Tenn.	6	5	8	3	4	8	4	8	5	6	4	7	7	6	38	43	.469
UAB	7	4	6	5	5	7	5	7	7	5	5	6	3	9	38	43	.469
Memphis	4	7	5	6	3	9	9	4	8	4	7	5	2	10	38	45	.458
Michigan St.	5	6	7	5	4	8	8	5	5	7	5	6	4	8	38	45	.458
Navy	1	10	0	10	2	10	8	5	10	2	8	4	9	4	38	45	.458
Connecticut	3	8	2	9	6	6	9	3	8	4	5	6	4	8	37	44	.457
Nevada	2	10	3	8	5	7	6	6	5	7	9	3	8	5	38	46	.452
Northwestern	8	4	4	7	3	9	6	7	6	6	7	5	4	8	38	46	.452
Syracuse	6	5	10	3	4	8	6	6	6	6	1	10	4	8	37	46	.446
North Texas	3	8	5	7	8	5	9	4	7	5	2	9	3	9	37	47	.440
UCF	7	4	6	5	7	5	3	9	0	11	8	5	4	8	35	47	.427
Tulsa	5	7	1	10	1	11	8	5	4	8	9	4	8	5	36	50	.419
Louisiana Tech	3	9	7	5	4	8	5	7	6	6	7	4	3	10	35	49	.417
UTEP	8	4	2	9	2	10	2	11	8	4	8	4	5	7	35	49	.417
Houston	3	8	0	11	5	7	7	6	3	8	6	6	10	4	34	50	.405
Rutgers	3	8	2	9	1	11	5	7	4	7	7	5	11	2	33	49	.402
Tulane	6	5	3	9	8	5	5	7	5	6	2	9	4	8	33	49	.402
East Caro.	8	4	6	6	4	8	1	11	2	9	5	6	7	6	33	50	.398
North Carolina	6	5	8	5	3	9	2	10	6	6	5	6	3	9	33	50	.398
San Jose St.	7	5	3	9	6	7	3	8	2	9	3	8	9	4	33	50	.398
Central Mich.	2	9	3	8	4	8	3	9	4	7	6	5	10	4	32	50	.390
Kansas	4	7	3	8	2	10	6	7	4	7	7	5	6	6	32	50	.390
Ball St.	5	6	5	6	6	6	4	8	2	9	4	7	5	7	31	49	.388
Rice	3	8	8	4	4	7	5	7	3	8	1	10	7	6	31	50	.383
Stanford	5	6	9	3	2	9	4	7	4	7	5	6	1	11	30	49	.380
Ohio	7	4	1	10	4	8	2	10	4	7	4	7	9	5	31	51	.378
Arkansas St.	1	10	2	9	6	7	5	7	3	8	6	6	6	6	29	53	.354
UNLV	8	5	4	7	5	7	6	6	2	9	2	9	2	10	29	53	.354
Arizona	5	6	5	6	4	8	2	10	3	8	3	8	6	6	28	52	.350
Illinois	5	6	10	2	5	7	1	11	3	8	2	9	2	10	28	53	.346
Kentucky	2	9	2	9	7	5	4	8	2	9	3	8	8	5	28	53	.346
San Diego St.	3	8	3	8	4	9	6	6	4	7	5	7	3	9	28	54	.341
Kent St.	1	10	6	5	3	9	5	7	5	6	1	10	6	6	27	53	.338
La.-Lafayette	1	10	3	8	3	9	4	8	4	7	6	5	6	6	27	53	.338
New Mexico St.	3	8	5	7	7	5	3	9	5	6	0	12	4	8	27	55	.329
Wyoming	1	10	2	9	2	10	4	8	7	5	4	7	6	6	26	55	.321
Indiana	3	8	5	6	3	9	2	10	3	8	4	7	5	7	25	55	.313
Mississippi St.	8	4	3	8	3	9	2	10	3	8	3	8	3	9	25	56	.309
SMU	3	9	4	7	3	9	0	12	3	8	5	6	6	6	24	57	.296
Utah St.	5	6	4	7	4	7	3	9	3	8	3	8	1	11	23	56	.291
Baylor	2	9	3	8	3	9	3	9	3	8	5	6	4	8	23	57	.288
Florida Int'l	-	-	-	-	5	6	2	10	3	7	5	6	0	12	15	41	.268
La.-Monroe	1	10	2	9	3	9	1	11	5	6	5	6	4	8	21	59	.263
Eastern Mich.	3	8	2	9	3	9	3	9	4	7	4	7	1	11	20	60	.250
Vanderbilt	3	8	2	9	2	10	2	10	2	9	5	6	4	8	20	60	.250
Idaho	5	6	1	10	2	10	3	9	3	9	2	9	4	8	20	61	.247
Temple	4	7	4	7	4	8	1	11	2	9	0	11	1	11	16	64	.200
Army	1	10	3	8	1	11	0	13	2	9	4	7	3	9	14	67	.173
Buffalo	2	9	3	8	1	11	1	11	2	9	1	10	2	10	12	68	.150
Duke	0	11	0	11	2	10	4	8	2	9	1	10	0	12	9	71	.113

BY VICTORIES

Team	Wins
Oklahoma	79
Boise St.	76
Texas	75
Miami (Fla.)	71
LSU	70
Ohio St.	70
Southern California	70
Georgia	69
Louisville	68
Virginia Tech	68
Auburn	66
Florida	65
Michigan	64
TCU	64
Florida St.	62
Tennessee	61
Boston College	60
Nebraska	60
Toledo	60
Wisconsin	60
Oregon	58
Fresno St.	57
West Virginia	57
Texas Tech	56
Hawaii	55
Kansas St.	55
Maryland	55
Clemson	54
Georgia Tech	54
Iowa	54
Notre Dame	54
Oregon St.	54
Utah	54
Marshall	53
Northern Ill.	53
Southern Miss.	53
Arkansas	50
Miami (Ohio)	50
Pittsburgh	50
Purdue	50
South Fla.	50
UCLA	50
Bowling Green	49
BYU	49
North Carolina St.	49
Washington St.	49
Colorado St.	48
Minnesota	48
South Carolina	48
Virginia	48
California	47
Alabama	46
Arizona St.	46
Penn St.	46
Texas A&M	46
Cincinnati	45
New Mexico	45
Troy	45
Colorado	44
Air Force	43
Iowa St.	43
Mississippi	42
Oklahoma St.	42
Missouri	40
Washington	40
Akron	39
Wake Forest	39
Western Mich.	39
UAB	38
Memphis	38
Michigan St.	38
Middle Tenn.	38
Navy	38
Nevada	38
Northwestern	38
Connecticut	37
North Texas	37
Syracuse	37
Tulsa	36
UCF	35
Louisiana Tech	35
UTEP	35
Houston	34
East Caro.	33
Fla. Atlantic	33
North Carolina	33
Rutgers	33
San Jose St.	33
Tulane	33
Central Mich.	32
Kansas	32
Ball St.	31
Ohio	31
Rice	31
Stanford	30
Arkansas St.	29
UNLV	29
Arizona	28
Illinois	28
Kentucky	28
San Diego St.	28
Kent St.	27
La.-Lafayette	27
New Mexico St.	27
Wyoming	26
Indiana	25
Mississippi St.	25
SMU	24
Baylor	23
Utah St.	23
La.-Monroe	21
Eastern Mich.	20
Idaho	20
Vanderbilt	20
Temple	16
Florida Int'l	15
Army	14
Buffalo	12
Duke	9

Records in the 1990s

(1990-91-92-93-94-95-96-97-98-99, Including Bowls and Playoffs; Tie-breaker Began 1996)

BY PERCENTAGE

Team	W-L-T	*Pct.
Florida St.	109-13-1	.890
Nebraska	108-16-1	.868
Marshall	114-25-0	.820
Florida	102-22-1	.820
Tennessee	99-22-2	.813
Penn St.	97-26-0	.789
Michigan	93-26-3	.775
Miami (Fla.)	92-27-0	.773
Texas A&M	94-28-2	.766
Ohio St.	91-29-3	.752
Colorado	87-29-4	.742
Kansas St.	87-30-1	.742
Notre Dame	84-35-2	.702
Washington	82-35-1	.699
Syracuse	82-35-3	.696
BYU	86-39-2	.685
Alabama	83-40-0	.675
Nevada	80-39-0	.672
North Carolina	78-39-1	.665
Virginia Tech	77-39-1	.662
Virginia	78-40-1	.660
Idaho	77-41-0	.653
Toledo	72-38-3	.650
Air Force	78-44-0	.639
Auburn	72-40-3	.639
Georgia	72-43-1	.625
Texas	74-44-2	.625
Colorado St.	74-46-0	.617
Miami (Ohio)	65-40-5	.614
Utah	71-46-0	.607
Arizona	71-46-1	.606
Wisconsin	69-45-4	.602
UCLA	69-46-0	.600
Wyoming	70-47-1	.597
Middle Tenn.	68-46-1	.596
Western Mich.	65-44-2	.595
Clemson	69-47-1	.594
Oregon	70-48-0	.593
UCF	67-46-0	.593
Southern Miss.	67-46-1	.592
East Caro.	67-47-0	.588
Mississippi	67-48-0	.583
Southern California	68-49-4	.579
Fresno St.	68-50-2	.575
Georgia Tech	66-49-1	.573
West Virginia	65-49-2	.569
Bowling Green	61-46-4	.568
North Carolina St.	66-51-1	.564
Mississippi St.	64-50-2	.560
Boise St.	67-53-0	.558
Louisiana Tech	61-48-3	.558
Arizona St.	62-51-0	.549
Oklahoma	61-51-3	.543
San Diego St.	62-52-2	.543
UAB	51-43-2	.542
Texas Tech	62-53-0	.539
Iowa	62-53-2	.538
Michigan St.	62-53-2	.538
Stanford	60-54-2	.526
Louisville	59-54-1	.522
La.-Monroe	58-56-1	.509
Central Mich.	54-53-5	.504
Boston College	57-57-2	.500
Kansas	56-57-1	.496
Arkansas	55-58-2	.487
California	55-59-1	.483
LSU	54-58-1	.482
Rice	52-57-1	.477
Ball St.	52-58-2	.473
Washington St.	53-61-0	.465
TCU	51-61-1	.456
Army	50-60-1	.455
Illinois	50-63-2	.443
Baylor	49-63-1	.438
Utah St.	48-63-1	.433
Purdue	47-64-3	.425
Indiana	47-64-2	.425
Memphis	45-64-1	.414
Hawaii	49-71-2	.410
San Jose St.	44-66-2	.402
Missouri	43-67-3	.394
Cincinnati	43-67-1	.392
South Carolina	42-66-3	.392
Kentucky	44-69-0	.389
New Mexico	45-71-0	.388
Navy	43-69-0	.384
Houston	42-68-1	.383
Northwestern	43-70-1	.382
Oklahoma St.	41-68-3	.379
Akron	40-68-2	.373
North Texas	40-69-2	.369
Tulsa	40-70-1	.365
La.-Lafayette	39-70-1	.359
Minnesota	40-72-0	.357
Maryland	38-72-1	.347
Rutgers	37-72-1	.341
Tulane	38-74-0	.339
Wake Forest	38-74-0	.339
Pittsburgh	37-74-1	.335
Eastern Mich.	35-74-1	.323
Ohio	34-74-3	.320
Vanderbilt	34-76-0	.309
Duke	33-77-1	.302
New Mexico St.	33-77-0	.300
SMU	31-76-3	.295
UNLV	33-79-0	.295
Northern Ill.	32-78-0	.291
Buffalo	30-77-0	.280
Oregon St.	29-81-1	.266
Arkansas St.	28-80-2	.264
Iowa St.	27-80-3	.259
UTEP	28-84-2	.254
Temple	22-88-0	.200
Kent St.	15-94-1	.141

**Ties counted as half won and half lost.*

BY VICTORIES

Team	Wins
Marshall	114
Florida St.	109
Nebraska	108
Florida	102
Tennessee	99
Penn St.	97
Texas A&M	94
Michigan	93
Miami (Fla.)	92
Ohio St.	91
Colorado	87
Kansas St.	87
BYU	86
Notre Dame	84
Alabama	83
Syracuse	82
Washington	82
Nevada	80
Air Force	78
North Carolina	78
Virginia	78
Idaho	77
Virginia Tech	77
Colorado St.	74
Texas	74
Auburn	72
Georgia	72
Toledo	72
Arizona	71
Utah	71
Oregon	70
Wyoming	70
Clemson	69
UCLA	69
Wisconsin	69
Fresno St.	68
Middle Tenn.	68
Southern California	68
Boise St.	67
UCF	67
East Caro.	67
Mississippi	67
Southern Miss.	67
Georgia Tech	66
North Carolina St.	66
Miami (Ohio)	65
West Virginia	65
Western Mich.	65
Mississippi St.	64
Arizona St.	62

Team	Wins
Iowa	62
Michigan St.	62
San Diego St.	62
Texas Tech	62
Bowling Green	61
Louisiana Tech	61
Oklahoma	61
Stanford	60
Louisville	59
La.-Monroe	58
Boston College	57
Kansas	56
Arkansas	55
California	55
Central Mich.	54
LSU	54
Washington St.	53
Ball St.	52
Rice	52
UAB	51
TCU	51
Army	50
Illinois	50
Baylor	49
Hawaii	49
Utah St.	48
Indiana	47
Purdue	47
Memphis	45
New Mexico	45
Kentucky	44
San Jose St.	44

Team	Wins
Cincinnati	43
Missouri	43
Navy	43
Northwestern	43
Houston	42
South Carolina	42
Oklahoma St.	41
Akron	40
Minnesota	40
North Texas	40
Tulsa	40
La.-Lafayette	39
Maryland	38
Tulane	38
Wake Forest	38
Pittsburgh	37
Rutgers	37
Eastern Mich.	35
Ohio	34
Vanderbilt	34
Duke	33
UNLV	33
New Mexico St.	33
Northern Ill.	32
SMU	31
Buffalo	30
Oregon St.	29
Arkansas St.	28
UTEP	28
Iowa St.	27
Temple	22
Kent St.	15

Winningest Teams by Decade

(By Percentage; Bowls and Playoffs Included, Unless Noted)

1980-89

Rank	Team	W-L-T	Pct.†
1.	Nebraska	103-20-0	.837
2.	Miami (Fla.)	98-20-0	.831
3.	BYU	102-26-0	.797
4.	Oklahoma	91-25-2	.780
5.	Clemson	86-25-4	.765
6.	Penn St.	89-27-2	.763
7.	Georgia	88-27-4	.756
8.	Florida St.	87-28-3	.750
	Michigan	89-29-2	.750
10.	Auburn	86-31-1	.733
11.	Alabama	85-32-2	.723
	Arkansas	85-32-2	.723
13.	UCLA	81-30-6	.718
14.	Washington	83-33-1	.714
15.	Fresno St.	80-34-1	.700
16.	Ohio St.	82-35-2	.697
17.	SMU	63-28-1	.690
18.	Southern California	78-35-3	.685
19.	Florida	76-37-3	.668
20.	Arizona St.	73-36-4	.664

1970-79

Rank	Team	W-L-T	Pct.†
1.	Oklahoma	102-13-3	.877
2.	Alabama	103-16-1	.863
3.	Michigan	96-16-3	.848
4.	Tennessee St.	85-17-2	.827
5.	Nebraska	98-20-4	.820
6.	Penn St.	96-22-0	.814
7.	Ohio St.	91-20-3	.811
8.	Notre Dame	91-22-0	.805
9.	Southern California	93-21-5	.803
10.	Texas	88-26-1	.770
11.	Arizona St.	90-28-0	.763
12.	Yale@	67-21-2	.756
13.	San Diego St.	82-26-2	.755
14.	Miami (Ohio)	80-26-2	.750
15.	Central Mich.	80-27-3	.741
16.	Arkansas	79-31-5	.709
17.	Houston	80-33-2	.704
18.	Louisiana Tech	77-34-2	.690
19.	McNeese St.@	75-33-4	.688
20.	Dartmouth@	60-27-3	.683

1960-69

(By Percentage; Bowls and Playoffs Not Included)

Rank	Team	W-L-T	Pct.†
1.	Alabama	85-12-3	.865
2.	Texas	80-18-2	.810
3.	Arkansas	80-19-1	.805
4.	Mississippi	72-20-6	.765
	Southern California	73-23-4	.750
5.	Bowling Green	71-22-2	.758
6.	Dartmouth@	68-22-0	.756
	Ohio St.	67-21-2	.756
8.	Missouri	72-22-6	.750
10.	Penn St.	73-26-0	.737
11.	Memphis	70-25-1	.734
12.	Arizona St.	72-26-1	.732
13.	LSU	70-25-5	.725
	Nebraska	72-27-1	.725
15.	Wyoming	69-26-4	.717
16.	Princeton@	64-26-0	.711
17.	Utah St.	68-29-3	.695
18.	Purdue	64-28-3	.689
19.	Syracuse	68-31-0	.687
20.	Florida	66-30-4	.680
	Miami (Ohio)	66-30-4	.680
	Tennessee	65-29-6	.680

1950-59

Rank	Team	W-L-T	Pct.†
1.	Oklahoma	93-10-2	.895
2.	Mississippi	80-21-5	.778
3.	Michigan St.	70-21-1	.766
4.	Princeton@	67-22-1	.750
5.	Georgia Tech	79-26-6	.739
6.	UCLA	68-26-3	.716
7.	Ohio St.	63-24-5	.712
8.	Tennessee	71-31-4	.692
9.	Penn St.	62-28-4	.681
10.	Maryland	67-31-3	.678
11.	Syracuse	62-29-2	.677
12.	Army	58-27-5	.672
13.	Cincinnati	64-30-7	.668
14.	Notre Dame	64-31-4	.667
15.	Clemson	64-32-5	.658
16.	Wisconsin	57-28-7	.658
17.	Colorado	62-33-6	.644
18.	Duke	62-33-7	.642
19.	Navy	55-30-8	.634
20.	Yale@	54-30-6	.633

†Ties computed as half won and half lost. @Now a member of the FCS.

National Poll Rankings

National Champion Major Selectors (1869 to Present)

The criteria for being included in this historical list of poll selectors is that the poll be national in scope, either through distribution in newspaper, television, radio and/or computer online. The list includes both former selectors, who were instrumental in the sport of college football, and selectors presently among the Bowl Championship Series (BCS) selectors.

Selector	Selection Format	Active Seasons First	Last	Total	Predated Seasons	Total Rankings
Caspar Whitney	Math	1905	1907	3		3
Frank Dickinson	Math	1926	1940	15	1924-25	17
Deke Houlgate	Math	1927	1958	32	1885-1926	72
Dunkel	Math	1929	2006	78		78
William Boand	Math	1930	1960	31	1919-29	42
Paul Williamson	Math	1932	1963	32		32
Parke Davis	Research	1933	1933	1	1869-1932	65
Edward Litkenhous	Math	1934	1984	51		51
Richard Poling	Math	1935	1984	50	1924-34	61
Associated Press	Poll	1936	2006	71		71
Helms Athletic Foundation	Poll	1941	1982	42	1883-1940	100
Harry DeVold	Math	1945	2006	62	1939-44	68
United Press International	Poll	1950	1995	44		44
International News Service	Poll	1952	1957	6		6
Football Writers Association	Poll	1954	2006	53		53
Football News	Poll	1958	2002	45		45
National Football Foundation	Poll	1959	2006	44		44
Herman Matthews	Math	1966	2006	41		41
David Rothman (FACT)	Math	1968	2006	39		39
Richard Billingsley*	Math	1970	2006	37	1869-70, 1872-1969	137

Selector	Selection Format	Active Seasons First	Last	Total	Predated Seasons	Total Rankings
Sporting News	Poll	1975	2006	32		32
Jeff Sagarin*	Math	1978	2006	29	1919-77	88
New York Times	Math	1979	2004	26		26
National Championship Foundation	Poll	1980	2000	21	1869-70, 1872-1979	131
College Football Researchers Association	Poll	1982	1992	11	1919-81	75
USA Today/CNN	Poll	1982	1996	15		15
Steve Eck	Math	1983	2005	22		22
Clyde Berryman	Math	1990	2006	17	1940-89	67
UPI/NFF	Poll	1991	1992	2		2
Wes Colley Matrix*	Math	1992	2006	15		15
Peter Wolfe*	Math	1992	2006	15		15
USA Today/National Football Foundation	Poll	1993	1994	2		2
Bob Alderson	Math	1994	1998	5		5
Kenneth Massey*	Math	1995	2006	12		12
USA Today/ESPN*	Poll	1997	2006	10		10
Anderson/Hester (Seattle Times)*	Math	1997	2006	10		10
Harris Interactive*	Poll	2005	2006	2		2

**Poll utilized in Bowl Championship Series Rankings for 2006.*

POLL SYSTEMS HISTORY

(Listed alphabetically)

Alderson System (1994-98), a mathematical rating system based strictly on a point value system reflecting competition and won-lost record. Developed by Bob Alderson of Muldrow, Oklahoma.

Anderson & Hester (1997-present), a mathematical rating system developed by Jeff Anderson and Chris Hester. Published weekly in The Seattle Times since 1993. Member of 2006 BCS.

Associated Press (1936-present), the first major nationwide poll for ranking college football teams was voted on by sportswriters and broadcasters. It continues to this day and is probably the most well-known and widely circulated among all of history's polls. The Associated Press annual national champions were awarded the Williams Trophy and the Reverend J. Hugh O'Donnell Trophy. In 1947, Notre Dame retired the Williams Trophy (named after Henry L. Williams, Minnesota coach, and sponsored by the M Club of Minnesota). In 1956, Oklahoma retired the O'Donnell Trophy (named for Notre Dame's president and sponsored by Notre Dame alumni). Beginning with the 1957 season, the award was known as the AP Trophy, and since 1983, has been known as the Paul "Bear" Bryant Trophy.

Berryman (QPRS) (1990-present), a mathematical rating system based on a quality point rating formula developed by Clyde P. Berryman. It takes into account a team's schedule strength, won-lost record, points scored and points allowed. Predated national champions from 1940-89.

Billingsley Report (1970-present), a mathematically based power rating system developed by Richard Billingsley of Hugo, Oklahoma. The main feature of his system is the inclusion of a unique rule for head-to-head competition, with the overall system consisting of a balanced approach to wins, losses, strength of schedule, and home-field advantage. A slight weight is given to most recent performance. The 2004 publication represents an updated list of champions based on his 'no margin of victory formula,' and supercedes any previous reports. Member of 2006 BCS.

Boand System (1930-60), known as the Azzi Ratem System developed by William Boand of Tucson, Arizona. He moved to Chicago in 1932. Appeared in many newspapers and Illustrated Football Annual (1932-42), and weekly in Football News (1942-44, 1951-60). Predated national champions from 1919-29.

Caspar Whitney (1905-07), one of the founders of the first all-American Football Team. Also selected national polls for Outing magazine.

College Football Researchers Association (1982-92), founded by Anthony Cusher of Reeder, North Dakota, and Robert Kirlin of Spokane, Washington. Announced its champion in its monthly bulletin and No. 1 team determined by top-10 vote of membership on a point system. Predated national champions from 1919-81, conducted on a poll by Harry Carson Frye.

Colley Matrix (1992-present), a mathematically based power rating developed by Wes Colley of Virginia. His work is published in the Atlanta Journal-Constitution. Colley is a graduate of Princeton University with a doctorate in astrophysical sciences. Member of 2006 BCS.

DeVold System (1945-present), a mathematical rating system developed by Harry DeVold from Minneapolis, Minnesota, a former football player at Cornell. He eventually settled in the Detroit, Michigan, area and worked in the real estate business. The ratings have appeared in The Football News since 1962. Predated national champions from 1939-44.

Dickinson System (1926-40), a mathematical point system devised by Frank Dickinson, a professor of economics at Illinois. The annual Dickinson ratings were emblematic of the national championship and the basis for awarding the Rissman National Trophy and the Knute K. Rockne Intercollegiate Memorial Trophy. Notre Dame gained permanent possession of the Rissman Trophy (named for Jack F. Rissman, a Chicago clothing manufacturer) after its third victory in 1930. Minnesota retired the Rockne Trophy (named in honor of the famous Notre Dame coach) after winning it for a third time in 1940.

Dunkel System (1929-present), a power index system devised by Dick Dunkel, Sr., Founder/Owner (1929-75); by Dick Dunkel Jr., Owner (1975-02); and by Bob Dunkel, Co-Owner (2002-present), Richard H. Dunkel, Jr., Co-Owner (2002-present) and John Duck, Executive Producer, of the Daytona (Fla.) Beach News-Journal.

Eck Ratings System (1983-05), a mathematical point system developed by Steve Eck, an aerospace worker with a master's degree from UCLA. The factors in the poll are game outcome, strength of opponent and location of game.

Football News (1958-02), weekly poll of its staff writers has named a national champion since 1958.

Football Writers Association of America (1954-present), the No. 1 team of the year is determined by a five-person panel representing the nation's football writers. The national championship team named receives the Grantland Rice Award.

Harris Interactive (2005-present), a panel of former players, coaches, administrators and current and former media, who committed to ranking college teams each week. Panelists were randomly selected from among more than 300 nominations submitted by FBS conference offices and Notre Dame. The panel has been designed to be a statistically valid representation of all 11 FBS conferences and independent institutions. Member of 2006 BCS.

Helms Athletic Foundation (1941-82), originally known by this name from 1936-69 and established by the founding sponsor, Paul H. Helms, Los Angeles sportsman and philanthropist. After Helms' death in 1957, United Savings & Loan Association became its benefactor during 1970-72. A merger of United Savings and Citizen Savings was completed in 1973, and the Athletic Foundation became known as Citizens Savings Athletic Foundation. In 1982, First Interstate Bank assumed sponsorship for its final rankings. In 1941, Bill Schroeder, managing director of the Helms Athletic Foundation, retroactively selected the national football champions for the period beginning in 1883 (the first year of a scoring system) through 1940. Thereafter, Schroeder, who died in 1988, then chose, with the assistance of a Hall Board, the annual national champion after the bowl games.

Houlgate System (1927-58), a mathematical rating system developed by Deke Houlgate of Los Angeles, California. His ratings were syndicated in newspapers and published in Illustrated Football and the Football Thesaurus (1946-58).

International News Service (1952-57), a poll conducted for six years by members of the International News Service (INS) before its merger with United Press in 1958.

Litkenhous (1934-84), a difference-by-score formula developed by Edward E. Litkenhous, a professor of chemical engineering at Vanderbilt, and his brother, Frank.

Massey College Football Ratings (1995-present), a mathematical rating system developed by Kenneth Massey, a graduate student at Virginia Tech in mathematics. His ratings account for homefield advantage. Member of 2006 BCS.

Matthews Grid Ratings (1966-present), a mathematical rating system developed by college mathematics professor Herman Matthews of Middlesboro, Kentucky. Has appeared in Scripps-Howard newspapers and The Football News.

National Championship Foundation (1980-00), established by Mike Riter of Hudson, New York. Issued annual report. Predated national champions from 1869-1979, with the exception of 1871.

National Football Foundation (1959-present), the National Football Foundation and Hall of Fame named its first national champion in 1959. Headquartered in Morristown, New Jersey, the present National Football Foundation was established in 1947 to promote amateur athletics in America. The national champion was awarded the MacArthur Bowl from 1959-90. In 1991 and 1992, the NFF/HOF joined with UPI to award the MacArthur Bowl, and in 1993, the NFF/HOF joined with USA Today to award the MacArthur Bowl.

New York Times (1979-04), a mathematical poll that combined the voting of a panel of sportswriters.

Parke Davis (1933), a noted college football historian and former Princeton lineman, Parke H. Davis went back and named the championship teams from 1869 through the 1932 season. He also named a national champion at the conclusion of the 1933 season. Interestingly, the years 1869-75 were identified by Davis as the Pioneer Period; the years 1876-93 were called the Period of the American Intercollegiate Football Association, and the years 1894-1933 were referred to as the Period of Rules Committees and Conferences. He also coached at Wisconsin, Amherst and Lafayette.

Poling System (1935-84), a mathematical rating system for college football teams developed by Richard Poling from Mansfield, Ohio, a former football player at Ohio Wesleyan. Poling's football ratings were published annually in the Football Review Supplement and in various newspapers. Predated national champions from 1924-34.

Rothman (FACT) (1968-present), a computerized mathematical ranking system developed by David Rothman of Hawthorne, California. FACT is the Foundation for the Analysis of Competitions and Tournaments, which began selecting a national champion in 1968. Rothman is a semiretired defense and aerospace statistician and was cochair of the Committee on Statistics in Sports and Competition of the American Statistical Association in the 1970s.

Sagarin Ratings (1978-present), a mathematical rating system developed by Jeff Sagarin of Bloomington, Indiana, a 1970 MIT mathematics graduate. Runs annually in USA Today newspaper. Predated national champions from 1919-77. Member of 2006 BCS.

Sporting News (1975-present), voted on annually by the staff of this St. Louis-based nationally circulated sports publication.

United Press International (1950-90, 1993-95), in 1950, the United Press news service began its poll of football coaches (replaced as coaches' poll after 1990 season). When the United Press merged with the International News Service in 1958, it became known as United Press International. The weekly UPI rankings were featured in newspapers and on radio and television nationwide. UPI and the National Football Foundation formed a coalition for 1991 and 1992 to name the MacArthur Bowl national champion. Returned to single poll in 1993-95.

USA Today/Cable News Network and ESPN (1982-96; 1997-present), introduced a weekly poll of sportswriters in 1982 and ranked the top 25 teams in the nation with a point system. The poll results were featured in USA Today, a national newspaper, and on the Cable News Network, a national cable television network. Took over as the coaches' poll in 1991. USA Today also formed a coalition with the National Football Foundation in 1993 to name the MacArthur Bowl national champion. Combined with ESPN in 1997 to distribute the coaches' poll nationally. Member of 2006 BCS.

Williamson System (1932-63), a power rating system chosen by Paul Williamson of New Orleans, Louisiana, a geologist and member of the Sugar Bowl committee.

Wolfe (1992-present), a mathematically based power rating matrix developed by Peter Wolfe and Ross Baker. Member of 2006 BCS.

Thanks from the NCAA Statistics Service to Robert A. Rosiek of Dearborn, Michigan, who researched much of the former polls' history, and to Tex Noel, who provided information about Parke H. Davis.

National Poll Champions

Over the last 137 years, there have been more than 30 selectors of national champions using polls, historical research and mathematical rating systems. Beginning in 1936, The Associated Press began the best-known and most widely circulated poll of sportswriters and broadcasters. Before 1936, national champions were determined by historical research and retroactive ratings and polls.

*Note: * indicates selectors that chose multiple schools. The national champion was selected before bowl games as follows: AP (1936-64 and 1966-67); UP-UPI (1950-73); FWAA (1954); NFF-HOF (1959-70). In all other latter-day polls, champions were selected after bowl games. The Sagarin Rating includes his actual rating that combines scores and pure won-lost records. Sagarin also now provides an ELO-Chess rating that uses only pure won-lost records, and is the one utilized in the Bowl Championship Series (BCS) rankings. The Billingsley Ratings were converted in 2003 to conform to his "no margin of victory" formula to match the requirements of the BCS.*

1869
Princeton: Billingsley, National Championship Foundation, Parke Davis*
Rutgers: Parke Davis*

1870
Princeton: Billingsley, National Championship Foundation, Parke Davis

1871
No national champions selected.

1872
Princeton: Billingsley, National Championship Foundation, Parke Davis*
Yale: Parke Davis*

1873
Princeton: Billingsley, National Championship Foundation, Parke Davis

1874
Harvard: Parke Davis*
Princeton: Billingsley, Parke Davis*
Yale: National Championship Foundation, Parke Davis*

1875
Colgate: Parke Davis*
Harvard: National Championship Foundation, Parke Davis*
Princeton: Billingsley, Parke Davis*

1876
Yale: Billingsley, National Championship Foundation, Parke Davis

1877
Princeton: Billingsley, Parke Davis*
Yale: National Championship Foundation, Parke Davis*

1878
Princeton: Billingsley, National Championship Foundation, Parke Davis

1879
Princeton: Billingsley, National Championship Foundation, Parke Davis*
Yale: Parke Davis*

1880
Princeton: National Championship Foundation*, Parke Davis*
Yale: Billingsley, National Championship Foundation*, Parke Davis*

1881
Princeton: Billingsley, Parke Davis*
Yale: National Championship Foundation, Parke Davis*

1882
Yale: Billingsley, National Championship Foundation, Parke Davis

1883
Yale: Billingsley, Helms, National Championship Foundation, Parke Davis

1884
Princeton: Billingsley, Parke Davis*
Yale: Helms, National Championship Foundation, Parke Davis*

1885
Princeton: Billingsley, Helms, Houlgate, National Championship Foundation, Parke Davis

1886
Princeton: Billingsley, Parke Davis*
Yale: Helms, National Championship Foundation, Parke Davis*

1887
Yale: Billingsley, Helms, Houlgate, National Championship Foundation, Parke Davis

1888
Yale: Billingsley, Helms, Houlgate, National Championship Foundation, Parke Davis

1889
Princeton: Billingsley, Helms, Houlgate, National Championship Foundation, Parke Davis

1890
Harvard: Billingsley, Helms, Houlgate, National Championship Foundation, Parke Davis

1891
Yale: Billingsley, Helms, Houlgate, National Championship Foundation, Parke Davis

1892
Yale: Billingsley, Helms, Houlgate, National Championship Foundation, Parke Davis

1893
Princeton: Billingsley, Helms, Houlgate, National Championship Foundation
Yale: Parke Davis

1894
Penn: Parke Davis*
Princeton: Houlgate
Yale: Billingsley, Helms, National Championship Foundation, Parke Davis*

1895
Penn: Billingsley, Helms, Houlgate, National Championship Foundation, Parke Davis*
Yale: Parke Davis*

1896
Lafayette: National Championship Foundation*, Parke Davis*
Princeton: Billingsley, Helms, Houlgate, National Championship Foundation*, Parke Davis*

1897
Penn: Billingsley, Helms, Houlgate, National Championship Foundation, Parke Davis*
Yale: Parke Davis*

1898
Harvard: Billingsley, Helms, Houlgate, National Championship Foundation
Princeton: Parke Davis

1899
Harvard: Helms, Houlgate, National Championship Foundation
Princeton: Billingsley, Parke Davis

1900
Yale: Billingsley, Helms, Houlgate, National Championship Foundation, Parke Davis

1901
Harvard: Billingsley
Michigan: Helms, Houlgate, National Championship Foundation
Yale: Parke Davis

1902
Michigan: Billingsley, Helms, Houlgate, National Championship Foundation, Parke Davis*
Yale: Parke Davis*

1903
Michigan: National Championship Foundation*
Princeton: Billingsley, Helms, Houlgate, National Championship Foundation*, Parke Davis

1904
Michigan: National Championship Foundation*
Minnesota: Billingsley
Penn: Helms, Houlgate, National Championship Foundation*, Parke Davis

1905
Chicago: Billingsley, Helms, Houlgate, National Championship Foundation
Yale: Parke Davis, Whitney

1906
Princeton: Helms, National Championship Foundation
Yale: Billingsley, Parke Davis, Whitney

1907
Yale: Billingsley, Helms, Houlgate, National Championship Foundation, Parke Davis, Whitney

1908
Harvard: Billingsley
LSU: National Championship Foundation*
Penn: Helms, Houlgate, National Championship Foundation*, Parke Davis

1909
Yale: Billingsley, Helms, Houlgate, National Championship Foundation, Parke Davis

1910
Harvard: Billingsley, Helms, Houlgate, National Championship Foundation*
Pittsburgh: National Championship Foundation*

1911
Penn St.: National Championship Foundation*
Princeton: Billingsley, Helms, Houlgate, National Championship Foundation*, Parke Davis

1912
Harvard: Billingsley, Helms, Houlgate, National Championship Foundation*, Parke Davis
Penn St.: National Championship Foundation*

1913
Auburn: Billingsley
Chicago: Parke Davis*
Harvard: Helms, Houlgate, National Championship Foundation, Parke Davis*

1914
Army: Helms, Houlgate, National Championship Foundation, Parke Davis*
Illinois: Parke Davis*
Texas: Billingsley

1915
Cornell: Helms, Houlgate, National Championship Foundation, Parke Davis*
Oklahoma: Billingsley
Pittsburgh: Parke Davis*

1916
Army: Parke Davis*
Pittsburgh: Billingsley, Helms, Houlgate, National Championship Foundation, Parke Davis*

1917
Georgia Tech: Billingsley, Helms, Houlgate, National Championship Foundation

1918
Michigan: Billingsley, National Championship Foundation*
Pittsburgh: Helms, Houlgate, National Championship Foundation*

1919
Harvard: Football Research*, Helms, Houlgate, National Championship Foundation*, Parke Davis*
Illinois: Boand, Football Research*, Parke Davis*, Sagarin (ELO-Chess)*
Notre Dame: National Championship Foundation*, Parke Davis*
Texas A&M: Billingsley, National Championship Foundation*
Centre (Ky.): Sagarin*

1920
California: Football Research, Helms, Houlgate, National Championship Foundation, Sagarin, Sagarin (ELO-Chess)
Harvard: Boand*
Notre Dame: Billingsley, Parke Davis*
Princeton: Boand*, Parke Davis*

1921
California: Billingsley, Boand*, Football Research, Sagarin, Sagarin (ELO-Chess)
Cornell: Helms, Houlgate, National Championship Foundation, Parke Davis*
Iowa: Parke Davis*
Lafayette: Boand*, Parke Davis*
Wash. & Jeff.: Boand*

1922
California: Billingsley, Houlgate, National Championship Foundation*, Sagarin*
Cornell: Helms, Parke Davis*
Princeton: Boand, Football Research, National Championship Foundation*, Parke Davis*, Sagarin (ELO-Chess)*

1923
California: Houlgate
Cornell: Sagarin*
Illinois: Boand, Football Research, Helms, National Championship Foundation*, Parke Davis, Sagarin (ELO-Chess)*
Michigan: Billingsley, National Championship Foundation*

1924
Notre Dame: Billingsley, Boand, Dickinson, Football Research, Helms, Houlgate, National Championship Foundation, Poling, Sagarin, Sagarin (ELO-Chess)
Penn: Parke Davis

1925
Alabama: Billingsley, Boand, Football Research, Helms, Houlgate, National Championship Foundation, Poling, Sagarin (ELO-Chess)*
Dartmouth: Dickinson, Parke Davis
Michigan: Sagarin*

1926
Alabama: Billingsley, Football Research, Helms*, National Championship Foundation*, Poling
Lafayette: Parke Davis
Michigan: Sagarin*
Navy: Boand, Houlgate
Stanford: Dickinson, Helms*, National Championship Foundation*, Sagarin (ELO-Chess)*

1927
Georgia: Boand, Poling
Illinois: Billingsley, Dickinson, Helms, National Championship Foundation, Parke Davis
Notre Dame: Houlgate
Texas A&M: Sagarin, Sagarin (ELO-Chess)
Yale: Football Research

1928
Detroit: Parke Davis*
Georgia Tech: Billingsley, Boand, Football Research, Helms, Houlgate, National Championship Foundation, Parke Davis*, Poling, Sagarin (ELO-Chess)*
Southern California: Dickinson, Sagarin*

1929
Notre Dame: Billingsley, Boand, Dickinson, Dunkel, Football Research, Helms, National Championship Foundation, Poling, Sagarin (ELO-Chess)*
Pittsburgh: Parke Davis
Southern California: Houlgate, Sagarin*

1930
Alabama: Football Research, Parke Davis*, Sagarin, Sagarin (ELO-Chess)
Notre Dame: Billingsley, Boand, Dickinson, Dunkel, Helms, Houlgate, National Championship Foundation, Parke Davis*, Poling

1931
Pittsburgh: Parke Davis*
Purdue: Parke Davis*
Southern California: Billingsley, Boand, Dickinson, Dunkel, Helms, Houlgate, Football Research, National Championship Foundation, Poling, Sagarin, Sagarin (ELO-Chess), Williamson

1932
Colgate: Parke Davis*
Michigan: Dickinson, Parke Davis*, Sagarin (ELO-Chess)*
Southern California: Billingsley, Boand, Dunkel, Football Research, Helms, Houlgate, National Championship Foundation, Parke Davis*, Poling, Sagarin*, Williamson

1933
Michigan: Billingsley, Boand, Dickinson, Helms, Houlgate, Football Research, National Championship Foundation, Parke Davis*, Poling, Sagarin, Sagarin (ELO-Chess)
Ohio St.: Dunkel
Princeton: Parke Davis*
Southern California: Williamson

1934
Alabama: Dunkel, Houlgate, Poling, Williamson
Minnesota: Billingsley, Boand, Dickinson, Football Research, Helms, Litkenhous, National Championship Foundation, Sagarin, Sagarin (ELO-Chess)

1935
LSU: Williamson*
Minnesota: Billingsley, Boand, Football Research, Helms, Litkenhous, National Championship Foundation, Poling
Princeton: Dunkel
SMU: Dickinson, Houlgate, Sagarin, Sagarin (ELO-Chess)
TCU: Williamson*

1936
LSU: Sagarin, Sagarin (ELO-Chess), Williamson
Minnesota: AP, Billingsley, Dickinson, Dunkel, Helms, Litkenhous, National Championship Foundation, Poling
Pittsburgh: Boand, Football Research, Houlgate

1937
California: Dunkel, Helms
Pittsburgh: AP, Billingsley, Boand, Dickinson, Football Research, Houlgate, Litkenhous, National Championship Foundation, Poling, Sagarin, Sagarin (ELO-Chess), Williamson

1938
Notre Dame: Dickinson
Tennessee: Billingsley, Boand, Dunkel, Football Research, Houlgate, Litkenhous, Poling, Sagarin, Sagarin (ELO-Chess)
TCU: AP, Helms, National Championship Foundation, Williamson

1939
Cornell: Litkenhous, Sagarin*
Southern California: Dickinson
Texas A&M: AP, Billingsley, Boand, DeVold, Dunkel, Football Research, Helms, Houlgate, National Championship Foundation, Poling, Sagarin (ELO-Chess)*, Williamson

1940
Minnesota: AP, Berryman, Boand, DeVold, Dickinson, Football Research, Houlgate, Litkenhous, National Championship Foundation, Sagarin, Sagarin (ELO-Chess)
Stanford: Billingsley, Helms, Poling
Tennessee: Dunkel, Williamson

1941
Alabama: Houlgate
Minnesota: AP, Billingsley, Boand, DeVold, Dunkel, Football Research, Helms, Litkenhous, National Championship Foundation, Poling, Sagarin, Sagarin (ELO-Chess)
Texas: Berryman, Williamson

1942
Georgia: Berryman, Billingsley, DeVold, Houlgate, Litkenhous, Poling, Sagarin, Sagarin (ELO-Chess), Williamson
Ohio St.: AP, Boand, Dunkel, Football Research, National Championship Foundation
Wisconsin: Helms

1943
Notre Dame: AP, Berryman, Billingsley, Boand, DeVold, Dunkel, Football Research, Helms, Houlgate, Litkenhous, National Championship Foundation, Poling, Sagarin, Sagarin (ELO-Chess), Williamson

1944
Army: AP, Berryman, Billingsley, Boand, DeVold, Dunkel, Football Research, Helms, Houlgate, Litkenhous, National Championship Foundation*, Poling, Sagarin*, Williamson
Ohio St.: National Championship Foundation*, Sagarin (ELO-Chess)*

1945
Alabama: National Championship Foundation*
Army: AP, Berryman, Billingsley, Boand, DeVold, Dunkel, Football Research, Helms, Houlgate, Litkenhous, National Championship Foundation*, Poling, Sagarin, Sagarin (ELO-Chess), Williamson

1946
Army: Billingsley, Boand*, Football Research, Helms*, Houlgate, Poling*
Georgia: Williamson
Notre Dame: AP, Berryman, Boand*, DeVold, Dunkel, Helms*, Litkenhous, National Championship Foundation, Poling*, Sagarin, Sagarin (ELO-Chess)

1947
Michigan: Berryman, Billingsley, Boand, DeVold, Dunkel, Football Research, Helms*, Houlgate, Litkenhous, National Championship Foundation, Poling, Sagarin, Sagarin (ELO-Chess)
Notre Dame: AP, Helms*, Williamson

1948
Michigan: AP, Berryman, Billingsley, Boand, DeVold, Dunkel, Football Research, Helms, Houlgate, Litkenhous, National Championship Foundation, Poling, Sagarin, Sagarin (ELO-Chess), Williamson

1949
Notre Dame: AP, Berryman, Billingsley, Boand, DeVold, Dunkel, Helms, Houlgate, Litkenhous, National Championship Foundation, Poling, Sagarin, Sagarin (ELO-Chess), Williamson
Oklahoma: Football Research

1950
Kentucky: Sagarin*
Oklahoma: AP, Berryman, Helms, Litkenhous, UPI, Williamson
Princeton: Boand, Poling
Tennessee: Billingsley, DeVold, Dunkel, Football Research, National Championship Foundation, Sagarin (ELO-Chess)*

1951
Georgia Tech: Berryman, Boand*
Illinois: Boand*
Maryland: DeVold, Dunkel, Football Research, National Championship Foundation, Sagarin, Sagarin (ELO-Chess)
Michigan St.: Billingsley, Helms, Poling
Tennessee: AP, Litkenhous, UPI, Williamson

1952
Georgia Tech: Berryman, Billingsley, INS, Poling, Sagarin (ELO-Chess)*
Michigan St.: AP, Boand, DeVold, Dunkel, Football Research, Helms, Litkenhous, National Championship Foundation, Sagarin*, UPI, Williamson

1953
Maryland: AP, INS, UPI
Notre Dame: Billingsley, Boand, DeVold, Dunkel, Helms, Litkenhous, National Championship Foundation, Poling, Sagarin, Sagarin (ELO-Chess), Williamson
Oklahoma: Berryman, Football Research

1954
Ohio St.: AP, Berryman, Billingsley, Boand, DeVold, Football Research*, Helms*, INS, National Championship Foundation*, Poling, Sagarin, Sagarin (ELO-Chess), Williamson
UCLA: Dunkel, Football Research*, FW, Helms*, Litkenhous, National Championship Foundation*, UPI

1955
Michigan St.: Boand
Oklahoma: AP, Berryman, Billingsley, DeVold, Dunkel, Football Research, FW, Helms, INS, Litkenhous, National Championship Foundation, Poling, Sagarin, Sagarin (ELO-Chess), UPI, Williamson

1956
Georgia Tech: Berryman, Sagarin*
Iowa: Football Research
Oklahoma: AP, Billingsley, Boand, DeVold, Dunkel, FW, Helms, INS, Litkenhous, National Championship Foundation, Sagarin, UPI, Williamson
Tennessee: Sagarin (ELO-Chess)*

1957
Auburn: AP, Billingsley, Football Research, Helms, National Championship Foundation, Poling, Sagarin, Sagarin (ELO-Chess), Williamson
Michigan St.: Dunkel
Ohio St.: Boand, DeVold, FW, INS, Litkenhous, UPI
Oklahoma: Berryman

1958
Iowa: FW
LSU: AP, Berryman, Billingsley, Boand, DeVold, Dunkel, FB News, Football Research, Helms, Litkenhous, National Championship Foundation, Poling, Sagarin, Sagarin (ELO-Chess), UPI, Williamson

1959
Mississippi: Berryman, Dunkel, Sagarin*
Syracuse: AP, Billingsley, Boand, DeVold, FB News, Football Research, FW, Helms, Litkenhous, National Championship Foundation, NFF, Poling, Sagarin (ELO-Chess)*, UPI, Williamson

1960
Iowa: Berryman, Boand, Litkenhous, Sagarin, Sagarin (ELO-Chess)
Minnesota: AP, FB News, NFF, UPI
Mississippi: Billingsley, DeVold, Dunkel, Football Research, FW, National Championship Foundation, Williamson
Missouri: Poling
Washington: Helms

1961
Alabama: AP, Berryman, Billingsley, DeVold, Dunkel, FB News, Football Research, Helms, Litkenhous, National Championship Foundation, NFF, Sagarin, Sagarin (ELO-Chess), UPI, Williamson
Ohio St.: FW, Poling

1962
LSU: Berryman*
Southern California: AP, Berryman*, DeVold, Dunkel, FB News, Football Research, FW, Helms, National Championship Foundation, NFF, Poling, UPI, Williamson
Mississippi: Billingsley, Litkenhous, Sagarin, Sagarin (ELO-Chess)

1963
Texas: AP, Berryman, Billingsley, DeVold, Dunkel, FB News, Football Research, FW, Helms, Litkenhous, National Championship Foundation, NFF, Poling, Sagarin, Sagarin (ELO-Chess), UPI, Williamson

1964
Alabama: AP, Berryman, Litkenhous, UPI
Arkansas: Billingsley, Football Research, FW, Helms, National Championship Foundation, Poling, Sagarin, Sagarin (ELO-Chess)
Michigan: Dunkel
Notre Dame: DeVold, FB News, NFF

1965
Alabama: AP, Football Research, FW*, National Championship Foundation
Michigan St.: Berryman, Billingsley, DeVold, Dunkel, FB News, FW*, Helms, Litkenhous, NFF, Poling, Sagarin, Sagarin (ELO-Chess), UPI

1966
Alabama: Berryman, Sagarin (ELO-Chess)*
Michigan St.: Football Research, Helms*, NFF*, Poling*
Notre Dame: AP, Billingsley, DeVold, Dunkel, FB News, FW, Helms*, Litkenhous, Matthews, National Championship Foundation, NFF*, Poling*, Sagarin*, UPI

1967
Notre Dame: Dunkel
Oklahoma: Poling
Southern California: AP, Berryman, Billingsley, DeVold, FB News, Football Research, FW, Helms, Matthews, National Championship Foundation, NFF, Sagarin, Sagarin (ELO-Chess), UPI
Tennessee: Litkenhous

1968
Georgia: Litkenhous
Ohio St.: AP, Berryman, Billingsley, Dunkel, FACT, FB News, Football Research, FW, Helms, National Championship Foundation, NFF, Poling, Sagarin (ELO-Chess)*, UPI
Texas: DeVold, Matthews, Sagarin*

1969
Ohio St.: Matthews
Penn St.: FACT*, Sagarin (ELO-Chess)*
Texas: AP, Berryman, Billingsley, DeVold, Dunkel, FACT*, FB News, Football Research, FW, Helms, Litkenhous, National Championship Foundation, NFF, Poling, Sagarin*, UPI

1970
Arizona St.: Poling
Nebraska: AP, Billingsley, DeVold, Dunkel, FACT*, FB News, Football Research, FW, Helms, National Championship Foundation, Sagarin (ELO-Chess)*
Notre Dame: FACT*, Matthews, Sagarin*
Ohio St.: NFF*
Texas: Berryman, FACT*, Litkenhous, NFF*, UPI

1971
Nebraska: AP, Berryman, Billingsley, DeVold, Dunkel, FACT, FB News, Football Research, FW, Helms, Litkenhous, Matthews, National Championship Foundation, NFF, Poling, Sagarin, Sagarin (ELO-Chess), UPI

1972
Southern California: AP, Berryman, Billingsley, DeVold, Dunkel, FACT, FB News, Football Research, FW, Helms, Litkenhous, Matthews, National Championship Foundation, NFF, Poling, Sagarin, Sagarin (ELO-Chess), UPI

1973
Alabama: Berryman, UPI
Michigan: National Championship Foundation*, Poling*
Notre Dame: AP, Billingsley, FB News, FW, Helms, National Championship Foundation*, NFF
Ohio St.: FACT, National Championship Foundation*, Poling*, Sagarin (ELO-Chess)*
Oklahoma: DeVold, Dunkel, Football Research, Sagarin*

1974
Ohio St.: Matthews
Oklahoma: AP, Berryman, Billingsley, DeVold, Dunkel, FACT, FB News, Football Research, Helms*, Litkenhous, National Championship Foundation*, Poling, Sagarin, Sagarin (ELO-Chess)
Southern California: FW, Helms*, National Championship Foundation*, NFF, UPI

1975
Alabama: Matthews*
Arizona St.: National Championship Foundation*, Sporting News
Ohio St.: Berryman, FACT*, Helms*, Matthews*, Poling
Oklahoma: AP, Billingsley, DeVold, Dunkel, FACT*, FB News, Football Research, FW, Helms*, National Championship Foundation*, NFF, Sagarin, Sagarin (ELO-Chess), UPI

1976
Pittsburgh: AP, FACT, FB News, FW, Helms, National Championship Foundation, NFF, Poling, Sagarin, Sagarin (ELO-Chess), Sporting News, UPI
Southern California: Berryman, Billingsley, DeVold, Dunkel, Football Research, Matthews

1977
Alabama: Football Research*
Arkansas: FACT*
Notre Dame: AP, Billingsley, DeVold, Dunkel, FACT*, FB News, Football Research*, FW, Helms, Matthews, National Championship Foundation, NFF, Poling, Sagarin*, Sporting News, UPI
Texas: Berryman, FACT*, Sagarin (ELO-Chess)*

1978
Alabama: AP, FACT*, Football Research, FW, Helms*, National Championship Foundation*, NFF
Oklahoma: DeVold, Dunkel, FACT*, Helms*, Litkenhous, Matthews, Poling, Sagarin*
Southern California: Berryman, Billingsley, FACT*, FB News, Helms*, National Championship Foundation*, Sagarin (ELO-Chess)*, Sporting News, UPI

1979
Alabama: AP, Berryman, Billingsley, DeVold, Dunkel, FACT, FB News, FW, Helms, Matthews, National Championship Foundation, NFF, NY Times, Poling, Sagarin, Sagarin (ELO-Chess), Sporting News, UPI
Southern California: Football Research

1980
Florida St.: FACT*
Georgia: AP, Berryman, Billingsley, FACT*, FB News, FW, Helms, National Championship Foundation, NFF, Poling, Sagarin (ELO-Chess)*, Sporting News, UPI
Nebraska: FACT*
Oklahoma: Dunkel, Matthews
Pittsburgh: DeVold, FACT*, Football Research, NY Times, Sagarin*

1981

Clemson: AP, Berryman, Billingsley, DeVold, FACT, FB News, Football Research, FW, Helms, Litkenhous, Matthews, National Championship Foundation*, NFF, NY Times, Poling, Sagarin, Sagarin (ELO-Chess), Sporting News, UPI
Nebraska: National Championship Foundation*
Penn St.: Dunkel
Pittsburgh: National Championship Foundation*
SMU: National Championship Foundation*
Texas: National Championship Foundation*

1982

Nebraska: Berryman
Penn St.: AP, Billingsley, DeVold, Dunkel, FACT, FB News, Football Research, FW, Helms*, Litkenhous, Matthews, National Championship Foundation, NFF, NY Times, Poling, Sagarin, Sagarin (ELO-Chess), Sporting News, UPI, USA/CNN
SMU: Helms*

1983

Auburn: Billingsley, FACT*, Football Research, NY Times, Sagarin (ELO-Chess)*
Miami (Fla.): AP, Dunkel, FB News, FW, National Championship Foundation, NFF, Sporting News, UPI, USA/CNN
Nebraska: Berryman, DeVold, FACT*, Litkenhous, Matthews, Poling, Sagarin*

1984

BYU: AP, Billingsley, Football Research, FW, National Championship Foundation*, NFF, Poling, Sagarin (ELO-Chess)*, UPI, USA/CNN
Florida: DeVold, Dunkel, FACT, Matthews, NY Times, Sagarin*, Sporting News
Nebraska: Litkenhous
Washington: Berryman, FB News, National Championship Foundation*

1985

Florida: Sagarin (ELO-Chess)*
Michigan: Matthews
Oklahoma: AP, Berryman, Billingsley, DeVold, Dunkel, FACT, FB News, Football Research, FW, National Championship Foundation, NFF, NY Times, Sagarin*, Sporting News, UPI, USA/CNN

1986

Miami (Fla.): FACT*
Oklahoma: Berryman, DeVold, Dunkel, Football Research, NY Times, Sagarin*
Penn St.: AP, Billingsley, FACT*, FB News, FW, Matthews, National Championship Foundation, NFF, Sagarin (ELO-Chess)*, Sporting News, UPI, USA/CNN

1987

Florida St.: Berryman
Miami (Fla.): AP, Billingsley, DeVold, Dunkel, Eck, FACT, FB News, Football Research, FW, Matthews, National Championship Foundation, NFF, NY Times, Sagarin, Sagarin (ELO-Chess), Sporting News, UPI, USA/CNN

1988

Miami (Fla.): Berryman, Sagarin*
Notre Dame: AP, Billingsley, DeVold, Dunkel, Eck, FACT, FB News, Football Research, FW, Matthews, National Championship Foundation, NFF, NY Times, Sagarin, (ELO-Chess)*, Sporting News, UPI, USA/CNN

1989

Miami (Fla.): AP, Billingsley, DeVold, Dunkel, FACT*, FB News, Football Research, FW, Matthews, National Championship Foundation, NFF, NY Times, Sporting News, UPI, USA/CNN
Notre Dame: Berryman, Eck, FACT*, Sagarin, Sagarin (ELO-Chess)

1990

Colorado: AP, Berryman, Billingsley, DeVold, FACT*, FB News, Football Research, FW, Matthews, National Championship Foundation*, NFF, Sporting News, USA/CNN
Georgia Tech: Dunkel, FACT*, National Championship Foundation*, Sagarin (ELO-Chess)*, UPI
Miami (Fla.): Eck, FACT*, NY Times, Sagarin*
Washington: FACT*

1991

Miami (Fla.): AP, Billingsley, Eck, Football Research, National Championship Foundation*, NY Times, Sagarin (ELO-Chess)*, Sporting News
Washington: Berryman, DeVold, Dunkel, FACT, FB News, FW, Matthews, National Championship Foundation*, Sagarin*, UPI/NFF, USA/CNN

1992

Alabama: AP, Berryman, Billingsley, DeVold, Dunkel, Eck, FACT, FB News, Football Research, FW, Matthews, National Championship Foundation, NY Times, Sagarin (ELO-Chess)*, Sporting News, UPI/NFF, USA/CNN
Florida St.: Sagarin*

1993

Auburn: National Championship Foundation*
Florida St.: AP, Berryman, Billingsley, DeVold, Dunkel, Eck, FACT, FB News, FW, National Championship Foundation*, NY Times, Sagarin, Sagarin (ELO-Chess), Sporting News, UPI, USA/CNN, USA/NFF
Nebraska: National Championship Foundation*
Notre Dame: Matthews, National Championship Foundation*

1994

Florida St.: Dunkel
Nebraska: Alderson, AP, Berryman, Billingsley, FACT*, FB News, FW, National Championship Foundation*, Sagarin (ELO-Chess)*, Sporting News, UPI, USA/CNN, USA/NFF
Penn St.: DeVold, Eck, FACT*, Matthews, National Championship Foundation*, NY Times, Sagarin*

1995

Nebraska: Alderson, AP, Berryman, Billingsley, DeVold, Dunkel, Eck, FACT, FB News, FW, Matthews, National Championship Foundation, NFF, NY Times, Sagarin, Sagarin (ELO-Chess), Sporting News, UPI, USA/CNN

1996

Florida: AP, Berryman, Billingsley, Eck, FACT, FB News, FW, NFF, Sagarin, Sagarin (ELO-Chess), Sporting News, USA/CNN, NY Times, National Championship Foundation, Dunkel, Matthews, DeVold
Florida St.: Alderson

1997

Michigan: AP, FB News, FW, National Championship Foundation*, NFF, Sporting News
Nebraska: Alderson, Berryman, Billingsley, DeVold, Dunkel, Eck, FACT, Matthews, National Championship Foundation*, NY Times, Sagarin, Sagarin (ELO-Chess), Seattle Times, USA/ESPN

1998

Tennessee: Alderson, AP, Berryman, Billingsley, DeVold, Dunkel, Eck, FACT, FB News, FW, Matthews, National Championship Foundation, NFF, NY Times, Sagarin, Sagarin (ELO-Chess), Seattle Times, Sporting News, USA/ESPN

1999

Florida St.: AP, Berryman, Billingsley, DeVold, Dunkel, Eck, FACT, FB News, FW, Massey, Matthews, National Championship Foundation, NFF, NY Times, Sagarin, Sagarin (ELO-Chess), Seattle Times, Sporting News, USA/ESPN

2000

Oklahoma: AP, Berryman, Billingsley, DeVold, Dunkel, Eck, FACT, FB News, FW, Massey, Matthews, National Championship Foundation, NFF, Sagarin, Sagarin (ELO-Chess), Seattle Times, Sporting News, USA/ESPN
Miami (Fla.): NY Times

2001

Miami (Fla.): AP, Berryman, Billingsley, Colley Matrix, DeVold, Dunkel, Eck, FACT, FB News, FW, Massey, Matthews, NFF, NY Times, Sagarin, Sagarin (ELO-Chess), Seattle Times, Sporting News, USA/ESPN, Wolfe

2002

Ohio St.: AP, Berryman, Billingsley, Colley Matrix, DeVold, Eck, FACT, FB News, FW, Massey, NFF, NY Times, Sagarin (ELO-Chess)*, Seattle Times, Sporting News, USA/ESPN, Wolfe
Southern California: Dunkel, Matthews, Sagarin*

2003

LSU: Billingsley, Colley Matrix, DeVold, Dunkel, FACT, Massey, NFF, Sagarin, Sagarin (ELO-Chess), Seattle Times, USA/ESPN, Wolfe
Oklahoma: Berryman
Southern California: AP, Eck, FW, Matthews, NY Times, Sporting News

2004

Southern California: AP, Berryman, Billingsley, Colley Matrix, DeVold, Dunkel, Eck, FACT, FW, Massey, Matthews, NY Times, NFF, Sagarin, Sagarin (ELO-Chess), Seattle Times, Sporting News, USA/ESPN, Wolfe

2005

Southern California: Harris
Texas: AP, Berryman, Billingsley, Colley Matrix, DeVold, Dunkel, Eck, FACT, FW, Massey, Matthews, NFF, Sagarin, Sagarin (ELO-Chess), Seattle Times, Sporting News, USA/ESPN, Wolfe

2006

Florida: AP, Berryman, Billingsley, Colley Matrix, Dunkel, FACT, FW, Massey, Matthews, NFF, Sagarin, Sagarin (ELO-Chess), Seattle Times, Sporting News, USA/ESPN, Wolfe
Ohio St.: DeVold, Harris

Legend of Present Major Selectors: Associated Press (AP) from 1936-present; Football Writers Association of America (FW) from 1954-present; National Football Foundation and Hall of Fame (NFF) from 1959-90 and 1995 to present; USA Today/ESPN (USA/ESPN) from 1997-present. The Associated Press has been the designated media poll since 1936. United Press International served as the coaches' poll from 1950 to 1991 when it was taken over by USA Today/Cable News Network and in 1997 became USA Today/ESPN. In 1991-92, the No. 1 team in the final UPI/NFF ratings received the MacArthur Bowl as the national champion by the NFF. In 1993-94 and again in 1996, the No. 1 team in the USA Today/NFF final poll received the MacArthur Bowl.

Major Selectors Since 1936

ASSOCIATED PRESS

Year	Team	Record
1936	Minnesota	7-1-0
1937	Pittsburgh	9-0-1
1938	TCU	11-0-0
1939	Texas A&M	11-0-0
1940	Minnesota	8-0-0
1941	Minnesota	8-0-0
1942	Ohio St.	9-1-0
1943	Notre Dame	9-1-0
1944	Army	9-0-0
1945	Army	9-0-0
1946	Notre Dame	8-0-1
1947	Notre Dame	9-0-0
1948	Michigan	9-0-0
1949	Notre Dame	10-0-0
1950	Oklahoma	10-1-0
1951	Tennessee	10-0-0
1952	Michigan St.	9-0-0
1953	Maryland	10-1-0
1954	Ohio St.	10-0-0
1955	Oklahoma	11-0-0
1956	Oklahoma	10-0-0
1957	Auburn	10-0-0
1958	LSU	11-0-0
1959	Syracuse	11-0-0
1960	Minnesota	8-2-0
1961	Alabama	11-0-0
1962	Southern California	11-0-0
1963	Texas	11-0-0
1964	Alabama	10-1-0
1965	Alabama	9-1-1
1966	Notre Dame	9-0-1
1967	Southern California	10-1-0
1968	Ohio St.	10-0-0
1969	Texas	11-0-0
1970	Nebraska	11-0-1
1971	Nebraska	13-0-0
1972	Southern California	12-0-0
1973	Notre Dame	11-0-0
1974	Oklahoma	11-0-0
1975	Oklahoma	11-1-0
1976	Pittsburgh	12-0-0
1977	Notre Dame	11-1-0
1978	Alabama	12-1-0
1979	Alabama	12-0-0
1980	Georgia	12-0-0
1981	Clemson	12-0-0
1982	Penn St.	11-1-0
1983	Miami (Fla.)	11-1-0
1984	BYU	13-0-0
1985	Oklahoma	11-1-0
1986	Penn St.	12-0-0
1987	Miami (Fla.)	12-0-0
1988	Notre Dame	12-0-0
1989	Miami (Fla.)	11-1-0
1990	Colorado	11-1-1
1991	Miami (Fla.)	12-0-0
1992	Alabama	13-0-0
1993	Florida St.	12-1-0
1994	Nebraska	13-0-0
1995	Nebraska	12-0-0
1996	Florida	12-1-0
1997	Michigan	12-0-0
1998	Tennessee	13-0-0
1999	Florida St.	12-0-0
2000	Oklahoma	13-0-0
2001	Miami (Fla.)	12-0-0
2002	Ohio St.	14-0-0
2003	Southern California	12-1-0
2004	Southern California	13-0-0
2005	Texas	13-0-0
2006	Florida	13-1-0

NATIONAL FOOTBALL FOUNDATION AND COLLEGE FOOTBALL HALL OF FAME (MacArthur Bowl)

Year	Team	Record
1959	Syracuse	11-0-0
1960	Minnesota	8-2-0
1961	Alabama	11-0-0
1962	Southern California	11-0-0
1963	Texas	11-0-0
1964	Notre Dame	9-1-0
1965	Michigan St.	10-1-0
1966	Michigan St. 9-0-1/Notre Dame	9-0-1
1967	Southern California	10-1-0
1968	Ohio St.	10-0-0
1969	Texas	11-0-0
1970	Ohio St. 10-1-0/Texas	10-1-0
1971	Nebraska	13-0-0
1972	Southern California	12-0-0
1973	Notre Dame	11-0-0
1974	Southern California	10-1-1
1975	Oklahoma	11-1-0
1976	Pittsburgh	12-0-0
1977	Notre Dame	11-1-0
1978	Alabama	11-1-0
1979	Alabama	12-0-0
1980	Georgia	12-0-0
1981	Clemson	12-0-0
1982	Penn St.	11-1-0
1983	Miami (Fla.)	11-1-0
1984	BYU	13-0-0
1985	Oklahoma	11-1-0
1986	Penn St.	12-0-0
1987	Miami (Fla.)	12-0-0
1988	Notre Dame	12-0-0
1989	Miami (Fla.)	11-1-0
1990	Colorado	11-1-1
1991	Wash. (UPI/NFF)	12-0-0
1992	Alabama (UPI/NFF)	13-0-0
1993	Florida St. (USA/NFF)	12-1-0
1994	Nebraska (USA/NFF)	13-0-0
1995	Nebraska (USA/NFF)	12-0-0
1996	Florida (USA/NFF)	12-1-0
1997	Michigan	12-0-0
1998	Tennessee	13-0-0
1999	Florida St.	12-0-0
2000	Oklahoma	13-0-0
2001	Miami (Fla.)	12-0-0
2002	Ohio St.	14-0-0
2003	LSU	13-1-0
2004	Southern California	13-0-0
2005	Texas	13-0-0
2006	Florida	13-1-0

UNITED PRESS

Year	Team	Record
1950	Oklahoma	10-1-0
1951	Tennessee	10-0-0
1952	Michigan St.	9-0-0
1953	Maryland	10-1-0
1954	UCLA	9-0-0
1955	Oklahoma	11-0-0
1956	Oklahoma	10-0-0
1957	Ohio St.	9-1-0
1958	LSU	11-0-0
1959	Syracuse	11-0-0
1960	Minnesota	8-2-0
1961	Alabama	11-0-0
1962	Southern California	11-0-0
1963	Texas	11-0-0
1964	Alabama	10-1-0
1965	Michigan St.	10-1-0
1966	Notre Dame	9-0-1
1967	Southern California	10-1-0
1968	Ohio St.	10-0-0
1969	Texas	11-0-0
1970	Texas	10-1-0
1971	Nebraska	13-0-0
1972	Southern California	12-0-0
1973	Alabama	11-1-0
1974	Southern California	10-1-1
1975	Oklahoma	11-1-0
1976	Pittsburgh	12-0-0
1977	Notre Dame	11-1-0
1978	Southern California	12-1-0
1979	Alabama	12-0-0
1980	Georgia	12-0-0
1981	Clemson	12-0-0
1982	Penn St.	11-1-0
1983	Miami (Fla.)	11-1-0
1984	BYU	13-0-0
1985	Oklahoma	11-1-0
1986	Penn St.	12-0-0
1987	Miami (Fla.)	12-0-0
1988	Notre Dame	12-0-0
1989	Miami (Fla.)	11-1-0
1990	Georgia Tech	11-0-1
1991	Washington	12-0-0
1992	Alabama	13-0-0
1993	Florida St.	12-1-0
1994	Nebraska	13-0-0
1995	Nebraska	12-0-0

FOOTBALL WRITERS'

Year	Team	Record
1954	UCLA	9-0-0
1955	Oklahoma	11-0-0
1956	Oklahoma	10-0-0
1957	Ohio St.	9-1-0
1958	Iowa	8-1-1
1959	Syracuse	11-0-0
1960	Mississippi	10-0-1
1961	Ohio St.	8-0-1
1962	Southern California	11-0-0
1963	Texas	11-0-0
1964	Arkansas	11-0-0
1965	Alabama	9-1-1/
	Michigan St.	10-1-0
1966	Notre Dame	9-0-1
1967	Southern California	10-1-0
1968	Ohio St.	10-0-0
1969	Texas	11-0-0
1970	Nebraska	11-0-1
1971	Nebraska	13-0-0
1972	Southern California	12-0-0
1973	Notre Dame	11-0-0
1974	Southern California	10-1-1
1975	Oklahoma	11-1-0
1976	Pittsburgh	12-0-0
1977	Notre Dame	11-1-0
1978	Alabama	11-1-0
1979	Alabama	12-0-0
1980	Georgia	12-0-0
1981	Clemson	12-0-0
1982	Penn St.	11-1-0
1983	Miami (Fla.)	11-1-0
1984	BYU	13-0-0
1985	Oklahoma	11-1-0
1986	Penn St.	12-0-0
1987	Miami (Fla.)	12-0-0
1988	Notre Dame	12-0-0
1989	Miami (Fla.)	11-1-0
1990	Colorado	11-1-1
1991	Washington	12-0-0
1992	Alabama	13-0-0
1993	Florida St.	12-1-0
1994	Nebraska	13-0-0
1995	Nebraska	12-0-0
1996	Florida	12-1-0
1997	Michigan	12-0-0
1998	Tennessee	13-0-0
1999	Florida St.	12-0-0
2000	Oklahoma	13-0-0
2001	Miami (Fla.)	12-0-0
2002	Ohio St.	14-0-0
2003	Southern California	12-1-0
2004	Southern California	13-0-0
2005	Texas	13-0-0
2006	Florida	13-1-0

USA TODAY/ESPN

Year	Team	Record
1982	Penn St.	11-1-0
1983	Miami (Fla.) (CNN)	11-1-0
1984	BYU (CNN)	13-0-0
1985	Oklahoma (CNN)	11-1-0
1986	Penn St. (CNN)	12-0-0
1987	Miami (Fla.) (CNN)	12-0-0
1988	Notre Dame (CNN)	12-0-0
1989	Miami (Fla.) (CNN)	11-1-0
1990	Colorado (CNN)	11-1-1
1991	Washington (CNN)	12-0-0
1992	Alabama (CNN)	13-0-0
1993	Florida St. (CNN)	12-1-0
1994	Nebraska (CNN)	13-0-0
1995	Nebraska (CNN)	12-0-0
1996	Florida (CNN)	12-1-0
1997	Nebraska (ESPN)	13-0-0
1998	Tennessee (ESPN)	13-0-0
1999	Florida St. (ESPN)	12-0-0
2000	Oklahoma (ESPN)	13-0-0
2001	Miami (Fla.) (ESPN)	12-0-0
2002	Ohio St. (ESPN)	14-0-0
2003	LSU (ESPN)	13-1-0
2004	Southern California (ESPN)	13-0-0
2005	Texas (ESPN)	13-0-0
2006	Florida (ESPN)	13-1-0

National Poll Champions in Bowl Games

Year	Team	Coach (Years†)	Record	Bowl (Result)
1900	Yale	Malcolm McBride	12-0-0	None
1901	Michigan	Fielding Yost	11-0-0	Rose (beat Stanford, 49-0)
	Harvard	William Reid	12-0-0	None
1902	Michigan	Fielding Yost	11-0-0	None
	Yale	Joseph Swan	11-0-1	None
1903	Princeton	Art Hillebrand	11-0-0	None
1904	Penn	Carl Williams	12-0-0	None
1905	Chicago	Amos Alonzo Stagg	11-0-0	None
	Yale	J.E. Owsley	10-0-0	None
1906	Princeton	Bill Roper	9-0-1	None
	Yale	Foster Rockwell	9-0-1	None
1907	Yale	William Knox	9-0-1	None
1908	Penn	Sol Metzer	11-0-1	None
	Harvard	Percy Haughton	9-0-1	None
1909	Yale	Howard Jones	10-0-0	None
1910	Harvard	Percy Haughton	8-0-1	None
1911	Princeton	Bill Roper	8-0-2	None
1912	Harvard	Percy Haughton	9-0-0	None
1913	Harvard	Percy Haughton	9-0-0	None
1914	Army	Charley Daly	9-0-0	None
	Harvard	Percy Haughton	7-0-2	None
1915	Cornell	Al Sharpe	9-0-0	None
1916	Pittsburgh	Glenn "Pop" Warner	8-0-0	None
1917	Georgia Tech	John Heisman	9-0-0	None
1918	Pittsburgh	Glenn "Pop" Warner	4-1-0	None
1919	Harvard	Robert Fisher	9-0-1	Rose (beat Oregon, 7-6)
	Penn St.	Hugo Bezdek	7-1-0	None
1920	California	Andy Smith	9-0-0	Rose (beat Ohio St., 28-0)
	Princeton	Bill Roper	6-0-1	None
1921	Cornell	Gil Dobie	8-0-0	None
	Penn St.	Hugo Bezdek	8-0-2	None
1922	Cornell	Gil Dobie	8-0-0	None
	Princeton	Bill Roper	8-0-0	None
1923	Illinois	Robert Zuppke	8-0-0	None
1924	Notre Dame	Knute Rockne	10-0-0	Rose (beat Stanford, 27-10)
1925	Alabama	Wallace Wade	10-0-0	Rose (beat Washington, 20-19)
	Dartmouth	Jesse Hawley	8-0-0	None
1926	Alabama	Wallace Wade	9-0-1	Rose (tied Stanford, 7-7)
	Stanford	Glenn "Pop" Warner	10-0-1	Rose (tied Alabama, 7-7)
1927	Illinois	Robert Zuppke	7-0-1	None
1928	Georgia Tech	Bill Alexander	10-0-0	Rose (beat California, 8-7)
	Southern California	Howard Jones	9-0-1	None
1929	Notre Dame	Knute Rockne	9-0-0	None
1930	Notre Dame	Knute Rockne	10-0-0	None
1931	Southern California	Howard Jones	10-1-0	Rose (beat Tulane, 21-12)
1932	Michigan	Harry Kipke	8-0-0	None
	Southern California	Howard Jones	10-0-0	Rose (beat Pittsburgh, 35-0)
1933	Michigan	Harry Kipke	7-0-1	None
1934	Minnesota	Bernie Bierman	8-0-0	None
1935	Minnesota	Bernie Bierman	8-0-0	None
	SMU	Matty Bell	12-1-0	Rose (lost to Stanford, 7-0)
1936	Minnesota	Bernie Bierman (5-15)	7-1-0	None
1937	Pittsburgh	Jock Sutherland (13-18)	9-0-1	None
1938	TCU	Dutch Meyer (5-5)	11-0-0	Sugar (beat Carnegie Mellon, 15-7)
1939	Texas A&M	Homer Norton (6-16)	11-0-0	Sugar (beat Tulane, 14-13)
1940	Minnesota	Bernie Bierman (9-19)	8-0-0	None
1941	Minnesota	Bernie Bierman (10-20)	8-0-0	None
1942	Ohio St.	Paul Brown (2-2)	9-1-0	None
1943	Notre Dame	Frank Leahy (3-5)	9-1-0	None
1944	Army	Earl "Red" Blaik (4-11)	9-0-0	None
1945	Army	Earl "Red" Blaik (5-12)	9-0-0	None
1946	Notre Dame	Frank Leahy (4-6)	8-0-1	None
1947	Notre Dame	Frank Leahy (5-7)	9-0-0	None
1948	Michigan	Bennie Oosterbaan (1-1)	9-0-0	None
1949	Notre Dame	Frank Leahy (7-9)	10-0-0	None
1950	Oklahoma	Bud Wilkinson (4-4)	10-1-0	Sugar (lost to Kentucky, 13-7)
1951	Tennessee	Robert Neyland (20-20)	10-0-0	Sugar (lost to Maryland, 28-13)
1952	Michigan St.	Clarence "Biggie" Munn (6-9)	9-0-0	None
1953	Maryland	Jim Tatum (7-9)	10-1-0	Orange (lost to Oklahoma, 7-0)
1954	Ohio St.	Woody Hayes (4-9)	10-0-0	Rose (beat Southern California, 20-7)
	UCLA	Red Sanders (6-12)	9-0-0	None
1955	Oklahoma	Bud Wilkinson (9-9)	11-0-0	Orange (beat Maryland, 20-6)
1956	Oklahoma	Bud Wilkinson (10-10)	10-0-0	None
1957	Auburn	Ralph "Shug" Jordan (7-7)	10-0-0	None
	Ohio St.	Woody Hayes (7-12)	9-1-0	Rose (beat Oregon, 10-7)
1958	LSU	Paul Dietzel (4-4)	11-0-0	Sugar (beat Clemson, 7-0)
	Iowa	Forest Evashevski (5-8)	8-1-1	Rose (beat California, 38-12)
1959	Syracuse	Ben Schwartzwalder (11-14)	11-0-0	Cotton (beat Texas, 23-14)
1960	Minnesota	Murray Warmath (7-9)	8-2-0	Rose (lost to Washington, 17-7)
	Mississippi	Johnny Vaught (14-14)	10-0-1	Sugar (beat Rice, 14-6)

Consensus National Champions

SINCE 1950

AP — Associated Press
UPI — United Press International (1950-95)
FWAA — Football Writers Association of America
NFF— National Football Foundation/College Football Hall of Fame
USA/CNN — USA Today/CNN
USA/ESPN — USA Today/ESPN

Year	Champion (Selectors)
1950	Oklahoma (AP, UPI)
1951	Tennessee (AP, UPI)
1952	Michigan St. (AP, UPI)
1953	Maryland (AP, UPI)
1954	UCLA (FWAA, UPI)
	Ohio St. (AP
1955	Oklahoma (AP, FWAA, UPI)
1956	Oklahoma (AP, FWAA, UPI)
1957	Ohio St. (FWAA, UPI)
	Auburn (AP)
1958	LSU (AP, UPI)
	Iowa (FWAA)
1959	Syracuse (AP, FWAA, NFF, UPI)
1960	Minnesota (AP, NFF, UPI)
	Mississippi (FWAA)
1961	Alabama (AP, NFF, UPI)
	Ohio St. (FWAA)
1962	Southern California (AP, FWAA, NFF, UPI)
1963	Texas (AP, FWAA, NFF, UPI)
1964	Alabama (AP, UPI)
	Arkansas (FWAA)
	Notre Dame (NFF)
1965	Michigan St. (FWAA, NFF, UPI)
	Alabama (AP, FWAA)
1966	Notre Dame (AP, FWAA, NFF, UPI)
	Michigan St. (NFF)
1967	Southern California (AP, FWAA, NFF, UPI)
1968	Ohio St. (AP, FWAA, NFF, UPI)
1969	Texas (AP, FWAA, NFF, UPI)
1970	Nebraska (AP, FWAA)
	Texas (NFF, UPI)
	Ohio St. (NFF)
1971	Nebraska (AP, FWAA, NFF, UPI)
1972	Southern California (AP, FWAA, NFF, UPI)
1973	Notre Dame (AP, FWAA, NFF)
	Alabama (UPI)
1974	Southern California (FWAA, NFF, UPI)
	Oklahoma (AP)
1975	Oklahoma (AP, FWAA, NFF, UPI)
1976	Pittsburgh (AP, FWAA, NFF, UPI)
1977	Notre Dame (AP, FWAA, NFF, UPI)
1978	Alabama (AP, FWAA, NFF)
	Southern California (UPI)
1979	Alabama (AP, FWAA, NFF, UPI)
1980	Georgia (AP, FWAA, NFF, UPI)
1981	Clemson (AP, FWAA, NFF, UPI)
1982	Penn St. (AP, FWAA, NFF, UPI, USA/CNN)
1983	Miami (Fla.) (AP, FWAA, NFF, UPI, USA/CNN)
1984	BYU (AP, FWAA, NFF, UPI, USA/CNN)
1985	Oklahoma (AP, FWAA, NFF, UPI, USA/CNN)
1986	Penn St. (AP, FWAA, NFF, UPI, USA/CNN)
1987	Miami (Fla.) (AP, FWAA, NFF, UPI, USA/CNN)
1988	Notre Dame (AP, FWAA, NFF, UPI, USA/CNN)
1989	Miami (Fla.) (AP, FWAA, NFF, UPI, USA/CNN)
1990	Colorado (AP, FWAA, NFF, USA/CNN)
	Georgia Tech (UPI)
1991	Washington (FWAA, NFF, USA/CNN, UPI)
	Miami (Fla.) (AP)
1992	Alabama (AP, FWAA, NFF, USA/CNN, UPI)
1993	Florida St. (AP, FWAA, NFF, USA/CNN, UPI)
1994	Nebraska (AP, FWAA, NFF, USA/CNN, UPI)
1995	Nebraska (AP, FWAA, NFF, USA/CNN, UPI)
1996	Florida (AP, FWAA, NFF, USA/CNN)
1997	Michigan (AP, FWAA, NFF)
	Nebraska (USA/ESPN)
1998	Tennessee (AP, FWAA, NFF, USA/ESPN)
1999	Florida St. (AP, FWAA, NFF, USA/ESPN)
2000	Oklahoma (AP, FWAA, NFF, USA/ESPN)

Year	Team	Coach (Years†)	Record	Bowl (Result)
1961	Alabama	Paul "Bear" Bryant (4-17)	11-0-0	Sugar (beat Arkansas, 10-3)
	Ohio St.	Woody Hayes (11-16)	8-0-1	None
1962	Southern California	John McKay (3-3)	11-0-0	Rose (beat Wisconsin, 42-37)
1963	Texas	Darrell Royal (7-10)	11-0-0	Cotton (beat Navy, 28-6)
1964	Alabama	Paul "Bear" Bryant (7-20)	10-1-0	Orange (lost to Texas, 21-17)
	Arkansas	Frank Broyles (3-4)	11-0-0	Cotton (beat Nebraska, 10-7)
	Notre Dame	Ara Parseghian (1-14)	9-1-0	None
1965	Alabama	Paul "Bear" Bryant (8-21)	9-1-1	Orange (beat Nebraska, 39-28)
	Michigan St.	Duffy Daugherty (12-12)	10-1-0	Rose (lost to UCLA, 14-12)
1966	Michigan St.	Duffy Daugherty (13-13)	9-0-1	None
	Notre Dame	Ara Parseghian (3-17)	9-0-1	None
1967	Southern California	John McKay (8-8)	10-1-0	Rose (beat Indiana, 14-3)
1968	Ohio St.	Woody Hayes (18-23)	10-0-0	Rose (beat Southern California, 27-16)
1969	Texas	Darrell Royal (13-16)	11-0-0	Cotton (beat Notre Dame, 21-17)
1970	Nebraska	Bob Devaney (9-14)	11-0-1	Orange (beat LSU, 17-12)
	Ohio St.	Woody Hayes (20-25)	9-1-0	Rose (lost to Stanford, 27-17)
	Texas	Darrell Royal (14-17)	10-1-0	Cotton (lost to Notre Dame, 24-11)
1971	Nebraska	Bob Devaney (10-15)	13-0-0	Orange (beat Alabama, 38-6)
1972	Southern California	John McKay (13-13)	12-0-0	Rose (beat Ohio St., 42-17)
1973	Alabama	Paul "Bear" Bryant (16-29)	11-1-0	Sugar (lost to Notre Dame, 24-23)
	Notre Dame	Ara Parseghian (10-23)	11-0-0	Sugar (beat Alabama, 24-23)
1974	Oklahoma	Barry Switzer (2-2)	11-0-0	None
	Southern California	John McKay (15-15)	10-1-1	Rose (beat Ohio St., 18-17)
1975	Oklahoma	Barry Switzer (3-3)	11-1-0	Orange (beat Michigan, 14-6)
1976	Pittsburgh	Johnny Majors (4-9)	12-0-0	Sugar (beat Georgia, 27-3)
1977	Notre Dame	Dan Devine (3-19)	11-1-0	Cotton (beat Texas, 38-10)
1978	Alabama	Paul "Bear" Bryant (21-34)	11-1-0	Sugar (beat Penn St., 14-7)
	Southern California	John Robinson (3-3)	12-1-0	Rose (beat Michigan, 17-10)
1979	Alabama	Paul "Bear" Bryant (22-35)	12-0-0	Sugar (beat Arkansas, 24-9)
1980	Georgia	Vince Dooley (17-17)	12-0-0	Sugar (beat Notre Dame, 17-10)
1981	Clemson	Danny Ford (4-4#)	12-0-0	Orange (beat Nebraska, 22-15)
1982	Penn St.	Joe Paterno (17-17)	11-1-0	Sugar (beat Georgia, 27-23)
1983	Miami (Fla.)	Howard Schnellenberger (5-5)	11-1-0	Orange (beat Nebraska, 31-30)
1984	BYU	LaVell Edwards (13-13)	13-0-0	Holiday (beat Michigan, 24-17)
1985	Oklahoma	Barry Switzer (13-13)	11-1-0	Orange (beat Penn St., 25-10)
1986	Penn St.	Joe Paterno (21-21)	12-0-0	Fiesta (beat Miami [Fla.], 14-10)
1987	Miami (Fla.)	Jimmy Johnson (3-9)	12-0-0	Orange (beat Oklahoma, 20-14)
1988	Notre Dame	Lou Holtz (3-19)	12-0-0	Fiesta (beat West Virginia, 34-21)
1989	Miami (Fla.)	Dennis Erickson (1-8)	11-1-0	Sugar (beat Alabama, 33-25)
1990	Colorado	Bill McCartney (9-9)	11-1-1	Orange (beat Notre Dame, 10-9)
	Georgia Tech	Bobby Ross (4-14)	11-0-1	Fla. Citrus (beat Nebraska, 45-21)
1991	Miami (Fla.)	Dennis Erickson (3-10)	12-0-0	Orange (beat Nebraska, 22-0)
	Washington	Don James (17-21)	12-0-0	Rose (beat Michigan, 34-14)
1992	Alabama	Gene Stallings (3-10)	13-0-0	Sugar (beat Miami [Fla.], 34-13)
1993	Florida St.	Bobby Bowden (18-28)	12-1-0	Orange (beat Nebraska, 18-16)
1994	Nebraska	Tom Osborne (22-22)	13-0-0	Orange (beat Miami [Fla.], 24-17)
1995	Nebraska	Tom Osborne (23-23)	12-0-0	Fiesta (beat Florida, 62-24)
1996	Florida	Steve Spurrier (7-10)	12-1-0	Sugar (beat Florida St., 52-20)
1997	Michigan	Lloyd Carr (3-3)	12-0-0	Rose (beat Washington St., 21-16)
	Nebraska	Tom Osborne (25-25)	13-0-0	Orange (beat Tennessee, 42-17)
1998*	Tennessee	Phillip Fulmer (7-7)	13-0-0	Fiesta (beat Florida St., 23-16)
1999	Florida St.	Bobby Bowden (25-35)	12-0-0	Sugar (beat Virginia Tech, 46-29)
2000	Oklahoma	Bob Stoops (2-2)	13-0-0	Orange (beat Florida St., 13-2)
2001	Miami (Fla.)	Larry Coker (1-1)	12-0-0	Rose (beat Nebraska, 37-14)
2002	Ohio St.	Jim Tressel (2-17)	14-0-0	Fiesta (beat Miami [Fla.] 31-24 [2ot])
2003	LSU	Nick Saban (4-10)	13-1-0	Sugar (beat Oklahoma, 21-14)
	Southern California	Pete Carroll (3-3)	12-1-0	Rose (beat Michigan, 28-14)
2004	Southern California	Pete Carroll (4-4)	13-0-0	Orange (beat Oklahoma, 55-19)
2005	Texas	Mack Brown (8-22)	13-0-0	Rose (beat Southern California, 41-38)
2006	Florida	Urban Meyer (2-6)	13-1-0	BCS National Championship (beat Ohio St., 41-14)

*†Years head coach at that college and total years at four-year colleges. #Includes last game of 1978 season. *First year of BCS ranking system.*

Year	Champion (Selectors)
2001	Miami (Fla.) (AP, FWAA, NFF, USA/ESPN)
2002	Ohio St. (AP, FWAA, NFF, USA/ESPN)
2003	LSU (NFF, USA/ESPN)
	Southern California (AP, FWAA)
2004	Southern California (AP, FWAA, NFF, USA/ESPN)
2005	Texas (AP, FWAA, NFF, USA/ESPN)
2006	Florida (AP, FWAA, NFF, USA/ESPN)

All-Time Associated Press National Poll Championships

(From 1936-Present)

Team	No.	Years No. 1 in Poll
Notre Dame	8	1943, 1946, 1947, 1949, 1966, 1973, 1977, 1988
Oklahoma	7	1950, 1955, 1956, 1974, 1975, 1985, 2000
Alabama	6	1961, 1964, 1965, 1978, 1979, 1992
Miami (Fla.)	5	1983, 1987, 1989, 1991, 2001
Southern California	5	1962, 1967, 1972, 2003, 2004
Minnesota	4	1936, 1940, 1941, 1960
Nebraska	4	1970, 1971, 1994, 1995
Ohio St.	4	1942, 1954, 1968, 2002
Texas	3	1963, 1969, 2005
Army	2	1944, 1945
Florida	2	1996, 2006
Florida St.	2	1993, 1999
Michigan	2	1948, 1997
Penn St.	2	1982, 1986
Pittsburgh	2	1937, 1976
Tennessee	2	1951, 1998
Auburn	1	1957
BYU	1	1984
Clemson	1	1981
Colorado	1	1990
Georgia	1	1980
LSU	1	1958
Maryland	1	1953
Michigan St.	1	1952
Syracuse	1	1959
Texas A&M	1	1939
TCU	1	1938
Total	**71**	

Associated Press Weekly Poll Leaders

The weekly dates are for Monday or Tuesday, the most frequent release dates of the poll, except when the final poll was taken after early January bowl games. A team's record includes its last game before the weekly poll. A new weekly leader's rank the previous week is indicated in parentheses after its record. Final poll leaders (annual champions) are in bold face. (Note: Only 10 teams were ranked in the weekly polls during 1962, 1963, 1964, 1965, 1966 and 1967; 20 were ranked in all other seasons until 1989, when 25 were ranked.)

1936

Date	Team	Record
10-20	Minnesota	(3-0-0)
10-27	Minnesota	(4-0-0)
11-3	Northwestern	(5-0-0) (3)
11-10	Northwestern	(6-0-0)
11-17	Northwestern	(7-0-0)
11-24	Minnesota	(7-1-0) (2)
12-1	**Minnesota**	**(7-1-0)**

1937

Date	Team	Record
10-20	California	(5-0-0)
10-27	California	(6-0-0)
11-2	California	(7-0-0)
11-9	Pittsburgh	(6-0-1) (3)
11-16	Pittsburgh	(7-0-1)
11-23	Pittsburgh	(8-0-1)
11-30	**Pittsburgh**	**(9-0-1)**

1938

Date	Team	Record
10-18	Pittsburgh	(4-0-0)
10-25	Pittsburgh	(5-0-0)
11-1	Pittsburgh	(6-0-0)
11-8	TCU	(7-0-0) (2)
11-15	Notre Dame	(7-0-0) (2)
11-22	Notre Dame	(8-0-0)
11-29	Notre Dame	(8-0-0)
12-6	**TCU**	**(10-0-0) (2)**

1939

Date	Team	Record
10-17	Pittsburgh	(3-0-0)
10-24	Tennessee	(4-0-0) (5)
10-31	Tennessee	(5-0-0)
11-7	Tennessee	(6-0-0)
11-14	Tennessee	(7-0-0)
11-21	Texas A&M	(9-0-0) (2)
11-28	(tie) Texas A&M	(9-0-0)
	(tie) Southern California	(6-0-1) (4)
12-5	Texas A&M	(10-0-0)
12-12	**Texas A&M**	**(10-0-0)**

1940

Date	Team	Record
10-15	Cornell	(2-0-0)
10-22	Cornell	(3-0-0)
10-29	Cornell	(4-0-0)
11-5	Cornell	(5-0-0)
11-12	Minnesota	(6-0-0) (2)
11-19	Minnesota	(7-0-0)
11-26	Minnesota	(8-0-0)
12-3	**Minnesota**	**(8-0-0)**

1941

Date	Team	Record
10-14	Minnesota	(2-0-0)
10-21	Minnesota	(3-0-0)
10-28	(tie) Minnesota	(4-0-0)
	(tie) Texas	(5-0-0) (2)
11-4	Texas	(6-0-0)
11-11	Minnesota	(6-0-0) (2)
11-18	Minnesota	(7-0-0)
11-25	Minnesota	(8-0-0)
12-2	**Minnesota**	**(8-0-0)**

1942

Date	Team	Record
10-13	Ohio St.	(3-0-0)
10-20	Ohio St.	(4-0-0)
10-27	Ohio St.	(5-0-0)
11-3	Georgia	(7-0-0) (2)
11-10	Georgia	(8-0-0)
11-17	Georgia	(9-0-0)
11-24	Boston College	(8-0-0) (3)
12-1	**Ohio St.**	**(9-1-0) (3)**

1943

Date	Team	Record
10-5	Notre Dame	(2-0-0)
10-12	Notre Dame	(3-0-0)
10-19	Notre Dame	(4-0-0)
10-26	Notre Dame	(5-0-0)
11-2	Notre Dame	(6-0-0)
11-9	Notre Dame	(7-0-0)
11-16	Notre Dame	(8-0-0)
11-23	Notre Dame	(9-0-0)
11-30	**Notre Dame**	**(9-1-0)**

1944

Date	Team	Record
10-10	Notre Dame	(2-0-0)
10-17	Notre Dame	(3-0-0)
10-24	Notre Dame	(4-0-0)
10-31	Army	(5-0-0) (2)
11-7	Army	(6-0-0)
11-14	Army	(7-0-0)
11-21	Army	(8-0-0)
11-28	Army	(8-0-0)
12-5	**Army**	**(9-0-0)**

1945

Date	Team	Record
10-9	Army	(2-0-0)
10-16	Army	(3-0-0)
10-23	Army	(4-0-0)
10-30	Army	(5-0-0)
11-6	Army	(6-0-0)
11-13	Army	(7-0-0)
11-20	Army	(8-0-0)
11-27	Army	(8-0-0)
12-4	**Army**	**(9-0-0)**

1946

Date	Team	Record
10-8	Texas	(3-0-0)
10-15	Army	(4-0-0) (2)
10-22	Army	(5-0-0)
10-29	Army	(6-0-0)
11-5	Army	(7-0-0)
11-12	Army	(7-0-1)
11-19	Army	(8-0-1)
11-26	Army	(8-0-1)
12-3	**Notre Dame**	**(8-0-1) (2)**

1947*

Date	Team	Record
10-7	Notre Dame	(1-0-0)
10-14	Michigan	(3-0-0) (2)
10-21	Michigan	(4-0-0)
10-28	Notre Dame	(4-0-0) (2)
11-4	Notre Dame	(5-0-0)
11-11	Notre Dame	(6-0-0)
11-18	Michigan	(8-0-0) (2)
11-25	Notre Dame	(8-0-0) (2)
12-2	Notre Dame	(8-0-0)
12-9	**Notre Dame**	**(9-0-0)**

1948

Date	Team	Record
10-5	Notre Dame	(2-0-0)
10-12	North Carolina	(3-0-0) (2)

10-19 Michigan (4-0-0) (4)
10-26 Michigan (5-0-0)
11-2 Notre Dame (6-0-0) (2)
11-9 Michigan (7-0-0) (2)
11-16 Michigan (8-0-0)
11-23 Michigan (9-0-0)
11-30 Michigan (9-0-0)

1949
10-4 Michigan (2-0-0)
10-11 Notre Dame (3-0-0) (2)
10-18 Notre Dame (4-0-0)
10-25 Notre Dame (4-0-0)
11-1 Notre Dame (5-0-0)
11-8 Notre Dame (6-0-0)
11-15 Notre Dame (7-0-0)
11-22 Notre Dame (8-0-0)
11-29 Notre Dame (9-0-0)

1950
10-3 Notre Dame (1-0-0)
10-10 Army (2-0-0) (4)
10-17 Army (3-0-0)
10-24 SMU (5-0-0) (3)
10-31 SMU (5-0-0)
11-7 Army (6-0-0) (2)
11-14 Ohio St. (6-1-0) (2)
11-21 Oklahoma (8-0-0) (2)
11-28 Oklahoma (9-0-0)

1951
10-2 Michigan St. (2-0-0)
10-9 Michigan St. (3-0-0)
10-16 California (4-0-0) (2)
10-23 Tennessee (4-0-0) (2)
10-30 Tennessee (5-0-0)
11-6 Tennessee (6-0-0)
11-13 Michigan St. (7-0-0)(5)
11-20 Tennessee (8-0-0) (2)
11-27 Tennessee (9-0-0)
12-4 Tennessee (10-0-0)

1952
9-30 Michigan St. (1-0-0)
10-7 Wisconsin (2-0-0) (8)
10-14 Michigan St. (3-0-0)(2)
10-21 Michigan St. (4-0-0)
10-28 Michigan St. (5-0-0)
11-4 Michigan St. (6-0-0)
11-11 Michigan St. (7-0-0)
11-18 Michigan St. (8-0-0)
11-25 Michigan St. (9-0-0)
12-1 Michigan St. (9-0-0)

1953
9-29 Notre Dame (1-0-0)
10-6 Notre Dame (2-0-0)
10-13 Notre Dame (2-0-0)
10-20 Notre Dame (3-0-0)
10-27 Notre Dame (4-0-0)
11-3 Notre Dame (5-0-0)
11-10 Notre Dame (6-0-0)
11-17 Notre Dame (7-0-0)
11-24 Maryland (10-0-0) (2)
12-1 Maryland (10-0-0)

1954
9-21 Oklahoma (1-0-0)
9-28 Notre Dame (1-0-0) (2)
10-5 Oklahoma (2-0-0) (2)
10-12 Oklahoma (3-0-0)
10-19 Oklahoma (4-0-0)
10-26 Ohio St. (5-0-0) (4)
11-2 UCLA (7-0-0) (3)
11-9 UCLA (8-0-0)
11-16 Ohio St. (8-0-0) (2)
11-23 Ohio St. (9-0-0)
11-30 Ohio St. (9-0-0)

1955
9-20 UCLA (1-0-0)
9-27 Maryland (2-0-0) (5)
10-4 Maryland (3-0-0)
10-11 Michigan (3-0-0) (2)
10-18 Michigan (4-0-0)
10-25 Maryland (6-0-0) (2)
11-1 Maryland (7-0-0)
11-8 Oklahoma (7-0-0) (2)
11-15 Oklahoma (8-0-0)
11-22 Oklahoma (9-0-0)
11-29 Oklahoma (10-0-0)

1956
9-25 Oklahoma (0-0-0)
10-2 Oklahoma (1-0-0)
10-9 Oklahoma (2-0-0)
10-16 Oklahoma (3-0-0)
10-23 Michigan St. (4-0-0) (2)
10-30 Oklahoma (5-0-0) (2)
11-6 Oklahoma (6-0-0)
11-13 Tennessee (7-0-0) (3)
11-20 Oklahoma (8-0-0) (2)
11-27 Oklahoma (9-0-0)
12-4 Oklahoma (10-0-0)

1957
9-24 Oklahoma (1-0-0)
10-1 Oklahoma (1-0-0)
10-8 Oklahoma (2-0-0)
10-15 Michigan St. (3-0-0) (2)
10-22 Oklahoma (4-0-0) (2)
10-29 Texas A&M (6-0-0) (2)
11-5 Texas A&M (7-0-0)
11-12 Texas A&M (8-0-0)
11-19 Michigan St. (7-1-0)(4)
11-26 Auburn (9-0-0) (2)
12-3 Auburn (10-0-0)

1958
9-23 Ohio St. (0-0-0)
9-30 Oklahoma (1-0-0) (2)
10-7 Auburn (2-0-0) (2)
10-14 Army (3-0-0) (3)
10-21 Army (4-0-0)
10-28 LSU (6-0-0) (3)
11-4 LSU (7-0-0)
11-11 LSU (8-0-0)
11-18 LSU (9-0-0)
11-25 LSU (10-0-0)
12-2 LSU (10-0-0)

1959
9-22 LSU (1-0-0)
9-29 LSU (2-0-0)
10-6 LSU (3-0-0)
10-13 LSU (4-0-0)
10-20 LSU (5-0-0)
10-27 LSU (6-0-0)
11-3 LSU (7-0-0)
11-10 Syracuse (7-0-0) (4)
11-17 Syracuse (8-0-0)
11-24 Syracuse (9-0-0)
12-1 Syracuse (9-0-0)
12-8 Syracuse (10-0-0)

1960
9-20 Mississippi (1-0-0)
9-27 Mississippi (2-0-0)
10-4 Syracuse (2-0-0) (2)
10-11 Mississippi (4-0-0) (2)
10-18 Iowa (4-0-0) (2)
10-25 Iowa (5-0-0)
11-1 Iowa (6-0-0)
11-8 Minnesota (7-0-0) (3)
11-15 Missouri (9-0-0) (2)
11-22 Minnesota (8-1-0) (4)
11-29 Minnesota (8-1-0)

1961
9-26 Iowa (0-0-0)
10-3 Iowa (1-0-0)
10-10 Mississippi (3-0-0) (2)
10-17 Michigan St. (3-0-0) (5)
10-24 Michigan St. (4-0-0)
10-31 Michigan St. (5-0-0)
11-7 Texas (7-0-0) (3)
11-14 Texas (8-0-0)
11-21 Alabama (9-0-0) (2)
11-28 Alabama (9-0-0)
12-5 Alabama (10-0-0)

1962
9-25 Alabama (1-0-0)
10-2 Ohio St. (1-0-0) (2)
10-9 Alabama (3-0-0) (2)
10-16 Texas (4-0-0) (2)
10-23 Texas (5-0-0)
10-30 Northwestern (5-0-0) (3)
11-6 Northwestern (6-0-0)
11-13 Alabama (8-0-0) (3)
11-20 Southern California (8-0-0) (2)
11-27 Southern California (9-0-0)
12-4 Southern California (10-0-0)

1963
9-24 Southern California (1-0-0)
10-1 Oklahoma (1-0-0) (3)
10-8 Oklahoma (2-0-0)
10-15 Texas (4-0-0) (3)
10-22 Texas (5-0-0)
10-29 Texas (6-0-0)
11-5 Texas (7-0-0)
11-12 Texas (8-0-0)
11-19 Texas (9-0-0)
11-26 Texas (9-0-0)
12-3 Texas (10-0-0)
12-10 Texas (10-0-0)

1964
9-29 Texas (2-0-0)
10-6 Texas (3-0-0)
10-13 Texas (4-0-0)
10-20 Ohio St. (4-0-0)(2)
10-27 Ohio St. (5-0-0)
11-3 Notre Dame (6-0-0)(2)
11-10 Notre Dame (7-0-0)
11-17 Notre Dame (8-0-0)
11-24 Notre Dame (9-0-0)
12-1 Alabama (10-0-0) (2)

1965
9-21 Notre Dame (1-0-0)
9-28 Texas (2-0-0) (3)
10-5 Texas (3-0-0)
10-12 Texas (4-0-0)
10-19 Arkansas (5-0-0) (3)
10-26 Michigan St. (6-0-0) (2)
11-2 Michigan St. (7-0-0)
11-9 Michigan St. (8-0-0)
11-16 Michigan St. (9-0-0)
11-23 Michigan St. (10-0-0)
11-30 Michigan St. (10-0-0)
1-4 Alabama (9-1-1) (4)

1966
9-20 Michigan St. (1-0-0)
9-27 Michigan St. (2-0-0)
10-4 Michigan St. (3-0-0)
10-11 Michigan St. (4-0-0)
10-18 Notre Dame (4-0-0) (2)
10-25 Notre Dame (5-0-0)
11-1 Notre Dame (6-0-0)
11-8 Notre Dame (7-0-0)
11-15 Notre Dame (8-0-0)
11-22 Notre Dame (8-0-1)
11-29 Notre Dame (9-0-1)
12-5 Notre Dame (9-0-1)

1967
9-19 Notre Dame (0-0-0)
9-26 Notre Dame (1-0-0)
10-3 Southern California (3-0-0) (2)
10-10 Southern California (4-0-0)
10-17 Southern California (5-0-0)
10-24 Southern California (6-0-0)
10-31 Southern California (7-0-0)
11-7 Southern California (8-0-0)
11-14 UCLA (7-0-1) (2)
11-21 Southern California (9-1-0) (4)
11-28 Southern California (9-1-0)

1968
9-17 Purdue (0-0-0)
9-24 Purdue (1-0-0)
10-1 Purdue (2-0-0)
10-8 Purdue (3-0-0)
10-15 Southern California (4-0-0) (2)
10-22 Southern California (5-0-0)
10-29 Southern California (5-0-0)
11-5 Southern California (6-0-0)
11-12 Southern California (7-0-0)
11-19 Southern California (8-0-0)
11-26 Ohio St. (9-0-0) (2)
12-2 Ohio St. (9-0-0)
1-4 Ohio St. (10-0-0)

1969
9-23 Ohio St. (0-0-0)
9-30 Ohio St. (1-0-0)
10-7 Ohio St. (2-0-0)
10-14 Ohio St. (3-0-0)
10-21 Ohio St. (4-0-0)
10-28 Ohio St. (5-0-0)
11-4 Ohio St. (6-0-0)
11-11 Ohio St. (7-0-0)
11-18 Ohio St. (8-0-0)

11-25 Texas (8-0-0) (2)
12-2 Texas (9-0-0)
12-9 Texas (10-0-0)
1-4 Texas (11-0-0)

1970
9-15 Ohio St. (0-0-0)
9-22 Ohio St. (0-0-0)
9-29 Ohio St. (1-0-0)
10-6 Ohio St. (2-0-0)
10-13 Ohio St. (3-0-0)
10-20 Ohio St. (4-0-0)
10-27 Texas (5-0-0) (2)
11-3 Texas (6-0-0)
11-10 Texas (7-0-0)
11-17 Texas (8-0-0)
11-24 Texas (8-0-0)
12-1 Texas (9-0-0)
12-8 Texas (10-0-0)
1-6 Nebraska (11-0-1) (3)

1971
9-14 Nebraska (1-0-0)
9-21 Nebraska (2-0-0)
9-28 Nebraska (3-0-0)
10-5 Nebraska (4-0-0)
10-12 Nebraska (5-0-0)
10-19 Nebraska (6-0-0)
10-26 Nebraska (7-0-0)
11-2 Nebraska (8-0-0)
11-9 Nebraska (9-0-0)
11-16 Nebraska (10-0-0)
11-23 Nebraska (10-0-0)
11-30 Nebraska (11-0-0)
12-7 Nebraska (12-0-0)
1-4 Nebraska (13-0-0)

1972
9-12 Southern California (1-0-0)
9-19 Southern California (2-0-0)
9-26 Southern California (3-0-0)
10-3 Southern California (4-0-0)
10-10 Southern California (5-0-0)
10-17 Southern California (6-0-0)
10-24 Southern California (7-0-0)
10-31 Southern California (8-0-0)
11-7 Southern California (9-0-0)
11-14 Southern California (9-0-0)
11-21 Southern California (10-0-0)
11-28 Southern California (10-0-0)
12-5 Southern California (11-0-0)
1-3 Southern California (12-0-0)

1973
9-11 Southern California (0-0-0)
9-18 Southern California (1-0-0)
9-25 Southern California (2-0-0)
10-2 Ohio St. (2-0-0) (3)
10-9 Ohio St. (3-0-0)
10-16 Ohio St. (4-0-0)
10-23 Ohio St. (5-0-0)
10-30 Ohio St. (6-0-0)
11-6 Ohio St. (7-0-0)
11-13 Ohio St. (8-0-0)
11-20 Ohio St. (9-0-0)
11-27 Alabama (10-0-0) (2)
12-4 Alabama (11-0-0)
1-3 Notre Dame (11-0-0) (3)

1974
9-10 Oklahoma (0-0-0)
9-17 Notre Dame (1-0-0) (2)
9-24 Ohio St. (2-0-0) (2)
10-1 Ohio St. (3-0-0)
10-8 Ohio St. (4-0-0)
10-15 Ohio St. (5-0-0)
10-22 Ohio St. (6-0-0)
10-29 Ohio St. (7-0-0)
11-5 Ohio St. (8-0-0)
11-12 Oklahoma (8-0-0) (2)
11-19 Oklahoma (9-0-0)
11-26 Oklahoma (10-0-0)
12-3 Oklahoma (11-0-0)
1-3 Oklahoma (11-0-0)

1975
9-9 Oklahoma (0-0-0)
9-16 Oklahoma (1-0-0)
9-23 Oklahoma (2-0-0)
9-30 Oklahoma (3-0-0)
10-7 Ohio St. (4-0-0) (2)
10-14 Ohio St. (5-0-0)
10-21 Ohio St. (6-0-0)
10-28 Ohio St. (7-0-0)
11-4 Ohio St. (8-0-0)
11-11 Ohio St. (9-0-0)
11-18 Ohio St. (10-0-0)
11-25 Ohio St. (11-0-0)
12-2 Ohio St. (11-0-0)
1-3 Oklahoma (11-1-0) (3)

1976
9-14 Michigan (1-0-0)
9-21 Michigan (2-0-0)
9-28 Michigan (3-0-0)
10-5 Michigan (4-0-0)
10-12 Michigan (5-0-0)
10-19 Michigan (6-0-0)
10-26 Michigan (7-0-0)
11-2 Michigan (8-0-0)
11-9 Pittsburgh (9-0-0) (2)
11-16 Pittsburgh (10-0-0)
11-23 Pittsburgh (10-0-0)
11-30 Pittsburgh (11-0-0)
1-5 Pittsburgh (12-0-0)

1977
9-13 Michigan (1-0-0)
9-20 Michigan (2-0-0)
9-27 Oklahoma (3-0-0) (3)
10-4 Southern California (4-0-0) (2)
10-11 Michigan (5-0-0) (3)
10-18 Michigan (6-0-0)
10-25 Texas (6-0-0) (2)
11-1 Texas (7-0-0)
11-8 Texas (8-0-0)
11-15 Texas (9-0-0)
11-22 Texas (10-0-0)
11-29 Texas (11-0-0)
1-4 Notre Dame (11-1-0) (5)

1978
9-12 Alabama (1-0-0)
9-19 Alabama (2-0-0)
9-26 Oklahoma (3-0-0) (tie 3)
10-3 Oklahoma (4-0-0)
10-10 Oklahoma (5-0-0)
10-17 Oklahoma (6-0-0)
10-24 Oklahoma (7-0-0)
10-31 Oklahoma (8-0-0)
11-7 Oklahoma (9-0-0)
11-14 Penn St. (10-0-0) (2)
11-21 Penn St. (10-0-0)
11-28 Penn St. (11-0-0)
12-5 Penn St. (11-0-0)
1-4 Alabama (11-1-0) (2)

1979
9-11 Southern California (1-0-0)
9-18 Southern California (2-0-0)
9-25 Southern California (3-0-0)
10-2 Southern California (4-0-0)
10-9 Southern California (5-0-0)
10-16 Alabama (5-0-0) (2)
10-23 Alabama (6-0-0)
10-30 Alabama (7-0-0)
11-6 Alabama (8-0-0)
11-13 Alabama (9-0-0)
11-20 Alabama (10-0-0)
11-27 Alabama (10-0-0)
12-4 Ohio St. (11-0-0) (3)
1-3 Alabama (12-0-0) (2)

1980
9-9 Ohio St. (0-0-0)
9-16 Alabama (1-0-0) (2)
9-23 Alabama (2-0-0)
9-30 Alabama (3-0-0)
10-7 Alabama (4-0-0)
10-14 Alabama (5-0-0)
10-21 Alabama (6-0-0)
10-28 Alabama (7-0-0)
11-4 Notre Dame (7-0-0) (3)
11-11 Georgia (9-0-0) (2)
11-18 Georgia (10-0-0)
11-25 Georgia (10-0-0)
12-2 Georgia (11-0-0)
12-9 Georgia (11-0-0)
1-4 Georgia (12-0-0)

1981
9-8 Michigan (0-0-0)
9-15 Notre Dame (1-0-0) (4)
9-22 Southern California (2-0-0) (2)
9-29 Southern California (3-0-0)
10-6 Southern California (4-0-0)
10-13 Texas (4-0-0) (3)
10-20 Penn St. (5-0-0) (2)
10-27 Penn St. (6-0-0)
11-3 Pittsburgh (7-0-0) (2)
11-10 Pittsburgh (8-0-0)
11-17 Pittsburgh (9-0-0)
11-24 Pittsburgh (10-0-0)
12-1 Clemson (11-0-0) (2)
1-3 Clemson (12-0-0)

1982
9-7 Pittsburgh (0-0-0)
9-14 Washington (1-0-0) (2)
9-21 Washington (2-0-0)
9-28 Washington (3-0-0)
10-5 Washington (4-0-0)
10-12 Washington (5-0-0)
10-19 Washington (6-0-0)
10-26 Pittsburgh (6-0-0) (2)
11-2 Pittsburgh (7-0-0)
11-9 Georgia (9-0-0) (3)
11-16 Georgia (10-0-0)
11-23 Georgia (10-0-0)
11-30 Georgia (11-0-0)
12-7 Georgia (11-0-0)
1-3 Penn St. (11-1-0) (2)

1983
9-6 Nebraska (1-0-0)
9-13 Nebraska (2-0-0)
9-20 Nebraska (3-0-0)
9-27 Nebraska (4-0-0)
10-4 Nebraska (5-0-0)
10-11 Nebraska (6-0-0)
10-18 Nebraska (7-0-0)
10-25 Nebraska (8-0-0)
11-1 Nebraska (9-0-0)
11-8 Nebraska (10-0-0)
11-15 Nebraska (11-0-0)
11-22 Nebraska (11-0-0)
11-29 Nebraska (12-0-0)
12-6 Nebraska (12-0-0)
1-3 Miami (Fla.) (11-1-0) (5)

1984
9-4 Miami (Fla.) (2-0-0)
9-11 Nebraska (1-0-0) (2)
9-18 Nebraska (2-0-0)
9-25 Nebraska (3-0-0)
10-2 Texas (2-0-0) (2)
10-9 Texas (3-0-0)
10-16 Washington (6-0-0) (2)
10-23 Washington (7-0-0)
10-30 Washington (8-0-0)
11-6 Washington (9-0-0)
11-13 Nebraska (9-1-0) (2)
11-20 BYU (11-0-0) (3)
11-27 BYU (12-0-0)
12-4 BYU (12-0-0)
1-3 BYU (13-0-0)

1985
9-3 Oklahoma (0-0-0)
9-10 Auburn (1-0-0) (2)
9-17 Auburn (2-0-0)
9-24 Auburn (2-0-0)
10-1 Iowa (3-0-0) (3)
10-8 Iowa (4-0-0)
10-15 Iowa (5-0-0)
10-22 Iowa (6-0-0)
10-29 Iowa (7-0-0)
11-5 Florida (7-0-1) (2)
11-12 Penn St. (9-0-0) (2)
11-19 Penn St. (10-0-0)
11-26 Penn St. (11-0-0)
12-3 Penn St. (11-0-0)
1-3 Oklahoma (11-1-0) (4)

1986
9-9 Oklahoma (1-0-0)
9-16 Oklahoma (1-0-0)
9-23 Oklahoma (2-0-0)
9-30 Miami (Fla.) (4-0-0) (2)
10-7 Miami (Fla.) (5-0-0)
10-14 Miami (Fla.) (6-0-0)
10-21 Miami (Fla.) (7-0-0)
10-28 Miami (Fla.) (7-0-0)
11-4 Miami (Fla.) (8-0-0)
11-11 Miami (Fla.) (9-0-0)

11-18 Miami (Fla.) (10-0-0)
11-25 Miami (Fla.) (10-0-0)
12-2 Miami (Fla.) (11-0-0)
1-4 Penn St. (12-0-0) (2)

1987
9-8 Oklahoma (1-0-0)
9-15 Oklahoma (2-0-0)
9-22 Oklahoma (2-0-0)
9-29 Oklahoma (3-0-0)
10-6 Oklahoma (4-0-0)
10-13 Oklahoma (5-0-0)
10-20 Oklahoma (6-0-0)
10-27 Oklahoma (7-0-0)
11-3 Oklahoma (8-0-0)
11-10 Oklahoma (9-0-0)
11-17 Nebraska (9-0-0) (2)
11-24 Oklahoma (11-0-0) (2)
12-1 Oklahoma (11-0-0)
12-8 Oklahoma (11-0-0)
1-3 Miami (Fla.) (12-0-0) (2)

1988
9-6 Miami (Fla.) (1-0-0)
9-13 Miami (Fla.) (1-0-0)
9-20 Miami (Fla.) (2-0-0)
9-27 Miami (Fla.) (3-0-0)
10-4 Miami (Fla.) (4-0-0)
10-11 Miami (Fla.) (4-0-0)
10-18 UCLA (6-0-0) (2)
10-25 UCLA (7-0-0)
11-1 Notre Dame (8-0-0) (2)
11-8 Notre Dame (9-0-0)
11-15 Notre Dame (9-0-0)
11-22 Notre Dame (10-0-0)
11-29 Notre Dame (11-0-0)
12-6 Notre Dame (11-0-0)
1-3 Notre Dame (12-0-0)

1989
9-5 Notre Dame (1-0-0)
9-12 Notre Dame (1-0-0)
9-19 Notre Dame (2-0-0)
9-26 Notre Dame (3-0-0)
10-3 Notre Dame (4-0-0)
10-10 Notre Dame (5-0-0)
10-17 Notre Dame (6-0-0)
10-24 Notre Dame (7-0-0)
10-31 Notre Dame (8-0-0)
11-7 Notre Dame (9-0-0)
11-14 Notre Dame (10-0-0)
11-21 Notre Dame (11-0-0)
11-28 Colorado (11-0-0) (2)
12-5 Colorado (11-0-0)
1-2 Miami (Fla.) (11-1-0) (2)

1990
9-4 Miami (Fla.) (0-0-0)
9-11 Notre Dame (0-0-0) (2)
9-18 Notre Dame (1-0-0)
9-25 Notre Dame (2-0-0)
10-2 Notre Dame (3-0-0)
10-9 Michigan (3-1-0) (3)
10-16 Virginia (6-0-0) (2)
10-23 Virginia (7-0-0)
10-30 Virginia (7-0-0)
11-6 Notre Dame (7-1-0) (2)
11-13 Notre Dame (8-1-0)
11-20 Colorado (10-1-1) (2)
11-27 Colorado (10-1-1)
12-4 Colorado (10-1-1)
1-2 Colorado (11-1-1)

1991
9-3 Florida St. (1-0-0)
9-10 Florida St. (2-0-0)
9-17 Florida St. (3-0-0)
9-23 Florida St. (3-0-0)
9-30 Florida St. (4-0-0)
10-7 Florida St. (5-0-0)
10-14 Florida St. (6-0-0)
10-21 Florida St. (7-0-0)
10-28 Florida St. (8-0-0)
11-4 Florida St. (9-0-0)
11-11 Florida St. (10-0-0)
11-18 Miami (Fla.) (9-0-0) (2)
11-25 Miami (Fla.) (10-0-0)
12-2 Miami (Fla.) (11-0-0)
1-2 Miami (Fla.) (12-0-0)

1992
9-8 Miami (Fla.) (1-0-0)
9-15 Miami (Fla.) (1-0-0)
9-22 Miami (Fla.) (2-0-0)
9-29 Washington (3-0-0) (2)
10-6 Washington (4-0-0)
10-13 Washington (5-0-0)
10-20 Miami (Fla.)† (6-0-0) (2)
10-27 Miami (Fla.) (7-0-0)
11-3 Washington (8-0-0) (2)
11-10 Miami (Fla.) (8-0-0) (2)
11-17 Miami (Fla.) (9-0-0)
11-24 Miami (Fla.) (10-0-0)
12-1 Miami (Fla.) (11-0-0)
12-8 Miami (Fla.) (11-0-0)
1-2 Alabama (13-0-0) (2)

1993
8-31 Florida St. (1-0-0)
9-7 Florida St. (2-0-0)
9-14 Florida St. (3-0-0)
9-21 Florida St. (4-0-0)
9-28 Florida St. (4-0-0)
10-5 Florida St. (5-0-0)
10-12 Florida St. (6-0-0)
10-19 Florida St. (7-0-0)
10-26 Florida St. (7-0-0)
11-2 Florida St. (8-0-0)
11-9 Florida St. (9-0-0)
11-16 Notre Dame (10-0-0) (2)
11-23 Florida St. (10-1-0) (2)
11-30 Florida St. (11-1-0)
12-7 Florida St. (11-1-0)
1-3 Florida St. (12-1-0)

1994
8-31 Florida (0-0-0)
9-6 Nebraska (1-0-0) (2)
9-13 Florida (2-0-0) (2)
9-20 Florida (3-0-0)
9-27 Florida (3-0-0)
10-4 Florida (4-0-0)
10-11 Florida (5-0-0)
10-18 Penn St. (6-0-0) (3)
10-25 Penn St. (6-0-0)
11-1 Nebraska (9-0-0) (3)
11-8 Nebraska (10-0-0)
11-15 Nebraska (11-0-0)
11-22 Nebraska (11-0-0)
11-29 Nebraska (12-0-0)
12-6 Nebraska (12-0-0)
1-3 Nebraska (13-0-0)

1995
8-29 Florida St. (0-0-0)
9-5 Florida St. (1-0-0)
9-12 Florida St. (2-0-0)
9-19 Florida St. (3-0-0)
9-26 Florida St. (4-0-0)
10-3 Florida St. (4-0-0)
10-10 Florida St. (5-0-0)
10-17 Florida St. (6-0-0)
10-24 Florida St. (7-0-0)
10-31 Nebraska (8-0-0) (2)
11-7 Nebraska (9-0-0)
11-14 Nebraska (10-0-0)
11-21 Nebraska (10-0-0)
11-28 Nebraska (11-0-0)
12-5 Nebraska (11-0-0)
1-3 Nebraska (12-0-0)

1996
8-26 Nebraska (0-0-0)
9-2 Nebraska (0-0-0)
9-9 Nebraska (1-0-0)
9-16 Nebraska (1-0-0)
9-23 Florida (3-0-0) (4)
9-30 Florida (4-0-0)
10-7 Florida (5-0-0)
10-14 Florida (6-0-0)
10-21 Florida (7-0-0)
10-28 Florida (7-0-0)
11-4 Florida (8-0-0)
11-11 Florida (9-0-0)
11-18 Florida (10-0-0)
11-25 Florida (10-0-0)
12-2 Florida St. (11-0-0) (2)
12-9 Florida St. (11-0-0)
1-3 Florida (12-1-0)

1997
8-25 Penn St. (0-0-0)
9-2 Penn St. (0-0-0)
9-8 Penn St. (1-0-0)
9-15 Penn St. (2-0-0)
9-22 Florida (3-0-0) (3)
9-29 Florida (4-0-0)
10-6 Florida (5-0-0)
10-13 Penn St. (5-0-0) (2)
10-20 Nebraska (6-0-0) (2)
10-27 Nebraska (7-0-0)
11-3 Nebraska (8-0-0)
11-10 Michigan (9-0-0) (4)
11-17 Michigan (10-0-0)
11-24 Michigan (11-0-0)
12-1 Michigan (11-0-0)
12-8 Michigan (11-0-0)
1-3 Michigan (12-0-0)

1998
9-7 Ohio St. (1-0-0)
9-14 Ohio St. (2-0-0)
9-21 Ohio St. (3-0-0)
9-28 Ohio St. (3-0-0)
10-5 Ohio St. (4-0-0)
10-12 Ohio St. (5-0-0)
10-19 Ohio St. (6-0-0)
10-26 Ohio St. (7-0-0)
11-2 Ohio St. (8-0-0)
11-9 Tennessee (8-0-0) (2)
11-16 Tennessee (9-0-0)
11-23 Tennessee (10-0-0)
11-30 Tennessee (11-0-0)
12-7 Tennessee (12-0-0)
1-5 Tennessee (13-0-0)

1999
8-30 Florida St. (1-0-0)
9-6 Florida St. (1-0-0)
9-13 Florida St. (2-0-0)
9-20 Florida St. (3-0-0)
9-27 Florida St. (4-0-0)
10-4 Florida St. (5-0-0)
10-11 Florida St. (6-0-0)
10-18 Florida St. (7-0-0)
10-25 Florida St. (8-0-0)
11-1 Florida St. (9-0-0)
11-8 Florida St. (9-0-0)
11-15 Florida St. (10-0-0)
11-22 Florida St. (11-0-0)
11-29 Florida St. (11-0-0)
12-6 Florida St. (11-0-0)
1-5 Florida St. (12-0-0)

2000
8-28 Nebraska (0-0-0)
9-4 Nebraska (1-0-0)
9-11 Nebraska (2-0-0)
9-18 Nebraska (2-0-0)
9-25 Nebraska (3-0-0)
10-2 Nebraska (4-0-0)
10-9 Nebraska (5-0-0)
10-16 Nebraska (6-0-0)
10-23 Nebraska (7-0-0)
10-30 Oklahoma (7-0-0) (3)
11-6 Oklahoma (8-0-0)
11-13 Oklahoma (9-0-0)
11-20 Oklahoma (10-0-0)
11-27 Oklahoma (11-0-0)
12-4 Oklahoma (12-0-0)
1-5 Oklahoma (13-0-0)

2001
8-27 Florida (0-0-0)
9-2 Florida (1-0-0)
9-9 Miami (Fla.) (2-0-0) (2)
9-23 Miami (Fla.) (2-0-0)
9-30 Miami (Fla.) (3-0-0)
10-7 Florida (4-0-0) (2)
10-14 Miami (Fla.) (5-0-0) (2)
10-21 Miami (Fla.) (6-0-0)
10-28 Miami (Fla.) (7-0-0)
11-4 Miami (Fla.) (7-0-0)
11-11 Miami (Fla.) (8-0-0)
11-18 Miami (Fla.) (9-0-0)
11-24 Miami (Fla.) (10-0-0)
12-2 Miami (Fla.) (11-0-0)
12-8 Miami (Fla.) (11-0-0)
1-4 Miami (Fla.) (12-0-0)

2002

8-26 Miami (Fla.) (0-0-0)
9-2 Miami (Fla.) (1-0-0)
9-9 Miami (Fla.) (2-0-0)
9-16 Miami (Fla.) (3-0-0)
9-23 Miami (Fla.) (4-0-0)
9-30 Miami (Fla.) (4-0-0)
10-7 Miami (Fla.) (5-0-0)
10-14 Miami (Fla.) (6-0-0)
10-21 Miami (Fla.) (6-0-0)
10-28 Miami (Fla.) (7-0-0)
11-4 Oklahoma (8-0-0) (2)
11-11 Miami (Fla.) (9-0-0) (2)
11-18 Miami (Fla.) (9-0-0)
11-25 Miami (Fla.) (10-0-0)
12-2 Miami (Fla.) (11-0-0)
12-9 Miami (Fla.) (12-0-0)
1-3 Ohio St. (14-0-0) (2)

2003

8-25 Oklahoma (0-0-0)
9-1 Oklahoma (1-0-0)
9-8 Oklahoma (2-0-0)
9-15 Oklahoma (3-0-0)
9-22 Oklahoma (4-0-0)
9-29 Oklahoma (4-0-0)
10-6 Oklahoma (5-0-0)
10-13 Oklahoma (6-0-0)
10-20 Oklahoma (7-0-0)
10-27 Oklahoma (8-0-0)
11-3 Oklahoma (9-0-0)
11-10 Oklahoma (10-0-0)
11-17 Oklahoma (11-0-0)
11-24 Oklahoma (12-0-0)
12-1 Oklahoma (12-0-0)
12-8 Southern California (11-1-0) (2)
1-5 Southern California (12-1-0)

2004

8-30 Southern California (0-0-0)
9-6 Southern California (1-0-0)
9-13 Southern California (2-0-0)
9-20 Southern California (3-0-0)
9-27 Southern California (4-0-0)
10-4 Southern California (4-0-0)
10-11 Southern California (5-0-0)
10-18 Southern California (6-0-0)
10-25 Southern California (7-0-0)
11-1 Southern California (8-0-0)
11-8 Southern California (9-0-0)
11-15 Southern California (9-0-0)
11-22 Southern California (10-0-0)
11-29 Southern California (11-0-0)
12-6 Southern California (12-0-0)
1-5 Southern California (13-0-0)

2005

Pre. Southern California (0-0-0)
9-4 Southern California (1-0-0)
9-11 Southern California (1-0-0)
9-18 Southern California (2-0-0)
9-25 Southern California (3-0-0)
10-2 Southern California (4-0-0)
10-9 Southern California (5-0-0)
10-16 Southern California (6-0-0)
10-23 Southern California (7-0-0)
10-30 Southern California (8-0-0)
11-6 Southern California (9-0-0)
11-13 Southern California (10-0-0)
11-20 Southern California (11-0-0)
11-27 Southern California (11-0-0)
12-4 Southern California (12-0-0)
1-6 Texas (13-0-0) (2)

2006

Pre. Ohio St. (0-0-0)
9-3 Ohio St. (1-0-0)
9-10 Ohio St. (2-0-0)
9-17 Ohio St. (3-0-0)
9-24 Ohio St. (4-0-0)
10-1 Ohio St. (5-0-0)
10-8 Ohio St. (6-0-0)
10-15 Ohio St. (7-0-0)
10-22 Ohio St. (8-0-0)
10-29 Ohio St. (9-0-0)
11-5 Ohio St. (10-0-0)
11-12 Ohio St. (11-0-0)
11-19 Ohio St. (12-0-0)
11-26 Ohio St. (12-0-0)
12-3 Ohio St. (12-0-0)
1-9 Florida (13-1-0) (2)

**On January 6, 1948, in a special postseason poll after the Rose Bowl, The Associated Press voted Michigan No. 1 and Notre Dame No. 2. However, the postseason poll did not supersede the final regular-season poll of December 9, 1947. †A first-place tie occurred in The Associated Press poll for the first time in 51 years, but Miami (Fla.) had one more first-place vote, 31-30, than Washington.*

Associated Press (AP) Poll Records

FULL SEASON AT NO. 1

1943 Notre Dame (Nine Weeks)
1945 Army (Nine Weeks)
1971 Nebraska (14 Weeks)
1972 Southern California (14 Weeks)
1999 Florida St. (16 Weeks)
2004 Southern California (16 Weeks)

MOST CONSECUTIVE WEEKS AT NO. 1

33 Southern California, Dec. 8, 2003 to Dec. 4, 2005
20 Miami (Fla.), Oct. 14, 2001 to Oct. 28, 2002
19 Notre Dame, Nov. 1, 1988 to Nov. 21, 1989
17 Southern California, Sept. 12, 1972 to Sept. 25, 1973
16 Florida St., Aug. 30, 1999 to Jan. 5, 2000
15 Army, Oct. 31, 1944 to Dec. 4, 1945
15 Nebraska, Jan. 1, 1971 to Jan. 4, 1972
14 Nebraska, Sept. 6, 1983 to Dec. 6, 1983
14 Oklahoma, Sept. 1, 2003 to Dec. 1, 2003
14 Ohio St., Sept. 3, 2006 to Dec. 3, 2006
13 LSU, Oct. 28, 1958 to Nov. 3, 1959
12 Notre Dame, Oct. 5, 1943 to Oct. 24, 1944
12 Texas, Oct. 15, 1963 to Oct. 13, 1964
12 Ohio St., Nov. 26, 1968 to Nov. 18, 1969

BIGGEST JUMP TO NO. 1 FROM PREVIOUS WEEK

8th Wisconsin, September 30 to October 7, 1952
5th Tennessee, October 17 to October 24, 1939
5th Michigan St., November 6 to November 13, 1951
5th Maryland, September 20 to September 27, 1955
5th Michigan St., October 10 to October 17, 1961
5th Notre Dame, November 29, 1977 to January 4, 1978
4th Southern California, November 21 to November 28, 1939
4th Michigan, October 12 to October 19, 1948
4th Army, October 3 to October 10, 1950
4th Ohio St., October 19 to October 26, 1954
4th Michigan St., November 12 to November 19, 1957
4th Syracuse, November 3 to November 10, 1959
4th Minnesota, November 15 to November 22, 1960
4th Alabama, November 30, 1965 to January 4, 1966
4th Southern California, November 21 to November 28, 1967
4th Notre Dame, September 8 to September 15, 1981
4th Oklahoma, December 3, 1985 to January 3, 1986
4th Florida, September 16 to September 23, 1996
4th Michigan, November 3 to November 10, 1997

PRESEASON NO. 1 TO NOT RANKED NO. 1 DURING REMAINDER OF THE SEASON
(From 1950)

1964 Mississippi
1965 Nebraska
1966 Alabama
1971 Notre Dame
1972 Nebraska
1976 Nebraska
1984 Auburn
1988 Florida St.
1989 Michigan

MOST TEAMS AT NO. 1 IN ONE SEASON

7 1981 (Michigan, Notre Dame, Southern California, Texas, Penn St., Pittsburgh, Clemson)
5 1950 (Notre Dame, Army, SMU, Ohio St., Oklahoma)
5 1958 (Ohio St., Oklahoma, Auburn, Army, LSU)
5 1960 (Mississippi, Syracuse, Iowa, Minnesota, Missouri)
5 1961 (Iowa, Mississippi, Michigan St., Texas, Alabama)
5 1962 (Alabama, Ohio St., Texas, Northwestern, Southern California)
5 1965 (Notre Dame, Texas, Arkansas, Michigan St., Alabama)
5 1977 (Michigan, Oklahoma, Southern California, Texas, Notre Dame)
5 1984 [Miami (Fla.), Nebraska, Texas, Washington, BYU]
5 1985 (Oklahoma, Auburn, Iowa, Florida, Penn St.)
5 1990 [Miami (Fla.), Notre Dame, Michigan, Virginia, Colorado]
4 1939 (Pittsburgh, Tennessee, Texas A&M, Southern California)
4 1954 (Oklahoma, Notre Dame, Ohio St., UCLA)
4 1957 (Oklahoma, Michigan St., Texas A&M, Auburn)
4 1964 (Texas, Ohio St., Notre Dame, Alabama)
4 1973 (Southern California, Ohio St., Alabama, Notre Dame)
4 1980 (Ohio St., Alabama, Notre Dame, Georgia)
4 1982 (Pittsburgh, Washington, Georgia, Penn St.)
4 1997 (Penn St., Florida, Nebraska, Michigan)

MOST CONSECUTIVE WEEKS WITH DIFFERENT NO. 1 TEAM

4 October 31 to November 21, 1950 (in order: SMU, Army, Ohio St., Oklahoma)
4 September 23 to October 14, 1958 (in order: Ohio St., Oklahoma, Auburn, Army)
3 November 1 to November 15, 1938 (in order: Pittsburgh, TCU, Notre Dame)
3 October 5 to October 19, 1948 (in order: Notre Dame, North Carolina, Michigan)
3 October 9 to October 23, 1951 (in order: Michigan St., California, Tennessee)
3 October 19 to November 2, 1954 (in order: Oklahoma, Ohio St., UCLA)
3 October 15 to October 29, 1957 (in order: Michigan St., Oklahoma, Texas A&M)
3 November 12 to November 26, 1957 (in order: Texas A&M, Michigan St., Auburn)
3 November 1 to November 15, 1960 (in order: Iowa, Minnesota, Missouri)
3 November 6 to November 20, 1962 (in order: Northwestern, Alabama, Southern California)
3 October 12 to October 26, 1965 (in order: Texas, Arkansas, Michigan St.)
3 September 10 to September 24, 1974 (in order: Oklahoma, Notre Dame, Ohio St.)
3 September 20 to October 4, 1977 (in order: Michigan, Oklahoma, Southern California)

3 September 8 to September 22, 1981 (in order: Michigan, Notre Dame, Southern California)
3 October 6 to October 20, 1981 (in order: Southern California, Texas, Penn St.)
3 November 6 to November 20, 1984 (in order: Washington, Nebraska, BYU)
3 October 29 to November 12, 1985 (in order: Iowa, Florida, Penn St.)
3 October 2 to October 16, 1990 (in order: Notre Dame, Michigan, Virginia)
3 October 6 to October 20, 1997 (in order: Florida, Penn St., Nebraska)

LARGEST WINNING MARGIN FOR A RANKED OPPONENT DEFEATING NO. 1

34 No. 11 Penn St. (48) vs. No. 1 Pittsburgh (14), Nov. 28, 1981
32 No. 3 Florida (52) vs. No. 1 Florida St. (20), Jan. 2, 1997 (Sugar Bowl)
29 No. 8 Wisconsin (37) vs. No. 1 Northwestern (6), Nov. 10, 1962
28 No. 5 Notre Dame (38) vs. No. 1 Texas (10), Jan. 2, 1978 (Cotton Bowl)
27 No. 2 Florida (41) vs. No. 1 Ohio St. (14), Jan. 8, 2007 (BCS Championship)
21 No. 2 Texas (28) vs. No. 1 Oklahoma (7), Oct. 12, 1963
21 No. 17 Georgia (24) vs. No. 1 Florida (3), Nov. 9, 1985
21 No. 2 Alabama (34) vs. No. 1 Miami (Fla.) (13), Jan. 1, 1993 (Sugar Bowl)
20 No. 11 Notre Dame (26) vs. No. 1 Northwestern (6), Nov. 21, 1936
19 No. 17 Arizona St. (19) vs. No. 1 Nebraska (0), Sept. 21, 1996
18 No. 11 Michigan (25) vs. No. 1 Notre Dame (7), Sept. 19, 1981
17 No. 3 Minnesota (27) vs. No. 1 Iowa (10), Nov. 5, 1950
17 No. 7 Miami (Fla.) (27) vs. No. 1 Notre Dame (10), Nov. 25, 1989
17 No. 3 Oklahoma (31) vs. No. 1 Nebraska (14), Oct. 28, 2000
15 No. 3 Maryland (28) vs. No. 1 Tennessee (13), Jan. 1, 1952 (Sugar Bowl)
15 No. 4 Oklahoma (25) vs. No. 1 Penn St. (10), Jan. 1, 1986 (Orange Bowl)
15 No. 4 Notre Dame (21) vs. No. 1 Colorado (6), Jan. 1, 1990 (Orange Bowl)

LARGEST WINNING MARGIN FOR AN UNRANKED OPPONENT DEFEATING NO. 1

43 Holy Cross (55) vs. No. 1 Boston College (12), Nov. 28, 1942
31 Arkansas (42) vs. No. 1 Texas (11), Oct. 17, 1981
18 Tennessee (38) vs. No. 1 Auburn (20), Sept. 28, 1985
16 Kansas (23) vs. No. 1 Missouri (7), Nov. 19, 1960
16 Minnesota (16) vs. No. 1 Michigan (0), Oct. 22, 1977
15 Notre Dame (31) vs. No. 1 Pittsburgh (16), Nov. 6, 1982
14 Auburn (27) vs. No. 1 Georgia (13), Nov. 21, 1942
14 Purdue (28) vs. No. 1 Notre Dame (14), Oct. 7, 1950

MOST WEEKS AT NO. 1 — ALL-TIME

(Complete List; Does not count preseason polls)

No.	Team, First Yr. as No. 1
89	Notre Dame, 1938
86	Oklahoma, 1954
81	Ohio St., 1942
77	Southern California, 1939
65	Nebraska, 1970
62	Miami (Fla.), 1983
53	Florida St., 1991
43	Texas, 1940
32	Michigan, 1947
29	Alabama, 1962
28	Michigan St., 1951
27	Army, 1944
25	Florida, 1985
20	Pittsburgh, 1937
19	Penn St., 1978
18	Minnesota, 1936
17	Tennessee, 1939
14	Georgia, 1942
14	Washington, 1982
13	LSU, 1958
10	Iowa, 1960
7	Texas A&M, 1939
6	Auburn, 1957
6	Colorado, 1989
6	Maryland, 1953
6	Syracuse, 1959
6	UCLA, 1954
5	Northwestern, 1936
4	BYU, 1984
4	California, 1937
4	*Cornell, 1940
4	Mississippi, 1960
4	Purdue, 1968
3	Virginia, 1990
2	Clemson, 1981
2	SMU, 1950
2	TCU, 1938
1	Arkansas, 1965
1	Boston College, 1942
1	Missouri, 1960
1	North Carolina, 1948
1	Wisconsin, 1952

No longer FBS.

MOST TIMES DEFEATING NO. 1

(Complete List)

(Since 1936)

8 Notre Dame
7 Miami (Fla.)
7 Purdue
7 Southern California
6 Oklahoma
4 Michigan
4 Ohio St.
4 Penn St.
4 Texas
3 Alabama
3 Arkansas
3 Auburn
3 Minnesota
3 UCLA
3 Wisconsin
2 Arizona
2 Florida
2 Georgia Tech
2 Illinois
2 Maryland
2 Michigan St.
2 Tennessee
1 Arizona St.
1 Army
1 Boston College
1 BYU
1 Florida St.
1 Georgia
1 Kansas
1 Kentucky
1 LSU
1 Mississippi St.
1 Nebraska
1 Northwestern
1 Oregon St.
1 Rice
1 Stanford
1 Syracuse
1 Texas A&M
1 TCU
1 Washington
1 Washington St.

LONGEST ACTIVE CONSECUTIVE STREAK OF WEEKS APPEARING IN THE AP POLL

No.	Team (Since Year)
109	Texas (2000)
82	Southern California (2002)
65	LSU (2003)
35	Ohio St. (2004)

LONGEST ACTIVE CONSECUTIVE STREAK OF WEEKS APPEARING IN THE AP TOP 10

No.	Team (Since Year)
56	Southern California (2002)

MOST WEEKLY APPEARANCES IN THE AP POLL

(Since 1936)

741 Michigan
716 Ohio St.
703 Notre Dame
642 Oklahoma
637 Southern California
632 Nebraska
621 Texas
605 Alabama
546 Tennessee
536 Penn St.

LOWEST FINAL RANKING OF NO. 1 IN FIRST RANKING

11th Oklahoma (2001)

2006 Associated Press Week-By-Week Polls

Team	Pre	S3	S10	S17	S24	O1	O8	O15	O22	O29	N5	N12	N19	N26	D3	J9
Ohio St.	1	1	1	1	1	1	1	1	1	1	1	1	1	1	1	2
Notre Dame	2	T-4	2	12	12	12	9	10	11	11	9	6	6	12	11	17
Texas	3	2	8	7	7	7	6	5	5	4	4	11	11	T-17	18	13
Auburn	4	T-4	3	2	2	2	11	8	7	6	5	15	14	11	10	9
West Virginia	5	6	5	4	4	4	5	4	4	3	10	8	7	15	13	10
Southern California	6	3	4	3	3	3	3	3	3	9	7	4	3	2	8	4
Florida	7	7	7	5	5	5	2	9	9	7	6	3	4	4	2	1
LSU	8	8	6	10	9	9	14	14	14	13	12	9	9	5	4	3
California	9	22	21	22	20	16	10	11	12	10	8	17	22	21	20	14
Oklahoma	10	15	15	17	16	14	23	20	19	18	17	16	13	T-8	7	11
Florida St.	11	9	9	18	19	17	NR	NR	NR	NR	NR	NR	NR	NR	NR	NR
Miami (Fla.)	12	17	17	NR	NR	NR	NR	NR	NR	NR	NR	NR	NR	NR	NR	NR
Louisville	13	13	12	8	8	8	7	6	6	5	3	10	8	6	5	6
Michigan	14	10	11	6	6	6	4	2	2	2	2	2	2	3	3	8
Georgia	15	12	10	9	10	10	16	NR	NR	NR	NR	NR	NR	NR	NR	23
Iowa	16	14	16	14	13	19	15	NR	NR	NR	NR	NR	NR	NR	NR	NR
Virginia Tech	17	16	14	11	11	21	22	NR	NR	23	20	19	17	14	14	19
Clemson	18	18	NR	19	18	15	12	12	10	19	NR	25	24	NR	NR	NR
Penn St.	19	19	25	24	NR	NR	NR	NR	NR	NR	NR	NR	NR	NR	NR	24
Nebraska	20	21	19	23	21	22	21	17	20	NR	NR	24	23	19	22	NR
Oregon	21	20	18	13	14	11	18	16	25	24	21	NR	NR	NR	NR	NR
TCU	22	23	20	16	17	NR	NR	NR	NR	NR	NR	NR	NR	NR	25	22
Tennessee	23	11	13	15	15	13	8	7	8	8	13	22	19	T-17	17	25
Arizona St.	24	25	22	20	NR	NR	NR	NR	NR	NR	NR	NR	NR	NR	NR	NR
Texas Tech	25	24	24	NR	NR	NR	NR	NR	NR	NR	NR	NR	NR	NR	NR	NR
Boston College	NR	NR	23	20	NR	25	NR	22	18	16	22	20	18	25	23	20
Boise St.	NR	NR	NR	25	22	20	20	18	15	14	14	13	12	10	9	5
Rutgers	NR	NR	NR	NR	23	24	24	19	16	15	15	7	15	13	16	12
Georgia Tech	NR	NR	NR	NR	24	18	13	13	21	20	19	18	16	23	NR	NR
Missouri	NR	NR	NR	NR	25	23	19	24	23	NR	NR	NR	NR	NR	NR	NR
Arkansas	NR	NR	NR	NR	NR	NR	17	15	13	12	11	5	5	T-8	12	15
Wisconsin	NR	NR	NR	NR	NR	NR	25	21	17	17	16	12	10	7	6	7
Texas A&M	NR	NR	NR	NR	NR	NR	NR	23	22	21	24	NR	NR	22	21	NR
Wake Forest	NR	NR	NR	NR	NR	NR	NR	25	24	22	18	14	20	16	15	18
Washington St.	NR	NR	NR	NR	NR	NR	NR	NR	NR	25	NR	NR	NR	NR	NR	NR
Maryland	NR	NR	NR	NR	NR	NR	NR	NR	NR	NR	23	21	NR	NR	NR	NR
BYU	NR	NR	NR	NR	NR	NR	NR	NR	NR	NR	25	23	21	20	19	16
Hawaii	NR	NR	NR	NR	NR	NR	NR	NR	NR	NR	NR	NR	25	24	NR	NR
Oregon St.	NR	NR	NR	NR	NR	NR	NR	NR	NR	NR	NR	NR	NR	NR	24	21

T-Tie for ranking.

No. 1 vs. No. 2

The No. 1 and No. 2 teams in The Associated Press poll (begun in 1936) have faced each other 36 times (20 in regular-season games and 16 in bowl games). The No. 1 team has won 21, with two games ending in ties.

Date	Score	Stadium (Site)
10-9-43	No. 1 Notre Dame 35, No. 2 Michigan 12	Michigan Stadium (Ann Arbor)
11-20-43	No. 1 Notre Dame 14, No. 2 Iowa Pre-Flight 13	Notre Dame (South Bend)
12-2-44	No. 1 Army 23, No. 2 Navy 7	Municipal (Baltimore)
11-10-45	No. 1 Army 48, No. 2 Notre Dame 0	Yankee (New York)
12-1-45	No. 1 Army 32, No. 2 Navy 13	Municipal (Philadelphia)
11-9-46	No. 1 Army 0, No. 2 Notre Dame 0 (tie)	Yankee (New York)
1-1-63	No. 1 Southern California 42, No. 2 Wisconsin 37 (Rose Bowl)	Rose Bowl (Pasadena)
10-12-63	No. 2 Texas 28, No. 1 Oklahoma 7	Cotton Bowl (Dallas)
1-1-64	No. 1 Texas 28, No. 2 Navy 6 (Cotton Bowl)	Cotton Bowl (Dallas)
11-19-66	No. 1 Notre Dame 10, No. 2 Michigan St. 10 (tie)	Spartan (East Lansing)
9-28-68	No. 1 Purdue 37, No. 2 Notre Dame 22	Notre Dame (South Bend)
1-1-69	No. 1 Ohio St. 27, No. 2 Southern California 16 (Rose Bowl)	Rose Bowl (Pasadena)
12-6-69	No. 1 Texas 15, No. 2 Arkansas 14	Razorback (Fayetteville)
11-25-71	No. 1 Nebraska 35, No. 2 Oklahoma 31	Owen Field (Norman)
1-1-72	No. 1 Nebraska 38, No. 2 Alabama 6 (Orange Bowl)	Orange Bowl (Miami)
1-1-79	No. 2 Alabama 14, No. 1 Penn St. 7 (Sugar Bowl)	Sugar Bowl (New Orleans)
9-26-81	No. 1 Southern California 28, No. 2 Oklahoma 24	Coliseum (Los Angeles)
1-1-83	No. 2 Penn St. 27, No. 1 Georgia 23 (Sugar Bowl)	Sugar Bowl (New Orleans)
10-19-85	No. 1 Iowa 12, No. 2 Michigan 10	Kinnick (Iowa City)
9-27-86	No. 2 Miami (Fla.) 28, No. 1 Oklahoma 16	Orange Bowl (Miami)
1-2-87	No. 2 Penn St. 14, No. 1 Miami (Fla.) 10 (Fiesta Bowl)	Sun Devil (Tempe)
11-21-87	No. 2 Oklahoma 17, No. 1 Nebraska 7	Memorial (Lincoln)
1-1-88	No. 2 Miami (Fla.) 20, No. 1 Oklahoma 14 (Orange Bowl)	Orange Bowl (Miami)
11-26-88	No. 1 Notre Dame 27, No. 2 Southern California 10	Coliseum (Los Angeles)
9-16-89	No. 1 Notre Dame 24, No. 2 Michigan 19	Michigan (Ann Arbor)
11-16-91	No. 2 Miami (Fla.) 17, No. 1 Florida St. 16	Doak Campbell (Tallahassee)
1-1-93	No. 2 Alabama 34, No. 1 Miami (Fla.) 13 (Sugar Bowl)	Superdome (New Orleans)

Date	Score	Stadium (Site)
11-13-93	No. 2 Notre Dame 31, No. 1 Florida St. 24	Notre Dame (South Bend)
1-1-94	No. 1 Florida St. 18, No. 2 Nebraska 16 (Orange Bowl)	Orange Bowl (Miami)
1-2-96	No. 1 Nebraska 62, No. 2 Florida 24 (Fiesta Bowl)	Sun Devil (Tempe)
11-30-96	No. 2 Florida St. 24, No. 1 Florida 21	Doak Campbell (Tallahassee)
1-4-99	No. 1 Tennessee 23, No. 2 Florida St. 16 (Fiesta Bowl)	Sun Devil (Tempe)
1-4-00	No. 1 Florida St. 46, No. 2 Virginia Tech 29	Superdome (New Orleans)
1-3-03	No. 2 Ohio St. 31, No. 1 Miami (Fla.) 24 (2 ot) (Fiesta Bowl)	Sun Devil (Tempe)
1-4-05	No. 1 Southern California 55, No. 2 Oklahoma 19 (Orange Bowl)	Dolphins Stadium (Miami)
1-5-06	No. 2 Texas 41, No. 1 Southern California 38 (Rose Bowl)	Rose Bowl (Pasadena)
9-9-06	No. 1 Ohio St. 24, No. 2 Texas 7	Darrell K. Royal-Texas Memorial (Austin)
11-18-06	No. 1 Ohio St. 42, No. 2 Michigan 39	Ohio Stadium (Columbus)
1-8-07	No. 2 Florida 41, No. 1 Ohio St. 14 (BCS Championship)	University of Phoenix (Glendale, Ariz.)

Games in Which a No. 1-Ranked Team Was Defeated or Tied

Listed here are 120 games in which the No. 1-ranked team in The Associated Press poll was defeated or tied. An asterisk (*) indicates the home team, an (N) or the name of the bowl game indicates a neutral site. In parentheses after the winning or tying team is its rank in the previous week's poll (NR indicates it was not ranked) and its won-lost record entering the game, followed by its score. The defeated or tied No. 1-ranked team follows with its score, and in parentheses is its rank in the poll the following week. Before 1965, the polls were final before bowl games. (Note: Only 10 teams were ranked in the weekly polls during 1962, 1963, 1964, 1965, 1966 and 1967; 20 teams all other seasons until 1989, when 25 teams were ranked.)

Date	Game
10-31-36	*Northwestern (3, 4-0-0) 6, Minnesota 0 (2)
11-21-36	*Notre Dame (11, 5-2-0) 26, Northwestern 6 (7)
10-30-37	(Tie) Washington (NR, 3-2-1) 0, *California 0 (2)
10-29-38	Carnegie Mellon (T19, 4-1-0) 20, *Pittsburgh 10 (3)
12-2-38	*Southern California (8, 7-2-0) 13, Notre Dame 0 (5)
10-14-39	Duquesne (NR, 3-0-0) 21, *Pittsburgh 13 (18)
11-8-41	(Tie) Baylor (NR, 3-4-0) 7, *Texas 7 (2)
10-31-42	*Wisconsin (6, 5-0-1) 17, Ohio St. 7 (6)
11-21-42	(N) Auburn (NR, 4-4-1) 27, Georgia 13 (5)
11-28-42	Holy Cross (NR, 4-4-1) 55, *Boston College 12 (8)
11-27-43	*Great Lakes NTS (NR, 9-2-0) 19, Notre Dame 14 (1)
11-9-46	(Tie) (N) Notre Dame (2, 5-0-0) 0, Army 0 (1)
10-8-49	Army (7, 2-0-0) 21, *Michigan 7 (7)
10-7-50	Purdue (NR, 0-1-0) 28, *Notre Dame 14 (10)
11-4-50	*Texas (7, 4-1-0) 23, SMU 20 (7)
11-18-50	*Illinois (10, 6-1-0) 14, Ohio St. 7 (8)
1-1-51	(Sugar Bowl) Kentucky (7, 10-1-0) 13, Oklahoma 7 (1)
10-20-51	Southern California (11, 4-1-0) 21, *California 14 (9)
1-1-52	(Sugar Bowl) Maryland (3, 9-0-0) 28, Tennessee 13 (1)
10-11-52	*Ohio St. (NR, 1-1-0) 23, Wisconsin 14 (12)
11-21-53	(Tie) Iowa (20, 5-3-0) 14, *Notre Dame 14 (2)
1-1-54	(Orange Bowl) Oklahoma (4, 8-1-1) 7, Maryland 0 (1)
10-2-54	Purdue (19, 1-0-0) 27, *Notre Dame 14 (8)
9-24-55	*Maryland (5, 1-0-0) 7, UCLA 0 (7)
10-27-56	*Illinois (NR, 1-3-0) 20, Michigan St. 13 (4)
10-19-57	Purdue (NR, 0-3-0) 20, *Michigan St. 13 (8)
11-16-57	*Rice (20, 4-3-0) 7, Texas A&M 6 (4)
10-25-58	(Tie) *Pittsburgh (NR, 4-1-0) 14, Army 14 (3)
11-7-59	*Tennessee (13, 4-1-1) 14, LSU 13 (3)
11-5-60	*Minnesota (3, 6-0-0) 27, Iowa 10 (5)
11-12-60	Purdue (NR, 2-4-1) 23, *Minnesota 14 (4)
11-19-60	Kansas (NR, 6-2-1) 23, *Missouri 7 (5)
1-1-61	(Rose Bowl) Washington (6, 9-1-0) 17, Minnesota 7 (1)
11-4-61	*Minnesota (NR, 4-1-0) 13, Michigan St. 0 (6)
11-18-61	TCU (NR, 2-4-1) 6, *Texas 0 (5)
10-6-62	*UCLA (NR, 0-0-0) 9, Ohio St. 7 (10)
10-27-62	(Tie) *Rice (NR, 0-3-1) 14, Texas 14 (5)
11-10-62	*Wisconsin (8, 5-1-0) 37, Northwestern 6 (9)
11-17-62	*Georgia Tech (NR, 5-2-1) 7, Alabama 6 (6)
9-28-63	Oklahoma (3, 1-0-0) 17, *Southern California 12 (8)
10-12-63	(N) Texas (2, 3-0-0) 28, Oklahoma 7 (6)
10-17-64	Arkansas (8, 4-0-0) 14, *Texas 13 (6)
11-28-64	*Southern California (NR, 6-3-0) 20, Notre Dame 17 (3)
1-1-65	(Orange Bowl) Texas (5, 9-1-0) 21, Alabama 17 (1)
9-25-65	*Purdue (6, 1-0-0) 25, Notre Dame 21 (8)
10-16-65	*Arkansas (3, 4-0-0) 27, Texas 24 (5)
1-1-66	(Rose Bowl) UCLA (5, 7-2-1) 14, Michigan St. 12 (2)
11-19-66	(Tie) *Michigan St. (2, 9-0-0) 10, Notre Dame 10 (1)
9-30-67	*Purdue (10, 1-0-0) 28, Notre Dame 21 (6)
11-11-67	*Oregon St. (NR, 5-2-1) 3, Southern California 0 (4)
11-18-67	*Southern California (4, 8-1-0) 21, UCLA 20 (4)
10-12-68	*Ohio St. (4, 2-0-0) 13, Purdue 0 (5)
11-22-69	*Michigan (12, 7-2-0) 24, Ohio St. 12 (4)
1-1-71	(Cotton Bowl) Notre Dame (6, 8-1-1) 24, Texas 11 (3)
9-29-73	(Tie) Oklahoma (8, 1-0-0) 7, *Southern California 7 (4)
11-24-73	(Tie) *Michigan (4, 10-0-0) 10, Ohio St. 10 (3)
12-31-73	(Sugar Bowl) Notre Dame (3, 10-0-0) 24, Alabama 23 (4)
11-9-74	*Michigan St. (NR, 4-3-1) 16, Ohio St. 13 (4)
1-1-76	(Rose Bowl) UCLA (11, 8-2-1) 23, Ohio St. 10 (4)
11-6-76	*Purdue (NR, 3-5-0) 16, Michigan 14 (4)
10-8-77	Alabama (T7, 3-1-0) 21, *Southern California 20 (6)
10-22-77	*Minnesota (NR, 4-2-0) 16, Michigan 0 (6)
1-2-78	(Cotton Bowl) Notre Dame (5, 10-1-0) 38, Texas 10 (4)
9-23-78	(N) Southern California (7, 2-0-0) 24, Alabama 14 (3)
11-11-78	*Nebraska (4, 8-1-0) 17, Oklahoma 14 (4)
1-1-79	(Sugar Bowl) Alabama (2, 10-1-0) 14, Penn St. 7 (4)
10-13-79	(Tie) Stanford (NR, 3-2-0) 21, *Southern California 21 (4)
1-1-80	(Rose Bowl) Southern California (3, 10-0-1) 17, Ohio St. 16 (4)
11-1-80	(N) Mississippi St. (NR, 6-2-0) 6, Alabama 3 (6)
11-8-80	(Tie) *Georgia Tech (NR, 1-7-0) 3, Notre Dame 3 (6)
9-12-81	*Wisconsin (NR, 0-0-0) 21, Michigan 14 (11)
9-19-81	*Michigan (11, 0-1-0) 25, Notre Dame 7 (13)
10-10-81	Arizona (NR, 2-2-0) 13, *Southern California 10 (7)
10-17-81	*Arkansas (NR, 4-1-0) 42, Texas 11 (10)
10-31-81	*Miami (Fla.) (NR, 4-2-0) 17, Penn St. 14 (5)
11-28-81	Penn St. (11, 8-2-0) 48, *Pittsburgh 14 (10)
11-6-82	Notre Dame (NR, 5-1-1) 31, *Pittsburgh 16 (8)
1-1-83	(Sugar Bowl) Penn St. (2, 10-1-0) 27, Georgia 23 (4)
1-2-84	(Orange Bowl) Miami (Fla.) (5, 10-1-0) 31, Nebraska 30 (4)
9-8-84	*Michigan (14, 0-0-0) 22, Miami (Fla.) 14 (5)
9-29-84	*Syracuse (NR, 2-1-0) 17, Nebraska 9 (8)
10-13-84	(N) (Tie) Oklahoma (3, 4-0-0) 15, Texas 15 (3)
11-10-84	*Southern California (12, 7-1-0) 16, Washington 7 (5)
11-17-84	Oklahoma (6, 7-1-1) 17, *Nebraska 7 (7)
9-28-85	*Tennessee (NR, 0-0-1) 38, Auburn 20 (14)
11-2-85	*Ohio St. (7, 6-1-0) 22, Iowa 13 (6)
11-9-85	(N) Georgia (17, 6-1-1) 24, Florida 3 (11)
1-1-86	(Orange Bowl) Oklahoma (4, 9-1-0) 25, Penn St. 10 (3)
9-27-86	*Miami (Fla.) (2, 3-0-0) 28, Oklahoma 16 (6)
1-2-87	(Fiesta Bowl) Penn St. (2, 11-0-0) 14, Miami (Fla.) 10 (2)
11-21-87	Oklahoma (2, 11-0-0) 17, *Nebraska 7 (5)
1-1-88	(Orange Bowl) Miami (Fla.) (2, 11-1-0) 20, Oklahoma 14 (3)
10-15-88	*Notre Dame (4, 5-0-0) 31, Miami (Fla.) 30 (4)
10-29-88	Washington St. (NR, 4-3-0) 34, *UCLA 30 (6)
11-25-89	*Miami (Fla.) (7, 9-1-0) 27, Notre Dame 10 (5)
1-1-90	(Orange Bowl) Notre Dame (4, 11-1-0) 21, Colorado 6 (4)
9-8-90	*BYU (16, 1-0-0) 28, Miami (Fla.) 21 (10)
10-6-90	Stanford (NR, 1-3-0) 36, *Notre Dame 31 (8)
10-13-90	Michigan St. (NR, 1-2-1) 28, *Michigan 27 (10)
11-3-90	Georgia Tech (16, 6-0-1) 41, *Virginia 38 (11)
11-17-90	Penn St. (18, 7-2-0) 24, *Notre Dame 21 (7)
11-16-91	Miami (Fla.) (2, 8-0-0) 17, *Florida St. 16 (3)
11-7-92	*Arizona (12, 5-2-1) 16, Washington 3 (6)
1-1-93	(Sugar Bowl) Alabama (2, 12-0) 34, Miami (Fla.) 13 (3)
11-13-93	*Notre Dame (2, 9-0-0) 31, Florida St. 24 (2)
11-20-93	Boston College (17, 7-2-0) 41, *Notre Dame 39 (4)
10-15-94	Auburn (6, 6-0-0) 36, *Florida 33 (5)
9-21-96	*Arizona St. (17, 2-0-0) 19, Nebraska 0 (8)
11-30-96	*Florida St. (2, 10-0-0) 24, Florida 21 (4)
1-2-97	(Sugar Bowl) Florida (3, 11-1-0) 52, Florida St. 20 (3)
10-11-97	*LSU (14, 4-1-0) 28, Florida 21 (7)
11-7-98	Michigan St. (NR, 4-4) 28, *Ohio St. 24 (7)
10-7-00	*Miami (Fla.) (7, 3-1) 27, Florida St. 24 (7)
10-28-00	*Oklahoma (3, 6-0) 31, Nebraska 14 (5)
10-13-01	*Auburn (NR, 4-1) 23, Florida 20 (7)
11-9-02	*Texas A&M (NR, 5-4) 30, Oklahoma 26 (4)
1-3-03	(Fiesta Bowl) Ohio St. (2, 13-0) 31, Miami (Fla.) 24 (2 ot) (2)
12-6-03	(N) Kansas St. (13, 10-3) 35, Oklahoma 7 (3)
1-5-06	(Rose Bowl) Texas (2, 12-0) 41, Southern California 38 (2)
1-8-07	(BCS Championship) Florida (2, 12-1) 41, Ohio St. 14 (2)

Associated Press Preseason No. 1 Teams

(The No. 1-ranked team in the annual Associated Press preseason college football poll. The preseason poll started in 1950.)

Year	Team+	Year	Team+	Year	Team+	Year	Team+
1950	Notre Dame	1965	Nebraska	1980	Ohio St.	1995	Florida St.
1951	Tennessee+	1966	Alabama	1981	Michigan	1996	Nebraska
1952	Michigan St.+	1967	Notre Dame	1982	Pittsburgh	1997	Penn St.
1953	Notre Dame	1968	Purdue	1983	Nebraska	1998	Ohio St.
1954	Notre Dame	1969	Ohio St.	1984	Auburn	1999	Florida St.+
1955	UCLA	1970	Ohio St.	1985	Oklahoma+	2000	Nebraska
1956	Oklahoma+	1971	Notre Dame	1986	Oklahoma	2001	Florida
1957	Oklahoma	1972	Nebraska	1987	Oklahoma	2002	Miami (Fla.)
1958	Ohio St.	1973	Southern California	1988	Florida St.	2003	Oklahoma
1959	LSU	1974	Oklahoma+	1989	Michigan	2004	Southern California+
1960	Syracuse	1975	Oklahoma+	1990	Miami (Fla.)	2005	Southern California
1961	Iowa	1976	Nebraska	1991	Florida St.	2006	Ohio St.
1962	Ohio St.	1977	Oklahoma	1992	Miami (Fla.)		
1963	Southern California	1978	Alabama+	1993	Florida St.+		
1964	Mississippi	1979	Southern California	1994	Florida		

+Indicated eventual national champion.

A Year-By-Year History of the Associated Press Poll

1936—The Associated Press Poll began with sports editors of AP newspapers voting for the top 20 teams nationally. Minnesota and Northwestern each had 7-1 records and, even though Northwestern whipped the Golden Gophers in the regular season, Minnesota was named No. 1 in the final poll.

1937—California began with a 5-0 record and was ranked No. 1 in the first three polls but Jock Sutherland's Pittsburgh Panthers took over the lead in November and finished 9-0-1 and No. 1.

1938—Previous year's AP leader Pittsburgh was ranked No. 1 to begin the season but Dutch Meyer's TCU Horned Frogs, behind legendary QB Davey O'Brien, posted an undefeated 10-0 regular season for the poll championship.

1939—Pittsburgh and Tennessee, two powerhouses, exchanged the No. 1 spot in the poll until Homer Norton's Texas A&M Aggies, behind big fullback John Kimbrough, took over the top spot late and finished 10-0 in the regular season for the mythical AP title.

1940—Eastern power Cornell led for the first four weeks until eventual champion Minnesota, behind coach Bernie Bierman and all-Americans George Franck and Urban Odson, finished No. 1. It was the second of three national poll champions for Bierman.

1941—Minnesota made it two in row behind Heisman Trophy winner Bruce Smith as the Gophers posted a perfect 8-0 record.

1942—Ohio State started the season as the No. 1 team until a mid-season loss dropped the Buckeyes back into the pack. Georgia and Boston College shared the No. 1 spot until the last week, when Ohio State, behind legendary coach Paul Brown, finished as the top team.

1943—Notre Dame led wire-to-wire, the first time a team had led every week since the poll originated in 1936. Coach Frank Leahy, in only his third year, had plenty of tools to work with, including backs Angelo Bertelli (Heisman Trophy winner and consensus all-America) and Creighton Miller (fourth in the Heisman voting and consensus all-America). The line was loaded also with end John Yonaker, tackle Jim White and guard Pat Filley, all consensus all-Americans.

1944—Notre Dame started off the year as the No. 1 team, but Red Blaik's Army team, behind consensus all-Americans Doc Blanchard (Mr. Inside) and Glenn Davis (Mr. Outside), rolled to an undefeated season and the first of two consecutive No. 1 finishes.

1945—During the war year of World War II, no team more personified America's determination than Army, which ran the table again behind Blanchard and Davis, and consensus all-America linemen John Green and Tex Coulter. The Cadets posted a perfect 9-0 record but service academies did not participate in bowl games then.

1946—This was a pivotal year for the AP poll in that Army was expected to sweep to the No. 1 spot easily, again behind Blanchard and Davis. During the season, Army finished 9-0-1, highlighted by a 0-0 tie at Yankee Stadium against Johnny Lujack-led Notre Dame (8-0-1) in the 'Game of the Decade.' However, Army barely beat an outclassed Navy team in its final game and the voters selected Notre Dame No. 1.

1947—Notre Dame and Michigan alternated No. 1 and 2 slots throughout the year with Notre Dame getting the final regular-season nod, even though both teams were 9-0. In the ensuing bowl game, Michigan rolled over Southern California, 49-0, and the public demanded that the voters release another post-bowl poll and the Wolverines won easily. AP decided, however, that the postseason poll did not supercede the final regular-season poll of December 6, 1947.

1948—Defending champion Notre Dame alternated with North Carolina and Michigan as No. 1 in the first few polls but the Wolverines took over in November and raced to a 9-0 record and a poll championship in coach Bennie Oosterbaan's first year as a head coach.

1949—Michigan was No. 1 the first week before Notre Dame took over and cruised to a perfect 9-0 mark and the national poll title. It was the last of four No. 1 finishes in seven years for coach Frank Leahy. The stars were end Leon Hart (Heisman Trophy winner and consensus all-America) and consensus all-America backs Emil Sitko and Bob Williams.

1950—This was another pivotal year as AP's rival United Press began its own top-20 poll, voted on by a panel of coaches. The two polls would go head-to-head for the next 45 years. On the field, Notre Dame, Army (behind Dan Foldberg), SMU (behind Kyle Rote) and Ohio State (led by Heisman winner Vic Janowicz) all led at least one week. But Oklahoma, behind coach Bud Wilkinson and consensus all-Americans Leon Heath and Jim Weatherall, posted a 9-0 record for the No. 1 spot and then promptly lost in the Sugar Bowl to Kentucky, led by Babe Parilli.

1951—Tennessee raced to a No. 1 ranking on the heels of Bob Neyland's coaching and the fleet feet of consensus all-American Hank Lauricella. Michigan State and California both mounted weekly challenges, but the Volunteers held on for Neyland's first title in 20 years of coaching.

1952—Michigan State took over in the third week and raced to a perfect 9-0 record behind coach Clarence "Biggie" Munn. The Spartans did not play in a bowl game.

1953—Notre Dame looked like a sure winner as the Irish led for the first eight weeks of the season behind Heisman Trophy winner Johnny Lattner. But Maryland, behind the coaching of Jim Tatum and the play of consensus all-America tackle Stan Jones, made a late bid with a 10-0 mark. The Terrapins lost in the Orange Bowl to Oklahoma, 7-0.

1954—The two polls split for the first time as Ohio State prevailed in the AP and UCLA in the UP. The two teams did not meet in the Rose Bowl to decide the "on-the-field" champion. UCLA had to stay behind because of the Pacific-8's "Rose Bowl no-repeater" rule since they had played in Pasadena the year before against Michigan. Ohio State gave coach Woody Hayes his first AP championship with a 10-0 record and the Buckeyes defeated Southern California, 20-7, in the Rose Bowl.

1955—Oklahoma continued with major college football's all-time 47-game winning streak by cruising to an AP No. 1 spot with a 10-0 mark and handing Bud Wilkinson the second of three national poll titles.

1956—This year was a continuation of Oklahoma's powerhouse team which posted a perfect 11-0 record in the all-time 47-game winning streak that lasted almost four years (1953-57). Led by center Jerry Tubbs and back Tommy McDonald, the Sooners gave Bud Wilkinson his final AP national title.

1957—Again there was a split vote in the two polls as AP selected as No. 1 unbeaten Auburn (10-0), under Shug Jordan, even though the Tigers were on probation. UP, the coaches' poll, threw out Auburn from poll consideration and went with Woody Hayes' Ohio State Buckeyes (9-1). Auburn did not go to a bowl and Ohio State beat Oregon, 10-7, in the Rose Bowl.

1958—1958 turned out to be the year of the Chinese Bandits in the AP poll. Led by consensus all-America back Billy Cannon on offense and a swarming defense called the Chinese Bandits, coach Paul Dietzel's surprising LSU Tigers took over the No. 1 spot in mid-season. LSU finished 11-0 and beat Clemson in the Sugar Bowl.

1959—Even though LSU had Heisman winner Billy Cannon returning, Syracuse took over the No. 1 slot in early November and posted an 11-0 mark to claim its first poll title. Coach Ben Schwartzwalder was rewarded with his only championship behind the all-America play of guard Roger Davis and Syracuse defeated Texas, 23-14, in the Cotton Bowl.

1960—Minnesota, under Murray Warmath, led in both polls before the bowl games but was upset by Washington, 17-7, in the Rose Bowl. That prompted the Football Writers Association of America (FWAA) to conduct a post-bowl poll that named Johnny Vaught's Mississippi Rebels as champion. Minnesota remained the official winner in both AP and UPI polls.

1961—Alabama avoided a minefield of upsets and raced to a 10-0 record to claim the AP title, even though Iowa, Mississippi, Michigan State and Texas all were No. 1 at one time during the year. It was Bear Bryant's first of six AP championships.

1962—Coach John McKay got his first national title as Southern California bided its time waiting for four other teams to share No. 1 during the year. The Trojans slipped into the top spot late with a 10-0 regular-season mark and then downed Wisconsin, 42-37, in the Rose Bowl.

1963—Texas, under Darrell Royal, was a unanimous choice of all of the polls as the Longhorns took over the No. 1 slot in October, finished 10-0 and then beat a Navy team, led by Heisman winner Roger Staubach, in the Cotton Bowl. The Longhorns' top player was tackle Scott Appleton.

1964—The 1964 season saw the AP and UPI polls both agree on Alabama as No. 1, while the other two consensus polls picked Arkansas (FWAA) and Notre Dame (National Football Foundation). It was Bear Bryant's second of six AP titles.

1965—AP had its first post-bowl poll while UPI remained with a pre-bowl selection. AP selected Alabama for the second straight year. UPI went with Michigan State, which then lost in the Rose Bowl to UCLA, 14-12. Alabama had a 9-1-1 record and then whipped Nebraska, 39-28, in the Orange Bowl.

1966—Both Notre Dame and Michigan State were unbeaten as they headed into the November 19 match-up. The Irish came back from a 10-0 deficit to tie the game in the fourth quarter. Ara Parseghian's Irish actually got the ball back with 1:30 remaining and decided to run the clock out rather than try to win. His strategy paid off the next week as Notre Dame crushed Southern California, 51-0, and the Irish were picked No. 1 in both final polls.

1967—Southern California rebounded from an early loss to post a 9-1 record and move into the No. 1 slot in late November. John McKay's Trojans beat Indiana, 14-3, in the Rose Bowl to cap off the season. USC stars were O.J. Simpson, Ron Yary, Tim Rossovich and Adrian Young, all consensus all-America selections.

1968—Ohio State overtook a crowded field of Purdue and defending champion Southern California to become No. 1 in late November. The Buckeyes finished 10-0 and drilled Southern California, 27-16, in the Rose Bowl.

1969—Defending champ Ohio State led the pack for most of the year before Darrell Royal's Texas Longhorns made a strong bid for No. 1 late. The Longhorns finished 11-0, including the first 'Game of the Century' vs. Arkansas, in which Texas scored a 15-14 victory after trailing 14-0. The team from the Lone Star State then beat Notre Dame, 21-17, in the Cotton Bowl. Texas had only one consensus all-America player, lineman Bob McKay, but had many productive players, such as James Street, Ted Koy and Steve Worster.

1970—It looked like this year might be a repeat of Texas' ascension in 1969. The Longhorns dominated the AP poll for the entire second half of the season, but a 24-11 loss to Notre Dame in the Cotton Bowl gave Nebraska a chance to take the final No. 1 spot. Bob Devaney's Cornhuskers had only a tie to mar their final record (11-0-1) and beat LSU, 17-12, in the Orange Bowl.

1971—Nebraska's 1971 team, which many say was the best squad of its era, held the No. 1 spot from wire to wire for Bob Devaney, the first team to do it since Army in 1945. The Cornhuskers were led by future Heisman winner Johnny Rodgers and defensive stalwarts Willie Harper and Larry Jacobson, all consensus all-America selections. The year's showdown for Nebraska was a match-up with Oklahoma in Norman in what many still consider the best 'Game of the Century.' Nebraska won the hyped contest, 35-31, to finish 13-0, including a 38-6 victory over Alabama in the Orange Bowl.

1972—It was all Southern California in 1972 as John McKay's Trojans became the second school in a row to take the No. 1 spot in the poll from first week to last. The 12-0 record included a 42-17 pounding of Ohio State in the Rose Bowl. Southern California was chosen the winner in all four consensus polls.

1973—First defending champion Southern California, and then Ohio State, combined to keep a lock on the No. 1 position throughout most of the season. But Alabama took over the last week of November and met No. 3 Notre Dame in the Sugar Bowl for the AP title. Notre Dame won a close 24-23 victory and captured the No. 1 final prize. Coach Ara Parseghian got his second of two championships behind such players as Dave Casper and Mike Townsend.

1974—In the year in which UPI finally moved its final poll until after the bowl games, Ohio State and Oklahoma led in the AP poll most of the year. Oklahoma, behind a crushing rushing attack headed by Joe Washington, was on probation and not ranked by UPI, but finished 11-0 to take the top AP poll spot. Oklahoma consensus all-America picks were Washington, guard John Roush and linebacker Rod Shoate. Coach Barry Switzer started his tenure with two AP titles in his first three seasons and a 32-1-1 record. UPI selected Southern California, which finished 10-1-1.

1975—Oklahoma looked unbeatable early, led the AP poll through September and seemed invincible. However, a roadblock cropped up in a surprise 23-3 loss to Kansas that snapped the Sooners' 28-game winning streak. That sent Ohio State into the No. 1 AP slot until the crucial bowl games behind Archie Griffin, who was on track for his second straight Heisman. While Oklahoma was beating Michigan, 14-6, in the Orange, Ohio State fell, 23-10, to UCLA in the Rose, and the Sooners had their second straight AP championship. The Oklahoma squad had big-time talent in Joe Washington, Billy Brooks, Dewey Selmon, Lee Roy Selmon and Tinker Owens, who all earned all-America mention. Arizona State finished 12-0 and was the only undefeated, untied team. The Sun Devils, however, played in the Western Athletic Conference, not known as a strong league at the time.

1976—Michigan raced to an 8-0 record and led the poll for the first eight weeks. Pittsburgh, under Johnny Majors, finished strong with a 12-0 mark, including a 27-3 victory over Georgia in the Sugar Bowl. The Panthers were on top at the end of the season and featured Heisman winner Tony Dorsett and defensive lineman Al Romano, both consensus all-America picks.

1977—Five teams alternated taking the No. 1 AP ranking during the year and five teams finished the season with 11-1 records, including pre-bowl leader Texas. However, Notre Dame (11-1) upset the No. 1 Longhorns, 38-10, in the Cotton Bowl by keeping Heisman winner Earl Campbell in check. Dan Devine's Irish, behind consensus all-America players Ross Browner, Ken MacAfee and Luther Bradley, were also voted No. 1 in the UPI poll.

1978—Penn State was No. 1 going into the bowl games but was upset, 14-7, by Alabama in the Sugar Bowl. The Crimson Tide (11-1) was voted No. 1 by AP, but Southern California got the nod in the UPI poll because it beat Alabama, 24-14, during the regular season. USC (12-1) was led by coach John Robinson and future Heisman winner Charles White. The Trojans whipped Michigan, 17-10, in the Rose Bowl.

1979—Alabama (12-0) made it two AP titles in a row and six overall for coach Bear Bryant as the Crimson Tide drilled Arkansas, 24-9, in the Sugar Bowl to forge ahead of pre-bowl No. 1 Ohio State. The Buckeyes (11-1) dropped out of contention when they lost in the Gator Bowl to Clemson, 17-15, in the famous "coach-slugging-player" incident by Ohio State coach Woody Hayes.

1980—Alabama seemed to be in charge early, taking over the No. 1 AP slot for seven straight weeks until Notre Dame grabbed the spot November 4. But the Irish dropped out the next week as Georgia pushed into the No. 1 spot behind the running of freshman sensation Herschel Walker. Vince Dooley's Bulldogs finished 12-0 and beat Notre Dame, 17-10, in the Sugar Bowl.

1981—Michigan began as the AP leader before giving way after one week to Notre Dame, which was passed by Southern California, which was overtaken for a week by Texas, which then surrendered the top spot to Penn State, which then saw Pittsburgh rise to No. 1. All six of these teams fell by the wayside as Clemson, under Danny Ford, finished strong with a 12-0 record, including a 22-15 victory over Nebraska in the Orange Bowl.

1982—Pittsburgh and Washington alternated sharing the No. 1 spot until Georgia took over November 9. The Bulldogs were still the leader going into the bowl games. However, No. 2 Penn State beat No. 1 Georgia, 27-23, in the Sugar Bowl for the AP poll championship. It was coach Joe Paterno's first of two AP national championships.

1983—It was a disappointing season for Nebraska, which held the No. 1 AP slot for 14 consecutive weeks, but was edged by fifth-ranked Miami (Florida), 31-30, in the Orange Bowl. Coach Howard Schnellenberger's Hurricanes took the AP title after winning a battle with a Nebraska team that had Heisman winner Mike Rozier and consensus all-America picks Irving Fryar and Dean Steinkuhler.

1984—In a year that saw four other teams alternate as No. 1, BYU (13-0) hung around until fortune pushed the Cougars into the final No. 1 slot. Coach LaVell Edwards' charges played no AP team in the top 20 in the regular season, but dispatched Michigan, 24-17, in the Holiday Bowl. When No. 1 Nebraska and No. 2 South Carolina both lost November 17, the No. 3 Cougars vaulted into the top spot and never gave it up.

1985—Oklahoma stayed the course after an early loss to beat No. 1 Penn State, 25-10, in the Orange Bowl and give Barry Switzer his second AP title. Brian Bosworth and Tony Casillas were the top players for the Sooners.

1986—Penn State had not been No. 1 all year, but the Nittany Lions finished 12-0, capped by a 14-10 victory over pre-bowl No. 1 Miami (Florida) in the Fiesta Bowl. The bowl was arranged to match No. 1 vs. No. 2 because the two top teams had no conference affiliation. It was Joe Paterno's second AP title.

1987—Oklahoma held the No. 1 spot for all but one week during the year, but Miami (Florida) grabbed the national poll title by downing the Sooners, 20-14, in the Orange Bowl. Miami featured a bruising defense with Daniel Stubbs and Bennie Blades topping the consensus all-America team. Coach Jimmy Johnson's 12-0 Hurricanes garnered the second of four AP titles in 10 years.

1988—Notre Dame made a late-season run for AP's No. 1 spot and finished a perfect 12-0 after a 34-21 win over West Virginia in the Fiesta Bowl to grab the title. Miami (Florida) had control of the No. 1 spot early before UCLA took over for a couple of weeks, followed by the Irish's push.

1989—Defending AP champion Notre Dame held the No. 1 slot for 12 consecutive weeks. Colorado took over when the Irish lost a game. The Buffaloes were No. 1 for only two weeks before Dennis Erickson's Miami (Florida) team moved into No. 1 in the final poll by beating Alabama, 33-25, in the Sugar Bowl. Colorado lost its chance by losing to Notre Dame, 21-6, in the Orange Bowl.

1990—This was another split between the polls with AP going with Colorado (11-1-1) while UPI went with undefeated Georgia Tech (10-0-1). In the ensuing bowl games, both teams won – Colorado beating Notre Dame, 10-9, in the Orange, and Georgia Tech downing Nebraska, 45-21, in the Florida Citrus. This was the season that critics of the bowl system began talking about creating another way to determine a national champion, indicating that the polls were not adequate.

1991—UPI, which fell on hard times financially, saw its coaches' poll switch affiliation to USA Today/CNN. With two teams each posting 12-0 records, the polls again split with AP naming Miami (Florida) No. 1 and the coaches' poll going with Washington. Again, the media and public grumbled about not having a clear-cut national titlist, and the Bowl Coalition people started to think about replacing the poll champions.

1992—The Bowl Coalition made its debut to decide a national champion, and Alabama, under Gene Stallings, upset Miami (Florida), 34-13, in the Sugar Bowl for the title. The Crimson Tide finished 13-0 to take No. 1 in both polls. Miami (Florida) was No. 1 in the AP poll for 10 of the season's 15 weeks.

1993—Florida State almost led the poll from first week to last, save for November 16 after a loss to Notre Dame, which took one quick week in the No. 1 roost. But Lou Holtz's Irish were upended by Boston College and Bobby Bowden's Seminoles regained the No. 1 spot the next week. The Seminoles posted a 12-1 record, including an 18-16 victory over Nebraska in the Orange Bowl. Florida State QB Charlie Ward was the Heisman Trophy winner and LB Derrick Brooks and DB Corey Sawyer were consensus all-America selections.

1994—Florida and Nebraska held the No. 1 spot for most of the first half of the season and Penn State went undefeated, but it was Nebraska (also unbeaten at 13-0) that took the championship. The Cornhuskers squeezed by Miami (Florida), 24-17, in the Orange Bowl to hand Tom Osborne his first AP title after 22 years as the head coach in Lincoln. Joe Paterno saw his Penn State squad go undefeated and uncrowned for the fourth time.

1995—Florida State was the team to beat as the Seminoles held the No. 1 slot for the first nine weeks, before giving way to defending champion Nebraska. The Cornhuskers ran their winning streak to 25 straight games with a 12-0 record. The Bowl Coalition matched No. 1 Nebraska with No. 2 Florida in the Fiesta Bowl. Nebraska whipped the Gators, 62-24, to remove any doubt about the No. 1 team and the Cornhuskers took the AP prize for the second straight year.

1996—This year marked a change from the Bowl Coalition to the Bowl Alliance, but it also proved less than satisfying as the top two teams – Florida State and Arizona State – did not meet because Arizona State was bound to the Rose Bowl and a game versus the Big Ten champion. Interestingly, both Florida State and Arizona State lost in their respective bowl games (Florida State lost to Florida, 52-20), which was enough to lift the Gators into the final No. 1 spot in both polls. Steve Spurrier got a measure of revenge over the Gator doubters from 1995, when Florida lost in the title game. Florida QB Danny Wuerffel was the Heisman winner and Ike Hilliard and Reidel Anthony were consensus all-Americans.

1997—ESPN replaced CNN in the USA Today coaches' poll that named Nebraska as its champion. Michigan finished No. 1 in the AP poll. The Wolverines and Nebraska were both unbeaten heading into the bowls, and the Cornhuskers finished 13-0 with a 41-21 win over Virginia Tech in the Orange Bowl. Meanwhile, Michigan (12-0) beat Washington, 21-16, in the Rose Bowl. Even though both teams won in the bowls, 21 coaches changed their votes in the USA Today/ESPN poll on the strength of Nebraska's margin of victory and handed Tom Osborne the third poll championship for Nebraska in four years. Lloyd Carr got his first AP title in only his third year as head coach of the Wolverines. Michigan DB Charles Woodson was the first defensive player ever selected as the Heisman Trophy winner.

1998—This was the first year of the Bowl Championship Series (BCS) and Ohio State, under John Cooper, was voted No. 1 in the AP poll for the first nine weeks. Phillip Fulmer's Tennessee Volunteers took over the top spot when the Buckeyes lost, and raced to a 13-0 record, including a 23-16 victory over No. 2 Florida State in the Fiesta Bowl. Tennessee was voted No. 1 in all four major polls – Associated Press (AP), USA Today/ESPN (USA/ESPN), National Football Foundation/College Football Hall of Fame (NFF) and Football Writers Association of America (FWAA).

1999—For the first time since Nebraska did so in 1983, Florida State led the AP poll from wire to wire. It was not easy for Bobby Bowden's Seminoles, as they posted a perfect 12-0 record, but had close calls in beating Georgia Tech, 41-35; Clemson, 17-14; and in-state rival Florida, 30-23. But Florida State ripped No. 2 Virginia Tech, 46-29, in the BCS Sugar Bowl. Peter Warrick, Jason Whitaker, Sebastian Janikowski and Corey Simon were all consensus all-America selections as Florida State finished No. 1 in all four major polls (AP, USA/ESPN, NFF and FWAA).

2000—Nebraska, 12-1 and No. 3 in the AP poll the previous year, looked strong and was voted No. 1 for nine consecutive weeks to begin the season. Oklahoma, unranked the previous year, took over the No. 1 spot October 30 and cruised into the BCS Orange Bowl to face No. 2 Florida State. The Seminoles had one loss but the second-best strength of schedule. Bob Stoops' Sooners clamped down on Florida State's offense to post a 13-2 victory. For Stoops, in only his second year as a head coach, it was the first Oklahoma AP poll title since 1985 under Barry Switzer. Oklahoma finished 13-0 behind QB Josh Heupel (Heisman runner-up to QB Chris Weinke of Florida State), LB Rocky Calmus and DB J.T. Thatcher, all consensus all-Americans.

2001—Florida and Miami (Florida) fought it out all year for a BCS crown and No. 1 spots in all four major polls. Miami finally came out on top by posting a perfect 12-0 mark and a decisive 37-14 victory over No. 2 Nebraska in the Rose Bowl, which finally became a part of the BCS process. Florida ended up fifth in the BCS rankings because of two regular-season season defeats. Associated Press' No. 2 Nebraska (11-2) overcame a 62-36 pounding by AP No. 14 Colorado in its final regular-season game to hold on to the No. 2 BCS ranking and the Rose Bowl date. Miami's Larry Coker was only the second first-year head coach to win a national title (Bennie Oosterbaan of Michigan in 1948) as the Hurricanes were No. 1 in all four major polls and BCS champion.

2002—Defending consensus champion Miami (Florida) held the AP No. 1 spot almost the entire year (Oklahoma was No. 1 during the week of November 4) and was No. 1 in the BCS rankings. The Hurricanes then faced undefeated Ohio State, No. 2 in both the BCS and AP poll, in the Fiesta Bowl. The Buckeyes, under second-year head coach Jim Tressel, held on for a double-overtime 31-24 victory, snapping the Hurricanes' 34-game winning streak, sixth longest of all-time. The Buckeyes had many talented players, including consensus all-Americas Mike Nugent (PK), Matt Wilhelm (LB) and Mike Doss (DB). It was the sixth straight year that the AP poll champion posted an undefeated season.

2003—Grumblings about the Bowl Championship Series (BCS) began after the season as the polls split yet again. AP selected Southern California (12-1) as No. 1 and USA Today/ESPN picked LSU (13-1) as champion. In a strange turn of events, Oklahoma was No. 1 in the AP poll for 14 consecutive weeks, and the Sooners looked unbeatable as they rolled to an 11-0 regular-season record. In the Big 12 Conference championship game, however, the Sooners were rocked, 35-7, by Kansas State. Oklahoma had built up such a lead in the BCS rankings, however, that it was still ranked No. 1 and faced BCS No. 2 LSU in the Sugar Bowl. Even though BCS No. 3 Southern California was ranked No. 1 in both the AP and USA Today/ESPN polls before the bowls, the Trojans were relegated to the Rose Bowl, in which they defeated Michigan, 28-14, to finish 12-1. LSU then edged Oklahoma, 21-14, in the Sugar Bowl in the BCS No. 1 vs. No. 2 match-up. The AP pollsters voted Southern California No. 1 and the USA Today/ESPN voters picked LSU No. 1 and split the nation again. Momentum began gathering toward a slightly tweaked BCS system that tentatively would add another BCS bowl to the mix in the future.

2004—Southern California left little doubt in the BCS-decided match-up with No. 2 Oklahoma that the Trojans were top dogs by racing to a 55-19 victory in the Orange Bowl. The Trojans were No. 1 in the weekly polls from wire to wire with Oklahoma No. 2, and both were 12-0 going into the bowl games. The only fans who had a problem with the BCS championship game were the Auburn supporters, who saw their Tigers post a perfect 13-0 record, yet not be included in the title match-up. Again, talk of a playoff system was heard, with Auburn not only having a perfect record playing in one of the toughest conferences (Southeastern), but finishing No. 2 in the final poll ahead of Oklahoma. Mountain West Conference power Utah also had an argument to be included after posting a 12-0 mark.

2005—For the first time in BCS history, and it was unanimous, the top two teams in the country faced each other in the national championship game, as Southern California and Texas met in the Rose Bowl. The game lived up to all its hype, as the Longhorns rallied from a 38-26 deficit with two touchdowns in the final five minutes of the fourth quarter, capped by Vince Young's eight-yard scamper with 19 seconds left for the 41-38 victory.

2006—Preseason No. 1 Ohio State played like a national champion from week one to earn a spot in the BCS Championship Game against the Gators of Florida. The Buckeyes had already taken care of another No. 2 in Texas in September, and after the opening kickoff, a 93-yard return for a touchdown by Ted Ginn Jr., it looked like they would hold off another challenge. However, the Gators answered quickly and often as Florida grabbed a 34-14 lead at halftime, coasted to a 41-14 win and was voted the 2006 AP championship.

Associated Press (Writers and Broadcasters) Final Polls

1936

Team
1. Minnesota
2. LSU
3. Pittsburgh
4. Alabama
5. Washington
6. Santa Clara
7. Northwestern
8. Notre Dame
9. Nebraska
10. Penn
11. Duke
12. Yale
13. Dartmouth
14. Duquesne
15. Fordham
16. TCU
17. Tennessee
18. Arkansas
Navy
20. Marquette

1937

Team
1. Pittsburgh
2. California
3. Fordham
4. Alabama
5. Minnesota
6. Villanova
7. Dartmouth
8. LSU
9. Notre Dame
Santa Clara
11. Nebraska
12. Yale
13. Ohio St.
14. Holy Cross
Arkansas
16. TCU
17. Colorado
18. Rice
19. North Carolina
20. Duke

1938

Team
1. TCU
2. Tennessee
3. Duke
4. Oklahoma
5. Notre Dame
6. Carnegie Mellon
7. Southern California
8. Pittsburgh
9. Holy Cross
10. Minnesota
11. Texas Tech
12. Cornell
13. Alabama
14. California
15. Fordham
16. Michigan
17. Northwestern
18. Villanova
19. Tulane
20. Dartmouth

1939

Team
1. Texas A&M
2. Tennessee
3. Southern California
4. Cornell
5. Tulane
6. Missouri
7. UCLA
8. Duke
9. Iowa
10. Duquesne
11. Boston College
12. Clemson
13. Notre Dame
14. Santa Clara
15. Ohio St.
16. Georgia Tech
17. Fordham
18. Nebraska
19. Oklahoma
20. Michigan

1940

Team
1. Minnesota
2. Stanford
3. Michigan
4. Tennessee
5. Boston College
6. Texas A&M
7. Nebraska
8. Northwestern
9. Mississippi St.
10. Washington
11. Santa Clara
12. Fordham
13. Georgetown
14. Penn
15. Cornell
16. SMU
17. Hardin-Simmons
18. Duke
19. Lafayette

1941

Team
1. Minnesota
2. Duke
3. Notre Dame
4. Texas
5. Michigan
6. Fordham
7. Missouri
8. Duquesne
9. Texas A&M
10. Navy
11. Northwestern
12. Oregon St.
13. Ohio St.
14. Georgia
15. Penn
16. Mississippi St.
17. Mississippi
18. Tennessee
19. Washington St.
20. Alabama

1942
Team
1. Ohio St.
2. Georgia
3. Wisconsin
4. Tulsa
5. Georgia Tech
6. Notre Dame
7. Tennessee
8. Boston College
9. Michigan
10. Alabama
11. Texas
12. Stanford
13. UCLA
14. William & Mary
15. Santa Clara
16. Auburn
17. Washington St.
18. Mississippi St.
19. Minnesota
    Holy Cross
    Penn St.

1943
Team
1. Notre Dame
2. Iowa Pre-Flight
3. Michigan
4. Navy
5. Purdue
6. Great Lakes
7. Duke
8. Del Monte P-F
9. Northwestern
10. March Field
11. Army
12. Washington
13. Georgia Tech
14. Texas
15. Tulsa
16. Dartmouth
17. Bainbridge NTS
18. Colorado Col.
19. Pacific
20. Penn

1944
Team
1. Army
2. Ohio St.
3. Randolph Field
4. Navy
5. Bainbridge NTS
6. Iowa Pre-Flight
7. Southern California
8. Michigan
9. Notre Dame
10. March Field
11. Duke
12. Tennessee
13. Georgia Tech
    Norman Pre-Flight
15. Illinois
16. El Toro Marines
17. Great Lakes
18. Fort Pierce
19. St. Mary's Pre-Flight
20. Second Air Force

1945
Team
1. Army
2. Alabama
3. Navy
4. Indiana
5. Oklahoma St.
6. Michigan
7. St. Mary's (Cal.)
8. Penn
9. Notre Dame
10. Texas
11. Southern California
12. Ohio St.
13. Duke
14. Tennessee
15. LSU
16. Holy Cross
17. Tulsa
18. Georgia
19. Wake Forest
20. Columbia

1946
Team
1. Notre Dame
2. Army
3. Georgia
4. UCLA
5. Illinois
6. Michigan
7. Tennessee
8. LSU
9. North Carolina
10. Rice
11. Georgia Tech
12. Yale
13. Penn
14. Oklahoma
15. Texas
16. Arkansas
17. Tulsa
18. North Carolina St.
19. Delaware
20. Indiana

*1947
Team
1. Notre Dame
2. Michigan
3. SMU
4. Penn St.
5. Texas
6. Alabama
7. Penn
8. Southern California
9. North Carolina
10. Georgia Tech
11. Army
12. Kansas
13. Mississippi
14. William & Mary
15. California
16. Oklahoma
17. North Carolina St.
18. Rice
19. Duke
20. Columbia

1948
Team
1. Michigan
2. Notre Dame
3. North Carolina
4. California
5. Oklahoma
6. Army
7. Northwestern
8. Georgia
9. Oregon
10. SMU
11. Clemson
12. Vanderbilt
13. Tulane
14. Michigan St.
15. Mississippi
16. Minnesota
17. William & Mary
18. Penn St.
19. Cornell
20. Wake Forest

1949
Team
1. Notre Dame
2. Oklahoma
3. California
4. Army
5. Rice
6. Ohio St.
7. Michigan
8. Minnesota
9. LSU
10. Pacific
11. Kentucky
12. Cornell
13. Villanova
14. Maryland
15. Santa Clara
16. North Carolina
17. Tennessee
18. Princeton
19. Michigan St.
20. Missouri
    Baylor

1950
Team
1. Oklahoma
2. Army
3. Texas
4. Tennessee
5. California
6. Princeton
7. Kentucky
8. Michigan St.
9. Michigan
10. Clemson
11. Washington
12. Wyoming
13. Illinois
14. Ohio St.
15. Miami (Fla.)
16. Alabama
17. Nebraska
18. Wash. & Lee
19. Tulsa
20. Tulane

1951
Team
1. Tennessee
2. Michigan St.
3. Maryland
4. Illinois
5. Georgia Tech
6. Princeton
7. Stanford
8. Wisconsin
9. Baylor
10. Oklahoma
11. TCU
12. California
13. Virginia
14. San Francisco
15. Kentucky
16. Boston U.
17. UCLA
18. Washington St.
19. Holy Cross
20. Clemson

1952
Team
1. Michigan St.
2. Georgia Tech
3. Notre Dame
4. Oklahoma
5. Southern California
6. UCLA
7. Mississippi
8. Tennessee
9. Alabama
10. Texas
11. Wisconsin
12. Tulsa
13. Maryland
14. Syracuse
15. Florida
16. Duke
17. Ohio St.
18. Purdue
19. Princeton
20. Kentucky

1953
Team
1. Maryland
2. Notre Dame
3. Michigan St.
4. Oklahoma
5. UCLA
6. Rice
7. Illinois
8. Georgia Tech
9. Iowa
10. West Virginia
11. Texas
12. Texas Tech
13. Alabama
14. Army
15. Wisconsin
16. Kentucky
17. Auburn
18. Duke
19. Stanford
20. Michigan

1954
Team
1. Ohio St.
2. UCLA
3. Oklahoma
4. Notre Dame
5. Navy
6. Mississippi
7. Army
8. Maryland
9. Wisconsin
10. Arkansas
11. Miami (Fla.)
12. West Virginia
13. Auburn
14. Duke
15. Michigan
16. Virginia Tech
17. Southern California
18. Baylor
19. Rice
20. Penn St.

1955
Team
1. Oklahoma
2. Michigan St.
3. Maryland
4. UCLA
5. Ohio St.
6. TCU
7. Georgia Tech
8. Auburn
9. Notre Dame
10. Mississippi
11. Pittsburgh
12. Michigan
13. Southern California
14. Miami (Fla.)
15. Miami (Ohio)
16. Stanford
17. Texas A&M
18. Navy
19. West Virginia
20. Army

1956
Team
1. Oklahoma
2. Tennessee
3. Iowa
4. Georgia Tech
5. Texas A&M
6. Miami (Fla.)
7. Michigan
8. Syracuse
9. Michigan St.
10. Oregon St.
11. Baylor
12. Minnesota
13. Pittsburgh
14. TCU
15. Ohio St.
16. Navy
17. George Washington
18. Southern California
19. Clemson
20. Colorado

1957
Team
1. Auburn
2. Ohio St.
3. Michigan St.
4. Oklahoma
5. Navy
6. Iowa
7. Mississippi
8. Rice
9. Texas A&M
10. Notre Dame
11. Texas
12. Arizona St.
13. Tennessee
14. Mississippi St.
15. North Carolina St.
16. Duke
17. Florida
18. Army
19. Wisconsin
20. VMI

1958
Team
1. LSU
2. Iowa
3. Army
4. Auburn
5. Oklahoma
6. Air Force
7. Wisconsin
8. Ohio St.
9. Syracuse
10. TCU
11. Mississippi
12. Clemson
13. Purdue
14. Florida
15. South Carolina
16. California
17. Notre Dame
18. SMU
19. Oklahoma St.
20. Rutgers

1959
Team
1. Syracuse
2. Mississippi
3. LSU
4. Texas
5. Georgia
6. Wisconsin
7. TCU
8. Washington
9. Arkansas
10. Alabama
11. Clemson
12. Penn St.
13. Illinois
14. Southern California
15. Oklahoma
16. Wyoming
17. Notre Dame
18. Missouri
19. Florida
20. Pittsburgh

1960
Team
1. Minnesota
2. Mississippi
3. Iowa
4. Navy
5. Missouri
6. Washington
7. Arkansas
8. Ohio St.
9. Alabama
10. Duke
11. Kansas
12. Baylor
13. Auburn
14. Yale
15. Michigan St.
16. Penn St.
17. New Mexico St.
18. Florida
19. Syracuse
Purdue

1961
Team
1. Alabama
2. Ohio St.
3. Texas
4. LSU
5. Mississippi
6. Minnesota
7. Colorado
8. Michigan St.
9. Arkansas
10. Utah St.
11. Missouri
12. Purdue
13. Georgia Tech
14. Syracuse
15. Rutgers
16. UCLA
17. Rice
Penn St.
Arizona
20. Duke

1962
Team
1. Southern California
2. Wisconsin
3. Mississippi
4. Texas
5. Alabama
6. Arkansas
7. LSU
8. Oklahoma
9. Penn St.
10. Minnesota
Only 10 ranked

1963
Team
1. Texas
2. Navy
3. Illinois
4. Pittsburgh
5. Auburn
6. Nebraska
7. Mississippi
8. Alabama
9. Oklahoma
10. Michigan St.
Only 10 ranked

1964
Team
1. Alabama
2. Arkansas
3. Notre Dame
4. Michigan
5. Texas
6. Nebraska
7. LSU
8. Oregon St.
9. Ohio St.
10. Southern California
Only 10 ranked

1965
Team
1. Alabama
2. Michigan St.
3. Arkansas
4. UCLA
5. Nebraska
6. Missouri
7. Tennessee
8. LSU
9. Notre Dame
10. Southern California
Only 10 ranked

1966
Team
1. Notre Dame
2. Michigan St.
3. Alabama
4. Georgia
5. UCLA
6. Nebraska
7. Purdue
8. Georgia Tech
9. Miami (Fla.)
10. SMU
Only 10 ranked

1967
Team
1. Southern California
2. Tennessee
3. Oklahoma
4. Indiana
5. Notre Dame
6. Wyoming
7. Oregon St.
8. Alabama
9. Purdue
10. Penn St.
Only 10 ranked

1968
Team
1. Ohio St.
2. Penn St.
3. Texas
4. Southern California
5. Notre Dame
6. Arkansas
7. Kansas
8. Georgia
9. Missouri
10. Purdue
11. Oklahoma
12. Michigan
13. Tennessee
14. SMU
15. Oregon St.
16. Auburn
17. Alabama
18. Houston
19. LSU
20. Ohio

1969
Team
1. Texas
2. Penn St.
3. Southern California
4. Ohio St.
5. Notre Dame
6. Missouri
7. Arkansas
8. Mississippi
9. Michigan
10. LSU
11. Nebraska
12. Houston
13. UCLA
14. Florida
15. Tennessee
16. Colorado
17. West Virginia
18. Purdue
19. Stanford
20. Auburn

1970
Team
1. Nebraska
2. Notre Dame
3. Texas
4. Tennessee
5. Ohio St.
6. Arizona St.
7. LSU
8. Stanford
9. Michigan
10. Auburn
11. Arkansas
12. Toledo
13. Georgia Tech
14. Dartmouth
15. Southern California
16. Air Force
17. Tulane
18. Penn St.
19. Houston
20. Oklahoma
Mississippi

1971
Team
1. Nebraska
2. Oklahoma
3. Colorado
4. Alabama
5. Penn St.
6. Michigan
7. Georgia
8. Arizona St.
9. Tennessee
10. Stanford
11. LSU
12. Auburn
13. Notre Dame
14. Toledo
15. Mississippi
16. Arkansas
17. Houston
18. Texas
19. Washington
20. Southern California

1972
Team
1. Southern California
2. Oklahoma
3. Texas
4. Nebraska
5. Auburn
6. Michigan
7. Alabama
8. Tennessee
9. Ohio St.
10. Penn St.
11. LSU
12. North Carolina
13. Arizona St.
14. Notre Dame
15. UCLA
16. Colorado
17. North Carolina St.
18. Louisville
19. Washington St.
20. Georgia Tech

1973
Team
1. Notre Dame
2. Ohio St.
3. Oklahoma
4. Alabama
5. Penn St.
6. Michigan
7. Nebraska
8. Southern California
9. Arizona St.
Houston
11. Texas Tech
12. UCLA
13. LSU
14. Texas
15. Miami (Ohio)
16. North Carolina St.
17. Missouri
18. Kansas
19. Tennessee
20. Maryland
Tulane

1974
Team
1. Oklahoma
2. Southern California
3. Michigan
4. Ohio St.
5. Alabama
6. Notre Dame
7. Penn St.
8. Auburn
9. Nebraska
10. Miami (Ohio)
11. North Carolina St.
12. Michigan St.
13. Maryland
14. Baylor
15. Florida
16. Texas A&M
17. Mississippi St.
Texas
19. Houston
20. Tennessee

1975
Team
1. Oklahoma
2. Arizona St.
3. Alabama
4. Ohio St.
5. UCLA
6. Texas
7. Arkansas
8. Michigan
9. Nebraska
10. Penn St.
11. Texas A&M
12. Miami (Ohio)
13. Maryland
14. California
15. Pittsburgh
16. Colorado
17. Southern California
18. Arizona
19. Georgia
20. West Virginia

1976
Team
1. Pittsburgh
2. Southern California
3. Michigan
4. Houston
5. Oklahoma
6. Ohio St.
7. Texas A&M
8. Maryland
9. Nebraska
10. Georgia
11. Alabama
12. Notre Dame
13. Texas Tech
14. Oklahoma St.
15. UCLA
16. Colorado
17. Rutgers
18. Kentucky
19. Iowa St.
20. Mississippi St.

1977
Team
1. Notre Dame
2. Alabama
3. Arkansas
4. Texas
5. Penn St.
6. Kentucky
7. Oklahoma
8. Pittsburgh
9. Michigan
10. Washington
11. Ohio St.
12. Nebraska
13. Southern California
14. Florida St.
15. Stanford
16. San Diego St.
17. North Carolina
18. Arizona St.
19. Clemson
20. BYU

1978
Team
1. Alabama
2. Southern California
3. Oklahoma
4. Penn St.
5. Michigan
6. Clemson
7. Notre Dame
8. Nebraska
9. Texas
10. Houston
11. Arkansas
12. Michigan St.
13. Purdue
14. UCLA
15. Missouri
16. Georgia
17. Stanford
18. North Carolina St.
19. Texas A&M
20. Maryland

1979
Team
1. Alabama
2. Southern California
3. Oklahoma
4. Ohio St.
5. Houston
6. Florida St.
7. Pittsburgh
8. Arkansas
9. Nebraska
10. Purdue
11. Washington
12. Texas
13. BYU
14. Baylor
15. North Carolina
16. Auburn
17. Temple
18. Michigan
19. Indiana
20. Penn St.

1980
Team
1. Georgia
2. Pittsburgh
3. Oklahoma
4. Michigan
5. Florida St.
6. Alabama
7. Nebraska
8. Penn St.
9. Notre Dame
10. North Carolina
11. Southern California
12. BYU
13. UCLA
14. Baylor
15. Ohio St.
16. Washington
17. Purdue
18. Miami (Fla.)
19. Mississippi St.
20. SMU

1981
Team
1. Clemson
2. Texas
3. Penn St.
4. Pittsburgh
5. SMU
6. Georgia
7. Alabama
8. Miami (Fla.)
9. North Carolina
10. Washington
11. Nebraska
12. Michigan
13. BYU
14. Southern California
15. Ohio St.
16. Arizona St.
17. West Virginia
18. Iowa
19. Missouri
20. Oklahoma

1982
Team
1. Penn St.
2. SMU
3. Nebraska
4. Georgia
5. UCLA
6. Arizona St.
7. Washington
8. Clemson
9. Arkansas
10. Pittsburgh
11. LSU
12. Ohio St.
13. Florida St.
14. Auburn
15. Southern California
16. Oklahoma
17. Texas
18. North Carolina
19. West Virginia
20. Maryland

1983
Team
1. Miami (Fla.)
2. Nebraska
3. Auburn
4. Georgia
5. Texas
6. Florida
7. BYU
8. Michigan
9. Ohio St.
10. Illinois
11. Clemson
12. SMU
13. Air Force
14. Iowa
15. Alabama
16. West Virginia
17. UCLA
18. Pittsburgh
19. Boston College
20. East Caro.

1984
Team
1. BYU
2. Washington
3. Florida
4. Nebraska
5. Boston College
6. Oklahoma
7. Oklahoma St.
8. SMU
9. UCLA
10. Southern California
11. South Carolina
12. Maryland
13. Ohio St.
14. Auburn
15. LSU
16. Iowa
17. Florida St.
18. Miami (Fla.)
19. Kentucky
20. Virginia

1985
Team
1. Oklahoma
2. Michigan
3. Penn St.
4. Tennessee
5. Florida
6. Texas A&M
7. UCLA
8. Air Force
9. Miami (Fla.)
10. Iowa
11. Nebraska
12. Arkansas
13. Alabama
14. Ohio St.
15. Florida St.
16. BYU
17. Baylor
18. Maryland
19. Georgia Tech
20. LSU

1986
Team
1. Penn St.
2. Miami (Fla.)
3. Oklahoma
4. Arizona St.
5. Nebraska
6. Auburn
7. Ohio St.
8. Michigan
9. Alabama
10. LSU
11. Arizona
12. Baylor
13. Texas A&M
14. UCLA
15. Arkansas
16. Iowa
17. Clemson
18. Washington
19. Boston College
20. Virginia Tech

1987
Team
1. Miami (Fla.)
2. Florida St.
3. Oklahoma
4. Syracuse
5. LSU
6. Nebraska
7. Auburn
8. Michigan St.
9. UCLA
10. Texas A&M
11. Oklahoma St.
12. Clemson
13. Georgia
14. Tennessee
15. South Carolina
16. Iowa
17. Notre Dame
18. Southern California
19. Michigan
20. Arizona St.

1988
Team
1. Notre Dame
2. Miami (Fla.)
3. Florida St.
4. Michigan
5. West Virginia
6. UCLA
7. Southern California
8. Auburn
9. Clemson
10. Nebraska
11. Oklahoma St.
12. Arkansas
13. Syracuse
14. Oklahoma
15. Georgia
16. Washington St.
17. Alabama
18. Houston
19. LSU
20. Indiana

†1989
Team
1. Miami (Fla.)
2. Notre Dame
3. Florida St.
4. Colorado
5. Tennessee
6. Auburn
7. Michigan
8. Southern California
9. Alabama
10. Illinois
11. Nebraska
12. Clemson
13. Arkansas
14. Houston
15. Penn St.
16. Michigan St.
17. Pittsburgh
18. Virginia
19. Texas Tech
20. Texas A&M
21. West Virginia
22. BYU
23. Washington
24. Ohio St.
25. Arizona

1990
Team
1. Colorado
2. Georgia Tech
3. Miami (Fla.)
4. Florida St.
5. Washington
6. Notre Dame
7. Michigan
8. Tennessee
9. Clemson
10. Houston
11. Penn St.
12. Texas
13. Florida
14. Louisville
15. Texas A&M
16. Michigan St.
17. Oklahoma
18. Iowa
19. Auburn
20. Southern California
21. Mississippi
22. BYU
23. Virginia
24. Nebraska
25. Illinois

1991
Team
1. Miami (Fla.)
2. Washington
3. Penn St.
4. Florida St.
5. Alabama
6. Michigan
7. Florida
8. California
9. East Caro.
10. Iowa
11. Syracuse
12. Texas A&M
13. Notre Dame
14. Tennessee
15. Nebraska
16. Oklahoma
17. Georgia
18. Clemson
19. UCLA
20. Colorado
21. Tulsa
22. Stanford
23. BYU
24. North Carolina St.
25. Air Force

1992
Team
1. Alabama
2. Florida St.
3. Miami (Fla.)
4. Notre Dame
5. Michigan
6. Syracuse
7. Texas A&M
8. Georgia
9. Stanford
10. Florida
11. Washington
12. Tennessee
13. Colorado
14. Nebraska
15. Washington St.
16. Mississippi
17. North Carolina St.
18. Ohio St.
19. North Carolina
20. Hawaii
21. Boston College
22. Kansas
23. Mississippi St.
24. Fresno St.
25. Wake Forest

1993
Team
1. Florida St.
2. Notre Dame
3. Nebraska
4. Auburn
5. Florida
6. Wisconsin
7. West Virginia
8. Penn St.
9. Texas A&M
10. Arizona
11. Ohio St.
12. Tennessee
13. Boston College
14. Alabama
15. Miami (Fla.)
16. Colorado
17. Oklahoma
18. UCLA
19. North Carolina
20. Kansas St.
21. Michigan
22. Virginia Tech
23. Clemson
24. Louisville
25. California

1994
Team
1. Nebraska
2. Penn St.
3. Colorado
4. Florida St.
5. Alabama
6. Miami (Fla.)
7. Florida
8. Texas A&M
9. Auburn
10. Utah
11. Oregon
12. Michigan
13. Southern California
14. Ohio St.
15. Virginia
16. Colorado St.
17. North Carolina St.
18. BYU
19. Kansas St.
20. Arizona
21. Washington St.
22. Tennessee
23. Boston College
24. Mississippi St.
25. Texas

1995
Team
1. Nebraska
2. Florida
3. Tennessee
4. Florida St.
5. Colorado
6. Ohio St.
7. Kansas St.
8. Northwestern
9. Kansas
10. Virginia Tech
11. Notre Dame
12. Southern California
13. Penn St.
14. Texas
15. Texas A&M
16. Virginia
17. Michigan
18. Oregon
19. Syracuse
20. Miami (Fla.)
21. Alabama
22. Auburn
23. Texas Tech
24. Toledo
25. Iowa

1996

Team (Record)
1. Florida (12-1)
2. Ohio St. (11-1)
3. Florida St. (11-1)
4. Arizona St. (11-1)
5. BYU (14-1)
6. Nebraska (11-2)
7. Penn St. (11-2)
8. Colorado (10-2)
9. Tennessee (10-2)
10. North Carolina (10-2)
11. Alabama (10-3)
12. LSU (10-2)
13. Virginia Tech (10-2)
14. Miami (Fla.) (9-3)
15. Northwestern (9-3)
16. Washington (9-3)
17. Kansas St. (9-3)
18. Iowa (9-3)
19. Notre Dame (8-3)
20. Michigan (8-4)
21. Syracuse (9-3)
22. Wyoming (10-2)
23. Texas (8-5)
24. Auburn (8-4)
25. Army (10-2)

1997

Team (Record)
1. Michigan (12-0)
2. Nebraska (13-0)
3. Florida St. (11-1)
4. Florida (10-2)
5. UCLA (10-2)
6. North Carolina (11-1)
7. Tennessee (11-2)
8. Kansas St. (11-1)
9. Washington St. (10-2)
10. Georgia (10-2)
11. Auburn (10-3)
12. Ohio St. (10-3)
13. LSU (9-3)
14. Arizona St. (9-3)
15. Purdue (9-3)
16. Penn St. (9-3)
17. Colorado St. (11-2)
18. Washington (8-4)
19. Southern Miss. (9-3)
20. Texas A&M (9-4)
21. Syracuse (9-4)
22. Mississippi (8-4)
23. Missouri (7-5)
24. Oklahoma St. (8-4)
25. Georgia Tech (7-5)

1998

Team (Record)
1. Tennessee (13-0)
2. Ohio St. (11-1)
3. Florida St. (11-2)
4. Arizona (12-1)
5. Florida (10-2)
6. Wisconsin (11-1)
7. Tulane (12-0)
8. UCLA (10-2)
9. Georgia Tech (10-2)
10. Kansas St. (11-2)
11. Texas A&M (11-3)
12. Michigan (10-3)
13. Air Force (12-1)
14. Georgia (9-3)
15. Texas (9-3)
16. Arkansas (9-3)
17. Penn St. (9-3)
18. Virginia (9-3)
19. Nebraska (9-4)
20. Miami (Fla.) (9-3)
21. Missouri (8-4)
22. Notre Dame (9-3)
23. Virginia Tech (9-3)
24. Purdue (9-4)
25. Syracuse (8-4)

1999

Team (Record)
1. Florida St. (12-0)
2. Virginia Tech (11-1)
3. Nebraska (12-1)
4. Wisconsin (10-2)
5. Michigan (10-2)
6. Kansas St. (11-1)
7. Michigan St. (10-2)
8. Alabama (10-3)
9. Tennessee (9-3)
10. Marshall (13-0)
11. Penn St. (10-3)
12. Florida (9-4)
13. Mississippi St. (10-2)
14. Southern Miss. (9-3)
15. Miami (Fla.) (9-4)
16. Georgia (8-4)
17. Arkansas (8-4)
18. Minnesota (8-4)
19. Oregon (9-3)
20. Georgia Tech (8-4)
21. Texas (9-5)
22. Mississippi (8-4)
23. Texas A&M (8-4)
24. Illinois (8-4)
25. Purdue (7-5)

2000

Team (Record)
1. Oklahoma (13-0)
2. Miami (Fla.) (11-1)
3. Washington (11-1)
4. Oregon St. (11-1)
5. Florida St. (11-2)
6. Virginia Tech (11-1)
7. Oregon (10-2)
8. Nebraska (10-2)
9. Kansas St. (11-3)
10. Florida (10-3)
11. Michigan (9-3)
12. Texas (9-3)
13. Purdue (8-4)
14. Colorado St. (10-2)
15. Notre Dame (9-3)
16. Clemson (9-3)
17. Georgia Tech (9-3)
18. Auburn (9-4)
19. South Carolina (8-4)
20. Georgia (8-4)
21. TCU (10-2)
22. LSU (8-4)
23. Wisconsin (9-4)
24. Mississippi St. (8-4)
25. Iowa St. (9-3)

2001

Team (Record)
1. Miami (Fla.) (12-0)
2. Oregon (11-1)
3. Florida (10-2)
4. Tennessee (11-2)
5. Texas (11-2)
6. Oklahoma (11-2)
7. LSU (10-3)
8. Nebraska (11-2)
9. Colorado (10-3)
10. Washington St. (10-2)
11. Maryland (10-2)
12. Illinois (10-2)
13. South Carolina (9-3)
14. Syracuse (10-3)
15. Florida St. (8-4)
16. Stanford (9-3)
17. Louisville (11-2)
18. Virginia Tech (8-4)
19. Washington (8-4)
20. Michigan (8-4)
21. Boston College (8-4)
22. Georgia (8-4)
23. Toledo (10-2)
24. Georgia Tech (8-5)
25. BYU (12-2)

2002

Team (Record)
1. Ohio St. (14-0)
2. Miami (Fla.) (12-1)
3. Georgia (13-1)
4. Southern California (11-2)
5. Oklahoma (12-2)
6. Texas (11-2)
7. Kansas St. (11-2)
8. Iowa (11-2)
9. Michigan (10-3)
10. Washington St. (10-3)
11. Alabama (10-3)
12. North Carolina St. (11-3)
13. Maryland (11-3)
14. Auburn (9-4)
15. Boise St. (12-1)
16. Penn St. (9-4)
17. Notre Dame (10-3)
18. Virginia Tech (10-4)
19. Pittsburgh (9-4)
20. Colorado (9-5)
21. Florida St. (9-5)
22. Virginia (9-5)
23. TCU (10-2)
24. Marshall (11-2)
25. West Virginia (9-4)

2003

Team (Record)
1. Southern California (12-1)
2. LSU (13-1)
3. Oklahoma (12-2)
4. Ohio St. (11-2)
5. Miami (Fla.) (11-2)
6. Michigan (10-3)
7. Georgia (11-3)
8. Iowa (10-3)
9. Washington St. (10-3)
10. Miami (Ohio) (13-1)
11. Florida St. (10-3)
12. Texas (10-3)
13. Mississippi (10-3)
14. Kansas St. (11-4)
15. Tennessee (10-3)
16. Boise St. (13-1)
17. Maryland (10-3)
18. Purdue (9-4)
19. Nebraska (10-3)
20. Minnesota (10-3)
21. Utah (10-2)
22. Clemson (9-4)
23. Bowling Green (11-3)
24. Florida (8-5)
25. TCU (11-2)

2004

Team (Record)
1. Southern California (13-0)
2. Auburn (13-0)
3. Oklahoma (12-1)
4. Utah (12-0)
5. Texas (11-1)
6. Louisville (11-1)
7. Georgia (10-2)
8. Iowa (10-2)
9. California (10-2)
10. Virginia Tech (10-3)
11. Miami (Fla.) (9-3)
12. Boise St. (11-1)
13. Tennessee (10-3)
14. Michigan (9-3)
15. Florida St. (9-3)
16. LSU (9-3)
17. Wisconsin (9-3)
18. Texas Tech (8-4)
19. Arizona St. (9-3)
20. Ohio St. (8-4)
21. Boston College (9-3)
22. Fresno St. (9-3)
23. Virginia (8-4)
24. Navy (10-2)
25. Pittsburgh (8-4)

2005

Team (Record)
1. Texas (13-0)
2. Southern California (12-1)
3. Penn St. (11-1)
4. Ohio St. (10-2)
5. West Virginia (11-1)
6. LSU (11-2)
7. Virginia Tech (11-2)
8. Alabama (10-2)
9. Notre Dame (9-3)
10. Georgia (10-3)
11. TCU (11-1)
12. Florida (9-3)
    Oregon (10-2)
14. Auburn (9-3)
15. Wisconsin (10-3)
16. UCLA (10-2)
17. Miami (Fla.) (9-3)
18. Boston College (9-3)
19. Louisville (9-3)
20. Texas Tech (9-3)
21. Clemson (8-4)
22. Oklahoma (8-5)
23. Florida St. (8-5)
24. Nebraska (8-4)
25. California (8-4)

2006

Team (Record)
1. Florida (13-1)
2. Ohio State (12-1)
3. Southern California (11-2)
4. USC (11-2)
5. Boise St. (13-0)
6. Louisville (12-1)
7. Wisconsin (12-1)
8. Michigan (11-2)
9. Auburn (11-2)
10. West Virginia (11-2)
11. Oklahoma (11-3)
12. Rutgers (11-2)
13. Texas (10-3)
14. California (10-3)
15. Arkansas (10-4)
16. BYU (11-2)
17. Notre Dame (10-3)
18. Wake Forest (11-3)
19. Virginia Tech (10-3)
20. Boston College (10-3)
21. Oregon St. (10-4)
22. TCU (11-2)
23. Georgia (9-4)
24. Penn St. (9-4)
25. Tennessee (9-4)

**On January 6, 1948, in a special postseason poll after the Rose Bowl, the Associated Press voted Michigan No. 1 and Notre Dame No. 2. However, the postseason poll did not supersede the final regular-season poll of December 6, 1947. †Beginning in 1989 season, AP selected top 25 teams instead of 20.*

United Press International Final Polls

United Press (UP), 1950-57; United Press International (UPI) from 1958-95 after merger with International News Service (INS). Served as the coaches' poll until 1991, when it was taken over by USA Today/Cable News Network (CNN)/ESPN poll.

1950
Team
1. Oklahoma
2. Texas
3. Tennessee
4. California
5. Army
6. Michigan
7. Kentucky
8. Princeton
9. Michigan St.
10. Ohio St.
11. Illinois
12. Clemson
13. Miami (Fla.)
14. Wyoming
15. Washington
    Baylor
17. Alabama
18. Wash. & Lee
19. Navy
20. Nebraska
    Wisconsin
    Cornell

1951
Team
1. Tennessee
2. Michigan St.
3. Illinois
4. Maryland
5. Georgia Tech
6. Princeton
7. Stanford
8. Wisconsin
9. Baylor
10. TCU
11. Oklahoma
12. California
13. Notre Dame
14. San Francisco
    Purdue
    Washington St.
17. Holy Cross
    UCLA
    Kentucky
20. Kansas

1952
Team
1. Michigan St.
2. Georgia Tech
3. Notre Dame
4. Oklahoma
    Southern California
6. UCLA
7. Mississippi
8. Tennessee
9. Alabama
10. Wisconsin
11. Texas
12. Purdue
13. Maryland
14. Princeton
15. Ohio St.
    Pittsburgh
17. Navy
18. Duke
19. Houston
    Kentucky

1953
Team
1. Maryland
2. Notre Dame
3. Michigan St.
4. UCLA
5. Oklahoma
6. Rice
7. Illinois
8. Texas
9. Georgia Tech
10. Iowa
11. Alabama
12. Texas Tech
13. West Virginia
14. Wisconsin
15. Kentucky
16. Army
17. Stanford
18. Duke
19. Michigan
20. Ohio St.

1954
Team
1. UCLA
2. Ohio St.
3. Oklahoma
4. Notre Dame
5. Navy
6. Mississippi
7. Army
8. Arkansas
9. Miami (Fla.)
10. Wisconsin
11. Southern California
    Maryland
    Georgia Tech
14. Duke
15. Michigan
16. Penn St.
17. SMU
18. Denver
19. Rice
20. Minnesota

1955
Team
1. Oklahoma
2. Michigan St.
3. Maryland
4. UCLA
5. Ohio St.
6. TCU
7. Georgia Tech
8. Auburn
9. Mississippi
10. Notre Dame
11. Pittsburgh
12. Southern California
13. Michigan
14. Texas A&M
15. Army
16. Duke
17. West Virginia
18. Miami (Fla.)
19. Iowa
20. Navy
    Stanford
    Miami (Ohio)

1956
Team
1. Oklahoma
2. Tennessee
3. Iowa
4. Georgia Tech
5. Texas A&M
6. Miami (Fla.)
7. Michigan
8. Syracuse
9. Minnesota
10. Michigan St.
11. Baylor
12. Pittsburgh
13. Oregon St.
14. TCU
15. Southern California
16. Wyoming
17. Yale
18. Colorado
19. Navy
20. Duke

1957
Team
1. Ohio St.
2. Auburn
3. Michigan St.
4. Oklahoma
5. Iowa
6. Navy
7. Rice
8. Mississippi
9. Notre Dame
10. Texas A&M
11. Texas
12. Arizona St.
13. Army
14. Duke
    Wisconsin
16. Tennessee
17. Oregon
18. Clemson
    UCLA
20. North Carolina St.

1958
Team
1. LSU
2. Iowa
3. Army
4. Auburn
5. Oklahoma
6. Wisconsin
7. Ohio St.
8. Air Force
9. TCU
10. Syracuse
11. Purdue
12. Mississippi
13. Clemson
14. Notre Dame
15. Florida
16. California
17. Northwestern
18. SMU

(Only 18 teams received votes)

1959
Team
1. Syracuse
2. Mississippi
3. LSU
4. Texas
5. Georgia
6. Wisconsin
7. Washington
8. TCU
9. Arkansas
10. Penn St.
11. Clemson
12. Illinois
13. Alabama
    Southern California
15. Auburn
16. Michigan St.
17. Oklahoma
18. Notre Dame
19. Pittsburgh
    Missouri
    Florida

1960
Team
1. Minnesota
2. Iowa
3. Mississippi
4. Missouri
5. Wisconsin
6. Navy
7. Arkansas
8. Ohio St.
9. Kansas
10. Alabama
11. Duke
    Baylor
    Michigan St.
14. Auburn
15. Purdue
16. Florida
17. Texas
18. Yale
19. New Mexico St.
    Tennessee

1961
Team
1. Alabama
2. Ohio St.
3. LSU
4. Texas
5. Mississippi
6. Minnesota
7. Colorado
8. Arkansas
9. Michigan St.
10. Utah St.
11. Purdue
    Missouri
13. Georgia Tech
14. Duke
15. Kansas
16. Syracuse
17. Wyoming
18. Wisconsin
19. Miami (Fla.)
    Penn St.

1962
Team
1. Southern California
2. Wisconsin
3. Mississippi
4. Texas
5. Alabama
6. Arkansas
7. Oklahoma
8. LSU
9. Penn St.
10. Minnesota
11. Georgia Tech
12. Missouri
13. Ohio St.
14. Duke
    Washington
16. Northwestern
    Oregon St.
18. Arizona St.
    Illinois
    Miami (Fla.)

1963
Team
1. Texas
2. Navy
3. Pittsburgh
4. Illinois
5. Nebraska
6. Auburn
7. Mississippi
8. Oklahoma
9. Alabama
10. Michigan St.
11. Mississippi St.
12. Syracuse
13. Arizona St.
14. Memphis
15. Washington
16. Penn St.
    Southern California
    Missouri
19. North Carolina
20. Baylor

1964
Team
1. Alabama
2. Arkansas
3. Notre Dame
4. Michigan
5. Texas
6. Nebraska
7. LSU
8. Oregon St.
9. Ohio St.
10. Southern California
11. Florida St.
12. Syracuse
13. Princeton
14. Penn St.
    Utah
16. Illinois
    New Mexico
18. Tulsa
    Missouri
20. Mississippi
    Michigan St.

1965
Team
1. Michigan St.
2. Arkansas
3. Nebraska
4. Alabama
5. UCLA
6. Missouri
7. Tennessee
8. Notre Dame
9. Southern California
10. Texas Tech
11. Ohio St.
12. Florida
13. Purdue
14. LSU
15. Georgia
16. Tulsa
17. Mississippi
18. Kentucky
19. Syracuse
20. Colorado

1966
Team
1. Notre Dame
2. Michigan St.
3. Alabama
4. Georgia
5. UCLA
6. Purdue
7. Nebraska
8. Georgia Tech
9. SMU
10. Miami (Fla.)
11. Florida
12. Mississippi
13. Arkansas
14. Tennessee
15. Wyoming
16. Syracuse
17. Houston
18. Southern California
19. Oregon St.
20. Virginia Tech

1967
Team
1. Southern California
2. Tennessee
3. Oklahoma
4. Notre Dame
5. Wyoming
6. Indiana
7. Alabama
8. Oregon St.
9. Purdue
10. UCLA
11. Penn St.
12. Syracuse
13. Colorado
14. Minnesota
15. Florida St.
16. Miami (Fla.)
17. North Carolina St.
18. Georgia
19. Houston
20. Arizona St.

1968
Team
1. Ohio St.
2. Southern California
3. Penn St.
4. Georgia
5. Texas
6. Kansas
7. Tennessee
8. Notre Dame
9. Arkansas
10. Oklahoma
11. Purdue
12. Alabama
13. Oregon St.
14. Florida St.
15. Michigan
16. SMU
17. Missouri
18. Ohio
    Minnesota
20. Houston
    Stanford

1969
Team
1. Texas
2. Penn St.
3. Arkansas
4. Southern California
5. Ohio St.
6. Missouri
7. LSU
8. Michigan
9. Notre Dame
10. UCLA
11. Tennessee
12. Nebraska
13. Mississippi
14. Stanford
15. Auburn
16. Houston
17. Florida
18. Purdue
    San Diego St.
    West Virginia

1970
Team
1. Texas
2. Ohio St.
3. Nebraska
4. Tennessee
5. Notre Dame
6. LSU
7. Michigan
8. Arizona St.
9. Auburn
10. Stanford
11. Air Force
12. Arkansas
13. Houston
    Dartmouth
15. Oklahoma
16. Colorado
17. Georgia Tech
    Toledo
19. Penn St.
    Southern California

1971
Team
1. Nebraska
2. Alabama
3. Oklahoma
4. Michigan
5. Auburn
6. Arizona St.
7. Colorado
8. Georgia
9. Tennessee
10. LSU
11. Penn St.
12. Texas
13. Toledo
14. Houston
15. Notre Dame
16. Stanford
17. Iowa St.
18. North Carolina
19. Florida St.
20. Arkansas
    Mississippi

1972
Team
1. Southern California
2. Oklahoma
3. Ohio St.
4. Alabama
5. Texas
6. Michigan
7. Auburn
8. Penn St.
9. Nebraska
10. LSU
11. Tennessee
12. Notre Dame
13. Arizona St.
14. Colorado
    North Carolina
16. Louisville
17. UCLA
    Washington St.
19. Utah St.
20. San Diego St.

1973
Team
1. Alabama
2. Oklahoma
3. Ohio St.
4. Notre Dame
5. Penn St.
6. Michigan
7. Southern California
8. Texas
9. UCLA
10. Arizona St.
11. Nebraska
    Texas Tech
13. Houston
14. LSU
15. Kansas
    Tulane
17. Miami (Ohio)
18. Maryland
19. San Diego St.
    Florida

*1974
Team
1. Southern California
2. Alabama
3. Ohio St.
4. Notre Dame
5. Michigan
6. Auburn
7. Penn St.
8. Nebraska
9. North Carolina St.
10. Miami (Ohio)
11. Houston
12. Florida
13. Maryland
14. Baylor
15. Texas A&M
    Tennessee
17. Mississippi St.
18. Michigan St.
19. Tulsa

1975
Team
1. Oklahoma
2. Arizona St.
3. Alabama
4. Ohio St.
5. UCLA
6. Arkansas
7. Texas
8. Michigan
9. Nebraska
10. Penn St.
11. Maryland
12. Texas A&M
13. Arizona
    Pittsburgh
15. California
16. Miami (Ohio)
17. Notre Dame
    West Virginia
19. Georgia
    Southern California

1976
Team
1. Pittsburgh
2. Southern California
3. Michigan
4. Houston
5. Ohio St.
6. Oklahoma
7. Nebraska
8. Texas A&M
9. Alabama
10. Georgia
11. Maryland
12. Notre Dame
13. Texas Tech
14. Oklahoma St.
15. UCLA
16. Colorado
17. Rutgers
18. Iowa St.
19. Baylor
    Kentucky

1977
Team
1. Notre Dame
2. Alabama
3. Arkansas
4. Penn St.
5. Texas
6. Oklahoma
7. Pittsburgh
8. Michigan
9. Washington
10. Nebraska
11. Florida St.
12. Ohio St.
    Southern California
14. North Carolina
15. Stanford
16. North Texas
    BYU
18. Arizona St.
19. San Diego St.
    North Carolina St.

1978
Team
1. Southern California
2. Alabama
3. Oklahoma
4. Penn St.
5. Michigan
6. Notre Dame
7. Clemson
8. Nebraska
9. Texas
10. Arkansas
11. Houston
12. UCLA
13. Purdue
14. Missouri
15. Georgia
16. Stanford
17. Navy
18. Texas A&M
19. Arizona St.
    North Carolina St.

1979
Team
1. Alabama
2. Southern California
3. Oklahoma
4. Ohio St.
5. Houston
6. Pittsburgh
7. Nebraska
8. Florida St.
9. Arkansas
10. Purdue
11. Washington
12. BYU
13. Texas
14. North Carolina
15. Baylor
16. Indiana
17. Temple
18. Penn St.
19. Michigan
20. Missouri

1980
Team
1. Georgia
2. Pittsburgh
3. Oklahoma
4. Michigan
5. Florida St.
6. Alabama
7. Nebraska
8. Penn St.
9. North Carolina
10. Notre Dame
11. BYU
12. Southern California
13. Baylor
14. UCLA
15. Ohio St.
16. Purdue
17. Washington
18. Miami (Fla.)
19. Florida
20. SMU

1981
Team
1. Clemson
2. Pittsburgh
3. Penn St.
4. Texas
5. Georgia
6. Alabama
7. Washington
8. North Carolina
9. Nebraska
10. Michigan
11. BYU
12. Ohio St.
13. Southern California
14. Oklahoma
15. Iowa
16. Arkansas
17. Mississippi St.
18. West Virginia
19. Southern Miss.
20. Missouri

1982
Team
1. Penn St.
2. SMU
3. Nebraska
4. Georgia
5. UCLA
6. Arizona St.
7. Washington
8. Arkansas
9. Pittsburgh
10. Florida St.
11. LSU
12. Ohio St.
13. North Carolina
14. Auburn
15. Michigan
16. Oklahoma
17. Alabama
18. Texas
19. West Virginia
20. Maryland

1983
Team
1. Miami (Fla.)
2. Nebraska
3. Auburn
4. Georgia
5. Texas
6. Florida
7. BYU
8. Ohio St.
9. Michigan
10. Illinois
11. SMU
12. Alabama
13. UCLA
14. Iowa
15. Air Force
16. West Virginia
17. Penn St.
18. Oklahoma St.
19. Pittsburgh
20. Boston College

1984
Team
1. BYU
2. Washington
3. Nebraska
4. Boston College
5. Oklahoma St.
6. Oklahoma
7. Florida
8. SMU
9. Southern California
10. UCLA
11. Maryland
12. Ohio St.
13. South Carolina
14. Auburn
15. Iowa
16. LSU
17. Virginia
18. West Virginia
19. Kentucky
    Florida St.

1985
Team
1. Oklahoma
2. Michigan
3. Penn St.
4. Tennessee
5. Air Force
6. UCLA
7. Texas A&M
8. Miami (Fla.)
9. Iowa
10. Nebraska
11. Ohio St.
12. Arkansas
13. Florida St.
14. Alabama
15. Baylor
16. Fresno St.
17. BYU
18. Georgia Tech
19. Maryland
20. LSU

1986
Team
1. Penn St.
2. Miami (Fla.)
3. Oklahoma
4. Nebraska
5. Arizona St.
6. Ohio St.
7. Michigan
8. Auburn
9. Alabama
10. Arizona
11. LSU
12. Texas A&M
13. Baylor
14. UCLA
15. Iowa
16. Arkansas
17. Washington
18. Boston College
19. Clemson
20. Florida St.

1987
Team
1. Miami (Fla.)
2. Florida St.
3. Oklahoma
4. Syracuse
5. LSU
6. Nebraska
7. Auburn
8. Michigan St.
9. Texas A&M
10. Clemson
11. UCLA
12. Oklahoma St.
13. Tennessee
14. Georgia
15. South Carolina
16. Iowa
17. Southern California
18. Michigan
19. Texas
20. Indiana

1988
Team
1. Notre Dame
2. Miami (Fla.)
3. Florida St.
4. Michigan
5. West Virginia
6. UCLA
7. Auburn
8. Clemson
9. Southern California
10. Nebraska
11. Oklahoma St.
12. Syracuse
13. Arkansas
14. Oklahoma
15. Georgia
16. Washington St.
17. North Carolina St.
    Alabama
19. Indiana
20. Wyoming

1989
Team
1. Miami (Fla.)
2. Florida St.
3. Notre Dame
4. Colorado
5. Tennessee
6. Auburn
7. Alabama
8. Michigan
9. Southern California
10. Illinois
11. Clemson
12. Nebraska
13. Arkansas
14. Penn St.
15. Virginia
16. Texas Tech
    Michigan St.
18. BYU
19. Pittsburgh
20. Washington

#1990
Team
1. Georgia Tech
2. Colorado
3. Miami (Fla.)
4. Florida St.
5. Washington
6. Notre Dame
7. Tennessee
8. Michigan
9. Clemson
10. Penn St.
11. Texas
12. Louisville
13. Texas A&M
14. Michigan St.
15. Virginia
16. Iowa
17. BYU
    Nebraska
19. Auburn
20. San Jose St.
21. Syracuse
22. Southern California
23. Mississippi
24. Illinois
25. Virginia Tech

¢1991
Team
1. Washington
2. Miami (Fla.)
3. Penn St.
4. Florida St.
5. Alabama
6. Michigan
7. Florida
8. California
9. East Caro.
10. Iowa
11. Syracuse
12. Notre Dame
13. Texas A&M
14. Tennessee
15. Nebraska
16. Oklahoma
17. Clemson
18. Colorado
19. UCLA
20. Georgia
21. Tulsa
22. Stanford
23. North Carolina St.
24. BYU
25. Ohio St.

1992
Team
1. Alabama
2. Florida St.
3. Miami (Fla.)
4. Notre Dame
5. Michigan
6. Syracuse
7. Texas A&M
8. Georgia
9. Stanford
10. Florida
11. Washington
12. Tennessee
13. Colorado
14. Nebraska
15. Washington St.
16. Mississippi
17. North Carolina St.
18. North Carolina
19. Ohio St.
20. Hawaii
21. Boston College
22. Kansas
23. Fresno St.
24. Penn St.
25. Mississippi St.

1993
Team
1. Florida St.
2. Notre Dame
3. Nebraska
4. Florida
5. Wisconsin
6. Texas A&M
7. Penn St.
8. West Virginia
9. Ohio St.
10. Arizona
11. Boston College
12. Tennessee
13. Alabama
14. Miami (Fla.)
15. Oklahoma
16. Colorado
17. UCLA
18. Kansas St.
19. Michigan
20. North Carolina
21. Virginia Tech
22. Louisville
23. Clemson
24. California
25. Southern California

1994
Team
1. Nebraska
2. Penn St.
3. Colorado
4. Florida St.
5. Alabama
6. Miami (Fla.)
7. Florida
8. Utah
9. Michigan
10. Ohio St.
11. Oregon
12. BYU
13. Southern California
14. Colorado St.
15. Virginia
16. Kansas St.
17. North Carolina St.
18. Tennessee
19. Washington St.
20. Arizona
21. North Carolina
22. Boston College
23. Texas
24. Virginia Tech
25. Mississippi St.

1995
Team
1. Nebraska
2. Florida
3. Tennessee
4. Colorado
5. Florida St.
6. Ohio St.
7. Kansas St.
8. Northwestern
9. Virginia Tech
10. Kansas
11. Southern California
12. Penn St.
13. Notre Dame
14. Texas A&M
15. Texas
16. Virginia
17. Syracuse
18. Oregon
19. Michigan
20. Texas Tech
21. Auburn
22. Toledo
23. Iowa
24. East Caro.
25. LSU

**Beginning in 1974, by agreement with the American Football Coaches Association, teams on probation by the NCAA were ineligible for ranking and national championship consideration by the UPI Board of Coaches. #Beginning in 1990 season, UPI selected top 25 teams instead of 20. ¢In 1991-92, the No. 1 team in the final UPI/NFF poll received the MacArthur Bowl, awarded by the NFF since 1959 to recognize its national champion. Beginning in 1993, the No. 1 team in the USA Today/Hall of Fame poll was awarded the MacArthur Bowl. The National Football Foundation and Hall of Fame MacArthur Bowl national champions before 1991 are listed in national polls section.*

USA Today/ESPN (Coaches) Weekly Poll Leaders

A team's record includes its last game before the weekly poll. A new weekly leader's rank the previous week is indicated in parentheses after its record. Final poll leaders (annual champions) are in bold face.

1992

9-8 Miami (Fla.) (1-0-0)
9-15 Miami (Fla.) (1-0-0)
9-22 Miami (Fla.) (2-0-0)
9-29 Washington (3-0-0) (2)
10-6 Washington (4-0-0)
10-13 Miami (Fla.) (5-0-0) (2)
10-20 Miami (Fla.) (6-0-0)
10-27 Miami (Fla.) (7-0-0)
11-3 Miami (Fla.) (8-0-0)
11-10 Miami (Fla.) (8-0-0)
11-17 Miami (Fla.) (9-0-0)
11-24 Miami (Fla.) (10-0-0)
12-1 Miami (Fla.) (11-0-0)
12-8 Miami (Fla.) (11-0-0)
1-2 Alabama (13-0-0) (2)

1993

8-31 Florida St. (1-0-0)
9-7 Florida St. (2-0-0)
9-14 Florida St. (3-0-0)
9-21 Florida St. (4-0-0)
9-28 Florida St. (4-0-0)
10-5 Florida St. (5-0-0)
10-12 Florida St. (6-0-0)
10-19 Florida St. (7-0-0)
10-26 Florida St. (7-0-0)
11-2 Florida St. (8-0-0)
11-9 Florida St. (9-0-0)
11-16 Notre Dame (10-0-0) (2)
11-23 Nebraska (10-0-0) (2)
11-30 Nebraska (11-0-0)
12-7 Nebraska (11-0-0)
1-3 Florida St. (12-1-0) (3)

1994

9-6 Nebraska (1-0-0)
9-13 Nebraska (2-0-0)
9-20 Nebraska (3-0-0)
9-27 Nebraska (4-0-0)
10-4 Florida (4-0-0) (2)
10-11 Florida (5-0-0)
10-18 Penn St. (6-0-0) (3)
10-25 Penn St. (6-0-0)
11-1 Penn St. (7-0-0)
11-8 Nebraska (10-0-0) (2)
11-15 Nebraska (11-0-0)
11-22 Nebraska (11-0-0)
11-29 Nebraska (12-0-0)
12-6 Nebraska (12-0-0)
1-3 Nebraska (13-0-0)

1995

9-5 Florida St. (1-0-0)
9-12 Florida St. (2-0-0)
9-19 Florida St. (3-0-0)
9-26 Florida St. (4-0-0)
10-3 Florida St. (4-0-0)
10-10 Florida St. (5-0-0)
10-17 Florida St. (6-0-0)
10-24 Florida St. (7-0-0)
10-31 Nebraska (8-0-0) (2)
11-7 Nebraska (9-0-0)
11-14 Nebraska (10-0-0)
11-21 Nebraska (10-0-0)
11-28 Nebraska (11-0-0)
12-5 Nebraska (11-0-0)
1-3 Nebraska (12-0-0)

1996

9-2 Nebraska (0-0-0)
9-9 Nebraska (1-0-0)
9-16 Nebraska (1-0-0)
9-23 Florida (3-0-0) (4)
9-30 Florida (4-0-0)
10-7 Florida (5-0-0)
10-14 Florida (6-0-0)
10-21 Florida (7-0-0)
10-28 Florida (7-0-0)
11-4 Florida (8-0-0)
11-11 Florida (9-0-0)
11-18 Florida (10-0-0)
11-25 Florida (10-0-0)
12-2 Florida St. (11-0-0) (2)
12-9 Florida St. (11-0-0)
1-3 Florida (12-1-0)

1997

9-2 Florida (1-0-0)
9-8 Florida (2-0-0)
9-15 Florida (2-0-0)
9-22 Florida (3-0-0)
9-29 Florida (4-0-0)
10-6 Florida (5-0-0)
10-13 Penn St. (5-0-0) (2)
10-20 Nebraska (6-0-0) (2)
10-27 Nebraska (7-0-0)
11-3 Nebraska (8-0-0)
11-10 Florida St. (9-0-0) (2)
11-17 Florida St. (10-0-0)
11-24 Michigan (11-0-0) (2)
12-1 Michigan (11-0-0)
12-8 Michigan (11-0-0)
1-3 Nebraska (13-0-0) (2)

1998

9-7 Ohio St. (1-0-0)
9-14 Ohio St. (2-0-0)
9-21 Ohio St. (3-0-0)
9-28 Ohio St. (3-0-0)
10-5 Ohio St. (4-0-0)
10-12 Ohio St. (5-0-0)
10-19 Ohio St. (6-0-0)
10-26 Ohio St. (7-0-0)
11-2 Ohio St. (8-0-0)
11-9 Tennessee (8-0-0) (3) & Kansas St. (9-0-0) (2)
11-16 Kansas St. (10-0-0)
11-23 Kansas St. (11-0-0)
11-30 Kansas St. (11-0-0)
12-7 Tennessee (12-0-0) (2)
1-5 Tennessee (13-0-0

1999

8-30 Florida St. (1-0-0)
9-6 Florida St. (1-0-0)
9-13 Florida St. (2-0-0)
9-20 Florida St. (3-0-0)
9-27 Florida St. (4-0-0)
10-4 Florida St. (5-0-0)
10-11 Florida St. (6-0-0)
10-18 Florida St. (7-0-0)
10-25 Florida St. (8-0-0)
11-1 Florida St. (9-0-0)
11-8 Florida St. (9-0-0)
11-15 Florida St. (10-0-0)
11-22 Florida St. (11-0-0)
11-29 Florida St. (11-0-0)
12-6 Florida St. (11-0-0)
1-5 Florida St. (12-0-0)

2000

8-28 Nebraska (0-0-0)
9-4 Nebraska (1-0-0)
9-11 Nebraska (2-0-0)
9-18 Nebraska (2-0-0)
9-25 Nebraska (3-0-0)
10-2 Nebraska (4-0-0)
10-9 Nebraska (5-0-0)
10-16 Nebraska (6-0-0)
10-23 Nebraska (7-0-0)
10-30 Oklahoma (7-0-0) (3)
11-6 Oklahoma (8-0-0)
11-13 Oklahoma (9-0-0)
11-20 Oklahoma (10-0-0)
11-27 Oklahoma (11-0-0)
12-4 Oklahoma (12-0-0)
1-5 Oklahoma (13-0-0)

2001

8-27 Florida (0-0-0)
9-2 Florida (1-0-0)
9-9 Miami (Fla.) (2-0-0) (2)
9-23 Miami (Fla.) (2-0-0)
9-30 Miami (Fla.) (3-0-0)
10-7 Miami (Fla.) (4-0-0)
10-14 Miami (Fla.) (5-0-0)
10-21 Miami (Fla.) (6-0-0)
10-28 Miami (Fla.) (7-0-0)
11-4 Miami (Fla.) (7-0-0)
11-11 Nebraska (8-0-0) (2)
11-18 Miami (Fla.) (9-0-0)
11-24 Miami (Fla.) (10-0-0)
12-2 Miami (Fla.) (11-0-0)
12-8 Miami (Fla.) (11-0-0)
1-4 Miami (Fla.) (12-0-0)

2002

8-26 Miami (Fla.) (0-0-0)
9-2 Miami (Fla.) (1-0-0)
9-9 Miami (Fla.) (2-0-0)
9-16 Miami (Fla.) (3-0-0)
9-23 Miami (Fla.) (4-0-0)
9-30 Miami (Fla.) (4-0-0)
10-7 Miami (Fla.) (5-0-0)
10-14 Miami (Fla.) (6-0-0)
10-21 Miami (Fla.) (6-0-0)
10-28 Miami (Fla.) (7-0-0)
11-4 Oklahoma (8-0-0) (2)
11-11 Miami (Fla.) (9-0-0) (2)
11-18 Miami (Fla.) (9-0-0)
11-25 Miami (Fla.) (10-0-0)
12-2 Miami (Fla.) (11-0-0)
12-9 Miami (Fla.) (12-0-0)
1-4 Ohio St. (14-0-0) (2)

2003

8-25 Oklahoma (0-0-0)
9-1 Oklahoma (1-0-0)
9-8 Oklahoma (2-0-0)
9-15 Oklahoma (3-0-0)
9-22 Oklahoma (4-0-0)
9-29 Oklahoma (4-0-0)
10-6 Oklahoma (5-0-0)
10-13 Oklahoma (6-0-0)
10-20 Oklahoma (7-0-0)
10-27 Oklahoma (8-0-0)
11-3 Oklahoma (9-0-0)
11-10 Oklahoma (10-0-0)
11-17 Oklahoma (11-0-0)
11-24 Oklahoma (12-0-0)
12-1 Oklahoma (12-0-0)
12-8 Southern California (11-1-0) (2)
1-5 LSU (13-1-0) (2)

2004

8-30 Southern California (0-0-0)
9-6 Southern California (1-0-0)
9-13 Southern California (2-0-0)
9-20 Southern California (3-0-0)
9-27 Southern California (4-0-0)
10-4 Southern California (4-0-0)
10-11 Southern California (5-0-0)
10-18 Southern California (6-0-0)
10-25 Southern California (7-0-0)
11-1 Southern California (8-0-0)
11-8 Southern California (9-0-0)
11-15 Southern California (9-0-0)
11-22 Southern California (10-0-0)
11-29 Southern California (11-0-0)
12-6 Southern California (12-0-0)
1-5 Southern California (13-0-0)

2005

Pre. Southern California (0-0-0)
9-4 Southern California (1-0-0)
9-11 Southern California (1-0-0)
9-18 Southern California (2-0-0)
9-25 Southern California (3-0-0)
10-2 Southern California (4-0-0)
10-9 Southern California (5-0-0)
10-16 Southern California (6-0-0)
10-23 Southern California (7-0-0)
10-30 Southern California (8-0-0)
11-6 Southern California (9-0-0)
11-13 Southern California (10-0-0)
11-20 Southern California (11-0-0)
11-27 Southern California (11-0-0)
12-4 Southern California (12-0-0)
1-5 Texas (13-0-0) (2)

2006

Pre.	Ohio St.	(0-0-0)
9-3	Ohio St.	(1-0-0)
9-10	Ohio St.	(2-0-0)
9-17	Ohio St.	(3-0-0)
9-24	Ohio St.	(4-0-0)
10-1	Ohio St.	(5-0-0)
10-8	Ohio St.	(6-0-0)
10-15	Ohio St.	(7-0-0)
10-22	Ohio St.	(8-0-0)
10-29	Ohio St.	(9-0-0)
11-5	Ohio St.	(10-0-0)
11-12	Ohio St.	(11-0-0)
11-19	Ohio St.	(12-0-0)
11-26	Ohio St.	(12-0-0)
12-3	Ohio St.	(12-0-0)
1-9	**Florida**	**(13-1-0) (2)**

2006 USA Today/ESPN Week-by-Week Polls

Team	Pre	S3	S10	S17	S24	O1	O8	O15	O22	O29	N5	N12	N19	N26	D3	J9
Ohio St.	1	1	1	1	1	1	1	1	1	1	1	1	1	1	1	2
Texas	2	2	8	8	7	7	6	5	5	4	3	11	10	17	16	13
Southern California	T-3	3	2	2	2	2	2	2	2	9	7	4	2	2	7	4
Notre Dame	T-3	T-5	3	13	14	12	8	8	10	10	8	5	6	12	11	19
Oklahoma	5	10	11	16	16	13	22	20	19	18	17	16	14	10	8	11
Auburn	6	4	4	3	3	3	10	7	7	6	5	15	13	11	10	8
West Virginia	7	T-5	5	4	4	4	4	4	4	3	10	7	7	15	12	10
Florida	8	7	6	5	5	5	3	10	8	7	6	3	4	4	2	1
LSU	9	8	7	11	T-10	10	16	14	13	13	12	9	8	5	4	3
Florida St.	10	9	10	17	17	16	NR	NR	NR	NR	NR	NR	NR	NR	NR	NR
Miami (Fla.)	11	16	15	NR	NR	NR	NR	NR	NR	NR	NR	NR	NR	NR	NR	NR
California	12	23	21	20	20	17	11	11	12	11	9	17	22	20	19	14
Louisville	13	12	12	9	8	8	7	6	6	5	4	12	11	7	6	7
Georgia	14	11	9	7	9	9	14	24	25	NR	NR	NR	NR	NR	NR	NR
Michigan	15	13	13	6	6	6	5	3	3	2	2	2	3	3	3	9
Virginia Tech	16	14	14	10	T-10	18	17	NR	NR	24	21	19	17	14	14	18
Iowa	17	15	16	14	13	19	13	23	NR	NR	NR	NR	NR	NR	NR	NR
Clemson	18	18	NR	23	19	15	12	12	11	19	NR	25	24	NR	NR	NR
Penn St.	19	19	NR	NR	NR	NR	NR	NR	NR	NR	NR	NR	NR	NR	NR	25
Oregon	20	20	18	12	12	11	18	15	24	22	20	NR	NR	NR	NR	NR
TCU	21	22	20	15	15	NR	NR	NR	NR	NR	NR	NR	NR	NR	24	21
Nebraska	22	21	19	24	21	22	20	16	20	NR	25	22	19	18	22	NR
Tennessee	23	17	17	19	18	14	9	9	9	8	15	23	21	19	18	23
Alabama	24	25	24	22	NR	NR	NR	NR	NR	NR	NR	NR	NR	NR	NR	NR
Texas Tech	25	24	22	NR	24	24	NR	NR	NR	NR	NR	NR	NR	NR	NR	NR
Arizona St.	NR	NR	23	18	NR	NR	NR	NR	NR	NR	NR	NR	NR	NR	NR	NR
Boston College	NR	NR	25	21	25	NR	25	21	17	16	22	20	18	25	23	20
Boise St.	NR	NR	NR	25	22	21	19	17	15	14	13	13	12	9	9	6
Rutgers	NR	NR	NR	NR	23	23	24	19	16	15	14	8	16	13	17	12
Georgia Tech	NR	NR	NR	NR	NR	20	15	13	21	20	18	18	15	22	T-25	NR
Missouri	NR	NR	NR	NR	NR	25	21	NR	23	25	NR	NR	NR	NR	NR	NR
Arkansas	NR	NR	NR	NR	NR	NR	23	18	14	12	11	6	5	8	13	16
Wisconsin	NR	NR	NR	NR	NR	NR	NR	22	18	17	16	10	9	6	5	5
Texas A&M	NR	NR	NR	NR	NR	NR	NR	25	22	21	23	NR	NR	24	21	NR
Wake Forest	NR	NR	NR	NR	NR	NR	NR	NR	NR	23	19	14	20	16	15	17
Maryland	NR	NR	NR	NR	NR	NR	NR	NR	NR	NR	24	21	NR	NR	NR	NR
BYU	NR	NR	NR	NR	NR	NR	NR	NR	NR	NR	NR	24	23	21	20	15
Hawaii	NR	NR	NR	NR	NR	NR	NR	NR	NR	NR	NR	NR	25	23	NR	24
Oregon St.	NR	NR	NR	NR	NR	NR	NR	NR	NR	NR	NR	NR	NR	NR	T-25	22

T-Tie for ranking.

USA Today/ESPN Preseason No. 1 Teams

(Since 1993)

Year	Team+
1993	Florida St.+
1994	Florida
1995	Florida St.
1996	Nebraska
1997	Florida
1998	Ohio St.
1999	Florida St.+
2000	Nebraska
2001	Florida
2002	Miami (Fla.)
2003	Oklahoma
2004	Southern California+
2005	Southern California
2006	Ohio St.

+Indicates eventual national champion.

USA Today/ESPN Final Polls (Coaches)

Took over as coaches poll in 1991. (Cable News Network, 1982-96; ESPN 1997-present)

1982
Team
1. Penn St.
2. SMU
3. Nebraska
4. Georgia
5. UCLA
6. Arizona St.
7. Pittsburgh
8. Arkansas
9. Clemson
10. Washington
11. LSU
12. Florida St.
13. Ohio St.
14. Southern California
15. Oklahoma
16. Auburn
17. West Virginia
18. Maryland
19. North Carolina
20. Texas
21. Michigan
22. Alabama
23. Tulsa
24. Iowa
25. Florida

1983
Team
1. Miami (Fla.)
2. Auburn
3. Nebraska
4. Georgia
5. Texas
6. BYU
7. Michigan
8. Ohio St.
9. Florida
10. Clemson
11. Illinois
12. SMU
13. Alabama
14. Air Force
15. West Virginia
16. Iowa
17. Tennessee
18. UCLA
19. Pittsburgh
20. Penn St.
21. Oklahoma
22. Boston College
23. Oklahoma St.
24. Maryland
25. East Caro.

1984
Team
1. BYU
2. Washington
3. Florida
4. Nebraska
5. Oklahoma
6. Boston College
7. Oklahoma St.
8. SMU
9. Maryland
10. South Carolina
11. Southern California
12. UCLA
13. LSU
14. Ohio St.
15. Auburn
16. Miami (Fla.)
17. Florida St.
18. Virginia
19. Kentucky
20. Iowa
21. West Virginia
22. Army
23. Georgia
24. Air Force
25. Notre Dame

1985
Team
1. Oklahoma
2. Penn St.
3. Michigan
4. Tennessee
5. Florida
6. Miami (Fla.)
7. Air Force
8. Texas A&M
9. UCLA
10. Iowa
11. Nebraska
12. Alabama
13. Ohio St.
14. Florida St.
15. Arkansas
16. BYU
17. Maryland
18. Georgia Tech
19. Baylor
20. Auburn
21. LSU
22. Army
23. Fresno St.
24. Georgia
25. Oklahoma St.

1986
Team
1. Penn St.
2. Miami (Fla.)
3. Oklahoma
4. Nebraska
5. Arizona St.
6. Ohio St.
7. Auburn
8. Michigan
9. Alabama
10. LSU
11. Arizona
12. Texas A&M
13. UCLA
14. Baylor
15. Boston College
16. Iowa
17. Arkansas
18. Clemson
19. Washington
20. Virginia Tech
21. Florida St.
22. Stanford
23. Georgia
24. North Carolina St.
25. San Diego St.

1987
Team
1. Miami (Fla.)
2. Florida St.
3. Oklahoma
4. Syracuse
5. Nebraska
6. LSU
7. Auburn
8. Michigan St.
9. Texas A&M
10. UCLA
11. Clemson
12. Oklahoma St.
13. Georgia
14. Tennessee
15. Iowa
16. Notre Dame
17. Southern California
18. South Carolina
19. Michigan
20. Texas
21. Pittsburgh
22. Indiana
23. Penn St.
24. Ohio St.
25. Alabama

1988
Team
1. Notre Dame
2. Miami (Fla.)
3. Florida St.
4. UCLA
5. Michigan
6. West Virginia
7. Southern California
8. Nebraska
9. Auburn
10. Clemson
11. Oklahoma St.
12. Syracuse
13. Oklahoma
14. Arkansas
15. Washington St.
16. Georgia
17. Alabama
18. North Carolina St.
19. Houston
20. Indiana
21. Wyoming
22. LSU
23. Colorado
24. Southern Miss.
25. BYU

1989
Team
1. Miami (Fla.)
2. Notre Dame
3. Florida St.
4. Colorado
5. Tennessee
6. Auburn
7. Southern California
8. Michigan
9. Alabama
10. Illinois
11. Nebraska
12. Clemson
13. Arkansas
14. Houston
15. Penn St.
16. Virginia
17. Michigan St.
18. Texas Tech
19. Pittsburgh
20. Texas A&M
21. West Virginia
22. BYU
23. Syracuse
24. Ohio St.
25. Washington

1990
Team
1. Colorado
2. Georgia Tech
3. Miami (Fla.)
4. Florida St.
5. Washington
6. Notre Dame
7. Tennessee
8. Michigan
9. Clemson
10. Texas
11. Penn St.
12. Houston
13. Florida
14. Louisville
15. Michigan St.
16. Texas A&M
17. Oklahoma
18. Iowa
19. Auburn
20. BYU
21. Mississippi
22. Southern California
23. Nebraska
24. Illinois
25. Virginia

1991
Team
1. Washington
2. Miami (Fla.)
3. Penn St.
4. Florida St.
5. Alabama
6. Michigan
7. California
8. Florida
9. East Caro.
10. Iowa
11. Syracuse
12. Notre Dame
13. Texas A&M
14. Oklahoma
15. Tennessee
16. Nebraska
17. Clemson
18. UCLA
19. Georgia
20. Colorado
21. Tulsa
22. Stanford
23. BYU
24. Air Force
25. North Carolina St.

1992
Team
1. Alabama
2. Florida St.
3. Miami (Fla.)
4. Notre Dame
5. Michigan
6. Texas A&M
7. Syracuse
8. Georgia
9. Stanford
10. Washington
11. Florida
12. Tennessee
13. Colorado
14. Nebraska
15. North Carolina St.
16. Mississippi
17. Washington St.
18. North Carolina
19. Ohio St.
20. Hawaii
21. Boston College
22. Fresno St.
23. Kansas
24. Penn St.
25. Wake Forest

1993
Team
1. Florida St.
2. Notre Dame
3. Nebraska
4. Florida
5. Wisconsin
6. West Virginia
7. Penn St.
8. Texas A&M
9. Arizona
10. Ohio St.
11. Tennessee
12. Boston College
13. Alabama
14. Oklahoma
15. Miami (Fla.)
16. Colorado
17. UCLA
18. Kansas St.
19. Michigan
20. Virginia Tech
21. North Carolina
22. Clemson
23. Louisville
24. California
25. Southern California

1994
Team
1. Nebraska
2. Penn St.
3. Colorado
4. Alabama
5. Florida St.
6. Miami (Fla.)
7. Florida
8. Utah
9. Ohio St.
10. BYU
11. Oregon
12. Michigan
13. Virginia
14. Colorado St.
15. Southern California
16. Kansas St.
17. North Carolina St.
18. Tennessee
19. Washington St.
20. Arizona
21. North Carolina
22. Boston College
23. Texas
24. Virginia Tech
25. Mississippi St.

1995
Team
1. Nebraska
2. Tennessee
3. Florida
4. Colorado
5. Florida St.
6. Kansas St.
7. Northwestern
8. Ohio St.
9. Virginia Tech
10. Kansas
11. Southern California
12. Penn St.
13. Notre Dame
14. Texas
15. Texas A&M
16. Syracuse
17. Virginia
18. Oregon
19. Michigan
20. Texas Tech
21. Auburn
22. Iowa
23. East Caro.
24. Toledo
25. LSU

1996
Team (Record)
1. Florida (12-1)
2. Ohio St. (11-1)
3. Florida St. (11-1)
4. Arizona St. (11-1)
5. BYU (14-1)
6. Nebraska (11-2)
7. Penn St. (11-2)
8. Colorado (10-2)
9. Tennessee (10-2)
10. North Carolina (10-2)
11. Alabama (10-3)
12. Virginia Tech (10-2)
13. LSU (10-2)
14. Miami (Fla.) (9-3)
15. Washington (9-3)
16. Northwestern (9-3)
17. Kansas St. (9-3)
18. Iowa (9-3)
19. Syracuse (9-3)
20. Michigan (8-4)
21. Notre Dame (8-3)
22. Wyoming (10-2)
23. Texas (8-5)
24. Army (10-2)
25. Auburn (8-4)

1997
Team (Record)
1. Nebraska (13-0)
2. Michigan (12-0)
3. Florida St. (11-1)
4. North Carolina (11-1)
5. UCLA (10-2)
6. Florida (10-2)
7. Kansas St. (11-1)
8. Tennessee (11-2)
9. Washington St. (10-2)
10. Georgia (10-2)
11. Auburn (10-3)
12. Ohio St. (10-3)
13. LSU (9-3)
14. Arizona St. (9-3)
15. Purdue (9-3)
16. Colorado St. (11-2)
17. Penn St. (9-3)
18. Washington (8-4)
19. Southern Miss. (9-3)
20. Syracuse (9-4)
21. Texas A&M (9-4)
22. Mississippi (8-4)
23. Missouri (7-5)
24. Oklahoma St. (8-4)
25. Air Force (10-3)

1998
Team (Record)
1. Tennessee (13-0)
2. Ohio St. (11-1)
3. Florida St. (11-2)
4. Arizona (12-1)
5. Wisconsin (11-1)
6. Florida (10-2)
7. Tulane (12-0)
8. UCLA (10-2)
9. Kansas St. (11-2)
10. Air Force (12-1)
11. Georgia Tech (10-2)
12. Michigan (10-3)
13. Texas A&M (11-3)
14. Georgia (9-3)
15. Penn St. (9-3)
16. Texas (9-3)
17. Arkansas (9-3)
18. Virginia (9-3)
19. Virginia Tech (9-3)
20. Nebraska (9-4)
21. Miami (Fla.) (9-3)
22. Notre Dame (9-3)
23. Purdue (9-4)
24. Syracuse (8-4)
25. Missouri (8-4)

1999
Team (Record)
1. Florida St. (12-0)
2. Nebraska (12-1)
3. Virginia Tech (11-1)
4. Wisconsin (10-2)
5. Michigan (10-2)
6. Kansas St. (11-1)
7. Michigan St. (10-2)
8. Alabama (10-3)
9. Tennessee (9-3)
10. Marshall (13-0)
11. Penn St. (10-3)
12. Mississippi St. (10-2)
13. Southern Miss. (9-3)
14. Florida (9-4)
15. Miami (Fla.) (9-4)
16. Georgia (8-4)
17. Minnesota (8-4)
18. Oregon (9-3)
19. Arkansas (8-4)
20. Texas A&M (8-4)
21. Georgia Tech (8-4)
22. Mississippi (8-4)
23. Texas (9-5)
24. Stanford (8-4)
25. Illinois (8-4)

2000

Team (Record)
1. Oklahoma (13-0)
2. Miami (Fla.) (11-1)
3. Washington (11-1)
4. Florida St. (11-2)
5. Oregon St. (11-1)
6. Virginia Tech (11-1)
7. Nebraska (10-2)
8. Kansas St. (11-3)
9. Oregon (10-2)
10. Michigan (9-3)
11. Florida (10-3)
12. Texas (9-3)
13. Purdue (8-4)
14. Clemson (9-3)
15. Colorado St. (10-2)
16. Notre Dame (9-3)
17. Georgia (8-4)
18. TCU (10-2)
19. Georgia Tech (9-3)
20. Auburn (9-4)
21. South Carolina (8-4)
22. Mississippi St. (8-4)
23. Iowa St. (9-3)
24. Wisconsin (9-4)
25. Tennessee (8-4)

2001

Team (Record)
1. Miami (Fla.) (12-0)
2. Oregon (11-1)
3. Florida (10-2)
4. Tennessee (11-2)
5. Texas (11-2)
6. Oklahoma (11-2)
7. Nebraska (11-2)
8. LSU (10-3)
9. Colorado (10-3)
10. Maryland (10-2)
11. Washington St. (10-2)
12. Illinois (10-2)
13. South Carolina (9-3)
14. Syracuse (10-3)
15. Florida St. (8-4)
16. Louisville (11-2)
17. Stanford (9-3)
18. Virginia Tech (8-4)
19. Washington (8-4)
20. Michigan (8-4)
21. Marshall (11-2)
22. Toledo (10-2)
23. Boston College (8-4)
24. BYU (12-2)
25. Georgia (8-4)

2002

Team (Record)
1. Ohio St. (14-0)
2. Miami (Fla.) (12-1)
3. Georgia (13-1)
4. Southern California (11-2)
5. Oklahoma (12-2)
6. Kansas St. (11-2)
7. Texas (11-2)
8. Iowa (11-2)
9. Michigan (10-3)
10. Washington St. (10-3)
11. North Carolina St. (11-3)
12. Boise St. (12-1)
13. Maryland (11-3)
14. Virginia Tech (10-4)
15. Penn St. (9-4)
16. Auburn (9-4)
17. Notre Dame (10-3)
18. Pittsburgh (9-4)
19. Marshall (11-2)
20. West Virginia (9-4)
21. Colorado (9-5)
22. TCU (10-2)
23. Florida St. (9-5)
24. Florida (8-5)
25. Virginia (9-5)

2003

Team (Record)
1. LSU (13-1)
2. Southern California (12-1)
3. Oklahoma (12-2)
4. Ohio St. (11-2)
5. Miami (Fla.) (11-2)
6. Georgia (11-3)
7. Michigan (10-3)
8. Iowa (10-3)
9. Washington St. (10-3)
10. Florida St. (10-3)
11. Texas (10-3)
12. Miami (Ohio) (13-1)
13. Kansas St. (11-4)
14. Mississippi (10-3)
15. Boise St. (13-1)
16. Tennessee (10-3)
17. Minnesota (10-3)
18. Nebraska (10-3)
19. Purdue (9-4)
20. Maryland (10-3)
21. Utah (10-2)
22. Clemson (9-4)
23. Bowling Green (11-3)
24. TCU (11-2)
25. Florida (8-5)

2004

Team (Record)
1. Southern California (13-0)
2. Auburn (13-0)
3. Oklahoma (12-1)
4. Texas (11-1)
5. Utah (12-0)
6. Georgia (10-2)
7. Louisville (11-1)
8. Iowa (10-2)
9. California (10-2)
10. Virginia Tech (10-3)
11. Miami (Fla.) (9-3)
12. Michigan (9-3)
13. Boise St. (11-1)
14. Florida St. (9-3)
15. Tennessee (10-3)
16. LSU (9-3)
17. Texas Tech (8-4)
18. Wisconsin (9-3)
19. Ohio St. (8-4)
20. Arizona St. (9-3)
21. Boston College (9-3)
22. Fresno St. (9-3)
23. Virginia (8-4)
24. Navy (10-2)
25. Florida (7-5)

2005

Team (Record)
1. Texas (13-0)
2. Southern California (12-1)
3. Penn St. (11-1)
4. Ohio St. (10-2)
5. LSU (11-2)
6. West Virginia (11-1)
7. Virginia Tech (11-2)
8. Alabama (10-2)
9. TCU (11-1)
10. Georgia (10-3)
11. Notre Dame (9-3)
12. Oregon (10-2)
13. UCLA (10-2)
14. Auburn (9-3)
15. Wisconsin (10-3)
16. Florida (9-3)
17. Boston College (9-3)
18. Miami (Fla.) (9-3)
19. Texas Tech (9-3)
20. Louisville (9-3)
21. Clemson (8-4)
22. Oklahoma (8-5)
23. Florida St. (8-5)
24. Nebraska (8-4)
25. California (8-4)

2006

Team (Record)
1. Florida (13-1)
2. Ohio St. (12-1)
3. LSU (11-2)
4. Southern California (11-2)
5. Wisconsin (12-1)
6. Boise St. (13-0)
7. Louisville (12-1)
8. Auburn (11-2)
9. Michigan (11-2)
10. West Virginia (11-2)
11. Oklahoma (11-3)
12. Rutgers (11-2)
13. Texas (10-3)
14. California (10-3)
15. BYU (11-2)
16. Arkansas (10-4)
17. Wake Forest (11-3)
18. Virginia Tech (10-3)
19. Notre Dame (10-3)
20. Boston College (10-3)
21. TCU (11-2)
22. Oregon St. (10-4)
23. Tennessee (9-4)
24. Hawaii (11-3)
25. Penn St. (9-4)

Bowl Coalition, Alliance and Bowl Championship Series History

BOWL COALITION

The history of the College Football Bowl Coalition began in 1992 and lasted for three years through the 1994 season. The Bowl Coalition featured four games – the Orange, Sugar, Cotton and Fiesta Bowls – with conference champions locked into the Orange (Big Eight), Sugar (Southeastern) and Cotton (Southwest) Bowls and the Fiesta Bowl pairing two at-large teams.

The Fiesta Bowl had the ability to select one Coalition-eligible team, that was not a conference champion, before the national selection date. The original Coalition also involved champions from the Big East and Atlantic Coast Conferences, as well as Notre Dame.

Selections were made on the basis of how the champions of the Big Eight, Southeastern and Southwest Conferences finished in the final regular-season poll, which was a combination of the Associated Press and CNN/USA Today rankings. Al selections were made by the Coalition as a group on the first Sunday in December following the final weekend of the regular season.

All teams had to have at least six wins against FBS opponents and Notre Dame was guaranteed a spot with seven wins and could still qualify with six wins given mutual agreement between the bowls.

There were 56 FBS members that were members of the original Coalition, which also included original involvement with the Gator and John Hancock Bowls. The remainder of the bowls remained in place, many with predetermined conference tie-ins. A second layer of bowls eventually was identified and came to be known as the Tier Two bowls.

BOWL COALITION (1992-94)

1992 SEASON

SUGAR BOWL
Alabama 34, Miami (Fla.) 13

[Had first selection, but had automatic matchup between SEC champion Alabama, which was ranked No. 2 in final regular-season AP poll, against Big East champion Miami (Florida), which was ranked No. 1.]

COTTON BOWL
Notre Dame 28, Texas A&M 3

(Has second selection based on SWC champion Texas A&M being ranked No. 4 at end of regular season and chose at-large selection Notre Dame.)

ORANGE BOWL
Florida St. 27, Nebraska 14

(Had third selection based on Big Eight champion Nebraska being ranked No. 11 at end of regular season and chose ACC champion Florida State.)

FIESTA BOWL
Syracuse 26, Colorado 22

(Had fourth selection and chose at-large selection Syracuse and at-large selection Colorado.)

1993 SEASON

ORANGE BOWL
Florida St. 18, Nebraska 14

(Had first selection, but had automatic matchup between Big Eight champion Nebraska, which was ranked No. 1 in final regular-season coalition poll, against ACC champion Florida State, which was ranked No. 2.)

SUGAR BOWL
Florida 41, West Virginia 7

(Had second selection based on Big East champion West Virginia being ranked No. 3 at end of regular season and chose SEC champion Florida.)

COTTON BOWL
Notre Dame 24, Texas A&M 21

(Had third selection based on SWC champion Texas A&M being ranked No. 7 at end of regular season and chose at-large selection Notre Dame.)

FIESTA BOWL
Arizona 29, Miami (Fla.) 0

[Had fourth selection and chose at-large selection Miami (Florida) and also picked at-large Arizona.]

1994 SEASON

ORANGE BOWL
Nebraska 24, Miami (Fla.) 17

[Had first selection based on Big Eight champion Nebraska being ranked No. 1 at end of regular season in coalition poll and chose Big East champion Miami (Florida).]

SUGAR BOWL
Florida St. 23, Florida 17

(Had second selection based on SEC champion Florida being ranked No. 5 and chose ACC champion Florida State.)

COTTON BOWL
Southern California 55, Texas Tech 14

(Had third selection based on SWC champion Texas Tech being unranked and chose at-large Southern California.)

FIESTA BOWL
Colorado 41, Notre Dame 24

(Had fourth selection and chose at-large Notre Dame and at-large Colorado.)

BOWL ALLIANCE

The Bowl Alliance lasted three seasons, 1995 through 1997, and involved three games – the Fiesta, Orange and Sugar Bowls. A predetermined rotation created a situation in which each year a different bowl had the first two choices, while a second bowl chose third and fifth and the third bowl chose fourth and sixth.

Conferences that were a part of the Alliance were the Big 12, Atlantic Coast, Big East and Southeastern, leaving two at-large slots.

The most noteworthy change from the Coalition to the Alliance was the elimination of the conference tie-ins which had been in existence for years. The goal was to provide the best opportunity to match the top two teams and provide the greatest flexibility in creating the postseason matchups between Alliance partners.

In 1995, the first season of the Alliance, there was only one at-large position since the merger of the Big Eight and Southwest Conferences into the Big 12 had not yet taken place, providing five guaranteed conference champions that season.

Notre Dame was guaranteed the at-large slot in 1995 by finishing in the top ten of either the Associated Press or CNN/USA Today poll.

BOWL ALLIANCE (1995-97)

1995 SEASON

FIESTA BOWL
Nebraska 62, Florida 24

(Had first and second selections and picked Big Eight champion Nebraska, which was ranked No. 1 in the regular-season AP poll, against SEC champion Florida, which was ranked No. 2. This pick was required through mandatory No. 1 vs. No. 2 matchup rules.)

ORANGE BOWL
Florida St. 31, Notre Dame 26

(Had third and fifth selections and picked ACC champion Florida State against at-large Notre Dame.)

SUGAR BOWL
Virginia Tech 28, Texas 10

(Had fourth and sixth selections and picked Big East champion Virginia Tech against SWC champion Texas.)

1996 SEASON

SUGAR BOWL
Florida 52, Florida St. 20

(Had first and second selections and picked SEC champion Florida and ACC champion Florida State.)

FIESTA BOWL
Penn State 38, Texas 15

(Had third and fifth selections and picked at-large Penn State and Big 12 champion Texas.)

ORANGE BOWL
Nebraska 41, Virginia Tech 21

(Had fourth and sixth selections and picked at-large selection Nebraska and Big East champion Virginia Tech.)

1997 SEASON

ORANGE BOWL
Nebraska 42, Tennessee 17

(Had first and second selections and picked Big 12 champion Nebraska and SEC champion Tennessee.)

SUGAR BOWL
Florida St. 31, Ohio St. 14

(Had third and fifth selections and picked ACC champion Florida State and at-large Ohio State.)

FIESTA BOWL
Kansas St. 35, Syracuse 18

(Had fourth and sixth selections and picked at-large Kansas State and Big East champion Syracuse.)

Bowl Championship Series

The Bowl Championship Series (BCS) was launched in 1998 to match the No. 1 and No. 2 teams in the BCS rankings in a bowl game to determine a national champion in the absence of NCAA-sponsored playoffs. The No.1 vs. No. 2 game rotates between the Fiesta, Orange, Rose and Sugar Bowls.

Top-ranked Tennessee beat Florida State, 23-16, in the Fiesta Bowl to cap the first BCS year. Florida State returned to the title game again in 1999, this time appearing in the Sugar Bowl as the No. 1 team. The Seminoles upended Virginia Tech, 46-29.

In 2000, it was the Orange Bowl's turn to host the final game, and Florida State kept its streak of appearances alive. However, Oklahoma's defense ruled the evening as the Sooners won, 13-2.

In 2001, Miami (Florida) was the only unbeaten team in the FBS through the regular season and earned the top spot in the BCS rankings. Nebraska edged Colorado for the second spot and joined the Hurricanes in the Rose Bowl. Miami exploded for 34 unanswered points in the first half on its way to a 37-14 triumph.

In 2002, Miami (Florida) again topped the BCS regular-season standings with a 2.93 mark and Ohio State was second at 3.97. However, the Buckeyes captured the No. 1 vs. No. 2 victory in the Fiesta Bowl, 31-24 in two overtimes, to take the national title.

In 2003, Oklahoma led the BCS rankings going in to the bowl games with a 5.11 mark, LSU was second at 5.99 and Southern California was third at 6.15. LSU captured the BCS title by defeating Oklahoma, 21-14, in the matchup of No. 1 against No. 2 in the Sugar Bowl. However, in the Associated Press (media) final poll, Southern California was voted No. 1 while LSU was No. 1 in the USA Today/ESPN (coaches) final poll.

In 2004, Southern California led from the opening bell to the final BCS game, in which the No. 1 Trojans demolished No. 2 Oklahoma, 55-19, in the Orange Bowl. The season was not without controversy, however, as many upset Auburn fans thought the Tigers should have been in the title game after posting a perfect 13-0 record.

In 2005, for the first time in BCS history, and it was unanimous, the top two teams in the country faced each other in the national championship game, as Southern California and Texas met in the Rose Bowl. The Longhorns rallied from a 38-26 deficit with two touchdowns in the final five minutes of the fourth quarter, capped by Vince Young's eight-yard scamper with 19 seconds left for the 41-38 victory.

2006—Preseason No. 1 Ohio State played like a national champion from week one to earn a spot in the BCS Championship Game against the Gators of Florida. The Buckeyes had already taken care of another No. 2 in Texas in September, and after the opening kickoff, a 93-yard return for a touchdown by Ted Ginn Jr., it looked like they would hold off another challenge. However, the Gators answered quickly and often as Florida grabbed a 34-14 lead at halftime, coasted to a 41-14 win and claimed the 2006 BCS Championship.

BCS CHAMPIONS

1998—Tennessee
1999—Florida St.
2000—Oklahoma
2001—Miami (Fla.)
2002—Ohio St.
2003—LSU
2004—Southern California
2005—Texas
2006—Florida

NOTE: The NCAA football certification subcommittee has not enacted, adopted or otherwise approved of the process described below. The NCAA has no role in the selection of the institutions that participate in postseason bowl games and does not sponsor an FBS championship.

2006 FINAL REGULAR-SEASON BOWL CHAMPIONSHIP SERIES RANKINGS

	Harris Interactive Pct.	USA Today/ ESPN Pct.	Computer Pct.	BCS Avg.
1. Ohio St.	.9996	1.0000	1.0000	1.000
2. Florida	.9451	.9484	.9400	.945
3. Michigan	.9317	.9316	.9400	.934
4. LSU	.8396	.8381	.8200	.833
5. Southern California	.7692	.7568	.8600	.795
6. Louisville	.8042	.7890	.7900	.794
7. Wisconsin	.7890	.8148	.6400	.748
8. Boise St.	.6903	.6794	.7600	.710
9. Auburn	.6106	.6452	.6900	.649
10. Oklahoma	.6998	.7194	.4700	.630
11. Notre Dame	.6106	.5955	.6800	.629
12. Arkansas	.5250	.5148	.5100	.517
13. West Virginia	.5257	.5161	.4800	.507
14. Wake Forest	.4835	.4806	.3300	.431
15. Virginia Tech	.4807	.5039	.3000	.428
16. Rutgers	.3834	.3658	.4800	.410
17. Tennessee	.3327	.3226	.5000	.385
18. California	.2605	.2813	.5400	.361
19. Texas	.3370	.3755	.1500	.288
20. BYU	.2966	.2381	.0900	.208
21. Texas A&M	.1950	.1955	.0500	.147
22. Oregon St.	.0450	.0465	.3400	.144
23. Nebraska	.1246	.1561	.0000	.094
24. Boston College	.1126	.1129	.0400	.089
25. UCLA	.0035	.0000	.1900	.065

EXPLANATION

To derive a team's poll percentages in the Harris Interactive and USA Today/ESPN polls, each team's point total is divided by a maximum 2,825 possible points in the Harris Interactive poll and 1,550 possible points in the USA Today/ESPN poll.

Teams are assigned an inverse point total (25 for No. 1, 24 for No. 2, etc.) for each of their respective computer poll rankings to determine the overall computer component. The highest and lowest ranking for each team is dropped, and the sum total of the remaining four rankings is divided by 100 (the maximum possible points).

This figure produces a Computer Rankings Percentage. The six computer ranking providers are Anderson and Hester, Richard Billingsley, Colley Matrix, Kenneth Massey, Jeff Sagarin, and Peter Wolfe. Each computer ranking accounts for schedule strength within its formula.

The BCS Average is calculated by averaging the percent totals of the Harris Interactive and USA Today/ESPN polls, and the computer rankings. The highest BCS Average receives the No. 1 ranking, the second highest receives No. 2, and so forth.

BCS RESULTS FOR 2006-07:
BCS Championship (Glendale, Ariz.)—Florida 41, Ohio St. 14
Fiesta Bowl—Boise St. 43, Oklahoma 42 (ot)
Orange Bowl—Louisville 24, Wake Forest 13
Rose Bowl—Southern California 32, Michigan 18
Sugar Bowl—LSU 41, Notre Dame 14

2005 FINAL REGULAR-SEASON BOWL CHAMPIONSHIP SERIES RANKINGS

	Harris Interactive Pct.	USA Today/ ESPN Pct.	Computer Pct.	BCS Avg.
1. Southern California	.9950	.9955	.970	.9868
2. Texas	.9650	.9645	.990	.9732
3. Penn St.	.9175	.9187	.920	.9187
4. Ohio St.	.8488	.8387	.880	.8559
5. Oregon	.7805	.7961	.820	.7989
6. Notre Dame	.8124	.7865	.600	.7329
7. Georgia	.7267	.7077	.720	.7182
8. Miami (Fla.)	.6874	.6935	.730	.7037
9. Auburn	.7381	.7361	.550	.6747
10. Virginia Tech	.6085	.6161	.790	.6715
11. West Virginia	.5922	.6187	.710	.6403
12. LSU	.6414	.6465	.600	.6293
13. Alabama	.5136	.5077	.340	.4538
14. TCU	.4701	.4735	.390	.4445
15. Texas Tech	.4060	.4103	.470	.4288

EXPLANATION

To derive a team's poll percentages in the Harris Interactive and USA Today/ESPN polls, each team's point total is divided by a maximum 2,825 possible points in the Harris Interactive poll and 1,550 possible points in the USA Today/ESPN poll.

Teams are assigned an inverse point total (25 for No. 1, 24 for No. 2, etc.) for each of their respective computer poll rankings to determine the overall computer component. The highest and lowest ranking for each team is dropped, and the sum total of the remaining four rankings is divided by 100 (the maximum possible points).

This figure produces a Computer Rankings Percentage. The six computer ranking providers are Anderson and Hester, Richard Billingsley, Colley Matrix, Kenneth Massey, Jeff Sagarin, and Peter Wolfe. Each computer ranking accounts for schedule strength within its formula.

The BCS Average is calculated by averaging the percent totals of the Harris Interactive and USA Today/ESPN polls, and the computer rankings. The highest BCS Average receives the No. 1 ranking, the second highest receives No. 2, and so forth.

BCS RESULTS FOR 2005-06:
Rose Bowl—Texas 41, Southern California 38
Orange Bowl—Penn St. 26, Florida St. 23 (3 ot)
Fiesta Bowl—Ohio St. 34, Notre Dame 20
Sugar Bowl—West Virginia 38, Georgia 35

2004 FINAL REGULAR-SEASON BOWL CHAMPIONSHIP SERIES RANKINGS

	AP Pct.	USA Today/ ESPN Pct.	Computer Pct.	BCS Avg.
1. Southern California	.9840	.9770	.970	.9770
2. Oklahoma	.9575	.9567	.990	.9681
3. Auburn	.9385	.9410	.920	.9331
4. Texas	.8228	.8400	.880	.8476
5. California	.8609	.8433	.800	.8347
6. Utah	.8277	.7967	.830	.8181
7. Georgia	.6874	.7325	.670	.6966
8. Virginia Tech	.6837	.6800	.650	.6712
9. Boise St.	.5908	.6184	.760	.6564
10. Louisville	.7280	.6990	.520	.6490
11. LSU	.5717	.6111	.650	.6109
12. Iowa	.5834	.5325	.550	.5553
13. Michigan	.5643	.5731	.380	.5058
14. Miami (Fla.)	.4775	.4839	.450	.4705
15. Tennessee	.4006	.3666	.450	.4057

EXPLANATION

Team percentages are derived by dividing a team's actual voting points by a maximum 1,625 possible points in the Associated Press (AP) poll and 1,525 possible points in the USA Today/ESPN Coaches' Poll.

Six computer rankings calculated in inverse points order (25 for #1, 24 for #2, etc.) are used to determine the overall computer component. The best and worst ranking for each team is dropped, and the remaining four are added and divided by 100 (the maximum possible points) to produce a Computer Rankings Percentage. The six computer ranking providers are Anderson & Hester, Richard Billingsley, Colley Matrix, Kenneth Massey, Jeff Sagarin and Peter Wolfe. Each computer ranking accounts for schedule strength in its formula.

The BCS Average is calculated by averaging the percent totals of the AP and USA Today/ESPN polls, and the computer rankings.

BCS RESULTS FOR 2004-05:
Rose Bowl—Texas 38, Michigan 37
Fiesta Bowl—Utah 35, Pittsburgh 7
Sugar Bowl—Auburn 16, Virginia Tech 13
Orange Bowl—Southern California 55, Oklahoma 19

2003 FINAL REGULAR-SEASON BOWL CHAMPIONSHIP SERIES RANKINGS

	Poll Avg.	Comp. Avg.	Sked Strength	Loss Record	Subtotal	Quality Win	Total
1. Oklahoma	3	1.17	11	1	5.61	-0.5	5.11
2. LSU	2	1.83	29	1	5.99		5.99
3. Southern California	1	2.67	37	1	6.15		6.15
4. Michigan	4	4.67	14	2	11.23	-0.6	10.63
5. Ohio St.	6.5	5.50	7	2	14.28		14.28
6. Texas	5	6.83	20	2	14.63	-0.1	14.53
7. Florida St.	8.5	6.83	15	2	17.93		17.93
8. Tennessee	6.5	9.50	46	2	19.84	-0.2	19.64
9. Miami (Fla.)	9.5	8.17	13	2	20.19	-0.4	19.79
10. Kansas St.	9	11.33	10	3	23.73	-1.0	22.73
11. Miami (Ohio)	14.5	6.00	68	1	24.22		24.22
12. Georgia	11	10.17	18	3	24.89	-0.3	24.59
13. Iowa	12.5	13.50	16	3	29.64	-0.7	28.94
14. Purdue	12.5	15.83	40	3	32.93		32.93
15. Florida	17	16.50	5	4	37.70	-0.9	36.80

EXPLANATION

Poll Average - Average of the AP Media Poll and USA Today/ESPN Coaches Poll. Others receiving votes calculated in order received.

Computer Average - Average of Anderson & Hester, Richard Billingsley, Colley Matrix, Kenneth Massey, New York Times, Jeff Sagarin's USA Today, and the Peter Wolfe rankings. The lowest (worst) computer ranking will be disregarded.

Schedule Rank - Rank of schedule strength compared to other FBS teams of actual games played divided by 25. This component is calculated by determining the cumulative won/loss records of the team's opponent (66 2/3 percent) and the cumulative won/loss records of the team's opponents' opponents (33 1/3 percent).

Losses - One point for each loss during the season.

Subtotal – The values from the four factors described above are added.

Quality Win Component - The quality win component will reward to varying degrees teams that defeat opponents ranked among the top 10 in the weekly standings. The bonus point scale will range from a high of 1.0 points for a win over the top ranked team to a low of 0.1 for a victory over the 10th-ranked BCS team. The BCS Standings at the end of the season will determine final quality win points. If a team registers a victory over a team more than once during the regular season, quality points will be awarded just once. Quality win points are based on the standings determined by the subtotal. The final standings are reconfigured to reflect the quality win point deduction.

Total – The value of the quality win component is subtracted from the subtotal.

Notes: 1. Teams on NCAA probation (i.e., not eligible for postseason competition) are not listed in the BCS standings. Teams with victories over teams on probation will receive appropriate quality win points. 2. The Nokia Sugar Bowl on January 4, 2004, was the host of the BCS national championship game and determined which team was presented the National Football Foundation and College Hall of Fame's MacArthur Trophy, awarded to college football's national champion since 1959.

BCS RESULTS FOR 2003-04:
Sugar Bowl—LSU 21, Oklahoma 14
Fiesta Bowl—Ohio St. 35, Kansas St. 28
Orange Bowl—Miami (Fla.) 16, Florida St. 14
Rose Bowl—Southern California 28, Michigan 14

2002 FINAL REGULAR-SEASON BOWL CHAMPIONSHIP SERIES RANKINGS

	Poll Avg.	Comp. Avg.	Sked Strength	Loss Record	Subtotal	Quality Win	Total
1. Miami (Fla.)	1	1.17	0.76	0	2.93		2.93
2. Ohio St.	2	1.67	0.80	0	4.47	-0.5	3.97
3. Georgia	4	3.17	0.20	1	8.37		8.37
4. Southern California	5	3.67	0.04	2	10.71	-0.2	10.51
5. Iowa	3	4.83	1.96	1	10.79		10.79
6. Washington St.	7	7.00	0.84	2	16.84	-0.7	16.14
7. Oklahoma	8	6.33	0.56	2	16.89	-0.1	16.79
8. Kansas St.	6	10.67	2.16	2	20.83	-0.7	20.13
9. Notre Dame	11.5	6.83	0.60	2	20.93		20.93
10. Texas	9	9.50	0.88	2	21.38	-0.3	21.08
11. Michigan	11.5	9.33	0.08	3	23.91		23.91
12. Penn St.	10	13.33	0.64	3	26.97		26.97
13. Colorado	14	15.17	0.40	4	33.57	-0.3	33.27
14. Florida St.	16	13.83	0.12	4	33.95		33.95
15. West Virginia	14	17.33	1.64	3	35.97		35.97

EXPLANATION

Poll Average - Average of the AP Media Poll and USA Today/ESPN Coaches Poll. Others receiving votes calculated in order received.

Computer Average - Average of Anderson & Hester, Richard Billingsley, Colley Matrix, Kenneth Massey, New York Times, Jeff Sagarin's USA Today, and the Peter Wolfe rankings. The lowest (worst) computer ranking will be disregarded.

Schedule Rank - Rank of schedule strength compared to other FBS teams of actual games played divided by 25. This component is calculated by determining the cumulative won/loss records of the team's opponent (66 ⅔ percent) and the cumulative won/loss records of the team's opponents' opponents (33 ⅓ percent).

Losses - One point for each loss during the season.

Subtotal – The values from the four factors described above are added.

Quality Win Component - The quality win component will reward to varying degrees teams that defeat opponents ranked among the top 10 in the weekly standings. The bonus point scale will range from a high of 1.0 points for a win over the top ranked team to a low of 0.1 for a victory over the 10th-ranked BCS team. The BCS Standings at the end of the season will determine final quality win points. If a team registers a victory over a team more than once during the regular season, quality points will be awarded just once. Quality win points are based on the standings determined by the subtotal. The final standings are reconfigured to reflect the quality win point deduction.

Total – The value of the quality win component is subtracted from the subtotal.

Notes: 1. Teams on NCAA probation (i.e., not eligible for postseason competition) are not listed in the BCS standings. Teams with victories over teams on probation will receive appropriate quality win points. 2. The Tostitos Fiesta Bowl on January 3, 2003, was the host of the BCS national championship game and determined which team was presented the National Football Foundation and College Hall of Fame's MacArthur Trophy, awarded to college football's national champion since 1959.

BCS RESULTS FOR 2002-03:
Fiesta Bowl—Ohio St. 31, Miami (Fla.) 24 (2 ot)
Orange Bowl—Southern California 38, Iowa 17
Sugar Bowl—Georgia 26, Florida St. 13
Rose Bowl—Oklahoma 34, Washington St. 14

2001 FINAL REGULAR-SEASON BOWL CHAMPIONSHIP SERIES RANKINGS

Rk	Team	AP	USA Today/ ESPN	Poll Avg.	And. & Hester	AJC Colley	Bill.	Massey	Roth.	Sagar.	Scripps-How.	Wolfe	Comp. Avg.	Sched. Strength	Sched. Rank	Losses	Subotal	Quality Win	Total
1.	Miami (Fla.)	1	1	1.0	1	1	1	1	1	1	1	1	1.00	18	0.72	0	2.72	-0.1	2.62
2.	Nebraska	4	4	4.0	2	2	2	3	2	3	2	2	2.17	14	0.56	1	7.73	-0.5	7.23
3.	Colorado	3	3	3.0	4	5	4	4	5	5	5	3	4.50	2	0.08	2	9.58	-2.3	7.28
4.	Oregon	2	2	2.0	3	3	3	2	8	7	6	7	4.83	31	1.24	1	9.07	-0.4	8.67
5.	Florida	5	5	5.0	9	8	7	8	4	2	3	5	5.83	19	0.76	2	13.59	-0.5	13.09
6.	Tennessee	8	8	8.0	5	4	8	6	7	8	7	4	6.17	3	0.12	2	16.29	-1.6	14.69
7.	Texas	9	9	9.0	8	9	10	9	3	4	4	6	6.67	33	1.32	2	18.99	-1.2	17.79
8.	Illinois	7	7	7.0	7	6	6	12	13	12	10	12	9.83	37	1.48	1	19.31	0.0	19.31
9.	Stanford	11	11	11.0	6	7	11	5	9	9	8	8	7.83	22	0.88	2	21.71	-1.3	20.41
10.	Maryland	6	6	6.0	14	10	5	10	11	11	14	11	11.17	78	3.12	1	21.29	0.0	21.29
11.	Oklahoma	10	10	10.0	10	11	9	13	6	6	9	9	9.00	36	1.44	2	22.44	-0.9	21.54
12.	Washington St.	13	13	13.0	12	12	12	7	10	10	11	10	10.83	42	1.68	2	27.51	-0.6	26.91
13.	LSU	12	12	12.0	11	13	14	14	12	18	13	14	13.33	10	0.40	3	28.73	-1.0	27.73
14.	South Carolina	14	14	14.0	20	19	19	17	17	23	23	17	19.17	40	1.60	3	37.77	0.0	37.77
15.	Washington	21	20	20.5	13	15	15	11	16	25	17	13	14.83	21	0.84	3	39.17	-1.0	38.17

Key: AP (Associated Press poll); USA/ESPN (USA Today/ESPN coaches poll); Poll Avg. (Average of two polls); Bill (Richard Billingsley); Dunk (Dunkel Index); Mass (Kenneth Massey); NYT (New York Times); Roth (David Rothman); SAG (Jeff Sagarin); SH (Scripps-Howard); ST (Seattle Times); Comp Avg. (Computer Services Average); SSch (Schedule Strength); SRk (Schedule Rank); L (Losses).

EXPLANATION

Poll Average - Average of the AP Media Poll and USA Today/ESPN Coaches Poll. Others receiving votes calculated in order received.

Computer Average - Average of Anderson & Hester (And. & Hester), Atlanta Journal-Constitution Colley Matrix (AJC Colley), Richard Billingsley (Bill.), Kenneth Massey (Massey), David Rothman (Roth.), Jeff Sagarin's USA Today (Sagar.), Matthews/Scripps-Howard (Scripps-How.), and the Peter Wolfe (Wolfe) rankings. The computer component will be determined by averaging six rankings. The highest and the lowest will be disregarded.

Schedule Rank - Rank of schedule strength compared to other FBS teams of actual games played divided by 25. This component is calculated by determining the cumulative won/loss records of the team's opponent (66 ⅔ percent) and the cumulative won/loss records of the team's opponents' opponents (33 ⅓ percent).

Losses - One point for each loss during the season.

Subtotal – The values from the four factors described above are added.

Quality Win Component - The quality win component will reward to varying degrees teams that defeat opponents ranked among the top 15 in the weekly standings. The bonus point scale will range from a high of 1.5 points for a win over the top ranked team to a low of 0.1 for a victory over the 15th-ranked BCS team. The BCS Standings at the end of the season will determine final quality win points. If a team registers a victory over a team more than once during the regular season, quality points will be awarded just once. Quality win points are based on the standings determined by the subtotal. The final standings are reconfigured to reflect the quality win point deduction.

Total – The value of the quality win component is subtracted from the subtotal.

BCS RESULTS FOR 2001-02:
Rose Bowl—Miami (Fla.) 37, Nebraska 14
Fiesta Bowl—Oregon 38, Colorado 16
Orange Bowl—Florida 56, Maryland 23
Sugar Bowl—LSU 47, Illinois 34

2000 FINAL REGULAR-SEASON BOWL CHAMPIONSHIP SERIES RANKINGS

Rk	Team	AP	USA/ ESPN	Poll Avg.	Bill	Dunk	MASS	NYT	Roth	SAG	SH	ST	Comp. Avg.	SSch	SRk	L	TOTAL
1.	Oklahoma	1	1	1.0	1	3	2	3	1	3	2	1	1.86	11	0.44	0	3.30
2.	Florida St.	3	3	3.0	2	1	1	1	2	1	1	3	1.29	2	0.08	1	5.37
3.	Miami (Fla.)	2	2	2.0	3	2	3	2	3	2	3	4	2.57	3	0.12	1	5.69
4.	Washington	4	4	4.0	10	11	5	5	4	8	4	2	5.43	6	0.24	1	10.67
5.	Virginia Tech	5	6	5.5	5	5	4	4	7	5	7	6	5.14	14	0.56	1	12.20
6.	Oregon St.	6	5	5.5	7	9	8	8	5	7	5	5	6.50	42	1.68	1	14.68
7.	Florida	7	7	7.0	4	4	7	6	9	6	6	7	5.71	1	0.04	2	14.75
8.	Nebraska	8	9	8.5	6	13	6	10	6	4	8	9	7.00	18	0.72	2	18.22
9.	Kansas St.	9	11	10.0	8	12	11	12	8	9	11	12	10.14	29	1.16	3	24.30
10.	Oregon	11	8	9.5	12	17	14	15	11	14	9	8	11.86	24	0.96	2	24.32
11.	Notre Dame	10	10	10.0	14	15	15	8	12	16	10	10	12.07	25	1.00	2	25.07
12.	Texas	12	12	12.0	11	6	9	11	10	10	12	15	9.86	84	3.36	2	27.22
13.	Georgia Tech	17	15	16.0	9	8	10	7	14	11	13	11	9.86	44	1.76	2	29.62
14.	TCU	16	13	14.5	16	7	12	20	15	12	14	20	13.71	95	3.80	1	33.01
15.	Clemson	13	16	14.5	13	21	13	19	13	15	15	13	14.43	56	2.24	2	33.17

Key: AP (Associated Press poll); USA/ESPN (USA Today/ESPN coaches poll); Poll Avg. (Average of two polls); Bill (Richard Billingsley); Dunk (Dunkel Index); Mass (Kenneth Massey); NYT (New York Times); Roth (David Rothman); SAG (Jeff Sagarin); SH (Scripps-Howard); ST (Seattle Times); Comp Avg. (Computer Services Average); SSch (Schedule Strength); SRk (Schedule Rank); L (Losses).

BCS RESULTS FOR 2000-01:
Orange Bowl—Oklahoma 13, Florida St. 2
Sugar Bowl—Miami (Fla.) 37, Florida 20
Fiesta Bowl—Oregon St. 41, Notre Dame 9
Rose Bowl—Washington 34, Purdue 34

1999 FINAL REGULAR-SEASON BCS RANKINGS

Team	Total Score
1. Florida St.	2.24
2. Virginia Tech	6.12
3. Nebraska	7.42
4. Alabama	12.11
5. Tennessee	13.71
6. Kansas St.	15.23
7. Wisconsin	16.71
8. Michigan	18.08
9. Michigan St.	19.11
10. Florida	23.06
11. Penn St.	28.75
12. Marshall	31.15
13. Minnesota	33.61
14. Texas A&M	34.76
15. Texas	34.81

BCS RESULTS FOR 1999-00:

SUGAR BOWL
Florida St. 46, Virginia Tech 29
(Had first and second selections and picked ACC champion Florida State and Big East champion Virginia Tech)

FIESTA BOWL
Nebraska 31, Tennessee 21
(Had third and fifth selections and selected Big 12 champion Nebraska and SEC Tennessee)

ORANGE BOWL
Michigan 35, Alabama 34 (ot)
(Had fourth and sixth selections and selected Big Ten Michigan and SEC champion Alabama)

ROSE BOWL
Wisconsin 17, Stanford 9
(Selected Big Ten champion Wisconsin and Pacific-10 champion Stanford)

1998 FINAL REGULAR-SEASON BCS RANKINGS

Team	Total Score
1. Tennessee	3.47
2. Florida St.	4.91
3. Kansas St.	9.96
4. Ohio St.	10.37
5. UCLA	10.90
6. Texas A&M	15.70
7. Arizona	16.49
8. Florida	19.95
9. Wisconsin	21.61
10. Tulane	26.67
11. Nebraska	29.06
12. Virginia	32.22
13. Arkansas	32.28
14. Georgia Tech	32.76
15. Syracuse	34.80

BCS RESULTS FOR 1998-99:

FIESTA BOWL
Tennessee 23, Florida St. 16
(Had first and second selections and picked SEC champion Tennessee and ACC champion Florida State)

SUGAR BOWL
Ohio St. 24, Texas A&M 14
(Had third and fifth selections and picked Big Ten Ohio State and Big 12 champion Texas A&M)

ORANGE BOWL
Florida 31, Syracuse 10
(Had fourth and sixth selections and chose SEC Florida and Big East champion Syracuse)

ROSE BOWL
Wisconsin 38, UCLA 31
(Selected Big Ten Wisconsin and Pacific-10 champion UCLA)

Undefeated, Untied Teams

(Regular-Season Games Only)

Minimum of five games played against opponents above the high-school level. Subsequent bowl win is indicated by (†), a bowl loss by (‡) and a bowl tie by ($). Unscored-on teams are indicated by (•). Beginning in 2002, all postseason games were counted in won-lost records and statistics. However, undefeated, untied teams will continue for regular-season only with postseason results indicated.

(Note: Following are undefeated, untied teams in regular-season games not included with major colleges at the time—Centre, 1919 & 1921; Lafayette, 1921, 1926 & 1937; Wash. & Jeff., 1921; Marquette, 1923; Louisville, 1925; Centenary (La.), 1927; Memphis, 1938; San Jose St., 1939; Hardin-Simmons, 1940; Arizona, 1945; Pacific, 1949; Fresno St., 1961; and San Diego St., 1966.) Beginning in 1996, tiebreaker procedures were in place for all FBS games.

Year	College	Wins
1878	Princeton	6
1882	Yale	8
1883	Yale	8
1885	Princeton	9
1887	Yale	9
1888	Yale	•13
1889	Princeton	10
1890	Harvard	11
1891	Yale	•13
1892	Minnesota	5
	Purdue	8
	Yale	•13
1893	Minnesota	6
	Princeton	11
1894	Penn	12
	VMI	5
	Yale	16
1895	Penn	14
1896	LSU	6
1897	Penn	15
1898	Harvard	11
	Kentucky	•7
	Michigan	10
	North Carolina	9
1899	Kansas	10
	Sewanee	12
1900	Clemson	6
	Texas	6
	Tulane	•5
	Yale	12
1901	Harvard	12
	Michigan	†•10
	Wisconsin	9
1902	Arizona	•5
	California	8
	Michigan	11
	Nebraska	•9
1903	Nebraska	10
	Princeton	11
1904	Auburn	5
	Michigan	10
	Minnesota	13
	Penn	12
	Pittsburgh	10
	Vanderbilt	9
1905	Chicago	10
	Stanford	8
	Yale	10
1906	New Mexico St.	5
	Washington St.	•6

Year	College	Wins
	Wisconsin	5
1907	Oregon St.	•6
1908	Kansas	9
	LSU	10
1909	Arkansas	7
	Colorado	•6
	Washington	7
	Yale	•10
1910	Colorado	6
	Illinois	•7
	Pittsburgh	•9
	Washington	6
1911	Colorado	6
	Oklahoma	8
	Utah St.	•5
	Washington	7
1912	Harvard	9
	Notre Dame	7
	Penn St.	8
	Washington	6
	Wisconsin	7
1913	Auburn	8
	Chicago	7
	Harvard	9
	Michigan St.	7
	Nebraska	8
	Notre Dame	7
	Washington	7
1914	Army	9
	Illinois	7
	Tennessee	9
	Texas	8
	Wash. & Lee	9
1915	Colorado St.	7
	Columbia	5
	Cornell	9
	Nebraska	8
	Oklahoma	10
	Pittsburgh	8
	Washington	7
	Washington St.	†6
1916	Army	9
	Ohio St.	7
	Pittsburgh	8
	Tulsa	10
1917	Denver	9
	Georgia Tech	9
	Pittsburgh	9
	Texas A&M	•8
	Washington St.	6
1918	Michigan	5
	Oklahoma	6
	Texas	9
	Virginia Tech	7
	Washington-St. Louis	6
1919	Notre Dame	9
	Texas A&M	•10
1920	Boston College	8
	California	†8
	Notre Dame	9
	Ohio St.	‡7
	Southern California	6
	Texas	9
	VMI	9
1921	California	$9
	Cornell	8
	Iowa	7
1922	California	9
	Cornell	8
	Drake	7
	Iowa	7
	Princeton	8
	Tulsa	7
1923	Colorado	9
	Cornell	8
	Illinois	8
	Michigan	8
	SMU	9
	Yale	8
1924	Notre Dame	†9
1925	Alabama	†9
	Dartmouth	8
1926	Alabama	$9
	Stanford	$10
	Utah	7
1927	(None)	
1928	Boston College	9
	Detroit	9
	Georgia Tech	†9
1929	Notre Dame	9

Year	College	Wins
	Pittsburgh	‡9
	Purdue	8
	Tulane	9
	Utah	7
1930	Alabama	†9
	Notre Dame	10
	Utah	8
	Washington St.	‡9
1931	Tulane	‡11
1932	Colgate	•9
	Michigan	8
	Southern California	†9
1933	Princeton	9
1934	Alabama	†9
	Minnesota	8
1935	Minnesota	8
	Princeton	9
	SMU.	‡12
1936	(None)	
1937	Alabama	‡9
	Colorado	‡8
	Santa Clara	†8
1938	Duke	‡•9
	Georgetown	8
	Oklahoma	‡10
	Tennessee	†10
	TCU	†10
	Texas Tech	‡10
1939	Cornell	8
	Tennessee	‡•10
	Texas A&M	†10
1940	Boston College	†10
	Lafayette	9
	Minnesota	8
	Stanford	†9
	Tennessee	‡10
1941	Duke	‡9
	Duquesne	8
	Minnesota	8
1942	Tulsa	‡10
1943	Purdue	9
1944	Army	9
	Ohio St.	9
1945	Alabama	†9
	Army	9
	Oklahoma St.	†8
1946	Georgia	†10
	Hardin-Simmons	†10
	UCLA	‡10
1947	Michigan	†9
	Notre Dame	9
	Penn St.	$9
1948	California	‡10
	Clemson	†10
	Michigan	9
1949	Army	9
	California	‡10
	Notre Dame	10
	Oklahoma	†10
1950	Oklahoma	‡10
	Princeton	9
	Wyoming	†9
1951	Maryland	†9
	Michigan St.	9
	Princeton	9
	San Francisco	9
	Tennessee	‡10
1952	Georgia Tech	†11
	Michigan St.	9
1953	Maryland	‡10
1954	Ohio St.	†9
	Oklahoma	10
	UCLA	9
1955	Maryland	‡10
	Oklahoma	†10
1956	Oklahoma	10
	Tennessee	‡10
	Wyoming	10
1957	Arizona St.	10
	Auburn	10
1958	LSU	†10
1959	Syracuse	†10
1960	New Mexico St.	†10
	Yale	9
1961	Alabama	†10
	Rutgers	9
1962	Dartmouth	9
	Mississippi	†9
	Southern California	†10
1963	Texas	†10

Year	College	Wins
1964	Alabama	‡10
	Arkansas	†10
	Princeton	9
1965	Arkansas	‡10
	Dartmouth	9
	Michigan St.	‡10
	Nebraska	‡10
1966	Alabama	†10
1967	Wyoming	‡10
1968	Ohio	‡10
	Ohio St.	†9
	Penn St.	†10
1969	Penn St.	†10
	San Diego St.	†10
	Texas	†10
	Toledo	†10
1970	Arizona St.	†10
	Dartmouth	9
	Ohio St.	‡9
	Texas	‡10
	Toledo	†11
1971	Alabama	‡11
	Michigan	‡11
	Nebraska	†12
	Toledo	†11
1972	Southern California	†11
1973	Alabama	‡11
	Miami (Ohio)	†10
	Notre Dame	†10
	Penn St.	†11
1974	Alabama	‡11
	Oklahoma	11
1975	Arizona St.	†11
	Arkansas St.	11
	Ohio St.	‡11
1976	Maryland	‡11
	Pittsburgh	†11
	Rutgers	11
1977	Texas	‡11
1978	Penn St.	‡11
1979	Alabama	†11
	BYU	‡11
	Florida St.	‡11
	McNeese St.	‡11
	Ohio St.	‡11
1980	Georgia	†11
1981	Clemson	†11
1982	Georgia	‡11
1983	Nebraska	‡12
	Texas	‡11
1984	BYU	†12
1985	Bowling Green	‡11
	Penn St.	‡11
1986	Miami (Fla.)	‡11
	Penn St.	†11
1987	Miami (Fla.)	†11
	Oklahoma	‡11
	Syracuse	$11
1988	Notre Dame	†11
	West Virginia	‡11
1989	Colorado	‡11
1990	(None)	
1991	Miami (Fla.)	†11
	Washington	†11
1992	Alabama	†12
	Miami (Fla.)	‡11
	Texas A&M	‡12
1993	Auburn	11
	Nebraska	‡11
	West Virginia	‡11
1994	Nebraska	†12
	Penn St.	†11
1995	Florida	‡12
	Nebraska	†11

Beginning in 1996, tiebreaker system added.

Year	College	Wins
1996	Arizona St.	‡11
	Florida St.	‡11
1997	Michigan	†12
	Nebraska	†13

FBS

Year	College	Wins
1998	Tennessee	†12
	Tulane	†11
1999	Florida St.	†11
	Marshall	†12
	Virginia Tech	‡11
2000	Oklahoma	†13
2001	Miami (Fla.)	†12

Beginning in 2002, postseason games included in won-lost records.

Year	College	Wins
2002	Miami (Fla.) (12-1 overall record)	‡12
	Ohio St. (14-0 overall record)	†12
2003	(None)	
2004	Auburn (13-0 overall record)	†12
	Oklahoma (12-1 overall record)	‡12
	Southern California (13-0 overall record)	†12
	Utah (12-0 overall record)	†11
2005	Southern California (12-1 overall record)	‡12
	Texas (13-0 overall record)	†12
2006	Boise St. (13-0 overall record)	†12
	Ohio St. (12-1 overall record)	‡12

The Spoilers

(From 1937 Season)

Following is a list of the spoilers of major-college teams that lost their perfect (undefeated, untied) record in their **final** game of the season, including a bowl game (in parentheses). Confrontations of two undefeated, untied teams at the time are in bold face. An asterisk (*) indicates the home team in a regular-season game, a dagger (†) indicates a neutral site.

Date	Spoiler	Victim	Score
1-1-38	California	Alabama (Rose)	13-0
1-1-38	Rice	Colorado (Cotton)	28-14
12-3-38	*Southern California	Notre Dame	13-0
1-2-39	Southern California	Duke (Rose)	7-3
1-2-39	**Tennessee**	**Oklahoma (Orange)**	17-0
1-2-39	St. Mary's (Cal.)	Texas Tech (Cotton)	20-13
12-2-39	*Duquesne	Detroit	tie 10-10
1-1-40	Southern California	Tennessee (Rose)	14-0
1-1-41	**Boston College**	**Tennessee (Sugar)**	19-13
1-1-42	Oregon St.	Duke (Rose)	20-16
1-1-43	Tennessee	Tulsa (Sugar)	14-7
11-27-43	*Great Lakes	Notre Dame	19-14
1-1-44	Southern California	Washington (Rose)	29-0
11-25-44	*Virginia	Yale	tie 6-6
1-1-47	Illinois	UCLA (Rose)	45-14
1-1-48	SMU	Penn St. (Cotton)	tie 13-13
11-27-48	†Navy	Army	tie 21-21
12-2-48	*Southern California	Notre Dame	tie 14-14
1-1-49	Northwestern	California (Rose)	20-14
1-2-50	Ohio St.	California (Rose)	17-14
12-2-50	†Navy	Army	14-2
1-1-51	Kentucky	Oklahoma (Sugar)	13-7
1-1-52	**Maryland**	**Tennessee (Sugar)**	28-13
11-22-52	Southern California	*UCLA	14-12
1-1-54	Oklahoma	Maryland (Orange)	7-0
1-2-56	**Oklahoma**	**Maryland (Orange)**	20-6
1-1-57	Baylor	Tennessee (Sugar)	13-7
11-28-64	*Southern California	Notre Dame	20-17
1-1-65	Texas	Alabama (Orange)	21-17
11-20-65	**Dartmouth**	***Princeton**	28-14
1-1-66	UCLA	Michigan St. (Rose)	14-12
1-1-66	Alabama	Nebraska (Orange)	39-28
1-1-66	LSU	Arkansas (Cotton)	14-7
11-19-66	**Notre Dame**	***Michigan St.**	tie 10-10
1-1-68	LSU	Wyoming (Sugar)	20-13
11-23-68	***Harvard**	**Yale**	tie 29-29
12-27-68	Richmond	Ohio (Tangerine)	49-42
11-22-69	*Michigan	Ohio St.	24-12
11-22-69	*Princeton	Dartmouth	35-7
11-21-70	***Ohio St.**	**Michigan**	20-9
1-1-71	Stanford	Ohio St. (Rose)	27-17
1-1-71	Notre Dame	Texas (Cotton)	24-11
1-1-72	Stanford	Michigan (Rose)	13-12
1-1-72	**Nebraska**	**Alabama (Orange)**	38-6
11-25-72	*Ohio St.	Michigan	14-11
11-24-73	**Ohio St.**	***Michigan**	tie 10-10
12-31-73	**Notre Dame**	**Alabama (Sugar)**	24-23
11-23-74	*Ohio St.	Michigan	12-10
11-23-74	*Harvard	Yale	21-16
1-1-75	Notre Dame	Alabama (Orange)	13-11
1-1-76	UCLA	Ohio St. (Rose)	23-10
1-1-77	Houston	Maryland (Cotton)	30-21
11-19-77	*Delaware	Colgate	21-3
1-2-78	Notre Dame	Texas (Cotton)	38-10
1-1-79	Alabama	Penn St. (Sugar)	14-7
11-17-79	Harvard	*Yale	22-7
12-15-79	Syracuse	McNeese St. (Independence)	31-7
12-21-79	Indiana	BYU (Holiday)	38-37
1-1-80	Southern California	Ohio St. (Rose)	17-16
1-1-80	Oklahoma	Florida St. (Orange)	24-7
1-1-83	Penn St.	Georgia (Sugar)	27-23
1-2-84	Georgia	Texas (Cotton)	10-9
1-2-84	Miami (Fla.)	Nebraska (Orange)	31-30
12-14-85	Fresno St.	Bowling Green (California)	51-7
1-1-86	Oklahoma	Penn St. (Orange)	25-10
1-2-87	**Penn St.**	**Miami (Fla.) (Fiesta)**	14-10
1-1-88	Auburn	Syracuse (Sugar)	tie 16-16
1-1-88	**Miami (Fla.)**	**Oklahoma (Orange)**	20-14
1-2-89	**Notre Dame**	**West Virginia (Fiesta)**	34-21
1-1-90	Notre Dame	Colorado (Orange)	21-6
1-1-93	Notre Dame	Texas A&M (Cotton)	28-3
1-1-93	**Alabama**	**Miami (Fla.) (Sugar)**	34-13
1-1-94	Florida St.	Nebraska (Orange)	18-16
1-1-94	Florida	West Virginia (Sugar)	41-7
1-2-96	**Nebraska**	**Florida (Fiesta)**	62-24
1-1-97	Ohio St.	Arizona St. (Rose)	20-17
1-2-97	Florida	Florida St. (Sugar)	52-20
1-4-00	Florida St.	Virginia Tech (Sugar)	46-29
1-4-00	Florida St.	Virginia Tech (Sugar)	46-29
1-3-03	**Ohio St.**	**Miami (Fla.) (Fiesta)**	**31-24 (2 ot)**
1-5-06	**Texas**	**Southern California (Rose)**	**41-38**
1-8-07	Florida	Ohio St. (BCS Championship)	41-14

Streaks and Rivalries

Longest Winning Streaks

(Includes Bowl Games)

Wins	Team	Years	Ended by	Score
47	Oklahoma	1953-57	Notre Dame	7-0
39	Washington	1908-14	Oregon St.	0-0
37	Yale	1890-93	Princeton	6-0
37	Yale	1887-89	Princeton	10-0
35	Toledo	1969-71	Tampa	21-0
34	Southern California	2003-05	Texas	*41-38
34	Miami (Fla.)	2000-03	Ohio St.	*31-24 (2 ot)
34	Penn	1894-96	Lafayette	6-4
31	Oklahoma	1948-50	Kentucky	*13-7
31	Pittsburgh	1914-18	Cleveland Naval Reserve	10-9
31	Penn	1896-98	Harvard	10-0
30	Texas	1968-70	Notre Dame	*24-11
29	Miami (Fla.)	1990-93	Alabama	*34-13
29	Michigan	1901-03	Minnesota	6-6
28	Alabama	1991-93	Tennessee	17-17
28	Alabama	1978-80	Mississippi St.	6-3
28	Oklahoma	1973-75	Kansas	23-3
28	Michigan St.	1950-53	Purdue	6-0
26	Nebraska	1994-96	Arizona St.	19-0
26	Cornell	1921-24	Williams	14-7
26	Michigan	1903-05	Chicago	2-0
25	BYU	1983-85	UCLA	27-24
25	San Diego St.	1965-67	Utah St.	31-25
25	Michigan	1946-49	Army	21-7
25	Army	1944-46	Notre Dame	0-0
25	Southern California	1931-33	Oregon St.	0-0
50	Michigan	1901-07	Penn	6-0
47	Nebraska	1991-98	Texas	20-16
44	Washington	1908-17	Oregon St.	0-0
42	Texas	1968-76	Houston	30-0
40	Notre Dame	1907-18	Great Lakes	7-7
38	Notre Dame	1919-27	Minnesota	7-7
37	Yale	1904-08	Brown	10-10
37	Yale	1900-03	Princeton	11-6
37	Florida St.	1992-01	Miami (Fla.)	49-27
*33	Southern California	2001-06		
33	Marshall	1995-00	Western Mich.	30-10
33	Nebraska	1901-06	Iowa St.	14-2
33	Harvard	1900-03	Amherst	5-0
31	Texas A&M	1990-95	Texas	16-6
31	Yale	1890-93	Princeton	6-0
30	Florida	1994-99	Alabama	40-39 (ot)
30	Auburn	1952-61	Kentucky	14-12
30	Tennessee	1928-33	Alabama	12-6

*Streak ended in bowl game. #Eight victories and one tie in 1993 forfeited by action of the NCAA Committee on Infractions.

Longest Unbeaten Streaks

(Includes Bowl Games; May Include Ties)

No.	Wins	Ties	Team	Years	Ended by	Score
63	59	4	Washington	1907-17	California	27-0
56	55	1	Michigan	1901-05	Chicago	2-0
50	46	4	California	1920-25	Olympic Club	15-0
48	47	1	Oklahoma	1953-57	Notre Dame	7-0
48	47	1	Yale	1885-89	Princeton	10-0
47	42	5	Yale	1879-85	Princeton	6-5
44	42	2	Yale	1894-96	Princeton	24-6
42	39	3	Yale	1904-08	Harvard	4-0
39	37	2	Notre Dame	1946-50	Purdue	28-14
37	37	0	Yale	1890-93	Princeton	6-0
37	36	1	Oklahoma	1972-75	Kansas	23-3
35	35	0	Toledo	1969-71	Tampa	21-0
35	34	1	Minnesota	1903-05	Wisconsin	16-12
34	34	0	Southern California	2003-05	Texas	41-38
34	34	0	Miami (Fla.)	2000-03	Ohio St.	31-24 (2 ot)
34	34	0	Penn	1894-96	Lafayette	6-4
34	33	1	Nebraska	1912-16	Kansas	7-3
34	32	2	Princeton	1884-87	Harvard	12-0
34	29	5	Princeton	1877-82	Harvard	1-0
33	31	2	Georgia Tech	1914-18	Pittsburgh	32-0
33	30	3	Tennessee	1926-30	Alabama	18-6
33	30	3	Harvard	1911-15	Cornell	10-0
32	31	1	Nebraska	1969-71	UCLA	20-17
32	31	1	Harvard	1898-00	Yale	28-0
32	30	2	Army	1944-47	Columbia	21-20
31	31	0	Oklahoma	1948-50	Kentucky	13-7
31	31	0	Pittsburgh	1914-18	Cleveland Naval	10-9
31	31	0	Penn	1896-98	Harvard	10-0
31	30	1	Penn St.	1967-70	Colorado	41-13
31	30	1	San Diego St.	1967-70	Long Beach St.	27-11
31	29	2	Georgia Tech	1950-53	Notre Dame	27-14

Longest Home Winning Streaks

(Includes Bowl Games)

Wins	Team	Years	Ended by	Score
58	Miami (Fla.)	1985-94	Washington	38-20
57	Alabama	1963-82	Southern Miss.	38-29
56	Harvard	1890-95	Boston AA	0-0

*Active streak.

Longest Losing Streaks

Losses	Team	Years	Ended with	Score
34	Northwestern	1979-82	Northern Ill.	31-6
28	Virginia	1958-61	William & Mary	21-6
28	Kansas St.	1945-48	Arkansas St.	37-6
27	New Mexico St.	1988-90	Cal St. Fullerton	43-9
27	Eastern Mich.	1980-82	Kent St.	9-7
26	Colorado St.	1960-63	Pacific	20-0
23	Duke	1999-02	East Caro.	23-16
23	Northern Ill.	1996-98	Central Mich.	16-6
21	Ball St.	1998-00	Miami (Ohio)	15-10
21	South Carolina	1998-00	New Mexico St.	31-0
21	Kent St.	1981-83	Eastern Mich.	37-13
21	New Mexico	1967-69	Kansas	16-7
*20	Duke	2005-06		
20	Temple	2004-06	Bowling Green	28-14
20	TCU	1974-75	Rice	28-21
20	Florida St.	1972-74	Miami (Fla.)	21-14
19	Hawaii	1997-99	Eastern Ill.	31-27
18	Illinois	1996-98	Middle Tenn.	48-20
18	Rice	1987-89	SMU	35-6
18	Wisconsin	1967-69	Iowa	23-17
18	Wake Forest	1962-63	South Carolina	20-19
18	Kansas St.	1961-62	BYU	24-7
17	Tulsa	2000-02	UTEP	20-0
17	Kent St.	1992-94	Akron	32-16
17	Kent St.	1989-90	Ohio	44-15
17	Memphis	1981-82	Arkansas St.	12-0
17	Kansas St.	1964-66	Kansas	3-3
17	Tulane	1961-63	South Carolina	20-7
17	Alabama	1954-56	Mississippi St.	13-12
17	Kansas	1953-55	Washington St.	13-0
16	UNLV	1997-98	North Texas	26-3
16	Kansas St.	1987-89	North Texas	20-17
16	Indiana	1983-85	Louisville	41-28
16	Vanderbilt	1961-62	Tulane	20-0
16	Iowa St.	1929-30	Simpson	6-0

*Active streak.

Most Consecutive Non-Losing Seasons

(All-Time and Current) (.500 percentage and above)

No.	School	Years
49	Penn St.	1939-87
42	Nebraska	1962-03
42	Notre Dame	1889-32#
40	Texas	1893-32
39	Michigan	1968-06*
38	Alabama	1911-50†
30	Florida St.	1977-06*
29	Oklahoma	1966-94
29	Texas	1957-85
29	Boston College	1916-44
28	BYU	1974-01
28	Virginia	1888-15
27	Florida	1980-06*
27	Washington	1977-03

No.	School	Years
27	Michigan	1892-18
26	Virginia Tech	1894-19
23	Syracuse	1913-35
23	Ohio St.	1899-21
21	Marshall	1984-04
21	Ohio St.	1967-87
21	Southern California	1962-82
21	Wyoming	1949-69
21	Northern Ill.	1929-49
21	Vanderbilt	1915-35
21	Minnesota	1899-19
20	Texas A&M	1983-02

**Active streak. #No teams in 1890 and 1891. †No teams in 1918 and 1943.*

Longest Streak of Games Without Being Shutout

No.	School	Years
361	BYU	1975-03
286	*Michigan	1984-present
282	Texas	1980-04
271	Washington	1981-04
261	*Washington St.	1984-present
257	*Oregon	1985-present
233	UCLA	1971-92
233	Nebraska	1974-91
232	Florida St.	1988-06
230	Florida	1988-present
222	*Colorado	1988-present
219	Hawaii	1976-95
195	Virginia	1984-00
186	Southern California	1967-83
177	*TCU	1992-present
175^	*Nevada	1992-present
168	*Air Force	1992-present
165	Central Mich.	1982-98
154	San Diego St.	1985-98

**Active streak. ^Games as a member of the FBS — total streak of 317 games includes 142 as a FCS member before 1992.*

Most-Played Rivalries

(Ongoing Unless Indicated)

Games	Opponents (Series leader listed first)	Rivalry Record	First Game
116	Minnesota-Wisconsin	59-49-8	1890
115	Kansas-Missouri	53-53-9	1891
113	Nebraska-Kansas	88-22-3	1892
113	Texas-Texas A&M	73-35-5	1894
111	Miami (Ohio)-Cincinnati	59-45-7	1888
111	*North Carolina-Virginia	57-50-4	1892
110	Auburn-Georgia	53-49-8	1892
110	Oregon-Oregon St.	55-45-10	1894
109	Purdue-Indiana	68-35-6	1891
109	Stanford-California	54-44-11	1892
107	Navy-Army	51-49-7	1890
106	Utah-Utah St.	74-28-4	1892
104	Clemson-South Carolina	63-37-4	1896
104	Baylor-TCU	49-48-7	1899
104	Kansas-Kansas St.	63-36-5	1902
103	Michigan-Ohio St.	57-40-6	1897
103	Mississippi-Mississippi St.	59-38-6	1901
102	North Carolina-Wake Forest	67-33-2	1888
102	Tennessee-Kentucky	70-23-9	1893
101	Georgia-Georgia Tech	58-38-5	1893
101	Nebraska-Iowa St.	83-16-2	1896
101	Texas-Oklahoma	57-39-5	1900
101	Oklahoma-Oklahoma St.	78-16-7	1904

**Disputed series record: Virginia claims North Carolina leads the series 56-49-4, based on a forfeited game in 1956.*

Additional Records

Longest Uninterrupted Series (Must have played every year)

101 games—Kansas-Nebraska (from 1906)
100 games—Minnesota-Wisconsin (from 1907)
98 games—Clemson-South Carolina (from 1909)
96 games—Kansas-Kansas St. (from 1911)
96 games—Kansas-Oklahoma (1903-97)
95 games—North Carolina-Virginia (from 1910)*
95 games—Wake Forest-North Carolina St. (1910-05)
92 games—Texas-Texas A&M (1915)
91 games—Mississippi-Mississippi St. (from 1915)**
89 games—Michigan-Ohio St. (from 1918)
89 games—Illinois-Ohio St. (1914-02)
88 games—Kansas-Missouri (from 1919)
88 games—Missouri-Iowa St. (from 1919)
87 games—Tennessee-Kentucky (from 1919)**
87 games—Auburn-Georgia (from 1919)**
87 games—Indiana-Purdue (from 1920)

**Neither school fielded a team in 1917-18 due to World War I. **Neither school fielded a team in 1943 due to World War II.*

Most Consecutive Wins Over a Major Opponent in an Uninterrupted Series (Must have played in consecutive years)

43—Notre Dame over Navy, 1964-06 (current)
36—Nebraska over Kansas, 1969-04
32—Oklahoma over Kansas St., 1937-68
29—Nebraska over Kansas St., 1969-97
28—Texas over Rice, 1966-93
26—Syracuse over Hobart, 1906-31
25—Penn St. over West Virginia, 1959-83
24—Nebraska over Missouri, 1979-02
22—Tennessee over Kentucky, 1985-06 (current)
22—Tennessee over Vanderbilt, 1983-04
22—Nebraska over Oklahoma St., 1974-95
22—Arkansas over TCU, 1959-80
22—Alabama over Mississippi St., 1958-79
20—Florida over Kentucky, 1987-06 (current)
20—Purdue over Iowa, 1961-80

Most Consecutive Wins Over a Major Opponent in a Nonconsecutive Series (Did not play in consecutive years)

29—Clemson over Virginia, 1955-90 (over 36-year period)
26—Southern California over Oregon St., 1968-99 (32-year period)
24—Nebraska over Oklahoma St., 1974-99 (26-year period)
21—Ohio St. over Northwestern, 1972-98 (27-year period)
19—Washington over California, 1977-01 (25-year period)
19—Michigan over Northwestern, 1966-92 (27-year period)
19—Vanderbilt over Mississippi, 1894-38 (45-year period)
17—Tulsa over Drake, 1939-85 (47-year period)
17—Mississippi over Memphis, 1921-62 (42-year period)
17—North Carolina over Wake Forest, 1893-23 (29-year period)

Most Consecutive Wins Over a Major Opponent in a Current Series (Must have played every year)

43—Notre Dame over Navy, 1964-06 (70-9-1 in rivalry)
36—Nebraska over Kansas, 1969-04 (88-22-3 in rivalry)
22—Tennessee over Kentucky, 1985-06 (70-23-9 in rivalry)
22—Tennessee over Vanderbilt, 1983-04 (68-27-5 in rivalry)

Most Consecutive Games Without a Loss Against a Major Opponent

43—Notre Dame over Navy, 1964-06 (0 ties) (current)
36—Nebraska over Kansas, 1969-04 (0 ties)
34—Oklahoma over Kansas St., 1935-68 (1 tie)

Cliffhangers

Regular-season FBS games won on the final play (since 1971, when first recorded). The extra point is listed when it provided the margin of victory after the winning touchdown on the game's final play. Overtime games are not included but follow Cliffhangers.

Date	Opponents, Score	Game-Winning Play
9-25-71	Marshall 15, Xavier (Ohio) 13	Terry Gardner 13 pass from Reggie Oliver
10-9-71	California 30, Oregon St. 27	Steve Sweeney 7 pass from Jay Cruze
10-23-71	Washington St. 24, Stanford 23	Don Sweet 27 FG
11-6-71	Kentucky 14, Vanderbilt 7	Darryl Bishop 43 interception return
11-4-72	LSU 17, Mississippi 16	Brad Davis 10 pass from Bert Jones (Rusty Jackson kick)
11-18-72	California 24, Stanford 21	Steve Sweeney 7 pass from Vince Ferragamo
9-15-73	Lamar 21, Howard Payne 17	Larry Spears 14 pass from Jabo Leonard
9-22-73	Hawaii 13, Fresno St. 10	Reinhold Stuprich 29 FG
11-17-73	New Mexico 23, Wyoming 21	Bob Berg 43 FG
11-23-74	Stanford 22, California 20	Mike Langford 50 FG
9-20-75	Indiana St. 23, Southern Ill. 21	Dave Vandercook 50 FG
10-18-75	Cal St. Fullerton 32, UC Riverside 31	John Choukair 52 FG
11-1-75	Yale 16, Dartmouth 14	Randy Carter 46 FG
11-8-75	West Virginia 17, Pittsburgh 14	Bill McKenzie 38 FG
11-8-75	Stanford 13, Southern California 10	Mike Langford 37 FG
11-15-75	North Carolina 17, Tulane 15	Tom Biddle 40 FG
11-6-76	Eastern Mich. 30, Central Mich. 27	Ken Dudal 38 FG
9-30-78	Virginia Tech 22, William & Mary 19	Ron Zollicoffer 50 pass from David Lamie
10-21-78	Arkansas St. 6, McNeese St. 3	Doug Dobbs 42 FG
11-9-78	San Jose St. 33, Pacific 31	Rick Parma 5 pass from Ed Luther
10-6-79	Stanford 27, UCLA 24	Ken Naber 56 FG
10-20-79	UNLV 43, Utah 41	Todd Peterson 49 FG
10-27-79	Michigan 27, Indiana 21	Anthony Carter 45 pass from John Wangler
11-10-79	Penn St. 9, North Carolina St. 7	Herb Menhardt 54 FG
11-17-79	Air Force 30, Vanderbilt 29	Andy Bark 14 pass from Dave Ziebart
11-24-79	Arizona 27, Arizona St. 24	Brett Weber 27 FG
9-13-80	Southern California 20, Tennessee 17	Eric Hipp 47 FG
9-13-80	Illinois 20, Michigan St. 17	Mike Bass 38 FG
9-20-80	Notre Dame 29, Michigan 27	Harry Oliver 51 FG
9-27-80	Tulane 26, Mississippi 24	Vince Manalla 29 FG
10-18-80	Connecticut 18, Holy Cross 17	Ken Miller 4 pass from Ken Sweitzer (Keith Hugger pass from Sweitzer)
10-18-80	Washington 27, Stanford 24	Chuck Nelson 25 FG
11-1-80	Tulane 24, Kentucky 22	Vince Manalla 22 FG
11-15-80	Florida 17, Kentucky 15	Brian Clark 34 FG
10-16-82	Arizona 16, Notre Dame 13	Max Zendejas 48 FG
10-23-82	Illinois 29, Wisconsin 28	Mike Bass 46 FG
11-20-82	California 25, Stanford 20	57 (5 laterals) kickoff return involving, in order: Kevin Moen, Richard Rodgers, Dwight Garner, Rodgers, Mariet Ford and Moen
10-8-83	Iowa St. 38, Kansas 35	Marc Bachrodt 47 FG
10-29-83	Bowling Green 15, Central Mich. 14	Stan Hunter 8 pass from Brian McClure
11-5-83	Baylor 24, Arkansas 21	Marty Jimmerson 24 FG
11-12-83	Pacific 30, San Jose St. 26	Ron Woods 85 pass from Mike Pitz
11-12-83	Miami (Fla.) 17, Florida St. 16	Jeff Davis 19 FG
11-26-83	Arizona 17, Arizona St. 15	Max Zendejas 45 FG
9-8-84	La.-Lafayette 17, Louisiana Tech 16	Patrick Broussard 21 FG
9-15-84	Syracuse 13, Northwestern 12	Jim Tait 2 pass from Todd Norley (Don McAulay kick)
10-13-84	UCLA 27, Washington St. 24	John Lee 47 FG
11-17-84	La.-Lafayette 18, Tulsa 17	Patrick Broussard 45 FG
11-17-84	Temple 19, West Virginia 17	Jim Cooper 36 FG
11-23-84	Boston College 47, Miami (Fla.) 45	Gerard Phelan 48 pass from Doug Flutie
9-14-85	Clemson 20, Virginia Tech 17	David Treadwell 36 FG
9-14-85	Oregon St. 23, California 20	Jim Nielsen 20 FG
9-14-85	Utah 29, Hawaii 27	Andre Guardi 19 FG
9-21-85	New Mexico St. 22, UTEP 20	Andy Weiler 32 FG
10-5-85	Mississippi St. 31, Memphis 28	Artie Cosby 54 FG
10-5-85	Illinois 31, Ohio St. 28	Chris White 38 FG
10-12-85	Tulsa 37, Long Beach St. 35	Jason Staurovsky 46 FG
10-19-85	Northwestern 17, Wisconsin 14	John Duvic 42 FG
10-19-85	Iowa 12, Michigan 10	Rob Houghtlin 29 FG
10-19-85	Utah 39, San Diego St. 37	Andre Guardi 42 FG
11-30-85	Alabama 25, Auburn 23	Van Tiffin 52 FG
9-13-86	Oregon 32, Colorado 30	Matt MacLeod 35 FG
9-13-86	Wyoming 23, Pacific 20	Greg Worker 38 FG
9-20-86	Clemson 31, Georgia 28	David Treadwell 46 FG
9-20-86	Southern California 17, Baylor 14	Don Shafer 32 FG
10-18-86	Michigan 20, Iowa 17	Mike Gillette 34 FG
10-25-86	Syracuse 27, Temple 24	Tim Vesling 32 FG
11-1-86	North Carolina St. 23, South Carolina 22	Danny Peebles 33 pass from Erik Kramer
11-1-86	North Carolina 32, Maryland 30	Lee Gliarmis 28 FG
11-8-86	Southern Miss. 23, East Caro. 21	Rex Banks 31 FG
11-15-86	Minnesota 20, Michigan 17	Chip Lohmiller 30 FG
11-29-86	Notre Dame 38, Southern California 37	John Carney 19 FG
9-12-87	Youngstown St. 20, Bowling Green 17	John Dowling 36 FG
9-19-87	Utah 31, Wisconsin 28	Scott Lieber 39 FG
10-10-87	Marshall 34, Louisville 31	Keith Baxter 31 pass from Tony Petersen
10-17-87	Texas 16, Arkansas 14	Tony Jones 18 pass from Bret Stafford

Date	Opponents, Score	Game-Winning Play
11-12-88	New Mexico 24, Colorado St. 23	Tony Jones 28 pass from Jeremy Leach
9-16-89	SMU 31, Connecticut 30	Mike Bowen 4 pass from Mike Romo
9-30-89	Kansas St. 20, North Texas 17	Frank Hernandez 12 pass from Carl Straw
10-7-89	Florida 16, LSU 13	Arden Czyzewski 41 FG
10-14-89	Southern Miss. 16, Louisville 10	Darryl Tillman 79 pass from Brett Favre
10-28-89	Virginia 16, Louisville 15	Jake McInerney 37 FG
11-4-89	Toledo 19, Western Mich. 18	Romauldo Brown 9 pass from Kevin Meger
11-4-89	Northern Ill. 23, La.-Lafayette 20	Stacey Robinson 7 run
9-8-90	Utah 35, Minnesota 29	Lavon Edwards 91 run of blocked FG
9-29-90	North Carolina St. 12, North Carolina 9	Damon Hartman 56 FG
10-6-90	Colorado 33, Missouri 31	Charles S. Johnson 1 run
10-20-90	Alabama 9, Tennessee 6	Philip Doyle 47 FG
11-3-90	Southern Miss. 14, La.-Lafayette 13	Michael Welch 11 pass from Brett Favre (Jim Taylor kick)
11-10-90	Ohio St. 27, Iowa 26	Bobby Olive 3 pass from Greg Frey
11-17-90	Stanford 27, California 25	John Hopkins 39 FG
11-24-90	Michigan 16, Ohio St. 13	J. D. Carlson 37 FG
9-7-91	Central Mich. 27, La.-Lafayette 24	L. J. Muddy 2 pass from Jeff Bender
9-21-91	California 23, Arizona 21	Doug Brien 33 FG
9-21-91	Georgia Tech 24, Virginia 21	Scott Sisson 33 FG
9-21-91	Louisiana Tech 17, Eastern Mich. 14	Chris Bonoil 54 FG
10-12-91	Ball St. 10, Eastern Mich. 8	Kenny Stucker 41 FG
11-2-91	Kentucky 20, Cincinnati 17	Doug Pelphrey 53 FG
11-2-91	Tulsa 13, Southern Miss. 10	Eric Lange 24 FG
9-5-92	Louisiana Tech 10, Baylor 9	Chris Bonoil 30 FG
9-19-92	Miami (Ohio) 17, Cincinnati 14	Chad Seitz 21 FG
9-19-92	Southern Miss. 16, Louisiana Tech 13	Johnny Lomoro 46 FG
10-3-92	Texas A&M 19, Texas Tech 17	Terry Venetoulias 21 FG
10-3-92	Georgia Tech 16, North Carolina St. 13	Scott Sisson 29 FG
10-3-92	San Jose St. 26, Wyoming 24	Joe Nedney 60 FG
10-24-92	Maryland 27, Duke 25	Marcus Badgett 38 pass from John Kaleo
10-31-92	Rutgers 50, Virginia Tech 49	Chris Brantley 15 pass from Bryan Fortay
11-14-92	UCLA 9, Oregon 6	Louis Perez 40 FG
10-2-93	Tulane 27, Navy 25	Bart Baldwin 43 FG
10-9-93	Ball St. 31, Toledo 30	Eric McCray 6 pass from Mike Neu (Matt Swart kick)
10-9-93	North Carolina St. 36, Texas Tech 34	Gary Downs 11 pass from Robert Hinton
10-16-93	Arizona 27, Stanford 24	Steve McLaughlin 27 FG
10-30-93	Missouri 37, Iowa St. 34	Kyle Pooler 40 FG
11-20-93	Maryland 33, Wake Forest 32	Russ Weaver 8 pass from Scott Milanovich (John Milligan kick)
11-20-93	Boston College 41, Notre Dame 39	David Gordon 41 FG
11-20-93	Arkansas St. 23, Nevada 21	Reginald Murphy 30 pass from Johnny Covington
9-10-94	Tulane 15, Rice 13	Bart Baldwin 47 FG
9-10-94	San Diego St. 22, California 20	Peter Holt 32 FG
9-24-94	Colorado 27, Michigan 26	Michael Westbrook 64 pass from Kordell Stewart
10-22-94	Central Mich. 32, Miami (Ohio) 30	Terrance McMillan 19 pass from Erik Timpf
10-22-94	Army 25, Citadel 24	Kurt Heiss 24 FG
11-19-94	Eastern Mich. 40, Toledo 37	Ontario Pryor 16 pass from Charlie Batch
9-16-95	Miami (Ohio) 30, Northwestern 28	Chad Seitz 20 FG
8-26-95	Michigan 18, Virginia 17	Mercury Hayes 15 pass from Scott Dreisbach
9-9-95	Kansas St. 23, Cincinnati 21	Kevin Lockett 22 pass from Matt Miller
10-21-95	Texas 17, Virginia 16	Phil Dawson 50 FG
10-28-95	East Caro. 36, Southern Miss. 34	Chad Holcomb 29 FG
8-31-96	Boston College 24, Hawaii 21	John Matich 42 FG
9-7-96	Arizona St. 45, Washington 42	Robert Nycz 38 FG
9-7-96	Air Force 20, Notre Dame 17	Dallas Thompson 27 FG
9-21-96	Notre Dame 27, Texas 24	Jim Sanson 39 FG
9-21-96	Navy 19, SMU 17	Tom Vanderhorst 38 FG
10-12-96	Louisville 23, Tulane 20	David Akers 39 FG
9-13-97	Toledo 38, Eastern Mich. 35	Chris Merrick 24 FG
9-27-97	Colorado 20, Wyoming 19	Jeremy Aldrich 18 FG
9-5-98	Tennessee 34, Syracuse 33	Jeff Hall 27 FG
9-5-98	Minnesota 17, Arkansas St. 14	Adam Bailey 17 FG
9-19-98	Marshall 24, South Carolina 21	Billy Malashevich 37 FG
9-19-98	Stanford 37, North Carolina 34	Kevin Miller 20 FG
10-17-98	Kentucky 39, LSU 36	Seth Hanson 33 FG
11-14-98	Akron 24, Eastern Mich. 21	Zac Derr 26 FG
11-14-98	Syracuse 28, Virginia Tech 26	Stephen Brominski 13 pass from Donovan McNabb
11-22-98	Toledo 17, Central Mich. 14	Todd France 29 FG
9-11-99	UNLV 27, Baylor 24	Kevin Thomas 100 fumble return
9-25-99	Western Mich. 24, Northern Ill. 21	Brad Selent 37 FG
9-25-99	Arizona 30, Washington St. 24	Bobby Wade 42 pass from Keith Smith
10-30-99	Texas 44, Iowa St. 41	Kris Stockton 18 FG
11-6-99	Minnesota 24, Penn St. 23	Dan Nystrom 32 FG
11-6-99	Virginia Tech 22, West Virginia 20	Shayne Graham 44 FG
11-27-99	Stanford 40, Notre Dame 37	Mike Biselli 22 FG
9-16-00	Notre Dame 23, Purdue 21	Nick Setta 38 FG
9-16-00	Arizona St. 13, Colorado St. 10	Mike Barth 41 FG
10-28-00	Northwestern 41, Minnesota 35	Sam Simmons 45 pass from Zak Kustok
11-24-00	Nebraska 34, Colorado 32	Josh Brown 29 FG
8-30-01	Akron 31, Ohio 29	Zac Derr 38 FG
9-29-01	Northwestern 27, Michigan St. 26	David Wasielewski 47 FG
10-6-01	Washington 27, Southern California 24	John Anderson 32 FG
10-13-01	Miami (Ohio) 30, Akron 27	Eddie Tillitz 70 pass from Ben Roethlisberger
10-27-01	Washington 33, Arizona St. 31	John Anderson 30 FG
11-3-01	Michigan St. 23, Michigan 21	T.J. Duckett 2 pass from Jeff Smoker

Date	Opponents, Score	Game-Winning Play
11-17-01	New Mexico St. 49, La.-Lafayette 46	Dario Aquiniga 29 FG
10-12-02	New Mexico St. 31, La.-Lafayette 28	Dario Aquiniga 41 FG
11-9-02	LSU 33, Kentucky 30	Devery Henderson 75 pass from Marcus Randall
11-8-03	Minnesota 37, Wisconsin 34	Rhyl Lloyd 35 FG

"CARDIAC SEASONS"

(From 1937; Won-Lost Record in Parentheses)

Games Decided by Two Points or Less

6—Kansas, 1973 (3-2-1): Tennessee 27-28, Nebraska 9-10, Iowa St. 22-20, Oklahoma St. 10-10, Colorado 17-15, Missouri 14-13 (season record: 7-3-1)

5—Illinois, 1992 (2-2-1): Minnesota 17-18, Ohio St. 18-16, Northwestern 26-27, Wisconsin 13-12, Michigan 22-22 (season record: 6-4-1)

5—Columbia, 1971 (4-1-0): Princeton 22-20, Harvard 19-21, Yale 15-14, Rutgers 17-16, Dartmouth 31-29 (season record: 6-3-0)

5—Missouri, 1957 (2-2-1): Vanderbilt 7-7, SMU 7-6, Nebraska 14-13, Kansas St. 21-23, Kansas 7-9 (season record: 5-4-1)

Games Decided by Three Points or Less

7—Bowling Green, 1980 (2-5-0): Ohio 20-21, Ball St. 24-21, Western Mich. 17-14, Kentucky 20-21, Long Beach St. 21-23, Eastern Mich. 16-18, Richmond 17-20 (season record: 4-7-0)

7—Columbia, 1971 (4-3-0): Lafayette 0-3, Princeton 22-20, Harvard 19-21, Yale 15-14, Rutgers 17-16, Cornell 21-24, Dartmouth 31-29 (season record: 6-3-0)

6—Illinois, 1992 (3-2-1): Minnesota 17-18, Ohio St. 18-16, Northwestern 26-27, Wisconsin 13-12, Purdue 20-17, Michigan 22-22 (season record: 6-4-1)

6—Central Mich., 1991 (2-0-4): Ohio 17-17, La.-Lafayette 27-24, Akron 31-29, Toledo 16-16, Miami (Ohio) 10-10, Eastern Mich. 14-14 (season record: 6-1-4)

6—Kansas, 1973 (3-2-1): Tennessee 27-28, Nebraska 9-10, Iowa St. 22-20, Oklahoma St. 10-10, Colorado 17-15, Missouri 14-13 (season record: 7-3-1)

6—Air Force, 1967 (2-2-2): Oklahoma St. 0-0, California 12-14, North Carolina 10-8, Tulane 13-10, Colorado St. 17-17, Army 7-10 (season record: 2-6-2)

6—Missouri, 1957 (3-2-1): Vanderbilt 7-7, SMU 7-6, Nebraska 14-13, Colorado 9-6, Kansas St. 21-23, Kansas 7-9 (season record: 5-4-1)

Overtime Games

In 1981, the NCAA Football Rules Committee approved an overtime tiebreaker system to decide a tie game for the purpose of determining a conference champion in regular-season play. In 1996, the tiebreaker became mandatory in all games tied after four periods.

2006 FBS Overtime Games

Date	Winner	Loser	Score	Number of OT Periods
Aug, 31	Iowa St.	Toledo	45-43	3
Aug. 31	Buffalo	Temple	9-3	1
Sept. 9	Bowling Green	Buffalo	48-40	4
Sept. 9	Iowa	Syracuse	20-13	2
Sept. 9	Boston College	Clemson	34-33	2
Sept. 9	Purdue	Miami (Ohio)	38-31	1
Sept. 9	Virginia	Wyoming	13-12	1
Sept. 9	Army	Kent St.	17-14	1
Sept. 9	Texas Tech	UTEP	38-35	1
Sept. 15	Toledo	Kansas	37-31	2
Sept. 16	Boston College	BYU	30-23	2
Sept. 23	Arkansas	Alabama	24-23	2
Sept. 23	Tulsa	Navy	24-23	1
Sept. 23	Central Mich.	Eastern Mich.	24-17	1
Sept. 23	Army	Baylor	27-20	1
Sept. 23	Mississippi St.	UAB	16-10	1
Sept. 30	Syracuse	Wyoming	40-34	2
Sept. 30	Nebraska	Kansas	39-32	1
Oct. 7	North Texas	Florida Int'l	25-22	7
Oct. 7	Penn St.	Minnesota	28-27	1
Oct. 7	Baylor	Colorado	34-31	1
Oct. 14	Alabama	Mississippi	26-23	1
Oct. 14	New Mexico	UNLV	39-36	1
Oct. 21	Texas A&M	Oklahoma St.	34-33	1
Oct. 21	California	Washington	31-24	1
Oct. 28	East Caro.	Southern Miss.	20-17	1
Oct. 28	Arizona St.	Washington	26-23	1
Nov. 11	Rice	Tulsa	41-38	2
Nov. 11	Connecticut	Pittsburgh	46-45	2
Nov. 18	LSU	Mississippi	23-20	1
Nov. 18	Houston	Memphis	23-20	1
Dec. 2	West Virginia	Rutgers	41-39	3
Dec. 29	Texas Tech	Minnesota	44-41	1
Jan. 1	Boise St.	Oklahoma	43-42	1

Note: 34 games with 55 extra periods (22 with one extra period, eight with two extra periods, two with three extra periods, one with four extra periods, one with seven extra periods) for an average of 1.62 extra periods per overtime game.

MOST OVERTIME GAMES IN A DAY

Date	OT Games
Sept. 9, 2006	7
Sept. 24, 2005	6
Nov. 6, 2004	6
Sept. 23, 2006	5

All-Time FBS Won-Lost Records in Overtime Games 1996-06

Team	1996	1997	1998	1999	2000	2001	2002	2003	2004	2005	2006	Overall W-L
Air Force	2-0	1-0	—	—	0-1	—	1-0	0-1	—	—	—	4-2
Akron	—	—	—	—	—	1-0	—	—	—	1-0	—	2-0
Alabama	—	0-1	1-0	1-1	—	—	—	0-2	—	0-1	1-1	3-6
UAB	—	—	0-1	1-0	0-1	—	—	—	—	—	0-1	1-3
Arizona	0-1	1-1	—	—	1-0	—	—	0-1	—	—	—	2-3
Arizona St.	1-0	—	1-0	—	1-2	—	—	—	—	—	1-0	4-2
Arkansas	1-0	—	—	—	1-0	1-0	0-1	2-0	—	—	1-0	6-1
Arkansas St.	—	—	1-0	0-1	0-2	—	—	—	—	1-0	—	2-3
Army	—	—	—	1-0	—	—	—	—	—	—	2-0	3-0
Auburn	0-1	—	—	0-1	1-0	1-0	1-1	—	—	0-1	—	3-4
Ball St.	1-0	1-0	—	—	—	—	1-0	—	0-1	1-1	—	4-2
Baylor	0-1	—	—	0-1	—	1-0	—	—	1-0	0-2	1-1	3-5
Boise St.	—	1-0	0-1	—	—	—	—	—	1-0	—	1-0	3-1
Boston College	—	0-1	—	1-0	—	—	0-1	—	0-1	1-0	2-0	4-3
Bowling Green	0-1	—	—	1-0	—	—	1-0	—	—	0-1	1-0	3-2
BYU	1-0	1-0	—	1-0	1-0	—	—	1-0	—	0-2	0-1	5-3
Buffalo	—	—	—	—	1-0	—	—	—	—	—	1-1	2-1
California	2-0	0-1	—	—	1-1	—	—	1-1	—	0-1	1-0	5-4
UCF	—	0-1	—	0-1	—	—	—	—	0-1	0-1	—	0-4
Central Mich.	—	0-1	1-0	—	0-1	—	—	—	1-1	1-1	1-0	4-4
Cincinnati	1-0	1-1	—	0-1	1-1	—	1-0	1-1	—	—	—	5-4
Clemson	—	1-0	—	—	—	1-0	—	1-0	2-0	0-2	0-1	5-3
Colorado	—	—	—	1-1	—	—	1-1	1-0	0-1	—	0-1	3-4
Colorado St.	—	—	—	—	—	0-1	—	—	—	—	—	0-1
Connecticut	*	*	*	*	*	*	0-1	1-0	—	—	1-0	2-1
Duke	—	0-1	0-1	1-2	—	—	—	1-0	—	—	—	2-4
East Caro.	—	—	—	—	—	0-1	1-0	0-1	—	—	1-0	2-2
Eastern Mich.	—	—	0-1	0-1	—	0-1	1-0	—	1-0	1-0	0-1	3-4
Florida	—	—	0-1	0-1	—	—	1-0	—	—	1-0	—	2-2
Fla. Atlantic	*	*	*	*	*	*	*	*	1-0	0-1	—	1-1
Florida Int'l	*	*	*	*	*	*	*	*	*	—	0-1	0-1
Florida St.	—	—	—	—	—	—	0-1	1-0	0-1	0-1	—	1-3
Fresno St.	0-2	0-1	—	2-1	—	1-0	—	—	1-0	—	—	4-4
Georgia	1-0	—	—	1-1	0-1	—	—	1-0	—	—	—	3-2
Georgia Tech	—	—	—	2-0	0-1	0-2	—	1-0	—	—	—	3-3
Hawaii	—	0-1	—	1-0	—	1-0	—	1-0	0-1	—	—	3-2
Houston	2-0	1-0	—	—	1-1	—	0-1	0-1	0-1	0-1	1-0	5-5
Idaho	—	0-1	1-0	1-0	1-0	0-1	—	0-1	—	1-0	—	4-3
Illinois	1-0	—	—	0-1	—	—	1-1	—	0-1	1-0	—	3-3
Indiana	0-1	—	0-1	1-0	—	—	—	0-1	0-1	—	—	1-4
Iowa	—	—	—	—	1-0	—	1-0	—	—	0-1	1-0	3-1
Iowa St.	0-1	—	—	—	—	—	—	—	0-1	0-3	1-0	1-5
Kansas	—	—	1-0	—	—	1-0	—	0-1	—	1-0	0-2	3-3
Kansas St.	—	—	0-1	—	—	—	—	—	—	—	—	0-1
Kent St.	—	—	—	—	1-1	—	—	0-1	—	—	0-1	1-3
Kentucky	—	1-0	—	—	0-1	—	—	0-1	—	—	—	1-2
La.-Lafayette	—	0-2	—	—	0-1	—	—	1-0	—	1-0	—	2-3
La.-Monroe	1-0	2-0	—	—	—	—	1-0	—	—	—	—	4-0
LSU	—	—	0-1	—	2-0	—	—	—	1-0	2-1	1-0	6-2
Louisiana Tech	—	—	—	—	0-1	1-1	—	—	—	—	—	1-2
Louisville	—	—	—	0-1	1-0	—	2-0	0-1	—	0-1	—	3-3
Marshall	—	—	—	—	—	1-0	—	—	—	1-1	—	2-1
Maryland	—	—	—	—	1-0	1-0	—	0-1	0-1	1-0	—	3-2
Memphis	—	—	—	—	0-2	—	—	—	—	0-1	0-1	0-4
Miami (Fla.)	—	1-0	0-1	—	—	—	0-1	—	1-1	1-0	—	3-3
Miami (Ohio)	0-1	0-1	—	—	—	—	—	—	—	—	0-1	0-3
Michigan	—	—	—	1-0	—	—	1-0	—	1-0	2-0	—	5-0
Michigan St.	—	—	1-0	—	—	—	—	—	0-1	1-1	—	2-2
Middle Tenn.	—	—	—	—	1-0	—	—	1-2	—	—	—	2-2
Minnesota	—	—	—	0-1	—	0-1	—	—	—	1-0	0-2	1-4
Mississippi	—	1-0	2-1	1-1	1-0	0-1	—	—	1-0	—	0-2	6-5
Mississippi St.	0-1	—	—	—	1-2	—	—	—	—	—	1-0	2-3
Missouri	2-0	1-1	—	0-1	—	1-0	1-1	1-0	1-0	1-0	—	8-3
Navy	—	—	—	—	—	—	—	—	—	—	0-1	0-1
Nebraska	—	1-0	—	1-0	1-0	—	—	—	—	1-0	1-0	5-0
Nevada	—	—	—	—	—	0-1	—	—	1-0	1-0	—	2-1
UNLV	—	0-2	0-1	—	0-1	—	1-0	0-1	0-1	—	0-1	1-7
New Mexico	—	—	1-1	—	—	0-1	1-2	—	—	—	1-0	3-4
New Mexico St.	—	0-1	0-2	—	1-1	—	—	—	—	0-1	—	1-5
North Carolina	—	—	1-0	0-1	—	—	—	0-1	—	0-1	—	1-3

Team	1996	1997	1998	1999	2000	2001	2002	2003	2004	2005	2006	Overall W-L
North Carolina St.	—	1-0	0-1	1-0	2-1	—	1-0	0-2	1-0	—	—	6-4
North Texas	—	—	—	—	—	—	—	—	—	—	1-0	1-0
Northern Ill.	—	—	—	—	—	—	1-0	2-0	1-0	0-1	—	4-1
Northwestern	—	—	—	1-0	1-0	—	—	1-0	3-1	—	—	6-1
Notre Dame	0-2	—	—	—	1-1	—	—	1-0	—	0-1	—	2-4
Ohio	0-1	—	—	—	—	—	—	0-1	1-0	1-0	—	2-2
Ohio St.	—	—	—	—	—	—	2-0	2-0	0-1	—	—	4-1
Oklahoma	1-0	—	—	—	—	—	—	—	—	1-0	0-1	2-1
Oklahoma St.	1-1	0-2	—	—	—	0-1	—	—	—	—	0-1	1-5
Oregon	1-1	1-0	0-2	1-0	—	2-0	—	—	—	1-0	—	6-3
Oregon St.	0-1	—	1-0	—	—	0-1	—	—	0-1	—	—	1-3
Penn St.	—	—	—	—	0-1	—	0-2	—	—	1-0	1-0	2-3
Pittsburgh	0-1	2-0	—	—	0-1	—	1-0	—	2-1	0-1	0-1	5-5
Purdue	—	—	—	0-1	1-0	1-0	0-1	0-2	—	0-1	1-0	3-5
Rice	—	—	1-0	—	1-0	1-1	—	0-1	0-1	—	1-0	4-3
Rutgers	—	0-1	—	1-0	0-1	—	—	—	—	0-1	0-1	1-4
San Diego St.	—	1-1	2-0	—	—	—	—	—	—	—	—	3-1
San Jose St.	—	1-0	—	—	—	—	—	—	0-1	—	—	1-1
South Carolina	—	—	—	—	—	—	—	0-1	—	—	—	0-1
South Fla.	—	—	—	—	—	—	—	3-0	1-0	—	—	4-0
Southern California	1-2	—	—	0-1	1-0	1-0	0-1	0-1	—	—	—	3-5
SMU	—	0-1	0-2	—	—	0-1	—	—	1-0	0-1	—	1-5
Southern Miss.	0-1	—	—	—	1-0	—	0-1	—	1-0	1-0	0-1	3-3
Stanford	1-0	—	0-1	—	1-0	—	—	—	—	0-1		2-2
Syracuse	—	0-1	—	0-1	1-0	—	1-1	1-0	1-0	—	1-1	5-4
Temple	—	—	—	—	—	—	—	0-3	—	—	0-1	0-4
Tennessee	—	—	1-0	—	0-1	—	1-0	2-0	—	1-0	—	5-1
Texas	0-1	—	—	—	—	—	—	—	—	—	—	0-1
UTEP	—	—	0-1	0-1	—	—	—	—	1-0	1-0	—	2-2
Texas A&M	—	1-0	1-0	—	0-1	—	0-2	—	2-1	1-0	1-0	6-4
TCU	—	—	1-0	0-1	—	0-1	0-1	1-0	1-1	2-0	0-1	5-5
Texas Tech	—	—	—	—	—	0-1	1-1	—	0-1	—	2-0	3-3
Toledo	1-0	—	—	—	—	—	—	—	—	1-0	1-1	3-1
Troy	*	*	*	*	*	*	0-1	—	—	0-1	—	0-2
Tulane	—	—	—	—	—	—	—	1-0	—	—	—	1-0
Tulsa	—	—	—	—	—	—	—	—	0-2	1-0	1-1	2-3
UCLA	1-0	—	1-0	1-0	0-1	—	—	1-0	—	2-0	—	6-1
Utah	—	—	1-1	—	—	—	0-1	1-0	—	1-1	—	3-3
Utah St.	—	—	1-1	0-1	—	0-1	2-1	—	—	—	—	3-4
Vanderbilt	—	—	1-1	—	—	—	—	0-1	0-1	0-1	—	1-4
Virginia	—	—	—	0-1	0-1	—	—	0-1	0-1	—	1-0	1-4
Virginia Tech	—	—	1-0	1-0	—	—	0-1	1-0	—	—	—	3-1
Wake Forest	—	—	—	—	—	—	0-1	—	0-2	—	—	0-3
Washington	1-0	—	—	0-1	—	—	1-0	—	—	—	0-2	2-3
Washington St.	0-1	1-0	—	—	0-3	—	1-1	0-1	—	0-1	—	2-7
West Virginia	—	0-1	—	—	1-0	—	—	—	1-0	1-0	1-0	4-1
Western Mich.	1-1	—	—	1-0	—	—	0-1	—	0-1	0-1	—	2-4
Wisconsin	—	—	—	1-0	1-2	—	1-0	—	—	—	—	3-2
Wyoming	1-1	—	1-0	—	—	—	0-1	—	1-0	—	0-2	3-4
I-AA, II Opponents	0-2	2-0	—	—	—	2-1	0-1	1-1	0-1	—	—	5-6
Totals	**26-26**	**25-25**	**24-24**	**27-27**	**36-36**	**18-18**	**31-31**	**34-34**	**32-32**	**39-39**	**34-34**	**326-326**

*Not an FBS member at the time.

BY CONFERENCE

Conference	1996	1997	1998	1999	2000	2001	2002	2003	2004	2005	2006	Overall W-L
Atlantic Coast	—	2-1	1-2	3-4	3-3	2-2	1-2	4-5	4-7	3-4	3-1	26-31
Big East	0-1	3-4	1-2	2-1	2-2	—	2-4	2-3	4-2	1-3	3-3	20-25
Big Ten	1-1	—	1-1	4-3	4-3	1-1	6-4	3-3	4-5	6-3	3-2	33-26
Big 12	4-4	3-3	2-1	2-3	1-1	3-2	3-5	2-1	4-4	5-5	6-6	35-35
Big West	—	1-2	3-4	1-2	2-3	—	—	—	—	—	—	7-11
Conference USA	3-1	2-1	—	2-2	4-5	0-2	4-3	6-4	3-2	4-5	4-5	32-30
Mid-American	3-4	1-2	1-0	2-1	2-2	2-1	4-1	2-2	4-4	6-5	4-5	31-27
Mountain West	—	—	—	1-0	1-2	0-2	3-4	2-2	1-1	3-3	1-4	12-18
Pacific-10	8-6	3-2	3-3	2-2	7-7	1-1	2-2	2-4	0-1	3-3	2-2	33-33
Southeastern	2-2	2-1	5-4	5-5	6-5	2-1	3-2	5-5	2-0	4-4	4-3	40-32
Sun Belt	—	—	—	—	—	0-1	1-0	2-3	—	2-2	1-1	6-7
Western Athletic	4-3	4-6	7-6	3-3	1-0	5-4	—	1-1	5-5	2-1	1-0	33-29
FBS Independents	1-2	2-3	0-1	0-1	2-3	—	2-3	2-0	1-0	0-1	2-2	12-16
FCS, Div. II Opponents	0-2	2-0	—	—	1-0	2-1	0-1	1-1	0-1	—	—	6-6
Totals	**26-26**	**25-25**	**24-24**	**27-27**	**36-36**	**18-18**	**31-31**	**34-34**	**32-32**	**39-39**	**34-34**	**326-326**

FBS Stadiums

LISTED ALPHABETICALLY BY SCHOOL

School	Stadium	Conference	Year Built	Cap.	Surface* (Year)
Air Force	Falcon	Mountain West	1962	52,480	Grass
Akron	^Rubber Bowl	Mid-American-E	1940	35,202	AstroTurf (94)
Alabama	Bryant-Denny	Southeastern-W	1929	83,818	PAT (S91)
UAB	^Legion Field	Conference USA	1927	83,091	Grass (S95)
Arizona	Arizona	Pacific-10	1928	57,803	Grass
Arizona St.	Sun Devil	Pacific-10	1959	73,656	Grass
Arkansas	Razorback	Southeastern-W	1938	72,000	Grass (S95)
Arkansas St.	Indian	Sun Belt	1974	33,410	Grass
Army	Michie	Independent	1924	39,929	AstroTurf (92)
Auburn	Jordan-Hare	Southeastern-W	1939	87,451	Grass
Ball St.	Scheumann	Mid-American-W	1967	22,500	Grass
Baylor	Floyd Casey	Big 12-S	1950	50,000	SportGrass (S98)
Boise St.	Bronco	Western Athletic	1970	30,000	Blue AstroTurf
Boston College	Alumni	Atlantic Coast	1957	44,500	AstroTurf (97)
Bowling Green	Doyt Perry	Mid-American-E	1966	30,599	Grass
BYU	LaVell Edwards	Mountain West	1964	65,000	FieldTurf (01)
Buffalo	UB Stadium	Mid-American-E	1993	30,000	Grass
California	Memorial	Pacific-10	1923	75,662	Momentum Turf (S03)
UCF	^Florida Citrus	Conference USA	1936	70,188	Grass
Central Mich.	Kelly-Shorts	Mid-American-W	1972	30,199	FieldTurf (04)
Cincinnati	Nippert	Big East	1916	35,000	FieldTurf (00)
Clemson	Memorial	Atlantic Coast	1942	81,473	Grass
Colorado	Folsom	Big 12-N	1924	50,942	Grass (S99)
Colorado St.	Hughes	Mountain West	1968	30,000	Grass
Connecticut	^Rentschler Field	Big East	2003	40,000	Grass
Duke	Wallace Wade	Atlantic Coast	1929	33,941	Grass
East Caro.	Dowdy-Ficklen	Conference USA	1963	43,000	Grass (83)
Eastern Mich.	Rynearson	Mid-American-W	1969	30,200	AstroTurf (98)
Florida	Florida Field	Southeastern-E	1929	83,000	Grass (S90)
Fla. Atlantic	Lockhart	Sun Belt	1987	20,450	Grass
Florida Int'l	FIU Stadium	Sun Belt	1995	17,000	AstroPlay (04)
Florida St.	Doak S. Campbell	Atlantic Coast	1950	80,000	PAT (88)
Fresno St.	Bulldog	Western Athletic	1980	41,031	Grass
Georgia	Sanford	Southeastern-E	1929	92,058	Grass
Georgia Tech	Bobby Dodd/Grant Field	Atlantic Coast	1913	55,000	Grass
Hawaii	^Aloha	Western Athletic	1975	50,000	FieldTurf (01)
Houston	Robertson	Conference USA	1942	22,000	Grass
Idaho	#Kibbie Dome	Western Athletic	1975	16,000	AstroTurf
Illinois	Memorial	Big Ten	1923	69,249	AstroPlay (01)
Indiana	Memorial	Big Ten	1960	52,354	AstroPlay (S03)
Iowa	Kinnick	Big Ten	1929	70,397	PAT (97)
Iowa St.	Cyclone-Jack Trice	Big 12-N	1975	43,000	Grass (S96)
Kansas	Memorial	Big 12-N	1921	50,250	AstroPlay (00)
Kansas St.	K S U-Wagner Field	Big 12-N	1968	51,000	FieldTurf (02)
Kent St.	Dix	Mid-American-E	1969	30,520	AstroTurf (S97)
Kentucky	Commonwealth	Southeastern-E	1973	67,530	Grass
La.-Lafayette	Cajun Field	Sun Belt	1971	31,000	Grass
La.-Monroe	Malone	Sun Belt	1978	30,427	Grass
LSU	Tiger	Southeastern-W	1924	91,600	Grass
Louisiana Tech	Joe Aillet	Western Athletic	1968	30,600	Grass
Louisville	Papa John's Cardinal	Big East	1998	42,000	FieldTurf (03)
Marshall	Marshall University	Conference USA	1991	38,019	PolyTurf
Maryland	Byrd/Chevy Chase Bank Field	Atlantic Coast	1950	48,055	FieldTurf (01)
Memphis	^Liberty Bowl	Conference USA	1965	62,380	Grass (87)
Miami (Fla.)	^Orange Bowl	Atlantic Coast	1935	72,319	PAT (94)
Miami (Ohio)	Fred C. Yager	Mid-American-E	1983	30,012	FieldTurf (S03)
Michigan	Michigan	Big Ten	1927	107,501	FieldTurf (03)
Michigan St.	Spartan	Big Ten	1957	72,027	Grass (02)
Middle Tenn.	Floyd/Jones Field	Sun Belt	1998	31,000	AstroTurf
Minnesota	^#Metrodome	Big Ten	1982	63,669	AstroTurf-8
Mississippi	Vaught-Hemingway	Southeastern-W	1941	60,580	Grass
Mississippi St.	Davis Wade at Scott Field	Southeastern-W	1914	55,082	PAT (86)
Missouri	Memorial/Faurot Field	Big 12-N	1926	68,349	FieldTurf (S03)
Navy	Navy-Marine Corps	Independent	1959	34,000	FieldTurf
Nebraska	Memorial/Osborne Field	Big 12-N	1923	81,067	FieldTurf (99)
Nevada	Mackay	Western Athletic	1967	31,545	FieldTurf (S00)
UNLV	^Sam Boyd	Mountain West	1971	36,800	Grass (S99)
New Mexico	University	Mountain West	1960	37,370	Grass
New Mexico St.	Aggie Memorial	Western Athletic	1978	30,343	Grass
North Carolina	Kenan Memorial	Atlantic Coast	1927	60,000	Grass
North Carolina St.	^Carter-Finley	Atlantic Coast	1966	51,500	Grass
North Texas	Fouts Field	Sun Belt	1952	30,500	All-Pro Turf
Northern Ill.	Huskie	Mid-American-W	1965	31,000	FieldTurf (01)
Northwestern	Ryan Field	Big Ten	1926	47,129	Grass (S97)
Notre Dame	Notre Dame	Independent	1930	80,795	Grass
Ohio	Peden	Mid-American-E	1929	24,000	FieldTurf (S02)
Ohio St.	Ohio	Big Ten	1922	101,568	FieldTurf (07)
Oklahoma	Memorial	Big 12-S	1923	72,765	Grass (S94)

School	Stadium	Conference	Year Built	Cap.	Surface* (Year)
Oklahoma St.	Boone Pickens	Big 12-S	1920	48,500	Football Pro (05)
Oregon	Autzen	Pacific-10	1967	41,698	FieldTurf (02)
Oregon St.	Reser	Pacific-10	1953	35,362	FieldTurf (01)
Penn St.	Beaver	Big Ten	1960	107,282	Grass
Pittsburgh	Heinz Field	Big East	2001	65,000	Grass
Purdue	Ross-Ade	Big Ten	1924	62,500	PAT (75)
Rice	Rice	Conference USA	1950	70,000	AstroTurf-12 (97)
Rutgers	Rutgers	Big East	1994	41,500	Grass
San Diego St.	^Qualcomm	Mountain West	1967	51,000	FieldTurf (03)
San Jose St.	Spartan	Western Athletic	1933	31,218	Grass
South Carolina	Williams-Brice	Southeastern-E	1934	80,250	Grass
South Fla.	^Raymond James	Big East	1998	41,441	Grass
Southern California	^L.A. Memorial Coliseum	Pacific-10	1923	92,000	Grass
SMU	Gerald J. Ford	Conference USA	2000	32,000	Grass
Southern Miss.	Roberts	Conference USA	1976	33,000	Grass
Stanford	Stanford	Pacific-10	1921	85,500	Grass
Syracuse	#Carrier Dome	Big East	1980	49,550	AstroTurf
Temple	Lincoln Financial Field	Independent	2003	68,532	Grass
Tennessee	Neyland	Southeastern-E	1921	102,038	Grass (S94)
Texas	Royal-Memorial	Big 12-S	1924	80,082	PAT (S99)
UTEP	^Sun Bowl	Conference USA	1963	52,000	AstroTurf (97)
Texas A&M	Kyle Field	Big 12-S	1925	82,600	Grass (S96)
TCU	Amon G. Carter	Mountain West	1929	44,008	FieldTurf (S04)
Texas Tech	Jones	Big 12-S	1947	50,500	AstroTurf-8 (88)
Toledo	Glass Bowl	Mid-American-W	1937	26,248	NexTurf (01)
Troy	Movie Gallery Veterans	Sun Belt	1950	30,000	AstroPlay (S03)
Tulane	^#Superdome	Conference USA	1975	69,767	AstroTurf (95)
Tulsa	Skelly	Conference USA	1930	40,385	FieldTurf (00)
UCLA	^Rose Bowl	Pacific-10	1922	95,000	Grass
Utah	Rice-Eccles	Mountain West	1927	45,634	FieldTurf (S02)
Utah St.	E.L. Romney	Western Athletic	1968	30,257	Grass
Vanderbilt	Vanderbilt	Southeastern-E	1981	41,600	Grass (S99)
Virginia	Scott/Harrison Field	Atlantic Coast	1931	61,500	PAT (S95)
Virginia Tech	Lane	Atlantic Coast	1965	65,115	Grass
Wake Forest	Groves	Atlantic Coast	1968	31,500	Grass
Washington	Husky	Pacific-10	1920	72,500	FieldTurf (00)
Washington St.	Clarence D. Martin	Pacific-10	1972	37,600	FieldTurf (00)
West Virginia	Mountaineer Field	Big East	1980	63,500	AstroTurf-12 (97)
Western Mich.	Waldo	Mid-American-W	1939	30,200	NexTurf (01)
Wisconsin	Camp Randall	Big Ten	1917	80,321	FieldTurf (S03)
Wyoming	War Memorial	Mountain West	1950	33,500	Grass

^Not located on campus. #Indoor facility.

Surface Notes: **This column indicates the type of surface (either artificial or natural grass) present this year in the stadium. The brand name of the artificial turf, if known, is listed as well as the year the last installation occurred. The "S" preceding the year indicates that the school has switched either from natural grass to artificial turf or vice-versa. Legend:* ***Turf****—Any of several types of artificial turfs (name brands include AstroTurf, All-Pro, Omni-Turf, SuperTurf, FieldTurf, etc.);* ***Grass****—Natural grass surface;* ***PAT****—Prescription Athletic Turf (a "natural-artificial" surface featuring a network of pipes connected to pumps capable of sucking water from the natural turf or watering it. The pipes are located 18 inches from the surface and covered with a mixture of sand and filler. The turf also is lined with heating coils to keep it from freezing in temperatures below 32 degrees).* ***SportGrass****—Combines natural grass with a below-the-surface system of synthetic elements.* ***FieldTurf****—Hybrid fibers made from a polyethlyene blend, treated and tufted into a unique porous surface. The infill is made from graded silica sand and ground rubber, and provides a non-compactible, resilient, natural earth feel. The current trends in college football field surfaces have been to switch back to a natural grass field or to a very safety-minded artificial hybrid surface.*

FBS Stadium Facts: Houston and Tulsa claim to be the first college football teams to play in an indoor stadium (the Astrodome on September 11, 1965). But actually, Utah and West Virginia met December 19, 1964, in the Liberty Bowl in the Atlantic City Convention Hall. Technically, the Astrodome was the first indoor stadium built specially for football and baseball. The first major-college football game ever played on artificial turf was between Houston and Washington State on September 23, 1966.

STADIUMS LISTED BY CAPACITY (TOP 30)

School	Stadium	Capacity
Michigan	Michigan	107,501
Penn St.	Beaver	107,282
Tennessee	Neyland	102,038
Ohio St.	Ohio	101,568
UCLA	^Rose Bowl	95,000
Georgia	Sanford	92,058
Southern California	L.A. Memorial Coliseum	92,000
LSU	Tiger	91,600
Auburn	Jordan-Hare	87,451
Stanford	Stanford	85,500
Alabama	Bryant-Denny	83,818
UAB	^Legion Field	83,091
Florida	Florida Field	83,000
Texas A&M	Kyle Field	82,600
Clemson	Memorial	81,473
Nebraska	Memorial/Osborne Field	81,067
Notre Dame	Notre Dame	80,795
Wisconsin	Camp Randall	80,321
South Carolina	Williams-Brice	80,250
Texas	Royal-Memorial	80,082
Florida St.	Doak S. Campbell	80,000
California	Memorial	75,662
Arizona St.	Sun Devil	73,656
Oklahoma	Memorial	72,765
Washington	Husky	72,500
Miami (Fla.)	^Orange Bowl	72,319
Michigan St.	Spartan	72,027
Arkansas	Razorback	72,000
Iowa	Kinnick	70,397
UCF	^Florida Citrus	70,188

^Not located on campus.

Major-College Statistics Trends†

(Average Per Game, One Team)

	Rushing			Passing					Total Offense			Scoring		
Year	**Plays**	**Yds.**	**Avg.**	**Att.**	**Cmp.**	**Pct.**	**Yds.**	**Av. Att.**	**Plays**	**Yds.**	**Avg.**	**TD**	**FG**	**Pts.**
1937	-	133.8	-	13.0	5.0	.381	64.5	4.96	-	198.4	-	-	-	10.1
1938	40.8	140.1	3.43	14.0	5.2	.371	70.1	5.01	54.8	210.2	3.85	1.75	0.06	11.8
1939	40.8	135.9	3.33	13.8	5.2	.374	66.4	4.81	54.6	202.3	3.70	1.66	0.09	11.4
1940	41.9	140.5	3.35	14.8	5.8	.386	77.8	5.26	56.7	218.5	3.85	1.97	0.08	13.3
1941	42.2	141.2	3.35	15.0	5.9	.392	80.7	5.38	57.2	221.8	3.88	2.03	0.06	13.8
1946	42.3	152.4	3.60	15.5	6.1	.389	88.2	5.69	57.8	240.7	4.16	2.39	0.04	16.1
1947	42.3	158.7	3.75	15.3	6.3	.414	90.3	5.91	57.6	248.8	4.32	2.37	0.04	15.9
1948	43.7	162.2	3.71	15.9	6.7	.423	94.6	5.95	59.5	256.5	4.31	2.52	0.05	17.1
1949	47.2	180.6	3.83	17.7	7.6	.431	110.4	6.24	64.9	290.7	4.48	2.86	0.04	19.4
1950	47.0	180.2	3.83	17.5	7.7	.438	108.5	6.19	64.5	288.6	4.47	2.79	0.04	18.9
1951	48.6	182.5	3.76	18.9	8.4	.446	113.7	6.02	67.5	296.1	4.39	2.86	0.05	19.4
1952	48.3	176.4	3.65	18.4	8.1	.441	111.9	6.09	66.7	288.2	4.32	2.68	0.07	18.4
1953	45.1	176.6	3.92	15.2	6.5	.428	91.7	6.03	60.3	268.2	4.45	2.54	0.05	17.1
1954	45.5	184.1	*4.05	14.9	6.5	.437	91.1	6.14	60.3	225.1	4.56	2.59	0.05	17.4
1955	46.1	176.7	3.83	13.6	5.9	.435	84.7	6.24	59.6	261.3	4.38	2.37	0.05	16.1
1956	49.2	193.1	3.93	14.1	6.2	.437	85.9	6.09	63.3	279.0	4.41	2.45	0.05	16.5
1957	49.3	177.5	3.60	14.4	6.4	.444	85.5	5.94	63.6	263.0	4.14	2.31	0.06	15.6
1958	47.1	170.7	3.62	16.1	7.4	.458	97.7	6.06	63.2	268.4	4.24	2.31	0.09	16.0
1959	46.2	166.0	3.59	16.5	7.5	.451	98.5	5.96	62.7	264.5	4.21	2.25	0.17	15.9
1960	45.3	169.9	3.75	15.8	7.2	.454	93.6	5.94	61.1	263.4	4.31	2.19	0.19	15.6
1961	45.6	166.7	3.66	15.9	7.2	.448	94.7	5.95	61.5	261.4	4.25	2.23	0.23	16.0
1962	45.3	164.0	3.63	17.2	8.0	.463	105.0	6.10	62.5	269.0	4.31	2.30	0.21	16.4
1963	44.1	160.0	3.63	17.6	8.1	.461	105.3	5.98	61.7	265.3	4.30	2.19	0.27	15.8
1964	43.7	149.7	3.43	17.9	8.5	.472	110.0	6.14	61.6	259.6	4.21	2.07	0.29	15.1
1965	45.1	149.4	3.31	20.8	9.7	.464	123.2	5.93	65.9	272.5	4.14	2.26	0.42	16.7
1966	44.3	148.7	3.36	22.0	10.3	.470	133.2	6.07	66.2	281.8	4.26	2.35	0.42	17.5
1967	47.3	154.7	3.27	22.9	10.7	.467	139.8	6.10	70.2	294.5	4.19	2.48	0.46	18.4
1968	49.7	170.8	3.44	25.4	12.1	.474	157.7	6.22	*75.1	328.5	4.38	2.89	0.46	21.2
1969	49.5	171.8	3.47	25.5	12.0	.471	157.1	6.17	74.9	328.9	4.39	2.90	0.54	21.6
1970	49.3	175.7	3.57	25.0	11.7	.467	152.7	6.12	74.2	328.3	4.42	2.83	0.57	21.3
1971	49.7	182.2	3.67	21.7	10.1	.463	132.3	6.10	71.3	314.5	4.41	2.69	0.54	20.2
1972	49.8	184.5	3.70	22.0	10.2	.462	136.9	6.24	71.8	321.4	4.48	2.71	0.61	20.6
1973	50.1	192.8	3.85	20.4	9.6	.472	130.9	6.41	70.5	323.6	4.59	2.75	0.65	21.0
1974	51.8	201.8	3.89	18.8	8.9	.474	122.3	6.50	70.7	324.1	4.59	2.64	0.63	20.2
1975	*51.9	*204.5	3.94	18.4	8.7	.473	119.6	6.52	70.3	324.1	4.61	2.57	0.74	20.1
1976	51.4	198.8	3.87	19.1	9.1	.474	123.5	6.49	70.4	322.2	4.58	2.57	0.75	20.0
1977	51.3	194.6	3.80	20.2	9.8	.483	134.5	6.67	71.5	329.1	4.61	2.67	0.73	20.8
1978	50.9	192.6	3.79	21.2	10.3	.486	138.9	6.55	72.1	331.5	4.60	2.64	0.76	20.6
1979	49.1	187.9	3.83	21.6	10.6	.491	139.3	6.47	70.6	327.2	4.63	2.55	0.77	20.0
1980	47.7	178.3	3.74	23.3	11.6	.500	151.9	6.52	71.0	330.2	4.65	2.61	0.81	20.5
1981	46.3	169.4	3.66	25.3	12.7	.502	164.7	6.51	71.6	334.1	4.67	2.57	0.87	20.5
1982	45.1	169.3	3.75	27.6	14.5	.522	182.4	6.61	72.7	351.7	4.84	2.71	1.02	21.9

Year	Rushing Plays	Rushing Yds.	Rushing Avg.	Passing Att.	Passing Cmp.	Passing Pct.	Passing Yds.	Passing Av. Att.	Total Offense Plays	Total Offense Yds.	Total Offense Avg.	Scoring TD	Scoring FG	Scoring Pts.
1983	44.6	169.5	3.80	27.0	14.4	.536	182.8	6.79	71.6	352.3	4.92	2.73	1.06	22.1
1984	44.7	168.1	3.76	26.8	14.1	.527	181.1	6.77	71.5	349.2	4.89	2.66	1.15	22.1
1985	44.6	169.2	3.80	27.3	14.7	.537	186.1	6.82	71.8	355.3	4.95	2.74	1.09	22.4
1986	44.2	167.9	3.80	27.2	14.6	.537	185.1	6.81	71.4	353.0	4.95	2.80	1.07	22.7
1987	44.4	174.2	3.92	27.1	14.2	.526	183.6	6.78	71.5	357.8	5.01	2.83	1.13	23.1
1988	44.0	174.6	3.97	27.1	14.3	.529	185.8	6.87	71.1	360.3	5.07	2.91	*1.16	23.8
1989	42.7	166.4	3.90	28.5	15.4	.540	200.9	7.05	71.2	367.3	5.16	2.97	1.13	24.1
1990	43.1	167.7	3.90	28.3	15.1	.534	197.2	6.96	71.4	364.8	5.11	3.04	1.08	24.4
1991	43.3	169.7	3.91	27.2	14.6	.535	189.6	6.98	70.5	359.4	5.10	2.95	0.89	23.1
1992	42.7	165.6	3.89	28.1	14.9	.530	190.5	6.77	70.8	356.1	5.03	2.84	1.04	22.9
1993	41.8	166.3	3.98	28.7	15.9	.551	204.9	7.13	70.5	371.2	5.27	3.09	0.97	24.4
1994	41.8	166.8	3.99	28.5	15.6	.547	198.3	6.96	70.3	365.1	5.19	3.11	0.99	24.6
1995	41.5	167.3	4.03	29.7	16.3	.547	205.5	6.92	71.2	372.8	5.24	3.21	0.93	25.1
1996	41.5	164.4	3.97	28.9	15.4	.533	202.0	6.99	70.4	366.3	5.21	3.26	0.94	25.5
1997	40.2	158.7	3.94	29.2	15.8	.543	207.6	7.12	69.4	366.3	5.28	3.25	0.97	25.5
1998	40.7	158.6	3.89	29.1	15.7	.540	209.5	*7.19	69.9	368.1	5.27	3.20	1.05	25.5
1999	39.8	152.8	3.83	30.6	16.7	.544	212.5	6.94	70.4	365.3	5.18	3.23	1.05	25.6
2000	39.5	154.0	3.90	31.5	17.0	.541	216.2	6.88	71.0	370.2	5.22	3.33	1.01	26.2
2001	39.8	158.9	3.99	31.6	17.6	.556	222.7	7.04	71.4	381.6	5.34	*3.47	1.01	27.2
2002	39.5	158.3	4.01	31.1	17.3	.554	217.5	6.98	70.6	375.8	5.32	3.46	1.07	*27.3
2003	39.6	158.7	4.01	31.4	17.8	.568	223.9	7.13	71.0	*382.6	5.39	3.40	1.06	26.9
2004	39.3	159.1	*4.05	30.9	17.6	.568	217.5	7.03	70.2	376.6	5.36	3.36	1.06	26.6
2005	38.6	155.2	4.03	*32.0	*18.5	.579	*224.6	7.01	70.6	379.8	5.39	3.36	1.11	26.8
2006	34.9	140.1	4.02	29.2	17.0	*.584	206.8	7.09	64.0	346.9	*5.42	3.07	1.00	24.4

**Record. †Records not compiled in 1942-45 except for Scoring Points Per Game: 1942 (15.7); 1943 (15.7); 1944 (16.3); 1945 (16.1).*

Additional Major-College Statistics Trends†

Rules changes and statistics changes affecting trends: PUNTING—Beginning in 1965, 20 yards not deducted from a punt into the end zone for a touchback. INTERCEPTIONS—Interception yards not compiled, 1958-65. KICKOFF RETURNS—During 1937-45, if a kickoff went out of bounds, the receiving team put the ball in play on its 35-yard line instead of a second kickoff; in 1984 (rescinded in 1985), a 30-yard-line touchback for kickoffs crossing the goal line in flight and first touching the ground out of the end zone; in 1986, kickoffs from the 35-yard line. PUNT RETURNS—In 1967, interior linemen restricted from leaving until the ball is kicked.

(Average Per Game, One Team)

Year	Punting No.	Punting Avg.	Punting Net Avg.	Interceptions No.	Interceptions Avg. Ret.	Interceptions Yds.	Punt Returns No.	Punt Returns Avg. Ret.	Punt Returns Yds.	Kickoff Returns No.	Kickoff Returns Avg. Ret.	Kickoff Returns Yds.
1937	9.2	36.3	-	1.68	-	-	-	-	-	-	-	-
1938	9.3	37.2	-	1.70	9.19	15.8	-	-	-	-	-	-
1939	*9.4	36.7	-	1.67	9.84	16.5	*4.42	9.40	41.6	2.14	19.3	41.3
1940	9.1	36.6	-	1.79	10.05	18.0	4.21	10.58	44.5	2.32	20.4	47.5
1941	8.9	36.1	-	*1.81	11.28	20.4	4.27	11.10	*47.4	2.41	20.2	48.6
1946	7.3	35.7	-	1.75	11.79	20.6	3.70	11.32	41.9	3.01	18.9	56.9
1947	6.7	36.4	30.3	1.61	11.93	19.2	3.47	11.73	40.7	3.04	18.9	57.3
1948	6.3	36.3	30.2	1.60	12.59	20.2	3.09	*12.16	37.6	3.17	18.5	58.6
1949	6.3	36.6	30.3	1.69	13.23	*22.3	3.21	12.13	38.9	3.51	17.9	62.8
1950	6.0	36.3	30.8	1.61	11.99	19.3	3.04	10.72	32.6	3.46	16.6	57.4
1951	6.4	35.9	30.7	1.67	12.00	20.1	3.10	10.58	32.8	3.53	17.0	59.9
1952	6.3	36.4	31.6	1.60	11.60	18.5	3.07	9.95	30.5	3.45	17.6	60.7
1953	5.2	34.9	29.7	1.37	12.12	16.6	2.57	10.66	27.4	3.27	17.8	58.2
1954	4.9	34.9	29.4	1.36	12.48	16.9	2.42	11.16	27.0	3.32	18.4	61.0
1955	4.9	34.9	29.8	1.26	12.96	16.8	2.39	10.54	25.2	3.09	18.5	57.2
1956	5.0	35.1	30.1	1.29	12.86	16.6	2.49	10.07	25.1	3.19	18.0	57.4
1957	5.3	34.8	30.2	1.26	11.95	15.0	2.53	9.57	24.2	3.05	18.7	57.1
1958	5.6	35.4	30.9	1.33	-	-	2.57	9.70	24.9	3.02	18.9	57.0
1959	5.5	35.9	31.5	1.33	-	-	2.67	9.06	24.2	3.09	18.7	57.8
1960	5.1	36.0	31.4	1.24	-	-	2.39	9.73	23.3	3.05	18.8	57.3
1961	5.2	35.5	35.5	1.22	-	-	2.43	9.44	22.9	3.06	18.3	56.1
1962	5.2	35.7	35.7	1.25	-	-	2.36	9.66	22.8	3.10	19.6	60.7
1963	5.2	36.3	32.5	1.19	-	-	2.34	9.71	22.7	3.08	20.1	61.9
1964	5.3	36.4	32.5	1.20	-	-	2.33	8.99	20.9	2.93	19.6	57.3
1965	5.9	38.5	38.5	1.42	-	-	2.73	9.99	27.3	3.15	18.8	59.3
1966	5.9	37.5	33.5	1.50	12.07	18.1	2.63	8.82	23.2	3.24	18.7	60.8
1967	6.5	36.8	31.6	1.52	11.39	17.3	3.42	9.92	33.9	3.31	18.7	61.7
1968	6.7	37.4	33.3	1.61	11.51	18.6	3.01	8.95	26.9	3.64	19.1	69.6
1969	6.6	37.5	33.4	1.70	11.07	18.8	3.00	9.00	27.0	3.67	18.9	69.4
1970	6.3	37.4	37.4	1.66	11.65	19.4	2.89	9.28	26.9	3.69	19.0	70.1
1971	6.2	37.6	33.4	1.49	11.75	17.5	2.89	9.04	26.2	3.57	19.2	68.6
1972	6.1	37.2	33.4	1.54	11.54	17.7	2.72	8.61	23.4	3.50	19.0	66.4
1973	5.8	37.8	34.1	1.36	11.30	15.4	2.52	8.65	21.8	3.54	19.6	69.2
1974	5.6	37.6	34.2	1.23	11.30	13.9	2.40	7.92	19.0	3.38	19.1	64.3
1975	5.4	38.1	35.0	1.21	11.26	13.6	2.39	7.19	17.2	3.20	19.3	61.7
1976	5.7	38.0	35.1	1.23	11.44	14.0	2.42	6.83	16.5	3.14	18.3	57.4
1977	5.8	38.0	35.0	1.26	11.05	13.9	2.45	7.10	17.3	3.16	18.4	58.1
1978	6.0	38.0	34.9	1.34	10.83	14.5	2.51	7.39	18.6	3.18	18.7	59.6
1979	5.8	37.7	34.8	1.31	10.66	14.0	2.38	7.09	16.9	3.02	18.8	56.9
1980	5.8	38.3	35.4	1.37	10.85	14.9	2.44	7.01	17.1	2.91	19.0	55.1
1981	6.0	38.9	35.9	1.38	10.22	14.1	2.45	7.22	17.7	2.86	18.8	53.9
1982	5.9	39.8	*36.5	1.39	10.70	14.9	2.40	8.00	19.2	2.69	19.3	51.9
1983	5.5	39.5	35.9	1.37	10.43	14.3	2.47	7.95	19.7	2.65	19.2	50.8
1984	5.6	39.7	36.3	1.31	10.07	13.2	2.47	7.61	18.8	3.03	18.6	56.2
1985	5.5	39.6	36.1	1.30	10.47	13.6	2.45	7.92	19.4	2.94	19.4	57.0

Year	Punting No.	Punting Avg.	Punting Net Avg.	Interceptions No.	Interceptions Avg. Ret.	Interceptions Yds.	Punt Returns No.	Punt Returns Avg. Ret.	Punt Returns Yds.	Kickoff Returns No.	Kickoff Returns Avg. Ret.	Kickoff Returns Yds.
1986	5.4	39.2	35.4	1.30	10.99	14.3	2.51	8.23	20.7	3.78	19.8	74.6
1987	5.4	38.6	34.7	1.32	10.82	14.3	2.48	8.31	20.6	3.89	19.1	74.5
1988	5.2	38.4	34.7	1.24	11.17	14.0	2.39	7.96	19.1	*3.97	19.4	77.1
1989	5.2	38.5	34.3	1.28	10.75	13.8	2.36	8.46	20.0	3.92	19.7	*77.2
1990	5.3	38.6	34.3	1.23	11.40	14.0	2.45	9.33	22.9	3.79	19.6	74.5
1991	5.3	38.4	34.3	1.18	11.30	13.3	2.50	8.74	21.9	3.43	19.4	66.6
1992	5.6	39.0	34.9	1.20	11.00	13.2	2.63	9.04	23.8	3.30	20.1	66.4
1993	5.2	38.8	35.1	1.14	11.00	12.5	2.28	8.28	18.9	3.43	20.0	68.7
1994	5.3	39.2	35.3	1.10	12.10	13.3	2.38	8.64	20.5	3.50	20.0	69.8
1995	5.3	38.7	34.9	1.12	11.67	13.1	2.23	8.98	20.0	3.57	19.5	69.7
1996	5.5	40.0	35.8	1.04	12.83	13.4	2.39	9.56	22.8	3.34	20.4	68.0
1997	5.4	*40.5	36.2	1.05	12.45	13.0	2.47	9.49	23.4	3.47	20.3	70.5
1998	5.5	39.8	35.5	1.05	12.80	13.4	2.53	9.45	23.9	3.52	20.6	72.4
1999	5.6	39.8	35.3	1.12	13.00	14.5	2.61	9.61	25.1	3.36	20.3	68.2
2000	5.6	39.0	34.2	1.12	*13.55	15.2	2.64	10.15	26.8	3.49	19.6	68.6
2001	5.3	39.8	35.0	1.12	12.66	14.2	2.59	9.84	25.4	3.43	20.7	71.0
2002	5.2	39.5	34.2	1.10	12.61	13.8	2.73	10.59	28.9	3.47	20.2	70.4
2003	5.3	40.4	34.7	1.06	12.69	13.4	2.67	9.84	26.3	3.30	20.6	67.8
2004	5.3	39.9	35.5	1.04	13.29	13.9	2.45	9.95	24.4	3.34	20.4	68.1
2005	5.2	39.9	^33.7	1.04	12.37	12.9	2.33	9.81	22.8	3.30	*20.8	68.6
2006	4.6	39.9	34.3	0.98	13.03	13.2	2.0	9.28	18.4	3.1	20.5	64.0

Record. †Records not compiled in 1942-45. ^Starting in 2005, touchbacks were included in net punting.

Field Goal Trends (1938-68)

Year	Made	Year	Made	Year	Made	Atts.	Pct.
1938	47	1951	53	1961	277		
1939	80	1952	83	1962	261		
1940	84	1953	50	1963	314		
1941	59	1954	48	1964	368		
1942-45	*	1955	57	1965	484	1,035	.468
1946	44	1956	53	1966	522	1,125	.464
1947	38	1957	64	1967	555	1,266	.438
1948	53	1958	103	1968	566	1,287	.440
1949	46	1959	†199				
1950	46	1960	224				

*Records not compiled. †Goal uprights widened from 18 feet, 6 inches to 23 feet, 4 inches in 1959.

Field Goal Trends (From 1969)

(Includes Field Goal Attempts by FCS, Divisions II and III Opponents)

Year	Totals Made	Totals Atts.	Totals Pct.	16-39	Pct.	16-49	Pct.	40-49	Pct.	50-59	Pct.	60 Plus
1969	669	1,402	.477	538-872	.617	654-1,267	.516	116-395	.294	15-135	.111	0-8
1970	754	1,548	.487	614-990	.620	740-1,380	.536	126-390	.323	14-168	.083	1-9
1971	780	1,625	.480	607-1,022	.594	760-1,466	.518	153-444	.345	20-159	.126	0-11
1972	876	1,828	.479	705-1,150	.613	855-1,641	.521	150-491	.305	21-187	.112	1-12
1973	958	1,920	.499	728-1,139	.639	914-1,670	.547	186-531	.350	44-250	.176	1-21
1974	947	1,905	.497	706-1,096	.644	906-1,655	.547	200-559	.358	41-250	.164	1-17
1975	1,164	2,237	.520	849-1,255	.676	1,088-1,896	.574	239-641	.373	76-341	.223	4-32
1976	1,187	2,330	.509	854-1,301	.656	1,131-1,997	.566	277-696	.398	56-333	.168	3-24
1977	1,238	2,514	.492	882-1,315	.671	1,160-2,088	.556	278-773	.360	78-426	.183	6-40
1978	1,229	2,113	.582	938-1,361	.689	1,193-1,982	.602	255-621	.411	36-131	.275	1-4

Year	Made	Atts.	Pct.	Under 20	Pct.	20-29	Pct.	30-39	Pct.	40-49	Pct.	50-59	Pct.	60 Plus	Pct.
1979	1,241	2,129	.583	34-43	.791	455-601	.757	425-706	.602	286-600	.477	41-173	.237	0-6	.000
1980	1,245	2,128	.585	31-39	.795	408-529	.771	452-696	.649	317-682	.465	37-175	.211	0-7	.000
1981	1,368	2,254	.607	42-48	.875	471-598	.788	461-731	.631	335-698	.480	58-169	.343	1-10	.100
1982	1,224	1,915	.639	31-34	.912	384-475	.808	415-597	.695	319-604	.528	73-190	.384	2-15	.133
1983	1,329	2,025	.656	34-37	.919	417-508	.821	477-636	.750	329-628	.524	72-201	.358	0-15	.000
1984	1,442	2,112	.683	44-49	.898	450-532	.846	503-681	.739	363-630	.576	80-206	.388	2-14	.143
1985	1,360	2,106	.646	40-47	.851	416-511	.814	478-657	.728	341-647	.527	84-227	.370	1-17	.059
1986	1,326	2,034	.652	45-48	.938	445-525	.848	448-641	.699	340-629	.541	44-182	.242	4-9	.444
1987	1,381	2,058	.671	45-48	.938	484-559	.866	469-638	.735	311-604	.515	72-200	.360	0-9	.000
1988	1,421	2,110	.673	33-35	.943	487-573	.850	495-664	.745	337-610	.552	68-217	.313	1-11	.091
1989#	1,389	2,006	.692	50-53	.943	497-565	.880	471-655	.719	319-573	.557	52-154	.338	0-6	.000
1990	1,348	2,011	.670	39-42	.929	477-546	.874	454-626	.725	319-625	.510	59-167	.353	0-5	.000
1991$	1,092	1,831	.596	31-32	.969	395-519	.761	366-612	.598	254-531	.478	45-132	.341	1-5	.200
1992	1,288	1,986	.649	32-38	.842	464-569	.815	447-673	.664	294-577	.510	49-126	.389	2-3	.667
1993§	1,182	1,832	.645	23-25	.920	490-599	.818	407-617	.660	224-488	.459	38-98	.388	0-5	.000
1994	1,220	1,877	.650	39-40	.975	458-528	.867	419-626	.669	263-547	.481	40-128	.313	1-8	.125
1995	1,150	1,759	.654	32-32	1.000	468-549	.852	373-587	.635	244-489	.499	31-100	.310	2-2	1.000
1996	1,207	1,899	.636	28-29	.966	431-509	.847	422-632	.668	277-581	.477	49-147	.333	0-1	.000
1997	1,255	1,895	.662	47-48	.979	445-524	.849	446-659	.677	272-540	.504	45-122	.369	0-2	.000
1998	1,376	2,075	.663	50-60	.833	475-563	.844	466-681	.684	336-622	.540	48-144	.333	1-5	.200
1999	1,387	2,074	.669	36-38	.947	499-608	.821	480-671	.715	321-611	.525	50-142	.352	1-4	.250
2000	1,285	1,906	.674	29-32	.906	442-517	.855	469-667	.703	297-539	.551	48-149	.322	0-2	.000
2001	1,302	1,941	.671	34-37	.919	459-530	.866	458-655	.699	306-572	.535	45-143	.315	0-4	.000
2002	*1,580	*2,355	.671	55-63	.873	541-637	.849	546-789	.692	389-717	.543	49-143	.343	0-6	.000
2003	1,560	2,260	.690	53-58	.914	552-650	.849	540-768	.703	359-608	.590	56-169	.331	0-7	.000

Year	Totals Made	Atts.	Pct.	Breakdown by Distances Under 20		20-29		30-39		40-49		50-59		60 Plus	
2004	1,435	2,131	.673	48-54	.889	460-538	.855	461-649	.710	422-752	.561	43-133	.323	1-5	.200
2005	1,525	2,209	.690	42-43	.977	572-666	.859	514-726	.708	346-647	.535	51-127	.402	0-0	.000
2006	1,500	2,127	*.705	47-50	.940	540-617	.875	535-748	.715	314-559	.562	64-149	.430	0-4	.000

**Record. #First year after kicking tee became illegal. $First year after goal-post width narrowed back to 18′6″ from 23′4″. §First year after hash marks narrowed to 60 feet from each sideline.*

Field Goal Trends by Soccer-Style and Conventional Kickers

(FBS Kickers Only)

(Pete Gogolak of Cornell was documented as the first soccer-style kicker in college football history. The Hungarian-born kicker played at Cornell from 1961 through 1963. He set a national major-college record of 44 consecutive extra-point conversions and finished 54 of 55 for his career. His younger brother, Charley, also a soccer-styler, kicked at Princeton from 1963 through 1965.)

SOCCER-STYLE

Year	†No.	Totals Made	Atts.	Pct.	Breakdown by Distances 16-39	Pct.	16-49	Pct.	40-49	Pct.	50-59	Pct.	60 Plus
1975	70	528	1,012	.522	370-540	.685	479-816	.587	109-276	.395	49-196	.250	1-17
1976	84	517	1,019	.507	350-517	.677	477-831	.574	127-314	.404	40-188	.213	3-16
1977	96	665	1,317	.505	450-649	.693	615-1,047	.587	165-398	.415	50-270	.185	2-27
1978	98	731	1,244	.588	540-768	.703	703-1,148	.612	163-380	.429	28-96	.292	1-3

Year	†No.	Made	Atts.	Pct.	Under 20	20-29	30-39	40-49	50-59	60 Plus
1979	116	839	1,413	.594	23-28	288-380	282-455	214-419	32-126	0-5
1980	121	988	1,657	.596	26-32	327-416	342-522	261-540	32-147	0-5
1981	138	1,108	1,787	.620	32-36	377-476	376-576	279-551	43-142	1-6
1982	105	1,026	1,548	.663	26-27	317-375	346-482	273-495	62-156	2-13
1983	110	1,139	1,724	.661	29-31	345-416	403-541	294-543	68-179	0-14
1984	127	1,316	1,898	.694	43-47	414-480	438-589	341-572	78-197	2-13
1985	133	1,198	1,838	.652	35-41	369-452	415-578	306-560	72-191	1-16
1986	128	1,201	1,829	.657	37-40	398-467	410-575	313-576	39-162	4-9
1987	122	1,275	1,892	.674	40-43	458-523	424-574	290-566	63-177	0-9
1988	140	1,317	1,947	.676	31-33	445-521	468-630	311-562	61-201	1-11
1989	138	1,313	1,897	.692	49-52	462-526	441-612	310-551	51-150	0-6
1990	135	1,282	1,890	.678	36-38	450-515	432-589	308-590	56-154	0-4
1991	132	1,048	1,763	.594	30-31	381-500	349-589	243-512	44-130	1-1
1992	135	1,244	1,926	.646	31-37	447-554	429-647	288-561	47-124	2-3
1993	132	1,153	1,776	.649	23-25	475-578	398-600	219-475	38-93	0-5
1994	138	1,203	1,856	.648	38-39	452-522	410-617	263-543	39-127	1-8
1995	148	1,150	1,759	.654	32-32	468-549	373-587	244-489	31-100	2-2
1996	149	1,207	1,899	.636	28-29	431-509	422-632	277-581	49-147	0-1
1997	146	1,255	1,895	.662	47-48	445-524	446-659	272-540	45-122	0-2
1998	149	1,376	2,075	.663	50-60	475-563	466-681	336-622	48-144	1-5
1999	153	1,387	2,074	.669	36-38	499-608	480-671	321-611	50-142	1-4
2000	147	1,285	1,906	.674	29-32	442-517	469-667	297-539	48-149	0-2
2001	151	1,302	1,941	.671	34-37	459-530	458-655	306-572	45-143	0-4
2002	159	*1,580	*2,355	.671	55-63	541-637	546-789	389-717	49-143	0-6
2003	162	1,560	2,260	.690	53-58	552-650	540-768	359-608	56-169	0-7
2004	169	1,435	2,131	.673	48-54	460-538	461-649	422-752	43-133	1-5
2005	NA	1,525	2,209	.690	42-43	572-666	514-726	346-647	51-127	0-0
2006	NA	1,500	2,127	*.705	47-50	540-617	535-748	314-559	64-149	0-4

CONVENTIONAL

Year	†No.	Totals Made	Atts.	Pct.	Breakdown by Distances 16-39	Pct.	16-49	Pct.	40-49	Pct.	50-59	Pct.	60 Plus
1975	116	564	1,085	.520	427-640	.667	541-959	.564	114-319	.357	23-126	.183	3-13
1976	101	608	1,192	.510	460-720	.639	594-1,065	.558	134-345	.388	14-127	.110	0-7
1977	98	513	1,054	.487	384-586	.655	487-916	.532	103-330	.312	26-138	.188	4-14
1978	86	440	761	.578	352-516	.682	434-729	.595	82-213	.385	6-32	.188	0-0

Year	†No.	Made	Atts.	Pct.	Under 20	20-29	30-39	40-49	50-59	60 Plus
1979	70	333	585	.569	10-14	140-185	111-198	63-150	9-37	0-1
1980	62	258	471	.548	5-7	81-113	110-174	56-142	6-33	0-2
1981	50	195	367	.531	8-9	70-97	69-126	41-112	7-22	0-1
1982	25	103	195	.528	3-4	36-50	34-62	25-59	5-18	0-2
1983	23	112	181	.619	4-5	40-55	46-58	22-50	0-12	0-1
1984	10	44	76	.579	0-1	17-26	20-33	7-15	0-1	0-0
1985	12	81	138	.587	3-4	22-29	29-40	19-44	8-20	0-1
1986	8	58	89	.652	4-4	21-28	17-27	14-24	2-6	0-0
1987	4	35	50	.700	4-4	10-14	14-16	6-9	1-7	0-0
1988	5	26	40	.650	0-0	17-21	5-7	4-10	0-2	0-0
1989	2	37	47	.787	1-1	19-20	12-16	5-9	0-1	0-0
1990	2	23	38	.605	1-1	8-10	8-9	4-13	2-5	0-0
1991	2	16	24	.667	0-0	5-9	6-7	5-7	0-1	0-0
1992	1	12	18	.667	0-0	5-6	6-8	1-4	0-0	0-0
1993	1	6	11	.545	0-0	4-5	2-3	0-3	0-0	0-0
1994	1	17	21	*.810	1-1	6-6	9-9	0-4	1-1	0-0
1995	0	0	0	.000	0-0	0-0	0-0	0-0	0-0	0-0
1996	0	0	0	.000	0-0	0-0	0-0	0-0	0-0	0-0
1997	0	0	0	.000	0-0	0-0	0-0	0-0	0-0	0-0
1998	0	0	0	.000	0-0	0-0	0-0	0-0	0-0	0-0
1999	0	0	0	.000	0-0	0-0	0-0	0-0	0-0	0-0
2000	0	0	0	.000	0-0	0-0	0-0	0-0	0-0	0-0
2001	0	0	0	.000	0-0	0-0	0-0	0-0	0-0	0-0

Year	†No.	Made	Atts.	Pct.	Under 20	20-29	30-39	40-49	50-59	60 Plus
	Totals				Breakdown by Distances					
2002	0	0	0	.000	0-0	0-0	0-0	0-0	0-0	0-0
2003	0	0	0	.000	0-0	0-0	0-0	0-0	0-0	0-0
2004	0	0	0	.000	0-0	0-0	0-0	0-0	0-0	0-0
2005	0	0	0	.000	0-0	0-0	0-0	0-0	0-0	0-0
2006	0	0	0	.000	0-0	0-0	0-0	0-0	0-0	0-0

**Record. †Number of kickers attempting at least one field goal.*

Average Yardage of Field Goals

(FBS Kickers Only)

Year	Soccer-Style Made	Soccer-Style Missed	Soccer-Style Total	Conventional Made	Conventional Missed	Conventional Total	Total Made	Total Missed	Total Total
1975	35.1	43.2	39.0	33.1	41.3	37.0	34.1	42.2	37.9
1976	35.0	43.1	39.0	33.2	40.7	36.9	34.0	41.8	37.9
1977	34.7	44.3	39.5	33.3	41.9	37.7	34.1	43.2	38.7
1978	34.0	39.9	36.4	31.9	38.3	34.6	33.2	39.3	35.7
1979	33.7	39.9	36.2	31.9	38.0	34.5	33.2	39.3	35.7
1980	34.0	40.7	36.7	33.4	39.6	36.2	33.8	40.4	36.6
1981	33.9	40.1	36.2	33.2	38.6	35.7	33.8	39.8	36.1
1982	34.8	41.8	37.2	34.0	39.8	36.7	34.7	41.5	37.1
1983	34.7	42.1	37.2	32.3	40.5	35.5	34.5	41.9	37.0
1984	34.4	41.8	36.7	32.3	34.9	33.4	34.3	41.5	36.5
1985	34.5	41.3	36.8	35.4	41.7	38.0	34.5	41.3	36.9
1986	33.9	41.6	36.6	32.5	38.6	34.7	33.9	41.4	36.5
1987	33.5	41.8	36.2	32.3	41.4	35.1	33.5	41.8	36.2
1988	33.9	41.7	36.4	30.0	37.6	32.7	32.0	39.3	34.4
1989	33.5	41.2	35.9	30.5	39.6	32.4	33.4	41.2	35.8
1990	33.4	41.3	36.0	33.4	42.0	36.7	33.4	41.3	36.0
1991	33.2	40.7	35.8	28.6	31.9	40.7	35.9	40.4	36.1
1992	34.1	41.2	36.7	30.1	37.8	32.7	37.2	41.3	37.8
1993	32.4	38.9	34.7	26.8	38.0	31.9	32.3	38.9	34.6
1994	32.9	40.6	35.6	31.4	45.5	34.0	32.9	40.7	35.6
1995	32.4	40.1	35.0	—	—	—	32.4	40.1	35.0
1996	33.4	40.5	36.0	—	—	—	33.4	40.5	36.0
1997	33.2	40.1	35.5	—	—	—	33.2	40.1	35.5
1998	33.4	40.6	36.1	—	—	—	33.4	40.6	36.1
1999	34.0	40.9	36.8	—	—	—	34.0	40.9	36.8
2000	33.8	40.3	36.2	—	—	—	33.8	40.3	36.2
2001	34.1	40.2	36.4	—	—	—	34.1	40.2	36.4
2002	34.9	40.5	36.6	—	—	—	34.9	40.5	36.6
2003	34.8	40.6	36.7	—	—	—	34.8	40.6	36.7
2004	34.4	40.8	36.8	—	—	—	34.4	40.8	36.8
2005	33.1	39.9	35.2	—	—	—	33.1	39.9	35.2
2006	33.1	39.8	35.1	—	—	—	33.1	39.8	35.1

FBS Extra-Point Trends

(From Start of Two-Point Attempts)

Year	Games	Percent of Total Tries Kick	Percent of Total Tries 2-Pt.	Kick Attempts Atts.	Kick Attempts Made	Kick Attempts Pct.	Two-Point Attempts Atts.	Two-Point Attempts Made	Two-Point Attempts Pct.
1958	578	#.486	*.514	1,295	889	.686	*1,371	*613	.447
1959	578	.598	.402	1,552	1,170	.754	1,045	421	.403
1960	596	.701	.299	1,849	1,448	.783	790	345	.437
1961	574	.723	.277	1,842	1,473	.800	706	312	.442
1962	602	.724	.276	1,987	1,549	.780	757	341	.450
1963	605	.776	.224	2,057	1,659	.807	595	256	.430
1964	613	.814	.186	2,053	1,704	.830	469	189	.403
1965	619	.881	.119	2,460	2,083	.847	331	134	.405
1966	626	.861	.139	2,530	2,167	.857	410	165	.402
1967	611	.869	.131	2,629	2,252	.857	397	160	.403
1968	615	.871	.129	3,090	2,629	.851	456	181	.397
1969	621	.880	.120	3,168	2,781	.878	432	170	.394
1970	667	.862	.138	3,255	2,875	.883	522	246	*.471
1971	726	.889	.111	3,466	3,081	.889	433	173	.400
1972	720	.872	.128	3,390	3,018	.890	497	219	.441
1973	741	.893	.107	3,637	3,258	.896	435	180	.414
1974	749	.885	.115	3,490	3,146	.901	455	211	.464
1975	785	.891	.109	3,598	3,266	.908	440	171	.389
1976	796	.877	.123	3,579	3,241	.906	502	203	.404
1977	849	.891	.109	4,041	3,668	.908	495	209	.422
1978	816	.884	.116	3,808	3,490	.916	498	208	.418
1979	811	.897	.103	3,702	3,418	.923	424	176	.415
1980	810	.895	.105	3,785	3,480	.919	442	170	.384
1981	788	.901	.099	3,655	3,387	.927	403	172	.427
1982	599	.901	.099	2,920	2,761	.946	320	120	.375
1983	631	.896	.104	3,080	2,886	.937	356	151	.424
1984	626	.889	.111	2,962	2,789	.942	370	173	.468
1985	623	.899	.101	3,068	2,911	.949	345	121	#.351
1986	619	.905	.095	3,132	2,999	.958	330	131	.397
1987	615	.892	.108	3,094	2,935	.949	375	163	.435
1988	616	.899	.101	3,215	3,074	.956	363	156	.430
1989	614	.888	.112	3,233	3,090	.956	409	179	.438
1990	623	.911	.089	3,429	3,291	*.960	335	138	.412
1991	617	.906	.094	3,279	3,016	.920	342	128	.374
1992	619	.899	.101	3,156	2,967	.940	353	159	.450
1993	613	.912	.088	3,455	3,251	.941	333	143	.429
1994	617	.897	.103	3,433	3,207	.934	395	163	.413
1995	622	.902	.098	3,594	3,354	.933	389	173	.445
1996	644	.923	.077	3,862	3,630	.940	322	144	.447
1997	646	.913	.087	3,828	3,572	.933	367	155	.422
1998	652	.919	.081	3,826	3,590	.938	339	146	.431
1999	663	.926	.074	3,957	3,725	.941	315	128	.406
2000	638	.934	.066	3,955	3,701	.936	278	114	.410
2001	645	.923	.077	4,125	3,897	.945	342	138	.404
2002	740	.930	.070	*4,744	4,452	.938	359	156	.435
2003	735	.943	.057	4,705	*4,482	.953	287	116	.404
2004	677	.950	.050	4,317	4,112	.953	229	97	.424
2005	691	*.953	#.047	4,361	4,160	.954	#215	98	.456
2006	753	.951	.049	4,370	4,158	.951	238	#88	.370

**Record high. #Record low.*

FBS Extra-Point Kick Attempts (1938-57)

Year	Pct. Made	Year	Pct. Made	Year	Pct. Made	Year	Pct. Made
1938	.608	1946	.657	1951	.711	1956	.666
1939	.625	1947	.657	1952	.744	1957	.653
1940	.607	1948	.708	1953	.650		
1941	.638	1949	.738	1954	.656		
1942-45	*	1950	.713	1955	.669		

**Not compiled.*

FBS Defensive Extra-Point Trends

In 1988, the NCAA Football Rules Committee adopted a rule that gave defensive teams an opportunity to score two points on point-after-touchdown tries. The two points were awarded for returning an interception or advancing a blocked kick for a touchdown on point-after tries.

Year	Games	Kick Ret./TDs	Int. Ret./TDs	Total Ret./TDs
1988	616	8/2	6/0	14/2
1989	614	12/3	9/2	21/5
1990	623	9/3	5/2	14/5
1991	617	9/3	10/3	19/6
1992	619	8/5	1/0	9/5
1993	613	5/2	6/1	11/3
1994	617	4/0	8/3	12/3
1995	622	12/5	5/3	17/8
1996	644	9/4	7/3	16/7
1997	646	13/3	6/1	19/4
1998	652	11/4	7/4	18/8
1999	663	8/2	3/0	11/2
2000	638	10/3	5/2	15/5
2001	645	11/4	7/3	18/7
2002	740	19/4	6/3	25/7
2003	735	16/5	5/3	21/8
2004	677	13/3	4/2	17/5
2005	691	17/7	8/2	25/9
2006	753	12/3	5/3	17/6
Totals	**12,425**	**206/65**	**113/40**	**319/105**

FBS Fumble-Recovery Returns

In 1990, the NCAA Football Rules Committee adopted a rule that gave the defense an opportunity to advance fumbles that occur beyond the neutral zone (or line of scrimmage). In 1992, the rule was changed to allow defenses to advance any fumble regardless of position behind or beyond the line of scrimmage. Here are the number of fumble recoveries by division that were advanced, and the number that resulted in a score.

Year	Games	Fumble Rec./TDs
1990	623	51/17
1991	617	60/16
1992	619	126/34
1993	613	117/24
1994	617	131/43
1995	622	148/49
1996	644	195/86
1997	646	206/76
1998	652	136/73
1999	663	150/84
2000	638	166/75
2001	645	152/78
2002	740	177/84
2003	735	194/88
2004	677	171/76
2005	691	211/78
2006	*792	242/92
Totals	**11,234**	**2,633/1,073**

Includes games against opponents from all divisions.

Major-College Tie Games

The record for most tie games in a single week is six—on October 27, 1962; September 28, 1963; and October 9, 1982.

Note: Tiebreaker procedures began with 1996 season.

Year	No.	Games	Pct.	Scoreless
1954	15	551	2.72	2
1955	22	536	4.10	1
1956	28	558	5.02	2
1957	24	570	4.21	4
1958*	19	578	3.29	2
1959	13	578	2.25	4
1960	23	596	3.86	4
1961	11	574	1.92	1
1962	20	602	3.32	2
1963	25	605	4.13	4
1964	19	613	3.10	2
1965	19	619	3.07	4
1966	13	626	2.08	0
1967	14	611	2.29	1
1968	17	615	2.76	1
1969	9	621	1.45	0
1970	7	667	1.05	0
1971	12	726	1.65	1
1972	14	720	1.94	1
1973	18	741	2.43	2
1974	18	749	2.40	0
1975	16	785	2.04	0
1976	13	796	1.63	1
1977	16	849	1.88	1
1978	16	816	1.96	1
1979	17	811	2.10	1
1980	12	810	1.48	0
1981	17	788	2.16	0
1982	14	599	2.34	0
1983	13	631	2.06	†1
1984	15	626	2.40	0
1985	13	623	2.09	0
1986	10	619	1.62	0
1987	13	615	2.11	0
1988	12	616	1.95	0
1989	15	614	2.44	0
1990	15	623	2.41	0
1991	14	617	2.27	0
1992	13	619	2.10	0
1993	11	613	1.79	0
1994	13	617	2.11	0
1995	9	622	1.45	0

**First year of two-point conversion rule. †Last scoreless tie game: Nov. 19, 1983, Oregon vs. Oregon St.*

Highest-Scoring Tie Games

(Home Team Listed First; Both Teams Classified Major-College or FBS at Time)

Note: Tiebreaker procedures began with 1996 season.

Score	Date	Opponents
52-52	11-16-91	San Diego St.-BYU
48-48	9-8-79	San Jose St.-Utah St.
43-43	11-12-88	Duke-North Carolina St.
41-41	9-10-94	Northwestern-Stanford
41-41	9-23-89	San Diego St.-Cal St. Fullerton
40-40	11-8-75	Idaho-Weber St.
39-39	11-7-82	Texas Tech-TCU
37-37	9-23-67	*Alabama-Florida St.
36-36	9-30-72	Georgia Tech-Rice
35-35	9-23-95	Michigan St.-Purdue
35-35	11-16-91	San Jose St.-Hawaii
35-35	12-9-89	Hawaii-Air Force
35-35	9-23-89	Colorado St.-Eastern Mich.
35-35	10-7-78	Ohio St.-SMU
35-35	10-19-74	Idaho-Montana
35-35	10-9-71	New Mexico-New Mexico St.
35-35	9-27-69	Minnesota-Ohio
35-35	9-21-68	Washington-Rice
35-35	11-18-67	Navy-Vanderbilt
35-35	12-11-48	†Pacific—Hardin-Simmons
34-34	10-6-90	Iowa St.-Kansas
33-33	10-1-83	California-Arizona
33-33	9-24-49	TCU-Oklahoma St.
33-33	10-31-31	Yale-Dartmouth

**At Birmingham. †Grape Bowl, Lodi, Calif.*

Home-Field Records

(Includes Host Teams at Neutral-Site Games)

Year	Games	Home Team Won	Lost	Tied	Pct.
1966	626	365	248	13	.594
1967	611	333	264	14	.557
1968	615	348	250	17	.580
1969	621	366	246	9	.596
1970	667	399	261	7	.603
1971	726	416	298	12	.581
1972	720	441	265	14	.622
1973	741	439	284	18	.605
1974	749	457	274	18	.622
1975	785	434	335	16	.563
1976	796	463	320	13	.590
1977	849	501	332	16	.600
1978	816	482	318	16	.601
1979	811	460	334	17	.578
1980	809	471	327	12	.589
1981	788	457	314	17	.591
1982	599	368	217	14	.626
1983	631	364	254	13	.587
1984	626	371	240	15	.605
1985	623	371	239	13	.606
1986	619	363	246	10	.595
1987	615	387	215	13	*.640
1988	616	370	234	12	.610
1989	614	365	234	15	.607
1990	623	373	235	15	.611
1991	617	362	241	14	.598
1992	619	388	218	13	.637
1993	613	375	227	11	.621
1994	617	357	247	13	.589
1995	622	354	259	9	.576
1996	644	389	255	0	.604
1997	646	392	254	0	.607
1998	652	399	253	0	.612
1999	663	403	260	0	.608
2000	638	391	247	0	.613
2001	645	401	244	0	.622
2002	734	456	278	0	.621
2003	728	452	276	0	.621
2004	677	419	258	0	.619
2005	708	418	290	0	.590
2006	#792	482	310	0	.609

**Record. #Includes games against opponents from all divisions.*

FBS Members Since 1978

The following list shows years of active membership for current and former FBS football-playing institutions. The lists are from 1978, the year Division I was divided into the FBS and FCS.

ACTIVE MEMBERS

Team	Year(s)
Air Force	1978-present
Akron	1987-present
Alabama	1978-present
UAB	1996-present
Arizona	1978-present
Arizona St.	1978-present
Arkansas	1978-present
Arkansas St.	1978-81, 92-present
Army	1978-present
Auburn	1978-present
Ball St.	1978-81, 83-present
Baylor	1978-present
Boise St.	1996-present
Boston College	1978-present
Bowling Green	1978-81, 83-present
BYU	1978-present
Buffalo	1999-present
California	1978-present
UCF	1996-present
Central Mich.	1978-present
Cincinnati	1978-81, 83-present
Clemson	1978-present
Colorado	1978-present
Colorado St.	1978-present
Connecticut	2002-present
Duke	1978-present
East Caro.	1978-present
Eastern Mich.	1978-81, 83-present
Florida	1978-present
Fla. Atlantic	2006-present
Florida Int'l	2006-present
Florida St.	1978-present
Fresno St.	1978-present
Georgia	1978-present
Georgia Tech	1978-present
Hawaii	1978-present
Houston	1978-present
Idaho	1996-present
Illinois	1978-present
Indiana	1978-present
Iowa	1978-present
Iowa St.	1978-present
Kansas	1978-present
Kansas St.	1978-present
Kent St.	1978-81, 83-present
Kentucky	1978-present
La.-Lafayette	1978-present
La.-Monroe	1978-81, 94-present
LSU	1978-present
Louisiana Tech	1978-81, 89-present
Louisville	1978-present

Team	Year(s)
Marshall	1978-81, 97-present
Maryland	1978-present
Memphis	1978-present
Miami (Fla.)	1978-present
Miami (Ohio)	1978-81, 83-present
Michigan	1978-present
Michigan St.	1978-present
Middle Tenn.	1999-present
Minnesota	1978-present
Mississippi	1978-present
Mississippi St.	1978-present
Missouri	1978-present
Navy	1978-present
Nebraska	1978-present
Nevada	1992-present
UNLV	1978-present
New Mexico	1978-present
New Mexico St.	1978-present
North Carolina	1978-present
North Carolina St.	1978-present
North Texas	1978-81, 95-present
Northern Ill.	1978-81, 83-present
Northwestern	1978-present
Notre Dame	1978-present
Ohio	1978-81, 83-present
Ohio St.	1978-present
Oklahoma	1978-present
Oklahoma St.	1978-present
Oregon	1978-present
Oregon St.	1978-present
Penn St.	1978-present
Pittsburgh	1978-present
Purdue	1978-present
Rice	1978-present
Rutgers	1978-present
San Diego St.	1978-present
San Jose St.	1978-present
South Carolina	1978-present
South Fla.	2001-present
Southern California	1978-present
SMU	1978-86, 89-present
Southern Miss.	1978-present
Stanford	1978-present
Syracuse	1978-present
Temple	1978-present
Tennessee	1978-present
Texas	1978-present
UTEP	1978-present
Texas A&M	1978-present
TCU	1978-present
Texas Tech	1978-present
Toledo	1978-present

Team	Year(s)
Troy	2002-present
Tulane	1978-present
Tulsa	1978-present
UCLA	1978-present
Utah	1978-present
Utah St.	1978-present
Vanderbilt	1978-present
Virginia	1978-present
Virginia Tech	1978-present
Wake Forest	1978-present
Washington	1978-present
Washington St.	1978-present
West Virginia	1978-present
Western Mich.	1978-81, 83-present
Wisconsin	1978-present
Wyoming	1978-present

FORMER MEMBERS

Team	Year(s)
Appalachian St.	1978-81
Brown	1978-81
Cal St. Fullerton	1978-92*
Chattanooga	1978-81
Citadel	1978-81
Colgate	1978-81
Columbia	1978-81
Cornell	1978-81
Dartmouth	1978-81
Drake	1978-80
East Tenn. St.	1978-81*
Furman	1978-81
Harvard	1978-81
Holy Cross	1978-81
Illinois St.	1978-81
Indiana St.	1978-81
Lamar	1978-81*
Long Beach St.	1978-91*
McNeese St.	1978-81
Pacific	1978-95*
Penn	1978-81
Princeton	1978-81
Richmond	1978-81
Southern Ill.	1978-81
Tennessee St.	1978-80
Texas-Arlington	1978-81*
Villanova	1978-80
VMI	1978-81
West Tex. A&M	1978-80
Western Caro.	1978-81
Wichita St.	1978-86*
William & Mary	1978-81
Yale	1978-81

**Dropped football program.*

College Football Rules Changes

The Ball

1869—Round, rubber Association ball.
1875—Egg-shaped, leather-covered Rugby ball.
1896—Prolate spheroid, without specific measurements.
1912—28-28 1/2 inches around ends, 22 1/2-23 inches around middle, weight 14-15 ounces.
1929—28-28 1/2 inches around ends, 22-22 1/2 inches around middle, weight 14-15 ounces.
1934—28-28 1/2 inches around ends, 21 1/4-21 1/2 inches around middle, weight 14-15 ounces.
1941—For night games, a white ball or other colored ball with two black stripes around the ball may be used at the discretion of the referee.
1952—Ball may be inclined no more than 45 degrees by snapper.
1956—Rubber-covered ball permitted.
1973—Teams allowed to use ball of their choice while in possession.
1978—Ball may not be altered, and new or nearly new balls added.
1982—10 7/8 to 11 7/16 inches long, 20 3/4 to 21 1/4 inches around middle, and 27 3/4 to 28 1/2 inches long-axis circumference.
1993—Rubber or composition ball ruled illegal.

The Field

1869—120 yards by 75 yards; uprights 24 feet apart.
1871—166 2/3 yards by 100 yards.
1872—133 1/3 yards by 83 1/3 yards.
1873—Uprights 25 feet apart.
1876—110 yards by 53 1/3 yards. Uprights 18 1/2 feet apart; crossbar 10 feet high.
1882—Field marked with transverse lines every five yards. This distance to be gained in three downs to retain possession.
1912—Field 120 yards by 53 1/3 yards, including two 10-yard end zones.
1927—Goal posts moved back 10 yards, to end line.
1957—Team area at 35-yard lines.
1959—Uprights widened to 23 feet, 4 inches apart.
1966—Pylons placed in corners of end zone and at goal lines mandatory in 1974.
1991—Uprights moved back to 18 feet, 6 inches apart.
1993—Hash marks moved six feet, eight inches closer to center of field to 60 feet from each sideline (40 feet apart).

Scoring

1869—All goals count 1 each.
1883—Safety 1, touchdown 4, goal after TD 4, goal from field 5.
1884—Safety 2, touchdown 4, goal from field 5.
1897—Touchdown 4, field goal 5, touchdown failing goal 5, safety 2.
1902—Teams change goals after every try at goal following a touchdown, after every goal from the field and also at the beginning of the half.
1904—Goal from field 4.
1909—Goal from field 3.
1912—Touchdown 4.
1921—Ball put in play at 30-yard line after a safety, 20-yard line after a touchback.
1922—Try-for-point by scrimmage play from 5-yard line.
1924—Try-for-point by scrimmage play from 3-yard line.
1927—Goal posts placed on end lines.
1929—Try-for-point by scrimmage play from 2-yard line.
1958—One-point & two-point conversion (from 3-yard line). One-point safety added.
1974—Ball must go between the uprights for a successful field goal, over the uprights previously scored.
1976—Forfeit score changed from 1-0 to score at time of forfeit if the offended team is ahead at time of forfeit.
1984—Try may be eliminated at end of game if both captains agree.
1995—Try at end of game mandatory unless team behind in score leaves field.

Scoring Values

1882—Touchdown 2 points; field goal 5 points; extra points 4 points
1883-87—Touchdown 4 points; field goal 5 points; extra points 4 points
1888-97—Touchdown 4 points; field goal 5 points; extra points 2 points
1898-1903—Touchdown 5 points; field goal 5 points; extra points 1 point
1904-08—Touchdown 5 points; field goal 4 points; extra points 1 point
1909-11—Touchdown 5 points; field goal 3 points; extra points 1 point
1912-57—Touchdown 6 points; field goal 3 points; extra points 1 point
1958-present—Touchdown 6 points; field goal 3 points; extra points 1 point/kick, 2 points/run or pass.
1988-present—Extra points 2 points/defense.

Note: Safety worth 1 point from 1882-1883, 2 points in all seasons since 1884.

Players

1869—Each team consisted of 25 players.
1873—Each team consisted of 20 players.
1876—Each team consisted of 15 players.
1880—Each team consisted of 11 players.
1895—Only one man in motion forward before the snap. No more than three players behind the line. One player permitted in motion toward own goal line.
1910—Seven players required on line.
1911—Illegal to conceal ball beneath a player's clothing.
1947—All players urged to be numbered in a uniform manner. Ends to wear numbers in the 80s; tackles, 70s; guards, 60s; centers, 50s; and backs, 10-49.
1966—Mandatory numbering of five players on the line 50-79.
1970—All players numbered 1-99.

Equipment

1894—No one wearing projecting nails or iron plates on his shoes, or any metal substance upon his person, is allowed to play. No greasy or sticky substance shall be used on the person of players.
1903—If head protectors are worn, there can be no sole leather or other hard or unyielding substances in their construction. Leather cleats on shoes allowed.
1908—First documented jersey numbers used by Washington & Jefferson.
1915—Numbers added to jerseys.
1927—Rubber cleats allowed, but under no conditions are cleats to be dangerously sharp.
1930—No player shall wear equipment that endangers players. The committee forbids the use of head protectors or jerseys that are so similar in color to the ball that they give the wearer an unfair and unsportsmanlike advantage over the opponent. Stripes may be used to break up the solid colors.
1933—Head protectors or helmets recommended to be worn by all players.
1937—All players must wear minimum 6-inch Arabic numerals on the front and minimum 8-inch Arabic numerals on the back of jerseys.
1939—All players must wear helmets.
1946—All players must wear minimum 8-inch Arabic numerals on front (changed from 6 inches) and minimum 10-inch Arabic numerals on back of jerseys (changed from 8 inches), of a single color which must be in sharp contrast with the color of the jerseys.
1948—One-inch kicking tees permitted.
1951—Any circular or ring cleat prohibited unless it has rounded edges and a wall at least 3/16-inch thick. Face masks added to helmet. Must be made of non-breakable, molded plastic with rounded edges.
1962—All players recommended to wear properly fitted mouth protectors.
1965—Two-inch kicking tees permitted.
1966—Players prohibited from wearing equipment with electronic, mechanical or other signal devices for the purpose of communicating with any source.
1968—Metal face masks having surfaces with material as resilient as rubber are allowed.
1970—Shoe cleats more than one-half inch in length (changed from three-quarters inch) prohibited.
1972—All players must wear mouth protectors, beginning with 1973 season.
1973—All players shall wear head protectors with a secured chin strap.
1974—All players shall wear shoulder pads.
1976—All players shall wear hip pads and thigh guards.
1979—Beginning in 1981, one team shall wear white jerseys.
1982—Tearaway jersey eliminated by charging a timeout.
1983—Mandatory white jersey for visiting teams.
1986—Therapeutic or preventive knee braces must be worn under the pants.
1989—Kicking tees eliminated for field goals and extra-point attempts.
1991—Rib and back pad covering mandatory.
1994—Standards established to limit glove stickiness. Jerseys that extend below the top of the pants must be tucked into the pants.
1995—Home team may wear white jerseys if both teams agree before the season.
1996—Cleats limited to one-half inch in length (see 1970). Violators disqualified for remainder of game and entire next game. Rule a dead ball when a ball carrier's helmet comes completely off, with the ball belonging to runner's team at that spot. Jerseys must extend to top of pants and must be tucked in if longer.
1997—Require all players on the same team to wear white or team-colored socks of the same design and length. Leg coverings, such as tights, if worn, must be in team colors and of a uniform design for all players on the same team.
1998—All eye shields, if worn, must be clear (transparent) and made from molded and rigid material. NCAA member institutions can, in the case of a death or catastrophic injury or illness, memorialize a player or person with a patch or decal not greater than 1 1/2 inches in diameter that displays the number, name or initials of the individual on the uniform or helmet.
1999—Visible bandanas are ruled an illegal uniform attachment. Eye shields that are not clear are permitted, only with proper documentation from the player's institution and approval from a medical doctor designated by the NCAA Committee on Competitive Safeguards and Medical Aspects of Sports.
2000—A maximum of two defensive players are allowed to wear 4-inch by 12-inch white towels without markings attached to the front belt.
2004—A glove cannot include any additional material that connects any of the fingers and/or thumb. On scrimmage plays, one white towel without markings may be worn by one interior offensive lineman, one offensive backfield player and a maximum of two defensive players. The towels of the offensive backfield and defensive players must be 4-inches by 12-inches and must be worn on the front or side belt. There are no restrictions on the size or location of the towel worn by the offensive lineman. On free kicks, one white towel without markings may be worn by a maximum of two Team A and two Team B players. The towels worn on free kicks must be 4-inches by 12-inches and must be worn on the front or side belt.
2006—The length of the kicking tee was shortened to one inch. Also, the use of eye shields that are not clear during games was eliminated.

Substitutions

1876—Fifteen players to a team and few if any substitutions.
1882—Replacements for disqualified or injured players.
1897—Substitutions may enter the game any time at discretion of captains.
1922—Players withdrawn during the first half may be returned during the second half. A player withdrawn in the second half may not return.

1941—A player may substitute any time but may not be withdrawn or the outgoing player returned to the game until one play had intervened. Platoon football made possible.
1948—Unlimited substitution on change of team possession.
1953—Two-platoon abolished and players allowed to enter the game only once in each quarter.
1954-64—Changes each year toward more liberalized substitution rule and platoon football.
1965—Platoon football returns. Unlimited substitutions between periods, after a score or try.
1974—Substitutes must be in for one play and replaced players out for one play.
1993—Players who are bleeding or whose uniforms are saturated with blood must come out of the game until their return has been approved by medical personnel.
2000—Offensive teams, while in the process of substitution or simulated substitution, are prohibited from rushing quickly to the line of scrimmage and snapping the ball with the obvious attempt to create a defensive disadvantage.
2004—The defensive team will be given the opportunity to complete its substitutions when offensive teams, while in the process of substitution or simulated substitution, rush quickly to the line of scrimmage with the obvious attempt to create a defensive disadvantage.

Passing Game

1906—One forward pass legalized behind the line if made five yards right or left of center. Ball went to opponents if it failed to touch a player of either side before touching the ground. Either team could recover a pass touched by an opponent. One pass each scrimmage down.
1910—Pass interference does not apply 20 yards beyond the line of scrimmage. Passer must be five yards behind the line of scrimmage. One forward pass permitted during each down.
1914—Roughing the passer added.
1923—Handing the ball forward is an illegal forward pass and receivers going out of bounds and returning prohibited.
1934—Three changes encourage use of pass. (1) First forward pass in series of downs can be incomplete in the end zone without loss of ball except on fourth down. (2) Circumference of ball reduced, making it easier to throw. (3) Five-yard penalty for more than one incomplete pass in same series of downs eliminated.
1941—Fourth-down forward pass incomplete in end zone no longer a touchback. Ball goes to opponent at spot where put in play.
1945—Forward pass may be thrown from anywhere behind the line, encouraging use of modern T formation.
1949—Intentional grounding of a pass shall result in a loss of down and a five-yard penalty from the spot of the foul.
1966—Compulsory numbering system makes only players numbered other than 50-79 eligible forward-pass receivers.
1976—Offensive blocking changed to provide half extension of arms to assist pass blocking.
1980—Retreat blocking added with full arm extension to assist pass blocking, and illegal use of hands reduced to five yards.
1982—Pass interference only on a catchable forward pass. Forward pass intentionally grounded to conserve time permitted.
1983—First down added to roughing the passer.
1985—Retreat block deleted and open hands and extended arms permitted anywhere on the field.
1990—Pass thrown immediately to the ground to conserve time legal.
1994—Ball must be catchable for offensive player to be charged with pass interference.
1996—Principle of "reasonable opportunity to catch the pass" applied to intentional grounding situations.
1998—A backward pass can be recovered and advanced by the defense.
1999—Intentional grounding of a pass shall result in a loss of down at the spot of the foul.
2000—Allowing a passer, who is five yards or more toward the sideline from the original position of the ball at the snap, to throw the ball so that it lands beyond the neutral zone to avoid loss of yardage without penalty.
2004—A defensive player who is blocked into the passer is exempt from being penalized for roughing the passer.

General Changes

1876—Holding and carrying the ball permitted.
1880—Eleven players on a side and a scrimmage line established.
1882—Downs and yards to gain enter the rules.
1883—Scoring system established.
1906—Forward passes permitted. Ten yards for first down.
1920—Clipping defined.
1922—Try-for-point introduced. Ball brought out five yards from goal line for scrimmage, allowing try for extra point by place kick, drop kick, run or forward pass.
1925—Kickoff returned to 40-yard line. Clipping made a violation, with penalty of 25 yards.
1927—One-second pause imposed on shift. Thirty seconds allowed for putting ball in play. Huddle limited to 15 seconds. To encourage use of lateral pass, missed backward pass other than from center declared dead ball when it hits the ground and cannot be recovered by opponents.
1929—All fumbles ruled dead at point of recovery.
1932—Most far-reaching changes in nearly a quarter of a century set up safeguards against hazards of game. (1) Ball declared dead when any portion of player in possession, except his hands or feet, touches ground. (2) Use of flying block and flying tackle barred under penalty of five yards. (3) Players on defense forbidden to strike opponents on head, neck or face. (4) Hard and dangerous equipment must be covered with padding.
1941—Legal to hand ball forward behind the neutral zone.
1949—Blockers required to keep hands against their chest.
1951—Fair catch restored.
1952—Penalty for striking with forearm, elbow or locked hands, or for flagrantly rough play or unsportsmanlike conduct, changed from 15 yards to mandatory suspension.
1957—Penalty for grabbing face mask.
1959—Distance penalties limited to one-half distance to offending team's goal line.
1967—Coaching from sideline permitted.
1970—Eleven-game schedule permitted.
1971—Crack-back block (blocking below waist) illegal.
1972—Freshman eligibility restored.
1977—Clock started on snap after a penalty.
1978—Unsuccessful field goal returned to the previous spot.
1983—Offensive encroachment changed...no offensive player permitted in or beyond the neutral zone after snapper touches ball.
1984—Defensive pass interference penalty changed from spot of foul to 15 yards from previous spot.
1985—One or both feet on ground required for blocking below waist foul.
1986—Kickoff from the 35-yard line.
1988—Defensive team allowed to score two points on return of blocked extra-point kick attempt or interception of extra-point pass attempt.
1990—Defense allowed to advance fumbles that occur beyond the neutral zone.
1991—Width between goal-post uprights reduced from 23 feet, 4 inches to 18 feet, 6 inches. Kickoffs out of bounds allow receiving team to elect to take ball 30 yards beyond yard line where kickoff occurred. Holding behind the neutral zone penalized 10 yards from the spot of the foul.
1992—Defense allowed to advance fumbles regardless of where they occur. Changes ruling of 1990 fumble advancement.
1993—Guard-around or "fumblerooski" play ruled illegal.
1994—Players involved in a fight after half time disqualified for first half of next game; substitutes and coaches who participate in a fight in their team area or leave the team area to join a fight disqualified for entire next game; squad members and coaches involved in a fight during half time disqualified for first half of next game.
1995—Defense penalized five yards for entering neutral zone before snap and causing offensive player to react immediately. Players prohibited from removing helmets on the field. Players disqualified after second unsportsmanlike-conduct foul in one game. Fight suspensions allowed to carry over to next season.
1996—NCAA tiebreaker system to be used in all games tied after four periods.
1997—In overtime tiebreaker system, require a team that scores a touchdown to attempt a two-point conversion in the third overtime period. Approved a rule requiring a game to be declared a tie if it is in overtime but cannot be finished due to weather, darkness or other conditions. Chop block redefined to be penalized if "obviously delayed" and added restrictions to the "crack-back" block to make it illegal up to five yards beyond line of scrimmage regardless of position of the ball. Officials prompted to enforce mouthpiece rule, charging a timeout to offending team if clock is stopped and player does not have mouthpiece in place. To prevent opponents from leveling punt returners with unnecessarily vicious hits, the penalty was increased from five to 15 yards.
1998—For the first time in history, a backward pass can be recovered and advanced by the defense. It is now consistent with the application of the rules similar to how the defense is allowed to advance a fumble.
1999—Holding behind the neutral zone will be penalized 10 yards from the previous line of scrimmage. Dead-ball fouls by both teams which are part of continuing action or of a retaliatory nature and reported at the same time will be canceled and the penalties disregarded. However, any disqualified player must leave the game. Teams may not break the huddle with 12 or more players.
2000—An illegal block shall now include any high-low, low-high or low-low combination block by any two offensive players beyond the neutral zone regardless of simultaneous contact by both. Also, blocking below the waist by offensive players ("crack-back block") now includes not only wide receivers or players in motion but any player in motion in any direction at the snap and the area is expanded to included the neutral zone and 10 yards beyond. Also, prohibiting a defensive player(s) aligned in a stationary position within one yard of the line of scrimmage from making quick or abrupt actions that are not part of normal player movement in an obvious attempt to cause an offensive player(s) to foul.
2001—A charged team timeout can be 30 seconds in duration if so desired by the team calling the timeout. Most penalties for offensive-team fouls that occur behind the neutral zone will be enforced from the previous spot.
2002—The penalty for interference with the opportunity to catch a kick, when no contact is involved, increased from five to 10 yards. Yardage enforcement of flagrant personal fouls during possession by the defensive team may carry from one extra period to the next.
2003—The game clock on all kickoffs will start when the ball is legally touched in the field of play. The two-yard restricted area around a player positioned to catch a free or scrimmage kick is deleted. Offensive linemen at the snap positioned more than seven yards in any direction from the middle lineman of the offensive formation are prohibited from blocking below the waist toward the original position of the ball in or behind the neutral zone and within 10 yards beyond the neutral zone. Backs at the snap positioned outside the normal tackle position in either direction toward a sideline, or in motion at the snap, are prohibited from blocking below the waist toward the original position of the ball in or behind the neutral zone and within 10 yards beyond the neutral zone.
2004—A camera, with no audio component, may be attached to cables that hang over the team area. The head coach may now request a charged team timeout when timeouts are not exhausted, and when the ball is dead. No defensive player who runs forward and leaps in an obvious attempt to block a field goal or try may land on an opponent. The referee, if he is equipped with a microphone, will announce the number of the player committing the foul. The receiving team has the option of assessing the penalty for encroachment by the kicking team during a free kick from either the previous spot or from the end of the receiving team's run.
2005—Expanded experimental use of in-game video officiating review to all member conferences and institutions for the 2005 season. The same parameters approved for 2004 for the Big Ten

Conference will be used. The video replay will not be allowed in postseason bowl games or in NCAA championships. Blocking from behind near the line of scrimmage was limited to contact above the knee. Another safety concern – helmet-to-helmet contact and spearing – was addressed by taking a player's intention out of the equation to assist officials in the proper enforcement of the rule governing that type of contact. The committee also defined regulation of unsportsmanlike conduct and celebration penalties to assist officials, players and coaches in understanding what type of action warrants a penalty. That means the committee does believe that spontaneous celebrations that are not prolonged or intended to bring attention to the individual should be allowed on a limited basis. A defined list of unacceptable behaviors was included in the 2005 rules book.

2006—After allowing instant replay to review a game official's call on the field for two seasons on an experimental basis, the committee approved one procedure for all institutions and conferences that choose to use it. The procedure calls for the replay official in the press box to review all plays on the field and stop the game. The committee also decided to allow each team one challenge during the course of a game, as long as the challenging team has a timeout. The head coach may request a review by signaling for a timeout. If the challenge overturns the call on the field, the challenging team is not charged a timeout. If the call is not overturned, the team is charged a timeout. If a team does not have any timeouts remaining, it is not allowed to request a review. In hopes of shortening the length of games, halftime is recommended to be 20 minutes in duration, but competing institutions are now permitted to shorten or lengthen halftime by mutual consent. Other changes include starting the game clock on kickoffs when the kicker's foot touches the ball, rather than when the returning team touches the ball, and starting the game clock when the ball is ready for play after a change of possession. In addition, the enforcement of all procedural fouls committed by the kicking team that occur before a scrimmage kick (except field goals) was changed. Now, the receiving team will have the option of accepting the penalty after the return or forcing the kicking team to kick again five yards from the original line of scrimmage.

2007—The committee altered its rule to have the clock start on the snap after a change in possession, as opposed to the 2006 rule that started the clock when the referee signaled the ball ready for play. Also, the committee returned its rules on free kicks to 2005 standards, starting the clock on kickoffs only when the ball is legally touched in the field of play. Other changes include limiting the play clock to 15 seconds after a television timeout. Kickoffs moved from the 35-yard line to 30-yard line. In addition, charged team timeouts were reduced by 30 seconds and penalties for all kicking team fouls that occur during the kick can be enforced at the end of the run. Finally, the play clock is started when the ball is handed to the kicker by the umpire on all free kicks and instant replay reviews are limited to two minutes to decide to overturn or confirm the ruling on the field.

Football Championship Subdivision Records

Individual Records

Total Offense

(Rushing Plus Passing)

MOST PLAYS
Quarter
33—Mickey Fein, Maine vs. Connecticut, Oct. 11, 1997 (4th)
Half
59—Joe Walland, Yale vs. Harvard, Nov. 20, 1999 (2nd)
Game
89—Thomas Leonard, Mississippi Val. vs. Texas Southern, Oct. 25, 1986 (440 yards)
Season
680—Bruce Eugene, Grambling, 2002 (5,018 yards)
Career
2,116—Marcus Brady, Cal St. Northridge, 1998-01 (13,095 yards)

MOST PLAYS PER GAME
Season
59.0—Steve McNair, Alcorn St., 1994 (649 in 11)
Career
49.5—Tom Proudian, Iona, 1993-95 (1,337 in 27)

MOST PLAYS BY A FRESHMAN
Game
81—Kevin Glenn, Illinois St. vs. Western Ill., Nov. 8, 1997 (470 yards)
Season
632—Martin Hankins, Southeastern La., 2003 (3,390 yards)
Also holds per-game record with 52.7 (632 in 12)

MOST YARDS GAINED
Quarter
278—Willie Totten, Mississippi Val. vs. Kentucky St., Sept. 1, 1984 (2nd)
Half
404—Todd Hammel, Stephen F. Austin vs. La.-Monroe, Nov. 11, 1989 (1st)
Game
668—Robert Kent, Jackson St. vs. Alabama St., Oct. 6, 2001 (595 passing, 73 rushing)
Season
5,799—Steve McNair, Alcorn St., 1994 (4,863 passing, 936 rushing)
2 Yrs
9,629—Steve McNair, Alcorn St., 1993-94 (8,060 passing, 1,569 rushing)
3 Yrs
13,686—Steve McNair, Alcorn St., 1992-94 (11,601 passing, 2,085 rushing)
Career
(4 yrs.) 16,823—Steve McNair, Alcorn St., 1991-94 (14,496 passing, 2,327 rushing)

MOST YARDS GAINED PER GAME
Season
527.2—Steve McNair, Alcorn St., 1994 (5,799 in 11)
Career
400.5—Steve McNair, Alcorn St., 1991-94 (16,823 in 42)

MOST SEASONS GAINING 3,000 YARDS OR MORE
4—Steve McNair, Alcorn St., 1991-94

MOST YARDS GAINED BY A FRESHMAN
Game
538—Ricky Santos, New Hampshire vs. Villanova, Oct. 2, 2004 (61 plays)
Season
3,601—Ricky Santos, New Hampshire, 2004 (550 plays)
Per-game record—313.7, Steve McNair, Alcorn St., 1991 (3,137 in 10)

MOST YARDS GAINED IN TWO, THREE AND FOUR CONSECUTIVE GAMES
2 Games
1,280—Steve McNair, Alcorn St., 1994 (633 vs. Grambling, Sept. 3; 647 vs. Chattanooga, Sept. 10)
3 Games
1,859—Steve McNair, Alcorn St., 1994 (649 vs. Samford, Oct. 29; 624 vs. Mississippi Val., Nov. 5; 586 vs. Troy, Nov. 12)
4 Games
2,423—Steve McNair, Alcorn St., 1994 (649 vs. Samford, Oct. 29; 624 vs. Mississippi Val., Nov. 5; 586 vs. Troy, Nov. 12; 564 vs. Jackson St., Nov. 19)

MOST GAMES GAINING 300 YARDS OR MORE
Season
11—Steve McNair, Alcorn St., 1994
Career
32—Steve McNair, Alcorn St., 1991-94

MOST CONSECUTIVE GAMES GAINING 300 YARDS OR MORE
Season
11—Steve McNair, Alcorn St., 1994
Career
13—Neil Lomax, Portland St., 1979-80; Willie Totten, Mississippi Val., 1984-85; Steve McNair, Alcorn St., 1992-93

MOST GAMES GAINING 400 YARDS OR MORE
Season
9—Steve McNair, Alcorn St., 1994
Career
15—Steve McNair, Alcorn St., 1991-94

MOST CONSECUTIVE GAMES GAINING 400 YARDS OR MORE
Season
5—Willie Totten, Mississippi Val., 1984; Steve McNair, Alcorn St., 1994

MOST GAMES GAINING 500 YARDS OR MORE
Season
6—Steve McNair, Alcorn St., 1994
Career
9—Steve McNair, Alcorn St., 1991-94

MOST YARDS GAINED AGAINST ONE OPPONENT
Career
1,772—Steve McNair, Alcorn St. vs. Jackson St., 1991-94
Also holds per-game record with 443.0 (1,772 in 4)

GAINING 1,000 YARDS RUSHING AND 1,000 YARDS PASSING
Season
Tracy Ham (QB), Ga. Southern, 1986 (1,048 rushing, 1,772 passing); Alcede Surtain (QB), Alabama St., 1995 (1,024 rushing, 1,224 passing); David Dinkins (QB), Morehead St., 1998 (1,169 rushing, 1,812 passing); Greg Hill (QB), Ga. Southern, 1998 (1,061 rushing, 1,193 passing); Greg Hill (QB), Ga. Southern, 1999 (1,084 rushing, 1,262 passing); David Dinkins (QB), Morehead St., 2000 (1,405 rushing, 1,704 passing); Chaz Williams (QB), Ga. Southern, 2002 (1,422 rushing, 1,022 passing); Allen Suber (QB), Bethune-Cookman, 2002 (1,035 rushing, 1,307 passing); Ryan Kuhn (QB), Cornell, 2005 (1,000 rushing, 1,008 passing)

GAINING 1,000 YARDS RUSHING AND 2,000 YARDS PASSING
Season
David Dinkins, Morehead St., 1999 (1,138 rushing, 2,011 passing); Barrick Nealy, Texas St., 2005 (1,057 rushing, 2,875 passing)

GAINING 1,000 YARDS RUSHING AND 1,000 YARDS RECEIVING
Season
Brian Westbrook (TB), Villanova, 1998 (1,046 rushing, 1,144 receiving) (first NCAA player to accomplish this feat)

GAINING 2,000 YARDS RUSHING AND 4,000 YARDS PASSING
Career
Tracy Ham (QB), Ga. Southern, 1984-86 (2,506 rushing, 4,871 passing); Bill Vergantino (QB), Delaware, 1989-92 (2,287 rushing, 6,177 passing); Steve McNair (QB), Alcorn St., 1991-94 (2,327 rushing, 14,496 passing); Ryan Vena (QB), Colgate, 1996-99 (2,008 rushing, 7,427 passing); David Dinkins (QB), Morehead St., 1997-00 (3,765 rushing, 5,572 passing); Travis Wilson (QB), Wofford, 1998-01 (2,488 rushing, 4,067 passing)

GAINING 3,000 YARDS RUSHING AND 3,000 YARDS PASSING
Career
Willie Taggart (QB), Western Ky., 1995-98 (3,957 rushing, 3,029 passing); Greg Hill (QB), Ga. Southern, 1996-99 (3,309 rushing, 3,369 passing); David Dinkins (QB), Morehead St., 1997-00 (3,765 rushing, 5,572 passing)

GAINING 3,000 YARDS RUSHING AND 5,000 YARDS PASSING
Career
David Dinkins (QB), Morehead St., 1997-00 (3,765 rushing, 5,572 passing)

TEAM HAVING A 200-YARD RUSHER AND A 200-YARD RECEIVER IN THE SAME GAME
Portland St., Charles Dunn (247 rushing yards) and Art Williams (208 receiving yards) vs. Sacramento St., Oct. 10, 1998 (Portland St. won, 58-31); Portland St., Charles Dunn (213 rushing yards) and Terry Charles (209 receiving yards) vs. Cal Poly, Oct. 30, 1999 (Portland St. won, 42-28)

HIGHEST AVERAGE GAIN PER PLAY
Game
(Min. 39-49 plays) 12.40—John Whitcomb, UAB vs. Prairie View, Nov. 19, 1994 (43 for 533)
(Min. 50-59 plays) 11.4—Steve McNair, Alcorn St. vs. Chattanooga, Sept. 10, 1994 (57 for 647)
(Min. 60 plays) 9.7—Steve McNair, Alcorn St. vs. Grambling, Sept. 3, 1994 (65 for 633)
Season
(Min. 2,500-3,299 yards) 9.6—Frank Baur, Lafayette, 1988 (285 for 2,727)
(Min. 3,300 yards) 8.9—Steve McNair, Alcorn St., 1994 (649 for 5,799)
Career
(Min. 4,000 yards) 8.2—Steve McNair, Alcorn St., 1991-94 (2,055 for 16,823)

MOST TOUCHDOWNS RESPONSIBLE FOR (TDs Scored and Passed For)
Game
9—Neil Lomax, Portland St. vs. Delaware St., Nov. 8, 1980 (passed for 8, scored 1); Willie Totten, Mississippi Val. vs. Kentucky St., Sept. 1, 1984 (passed for 9) & vs. Prairie View, Oct. 27, 1984 (passed for 8, scored 1)
Season
61—Willie Totten, Mississippi Val., 1984 (passed for 56, scored 5)
Also holds per-game record with 6.1 (61 in 10)
Career
159—Bruce Eugene, Grambling, $2001-05 (passed for 140, scored 19)
Per-game record—3.9, Willie Totten, Mississippi Val., 1982-85 (157 in 40)

$See page 10 for explanation.

MOST POINTS RESPONSIBLE FOR (Points Scored and Passed For)
Game
56—Willie Totten, Mississippi Val. vs. Kentucky St., Sept. 1, 1984 (passed for 9 TDs and 1 two-point conversion)
Season
368—Willie Totten, Mississippi Val., 1984 (passed for 56 TDs, scored 5 TDs and passed for 1 two-point conversion)
Also holds per-game record with 36.8 (368 in 10)
Career
946—Willie Totten, Mississippi Val., 1982-85 (passed for 139 TDs, scored 18 TDs and passed for 1 two-point conversion)
Also holds per-game record with 23.7 (946 in 40)

Rushing

MOST RUSHES
Quarter
20—Arnold Mickens, Butler vs. Dayton, Oct. 15, 1994 (4th)
Half
32—David Clark, Dartmouth vs. Penn, Nov. 18, 1989 (2nd); Arnold Mickens, Butler vs. Valparaiso, Oct. 8, 1994 (1st)

Game
56—Arnold Mickens, Butler vs. Valparaiso, Oct. 8, 1994 (295 yards)
Season
450—Jamaal Branch, Colgate, 2003 (2,326 yards) (16 games)
Career
1,124—Charles Roberts, Sacramento St., 1997-00 (6,553 yards)

MOST RUSHES PER GAME
Season
40.9—Arnold Mickens, Butler, 1994 (409 in 10)
Career
38.2—Arnold Mickens, Butler, 1994-95 (763 in 20)

MOST RUSHES IN TWO CONSECUTIVE GAMES
110—Arnold Mickens, Butler, 1994 (56 vs. Valparaiso, Oct. 8; 54 vs. Dayton, Oct. 15)

MOST CONSECUTIVE CARRIES BY SAME PLAYER
Game
26—Arnold Mickens, Butler vs. Valparaiso, Oct. 8, 1994 (during six series)

MOST YARDS GAINED
Quarter
194—Otto Kelly, Nevada vs. Idaho, Nov. 12, 1983 (3rd, 8 rushes)
Half
282—Herb Donaldson, Western Ill. vs. Indiana St., Nov. 4, 2006 (2nd, 26 rushes)
Game
437—Maurice Hicks, N.C. A&T vs. Morgan St., Oct. 6, 2001 (34 rushes)
Season
2,326—Jamaal Branch, Colgate, 2003 (450 rushes) (16 games)
Career
6,559—Adrian Peterson, Ga. Southern, 1998-01 (996 rushes)

MOST YARDS GAINED PER GAME
Season
225.5—Arnold Mickens, Butler, 1994 (2,255 in 10)
Career
(2 yrs.) 190.7—Arnold Mickens, Butler, 1994-95 (3,813 in 20)
(3 yrs.) 164.5—Adrian Peterson, Ga. Southern, 1998-00 (5,100 in 31)
(4 yrs.) 156.2—Adrian Peterson, Ga. Southern, 1998-01 (6,559 in 42)

MOST YARDS GAINED BY A FRESHMAN
Game
393—Ryan Fuqua, Portland St. vs. Eastern Wash., Nov. 10, 2001 (45 rushes)
Season
1,932—Adrian Peterson, Ga. Southern, 1998 (257 rushes)
Also holds per-game record with 175.6 (1,932 in 11)

MOST YARDS GAINED BY A QUARTERBACK
Game
309—Eddie Thompson, Western Ky. vs. Southern Ill., Oct. 31, 1992 (28 rushes)
Season
1,602—Matt Cannon, Southern Utah, 2000 (218 rushes)
Per-game record—156.1, David Dinkins, Morehead St., 2000 (1,405 in 9)
Career
4,852—Matt Cannon, Southern Utah, 1997-00 (674 rushes)
Also played as a slotback in 1997 and those statistics are not included

MOST GAMES GAINING 100 YARDS OR MORE
Season
12—Jamaal Branch, Colgate, 2003
Career
40—Adrian Peterson, Ga. Southern, 1998-01 (42 games)

MOST CONSECUTIVE GAMES GAINING 100 YARDS OR MORE
Season
11—Frank Hawkins, Nevada, 1980; Rich Lemon, Bucknell, 1994; Charles Roberts, Sacramento St., 1998; Adrian Peterson, Ga. Southern, 1998-99; Jamaal Branch, Colgate, 2003
Career
36—Adrian Peterson, Ga. Southern, 1998-01

MOST GAMES GAINING 100 YARDS OR MORE BY A FRESHMAN
11—Adrian Peterson, Ga. Southern, 1998

MOST GAMES GAINING 200 YARDS OR MORE
Season
8—Arnold Mickens, Butler, 1994
Career
13—Charles Roberts, Sacramento St., 1997-00

MOST CONSECUTIVE GAMES GAINING 200 YARDS OR MORE
Season
8—Arnold Mickens, Butler, 1994

MOST YARDS GAINED IN TWO, THREE AND FOUR CONSECUTIVE GAMES
2 Games
691—Tony Vinson, Towson, 1993 (364 vs. Bucknell, Nov. 13; 327 vs. Morgan St., Nov. 20)
3 Games
906—Ryan Fuqua, Portland St., 2001 (393 vs. Eastern Wash., Nov. 10; 270 vs. Cal St. Northridge, Nov. 17; 243 vs. Sacramento St., Nov. 24)
4 Games
1,109—Arnold Mickens, Butler, 1994 (233 vs. Georgetown [Ky.], Sept. 17; 288 vs. Wis.-Stevens Point, Sept. 24; 293 vs. Drake, Oct. 1; 295 vs. Valparaiso, Oct. 8)

MOST SEASONS GAINING 1,000 YARDS OR MORE
Career
4—Jerry Azumah, New Hampshire, 1995-98; Adrian Peterson, Ga. Southern, 1998-01; Alonzo Coleman, Hampton, 2003-06

TWO PLAYERS, SAME TEAM, EACH GAINING 1,000 YARDS OR MORE
Jackson St., 1978—Perry Harrington (1,105) & Jeffrey Moore (1,094); Nevada, 1983—Otto Kelly (1,090) & Tony Corley (1,006); Eastern Ky., 1985—James Crawford (1,282) & Elroy Harris (1,134); Eastern Ky., 1986—Elroy Harris (1,152) & James Crawford (1,070); Citadel, 1988—Adrian Johnson (1,091) & Gene Brown (1,006); William & Mary, 1990—Robert Green (1,185) & Tyrone Shelton (1,020); Yale, 1991—Chris Kouri (1,101) & Nick Crawford (1,024); La.-Monroe, 1992—Greg Robinson (1,011) & Roosevelt Potts (1,004); Eastern Ky., 1993—Mike Penman (1,139) & Leon Brown (1,046); South Carolina St., 1994—Michael Hicks (1,368) & Marvin Marshall (1,201); Massachusetts, 1995—Frank Alessio (1,276) & Rene Ingoglia (1,178); Southern Utah, 1996—Brook Madsen (1,405) & Joe Dupaix (1,246); Colgate, 1997—Ed Weiss (1,069) & Daymon Smith (1,012); Cal Poly, 1997—Antonio Warren (1,151) & Craig Young (1,038); Southern Utah, 1997—Brook Madsen (1,214) & Matt Cannon (1,024); Ga. Southern, 1998—Adrian Peterson (1,932) & Greg Hill (1,061); Texas Southern, 1998—D.J. Bradley (1,219) & Thomas Sieh (1,202); Southern Utah, 1999—Matt Cannon (1,310) & Brook Madsen (1,046); Ga. Southern, 1999—Adrian Peterson (1,807) & Greg Hill (1,084); Ga. Southern, 2002—Chaz Williams (1,422) & Jermaine Austin (1,416); Hampton, 2004—Alonzo Coleman (1,133) & Ardell Daniels (1,098); Ga. Southern, 2005—Jermaine Austin (1,546) & Jayson Foster (1,481); Hampton, 2006—Alonzo Coleman (1,326) & Ardell Daniels (1,044)

MOST YARDS GAINED BY TWO PLAYERS, SAME TEAM
Game
473—Jovan Griffith (262) & Jesse Chatman (211), Eastern Wash. vs. Cal St. Northridge, Sept. 25, 1999
Season
3,027—Jermaine Austin (1,546) & Jayson Foster (1,481), Ga. Southern, 2005

EARLIEST GAME GAINING 1,000 YARDS OR MORE
Season
5th—Arnold Mickens, Butler, 1994 (1,106); Charles Roberts, Sacramento St., 1999 (1,018)

MOST YARDS GAINED IN OPENING GAME OF SEASON
304—Tony Citizen, McNeese St. vs. Prairie View, Sept. 6, 1986 (30 rushes)

MOST YARDS GAINED IN FIRST GAME OF CAREER
304—Tony Citizen, McNeese St. vs. Prairie View, Sept. 6, 1986 (30 rushes)

HIGHEST AVERAGE GAIN PER RUSH
Game
(Min. 15-19 rushes) 19.1—Gene Brown, Citadel vs. VMI, Nov. 12, 1988 (15 for 286)
(Min. 20 rushes) 17.3—Russell Davis, Idaho vs. Portland St., Oct. 3, 1981 (20 for 345)
Season
(Min. 150-199 rushes) 8.7—Tim Hall, Robert Morris, 1994 (154 for 1,336)
(Min. 200 rushes) 7.6—Ryan Fuqua, Portland St., 2001 (210 for 1,586)
Career
(Min. 350-599 rushes) 7.4—Tim Hall, Robert Morris, 1994-95 (393 for 2,908)
(Min. 600 rushes) 7.3—Matt Cannon, Southern Utah, 1997-00 (757 for 5,489)

MOST TOUCHDOWNS SCORED BY RUSHING
Game
7—Archie Amerson, Northern Ariz. vs. Weber St., Oct. 5, 1996
Season
30—Kevin Richardson, Appalachian St., 2006 (15 games)
Career
84—Adrian Peterson, Ga. Southern, 1998-01

MOST TOUCHDOWNS SCORED PER GAME BY RUSHING
Season
2.5—Adrian Peterson, Ga. Southern, 1999 (28 in 11)
Career
2.0—Adrian Peterson, Ga. Southern, 1998-01 (84 in 42)

MOST TOUCHDOWNS SCORED BY RUSHING BY A QUARTERBACK
Season
27—Chaz Williams, Ga. Southern, 2002
Career
64—Matt Cannon, Southern Utah, 1997-00
Per-game record—1.7, David Dinkins, Morehead St., 1997-00 (63 in 37)

LONGEST PLAY
99—Hubert Owens, Mississippi Val. vs. Ark.-Pine Bluff, Sept. 20, 1980; Pedro Bacon, Western Ky. vs. West Ala., Sept. 13, 1986 (only rush of the game); Phillip Collins, Missouri St. vs. Western Ill., Sept. 16, 1989; Jim Varick, Monmouth vs. Sacred Heart, Oct. 29, 1994; Jermaine Creighton, St. John's (N.Y.) vs. Siena, Nov. 2, 1996; Michael Hobbs, Wofford vs. Ga. Southern, Nov. 4, 2006

Passing

HIGHEST PASSING EFFICIENCY RATING POINTS
Game
(Min. 15-24 atts.) 389.9—Mark Washington, Jackson St. vs. Alcorn St., Nov. 20, 1999 (17 attempts, 16 completions, 0 interceptions, 363 yards, 6 TD passes)
(Min. 25-44 atts.) 287.2—Doug Turner, Morehead St. vs. Miles, Oct. 18, 1997 (26 attempts, 20 completions, 0 interceptions, 415 yards, 6 TD passes)
(Min. 45 atts.) 220.8—Todd Hammel, Stephen F. Austin vs. La.-Monroe, Nov. 11, 1989 (45 attempts, 31 completions, 3 interceptions, 571 yards, 8 TD passes)
Season
(Min. 15 atts. per game) 204.6—Shawn Knight, William & Mary, 1993 (177 attempts, 125 completions, 4 interceptions, 2,055 yards, 22 TD passes)
Career
(Min. 300-399 comps.) 170.8—Shawn Knight, William & Mary, 1991-94 (558 attempts, 367 completions, 15 interceptions, 5,527 yards, 46 TD passes)
(Min. 400 comps.) 166.3—Dave Dickenson, Montana, 1992-95 (1,208 attempts, 813 completions, 26 interceptions, 11,080 yards, 96 TD passes)

MOST PASSES ATTEMPTED
Quarter
33—Joe Walland, Yale vs. Harvard, Nov. 20, 1999 (3rd, completed 20)

Half
51—Joe Walland, Yale vs. Harvard, Nov. 20, 1999 (2nd, completed 33)
Game
77—Neil Lomax, Portland St. vs. Northern Colo., Oct. 20, 1979 (completed 44)
Season
592—Martin Hankins, Southeastern La., 2003 (completed 353)
Per-game record—52.5, Joe Lee, Towson, 1999 (577 in 11)
Career
1,680—Steve McNair, Alcorn St., 1991-94 (completed 927); Marcus Brady, Cal St. Northridge, 1998-01 (completed 1,039)
Per-game record—42.9, Stan Greene, Boston U., 1989-90 (944 in 22)

MOST PASSES ATTEMPTED BY A FRESHMAN
Game
66—Chris Swartz, Morehead St. vs. Tennessee Tech, Oct. 17, 1987 (completed 35); Kevin Glenn, Illinois St. vs. Western Ill., Nov. 8, 1997 (completed 41)
Season
592—Martin Hankins, Southeastern La., 2003 (completed 353)
Also holds per-game record with 49.3 (592 in 12)

MOST PASSES COMPLETED
Quarter
20—Joe Walland, Yale vs. Harvard, Nov. 20, 1999 (3rd, attempted 33)
Half
33—Joe Walland, Yale vs. Harvard, Nov. 20, 1999 (2nd, attempted 51)
Game
50—Martin Hankins, Southeastern La. vs. Jacksonville, Nov. 6, 2004 (attempted 61)
Season
385—Brett Gordon, Villanova, 2002 (attempted 578)
Per-game record—32.4, Willie Totten, Mississippi Val., 1984 (324 in 10)
Career
1,039—Marcus Brady, Cal St. Northridge, 1998-01 (attempted 1,680)
Per-game record—26.5, Chris Sanders, Chattanooga, 1999-00 (584 in 22)

MOST PASSES COMPLETED BY A FRESHMAN
Game
42—Travis Brown, Northern Ariz. vs. Montana, Oct. 26, 1996 (attempted 65); Martin Hankins, Southeastern La. vs. Jacksonville, Nov. 8, 2003 (attempted 57)
Season
353—Martin Hankins, Southeastern La., 2003 (attempted 592)
Also holds per-game record with 29.4 (353 in 12)

MOST PASSES COMPLETED IN FRESHMAN AND SOPHOMORE SEASONS
710—Martin Hankins, Southeastern La., 2003-04 (attempted 1,132)

MOST CONSECUTIVE PASSES COMPLETED
Game
20—Austin Moherman, Missouri St. vs. Indiana St., Oct. 7, 2000; Kyle Slager, Brown vs. Rhode Island, Oct. 5, 2002

MOST CONSECUTIVE PASSES COMPLETED TO START GAME
20—Austin Moherman, Missouri St. vs. Indiana St., Oct. 7, 2000; Kyle Slager, Brown vs. Rhode Island, Oct. 5, 2002

MOST CONSECUTIVE PASSES COMPLETED TO START FIRST GAME AS A FRESHMAN
12—Daunte Culpepper, UCF vs. Eastern Ky., Aug. 31, 1995

HIGHEST PERCENTAGE OF PASSES COMPLETED
Game
(Min. 20-29 comps.) 95.7%—Butch Mosby, Murray St. vs. Tenn.-Martin, Oct. 2, 1993 (22 of 23)
(Min. 30 comps.) 85.0%—Marcus Brady, Cal St. Northridge vs. Missouri St., Nov. 14, 1998 (34 of 40)
Season
(Min. 200 atts.) 70.6%—Giovanni Carmazzi, Hofstra, 1997 (288 of 408)
Career
(Min. 750 atts.) 67.3%—Dave Dickenson, Montana, 1992-95 (813 of 1,208)

MOST PASSES HAD INTERCEPTED
Game
7—Mick Spoon, Idaho St. vs. Montana, Oct. 21, 1978 (attempted 35); Charles Hebert, Southeastern La. vs. Northwestern St., Nov. 12, 1983 (23 attempts); Carlton Jenkins, Mississippi Val. vs. Prairie View, Oct. 31, 1987 (34 attempts); Dan Crowley, Towson vs. Maine, Nov. 16, 1991 (53 attempts)
Season
29—Willie Totten, Mississippi Val., 1985 (492 attempts)
Also holds per-game record with 2.6 (29 in 11)
Career
75—Willie Totten, Mississippi Val., 1982-85
Per-game record—2.0, John Witkowski, Columbia, 1981-83 (60 in 30)

LOWEST PERCENTAGE OF PASSES HAD INTERCEPTED
Season
(Min. 175-324 atts.) 0.36%—Eric Rasmussen, San Diego, 2002 (1 of 279)
(Min. 325 atts.) 0.84%—Jimmy Blanchard, Portland St., 1999 (3 of 355)
Career
(Min. 750 atts.) 1.57%—Lang Campbell, William & Mary, 2001-04 (12 of 763)

MOST PASSES ATTEMPTED WITHOUT AN INTERCEPTION
Regulation Game
68—Tony Petersen, Marshall vs. Western Caro., Nov. 14, 1987 (completed 34)
Overtime Game
69—Chris Boden, Villanova vs. Connecticut, Oct. 16, 1999 (completed 43) (3 ot)
Entire Season
150—Ryan Fitzpatrick, Harvard, 2002 (completed 94)

MOST CONSECUTIVE PASSES ATTEMPTED WITHOUT AN INTERCEPTION
Season
342—Jimmy Blanchard, Portland St., 1999 (in 11 games, from Sept. 4 through Nov. 13)
Career
342—Jimmy Blanchard, Portland St., began Sept. 4, 1999, ended Nov. 13, 1999

MOST YARDS GAINED
Quarter
284—Sam Clemons, Western Ill. vs. Indiana St., Nov. 17, 2001 (2nd)
Half
383—Michael Payton, Marshall vs. VMI, Nov. 16, 1991 (1st)
Game
624—Jamie Martin, Weber St. vs. Idaho St., Nov. 23, 1991
Season
4,863—Steve McNair, Alcorn St., 1994
Career
14,496—Steve McNair, Alcorn St., 1991-94

MOST YARDS GAINED PER GAME
Season
455.7—Willie Totten, Mississippi Val., 1984 (4,557 in 10)
Career
350.0—Neil Lomax, Portland St., 1978-80 (11,550 in 33)

MOST YARDS GAINED BY A FRESHMAN
Game
540—Brad Otton, Weber St. vs. Northern Ariz., Nov. 6, 1993
Season
3,537—Martin Hankins, Southeastern La., 2003 (12 games)
Per-game record—308.9, Travis Brown, Northern Ariz., 1996 (3,398 in 11)

MOST YARDS GAINED IN FRESHMAN AND SOPHOMORE SEASONS
7,777—Martin Hankins, Southeastern La., 2003-04 (23 games)
Also holds per-game record with 338.1 (7,777 in 23)

MOST YARDS GAINED IN TWO, THREE AND FOUR CONSECUTIVE GAMES
2 Games
1,150—Steve McNair, Alcorn St., 1994 (587 vs. Samford, Oct. 29; 563 vs. Mississippi Val., Nov. 5)
3 Games
1,626—Steve McNair, Alcorn St., 1994 (587 vs. Samford, Oct. 29; 563 vs. Mississippi Val., Nov. 5; 476 vs. Troy, Nov. 12)
4 Games
2,159—Steve McNair, Alcorn St., 1994 (587 vs. Samford, Oct. 29; 563 vs. Mississippi Val., Nov. 5; 476 vs. Troy, Nov. 12; 533 vs. Jackson St., Nov. 19)

MOST GAMES GAINING 200 YARDS OR MORE
Season
11—By 18 players. Most recent: Lang Campbell, William & Mary, 2004; Martin Hankins, Southeastern La., 2004; Chris Sanders, Chattanooga, 2000; Chris Sanders, Chattanooga, 1999; Joe Lee, Towson, 1999; Steve McNair, Alcorn St., 1994; Chris Hakel, William & Mary, 1991; Jamie Martin, Weber St., 1991
Career
41—Steve McNair, Alcorn St., 1991-94 (42 games)

MOST CONSECUTIVE GAMES GAINING 200 YARDS OR MORE
Season
11—By 14 players. Most recent: Martin Hankins, Southeastern La., 2004; Chris Sanders, Chattanooga, 2000; Chris Sanders, Chattanooga, 1999; Steve McNair, Alcorn St., 1994; Chris Hakel, William & Mary, 1991; Jamie Martin, Weber St., 1991
Career
28—Steve McNair, Alcorn St., 1991-93; Neil Lomax, Portland St., 1978-80

MOST GAMES GAINING 300 YARDS OR MORE
Season
10—Willie Totten, Mississippi Val., 1984; John Friesz, Idaho, 1989; Steve McNair, Alcorn St., 1994
Career
28—Neil Lomax, Portland St., 1978-80

MOST CONSECUTIVE GAMES GAINING 300 YARDS OR MORE
Season
10—Willie Totten, Mississippi Val., 1984; John Friesz, Idaho, 1989
Career
13—Neil Lomax, Portland St., 1979-80

MOST YARDS GAINED AGAINST ONE OPPONENT
Career
1,675—Willie Totten, Mississippi Val. vs. Prairie View, 1982-85
Also holds per-game record with 418.8 (1,675 in 4)

MOST YARDS PER ATTEMPT
Game
(Min. 30-44 atts.) 16.1—Gilbert Renfroe, Tennessee St. vs. Dist. Columbia, Nov. 5, 1983 (30 for 484)
(Min. 45 atts.) 12.7—Todd Hammel, Stephen F. Austin vs. La.-Monroe, Nov. 11, 1989 (45 for 571)
Season
(Min. 250-324 atts.) 10.3—Mike Smith, UNI, 1986 (303 for 3,125)
(Min. 325 atts.) 9.88—Rocky Butler, Hofstra, 2001 (335 for 3,311)
Career
(Min. 500-999 atts.) 9.5—Jay Johnson, UNI, 1989-92 (744 for 7,049)
(Min. 1,000 atts.) 9.2—Dave Dickenson, Montana, 1992-95 (1,208 for 11,080)

MOST YARDS GAINED PER COMPLETION
Game
(Min. 15-19 comps.) 28.5—Kendrick Nord, Grambling vs. Alcorn St., Sept. 3, 1994 (17 for 485)
(Min. 20 comps.) 24.2—Matt Nagy, Delaware vs. Connecticut, Nov. 7, 1998 (23 for 556)
Season
(Min. 200 comps.) 16.7—Bruce Eugene, Grambling, 2002 (269 for 4,483)

Career
(Min. 350-399 comps.) 17.8—Jay Johnson, UNI, 1989-92 (397 for 7,049)
(Min. 400 comps.) 16.0—Shane Stafford, Connecticut, 1995-98 (522 for 8,368)

MOST TOUCHDOWN PASSES
Quarter
7—Neil Lomax, Portland St. vs. Delaware St., Nov. 8, 1980 (1st)
Half
7—Neil Lomax, Portland St. vs. Delaware St., Nov. 8, 1980 (1st)
Game
9—Willie Totten, Mississippi Val. vs. Kentucky St., Sept. 1, 1984
Season
56—Willie Totten, Mississippi Val., 1984; Bruce Eugene, Grambling, 2005
Totten holds per-game record with 5.6 (56 in 10)
Career
140—Bruce Eugene, Grambling, $2001-05
Per-game record—3.5, Willie Totten, Mississippi Val., 1982-85 (139 in 40)

$See page 10 for explanation.

MOST TOUCHDOWN PASSES BY A FRESHMAN
Season
31—Ricky Santos, New Hampshire, 2004 (13 games)

MOST CONSECUTIVE GAMES THROWING A TOUCHDOWN PASS
Career
36—Steve McNair, Alcorn St., 1991-94

MOST TOUCHDOWN PASSES, SAME PASSER AND RECEIVER
Season
27—Willie Totten to Jerry Rice, Mississippi Val., 1984
Career
47—Willie Totten to Jerry Rice, Mississippi Val., 1982-84

HIGHEST PERCENTAGE OF PASSES FOR TOUCHDOWNS
Season
(Min. 200-299 atts.) 12.5%—Ted White, Howard, 1996 (36 of 289)
(Min. 300 atts.) 10.9%—Doug Nussmeier, Idaho, 1993 (33 of 304)
Career
(Min. 500-749 atts.) 8.5%—Mike Williams, Grambling, 1977-80 (44 of 520)
(Min. 750 atts.) 8.2%—Tony Zimmerman, Duquesne, 1998-00 (73 of 889)

Receiving

MOST PASSES CAUGHT
Game
24—Jerry Rice, Mississippi Val. vs. Southern U., Oct. 1, 1983 (219 yards); Chas Gessner, Brown vs. Rhode Island, Oct. 5, 2002 (206 yards)
Season
120—Stephen Campbell, Brown, 2000 (1,332 yards)
Also holds per-game record with 12.0 (120 in 10)
Career
317—Jacquay Nunnally, Florida A&M, 1997-00 (4,239 yards)
Per-game record—7.3, Jerry Rice, Mississippi Val., 1981-84 (301 in 41)

MOST PASSES CAUGHT BY A TIGHT END
Game
18—Brian Forster, Rhode Island vs. Brown, Sept. 28, 1985 (327 yards)
Season
120—Stephen Campbell, Brown, 2000 (1,332 yards)
Also holds per-game record with 12.0 (120 in 10)
Career
245—Brian Forster, Rhode Island, 1983-85, 1987 (3,410 yards)

MOST PASSES CAUGHT BY A RUNNING BACK
Game
21—David Pandt, Montana St. vs. Eastern Wash., Sept. 21, 1985 (169 yards)
Season
89—Brian Westbrook, Villanova, 1998 (1,144 yards)
2 Yrs
135—Gordie Lockbaum, Holy Cross, 1986-87 (2,012 yards)
Also holds per-game record with 6.1 (135 in 22)
Career
188—Jason Corle, Towson, 1996-99 (1,725 yards)

MOST PASSES CAUGHT BY A FRESHMAN
Game
15—Emerson Foster, Rhode Island vs. Northeastern, Nov. 9, 1985 (205 yards); Drew Amerson, Cal St. Northridge vs. Weber St., Oct. 30, 1999 (147 yards)
Season
71—Drew Amerson, Cal St. Northridge, 1999 (897 yards)

MOST PASSES CAUGHT BY TWO PLAYERS, SAME TEAM
Season
183—Jerry Rice (103 for 1,682 yards and 27 TDs) & Joe Thomas (80 for 1,119 yards and 11 TDs), Mississippi Val., 1984
Career
420—Darrell Colbert (217 for 3,177 yards and 33 TDs) & Donald Narcisse (203 for 2,429 yards and 26 TDs), Texas Southern, 1983-86

MOST YARDS GAINED
Game
376—Kassim Osgood, Cal Poly vs. UNI, Nov. 4, 2000 (caught 17)
Season
1,712—Eddie Conti, Delaware, 1998 (caught 91)
Career
4,693—Jerry Rice, Mississippi Val., 1981-84 (caught 301)

MOST YARDS GAINED PER GAME
Season
168.2—Jerry Rice, Mississippi Val., 1984 (1,682 in 10)
Career
(Min. 2,000-2,999 yds.) 116.9—Derrick Ingram, UAB, 1993-94 (2,572 in 22)
(Min. 3,000 yds.) 114.5—Jerry Rice, Mississippi Val., 1981-84 (4,693 in 41)

MOST YARDS GAINED BY A TIGHT END
Game
327—Brian Forster, Rhode Island vs. Brown, Sept. 28, 1985 (caught 18)
Season
1,617—Brian Forster, Rhode Island, 1985 (caught 115)
Also holds per-game record with 161.7 (1,617 in 10)
Career
3,410—Brian Forster, Rhode Island, 1983-85, 1987 (caught 245)

MOST YARDS GAINED BY A RUNNING BACK
Game
228—T.J. Stallings, Morgan St. vs. N.C. A&T, Oct. 6, 2001 (caught 8)
Season
1,152—Gordie Lockbaum, Holy Cross, 1987 (caught 78)
Also holds per-game record with 104.7 (1,152 in 11)

MOST YARDS GAINED BY A FRESHMAN
Game
284—Jacquay Nunnally, Florida A&M vs. N.C. A&T, Oct. 11, 1997 (caught 13)
Season
1,073—Randy Moss, Marshall, 1996 (caught 55)

MOST YARDS GAINED BY TWO PLAYERS, SAME TEAM
Season
2,801—Jerry Rice (1,682, 103 caught and 27 TDs) & Joe Thomas (1,119, 80 caught and 11 TDs), Mississippi Val., 1984
Career
5,806—Roy Banks (3,177, 184 caught and 38 TDs) & Cal Pierce (2,629, 163 caught and 13 TDs), Eastern Ill., 1983-86

HIGHEST AVERAGE GAIN PER RECEPTION
Game
(Min. 5-9 receps.) 44.6—John Taylor, Delaware St. vs. St. Paul's, Sept. 21, 1985 (5 for 223)
(Min. 10 receps.) 29.0—Jason Cristino, Lehigh vs. Lafayette, Nov. 21, 1992 (11 for 319)
Season
(Min. 35-59 receps.) 28.9—Mikhael Ricks, Stephen F. Austin, 1997 (47 for 1,358)
(Min. 60 receps.) 20.7—Golden Tate, Tennessee St., 1983 (63 for 1,307)
Career
(Min. 90-124 receps.) 24.3—John Taylor, Delaware St., 1982-85 (100 for 2,426)
(Min. 125 receps.) 22.0—Dedric Ward, UNI, 1993-96 (176 for 3,876)

MOST GAMES GAINING 100 YARDS OR MORE
Career
23—Jerry Rice, Mississippi Val., 1981-84 (41 games)

MOST TOUCHDOWN PASSES CAUGHT
Game
6—Cos DeMatteo, Chattanooga vs. Mississippi Val., Sept. 16, 2000 (9 total catches for 203 yards)
Season
27—Jerry Rice, Mississippi Val., 1984
Career
50—Jerry Rice, Mississippi Val., 1981-84

MOST TOUCHDOWN PASSES CAUGHT BY A FRESHMAN
Season
19—Randy Moss, Marshall, 1996

MOST TOUCHDOWN PASSES CAUGHT PER GAME
Season
2.7—Jerry Rice, Mississippi Val., 1984 (27 in 10)
Career
1.2—Jerry Rice, Mississippi Val., 1981-84 (50 in 41)

MOST GAMES CATCHING A TOUCHDOWN PASS
Season
11—Randy Moss, Marshall, 1996
Also holds consecutive record with 11, 1996
Career
26—Jerry Rice, Mississippi Val., 1981-84
Also holds consecutive record with 17, 1983-84

Punting

MOST PUNTS
Game
16—Matt Stover, Louisiana Tech vs. La.-Monroe, Nov. 18, 1988 (567 yards)
Season
98—Barry Hickingbotham, Louisiana Tech, 1987 (3,821 yards)
Career
301—Barry Bowman, Louisiana Tech, 1983-86 (11,441 yards)

HIGHEST AVERAGE PER PUNT
Game
(5-9 punts) 61.5—Eddie Johnson, Idaho St. vs. Cal Poly, Nov. 16, 2002 (6 for 369)
(Min. 10 punts) 52.2—Stuart Dodds, Montana St. vs. Northern Ariz., Oct. 20, 1979 (10 for 522)
Season
(Min. 60 punts) 48.2—Mark Gould, Northern Ariz., 2002 (62 for 2,987)
Career
(Min. 150 punts) 44.8—Mark Gould, Northern Ariz., 2000-03 (211 for 9,443)

LONGEST PUNT
93—Tyler Grogan, Northeastern vs. Villanova, Sept. 8, 2001

Interceptions

MOST PASSES INTERCEPTED
Game
5—Karl Johnson, Jackson St. vs. Grambling, Oct. 23, 1982 (29 yards); Michael Richardson, Northwestern St. vs. Southeastern La., Nov. 12, 1983 (128 yards); Mark Cordes, Eastern Wash. vs. Boise St., Sept. 6, 1986 (48 yards)
Season
14—Rashean Mathis, Bethune-Cookman, 2002 (455 yards)
Per-game record—1.2, Dean Cain, Princeton, 1987 (12 in 10)
Career
31—Rashean Mathis, Bethune-Cookman, 1999-02 (682 yards)
Per-game record—0.73, Dean Cain, Princeton, 1985-87 (22 in 30)

MOST YARDS ON INTERCEPTION RETURNS
Game
216—Keiron Bigby, Brown vs. Yale, Sept. 29, 1984 (3 interceptions) (first career game)
Season
455—Rashean Mathis, Bethune-Cookman, 2002 (14 interceptions)
Career
682—Rashean Mathis, Bethune-Cookman, 1999-02 (31 interceptions)

MOST TOUCHDOWNS SCORED ON INTERCEPTION RETURNS
Game
2—By 22 players. Most recent: Kellin White, Southeast Mo. St. vs. Tenn.-Martin, Oct. 30, 2004; Kevin Gerard, Northern Ariz. vs. Weber St., Sept. 25, 2004; Travis Hill, Western Caro. vs. West Virginia St., Sept. 2, 2004; Davon Telp, Towson vs. Georgetown, Nov. 8, 2003; Tony Tiller, East Tenn. St. vs. Liberty, Oct. 18, 2003; Bruce Woods, Northwestern St. vs. Southeastern La., Oct. 11, 2003
Season
4—Robert Turner, Jackson St., 1990 (9 interceptions, 212 yards); Joseph Vaughn, Cal St. Northridge, 1994 (9 interceptions, 265 yards); William Hampton, Murray St., 1995 (8 interceptions, 280 yards)
Career
6—William Hampton, Murray St., 1993-96 (20 interceptions)

HIGHEST AVERAGE GAIN PER INTERCEPTION
Game
(Min. 3 ints.) 72.0—Keiron Bigby, Brown vs. Yale, Sept. 29, 1984 (3 for 216)
Season
(Min. 3 ints.) 72.0—Keiron Bigby, Brown, 1984 (3 for 216)
Career
(Min. 12 ints.) 25.9—Michael Ford, Duquesne, 2003-05 (13 for 337)

MOST SEASONS INTERCEPTING AT LEAST ONE PASS
5—Rayshun Reed, Troy, $1999-03 (Note: Troy was an FBS member for 2002-03)

$See page 10 for explanation.

Punt Returns

MOST PUNT RETURNS
Game
11—Peter Athans, Sacred Heart vs. Siena, Nov. 9, 2002 (98 yards)
Season
55—Tommy Houk, Murray St., 1980 (442 yards)
Also holds per-game record with 5.0 (55 in 11)
Career
143—Levander Segars, Montana, 2001-04 (1,441 yards)
Per-game record—3.8, Tommy Houk, Murray St., 1979-80 (84 in 22)

MOST YARDS ON PUNT RETURNS
Game
227—Leonard Goolsby, South Carolina St. vs. Norfolk St., Oct. 11, 2003 (7 returns)
Season
662—Dan McGrath, Fordham, 2002 (48 returns)
Per-game record—54.7, Joe Rosato, Duquesne, 1996 (547 in 10)
Career
1,668—Marquay McDaniel, Hampton, 2002-05 (116 returns)

HIGHEST AVERAGE GAIN PER RETURN
Game
(Min. 5 rets.) 43.2—Ricky Pearsall, Northern Ariz. vs. Western N.M., Aug. 29, 1996 (5 for 216)
Season
(Min. 1.2 rets. per game) 26.5—Curtis DeLoatch, N.C. A&T, 2001 (20 for 530)
Career
(Min. 1.2 rets. per game) 17.4—Terrence McGee, Northwestern St., 1999-02 (56 for 972)

MOST TOUCHDOWNS SCORED ON PUNT RETURNS
Game
3—Aaron Fix, Canisius vs. Siena, Sept. 24, 1994 (5 returns); Zuriel Smith, Hampton vs. Virginia St., Sept. 22, 2001 (3 returns)
Season
5—Curtis DeLoatch, N.C. A&T, 2001 (20 returns)
Career
7—Kenny Shedd, UNI, 1989-92

LONGEST PUNT RETURN
98—Barney Bussey, South Carolina St. vs. Johnson C. Smith, Oct. 10, 1981; Willie Ware, Mississippi Val. vs. Bishop, Sept. 21, 1985

MOST CONSECUTIVE GAMES RETURNING PUNT FOR TOUCHDOWN
3—Troy Jones, McNeese St., 1989 (vs. Mississippi Col., Sept. 2; vs. Samford, Sept. 9; vs. La.-Monroe, Sept. 16)

Kickoff Returns

MOST KICKOFF RETURNS
Game
10—Merril Hoge, Idaho St. vs. Weber St., Oct. 25, 1986 (179 yards); Ryan Steen, Cal Poly vs. Eastern Wash., Sept. 10, 1994 (203 yards); Keylam Davis, Southeastern La. vs. Northwestern St., Oct. 11, 2003 (282 yards)
Season
50—David Primus, Samford, 1989 (1,411 yards); Kijana Thomas, Charleston So., 2003 (1,148 yards)
Primus holds per-game record with 4.5 (50 in 11)
Career
155—Lonnie Teagle, Alcorn St., 2001-04 (2,734 yards)
Also holds per-game record with 3.4 (155 in 45)

MOST YARDS ON KICKOFF RETURNS
Game
326—Bashir Levingston, Eastern Wash. vs. Sacramento St., Oct. 31, 1998 (5 returns)
Season
1,411—David Primus, Samford, 1989 (50 returns)
Also holds per-game record with 128.3 (1,411 in 11)
Career
2,734—Lonnie Teagle, Alcorn St., 2001-04 (155 returns)
Per-game record—73.5, Justin Campbell, Butler, 2002-04 (2,498 in 34)

HIGHEST AVERAGE GAIN PER RETURN
Game
(Min. 5 rets.) 65.2—Bashir Levingston, Eastern Wash. vs. Sacramento St., Oct. 31, 1998 (5 for 326)
Season
(Min. 1.2 rets. per game) 37.3—David Fraterrigo, Canisius, 1993 (13 for 485)
Career
(Min. 45 rets. and 1.2 rets. per game) 30.0—Lamont Brightful, Eastern Wash., 1998-01 (65 for 1,949)

MOST TOUCHDOWNS SCORED ON KICKOFF RETURNS
Game
3—Bashir Levingston, Eastern Wash. vs. Sacramento St., Oct. 31, 1998
Season
5—Jerome Mathis, Hampton, 2004
Career
6—Jerome Mathis, Hampton, 2001-04

Total Kick Returns

(Combined Punt and Kickoff Returns)

MOST KICK RETURNS
Game
12—Craig Hodge, Tennessee St. vs. Morgan St., Oct. 24, 1987 (8 punts, 4 kickoffs; 319 yards)
Season
64—Joe Markus, Connecticut, 1981 (34 punts, 30 kickoffs; 939 yards)
Career
199—Herman Hunter, Tennessee St., 1981-84 (103 punts, 96 kickoffs; 3,232 yards)

MOST YARDS ON KICK RETURNS
Game
349—Bashir Levingston, Eastern Wash. vs. Sacramento St., Oct. 31, 1998 (8 returns, 23 on punt returns, 326 on kickoff returns)
Season
1,469—David Primus, Samford, 1989 (1,411 on kickoffs, 58 on punts)
Also holds per-game record with 133.5 (1,469 in 11)
Career
3,318—Delvin Joyce, James Madison, 1997-00 (1,488 on punts, 1,830 on kickoffs)
Also holds per-game record with 85.1 (3,318 in 39)

GAINING 1,000 YARDS ON PUNT RETURNS AND 1,000 YARDS ON KICKOFF RETURNS
Career
Joe Markus, Connecticut, 1979-82 (1,012 on punts and 1,185 on kickoffs); Kenny Shedd, UNI, 1989-92 (1,081 on punts and 1,359 on kickoffs); Joe Rosato, Duquesne, 1994-97 (1,036 on punts and 1,661 on kickoffs); Delvin Joyce, James Madison, 1997-00 (1,488 on punts and 1,830 on kickoffs)

HIGHEST AVERAGE PER KICK RETURN
Game
(Min. 6 rets.) 44.7—Jay Jones, James Madison vs. Richmond, Oct. 19, 1996 (6 for 268)
Season
(Min. 40 rets.) 26.7—David Primus, Samford, 1989 (55 for 1,469)
Career
(Min. 60 rets.) 26.4—Lamont Brightful, Eastern Wash., 1998-01 (80 for 2,115)

MOST TOUCHDOWNS SCORED ON KICK RETURNS
Game
3—Aaron Fix, Canisius vs. Siena, Sept. 24, 1994 (3 punt returns); Bashir Levingston, Eastern Wash. vs. Sacramento St., Oct. 31, 1998 (3 kickoffs); Zuriel Smith, Hampton vs. Virginia St., Sept. 22, 2001 (3 punt returns)
Season
6—Bashir Levingston, Eastern Wash., 1998 (3 punt returns and 3 kickoff returns); Corey Smith, Montana St., 2003 (4 punt returns and 2 kickoff returns)
Career
7—Willie Ware, Mississippi Val., 1982-85 (5 punts and 2 kickoffs); Kenny Shedd, UNI, 1989-92 (7 punts); Kerry Hayes, Western Caro., 1991-94 (2 punts and 5 kickoffs); Joe Rosato, Duquesne, 1994-97 (4 punts and 3 kickoffs); Darrell Jones, Cal Poly, 2000-03 (4 punts and 3 kickoffs)

Blocked Kicks

MOST BLOCKED PUNTS
Game
3—Ben Duhon, McNeese St. vs. Ark.-Monticello, Sept. 29, 1998; Brandon Tinson, Colgate vs. Towson, Sept. 30, 2000
Season
4—Ryan Crawford, Davidson, 2000; Robert Herron, Sam Houston St., 2004
Career
8—Trey Woods, Sam Houston St., 1992-95

MOST BLOCKED FIELD GOALS
Game
2—Rod Gulky, McNeese St. vs. Henderson St., Aug. 30, 2003; Chris Mooney, Delaware vs. Massachusetts, Nov. 15, 2003
Season
4—Leonard Smith, McNeese St., 1981; Mark Weivoda, Idaho St., 2001; Clayton Smith, Dartmouth, 2004
Career
10—Leonard Smith, McNeese St., 1980-82

MOST BLOCKED EXTRA POINTS
Game
1—By many players
Season
4—Tim Hauck, Montana, 1988; Ed Groszewski, Cornell, 1991

Career
7—Tim Hauck, Montana, 1987-89

MOST COMBINED BLOCKED KICKS (Includes Punts, PAT Attempts, FG Attempts)
Game
3—Ben Duhon, McNeese St. vs. Ark.-Monticello, Sept. 29, 1998 (3 punts); Michael Adams, Stephen F. Austin vs. Central Okla., Aug. 30, 2000 (2 punts, 1 PAT); Brandon Tinson, Colgate vs. Towson, Sept. 30, 2000 (3 punts)
Season
6—Leonard Smith, McNeese St., 1981 (4 FGs, 2 punts); Ryan Crawford, Davidson, 2000 (4 punts, 2 FGs); Mark Weivoda, Idaho St., 2001 (4 FGs, 2 PATs)
Career
17—Leonard Smith, McNeese St., 1980-82 (10 FGs, 4 PATs, 3 punts)

All-Purpose Yards

(Yardage Gained From Rushing, Receiving and All Runbacks; Must Have One Attempt From at Least Two Categories)

MOST PLAYS
Game
54—Ron Darby, Marshall vs. Western Caro., Nov. 12, 1988 (47 rushes, 4 receptions, 3 kickoff returns; 329 yards)
(Note: 56—Arnold Mickens, Butler vs. Valparaiso, Oct. 8, 1994; all rushes)
Season
453—Jamaal Branch, Colgate, 2003 (450 rushes, 3 receptions; 2,350 yards)
Career
1,178—Charles Roberts, Sacramento St., 1997-00 (1,124 rushes, 44 receptions, 1 punt return, 9 kickoff returns; 7,112 yards)

MOST YARDS GAINED
Game
467—Joey Stockton, Western Ky. vs. Austin Peay, Sept. 16, 1995 (29 rushing, 276 receiving, 18 punt returns, 144 kickoff returns; 14 plays)
Season
3,026—Brian Westbrook, Villanova, 1998 (1,046 rushing, 1,144 receiving, 192 punt returns, 644 kickoff returns; 329 plays)
Also holds per-game record with 275.1 (3,026 in 11)
Career
9,512—Brian Westbrook, Villanova, 1997-98, 00-01 (4,298 rushing, 2,582 receiving, 343 punt returns, 2,289 kickoff returns; 1,022 plays)
Also holds per-game record with 216.2 (9,512 in 44)

MOST YARDS GAINED BY A FRESHMAN
Game
437—Ryan Fuqua, Portland St. vs. Eastern Wash., Nov. 10, 2001 (393 rushing, 44 kickoff returns)
Season
2,014—David Wright, Indiana St., 1992 (1,313 rushing, 108 receiving, 593 kickoff returns; 254 plays)

HIGHEST AVERAGE GAIN PER PLAY
Game
(Min. 20 plays) 20.6—Herman Hunter, Tennessee St. vs. Mississippi Val., Nov. 13, 1982 (453 on 22)
Season
(Min. 1,000 yards, 100 plays) 19.7—Otis Washington, Western Caro., 1988 (2,086 on 106)
Career
(Min. 4,000 yards, 350 plays) 17.2—Eddie Conti, Delaware, 1994-98 (6,096 on 355)

GAINING 1,000 YARDS RUSHING AND 1,000 YARDS RECEIVING
Season
Brian Westbrook, Villanova, 1998 (1,046 rushing, 1,144 receiving)

TEAM HAVING A 200-YARD RUSHER AND A 200-YARD RECEIVER IN THE SAME GAME
Portland St., Charles Dunn (247 rushing yards) and Art Williams (208 receiving yards) vs. Sacramento St., Oct. 10, 1998 (Portland St. won, 58-31); Portland St., Charles Dunn (213 rushing yards) and Terry Charles (209 receiving yards) vs. Cal Poly, Oct. 30, 1999 (Portland St. won, 42-28)

Scoring

MOST POINTS SCORED
Game
42—Archie Amerson, Northern Ariz. vs. Weber St., Oct. 5, 1996 (7 TDs); Jessie Burton, McNeese St. vs. Southern Utah, Sept. 19, 1998 (7 TDs)
Season
186—Kevin Richardson, Appalachian St., 2006 (31 TDs)
Career
544—Brian Westbrook, Villanova, 1997-98, 00-01 (89 TDs, 10 PATs)

MOST POINTS SCORED PER GAME
Season
16.2—Jerry Rice, Mississippi Val., 1984 (162 in 10)
Career
(Min. 200-299 pts.) 11.7—Aaron Stecker, Western Ill., 1997-98 (234 in 20)
(Min. 300 pts.) 12.5—Adrian Peterson, Ga. Southern, 1998-01 (524 in 42)

MOST TOUCHDOWNS SCORED
Game
7—Archie Amerson, Northern Ariz. vs. Weber St., Oct. 5, 1996; Jessie Burton, McNeese St. vs. Southern Utah, Sept. 19, 1998
Season
31—Kevin Richardson, Appalachian St., 2006
Career
89—Brian Westbrook, Villanova, 1997-98, 00-01

MOST TOUCHDOWNS SCORED PER GAME
Season
2.7—Jerry Rice, Mississippi Val., 1984 (27 in 10)
Career
(Min. 30 games) 2.07—Adrian Peterson, Ga. Southern, 1998-01 (87 in 42)

MOST TOUCHDOWNS SCORED BY A FRESHMAN
Season
26—Adrian Peterson, Ga. Southern, 1998
Also holds per-game record with 2.4 (26 in 11)

PASSING FOR A TOUCHDOWN AND SCORING TOUCHDOWNS BY RUSHING, RECEIVING AND PUNT RETURN
WR Sean Beckton, UCF, threw a 33-yard touchdown pass, rushed for an 11-yard touchdown, caught a 17-yard touchdown pass and returned a punt 60 yards for a touchdown vs. Texas Southern, Nov. 17, 1990

MOST EXTRA POINTS ATTEMPTED BY KICKING
Game
15—John Kincheloe, Portland St. vs. Delaware St., Nov. 8, 1980 (15 made)
Season
74—John Kincheloe, Portland St., 1980 (70 made)
Per-game record—7.2, Jonathan Stokes, Mississippi Val., 1984 (72 in 10)
Career
239—Craig Coffin, Southern Ill., $2002-06 (229 made)
$*See page 10 for explanation.*

MOST EXTRA POINTS MADE BY KICKING
Game
15—John Kincheloe, Portland St. vs. Delaware St., Nov. 8, 1980 (15 attempts)
Season
70—John Kincheloe, Portland St., 1980 (74 attempts)
Per-game record—6.8, Jonathan Stokes, Mississippi Val., 1984 (68 in 10)
Career
229—Craig Coffin, Southern Ill., $2002-06 (239 attempts)
Per-game record—4.8, Tim Openlander, Marshall, 1994-96 (159 in 33)
$*See page 10 for explanation.*

BEST PERFECT RECORD OF EXTRA POINTS MADE
Season
68 of 68—Mike Hollis, Idaho, 1993

HIGHEST PERCENTAGE OF EXTRA POINTS MADE
Season
(Min. 50 atts.) 100%—Billy Hayes, Sam Houston St., 1987 (50 of 50); Jim Hodson, Lafayette, 1988 (51 of 51); Mike Hollis, Idaho, 1993 (68 of 68); Chris Dill, Murray St., 1995 (56 of 56); Tim Openlander, Marshall, 1996 (58 of 58); Chris Snyder, Montana, 2002 (50 of 50); Craig Coffin, Southern Ill., 2004 (66 of 66); Dan Carpenter, Montana, 2004 (63 of 63); Lance Garner, Sam Houston St., 2004 (57 of 57) ; Craig Coffin, Southern Ill., 2006 (55 of 55)
Career
(Min. 100-119 atts.) 100%—Anders Larsson, Montana St., 1985-88 (101 of 101)
(Min. 120 atts.) 99.2%—Brian Mitchell, Marshall/UNI, 1987, 1989-91 (130 of 131)

MOST CONSECUTIVE EXTRA POINTS MADE
Game
15—John Kincheloe, Portland St. vs. Delaware St., Nov. 8, 1980
Season
68—Mike Hollis, Idaho, 1993
Career
126—Chris Snyder, Montana, 2000-03

MOST POINTS SCORED BY KICKING
Game
24—Goran Lingmerth, Northern Ariz. vs. Idaho, Oct. 25, 1986 (8 FGs)
Season
122—Chris Snyder, Montana, 2003 (25 of 30 FGs, 47 of 48 PATs)
Career
392—Chris Snyder, Montana, 2000-03 (70 FGs, 182 PATs)

MOST POINTS SCORED BY KICKING PER GAME
Season
10.1—Rob Hart, Murray St., 1996 (112 in 11)
Career
9.1—Tony Zendejas, Nevada, 1981-83 (300 in 33)

MOST TWO-POINT ATTEMPTS
Season
11—Brent Woods, Princeton, 1982; Jamie Martin, Weber St., 1990

MOST SUCCESSFUL TWO-POINT PASSES
Game
3—Brent Woods, Princeton vs. Lafayette, Nov. 6, 1982 (attempted 3)
Season
7—Jamie Martin, Weber St., 1992 (attempted 7)
Career
15—Jamie Martin, Weber St., 1989-92 (attempted 28)

Defensive Extra Points

MOST DEFENSIVE EXTRA-POINT RETURNS
Game
2—Joe Lee Johnson, Western Ky. vs. Indiana St., Nov. 10, 1990 (both kick returns, scored on neither)

MOST DEFENSIVE EXTRA POINTS SCORED
Game
1—By many players
Season
2—Jackie Kellogg, Eastern Wash. vs. Weber St., Oct. 6, 1990 (90-yard interception return) & vs. Portland St., Oct. 27, 1990 (94-yard interception return)

LONGEST RETURN OF A DEFENSIVE EXTRA POINT
100—Morgan Ryan (DB), Montana St. vs. Sam Houston St., Sept. 7, 1991 (interception return); Rich Kinsman (DB), William & Mary vs. Lehigh, Nov. 14, 1992

FIRST DEFENSIVE EXTRA-POINT ATTEMPTS
Mike Rogers (DB), Davidson vs. Lehigh, Sept. 10, 1988 (30-yard interception return); Dave Benna (LB), Towson vs. Northeastern, Sept. 10, 1988 (35-yard interception return)

Defensive Records

(Since 2000)

TOTAL TACKLES

Game

30—Josh Cain, Chattanooga vs. Citadel, Nov. 3, 2001

Season

195—Kevin Talley, Norfolk St., 2003

Per-game record—16.3, Boomer Grigsby, Illinois St., 2002 (179 in 11); Kevin Talley, Norfolk St., 2003 (195 in 12)

Career

550—Boomer Grigsby, Illinois St., 2001-04 (44 games)

Per-game record—13.2, Josh Cain, Chattanooga, 2000-02 (450 in 34)

SOLO TACKLES

Game

21—Dan Adams, Holy Cross vs. Colgate, Oct. 22, 2005

Season

113—Josh Cain, Chattanooga, 2002

Per-game record—9.8, Boomer Grigsby, Illinois St., 2002 (108 in 11)

Career

325—Boomer Grigsby, Illinois St., 2001-04 (44 games)

Per-game record—8.0, Josh Cain, Chattanooga, 2000-02 (273 in 34)

ASSISTED TACKLES

Game

12—Chris Carey, Columbia vs. Harvard, Nov. 3, 2001; Boomer Grigsby, Illinois St. vs. Youngstown St., Nov. 9, 2002; Maurice Bennett, Lafayette vs. Fordham, Sept. 24, 2005

Season

120—Kevin Talley, Norfolk St., 2003

Also holds per-game record with 10.0 (120 in 12)

Career

271—Liam Ezekiel, Northeastern, 2001-04 (44 games)

Also holds per-game record with 6.4 (271 in 44)

TACKLES FOR LOSS

Game

8.0—Sherrod Coates, Western Ky. vs. Indiana St., Oct. 26, 2002

Season

36.0—Steve Baggs, Bethune-Cookman, 2003

Also holds per-game record with 3.0 (36.0 in 12)

Career

67.0—Sherrod Coates, Western Ky., 2000-02 (40 games)

Per-game record—2.5, Steve Baggs, Bethune-Cookman, 2002-03 (62.0 in 25)

PASS SACKS

Game

6.0—Damien Huren, Southeastern La. vs. Northern Colo., Oct. 9, 2004

Season

23.5—Chris Gocong, Cal Poly, 2005

Per-game record—1.89, Andrew Hollingsworth, Towson, 2000 (17 in 9)

Career

42.0—Chris Gocong, Cal Poly, 2001, 03-05 (41 games)

Per-game record—1.05, Brent Hawkins, Illinois St., 2004-05 (20.0 in 19)

PASSES DEFENDED

Game

6—Sam Young, Illinois St. vs. Youngstown St., Oct. 7, 2000; Marcus Gray, Norfolk St. vs. Florida A&M, Oct. 26, 2002; James Young, Ga. Southern vs. Bethune-Cookman, Nov. 30, 2002; Robson Noel, Jacksonville vs. Dayton, Oct. 14, 2006

Season

27—Bobby Sippio, Western Ky., 2000

Also holds per-game record with 2.7 (27 in 10)

Career

51—Billy Parker, William & Mary, 2000-03 (44 games)

Per-game record—1.54, Benny Sapp, UNI, 2002-03 (37 in 24)

FORCED FUMBLES

Game

3—Sterling Rogers, Texas St. vs. Portland St., Oct. 6, 2001; Lee Basinger, Wofford vs. Elon, Nov. 23, 2002; Sam Harper, Coastal Caro. vs. Jacksonville, Nov. 13, 2004; Brent Hawkins, Illinois St. vs. Murray St., Sept. 24, 2005

Season

10—Robert Mathis, Alabama A&M, 2002

Also holds per-game record with 0.91 (10 in 11)

Career

13—Sherrod Coates, Western Ky., 2000-02 (40 games); Robert Mathis, Alabama A&M, 2001-02 (22 games)

Mathis holds per-game record with 0.59 (13 in 22)

Field Goals

MOST FIELD GOALS ATTEMPTED

Game

8—Goran Lingmerth, Northern Ariz. vs. Idaho, Oct. 25, 1986 (made 8)

Season

33—Tony Zendejas, Nevada, 1982 (made 26); David Ettinger, Hofstra, 1995 (made 22)

Career

105—Chris Snyder, Montana, 2000-03 (made 70)

MOST FIELD GOALS MADE

Quarter

4—Tony Zendejas, Nevada vs. Northern Ariz., Oct. 16, 1982 (4th); Ryan Weeks, Tennessee Tech vs. Chattanooga, Sept. 9, 1989 (3rd)

Half

5—Dean Biasucci, Western Caro. vs. Mars Hill, Sept. 18, 1982 (1st); Tony Zendejas, Nevada vs. Northern Ariz., Oct. 16, 1982 (2nd); Ryan Weeks, Tennessee Tech vs. Chattanooga, Sept. 9, 1989 (2nd)

Game

8—Goran Lingmerth, Northern Ariz. vs. Idaho, Oct. 25, 1986 (39, 18, 20, 33, 46, 27, 22, 35 yards; by quarters—1, 3, 2, 2), 8 attempts

Season

26—Tony Zendejas, Nevada, 1982 (33 attempts); Brian Mitchell, UNI, 1990 (27 attempts)

Also share per-game record with 2.4 (26 in 11)

Career

72—Marty Zendejas, Nevada, 1984-87 (90 attempts)

Per-game record—2.1, Tony Zendejas, Nevada, 1981-83 (70 in 33)

HIGHEST PERCENTAGE OF FIELD GOALS MADE

Season

(Min. 20 atts.) 96.3%—Brian Mitchell, UNI, 1990 (26 of 27)

Career

(Min. 50 atts.) 82.0%—Juan Toro, Florida A&M, 1995-98 (41 of 50)

BEST PERFECT RECORD OF FIELD GOALS MADE

Season

100%—Jon Scifres, Missouri St., 2004 (15 of 15)

MOST CONSECUTIVE FIELD GOALS MADE

Game

8—Goran Lingmerth, Northern Ariz. vs. Idaho, Oct. 25, 1986

Season

21—Brian Mitchell, UNI, 1990

Career

26—Brian Mitchell, UNI, 1990-91

MOST CONSECUTIVE GAMES KICKING A FIELD GOAL

Career

33—Tony Zendejas, Nevada, 1981-83 (at least one in every game played)

MOST FIELD GOALS MADE, 50 YARDS OR MORE

Game

3—Jesse Garcia, La.-Monroe vs. McNeese St., Oct. 29, 1983 (52, 56, 53 yards); Terry Belden, Northern Ariz. vs. Cal St. Northridge, Sept. 18, 1993 (60, 50, 54 yards)

Season

7—Jesse Garcia, La.-Monroe, 1983 (12 attempts); Kirk Roach, Western Caro., 1987 (12 attempts)

Career

11—Kirk Roach, Western Caro., 1984-87 (26 attempts); Pete Garces, Idaho St., 1998-99 (16 attempts)

HIGHEST PERCENTAGE OF FIELD GOALS MADE, 50 YARDS OR MORE

Season

(Min. 5 atts.) 100.0%—Wayne Boyer, Missouri St., 1996 (5 of 5)

Career

(Min. 10 atts.) 90.9%—Tim Foley, Ga. Southern, 1984-87 (10 of 11)

MOST FIELD GOALS MADE, 40 YARDS OR MORE

Season

12—Marty Zendejas, Nevada, 1985 (15 attempts)

Career

30—Marty Zendejas, Nevada, 1984-87 (45 attempts)

HIGHEST PERCENTAGE OF FIELD GOALS MADE, 40 YARDS OR MORE

Season

(Min. 8 made) 100.0%—Tim Foley, Ga. Southern, 1985 (8 of 8)

Career

(Min. 15 made) 72.0%—Tim Foley, Ga. Southern, 1984-87 (18 of 25)

HIGHEST PERCENTAGE OF FIELD GOALS MADE, 40-49 YARDS

Season

(Min. 8 made) 90.0%—Marty Zendejas, Nevada, 1985 (9 of 10)

Career

(Min. 12 made) 72.0%—Tony Zendejas, Nevada, 1981-83 (18 of 25)

HIGHEST PERCENTAGE OF FIELD GOALS MADE, UNDER 40 YARDS

Season

(Min. 15 made) 100.0%—Matt Stover, Louisiana Tech, 1986 (15 of 15); Kirk Roach, Western Caro., 1986 (17 of 17); Brian Mitchell, UNI, 1990 (23 of 23)

Career

(Min. 25 made) 93.3%—Marty Zendejas, Nevada, 1984-87 (42 of 45)

MOST TIMES KICKING TWO OR MORE FIELD GOALS IN A GAME

Season

10—Brian Mitchell, UNI, 1991

Career

25—Kirk Roach, Western Caro., 1984-87

MOST TIMES KICKING THREE OR MORE FIELD GOALS IN A GAME

Season

7—Brian Mitchell, UNI, 1991

Career

11—Brian Mitchell, Marshall/UNI, 1987, 1989-91

MOST CONSECUTIVE QUARTERS KICKING A FIELD GOAL

Season

7—Scott Roper, Arkansas St., 1986 (last 3 vs. McNeese St., Oct. 25; all 4 vs. North Texas, Nov. 1)

LONGEST AVERAGE DISTANCE FIELD GOALS MADE

Game

(Min. 3 made) 54.7—Terry Belden, Northern Ariz. vs. Sacramento St., Sept. 18, 1993 (60, 50, 54 yards)

Season

(Min. 14 made) 45.0—Jesse Garcia, La.-Monroe, 1983 (15 made)

Career

(Min. 35 made) 37.5—Roger Ruzek, Weber St., 1979-82 (46 made)

LONGEST AVERAGE DISTANCE FIELD GOALS ATTEMPTED

Game

(Min. 4 atts.) 55.5—Pete Garces, Idaho St. vs. Sacramento St., Nov. 7, 1998 (made 53, 54; missed 54, 61)

Season

(Min. 20 atts.) 45.9—Jesse Garcia, La.-Monroe, 1983 (26 attempts)

Career

(Min. 60 atts.) 40.5—Kirk Roach, Western Caro., 1984-87 (102 attempts)

LONGEST FIELD GOAL MADE

63—Scott Roper, Arkansas St. vs. North Texas, Nov. 7, 1987; Tim Foley, Ga. Southern vs. James Madison, Nov. 7, 1987; Bill Gramatica, South Fla. vs. Austin Peay, Nov. 18, 2000

LONGEST FIELD GOAL MADE BY A FRESHMAN

60—David Cool, Ga. Southern vs. James Madison, Nov. 5, 1988

MOST FIELD GOALS MADE BY A FRESHMAN

Game

5—Mike Powers, Colgate vs. Army, Sept. 10, 1983 (6 attempts); Marty Zendejas, Nevada vs. Idaho St., Nov. 17, 1984 (5 attempts); Chuck Rawlinson, Stephen F. Austin vs. Prairie View, Sept. 10, 1988 (5 attempts); Juan Vasquez, Florida A&M vs. Morgan St., Sept. 9, 2000 (5 attempts)

Season

22—Marty Zendejas, Nevada, 1984 (27 attempts)

MOST FIELD GOALS MADE IN FIRST GAME OF CAREER

5—Mike Powers, Colgate vs. Army, Sept. 10, 1983 (6 attempts)

MOST GAMES IN WHICH FIELD GOAL(S) PROVIDED WINNING MARGIN

Career

11—John Dowling, Youngstown St., 1984-87

LONGEST RETURN OF A MISSED FIELD GOAL

89—Pat Bayers, Western Ill. vs. Youngstown St., Nov. 6, 1982 (TD)

FCS

Team Records

Single Game—Offense

Total Offense

MOST PLAYS

115—Buffalo vs. Connecticut, Oct. 4, 1997 (437 yards)

MOST PLAYS, BOTH TEAMS

196—Villanova (113) & Connecticut (83), Oct. 7, 1989 (904 yards)

MOST YARDS GAINED

876—Weber St. vs. Idaho St., Nov. 23, 1991 (252 rushing, 624 passing)

MOST YARDS GAINED, BOTH TEAMS

1,418—Howard (740) & Bethune-Cookman (678), Sept. 19, 1987 (161 plays)

MOST YARDS GAINED BY A LOSING TEAM

756—Alcorn St. vs. Grambling, Sept. 3, 1994 (lost 62-56)

FEWEST YARDS GAINED BY A WINNING TEAM

31—Middle Tenn. vs. Murray St., Oct. 17, 1981 (won 14-9)

HIGHEST AVERAGE GAIN PER PLAY (Min. 55 Plays)

13.1—Northeastern vs. Stonehill, Aug. 30, 2003 (57 for 745)

MOST TOUCHDOWNS SCORED BY RUSHING AND PASSING

14—Portland St. vs. Delaware St., Nov. 8, 1980 (10 passing, 4 rushing)

Rushing

MOST RUSHES

90—VMI vs. East Tenn. St., Nov. 17, 1990 (311 yards)

MOST RUSHES, BOTH TEAMS

127—Western Ky. (73) & Elon (54), Oct. 24, 1998 (718 yards)

FEWEST RUSHES

11—Mississippi Val. vs. Kentucky St., Sept. 1, 1984 (17 yards); Western Ill. vs. UNI, Oct. 24, 1987 (-11 yards)

MOST YARDS GAINED

681—Missouri St. vs. Mo. Southern St., Sept. 10, 1988 (83 rushes)

MOST YARDS GAINED, BOTH TEAMS

781—Dayton (462) & Morehead St. (319), Sept. 23, 2000 (109 rushes)

MOST YARDS GAINED BY A LOSING TEAM

515—Nicholls St. vs. Portland St., Sept. 13, 2003 (lost 44-37; 74 rushes)

HIGHEST AVERAGE GAIN PER RUSH (Min. 45 Rushes)

12.89—Northeastern vs. Stonehill, Aug. 30, 2003 (46 for 593)

MOST TOUCHDOWNS SCORED BY RUSHING

11—Ga. Southern vs. Johnson C. Smith, Sept. 11, 2004

Passing

MOST PASSES ATTEMPTED

79—Idaho St. vs. Portland St., Nov. 6, 2004 (completed 43 for 465 yards)

MOST PASSES ATTEMPTED, BOTH TEAMS

122—Idaho (62) & Idaho St. (60), Sept. 24, 1983 (completed 48 for 639 yards)

FEWEST PASSES ATTEMPTED

1—By many teams. Most recent: Northeastern vs. Towson, Sept. 9, 1989 (completed 1)

FEWEST PASSES ATTEMPTED, BOTH TEAMS

11—Memphis (3) & Arkansas St. (8), Nov. 27, 1982 (completed 6); N.C. A&T (5) & Western Ky. (6), Nov. 19, 1988 (completed 2); Citadel (3) & Ga. Southern (8), Nov. 19, 1994 (completed 6)

MOST PASSES ATTEMPTED WITHOUT INTERCEPTION

72—Marshall vs. Western Caro., Nov. 14, 1987 (completed 35)

MOST PASSES COMPLETED

59—Southeastern La. vs. Jacksonville, Nov. 6, 2004 (attempted 72 for 551 yards)

MOST PASSES COMPLETED, BOTH TEAMS FCS

77—La.-Monroe (46) & Stephen F. Austin (31), Nov. 11, 1989 (attempted 116 for 1,190 yards)

MOST PASSES COMPLETED, BOTH TEAMS

80—Hofstra (50) & Fordham (30), Oct. 19, 1991 (attempted 120 for 987 yards)

FEWEST PASSES COMPLETED

0—By many teams. Most recent: Monmouth vs. Towson, Oct. 27, 2001

FEWEST PASSES COMPLETED, BOTH TEAMS

2—N.C. A&T (0) & Western Ky. (2), Nov. 19, 1988 (attempted 11)

HIGHEST PERCENTAGE COMPLETED

(Min. 30-44 atts.) 85.4%—Cal St. Northridge vs. Missouri St., Nov. 14, 1998 (35 of 41)

(Min. 45 atts.) 81.9%—Southeastern La. vs. Jacksonville, Nov. 6, 2004 (59 of 72)

LOWEST PERCENTAGE COMPLETED (Min. 20 Attempts)

9.5%—Florida A&M vs. Central St., Oct. 11, 1986 (2 of 21)

MOST PASSES HAD INTERCEPTED

10—Mississippi Val. vs. Grambling, Oct. 17, 1987 (47 attempts); Boise St. vs. Montana, Oct. 28, 1989 (55 attempts)

MOST YARDS GAINED

699—Mississippi Val. vs. Kentucky St., Sept. 1, 1984

MOST YARDS GAINED, BOTH TEAMS

1,190—La.-Monroe (619) & Stephen F. Austin (571), Nov. 11, 1989

MOST YARDS GAINED PER ATTEMPT (Min. 25 Attempts)

20.1—Delaware vs. Connecticut, Nov. 7, 1998 (29 for 584)

MOST YARDS GAINED PER COMPLETION

(Min. 10-24 comps.) 33.0—Jackson St. vs. Southern U., Oct. 13, 1990 (14 for 462)

(Min. 25 comps.) 22.9—Marshall vs. VMI, Nov. 16, 1991 (28 for 642)

MOST TOUCHDOWN PASSES

11—Mississippi Val. vs. Kentucky St., Sept. 1, 1984

MOST TOUCHDOWN PASSES, BOTH TEAMS

14—Mississippi Val. (8) & Texas Southern (6), Oct. 26, 1985

Punting

MOST PUNTS

16—Louisiana Tech vs. La.-Monroe, Nov. 19, 1988 (567 yards)

MOST PUNTS, BOTH TEAMS

26—Hofstra (14) vs. Buffalo (12), Nov. 2, 1996

HIGHEST AVERAGE PER PUNT

(5-9 punts) 61.5—Idaho St. vs. Cal Poly, Nov. 16, 2002 (6 for 369)

(Min. 10 punts) 52.2—Montana St. vs. Northern Ariz., Oct. 20, 1979 (10 for 522)

FEWEST PUNTS

0—By many teams. Most recent: Ga. Southern vs. South Dakota St., Oct. 30, 2004

FEWEST PUNTS, BOTH TEAMS

0—Ga. Southern & James Madison, Nov. 15, 1986

MOST OPPONENT'S PUNTS BLOCKED BY

4—Montana vs. Montana St., Oct. 31, 1987 (13 punts); Middle Tenn. vs. Mississippi Val., Oct. 8, 1988 (7 punts)

Punt Returns

MOST PUNT RETURNS

12—UNI vs. Youngstown St., Oct. 20, 1984 (83 yards)

MOST YARDS ON PUNT RETURNS

322—Northern Ariz. vs. Western N.M., Aug. 29, 1996 (10 returns)

HIGHEST AVERAGE GAIN PER RETURN (Min. 6 Returns)

32.2—Northern Ariz. vs. Western N.M., Aug. 29, 1996 (10 for 322, 2 TDs)

MOST TOUCHDOWNS SCORED ON PUNT RETURNS

3—Canisius vs. Siena, Sept. 24, 1994; Northern Ariz. vs. Western N.M., Aug. 29, 1996

Kickoff Returns

MOST KICKOFF RETURNS
15—Delaware St. vs. Portland St., Nov. 8, 1980 (209 yards)

MOST YARDS ON KICKOFF RETURNS
326—Eastern Wash. vs. Sacramento St., Oct. 31, 1998 (5 returns)

HIGHEST AVERAGE GAIN PER RETURN
(Min. 3-5 rets.) 65.2—Eastern Wash. vs. Sacramento St., Oct. 31, 1998 (5 for 326)
(Min. 6 rets.) 46.3—Western Caro. vs. VMI, Oct. 10, 1992 (6 for 278)

MOST TOUCHDOWNS SCORED ON KICKOFF RETURNS
3—Eastern Wash. vs. Sacramento St., Oct. 31, 1998

Total Kick Returns

(Combined Punt and Kickoff Returns)

MOST YARDS ON KICK RETURNS
349—Eastern Wash. vs. Sacramento St., Oct. 31, 1998 (23 punt returns, 326 kickoff returns)

HIGHEST AVERAGE GAIN PER RETURN (Min. 6 Returns)
46.8—Connecticut vs. Yale, Sept. 24, 1983 (6 for 281)

MOST TOUCHDOWNS SCORED ON TOTAL KICK RETURNS
5—Hampton vs. Virginia St., Sept. 22, 2001 (3 punt returns, 2 kickoff returns)

Scoring

MOST POINTS SCORED
105—Portland St. vs. Delaware St., Nov. 8, 1980 (15 TDs, 15 PATs)

MOST POINTS SCORED, BOTH TEAMS
125—Sacramento St. (64) & Cal St. Northridge (61), Nov. 4, 2000 (18 TDs, 11 PATs, 3 2-pt. extra points)

MOST POINTS SCORED BY A LOSING TEAM
61—Cal St. Northridge vs. Sacramento St. (64), Nov. 4, 2000

MOST POINTS SCORED EACH QUARTER
1st: 49—Portland St. vs. Delaware St., Nov. 8, 1980
2nd: 50—Alabama St. vs. Prairie View, Oct. 26, 1991
3rd: 35—Portland St. vs. Delaware St., Nov. 8, 1980; La.-Monroe vs. Arkansas St., Nov. 6, 1993
4th: 39—Montana vs. South Dakota St., Sept. 4, 1993

MOST POINTS SCORED EACH HALF
1st: 73—Montana St. vs. Eastern Ore., Sept. 14, 1985
2nd: 56—Brown vs. Columbia, Nov. 19, 1994

MOST TOUCHDOWNS SCORED
15—Portland St. vs. Delaware St., Nov. 8, 1980

MOST POINTS SCORED IN FOURTH QUARTER, BOTH TEAMS
58—Brown (30) vs. Penn (28), Oct. 10, 1998

MOST TOUCHDOWNS SCORED, BOTH TEAMS
17—Furman (9) & Davidson (8), Nov. 3, 1979; Weber St. (9) & Eastern Wash. (8), Sept. 28, 1991; Grambling (9) & Alcorn St. (8), Sept. 3, 1994

MOST EXTRA POINTS MADE BY KICKING
15—Portland St. vs. Delaware St., Nov. 8, 1980 (15 attempts)

MOST TWO-POINT ATTEMPTS MADE
5—Weber St. vs. Eastern Wash., Oct. 6, 1990 (5 passes attempted)

MOST FIELD GOALS MADE
8—Northern Ariz. vs. Idaho, Oct. 25, 1986 (8 attempts)

MOST FIELD GOALS ATTEMPTED
8—Northern Ariz. vs. Idaho, Oct. 25, 1986 (made 8)

MOST FIELD GOALS MADE, BOTH TEAMS
9—Nevada (5) & Northern Ariz. (4), Oct. 9, 1982 (12 attempts); Nevada (5) & Weber St. (4), Nov. 6, 1982 (11 attempts, 3 ot)

MOST SAFETIES SCORED
3—Alabama St. vs. Albany St. (Ga.), Oct. 15, 1988

MOST DEFENSIVE EXTRA POINTS SCORED
2—VMI vs. Davidson, Nov. 4, 1989 (Jeff Barnes, 95-yard interception return, and Wayne Purcell, 90-yard interception return); Duquesne vs. Fairfield, Nov. 3, 2001 (Leigh Bodden, 88-yard fumble return on two-point attempt, and Armar Watson, blocked extra point return)

MOST DEFENSIVE EXTRA-POINT ATTEMPTS
2—VMI vs. Davidson, Nov. 4, 1989 (2 interception returns); Western Ky. vs. Indiana St., Nov. 10, 1990 (2 interception returns); Duquesne vs. Fairfield, Nov. 3, 2001

First Downs

MOST FIRST DOWNS
46—Weber St. vs. Idaho St., Nov. 23, 1991 (12 rushing, 31 passing, 3 penalty)

MOST FIRST DOWNS, BOTH TEAMS
72—Bethune-Cookman (40) & Howard (32), Sept. 19, 1987

MOST FIRST DOWNS BY RUSHING
31—Ga. Southern vs. Glenville St., Nov. 12, 1994

MOST FIRST DOWNS BY PASSING
32—Montana vs. Weber St., Sept. 25, 1999

MOST FIRST DOWNS BY PENALTY
11—Towson vs. Liberty, Oct. 21, 1990

Fumbles

MOST FUMBLES
16—Delaware St. vs. Portland St., Nov. 8, 1980 (lost 6)

MOST FUMBLES, BOTH TEAMS
21—N.C. A&T (15) & Lane (6), Nov. 11, 1995 (lost 12)

MOST FUMBLES LOST
9—N.C. A&T vs. Lane, Nov. 11, 1995 (15 fumbles)

MOST FUMBLES LOST, BOTH TEAMS
12—Virginia St. (7) & Howard (5), Oct. 13, 1979 (16 fumbles); Austin Peay (8) & Mars Hill (4), Nov. 17, 1979 (18 fumbles); N.C. A&T (9) & Lane (3), Nov. 11, 1995 (21 fumbles)

Penalties

MOST PENALTIES AGAINST
23—Idaho vs. Idaho St., Oct. 10, 1992 (204 yards)

MOST PENALTIES, BOTH TEAMS
39—In four games. Most recent: Jackson St. (22) & Grambling (17), Oct. 24, 1987 (370 yards)

MOST YARDS PENALIZED
260—Southern U. vs. Howard, Nov. 4, 1978 (22 penalties)

MOST YARDS PENALIZED, BOTH TEAMS
423—Southern U. (260) & Howard (163), Nov. 4, 1978 (37 penalties)

Turnovers

(Passes Had Intercepted and Fumbles Lost)

MOST TURNOVERS
12—Texas Southern vs. Lamar, Sept. 6, 1980 (4 interceptions, 8 fumbles lost)

MOST TURNOVERS, BOTH TEAMS
15—Bucknell (8) & Hofstra (7), Sept. 8, 1990 (10 interceptions, 5 fumbles lost); Stephen F. Austin (8) & Nicholls St. (7), Sept. 22, 1990 (8 interceptions, 7 fumbles lost)

Overtimes

MOST OVERTIME PERIODS, BOTH TEAMS I-AA
6—Rhode Island (58) vs. Maine (55), Sept. 18, 1982; Villanova (41) vs. Connecticut (35), Oct. 7, 1989; Florida A&M (59) vs. Hampton (58), Oct. 5, 1996

MOST OVERTIME PERIODS
8—Bethune-Cookman (63) vs. Virginia St. (Division II) (57), Sept. 26, 1998

MOST POINTS SCORED IN OVERTIME PERIODS
39—Florida A&M (59) vs. Hampton (58), Oct. 5, 1996 (6 overtime periods)

MOST POINTS SCORED IN OVERTIME PERIODS, BOTH TEAMS
77—Florida A&M (39) vs. Hampton (38), Oct. 5, 1996 (6 overtime periods; Florida A&M won, 59-58)

LARGEST WINNING MARGIN IN OVERTIME
13—Nicholls St. (49) vs. Texas St. (36), Oct. 26, 1996 (5 overtime periods)

MOST CONSECUTIVE OVERTIME GAMES PLAYED
2—Maine, 1982 (Rhode Island 58, Maine 55, 6 ot, Sept. 18; and Boston U. 48, Maine 45, 4 ot, Sept. 25); Connecticut, 1989 (Villanova 41, Connecticut 35, 6 ot, Oct. 7; and Connecticut 39, Massachusetts 33, Oct. 14); Montana, 1991 (Nevada 35, Montana 28, 2 ot, Nov. 9; and Montana 35, Idaho 34, Nov. 16); Tennessee Tech, 1998 (Tennessee Tech 31, Tenn.-Martin 24, Oct. 17 and Tennessee Tech 31, Eastern Ky. 29, 3 ot, Oct. 24); Wagner, 2004 (Central Conn. St. 28, Wagner 21, 2 ot, Sept. 25 and Sacred Heart 30, Wagner 24, Oct. 2); Howard, 2004 (Howard 42, Morgan St. 35, Oct. 16 and N.C. A&T 14, Howard 13, Oct. 23); Tennessee Tech, 2004 (Tennessee Tech 40, Eastern Ill. 37, Nov. 6 and Southeast Mo. St. 31, Tennessee Tech 28, Nov. 13); Coastal Caro., 2005 (Coastal Caro. 34, Gardner-Webb 31, Oct. 15 and Coastal Caro. 27, Liberty 21, 3 ot, Oct. 22); Gardner-Webb, 2005 (Coastal Caro. 34, Gardner-Webb 31, Oct. 15 and Gardner-Webb 55, VMI 52, Oct. 22); Grambling, 2006 (Hampton 27, Grambling 26, Sept. 2 and Alabama A&M 30, Grambling 27, Sept. 9); Yale, 2006 (Yale 26, Lehigh 20, Oct. 14 and Yale 17, Penn 14, Oct. 21); Penn, 2006 (Brown 30, Penn 27, Oct. 28 and Princeton 31, Penn 30, Nov. 4)

Single Game—Defense

Total Defense

FEWEST PLAYS ALLOWED
31—Howard vs. Dist. Columbia, Sept. 2, 1989 (32 yards)

FEWEST YARDS ALLOWED
Minus 12—Eastern Ill. vs. Kentucky St., Nov. 13, 1982 (-67 rushing, 55 passing)

Rushing Defense

FEWEST RUSHES ALLOWED
9—Mississippi Val. vs. Alcorn St., Nov. 6, 1999 (4 yards)

FEWEST RUSHING YARDS ALLOWED
Minus 90—Sacred Heart vs. Iona, Nov. 16, 2002 (42 rushes)

Pass Defense

FEWEST ATTEMPTS ALLOWED
1—By six teams. Most recent: Western Caro. vs. Wofford, Oct. 17, 1998

FEWEST COMPLETIONS ALLOWED
0—By many teams. Most recent: N.C. A&T vs. Wofford, Nov. 29, 2003 (2 attempts)

LOWEST COMPLETION PERCENTAGE ALLOWED (Min. 30 Attempts)
11.8%—Southern U. vs. Nicholls St., Oct. 11, 1980 (4 of 34)

FEWEST YARDS ALLOWED
Minus 2—Florida A&M vs. Albany St. (Ga.), Oct. 16, 1982

MOST PASSES INTERCEPTED BY
10—Grambling vs. Mississippi Val., Oct. 17, 1987 (47 attempts); Montana vs. Boise St., Oct. 28, 1989 (55 attempts)

MOST TIMES OPPONENT TACKLED FOR LOSS ATTEMPTING TO PASS
14—Duquesne vs. Iona, Oct. 31, 1998 (92 yards)

MOST INTERCEPTIONS RETURNED FOR TOUCHDOWNS
4—Northwestern St. vs. Southeastern La., Oct. 11, 2003 (6 for 195 yards)

Opponent's Kicks Blocked

MOST OPPONENT'S PUNTS BLOCKED
4—Montana vs. Montana St., Oct. 31, 1987 (13 punts); Middle Tenn. vs. Mississippi Val., Oct. 8, 1988 (7 punts)

MOST OPPONENT'S TOTAL KICKS BLOCKED (Includes punts, field goals, PATs)
4—Montana vs. Montana St., Oct. 31, 1987 (all punts); Middle Tenn. vs. Mississippi Val., Oct. 8, 1988 (all punts); Colgate vs. Towson, Sept. 30, 2000 (3 punts, 1 PAT)

Fumble Returns

(Since 1992)

MOST FUMBLES RETURNED FOR TOUCHDOWNS
2—Marshall vs. VMI, Oct. 9, 1993; Idaho vs. Weber St., Nov. 12, 1994; Texas St. vs. Nicholls St., Oct. 7, 2000; Harvard vs. Northeastern, Oct. 6, 2001

Safeties

MOST SAFETIES
3—Alabama St. vs. Albany St. (Ga.), Oct. 15, 1988

SEASON—Offense

Total Offense

MOST YARDS GAINED PER GAME
640.1—Mississippi Val., 1984 (6,401 in 10)

HIGHEST AVERAGE GAIN PER PLAY
7.8—Alcorn St., 1994 (848 for 6,577)

MOST PLAYS PER GAME
89.6—Weber St., 1991 (986 in 11)

MOST TOUCHDOWNS BY RUSHING AND PASSING PER GAME
8.4—Mississippi Val., 1984 (84 in 10)

Rushing

MOST YARDS GAINED PER GAME
419.0—Ga. Southern, 1999 (4,609 in 11)

HIGHEST AVERAGE GAIN PER RUSH
7.0—Ga. Southern, 1999 (654 for 4,609)

MOST RUSHES PER GAME
69.8—Northeastern, 1986 (698 in 10)

MOST TOUCHDOWNS BY RUSHING PER GAME
5.5—Ga. Southern, 1999 (61 in 11)

Passing

MOST YARDS GAINED PER GAME
496.8—Mississippi Val., 1984 (4,968 in 10)

HIGHEST AVERAGE GAIN PER ATTEMPT
(Min. 250-399 atts.) 10.7—UNI, 1996 (252 for 2,700)
(Min. 400 atts.) 9.5—Grambling, 2005 (465 for 4,408)

HIGHEST AVERAGE GAIN PER COMPLETION
(Min. 125-199 comps.) 19.3—Jackson St., 1990 (156 for 3,006)
(Min. 200 comps.) 17.2—Grambling, 2005 (256 for 4,408)

MOST PASSES ATTEMPTED PER GAME
55.8—Mississippi Val., 1984 (558 in 10)

MOST PASSES COMPLETED PER GAME
35.1—Mississippi Val., 1984 (351 in 10)

HIGHEST PERCENTAGE COMPLETED
(Min. 200-449 atts.) 70.6%—Hofstra, 1997 (293 of 415)
(Min. 450 atts.) 67.8%—Montana, 2004 (331 of 488)

LOWEST PERCENTAGE HAD INTERCEPTED
(Min. 200-399 atts.) 0.78%—Portland St., 1999 (3 of 383)
(Min. 400 atts.) 1.06%—William & Mary, 2004 (5 of 473)

MOST CONSECUTIVE PASSES ATTEMPTED WITHOUT AN INTERCEPTION
275—Lamar, 1988 (during 8 games, Sept. 3 to Oct. 29)

MOST TOUCHDOWN PASSES PER GAME
6.4—Mississippi Val., 1984 (64 in 10)

HIGHEST PASSING EFFICIENCY RATING POINTS
190.6—William & Mary, 1993 (232 attempts, 161 completions, 4 interceptions, 2,499 yards, 24 TDs)

Punting

MOST PUNTS PER GAME
9.6—Louisiana Tech, 1987 (106 in 11)

FEWEST PUNTS PER GAME
2.1—Ga. Southern, 1999 (23 in 11)

HIGHEST PUNTING AVERAGE
48.0—Northern Ariz., 2004 (57 for 2,736)

HIGHEST NET PUNTING AVERAGE
(Min. 46 atts.) 44.9—Northern Ariz., 2004 (57 for 2,736; 178 yards returned)

MOST PUNTS HAD BLOCKED
8—Western Ky., 1982

Punt Returns

MOST PUNT RETURNS PER GAME
5.4—Murray St., 1980 (59 in 11)

FEWEST PUNT RETURNS PER GAME
0.45—Tenn.-Martin, 2000 (5 in 11); Butler, 2004 (5 in 11)

MOST PUNT-RETURN YARDS PER GAME
64.8—Duquesne, 1996 (648 in 10)

HIGHEST AVERAGE GAIN PER PUNT RETURN
(Min. 20-29 rets.) 23.0—N.C. A&T, 2001 (25 for 576)
(Min. 30 rets.) 18.1—Mississippi Val., 1985 (31 for 561)

MOST TOUCHDOWNS SCORED ON PUNT RETURNS
7—N.C. A&T, 2001 (25 returns)

Kickoff Returns

MOST KICKOFF RETURNS PER GAME
7.7—Morehead St., 1994 (85 in 11; 1,582 yards)

FEWEST KICKOFF RETURNS PER GAME
1.2—McNeese St., 1997 (13 in 11)

MOST KICKOFF-RETURN YARDS PER GAME
143.8—Morehead St., 1994 (1,582 in 11; 85 returns)

HIGHEST AVERAGE GAIN PER KICKOFF RETURN (Min. 20 Returns)
30.5—Hampton, 2004 (38 for 1,157)

MOST TOUCHDOWNS SCORED ON KICKOFF RETURNS
6—Hampton, 2004 (38 returns)

Combined Returns

(Interceptions, Punt Returns, Fumble Returns and Kickoff Returns)

MOST TOUCHDOWNS SCORED
9—Delaware St., 1987 (5 interceptions, 3 punt returns, 1 kickoff return)

Scoring

MOST POINTS PER GAME
60.9—Mississippi Val., 1984 (609 in 10)

MOST TOUCHDOWNS PER GAME
8.7—Mississippi Val., 1984 (87 in 10)

MOST EXTRA POINTS MADE BY KICKING PER GAME
7.7—Mississippi Val., 1984 (77 in 10)

MOST CONSECUTIVE EXTRA POINTS MADE BY KICKING
68—Idaho, 1993

MOST TWO-POINT ATTEMPTS MADE
9—Weber St., 1992 (11 attempts)

MOST DEFENSIVE EXTRA-POINT ATTEMPTS
2—VMI, 1989; Eastern Wash., 1990; Western Ky., 1990

MOST DEFENSIVE EXTRA POINTS SCORED
2—VMI, 1989 (2 interception returns); Eastern Wash., 1990 (2 interception returns)

MOST FIELD GOALS MADE PER GAME
2.4—Nevada, 1982 (26 in 11); UNI, 1990 (26 in 11)

MOST SAFETIES SCORED
5—Jackson St., 1986; Monmouth, 2005

First Downs

MOST FIRST DOWNS PER GAME
31.7—Mississippi Val., 1984 (317 in 10)

MOST RUSHING FIRST DOWNS PER GAME
18.6—Ga. Southern, 1999 (205 in 11)

MOST PASSING FIRST DOWNS PER GAME
21.4—Mississippi Val., 1984 (214 in 10)

MOST FIRST DOWNS BY PENALTY PER GAME
3.7—Alabama St., 1984 (41 in 11; 109 penalties by opponents); Texas Southern, 1987 (41 in 11; 134 penalties by opponents)

Fumbles

MOST FUMBLES PER GAME
5.3—Prairie View, 1984 (58 in 11)

MOST FUMBLES LOST PER GAME
3.1—Idaho, 1978 (31 in 10); Delaware St., 1980 (31 in 10)

FEWEST OWN FUMBLES LOST
1—Yale, 1999 (5 fumbles)

Penalties

MOST PENALTIES
152—Alabama St., 2001

MOST PENALTIES PER GAME
13.7—Grambling, 1984 (151 in 11; 1,206 yards)

MOST YARDS PENALIZED PER GAME
125.5—Tennessee St., 1982 (1,255 in 10; 132 penalties)

Turnovers

FEWEST TURNOVERS LOST
9—Hofstra, 1995 (6 fumbles, 3 interceptions); Yale, 1999 (1 fumble, 8 interceptions); Harvard, 2001 (3 fumbles, 6 interceptions)

MOST TURNOVERS LOST
59—Texas Southern, 1980 (27 fumbles, 32 interceptions)

HIGHEST TURNOVER MARGIN PER GAME OVER OPPONENTS
3.18—St. Peter's, 2001 (47 gained, 12 lost; 11 games)

SEASON—Defense

Total Defense

FEWEST YARDS ALLOWED PER GAME
149.9—Florida A&M, 1978 (1,649 in 11)

FEWEST RUSHING AND PASSING TOUCHDOWNS ALLOWED PER GAME
0.7—Western Mich., 1982 (8 in 11)

LOWEST AVERAGE YARDS ALLOWED PER PLAY
2.4—South Carolina St., 1978 (719 for 1,736)

Rushing Defense

FEWEST YARDS ALLOWED PER GAME
39.7—Alabama A&M, 2000 (476 in 12)

LOWEST AVERAGE YARDS ALLOWED PER RUSH
1.3—Marist, 1997 (319 for 404)

FEWEST RUSHING TOUCHDOWNS ALLOWED PER GAME
0.3—Florida A&M, 1978 (3 in 11)

Pass Defense

FEWEST YARDS ALLOWED PER GAME
59.9—Bethune-Cookman, 1981 (659 in 11)

FEWEST YARDS ALLOWED PER ATTEMPT (Min. 200 Attempts)
4.0—Middle Tenn., 1988 (251 for 999)

FEWEST YARDS ALLOWED PER COMPLETION (Min. 100 Completions)
9.1—Middle Tenn., 1988 (110 for 999)

LOWEST COMPLETION PERCENTAGE ALLOWED
(Min. 200-299 atts.) 32.3%—Alcorn St., 1979 (76 of 235)
(Min. 300 atts.) 34.2%—Tennessee St., 1986 (107 of 313)

FEWEST TOUCHDOWNS ALLOWED BY PASSING
1—Nevada, 1978; Middle Tenn., 1990; Penn, 1994

LOWEST PASSING EFFICIENCY DEFENSE RATING (Since 1990)
61.0—Sacred Heart, 2002 (252 attempts, 87 completions, 19 interceptions, 1,019 yards, 4 TDs)

MOST PASSES INTERCEPTED BY, PER GAME
3.2—Florida A&M, 1981 (35 in 11)

HIGHEST PERCENTAGE INTERCEPTED BY
13.4%—Florida A&M, 1981 (35 of 262)

MOST YARDS GAINED ON INTERCEPTIONS
689—N.C. A&T, 2001 (20 interceptions)

MOST YARDS GAINED PER GAME ON INTERCEPTIONS
62.6—N.C. A&T, 2001 (689 in 11)

HIGHEST AVERAGE PER INTERCEPTION RETURN (Min. 15 Returns)
34.5—N.C. A&T, 2001 (20 for 689)

MOST TOUCHDOWNS ON INTERCEPTION RETURNS
7—Jackson St., 1985; Northeastern, 1996

Opponents' Kicks Blocked

MOST OPPONENTS' TOTAL KICKS BLOCKED (Includes punts, field goals, PATs)
13—Davidson, 1999 (6 punts, 4 field goals, 3 PATs)

Punting

MOST OPPONENTS' PUNTS BLOCKED BY
9—Middle Tenn., 1988 (73 punts)

Punt Returns

LOWEST AVERAGE YARDS ALLOWED PER PUNT RETURN
1.0—Yale, 1988 (24 for 23)

FEWEST RETURNS ALLOWED
7—Furman, 1984 (11 games, 8 yards); Cal Poly, 1997 (11 games, 108 yards)

Kickoff Returns

LOWEST AVERAGE YARDS ALLOWED PER KICKOFF RETURN
10.6—Southern Utah, 1996 (33 for 350)

Scoring

FEWEST POINTS ALLOWED PER GAME
6.5—South Carolina St., 1978 (72 in 11)

Fumbles

MOST OPPONENTS' FUMBLES RECOVERED
29—Western Ky., 1982 (43 fumbles)

Fumble Returns

(Since 1992)

MOST FUMBLES RETURNED FOR TOUCHDOWNS
3—Texas St., 2000 (2 vs. Nicholls St., Oct. 7 & 1 vs. Northwestern St., Oct. 31)

Turnovers

MOST OPPONENTS' TURNOVERS PER GAME
4.9—Canisius, 1996 (44 in 9)

Additional Records

MOST CONSECUTIVE VICTORIES
24—Penn, from Nov. 14, 1992, through Sept. 30, 1995 (ended Oct. 7, 1995, with 24-14 loss to Columbia); Montana, from Sept. 22, 2001, through November 9, 2002 (ended Nov. 16, 2002, with 30-21 loss to Eastern Wash.)

MOST CONSECUTIVE HOME VICTORIES
39—Ga. Southern, from Sept. 27, 1997 through Dec. 15, 2001 (includes 11 FCS playoff games)

MOST CONSECUTIVE LOSSES
80—Prairie View, from Nov. 4, 1989, until Sept. 26, 1998

MOST CONSECUTIVE GAMES WITHOUT A WIN
80—Prairie View, from Nov. 4, 1989, until Sept. 26, 1998

MOST CONSECUTIVE GAMES WITHOUT BEING SHUT OUT
338—Dayton, from Oct. 23, 1976, through present

(Note: Dayton has been an FCS member since 1993. Boise State had a 193-game streak from Sept. 21, 1968, through Nov. 10, 1984)

MOST SHUTOUTS IN A SEASON
5—South Carolina St., 1978

MOST CONSECUTIVE QUARTERS HOLDING OPPONENTS SCORELESS
15—Robert Morris, 1996

MOST CONSECUTIVE GAMES WITHOUT A TIE
343—Richmond, from Nov. 2, 1963, to Oct. 14, 1995 (ended Oct. 21, 1995, with 3-3 tie with Fordham)

LAST TIE GAME
Nov. 18, 1995—Dartmouth 10, Princeton 10

LAST SCORELESS-TIE GAME
Oct. 26, 1985—McNeese St. & North Texas

MOST CONSECUTIVE PASSES ATTEMPTED WITHOUT AN INTERCEPTION
370—Portland St. (in 11 games from Sept 4, 1999, to Nov. 13, 1999)

MOST POINTS OVERCOME IN SECOND HALF TO WIN A GAME
35—Nevada (55) vs. Weber St. (49), Nov. 2, 1991 (trailed 49-14 with 12:16 remaining in 3rd quarter)
32—Morehead St. (36) vs. Wichita St. (35), Sept. 20, 1986 (trailed 35-3 with 9:03 remaining in 3rd quarter)
31—Montana (52) vs. South Dakota St. (48), Sept. 4, 1993 (trailed 38-7 with 8:12 remaining in 3rd quarter)

MOST POINTS OVERCOME IN FOURTH QUARTER TO WIN A GAME
28—Delaware St. (38) vs. Liberty (37), Oct. 6, 1990 (trailed 37-9 with 13:00 remaining in 4th quarter)

MOST POINTS SCORED IN FOURTH QUARTER TO WIN A GAME
39—Montana (52) vs. South Dakota St. (48), Sept. 4, 1993 (trailed 38-13 to begin 4th quarter)
33—Missouri St. (40) vs. Illinois St. (28), Oct. 9, 1993 (trailed 21-7 with 11:30 remaining in 4th quarter)

MOST CONSECUTIVE EXTRA-POINT KICKS MADE
134—Boise St. (began Oct. 27, 1984; ended Nov. 12, 1988)

MOST CONSECUTIVE WINNING SEASONS
27—Grambling (1960-86)

MOST IMPROVED WON-LOST RECORD
9 1/2 games—Montana St., 1984 (12-2-0, including 3 FCS playoff games) from 1983 (1-10-0)

Annual Champions, All-Time Leaders

Total Offense

CAREER YARDS PER GAME

(Minimum 5,500 Yards; Player must have concluded his career)

Player, Team	Years	G	Plays	Yards	TDR‡	Yd. PG
Steve McNair, Alcorn St.	1991-94	42	2,055	*16,823	152	400.5
Neil Lomax, Portland St.	1978-80	33	1,680	11,647	100	352.9
Aaron Flowers, Cal St. Northridge	1996-97	20	944	6,754	60	337.7
David Macchi, Valparaiso	2002-03	23	1,047	7,628	65	331.7
Chris Sanders, Chattanooga	1999-00	22	1,044	7,247	52	329.4
Dave Dickenson, Montana	1992-95	35	1,539	11,523	116	329.2
Willie Totten, Mississippi Val.	1982-85	40	1,812	13,007	157	325.2
Bruce Eugene, Grambling	$2001-05	46	1,998	14,720	*159	320.0
Drew Miller, Montana	1999-00	18	708	5,628	47	312.7
Tom Ehrhardt, Rhode Island	1984-85	21	1,010	6,492	66	309.1
Doug Nussmeier, Idaho	1990-93	39	1,556	12,054	109	309.1
Oteman Sampson, Florida A&M	1996-97	22	906	6,751	57	306.9
Marcus Brady, Cal St. Northridge	1998-01	43	*2,116	13,095	123	304.5
Jamie Martin, Weber St.	1989-92	41	1,838	12,287	93	299.7
Tom Proudian, Iona	1993-95	27	1,337	7,939	61	294.0
Robert Dougherty, Boston U.	1993-94	21	918	6,135	56	292.1
Stan Greene, Boston U.	1989-90	22	1,167	6,408	49	291.3
John Friesz, Idaho	1986-89	35	1,459	10,187	79	291.1
Ben Dougherty, Florida A&M	2003-04	22	1,044	6,212	46	282.4
Robert Kent, Jackson St.	2000-03	45	1,982	12,538	104	278.6
Travis Brown, Northern Ariz.	1996-99	41	1,732	11,267	95	274.8
Grady Bennett, Montana	1988-90	31	1,389	8,304	69	267.9
John Sciarra, Wagner	2004-05	22	971	5,815	44	264.3
Sean Payton, Eastern Ill.	1983-86	39	1,690	10,298	91	264.1
James Perry, Brown	1996-99	35	1,408	9,225	75	263.6
Eric Rasmussen, San Diego	2001-03	29	1,048	7,570	75	261.0
Erik Meyer, Eastern Wash.	2002-05	42	1,373	10,942	91	260.5
Giovanni Carmazzi, Hofstra	1996-99	40	1,564	10,416	103	260.4
Travis Lulay, Montana St.	2002-05	47	2,006	12,190	81	259.4
Brian Ah Yat, Montana	1995-98	36	1,365	9,319	98	258.9
John Witkowski, Columbia	1981-83	30	1,330	7,748	58	258.3
John Whitcomb, UAB	1993-94	22	800	5,683	43	258.3

*Record. ‡Touchdowns-responsible-for are player's TDs scored and passed for. $See page 10 for explanation.

SEASON YARDS PER GAME

Player, Team	Year	G	Plays	Yards	TDR‡	Yd. PG
Steve McNair, Alcorn St.	†1994	11	649	*5,799	53	527.2
Willie Totten, Mississippi Val.	†1984	10	564	4,572	*61	457.2
Steve McNair, Alcorn St.	†1992	10	519	4,057	39	405.7
Jamie Martin, Weber St.	†1991	11	591	4,337	37	394.3
Bruce Eugene, Grambling	†2002	13	*680	5,018	43	386.0
Martin Hankins, Southeastern La.	†2004	11	596	4,221	38	383.7
Dave Dickenson, Montana	†1995	11	544	4,209	41	382.6
Neil Lomax, Portland St.	†1980	11	550	4,157	42	377.9
Bruce Eugene, Grambling	†2005	12	536	4,517	59	376.4
Joe Lee, Towson	†1999	11	608	4,031	22	366.5
Marcus Brady, Cal St. Northridge	†2001	10	532	3,632	40	363.2
Dave Dickenson, Montana	†1993	11	530	3,978	46	361.6
Neil Lomax, Portland St.	†1979	11	611	3,966	31	360.5
Erik Meyer, Eastern Wash.	2005	12	502	4,224	32	352.0
Bruce Eugene, Grambling	†2003	12	622	4,220	36	351.7
Travis Lulay, Montana St.	2004	11	602	3,856	23	350.5
John Friesz, Idaho	†1989	11	464	3,853	31	350.3
Steve McNair, Alcorn St.	1993	11	493	3,830	30	348.2
Aaron Flowers, Cal St. Northridge	†1997	9	456	3,132	26	348.0
Todd Hammel, Stephen F. Austin	1989	11	487	3,822	38	347.5
Tom Ehrhardt, Rhode Island	†1985	10	529	3,460	35	346.0
Ken Hobart, Idaho	†1983	11	578	3,800	37	345.5
David Dinkins, Morehead St.	†2000	9	408	3,109	38	345.4
Dave Dickenson, Montana	1994	9	431	3,108	27	345.3

*Record. †National champion. ‡Touchdowns-responsible-for are player's TDs scored and passed for.

CAREER YARDS

Player, Team	Years	Plays	Yards	Avg.
Steve McNair, Alcorn St.	1991-94	2,055	16,823	*8.19
Bruce Eugene, Grambling	$2001-05	1,998	14,720	7.37
Marcus Brady, Cal St. Northridge	1998-01	*2,116	13,095	6.19
Willie Totten, Mississippi Val.	1982-85	1,812	13,007	7.18
Robert Kent, Jackson St.	2000-03	1,982	12,538	6.33
Jamie Martin, Weber St.	1989-92	1,838	12,287	6.68
Travis Lulay, Montana St.	2002-05	2,006	12,190	6.08
Doug Nussmeier, Idaho	1990-93	1,556	12,054	7.75
Neil Lomax, Portland St.	1978-80	1,680	11,647	6.93
Dave Dickenson, Montana	1992-95	1,539	11,523	7.49
Travis Brown, Northern Ariz.	1996-99	1,732	11,267	6.51
Ken Hobart, Idaho	1980-83	1,847	11,127	6.02
David Corley Jr., William & Mary	1999-02	1,611	10,948	6.80
Erik Meyer, Eastern Wash.	2002-05	1,373	10,942	7.97
Jason Murrietta, Northern Ariz.	2003-06	1,805	10,593	5.87
Collin Drafts, Charleston So.	2003-06	1,848	10,571	5.72
Giovanni Carmazzi, Hofstra	1996-99	1,564	10,416	6.66
Sean Payton, Eastern Ill.	1983-86	1,690	10,298	6.09
Greg Wyatt, Northern Ariz.	1986-89	1,753	10,277	5.86
John Friesz, Idaho	1986-89	1,459	10,187	6.98
Marko Glavic, Lafayette	2000-03	1,745	10,169	5.83
Niel Loebig, Duquesne	2001-04	1,469	10,039	6.83
Donald Carrie, Alcorn St.	2001-04	1,606	10,026	6.24
Michael Proctor, Murray St.	1986-89	1,577	9,886	6.27
Jeff Wiley, Holy Cross	1985-88	1,428	9,877	6.92
Jeff Lewis, Northern Ariz.	1992-95	1,654	9,769	5.91
Ted White, Howard	1995-98	1,377	9,669	7.02
Ryan Vena, Colgate	1996-99	1,404	9,435	6.72
Chris Boden, Villanova	1996-99	1,514	9,369	6.19
David Dinkins, Morehead St.	1997-00	1,260	9,337	7.41
Brian Ah Yat, Montana	1995-98	1,365	9,319	6.83
Matt DeGennaro, Connecticut	1987-90	1,619	9,269	5.73

*Record. $See page 10 for explanation.

SEASON YARDS

Player, Team	Year	G	Plays	Yards	Avg.
Steve McNair, Alcorn St.	†1994	11	649	5,799	*8.94
Bruce Eugene, Grambling	†2002	13	*680	5,018	7.38
Dustin Long, Sam Houston St.	2004	14	576	4,576	7.94
Willie Totten, Mississippi Val.	†1984	10	564	4,572	8.11
Bruce Eugene, Grambling	†2005	12	456	4,517	8.43
Jamie Martin, Weber St.	†1991	11	591	4,337	7.34
Lang Campbell, William & Mary	2004	14	556	4,305	7.74
Martin Hankins, Southeastern La.	†2004	11	596	4,221	7.08
Bruce Eugene, Grambling	†2003	12	622	4,220	6.78
Dave Dickenson, Montana	†1995	11	544	4,209	7.74
Neil Lomax, Portland St.	†1980	11	550	4,157	7.56
Brett Gordon, Villanova	2002	15	665	4,155	6.25
David Macchi, Valparaiso	2003	12	525	4,079	7.77
Steve McNair, Alcorn St.	†1992	10	519	4,057	7.82
Josh Johnson, San Diego	†2006	12	478	4,040	8.45
Joe Lee, Towson	†1999	11	608	4,031	6.63
Erik Meyer, Eastern Wash.	2005	12	410	4,003	8.41
Craig Ochs, Montana	2004	15	545	3,992	7.32
Dave Dickenson, Montana	†1993	11	530	3,978	7.51
Neil Lomax, Portland St.	†1979	11	611	3,966	6.49
Tyler Thigpen, Coastal Caro.	2006	12	452	3,952	8.74
Erik Meyer, Eastern Wash.	2004	13	478	3,934	8.23
Travis Lulay, Montana St.	2004	11	602	3,856	6.41
John Friesz, Idaho	†1989	11	464	3,853	8.30
Steve McNair, Alcorn St.	1993	11	493	3,830	7.77
Todd Hammel, Stephen F. Austin	1989	11	487	3,822	7.85
Ken Hobart, Idaho	†1983	11	578	3,800	6.57

*Record. †National champion.

SINGLE-GAME YARDS

Yds.	Player, Team (Opponent)	Date
668	Robert Kent, Jackson St. (Alabama St.)	Oct. 6, 2001
649	Steve McNair, Alcorn St. (Southern U.)	Oct. 22, 1994
647	Steve McNair, Alcorn St. (Chattanooga)	Sept. 10, 1994
643	Jamie Martin, Weber St. (Idaho St.)	Nov. 23, 1991
641	Bruce Eugene, Grambling (Prairie View)	Oct. 1, 2005
633	Steve McNair, Alcorn St. (Grambling)	Sept. 3, 1994
624	Steve McNair, Alcorn St. (Samford)	Oct. 29, 1994
621	Willie Totten, Mississippi Val. (Prairie View)	Oct. 27, 1984
614	Bryan Martin, Weber St. (Cal Poly)	Sept. 23, 1995
604	Steve McNair, Alcorn St. (Jackson St.)	Nov. 21, 1992
598	Robert Kent, Jackson St. (N.C. A&T)	Sept. 7, 2002
598	Dustin Long, Sam Houston St. (McNeese St.)	Nov. 6, 2004
595	Doug Pederson, La.-Monroe (Stephen F. Austin)	Nov. 11, 1989
587	Vern Harris, Idaho St. (Montana)	Oct. 12, 1985
586	Steve McNair, Alcorn St. (Troy St.)	Nov. 12, 1994
582	Martin Hankins, Southeastern La. (Ark.-Monticello)	Sept. 2, 2004
574	Dave Dickenson, Montana (Idaho)	Oct. 21, 1995
570	Steve McNair, Alcorn St. (Texas Southern)	Sept. 11, 1993
570	Cedric Stevens, Chattanooga (Appalachian St.)	Oct. 30, 2004
569	Jimmy Blanchard, Portland St. (Montana)	Oct. 2, 1999

Yds.	Player, Team (Opponent)	Date
566	Tom Ehrhardt, Rhode Island (Connecticut)	Nov. 16, 1985
566	Brian Ah Yat, Montana (Eastern Wash.)	Oct. 19, 1996

ANNUAL CHAMPIONS

Year	Player, Team	Class	G	Plays	Yards	Avg.
1978	Neil Lomax, Portland St.	So.	11	519	3,524	320.4
1979	Neil Lomax, Portland St.	Jr.	11	611	3,966	360.5
1980	Neil Lomax, Portland St.	Sr.	11	550	4,157	377.9
1981	Mike Machurek, Idaho St.	Sr.	9	363	2,645	293.9
1982	Brent Woods, Princeton	Sr.	10	577	3,079	307.9
1983	Ken Hobart, Idaho	Sr.	11	578	3,800	345.5
1984	Willie Totten, Mississippi Val.	Jr.	10	564	4,572	457.2
1985	Tom Ehrhardt, Rhode Island	Sr.	10	529	3,460	346.0
1986	Brent Pease, Montana	Sr.	10	499	3,094	309.4
1987	Jeff Wiley, Holy Cross	Jr.	11	445	3,722	338.4
1988	John Friesz, Idaho	Jr.	10	424	2,751	275.1
1989	John Friesz, Idaho	Sr.	11	464	3,853	350.3
1990	Jamie Martin, Weber St.	So.	11	508	3,713	337.6
1991	Jamie Martin, Weber St.	Jr.	11	591	4,337	394.3
1992	Steve McNair, Alcorn St.	So.	10	519	4,057	405.7
1993	Dave Dickenson, Montana	So.	11	530	3,978	361.6
1994	Steve McNair, Alcorn St.	Sr.	11	649	*5,799	*527.2
1995	Dave Dickenson, Montana	Sr.	11	544	4,209	382.6
1996	Brian Ah Yat, Montana	So.	11	501	3,744	340.4
1997	Aaron Flowers, Cal St. Northridge	Sr.	9	456	3,132	348.0
1998	Patrick Bonner, Florida A&M	Sr.	11	488	3,568	324.4
1999	Joe Lee, Towson	Sr.	11	608	4,031	366.5
2000	David Dinkins, Morehead St.	Sr.	9	408	3,109	345.4
2001	Marcus Brady, Cal St. Northridge	Sr.	10	532	3,632	363.2
2002	Bruce Eugene, Grambling	So.	13	*680	5,018	386.0
2003	Bruce Eugene, Grambling	Jr.	12	622	4,220	351.7
2004	Martin Hankins, Southeastern La.	So.	11	596	4,221	383.7
2005	Bruce Eugene, Grambling	Sr.	12	536	4,517	376.4
2006	Josh Johnson, San Diego	Jr.	12	478	4,040	336.7

**Record.*

Rushing

CAREER YARDS PER GAME

(Minimum 2,500 Yards; Player must have concluded his career)

Player, Team	Years	G	Plays	Carries	TD	Yd. PG
Arnold Mickens, Butler	1994-95	20	763	3,813	29	190.7
Adrian Peterson, Ga. Southern	1998-01	42	996	*6,559	*84	156.2
Aaron Stecker, Western Ill.	1997-98	20	550	3,081	36	154.1
Tim Hall, Robert Morris	1994-95	19	393	2,908	27	153.1
Jerry Azumah, New Hampshire	1995-98	41	1,044	6,193	60	151.0
Reggie Greene, Siena	1994-97	36	890	5,415	45	150.4
Nick Hartigan, Brown	2003-05	30	912	4,488	52	149.6
Charles Roberts, Sacramento St.	1997-00	44	*1,124	6,553	56	148.9
Charles Dunn, Portland St.	1998-00	33	872	4,831	46	146.4
Archie Amerson, Northern Ariz.	1995-96	22	526	3,196	37	145.3
Keith Elias, Princeton	1991-93	30	736	4,208	49	140.3
Jesse Chatman, Eastern Wash.	1999-01	31	627	4,173	48	134.6
Mike Clark, Akron	1984-86	32	804	4,257	24	133.0
Gary Jones, Albany (N.Y.)	2002-03	23	442	3,033	40	131.9
Corey Holmes, Mississippi Val.	1999-00	22	526	2,897	21	131.7
Marcus Mason, Youngstown St.	2005-06	21	478	2,739	31	130.4
Rick Sarille, Wagner	$1995-99	41	965	5,290	50	129.0
Charles Tharp, Western Ill.	1999-00	22	520	2,834	29	128.8
Michael Hicks, South Carolina St.	1993-95	32	701	4,093	51	127.9
Louis Ivory, Furman	1998-01	42	847	5,353	53	127.5
Marcel Shipp, Massachusetts	1997-00	43	1,042	5,383	49	125.2
Matt Cannon (QB), Southern Utah	1997-00	44	757	5,489	69	124.8
Rich Erenberg, Colgate	1982-83	21	464	2,618	22	124.7
Kenny Gamble, Colgate	1984-87	42	963	5,220	55	124.3
Clifton Dawson, Harvard	2003-06	39	958	4,841	60	124.1
Frank Hawkins, Nevada	1977-80	43	945	5,333	39	124.0
Curtis Keaton, James Madison	1998-99	22	513	2,723	29	123.8
Elroy Harris, Eastern Ky.	1985, 87-88	31	648	3,829	47	123.5
Chad Levitt, Cornell	1993-96	38	922	4,657	44	122.6
Thomas Haskins, VMI	1993-96	44	899	5,355	50	121.7
Gill Fenerty, Holy Cross	1983-85	30	622	3,618	26	120.6
Markus Thomas, Eastern Ky.	1989-92	43	784	5,149	51	119.7

**Record. $See page 10 for explanation.*

SEASON YARDS PER GAME

Player, Team	Year	G	Carries	Yards	TD	Yd. PG
Arnold Mickens, Butler	†1994	10	409	2,255	18	225.5
Charles Roberts, Sacramento St.	†1998	11	386	2,260	19	205.5
Tony Vinson, Towson	†1993	10	293	2,016	23	201.6
Jerry Azumah, New Hampshire	1998	11	342	2,195	22	199.6
Reggie Greene, Siena	†1997	9	256	1,778	18	197.6
Reggie Greene, Siena	†1996	9	280	1,719	12	191.0
Jesse Chatman, Eastern Wash.	†2001	11	285	2,096	24	190.6
Charles Roberts, Sacramento St.	†1999	11	303	2,082	22	189.3
Archie Amerson, Northern Ariz.	1996	11	333	2,079	25	189.0
Louis Ivory, Furman	†2000	11	286	2,079	16	189.0
Aaron Stecker, Western Ill.	1997	11	298	1,957	24	177.9
Marcel Shipp, Massachusetts	1998	11	319	1,949	13	177.2
Adrian Peterson, Ga. Southern	1998	11	257	1,932	25	175.6
Keith Elias, Princeton	1993	10	305	1,731	19	173.1
Nick Hartigan, Brown	†2005	10	314	1,727	20	172.7
Gene Lake, Delaware St.	†1984	10	238	1,722	20	172.2
Karlton Carpenter, Southern Ill.	1998	11	323	1,892	16	172.0
Rich Erenberg, Colgate	†1983	11	302	1,883	20	171.2
Justise Hairston, Central Conn. St.	†2006	11	277	1,847	20	167.9
Sean Bennett, Evansville	1997	10	235	1,668	16	166.8
Kenny Gamble, Colgate	†1986	11	307	1,816	21	165.1

†National champion.

CAREER YARDS

Player, Team	Years	Carries	Yards	Avg.	Long
Adrian Peterson, Ga. Southern	1998-01	996	6,559	6.59	91
Charles Roberts, Sacramento St.	1997-00	*1,124	6,553	5.83	70
Jerry Azumah, New Hampshire	1995-98	1,044	6,193	5.93	96
Matt Cannon, Southern Utah (QB)	1997-00	757	5,489	‡7.25	93
Reggie Greene, Siena	1994-97	890	5,415	6.08	82
Jermaine Austin, Ga. Southern	2002-05	857	5,411	6.31	78
Marcel Shipp, Massachusetts	1997-00	1,042	5,383	5.17	82
Thomas Haskins, VMI	1993-96	899	5,355	5.96	80
Louis Ivory, Furman	1998-01	847	5,353	6.32	88
Frank Hawkins, Nevada	1977-80	945	5,333	5.64	50
Steve Baylark, Massachusetts	2003-06	1,104	5,332	4.83	50
Rick Sarille, Wagner	$1995-99	965	5,290	5.48	80
Kenny Gamble, Colgate	1984-87	963	5,220	5.42	91
Markus Thomas, Eastern Ky.	1989-92	784	5,149	6.57	90
Charles Anthony, Tennessee St.	2001-04	910	5,057	5.56	80
Clifton Dawson, Harvard	2003-06	958	4,841	5.05	93
Erik Marsh, Lafayette	1991-94	1,027	4,834	4.71	62
Charles Dunn, Portland St.	1998-00	872	4,831	5.54	67
Rich Lemon, Bucknell	1993-96	994	4,742	4.77	83
Ryan Fuqua, Portland St.	2001-04	915	4,730	5.17	80
Claude Mathis, Texas St.	1994-97	882	4,691	5.32	79
Alonzo Coleman, Hampton	2003-06	827	4,658	5.63	65
Chad Levitt, Cornell	1993-96	922	4,657	5.05	88
Rene Ingoglia, Massachusetts	1992-95	905	4,623	5.11	84
Chris Parker, Marshall	1992-95	780	4,571	5.86	89
Ralph Saldiveri, Iona	1997-00	986	4,488	4.55	91
Nick Hartigan, Brown	2003-05	912	4,488	4.92	82
Cedric Minter, Boise St.	1977-80	752	4,475	5.95	77
Joe McCourt, Lafayette	2001-04	955	4,474	4.68	58
John Settle, Appalachian St.	1983-86	891	4,409	4.95	88
Lerron Moore, Western Ky.	2003-06	828	4,396	5.31	37
Brian Westbrook, Villanova	1997-98, 00-01	691	4,298	6.22	52
Jermaine Creighton, St. John's (N.Y.)	1994-97	948	4,271	4.51	99
Donte Small, Duquesne	1998-01	843	4,260	5.05	68

**Record. †Did not score. $See page 10 for explanation. ‡Record for minimum 600 carries.*

CAREER RUSHING TOUCHDOWNS

Player, Team	Years	G	TDs
Adrian Peterson, Ga. Southern	1998-01	42	84
Matt Cannon, Southern Utah (QB)	1997-00	44	69
David Dinkins, Morehead St. (QB)	1997-00	37	63
Chaz Williams, Ga. Southern (QB)	2001-04	45	62
Alonzo Colman, Hampton	2003-06	46	62
Jerry Azumah, New Hampshire	1995-98	41	60
Clifton Dawson, Harvard	2003-06	39	60
Charles Roberts, Sacramento St.	1997-00	44	56
Kenny Gamble, Colgate	1984-87	42	55
Rene Ingoglia, Massachusetts	1992-95	41	54
Louis Ivory, Furman	1998-01	42	53
Charvez Foger, Nevada	1985-88	42	52
Brian Westbrook, Villanova	1997-98, 00-01	44	52
Nick Hartigan, Brown	2003-05	30	52
Markus Thomas, Eastern Ky.	1989-92	43	51
Michael Hicks, South Carolina St.	1993-95	32	51
Arkee Whitlock, Southern Ill.	2003-06	37	51
Paul Lewis, Boston U.	1981-84	37	50
Sherriden May, Idaho	1992-94	33	50
Thomas Haskins, VMI	1993-96	44	50

Player, Team	Years	G	TDs
Rick Sarille, Wagner	$1995-99	41	50
Joe McCourt, Lafayette	2001-04	45	50

[Note: Anthony Russo of St. John's (N.Y.) scored 16 TDs in 1993 at the FCS level but had 57 total touchdowns during 1990-94.] $See page 10 for explanation.

SEASON YARDS

Player, Team	Year	G	Carries	Yards	Avg.
Jamaal Branch, Colgate	2003	16	*450	2,326	5.17
Charles Roberts, Sacramento St.	†1998	11	386	2,260	5.85
Arnold Mickens, Butler	†1994	10	409	2,255	5.51
Jerry Azumah, New Hampshire	1998	11	342	2,195	6.42
Jesse Chatman, Eastern Wash.	†2001	11	285	2,096	7.35
Charles Roberts, Sacramento St.	†1999	11	303	2,082	6.87
Archie Amerson, Northern Ariz.	1996	11	333	2,079	6.24
Louis Ivory, Furman	†2000	11	286	2,079	7.27
Tony Vinson, Towson	†1993	10	293	2,016	6.89
Steve Baylark, Massachusetts	2006	15	338	1,960	5.80
Aaron Stecker, Western Ill.	1997	11	298	1,957	6.57
Marcel Shipp, Massachusetts	1998	11	319	1,949	6.11
Adrian Peterson, Ga. Southern	1998	11	257	1,932	7.52
Karlton Carpenter, Southern Ill.	1998	11	323	1,892	5.86
Rich Erenberg, Colgate	†1983	11	302	1,883	6.24
Justise Hairston, Central Conn. St.	†2006	11	277	1,847	6.67
Marcus Mason, Youngstown St.	2006	12	302	1,847	6.12
Arkee Whitlock, Southern Ill.	2006	13	317	1,828	5.77
Kenny Gamble, Colgate	†1986	11	307	1,816	5.92
Adrian Peterson, Ga. Southern	1999	11	248	1,807	7.29
Charles Dunn, Portland St.	2000	11	302	1,792	5.93
Mike Clark, Akron	1986	11	245	1,786	‡7.29
Reggie Greene, Siena	†1997	9	256	1,778	6.95
Derrick Cullors, Murray St.	1995	11	269	1,765	6.56
L.J. McKanas, Northeastern	2001	11	342	1,756	5.13
Pierre Rembert, Illinois St.	2006	13	355	1,743	4.91
Charles Anthony, Tennessee St.	†2004	11	306	1,739	5.68
Keith Elias, Princeton	1993	10	305	1,731	5.68
Nick Hartigan, Brown	†2005	10	314	1,727	5.50
Gene Lake, Delaware St.	†1984	10	238	1,722	7.24
Frank Hawkins, Nevada	†1980	11	307	1,719	5.60
Reggie Greene, Siena	†1996	9	280	1,719	6.14
Charles Anthony, Tennessee St.	2003	12	322	1,708	5.30
Brad Baxter, Alabama St.	1986	11	302	1,705	5.65
Thomas Haskins, VMI	1996	11	287	1,704	5.94
Joe Rubin, Portland St.	2005	11	345	1,702	4.93

**Record. †National champion. ‡Record for minimum of 200 carries.*

SINGLE-GAME YARDS

Yds.	Player, Team (Opponent)	Date
437	Maurice Hicks, N.C. A&T (Morgan St.)	Oct. 6, 2001
409	Charles Roberts, Sacramento St. (Idaho St.)	Nov. 6, 1999
393	Ryan Fuqua, Portland St. (Eastern Wash.)	Nov. 10, 2001
379	Reggie Greene, Siena [St. John's (N.Y.)]	Nov. 2, 1996
364	Tony Vinson, Towson (Bucknell)	Nov. 13, 1993
356	Joe Rubin, Portland St. (Northern Colo.)	Sept. 24, 2005
353	Maurice Hicks, N.C. A&T (South Carolina St.)	Nov. 18, 2000
346	William Arnold, Jackson St. (Texas Southern)	Nov. 6, 1993
345	Russell Davis, Idaho (Portland St.)	Oct. 3, 1981
337	Gill Fenerty, Holy Cross (Columbia)	Oct. 29, 1983
337	Frank Alessio, Massachusetts (Boston U.)	Nov. 11, 1995
336	Gene Lake, Delaware St. (Liberty)	Nov. 10, 1984
332	Justise Hairston, Central Conn. St. [St. Francis (Pa.)]	Oct. 7, 2006
331	Cory Harge, Central Conn. St. (Stony Brook)	Nov. 6, 2004
329	Jerry Azumah, New Hampshire (Hofstra)	Nov. 7, 1998
328	Herb Donaldson, Western Ill. (Indiana St.)	Nov. 4, 2006
327	Tony Vinson, Towson (Morgan St.)	Nov. 20, 1993
324	Robert Vaughn, Alabama St. (Tuskegee)	Nov. 24, 1994
324	John Campbell, Wagner (Jacksonville)	Nov. 14, 1998
324	Charles Dunn, Portland St. (Hofstra)	Oct. 7, 2000
323	Matt Johnson, Harvard (Brown)	Nov. 9, 1991
323	Mike Hilliard, Duquesne (La Salle)	Sept. 27, 2003

Note: There have been 45 300-yard rushing games in FCS history.

ANNUAL CHAMPIONS

Year	Player, Team	Class	G	Carries	Yards	Avg.
1978	Frank Hawkins, Nevada	So.	10	259	1,445	144.5
1979	Frank Hawkins, Nevada	Jr.	11	293	1,683	153.0
1980	Frank Hawkins, Nevada	Sr.	11	307	1,719	156.3
1981	Gregg Drew, Boston U.	Jr.	10	309	1,257	125.7
1982	Garry Pearson, Massachusetts	Sr.	11	312	1,631	148.3
1983	Rich Erenberg, Colgate	Sr.	11	302	1,883	171.2
1984	Gene Lake, Delaware St.	Jr.	10	238	1,722	172.2
1985	Burton Murchison, Lamar	So.	11	265	1,547	140.6
1986	Kenny Gamble, Colgate	Jr.	11	307	1,816	165.1
1987	Harvey Reed, Howard	Sr.	10	211	1,512	151.2
1988	Elroy Harris, Eastern Ky.	Jr.	10	277	1,543	154.3
1989	Carl Smith, Maine	So.	11	305	1,680	152.7
1990	Walter Dean, Grambling	Sr.	11	221	1,401	127.4
1991	Al Rosier, Dartmouth	Sr.	10	258	1,432	143.2
1992	Keith Elias, Princeton	Jr.	10	245	1,575	157.5
1993	Tony Vinson, Towson	Sr.	10	293	2,016	201.6
1994	Arnold Mickens, Butler	Jr.	10	409	2,255	*225.5
1995	Reggie Greene, Siena	So.	9	273	1,461	162.3
1996	Reggie Greene, Siena	Jr.	9	280	1,719	191.0
1997	Reggie Greene, Siena	Sr.	9	256	1,778	197.6
1998	Charles Roberts, Sacramento St.	So.	11	386	2,260	205.5
1999	Charles Roberts, Sacramento St.	Jr.	11	303	2,082	189.3
2000	Louis Ivory, Furman	Jr.	11	286	2,079	189.0
2001	Jesse Chatman, Eastern Wash.	Sr.	11	285	2,096	190.6
2002	Jay Bailey, Austin Peay	Sr.	12	319	1,687	140.6
2003	Nick Hartigan, Brown	So.	10	275	1,498	149.8
2004	Charles Anthony, Tennessee St.	Sr.	11	306	1,739	158.1
2005	Nick Hartigan, Brown	Sr.	10	314	1,727	172.7
2006	Justise Hairston, Central Conn. St.	Sr.	11	277	1,847	6.67

**Record.*

Quarterback Rushing

CAREER YARDS

(Since 1978)

Player, Team	Years	G	Carries	Yards	TD	Yd. PG
#Matt Cannon, Southern Utah	1997-00	44	674	4,852	*64	*110.3
Willie Taggart, Western Ky.	1995-98	41	684	3,957	46	96.5
David Dinkins, Morehead St.	1997-00	37	553	3,765	63	101.8
Jack Douglas, Citadel	1989-92	44	*832	3,674	48	83.5
Greg Hill, Ga. Southern	1996-99	41	575	3,309	49	80.7
Allen Suber, Bethune-Cookman	2000-03	45	578	2,897	39	64.4
Chaz Williams, Ga. Southern	2001-04	40	603	2,768	62	69.2
Jayson Davis, Rhode Island	2002-05	42	684	2,717	42	64.7
Josh Non, Nicholls St.	2000-03	44	664	2,658	29	60.4
Tracy Ham, Ga. Southern	1984-86	33	511	2,506	32	75.9
Travis Wilson, Wofford	1998-01	44	550	2,488	18	56.5
Tony Scales, VMI	1989-92	44	561	2,475	19	56.3
Eddie Thompson, Western Ky.	1991-93	27	387	2,349	19	87.0
Steve McNair, Alcorn St.	1991-94	42	375	2,327	33	55.4
Eriq Williams, James Madison	1989-92	43	642	2,321	32	54.0
Raymond Gross, Ga. Southern	1987-90	42	695	2,290	20	54.5
Bill Vergantino, Delaware	1989-92	44	656	2,287	34	52.0
Dwane Brown, Arkansas St.	1984-87	42	595	2,192	33	52.2
Roy Johnson, Arkansas St.	1988-91	43	558	2,182	22	50.7
DeAndre Smith, Missouri St.	1987-90	42	558	2,140	36	50.9
Daris Wilson, Bucknell	2001-04	40	477	2,046	23	51.2
Ryan Vena, Colgate	1996-99	40	585	2,008	33	50.2

**Record. #Does not include statistics as a slotback in 1997.*

SEASON YARDS

(Since 1978)

Player, Team	Year	G	Carries	Yards	TD	Avg.
Matt Cannon, Southern Utah	2000	11	218	1,602	22	7.35
Matt Cannon, Southern Utah	1998	11	199	1,533	14	7.80
Jayson Foster, Ga. Southern	2005	12	239	1,481	21	6.20
Chaz Williams, Ga. Southern	2002	14	*290	1,422	*27	4.90
David Dinkins, Morehead St.	2000	9	190	1,405	21	7.39
Willie Taggart, Western Ky.	1998	11	210	1,313	15	6.25
Matt Cannon, Southern Utah	1999	11	203	1,310	23	6.45
Joe Dupaix, Southern Utah	1996	11	271	1,246	12	4.60
Willie Taggart, Western Ky.	1997	10	152	1,217	15	*8.01
Marvin Marshall, South Carolina St.	1994	11	160	1,201	10	7.51
David Dinkins, Morehead St.	1998	11	147	1,169	20	7.95
Jack Douglas, Citadel	1991	11	266	1,152	13	4.33
Daris Wilson, Bucknell	2004	11	254	1,149	17	4.52
David Dinkins, Morehead St.	1999	10	200	1,138	20	5.69
Tony Scales, VMI	1991	11	185	1,105	8	5.97
Pa'tel Troutman, Bethune-Cookman	1999	11	220	1,089	9	4.95
Greg Hill, Ga. Southern	1999	11	152	1,084	16	7.13
Greg Hill, Ga. Southern	1998	11	202	1,061	16	5.25
Pa'tel Troutman, Bethune-Cookman	1998	10	183	1,054	15	5.76
Tracy Ham, Ga. Southern	1986	11	207	1,048	18	5.06
Nicholas Bazan, Albany (N.Y.)	2004	11	194	1,043	12	5.38
Allen Suber, Bethune-Cookman	2002	12	158	1,035	15	6.55
Sheraton Fox, Indiana St.	1999	11	228	1,034	8	4.54
Nick Crawford, Yale	1991	10	210	1,024	8	4.98
Alcede Surtain, Alabama St.	1995	11	178	1,024	21	5.75
Matt Cannon, Southern Utah	1997	11	137	1,024	10	7.47
Gene Brown, Citadel	1988	9	152	1,006	13	6.62

Player, Team	Year	G	Carries	Yards	TD	Avg.
Ryan Kuhn, Cornell	2005	10	199	1,000	12	5.03
Willie Taggart, Western Ky.	1996	10	167	997	8	5.97
Allen Suber, Bethune-Cookman	2003	12	179	987	14	5.51
Kharon Brown, Hofstra	1995	11	151	977	7	6.47
Gus Papanikolas, St. Mary's (Cal.)	2000	11	194	966	8	4.98
Corey Thomas, Nicholls St.	1994	11	158	962	8	6.09

**Record.*

Passing

CAREER PASSING EFFICIENCY

(Minimum 300 Completions; Player must have concluded his career)

Player, Team	Years	Att.	Cmp.	Int.	Pct.	Yards	TD	Pts.
Shawn Knight, William & Mary	1991-94	558	367	15	.658	5,527	46	170.8
Erik Meyer, Eastern Wash.	2002-05	1,097	721	17	.657	10,261	84	166.5
Dave Dickenson, Montana	1992-95	1,208	813	26	*.673	11,080	96	166.3
Drew Miller, Montana	1999-00	654	430	14	.657	5,900	46	160.5
Eric Rasmussen, San Diego	2001-03	851	512	13	.602	7,490	75	160.1
Lang Campbell, William & Mary	2001-04	763	495	12	.649	6,494	54	156.6
Doug Nussmeier, Idaho	1990-93	1,225	746	32	.609	10,824	91	154.4
Justin Rascati, James Madison	2003-06	728	487	16	.669	5,912	51	153.8
Mark Washington, Jackson St.	1996-99	724	384	24	.530	6,561	68	153.5
Craig Ochs, Montana	2003-04	654	430	16	.657	5,419	42	151.7
Mike Simpson, Eastern Ill.	1996-97	493	331	15	.671	3,901	32	148.9
Jay Johnson, UNI	1989-92	744	397	25	.534	7,049	51	148.9
Matt Nagy, Delaware	1997-00	771	433	32	.562	7,220	52	148.8
Joel Sambursky, Southern Ill.	2002-05	933	559	25	.563	7,894	65	148.6
Ryan Vena, Colgate	1996-99	819	482	46	.589	7,427	61	148.4
Mike Cook, William & Mary	1995-98	804	495	21	.616	6,644	55	148.3
Michael Payton, Marshall	1989-92	876	542	32	.619	7,530	57	148.2
Bryan Martin, Weber St.	1992-95	606	365	14	.602	5,211	37	148.0
David Macchi, Valparaiso	2002-03	802	450	28	.561	7,089	59	147.7
Ingle Martin, Furman	2002-05	669	410	22	.613	5,751	42	147.6
Aaron Flowers, Cal St. Northridge	1996-97	819	502	21	.613	6,766	54	147.3
Willie Totten, Mississippi Val.	1982-85	1,555	907	*75	.583	12,711	139	146.8
Kenneth Biggles, Tennessee St.	1981-84	701	397	28	.566	5,933	57	146.6
Shane Stafford, Connecticut	1995-98	951	522	29	.549	8,368	67	146.0
Mark Borda, Lehigh	2002-05	562	351	14	.625	4,469	37	146.0
Oteman Sampson, Florida A&M	1996-97	686	387	26	.564	6,104	46	145.7
Brian Ah Yat, Montana	1995-98	1,190	735	39	.618	9,315	89	145.6
Russ Michna, Western Ill.	2000-03	733	418	20	.570	6,434	44	145.1
Giovanni Carmazzi, Hofstra	1996-99	1,187	764	32	.644	9,371	71	145.0
Bruce Eugene, Grambling	$2001-05	1,657	872	38	.526	13,513	*140	144.4
Jimmy Blanchard, Portland St.	1997-00	1,038	618	19	.595	8,455	63	144.3
Ted White, Howard	1995-98	1,163	635	34	.546	9,611	92	144.3

**Record. $See page 10 for explanation.*

SEASON PASSING EFFICIENCY

(Minimum 15 Attempts Per Game)

Player, Team	Year	G	Att.	Cmp.	Int.	Pct.	Yards	TD	Pts.
Shawn Knight, William & Mary	†1993	10	177	125	4	.706	2,055	22	204.6
Michael Payton, Marshall	†1991	9	216	143	5	.622	2,333	19	181.3
Alli Abrew, Cal Poly	†1997	11	191	130	4	.681	1,961	17	179.5
Tony Romo, Eastern Ill.	†2001	10	207	138	6	.667	2,068	21	178.3
Doug Turner, Morehead St.	1997	10	290	190	6	.655	2,869	29	177.5
Ted White, Howard	†1996	11	289	174	10	.602	2,814	36	176.2
Doug Nussmeier, Idaho	1993	11	304	185	5	.609	2,960	33	175.2
Brian Kadel, Dayton	†1995	11	183	115	6	.628	1,880	18	175.0
Eric Rasmussen, San Diego	†2003	10	318	195	3	.613	2,982	35	174.5
Chris Boden, Villanova	1997	11	345	231	4	.670	3,079	36	174.0
Bruce Eugene, Grambling	†2005	12	456	254	6	.557	4,360	*56	173.9
Kelvin Simmons, Troy	1993	11	224	143	6	.638	2,144	23	172.8
Rocky Butler, Hofstra	2001	11	335	206	4	.615	3,311	30	171.7
Josh Johnson, San Diego	2005	12	371	260	8	.701	3,256	36	171.5
Erik Meyer, Eastern Wash.	†2004	13	382	259	9	.678	3,707	31	171.4
Frank Baur, Lafayette	†1988	10	256	164	11	.641	2,621	23	171.1
Bobby Lamb, Furman	†1985	11	181	106	6	.586	1,856	18	170.9
Ricky Santos, New Hampshire	2005	13	429	301	9	.702	3,797	39	170.3
Harry Leons, Eastern Wash.	1997	10	257	159	5	.619	2,588	21	169.5
Steven Beard, UNI	1996	11	238	140	9	.588	2,526	21	169.5

**Record. †National champion.*

CAREER YARDS PER GAME

(Minimum 5,000 Yards; Player must have concluded his career)

Player, Team	Years	G	Att.	Cmp.	Yards	TD	Yd. PG
Neil Lomax, Portland St.	1978-80	33	1,425	836	11,550	88	350.0
Steve McNair, Alcorn St.	1991-94	42	*1,680	927	*14,496	119	345.1
Aaron Flowers, Cal St. Northridge	1996-97	20	819	502	6,766	54	338.3
Chris Sanders, Chattanooga	1999-00	22	953	584	7,230	49	328.6
Drew Miller, Montana	1999-00	18	654	430	5,900	46	327.8
Willie Totten, Mississippi Val.	1982-85	40	1,555	907	12,711	139	317.8
Dave Dickenson, Montana	1992-95	35	1,208	813	11,080	96	316.6

Player, Team	Years	G	Att.	Cmp.	Yards	TD	Yd. PG
David Macchi, Valparaiso	2002-03	23	802	450	7,089	59	308.2
John Friesz, Idaho	1986-89	35	1,350	801	10,697	77	305.6
James Perry, Brown	1996-99	31	1,309	789	9,294	74	299.8
Tom Proudian, Iona	1993-95	27	1,134	656	8,088	58	299.6
Jamie Martin, Weber St.	1989-92	41	1,544	934	12,207	87	297.7
Bruce Eugene, Grambling	$2001-05	46	1,657	872	13,513	*140	293.8
Marcus Brady, Cal St. Northridge	1998-01	43	*1,680	*1,039	12,479	109	290.2
Sean Payton, Eastern Ill.	1983-86	37	1,408	756	10,655	75	288.0
Travis Brown, Northern Ariz.	1996-99	41	1,577	888	11,400	86	278.0
Doug Nussmeier, Idaho	1990-93	39	1,225	746	10,824	91	277.5
Oteman Sampson, Florida A&M	1996-97	22	686	387	6,104	46	277.5
John Sciarra, Wagner	2004-05	22	847	473	5,902	40	268.3
Robert Dougherty, Boston U.	1993-94	21	705	405	5,608	41	267.0
Robert Kent, Jackson St.	2000-03	45	1,540	826	11,784	104	261.9
Gavin Hoffman, Penn	1999-01	29	1,004	651	7,542	50	260.0

**Record. $See page 10 for explanation.*

SEASON YARDS PER GAME

Player, Team	Year	G	Att.	Cmp.	Int.	Pct.	Yards	TD	Yd.PG
Willie Totten, Mississippi Val.	†1984	10	518	324	22	.626	4,557	*56	455.7
Steve McNair, Alcorn St.	1994	11	530	304	17	.574	*4,863	44	442.1
Martin Hankins, Southeastern La.	2004	11	540	357	12	.661	4,240	35	385.5
Dave Dickenson, Montana	1995	11	455	309	9	.679	4,176	38	379.6
Joe Lee, Towson	1999	11	577	322	13	.558	4,168	22	378.9
Jamie Martin, Weber St.	1991	11	500	310	17	.620	4,125	35	375.0
Neil Lomax, Portland St.	1980	11	473	296	12	.626	4,094	37	372.2
John Friesz, Idaho	1989	11	425	260	8	.612	4,041	31	367.4
Bruce Eugene, Grambling	†2005	12	456	254	6	.557	4,360	*56	363.3
Neil Lomax, Portland St.	1979	11	516	299	16	.579	3,950	26	359.1
Aaron Flowers, Cal St. Northridge	1997	9	404	255	10	.631	3,226	24	358.4
Todd Hammel, Stephen F. Austin	†1989	11	401	238	13	.594	3,914	34	355.8
Tom Ehrhardt, Rhode Island	1985	10	497	283	19	.569	3,542	35	354.2
Steve McNair, Alcorn St.	1992	10	427	231	11	.541	3,541	29	354.1
Sean Payton, Eastern Ill.	1984	11	473	270	15	.571	3,843	28	349.4
Drew Miller, Montana	1999	10	368	240	8	.652	3,461	32	346.1
Bruce Eugene, Grambling	2002	13	543	269	16	.495	4,483	43	344.8
Dave Dickenson, Montana	†1994	9	336	229	6	.682	3,053	24	339.2
Tom Proudian, Iona	1993	10	440	262	13	.595	3,368	29	336.8
Jamie Martin, Weber St.	1990	11	428	256	15	.598	3,700	23	336.4

**Record. †National pass-efficiency champion.*

CAREER YARDS

Player, Team	Years	Att.	Cmp.	Int.	Pct.	Yards	TD
Steve McNair, Alcorn St.	1991-94	*1,680	927	58	.552	14,496	119
Bruce Eugene, Grambling	$2001-05	1,657	872	38	.526	13,513	*140
Willie Totten, Mississippi Val.	1982-85	1,555	907	*75	.583	12,711	139
Marcus Brady, Cal St. Northridge	1998-01	*1,680	*1,039	47	.618	12,479	109
Jamie Martin, Weber St.	1989-92	1,544	934	56	.605	12,207	87
Robert Kent, Jackson St.	2000-03	1,540	826	58	.536	11,784	104
Neil Lomax, Portland St.	1978-80	1,425	836	50	.587	11,550	88
Travis Brown, Northern Ariz.	1996-99	1,577	888	42	.563	11,400	86
Dave Dickenson, Montana	1992-95	1,208	813	26	*.673	11,080	96
Doug Nussmeier, Idaho	1990-93	1,225	746	32	.609	10,824	91
Travis Lulay, Montana St.	2002-05	1,559	889	35	.570	10,746	58
Jason Murrietta, Northern Ariz.	2003-06	1,516	878	49	.579	10,726	94
John Friesz, Idaho	1986-89	1,350	801	40	.593	10,697	77
Greg Wyatt, Northern Ariz.	1986-89	1,510	926	49	.613	10,697	70
Sean Payton, Eastern Ill.	1983-86	1,408	756	55	.537	10,655	75
Donald Carrie, Alcorn St.	2001-04	1,369	695	61	.508	10,329	82
Erik Meyer, Eastern Wash.	2002-05	1,097	721	17	.657	10,261	84
Niel Loebig, Duquesne	2001-04	1,316	705	72	.536	10,254	103
Marko Glavic, Lafayette	2000-03	1,459	820	56	.562	9,819	62
David Corley Jr., William & Mary	1999-02	1,168	676	38	.579	9,805	73
Collin Drafts, Charleston So.	2003-06	1,344	833	44	.620	9,768	73
Jeff Wiley, Holy Cross	1985-88	1,208	723	63	.599	9,698	71
Phil Stambaugh, Lehigh	1996-99	1,284	816	43	.636	9,669	78
Jeff Lewis, Northern Ariz.	1992-95	1,316	785	24	.597	9,655	67
Ted White, Howard	1995-98	1,163	635	34	.546	9,611	92
Robbie Justino, Liberty	1989-92	1,267	769	51	.607	9,548	64
Chris Boden, Villanova	1996-99	1,338	818	30	.611	9,538	93
Giovanni Carmazzi, Hofstra	1996-99	1,187	764	32	.644	9,371	71
Brian Ah Yat, Montana	1995-98	1,190	735	39	.618	9,315	89
Kirk Schulz, Villanova	1986-89	1,297	774	70	.597	9,305	70
Ken Hobart, Idaho	1980-83	1,219	629	42	.516	9,300	79
James Perry, Brown	1996-99	1,309	789	48	.603	9,294	74

**Record. $See page 10 for explanation.*

SEASON YARDS

Player, Team	Year	G	Att.	Cmp.	Int.	Pct.	Yards	TD
Steve McNair, Alcorn St.	1994	11	530	304	17	.574	4,863	44
Dustin Long, Sam Houston St.	2004	14	531	333	18	.627	4,588	39
Willie Totten, Mississippi Val.	†1984	10	518	324	22	.626	4,557	*56

Player, Team	Year	G	Att.	Cmp.	Int.	Pct.	Yards	TD
Bruce Eugene, Grambling	2002	13	543	269	16	.495	4,483	43
Bruce Eugene, Grambling	†2005	12	456	254	6	.557	4,360	*56
Brett Gordon, Villanova	2002	15	578	*385	14	.666	4,305	36
Martin Hankins, Southeastern La.	2004	11	540	357	12	.661	4,240	35
Dave Dickenson, Montana	1995	11	455	309	9	.679	4,176	38
Joe Lee, Towson	1999	11	577	322	13	.558	4,168	22
Jamie Martin, Weber St.	1991	11	500	310	17	.620	4,125	35
Neil Lomax, Portland St.	1980	11	473	296	12	.626	4,094	37
John Friesz, Idaho	1989	11	425	260	8	.612	4,041	31
Erik Meyer, Eastern Wash.	2005	12	410	269	5	.656	4,003	30
Lang Campbell, William & Mary	2004	14	455	298	5	.655	3,988	30
Neil Lomax, Portland St.	1979	11	516	299	16	.579	3,950	26
Todd Hammel, Stephen F. Austin	†1989	11	401	238	13	.594	3,914	34
Sean Payton, Eastern Ill.	1984	11	473	270	15	.571	3,843	28
Bruce Eugene, Grambling	2003	12	528	285	13	.540	3,808	34
Craig Ochs, Montana	2004	15	450	309	8	.687	3,807	33
Ricky Santos, New Hampshire	2005	13	429	301	9	.702	3,797	39

**Record. †National pass-efficiency champion.*

CAREER TOUCHDOWN PASSES

Player, Team	Years	G	TD Passes
Bruce Eugene, Grambling	$2001-05	46	140
Willie Totten, Mississippi Val.	1982-85	40	139
Steve McNair, Alcorn St.	1991-94	42	119
Marcus Brady, Cal St. Northridge	1998-01	43	109
Robert Kent, Jackson St.	2000-03	45	104
Niel Loebig, Duquesne	2001-04	43	103
Dave Dickenson, Montana	1992-95	35	96
Jason Murrietta, Northern Ariz.	2003-06	46	94
Chris Boden, Villanova	1996-99	39	93
Ted White, Howard	1995-98	41	92
Doug Nussmeier, Idaho	1990-93	39	91
Brian Ah Yat, Montana	1995-98	36	89
Neil Lomax, Portland St.	1978-80	33	88
Jamie Martin, Weber St.	1989-92	41	87
Travis Brown, Northern Ariz.	1996-99	41	86
Erik Meyer, Eastern Wash.	2002-05	42	84
Jim Lopusznick, Fairfield	1996-99	39	83
Darin Hinshaw, UCF	1991-94	40	82
Donald Carrie, Alcorn St.	2001-04	45	82
Dan Crowley, Towson	1991-94	40	81
Ken Hobart, Idaho	1980-83	44	79
Phil Stambaugh, Lehigh	1996-99	44	78
Eric Beavers, Nevada	1983-86	40	77
John Friesz, Idaho	1986-89	35	77
Ryan Helming, UNI	1997-00	44	77
Sean Payton, Eastern Ill.	1983-86	39	75
Eric Rasmussen, San Diego	2002-03	29	75
James Perry, Brown	1996-99	31	74
Matt DeGennaro, Connecticut	1987-90	43	73
Tony Zimmerman, Duquesne	1998-00	33	73
David Corley Jr., William & Mary	1999-02	45	73
Collin Drafts, Charleston So.	2003-06	44	73

$See page 10 for explanation.

SEASON TOUCHDOWN PASSES

Player, Team	Year	G	TD Passes
Willie Totten, Mississippi Val.	1984	10	56
Bruce Eugene, Grambling	2005	12	56
Steve McNair, Alcorn St.	1994	11	44
Bruce Eugene, Grambling	2002	13	43
Brian Ah Yat, Montana	1996	11	42
Willie Totten, Mississippi Val.	1985	11	39
Dustin Long, Sam Houston St.	2004	14	39
Ricky Santos, New Hampshire	2005	13	39
Dave Dickenson, Montana	1995	11	38
David Macchi, Valparaiso	2003	12	38
Neil Lomax, Portland St.	1980	11	37
Patrick Bonner, Florida A&M	1998	11	37
Ted White, Howard	1996	11	36
Chris Boden, Villanova	1997	11	36
Brett Gordon, Villanova	2002	15	36
Josh Johnson, San Diego	2005	12	36
Tom Ehrhardt, Rhode Island	1985	10	35
Jamie Martin, Weber St.	1991	11	35
Eric Rasmussen, San Diego	2003	10	35
Martin Hankins, Southeastern La.	2004	11	35

SINGLE-GAME YARDS

Yds.	Player, Team (Opponent)	Date
624	Jamie Martin, Weber St. (Idaho St.)	Nov. 23, 1991
619	Doug Pederson, La.-Monroe (Stephen F. Austin)	Nov. 11, 1989
618	Bruce Eugene, Grambling (Prairie View)	Oct. 1, 2005

Yds.	Player, Team (Opponent)	Date
599	Willie Totten, Mississippi Val. (Prairie View)	Oct. 27, 1984
595	Robert Kent, Jackson St. (Alabama St.)	Oct. 6, 2001
589	Vern Harris, Idaho St. (Montana)	Oct. 12, 1985
588	Martin Hankins, Southeastern La. (Ark.-Monticello)	Sept. 2, 2004
587	Steve McNair, Alcorn St. (Southern U.)	Oct. 22, 1994
577	Dustin Long, Sam Houston St. (McNeese St.)	Nov. 6, 2004
571	Todd Hammel, Stephen F. Austin (La.-Monroe)	Nov. 11, 1989
567	Joe Lee, Towson (Lehigh)	Oct. 30, 1999
566	Tom Ehrhardt, Rhode Island (Connecticut)	Nov. 16, 1985
566	Seth Burford, Cal Poly (UNI)	Nov. 4, 2000
563	Steve McNair, Alcorn St. (Samford)	Oct. 29, 1994
560	Brian Ah Yat, Montana (Eastern Wash.)	Oct. 19, 1996
560	Bobby Seck, Hofstra (Rhode Island)	Sept. 25, 2004
558	Dave Dickenson, Montana (Idaho)	Oct. 21, 1995
556	Matt Nagy, Delaware (Connecticut)	Nov. 7, 1998
553	Willie Totten, Mississippi Val. (Southern U.)	Sept. 29, 1984
553	Justin Fuente, Murray St. (Southern Ill.)	Sept. 11, 1999
553	Kevin McCarthy, Idaho St. (Southern Utah)	Oct. 23, 1999
552	Quincy Richard, Southern U. (Grambling)	Nov. 29, 2003
551	Lejominick Washington, Morgan St. (N.C. A&T)	Oct. 6, 2001
550	Jimmy Blanchard, Portland St. (Montana)	Oct. 2, 1999

SINGLE-GAME ATTEMPTS

No.	Player, Team (Opponent)	Date
77	Neil Lomax, Portland St. (Northern Colo.)	Oct. 20, 1979
76	Joe Lee, Towson (Lehigh)	Oct. 30, 1999
74	Paul Peterson, Idaho St. (Nevada)	Oct. 1, 1983
72	Dave Dickenson, Montana (Idaho)	Oct. 21, 1995
72	Val Troiani, Towson [St. Mary's (Cal.)]	Nov. 4, 2000
71	Doug Pederson, La.-Monroe (Stephen F. Austin)	Nov. 11, 1989
71	Bobby Townsend, Howard (Morgan St.)	Nov. 13, 1999
71	Josh Greco, Eastern Ky. (Eastern Ill.)	Oct. 15, 2005
70	Greg Farland, Rhode Island (Boston U.)	Oct. 18, 1986
70	Joe Lee, Towson (Dayton)	Nov. 6, 1999

SINGLE-GAME COMPLETIONS

No.	Player, Team (Opponent)	Date
50	Martin Hankins, Southeastern La. (Jacksonville)	Nov. 6, 2004
48	Clayton Millis, Cal St. Northridge [St. Mary's (Cal.)]	Nov. 11, 1995
47	Jamie Martin, Weber St. (Idaho St.)	Nov. 23, 1991
47	Joe Lee, Towson (Lehigh)	Oct. 30, 1999
46	Willie Totten, Mississippi Val. (Southern U.)	Sept. 29, 1984
46	Doug Pederson, La.-Monroe (Stephen F. Austin)	Nov. 11, 1989
45	Willie Totten, Mississippi Val. (Prairie View)	Oct. 27, 1984
45	Ben Dougherty, Florida A&M (Florida Int'l)	Nov. 27, 2004
44	Neil Lomax, Portland St. (Northern Colo.)	Oct. 20, 1979
44	Kyle Slager, Brown (Rhode Island)	Oct. 5, 2002
44	Brady Wahlberg, Tenn.-Martin (Jacksonville St.)	Oct. 11, 2003

ALL-TIME BEST RECORDS BY A STARTING QUARTERBACK

(Minimum 25 Starts; Player must have completed his career)

Name, Team, Years	Starting Record	Winning #Pct.
Tom Ciaccio, Holy Cross, 1989-91	30-2-1	.924
Dave Dickenson, Montana, 1993-95	27-3-0	.900
Greg Hill, Ga. Southern, 1996-99	32-4-0	.889
John Edwards, Montana, 2001-02	27-4-0	.871
Chris Brown, Colgate, 2001-04	25-5-0	.833
Rick Scully, Delaware, 1980-82	26-6-0	.813
Jeff Zolman, Wofford, 2001-04	26-6-0	.813
Demond Tidwell, Youngstown St., 1996-97	21-5-0	.808
T.J. Mont, Georgetown, 1996, 98-99	21-5-0	.808
Ray Isaac, Youngstown St., 1988-91	32-8-0	.800
Jay Johnson, UNI, 1989-92	31-8-0	.795
Niel Loebig, Duquesne, 2001-04	34-9-0	.791
Tony Zimmerman, Duquesne, 1998-00	26-7-0	.788
Paul Nichols, Davidson, 1999-02	22-6-0	.786
Jeff Wiley, Holy Cross, 1985-88	30-8-1	.782
Andy Hall, Delaware, 2002-03	21-6-0	.778
Russ Michna, Western Ill., 2000-03	20-6-0	.769
Chaz Williams, Ga. Southern, 2001-04	25-8-0	.758
Peter Muldoon, Holy Cross, 1982-84	25-8-1	.750
Mike Smith, UNI, 1985-87	28-9-1	.750
Jay Fiedler, Dartmouth, 1991-93	22-7-1	.750
Todd Bankhead, Massachusetts, 1998-99	21-7-0	.750
Scott Pendarvis, McNeese St., 2001-04	27-9-0	.750
Others (Did not meet minimum of 25 starts):		
Mark Derosa, Penn, 1994-95	16-3-0	.842

#Ties are counted as half won, half lost.

ANNUAL CHAMPIONS

Year	Player, Team	Class	G	Att.	Cmp.	Avg.	Int.	Pct.	Yds.	TD
1978	Neil Lomax, Portland St.	So.	11	436	241	21.9	22	.553	3,506	25

Beginning in 1979, ranked on passing efficiency rating points (instead of per-game completions)

Year	Player, Team	Cl.	G	Att.	Cmp.	Int.	Pct.	Yards	TD	Pts.
1979	Joe Aliotti, Boise St.	Jr.	11	219	144	7	.658	1,870	19	159.7
1980	Mike Williams, Grambling	Sr.	11	239	127	5	.531	2,116	28	162.0
1981	Mike Machurek, Idaho St.	Sr.	9	313	188	11	.601	2,752	22	150.1
1982	Frank Novak, Lafayette	Jr.	10	257	154	12	.599	2,257	20	150.0
1983	Willie Totten, Mississippi Val.	So.	9	279	174	9	.624	2,566	29	167.5
1984	Willie Totten, Mississippi Val.	Jr.	10	518	324	22	.626	4,557	*56	163.6
1985	Bobby Lamb, Furman	Sr.	11	181	106	6	.586	1,856	18	170.9
1986	Mike Smith, UNI	Jr.	11	303	190	16	.627	3,125	27	168.2
1987	Jeff Wiley, Holy Cross	Jr.	11	400	265	17	.663	3,677	34	163.0
1988	Frank Baur, Lafayette	Jr.	10	256	164	11	.641	2,621	23	171.1
1989	Todd Hammel, Stephen F. Austin	Sr.	11	401	238	13	.594	3,914	34	162.8
1990	Connell Maynor, N.C. A&T	Jr.	11	191	123	10	.644	1,699	16	156.3
1991	Michael Payton, Marshall	Jr.	9	216	143	5	.662	2,333	19	181.3
1992	Jay Fiedler, Dartmouth	Jr.	10	273	175	13	.641	2,748	25	169.4
1993	Shawn Knight, William & Mary	Jr.	10	177	125	4	.706	2,055	22	*204.6
1994	Dave Dickenson, Montana	Jr.	9	336	229	6	.682	3,053	24	164.5
1995	Brian Kadel, Dayton	Sr.	11	183	115	6	.628	1,880	18	175.0
1996	Ted White, Howard	So.	11	289	174	10	.602	2,814	36	176.2
1997	Alli Abrew, Cal Poly	Sr.	11	191	130	4	.681	1,961	17	179.5
1998	Jim Blanchard, Portland St.	So.	9	169	112	1	.663	1,512	14	167.6
1999	Drew Miller, Montana	Jr.	10	368	240	8	.652	3,461	32	168.6
2000	Terrance Ley, Southern U.	Jr.	11	233	139	6	.597	2,249	23	168.2
2001	Tony Romo, Eastern Ill.	Jr.	10	207	138	6	.667	2,068	21	178.3
2002	Eric Rasmussen, San Diego	Jr.	10	279	170	1	.609	2,473	25	164.2
2003	Eric Rasmussen, San Diego	Sr.	10	318	195	3	.613	2,982	35	174.5
2004	Erik Meyer, Eastern Wash.	Jr.	13	382	259	9	.678	3,707	31	171.4
2005	Bruce Eugene, Grambling	Sr.	12	456	254	6	.557	4,360	*56	173.9
2006	Josh Johnson, San Diego	Jr.	12	371	246	5	.663	3,320	34	169.0

**Record.*

Receiving

CAREER RECEPTIONS PER GAME

(Minimum 125 Receptions; Player must have concluded his career)

Player, Team	Years	G	Rec.	Yards	TD	Rec. PG
Tramon Douglas, Grambling	2002-03	22	169	2,621	28	7.7
Stephen Campbell, Brown	1997-00	40	305	3,555	31	7.6
Chas Gessner, Brown	1999-02	39	292	3,408	36	7.5
Jerry Rice, Mississippi Val.	1981-84	41	301	*4,693	50	7.3
Mike Furrey, UNI	1997-99	33	242	3,544	27	7.3
Ralph Plumb, Yale	2003-04	19	138	1,752	12	7.3
Drew Amerson, Cal St. Northridge	1999-01	33	239	3,190	20	7.2
Derrick Ingram, UAB	1993-94	22	159	2,572	21	7.2
Jacquay Nunnally, Florida A&M	1997-00	44	*317	4,239	38	7.2
Jeff Johnson, East Tenn. St.	1993-94	20	142	1,772	19	7.1
Miles Macik, Penn	1993-95	29	200	2,364	26	6.9
Ricky Gatewood, Montana St.	2004-05	19	131	1,759	13	6.9
Kevin Guthrie, Princeton	1981-83	28	193	2,645	16	6.9
A.J. Smith, Southern Utah	2003-04	21	143	1,358	6	6.8
Eric Yarber, Idaho	1984-85	19	129	1,920	17	6.8
Joe Douglass, Montana	1995-96	22	145	2,301	25	6.6
Rob Milanese, Penn	1999-02	39	259	3,405	21	6.6
Alonzo Nix, Chattanooga	2003-04	23	150	1,879	14	6.5
Brian Forster, Rhode Island (TE)	1983-85, 87	38	245	3,410	31	6.5
Jarrod Fuller, Sam Houston St.	2003-04	23	147	2,019	9	6.4
Kasey Dunn, Idaho	1988-91	42	268	3,847	25	6.4
Carl Morris, Harvard	1999-02	39	245	3,488	28	6.3
Javarus Dudley, Fordham	2000-03	47	295	4,197	34	6.3
Sean Morey, Brown	1995-98	40	251	3,850	39	6.3
Gordie Lockbaum, Holy Cross (RB)	‡1986-87	22	135	2,012	17	6.1
Efrem Hill, Samford	2002-04	33	202	2,940	31	6.1
David Ball, New Hampshire	2003-06	50	304	4,655	*58	6.1
Derek Graham, Princeton	1981, 83-84	29	176	2,819	19	6.1

**Record. ‡Defensive back in 1984-85.*

SEASON RECEPTIONS PER GAME

Player, Team	Year	G	Rec.	Yards	TD	Rec. PG
Stephen Campbell, Brown	†2000	10	*120	1,332	11	12.0
Brian Forster, Rhode Island (TE)	†1985	10	115	1,617	12	11.5
Chas Gessner, Brown	†2002	10	114	1,166	11	11.4
Jerry Rice, Mississippi Val.	†1984	10	103	1,682	*27	10.3
Jerry Rice, Mississippi Val.	†1983	10	102	1,450	14	10.2
Stuart Gaussoin, Portland St.	†1979	9	90	1,132	8	10.0
Drew Amerson, Cal St. Northridge	†2001	10	97	1,244	5	9.7
DaVon Fowlkes, Appalachian St.	†2004	11	103	1,618	14	9.4
Maurice Price, Charleston So.	†2006	11	103	985	10	9.4
Chas Gessner, Brown	2001	9	83	1,182	12	9.2
Carl Morris, Harvard	2002	10	90	1,288	8	9.0
Murle Sango, Villanova	†1999	11	98	1,064	10	8.9
Eric Krawczyk, Cornell	†1997	10	89	1,042	11	8.9
Stephen Campbell, Brown	1999	10	89	1,107	11	8.9
Kevin Guthrie, Princeton	1983	10	88	1,259	9	8.8
David Romines, Cal St. Northridge	†1996	10	87	1,300	12	8.7
Eric Johnson, Yale	2000	10	87	1,017	14	8.7
Jacquay Nunnally, Florida A&M	2000	11	95	1,082	9	8.6
Rob Milanese, Penn	2002	10	85	1,112	8	8.5
Alfred Pupunu, Weber St. (TE)	†1991	11	93	1,204	12	8.5
Jacquay Nunnally, Florida A&M	†1998	11	93	1,316	12	8.5

**Record. †National champion.*

CAREER RECEPTIONS

Player, Team	Years	Rec.	Yards	Avg.	TD
Jacquay Nunnally, Florida A&M	1997-00	317	4,239	13.4	38
Stephen Campbell, Brown	1997-00	305	3,555	11.7	31
David Ball, New Hampshire	2003-06	304	4,655	15.3	*58
Jerry Rice, Mississippi Val.	1981-84	301	*4,693	15.6	50
Javarus Dudley, Fordham	2000-03	295	4,197	14.2	34
Chas Gessner, Brown	1999-02	292	3,408	11.7	36
Kasey Dunn, Idaho	1988-91	268	3,847	14.4	25
Rob Milanese, Penn	1999-02	259	3,405	13.1	21
Eric Kimble, Eastern Wash.	2002-05	253	4,410	16.4	46
Sean Morey, Brown	1995-98	251	3,850	15.3	39
Eddie Berlin, UNI	1997-00	249	3,735	15.0	34
Fred Amey, Sacramento St.	2001-04	248	4,049	16.3	27
Adam Hannula, San Diego	2002-05	248	3,465	14.0	36
Brian Forster, Rhode Island (TE)	1983-85, 87	245	3,410	13.9	31
Carl Morris, Harvard	1999-02	245	3,488	14.2	28
Michael Caputo, St. Francis (Pa.)	2003-06	245	3,464	14.1	31
Mike Furrey, UNI	1997-99	242	3,544	14.6	27
Mark Didio, Connecticut	1988-91	239	3,535	14.8	21
Drew Amerson, Cal St. Northridge	1999-01	239	3,190	13.3	20
Rennie Benn, Lehigh	1982-85	237	3,662	15.5	44
Daren Altieri, Boston U.	1987-90	225	2,518	11.2	15
Luke Palko, St. Francis (Pa.)	2003-06	225	2,020	9.0	13
Orshawante Bryant, Portland St.	1997-00	223	3,449	15.5	25
Luke Graham, Colgate	2001-04	221	3,381	15.3	21
Jamal White, Towson	1998-00, 02	219	3,156	14.4	21
Rich Musinski, William & Mary	2000-03	219	4,017	18.3	30
Darrell Colbert, Texas Southern	1983-86	217	3,177	14.6	33

Player, Team	Years	Rec.	Yards	Avg.	TD
Deron Braswell, Lehigh	1995-98	217	3,292	15.2	28
Brian Westbrook, Villanova	1997-98, 00-01	217	2,582	11.9	30
Jay Barnard, Dartmouth	2000-03	216	2,392	11.1	17
David Rhodes, UCF	1991-94	213	3,618	17.0	29
Chris Turner, Wagner	2003-06	213	2,853	13.4	33
Corey Hill, Colgate	1995-98	212	3,434	16.2	34
Eric Wise, Fairfield	1996-99	211	2,139	10.1	20

**Record.*

SEASON RECEPTIONS

Player, Team	Year	G	Rec.	Yards	TD
Stephen Campbell, Brown	†2000	10	120	1,332	11
Brian Forster, Rhode Island (TE)	†1985	10	115	1,617	12
Chas Gessner, Brown	†2002	10	114	1,166	11
Jerry Rice, Mississippi Val.	†1984	10	103	1,682	*27
DaVon Fowlkes, Appalachian St.	†2004	11	103	1,618	14
Maurice Price, Charleston So.	†2006	11	103	985	10
Jerry Rice, Mississippi Val.	†1983	10	102	1,450	14
Javarus Dudley, Fordham	†2003	12	101	1,439	14
Jarrod Fuller, Sam Houston St.	2004	14	99	1,383	8
Murle Sango, Villanova	†1999	11	98	1,064	10
Drew Amerson, Cal St. Northridge	†2001	10	97	1,244	5
Jacquay Nunnally, Florida A&M	2000	11	95	1,082	9
Alfred Pupunu, Weber St. (TE)	†1991	11	93	1,204	12
Jacquay Nunnally, Florida A&M	†1998	11	93	1,316	12
Peter Macon, Weber St.	†1989	11	92	1,047	6
Tramon Douglas, Grambling	2002	12	92	1,704	18
Efrem Hill, Samford	2003	11	92	1,387	15
Michael Caputo, St. Francis (Pa.)	†2005	11	92	1,433	12
Marvin Walker, North Texas	1982	11	91	934	11
Eddie Conti, Delaware	1998	11	91	*1,712	10
Stuart Gaussoin, Portland St.	†1979	9	90	1,132	8
Carl Morris, Harvard	2002	10	90	1,288	8
Alonzo Nix, Chattanooga	2003	12	90	1,060	7
Ari Confesor, Holy Cross	2003	12	90	1,213	9

**Record. †National champion.*

SINGLE-GAME RECEPTIONS

No.	Player, Team (Opponent)	Date
24	Jerry Rice, Mississippi Val. (Southern U.)	Oct. 1, 1983
24	Chas Gessner, Brown (Rhode Island)	Oct. 5, 2002
22	Marvin Walker, North Texas (Tulsa)	Nov. 20, 1982
21	David Pandt, Montana St. (Eastern Wash.)	Sept. 21, 1985
21	Eric Johnson, Yale (Harvard)	Nov. 20, 1999
21	Carl Morris, Harvard (Dartmouth)	Nov. 2, 2002
20	Tim Hilton, Cal St. Northridge [St. Mary's (Cal.)]	Nov. 11, 1995
19	Stephen Campbell, Brown (Rhode Island)	Sept. 30, 2000
19	Chas Gessner, Brown (Rhode Island)	Sept. 29, 2001
19	Rickey Gatewood, Montana St. (Portland St.)	Oct. 15, 2005
18	Brian Forster, Rhode Island (Brown)	Sept. 28, 1985
18	Jerome Williams, Morehead St. (Eastern Ky.)	Nov. 18, 1989
18	David Romines, Cal St. Northridge (UC Davis)	Sept. 14, 1996
18	Jeremy Nunamaker, St. Francis (Pa.) (Sacred Heart)	Oct. 2, 1999
18	Stephen Campbell, Brown (Penn)	Oct. 28, 2000
18	Alonzo Nix, Chattanooga (Wofford)	Oct. 4, 2003
18	Ralph Plumb, Yale (Brown)	Nov. 6, 2004

CAREER TOUCHDOWN RECEPTIONS

Player, Team	Years	G	TD
David Ball, New Hampshire	2003-06	50	58
Jerry Rice, Mississippi Val.	1981-84	41	50
Eric Kimble, Eastern Wash.	2002-05	46	46
Rennie Benn, Lehigh	1982-85	41	44
Dedric Ward, UNI	1993-96	43	41
Rob Giancola, Valparaiso	2001-04	53	40
Sean Morey, Brown	1995-98	40	39
Gharun Hester, Georgetown	1997-00	36	39
Mike Jones, Tennessee St.	1979-82	42	38
Roy Banks, Eastern Ill.	1983-86	38	38
Jacquay Nunnally, Florida A&M	1997-00	44	38
Cornell Craig, Southern Ill.	1996-99	44	37
Vincent Jackson, Northern Colo.	2001-04	46	37
Joe Thomas, Mississippi Val.	1982-85	41	36
Chas Gessner, Brown	1999-02	39	36
Adam Hannula, San Diego	2002-05	43	36
Dameon Reilly, Rhode Island	1983-85	32	35

SEASON TOUCHDOWN RECEPTIONS

Player, Team	Year	G	TD
Jerry Rice, Mississippi Val.	1984	10	27
David Ball, New Hampshire	2005	13	24
Rob Giancola, Valparaiso	2003	12	23
Randy Moss, Marshall	1996	11	19
Eric Kimble, Eastern Wash.	2004	13	19
Henry Tolbert, Grambling	2005	12	19
Joe Douglass, Montana	1996	11	18
Tramon Douglas, Grambling	2002	12	18
Roy Banks, Eastern Ill.	1984	11	17
Joe Thomas, Mississippi Val.	1985	11	17
Dameon Reilly, Rhode Island	1985	11	17
Mark Carrier, Nicholls St.	1986	11	17
Sylvester Morris, Jackson St.	1995	11	17
Brian Finneran, Villanova	1997	11	17
Jonathon Cooper, Sam Houston St.	2001	11	17
David Ball, New Hampshire	2004	12	17

CAREER YARDS PER GAME

(Minimum 2,000 Yards; Player must have concluded his career)

Player, Team	Years	G	Yards	Yds. PG
Tramon Douglas, Grambling	2002-03	22	2,621	119.1
Derrick Ingram, UAB	1993-94	22	2,572	116.9
Jerry Rice, Mississippi Val.	1981-84	41	*4,693	114.5
Mike Furrey, UNI	1997-99	33	3,544	107.4
Joe Douglass, Montana	1995-96	22	2,301	104.6
Eddie Conti, Delaware	1994-98	35	3,496	99.9
Derek Graham, Princeton	1981, 83-84	29	2,819	97.2
Drew Amerson, Cal St. Northridge	1999-01	33	3,190	96.7
Jacquay Nunnally, Florida A&M	1997-00	44	4,239	96.3
Sean Morey, Brown	1995-98	40	3,850	96.3
Kevin Guthrie, Princeton	1981-83	28	2,645	94.5
Fred Amey, Sacramento St.	2001-04	43	4,049	94.2
Tracy Singleton, Howard	1979-82	34	3,187	93.7
Maurice Price, Charleston So.	2004-06	26	2,429	93.4
Rich Musinski, William & Mary	2000-03	43	4,017	93.4
David Ball, New Hampshire	2003-06	50	4,655	93.1
David Rhodes, UCF	1991-94	39	3,618	92.8
Kasey Dunn, Idaho	1988-91	42	3,847	91.6
Gordie Lockbaum, Holy Cross	‡1986-87	22	2,012	91.5
Bryan Calder, Nevada	1984-86	28	2,559	91.4
Mike Barber, Marshall	1985-88	36	3,520	90.3
Dedric Ward, UNI	1993-96	43	3,876	90.1
Eric Kimble, Eastern Wash.	2002-05	46	4,140	90.0

**Record. ‡Defensive back in 1984-85.*

CAREER YARDS

Player, Team	Years	Rec.	Yards	Avg.	TD
Jerry Rice, Mississippi Val.	1981-84	301	4,693	15.6	50
David Ball, New Hampshire	2003-06	304	4,655	15.3	*58
Jacquay Nunnally, Florida A&M	1997-00	*317	4,239	13.4	38
Javarus Dudley, Fordham	2000-03	295	4,197	14.2	34
Eric Kimble, Eastern Wash.	2002-05	253	4,140	16.4	46
Fred Amey, Sacramento St.	2001-04	248	4,049	16.3	27
Rich Musinski, William & Mary	2000-03	219	4,017	18.3	30
C.J. Johnson, Tennessee St.	2000-03	194	3,903	20.1	32
Dedric Ward, UNI	1993-96	176	3,876	22.0	41
Sean Morey, Brown	1995-98	251	3,850	15.3	39
Kasey Dunn, Idaho	1988-91	268	3,847	14.4	25
Rob Giancola, Valparaiso	2001-04	176	3,833	21.8	40
Eddie Berlin, UNI	1997-00	249	3,735	15.0	34
Rennie Benn, Lehigh	1982-85	237	3,662	15.5	44
David Rhodes, UCF	1991-94	213	3,618	17.0	29
Stephen Campbell, Brown	1997-00	305	3,555	11.7	31
Correll Craig, Southern Ill.	1996-99	207	3,550	17.1	37
Vincent Jackson, Northern Colo.	2001-04	177	3,548	20.0	37
Mike Furrey, UNI	1997-99	242	3,544	14.6	27
Mark Didio, Connecticut	1988-91	239	3,535	14.8	21
Mike Barber, Marshall	1985-88	209	3,520	16.8	20

**Record.*

SEASON YARDS

Player, Team	Year	Rec.	Yards	Avg.	TD
Eddie Conti, Delaware	†1998	91	1,712	18.8	10
Tramon Douglas, Grambling	†2002	92	1,704	18.5	18
Jerry Rice, Mississippi Val.	1984	103	1,682	16.3	*27
DaVon Fowlkes, Appalachian St.	†2004	103	1,618	15.7	14
Brian Forster, Rhode Island	1985	115	1,617	14.1	12
Dominique Thompson, William & Mary	2004	79	1,585	20.1	13
David Ball, New Hampshire	2005	87	1,551	17.8	24
David Ball, New Hampshire	2004	86	1,504	17.5	17
Rob Giancola, Valparaiso	2003	57	1,496	26.3	23
Joe Douglass, Montana	1996	82	1,469	17.9	18
Laurent Robinson, Illinois St.	†2005	86	1,465	17.0	12
Derrick Ingram, UAB	1994	83	1,457	17.6	13

Player, Team	Year	Rec.	Yards	Avg.	TD
Willie Ponder, Southeast Mo. St.	2002	87	1,453	16.7	15
Eric Kimble, Eastern Wash.	2004	83	1,453	17.5	19
Jerry Rice, Mississippi Val.	1983	102	1,450	14.2	14
Javarus Dudley, Fordham	2003	101	1,439	14.3	14
Michael Caputo, St. Francis (Pa.)	2005	92	1,433	15.6	12
Sean Morey, Brown	†1997	73	1,427	19.6	15
Cornell Craig, Southern Ill.	†1999	77	1,419	18.4	15
Eric Kimble, Eastern Wash.	2005	87	1,419	16.3	12

**Record. †National champion.*

SINGLE-GAME YARDS

Yds.	Player, Team (Opponent)	Date
376	Kassim Osgood, Cal Poly (UNI)	Nov. 4, 2000
370	Michael Lerch, Princeton (Brown)	Oct. 12, 1991
354	Eddie Conti, Delaware (Connecticut)	Nov. 7, 1998
330	Nate Singleton, Grambling (Virginia Union)	Sept. 14, 1991
327	Brian Forster, Rhode Island (Brown)	Sept. 28, 1985
319	Jason Cristino, Lehigh (Lafayette)	Nov. 21, 1992
316	Marcus Hinton, Alcorn St. (Chattanooga)	Sept. 10, 1994
305	Howard Gilmore, Norfolk St. (Morgan St.)	Nov. 22, 2003
299	Brian Forster, Rhode Island (Lehigh)	Oct. 12, 1985
299	Treamelle Taylor, Nevada (Montana)	Oct. 14, 1989
294	Jerry Rice, Mississippi Val. (Kentucky St.)	Sept. 1, 1984
294	Michael Caputo, St. Francis (Pa.) (Sacred Heart)	Oct. 29, 2005
292	Laurent Robinson, Illinois St. (Indiana St.)	Nov. 12, 2005

ANNUAL CHAMPIONS

Year	Player, Team	Class	G	Rec.	Avg.	Yards	TD
1978	Dan Ross, Northeastern	Sr.	11	68	6.2	988	7
1979	Stuart Gaussoin, Portland St.	Jr.	9	90	10.0	1,132	8
1980	Kenny Johnson, Portland St.	So.	11	72	6.5	1,011	11
1981	Ken Harvey, UNI	Sr.	11	78	7.1	1,161	15
1982	Don Lewis, Columbia	Jr.	10	84	8.4	1,000	6
1983	Jerry Rice, Mississippi Val.	Jr.	10	102	10.2	1,450	14
1984	Jerry Rice, Mississippi Val.	Sr.	10	103	10.3	1,682	*27
1985	Brian Forster, Rhode Island (TE)	Jr.	10	115	11.5	1,617	12
1986	Donald Narcisse, Texas Southern	Sr.	11	88	8.0	1,074	15
1987	Mike Barber, Marshall	Jr.	11	78	7.1	1,237	7
	Gordie Lockbaum, Holy Cross (RB)	Sr.	11	78	7.1	1,152	9
1988	Glenn Antrum, Connecticut	Sr.	11	77	7.0	1,130	7
1989	Peter Macon, Weber St.	Sr.	11	92	8.4	1,047	6

Beginning in 1990, ranked on both per-game catches and yards per game

PER-GAME RECEPTIONS

Year	Player, Team	Class	G	Rec.	Avg.	Yards	TD
1990	Kasey Dunn, Idaho	Jr.	11	88	8.0	1,164	7
1991	Alfred Pupunu, Weber St. (TE)	Sr.	11	93	8.5	1,204	12
1992	Glenn Krupa, Southeast Mo. St.	Sr.	11	77	7.0	773	4
1993	Dave Cecchini, Lehigh	Sr.	11	88	8.0	1,318	16
1994	Jeff Johnson, East Tenn. St.	Sr.	9	73	8.1	857	8
1995	Ed Mantie, Boston U.	Sr.	11	81	7.4	943	1
1996	David Romines, Cal St. Northridge	Sr.	10	87	8.7	1,300	12
1997	Eric Krawczyk, Cornell	Sr.	10	89	8.9	1,042	11
1998	Jacquay Nunnally, Florida A&M	So.	11	93	8.5	1,316	12
1999	Murle Sango, Villanova	So.	11	98	8.9	1,064	10
2000	Stephen Campbell, Brown	Sr.	10	*120	*12.0	1,332	11
2001	Drew Amerson, Cal St. Northridge	Jr.	10	97	9.7	1,244	5
2002	Chas Gessner, Brown	Sr.	10	114	11.4	1,166	11
2003	Javarus Dudley, Fordham	Sr.	12	101	8.4	1,439	14
2004	DaVon Fowlkes, Appalachian St.	Sr.	11	103	9.4	1,618	14
2005	Michael Caputo, St. Francis (Pa.)	Jr.	11	92	8.4	1,433	12
2006	Maurice Price, Charleston So.	Jr.	11	103	9.4	985	10

YARDS PER GAME

Year	Player, Team	Class	G	Rec.	Yards	Avg.	TD
1990	Kasey Dunn, Idaho	Jr.	11	88	1,164	105.8	7
1991	Mark Didio, Connecticut	Sr.	11	88	1,354	123.1	8
1992	Jason Cristino, Lehigh	Sr.	11	65	1,282	116.5	9
1993	Dave Cecchini, Lehigh	Sr.	11	88	1,318	119.8	16
1994	Mark Orlando, Towson	Sr.	9	55	1,223	135.9	12
1995	Dedric Ward, UNI	Jr.	10	44	1,164	116.4	12
1996	Joe Douglass, Montana	Sr.	11	82	1,469	133.6	18
1997	Sean Morey, Brown	Jr.	10	73	1,427	142.7	15
1998	Eddie Conti, Delaware	Sr.	11	91	*1,712	*155.6	10
1999	Cornell Craig, Southern Ill.	Sr.	11	77	1,419	129.0	15
2000	Stephen Campbell, Brown	Sr.	10	*120	1,332	133.2	11
2001	Chas Gessner, Brown	Jr.	9	83	1,182	131.3	12
2002	Tramon Douglas, Grambling	Jr.	12	92	1,704	142.0	18
2003	Efrem Hill, Samford	Jr.	11	92	1,387	126.1	15
2004	DaVon Fowlkes, Appalachian St.	Sr.	11	103	1,618	147.1	14
2005	Laurent Robinson, Illinois St.	Jr.	11	86	1,465	133.2	12
2006	Bruce Hocker, Duquesne	Jr.	10	61	1,070	107.0	16

**Record.*

Scoring

CAREER POINTS PER GAME

(Minimum 225 Points; Player must have concluded his career)

Player, Team	Years	G	TD	Extra Pts. Scored	FG	Pts.	Pt. PG
Adrian Peterson, Ga. Southern	1998-01	42	87	2	0	524	12.5
Brian Westbrook, Villanova	1997-98, 00-01	44	*89	10	0	*544	12.4
Aaron Stecker, Western Ill.	1997-98	20	39	0	0	234	11.7
Gary Jones, Albany (N.Y.)	2002-03	23	42	0	0	252	11.0
Nick Hartigan, Brown	2003-05	30	54	0	0	324	10.8
Keith Elias, Princeton	1991-93	30	52	8	0	320	10.7
Kevin Richardson, Appalachian St.	2003-06	30	52	0	0	312	10.4
Jesse Chatman, Eastern Wash.	1999-01	31	53	4	0	322	10.4
David Dinkins, Morehead St.	1997-00	37	63	6	0	384	10.4
Archie Amerson, Northern Ariz.	1995-96	22	38	0	0	228	10.4
Clifton Dawson, Harvard	2003-06	39	66	2	0	398	10.2
Jerry Azumah, New Hampshire	1995-98	41	69	4	0	418	10.2
Michael Hicks, South Carolina St.	1993-95	32	52	4	0	316	9.9
Matt Cannon, Southern Utah	1997-00	44	69	6	0	420	9.5
Chaz Williams, Ga. Southern	2001-04	40	62	2	0	374	9.4
Joel Sigel, Portland St.	1978-80	30	46	2	0	278	9.3
Elroy Harris, Eastern Ky.	1985, 87-88	31	47	6	0	288	9.3
Charles Dunn, Portland St.	1998-00	33	51	0	0	306	9.3
Tony Zendejas, Nevada	1981-83	33	0	90	70	300	9.1
Gerald Harris, Ga. Southern	1984-86	31	45	2	0	272	8.8
Marty Zendejas, Nevada	1984-87	44	0	169	*72	385	8.8
Charvez Foger, Nevada	1985-88	42	60	2	0	362	8.6
Arkee Whitlock, Southern Ill.	2003-06	37	52	0	0	312	8.4
Paul Lewis, Boston U.	1981-84	37	51	2	0	308	8.3
Judd Garrett, Princeton	1987-89	30	41	2	0	248	8.3
Sherriden May, Idaho	1991-94	44	61	0	0	366	8.3
Andre Garron, New Hampshire	1982-85	30	41	0	0	246	8.2
Kenny Gamble, Colgate	1984-87	42	57	0	0	342	8.1
Rene Ingoglia, Massachusetts	1992-95	41	55	2	0	332	8.1
Reggie Greene, Siena	1994-97	36	48	2	0	290	8.1
Rick Sarille, Wagner	$1995-99	41	55	4	0	334	8.1
Charles Roberts, Sacramento St.	1997-00	44	57	10	0	352	8.0

**Record. $See page 10 for explanation.*

SEASON POINTS PER GAME

Player, Team	Year	G	TD	Extra Pts. Scored	FG	Pts.	Pt. PG
Jerry Rice, Mississippi Val.	†1984	10	27	0	0	162	16.2
Brian Westbrook, Villanova	†2001	11	*29	2	0	*176	16.0
Adrian Peterson, Ga. Southern	†1999	11	*29	0	0	174	15.8
Montrell Coley, Hampton	†2000	11	28	4	0	172	15.6
Jesse Chatman, Eastern Wash.	2001	11	28	4	0	172	15.6
Geoff Mitchell, Weber St.	†1991	11	28	2	0	170	15.5
Brian Westbrook, Villanova	†1998	11	26	4	0	160	14.6
Tony Vinson, Towson	†1993	10	24	0	0	144	14.4
David Dinkins, Morehead St.	2000	9	21	2	0	128	14.2
Archie Amerson, Northern Ariz.	†1996	11	26	0	0	156	14.2
Adrian Peterson, Ga. Southern	1998	11	26	0	0	156	14.2
Ronald Jean, Lehigh	1999	11	26	0	0	156	14.2
Sherriden May, Idaho	†1992	11	25	0	0	150	13.6
Aaron Stecker, Western Ill.	†1997	11	25	0	0	150	13.6
Chris Reed, Monmouth	1998	10	22	0	0	132	13.2
Clifton Dawson, Harvard	†2006	10	22	0	0	132	13.2
Keith Elias, Princeton	1993	10	21	4	0	130	13.0
Elroy Harris, Eastern Ky.	†1988	10	21	2	0	128	12.8
Jerry Azumah, New Hampshire	1998	11	23	2	0	140	12.7
Jessie Burton, McNeese St.	1998	9	19	0	0	114	12.7
Chaz Williams, Ga. Southern	†2004	12	25	2	0	152	12.7

**Record. †National champion.*

CAREER POINTS

(Non-Kickers)

Player, Team	Years	TD	Extra Pts. Scored	Pts.
Brian Westbrook, Villanova	1997-98, 00-01	*89	10	544
Adrian Peterson, Ga. Southern	1998-01	87	2	524
Matt Cannon (QB), Southern Utah	1997-00	69	6	420

Player, Team	Years	TD	Extra Pts. Scored	Pts.
Jerry Azumah, New Hampshire	1995-98	69	4	418
Clifton Dawson, Harvard	2003-06	66	2	398
David Dinkins, Morehead St.	1997-00	63	6	384
Alonzo Coleman, Hampton	2003-06	64	0	384
Chaz Williams (QB), Ga. Southern	2001-04	62	2	374
Sherriden May, Idaho	1991-94	61	0	366
Charvez Foger, Nevada	1985-88	60	2	362
Charles Roberts, Sacramento St.	1997-00	57	10	352
David Ball, New Hampshire	2003-06	58	0	348
Kenny Gamble, Colgate	1984-87	57	0	342
Rick Sarille, Wagner	$1995-99	55	4	334
Rene Ingoglia, Massachusetts	1992-95	55	2	332
Travis Glasford, Western Ill.	2002-05	55	2	332
Montrell Coley, Hampton	1997-00	53	8	326
Joe McCourt, Lafayette	2001-04	54	2	326
Eric Kimble, Eastern Wash.	2002-05	54	2	326
Marcel Shipp, Massachusetts	1997-00	54	0	324
Nick Hartigan, Brown	2003-05	54	0	324
Markus Thomas, Eastern Ky.	1989-92	53	4	322
Jesse Chatman, Eastern Wash.	1999-01	53	4	322
Keith Elias, Princeton	1991-93	52	8	320

**Record. $See page 10 for explanation.*

CAREER POINTS

(Kickers)

Player, Team	Years	PAT	PAT Att.	FG	FG Att.	Pts.
Chris Snyder, Montana	2000-03	182	187	70	*105	^394
Marty Zendejas, Nevada	1984-87	169	175	*72	90	385
Craig Coffin, Southern Ill.	$2002-06	*229	*239	50	63	379
Andrew Paterini, Hampton	2003-06	184	204	59	90	361
Greg Kuehn, William & Mary	2002-05	166	171	59	89	343
Justin Langan, Western Ill.	2001-04	174	182	53	78	@335
Brian Wingert, UNI	2003-06	151	157	60	79	331
Dave Ettinger, Hofstra	1994-97	140	155	62	93	326
Brian Morgan, Grambling	2001-04	174	197	50	87	324
Brian Mitchell, Marshall/UNI	1987, 89-91	130	131	64	81	322
Scott Shields, Weber St.	1995-98	109	118	67	90	#322
Thayne Doyle, Idaho	1988-91	160	174	49	75	307
Miro Kesic, Northeastern	2002-05	162	168	48	71	306
Jose Larios, McNeese St.	1992-95	133	136	57	89	304
Kirk Roach, Western Caro.	1984-87	89	91	71	102	302
Tim Foley, Ga. Southern	1984-87	151	156	50	62	301
Tony Zendejas, Nevada	1981-83	90	96	70	86	300
Dewey Klein, Marshall	1988-91	156	165	48	66	300
Josh Hoke, Coastal Caro.	2003-06	177	183	40	63	297
Chris Onorato, Hofstra	2001-04	145	153	50	77	295
Connor McCormick, New Hampshire	2002-05	174	185	40	61	294
Jeff Wilkins, Youngstown St.	1990-93	134	136	50	73	286
Danny Marshall, Furman	2000-03	149	157	45	57	284
Garth Petrilli, Middle Tenn.	1991-94	166	170	38	60	280

**Record. #Includes 2 TDs. ^Includes one two-point conversion made in two attempts. @Includes one two-point conversion made in one attempt.*

SEASON POINTS

Player, Team	Year	TD	Extra Pts. Scored	FG	Pts.
Kevin Richardson, Appalachian St.	2006	*31	0	0	186
Brian Westbrook, Villanova	†2001	29	2	0	176
Adrian Peterson, Ga. Southern	†1999	29	0	0	174
Jamaal Branch, Colgate	2003	29	0	0	174
Montrell Coley, Hampton	†2000	28	4	0	172
Jesse Chatman, Eastern Wash.	2001	28	4	0	172
Geoff Mitchell, Weber St.	†1991	28	2	0	170
Jerry Rice, Mississippi Val.	†1984	27	0	0	162
Chaz Williams, Ga. Southern	2002	27	0	0	162
Brian Westbrook, Villanova	†1998	26	4	0	160
Archie Amerson, Northern Ariz.	†1996	26	0	0	156
Adrian Peterson, Ga. Southern	1998	26	0	0	156
Ronald Jean, Lehigh	1999	26	0	0	156
Chaz Williams, Ga. Southern	†2004	25	2	0	152
Sherriden May, Idaho	†1992	25	0	0	150
Aaron Stecker, Western Ill.	†1997	25	0	0	150
Arkee Whitlock, Southern Ill.	2006	25	0	0	150
Tony Vinson, Towson	†1993	24	0	0	144
T.J. Stallings, Morgan St.	†2002	23	6	0	144
David Ball, New Hampshire	2005	24	0	0	144
Jerry Azumah, New Hampshire	1998	23	2	0	140
Rob Giancola, Valparaiso	2003	23	2	0	140
Jerome Felton, Furman	2006	23	2	0	140

**Record. †National champion.*

ANNUAL CHAMPIONS

Year	Player, Team	Class	G	TD	Extra Pts. Scored	FG	Pts.	Avg.
1978	Frank Hawkins, Nevada	So.	10	17	0	0	102	10.2
1979	Joel Sigel, Portland St.	Jr.	10	16	0	0	96	9.6
1980	Ken Jenkins, Bucknell	Jr.	10	16	0	0	96	9.6
1981	Paris Wicks, Youngstown St.	Jr.	11	17	2	0	104	9.5
1982	Paul Lewis, Boston U.	So.	10	18	0	0	108	10.8
1983	Rich Erenberg, Colgate	Sr.	11	21	10	0	136	12.4
1984	Jerry Rice, Mississippi Val.	Sr.	10	27	0	0	162	*16.2
1985	Charvez Foger, Nevada	Fr.	10	18	0	0	108	10.8
1986	Gordie Lockbaum, Holy Cross	Jr.	11	22	0	0	132	12.0
1987	Sean Sanders, Weber St.	Sr.	10	21	0	0	126	12.6
1988	Elroy Harris, Eastern Ky.	Jr.	10	21	2	0	128	12.8
1989	Carl Smith, Maine	So.	11	20	0	0	120	10.9
1990	Barry Bourassa, New Hampshire	So.	9	16	0	0	96	10.7
1991	Geoff Mitchell, Weber St.	Sr.	11	28	2	0	170	15.5
1992	Sherriden May, Idaho	So.	11	25	0	0	150	13.6
1993	Tony Vinson, Towson	Sr.	10	24	0	0	144	14.4
1994	Michael Hicks, South Carolina St.	Jr.	11	22	0	0	132	12.0
1995	Alcede Surtain, Alabama St.	Sr.	11	21	6	0	132	12.0
	Tim Hall, Robert Morris	Sr.	10	20	0	0	120	12.0
1996	Archie Amerson, Northern Ariz.	Sr.	11	26	0	0	156	14.2
1997	Aaron Stecker, Western Ill.	Jr.	11	25	0	0	150	13.6
1998	Brian Westbrook, Villanova	So.	11	26	4	0	160	14.6
1999	Adrian Peterson, Ga. Southern	So.	11	29	0	0	174	15.8
2000	Montrell Coley, Hampton	Sr.	11	28	4	0	172	15.6
2001	Brian Westbrook, Villanova	Sr.	11	29	2	0	176	16.0
2002	T.J. Stallings, Morgan St.	Sr.	12	23	6	0	144	12.0
	Dale Jennings, Butler	Sr.	10	20	0	0	120	12.0
2003	Evan Harney, San Diego	Fr.	10	20	2	0	122	12.2
2004	Chaz Williams, Ga. Southern	Sr.	12	25	2	0	152	12.7
2005	Nick Hartigan, Brown	Sr.	10	21	0	0	126	12.6
2006	Clifton Dawson, Harvard	Sr.	10	22	0	0	132	13.2

**Record.*

Interceptions

CAREER INTERCEPTIONS

Player, Team	Years	No.	Yards	Avg.
Rashean Mathis, Bethune-Cookman	1999-02	31	*682	22.0
Dave Murphy, Holy Cross	1986-89	28	309	11.0
Leigh Bodden, Duquesne	1999-02	28	297	10.6
Cedric Walker, Stephen F. Austin	1990-93	25	230	9.2
Issiac Holt, Alcorn St.	1981-84	24	319	13.3
Bill McGovern, Holy Cross	1981-84	24	168	7.0
Darren Sharper, William & Mary	1993-96	24	488	20.3
Mike Prior, Illinois St.	1981-84	23	211	9.2
Kevin Smith, Rhode Island	1987-90	23	287	12.5
William Carroll, Florida A&M	1989-92	23	328	14.3
Adrion Smith, Missouri St.	1990-93	23	219	9.5
Scott Shields, Weber St.	1995-98	23	278	12.1
Dean Cain, Princeton	1985-87	22	203	9.2
Derrick Harris, East Tenn. St.	1986-89	22	453	20.6
Frank Robinson, Boise St.	1988-91	22	203	9.2
Dave Roberts, Youngstown St.	1989-92	22	131	6.0
Morgan Ryan, Montana St.	1990-93	22	245	11.1
Chris Helon, Boston U.	1991-94	22	110	5.0
Robert Taylor, Tennessee Tech	1993-96	22	267	12.1
George Floyd, Eastern Ky.	1978-81	21	318	15.1
Greg Greely, Nicholls St.	1981-84	21	218	10.4
Chris Demarest, Northeastern	1984-87	21	255	12.1
Mark Seals, Boston U.	1985-88	21	169	8.0
Jeff Smith, Illinois St.	1985-88	21	152	7.2
Kevin Dent, Jackson St.	1985-88	21	280	13.3
Brian Randall, Delaware St.	1990-93	21	367	17.4
Derek Carter, Maine	1994-97	21	301	14.3
Paul Serie, Siena	1995-98	21	107	5.1
Steve Dogmanits, Fairfield	1997-00	21	231	11.0
Tyrone Parsons, Alcorn St.	2000-03	21	270	12.9

**Record.*

SEASON INTERCEPTIONS

Player, Team	Year	No.	Yards
Rashean Mathis, Bethune-Cookman	†2002	14	*455
Dean Cain, Princeton	†1987	12	98
Anthony Young, Jackson St.	†1978	11	108
Everson Walls, Grambling	†1980	11	145
Bill McGovern, Holy Cross	†1984	11	102
Claude Pettaway, Maine	‡1990	11	161
Aeneas Williams, Southern U.	‡1990	11	173

Player, Team	Year	No.	Yards
Rashean Mathis, Bethune-Cookman	2000	11	157
Steve Dogmanits, Fairfield	†2000	11	113
Jon Ambrose, St. Peter's	†2001	11	222
Bob Mahr, Lafayette	1981	10	48
Mike Genetti, Northeastern	†1981	10	144
George Schmitt, Delaware	†1982	10	186
Mike Armentrout, Missouri St.	†1983	10	42
Anthony Anderson, Grambling	‡1986	10	37
Kevin Dent, Jackson St.	‡1986	10	192
Eric Thompson, New Hampshire	‡1986	10	94
Chris Demarest, Northeastern	1987	10	129
Cedric Walker, Stephen F. Austin	1990	10	11
Chris Helon, Boston U.	†1993	10	42
Scott Shields, Weber St.	1996	10	101
Darren Sharper, William & Mary	1996	10	228

**Record. †National champion. ‡National championship shared.*

ANNUAL CHAMPIONS

(Ranked on Per-Game Average)

Year	Player, Team	Class	G	No.	Avg.	Yards
1978	Anthony Young, Jackson St.	Sr.	11	11	1.00	108
1979	Neale Henderson, Southern U.	Sr.	11	10	0.91	151
1980	Everson Walls, Grambling	Sr.	11	11	1.00	145
1981	Mike Genetti, Northeastern	So.	10	10	1.00	144
1982	George Schmitt, Delaware	Sr.	11	10	0.91	186
1983	Mike Armentrout, Missouri St.	Jr.	11	10	0.91	42
1984	Bill McGovern, Holy Cross	Sr.	11	11	1.00	102
1985	Mike Cassidy, Rhode Island	Sr.	10	9	0.90	169
	George Duarte, Northern Ariz.	Jr.	10	9	0.90	150
1986	Kevin Dent, Jackson St.	So.	11	10	0.91	192
	Eric Thompson, New Hampshire	Sr.	11	10	0.91	94
	Anthony Anderson, Grambling	Sr.	11	10	0.91	37
1987	Dean Cain, Princeton	Sr.	10	12	*1.20	98
1988	Kevin Smith, Rhode Island	So.	10	9	0.90	94
1989	Mike Babb, Weber St.	Sr.	11	9	0.82	90
1990	Aeneas Williams, Southern U.	Sr.	11	11	1.00	173
	Claude Pettaway, Maine	Sr.	11	11	1.00	161
1991	Warren McIntire, Delaware	Jr.	11	9	0.82	208
1992	Dave Roberts, Youngstown St.	Sr.	11	9	0.82	39
1993	Chris Helon, Boston U.	Jr.	11	10	0.91	42
1994	Joseph Vaughn, Cal St. Northridge	Sr.	10	9	0.90	265
	Brian Clark, Hofstra	Jr.	10	9	0.90	56
1995	Picasso Nelson, Jackson St.	Sr.	9	8	0.89	101
1996	Shane Hurd, Canisius	Jr.	7	7	1.00	198
1997	Roderic Parson, Brown	Sr.	8	8	1.00	93
1998	Ken Krapf, St. John's (N.Y.)	Jr.	11	9	0.82	144
	Eric Kenesie, Valparaiso	Jr.	11	9	0.82	88
1999	Ryan Crawford, Davidson	Jr.	11	8	0.73	63
2000	Steve Dogmanits, Fairfield	Sr.	10	11	1.10	113
2001	Jon Ambrose, St. Peter's	Jr.	11	11	1.00	222
2002	Rashean Mathis, Bethune-Cookman	Sr.	13	*14	1.08	*455
2003	Brandon Martin, Butler	Sr.	11	8	0.73	76
2004	Ahmad Treaudo, Southern U.	Sr.	11	9	0.82	166
2005	Jay McCareins, Princeton	Jr.	10	9	0.90	236
2006	Dre Dokes, UNI	Sr.	11	7	0.64	116

**Record.*

DEFENSIVE RECORDS

(Since 2000)

Total Tackles

CAREER TOTAL TACKLES PER GAME

(Min. 250 Total Tackles; Player must have concluded his career)

Player, Team	Years	G	Solo	Ast.	Total	Avg.
Josh Cain, Chattanooga	2000-02	34	273	177	450	13.2
Boomer Grigsby, Illinois St.	2001-04	44	*325	225	*550	12.5
Liam Ezekiel, Northeastern	2001-04	44	218	*271	489	11.1
James Noel, Robert Morris	2002-05	41	179	258	437	10.7
Jordan Beck, Cal Poly	2001-04	43	270	179	449	10.4
Nick Ricks, Eastern Ill.	2000-03	47	298	180	478	10.2
Lee Russell, Western Ill.	2000-03	48	317	163	480	10.0
Matt Nelson, Wofford	2000-03	47	296	156	452	9.6
Erik Dandy, Western Ky.	2000-03	45	241	183	424	9.4
Mario Williams, Gardner-Webb	2001-04	35	181	145	326	9.3
Henry Carter, Duquesne	2002-05	43	207	187	394	9.2
Stephen Cooper, Maine	2000-02	33	199	101	300	9.1
Dante Balestracci, Harvard	2000-03	38	200	143	343	9.0
Maurice Bennett, Lafayette	2002-05	46	161	242	403	8.8
Matt McFadden, Weber St.	2000-03	41	152	198	350	8.5
Jamar Leath, Coastal Caro.	2003-06	43	154	210	364	8.5
Robert Mason, VMI	2002-05	44	186	185	371	8.4
Maurice Simpkins, Coastal Caro.	2003-05	33	171	101	272	8.2
David Dugan, Holy Cross	2000-02	33	140	125	265	8.0
Keppy Baucom, Gardner-Webb	2002-05	39	111	195	306	7.8
Justin Huggard, VMI	2002-05	43	149	188	337	7.8
Manny Rojas, Liberty	2003-06	45	140	208	348	7.7
Todd Baldwin, VMI	2002-05	45	140	206	346	7.7
Anton McKenzie, Massachusetts	2000-03	42	234	86	320	7.6
Ryan Garrison, McNeese St.	2000-03	52	236	155	391	7.5
Casey Tierney, UNI	2000-03	38	171	109	280	7.4
John Mohring, Ga. Southern	2003-06	44	135	181	316	7.2
Mark Kimener, Massachusetts	2000-03	45	214	99	313	7.0

**Record.*

SEASON TOTAL TACKLES PER GAME

Player, Team	Year	G	Solo	Ast.	Total	Avg.
Boomer Grigsby, Illinois St.	†2002	11	108	71	179	16.3
Kevin Talley, Norfolk St.	†2003	12	75	*120	*195	16.3
Josh Cain, Chattanooga	2002	12	*113	79	192	16.0
Edgerton Hartwell, Western Ill.	†2000	11	107	62	169	15.4
Kevin Talley, Norfolk St.	†2004	9	58	77	135	15.0
Boomer Grigsby, Illinois St.	2003	12	109	70	179	14.9
Tim Johnson, Youngstown St.	2000	11	83	80	163	14.8
P.J. Jones, Missouri St.	†2001	11	66	95	161	14.6
Derrick Lloyd, James Madison	2001	11	94	63	157	14.3
Dietrich Lapsley, Indiana St.	2002	12	103	68	171	14.3
Aden Smith, Stony Brook	2002	10	57	83	140	14.0
Bobby Rosenberg, St. John's (N.Y.)	2002	10	80	60	140	14.0
Chad Nkang, Elon	†2005	11	73	79	152	13.8
Melvin Wisham, Western Ky.	2000	11	92	58	150	13.6

**Record. †National champion.*

CAREER TOTAL TACKLES

Player, Team	Years	G	Solo	Ast.	Total
Boomer Grigsby, Illinois St.	2001-04	44	*325	225	550
Liam Ezekiel, Northeastern	2001-04	44	218	*271	489
Lee Russell, Western Ill.	2000-03	48	317	163	480
Nick Ricks, Eastern Ill.	2000-03	47	298	180	478
Matt Nelson, Wofford	2000-03	47	296	156	452
Josh Cain, Chattanooga	2000-02	34	273	177	450
Jordan Beck, Cal Poly	2001-04	43	270	179	449
James Noel, Robert Morris	2002-05	41	179	258	437
Erik Dandy, Western Ky.	2000-03	45	241	183	424
Charles Thompson, Western Ky.	2001-04	49	208	203	411
Maurice Bennett, Lafayette	2002-05	46	161	242	403
Henry Carter, Duquesne	2002-05	43	207	187	394
Ryan Garrison, McNeese St.	2000-03	52	236	155	391
Robert Mason, VMI	2002-05	44	186	185	371
Jamar Leath, Coastal Caro.	2003-06	43	154	210	364
Matt McFadden, Weber St.	2000-03	41	152	198	350
Manny Rojas, Liberty	2003-06	45	140	208	348
Todd Baldwin, VMI	2002-05	45	140	206	346
Sam Smalls, Appalachian St.	2000-03	46	185	158	343
Dante Balestracci, Harvard	2000-03	38	200	143	343
Justin Huggard, VMI	2002-05	43	149	188	337
Mario Williams, Gardner-Webb	2001-04	35	181	145	326
Anton McKenzie, Massachusetts	2000-03	42	234	86	320
John Mohring, Ga. Southern	2003-06	44	135	181	316
Mark Kimener, Massachusetts	2000-03	45	214	99	313
Matt Logue, Sacramento St.	2002-05	45	181	125	306
Keppy Baucom, Gardner-Webb	2002-05	39	111	195	306
Stephen Cooper, Maine	2000-02	33	199	101	300

**Record.*

SEASON TOTAL TACKLES

Player, Team	Year	G	Solo	Ast.	Total
Kevin Talley, Norfolk St.	2002	12	*113	79	192
Boomer Grigsby, Illinois St.	†2002	11	108	71	179
Boomer Grigsby, Illinois St.	2003	12	109	70	179
Dietrich Lapsley, Indiana St.	2002	12	103	68	171
Edgerton Hartwell, Western Ill.	†2000	11	107	62	169
Erik Dandy, Western Ky.	2003	13	101	66	167
Tim Johnson, Youngstown St.	2000	11	83	80	163
P.J. Jones, Missouri St.	†2001	11	66	95	161
Dennard Melton, James Madison	2003	12	101	60	161
Charles Thompson, Western Ky.	2002	15	93	66	159
Kyle Shotwell, Cal Poly	2005	13	84	74	158
Derrick Lloyd, James Madison	2001	11	94	63	157
Cornell Middlebrook, Western Ill.	2002	13	101	53	154
Chad Nkang, Elon	†2005	11	73	79	152
Melvin Wisham, Western Ky.	2000	11	92	58	150

**Record. †National champion.*

SINGLE-GAME TOTAL TACKLES
(Since 2000)

Tackles	Player, Team (Opponent)	Date
30	Josh Cain, Chattanooga (Citadel)	Nov. 3, 2001
26	Boomer Grigsby, Illinois St. (Youngstown St.)	Nov. 9, 2002
26	Adam Goloboski, Richmond (Delaware)	Nov. 13, 2004
25	Tim Johnson, Youngstown St. (Hofstra)	Nov. 4, 2000
25	Nick Ricks, Eastern Ill. (Eastern Ky.)	Oct. 12, 2002
25	Kevin Talley, Norfolk St. (N.C. A&T)	Oct. 4, 2003
25	Chad Nkang, Elon (Chattanooga)	Oct. 15, 2005
25	Mario Brown, Gardner-Webb (Southeastern La.)	Sept. 30, 2006
25	Cory Weaver, Elon (Appalachian St.)	Sept. 30, 2006
24	Neil Morrissey, Cornell (Colgate)	Oct. 4, 2003
24	Mike Pavelko, Gardner-Webb (VMI)	Oct. 22, 2005
23	Marty Magerko, William & Mary (Rhode Island)	Oct. 13, 2001
23	Matt McFadden, Weber St. (Idaho St.)	Oct. 27, 2001
23	Andrew Clarke, Georgetown (Colgate)	Nov. 16, 2002
23	Jordan Beck, Cal Poly (Montana)	Oct. 4, 2003
22	Adam Vogt, UNI (Youngstown St.)	Oct. 14, 2000
22	Liam Ezekiel, Northeastern (Delaware)	Oct. 5, 2002
22	Dietrich Lapsley, Indiana St. (Missouri St.)	Oct. 12, 2002
22	Mario Williams, Gardner-Webb (Savannah St.)	Nov. 16, 2002
22	Jordan Beck, Cal Poly (Eastern Wash.)	Nov. 6, 2004
22	Cameron Siskowic, Illinois St. (Eastern Ill.)	Sept. 16, 2006
22	Tad Crawford, Columbia (Penn)	Oct. 14, 2006
21	Boomer Grigsby, Illinois St. (UNI)	Oct. 4, 2003
21	Kevin Talley, Norfolk St. (Hampton)	Oct. 18, 2003
21	Erik Dandy, Western Ky. (Illinois St.)	Oct. 18, 2003
21	Karl Maslowski, Western Ky. (Illinois St.)	Oct. 18, 2003
21	Kane Ioane, Montana St. (Northern Ariz.)	Oct. 25, 2003
21	Dennard Melton, James Madison (Northeastern)	Nov. 22, 2003
21	Dan Adams, Holy Cross (Colgate)	Oct. 22, 2005
21	Pago Togafau, Idaho St. (Northern Ariz.)	Sept. 23, 2006
21	Cyrus Mulitalo, Sacramento St. (Northern Colo.)	Oct. 28, 2006

ANNUAL CHAMPIONS

Year	Player, Team	Class	G	Solo	Ast.	Total	Avg.
2000	Edgerton Hartwell, Western Ill.	Sr.	11	107	62	169	15.4
2001	P.J. Jones, Missouri St.	Sr.	11	66	95	161	14.6
2002	Boomer Grigsby, Illinois St.	So.	11	108	71	179	*16.3
2003	Kevin Talley, Norfolk St.	Jr.	12	75	*120	*195	*16.3
2004	Kevin Talley, Norfolk St.	Sr.	9	58	77	135	15.0
2005	Chad Nkang, Elon	Jr.	11	73	79	152	13.8
2006	Mike Gallihugh, Colgate	Jr.	11	84	56	140	12.7

**Record.*

Solo Tackles

CAREER SOLO TACKLES PER GAME
(Min. 200 Solo Tackles; Player must have concluded his career)

Player, Team	Years	G	Solo	Avg.
Josh Cain, Chattanooga	2000-02	34	273	8.0
Boomer Grigsby, Illinois St.	2001-04	44	*325	7.4
Lee Russell, Western Ill.	2000-03	48	317	6.6
Nick Ricks, Eastern Ill.	2000-03	47	298	6.3
Matt Nelson, Wofford	2000-03	47	296	6.3
Jordan Beck, Cal Poly	2001-04	43	270	6.3
Anton McKenzie, Massachusetts	2000-03	42	234	5.6
Erik Dandy, Western Ky.	2000-03	45	241	5.4
Dante Balestracci, Harvard	2000-03	38	200	5.3
Liam Ezekiel, Northeastern	2001-04	44	218	5.0
Henry Carter, Duquesne	2002-05	43	207	4.8
Mark Kimener, Massachusetts	2000-03	45	214	4.8
Ryan Garrison, McNeese St.	2000-03	52	236	4.5

**Record.*

SEASON SOLO TACKLES PER GAME

Player, Team	Year	G	Solo	Avg.
Boomer Grigsby, Illinois St.	†2002	11	108	9.82
Edgerton Hartwell, Western Ill.	2000	11	107	9.73
Josh Cain, Chattanooga	2002	12	*113	9.42
Brian Hulea, Villanova	†2003	11	101	9.18
Boomer Grigsby, Illinois St.	2003	12	109	9.08
Derick Pack, James Madison	2000	11	97	8.82
Jordan Beck, Cal Poly	†2004	11	97	8.82
Dietrich Lapsley, Indiana St.	2002	12	103	8.58
Derrick Lloyd, James Madison	†2001	11	94	8.55
Nick Ricks, Eastern Ill.	2001	10	85	8.50
Dennard Melton, James Madison	2003	12	101	8.42
Melvin Wisham, Western Ky.	2000	11	92	8.36
Dan Adams, Holy Cross	†2005	11	91	8.27
Nick Ricks, Eastern Ill.	2002	12	98	8.17

**Record. †National champion.*

CAREER SOLO TACKLES

Player, Team	Years	G	Solo
Boomer Grigsby, Illinois St.	2001-04	44	325
Lee Russell, Western Ill.	2000-03	48	317
Nick Ricks, Eastern Ill.	2000-03	47	298
Matt Nelson, Wofford	2000-03	47	296
Josh Cain, Chattanooga	2000-02	34	273
Jordan Beck, Cal Poly	2001-04	43	270
Erik Dandy, Western Ky.	2000-03	45	241
Ryan Garrison, McNeese St.	2000-03	52	236
Anton McKenzie, Massachusetts	2000-03	42	234
Liam Ezekiel, Northeastern	2001-04	44	218
Mark Kimener, Massachusetts	2000-03	45	214
Charles Thompson, Western Ky.	2001-04	49	208
Henry Carter, Duquesne	2002-05	43	207
Dante Balestracci, Harvard	2000-03	38	200
Stephen Cooper, Maine	2000-02	33	199
Zak DeOssie, Brown	2003-06	37	187
Robert Mason, VMI	2002-05	44	186
Sam Smalls, Appalachian St.	2000-03	46	185
Mario Williams, Gardner-Webb	2001-04	35	181
Matt Logue, Sacramento St.	2002-05	45	181
John Mohring, Ga. Southern	2003-06	44	181
Ben Koller, Holy Cross	2000-03	38	174
Casey Tierney, UNI	2000-03	38	171
Maurice Simpkins, Coastal Caro.	2003-05	33	171
Matt Mitchell, UNI	2000-03	46	169

SEASON SOLO TACKLES

Player, Team	Year	G	Solo
Josh Cain, Chattanooga	2002	12	113
Boomer Grigsby, Illinois St.	2003	12	109
Boomer Grigsby, Illinois St.	†2002	11	108
Edgerton Hartwell, Western Ill.	2000	11	107
Dietrich Lapsley, Indiana St.	2002	12	103
Lee Russell, Western Ill.	2003	13	102
Phil Archer, Western Ill.	2003	13	102
Cornell Middlebrook, Western Ill.	2002	13	101
Dennard Melton, James Madison	2003	12	101
Brian Hulea, Villanova	†2003	11	101
Erik Dandy, Western Ky.	2003	13	101
Nick Ricks, Eastern Ill.	2002	12	98
Derick Pack, James Madison	2000	11	97
Jeremy Cain, Massachusetts	2002	12	97
Lee Russell, Western Ill.	2002	13	97
Derrick Lloyd, James Madison	†2001	11	94

†National champion.

SINGLE-GAME SOLO TACKLES
(Since 2000)

Solo	Player, Team (Opponent)	Date
21	Dan Adams, Holy Cross (Colgate)	Oct. 22, 2005
18	Nick Ricks, Eastern Ill. (Eastern Ky.)	Oct. 12, 2002
18	Jordan Beck, Cal Poly (Eastern Wash.)	Nov. 6, 2004
17	Josh Cain, Chattanooga (Citadel)	Nov. 3, 2001
16	Marty Magerko, William & Mary (Rhode Island)	Oct. 13, 2001
15	Matt McFadden, Weber St. (Idaho St.)	Oct. 27, 2001
15	Andrew Clarke, Georgetown (Colgate)	Nov. 16, 2002
15	Karl Maslowski, Western Ky. (Illinois St.)	Oct. 18, 2003
15	Markeseo Jackson, Tenn.-Martin (Murray St.)	Nov. 13, 2004
15	Vincent Dancy, Jackson St. (Alabama St.)	Oct. 8, 2005
15	Farod Muhammad, Central Conn. St. (Southern Conn. St.)	Sept. 15, 2006
15	J.R. Webber, Murray St. (Illinois St.)	Sept. 23, 2006
15	Mario Brown, Gardner-Webb (Southeastern La.)	Sept. 30, 2006

ANNUAL CHAMPIONS

Year	Player, Team	Class	G	Solo	Avg.
2001	Derrick Lloyd, James Madison	Sr.	11	94	8.55
2002	Boomer Grigsby, Illinois St.	So.	11	108	*9.82
2003	Brian Hulea, Villanova	Jr.	11	101	9.18
2004	Jordan Beck, Cal Poly	Sr.	11	97	8.82
2005	Dan Adams, Holy Cross	Jr.	11	91	8.27
2006	Mike Gallihugh, Colgate	Jr.	11	84	7.64

**Record.*

Tackles for Loss

CAREER TACKLES FOR LOSS PER GAME

(Min. 20 Tackles For Loss; Player must have concluded his career)

Player, Team	Years	G	Solo	Ast	Total	Avg.
Steve Baggs, Bethune-Cookman	2002-03	25	53	18	62.0	2.5
Anthony Jones, Wofford	2000-02	32	60	0	60.0	1.9
Sherrod Coates, Western Ky.	2000-02	40	67	0	*67.0	1.7
Mike O'Brien, Western Ill.	2000-03	35	54	0	54.0	1.5
Chris Gocong, Cal Poly	2001, 03-05	41	60	3	61.5	1.5
Valdamar Brower, Massachusetts	2000-03	46	63	0	63.0	1.4
Lee Basinger, Wofford	2001-04	46	61	0	61.0	1.3
Ryan Tennis, Davidson	2000-02	29	34	7	37.5	1.3
Lee Russell, Western Ill.	2000-03	48	58	0	58.0	1.2
Doran Davis, Massachusetts	2000-03	34	40	0	40.0	1.2
Derik Screen, VMI	2000-03	42	47	1	47.5	1.1
Dante Balestracci, Harvard	2000-03	38	42	0	42.0	1.1
Maurice Simpkins, Coastal Caro.	2003-05	33	36	0	36.0	1.1
Kelvin McIver, Coastal Caro.	2004-05	22	24	0	24.0	1.1
Josh Cain, Chattanooga	2000-02	34	37	0	37.0	1.1
Aaron DeBerry, Liberty	2000-03	42	45	0	45.0	1.1
Erik Dandy, Western Ky.	2000-03	45	45	0	45.0	1.0
K.T. Stovall, Appalachian St.	2000-03	50	40	18	49.0	1.0
Brendan Dete, Davidson	2001-04	39	29	17	37.5	1.0
Matt Logue, Sacramento St.	2002-05	45	42	9	46.5	1.0
Zak DeOssie, Brown	2003-06	36	34	3	35.5	1.0
Antoine Bullock, Duquesne	2002-05	43	41	1	41.5	1.0
Tim Bush, Montana	2000-03	48	40	9	44.5	0.9
Darryl Childers, Davidson	2000-03	40	36	2	37.0	0.9
Liam Ezekiel, Northeastern	2001-04	44	40	1	40.5	0.9
Harry Carter, Duquesne	2002-05	43	40	1	40.5	0.9
Steve Lhotak, Penn	2000-03	36	28	1	28.5	0.8
Matt Mitchell, UNI	2000-03	46	36	0	36.0	0.8
Philip Polony, Duquesne	2000-03	44	37	0	37.0	0.8
Seth Reichert, Liberty	2001-04	45	37	1	37.5	0.8
Tom Parks, Delaware	2002-05	45	37	1	37.5	0.8
Vicheal Foxx, VMI	2001-03	41	32	1	32.5	0.8
Harold Wells, Gardner-Webb	2001-04	41	32	1	32.5	0.8

**Record.*

SEASON TACKLES FOR LOSS PER GAME

Player, Team	Year	G	Solo	Ast.	Total	Avg.
Steve Baggs, Bethune-Cookman	†2003	12	28	16	*36.0	3.00
Robert Mathis, Alabama A&M	†2002	11	30	1	30.5	2.77
Odain Mitchell, Sacred Heart	2002	10	20	11	25.5	2.55
Joseph Crear, Mississippi Val.	2002	11	27	2	28.0	2.55
Leonard Mack, Texas Southern	2002	11	25	5	27.5	2.50
Andy Petek, Montana	†2000	11	27	0	27.0	2.45
Jamal Naji, Norfolk St.	2002	11	23	8	27.0	2.45
Brent Hawkins, Illinois St.	†2005	11	22	9	26.5	2.41
D.J. Bleisath, Tennessee Tech.	†2001	10	24	0	24.0	2.40
Isaac Hilton, Hampton	2002	12	27	3	28.5	2.38
Chris Gocong, Cal Poly	2005	13	27	7	30.5	2.35
Anthony Jones, Wofford	2002	12	28	0	28.0	2.33
Steve Watson, Missouri St.	2002	9	21	0	21.0	2.33

**Record. †National champion.*

CAREER TACKLES FOR LOSS

Player, Team	Years	G	Solo	Ast.	Total
Sherrod Coates, Western Ky.	2000-02	40	67	0	67.0
Valdamar Brower, Massachusetts	2000-03	46	63	0	63.0
Steve Baggs, Bethune-Cookman	2002-03	25	53	18	62.0
Chris Gocong, Cal Poly	2001, 03-05	41	60	3	61.5
Lee Basinger, Wofford	2001-04	46	61	0	61.0
Anthony Jones, Wofford	2000-02	32	60	0	60.0
Lee Russell, Western Ill.	2000-03	48	58	0	58.0
Mike O'Brien, Western Ill.	2000-03	35	54	0	54.0
K.T. Stovall, Appalachian St.	2000-03	50	40	18	49.0
Derik Screen, VMI	2000-03	42	47	1	47.5
Matt Logue, Sacramento St.	2002-05	45	42	9	46.5
Aaron DeBerry, Liberty	2000-03	42	45	0	45.0
Erik Dandy, Western Ky.	2000-03	45	45	0	45.0
Tim Bush, Montana	2000-03	48	40	9	44.5
Dante Balestracci, Harvard	2000-03	38	42	0	42.0
Antoine Bullock, Duquesne	2002-05	43	41	1	41.5
Liam Ezekiel, Northeastern	2001-04	44	40	1	40.5
Harry Carter, Duquesne	2002-05	43	40	1	40.5
Dorna Davis, Massachusetts	2000-03	34	40	0	40.0
Ryan Tennis, Davidson	2000-02	29	34	7	37.5
Brendan Dete, Davidson	2001-04	39	29	17	37.5
Tom Parks, Delaware	2002-05	45	37	1	37.5
Josh Cain, Chattanooga	2000-02	34	37	0	37.0
Darryl Childers, Davidson	2000-03	40	36	2	37.0
Philip Polony, Duquesne	2000-03	44	37	0	37.0
Matt Mitchell, UNI	2000-03	46	36	0	36.0
Maurice Simpkins, Coastal Caro.	2003-05	33	36	0	36.0

SEASON TACKLES FOR LOSS

Player, Team	Years	G	Solo	Ast.	Total
Steve Baggs, Bethune-Cookman	†2003	12	28	16	36.0
Sherrod Coates, Western Ky.	2002	15	31	0	31.0
Robert Mathis, Alabama A&M	†2002	11	30	1	30.5
Chris Gocong, Cal Poly	2005	13	27	7	30.5
Isaac Hilton, Hampton	2002	12	27	3	28.5
Joseph Crear, Mississippi Val.	2002	11	27	2	28.0
Anthony Jones, Wofford	2002	12	28	0	28.0
Leonard Mack, Texas Southern	2002	11	25	5	27.5
Andy Petek, Montana	†2000	11	27	0	27.0
Jamal Naji, Norfolk St.	2002	11	23	8	27.0
Brent Hawkins, Illinois St.	†2005	11	22	9	26.5
Marques Murrell, Appalachian St.	2005	15	21	11	26.5
Steve Baggs, Bethune-Cookman	2002	13	25	2	26.0
Shawn Johnson, Delaware	2003	16	22	8	26.0

†National champion.

SINGLE-GAME TACKLES FOR LOSS

(Since 2000)

TFL	Player, Team (Opponent)	Date
8.0	Sherrod Coates, Westerm Ky. (Indiana St.)	Oct. 26, 2002
7.0	Greg Pitts, Texas St. (Texas Southern)	Sept. 21, 2002
6.0	Eric Allen, Tennessee Tech (Eastern Ill.)	Nov. 21, 2000
6.0	Valdamar Brower, Masschusetts (Rhode Island)	Nov. 17, 2001
6.0	Michael Young, Nicholls St. [Bethel (Tenn.)]	Aug. 28, 2003
6.0	Jerame Southern, James Madison (Hofstra)	Sept. 20, 2003
6.0	Erik Dandy, Western Ky. (Southern Ill.)	Nov. 1, 2003
6.0	Chad Kincaid, Western Ky. (Youngstown St.)	Nov. 15, 2003
6.0	Lee Basinger, Wofford (N.C. A&T)	Nov. 29, 2003
5.5	Isaac Hilton, Hampton (Howard)	Sept. 13, 2003
5.5	Brady Fosmark, Weber St. (Eastern Wash.)	Sept. 27, 2003
5.5	John Hermann, UNI (Northern Ariz.)	Nov. 19, 2005
5.0	Ryan Hutto, Davidson (Jacksonville)	Sept. 9, 2000
5.0	Phil Tolliver, Stony Brook [St. John's (N.Y.)]	Sept. 21, 2001
5.0	Kyle Mitchell, Indiana St. (Western Mich.)	Aug. 29, 2002
5.0	Kyle Mitchell, Indiana St. (Illinois St.)	Nov. 16, 2002
5.0	Odi Anyanwu, Morehead St. (Dayton)	Sept. 6, 2003
5.0	Johnnie Sloan, Fla. Atlantic (Youngstown St.)	Sept. 20, 2003
5.0	Brendan Summers, James Madison (Hofstra)	Sept. 20, 2003
5.0	Carlos Stephens, Northwestern St. (Texas St.)	Oct. 18, 2003
5.0	Matt Palmer, East Tenn. St. (Furman)	Oct. 25, 2003
5.0	Kevin Mack, Southern U. (Alcorn St.)	Oct. 25, 2003
5.0	Robert Watson, Texas Southern (Mississippi Val.)	Oct. 25, 2003
5.0	Darrell Adams, Villanova (Massachusetts)	Oct. 25, 2003
5.0	Steve Baggs, Bethune-Cookman (N.C. A&T)	Nov. 1, 2003
5.0	Paul White, Hampton (Florida A&M)	Nov. 1, 2003
5.0	Aaron DeBerry, Liberty (Charleston So.)	Nov. 1, 2003
5.0	Steven Nance, Towson [Albany (N.Y.)]	Nov. 15, 2003
5.0	Colby Khuns, Fordham (Towson)	Nov. 22, 2003
5.0	Jacob Houston, Sacramento St. (Weber St.)	Oct. 16, 2004
5.0	Brent Hawkins, Illinois St. (UNI)	Oct. 22, 2005

ANNUAL CHAMPIONS

Year	Player, Team	G	Solo	Ast.	Total	Avg.
2000	Andy Petek, Montana	11	27	0	27.0	2.45
2001	D.J. Bleisath, Tennessee Tech	10	24	0	24.0	2.40
2002	Robert Mathis, Alabama A&M	11	30	1	30.5	2.77
2003	Steve Baggs, Bethune-Cookman	12	28	16	*36.0	*3.00
2004	Harold Wells, Gardner-Webb	11	17	11	22.5	2.05
2005	Brent Hawkins, Illinois St.	11	22	9	26.5	2.41
2006	Chris Hunsaker, Northern Ariz.	11	17	8	21.0	1.91

**Record.*

Pass Sacks

CAREER PASS SACKS PER GAME

(Min. 15 Pass Sacks; Player must have concluded his career)

Player, Team	Years	G	Solo	Ast.	Total	Avg.
Brent Hawkins, Illinois St.	2004-05	19	19	2	20.0	1.05
Chris Gocong, Cal Poly	2001, 03-05	41	36	12	*42.0	1.02
Anthony Jones, Wofford	2000-02	32	29	1	29.5	0.92
Anthony Gargiulo, Dartmouth	2002-05	31	25	0	25.0	0.81
Sherrod Coates, Western Ky.	2000-02	40	29	0	29.0	0.73

Player, Team	Years	G	Solo	Ast.	Total	Avg.
Matt Mitchell, UNI	2000-03	46	33	0	33.0	0.72
Tim Bush, Montana	2000-03	48	28	7	31.5	0.66
Antoine Bullock, Duquesne	2002-05	43	27	1	27.5	0.64
Ryan Tennis, Davidson	2000-02	29	14	8	18.0	0.62
K.T. Stovall, Appalachian St.	2000-03	50	28	5	30.5	0.61
Stephen Cooper, Maine	2000-02	33	19	2	20.0	0.61
Keith O'Neil, Northern Ariz.	2000-02	33	20	0	20.0	0.60
Darryl Childers, Davidson	2000-03	40	21	4	23.0	0.58
Dennis Dottin-Carter, Maine	2000-03	43	21	6	24.0	0.56
Steve Lhotak, Penn	2000-03	36	19	0	19.0	0.53
Aaron DeBerry, Liberty	2000-03	42	22	0	22.0	0.52
Valdamar Brower, Massachusetts	2000-03	46	22	4	24.0	0.52
Ryan Conger, Dartmouth	2001-04	39	20	0	20.0	0.51
Josh Antinopoulos, Duquesne	2002-05	43	22	0	22.0	0.51
Philip Polony, Duquesne	2000-03	44	22	1	22.5	0.51
Jon Drummond, Western Ky.	2000-02	40	20	0	20.0	0.50
Dante Balestracci, Harvard	2000-03	38	16	0	16.0	0.42

**Record.*

SEASON PASS SACKS PER GAME

Player, Team	Year	G	Solo	Ast.	Total	Avg.
Andrew Hollingsworth, Towson	†2000	9	16	2	17.0	1.89
Robert Mathis, Alabama A&M	†2002	11	19	2	20.0	1.82
Chris Gocong, Cal Poly	†2005	13	19	9	*23.5	1.81
Andy Petek, Montana	2000	11	19	0	19.0	1.73
Odain Mitchell, Sacred Heart	2002	10	13	6	16.0	1.60
Chris Gocong, Cal Poly	†2004	11	16	3	17.5	1.59
Brent Hawkins, Illinois St.	2005	11	16	2	17.0	1.55
Jared Allen, Idaho St.	†2003	12	16	3	17.5	1.46
Brady Fosmark, Weber St.	2003	9	11	3	12.5	1.39
Joseph Crear, Mississippi Val.	2002	11	13	3	14.5	1.32
Mike Foster, Drake	2000	10	13	0	13.0	1.30
Kevin Fales, Iona	2003	11	13	2	14.0	1.27
Renauld Williams, Hofstra	2002	12	15	0	15.0	1.25
Steve Baggs, Bethune-Cookman	2003	12	13	4	15.0	1.25

**Record. †National champion.*

CAREER PASS SACKS

Player, Team	Years	G	Solo	Ast.	Total
Chris Gocong, Cal Poly	2001, 03-05	41	36	12	42.0
Matt Mitchell, UNI	2000-03	46	33	0	33.0
Tim Bush, Montana	2000-03	48	28	7	31.5
K.T. Stovall, Appalachian St.	2000-03	50	28	5	30.5
Anthony Jones, Wofford	2000-02	32	29	1	29.5
Sherrod Coates, Western Ky.	2000-02	40	29	0	29.0
Antoine Bullock, Duquesne	2002-05	43	27	1	27.5
Anthony Gargiulo, Dartmouth	2002-05	31	25	0	25.0
Valdamar Brower, Massachusetts	2000-03	46	22	4	24.0
Dennis Dottin-Carter, Maine	2000-03	43	21	6	24.0
Darryl Childers, Davidson	2000-03	40	21	4	23.0
Philip Polony, Duquesne	2000-03	44	22	1	22.5
Aaron DeBerry, Liberty	2000-03	42	22	0	22.0
John Perrigo, Northern Ariz.	2001-03	36	21	0	21.0
Keith O'Neil, Northern Ariz.	2000-02	33	20	0	20.0
Jon Drummond, Western Ky.	2000-02	40	20	0	20.0
Stephen Cooper, Maine	2000-02	33	19	2	20.0
Ryan Conger, Dartmouth	2001-04	39	20	0	20.0
Brent Hawkins, Illinois St.	2004-05	19	19	2	20.0

SEASON PASS SACKS

Player, Team	Year	G	Solo	Ast.	Total
Chris Gocong, Cal Poly	†2005	13	19	9	23.5
Robert Mathis, Alabama A&M	†2002	11	19	2	20.0
Andy Petek, Montana	2000	11	19	0	19.0
Jared Allen, Idaho St.	†2003	12	16	3	17.5
Chris Gocong, Cal Poly	†2004	11	16	3	17.5
Andrew Hollingsworth, Towson	†2000	9	16	2	17.0
Brent Hawkins, Illinois St.	2005	11	16	2	17.0
Odain Mitchell, Sacred Heart	2002	10	13	6	16.0
Renauld Williams, Hofstra	2002	12	15	0	15.0
Steve Baggs, Bethune-Cookman	2003	12	13	4	15.0
Joseph Crear, Mississippi Val.	2002	11	13	3	14.5
Anthony Jones, Wofford	2002	12	13	3	14.5
Kevin Fales, Iona	2003	11	13	2	14.0
Ray Robinson, Illinois St.	2003	12	14	0	14.0

†National champion.

SINGLE-GAME PASS SACKS
(Since 2000)

PS	Player, Team (Opponent)	Date
6.0	Damien Huren, Southeastern La. (Northern Colo.)	Oct. 9, 2004
5.0	Maurice Troutman, Ark.-Pine Bluff (Mississippi Val.)	Sept. 6, 2003
5.0	Brent Hawkins, Illinois St. (UNI)	Oct. 22, 2005
4.5	Michael Young, Nicholls St. [Bethel (Tenn.)]	Aug. 28, 2003
4.5	Tyree Broden, McNeese St. (Sam Houston St.)	Oct. 25, 2003
4.5	Steve Lhotak, Penn (Harvard)	Nov. 15, 2003
4.0	Bo Henderson, Davidson (San Diego)	Oct. 14, 2000
4.0	Valdamar Brower, Massachusetts (Maine)	Oct. 14, 2000
4.0	Galen Scott, Illinois St. (Indiana St.)	Oct. 14, 2000
4.0	C.J. Carroll, Texas St. (Sam Houston St.)	Nov. 22, 2000
4.0	Adam Chambers, Eastern Wash. (Central Wash.)	Nov. 17, 2001
4.0	Valdamar Brower, Massachusetts (American Int'l)	Sept. 14, 2002
4.0	Erik Yngstrom, Monmouth (Iona)	Oct. 4, 2003
4.0	Andre Plummer, Tenn.-Martin (Tennessee Tech)	Oct. 4, 2003
4.0	Ryan Roth, Southeast Mo. St. (Eastern Ky.)	Oct. 18, 2003
4.0	Ray Robinson, Illinois St. (Youngstown St.)	Oct. 25, 2003
4.0	Aaron DeBerry, Liberty (Charleston So.)	Nov. 1, 2003
4.0	Marcus White, Murray St. (Eastern Ky.)	Nov. 1, 2003
4.0	Kory Lothe, Eastern Ill. (Tennessee Tech)	Nov. 8, 2003
4.0	Josh Antinopoulos, Duquesne (Marist)	Oct. 30, 2004
4.0	Anthony Gargialo, Dartmouth (Cornell)	Nov. 6, 2004
4.0	John Hermann, UNI (Northern Ariz.)	Nov. 19, 2005

ANNUAL CHAMPIONS

Year	Player, Team	G	Solo	Ast.	Total	Avg.
2000	Andrew Hollingsworth, Towson	9	16	2	17.0	*1.89
2001	Marc Laborsky, Harvard	9	9	2	10.0	1.11
2002	Robert Mathis, Alabama A&M	11	19	2	20.0	1.82
2003	Jared Allen, Idaho St.	12	16	3	17.5	1.46
2004	Chris Gocong, Cal Poly	11	16	3	17.5	1.59
2005	Chris Gocong, Cal Poly	13	19	9	*23.5	1.81
2006	Edgar Jones, Southeast Mo. St.	10	11	2	12.0	1.20

**Record.*

FCS

Passes Defended

CAREER PASSES DEFENDED PER GAME
(Min. 20 Passes Defended; Player must have concluded his career)

Player, Team	Years	G	PBU	Int.	Total	Avg.
Benny Sapp, UNI	2002-03	24	30	7	37	1.54
Bobby Sippio, Western Ky.	2000-01	22	18	15	33	1.50
Vernell Shaw, Holy Cross	2000-01	17	20	1	21	1.24
Mario Williams, Gardner-Webb	2001-04	35	35	8	43	1.23
Michael Blake, Holy Cross	2000-01	21	20	5	25	1.19
Billy Parker, William & Mary	2000-03	44	40	11	*51	1.16
Michael Ford, Duquesne	2003-05	31	21	13	34	1.10
Quinton Teal, Coastal Caro.	2003-06	44	31	17	48	1.09
Jay Lyles, Appalachian St.	2000-03	37	35	3	38	1.03
Jesse Hendrix, Eastern Wash.	2002-05	47	41	5	46	0.98
Joseph Jefferson, Western Ky.	2000-01	25	16	7	23	0.92
Isaiah Trufant, Eastern Wash.	2002-05	39	24	11	35	0.90
Matt Nelson, Wofford	2000-03	47	32	9	41	0.87
Devon Goree, Maine	2000-03	31	20	7	27	0.87
Kenny Heatley, Bethune-Cookman	2000-03	44	37	4	41	0.84
Justin Sandy, Northern Iowa	2001-03	34	20	7	27	0.79
Dante Balestracci, Harvard	2000-03	38	23	6	29	0.76
David Cusano, Maine	2000-02	32	17	7	24	0.75

**Record.*

SEASON PASSES DEFENDED PER GAME

Player, Team	Year	G	PBU	Int.	Total	Avg.
Bobby Sippio, Western Ky.	†2000	10	18	9	*27	2.70
Santino Hall, Texas Southern	†2001	10	20	6	26	2.60
Leigh Bodden, Duquesne	2000	11	17	9	26	2.36
Brandon Phillips, Morehead St.	2001	11	21	5	26	2.36
Brandon Phillips, Morehead St.	†2002	10	18	5	23	2.30
Harry Sutton, Iona	2000	11	24	1	25	2.27
Jon Ambrose, St. Peter's	2001	11	15	10	25	2.27
Charles Byrd, Morehead St.	†2003	11	23	2	25	2.27
Yeremiah Bell, Eastern Ky.	2001	10	16	6	22	2.20
Brian Sawyer, Hampton	2002	12	23	3	26	2.17
Steve Dogmanits, Fairfield	2000	10	10	11	21	2.10
Don Milligan, Fairfield	2000	10	12	9	21	2.10

**Record. †National champion.*

CAREER PASSES DEFENDED

Player, Team	Years	G	PBU	Int.	Total
Billy Parker, William & Mary	2000-03	44	40	11	51
Quinton Teal, Coastal Caro.	2003-06	44	31	17	48
Jesse Hendrix, Eastern Wash.	2002-05	47	41	5	46
Mario Williams, Gardner-Webb	2001-04	37	35	8	43
Kenny Heatley, Bethune-Cookman	2000-03	44	37	4	41

Player, Team	Years	G	PBU	Int.	Total
Matt Nelson, Wofford	2000-03	47	32	9	41
Jay Lyles, Appalachian St.	2000-03	37	35	3	38
Benny Sapp, UNI	2002-03	24	30	7	37
Sidney Haugabrook, Delaware	2001-04	50	25	12	37
Isaiah Trufant, Eastern Wash.	2002-05	39	24	11	35
Michael Ford, Duquesne	2003-05	31	21	13	34
Bobby Sippio, Western Ky.	2000-01	22	18	15	33
Larry Johnson, Lafayette	2002-05	46	26	4	30
Dante Balestracci, Harvard	2000-03	38	23	6	29
Devon Goree, Maine	2000-03	31	20	7	27
Justin Sandy, UNI	2001-03	34	20	7	27
Willie Hughley, Fla. Atlantic	2002-03	24	18	8	26
Michael Blake, Holy Cross	2000-01	21	20	5	25
David Cusano, Maine	2000-02	32	17	7	24
Gary Bordelon, Holy Cross	2000-03	30	23	1	24
Aaron Whitaker, Ga. Southern	2001-03	35	19	5	24
Derrick Black, Appalachian St.	2002-03	23	19	5	24
Dewitt Myers, Coastal Caro.	2003-06	37	14	10	24
James Young, Ga. Southern	2001-03	35	19	4	23
Shannon James, Massachusetts	2002-03	25	15	8	23
Tavares Shorter, Charleston So.	2003-05	31	16	7	23

SEASON PASSES DEFENDED

Player, Team	Year	G	PBU	Int.	Total
Bobby Sippio, Western Ky.	†2000	10	18	9	27
Leigh Bodden, Duquesne	2000	11	17	9	26
Brandon Phillips, Morehead St.	2001	11	21	5	26
Santino Hall, Texas Southern	†2001	10	20	6	26
Brian Sawyer, Hampton	2002	12	23	3	26
Harry Sutton, Iona	2000	11	24	1	25
Jon Ambrose, St. Peter's	2001	11	15	10	25
Charles Byrd, Morehead St.	†2003	11	23	2	25
Gary Johnson, Villanova	2001	11	21	2	23
Brandon Phillips, Morehead St.	†2002	10	18	5	23
Yeremiah Bell, Eastern Ky.	2001	10	16	6	22
LeVar Greene, Youngstown St.	2001	11	15	7	22
Antwan Hill, Alabama St.	2002	12	12	10	22
Scott Cunningham, Tennessee St.	2002	12	19	3	22
Kenny Heatley, Bethune-Cookman	2003	12	21	1	22
Allen Davis, Gardner-Webb	†2004	11	17	5	22
Calvin Bannister, Hampton	†2004	11	19	3	22

†National champion.

SINGLE-GAME PASSES DEFENDED
(Since 2000)

PD	Player, Team (Opponent)	Date
6	Sam Young, Illinois St. (Youngstown St.)	Oct. 7, 2000
6	Marcus Gray, Norfolk St. (Florida A&M)	Oct. 26, 2002
6	James Young, Ga. Southern (Bethune-Cookman)	Nov. 30, 2002
6	Robson Noel, Jacksonville (Dayton)	Oct. 14, 2006
5	Sidney Haugabrook, Delaware (Northeastern)	Sept. 29, 2001
5	Marcus Thurmond, Weber St. (Idaho St.)	Oct. 27, 2001
5	Billy Parker, William & Mary (Villanova)	Nov. 24, 2001
5	A.J. Bryant, Ga. Southern (Chattanooga)	Sept. 27, 2003
5	Isaiah Trufant, Eastern Wash. (Idaho St.)	Sept. 25, 2004
5	Greg Ambrogi, Penn (Columbia)	Oct. 14, 2006
5	Ricky Wilson, Northern Ariz. (Portland St.)	Nov. 4, 2006

ANNUAL CHAMPIONS

Year	Player, Team	G	PBU	Int.	Total	Avg.
2000	Bobby Sippio, Western Ky.	10	18	9	*27	*2.70
2001	Santino Hall, Texas Southern	10	20	6	26	2.60
2002	Brandon Phillips, Morehead St.	10	18	5	23	2.30
2003	Charles Byrd, Morehead St.	11	23	2	25	2.27
2004	Calvin Bannister, Hampton	11	19	3	22	2.00
	Allen Davis, Gardner-Webb	11	17	5	22	2.00
2005	Jay McCareins, Princeton	10	11	9	20	2.00
2006	Tim Strickland, Princeton	10	14	3	17	1.70

**Record.*

Forced Fumbles

CAREER FORCED FUMBLES PER GAME
(Min. 20 Games Played; Player must have concluded his career)

Player, Team	Years	G	FF	Avg.
Robert Mathis, Alabama A&M	2001-02	22	*13	0.59
Sherrod Coates, Western Ky.	2000-02	40	*13	0.33
Antoine Bullock, Duquesne	2002-05	43	9	0.21
Lee Russell, Western Ill.	2000-03	48	10	0.21
Brendan Curry, Maine	2000-02	34	7	0.21
K.T. Stovall, Appalachian St.	2000-03	50	10	0.20
Wes Erbe, Lafayette	2001-04	30	6	0.20
Eric Speron, Georgetown	2000-01	21	4	0.19
Ryan Arnold, UNI	2001-04	38	7	0.18
Keith O'Neil, Northern Ariz.	2000-02	33	6	0.18
Ryan Tennis, Davidson	2000-02	29	5	0.17
Matt McFadden, Weber St.	2000-03	41	7	0.17
Anton McKenzie, Massachusetts	2000-03	42	7	0.17
Mondoe Davis, Delaware	2001-04	49	8	0.16
Raleigh Robinson, Davidson	2001-04	37	6	0.16
Matt Mitchell, UNI	2000-03	46	7	0.15
Lee Basinger, Wofford	2001-04	46	7	0.15
Marcus Green, Portland St.	2000-02	33	5	0.15
Darryl Childers, Davidson	2000-03	40	6	0.15
Marques Bobo, William & Mary	2000-03	41	6	0.15

**Record.*

SEASON FORCED FUMBLES PER GAME

Player, Team	Year	G	FF	Avg.
Robert Mathis, Alabama A&M	†2002	11	*10	0.91
Brent Hawkins, Illinois St.	†2005	11	7	0.64
Nick Ricks, Eastern Ill.	2002	12	7	0.58
Andy Petek, Montana	†2000	11	6	0.55
Jordan Beck, Cal Poly	†2004	11	6	0.55
Lee Basinger, Wofford	2002	12	6	0.50
Raleigh Robinson, Davidson	2002	10	5	0.50
Steve Baggs, Bethune-Cookman	†2003	12	6	0.50
Jared Allen, Idaho St.	†2003	12	6	0.50
Tim Heaney, Wagner	†2003	10	5	0.50
Jonathan Corto, Sacred Heart	2005	10	5	0.50
Jerome Bennett, Western Ill.	†2006	10	5	0.50

**Record. †National champion.*

CAREER FORCED FUMBLES

Player, Team	Years	G	FF
Sherrod Coates, Western Ky.	2000-02	40	13
Robert Mathis, Alabama A&M	2001-02	22	13
Lee Russell, Western Ill.	2000-03	48	10
K.T. Stovall, Appalachian St.	2000-03	50	10
Antoine Bullock, Duquesne	2002-05	43	9
Mondoe Davis, Delaware	2001-04	49	8
Brendan Curry, Maine	2000-02	34	7
Nick Ricks, Eastern Ill.	2002	12	7
Quentin Swain, Fla. Atlantic	2002-03	25	7
Lee Basinger, Wofford	2001-03	35	7
Matt McFadden, Weber St.	2000-03	41	7
Anton McKenzie, Massachusetts	2000-03	42	7
Matt Mitchell, UNI	2000-03	46	7
Ryan Arnold, UNI	2001-04	38	7
Lee Basinger, Wofford	2001-04	46	7
Brent Hawkins, Illinois St.	2004-05	19	7

SEASON FORCED FUMBLES

Player, Team	Year	G	FF
Robert Mathis, Alabama A&M	†2002	11	10
Nick Ricks, Eastern Ill.	2002	12	7
Brent Hawkins, Illinois St.	†2005	11	7
Marques Murrell, Appalachian St.	2005	15	7
Andy Petek, Montana	†2000	11	6
Lee Basinger, Wofford	2002	12	6
Jared Allen, Idaho St.	†2003	12	6
Steve Baggs, Bethune-Cookman	†2003	12	6
Ryan Arnold, UNI	2003	13	6
Jordan Beck, Cal Poly	†2004	11	6

†National champion.

SINGLE-GAME FORCED FUMBLES
(Since 2000)

FF	Player, Team (Opponent)	Date
3	Sterling Rogers, Texas St. (Portland St.)	Oct. 6, 2001
3	Lee Basinger, Wofford (Elon)	Nov. 23, 2002
3	Sam Harper, Coastal Caro. (Jacksonville)	Nov. 13, 2004
3	Brent Hawkins, Illinois St. (Murray St.)	Sept. 24, 2005

ANNUAL CHAMPIONS

Year	Player, Team	G	FF	Avg.
2000	Tommy Swindell, Jacksonville	11	‡9	0.82
	C.J. Carroll, Texas St.	11	‡9	0.82
	Andy Petek, Montana	11	‡9	0.82

‡In 2000, the total was forced fumbles plus fumbles recovered. Beginning in 2001, FF was forced fumbles only.

Year	Player, Team	G	FF	Avg.
2001	Jeran Crawford, St. Peter's	11	5	0.45
	Jamison Young, Villanova	11	5	0.45
2002	Robert Mathis, Alabama A&M	11	*10	*0.91
2003	Jared Allen, Idaho St.	12	6	0.50
	Steve Baggs, Bethune-Cookman	12	6	0.50
	Tim Heaney, Wagner	10	5	0.50
2004	Jordan Beck, Cal Poly	11	6	0.55
2005	Brent Hawkins, Illinois St.	11	7	0.64
2006	Jerome Bennett, Western Ill.	10	5	0.50

*Record.

BLOCKED KICKS RECORDS

Special Note About Blocked-Kick Records:
The blocked-kick records include players from the beginning of FCS play in 1978.

Even though the other defensive statistics and records began in 2000, blocked-kick records are compiled by most institutions and those records are more reliable than tackles, assists, tackles for loss, pass sacks, passes defended and forced fumbles.

Blocked Punts

CAREER BLOCKED PUNTS

Player, Team	Years	BP
Trey Woods, Sam Houston St.	1992-95	8
Ryan Crawford, Davidson	1997-00	7
Mike Pierce, McNeese St.	1987-90	6
Lamont Watson, Delaware	1997-98	5

SEASON BLOCKED PUNTS

Player, Team	Year	BP
Ryan Crawford, Davidson	2000	4
Robert Herron, Sam Houston St.	2004	4
Trey Woods, Sam Houston St.	1993	3
Ben Duhon, McNeese St.	1998	3
Jamin Elliott, Delaware	1998	3
Lamont Watson, Delaware	1998	3
Carlos Dallis, UNI	2000	3
Brandon Tinson, Colgate	2000	3
Germaine Bennett, Delaware	2002	3
DeJuan Davis, Sam Houston St.	2002	3

SINGLE-GAME BLOCKED PUNTS

No.	Player, Team (Opponent)	Date
3	Ben Duhon, McNeese St. (Ark.-Monticello)	Sept. 29, 1998
3	Brandon Tinson, Colgate (Towson)	Sept. 30, 2000
2	Demetrius Pope, Sam Houston St. (Tex. A&M-Kingsville)	Sept. 14, 1996
2	Fabian Johnson, Sam Houston St. (Troy)	Oct. 11, 1997
2	Ryan Crawford, Davidson (Sewanee)	Sept. 16, 2000
2	DeJuan Davis, Sam Houston St. (Mississippi Val.)	Sept. 29, 2001
2	Robert Herron, Sam Houston St. (Ouachita Baptist)	Sept. 4, 2004
2	Tim Camp, Ga. Southern (Morehead St.)	Nov. 12, 2005

Blocked Field Goals

CAREER BLOCKED FIELD GOALS

Player, Team	Years	BFG
Leonard Smith, McNeese St.	1980-82	10
Mark Weivoda, Idaho St.	2000-03	8
Clayton Smith, Dartmouth	2001-04	6
Ryan Crawford, Davidson	1997-00	5
Bryan Cox, Western Ill.	1987-90	4
Brent Browner, UNI	1998-01	4
DeJuan Davis, Sam Houston St.	2001-02	3
Tom Parks, Delaware	2002-05	3

SEASON BLOCKED FIELD GOALS

Player, Team	Year	BFG
Leonard Smith, McNeese St.	1981	4
Mark Weivoda, Idaho St.	2001	4
Clayton Smith, Dartmouth	2004	4
Bryan Cox, Western Ill.	1990	3
Ryan Crawford, Davidson	1999	3
Brent Browner, UNI	2001	3
Tom Parks, Delaware	2005	3
Bo Black, Sam Houston St.	1994	2
Ryan Crawford, Davidson	2000	2
Mark Weivoda, Idaho St.	2002	2
DeJuan Davis, Sam Houston St.	2002	2
Chris Mooney, Delaware	2003	2
Rod Gulky, McNeese St.	2003	2

SINGLE-GAME BLOCKED FIELD GOALS

No.	Player, Team (Opponent)	Date
2	Rod Gulky, McNeese St. (Henderson St.)	Aug. 30, 2003
2	Chris Mooney, Delaware (Massachusetts)	Nov. 15, 2003

Blocked Extra Points

CAREER BLOCKED EXTRA POINTS

Player, Team	Years	BXP
Tim Hauck, Montana	1987-89	7
Joel Sussman, Cornell	2001-04	6
Bryan Cox, Western Ill.	1987-90	5
Leonard Smith, McNeese St.	1980-82	4
Ed Groszewski, Cornell	1990-93	4
Brent Browner, UNI	1998-01	3
Mark Weivoda, Idaho St.	2000-03	3

SEASON BLOCKED EXTRA POINTS

Player, Team	Year	BXP
Tim Hauck, Montana	1988	4
Ed Groszewski, Cornell	1991	4
Leonard Smith, McNeese St.	1982	2
Bryan Cox, Western Ill.	1990	2
David Gunn, UNI	2000	2
Brent Browner, UNI	2000	2
Mark Weivoda, Idaho St.	2001	2

SINGLE-GAME BLOCKED EXTRA POINTS

No.	Player, Team (Opponent)	Date
1	By many players	

Combined Blocked Kicks

CAREER COMBINED BLOCKED KICKS

Player, Team	Years	BK (#Breakdown)
Leonard Smith, McNeese St.	1980-82	17 (10 FGs, 4 PATs, 3 Punts)
Trey Woods, Sam Houston St.	1992-95	12 (8 Punts, 2 PATs, 2 FGs)
Ryan Crawford, Davidson	1997-00	12 (7 Punts, 5 FGs)
Mark Weivoda, Idaho St.	2000-03	11 (8 FGs, 3 PATs)
Bryan Cox, Western Ill.	1987-90	10 (5 PATs, 4 FGs, 1 Punt)
Tim Hauck, Montana	1987-89	9 (7 PATs, 2 FGs)
Brent Browner, UNI	1998-01	7 (4 FGs, 3 PATs)
Mike Pierce, McNeese St.	1987-90	6 (6 Punts)
Clayton Smith, Dartmouth	2001-04	6 (6 FGs)
Joel Sussman, Cornell	2001-04	6 (6 PATs)

SEASON COMBINED BLOCKED KICKS

Player, Team	Year	BK (#Breakdown)
Leonard Smith, McNeese St.	1981	6 (4 FGs, 2 Punts)
Ryan Crawford, Davidson	2000	6 (4 Punts, 2 FGs)
Mark Weivoda, Idaho St.	2001	6 (4 FGs, 2 PATs)
Bryan Cox, Western Ill.	1990	5 (3 FGs, 2 PATs)
Trey Woods, Sam Houston St.	1993	5 (3 Punts, 1 FG, 1 PAT)
DeJuan Davis, Sam Houston St.	2002	5 (3 Punts, 2 FGs)
Cy Kaplowitz, Delaware	1949	4 (3 Punts, 1 PAT)
Tim Hauck, Montana	1988	4 (4 PATs)
Ed Groszewski, Cornell	1991	4 (4 PATs)
Brent Browner, UNI	2001	4 (3 FGs, 1 PAT)
Clayton Smith, Dartmouth	2004	4 (4 FGs)

SINGLE-GAME COMBINED BLOCKED KICKS

BK	Player, Team	Opponent	Date	BK (#Breakdown)
3	Ben Duhon, McNeese St.	Ark.-Monticello	Sept. 29, 1998	3 Punts
3	Michael Adams, Stephen F. Austin	Central Okla.	Aug. 30, 2000	2 Punts; 1 PAT
3	Brandon Tinson, Colgate	Towson	Sept. 30, 2000	3 Punts
2	By many players			

#Breakdown=No. of Punts, No. of FGs and No. of Extra Points Blocked.

Punting

CAREER AVERAGE

(Minimum 150 Punts; Player must have concluded his career)

Player, Team	Years	No.	Yards	Long	Avg.
Mark Gould, Northern Ariz.	2000-03	211	9,443	78	44.8
Pumpy Tudors, Chattanooga	1989-91	181	8,041	79	44.4
David Simonhoff, Southeast Mo. St.	2003-06	237	10,402	75	43.9

Player, Team	Years	No.	Yards	Long	Avg.
Case de Bruijn, Idaho St.	1978-81	256	11,184	76	43.7
Mike Scifres, Western Ill.	1999-02	203	8,842	89	43.6
Terry Belden, Northern Ariz.	1990-93	225	9,760	76	43.4
Chad Stanley, Stephen F. Austin	1996-98	178	7,709	79	43.3
George Cimadevilla, East Tenn. St.	1983-86	225	9,676	72	43.0
Harold Alexander, Appalachian St.	1989-92	259	11,100	78	42.9
Ken Hinsley, Western Caro.	1995-98	199	8,512	85	42.8
Brad Costello, Boston U.	1995-97	193	8,206	73	42.5
John Christopher, Morehead St.	1979-82	298	12,633	62	42.4
Matthew Peot, Montana St.	1997-99	155	6,578	61	42.4
Colin Godfrey, Tennessee St.	1989-92	213	9,012	69	42.3
Bret Wright, Southeastern La.	1981-83	165	6,963	66	42.2
Richie Rhodes, Jacksonville St.	2001-04	218	9,208	74	42.2
Ryan Hoffman, Illinois St.	$2001-05	191	8,057	70	42.2
Jeff Kaiser, Idaho St.	1982-84	156	6,571	88	42.1
Greg Davis, Citadel	1983-86	263	11,076	81	42.1
Mark Royals, Appalachian St.	1983-85	223	9,372	67	42.0

$See page 10 for explanation.

SEASON AVERAGE

(Qualifiers for Championship)

Player, Team	Year	No.	Yards	Avg.
Mark Gould, Northern Ariz.	†2002	62	2,987	48.2
Mike Scifres, Western Ill.	2002	53	2,545	48.0
Paul Ernster, Northern Ariz.	†2004	55	2,631	47.8
Brent Barth, VMI	2002	64	3,032	47.4
Harold Alexander, Appalachian St.	†1991	64	3,009	47.0
Chad Stanley, Stephen F. Austin	†1998	58	2,703	46.6
Eddie Johnson, Idaho St.	†2001	49	2,270	46.3
Eddie Johnson, Idaho St.	2002	51	2,357	46.2
David Simonhoff, Southeast Mo. St.	2004	69	3,174	46.0
Terry Belden, Northern Ariz.	†1993	59	2,712	46.0
Case de Bruijn, Idaho St.	†1981	42	1,928	45.9
Wesley Taylor, Florida A&M	†2005	59	2,707	45.9
Colin Godfrey, Tennessee St.	†1990	57	2,614	45.9
Barry Cantrell, Fordham	†1997	65	2,980	45.9
Matthew Peot, Montana St.	†1999	48	2,195	45.7
Stuart Dodds, Montana St.	†1979	59	2,689	45.6
Pumpy Tudors, Chattanooga	1991	53	2,414	45.5
Graham Whitlock, Gardner-Webb	†2003	57	2,593	45.5
Matt Bushart, Southern U.	1998	50	2,260	45.2
Mark Gagliano, Southern Ill.	†1996	54	2,432	45.0
Mark Gould, Northern Ariz.	2003	58	2,610	45.0

†National champion.

ANNUAL CHAMPIONS

Year	Player, Team	Class	No.	Yards	Avg.
1978	Nick Pavich, Nevada	So.	47	1,939	41.3
1979	Stuart Dodds, Montana St.	Sr.	59	2,689	45.6
1980	Case de Bruijn, Idaho St.	Jr.	67	2,945	44.0
1981	Case de Bruijn, Idaho St.	Sr.	42	1,928	45.9
1982	John Christopher, Morehead St.	Sr.	93	4,084	43.9
1983	Pat Velarde, Marshall	Sr.	64	2,852	44.6
1984	Steve Kornegay, Western Caro.	Jr.	49	2,127	43.4
1985	Mike Rice, Montana	Jr.	62	2,771	44.7
1986	Greg Davis, Citadel	Sr.	61	2,723	44.6
1987	Eric Stein, Eastern Wash.	Sr.	74	3,193	43.2
1988	Mike McCabe, Illinois St.	Sr.	69	3,042	44.1
1989	Pumpy Tudors, Chattanooga	So.	65	2,817	43.3
1990	Colin Godfrey, Tennessee St.	So.	57	2,614	45.9
1991	Harold Alexander, Appalachian St.	Jr.	64	3,009	47.0
1992	Harold Alexander, Appalachian St.	Sr.	55	2,445	44.5
1993	Terry Belden, Northern Ariz.	Sr.	59	2,712	46.0
1994	Scott Holmes, Samford	Jr.	49	2,099	42.8
1995	Kevin O'Leary, Northern Ariz.	Sr.	44	1,881	42.8
1996	Mark Gagliano, Southern Ill.	Sr.	54	2,432	45.0
1997	Barry Cantrell, Fordham	Sr.	65	2,980	45.9
1998	Chad Stanley, Stephen F. Austin	Sr.	58	2,703	46.6
1999	Matthew Peot, Montana St.	Jr.	48	2,195	45.7
2000	David Beckford, Alabama St.	So.	48	2,121	44.2
2001	Eddie Johnson, Idaho St.	Jr.	49	2,270	46.3
2002	Mark Gould, Northern Ariz.	Jr.	62	2,987	*48.2
2003	Graham Whitlock, Gardner-Webb	Jr.	57	2,593	45.5
2004	Paul Ernster, Northern Ariz.	Sr.	55	2,631	47.8
2005	Wesley Taylor, Florida A&M	So.	59	2,707	45.9
2006	Breck Ackley, Southern U.	Sr.	49	2,228	45.5

**Record.*

Punt Returns

CAREER AVERAGE

(Minimum 1.2 Returns Per Game; Minimum 30 Returns; Player must have concluded his career)

Player, Team	Years	No.	Yards	Avg.
Terrence McGee, Northwestern St.	1999-02	56	972	17.4
Willie Ware, Mississippi Val.	1982-85	61	1,003	16.4
Buck Phillips, Western Ill.	1994-95	40	656	16.4
Tim Egerton, Delaware St.	1986-89	59	951	16.1
Mark Orlando, Towson	1991-94	41	644	15.7
Joseph Jefferson, Western Ky.	1998-01	53	809	15.3
Emery Beckles, Idaho St.	2002-03	60	903	15.1
Corey Smith, Montana St.	2000-03	63	938	14.9
Toby Zeigler, Northwestern St.	2002-05	93	1,363	14.7
John Armstrong, Richmond	1984-85	31	449	14.5
Joey Jamison, Texas Southern	1997-99	88	1,269	14.4
Darrick Brown, Maine	1995-98	56	807	14.4
Marquay McDaniel, Hampton	2002-05	116	*1,668	14.4
Delvin Joyce, James Madison	1997-00	104	1,488	14.3
James Norris, Western Ill.	2001-04	33	467	14.2
Ricky Pearsall, Northern Ariz.	1994-97	39	546	14.0

**Record.*

SEASON AVERAGE

(Minimum 1.2 Returns Per Game and Qualifiers for Championship)

Player, Team	Year	No.	Yards	Avg.
Curtis DeLoatch, N.C. A&T	†2001	20	530	26.5
Derrick Harris, Sam Houston St.	†2006	15	366	24.4
Terrence McGee, Northwestern St.	†2000	18	427	23.7
Tim Egerton, Delaware St.	†1988	16	368	23.0
Ryan Priest, Lafayette	†1982	12	271	22.6
Craig Hodge, Tennessee St.	†1987	19	398	21.0
Chris Berry, Morehead St.	†1997	13	273	21.0
Nate Hughes, Alcorn St.	2006	22	460	20.9
Reggie Barlow, Alabama St.	†1995	12	249	20.8
Bashir Levingston, Eastern Wash.	†1998	16	333	20.8
John Armstrong, Richmond	†1985	19	391	20.6
KaRon Coleman, Stephen F. Austin	†1999	17	348	20.5
Craig Agee, Jacksonville St.	†2004	18	369	20.5
Mark Orlando, Towson	†1994	19	377	19.8
Willie Ware, Mississippi Val.	†1984	19	374	19.7
Buck Phillips, Western Ill.	1994	24	464	19.3
Junior Adams, Montana St.	2001	20	381	19.1
James Norris, Western Ill.	†2003	15	287	19.1

†National champion.

ANNUAL CHAMPIONS

Year	Player, Team	Class	No.	Yards	Avg.
1978	Ray Smith, Northern Ariz.	Sr.	13	181	13.9
1979	Joseph Markus, Connecticut	Fr.	17	219	12.9
1980	Trumaine Johnson, Grambling	So.	††13	226	17.4
1981	Barney Bussey, South Carolina St.	So.	14	255	18.2
1982	Ryan Priest, Lafayette	Fr.	12	271	22.6
1983	Joe Fuller, UNI	So.	22	344	15.6
1984	Willie Ware, Mississippi Val.	Jr.	19	374	19.7
1985	John Armstrong, Richmond	Sr.	19	391	20.6
1986	Chris Darrington, Weber St.	Sr.	16	290	18.1
1987	Craig Hodge, Tennessee St.	Sr.	19	398	21.0
1988	Tim Egerton, Delaware St.	Jr.	16	368	23.0
1989	Henry Richard, La.-Monroe	Jr.	15	258	17.2
1990	Gary Harrell, Howard	Fr.	26	417	16.0
1991	Ashley Ambrose, Mississippi Val.	Sr.	28	514	18.4
1992	Quincy Miller, South Carolina St.	Jr.	17	311	18.3
1993	Ray Marshall, St. Peter's	Jr.	10	171	17.1
1994	Mark Orlando, Towson	Sr.	19	377	19.8
1995	Reggie Barlow, Alabama St.	Sr.	12	249	20.8
1996	Ricky Pearsall, Northern Ariz.	Jr.	29	490	16.9
1997	Chris Berry, Morehead St.	Sr.	13	273	21.0
1998	Bashir Levingston, Eastern Wash.	Sr.	16	333	20.8
1999	KaRon Coleman, Stephen F. Austin	Sr.	17	348	20.5
2000	Terrence McGee, Northwestern St.	So.	18	427	23.7
2001	Curtis DeLoatch, N.C. A&T	So.	20	530	*26.5
2002	Zuriel Smith, Hampton	Sr.	27	500	18.5
2003	James Norris, Western Ill.	Jr.	15	287	19.1
2004	Craig Agee, Jacksonville St.	So.	18	369	20.5
2005	Nick Feldman, Morehead St.	So.	27	512	18.9
2006	Derrick Harris, Sam Houston St.	Sr.	15	366	24.4

**Record. ††Declared champion; with one more return (making 1.3 per game) for zero yards, still would have highest average.*

Kickoff Returns

CAREER AVERAGE

(Minimum 1.2 Returns Per Game; Minimum 30 Returns; Player must have concluded his career)

Player, Team	Years	No.	Yards	Avg.
Lamont Brightful, Eastern Wash.	1998-01	65	1,949	30.0
Troy Brown, Marshall	1991-92	32	950	29.7
Cedric Bowen, Ark.-Pine Bluff	2001-04	38	1,124	29.6
Charles Swann, Indiana St.	1989-91	45	1,319	29.3
Craig Richardson, Eastern Wash.	1983-86	71	2,021	28.5
Cortland Finnegan, Samford	2002-05	70	1,980	28.3
Ramondo North, N.C. A&T	1998-00	48	1,356	28.3
Kenyatta Sparks, Southern U.	1992-95	39	1,100	28.2
Kerry Hayes, Western Caro.	1991-94	73	2,058	28.2
Daryl Holcombe, Eastern Ill.	1986-89	49	1,379	28.1
Dwight Robinson, James Madison	1990-93	51	1,434	28.1
Curtis Chappell, Howard	1984-87	42	1,177	28.0
Leon Brown, Eastern Ky.	1990-93	44	1,230	28.0
Josh Cole, Furman	1993-96	65	1,808	27.8
Tyree Talton, UNI	1995-98	72	1,999	27.8
Joe Rosato, Duquesne	1994-97	60	1,661	27.7
Marcus Durgin, Samford	1990-93	44	1,218	27.7
Cornelius Turner, Mississippi Val.	1992-94	50	1,379	27.6
Corey Graham, New Hampshire	2003-06	65	1,787	27.5
Anthony Taylor, UNI	1992-95	30	821	27.4
Jerry Parrish, Eastern Ky.	1978-81	61	1,668	27.3
Steven Rush, Missouri St.	2001-04	41	1,120	27.3
Tony James, Eastern Ky.	1982-84	57	1,552	27.2
Ricky Ellis, St. Mary's (Cal.)	1994-96	31	836	27.0

$See page 10 for explanation.

SEASON AVERAGE

(Minimum 1.2 Returns Per Game and Qualifiers for Championship)

Player, Team	Year	No.	Yards	Avg.
David Fraterrigo, Canisius	†1993	13	485	37.3
Brian Bratton, Furman	†2001	14	521	37.2
Kerry Hayes, Western Caro.	1993	16	584	36.5
Cordell Roane, Richmond	†1999	13	470	36.2
Jerome Mathis, Hampton	†2004	25	888	35.5
Ulysses Banks, Alabama A&M	†2006	13	454	34.9
Craig Richardson, Eastern Wash.	†1984	21	729	34.7
Ryan Zimpleman, Butler	†1998	28	972	34.7
Randy Moss, Marshall	†1996	14	484	34.6
Avion Black, Tennessee St.	1999	23	786	34.2
Lamont Brightful, Eastern Wash.	1999	26	882	33.9
Errin Hatwood, St. John's (N.Y.)	†1994	12	401	33.4
Marcus Durgin, Samford	†1992	15	499	33.3
Corey Smith, Montana St.	†2003	20	664	33.2
Richard Holland, VMI	†2000	19	628	33.1
Rory Lee, Western Ill.	1993	16	527	32.9
Corey Alexander, Texas Southern	†2002	19	615	32.4
Dave Meggett, Towson	†1988	13	418	32.2
Lamont Brightful, Eastern Wash.	2000	15	483	32.2
Cortland Finnegan, Samford	2002	23	741	32.2
Chris Crawford, Nicholls St.	2003	20	646	32.3
Charles Swann, Indiana St.	†1990	20	642	32.1
Josh Cole, Furman	†1995	17	546	32.1
Tyree Talton, UNI	1996	22	703	32.0

†National champion.

ANNUAL CHAMPIONS

Year	Player, Team	Class	No.	Yards	Avg.
1978	Dave Loehle, New Hampshire	Jr.	15	460	30.7
1979	Garry Pearson, Massachusetts	Fr.	12	348	29.0
1980	Danny Thomas, N.C. A&T	Fr.	15	381	25.4
1981	Jerry Parrish, Eastern Ky.	Sr.	18	534	29.7
1982	Davlin Mullen, Western Ky.	Sr.	18	574	31.9
1983	Tony James, Eastern Ky.	Jr.	17	511	30.1
1984	Craig Richardson, Eastern Wash.	So.	21	729	34.7
1985	Rodney Payne, Murray St.	Fr.	16	464	29.0
1986	Danny Copeland, Eastern Ky.	Jr.	26	812	31.2
1987	Howard Huckaby, Florida A&M	So.	20	602	30.1
1988	Dave Meggett, Towson	Sr.	13	418	32.2
1989	Scott Thomas, Liberty	Fr.	13	373	28.7
1990	Charles Swann, Indiana St.	Jr.	20	642	32.1
1991	Paul Ashby, Alabama St.	Jr.	17	520	30.6
1992	Marcus Durgin, Samford	Jr.	15	499	33.3
1993	David Fraterrigo, Canisius	Sr.	13	485	*37.3
1994	Errin Hatwood, St. John's (N.Y.)	Sr.	12	401	33.4
1995	Josh Cole, Furman	Jr.	17	546	32.1
1996	Randy Moss, Marshall	Fr.	14	484	34.6
1997	Andy Swafford, Troy	Sr.	14	440	31.4
1998	Ryan Zimpleman, Butler	So.	28	972	34.7
1999	Cordell Roane, Richmond	Fr.	13	470	36.2
2000	Richard Holland, VMI	Sr.	19	628	33.1
2001	Brian Bratton, Furman	Fr.	14	521	37.2
2002	Corey Alexander, Texas Southern	So.	19	615	32.4
2003	Corey Smith, Montana St.	Sr.	20	664	33.2
2004	Jerome Mathis, Hampton	Sr.	25	888	35.5
2005	Ricky Williams, Bethune-Cookman	Sr.	21	659	31.4
2006	Ulysses Banks, Alabama A&M	Fr.	13	454	34.9

**Record.*

All-Purpose Yards

CAREER YARDS PER GAME

(Minimum 3,200 Yards; Player must have concluded his career)

Player, Team	Years	G	Rush	Rcv.	Int.	PR	KOR	Yds.	Yd. PG
Brian Westbrook, Villanova	1997-98, 00-01	44	4,298	2,582	0	343	2,289	*9,512	216.2
Jerry Azumah, New Hampshire	1995-98	41	6,193	1,153	0	5	1,025	8,376	204.3
Arnold Mickens, Butler	1994-95	20	3,813	47	0	0	87	3,947	197.4
Tim Hall, Robert Morris	1994-95	19	2,908	793	0	0	0	3,701	194.8
Reggie Greene, Siena	1994-97	36	5,415	274	0	53	1,217	6,959	193.3
Dave Meggett, Towson	1987-88	18	1,658	788	0	212	745	3,403	189.1
Archie Amerson, Northern Ariz.	1995-96	22	3,196	484	0	0	382	4,062	184.6
Kenny Gamble, Colgate	1984-87	42	5,220	536	0	104	1,763	7,623	181.5
Rick Sarille, Wagner	$1995-99	41	5,290	365	0	0	1,682	7,337	179.0
Aaron Stecker, Western Ill.	1997-98	20	3,081	427	0	0	0	3,508	175.4
Rich Erenberg, Colgate	1982-83	21	2,618	423	0	268	315	3,624	172.6
Claude Mathis, Texas St.	1994-97	44	4,691	744	0	635	1,353	7,423	168.7
Thomas Haskins, VMI	1993-96	44	5,355	179	0	216	1,661	7,411	168.4
Ozzie Young, Valparaiso	1993-95	29	1,576	1,123	0	418	1,728	4,845	167.1
Nick Hartigan, Brown	2003-05	30	4,488	510	0	0	0	4,998	166.6
Fine Unga, Weber St.	1987-88	22	2,298	391	0	7	967	3,663	166.5
Adrian Peterson, Ga. Southern	1998-01	42	*6,559	225	0	0	0	6,784	161.5
Charles Dunn, Portland St.	1998-00	33	4,831	489	0	0	0	5,320	161.2
Gill Fenerty, Holy Cross	1983-85	30	3,618	477	0	1	731	4,827	160.9
Gary Jones, Albany (N.Y.)	2002-03	23	3,033	227	0	0	379	3,639	158.2
Keith Elias, Princeton	1991-93	30	4,208	508	0	0	25	4,741	158.0
Clifton Dawson, Harvard	2003-06	39	4,841	759	0	0	538	6,138	157.4
Don Wilkerson, Texas St.	1993-94	22	2,356	255	0	83	757	3,451	156.9
Marcel Shipp, Massachusetts	1997-00	43	5,383	932	0	0	392	6,707	156.0
Kito Lockwood, Wagner	1993-95	25	2,576	891	0	0	420	3,887	155.5

Player, Team	Years	G	Rush	Rcv.	Int.	PR	KOR	Yds.	Yd. PG
Tyrone Butterfield, Tennessee St.	1997-98	22	12	2,182	0	44	1,164	3,402	154.6
Jesse Chatman, Eastern Wash.	1999-01	31	4,173	614	0	0	4	4,791	154.5
Barry Bourassa, New Hampshire	1989-92	39	2,960	1,307	0	306	1,370	5,943	152.4
Ryan Fuqua, Portland St.	2001-04	43	4,730	819	0	0	982	6,531	151.9
Javarus Dudley, Fordham	2000-03	47	58	4,197	0	192	2,668	7,115	151.4
Charles Tharp, Western Ill.	1999-00	22	2,834	454	0	23	0	3,311	150.5

Record. $See page 10 for explanation.

SEASON YARDS PER GAME

Player, Team	Year	Rush	Rcv.	Int.	PR	KOR	Yds.	Yd. PG
Brian Westbrook, Villanova	†1998	1,046	1,144	0	192	644	*3,026	275.1
Brian Westbrook, Villanova	†2000	1,220	724	0	0	1,048	2,992	272.0
Brian Westbrook, Villanova	†2001	1,603	658	0	122	440	2,823	256.6
Jerry Azumah, New Hampshire	1998	2,195	218	0	5	308	2,726	247.8
Reggie Greene, Siena	†1996	1,719	50	0	0	337	2,106	234.0
Jesse Chatman, Eastern Wash.	2001	2,096	424	0	0	0	2,520	229.1
Arnold Mickens, Butler	†1994	2,255	7	0	0	0	2,262	226.2
Reggie Greene, Siena	†1997	1,719	50	0	0	158	2,009	223.2
Charles Roberts, Sacramento St.	1998	2,260	79	0	0	91	2,430	220.9
Archie Amerson, Northern Ariz.	1996	2,079	262	0	0	88	2,429	220.8
Kenny Gamble, Colgate	†1986	1,816	178	0	40	391	2,425	220.5
Reggie Greene, Siena	†1995	1,461	77	0	53	363	1,954	217.1
Stephan Lewis, New Hampshire	2001	1,390	527	0	0	471	2,388	217.1
Johnnie Gray, Weber St.	2001	1,571	446	0	0	369	2,386	216.9
Eddie Conti, Delaware	1998	-2	*1,712	0	156	502	2,368	215.3
Steve Silva, Holy Cross	†2005	912	364	0	395	462	2,133	213.3
Marcel Shipp, Massachusetts	1998	1,949	288	0	0	100	2,337	212.5
Michael Clemons, William & Mary	1986	1,065	516	0	330	423	2,334	212.2
DaVon Fowlkes, Appalachian St.	†2004	82	1,618	0	194	419	2,313	210.3

**Record. †National champion.*

CAREER YARDS

Player, Team	Years	Rush	Rcv.	Int.	PR	KOR	Yds.	Yd. PP
Brian Westbrook, Villanova	1997-98, 00-01	4,298	2,582	0	343	2,289	9,512	9.3
Jerry Azumah, New Hampshire	1995-98	6,193	1,153	0	5	1,025	8,376	7.4
Kenny Gamble, Colgate	1984-87	5,220	536	0	104	1,763	7,623	7.0
Claude Mathis, Texas St.	1994-97	4,691	744	0	635	1,353	7,423	7.0
Thomas Haskins, VMI	1993-96	5,355	179	0	216	1,661	7,411	7.2
Rick Sarille, Wagner	$1995-99	5,290	365	0	0	1,682	7,337	6.9
Javarus Dudley, Fordham	2000-03	58	4,197	0	192	2,668	7,115	16.3
Charles Roberts, Sacramento St.	1997-00	6,553	382	0	12	165	7,112	6.0
Reggie Greene, Siena	1994-97	5,415	274	0	53	1,217	6,959	7.1
Adrian Peterson, Ga. Southern	1998-01	*6,559	225	0	0	0	6,784	6.7
Marcel Shipp, Massachusetts	1997-00	5,383	932	0	0	392	6,707	5.7
Ryan Fuqua, Portland St.	2001-04	4,730	819	0	0	982	6,531	6.2
Fred Amey, Sacramento St.	2001-04	34	4,049	0	573	1,687	6,343	15.7
Clifton Dawson, Harvard	2003-06	4,841	759	0	0	538	6,138	5.8
Joe McCourt, Lafayette	2001-04	4,474	1,135	0	103	335	6,047	5.4
Donte Small, Duquesne	1998-01	4,260	306	0	0	1,426	5,992	6.4
Rich Lemon, Bucknell	1993-96	4,742	961	0	99	150	5,952	5.2
Barry Bourassa, New Hampshire	1989-92	2,960	1,307	0	306	1,370	5,943	7.5
Eric Kimble, Eastern Wash.	2002-05	339	4,140	0	990	465	5,934	14.1
Pete Mandley, Northern Ariz.	1979-80, 82-83	436	2,598	11	901	1,979	5,925	14.8
Charles Anthony, Tennessee St.	2001-04	5,057	851	0	0	0	5,908	6.0
Frank Hawkins, Nevada	1977-80	5,333	519	0	0	0	5,852	5.8
Vincent Jackson, Northern Colo.	2001-04	0	3,548	0	1,024	1,238	5,810	18.3
Erik Marsh, Lafayette	1991-94	4,834	383	0	76	490	5,783	5.2
Darrell Jones, Cal Poly	2001-04	173	2,460	0	1,328	1,807	5,768	14.3
Matt Cannon, Southern Utah	1997-00	5,489	236	0	0	17	5,742	7.5
Eddie Conti, Delaware	1994-98	-7	3,496	0	802	1,446	5,737	17.1
Sean Morey, Brown	1995-98	131	3,850	0	9	1,736	5,726	15.7
Sean Mizzer, VMI	2002-06	3,723	753	0	150	1,100	5,726	6.4
Andre Raymond, Eastern Ill.	2000-03	2,342	1,256	0	112	1,968	5,678	8.7
Kerry Hayes, Western Caro.	1991-94	5	2,594	0	876	2,058	5,603	*19.1
Jamie Jones, Eastern Ill.	1988-91	3,466	816	0	66	1,235	5,583	6.2

Record. $See page 10 for explanation.

SEASON YARDS

Player, Team	Year	Rush	Rcv.	Int.	PR	KOR	Yds.	Yd. PP
Brian Westbrook, Villanova	†1998	1,046	1,144	0	192	644	3,026	9.2
Brian Westbrook, Villanova	†2000	1,220	724	0	0	1,048	2,992	10.8
Brian Westbrook, Villanova	†2001	1,603	658	0	122	440	2,823	8.5
Jerry Azumah, New Hampshire	1998	2,195	218	0	5	308	2,726	7.3
Jesse Chatman, Eastern Wash.	2001	2,096	424	0	0	0	2,520	7.8
Charles Roberts, Sacramento St.	1998	2,260	79	0	0	91	2,430	6.1
Archie Amerson, Northern Ariz.	1996	2,079	262	0	0	88	2,429	6.9
Kenny Gamble, Colgate	†1986	1,816	178	0	40	391	2,425	7.1
Stephan Lewis, New Hampshire	2001	1,390	527	0	0	471	2,388	7.4
Johnnie Gray, Weber St.	2001	1,571	446	0	0	369	2,386	6.5
Eddie Conti, Delaware	1998	-2	*1,712	0	156	502	2,368	18.2
Jamaal Branch, Colgate	2003	*2,326	24	0	0	0	2,350	5.2
Marcel Shipp, Massachusetts	1998	1,949	288	0	0	100	2,337	6.6

Player, Team	Year	Rush	Rcv.	Int.	PR	KOR	Yds.	Yd. PP
Michael Clemons, William & Mary	1986	1,065	516	0	330	423	2,334	6.7
Arkee Whitlock, Southern Ill.	2006	1,828	63	0	0	439	2,330	6.8
DaVon Fowlkes, Appalachian St.	†2004	82	1,618	0	194	419	2,313	15.2
Derrick Cullors, Murray St.	1995	1,765	312	0	0	201	2,278	7.6
Clarence Matthews, Northwestern St.	1995	1,384	194	0	145	554	2,277	7.7
Andre Raymond, Eastern Ill.	2002	612	672	0	112	872	2,268	9.3
Arnold Mickens, Butler	†1994	2,255	7	0	0	0	2,262	5.5
Claude Mathis, Texas St.	1995	1,286	315	0	352	308	2,261	7.3
Anthony Jordan, Samford	1994	924	400	0	169	767	2,260	10.8
Aaron Stecker, Western Ill.	1997	1,957	288	0	0	0	2,245	6.9
Rich Erenberg, Colgate	†1983	1,883	214	0	126	18	2,241	6.7
Stephan Lewis, New Hampshire	†2002	1,152	419	0	13	645	2,229	7.1
Jerry Azumah, New Hampshire	1997	1,572	297	0	0	351	2,220	7.2
Charles Roberts, Sacramento St.	1999	2,082	108	0	12	0	2,202	6.9

**Record. †National champion.*

ALL-PURPOSE SINGLE-GAME HIGHS

Yds.	Player, Team (Opponent)	Date
467	Joey Stockton, Western Ky. (Austin Peay)	Sept. 16, 1995
463	Michael Lerch, Princeton (Brown)	Oct. 12, 1991
458	Brian Westbrook, Villanova (Delaware)	Nov. 18, 2000
453	Herman Hunter, Tennessee St. (Mississippi Val.)	Nov. 13, 1982
447	Maurice Hicks, N.C. A&T (Morgan St.)	Oct. 6, 2001
437	Ryan Fuqua, Portland St. (Eastern Wash.)	Nov. 10, 2001
428	Brian Westbrook, Villanova (Pittsburgh)	Sept. 5, 1998
420	Reggie Greene, Siena [St. John's (N.Y.)]	Nov. 2, 1996
410	Steven Rush, Missouri St. (Illinois St.)	Nov. 8, 2003
409	Charles Roberts, Sacramento St. (Idaho St.)	Nov. 6, 1999
409	Josh Rue, Duquesne (Canisius)	Nov. 17, 2001
405	Brian Westbrook, Villanova (James Madison)	Oct. 6, 2001
401	Eddie Conti, Delaware (Northeastern)	Oct. 3, 1998
401	Eddie Conti, Delaware (Connecticut)	Nov. 7, 1998

ANNUAL CHAMPIONS

Year	Player, Team	Class	Rush	Rcv.	Int.	PR	KOR	Yds.	Yd. PG
1978	Frank Hawkins, Nevada	So.	1,445	211	0	0	0	1,656	165.6
1979	Frank Hawkins, Nevada	Jr.	1,683	123	0	0	0	1,806	164.2
1980	Ken Jenkins, Bucknell	Jr.	1,270	293	0	65	256	1,884	188.4
1981	Garry Pearson, Massachusetts	Jr.	1,026	105	0	0	450	1,581	175.7
1982	Pete Mandley, Northern Ariz.	Jr.	36	1,067	0	344	532	1,979	179.9
1983	Rich Erenberg, Colgate	Sr.	1,883	214	0	126	18	2,241	203.7
1984	Gene Lake, Delaware St.	Jr.	1,722	37	0	0	0	1,759	175.9
1985	Gill Fenerty, Holy Cross	Sr.	1,368	187	0	1	414	1,970	197.0
1986	Kenny Gamble, Colgate	Jr.	1,816	178	0	40	391	2,425	220.5
1987	Dave Meggett, Towson	Jr.	814	572	0	78	327	1,791	199.0
1988	Otis Washington, Western Caro.	Sr.	66	907	0	0	1,113	2,086	189.6
1989	Dominic Corr, Eastern Wash.	Sr.	796	52	0	0	807	1,655	183.9
1990	Barry Bourassa, New Hampshire	So.	957	276	0	133	368	1,734	192.7
1991	Barry Bourassa, New Hampshire	Jr.	1,130	426	0	0	596	2,152	195.6
1992	David Wright, Indiana St.	Fr.	1,313	108	0	0	593	2,014	183.1
1993	Tony Vinson, Towson	Sr.	2,016	57	0	0	0	2,073	207.3
1994	Arnold Mickens, Butler	Jr.	2,255	7	0	0	0	2,262	226.2
1995	Reggie Greene, Siena	So.	1,461	77	0	53	363	1,954	217.1
1996	Reggie Greene, Siena	Jr.	1,719	50	0	0	337	2,106	234.0
1997	Reggie Greene, Siena	Sr.	1,778	73	0	0	158	2,009	223.2
1998	Brian Westbrook, Villanova	So.	1,046	1,144	0	192	644	*3,026	*275.1
1999	Rick Sarille, Wagner	Sr.	1,373	226	0	0	475	2,074	207.4
2000	Brian Westbrook, Villanova	Jr.	1,220	724	0	0	1,048	2,992	272.0
2001	Brian Westbrook, Villanova	Sr.	1,603	658	0	122	440	2,823	256.6
2002	Stephan Lewis, New Hampshire	Sr.	1,152	419	0	13	645	2,229	202.6
2003	Luke McArdle, Georgetown	Sr.	0	1,118	0	506	407	2,031	184.6
2004	DaVon Fowlkes, Appalachian St.	Sr.	82	1,618	0	194	419	2,313	210.3
2005	Steve Silva, Holy Cross	Sr.	912	364	0	395	462	2,133	213.3
2006	Justise Hairston, Central Conn. St.	Sr.	1,847	58	0	123	170	2,198	199.8

**Record.*

Field Goals

CAREER FIELD GOALS

Player, Team	Years	Total	Pct.	Under 40 Yds.	40 Plus	Long
Marty Zendejas, Nevada (S)	1984-87	72-90	.800	42-45	30-45	54
Kirk Roach, Western Caro. (S)	1984-87	71-102	.696	45-49	26-53	57
Tony Zendejas, Nevada (S)	1981-83	70-86	*.814	45-49	25-37	58
Chris Snyder, Montana (S)	2000-03	70-*105	.667	43-53	27-52	57
Scott Shields, Weber St. (S)	1995-98	67-90	.744	48-55	19-35	55
Brian Mitchell, Marshall/UNI (S)	1987, 89-91	64-81	.790	48-55	16-26	57
Dave Ettinger, Hofstra (S)	1994-97	62-93	.667	37-48	24-45	54
Brian Wingert, UNI (S)	2003-06	60-79	.759	42-47	18-32	56
Todd Kurz, Illinois St. (S)	1993-96	59-87	.678	40-53	19-34	51
Greg Kuehn, William & Mary (S)	2002-05	59-89	.663	44-62	15-27	51
Andrew Paterini, Hampton (S)	2003-06	59-90	.656	46-63	13-27	55
Steve Christie, William & Mary (S)	1986-89	57-83	.686	39-49	18-34	53

Player, Team	Years	Total	Pct.	Under 40 Yds.	40 Plus	Long
Jose Larios, McNeese St. (S)	1992-95	57-89	.640	47-57	10-32	47
Teddy Garcia, La.-Monroe (S)	1984-87	56-88	.636	35-43	21-45	55
Bjorn Nittmo, Appalachian St. (S)	1985-88	55-74	.743	35-40	20-34	54
Justin Langan, Western Ill. (S)	2001-04	53-78	.679	36-44	17-34	53
Paul McFadden, Youngstown St. (S)	1980-83	52-90	.578	28-42	24-48	54
Kelly Potter, Middle Tenn. (S)	1981-84	52-78	.667	37-49	15-29	57
Shonz LaFrenz, McNeese St. (S)	1996-99	52-78	.667	44-65	8-13	46
Mike Black, Boise St. (S)	1988-91	51-75	.680	35-43	16-32	48
Paul Politi, Illinois St. (S)	1983-86	50-78	.641	34-48	16-30	50
Tim Foley, Ga. Southern (S)	1984-87	50-62	.806	32-37	18-25	**63
Jeff Wilkins, Youngstown St. (S)	1990-93	50-73	.685	33-38	17-35	54
Chris Onorato, Hofstra (S)	2001-04	50-77	.649	42-58	8-19	52
Brian Morgan, Grambling (S)	2001-04	50-87	.575	39-64	11-23	52
Craig Coffin, Southern Ill. (S)	$2002-06	50-63	.794	39-47	11-16	52
Scott Roper, Texas-Arlington/Arkansas St. (S)	1985, 86-87	49-75	.653	35-43	14-32	**63
Paul Hickert, Murray St. (S)	1984-87	49-79	.620	34-48	15-31	62
Matt Stover, Louisiana Tech (S)	1986-88	49-68	.721	29-34	20-34	57
Chuck Rawlinson, Stephen F. Austin (S)	1988-91	49-69	.710	34-43	15-26	58
Thayne Doyle, Idaho (S)	1988-91	49-75	.653	35-51	14-24	52
Wayne Boyer, Missouri St. (S)	1993-96	49-71	.690	36-45	13-26	57

**Record. **Record tied. (S)Soccer-style kicker. $See page 10 for explanation.*

SEASON FIELD GOALS

Player, Team	Year	Total	Pct.	Under 40 Yds.	40 Plus	Long
Tony Zendejas, Nevada (S)	†1982	26-**33	.788	18-20	8-13	52
Brian Mitchell, UNI (S)	†1990	26-27	*.963	23-23	3-4	45
Wayne Boyer, Missouri St. (S)	†1996	25-30	.833	16-18	9-12	57
MacKenzie Hoambrecker, UNI (S)	†2002	25-28	.893	17-19	8-9	59
Chris Snyder, Montana (S)	†2003	25-30	.833	17-18	8-12	54
George Benyola, Louisiana Tech (S)	†1985	24-31	.774	15-18	9-13	53
Kirk Roach, Western Caro. (S)	†1986	24-28	.857	17-17	7-11	52
Tony Zendejas, Nevada (S)	†1983	23-29	.793	14-15	9-14	58
Goran Lingmerth, Northern Ariz. (S)	1986	23-29	.793	16-19	7-10	55
Matt Lange, Western Ky. (S)	2003	23-28	.821	17-18	6-10	46
Marty Zendejas, Nevada (S)	†1984	22-27	.815	12-13	10-14	52
Mike Dodd, Boise St. (S)	†1992	22-31	.710	16-21	6-10	50
Jose Larios, McNeese St. (S)	†1993	22-28	.786	19-21	3-7	47
David Ettinger, Hofstra (S)	†1995	22-**33	.667	17-22	5-11	54
Rob Hart, Murray St. (S)	1996	22-27	.815	18-20	4-7	52
Matt Vick, Chattanooga (S)	†2000	22-26	.846	17-19	5-7	42
Tony Zendejas, Nevada (S)	†1981	21-24	.875	13-14	8-10	55
Scott Roper, Arkansas St. (S)	1986	21-28	.750	15-17	6-11	50
Matt Stover, Louisiana Tech (S)	1986	21-25	.840	15-15	6-10	53
Kevin McKelvie, Nevada (S)	1990	21-24	.875	16-17	5-7	52
Travis Brawner, Missouri St. (S)	†1997	21-28	.750	15-17	6-11	52

**Record. **Record tied. †National champion. (S) Soccer-style kicker.*

ANNUAL CHAMPIONS

(Ranked on Per-Game Average)

Year	Player, Team	Total	PG	Pct.
1978	Tom Sarette, Boise St. (S)	12-20	1.2	.600
1979	Wilfredo Rosales, Alcorn St. (S)	13-20	1.3	.650
	Sandro Vitiello, Massachusetts (S)	13-22	1.3	.591
1980	Scott Norwood, James Madison (S)	15-21	1.5	.714
1981	Tony Zendejas, Nevada (S)	21-24	1.9	.875
1982	Tony Zendejas, Nevada (S)	**26-**33	**2.4	.788
1983	Tony Zendejas, Nevada (S)	23-29	2.1	.793
1984	Marty Zendejas, Nevada (S)	22-27	2.0	.815
1985	George Benyola, Louisiana Tech (S)	24-31	2.2	.774
1986	Kirk Roach, Western Caro. (S)	24-28	2.2	.857
1987	Micky Penaflor, Northern Ariz. (S)	19-27	1.9	.704
1988	Chris Lutz, Princeton (S)	19-24	1.9	.792
1989	Steve Christie, William & Mary (S)	20-29	1.8	.690
1990	Brian Mitchell, UNI (S)	**26-27	**2.4	*.963
1991	Brian Mitchell, UNI (S)	19-24	1.7	.792
1992	Mike Dodd, Boise St. (S)	22-31	2.0	.710
1993	Jose Larios, McNeese St. (S)	22-28	2.0	.786
1994	Andy Glockner, Penn (S)	14-20	1.6	.700
1995	David Ettinger, Hofstra (S)	22-**33	2.0	.667
1996	Wayne Boyer, Missouri St. (S)	25-30	2.3	.833
1997	Travis Brawner, Missouri St. (S)	21-28	1.9	.750
1998	Mike Goldstein, Northern Ariz. (S)	16-23	1.5	.696
	Scott Shields, Weber St. (S)	16-23	1.5	.696
	Bill Gramatica, South Fla. (S)	16-24	1.5	.667
	Chad Johnson, Hofstra (S)	16-27	1.5	.593
	Joe Lopez, Western Ill. (S)	16-28	1.5	.571
1999	Brett Sterba, William & Mary (S)	18-23	1.6	.783
2000	Matt Vick, Chattanooga (S)	22-26	2.0	.846
2001	Brian Morgan, Grambling (S)	18-25	1.64	.720
2002	MacKenzie Hoambrecker, UNI (S)	25-28	2.3	.893
2003	Chris Snyder, Montana (S)	25-30	1.92	.833
2004	Joe Johnson, Weber St. (S)	17-22	1.55	.773
2005	Steve Morgan, Brown (S)	18-23	1.80	.783
2006	Dan Carpenter, Montana (S)	24-30	1.71	.800

**Record. **Record tied. (S) Soccer-style kicker.*

All-Time Longest Plays

(Since 1978 for FCS records)

Since 1941, official maximum length of all plays fixed at 100 yards for every division.

RUSHING

Yds.	Player, Team (Opponent)	Year
99	Michael Hobbs, Wofford (Ga. Southern)	2006
99	Jermaine Creighton, St. John's (N.Y.) (Siena)	1996
99	Jim Varick, Monmouth (Sacred Heart)	1994
99	Phillip Collins, Missouri St. (Western Ill.)	1989
99	Pedro Bacon, Western Ky. (West Ala.)	1986
99	Hubert Owens, Mississippi Val. (Ark.-Pine Bluff)	1980
98	Jon Underhill, Jacksonville (Greensboro)	1998
98	Johnny Gordon, Nevada (Montana St.)	1984
97	Dedrick Poole, Ark.-Pine Bluff (Grambling)	2006
97	Stevie Chaney, Murray St. (Austin Peay)	2005
97	Dane Romero, Wofford (Gardner-Webb)	2005
97	Pat Williams, Delaware (West Chester)	1995
97	Norman Bradford, Grambling (Prairie View)	1992

Yds.	Player, Team (Opponent)	Year
97	David Clark, Dartmouth (Harvard)	1989
97	David Clark, Dartmouth (Princeton)	1988
96	Jerry Azumah, New Hampshire (Connecticut)	1996
96	Jim Pizano, Massachusetts (Rhode Island)	1996
96	Kelvin Anderson, Southeast Mo. St. (Murray St.)	1992
96	Andre Lockhart, Chattanooga (East Tenn. St.)	1986
95	Marcus Mason, Youngstown St. (Western Ill.)	2006
95	Wendall Williams, Rhode Island (Villanova)	2003
95	Corey Hill, Colgate (Brown)	1996
95	Brett Chappell, Western Caro. (Elon)	1995
95	Tim Hall, Robert Morris (Gannon)	1994
95	Jeff Sawulski, Siena (Iona)	1993
95	Jerry Ellison, Chattanooga (Boise St.)	1992
95	John McNiff, Cornell (Columbia)	1990
95	Joe Sparksman, James Madison (William & Mary)	1990

PASSING

Yds.	Passer-Receiver, Team (Opponent)	Year
99	Riley Walker-Fred Burnette, Tennessee St. (Jacksonville St.)	2004
99	Matt Verbit-Clinton Wu, Princeton (Brown)	2003
99	Jimmy Blanchard-Terry Charles, Portland St. (Eastern Wash.)	1999
99	Michael Moore-Otis Covington, Morgan St. (Florida A&M)	1995
99	Todd Bernett-Jason Anderson, Eastern Wash. (Montana)	1994
99	Aaron Garcia-Greg Ochoa, Sacramento St. (Cal Poly)	1993
99	Todd Donnan-Troy Brown, Marshall (East Tenn. St.)	1991
99	Antoine Ezell-Tyrone Davis, Florida A&M (Bethune-Cookman)	1991
99	Jay Johnson-Kenny Shedd, UNI (Oklahoma St.)	1990
99	John Bonds-Hendricks Johnson, Northern Ariz. (Boise St.)	1990
99	Scott Stoker-Victor Robinson, Northwestern St. (La.-Monroe)	1989
98	Chris Wallace-Jason Jones, Ark.-Pine Bluff (Southern Ill.)	2006
98	Steve LaFalce-Marco Thomas, Western Ill. (Illinois St.)	2005
98	Princeton Shepherd-Jerome Mathis, Hampton (South Carolina St.)	2004
98	Ben Anderson-Courtney Freeman, Liberty (Charleston So.)	1996
98	Derek Jensen-Jason Cannon, Missouri St. (Eastern Ill.)	1995
98	Jonathan Quinn-Dee Mostiller, Middle Tenn. (Tennessee Tech)	1995
98	Antoine Ezell-Tim Daniel, Florida A&M (Delaware St.)	1991
98	John Friesz-Lee Allen, Idaho (Northern Ariz.)	1989
98	Fred Gatlin-Treamelle Taylor, Nevada (Montana)	1989
98	Steve Monaco-Emerson Foster, Rhode Island (Holy Cross)	1988
98	Frank Baur-Maurice Caldwell, Lafayette (Columbia)	1988
98	David Gabianelli-Craig Morton, Dartmouth (Columbia)	1986
98	Joe Pizzo-Bryan Calder, Nevada (Eastern Wash.)	1984
98	Bobby Hebert-Randy Liles, Northwestern St. (Southeastern La.)	1980
97	Jeff Krohn-Jimmie Howard, Masschusetts (Villanova)	2003
97	Dontrell Leonard-Howard Gilmore, Norfolk St. (Liberty)	2003
97	Scott Dolch-Akeen Watson, Central Conn. St. (Monmouth)	2003
97	Brad Smith-Sullivan Beard, Nicholls St. (Jacksonville St.)	1999
97	Peyton Jones-Mikhael Ricks, Stephen F. Austin (Troy)	1997
97	Lester Anderson-Kevin Glenn, Illinois St. (Ball St.)	1993
97	Nate Harrison-Brian Thomas, Southern U. (Dist. Columbia)	1989
97	Jerome Baker-John Taylor, Delaware St. (St. Paul's)	1985
97	John McKenzie-Chris Burkett, Jackson St. (Mississippi Val.)	1983

INTERCEPTION RETURNS

Yds.	Player, Team (Opponent)	Year
100	Brian Jackson, Indiana St. (Eastern Ill.)	2006
100	Antonio Nelson, Alabama A&M (Tennessee St.)	2005
100	Tony LeZotte, James Madison (Towson)	2005
100	Mark Johnson, San Diego (Valparaiso)	2005
100	Ricky Williamson, Harvard (Yale)	2004
100	Giovanni Benson, New Hampshire (Dartmouth)	2003
100	Ernie James, Idaho St. (Northern Colo.)	2003
100	Timmy Thrift, Wofford (Chattanooga)	2003
100	Ricardo Walker, Delaware (Villanova)	2000
100	Jacori Rufus, Idaho St. (Southern Utah)	1998
100	Sean Gorius, Dayton (Morehead St.)	1997
100	Tehran Hunter, Massachusetts (Buffalo)	1997
100	Derek Grier, Marshall (East Tenn. St.)	1991
100	Ricky Fields, Samford (Concord)	1990
100	Warren Smith, Stephen F. Austin (Nicholls St.)	1990
100	Rob Pouliot, Montana St. (Boise St.)	1988
100	Rick Harris, East Tenn. St. (Davidson)	1986
100	Bruce Alexander, Stephen F. Austin (Lamar)	1986
100	Guy Carbone, Rhode Island (Lafayette)	1985
100	Moses Aimable, UNI (Western Ill.)	1985
100	Kervin Fontennette, Southeastern La. (Nicholls St.)	1985
100	Jim Anderson, Princeton (Cornell)	1984
100	Keiron Bigby, Brown (Yale)	1984
100	Vencie Glenn, Indiana St. [Wayne St. (Mich.)]	1984
100	George Floyd, Eastern Ky. (Youngstown St.)	1980

PUNT RETURNS

Yds.	Player, Team (Opponent)	Year
98	Willie Ware, Mississippi Val. (Bishop)	1985
98	Barney Bussey, South Carolina St. (Johnson C. Smith)	1981
96	Cletis Gordon, Jackson St. (Hampton)	2004
96	Carl Williams, Texas Southern (Grambling)	1981
95	James Norris, Western Ill. (Eastern Mich.)	2003
95	Joseph Jefferson, Western Ky. (Illinois St.)	2001
95	Clarence Weathers, Delaware St. (Salisbury)	1980
94	Tuff Harris, Montana (Eastern Wash.)	2006
94	Jayson Foster, Ga. Southern (Appalachian St.)	2004
94	Drew Haddad, Buffalo (Cornell)	1998
94	Brad Friedman, Towson [St. Francis (Pa.)]	1996
93	Andrew McFadden, Liberty (Delaware St.)	1995
93	Patrick Plott, Jacksonville St. (Missouri St.)	1995
93	Joe Fuller, UNI (Wis.-Whitewater)	1984

KICKOFF RETURNS

Sixty-nine players have returned kickoffs 100 yards. The most recent:

Yds.	Player, Team (Opponent)	Year
100	Davin Walker, Eastern Ky. (Murray St.)	2006
100	Jesse Burton, Tenn. Martin (Southeast Mo. St.)	2006
100	Bryant Eteuati, Weber St. (Montana)	2006
100	Isiejah Allen, Fordham (Holy Cross)	2006
100	William Middleton, Furman (Wofford)	2006
100	Charlie Spiller, Alcorn St. (Mississippi Val.)	2005
100	Charlie Spiller, Alcorn St. (Mississippi Val.)	2005
100	Ricky Williams, Bethune-Cookman (Ark.-Pine Bluff)	2004
100	Steven Rush, Missouri St. (Illinois St.)	2004
100	Arel Gordon, Maine (Morgan St.)	2003
100	Corey Smith, Montana St. (Gardner-Webb)	2003
100	Steven Rush, Missouri St. (Western Ill.)	2003
100	Xavier Godard, Western Caro. (Ga. Southern)	2003
100	Chris Crawford, Nicholls St. (Texas St.)	2003
100	Cedric Bowen, Ark.-Pine Bluff (Alcorn St.)	2003
100	Art Smith, Northeastern (Villanova)	2002
100	James McCowan, Weber St. (Eastern Ore.)	2002
100	Terrance Patrick, Hampton (Alcorn St.)	2002
100	John Leverett, Davidson (Randolph-Macon)	2001
100	R.J. Harvey, New Hampshire (Maine)	2001
100	Terry Tharps, Western Ill. (Sam Houston St.)	2001
100	Brian Bratton, Furman (Appalachian St.)	2001
100	Brian Bratton, Furman (Wofford)	2001
100	Lamont Brightful, Eastern Wash. (Montana)	2000
100	Kunle Williams, Penn (Princeton)	1999
100	Joey Hamilton, Jacksonville St. (Samford)	1999
100	Lamont Brightful, Eastern Wash. (Central Wash.)	1999
100	Darriel Ruffin, Tenn.-Martin (Murray St.)	1997
100	Corey Joyner, Ga. Southern (East Tenn. St.)	1997

PUNTS

Yds.	Player, Team (Opponent)	Year
93	Tyler Grogan, Northeastern (Villanova)	2001
91	Bart Helsley, North Texas (La.-Monroe)	1990
89	Steve Bulcavage, Towson (Colgate)	2003
89	Mike Scifres, Western Ill. (Missouri St.)	2000
89	Jim Carriere, Connecticut (Maine)	1987
88	Jeff Kaiser, Idaho St. (UTEP)	1983
87	John Starnes, North Texas (Texas-Arlington)	1983
86	Jesse Ohliger, Murray St. (Eastern Ky.)	2003
86	Cory Elolf, Texas St. (McNeese St.)	2003
86	Andy Dorsey, Tennessee Tech (Eastern Ill.)	1998
85	Troy LeFever, Youngstown St. (UNI)	2000
85	Ken Hinsley, Western Caro. (Chattanooga)	1998
85	Don Alonzo, Nicholls St. (Northwestern St.)	1980
84	Sean Dennis, Monmouth (Central Conn. St.)	2003
84	Billy Smith, Chattanooga (Appalachian St.)	1988
83	David Simonhoff, Southeast Mo. St. (Eastern Ill.)	2003
83	Jason Harkins, Appalachian St. (Citadel)	1986
82	David Simonhoff, Southeast Mo. St. (Tenn.-Martin)	2004
82	Dan Frantz, Portland St. (Montana)	2000
82	Scott White, Delaware (Maine)	1996
82	Scott Shields, Weber St. (Cal St. Northridge)	1996
82	Tim Healy, Delaware (Boston U.)	1987
82	John Howell, Chattanooga (Vanderbilt)	1982

FUMBLE RETURNS

Yds.	Player, Team (Opponent)	Year
99	Jarrell Guyton (20 yds.) and Everette Baker (79 yds. after lateral), Morgan St. (Howard)	2006
99	Randall State, Liberty (Akron)	2002
90	Cornell Middlebrook, Western Ill. (UNI)	2002
87	Garron Bible, Delaware (Lafayette)	2004
82	Brendan Dete, Davidson (Newberry)	2002
79	Al Clark, Wofford (Middle Tenn. St.)	1999

FCS

FIELD GOALS

Yds.	Player, Team (Opponent)	Year
63	Bill Gramatica, South Fla. (Austin Peay)	2000
63	Scott Roper, Arkansas St. (North Texas)	1987
63	Tim Foley, Ga. Southern (James Madison)	1987
62	Billy Cundiff, Drake (San Diego)	2000
62	Paul Hickert, Murray St. (Eastern Ky.)	1986
60	Pete Garces, Idaho St. (Cal St. Northridge)	1998
60	Terry Belden, Northern Ariz. (Cal St. Northridge)	1993
60	David Cool, Ga. Southern (James Madison)	1988
59	MacKenzie Hoambrecker, UNI (Missouri St.)	2002
58	Rich Emke, Eastern Ill. (UNI)	1986
58	Tony Zendejas, Nevada (Boise St.)	1983

Team Champions

Annual Offense Champions

TOTAL OFFENSE

Year	Team	Avg.
1978	Portland St.	477.4
1979	Portland St.	460.7
1980	Portland St.	504.3
1981	Idaho	438.8
1982	Drake	444.8
1983	Idaho	479.5
1984	Mississippi Val.	*640.1
1985	Weber St.	516.1
1986	Nevada	492.0
1987	Holy Cross	552.2
1988	Lehigh	485.6
1989	Idaho	495.9
1990	William & Mary	498.7
1991	Weber St.	581.4
1992	Alcorn St.	502.9
1993	Idaho	532.0
1994	Alcorn St.	597.9
1995	Montana	512.5
1996	Northern Ariz.	522.8
1997	Eastern Wash.	505.6
1998	Florida A&M	535.7
1999	Ga. Southern	551.7
2000	Morehead St.	523.9
2001	Eastern Wash.	514.5
2002	Jackson St.	485.5
2003	San Diego	483.3
2004	Southeastern La.	537.1
2005	Grambling	495.6
2006	San Diego	494.3

*Record.

RUSHING OFFENSE

Year	Team	Avg.
1978	Jackson St.	314.5
1979	Jackson St.	288.4
1980	N.C. A&T	322.1
1981	Idaho	266.3
1982	Delaware	258.4
1983	Furman	287.1
1984	Delaware St.	377.3
1985	Missouri St.	298.7
1986	Northeastern	336.0
1987	Howard	381.6
1988	Eastern Ky.	303.0
1989	Ga. Southern	329.2
1990	Delaware St.	298.7
1991	VMI	316.9
1992	Citadel	345.5
1993	Western Ky.	300.1
1994	Citadel	382.0
1995	Massachusetts	302.5
1996	Southern Utah	330.8
1997	Western Ky.	366.0
1998	Southern Utah	386.0
1999	Ga. Southern	*419.0
2000	Southern Utah	394.2
2001	Ga. Southern	323.6
2002	Ga. Southern	386.2
2003	Ga. Southern	335.6
2004	Ga. Southern	369.9
2005	Ga. Southern	386.8
2006	Central Conn. St.	284.9

*Record.

PASSING OFFENSE

Year	Team	Avg.
1978	Portland St.	367.1
1979	Portland St.	368.9
1980	Portland St.	434.9
1981	Idaho St.	325.7
1982	West Tex. A&M	313.7
1983	Idaho	336.1
1984	Mississippi Val.	*496.8
1985	Rhode Island	384.3
1986	Eastern Ill.	326.1
1987	Holy Cross	358.4
1988	Lehigh	330.1
1989	Idaho	374.3
1990	Weber St.	342.2
1991	Weber St.	389.1
1992	Alcorn St.	360.5
1993	Montana	359.0
1994	Alcorn St.	442.3
1995	Montana	408.2
1996	Montana	339.6
1997	Cal. St. Northridge	358.1
1998	Florida A&M	400.6
1999	Towson	381.2
2000	Penn	342.7
2001	Jackson St.	344.4
2002	Grambling	360.7
2003	Grambling	321.8
2004	Southeastern La.	408.0
2005	Grambling	367.3
2006	San Diego	293.3

*Record.

SCORING OFFENSE

Year	Team	Avg.
1978	Nevada	35.6
1979	Portland St.	34.3
1980	Portland St.	49.2
1981	Delaware	34.1
1982	Delaware	34.1
1983	Mississippi Val.	39.2
1984	Mississippi Val.	*60.9
1985	Mississippi Val.	41.5
1986	Nevada	39.4
1987	Holy Cross	46.5
1988	Lafayette	38.2
1989	Grambling	37.1
1990	Jackson St.	38.0
1991	Nevada	45.1
1992	Marshall	42.4
1993	Idaho	47.5
1994	Alcorn St.	45.7
1995	Montana	42.5
1996	Northern Ariz.	43.2
1997	Morehead St.	41.9
1998	Florida A&M	49.6
1999	Ga. Southern	50.0
2000	Morehead St.	41.6
2001	Eastern Wash.	41.9
2002	Grambling	38.9
2003	Southern U.	40.0
2004	Ga. Southern	47.0
2005	Grambling	44.1
2006	San Diego	42.8

*Record.

Annual Defense Champions

TOTAL DEFENSE

Year	Team	Avg.
1978	Florida A&M	*149.9
1979	Alcorn St.	166.3
1980	Massachusetts	193.5
1981	South Carolina St.	204.0
1982	South Carolina St.	191.4
1983	Grambling	206.0
1984	Tennessee St.	187.0
1985	Arkansas St.	258.8
1986	Tennessee St.	178.5
1987	Southern U.	202.8
1988	Alcorn St.	215.4
1989	Howard	220.0
1990	Middle Tenn.	244.8
1991	South Carolina St.	208.9
1992	South Carolina St.	250.9
1993	McNeese St.	249.5
1994	Penn	218.9
1995	Georgetown	216.4
1996	Georgetown	218.2
1997	Marist	213.6
1998	Fairfield	213.8
1999	St. John's (N.Y.)	199.7
2000	Monmouth	232.1
2001	St. Peter's	157.7
2002	Duquesne	188.0
2003	Monmouth	244.3
2004	Dayton	263.1
2005	Duquesne	205.9
2006	Robert Morris	228.4

*Record.

RUSHING DEFENSE

Year	Team	Avg.
1978	Florida A&M	48.6
1979	Alcorn St.	56.7
1980	South Carolina St.	61.8
1981	South Carolina St.	60.8
1982	South Carolina St.	59.4
1983	Jackson St.	79.2
1984	Grambling	44.5
1985	Jackson St.	63.0
1986	Eastern Ky.	62.8
1987	Southern U.	64.5
1988	Stephen F. Austin	83.5
1989	Montana	70.2

Year	Team	Avg.
1990	Delaware St.	77.2
1991	Boise St.	84.4
1992	Villanova	77.8
1993	Wagner	87.0
1994	Idaho	65.3
1995	McNeese St.	60.9
1996	Georgetown	53.2
1997	Marist	40.4
1998	Fairfield	61.7
1999	Jackson St.	67.8
2000	Alabama A&M	*39.7
2001	Penn	58.4
2002	Penn	55.8
2003	Monmouth	64.3
2004	Cal Poly	84.3
2005	Duquesne	72.5
2006	Maine	63.9

*Record.

PASSING DEFENSE

Year	Team	$Avg.
1978	Southern U.	85.6
1979	Mississippi Val.	64.2
1980	Howard	93.8
1981	Bethune-Cookman	*59.9
1982	Northeastern	98.8
1983	Louisiana Tech	111.4
1984	Louisiana Tech	105.5
1985	Dartmouth	110.3
1986	Bethune-Cookman	99.8
1987	Alcorn St.	101.3
1988	Middle Tenn.	90.8
1989	Chattanooga	104.4
1990	Middle Tenn.	78.83
1991	South Carolina St.	70.01
1992	Middle Tenn.	76.93
1993	Georgetown	76.92
1994	Penn	63.15
1995	Canisius	69.13
1996	Canisius	71.99
1997	McNeese St.	79.05
1998	Davidson	74.64
1999	Robert Morris	80.80
2000	Bethune-Cookman	76.39
2001	St. Peter's	63.26
2002	Sacred Heart	*61.03
2003	South Carolina St.	93.14
2004	Coastal Caro.	86.79
2005	Duquesne	79.76
2006	Robert Morris	88.70

Record. $Beginning in 1990, ranked on passing-efficiency defense rating points instead of per-game yardage allowed.

SCORING DEFENSE

Year	Team	Avg.
1978	South Carolina St.	*6.5
1979	Lehigh	7.2
1980	Murray St.	9.1
1981	Jackson St.	9.4
1982	Western Mich.	7.1
1983	Grambling	8.6
1984	Northwestern St.	9.0
1985	Appalachian St.	9.9
1986	Tennessee St.	8.3
1987	Holy Cross	10.0
1988	Furman	9.7
1989	Howard	10.5
1990	Middle Tenn.	9.2
1991	Villanova	12.0
1992	Citadel	13.0
1993	Marshall	11.2
1994	Penn	7.6
1995	McNeese St.	8.9
1996	Duquesne	10.1
1997	McNeese St.	10.5
1998	Western Ill.	9.4
1999	St. John's (N.Y.)	12.9
2000	Western Ky.	11.6
2001	St. Peter's	8.2
2002	Duquesne	9.6
2003	Monmouth	8.5
2004	Southern Ill.	13.2
2005	Massachusetts	13.3
2006	Monmouth	12.7

*Record.

Other Annual Team Champions

NET PUNTING

Year	Team	Avg.
1992	Stephen F. Austin	38.2
1993	Northern Ariz.	40.1
1994	Marshall	42.9
1995	Eastern Ky.	40.4
1996	Marshall	44.5
1997	James Madison	40.5
1998	Western Ill.	41.5
	Western Caro.	41.5
1999	Missouri St.	40.0
2000	Idaho St.	39.2
2001	Idaho St.	44.3
2002	Idaho St.	42.7
2003	Illinois St.	39.2
2004	Northern Ariz.	44.9
2005	Massachusetts	38.4
2006	Northern Ariz.	43.0

PUNT RETURNS

Year	Team	Avg.
1992	South Carolina St.	17.9
1993	Montana	14.6
1994	Towson	19.5
1995	Texas St.	19.3
1996	Northern Ariz.	16.6
1997	Morehead St.	19.4
1998	Buffalo	17.8
1999	Stephen F. Austin	19.1
2000	Northwestern St.	19.4
2001	N.C. A&T	23.0
2002	Hampton	17.8
2003	Eastern Ky.	16.5
2004	Jacksonville St.	18.6
2005	Southern U.	19.1
2006	Norfolk St.	20.7

KICKOFF RETURNS

Year	Team	Avg.
1992	Penn	25.0
1993	Western Caro.	26.8
1994	Youngstown St.	27.3
1995	Southern U.	27.0
1996	Monmouth	27.2
1997	Furman	27.1
1998	Butler	28.8
1999	Tennessee St.	27.9
2000	Weber St.	25.2
2001	Hampton	28.2
2002	Portland St.	25.2
2003	Montana	28.1
2004	Hampton	30.5
2005	Western Caro.	27.4
2006	James Madison	27.1

TURNOVER MARGIN

Year	Team	Avg.
1992	Howard	1.64
	Youngstown St.	1.64
1993	St. John's (N.Y.)	1.91
1994	Robert Morris	1.89
1995	Princeton	2.20
1996	Canisius	2.44
1997	Texas Southern	1.91
1998	Yale	1.70
1999	Grambling	1.45
	Valparaiso	1.45
2000	Western Ky.	2.73
2001	St. Peter's	3.18
2002	Dayton	1.92
2003	Wofford	1.64
2004	Coastal Caro.	2.00
2005	New Hampshire	1.54
2006	Wofford	1.91

Defensive Single-Game Records

(Since 2000)

TACKLES FOR LOSS

TFL	Team (Opponent)	Date
22	Illinois St. (Western Ill.)	Nov. 4, 2000
21	Eastern Wash. (Montana St.)	Oct. 7, 2000
21	Duquesne (Iona)	Oct. 9, 2004
20	Western Ky. (Youngstown St.)	Nov. 15, 2003
19	Fla. Atlantic (Bethune-Cookman)	Sept. 7, 2002
19	Massachusetts (American Int'l)	Sept. 14, 2002
19	Penn (Brown)	Nov. 2, 2002
19	Massachusetts (Central Conn. St.)	Sept. 6, 2003
18	Holy Cross (Bucknell)	Nov. 4, 2000
17	Stony Brook [St. John's (N.Y.)]	Sept. 21, 2002
17	Ga. Southern (East Tenn. St.)	Nov. 2, 2002
16	Western Ill. [Wayne St. (Mich.)]	Aug. 29, 2003
16	Western Ill. (Eastern Mich.)	Sept. 4, 2003
16	Fla. Atlantic (Colgate)	Dec. 13, 2003
16	UNI (Northern Ariz.)	Nov. 19, 2005

PASS SACKS

Sacks	Team (Opponent)	Date
12	Illinois St. (Western Ill.)	Nov. 4, 2000
11	Fla. Atlantic (Bethune-Cookman)	Sept. 7, 2002
11	Massachusetts (American Int'l)	Sept. 14, 2002
11	Duquesne (La Salle)	Nov. 5, 2005
10	Grambling (Alabama A&M)	Sept. 10, 2005
10	New Hampshire (Dartmouth)	Sept. 24, 2005
10	Cal Poly (Southern Utah)	Nov. 12, 2005
9	Eight times, including four times in 2005	

PASSES DEFENDED

(Pass Interceptions and Pass Break-ups)

PD	Team (Opponent)	Date
17	Penn (Lafayette)	Sept. 21, 2002
14	Holy Cross (Penn)	Oct. 7, 2000
14	Massachusetts (Maine)	Oct. 12, 2002
13	Ga. Southern (Chattanooga)	Sept. 27, 2003
13	Harvard (Princeton)	Oct. 23, 2003
13	Weber St. (Idaho St.)	Oct. 23, 2003
12	Norfolk St. (Hampton)	Oct. 19, 2002
12	Massachusetts (Hofstra)	Oct. 18, 2003
12	Lafayette (Columbia)	Oct. 15, 2005
11	UNI (Illinois St.)	Oct. 4, 2003
11	Cal Poly (Southern Utah)	Nov. 1, 2003
10	Delaware (New Hampshire)	Nov. 4, 2000
10	Delaware (West Chester)	Sept. 21, 2002
10	Ga. Southern (Citadel)	Oct. 26, 2002
10	Ga. Southern (Bethune-Cookman)	Nov. 30, 2002
10	Ga. Southern (Maine)	Dec. 7, 2002
10	Wofford (Western Ky.)	Dec. 6, 2003

FORCED FUMBLES

FF	Team (Opponent)	Date
6	Delaware (Ga. Southern)	Dec. 9, 2000
6	Delaware (Citadel)	Sept. 9, 2002
6	Fla. Atlantic (Troy)	Oct. 26, 2002
6	Jacksonville (Valparaiso)	Sept. 27, 2003
5	Ga. Southern (Savannah St.)	Sept. 1, 2001
5	Illinois St. (Missouri St.)	Oct. 5, 2002
5	Delaware (Massachusetts)	Nov. 15, 2003
5	Fla. Atlantic (Bethune-Cookman)	Nov. 29, 2003
4	Holy Cross (Towson)	Sept. 22, 2001
4	Massachusetts (Northeastern)	Nov. 3, 2001
4	Massachusetts (Rhode Island)	Nov. 17, 2001
4	Davidson (Newberry)	Sept. 21, 2002
4	Massachusetts (Richmond)	Oct. 5, 2002
4	Maine (Hofstra)	Sept. 6, 2003
4	UNI (Northwestern St.)	Sept. 27, 2003
4	Davidson (Dayton)	Oct. 4, 2003
4	Massachusetts (New Hampshire)	Oct. 4, 2003
4	Penn (Princeton)	Nov. 8, 2003
4	UNI (Montana St.)	Nov. 29, 2003
4	Western Ill. (Montana)	Nov. 29, 2003
4	Lafayette (Bucknell)	Oct. 16, 2004

Toughest-Schedule Annual Leaders

The FCS toughest-schedule program, which began in 1982, is based on what all FCS opponents did against other FCS and Division I-A teams when not playing the team in question. Games against non-I-AA and I-A teams are deleted. (All playoff or postseason games were included for the first time in 2002.) The top two leaders by year:

Year	Team (Record†)	¢Opponents' Record W	L	T	Pct.
1982	Massachusetts (5-6-0)	50	30	1	.623
	Lehigh (4-6-0)	44	31	0	.587
1983	Florida A&M (7-4-0)	42	23	3	.640
	Grambling (8-1-2)	49	31	0	.613
1984	North Texas (2-9-0)	55	35	2	.609
	VMI (1-9-0)	53	37	2	.587
1985	South Carolina St. (5-6-0)	43	20	1	.680
	Lehigh (5-6-0)	47	33	1	.586
1986	James Madison (5-5-1)	46	28	1	.620
	Bucknell (3-7-0)	43	27	0	.614
1987	Ga. Southern (8-3-0)	47	31	0	.603
	Northeastern (6-5-0)	50	37	0	.575
1988	Northwestern St. (9-2-0)	54	36	2	.598
	Ga. Southern (9-2-0)	43	31	1	.580
1989	Liberty (7-3-0)	39	22	2	.635
	Western Caro. (3-7-1)	46	34	2	.573
1990	Ga. Southern (8-3-0)	53	25	1	.677
	Western Ky. (2-8-0)	55	36	1	.603
1991	Bucknell (1-9-0)	53	29	1	.645
	William & Mary (5-6-0)	62	43	0	.590
1992	VMI (3-8-0)	46	36	0	.561
	Harvard (3-7-0)	51	40	0	.560
1993	Samford (5-6-0)	55	26	0	.679
	Delaware St. (6-5-0)	44	30	0	.595
1994	Montana (9-2-0)	46	30	1	.604
	McNeese St. (9-2-0)	44	29	5	.596
1995	Western Ky. (2-8-0)	59	32	0	.648
	Nicholls St. (0-11-0)	61	38	0	.616
1996	Indiana St. (6-5)	50	32	0	.610
	Towson (6-4)	42	29	0	.592
1997	Lehigh (4-7)	65	39	0	.625
	William & Mary (7-4)	65	42	0	.607
1998	Connecticut (9-2)	66	41	0	.617
	New Hampshire (4-7)	54	40	0	.596
1999	Elon (9-2)	50	26	0	.658
	Cal Poly (3-8)	52	32	0	.619
2000	Elon (7-4)	59	31	0	.656
	Indiana St. (1-10)	62	38	0	.620
2001	Elon (2-9)	63	36	0	.636
	Nicholls St. (3-8)	55	34	0	.618
2002	McNeese St. (13-2)	104	45	0	.698
	Western Ky. (12-3)	98	49	0	.667
2003	Delaware (15-1)	104	60	0	.634
	Western Ky. (9-4)	68	46	0	.596
2004	Delaware (9-4)	84	46	0	.646
	Villanova (6-5)	73	44	0	.624
2005	Appalachian St. (12-3)	106	51	0	.675
	Princeton (7-3)	55	37	0	.598
2006	Youngstown St. (11-3)	83	51	0	.619
	Northeastern (5-6)	70	44	0	.614

†Beginning in 2002, all playoff or postseason games are included in the record. ¢When not playing the team listed.

Top 10 Toughest-Schedule Leaders for 2002-06

2002

	Team	¢Opp. Record	Pct.
1.	McNeese St.	104-45	.698
2.	Western Ky.	98-49	.667
3.	Villanova	103-54	.656
4.	Sam Houston St.	61-38	.616
5.	Montana St.	66-43	.606
6.	Missouri St.	63-43	.594
	Southern Ill.	63-43	.594
8.	Florida Int'l	70-48	.593
9.	Indiana St.	59-41	.590
10.	Ga. Southern	98-70	.583

2003

	Team	¢Opp. Record	Pct.
1.	Delaware	104-60	.634
2.	Western Ky.	68-46	.596
3.	Princeton	58-40	.592
4.	Wofford	81-57	.587
5.	Idaho St.	58-41	.586
6.	Western Ill.	75-54	.581
7.	Massachusetts	84-62	.575
8.	Portland St.	57-44	.564
9.	Northeastern	66-51	.564
10.	Richmond	67-52	.563

2004

	Team	¢Opp. Record	Pct.
1.	Delaware	84-46	.646
2.	Villanova	73-44	.624
3.	Sam Houston St.	71-45	.612
4.	James Madison	92-59	.609
5.	Northeastern	63-41	.606
6.	William & Mary	85-60	.586
7.	Massachusetts	66-49	.574
8.	Yale	52-40	.565
9.	Jackson St.	57-44	.564
10.	Texas St.	51-40	.560

2005

	Team	¢Opp. Record	Pct.
1.	Appalachian St.	106-51	.675
2.	Princeton	55-37	.598
3.	Furman	83-56	.597
4.	Dartmouth	57-39	.594
5.	Yale	53-37	.589
6.	Richmond	77-54	.588
7.	UNI	81-58	.583
8.	Hofstra	66-48	.579
9.	James Madison	56-41	.577
10.	Harvard	54-40	.575

¢When not playing the team listed.

2006

	Team	¢Opp. Record	Pct.
1.	Youngstown St.	83-51	.619
2.	Northeastern	70-44	.614
3.	Massachusetts	96-63	.603
4.	Yale	55-38	.591
5.	Appalachian St.	85-61	.582
6.	Maine	63-46	.578
7.	Ga. Southern	61-45	.575
8.	Dartmouth	54-41	.568
9.	San Diego	46-35	.568
10.	Harvard	53-41	.563

Annual Most-Improved Teams

Year	Team	$Games Improved	From		To		Coach
1978	Western Ky.	6½	1977	1-8-1	1978	8-2-0	Jimmy Feix
1979	Murray St.	5	1978	4-7-0	1979	*9-2-1	Mike Gottfried
1980	Idaho St.	6	1979	0-11-0	1980	6-5-0	#Dave Kragthorpe
1981	Lafayette	5½	1980	3-7-0	1981	9-2-0	#Bill Russo
1982	Penn	6	1981	1-9-0	1982	7-3-0	Jerry Berndt
1983	North Texas	5½	1982	2-9-0	1983	*8-4-0	Corky Nelson
	Southern Ill.	5½	1982	6-5-0	1983	*13-1-0	Rey Dempsey
1984	Montana St.	9½	1983	1-10-0	1984	*12-2-0	Dave Arnold
1985	Appalachian St.	4	1984	4-7-0	1985	8-3-0	Sparky Woods
	Massachusetts	4	1984	3-8-0	1985	7-4-0	Bob Stull
	West Tex. A&M	4	1984	3-8-0	1985	6-3-1	#Bill Kelly
1986	Morehead St.	6	1985	1-10-0	1986	7-4-0	Bill Baldridge
1987	Weber St.	6	1986	3-8-0	1987	*10-3-0	Mike Price
1988	Stephen F. Austin	5½	1987	3-7-1	1988	*10-3-0	Jim Hess
1989	Yale	4½	1988	3-6-1	1989	8-2-0	Carmen Cozza
1990	Nevada	4	1989	7-4-0	1990	*13-2-0	Chris Ault
	N.C. A&T	4	1989	5-6-0	1990	9-2-0	Bill Hayes
1991	Alcorn St.	5	1990	2-7-0	1991	7-2-1	#Cardell Jones
	Austin Peay	5	1990	0-11-0	1991	5-6-0	#Roy Gregory
	Princeton	5	1990	3-7-0	1991	8-2-0	Steve Tosches
	Southern Ill.	5	1990	2-9-0	1991	7-4-0	Bob Smith
1992	Howard	5	1991	2-9-0	1992	7-4-0	Steve Wilson
	Penn	5	1991	2-8-0	1992	7-3-0	#Al Bagnoli
	Richmond	5	1991	2-9-0	1992	7-4-0	Jim Marshall
	Tennessee Tech	5	1991	2-9-0	1992	7-4-0	Jim Ragland

Year	Team	$Games Improved	From		To		Coach
	Western Caro.	5	1991	2-9-0	1992	7-4-0	Steve Hodgin
1993	Boston U.	8	1992	3-8-0	1993	*12-1-0	Dan Allen
1994	Boise St.	8	1993	3-8-0	1994	*13-2-0	Pokey Allen
1995	Murray St.	5½	1994	5-6-0	1995	*11-1-0	Houston Nutt
1996	Nicholls St.	7½	1995	0-11	1996	*8-4	Darren Barbier
1997	McNeese St.	8	1996	3-8	1997	*13-2	Bobby Keasler
1998	Massachusetts	8	1997	2-9	1998	*12-3	#Mark Whipple
1999	Stephen F. Austin	5	1998	3-8	1999	8-3	#Mike Santiago
2000	Sacred Heart	8	1999	2-9	2000	10-1	#Jim Fleming
2001	Alcorn St.	6	2000	0-11	2001	6-5	Johnny Thomas
	St. Peter's	6	2000	4-7	2001	10-1	Rob Stern
2002	Mississippi Val.	5	2001	0-11	2002	5-6	#Willie Totten
2003	Fla. Atlantic	7½	2002	2-9	2003	*11-3	Howard Schnellenberger
2004	Sam Houston St.	7½	2003	2-9	2004	*11-3	Ron Randleman
2005	Richmond	5	2004	3-8	2005	*9-4	Dave Clawson
	Weber St.	5	2004	1-10	2005	6-5	#Ron McBride
2006	Bucknell	5	2005	1-10	2006	6-5	Tim Landis
	Liberty	5	2005	1-10	2006	6-5	Danny Rocco

*$To determine games improved, add the difference in victories between the two seasons to the difference in losses, then divide by two; ties not counted. *FCS playoff included. #First year as head coach at that college.*

ALL-TIME MOST-IMPROVED TEAMS

Games	Team (Year)
9½	Montana St. (1984)
8	Boston U. (1993)
8	Boise St. (1994)
8	McNeese St. (1997)
8	Massachusetts (1998)
8	Sacred Heart (2000)
7½	Nicholls St. (1996)
7½	Fla. Atlantic (2003)
7½	Sam Houston St. (2004)
7	Lehigh (1998)
7	Delaware (2003)
7	Monmouth (2003)
6½	Western Ky. (1978)
6½	Valparaiso (2003)
6	Idaho St. (1980)
6	Penn (1982)
6	Morehead St. (1986)
6	Weber St. (1987)
6	Colgate (1996)
6	Jacksonville St. (1998)
6	Alcorn St. (2001)
6	St. Peter's (2001)
6	Southern Ill. (2003)

2006 MOST-IMPROVED TEAMS

(Includes Playoff Games)

Team	2005	2006	$Games Improved
Bucknell	1-10	6-5	5
Liberty	1-10	6-5	5
Ark.-Pine Bluff	3-8	8-4	4½
Robert Morris	2-8	7-4	4½
Massachusetts	7-4	13-2	4
Tennessee St.	2-9	6-5	4
Yale	4-6	8-2	4
Jackson St.	2-9	5-5	3½

$To determine games improved, add the difference in victories between the two seasons to the difference in losses, then divide by two.

All-Time Team Won-Lost Records

BY PERCENTAGE (TOP 25)

Team	Yrs.	Won	Lost	Tied	Pct.	Total Games
Coastal Caro.	4	34	12	0	.739	46
Ga. Southern	25	238	84	1	.737	323
Yale	134	838	328	55	.709	1,221
Grambling	64	480	197	15	.704	692
Florida A&M	74	519	223	18	.695	760
Princeton	137	772	351	50	.680	1,173
Harvard	132	781	371	50	.671	1,202
Penn	130	786	445	42	.634	1,273
Tennessee St.	79	490	231	30	@.632	751
Southern U.	85	517	296	25	.632	838
Dayton	99	583	336	26	.631	945
Eastern Ky.	83	512	295	27	.630	834
Appalachian St.	77	504	292	29	.628	825
Jackson St.	61	389	230	13	.626	632
Robert Morris	13	82	49	1	.625	132
Fordham	108	725	428	53	.623	1,206
North Dakota St. (Reclassifying)	110	585	344	34	.625	963
McNeese St.	56	373	225	14	.621	612
South Carolina St.	79	447	271	27	.618	745
Dartmouth	125	640	403	46	.609	1,089
Hofstra	66	387	250	11	.606	648
Albany (N.Y.)	34	208	136	0	.605	344
Delaware	115	618	395	44	.605	1,057
Western Ky.	88	501	322	31	.605	854
Gardner-Webb	7	45	30	0	.600	75

Includes records as senior college only. Bowl and playoff games are included, and each tie game is computed as half won and half lost. Note: Tiebreaker rule began with 1996 season.

@Tennessee State's participation in the 1981 and 1982 FCS championships (1-2 record) voided.

BY VICTORIES

Team	Yrs.	Won	Lost	Tied	Pct.	Total Games
Yale	134	838	328	55	.709	1,221
Penn	130	786	445	42	.634	1,273
Harvard	132	781	371	50	.671	1,202
Princeton	137	772	351	50	.679	1,173
Fordham	108	725	428	53	.623	1,206
Dartmouth	125	640	403	46	.609	1,089
Lafayette	125	626	532	39	.539	1,197
Delware	115	618	395	44	.605	1,057
Lehigh	123	615	544	45	.529	1,204
Cornell	119	607	447	34	.574	1,088
North Dakota St. (Reclassifying)	109	585	344	34	.625	963
Dayton	99	583	336	26	.631	945
UNI	108	571	368	47	.603	986
Colgate	116	571	434	50	.565	1,055
Holy Cross	111	569	457	55	.552	1,081
Brown	121	553	527	40	.512	1,120
Bucknell	121	551	511	51	.518	1,113
Furman	93	537	392	37	.575	966
Drake	113	537	467	29	.534	1,033
Villanova	109	531	431	41	.550	1,003
Massachusetts	124	522	503	51	.509	1,076
Florida A&M	74	519	223	18	.695	760
Butler	117	517	405	35	.559	957
Southern U.	85	516	296	25	.631	837
Eastern Ky.	83	512	295	27	.630	834
William & Mary	111	512	499	37	.506	1,048
Hampton	105	506	358	34	.582	898
South Dakota St. (Reclassifying)	109	506	410	38	.550	954
Appalachian St.	77	504	292	29	.628	825
Western Ky.	88	501	322	31	.605	854

Team	Yrs.	Won	Lost	Tied	Pct.	Total Games
Montana	107	491	458	26	.517	975
Tennessee St.	79	490	231	30	.672	751
Central Ark. (Reclassifying)	95	490	338	42	.587	870
New Hampshire	110	488	411	54	.540	953
Northwestern St.	98	481	384	33	.554	898
Grambling	64	480	197	15	.704	692
Maine	115	469	438	38	.516	945
Western Ill.	103	468	388	37	.545	893
Chattanooga	99	467	464	33	.502	964
UC Davis	88	461	336	33	.575	830
Georgetown	95	459	335	31	.575	825
Texas St.	92	458	372	27	.550	857
Howard	110	458	383	42	.542	883
Richmond	123	455	593	53	.437	1,101
South Carolina St.	79	447	271	27	.618	745
Eastern Ill.	106	447	460	44	.493	951
VMI	116	447	596	43	.431	1,086
Elon	85	446	374	18	.543	838
Wofford	98	442	453	36	.494	931
Citadel	99	440	491	32	.474	963
Idaho St.	102	438	419	20	.511	877
Eastern Wash.	96	436	364	23	.544	823
Murray St.	82	430	355	34	.546	819
Alabama St.	101	429	408	43	.512	880
Illinois St.	107	426	483	65	.471	974
Missouri St.	95	422	422	40	.500	884
Montana St.	103	416	435	34	.489	885
Samford	91	415	421	34	.497	870
N.C. A&T	83	412	354	39	.536	805
Alcorn St.	83	410	295	39	.577	744
Northern Colo.	94	410	380	24	.518	814
Youngstown St.	66	404	262	17	.604	683
Southeast Mo. St.	94	397	429	37	.481	863
Morgan St.	86	394	350	30	.528	774
Davidson	109	394	530	45	.430	969
Jacksonville St.	74	393	295	27	.569	715
Jackson St.	61	389	230	13	.626	632
Hofstra	66	387	250	11	.606	648
Sam Houston St.	90	384	382	47	.501	813
Bethune-Cookman	68	377	256	22	.592	655
Southern Ill.	91	377	458	33	.453	868
Northern Ariz.	82	374	376	22	.499	772
McNeese St.	56	373	225	14	.621	612
Tennessee Tech	85	370	431	31	.463	832
Rhode Island	106	366	505	41	.424	912
Cal Poly	66	359	283	9	.558	651
Columbia	116	358	588	43	.384	989
Wagner	76	352	296	17	.542	665
Valparaiso	86	351	406	24	.465	781
Prairie View	80	347	424	31	.452	802
Stephen F. Austin	80	343	436	30	.443	809
Indiana St.	90	340	430	20	.443	790
Alabama A&M	69	339	289	26	.538	654
Winston-Salem (Reclassifying)	65	334	245	21	.574	600
Ark.-Pine Bluff	75	326	366	42	.473	734
Western Caro.	73	305	405	23	.432	733
Portland St.	60	302	304	10	.498	616
Duquesne	59	296	230	18	.561	544
Morehead St.	77	295	400	22	.427	717
Southeastern La.	57	293	246	17	.542	556
Texas Southern	61	283	328	27	.465	638
Northeastern	71	281	339	17	.454	637
Delaware St.	61	271	318	8	.461	597
Central Conn. St.	68	264	307	22	.464	593
Austin Peay	70	254	440	16	.369	710
Ga. Southern	25	238	84	1	.738	323
Weber St.	45	228	250	3	.477	481
Sacramento St.	53	228	308	8	.426	544
Norfolk St.	46	216	232	7	.482	455
Towson	38	214	178	4	.545	396
Mississippi Val.	54	214	300	11	.418	525
James Madison	34	209	167	3	.555	379
Albany (N.Y.)	34	208	136	0	.605	344
Southern Utah	44	205	230	6	.472	441
Tenn.-Martin	50	205	315	5	.395	525
San Diego	39	200	171	8	.538	379
Liberty	34	164	187	4	.468	355
St. Francis (Pa.)	58	164	313	13	.348	490
Nicholls St.	35	163	219	4	.427	386
Marist	29	126	147	3	.462	276
Iona	29	117	169	3	.410	289
Stony Brook	24	111	118	2	.485	231
Monmouth	13	83	51	0	.619	134
Robert Morris	13	82	49	1	.625	132
St. Peter's	35	82	219	1	.273	302
Sacred Heart	16	68	92	0	.425	160
Charleston So.	16	55	115	0	.324	170
Gardner-Webb	7	45	30	0	.600	75
Coastal Caro.	4	34	11	0	.756	45
Jacksonville	9	34	54	0	.386	88
La Salle	10	33	66	0	.333	99
Savannah St.	7	9	64	0	.123	73

Also includes any participation in major bowl games. Ties computed as half won and half lost. #Northern Arizona's participation in the 1999 FCS championship (0-1 record) voided. %Stephen F. Austin's participation in the 1989 FCS championship (3-1 record) voided. @Tennessee State's participation in the 1981 and 1982 FCS championships (1-2 record) voided.

ALPHABETICAL LISTING

Team	Yrs.	Won	Lost	Tied	Pct.	Total Games
Alabama A&M	69	339	289	26	.538	654
Alabama St.	101	429	408	43	.512	880
Albany (N.Y.)	34	208	136	0	.605	344
Alcorn St.	83	410	295	39	.577	744
Appalachian St.	77	504	292	29	.628	825
Ark.-Pine Bluff	75	326	366	42	.473	734
Austin Peay	70	254	440	16	.369	710
Bethune-Cookman	68	377	256	22	.592	655
Brown	121	553	527	40	.512	1,120
Bucknell	121	551	511	51	.518	1,113
Butler	117	517	405	35	.559	957
UC Davis	66	359	283	9	.558	651
Cal Poly	95	490	338	42	.587	870
Central Ark. (Reclassifying)	95	490	338	42	.587	870
Central Conn. St.	68	264	307	22	.464	593
Charleston So.	16	55	115	0	.324	170
Chattanooga	99	467	464	33	.502	964
Citadel	99	440	491	32	.474	963
Coastal Carolina	4	34	11	0	.756	45
Colgate	116	571	434	50	.565	1,055
Columbia	116	358	588	43	.384	989
Cornell	119	607	447	34	.574	1,088
Dartmouth	125	640	403	46	.609	1,089
Davidson	109	394	530	45	.430	969
Dayton	99	583	336	26	.631	945
Delaware	115	618	395	44	.605	1,057
Delaware St.	61	271	318	8	.461	597
Drake	113	537	467	29	.534	1,033
Duquesne	59	296	230	18	.561	544
Eastern Ill.	106	447	460	44	.493	951
Eastern Ky.	83	512	295	27	.630	834
Eastern Wash.	96	436	364	23	.544	823
Elon	85	446	374	18	.543	838
Florida A&M	74	519	223	18	.695	760
Fordham	108	725	428	53	.623	1,206
Furman	93	537	392	37	.575	966
Gardner-Webb	25	238	84	1	.738	323
Georgetown	7	45	30	0	.600	75
Ga. Southern	95	459	335	31	.575	825
Grambling	64	480	197	15	.704	692
Hampton	105	506	358	34	.582	898
Harvard	132	781	371	50	.671	1,202
Hofstra	66	387	250	11	.606	648
Holy Cross	111	569	457	55	.552	1,081
Howard	110	458	383	42	.542	883
Idaho St.	102	438	419	20	.511	877
Illinois St.	107	426	483	65	.471	974
Indiana St.	90	340	430	20	.443	790
Iona	29	117	169	3	.410	289
Jackson St.	61	389	230	13	.626	632
Jacksonville	9	34	54	0	.386	88
Jacksonville St.	74	393	295	27	.569	715
James Madison	34	209	167	3	.555	379
La Salle	10	33	66	0	.333	99
Lafayette	125	626	532	39	.539	1,197
Lehigh	123	615	544	45	.529	1,204
Liberty	34	164	187	4	.468	355
Maine	115	469	438	38	.516	945
Marist	29	126	147	3	.462	276
Massachusetts	124	522	503	51	.509	1,076
McNeese St.	56	373	225	14	.621	612
Mississippi Val.	54	214	300	11	.418	525
Missouri St.	95	422	422	40	.500	884
Monmouth	13	83	51	0	.619	134
Montana	107	491	458	26	.517	975

Team	Yrs.	Won	Lost	Tied	Pct.	Total Games
Montana St.	103	416	435	34	.489	885
Morehead St.	77	295	400	22	.427	717
Morgan St.	86	394	350	30	.528	774
Murray St.	82	430	355	34	.546	819
New Hampshire	110	488	411	54	.540	953
Nicholls St.	35	163	219	4	.427	386
Norfolk St.	46	216	232	7	.482	455
N.C. A&T	83	412	354	39	.536	805
North Dakota St. (Reclassifying)	109	585	344	34	.625	963
Northeastern	71	281	339	17	.454	637
Northern Ariz.	82	374	376	22	.499	772
Northern Colo.	94	410	380	24	.518	814
UNI	108	571	368	47	.603	986
Northwestern St.	98	481	384	33	.554	898
Penn	130	786	445	42	.634	1,273
Portland St.	60	302	304	10	.498	616
Prairie View	80	347	424	31	.452	802
Princeton	137	772	351	50	.679	1,173
Rhode Island	106	366	505	41	.424	912
Richmond	123	455	593	53	.437	1,101
Robert Morris	13	82	49	1	.625	132
Sacramento St.	53	228	308	8	.426	544
Sacred Heart	16	68	92	0	.425	160
Sam Houston St.	90	384	382	47	.501	813
Samford	91	415	421	34	.497	870
San Diego	39	200	171	8	.538	379
Savannah St.	7	9	64	0	.123	73
South Carolina St.	79	447	271	27	.618	745
South Dakota St. (Reclassifying)	109	506	410	38	.550	954
Southeast Mo. St.	94	397	429	37	.481	863

Team	Yrs.	Won	Lost	Tied	Pct.	Total Games
Southeastern La.	57	293	246	17	.542	556
Southern Ill.	91	377	458	33	.453	868
Southern U.	85	516	296	25	.631	837
Southern Utah	44	205	230	6	.472	441
St. Francis (Pa.)	58	164	313	13	.348	490
Stephen F. Austin	80	343	436	30	.443	809
Stony Brook	24	111	118	2	.485	231
Tenn. Martin	50	205	315	5	.395	525
Tennessee St.	79	490	231	30	.672	751
Tennessee Tech	85	370	431	31	.463	832
Texas Southern	61	283	328	27	.465	638
Texas St.	92	458	372	27	.550	857
Towson	38	214	178	4	.545	396
UC Davis	88	461	336	33	.575	830
Valparaiso	86	351	406	24	.465	781
Villanova	109	531	431	41	.550	1,003
VMI	116	447	596	43	.431	1,086
Wagner	76	352	296	17	.542	665
Weber St.	45	228	250	3	.477	481
Western Caro.	73	305	405	23	.432	733
Western Ill.	103	468	388	37	.545	893
Western Ky.	88	501	322	31	.605	854
William & Mary	111	512	499	37	.506	1,048
Winston-Salem (Reclassifying)	65	334	245	21	.574	600
Wofford	98	442	453	36	.494	931
Yale	134	838	328	55	.709	1,221
Youngstown St.	66	404	262	17	.604	683

Also includes any participation in major bowl games. Ties computed as half won and half lost. #Northern Arizona's participation in the 1999 FCS championship (0-1 record) voided. %Stephen F. Austin's participation in the 1989 FCS championship (3-1 record) voided. @Tennessee State's participation in the 1981 and 1982 FCS championships (1-2 record) voided.

FCS

Records in the 2000s

(2000-01-02-03-04-05-06, Including playoffs)

BY PERCENTAGE

Team	2000 W	2000 L	2001 W	2001 L	2002 W	2002 L	2003 W	2003 L	2004 W	2004 L	2005 W	2005 L	2006 W	2006 L	Total W	Total L	Pct.
Montana	13	2	15	1	11	3	9	4	12	3	8	4	12	2	80	19	.808
Dayton	8	3	10	1	11	1	9	2	7	3	9	1	4	6	58	17	.773
Duquesne	10	1	8	3	11	1	8	3	7	3	7	3	7	3	58	17	.773
Lehigh	12	1	11	1	8	4	8	3	9	3	8	3	6	5	62	20	.756
Coastal Caro.	–	–	–	–	–	–	6	5	10	1	9	2	9	3	34	11	.756
Harvard	5	5	9	0	7	3	7	3	10	0	7	3	7	3	52	17	.754
Penn	7	3	8	1	9	1	10	0	8	2	5	5	5	5	52	17	.754
Grambling	10	2	10	1	11	2	9	3	6	5	11	1	3	8	60	22	.732
Hampton	7	4	7	4	7	5	7	4	10	2	11	1	10	2	59	22	.728
Appalachian St.	10	4	9	4	8	4	7	4	6	5	12	3	14	1	66	25	.725
Furman	9	3	12	3	8	4	6	5	10	3	11	3	8	4	64	25	.719
Ga. Southern	13	2	12	2	11	3	7	4	9	3	8	4	3	8	63	26	.708
San Diego	4	6	6	3	5	5	8	2	7	4	11	1	11	1	52	22	.703
Western Ky.	11	2	8	4	12	3	9	4	9	3	6	5	6	5	61	26	.701
North Dakota St. (Reclassifying)	12	2	7	3	2	8	8	3	8	3	7	4	10	1	54	24	.692
UC Davis	12	1	10	3	9	3	6	4	6	4	6	5	6	5	55	25	.688
Colgate	7	4	7	3	9	3	15	1	7	4	8	4	4	7	57	26	.687
Bethune-Cookman	9	2	6	4	11	2	9	3	6	4	7	4	5	6	53	25	.679
UNI	7	4	11	3	5	6	10	3	7	4	11	4	7	4	58	28	.674
McNeese St.	8	4	8	4	13	2	10	2	4	7	5	4	7	5	55	28	.663
Monmouth	5	6	7	3	2	8	10	2	10	1	6	4	10	2	50	26	.658
Delaware	12	2	4	6	6	6	15	1	9	4	6	5	5	6	57	30	.655
Wofford	7	4	4	7	9	3	12	2	8	3	6	5	7	4	53	28	.654
Alabama A&M	7	5	4	5	8	4	8	4	7	4	9	3	9	3	52	28	.650
Massachusetts	7	4	3	8	8	4	10	3	6	5	7	4	13	2	54	30	.643
Central Ark. (Reclassifying)	3	8	9	3	8	3	5	6	8	3	11	3	8	3	52	29	.642
Youngstown St.	9	3	8	3	7	4	5	7	4	7	8	3	11	3	52	30	.634
Drake	7	4	5	5	5	6	6	6	10	2	6	4	9	2	48	29	.623
South Carolina St.	3	8	6	5	7	5	8	4	9	2	9	2	7	4	49	30	.620
Sacred Heart	10	1	10	0	7	3	6	5	6	4	4	6	2	9	45	28	.616
Eastern Ky.	6	5	8	2	8	4	7	5	6	5	7	4	6	5	48	30	.615
Eastern Ill.	8	4	9	2	8	4	4	8	5	6	9	3	8	5	51	32	.614
Southern U.	6	5	7	4	6	6	12	1	8	4	4	5	4	6	47	31	.603
Gardner-Webb	6	4	6	4	9	1	8	4	5	6	5	6	6	5	45	30	.600
Alabama St.	6	5	8	4	6	6	8	5	10	2	6	5	5	6	49	33	.598
Western Ill.	9	3	5	5	11	2	9	4	4	7	5	6	5	6	48	33	.593
Morehead St.	6	3	6	4	9	3	8	3	6	6	8	4	2	9	45	32	.584
Maine	5	6	9	3	11	3	6	5	5	6	5	6	6	5	47	34	.580
Villanova	5	6	8	3	11	4	7	4	6	5	4	7	6	5	47	34	.580
Portland St.	8	4	7	4	6	5	4	7	7	4	6	5	7	4	45	33	.577

Team	2000 W	2000 L	2001 W	2001 L	2002 W	2002 L	2003 W	2003 L	2004 W	2004 L	2005 W	2005 L	2006 W	2006 L	Total W	Total L	Pct.
James Madison	6	5	2	9	5	7	6	6	13	2	7	4	9	3	48	36	.571
New Hampshire	6	5	4	7	3	8	5	7	10	3	11	2	9	4	48	36	.571
Northwestern St.	6	5	8	4	9	4	6	6	8	4	5	5	4	7	46	35	.568
Winston-Salem (Reclassifying)	9	3	8	3	4	6	7	3	4	6	6	4	4	7	42	32	.568
South Dakota St. (Reclassifying)	6	5	5	6	6	4	7	4	6	5	6	5	7	4	43	33	.566
Yale	7	3	3	6	6	4	6	4	5	5	4	6	8	2	39	30	.565
Robert Morris	10	0	6	3	3	7	6	4	6	5	2	8	7	4	40	31	.563
Florida A&M	9	3	7	4	7	5	6	6	3	8	6	5	7	4	45	35	.563
Southern Ill.	4	7	1	10	4	8	10	2	10	2	9	4	9	4	47	37	.560
Albany (N.Y.)	5	6	7	3	8	4	7	4	4	7	5	6	7	4	43	34	.558
Jacksonville St.	4	6	5	6	5	6	8	4	9	2	6	5	6	5	43	34	.558
Cal Poly	3	8	6	5	3	8	7	4	9	2	9	4	7	4	44	35	.557
Brown	7	3	6	3	2	8	5	5	6	4	9	1	3	7	38	31	.551
Eastern Wash.	6	5	7	4	6	5	6	5	9	4	7	5	3	8	44	36	.550
William & Mary	5	6	8	4	6	5	5	5	11	3	5	6	3	8	43	37	.538
Davidson	10	0	5	4	7	3	3	8	2	7	4	6	6	4	37	32	.536
Sam Houston St.	7	4	10	3	4	7	2	9	11	3	3	7	6	5	43	38	.531
Stephen F. Austin	6	5	6	5	6	5	7	4	6	5	5	6	4	7	40	37	.519
Illinois St.	7	4	2	9	6	5	6	6	4	7	7	4	9	4	41	39	.513
Princeton	3	7	3	6	6	4	2	8	5	5	7	3	9	1	35	34	.507
Central Conn. St.	4	6	2	7	5	6	3	8	8	2	7	4	8	3	37	36	.507
Wagner	6	5	3	6	7	4	6	5	6	5	6	5	4	7	38	37	.507
Texas St.	7	4	4	7	4	7	4	8	5	6	11	3	5	6	40	41	.494
Alcorn St.	0	11	6	5	6	5	7	5	7	4	6	5	6	4	38	39	.494
Towson	7	4	3	7	6	5	6	6	3	8	6	5	7	4	38	39	.494
Hofstra	9	4	9	3	6	6	2	10	5	6	7	4	2	9	40	42	.488
Fordham	3	8	7	4	10	3	9	3	5	6	2	9	3	8	39	41	.488
Northeastern	4	7	5	6	10	3	8	4	5	6	2	9	5	6	39	41	.488
Northern Ariz.	3	8	8	4	6	5	9	4	4	7	3	8	6	5	39	41	.488
Northern Colo.	4	7	7	4	12	2	9	2	2	9	4	7	1	10	39	41	.488
Montana St.	0	11	5	6	7	6	7	6	6	5	7	4	8	5	40	43	.482
Marist	6	4	3	6	7	4	4	6	3	6	7	4	4	7	34	37	.479
Lafayette	2	9	2	8	7	5	5	6	8	4	8	4	6	6	38	42	.475
Tennessee Tech	8	3	7	3	5	7	2	9	6	5	4	7	4	7	36	41	.468
Stony Brook	2	8	3	6	8	2	6	4	3	7	6	5	5	6	33	38	.465
Charleston So.	5	6	5	6	4	8	1	11	5	5	7	4	9	2	36	42	.462
Delaware St.	7	4	5	6	4	8	1	10	4	7	7	4	8	3	36	42	.462
Idaho St.	6	5	4	7	8	3	8	4	3	8	5	6	2	9	36	42	.462
Richmond	10	3	3	8	4	7	2	9	3	8	9	4	6	5	37	44	.457
Ark.-Pine Bluff	6	5	4	7	3	8	4	7	6	3	3	8	8	4	34	42	.447
Bucknell	6	5	6	4	2	9	6	6	7	4	1	10	6	5	34	43	.442
Jackson St.	7	4	7	4	7	4	2	10	4	7	2	9	5	5	34	43	.442
N.C. A&T	8	3	8	3	4	8	10	3	3	8	2	9	0	11	35	45	.438
Samford	4	7	5	5	4	7	7	4	4	7	5	6	3	8	32	44	.421
Western Caro.	4	7	7	4	5	6	5	7	4	7	5	4	2	9	32	44	.421
Nicholls St.	1	10	3	8	7	4	5	6	5	5	6	4	4	7	31	44	.413
Holy Cross	7	4	4	6	4	8	1	11	3	8	6	5	7	4	32	46	.410
Weber St.	7	4	3	8	3	8	8	4	1	10	6	5	4	7	32	46	.410
Southeastern La.	–	–	–	–	–	–	5	7	7	4	4	6	2	9	18	26	.409
Missouri St.	5	6	6	5	4	7	4	7	6	5	4	6	2	9	31	45	.408
Tennessee St.	3	8	8	3	2	10	7	5	4	7	2	9	6	5	32	47	.405
Murray St.	6	5	4	6	7	5	4	8	7	4	2	9	1	10	31	47	.397
Cornell	5	5	2	7	4	6	1	9	4	6	6	4	5	5	27	42	.391
Howard	3	8	2	9	6	5	4	7	6	5	4	7	5	6	30	47	.390
Jacksonville	3	8	5	5	3	7	5	6	3	7	4	4	4	6	27	43	.386
Valparaiso	7	4	3	8	1	10	8	4	5	6	3	8	3	8	30	48	.385
St. Peter's	4	7	10	1	6	5	2	8	3	7	1	9	2	8	28	45	.384
Rhode Island	3	8	8	3	3	9	4	8	4	7	4	7	4	7	30	49	.380
Iona	4	7	4	5	5	6	6	5	2	8	3	7	3	7	27	45	.375
Southeast Mo. St.	3	8	4	7	8	4	5	7	3	8	2	9	4	7	29	50	.367
La Salle	6	4	5	4	2	9	3	8	3	7	4	7	3	7	26	46	.361
Morgan St.	1	10	2	9	7	5	6	5	5	6	2	9	5	6	28	50	.359
Liberty	3	8	3	8	2	9	6	6	6	5	1	10	6	5	27	51	.346
Citadel	2	9	3	7	3	9	6	6	3	7	4	7	5	6	26	51	.338
Georgetown	5	6	3	7	5	6	4	8	3	8	4	7	2	9	26	51	.338
Elon	7	4	2	9	4	7	2	10	3	8	3	8	5	6	26	52	.333
Sacramento St.	7	4	2	9	5	7	2	9	3	8	2	9	4	7	25	53	.321
Southern Utah	7	4	2	9	1	10	4	7	6	5	1	9	3	8	24	52	.316
Texas Southern	8	3	3	7	4	7	5	6	0	11	1	10	3	8	24	52	.316
Mississippi Val.	2	9	0	11	5	6	2	9	3	8	6	5	6	5	24	53	.312
Chattanooga	5	6	3	8	2	10	3	9	2	9	6	5	3	8	24	55	.304
Norfolk St.	3	8	5	6	5	6	1	11	1	8	4	7	4	7	23	53	.303
Tenn.-Martin	2	9	1	10	2	10	2	10	2	9	6	5	9	3	24	56	.300
Austin Peay	2	9	3	7	7	5	4	7	2	9	2	9	3	8	23	54	.299
Columbia	3	7	3	7	1	9	4	6	1	9	2	8	5	5	19	51	.271
VMI	2	9	1	10	6	6	6	6	0	11	3	8	1	10	19	60	.241
Dartmouth	2	8	1	8	3	7	5	5	1	9	2	8	2	8	16	53	.232
Butler	2	8	5	5	4	6	2	9	1	10	0	11	3	8	17	57	.230
Prairie View	1	10	3	7	1	10	1	9	3	8	5	6	3	7	17	57	.230
Indiana St.	1	10	3	8	5	7	3	9	4	7	0	11	1	10	17	62	.215
St. Francis (Pa.)	0	11	0	10	2	8	1	9	3	8	3	8	3	8	12	62	.162
Savannah St.	2	8	2	7	1	9	0	12	2	8	0	11	2	9	9	64	.123

BY VICTORIES

Team	Wins
Montana	80
Appalachian St.	66
Furman	64
Ga. Southern	63
Lehigh	62
Western Ky.	61
Grambling	60
Hampton	59
Dayton	58
Duquesne	58
UNI	58
Colgate	57
Delaware	57
UC Davis	55
McNeese St.	55
North Dakota St. (Reclassifying)	54
Massachusetts	54
Bethune-Cookman	53
Wofford	53
Harvard	52
Penn	52
San Diego	52
Alabama A&M	52
Central Ark. (Reclassifying)	52
Youngstown St.	52
Eastern Ill.	51
Monmouth	50
South Carolina St	49
Alabama St.	49
Drake	48
Eastern Ky.	48
Western Ill.	48
James Madison	48
New Hampshire	48
Southern U.	47
Maine	47
Villanova	47
Southern Ill.	47
Northwestern St.	46
Sacred Heart	45
Gardner-Webb	45
Morehead St.	45
Portland St.	45
Florida A&M	45
Cal Poly	44
Eastern Wash.	44
South Dakota St. (Reclassifying)	43
Albany (N.Y.)	43
Jacksonville St.	43
William & Mary	43
Sam Houston St.	43
Winston-Salem (Reclassifying)	42
Illinois St.	41
Robert Morris	40
Stephen F. Austin	40
Texas St.	40
Hofstra	40
Montana St.	40
Yale	39
Fordham	39
Northeastern	39
Northern Ariz.	39
Northern Colo.	39
Brown	38
Wagner	38
Alcorn St.	38
Towson	38
Lafayette	38
Davidson	37
Central Conn. St.	37
Richmond	37
Tennessee Tech	36
Charleston So.	36
Delaware St.	36
Idaho St.	36
Princeton	35
N.C. A&T	35
Coastal Caro.	34
Marist	34
Ark.-Pine Bluff	34
Bucknell	34
Jackson St.	34
Stony Brook	33
Samford	32
Western Caro.	32
Holy Cross	32
Weber St.	32
Tennessee St.	32
Nicholls St.	31
Missouri St.	31
Murray St.	31
Howard	30
Valparaiso	30
Rhode Island	30
Southeast Mo. St.	29
St. Peter's	28
Morgan St.	28
Cornell	27
Jacksonville	27
Iona	27
Liberty	27
La Salle	26
Citadel	26
Georgetown	26
Elon	26
Sacramento St.	25
Southern Utah	24
Texas Southern	24
Mississippi Val.	24
Chattanooga	24
Tenn.-Martin	24
Norfolk St.	23
Austin Peay	23
Columbia	19
VMI	19
Southeastern La.	18
Butler	17
Prairie View	17
Indiana St.	17
Dartmouth	16
St. Francis (Pa.)	12
Savannah St.	9

FCS

Records in the 1990s

(1990-91-92-93-94-95-96-97-98-99, Playoffs Included; tiebreaker began in 1996)

BY PERCENTAGE

Team	W-L-T	*Pct.
Dayton	92-17-0	.844
Youngstown St.	103-30-2	.770
Montana	93-32-0	.744
Hofstra	81-29-2	.732
Troy	87-32-1	.729
Delaware	88-33-1	.725
UNI	89-34-0	.724
Ga. Southern	92-36-0	.719
Eastern Ky.	85-35-0	.708
Robert Morris	42-18-1	.697
N.C. A&T	79-35-0	.693
Drake	70-31-2	.689
Hampton	78-36-1	.683
McNeese St.	84-39-2	.680
William & Mary	78-37-0	.678
Jackson St.	76-37-1	.671
Appalachian St.	79-40-0	.664
Florida A&M	79-40-0	.664
Ark.-Pine Bluff	56-31-0	.644
Dartmouth	62-35-3	.635
Fairfield	26-15-0	.634
Georgetown	63-37-0	.630
Southern Utah	66-39-0	.629
Penn	62-37-0	.626
Lehigh	70-42-1	.624
Wagner	63-38-0	.624
St. John's (N.Y.)	65-40-0	.619
Marist	61-38-2	.614
Samford	69-43-2	.614
Western Ill.	71-45-1	.611
Albany (N.Y.)	62-40-0	.608
South Fla.	20-13-0	.606
Villanova	69-46-0	.600
Portland St.	70-47-0	.598
New Hampshire	65-45-2	.589
Massachusetts	67-47-1	.587
South Carolina St.	64-45-0	.587
Princeton	58-41-1	.585
Duquesne	59-42-1	.583
Howard	65-47-0	.580
Furman	66-48-1	.578
San Diego	57-42-1	.575
Missouri St.	57-43-1	.569
Monmouth	33-25-0	.569
Elon	61-47-0	.565
James Madison	65-51-0	.560
Grambling	62-50-0	.554
Northern Ariz.	62-50-0	.554
Northwestern St.	63-51-0	.553
Cornell	55-45-0	.550
Eastern Wash.	61-51-0	.545
Liberty	60-50-0	.545
St. Mary's (Cal.)	54-46-1	.540
Wofford	59-51-1	.536
Cal Poly	57-50-1	.532
Weber St.	59-52-0	.532
Stephen F. Austin	58-52-3	.527
Butler	53-48-1	.525
Bucknell	57-52-0	.523
Murray St.	59-54-0	.522
Alabama St.	55-51-4	.518
Connecticut	57-54-0	.514
Jacksonville St.	58-55-1	.513
Eastern Ill.	57-55-1	.509
Stony Brook	50-49-2	.505
Alcorn St.	52-52-3	.500
Davidson	49-49-1	.500
Western Ky.	54-54-0	.500
Illinois St.	55-57-2	.491
Towson	51-53-0	.490
Citadel	55-58-0	.487
Tennessee St.	54-58-0	.482
Alabama A&M	52-57-1	.477
Sam Houston St.	51-56-3	.477
Tennessee Tech	51-58-0	.468
Norfolk St.	48-55-1	.466
Colgate	52-60-1	.465
Cal St. Northridge	49-57-0	.462
Brown	46-54-0	.460
Delaware St.	50-59-0	.459
Yale	45-55-0	.450
East Tenn. St.	50-62-0	.446
Lafayette	47-59-3	.445
Harvard	43-56-1	.435
Sacramento St.	45-59-1	.433
Iona	42-56-1	.429
Richmond	47-63-1	.428
Montana St.	47-63-0	.427
Texas Southern	46-62-1	.427
Valparaiso	43-59-1	.422
Chattanooga	46-64-0	.418
Indiana St.	46-64-0	.418
Morehead St.	44-62-0	.415
Bethune-Cookman	44-64-0	.407
Holy Cross	44-65-1	.405
Mississippi Val.	40-62-3	.395
Western Caro.	43-66-0	.394
Maine	43-67-0	.391
Jacksonville	7-11-0	.389
Southern U.	38-63-1	.377
Southeast Mo. St.	40-70-0	.364
Northeastern	39-70-1	.359
Morgan St.	20-37-0	.351
Canisius	34-64-1	.348
Columbia	33-65-2	.340
Southern Ill.	37-73-0	.336
Idaho St.	36-73-1	.332
Central Conn. St.	31-66-1	.321
Nicholls St.	35-75-1	.320
Rhode Island	34-75-0	.312
St. Francis (Pa.)	29-70-1	.295
Tenn.-Martin	31-79-0	.282
Sacred Heart	23-64-0	.264
La Salle	7-20-0	.259
Texas St.	23-68-0	.253
Siena	22-69-0	.242
St. Peter's	21-70-0	.231
Austin Peay	24-85-0	.220
Charleston So.	19-73-0	.207
VMI	22-88-0	.200
Fordham	20-85-1	.193
Prairie View	3-93-0	.031

**Ties counted as half won and half lost.*

BY VICTORIES

(Minimum 55 Wins; Playoffs Included)

Team	Wins
Youngstown St.	103
Montana	93
Dayton	92
Ga. Southern	92
UNI	89
Delaware	88
Troy	87
Eastern Ky.	85
McNeese St.	84
Hofstra	81
Appalachian St.	79
Florida A&M	79
N.C. A&T	79
Hampton	78
William & Mary	78
Jackson St.	76
Western Ill.	71
Drake	70
Lehigh	70
Portland St.	70

Team	Wins
Samford	69
Villanova	69
Massachusetts	67
Furman	66
Southern Utah	66
Howard	65
James Madison	65
New Hampshire	65
St. John's (N.Y.)	65
South Carolina St.	64
Georgetown	63
Northwestern St.	63
Wagner	63
Albany (N.Y.)	62
Dartmouth	62
Grambling	62
Northern Ariz.	62
Penn	62
Eastern Wash.	61
Elon	61
Marist	61
Liberty	60
Duquesne	59
Murray St.	59
Weber St.	59
Wofford	59
Jacksonville St.	58
Princeton	58
Stephen F. Austin	58
Bucknell	57
Cal Poly	57
Connecticut	57
Eastern Ill.	57
San Diego	57
Missouri St.	57
Ark.-Pine Bluff	56
Alabama St.	55
Citadel	55
Cornell	55
Illinois St.	55

Records in the 1980s

(Playoffs Included)

BY PERCENTAGE

Team	W-L-T	Pct.†
Eastern Ky.	88-24-2	.781
Furman	83-23-4	.773
Ga. Southern	68-22-1	*.753
Jackson St.	71-25-5	.728
Grambling	68-30-3	.688
Nevada	71-35-1	.668
Holy Cross	67-33-2	.667
Tennessee St.	64-32-4	.660
Eastern Ill.	70-36-1	.659
Idaho	69-36-0	.657
Delaware	68-36-0	.654
Middle Tenn.	65-36-0	.644
Boise St.	66-38-0	.635
Texas St.	66-39-0	.629
Murray St.	61-36-2	.626
UNI	64-38-2	.625
Towson	60-36-2	.622
Alcorn St.	56-34-0	.622
La.-Monroe	64-39-0	.621
South Carolina St.	55-34-1	.617

*†Ties counted as half won and half lost. *Includes two nonvarsity seasons and five varsity seasons; varsity record, 55-14-0 for .797.*

National Poll Rankings

Final Poll Leaders

(Released before division championship playoffs before 2001 and released after the championship playoffs beginning with 2001. Both the Sports Network/CSTV and CollegeSportingNews.com polls select final poll leaders after the playoffs.)

Year	Team, Record*	Coach	Record in Championship†
1978	Nevada (10-0-0)	Chris Ault	0-1 Lost in semifinals
1979	Grambling (8-2-0)	Eddie Robinson	Did not compete
1980	Lehigh (9-0-2)	John Whitehead	0-1 Lost in semifinals
1981	Eastern Ky. (9-1-0)	Roy Kidd	2-1 Lost in championship
1982	Eastern Ky. (10-0-0)	Roy Kidd	3-0 Champion
1983	Southern Ill. (10-1-0)	Rey Dempsey	3-0 Champion
1984	Alcorn St. (9-0-0)	Marino Casem	0-1 Lost in quarterfinals
1985	Middle Tenn. (11-0-0)	James Donnelly	0-1 Lost in quarterfinals
1986	Nevada (11-0-0)	Chris Ault	2-1 Lost in semifinals
1987	Holy Cross (11-0-0)	Mark Duffner	Did not compete
1988	Idaho (9-1-0)	Keith Gilbertson	2-1 Lost in semifinals
1989	Ga. Southern (11-0-0)	Erk Russell	4-0 Champion
1990	Middle Tenn. (10-1-0)	James Donnelly	1-1 Lost in quarterfinals
1991	Nevada (11-0-0)	Chris Ault	1-1 Lost in quarterfinals
1992	(tie) Citadel (10-1-0)	Charlie Taaffe	1-1 Lost in quarterfinals
	La.-Monroe (9-2-0)	Dave Roberts	1-1 Lost in quarterfinals
1993	Troy (10-0-1)	Larry Blakeney	2-1 Lost in semifinals
1994	Youngstown St. (10-0-1)	Jim Tressel	4-0 Champion
1995	McNeese St. (11-0-0)	Bobby Keasler	2-1 Lost in semifinals
1996	Marshall (11-0)	Bob Pruett	4-0 Champion
1997	Villanova (11-0)	Andy Talley	1-1 Lost in quarterfinals
1998	Ga. Southern (11-0)	Paul Johnson	3-1 Lost in championship
1999	Tennessee St. (11-0)	L.C. Cole	0-1 Lost in first round
2000	Montana (10-1)	Joe Glenn	3-1 Lost in championship
2001	Montana (11-1)	Joe Glenn	4-0 Champion
2002	Western Ky. (12-3)	Jack Harbaugh	4-0 Champion
2003	Delaware (15-1)	K.C. Keeler	4-0 Champion
2004	James Madison (13-2)	Mickey Matthews	4-0 Champion
2005	Appalachian St. (12-3)	Jerry Moore	4-0 Champion
2006	Appalachian St. (14-1)	Jerry Moore	4-0 Champion

**Final poll record; in some cases, a team had one or two games remaining before the championship playoffs. †Number of teams in the championship: 4 (1978-80); 8 (1981); 12 (1982-85); 16 (1986-present).*

2006 CollegeSportingNews.com Week-By-Week Polls

School	S10	S17	S24	O3	O10	O17	O24	O31	N7	N14	N21	D18
New Hampshire	1	1	1	1	1	7	11	8	13	10	8	6
Appalachian St.	2	2	2	2	2	1	1	1	1	1	1	1
Cal Poly	3	3	7	6	4	4	9	6	9	16	14	14
Montana	4	4	4	4	3	2	3	2	2	2	2	3
Furman	5	6	3	3	12	12	8	11	10	7	7	12
Youngstown St.	6	8	8	8	6	5	10	7	6	5	5	4
Illinois St.	7	5	5	5	5	3	2	9	7	6	11	8
Richmond	8	7	6	7	11	10	13	16	24	-	-	-
Massachusetts	9	9	10	10	9	6	4	3	3	3	3	2
North Dakota St.	10	10	12	11	8	8	6	5	5	4	4	5
Delaware	11	19	16	19	-	-	25	-	-	-	-	-
UNI	12	13	13	13	14	13	7	12	11	21	15	19
McNeese St.	13	11	18	-	-	-	-	-	-	-	22	22
Portland St.	14	16	14	15	-	23	19	-	23	20	20	20
Hampton	15	14	11	12	10	11	18	14	12	9	9	10

School	S10	S17	S24	O3	O10	O17	O24	O31	N7	N14	N21	D18
James Madison	16	17	15	14	13	9	5	4	4	8	6	9
Eastern Ill.	17	18	17	20	16	16	14	20	20	17	16	16
Southern Ill.	18	12	9	9	7	14	20	13	18	11	10	7
UC Davis	19	15	20	16	21	18	17	-	-	-	-	24
Montana St.	20	-	-	-	-	25	24	19	16	14	19	11
Lafayette	21	-	-	-	-	-	-	-	-	-	-	-
Eastern Ky.	22	-	-	-	-	-	-	-	-	-	-	-
Nicholls St.	23	24	-	-	-	-	-	-	-	-	-	-
Idaho St.	24	-	-	-	-	-	-	-	-	-	-	-
Ga. Southern	25	T-21	25	21	-	-	-	-	-	-	-	-
Western Caro.	-	20	-	-	-	-	-	-	-	-	-	-
Towson	-	T-21	19	17	25	-	-	22	-	25	-	-
Harvard	-	23	21	18	15	15	22	18	17	23	-	-
Central Conn. St.	-	25	-	25	20	-	-	-	-	-	-	-
Western Ill.	-	-	22	-	-	-	-	-	-	-	-	-
Albany (N.Y.)	-	-	23	-	-	-	-	-	-	-	-	-
Alabama A&M	-	-	24	23	18	22	-	-	-	-	-	-
Princeton	-	-	-	22	22	21	15	23	22	19	18	17
San Diego	-	-	-	24	19	20	21	15	15	15	17	18
Tenn.-Martin	-	-	-	-	17	17	12	10	8	13	12	13
Maine	-	-	-	-	23	19	16	24	19	22	-	-
Coastal Caro.	-	-	-	-	24	24	23	17	14	12	13	15
South Dakota St.	-	-	-	-	-	-	-	21	21	18	21	21
Charleston So.	-	-	-	-	-	-	-	25	25	-	-	-
Delaware St.	-	-	-	-	-	-	-	-	-	24	-	-
Monmouth	-	-	-	-	-	-	-	-	-	-	23	-
Wofford	-	-	-	-	-	-	-	-	-	-	24	23
Yale	-	-	-	-	-	-	-	-	-	-	25	-
Northern Ariz.	-	-	-	-	-	-	-	-	-	-	-	25

T-Tie for ranking.

2006 Sports Network/CSTV Week-By-Week Polls

School	Pre	S5	S12	S19	S26	O3	O10	O17	O24	O31	N7	N14	N21	D18
Appalachian St.	1	1	2	2	2	2	2	1	1	1	1	1	1	1
New Hampshire	2	2	1	1	1	1	1	7	11	9	13	10	9	6
Montana	3	6	5	5	4	4	3	2	2	2	2	2	2	3
UNI	4	3	12	12	13	14	14	14	7	14	12	20	17	17
Furman	5	4	4	4	3	3	11	12	8	11	10	8	7	12
Cal Poly	6	5	3	3	5	5	4	4	9	6	9	16	15	16
Youngstown St.	7	8	6	8	8	8	6	5	10	7	6	5	5	4
James Madison	8	12	15	17	15	13	13	8	5	4	4	7	6	9
Illinois St.	9	7	7	6	6	6	5	3	3	8	7	6	11	8
Massachusetts	10	9	9	9	9	10	8	6	4	3	3	3	3	2
McNeese St.	11	16	14	13	16	-	-	-	-	-	-	-	22	21
Ga. Southern	12	13	24	19	-	21	-	-	-	-	-	-	-	-
Hampton	13	14	10	11	12	12	12	11	17	13	11	9	8	11
Eastern Ill.	14	20	18	20	20	20	16	17	14	20	20	17	14	15
Richmond	15	10	8	7	7	7	10	10	13	15	25	-	-	-
Delaware	16	15	11	18	17	18	-	-	25	-	-	-	-	-
Southern Ill.	17	17	16	10	10	9	7	13	19	12	14	11	10	7
Texas St.	18	22	23	-	-	-	-	-	-	-	-	-	-	-
North Dakota St.	19	18	17	14	11	11	9	9	6	5	5	4	4	5
Eastern Ky.	20	23	19	24	-	-	-	-	-	-	-	-	-	-
UC Davis	21	19	21	16	18	16	18	18	16	-	-	-	-	-
Montana St.	22	11	20	-	-	-	-	-	24	19	18	15	18	10
Grambling St.	23	-	-	-	-	-	-	-	-	-	-	-	-	-
Nicholls St.	24	24	-	-	-	-	-	-	-	-	-	-	-	-
Coastal Caro.	25	-	-	-	-	-	-	24	22	17	16	13	13	14
Portland St.	-	21	13	15	14	15	25	23	21	25	23	21	20	19
Lafayette	-	25	22	-	-	-	-	-	-	-	-	-	-	-
Alabama A&M	-	-	25	-	-	24	20	20	-	-	-	25	-	-
Towson	-	-	-	21	-	17	22	-	-	21	-	24	-	-
Western Caro.	-	-	-	22	24	-	-	-	-	-	-	-	-	-
Central Conn. St.	-	-	-	23	-	23	19	-	-	-	-	-	-	-
Jacksonville St.	-	-	-	25	-	-	-	-	-	-	-	-	-	-
Western Ill.	-	-	-	-	21	-	-	-	-	-	-	-	-	-
Harvard	-	-	-	-	22	19	15	15	23	18	17	-	-	-
Albany (N.Y.)	-	-	-	-	23	-	-	-	-	-	-	-	-	-
Northern Ariz.	-	-	-	-	25	-	-	-	-	-	-	-	-	-
Tenn.-Martin	-	-	-	-	-	22	17	16	12	10	8	12	12	13
San Diego	-	-	-	-	-	25	21	21	20	16	15	14	16	20
Maine	-	-	-	-	-	-	23	19	15	22	19	22	24	-
Princeton	-	-	-	-	-	-	24	22	18	23	21	18	19	18
Sam Houston St.	-	-	-	-	-	-	-	25	-	-	-	-	-	-
South Dakota St.	-	-	-	-	-	-	-	-	-	24	22	19	21	22
Charleston So.	-	-	-	-	-	-	-	-	-	-	24	-	-	-
Delaware St.	-	-	-	-	-	-	-	-	-	-	-	23	-	-
Wofford	-	-	-	-	-	-	-	-	-	-	-	-	23	23
Central Ark.	-	-	-	-	-	-	-	-	-	-	-	-	25	24
Yale	-	-	-	-	-	-	-	-	-	-	-	-	-	25

Final Regular-Season Polls

1978
(NCAA)

Team
1. Nevada
2. Jackson St.
3. Florida A&M
4. Massachusetts
5. Western Ky.
6. South Carolina St.
7. Northern Ariz.
   Montana St.
   Eastern Ky.
   Lehigh
   Rhode Island

1979
(NCAA)

Team
1. Grambling
2. Murray St.
3. Eastern Ky.
   Lehigh
5. Nevada
6. Alcorn St.
7. Boston U.
8. Jackson St.
9. Montana St.
10. Northern Ariz.
    Southern U.

1980
(NCAA)

Team
1. Lehigh
2. Grambling
3. Eastern Ky.
4. South Carolina St.
5. Western Ky.
6. Delaware
7. Boise St.
8. Northwestern St.
9. Boston U.
10. Connecticut
    Massachusetts
    Murray St.

1981
(NCAA)

Team
1. Eastern Ky.
2. Idaho St.
3. South Carolina St.
4. Jackson St.
5. Boise St.
6. Tennessee St.
7. Delaware
8. Lafayette
9. Murray St.
10. New Hampshire

1982
(NCAA)

Team
1. Eastern Ky.
2. Louisiana Tech
3. Delaware
4. Tennessee St.
5. Eastern Ill.
6. Furman
7. South Carolina St.
8. Jackson St.
9. Colgate
10. Grambling
11. Idaho
12. Northern Ill.
13. Holy Cross
14. Bowling Green
15. Boise St.
16. Western Mich.
17. Chattanooga
18. Northwestern St.
19. Montana
20. Lafayette

1983
(NCAA)

Team
1. Southern Ill.
2. Furman
3. Holy Cross
4. North Texas
5. Indiana St.
6. Eastern Ill.
7. Colgate
8. Eastern Ky.
9. Western Caro.
10. Grambling
11. Nevada
12. Idaho St.
13. Boston U.
    La.-Monroe
15. Jackson St.
16. Middle Tenn.
17. Tennessee St.
18. South Carolina St.
19. Mississippi Val.
20. New Hampshire

1984
(NCAA)

Team
1. Alcorn St.
2. Montana St.
   Rhode Island
4. Boston U.
5. Indiana St.
6. Middle Tenn.
   Mississippi Val.
8. Eastern Ky.
9. Louisiana Tech
10. Arkansas St.
11. New Hampshire
12. Richmond
13. Murray St.
14. Western Caro.
15. Holy Cross
16. Furman
17. Chattanooga
18. UNI
19. Delaware
20. McNeese St.

1985
(NCAA)

Team
1. Middle Tenn.
2. Furman
   Nevada
4. UNI
5. Idaho
6. Arkansas St.
7. Rhode Island
8. Grambling
9. Ga. Southern
10. Akron
11. Eastern Wash.
12. Appalachian St.
    Delaware St.
14. Louisiana Tech
15. Jackson St.
16. William & Mary
17. Murray St.
18. Richmond
19. Eastern Ky.
20. Alcorn St.

1986
(NCAA)

Team
1. Nevada
2. Arkansas St.
3. Eastern Ill.
4. Ga. Southern
5. Holy Cross
6. Appalachian St.
7. Penn
8. William & Mary
9. Jackson St.
10. Eastern Ky.
11. Sam Houston St.
12. Nicholls St.
13. Delaware
14. Tennessee St.
15. Furman
16. Idaho
17. Southern Ill.
18. Murray St.
19. Connecticut
20. N.C. A&T

1987
(NCAA)

Team
1. Holy Cross
2. Appalachian St.
3. La.-Monroe
4. UNI
5. Idaho
6. Ga. Southern
7. Eastern Ky.
8. James Madison
9. Jackson St.
10. Weber St.
11. Western Ky.
12. Arkansas St.
13. Maine
14. Marshall
15. Youngstown St.
16. North Texas
17. Richmond
18. Howard
19. Sam Houston St.
20. Delaware St.

1988
(NCAA)

Team
1. Stephen F. Austin
2. Idaho
3. Ga. Southern
4. Western Ill.
5. Furman
6. Jackson St.
7. Marshall
8. Eastern Ky.
9. Citadel
10. Northwestern St.
11. Massachusetts
12. North Texas
13. Boise St.
14. Florida A&M
    Penn
16. Western Ky.
17. Connecticut
18. Grambling
19. Montana
20. New Hampshire

1989
(NCAA)

Team
1. Ga. Southern
2. Furman
3. Stephen F. Austin
4. Holy Cross
   Idaho
6. Montana
7. Appalachian St.
8. Maine
9. Missouri St.
10. Middle Tenn.
    William & Mary
12. Eastern Ky.
13. Grambling
14. Youngstown St.
15. Eastern Ill.
16. Villanova
17. Jackson St.
18. Connecticut
19. Nevada
20. UNI

1990
(NCAA)

Team
1. Middle Tenn.
2. Youngstown St.
3. Ga. Southern
4. Nevada
5. Eastern Ky.
6. Missouri St.
7. William & Mary
8. Holy Cross
9. Massachusetts
10. Boise St.
11. UNI
12. Furman
13. Idaho
14. La.-Monroe
15. Citadel
16. Jackson St.
17. Dartmouth
18. UCF
19. New Hampshire
    N.C. A&T

1991
(NCAA)

Team
1. Nevada
2. Eastern Ky.
3. Holy Cross
4. UNI
5. Alabama St.
6. Delaware
7. Villanova
8. Marshall
9. Middle Tenn.
10. Samford
11. New Hampshire
12. Sam Houston St.
13. Youngstown St.
14. Western Ill.
15. Weber St.
16. James Madison
17. Appalachian St.
18. La.-Monroe
19. McNeese St.
20. Citadel
    Furman

1992
(NCAA)

Team
1. Citadel
   La.-Monroe
3. UNI
4. Middle Tenn.
5. Idaho
6. Marshall
7. Youngstown St.
8. Delaware
9. Samford
10. Villanova
11. McNeese St.
12. Eastern Ky.
13. William & Mary
14. Eastern Wash.
15. Florida A&M
16. Appalachian St.
17. N.C. A&T
18. Alcorn St.
19. Liberty
20. Western Ill.

1993
(Sports Network)

Team
1. Troy
2. Ga. Southern
3. Montana
4. La.-Monroe
5. McNeese St.
6. Boston U.
7. Youngstown St.
8. Howard
9. Marshall
10. William & Mary
11. Idaho
12. UCF
13. UNI
14. Stephen F. Austin
15. Southern U.
16. Penn
17. Eastern Ky.
18. Delaware
19. Western Ky.
20. Eastern Wash.
21. N.C. A&T
22. Tennessee Tech
23. Alcorn St.
24. Towson
25. Massachusetts

1994
(Sports Network)

Team
1. Youngstown St.
2. Marshall
3. Boise St.
4. Eastern Ky.
5. McNeese St.
6. Idaho
7. Grambling
8. Montana
9. Boston U.
10. Troy
11. UNI
12. New Hampshire
13. James Madison
14. Penn
15. Alcorn St.
16. Middle Tenn.
17. Appalachian St.
18. North Texas
19. William & Mary
20. UCF
21. Stephen F. Austin
22. South Carolina St.
23. Hofstra
24. Western Ill.
25. Northern Ariz.

1995
(Sports Network)

Team
1. McNeese St.
2. Appalachian St.
3. Troy
4. Murray St.
5. Stephen F. Austin
6. Marshall
7. Delaware
8. Montana
9. Hofstra
10. Eastern Ky.
11. Southern U.
12. Eastern Ill.
13. James Madison
14. Jackson St.
15. Ga. Southern
16. Florida A&M
17. Idaho
18. UNI
19. William & Mary
20. Richmond
21. Boise St.
22. Northern Ariz.
23. Connecticut
24. Indiana St.
25. Middle Tenn.

1996
(Sports Network)

Team
1. Marshall
2. Montana
3. UNI
4. Murray St.
5. Troy
6. Northern Ariz.
7. William & Mary
8. Jackson St.
   (tie) East Tenn. St.
10. Western Ill.
11. Delaware
12. Florida A&M
13. Furman
14. Villanova
15. Youngstown St.
16. Eastern Ill.
17. Dartmouth
18. New Hampshire
19. Nicholls St.
20. Howard
21. Missouri St.
22. Stephen F. Austin
23. James Madison
24. Dayton
25. Appalachian St.

1997
(Sports Network)

Team
1. Villanova
2. Western Ill.
3. Delaware
4. Eastern Wash.
5. Western Ky.
6. McNeese St.
7. Hampton
8. Ga. Southern
9. Youngstown St.
10. Florida A&M
11. Montana
12. Southern U.
13. Jackson St.
14. Hofstra
15. Eastern Ky.
16. Cal Poly
17. Northwestern St.
18. Stephen F. Austin
19. South Carolina St.
20. Liberty
21. Eastern Ill.
22. Appalachian St.
23. Dayton
24. Northeastern
25. Colgate

1997
(USA Today/ESPN)

Team
1. Youngstown St.
2. McNeese St.
3. Delaware
4. Eastern Wash.
5. Villanova
6. Western Ill.
7. Western Ky.
8. Ga. Southern
9. Montana
10. Hampton
11. Southern U.
12. Florida A&M
13. Jackson St.
14. Northwestern St.
15. Eastern Ky.
16. Hofstra
17. Cal Poly
18. Stephen F. Austin
19. Liberty
20. South Carolina St.
21. Colgate
22. Eastern Ill.
23. Appalachian St.
24. Northeastern
25. Dayton

1998
(USA Today/ESPN)
(After Playoffs)

Team
1. Massachusetts
2. Ga. Southern

Team
3. Northwestern St.
4. Western Ill.
5. Florida A&M
6. Appalachian St.
7. Connecticut
8. McNeese St.
9. Richmond
10. Hampton
11. Troy
12. Lehigh
13. Tennessee St.
14. Montana
15. Illinois St.
16. Southern U.
17. South Fla.
18. Hofstra
19. William & Mary
20. Murray St.
21. Colgate
22. Western Ky.
23. Bethune-Cookman
24. Delaware
25. Montana St.

1998

(Sports Network)

Team
1. Ga. Southern
2. Northwestern St.
3. Florida A&M
4. Western Ill.
5. Richmond
6. McNeese St.
7. Appalachian St.
8. Connecticut
9. Hampton
10. Tennessee St.
11. Troy
12. Massachusetts
13. Lehigh
14. Montana
15. Southern U.
16. William & Mary
17. Western Ky.
18. Hofstra
19. South Fla.
20. Bethune-Cookman
21. Illinois St.
22. Delaware
23. Murray St.
24. Montana St.
25. UNI

1999

(USA Today/ESPN)

Team (Record)
1. Tennessee St. (11-0)
2. Ga. Southern (9-2)
3. Appalachian St. (8-2)
4. Hofstra (10-1)
5. Illinois St. (9-2)
6. Troy (10-1)
7. Montana (9-2)
8. Furman (9-2)
9. Youngstown St. (9-2)
10. Southern U. (9-1)
11. Massachusetts (8-3)
12. James Madison (8-3)
13. Lehigh (10-1)
14. Jackson St. (9-2)
15. Florida A&M (8-3)
16. N.C. A&T (10-1)
17. UNI (8-3)
18. Colgate (10-1)
19. Northern Ariz. (8-3)
20. Elon (9-2)
21. Portland St. (8-3)
22. Stephen F. Austin (8-3)
23. South Fla. (7-4)
24. Southern Utah (8-3)
25. Villanova (7-4)

1999

(Sports Network) (After Playoffs)

Team (Record)
1. Ga. Southern (13-2)
2. Youngstown St. (12-3)
3. Illinois St. (11-3)
4. Florida A&M (10-4)
5. Hofstra (11-2)
6. Troy (11-2)
7. Massachusetts (9-4)
8. Montana (9-3)
9. Appalachian St. (9-3)
(tie) N.C. A&T (11-2)
11. Tennessee St. (11-1)
12. Furman (9-3)
13. James Madison (8-4)
14. Lehigh (10-2)
15. UNI (8-3)
16. Northern Ariz. (8-4)
17. Southern U. (11-2)
18. Colgate (10-2)
19. Jackson St. (9-3)
20. Portland St. (8-3)
21. Elon (9-2)
22. Stephen F. Austin (8-3)
23. South Fla. (7-4)
24. Villanova (7-4)
25. Brown (9-1)

2000

(USA Today/ESPN)

Team (Record)
1. Montana (9-1)
2. Delaware (9-1)
3. Troy (8-2)
4. Ga. Southern (9-2)
5. Furman (8-2)
6. Western Ill. (8-2)
7. Western Ky. (9-1)
8. Richmond (8-2)
9. Youngstown St. (8-2)
10. Appalachian St. (7-3)
11. Lehigh (10-0)
12. Hofstra (7-3)
13. Grambling (9-1)
14. Florida A&M (8-2)
15. Portland St. (7-3)
16. McNeese St. (7-3)
17. Bethune-Cookman (9-1)
18. UNI (6-3)
19. Weber St. (7-4)
20. N.C. A&T (7-3)
21. Sam Houston St. (7-3)
22. Eastern Ill. (7-3)
23. James Madison (6-4)
24. Tennessee Tech (7-3)
25. Northwestern St. (6-4)

2000

(Sports Network) (After Playoffs)

Team (Record)
1. Ga. Southern (13-2)
2. Montana (13-2)
3. Delaware (12-2)
4. Appalachian St. (10-4)
5. Western Ky. (11-2)
6. Richmond (10-3)
7. Hofstra (9-4)
8. Lehigh (12-1)
9. Troy (9-3)
10. Furman (9-3)
11. Youngstown St. (9-3)
12. Western Ill. (9-3)
13. Grambling (10-2)
14. Florida A&M (9-3)
15. Portland St. (8-4)
16. McNeese St. (8-4)
17. Eastern Ill. (8-4)

Team (Record)
18. Weber St. (7-4)
19. UNI (7-4)
20. Bethune-Cookman (9-2)
21. N.C. A&T (8-3)
22. Tennessee Tech (8-3)
23. Wofford (7-4)
24. Illinois St. (7-4)
25. Texas St. (7-4)

2001

(USA Today/ESPN) (After Playoffs)

Team (Record)
1. Montana (15-1)
2. Furman (12-3)
3. Ga. Southern (12-2)
4. UNI (11-3)
5. Lehigh (11-1)
6. Appalachian St. (9-4)
7. Hofstra (9-3)
8. Sam Houston St. (10-3)
9. Eastern Ill. (9-2)
10. Western Ky. (8-4)
11. Grambling (10-1)
12. Maine (9-3)
13. McNeese St. (8-4)
14. Northwestern St. (8-4)
15. Northern Ariz. (8-4)
16. Youngstown St. (8-3)
17. William & Mary (8-4)
18. Eastern Ky. (8-2)
19. Villanova (8-3)
20. Rhode Island (8-3)
21. Harvard (9-0)
22. Florida A&M (7-4)
23. Tennessee Tech (7-3)
24. Penn (8-1)
25. Portland St. (7-4)

2001

(Sports Network) (After Playoffs)

Team (Record)
1. Montana (15-1)
2. Furman (12-3)
3. Ga. Southern (12-2)
4. UNI (11-3)
5. Lehigh (11-1)
6. Appalachian St. (9-4)
7. Sam Houston St. (10-3)
8. Grambling (10-1)
9. Eastern Ill. (9-2)
10. Maine (9-3)
11. Hofstra (9-3)
12. Western Ky. (8-4)
13. McNeese St. (8-4)
14. Northwestern St. (8-4)
15. Youngstown St. (8-3)
16. Northern Ariz. (8-4)
17. William & Mary (8-4)
18. Eastern Ky. (8-2)
19. Harvard (9-0)
20. Villanova (8-3)
21. Rhode Island (8-3)
22. Florida A&M (7-4)
23. Tennessee Tech (7-3)
24. Penn (8-1)
25. Tennessee St. (8-3)

2002

(USA Today/ESPN) (After Playoffs)

Team (Record)
1. Western Ky. (12-3)
2. McNeese St. (13-2)
3. Ga. Southern (11-3)
4. Villanova (11-4)
5. Western Ill. (11-2)
6. Maine (11-3)
(tie) Montana (11-3)

Team (Record)
8. Grambling (11-2)
9. Furman (8-4)
10. Northeastern (10-3)
11. Wofford (9-3)
12. Bethune-Cookman (11-2)
(tie) Eastern Ill. (8-4)
14. Appalachian St. (8-4)
15. Fordham (10-3)
16. Northwestern St. (9-4)
17. Idaho St. (8-3)
(tie) Penn (9-1)
19. Montana St. (7-6)
20. Eastern Ky. (8-4)
21. Nicholls St. (7-4)
22. Murray St. (7-5)
23. Southeast Mo. St. (8-4)
24. Gardner-Webb (9-1)
25. Colgate (9-3)

2002

(Sports Network) (After Playoffs)

Team (Record)
1. Western Ky. (12-3)
2. McNeese St. (13-2)
3. Ga. Southern (11-3)
4. Villanova (11-4)
5. Western Ill. (11-2)
6. Maine (11-3)
7. Montana (11-3)
8. Grambling (11-2)
9. Furman (8-4)
10. Appalachian St. (8-4)
11. Northeastern (10-3)
12. Fordham (10-3)
13. Eastern Ill. (8-4)
14. Wofford (9-3)
15. Bethune-Cookman (11-2)
16. Northwestern St. (9-4)
17. Penn (9-1)
18. Idaho St. (8-3)
19. Montana St. (7-6)
20. Murray St. (7-5)
21. Eastern Ky. (8-4)
22. Gardner-Webb (9-1)
23. Nicholls St. (7-4)
24. Southeast Mo. St. (8-4)
25. Colgate (9-3)

2003

(USA Today/ESPN) (After Playoffs)

Team (Record)
1. Delaware (15-1)
2. Colgate (15-1)
3. Wofford (12-2)
4. Fla. Atlantic (11-3)
5. Western Ill. (9-4)
6. UNI (10-3)
7. McNeese St. (10-2)
8. Western Ky. (9-4)
9. Northern Ariz. (9-4)
10. Southern Ill. (10-2)
11. Massachusetts (10-3)
12. Penn (10-0)
13. Montana (9-4)
14. Southern U. (12-1)
15. Bethune-Cookman (9-3)
16. N.C. A&T (10-3)
17. Grambling (9-3)
18. Jacksonville St. (8-4)
19. Northeastern (8-4)
20. Northern Colo. (9-2)
21. Montana St. (7-6)
22. Idaho St. (8-4)

Team (Record)
23. Villanova (7-4)
24. Lehigh (8-3)
25. Ga. Southern (7-4)

2003

(Sports Network/ CSTV) (After Playoffs)

Team (Record)
1. Delaware (15-1)
2. Colgate (15-1)
3. Wofford (12-2)
4. Fla. Atlantic (11-3)
5. UNI (10-3)
6. Western Ill. (9-4)
7. Western Ky. (9-4)
8. McNeese St. (10-2)
9. Southern Ill. (10-2)
10. Northern Ariz. (9-4)
11. Massachusetts (10-3)
12. Penn (10-0)
13. Southern U. (12-1)
14. Montana (9-4)
15. Bethune-Cookman (9-3)
16. N.C. A&T (10-3)
17. Grambling (9-3)
18. Jacksonville St. (8-4)
19. Northern Colo. (9-2)
20. Northeastern (8-4)
21. Montana St. (7-6)
22. Idaho St. (8-4)
23. Lehigh (8-3)
24. Ga. Southern (7-4)
25. Villanova (7-4)

2004

(USA Today/ESPN) (After Playoffs)

Team (Record)
1. James Madison (13-2)
2. Montana (12-3)
3. William & Mary (11-3)
4. Sam Houston St. (11-3)
5. Furman (10-3)
6. New Hampshire (10-3)
7. Eastern Wash. (9-4)
8. Delaware (9-4)
9. Southern Ill. (10-2)
10. Ga. Southern (9-3)
11. Western Ky. (9-3)
12. Hampton (10-2)
13. Harvard (10-0)
14. Lehigh (9-3)
15. Cal Poly (9-2)
16. Jacksonville St. (9-2)
17. Northwestern St. (8-4)
18. Wofford (8-3)
19. Lafayette (8-4)
20. Alabama St. (10-2)
21. Penn (8-2)
22. South Carolina St. (9-2)
23. North Dakota St. (8-3)
24. Coastal Caro. (10-1)
25. UNI (7-4)

2004

(Sports Network/ CSTV) (After Playoffs)

Team (Record)
1. James Madison (13-2)
2. Montana (12-3)
3. William & Mary (11-3)
4. Sam Houston St. (11-3)
5. Furman (10-3)
6. New Hampshire (10-3)

Team (Record)
7. Delaware (9-4)
8. Eastern Wash. (9-4)
9. Southern Ill. (10-2)
10. Ga. Southern (9-3)
11. Western Ky. (9-3)
12. Hampton (10-2)
13. Harvard (10-0)
14. Jacksonville St. (9-2)
15. Lehigh (9-3)
16. Cal Poly (9-2)
17. Northwestern St. (8-4)
18. Wofford (8-3)
19. Lafayette (8-4)
20. Alabama St. (10-2)
21. Penn (8-2)
22. South Carolina St. (9-2)
23. North Dakota St. (8-3)
24. Coastal Caro. (10-1)
25. UNI (7-4)

2005

(USA Today/ESPN) (After Playoffs)

Team (Record)
1. Appalachian St. (12-3)
2. UNI (11-4)
3. Furman (11-3)
4. Texas St. (11-3)
5. New Hampshire (11-2)
6. Cal Poly (9-4)
7. Southern Ill. (9-4)
8. Richmond (9-4)
9. Ga. Southern (8-4)
10. Hampton (11-1)
11. Montana (8-4)
12. Grambling (11-1)
13. Eastern Wash. (7-5)
14. Youngstown St. (8-3)
15. Eastern Ill. (9-3)
16. Nicholls St. (6-4)
17. Montana St. (7-4)
18. Brown (9-1)
19. South Carolina St. (9-2)
20. Lafayette (8-4)
21. Massachusetts (7-4)
22. Colgate (8-4)
23. Coastal Caro. (9-2)
24. Illinois St. (7-4)
25. Lehigh (8-3)

2005

(Sports Network/ CSTV) (After Playoffs)

Team (Record)
1. Appalachian St. (12-3)
2. UNI (11-4)
3. Furman (11-3)
4. Texas St. (11-3)
5. New Hampshire (11-2)
6. Cal Poly (9-4)
7. Southern Ill. (9-4)
8. Richmond (9-4)
9. Ga. Southern (8-4)
10. Hampton (11-1)
11. Grambling (11-1)
12. Montana (8-4)
13. Eastern Wash. (7-5)
14. Youngstown St. (8-3)
15. Brown (9-1)
16. Eastern Ill. (9-3)
17. Nicholls St. (6-4)
18. Montana St. (7-4)
19. Massachusetts (7-4)
20. South Carolina St. (9-2)
21. Lafayette (8-4)
22. Illinois St. (7-4)
23. Colgate (8-4)
24. Coastal Caro. (9-2
25. James Madison (7-4)

2006
(CollegeSporting News.com)
(After Playoffs)

Team (Record)	Team (Record)	Team (Record)
1. Appalachian St. (14-1)	6. New Hampshire (9-4)	16. Eastern Ill. (8-5)
2. Massachusetts (13-2)	7. Southern Ill. (9-4)	17. Princeton (9-1)
3. Montana (12-2)	8. Illinois St. (9-4)	18. San Diego (11-1)
4. Youngstown St. (11-3)	9. James Madison (9-3)	19. UNI (7-4)
5. North Dakota St. (10-1)	10. Hampton (10-2)	20. Portland St. (7-4)
	11. Montana St. (8-5)	21. South Dakota St. (7-4)
	12. Furman (8-4)	22. McNeese St. (7-5)
	13. Tenn.-Martin (9-3)	23. Wofford (7-4)
	14. Cal Poly (7-4)	24. UC Davis (6-5)
	15. Coastal Caro. (9-3)	25. Northern Ariz. (6-5)

2006
(Sports Network/ CSTV)
(After Playoffs)

Team (Record)	Team (Record)	Team (Record)
1. Appalachian St. (14-1)	6. New Hampshire (9-4)	16. Cal Poly (7-4)
2. Massachusetts (13-2)	7. Southern Ill. (9-4)	17. UNI (7-4)
3. Montana (12-2)	8. Illinois St. (9-4)	18. Princeton (9-1)
4. Youngstown St. (11-3)	9. James Madison (9-3)	19. Portland St. (7-4)
5. North Dakota St. (10-1)	10. Montana St. (8-5)	20. San Diego (11-1)
	11. Hampton (10-2)	21. McNeese St. (7-5)
	12. Furman (8-4)	22. South Dakota St. (7-4)
	13. Tenn.-Martin (9-3)	23. Wofford (7-4)
	14. Coastal Caro. (9-3)	24. Central Ark. (8-3)
	15. Eastern Ill. (8-5)	25. Yale (8-2)

Undefeated, Untied Teams

Regular-season games only, from 1978. Subsequent loss in FCS championship is indicated by (††).

Year	Team	Wins
1978	Nevada	††11
1979	(None)	
1980	(None)	
1981	(None)	
1982	*Eastern Ky.	10
1983	(None)	
1984	Tennessee St.	11
	Alcorn St.	††9
1985	Middle Tenn.	††11
1986	Nevada	††11
	Penn	10
1987	Holy Cross	11
1988	(None)	
1989	*Ga. Southern	11
1990	Youngstown St.	††11
1991	Holy Cross	11
	Nevada	††11
1992	(None)	
1993	Boston U.	††11
	Howard	††11
	Penn	10
1994	Penn	9
1995	Appalachian St.	††11
	McNeese St.	††11
	Murray St.	††11
	Troy	††11
1996	Dartmouth	10
	Dayton	11
	*Marshall	11
	Montana	††11
1997	Villanova	††11
1998	Ga. Southern	††11
	Lehigh	††11
1999	(None)	
2000	Davidson	10
	Robert Morris	10
2001	Sacred Heart	10
	Harvard	9
2002	(None)	
2003	Penn	10
2004	Harvard	10
2005	Hampton	††11

**Won FCS championship.*

The Spoilers

(From 1978 Season)

Following is a list of the spoilers of FCS teams that lost their perfect (undefeated, untied) record in their **season-ending** game, including the FCS championship playoffs. An asterisk (*) indicates a championship playoff game and a dagger (†) indicates the home team in a regular-season game.

Date	Spoiler	Victim	Score
12-9-78	*Massachusetts	Nevada	44-21
11-15-80	†Grambling	South Carolina St.	26-3
11-22-80	†Murray St.	Western Ky.	49-0
12-1-84	*Louisiana Tech	Alcorn St.	44-21
12-7-85	*Ga. Southern	Middle Tenn.	28-21
11-22-86	Boston College	†Holy Cross	56-26
12-19-86	*Ga. Southern	Nevada	48-38
11-19-88	*Cornell	Penn	19-6
11-24-90	*UCF	Youngstown St.	20-17
12-7-91	*Youngstown St.	Nevada	30-28
11-27-93	*Marshall	Howard	28-14
12-4-93	*Idaho	Boston U.	21-14
11-25-95	*Ga. Southern	Troy	24-21
11-25-95	*UNI	Murray St.	35-34
12-2-95	*Stephen F. Austin	Appalachian St.	27-17
12-9-95	*Marshall	McNeese St.	25-13
11-23-96	Robert Morris	Duquesne	28-26
12-21-96	*Marshall	Montana	49-29
11-22-97	†Colgate	Bucknell	48-14
12-6-97	*Youngstown St.	Villanova	37-34
12-5-98	*Massachusetts	Lehigh	27-21
12-19-98	*Massachusetts	Ga. Southern	55-43
11-27-99	*N.C. A&T	Tennessee St.	24-10
12-2-00	*Delaware	Lehigh	47-22
12-8-01	*Furman	Lehigh	34-17
12-19-03	*Delaware	Colgate	40-0
11-26-05	*Richmond	Hampton	38-10

Streaks and Rivalries

Because FCS began in 1978, only those streaks from the period (1978-present) are listed. Only schools that have been FCS members for five years are eligible for inclusion.

Longest Winning Streaks

(From 1978; Includes Playoff Games)

Wins	Team	Year(s)	Ended by	Score
24	Montana	2001-02	Eastern Wash.	21-30
24	Penn	1992-95	Columbia	14-24
21	Colgate	2002-03	Delaware	0-40
21	Montana	1995-96	Marshall	29-49
20	Dayton	1996-97	Cal Poly	24-44
20	Holy Cross	1990-92	Army	7-17
19	Duquesne	1995-96	Robert Morris	26-28
18	Davidson	1999-01	Jacksonville	3-45
18	Eastern Ky.	1982-83	Western Ky.	10-10
18	San Diego	2005-06	UC Davis	27-37
17	Penn	2002-04	Villanova	13-16
17	Robert Morris	1999-00	Buffalo	27-33
16	Ga. Southern	1989-90	Middle Tenn.	13-16
15	Dartmouth	1996-97	Lehigh	26-46
15	Marshall	1996	Moved to FBS	
14	Appalachian St.	2006	current	
14	Charleston So.	2005-06	Liberty	20-34
14	Ga. Southern	1998	Massachusetts	43-55
14	Youngstown St.	1994	Kent St.	14-17
14	Delaware	1979-80	Lehigh	20-27
13	Montana	2000	Ga. Southern	25-27
13	Fairfield	1998-99	Holy Cross	23-24
13	Lehigh	1997-98	Massachusetts	21-27
13	McNeese St.	1995	Marshall	13-25
13	Holy Cross	1988-89	Army	9-45
13	Nevada	1986	Ga. Southern	38-48
13	Tennessee St.	1983-85	Western Ky.	17-22
13	Eastern Ill.	1978-79	Western Ill.	7-10
12	Wofford	2003	Delaware	9-24
12	Harvard	2001-02	Lehigh	35-36
12	Sacred Heart	2000-02	Marist	27-38
12	Lehigh	2000	Delaware	22-47
12	Bucknell	1996-97	Colgate	14-48
12	Appalachian St.	1995	Stephen F. Austin	17-27
12	Nevada	1989-90	Boise St.	14-30
12	Furman	1989	Stephen F. Austin	19-21
12	Holy Cross	1987-88	Army	3-23
12	Southern Ill.	1982-83	Wichita St.	6-28
12	Florida A&M	1978-79	Tennessee St.	3-20

Longest Unbeaten Streaks

(From 1978; Includes Playoff Games and Ties)

No.	Wins	Ties	Team	Year(s)	Ended by
24	24	0	Montana	2001-02	Eastern Wash.
24	24	0	Penn	1992-95	Columbia
22	21	1	Dartmouth	1995-97	Lehigh
21	21	0	Colgate	2002-03	Delaware
21	21	0	Montana	1995-96	Marshall
20	20	0	Dayton	1996-97	Cal Poly
20	20	0	Holy Cross	1990-92	Army
20	19	1	Youngstown St.	1993-94	Kent St.
19	19	0	Duquesne	1995-96	Robert Morris
19	18	1	Eastern Ky.	1982-83	Murray St.
18	18	0	Davidson	1999-01	Jacksonville
17	17	0	Penn	2002-04	Villanova
17	17	0	Robert Morris	1999-00	Buffalo
17	16	1	Alabama St.	1990-92	Alcorn St.
17	16	1	Grambling	1977-78	Florida A&M
16	16	0	Ga. Southern	1989-90	Middle Tenn.
15	15	0	Marshall	1996	Moved to FBS
15	14	1	Delaware	1994-95	Navy
14	14	0	Appalachian St.	2006	current
14	14	0	Ga. Southern	1998	Massachusetts
13	13	0	Montana	2000	Ga. Southern
13	13	0	Fairfield	1998-99	Holy Cross
13	13	0	Lehigh	1997-98	Massachusetts
13	13	0	McNeese St.	1995	Marshall
13	13	0	Holy Cross	1988-89	Army
13	13	0	Nevada	1986	Ga. Southern
13	13	0	Tennessee St.	1983-85	Western Ky.
13	13	0	Eastern Ill.	1978-79	Western Ill.
13	12	1	Mississippi Val.	1983-84	Alcorn St.
13	12	1	Eastern Ill.	1981-82	Tennessee St.
12	12	0	Wofford	2003	Delaware
12	12	0	Harvard	2001-02	Lehigh
12	12	0	Sacred Heart	2000-02	Marist
12	12	0	Lehigh	2000	Delaware
12	12	0	Bucknell	1996-97	Colgate
12	12	0	Appalachian St.	1995	Stephen F. Austin
12	12	0	Nevada	1989-90	Boise St.
12	12	0	Furman	1989	Stephen F. Austin
12	12	0	Holy Cross	1987-88	Army
12	12	0	Southern Ill.	1982-83	Wichita St.
12	12	0	Florida A&M	1978-79	Tennessee St.
12	11	1	Tennessee St.	1985-86	Alabama St.
12	11	1	Tennessee St.	1981-83	Jackson St.

Longest Home Winning Streaks

(From 1978; Includes Playoff Games)

Wins	Team	Years	Ended by
39	Ga. Southern	1997-01	Furman
38	Ga. Southern	1985-90	Eastern Ky.
34	Eastern Ky.	1978-84	Western Ky.
31	Middle Tenn.	1987-94	Eastern Ky.
30	Montana	1994-97	Eastern Wash.
27	Appalachian St.	2002-06	Current
25	Montana	2000-02	Montana St.
25	UNI	1989-92	Youngstown St.
23	UNI	1983-87	Montana
22	Nevada	1989-91	Youngstown St.
20	Arkansas St.	1984-87	Northwestern St.
19	San Diego	2004-06	current
19	Penn	2000-03	Villanova
17	Colgate	2003-05	Central Conn. St.
16	Penn	1992-95	Princeton
16	Texas St.	1981-83	Central St.
16	Citadel	1980-82	East Tenn. St.
15	Davidson	1999-02	Morehead St.
15	Holy Cross	1987-89	Massachusetts

Longest Losing Streaks

(From 1978; Can Include Playoff Games)

Losses	Team	Years	Ended Against
80	Prairie View	1989-98	Langston
44	Columbia	1983-88	Princeton
30	St. Francis (Pa.)	1999-02	La Salle
24	Canisius	1999-01	Siena
19	Indiana St.	2004-06	Missouri St.
19	Delaware St.	1997-99	Norfolk St.
19	Charleston So.	1993-95	Morehead St.
19	Idaho St.	1978-80	Portland St.
18	Davidson	1985-87	Wofford
17	Butler	2004-05	Hanover
17	Tennessee Tech	1984-85	Morehead St.
16	Colgate	1994-96	Brown
16	Siena	1994-96	Iona
16	Middle Tenn.	1978-79	Tennessee Tech
15	Savannah St.	2003-04	Norfolk St.

Longest Active Home Winning Streaks

No.	Team	2006 Overall Record
27	Appalachian St.	14-1
19	San Diego	11-1

Longest Active Conference Winning Streaks

No.	Team	Conference	2006 Conference Record
16	San Diego	Pioneer	7-0
12	Appalachian St.	Southern	7-0

Longest Streak of Games Without Being Shut Out

No.	School	Years
258	*Hampton	1984-present
240	*Montana	1989-present
199	Eastern Wash.	1988-2006
165	UNI	1983-96
158	McNeese St.	1988-01
154	Delaware	1983-96
150	*Western Ill.	1994-present
143	*Ga. Southern	1996-present
133	*Delaware	1996-present
132	William & Mary	1981-93
105	Texas St.	1987-96

**Active streak.*

Before FCS was formed in 1978:

No.	School	Years
197	Eastern Ill.	1977-96
124	Western Ill.	1968-80
109	Dartmouth	1961-73
89	Weber St.	1964-73

Most-Played Rivalries

(Ongoing Unless Indicated)

Games	Opponents (Series leader listed first)	Rivalry Record	First Game
142	Lafayette-Lehigh	75-62-5	1884
129	Yale-Princeton	70-49-10	1873
123	Yale-Harvard	65-50-8	1875
116	William & Mary-Richmond	59-52-5	1898
113	Penn-Cornell	64-44-5	1893
111	Yale-Brown	75-31-5	1880
110	Harvard-Dartmouth	61-44-5	1882
106	Harvard-Brown	76-28-2	1893
106	Montana-Montana St.	66-45-5	1897
99	Princeton-Harvard	51-41-7	1877
98	Princeton-Penn	62-35-1	1876
94	Cornell-Columbia	59-32-3	1889
94	#Illinois St.-Eastern Ill.	48-37-9	1901
94	New Hampshire-Maine	44-42-8	1903
90	$@Connecticut-Rhode Island	48-34-8	1897
90	Western Ill.-Illinois St.	47-38-5	1904
89	Cornell-Colgate	47-39-3	1896

#Did not play in 2001. $Have not played since 2000. @Connecticut moved to Division I-A in 2002.

Additional Rivalry Records

LONGEST UNINTERRUPTED SERIES
(Must have played every year; current unless indicated)

117 games—Lafayette-Lehigh (from 1897)$
88 games—Cornell-Dartmouth (from 1919)
87 games—Cornell-Penn (from 1919)

FCS

81 games—Dartmouth-Yale (from 1926)
75 games—Brown-Yale (from 1932)

74 games—Dartmouth-Princeton (from 1933)
65 games—Columbia-Dartmouth (from 1942)
64 games—Columbia-Yale (from 1943)
63 games—Richmond-William & Mary (from 1944)
63 games—VMI-William & Mary (from 1944)

62 games—Brown-Harvard (from 1945)
62 games—Bucknell-Lafayette (from 1945)
62 games—Harvard-Yale (from 1945)
62 games—Princeton-Yale (from 1945)
61 games—Harvard-Princeton (from 1946)

61 games—Massachusetts-Rhode Island (from 1946)
61 games—Sam Houston St.-Texas St. (from 1946)
61 games—Stephen F. Austin-Texas St. (from 1946)
61 games—Montana-Montana St. (from 1946)

$*Played twice in 1897-1901 and 1943-44.*

MOST CONSECUTIVE WINS OVER AN OPPONENT IN AN UNINTERRUPTED SERIES
(Must have played in consecutive years)
30—Grambling over Prairie View, 1977-06 (current)
22—Eastern Ky. over Tennessee Tech, 1976-97
21—William & Mary over VMI, 1986-06 (current)
20—Eastern Ky. over Austin Peay, 1978-97
18—Western Ill. over Southern Ill., 1984-01

18—Eastern Ky. over Morehead St., 1972-89
18—Southeast Mo. St. over Lincoln (Mo.), 1972-89
17—Princeton over Columbia, 1954-70
16—Montana over Montana St., 1986-01
16—Harvard over Columbia, 1979-94

16—Middle Tenn. over Morehead St., 1951-66
15—Delaware over West Chester, 1968-82
15—Dartmouth over Brown, 1960-74
15—Evansville over Ky. Wesleyan, 1983-97
14—Appalachian St. over East Tenn. St., 1982-95

14—Yale over Princeton, 1967-80
14—Marshall over VMI, 1983-96
14—Dartmouth over Columbia, 1984-97
13—Appalachian St. over Western Caro., 1985-97
13—Duquesne over St. Francis (Pa.), 1977-89

13—Massachusetts over Northeastern, 1984-96
13—Duquesne over St. Peter's, 1994-06 (current)
12—Idaho over Boise St., 1982-93
12—Cornell over Columbia, 1977-88
11—Wofford over Newberry, 1960-70

11—Tennessee Tech over Morehead St., 1951-61
11—William & Mary over Richmond, 1944-54
11—Davidson over Elon, 1921-31

MOST CONSECUTIVE WINS OVER AN OPPONENT IN A SERIES
(Did not have to play in consecutive years)
46—Yale over Wesleyan (Conn.), 1875-1913
30—Harvard over Williams, 1883-1920
23—Grambling over Prairie View, 1977-06 (current)
23—Harvard over Bates, 1899-1944
23—Brown over Rhode Island, 1909-34

21—Grambling over Mississippi Val., 1957-77
21—William & Mary over VMI, 1986-06 (current)
16—Montana over Montana St., 1986-01
16—Massachusetts over Northeastern, 1984-01
16—Harvard over Columbia, 1979-94

16—Yale over Connecticut, 1948-64
16—Davidson over Elon, 1921-48
14—Delaware over Massachusetts, 1958-89
13—Delaware over West Chester, 1993-06 (current)
12—Idaho over Ricks College, 1919-33

12—Yale over Penn, 1879-92

MOST CONSECUTIVE CURRENT WINS OVER AN OPPONENT IN AN UNINTERRUPTED SERIES
(Must have played in consecutive years)
30—Grambling over Prairie View, 1977-06
21—William & Mary over VMI, 1986-06

Cliffhangers

Regular-season FCS games won on the final play in regulation time. The extra point is listed when it provided the margin of victory after the winning touchdown on the game's final play.

Date	Opponents, Score	Game-Winning Play
10-21-78	Western Ky. 17, Eastern Ky. 16	Kevin McGrath 25 FG
9-8-79	Northern Ariz. 22, Portland St. 21	Ken Fraser 15 pass from Brian Potter (Mike Jenkins pass from Potter)
11-15-80	Morris Brown 19, Bethune-Cookman 18	Ray Mills 1 run (Carlton Johnson kick)
9-26-81	Abilene Christian 41, Northwestern St. 38	David Russell 17 pass from Loyal Proffitt
10-10-81	C.W. Post 37, James Madison 36	Tom DeBona 10 pass from Tom Ehrhardt
11-13-82	Penn 23, Harvard 21	Dave Shulman 27 FG
10-1-83	Connecticut 9, New Hampshire 7	Larry Corn 7 run
9-8-84	La.-Lafayette 17, Louisiana Tech 16	Patrick Broussard 21 FG
9-15-84	Lehigh 10, Connecticut 7	Dave Melick 45 FG
9-15-84	William & Mary 23, Delaware 21	Jeff Sanders 18 pass from Stan Yagiello
10-13-84	Lafayette 20, Connecticut 13	Ryan Priest 2 run
10-20-84	UCF 28, Illinois St. 24	Jeff Farmer 30 punt return
10-27-84	Western Ky. 33, Morehead St. 31	Arnold Grier 50 pass from Jeff Cesarone
9-7-85	UCF 39, Bethune-Cookman 37	Ed O'Brien 55 FG
10-26-85	VMI 39, William & Mary 38	Al Comer 3 run (James Wright run)
8-30-86	Texas Southern 38, Prairie View 35	Don Espinoza 23 FG
9-20-86	Delaware 33, West Chester 31	Fred Singleton 3 run
10-4-86	Northwestern St. 17, La.-Monroe 14	Keith Hodnett 27 FG
10-11-86	Eastern Ill. 31, UNI 30	Rich Ehmke 58 FG
9-12-87	Youngstown St. 20, Bowling Green 17	John Dowling 36 FG
10-3-87	La.-Monroe 33, Northwestern St. 31	Jackie Harris 48 pass from Stan Humphries
10-10-87	Marshall 34, Louisville 31	Keith Baxter 31 pass from Tony Petersen
10-17-87	Princeton 16, Lehigh 15	Rob Goodwin 38 FG
11-12-87	South Carolina St. 15, Grambling 13	William Wrighten 23 FG
9-24-88	Holy Cross 30, Princeton 26	70 kickoff return; Tim Donovan 55 on lateral from Darin Cromwell (15)
10-15-88	Weber St. 37, Nevada 31	Todd Beightol 57 pass from Jeff Carlson
10-29-88	Nicholls St. 13, Texas St. 10	Jim Windham 33 FG
9-2-89	Alabama St. 16, Troy 13	Reggie Brown 28 pass from Antonius Smith
9-16-89	Western Caro. 26, Chattanooga 20	Terrell Wagner 68 interception return
9-23-89	Northwestern St. 18, McNeese St. 17	Chris Hamler 25 FG
10-14-89	East Tenn. St. 24, Chattanooga 23	George Searcy 1 run
9-29-90	Texas St. 33, Nicholls St. 30	Robbie Roberson 32 FG
10-6-90	Grambling 27, Alabama A&M 20	Dexter Butcher 28 pass from Shawn Burras
11-2-91	Grambling 30, Texas Southern 27	Gilad Landau 37 FG
9-19-92	Eastern Ky. 26, La.-Monroe 21	Sean Little recovered fumble in end zone
10-10-92	Appalachian St. 27, James Madison 21	Craig Styron 44 pass from D.J. Campbell
11-14-92	Towson 33, Northeastern 32	Mark Orlando 10 pass from Dan Crowley

Date	Opponents, Score	Game-Winning Play
9-4-93	Delaware St. 31, Fayetteville St. 28	Jon Jensen 17 FG
9-11-93	Connecticut 24, New Hampshire 23	Wilbur Gilliard 14 run (Nick Sosik kick)
10-16-93	Howard 44, Towson 41	Germaine Kohn 9 pass from Jay Walker
10-7-95	Valparaiso 44, Butler 42	Cameron Hatten 27 FG
10-14-95	Montana 24, Northern Ariz. 21	Andy Larson 29 FG
10-14-95	Connecticut 31, Maine 30	David DeArmas 38 FG
10-28-95	UNI 19, Missouri St. 17	Matt Waller 39 FG
10-28-95	William & Mary 18, Villanova 15	Brian Shallcross 49 FG
9-7-96	Valparaiso 23, Hope 22	Cameron Hatten 37 FG
9-21-96	Charleston So. 17, West Virginia St. 14	Clint Kelly 20 FG
11-2-96	Butler 33, Evansville 31	Shawn Wood 32 FG
11-2-96	Wagner 38, Robert Morris 35	Carl Franke 41 FG
11-9-96	Murray St. 17, Eastern Ky. 14	Rob Hart 36 FG
9-6-97	Butler 10, Howard Payne 9	Jeremy Harkin 26 pass from Eli Stoddard (Shawn Wood kick)
9-13-97	Southern U. 36, Ark.-Pine Bluff 33	Chris Diaz 23 FG
9-20-97	Dayton 16, Robert Morris 13	Ryan Hulme 18 FG
10-4-97	Missouri St. 36, Southern Ill. 35	Travis Brawner 32 FG
11-8-97	Cal Poly 20, Montana St. 19	Alan Beilke 50 FG
11-15-97	James Madison 39, Rhode Island 37	Lindsay Fleshman 3 pass from Greg Maddox
11-22-97	Montana 27, Montana St. 25	Kris Heppner 37 FG
9-19-98	South Fla. 24, Liberty 21	Bill Gramatica 44 FG
9-19-98	Yale 30, Brown 28	Jake Borden 27 pass from Joe Walland (run failed)
10-2-99	Robert Morris 23, Wagner 21	J.T. Kirk 14 pass from Steve Tryon
11-6-99	Ga. Southern 41, Furman 38	Chris Chambers 28 FG
10-21-00	Sacramento St. 25, Eastern Wash. 22	Jimmie Sanchez 23 FG
11-4-00	Holy Cross 10, Bucknell 9	Ryan Rolfert 39 FG
11-18-00	Western Ill. 44, UNI 41	Mike Scifres 56 FG
9-22-01	Grambling 30, Portland St. 29	Randy Hymes 2 run (Brian Morgan kick)
9-29-01	Portland St. 33, Northern Ariz. 30	Mike Cajal-Willis 27 FG
9-29-01	Montana 29, Eastern Wash. 26	Etu Molden 20 pass from John Edwards
10-6-01	East Tenn. St. 23, Citadel 21	Con Chellis 41 FG
10-5-02	Southern Ill. 54, Western Ill. 52	Brandon Robinson 6 pass from Joel Sambursky
11-02-02	Portland St. 27, Idaho St. 24	Mike Cajal-Willis 20 FG
8-28-03	Fla. Atlantic 20, Middle Tenn. 19	Roosevelt Bynes 63 pass from Jared Allen
10-4-03	Columbia 33, Princeton 27	Wade Fletcher 49 pass from Jeff Otis
10-16-04	UNI 22, Youngstown St. 20	Brian Wingert 31 FG
11-13-04	William & Mary 27, James Madison 24	Greg Kuehn 42 FG
12-4-04	Sam Houston St. 35, Eastern Wash. 34	Jason Mathenia 7 pass from Dustin Long (Lance Gainer kick)
9-23-06	Chattanooga 27, Ga. Southern 26	Esteban Lopex 38 FG
10-14-06	Davidson 27, Morehead St. 24	Brad Smith 39 FG

FCS

Overtime Games

Regular-Season Overtime Games Before 1996

In 1981, the NCAA Football Rules Committee approved an overtime tiebreaker system to decide a tie game for the purpose of determining a conference champion. The following conferences used the tiebreaker system to decide conference-only tie games. (Beginning in 1996, all college football games used the tiebreaker if the score was tied after four periods.) In an overtime period, one end of the field is used and each team gets an offensive possession beginning at the 25-yard line. Each team shall have possession until it has scored, failed to gain a first down or lost possession. The team scoring the greater number of points after completion of both possessions is declared the winner. The periods continue until a winner is determined.

NUMBER OF FCS OVERTIME GAMES SINCE 1981

Year	Games	Year	Games	Year	Games	Year	Games
1981	2	1988	6	1995	8	*2001	18
1982	4	1989	2	*1996	23	*2002	26
1983	0	1990	6	*1997	23	*2003	23
1984	4	1991	5	*1998	25	*2004	34
1985	2	1992	2	*1999	21	*2005	33
1986	4	1993	4	*2000	24	*2006	31
1987	6	1994	6				

**All games tied at end of four periods use tiebreaker system.*

BIG SKY CONFERENCE

Date	Opponents, Score	No. OTs	Score, Reg.
10-31-81	‡Weber St. 24, Northern Ariz. 23	1	17-17
11-21-81	‡Idaho St. 33, Weber St. 30	3	23-23
10-2-82	‡Montana St. 30, Idaho St. 27	3	17-17
11-6-82	Nevada 46, ‡Weber St. 43	3	30-30
10-13-84	‡Montana St. 44, Nevada 41	4	21-21
9-17-88	Boise St. 24, ‡Northern Ariz. 21	2	14-14
10-15-88	‡Montana 33, Northern Ariz. 26	2	26-26
9-15-90	‡Weber St. 45, Idaho St. 38	2	31-31
9-29-90	‡Nevada 31, Idaho 28	1	28-28
11-3-90	Eastern Wash. 33, ‡Idaho St. 26	1	26-26
11-10-90	Montana St. 28, ‡Eastern Wash. 25	1	25-25
10-26-91	Eastern Wash. 34, ‡Idaho 31	2	24-24
11-16-91	Montana 35, ‡Idaho 34	1	28-28
10-29-94	‡Eastern Wash. 34, Montana St. 31	3	31-31

GATEWAY CONFERENCE

Date	Opponents, Score	No. OTs	Score, Reg.
9-24-94	Western Ill. 31, ‡Missouri St. 24	1	24-24
9-30-95	Illinois St. 20, ‡Missouri St. 17	1	17-17
10-14-95	‡Southern Ill. 33, Missouri St. 30	1	30-30

MID-EASTERN ATHLETIC CONFERENCE

Date	Opponents, Score	No. OTs	Score, Reg.
11-1-86	‡N.C. A&T 30, Bethune-Cookman 24	1	24-24
10-22-93	Howard 41, ‡N.C. A&T 35	1	35-35
11-20-93	‡South Carolina St. 58, N.C. A&T 52	1	52-52

OHIO VALLEY CONFERENCE

Date	Opponents, Score	No. OTs	Score, Reg.
10-13-84	Youngstown St. 17, ‡Austin Peay 13	1	10-10
11-3-84	‡Murray St. 20, Austin Peay 13	2	10-10
10-19-85	‡Middle Tenn. 31, Murray St. 24	2	17-17
11-2-85	‡Middle Tenn. 28, Youngstown St. 21	2	14-14
10-4-86	‡Austin Peay 7, Middle Tenn. 0	1	0-0
10-10-87	‡Austin Peay 20, Morehead St. 13	1	13-13
11-7-87	‡Youngstown St. 20, Murray St. 13	1	13-13
10-1-88	Tennessee Tech 16, ‡Murray St. 13	1	10-10
10-29-88	Eastern Ky. 31, ‡Murray St. 24	1	24-24
11-18-89	Eastern Ky. 38, ‡Morehead St. 31	3	24-24
11-10-90	‡Tennessee Tech 20, Austin Peay 14	1	14-14
11-17-90	Murray St. 31, ‡Austin Peay 24	3	24-24
11-7-92	‡Eastern Ky. 21, Murray St. 18	1	18-18

Date	Opponents, Score	No. OTs	Score, Reg.
10-2-93	Murray St. 28, ‡Tenn.-Martin 21	1	21-21
11-20-93	Tenn.-Martin 39, ‡Austin Peay 33	2	26-26

PATRIOT LEAGUE

Date	Opponents, Score	No. OTs	Score, Reg.
11-11-95	Bucknell 21, ‡Colgate 14	1	14-14
11-11-95	‡Lafayette 24, Fordham 21	2	21-21
11-18-95	‡Lehigh 37, Lafayette 30	2	30-30

SOUTHERN CONFERENCE

Date	Opponents, Score	No. OTs	Score, Reg.
110-19-91	Appalachian St. 26, Furman 23	3	20-20
11-2-91	Marshall 27, Western Caro. 24	3	20-20
11-21-92	VMI 37, Chattanooga 34	1	34-34
10-16-93	VMI 35, Chattanooga 29		
11-19-94	VMI 26, Appalachian St. 23	1	20-20

YANKEE CONFERENCE

Date	Opponents, Score	No. OTs	Score, Reg.
9-18-82	Rhode Island 58, ‡Maine 55	6	21-21
9-25-82	‡Boston U. 48, Maine 45	4	24-24
10-27-84	Maine 13, ‡Connecticut 10	1	10-10
9-13-86	New Hampshire 28, ‡Delaware 21	1	21-21
11-15-86	‡Connecticut 21, Rhode Island 14	1	14-14
9-19-87	‡Richmond 52, Massachusetts 51	4	28-28
9-19-87	New Hampshire 27, ‡Boston U. 20	3	17-17
10-31-87	Maine 59, ‡Delaware 56	2	49-49
11-21-87	‡Delaware 17, Boston U. 10	1	10-10
9-24-88	Villanova 31, ‡Boston U. 24	1	24-24
10-8-88	‡Richmond 23, New Hampshire 17	1	17-17
10-7-89	‡Villanova 41, Connecticut 35	6	21-21
11-16-91	Boston U. 29, ‡Connecticut 26	2	23-23
9-11-93	‡Connecticut 24, New Hampshire 23	1	17-17
10-16-93	Maine 26, ‡Rhode Island 23	2	17-17
9-17-94	Delaware 38, ‡Villanova 31	1	31-31
11-19-94	Northeastern 9, ‡James Madison 6	1	6-6
9-23-95	James Madison 28, ‡Villanova 27	1	21-21
10-7-95	‡Richmond 26, Northeastern 23	1	23-23
11-4-95	‡Maine 24, Massachusetts 21	1	21-21
11-19-94	New Hampshire 52, ‡Boston U. 51	2	45-45

‡Home team.

2006 FCS Overtime Games

Date	Winner	Loser	Score	Number of OT Periods
Sept. 2	Bucknell	Duquesne	31-28	1
Sept. 2	Hampton	Grambling	27-26	2
Sept. 9	Alabama A&M	Grambling	30-27	1
Sept. 9	Charleston So.	Citadel	38-35	2
Sept. 9	Wingate	Davidson	22-16	1
Sept. 16	Prairie View	Southern U.	26-23	1
Sept. 16	Tennessee St.	Jackson St.	31-30	1
Sept. 30	Tennessee Tech	Murray St.	20-14	1
Sept. 30	Florida A&M	Tennessee St.	25-22	1
Oct. 7	Princeton	Colgate	27-26	1
Oct. 14	Holy Cross	Dartmouth	24-21	1
Oct. 14	Robert Morris	Central Conn. St.	23-17	1
Oct. 14	Chattanooga	Western Caro.	17-14	1
Oct. 14	Morgan St.	Howard	18-12	1
Oct. 14	Jackson St.	Southern U.	31-28	1
Oct. 14	Southeastern La.	Northwestern St.	31-24	1
Oct. 14	Yale	Lehigh	26-20	1
Oct. 21	Yale	Penn	17-14	1
Oct. 21	Appalachian St.	Ga. Southern	27-20	2
Oct. 21	Cumberland (Ky.)	Austin Peay	27-26	1
Oct. 21	Citadel	Western Caro.	30-27	1
Oct. 21	Florida A&M	Norfolk St.	36-33	1
Oct. 21	Furman	Chattanooga	28-22	1
Oct. 21	Northeastern	New Hampshire	36-35	1
Oct. 28	Brown	Penn	30-27	1
Oct. 28	Jacksonville St.	Tennessee Tech	17-10	1
Nov. 4	Princeton	Penn	31-30	1
Nov. 11	Dartmouth	Brown	19-13	1
Nov. 11	McNeese St.	Northwestern St.	29-26	1
Nov. 18	Central Ark.	Ga. Southern	34-31	1
Nov. 18	New Hampshire	Maine	19-13	1

Note: *31 games with 34 extra periods (28 with one extra period, three with two extra periods) for an average of 1.10 extra periods per overtime game.*

FCS Stadiums

LISTED ALPHABETICALLY BY SCHOOL

School	Stadium	Conference	Year Built	Cap.	Surface*
Alabama A&M	Louis Crews	SWAC-E	1996	21,000	Grass
Alabama St. ^	Cramton	SWAC-E	1922	24,600	Grass
Albany (N.Y.)	University Field	Northeast	1967	10,000	Grass
Alcorn St.	Jack Spinks	SWAC-E	1992	25,000	Grass
Appalachian St.	Kidd Brewer	Southern	1962	16,650	FieldTurf (04)
Ark.-Pine Bluff	Pumphrey	SWAC-W	1951	6,000	Grass
Austin Peay	Governors	Pioneer-S	1946	10,000	Stadia Turf
Bethune-Cookman	Municipal	MEAC	NA	10,000	Grass
Brown	Brown	Ivy	1925	20,000	Grass
Bucknell	Christy Mathewson	Patriot	1924	13,100	Grass
Butler	Butler Bowl	Pioneer-N	1927	19,000	Grass
UC Davis%	Toomey Field	Great West	1949	10,111	Grass
Cal Poly	Mustang	Great West	1935	8,500	Grass
Central Ark.%	Estes	Southland	1939	8,500	Grass
Central Conn. St.	Arute Field	Northeast	1969	5,000	Grass
Charleston So.	Buccaneer Field	Big South	1970	4,000	Grass
Chattanooga ^	Finley	Southern	1997	20,668	Polyethylene turf (05)
Citadel	Johnson Hagood	Southern	1948	22,500	Grass
Coastal Caro.	Brooks Stadium	Big South	2003	7,332	Grass
Colgate	Andy Kerr	Patriot	1937	10,221	Grass
Columbia	Lawrence A. Wien	Ivy	1984	17,000	Grass
Cornell	Schoellkopf	Ivy	1915	27,000	All-Pro Turf
Dartmouth	Memorial Field	Ivy	1923	20,416	Grass
Davidson	Richardson	Pioneer-S	1924	4,000	Grass
Dayton	Welcome	Pioneer-N	1949	11,000	AstroTurf
Delaware	Delaware	Atlantic 10	1952	22,000	Grass
Delaware St.	Alumni Field	MEAC	1957	5,000	Grass
Drake	Drake	Pioneer-N	1925	18,000	Grass
Duquesne	Arthur J. Rooney Field	MAAC	1993	4,500	AstroPlay
Eastern Ill.	O'Brien	Ohio Valley	1970	10,000	Grass
Eastern Ky.	Roy Kidd	Ohio Valley	1969	20,000	Grass
Eastern Wash.	Woodward	Big Sky	1967	8,600	Grass
Elon	Rhodes	Southern	2001	11,250	Grass
Florida A&M	Bragg Memorial	MEAC	1957	25,500	Grass
Fordham	Jack Coffey Field	Patriot	1930	7,000	Grass
Furman	Paladin	Southern	1981	16,000	Grass
Gardner-Webb	Ernest W. Spangler	Big South	1969	5,000	Grass
Georgetown	Harbin Field	Patriot	2003	2,400	Grass
Ga. Southern	Paulson	Southern	1984	18,000	PAT
Grambling	Robinson	SWAC-W	1983	19,600	Grass
Hampton	Armstrong	MEAC	1928	17,000	Grass
Harvard	Harvard	Ivy	1903	30,898	Grass
Hofstra	James M. Shuart	Atlantic 10	1963	15,000	AstroTurf
Holy Cross	Fitton Field	Patriot	1924	23,500	Grass
Howard	Greene	MEAC	1986	8,890	AstroTurf
Idaho St. #	Holt Arena	Big Sky	1970	12,000	AstroTurf
Illinois St.	Hancock	Gateway	1967	15,000	AstroTurf
Indiana St.	Memorial	Gateway	1970	12,764	All-Pro Turf
Iona	Mazzella Field	MAAC	1989	1,200	AstroTurf
Jackson St.	^Mississippi Memorial	SWAC-E	1949	62,512	Grass
Jacksonville	Milne Field	Pioneer-S	1998	4,500	Grass
Jacksonville St.	Paul Snow	Southland	1947	15,000	Grass
James Madison	Bridgeforth	Atlantic 10	1974	12,500	AstroTurf
La Salle	McCarthy	MAAC	1936	7,500	Grass
Lafayette	Fisher Field	Patriot	1926	13,750	Grass
Lehigh	Goodman	Patriot	1988	16,000	Grass
Liberty	Williams	Big South	1989	12,000	FieldTurf
Maine	Alumni	Atlantic 10	1942	10,000	Grass
Marist	Leonidoff Field	MAAC	1972	2,500	Grass
Massachusetts	Warren McGuirk	Atlantic 10	1965	17,000	Grass
McNeese St.	Cowboy	Southland	1965	17,500	Grass
Mississippi Val.	Rice-Totten	SWAC-E	1958	10,500	Grass
Missouri St.	Plaster Field	Gateway	1941	16,300	FieldTurf
Monmouth	Kessler Field	Northeast	1993	4,600	Grass
Montana	Washington-Grizzly	Big Sky	1986	23,117	SprinTurf
Montana St.	Reno H. Sales	Big Sky	1973	15,197	Grass
Morehead St.	Jayne	Pioneer-S	1964	10,000	OmniTurf
Morgan St.	Hughes	MEAC	1934	10,000	Grass
Murray St.	Stewart	Ohio Valley	1973	16,800	AstroTurf
New Hampshire	Cowell	Atlantic 10	1936	9,571	Grass
Nicholls St.	John L. Guidry	Southland	1972	12,800	Grass
Norfolk St.	Price	MEAC	1997	27,700	Grass
N.C. A&T	Aggie	MEAC	1981	21,000	Grass
North Dakota St.% #	FargoDome	Great West	1992	18,700	AstroTurf
Northeastern	E.S. Parsons	Atlantic 10	1933	7,000	AstroTurf
Northern Ariz. #	Walkup Skydome	Big Sky	1977	15,300	AstroTurf
Northern Colo.%	Nottingham Field	Great West	1995	7,000	Grass
UNI #	U.N.I.-Dome	Gateway	1976	16,324	AstroTurf

FCS

School	Stadium	Conference	Year Built	Cap.	Surface*
Northwestern St.	Turpin	Southland	1976	15,971	AstroTurf
Penn	Franklin Field	Ivy	1895	53,000	AstroTurf
Portland St.	^ PGE Park	Big Sky	1928	23,000	NexTurf
Prairie View	Blackshear	SWAC-W	1960	6,000	Grass
Princeton	Princeton	Ivy	1998	30,000	Grass
Rhode Island	Meade	Atlantic 10	1928	8,000	Grass
Richmond	Richmond	Atlantic 10	1929	21,319	SuperTurf
Robert Morris	Moon	Northeast	1950	7,000	Grass
Sacramento St.	Hornet Field	Big Sky	1964	21,418	Grass
Sacred Heart	Campus Field	Northeast	1993	3,500	AstroTurf
St. Francis (Pa.)	Pine Bowl	Northeast	1979	1,500	Grass
Sam Houston St.	Bowers	Southland	1986	14,000	All-Pro Turf
Samford	Seibert	Independent	1960	6,700	Grass
San Diego	USD Torero	Pioneer-N	1955	4,000	Grass
South Carolina St.	Dawson Bulldog	MEAC	1955	22,000	Grass
South Dakota St.%	Coughlin-Alumni	Independent	1962	12,323	Grass
Southeast Mo. St.	Houck	Ohio Valley	1930	10,000	Grass
Southeastern La.	Strawberry	Southland	1936	7,400	SprinTurf
Southern Ill.	McAndrew	Gateway	1975	17,324	OmniTurf
Southern U.	A.W. Mumford	SWAC-W	1928	24,000	Grass
Southern Utah	Col. of Southern Utah	Great West	1967	6,500	Grass
Stephen F. Austin	Homer Bryce	Southland	1973	14,575	AstroTurf-12
Stony Brook	Seawolves Field	Northeast	1978	2,000	Grass
Tenn.-Martin	Skyhawk	Ohio Valley	1964	7,500	Grass
Tennessee St.	The Coliseum	Ohio Valley	1999	67,500	Grass
Tennessee Tech	Tucker	Ohio Valley	1966	16,500	Stadia Turf
Texas Southern	^ Robertson	SWAC-W	1965	22,000	Grass
Texas St.	Bobcat	Southland	1981	15,218	Grass
Towson	Johnny Unitas	Atlantic 10	1978	11,000	Turf
Valparaiso	Brown Field	Pioneer-N	1947	5,000	Grass
Villanova	Villanova	Atlantic 10	1927	12,000	AstroTurf
VMI	Alumni Field	Big South	1962	10,000	Grass
Wagner	Fischer Memorial Field	Northeast	1967	5,000	Grass
Weber St.	Elizabeth Dee Shaw Stewart	Big Sky	1966	17,500	Grass
Western Caro.	E.J. Whitmire	Southern	1974	12,000	AstroTurf
Western Ill.	Hanson Field	Gateway	1948	15,168	Grass
Western Ky.	L.T. Smith	Gateway	1968	17,500	AstroPlay (S03)
William & Mary	Walter Zable	Atlantic 10	1935	15,000	FieldTurf (S03)
Winston-Salem%	Bowman-Gray	MEAC	1940	18,000	Grass
Wofford	Gibbs	Southern	1996	13,000	Grass
Yale	Yale Bowl	Ivy	1914	64,269	Grass
Youngstown St.	Arnold D. Stambaugh	Gateway	1982	20,630	SprinTurf

%These teams are in the process of reclassifying to FCS from Division II, but all play an FCS schedule and are listed here. ^Not located on campus. #Indoor facility.

STADIUMS LISTED BY CAPACITY (TOP 33)

School	Stadium	Capacity	Surface*
Tennessee St.	The Coliseum	67,500	Grass
Yale	Yale Bowl	64,269	Grass
Jackson St.	^Mississippi Memorial	62,512	Grass
Penn	Franklin Field	53,000	AstroTurf
Harvard	Harvard	30,898	Grass
Princeton	Princeton	30,000	Grass
Norfolk St.	Price	27,700	Grass
Cornell	Schoellkopf	27,000	All-Pro Turf
Florida A&M	Bragg Memorial	25,500	Grass
Alcorn St.	Jack Spinks	25,000	Grass
Alabama St.	^Cramton	24,600	Grass
Southern U.	A.W. Mumford	24,000	Grass
Holy Cross	Fitton Field	23,500	Grass
Montana	Washington-Grizzly	23,117	SprinTurf
Portland St.	^PGE Park	23,000	NexTurf
Citadel	Johnson Hagood	22,500	Grass
Delaware	Delaware	22,000	Grass
South Carolina St.	Dawson Bulldog	22,000	Grass
Texas Southern	^Robertson	22,000	Grass
Sacramento St.	Hornet Field	21,418	Grass
Richmond	Richmond	21,319	SuperTurf
Alabama A&M	Louis Crews	21,000	Grass
N.C. A&T	Aggie	21,000	Grass
Chattanooga	^Finley	20,668	Polyethylene turf
Youngstown St.	Stambaugh	20,630	SprinTurf
Dartmouth	Memorial Field	20,416	Grass
Brown	Brown	20,000	Grass
Eastern Ky.	Roy Kidd	20,000	Grass
Grambling	Robinson	19,600	Grass
Butler	Butler Bowl	19,000	Grass
Drake	Drake	18,000	Grass
Ga. Southern	Paulson	18,000	PAT
Winston-Salem%	Bowman-Gray	18,000	Grass

^Not located on campus. %Reclassifying to FCS from Division II.

Surface Notes: **This column indicates the type of surface (either artificial or natural grass) present this year in the stadium. The brand name of the artificial turf, if known, is listed. Legend: Turf—Any of several types of artificial turfs (name brands include AstroTurf, FieldTurf, All-Pro, Omni-Turf, SuperTurf, Sprinturf, etc.); Grass—Natural grass surface; PAT—Prescription Athletic Turf (a "natural-artificial" surface featuring a network of pipes connected to pumps capable of sucking water from the natural turf or watering it. The pipes are located 18 inches from the surface and covered with a mixture of sand and filler. The turf also is lined with heating coils to keep it from freezing in temperatures below 32 degrees).*

FCS Statistics Trends

(Average Per Game, One Team)

Year	Rushing Plays	Rushing Yds.	Rushing Avg.	Passing Att.	Passing Cmp.	Passing Pct.	Passing Yds.	Passing Av. Att.	Total Offense Plays	Total Offense Yds.	Total Offense Avg.	Scoring TD	Scoring FG	Scoring Pts.
1978	*48.4	171.8	3.55	20.7	9.5	46.2	129.3	6.24	69.1	301.1	4.36	2.60	0.52	19.5
1979	47.1	164.7	3.50	20.5	9.2	45.0	125.2	6.13	67.5	289.9	4.30	2.40	0.62	18.5
1980	45.2	164.8	3.65	22.4	10.4	46.5	144.4	6.45	67.6	309.2	4.58	2.58	0.59	19.6
1981	44.3	155.0	3.50	24.9	11.9	47.7	161.5	6.49	69.1	316.4	4.58	2.71	0.69	20.9
1982	44.4	156.6	3.53	26.1	12.8	48.9	166.0	6.35	70.5	322.6	4.57	2.62	0.80	20.5
1983	43.9	155.2	3.54	26.2	13.0	49.4	167.3	6.38	70.1	322.4	4.60	2.69	0.79	21.1
1984	42.9	152.6	3.56	27.9	14.0	50.0	181.0	6.49	70.7	333.5	4.72	2.80	0.80	21.8
1985	42.4	157.6	3.72	28.9	14.6	50.4	187.3	6.49	*71.2	344.9	4.84	2.84	0.81	22.1
1986	42.4	157.9	3.72	28.3	14.1	49.7	186.4	6.60	70.7	344.3	4.87	2.90	0.86	22.7
1987	43.1	158.6	3.68	27.1	13.6	50.1	175.6	6.48	70.2	334.2	4.76	2.78	0.91	22.0
1988	43.2	161.3	3.74	26.5	13.3	50.2	172.7	6.53	69.6	334.0	4.80	2.80	*0.92	22.1
1989	42.5	160.2	3.77	27.7	14.2	51.3	186.0	6.71	70.2	346.2	4.93	2.72	0.75	22.8
1990	42.7	161.5	3.79	27.8	14.1	50.6	187.0	6.73	70.5	348.5	4.95	2.98	0.84	23.2
1991	43.2	170.6	3.95	26.9	14.0	51.9	184.7	6.87	70.1	355.3	5.07	3.19	0.67	24.1
1992	43.0	171.4	3.99	26.0	13.5	51.7	179.4	6.89	69.0	350.8	5.08	3.16	0.68	23.9
1993	42.4	168.3	3.97	27.0	14.0	51.8	186.4	6.90	69.4	354.7	5.11	3.20	0.70	24.2
1994	41.6	164.1	3.95	27.5	14.3	51.9	188.1	6.85	69.0	352.1	5.10	3.18	0.70	24.1
1995	42.0	165.1	3.94	27.1	13.9	51.3	177.7	6.57	69.0	342.8	4.97	3.06	0.68	23.2
1996	42.0	162.0	3.86	26.9	13.7	51.1	177.6	6.62	68.8	339.6	4.94	3.05	0.72	23.2
1997	40.2	153.2	3.81	27.8	14.3	51.3	185.2	6.67	68.0	338.4	4.98	3.06	0.72	23.3
1998	40.8	162.7	3.98	27.2	14.3	52.6	187.8	*6.91	68.0	350.5	5.15	3.26	0.71	24.7
1999	40.8	162.9	4.02	28.8	15.1	52.5	197.1	6.83	69.4	360.0	5.19	*3.45	0.71	25.9
2000	41.2	164.9	4.00	27.8	14.5	52.3	191.1	6.88	69.0	356.0	5.16	3.40	0.75	25.8
2001	40.6	160.4	3.95	28.1	14.8	52.6	193.7	6.89	68.7	354.1	5.15	3.34	0.72	25.3
2002	41.0	155.6	3.80	27.5	14.5	52.7	187.5	6.81	68.5	343.1	5.01	3.19	0.75	24.3
2003	40.5	159.5	3.94	28.7	15.6	54.2	197.4	6.87	69.2	356.9	5.16	3.32	0.81	25.4
2004	40.0	159.5	3.99	*29.6	*16.2	54.7	*201.7	6.83	69.6	*361.2	5.19	3.42	0.75	*26.0
2005	41.3	162.8	4.04	28.7	15.9	55.5	198.1	6.90	69.0	360.9	5.23	3.37	0.82	25.8
2006	36.1	*172.2	*4.77	26.7	15.0	*56.2	183.4	6.87	62.8	330.7	*5.27	2.76	0.77	22.8

**Record.*

Additional FCS Statistics Trends

(Average Per Game, One Team)

Year	Punting No.	Punting Avg.	Punting Net Avg.	Interceptions No.	Interceptions Avg. Ret.	Interceptions Yds.	Punt Returns No.	Punt Returns Avg. Ret.	Punt Returns Yds.	Kickoff Returns No.	Kickoff Returns Avg. Ret.	Kickoff Returns Yds.
1978	*6.1	36.5	33.6	1.42	11.92	17.0	2.39	7.49	17.9	3.23	18.4	59.2
1979	6.0	36.5	33.4	1.44	11.39	16.4	2.41	7.46	18.0	3.06	18.4	56.2
1980	5.8	37.0	33.7	1.37	10.06	13.8	2.44	7.94	19.4	3.09	17.4	53.7
1981	5.9	37.2	33.9	*1.60	10.63	*17.0	2.50	7.77	19.4	3.27	18.4	60.1
1982	6.0	37.1	34.0	1.50	10.15	15.2	2.44	7.63	18.6	3.08	19.0	58.4
1983	6.0	37.3	34.1	1.52	9.99	15.1	2.59	7.58	19.6	3.06	18.6	56.9
1984	5.8	37.3	33.9	1.53	10.40	15.9	2.55	7.84	20.0	3.23	18.6	60.0
1985	5.7	37.6	*34.2	1.51	10.56	16.0	2.55	7.52	19.2	3.20	18.1	57.9
1986	5.6	37.6	34.0	1.51	10.90	16.4	2.55	7.92	20.2	*4.02	19.4	*77.9
1987	5.6	36.8	33.4	1.40	10.57	14.9	2.48	7.51	18.7	3.96	19.0	74.6
1988	5.5	36.3	32.8	1.34	10.61	14.2	2.40	7.96	19.2	3.95	18.8	74.3
1989	5.5	36.1	32.8	1.31	10.40	13.7	2.32	7.93	18.4	3.96	18.9	74.7
1990	5.4	36.7	32.7	1.38	11.94	16.5	2.49	8.46	21.0	4.02	18.9	75.9
1991	5.3	36.6	32.6	1.35	10.81	14.6	2.46	8.57	21.1	3.84	19.1	73.4
1992	5.3	36.6	32.2	1.21	10.24	12.3	2.53	9.35	23.6	3.82	19.5	74.4
1993	5.2	36.0	32.3	1.23	10.79	13.2	2.35	8.26	19.5	3.72	19.3	71.7
1994	5.2	36.3	32.1	1.27	10.94	13.8	2.38	9.20	21.9	3.83	*19.9	76.0
1995	5.4	35.8	32.0	1.16	12.20	14.1	2.36	8.57	20.2	3.73	18.6	69.4
1996	5.5	36.6	32.8	1.22	12.25	15.0	2.44	8.54	20.9	3.60	19.0	68.4
1997	5.6	37.3	33.3	1.18	12.32	14.5	2.53	8.90	22.5	3.60	19.1	68.8
1998	5.3	*37.6	33.3	1.12	12.33	13.8	2.54	8.98	22.8	3.90	19.5	75.9
1999	5.4	37.2	32.8	1.18	12.55	14.8	2.46	9.40	23.1	3.91	19.1	74.7
2000	5.3	36.5	32.2	1.19	12.25	14.6	2.49	9.20	22.9	3.94	19.3	76.0
2001	5.4	36.5	32.1	1.16	12.45	14.4	2.45	*9.82	24.0	3.96	19.2	75.9
2002	5.5	36.7	32.2	1.11	12.10	13.4	*2.63	9.38	*24.7	3.85	19.3	74.4
2003	5.3	37.1	32.8	1.12	*13.33	14.9	2.53	9.20	23.3	3.86	*19.9	76.8
2004	5.3	36.9	32.9	1.17	13.02	15.2	2.40	9.11	21.8	3.87	19.6	75.8
2005	5.1	37.2	33.1	1.07	12.34	13.2	2.20	9.57	21.0	3.77	19.3	72.6
2006	4.7	37.3	33.2	0.95	10.97	11.5	2.00	9.16	18.3	3.59	19.5	70.1

**Record.*

Rules changes and statistics changes affecting trends: PUNTING–Beginning in 1965, 20 yards not deducted from a punt into the end zone for a touchback. INTERCEPTIONS–Interceptions yards not compiled, 1958-65. KICKOFF RETURNS–During 1937-45, if a kickoff went out of bounds, the receiving team put the ball in play on its 35-yard line instead of a second kickoff; in 1984 (rescinded in 1985), a 30-yard-line touchback for kickoffs crossing the goal line in flight and first touching the ground out of the end zone; in 1986, kickoffs from the 35-yard line. PUNT RETURNS–In 1967, interior linemen restricted from leaving until the ball is kicked.

Classification History

SINCE 1978

The following lists show years of active membership for current and former FCS football-playing institutions. The lists are from 1978, the year that Division I was divided into FBS and FCS.

ACTIVE MEMBERS (119)

Team	Year(s)
Alabama A&M	1999-current
Alabama St.	1982-current
Albany (N.Y.)	1999-current
Alcorn St.	1978-current
Appalachian St.	1982-current
Ark.-Pine Bluff	1998-current
Austin Peay	1978-current
Bethune-Cookman	1980-current
Brown	1982-current
Bucknell	1978-current
Butler	1993-current
UC Davis	2007-current
Cal Poly	1994-current
Central Conn. St.	1993-current
Charleston So.	1993-current
Chattanooga	1982-current
Citadel	1982-current
Coastal Caro.	2003-current
Colgate	1982-current
Columbia	1982-current
Cornell	1982-current
Dartmouth	1982-current
Davidson	1978-90, 93-current
Dayton	1993-current
Delaware	1980-current
Delaware St.	1978, 80-current
Drake	1992-85, 93-current
Duquesne	1993-current
Eastern Ill.	1981-current
Eastern Ky.	1978-current
Eastern Wash.	1984-current
Elon	1999-current
Florida A&M	1979-current
Fordham	1989-current
Furman	1982-current
Gardner-Webb	2002-current
Georgetown	1993-current
Ga. Southern	1984-current
Grambling	1978-current
Hampton	1997-current
Harvard	1982-current
Hofstra	1993-current
Holy Cross	1982-current
Howard	1978, 80-current
Idaho St.	1978-current
Illinois St.	1982-current
Indiana St.	1982-current
Iona	1993-current
Jackson St.	1978-current
Jacksonville	1998-current
Jacksonville St.	1997-current
James Madison	1980-current
La Salle	1997-current
Lafayette	1978-current
Lehigh	1978-current

Team	Year(s)
Liberty	1989-current
Team	Year(s)
Maine	1978-current
Marist	1993-current
Massachusetts	1978-current
McNeese St.	1982-current
Mississippi Val.	1980-current
Missouri St.	1982-current
Monmouth	1994-current
Montana	1978-current
Montana St.	1978-current
Morehead St.	1978-current
Morgan St.	1986-current
Murray St.	1978-current
New Hampshire	1978-current
Nicholls St.	1980-current
Norfolk St.	1997-current
N.C. A&T	1978, 80-current
Northeastern	1978-current
Northern Colo.	2007-current
Northern Ariz.	1978-current
UNI	1981-current
Northwestern St.	1978-current
Penn	1982-current
Portland St.	1978-80, 98-current
Prairie View	1978-current
Princeton	1982-current
Rhode Island	1978-current
Richmond	1982-current
Robert Morris	1998-current
Sacramento St.	1993-current
Sacred Heart	1999-current
St. Francis (Pa.)	1993-current
Sam Houston St.	1986-current
Samford	1989-current
San Diego	1993-current
Savannah St.	2002-current
South Carolina St.	1978, 80-current
Southeast Mo. St.	1990-current
Southeastern La.	1980-85; 2003-current
Southern Ill.	1982-current
Southern U.	1978-current
Southern Utah	1993-current
Stephen F. Austin	1986-current
Stony Brook	1999-current
Tenn.-Martin	1992-current
Tennessee St.	1981-current
Tennessee Tech	1978-current
Texas Southern	1978-current
Texas St.	1984-current
Towson	1987-current
Valparaiso	1993-current
Villanova	1987-current
VMI	1982-current
Wagner	1993-current
Weber St.	1978-current
Western Caro.	1982-current

Team	Year(s)
Western Ill.	1981-current
Western Ky.	1978-current
William & Mary	1982-current
Team	Year(s)
Wofford	1995-current
Yale	1982-current
Youngstown St.	1981-current

RECLASSIFYING TEAMS

Team	First Year as Full Div. I-AA Member
Central Ark. (from Div. II)	2010
North Dakota St. (from Div. II)	2008
South Dakota St. (from Div. II)	2008
Winston-Salem (from Div. II)	2010

FORMER MEMBERS

Team	Year(s)
UAB	1993-95
Akron	1980-86
Arkansas St.	1982-91
Ball St.	1982
Boise St.	1978-98
Boston U.	1978-97
Bowling Green	1982
Buffalo	1993-98
Cal St. Northridge*	1993-01
Canisius*	1993-02
UCF	1990-95
Connecticut	1978-01
East Tenn. St.*	1982-03
Eastern Mich.	1982
Evansville*	1993-97
Fairfield*	1997-02
Fla. Atlantic	2001-04
Florida Int'l	2003-05
Idaho	1978-96
Kent St.	1982
Lamar*	1982-89
La.-Monroe	1982-93
Louisiana Tech	1982-88
Marshall	1982-96
Middle Tenn.	1978-98
Morris Brown*	2001-03
Nevada	1978-91
North Texas	1982-94
Northern Ill.	1982
Ohio U.	1982
St. John's (N.Y.)*	1993-02
St. Mary's (Cal.)*	1993-03
St. Peter's*	1993-06
Siena*	1993-03
South Fla.	1997-00
Tex.-Arlington*	1982-85
Troy	1993-01
West Tex. A&M	1982-85

Dropped football program.

Black College National Champions

Sheridan Poll

Selected by the Pittsburgh Courier, 1920-80, and compiled by Collie Nicholson, former Grambling sports information director; William Nunn Jr., Pittsburgh Courier sports editor; and Eric "Ric" Roberts, Pittsburgh Courier sports writer and noted black college sports historian. Selected from 1981 by the Sheridan Broadcasting Network. Records include postseason games.

Year	Team	Won	Lost	Tied	Coach
1920	Howard	7	0	0	Edward Morrison
	Talladega	5	0	1	Jubie Bragg
1921	Talladega	6	0	1	Jubie Bragg
	Wiley	7	0	1	Jason Grant
1922	Hampton	6	1	0	Gideon Smith
1923	Virginia Union	6	0	1	Harold Martin
1924	Tuskegee	9	0	1	Cleve Abbott
	Wiley	8	0	1	Fred Long
1925	Tuskegee	8	0	1	Cleve Abbott
	Howard	6	0	2	Louis Watson
1926	Tuskegee	10	0	0	Cleve Abbott
	Howard	7	0	0	Louis Watson
1927	Tuskegee	9	0	1	Cleve Abbott
	Bluefield St.	8	0	1	Harry Jefferson
1928	Bluefield St.	8	0	1	Harry Jefferson
	Wiley	8	0	1	Fred Long
1929	Tuskegee	10	0	0	Cleve Abbott
1930	Tuskegee	11	0	1	Cleve Abbott
1931	Wilberforce	9	0	0	Harry Graves
1932	Wiley	9	0	0	Fred Long
1933	Morgan St.	9	0	0	Edward Hurt
1934	Kentucky St.	9	0	0	Henry Kean
1935	Texas College	9	0	0	Arnett Mumford
1936	West Virginia St.	8	0	0	Adolph Hamblin
	Virginia St.	7	0	2	Harry Jefferson
1937	Morgan St.	7	0	0	Edward Hurt
1938	Florida A&M	8	0	0	Bill Bell
1939	Langston	9	0	0	Felton "Zip" Gayles
1940	Morris Brown	9	1	0	Artis Graves
1941	Morris Brown	8	1	0	William Nicks
1942	Florida A&M	9	0	0	Bill Bell
1943	Morgan St.	5	0	0	Edward Hurt
1944	Morgan St.	6	1	0	Edward Hurt
1945	Wiley	10	0	0	Fred Long
1946	Tennessee St.	10	1	0	Henry Kean
	Morgan St.	8	0	0	Edward Hurt
1947	Tennessee St.	10	0	0	Henry Kean
	Shaw	10	0	0	Brutus Wilson
1948	Southern U.	12	0	0	Arnett Mumford
1949	Southern U.	10	0	1	Arnett Mumford
	Morgan St.	8	0	0	Edward Hurt
1950	Southern U.	10	0	1	Arnett Mumford
	Florida A&M	8	1	1	Alonzo "Jake" Gaither
1951	Morris Brown	10	1	0	Edward "Ox" Clemons
1952	Florida A&M	8	2	0	Alonzo "Jake" Gaither
	Texas Southern	10	0	1	Alexander Durley
	Lincoln (Mo.)	8	0	1	Dwight Reed
	Virginia St.	8	1	0	Sylvester "Sal" Hall
1953	Prairie View	12	0	0	William Nicks
1954	Tennessee St.	10	1	0	Henry Kean
	Southern U.	10	1	0	Arnett Mumford
	Florida A&M	8	1	0	Alonzo "Jake" Gaither
	Prairie View	10	1	0	William Nicks
1955	Grambling	10	0	0	Eddie Robinson
1956	Tennessee St.	10	0	0	Howard Gentry
1957	Florida A&M	9	0	0	Alonzo "Jake" Gaither
1958	Prairie View	10	0	1	William Nicks
1959	Florida A&M	10	0	0	Alonzo "Jake" Gaither
1960	Southern U.	9	1	0	Arnett Mumford
1961	Florida A&M	10	0	0	Alonzo "Jake" Gaither
1962	Jackson St.	10	1	0	John Merritt
1963	Prairie View	10	1	0	William Nicks
1964	Prairie View	9	0	0	William Nicks
1965	Tennessee St.	9	0	1	John Merritt
1966	Tennessee St.	10	0	0	John Merritt
1967	Morgan St.	8	0	0	Earl Banks
	Grambling	9	1	0	Eddie Robinson
1968	Alcorn St.	9	1	0	Marino Casem
	N.C. A&T	8	1	0	Hornsby Howell
1969	Alcorn St.	8	0	1	Marino Casem
1970	Tennessee St.	11	0	0	John Merritt
1971	Tennessee St.	9	1	0	John Merritt
1972	Grambling	11	2	0	Eddie Robinson
1973	Tennessee St.	10	0	0	John Merritt
1974	Grambling	11	1	0	Eddie Robinson
	Alcorn St.	9	2	0	Marino Casem
1975	Grambling	10	2	0	Eddie Robinson
1976	South Carolina St.	10	1	0	Willie Jeffries
1977	South Carolina St.	9	1	1	Willie Jeffries
	Grambling	10	1	0	Eddie Robinson
	Florida A&M	11	0	0	Rudy Hubbard
1978	Florida A&M	12	1	0	Rudy Hubbard
1979	Tennessee St.	8	3	0	John Merritt
1980	Grambling	10	2	0	Eddie Robinson
1981	South Carolina St.	10	3	0	Bill Davis
1982	* Tennessee St.	9	0	1	John Merritt
1983	Grambling	8	1	2	Eddie Robinson
1984	Alcorn St.	9	1	0	Marino Casem
1985	Jackson St.	8	3	0	W.C. Gorden
1986	Central St.	10	1	1	Billy Joe
1987	Central St.	10	1	1	Billy Joe
1988	Central St.	11	2	0	Billy Joe
1989	Central St.	10	2	0	Billy Joe
1990	# Central St.	11	1	0	Billy Joe
1991	Alabama St.	11	0	1	Houston Markham
1992	Grambling	10	2	0	Eddie Robinson
1993	Southern U.	11	1	0	Pete Richardson
1994	Hampton	10	1	0	Joe Taylor
1995	Southern U.	11	1	0	Pete Richardson
1996	Jackson St.	10	2	0	James Carson
1997	Southern U.	11	1	0	Pete Richardson
1998	Florida A&M	11	2	0	Billy Joe
1999	N.C. A&T	11	2	0	Bill Hayes
2000	Tuskegee	12	0	0	Rick Comegy
2001	Grambling	10	1	0	Doug Williams
2002	Grambling	11	2	0	Doug Williams
2003	Southern U.	12	1	0	Pete Richardson
2004	Hampton	10	2	0	Joe Taylor
2005	Grambling	11	1	0	Melvin Spears
2006	N.C. Central	11	1	0	Rod Broadway

**Tennessee State's participation in the 1982 FCS championship (1-1 record) voided.*
#NAIA Division I national champion.

American Sports Wire

Selected by American Sports Wire and compiled by Dick Simpson, Executive Director. Selected from 1990 by the American Sports Wire, P.O. Box 802031, Santa Clarita, Calif. 91380-2031. Record includes postseason games.

Year	Team	Won	Lost	Tied	Coach
1990	N.C. A&T	9	2	0	Bill Hayes
1991	Alabama St.	11	0	1	Houston Markham
1992	Grambling	10	2	0	Eddie Robinson
1993	Southern U.	11	1	0	Pete Richardson
1994	Hampton	10	1	0	Joe Taylor
1995	Southern U.	11	1	0	Pete Richardson
1996	Jackson St.	10	2	0	James Carson
1997	Southern U.	11	1	0	Pete Richardson
1998	Florida A&M	11	2	0	Billy Joe
1999	N.C. A&T	11	2	0	Bill Hayes
2000	Grambling	10	2	0	Doug Williams
2001	Grambling	10	1	0	Doug Williams
2002	Grambling	11	2	0	Doug Williams
2003	Southern U.	12	1	0	Pete Richardson
2004	Hampton	10	2	0	Joe Taylor
2005	Hampton	11	1	0	Joe Taylor
2006	Hampton	10	2	0	Joe Taylor

Heritage Bowl

The first bowl game matching historically black schools in FCS. The champion of the Southwestern Athletic Conference met the champion of the Mid-Eastern Athletic Conference.

Date	Score (Attendance)	Site
12-21-91	Alabama St. 36, N.C. A&T 13 (7,724)	Miami, Fla.
1-2-93	Grambling 45, Florida A&M 15 (11,273)	Tallahassee, Fla.
1-1-94	Southern U. 11, South Carolina St. 0 (36,128)	Atlanta, Ga.
12-30-94	South Carolina St. 31, Grambling 27 (22,179)	Atlanta, Ga.
12-29-95	Southern U. 30, Florida A&M 25 (25,164)	Atlanta, Ga.
12-31-96	Howard 27, Southern U. 24 (18,126)	Atlanta, Ga.
12-27-97	Southern U. 34, South Carolina St. 28 (32,629)	Atlanta, Ga.
12-26-98	Southern U. 28, Bethune-Cookman 2 (32, 955)	Atlanta, Ga.
12-18-99	Hampton 24, Southern U. 3 (29,561)	Atlanta, Ga.

All-Time Black College Football Team

(Selected by the Sheridan Broadcasting Network in 1993)

OFFENSE

Pos.	Player	School
QB	Doug Williams	Grambling
RB	Walter Payton	Jackson St.
RB	Tank Younger	Grambling
WR	Jerry Rice	Mississippi Val.
WR	John Stallworth	Alabama A&M
WR	Charlie Joiner	Grambling
OL	Art Shell	Md.-East. Shore
OL	Rayfield Wright	Fort Valley St.
OL	Jackie Slater	Jackson St.
OL	Larry Little	Bethune-Cookman
OL	Ernie Barnes	N.C. Central

DEFENSE

Pos.	Player	School
DL	Willie Davis	Grambling
DL	Ed "Too Tall" Jones	Tennessee St.
DL	Deacon Jones	South Carolina St.
DL	L.C. Greenwood	Ark.-Pine Bluff
LB	Robert Brazile	Jackson St.
LB	Harry Carson	South Carolina St.
LB	Willie Lanier	Morgan St.
DB	Mel Blount	Southern U.
DB	Lem Barney	Jackson St.
DB	Donnie Shell	South Carolina St.
DB	Everson Walls	Grambling

Individual and Team Collegiate Records

Individual Collegiate Records

Individual collegiate records are determined by comparing the best records in all four divisions (Football Bowl Subdivision, Football Championship Subdivision, II and III) in comparable categories. Before 2002, postseason games were not included in NCAA final football statistics or records. Beginning with the 2002 season, all postseason games were included in NCAA final football statistics and records. Included are career records of players who played in two divisions (e.g., Dennis Shaw of San Diego St., Howard Stevens of Randolph-Macon and Louisville, and Tom Ehrhardt of C.W. Post and Rhode Island). Players who played seasons other than in the NCAA will have statistics only including NCAA seasons.

Total Offense

CAREER YARDS PER GAME

(Minimum 5,500 Yards; Player must have concluded his career)

Player, Team (Division[s])	Years	G	Plays	Yards	TDR‡	Yd. PG
Steve McNair, Alcorn St. (FCS)	1991-94	42	2,055	16,823	152	400.5
Tim Rattay, Louisiana Tech (FBS)	1997-99	33	1,705	12,618	117	382.4
Justin Peery, Westminster (Mo.) (III)	1996-99	39	2,001	13,645	*166	349.9
Josh Brehm, Alma (III)	2003-06	36	1,946	12,247	107	340.2
Aaron Flowers, Cal St. Northridge (FCS)	1996-97	20	944	6,754	60	337.7
Jimmy Terwilliger, East Stroudsburg (II)	2003-06	48	1,902	16,064	161	334.7
Terry Peebles, Hanover (III)	1992-95	23	1,140	7,672	89	333.6
David Macchi, Valparaiso (FCS)	2002-03	23	1,047	7,628	65	331.7
Dave Dickenson, Montana (FCS)	1992-95	35	1,539	11,523	116	329.2
Willie Totten, Mississippi Val. (FCS)	1982-85	40	1,812	13,007	157	325.2
Grady Benton, West Tex. A&M (II)	1994-95	18	844	5,831	55	323.9
Bruce Eugene, Grambling (FCS)	$2001-05	46	1,998	14,720	159	320.0
Timmy Chang, Hawaii (FBS)	$2000-04	53	*2,587	*16,910	123	319.1
Ty Detmer, BYU (FBS)	1988-91	46	1,795	14,665	135	318.8
Neil Lomax, Portland St. (II; FCS)	1977; 78-80	42	1,901	13,345	120	317.7
Brett Dietz, Hanover (III)	2002-03	22	1,054	6,969	72	316.7
Drew Miller, Montana (FCS)	1999-00	18	708	5,628	47	312.7
Adam Ryan, Wilmington (Ohio) (III)	1998-01	33	1,520	10,314	47	312.5
Kirk Baumgartner, Wis.-Stevens Point (III)	1986-89	41	2,007	12,767	110	311.4
Mike Perez, San Jose St. (FBS)	1986-87	20	875	6,182	37	309.1
Doug Nussmeier, Idaho (FCS)	1990-93	39	1,556	12,054	109	309.1
Josh Wallwork, Wyoming (FBS)	1995-96	22	845	6,753	60	307.0
Oteman Sampson, Florida A&M (FCS)	1996-97	22	906	6,751	57	306.9
Dan Cole, Rensselaer (III)	2001-03	31	1,488	9,487	100	306.0
Doug Gaynor, Long Beach St. (FBS)	1984-85	22	1,067	6,710	45	305.0
Tod Mayfield, West Tex. A&M (FCS; II)	1984-85; 86	24	1,165	7,316	58	304.8
Marcus Brady, Cal St. Northridge (FCS)	1998-01	43	2,116	13,095	123	304.5
J.T. O'Sullivan, UC Davis (II)	1998-01	29	987	8,743	78	301.5
Zamir Amin, Menlo (III)	1999-01	26	1,015	7,836	87	301.4
Jamie Martin, Weber St. (FCS)	1989-92	41	1,838	12,287	93	299.7

**Record. $See Page 10 for explanation. ‡Touchdowns-responsible-for are player's TDs scored and passed for.*

SEASON YARDS PER GAME

Player, Team (Division)	Year	G	Plays	Yards	TDR‡	Yd. PG
Steve McNair, Alcorn St. (FCS)	†1994	11	649	5,799	53	527.2
David Klingler, Houston (FBS)	†1990	11	704	5,221	55	474.6
Justin Peery, Westminster (Mo.) (III)	†1998	10	645	4,651	57	465.1
B.J. Symons, Texas Tech (FBS)	†2003	13	798	*5,976	52	459.7
Willie Totten, Mississippi Val. (FCS)	†1984	10	564	4,572	61	457.2
Justin Peery, Westminster (Mo.) (III)	†1999	10	599	4,419	60	441.9
Danny Ragsdale, Redlands (III)	1999	9	464	3,855	35	428.3
Andre Ware, Houston (FBS)	†1989	11	628	4,661	49	423.7
Zamir Amin, Menlo (III)	†2000	10	511	4,231	43	423.1
Colt Brennan, Hawaii (FBS)	†2006	14	645	5,915	*63	422.5
Ty Detmer, BYU (FBS)	1990	12	635	5,022	45	418.5
Grady Benton, West Tex. A&M (II)	†1994	9	505	3,699	35	411.0
Josh Brehm, Alma (III)	†2006	10	616	4,084	39	408.4
Steve McNair, Alcorn St. (FCS)	†1992	10	519	4,057	39	405.7
Perry Klein, C.W. Post (II)	†1993	10	499	4,052	41	405.2
Tim Rattay, Louisiana Tech (FBS)	†1998	12	602	4,840	47	403.3
Mike Maxwell, Nevada (FBS)	†1995	9	443	3,623	34	402.6
Chris Redman, Louisville (FBS)	1998	10	513	4,009	31	400.9
Terry Peebles, Hanover (III)	†1995	10	572	3,981	43	398.1
Steve Young, BYU (FBS)	†1983	11	531	4,346	41	395.1
Jamie Martin, Weber St. (FCS)	†1991	11	591	4,337	37	394.3
Chris Vargas, Nevada (FBS)	†1993	11	535	4,332	35	393.8

**Record. †National total-offense champion. ‡Touchdowns-responsible-for are player's TDs scored and passed for.*

CAREER YARDS

Player, Team (Division[s])	Years	Plays	Yards	Avg.
Timmy Chang, Hawaii (FBS)	$2000-04	*2,587	16,910	6.54
Steve McNair, Alcorn St. (FCS)	1991-94	2,055	16,823	8.19
Jimmy Terwilliger, East Stroudsburg (II)	2003-06	1,902	16,064	8.45
Bruce Eugene, Grambling (FCS)	$2001-05	1,998	14,720	7.37
Ty Detmer, BYU (FBS)	1988-91	1,795	14,665	8.17
Scott Eyster, Delta St. (II)	2003-06	1,897	14,319	7.55
Kevin Kolb, Houston (FBS)	2003-06	2,037	13,715	6.73
Justin Peery, Westminster (Mo.) (III)	1996-99	2,001	13,645	6.82
Philip Rivers, North Carolina St. (FBS)	2000-03	1,422	13,582	*9.55
Neil Lomax, Portland St. (II; FCS)	1977; 78-80	1,901	13,345	7.02
Cullen Finnerty, Grand Valley St. (II)	2003-06	1,881	13,275	7.06
Marcus Brady, Cal St. Northridge (FCS)	1998-01	2,116	13,095	6.19
Brad Smith, Missouri (FBS)	2002-05	2,283	13,088	5.73
Willie Totten, Mississippi Val. (FCS)	1982-85	1,812	13,007	7.18
Adam Knoblauch, Delaware Valley (III)	2002-05	1,985	12,833	6.46
Kirk Baumgartner, Wis.-Stevens Point (III)	1986-89	2,007	12,767	6.36
Luke McCown, Louisiana Tech (FBS)	2000-03	2,049	12,731	6.21
Tim Rattay, Louisiana Tech (FBS)	1997-99	1,705	12,618	7.40
Robert Kent, Jackson St. (FCS)	2000-03	1,928	12,538	6.33
Joey Conrad, Glenville St. (II)	2002-05	1,898	12,491	6.58
James McNear, Concordia-St. Paul (II)	2002-05	1,746	12,446	7.13
Daunte Culpepper, UCF (FCS; FBS)	1995-98	1,847	12,432	6.73
Chad Pennington, Marshall (FCS; FBS)	1995, 97-99	1,719	12,313	7.16
Jamie Martin, Weber St. (FCS)	1989-92	1,838	12,287	6.68
Kliff Kingsbury, Texas Tech (FBS)	1999-02	2,156	12,263	5.69
Josh Brehm, Alma (III)	2003-06	1,946	12,247	6.29
John Port, Albright (III)	$2001-05	1,816	12,195	6.72
Travis Lulay, Montana St. (FCS)	2002-05	2,006	12,190	6.08
Chris Redman, Louisville (FBS)	1996-99	1,846	12,129	6.57
Rocky Pentello, Capital (III)	$2002-06	1,770	12,126	6.85

**Record. ¢Active player. $See Page 10 for explanation.*

SEASON YARDS

Player, Team (Division)	Year	G	Plays	Yards	Avg.
B.J. Symons, Texas Tech (FBS)	†2003	13	798	5,976	7.49
Colt Brennan, Hawaii (FBS)	†2006	14	645	5,915	9.17
Steve McNair, Alcorn St. (FCS)	†1994	11	649	5,799	8.94
Chad Friehauf, Colorado Mines (II)	†2004	13	660	5,363	8.13
David Klingler, Houston (FBS)	†1990	11	704	5,221	7.42
Ty Detmer, BYU (FBS)	1990	12	635	5,022	7.91
Bruce Eugene, Grambling (FCS)	2002	13	680	5,018	7.38
Jimmy Terwilliger, East Stroudsburg (II)	†2005	14	551	4,960	9.00
Kliff Kingsbury, Texas Tech (FBS)	2002	14	*814	4,903	6.02
Tim Rattay, Louisiana Tech (FBS)	†1998	12	602	4,840	8.04
Brett Elliott, Linfield (III)	†2004	13	472	4,663	9.88
Andre Ware, Houston (FBS)	†1989	11	628	4,661	7.42
Justin Peery, Westminster (Mo.) (III)	†1998	10	645	4,651	6.58
Josh Harris, Bowling Green (FBS)	2003	14	709	4,643	6.55
Jim McMahon, BYU (FBS)	†1980	12	540	4,627	8.57
Philip Rivers, North Carolina St. (FBS)	2003	13	561	4,600	8.20
Ben Roethlisberger, Miami (Ohio) (FBS)	2003	14	562	4,597	8.18
Dustin Long, Sam Houston St. (FCS)	2004	14	576	4,576	7.94
Sonny Cumbie, Texas Tech (FBS)	†2004	12	694	4,575	6.59
Willie Totten, Mississippi Val. (FCS)	†1984	10	564	4,572	8.11
Chase Holbrook, New Mexico St. (FBS)	2006	12	647	4,541	7.02

**Record. †National total-offense champion.*

SINGLE-GAME YARDS

Yds.	Div.	Player, Team (Opponent)	Date
732	FBS	David Klingler, Houston (Arizona St.)	Dec. 2, 1990
723	III	Zamir Amin, Menlo (Cal Lutheran)	Oct. 7, 2000
696	FBS	Matt Vogler, TCU (Houston)	Nov. 3, 1990
681	FBS	B.J. Symons, Texas Tech (Mississippi)	Sept. 27, 2003
668	FCS	Robert Kent, Jackson St. (Alabama St.)	Oct. 6, 2001
660	II	Andrew Webb, Fort Lewis (Mesa St.)	Nov. 16, 2002
657	FBS	Brian Lindgren, Idaho (Middle Tenn.)	Oct. 6, 2001
652	II	Matt Kohn, Indianapolis (Michigan Tech)	Sept. 20, 2003
651	II	Wilkie Perez, Glenville St. (Concord)	Oct. 25, 1997
649	FCS	Steve McNair, Alcorn St. (Southern U.)	Oct. 22, 1994
647	FCS	Steve McNair, Alcorn St. (Chattanooga)	Sept. 10, 1994
643	FCS	Jamie Martin, Weber St. (Idaho St.)	Nov. 23, 1991
641	FCS	Bruce Eugene, Grambling (Prairie View)	Oct. 1, 2005
633	FCS	Steve McNair, Alcorn St. (Grambling)	Sept. 3, 1994
631	II	Jayce Goree, Glenville St. (Concord)	Oct. 24, 1998
630	III	Justin Peery, Westminster (Mo.) (Colorado Col.)	Oct. 30, 1999
628	III	Justin Peery, Westminster (Mo.) (MacMurray)	Nov. 14, 1998
625	FBS	David Klingler, Houston (TCU)	Nov. 3, 1990
625	FBS	Scott Mitchell, Utah (Air Force)	Oct. 15, 1988
624	FCS	Steve McNair, Alcorn St. (Samford)	Oct. 29, 1994
623	II	Perry Klein, C.W. Post (Salisbury)	Nov. 6, 1993
621	FCS	Willie Totten, Mississippi Val. (Prairie View)	Oct. 27, 1984
618	FBS	B.J. Symons, Texas Tech (North Carolina St.)	Sept. 20, 2003
617	III	Justin Peery, Westminster (Mo.) (Principia)	Oct. 17, 1998
614	FCS	Bryan Martin, Weber St. (Cal Poly)	Sept. 23, 1995
614	II	Alfred Montez, Western N.M. (West Tex. A&M)	Oct. 8, 1994
612	FBS	Jimmy Klingler, Houston (Rice)	Nov. 28, 1992
610	II	Andrew Webb, Fort Lewis (Western N.M.)	Nov. 2, 2002
604	FBS	Cody Hodges, Texas Tech (Kansas St.)	Oct. 15, 2005
604	FCS	Steve McNair, Alcorn St. (Jackson St.)	Nov. 21, 1992
603	FBS	Ty Detmer, Brigham Young (San Diego St.)	Nov. 16, 1991
601	FBS	Troy Kopp, Pacific (New Mexico St.)	Oct. 20, 1990

Rushing

CAREER YARDS PER GAME

(Minimum 2,500 Yards; Player must have concluded his career)

Player, Team (Division[s])	Years	G	Carries	Yards	TD	Yd. PG
Arnold Mickens, Butler (FCS)	1994-95	20	763	3,813	29	190.7
R.J. Bowers, Grove City (III)	1997-00	40	1,188	*7,353	91	183.8
Anthony Gray, Western N.M. (II)	1997-98	19	503	3,484	19	183.4
Ed Marinaro, Cornell (FBS)	1969-71	27	918	4,715	50	174.6
Antoine Bagwell, California (Pa.) (II)	2004-05	20	432	3,353	41	167.7
Damian Beane, Shepherd (II)	1996-99	38	1,065	6,346	58	167.0
Rob Marchitello, Maine Maritime (III)	1993-95	26	879	4,300	59	165.4
O.J. Simpson, Southern California (FBS)	1967-68	19	621	3,214	33	164.4
Kelvin Gladney, Millsaps (III)	1993-94	19	510	3,085	36	162.4
Johnny Bailey, Tex. A&M-Kingsville (II)	1986-89	39	885	6,320	66	162.1
Brett Trichilo, Wilkes (III)	2001-04	36	981	5,837	63	162.1
Tyrone Morgan, Northern St. (II)	1998-00	30	830	4,816	56	160.5
Herschel Walker, Georgia (FBS)	1980-82	33	994	5,259	49	159.4
Brian Shay, Emporia St. (II)	1995-98	44	1,007	6,958	81	158.1
Carey Bender, Coe (III)	1991-94	39	926	6,125	71	157.1
Brad Olson, Lawrence (III)	1994-97	34	792	5,325	44	156.6
Garrett Wolfe, Northern Ill. (FBS)	2004-06	33	807	5,164	52	156.5
Steve Tardif, Maine Maritime (III)	1996-99	39	1,190	6,093	50	156.2
Adrian Peterson, Ga. Southern (FCS)	1998-01	42	996	6,559	84	156.2
Kirk Matthieu, Maine Maritime (III)	$1989-93	33	964	5,107	41	154.8
Josh Ranek, South Dakota St. (II)	$1997-01	44	1,131	6,794	62	154.4
Aaron Stecker, Western Ill. (FCS)	1997-98	20	550	3,081	36	154.1
Tim Hall, Robert Morris (FCS)	1994-95	19	393	2,908	27	153.1
Fred Lane, Lane (II)	1994-96	29	700	4,433	41	152.9
Terry Underwood, Wagner (III)	1985-88	33	742	5,010	52	151.8
Kavin Gailliard, American Int'l (II)	1996-99	43	950	6,523	69	151.7
Jerry Azumah, New Hampshire (FCS)	1995-98	41	1,044	6,193	60	151.0
LeShon Johnson, Northern Ill. (FBS)	1992-93	22	592	3,314	18	150.6
Reggie Greene, Siena (FCS)	1994-97	36	890	5,415	45	150.4
Ole Gunderson, St. Olaf (II)	1969-71	27	639	4,060	56	150.4
Richard Huntley, Winston-Salem (II)	1992-95	42	932	6,286	57	149.7

**Record. $See Page 10 for explanation.*

SEASON YARDS PER GAME

Player, Team (Division)	Year	G	Carries	Yards	TD	Yd. PG
Barry Sanders, Oklahoma St. (FBS)	†1988	11	344	2,628	*37	238.9
Dante Brown, Marietta (III)	†1996	10	314	2,385	25	238.5
R.J. Bowers, Grove City (III)	†1998	10	329	2,283	34	228.3
Arnold Mickens, Butler (FCS)	†1994	10	409	2,255	18	225.5
Carey Bender, Coe (III)	†1994	10	295	2,243	29	224.3
Anthony Gray, Western N.M. (II)	†1997	10	277	2,220	12	222.0
Kavin Gailliard, American Int'l (II)	†1999	12	320	2,653	32	221.1
Tony Sutton, Wooster (III)	†2003	9	271	1,955	30	217.2
Marcus Allen, Southern California (FBS)	†1981	11	403	2,342	22	212.9
Danny Woodhead, Chadron St. (II)	†2006	13	344	*2,756	34	212.0
Ian Smart, C.W. Post (II)	†2001	12	308	2,536	33	211.3
R.J. Bowers, Grove City (III)	†1999	10	344	2,098	25	209.8
Ed Marinaro, Cornell (FBS)	†1971	9	356	1,881	24	209.0
Brian Shay, Emporia St. (II)	†1998	11	293	2,265	29	205.9
Charles Roberts, Sacramento St. (FCS)	†1998	11	386	2,260	19	205.5
Irv Sigler, Bloomsburg (II)	1997	10	299	2,038	20	203.8
Ricky Gales, Simpson (III)	†1989	10	297	2,035	26	203.5
Tony Vinson, Towson (FCS)	†1993	10	293	2,016	23	201.6
Terry Underwood, Wagner (III)	†1988	9	245	1,809	21	201.0
Jerry Azumah, New Hampshire (FCS)	1998	11	342	2,195	22	199.6

**Record. †National champion.*

CAREER YARDS

Player, Team (Division[s])	Years	Carries	Yards	Avg.
R.J. Bowers, Grove City (III)	1997-00	1,188	7,353	6.19
Germaine Race, Pittsburg St. (II)	2003-06	941	6,985	7.42
Brian Shay, Emporia St. (II)	1995-98	1,007	6,958	6.91

COLLEGIATE RECORDS

Player, Team (Division[s])	Years	Carries	Yards	Avg.
Josh Ranek, South Dakota St. (II)	$1997-01	1,131	6,794	6.01
Ian Smart, C.W. Post (II)	1999-02	877	6,647	++7.58
Adrian Peterson, Ga. Southern (FCS)	1998-01	996	6,559	6.59
Charles Roberts, Sacramento St. (FCS)	1997-00	1,124	6,553	5.83
Kavin Gailliard, American Int'l (II)	1996-99	950	6,523	6.87
Ron Dayne, Wisconsin (FBS)	1996-99	1,115	6,397	5.74
¢Danny Woodhead, Chadron St. (II)	2004-06	906	6,365	7.03
Damian Beane, Shepherd (II)	1996-99	1,065	6,346	5.96
Johnny Bailey, Tex. A&M-Kingsville (II)	1986-89	885	6,320	7.14
Richard Huntley, Winston-Salem (II)	1992-95	932	6,286	6.74
Ricky Williams, Texas (FBS)	1995-98	1,011	6,279	6.21
Jerry Azumah, New Hampshire (FCS)	1995-98	1,044	6,193	5.93
Jarrett Anderson, Truman (II)	1993-96	979	6,166	6.30
Carey Bender, Coe (III)	1991-94	926	6,125	6.61
Steve Tardif, Maine Maritime (III)	1996-99	1,190	6,093	5.12
Tony Dorsett, Pittsburgh (FBS)	1973-76	1,074	6,082	5.66
DeAngelo Williams, Memphis (FBS)	2002-05	969	6,026	6.22
Charles Dunn, Portland St. (II;FCS)	1997; 98-00	1,098	6,007	5.47
Stefan Logan, South Dakota (II)	2003-06	808	5,958	7.37
Roger Graham, New Haven (II)	1991-94	821	5,953	7.25
Brett Trichilo, Wilkes (III)	2001-04	981	5,837	5.95
Anthony Russo, St. John's (N.Y.) (III)	1990-93	1,152	5,834	5.06
Eddie Acosta, Bemidji St. (II)	$1999-03	1,038	5,792	5.58
Tony Sutton, Findlay (II); Wooster (III)	2001; 2002-04	851	5,685	6.68
Wesley Cates, California (Pa.) (II)	1998-01	937	5,647	6.03
Charles White, Southern California (FBS)	1976-79	1,023	5,598	5.47
Travis Prentice, Miami (Ohio) (FBS)	1996-99	1,138	5,596	4.92

++Record for minimum 600 carries. ¢Active player. $See Page 10 for explanation.

SEASON YARDS

Player, Team (Division)	Year	G	Carries	Yards	Avg.
Danny Woodhead, Chadron St. (II)	†2006	13	344	2,756	8.01
Kavin Gailliard, American Int'l (II)	†1999	12	320	2,653	8.29
Barry Sanders, Oklahoma St. (FBS)	†1988	11	344	2,628	7.64
Ian Smart, C.W. Post (II)	†2001	12	308	2,536	8.23
Justin Beaver, Wis.-Whitewater (III)	†2005	14	428	2,420	5.65
Dante Brown, Marietta (III)	†1996	10	314	2,385	7.60
Nate Kmic, Mount Union (III)	2006	15	336	2,365	7.04
Marcus Allen, Southern California (FBS)	†1981	11	403	2,342	5.81
Jamaal Branch, Colgate (FCS)	†2003	16	*450	2,326	5.17
Dan Pugh, Mount Union (III)	†2002	14	384	2,300	5.99
R.J. Bowers, Grove City (III)	†1998	10	329	2,283	6.94
Brian Shay, Emporia St. (II)	†1998	11	293	2,265	7.73
Charles Roberts, Sacramento St. (FCS)	†1998	11	386	2,260	5.85
Jamar Brittingham, Bloomsburg (II)	†2005	12	316	2,260	7.15
Arnold Mickens, Butler (FCS)	†1994	10	409	2,255	5.51
Carey Bender, Coe (III)	†1994	10	295	2,243	7.60
Tony Sutton, Wooster (III)	†2004	12	352	2,240	6.36
Anthony Gray, Western N.M. (II)	†1997	10	277	2,220	8.01
Germaine Race, Pittsburg St. (II)	2004	15	247	2,213	††8.96
Jerry Azumah, New Hampshire (FCS)	1998	11	342	2,195	6.42
Mark Robinson, St. John Fisher (III)	2004	12	386	2,194	5.68
Troy Davis, Iowa St. (FBS)	†1996	11	402	2,185	5.44

**Record. †National champion. ††Record for minimum 214 carries.*

SINGLE-GAME YARDS

Yds.	Div.	Player, Team (Opponent)	Date
441	III	Dante Brown, Marietta (Baldwin-Wallace)	Oct. 5, 1996
437	FCS	Maurice Hicks, N.C. A&T (Morgan St.)	Oct. 6, 2001
436	III	A.J. Pittorino, Hartwick (Waynesburg)	Nov. 2, 1996
417	III	Carey Bender, Coe (Grinnell)	Oct. 9, 1993
413	III	Dante Brown, Marietta (Heidelberg)	Nov. 9, 1996
410	II	Andrew Terry, Ferris St. (Findlay)	Oct. 2, 2004
409	FCS	Charles Roberts, Sacramento St. (Idaho St.)	Nov. 6, 1999
406	FBS	LaDainian Tomlinson, TCU (UTEP)	Nov. 20, 1999
405	II	Alvon Brown, Kentucky St. (Ky. Wesleyan)	Sept. 16, 2000
403	II	Rob Davidson, Fairmont St. (Concord)	Nov. 14, 1998
396	FBS	Tony Sands, Kansas (Missouri)	Nov. 23, 1991
393	FCS	Ryan Fuqua, Portland St. (Eastern Wash.)	Nov. 10, 2001
391	III	Andrew Mocadlo, Wis.-La Crosse (Wis.-Stout)	Nov. 1, 2003
390	III	Paul Smith, Gettysburg (Muhlenberg)	Oct. 23, 1999
386	FBS	Marshall Faulk, San Diego St. (Pacific)	Sept. 14, 1991
385	III	Jason Meyers, St. John Fisher (Rochester)	Sept. 13, 2003
384	II	R.J. Rollins, Minn.-Crookston (Minn. St. Moorhead)	Nov. 6, 2004
382	III	Shane Davis, Loras (Dubuque)	Nov. 8, 1997
382	III	Pete Baranek, Carthage [North Central (Ill.)]	Oct. 5, 1985
382	II	Kelly Ellis, UNI (Western Ill.)	Oct. 13, 1979
380	II	Garrion Corbin, Tiffin (Quincy)	Nov. 16, 2002
379	FCS	Reggie Greene, Siena [St. John's (N.Y.)]	Nov. 2, 1996
378	II	Jason Broom, Fort Hays St. (Okla. Panhandle)	Oct. 6, 2001
378	FBS	Troy Davis, Iowa St. (Missouri)	Sept. 28, 1996
377	III	Antwan Harris, Mount Ida (Becker)	Sept. 24, 2005
377	FBS	Robbie Mixon, Central Mich. (Eastern Mich.)	Nov. 2, 2002
377	FBS	Anthony Thompson, Indiana (Wisconsin)	Nov. 11, 1989
376	FBS	Travis Prentice, Miami (Ohio) (Akron)	Nov. 6, 1999
373	FBS	Astron Whatley, Kent St. (Eastern Mich.)	Sept. 20, 1997
373	II	Dallas Garber, Marietta (Wash. & Jeff.)	Nov. 7, 1959
371	III	Nate Kmic, Mount Union (St. John Fisher)	Dec. 9, 2006
370	II	Jim Baier, Wis.-River Falls (Wis.-Stevens Point)	Nov. 5, 1966
370	II	Jim Hissam, Marietta [Bethany (W.V.)]	Nov. 15, 1958

Passing

CAREER PASSING EFFICIENCY

(Minimum 475 Completions; Player must have concluded his career)

Player, Team (Division[s])	Years	Att.	Cmp.	Int.	Pct.	Yds.	TD	Pts.
Bill Borchert, Mount Union (III)	1994-97	1,009	671	17	.665	10,201	141	194.2
Gary Smeck, Mount Union (III)	1997-00	752	504	15	.670	7,764	83	186.2
Brett Elliott, Utah (FBS); Linfield (III)	$2001-03, 04-05	1,113	726	30	.652	10,626	122	174.9
Jimmy Terwilliger, East Stroudsburg (II)	2003-06	1,481	906	36	.612	14,350	148	170.7
Roy Hampton, Trinity (Tex.) (III)	$1998-02	942	600	26	.637	8,869	94	170.2
Dusty Bonner, Kentucky (FBS); Valdosta St. (II)	1997,99-01	1,233	861	27	.698	10,501	123	169.9
J.T. O'Sullivan, UC Davis (II)	1998-01	808	510	32	.631	8,143	72	169.3
J.D. Ricca, Hampden-Sydney (III)	2002-05	920	584	28	.635	8,626	91	168.8
Ryan Dinwiddie, Boise St. (FBS)	2000-03	992	622	21	.627	9,819	82	168.4
Erik Meyer, Eastern Wash. (FCS)	2002-05	1,097	721	17	.657	10,261	84	166.5
Dave Dickenson, Montana (FCS)	1992-95	1,208	813	26	.673	11,080	96	166.3
Corte McGuffey, Northern Colo. (II)	1996-99	768	484	23	.630	6,975	75	165.6
Jordan Neal, Hardin-Simmons (III)	$2001, 03-06	907	620	31	.684	8,347	72	165.0
Curt Anes, Grand Valley St. (II)	1999-02	1,186	741	27	.625	10,581	114	164.6
Danny Wuerffel, Florida (FBS)	1993-96	1,170	708	42	.605	10,875	114	163.6
Omar Jacobs, Bowling Green (FBS)	2003-05	811	523	11	.645	6,937	71	163.5
Chad Johnson, Pacific Lutheran (III)	1998-00	699	491	20	.702	6,292	48	162.8
Ty Detmer, BYU (FBS)	1988-91	1,530	958	65	.626	15,031	121	162.7
Steve Sarkisian, BYU (FBS)	1995-96	789	528	26	.669	7,464	53	162.0
Chris Edwards, Wash. & Jeff. (III)	2002-05	923	561	30	.608	8,303	87	160.9
Zamir Amin, Menlo (III)	1999-01	905	566	29	.625	7,982	83	160.5
Mike Simpson, Eureka (III)/ Eastern Ill. (FCS)	1993-94, 96-97	724	481	25	.664	6,402	58	160.3
Eric Rasmussen, San Diego (FCS)	2001-03	851	512	13	.602	7,490	75	160.1

Player, Team (Division[s])	Years	Att.	Cmp.	Int.	Pct.	Yds.	TD	Pts.
Jim Ballard, Wilmington (Ohio)/ Mount Union (III)	1990, 91-93	1,199	743	41	.620	10,379	115	159.5
Matt Leinart, Southern California (FBS)	2002-05	1,245	807	23	.648	10,693	99	159.5
Justin Coleman, Neb.-Kearney (II)	1997-00	1,193	706	42	.592	11,213	99	158.5
Troy Dougherty, Grinnell (III)	1994, 97-99	1,192	734	33	.616	10,140	109	157.7
Bruce Gradkowski, Toledo (FBS)	2002-05	1,123	766	27	.682	9,225	85	157.4
Billy Blanton, San Diego St. (FBS)	1993-96	920	588	25	.639	8,165	67	157.1
Jim McMahon, BYU (FBS)	1977-78, 80-81	1,060	653	34	.616	9,536	84	156.9

$See Page 10 for explanation.

CAREER PASSING EFFICIENCY

(Minimum 375-474 Completions)

Player, Team (Division)	Years	Att.	Cmp.	Int.	Pct.	Yds.	TD	Pts.
Wesley Beschorner, South Dakota (II)	2002-05	673	415	18	.617	6,240	64	165.6
Alex Smith, Utah (FBS)	2002-04	587	389	8	.663	5,203	47	164.4
Chris Petersen, UC Davis (II)	1985-86	553	385	13	*.696	4,988	39	164.0
Kurt Ramler, St. John's (Minn.) (III)	1994-96	722	420	16	.582	6,475	75	163.4
Danny Ragsdale, Redlands (III)	1997-99	610	386	17	.633	5,560	51	161.9
Dan DesPlaines, Trinity (Tex.) (III)	2001-04	720	461	19	.640	6,374	60	160.6
Drew Miller, Montana (FCS)	1999-00	654	430	14	.657	5,900	46	160.5
Kyle Adamson, Allegheny (III)	1995-97	608	388	18	.638	5,506	48	160.0
Troy Smith, Ohio St. (FBS)	2002-06	670	420	13	.627	5,720	54	157.1
Will Hall, North Ala. (II)	2002-03	693	471	21	.680	6,166	42	156.7
Jason Baer, Wash. & Jeff. (III)	1993-96	671	406	24	.605	5,632	66	156.3
Tony Racioppi, Rowan (III)	2000-02	669	386	28	.577	5,881	66	155.7
Joe Germaine, Ohio St. (FBS)	1996-98	660	399	18	.605	5,844	52	155.4
Chad Johnson, Pacific Lutheran (III)	1998-00	699	433	20	.619	6,292	48	154.5
Joel Parrett, Bluffton (III)	1996-99	633	412	28	.651	5,684	43	154.1
Rick Hebert, American Int'l (II)	1996-99	699	423	16	.605	5,990	55	153.9
Mark Washington, Jackson St. (FCS)	1996-99	724	384	24	.530	6,561	68	153.5
Joe Blake, Simpson (III)	1987-90	672	399	15	.594	6,183	43	153.3
Vinny Testaverde, Miami (Fla.) (FBS)	1982, 84-86	674	413	25	.613	6,058	48	152.9
Jim McMillan, Boise St. (II)	1971-74	640	382	29	.597	5,508	58	152.8
Sean Hoolihan, Wis.-Eau Claire (III)	1996-98	686	413	23	.602	6,301	46	152.8
Josh Wallwork, Wyoming (FBS)	1995-96	729	449	28	.616	6,453	54	152.7
Brian Eyerman, Indiana (Pa.) (II)	1999-02	837	467	32	.558	7,409	76	152.5
Trent Dilfer, Fresno St. (FBS)	1991-93	774	461	21	.596	6,944	51	151.2
Chris Greisen, Northwest Mo. St. (II)	1995-98	653	379	22	.580	5,741	51	150.9
Greg Lister, Rowan (III)	1994-97	773	454	29	.587	6,553	66	150.6
Aaron Rodgers, California (FBS)	2002-04	665	424	13	.638	5,469	43	150.3
Troy Aikman, Oklahoma/UCLA (FBS)	1984-85, 87-88	637	401	18	.630	5,436	40	149.7
Chuck Hartlieb, Iowa (FBS)	1985-88	716	461	17	.643	6,269	34	148.9
Jay Johnson, UNI (FCS)	1989-92	744	397	25	.534	7,049	51	148.9

**Record.*

SEASON PASSING EFFICIENCY

(Minimum 30 Attempts Per Game)

Player, Team (Division)	Year	G	Att.	Cmp.	Int.	Pct.	Yds.	TD	Pts.
Brett Elliott, Linfield (III)	†2004	13	437	290	11	.664	4,595	*61	195.7
Jim Ballard, Mount Union (III)	1993	10	314	229	11	.729	3,304	37	193.2
Brett Elliott, Linfield (III)	†2005	11	396	277	9	.699	4,019	49	191.5
Jayson Merrill, Western St. (II)	†1991	10	309	195	11	.631	3,484	35	188.1
Dusty Bonner, Valdosta St. (II)	2000	11	435	317	6	.728	3,907	54	186.5
Jimmy Terwilliger, East Stroudsburg (II)	2005	14	424	262	11	.618	4,571	50	186.1
Colt Brennan, Hawaii (FBS)	†2006	14	559	406	12	.726	5,549	58	186.0
Kevin Ricca, Catholic (III)	1997	10	306	208	6	.679	2,990	35	183.9
John Charles, Portland St. (II)	1992	8	263	179	7	.681	2,770	24	181.3
Chad Johnson, Pacific Lutheran (III)	2000	9	274	185	6	.675	2,839	24	179.1
Chris Hatcher, Valdosta St. (II)	†1994	11	430	321	9	*.747	3,591	50	179.0
Wilkie Perez, Glenville St. (II)	†1997	11	425	280	12	.658	4,189	45	178.0
Jim McMahon, BYU (FBS)	†1980	12	445	284	18	.638	4,571	47	176.9
Ty Detmer, BYU (FBS)	†1989	12	412	265	15	.643	4,560	32	175.6
Eric Rasmussen, San Diego (FCS)	†2003	10	318	195	3	.613	2,982	35	174.5
Jimmy Terwilliger, East Stroudsburg (II)	†2004	12	362	222	11	.613	3,826	33	174.1
Chris Boden, Villanova (FCS)	1997	11	345	231	4	.670	3,079	36	174.0
Trent Dilfer, Fresno St. (FBS)	†1993	11	333	217	4	.652	3,276	28	173.1
Jerry Rhome, Tulsa (FBS)	†1964	10	326	224	4	.687	2,870	32	172.6
Rocky Butler, Hofstra (FCS)	2001	11	335	206	4	.615	3,311	30	171.7
Rex Grossman, Florida (FBS)	†2001	11	395	259	12	.656	3,896	34	170.8

**Record. †National pass-efficiency champion.*

SEASON PASSING EFFICIENCY

(Minimum 15 Attempts Per Game)

Player, Team (Division)	Year	G	Att.	Cmp.	Int.	Pct.	Yds.	TD	Pts.
Mike Simpson, Eureka (III)	†1994	10	158	116	5	.734	1,988	25	225.0
Willie Seiler, St. John's (Minn.) (III)	†1993	10	205	141	6	.687	2,648	33	224.6
Curt Anes, Grand Valley St. (II)	†2001	10	271	189	3	.697	3,086	48	221.6
Dustin Proctor, Hardin-Simmons (III)	†2001	9	178	116	3	.652	2,194	28	217.2
Bill Borchert, Mount Union (III)	†1997	10	272	190	1	.698	2,933	47	216.7
Wesley Beschorner, South Dakota (II)	†2005	11	255	172	4	.675	3,049	39	215.2
Boyd Crawford, Albertson (II)	†1953	8	120	72	6	.600	1,462	21	210.1

Player, Team (Division)	Year	G	Att.	Cmp.	Int.	Pct.	Yds.	TD	Pts.
Bill Borchert, Mount Union (III)	†1996	10	240	165	6	.687	2,655	38	208.9
Gary Smeck, Mount Union (III)	†1999	10	199	131	3	.658	2,274	30	208.6
Shawn Knight, William & Mary (FCS)	†1993	10	177	125	4	.706	2,055	22	204.6
Matt LeFever, Western Conn. St. (III)	1999	10	158	95	7	.601	1,874	25	203.1
Brian Dawson, Wash. & Jeff. (III)	†2000	10	227	149	6	.656	2,675	29	201.5
Troy Dougherty, Grinnell (III)	†1998	10	293	198	5	.675	3,310	36	199.6
Dusty Bonner, Valdosta St. (II)	2001	11	319	231	8	.724	3,214	43	196.5
Bill Borchert, Mount Union (III)	†1995	10	225	160	4	.711	2,270	30	196.3
Jason Baer, Wash. & Jeff. (III)	1995	8	146	95	3	.650	1,536	19	192.3
Greg Lister, Rowan (III)	1997	9	162	111	4	.685	1,688	20	191.9
Gary Smeck, Mount Union (III)	2000	10	266	184	3	.691	2,773	30	191.7
J.T. O'Sullivan, UC Davis (II)	†2000	9	226	141	7	.623	2,648	25	191.1
Chuck Green, Wittenberg (II)	†1963	9	182	114	8	.626	2,181	19	189.0

†National pass-efficiency champion.

CAREER YARDS

Player, Team (Division[s])	Years	Att.	Cmp.	Int.	Pct.	Yds.	TD
Timmy Chang, Hawaii (FBS)	$2000-04	*2,436	*1,388	80	.570	17,072	117
Ty Detmer, BYU (FBS)	1988-91	1,530	958	65	.626	15,031	121
Steve McNair, Alcorn St. (FCS)	1991-94	1,680	929	58	.553	14,496	119
Jimmy Terwilliger, East Stroudsburg (II)	2003-06	1,481	906	36	.612	14,350	*148
Scott Eyster, Delta St. (II)	2003-06	1,644	1,001	37	.609	13,887	116
Bruce Eugene, Grambling (FCS)	$2001-05	1,657	872	38	.526	13,513	140
Philip Rivers, North Carolina St. (FBS)	2000-03	1,710	1,147	34	.671	13,484	95
Justin Peery, Westminster (Mo.) (III)	1996-99	1,669	1,012	57	.606	13,262	*148
Neil Lomax, Portland St. (II; FCS)	1977, 78-80	1,606	938	55	.584	13,220	106
Kirk Baumgartner, Wis.-Stevens Point (III)	1986-89	1,696	883	57	.521	13,028	110
Kevin Kolb, Houston (FBS)	2003-06	1,565	964	31	.616	12,964	85
Tim Rattay, Louisiana Tech (FBS)	1997-99	1,552	1,015	35	.654	12,746	115
Willie Totten, Mississippi Val. (FCS)	1982-85	1,555	907	75	.583	12,711	139
Luke McCown, Louisiana Tech (FBS)	2000-03	1,775	1,063	62	.599	12,666	87
Rocky Pentello, Capital (III)	$2002-06	1,568	1,011	38	.645	12,569	111
Chris Redman, Louisville (FBS)	1996-99	1,679	1,031	51	.614	12,541	84
Marcus Brady, Cal St. Northridge (FCS)	1998-01	1,680	1,039	47	.618	12,479	109
John Port, Albright (III)	$2001-05	1,585	966	46	.610	12,470	110
Kliff Kingsbury, Texas Tech (FBS)	1999-02	1,883	1,231	40	.654	12,429	95
Chad Pennington, Marshall (FCS; FBS)	1995, 97-99	1,501	947	39	.631	12,348	110
Jamie Martin, Weber St. (FCS)	1989-92	1,544	934	56	.605	12,207	87
Byron Leftwich, Marshall (FBS)	$1998-02	1,442	939	28	.651	11,903	89
Joey Conrad, Glenville St. (II)	2002-05	1,655	954	58	.576	11,884	104
Robert Kent, Jackson St. (FCS)	2000-03	1,540	826	58	.536	11,784	104
Brady Quinn, Notre Dame (FBS)	2003-06	1,602	929	39	.580	11,762	95
Andrew Webb, Fort Lewis (II)	2000-03	1,898	1,007	66	.531	11,742	82
David Greene, Georgia (FBS)	2001-04	1,440	849	32	.590	11,528	72
Joel Steele, Anderson (Ind.) (III)	2000-03	1,480	900	52	.608	11,523	110
Gino Guidugli, Cincinnati (FBS)	2001-04	1,556	880	48	.566	11,453	78
Todd Santos, San Diego St. (FBS)	1984-87	1,484	910	57	.613	11,425	70

**Record. $See Page 10 for explanation.*

CAREER YARDS PER GAME

(Minimum 5,000 Yards; Player must have concluded his career)

Player, Team (Division[s])	Years	G	Att.	Cmp.	Int.	Pct.	Yds.	TD	Yd. PG
Tim Rattay, Louisiana Tech (FBS)	1997-99	33	1,552	1,015	35	.654	12,746	115	386.2
Steve McNair, Alcorn St. (FCS)	1991-94	42	1,680	929	58	.553	14,496	119	345.1
Justin Peery, Westminster (Mo.) (III)	1996-99	39	1,669	1,012	57	.606	13,262	*148	340.1
Aaron Flowers, Cal St. Northridge (FCS)	1996-97	20	819	502	21	.613	6,766	54	338.3
Drew Miller, Montana (FCS)	1999-00	18	654	430	14	.657	5,900	46	327.8
Ty Detmer, Brigham Young (FBS)	1988-91	46	1,530	958	65	.626	15,031	121	326.8
Timmy Chang, Hawaii (FBS)	$2000-04	53	*2,436	*1,388	80	.570	*17,072	117	322.1
Willie Totten, Mississippi Val. (FCS)	1982-85	40	1,555	907	75	.583	12,711	139	317.8
Kirk Baumgartner, Wis.-Stevens Point (III)	1986-89	41	1,696	883	57	.521	13,028	110	317.8
Dave Dickenson, Montana (FCS)	1992-95	35	1,208	813	26	.673	11,080	96	316.6
Neil Lomax, Portland St. (II; FCS)	1977; 78-80	42	1,606	938	55	.584	13,220	106	314.8
Grady Benton, West Tex. A&M (II)	1994-95	18	686	421	22	.614	5,618	49	312.1
Mike Perez, San Jose St. (FBS)	1986-87	20	792	471	30	.595	6,194	36	309.7
Keith Bishop, Ill. Wes./Wheaton (Ill.) (III)	1981, 83-85	31	1,311	772	65	.589	9,579	71	309.0
Doug Gaynor, Long Beach St. (FBS)	1984-85	22	837	569	35	.680	6,793	35	308.8
David Macchi, Valparaiso (FCS)	2002-03	23	802	450	28	.561	7,089	59	308.2
Zamir Amin, Menlo (III)	1999-01	26	905	566	29	.625	7,982	83	307.0
Adam Ryan, Wilmington (Ohio) (III)	1998-01	33	1,223	693	43	.567	10,095	88	305.9
John Friesz, Idaho (FCS)	1986-89	35	1,350	801	40	.593	10,697	77	305.6
Brett Dietz, Hanover (III)	2002-03	22	940	579	31	.616	6,663	67	302.9
Tony Eason, Illinois (FBS)	1981-82	22	856	526	29	.615	6,608	37	300.4

**Record.*

CAREER TOUCHDOWN PASSES

Player, Team (Division[s])	Years	Att.	Cmp.	Int.	Pct.	Yds.	TD
Jimmy Terwilliger, East Stroudsburg (II)	2003-06	1,481	906	36	.612	14,350	148
Justin Peery, Westminster (Mo.) (III)	1996-99	1,669	1,012	57	.606	13,262	148
Bill Borchert, Mount Union (III)	1994-97	1,009	671	17	.665	10,201	141
Bruce Eugene, Grambling (FCS)	$2001-05	1,657	872	38	.526	13,513	140
Willie Totten, Mississippi Val. (FCS)	1982-85	1,555	907	75	.583	12,711	139

Player, Team (Division[s])	Years	Att.	Cmp.	Int.	Pct.	Yds.	TD
Dusty Bonner, Kentucky (FBS); Valdosta St. (II)	1997, 99-01	1,233	861	27	.698	10,501	123
Brett Elliott, Utah (FBS); Linfield (III)	2001-03, 04-05	1,113	726	30	.652	10,447	122
Marc Eddy, Bentley (II)	2001-04	1,391	785	44	.564	11,035	121
Ty Detmer, BYU (FBS)	1988-91	1,530	958	65	.626	15,031	121
Steve McNair, Alcorn St. (FCS)	1991-94	1,680	929	58	.553	14,496	119
Timmy Chang, Hawaii (FBS)	$2000-04	*2,436	*1,388	80	.570	*17,072	117
Scott Eyster, Delta St. (II)	2003-06	1,644	1,001	37	.609	13,887	116
Chris Hatcher, Valdosta St. (II)	1991-94	1,451	1,001	38	.690	10,878	116
Tim Rattay, Louisiana Tech (FBS)	1997-99	1,552	1,015	35	.654	12,746	115
Jim Ballard, Wilmington (Ohio)/Mount Union (III)	1990, 91-93	1,199	743	41	.620	10,379	115
Curt Anes, Grand Valley St. (II)	1999-02	1,186	741	27	.625	10,581	114
Danny Wuerffel, Florida (FBS)	1993-96	1,170	708	42	.605	10,875	114
Toby Korrodi, Central Mo./Northern St. (II)	2003-06	1,332	804	34	.604	10,843	112
Rocky Pentello, Capital (III)	$2002-06	1,568	1,011	38	.645	12,569	111
Todd Cunningham, Presbyterian (II)	1998-01	1,376	834	47	.606	10,937	111
Cullen Finnerty, Grand Valley St. (II)	2003-06	1,312	774	31	.590	10,905	110
John Port, Albright (III)	$2001-05	1,585	966	46	.610	12,470	110
Joel Steele, Anderson (Ind.) (III)	2000-03	1,480	900	52	.608	11,523	110
Dan Pincelli, Hartwick (III)	1999-02	1,122	553	56	.493	9,264	110
Chad Pennington, Marshall (FCS; FBS)	1995, 97-99	1,501	947	39	.631	12,348	110
Kirk Baumgartner, Wis.-Stevens Point (III)	1986-89	1,696	883	57	.521	13,028	110
Marcus Brady, Cal St. Northridge (FCS)	1998-01	1,680	1,039	47	.618	12,479	109
Troy Dougherty, Grinnell (III)	1994, 97-99	1,192	734	33	.616	10,140	109
Neil Lomax, Portland St. (II; FCS)	1977; 78-80	1,606	938	55	.584	13,220	106
Joey Conrad, Glenville St. (II)	2002-05	1,655	954	58	.576	11,884	104
Robert Kent, Jackson St. (FCS)	2000-03	1,540	826	58	.536	11,784	104

**Record. $See Page 10 for explanation.*

SEASON YARDS

Player, Team (Division)	Year	G	Att.	Cmp.	Int.	Pct.	Yds.	TD
B.J. Symons, Texas Tech (FBS)	2003	13	*719	470	22	.654	5,833	52
Colt Brennan, Hawaii (FBS)	†2006	14	559	406	12	.726	5,549	58
Ty Detmer, BYU (FBS)	†1990	12	562	361	28	.642	5,188	41
David Klingler, Houston (FBS)	1990	11	643	374	20	.582	5,140	54
Kliff Kingsbury, Texas Tech (FBS)	2002	14	712	*479	13	.673	5,017	45
Tim Rattay, Louisiana Tech (FBS)	1998	12	559	380	13	.680	4,943	46
Steve McNair, Alcorn St. (FCS)	1994	11	530	304	17	.574	4,863	44
Sonny Cumbie, Texas Tech (FBS)	2004	12	642	421	18	.656	4,742	32
Andre Ware, Houston (FBS)	†1989	11	578	365	15	.631	4,699	46
Chad Friehauf, Colorado Mines (II)	2004	13	516	384	11	.744	4,646	39
Chase Holbrook, New Mexico St. (FBS)	2006	12	567	397	9	.700	4,619	34
Brett Elliott, Linfield (III)	†2004	13	437	290	11	.664	4,595	*61
Dustin Long, Sam Houston St. (FCS)	2004	14	531	333	18	.627	4,588	39
Jimmy Terwilliger, East Stroudsburg (II)	2005	14	424	262	11	.618	4,571	50
Jim McMahon, BYU (FBS)	†1980	12	445	284	18	.638	4,571	47
Ty Detmer, BYU (FBS)	1989	12	412	265	15	.643	4,560	32
Willie Totten, Mississippi Val. (FCS)	†1984	10	518	324	22	.626	4,557	56
Graham Harrell, Texas Tech (FBS)	2006	13	616	412	11	.669	4,555	38
Justin Peery, Westminster (Mo.) (III)	1998	10	526	319	21	.606	4,501	51
Philip Rivers, North Carolina St. (FBS)	†2003	13	483	348	7	.721	4,491	34
Ben Roethlisberger, Miami (Ohio) (FBS)	2003	14	495	342	10	.691	4,486	37
Bruce Eugene, Grambling (FCS)	2002	13	543	269	16	.495	4,483	43
Timmy Chang, Hawaii (FBS)	2002	14	624	349	22	.559	4,474	25

**Record. †National pass-efficiency champion.*

SEASON YARDS PER GAME

Player, Team (Division)	Year	G	Att.	Cmp.	Int.	Pct.	Yds.	TD	Yd. PG
David Klingler, Houston (FBS)	1990	11	643	374	20	.582	5,140	54	467.3
Willie Totten, Mississippi Val. (FCS)	1984	10	518	324	22	.626	4,557	56	455.7
Justin Peery, Westminster (Mo.) (III)	1998	10	526	319	21	.606	4,501	51	450.1
B.J. Symons, Texas Tech (FBS)	2003	13	*719	470	22	.654	*5,833	52	448.7
Steve McNair, Alcorn St. (FCS)	1994	11	530	304	17	.574	4,863	44	442.1
Ty Detmer, BYU (FBS)	1990	12	562	361	28	.642	5,188	41	432.3
Zamir Amin, Menlo (III)	2000	10	458	309	17	.674	4,320	43	432.0
Andre Ware, Houston (FBS)	1989	11	578	365	15	.631	4,699	46	427.2
Tim Rattay, Louisiana Tech (FBS)	1998	12	559	380	13	.680	4,943	46	411.9
Justin Peery, Westminster (Mo.) (III)	1999	10	498	329	15	.660	4,092	54	409.2
Danny Ragsdale, Redlands (III)	1999	9	380	247	7	.650	3,639	33	404.3
Chris Redman, Louisville (FBS)	1998	10	473	309	15	.653	4,042	29	404.2
Mike Maxwell, Nevada (FBS)	1995	9	409	277	17	.677	3,611	33	401.2
Colt Brennan, Hawaii (FBS)	2006	14	559	406	12	.726	5,549	58	396.4
Sonny Cumbie, Texas Tech (FBS)	2004	12	642	421	18	.656	4,742	32	395.2
Grady Benton, West Tex. A&M (II)	1994	9	409	258	13	.631	3,541	30	393.4
Scott Mitchell, Utah (FBS)	1988	11	533	323	15	.606	4,322	29	392.9
Tim Rattay, Louisiana Tech (FBS)	1999	10	516	342	12	.663	3,922	35	392.2
Tim Couch, Kentucky (FBS)	1998	11	553	400	15	.723	4,275	36	388.6
Chris Vargas, Nevada (FBS)	1993	11	490	331	18	.676	4,265	34	387.7

**Record.*

SEASON TOUCHDOWN PASSES

Player, Team (Division)	Year	Att.	Cmp.	Int.	Pct.	Yds.	TD
Brett Elliott, Linfield (III)	†2004	437	290	11	.664	4,595	61
Colt Brennan, Hawaii (FBS)	†2006	559	406	12	.726	5,549	58
Willie Totten, Mississippi Val. (FCS)	1984	518	324	22	.626	4,557	56
Bruce Eugene, Grambling (FCS)	†2005	456	254	6	.557	4,360	56
Dusty Bonner, Valdosta St. (II)	2000	435	317	6	.728	3,907	54
Justin Peery, Westminster (Mo.) (III)	1999	498	329	15	.660	4,092	54
David Klingler, Houston (FBS)	1990	643	374	20	.582	5,140	54
B.J. Symons, Texas Tech (FBS)	2003	*719	470	22	.654	*5,833	52
Justin Peery, Westminster (Mo.) (III)	1998	526	319	21	.606	4,501	51
Jimmy Terwilliger, East Stroudsburg (II)	2005	424	262	11	.618	4,571	50
Chris Hatcher, Valdosta St. (II)	†1994	430	321	9	*.747	3,591	50
Brett Elliott, Linfield (III)	2005	396	277	9	.699	4,019	49
Curt Anes, Grand Valley St. (II)	†2001	271	189	3	.697	3,086	48
Curt Anes, Grand Valley St. (II)	†2002	414	278	6	.671	3,692	47
Bill Borchert, Mount Union (III)	†1997	272	190	1	.698	2,933	47
Jim McMahon, BYU (FBS)	1980	445	284	18	.638	4,571	47
Tim Rattay, Louisiana Tech (FBS)	1998	559	380	13	.680	4,943	46
Andre Ware, Houston (FBS)	1989	578	365	15	.631	4,699	46
Kliff Kingsbury, Texas Tech (FBS)	2002	712	*479	13	.673	5,017	45
Wilkie Perez, Glenville St. (II)	†1997	425	280	12	.658	4,189	45
Bob Toledo, San Fran. St. (II)	1967	396	211	24	.533	3,513	45

**Record. †National pass-efficiency champion.*

SINGLE-GAME YARDS

Yds.	Div.	Player, Team (Opponent)	Date
731	III	Zamir Amin, Menlo (Cal Lutheran)	Oct. 7, 2000
716	FBS	David Klingler, Houston (Arizona St.)	Dec. 2, 1990
690	FBS	Matt Vogler, TCU (Houston)	Nov. 3, 1990
661	FBS	B.J. Symons, Texas Tech (Mississippi)	Sept. 27, 2003
645	II	Matt Kohn, Indianapolis (Michigan Tech)	Sept. 20, 2003
643	FBS	Cody Hodges, Texas Tech (Kansas St.)	Oct. 15, 2005
642	II	Wilkie Perez, Glenville St. (Concord)	Oct. 25, 1997
638	II	Andrew Webb, Fort Lewis (Mesa St.)	Nov. 16, 2002
637	FBS	Brian Lindgren, Idaho (Middle Tenn.)	Oct. 6, 2001
631	FBS	Scott Mitchell, Utah (Air Force)	Oct. 15, 1988
624	FCS	Jamie Martin, Weber St. (Idaho St.)	Nov. 23, 1991
622	FBS	Jeremy Leach, New Mexico (Utah)	Nov. 11, 1989
621	FBS	Dave Wilson, Illinois (Ohio St.)	Nov. 8, 1980
619	III	Justin Peery, Westminster (Mo.) (MacMurray)	Nov. 14, 1998
619	FBS	John Walsh, BYU (Utah St.)	Oct. 30, 1993
619	FCS	Doug Pederson, La.-Monroe (Stephen F. Austin)	Nov. 11, 1989
618	FCS	Bruce Eugene, Grambling (Prairie View)	Oct. 1, 2005
618	III	Justin Peery, Westminster (Mo.) (Principia)	Oct. 17, 1998
616	II	Damian Poalucci, East Stroudsburg (Mansfield)	Nov. 2, 1996
614	II	Alfred Montez, Western N.M. (West Tex. A&M)	Oct. 8, 1994
614	II	Perry Klein, C.W. Post (Salisbury)	Nov. 6, 1993
613	II	Jayce Goree, Glenville St. (Concord)	Oct. 24, 1998
613	FBS	Jimmy Klingler, Houston (Rice)	Nov. 28, 1992
611	FBS	David Neill, Nevada (New Mexico St.)	Oct. 10, 1998
602	III	Danny Ragsdale, Redlands (Azusa Pacific)	Sept. 25, 1999
602	III	Tom Stallings, St. Thomas (Minn.) [Bethel (Minn.)]	Nov. 13, 1993

SINGLE-GAME ATTEMPTS

Atts.	Div.	Player, Team (Opponent)	Date
83	FBS	Drew Brees, Purdue (Wisconsin)	Oct. 10, 1998
81	III	Jordan Poznick, Principia (Blackburn)	Oct. 10, 1992
80	III	Scott Kello, Sul Ross St. (Howard Payne)	Oct. 5, 2002
79	FBS	Matt Vogler, TCU (Houston)	Nov. 3, 1990
79	III	Mike Wallace, Ohio Wesleyan (Denison)	Oct. 3, 1981
78	III	Brett Dietz, Hanover (Baldwin-Wallace)	Nov. 22, 2003
78	III	Shawn Wheeler, Capital (Ohio Northern)	Nov. 13, 1999
78	FBS	Rusty LaRue, Wake Forest (Duke)	Oct. 28, 1995
77	III	Justin Peery, Westminster (Mo.) (MacMurray)	Nov. 14, 1998
77	FCS	Neil Lomax, Portland St. (Northern Colo.)	Oct. 20, 1979
76	II	Evan Gray, Mo.-Rolla (Mo. Western St.)	Nov. 15, 2003
76	FCS	Joe Lee, Towson (Lehigh)	Oct. 30, 1999
76	II	Jarrod DeGeorgia, Wayne St. (Neb.) (Drake)	Nov. 9, 1996
76	FBS	David Klingler, Houston (SMU)	Oct. 20, 1990
75	FBS	Chris Vargas, Nevada (McNeese St.)	Sept. 19, 1992

SINGLE-GAME COMPLETIONS

Cmp.	Div.	Player, Team (Opponent)	Date
56	II	Jarrod DeGeorgia, Wayne St. (Neb.) (Drake)	Nov. 9, 1996
55	FBS	Drew Brees, Purdue (Wisconsin)	Oct. 10, 1998
55	FBS	Rusty LaRue, Wake Forest (Duke)	Oct. 28, 1995
51	III	Scott Kello, Sul Ross St. (Howard Payne)	Oct. 5, 2002
50	FCS	Martin Hankins, Southeastern La. (Jacksonville)	Nov. 6, 2004
50	II	Todd Cunningham, Presbyterian (Tusculum)	Nov. 3, 2001
50	III	Justin Peery, Westminster (Mo.) (MacMurray)	Nov. 14, 1998
50	FBS	Rusty LaRue, Wake Forest (North Carolina St.)	Nov. 18, 1995
50	III	Tim Lynch, Hofstra (Fordham)	Oct. 19, 1991
49	FBS	Chase Holbrook, New Mexico St. (Boise St.)	Oct. 15, 2006
49	FBS	Bruce Gradkowski, Toledo (Pittsburgh)	Sept. 20, 2003
49	FBS	Kliff Kingsbury, Texas Tech (Missouri)	Oct. 19, 2002
49	FBS	Kliff Kingsbury, Texas Tech (Texas A&M)	Oct. 5, 2002
49	FBS	Brian Lindgren, Idaho (Middle Tenn.)	Oct. 6, 2001
48	FBS	Chase Holbrook, New Mexico St. (UTEP)	Sept. 30, 2006
48	FCS	Clayton Millis, Cal St. Northridge [St. Mary's (Cal.)]	Nov. 11, 1995
48	III	Jordan Poznick, Principia (Blackburn)	Oct. 10, 1992
48	FBS	David Klingler, Houston (SMU)	Oct. 20, 1990
47	III	Brett Elliott, Linfield (Wis.-Whitewater)	Dec. 3, 2005
47	II	Evan Gray, Mo.-Rolla (Mo. Western St.)	Nov. 15, 2003
47	FBS	Luke McCown, Louisiana Tech (Auburn)	Oct. 21, 2000
47	FCS	Joe Lee, Towson (Lehigh)	Oct. 30, 1999
47	FBS	Tim Couch, Kentucky (Arkansas)	Oct. 3, 1998
47	FCS	Jamie Martin, Weber St. (Idaho St.)	Nov. 23, 1991
47	III	Mike Wallace, Ohio Wesleyan (Denison)	Oct. 3, 1981

Receiving

CAREER RECEPTIONS

Player, Team (Division)	Years	Rec.	Yards	Avg.	TD
Scott Pingel, Westminster (Mo.) (III)	1996-99	436	*6,108	14.0	75
Blake Elliott, St. John's (Minn.) (III)	2000-03	327	4,200	12.8	56
Clarence Coleman, Ferris St. (II)	1998-01	323	4,983	15.4	42
Jacquay Nunnally, Florida A&M (FCS)	1997-00	317	4,239	13.4	38
Taylor Stubblefield, Purdue (FBS)	2001-04	316	3,433	10.9	19
Josh Davis, Marshall (FBS)	2001-04	306	3,889	12.7	23
Stephen Campbell, Brown (FCS)	1997-00	305	3,555	11.7	31
David Ball, New Hampshire (FCS)	2003-06	304	4,655	15.3	58
Taurean Henderson, Texas Tech (FBS)	2002-05	303	2,058	6.8	19
Jerry Rice, Mississippi Val. (FCS)	1981-84	301	4,693	15.6	50
Andrew Blakely, Truman (II)	1999-02	300	3,458	11.5	22
Arnold Jackson, Louisville (FBS)	1997-00	300	3,670	12.2	31
Trevor Insley, Nevada (FBS)	1996-99	298	5,005	16.8	35
Javarus Dudley, Fordham (FCS)	2000-03	295	4,197	14.2	34
Geoff Noisy, Nevada (FBS)	1995-98	295	4,249	14.4	21
Rashaun Woods, Oklahoma St. (FBS)	2000-03	293	4,412	15.1	42
Chas Gessner, Brown (FCS)	1999-02	292	3,408	11.7	36
Jamaica Rector, Northwest Mo. St. (II)	2001-04	289	4,497	15.6	38
Brad Duesing, Washington-St. Louis (III)	2002-05	287	4,249	14.8	36
Conrad Singh, Hampden-Sydney (III)	2000-03	287	3,289	11.5	23
Matt Newton, Principia (III)	1990-93	287	3,646	12.7	32
Scott Hvistendahl, Augsburg (III)	1995-98	285	4,696	16.5	40
Brian Potucek, Central Wash. (II)	$2001-05	283	3,889	13.7	33
Dallas Mall, Bentley (II)	2001-04	283	4,347	15.4	*78
Matt Holmlund, Augustana (S.D.) (II)	1998-01	282	3,522	12.5	35
Carlos Ferralls, Glenville St. (II)	1994-97	282	4,091	14.5	53
Troy Edwards, Louisiana Tech (FBS)	1996-98	280	4,352	15.5	50
Mark Bartosic, Susquehanna (III)	2000-03	275	4,733	17.2	55
Michael Becker, Randolph-Macon (III)	1997-00	273	3,683	13.5	19
Damien Hoffman, Minn.-Morris (II)	1997-00	273	3,128	11.5	21

**Record. $See Page 10 for explanation.*

CAREER RECEPTIONS PER GAME

(Minimum 125 Receptions; Player must have concluded his career)

Player, Team (Division[s])	Years	G	Rec.	Yards	TD	Rec. PG
Chris George, Glenville St. (II)	1993-94	20	230	3,215	30	11.5
Scott Pingel, Westminster (Mo.) (III)	1996-99	39	*436	*6,108	75	11.2
Manny Hazard, Houston (FBS)	1989-90	21	220	2,635	31	10.5
Alex Van Dyke, Nevada (FBS)	1994-95	22	227	3,100	26	10.3
Howard Twilley, Tulsa (FBS)	1963-65	26	261	3,343	32	10.0
Jason Phillips, Houston (FBS)	1987-88	22	207	2,319	18	9.4
Nate Jackson, Menlo (III)	1999-01	29	261	3,976	43	9.0
Matt Newton, Principia (III)	1990-93	33	287	3,646	32	8.7
Ed Bell, Idaho St. (II)	1968-69	19	163	2,608	30	8.6
Darryl DeShields, Greenville (III)	1999-01	29	248	4,051	39	8.6
Byron Chamberlain, Wayne St. (Neb.) (II)	1993-94	19	161	1,941	14	8.5
Todd Bloom, Hardin-Simmons (III)	1995-97	28	233	2,621	14	8.3
Troy Edwards, Louisiana Tech (FBS)	1996-98	34	280	4,352	50	8.2
Carlos Ferralls, Glenville St. (II)	1994-97	35	282	4,091	53	8.1
Kevin Curtis, Utah St. (FBS)	2001-02	22	174	2,789	19	7.9
Nate Burleson, Nevada (FBS)	2000-02	32	248	3,293	22	7.8
Clarence Coleman, Ferris St. (II)	1998-01	42	323	4,982	42	7.7
Tramon Douglas, Grambling (FCS)	2002-03	22	169	2,621	28	7.7
Jerry Hendren, Idaho (II)	1967-69	30	230	3,435	27	7.7
Stephen Campbell, Brown (FCS)	1997-00	40	305	3,555	31	7.6
Conrad Singh, Hampden-Sydney (III)	2000-03	38	287	3,289	23	7.6
Bryan Reeves, Nevada (FCS; FBS)	1991; 92-93	31	234	3,407	32	7.6
Siaha Burley, UCF (FBS)	1997-98	22	165	2,248	15	7.5

Player, Team (Division[s])	Years	G	Rec.	Yards	TD	Rec. PG
Chas Gessner, Brown (FCS)	1999-02	39	292	3,408	36	7.5
Jeff Clay, Catholic (III)	1994-97	36	269	4,101	44	7.5
Geoff Noisy, Nevada (FBS)	1995-98	40	295	4,249	21	7.4
David Williams, Illinois (FBS)	1983-85	33	245	3,195	22	7.4
Gary Garrison, San Diego St. (II)	1964-65	20	148	2,188	26	7.4
Brad Bailey, West Tex. A&M (II)	1992-94	30	221	2,677	22	7.4
Jerry Rice, Mississippi Val. (FCS)	1981-84	41	301	4,693	50	7.3

**Record.*

CAREER TOUCHDOWN RECEPTIONS

Player, Team (Division[s])	Years	G	TD
Dallas Mall, Bentley (II)	2001-04	44	78
David Kircus, Grand Valley St. (II)	1999-02	43	76
Scott Pingel, Westminster (Mo.) (III)	1996-99	39	75
Casey Allen, Linfield (III)	2002-05	44	59
David Ball, New Hampshire (FCS)	2003-06	50	58
Blake Elliott, St. John's (Minn.) (III)	2000-03	47	56
Mark Bartosic, Susquehanna (III)	2000-03	40	55
Chris Bisaillon, Ill. Wesleyan (III)	1989-92	36	55
Chris Samp, Winona St. (II)	2001-04	49	53
Kurt Barth, Eureka (III)	1994-97	39	51
Evan Prall, East Stroudsburg (II)	2003-06	48	50
Richie Ross, Neb.-Kearney (II)	2002-05	44	50
Troy Edwards, Louisiana Tech (FBS)	1996-98	34	50
Jerry Rice, Mississippi Val. (FCS)	1981-84	41	50
R.J. Hoppe, Carroll (Wis.) (III)	1993-96	37	49
Bruce Cerone, Yankton/Emporia St. (II)	1965-66, 68-69	36	49
Darius Watts, Marshall (FBS)	2000-03	48	47
Eric Kimble, Eastern Wash. (FCS)	2002-05	46	46
James Roe, Norfolk St. (II)	1992-95	41	46
Ryan Short, Wabash (III)	1999-02	41	45
Kevin Ingram, West Chester (II)	1995-96, 98-99	39	45
Michael Coleman, Widener (III)	1998-01	40	44
Randy Moss, Marshall (FCS; FBS)	1996-97	23	44
Jeff Clay, Catholic (III)	1994-97	36	44
Rennie Benn, Lehigh (FCS)	1982-85	41	44
Nick Bublavi, Catholic (III)	2001-03, 05	40	43
Ben Nelson, St. Cloud St. (II)	1999-02	41	43
Nate Jackson, Menlo (III)	1999-01	29	43
Steve Vagedes, Ohio Northern (III)	1995, 97-99	40	43
Carlos Ferralls, Glenville St. (II)	1994-97	35	43
Mark Loeffler, Wheaton (Ill.) (III)	1993-96	38	43
Bill Schultz, Ripon (III)	1993-96	38	43
Aaron Turner, Pacific (FBS)	1989-92	44	43

SEASON RECEPTIONS

Player, Team (Division)	Year	G	Rec.	Yards	TD
Manny Hazard, Houston (FBS)	†1989	11	142	1,689	22
Troy Edwards, Louisiana Tech (FBS)	†1998	12	140	1,996	27
Nate Burleson, Nevada (FBS)	†2002	12	138	1,629	12
Scott Pingel, Westminster (Mo.) (III)	†1999	10	136	1,648	24
Trevor Insley, Nevada (FBS)	†1999	11	134	2,060	13
Howard Twilley, Tulsa (FBS)	†1965	10	134	1,779	16
Scott Pingel, Westminster (Mo.) (III)	†1998	10	130	*2,157	26
Alex Van Dyke, Nevada (FBS)	†1995	11	129	1,854	16
J.R. Tolver, San Diego St. (FBS)	2002	13	128	1,785	13
Stephen Campbell, Brown (FCS)	†2000	10	120	1,332	11
Brad Bailey, West Tex. A&M (II)	1994	11	119	1,552	16
Blake Elliott, St. John's (Minn.) (III)	2003	14	117	1,319	13
Chris George, Glenville St. (II)	†1993	10	117	1,876	15
Kevin Ingram, West Chester (II)	†1998	11	115	1,673	21
Brian Forster, Rhode Island (FCS) (TE)	†1985	10	115	1,617	12
Chas Gessner, Brown (FCS)	†2002	10	114	1,166	11
Damond Wilkins, Nevada (FBS)	†1996	11	114	1,121	4
Chris George, Glenville St. (II)	†1994	10	113	1,339	15
Scott Hvistendahl, Augsburg (III)	1998	10	112	1,860	15
Jeff Clay, Catholic (III)	†1997	10	112	1,625	20
Sean Pender, Valdosta St. (II)	†1995	11	111	983	2
Flynn Cochran, Rensselaer (III)	2003	12	109	1,274	15
James Jordan, Louisiana Tech (FBS)	†2000	12	109	1,003	4
Chris Daniels, Purdue (FBS)	1999	11	109	1,133	5
Marcus Harris, Wyoming (FBS)	1996	12	109	1,650	13
Kassim Osgood, San Diego St. (FBS)	2002	13	108	1,552	8
Rashaun Woods, Oklahoma St. (FBS)	2002	13	107	1,695	17
Jamal Allen, Fort Lewis (II)	†2001	11	106	1,086	7
Fred Gilbert, Houston (FBS)	†1991	11	106	957	7
Barry Wagner, Alabama A&M (II)	†1989	11	106	1,812	17
Theo Blanco, Wis.-Stevens Point (III) (RB)	1987	11	#106	#1,616	8

**Record. †National champion. #Record for a running back.*

SEASON RECEPTIONS PER GAME

Player, Team (Division)	Year	G	Rec.	Yards	TD	Rec. PG
Scott Pingel, Westminster (Mo.) (III)	†1999	10	136	1,648	24	13.6
Howard Twilley, Tulsa (FBS)	†1965	10	134	1,779	16	13.4
Scott Pingel, Westminster (Mo.) (III)	†1998	10	130	*2,157	26	13.0
Manny Hazard, Houston (FBS)	†1989	11	*142	1,689	22	12.9
Matt Newton, Principia (III)	†1992	8	98	1,487	14	12.3
Trevor Insley, Nevada (FBS)	†1999	11	134	2,060	13	12.2
Stephen Campbell, Brown (FCS)	†2000	10	120	1,332	11	12.0
Matt Newton, Principia (III)	†1993	8	96	1,080	11	12.0
Nate Burleson, Nevada (FBS)	†2002	12	138	1,629	12	11.8
Alex Van Dyke, Nevada (FBS)	†1995	11	129	1,854	16	11.7
Chris George, Glenville St. (II)	†1993	10	117	1,876	15	11.7
Troy Edwards, Louisiana Tech (FBS)	†1998	12	140	1,996	27	11.7
Brian Forster, Rhode Island (FCS) (TE)	†1985	10	115	1,617	12	11.5
Chas Gessner, Brown (FCS)	†2002	10	114	1,166	11	11.4
Chris George, Glenville St. (II)	†1994	10	113	1,339	15	11.3
Scott Hvistendahl, Augsburg (III)	1998	10	112	1,860	15	11.2
Jeff Clay, Catholic (III)	†1997	10	112	1,625	20	11.2
Brad Bailey, West Tex. A&M (II)	1994	11	119	1,552	16	10.8
Ben Fox, Hanover (III)	†1995	9	95	1,087	15	10.6
Sean Munroe, Mass.-Boston (III)	1992	9	95	1,693	17	10.6

**Record. †National champion.*

SINGLE-GAME RECEPTIONS

No.	Div.	Player, Team (Opponent)	Date
24	FCS	Chas Gessner, Brown (Rhode Island)	Oct. 5, 2002
24	FCS	Jerry Rice, Mississippi Val. (Southern U.)	Oct. 1, 1983
23	II	Chris George, Glenville St. (West Va. Wesleyan)	Oct. 15, 1994
23	FBS	Randy Gatewood, UNLV (Idaho)	Sept. 17, 1994
23	III	Sean Munroe, Mass.-Boston (Mass. Maritime)	Oct. 10, 1992
23	II	Barry Wagner, Alabama A&M (Clark Atlanta)	Nov. 4, 1989
22	III	Kevin Holland, Tufts (Bowdoin)	Oct. 9, 2004
22	FCS	Marvin Walker, North Texas (Tulsa)	Nov. 20, 1982
22	FBS	Jay Miller, BYU (New Mexico)	Nov. 3, 1973
21	FCS	Carl Morris, Harvard (Dartmouth)	Nov. 2, 2002
21	FCS	Eric Johnson, Yale (Harvard)	Nov. 20, 1999
21	FBS	Chris Daniels, Purdue (Michigan St.)	Oct. 16, 1999
21	FBS	Troy Edwards, Louisiana Tech (Nebraska)	Aug. 29, 1998
21	II	Kevin Swayne, Wayne St. (Neb.) (Drake)	Nov. 9, 1996
21	II	Jarett Vito, Emporia St. (Truman)	Nov. 4, 1995
21#	FCS	David Pandt, Montana St. (Eastern Wash.)	Sept. 21, 1985
20	FBS	Kenny Christian, Eastern Mich. (Temple)	Sept. 23, 2000
20	III	Scott Pingel, Westminster (Mo.) (Colorado Col.)	Oct. 30, 1999
20	III	Todd Bloom, Hardin-Simmons (Mississippi Col.)	Oct. 12, 1996
20	III	Kurt Barth, Eureka [Concordia (Wis.)]	Sept. 28, 1996
20	FCS	Tim Hilton, Cal St. Northridge [St. Mary's (Cal.)]	Nov. 11, 1995
20	II	Sean Pender, Valdosta St. (Mississippi Col.)	Nov. 4, 1995
20	II	Keylie Martin, N.M. Highlands (Western St.)	Nov. 5, 1994
20	III	Rich Johnson, Pace (Fordham)	Nov. 7, 1987
20	III	Pete Thompson, Carroll (Wis.) [Augustana (Ill.)]	Nov. 4, 1978
20	II	Harold "Red" Roberts, Austin Peay (Murray St.)	Nov. 8, 1969
20	FBS	Rick Eber, Tulsa (Idaho St.)	Oct. 7, 1967

#Record for a running back.

CAREER YARDS

Player, Team (Division)	Years	Rec.	Yards	Avg.	TD
Scott Pingel, Westminster (Mo.) (III)	1996-99	*436	6,108	14.0	75
Trevor Insley, Nevada (FBS)	1996-99	298	5,005	16.8	35
Clarence Coleman, Ferris St. (II)	1998-01	323	4,983	15.4	42
Richie Ross, Neb.-Kearney (II)	2002-05	248	4,882	19.7	50
Mark Bartosic, Susquehanna (III)	2000-03	275	4,733	17.2	55
Scott Hvistendahl, Augsburg (III)	1995-98	285	4,696	16.5	40
Jerry Rice, Mississippi Val. (FCS)	1981-84	301	4,693	15.6	50
David Ball, New Hampshire (FCS)	2003-06	304	4,655	15.3	58
Marcus Harris, Wyoming (FBS)	1993-96	259	4,518	17.4	38
Jamaica Rector, Northwest Mo. St. (II)	2001-04	289	4,497	15.6	38
Nick Bublavi, Catholic (III)	2001-03, 05	255	4,485	17.6	43
Chris Samp, Winona St. (II)	2001-04	222	4,471	20.1	53
James Roe, Norfolk St. (II)	1992-95	239	4,468	18.7	46
Rashaun Woods, Oklahoma St. (FBS)	2000-03	293	4,412	15.1	42
Damon Thompson, Virginia St. (II)	1997-00	268	4,387	16.4	37
Ryan Yarborough, Wyoming (FBS)	1990-93	229	4,357	19.0	42
Bruce Cerone, Yankton/Emporia St. (II)	1965-66, 68-69	241	4,354	18.1	49
Troy Edwards, Louisiana Tech (FBS)	1996-98	280	4,352	15.5	50
Dallas Mall, Bentley (II)	2001-04	283	4,347	15.4	*78
Aaron Turner, Pacific (FBS)	1989-92	266	4,345	16.3	43
Kurt Barth, Eureka (III)	1994-97	256	4,311	16.8	51
Brad Musso, Wheaton (Ill.) (III)	2001-04	255	4,287	16.8	36
Terance Mathis, New Mexico (FBS)	1985-87, 89	263	4,254	16.2	36
Brad Duesing, Washington-St. Louis (III)	2002-05	287	4,249	14.8	36
Geoff Noisy, Nevada (FBS)	1995-98	295	4,249	14.4	21

Player, Team (Division)	Years	Rec.	Yards	Avg.	TD
Jacquay Nunnally, Florida A&M (FCS)	1997-00	317	4,239	13.4	38
Robert Clark, N.C. Central (II)	1983-86	210	4,231	‡20.1	38
Blake Elliott, St. John's (Minn.) (III)	2000-03	327	4,200	12.8	56
Javarus Dudley, Fordham (FCS)	2000-03	295	4,197	14.2	34
David Kircus, Grand Valley St. (II)	1999-02	222	4,142	18.7	76

**Record. ‡Record for minimum 180 catches.*

CAREER YARDS PER GAME

(Minimum 2,200 Yards; Player must have concluded his career)

Player, Team (Division[s])	Years	G	Yards	Yd. PG
Chris George, Glenville St. (II)	1993-94	20	3,215	160.8
Scott Pingel, Westminster (Mo.) (III)	1996-99	39	*6,108	156.6
Alex Van Dyke, Nevada (FBS)	1994-95	22	3,100	140.9
Darryl DeShields, Greenville (III)	1999-01	29	4,051	139.7
Ed Bell, Idaho St. (II)	1968-69	19	2,608	137.3
Nate Jackson, Menlo (III)	1999-01	29	3,976	137.1
Troy Edwards, Louisiana Tech (FBS)	1996-98	34	4,352	128.0
Kevin Curtis, Utah St. (FBS)	2001-02	22	2,789	126.8
Manny Hazard, Houston (FBS)	1989-90	21	2,635	125.5
Bruce Cerone, Yankton/Emporia St. (II)	1965-66, 68-69	36	4,354	120.9
Ron Sellers, Florida St. (FBS)	1966-68	30	3,598	119.9
Tramon Douglas, Grambling (FCS)	2002-03	22	2,621	119.1
Clarence Coleman, Ferris St. (II)	1998-01	42	4,983	118.6
Mark Bartosic, Susquehanna (III)	2000-03	40	4,733	118.3
Randy Moss, Marshall (FCS; FBS)	1996-97	23	2,720	118.3
Jim Jones, Widener (III)	1999-01	30	3,523	117.4
Scott Hvistendahl, Augsburg (III)	1995-98	40	4,696	117.4
Derrick Ingram, UAB (FCS)	1993-94	22	2,572	116.9
Carlos Ferralls, Glenville St. (II)	1994-97	35	4,091	116.9
Damon Thompson, Virginia St. (II)	1997-00	38	4,387	115.4
Adam Marino, Mount Union (III)	1998-00	30	3,436	114.5
Jerry Rice, Mississippi Val. (FCS)	1981-84	41	4,693	114.5
Jerry Hendren, Idaho (II)	1967-69	30	3,435	114.5
Jeff Clay, Catholic (III)	1994-97	36	4,101	113.9
Trevor Insley, Nevada (FBS)	1996-99	44	5,005	113.8
Nakia Jenkins, Utah St. (FBS)	1996-97	22	2,483	112.9
Nick Bublavi, Catholic (III)	2001-03, 05	40	4,485	112.1
Elmo Wright, Houston (FBS)	1968-70	30	3,347	111.6
Howard Twilley, Tulsa (FBS)	1963-65	30	3,343	111.4
Chris Myers, Kenyon (II)	1967-70	35	3,897	111.3

**Record.*

SEASON YARDS

Player, Team (Division)	Year	Rec.	Yards	Avg.	TD
Scott Pingel, Westminster (Mo.) (III)	†1998	130	2,157	16.6	26
Trevor Insley, Nevada (FBS)	†1999	134	2,060	15.4	13
Troy Edwards, Louisiana Tech (FBS)	†1998	140	1,996	14.3	27
Chris George, Glenville St. (II)	†1993	117	1,876	16.0	15
Scott Hvistendahl, Augsburg (III)	1998	112	1,860	16.6	15
Alex Van Dyke, Nevada (FBS)	†1995	129	1,854	14.4	16
Barry Wagner, Alabama A&M (II)	†1989	106	1,812	17.1	17
Nick Bublavi, Catholic (III)	†2005	101	1,797	17.8	15
J.R. Tolver, San Diego St. (FBS)	†2002	128	1,785	14.0	13
Howard Twilley, Tulsa (FBS)	†1965	134	1,779	13.3	16
Evan Prall, East Stroudsburg (II)	2005	88	1,766	20.1	23
Josh Reed, LSU (FBS)	†2001	94	1,740	18.5	7
Chris Perry, Adams St. (II)	†1995	88	1,719	19.5	21
Ashley Lelie, Hawaii (FBS)	2001	84	1,713	20.4	19
Eddie Conti, Delaware (FCS)	†1998	91	1,712	18.8	10
Troy Edwards, Louisiana Tech (FBS)	†1997	102	1,707	16.7	13
Tramon Douglas, Grambling (FCS)	†2002	92	1,704	18.5	18
Rashaun Woods, Oklahoma St. (FBS)	2002	107	1,695	15.8	17
Eric Fowler, Grand Valley St. (II)	†2006	83	1,694	20.4	22
Sean Munroe, Mass.-Boston (III)	†1992	95	1,693	17.8	17
Manny Hazard, Houston (FBS)	†1989	*142	1,689	11.9	22
Nick Cushman, Albright (III)	†2004	101	1,682	16.6	17
Jerry Rice, Mississippi Val. (FCS)	†1984	103	1,682	16.3	27
Kevin Ingram, West Chester (II)	†1998	115	1,673	14.5	21
Larry Fitzgerald, Pittsburgh (FBS)	†2003	92	1,672	18.2	22
Marcus Harris, Wyoming (FBS)	†1996	109	1,650	15.1	13
Scott Pingel, Westminster (Mo.) (III)	†1999	136	1,648	12.1	24
Randy Moss, Marshall (FBS)	1997	90	1,647	18.3	25
Ellis Debrow, Delta St. (II)	†2003	77	1,637	21.3	18
Mark DeBrito, Bentley (II)	1999	101	1,637	16.2	19
Nate Burleson, Nevada (FBS)	2002	138	1,629	11.8	12
Jeff Clay, Catholic (III)	†1997	112	1,625	14.5	25
DaVon Fowlkes, Appalachian St. (FCS)	†2004	103	1,618	15.7	14
Brian Forster, Rhode Island (FCS) (TE)	†1985	115	1,617	14.1	12
Theo Blanco, Wis.-Stevens Point (III) (RB)	1987	#106	#1,616	15.2	8

**Record. †National champion. #Record for a running back.*

SEASON YARDS PER GAME

Player, Team (Division)	Year	G	Rec.	Yards	Yd. PG
Scott Pingel, Westminster (Mo.) (III)	†1998	10	130	*2,157	215.7
Sean Munroe, Mass.-Boston (III)	†1992	9	95	1,693	188.1
Chris George, Glenville St. (II)	†1993	10	117	1,876	187.6
Trevor Insley, Nevada (FBS)	†1999	11	134	2,060	187.3
Scott Hvistendahl, Augsburg (III)	1998	10	112	1,860	186.0
Matt Newton, Principia (III)	†1992	8	98	1,487	185.9
Nick Bublavi, Catholic (III)	†2005	10	101	1,797	179.7
Howard Twilley, Tulsa (FBS)	†1965	10	134	1,779	177.9
Chris Perry, Adams St. (II)	†1995	10	88	1,719	171.9
Alex Van Dyke, Nevada (FBS)	†1995	11	129	1,854	168.5
Jerry Rice, Mississippi Val. (FCS)	†1984	10	103	1,682	168.2
Troy Edwards, Louisiana Tech (FBS)	†1998	12	140	1,996	166.3
Scott Pingel, Westminster (Mo.) (III)	†1999	10	136	1,648	164.8
Barry Wagner, Alabama A&M (II)	†1989	11	106	1,812	164.7
Bruce Cerone, Emporia St. (II)	†1968	9	91	1,479	164.3
Jeff Clay, Catholic (III)	†1997	10	112	1,625	162.5
Jeff Clay, Catholic (III)	†1996	9	81	1,460	162.2
Brian Forster, Rhode Island (FCS)	†1985	10	115	1,617	161.7

**Record. †National champion.*

SEASON TOUCHDOWN RECEPTIONS

Player, Team (Division)	Year	G	TD
David Kircus, Grand Valley St. (II)	2002	14	35
David Kircus, Grand Valley St. (II)	2001	10	28
Troy Edwards, Louisiana Tech (FBS)	1998	12	27
Jerry Rice, Mississippi Val. (FCS)	1984	10	27
Scott Pingel, Westminster (Mo.) (III)	1998	10	26
Randy Moss, Marshall (FBS)	1997	12	25
David Ball, New Hampshire (FCS)	2005	13	24
Dallas Mall, Bentley (II)	2001	12	24
Scott Pingel, Westminster (Mo.) (III)	1999	10	24
Evan Prall, East Stroudsburg (II)	2005	14	23
Rob Giancola, Valparaiso (FCS)	2003	12	23
Ben Nelson, St. Cloud St. (II)	2002	11	23
Eric Fowler, Grand Valley St. (II)	2006	15	22
Matt Willis, Hartwick (III)	2005	10	22
Casey Allen, Linfield (III)	2005	11	22
Chris Samp, Winona St. (II)	2004	12	22
Larry Fitzgerald, Pittsburgh (FBS)	2003	13	22
Blake Elliott, St. John's (Minn.) (III)	2002	14	22
Manny Hazard, Houston (FBS)	1989	11	22
Dallas Mall, Bentley (II)	2004	10	21
Vincent Jackson, Northern Colo. (II)	2003	11	21
David Snider, Grinnell (III)	1998	10	21
Chris Perry, Adams St. (II)	1995	10	21
Brandon Simmons, West Chester (II)	2004	15	20
Ryan Soule, Hartwick (III)	2002	10	20
Ryan Johnson, Hartwick (III)	2001	10	20
Brian Dolph, Saginaw Valley (II)	2000	11	20
Kirk Aikens, Hartwick (III)	1998	10	20
Steve Vagades, Ohio Northern (III)	1998	10	20
Jeff Clay, Catholic (III)	1997	10	20
John Aromando, TCNJ (III)	1983	10	20
Ed Bell, Idaho St. (II)	1969	10	20

SINGLE-GAME YARDS

Yds.	Div.	Player, Team (Opponent)	Date
418	III	Lewis Howes, Principia (Martin Luther)	Oct. 12, 2002
405	FBS	Troy Edwards, Louisiana Tech (Nebraska)	Aug. 29, 1998
401	II	Kevin Ingram, West Chester (Clarion)	Oct. 31, 1998
397	III	Matt Eisenberg, Juniata (Widener)	Nov. 13, 1999
395	III	Scott Pingel, Westminster (Mo.) [Bethel (Tenn.)]	Nov. 7, 1998
386	III	Nick Bublavi, Catholic (La Salle)	Sept. 15, 2005
376	FCS	Kassim Osgood, Cal Poly (UNI)	Nov. 4, 2000
370	FCS	Michael Lerch, Princeton (Brown)	Oct. 12, 1991
370	II	Barry Wagner, Alabama A&M (Clark Atlanta)	Nov. 4, 1989
364	III	Jeff Clay, Catholic (Albright)	Nov. 16, 1996
363	FBS	Randy Gatewood, UNLV (Idaho)	Sept. 17, 1994
363	II	Tom Nettles, San Diego St. (Southern Miss.)	Nov. 9, 1968
362	III	Matt Surette, WPI (Springfield)	Oct. 25, 1997
354	FCS	Eddie Conti, Delaware (Connecticut)	Nov. 7, 1998
354	II	Robert Clark, N.C. Central (Jackson St.)	Aug. 30, 1986
352	II	Chad Luttrell, Henderson St. (Arkansas Tech)	Oct. 28, 2000
349	FBS	Chuck Hughes, UTEP (North Texas)	Sept. 18, 1965
337	III	Adam Brossman, Lebanon Valley (Albright)	Nov. 11, 2006
332	III	Ryan Pifer, Heidelberg (Marietta)	Nov. 8, 1997
332	III	Sean Munroe, Mass.-Boston (Mass. Maritime)	Oct. 10, 1992
330	FCS	Nate Singleton, Grambling (Virginia Union)	Sept. 14, 1991
327	III	Harrison Dull, Chapman (Pacific Lutheran)	Sept. 23, 2006
327@	FCS	Brian Forster, Rhode Island (Brown)	Sept. 28, 1985

Yds.	Div.	Player, Team (Opponent)	Date
326	FBS	Nate Burleson, Nevada (San Jose St.)	Nov. 10, 2001
325	II	Paul Zaeske, North Park [North Central (Ill.)]	Oct. 12, 1968
322	FBS	Rick Eber, Tulsa (Idaho St.)	Oct. 7, 1967
319	II	Kyle Henderson, West Ala. (Valdosta St.)	Oct. 26, 2002
319	FCS	Jason Cristino, Lehigh (Lafayette)	Nov. 21, 1992
318	FBS	Harry Wood, Tulsa (Idaho St.)	Oct. 7, 1967
317	II	Richie Ross, Neb.-Kearney (Fort Hays St.)	Nov. 1, 2003
317	II	Dan Fulton, Neb.-Omaha (South Dakota)	Sept. 4, 1976
316	FCS	Marcus Hinton, Alcorn St. (Chattanooga)	Sept. 10, 1994
316	FBS	Jeff Evans, New Mexico St. (Southern Ill.)	Sept. 30, 1978
314	III	Matt Eisenberg, Juniata (Albright)	Oct. 2, 1999
314	FBS	Alex Van Dyke, Nevada (San Jose St.)	Nov. 18, 1995
310	III	Randell Knapp, Mount Union (Wis.-Whitewater)	Sept. 6, 2003
310	III	Jace Metzner, Ohio Northern (John Carroll)	Oct. 20, 2001
310	III	Jeff Clay, Catholic (La Salle)	Oct. 11, 1997
310	FBS	Chad Mackey, Louisiana Tech (Toledo)	Oct. 19, 1996
310	II	Mike Collodi, Colorado Mines [Westminster (Utah)]	Oct. 3, 1970

@Record for a tight end.

Defensive Records

Interceptions

CAREER INTERCEPTIONS

Player, Team (Division[s])	Years	No.	Yards	Avg.
Tom Collins, Indianapolis (II)	1982-85	37	390	10.5
Ralph Gebhardt, Rochester (II; III)	1972; 73-75	34	406	11.9
Dan Peters, Shepherd (II)	2003-06	32	505	15.8
Dean Diaz, Humboldt St. (II)	1980-83	31	328	10.6
Bill Grantham, Mo.-Rolla (II)	1977-80	29	263	9.1
Eugene Hunter, Fort Valley St. (II; III)	1972; 73-74	29	479	16.5
Al Brosky, Illinois (FBS)	1950-52	29	356	12.3
Leigh Bodden, Duquesne (FCS)	1999-02	28	297	10.6
Jason Johnson, Shepherd (II)	1991-94	28	321	11.5
Rick Bealer, Lycoming (III)	1987-90	28	279	10.0
Brian Fetterolf, Aurora (III)	1986-89	28	390	13.9
Dave Murphy, Holy Cross (FCS)	1986-89	28	309	11.0
Brent Grimes, Shippensburg (II)	2002-05	27	314	11.6
Andrew Ostrand, Carroll (Wis.) (III)	1990-93	27	258	9.6
Tim Lennon, Curry (III)	1986-89	27	190	7.0
Scott Stanitous, Moravian (III)	1985-88	27	178	6.6
Mike Hintz, Wis.-Platteville (III)	1983-86	27	183	6.8
Martin Bayless, Bowling Green (FBS)	1980-83	27	266	9.9
John Provost, Holy Cross (FBS)	1972-74	27	470	17.4
Cory Mabry, Susquehanna (III)	1988-91	26	400	15.4
Mark Dorner, Juniata (III)	1984-87	26	443	17.0
Tony Woods, Bloomsburg (II)	1982-85	26	105	4.0
Jeff Hughes, Ripon (III)	1975-78	26	333	12.8
Buster West, Gust. Adolphus (II)	1967-70	26	192	7.4

SEASON INTERCEPTIONS

Player, Team (Division)	Year	No.	Yards
Ben Matthews, Bethel (Minn.) (III)	†2000	15	134
Mark Dorner, Juniata (III)	†1987	15	202
Dan Peters, Shepherd (II)	†2006	14	219
Pierre Thomas, Mo. Western St. (II)	2003	14	362
Rashean Mathis, Bethune-Cookman (FCS)	†2002	14	*455
Eugene Hunter, Fort Valley St. (II)	†1972	14	211
Luther Howard, Delaware St. (II)	†1972	14	99
Tom Rezzuti, Northeastern (II)	†1971	14	153
Jim Blackwell, Southern U. (II)	†1970	14	196
Carl Ray Harris, Fresno St. (II)	†1970	14	98
Al Worley, Washington (FBS)	†1968	14	130

**Record. †National champion.*

Total Tackles

(Since 2000)

CAREER TOTAL TACKLES PER GAME

(Min. 275 Total Tackles; Player must have concluded his career)

Player, Team (Division)	Years	G	Solo	Ast	Total	Avg.
Jason Ocean, Livingstone (II)	2000-03	37	193	323	516	13.95
Tavarski Wallace, Adrian (III)	2003-06	32	227	202	429	13.4
Josh Cain, Chattanooga (FCS)	2000-02	34	273	177	450	13.2
Boomer Grigsby, Illinois St. (FCS)	2001-04	44	325	225	*550	12.5
E.J. Henderson, Maryland (FBS)	2000-02	35	308	126	434	12.4
Ron Swearingin, Capital (III)	2000-03	40	282	217	499	12.5
Matt O'Bryant, Millsaps (III)	2000-03	38	236	226	462	12.2
Hanik Milligan, Houston (FBS)	2000-02	34	235	170	405	11.9
Casey Urlacher, Lake Forest (III)	2000-02	31	158	197	355	11.5
Tim McGarigle, Northwestern (FBS)	2002-05	48	319	226	545	11.4
Rod Davis, Southern Miss. (FBS)	2000-03	47	*360	166	526	11.2
Liam Ezekiel, Northeastern (FCS)	2001-04	44	218	271	489	11.1
Justin Beriault, Ball St. (FBS)	2001-04	46	267	241	508	11.0
Eric Walker, Mo. Western St. (II)	2000-02	31	168	168	336	10.8
Ryan Fowler, Duke (FBS)	2000-03	46	286	209	495	10.8
Dantonio Burnette, North Carolina St. (FBS)	2000-02	34	185	178	363	10.7
Deric Sieck, Winona St. (II)	2000-03	49	275	242	517	10.6
Bruce Renner, Indianapolis (II)	2002-05	42	242	198	440	10.5
Grant Wiley, West Virginia (FBS)	2000-03	47	298	194	492	10.5
Jordan Beck, Cal Poly (FCS)	2001-04	43	270	179	449	10.4
Josh Smith, Navy (FBS)	2002-04	34	164	190	354	10.4
Nick Ricks, Eastern Ill. (FCS)	2000-03	47	298	180	478	10.2
Jerry Schumacher, Illinois (FBS)	2000-02	35	236	115	351	10.0
Lee Russell, Western Ill. (FCS)	2000-03	48	317	163	480	10.0
Grant Gould, Washburn (II)	2002-05	46	207	252	459	10.0
Dexter Reid, North Carolina (FBS)	2000-03	47	304	162	466	9.9
Steve Sheeler, Stonehill (II)	2000-03	41	230	172	402	9.8
Daniel Leger, Colorado Mines (II)	2001-04	46	236	210	446	9.7
Alfred Fincher, Connecticut (FBS)	2002-04	36	181	166	347	9.6
Matt Nelson, Wofford (FCS)	2000-03	47	296	156	452	9.6
Kevin Jones, St. Augustine's (II)	2003-06	38	162	201	363	9.6

**Record.*

SEASON TOTAL TACKLES PER GAME

Player, Team (Division)	Year	G	Solo	Ast	Total	Avg.
Robert Gunn, Earlham (III)	†2000	10	106	72	178	17.8
Donnie Hohman, Chapman (III)	†2002	10	77	95	172	17.2
Boomer Grigsby, Illinois St. (FCS)	†2002	11	108	71	179	16.3
Kevin Talley, Norfolk St. (FCS)	†2003	12	75	120	*195	16.3
Robert Aguilar, Greenville (III)	2000	10	101	61	162	16.2
Josh Cain, Chattanooga (FCS)	2002	12	113	79	192	16.0
Allen Minus, Lincoln (Mo.) (II)	†2004	10	73	86	159	15.9
Bryan Meuse, Nichols (III)	†2005	9	72	71	143	15.9
Jeremy Vanisacker, Kalamazoo (III)	†2004	8	76	50	126	15.8
Isaac Sieling, Gust. Adolphus (III)	2004	10	55	102	157	15.7
Jason Ocean, Livingstone (II)	†2001	9	50	91	141	15.7
Mike Matson, Augsburg (III)	2005	10	75	81	156	15.6
Rick Sherrod, West Virginia (FBS)	†2001	10	102	54	156	15.6
Lance Ramer, Rochester (III)	2000	10	87	69	156	15.6
Tavarski Wallace, Adrian (III)	2004	10	100	55	155	15.5
Kelvin Hutcheson, Averett (III)	†2001	8	56	68	124	15.5
Graham Goldwasser, Williams (III)	†2003	8	43	80	123	15.4
Edgerton Hartwell, Western Ill. (FCS)	†2000	11	107	62	169	15.4

**Record. †National champion.*

CAREER TOTAL TACKLES

Player, Team (Division)	Years	G	Solo	Ast	Total
Boomer Grigsby, Illinois St. (FCS)	2001-04	44	325	225	550
Tim McGarigle, Northwestern (FBS)	2002-05	48	319	226	545
Casey McConnell, Kenyon (III)	2001-03, 05	40	294	237	531
Rod Davis, Southern Miss. (FBS)	2000-03	47	*360	166	526
Deric Sieck, Winona St. (II)	2000-03	49	275	242	517
Jason Ocean, Livingstone (II)	2000-03	37	193	*323	516
Justin Beriault, Ball St. (FBS)	2001-04	46	267	241	508
Ron Swearingin, Capital (III)	2000-03	40	282	217	499
Ryan Fowler, Duke (FBS)	2000-03	46	286	209	495
Grant Wiley, West Virginia (FBS)	2000-03	47	298	194	492
Liam Ezekiel, Northeastern (FCS)	2001-04	44	218	271	489
Matt Pusateri, Miami (Ohio) (FBS)	2001-04	51	313	172	485
Lee Russell, Western Ill. (FCS)	2000-03	48	317	163	480
Mike Fox, St. John Fisher (III)	2001-04	42	221	257	478
Nick Ricks, Eastern Ill. (FCS)	2000-03	47	298	180	478
Matt O'Bryant, Millsaps (III)	2000-03	38	236	226	472
Dexter Reid, North Carolina (FBS)	2000-03	47	304	162	466
Grant Gould, Washburn (II)	2002-05	46	207	252	459
Derrick Johnson, Texas (FBS)	2001-04	49	281	177	458
Abdul Hodge, Iowa (FBS)	2002-05	50	289	164	453
Josh Cain, Chattanooga (FCS)	2000-02	34	273	177	450
Jordan Beck, Cal Poly (FCS)	2001-04	43	270	179	449
Daniel Leger, Colorado Mines (II)	2001-04	46	236	210	446
John Leake, Clemson (FBS)	2000-03	49	244	199	443
Bruce Renner, Indianapolis (II)	2002-05	42	242	198	440
E.J. Henderson, Maryland (FBS)	2000-02	35	308	126	434
Adam Seward, UNLV (FBS)	2001-04	46	215	218	433
Barrett Ruud, Nebraska (FBS)	2001-04	50	218	214	432
Erik Dandy, Western Ky. (FCS)	2000-03	45	241	183	424
Terrell Jones, Miami (Ohio) (FBS)	2000-03	47	258	166	424

**Record.*

SEASON TOTAL TACKLES

Player, Team (Division)	Year	G	Solo	Ast	Total
Kevin Talley, Norfolk St. (FCS)	†2003	12	75	120	195
Lawrence Flugence, Texas Tech (FBS)	2002	14	124	69	193
Josh Cain, Chattanooga (FCS)	2002	12	113	79	192
Josh Buhl, Kansas St. (FBS)	2003	15	109	75	184
Tom Ward, Toledo (FBS)	2002	14	107	73	180
Jimmy Cottrell, New Mexico St. (FBS)	†2005	12	90	89	179
Boomer Grigsby, Illinois St. (FCS)	2003	12	109	70	179
Boomer Grigsby, Illinois St. (FCS)	†2002	11	108	71	179
Robert Gunn, Earlham (III)	†2000	10	106	72	178
E.J. Henderson, Maryland (FBS)	2002	14	*135	40	175
Donnie Hohman, Chapman (III)	†2002	10	77	95	172
Dietrich Lapsley, Indiana St. (FCS)	2002	12	103	68	171
B.J. Russell, Mesa St. (II)	2004	11	71	98	169
John Leake, Clemson (FBS)	2002	13	81	88	169
Edgerton Hartwell, Western Ill. (FCS)	†2000	11	107	62	169

**Record. †National champion.*

SINGLE-GAME TOTAL TACKLES

Tkls.	Div.	Player, Team (Opponent)	Date
30	III	Bryan Meuse, Nichols (Endicott)	Oct. 29, 2005
30	II	Shaun Maloney, Minn.-Morris (Minn. St. Moorhead)	Oct. 27, 2001
30	FCS	Josh Cain, Chattanooga (Citadel)	Nov. 3, 2001
29	III	Adam Neitzel, Wis.-La Crosse (Wis.-Eau Claire)	Oct. 22, 2005
29	II	Jim Couretas, Northern Mich. (Findlay)	Sept. 10, 2005
28	III	Mike Matson, Augsburg [Bethel (Minn.)]	Nov. 4, 2005
28	II	Brent Russell, Mesa St. (Fort Lewis)	Sept. 11, 2004
27	III	Casey McConnell, Kenyon (Centre)	Sept. 7, 2002
26	FCS	Adam Goloboski, Richmond (Delaware)	Nov. 13, 2004
26	III	Chris Kern, Simpson (Luther)	Nov. 13, 2004
26	FCS	Boomer Grigsby, Illinois St. (Youngstown St.)	Nov. 9, 2002
26	FBS	Doug Szymul, Northwestern (Navy)	Sept. 21, 2002
26	FBS	Brian Leigeb, Central Mich. (Northern Ill.)	Nov. 17, 2000
25	III	Brick Crowder, Greensboro (Shenandoah)	Oct. 14, 2006
25	FCS	Chad Nkang, Elon (Chattanooga)	Oct. 15, 2005
25	FBS	Tim McGarigle, Northwestern (Wisconsin)	Oct. 8, 2005
25	FCS	Kevin Talley, Norfolk St. (N.C. A&T)	Oct. 4, 2003
25	FBS	DeMeco Ryans, Alabama (Arkansas)	Sept. 27, 2003
25	FCS	Nick Ricks, Eastern Ill. (Eastern Ky.)	Oct. 12, 2002
25	FBS	Bob Sanders, Iowa (Indiana)	Oct. 20, 2001
25	FCS	Tim Johnson, Youngstown St. (Hofstra)	Nov. 4, 2000
25	II	Alan Slaughter, Tusculum (Lenoir-Rhyne)	Sept. 30, 2000

Solo Tackles

CAREER SOLO TACKLES PER GAME

(Min. 225 Solo Tackles; Player must have concluded his career)

Player, Team (Division)	Years	G	Solo	Avg.
E.J. Henderson, Maryland (FBS)	2000-02	35	308	8.80
Josh Cain, Chattanooga (FCS)	2000-02	34	273	8.03
Rod Davis, Southern Miss. (FBS)	2000-03	47	*360	7.66
Boomer Grigsby, Illinois St. (FCS)	2001-04	44	325	7.39
Casey McConnell, Kenyon (III)	2001-03, 05	40	294	7.35
Ron Swearingin, Capital (III)	2000-03	40	282	7.05
Hanik Milligan, Houston (FBS)	2000-02	34	235	6.91
Jerry Schumacher, Illinois (FBS)	2000-02	35	236	6.74
Tim McGarigle, Northwestern (FBS)	2002-05	48	319	6.65
Lee Russell, Western Ill. (FCS)	2000-03	48	317	6.60
Dexter Reid, North Carolina (FBS)	2000-03	47	304	6.47
Grant Wiley, West Virginia (FBS)	2000-03	47	298	6.34
Nick Ricks, Eastern Ill. (FCS)	2000-03	47	298	6.34
Matt Nelson, Wofford (FCS)	2000-03	47	296	6.30
Jordan Beck, Cal Poly (FCS)	2001-04	43	270	6.28
Ryan Fowler, Duke (FBS)	2000-03	46	286	6.22
Matt O'Bryant, Millsaps (III)	2000-03	38	236	6.21
Nick Duffy, Northern Ill. (FBS)	2000-03	39	236	6.05
James King, Central Mich. (FBS)	2001-04	45	268	5.96
Akil Grant, Northern Ill. (FBS)	2000-03	42	246	5.86

**Record.*

SEASON SOLO TACKLES PER GAME

Player, Team (Division)	Year	G	Solo	Avg.
Robert Gunn, Earlham (III)	†2000	10	106	10.6
Rick Sherrod, West Virginia (FBS)	†2001	10	102	10.2
Robert Aguilar, Greenville (III)	2000	10	101	10.1
Boomer Grigsby, Illinois St. (FCS)	†2002	11	108	9.82
Edgerton Hartwell, Western Ill. (FCS)	†2000	11	107	9.73
Hunter Hillenmeyer, Vanderbilt (FBS)	†2002	12	116	9.67
E.J. Henderson, Maryland (FBS)	2002	14	*135	9.64
E.J. Henderson, Maryland (FBS)	2001	11	104	9.45
Josh Cain, Chattanooga (FCS)	2002	12	113	9.42
Brenden Givan, Stillman (III)	2000	9	84	9.33

**Record. †National champion.*

CAREER SOLO TACKLES

Player, Team (Division)	Years	G	Solo
Rod Davis, Southern Miss. (FBS)	2000-03	47	360
Boomer Grigsby, Illinois St. (FCS)	2001-04	44	325
Tim McGarigle, Northwestern (FBS)	2002-05	48	319
Lee Russell, Western Ill. (FCS)	2000-03	48	317
Matt Pusateri, Miami (Ohio) (FBS)	2001-04	51	313
E.J. Henderson, Maryland (FBS)	2000-02	35	308
Dexter Reid, North Carolina (FBS)	2000-03	47	304
Grant Wiley, West Virginia (FBS)	2000-03	47	298
Nick Ricks, Eastern Ill. (FCS)	2000-03	47	298
Matt Nelson, Wofford (FCS)	2000-03	47	296
Casey McConnell, Kenyon (III)	2001-03, 05	40	294
Abdul Hodge, Iowa (FBS)	2002-05	50	289
Ryan Fowler, Duke (FBS)	2000-03	46	286
Ron Swearingin, Capital (III)	2000-03	40	282
Derrick Johnson, Texas (FBS)	2001-04	49	281
Deric Sieck, Winona St. (II)	2000-03	49	275
Josh Cain, Chattanooga (FCS)	2000-02	34	273
Jordan Beck, Cal Poly (FCS)	2001-04	43	270
James King, Central Mich. (FBS)	2001-04	45	268
Justin Beriault, Ball St. (FBS)	2001-04	46	267
Terrell Jones, Miami (Ohio) (FBS)	2000-03	47	258
Chad Greenway, Iowa (FBS)	2002-05	50	252
Akil Grant, Northern Ill. (FBS)	2000-03	42	246
Bruce Renner, Indianapolis (II)	2002-05	42	242
Kirk Morrison, San Diego St. (FBS)	2000-04	47	241
Charleston Hughes, Northwood (Mich.) (II)	2003-06	45	237
Daniel Leger, Colorado Mines (II)	2001-04	46	236
Matt O'Bryant, Millsaps (III)	2000-03	38	236
Jerry Schumacher, Illinois (FBS)	2000-02	35	236

SEASON SOLO TACKLES

Player, Team (Division)	Year	G	Solo
E.J. Henderson, Maryland (FBS)	2002	14	135
Lawrence Flugence, Texas Tech (FBS)	2002	14	124
Rod Davis, Southern Miss. (FBS)	2002	13	121
Hunter Hillenmeyer, Vanderbilt (FBS)	†2002	12	116
Andre Maddox, North Carolina St. (FBS)	2003	13	113
Josh Cain, Chattanooga (FCS)	2002	12	113
Rod Davis, Southern Miss. (FBS)	†2003	12	111
Leroy Hill, Clemson (FBS)	2003	13	110
Josh Buhl, Kansas St. (FBS)	2003	15	109
Boomer Grigsby, Illinois St. (FCS)	2003	12	109
Boomer Grigsby, Illinois St. (FCS)	†2002	11	108
Dexter Reid, North Carolina (FBS)	2002	12	107
Tom Ward, Toledo (FBS)	2002	14	107
Edgerton Hartwell, Western Ill. (FCS)	†2000	11	107
Robert Gunn, Earlham (III)	†2000	10	106

†National champion.

SINGLE-GAME SOLO TACKLES

Solo	Div	Player, Team (Opponent)	Date
21	FCS	Dan Adams, Holy Cross (Colgate)	Oct. 22, 2005
21	III	Tim Rotenberry, North Park (Millikin)	Oct. 16, 2004
20	FBS	Tyrell Johnson, Arkansas St. (North Texas)	Nov. 26, 2005
20	III	Anthony Venturino, Utica (Springfield)	Oct. 2, 2004
19	II	Eric Portley, Fayetteville St. (N.C. Central)	Oct. 8, 2005
19	FBS	Doug Szymul, Northwestern (Navy)	Sept. 21, 2002
18	II	Kevin Jones, St. Augustine's (Johnson C. Smith)	Oct. 8, 2005
18	II	DeLaurence Walker, Fayetteville St. (Winston-Salem)	Oct. 1, 2005
18	FCS	Jordan Beck, Cal Poly (Eastern Wash.)	Nov. 6, 2004
18	II	Todd Lowe, Merrimack (C.W. Post)	Oct. 30, 2004
18	III	Tim Rotenberry, North Park [Augustana (Ill.)]	Oct. 2, 2004
18	FCS	Nick Ricks, Eastern Ill. (Eastern Ky.)	Oct. 12, 2002
18	FBS	Nick Duffy, Northern Ill. (Ball St.)	Nov. 17, 2001
18	FBS	Brian Leigeb, Central Mich. (Northern Ill.)	Nov. 17, 2000
17	FBS	Nelson Coleman, Tulsa (Rice)	Oct. 15, 2005
17	III	Ron Ringgold, McDaniel (Dickinson)	Oct. 15, 2005
17	FBS	A.J. Nicholson, Florida St. (Boston College)	Sept. 17, 2005
17	III	Ward Brady, Elmhurst (Ill. Wesleyan)	Oct. 2, 2004
17	FBS	Matt McCoy, San Diego St. (Michigan)	Sept. 18, 2004
17	FBS	Tom Ward, Toledo (UNLV)	Sept. 21, 2002
17	III	Casey McConnell, Kenyon (Centre)	Sept. 7, 2002
17	FCS	Josh Cain, Chattanooga (Citadel)	Nov. 3, 2001

Tackles for Loss

CAREER TACKLES FOR LOSS PER GAME

(Min. 25 Tackles for Loss; Player must have concluded his career)

Player, Team (Division)	Years	G	Solo	Ast	Total	Avg.
Steven Wilson, King's (Pa.) (III)	2000-02	32	105	3	*106.5	3.33
Brenden Givan, Stillman (III)	2000-02	28	74	3	75.5	2.70
Charlie Cook, C.W. Post (II)	2000-01	19	49	0	49.0	2.58
Steve Baggs, Bethune-Cookman (FCS)	2002-03	25	53	18	62.0	2.48
Vince King, Wartburg (III)	2000-03	37	83	0	83.0	2.24
Brandon Tisdale, Wilmington (Ohio) (III)	2001-04	40	88	3	89.5	2.24
Kevin Culbert, Frostburg St. (III)	2002-05	42	84	7	87.5	2.08
Jason Trusnik, Ohio Northern (III)	$2002-06	41	78	8	82.0	2.00
Jason Ocean, Livingstone (II)	2000-03	37	68	12	74.0	2.00
Anthony Jones, Wofford (FCS)	2000-02	32	60	0	60.0	1.88
Julius Peppers, North Carolina (FBS)	2000-01	23	43	0	43.0	1.87
Terrell Suggs, Arizona St. (FBS)	2000-02	36	61	9	65.5	1.82
E.J. Henderson, Maryland (FBS)	2000-02	35	59	4	61.0	1.74
Mike Lewis, Adrian (III)	2002-05	35	58	5	60.5	1.73
Matt O'Bryant, Millsaps (III)	2000-03	38	64	0	64.0	1.68
Dustin Hertel, DePauw (III)	2002, 04-06	39	65	1	65.5	1.68
Willie Thompson, Illinois Col. (III)	2001-04	40	67	0	67.0	1.68
Sherrod Coates, Western Ky. (FCS)	2000-02	40	67	0	67.0	1.68
Antwan Peek, Cincinnati (FBS)	2000-02	34	56	0	56.0	1.65
Alton Pettway, Albany St. (Ga.) (II)	2004-06	22	30	12	36.0	1.64
Dan Klecko, Temple (FBS)	2000-02	30	49	0	49.0	1.63
Ron Swearingin, Capital (III)	2000-03	40	64	0	64.0	1.60
Jason Babin, Western Mich. (FBS)	2000-03	47	73	4	75.0	1.60
Paul Hubbard, Northern Colo. (II)	2002-03	25	40	0	40.0	1.60
Michael Holbok, Buffalo St. (III)	2001-04	32	49	4	51.0	1.59
Anthony Silver, Delaware Valley (III)	2003-06	48	75	0	75.0	1.56
Mike O'Brien, Western Ill. (FCS)	2000-03	35	54	0	54.0	1.54
Calvin Pace, Wake Forest (FBS)	2000-02	34	52	0	52.0	1.53
Tully Banta-Cain, California (FBS)	2000-02	34	49	5	51.5	1.51

**Record. $See page 10 for explanation.*

SEASON TACKLES FOR LOSS PER GAME

Player, Team (Division)	Year	G	Solo	Ast	Total	Avg.
Steven Wilson, King's (Pa.) (III)	†2001	10	37	3	38.5	3.85
Russ Watson, Worcester St. (III)	†2000	9	32	0	32.0	3.56
Robert Aguilar, Greenville (III)	2000	10	35	0	35.0	3.50
Quincy Malloy, Methodist (III)	2001	10	34	0	34.0	3.40
Patrick Ryan, Benedictine (Ill.) (III)	†2002	10	33	0	33.0	3.30
Steven Wilson, King's (Pa.) (III)	2002	12	38	2	*39.0	3.25
Brenden Givan, Stillman (III)	2001	9	29	0	29.0	3.22
Brenden Givan, Stillman (III)	2000	9	25	7	28.5	3.17
Jason Trusnik, Ohio Northern (III)	†2004	10	27	8	31.0	3.10
Jason Ripke, Simpson (III)	†2004	10	26	10	31.0	3.10
Adam Frantz, Lebanon Valley (III)	2001	10	31	0	31.0	3.10
Jeff Heinz, Ill. Wesleyan (III)	2000	10	31	0	31.0	3.10

**Record. †National champion.*

CAREER TACKLES FOR LOSS

Player, Team (Division)	Years	G	Solo	Ast	Total
Steven Wilson, King's (Pa.) (III)	2000-02	32	105	3	106.5
Brandon Tisdale, Wilmington (Ohio) (III)	2001-04	40	88	3	89.5
Kevin Culbert, Frostburg St. (III)	2002-05	42	84	7	87.5
Vince King, Wartburg (III)	2000-03	37	83	0	83.0
Jason Trusnik, Ohio Northern (III)	$2002-06	41	78	8	82.0
Brenden Givan, Stillman (III)	2000-02	28	74	3	75.5
Anthony Silver, Delaware Valley (III)	2003-06	48	75	0	75.0
Jason Babin, Western Mich. (FBS)	2000-03	47	73	4	75.0
Jason Ocean, Livingstone (II)	2000-03	37	68	12	74.0
Aaron McConnell, Pittsburg St. (II)	2000-03	48	69	6	72.0
Willie Thompson, Illinois Col. (III)	2001-04	40	67	0	67.0
Sherrod Coates, Western Ky. (FCS)	2000-02	40	67	0	67.0
Dustin Hertel, DePauw (III)	2002, 04-06	39	65	1	65.5
Jonathan Goddard, Marshall (FBS)	2001-04	48	60	11	65.5
Terrell Suggs, Arizona St. (FBS)	2000-02	36	61	9	65.5
Derrick Johnson, Texas (FBS)	2001-04	49	65	0	65.0
Terrance Lee, Concord (II)	2003-06	43	52	25	64.5
Ron Swearingin, Capital (III)	2000-03	40	64	0	64.0
Matt O'Bryant, Millsaps (III)	2000-03	38	64	0	64.0
Valdamar Brower, Masschusetts (FCS)	2000-03	46	63	0	63.0
Adam McGurk, Adams St. (II)	2002-05	44	49	27	62.5
Steve Baggs, Bethune-Cookman (FCS)	2002-03	25	53	18	62.0
Chris Gocong, Cal Poly (FCS)	2001, 03-05	41	60	3	61.5
Lee Basinger, Wofford (FCS)	2001-04	46	61	0	61.0
E.J. Henderson, Maryland (FBS)	2000-02	35	59	4	61.0
Mike Lewis, Adrian (III)	2002-05	35	58	5	60.5
Rod Davis, Southern Miss. (FBS)	2000-03	47	60	1	60.5
Adam Haas, Cortland St. (III)	2003-06	40	60	0	60.0
Anthony Jones, Wofford (FCS)	2000-02	32	60	0	60.0
Eric Henderson, Georgia Tech (FBS)	2002-05	42	57	5	59.5
Shaun Phillips, Purdue (FBS)	2000-03	47	53	13	59.5

$See page 10 for explanation.

SEASON TACKLES FOR LOSS

Player, Team (Division)	Year	G	Solo	Ast	Total
Steven Wilson, King's (Pa.) (III)	†2002	12	38	2	39.0
Steven Wilson, King's (Pa.) (III)	†2001	10	37	3	38.5
Charlie Cook, C.W. Post (II)	†2001	12	36	2	37.0
Steve Baggs, Bethune-Cookman (FCS)	†2003	12	28	16	36.0
Robert Aguilar, Greenville (III)	2000	10	35	0	35.0
Quincy Malloy, Methodist (III)	2001	10	34	0	34.0
Kevin Culbert, Frostburg St. (III)	†2005	11	30	6	33.0
Patrick Ryan, Benedictine (Ill.) (III)	†2002	10	33	0	33.0
Bryan Robinson, Wesley (III)	2006	14	28	9	32.5
Jason Babin, Western Mich. (FBS)	†2003	12	31	2	32.0
Russ Watson, Worcester St. (III)	†2000	9	32	0	32.0
Terrell Suggs, Arizona St. (FBS)	†2002	14	27	9	31.5
Jason Trusnik, Ohio Northern (III)	†2004	10	27	8	31.0
Jason Ripke, Simpson (III)	†2004	10	26	10	31.0
Sherrod Coates, Western Ky. (FCS)	2002	15	31	0	31.0
Adam Frantz, Lebanon Valley (III)	2001	10	31	0	31.0
Jeff Heinz, Ill. Wesleyan (III)	2000	10	31	0	31.0

†National champion.

SINGLE-GAME TACKLES FOR LOSS

TFL	Div.	Player, Team (Opponent)	Date
9.0	II	Darryl Wilson, Concord (West Virginia St.)	Oct. 8, 2005
9.0	II	Ron Ellington, Catawba (Mars Hill)	Oct. 1, 2005
8.5	III	Kevin McNamara, St. John's (Minn.) [Monmouth (Ill.)]	Nov. 19, 2005
8.0	FCS	Sherrod Coates, Western Ky. (Indiana St.)	Oct. 26, 2002
8.0	III	Brenden Givan, Stillman (Pikeville)	Sept. 1, 2001
7.5	III	Matt Rugenstein, Hope (DePauw)	Sept. 16, 2006
7.0	FBS	Elvis Dumervil, Louisville (Kentucky)	Sept. 4, 2005
7.0	III	Ben Hare, North Central (Ill.) (Augsburg)	Sept. 18, 2004
7.0	FCS	Greg Pitts, Texas St. (Texas Southern)	Sept. 21, 2002
7.0	FBS	Larry Foote, Michigan (Iowa)	Oct. 27, 2001
7.0	FBS	Richard Seigler, Oregon St. (Arizona St.)	Oct. 20, 2001
7.0	III	Jon Foss, Bethel (Minn.) (Gust. Adolphus)	Sept. 22, 2001
7.0	FBS	Chris Johnson, Kansas St. (Kansas)	Oct. 7, 2000
6.5	III	Chris Tetje, Defiance (Mt. St. Joseph)	Oct. 28, 2006
6.5	FBS	Ameer Ismail, Western Mich. (Ball St.)	Oct. 21, 2006
6.5	III	Vance Murphy, Oberlin (Hiram)	Nov. 12, 2005
6.5	II	David Heiner, St. Anselm (Stonehill)	Oct. 2, 2004
6.5	III	Brandon Clum, Muskingum [Wilmington (Ohio)]	Sept. 18, 2004
6.5	FBS	Alex Lewis, Wisconsin (Purdue)	Oct. 18, 2003
6.5	III	Daniel McCall, Muhlenberg (Ursinus)	Oct. 18, 2003
6.5	III	Dylan Tarr, Rose-Hulman (Millsaps)	Oct. 18, 2003
6.5	FBS	Terrell Suggs, Arizona St. (Washington)	Oct. 26, 2002
6.5	III	Steven Wilson, King's (Pa.) (Delaware Valley)	Sept. 15, 2001

Pass Sacks

CAREER PASS SACKS PER GAME

(Min. 18 Pass Sacks; Player must have concluded his career)

Player, Team (Division)	Years	G	Solo	Ast	Total	Avg.
Dwight Freeney, Syracuse (FBS)	2000-01	19	30	1	30.5	1.61
Steven Wilson, King's (Pa.) (III)	2000-02	32	49	0	*49.0	1.52
Brenden Givan, Stillman (III)	2000-02	28	41	0	41.0	1.46
Charlie Cook, C.W. Post (II)	2000-01	19	27	0	27.0	1.42
Terrell Suggs, Arizona St. (FBS)	2000-02	36	43	2	44.0	1.22
Walter Curry, Albany St. (Ga.) (II)	2001-04	24	24	10	29.0	1.21
Mike Lewis, Adrian (III)	2002-05	35	35	5	37.5	1.07
Alton Pettway, Albany St. (Ga.) (II)	2004-06	22	20	7	23.5	1.07
Julius Peppers, North Carolina (FBS)	2000-01	23	24	1	24.5	1.07
Brandon Tisdale, Wilmington (Ohio) (III)	2001-04	40	41	3	42.5	1.06
Brent Hawkins, Illinois St. (FCS)	2004-05	19	19	2	20.0	1.05
Jason Trusnik, Ohio Northern (III)	$2002-06	41	42	2	43.0	1.05
Chris Gocong, Cal Poly (FCS)	2001, 03-05	41	36	12	42.0	1.02
Dustin Hertel, DePauw (III)	2002, 04-06	39	37	0	37.0	0.95
Casey Carlson, Pacific Lutheran (III)	2000-03	36	34	0	34.0	0.94
Greg Gathers, Georgia Tech (FBS)	2000-02	26	24	0	24.0	0.92
Anthony Jones, Wofford (FCS)	2000-02	32	29	1	29.5	0.92
Kevin Culbert, Frostburg St. (III)	2002-05	42	35	7	38.5	0.92
Dan Klecko, Temple (FBS)	2000-02	30	26	0	26.0	0.87
Ameer Ismail, Western Mich. (FBS)	2004-06	29	24	2	25.0	0.86
Joe Peters, Concordia-St. Paul (II)	2001-03	34	29	0	29.0	0.85
Adam Haas, Cortland St. (III)	2003-06	40	34	0	34.0	0.85

Player, Team (Division)	Years	G	Solo	Ast	Total	Avg.
Jason Babin, Western Mich. (FBS)	2000-03	47	37	2	38.0	0.81
Dave Tollefson, Northwest Mo. St. (II)	2004-05	26	19	4	21.0	0.81
Anthony Gargiulo, Dartmouth (FCS)	2002-05	31	25	0	25.0	0.81
Michael Holbok, Buffalo St. (III)	2001-04	32	24	3	25.5	0.80

**Record. $See page 10 for explanation.*

SEASON PASS SACKS PER GAME

Player, Team (Division)	Year	G	Solo	Ast	Total	Avg.
Russ Watson, Worcester St. (III)	†2000	9	24	0	*24.0	2.67
Steven Wilson, King's (Pa.) (III)	†2001	10	18	3	19.5	1.95
Kevin Ryan, Middlebury (III)	†2006	8	14	3	15.5	1.94
Josh Stinehour, Union (N.Y.) (III)	2001	10	18	2	19.0	1.90
Michael Gardner, Benedictine (Ill.) (III)	2000	10	19	0	19.0	1.90
Andrew Hollingsworth, Towson (FCS)	†2000	9	16	2	17.0	1.89
Brenden Givan, Stillman (III)	2000	9	16	2	17.0	1.89
Mark Seagraves, Lycoming (III)	2000	9	17	0	17.0	1.89
Robert Mathis, Alabama A&M (FCS)	†2002	11	19	2	20.0	1.82
Chris Gocong, Cal Poly (FCS)	†2005	13	19	9	23.5	1.81
Jason Trusnik, Ohio Northern (III)	†2004	10	17	2	18.0	1.80
Edith Forestal, Defiance (III)	2000	10	18	0	18.0	1.80
Lance Ramer, Rochester (III)	2000	10	17	2	18.0	1.80

**Record. †National champion.*

CAREER PASS SACKS

Player, Team (Division)	Years	G	Solo	Ast	Total
Steven Wilson, King's (Pa.) (III)	2000-02	32	49	0	49.0
Terrell Suggs, Arizona St. (FBS)	2000-02	36	43	2	44.0
Jason Trusnik, Ohio Northern (III)	$2002-06	41	42	2	43.0
Brandon Tisdale, Wilmington (Ohio) (III)	2001-04	40	41	3	42.5
Chris Gocong, Cal Poly (FCS)	2001, 03-05	41	36	12	42.0
Brenden Givan, Stillman (III)	2000-02	28	41	0	41.0
Kevin Culbert, Frostburg St. (III)	2002-05	42	35	7	38.5
Jason Babin, Western Mich. (FBS)	2000-03	47	37	2	38.0
Jeremy Hood, St. John's (Minn.) (III)	2000-03	47	38	0	38.0
Mike Lewis, Adrian (III)	2002-05	35	35	5	37.5
Dustin Hertel, DePauw (III)	2002, 04-06	39	37	0	37.0
David Pollack, Georgia (FBS)	2001-04	50	35	2	36.0
Adam Haas, Cortland St. (III)	2003-06	40	34	0	34.0
Casey Carlson, Pacific Lutheran (III)	2000-03	36	34	0	34.0
Shaun Phillips, Purdue (FBS)	2000-03	47	31	5	33.5
Matt Mitchell, UNI (FCS)	2000-03	46	33	0	33.0
Adam McGurk, Adams St. (II)	2002-05	44	28	9	32.5
Elvis Dumervil, Louisville (FBS)	2002-05	44	31	2	32.0
¢Casey Larson, St. Anselm (II)	2004-06	29	29	5	31.5
Tim Bush, Montana (FCS)	2000-03	48	28	7	31.5
Mike McFadden, Grand Valley St. (II)	2003-06	53	24	14	31.0
Dave Ball, UCLA (FBS)	2000-03	49	30	1	30.5
K.T. Stovall, Appalachian St. (FCS)	2000-03	50	28	5	30.5
Dwight Freeney, Syracuse (FBS)	2000-01	19	30	1	30.5
Terrance Lee, Concord (II)	2003-06	43	26	8	30.0
Matt Roth, Iowa (FBS)	2001-04	50	30	0	30.0
Anthony Jones, Wofford (FCS)	2000-02	32	29	1	29.5
Russ Rabe, Minn.-Duluth (II)	2001-04	40	29	0	29.0
Walter Curry, Albany St. (Ga.) (II)	2001-04	24	24	10	29.0
Joe Peters, Concordia-St. Paul (II)	2001-03	34	29	0	29.0
Jorge Cordova, Nevada (FBS)	2000-03	42	28	2	29.0
Bo Schobel, TCU (FBS)	2000-03	37	27	4	29.0
Sherrod Coates, Western Ky. (FCS)	2000-02	40	29	0	29.0

¢Active player. $See page 10 for explanation.

SEASON PASS SACKS

Player, Team (Division)	Year	G	Solo	Ast	Total
Terrell Suggs, Arizona St. (FBS)	†2002	14	23	2	24.0
Russ Watson, Worcester St. (III)	†2000	9	24	0	24.0
Chris Gocong, Cal Poly (FCS)	†2005	13	19	9	23.5
Charlie Cook, C.W. Post (II)	†2001	12	20	1	20.5
Robert Mathis, Alabama A&M (FCS)	†2002	11	19	2	20.0
Elvis Dumervil, Louisville (FBS)	†2005	12	19	2	20.0
Damien Gilyard, C.W. Post (II)	†2004	11	18	3	19.5
Steven Wilson, King's (Pa.) (III)	†2001	10	18	3	19.5
Josh Stinehour, Union (N.Y.) (III)	2001	10	18	2	19.0
Andy Petek, Montana (FCS)	2000	11	19	0	19.0
Michael Gardner, Benedictine (Ill.) (III)	2000	10	19	0	19.0
Andrew Schable, South Dakota (II)	†2005	11	18	1	18.5
Jason Trusnik, Ohio Northern (III)	†2004	10	17	2	18.0
Walter Curry, Albany St. (Ga.) (II)	†2003	12	13	10	18.0
Edith Forestal, Defiance (III)	2000	10	18	0	18.0
Lance Ramer, Rochester (III)	2000	10	17	2	18.0

†National champion.

SINGLE-GAME PASS SACKS

PS	Div.	Player, Team (Opponent)	Date
7.5	III	Kevin McNamara, St. John's (Minn.) [Monmouth (Ill.)]	Nov. 19, 2005
7.0	II	Ron Ellington, Catawba (Mars Hill)	Oct. 1, 2005
6.0	FBS	Ameer Ismail, Western Mich. (Ball St.)	Oct. 21, 2006
6.0	FBS	Elvis Dumervil, Louisville (Kentucky)	Sept. 4, 2005
6.0	FCS	Damien Huren, Southeastern La. (Northern Colo.)	Oct. 9, 2004
5.5	II	Brandon Beard, Lincoln (Mo.) (Paul Quinn)	Nov. 6, 2004
5.5	II	Shant Banosian, Bentley (Assumption)	Oct. 27, 2001
5.0	III	Andrew Eisentrout, Pacific Lutheran (Willamette)	Nov. 11, 2006
5.0	III	Adam Jordison, Coe (Buena Vista)	Sept. 23, 2006
5.0	II	Victor Adesanya, Merrimack (Stonehill)	Sept. 1, 2006
5.0	III	Randy Tosh, Rowan (Montclair St.)	Nov. 12, 2005
5.0	FCS	Brent Hawkins, Illinois St. (UNI)	Oct. 22, 2005
5.0	II	Bryan Biggs, Catawba (Tusculum)	Oct. 22, 2005
5.0	II	Damien Gilyard, C.W. Post (Pace)	Sept. 4, 2004
5.0	II	Matt Sola, Kutztown (Millersville)	Oct. 25, 2003
5.0	FBS	Alex Lewis, Wisconsin (Purdue)	Oct. 18, 2003
5.0	III	Daniel McCall, Muhlenberg (Ursinus)	Oct. 18, 2003
5.0	FCS	Maurice Troutman, Ark.-Pine Bluff (Mississippi Val.)	Sept. 6, 2003
5.0	III	Aaron Brennan, Fitchburg St. (Maine Maritime)	Oct. 19, 2002
5.0	III	J.J. Zearley, Wartburg (Loras)	Oct. 5, 2002
5.0	FBS	James Harrison, Kent St. [Miami (Ohio)]	Nov. 24, 2001
5.0	II	Luke Larson, Quincy [Westminster (Mo.)]	Oct. 6, 2001
5.0	FBS	Wendell Bryant, Wisconsin (Penn St.)	Sept. 22, 2001
5.0	III	Steven Wilson, King's (Pa.) (Delaware Valley)	Sept. 15, 2001

Passes Defended

CAREER PASSES DEFENDED PER GAME

(Min. 30 Passes Defended; Player must have concluded his career)

Player, Team (Division)	Years	G	PBU	Int	Total	Avg.
Kip Daniels, Aurora (III)	2000-01	19	37	13	50	2.63
Jarrod Pence, Moravian (III)	2001-02	21	46	8	54	2.57
Chris Spiegel, Benedictine (Ill.) (III)	2001-02	20	36	15	51	2.55
Evan Zupancic, Tufts (III)	2000-02	24	44	15	60	2.50
Eric Moe, Wis.-Stout (III)	2001-02	19	30	13	43	2.26
Kory Schramm, Hartwick (III)	2000-02	30	45	20	65	2.17
Eugene Wilson, Illinois (FBS)	2000-02	33	60	11	71	2.15
Ricardo Colclough, Tusculum (II)	2002-03	20	22	15	37	1.85
Joey Flora, Indiana (Pa.) (II)	2000-01	17	20	10	30	1.76
Rayshun Reed, Troy (FBS)	2000-03	31	43	10	53	1.71
Nathan Vasher, Texas (FBS)	2000-03	46	61	17	*78	1.70
Kennard Davis, Thiel (III)	2001-04	40	42	24	66	1.65
Kyle Westphal, Simpson (III)	2001-04	39	45	19	64	1.64
Phil Crumb, Fayetteville St. (II)	2000-01	20	27	5	32	1.60
Michael Jolivette, Arizona (FBS)	2000-03	36	44	12	56	1.56
Benny Sapp, UNI (FCS)	2002-03	24	30	7	37	1.54
Charles Allgood, Adams St. (II)	2003-04	21	26	6	32	1.52
Fletcher Terrell, Washburn (II)	2003-06	46	48	22	70	1.52
Bobby Sippio, Western Ky. (FCS)	2000-01	22	18	15	33	1.50
Aharon Kiett, Kean (III)	2003-06	39	44	12	56	1.44
Rob Keefe, Mercyhurst (II)	2000-03	40	48	8	56	1.40
Christian Morton, Illinois (FBS)	2000-03	33	41	5	46	1.39
Brian King, West Virginia (FBS)	2000-03	46	54	10	64	1.39
Greg Brooks, Southern Miss. (FBS)	2000-03	43	47	9	56	1.30
Kyle Hausler, Capital (III)	2002, 04-06	39	27	23	50	1.28
Mario Williams, Gardner-Webb (FBS; II)	2001-04	35	35	8	43	1.23
Dan Peters, Shepherd (II)	2003-06	44	22	32	54	1.23

**Record.*

SEASON PASSES DEFENDED PER GAME

Player, Team (Division)	Year	G	PBU	Int	Total	Avg.
Jarrod Pence, Moravian (III)	†2001	10	31	5	*36	3.60
Anthony Cooks, Fairmont St. (II)	†2001	9	28	4	32	3.56
Kip Daniels, Aurora (III)	2001	9	23	9	32	3.56
Johnny Kelly, Williams (III)	2001	8	23	4	27	3.38
Kennard Davis, Thiel (III)	2001	10	23	9	32	3.20
Chris Speigel, Benedictine (Ill.) (III)	2001	10	25	7	32	3.20
James Patrick, Stillman (III)	†2002	10	20	11	31	3.10
B.J. Harvey, Illinois Col. (III)	2001	10	25	6	31	3.10
Evan Zupancic, Tufts (III)	†2000	8	18	6	24	3.00

**Record. †National champion.*

CAREER PASSES DEFENDED

Player, Team (Division)	Years	G	PBU	Int	Total
Nathan Vasher, Texas (FBS)	2000-03	46	61	17	78
Eugene Wilson, Illinois (FBS)	2000-02	33	60	11	71
Fletcher Terrell, Washburn (II)	2003-06	46	48	22	70
Kennard Davis, Thiel (III)	2001-04	40	42	24	66

Player, Team (Division)	Years	G	PBU	Int	Total
Kory Schramm, Hartwick (III)	2000-02	30	45	20	65
Kyle Westphal, Simpson (III)	2001-04	39	45	19	64
Brian King, West Virginia (FBS)	2000-03	46	54	10	64
Evan Zupancic, Tufts (III)	2000-02	24	44	16	60
B.J. Harvey, Illinois Col. (III)	2000-03	39	45	13	58
Aharon Kiett, Kean (III)	2003-06	39	44	12	56
Michael Jolivette, Arizona (FBS)	2000-03	36	44	12	56
Rob Keefe, Mercyhurst (II)	2000-03	40	48	8	56
Blake Farris, North Ala. (II)	2002-05	52	39	16	55
Dan Peters, Shepherd (II)	2003-06	44	22	32	54
Jarrod Pence, Moravian (III)	2001-02	21	46	8	54
Greg Brooks, Southern Miss. (FBS)	2000-03	43	47	6	53
Rayshun Reed, Troy (FBS)	2000-03	31	43	10	53
Scott Starks, Wisconsin (FBS)	2001-04	51	46	6	52
Randee Drew, Northern Ill. (FBS)	2000-03	44	38	14	52
Billy Parker, William & Mary (FCS)	2000-03	44	40	11	51
Eric Mickelson, St. Cloud St. (II)	2000-03	42	45	6	51
Chris Spiegel, Benedictine (Ill.) (III)	2001-02	20	36	15	51
Kyle Hausler, Capital (III)	2002, 04-06	39	27	23	50
Robert Towns, Harding (II)	2003-06	42	32	18	50
Jim Leonhard, Wisconsin (FBS)	2001-04	51	29	21	50
Kip Daniels, Aurora (III)	2000-01	19	37	13	50
Quinton Teal, Coastal Caro. (FBS)	2003-06	44	31	17	48
Jeff Molesso, Bentley (II)	2002-05	40	33	14	47
Jesse Hendrix, Eastern Wash. (FCS)	2002-05	47	41	5	46
Kelvin Millhouse, Hawaii (FBS)	2001-03	40	23	13	46
Christian Morton, Illinois (FBS)	2000-03	33	41	5	46
¢Deqwan Young, St. Joseph's (Ind.) (II)	2004-06	33	34	11	45

¢Active player.

SEASON PASSES DEFENDED

Player, Team (Division)	Year	G	PBU	Int	Total
Jarrod Pence, Moravian (III)	†2001	10	31	5	36
Nathan Vasher, Texas (FBS)	†2003	13	26	6	32
Corey Webster, LSU (FBS)	2003	14	25	7	32
Jason Goss, TCU (FBS)	†2002	12	24	8	32
Anthony Cooks, Fairmont St. (II)	†2001	9	28	4	32
Kip Daniels, Aurora (III)	2001	9	23	9	32
Kennard Davis, Thiel (III)	2001	10	23	9	32
Chris Speigel, Benedictine (Ill.) (III)	2001	10	25	7	32
Lynaris Elpheage, Tulane (FBS)	2002	13	23	8	31
James Patrick, Stillman (III)	†2002	10	20	11	31
B.J. Harvey, Illinois Col. (III)	2001	10	25	6	31
Jason Patterson, Central Wash. (II)	2001	11	19	11	30

†National champion.

SINGLE-GAME PASSES DEFENDED

PD	Div.	Player, Team (Opponent)	Date
10	III	James Patrick, Stillman (Edward Waters)	Nov. 2, 2002
8	FBS	Joselio Hanson, Texas Tech (Oklahoma St.)	Nov. 9, 2002
7	III	Dan Medlock, Alfred (Ithaca)	Nov. 4, 2006
7	III	D.J. Moore, Dubuque [Central (Iowa)]	Oct. 29, 2005
7	FBS	Fabian Washington, Nebraska (Kansas)	Oct. 2, 2004
7	II	Taiwan Russell, Tiffin (Alma)	Sept. 25, 2004
7	II	Rob Keefe, Mercyhurst (Indianapolis)	Oct. 25, 2003
7	FBS	Jason Goss, TCU (Tulane)	Nov. 9, 2002
7	FBS	Korey Banks, Mississippi St. (Memphis)	Oct. 19, 2002
7	III	Kyle Westphal, Simpson (Washington-St. Louis)	Sept. 7, 2002
7	III	Derrick Brantley, Wesleyan (Conn.) (Colby)	Oct. 6, 2001
7	FBS	Nashville Dyer, Kent St. (Bucknell)	Sept. 8, 2001
7	FBS	Demerist Whitfield, Northern Ill. (Illinois St.)	Sept. 9, 2000

Forced Fumbles

CAREER FORCED FUMBLES PER GAME

(Min. 20 Games Played; Player must have concluded his career)

Player, Team (Division)	Years	G	FF	Avg.
Robert Mathis, Alabama A&M (FCS)	2001-02	22	13	0.59
Antwan Peek, Cincinnati (FBS)	2000-02	34	*14	0.41
Tom Canada, California (FBS)	2001-02	20	8	0.40
Terrell Suggs, Arizona St. (FBS)	2000-02	36	*14	0.39
Kenechi Udeze, Southern California (FBS)	2001-03	37	*14	0.38
Sherrod Coates, Western Ky. (FCS)	2000-02	40	13	0.33
Adam McGurk, Adams St. (II)	2002-05	44	*14	0.32
James Ward, St. Anselm (II)	2000-03	38	11	0.29
Jared Ziemke, Minn. St. Mankato (II)	$1999-03	45	13	0.29
Neal Wood, Indiana (Pa.) (II)	2002-03	21	6	0.29
Nate Jackson, Hawaii (FBS)	2000-01	23	6	0.26
Heath Farwell, San Diego St. (FBS)	2001-03	36	9	0.25
D.J. Starling, Tusculum (II)	2000-03	34	8	0.24
Kris Griffin, Indiana (Pa.) (II)	2002, 2004	22	5	0.23
Derrick Johnson, Texas (FBS)	2001-04	49	11	0.22
Guss Scott, Florida (FBS)	2000-03	49	11	0.22
Ryan Claridge, UNLV (FBS)	2000-01, 03-04	46	10	0.22
Emanuel Plummer, Elizabeth City St. (II)	2003-06	38	8	0.21
Antoine Bullock, Duquesne (FCS)	2002-05	43	9	0.21
Johnathan Goddard, Marshall (FBS)	2001-04	48	10	0.21
Lee Russell, Western Ill. (FCS)	2000-03	48	10	0.21
Josh Smith, Navy (FBS)	2002-04	34	7	0.21
Brendan Curry, Maine (FCS)	2000-02	34	7	0.21
K.T. Stovall, Appalachian St. (FCS)	2000-03	50	10	0.20
Osi Umenyiora, Troy (FBS)	2000-02	35	7	0.20
Wes Erbe, Lafayette (FCS)	2001-04	30	6	0.20
Garrett Padgett, Tiffin (II)	2000-03	41	8	0.20

**Record. $See Page 10 for explanation.*

SEASON FORCED FUMBLES PER GAME

Player, Team (Division)	Year	G	FF	Avg.
Robert Mathis, Alabama A&M (FCS)	†2002	11	*10	0.91
Curtis Johnson, Clark Atlanta (II)	†2006	10	9	0.90
Tony Pate, Concordia (Ill.) (III)	†2000	9	8	0.89
Peter Sherman, Colby (III)	†2004	7	6	0.86
Elvis Dumervil, Louisville (FBS)	†2005	12	*10	0.83
Jared Ziemke, Minn. St. Mankato (II)	†2003	11	8	0.73
Bryan Eakin, Neb.-Kearney (II)	†2001	10	7	0.70
Bryan Sandry, Maranatha Baptist (III)	†2006	9	6	0.67
Dwayne Slay, Texas Tech (FBS)	2005	12	8	0.67
Casey Carlson, Pacific Lutheran (III)	†2003	9	6	0.67
Tom Canada, California (FBS)	†2002	9	6	0.67
Courtney Johnson, Fairmont St. (II)	2001	9	6	0.67
Dwight Freeney, Syracuse (FBS)	†2001	12	8	0.67
Erik Tinsley, Concordia (Ill.) (III)	2000	9	6	0.67
Brent Hawkins, Illinois St. (FCS)	†2005	11	7	0.64
Al Sullivan, Midwestern St. (II)	†2002	11	7	0.64
Roderick Hutchins, McMurry (III)	2003	8	5	0.63
Greg Boucher, Western Conn. St. (III)	†2001	8	5	0.63

**Record. †National champion.*

CAREER FORCED FUMBLES

Player, Team (Division)	Years	G	FF
Adam McGurk, Adams St. (II)	2002-05	44	14
Kenechi Udeze, Southern California (FBS)	2001-03	37	14
Terrell Suggs, Arizona St. (FBS)	2000-02	36	14
Antwan Peek, Cincinnati (FBS)	2000-02	34	14
Jared Ziemke, Minn. St. Mankato (II)	$1999-03	45	13
Robert Mathis, Alabama A&M (FCS)	2001-02	22	13
Sherrod Coates, Western Ky. (FCS)	2000-02	40	13
Elvis Dumervil, Louisville (FBS)	2002-05	44	11
Derrick Johnson, Texas (FBS)	2001-04	49	11
James Ward, St. Anselm (II)	2000-03	38	11
Guss Scott, Florida (FBS)	2000-03	49	11
¢Casey Larson, St. Anselm (II)	2004-06	29	10
Ryan Claridge, UNLV (FBS)	2000-01, 03-04	46	10
Johnathan Goddard, Marshall (FBS)	2001-04	48	10
K.T. Stovall, Appalachian St. (FCS)	2000-03	50	10
Lee Russell, Western Ill. (FCS)	2000-03	48	10
¢Curtis Johnson, Clark Atlanta (II)	2006	10	9
Antoine Bullock, Duquesne (FCS)	2002-05	43	9
Heath Farwell, San Diego St. (FBS)	2001-03	36	9
Shaun Phillips, Purdue (FBS)	2000-03	47	9

¢Active player. $See Page 10 for explanation.

SEASON FORCED FUMBLES

Player, Team (Division)	Year	G	FF
Elvis Dumervil, Louisville (FBS)	†2005	12	10
Robert Mathis, Alabama A&M (FCS)	†2002	11	10
Curtis Johnson, Clark Atlanta (II)	†2006	10	9
Dwayne Slay, Texas Tech (FBS)	2005	12	8
Jared Ziemke, Minn. St. Mankato (II)	†2003	11	8
Quintin Mikell, Boise St. (FBS)	2002	13	8
Dwight Freeney, Syracuse (FBS)	†2001	12	8
Tony Pate, Concordia (Ill.) (III)	†2000	9	8
Brent Hawkins, Illinois St. (FCS)	†2005	11	7
Randy Tosh, Rowan (III)	2005	13	7
Jacob Ford, Central Ark. (II)	2005	14	7
Marques Murrell, Appalachian St. (FCS)	2005	15	7
Derrick Johnson, Texas (FBS)	†2004	12	7
Grant Wiley, West Virginia (FBS)	2003	13	7
Al Sullivan, Midwestern St. (II)	†2002	11	7
Nick Ricks, Eastern Ill. (FCS)	2002	12	7
Claude Harriott, Pittsburgh (FBS)	2002	13	7
Michael Haynes, Penn St. (FBS)	2002	13	7

Player, Team (Division)	Year	G	FF
Phillip Perry, San Jose St. (FBS)	2002	13	7
Antwan Peek, Cincinnati (FBS)	2002	14	7
Bryan Eakin, Neb.-Kearney (II)	†2001	10	7

†*National champion.*

SINGLE-GAME FORCED FUMBLES

FF	Div.	Player, Team (Opponent)	Date
4	III	Nick Rice, Thomas More (Franklin)	Oct. 11, 2002
4	II	Rob White, Western Wash. (Fort Lewis)	Sept. 14, 2002
3	III	Jamie Edlow, Hampden-Sydney (Catholic)	Oc. 21, 2006
3	III	Michael Tuertscher, Case Reserve (Washington-St. Louis)	Oct. 21, 2006
3	FBS	Ramel Meekins, Rutgers (Navy)	Oct. 14, 2006
3	II	Jimmy Lewis, West Chester (East Stroudsburg)	Oct. 22, 2005
3	FCS	Brent Hawkins, Illinois St. (Murray St.)	Sept. 24, 2005
3	III	Jake Dearing, Texas Lutheran (McMurry)	Sept. 24, 2005
3	II	Jim Couretas, Northern Mich. (Findlay)	Sept. 10, 2005
3	FCS	Sam Harper, Coastal Caro. (Jacksonville)	Nov. 13, 2004
3	III	Matt Chiles, Bluffton [Anderson (Ind.)]	Oct. 16, 2004
3	II	Antonio Knox, Tuskegee [Albany St. (Ga.)]	Oct. 2, 2004
3	III	Brooks Klosterman, Mt. St. Joseph (Rose-Hulman)	Sept. 11, 2004
3	FBS	Derrick Johnson, Texas (North Texas)	Sept. 4, 2004
3	II	Colin Tozer, Millersville (West Chester)	Nov. 8, 2003
3	II	Javon Allen, Western Ore. (Central Wash.)	Nov. 1, 2003
3	FBS	Grant Wiley, West Virginia (Cincinnati)	Sept. 13, 2003
3	III	Joe Sollitt, Concordia (Ill.) [Benedictine (Ill.)]	Nov. 2, 2002
3	FBS	Quintin Mikell, Boise St. (Hawaii)	Oct. 5, 2002
3	FBS	Mason Unck, Arizona St. (Stanford)	Sept. 28, 2002
3	FBS	Antwan Peek, Cincinnati (La.-Monroe)	Dec. 1, 2001
3	FCS	Sterling Rogers, Texas St. (Portland St.)	Oct. 6, 2001
3	III	Greg Boucher, Western Conn. St. (Mount Ida)	Sept. 8, 2001
3	II	Roger Williams, Indiana (Pa.) (Millersville)	Nov. 11, 2000
3	FBS	DeLawrence Grant, Oregon St. (San Diego St.)	Sept. 23, 2000

Punt Returns

CAREER AVERAGE

(Minimum 1.2 Returns Per Game; Minimum 30 Returns)

Player, Team (Division[s])	Years	No.	Yards	Avg.
Billy Johnson, Widener (II; III)	1971-72; 73	40	989	24.7
Jack Mitchell, Oklahoma (FBS)	1946-48	39	922	23.6
Keith Winston, Knoxville (III)	1986-87	30	686	22.9
Kevin Doherty, Mass. Maritime (III)	1976-78, 80	45	939	20.9
James Rooths, Shepherd (II)	1997-00	59	1,223	*20.7
Chuck Downey, Stony Brook (III)	1984-87	59	1,198	20.3
Chuck Goehl, Monmouth (Ill.) (II)	1970-72	48	911	19.0
Eddie Macon, Pacific (FBS)	1949-51	48	907	18.9
Jackie Robinson, UCLA (FBS)	1939-40	37	694	18.8
Willie Canady, Fort Valley St. (III)	1979-82	41	772	18.8

**Record for minimum 50 returns.*

SEASON AVERAGE

(Minimum 1.2 Returns Per Game and Qualifiers for Championship)

Player, Team (Division)	Year	No.	Yards	Avg.
Billy Johnson, Widener (II)	†1972	15	511	34.1
Chuck Downey, Stony Brook (III)	†1986	17	530	31.2
Kevin Doherty, Mass. Maritime (III)	†1976	11	332	30.2
Dennis Robinson, Wesleyan (Conn.) (III)	†1978	9	263	29.2
Robert Middlebrook, Knoxville (III)	†1984	9	260	28.9
Joe Troise, Kean (III)	†1974	12	342	28.5
Maurice Drew, UCLA (FBS)	†2005	15	427	28.5
William Williams, Livingstone (II)	†1976	16	453	28.3
Terry Egerdahl, Minn. Duluth (II)	†1975	13	360	27.7
Melvin Dillard, Ferrum (III)	†1990	25	688	27.5
Elliot Turner, Greenville (III)	†2000	14	385	27.5
Chris McKinney, Guilford (III)	†2001	20	533	26.7
Eric Green, Benedictine (Ill.) (III)	†1993	13	346	26.6
Curtis DeLoatch, N.C. A&T (FCS)	†2001	20	530	26.5
Bill Blackstock, Tennessee (FBS)	1951	12	311	25.9
Ted Ginn Jr., Ohio St. (FBS)	†2004	15	384	25.6
Rodney Woodruff, Arkansas Tech (II)	†2000	12	305	25.4
George Sims, Baylor (FBS)	1948	15	375	25.0
Ennis Thomas, Bishop (II)	†1971	18	450	25.0

†*National champion.*

Kickoff Returns

CAREER AVERAGE

(Minimum 1.2 Returns Per Game; Minimum 30 Returns)

Player, Team (Division)	Years	No.	Yards	Avg.
Anthony Davis, Southern California (FBS)	1972-74	37	1,299	35.1
Eric Booth, Southern Miss. (FBS)	1994	35	1,135	32.4
Overton Curtis, Utah St. (FBS)	1957-58	32	991	31.0
Fred Montgomery, New Mexico St. (FBS)	1991-92	39	1,191	30.5
Lamont Brightful, Eastern Wash. (FCS)	1998-01	65	1,949	30.0
Karl Evans, Mo. Southern St. (II)	1991-92	32	959	30.0
Kevin Cannon, Millersville (II)	1992-95	67	1,999	29.8
Troy Brown, Marshall (FCS)	1991-92	32	950	29.7
Cedric Bowen, Ark.-Pine Bluff (FCS)	2001-04	38	1,124	29.6
Dave Ludy, Winona St. (II)	1991-94	89	2,630	29.6
Charles Swann, Indiana St. (FCS)	1989-91	45	1,319	29.3
Joe Krile, Mesa St. (II)	2002-05	79	2,312	29.3
Altie Taylor, Utah St. (FBS)	1966-68	40	1,170	29.3
Daryl Brown, Tufts (III)	1974-76	38	1,111	29.2
Joshua Carter, Muhlenberg (III)	1998-01	75	2,189	29.2
Stan Brown, Purdue (FBS)	1968-70	49	1,412	28.8
Henry White, Colgate (FBS)	1974-77	41	1,180	28.8
Kevin Johnson, Syracuse (FBS)	1995-98	50	1,437	28.7
Doug Parrish, San Fran. St. (II)	1990	35	1,002	28.6
Jeremiah Pope, C.W. Post (II)	2000-03	58	1,656	28.6
Craig Richardson, Eastern Wash. (FCS)	1983-86	71	2,021	28.5

SEASON AVERAGE

(Minimum 1.2 Returns Per Game and Qualifiers for Championship)

Player, Team (Division)	Year	No.	Yards	Avg.
Brandon Steinheim, Wesley (III)	†1994	10	422	42.2
Andrew Jackson, Merrimack (II)	†2005	17	707	41.6
Paul Allen, BYU (FBS)	1961	12	481	40.1
D.J. Flick, Slippery Rock (II)	†2000	14	558	39.9
Jason Martin, Coe (III)	†1992	11	438	39.8
Tremain Mack, Miami (Fla.) (FBS)	†1996	13	514	39.5
LaVon Reis, Western St. (II)	†1993	14	552	39.4
Danny Lee, Jacksonville St. (II)	†1992	12	473	39.4
Leeland McElroy, Texas A&M (FBS)	†1993	15	590	39.3
Tony Hill, Salisbury (III)	†1998	14	549	39.2
Fran DeFalco, Assumption (II)	1993	12	461	38.4
Forrest Hall, San Francisco (FBS)	1946	15	573	@38.2
Marcus Washington, Bridgewater (Va.) (III)	†2004	11	420	38.2
David Fraterrigo, Canisius (FCS)	†1993	13	485	37.3
Brian Bratton, Furman (FCS)	†2001	14	521	37.2
Brian Sump, Colorado Mines (II)	†2001	21	780	37.1
Derek Stanley, Wis.-Whitewater (III)	†2003	12	443	36.9
Nate Kirtman, Pomona-Pitzer (III)	†1990	14	515	36.8
Kendall James, Carson-Newman (II)	1993	15	549	36.6
Kerry Hayes, Western Caro. (FCS)	1993	16	584	36.5
Tom Myers, Coe (III)	†1983	11	401	36.5

†*National champion. @ Record for minimum 1.5 returns per game.*

Field Goals

(One-inch tees were permitted in 1949, two-inch tees were permitted in 1965, and use of tees was eliminated before the 1989 season. The goal posts were widened from 18 feet, 6 inches to 23 feet, 4 inches in 1959 and were narrowed back to 18 feet, 6 inches before the 1991 season. The hash marks were moved six feet, eight inches closer to the center of the field to 60 feet from each sideline in 1993.)

CAREER FIELD GOALS

Player, Team (Division)	Years	FGM	FGA	Pct.
Billy Bennett, Georgia (S) (FBS)	2000-03	87	110	.791
Jeff Glas, North Dakota (S) (II)	2002-05	82	*122	.672
Jeff Jaeger, Washington (S) (FBS)	1983-86	80	99	.808
Nick Novak, Maryland (S) (FBS)	2001-04	80	107	.748
John Lee, UCLA (S) (FBS)	1982-85	79	92	*.859
Philip Doyle, Alabama (S) (FBS)	1987-90	78	105	.743
Luis Zendejas, Arizona St. (S) (FBS)	1981-84	78	105	.743
Max Zendejas, Arizona (S) (FBS)	1982-85	77	104	.740
Kevin Butler, Georgia (S) (FBS)	1981-84	77	98	.786
Steve Azar, Northern Ill. (S) (FBS)	2000-03	73	92	.793
Carlos Huerta, Miami (Fla.) (S) (FBS)	1988-91	73	91	.802
Derek Schmidt, Florida St. (S) (FBS)	1984-87	73	104	.702
Marty Zendejas, Nevada (S) (FCS)	1984-87	72	90	.800
Mason Crosby, Colorado (S (FBS)	2003-06	71	95	.747
Kirk Roach, Western Caro. (S) (FCS)	1984-87	71	102	.696

Player, Team (Division)	Years	FGM	FGA	Pct.
Fuad Reveiz, Tennessee (S) (FBS)	1981-84	71	95	.747
Stephen Gostkowski, Memphis (S) (FBS)	2002-05	70	92	.761
Chris Snyder, Montana (S) (FCS)	2000-03	70	105	.667
Roman Anderson, Houston (S) (FBS)	1988-91	70	101	.693
Barry Belli, Fresno St. (S) (FBS)	1984-87	70	99	.707
Tony Zendejas, Nevada (S) (FCS)	1981-83	70	86	.814
Andrew Wellock, Eastern Mich. (S) (FCS)	2003-06	69	87	.793
Darren McCaleb, Southern Miss. (S) (FCS)	2003-06	69	88	.784
Collin Mackie, South Carolina (S) (FBS)	1987-90	69	95	.726
Shayne Graham, Virginia Tech (S) (FBS)	1996-99	68	93	.731
Gary Gussman, Miami (Ohio) (S) (FBS)	1984-87	68	94	.723
Larry Roach, Oklahoma St. (S) (FBS)	1981-84	68	101	.673

**Record. (S) Soccer-style kicker.*

SEASON FIELD GOALS

Player, Team (Division)	Year	FGM	FGA	Pct.
Billy Bennett, Georgia (S) (FBS)	2003	31	*38	.816
Jeff Glas, North Dakota (S) (II)	2005	30	36	.833
John Lee, UCLA (S) (FBS)	1984	29	33	.879
Justin Medlock, UCLA (S) (FBS)	2006	28	32	.875
Nick Browne, TCU (S) (FBS)	2003	28	33	.848
Luis Zendejas, Arizona St. (S) (FBS)	1983	28	37	.757
Paul Woodside, West Virginia (S) (FBS)	1982	28	31	.903
Drew Dunning, Washington St. (S) (FBS)	2003	27	31	.871
Sebastian Janikowski, Florida St. (S) (FBS)	1998	27	32	.844
Fuad Reveiz, Tennessee (S) (FBS)	1982	27	31	.871
Billy Bennett, Georgia (S) (FBS)	2002	26	33	.788
Jonathan Ruffin, Cincinnati (S) (FBS)	2000	26	29	.897
Brian Mitchell, UNI (S) (FCS)	1990	26	27	*.963
Tony Zendejas, Nevada (S) (FCS)	1982	26	33	.788
Jonathan Nichols, Mississippi (S) (FBS)	2003	25	29	.862
Ben Jones, Purdue (S) (FBS)	2003	25	30	.833
Chris Snyder, Montana (S) (FCS)	2003	25	30	.833
David Hendrix, Grand Valley St. (S) (II)	2003	25	32	.781
Mike Nugent, Ohio St. (S) (FBS)	2002	25	28	.893
MacKenzie Hoambrecker, UNI (S) (FCS)	2002	25	28	.893
Wayne Boyer, Missouri St. (S) (FCS)	1996	25	30	.833
Chris Jacke, UTEP (S) (FBS)	1988	25	27	.926
John Diettrich, Ball St. (S) (FBS)	1985	25	29	.862
Chuck Nelson, Washington (S) (FBS)	1982	25	26	.962

**Record. (S) Soccer-style kicker.*

LONGEST FIELD GOALS

Yds.	Div.	Player, Team (Opponent)	Year
67	II	Tom Odle, Fort Hays St. (Washburn)	1988
67	FBS	Joe Williams, Wichita St. (Southern Ill.)	1978
67	FBS	Russell Erxleben, Texas (Rice)	1977
67	FBS	Steve Little, Arkansas (Texas)	1977
65*	FBS	Martin Gramatica, Kansas St. (Northern Ill.)	1998
65	FBS	Tony Franklin, Texas A&M (Baylor)	1976
64	FBS	Russell Erxleben, Texas (Oklahoma)	1977
64	FBS	Tony Franklin, Texas A&M (Baylor)	1976
63	FCS	Bill Gramatica, South Fla. (Austin Peay)	2000
63	FCS	Tim Foley, Ga. Southern (James Madison)	1987
63	FCS	Scott Roper, Arkansas St. (North Texas)	1987
63	FBS	Morten Andersen, Michigan St. (Ohio St.)	1981
63	FBS	Clark Kemble, Colorado St. (Arizona)	1975
63	II	Joe Duren, Arkansas St. (McNeese St.)	1974
62	FCS	Billy Cundiff, Drake (San Diego)	2000
62	FBS	Terance Kitchens, Texas A&M (Southern Miss.)	1999
62	II	Doc Proctor, Ferris St. (Michigan Tech)	1999
62	FBS	Jason Hanson, Washington St. (UNLV)	1991
62	FBS	John Diettrich, Ball St. (Ohio)	1986
62	FCS	Paul Hickert, Murray St. (Eastern Ky.)	1986
62#	FBS	Chip Lohmiller, Minnesota (Iowa)	1986
62	FBS	Tom Whelihan, Missouri (Colorado)	1986
62	FBS	Dan Christopulos, Wyoming (Colorado St.)	1977
62	FBS	Iseed Khoury, North Texas (Richmond)	1977
62	III	Dom Antonini, Rowan (Salisbury)	1976
62	FBS	Dave Lawson, Air Force (Iowa St.)	1975
62	II	Mike Flater, Colorado Mines (Western St.)	1973

**Longest collegiate field goal without use of a tee and also longest collegiate field goal with narrower goal posts (18 feet, 6 inches). #Longest field goal made indoors.*

Special Reference: Ove Johansson, Abilene Christian (not an NCAA-member college at the time), kicked a 69-yard field goal against East Texas St. (now Tex. A&M-Commerce), Oct. 16, 1976, the longest collegiate field goal.

Punting

CAREER PUNTING AVERAGE

(Minimum 150 Punts)

Player, Team (Division)	Years	No.	Yards	Avg.
Todd Sauerbrun, West Virginia (FBS)	1991-94	167	7,733	46.3
Reggie Roby, Iowa (FBS)	1979-82	172	7,849	45.6
Greg Montgomery, Michigan St. (FBS)	1985-87	170	7,721	45.4
Ryan Plackemeier, Wake Forest (FBS)	2002-05	220	9,957	45.3
Daniel Sepulveda, Baylor (FBS)	2003-06	277	12,531	45.2
Tom Tupa, Ohio St. (FBS)	1984-87	196	8,854	45.2
Brandon Fields, Michigan St. (FBS)	2003-06	209	9,405	45.0
Barry Helton, Colorado (FBS)	1984-87	153	6,873	44.9
Jeff Williams, Adams St. (II)	2002-05	240	10,780	44.9
Mark Gould, Northern Ariz. (FCS)	2000-03	211	9,443	44.8
Aron Langley, Wyoming (FBS)	1996-98	171	7,649	44.7
Shane Lechler, Texas A&M (FBS)	1996-99	268	11,977	44.7
Ray Guy, Southern Miss. (FBS)	1970-72	200	8,934	44.7
Dave Zastudil, Ohio (FBS)	1998-01	207	9,225	44.6
Bucky Scribner, Kansas (FBS)	1980-82	217	9,670	44.6
Terry Daniel, Auburn (FBS)	1992-94	169	7,522	44.5
Greg Horne, Arkansas (FBS)	1983-86	180	8,002	44.5
Ray Criswell, Florida (FBS)	1982-85	161	7,153	44.4
Pumpy Tudors, Chattanooga (FCS)	1988-91	181	8,041	44.4
Mark Simon, Air Force (FBS)	1984-86	164	7,283	44.4
Brian Schmitz, North Carolina (FBS)	1996-99	208	9,233	44.4
Bill Smith, Mississippi (FBS)	1983-86	254	11,260	44.3
Jason Van Dyke, Adams St. (II)	1995-98	242	10,720	44.3
Tim Baer, Colorado Mines (II)	1986-89	235	10,406	44.3
Russell Erxleben, Texas (FBS)	1975-78	214	9,467	44.2
Brad Maynard, Ball St. (FBS)	1993-96	242	10,702	44.2
Mark Simon, Air Force (FBS)	1984-86	156	6,898	44.2
Johnny Evans, North Carolina St. (FBS)	1974-77	185	8,143	44.0
Brian Moorman, Pittsburg St. (II)	1995-98	157	6,903	44.0
Chuck Ramsey, Wake Forest (FBS)	1971-73	205	9,010	44.0

SEASON PUNTING AVERAGE

(Qualifiers for Championship)

Player, Team (Division)	Year	No.	Yards	Avg.
Chad Kessler, LSU (FBS)	†1997	39	1,961	50.3
Reggie Roby, Iowa (FBS)	†1981	44	2,193	49.8
Kirk Wilson, UCLA (FBS)	†1956	30	1,479	49.3
Steve Ecker, Shippensburg (II)	†1965	32	1,570	49.1
Todd Sauerbrun, West Virginia (FBS)	†1994	72	3,486	48.4
Travis Dorsch, Purdue (FBS)	†2001	49	2,370	48.4
Mark Gould, Northern Ariz. (FCS)	†2002	62	2,987	48.2
Zack Jordan, Colorado (FBS)	†1950	38	1,830	48.2
Ricky Anderson, Vanderbilt (FBS)	†1984	58	2,793	48.2
Reggie Roby, Iowa (FBS)	†1982	52	2,501	48.1
Marv Bateman, Utah (FBS)	†1971	68	3,269	48.1
Andrew Bayes, East Caro. (FBS)	†1999	47	2,259	48.1
Mike Scifres, Western Ill. (FCS)	2002	53	2,545	48.0
Don Cockroft, Adams St. (II)	†1966	36	1,728	48.0
Owen Price, UTEP (FBS)	†1940	30	1,440	48.0
Matt Prater, UCF (FBS)	†2003	58	2,781	48.0
Jeff Williams, Adams St. (II)	†2004	71	3,405	48.0
Brandon Fields, Michigan St. (FBS)	†2004	50	2,394	47.9
Jack Jacobs, Oklahoma (FBS)	1940	31	1,483	47.8
Paul Ernster, Northern Ariz. (FCS)	†2004	55	2,631	47.8
Brian Schmitz, North Carolina (FBS)	1999	74	3,538	47.8

†National champion.

LONGEST PUNTS

Yds.	Div.	Player, Team (Opponent)	Year
99	FBS	Pat Brady, Nevada (Loyola Marymount)	1950
97	II	Earl Hurst, Emporia St. (Central Mo.)	1964
96	II	Alex Campbell, Morris Brown (Clark Atlanta)	1994
96	II	Gary Frens, Hope (Olivet)	1966
96	II	Jim Jarrett, North Dakota (South Dakota)	1957
96	FBS	George O'Brien, Wisconsin (Iowa)	1952
94	FBS	John Hadl, Kansas (Oklahoma)	1959
94	FBS	Carl Knox, TCU (Oklahoma St.)	1947
94	FBS	Preston Johnson, SMU (Pittsburgh)	1940
93	FCS	Tyler Grogan, Northeastern (Villanova)	2001
93	FBS	Ray Guy, Southern Miss. (Mississippi)	1972
93	II	Elliot Mills, Carleton [Monmouth (Ill.)]	1970
93	II	Kasper Fitins, Taylor [Georgetown (Ky.)]	1966
93	II	Leeroy Sweeney, Pomona-Pitzer (UC Riverside)	1960
93	FBS	Bob Handke, Drake (Wichita St.)	1949

COLLEGIATE RECORDS

All-purpose yardage *is the combined net yards gained by rushing, receiving, interception (and fumble) returns, punt returns, kickoff returns and runbacks of field goal attempts. All-purpose yardage does not include forward passing yardage.*

Total offense *is the total of net gain rushing and net gain forward passing. Receiving and runback yards are not included in total offense.*

All-Purpose Yards

CAREER YARDS

Player, Team (Division[s])	Years	Rush	Rcv.	Int.	PR	KO	Yds.
Brian Westbrook, Villanova (FCS)	1997-98, 00-01	4,298	2,528	0	343	2,289	9,512
Brian Shay, Emporia St. (II)	1995-98	6,958	1,032	0	104	1,207	9,301
R.J. Bowers, Grove City (III)	1997-00	*7,353	397	0	50	1,453	9,253
Paul Smith, Gettysburg (III)	1996-99	5,205	758	0	959	2,182	9,104
Kavin Gailliard, American Int'l (II)	1996-99	6,523	1,049	0	472	814	8,858
Jerry Azumah, New Hampshire (FCS)	1995-98	6,193	1,153	0	5	1,025	8,376
Clarence Coleman, Ferris St. (II)	1998-01	49	4,983	0	1,494	1,483	8,009
Damon Thompson, Virginia St. (II)	1997-00	303	4,387	0	1,153	2,143	7,986
Carey Bender, Coe (III)	1991-94	6,125	1,751	0	7	87	7,970
Steve Tardif, Maine Maritime (III)	1996-99	6,093	643	8	65	1,151	7,960
Josh Ranek, South Dakota St. (II)	$1997-01	6,794	857	0	0	295	7,946
Stefan Logan, South Dakota (II)	2003-06	5,958	878	0	305	718	7,859
Johnny Bailey, Tex. A&M-Kingsville (II)	1986-89	6,320	452	0	20	1,011	7,803
Kenny Gamble, Colgate (FCS)	1984-87	5,220	536	0	104	1,763	7,623
Kevin Curtin, Winona St. (II)	2000-03	3,702	698	0	1,219	1,993	7,612
Blake Elliott, St. John's (Minn.) (III)	2000-03	688	4,200	0	1,209	1,508	7,605
DeAngelo Williams, Memphis (FBS)	2002-05	6,026	723	0	0	824	7,573
Howard Stevens, Randolph-Macon (II); Louisville (FBS)	1968-69; 71-72	5,297	738	0	781	748	7,564
Claude Mathis, Texas St. (FCS)	1994-97	4,691	744	0	635	1,353	7,423
Thomas Haskins, VMI (FCS)	1993-96	5,355	179	0	216	1,661	7,411
¢Danny Woodhead, Chadron St. (II)	2004-06	6,365	933	0	0	101	7,399
Jamaica Rector, Northwest Mo. St. (II)	2001-04	232	4,497	0	1,494	1,138	7,361
Ian Smart, C.W. Post (II)	1999-02	6,647	293	0	33	383	7,356
Rick Sarille, Wagner (FCS)	$1995-99	5,290	365	0	0	1,682	7,337
Roger Graham, New Haven (II)	1991-94	5,953	393	0	0	870	7,216
Ricky Williams, Texas (FBS)	1995-98	6,279	927	0	0	0	7,206
Napoleon McCallum, Navy (FBS)	$1981-85	4,179	796	0	858	1,339	7,172
Germaine Race, Pittsburg St. (II)	2003-06	6,985	137	0	0	0	7,122
Javarus Dudley, Fordham (FCS)	2000-03	58	4,197	0	192	2,668	7,115
Charles Roberts, Sacramento St. (FCS)	1997-00	6,553	382	0	12	165	7,112
Dave Ludy, Winona St. (II)	1991-94	3,501	906	0	34	2,630	7,071
Albert Fann, Cal St. Northridge (II)	1987-90	4,090	803	0	0	2,141	7,032
Reggie Greene, Siena (FCS)	1994-97	5,415	274	0	53	1,217	6,959

**Record. $See Page 10 for explanation. ¢Active player.*

CAREER YARDS PER GAME

(Minimum 3,500 Yards)

Player, Team (Division[s])	Years	G	Rush	Rcv.	Int.	PR	KO	Yds.	Yd. PG
Ryan Benjamin, Pacific (FBS)	1990-92	24	3,119	1,063	0	100	1,424	5,706	237.8
Chris George, Glenville St. (II)	1993-94	20	23	3,215	0	391	1,050	4,679	234.0
R.J. Bowers, Grove City (III)	1997-00	40	*7,353	397	0	50	1,453	9,253	231.3
Paul Smith, Gettysburg (III)	1996-99	40	5,205	758	0	959	2,182	9,104	227.6
Brian Westbrook, Villanova (FCS)	1997-98, 00-01	44	4,298	2,582	0	343	2,289	*9,512	216.2
Brian Shay, Emporia St. (II)	1995-98	44	6,958	1,032	0	104	1,207	9,301	211.4
Kirk Matthieu, Maine Maritime (III)	$1989-93	33	5,107	315	0	254	1,279	6,955	210.8
Damon Thompson, Virginia St. (II)	1997-00	38	303	4,387	0	1,153	2,143	7,986	210.2
Anthony Gray, Western N.M. (II)	1997-98	19	3,484	499	0	0	8	3,991	210.1
Kavin Gailliard, American Int'l (II)	1996-99	43	6,523	1,049	0	472	814	8,858	206.0
Sheldon Canley, San Jose St. (FBS)	1988-90	25	2,513	828	0	5	1,800	5,146	205.8
Carey Bender, Coe (III)	1991-94	39	6,125	1,751	0	7	87	7,970	204.4
Jerry Azumah, New Hampshire (FCS)	1995-98	41	6,193	1,153	0	5	1,025	8,376	204.3
Steve Tardif, Maine Maritime (III)	1996-99	39	6,093	643	8	65	1,151	7,960	204.1
Johnny Bailey, Tex. A&M-Kingsville (II)	1986-89	39	6,320	452	0	20	1,011	7,803	200.1
Howard Stevens, Randolph-Macon (II); Louisville (FBS)	1968-69; 71-72	38	5,297	738	0	781	748	7,564	199.1
Antoine Bagwell, California (Pa.) (II)	2004-05	20	3,353	549	0	0	54	3,956	197.8
Gary Trettel, St. Thomas (Minn.) (III)	1988-90	29	3,483	834	0	0	1,407	5,724	197.4
Arnold Mickens, Butler (FCS)	1994-95	22	3,813	47	0	0	87	3,947	197.4
Tim Hall, Robert Morris (FCS)	1994-95	19	2,908	793	0	0	0	3,701	194.8
Reggie Greene, Siena (FCS)	1994-97	36	5,415	274	0	53	1,217	6,959	193.3
Billy Johnson, Widener (II; III)	1971-72; 73	28	3,737	27	0	43	989	5,404	193.0
O.J. Simpson, Southern California (FBS)	1967-68	19	3,124	235	0	0	307	3,666	192.9
Clarence Coleman, Ferris St. (II)	1998-01	42	49	4,983	0	1,494	1,483	8,009	190.7
Steve Roberts, Butler (II)	1986-89	35	4,623	1,201	0	272	578	6,674	190.7

**Record. $See Page 10 for explanation.*

SEASON YARDS

Player, Team (Division)	Year	Rush	Rcv.	Int.	PR	KO	Yds.
Barry Sanders, Oklahoma St. (FBS)	†1988	2,628	106	0	95	421	3,250
Danny Woodhead, Chadron St. (II)	†2006	*2,756	403	0	0	0	3,159
Kavin Gailliard, American Int'l (II)	†1999	2,653	289	0	0	122	3,064
Brian Westbrook, Villanova (FCS)	†1998	1,046	1,144	0	192	644	3,026
Ryan Benjamin, Pacific (FBS)	†1991	1,581	612	0	4	798	2,995
Brian Westbrook, Villanova (FCS)	†2000	1,220	724	0	0	1,048	2,992
Dante Brown, Marietta (III)	†1996	2,385	174	0	46	368	2,973
Reggie Bush, Southern California (FBS)	†2005	1,740	478	0	179	493	2,890
R.J. Bowers, Grove City (III)	†1998	2,283	51	0	4	538	2,876
Nate Kmic, Mount Union (III)	2006	2,365	173	0	0	333	2,871

Player, Team (Division)	Year	Rush	Rcv.	Int.	PR	KO	Yds.
Brian Westbrook, Villanova (FCS)	†2001	1,603	658	0	122	440	2,823
Brian Shay, Emporia St. (II)	†1998	2,265	165	0	0	389	2,819
Troy Edwards, Louisiana Tech (FBS)	†1998	227	1,996	0	235	326	2,784
Blake Elliott, St. John's (Minn.) (III)	2003	586	1,319	0	223	621	2,749
Brian Shay, Emporia St. (II)	†1996	2,103	247	0	48	340	2,738
Darren Sproles, Kansas St. (FBS)	2003	1,986	287	0	190	272	2,735
Jerry Azumah, New Hampshire (FCS)	1998	2,195	218	0	5	308	2,726
Brian Shay, Emporia St. (II)	†1997	1,912	277	0	56	478	2,723
Paul Smith, Gettysburg (III)	†1999	1,546	301	0	255	615	2,717
Mike Pringle, Cal St. Fullerton (FBS)	†1989	1,727	249	0	0	714	2,690
Ian Smart, C.W. Post (II)	2001	2,536	135	0	0	0	2,671
Stefan Logan, South Dakota (II)	2006	1,707	153	0	302	508	2,670
Steve Roberts, Butler (II)	†1989	1,450	532	0	272	415	2,669

**Record. †National champion.*

SEASON YARDS PER GAME

Player, Team (Division)	Year	G	Rush	Rcv.	Int.	PR	KO	Yds.	Yd.PG
Dante Brown, Marietta (III)	†1996	10	2,385	174	0	46	368	2,973	297.3
Barry Sanders, Oklahoma St. (FBS)	†1988	11	2,628	106	0	0	95	*3,250	295.5
R.J. Bowers, Grove City (III)	†1998	10	2,283	51	0	4	538	2,876	287.6
Brian Westbrook, Villanova (FCS)	†1998	11	1,046	1,144	0	192	644	3,026	275.1
Brian Westbrook, Villanova (FCS)	†2000	11	1,220	724	0	0	1,048	2,992	272.0
Paul Smith, Gettysburg (III)	†1999	10	1,546	301	0	255	615	2,717	271.7
Steve Roberts, Butler (II)	†1989	10	1,450	532	0	272	415	2,669	266.9
Carey Bender, Coe (III)	†1994	10	2,243	319	0	7	87	2,656	265.6
Bobby Felix, Western N.M. (II)	†1994	8	439	853	0	150	667	2,109	263.6
Chris George, Glenville St. (II)	†1993	10	23	1,876	0	157	562	2,618	261.8
Brian Westbrook, Villanova (FCS)	†2001	11	1,603	658	0	122	440	2,823	256.6
Brian Shay, Emporia St. (II)	†1998	11	2,265	165	0	0	389	2,819	256.3
Kavin Gailliard, American Int'l (II)	†1999	12	*2,653	289	0	0	122	3,064	255.3
Damon Thompson, Virginia St. (II)	1998	10	127	1,330	0	292	770	2,519	251.9
Billy Johnson, Widener (II)	1972	9	1,556	40	43	511	115	2,265	251.7
Ryan Benjamin, Pacific (FBS)	†1991	12	1,581	612	0	4	798	2,995	249.6
Brian Shay, Emporia St. (II)	†1996	11	2,103	247	0	48	340	2,738	248.9
Damon Thompson, Virginia St. (II)	1999	10	88	1,517	0	410	465	2,480	248.0
Jerry Azumah, New Hampshire (FCS)	1998	11	2,195	218	0	5	308	2,726	247.8
Brian Shay, Emporia St. (II)	†1997	11	1,912	277	0	56	478	2,723	247.5

**Record. †National champion.*

Scoring

CAREER POINTS

Player, Team (Division[s])	Years	TD	Extra Pts. Scored	FG	Pts.
Germaine Race, Pittsburg St. (II)	2003-06	*109	2	0	656
Ian Smart, C.W. Post (II)	1999-02	95	0	0	570
R.J. Bowers, Grove City (III)	1997-00	92	10	0	562
Brian Westbrook, Villanova (FCS)	1997-98, 00-01	89	10	0	544
Brian Shay, Emporia St. (II)	1995-98	88	16	0	544
Carey Bender, Coe (III)	1991-94	86	12	0	528
Adrian Peterson, Ga. Southern (FCS)	1998-01	87	2	0	524
¢Danny Woodhead, Chadron St. (II)	2004-06	86	0	0	516
Tony Sutton, Findlay (II); Wooster (III)	2001; 2002-04	81	0	0	486
Scott Pingel, Westminster (Mo.) (III)	1996-99	75	34	0	484
Trevor Shannon, Wartburg (III)	1995-98	79	10	0	484
Dallas Mall, Bentley (II)	2001-04	78	10	0	478
Kavin Gailliard, American Int'l (II)	1996-99	78	8	0	476
Joe Dudek, Plymouth St. (III)	1982-85	79	0	0	474
Travis Prentice, Miami (Ohio) (FBS)	1996-99	78	0	0	468
David Kircus, Grand Valley St. (II)	1999-02	77	2	0	464
Walter Payton, Jackson St. (II)	1971-74	66	53	5	464
Ricky Williams, Texas (FBS)	1995-98	75	2	0	452
Dan Pugh, Mount Union (III)	1999-02	73	2	0	440
Jarrett Anderson, Truman (II)	1993-96	73	2	0	440
Chuck Moore, Mount Union (III)	1998-01	73	0	0	438
Shawn Graves, Wofford (QB) (II)	1989-92	72	3	0	438
Rashaan Dumas, Southern Conn. St. (II)	1996-99	72	0	0	432
Josh Ranek, South Dakota St. (II)	$1997-01	69	12	0	426
Johnny Bailey, Tex. A&M-Kingsville (II)	1986-89	70	3	0	426
Roger Graham, New Haven (II)	1991-94	70	2	0	424
Roman Anderson, Houston (FBS)	1988-91	0	213	70	423
Mark Kacmarynski, Central (Iowa) (III)	$1992-96	70	2	0	422
Jeff Glas, North Dakota (II)	2002-05	0	174	82	420
Matt Cannon, Southern Utah (FCS)	1997-00	69	3	0	420
Jerry Azumah, New Hampshire (FCS)	1995-98	69	4	0	418

**Record. $See Page 10 for explanation. ¢Active player.*

CAREER POINTS PER GAME

(Minimum 225 Points; Player must have concluded his career)

Player, Team (Division[s])	Years	G	TD	Extra Pts. Scored	FG	Pts.	Pt.PG
R.J. Bowers, Grove City (III)	1997-00	40	92	10	0	562	14.1
Cory Christensen, Simpson (III)	1996-97	19	44	0	0	264	13.9
Rob Marchitello, Maine Maritime (III)	1993-95	26	59	4	0	358	13.8
Carey Bender, Coe (III)	1991-94	39	86	12	0	528	13.5
Antoine Bagwell, California (Pa.) (II)	2004-05	20	45	0	0	270	13.5
Ole Gunderson, St. Olaf (II)	1969-71	27	60	2	0	362	13.4
Billy Johnson, Widener (II; III)	1971-72; 73	28	62	0	0	372	13.3
Leon Burns, Long Beach St. (II)	1969-70	22	47	2	0	284	12.9
Tony Sutton, Findlay (II); Wooster (III)	2001; 2002-04	38	81	0	0	486	12.8
Ian Smart, C.W. Post (II)	1999-02	45	95	0	0	570	12.7
Germaine Race, Pittsburg St. (II)	2003-06	52	*109	2	0	*656	12.6
Adrian Peterson, Ga. Southern (FCS)	1998-01	42	87	2	0	524	12.5
Trevor Shannon, Wartburg (III)	1995-98	39	79	10	0	484	12.4
Brian Westbrook, Villanova (FCS)	1997-98, 00-01	44	89	10	0	544	12.4
Brian Shay, Emporia St. (II)	1995-98	44	88	16	0	544	12.4
Scott Pingel, Westminster (Mo.) (III)	1996-99	39	75	34	0	484	12.4
Marshall Faulk, San Diego St. (FBS)	1991-93	31	62	4	0	376	12.1
Jim Regan, Pomona-Pitzer (III)	1995-98	30	37	93	15	360	12.0
Tyrone Morgan, Northern St. (II)	1998-00	30	59	0	0	354	11.8
Ed Marinaro, Cornell (FBS)	1969-71	27	52	6	0	318	11.8
Aaron Stecker, Western Ill. (FCS)	1997-98	20	39	0	0	234	11.7
Rashaan Dumas, Southern Conn. St. (II)	1996-99	37	72	0	0	432	11.7
Chad Hoiska, Wis.-Eau Claire (III)	1995-97	30	58	2	0	350	11.7
Joe Dudek, Plymouth St. (III)	1982-85	41	79	0	0	474	11.6
Bill Burnett, Arkansas (FBS)	1968-70	26	49	0	0	294	11.3
Dale Mills, Truman (II)	1957-60	36	64	23	0	407	11.3
Steve Owens, Oklahoma (FBS)	1967-69	30	56	0	0	336	11.2
Kavin Gailliard, American Int'l (II)	1996-99	43	78	8	0	476	11.1
Walter Payton, Jackson St. (II)	1971-74	42	66	53	5	464	11.0
Steve Roberts, Butler (II)	1986-89	35	63	4	0	386	11.0
Jeff Bentrim, North Dakota St. (II)	1983-86	35	64	2	0	386	11.0

Player, Team (Division[s])	Years	G	TD	Extra Pts. Scored	FG	Pts.	Pt.PG
Gary Jones, Albany (N.Y.) (FCS)	2002-03	23	42	0	0	252	11.0
Chuck Moore, Mount Union (III)	1998-01	40	73	0	0	438	11.0
Shawn Graves, Wofford (II)	1989-92	40	72	3	0	438	11.0

**Record.*

SEASON POINTS

Player, Team (Division[s])	Year	TD	Extra Pts. Scored	FG	Pts.
Dan Pugh, Mount Union (III)	†2002	*41	2	0	248
Barry Sanders, Oklahoma St. (FBS)	†1988	39	0	0	234
Danny Woodhead, Chadron St. (II)	†2006	38	0	0	228
Chris Sharpe, Springfield (III)	†2006	35	2	0	212
David Kircus, Grand Valley St. (II)	†2002	35	2	0	212
Kavin Gailliard, American Int'l (II)	†1999	34	2	0	206
R.J. Bowers, Grove City (III)	†1998	34	2	0	206
Jamar Brittingham, Bloomsburg (II)	†2005	34	0	0	204
Germaine Race, Pittsburg St. (II)	2005	33	0	0	198
Tony Sutton, Wooster (III)	†2004	33	0	0	198
Ian Smart, C.W. Post (II)	2001	33	0	0	198
Brian Shay, Emporia St. (II)	†1997	32	6	0	198
Guy Leman, Simpson (III)	1998	33	0	0	198
Carey Bender, Coe (III)	†1994	32	2	0	194
Brock Forsey, Boise St. (FBS)	†2002	32	0	0	192
Kevin Richardson, Appalachian St. (FCS)	2006	31	0	0	186
Tony Sutton, Wooster (III)	†2003	31	0	0	186
Troy Edwards, Louisiana Tech (FBS)	†1998	31	0	0	186
Travis Walch, Winona St. (II)	1997	30	2	0	182
Ian Smart, C.W. Post (II)	2002	30	0	0	180
David Russell, Linfield (III)	2002	30	0	0	180
Shane Ream, Allegheny (III)	†2000	30	0	0	180
Terry Metcalf, Long Beach St. (II)	1971	29	4	0	178
Brian Westbrook, Villanova (FCS)	†2001	29	2	0	176
Andre Braxton, Virginia Union (II)	†2000	27	14	0	176
Brian Shay, Emporia St. (II)	†1998	29	2	0	176
Chad Hoiska, Wis.-Eau Claire (III)	1997	29	2	0	176
Jamaal Branch, Colgate (FCS)	2003	29	0	0	174
Fredrick Jackson, Coe (III)	2002	29	0	0	174
Adrian Peterson, Ga. Southern (FCS)	†1999	29	0	0	174
Jim Mormino, Allegheny (III)	1997	29	0	0	174
Doug Steiner, Grove City (III)	1997	29	0	0	174
Mike Rozier, Nebraska (FBS)	†1983	29	0	0	174
Lydell Mitchell, Penn St. (FBS)	1971	29	0	0	174

**Record. †National champion.*

SEASON POINTS PER GAME

Player, Team (Division[s])	Year	G	TD	Extra Pts. Scored	FG	Pts.	Pt.PG
Barry Sanders, Oklahoma St. (FBS)	†1988	11	39	0	0	234	21.3
Carl Herakovich, Rose-Hulman (II)	†1958	8	25	18	0	168	21.0
James Regan, Pomona-Pitzer (III)	†1997	8	21	34	2	166	20.8
Tony Sutton, Wooster (III)	†2003	9	31	0	0	186	20.7
R.J. Bowers, Grove City (III)	†1998	10	34	2	0	206	20.6
Guy Leman, Simpson (III)	1998	10	33	0	0	198	19.8
Carey Bender, Coe (III)	†1994	10	32	2	0	194	19.4
Jim Switzer, Col. of Emporia (II)	†1963	9	28	0	0	168	18.7
Shane Ream, Allegheny (III)	†2000	10	30	0	0	180	18.0
Brian Shay, Emporia St. (II)	†1997	11	32	6	0	198	18.0
Billy Johnson, Widener (II)	†1972	9	27	0	0	162	18.0
Dan Pugh, Mount Union (III)	†2002	14	*41	2	0	*248	17.7
Chris Sharpe, Springfield (III)	†2006	12	35	2	0	212	17.7
Chad Hoiska, Wis.-Eau Claire (III)	1997	10	29	2	0	176	17.6
Carl Garrett, N.M. Highlands (II)	†1966	9	26	2	0	158	17.6
Danny Woodhead, Chadron St. (II)	†2006	13	38	0	0	228	17.5
Jim Mormino, Allegheny (III)	1997	10	29	0	0	174	17.4
Doug Steiner, Grove City (III)	1997	10	29	0	0	174	17.4
Bobby Reynolds, Nebraska (FBS)	†1950	9	22	25	0	157	17.4
Kavin Gailliard, American Int'l (II)	†1999	12	34	2	0	206	17.2
Rob Marchitello, Maine Maritime (III)	1994	9	25	4	0	154	17.1

**Record. †National champion.*

SINGLE-GAME POINTS

Pts.	Div.	Player, Team (Opponent)	Date
48	III	Carey Bender, Coe (Beloit)	Nov. 12, 1994
48	FBS	Howard Griffith, Illinois (Southern Ill.)	Sept. 22, 1990
48	II	Paul Zaeske, North Park [North Central (Ill.)]	Oct. 12, 1968
48	II	Junior Wolf, Okla. Panhandle [St. Mary (Kan.)]	Nov. 8, 1958
44	FBS	Marshall Faulk, San Diego St. (Pacific)	Sept. 14, 1991
43	FBS	Jim Brown, Syracuse (Colgate)	Nov. 17, 1956
42	FBS	Rashaun Woods, Oklahoma St. (SMU)	Sept. 20, 2003
42	FBS	Arnold "Showboat" Boykin, Mississippi (Mississippi St.)	Dec. 1, 1951
42	FBS	Fred Wendt, UTEP (New Mexico St.)	Nov. 25, 1948

Team Collegiate Records

Explanation: These team collegiate records were compiled by taking the record holder from each division and comparing them. There are some categories in which a division did not have a team record. In those cases, the records from the other divisions are listed.

Single Game—Offense

Total Offense

MOST PLAYS

117—Tex. A&M-Kingsville vs. Angelo St., Oct. 30, 1982 (546 yards) (II)

Other Division records:

112—Montana vs. Montana St., Nov. 1, 1952 (457 yards) (FBS)

115—Buffalo vs. Connecticut, Oct. 4, 1997 (437 yards) (FCS)

112—Gust. Adolphus vs. Bethel (Minn.), Nov. 2, 1985 (493 yards) (III)

MOST YARDS GAINED

1,021—Houston vs. SMU, Oct. 21, 1989 (250 rushing, 771 passing, 86 plays) (FBS)

Other Division records:

876—Weber St. vs. Idaho St., Nov. 23, 1991 (252 rushing, 624 passing) (FCS)

910—Hanover vs. Franklin, Oct. 30, 1948 (426 rushing, 484 passing, 75 plays) (II)

823—Westminster (Mo.) vs. Principia, Oct. 17, 1998 (176 rushing, 647 passing) (III)

MOST YARDS GAINED, BOTH TEAMS

1,640—San Jose St. (849) & Nevada (791), Nov. 10, 2001 (168 plays) (FBS)

Other Division records:

1,418—Howard (740) & Bethune-Cookman (678), Sept. 19, 1987 (161 plays) (FCS)

1,353—East Stroudsburg (712) & Southern Conn. St. (641), Nov. 12, 2005 (II)

1,395—Occidental (753) & Claremont-M-S (642), Oct. 30, 1993 (136 plays) (III)

MOST TOUCHDOWNS SCORED BY RUSHING AND PASSING

16—Arkansas vs. Mississippi, Nov. 3, 2001 (9 rushing, 7 passing) (7 ot) (FBS)

Other Division records:

14—Portland St. vs. Delaware St., Nov. 8, 1980 (4 rushing, 10 passing) (FCS)

15—North Park vs. North Central (Ill.), Oct. 12, 1968 (4 rushing, 11 passing) (II)

14—Concordia-M'head vs. Macalester, Sept. 24, 1977 (12 rushing, 2 passing) (III)

Rushing

MOST RUSHES

99—Missouri vs. Colorado, Oct. 12, 1968 (421 yards) (FBS)

Other Division records:

90—VMI vs. East Tenn. St., Nov. 17, 1990 (311 yards) (FCS)

97—Hobart vs. Union (N.Y.), Oct. 23, 1971 (444 yards) (II)

92—Wis.-River Falls vs. Wis.-Platteville, Oct. 21, 1989 (464 yards) (III)

MOST YARDS GAINED

768—Oklahoma vs. Kansas St., Oct. 15, 1988 (72 rushes) (FBS)

Other Division records:

681—Missouri St. vs. Mo. Southern St., Sept. 10, 1988 (83 rushes) (FCS)

719—Coe vs. Beloit, Oct. 16, 1971 (73 rushes) (II)

670—Olivet vs. Ohio Wesleyan, Sept. 18, 2004 (84 rushes) (III)

MOST TOUCHDOWNS SCORED BY RUSHING

12—UTEP vs. New Mexico St., Nov. 25, 1948 (FBS)

12—Coe vs. Beloit, Oct. 16, 1971 (II)
12—Concordia-M'head vs. Macalester, Sept. 24, 1977 (III)
Other Division record:
11—Ga. Southern vs. Johnson C. Smith, Sept. 11, 2004 (FCS)

Passing

MOST PASSES ATTEMPTED
85—West Tex. A&M vs. Eastern N.M., Nov. 5, 1994 (completed 47) (II)
Other Division records:
83—Purdue vs. Wisconsin, Oct. 10, 1998 (completed 55) (FBS)
79—Idaho St. vs. Portland St., Nov. 6, 2004 (completed 43) (FCS)
82—Sul Ross St. vs. Howard Payne, Oct. 5, 2002 (completed 52) (III)

MOST PASSES ATTEMPTED, BOTH TEAMS
143—Bethel (Minn.) (78) & Gust. Adolphus (65), Nov. 2, 1985 (completed 65) (III)
Other Division records:
135—TCU (79) & Houston (56), Nov. 3, 1990 (completed 81) (FBS)
122—Idaho (62) & Idaho St. (60), Sept. 24, 1983 (completed 48) (FCS)
131—Presbyterian (70) & Tusculum (61), Nov. 3, 2001 (completed 82) (II)

MOST PASSES ATTEMPTED WITHOUT AN INTERCEPTION
77—Westminster (Mo.) vs. MacMurray, Nov. 14, 1998 (completed 50) (III)
Other Division records:
72—Houston vs. TCU, Nov. 4, 1989 (completed 47) (FBS)
72—Marshall vs. Western Caro., Nov. 14, 1987 (completed 35) (FCS)
73—Concord vs. Fairmont St., Oct. 27, 2001 (completed 35) (II)

MOST PASSES COMPLETED
59—Southeastern La. vs. Jacksonville, Nov. 6, 2004 (attempted 72) (FCS)
Other Division records:
55—Wake Forest vs. Duke, Oct. 28, 1995 (attempted 78); Purdue vs. Wisconsin, Oct. 10, 1998 (attempted 83) (FBS)
56—Wayne St. (Neb.) vs. Drake, Nov. 9, 1996 (attempted 76) (II)
52—Sul Ross St. vs. Howard Payne, Oct. 5, 2002 (attempted 82) (III)

MOST PASSES COMPLETED, BOTH TEAMS
87—Sul Ross St. (52) & Howard Payne (35), Oct. 5, 2002 (attempted 128) (III)
Other Division records:
81—TCU (44) & Houston (37), Nov. 3, 1990 (attempted 135) (FBS)
80—Hofstra (50) & Fordham (30), Oct. 19, 1991 (attempted 120) (FCS)
82—Presbyterian (50) & Tusculum (32), Nov. 3, 2001 (attempted 131) (II)

HIGHEST PERCENTAGE OF PASSES COMPLETED (Min. 20 Attempts)
96.0%—Tennessee vs. South Carolina, Oct. 31, 1998 (24 of 25) (FBS)
Other Division records:
85.4%—Cal St. Northridge vs. Missouri St., Nov. 14, 1998 (35 of 41) (FCS)
90.9%—Northwestern St. vs. La.-Lafayette, Nov. 12, 1966 (20 of 22) (II)
86.1%—Howard Payne vs. East Tex. Baptist, Sept. 28, 2002 (31 of 36) (III)

MOST YARDS GAINED
771—Houston vs. SMU, Oct. 21, 1989 (completed 40 of 61) (FBS)
Other Division records:
699—Mississippi Val. vs. Kentucky St., Sept. 1, 1984 (FCS)
678—Portland St. vs. Mont. St.-Billings, Nov. 20, 1976 (II)
731—Menlo vs. Cal Lutheran, Oct. 7, 2000 (III)

MOST YARDS GAINED, BOTH TEAMS
1,253—TCU (690) & Houston (563), Nov. 3, 1990 (FBS)
Other Division records:
1,190—La.-Monroe (619) & Stephen F. Austin (571), Nov. 11, 1989 (FCS)
1,065—Western N.M. (614) & West Tex. A&M (451), Oct. 8, 1994 (II)
1,180—Guilford (606) & Catholic (574), Nov. 9, 2005

MOST TOUCHDOWN PASSES
11—Houston vs. Eastern Wash., Nov. 17, 1990 (FBS)
11—Mississippi Val. vs. Kentucky St., Sept. 1, 1984 (FCS)
11—North Park vs. North Central (Ill.), Oct. 12, 1968 (II)
Other Division record:
9—Westminster (Mo.) vs. Principia, Oct. 17, 1998; Ohio Northern vs. Capital, Nov. 14, 1998 (III)

MOST TOUCHDOWN PASSES, BOTH TEAMS
14—Houston (11) & Eastern Wash. (3), Nov. 17, 1990 (FBS)
14—Mississippi Val. (8) & Texas Southern (6), Oct. 26, 1985 (FCS)
14—North Park (11) & North Central (Ill.) (3), Oct. 12, 1968 (II)
Other Division record:
12—St. Thomas (Minn.) (6) & Bethel (Minn.) (6), Nov. 13, 1993 (III)

Scoring

MOST POINTS SCORED
106—Fort Valley St. vs. Knoxville, Oct. 11, 1969 (14 TDs, 2 PATs, 9 two-point conversions,1 safety) (II)
Other Division records:
103—Wyoming vs. Northern Colo. (0), Nov. 5, 1949 (FBS)
105—Portland St. vs. Delaware St., Nov. 8, 1980 (15 TDs, 15 PATs) (FCS)
105—Rockford vs. Trinity Bible, Sept. 6, 2003 (III)
Historical Notes:
100—Houston vs. Tulsa (6), Nov. 23, 1968 (FBS) (Record for game involving two major-college opponents)
222—Georgia Tech vs. Cumberland (0), Oct. 7, 1916 (FBS) (Before beginning of NCAA records in 1937)
125—Southeastern Okla. vs. Northeastern St., 1916 (II) (Before beginning of NCAA records in 1937)

MOST POINTS SCORED, BOTH TEAMS
136—North Park (104) & North Central (Ill.) (32), Oct. 12, 1968 (II)
Other Division records:
133—San Jose St. (70) & Rice (63), Oct. 2, 2004 (FBS)
125—Sacramento St. (64) & Cal St. Northridge (61), Nov. 4, 2000 (FCS)
131—Earlham (69) & Manchester (62), Sept. 10, 2005 (III)

MOST POINTS SCORED BY A LOSING TEAM
66—Western N.M. vs. Fort Lewis (67), Nov. 2, 2002 (2 ot) (II)
Other Division records:
63—Kentucky vs. Arkansas (71), Nov. 1, 2003 (7 ot); Rice vs. San Jose St. (70), Oct. 2, 2004 (FBS)
61—Cal St. Northridge vs. Sacramento St. (64), Nov. 4, 2000 (FCS)
63—Cornell College vs. Coe (66), Oct. 25, 2003 (III)

MOST TOUCHDOWNS SCORED
15—Wyoming vs. Northern Colo., Nov. 5, 1949 (9 rushing, 6 passing) (FBS)
15—Portland St. vs. Delaware St., Nov. 8, 1980 (FCS)
15—Iowa Wesleyan vs. William Penn, Oct. 31, 1953; Alcorn St. vs. Paul Quinn, Sept. 9, 1967; North Park vs. North Central (Ill.), Oct. 12, 1968 (II)
15—Rockford vs. Trinity Bible, Sept. 6, 2003 (III)
Historical Note:
17—Connecticut vs. Newport Naval Training, Oct. 22, 1949 (Record for Division II or small-college in game not involving two Division II or small-college teams)

MOST EXTRA-POINT KICKS ATTEMPTED
15—Wyoming vs. Northern Colo., Nov. 5, 1949 (FBS)
15—Portland St. vs. Delaware St., Nov. 8, 1980 (FCS)
15—North Park vs. North Central (Ill.), Oct. 12, 1968 (II)
Other Division record:
14—Concordia-M'head vs. Macalester, Sept. 24, 1977 (III)

MOST EXTRA-POINT KICKS MADE
15—Portland St. vs. Delaware St., Nov. 8, 1980 (FCS)
Other Division records:
13—Wyoming vs. Northern Colo., Nov. 5, 1949; Houston vs. Tulsa, Nov. 23, 1968; Fresno St. vs. New Mexico, Oct. 5, 1991 (FBS)
14—North Park vs. North Central (Ill.), Oct. 12, 1968 (II)
13—Concordia-M'head vs. Macalester, Sept. 24, 1977; Rockford vs. Trinity Bible, Sept. 6, 2003 (III)

MOST FIELD GOALS ATTEMPTED
9—Western Mich. vs. Marshall, Sept. 29, 1984 (made 7) (FBS); North Texas vs. Florida Int'l, Oct. 7, 2006 (made 5) (FBS)
Other Division records:
8—Northern Ariz. vs. Idaho, Oct. 25, 1986 (made 8) (FCS)
7—Mississippi Col. vs. Troy, Oct. 3, 1981 (made 2) (II)
8—Rhodes vs. Millsaps, Sept. 22, 1984 (made 6) (III)

MOST FIELD GOALS MADE
8—Northern Ariz. vs. Idaho, Oct. 25, 1986 (attempted 8) (FCS)
Other Division records:
7—Western Mich. vs. Marshall, Sept. 29, 1984 (attempted 9); Nebraska vs. Missouri, Oct. 19, 1985 (attempted 7) (FBS)
6—Central Mo. vs. Southeast Mo. St., Nov. 2, 1985 (attempted 6); Ashland vs. Wayne St. (Mich.), Oct. 5, 2002 (attempted 6) (II)
6—Rhodes vs. Millsaps, Sept. 22, 1984 (attempted 8) (III)

Miscellaneous Records

TOTAL FIRST DOWNS
46—Weber St. vs. Idaho St., Nov. 23, 1991 (12 rushing, 31 passing, 3 penalty) (FCS)
Other Division records:
45—Texas Tech vs. Iowa St., Oct. 11, 2003 (16 rushing, 28 passing, 1 penalty) (FBS)
42—Delaware vs. Baldwin-Wallace, Oct. 6, 1973 (II)
40—Upper Iowa vs. Loras, Nov. 7, 1992 (19 rushing, 17 passing, 4 penalty); Mount Union vs. Marietta, Oct. 15, 2005 (25 rushing, 15 passing) (III)

MOST PENALTIES AGAINST
28—Northern Ariz. vs. La Verne, Oct. 11, 1958 (155 yards) (II)
Other Division records:
24—San Jose St. vs. Fresno St., Oct. 4, 1986 (199 yards) (FBS)
23—Idaho vs. Idaho St., Oct. 10, 1992 (204 yards) (FCS)
25—Norwich vs. Coast Guard, Sept. 29, 1985 (192 yards) (III)

MOST POINTS OVERCOME TO WIN A GAME
35—Michigan St. (41) vs. Northwestern (38), Oct. 21, 2006 (trailed 38-3 with 9:54 remaining in third quarter) (FBS)
35—Nevada vs. Weber St., Nov. 2, 1991 (trailed 49-14 with 12:16 remaining in third quarter; won 55-49) (FCS)
Other Division records:
28—Ferris St. vs. Saginaw Valley, Nov. 11, 1995 (trailed 28-0 with 11:17 remaining in second quarter; won 46-42) (II)

33—Wis.-Platteville vs. Wis.-Eau Claire, Nov. 8, 1980 (trailed 33-0 with 7:00 remaining in second quarter; won 52-43); Salisbury vs. Randolph-Macon, Sept. 15, 1984 (trailed 33-0 with 14:18 remaining in second quarter; won 34-33); Lakeland vs. Concordia (Wis.), Oct. 11, 1997 (trailed 33-0 with 7:53 remaining in third quarter; won 41-33) (III)

Single Game—Defense

Total Defense

FEWEST PLAYS ALLOWED
12—Centenary (La.) vs. Texas Tech, Nov. 11, 1939 (FBS)
Other Division records:
31—Howard vs. Dist. Columbia, Sept. 2, 1989 (FCS)
29—North Park vs. Concordia (Ill.), Sept. 26, 1964 (II)

FEWEST YARDS ALLOWED
Minus 69—Fort Valley St. vs. Miles, Oct. 16, 1993 (II)
Other Division records:
Minus 47—Penn St. vs. Syracuse, Oct. 18, 1947 (FBS)
Minus 12—Eastern Ill. vs. Kentucky St., Nov. 13, 1982 (FCS)
Minus 52—Worcester St. vs. Maine Maritime, Sept. 28, 1996 (III)

Rushing Defense

FEWEST RUSHES ALLOWED
5—Texas Tech vs. Houston, Nov. 25, 1989 (FBS)
Other Division records:
9—Mississippi Val. vs. Alcorn St., Nov. 6, 1999 (FCS)
7—Indianapolis vs. Valparaiso, Oct. 30, 1982 (II)
9—Wis.-La Crosse vs. Huron, Sept. 21, 1996 (III)

FEWEST RUSHING YARDS ALLOWED
Minus 112—Coast Guard vs. Wesleyan (Conn.), Oct. 7, 1989 (III)
Other Division records:
Minus 109—Toledo vs. Northern Ill., Nov. 11, 1967 (FBS)
Minus 90—Sacred Heart vs. Iona, Nov. 16, 2002 (FCS)
Minus 95—San Diego St. vs. Alliant Int'l, Nov. 27, 1965 (II)

Passing Defense

FEWEST PASS ATTEMPTS ALLOWED
0—By many teams (FBS)
0—By many teams (II)
0—By many teams (III)
Other Division record:
1—By six teams (FCS)

FEWEST PASS COMPLETIONS ALLOWED
0—By many teams (FBS)
0—By many teams (FCS)
0—By many teams (II)
0—By many teams (III)

FEWEST PASSING YARDS ALLOWED
Minus 19—Ashland vs. Heidelberg, Sept. 25, 1948 (II)
Other Division records:
Minus 16—VMI vs. Richmond, Oct. 5, 1957 (FBS)
Minus 2—Florida A&M vs. Albany St. (Ga.), Oct. 16, 1982 (FCS)
Minus 6—Central (Iowa) vs. Simpson, Oct. 19, 1985; Wittenberg vs. Hiram, Oct. 27, 2001 (III)

MOST PASSES INTERCEPTED BY
11—Brown vs. Rhode Island, Oct. 8, 1949 (FBS)
11—Concordia-M'head vs. Hamline, Nov. 5, 1955; St. Cloud St. vs. Bemidji St., Oct. 31, 1970 (II)
Other Division records:
10—Grambling vs. Mississippi Val., Oct. 17, 1987; Montana vs. Boise St., Oct. 28, 1989 (FCS)
10—St. Thomas (Minn.) vs. St. Olaf, Oct. 12, 1985 (III)
Historical Note:
10—Oklahoma St. vs. Detroit, Nov. 28, 1942; UCLA vs. California, Oct. 21, 1978 (Record for game involving two major-college opponents) (FBS)

MOST PASS INTERCEPTIONS RETURNED FOR TOUCHDOWNS
4—Houston vs. Texas, Nov. 7, 1987 (FBS)
4—Northwestern St. vs. Southeastern La., Oct. 11, 2003 (FCS)
4—Millikin vs. Ill. Wesleyan, Nov. 6, 1999 (III)
Other Division records:
3—By many teams (II)

Opponent's Kicks Blocked

MOST OPPONENT'S PUNTS BLOCKED
5—Southeastern La. vs. Troy, Oct. 7, 1978; Winston-Salem vs. N.C. Central, Oct. 4, 1986 (II)
Other Division records:
4—SMU vs. Texas-Arlington, Sept. 30, 1944; Michigan vs. Ohio St., Nov. 25, 1950; Memphis vs. Arkansas, Sept. 26, 1992; Central Mich. vs. Michigan St., Sept. 8, 2001 (FBS)
4—Montana vs. Montana St., Oct. 31, 1987; Middle Tenn. vs. Mississippi Val., Oct. 8, 1988 (FCS)
4—Benedictine (Ill.) vs. Olivet Nazarene, Oct. 22, 1988; Benedictine (Ill.) vs. Aurora, Oct. 29, 1988 (III)

Defensive Records

(Since 2000)

MOST TACKLES FOR LOSS
25—Adams St. vs. Okla. Panhandle, Oct. 13, 2001 (II)
Other Division records:
24—North Carolina St. vs. Georgia Tech, Oct. 4, 2003 (FBS)
22—Illinois St. vs. Western Ill., Nov. 4, 2000 (FCS)
22—King's (Pa.) vs. Salisbury, Nov. 23, 2002; St. John's (Minn.) vs. Monmouth (Ill.), Nov. 19, 2005 (III)

MOST PASS SACKS
15—TCU vs. Nevada, Sept. 9, 2000 (FBS)
Other Division records:
12—Illinois St. vs. Western Ill., Nov. 4, 2000 (FCS)
14—North Dakota vs. New Haven, Sept. 21, 2001 (II)
13—St. John's (Minn.) vs. Monmouth (Ill.), Nov. 19, 2005

MOST PASSES DEFENDED
21—Stillman vs. Edward Waters, Nov. 2, 2002 (III)
Other Division records:
19—South Carolina vs. Alabama, Oct. 2, 2000 (FBS)
17—Penn vs. Lafayette, Sept. 21, 2002 (FCS)
18—Winona St. vs. Concordia-St. Paul, Oct. 27, 2001; Adams St. vs. N.M. Highlands, Oct. 11, 2003 (II)

MOST FORCED FUMBLES
8—Simpson vs. William Penn, Nov. 11, 2000 (III)
Other Division records:
7—Miami (Ohio) vs. North Carolina, Aug. 31, 2002; Virginia vs. South Carolina, Sept. 7, 2002; West Virginia vs. Cincinnati, Sept. 13, 2003; Miami (Ohio) vs. Buffalo, Nov. 5, 2005 (FBS)
6—Delaware vs. Ga. Southern, Dec. 9, 2000; Delaware vs. Citadel, Sept. 9, 2002; Fla. Atlantic vs. Troy, Oct. 26, 2002; Jacksonville vs. Valparaiso, Sept. 27, 2003 (FCS)
5—Harding vs. Tarleton St., Sept. 2, 2000; Harding vs. Central Ark., Oct. 7, 2000; Winona St. vs. Minn. Duluth, Nov. 15, 2003 (II)

Season—Offense

Total Offense

MOST PLAYS PER GAME
92.4—Notre Dame, 1970 (924 in 10) (FBS)
Other Division records:
89.6—Weber St., 1991 (986 in 11) (FCS)
88.7—Cal St. Chico, 1967 (887 in 10) (II)
85.6—Hampden-Sydney, 1978 (856 in 10) (III)

MOST YARDS GAINED
8,976—Pittsburg St., 2004 (II)
Other Division records:
7,829—Hawaii, 2006 (FBS)
6,577—Alcorn St., 1994 (FCS)
7,800—Mount Union, 2005 (III)

MOST YARDS GAINED PER GAME
640.1—Mississippi Val., 1984 (6,401 in 10) (FCS)
Other Division records:
624.9—Houston, 1989 (6,874 in 11) (FBS)
624.1—Hanover, 1948 (4,993 in 8) (II)
561.2—Westminster (Mo.), 1998 (5,612 in 10) (III)

HIGHEST AVERAGE GAIN PER PLAY
9.2—Hanover, 1948 (543 for 4,993) (II)
Other Division records:
8.6—Hawaii, 2006 (913 for 7,829) (FBS)
7.8—Alcorn St., 1994 (848 for 6,577) (FCS)
8.1—Ferrum, 1990 (534 for 4,350) (III)

MOST TOUCHDOWNS SCORED BY RUSHING AND PASSING
113—Pittsburg St., 2004 (II)
Other Division records:
84—Nebraska, 1983; Hawaii, 2006 (FBS)
84—Mississippi Val., 1984 (FCS)
84—St. John's (Minn.), 1993 (III)

Rushing

MOST RUSHES PER GAME
78.9—Okla. Panhandle, 1963 (789 in 10) (II)
Other Division records:
73.9—Oklahoma, 1974 (813 in 11) (FBS)
69.8—Northeastern, 1986 (698 in 10) (FCS)
71.4—Wis.-River Falls, 1988 (714 in 10) (III)

MOST YARDS GAINED RUSHING
5,320—Pittsburg St., 2004 (II)
Other Division records:
5,196—Oklahoma, 1971 (FBS)
4,609—Ga. Southern, 1999 (FCS)
4,496—Springfield, 2006 (III)

MOST YARDS GAINED RUSHING PER GAME
472.4—Oklahoma, 1971 (5,196 in 11) (FBS)
Other Division records:
419.0—Ga. Southern, 1999 (4,609 in 11) (FCS)
404.8—Col. of Emporia, 1954 (3,643 in 9) (II)
434.7—Ferrum, 1990 (3,912 in 9) (III)

HIGHEST GAIN PER RUSH
8.4—Hanover, 1948 (382 for 3,203) (II)
Other Division records:
7.6—Army, 1945 (424 for 3,238) (FBS)
7.0—Ga. Southern, 1999 (654 for 4,609) (FCS)
8.3—Ferrum, 1990 (470 for 3,912) (III)

Passing

MOST PASSES ATTEMPTED PER GAME
63.1—Houston, 1989 (694 in 11) (FBS)
Other Division records:
55.8—Mississippi Val., 1984 (558 in 10) (FCS)
56.6—Emporia St., 1995 (623 in 11) (II)
59.9—Sul Ross St., 2002 (599 in 10) (III)

MOST PASSES COMPLETED PER GAME
39.4—Houston, 1989 (434 in 11) (FBS)
Other Division records:
35.1—Mississippi Val., 1984 (351 in 10) (FCS)
33.9—Valdosta St., 1995 (373 in 11) (II)
35.8—Sul Ross St., 2002 (358 in 10) (III)

HIGHEST PASS COMPLETION PERCENTAGE (Min. 300 Attempts)
73.5%—UCF, 1998 (completed 302 of 411) (FBS)
Other Division records:
70.6%—Hofstra, 1997 (completed 293 of 415) (FCS)
73.2%—Colorado Mines, 2004 (completed 401 of 548) (II)
71.2%—Monmouth (Ill.), 2005 (completed 222 of 312) (III)

HIGHEST AVERAGE GAIN PER ATTEMPTED PASS (Min. 250 Attempts)
11.5—Grand Valley St., 2001 (291 for 3,346) (II)
Other Division records:
10.9—BYU, 1989 (433 for 4,732) (FBS)
10.7—UNI, 1996 (252 for 2,700) (FCS)
11.1—Grinnell, 1998 (301 for 3,354) (III)

HIGHEST AVERAGE GAIN PER COMPLETION (Min. 100 Completions)
19.4—California (Pa.), 1966 (116 for 2,255) (II)
Other Division records:
19.1—Houston, 1968 (105 for 2,003) (FBS)
19.3—Jackson St., 1990 (156 for 3,006) (FCS)
17.1—Mount Union, 2003 (240 for 4,103) (III)

MOST PASSING YARDS GAINED PER GAME
511.3—Houston, 1989 (5,624 in 11) (FBS)
Other Division records:
496.8—Mississippi Val., 1984 (4,968 in 10) (FCS)
454.5—West Tex. A&M, 1994 (5,000 in 11) (II)
488.8—Westminster (Mo.), 1998 (4,888 in 10) (III)

MOST PASSING YARDS GAINED
6,179—Texas Tech, 2003 (13 games) (FBS)
Other Division records:
4,968—Mississippi Val., 1984 (10 games) (FCS)
5,000—West Tex. A&M, 1994 (11 games) (II)
4,888—Westminster (Mo.), 1998 (10 games) (III)

MOST TOUCHDOWN PASSES PER GAME
6.4—Mississippi Val., 1984 (64 in 10) (FCS)
Other Division records:
5.0—Houston, 1989 (55 in 11) (FBS)
5.1—Grand Valley St., 2001 (51 in 10) (II)
5.7—Westminster (Mo.), 1998 (57 in 10) (III)

HIGHEST PASS EFFICIENCY RATING POINTS (Min. 200 Attempts)
222.5—Grand Valley St., 2001 (291 attempts, 204 completions, 3 interceptions, 3,346 yards, 51 TD passes) (II)
Other Division records:
185.9—Hawaii, 2006 (615 attempts, 444 completions, 12 interceptions, 6,178 yards, 62 TD passes) (FBS)
190.6—William & Mary, 1993 (232 attempts, 161 completions, 4 interceptions, 2,499 yards, 24 TD passes) (FCS)
211.3—Eureka, 1994 (205 attempts, 142 completions, 8 interceptions, 2,478 yards, 30 TD passes) (III)

Scoring

MOST POINTS SCORED PER GAME
61.5—St. John's (Minn.), 1993 (615 in 10) (III)
Other Division records:
56.0—Army, 1944 (509 in 9) (FBS)
60.9—Mississippi Val., 1984 (609 in 10) (FCS)
58.4—Grand Valley St., 2001 (584 in 10) (II)

MOST POINTS SCORED
837—Pittsburg St., 2004 (15 games) (II)
Other Division records:
656—Hawaii, 2006 (14 games) (FBS)
609—Mississppi Val., 1984 (10 games) (FCS)
615—St. John's (Minn.), 1993 (10 games) (III)

MOST CONSECUTIVE EXTRA POINTS MADE BY KICKING
77—Louisville, 2004 (Entire Season) (FBS)
Other Division records:
68—Idaho, 1993 (FCS)
70—Pittsburg St., 2006 (Entire Season) (II)
49—Dayton, 1989 (Entire Season) (III)

MOST FIELD GOALS MADE PER GAME
2.6—UCLA, 1984 (29 in 11) (FBS)
Other Division records:
2.4—Nevada, 1982 (26 in 11); UNI, 1990 (26 in 11) (FCS)
2.3—North Dakota, 2005 (30 in 13)
2.0—Mount Union, 1990 (20 in 10) (III)

Penalties

MOST PENALTIES PER GAME
14.6—Portland St., 1994 (146 in 10) (II)
Other Division records:
12.9—Grambling, 1977 (142 in 11) (FBS)
13.7—Grambling, 1984 (151 in 11) (FCS)
13.3—Kean, 1990 (133 in 10) (III)

MOST TOTAL PENALTIES
152—Alabama St., 2001 (12 games) (FCS)
Other Division records:
142—Grambling, 1977 (11 games) (FBS)
146—Gardner-Webb, 1992 (11 games); Portland St., 1994 (10 games) (II)
133—Kean, 1990 (10 games) (III)

MOST YARDS PENALIZED PER GAME
134.2—Grambling, 1977 (1,476 in 11) (FBS)
Other Division records:
125.5—Tennessee St., 1982 (1,255 in 10) (FCS)
123.3—Hampton, 1977 (1,356 in 11) (II)
121.9—Hofstra, 1991 (1,219 in 10) (III)

Turnovers

MOST TURNOVERS LOST PER GAME
6.1—Mississippi St., 1949 (55 in 9) (FBS)
Other Division records:
5.9—Texas Southern, 1980 (59 in 10) (FCS)
5.8—Livingstone, 1986 (58 in 10) (II)
5.2—William Penn, 1985 (52 in 10) (III)

MOST TURNOVERS LOST
61—North Texas, 1971; Tulsa, 1976 (FBS)
61—Cheyney, 1990 (II)
Other Division records:
59—Texas Southern, 1980 (FCS)
52—William Penn, 1985 (III)

Miscellaneous All-Time Records

MOST IMPROVED TEAMS
11 games—Northern Mich., 1975 (from 0-10-0 to 13-1-0) (II)
Other Division records:
$8^1/2$ games—Hawaii, 1999 (from 0-12-0 to 9-4-0) (FBS)
$9^1/2$ games—Montana St., 1984 (from 1-10-0 to 12-2-0) (FCS)
$7^1/2$ games—Wis.-Stout, 2000 (from 2-8-0 to 10-1-0) (III)

LONGEST WINNING STREAKS
55 games—Mount Union, 2000-03 (III)
Other Division records:
47 games—Oklahoma, 1953-57 (FBS)
24 games—Penn, 1992-95; Montana, 2001-02 (FCS)
34 games—Hillsdale, 1954-57 (II)

LONGEST UNBEATEN STREAKS (Includes Ties)
63 games—Washington, 1907-17 (59-0-4 record) (FBS)
Other Division records:
24 games—Penn, 1992-95 (24-0-0 record); Montana, 2001-02 (24-0-0 record) (FCS)
54 games—Morgan St., 1931-38 (47-0-7 record) (II)
60 games—Augustana (Ill.), 1983-87 (59-0-1 record) (III)

LONGEST LOSING STREAKS
80 games—Prairie View, 1989-98 (FCS)
Other Division records:
34 games—Northwestern, 1979-82 (FBS)
46 games—Minn.-Morris, 1998-03 (II)
50 games—Macalester, 1974-79 (III)

LONGEST HOME WINNING STREAKS
58 games—Miami (Fla.), 1985-94 (FBS)
Other Division records:
39 games—Ga. Southern, 1997-01 (FCS)
31 games—Indiana (Pa.), 1986-92 (II)
52 games—Augustana (Ill.), 1980-89 (III)

Longest Plays

RUSHING
99 Yards—Six players tied (Most recent: Terry Caulley, Connecticut vs. Army, 2006) (FBS)
99 Yards—Six players tied (Most recent: Michael Hobbs, Wofford vs. Ga. Southern, 2006) (FCS)
99 Yards—22 players tied (Most recent: Isaac Redman, Bowie St. vs. Morgan St., 2005) (II)
99 Yards—13 players tied (Most recent: Jay Bernardo, Rensselaer vs. Endicott, 2005; Neil Suckow, Coe vs. Simpson, 2005) (III)

PASSING
99 Yards—15 passers-receivers tied (Most recent: Dondrial Pinkins-Troy Williamson, South Carolina vs. Virginia, 2003; Jim Sorgi-Lee Evans, Wisconsin vs. Akron, 2003) (FBS)
99 Yards—11 passers-receivers tied (Most recent: Riley Walker-Fred Burnette, Tennessee St. vs. Jacksonville St., 2004) (FCS)
99 Yards—27 passers-receivers tied (Most recent: Lamar Little-Michael Hampton, Virginia Union vs. West Va. Wesleyan, 2006; Mark Smith-Brian Pray, Pittsburg St. vs. Mo. Southern St., 2006) (II)
99 Yards—26 passers-receivers tied [Most recent: Alex Kiel-Dustin Stewart, Hanover vs. Manchester, 2006; Nick Maxam-Aljay Wren, Lawrence vs. Monmouth (Ill.), 2006] (III)

INTERCEPTION RETURNS
100 Yards—75 players tied (Most recent: Josh Gordy, Central Mich. vs. Akron, 2006) (FBS)
100 Yards—25 players tied (Most recent: Brian Jackson, Indiana St. vs. Eastern Ill., 2006) (FCS)
100 Yards—20 players tied (Most recent: Mike DeBye, Stonehill vs. Assumption, 2005; Ian Whittington, West Liberty St. vs. Concord, 2005) (II)
100 Yards—45 players tied [Most recent: Steve Stepnick, St. John Fisher vs. Union (N.Y.), 2006; Stephon Anderson, Wm. Paterson vs. Buffalo St., 2006] (III)

PUNT RETURNS
100 Yards—Nine players tied (Most recent: Courtney Davis, Bowling Green vs. Kent St., 1996) (FBS)
100 Yards—Randy Ladson, Fayetteville St. vs. St. Paul's, 1987 (II)
Other Division records:
98 Yards—Barney Bussey, South Carolina St. vs. Johnson C. Smith, 1981; Willie Ware, Mississippi Val. vs. Bishop, 1985 (FCS)
99 Yards—Robert Middlebrook, Knoxville vs. Miles, 1985 (III)

KICKOFF RETURNS
100 Yards—251 players tied (Most recent: Gerald Lawson, Oregon St. vs. Hawaii, 2006; Patric Jackson, Louisiana Tech vs. Fresno St., 2006; JaJua Spillman, Louisville vs. Rutgers, 2006; Ross Dickerson, Hawaii vs. Idaho, 2006; Felix Jones, Arkansas vs. Mississippi, 2006; Josh Wilson, Maryland vs. Georgia Tech, 2006; Terry Richardson, Arizona St. vs. Oregon, 2006; Marcus Thigpen, Indiana vs. Ball St., 2006; Keenan Burton, Kentucky vs. Louisville, 2006) (FBS)
100 Yards—69 players tied (Most recent: Davin Walker, Eastern Ky. vs. Murray St., 2006; Jesse Burton, Tenn.-Martin vs. Southeast Mo. St., 2006; Bryant Eteuati, Weber St. vs. Montana, 2006; Isiejah Allen, Fordham vs. Holy Cross, 2006; William Middleton, Furman vs. Wofford, 2006) (FCS)
100 Yards—34 players tied [Most recent: Jonathon Hawks, Bemidji St. vs. Northern St., 2006; Marc Huddleston, California (Pa.) vs. Slippery Rock, 2006] (II)
100 Yards—54 players tied (Most recent: Brian Williams, Kean vs. Wm. Paterson, 2006) (III)

PUNTS
99 Yards—Pat Brady, Nevada vs. Loyola Marymount, 1950 (FBS)
Other Division records:
93 Yards—Tyler Grogan, Northeastern vs. Villanova, 2001 (FCS)
97 Yards—Earl Hurst, Emporia St. vs. Central Mo., 1964 (II)
90 Yards—Dan Heeren, Coe vs. Lawrence, 1974; Sean Lipscomb, Redlands vs. Pomona-Pitzer, 2002 (III)

FIELD GOALS
67 Yards—Russell Erxleben, Texas vs. Rice, 1977; Steve Little, Arkansas vs. Texas, 1977; Joe Williams, Wichita St. vs. Southern Ill., 1978 (FBS)
67 Yards—Tom Odle, Fort Hays St. vs. Washburn, 1988 (II)

Other Division records:
63 Yards—Tim Foley, Ga. Southern vs. James Madison, 1987; Scott Roper, Arkansas St. vs. North Texas, 1987; Bill Gramatica, South Fla. vs. Austin Peay, 2000 (FCS)
62 Yards—Dom Antonini, Rowan vs. Salisbury, 1976 (III)

All-Time Won-Lost-Tied Records

MOST GAMES PLAYED
1,273—Penn (786-445-42 in 130 seasons) (FCS)
Other Division records:
1,202—Rutgers (580-580-42 in 137 seasons) (FBS)
1,044—Washburn (472-528-44 in 115 seasons) (II)
1,050—Frank. & Marsh. (559-434-47 in 119 seasons) (III)

MOST SEASONS PLAYED
137—Rutgers (FBS)
137—Princeton (FCS)
Other Division records:
117—Colorado Mines (II)
127—Amherst (III)

MOST VICTORIES
860—Michigan, 127 seasons (282 losses, 36 ties) (FBS)
Other Division records:
838—Yale, 134 seasons (328 losses, 55 ties) (FCS)
611—Pittsburg St., 99 seasons (311 losses, 47 ties) (II)
663—Wittenberg, 113 seasons (338 losses, 31 ties) (III)

MOST LOSSES
605—Northwestern (119 seasons) (FBS)
Other Division records:
593—Richmond (123 seasons) (FCS)
528—Washburn (115 seasons) (II)
568—Hiram (108 seasons) (III)

MOST TIED GAMES
65—Illinois St. (107 seasons, 426-483-65) (FCS)
Other Division records:
58—Kansas (117 seasons, 542-537-58) (FBS)
51—Central Mo. (110 seasons, 464-471-51) (II)
62—Union (N.Y.) (118 seasons, 486-415-62) (III)

BEST WINNING PERCENTAGE (Min. 20 Seasons)
.745—Michigan (860-282-36, 127 seasons) (FBS)
Other Division records:
.737—Ga. Southern (238-84-1, 25 seasons) (FCS)
.711—Grand Valley St. (275-111-3, 36 seasons) (II)
.705—St. John's (Minn.) (539-219-24, 96 seasons) (III)

Winningest Teams by Decade

BY PERCENTAGE
2000s (2000-01-02-03-04-05-06)
.970—Mount Union (96-3) (III)
Other Division records:
.854—Boise St. (76-13) (FBS)
.808—Montana (80-19) (FCS)
.905—Grand Valley St. (86-9) (II)

1990s (1990-99)
.941—Mount Union (120-7-1) (III)
Other Division records:
.890—Florida St. (109-13-1) (FBS)
.844—Dayton (92-17-0) (FCS) (FCS)
.846—Pittsburg St. (103-18-2) (II)

BY VICTORIES
2000s (2000-01-02-03-04-05-06)
96—Mount Union (96-3) (III)
Other Division records:
79—Oklahoma (79-14) (FBS)
80—Montana (80-19) (FCS)
86—Grand Valley St. (86-9) (II)

1990s (1990-99)
120—Mount Union (120-7-1) (III)
Other Division records:
114—Marshall (114-25-0) (FBS)
103—Youngstown St. (103-30-2) (FCS)
103—Pittsburg St. (103-18-2) (II)

All-Time Longest Rivalries

MOST GAMES PLAYED (Series leader listed first)
142 games—Lafayette-Lehigh (75-62-5 record, first meeting in 1884) (FCS)
Other Division records:
116 games—Minnesota-Wisconsin (59-49-8 record, first meeting in 1890) (FBS)
110 games—North Dakota-North Dakota St. (62-45-3 record, first meeting in 1894) (Last met in 2003) (II)
121 games—Williams-Amherst (68-48-5 record, first meeting in 1881) (III)

EARLIEST YEAR PLAYED (Series leader listed first)
1873—Yale-Princeton (129 meetings, 70-49-10 record) (FCS)
Other Division records:
1888—Miami (Ohio)-Cincinnati (111 meetings, 59-45-7 record); North Carolina-Wake Forest (102 meetings, 67-33-2 record) (FBS)
1889—South Dakota-South Dakota St. (104 meetings, 50-47-7 record) (Last met in 2003); Colorado Mines-Colorado Col. (88 meetings, 46-37-5 record) (Last met in 2000) (II)
1881—Williams-Amherst (121 meetings, 68-48-5 record); Williams-Wesleyan (Conn.) (112 meetings, 70-37-5 record) (III)

Award Winners

Consensus All-America Selections, 1889-2006

In 1950, the National Collegiate Athletic Bureau (the NCAA's service bureau) compiled the first official comprehensive roster of all-time All-Americans. The compilation of the All-American roster was supervised by a panel of analysts working in large part with the historical records contained in the files of the Dr. Baker Football Information Service.

The roster consists of only those players who were first-team selections on one or more of the All-America teams that were selected for the national audience and received nationwide circulation. Not included are the thousands of players who received mention on All-America second or third teams, nor the numerous others who were selected by newspapers or agencies with circulations that were not primarily national and with viewpoints, therefore, that were not normally nationwide in scope.

The following chart indicates, by year (in left column), which national media and organizations selected All-America teams. The headings at the top of each column refer to the selector (see legend after chart).

All-America Selectors

	AA	AP	C	CNN	COL	CP	FBW	FC	FN	FW	INS	L	LIB	M	N	NA	NEA	SN	UP	UPI	W	WCF
1889	-	-	-	-	-	-	-	-	-	-	-	-	-	-	-	-	-	-	-	-	√	-
1890	-	-	-	-	-	-	-	-	-	-	-	-	-	-	-	-	-	-	-	-	√	-
1891	-	-	-	-	-	-	-	-	-	-	-	-	-	-	-	-	-	-	-	-	√	-
1892	-	-	-	-	-	-	-	-	-	-	-	-	-	-	-	-	-	-	-	-	√	-
1893	-	-	-	-	-	-	-	-	-	-	-	-	-	-	-	-	-	-	-	-	√	-
1894	-	-	-	-	-	-	-	-	-	-	-	-	-	-	-	-	-	-	-	-	√	-
1895	-	-	-	-	-	-	-	-	-	-	-	-	-	-	-	-	-	-	-	-	√	-
1896	-	-	-	-	-	-	-	-	-	-	-	-	-	-	-	-	-	-	-	-	√	-
1897	-	-	-	-	-	-	-	-	-	-	-	-	-	-	-	-	-	-	-	-	√	-
1898	-	-	√	-	-	-	-	-	-	-	-	-	-	-	-	-	-	-	-	-	√	-
1899	-	-	√	-	-	-	-	-	-	-	-	-	-	-	-	-	-	-	-	-	√	-
1900	-	-	√	-	-	-	-	-	-	-	-	-	-	-	-	-	-	-	-	-	√	-
1901	-	-	√	-	-	-	-	-	-	-	-	-	-	-	-	-	-	-	-	-	√	-
1902	-	-	√	-	-	-	-	-	-	-	-	-	-	-	-	-	-	-	-	-	√	-
1903	-	-	√	-	-	-	-	-	-	-	-	-	-	-	-	-	-	-	-	-	√	-
1904	-	-	√	-	-	-	-	-	-	-	-	-	-	-	-	-	-	-	-	-	√	-
1905	-	-	√	-	-	-	-	-	-	-	-	-	-	-	-	-	-	-	-	-	√	-
1906	-	-	√	-	-	-	-	-	-	-	-	-	-	-	-	-	-	-	-	-	√	-
1907	-	-	√	-	-	-	-	-	-	-	-	-	-	-	-	-	-	-	-	-	√	-
1908	-	-	√	-	-	-	-	-	-	-	-	-	-	-	-	-	-	-	-	-	√	-
1909	-	-	√	-	-	-	-	-	-	-	-	-	-	-	-	-	-	-	-	-	-	-
1910	-	-	√	-	-	-	-	-	-	-	-	-	-	-	-	-	-	-	-	-	-	-
1911	-	-	√	-	-	-	-	-	-	-	-	-	-	-	-	-	-	-	-	-	-	-
1912	-	-	√	-	-	-	-	-	-	-	-	-	-	-	-	-	-	-	-	-	-	-
1913	-	-	√	-	-	-	-	-	-	-	√	-	-	-	-	-	-	-	-	-	-	-
1914	-	-	√	-	-	-	-	-	-	-	√	-	-	-	-	-	-	-	-	-	-	-
1915	-	-	√	-	-	-	-	-	-	-	√	-	-	-	-	-	-	-	-	-	-	-
1916	-	-	√	-	-	-	-	-	-	-	√	-	-	√	-	-	-	-	-	-	-	-
1917	-	-	(*)	-	-	-	-	-	-	-	√	-	-	√	-	-	√	-	-	-	-	-
1918	-	-	√	-	-	-	-	-	-	-	-	-	-	√	-	-	-	-	-	-	-	-
1919	-	-	√	-	-	-	-	-	-	-	-	-	-	√	-	-	-	-	-	-	-	-
1920	-	-	√	-	-	-	√	-	-	-	√	-	-	√	-	-	-	-	-	-	-	-
1921	-	-	√	-	-	-	-	-	-	-	-	-	-	-	-	-	-	-	-	-	-	-
1922	-	-	√	-	-	-	-	-	-	-	-	-	-	-	-	-	-	-	-	-	-	-
1923	-	-	√	-	-	-	√	-	-	-	-	-	-	-	-	-	-	-	-	-	-	-
1924	√	-	√	-	-	-	√	-	-	-	√	-	√	-	-	-	√	-	-	-	-	-
1925	√	√	-	-	√	-	√	-	-	-	√	-	√	-	-	-	√	-	√	-	-	-
1926	√	√	-	-	√	-	-	-	-	-	√	-	-	-	-	-	√	-	√	-	-	-
1927	√	√	-	-	√	-	-	-	-	-	√	-	-	-	-	√	√	-	√	-	-	-
1928	√	√	-	-	√	-	-	-	-	-	√	-	-	-	-	√	√	-	√	-	-	-
1929	√	√	-	-	√	-	-	-	-	-	√	-	-	-	-	√	√	-	√	-	-	-
1930	√	√	-	-	√	-	-	-	-	-	√	-	-	-	-	√	√	-	√	-	-	-
1931	√	√	-	-	√	-	-	-	-	-	√	-	√	-	-	-	√	-	√	-	-	-
1932	√	√	-	-	√	-	-	-	-	-	√	-	√	-	-	√	√	-	√	-	-	-
1933	√	√	-	-	√	-	-	-	-	-	√	-	√	-	-	√	√	-	√	-	-	-
1934	√	√	-	-	√	-	-	-	-	-	√	-	√	-	-	√	√	√	√	-	-	-
1935	√	√	-	-	√	-	-	-	-	-	√	-	√	-	-	√	√	√	√	-	-	-
1936	√	√	-	-	√	-	-	-	-	-	√	-	√	-	-	√	√	√	√	-	-	-
1937	√	√	-	-	√	-	-	-	-	-	√	-	√	-	√	√	√	√	√	-	-	-
1938	√	√	-	-	√	-	-	-	-	-	√	-	√	-	√	-	√	√	√	-	-	-
1939	√	√	-	-	√	-	-	-	-	-	√	-	√	-	√	-	√	√	√	-	-	-
1940	√	√	-	-	√	-	-	-	-	-	√	-	√	-	√	-	√	√	√	-	-	-
1941	√	√	-	-	√	-	-	-	-	-	√	-	√	-	√	-	√	√	√	-	-	-
1942	√	√	-	-	√	-	-	-	-	-	√	√	-	-	√	-	√	√	√	-	-	-
1943	√	√	-	-	√	-	-	-	√	-	√	√	-	-	-	-	-	√	√	-	-	-
1944	√	√	-	-	√	-	-	-	√	√	√	√	-	-	-	-	√	√	√	-	-	-
1945	√	√	-	-	√	-	-	√	-	√	√	√	-	-	-	-	√	√	√	-	-	-
1946	√	√	-	-	√	-	-	√	-	√	√	(†)	-	-	-	-	√	√	√	-	-	-
1947	-	√	-	-	√	-	-	√	-	√	√	-	-	-	-	-	√	√	√	-	-	-
1948	-	√	-	-	(§)	-	-	√	-	√	(#)√	-	-	-	-	-	√	√	√	-	-	-
1949	√	√	-	-	-	-	-	√	-	√	√	-	-	-	-	-	√	√	√	-	-	-
1950	√	√	-	-	-	-	-	√	-	√	√	-	-	-	-	-	√	√	√	-	-	-
1951	√	√	-	-	-	-	-	√	-	√	√	-	-	-	-	-	√	√	√	-	-	-
1952	√	√	-	-	-	-	-	√	-	√	√	-	-	-	-	-	√	√	√	-	-	-
1953	√	√	-	-	-	-	-	√	-	√	√	-	-	-	-	-	√	√	√	-	-	-

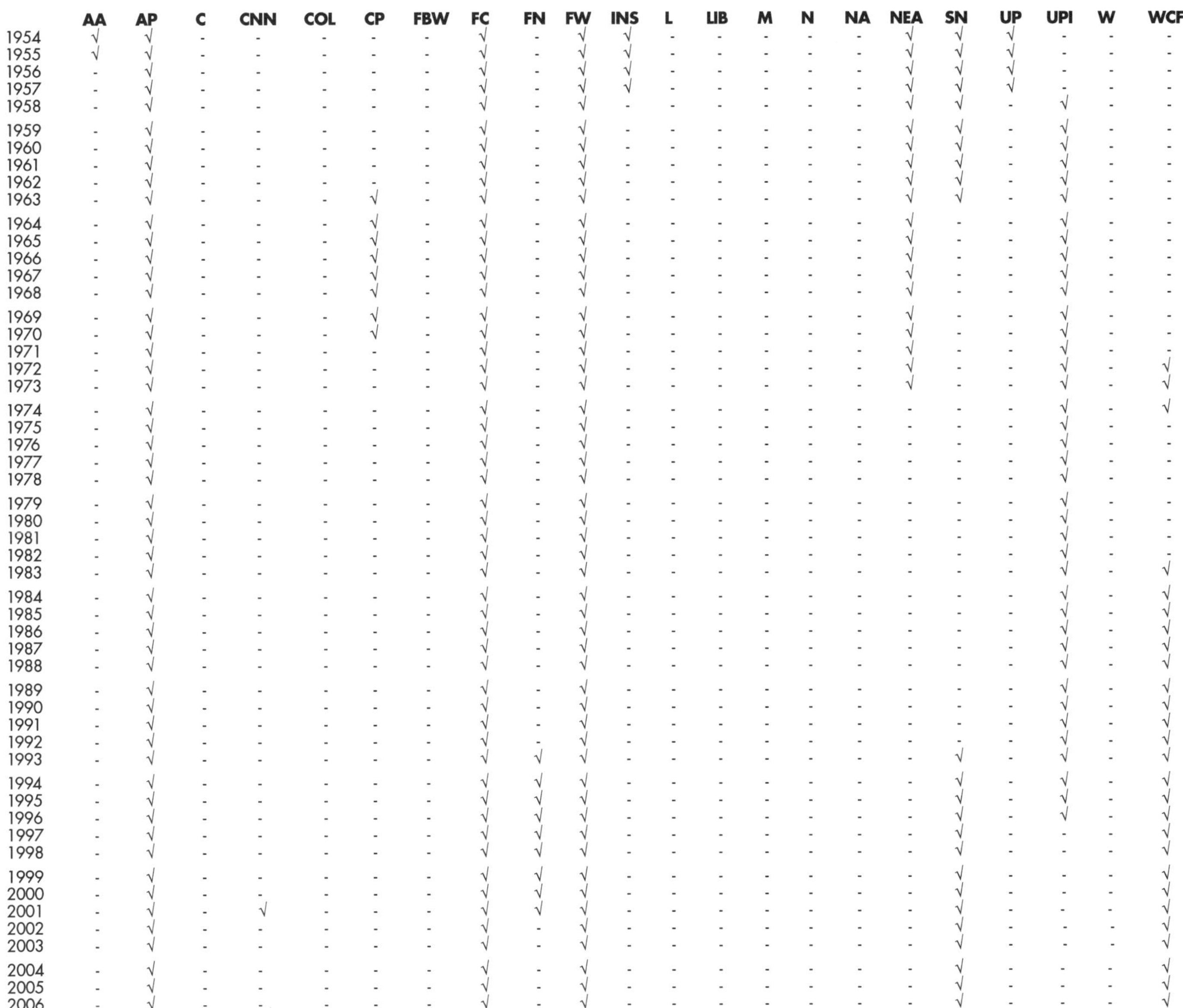

	AA	AP	C	CNN	COL	CP	FBW	FC	FN	FW	INS	L	LIB	M	N	NA	NEA	SN	UP	UPI	W	WCF
1954	√	√	-	-	-	-	-	√	-	√	√	-	-	-	-	-	√	√	√	-	-	-
1955	√	√	-	-	-	-	-	√	-	√	√	-	-	-	-	-	√	√	√	-	-	-
1956	-	√	-	-	-	-	-	√	-	√	√	-	-	-	-	-	√	√	√	-	-	-
1957	-	√	-	-	-	-	-	√	-	√	√	-	-	-	-	-	√	√	√	-	-	-
1958	-	√	-	-	-	-	-	√	-	√	-	-	-	-	-	-	√	√	-	√	-	-
1959	-	√	-	-	-	-	-	√	-	√	-	-	-	-	-	-	√	√	-	√	-	-
1960	-	√	-	-	-	-	-	√	-	√	-	-	-	-	-	-	√	√	-	√	-	-
1961	-	√	-	-	-	-	-	√	-	√	-	-	-	-	-	-	√	√	-	√	-	-
1962	-	√	-	-	-	-	-	√	-	√	-	-	-	-	-	-	√	√	-	√	-	-
1963	-	√	-	-	-	√	-	√	-	√	-	-	-	-	-	-	√	√	-	√	-	-
1964	-	√	-	-	-	√	-	√	-	√	-	-	-	-	-	-	√	-	-	√	-	-
1965	-	√	-	-	-	√	-	√	-	√	-	-	-	-	-	-	√	-	-	√	-	-
1966	-	√	-	-	-	√	-	√	-	√	-	-	-	-	-	-	√	-	-	√	-	-
1967	-	√	-	-	-	√	-	√	-	√	-	-	-	-	-	-	√	-	-	√	-	-
1968	-	√	-	-	-	√	-	√	-	√	-	-	-	-	-	-	√	-	-	√	-	-
1969	-	√	-	-	-	√	-	√	-	√	-	-	-	-	-	-	√	-	-	√	-	-
1970	-	√	-	-	-	√	-	√	-	√	-	-	-	-	-	-	√	-	-	√	-	-
1971	-	√	-	-	-	-	-	√	-	√	-	-	-	-	-	-	√	-	-	√	-	-
1972	-	√	-	-	-	-	-	√	-	√	-	-	-	-	-	-	√	-	-	√	-	√
1973	-	√	-	-	-	-	-	√	-	√	-	-	-	-	-	-	√	-	-	√	-	√
1974	-	√	-	-	-	-	-	√	-	√	-	-	-	-	-	-	-	-	-	√	-	√
1975	-	√	-	-	-	-	-	√	-	√	-	-	-	-	-	-	-	-	-	√	-	-
1976	-	√	-	-	-	-	-	√	-	√	-	-	-	-	-	-	-	-	-	√	-	-
1977	-	√	-	-	-	-	-	√	-	√	-	-	-	-	-	-	-	-	-	√	-	-
1978	-	√	-	-	-	-	-	√	-	√	-	-	-	-	-	-	-	-	-	√	-	-
1979	-	√	-	-	-	-	-	√	-	√	-	-	-	-	-	-	-	-	-	√	-	-
1980	-	√	-	-	-	-	-	√	-	√	-	-	-	-	-	-	-	-	-	√	-	-
1981	-	√	-	-	-	-	-	√	-	√	-	-	-	-	-	-	-	-	-	√	-	-
1982	-	√	-	-	-	-	-	√	-	√	-	-	-	-	-	-	-	-	-	√	-	-
1983	-	√	-	-	-	-	-	√	-	√	-	-	-	-	-	-	-	-	-	√	-	√
1984	-	√	-	-	-	-	-	√	-	√	-	-	-	-	-	-	-	-	-	√	-	√
1985	-	√	-	-	-	-	-	√	-	√	-	-	-	-	-	-	-	-	-	√	-	√
1986	-	√	-	-	-	-	-	√	-	√	-	-	-	-	-	-	-	-	-	√	-	√
1987	-	√	-	-	-	-	-	√	-	√	-	-	-	-	-	-	-	-	-	√	-	√
1988	-	√	-	-	-	-	-	√	-	√	-	-	-	-	-	-	-	-	-	√	-	√
1989	-	√	-	-	-	-	-	√	-	√	-	-	-	-	-	-	-	-	-	√	-	√
1990	-	√	-	-	-	-	-	√	-	√	-	-	-	-	-	-	-	-	-	√	-	√
1991	-	√	-	-	-	-	-	√	-	√	-	-	-	-	-	-	-	-	-	√	-	√
1992	-	√	-	-	-	-	-	√	-	√	-	-	-	-	-	-	-	-	-	√	-	√
1993	-	√	-	-	-	-	-	√	√	√	-	-	-	-	-	-	-	√	-	√	-	√
1994	-	√	-	-	-	-	-	√	√	√	-	-	-	-	-	-	-	√	-	√	-	√
1995	-	√	-	-	-	-	-	√	√	√	-	-	-	-	-	-	-	√	-	√	-	√
1996	-	√	-	-	-	-	-	√	√	√	-	-	-	-	-	-	-	√	-	√	-	√
1997	-	√	-	-	-	-	-	√	√	√	-	-	-	-	-	-	-	√	-	-	-	√
1998	-	√	-	-	-	-	-	√	√	√	-	-	-	-	-	-	-	√	-	-	-	√
1999	-	√	-	-	-	-	-	√	√	√	-	-	-	-	-	-	-	√	-	-	-	√
2000	-	√	-	-	-	-	-	√	√	√	-	-	-	-	-	-	-	√	-	-	-	√
2001	-	√	-	√	-	-	-	√	√	√	-	-	-	-	-	-	-	√	-	-	-	√
2002	-	√	-	-	-	-	-	√	-	√	-	-	-	-	-	-	-	√	-	-	-	√
2003	-	√	-	-	-	-	-	√	-	√	-	-	-	-	-	-	-	√	-	-	-	√
2004	-	√	-	-	-	-	-	√	-	√	-	-	-	-	-	-	-	√	-	-	-	√
2005	-	√	-	-	-	-	-	√	-	√	-	-	-	-	-	-	-	√	-	-	-	√
2006	-	√	-	-	-	-	-	√	-	√	-	-	-	-	-	-	-	√	-	-	-	√

**In 1917, Walter Camp selected an all-Service, All-America team composed of military personnel. †During 1946-70, Look Magazine published the Football Writers Association of America's selections, listed under FW. §During 1948-56, Collier's Magazine published the American Football Coaches Association's selections, listed under FC. #International News Service was the first to select offensive and defensive teams.*

LEGEND FOR SELECTORS

AA—All-America Board
AP—Associated Press
C—Walter Camp (published in Harper's Weekly, 1897; in Collier's Magazine, 1898-1924)
CNN—Cable News Network-Sports Illustrated.com
COL—Collier's Magazine (selections by Grantland Rice, 1925-47; published American Football Coaches Association teams, 1948-56, listed under FC)
CP—Central Press
FBW—Football World Magazine
FC—American Football Coaches Association (published in Saturday Evening Post Magazine, 1945-47; in Collier's Magazine, 1948-56; sponsored by General Mills in 1957-59 and by Eastman Kodak from 1960-93)
FN—Football News
FW—Football Writers Association of America (published in Look Magazine, 1946-70)
INS—International News Service (merged with United Press in 1958 to form UPI)
L—Look Magazine (published Football Writers Association of America teams, 1946-70, listed under FW)
LIB—Liberty Magazine
M—Frank Menke Syndicate
N—Newsweek
NA—North American Newspaper Alliance
NEA—Newspaper Enterprise Association
SN—Sporting News
UP—United Press (merged with International News Service in 1958 to form UPI)
UPI—United Press International
W—Caspar Whitney (published in The Week's Sport in association with Walter Camp, 1889-90; published in Harper's Weekly, 1891-96, and in Outing Magazine, which he owned, 1898-1908; Walter Camp substituted for Whitney, who was on a world sports tour, and selected Harper's Weekly's team for 1897)
WCF—Walter Camp Foundation

All-America Selections

Listed on the following pages are the consensus All-Americans (i.e., the players who were accorded a majority of votes at their positions by the selectors). Included are the selections of 1889-97, 1909-12 and 1921-22 when there was only one selector.

1889
E—Amos Alonzo Stagg, Yale; Arthur Cumnock, Harvard; T—Hector Cowan, Princeton; Charles Gill, Yale; G—Pudge Heffelfinger, Yale; John Cranston, Harvard; C—William George, Princeton; B—Edgar Allan Poe, Princeton; Roscoe Channing, Princeton; Knowlton Ames, Princeton; James Lee, Harvard.

1890
E—Frank Hallowell, Harvard; Ralph Warren, Princeton; T—Marshall Newell, Harvard; William Rhodes, Yale; G—Pudge Heffelfinger, Yale; Jesse Riggs, Princeton; C—John Cranston, Harvard; B—Thomas McClung, Yale; Sheppard Homans, Princeton; Dudley Dean, Harvard; John Corbett, Harvard.

1891
E—Frank Hinkey, Yale; John Hartwell, Yale; T—Wallace Winter, Yale; Marshall Newell, Harvard; G—Pudge Heffelfinger, Yale; Jesse Riggs, Princeton; C—John Adams, Penn; B—Philip King, Princeton; Everett Lake, Harvard; Thomas McClung, Yale; Sheppard Homans, Princeton.

1892
E—Frank Hinkey, Yale; Frank Hallowell, Harvard; T—Marshall Newell, Harvard; A. Hamilton Wallis, Yale; G—Arthur Wheeler, Princeton; Bertram Waters, Harvard; C—William Lewis, Harvard; B—Charles Brewer, Harvard; Vance McCormick, Yale; Philip King, Princeton; Harry Thayer, Penn.

1893
E—Frank Hinkey, Yale; Thomas Trenchard, Princeton; T—Langdon Lea, Princeton; Marshall Newell, Harvard; G—Arthur Wheeler, Princeton; William Hickok, Yale; C—William Lewis, Harvard; B—Philip King, Princeton; Charles Brewer, Harvard; Franklin Morse, Princeton; Frank Butterworth, Yale.

1894
E—Frank Hinkey, Yale; Charles Gelbert, Penn; T—Bertram Waters, Harvard; Langdon Lea, Princeton; G—Arthur Wheeler, Princeton; William Hickok, Yale; C—Philip Stillman, Yale; B—George Adee, Yale; Arthur Knipe, Penn; George Brooke, Penn; Frank Butterworth, Yale.

1895
E—Norman Cabot, Harvard; Charles Gelbert, Penn; T—Langdon Lea, Princeton; Fred Murphy, Yale; G—Charles Wharton, Penn; Dudley Riggs, Princeton; C—Alfred Bull, Penn; B—Clinton Wyckoff, Cornell; Samuel Thorne, Yale; Charles Brewer, Harvard; George Brooke, Penn.

1896
E—Norman Cabot, Harvard; Charles Gelbert, Penn; T—William Church, Princeton; Fred Murphy, Yale; G—Charles Wharton, Penn; Wylie Woodruff, Penn; C—Robert Gailey, Princeton; B—Clarence Fincke, Yale; Edgar Wrightington, Harvard; Addison Kelly, Princeton; John Baird, Princeton.

1897
E—Garrett Cochran, Princeton; John Hall, Yale; T—Burr Chamberlain, Yale; John Outland, Penn; G—T. Truxton Hare, Penn; Gordon Brown, Yale; C—Alan Doucette, Harvard; B—Charles DeSaulles, Yale; Benjamin Dibblee, Harvard; Addison Kelly, Princeton; John Minds, Penn.

1898
E—Lew Palmer, Princeton; John Hallowell, Harvard; T—Arthur Hillebrand, Princeton; Burr Chamberlain, Yale; G—T. Truxton Hare, Penn; Gordon Brown, Yale; Walter Boal, Harvard; C—Pete Overfield, Penn; William Cunningham, Michigan; B—Charles Daly, Harvard; Benjamin Dibblee, Harvard; John Outland, Penn; Clarence Herschberger, Chicago; Malcolm McBride, Yale; Charles Romeyn, Army.

1899
E—David Campbell, Harvard; Arthur Poe, Princeton; T—Arthur Hillebrand, Princeton; George Stillman, Yale; G—T. Truxton Hare, Penn; Gordon Brown, Yale; C—Pete Overfield, Penn; B—Charles Daly, Harvard; Josiah McCracken, Penn; Malcolm McBride, Yale; Isaac Seneca, Carlisle; Albert Sharpe, Yale; Howard Reiter, Princeton.

1900
E—John Hallowell, Harvard; David Campbell, Harvard; William Smith, Army; T—George Stillman, Yale; James Bloomer, Yale; G—Gordon Brown, Yale; T. Truxton Hare, Penn; C—Herman Olcott, Yale; Walter Bachman, Lafayette; B—Bill Morley, Columbia; George Chadwick, Yale; Perry Hale, Yale; William Fincke, Yale; Charles Daly, Harvard; Raymond Starbuck, Cornell.

1901
E—David Campbell, Harvard; Ralph Davis, Princeton; Edward Bowditch, Harvard; Neil Snow, Michigan; T—Oliver Cutts, Harvard; Paul Bunker, Army; Crawford Blagden, Harvard; G—William Warner, Cornell; William Lee, Harvard; Charles Barnard, Harvard; Sanford Hunt, Cornell; C—Henry Holt, Yale; Walter Bachman, Lafayette; B—Robert Kernan, Harvard; Charles Daly, Army; Thomas Graydon, Harvard; Harold Weekes, Columbia; Bill Morley, Columbia.

1902
E—Thomas Shevlin, Yale; Edward Bowditch, Harvard; T—Ralph Kinney, Yale; James Hogan, Yale; Paul Bunker, Army; G—Edgar Glass, Yale; John DeWitt, Princeton; William Warner, Cornell; C—Henry Holt, Yale; Robert Boyers, Army; B—Foster Rockwell, Yale; George Chadwick, Yale; Thomas Graydon, Harvard; Thomas Barry, Brown.

1903
E—Howard Henry, Princeton; Charles Rafferty, Yale; T—Daniel Knowlton, Harvard; James Hogan, Yale; Fred Schacht, Minnesota; G—John DeWitt, Princeton; Andrew Marshall, Harvard; James Bloomer, Yale; C—Henry Hooper, Dartmouth; B—Willie Heston, Michigan; J. Dana Kafer, Princeton; James Johnson, Carlisle; Richard Smith, Columbia; Myron Witham, Dartmouth; W. Ledyard Mitchell, Yale.

1904
E—Thomas Shevlin, Yale; Fred Speik, Chicago; T—James Hogan, Yale; James Cooney, Princeton; G—Frank Piekarski, Penn; Joseph Gilman, Dartmouth; Ralph Kinney, Yale; C—Arthur Tipton, Army; B—Daniel Hurley, Harvard; Walter Eckersall, Chicago; Vincent Stevenson, Penn; Willie Heston, Michigan; Andrew Smith, Penn; Foster Rockwell, Yale; Henry Torney, Army.

1905
E—Thomas Shevlin, Yale; Ralph Glaze, Dartmouth; Mark Catlin, Chicago; T—Otis Lamson, Penn; Beaton Squires, Harvard; Karl Brill, Harvard; G—Roswell Tripp, Yale; Francis Burr, Harvard; C—Robert Torrey, Penn; B—Walter Eckersall, Chicago; Howard Roome, Yale; John Hubbard, Amherst; James McCormick, Princeton; Guy Hutchinson, Yale; Daniel Hurley, Harvard; Henry Torney, Army.

1906
E—Robert Forbes, Yale; L. Casper Wister, Princeton; T—L. Horatio Biglow, Yale; James Cooney, Princeton; Charles Osborne, Harvard; G—Francis Burr, Harvard; Elmer Thompson, Cornell; August Ziegler, Penn; C—William Dunn, Penn St.; William Newman, Cornell; B—Walter Eckersall, Chicago; Hugh Knox, Yale; Edward Dillon, Princeton; John Mayhew, Brown; William Hollenback, Penn; Paul Veeder, Yale.

1907
E—Bill Dague, Navy; Clarence Alcott, Yale; Albert Exendine, Carlisle; L. Casper Wister, Princeton; T—Dexter Draper, Penn; L. Horatio Biglow, Yale; G—August Ziegler, Penn; William Erwin, Army; C—Adolph Schulz, Michigan; Patrick Grant, Harvard; B—John Wendell, Harvard; Thomas A. D. Jones, Yale; Edwin Harlan, Princeton; James McCormick, Princeton; Edward Coy, Yale; Peter Hauser, Carlisle.

1908
E—Hunter Scarlett, Penn; George Schildmiller, Dartmouth; T—Hamilton Fish, Harvard; Frank Horr, Syracuse; Percy Northcroft, Navy; G—Clark Tobin, Dartmouth; William Goebel, Yale; Hamlin Andrus, Yale; Bernard O'Rourke, Cornell; C—Charles Nourse, Harvard; B—Edward Coy, Yale; Frederick Tibbott, Princeton; William Hollenback, Penn; Walter Steffen, Chicago; Ed Lange, Navy; Hamilton Corbett, Harvard.

1909
E—Adrian Regnier, Brown; John Kilpatrick, Yale; T—Hamilton Fish, Harvard; Henry Hobbs, Yale; G—Albert Benbrook, Michigan; Hamlin Andrus, Yale; C—Carroll Cooney, Yale; B—Edward Coy, Yale; John McGovern, Minnesota; Stephen Philbin, Yale; Wayland Minot, Harvard.

1910
E—John Kilpatrick, Yale; Stanfield Wells, Michigan; T—Robert McKay, Harvard; James Walker, Minnesota; G—Robert Fisher, Harvard; Albert Benbrook, Michigan; C—Ernest Cozens, Penn; B—E. LeRoy Mercer, Penn; Percy Wendell, Harvard; Earl Sprackling, Brown; Talbot Pendleton, Princeton.

1911
E—Douglass Bomeisler, Yale; Sanford White, Princeton; T—Edward Hart, Princeton; Leland Devore, Army; G—Robert Fisher, Harvard; Joseph Duff, Princeton; C—Henry Ketcham, Yale; B—Jim Thorpe, Carlisle; Percy Wendell, Harvard; Arthur Howe, Yale; Jack Dalton, Navy.

1912
E—Samuel Felton, Harvard; Douglass Bomeisler, Yale; T—Wesley Englehorn, Dartmouth; Robert Butler, Wisconsin; G—Stanley Pennock, Harvard; John Logan, Princeton; C—Henry Ketcham, Yale; B—Charles Brickley, Harvard; Jim Thorpe, Carlisle; George Crowther, Brown; E. LeRoy Mercer, Penn.

1913
E—Robert Hogsett, Dartmouth; Louis Merrillat, Army; T—Harold Ballin, Princeton; Nelson Talbott, Yale; Miller Pontius, Michigan; Harvey Hitchcock, Harvard; G—John Brown, Navy; Stanley Pennock, Harvard; Ray Keeler, Wisconsin; C—Paul Des Jardien, Chicago; B—Charles Brickley, Harvard; Edward Mahan, Harvard; Jim Craig, Michigan; Ellery Huntington, Colgate; Gus Dorais, Notre Dame.

1914
E—Huntington Hardwick, Harvard; John O'Hearn, Cornell; Perry Graves, Illinois; T—Harold Ballin, Princeton; Walter Trumbull, Harvard; G—Stanley Pennock, Harvard; Ralph Chapman, Illinois; Clarence Spears, Dartmouth; C—John McEwan, Army; B—John Maulbetsch, Michigan; Edward Mahan, Harvard; Charles Barrett, Cornell; John Spiegel, Wash. & Jeff.; Harry LeGore, Yale.

1915
E—Murray Shelton, Cornell; Guy Chamberlin, Nebraska; T—Joseph Gilman, Harvard; Howard Buck, Wisconsin; G—Clarence Spears, Dartmouth; Harold White, Syracuse; C—Robert Peck, Pittsburgh; B—Charles Barrett, Cornell; Edward Mahan, Harvard; Richard King, Harvard; Bart Macomber, Illinois; Eugene Mayer, Virginia; Neno Jerry DaPrato, Michigan St.

1916
E—Bert Baston, Minnesota; James Herron, Pittsburgh; T—Clarence Horning, Colgate; D. Belford West, Colgate; G—Clinton Black, Yale; Harrie Dadmun, Harvard; Frank Hogg, Princeton; C—Robert Peck, Pittsburgh; B—Elmer Oliphant, Army; Oscar Anderson, Colgate; Fritz Pollard, Brown; Charles Harley, Ohio St.

1917
E—Charles Bolen, Ohio St.; Paul Robeson, Rutgers; Henry Miller, Penn; T—Alfred Cobb, Syracuse; George Hauser, Minnesota; G—Dale Seis, Pittsburgh; John Sutherland, Pittsburgh; Eugene Neely, Dartmouth; C—Frank Rydzewski, Notre Dame; B—Elmer Oliphant, Army; Ben Boynton, Williams; Everett Strupper, Georgia Tech; Charles Harley, Ohio St.

1918
E—Paul Robeson, Rutgers; Bill Fincher, Georgia Tech; T—Wilbur Henry, Wash. & Jeff.; Leonard Hilty, Pittsburgh; Lou Usher, Syracuse; Joe Guyon, Georgia Tech; G—Joe Alexander, Syracuse; Lyman Perry, Navy; C—Ashel Day, Georgia Tech; John Depler, Illinois; B—Frank Murrey, Princeton; Tom Davies, Pittsburgh; Wolcott Roberts, Navy; George McLaren, Pittsburgh.

1919
E—Bob Higgins, Penn St.; Henry Miller, Penn; Lester Belding, Iowa; T—Wilbur Henry, Wash. & Jeff.; D.

Belford West, Colgate; G—Joe Alexander, Syracuse; Adolph Youngstrom, Dartmouth; C—James Weaver, Centre; Charles Carpenter, Wisconsin; B—Charles Harley, Ohio St.; Ira Rodgers, West Virginia; Edward Casey, Harvard; Bo McMillin, Centre; Ben Boynton, Williams.

1920

E—Luke Urban, Boston College; Charles Carney, Illinois; Bill Fincher, Georgia Tech; T—Stan Keck, Princeton; Ralph Scott, Wisconsin; G—Tim Callahan, Yale; Tom Woods, Harvard; Iolas Huffman, Ohio St.; C—Herb Stein, Pittsburgh; B—George Gipp, Notre Dame; Donold Lourie, Princeton; Gaylord Stinchcomb, Ohio St.; Charles Way, Penn St.

1921

E—Brick Muller, California; Eddie Anderson, Notre Dame; T—Dan McMillan, California; Iolas Huffman, Ohio St.; G—Frank Schwab, Lafayette; John Brown, Harvard; Stan Keck, Princeton; C—Herb Stein, Pittsburgh; B—Aubrey Devine, Iowa; Glenn Killinger, Penn St.; Bo McMillin, Centre; Malcolm Aldrich, Yale; Edgar Kaw, Cornell.

1922

E—Brick Muller, California; Wendell Taylor, Navy; T—C. Herbert Treat, Princeton; John Thurman, Penn; G—Frank Schwab, Lafayette; Charles Hubbard, Harvard; C—Ed Garbisch, Army; B—Harry Kipke, Michigan; Gordon Locke, Iowa; John Thomas, Chicago; Edgar Kaw, Cornell.

1923

E—Pete McRae, Syracuse; Ray Ecklund, Minnesota; Lynn Bomar, Vanderbilt; T—Century Milstead, Yale; Marty Below, Wisconsin; G—Charles Hubbard, Harvard; James McMillen, Illinois; C—Jack Blott, Michigan; B—George Pfann, Cornell; Red Grange, Illinois; William Mallory, Yale; Harry Wilson, Penn St.

Beginning in 1924, unanimous selections are indicated by (*).

1924

E—Jim Lawson, Stanford, 5-11, 190, Long Beach, Calif.; (tie) E—Dick Luman, Yale, 6-1, 176, Pinedale, Wyo.; Henry Wakefield, Vanderbilt, 5-10, 160, Petersburg, Tenn.; T—Ed McGinley, Penn, 5-11, 185, Swarthmore, Pa.; T—Ed Weir, Nebraska, 6-1, 194, Superior, Neb.; G—Joe Pondelik, Chicago, 5-11, 215, Cicero, Ill.; G—Carl Diehl, Dartmouth, 6-1, 205, Chicago, Ill.; C—Edwin Horrell, California, 5-11, 185, Pasadena, Calif.; B—*Red Grange, Illinois, 5-10, 170, Wheaton, Ill.; B—Harry Stuhldreher, Notre Dame, 5-7, 151, Massillon, Ohio; B—Jimmy Crowley, Notre Dame, 5-11, 162, Green Bay, Wis.; B—Elmer Layden, Notre Dame, 6-0, 162, Davenport, Iowa.

1925

E—Bennie Oosterbaan, Michigan, 6-0, 180, Muskegon, Mich.; E—George Tully, Dartmouth, 5-10, 175, Orange, N.J.; T—*Ed Weir, Nebraska, 6-1, 194, Superior, Neb.; T—Ralph Chase, Pittsburgh, 6-3, 202, Easton, Pa.; G—Carl Diehl, Dartmouth, 6-1, 205, Chicago, Ill.; G—Ed Hess, Ohio St., 6-1, 190, Cincinnati, Ohio; C—Ed McMillan, Princeton, 6-0, 208, Pittsburgh, Pa.; B—*Andy Oberlander, Dartmouth, 6-0, 197, Everett, Mass.; B—Red Grange, Illinois, 5-10, 170, Wheaton, Ill.; B—Ernie Nevers, Stanford, 6-0, 200, Superior, Wis.; (tie) B—Benny Friedman, Michigan, 5-8, 170, Cleveland, Ohio; George Wilson, Washington, 5-11, 190, Everett, Wash.

1926

E—Bennie Oosterbaan, Michigan, 6-0, 186, Muskegon, Mich.; E—Vic Hanson, Syracuse, 5-10, 174, Syracuse, N.Y.; T—*Frank Wickhorst, Navy, 6-0, 218, Oak Park, Ill.; T—Bud Sprague, Army, 6-2, 210, Dallas, Texas; G—Harry Connaughton, Georgetown, 6-2, 275, Philadelphia, Pa.; G—Bernie Shively, Illinois, 6-4, 208, Oliver, Ill.; C—Bud Boeringer, Notre Dame, 6-1, 186, St. Paul, Minn.; B—Benny Friedman, Michigan, 5-8, 172, Cleveland, Ohio; B—Mort Kaer, Southern California, 5-11, 167, Red Bluff, Calif.; B—Ralph Baker, Northwestern, 5-10, 172, Rockford, Ill.; B—Herb Joesting, Minnesota, 6-1, 192, Owatonna, Minn.

1927

E—*Bennie Oosterbaan, Michigan, 6-0, 186, Muskegon, Mich.; E—Tom Nash, Georgia, 6-3, 200, Washington, Ga.; T—Jesse Hibbs, Southern California, 5-11, 185, Glendale, Calif.; T—Ed Hake, Penn, 6-0, 190, Philadelphia, Pa.; G—Bill Webster, Yale, 6-0, 200, Shelton, Conn.; G—John Smith, Notre Dame, 5-9, 164, Hartford, Conn.; (tie) C—Larry Bettencourt, St. Mary's (Cal.), 5-10, 187, Centerville, Calif.; John Charlesworth, Yale, 5-11, 198, North Adams, Mass.; B—*Gibby Welch, Pittsburgh, 5-11, 170, Parkersburg, W. Va.; B—Morley Drury, Southern California, 6-0, 185, Long Beach, Calif.; B—Red Cagle, Army, 5-9, 167, Merryville, La.; B—Herb Joesting, Minnesota, 6-1, 192, Owatonna, Minn.

1928

E—Irv Phillips, California, 6-1, 188, Salinas, Calif.; E—Wes Fesler, Ohio St., 6-0, 173, Youngstown, Ohio; T—Otto Pommerening, Michigan, 6-0, 178, Ann Arbor, Mich.; T—Mike Getto, Pittsburgh, 6-2, 198, Jeannette, Pa.; G—Seraphim Post, Stanford, 6-0, 190, Berkeley, Calif.; (tie) G—Don Robesky, Stanford, 5-11, 198, Bakersfield, Calif.; Edward Burke, Navy, 6-0, 180, Larksville, Pa.; C—Pete Pund, Georgia Tech, 6-0, 195, Augusta, Ga.; B—*Red Cagle, Army, 5-9, 167, Merryville, La.; B—Paul Scull, Penn, 5-8, 187, Bala, Pa.; (tie) B—Ken Strong, New York U., 6-0, 201, West Haven, Conn.; Howard Harpster, Carnegie Mellon, 6-1, 160, Akron, Ohio; B—Charles Carroll, Washington, 6-0, 190, Seattle, Wash.

1929

E—*Joe Donchess, Pittsburgh, 6-0, 175, Youngstown, Ohio; E—Wes Fesler, Ohio St., 6-0, 183, Youngstown, Ohio; T—Bronko Nagurski, Minnesota, 6-2, 217, International Falls, Minn.; T—Elmer Sleight, Purdue, 6-2, 193, Morris, Ill.; G—Jack Cannon, Notre Dame, 5-11, 193, Columbus, Ohio; G—Ray Montgomery, Pittsburgh, 6-1, 188, Wheeling, W.Va.; C—Ben Ticknor, Harvard, 6-2, 193, New York, N.Y.; B—*Frank Carideo, Notre Dame, 5-7, 175, Mount Vernon, N.Y.; B—Ralph Welch, Purdue, 6-1, 189, Whitesboro, Texas; B—Red Cagle, Army, 5-9, 167, Merryville, La.; B—Gene McEver, Tennessee, 5-10, 185, Bristol, Va.

1930

E—*Wes Fesler, Ohio St., 6-0, 185, Youngstown, Ohio; E—Frank Baker, Northwestern, 6-2, 175, Cedar Rapids, Iowa; T—*Fred Sington, Alabama, 6-2, 215, Birmingham, Ala.; T—Milo Lubratovich, Wisconsin, 6-2, 216, Duluth, Minn.; G—Ted Beckett, California, 6-1, 190, Oroville, Calif.; G—Barton Koch, Baylor, 5-10, 195, Temple, Texas; C—*Ben Ticknor, Harvard, 6-2, 193, New York, N.Y.; B—*Frank Carideo, Notre Dame, 5-7, 175, Mount Vernon, N.Y.; B—Marchy Schwartz, Notre Dame, 5-11, 172, Bay St. Louis, Miss.; B—Erny Pinckert, Southern California, 6-0, 189, San Bernardino, Calif.; B—Leonard Macaluso, Colgate, 6-2, 210, East Aurora, N.Y.

1931

E—*Jerry Dalrymple, Tulane, 5-10, 175, Arkadelphia, Ark.; E—Vernon Smith, Georgia, 6-2, 190, Macon, Ga.; T—Jesse Quatse, Pittsburgh, 5-8, 198, Greensburg, Pa.; (tie) T—Jack Riley, Northwestern, 6-2, 218, Wilmette, Ill.; Dallas Marvil, Northwestern, 6-3, 227, Laurel, Del.; G—Biggie Munn, Minnesota, 5-10, 217, Minneapolis, Minn.; G—John Baker, Southern California, 5-10, 185, Kingsburg, Calif.; C—Tommy Yarr, Notre Dame, 5-11, 197, Chimacum, Wash.; B—Gus Shaver, Southern California, 5-11, 185, Covina, Calif.; B—Marchy Schwartz, Notre Dame, 5-11, 178, Bay St. Louis, Miss.; B—Pug Rentner, Northwestern, 6-1, 185, Joliet, Ill.; B—Barry Wood, Harvard, 6-1, 173, Milton, Mass.

1932

E—*Paul Moss, Purdue, 6-2, 185, Terre Haute, Ind.; E—Joe Skladany, Pittsburgh, 5-10, 185, Larksville, Pa.; T—*Joe Kurth, Notre Dame, 6-2, 204, Madison, Wis.; T—*Ernie Smith, Southern California, 6-2, 215, Los Angeles, Calif.; G—Milt Summerfelt, Army, 6-0, 181, Benton Harbor, Mich.; G—Bill Corbus, Stanford, 5-11, 188, Vallejo, Calif.; C—Pete Gracey, Vanderbilt, 6-0, 188, Franklin, Tenn.; B—*Harry Newman, Michigan, 5-7, 175, Detroit, Mich.; B—*Warren Heller, Pittsburgh, 6-0, 170, Steelton, Pa.; B—Don Zimmerman, Tulane, 5-10, 190, Lake Charles, La.; B—Jimmy Hitchcock, Auburn, 5-11, 172, Union Springs, Ala.

1933

E—Joe Skladany, Pittsburgh, 5-10, 190, Larksville, Pa.; E—Paul Geisler, Centenary (La.), 6-2, 189, Berwick, La.; T—Fred Crawford, Duke, 6-2, 195, Waynesville, N.C.; T—Francis Wistert, Michigan, 6-3, 212, Chicago, Ill.; G—Bill Corbus, Stanford, 5-11, 195, Vallejo, Calif.; G—Aaron Rosenberg, Southern California, 6-0, 210, Los Angeles, Calif.; C—*Chuck Bernard, Michigan, 6-2, 215, Benton Harbor, Mich.; B—*Cotton Warburton, Southern California, 5-7, 147, San Diego, Calif.; B—George Sauer, Nebraska, 6-2, 195, Lincoln, Neb.; B—Beattie Feathers, Tennessee, 5-10, 180, Bristol, Va.; B—Duane Purvis, Purdue, 6-1, 190, Mattoon, Ill.

1934

E—Don Hutson, Alabama, 6-1, 185, Pine Bluff, Ark.; E—Frank Larson, Minnesota, 6-3, 190, Duluth, Minn.; T—Bill Lee, Alabama, 6-2, 225, Eutaw, Ala.; T—Bob Reynolds, Stanford, 6-4, 220, Okmulgee, Okla.; G—Chuck Hartwig, Pittsburgh, 6-0, 190, Benwood, W.Va.; G—Bill Bevan, Minnesota, 5-11, 194, St. Paul, Minn.; (tie) C—Jack Robinson, Notre Dame, 6-3, 195, Huntington, N.Y.; Darrell Lester, TCU, 6-4, 218, Jacksboro, Texas; George Shotwell, Pittsburgh; B—Bobby Grayson, Stanford, 5-11, 186, Portland, Ore.; B—Pug Lund, Minnesota, 5-11, 185, Rice Lake, Wis.; B—Dixie Howell, Alabama, 5-10, 164, Hartford, Ala.; B—Fred Borries, Navy, 6-0, 175, Louisville, Ky.

1935

E—Wayne Millner, Notre Dame, 6-0, 184, Salem, Mass.; (tie) E—James Moscrip, Stanford, 6-0, 186, Adena, Ohio; Gaynell Tinsley, LSU, 6-0, 188, Homer, La.; T—Ed Widseth, Minnesota, 6-2, 220, McIntosh, Minn.; T—Larry Lutz, California, 6-0, 201, Santa Ana, Calif.; G—John Weller, Princeton, 6-0, 195, Wynnewood, Pa.; (tie) G—Sidney Wagner, Michigan St., 5-11, 186, Lansing, Mich.; J.C. Wetsel, SMU, 5-10, 185, Dallas, Texas; (tie) C—Gomer Jones, Ohio St., 5-8, 210, Cleveland, Ohio; Darrell Lester, TCU, 6-4, 218, Jacksboro, Texas; B—*Jay Berwanger, Chicago, 6-0, 195, Dubuque, Iowa; B—*Bobby Grayson, Stanford, 5-11, 190, Portland, Ore.; B—Bobby Wilson, SMU, 5-10, 147, Corsicana, Texas; B—Riley Smith, Alabama, 6-1, 195, Columbus, Miss.

1936

E—*Larry Kelley, Yale, 6-1, 190, Williamsport, Pa.; E—*Gaynell Tinsley, LSU, 6-0, 196, Homer, La.; T—*Ed Widseth, Minnesota, 6-2, 220, McIntosh, Minn.; T—Averell Daniell, Pittsburgh, 6-3, 200, Mt. Lebanon, Pa.; G—Steve Reid, Northwestern, 5-9, 192, Chicago, Ill.; G—Max Starcevich, Washington, 5-10, 198, Duluth, Minn.; (tie) C—Alex Wojciechowicz, Fordham, 6-0, 192, South River, N.J.; Mike Basrak, Duquesne, 6-1, 210, Bellaire, Ohio; B—Sammy Baugh, TCU, 6-2, 180, Sweetwater, Texas; B—Ace Parker, Duke, 5-11, 175, Portsmouth, Va.; B—Ray Buivid, Marquette, 6-1, 193, Port Washington, Wis.; B—Sam Francis, Nebraska, 6-1, 207, Oberlin, Kan.

1937

E—Chuck Sweeney, Notre Dame, 6-0, 190, Bloomington, Ill.; E—Andy Bershak, North Carolina, 6-0, 190, Clairton, Pa.; T—Ed Franco, Fordham, 5-8, 196, Jersey City, N.J.; T—Tony Matisi, Pittsburgh, 6-0, 224, Endicott, N.Y.; G—Joe Routt, Texas A&M, 6-0, 193, Chappel Hill, Texas; G—Leroy Monsky, Alabama, 6-0, 198, Montgomery, Ala.; C—Alex Wojciechowicz, Fordham, 6-0, 196, South River, N.J.; B—*Clint Frank, Yale, 5-10, 190, Evanston, Ill.; B—Marshall Goldberg, Pittsburgh, 5-11, 185, Elkins, W.Va.; B—Byron "Whizzer" White, Colorado, 6-1, 185, Wellington, Colo.; B—Sam Chapman, California, 6-0, 190, Tiburon, Calif.

1938

E—Waddy Young, Oklahoma, 6-2, 203, Ponca City, Okla.; (tie) E—Brud Holland, Cornell, 6-1, 205, Auburn, N.Y.; Bowden Wyatt, Tennessee, 6-1, 190, Kingston, Tenn.; T—*Ed Beinor, Notre Dame, 6-2, 207, Harvey, Ill.; T—Alvord Wolff, Santa Clara, 6-2, 220, San Francisco, Calif.; G—*Ralph Heikkinen, Michigan, 5-10, 185, Ramsey, Mich.; G—Ed Bock, Iowa St., 6-0, 202, Fort Dodge, Iowa; C—Ki Aldrich, TCU, 5-11, 195, Temple, Texas; B—*Davey O'Brien, TCU, 5-7, 150, Dallas, Texas; B—*Marshall Goldberg, Pittsburgh, 6-0, 190, Elkins, W.Va.; B—Bob MacLeod, Dartmouth, 6-0, 190, Glen Ellyn, Ill.; B—Vic Bottari, California, 5-9, 182, Vallejo, Calif.

1939

E—Esco Sarkkinen, Ohio St., 6-0, 192, Fairport Harbor, Ohio; E—Ken Kavanaugh, LSU, 6-3, 203, Little Rock, Ark.; T—Nick Drahos, Cornell, 6-3, 200, Cedarhurst, N.Y.; T—Harley McCollum, Tulane, 6-4, 235, Wagoner, Okla.; G—*Harry Smith, Southern California, 5-11, 218, Ontario, Calif.; G—Ed Molinski, Tennessee, 5-10, 190, Massillon, Ohio; C—John Schiechl, Santa Clara, 6-2, 220, San Francisco, Calif.; B—Nile Kinnick, Iowa, 5-8,

167, Omaha, Neb.; B—Tom Harmon, Michigan, 6-0, 195, Gary, Ind.; B—John Kimbrough, Texas A&M, 6-2, 210, Haskell, Texas; B—George Cafego, Tennessee, 6-0, 174, Scarbro, W.Va.

1940

E—Gene Goodreault, Boston College, 5-10, 184, Haverhill, Mass.; E—Dave Rankin, Purdue, 6-1, 190, Warsaw, Ind.; T—Nick Drahos, Cornell, 6-3, 212, Cedarhurst, N.Y.; (tie) T—Alf Bauman, Northwestern, 6-1, 210, Chicago, Ill.; Urban Odson, Minnesota, 6-3, 247, Clark, S.D.; G—*Bob Suffridge, Tennessee, 6-0, 190, Knoxville, Tenn.; G—Marshall Robnett, Texas A&M, 6-1, 205, Klondike, Texas; C—Rudy Mucha, Washington, 6-2, 210, Chicago, Ill.; B—*Tom Harmon, Michigan, 6-0, 195, Gary, Ind.; B—*John Kimbrough, Texas A&M, 6-2, 221, Haskell, Texas; B—Frank Albert, Stanford, 5-9, 170, Glendale, Calif.; B—George Franck, Minnesota, 6-0, 175, Davenport, Iowa.

1941

E—Holt Rast, Alabama, 6-1, 185, Birmingham, Ala.; E—Bob Dove, Notre Dame, 6-2, 195, Youngstown, Ohio; T—Dick Wildung, Minnesota, 6-0, 210, Luverne, Minn.; T—Ernie Blandin, Tulane, 6-3, 245, Keighley, Kan.; G—*Endicott Peabody, Harvard, 6-0, 181, Syracuse, N.Y.; G—Ray Frankowski, Washington, 5-10, 210, Hammond, Ind.; C—Darold Jenkins, Missouri, 6-0, 195, Higginsville, Mo.; B—Bob Westfall, Michigan, 5-8, 190, Ann Arbor, Mich.; B—Bruce Smith, Minnesota, 6-0, 193, Faribault, Minn.; B—Frank Albert, Stanford, 5-9, 173, Glendale, Calif.; (tie) B—Bill Dudley, Virginia, 5-10, 175, Bluefield, Va.; Frank Sinkwich, Georgia, 5-8, 180, Youngstown, Ohio.

1942

E—*Dave Schreiner, Wisconsin, 6-2, 198, Lancaster, Wis.; E—Bob Dove, Notre Dame, 6-2, 195, Youngstown, Ohio; T—Dick Wildung, Minnesota, 6-0, 215, Luverne, Minn.; T—Albert Wistert, Michigan, 6-2, 205, Chicago, Ill.; G—Chuck Taylor, Stanford, 5-11, 200, San Jose, Calif.; (tie) G—Harvey Hardy, Georgia Tech, 5-10, 185, Thomaston, Ga.; Julie Franks, Michigan, 6-0, 187, Hamtramck, Mich.; C—Joe Domnanovich, Alabama, 6-1, 200, South Bend, Ind.; B—*Frank Sinkwich, Georgia, 5-8, 185, Youngstown, Ohio; B—Paul Governali, Columbia, 5-11, 186, New York, N.Y.; B—Mike Holovak, Boston College, 6-2, 214, Lansford, Pa.; B—Billy Hillenbrand, Indiana, 6-0, 195, Evansville, Ind.

1943

E—Ralph Heywood, Southern California, 6-2, 195, Huntington Park, Calif.; E—John Yonakor, Notre Dame, 6-4, 220, Dorchester, Mass.; T—Jim White, Notre Dame, 6-2, 210, Edgewater, N.J.; T—Don Whitmire, Navy, 5-11, 215, Decatur, Ala.; G—Alex Agase, Purdue, 5-10, 190, Evanston, Ill.; G—Pat Filley, Notre Dame, 5-8, 175, South Bend, Ind.; C—*Casimir Myslinski, Army, 5-11, 186, Steubenville, Ohio; B—*Bill Daley, Michigan, 6-2, 206, St. Cloud, Minn.; B—Angelo Bertelli, Notre Dame, 6-1, 173, West Springfield, Mass.; B—Creighton Miller, Notre Dame, 6-0, 185, Wilmington, Del.; B—Bob Odell, Penn, 5-11, 182, Sioux City, Iowa.

1944

E—Phil Tinsley, Georgia Tech, 6-1, 188, Bessemer, Ala.; (tie) E—Paul Walker, Yale, 6-3, 203, Oak Park, Ill.; Jack Dugger, Ohio St., 6-3, 210, Canton, Ohio; T—*Don Whitmire, Navy, 5-11, 215, Decatur, Ala.; T—John Ferraro, Southern California, 6-3, 235, Maywood, Calif.; G—Bill Hackett, Ohio St., 5-9, 191, London, Ohio; G—Ben Chase, Navy, 6-1, 195, San Diego, Calif.; C—John Tavener, Indiana, 6-0, 220, Granville, Ohio; B—*Les Horvath, Ohio St., 5-10, 167, Parma, Ohio; B—Glenn Davis, Army, 5-9, 170, Claremont, Calif.; B—Doc Blanchard, Army, 6-0, 205, Bishopville, S.C.; B—Bob Jenkins, Navy, 6-1, 195, Talladega, Ala.

1945

E—Dick Duden, Navy, 6-2, 203, New York, N.Y.; (tie) E—Hubert Bechtol, Texas, 6-2, 190, Lubbock, Texas; Bob Ravensberg, Indiana, 6-1, 180, Bellevue, Ky.; Max Morris, Northwestern, 6-2, 195, West Frankfort, Ill.; T—Tex Coulter, Army, 6-3, 220, Fort Worth, Texas; T—George Savitsky, Penn, 6-3, 250, Camden, N.J.; G—*Warren Amling, Ohio St., 6-0, 197, Pana, Ill.; G—John Green, Army, 5-11, 190, Shelbyville, Ky.; C—Vaughn Mancha, Alabama, 6-0, 235, Birmingham, Ala.; B—*Glenn Davis, Army, 5-9, 170, Claremont, Calif.; B—*Doc Blanchard, Army, 6-0, 205, Bishopville, S.C.; B—*Herman Wedemeyer, St. Mary's (Cal.), 5-10, 173, Honolulu, Hawaii; B—Bob Fenimore, Oklahoma St., 6-2, 188, Woodward, Okla.

1946

E—*Burr Baldwin, UCLA, 6-1, 196, Bakersfield, Calif.; (tie) E—Hubert Bechtol, Texas, 6-2, 201, Lubbock, Texas; Hank Foldberg, Army, 6-1, 200, Dallas, Texas; T—George Connor, Notre Dame, 6-3, 225, Chicago, Ill.; (tie) T—Warren Amling, Ohio St., 6-0, 197, Pana, Ill.; Dick Huffman, Tennessee, 6-2, 230, Charleston, W.Va.; G—Alex Agase, Illinois, 5-10, 191, Evanston, Ill.; G—Weldon Humble, Rice, 6-1, 214, San Antonio, Texas; C—Paul Duke, Georgia Tech, 6-1, 210, Atlanta, Ga.; B—*John Lujack, Notre Dame, 6-0, 180, Connellsville, Pa.; B—*Charley Trippi, Georgia, 5-11, 185, Pittston, Pa.; B—*Glenn Davis, Army, 5-9, 170, Claremont, Calif.; B—*Doc Blanchard, Army, 6-0, 205, Bishopville, S.C.

1947

E—Paul Cleary, Southern California, 6-1, 195, Santa Ana, Calif.; E—Bill Swiacki, Columbia, 6-2, 198, Southbridge, Mass.; T—Bob Davis, Georgia Tech, 6-4, 220, Columbus, Ga.; T—George Connor, Notre Dame, 6-3, 225, Chicago, Ill.; G—Joe Steffy, Army, 5-11, 190, Chattanooga, Tenn.; G—Bill Fischer, Notre Dame, 6-2, 230, Chicago, Ill.; C—Chuck Bednarik, Penn, 6-3, 220, Bethlehem, Pa.; B—*John Lujack, Notre Dame, 6-0, 180, Connellsville, Pa.; B—*Bob Chappuis, Michigan, 6-0, 180, Toledo, Ohio; B—Doak Walker, SMU, 5-11, 170, Dallas, Texas; (tie) B—Charley Conerly, Mississippi, 6-0, 184, Clarksdale, Miss.; Bobby Layne, Texas, 6-0, 191, Dallas, Texas.

1948

E—Dick Rifenburg, Michigan, 6-3, 197, Saginaw, Mich.; E—Leon Hart, Notre Dame, 6-4, 225, Turtle Creek, Pa.; T—Leo Nomellini, Minnesota, 6-2, 248, Chicago, Ill.; T—Alvin Wistert, Michigan, 6-3, 218, Chicago, Ill.; G—Buddy Burris, Oklahoma, 5-11, 214, Muskogee, Okla.; G—Bill Fischer, Notre Dame, 6-2, 233, Chicago, Ill.; C—Chuck Bednarik, Penn, 6-3, 220, Bethlehem, Pa.; B—*Doak Walker, SMU, 5-11, 168, Dallas, Texas; B—Charlie Justice, North Carolina, 5-10, 165, Asheville, N.C.; B—Jackie Jensen, California, 5-11, 195, Oakland, Calif.; (tie) B—Emil Sitko, Notre Dame, 5-8, 180, Fort Wayne, Ind.; Clyde Scott, Arkansas, 6-0, 175, Smackover, Ark.

1949

E—*Leon Hart, Notre Dame, 6-5, 260, Turtle Creek, Pa.; E—James Williams, Rice, 6-0, 197, Waco, Texas; T—Leo Nomellini, Minnesota, 6-2, 255, Chicago, Ill.; T—Alvin Wistert, Michigan, 6-3, 223, Chicago, Ill.; G—*Rod Franz, California, 6-1, 198, San Francisco, Calif.; G—Ed Bagdon, Michigan St., 5-10, 200, Dearborn, Mich.; C—*Clayton Tonnemaker, Minnesota, 6-3, 240, Minneapolis, Minn.; B—*Emil Sitko, Notre Dame, 5-8, 180, Fort Wayne, Ind.; B—Doak Walker, SMU, 5-11, 170, Dallas, Texas; B—Arnold Galiffa, Army, 6-2, 190, Donora, Pa.; B—Bob Williams, Notre Dame, 6-1, 180, Baltimore, Md.

1950

E—*Dan Foldberg, Army, 6-1, 185, Dallas, Texas; E—Bill McColl, Stanford, 6-4, 225, San Diego, Calif.; T—Bob Gain, Kentucky, 6-3, 230, Weirton, W.Va.; T—Jim Weatherall, Oklahoma, 6-4, 220, White Deer, Texas; G—Bud McFadin, Texas, 6-3, 225, Iraan, Texas; G—Les Richter, California, 6-2, 220, Fresno, Calif.; C—Jerry Groom, Notre Dame, 6-3, 215, Des Moines, Iowa; B—*Vic Janowicz, Ohio St., 5-9, 189, Elyria, Ohio; B—Kyle Rote, SMU, 6-0, 190, San Antonio, Texas; B—Babe Parilli, Kentucky, 6-1, 183, Rochester, Pa.; B—Leon Heath, Oklahoma, 6-1, 195, Hollis, Okla.

1951

E—*Bill McColl, Stanford, 6-4, 225, San Diego, Calif.; E—Bob Carey, Michigan St., 6-5, 215, Charlevoix, Mich.; T—*Don Coleman, Michigan St., 5-10, 185, Flint, Mich.; T—*Jim Weatherall, Oklahoma, 6-4, 230, White Deer, Texas; G—*Bob Ward, Maryland, 5-10, 185, Elizabeth, N.J.; G—Les Richter, California, 6-2, 230, Fresno, Calif.; C—Dick Hightower, SMU, 6-1, 215, Tyler, Texas; B—*Dick Kazmaier, Princeton, 5-11, 171, Maumee, Ohio; B—*Hank Lauricella, Tennessee, 5-10, 169, New Orleans, La.; B—Babe Parilli, Kentucky, 6-1, 188, Rochester, Pa.; B—Johnny Karras, Illinois, 5-11, 171, Argo, Ill.

1952

E—Frank McPhee, Princeton, 6-3, 203, Youngstown, Ohio; E—Bernie Flowers, Purdue, 6-1, 189, Erie, Pa.; T—Dick Modzelewski, Maryland, 6-0, 235, West Natrona, Pa.; T—Hal Miller, Georgia Tech, 6-4, 235, Kingsport, Tenn.; G—John Michels, Tennessee, 5-10, 195, Philadelphia, Pa.; G—Elmer Wilhoite, Southern California, 6-2, 216, Winton, Calif.; C—Donn Moomaw, UCLA, 6-4, 220, Santa Ana, Calif.; B—*Jack Scarbath, Maryland, 6-1, 190, Baltimore, Md.; B—*Johnny Lattner, Notre Dame, 6-1, 190, Chicago, Ill.; B—Billy Vessels, Oklahoma, 6-0, 185, Cleveland, Okla.; B—Jim Sears, Southern California, 5-9, 167, Inglewood, Calif.

1953

E—Don Dohoney, Michigan St., 6-1, 193, Ann Arbor, Mich.; E—Carlton Massey, Texas, 6-4, 210, Rockwall, Texas; T—*Stan Jones, Maryland, 6-0, 235, Lemoyne, Pa.; T—Art Hunter, Notre Dame, 6-2, 226, Akron, Ohio; G—J.D. Roberts, Oklahoma, 5-10, 210, Dallas, Texas; G—Crawford Mims, Mississippi, 5-10, 200, Greenwood, Miss.; C—Larry Morris, Georgia Tech, 6-0, 205, Decatur, Ga.; B—*Johnny Lattner, Notre Dame, 6-1, 190, Chicago, Ill.; B—*Paul Giel, Minnesota, 5-11, 185, Winona, Minn.; B—Paul Cameron, UCLA, 6-0, 185, Burbank, Calif.; B—J.C. Caroline, Illinois, 6-0, 184, Columbia, S.C.

1954

E—Max Boydston, Oklahoma, 6-2, 207, Muskogee, Okla.; E—Ron Beagle, Navy, 6-0, 185, Covington, Ky.; T—Jack Ellena, UCLA, 6-3, 214, Susanville, Calif.; T—Sid Fournet, LSU, 5-11, 225, Baton Rouge, La.; G—*Bud Brooks, Arkansas, 5-11, 200, Wynne, Ark.; G—Calvin Jones, Iowa, 6-0, 200, Steubenville, Ohio; C—Kurt Burris, Oklahoma, 6-1, 209, Muskogee, Okla.; B—*Ralph Guglielmi, Notre Dame, 6-0, 185, Columbus, Ohio; B—*Howard Cassady, Ohio St., 5-10, 177, Columbus, Ohio; B—*Alan Ameche, Wisconsin, 6-0, 215, Kenosha, Wis.; B—Dicky Maegle, Rice, 6-0, 175, Taylor, Texas.

1955

E—*Ron Beagle, Navy, 6-0, 186, Covington, Ky.; E—Ron Kramer, Michigan, 6-3, 218, East Detroit, Mich.; T—Norman Masters, Michigan St., 6-2, 225, Detroit, Mich.; T—Bruce Bosley, West Virginia, 6-2, 225, Green Bank, W.Va.; G—Bo Bolinger, Oklahoma, 5-10, 206, Muskogee, Okla.; (tie) G—Calvin Jones, Iowa, 6-0, 220, Steubenville, Ohio; Hardiman Cureton, UCLA, 6-0, 213, Duarte, Calif.; C—*Bob Pellegrini, Maryland, 6-2, 225, Yatesboro, Pa.; B—*Howard Cassady, Ohio St., 5-10, 172, Columbus, Ohio; B—*Jim Swink, TCU, 6-1, 180, Rusk, Texas; B—Earl Morrall, Michigan St., 6-1, 180, Muskegon, Mich.; B—Paul Hornung, Notre Dame, 6-2, 205, Louisville, Ky.

1956

E—*Joe Walton, Pittsburgh, 5-11, 205, Beaver Falls, Pa.; E—*Ron Kramer, Michigan, 6-3, 220, East Detroit, Mich.; T—John Witte, Oregon St., 6-2, 232, Klamath Falls, Ore.; T—Lou Michaels, Kentucky, 6-2, 229, Swoyersville, Pa.; G—*Jim Parker, Ohio St., 6-2, 251, Toledo, Ohio; G—*Bill Glass, Baylor, 6-4, 220, Corpus Christi, Texas; C—*Jerry Tubbs, Oklahoma, 6-2, 205, Breckenridge, Texas; B—*Jim Brown, Syracuse, 6-2, 212, Manhasset, N.Y.; B—*John Majors, Tennessee, 5-10, 162, Huntland, Tenn.; B—Tommy McDonald, Oklahoma, 5-9, 169, Albuquerque, N.M.; B—John Brodie, Stanford, 6-1, 190, Oakland, Calif.

1957

E—*Jimmy Phillips, Auburn, 6-2, 205, Alexander City, Ala.; E—Dick Wallen, UCLA, 6-0, 185, Alhambra, Calif.; T—Lou Michaels, Kentucky, 6-2, 235, Swoyersville, Pa.; T—Alex Karras, Iowa, 6-2, 233, Gary, Ind.; G—Bill Krisher, Oklahoma, 6-1, 213, Midwest City, Okla.; G—Al Ecuyer, Notre Dame, 5-10, 190, New Orleans, La.; C—Dan Currie, Michigan St., 6-3, 225, Detroit, Mich.; B—*John David Crow, Texas A&M, 6-2, 214, Springhill, La.; B—Walt Kowalczyk, Michigan St., 6-0, 205, Westfield, Mass.; B—Bob Anderson, Army, 6-2, 200, Cocoa, Fla.; B—Clendon Thomas, Oklahoma, 6-2, 188, Oklahoma City, Okla.

1958

E—Buddy Dial, Rice, 6-1, 185, Magnolia, Texas; E—Sam Williams, Michigan St., 6-5, 225, Dansville, Mich.; T—Ted Bates, Oregon St., 6-2, 215, Los Angeles, Calif.; T—Brock Strom, Air Force, 6-0, 217, Ironwood, Mich.; G—John Guzik, Pittsburgh, 6-3, 223, Lawrence, Pa.; (tie) G—Zeke Smith, Auburn, 6-2, 210, Uniontown, Ala.; George Deiderich, Vanderbilt, 6-1, 198, Toronto, Ohio; C—Bob Harrison, Oklahoma, 6-2, 206, Stamford, Texas; B—

*Randy Duncan, Iowa, 6-0, 180, Des Moines, Iowa; B—*Pete Dawkins, Army, 6-1, 197, Royal Oak, Mich.; B—*Billy Cannon, LSU, 6-1, 200, Baton Rouge, La.; B—Bob White, Ohio St., 6-2, 212, Covington, Ky.

1959

E—Bill Carpenter, Army, 6-2, 210, Springfield, Pa.; E—Monty Stickles, Notre Dame, 6-4, 225, Poughkeepsie, N.Y.; T—*Dan Lanphear, Wisconsin, 6-2, 214, Madison, Wis.; T—Don Floyd, TCU, 6-3, 215, Midlothian, Texas; G—*Roger Davis, Syracuse, 6-2, 228, Solon, Ohio; G—Bill Burrell, Illinois, 6-0, 210, Chebanse, Ill.; C—Maxie Baughan, Georgia Tech, 6-1, 212, Bessemer, Ala.; B—Richie Lucas, Penn St., 6-1, 185, Glassport, Pa.; B—Billy Cannon, LSU, 6-1, 208, Baton Rouge, La.; B—Charlie Flowers, Mississippi, 6-0, 198, Marianna, Ark.; B—Ron Burton, Northwestern, 5-9, 185, Springfield, Ohio.

1960

E—*Mike Ditka, Pittsburgh, 6-3, 215, Aliquippa, Pa.; E—*Danny LaRose, Missouri, 6-4, 220, Crystal City, Mo.; T—*Bob Lilly, TCU, 6-5, 250, Throckmorton, Texas; T—Ken Rice, Auburn, 6-3, 250, Bainbridge, Ga.; G—*Tom Brown, Minnesota, 6-0, 225, Minneapolis, Minn.; G—Joe Romig, Colorado, 5-10, 197, Lakewood, Colo.; C—E.J. Holub, Texas Tech, 6-4, 215, Lubbock, Texas; B—*Jake Gibbs, Mississippi, 6-0, 185, Grenada, Miss.; B—*Joe Bellino, Navy, 5-9, 181, Winchester, Mass.; B—*Bob Ferguson, Ohio St., 6-0, 217, Troy, Ohio; B—Ernie Davis, Syracuse, 6-2, 205, Elmira, N.Y.

1961

E—Gary Collins, Maryland, 6-3, 205, Williamstown, Pa.; E—Bill Miller, Miami (Fla.), 6-0, 188, McKeesport, Pa.; T—*Billy Neighbors, Alabama, 5-11, 229, Tuscaloosa, Ala.; T—Merlin Olsen, Utah St., 6-5, 265, Logan, Utah; G—*Roy Winston, LSU, 6-1, 225, Baton Rouge, La.; G—Joe Romig, Colorado, 5-10, 199, Lakewood, Colo.; C—Alex Kroll, Rutgers, 6-2, 228, Leechburg, Pa.; B—*Ernie Davis, Syracuse, 6-2, 210, Elmira, N.Y.; B—*Bob Ferguson, Ohio St., 6-0, 217, Troy, Ohio; B—*Jimmy Saxton, Texas, 5-11, 160, Palestine, Texas; B—Sandy Stephens, Minnesota, 6-0, 215, Uniontown, Pa.

1962

E—Hal Bedsole, Southern California, 6-5, 225, Northridge, Calif.; E—Pat Richter, Wisconsin, 6-5, 229, Madison, Wis.; T—*Bobby Bell, Minnesota, 6-4, 214, Shelby, N.C.; T—Jim Dunaway, Mississippi, 6-4, 260, Columbia, Miss.; G—*Johnny Treadwell, Texas, 6-1, 194, Austin, Texas; G—Jack Cvercko, Northwestern, 6-0, 230, Campbell, Ohio; C—*Lee Roy Jordan, Alabama, 6-2, 207, Monroeville, Ala.; B—*Terry Baker, Oregon St., 6-3, 191, Portland, Ore.; B—*Jerry Stovall, LSU, 6-2, 195, West Monroe, La.; B—Mel Renfro, Oregon, 5-11, 190, Portland, Ore.; B—George Saimes, Michigan St., 5-10, 186, Canton, Ohio.

1963

E—Vern Burke, Oregon St., 6-4, 195, Bakersfield, Calif.; E—Lawrence Elkins, Baylor, 6-1, 187, Brownwood, Texas; T—*Scott Appleton, Texas, 6-3, 235, Brady, Texas; T—Carl Eller, Minnesota, 6-6, 241, Winston-Salem, N.C.; G—*Bob Brown, Nebraska, 6-5, 259, Cleveland, Ohio; G—Rick Redman, Washington, 5-11, 210, Seattle, Wash.; C—*Dick Butkus, Illinois, 6-3, 234, Chicago, Ill.; B—*Roger Staubach, Navy, 6-2, 190, Cincinnati, Ohio; B—Sherman Lewis, Michigan St., 5-8, 154, Louisville, Ky.; B—Jim Grisham, Oklahoma, 6-2, 205, Olney, Texas; (tie) B—Gale Sayers, Kansas, 6-0, 196, Omaha, Neb.; Paul Martha, Pittsburgh, 6-1, 180, Wilkinsburg, Pa.

1964

E—Jack Snow, Notre Dame, 6-2, 210, Long Beach, Calif.; E—Fred Biletnikoff, Florida St., 6-1, 186, Erie, Pa.; T—*Larry Kramer, Nebraska, 6-2, 240, Austin, Minn.; T—Ralph Neely, Oklahoma, 6-5, 243, Farmington, N.M.; G—Rick Redman, Washington, 5-11, 215, Seattle, Wash.; G—Glenn Ressler, Penn St., 6-2, 230, Dornsife, Pa.; C—Dick Butkus, Illinois, 6-3, 237, Chicago, Ill.; B—John Huarte, Notre Dame, 6-0, 180, Anaheim, Calif.; B—Gale Sayers, Kansas, 6-0, 194, Omaha, Neb.; B—Lawrence Elkins, Baylor, 6-1, 187, Brownwood, Texas; B—Tucker Frederickson, Auburn, 6-2, 210, Hollywood, Fla.

Beginning in 1965, offense and defense selected.

1965

Offense E—*Howard Twilley, Tulsa, 5-10, 180, Galena Park, Texas; E—Freeman White, Nebraska, 6-5, 220, Detroit, Mich.; T—Sam Ball, Kentucky, 6-4, 241, Henderson, Ky.; T—Glen Ray Hines, Arkansas, 6-5, 235, El Dorado, Ark.; G—*Dick Arrington, Notre Dame, 5-11, 232, Erie, Pa.; G—Stas Maliszewski, Princeton, 6-1, 215, Davenport, Iowa; C—Paul Crane, Alabama, 6-2, 188, Prichard, Ala.; B—*Mike Garrett, Southern California, 5-9, 185, Los Angeles, Calif.; B—*Jim Grabowski, Illinois, 6-2, 211, Chicago, Ill.; B—Bob Griese, Purdue, 6-1, 185, Evansville, Ind.; B—Donny Anderson, Texas Tech, 6-3, 210, Stinnett, Texas.

Defense E—Aaron Brown, Minnesota, 6-4, 230, Port Arthur, Texas; E—Bubba Smith, Michigan St., 6-7, 268, Beaumont, Texas; T—Walt Barnes, Nebraska, 6-3, 235, Chicago, Ill.; T—Loyd Phillips, Arkansas, 6-3, 221, Longview, Texas; T—Bill Yearby, Michigan, 6-3, 222, Detroit, Mich.; LB—Carl McAdams, Oklahoma, 6-3, 215, White Deer, Texas; LB—Tommy Nobis, Texas, 6-2, 230, San Antonio, Texas; LB—Frank Emanuel, Tennessee, 6-3, 228, Newport News, Va.; B—George Webster, Michigan St., 6-4, 204, Anderson, S.C.; B—Johnny Roland, Missouri, 6-2, 198, Corpus Christi, Texas; B—Nick Rassas, Notre Dame, 6-0, 185, Winnetka, Ill.

1966

Offense E—*Jack Clancy, Michigan, 6-1, 192, Detroit, Mich.; E—Ray Perkins, Alabama, 6-0, 184, Petal, Miss.; T—*Cecil Dowdy, Alabama, 6-0, 206, Cherokee, Ala.; T—Ron Yary, Southern California, 6-6, 265, Bellflower, Calif.; G—Tom Regner, Notre Dame, 6-1, 245, Kenosha, Wis.; G—LaVerne Allers, Nebraska, 6-0, 209, Davenport, Iowa; C—Jim Breland, Georgia Tech, 6-2, 223, Blacksburg, Va.; B—*Steve Spurrier, Florida, 6-2, 203, Johnson City, Tenn.; B—*Nick Eddy, Notre Dame, 6-0, 195, Lafayette, Calif.; B—Mel Farr, UCLA, 6-2, 208, Beaumont, Texas; B—Clint Jones, Michigan St., 6-0, 206, Cleveland, Ohio.

Defense E—*Bubba Smith, Michigan St., 6-7, 283, Beaumont, Texas; E—Alan Page, Notre Dame, 6-5, 238, Canton, Ohio; T—*Loyd Phillips, Arkansas, 6-3, 230, Longview, Texas; T—Tom Greenlee, Washington, 6-0, 195, Seattle, Wash.; MG—Wayne Meylan, Nebraska, 6-0, 239, Bay City, Mich.; MG—John LaGrone, SMU, 5-10, 232, Borger, Texas; LB—*Jim Lynch, Notre Dame, 6-1, 225, Lima, Ohio; LB—Paul Naumoff, Tennessee, 6-1, 209, Columbus, Ohio; B—*George Webster, Michigan St., 6-4, 218, Anderson, S.C.; B—Tom Beier, Miami (Fla.), 5-11, 197, Fremont, Ohio; B—Nate Shaw, Southern California, 6-2, 205, San Diego, Calif.

1967

Offense E—Dennis Homan, Alabama, 6-0, 182, Muscle Shoals, Ala.; E—Ron Sellers, Florida St., 6-4, 187, Jacksonville, Fla.; T—*Ron Yary, Southern California, 6-6, 245, Bellflower, Calif.; T—Ed Chandler, Georgia, 6-2, 222, Cedartown, Ga.; G—Harry Olszewski, Clemson, 5-11, 237, Baltimore, Md.; G—Rich Stotter, Houston, 5-11, 225, Shaker Heights, Ohio; C—*Bob Johnson, Tennessee, 6-4, 232, Cleveland, Tenn.; B—Gary Beban, UCLA, 6-0, 191, Redwood City, Calif.; B—*Leroy Keyes, Purdue, 6-3, 199, Newport News, Va.; B—*O.J. Simpson, Southern California, 6-2, 205, San Francisco, Calif.; B—*Larry Csonka, Syracuse, 6-3, 230, Stow, Ohio.

Defense E—*Ted Hendricks, Miami (Fla.), 6-8, 222, Miami Springs, Fla.; E—Tim Rossovich, Southern California, 6-5, 235, Mountain View, Calif.; T—Dennis Byrd, North Carolina St., 6-4, 250, Lincolnton, N.C.; MG—*Granville Liggins, Oklahoma, 5-11, 216, Tulsa, Okla.; MG—Wayne Meylan, Nebraska, 6-0, 231, Bay City, Mich.; LB—Adrian Young, Southern California, 6-1, 210, La Puente, Calif.; LB—Don Manning, UCLA, 6-2, 204, Culver City, Calif.; B—Tom Schoen, Notre Dame, 5-11, 178, Euclid, Ohio; B—Frank Loria, Virginia Tech, 5-9, 174, Clarksburg, W.Va.; B—Bobby Johns, Alabama, 6-1, 180, Birmingham, Ala.; B—Dick Anderson, Colorado, 6-2, 204, Boulder, Colo.

1968

Offense E—*Ted Kwalick, Penn St., 6-4, 230, McKees Rocks, Pa.; E—Jerry LeVias, SMU, 5-10, 170, Beaumont, Texas; T—*Dave Foley, Ohio St., 6-5, 246, Cincinnati, Ohio; T—George Kunz, Notre Dame, 6-5, 240, Arcadia, Calif.; G—*Charles Rosenfelder, Tennessee, 6-1, 220, Humboldt, Tenn.; (tie) G—Jim Barnes, Arkansas, 6-4, 227, Pine Bluff, Ark.; Mike Montler, Colorado, 6-4, 235, Columbus, Ohio; C—*John Didion, Oregon St., 6-4, 242, Woodland, Calif.; B—*O.J. Simpson, Southern California, 6-2, 205, San Francisco, Calif.; B—*Leroy Keyes, Purdue, 6-3, 205, Newport News, Va.; B—Terry Hanratty, Notre Dame, 6-1, 200, Butler, Pa.; B—Chris Gilbert, Texas, 5-11, 176, Spring, Texas.

Defense E—*Ted Hendricks, Miami (Fla.), 6-8, 222, Miami Springs, Fla.; E—John Zook, Kansas, 6-4, 230, Larned, Kan.; T—Bill Stanfill, Georgia, 6-5, 245, Cairo, Ga.; T—Joe Greene, North Texas, 6-4, 274, Temple, Texas; MG—Ed White, California, 6-3, 245, Palm Desert, Calif.; MG—Chuck Kyle, Purdue, 6-1, 225, Fort Thomas, Ky.; LB—Steve Kiner, Tennessee, 6-1, 205, Tampa, Fla.; LB—Dennis Onkotz, Penn St., 6-2, 205, Northampton, Pa.; B—Jake Scott, Georgia, 6-1, 188, Arlington, Va.; B—Roger Wehrli, Missouri, 6-0, 184, King City, Mo.; B—Al Worley, Washington, 6-0, 175, Wenatchee, Wash.

1969

Offense E—Jim Mandich, Michigan, 6-3, 222, Solon, Ohio; (tie) E—Walker Gillette, Richmond, 6-5, 200, Capron, Va.; Carlos Alvarez, Florida, 5-11, 180, Miami, Fla.; T—Bob McKay, Texas, 6-6, 245, Crane, Texas; T—John Ward, Oklahoma St., 6-5, 248, Tulsa, Okla.; G—Chip Kell, Tennessee, 6-0, 255, Decatur, Ga.; G—Bill Bridges, Houston, 6-2, 230, Carrollton, Texas; C—Rodney Brand, Arkansas, 6-2, 218, Newport, Ark.; B—*Mike Phipps, Purdue, 6-3, 206, Columbus, Ind.; B—*Steve Owens, Oklahoma, 6-2, 215, Miami, Okla.; B—Jim Otis, Ohio St., 6-0, 214, Celina, Ohio; B—Bob Anderson, Colorado, 6-0, 208, Boulder, Colo.

Defense E—Jim Gunn, Southern California, 6-1, 210, San Diego, Calif.; E—Phil Olsen, Utah St., 6-5, 255, Logan, Utah; T—*Mike Reid, Penn St., 6-3, 240, Altoona, Pa.; T—*Mike McCoy, Notre Dame, 6-5, 274, Erie, Pa.; MG—Jim Stillwagon, Ohio St., 6-0, 216, Mount Vernon, Ohio; LB—*Steve Kiner, Tennessee, 6-1, 215, Tampa, Fla.; LB—Dennis Onkotz, Penn St., 6-2, 212, Northampton, Pa.; LB—Mike Ballou, UCLA, 6-3, 230, Los Angeles, Calif.; B—Jack Tatum, Ohio St., 6-0, 204, Passaic, N.J.; B—Buddy McClinton, Auburn, 5-11, 190, Montgomery, Ala.; B—Tom Curtis, Michigan, 6-1, 190, Aurora, Ohio.

1970

Offense E—Tom Gatewood, Notre Dame, 6-2, 208, Baltimore, Md.; E—Ernie Jennings, Air Force, 6-0, 172, Kansas City, Mo.; E—Elmo Wright, Houston, 6-0, 195, Brazoria, Texas; T—Dan Dierdorf, Michigan, 6-4, 250, Canton, Ohio; (tie) T—Bobby Wuensch, Texas, 6-3, 230, Houston, Texas; Bob Newton, Nebraska, 6-4, 248, LaMirada, Calif.; G—*Chip Kell, Tennessee, 6-0, 240, Decatur, Ga.; G—Larry DiNardo, Notre Dame, 6-1, 235, New York, N.Y.; C—Don Popplewell, Colorado, 6-2, 240, Raytown, Mo.; QB—Jim Plunkett, Stanford, 6-3, 204, San Jose, Calif.; RB—Steve Worster, Texas, 6-0, 210, Bridge City, Texas; RB—Don McCauley, North Carolina, 6-0, 211, Garden City, N.Y.

Defense E—Bill Atessis, Texas, 6-3, 255, Houston, Texas; E—Charlie Weaver, Southern California, 6-2, 214, Richmond, Calif.; T—Rock Perdoni, Georgia Tech, 5-11, 236, Wellesley, Mass.; T—Dick Bumpas, Arkansas, 6-1, 225, Fort Smith, Ark.; MG—*Jim Stillwagon, Ohio St., 6-0, 220, Mount Vernon, Ohio; LB—Jack Ham, Penn St., 6-3, 212, Johnstown, Pa.; LB—Mike Anderson, LSU, 6-3, 225, Baton Rouge, La.; B—*Jack Tatum, Ohio St., 6-0, 208, Passaic, N.J.; B—Larry Willingham, Auburn, 6-1, 185, Birmingham, Ala.; B—Dave Elmendorf, Texas A&M, 6-1, 190, Houston, Texas; B—Tommy Casanova, LSU, 6-1, 191, Crowley, La.

1971

Offense E—*Terry Beasley, Auburn, 5-11, 184, Montgomery, Ala.; E—Johnny Rodgers, Nebraska, 5-10, 171, Omaha, Neb.; T—*Jerry Sisemore, Texas, 6-4, 255, Plainview, Texas; T—Dave Joyner, Penn St., 6-0, 235, State College, Pa.; G—*Royce Smith, Georgia, 6-3, 240, Savannah, Ga.; G—Reggie McKenzie, Michigan, 6-4, 232, Highland Park, Mich.; C—Tom Brahaney, Oklahoma, 6-2, 231, Midland, Texas; QB—*Pat Sullivan, Auburn, 6-0, 191, Birmingham, Ala.; RB—*Ed Marinaro, Cornell, 6-3, 210, New Milford, N.J.; RB—*Greg Pruitt, Oklahoma, 5-9, 176, Houston, Texas; RB—Johnny Musso, Alabama, 5-11, 194, Birmingham, Ala.

Defense E—*Walt Patulski, Notre Dame, 6-5, 235, Liverpool, N.Y.; E—Willie Harper, Nebraska, 6-3, 207, Toledo, Ohio; T—Larry Jacobson, Nebraska, 6-6, 250, Sioux Falls, S.D.; T—Mel Long, Toledo, 6-1, 230, Toledo, Ohio; T—Sherman White, California, 6-5, 250, Portsmouth, N.H.; LB—*Mike Taylor, Michigan, 6-2, 224, Detroit, Mich.; LB—Jeff Siemon, Stanford, 6-2, 225, Bakersfield, Calif.; B—*Bobby Majors, Tennessee, 6-1, 197, Sewanee, Tenn.; B—Clarence Ellis, Notre Dame, 6-0, 178, Grand Rapids, Mich.; B—Ernie Jackson, Duke, 5-10, 170, Hopkins, S.C.; B—Tommy Casanova, LSU, 6-2, 195, Crowley, La.

1972

Offense WR—*Johnny Rodgers, Nebraska, 5-9, 173, Omaha, Neb.; TE—*Charles Young, Southern California, 6-4, 228, Fresno, Calif.; T—*Jerry Sisemore, Texas, 6-4, 260, Plainview, Texas; T—Paul Seymour, Michigan, 6-5, 250, Berkley, Mich.; G—*John Hannah, Alabama, 6-3, 282, Albertville, Ala.; G—Ron Rusnak, North Carolina, 6-1, 223, Prince George, Va.; C—Tom Brahaney, Oklahoma, 6-2, 227, Midland, Texas; QB—Bert Jones, LSU, 6-3, 205, Ruston, La.; RB—*Greg Pruitt, Oklahoma, 5-9, 177, Houston, Texas; RB—Otis Armstrong, Purdue, 5-11, 197, Chicago, Ill.; RB—Woody Green, Arizona St., 6-1, 190, Portland, Ore.

Defense E—Willie Harper, Nebraska, 6-2, 207, Toledo, Ohio; E—Bruce Bannon, Penn St., 6-3, 224, Rockaway, N.J.; T—*Greg Marx, Notre Dame, 6-5, 265, Redford, Mich.; T—Dave Butz, Purdue, 6-7, 279, Park Ridge, Ill.; MG—*Rich Glover, Nebraska, 6-1, 234, Jersey City, N.J.; LB—Randy Gradishar, Ohio St., 6-3, 232, Champion, Ohio; LB—John Skorupan, Penn St., 6-2, 208, Beaver, Pa.; B—*Brad VanPelt, Michigan St., 6-5, 221, Owosso, Mich.; B—Cullen Bryant, Colorado, 6-2, 215, Colorado Springs, Colo.; B—Robert Popelka, SMU, 6-1, 190, Temple, Texas; B—Randy Logan, Michigan, 6-2, 192, Detroit, Mich.

1973

Offense WR—Lynn Swann, Southern California, 6-0, 180, Foster City, Calif.; TE—Dave Casper, Notre Dame, 6-3, 252, Chilton, Wis.; T—*John Hicks, Ohio St., 6-3, 258, Cleveland, Ohio; T—Booker Brown, Southern California, 6-3, 270, Santa Barbara, Calif.; G—Buddy Brown, Alabama, 6-2, 242, Tallahassee, Fla.; G—Bill Yoest, North Carolina St., 6-0, 235, Pittsburgh, Pa.; C—Bill Wyman, Texas, 6-2, 235, Spring, Texas; QB—Dave Jaynes, Kansas, 6-2, 212, Bonner Springs, Kan.; RB—*John Cappelletti, Penn St., 6-1, 206, Upper Darby, Pa.; RB—Roosevelt Leaks, Texas, 5-11, 209, Brenham, Texas; RB—Woody Green, Arizona St., 6-1, 202, Portland, Ore.; RB—Kermit Johnson, UCLA, 6-0, 185, Los Angeles, Calif.

Defense L—*John Dutton, Nebraska, 6-7, 248, Rapid City, S.D.; L—Dave Gallagher, Michigan, 6-4, 245, Piqua, Ohio; L—*Lucious Selmon, Oklahoma, 5-11, 236, Eufaula, Okla.; L—Tony Cristiani, Miami (Fla.), 5-10, 215, Brandon, Fla.; LB—*Randy Gradishar, Ohio St., 6-3, 236, Champion, Ohio; LB—Rod Shoate, Oklahoma, 6-1, 214, Spiro, Okla.; LB—Richard Wood, Southern California, 6-2, 217, Elizabeth, N.J.; B—Mike Townsend, Notre Dame, 6-3, 183, Hamilton, Ohio; B—Artimus Parker, Southern California, 6-3, 215, Sacramento, Calif.; B—Dave Brown, Michigan, 6-1, 188, Akron, Ohio; B—Randy Rhino, Georgia Tech, 5-10, 179, Charlotte, N.C.

1974

Offense WR—Pete Demmerle, Notre Dame, 6-1, 190, New Canaan, Conn.; TE—Bennie Cunningham, Clemson, 6-5, 252, Seneca, S.C.; T—*Kurt Schumacher, Ohio St., 6-4, 250, Lorain, Ohio; T—Marvin Crenshaw, Nebraska, 6-6, 240, Toledo, Ohio; G—Ken Huff, North Carolina, 6-4, 261, Coronado, Calif.; G—John Roush, Oklahoma, 6-0, 252, Arvada, Colo.; G—Gerry DiNardo, Notre Dame, 6-1, 237, New York, N.Y.; C—Steve Myers, Ohio St., 6-2, 244, Kent, Ohio; QB—Steve Bartkowski, California, 6-4, 215, Santa Clara, Calif.; RB—*Archie Griffin, Ohio St., 5-9, 184, Columbus, Ohio; RB—*Joe Washington, Oklahoma, 5-10, 178, Port Arthur, Texas; RB—*Anthony Davis, Southern California, 5-9, 183, San Fernando, Calif.

Defense L—*Randy White, Maryland, 6-4, 238, Wilmington, Del.; L—Mike Hartenstine, Penn St., 6-4, 233, Bethlehem, Pa.; L—Pat Donovan, Stanford, 6-5, 240, Helena, Mont.; L—Jimmy Webb, Mississippi St., 6-5, 245, Florence, Miss.; L—Leroy Cook, Alabama, 6-4, 205, Abbeville, Ala.; MG—Louie Kelcher, SMU, 6-5, 275, Beaumont, Texas; MG—Rubin Carter, Miami (Fla.), 6-3, 260, Fort Lauderdale, Fla.; LB—*Rod Shoate, Oklahoma, 6-1, 213, Spiro, Okla.; LB—Richard Wood, Southern California, 6-2, 213, Elizabeth, N.J.; LB—Ken Bernich, Auburn, 6-2, 240, Gretna, La.; LB—Woodrow Lowe, Alabama, 6-0, 211, Phenix City, Ala.; B—*Dave Brown, Michigan, 6-1, 188, Akron, Ohio; B—Pat Thomas, Texas A&M, 5-9, 180, Plano, Texas; B—John Provost, Holy Cross, 5-10, 180, Quincy, Mass.

1975

Offense E—Steve Rivera, California, 6-0, 185, Wilmington, Calif.; E—Larry Seivers, Tennessee, 6-4, 198, Clinton, Tenn.; T—Bob Simmons, Texas, 6-5, 245, Temple, Texas; T—Dennis Lick, Wisconsin, 6-3, 262, Chicago, Ill.; G—Randy Johnson, Georgia, 6-2, 250, Rome, Ga.; G—Ted Smith, Ohio St., 6-1, 242, Gibsonburg, Ohio; C—*Rik Bonness, Nebraska, 6-4, 223, Bellevue, Neb.; QB—John Sciarra, UCLA, 5-10, 178, Alhambra, Calif.; RB—*Archie Griffin, Ohio St., 5-9, 182, Columbus, Ohio; RB—*Ricky Bell, Southern California, 6-2, 215, Los Angeles, Calif.; RB—Chuck Muncie, California, 6-3, 220, Uniontown, Pa.

Defense E—*Leroy Cook, Alabama, 6-4, 205, Abbeville, Ala.; E—Jimbo Elrod, Oklahoma, 6-0, 210, Tulsa, Okla.; T—*Lee Roy Selmon, Oklahoma, 6-2, 256, Eufaula, Okla.; T—*Steve Niehaus, Notre Dame, 6-5, 260, Cincinnati, Ohio; MG—Dewey Selmon, Oklahoma, 6-1, 257, Eufaula, Okla.; LB—*Ed Simonini, Texas A&M, 6-0, 215, Las Vegas, Nev.; LB—Greg Buttle, Penn St., 6-3, 220, Linwood, N.J.; LB—Sammy Green, Florida, 6-2, 228, Fort Meade, Fla.; B—*Chet Moeller, Navy, 6-0, 189, Kettering, Ohio; B—Tim Fox, Ohio St., 6-0, 186, Canton, Ohio; B—Pat Thomas, Texas A&M, 5-10, 180, Plano, Texas.

1976

Offense SE—Larry Seivers, Tennessee, 6-4, 200, Clinton, Tenn.; TE—Ken MacAfee, Notre Dame, 6-4, 251, Brockton, Mass.; T—Mike Vaughan, Oklahoma, 6-5, 275, Ada, Okla.; T—Chris Ward, Ohio St., 6-4, 274, Dayton, Ohio; G—Joel Parrish, Georgia, 6-3, 232, Douglas, Ga.; G—Mark Donahue, Michigan, 6-3, 245, Oak Lawn, Ill.; C—Derrel Gofourth, Oklahoma St., 6-2, 250, Parsons, Kan.; QB—Tommy Kramer, Rice, 6-2, 190, San Antonio, Texas; RB—*Tony Dorsett, Pittsburgh, 5-11, 192, Aliquippa, Pa.; RB—*Ricky Bell, Southern California, 6-2, 218, Los Angeles, Calif.; RB—Rob Lytle, Michigan, 6-1, 195, Fremont, Ohio; PK—Tony Franklin, Texas A&M, 5-10, 170, Fort Worth, Texas.

Defense E—*Ross Browner, Notre Dame, 6-3, 248, Warren, Ohio; E—Bob Brudzinski, Ohio St., 6-4, 228, Fremont, Ohio; T—Wilson Whitley, Houston, 6-3, 268, Brenham, Texas; T—Gary Jeter, Southern California, 6-5, 255, Cleveland, Ohio; T—Joe Campbell, Maryland, 6-6, 255, Wilmington, Del.; MG—Al Romano, Pittsburgh, 6-3, 230, Solvay, N.Y.; LB—*Robert Jackson, Texas A&M, 6-2, 228, Houston, Texas; LB—Jerry Robinson, UCLA, 6-3, 208, Santa Rosa, Calif.; B—*Bill Armstrong, Wake Forest, 6-4, 205, Randolph, N.J.; B—Gary Green, Baylor, 5-11, 182, San Antonio, Texas; B—Dennis Thurman, Southern California, 5-11, 170, Santa Monica, Calif.; B—Dave Butterfield, Nebraska, 5-10, 182, Kersey, Colo.

1977

Offense WR—John Jefferson, Arizona St., 6-1, 184, Dallas, Texas; WR—Ozzie Newsome, Alabama, 6-4, 210, Leighton, Ala.; TE—*Ken MacAfee, Notre Dame, 6-4, 250, Brockton, Mass.; T—*Chris Ward, Ohio St., 6-4, 272, Dayton, Ohio; T—Dan Irons, Texas Tech, 6-7, 260, Lubbock, Texas; G—*Mark Donahue, Michigan, 6-3, 245, Oak Lawn, Ill.; G—Leotis Harris, Arkansas, 6-1, 254, Little Rock, Ark.; C—Tom Brzoza, Pittsburgh, 6-3, 240, New Castle, Pa.; QB—Guy Benjamin, Stanford, 6-4, 202, Sepulveda, Calif.; RB—*Earl Campbell, Texas, 6-1, 220, Tyler, Texas; RB—*Terry Miller, Oklahoma St., 6-0, 196, Colorado Springs, Colo.; RB—Charles Alexander, LSU, 6-1, 215, Galveston, Texas; K—Steve Little, Arkansas, 6-0, 179, Overland Park, Kan.

Defense L—*Ross Browner, Notre Dame, 6-3, 247, Warren, Ohio; L—*Art Still, Kentucky, 6-8, 247, Camden, N.J.; L—*Brad Shearer, Texas, 6-4, 255, Austin, Texas; L—Randy Holloway, Pittsburgh, 6-6, 228, Sharon, Pa.; L—Dee Hardison, North Carolina, 6-4, 252, Newton Grove, N.C.; LB—*Jerry Robinson, UCLA, 6-3, 208, Santa Rosa, Calif.; LB—Tom Cousineau, Ohio St., 6-3, 228, Fairview Park, Ohio; LB—Gary Spani, Kansas St., 6-2, 222, Manhattan, Kan.; B—*Dennis Thurman, Southern California, 5-11, 173, Santa Monica, Calif.; B—*Zac Henderson, Oklahoma, 6-1, 184, Burkburnett, Texas; B—Luther Bradley, Notre Dame, 6-2, 204, Muncie, Ind.; B—Bob Jury, Pittsburgh, 6-0, 190, Library, Pa.

1978

Offense WR—Emanuel Tolbert, SMU, 5-10, 180, Little Rock, Ark.; TE—Kellen Winslow, Missouri, 6-6, 235, East St. Louis, Ill.; T—*Keith Dorney, Penn St., 6-5, 257, Allentown, Pa.; T—Kelvin Clark, Nebraska, 6-4, 275, Odessa, Texas; G—*Pat Howell, Southern California, 6-6, 255, Fresno, Calif.; G—*Greg Roberts, Oklahoma, 6-3, 238, Nacogdoches, Texas; C—Dave Huffman, Notre Dame, 6-5, 245, Dallas, Texas; C—Jim Ritcher, North Carolina St., 6-3, 242, Hinckley, Ohio; QB—*Chuck Fusina, Penn St., 6-1, 195, McKees Rocks, Pa.; RB—*Billy Sims, Oklahoma, 6-0, 205, Hooks, Texas; RB—*Charles White, Southern California, 5-11, 183, San Fernando, Calif.; RB—Ted Brown, North Carolina St., 5-10, 195, High Point, N.C.; RB—Charles Alexander, LSU, 6-1, 214, Galveston, Texas.

Defense L—*Al Harris, Arizona St., 6-5, 240, Wheeler AFB, Hawaii; L—*Bruce Clark, Penn St., 6-3, 246, New Castle, Pa.; L—Hugh Green, Pittsburgh, 6-2, 215, Natchez, Miss.; L—Mike Bell, Colorado St., 6-5, 265, Wichita, Kan.; L—Marty Lyons, Alabama, 6-6, 250, St. Petersburg, Fla.; LB—*Bob Golic, Notre Dame, 6-3, 244, Willowick, Ohio; LB—*Jerry Robinson, UCLA, 6-3, 209, Santa Rosa, Calif.; LB—Tom Cousineau, Ohio St., 6-3, 227, Fairview Park, Ohio; B—*Johnnie Johnson, Texas, 6-2, 183, LaGrange, Texas; B—Kenny Easley, UCLA, 6-2, 202, Chesapeake, Va.; B—Jeff Nixon, Richmond, 6-4, 195, Glendale, Ariz.

1979

Offense WR—Ken Margerum, Stanford, 6-1, 175, Fountain Valley, Calif.; TE—*Junior Miller, Nebraska, 6-4, 222, Midland, Texas; T—*Greg Kolenda, Arkansas, 6-1, 258, Kansas City, Kan.; T—Jim Bunch, Alabama, 6-2, 240, Mechanicsville, Va.; G—*Brad Budde, Southern California, 6-5, 253, Kansas City, Mo.; G—Ken Fritz, Ohio St., 6-3, 238, Ironton, Ohio; C—*Jim Ritcher, North Carolina St., 6-3, 245, Hinckley, Ohio; QB—*Marc Wilson, Brigham Young, 6-5, 204, Seattle, Wash.; RB—*Charles White, Southern California, 6-0, 185, San Fernando, Calif.; RB—*Billy Sims, Oklahoma, 6-0, 205, Hooks, Texas; RB—Vagas Ferguson, Notre Dame, 6-1, 194, Richmond, Ind.; PK—Dale Castro, Maryland, 6-1, 170, Shady Side, Md.

Defense L—*Hugh Green, Pittsburgh, 6-2, 220, Natchez, Miss.; L—*Steve McMichael, Texas, 6-2, 250, Freer, Texas; L—Bruce Clark, Penn St., 6-3, 255, New Castle, Pa.; L—Jim Stuckey, Clemson, 6-5, 241, Cayce, S.C.; MG—Ron Simmons, Florida St., 6-1, 235, Warner Robins, Ga.; LB—*George Cumby, Oklahoma, 6-0, 205, Tyler, Texas; LB—Ron Simpkins, Michigan, 6-2, 220, Detroit, Mich.; LB—Mike Singletary, Baylor, 6-1, 224, Houston, Texas; B—*Kenny Easley, UCLA, 6-3, 204, Chesapeake, Va.; B—*Johnnie Johnson, Texas, 6-2, 190, LaGrange, Texas; B—Roland James, Tennessee, 6-2, 182, Jamestown, Ohio; P—Jim Miller, Mississippi, 5-11, 183, Ripley, Miss.

1980

Offense WR—*Ken Margerum, Stanford, 6-1, 175, Fountain Valley, Calif.; TE—*Dave Young, Purdue, 6-6, 242, Akron, Ohio; L—*Mark May, Pittsburgh, 6-6, 282, Oneonta, N.Y.; L—Keith Van Horne, Southern California, 6-7, 265, Fullerton, Calif.; L—Nick Eyre, Brigham Young, 6-5, 276, Las Vegas, Nev.; L—Louis Oubre, Oklahoma, 6-4, 262, New Orleans, La.; L—Randy Schleusener, Nebraska, 6-7, 242, Rapid City, S.D.; C—*John Scully, Notre Dame, 6-5, 255, Huntington, N.Y.; QB—*Mark Herrmann, Purdue, 6-4, 187, Carmel, Ind.; RB—*George Rogers, South Carolina, 6-2, 220, Duluth, Ga.; RB—*Herschel Walker, Georgia, 6-2, 220, Wrightsville, Ga.; RB—Jarvis Redwine, Nebraska, 5-11, 204, Inglewood, Calif.

Defense L—*Hugh Green, Pittsburgh, 6-2, 222, Natchez, Miss.; L—*E.J. Junior, Alabama, 6-3, 227, Nashville, Tenn.; L—Kenneth Sims, Texas, 6-6, 265, Groesbeck, Texas; L—Leonard Mitchell, Houston, 6-7, 270, Houston, Texas; MG—Ron Simmons, Florida St., 6-1, 230, Warner Robins, Ga.; LB—*Mike Singletary, Baylor, 6-1, 232, Houston, Texas; LB—*Lawrence Taylor, North Carolina, 6-3, 237, Williamsburg, Va.; LB—David Little, Florida, 6-1, 228, Miami, Fla.; LB—Bob Crable, Notre Dame, 6-3, 222, Cincinnati, Ohio; B—*Kenny Easley, UCLA, 6-3, 206, Chesapeake, Va.; B—*Ronnie Lott, Southern California, 6-2, 200, Rialto, Calif.; B—John Simmons, SMU, 5-11, 188, Little Rock, Ark.

1981

Offense WR—*Anthony Carter, Michigan, 5-11, 161, Riviera Beach, Fla.; TE—*Tim Wrightman, UCLA, 6-3, 237, San Pedro, Calif.; L—*Sean Farrell, Penn St., 6-3, 266, Westhampton Beach, N.Y.; L—Roy Foster, Southern California, 6-4, 265, Overland Park, Kan.; L—Terry Crouch, Oklahoma, 6-1, 275, Dallas, Texas; L—Ed Muransky, Michigan, 6-7, 275, Youngstown, Ohio; L—Terry Tausch, Texas, 6-4, 265, New Braunfels, Texas; L—Kurt Becker, Michigan, 6-6, 260, Aurora, Ill.; C—*Dave Rimington, Nebraska, 6-3, 275, Omaha, Neb.; QB—*Jim McMahon, Brigham Young, 6-0, 185, Roy, Utah; RB—*Marcus Allen, Southern California, 6-2, 202, San Diego, Calif.; RB—*Herschel Walker, Georgia, 6-2, 222, Wrightsville, Ga.

Defense L—*Billy Ray Smith, Arkansas, 6-4, 228, Plano, Texas; L—*Kenneth Sims, Texas, 6-6, 265, Groesbeck, Texas; L—Andre Tippett, Iowa, 6-4, 235, Newark, N.J.; L—Tim Krumrie, Wisconsin, 6-3, 237, Mondovi, Wis.; LB—Bob Crable, Notre Dame, 6-3, 225, Cincinnati, Ohio; LB—Jeff Davis, Clemson, 6-0, 223, Greensboro, N.C.; LB—Sal Sunseri, Pittsburgh, 6-0, 220, Pittsburgh, Pa.; DB—Tommy Wilcox, Alabama, 5-11, 187, Harahan, La.; DB—Mike Richardson, Arizona St., 6-1, 192, Compton, Calif.; DB—Terry Kinard, Clemson, 6-1, 183, Sumter, S.C.; DB—Fred Marion, Miami (Fla.), 6-3, 194, Gainesville, Fla.; P—Reggie Roby, Iowa, 6-3, 215, Waterloo, Iowa.

1982

Offense WR—*Anthony Carter, Michigan, 5-11, 161, Riviera Beach, Fla.; TE—*Gordon Hudson, Brigham Young, 6-4, 224, Salt Lake City, Utah; L—*Don Mosebar, Southern California, 6-7, 270, Visalia, Calif.; L—*Steve Korte, Arkansas, 6-2, 270, Littleton, Colo.; L—Jimbo Covert, Pittsburgh, 6-5, 279, Conway, Pa.; L—Bruce Matthews, Southern California, 6-5, 265, Arcadia, Calif.; C—*Dave Rimington, Nebraska, 6-3, 290, Omaha, Neb.; QB—*John Elway, Stanford, 6-4, 202, Northridge, Calif.; RB—*Herschel Walker, Georgia, 6-2, 222, Wrightsville, Ga.; RB—*Eric Dickerson, SMU, 6-2, 215, Sealy, Texas; RB—Mike Rozier, Nebraska, 5-11, 210, Camden, N.J.; PK—*Chuck Nelson, Washington, 5-11, 178, Everett, Wash.

Defense L—*Billy Ray Smith, Arkansas, 6-3, 228, Plano, Texas; L—Vernon Maxwell, Arizona St., 6-2, 225, Carson, Calif.; L—Mike Pitts, Alabama, 6-5, 255, Baltimore, Md.; L—Wilber Marshall, Florida, 6-1, 230, Titusville, Fla.; L—Gabriel Rivera, Texas Tech, 6-3, 270, San Antonio, Texas; L—Rick Bryan, Oklahoma, 6-4, 260, Coweta, Okla.; MG—George Achica, Southern California, 6-5, 260, San Jose, Calif.; LB—*Darryl Talley, West Virginia, 6-4, 210, East Cleveland, Ohio; LB—Ricky Hunley, Arizona, 6-1, 230, Petersburg, Va.; LB—Marcus Marek, Ohio St., 6-2, 224, Masury, Ohio; DB—*Terry Kinard, Clemson, 6-1, 189, Sumter, S.C.; DB—Mike Richardson, Arizona St., 6-0, 190, Compton, Calif.; DB—Terry Hoage, Georgia, 6-3, 196, Huntsville, Texas; P—*Jim Arnold, Vanderbilt, 6-3, 205, Dalton, Ga.

1983

Offense WR—*Irving Fryar, Nebraska, 6-0, 200, Mount Holly, N.J.; TE—*Gordon Hudson, Brigham Young, 6-4, 231, Salt Lake City, Utah; L—*Bill Fralic, Pittsburgh, 6-5, 270, Penn Hills, Pa.; L—Terry Long, East Carolina, 6-0, 280, Columbia, S.C.; L—Dean Steinkuhler, Nebraska, 6-3, 270, Burr, Neb.; L—Doug Dawson, Texas, 6-3, 263, Houston, Texas; C—Tony Slaton, Southern California, 6-4, 260, Merced, Calif.; QB—*Steve Young, Brigham Young, 6-1, 198, Greenwich, Conn.; RB—*Mike Rozier, Nebraska, 5-11, 210, Camden, N.J.; RB—Bo Jackson, Auburn, 6-1, 222, Bessemer, Ala.; RB—Greg Allen, Florida St., 6-0, 200, Milton, Fla.; RB—Napoleon McCallum, Navy, 6-2, 208, Milford, Ohio; PK—Luis Zendejas, Arizona St., 5-9, 186, Chino, Calif.

Defense L—*Rick Bryan, Oklahoma, 6-4, 260, Coweta, Okla.; L—*Reggie White, Tennessee, 6-5, 264, Chattanooga, Tenn.; L—William Perry, Clemson, 6-3, 320, Aiken, S.C.; L—William Fuller, North Carolina, 6-4, 250, Chesapeake, Va.; LB—*Ricky Hunley, Arizona, 6-2, 230, Petersburg, Va.; LB—Wilber Marshall, Florida, 6-1, 230, Titusville, Fla.; LB—Ron Rivera, California, 6-3, 225, Monterey, Calif.; LB—Jeff Leiding, Texas, 6-4, 240, Tulsa, Okla.; DB—*Russell Carter, SMU, 6-3, 193, Ardmore, Pa.; DB—Jerry Gray, Texas, 6-1, 183, Lubbock, Texas; DB—Terry Hoage, Georgia, 6-3, 196, Huntsville, Texas; DB—Don Rogers, UCLA, 6-2, 208, Sacramento, Calif.; P—Jack Weil, Wyoming, 5-11, 171, Northglenn, Colo.

1984

Offense WR—*David Williams, Illinois, 6-3, 195, Los Angeles, Calif.; WR—Eddie Brown, Miami (Fla.), 6-0, 185, Miami, Fla.; TE—Jay Novacek, Wyoming, 6-4, 211, Gothenburg, Neb.; T—*Bill Fralic, Pittsburgh, 6-5, 285, Penn Hills, Pa.; T—Lomas Brown, Florida, 6-5, 277, Miami, Fla.; G—Del Wilkes, South Carolina, 6-3, 255, Columbia, S.C.; G—Jim Lachey, Ohio St., 6-6, 274, St. Henry, Ohio; G—Bill Mayo, Tennessee, 6-3, 280, Dalton, Ga.; C—*Mark Traynowicz, Nebraska, 6-6, 265, Bellevue, Neb.; QB—*Doug Flutie, Boston College, 5-9, 177, Natick, Mass.; RB—*Keith Byars, Ohio St., 6-2, 233, Dayton, Ohio; RB—*Kenneth Davis, TCU, 5-11, 205, Temple, Texas; RB—Rueben Mayes, Washington St., 6-0, 200, North Battleford, Saskatchewan, Canada; PK—Kevin Butler, Georgia, 6-1, 190, Stone Mountain, Ga.

Defense DL—Bruce Smith, Virginia Tech, 6-4, 275, Norfolk, Va.; DL—Tony Degrate, Texas, 6-4, 280, Snyder, Texas; DL—Ron Holmes, Washington, 6-4, 255, Lacey, Wash.; DL—Tony Casillas, Oklahoma, 6-3, 272, Tulsa, Okla.; LB—Gregg Carr, Auburn, 6-2, 215, Birmingham, Ala.; LB—Jack Del Rio, Southern California, 6-4, 235, Hayward, Calif.; LB—Larry Station, Iowa, 5-11, 233, Omaha, Neb.; DB—*Jerry Gray, Texas, 6-1, 183, Lubbock, Texas; DB—Tony Thurman, Boston College, 6-0, 179, Lynn, Mass.; DB—Jeff Sanchez, Georgia, 6-0, 183, Yorba Linda, Calif.; DB—David Fulcher, Arizona St., 6-3, 220, Los Angeles, Calif.; DB—Rod Brown, Oklahoma St., 6-3, 188, Gainesville, Texas; P—*Ricky Anderson, Vanderbilt, 6-2, 190, St. Petersburg, Fla.

1985

Offense WR—*David Williams, Illinois, 6-3, 195, Los Angeles, Calif.; WR—Tim McGee, Tennessee, 5-10, 181, Cleveland, Ohio; TE—Willie Smith, Miami (Fla.), 6-2, 230, Jacksonville, Fla.; L—*Jim Dombrowski, Virginia, 6-5, 290, Williamsville, N.Y.; L—Jeff Bregel, Southern California, 6-4, 280, Granada Hills, Calif.; L—Brian Jozwiak, West Virginia, 6-6, 290, Catonsville, Md.; L—John Rienstra, Temple, 6-4, 280, Colorado Springs, Colo.; L—J.D. Maarleveld, Maryland, 6-5, 300, Rutherford, N.J.; L—Jamie Dukes, Florida St., 6-0, 272, Orlando, Fla.; C—Pete Anderson, Georgia, 6-3, 264, Glen Ridge, N.J.; QB—*Chuck Long, Iowa, 6-4, 213, Wheaton, Ill.; RB—*Bo Jackson, Auburn, 6-1, 222, Bessemer, Ala.; RB—*Lorenzo White, Michigan St., 5-11, 205, Fort Lauderdale, Fla.; RB—Thurman Thomas, Oklahoma St., 5-11, 186, Missouri City, Texas; RB—Reggie Dupard, SMU, 6-0, 201, New Orleans, La.; RB—Napoleon McCallum, Navy, 6-2, 214, Milford, Ohio; PK—*John Lee, UCLA, 5-11, 187, Downey, Calif.

Defense L—*Tim Green, Syracuse, 6-2, 246, Liverpool, N.Y.; L—*Leslie O'Neal, Oklahoma St., 6-3, 245, Little Rock, Ark.; L—Tony Casillas, Oklahoma, 6-3, 280, Tulsa, Okla.; L—Mike Ruth, Boston College, 6-2, 250, Norristown, Pa.; L—Mike Hammerstein, Michigan, 6-4, 240, Wapakoneta, Ohio; LB—*Brian Bosworth, Oklahoma, 6-2, 234, Irving, Texas; LB—*Larry Station, Iowa, 5-11, 227, Omaha, Neb.; LB—Johnny Holland, Texas A&M, 6-2, 219, Hempstead, Texas; DB—David Fulcher, Arizona St., 6-3, 228, Los Angeles, Calif.; DB—Brad Cochran, Michigan, 6-3, 219, Royal Oak, Mich.; DB—Scott Thomas, Air Force, 6-0, 185, San Antonio, Texas; P—Barry Helton, Colorado, 6-3, 195, Simla, Colo.

1986

Offense WR—Cris Carter, Ohio St., 6-3, 194, Middletown, Ohio; TE—*Keith Jackson, Oklahoma, 6-3, 241, Little Rock, Ark.; L—Jeff Bregel, Southern California, 6-4, 280, Granada Hills, Calif.; L—Randy Dixon, Pittsburgh, 6-4, 286, Clewiston, Fla.; L—Danny Villa, Arizona St., 6-5, 284, Nogales, Ariz.; L—John Clay, Missouri, 6-5, 285, St. Louis, Mo.; C—*Ben Tamburello, Auburn, 6-3, 268, Birmingham, Ala.; QB—*Vinny Testaverde, Miami (Fla.), 6-5, 218, Elmont, N.Y.; RB—*Brent Fullwood, Auburn, 5-11, 209, St. Cloud, Fla.; RB—*Paul Palmer, Temple, 5-10, 180, Potomac, Md.; RB—Terrence Flagler, Clemson, 6-1, 200, Fernandina Beach, Fla.; RB—Brad Muster, Stanford, 6-3, 226, Novato, Calif.; RB—D.J. Dozier, Penn St., 6-1, 204, Virginia Beach, Va.; PK—Jeff Jaeger, Washington, 5-11, 191, Kent, Wash.

Defense L—*Jerome Brown, Miami (Fla.), 6-2, 285, Brooksville, Fla.; L—*Danny Noonan, Nebraska, 6-4, 280, Lincoln, Neb.; L—Tony Woods, Pittsburgh, 6-4, 240, Newark, N.J.; L—Jason Buck, Brigham Young, 6-6, 270, St. Anthony, Idaho; L—Reggie Rogers, Washington, 6-6, 260, Sacramento, Calif.; LB—*Cornelius Bennett, Alabama, 6-4, 235, Birmingham, Ala.; LB—Shane Conlan, Penn St., 6-3, 225, Frewsburg, N.Y.; LB—Brian Bosworth, Oklahoma, 6-2, 240, Irving, Texas; LB—Chris Spielman, Ohio St., 6-2, 227, Massillon, Ohio; DB—*Thomas Everett, Baylor, 5-9, 180, Daingerfield, Texas; DB—Tim McDonald, Southern California, 6-3, 205, Fresno, Calif.; DB—Bennie Blades, Miami (Fla.), 6-0, 207, Fort Lauderdale, Fla.; DB—Rod Woodson, Purdue, 6-0, 195, Fort Wayne, Ind.; DB—Garland Rivers, Michigan, 6-1, 187, Canton, Ohio; P—Barry Helton, Colorado, 6-4, 200, Simla, Colo.

1987

Offense WR—*Tim Brown, Notre Dame, 6-0, 195, Dallas, Texas; WR—Wendell Davis, LSU, 6-0, 186, Shreveport, La.; TE—*Keith Jackson, Oklahoma, 6-3, 248, Little Rock, Ark.; L—*Mark Hutson, Oklahoma, 6-4, 282, Fort Smith, Ark.; L—Dave Cadigan, Southern California, 6-5, 280, Newport Beach, Calif.; L—John Elliott, Michigan, 6-7, 306, Lake Ronkonkoma, N.Y.; L—Randall McDaniel, Arizona St., 6-5, 261, Avondale, Ariz.; C—*Nacho Albergamo, LSU, 6-2, 257, Marrera, La.; QB—*Don McPherson, Syracuse, 6-0, 182, West Hempstead, N.Y.; RB—Lorenzo White, Michigan St., 5-11, 211, Fort Lauderdale, Fla.; RB—Craig Heyward, Pittsburgh, 6-0, 260, Passaic, N.J.; PK—David Treadwell, Clemson, 6-1, 165, Jacksonville, Fla.

Defense L—*Daniel Stubbs, Miami (Fla.), 6-4, 250, Red Bank, N.J.; L—*Chad Hennings, Air Force, 6-5, 260, Elboron, Iowa; L—Tracy Rocker, Auburn, 6-3, 258, Atlanta, Ga.; L—Ted Gregory, Syracuse, 6-1, 260, East Islip, N.Y.; L—John Roper, Texas A&M, 6-2, 215, Houston, Texas; LB—*Chris Spielman, Ohio St., 6-2, 236, Massillon, Ohio; LB—Aundray Bruce, Auburn, 6-6, 236, Montgomery, Ala.; LB—Dante Jones, Oklahoma, 6-2, 235, Dallas, Texas; DB—*Bennie Blades, Miami (Fla.), 6-0, 215, Fort Lauderdale, Fla.; DB—*Deion Sanders, Florida St., 6-0, 192, Fort Myers, Fla.; DB—Rickey Dixon, Oklahoma, 5-10, 184, Dallas, Texas; DB—Chuck Cecil, Arizona, 6-0, 185, Red Bluff, Calif.; P—*Tom Tupa, Ohio St., 6-5, 215, Brecksville, Ohio.

1988

Offense WR—Jason Phillips, Houston, 5-9, 175, Houston, Texas; WR—Hart Lee Dykes, Oklahoma St., 6-4, 220, Bay City, Texas; TE—Marv Cook, Iowa, 6-4, 243, West Branch, Iowa; L—*Tony Mandarich, Michigan St., 6-6, 315, Oakville, Ontario, Canada; L—*Anthony Phillips, Oklahoma, 6-3, 286, Tulsa, Okla.; L—Mike Utley, Washington St., 6-6, 302, Seattle, Wash.; L—Mark Stepnoski, Pittsburgh, 6-3, 265, Erie, Pa.; C—Jake Young, Nebraska, 6-5, 260, Midland, Texas; C—John Vitale, Michigan, 6-1, 273, Detroit, Mich.; QB—Steve Walsh, Miami (Fla.), 6-3, 195, St. Paul, Minn.; QB—Troy Aikman, UCLA, 6-4, 217, Henryetta, Okla.; RB—*Barry Sanders, Oklahoma St., 5-8, 197, Wichita, Kan.; RB—Anthony Thompson, Indiana, 6-0, 205, Terre Haute, Ind.; RB—Tim Worley, Georgia, 6-2, 216, Lumberton, N.C.; PK—Kendall Trainor, Arkansas, 6-2, 205, Fredonia, Kan.

Defense L—*Mark Messner, Michigan, 6-3, 244, Hartland, Mich.; L—*Tracy Rocker, Auburn, 6-3, 278, Atlanta, Ga.; L—Wayne Martin, Arkansas, 6-5, 263, Cherry Valley, Ark.; L—Frank Stams, Notre Dame, 6-4, 237, Akron, Ohio; L—Bill Hawkins, Miami (Fla.), 6-6, 260, Hollywood, Fla.; LB—*Derrick Thomas, Alabama, 6-4, 230, Miami, Fla.; LB—*Broderick Thomas, Nebraska, 6-3, 235, Houston, Texas; LB—Michael Stonebreaker, Notre Dame, 6-1, 228, River Ridge, La.; DB—*Deion Sanders, Florida St., 6-0, 195, Fort Myers, Fla.; DB—Donnell Woolford, Clemson, 5-10, 195, Fayetteville, N.C.; DB—Louis Oliver, Florida, 6-2, 222, Bell Glade, Fla.; DB—Darryl Henley, UCLA, 5-10, 165, Ontario, Calif.; P—Keith English, Colorado, 6-3, 215, Greeley, Colo.

1989

Offense WR—*Clarkston Hines, Duke, 6-1, 170, Chapel Hill, N.C.; WR—Terance Mathis, New Mexico, 5-9, 167, Stone Mountain, Ga.; TE—Mike Busch, Iowa St., 6-5, 252, Donahue, Iowa; L—Jim Mabry, Arkansas, 6-4, 262, Memphis, Tenn.; L—Bob Kula, Michigan St., 6-4, 282, West Bloomfield, Mich.; L—Mohammed Elewonibi, Brigham Young, 6-5, 290, Kamloops, British Columbia, Canada; L—Joe Garten, Colorado, 6-3, 280, Placentia, Calif.; L—*Eric Still, Tennessee, 6-3, 283, Germantown, Tenn.; C—Jake Young, Nebraska, 6-4, 270, Midland, Texas; QB—Andre Ware, Houston, 6-2, 205, Dickinson, Texas; RB—*Anthony Thompson, Indiana, 6-0, 209, Terre Haute, Ind.; RB—*Emmitt Smith, Florida, 5-10, 201, Pensacola, Fla.; PK—*Jason Hanson, Washington St., 6-0, 164, Spokane, Wash.

Defense L—Chris Zorich, Notre Dame, 6-1, 268, Chicago, Ill.; L—Greg Mark, Miami (Fla.), 6-4, 255, Pennsauken, N.J.; L—Tim Ryan, Southern California, 6-5, 260, San Jose, Calif.; L—*Moe Gardner, Illinois, 6-2, 250, Indianapolis, Ind.; LB—*Percy Snow, Michigan St., 6-3, 240, Canton, Ohio; LB—*Keith McCants, Alabama, 6-5, 256, Mobile, Ala.; LB—Alfred Williams, Colorado, 6-6, 230, Houston, Texas; DB—*Todd Lyght, Notre Dame, 6-1, 181, Flint, Mich.; DB—*Mark Carrier, Southern California, 6-1, 185, Long Beach, Calif.; DB—*Tripp Welborne, Michigan, 6-1, 193, Greensboro, N.C.; DB—LeRoy Butler, Florida St., 6-0, 194, Jacksonville, Fla.; P—Tom Rouen, Colorado, 6-3, 220, Littleton, Colo.

1990

Offense WR—*Raghib Ismail, Notre Dame, 5-10, 175, Wilkes-Barre, Pa.; WR—Herman Moore, Virginia, 6-5, 197, Danville, Va.; TE—*Chris Smith, Brigham Young, 6-4, 230, La Canada, Calif.; OL—*Antone Davis, Tennessee, 6-4, 310, Fort Valley, Ga.; OL—*Joe Garten, Colorado, 6-3, 280, Placentia, Calif.; OL—*Ed King, Auburn, 6-4, 284, Phenix City, Ala.; OL—Stacy Long, Clemson, 6-2, 275, Griffin, Ga.; C—John Flannery, Syracuse, 6-4, 301, Pottsville, Pa.; QB—Ty Detmer, Brigham Young, 6-0, 175, San Antonio, Texas; RB—*Eric Bieniemy, Colorado, 5-7, 195, West Covina, Calif.; RB—Darren Lewis, Texas A&M, 6-0, 220, Dallas, Texas; PK—*Philip Doyle, Alabama, 6-1, 190, Birmingham, Ala.

Defense DL—*Russell Maryland, Miami (Fla.), 6-2, 273, Chicago, Ill.; DL—*Chris Zorich, Notre Dame, 6-1, 266, Chicago, Ill.; DL—Moe Gardner, Illinois, 6-2, 258, Indianapolis, Ind.; DL—David Rocker, Auburn, 6-4, 264, Atlanta, Ga.; LB—*Alfred Williams, Colorado, 6-6, 236, Houston, Texas; LB—*Michael Stonebreaker, Notre Dame, 6-1, 228, River Ridge, La.; LB—Maurice Crum, Miami (Fla.), 6-0, 222, Tampa, Fla.; DB—*Tripp Welborne, Michigan, 6-1, 201, Greensboro, N.C.; DB—*Darryll Lewis, Arizona, 5-9, 186, West Covina, Calif.; DB—*Ken Swilling, Georgia Tech, 6-3, 230, Toccoa, Ga.; DB—Todd Lyght, Notre Dame, 6-1, 184, Flint, Mich.; P—Brian Greenfield, Pittsburgh, 6-1, 210, Sherman Oaks, Calif.

1991

Offense WR—*Desmond Howard, Michigan, 5-9, 176, Cleveland, Ohio; WR—Mario Bailey, Washington, 5-9, 167, Seattle, Wash.; TE—Kelly Blackwell, TCU, 6-2, 242, Fort Worth, Texas; OL—*Greg Skrepenak, Michigan, 6-8, 322, Wilkes-Barre, Pa.; OL—Bob Whitfield, Stanford, 6-7, 300, Carson, Calif.; OL—Jeb Flesch, Clemson, 6-3, 266, Morrow, Ga.; (tie) OL—Jerry Ostroski, Tulsa, 6-4, 305, Collegeville, Pa.; Mirko Jurkovic, Notre Dame, 6-4, 289, Calumet City, Ill.; C—*Jay Leeuwenburg, Colorado, 6-3, 265, Kirkwood, Mo.; QB—Ty Detmer, Brigham Young, 6-0, 175, San Antonio, Texas; RB—*Vaughn Dunbar, Indiana, 6-0, 207, Fort Wayne, Ind.; (tie) RB—Trevor Cobb, Rice, 5-9, 180, Houston, Texas; Russell White, California, 6-0, 210, Van Nuys, Calif.; PK—Carlos Huerta, Miami (Fla.), 5-9, 186, Miami, Fla.

Defense DL—*Steve Emtman, Washington, 6-4, 280, Cheney, Wash.; DL—*Santana Dotson, Baylor, 6-5, 264, Houston, Texas; DL—Brad Culpepper, Florida, 6-2, 263, Tallahassee, Fla.; DL—Leroy Smith, Iowa, 6-2, 214, Sicklerville, N.J.; LB—*Robert Jones, East Caro., 6-3, 234, Blackstone, Va.; LB—Marvin Jones, Florida St., 6-2, 220, Miami, Fla.; LB—Levon Kirkland, Clemson, 6-2, 245, Lamar, S.C.; DB—*Terrell Buckley, Florida St., 5-10, 175, Pascagoula, Miss.; DB—Dale Carter, Tennessee, 6-2, 182, Oxford, Ga.; DB—Kevin Smith, Texas A&M, 6-0, 180, Orange, Texas; DB—Darryl Williams, Miami (Fla.), 6-2, 190, Miami, Fla.; P—*Mark Bounds, Texas Tech, 5-11, 185, Stamford, Texas.

1992

Offense WR—O.J. McDuffie, Penn St., 5-11, 185, Warrensville Heights, Ohio; WR—Sean Dawkins, California, 6-4, 205, Sunnyvale, Calif.; TE—*Chris Gedney, Syracuse, 6-5, 256, Liverpool, N.Y.; OL—*Lincoln Kennedy, Washington, 6-7, 325, San Diego, Calif.; OL—*Will Shields, Nebraska, 6-1, 305, Lawton, Okla.; OL—Aaron Taylor, Notre Dame, 6-4, 294, Concord, Calif.; (tie) OL—Willie Roaf, Louisiana Tech, 6-5, 300, Pine Bluff, Ark.; Everett Lindsay, Mississippi, 6-5, 290, Raleigh, N.C.; C—Mike Compton, West Virginia, 6-7, 289, Richlands, Va.; QB—*Gino Torretta, Miami (Fla.), 6-3, 205, Pinole, Calif.; RB—*Marshall Faulk, San Diego St., 5-10, 200, New Orleans, La.; RB—*Garrison Hearst, Georgia, 5-11, 202, Lincolnton, Ga.; PK—Joe Allison, Memphis, 6-0, 184, Atlanta, Ga.

Defense DL—Eric Curry, Alabama, 6-6, 265, Thomasville, Ga.; DL—John Copeland, Alabama, 6-3, 261, Lanett, Ala.; DL—Chris Slade, Virginia, 6-5, 235, Tabb, Va.; DL—Rob Waldrop, Arizona, 6-2, 265, Phoenix, Ariz.; LB—*Marcus Buckley, Texas A&M, 6-4, 230, Fort Worth, Texas; LB—*Marvin Jones, Florida St., 6-2, 235, Miami, Fla.; LB—Micheal Barrow, Miami (Fla.), 6-2, 230, Homestead, Fla.; DB—*Carlton McDonald, Air Force, 6-0, 185, Jacksonville, Fla.; DB—Carlton Gray, UCLA, 6-0, 194, Cincinnati, Ohio; DB—Deon Figures, Colorado, 6-1, 195, Compton, Calif.; DB—Ryan McNeil, Miami (Fla.), 6-2, 185, Fort Pierce, Fla.; P—Sean Snyder, Kansas St., 6-1, 190, Greenville, Texas.

1993

Offense WR—*J.J. Stokes, UCLA, 6-5, 214, San Diego, Calif.; WR—Johnnie Morton, Southern California, 6-0, 190, Torrance, Calif.; OL—Mark Dixon, Virginia, 6-4, 283, Jamestown, N.C.; OL—Stacy Seegars, Clemson, 6-4, 320, Kershaw, S.C.; OL—*Aaron Taylor, Notre Dame, 6-4, 299, Concord, Calif.; OL—Wayne Gandy, Auburn, 6-5, 275, Haines City, Fla.; C—*Jim Pyne, Virginia Tech, 6-2, 280, Milford, Mass.; QB—*Charlie Ward, Florida St., 6-2, 190, Thomasville, Ga.; RB—*Marshall Faulk, San Diego St., 5-10, 200, New Orleans, La.; RB—*LeShon Johnson, Northern Ill., 6-0, 201, Haskell, Okla.; PK—Bjorn Merten, UCLA, 6-0, 203, Centreville, Va.; KR—David Palmer, Alabama, 5-9, 170, Birmingham, Ala.

Defense DL—*Rob Waldrop, Arizona, 6-2, 275, Phoenix, Ariz.; DL—Dan Wilkinson, Ohio St., 6-5, 300, Dayton, Ohio; DL—Sam Adams, Texas A&M, 6-4, 269, Cypress, Texas; LB—*Trev Alberts, Nebraska, 6-4, 240, Cedar Falls, Iowa; LB—*Derrick Brooks, Florida St., 6-1, 225, Pensacola, Fla.; LB—Jamir Miller, UCLA, 6-4, 233, El Cerrito, Calif.; DB—*Antonio Langham, Alabama, 6-1, 170, Town Creek, Ala.; DB—Aaron Glenn, Texas A&M, 5-10, 182, Aldine, Texas; DB—Jeff Burris, Notre Dame, 6-0, 204, Rock Hill, S.C.; DB—Corey Sawyer, Florida St., 5-11, 171, Key West, Fla.; P—Terry Daniel, Auburn, 6-1, 226, Valley, Ala.

1994

Offense WR—Jack Jackson, Florida, 5-9, 171, Moss Point, Miss.; WR—Michael Westbrook, Colorado, 6-4, 210, Detroit, Mich.; TE—Pete Mitchell, Boston College, 6-2, 238, Bloomfield Hills, Mich.; OL—*Zach Wiegert, Nebraska, 6-5, 300, Fremont, Neb.; OL—Tony Boselli, Southern California, 6-8, 305, Boulder, Colo.; OL—Korey Stringer, Ohio St., 6-5, 315, Warren, Ohio; OL—Brenden Stai, Nebraska, 6-4, 300, Yorba Linda, Calif.; C—Cory Raymer, Wisconsin, 6-4, 290, Fond du Lac, Wis.; QB—Kerry Collins, Penn St., 6-5, 235, West Lawn, Pa.; RB—*Rashaan Salaam, Colorado, 6-1, 210, San Diego, Calif.; RB—*Ki-Jana Carter, Penn St., 5-10, 212, Westerville, Ohio; PK—Steve McLaughlin, Arizona, 6-1, 175, Tucson, Ariz.; KR—Leeland McElroy, Texas A&M, 5-11, 200, Beaumont, Texas.

Defense DL—*Warren Sapp, Miami (Fla.), 6-3, 284, Plymouth, Fla.; DL—Tedy Bruschi, Arizona, 6-1, 255, Roseville, Calif.; DL—Luther Elliss, Utah, 6-6, 288, Mancos, Colo.; DL—Kevin Carter, Florida, 6-6, 265, Tallahassee, Fla.; LB—*Dana Howard, Illinois, 6-0, 235, East St. Louis, Ill.; LB—Ed Stewart, Nebraska, 6-1, 215, Chicago, Ill.; LB—Derrick Brooks, Florida St., 6-1, 226, Pensacola, Fla.; DB—Clifton Abraham, Florida St., 5-9, 185, Dallas, Texas; DB—Bobby Taylor, Notre Dame, 6-3, 201, Longview, Texas; DB—Chris Hudson, Colorado, 5-11, 195, Houston, Texas; DB—Brian Robinson, Auburn, 6-3, 194, Fort Lauderdale, Fla.; DB—Tony Bouie, Arizona, 5-10, 183, New Orleans, La.; P—*Todd Sauerbrun, West Virginia, 6-0, 205, Setauket, N.Y.

1995

Offense WR—Terry Glenn, Ohio St., 5-11, 185, Columbus, Ohio; WR—*Keyshawn Johnson, Southern California, 6-4, 210, Los Angeles, Calif.; TE—*Marco Battaglia, Rutgers, 6-3, 240, Queens, N.Y.; OL—*Jonathan Ogden, UCLA, 6-8, 310, Washington, D.C.; OL—*Jason Odom, Florida, 6-5, 291, Bartow, Fla.; OL—*Orlando Pace, Ohio St., 6-6, 320, Sandusky, Ohio; OL—Jeff Hartings, Penn St., 6-3, 278, St. Henry, Ohio; (tie) C—Clay Shiver, Florida St., 6-2, 285, Tifton, Ga.; Bryan Stoltenberg, Colorado, 6-2, 280, Sugarland, Texas; QB—Tommie Frazier, Nebraska, 6-2, 205, Bradenton, Fla.; RB—*Eddie George, Ohio St., 6-3, 230, Philadelphia, Pa.; RB—Troy Davis, Iowa St., 5-8, 182, Miami, Fla.; PK—Michael Reeder, TCU, 6-0, 160, Sulphur, La.

Defense DL—*Tedy Bruschi, Arizona, 6-1, 253, Roseville, Calif.; DL—Cornell Brown, Virginia Tech, 6-2, 240, Lynchburg, Va.; DL—Marcus Jones, North Carolina, 6-6, 270, Jacksonville, N.C.; DL—Tony Brackens, Texas, 6-4, 250, Fairfield, Texas; LB—*Zach Thomas, Texas Tech, 6-0, 232, Pampa, Texas; LB—Kevin Hardy, Illinois, 6-4, 243, Evansville, Ind.; LB—Pat Fitzgerald, Northwestern, 6-4, 228, Orland Park, Ill.; DB—Chris Canty, Kansas St., 5-10, 190, Voorhees, N.J.; DB—*Lawyer Milloy, Washington, 6-2, 200, Tacoma, Wash.; DB—Aaron Beasley, West Virginia, 6-0, 190, Pottstown, Pa.; DB—Greg Myers, Colorado St., 6-2, 191, Windsor, Colo.; P—Brad Maynard, Ball St., 6-1, 175, Atlanta, Ind.

1996

Offense WR—Marcus Harris, Wyoming, 6-2, 216, Senior, Minneapolis, Minn.; (tie) WR—Ike Hilliard, Florida, 5-11, 182, Junior, Patterson, La.; Reidel Anthony, Florida, 6-0, 181, Junior, South Bay, Fla.; TE—Tony Gonzalez, California, 6-6, 235, Junior, Huntington Beach, Calif.; OL—*Orlando Pace, Ohio St., 6-6, 330, Junior, Sandusky, Ohio; OL—Juan Roque, Arizona St., 6-8, 319, Senior, Ontario, Calif.; OL—Chris Naeole, Colorado, 6-4, 310, Senior, Kaaava, Hawaii; OL—Dan Neil, Texas, 6-2, 283, Senior, Cypress Creek, Texas; OL—Benji Olson, Washington, 6-4, 310, Sophomore, Port Orchard, Wash.; C—Aaron Taylor, Nebraska, 6-1, 305, Junior, Wichita Falls, Texas; QB—Danny Wuerffel, Florida, 6-2, 209, Senior, Fort Walton Beach, Fla.; RB—*Byron Hanspard, Texas Tech, 6-0, 193, Junior, DeSoto, Texas; RB—Troy Davis, Iowa St., 5-8, 185, Junior, Miami, Fla.; PK—Marc Primanti, North Carolina St., 5-7, 171, Senior, Thorndale, Pa.

Defense DL—Grant Wistrom, Nebraska, 6-5, 250, Junior, Webb City, Mo.; DL—Peter Boulware, Florida St., 6-5, 255, Junior, Columbia, S.C.; DL—Reinard Wilson, Florida St., 6-2, 255, Senior, Lake City, Fla.; (tie) DL—Derrick Rodgers, Arizona St., 6-2, 220, Junior, Cordova, Tenn.; Mike Vrabel, Ohio St., 6-4, 260, Senior, Akron, Ohio; LB—Canute Curtis, West Virginia, 6-2, 250, Senior, Amityville, N.Y.; LB—Pat Fitzgerald, Northwestern, 6-2, 243, Senior, Orland Park, Ill.; LB—Matt Russell, Colorado, 6-2, 245, Senior, Fairview Heights, Ill.; LB—Jarrett Irons, Michigan, 6-2, 234, Senior, The Woodlands, Texas; DB—*Chris Canty, Kansas St., 5-10, 190, Junior, Voorhees, N.J.; DB—*Kevin Jackson, Alabama, 6-2, 206, Senior, Dothan, Ala.; DB—Dre' Bly, North Carolina, 5-10, 180, Freshman, Chesapeake, Va.; DB—Shawn Springs, Ohio St., 6-0, 188, Junior, Silver Spring, Md.; P—Brad Maynard, Ball St., 6-1, 176, Senior, Atlanta, Ind.

1997

Offense WR—*Randy Moss, Marshall, 6-5, 210, Sophomore, Rand, W.Va.; WR—Jacquez Green, Florida, 5-9, 168, Junior, Fort Valley, Ga.; TE—Alonzo Mayes, Oklahoma St., 6-6, 265, Senior, Oklahoma City, Okla.; OL—*Aaron Taylor, Nebraska, 6-1, 305, Senior, Wichita Falls, Texas; OL—Alan Faneca, LSU, 6-5, 310, Junior, Rosenberg, Texas; OL—Kyle Turley, San Diego St., 6-6, 305, Senior, Moreno Valley, Calif.; OL—Chad Overhauser, UCLA, 6-6, 304, Senior, Sacramento, Calif.; C—Olin Kreutz, Washington, 6-4, 290, Junior, Honolulu, Hawaii; QB—Peyton Manning, Tennessee, 6-5, 222, Senior, New Orleans, La.; RB—*Ricky Williams, Texas, 6-0, 220, Junior, San Diego, Calif.; RB—Curtis Enis, Penn St., 6-1, 233, Junior, Union City, Ohio; PK—Martin Gramatica, Kansas St., 5-9, 170, Junior, Buenos Aires, Argentina; KR—Tim Dwight, Iowa, 5-9, 185, Senior, Iowa City, Iowa.

Defense DL—Grant Wistrom, Nebraska, 6-5, 255, Senior, Webb City, Mo.; DL—Andre Wadsworth, Florida St., 6-4, 282, Senior, Miami, Fla.; DL—Greg Ellis, North Carolina, 6-6, 265, Senior, Wendell, N.C.; DL—Jason Peter, Nebraska, 6-5, 285, Senior, Locust, N.J.; LB—Andy Katzenmoyer, Ohio St., 6-4, 260, Sophomore, Westerville, Ohio; LB—Sam Cowart, Florida St., 6-3, 239, Senior, Jacksonville, Fla.; LB—Anthony Simmons, Clemson, 6-1, 225, Junior, Spartanburg, S.C.; LB—Brian Simmons, North Carolina, 6-4, 230, Senior, New Bern, N.C.; DB—*Charles Woodson, Michigan, 6-1, 198, Junior, Fremont, Ohio; DB—Dre' Bly, North Carolina, 5-10, 185, Sophomore, Chesapeake, Va.; DB—Fred Weary, Florida, 5-10, 180, Senior, Jacksonville, Fla.; DB—Brian Lee, Wyoming, 6-2, 200, Senior, Arvada, Colo.; P—Chad Kessler, LSU, 6-1, 197, Senior, Longwood, Fla.

1998

Offense WR—Torry Holt, North Carolina St., 6-2, 188, Senior, Gibsonville, N.C. (Eastern Guilford HS); WR—Peter Warrick, Florida St., 6-0, 190, Junior, Bradenton, Fla. (Southeast HS); WR—Troy Edwards, Louisiana Tech, 5-10, 195, Senior, Shreveport, La. (Huntington HS); TE—*Rufus French, Mississippi, 6-4, 245, Junior, Amory, Miss. (Amory HS); OL—Kris Farris, UCLA, 6-9, 310, Junior, Mission Viejo, Calif. (Santa Margarita HS); OL—Aaron Gibson, Wisconsin, 6-7, 372, Senior, Indianapolis, Ind. (Decatur Central HS); OL—Matt Stinchcomb, Georgia, 6-6, 291, Senior, Lilburn, Ga. (Lilburn HS); OL—Rob Murphy, Ohio St., 6-5, 300, Junior, Cincinnati, Ohio (Moeller HS); C—Craig Page, Georgia Tech, 6-3, 288, Senior, Jupiter, Fla. (Jupiter HS); (tie) QB—Cade McNown, UCLA, 6-1, 214, Senior, West Linn, Ore.

(West Linn HS); Michael Bishop, Kansas St., 6-1, 205, Senior, Willis, Texas (Willis HS); Tim Couch, Kentucky, 6-5, 225, Junior, Hyden, Ky. (Leslie County HS); RB—*Ricky Williams, Texas, 6-0, 225, Senior, San Diego, Calif. (Patrick Henry HS); RB—Mike Cloud, Boston College, 5-11, 201, Senior, Portsmouth, R.I. (Portsmouth HS); PK—Sebastian Janikowski, Florida St., 6-2, 255, Sophomore, Daytona Beach, Fla. (Seabreeze HS); KR—David Allen, Kansas St., 5-9, 185, Sophomore, Liberty, Mo. (Liberty HS).

Defense DL—*Tom Burke, Wisconsin, 6-4, 249, Senior, Poplar, Wis. (Northwestern HS); DL—Montae Reagor, Texas Tech, 6-2, 254, Senior, Waxahachie, Texas (Waxahachie HS); DL—Jared DeVries, Iowa, 6-4, 284, Senior, Aplington, Iowa (Aplington-Parkersburg HS); LB—*Chris Claiborne, Southern California, 6-3, 250, Junior, Riverside, Calif. (North HS); LB—*Dat Nguyen, Texas A&M, 6-0, 216, Senior, Rockport, Texas (Rockport-Fulton HS); LB—Jeff Kelly, Kansas St., 6-0, 250, Senior, LaGrange, Texas (LaGrange HS); LB—Al Wilson, Tennessee, 6-0, 226, Senior, Jackson, Tenn. (Central Merry HS); DB—*Chris McAlister, Arizona, 6-2, 185, Senior, Pasadena, Calif. (Pasadena HS); DB—*Antoine Winfield, Ohio St., 5-9, 180, Senior, Akron, Ohio (Garfield HS); DB—Champ Bailey, Georgia, 6-1, 186, Junior, Folkston, Ga. (Folkston HS); DB—Anthony Poindexter, Virginia, 6-1, 220, Senior, Forest, Va. (Jefferson Forest HS); P—Joe Kristosik, UNLV, 6-3, 220, Junior, Las Vegas, Nev. (Bishop Gorman HS).

1999

Offense WR—Troy Walters, Stanford, 5-8, 170, Senior, College Station, Texas (A&M Consolidated HS); WR—*Peter Warrick, Florida St., 6-0, 195, Senior, Bradenton, Fla. (Southeast HS); TE—James Whalen, Kentucky, 6-4, 231, Senior, Portland, Ore. (LaSalle HS); OL—*Chris McIntosh, Wisconsin, 6-7, 310, Senior, Pewaukee, Wis. (Pewaukee HS); OL—*Chris Samuels, Alabama, 6-6, 291, Senior, Mobile, Ala. (Shaw HS); OL—Cosey Coleman, Tennessee, 6-5, 315, Junior, Clarkston, Ga. (Southwest DeKalb HS); OL—Jason Whitaker, Florida St., 6-5, 300, Senior, Panama City, Fla. (Moseley HS); C—Ben Hamilton, Minnesota, 6-5, 271, Junior, Plymouth, Minn. (Wayzata HS); C—Rob Riti, Missouri, 6-3, 289, Senior, Florissant, Mo. (Hazelwood West HS); QB—Joe Hamilton, Georgia Tech, 5-10, 189, Senior, Alvin, S.C. (Macedonia HS); RB—*Ron Dayne, Wisconsin, 5-10, 254, Senior, Berlin, N.J. (Overbrook HS); RB—Thomas Jones, Virginia, 5-10, 205, Senior, Big Stone Gap, Va. (Powell Valley HS); PK—*Sebastian Janikowski, Florida St., 6-2, 255, Junior, Daytona Beach, Fla. (Seabreeze HS); AP—Dennis Northcutt, Arizona, 5-11, 178, Senior, Los Angeles, Calif. (Dorsey HS).

Defense DL—*Courtney Brown, Penn St., 6-5, 270, Senior, Alvin, S.C. (Macedonia HS); DL—*Corey Moore, Virginia Tech, 6-0, 225, Senior, Brownsville, Tenn. (Haywood HS); DL—Corey Simon, Florida St., 6-4, 275, Senior, Pompano Beach, Fla. (Ely HS); LB—*LaVar Arrington, Penn St., 6-3, 242, Junior, Pittsburgh, Pa. (North Hills HS); LB—Mark Simoneau, Kansas St., 6-0, 240, Senior, Smith Center, Kan. (Smith Center HS); LB—Brandon Short, Penn St., 6-3, 252, Senior, McKeesport, Pa. (McKeesport HS); DB—Tyrone Carter, Minnesota, 5-9, 184, Senior, Pompano Beach, Fla. (Ely HS); DB—Brian Urlacher, New Mexico, 6-4, 240, Senior, Lovington, N.M. (Lovington HS); DB—Ralph Brown, Nebraska, 5-10, 180, Senior, Hacienda Heights, Calif. (Bishop Amat HS); DB—Deon Grant, Tennessee, 6-3, 205, Junior, Augusta, Ga. (Josey HS); DB—Deltha O'Neal, California, 5-11, 195, Senior, Milpitas, Calif. (Milpitas HS); P—Andrew Bayes, East Caro., 6-3, 200, Senior, Hyattsville, Md. (DeMatha HS).

2000

Offense WR—Marvin Minnis, Florida St., 6-1, 185, Senior, Miami, Fla. (Northwestern HS); (tie) WR—Antonio Bryant, Pittsburgh, 6-2, 185, Sophomore, Miami, Fla. (Northwestern HS); Fred Mitchell, UCLA, 6-0, 188, Junior, Lakeland, Fla. (Kathleen HS); TE—*Brian Natkin, UTEP, 6-4, 245, Senior, San Antonio, Texas (Churchill HS); OL—*Steve Hutchinson, Michigan, 6-5, 299, Senior, Coral Springs, Fla. (Coral Springs HS); OL—Ben Hamilton, Minnesota, 6-5, 285, Senior, Plymouth, Minn. (Wayzata HS); OL—Chris Brown, Georgia Tech, 6-6, 315, Senior, Augusta, Ga. (Butler HS); OL—Leonard Davis, Texas, 6-6, 365, Senior, Wortham, Texas (Wortham HS); C—Dominic Raiola, Nebraska, 6-2, 300, Junior, Honolulu, Hawaii (St. Louis HS); QB—Josh Heupel, Oklahoma, 6-2, 214, Senior, Aberdeen, S.D. (Central HS); RB—*LaDainian Tomlinson, TCU, 5-11, 220, Senior, Waco, Texas (University HS); RB—Damien Anderson, Northwestern, 5-11, 202, Junior, Wilmington, Ill. (Wilmington HS); PK—Jonathan Ruffin, Cincinnati, 5-10, 184, Sophomore, Metairie, La. (Ridgewood Prep HS); AP—Santana Moss, Miami (Fla.), 5-10, 180, Senior, Miami, Fla. (Carol City HS).

Defense DL—*Jamal Reynolds, Florida St., 6-4, 254, Senior, Aiken, S.C. (Aiken HS); DL—*Andre Carter, California, 6-5, 265, Senior, San Jose, Calif. (Oak Grove HS); DL—Casey Hampton, Texas, 6-1, 310, Senior, Galveston, Texas (Ball HS); DL—John Henderson, Tennessee, 6-7, 290, Junior, Nashville, Tenn. (Pearl Cohn HS); LB—*Dan Morgan, Miami (Fla.), 6-3, 245, Senior, Coral Springs, Fla. (Taravella HS); LB—Rocky Calmus, Oklahoma, 6-3, 240, Junior, Jenks, Okla. (Jenks HS); LB—Keith Adams, Clemson, 5-11, 220, Junior, College Park, Ga. (Westlake HS); DB—Dwight Smith, Akron, 5-11, 205, Senior, Detroit, Mich. (Central HS); DB—Jamar Fletcher, Wisconsin, 5-10, 175, Junior, St. Louis, Mo. (Hazelwood East HS); DB—Fred Smoot, Mississippi St., 6-1, 179, Senior, Jackson, Miss. (Provine HS); (tie) DB—Tay Cody, Florida St., 5-11, 180, Senior, Blakely, Ga. (Early County HS); Edward Reed, Miami (Fla.), 6-0, 190, Junior, St. Rose, La. (Destrehan HS); J.T. Thatcher, Oklahoma, 6-0, 225, Senior, Norman, Okla. (Norman HS); P—Nick Harris, California, 6-3, 225, Senior, Avondale, Ariz. (Westview HS).

2001

Offense WR—*Jabar Gaffney, Florida, 6-1, 197, Sophomore, Jacksonville, Fla. (Raines HS); WR—Josh Reed, LSU, 5-11, 205, Junior, Rayne, La. (Rayne HS); TE—Dan Graham, Colorado, 6-3, 245, Senior, Denver, Colo. (Thomas Jefferson HS); OL—*Bryant McKinnie, Miami (Fla.), 6-9, 335, Senior, Woodbury, N.J. (Woodbury HS); OL—Toniu Fonoti, Nebraska, 6-4, 340, Junior, Hauula, Hawaii (Kahuku HS); (tie) OL—Andre Gurode, Colorado, 6-4, 320, Senior, Houston, Texas (North Shore HS); Mike Williams, Texas, 6-6, 339, Senior, The Colony, Texas (The Colony HS); Mike Pearson, Florida, 6-7, 300, Junior, Seffner, Fla. (Armwood HS); Terrence Metcalf, Mississippi, 6-4, 315, Senior, Clarksdale, Miss. (Clarksdale HS); C—LeCharles Bentley, Ohio St., 6-2, 300, Senior, Cleveland, Ohio (St. Ignatius HS); QB—Rex Grossman, Florida, 6-1, 223, Sophomore, Bloomington, Ind. (Bloomington South HS); RB—Luke Staley, Brigham Young, 6-2, 225, Junior, Tualatin, Ore. (Tualatin HS); RB—William Green, Boston College, 6-1, 217, Junior, Atlantic City, N.J. (Holy Spirit HS); PK—Damon Duval, Auburn, 6-1, 186, Junior, Chattanooga, Tenn. (Central HS).

Defense DL—Alex Brown, Florida, 6-4, 254, Senior, White Springs, Fla. (Hamilton County HS); DL—*Dwight Freeney, Syracuse, 6-1, 250, Senior, Bloomfield, Conn. (Bloomfield HS); DL—John Henderson, Tennessee, 6-7, 290, Senior, Nashville, Tenn. (Pearl Cohn HS); DL—*Julius Peppers, North Carolina, 6-6, 285, Junior, Bailey, N.C. (Southern Nash HS); LB—Rocky Calmus, Oklahoma, 6-3, 235, Senior, Jenks, Okla. (Jenks HS); LB—Robert Thomas, UCLA, 6-2, 237, Senior, Imperial, Calif. (Imperial HS); LB—E.J. Henderson, Maryland, 6-2, 238, Junior, Aberdeen, Md. (Aberdeen HS); DB—*Quentin Jammer, Texas, 6-1, 200, Senior, Angleton, Tex. (Angleton HS); DB—*Edward Reed, Miami (Fla.), 6-0, 198, Senior, St. Rose, La. (Destrehan HS); DB—*Roy Williams, Oklahoma, 6-0, 215, Junior, Union City, Calif. (James Logan HS); P—Travis Dorsch, Purdue, 6-6, 222, Junior, Bozeman, Mont. (Bozeman HS).

2002

Offense WR—*Charles Rogers, Michigan St., 6-4, 205, Junior, Saginaw, Mich. (Saginaw HS); (tie) WR—Reggie Williams, Washington, 6-4, 200, Sophomore, Tacoma, Wash. (Lakes HS); Rashaun Woods, Oklahoma St., 6-2, 187, Junior, Oklahoma City, Okla. (Millwood HS); TE—*Dallas Clark, Iowa, 6-4, 244, Junior, Livermore, Iowa (Twin River Valley HS); OL—Shawn Andrews, Arkansas, 6-5, 345, Sophomore, Camden, Ark. (Fairview HS); OL—Eric Steinbach, Iowa, 6-7, 284, Senior, Lockport, Ill. (Providence Catholic HS); OL—Derrick Dockery, Texas, 6-6, 345, Senior, Garland, Texas (Lakeview Centennial HS); OL—Jordan Gross, Utah, 6-5, 306, Senior, Fruitland, Idaho (Fruitland HS); C—Brett Romberg, Miami (Fla.), 6-3, 290, Senior, Windsor, Ontario, Canada (Belle River HS); QB—Carson Palmer, Southern California, 6-5, 225, Senior, Laguna Niguel, Calif. (Santa Margarita HS); RB—*Larry Johnson, Penn St., 6-2, 222, Senior, State College, Pa. (State College Area HS); RB—Willis McGahee, Miami (Fla.), 6-1, 224, Sophomore, Miami, Fla. (Central HS); PK—Mike Nugent, Ohio St., 5-10, 170, Sophomore, Centerville, Ohio (Centerville HS); AP/KR—Derek Abney, Kentucky, 5-10, 175, Junior, Mosinee, Wis. (Everest HS).

Defense DL—*Terrell Suggs, Arizona St., 6-3, 251, Junior, Chandler, Ariz. (Hamilton HS); DL—David Pollack, Georgia, 6-2, 275, Sophomore, Snellville, Ga. (Shiloh HS); DL—Rien Long, Washington St., 6-6, 287, Junior, Anacortes, Wash. (Anacortes HS); DL—Tommie Harris, Oklahoma, 6-3, 280, Sophomore, Killeen, Texas (Ellison HS); LB—E.J. Henderson, Maryland, 6-2, 250, Senior, Aberdeen, Md. (Aberdeen HS); LB—Teddy Lehman, Oklahoma, 6-2, 235, Junior, Fort Gibson, Okla. (Fort Gibson HS); LB—Matt Wilhelm, Ohio St., 6-5, 245, Senior, Lorain, Ohio (Elyria Catholic HS); DB—*Mike Doss, Ohio St., 5-11, 204, Senior, Canton, Ohio (McKinley HS); DB—*Terence Newman, Kansas St., 5-11, 185, Senior, Salina, Kan. (Central HS); DB—*Shane Walton, Notre Dame, 5-11, 185, Senior, San Diego, Calif. (Bishops School HS); DB—Troy Polamalu, Southern California, 5-10, 215, Senior, Tenmile, Ore. (Douglas HS); P—Mark Mariscal, Colorado, 6-2, 200, Senior, Tallahassee, Fla. (Lincoln HS).

2003

Offense WR—*Larry Fitzgerald, Pittsburgh, 6-3, 225, Sophomore, Minneapolis, Minn. (Valley Forge Military); WR—Mike Williams, Southern California, 6-5, 230, Sophomore, Tampa, Fla. (Plant HS); TE—*Kellen Winslow, Miami (Fla.), 6-5, 250, Junior, San Diego, Calif. (Scripps Ranch HS); OL—*Shawn Andrews, Arkansas, 6-6, 353, Junior, Camden, Ark. (Fairview HS); OL—*Robert Gallery, Iowa, 6-7, 321, Senior, Masonville, Iowa (East Buchanan HS); OL—Jacob Rogers, Southern California, 6-6, 305, Senior, Oxnard, Calif. (Oxnard HS); OL—Alex Barron, Florida St., 6-6, 316, Junior, Orangeburg, S.C. (Wilkinson HS); C—*Jake Grove, Virginia Tech, 6-3, 300, Senior, Forest, Va. (Jefferson Forest HS); QB—*Jason White, Oklahoma, 6-3, 221, Senior, Tuttle, Okla. (Tuttle HS); RB—Chris Perry, Michigan, 6-1, 218, Senior, Advance, N.C. (Fork Union Military); RB—Kevin Jones, Virginia Tech, 6-0, 221, Junior, Chester, Pa. (Cardinal O'Hara HS); (tie) PK—Nate Kaeding, Iowa, 6-0, 180, Senior, Coralville, Iowa (Iowa City West HS); Nick Browne, TCU, 5-10, 172, Senior, Garland, Texas (Naaman Forest HS); AP/KR—*Antonio Perkins, Oklahoma, 6-0, 188, Junior, Lawton, Okla. (Lawton HS).

Defense DL—*Dave Ball, UCLA, 6-6, 269, Senior, Dixon, Calif. (Dixon HS); DL—*Tommie Harris, Oklahoma, 6-3, 289, Junior, Killeen, Texas (Ellison HS); DL—Chad Lavalais, LSU, 6-3, 292, Senior, Marksville, La. (Marksville HS); DL—Kenechi Udeze, Southern California, 6-4, 285, Junior, Los Angeles, Calif. (Verbum Dei HS); LB—*Teddy Lehman, Oklahoma, 6-2, 243, Senior, Fort Gibson, Okla. (Fort Gibson HS); LB—Derrick Johnson, Texas, 6-4, 230, Junior, Waco, Texas (Waco HS); LB—Grant Wiley, West Virginia, 6-1, 235, Senior, Trappe, Pa. (Perkiomen Valley HS); DB—*Derrick Strait, Oklahoma, 5-11, 195, Senior, Austin, Texas (Lanier HS); DB—*Sean Taylor, Miami (Fla.), 6-3, 230, Junior, Miami, Fla. (Gulliver Prep HS); DB—Keiwan Ratliff, Florida, 5-10, 178, Senior, Columbus, Ohio (Whitehall-Yearling HS); DB—Will Allen, Ohio St., 6-2, 190, Senior, Dayton, Ohio (Huber Heights Wayne HS); P—Dustin Colquitt, Tennessee, 6-2, 196, Junior, Knoxville, Tenn. (Bearden HS).

2004

Offense WR—*Braylon Edwards, Michigan, 6-3, 208, Senior, Detroit, Mich. (Bishop Gallagher HS); WR—Taylor Stubblefield, Purdue, 6-1, 182, Senior, Yakima, Wash. (Davis HS); TE—*Heath Miller, Virginia, 6-5, 255, Junior, Swords Creek, Va. (Honaker HS); OL—*Jammal Brown, Oklahoma, 6-6, 313, Senior, Lawton, Okla. (MacArthur HS); OL—*Alex Barron, Florida St., 6-6, 308, Senior, Orangeburg, S.C. (Wilkinson HS); OL—David Baas, Michigan, 6-5, 323, Senior, Sarasota, Fla. (Riverview HS); OL—Elton Brown, Virginia, 6-6, 338, Senior, Hampton, Va. (Hampton HS); OL—Michael Munoz, Tennessee, 6-6, 315, Senior, Mason, Ohio (Moeller HS); C—Ben Wilkerson, LSU, 6-4, 297, Senior, Hemphill, Texas (Hemphill HS); QB—Matt Leinart, Southern California, 6-5, 225, Junior, Santa Ana, Calif. (Mater Dei HS); RB—*Adrian Peterson, Oklahoma, 6-2, 210, Freshman, Palestine, Texas (Palestine HS); RB—J.J. Arrington, California, 5-10, 210, Senior, Rocky Mount, N.C. (Northern Nash HS); PK—*Mike Nugent, Ohio St., 5-10, 180, Senior, Centerville, Ohio (Centerville HS); AP/KR—Reggie Bush, Southern California, 6-0, 200, Sophomore, Spring Valley, Calif. (Helix HS).

Defense DL—David Pollack, Georgia, 6-3, 261, Senior, Snellville, Ga. (Shiloh HS); DL—Erasmus James, Wisconsin, 6-4, 263, Senior, Pembroke Pines, Fla. (McArthur HS); DL—Shaun Cody, Southern California, 6-4, 295, Senior, Hacienda, Calif. (Los Altos HS); DL—Marcus Spears, LSU, 6-4, 298, Senior, Baton Rouge, La. (Southern Lab HS); LB—*Derrick Johnson, Texas, 6-4, 235, Senior, Waco, Texas (Waco HS); LB—Matt Grootegoed, Southern California, 5-11, 215, Senior, Huntington Beach, Calif. (Mater Dei HS); LB—A.J. Hawk, Ohio St., 6-1, 238, Junior, Centerville, Ohio (Centerville HS); DB—*Antrel Rolle, Miami (Fla.), 6-1, 202, Senior, Homestead, Fla. (South Dade HS); DB—Marlin Jackson, Michigan, 6-1, 196, Senior, Sharon, Pa. (Sharon HS); DB—Carlos Rogers, Auburn, 6-1, 200, Senior, Augusta, Ga. (Butler HS); DB—Ernest Shazor, Michigan, 6-4, 229, Senior, Detroit, Mich. (Martin Luther King HS); DB—Thomas Davis, Georgia, 6-1, 230, Junior, Shellman, Ga. (Randolph-Clay HS); P—Brandon Fields, Michigan St., 6-6, 234, Sophomore, Toledo, Ohio (St. John's HS).

2005

Offense WR—*Dwayne Jarrett, Southern California, 6-5, 195, Sophomore; WR—Jeff Samardzija, Notre Dame, 6-5, 215, Junior; TE—Marcedes Lewis, UCLA, 6-6, 255, Senior; OL—*Jonathan Scott, Texas, 6-7, 310, Senior; OL—Marcus McNeill, Auburn, 6-9, 337, Senior; OL—Max Jean-Gilles, Georgia, 6-4, 340, Senior; OL—Taitusi Lutui, Southern California, 6-6, 365, Senior; C—*Greg Eslinger, Minnesota, 6-3, 285, Senior; QB—Vince Young, Texas, 6-5, 230, Junior; RB—*Reggie Bush, Southern California, 6-0, 200, Junior; RB—Jerome Harrison, Washington St., 5-9, 192, Senior; PK—Mason Crosby, Colorado, 6-2, 210, Junior; AP/KR—*Maurice Drew, UCLA, 5-8, 198, Junior.

Defense DL—*Elvis Dumervil, Louisville, 6-0, 256, Senior; DL—*Tamba Hali, Penn St., 6-3, 258, Senior; DL—Haloti Ngata, Oregon, 6-5, 338, Junior; DL—Rodrique Wright, Texas, 6-5, 305, Senior; LB—*A.J. Hawk, Ohio St., 6-1, 238, Senior; LB—*DeMeco Ryans, Alabama, 6-2, 232, Senior; LB—Paul Posluszny, Penn St., 6-2, 230, Junior; DB—*Jimmy Williams, Virginia Tech, 6-3, 206, Senior; DB—*Michael Huff, Texas, 6-1, 205, Senior; DB—Greg Blue, Georgia, 6-2, 214, Senior; DB—Tye Hill, Clemson, 5-10, 178, Senior; P—*Ryan Plackemeier, Wake Forest, 6-4, 235, Senior.

2006

The 26-man NCAA Consensus All-America Football Team features 13 players on offense and 13 on defense. The players listed had the majority of votes competing against players at that position only. The points system was used for the selection of the All-America team (three points for first team, two points for second team and one point for third team). Eight players were unanimous choices by the five organizations used in the consensus chart — American Football Coaches Association (First Team), Associated Press (First, Second and Third Teams), Football Writers Association of America (First Team), The Sporting News (First and Second Teams) and Walter Camp Foundation (First and Second Teams).

Offense WR—*Calvin Johnson, Georgia Tech, 6-5, 235, Junior; **WR—Dwayne Jarrett, Southern California, 6-5, 210, Junior**; TE—Zach Miller, Arizona St., 6-5, 260, Junior; OL—Sam Baker, Southern California, 6-5, 305, Junior; OL—Justin Blalock, Texas, 6-4, 335, Senior; OL—Jake Long, Michigan, 6-7, 313, Senior; OL—*Joe Thomas, Wisconsin, 6-8, 313, Senior; C—*Dan Mozes, West Virginia, 6-4, 290; Senior; QB—*Troy Smith, Ohio St., 6-1, 215, Senior; RB/AP—Darren McFadden, Arkansas, 6-2, 205, Sophomore; RB—*Steve Slaton, West Virginia, 5-10, 195, Sophomore; PK—Justin Medlock, UCLA, 6-0, 197, Senior; KR—DeSean Jackson, California, 6-0, 166, Sophomore.

Defense DL—*Gaines Adams, Clemson, 6-5, 265, Senior; DL—Justin Hickman, UCLA, 6-2, 263, Senior; DL—Quinn Pitcock, Ohio St., 6-3, 295, Senior; DL—*LaMarr Woodley, Michigan, 6-2, 269, Senior; LB—James Laurinaitis, Ohio St., 6-3, 244, Sophomore; LB—Patrick Willis, Mississippi, 6-2, 240, Senior; **LB—Paul Posluszny, Penn St., 6-2, 238, Senior**; DB—Leon Hall, Michigan, 5-11, 193, Senior; DB—Daymeion Hughes, California, 6-0, 188, Senior; DB—LaRon Landry, LSU, 6-2, 202, Senior; DB—Reggie Nelson, Florida, 6-1, 193, Junior; DB—Eric Weddle, Utah, 6-0, 200, Senior; P—*Daniel Sepulveda, Baylor, 6-3, 230, Senior.

*Indicates unanimous selection. **Boldface indicates consensus repeater from 2005.**

2006 Consensus Team Class Makeup: 17 seniors, 5 juniors and 4 sophomores.

Consensus All-Americans by College

Beginning in 1924, unanimous selections are indicated by (*).

AIR FORCE
58— Brock Strom, T
70— Ernie Jennings, E
85— Scott Thomas, DB
87— *Chad Hennings, DL
92— *Carlton McDonald, DB

AKRON
2000— Dwight Smith, DB

ALABAMA
30— *Fred Sington, T
34— Don Hutson, E
Bill Lee, T
Dixie Howell, B
35— Riley Smith, B
37— Leroy Monsky, G
41— Holt Rast, E
42— Joe Domnanovich, C
45— Vaughn Mancha, C
61— *Billy Neighbors, T
62— *Lee Roy Jordan, C
65— Paul Crane, C
66— Ray Perkins, E
*Cecil Dowdy, T
67— Dennis Homan, E
Bobby Johns, DB
71— Johnny Musso, B
72— *John Hannah, G
73— Buddy Brown, G
74— Leroy Cook, DL
Woodrow Lowe, LB
75— *Leroy Cook, DE
77— Ozzie Newsome, WR
78— Marty Lyons, DL
79— Jim Bunch, T
80— *E.J. Junior, DL
81— Tommy Wilcox, DB
82— Mike Pitts, DL
86— *Cornelius Bennett, LB
88— *Derrick Thomas, LB
89— *Keith McCants, LB
90— *Philip Doyle, PK
92— John Copeland, DL
Eric Curry, DL
93— David Palmer, KR
*Antonio Langham, DB
96— *Kevin Jackson, DB
99— *Chris Samuels, OL
2005—*DeMeco Ryans, LB

AMHERST
05— John Hubbard, B

ARIZONA
82— Ricky Hunley, LB
83— *Ricky Hunley, LB
87— Chuck Cecil, DB
90— *Darryll Lewis, DB
92— Rob Waldrop, DL
93— *Rob Waldrop, DL
94— Steve McLaughlin, PK
Tedy Bruschi, DL
Tony Bouie, DB
95— *Tedy Bruschi, DL
98— *Chris McAlister, DB
99— Dennis Northcutt, AP

ARIZONA ST.
72— Woody Green, B
73— Woody Green, B
77— John Jefferson, WR
78— *Al Harris, DL
81— Mike Richardson, DB
82— Mike Richardson, DB
Vernon Maxwell, DL
83— Luis Zendejas, PK
84— David Fulcher, DB
85— David Fulcher, DB
86— Danny Villa, OL
87— Randall McDaniel, OL
96— Juan Rogue, OL
Derrick Rodgers, DL
2002—*Terrell Suggs, DL
06— Zach Miller, TE

ARKANSAS
48— Clyde Scott, B
54— *Bud Brooks, G
65— Glen Ray Hines, T
Loyd Phillips, DT
66— *Loyd Phillips, DT
68— Jim Barnes, G
69— Rodney Brand, C
70— Dick Bumpas, DT
77— Leotis Harris, G
Steve Little, K
79— *Greg Kolenda, T
81— *Billy Ray Smith, DL
82— *Billy Ray Smith, DL
*Steve Korte, OL
88— Kendall Trainor, PK
Wayne Martin, DL
89— Jim Mabry, OL
2002— Shawn Andrews, OL
03— *Shawn Andrews, OL
06— Darren McFadden, RB/AP

ARMY
1898— Charles Romeyn, B
00— William Smith, E
01— Paul Bunker, T
Charles Daly, B
02— Paul Bunker, T-B
Robert Boyers, C
04— Arthur Tipton, C
Henry Torney, B
05— Henry Torney, B
07— William Erwin, G
11— Leland Devore, T
13— Louis Merillat, E
14— John McEwan, C
16— Elmer Oliphant, B
17— Elmer Oliphant, B
22— Ed Garbisch, C
26— Bud Sprague, T
27— Red Cagle, B
28— *Red Cagle, B
29— Red Cagle, B
32— Milt Summerfelt, G
43— *Casimir Myslinski, C
44— Glenn Davis, B
Doc Blanchard, B
45— Tex Coulter, T
John Green, G
*Glenn Davis, B
*Doc Blanchard, B
46— Hank Foldberg, E
*Glenn Davis, B
*Doc Blanchard, B
47— Joe Steffy, G
49— Arnold Galiffa, B
50— *Dan Foldberg, E
57— Bob Anderson, B
58— *Pete Dawkins, B
59— Bill Carpenter, E

AUBURN
32— Jimmy Hitchcock, B
57— *Jimmy Phillips, E
58— Zeke Smith, G
60— Ken Rice, T
64— Tucker Frederickson, B
69— Buddy McClinton, DB
70— Larry Willingham, DB
71— *Pat Sullivan, QB
*Terry Beasley, E
74— Ken Bernich, LB
83— Bo Jackson, RB
84— Gregg Carr, LB
85— *Bo Jackson, RB
86— *Ben Tamburello, C
*Brent Fullwood, RB
87— Tracy Rocker, DL
Aundray Bruce, LB
88— *Tracy Rocker, DL
90— *Ed King, OL
David Rocker, DL
93— Wayne Gandy, OL
Terry Daniel, P
94— Brian Robinson, DB
2001— Damon Duval, PK
04— Carlos Rogers, DB
05— Marcus McNeill, OL

BALL ST.
95— Brad Maynard, P
96— Brad Maynard, P

BAYLOR
30— Barton Koch, G
56— *Bill Glass, G
63— Lawrence Elkins, E
64— Lawrence Elkins, B
76— Gary Green, DB
79— Mike Singletary, LB
80— *Mike Singletary, LB
86— *Thomas Everett, DB
91— *Santana Dotson, DL
2006—*Daniel Sepulveda, P

BOSTON COLLEGE
20— Luke Urban, E
40— Gene Goodreault, E
42— Mike Holovak, B
84— *Doug Flutie, QB
Tony Thurman, DB
85— Mike Ruth, DL
94— Pete Mitchell, TE
98— Mike Cloud, RB
2001— William Green, RB

BRIGHAM YOUNG
79— *Marc Wilson, QB
80— Nick Eyre, OL
81— *Jim McMahon, QB
82— *Gordon Hudson, TE
83— *Gordon Hudson, TE
*Steve Young, QB
86— Jason Buck, DL
89— Mohammed Elewonibi, OL
90— Ty Detmer, QB
*Chris Smith, TE
91— Ty Detmer, QB
2001— Luke Staley, RB

BROWN
02— Thomas Barry, B
06— John Mayhew, B

09— Adrian Regnier, E
10— Earl Sprackling, B
12— George Crowther, B
16— Fritz Pollard, B

CALIFORNIA
21— Brick Muller, E
Dan McMillan, T
22— Brick Muller, E
24— Edwin Horrell, C
28— Irv Phillips, E
30— Ted Beckett, G
35— Larry Lutz, T
37— Sam Chapman, B
38— Vic Bottari, B
48— Jackie Jensen, B
49— *Rod Franz, G
50— Les Richter, G
51— Les Richter, G
68— Ed White, MG
71— Sherman White, DT
74— Steve Bartkowski, QB
75— Chuck Muncie, RB
Steve Rivera, E
83— Ron Rivera, LB
91— Russell White, RB
92— Sean Dawkins, WR
96— Tony Gonzalez, TE
99— Deltha O'Neal, DB
2000—*Andre Carter, DL
Nick Harris, P
04— J.J. Arrington, RB
06— Daymeion Hughes, DB
DeSean Jackson, KR

CARLISLE
1899— Isaac Seneca, B
03— James Johnson, B
07— Albert Exendine, E
Peter Hauser, B
11— Jim Thorpe, B
12— Jim Thorpe, B

CARNEGIE MELLON
28— Howard Harpster, B

CENTENARY (LA.)
33— Paul Geisler, E

CENTRE
19— James Weaver, C
Bo McMillin, B
21— Bo McMillin, B

CHICAGO
1898— Clarence Herschberger, B
04— Fred Speik, E
Walter Eckersall, B
05— Mark Catlin, E
Walter Eckersall, B
06— Walter Eckersall, B
08— Walter Steffen, B
13— Paul Des Jardien, C
22— John Thomas, B
24— Joe Pondelik, G
35— *Jay Berwanger, B

CINCINNATI
2000— Jonathan Ruffin, PK

CLEMSON
67— Harry Olszewski, G
74— Bennie Cunningham, TE
79— Jim Stuckey, DL
81— Jeff Davis, LB
Terry Kinard, DB
82— *Terry Kinard, DB
83— William Perry, DL
86— Terrence Flagler, RB
87— David Treadwell, PK
88— Donnell Woolford, DB
90— Stacy Long, OL
91— Jeb Flesch, OL
Levon Kirkland, LB
93— Stacy Seegars, OL
97— Anthony Simmons, LB
2000— Keith Adams, LB
05— Tye Hill, DB
06— *Gaines Adams, DL

COLGATE
13— Ellery Huntington, B
16— Clarence Horning, T
D. Belford West, T
Oscar Anderson, B
19— D. Belford West, T
30— Leonard Macaluso, B

COLORADO
37— Byron White, B
60— Joe Romig, G
61— Joe Romig, G
67— Dick Anderson, DB
68— Mike Montler, G
69— Bob Anderson, B
70— Don Popplewell, C
72— Cullen Bryant, DB
85— Barry Helton, P
86— Barry Helton, P
88— Keith English, P
89— Joe Garten, OL
Alfred Williams, LB
Tom Rouen, P
90— *Eric Bieniemy, RB
*Joe Garten, OL
*Alfred Williams, LB
91— *Jay Leeuwenburg, OL
92— Deon Figures, DB
94— Michael Westbrook, WR
*Rashaan Salaam, RB
Chris Hudson, DB
95— Bryan Stoltenberg, C
96— Matt Russell, LB
Chris Naeole, OL
2001— Dan Graham, TE
Andre Gurode, OL
02— Mark Mariscal, P
05— Mason Crosby, PK

COLORADO ST.
78— Mike Bell, DL
95— Greg Myers, DB

COLUMBIA
00— Bill Morley, B
01— Harold Weekes, B
Bill Morley, B
03— Richard Smith, B
42— Paul Governali, B
47— Bill Swiacki, E

CORNELL
1895— Clinton Wyckoff, B
00— Raymond Starbuck, B
01— William Warner, G
Sanford Hunt, G
02— William Warner, G
06— Elmer Thompson, G
William Newman, C
08— Bernard O'Rourke, G
14— John O'Hearn, E
Charles Barrett, B
15— Murray Shelton, E
Charles Barrett, B
21— Edgar Kaw, B
22— Edgar Kaw, B
23— George Pfann, B
38— Brud Holland, E
39— Nick Drahos, T
40— Nick Drahos, T
71— *Ed Marinaro, B

DARTMOUTH
03— Henry Hooper, C
Myron Witham, B
04— Joseph Gilman, G
05— Ralph Glaze, E
08— George Schildmiller, E
Clark Tobin, G
12— Wesley Englehorn, T
13— Robert Hogsett, E
14— Clarence Spears, G
15— Clarence Spears, G
17— Eugene Neely, G
19— Adolph Youngstrom, G
24— Carl Diehl, G
25— Carl Diehl, G
George Tully, E
*Andy Oberlander, B
38— Bob MacLeod, B

DUKE
33— Fred Crawford, T
36— Ace Parker, B
71— Ernie Jackson, DB
89— *Clarkston Hines, WR

DUQUESNE
36— Mike Basrak, C

EAST CARO.
83— Terry Long, OL

91— *Robert Jones, LB
99— Andrew Bayes, P

FLORIDA
66— *Steve Spurrier, B
69— Carlos Alvarez, E
75— Sammy Green, LB
80— David Little, LB
82— Wilber Marshall, DL
83— Wilber Marshall, LB
84— Lomas Brown, OT
88— Louis Oliver, DB
89— *Emmitt Smith, RB
91— Brad Culpepper, DL
94— Jack Jackson, WR
Kevin Carter, DL
95— *Jason Odom, OL
96— Danny Wuerffel, QB
Ike Hilliard, WR
Reidel Anthony, WR
97— Jacquez Green, WR
Fred Weary, DB
2001—*Jabar Gaffney, WR
Mike Pearson, OL
Rex Grossman, QB
Alex Brown, DL
03— Keiwan Ratliff, DB
06— Reggie Nelson, DB

FLORIDA ST.
64— Fred Biletnikoff, E
67— Ron Sellers, E
79— Ron Simmons, MG
80— Ron Simmons, MG
83— Greg Allen, RB
85— Jamie Dukes, OL
87— *Deion Sanders, DB
88— *Deion Sanders, DB
89— LeRoy Butler, DB
91— *Terrell Buckley, DB
Marvin Jones, LB
92— *Marvin Jones, LB
93— *Charlie Ward, QB
*Derrick Brooks, LB
Corey Sawyer, DB
94— Derrick Brooks, LB
Clifton Abraham, DB
95— Clay Shiver, C
96— Peter Boulware, DL
Reinard Wilson, DL
97— Andre Wadsworth, DL
Sam Cowart, LB
98— Peter Warrick, WR
Sebastian Janikowski, PK
99— *Sebastian Janikowski, PK
*Peter Warrick, WR
Jason Whitaker, OL
Corey Simon, DL
2000— Marvin Minnis, WR
*Jamal Reynolds, DL
Tay Cody, DB
03— Alex Barron, OL
04— *Alex Barron, OL

FORDHAM
36— Alex Wojciechowicz, C
37— Ed Franco, T
Alex Wojciechowicz, C

GEORGETOWN
26— Harry Connaughton, G

GEORGIA
27— Tom Nash, E
31— Vernon Smith, E
41— Frank Sinkwich, B
42— *Frank Sinkwich, B
46— *Charley Trippi, B
67— Ed Chandler, T
68— Bill Stanfill, DT
Jake Scott, DB
71— *Royce Smith, G
75— Randy Johnson, G
76— Joel Parrish, G
80— *Herschel Walker, RB
81— *Herschel Walker, RB
82— *Herschel Walker, RB
Terry Hoage, DB
83— Terry Hoage, DB
84— Kevin Butler, PK
Jeff Sanchez, DB
85— Pete Anderson, C
88— Tim Worley, RB
92— *Garrison Hearst, RB

98— Champ Bailey, DB
Matt Stinchcomb, OL
2002— David Pollack, DL
04— Thomas Davis, DB
David Pollack, DL
05— Max Jean-Gilles, OL
Greg Blue, DB

GEORGIA TECH
17— Everett Strupper, B
18— Bill Fincher, E
Joe Guyon, T
Ashel Day, C
20— Bill Fincher, E
28— Pete Pund, C
42— Harvey Hardy, G
44— Phil Tinsley, E
46— Paul Duke, C
47— Bob Davis, T
52— Hal Miller, T
53— Larry Morris, C
59— Maxie Baughan, C
66— Jim Breland, C
70— Rock Perdoni, DT
73— Randy Rhino, DB
90— *Ken Swilling, DB
98— Craig Page, C
99— Joe Hamilton, QB
2000— Chris Brown, OL
06— *Calvin Johnson, WR

HARVARD
1889— Arthur Cumnock, E
John Cranston, G
James Lee, B
1890— Frank Hallowell, E
Marshall Newell, T
John Cranston, C
Dudley Dean, B
John Corbett, B
1891— Marshall Newell, T
Everett Lake, B
1892— Frank Hallowell, E
Marshall Newell, T
Bertram Waters, G
William Lewis, C
Charles Brewer, B
1893— Marshall Newell, T
William Lewis, C
Charles Brewer, B
1894— Bertram Waters, T
1895— Norman Cabot, E
Charles Brewer, B
1896— Norman Cabot, E
Edgar Wrightington, B
1897— Alan Doucette, C
Benjamin Dibblee, B
1898— John Hallowell, E
Walter Boal, G
Charles Daly, B
Benjamin Dibblee, B
1899— David Campbell, E
Charles Daly, B
1900— John Hallowell, E
David Campbell, E
Charles Daly, B
01— David Campbell, E
Edward Bowditch, E
Oliver Cutts, T
Crawford Blagden, T
William Lee, G
Charles Barnard, G
Robert Kernan, B
Thomas Graydon, B
02— Edward Bowditch, E
Thomas Graydon, B
03— Daniel Knowlton, T
Andrew Marshall, G
04— Daniel Hurley, B
05— Beaton Squires, T
Karl Brill, T
Francis Burr, G
Daniel Hurley, B
06— Charles Osborne, T
Francis Burr, G
07— Patrick Grant, C
John Wendell, B
08— Hamilton Fish, T
Charles Nourse, C
Hamilton Corbett, B
09— Hamilton Fish, T
Wayland Minot, B

10— Robert McKay, T
Robert Fisher, G
Percy Wendell, B
11— Robert Fisher, G
Percy Wendell, B
12— Samuel Felton, E
Stanley Pennock, G
Charles Brickley, B
13— Harvey Hitchcock, T
Stanley Pennock, G
Charles Brickley, B
Edward Mahan, B
14— Huntington Hardwick, E
Walter Trumbull, T
Stanley Pennock, G
Edward Mahan, B
15— Joseph Gilman, T
Edward Mahan, B
Richard King, B
16— Harrie Dadmun, G
19— Edward Casey, B
20— Tom Woods, G
21— John Brown, G
22— Charles Hubbard, G
23— Charles Hubbard, G
29— Ben Ticknor, C
30— *Ben Ticknor, C
31— Barry Wood, B
41— *Endicott Peabody, G

HOLY CROSS
74— John Provost, DB

HOUSTON
67— Rich Stotter, G
69— Bill Bridges, G
70— Elmo Wright, E
76— Wilson Whitley, DT
80— Leonard Mitchell, DL
88— Jason Phillips, WR
89— Andre Ware, QB

ILLINOIS
14— Perry Graves, E
Ralph Chapman, G
15— Bart Macomber, B
18— John Depler, C
20— Charles Carney, E
23— James McMillen, G
Red Grange, B
24— *Red Grange, B
25— Red Grange, B
26— Bernie Shively, G
46— Alex Agase, G
51— Johnny Karras, B
53— J.C. Caroline, B
59— Bill Burrell, G
63— *Dick Butkus, C
64— Dick Butkus, C
65— *Jim Grabowski, B
84— *David Williams, WR
85— *David Williams, WR
89— *Moe Gardner, DL
90— Moe Gardner, DL
94— *Dana Howard, LB
95— Kevin Hardy, LB

INDIANA
42— Billy Hillenbrand, B
44— John Tavener, C
45— Bob Ravensberg, E
88— Anthony Thompson, RB
89— *Anthony Thompson, RB
91— *Vaughn Dunbar, RB

IOWA
19— Lester Belding, E
21— Aubrey Devine, B
22— Gordon Locke, B
39— Nile Kinnick, B
54— Calvin Jones, G
55— Calvin Jones, G
57— Alex Karras, T
58— *Randy Duncan, B
81— Andre Tippett, DL
Reggie Roby, P
84— Larry Station, LB
85— *Chuck Long, QB
*Larry Station, LB
88— Marv Cook, TE
91— Leroy Smith, DL
97— Tim Dwight, KR
98— Jared DeVries, DL
2002—*Dallas Clark, TE
Eric Steinbach, OL
03— *Robert Gallery, OL
Nate Kaeding, PK

IOWA ST.
38— Ed Bock, G
89— Mike Busch, TE
95— Troy Davis, RB
96— Troy Davis, RB

KANSAS
63— Gale Sayers, B
64— Gale Sayers, B
68— John Zook, DE
73— David Jaynes, QB

KANSAS ST.
77— Gary Spani, LB
92— Sean Snyder, P
95— Chris Canty, DB
96— *Chris Canty, DB
97— Martin Gramatica, PK
98— Jeff Kelly, LB
Michael Bishop, QB
David Allen, KR
99— Mark Simoneau, LB
2002—*Terence Newman, DB

KENTUCKY
50— Bob Gain, T
Babe Parilli, B
51— Babe Parilli, B
56— Lou Michaels, T
57— Lou Michaels, T
65— Sam Ball, T
77— *Art Still, DL
98— Tim Couch, QB
99— James Whalen, TE
2002— Derek Abney, AP/KR

LAFAYETTE
00— Walter Bachman, C
01— Walter Bachman, C
21— Frank Schwab, G
22— Frank Schwab, G

LSU
35— Gaynell Tinsley, E
36— *Gaynell Tinsley, E
39— Ken Kavanaugh, E
54— Sid Fournet, T
58— *Billy Cannon, B
59— Billy Cannon, B
61— *Roy Winston, G
62— *Jerry Stovall, B
70— Mike Anderson, LB
Tommy Casanova, DB
71— Tommy Casanova, DB
72— Bert Jones, QB
77— Charles Alexander, RB
78— Charles Alexander, RB
87— Wendell Davis, WR
*Nacho Albergamo, C
97— Alan Faneca, OL
Chad Kessler, P
2001— Josh Reed, WR
03— Chad Lavalais, DL
04— Ben Wilkerson, C
Marcus Spears, DL
06— LaRon Landry, DB

LOUISIANA TECH
92— Willie Roaf, OL
98— Troy Edwards, WR

LOUISVILLE
2005—*Elvis Dumervil, DL

MARQUETTE
36— Ray Buivid, B

MARSHALL
97— *Randy Moss, WR

MARYLAND
51— *Bob Ward, G
52— Dick Modzelewski, T
*Jack Scarbath, B
53— *Stan Jones, T
55— *Bob Pellegrini, C
61— Gary Collins, E
74— *Randy White, DL
76— Joe Campbell, DT
79— Dale Castro, PK
85— J.D. Maarleveld, OL
2001— E.J. Henderson, LB
02— E.J. Henderson, LB

MEMPHIS
92— Joe Allison, PK

MIAMI (FLA.)
61— Bill Miller, E
66— Tom Beier, DB
67— *Ted Hendricks, DE
68— *Ted Hendricks, DE
73— Tony Cristiani, DL
74— Rubin Carter, MG
81— Fred Marion, DB
84— Eddie Brown, WR
85— Willie Smith, TE
86— *Vinny Testaverde, QB
*Jerome Brown, DL
Bennie Blades, DB
87— *Daniel Stubbs, DL
*Bennie Blades, DB
88— Steve Walsh, QB
Bill Hawkins, DL
89— Greg Mark, DL
90— Maurice Crum, LB
*Russell Maryland, DL
91— Carlos Huerta, PK
Darryl Williams, DB
92— *Gino Torretta, QB
Micheal Barrow, LB
Ryan McNeil, DB
94— *Warren Sapp, DL
2000— Santana Moss, AP
*Dan Morgan, LB
Edward Reed, DB
01— *Bryant McKinnie, OL
*Edward Reed, DB
02— Willis McGahee, RB
Brett Romberg, C
03— *Kellen Winslow, TE
*Sean Taylor, DB
04— *Antrel Rolle, DB

MICHIGAN
1898— William Cunningham, C
01— Neil Snow, E
03— Willie Heston, B
04— Willie Heston, B
07— Adolph Schulz, C
09— Albert Benbrook, G
10— Stanfield Wells, E
Albert Benbrook, G
13— Miller Pontius, T
Jim Craig, B
14— John Maulbetsch, B
22— Harry Kipke, B
23— Jack Blott, C
25— Bennie Oosterbaan, E
Benny Friedman, B
26— Bennie Oosterbaan, E
Benny Friedman, B
27— *Bennie Oosterbaan, E
28— Otto Pommerening, T
32— *Harry Newman, B
33— Francis Wistert, T
*Chuck Bernard, C
38— *Ralph Heikkinen, G
39— Tom Harmon, B
40— *Tom Harmon, B
41— Bob Westfall, B
42— Albert Wistert, T
Julie Franks, G
43— *Bill Daley, B
47— *Bob Chappuis, B
48— Dick Rifenburg, E
Alvin Wistert, T
49— Alvin Wistert, T
55— Ron Kramer, E
56— *Ron Kramer, E
65— Bill Yearby, DT
66— *Jack Clancy, E
69— *Jim Mandich, E
Tom Curtis, DB
70— Dan Dierdorf, T
71— Reggie McKenzie, G
*Mike Taylor, LB
72— Paul Seymour, T
Randy Logan, DB
73— Dave Gallagher, DL
Dave Brown, DB
74— *Dave Brown, DB
76— Rob Lytle, RB
Mark Donahue, G
77— *Mark Donahue, G
79— Ron Simpkins, LB
81— *Anthony Carter, WR
Ed Muransky, OL
Kurt Becker, OL
82— *Anthony Carter, WR
85— Mike Hammerstein, DL
Brad Cochran, DB
86— Garland Rivers, DB
87— John Elliott, OL
88— John Vitale, C
*Mark Messner, DL
89— *Tripp Welborne, DB
90— *Tripp Welborne, DB
91— *Desmond Howard, WR
*Greg Skrepenak, OL
96— Jarrett Irons, LB
97— *Charles Woodson, DB
2000—*Steve Hutchinson, OL
03— Chris Perry, RB
04— David Baas, OL
*Braylon Edwards, WR
Marlin Jackson, DB
Ernest Shazor, DB
06— Leon Hall, DB
Jake Long, OL
*LaMarr Woodley, DL

MICHIGAN ST.
15— Neno Jerry DaPrato, B
35— Sidney Wagner, G
49— Ed Bagdon, G
51— Bob Carey, E
*Don Coleman, T
53— Don Dohoney, E
55— Norman Masters, T
Earl Morrall, B
57— Dan Currie, C
Walt Kowalczyk, B
58— Sam Williams, E
62— George Saimes, B
63— Sherman Lewis, B
65— Bubba Smith, DE
*George Webster, DB
66— Clint Jones, B
*Bubba Smith, DE
*George Webster, DB
72— *Brad VanPelt, DB
85— *Lorenzo White, RB
87— Lorenzo White, RB
88— Tony Mandarich, OL
89— *Percy Snow, LB
Bob Kula, OL
2002—*Charles Rogers, WR
04— Brandon Fields, P

MINNESOTA
03— Fred Schacht, T
09— John McGovern, B
10— James Walker, T
16— Bert Baston, E
17— George Hauser, T
23— Ray Ecklund, E
26— Herb Joesting, B
27— Herb Joesting, B
29— Bronko Nagurski, T
31— Biggie Munn, G
34— Frank Larson, E
Bill Bevan, G
Pug Lund, B
35— Ed Widseth, T
36— *Ed Widseth, T
40— Urban Odson, T
George Franck, B
41— Dick Wildung, T
Bruce Smith, B
42— Dick Wildung, T
48— Leo Nomellini, T
49— Leo Nomellini, T
*Clayton Tonnemaker, C
53— *Paul Giel, B
60— *Tom Brown, G
61— Sandy Stephens, B
62— *Bobby Bell, T
63— Carl Eller, T
65— Aaron Brown, DE
99— Tyrone Carter, DB
Ben Hamilton, C
2000— Ben Hamilton, OL
05— *Greg Eslinger, C

MISSISSIPPI
47— Charley Conerly, B
53— Crawford Mims, G
59— Charlie Flowers, B
60— *Jake Gibbs, B

62— Jim Dunaway, T
79— Jim Miller, P
92— Everett Lindsay, OL
98— *Rufus French, TE
2001— Terrence Metcalf, OL
06— Patrick Willis, LB

MISSISSIPPI ST.
74— Jimmy Webb, DL
2000— Fred Smoot, DB

MISSOURI
41— Darold Jenkins, C
60— *Danny LaRose, E
65— Johnny Roland, DB
68— Roger Wehrli, DB
78— Kellen Winslow, TE
86— John Clay, OL
99— Rob Riti, C

NAVY
07— Bill Dague, E
08— Percy Northcroft, T
Ed Lange, B
11— Jack Dalton, B
13— John Brown, G
18— Lyman Perry, G
Wolcott Roberts, B
22— Wendell Taylor, T
26— *Frank Wickhorst, T
28— Edward Burke, G
34— Fred Borries, B
43— Don Whitmire, T
44— *Don Whitmire, T
Ben Chase, G
Bob Jenkins, B
45— Dick Duden, E
54— Ron Beagle, E
55— *Ron Beagle, E
60— *Joe Bellino, B
63— *Roger Staubach, B
75— *Chet Moeller, DB
83— Napoleon McCallum, RB
85— Napoleon McCallum, RB

NEBRASKA
15— Guy Chamberlin, E
24— Ed Weir, T
25— *Ed Weir, T
33— George Sauer, B
36— Sam Francis, B
63— *Bob Brown, G
64— *Larry Kramer, T
65— Freeman White, E
Walt Barnes, DT
66— LaVerne Allers, G
Wayne Meylan, MG
67— Wayne Meylan, MG
70— Bob Newton, T
71— Johnny Rodgers, FL
Willie Harper, DE
Larry Jacobson, DT
72— *Johnny Rodgers, FL
Willie Harper, DE
*Rich Glover, MG
73— *John Dutton, DL
74— Marvin Crenshaw, OT
75— *Rik Bonness, C
76— Dave Butterfield, DB
78— Kelvin Clark, OT
79— *Junior Miller, TE
80— Randy Schleusener, OL
Jarvis Redwine, RB
81— *Dave Rimington, C
82— *Dave Rimington, C
Mike Rozier, RB
83— *Irving Fryar, WR
Dean Steinkuhler, OL
*Mike Rozier, RB
84— *Mark Traynowicz, C
86— *Danny Noonan, DL
88— Jake Young, C
*Broderick Thomas, LB
89— Jake Young, C
92— *Will Shields, OL
93— *Trev Alberts, LB
94— *Zach Wiegert, OL
Brenden Stai, OL
Ed Stewart, LB
95— Tommie Frazier, QB
96— Aaron Taylor, C
Grant Wistrom, DL
97— *Aaron Taylor, OL
Grant Wistrom, DL
Jason Peter, DL
99— Ralph Brown, DB
2000— Dominic Raiola, C
01— Toniu Fonoti, OL

UNLV
98— Joe Kristosik, P

NEW MEXICO
89— Terance Mathis, WR
99— Brian Urlacher, DB

NEW YORK U.
28— Ken Strong, B

NORTH CAROLINA
37— Andy Bershak, E
48— Charlie Justice, B
70— Don McCauley, B
72— Ron Rusnak, G
74— Ken Huff, G
77— Dee Hardison, DL
80— *Lawrence Taylor, LB
83— William Fuller, DL
95— Marcus Jones, DL
96— Dre' Bly, DB
97— Greg Ellis, DL
Brian Simmons, LB
Dre' Bly, DB
2001—*Julius Peppers, DL

NORTH CAROLINA ST.
67— Dennis Byrd, DT
73— Bill Yoest, G
78— Jim Ritcher, C
Ted Brown, RB
79— *Jim Ritcher, C
96— Marc Primanti, PK
98— Torry Holt, WR

NORTH TEXAS
68— Joe Greene, DT

NORTHERN ILL.
93— *LeShon Johnson, RB

NORTHWESTERN
26— Ralph Baker, B
30— Frank Baker, E
31— Jack Riley, T
Dallas Marvil, T
Pug Rentner, B
36— Steve Reid, G
40— Alf Bauman, T
45— Max Morris, E
59— Ron Burton, B
62— Jack Cvercko, G
95— Pat Fitzgerald, LB
96— Pat Fitzgerald, LB
2000— Damien Anderson, RB

NOTRE DAME
13— Gus Dorais, B
17— Frank Rydzewski, C
20— George Gipp, B
21— Eddie Anderson, E
24— Harry Stuhldreher, B
Jimmy Crowley, B
Elmer Layden, B
26— Bud Boeringer, C
27— John Smith, G
29— Jack Cannon, G
*Frank Carideo, B
30— *Frank Carideo, B
Marchy Schwartz, B
31— Tommy Yarr, C
Marchy Schwartz, B
32— *Joe Kurth, T
34— Jack Robinson, C
35— Wayne Millner, E
37— Chuck Sweeney, E
38— *Ed Beinor, T
41— Bob Dove, E
42— Bob Dove, E
43— John Yonakor, E
Jim White, T
Pat Filley, G
Angelo Bertelli, B
Creighton Miller, B
46— George Connor, T
*John Lujack, B
47— George Connor, T
Bill Fischer, G
*John Lujack, B
48— Leon Hart, E
Bill Fischer, G
Emil Sitko, B
49— *Leon Hart, E
*Emil Sitko, B
Bob Williams, B
50— Jerry Groom, C
52— *Johnny Lattner, B
53— Art Hunter, T
*Johnny Lattner, B
54— *Ralph Guglielmi, B
55— Paul Hornung, B
57— Al Ecuyer, G
59— Monty Stickles, E
64— Jack Snow, E
John Huarte, B
65— *Dick Arrington, G
Nick Rassas, B
66— Tom Regner, G
*Nick Eddy, B
Alan Page, DE
*Jim Lynch, LB
67— Tom Schoen, DB
68— George Kunz, T
Terry Hanratty, QB
69— *Mike McCoy, DT
70— Tom Gatewood, E
Larry DiNardo, G
71— *Walt Patulski, DE
Clarence Ellis, DB
72— *Greg Marx, DT
73— Dave Casper, TE
Mike Townsend, DB
74— Pete Demmerle, WR
Gerry DiNardo, G
75— *Steve Niehaus, DT
76— Ken MacAfee, TE
*Ross Browner, DE
77— *Ken MacAfee, TE
*Ross Browner, DL
Luther Bradley, DB
78— Dave Huffman, C
*Bob Golic, LB
79— Vagas Ferguson, RB
80— *John Scully, C
Bob Crable, LB
81— Bob Crable, LB
87— *Tim Brown, WR
88— Frank Stams, DL
Michael Stonebreaker, LB
89— *Todd Lyght, DB
Chris Zorich, DL
90— *Raghib Ismail, WR
Todd Lyght, DB
*Michael Stonebreaker, LB
*Chris Zorich, DL
91— Mirko Jurkovic, OL
92— Aaron Taylor, OL
93— *Aaron Taylor, OL
Jeff Burris, DB
94— Bobby Taylor, DB
2002—*Shane Walton, DB
05— Jeff Samardzija, WR

OHIO ST.
16— Charles Harley, B
17— Charles Bolen, E
Charles Harley, B
19— Charles Harley, B
20— Iolas Huffman, G
Gaylord Stinchcomb, B
21— Iolas Huffman, T
25— Ed Hess, G
28— Wes Fesler, E
29— Wes Fesler, E
30— *Wes Fesler, E
35— Gomer Jones, C
39— Esco Sarkkinen, E
44— Jack Dugger, E
Bill Hackett, G
*Les Horvath, B
45— *Warren Amling, G
46— Warren Amling, T
50— *Vic Janowicz, B
54— *Howard Cassady, B
55— *Howard Cassady, B
56— *Jim Parker, G
58— Bob White, B
60— *Bob Ferguson, B
61— *Bob Ferguson, B
68— *Dave Foley, T
69— Jim Otis, B
Jim Stillwagon, MG
Jack Tatum, DB
70— *Jim Stillwagon, MG
*Jack Tatum, DB
72— Randy Gradishar, LB
73— *John Hicks, OT
*Randy Gradishar, LB
74— Kurt Schumacher, OT
Steve Myers, C
*Archie Griffin, RB
75— *Archie Griffin, RB
Ted Smith, G
Tim Fox, DB
76— Chris Ward, T
Bob Brudzinski, DE
77— *Chris Ward, T
Tom Cousineau, LB
78— Tom Cousineau, LB
79— Ken Fritz, G
82— Marcus Marek, LB
84— Jim Lachey, OG
*Keith Byars, RB
86— Cris Carter, WR
Chris Spielman, LB
87— *Chris Spielman, LB
*Tom Tupa, P
93— Dan Wilkinson, DL
94— Korey Stringer, OL
95— Terry Glenn, WR
*Orlando Pace, OL
*Eddie George, RB
96— *Orlando Pace, OL
Mike Vrabel, DL
Shawn Springs, DB
97— Andy Katzenmoyer, LB
98— *Antoine Winfield, DB
Rob Murphy, OL
2001— LeCharles Bentley, C
02— Mike Nugent, PK
*Mike Doss, DB
Matt Wilhelm, LB
03— Will Allen, DB
04— *Mike Nugent, PK
A.J. Hawk, LB
05— *A.J. Hawk, LB
06— James Laurinaitis, LB
Quinn Pitcock, DL
*Troy Smith, QB

OKLAHOMA
38— Waddy Young, E
48— Buddy Burris, G
50— Jim Weatherall, T
Leon Heath, B
51— *Jim Weatherall, T
52— Billy Vessels, B
53— J.D. Roberts, G
54— Max Boydston, E
Kurt Burris, C
55— Bo Bolinger, G
56— *Jerry Tubbs, C
Tommy McDonald, B
57— Bill Krisher, G
Clendon Thomas, B
58— Bob Harrison, C
63— Jim Grisham, B
64— Ralph Neely, T
65— Carl McAdams, LB
67— *Granville Liggins, MG
69— *Steve Owens, B
71— *Greg Pruitt, B
Tom Brahaney, C
72— *Greg Pruitt, B
Tom Brahaney, C
73— *Lucious Selmon, DL
Rod Shoate, LB
74— John Roush, G
*Joe Washington, RB
*Rod Shoate, LB
75— *Lee Roy Selmon, DT
Dewey Selmon, MG
Jimbo Elrod, DE
76— *Mike Vaughan, OT
77— *Zac Henderson, DB
78— *Greg Roberts, G
*Billy Sims, RB
79— *Billy Sims, RB
*George Cumby, LB
80— Louis Oubre, OL
81— Terry Crouch, OL
82— Rick Bryan, DL
83— *Rick Bryan, DL
84— Tony Casillas, DL
85— Tony Casillas, DL

*Brian Bosworth, LB
86— *Keith Jackson, TE
*Brian Bosworth, LB
87— *Keith Jackson, TE
*Mark Hutson, OL
Dante Jones, LB
Rickey Dixon, DB
88— *Anthony Phillips, OL
2000— Josh Heupel, QB
Rocky Calmus, LB
J.T. Thatcher, DB
01— Rocky Calmus, LB
*Roy Williams, DB
02— Tommie Harris, DL
Teddy Lehman, LB
03— *Jason White, QB
*Antonio Perkins, AP/KR
*Tommie Harris, DL
*Teddy Lehman, LB
*Derrick Strait, DB
04— *Jammal Brown, OL
*Adrian Peterson, RB

OKLAHOMA ST.
45— Bob Fenimore, B
69— John Ward, T
76— Derrel Gofourth, C
77— *Terry Miller, RB
84— Rod Brown, DB
85— Thurman Thomas, RB
*Leslie O'Neal, DL
88— Hart Lee Dykes, WR
*Barry Sanders, RB
97— Alonzo Mayes, TE
2002— Rashaun Woods, WR

OREGON
62— Mel Renfro, B
2005— Haloti Ngata, DL

OREGON ST.
56— John Witte, T
58— Ted Bates, T
62— *Terry Baker, B
63— Vern Burke, E
68— *John Didion, C

PENN
1891— John Adams, C
1892— Harry Thayer, B
1894— Charles Gelbert, E
Arthur Knipe, B
George Brooke, B
1895— Charles Gelbert, E
Charles Wharton, G
Alfred Bull, C
George Brooke, B
1896— Charles Gelbert, E
Charles Wharton, G
Wylie Woodruff, G
1897— John Outland, T
T. Truxton Hare, G
John Minds, B
1898— T. Truxton Hare, G
Pete Overfield, C
John Outland, B
1899— T. Truxton Hare, G
Pete Overfield, C
Josiah McCracken, B
00— T. Truxton Hare, G
04— Frank Piekarski, G
Vincent Stevenson, B
Andrew Smith, B
05— Otis Lamson, T
Robert Torrey, C
06— August Ziegler, G
William Hollenback, B
07— Dexter Draper, T
August Ziegler, G
08— Hunter Scarlett, E
William Hollenback, B
10— Ernest Cozens, C
E. LeRoy Mercer, B
12— E. LeRoy Mercer, B
17— Henry Miller, E
19— Henry Miller, E
22— John Thurman, T
24— Ed McGinley, T
27— Ed Hake, T
28— Paul Scull, B
43— Bob Odell, B
45— George Savitsky, T
47— Chuck Bednarik, C
48— Chuck Bednarik, C

PENN ST.
06— William Dunn, C
19— Bob Higgins, E
20— Charles Way, B
21— Glenn Killinger, B
23— Harry Wilson, B
59— Richie Lucas, B
64— Glenn Ressler, G
68— *Ted Kwalick, E
Dennis Onkotz, LB
69— *Mike Reid, DT
Dennis Onkotz, LB
70— Jack Ham, LB
71— Dave Joyner, T
72— Bruce Bannon, DE
John Skorupan, LB
73— *John Cappelletti, B
74— Mike Hartenstine, DL
75— Greg Buttle, LB
78— *Keith Dorney, OT
*Chuck Fusina, QB
*Bruce Clark, DL
79— Bruce Clark, DL
81— *Sean Farrell, OL
86— D.J. Dozier, RB
Shane Conlan, LB
92— O.J. McDuffie, WR
94— Kerry Collins, QB
*Ki-Jana Carter, RB
95— Jeff Hartings, OL
97— Curtis Enis, RB
99— *LaVar Arrington, LB
*Courtney Brown, DL
Brandon Short, LB
2002—*Larry Johnson, RB
05— *Tamba Hali, DL
Paul Posluszny, LB
06— Paul Posluszny, LB

PITTSBURGH
15— Robert Peck, C
16— James Herron, E
Robert Peck, C
17— Dale Seis, G
John Sutherland, G
18— Leonard Hilty, T
Tom Davies, B
George McLaren, B
20— Herb Stein, C
21— Herb Stein, C
25— Ralph Chase, T
27— *Gibby Welch, B
28— Mike Getto, T
29— *Joe Donchess, E
Ray Montgomery, G
31— Jesse Quatse, T
32— Joe Skladany, E
*Warren Heller, B
33— Joe Skladany, E
34— Chuck Hartwig, G
George Shotwell, C
36— Averell Daniell, T
37— Tony Matisi, T
Marshall Goldberg, B
38— *Marshall Goldberg, B
56— *Joe Walton, E
58— John Guzik, G
60— *Mike Ditka, E
63— Paul Martha, B
76— *Tony Dorsett, RB
Al Romano, MG
77— Tom Brzoza, C
Randy Holloway, DL
Bob Jury, DB
78— Hugh Green, DL
79— *Hugh Green, DL
80— *Hugh Green, DL
*Mark May, OL
81— Sal Sunseri, LB
82— Jimbo Covert, OL
83— *Bill Fralic, OL
84— *Bill Fralic, OT
86— Randy Dixon, OL
Tony Woods, DL
87— Craig Heyward, RB
88— Mark Stepnoski, OL
90— Brian Greenfield, P
2000— Antonio Bryant, WR
03— *Larry Fitzgerald, WR

PRINCETON
1889— Hector Cowan, T
William George, C
Edgar Allan Poe, B
Roscoe Channing, B
Knowlton Ames, B
1890— Ralph Warren, E
Jesse Riggs, G
Sheppard Homans, B
1891— Jesse Riggs, G
Philip King, B
Sheppard Homans, B
1892— Arthur Wheeler, G
Philip King, B
1893— Thomas Trenchard, E
Langdon Lea, T
Arthur Wheeler, G
Philip King, B
Franklin Morse, B
1894— Langdon Lea, T
Arthur Wheeler, G
1895— Langdon Lea, T
Dudley Riggs, G
1896— William Church, T
Robert Gailey, C
Addison Kelly, B
John Baird, B
1897— Garrett Cochran, E
Addison Kelly, B
1898— Lew Palmer, E
Arthur Hillebrand, T
1899— Arthur Hillebrand, T
Arthur Poe, E
Howard Reiter, B
01— Ralph Davis, E
02— John DeWitt, G
03— Howard Henry, E
John DeWitt, G
J. Dana Kafer, B
04— James Cooney, T
05— James McCormick, B
06— L. Casper Wister, E
James Cooney, T
Edward Dillon, B
07— L. Casper Wister, E
Edwin Harlan, B
James McCormick, B
08— Frederick Tibbott, B
10— Talbot Pendleton, B
11— Sanford White, E
Edward Hart, T
Joseph Duff, G
12— John Logan, G
13— Harold Ballin, T
14— Harold Ballin, T
16— Frank Hogg, G
18— Frank Murrey, B
20— Stan Keck, T
Donold Lourie, B
21— Stan Keck, G
22— C. Herbert Treat, T
25— Ed McMillan, C
35— John Weller, G
51— *Dick Kazmaier, B
52— Frank McPhee, E
65— Stas Maliszewski, G

PURDUE
29— Elmer Sleight, T
Ralph Welch, B
32— *Paul Moss, E
33— Duane Purvis, B
40— Dave Rankin, E
43— Alex Agase, G
52— Bernie Flowers, E
65— Bob Griese, QB
67— *Leroy Keyes, B
68— *Leroy Keyes, B
Chuck Kyle, MG
69— *Mike Phipps, QB
72— Otis Armstrong, B
Dave Butz, DT
80— *Dave Young, TE
*Mark Herrmann, QB
86— Rod Woodson, DB
2001— Travis Dorsch, P
04— Taylor Stubblefield, WR

RICE
46— Weldon Humble, G
49— James Williams, E
54— Dicky Maegle, B
58— Buddy Dial, E
76— Tommy Kramer, QB
91— Trevor Cobb, RB

RICHMOND
69— Walker Gillette, E
78— Jeff Nixon, DB

RUTGERS
17— Paul Robeson, E
18— Paul Robeson, E
61— Alex Kroll, C
95— *Marco Battaglia, TE

ST. MARY'S (CAL.)
27— Larry Bettencourt, C
45— *Herman Wedemeyer, B

SAN DIEGO ST.
92— *Marshall Faulk, RB
93— *Marshall Faulk, RB
97— Kyle Turley, OL

SANTA CLARA
38— Alvord Wolff, T
39— John Schiechl, C

SOUTH CAROLINA
80— *George Rogers, RB
84— Del Wilkes, OG

SOUTHERN CALIFORNIA
26— Mort Kaer, B
27— Jesse Hibbs, T
Morley Drury, B
30— Erny Pinckert, B
31— John Baker, G
Gus Shaver, B
32— *Ernie Smith, T
33— Aaron Rosenberg, G
*Cotton Warburton, B
39— *Harry Smith, G
43— Ralph Heywood, E
44— John Ferraro, T
47— Paul Cleary, E
52— Elmer Willhoite, G
Jim Sears, B
62— Hal Bedsole, E
65— *Mike Garrett, B
66— Ron Yary, T
Nate Shaw, DB
67— *Ron Yary, T
*O.J. Simpson, B
Tim Rossovich, DE
Adrian Young, LB
68— *O.J. Simpson, B
69— Jim Gunn, DE
70— Charlie Weaver, DE
72— *Charles Young, TE
73— Lynn Swann, WR
Booker Brown, OT
Richard Wood, LB
Artimus Parker, DB
74— *Anthony Davis, RB
Richard Wood, LB
75— *Ricky Bell, RB
76— *Ricky Bell, RB
Gary Jeter, DT
Dennis Thurman, DB
77— *Dennis Thurman, DB
78— *Pat Howell, G
*Charles White, RB
79— *Brad Budde, G
*Charles White, RB
80— Keith Van Horne, OL
*Ronnie Lott, DB
81— Roy Foster, OL
*Marcus Allen, RB
82— *Don Mosebar, OL
Bruce Matthews, OL
George Achica, MG
83— Tony Slaton, C
84— Jack Del Rio, LB
85— Jeff Bregel, OL
86— Jeff Bregel, OL
Tim McDonald, DB
87— Dave Cadigan, OL
89— *Mark Carrier, DB
Tim Ryan, DL
93— Johnnie Morton, WR
94— Tony Boselli, OL
95— *Keyshawn Johnson, WR
98— *Chris Claiborne, LB
2002— Carson Palmer, QB
Troy Polamalu, DB

03— Mike Williams, WR
Jacob Rogers, OL
Kenechi Udeze, DL
04— Reggie Bush, AP/KR
Matt Leinart, QB
Shaun Cody, DL
Matt Grootegoed, LB
05— *Reggie Bush, RB
*Dwayne Jarrett, WR
Taitusi Lutui, OL
06— Sam Baker, OL
Dwayne Jarrett, WR

SMU
35— J.C. Wetsel, G
Bobby Wilson, B
47— Doak Walker, B
48— *Doak Walker, B
49— Doak Walker, B
50— Kyle Rote, B
51— Dick Hightower, C
66— John LaGrone, MG
68— Jerry LeVias, E
72— Robert Popelka, DB
74— Louie Kelcher, G
78— Emanuel Tolbert, WR
80— John Simmons, DB
82— *Eric Dickerson, RB
83— *Russell Carter, DB
85— Reggie Dupard, RB

STANFORD
24— Jim Lawson, E
25— Ernie Nevers, B
28— Seraphim Post, G
Don Robesky, G
32— Bill Corbus, G
33— Bill Corbus, G
34— Bob Reynolds, T
Bobby Grayson, B
35— James Moscrip, E
*Bobby Grayson, B
40— Frank Albert, B
41— Frank Albert, B
42— Chuck Taylor, G
50— Bill McColl, E
51— *Bill McColl, E
56— John Brodie, QB
70— Jim Plunkett, QB
71— Jeff Siemon, LB
74— Pat Donovan, DL
77— Guy Benjamin, QB
79— Ken Margerum, WR
80— *Ken Margerum, WR
82— *John Elway, QB
86— Brad Muster, RB
91— Bob Whitfield, OL
99— Troy Walters, WR

SYRACUSE
08— Frank Horr, T
15— Harold White, G
17— Alfred Cobb, T
18— Lou Usher, T
Joe Alexander, G
19— Joe Alexander, G
23— Pete McRae, E
26— Vic Hanson, E
56— *Jim Brown, B
59— *Roger Davis, G
60— Ernie Davis, B
61— *Ernie Davis, B
67— *Larry Csonka, B
85— *Tim Green, DL
87— *Don McPherson, QB
Ted Gregory, DL
90— John Flannery, C
92— *Chris Gedney, TE
2001—*Dwight Freeney, DL

TEMPLE
85— John Rienstra, OL
86— *Paul Palmer, RB

TENNESSEE
29— Gene McEver, B
33— Beattie Feathers, B
38— Bowden Wyatt, E
39— Ed Molinski, G
George Cafego, B
40— *Bob Suffridge, G
46— Dick Huffman, T
51— *Hank Lauricella, B
52— John Michels, G
56— *John Majors, B
65— Frank Emanuel, LB
66— Paul Naumoff, LB
67— *Bob Johnson, C
68— *Charles Rosenfelder, G
Steve Kiner, LB
69— Chip Kell, G
*Steve Kiner, LB
70— *Chip Kell, G
71— *Bobby Majors, DB
75— Larry Seivers, E
76— Larry Seivers, SE
79— Roland James, DB
83— *Reggie White, DL
84— Bill Mayo, OG
85— Tim McGee, WR
89— *Eric Still, OL
90— *Antone Davis, OL
91— Dale Carter, DB
97— Peyton Manning, QB
98— Al Wilson, LB
99— Cosey Coleman, OL
Deon Grant, DB
2000— John Henderson, DL
01— John Henderson, DL
03— Dustin Colquitt, P
04— Michael Munoz, OL

TEXAS
45— Hubert Bechtol, E
46— Hubert Bechtol, E
47— Bobby Layne, B
50— *Bud McFadin, G
53— Carlton Massey, E
61— *Jimmy Saxton, B
62— *Johnny Treadwell, G
63— *Scott Appleton, T
65— Tommy Nobis, LB
68— Chris Gilbert, B
69— Bob McKay, T
70— Bobby Wuensch, T
Steve Worster, B
Bill Atessis, DE
71— *Jerry Sisemore, T
72— *Jerry Sisemore, T
73— *Bill Wyman, C
Roosevelt Leaks, B
75— Bob Simmons, T
77— *Earl Campbell, RB
*Brad Shearer, DL
78— *Johnnie Johnson, DB
79— *Steve McMichael, DL
*Johnnie Johnson, DB
80— Kenneth Sims, DL
81— Terry Tausch, OL
*Kenneth Sims, DL
83— Doug Dawson, OL
Jeff Leiding, LB
Jerry Gray, DB
84— Tony Degrate, DL
*Jerry Gray, DB
95— Tony Brackens, DL
96— Dan Neil, OL
97— *Ricky Williams, RB
98— *Ricky Williams, RB
2000— Leonard Davis, OL
Casey Hampton, DL
01— Mike Williams, OL
*Quentin Jammer, DB
02— Derrick Dockery, OL
03— Derrick Johnson, LB
04— *Derrick Johnson, LB
05— *Jonathan Scott, OL
Vince Young, QB
*Michael Huff, DB
Rodrique Wright, DL
06— Justin Blalock, OL

UTEP
2000— *Brian Natkin, TE

TEXAS A&M
37— Joe Routt, G
39— John Kimbrough, B
40— Marshall Robnett, G
*John Kimbrough, B
57— *John David Crow, B
70— Dave Elmendorf, DB
74— Pat Thomas, DB
75— *Ed Simonini, LB
Pat Thomas, DB
76— Tony Franklin, PK
*Robert Jackson, LB
85— Johnny Holland, LB
87— John Roper, DL
90— Darren Lewis, RB
91— Kevin Smith, DB
92— *Marcus Buckley, LB
93— Aaron Glenn, DB
Sam Adams, DL
94— Leeland McElroy, KR
98— *Dat Nguyen, LB

TCU
34— Darrell Lester, C
35— Darrell Lester, C
36— Sammy Baugh, B
38— Ki Aldrich, C
*Davey O'Brien, B
55— *Jim Swink, B
59— Don Floyd, T
60— *Bob Lilly, T
84— *Kenneth Davis, RB
91— Kelly Blackwell, TE
95— Michael Reeder, PK
2000—*LaDainian Tomlinson, RB
03— Nick Browne, PK

TEXAS TECH
60— E.J. Holub, C
65— Donny Anderson, B
77— Dan Irons, T
82— Gabriel Rivera, DL
91— *Mark Bounds, P
95— *Zach Thomas, LB
96— *Byron Hanspard, RB
98— Montae Reagor, DL

TOLEDO
71— Mel Long, DT

TULANE
31— *Jerry Dalrymple, E
32— Don Zimmerman, B
39— Harley McCollum, T
41— Ernie Blandin, T

TULSA
65— *Howard Twilley, E
91— Jerry Ostroski, OL

UCLA
46— *Burr Baldwin, E
52— Donn Moomaw, C
53— Paul Cameron, B
54— Jack Ellena, T
55— Hardiman Cureton, G
57— Dick Wallen, E
66— Mel Farr, B
67— *Gary Beban, B
Don Manning, LB
69— Mike Ballou, LB
73— Kermit Johnson, B
75— John Sciarra, QB
76— Jerry Robinson, LB
77— *Jerry Robinson, LB
78— *Jerry Robinson, LB
Kenny Easley, DB
79— *Kenny Easley, DB
80— *Kenny Easley, DB
81— *Tim Wrightman, TE
83— Don Rogers, DB
85— *John Lee, PK
88— Troy Aikman, QB
Darryl Henley, DB
92— Carlton Gray, DB
93— *J.J. Stokes, WR
Bjorn Merten, PK
Jamir Miller, LB
95— *Jonathan Ogden, OL
97— Chad Overhauser, OL
98— Cade McNown, QB
Kris Farris, OL
2000— Fred Mitchell, WR
01— Robert Thomas, LB
03— *Dave Ball, DL
05— *Maurice Drew, AP/KR
Marcedes Lewis, TE
06— Justin Hickman, DL
Justin Medlock, PK

UTAH
94— Luther Elliss, DL
2002— Jordan Gross, OL
06— Eric Weddle, DB

UTAH ST.
61— Merlin Olsen, T
69— Phil Olsen, DE

VANDERBILT
23— Lynn Bomar, E
24— Henry Wakefield, E
32— Pete Gracey, C
58— George Deiderich, G
82— *Jim Arnold, P
84— *Ricky Anderson, P

VIRGINIA
15— Eugene Mayer, B
41— Bill Dudley, B
85— *Jim Dombrowski, OL
90— Herman Moore, WR
92— Chris Slade, DL
93— Mark Dixon, OL
98— Anthony Poindexter, DB
99— Thomas Jones, RB
2004— Elton Brown, OL
*Heath Miller, TE

VIRGINIA TECH
67— Frank Loria, DB
84— Bruce Smith, DL
93— *Jim Pyne, C
95— Cornell Brown, DL
99— *Corey Moore, DL
2003—*Jake Grove, C
Kevin Jones, RB
05— *Jimmy Williams, DB

WAKE FOREST
76— *Bill Armstrong, DB
2005—*Ryan Plackemeier, P

WASH. & JEFF.
14— John Spiegel, B
18— Wilbur Henry, T
19— Wilbur Henry, T

WASHINGTON
25— George Wilson, B
28— Charles Carroll, B
36— Max Starcevich, G
40— Rudy Mucha, C
41— Ray Frankowski, G
63— Rick Redman, G
64— Rick Redman, G
66— Tom Greenlee, DT
68— Al Worley, DB
82— *Chuck Nelson, PK
84— Ron Holmes, DL
86— Jeff Jaeger, PK
Reggie Rogers, DL
91— *Steve Emtman, DL
Mario Bailey, WR
92— *Lincoln Kennedy, OL
95— *Lawyer Milloy, DB
96— Benji Olson, OL
97— Olin Kreutz, C
2002— Reggie Williams, WR

WASHINGTON ST.
84— Rueben Mayes, RB
88— Mike Utley, OL
89— *Jason Hanson, PK
2002— Rien Long, DL
05— Jerome Harrison, RB

WEST VIRGINIA
19— Ira Rodgers, B
55— Bruce Bosley, T
82— *Darryl Talley, LB
85— Brian Jozwiak, OL
92— Mike Compton, C
94— *Todd Sauerbrun, P
95— Aaron Beasley, DB
96— Canute Curtis, LB
2003— Grant Wiley, LB
06— *Dan Mozes, C
*Steve Slaton, RB

WILLIAMS
17— Ben Boynton, B
19— Ben Boynton, B

WISCONSIN
12— Robert Butler, T
13— Ray Keeler, G
15— Howard Buck, T
19— Charles Carpenter, C
20— Ralph Scott, T
23— Marty Below, T
30— Milo Lubratovich, T
42— *Dave Schreiner, E
54— *Alan Ameche, B
59— *Dan Lanphear, T
62— Pat Richter, E

75— Dennis Lick, T
81— Tim Krumrie, DL
94— Cory Raymer, C
98— Aaron Gibson, OL
*Tom Burke, DL
99— *Chris McIntosh, OL
*Ron Dayne, RB
2000— Jamar Fletcher, DB
04— Erasmus James, DL
06— *Joe Thomas, OL

WYOMING
83— Jack Weil, P
84— Jay Novacek, TE
96— Marcus Harris, WR
97— Brian Lee, DB

YALE
1889— Amos Alonzo Stagg, E
Charles Gill, T
Pudge Heffelfinger, G
1890— William Rhodes, T
Pudge Heffelfinger, G
Thomas McClung, B
1891— Frank Hinkey, E
John Hartwell, E
Wallace Winter, T
Pudge Heffelfinger, G
Thomas McClung, B
1892— Frank Hinkey, E
A. Hamilton Wallis, T
Vance McCormick, B
1893— Frank Hinkey, E
William Hickok, G
Frank Butterworth, B
1894— Frank Hinkey, E
William Hickok, G
Philip Stillman, C
George Adee, B
Frank Butterworth, B
1895— Fred Murphy, T
Samuel Thorne, B
1896— Fred Murphy, T
Clarence Fincke, B
1897— John Hall, E
Burr Chamberlin, T
Gordon Brown, G
Charles DeSaulles, B
1898— Burr Chamberlin, T
Gordon Brown, G
Malcolm McBride, B
1899— George Stillman, T
Gordon Brown, G
Malcolm McBride, B
Albert Sharpe, B
00— George Stillman, T
James Bloomer, T
Gordon Brown, G
Herman Olcott, C
George Chadwick, B
Perry Hale, B
William Fincke, B
01— Henry Holt, C
02— Thomas Shevlin, E
Ralph Kinney, T
James Hogan, T
Edgar Glass, G
Henry Holt, C
Foster Rockwell, B
George Chadwick, B
03— Charles Rafferty, E
James Hogan, T
James Bloomer, G
W. Ledyard Mitchell, B
04— Thomas Shevlin, E
James Hogan, T
Ralph Kinney, G
Foster Rockwell, B
05— Thomas Shevlin, E
Roswell Tripp, G
Howard Roome, B
Guy Hutchinson, B
06— Robert Forbes, E
L. Horatio Biglow, T
Hugh Knox, B
Paul Veeder, B
07— Clarence Alcott, E
L. Horatio Biglow, T
Thomas A. D. Jones, B
Edward Coy, B
08— William Goebel, G
Hamlin Andrus, G
Edward Coy, B
09— John Kilpatrick, E
Henry Hobbs, T
Hamlin Andrus, G
Carroll Cooney, C
Edward Coy, B
Stephen Philbin, B
10— John Kilpatrick, E
11— Douglass Bomeisler, E
Henry Ketcham, C
Arthur Howe, B
12— Douglass Bomeisler, E
Henry Ketcham, C
13— Nelson Talbott, T
14— Harry LeGore, B
16— Clinton Black, G
20— Tim Callahan, G
21— Malcolm Aldrich, B
23— Century Milstead, T
William Mallory, B
24— Dick Luman, E
27— Bill Webster, G
John Charlesworth, C
36— Larry Kelley, E
37— *Clint Frank, B
44— Paul Walker, E

Team Leaders in Consensus All-Americans

(Ranked on Total Number of Selections; Minimum 5 Selections)

Team	No.	Players
Yale	100	69
Notre Dame	95	79
Harvard	89	59
Michigan	76	64
Southern California	75	66
Ohio St.	75	58
Oklahoma	66	54
Princeton	65	49
Nebraska	52	43
Pittsburgh	49	42
Texas	48	42
Penn	46	32
Alabama	39	38
Penn St.	37	34
UCLA	37	33
Army	37	28
Tennessee	36	27
Miami (Fla.)	35	32
Minnesota	33	28
Florida St.	33	26
Colorado	29	25
Georgia	28	23
California	27	25
Auburn	26	24
Michigan St.	26	23
Stanford	26	21
Florida	24	23
Navy	23	20
LSU	23	19
Illinois	23	18
Wisconsin	21	21
Georgia Tech	21	20
Iowa	21	19
Washington	20	19
Texas A&M	20	18
Arkansas	20	17
Purdue	19	18
Syracuse	19	17
Cornell	19	15
Clemson	18	17
Dartmouth	17	15
SMU	16	14
Arizona St.	16	13
North Carolina	14	13
Northwestern	13	13
TCU	13	12
Maryland	12	11
Brigham Young	12	10
Arizona	12	9
Oklahoma St.	11	11
West Virginia	11	11
Chicago	11	9
Mississippi	10	10
Virginia	10	10
Kansas St.	10	9
Baylor	10	8
Kentucky	10	8
Boston College	9	9
Texas Tech	8	8
Virginia Tech	8	8
Houston	7	7
Missouri	7	7
North Carolina St.	7	6
Brown	6	6
Rice	6	6
Vanderbilt	6	6
Carlisle	6	5
Colgate	6	5
Columbia	6	5
Indiana	6	5
Air Force	5	5
Oregon St.	5	5
Washington St.	5	5

Special Awards

HEISMAN MEMORIAL TROPHY

Originally presented in 1935 as the DAC Trophy by the Downtown Athletic Club of New York City to the best college player east of the Mississippi River. In 1936, players across the country were eligible and the award was renamed the Heisman Memorial Trophy to honor former college coach and DAC athletics director John W. Heisman. The award now goes to the outstanding college football player in the United States. The bronze trophy was sculpted by Frank Eliscu, with the aid of Jim Crowley, one of Notre Dame's famed Four Horsemen. Crowley was then coach at Fordham, and some of his players posed as models for the trophy.

Year	Player (Winner Bold), School, Position	Points
1935	**Jay Berwanger,** Chicago, HB	84
	2nd—Monk Meyer, Army	29
	3rd—Bill Shakespeare, Notre Dame, HB	23
	4th—Pepper Constable, Princeton, FB	20
1936	**Larry Kelley,** Yale, E	219
	2nd—Sam Francis, Nebraska, FB	47
	3rd—Ray Buivid, Marquette, HB	43
	4th—Sammy Baugh, TCU, HB	39
1937	**Clint Frank,** Yale, HB	524
	2nd—Byron White, Colorado, HB	264
	3rd—Marshall Goldberg, Pittsburgh, HB	211
	4th—Alex Wojciechowicz, Fordham, C	85
1938	**Davey O'Brien,** TCU, QB	519
	2nd—Marshall Goldberg, Pittsburgh, HB	294
	3rd—Sid Luckman, Columbia, QB	154
	4th—Bob MacLeod, Dartmouth, HB	78
1939	**Nile Kinnick,** Iowa, HB	651
	2nd—Tom Harmon, Michigan, HB	405
	3rd—Paul Christman, Missouri, QB	391
	4th—George Cafego, Tennessee, QB	296
1940	**Tom Harmon,** Michigan, HB	1,303
	2nd—John Kimbrough, Texas A&M, FB	841
	3rd—George Franck, Minnesota, HB	102
	4th—Frankie Albert, Stanford, QB	90
1941	**Bruce Smith,** Minnesota, HB	554
	2nd—Angelo Bertelli, Notre Dame, QB	345
	3rd—Frankie Albert, Stanford, QB	336
	4th—Frank Sinkwich, Georgia, HB	249
1942	**Frank Sinkwich,** Georgia, HB	1,059
	2nd—Paul Governali, Columbia, QB	218
	3rd—Clint Castleberry, Georgia Tech, HB	99
	4th—Mike Holovak, Boston College, FB	95
1943	**Angelo Bertelli,** Notre Dame, QB	648
	2nd—Bob Odell, Penn, HB	177
	3rd—Otto Graham, Northwestern, QB	140
	4th—Creighton Miller, Notre Dame, HB	134
1944	**Les Horvath,** Ohio St., QB/HB	412
	2nd—Glenn Davis, Army, HB	287
	3rd—Doc Blanchard, Army, FB	237
	4th—Don Whitmire, Navy, T	115
1945	***Doc Blanchard,** Army, FB	860
	2nd—Glenn Davis, Army, HB	638
	3rd—Bob Fenimore, Oklahoma St., HB	187
	4th—Herman Wedermeyer, St. Mary's (Cal.), HB	152
1946	**Glenn Davis,** Army, HB	792
	2nd—Charlie Trippi, Georgia, HB	435
	3rd—Johnny Lujack, Notre Dame, QB	379
	4th—Doc Blanchard, Army, FB	267
1947	**Johnny Lujack,** Notre Dame, QB	742
	2nd—Bob Chappius, Michigan, HB	555
	3rd—Doak Walker, SMU, HB	196
	4th—Charlie Conerly, Mississippi, QB	186
1948	***Doak Walker,** SMU, HB	778
	2nd—Charlie Justice, North Carolina, HB	443
	3rd—Chuck Bednarik, Penn, C	336
	4th—Jackie Jensen, California, HB	143
1949	**Leon Hart,** Notre Dame, E	995
	2nd—Charlie Justice, North Carolina, HB	272
	3rd—Doak Walker, SMU, HB	229
	4th—Arnold Galiffa, Army, QB	196

Year	Player (Winner Bold), School, Position	Points
1950	* **Vic Janowicz,** Ohio St., HB	633
	2nd—Kyle Rote, SMU, HB	280
	3rd—Reds Bagnell, Penn, HB	231
	4th—Babe Parilli, Kentucky, QB	214
1951	**Dick Kazmaier,** Princeton, HB	1,777
	2nd—Hank Lauricella, Tennessee, HB	424
	3rd—Babe Parilli, Kentucky, QB	344
	4th—Bill McColl, Stanford, E	313
1952	**Billy Vessels,** Oklahoma, HB	525
	2nd—Jack Scarbath, Maryland, QB	367
	3rd—Paul Giel, Minnesota, HB	329
	4th—Donn Moomaw, UCLA, C	257
1953	**Johnny Lattner,** Notre Dame, HB	1,850
	2nd—Paul Giel, Minnesota, HB	1,794
	3rd—Paul Cameron, UCLA, HB	444
	4th—Bernie Faloney, Maryland, QB	258
1954	**Alan Ameche,** Wisconsin, FB	1,068
	2nd—Kurt Burris, Oklahoma, C	838
	3rd—Howard Cassady, Ohio St., HB	810
	4th—Ralph Guglielmi, Notre Dame, QB	691
1955	**Howard Cassady,** Ohio St., HB	2,219
	2nd—Jim Swink, TCU, HB	742
	3rd—George Welsh, Navy, QB	383
	4th—Earl Morrall, Michigan St., QB	323
1956	**Paul Hornung,** Notre Dame, QB	1,066
	2nd—Johnny Majors, Tennessee, HB	994
	3rd—Tommy McDonald, Oklahoma, HB	973
	4th—Jerry Tubbs, Oklahoma, C	724
1957	**John David Crow,** Texas A&M, HB	1,183
	2nd—Alex Karras, Iowa, T	693
	3rd—Walt Kowalczyk, Michigan St., HB	630
	4th—Lou Michaels, Kentucky, T	330
1958	**Pete Dawkins,** Army, HB	1,394
	2nd—Randy Duncan, Iowa, QB	1,021
	3rd—Billy Cannon, LSU, HB	975
	4th—Bob White, Ohio St., HB	365
1959	**Billy Cannon,** LSU, HB	1,929
	2nd—Richie Lucas, Penn St., QB	613
	3rd—Don Meredith, SMU, QB	286
	4th—Bill Burrell, Illinois, G	196
1960	**Joe Bellino,** Navy, HB	1,793
	2nd—Tom Brown, Minnesota, G	731
	3rd—Jake Gibbs, Mississippi, QB	453
	4th—Ed Dyas, Auburn, HB	319
1961	**Ernie Davis,** Syracuse, HB	824
	2nd—Bob Ferguson, Ohio St., HB	771
	3rd—Jimmy Saxton, Texas, HB	551
	4th—Sandy Stephens, Minnesota, QB	543
1962	**Terry Baker,** Oregon St., QB	707
	2nd—Jerry Stovall, LSU, HB	618
	3rd—Bobby Bell, Minnesota, T	429
	4th—Lee Roy Jordan, Alabama, C	321
1963	* **Roger Staubach,** Navy, QB	1,860
	2nd—Billy Lothridge, Georgia Tech, QB	504
	3rd—Sherman Lewis, Michigan St., HB	369
	4th—Don Trull, Baylor, QB	253
1964	**John Huarte,** Notre Dame, QB	1,026
	2nd—Jerry Rhome, Tulsa, QB	952
	3rd—Dick Butkus, Illinois, C	505
	4th—Bob Timberlake, Michigan, QB	361
1965	**Mike Garrett,** Southern California, HB	926
	2nd—Howard Twilley, Tulsa, E	528
	3rd—Jim Grabowski, Illinois, FB	481
	4th—Donny Anderson, Texas Tech, HB	408
1966	**Steve Spurrier,** Florida, QB	1,679
	2nd—Bob Griese, Purdue, QB	816
	3rd—Nick Eddy, Notre Dame, HB	456
	4th—Gary Beban, UCLA, QB	318
1967	**Gary Beban,** UCLA, QB	1,968
	2nd—O.J. Simpson, Southern California, HB	1,722
	3rd—Leroy Keyes, Purdue, HB	1,366
	4th—Larry Csonka, Syracuse, FB	136
1968	**O.J. Simpson,** Southern California, HB	2,853
	2nd—Leroy Keyes, Purdue, HB	1,103
	3rd—Terry Hanratty, Notre Dame, QB	387
	4th—Ted Kwalik, Penn St., TE	254
1969	**Steve Owens,** Oklahoma, HB	1,488
	2nd—Mike Phipps, Purdue, QB	1,344
	3rd—Rex Kern, Ohio St., QB	856
	4th—Archie Manning, Mississippi, QB	582
1970	**Jim Plunkett,** Stanford, QB	2,229
	2nd—Joe Theismann, Notre Dame, QB	1,410
	3rd—Archie Manning, Mississippi, QB	849
	4th—Steve Worster, Texas, RB	398
1971	**Pat Sullivan,** Auburn, QB	1,597
	2nd—Ed Marinaro, Cornell, RB	1,445
	3rd—Greg Pruitt, Oklahoma, RB	586
	4th—Johnny Musso, Alabama, RB	365
1972	**Johnny Rodgers,** Nebraska, WR	1,310
	2nd—Greg Pruitt, Oklahoma, RB	966
	3rd—Rich Glover, Nebraska, MG	652
	4th—Bert Jones, LSU, QB	351
1973	**John Cappelletti,** Penn St., RB	1,057
	2nd—John Hicks, Ohio St., OT	524
	3rd—Roosevelt Leaks, Texas, RB	482
	4th—David Jaynes, Kansas, QB	394
1974	* **Archie Griffin,** Ohio St., RB	1,920
	2nd—Anthony Davis, Southern California, RB	819
	3rd—Joe Washington, Oklahoma, RB	661
	4th—Tom Clements, Notre Dame, QB	244
1975	**Archie Griffin,** Ohio St., RB	1,800
	2nd—Chuck Muncie, California, RB	730
	3rd—Ricky Bell, Southern California, RB	708
	4th—Tony Dorsett, Pittsburgh, RB	616
1976	**Tony Dorsett,** Pittsburgh, RB	2,357
	2nd—Ricky Bell, Southern California, RB	1,346
	3rd—Rob Lytle, Michigan, RB	413
	4th—Terry Miller, Oklahoma St., RB	197
1977	**Earl Campbell,** Texas, RB	1,547
	2nd—Terry Miller, Oklahoma St., RB	812
	3rd—Ken MacAfee, Notre Dame, TE	343
	4th—Doug Williams, Grambling, QB	266
1978	* **Billy Sims,** Oklahoma, RB	827
	2nd—Chuck Fusina, Penn St., QB	750
	3rd—Rick Leach, Michigan, QB	435
	4th—Charles White, Southern California, RB	354
1979	**Charles White,** Southern California, RB	1,695
	2nd—Billy Sims, Oklahoma, RB	773
	3rd—Marc Wilson, Brigham Young, QB	589
	4th—Art Schlichter, Ohio St., QB	251
1980	**George Rogers,** South Carolina, RB	1,128
	2nd—Hugh Green, Pittsburgh, DE	861
	3rd—Herschel Walker, Georgia, RB	683
	4th—Mark Herrmann, Purdue, QB	405
1981	**Marcus Allen,** Southern California, RB	1,797
	2nd—Herschel Walker, Georgia, RB	1,199
	3rd—Jim McMahon, Brigham Young, QB	706
	4th—Dan Marino, Pittsburgh, QB	256
1982	* **Herschel Walker,** Georgia, RB	1,926
	2nd—John Elway, Stanford, QB	1,231
	3rd—Eric Dickerson, SMU, RB	465
	4th—Anthony Carter, Michigan, WR	142
1983	**Mike Rozier,** Nebraska, RB	1,801
	2nd—Steve Young, Brigham Young, QB	1,172
	3rd—Doug Flutie, Boston College, QB	253
	4th—Turner Gill, Nebraska, QB	190
1984	**Doug Flutie,** Boston College, QB	2,240
	2nd—Keith Byars, Ohio St., RB	1,251
	3rd—Robbie Bosco, Brigham Young, QB	443
	4th—Bernie Kosar, Miami (Fla.), QB	320
1985	**Bo Jackson,** Auburn, RB	1,509
	2nd—Chuck Long, Iowa, QB	1,464
	3rd—Robbie Bosco, Brigham Young, QB	459
	4th—Lorenzo White, Michigan St., RB	391
1986	**Vinny Testaverde,** Miami (Fla.), QB	2,213
	2nd—Paul Palmer, Temple, RB	672
	3rd—Jim Harbaugh, Michigan, QB	458
	4th—Brian Bosworth, Oklahoma, LB	395
1987	**Tim Brown,** Notre Dame, WR	1,442
	2nd—Don McPherson, Syracuse, QB	831
	3rd—Gordie Lockbaum, Holy Cross, WR/DB	657
	4th—Lorenzo White, Michigan St., RB	632
1988	* **Barry Sanders,** Oklahoma St., RB	1,878
	2nd—Rodney Peete, Southern California, QB	912
	3rd—Troy Aikman, UCLA, QB	582
	4th—Steve Walsh, Miami (Fla.), QB	341
1989	* **Andre Ware,** Houston, QB	1,073
	2nd—Anthony Thompson, Indiana, RB	1,003
	3rd—Major Harris, West Virginia, QB	709
	4th—Tony Rice, Notre Dame, QB	523
1990	* **Ty Detmer,** Brigham Young, QB	1,482
	2nd—Raghib Ismail, Notre Dame, WR	1,177
	3rd—Eric Bieniemy, Colorado, RB	798
	4th—Shawn Moore, Virginia, QB	465
1991	# **Desmond Howard,** Michigan, WR	2,077
	2nd—Casey Weldon, Florida St., QB	503
	3rd—Ty Detmer, Brigham Young, QB	445
	4th—Steve Emtman, Washington, DT	357
1992	**Gino Torretta,** Miami (Fla.), QB	1,400
	2nd—Marshall Faulk, San Diego St., RB	1,080
	3rd—Garrison Hearst, Georgia, RB	982
	4th—Marvin Jones, Florida St., LB	392
1993	**Charlie Ward,** Florida St., QB	2,310
	2nd—Heath Shuler, Tennessee, QB	688
	3rd—David Palmer, Alabama, RB	292
	4th—Marshall Faulk, San Diego St., RB	250
1994	* **Rashaan Salaam,** Colorado, RB	1,743
	2nd—Ki-Jana Carter, Penn St., RB	901
	3rd—Steve McNair, Alcorn St., QB	655
	4th—Kerry Collins, Penn St., QB	639
1995	**Eddie George,** Ohio St., RB	1,460
	2nd—Tommie Frazier, Nebraska, QB	1,196
	3rd—Danny Wuerffel, Florida, QB	987
	4th—Darnell Autry, Northwestern, RB	535
1996	**Danny Wuerffel,** Florida, QB	1,363
	2nd—Troy Davis, Iowa St., RB	1,174
	3rd—Jake Plummer, Arizona St., QB	685
	4th—Orlando Pace, Ohio St., OL	599
1997	* **Charles Woodson,** Michigan, DB	1,815
	2nd—Peyton Manning, Tennessee, QB	1,543
	3rd—Ryan Leaf, Washington St., QB	861
	4th—Randy Moss, Marshall, WR	253
1998	**Ricky Williams,** Texas, RB	2,355
	2nd—Michael Bishop, Kansas St., QB	792
	3rd—Cade McNown, UCLA, QB	696
	4th—Tim Couch, Kentucky, QB	527
1999	**Ron Dayne,** Wisconsin, RB	2,042
	2nd—Joe Hamilton, Georgia Tech, QB	994
	3rd—Michael Vick, Virginia Tech, QB	319
	4th—Drew Brees, Purdue, QB	308
2000	**Chris Weinke,** Florida St., QB	1,628
	2nd—Josh Heupel, Oklahoma, QB	1,552
	3rd—Drew Brees, Purdue, QB	619
	4th—LaDainian Tomlinson, TCU, RB	566
2001	**Eric Crouch,** Nebraska, QB	770
	2nd—Rex Grossman, Florida, QB	708
	3rd—Ken Dorsey, Miami (Fla.), QB	638
	4th—Joey Harrington, Oregon, QB	364
2002	**Carson Palmer**, Southern California, QB	1,328
	2nd—Brad Banks, Iowa, QB	1,095
	3rd—Larry Johnson, Penn St., RB	726
	4th—Willis McGahee, Miami (Fla.), RB	660
2003	* **Jason White**, Oklahoma, QB	1,481
	2nd—Larry Fitzgerald, Pittsburgh, WR	1,353
	3rd—Eli Manning, Mississippi, QB	710
	4th—Chris Perry, Michigan, RB	341
2004	* **Matt Leinart**, Southern California, QB	1,325
	2nd—Adrian Peterson, Oklahoma, RB	997
	3rd—Jason White, Oklahoma, QB	957
	4th—Alex Smith, Utah, QB	635
2005	* **Reggie Bush**, Southern California, RB	2,541
	2nd—Vince Young, Texas, QB	1,608
	3rd—Matt Leinart, Southern California, QB	797
	4th—Brady Quinn, Notre Dame, QB	191

**Winner as junior (all others seniors). #Had one year of eligibility remaining.*

2006 Heisman Voting

(First-, second- and third-place votes, and total points; voting on a 3-2-1 basis)

	1st	2nd	3rd	Total
1. Troy Smith, QB, Ohio St.	801	62	13	2,540
2. ^Darren McFadden, RB Arkansas	45	298	147	878
3. Brady Quinn, QB, Notre Dame	13	276	191	782
4. ^Steve Slaton, RB, West Virginia	6	51	94	214
5. *Mike Hart, RB, Michigan	5	58	79	210
6. Colt Brennan, QB, Hawaii	6	44	96	202
7. ^Ray Rice, RB, Rutgers	1	16	44	79
8. ^Ian Johnson, RB, Boise St.	1	13	44	73

	1st	2nd	3rd	Total
9. *Dwayne Jarrett, WR, Southern California	1	11	22	47
10. *Calvin Johnson, WR, Georgia Tech................	1	8	24	43

**Junior. ^Sophomore. All others seniors.*

Heisman Trophy Winners by Position

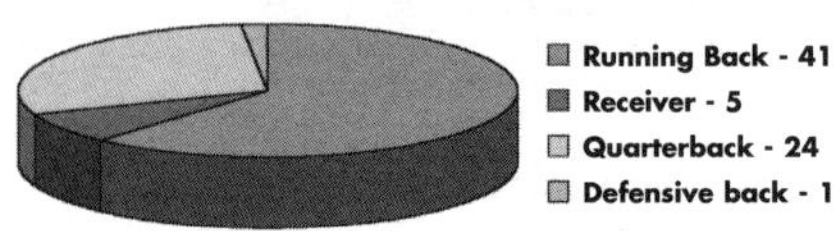

MAXWELL AWARD

First presented in 1937 to honor the nation's outstanding college football player by the Maxwell Memorial Football Club of Philadelphia. The award is named after Robert "Tiny" Maxwell, a Philadelphia native who played at the University of Chicago as a lineman near the turn of the century.

Year	Player, College, Position
1937	Clint Frank, Yale, HB
1938	Davey O'Brien, TCU, QB
1939	Nile Kinnick, Iowa, HB
1940	Tom Harmon, Michigan, HB
1941	Bill Dudley, Virginia, HB
1942	Paul Governali, Columbia, QB
1943	Bob Odell, Penn, HB
1944	Glenn Davis, Army, HB
1945	Doc Blanchard, Army, FB
1946	Charley Trippi, Georgia, HB
1947	Doak Walker, SMU, HB
1948	Chuck Bednarik, Penn, C
1949	Leon Hart, Notre Dame, E
1950	Reds Bagnell, Penn, HB
1951	Dick Kazmaier, Princeton, HB
1952	Johnny Lattner, Notre Dame, HB
1953	Johnny Lattner, Notre Dame, HB
1954	Ron Beagle, Navy, E
1955	Howard Cassady, Ohio St., HB
1956	Tommy McDonald, Oklahoma, HB
1957	Bob Reifsnyder, Navy, T
1958	Pete Dawkins, Army, HB
1959	Rich Lucas, Penn St., QB
1960	Joe Bellino, Navy, HB
1961	Bob Ferguson, Ohio St., FB
1962	Terry Baker, Oregon St., QB
1963	Roger Staubach, Navy, QB
1964	Glenn Ressler, Penn St., C
1965	Tommy Nobis, Texas, LB
1966	Jim Lynch, Notre Dame, LB
1967	Gary Beban, UCLA, QB
1968	O.J. Simpson, Southern California, RB
1969	Mike Reid, Penn St., DT
1970	Jim Plunkett, Stanford, QB
1971	Ed Marinaro, Cornell, RB
1972	Brad VanPelt, Michigan St., DB
1973	John Cappelletti, Penn St., RB
1974	Steve Joachim, Temple, QB
1975	Archie Griffin, Ohio St., RB
1976	Tony Dorsett, Pittsburgh, RB
1977	Ross Browner, Notre Dame, DE
1978	Chuck Fusina, Penn St., QB
1979	Charles White, Southern California, RB
1980	Hugh Green, Pittsburgh, DE
1981	Marcus Allen, Southern California, RB
1982	Herschel Walker, Georgia, RB
1983	Mike Rozier, Nebraska, RB
1984	Doug Flutie, Boston College, QB
1985	Chuck Long, Iowa, QB
1986	Vinny Testaverde, Miami (Fla.), QB
1987	Don McPherson, Syracuse, QB
1988	Barry Sanders, Oklahoma St., RB
1989	Anthony Thompson, Indiana, RB
1990	Ty Detmer, Brigham Young, QB
1991	Desmond Howard, Michigan, WR
1992	Gino Torretta, Miami (Fla.), QB
1993	Charlie Ward, Florida St., QB
1994	Kerry Collins, Penn St., QB
1995	Eddie George, Ohio St., RB
1996	Danny Wuerffel, Florida, QB
1997	Peyton Manning, Tennessee, QB
1998	Ricky Williams, Texas, RB
1999	Ron Dayne, Wisconsin, RB
2000	Drew Brees, Purdue, QB
2001	Ken Dorsey, Miami (Fla.), QB
2002	Larry Johnson, Penn St., RB
2003	Eli Manning, Mississippi, QB
2004	Jason White, Oklahoma, QB
2005	Vince Young, Texas, QB
2006	Brady Quinn, Notre Dame, QB

JOHN OUTLAND TROPHY

First presented in 1946 to honor the outstanding interior lineman in the nation by the Football Writers Association of America. The award is named for its benefactor, Dr. John H. Outland.

Year	Player, College, Position
1946	George Connor, Notre Dame, T
1947	Joe Steffy, Army, G
1948	Bill Fischer, Notre Dame, G
1949	Ed Bagdon, Michigan St., G
1950	Bob Gain, Kentucky, T
1951	Jim Weatherall, Oklahoma, T
1952	Dick Modzelewski, Maryland, T
1953	J.D. Roberts, Oklahoma, G
1954	Bill Brooks, Arkansas, G
1955	Calvin Jones, Iowa, G
1956	Jim Parker, Ohio St., G
1957	Alex Karras, Iowa, T
1958	Zeke Smith, Auburn, G
1959	Mike McGee, Duke, T
1960	Tom Brown, Minnesota, G
1961	Merlin Olsen, Utah St., T
1962	Bobby Bell, Minnesota, T
1963	Scott Appleton, Texas, T
1964	Steve DeLong, Tennessee, T
1965	Tommy Nobis, Texas, G
1966	Loyd Phillips, Arkansas, T
1967	Ron Yary, Southern California, T
1968	Bill Stanfill, Georgia, T
1969	Mike Reid, Penn St., DT
1970	Jim Stillwagon, Ohio St., MG
1971	Larry Jacobson, Nebraska, DT
1972	Rich Glover, Nebraska, MG
1973	John Hicks, Ohio St., OT
1974	Randy White, Maryland, DE
1975	Lee Roy Selmon, Oklahoma, DT
1976	*Ross Browner, Notre Dame, DE
1977	Brad Shearer, Texas, DT
1978	Greg Roberts, Oklahoma, G
1979	Jim Ritcher, North Carolina St., C
1980	Mark May, Pittsburgh, OT
1981	*Dave Rimington, Nebraska, C
1982	Dave Rimington, Nebraska, C
1983	Dean Steinkuhler, Nebraska, G
1984	Bruce Smith, Virginia Tech, DT
1985	Mike Ruth, Boston College, NG
1986	Jason Buck, Brigham Young, DT
1987	Chad Hennings, Air Force, DT
1988	Tracy Rocker, Auburn, DT
1989	Mohammed Elewonibi, Brigham Young, G
1990	Russell Maryland, Miami (Fla.), DT
1991	*Steve Emtman, Washington, DT
1992	Will Shields, Nebraska, G
1993	Rob Waldrop, Arizona, NG
1994	Zach Wiegert, Nebraska, OT
1995	Jonathan Ogden, UCLA, OT
1996	*Orlando Pace, Ohio St., OT
1997	Aaron Taylor, Nebraska, OG
1998	*Kris Farris, UCLA, OT
1999	Chris Samuels, Alabama, OT
2000	*John Henderson, Tennessee, DL
2001	Bryant McKinnie, Miami (Fla.), OT
2002	Rien Long, Washington St., DT
2003	Robert Gallery, Iowa, OT
2004	Jammal Brown, Oklahoma, OT
2005	Greg Eslinger, Minnesota, C
2006	Joe Thomas, Wisconsin, OT

**Junior (all others seniors).*

WALTER CAMP AWARD

First presented in 1967 to honor the nation's outstanding college football player by the Walter Camp Foundation in balloting by Football Bowl Subdivision coaches and sports information directors. The award is named after Walter Camp, one of the founders of modern American football.

Year	Player, College, Position
1967	O.J. Simpson, Southern California, RB
1968	O.J. Simpson, Southern California, RB
1969	Steve Owens, Oklahoma, RB
1970	Jim Plunkett, Stanford, QB
1971	Pat Sullivan, Auburn, QB
1972	Johnny Rodgers, Nebraska, WR
1973	John Cappelletti, Penn St., RB
1974	Archie Griffin, Ohio St., RB
1975	Archie Griffin, Ohio St., RB
1976	Tony Dorsett, Pittsburgh, RB
1977	Ken MacAfee, Notre Dame, TE
1978	Billy Sims, Oklahoma, RB
1979	Charles White, Southern California, RB
1980	Hugh Green, Pittsburgh, DE
1981	Marcus Allen, Southern California, RB
1982	Herschel Walker, Georgia, RB
1983	Mike Rozier, Nebraska, RB
1984	Doug Flutie, Boston College, QB
1985	Bo Jackson, Auburn, RB
1986	Vinny Testaverde, Miami (Fla.), QB
1987	Tim Brown, Notre Dame, WR
1988	Barry Sanders, Oklahoma St., RB
1989	Andre Ware, Houston, QB
1990	Raghib Ismail, Notre Dame, RB/WR
1991	Desmond Howard, Michigan, WR
1992	Gino Torretta, Miami (Fla.), QB
1993	Charlie Ward, Florida St., QB
1994	Rashaan Salaam, Colorado, RB
1995	Eddie George, Ohio St., RB
1996	Danny Wuerffel, Florida, QB
1997	Charles Woodson, Michigan, DB
1998	Ricky Williams, Texas, RB
1999	Ron Dayne, Wisconsin, RB
2000	Josh Heupel, Oklahoma, QB
2001	Eric Crouch, Nebraska, QB
2002	Larry Johnson, Penn St., RB
2003	Larry Fitzgerald, Pittsburgh, WR
2004	Matt Leinart, Southern California, QB
2005	Reggie Bush, Southern California, RB
2006	Troy Smith, Ohio St., QB

VINCE LOMBARDI/ ROTARY AWARD

First presented in 1970 to honor the outstanding college lineman or linebacker of the year by the Rotary Club of Houston, Texas. The award is named after professional football coach Vince Lombardi, a member of the legendary "Seven Blocks of Granite" at Fordham in the 1930s.

Year	Player, College, Position
1970	Jim Stillwagon, Ohio St., MG
1971	Walt Patulski, Notre Dame, DE
1972	Rich Glover, Nebraska, MG
1973	John Hicks, Ohio St., OT
1974	Randy White, Maryland, DT
1975	Lee Roy Selmon, Oklahoma, DT
1976	Wilson Whitley, Houston, DT
1977	Ross Browner, Notre Dame, DE
1978	Bruce Clark, Penn St., DT
1979	Brad Budde, Southern California, G
1980	Hugh Green, Pittsburgh, DE
1981	Kenneth Sims, Texas, DT
1982	Dave Rimington, Nebraska, C
1983	Dean Steinkuhler, Nebraska, G
1984	Tony Degrate, Texas, DT
1985	Tony Casillas, Oklahoma, NG
1986	Cornelius Bennett, Alabama, LB
1987	Chris Spielman, Ohio St., LB
1988	Tracy Rocker, Auburn, DT
1989	Percy Snow, Michigan St., LB
1990	Chris Zorich, Notre Dame, NT
1991	Steve Emtman, Washington, DT
1992	Marvin Jones, Florida St., LB
1993	Aaron Taylor, Notre Dame, OT
1994	Warren Sapp, Miami (Fla.), DT
1995	Orlando Pace, Ohio St., OT
1996	Orlando Pace, Ohio St., OT

Year	Player, College, Position
1997	Grant Wistrom, Nebraska, DE
1998	Dat Nguyen, Texas A&M, LB
1999	Corey Moore, Virginia Tech, DE
2000	Jamal Reynolds, Florida St., DE
2001	Julius Peppers, North Carolina, DE
2002	Terrell Suggs, Arizona St., DE
2003	Tommie Harris, Oklahoma, DT
2004	David Pollack, Georgia, DE
2005	A.J. Hawk, Ohio St., LB
2006	LaMarr Woodley, Michigan, DE

DAVEY O'BRIEN NATIONAL QUARTERBACK AWARD

First presented in 1977 as the O'Brien Memorial Trophy to the outstanding player in the Southwest. In 1981, the Davey O'Brien Educational and Charitable Trust of Fort Worth, Texas, renamed the award the Davey O'Brien National Quarterback Award, and it now honors the nation's best quarterback.

MEMORIAL TROPHY

Year	Player, College, Position
1977	Earl Campbell, Texas, RB
1978	Billy Sims, Oklahoma, RB
1979	Mike Singletary, Baylor, LB
1980	Mike Singletary, Baylor, LB

NATIONAL QB AWARD

Year	Player, College
1981	Jim McMahon, Brigham Young
1982	Todd Blackledge, Penn St.
1983	Steve Young, Brigham Young
1984	Doug Flutie, Boston College
1985	Chuck Long, Iowa
1986	Vinny Testaverde, Miami (Fla.)
1987	Don McPherson, Syracuse
1988	Troy Aikman, UCLA
1989	Andre Ware, Houston
1990	Ty Detmer, Brigham Young
1991	Ty Detmer, Brigham Young
1992	Gino Torretta, Miami (Fla.)
1993	Charlie Ward, Florida St.
1994	Kerry Collins, Penn St.
1995	Danny Wuerffel, Florida
1996	Danny Wuerffel, Florida
1997	Peyton Manning, Tennessee
1998	Michael Bishop, Kansas St.
1999	Joe Hamilton, Georgia Tech
2000	Chris Weinke, Florida St.
2001	Eric Crouch, Nebraska
2002	Brad Banks, Iowa
2003	Jason White, Oklahoma
2004	Jason White, Oklahoma
2005	Vince Young, Texas
2006	Troy Smith, Ohio St.

DICK BUTKUS AWARD

First presented in 1985 to honor the nation's best collegiate linebacker by the Downtown Athletic Club of Orlando, Fla. The award is named after Dick Butkus, two-time consensus All-American at Illinois and six-time all-Pro linebacker with the Chicago Bears.

Year	Player, College
1985	Brian Bosworth, Oklahoma
1986	Brian Bosworth, Oklahoma
1987	Paul McGowan, Florida St.
1988	Derrick Thomas, Alabama
1989	Percy Snow, Michigan St.
1990	Alfred Williams, Colorado
1991	Erick Anderson, Michigan
1992	Marvin Jones, Florida St.
1993	Trev Alberts, Nebraska
1994	Dana Howard, Illinois
1995	Kevin Hardy, Illinois
1996	Matt Russell, Colorado
1997	Andy Katzenmoyer, Ohio St.
1998	Chris Claiborne, Southern California
1999	LaVar Arrington, Penn St.
2000	Dan Morgan, Miami (Fla.)
2001	Rocky Calmus, Oklahoma
2002	E.J. Henderson, Maryland
2003	Teddy Lehman, Oklahoma
2004	Derrick Johnson, Texas
2005	Paul Posluszny, Penn St.
2006	Patrick Willis, Mississippi

JIM THORPE AWARD

First presented in 1986 to honor the nation's best defensive back by the Jim Thorpe Athletic Club of Oklahoma City. The award is named after Jim Thorpe, Olympic champion, two-time consensus All-American halfback at Carlisle and professional football player.

Year	Player, College
1986	Thomas Everett, Baylor
1987	Bennie Blades, Miami (Fla.)
	Rickey Dixon, Oklahoma
1988	Deion Sanders, Florida St.
1989	Mark Carrier, Southern California
1990	Darryll Lewis, Arizona
1991	Terrell Buckley, Florida St.
1992	Deon Figures, Colorado
1993	Antonio Langham, Alabama
1994	Chris Hudson, Colorado
1995	Greg Myers, Colorado St.
1996	Lawrence Wright, Florida
1997	Charles Woodson, Michigan
1998	Antoine Winfield, Ohio St.
1999	Tyrone Carter, Minnesota
2000	Jamar Fletcher, Wisconsin
2001	Roy Williams, Oklahoma
2002	Terence Newman, Kansas St.
2003	Derrick Strait, Oklahoma
2004	Carlos Rogers, Auburn
2005	Michael Huff, Texas
2006	Aaron Ross, Texas

JOHNNY UNITAS GOLDEN ARM AWARD

First presented in 1987 to honor the nation's top senior quarterback by the Frank Camp Chapter of the Johnny Unitas Golden Arm Educational Foundation. Each year, a committee composed of NFL executives, coaches, scouts and media members selects the winner based on citizenship, scholarship, leadership and athletic accomplishments. The award, formerly presented by the Kentucky Chapter of the National Football Foundation and College Football Hall of Fame, Inc., is named after Pro Football Hall of Fame quarterback Johnny Unitas.

Year	Player, College
1987	Don McPherson, Syracuse
1988	Rodney Peete, Southern California
1989	Tony Rice, Notre Dame
1990	Craig Erickson, Miami (Fla.)
1991	Casey Weldon, Florida St.
1992	Gino Torretta, Miami (Fla.)
1993	Charlie Ward, Florida St.
1994	Jay Barker, Alabama
1995	Tommy Frazier, Nebraska
1996	Danny Wuerffel, Florida
1997	Peyton Manning, Tennessee
1998	Cade McNown, UCLA
1999	Chris Redman, Louisville
2000	Chris Weinke, Florida St.
2001	David Carr, Fresno St.
2002	Carson Palmer, Southern California
2003	Eli Manning, Mississippi
2004	Jason White, Oklahoma
2005	Matt Leinart, Southern California
2006	Brady Quinn, Notre Dame

DOAK WALKER NATIONAL RUNNING BACK AWARD

First presented in 1990 to honor the nation's best running back among Football Bowl Subdivision juniors or seniors who combine outstanding achievements on the field, in the classroom and in the community, by the GTE/SMU Athletic Forum in Dallas, Texas, and sponsored by Dr. Pepper, a $10,000 scholarship is donated to the recipient's university in his name. It is voted on by a panel of media and former college football standouts. The award is named after Doak Walker, SMU's three-time consensus All-America halfback and 1948 Heisman Trophy winner.

Year	Player, College
1990	Greg Lewis, Washington
1991	Trevor Cobb, Rice
1992	Garrison Hearst, Georgia
1993	Byron Morris, Texas Tech
1994	Rashaan Salaam, Colorado
1995	Eddie George, Ohio St.
1996	Byron Hanspard, Texas Tech
1997	Ricky Williams, Texas
1998	Ricky Williams, Texas
1999	Ron Dayne, Wisconsin
2000	LaDainian Tomlinson, TCU
2001	Luke Staley, Brigham Young
2002	Larry Johnson, Penn St.
2003	Chris Perry, Michigan
2004	Cedric Benson, Texas
2005	Reggie Bush, Southern California
2006	Darren McFadden, Arkansas

LOU GROZA COLLEGIATE PLACE-KICKER AWARD

First presented in 1992 to honor the nation's top collegiate place-kicker by the Palm Beach County Sports Commission in conjunction with the Orange Bowl Committee. The award is named after Pro Football Hall of Fame kicker Lou Groza.

Year	Player, College
1992	Joe Allison, Memphis
1993	Judd Davis, Florida
1994	Steve McLaughlin, Arizona
1995	Michael Reeder, TCU
1996	Marc Primanti, North Carolina St.
1997	Martin Gramatica, Kansas St.
1998	Sebastian Janikowski, Florida St.
1999	Sebastian Janikowski, Florida St.
2000	Jonathan Ruffin, Cincinnati
2001	Seth Marler, Tulane
2002	Nate Kaeding, Iowa
2003	Jonathan Nichols, Mississippi
2004	Mike Nugent, Ohio St.
2005	Alexis Serna, Oregon St.
2006	Arthur Carmody, Louisville

BRONKO NAGURSKI AWARD

First presented in 1993 to honor the nation's top collegiate defensive player by the Football Writers Association of America and the Charlotte (N.C.) Touchdown Club. The award is named after Bronko Nagurski, consensus All-America tackle and running back at Minnesota in 1929, and a member of both the College Football Hall of Fame and Pro Football Hall of Fame.

Year	Player, College, Position
1993	Rob Waldrop, Arizona, DL
1994	Warren Sapp, Miami (Fla.), DT
1995	Pat Fitzgerald, Northwestern, LB
1996	Pat Fitzgerald, Northwestern, LB
1997	Charles Woodson, Michigan, CB
1998	Champ Bailey, Georgia, DB
1999	Corey Moore, Virginia Tech, DE
2000	Dan Morgan, Miami (Fla.), LB
2001	Roy Williams, Oklahoma, DB
2002	Terrell Suggs, Arizona St., DE
2003	Derrick Strait, Oklahoma, CB
2004	Derrick Johnson, Texas, LB
2005	Elvis Dumervil, Louisville, DE
2006	James Laurinaitis, Ohio St., LB

FRED BILETNIKOFF RECEIVER AWARD

First presented in 1994 to honor the nation's top collegiate pass receiver by the Quarterback Club of Tallahassee, Fla. The award is named after Fred Biletnikoff, former Florida State All-American and NFL Oakland Raider receiver, a member of both the College Football Hall of Fame and Pro Football Hall of Fame.

Year	Player, College
1994	Bobby Engram, Penn St.
1995	Terry Glenn, Ohio St.
1996	Marcus Harris, Wyoming
1997	Randy Moss, Marshall
1998	Troy Edwards, Louisiana Tech
1999	Troy Walters, Stanford
2000	Antonio Bryant, Pittsburgh

Year	Player, College
2001	Josh Reed, LSU
2002	Charles Rogers, Michigan St.
2003	Larry Fitzgerald, Pittsburgh
2004	Braylon Edwards, Michigan
2005	Mike Hass, Oregon St.
2006	Calvin Johnson, Georgia Tech

CHUCK BEDNARIK AWARD

First presented in 1995 to honor the collegiate defensive player of the year by the Maxwell Memorial Football Club of Philadelphia. The award is named after Chuck Bednarik, consensus All-America center at Penn in 1947-48 and a member of both the College Football Hall of Fame and Pro Football Hall of Fame.

Year	Player, College
1995	Pat Fitzgerald, Northwestern
1996	Pat Fitzgerald, Northwestern
1997	Charles Woodson, Michigan
1998	Dat Nguyen, Texas A&M
1999	LaVar Arrington, Penn St.
2000	Dan Morgan, Miami (Fla.)
2001	Julius Peppers, North Carolina
2002	E.J. Henderson, Maryland
2003	Teddy Lehman, Oklahoma
2004	David Pollack, Georgia
2005	Paul Posluszny, Penn St.
2006	Paul Posluszny, Penn St.

RAY GUY PUNTING AWARD

First presented in 2000 to honor the nation's top collegiate punter by the Greater Augusta (Ga.) Sports Council. The winner will display leadership, self-discipline and have a significant impact on the team's success. Voted upon by a panel of sports writers, college football coaches and former punters. The award is named after Ray Guy, former punter at Southern Mississippi and NFL all-Pro punter for the Oakland Raiders.

Year	Player, College
2000	Kevin Stemke, Wisconsin
2001	Travis Dorsch, Purdue
2002	Mark Mariscal, Colorado
2003	B.J. Sander, Ohio St.
2004	Daniel Sepulveda, Baylor
2005	Ryan Plackemeier, Wake Forest
2006	Daniel Sepulveda, Baylor

JOHN MACKEY TIGHT END AWARD

First presented in 2000 to honor the nation's top collegiate tight end by the Nassau County (N.Y.) Sports Commission. The award is named after John Mackey, the first tight end inducted into the Pro Football Hall of Fame.

Year	Player, College
2000	Tim Stratton, Purdue
2001	Dan Graham, Colorado
2002	Dallas Clark, Iowa
2003	Kellen Winslow, Miami (Fla.)
2004	Heath Miller, Virginia
2005	Marcedes Lewis, UCLA
2006	Matt Spaeth, Minnesota

DAVE RIMINGTON CENTER TROPHY (FBS)

First presented in 2000 to honor the nation's top Football Bowl Subdivision offensive center by the Boomer Esiason Foundation. The award is named after Dave Rimington, a consensus All-America center at Nebraska in 1981-82 who was inducted into the College Football Hall of Fame in 1997.

Year	Player, College
2000	Dominic Raiola, Nebraska
2001	LeCharles Bentley, Ohio St.
2002	Brett Romberg, Miami (Fla.)
2003	Jake Grove, Virginia Tech
2004	David Baas, Michigan
	Ben Wilkerson, LSU
2005	Greg Eslinger, Minnesota
2006	Dan Mozes, West Virginia

TED HENDRICKS DEFENSIVE END AWARD

First presented in 2002 to honor the nation's top defensive end by the Miami (Florida) Touchdown Club. The award is named after Ted Hendricks, College Football Hall of Fame member from Miami (Florida) and a member of the Pro Football Hall of Fame.

Year	Player, College
2002	Terrell Suggs, Arizona St.
2003	David Pollack, Georgia
2004	David Pollack, Georgia
2005	Elvis Dumervil, Louisville
2006	LaMarr Woodley, Michigan

BOBBY BOWDEN AWARD

First presented in 2003 by the Fellowship of Christian Athletes (FCA) to the collegiate football player who best epitomizes the term student-athlete. The person selected will be one of character, classroom excellence, athletic achievement and community involvement. Presented at the site of the Bowl Championship Series national championship game.

Year	Player, College
2003	Jason Wright, Northwestern
2004	Billy Bajema, Oklahoma St.
2005	D.J. Shockley, Georgia
2006	Carl Pendleton, Oklahoma

RONNIE LOTT TROPHY

First presented in 2004 by the Pacific Club of Newport Beach, California, to the IMPACT Defensive Player of the Year. It recognizes a player's success both on and off the field. IMPACT is an acronym for Integrity, Maturity, Performance, Academics, Community and Tenacity.

Year	Player, College, Position
2004	David Pollack, Georgia, DE
2005	DeMeco Ryans, Alabama, LB
2006	Daymeion Hughes, California, CB

MANNING AWARD

First presented in 2004 by the Nokia Sugar Bowl to the nation's top Football Bowl Subdivision quarterback. The award is named for the Manning family – former New Orleans Saints quarterback Archie Manning and his sons Peyton and Eli, both NFL quarterbacks and former collegiate All-Americans.

Year	Player, College
2004	Matt Leinart, Southern California
2005	Vince Young, Texas
2006	JaMarcus Russell, LSU

WUERFFEL TROPHY

First presented in 2005 by the All Sports Association of Fort Walton Beach, Florida, and named after Danny Wuerffel, Heisman Trophy-winning quarterback at Florida, NFL veteran and graduate of Fort Walton Beach High School. In addition to being a great college quarterback, Wuerffel is also recognized for his work off the field, including running Desire Street Ministries, a faith-based organization for underprivileged children in New Orleans.

Year	Player, College
2005	Rudy Niswanger, LSU
2006	Joel Penton, Ohio St.

Discontinued Awards

MOSI TATUPU SPECIAL TEAMS PLAYER OF THE YEAR AWARD

First presented in 1997 to the top special teams player in the country by the Maui (Hawaii) Touchdown Club. The award is named after Mosi Tatupu, who played high school football in Honolulu and collegiate football at Southern California. He went on to a 14-year playing career in the NFL.

Year	Player, College
1997	Brock Olivo, Missouri
1998	Chris McAlister, Arizona
1999	Deltha O'Neal, California
2000	J.T. Thatcher, Oklahoma
2001	Kahlil Hill, Iowa
2002	Glenn Pakulak, Kentucky
2003	Wes Welker, Texas Tech
2004	Chad Owens, Hawaii

Football Championship Subdivision

WALTER PAYTON PLAYER OF THE YEAR AWARD

First presented in 1987 to honor the top Football Championship Subdivision football player by the Sports Network and voted on by Football Championship Subdivision sports information directors. The award is named after Walter Payton, former Jackson State player and the National Football League's second all-time leading rusher.

Year	Player, College, Position
1987	Kenny Gamble, Colgate, RB
1988	Dave Meggett, Towson, RB
1989	John Friesz, Idaho, QB
1990	Walter Dean, Grambling, RB
1991	Jamie Martin, Weber St., QB
1992	Michael Payton, Marshall, QB
1993	Doug Nussmeier, Idaho, QB
1994	Steve McNair, Alcorn St., QB
1995	Dave Dickenson, Montana, QB
1996	Archie Amerson, Northern Ariz., RB
1997	Brian Finneran, Villanova, WR
1998	Jerry Azumah, New Hampshire, RB
1999	Adrian Peterson, Ga. Southern, RB
2000	Louis Ivory, Furman, RB
2001	Brian Westbrook, Villanova, RB
2002	Tony Romo, Eastern Ill., QB
2003	Jamaal Branch, Colgate, RB
2004	Lang Campbell, William & Mary, QB
2005	Erik Meyer, Eastern Wash., QB
2006	Ricky Santos, New Hampshire, QB

ERNIE DAVIS AWARD

First presented in 1992 to honor a Football Championship Subdivision college football player who has overcome personal, athletic or academic adversity and performs in an exemplary manner by the American Sports Wire. The award is named after the late Ernie Davis, Syracuse halfback who won the Heisman Trophy in 1961.

Year	Player, College, Position
1992	Gilad Landau, Grambling, PK
1993	Jay Walker, Howard, QB
1994	Steve McNair, Alcorn St., QB
1995	Earl Holmes, Florida A&M, LB
1996	Jason DeCuir, Howard, PK
1997	DeMingo Graham, Hofstra, OL
1998	Chris Boden, Villanova, QB
1999	Matt Bushart, Southern U., P
2000	Charles Roberts, Sacramento St., RB
2001	Mark Leyenaar, Robert Morris, OL
2002	Kayode Mayowa, Sacred Heart, LB
2003	Steve Baggs, Bethune-Cookman, LB
2004	Jamaal Branch, Colgate, RB
2005	Bruce Eugene, Grambling, QB
2006	Ricky Santos, New Hampshire, QB

BUCK BUCHANAN AWARD

First presented in 1995 to the nation's outstanding Football Championship Subdivision defensive player by The Sports Network. The award is named after Junious 'Buck' Buchanan, NAIA All-America defensive lineman at Grambling from 1959 through 1962 and Pro Football Hall of Fame inductee after an outstanding 13-year career.

Year	Player, College, Position
1995	Dexter Coakley, Appalachian St., LB
1996	Dexter Coakley, Appalachian St., LB
1997	Chris McNeil, N.C. A&T, DE
1998	James Milton, Western Ill., LB
1999	Al Lucas, Troy, DT
2000	Edgerton Hartwell, Western Ill., DL
2001	Derrick Lloyd, James Madison, LB
2002	Rashean Mathis, Bethune-Cookman, DB

Year	Player, College, Position
2003	Jared Allen, Idaho St., DE
2004	Jordan Beck, Cal Poly, LB
2005	Chris Gocong, Cal Poly, DE
2006	Kyle Shotwell, Cal Poly, LB

DAVE RIMINGTON AWARD (FCS)

First presented in 2003 to honor the best Football Championship Subdivision center by the Boomer Esiason Foundation. The award is named after Dave Rimington, a College Football Hall of Fame center from Nebraska and the only player to win the John Outland Trophy twice (1981-82).

Year	Player, College
2003	Eugene Amano, Southeast Mo. St.
2004	Rob Hunt, North Dakota St.
2005	Jeff Bolton, Montana St.
2006	Jackie Skipper, Ark.-Pine Bluff

Division II

HARLON HILL TROPHY

First presented in 1986 to honor the best Division II player by the Harlon Hill Award Committee of Florence, Alabama. The award is named after Harlon Hill, former receiver at North Alabama and the National Football League's most valuable player for the Chicago Bears in 1955.

Year	Player, College
1986	Jeff Bentrim, North Dakota St., QB
1987	Johnny Bailey, Tex. A&M-Kingsville, RB
1988	Johnny Bailey, Tex. A&M-Kingsville, RB
1989	Johnny Bailey, Tex. A&M-Kingsville, RB
1990	Chris Simdorn, North Dakota St., QB
1991	Ronnie West, Pittsburg St., WR
1992	Ronald Moore, Pittsburg St., RB
1993	Roger Graham, New Haven, RB
1994	Chris Hatcher, Valdosta St., QB
1995	Ronald McKinnon, North Ala., LB
1996	Jarrett Anderson, Truman, RB
1997	Irv Sigler, Bloomsburg, RB
1998	Brian Shay, Emporia St., RB
1999	Corte McGuffey, Northern Colo., QB
2000	Dusty Bonner, Valdosta St., QB
2001	Dusty Bonner, Valdosta St., QB
2002	Curt Anes, Grand Valley St., QB
2003	Will Hall, North Ala., QB
2004	Chad Friehauf, Colorado Mines, QB
2005	Jimmy Terwilliger, East Stroudsburg, QB
2006	Danny Woodhead, Chadron St., RB

DAVE RIMINGTON AWARD (NCAA II)

First presented in 2003 to honor the best Division II center by the Boomer Esiason Foundation. The award is named after Dave Rimington, a College Football Hall of Fame center from Nebraska and the only player to win the John Outland Trophy twice (1981-82).

Year	Player, College
2003	Kevin Palmer, Tex. A&M-Kingsville
2004	Kevin Burton, Southeastern Okla.
2005	Lance Ancar, North Ala.
2006	Christian Morton, South Dakota

GENE UPSHAW AWARD

First presented in 2004 by the Manheim (Pa.) Touchdown Club to the Division II lineman of the year. The award is named for Gene Upshaw, an all-Pro offensive lineman during his 15-year Hall-of-Fame career with the Oakland Raiders, and currently the executive director of the National Football League Players Association.

Year	Player, College
2004	Nathan Baker, Pittsburg St.
2005	Mike McFadden, Grand Valley St.
2006	Mike McFadden, Grand Valley St.

Discontinued Awards

JIM LANGER AWARD

First presented in 1994 to the top offensive lineman in Division II by the American Football Coaches Association Division II membership. The award is named after former South Dakota State standout Jim Langer, a five-time NFL all-Pro center and 1987 Pro Football Hall of Fame inductee.

Year	Player, College
1994	Kevin Robson, North Dakota
1995	Adam Timmerman, South Dakota St.
1996	Chris Villarrial, Indiana (Pa.)
1997	Andy Mazurek, Minn. St. Mankato
1998	Sean McNamara, Pittsburg St.
1999	Greg Lotyse, North Dakota
2000	Nick O'Brien, Tex. A&M-Kingsville
2001	Brian Crawford, Western Ore.
2002	Peter Campion, North Dakota St.
2003	Phillip Bogle, New Haven
2004	Alan Dunn, Tusculum
2005	Nick Hageman, South Dakota

Division III

JOHN GAGLIARDI TROPHY

First presented in 1993 to the nation's outstanding Division III player by the St. John's (Minn.) University J-Club. The award is named after John Gagliardi, St. John's head coach for 53 seasons and one of only two coaches in college football history to win 400 games.

Year	Player, College, Position
1993	Jim Ballard, Mount Union, QB
1994	Carey Bender, Coe, RB
1995	Chris Palmer, St. John's (Minn.), WR
1996	Lon Erickson, Ill. Wesleyan, QB
1997	Bill Borchert, Mount Union, QB
1998	Scott Hvistendahl, Augsburg, WR/P
1999	Danny Ragsdale, Redlands, QB
2000	Chad Johnson, Pacific Lutheran, QB
2001	Chuck Moore, Mount Union, RB
2002	Dan Pugh, Mount Union, RB
2003	Blake Elliott, St. John's (Minn.), WR
2004	Rocky Myers, Wesley, DB
2005	Brett Elliott, Linfield, QB
2006	Josh Brehm, Alma, QB

CLIFF MELBERGER AWARD

First presented in 1993 to the nation's outstanding Division III player by the Downtown Wilkes-Barre (Pa.) Touchdown Club. The award is named after Clifford K. Melberger, captain of the 1960 Bucknell football team that won the Lambert Cup and a member of the Touchdown Club's board of directors.

Year	Player, College, Position
1993	Jim Ballard, Mount Union, QB
1994	Carey Bender, Coe, RB
1995	Craig Kusick, Wis.-La Crosse, QB
1996	Bill Borchert, Mount Union, QB
1997	Bill Borchert, Mount Union, QB
1998	Mike Burton, Trinity (Tex.), QB
1999	Scott Pingel, Westminster (Mo.), WR
2000	R.J. Bowers, Grove City, RB
2001	Chuck Moore, Mount Union, RB
2002	Dan Pincelli, Hartwick, QB
2003	Brett Trichilo, Wilkes, RB
2004	Brett Trichilo, Wilkes, RB
2005	Brett Elliott, Linfield, QB
2006	Chris Sharpe, Springfield, QB

DAVE RIMINGTON AWARD (NCAA III)

First presented in 2003 to honor the best Division III center by the Boomer Esiason Foundation. The award is named after Dave Rimington, a College Football Hall of Fame center from Nebraska and the only player to win the John Outland Trophy twice (1981-82).

Year	Player, College
2003	Tom Doyle, Capital
2004	Matthew Bush, Mary Hardin-Baylor
2005	Damien Ciecwisz, Delaware Valley
2006	Josh Knox, Hardin-Simmons

COLLEGE FOOTBALL HALL OF FAME

Established: In 1947, by the National Football Foundation and College Hall of Fame, Inc. The first class of enshrinement of Division I or major-college players was in 1951. In 1996, the yearly classes elected were expanded to include other than Division I players. **Eligibility:** A nominated player must be out of college at least 10 years and a first-team All-America selection by a major selector during his career. For divisional (college-division) players, the player must have been a first-team selection on a recognized All-America team in the Football Championship Subdivision, Divisions II or III, or the NAIA. Coaches must be retired three years or are eligible immediately after retirement provided they are at least 70 years of age. Active coaches become eligible at 75 years of age. Coaches must have been a head coach for a minimum of 10 years and have coached at least 100 games with a .600 winning percentage. The voting is done by a 12-member panel made up of athletics directors, conference and bowl officials, and media representatives.

Member players are listed with the final year they played in college, and member coaches are listed with the year they were inducted. ($) Indicates college-division member. (†) Indicates deceased members. (#) Indicates dual member of the Pro Football Hall of Fame.

COLLEGE FOOTBALL HALL OF FAME CLASS OF 2007

(Football Bowl Subdivision Class to be inducted at the 50th annual awards dinner December 4, 2007, and enshrined at the Hall, in South Bend, Ind., in the summer of 2008; Divisional Class to be enshrined during ceremonies at the Hall July 19-21, 2007)

FOOTBALL BOWL SUBDIVISION CLASS

Player, School	Pos.	Years
Tom Brahaney, Oklahoma	C	1970-72
Dave Brown, Michigan (†)	DB	1972-74
Jeff Davis, Clemson	LB	1978-81
Doug Flutie, Boston College	QB	1981-84
Johnnie Johnson, Texas	DB	1976-79
Rex Kern, Ohio St.	QB	1968-70
Ahmad Rashad, Oregon	RB/WR	1969-71
Anthony Thompson, Indiana	RB	1986-89
Wilson Whitley, Houston (†)	DT	1973-76
Reggie Williams, Dartmouth	LB	1973-75
Richard Wood, Southern California	LB	1972-74
Chris Zorich, Notre Dame	DT	1988-90

Coach, School	Years	Record
Herb Deromedi, Central Mich.	1978-93	110-55-10
Joe Paterno, Penn St.	1966-present	363-121-3

DIVISIONAL CLASS (FCS, DIVISIONS II AND III, NAIA)

Player, School	Pos.	Years
Tracy Ham, Ga. Southern	QB	1983-86
Joe Kendall, Kentucky St. (†)	QB	1934-36
Frank Sheptock, Bloomsburg	LB	1982-85
Jessie Tuggle, Vadosta St.	LB	1983-86

Coach, School	Years	Record
Jim Christopherson, Concordia-M'head	1969-00	218-101-7
William "Billy" Joe, Cheyney	1972-78	237-108-4
Central St. (Ohio)	1981-93	
Florida A&M	1994-04	

PLAYERS

Player, College	Year
†Earl Abell, Colgate	1915
†Alex Agase, Purdue/Illinois	1946
†Harry Agganis, Boston U.	1952
†Frank Albert, Stanford	1941
†Ki Aldrich, TCU	1938
†Malcolm Aldrich, Yale	1921
Marcus Allen, Southern California#	1981
†Joe Alexander, Syracuse	1920
Lance Alworth, Arkansas#	1961
†Alan Ameche, Wisconsin	1954

AWARD WINNERS

Player, College	Year
†Knowlton Ames, Princeton	1889
Warren Amling, Ohio St.	1946
Bob P. Anderson, Army	1959
Bobby Anderson, Colorado	1969
Dick Anderson, Colorado	1967
Donny Anderson, Texas Tech	1965
†Hunk Anderson, Notre Dame	1921
Jon Arnett, Southern California	1956
Doug Atkins, Tennessee#	1952
Bob Babich, Miami (Ohio)	1968
†Everett Bacon, Wesleyan (Conn.)	1912
†Reds Bagnell, Penn	1950
Johnny Bailey, Tex. A&M-Kingsville ($)	1989
†Hobey Baker, Princeton	1913
†John Baker, Southern California	1931
†Moon Baker, Northwestern	1926
Terry Baker, Oregon St.	1962
†Harold Ballin, Princeton	1914
†Bill Banker, Tulane	1929
Vince Banonis, Detroit	1941
Mike Barber, Marshall ($)	1988
†Stan Barnes, California	1921
†Charles Barrett, Cornell	1915
†Bert Baston, Minnesota	1916
†Cliff Battles, West Va. Wesleyan#	1931
Sammy Baugh, TCU#	1936
Maxie Baughan, Georgia Tech	1959
Kirk Baumgartner, Wis.-Stevens Point ($)	1989
†James Bausch, Wichita St./Kansas	1930
Ron Beagle, Navy	1955
Terry Beasley, Auburn	1971
Gary Beban, UCLA	1967
Hub Bechtol, Texas Tech/Texas	1946
†Ray Beck, Georgia Tech	1951
†John Beckett, Oregon	1916
Chuck Bednarik, Penn#	1948
Forrest Behm, Nebraska	1940
Bobby Bell, Minnesota#	1962
†Ricky Bell, Southern California	1976
Joe Bellino, Navy	1960
†Marty Below, Wisconsin	1923
†Al Benbrook, Michigan	1910
Cornelius Bennett, Alabama	1986
Jeff Bentrim, North Dakota St. ($)	1986
†Charlie Berry, Lafayette	1924
Angelo Bertelli, Notre Dame	1943
†Jay Berwanger, Chicago	1935
†Lawrence Bettencourt, St. Mary's (Cal.)	1927
Fred Biletnikoff, Florida St.#	1964
Bennie Blades, Miami (Fla.)	1987
Doc Blanchard, Army	1946
Tony Blazine, Ill. Wesleyan ($)	1934
†Al Blozis, Georgetown	1941
†Ed Bock, Iowa St.	1938
†Lynn Bomar, Vanderbilt	1924
†Douglas Bomeisler, Yale	1912
†Albie Booth, Yale	1931
George Bork, Northern Ill. ($)	1963
†Fred Borries, Navy	1934
Bruce Bosley, West Virginia	1955
Don Bosseler, Miami (Fla.)	1956
†Vic Bottari, California	1938
Murry Bowden, Dartmouth	1970
†Ben Boynton, Williams	1920
Terry Bradshaw, Louisiana Tech# ($)	1969
†Charles Brewer, Harvard	1895
†Johnny Bright, Drake	1951
John Brodie, Stanford	1956
†George Brooke, Swarthmore/Penn	1895
Al Brosky, Illinois	1952
Bob Brown, Nebraska#	1963
George Brown, Navy/San Diego St.	1947
†Gordon Brown, Yale	1900
Jim Brown, Syracuse#	1956
†John Brown Jr., Navy	1913
†Johnny Mack Brown, Alabama	1925
†Tay Brown, Southern California	1932
Tom Brown, Minnesota	1960
Ross Browner, Notre Dame	1977
Tel Bruner, Centre ($)	1985
†Buck Buchanan, Grambling# ($)	1962
Brad Budde, Southern California	1979
†Paul Bunker, Army	1902
Chris Burford, Stanford	1959
Kurt Burris, Oklahoma	1954
†Ron Burton, Northwestern	1959
Dick Butkus, Illinois#	1964
†Robert Butler, Wisconsin	1913
Kevin Butler, Georgia	1984
†George Cafego, Tennessee	1939
†Red Cagle, La.-Lafayette/Army	1929
†John Cain, Alabama	1932
Brad Calip, East Central ($)	1984
Ed Cameron, Wash. & Lee	1924
†David Campbell, Harvard	1901
Earl Campbell, Texas#	1977
†Jack Cannon, Notre Dame	1929
John Cappelletti, Penn St.	1973
†Frank Carideo, Notre Dame	1930
†Charles Carney, Illinois	1921
J.C. Caroline, Illinois	1954
Bill Carpenter, Army	1959
†Hunter Carpenter, Virginia Tech/North Carolina	1905
Charles Carroll, Washington	1928
Harry Carson, South Carolina St.# ($)	1975
Anthony Carter, Michigan	1982
Tommy Casanova, LSU	1971
†Edward Casey, Harvard	1919
Tony Casillas, Oklahoma	1985
Rod Cason, Angelo St. ($)	1971
Howard Cassady, Ohio St.	1955
†Guy Chamberlin, Neb. Wesleyan/Nebraska#	1915
Sam Chapman, California	1937
Bob Chappuis, Michigan	1947
†Paul Christman, Missouri	1940
Joe Cichy, North Dakota St. ($)	1970
†Dutch Clark, Colorado Col.#	1929
Paul Cleary, Southern California	1947
†Zora Clevenger, Indiana	1903
Jack Cloud, William & Mary	1949
†Gary Cochran, Princeton	1897
†Josh Cody, Vanderbilt	1919
Don Coleman, Michigan St.	1951
†Charlie Conerly, Mississippi	1947
†George Connor, Holy Cross/Notre Dame#	1947
Bill Cooper, Muskingum ($)	1960
†William Corbin, Yale	1888
William Corbus, Stanford	1933
Jimbo Covert, Pittsburgh	1983
†Hector Cowan, Princeton	1889
†Edward Coy, Yale	1909
Brad Crawford, Franklin ($)	1977
†Fred Crawford, Duke	1933
John David Crow, Texas A&M	1957
†Jim Crowley, Notre Dame	1924
Larry Csonka, Syracuse#	1967
Tom Curtis, Michigan	1969
†Slade Cutter, Navy	1934
†Ziggie Czarobski, Notre Dame	1947
Carroll Dale, Virginia Tech	1959
†Gerald Dalrymple, Tulane	1931
†John Dalton, Navy	1911
†Charles Daly, Harvard/Army	1902
Averell Daniell, Pittsburgh	1936
†James Daniell, Ohio St.	1941
†Tom Davies, Pittsburgh	1921
Anthony Davis, Southern California	1974
†Ernie Davis, Syracuse	1961
†Glenn Davis, Army	1946
Harold Davis, Westminster (Pa.) ($)	1956
Robert Davis, Georgia Tech	1947
Pete Dawkins, Army	1958
Tom Deery, Widener ($)	1981
†Joe Delaney, Northwestern St. ($)	1980
Steve DeLong, Tennessee	1964
Vern Den Herder, Central (Iowa) ($)	1970
Kevin Dent, Jackson St. ($)	1988
Al DeRogatis, Duke	1948
†Paul DesJardien, Chicago	1914
†Aubrey Devine, Iowa	1921
†John DeWitt, Princeton	1903
Buddy Dial, Rice	1958
Chuck Dicus, Arkansas	1970
Don Dierdorf, Michigan#	1970
Mike Ditka, Pittsburgh#	1960
†Glenn Dobbs, Tulsa	1942
†Bobby Dodd, Tennessee	1930
Holland Donan, Princeton	1950
†Joseph Donchess, Pittsburgh	1929
Keith Dorney, Penn St.	1978
Tony Dorsett, Pittsburgh#	1976
†Nathan Dougherty, Tennessee	1909
†Bob Dove, Notre Dame	1942
Nick Drahos, Cornell	1940
†Paddy Driscoll, Northwestern#	1916
†Morley Drury, Southern California	1927
Fred Dryer, San Diego St. ($)	1968
Joe Dudek, Plymouth St. ($)	1985
Dick Duden, Navy	1945
Bill Dudley, Virginia#	1941
Randy Duncan, Iowa	1958
Kenny Easley, UCLA	1980
†Walter Eckersall, Chicago	1906
†Turk Edwards, Washington St.#	1931
†William Edwards, Princeton	1899
†Ray Eichenlaub, Notre Dame	1914
Steve Eisenhauer, Navy	1953
Lawrence Elkins, Baylor	1964
Carl Eller, Minnesota#	1963
Bump Elliott, Michigan/Purdue	1947
Pete Elliott, Michigan	1948
Dave Elmendorf, Texas A&M	1970
John Elway, Stanford#	1982
Frank Emanuel, Tennessee	1965
Steve Emtman, Washington	1991
Ray Evans, Kansas	1947
Thomas Everett, Baylor	1986
†Albert Exendine, Carlisle	1907
†Nello Falaschi, Santa Clara	1936
†Tom Fears, Santa Clara/UCLA#	1947
†Beattie Feathers, Tennessee	1933
Bob Fenimore, Oklahoma St.	1946
†Doc Fenton, LSU	1909
Bob Ferguson, Ohio St.	1961
John Ferraro, Southern California	1947
†Wes Fesler, Ohio St.	1930
†Bill Fincher, Davidson/Georgia Tech	1920
Bill Fischer, Notre Dame	1948
†Hamilton Fish, Harvard	1909
†Robert Fisher, Harvard	1911
†Allen Flowers, Davidson/Georgia Tech	1920
Charlie Flowers, Mississippi	1959
George Floyd, Eastern Ky. ($)	1981
†Danny Fortmann, Colgate#	1935
Bill Fralic, Pittsburgh	1984
†Sam Francis, Nebraska	1936
George "Sonny" Franck, Minnesota	1940
†Ed Franco, Fordham	1937
†Clint Frank, Yale	1937
Rodney Franz, California	1949
Tucker Frederickson, Auburn	1964
†Benny Friedman, Michigan#	1926
John Friesz, Idaho ($)	1989
Roman Gabriel, North Carolina St.	1961
Bob Gain, Kentucky	1950
†Arnold Galiffa, Army	1949
Willie Galimore, Florida A&M ($)	1956
Hugh Gallarneau, Stanford	1940
Kenny Gamble, Colgate ($)	1987
†Edgar Garbisch, Wash. & Jeff./Army	1924
Mike Garrett, Southern California	1965
†Charles Gelbert, Penn	1896
†Forest Geyer, Oklahoma	1915
Jake Gibbs, Mississippi	1960
†Paul Giel, Minnesota	1953
Frank Gifford, Southern California#	1951
Chris Gilbert, Texas	1968
†Walter Gilbert, Auburn	1936
Harry Gilmer, Alabama	1947
†George Gipp, Notre Dame	1920
†Chet Gladchuk, Boston College	1940
Bill Glass, Baylor	1956
Rich Glover, Nebraska	1972
†Marshall Goldberg, Pittsburgh	1938
Gene Goodreault, Boston College	1940
†Walter Gordon, California	1918
†Paul Governali, Columbia	1942
Jim Grabowski, Illinois	1965

Player, College	Year
Randy Gradishar, Ohio St.	1973
†Otto Graham, Northwestern#	1943
†Red Grange, Illinois#	1925
†Bobby Grayson, Stanford	1935
Charlie Green, Wittenberg ($)	1964
Darrell Green, Tex. A&M-Kingsville ($)	1982
Hugh Green, Pittsburgh	1980
†Jack Green, Tulane/Army	1945
Tim Green, Syracuse	1985
Joe Greene, North Texas#	1968
Bob Griese, Purdue#	1966
Archie Griffin, Ohio St.	1975
William Grinnell, Tufts ($)	1934
Jerry Groom, Notre Dame	1950
Ralph Guglielmi, Notre Dame	1954
†Merle Gulick, Toledo/Hobart	1929
Ray Guy, Southern Miss.	1972
†Joe Guyon, Carlisle/Georgia Tech#	1918
John Hadl, Kansas	1961
†Edwin Hale, Mississippi Col.	1921
L. Parker Hall, Mississippi	1938
Jack Ham, Penn St.#	1970
Bob Hamilton, Stanford	1935
†Tom Hamilton, Navy	1926
John Hannah, Alabama#	1972
†Vic Hanson, Syracuse	1926
†Pat Harder, Wisconsin	1942
†Tack Hardwick, Harvard	1914
†T. Truxton Hare, Penn	1900
†Chick Harley, Ohio St.	1919
†Tom Harmon, Michigan	1940
†Howard Harpster, Carnegie Mellon	1928
Wayne Harris, Arkansas	1960
†Edward Hart, Princeton	1911
†Leon Hart, Notre Dame	1949
Bill Hartman, Georgia	1937
Jim Haslett, Indiana (Pa.) ($)	1978
Frank Hawkins, Nevada ($)	1980
Michael Haynes, Arizona St.#	1975
†Homer Hazel, Rutgers	1924
†Matt Hazeltine, California	1954
†Ed Healey, Holy Cross/Dartmouth#	1919
†Pudge Heffelfinger, Yale	1891
†Mel Hein, Washington St.#	1930
†Don Heinrich, Washington	1952
Ted Hendricks, Miami (Fla.)#	1968
Garney Henley, Huron (S.D.) ($)	1959
†Wilbur Henry, Wash. & Jeff.#	1919
†Clarence Herschberger, Chicago	1898
†Robert Herwig, California	1937
Chad Hennings, Air Force	1987
†Willie Heston, San Jose St./Michigan	1904
†Herman Hickman, Tennessee	1931
†William Hickok, Yale	1894
John Hicks, Ohio St.	1973
†Dan Hill, Duke	1938
†Art Hillebrand, Princeton	1899
†Frank Hinkey, Yale	1894
†Carl Hinkle, Vanderbilt	1937
†Clarke Hinkle, Bucknell#	1931
†Elroy Hirsch, Wisconsin/Michigan#	1943
†James Hitchcock, Auburn	1932
Terry Hoage, Georgia	1983
†Frank Hoffmann, Notre Dame	1931
†James J. Hogan, Yale	1904
†Brud Holland, Cornell	1938
†Don Holleder, Army	1955
†Bill Hollenback, Penn	1908
Mike Holovak, Boston College	1942
Pierce Holt, Angelo St. ($)	1987
E.J. Holub, Texas Tech	1960
Paul Hornung, Notre Dame#	1956
†Edwin Horrell, California	1924
†Les Horvath, Ohio St.	1944
Jim Houston, Ohio St.	1959
†Arthur Howe, Yale	1911
†Dixie Howell, Alabama	1934
John Huarte, Notre Dame	1964
†Cal Hubbard, Geneva/Centenary (La.)#	1926
†John Hubbard, Amherst	1906
†Pooley Hubert, Alabama	1925
Sam Huff, West Virginia#	1955
Weldon Humble, La.-Lafayette/Rice	1946
Ricky Hunley, Arizona	1983
Jackie Hunt, Marshall ($)	1941
†Joel Hunt, Texas A&M	1927
†Ellery Huntington, Colgate	1913
†Don Hutson, Alabama#	1934
Cosmo Iacavazzi, Princeton	1964
†Jonas Ingram, Navy	1906
†Cecil Isbell, Purdue	1937
†Harvey Jablonsky, Army/Washington-St. Louis	1933
Bo Jackson, Auburn	1985
Keith Jackson, Oklahoma	1987
†Vic Janowicz, Ohio St.	1951
John Jefferson, Arizona St.	1977
†Darold Jenkins, Missouri	1941
†Jackie Jensen, California	1948
†Herbert Joesting, Minnesota	1927
Billy Johnson, Widener ($)	1972
Bob Johnson, Tennessee	1967
Gary Johnson, Grambling ($)	1974
†Jimmie Johnson, Carlisle/Northwestern	1905
Ron Johnson, Michigan	1968
Brent Jones, Santa Clara ($)	1985
†Calvin Jones, Iowa	1955
†Gomer Jones, Ohio St.	1935
Stan Jones, Maryland#	1953
Lee Roy Jordan, Alabama	1962
†Frank Juhan, Sewanee	1910
†Charlie Justice, North Carolina	1949
†Mort Kaer, Southern California	1926
Joe Kapp, California	1958
Alex Karras, Iowa	1957
Ken Kavanaugh, LSU	1939
†Edgar Kaw, Cornell	1922
Dick Kazmaier, Princeton	1951
†Stan Keck, Princeton	1921
Chip Kell, Tennessee	1970
Larry Kelley, Yale	1936
†Wild Bill Kelly, Montana	1926
Doug Kenna, Army	1944
†George Kerr, Boston College	1940
†Henry Ketcham, Yale	1913
Leroy Keyes, Purdue	1968
†Glenn Killinger, Penn St.	1921
Billy Kilmer, UCLA	1960
†John Kilpatrick, Yale	1910
†John Kimbrough, Texas A&M	1940
†Frank Kinard, Mississippi#	1937
Terry Kinard, Clemson	1982
Steve Kiner, Tennessee	1969
†Phillip King, Princeton	1893
†Nile Kinnick, Iowa	1939
†Harry Kipke, Michigan	1923
†John Kitzmiller, Oregon	1930
†Barton Koch, Baylor	1930
†Walt Koppisch, Columbia	1924
Ron Kramer, Michigan	1956
Alex Kroll, Yale/Rutgers	1961
Charlie Krueger, Texas A&M	1957
Malcolm Kutner, Texas	1941
Ted Kwalick, Penn St.	1968
†Steve Lach, Duke	1941
†Myles Lane, Dartmouth	1927
Willie Lanier, Morgan St.# ($)	1966
Johnny Lattner, Notre Dame	1953
Hank Lauricella, Tennessee	1951
†Lester Lautenschlaeger, Tulane	1925
†Elmer Layden, Notre Dame	1924
†Bobby Layne, Texas#	1947
†Langdon Lea, Princeton	1895
Roosevelt Leaks, Texas	1974
Eddie LeBaron, Pacific	1949
Jim LeClair, North Dakota ($)	1971
†James Leech, VMI	1920
†Darrell Lester, TCU	1935
Jerry LeVias, SMU	1968
D.D. Lewis, Mississippi St.	1968
Leo Lewis, Lincoln (Mo.) ($)	1954
Bob Lilly, TCU#	1960
†Augie Lio, Georgetown	1940
Floyd Little, Syracuse	1966
Gordie Lockbaum, Holy Cross ($)	1987
†Gordon Locke, Iowa	1922
Neil Lomax, Portland St. ($)	1980
Chuck Long, Iowa	1985
Mel Long, Toledo	1971
†Frank Loria, Virginia Tech	1967
Ronnie Lott, Southern California#	1980
†Don Lourie, Princeton	1921
Richie Lucas, Penn St.	1959
†Sid Luckman, Columbia#	1938
Johnny Lujack, Notre Dame	1947
†Pug Lund, Minnesota	1934
Jim Lynch, Notre Dame	1966
Ken MacAfee, Notre Dame	1977
†Robert MacLeod, Dartmouth	1938
†Bart Macomber, Illinois	1916
Dicky Maegle, Rice	1954
†Ned Mahon, Harvard	1915
Johnny Majors, Tennessee	1956
Ronnie Mallett, Central Ark. ($)	1981
†William Mallory, Yale	1923
Vaughn Mancha, Alabama	1947
James Mandich, Michigan	1969
†Gerald Mann, SMU	1927
Archie Manning, Mississippi	1970
Edgar Manske, Northwestern	1933
Ed Marinaro, Cornell	1971
Dan Marino, Pittsburgh#	1982
†Vic Markov, Washington	1937
†Bobby Marshall, Minnesota	1906
Jim Martin, Notre Dame	1949
Ollie Matson, San Francisco#	1951
Ray Matthews, TCU	1927
†John Maulbetsch, Adrian/Michigan	1916
†Pete Mauthe, Penn St.	1912
†Robert Maxwell, Chicago/Swarthmore	1905
Mark May, Pittsburgh	1980
George McAfee, Duke#	1939
Napoleon McCallum, Navy	1985
Don McCauley, North Carolina	1970
†Thomas McClung, Yale	1891
Bill McColl, Stanford	1951
†Jim McCormick, Princeton	1907
Tommy McDonald, Oklahoma#	1956
†Jack McDowall, North Carolina St.	1927
Hugh McElhenny, Washington#	1951
†Gene McEver, Tennessee	1931
†John McEwan, Army	1916
†Banks McFadden, Clemson	1939
Bud McFadin, Texas	1950
Mike McGee, Duke	1959
†Edward McGinley, Penn	1924
†John McGovern, Minnesota	1910
Thurman McGraw, Colorado St.	1949
Tyrone McGriff, Florida A&M ($)	1979
†Mike McKeever, Southern California	1960
Reggie McKenzie, Michigan	1971
†George McLaren, Pittsburgh	1918
Jim McMahon, Brigham Young	1981
†Dan McMillan, Southern California/California	1921
†Bo McMillin, Centre	1921
†Bob McWhorter, Georgia	1913
†Roy Mercer, Penn	1912
Don Meredith, SMU	1959
Frank Merritt, Army	1943
†Bert Metzger, Notre Dame	1930
†Wayne Meylan, Nebraska	1967
Lou Michaels, Kentucky	1957
John Michels, Tennessee	1952
Abe Mickal, LSU	1935
†Creighton Miller, Notre Dame	1943
†Don Miller, Notre Dame	1924
†Eugene Miller, Penn St.	1913
†Fred Miller, Notre Dame	1928
†Rip Miller, Notre Dame	1924
†Wayne Millner, Notre Dame#	1935
†Century Milstead, Wabash/Yale	1923
†John Minds, Penn	1897
†Skip Minisi, Penn/Navy	1947
Lydell Mitchell, Penn St.	1971
Dick Modzelewski, Maryland	1952
†Alex Moffat, Princeton	1883
†Ed Molinski, Tennessee	1940
†Cliff Montgomery, Columbia	1933

Player, College	Year
Wilbert Montgomery, Abilene Christian ($)	1976
Donn Moomaw, UCLA	1952
†William Morley, Columbia	1901
George Morris, Georgia Tech	1952
Larry Morris, Georgia Tech	1954
†Bill Morton, Dartmouth	1931
Craig Morton, California	1964
†Monk Moscrip, Stanford	1935
†Brick Muller, California	1922
Johnny Musso, Alabama	1971
†Bronko Nagurski, Minnesota#	1929
Billy Neighbors, Alabama	1961
†Ernie Nevers, Stanford#	1925
†Marshall Newell, Harvard	1893
Harry Newman, Michigan	1932
Ozzie Newsome, Alabama#	1977
Gifford Nielsen, Brigham Young	1977
Dwayne Nix, Tex. A&M-Kingsville ($)	1968
Tommy Nobis, Texas	1965
Leo Nomellini, Minnesota#	1949
†Andrew Oberlander, Dartmouth	1925
†Davey O'Brien, TCU	1938
Ken O'Brien, UC Davis ($)	1982
†Pat O'Dea, Wisconsin	1899
Bob Odell, Penn	1943
†Jack O'Hearn, Cornell	1914
†Robin Olds, Army	1942
†Elmer Oliphant, Army/Purdue	1917
Merlin Olsen, Utah St.#	1961
Dennis Onkotz, Penn St.	1969
†Bennie Oosterbaan, Michigan	1927
Charles O'Rourke, Boston College	1940
†John Orsi, Colgate	1931
†Win Osgood, Cornell/Penn	1894
Bill Osmanski, Holy Cross	1938
†John Outland, Kansas/Penn	1899
†George Owen, Harvard	1922
Jim Owens, Oklahoma	1949
Steve Owens, Oklahoma	1969
Alan Page, Notre Dame#	1966
Joe Palumbo, Virginia	1951
Jack Pardee, Texas A&M	1956
Babe Parilli, Kentucky	1951
Ace Parker, Duke#	1936
Jackie Parker, Mississippi St.	1953
†Jim Parker, Ohio St.#	1956
†Walter Payton, Jackson St.# ($)	1974
†Vince Pazzetti, Wesleyan/Lehigh	1912
Chub Peabody, Harvard	1941
†Robert Peck, Pittsburgh	1916
Bob Pellegrini, Maryland	1955
†Stan Pennock, Harvard	1914
George Pfann, Cornell	1923
†H.D. Phillips, Sewanee	1905
Loyd Phillips, Arkansas	1966
Mike Phipps, Purdue	1969
Pete Pihos, Indiana#	1946
†Erny Pinckert, Southern California	1931
†John Pingel, Michigan St.	1938
Jim Plunkett, Stanford	1970
†Arthur Poe, Princeton	1899
†Fritz Pollard, Brown#	1916
†George Poole, Mississippi/North Carolina/Army	1948
Marvin Powell, Southern California	1976
Merv Pregulman, Michigan	1943
†Eddie Price, Tulane	1949
Ron Pritchard, Arizona St.	1968
Greg Pruitt, Oklahoma	1972
Larry Pugh, Westminster (Pa.) ($)	1964
†Peter Pund, Georgia Tech	1928
Garrard Ramsey, William & Mary	1942
John Rauch, Georgia	1948
Gary Reasons, Northwestern St. ($)	1983
Bill Redell, Occidental ($)	1963
Rick Redman, Washington	1964
†Claude Reeds, Oklahoma	1913
Mike Reid, Penn St.	1969
Steve Reid, Northwestern	1936
†William Reid, Harvard	1899
Bob Reifsnyder, Navy	1958
Mel Renfro, Oregon#	1963
†Pug Rentner, Northwestern	1932
Scott Reppert, Lawrence ($)	1982

Player, College	Year
Glenn Ressler, Penn St.	1969
†Bob Reynolds, Stanford	1935
†Bobby Reynolds, Nebraska	1952
Randy Rhino, Georgia Tech	1974
Jerry Rhome, SMU/Tulsa	1964
Jerry Rice, Mississippi Val. ($)	1984
Willie Richardson, Jackson St. ($)	1962
Les Richter, California	1951
Pat Richter, Wisconsin	1962
†Jack Riley, Northwestern	1931
Dave Rimington, Nebraska	1982
†Charles Rinehart, Lafayette	1897
Jim Ritcher, North Carolina St.	1979
Richard Ritchie, Tex. A&M-Kingsville ($)	1976
Calvin Roberts, Gust. Adolphus ($)	1952
J.D. Roberts, Oklahoma	1953
†Paul Robeson, Rutgers	1918
Dave Robinson, Penn St.	1962
Jerry Robinson, UCLA	1978
Tracy Rocker, Auburn	1988
†Ira Rodgers, West Virginia	1919
Johnny Rodgers, Nebraska	1972
†Edward Rogers, Carlisle/Minnesota	1903
George Rogers, South Carolina	1980
Johnny Roland, Missouri	1965
Joe Romig, Colorado	1961
†Aaron Rosenberg, Southern California	1933
†Dan Ross, Northeastern ($)	1978
†Kyle Rote, SMU	1950
†Joe Routt, Texas A&M	1937
Mike Rozier, Nebraska	1983
†Red Salmon, Notre Dame	1903
Barry Sanders, Oklahoma St.#	1988
Alex Sarkisian, Northwestern	1948
†George Sauer, Nebraska	1933
George Savitsky, Penn	1947
James Saxton, Texas	1961
Gale Sayers, Kansas#	1964
Jack Scarbath, Maryland	1952
†Hunter Scarlett, Penn	1908
Bob Schloredt, Washington	1960
Joe Schmidt, Pittsburgh#	1952
†Wear Schoonover, Arkansas	1929
†Dave Schreiner, Wisconsin	1942
†Germany Schultz, Michigan	1908
†Dutch Schwab, Lafayette	1922
†Marchy Schwartz, Notre Dame	1931
†Paul Schwegler, Washington	1931
Clyde Scott, Navy/Arkansas	1948
Freddie Scott, Amherst ($)	1973
Richard Scott, Navy	1947
Tom Scott, Virginia	1952
†Henry Seibels, Sewanee	1900
Ron Sellers, Florida St.	1968
Lee Roy Selmon, Oklahoma#	1975
Harley Sewell, Texas	1952
†Bill Shakespeare, Notre Dame	1935
Donnie Shell, South Carolina St. ($)	1973
†Murray Shelton, Cornell	1915
†Tom Shevlin, Yale	1905
†Bernie Shively, Illinois	1926
Jeff Siemon, Stanford	1981
†Monk Simons, Tulane	1934
O.J. Simpson, Southern California#	1968
Billy Sims, Oklahoma	1979
Mike Singletary, Baylor#	1980
Fred Sington, Alabama	1930
†Frank Sinkwich, Georgia	1942
Jerry Sisemore, Texas	1972
†Emil Sitko, Notre Dame	1949
†Joe Skladany, Pittsburgh	1933
†Duke Slater, Iowa	1921
Billy Ray Smith, Arkansas	1982
†Bruce Smith, Minnesota	1941
Bruce Smith, Virginia Tech	1984
Bubba Smith, Michigan St.	1966
†Clipper Smith, Notre Dame	1927
Emmitt Smith, Florida	1989
†Ernie Smith, Southern California	1932
Harry Smith, Southern California	1939
Jim Ray Smith, Baylor	1954
Riley Smith, Alabama	1935

Player, College	Year
†Vernon Smith, Georgia	1931
†Neil Snow, Michigan	1901
Gary Spani, Kansas St.	1977
Al Sparlis, UCLA	1945
†Clarence Spears, Knox/Dartmouth	1915
†W.D. Spears, Vanderbilt	1927
†William Sprackling, Brown	1911
†Bud Sprague, Army/Texas	1928
Steve Spurrier, Florida	1966
Harrison Stafford, Texas	1932
†Amos Alonzo Stagg, Yale	1889
Bill Stanfill, Georgia	1968
†Max Starcevich, Washington	1936
Roger Staubach, Navy#	1964
†Walter Steffen, Chicago	1908
Joe Steffy, Tennessee/Army	1947
†Herbert Stein, Pittsburgh	1921
Bob Steuber, DePauw/Missouri	1943
†Mal Stevens, Washburn/Yale	1923
Ben Stevenson, Tuskegee ($)	1930
†Vincent Stevenson, Penn	1905
Jim Stillwagon, Ohio St.	1970
†Pete Stinchcomb, Ohio St.	1920
Brock Strom, Air Force	1958
William Stromberg, Johns Hopkins ($)	1981
†Ken Strong, New York U.#	1928
†George Strupper, Georgia Tech	1917
†Harry Stuhldreher, Notre Dame	1924
†Herb Sturhahn, Yale	1926
†Joe Stydahar, West Virginia#	1935
†Bob Suffridge, Tennessee	1940
†Steve Suhey, Penn St.	1947
Pat Sullivan, Auburn	1971
†Frank Sundstrom, Cornell	1923
Lynn Swann, Southern California#	1973
†Clarence Swanson, Nebraska	1921
†Bill Swiacki, Holy Cross/Columbia	1947
Jim Swink, TCU	1956
†Eddie Talboom, Wyoming	1950
George Taliaferro, Indiana	1948
Fran Tarkenton, Georgia#	1960
Jack Tatum, Ohio St.	1970
John Tavener, Indiana	1944
Bruce Taylor, Boston U. ($)	1969
†Chuck Taylor, Stanford	1942
Joe Theismann, Notre Dame	1970
Aurelius Thomas, Ohio St.	1957
†Joe Thompson, Geneva/Pittsburgh	1906
Lynn Thomsen, Augustana (Ill.)$	1986
†Samuel Thorne, Yale	1895
†Jim Thorpe, Carlisle#	1912
†Ben Ticknor, Harvard	1930
†John Tigert, Vanderbilt	1903
Gaynell Tinsley, LSU	1936
Eric Tipton, Duke	1938
†Clayton Tonnemaker, Minnesota	1949
†Bob Torrey, Penn	1905
Willie Totten, Mississippi Val. ($)	1985
Randy Trautman, Boise St. ($)	1981
†Brick Travis, Tarkio/Missouri	1920
Charley Trippi, Georgia#	1946
†Edward Tryon, Colgate	1925
Jerry Tubbs, Oklahoma	1956
Bulldog Turner, Hardin-Simmons#	1939
Howard Twilley, Tulsa	1965
†Joe Utay, Texas A&M	1907
†Norm Van Brocklin, Oregon#	1948
Brad Van Pelt, Michigan St.	1972
†Dale Van Sickel, Florida	1929
†H. Van Surdam, Wesleyan (Conn.)	1905
†Dexter Very, Penn St.	1912
†Billy Vessels, Oklahoma	1952
†Ernie Vick, Michigan	1921
†Hube Wagner, Pittsburgh	1913
†Doak Walker, SMU#	1949
Herschel Walker, Georgia	1982
†Bill Wallace, Rice	1935
†Adam Walsh, Notre Dame	1924
†Cotton Warburton, Southern California	1934
†Bob Ward, Maryland	1951
Charlie Ward, Florida St.	1993
Andre Ware, Houston	1989
†William Warner, Cornell	1902

Player, College	Year
Joe Washington, Oklahoma	1975
†Kenny Washington, UCLA	1939
†Jim Weatherall, Oklahoma	1951
†George Webster, Michigan St.	1966
Herman Wedemeyer, St. Mary's (Cal.)	1947
†Harold Weekes, Columbia	1902
Roger Wehrli, Missouri#	1968
Art Weiner, North Carolina	1949
†Ed Weir, Nebraska	1925
†Gus Welch, Carlisle	1914
†John Weller, Princeton	1935
†Percy Wendell, Harvard	1912
†Belford West, Colgate	1919
†Bob Westfall, Michigan	1941
†Babe Weyand, Army	1915
†Buck Wharton, Penn	1896
†Arthur Wheeler, Princeton	1894
†Byron White, Colorado	1937
Charles White, Southern California	1979
Danny White, Arizona St.	1973
Ed White, California	1968
Randy White, Maryland#	1974
†Reggie White, Tennessee#	1983
†Don Whitmire, Navy/Alabama	1944
†Frank Wickhorst, Navy	1926
Ed Widseth, Minnesota	1936
Paul Wiggin, Stanford	1956
†Dick Wildung, Minnesota	1942
Bob Williams, Notre Dame	1950
David Williams, Illinois	1985
Doug Williams, Grambling ($)	1977
Froggie Williams, Rice	1949
Bill Willis, Ohio St.#	1944
Bobby Wilson, SMU	1935
†George Wilson, Washington	1925
†Harry Wilson, Army/Penn St.	1927
Marc Wilson, Brigham Young	1979
Mike Wilson, Lafayette	1928
Kellen Winslow, Missouri#	1978
Albert Wistert, Michigan	1942
Alvin Wistert, Boston U./Michigan	1949
†Whitey Wistert, Michigan	1933
†Alex Wojciechowicz, Fordham#	1937
†Barry Wood, Harvard	1931
†Andy Wyant, Bucknell/Chicago	1894
†Bowden Wyatt, Tennessee	1938
†Clint Wyckoff, Cornell	1895
†Tommy Yarr, Notre Dame	1931
Ron Yary, Southern California#	1967
†Lloyd Yoder, Carnegie Mellon	1926
†Buddy Young, Illinois	1946
Charles Young, Southern California	1972
†Harry Young, Wash. & Lee	1916
Steve Young, Brigham Young#	1983
†Waddy Young, Oklahoma	1938
Jack Youngblood, Florida#	1970
Jim Youngblood, Tennessee Tech ($)	1972
Paul Younger, Grambling ($)	1948
Gust Zarnas, Ohio St.	1937

COACHES

Coach	Year
†Joe Aillet	1989
†Bill Alexander	1951
†Eddie Anderson	1971
†Ike Armstrong	1957
Chris Ault ($)	2002
†Charlie Bachman	1978
Earl Banks	1992
†Harry Baujan	1990
Thomas Beck ($)	2004
†Matty Bell	1955
†Hugo Bezdek	1954
†Dana X. Bible	1951
†Bernie Bierman	1955
†Bob Blackman	1987
†Earl "Red" Blaik	1964
Bobby Bowden	2006
Frank Broyles	1983
Earle Bruce	2002
†Paul "Bear" Bryant	1986
Harold Burry ($)	1996
Jim Butterfield ($)	1997
†Wally Butts	1997
†Charlie Caldwell	1961
†Walter Camp	1951
†Len Casanova	1977
Marino Casem ($)	2003
†Frank Cavanaugh	1954
Jerry Claiborne	1999
†Dick Colman	1990
Don Coryell ($)	1999
Carmen Cozza	2002
†Fritz Crisler	1954
†Duffy Daugherty	1984
†Bob Devaney	1981
†Dan Devine	1985
Doug Dickey	2003
†Gil Dobie	1951
†Bobby Dodd	1993
†Michael Donahue	1951
Terry Donahue	2000
Vince Dooley	1994
†Gus Dorais	1954
Pat Dye	2005
†Bill Edwards	1986
LaVell Edwards	2004
†Rip Engle	1973
Forest Evashevski	2000
Dick Farley ($)	2006
†Don Faurot	1961
Hayden Fry	2003
Joseph Fusco ($)	2001
John Gagliardi ($)	2006
†Jake Gaither	1975
†Sid Gillman#	1989
†Ernest Godfrey	1972
Ray Graves	1990
†Andy Gustafson	1985
†Edward Hall	1951
†Jack Hardin	1980
†Richard Harlow	1954
†Harvey Harman	1981
†Jesse Harper	1971
Roger Harring ($)	2005
†Percy Haughton	1951
†Woody Hayes	1983
†John W. Heisman	1954
†Robert Higgins	1954
†Paul Hoernemann ($)	1997
†Babe Hollingberry	1979
†Frank Howard	1989
Marcelino Huerta ($)	2002
†Bill Ingram	1973
Don James	1997
†Morley Jennings	1973
†Biff Jones	1954
†Howard Jones	1951
†Tad Jones	1958
†Lloyd Jordan	1978
†Ralph "Shug" Jordan	1982
†Andy Kerr	1951
Roy Kidd ($)	2003
Chuck Klausing ($)	1998
Frank Kush	1995
†Frank Leahy	1970
†George Little	1955
†Lou Little	1960
†Slip Madigan	1974
Fred Martinelli ($)	2002
Dave Maurer	1991
Vernon "Skip" McCain ($)	2006
†Charlie McClendon	1986
Herb McCracken	1973
†Dan McGugin	1951
†John McKay	1988
Allyn McKeen	1991
†Tuss McLaughry	1962
†John Merritt	1994
†Dutch Meyer	1956
†Jack Mollenkopf	1988
†Bernie Moore	1954
†Scrappy Moore	1980
†Ray Morrison	1954
Darrell Mudra ($)	2000
†Arnett "Ace" Mumford ($)	2001
†George Munger	1976
†Clarence "Biggie" Munn	1959
†Bill Murray	1974
†Frank Murray	1974
†Ed "Hook" Mylin	1974
†Earle "Greasy" Neale #	1967
†Jess Neely	1971
Don Nehlen	2005
†David Nelson	1987
†Robert Neyland	1956
Billy Nicks ($)	1999
†Homer Norton	1971
†Frank "Buck" O'Neill	1951
Tom Osborne	1998
†Bennie Owen	1951
Ara Parseghian	1980
†Doyt Perry	1988
†Jimmy Phelan	1973
†Tommy Prothro	1991
John Ralston	1992
Harold "Tubby" Raymond ($)	2003
Bob Reade ($)	1998
Charlie Richard ($)	2004
†E.N. Robinson	1955
Eddie Robinson ($)	1997
†Knute Rockne	1951
†Dick Romney	1954
†Bill Roper	1951
Darrell Royal	1983
Adolph Rutschman ($)	1998
†Henry "Red" Sanders	1996
†George Sanford	1971
Glenn "Bo" Schembechler	1993
†Ron Schipper ($)	2000
†Francis Schmidt	1971
†Ben Schwartzwalder	1982
†Clark Shaughnessy	1968
†Buck Shaw	1972
Edgar Sherman ($)	1996
†Andy Smith	1951
†Carl Snavely	1965
Jim Sochor ($)	1999
†Amos Alonzo Stagg	1951
†Gil Steinke ($)	1996
Dick Strahm ($)	2004
†Jock Sutherland	1951
Barry Switzer	2001
†Jim Tatum	1984
Grant Teaff	2001
†Frank Thomas	1951
†Lee Tressel ($)	1996
†Thad "Pie" Vann	1987
†Johnny Vaught	1979
†Wallace Wade	1955
†Lynn "Pappy" Waldorf	1966
†Glenn "Pop" Warner	1951
†Frank "Muddy" Waters ($)	2000
George Welsh	2004
Frosty Westering ($)	2005
†E.E. "Tad" Wieman	1956
†John Wilce	1954
†Bud Wilkinson	1969
†Henry Williams	1951
†George Woodruff	1963
†Warren Woodson	1989
†Bowden Wyatt	1997
Bill Yeoman	2001
†Fielding "Hurry Up" Yost	1951
Jim Young	1999
†Bob Zuppke	1951

† *Deceased*

DIVISION II NATIONAL HALL OF FAME
(at Florence, Alabama)

1999
Johnny Bailey, Tex. A&M-Kingsville, RB
Jeff Bentrim, North Dakota St., QB
Walter Payton, Jackson St., RB

2000
Harry Carson, South Carolina St., LB
Pierce Holt, Angelo St., DL
John Stallworth, Alabama A&M, WR

2001
Brent Jones, Santa Clara, TE
Greg Lloyd, Fort Valley St., LB
Ken Davis, UC Davis, QB

2002
Scott Brunner, Delaware, QB
Andre Reed, Kutztown, WR
Jessie Tuggle, Valdosta St., LB

2003
Darrell Green, Tex. A&M-Kingsville, DB

2004
Phil Hansen, North Dakota St., DL

2005
Chris Hatcher, Valdosta St., QB
Ronald Moore, Pittsburg St., RB
Donnie Shell, South Carolina St., LB/DB

2006
Cody Gross, North Ala., QB
Sean Landeta, Towson, K/P
John Randle, Tex. A&M-Kingsville, DE

First-Team All-Americans Below Football Bowl Subdivision

2006 Selectors (and division[s]): American Football Coaches Association (FCS, II, III); Associated Press (FCS); Football Gazette (FCS, II, III); The Sports Network (FCS); Daktronics (II); D2 Football.com (II); D3 Football.com (III).

Selection of Associated Press Little All-America Teams began in 1934. Early AP selectors were not bound by NCAA membership classifications; therefore, several current Football Bowl Subdivision (FBS) teams are included in this list.

The American Football Coaches Association began selecting All-America teams below the FBS in 1967 for two College Division classifications. Its College Division I team included NCAA Division II and National Association of Intercollegiate Athletics (NAIA) Division I players. The AFCA College Division II team included NCAA Division III and NAIA Division II players. The AFCA renamed the College Division I team to Division II, and the College Division II team to Division III, in 1996; players at NAIA institutions are no longer eligible for these teams.

The AFCA added a Football Championship Subdivision (FCS) team in 1979; AP began selecting an FCS team in 1982; the Sports Network added an FCS team in 1994; and these players are included. In 1993, the College Sports Information Directors of America Division II team was added, selected by sports information directors from every NCAA Division II institution. In 1997, the Daktronics team for Division II was added. In 1990, the Champion USA Division III team was added, selected by a panel of 25 sports information directors and replaced by the Hewlett-Packard Division III team in 1995. It was then replaced by College Sports Information Directors Team in 2003. In 1993, Football Gazette's team was added for the FCS and Divisions II and III. In 2002, D2 Football.com and D3 Football.com were added for Divisions II and III, respectively.

Nonmembers of the NCAA are included in this list, as are colleges that no longer play varsity football.

Players selected to an FCS All-America team are indicated by (†). Current members of the FBS are indicated by (*).

All-Americans are listed by college, year selected and position.

ABILENE CHRISTIAN (23)
48— V.T. Smith, B
51— Lester Wheeler, OT
52— Wallace Bullington, DB
65— Larry Cox, OT
69— Chip Bennett, LB
70— Jim Lindsey, QB
73— Wilbert Montgomery, RB
74— Chip Martin, DL
77— Chuck Sitton, DB
82— Grant Feasel, C
83— Mark Wilson, DB
84— Dan Remsberg, OT
87— Richard Van Druten, OT
89— John Layfield, OG
90— Dennis Brown, PK
91— Jay Jones, LB
97— Junior Filikitonga, DL
Victor Burke, DB
2001— Brad Raphelt, P
03— Britt Lively, OL
04— Danieal Manning, RS
05— Clayton Farrell, DL
Danieal Manning, DB

ADAMS ST. (9)
79— Ronald Johnson, DB
84— Bill Stone, RB
87— Dave Humann, DB
95— Chris Perry, WR
97— Jason Van Dyke, P
98— Jason Van Dyke, P
2004— Adam McGurk, LB
Jeff Williams, P
05— Jeff Williams, P

ADRIAN (3)
2004— Dan McKeown, DB
05— Mike Lewis, DL
06— Taz Wallace, LB

AKRON* (9)
69— John Travis, OG
71— Michael Hatch, DB
76— Mark Van Horn, OG
Steve Cockerham, LB
77— Steve Cockerham, LB
80— †Brad Reece, LB
81— †Brad Reece, LB
85— †Wayne Grant, DL
86— †Mike Clark, RB

UAB* (1)
94— †Derrick Ingram, WR

ALABAMA A&M (4)
87— Howard Ballard, OL
88— Fred Garner, DB
89— Barry Wagner, WR
2002—†Robert Mathis, DL

ALABAMA ST. (6)
90— †Eddie Robinson, LB
91— †Patrick Johnson, OL
†Eddie Robinson, LB
2000—†David Beckford, P
01— †David Beckford, P
†Chris Coleman, TE

ALBANY (N.Y.) (6)
92— Scott Turrin, OL
94— Scott Turrin, OL
98— Matt Caliandro, DL
2000—†J.T. Herfurth, OL
04— †Geir Gudmundsen, OL
06— †Colin Disch, LB

ALBANY ST. (GA.) (3)
72— Harold Little, DE
2004— Walter Curry, DL
06— Alton Pettway, DL

ALBION (16)
40— Walter Ptak, G
58— Tom Taylor, E
76— Steve Spencer, DL
86— Joe Felton, OG
Mike Grant, DB
91— Hank Wineman, RB
93— Ron Dawson, OL
Jeff Brooks, OL
94— Jeff Robinson, RB
Martin Heyboer, C
David Lefere, DB
95— David Lefere, DB
96— Jason Carriveau, OG
98— Pat Sloane, DL
Jason Carriveau, OL
2000— Keith Debbaudt, PK

ALBRIGHT (8)
36— Richard Riffle, B
37— Richard Riffle, B
75— Chris Simcic, OL
95— Dennis Unger, PK
96— Ryan Ditze, WR
Bob Maro, DB
98— Chris Morehouse, P
2004— Nick Cushman, WR

ALCORN ST. (16)
69— David Hadley, DB
70— Fred Carter, DT
71— Harry Gooden, LB
72— Alex Price, DT
73— Leonard Fairley, DB
74— Jerry Dismuke, OG
75— Lawrence Pillers, DE
76— Augusta Lee, RB
Larry Warren, DT
79— †Leslie Frazier, DB
84— †Issiac Holt, DB
93— †Goree White, KR
94— †Steve McNair, QB
99— †Chad Slaughter, OL
2003—†Tyrone Parsons, DB
06— †Nate Hughes, PR

ALFRED (9)
51— Ralph DiMicco, B
52— Ralph DiMicco, B
55— Charles Schultz, E
56— Charles Schultz, E
75— Joseph Van Cura, DE
82— Brian O'Neil, DB
92— Mark Obuszewski, DB
2005— Brenton Brady, LB
06— Don Miller, DL

ALLEGHENY (22)
75— Charles Slater, OL
87— Mike Mates, OL
88— Mike Parker, DL
90— Jeff Filkovski, QB
David LaCarte, DB
John Marzca, C
91— Ron Bendekovic, OT
Stanley Drayton, RB
Tony Bifulco, DB
92— Ron Bendekovic, OT
Stanley Drayton, RB
94— Matt Allison, OL
Paul Bell, QB
Marvin Farr, DB
95— Brian Adams, C
Nick Reiser, DE
Anson Park, OL
96— Chris Conrad, KR
Nick Reiser, DL
Bob Tatsch, DL
97— Jim Mormino, RB
2000— Bill Andrews, OL

ALLIANT INT'L (2)
72— Jerry Robinson, DB
75— Steve Matson, FL

ALMA (2)
2002— David Simpson, DB
06— Josh Brehm, QB

AMERICAN INT'L (14)
71— Bruce Laird, RB

80— Ed Cebula, C
82— Paul Thompson, DT
85— Keith Barry, OL
86— Jon Provost, OL
87— Jon Provost, OL
88— Greg Doherty, OL
89— Lamont Cato, DB
90— George Patterson, DL
91— Gabe Mokwuah, DL
98— Ray Shuster, OL
99— Kavin Gailliard, RB
2000— Bob Parker, DB
01— Dan Porter, OL

AMHERST (5)
42— Adrian Hasse, E
72— Richard Murphy, QB
73— Fred Scott, FL
96— Alex Bernstein, DL
97— Devin Moriarty, DL

ANDERSON (IND.) (1)
97— Justin Shively, P

ANGELO ST. (14)
75— James Cross, DB
78— Jerry Aldridge, RB
Kelvin Smith, LB
81— Clay Weishuhn, LB
82— Mike Elarms, WR
83— Mike Thomas, K
85— Henry Jackson, LB
86— Pierce Holt, DL
87— Pierce Holt, DL
88— Henry Alsbrooks, LB
92— Jimmy Morris, P
93— Anthony Hooper, DB
95— Greg Stokes, LB
2001— Dan Krager, DL

APPALACHIAN ST. (35)
48— John Caskey, E
63— Greg Van Orden, G
85— †Dino Hackett, LB
87— †Anthony Downs, DE
88— †Bjorn Nittmo, PK
89— †Derrick Graham, OL
†Keith Collins, DB
91— †Harold Alexander, P
92— †Avery Hall, DL
†Harold Alexander, P
94— †Chip Miller, DL
†William Peebles, DL
†Brad Ohrt, OL
†Dexter Coakley, LB
†Matt Stevens, DB
95— †Dexter Coakley, LB
†Matt Stevens, DB
†Chip Miller, DL
†Scott Kadlub, C
96— †Scott Kadlub, C
†Dexter Coakley, LB
97— †Jackie Avery, DL
99— †Corey Hall, DB
2000—†Corey Hall, DB
01— †Josh Jeffries, DL
02— †Josh Jeffries, DL
03— †K.T. Stovall, DL
04— †DaVon Fowlkes, WR
05— †Jason Hunter, DL
†Marques Murrell, DL
06— †Kerry Brown, OL
†Matt Isenhour, OL
†Corey Lynch, DB
†Marques Murrell, DL
†Jeremy Wiggins, DB

ARIZONA* (1)
41— Henry Stanton, E

ARK.-MONTICELLO (1)
2003— Devon Stewart, TE

ARK.-PINE BLUFF (1)
2006—†Jackie Skipper, OL

ARKANSAS ST.* (17)
53— Richard Woit, B
64— Dan Summers, OG
65— Dan Summers, OG
68— Bill Bergey, LB
69— Dan Buckley, C
Clovis Swinney, DT
70— Bill Phillips, OG
Calvin Harrell, HB
71— Calvin Harrell, RB
Dennis Meyer, DB
Wayne Dorton, OG
73— Doug Lowrey, OG
84— †Carter Crawford, DL
85— †Carter Crawford, DL
86— †Randy Barnhill, OG
87— †Jim Wiseman, C
†Charlie Fredrick, DT

ARKANSAS TECH (7)
58— Edward Meador, B
61— Powell McClellan, E
95— Piotr Styczen, PK
99— Todd Matthews, OG
2002— Tommy Edwards, DL
03— Tommy Edwards, DL
06— Quincy Skinner, DB

ASHLAND (10)
70— Len Pettigrew, LB
78— Keith Dare, DL
85— Jeff Penko, OL
86— Vince Mazza, PK
89— Douglas Powell, DB
90— Morris Furman, LB
91— Ron Greer, LB
93— Bill Royce, DL
94— Sam Hohler, DE
2003— Toure Carter, DB

AUGUSTANA (ILL.) (19)
72— Willie Van, DT
73— Robert Martin, OT
83— Kurt Kapischke, OL
84— Greg King, C
86— Lynn Thomsen, DL
87— Carlton Beasley, DL
88— John Bothe, OL
90— Barry Reade, PK
91— Mike Hesler, DB
92— George Annang, DL
95— Rusty Van Wetzinga, LB
2000— Mack Hay, OG
01— J.D. Sheldon, OL
02— J.D. Sheldon, OL
03— Mike Clark, PK
Mike Hansen, DL
04— Mike Clark, PK
05— Mike Zeifert, OL
Tom Anthony, DB

AUGUSTANA (S.D.) (6)
60— John Simko, E
87— Tony Adkins, DL
88— Pete Jaros, DB
94— Bryan Schwartz, LB
2000— Matt Holmlund, WR
01— Matt Holmlund, WR

AUGSBURG (2)
97— Scott Hvistendahl, WR
98— Scott Hvistendahl, WR

AURORA (3)
99— Jeremy Benson, DL
2000— Jeremy Benson, DL
01— Kip Daniels, DB

AUSTIN (10)
37— Wallace Johnson, C
79— Price Clifford, LB
80— Chris Luper, DB
81— Larry Shillings, QB
83— Ed Holt, DL
84— Jeff Timmons, PK
87— Otis Amy, WR
88— Otis Amy, WR
90— Jeff Cordell, DB
94— Brent Badger, P

AUSTIN PEAY (10)
65— Tim Chilcutt, DB
66— John Ogles, FB
70— Harold Roberts, OE
77— Bob Bible, LB
78— Mike Betts, DB
80— Brett Williams, DE
82— Charlie Tucker, OL
92— †Richard Darden, DL
2001—†Dustin Wilson, LB
02— †Jay Bailey, RB

AZUSA PACIFIC (3)
86— Christian Okoye, RB
95— Jake Wiersma, OL
2001— Jeremiah Beery, LB

BAKER (3)
83— Chris Brown, LB
85— Kevin Alewine, RB
90— John Campbell, OL

BALDWIN-WALLACE (17)
50— Norbert Hecker, E
68— Bob Quackenbush, DT
78— Jeff Jenkins, OL
80— Dan Delfino, DE
82— Pete Primeau, DL
83— Steve Varga, K
89— Doug Halbert, DL
91— John Koz, QB
Jim Clardy, LB
94— Chris Kondik, PK
Phil Sahley, DL
97— Fred Saylor, DL
2003— Ian Formaz, OG
Nate Mitchell, DL
Greg Koch, DB
04— Kevin Soflkiancs, P
06— Kevin Soflkiancs, P

BALL ST.* (4)
67— Oscar Lubke, OT
68— Amos Van Pelt, HB
72— Douglas Bell, C
73— Terry Schmidt, DB

BATES (1)
81— Larry DiGammarino, WR

BELOIT (1)
95— Maurice Redd, DB

BEMIDJI ST. (1)
83— Bruce Ecklund, TE

BENEDICTINE (ILL.) (3)
72— Mike Rogowski, LB
92— Bob McMillen, TE
93— Eric Green, KR

BENEDICTINE (KAN.) (1)
36— Leo Deutsch, E

BENTLEY (3)
99— Mark DeBrito, WR
2001— Gregg Albano, DB
04— Dallas Mall, WR

BETHANY (W.V.) (2)
77— Scott Lanz, P
93— Brian Darden, PK

BETHEL (KAN.) (1)
80— David Morford, C

BETHEL (MINN.) (5)
99— Chico Rowland, OL
2000— Ben Matthews, DB
03— Sam Lacy, DB
06— Kirby Carr, LB
Phil Porta, RB

BETHUNE-COOKMAN (6)
75— Willie Lee, DE
81— Booker Reese, DE
98— †James Souder, LB
2002—†Rashean Mathis, DB
03— †Steve Baggs, DL
05— †Ricky Williams, AP

BIRMINGHAM-SO. (1)
37— Walter Riddle, T

BISHOP (1)
81— Carlton Nelson, DL

BLOOMSBURG (16)
79— Mike Morucci, RB
82— Mike Blake, TE
83— Frank Sheptock, LB
84— Frank Sheptock, LB
85— Frank Sheptock, LB
Tony Woods, DB
91— Eric Jonassen, OL
96— Ron Lelko, WR
Sean Smith, KR
97— Tim Baer, OL
Irvin Sigler, RB
98— Tim Baer, OG
2000— Jeff Smith, OT
04— Jhari Evans, OL
05— Jamar Brittingham, RB
Jahri Evans, OL

BOISE ST.* (23)
72— Al Marshall, OE
73— Don Hutt, WR
74— Jim McMillan, QB
75— John Smith, FL
77— Chris Malmgren, DT
Terry Hutt, WR
Harold Cotton, OT
79— †Joe Aliotti, QB
†Doug Scott, DT
80— †Randy Trautman, DT
81— †Randy Trautman, DT
†Rick Woods, DB
82— †John Rade, DL
†Carl Keever, LB
84— †Carl Keever, LB
85— †Marcus Koch, DL
87— †Tom DeWitz, OG
†Pete Kwiatkowski, DT
90— †Erik Helgeson, DL
91— †Frank Robinson, DB
92— †Michael Dodd, PK
94— †Joe O'Brien, DL
†Rashid Gayle, DB

BOSTON U. (19)
67— Dick Farley, DB
68— Bruce Taylor, DB
69— Bruce Taylor, DB
79— †Mal Najarian, RB
†Tom Pierzga, DL
81— †Bob Speight, OT
†Gregg Drew, RB
82— †Mike Mastrogiacomo, OG
83— †Paul Lewis, RB
84— †Paul Lewis, RB
86— †Kevin Murphy, DT
87— †Mark Seals, DB
88— †Mark Seals, DB
89— †Daren Altieri, WR
93— †Chris Helon, DB
†Andre Maksimov, C
94— †Andre Maksimov, C
96— †Brad Costello, P
97— †Brad Costello, P

BOWDOIN (1)
77— Steve McCabe, OL

BOWIE ST. (3)
80— Victor Jackson, CB
81— Marco Tongue, DB
2002— Charles Alston, DL

BOWLING GREEN* (2)
59— Bob Zimpfer, T
82— †Andre Young, DL

BRADLEY (1)
38— Ted Panish, B

BRANDEIS (2)
54— William McKenna, E
56— James Stehlin, B

BRIDGEPORT (1)
72— Dennis Paldin, DB

BRIDGEWATER (VA.) (8)
75— C.J. DeWitt, SE
98— Mike Padgett, PK
2001— Michael Day, OL
Davon Cruz, RB
02— Michael Day, OL
Jermaine Taylor, LB
03— Jermaine Taylor, LB
04— Lawrence Frierson, DL

BRIDGEWATER ST. (2)
92— Erik Arthur, DL
2005— Brenden Kavey, RB

BROCKPORT ST. (6)
90— Ed Smart, TE
93— Steve Milne, PK
97— Tom Massey, DB
2000— Josh Warner, OL
01— Jason Johnson, LB
02— Mike Condello, DL

BROWN (7)
96— †Paul Choquette, TE
97— †Sean Morey, WR
†Roderic Parson, DB
98— †Zach Burns, TE
2000—†Stephen Campbell, WR
01— †Chas Gassner, WR
05— †Nick Hartigan, RB

BUCKNELL (13)
51— George Young, DT
60— Paul Terhes, B
64— Tom Mitchell, OE
65— Tom Mitchell, OE
74— Larry Schoenberger, LB
80— Mike McDonald, OT
90— †Mike Augsberger, DB
95— †Ed Burman, DL
96— †Brandon Little, LB
97— †Willie Hill, LB
2000—†Kevin Eiben, DB
01— †Adam Lord, DL
02— †Adam Lord, DL

BUENA VISTA (5)
72— Joe Kotval, OG
73— Joe Kotval, OG
76— Keith Kerkhoff, DL
87— Jim Higley, LB
2001— Carlos Martinez, PK

BUFFALO* (4)
84— Gerry Quinlivan, LB
87— Steve Wojciechowski, LB
95— †Pete Conley, LB
96— †Michael Chichester, DB

BUFFALO ST. (3)
93— John Mattey, OL
98— Dan Lauta, OL
99— Jon Crumley, LB

BUTLER (3)
88— Steve Roberts, RB
94— †Arnold Mickens, RB
2003—† Brandon Martin, DB

C.W. POST (10)
71— Gary Wichard, QB
77— John Mohring, DE
78— John Mohring, DE
81— Tom DeBona, WR
89— John Levelis, DL
2000— William Yarocki, DL
01— Ian Smart, RB
02— Jon Isopo, OG
Ian Smart, RB
04— Joe Gangemi, LB

UC DAVIS (19)
72— Bob Biggs, QB
David Roberts, OT
76— Andrew Gagnon, OL
77— Chuck Fomasi, DT
78— Casey Merrill, DL
79— Jeffrey Allen, DB
82— Ken O'Brien, QB
83— Bo Eason, DB
84— Scott Barry, QB
85— Mike Wise, DL
94— Aaron Bennetts, TE
96— Josh Antstey, DE
97— Wes Terrell, TE
Kevin Daft, QB
98— Wes Terrell, TE
99— Troy Larkin, OL
Joe Caviglia, DB
2000— Eric Friend, PK
02— Forrest Vance, OL

UC RIVERSIDE (1)
75— Michael Johnson, SE

UC SANTA BARB. (3)
36— Douglas Oldershaw, G
37— Douglas Oldershaw, G
67— Paul Vallerga, DB

CALIFORNIA (PA.) (5)
83— Perry Kemp, WR
2001— Wesley Cates, RB
02— R.J. Abercrombie, KR
05— Antoine Bagwell, RB
06— Tim McCutcheon, OL

CAL LUTHERAN (6)
72— Brian Kelley, LB
79— Mike Hagen, SE
95— Jeff Shea, P
96— Jeff Shea, P
97— Jeff Shea, P
99— Ryan Geisler, PK

CAL POLY (23)
53— Stan Sheriff, C
58— Charles Gonzales, G
66— David Edmondson, C
72— Mike Amos, DB
73— Fred Stewart, OG
78— Louis Jackson, RB
80— Louis Jackson, RB
Robbie Martin, FL
81— Charles Daum, OL
84— Nick Frost, DB
89— Robert Morris, DL
90— Pat Moore, DL
91— Doug O'Neill, P
2000—† Kassim Osgood, WR
03— †David Richardson, DB
04— †Jordan Beck, LB
†Kenny Chicoine, DB
†Chris Gocong, DL
05— †James Noble, RB
†Chris Gocong, DL
†Kyle Shotwell, LB
06— †Kyle Shotwell, LB
†Chris White, DL

CAL ST. CHICO (1)
87— Chris Verhulst, TE

CAL ST. EAST BAY (4)
75— Greg Blankenship, LB
84— Ed Lively, DT
86— Fred Williams, OL
93— Jeff Williamson, TE

CAL ST. NORTHRIDGE (9)
75— Mel Wilson, DB
82— Pat Hauser, OT
83— Pat Hauser, OT
87— Kip Dukes, DB
91— Don Goodman, OL
94— †Joe Vaughn, DB
99— †Brennen Swanson, DE
2001—†Drew Amerson, WR
†Marcus Brady, QB

CANISIUS (3)
87— Tom Doctor, LB
88— Marty Hurley, DB
94— †Aaron Fix, PR

CAPITAL (11)
74— Greg Arnold, OG
80— John Phillips, DL
Steve Wigton, C
2001— Ron Swearingin, LB
02— Ron Swearingin, LB
03— Tom Doyle, C
Ron Swearingin, LB
05— Shawn Papp, OL
Kyle Hausler, DB
06— Derick Alexander, WR
Rocky Pentello, QB

CARLETON (1)
90— Jim Bradford, WR

CARNEGIE MELLON (5)
81— Ken Murawski, LB
85— Robert Butts, OL
91— Chuck Jackson, OT
93— Chad Wilson, LB
2000— Nick Zitelli, LB

CARROLL (MONT.) (8)
76— Richard Dale, DB
79— Don Diggins, DL
87— Jeff Beaudry, DB
88— Paul Petrino, QB
89— Suitoa Keleti, OL
2002— Casey Fitzsimmons, TE
03— Mark Gallik, WR
05— Tyler Emmert, QB

CARROLL (WIS.) (3)
74— Robert Helf, TE
90— Bill Nolan, P
93— Andy Ostrand, DB

CARSON-NEWMAN (21)
78— Tank Black, FL
80— Brad Payne, S
83— Dwight Wilson, OL
90— Robert Hardy, RB
92— Darryl Gooden, LB
93— Kendall James, KR
95— Steve Mellon, DL
Anthony Davis, LB
96— Mike Clowney, LB
97— Cedric Killings, DL
Jacques Rumph, RS
Jon Jon Simmons, DB
98— Ques Rumph, RS
Cedric Killings, DL
Montrae Ford, DB
99— Cedric Killings, DL
2000— Clay Clevenger, OL
02— Leonard Guyton, QB
03— Reggie Perkins, OG
04— Leonard Weaver, TE
05— Deonte Bolden, DB

CARTHAGE (2)
80— Rick Kehr, OL
2004— Dante Washington, RB

CASE RESERVE (5)
41— Mike Yurcheshen, E
52— Al Feeny, DE
84— Fred Manley, DE
85— Mark Raiff, OL
2006— Tom Brew, LB

CATAWBA (15)
34— Charles Garland, T
35— Charles Garland, T
45— Carroll Bowen, B
72— David Taylor, OT
74— Mike McDonald, LB
96— Greg Payne, PK
97— Maurice Miller, DL
98— Brian Hinson, OL
99— Brian Hinson, OL
2000— Radell Lockhart, DL
DeVonte Peterson, DL
02— Todd McComb, LB
03— Cole Beane, OG
Khanis Hubbard, DE
06— Ron Ellington, DL

CATHOLIC (9)
84— Chris McMahon, DB
94— Steve Wilkerson, WR
96— Matt Taylor, FB
Jeff Clay, WR
97— Jeff Clay, WR
Tony Faison, OL
99— Brian Hee, LB
2000— Dan Riely, OL
05— Nick Bublavi, WR

CENTRAL (IOWA) (19)
70— Vernon Den Herder, DT
74— Al Dorenkamp, LB
77— Donald Taylor, RB
84— Scott Froehle, DB
85— Rich Thomas, DL
88— Mike Stumberg, DL
89— Mike Estes, DL
Kris Reis, LB
92— Bill Maulder, LB
93— Jeff Helle, OL
94— Jeff Helle, OL
Mark Kacmarynski, RB
Rick Sanger, LB
95— Rick Sanger, LB
96— Mark Kacmarynski, RB
97— Matt Paulson, DB
98— Andrew Paulsen, DB
2000— Jeff Sanger, LB
05— Ryan Johnson, OL

CENTRAL ARK. (7)
80— Otis Chandler, MG
84— David Burnette, DT
91— David Henson, DL
95— Bart Reynolds, DL
96— Don Struebing, C
99— Scott Stephens, P
2005— Aaron Fairooz, WR

CENTRAL CONN. ST. (5)
74— Mike Walton, C
84— Sal Cintorino, LB
88— Doug Magazu, DL
89— Doug Magazu, DL
2006—†Justise Hairston, RB

UCF* (4)
87— Bernard Ford, WR
Ed O'Brien, PK
93— †David Rhodes, WR
94— †Charlie Pierce, PK

CENTRAL MICH.* (4)
42— Warren Schmakel, G
59— Walter Beach, B
62— Ralph Soffredine, G
74— Rick Newsome, DL

CENTRAL MO. (10)
68— Jim Urczyk, OT
85— Steve Huff, PK
88— Jeff Wright, DL
92— Bart Woods, DL
93— Bart Woods, DL
97— Shane Meyer, PK
99— Colston Weatherington, DL
2003— Rod Green, DL
Kegan Coleman, AP
05— Darryl Grace, OL

CENTRAL OKLA. (11)
65— Jerome Bell, OE
78— Gary Smith, TE
94— Elton Rhoades, DB
Joe Aska, RB
96— Johnny Luter, LB
97— Dustin McNeal, OL
98— Johnny Luter, LB
John Fitzgerald, OG
Reggie Donner, RB
Brandon Carder, DB
99— Johnnie Jones, DB

CENTRAL ST. (OHIO) (9)
83— Mark Corbin, RB
84— Dave Dunham, OT
85— Mark Corbin, RB
86— Terry Morrow, RB
89— Kenneth Vines, OG
90— Eric Williams, OL
92— Marvin Coleman, DB
93— Marvin Coleman, DB
94— Hugh Douglas, DL

CENTRAL WASH. (10)
48— Robert Osgood, G
50— Jack Hawkins, G
88— Mike Estes, DL
91— Eric Lamphere, OL
2001— Jason Patterson, DB
02— Brian Potucek, WR
Rob Williams, C
Lance Gibson, DL
03— Joe Smith, P
04— Jacob Galloway, DL

CENTRE (8)
55— Gene Scott, B
84— Teel Bruner, DB
85— Teel Bruner, DB
86— Jeff Leonard, OL
88— John Gohmann, DL
89— Jeff Bezold, LB
97— Montas Allen, RS
2001— Brian Britt, RS

CHADRON ST. (13)
74— Dennis Fitzgerald, DB
78— Rick Mastey, OL
90— David Jones, RB
94— Scott Doyle, PK
97— Kevin Homer, LB
99— Jess Clarke, TE
Casey Beran, DL
2001— Jeremy Eardley, OL
02— Marvin Jackson, DB
03— Marvin Jackson, DB
04— Danny Woodhead, RB
06— Robbie Klinetrobe, OL
Danny Woodhead, RB

CHAPMAN (1)
98— Keith Dykes, LB

CHATTANOOGA (23)
35— Robert Klein, E
38— Robert Sutton, G
39— Jack Gregory, T
45— Thomas Stewart, T
46— Gene Roberts, B
48— Ralph Hutchinson, T
49— Vincent Sarratore, G
51— Chester LaGod, DT
52— Chester LaGod, DT
54— Richard Young, B
57— Howard Clark, E
58— John Green, B
60— Charles Long, T
64— Jerry Harris, S
66— Harry Sorrell, OG

76— Tim Collins, LB
86— †Mike Makins, DL
89— †Pumpy Tudors, P
†Junior Jackson, LB
90— †Troy Boeck, DL
†Tony Hill, DL
†Pumpy Tudors, P
2000—†Matt Vick, PK

CHICAGO (4)
91— Neal Cawi, DE
Jeff Stolte, P
93— Frank Baker, FB
95— Derrick Brooms, KR

CHRIS. NEWPORT (3)
2004— Tommy Fitzgerald, OL
05— Justin Wood, LB
06— Rob Rodriguez, AP

CITADEL (11)
82— Jim Ettari, DL
84— Jim Gabrish, OL
85— Jim Gabrish, OL
86— Scott Thompson, DT
88— †Carlos Avalos, OL
90— †DeRhon Robinson, OL
92— †Corey Cash, OL
†Lester Smith, DB
94— †Levi Davis, OL
95— †Brad Keeney, DL
97— †Carlos Frank, KR

CLARION (14)
78— Jeff Langhans, OL
80— Steve Scillitani, MG
Gary McCauley, TE
81— Gary McCauley, TE
83— Elton Brown, RB
85— Chuck Duffy, OL
87— Lou Weiers, DL
93— Tim Brown, TE
95— Kim Niedbala, DB
96— Chris Martin, OL
Kim Niedbala, DB
2002— Reggie Wells, OL
Troy Bowers, DL
03— Troy Bowers, DL

CLARK ATLANTA (1)
79— Curtis Smith, OL

CLINCH VALLEY (1)
95— Shonn Bell, TE

COAST GUARD (5)
90— Ron Davies, DB
91— Ron Davies, DB
97— Ed Hernaez, LB
2000— Mike Benson, RS
02— Brad Brunaugh, OL

COASTAL CARO. (1)
2006—†Tyler Thigpen, QB

COE (9)
74— Dan Schmidt, OG
76— Paul Wagner, OT
85— Mike Matzen, P
90— Richard Matthews, DB
93— Carey Bender, RB
Craig Chmelicek, OL
94— Carey Bender, RB
99— Zak Gordon, DB
2002— Fredrick Jackson, RB/RS

COLGATE (14)
82— †Dave Wolf, LB
83— †Rich Erenberg, RB
84— †Tom Stenglein, WR
85— †Tom Stenglein, WR
86— †Kenny Gamble, RB
87— †Kenny Gamble, RB
†Greg Manusky, LB
96— †Adam Sofran, LB
97— †Tim Girard, OL
98— †Corey Hill, WR
99— †Paul Clasby, OL
2003—†Jamaal Branch, RB
†Marc Sclafani, OL
05— †Jared Nepa, LB

COL. OF EMPORIA (1)
51— William Chai, OG

COL. OF IDAHO (2)
53— Norman Hayes, T
54— R.C. Owens, E

COLORADO COL. (4)
72— Ed Smith, DE
73— Darryl Crawford, DB
82— Ray Bridges, DL
93— Todd Mays, DL

COLORADO MINES (9)
39— Lloyd Madden, B
41— Dick Moe, T
59— Vince Tesone, B
72— Roger Cirimotich, DB
86— Tim Baer, P
94— Pat Hogelin, P
2004— Chad Friehauf, QB
Daniel Leger, DB
05— Justin Gallas, WR/AP

CONCORD (3)
86— Kevin Johnson, LB
92— Chris Hairston, RB
2002— Kory Wright, TE

CONCORDIA-M'HEAD (6)
77— Barry Bennett, DT
90— Mike Gindorff, DT
Shayne Lindsay, NG
95— Tim Lowry, OL
2004— Nick Didier, OL
Jordan Talge, DB

CONCORDIA (WIS.) (2)
2003— Jacob Knighton, LB
06— Mike Steinmetz, PR

CONNECTICUT* (8)
45— Walter Trojanowski, B
73— Richard Foye, C
80— †Reggie Eccleston, WR
83— †John Dorsey, LB
88— †Glenn Antrum, WR
89— †Troy Ashley, LB
91— †Mark Didio, WR
97— †TaVarr Closs, OL

CORNELL (5)
82— †Dan Suren, TE
86— †Tom McHale, DE
93— †Chris Zingo, LB
96— †Chad Levitt, RB
2005—†Kevin Boothe, OL

CORNELL COLLEGE (2)
82— John Ward, WR
92— Brent Sands, DB

CORTLAND ST. (9)
67— Rodney Verkey, DE
89— Jim Cook, OL
90— Chris Lafferty, OG
Vinny Swanda, LB
91— Vinny Swanda, LB
96— Pat Lalley, OL
97— Brian McAvan, OL
2005— Adam Haas, DL
06— Adam Haas, DL

CUMBERLAND (KY.) (4)
87— David Carmichael, DB
89— Ralph McWilliams, OL
93— Doug Binkley, DB
94— Doug Binkley, LB

CURRY (1)
2004— Brian Robitaille, LB

DAKOTA WESLEYAN (1)
45— Robert Kirkman, T

DARTMOUTH (5)
91— †Al Rosier, RB
92— †Dennis Durkin, PK
96— †Brian Larsen, OL
97— †Zach Walz, LB
2002—†Casey Cramer, TE

DAVIDSON (3)
34— John Mackorell, B
99— †Ryan Crawford, DB
2003—†Chris Costello, PK

DAYTON (13)
36— Ralph Niehaus, T
78— Rick Chamberlin, LB
81— Chris Chaney, DB
84— David Kemp, LB
86— Gerry Meyer, OL
89— Mike Duvic, PK
90— Steve Harder, OL
91— Brian Olson, OG
92— Andy Pellegrino, OL
94— †Tim Duvic, PK
2001—†Eric Willman, OL
02— †Mark Kasmer, DB
04— †Doug Jones, DB

DEFIANCE (1)
93— Sammy Williams, WR

DELAWARE (44)
42— Hugh Bogovich, G
46— Tony Stalloni, T
54— Don Miller, B
63— Mike Brown, B
66— Herb Slattery, OT
69— John Favero, LB
70— Conway Hayman, OG
71— Gardy Kahoe, RB
72— Joe Carbone, DE
Dennis Johnson, DT
73— Jeff Cannon, DT
74— Ed Clark, LB
Ray Sweeney, OG
75— Sam Miller, DE
76— Robert Pietuszka, DB
78— Jeff Komlo, QB
79— †Herb Beck, OG
†Scott Brunner, QB
80— †Gary Kuhlman, OT
81— †Gary Kuhlman, OL
82— †George Schmitt, DB
85— †Jeff Rosen, OL
86— †Darrell Booker, LB
87— †James Anderson, WR
88— †Mike Renna, DL
89— †Mike Renna, DL
91— †Warren McIntire, DB
92— †Matt Morrill, DL
93— †Matt Morrill, DL
94— †Daryl Brown, RB
95— †Kenny Bailey, DB
96— †Kenny Bailey, DB
97— †Brian Smith, LB
98— †Eddie Conti, WR
2000—†Jamin Elliott, WR
†Jeff Fiss, OL
†Brian McKenna, LB
03— †Germaine Bennett, RB
†Andy Hall, QB
†Jason Nerys, OL
†Sidney Haugabrook, DB
†Shawn Johnson, DL
04— †Sidney Haugabrook, DB
06— †Ben Patrick, TE

DELAWARE ST. (7)
84— Gene Lake, RB
86— Joe Burton, DB
91— †Rod Milstead, OL
92— †LeRoy Thompson, DL
2000—†Darnerien McCants, TE
02— †DaShaun Morris, RS
05— †Eric Conyos, P

DELAWARE VALLEY (1)
2005— Damien Ciecwisz, C

DELTA ST. (11)
67— Leland Hughes, OG
95— Jerome Williams, DB
2000— Chris Booker, OG
Rory Bell, DB
01— Chris Booker, OL
02— Chris Booker, OL
03— Mark Barron, OT
Ellis Debrow, WR
Anthony Maddox, DL
04— Ellis Debrow, WR
06— Michael Eubanks, LB

DENISON (5)
47— William Hart, E
48— William Wehr, C
75— Dennis Thome, DL
79— Clay Sampson, RB
86— Dan Holland, DL

DEPAUW (6)
63— Richard Dean, C
96— Scott Farnham, DB
Jay Pettigrew, TE
2003— Jamarcus Shephard, RS
04— Jamarcus Shephard, RS
06— Dustin Hertel, DL

DETROIT TECH (1)
39— Mike Kostiuk, T

DICKINSON (4)
91— Shaughn White, DB
92— Brian Ridgway, DL
94— Jason Fox, LB
98— Jason Shoff, DL

DICKINSON ST. (2)
81— Tony Moore, DL
92— Rory Farstveet, OL

DOANE (1)
66— Fred Davis, OT

DRAKE (6)
72— Mike Samples, DT
82— Pat Dunsmore, TE
Craig Wederquist, OT
95— †Matt Garvis, LB
99— †Mike Foster, DL
2000—†Mike Foster, DL

DREXEL (2)
55— Vincent Vidas, T
56— Vincent Vidas, T

DUBUQUE (1)
96— Matt Plummer, WR

DUQUESNE (5)
2001—†Leigh Bodden, DB
02— †Jeremy Conley, WR
†Leigh Bodden, DB
04— †Ryan Tolan, DL
06— †Bruce Hocker, WR

EAST CARO.* (1)
64— Bill Cline, HB

EAST CENTRAL (4)
84— Don Wilson, C
2002— Kwame Ferguson, LB
04— Justin Brown, DL
06— Curtis Lilly, P

EAST STROUDSBURG (13)
65— Barry Roach, DB
75— William Stem, DB
79— Ronald Yakavonis, DL
83— Mike Reichenbach, LB
84— Andy Baranek, QB
91— Curtis Bunch, DB
94— Steve Hynes, OL
2000— Kevin Nagle, LB
01— Adam Hostetter, P
04— Matt Crispell, DB
Ken Parrish, P
05— Evan Prall, WR
Jimmy Terwilliger, QB

EAST TENN. ST. (10)
53— Hal Morrison, E
68— Ron Overbay, DB
70— William Casey, DB
85— George Cimadevilla, P
86— George Cimadevilla, P
94— †Jeff Johnson, WR
96— †James Russell, DL
97— †B.J. Adigun, WR
†Mario Hankerson, LB
2003—†Brandon Calton, DL

EAST TEX. BAPTIST (3)
2001— Scott Verhalen, P
02— Scott Verhalen, P
05— Chad Glover, DL

EASTERN ILL. (25)
72— Nate Anderson, RB
76— Ted Petersen, C
78— James Warring, WR
79— Chris Cobb, RB
Pete Catan, DE
80— Pete Catan, DE
81— †Kevin Grey, DB
82— †Robert Williams, DB
†Bob Norris, OG
83— †Robert Williams, DB
†Chris Nicholson, DT
84— †Jerry Wright, WR
86— †Roy Banks, WR
88— †John Jurkovic, DL
89— †John Jurkovic, DL
90— †Tim Lance, DB
95— †Willie High, RB
†Tim Carver, LB

2002—†Kevin Hill, OL
†Tony Romo, QB
†J.R. Taylor, RB
†Nick Ricks, LB
05— †Clint Sellers, LB
06— †Tristan Burge, DB
†Donald Thomas, LB

EASTERN KY. (32)
69— Teddy Taylor, MG
74— Everett Talbert, RB
75— Junior Hardin, MG
76— Roosevelt Kelly, OL
79— †Bob McIntyre, LB
80— †George Floyd, DB
81— †George Floyd, DB
†Kevin Greve, OG
82— †Steve Bird, WR
83— †Chris Sullivan, OL
84— †Chris Sullivan, C
85— †Joe Spadafino, OL
86— †Fred Harvey, LB
87— †Aaron Jones, DL
88— †Elroy Harris, RB
†Jessie Small, DL
89— †Al Jacevicius, OL
90— †Kelly Blount, LB
†Al Jacevicius, OL
91— †Carl Satterly, OL
†Ernest Thompson, DL
92— †Markus Thomas, RB
93— †Chad Bratzke, DL
94— †James Hand, OL
95— †James Hand, OL
†Marc Collins, P
96— †Tony McCombs, LB
98— †Tyrone Hopson, OL
2000—†Alex Bannister, WR
01— †Yeremiah Bell, DB
04— †Pierre Wright, DB
05— †Patrick Bugg, TE

EASTERN MICH.* (5)
68— John Schmidt, C
69— Robert Lints, MG
70— Dave Pureifory, DT
71— Dave Pureifory, DT
73— Jim Pietrzak, OT

EASTERN N.M. (10)
81— Brad Beck, RB
83— Kevin Kott, QB
87— Earl Jones, OL
89— Murray Garrett, DL
90— Anthony Pertile, DB
94— Conrad Hamilton, DB
95— Conrad Hamilton, DB
98— Michael Walton, LB
99— Michael Walton, LB
2004— Jeff Howard, LB

EASTERN ORE. (1)
96— Shea Little, OL

EASTERN WASH. (21)
57— Richard Huston, C
65— Mel Stanton, HB
73— Scott Garske, TE
81— John Tighe, OL
86— Ed Simmons, OT
87— †Eric Stein, P
91— †Kevin Sargent, OL
97— †Harry Leons, QB
†Chris Scott, DL
†Jim Buzzard, OL
98— †Bashir Levingston, RS
99— †Lance Knaevelsrud, OL
2000—†Jeff Allen, DL
01— †Jesse Chatman, RB
†Chris Polinder, OL
†Lamont Brightful, RS
04— †Eric Kimble, WR
†Mike Roos, OL
05— †Matt Alfred, OL
†Eric Kimble, WR
†Erik Meyer, QB

EDINBORO (8)
82— Rick Ruszkiewicz, K
89— Elbert Cole, RB
90— Ernest Priester, WR
93— Mike Kegarise, OL
95— Pat Schuster, DL
2002— Sean McNicholas, P
03— Joe Valvoda, OL
06— Ben Stroup, LB

ELIZABETH CITY ST. (2)
2004— Howard Williams, DB
06— Maceo Thomas, DL

ELMHURST (1)
82— Lindsay Barich, OL

ELON (12)
50— Sal Gero, T
68— Richard McGeorge, OE
69— Richard McGeorge, OE
73— Glenn Ellis, DT
76— Ricky Locklear, DT
Dan Bass, OL
77— Dan Bass, OL
80— Bobby Hedrick, RB
86— Ricky Sigmon, OL
2001— Scott McLain, OL
05— †Chad Nkang, LB
06— †Chad Nkang, LB

EMORY & HENRY (18)
50— Robert Miller, B
51— Robert Miller, B
56— William Earp, C
68— Sonny Wade, B
85— Keith Furr, DB
Rob McMillen, DL
86— Sandy Rogers, RB
87— Gary Collier, QB
88— Steve Bowman, DL
89— Doug Reavis, DB
90— Billy Salyers, OL
91— Jason Grooms, DL
92— Pat Buchanan, OL
Scott Pruner, DL
97— Jamie Harless, DL
98— Mike Kassnove, DL
99— Charles Peterson, DB
2001— Jelani Patterson, DL

EMPORIA ST. (11)
35— James Fraley, B
37— Harry Klein, E
68— Bruce Cerone, OE
69— Bruce Cerone, OE
91— Quincy Tillmon, RB
96— Brian Shay, RB
97— Brian Shay, RB
98— John Hesse, OL
Brian Shay, RB
2002— Dontaye McCoy, DB
03— Tyler Paul, RB

EUREKA (1)
95— Kurt Barth, WR

EVANSVILLE (3)
46— Robert Hawkins, T
93— †Hanz Hoag, TE
94— †Hanz Hoag, TE

FAIRFIELD (1)
2000—†Steve Dogmanits, DB

FDU-FLORHAM (4)
84— Ira Epstein, DL
86— Eric Brey, DB
87— Frank Illidge, DL
93— Vic Moncato, P

FAIRMONT ST. (4)
67— Dave Williams, DT
84— Ed Coleman, WR
88— Lou Mabin, DB
99— Nathan White, P

FAYETTEVILLE ST. (3)
90— Terrence Smith, LB
2004— Charles Roberts, LB
Walt Williams, DB

FERRIS ST. (13)
76— Charles Evans, RB
92— Monty Brown, LB
93— Ed Phillion, DL
94— Tyree Dye, RB
95— Bill Love, QB
96— Kelly Chisholm, DL
99— Doc Proctor, PK
2000— Clarence Coleman, WR
01— Clarence Coleman, WR/AP
03— Kevin Myers, LB
04— Kevin Myers, LB
05— Carlton Brewster, WR
06— Mike Klobucher, LB

FERRUM (7)
87— Dave Harper, LB
88— Dave Harper, LB
89— Chris Warren, RB
90— Melvin Dillard, DB/KR
91— John Sheets, OG
2000— Toné Dancy, DL
01— Tim Carter, DB

FINDLAY (5)
65— Allen Smith, HB
80— Nelson Bolden, FB
85— Dana Wright, RB
90— Tim Russ, OL
2002— Robert Campbell, RB

FLORIDA A&M (22)
61— Curtis Miranda, C
62— Robert Paremore, B
67— Major Hazelton, DB
John Eason, OE
73— Henry Lawrence, OT
75— Frank Poole, LB
77— Tyrone McGriff, OG
78— Tyrone McGriff, OG
79— †Tyrone McGriff, OG
†Kiser Lewis, C
80— †Gifford Ramsey, DB
83— †Ray Alexander, WR
95— †Earl Holmes, LB
96— †Jamie Nails, OL
97— †Oteman Sampson, QB
†Juan Toro, PK
98— †Patrick Bonner, QB
†Jacquay Nunnally, WR
†Juan Toro, PK
†Olrick Johnson, LB
2000—†Freddie Moore, OL
05— †Wes Taylor, P

FLA. ATLANTIC* (1)
2003—†Anthony Crissinger-Hill, TE

FLORIDA ST.* (1)
51— William Dawkins, OG

FORDHAM (4)
97— †Barry Cantrell, P
2003—†Javarus Dudley, WR
04— †Tad Kornegay, DB
06— †Marcus Taylor, LB

FORT HAYS ST. (4)
95— Lance Schwindt, TE
Shawn Behr, QB
2000— Adam Ryan, P
03— Tyler Strong, OL

FORT LEWIS (3)
89— Eric Fadness, P
92— Johnny Cox, WR
93— Johnny Cox, AP

FORT VALLEY ST. (10)
74— Fred Harris, OT
80— Willie Canady, DB
81— Willie Canady, DB
83— Tugwan Taylor, DB
92— Joseph Best, DB
93— Joseph Best, DB
94— Tyrone Poole, DB
2002— Duron Croson, RB
Rico Cody, DB
04— Derrick Wimbush, RB

FRANKLIN (3)
82— Joe Chester, WR
95— Michael Brouwer, DB
2001— Josh McMillin, DL

FRANK. & MARSH. (10)
35— Woodrow Sponaugle, C
38— Sam Roeder, B
40— Alex Schibanoff, T
47— William Iannicelli, E
50— Charles Cope, C
81— Vin Carioscia, OL
82— Vin Carioscia, OL
89— Dale Amos, WR
95— Steve DeLuca, LB
2004— Dan Eggertsson, P

FRESNO ST.* (5)
39— Jack Mulkey, E
40— Jack Mulkey, E
60— Douglas Brown, G
68— Tom McCall, LB
Erv Hunt, DB

FROSTBURG ST. (12)
80— Terry Beamer, LB
82— Steve Forsythe, WR
83— Kevin Walsh, DL
85— Bill Bagley, WR
86— Marcus Wooley, LB
88— Ken Boyd, DB
89— Ken Boyd, DB
93— Russell Williams, DB
94— Joe Holland, DL
Ariel Bell, KR
96— Ron Wallace, DB
2002— George O'Brien II, DL

FURMAN (24)
82— †Ernest Gibson, DB
83— †Ernest Gibson, DB
84— †Rock Hurst, LB
85— †Gene Reeder, C
88— †Jeff Blankenship, LB
89— †Kelly Fletcher, DL
90— †Steve Duggan, C
†Kevin Kendrick, LB
91— †Eric Walter, OL
92— †Kota Suttle, LB
94— †Jim Richter, PK
97— †Bryan Dailer, DL
98— †Orlando Ruff, LB
99— †John Keith, DB
2000—†Louis Ivory, RB
†Josh Moore, OL
†Marty Priore, OL
†Will Bouton, LB
01— †Donnie Littlejohn, OL
†Will Bouton, LB
02— †Trevor Kruger, OL
04— †Ben Bainbridge, OL
05— †Patrick Covington, OL
†Willie Freeman, LB

GALLAUDET (1)
87— Shannon Simon, OL

GARDNER-WEBB (7)
73— Richard Grissom, LB
87— Jeff Parker, PK
92— Rodney Robinson, WR
93— Gabe Wilkins, DL
2003—†Graham Whitlock, P
†Mario Williams, DB
04— †Harold Wells, DL

GEORGETOWN (6)
73— Robert Morris, DE
74— Robert Morris, DE
91— Chris Murphy, DE
2004—†Michael Ononibaku, DL
05— †Michael Ononibaku, DL
06— †Kenny Mitchell, KR

GEORGETOWN (KY.) (12)
74— Charles Pierson, DL
78— John Martinelli, OL
85— Rob McCrary, RB
87— Chris Reed, C
88— Chris Reed, OL
89— Steve Blankenbaker, DL
91— Chris Hogan, DL
92— Chris Hogan, DL
2000— Shane Pearson, LB
01— Walt DeLong, OL
02— Shan Housekeeper, LB
03— John Sullivan, LB

GA. SOUTHERN (37)
85— †Vance Pike, OL
†Tim Foley, PK
86— †Fred Stokes, OT
†Tracy Ham, QB
87— †Flint Matthews, LB
†Dennis Franklin, C
†Tim Foley, PK
88— †Dennis Franklin, C
†Darren Alford, DL
89— †Joe Ross, RB
†Giff Smith, DL
90— †Giff Smith, DL
91— †Rodney Oglesby, DB
92— †Alex Mash, DL
93— †Alex Mash, DL
†Franklin Stephens, OL

94— †Franklin Stephens, OL
96— †Edward Thomas, DL
97— †Roderick Russell, FB
98— †Matt Winslette, C
†Adrian Peterson, RB
†Mark Williams, OL
†Voncellies Allen, DL
†Arkee Thompson, DB
99— †Adrian Peterson, RB
†Mark Williams, OL
†Voncellies Allen, DL
2000—†Adrian Peterson, RB
†Freddy Pesqueira, DL
01— †Adrian Peterson, RB
†Freddy Pesqueira, DL
02— †Charles Clarke, OL
†Freddy Pesqueira, DL
04— †Chad Motte, OL
†Ahmad Treaudo, DB
05— †Chad Motte, OL
06— †John Mohring, LB

GA. SOUTHWESTERN (2)
85— Roger Glover, LB
86— Roger Glover, LB

GETTYSBURG (7)
66— Joseph Egresitz, DE
83— Ray Condren, RB
84— Ray Condren, RB
85— Brian Barr, DB
94— Dwayne Marcus, FB
98— Paul Smith, RS
99— Paul Smith, RS

GLENVILLE ST. (8)
73— Scotty Hamilton, DB
83— Byron Brooks, RB
84— Mike Payne, DB
93— Chris George, WR
94— Chris George, WR
96— Carlos Ferralls, WR
97— Carlos Ferralls, WR
2003— Antonio Carter, WR

GONZAGA (2)
34— Ike Peterson, B
39— Tony Canadeo, B

GRAMBLING (36)
62— Junious Buchanan, T
64— Alphonse Dotson, OT
65— Willie Young, OG
Frank Cornish, DT
69— Billy Manning, C
70— Richard Harris, DE
Charles Roundtree, DT
71— Solomon Freelon, OG
John Mendenhall, DE
72— Steve Dennis, DB
Gary Johnson, DT
73— Gary Johnson, DT
Willie Bryant, DB
74— Gary Johnson, DT
75— Sammie White, WR
James Hunter, DB
79— †Joe Gordon, DT
†Aldrich Allen, LB
†Robert Salters, DB
80— †Trumaine Johnson, WR
†Mike Barker, DT
81— †Andre Robinson, LB
82— †Trumaine Johnson, WR
83— †Robert Smith, DL
85— †James Harris, LB
90— †Walter Dean, RB
†Jake Reed, WR
94— †Curtis Ceaser, WR
2001—†Robert Taylor, LB
02— †Tramon Douglas, WR
†Bruce Eugene, QB
†Terry Riley, OL
03— †Bruce Eugene, QB
05— †Jonathan Banks, OT
†Bruce Eugene, QB
†Henry Tolbert, WR

GRAND VALLEY ST. (31)
79— Ronald Essink, OL
89— Todd Tracey, DL
91— Chris Tiede, C
94— Mike Sheldon, OL
95— Diriki Mose, WR
96— Matt Potter, DE
2001— Curt Anes, QB
David Kircus, WR
Dale Westrick, OL
02— Curt Anes, QB
David Kircus, WR
Reggie Spearmon, RB
Dale Westrick, OL
Scott Mackey, DB
Keyonta Marshall, DL
03— David Hendrix, PK
Michael Tennessee, RB
Mike Wilford, OT
Scott Mackey, S
Keyonta Marshall, DL
04— DeJuane Boone, DB
Lucius Hawkins, DB
Keyonta Marshall, DL
05— Josh Bourke, OL
Michael McFadden, DL
06— Anthony Adams, LB
Brandon Barnes, OL
Brandon Carr, DB
Cullen Finnerty, QB
Eric Fowler, WR
Michael McFadden, DL

GRINNELL (1)
99— Jeff Pedersen, TE

GROVE CITY (6)
87— Doug Hart, PK
97— Doug Steiner, FB
98— R.J. Bowers, FB
99— R.J. Bowers, FB
2000— R.J. Bowers, FB
05— Aaron Margo, DB

GUILFORD (5)
75— Steve Musulin, OT
91— Rodney Alexander, DE
94— Bryan Garland, OL
2001— Chris McKinney, KR
06— Chris Barnette, WR

GUST. ADOLPHUS (9)
37— Wendell Butcher, B
50— Calvin Roberts, T
51— Haldo Norman, OE
52— Calvin Roberts, DT
54— Gene Nei, G
67— Richard Jaeger, LB
84— Kurt Ploeger, DL
97— Ryan Boutwell, PK
2004— Isaac Sieling, LB

HAMILTON (2)
86— Joe Gilbert, OL
91— Eric Grey, RB

HAMLINE (4)
55— Dick Donlin, E
84— Kevin Graslewicz, WR
85— Ed Hitchcock, OL
89— Jon Voss, TE

HAMPDEN-SYDNEY (10)
48— Lynn Chewning, B
54— Stokeley Fulton, C
72— Michael Leidy, LB
74— Ed Kelley, DE
75— Ed Kelley, DE
77— Robert Wilson, OL
78— Tim Smith, DL
86— Jimmy Hondroulis, PK
2003— Lee Bailey, C
Conrad Singh, WR

HAMPTON (19)
84— Ike Readon, MG
85— Ike Readon, DL
93— Emerson Martin, OL
Christopher Williams, DL
94— John Meredith, LB
95— †Hugh Hunter, DL
96— †Darrell Flythe, LB
97— †Cordell Taylor, DB
98— †Charles Preston, DL
99— †Deon Hunt, LB
2002—†Zuriel Smith, RS
†Erik Steiner, OL
03— †Jelani Clement, OL
04— †Jelani Clement, OL
†Jerome Mathis, KR
05— †Gerell Golightly, OL
†Andrew Paterini, PK
†Justin Durant, LB
06— †Andrew Paterini, PK

HANOVER (6)
86— Jon Pinnick, QB
88— Mike Luker, WR
95— Ben Fox, WR
Terry Peebles, QB
97— Kevin O'Donohue, LB
99— Anthony Weigleb, OL

HARDIN-SIMMONS (19)
37— Burns McKinney, B
39— Clyde Turner, C
40— Owen Goodnight, B
42— Rudy Mobley, B
46— Rudy Mobley, B
94— Colin McCormick, WR
99— Gary Gutierrez, OL
2002— Thomas Anderson, OL
Alex Hansen, DB
03— Adam Hernandez, OL
Alex Hansen, DB
04— Adam Hernandez, OL
Will Galusha, DB
Brent Geiley, LB
Alex Hansen, DB
Reggie Robinson, DL
05— Tye Conry, OL
Will Galusha, DB
06— Josh Knox, OL

HARDING (4)
74— Barney Crawford, DL
91— Pat Gill, LB
94— Paul Simmons, LB
2006— Robert Towns, DB

HARTWICK (2)
2002— Ryan Soule, WR
06— Lindy Crea, AP

HARVARD (8)
82— †Mike Corbat, OL
84— †Roger Caron, OL
99— †Isaiah Kacyvenski, LB
2000—†Mike Clare, OL
02— †Carl Morris, WR
03— †Dante Balestracci, LB
04— †Clifton Dawson, RB
06— †Mike Berg, DL

HASTINGS (2)
84— Dennis Sullivan, OL
94— Jeff Drake, DL

HAWAII* (2)
41— Nolle Smith, B
68— Tim Buchanan, LB

HENDERSON ST. (3)
90— Todd Jones, OL
93— Chris Carter, P
96— Robert Thomas, LB

HILLSDALE (11)
49— William Young, B
55— Nate Clark, B
56— Nate Clark, B
75— Mark Law, OG
81— Mike Broome, OG
82— Ron Gladnick, DE
86— Al Huge, DL
87— Al Huge, DL
88— Rodney Patterson, LB
2000— Todd DeVree, DL
Tim Mustapha, DB

HOBART (7)
72— Don Aleksiewicz, RB
75— Rich Kowalski, RB
86— Brian Verdon, DB
93— Bill Palmer, DB
96— Nico Karagosian, TE
97— David Russell, DL
2004— Alex Bell, OL

HOFSTRA (23)
83— Chuck Choinski, DL
86— Tom Salamone, P
88— Tom Salamone, DB
90— George Tischler, LB
94— †Brian Clark, DB
95— †Dave Fiore, OL
†Dave Ettinger, PK
†Buck Buchanan, LB
96— †Eugene McAleer, LB
97— †Dave Ettinger, PK
†Lance Schulters, DB
99— †Giovanni Carmazzi, QB
†Jim Magda, DL
2000—†Rocky Butler, QB
†Doug Shanahan, DB
†Khary Williams, DL
01— †Rocky Butler, QB
†Kahmal Roy, WR
†Dan Zorger, OL
†Ryan Fletcher, DL
04— †Dan Garay, DL
†Gian Villante, LB
05— †Willie Colon, OL

HOLY CROSS (16)
83— †Bruce Kozerski, OT
†Steve Raquet, DL
84— †Bill McGovern, DB
†Kevin Garvey, OG
85— †Gill Fenerty, RB
86— †Gordie Lockbaum, RB-DB
87— †Jeff Wiley, QB
†Gordie Lockbaum, WR-SP
88— †Dennis Golden, OL
89— †Dave Murphy, DB
90— †Craig Callahan, LB
91— †Jerome Fuller, RB
93— †Rob Milanette, LB
95— †Tom Claro, OL
2004—†Steve Silva, AP
05— †Steve Silva, AP

HOPE (2)
79— Craig Groendyk, OL
82— Kurt Brinks, C

HOWARD (5)
75— Ben Harris, DL
87— †Harvey Reed, RB
98— †Marques Douglas, DL
99— †Elijah Thurmon, WR
2001—†Tracy White, LB

HOWARD PAYNE (8)
61— Ray Jacobs, T
72— Robert Woods, LB
73— Robert Woods, LB
92— Scott Lichner, QB
94— Steven Seale, OL
95— Sean Witherwax, DL
97— Sedrick Medlock, DB
98— Sedrick Medlock, DB

HUMBOLDT ST. (7)
61— Drew Roberts, E
62— Drew Roberts, E
76— Michael Gooing, OL
82— David Rush, MG
83— Dean Diaz, DB
95— Randy Matyshock, TE
2006— Kyle Killingsworth, RS

HURON (1)
76— John Aldridge, OL

IDAHO* (14)
83— †Ken Hobart, QB
85— †Eric Yarber, WR
88— †John Friesz, QB
89— †John Friesz, QB
†Lee Allen, WR
90— †Kasey Dunn, WR
91— †Kasey Dunn, WR
92— †Yo Murphy, WR
†Jeff Robinson, DL
93— †Doug Nussmeier, QB
†Mat Groshong, C
94— †Sherriden May, RB
†Jim Mills, OL
95— †Ryan Phillips, DL

IDAHO ST. (11)
69— Ed Bell, OE
77— Ray Allred, MG
81— †Case de Bruijn, P
†Mike Machurek, QB
83— †Jeff Kaiser, P
84— †Steve Anderson, DL
97— †Trevor Bell, DB
2001—†Eddie Johnson, P
03— †Jared Allen, DL
05— †Jarrett Johnson, PK
†Jeff Charleston, DL

ILLINOIS COL. (2)
81— Joe Aiello, DL
2002— B.J. Harvey, KR

ILLINOIS ST. (17)
68— Denny Nelson, OT
85— †Jim Meyer, OL
86— †Brian Gant, LB
88— †Mike McCabe, P
93— †Todd Kurz, PK
98— †Chad Pegues, DL
†Galen Scott, LB
99— †Damien Gregory, DL
†Mike Rodbro, OG
†Sam Young, DB
2002—†Boomer Grigsby, LB
03— †Boomer Grigsby, LB
04— †Boomer Grigsby, LB
05— †Stafford Davis, OL
†Laurent Robinson, WR
†Brent Hawkins, DL
06— †Cameron Siskowic, LB

ILL. WESLEYAN (10)
34— Tony Blazine, T
74— Caesar Douglas, OT
91— Chris Bisaillon, WR
92— Chris Bisaillon, WR
96— Adam Slotkus, C
John Munch, LB
97— John Munch, LB
98— Kevin Fahey, DB
2000— Jeff Heinzl, DL
04— Eric Esch, RS

INDIANA (PA.) (25)
75— Lynn Hieber, QB
76— Jim Haslett, DE
77— Jim Haslett, DE
78— Jim Haslett, DE
79— Terrence Skelley, OE
80— Joe Cuigari, DT
84— Gregg Brenner, WR
86— Jim Angelo, OL
87— Troy Jackson, LB
88— Dean Cottrill, LB
90— Andrew Hill, WR
91— Tony Aliucci, QB
93— Matt Dalverny, OL
Mike Geary, PK
Michael Mann, RB
94— Jeff Turnage, DL
95— Jon Ruff, PK
Jeff Turnage, DL
97— Barry Threats, DB
98— Barry Threats, DB
99— Leander Jordan, OL
2000— Mike Borisenko, LB
01— Joey Flora, DB
03— Khiawatha Downey, OL
06— Jason Capizzi, OL

INDIANA ST. (13)
69— Jeff Keller, DE
75— Chris Hicks, OL
Vince Allen, RB
83— †Ed Martin, DE
84— †Wayne Davis, DB
85— †Vencie Glenn, DB
86— †Mike Simmonds, OL
93— †Shawn Moore, OL
94— †Dan Brandenburg, DL
95— †Dan Bradenburg, DL
†Tom Allison, PK
98— †Troy Lefevra, DE
99— †DeJuan Alfonzo, DB/KR

INDIANAPOLIS (9)
83— Mark Bless, DL
84— Paul Loggan, DB
85— Tom Collins, DB
86— Dan Jester, TE
87— Thurman Montgomery, DL
91— Greg Matheis, DL
98— Ted Liette, LB
99— Josh Gentry, LB
2001— Neal Blank, DL

IONA (1)
2003—†Kevin Fales, DL

IOWA WESLEYAN (1)
87— Mike Wiggins, P

ITHACA (17)
72— Robert Wojnar, OT
74— David Remick, RB
75— Larry Czarnecki, DT
79— John Laper, LB
80— Bob Ferrigno, HB
84— Bill Sheerin, DL
85— Tim Torrey, LB
90— Jeff Wittman, FB
91— Jeff Wittman, FB
92— Jeff Wittman, FB
Dave Brumfield, OL
95— Scott Connolly, DL
98— Matt Buddenhagen, KR
Mike Sansone, LB
2000— Ron Amato, DB
04— Vince Dargush, TE
05— Joe Scalice, OL

JACKSON ST. (26)
62— Willie Richardson, E
69— Joe Stephens, OG
71— Jerome Barkum, OE
74— Walter Payton, RB
Robert Brazile, LB
78— Robert Hardy, DT
80— †Larry Werts, LB
81— †Mike Fields, OT
85— †Jackie Walker, LB
86— †Kevin Dent, DB
87— †Kevin Dent, DB
88— †Lewis Tillman, RB
†Kevin Dent, DB
89— †Darion Conner, LB
90— †Robert Turner, DB
91— †Deltrich Lockridge, OL
92— †Lester Holmes, OL
95— †Picasso Nelson, DB
96— †Sean Woodson, DB
†Grailyn Pratt, QB
†Otha Evans, LB
97— †Toby Myles, OL
98— †Sylvester Morris, WR
99— †Tommie Head, LB
†Sylvester Morris, WR
2002—†Elgin Andrews, LB

JACKSONVILLE ST. (11)
52— Jodie Connell, OG
66— Ray Vinson, DB
70— Jimmy Champion, C
77— Jesse Baker, DT
78— Jesse Baker, DT
82— Ed Lett, QB
86— Joe Billingsley, OT
88— Joe Billingsley, OT
95— †Darron Edwards, DB
2002—†Deon White, OL
04— †Oscar Bonds, RB

JAMES MADISON (22)
77— Woody Bergeria, DT
78— Rick Booth, OL
85— †Charles Haley, LB
86— †Carlo Bianchini, OG
89— †Steve Bates, DL
90— †Eupton Jackson, DB
93— †David McLeod, WR
94— †Dwight Robinson, DB
95— †John Coursey, PK
†David Bailey, C
†Ed Perry, TE
96— †Ed Perry, TE
97— †Tony Booth, DB
99— †Curtis Keaton, RB
2000—†Chris Morant, DL
†Derick Pack, LB
01— †Derrick Lloyd, LB
04— †Matt Magerko, OL
05— †Matt Magerko, OL
†Tony LeZotte, DB
06— †Akeem Jordan, LB
†Kevin Winston, DL

JAMESTOWN (2)
76— Brent Tischer, OL
81— Ron Hausauer, OL

JOHN CARROLL (15)
50— Carl Taseff, B
74— Tim Barrett, RB
94— Jason Goldberg, PK
Ryan Haley, P
95— Chris Anderson, LB
96— London Fletcher, LB
Scott O'Donnell, DL
Chris Anderson, LB
97— London Fletcher, LB
David Ziegler, R
98— David Vitatoe, PK
99— Tom Rini, DB
2002— Tom Arth, QB
Chris Cubero, LB
04— Scott Greenberg, DB

JOHNS HOPKINS (5)
80— Bill Stromberg, WR
81— Bill Stromberg, WR
96— Jim Wilson, DL
2003— Matt Campbell, DB
06— Ben Scott, P

JOHNSON C. SMITH (2)
82— Dan Beauford, DE
88— Ronald Capers, LB

JUNIATA (4)
54— Joe Veto, T
86— Steve Yerger, OL
87— Mark Dorner, DB
99— Matt Eisenberg, WR

KANSAS WESLEYAN (2)
35— Virgil Baker, G
56— Larry Houdek, B

KEAN (1)
87— Kevin McGuirl, TE

KENTUCKY ST. (4)
72— Wiley Epps, LB
98— Cletidus Hunt, DL
99— Ike Ihejeto, TE
2005— Marcus Wright, KR

KENYON (1)
74— Jim Myers, WR

KING'S (PA.) (5)
2000— Damon Saxon, RB
01— Steven Wilson, DL
02— Steven Wilson, DL
05— Geoff Troy, PK
06— Craig Haywood, DB

KNOX (4)
86— Rich Schiele, TE
87— Chris Vogel, WR
96— Chris Warwick, PK
98— Josh Fourdyce, DL

KNOXVILLE (1)
77— Dwight Treadwell, OL

KUTZTOWN (5)
77— Steve Head, OG
95— John Mobley, LB
97— Denauld Brown, DL
2001— Pete Mendez, DB
02— Pete Mendez, DB

LA SALLE (2)
38— George Somers, T
39— Frank Loughney, G

LA VERNE (3)
72— Dana Coleman, DT
91— Willie Reyna, QB
95— Anthony Jones, RB

LAFAYETTE (10)
79— †Rich Smith, TE
81— †Joe Skladany, LB
82— †Tony Green, DL
88— †Frank Baur, QB
92— †Edward Hudak, OL
96— †B.J. Galles, DB
97— †Dan Bengele, LB
2004—†Joe McCourt, RB
05— †Maurice Bennett, LB
06— †Mike Saint Germain, OL

LAKE FOREST (1)
2002— Casey Urlacher, LB

LAKELAND (1)
89— Jeff Ogiego, P

LAMAR (5)
57— Dudley Meredith, T
61— Bobby Jancik, B
67— Spergon Wynn, OG
83— †Eugene Seale, LB
85— †Burton Murchison, RB

LAMBUTH (3)
93— Jo Jo Jones, RB
94— Jo Jo Jones, RB
2005— Evan Granier, PK

LANE (1)
73— Edward Taylor, DT

LANGSTON (2)
73— Thomas Henderson, DE
94— Paul Reed, DB

LAWRENCE (11)
49— Claude Radtke, E
67— Charles McKee, QB
77— Frank Bouressa, C
78— Frank Bouressa, C
80— Scott Reppert, HB
81— Scott Reppert, HB
82— Scott Reppert, RB
83— Murray McDonough, DB
86— Dan Galante, DL
95— Brad Olson, RB
97— Brad Olson, FB

LEBANON VALLEY (1)
2003— Scott Marek, TE

LEHIGH (28)
49— Robert Numbers, C
50— Dick Doyne, B
57— Dan Nolan, B
59— Walter Meincke, T
69— Thad Jamula, OT
71— John Hill, C
73— Kim McQuilken, QB
75— Joe Sterrett, QB
77— Steve Kreider, WR
Mike Reiker, QB
79— †Dave Melone, OT
†Jim McCormick, DL
80— †Bruce Rarig, LB
83— †John Shigo, LB
85— †Rennie Benn, WR
90— †Keith Petzold, OL
93— †Dave Cecchini, WR
95— †Brian Klingerman, WR
†Rabih Abdullah, RB
96— †Ben Talbott, P
98— †Nick Martucci, DL
99— †Ian Eason, LB
2000—†Brian McDonald, OL
01— †Abdul Byron, DB
†Josh Snyder, WR
02— †Jeff Santacroce, OL
03— †Adam Bergen, TE
04— †Adam Bergen, TE

LENOIR-RHYNE (5)
52— Steve Trudnak, B
62— Richard Kemp, B
67— Eddie Joyner, OT
92— Jason Monday, PK
94— Leonard Davis, RB

LEWIS & CLARK (2)
68— Bill Bailey, DT
91— Dan Ruhl, RB

LIBERTY (6)
82— John Sanders, LB
86— Mark Mathis, DB
95— †Andrew McFadden, KR
†Tony Dews, TE
98— †Jesse Riley, LB
2000—†Jason Wells, DL

LINCOLN (MO.) (3)
53— Leo Lewis, B
54— Leo Lewis, B
2004— Brandon Beard, DL

LINFIELD (20)
57— Howard Morris, G
64— Norman Musser, C
72— Bernard Peterson, OE
75— Ken Cutcher, OL
78— Paul Dombroski, DB
80— Alan Schmidlin, QB
83— Steve Lopes, OL
84— Steve Boyea, OL
94— Darrin Causey, LB
2002— Daryl Agpalsa, OL
David Russell, RB
Ray Lions, DB
03— Tyler Matthews, QB
James Wilson, P

04— Casey Allen, WR
Brett Elliott, QB
Brandon Hazenberg, RS
05— Casey Allen, WR
Brett Elliott, QB
Josh Ort, DB

LIVINGSTONE (4)
84— Jo Jo White, RB
98— Charles Cooley, OL
2003— Jason Ocean, LB
04— Moises Gordon, LB

LOCK HAVEN (1)
45— Robert Eyer, E

LONG BEACH ST. (4)
68— Bill Parks, OE
69— Leon Burns, FB
70— Leon Burns, RB
71— Terry Metcalf, RB

LORAS (4)
47— Robert Hanlon, B
84— James Drew, P
97— Shane Davis, RB
2005— Ross Dillavou, DL

LOS ANGELES ST. (1)
64— Walter Johnson, OG

LOUISIANA (1)
50— Bernard Calendar, E

LA.-LAFAYETTE* (1)
69— Glenn LaFleur, LB

LA.-MONROE* (19)
67— Vic Bender, C
70— Joe Profit, RB
72— Jimmy Edwards, RB
73— Glenn Fleming, MG
74— Glenn Fleming, MG
82— †Arthur Christophe, C
†Bruce Daigle, DB
83— †Mike Grantham, OG
84— †Mike Grantham, OG
85— †Mike Turner, DB
87— †John Clement, OT
†Claude Brumfield, DT
88— †Cyril Crutchfield, DB
89— †Jackie Harris, E
92— †Jeff Blackshear, OL
†Vic Zordan, OL
†Roosevelt Potts, RB
93— †Raymond Batiste, OL
†James Folston, DL

LOUISIANA TECH* (15)
41— Garland Gregory, G
46— Mike Reed, G
68— Terry Bradshaw, QB
69— Terry Bradshaw, QB
72— Roger Carr, WR
73— Roger Carr, FL
74— Mike Barber, TE
Fred Dean, DT
82— †Matt Dunigan, QB
84— †Doug Landry, LB
†Walter Johnson, DE
85— †Doug Landry, LB
86— †Walter Johnson, LB-DE
87— †Glenell Sanders, LB
88— †Glenell Sanders, LB

LOUISVILLE* (1)
57— Leonard Lyles, B

LOYOLA (ILL.) (2)
35— Billy Roy, B
37— Clay Calhoun, B

LOYOLA MARYMOUNT (1)
42— Vince Pacewic, B

LUTHER (1)
57— Bruce Hartman, T

LYCOMING (10)
83— John Whalen, OL
85— Walt Zataveski, OL
89— Rick Bealer, DB
90— Rick Bealer, DB
91— Darrin Kenney, OT
Don Kinney, DL
Bill Small, LB
96— Michael Downey, OL
98— Jason Marraccini, QB
99— Cameron Coleman, DL

MacMURRAY (3)
97— Jamie Lee, RB
98— Jamie Lee, RB
2001— Curtis Fisher, OL

MAINE (12)
65— John Huard, LB
66— John Huard, LB
80— †Lorenzo Bouier, RB
89— †Carl Smith, RB
†Scott Hough, OL
90— †Claude Pettaway, DB
99— †Jojo Oliphant, DL
2001—†Chad Hayes, TE
†Stephen Cooper, LB
†Lennard Byrd, KR
02— †Stephan Cooper, LB
06— †Matt King, DL

MAINE MARITIME (2)
92— Kirk Matthieu, RB
95— Rob Marchitello, RB

MANSFIELD (2)
2002— Dan Holland, LB
03— Dan Holland, LB

MARIETTA (1)
96— Dante Brown, RB

MARS HILL (6)
78— Alan Rice, OL
79— Steven Campbell, DB
87— Lee Marchman, LB
2000— Terrence Stokes, RB
01— David Cassell, TE
02— Khalid Abdullah, LB

MARSHALL* (29)
37— William Smith, E
40— Jackie Hunt, B
41— Jackie Hunt, B
87— †Mike Barber, WR
†Sean Doctor, TE
88— †Mike Barber, WR
†Sean Doctor, TE
90— †Eric Ihnat, TE
91— †Phil Ratliff, OL
92— †Michael Payton, QB
†Troy Brown, WR
†Phil Ratliff, OL
93— †Chris Deaton, OL
†William King, LB
†Roger Johnson, DB
94— †Roger Johnson, DB
†William Pannell, OL
†Travis Colquitt, P
95— †Chris Parker, RB
†William Pannell, OL
†Billy Lyon, DL
†Melvin Cunningham, DB
96— †Randy Moss, WR
†Billy Lyon, DL
†Aaron Ferguson, OL
†B.J. Cohen, DL
†Jermaine Swafford, LB
†Eugene McAleer, LB
†Melvin Cunningham, DB

MARTIN LUTHER (1)
97— John Feuersthaler, DB

MARY HARDIN-BAYLOR (10)
2001— Preston Meyer, LB
02— Ryan Harris, OL
Preston Meyer, LB
03— Tony Salazar, DB
04— Matt Bush, C
Jeff Oliver, OL
05— Hunter Hamrick, P
06— Jerrell Freeman, LB
Josh Kubiak, DB
Zach Newcomb, PK

MD.-EAST. SHORE (2)
64— John Smith, DT
68— Bill Thompson, DB

MARYVILLE (TENN.) (5)
67— Steve Dockery, DB
73— Earl McMahon, OG
77— Wayne Dunn, LB
92— Tom Smith, OL
93— Tom Smith, OL

MASSACHUSETTS (35)
52— Tony Chambers, OE
63— Paul Graham, T
64— Milt Morin, DE
67— Greg Landry, QB
71— William DeFlavio, MG
72— Steve Schubert, OE
73— Tim Berra, OE
75— Ned Deane, OL
76— Ron Harris, DB
77— Kevin Cummings, TE
Bruce Kimball, OL
78— Bruce Kimball, OG
80— †Bob Manning, DB
81— †Garry Pearson, RB
82— †Garry Pearson, RB
85— †Mike Dwyer, DL
88— †John McKeown, LB
90— †Paul Mayberry, OL
92— †Don Caparotti, DB
93— †Bill Durkin, OL
94— †Breon Parker, DB
95— †Rene Ingoglia, RB
98— †Marcel Shipp, RB
†Khari Samuel, LB
†Kerry Taylor, TE
99— †Jeremy Robinson, DB
†Kole Ayi, LB
†Jerard White, DB
†Sean Higgins, TE
2000—†Kole Ayi, LB
01— †Valdamar Brower, DL
04— †Shannon James, DB
05— †Shannon James, DB
06— †James Ihedigbo, DB
†Alex Miller, OL

MASS.-BOSTON (1)
92— Sean Munroe, WR

MASS.-DARTMOUTH (1)
98— Mike Cotton, DB

MIT (1)
97— Duane Stevens, DB

MASS. MARITIME (1)
95— Paul Diamantopoulos, DE

McDANIEL (5)
51— Victor Makovitch, DG
78— Ricci Bonaccorsy, DL
79— Ricci Bonaccorsy, DL
98— Mat Mathias, OL
2001— Jason Wingeart, DB

McMURRY (6)
49— Brad Rowland, B
50— Brad Rowland, B
58— Charles Davis, G
68— Telly Windham, DE
74— Randy Roemisch, OT
80— Rick Nolly, OL

McNEESE ST. (32)
52— Charles Kuehn, DE
69— Glenn Kidder, OG
72— James Moore, TE
74— James Files, OT
82— †Leonard Smith, DB
92— †Terry Irving, LB
93— †Jose Larios, PK
†Terry Irving, LB
94— †Ronald Cherry, OL
95— †Kavika Pittman, DL
†Marsh Buice, DL
†Zack Bronson, DB
†Vincent Landrum, LB
96— †Zack Bronson, DB
97— †Reggie Nelson, OL
†Chris Fontenot, TE
†Donnie Ashley, PR
98— †Reggie Nelson, OL
†Charles Ayro, LB
2000—†Wes Hines, OL
†Jake Morrison, DL
01— †Joe Judge, DB
02— †Jason Davis, OL
†B.J. McNutt, DL
†Hadley Prince, DB
†Roderick Royal, LB
03— †Dwight Hudler, OL
†Roderick Royal, LB
†B.J. Sams, AP
†Keith Smith, DB
06— †Bryan Smith, DL
†Steven Whitehead, RS

MEMPHIS* (1)
54— Robert Patterson, G

MENLO (3)
2000— Nate Jackson, WR
01— Nate Jackson, WR
06— Jihad Mahasin, KR

MERCHANT MARINE (5)
52— Robert Wiechard, LB
69— Harvey Adams, DE
90— Harold Krebs, DB
97— Anthony Jacobs, OL
2002— David McNeal, RB

MESA ST. (9)
82— Dean Haugum, DT
83— Dean Haugum, DL
84— Don Holmes, DB
85— Mike Berk, OL
86— Mike Berk, OL
88— Tracy Bennett, PK
89— Jeff Russell, OT
90— Brian Johnson, LB
2003— DeMeco Moore, LB

METHODIST (1)
97— Trayfer Monroe, DB

MIAMI (FLA.)* (2)
45— Ed Cameron, G
William Levitt, C

MIAMI (OHIO)* (1)
82— †Brian Pillman, MG

MICHIGAN TECH (2)
76— Jim VanWagner, RB
2004— Joe Berger, OL

MIDDLE TENN.* (12)
64— Jimbo Pearson, S
65— Keith Atchley, LB
83— †Robert Carroll, OL
84— †Kelly Potter, PK
85— †Don Griffin, DB
88— †Don Thomas, LB
90— †Joe Campbell, RB
91— †Steve McAdoo, OL
†Joe Campbell, RB
92— †Steve McAdoo, OL
93— †Pat Hicks, OL
95— †Nathaniel Claybrooks, DL

MIDDLEBURY (3)
36— George Anderson, G
83— Jonathan Good, DL
2000— Andy Steele, LB

MIDLAND LUTHERAN (2)
76— Dave Marreel, DE
79— Scott Englehardt, OL

MILLERSVILLE (8)
76— Robert Parr, DB
80— Rob Riddick, RB
81— Mark Udovich, C
86— Jeff Hannis, DL
93— Scott Martin, DL
Greg Faulkner, OL
95— Kevin Cannon, AP
98— Mike McFetridge, WR

MILLIKIN (3)
42— Virgil Wagner, B
92— Mike Hall, KR
2003— Andy Beals, PK

MILLSAPS (14)
72— Rowan Torrey, DB
73— Michael Reams, LB
76— Rickie Haygood, QB
78— David Culpepper, LB
79— David Culpepper, LB
83— Edmond Donald, RB
85— Tommy Powell, LB
90— Sean Brewer, DL
91— Sean Brewer, DL
92— Sean Brewer, DL
93— Mitch Holloway, P
94— Kelvin Gladney, RB
2003— Matt O'Bryant, LB
06— Chris Jackson, KR

MINN. DULUTH (5)
74— Mark Johnson, DB
75— Terry Egerdahl, RB
76— Ted McKnight, RB

82— Gary Birkholz, OG
2003— Russ Rabe, DE

MINN. ST. MANKATO (13)
73— Marty Kranz, DB
87— Duane Goldammer, OG
91— John Kelling, DB
93— Jamie Pass, QB
94— Josh Nelsen, WR
95— Mark Erickson, AP
96— Tywan Mitchell, WR
Greg Janacek, PK
97— Tywan Mitchell, WR
98— Tywan Mitchell, WR
2002— Andrew Tippins, DL
03— Jared Ziemke, DB
06— Melvin Matlock, RS

MINN. ST. MOORHEAD (3)
76— Rocky Gullickson, OG
84— Randy Sullivan, DB
2006— Josh Jones, DB

MISSISSIPPI COL. (12)
72— Ricky Herzog, FL
79— Calvin Howard, RB
80— Bert Lyles, DE
82— Major Everett, RB
83— Wayne Frazier, OL
85— Earl Conway, DL
88— Terry Fleming, DL
89— Terry Fleming, DL
90— Fred McAfee, RB
92— Johnny Poole, OL
93— Kelly Ray, C
2000— Wilson Hillman, P

MISSISSIPPI VAL. (9)
79— †Carl White, OG
83— †Jerry Rice, WR
84— †Jerry Rice, WR
†Willie Totten, QB
87— †Vincent Brown, LB
91— †Ashley Ambrose, DB
97— †Terry Houzah, LB
98— †Terry Houzah, LB
2005—†Tyler Knight, LB

MO.-ROLLA (6)
41— Ed Kromka, T
69— Frank Winfield, OG
74— Merle Dillow, TE
80— Bill Grantham, S
93— Elvind Listerud, PK
2004— Cole Drussa, TE

MO. SOUTHERN ST. (4)
93— Rod Smith, WR
Ron Burton, LB
95— Yancy McKnight, OL
2006— Allen Barbre, OL

MISSOURI ST. (13)
66— William Stringer, OG
87— †Matt Soraghan, LB
89— †Mark Christenson, OL
90— †DeAndre Smith, QB
91— †Bill Walter, DL
93— †Adrion Smith, DB
95— †DeLaun Fowler, LB
96— †Michael Cosey, RB
†Wayne Boyer, PK
†Mike Miano, DL
97— †Travis Brawner, PK
2001—†P.J. Jones, LB
04— †Jon Scifres, PK

MISSOURI VALLEY (3)
47— James Nelson, G
48— James Nelson, G
49— Herbert McKinney, T

MO. WESTERN ST. (2)
2003— Pierre Thomas, DB
05— Jeremiah White, RB

MONMOUTH (2)
2002—†Joe Sentipal, LB
03— †Joe Sentipal, LB

MONMOUTH (ILL.) (1)
75— Ron Baker, RB

MONTANA (37)
67— Bob Beers, LB
70— Ron Stein, DB
76— Greg Anderson, DB
79— †Jim Hard, FL
83— †Brian Salonen, TE
85— †Mike Rice, P
87— †Larry Clarkson, OL
88— †Tim Hauck, DB
89— †Kirk Scafford, OL
†Tim Hauck, DB
93— †Dave Dickenson, QB
†Todd Ericson, DB
94— †Scott Gragg, OL
95— †Dave Dickenson, QB
†Matt Wells, WR
†Mike Agee, OL
†Eric Simonson, OL
96— †Joe Douglass, WR
†Mike Agee, OL
†Brian Ah Yat, QB
†Jason Crebo, LB
†David Kempfert, OL
97— †Jason Crebo, LB
99— †Kelley Bryant, DL
2000—†Drew Miller, QB
†Thatcher Szalay, OL
†Andy Petek, DL
01— †Thatcher Szalay, OL
†Vince Huntsberger, DB
†Mark Spencer, P
02— †Dylan McFarland, OL
†Trey Young, DB
03— †Dylan McFarland, OL
†Chris Snyder, PK
04— †Cory Proctor, OL
06— †Dan Carpenter, PK
†Mike Murphy, DL

MONTANA ST. (16)
66— Don Hass, HB
67— Don Hass, HB
70— Gary Gustafson, LB
73— Bill Kollar, DT
75— Steve Kracher, RB
76— Lester Leininger, DL
78— Jon Borchardt, OT
81— †Larry Rubens, OL
84— †Mark Fellows, LB
†Dirk Nelson, P
93— †Sean Hill, DB
97— †Neal Smith, DL
99— †Matthew Peot, P
2003—†Corey Smith, RS
†Kane Ioane, DB
05— †Jeff Bolton, OL

MONTANA TECH (3)
73— James Persons, OT
80— Steve Hossler, HB
81— Craig Opatz, OL

MONTCLAIR ST. (14)
75— Barry Giblin, DB
77— Mario Benimeo, DT
79— Tom Morton, OL
80— Sam Mills, LB
81— Terrance Porter, WR
82— Mark Casale, QB
84— Jim Rennae, OL
85— Dan Zakashefski, DL
86— Dan Zakashefski, DL
89— Paul Cioffi, LB
90— Paul Cioffi, LB
93— Jeff Bargiel, DL
95— Jeff Bargiel, DL
96— Jeff Bargiel, DL

MORAVIAN (1)
2002— Jarrod Pence, DB

MOREHEAD ST. (5)
38— John Horton, C
42— Vincent Zachem, C
69— Dave Haverdick, DT
82— †John Christopher, P
86— †Randy Poe, OG

MORGAN ST. (8)
65— Willie Lanier, LB
67— Jeff Queen, DE
70— Willie Germany, DB
72— Stan Cherry, LB
73— Eugene Simms, LB
78— Joe Fowlkes, DB
80— Mike Holston, WR
93— †Matthew Steeple, DL

MORNINGSIDE (2)
49— Connie Callahan, B
91— Jorge Diaz, PK

MT. ST. JOSEPH (1)
2006— Matt Lawless, LB

MOUNT UNION (52)
84— Troy Starr, LB
87— Russ Kring, RB
90— Ken Edelman, PK
Dave Lasecki, LB
92— Mike Elder, OL
Jim Ballard, QB
Chris Dattilio, LB
93— Rob Atwood, TE
Jim Ballard, QB
Ed Bubonics, WR
Mike Hallet, DL
94— Rob Rodgers, LB
95— Mike Wonderfer, OG
Matt Liggett, DL
96— Bill Borchert, QB
Joe Weimer, OL
Josh Weber, OT
Brian Wervey, LB
97— Bill Borchert, QB
Joe Weimer, OL
Vic Ricketts, G
98— Jason Hall, LB
Kris Bugara, DB
99— Tom Bauer, OL
2000— Jason Gerber, OT
Adam Marino, WR
Gary Smeck, QB
01— Chuck Moore, RB
Adam Indorf, OL
Todd Bhraden, DL
Matt Campbell, DL
Chris Kern, DB
02— Larry Kinnard, OT
Dan Pugh, RB
Matt Campbell, DE
Chris Kern, DB
03— Robert Bradley, OL
Larry Kinnard, OL
Randell Knapp, WR
Shaun Spisak, LB
04— Jesse Clum, DB
Johnny Josef, DL
Shaun Spisak, LB
05— Jason Lewis, OL
Mike Gibbons, LB
Ross Watson, DB
06— Derek Blanchard, OL
Pierre Garcon, WR
Nate Knic, RB
Matt Kostelnik, DB
Jason Lewis, OL
Justen Stickley, DE

MUHLENBERG (6)
46— George Bibighaus, E
47— Harold Bell, B
93— Rob Lokerson, WR
99— Joshua Carter, KR
2000— Joshua Carter, KR
02— Chris Reed, PK

MURRAY ST. (8)
37— Elmer Cochran, G
73— Don Clayton, RB
79— †Terry Love, DB
86— †Charley Wiles, OL
95— †Derrick Cullors, RB
†William Hampton, DB
96— †William Hampton, DB
2001—†Shane Andrus, PK

MUSKINGUM (5)
40— Dave Evans, T
60— Bill Cooper, B
66— Mark DeVilling, DT
75— Jeff Heacock, DB
95— Connon Thompson, DB

NEB.-KEARNEY (8)
76— Dale Mitchell Johnson, DB
78— Doug Peterson, DL
95— Matt Bruggeman, DL
97— Mike Smith, RT
2002— Henrik Juul-Nielson, PK
Mike Miller, RB
03— Richie Ross, WR
05— Richie Ross, WR

NEB.-OMAHA (20)
64— Gerald Allen, HB
68— Dan Klepper, OG
76— Dan Fulton, WR
77— Dan Fulton, OE
80— Tom Sutko, LB
82— John Walker, DT
83— Tim Carlson, LB
84— Ron Petersen, OT
86— Keith Coleman, LB
98— Chris Bober, OT
99— Chris Bober, OL
2000— Chris Cooper, DL
01— Chad Geiger, DB
02— Conor Riley, OL
03— Justin Kammrad, RB
04— Taiwo Onatolu, LB
05— Zach Herold, TE
06— Zach Herold, TE
Ben Hochstein, OL
Randall Jantzen, OL

NEB. WESLEYAN (4)
90— Brad Bohn, DB
91— Darren Stohlmann, TE
92— Darren Stohlmann, TE
2000— Noland Urban, LB

NEVADA* (23)
52— Neil Garrett, DB
74— Greg Grouwinkel, DB
78— James Curry, MG
Frank Hawkins, RB
79— †Frank Hawkins, RB
†Lee Fobbs, DB
80— †Frank Hawkins, RB
†Bubba Puha, DL
81— †John Ramatici, LB
†Tony Zendejas, K
82— †Tony Zendejas, K
†Charles Mann, DT
83— †Tony Zendejas, K
†Jim Werbeckes, OG
†Tony Shaw, DB
85— †Greg Rea, OL
†Marty Zendejas, PK
†Pat Hunter, DB
86— †Henry Rolling, DE-LB
88— †Bernard Ellison, DB
90— †Bernard Ellison, DB
†Treamelle Taylor, KR
91— †Matt Clafton, LB

UNLV* (3)
73— Mike Thomas, RB
74— Mike Thomas, RB
75— Joseph Ingersoll, DL

NEW HAMPSHIRE (20)
50— Ed Douglas, G
68— Al Whittman, DT
75— Kevin Martell, C
76— Bill Burnham, RB
77— Bill Burnham, RB
Grady Vigneau, OT
85— †Paul Dufault, OL
87— †John Driscoll, OL
91— †Barry Bourassa, RB
†Dwayne Sabb, LB
94— †Mike Foley, DL
97— †Jerry Azumah, RS/RB
98— †Jerry Azumah, RB
†Walter Jones, OL
2002—†Stephan Lewis, RB
04— †David Ball, WR
05— †David Ball, WR
†Jonathan Williams, TE
06— †David Ball, WR
†Ricky Santos, QB

NEW HAVEN (17)
85— David Haubner, OL
87— Erik Lesinski, LB
88— Rob Thompson, OL
90— Jay McLucas, QB
92— Scott Emmert, OL
Roger Graham, RB
93— Roger Graham, RB
George Byrd, DB
Tony Willis, WR
94— Roger Graham, RB
95— Scott Riggs, LB
96— Jesse Showerda, QB

97— Mario DiDino, OL
Cazzie Kosciolek, QB
2000— Steve Cedor, LB
01— Idris Price, LB
02— Phil Bogle, OL

TCNJ (7)
74— Eric Hamilton, C
83— John Aromando, WR
91— Chris Shaw, C
97— Jim Haines, OL
Tom Ruggia, DL
98— Tom Ruggia, DL
2003— Michael Sykes, DL

N.M. HIGHLANDS (8)
66— Carl Garrett, HB
67— Carl Garrett, HB
68— Carl Garrett, HB
81— Jay Lewis, DL
85— Neil Windham, LB
86— Tim Salz, PK
93— Rus Bailey, WR
96— Jamar Nailor, WR

NEWBERRY (4)
40— Dominic Collangelo, B
81— Stan Stanton, DL
97— Anthony Heatley, OL
2006— Heath Benedict, OL

NICHOLLS ST. (9)
76— Gerald Butler, OE
77— Rusty Rebowe, LB
81— †Dwight Walker, WR
82— †Clint Conque, LB
84— †Dewayne Harrison, TE
86— †Mark Carrier, WR
94— †Darryl Pounds, DB
2002—†LeJuan Walker, RS
03— †Chris Crawford, RS

NICHOLS (1)
81— Ed Zywien, LB

NORFOLK ST. (6)
79— Mike Ellis, DB
89— Arthur Jimmerson, LB
94— James Roe, WR
95— James Roe, WR
Aaron Sparrow, QB
2004—†Kevin Talley, LB

NORTH ALA. (29)
82— Don Smith, C
84— Daryl Smith, DB
85— Bruce Jones, DB
90— James Davis, LB
Mike Nord, OL
92— Harvey Summerhill, DB
93— Jeff Redcross, DL
Tyrone Rush, RB
Jeff Surbaugh, OL
Ronald McKinnon, LB
94— Jon Thompson, OL
Ronald McKinnon, LB
Marcus Keyes, DL
95— Jon Thompson, OL
Israel Raybon, DE
Ronald McKinnon, LB
Marcus Keyes, DL
96— Gerald Smith, DB
97— Reginald Ruffin, LB
Marcus Hill, DB
2003— Will Hall, QB
Evan Oglesby, CB
04— Evan Oglesby, DB
Kendrick Triplett, DL
Anthony Merritt, RS
05— Lance Ancar, C
Anthony Merritt, KR
Blake Farris, DL
06— Anthony Merritt, WR

N.C. A&T (10)
69— Merl Code, DB
70— Melvin Holmes, OT
81— †Mike West, OL
86— †Ernest Riddick, NG
88— †Demetrius Harrison, LB
93— †Ronald Edwards, OL
95— †Jamain Stephens, OL
97— †Chris McNeil, DL
2001—†Curtis DeLoatch, RS
†Qasim Mitchell, OL

N.C. CENTRAL (6)
68— Doug Wilkerson, MG
69— Doug Wilkerson, OT
74— Charles Smith, DE
88— Earl Harvey, QB
96— Tommy Dorsey, LB
2006— Craig Amos, DB

NORTH CENTRAL (ILL.) (2)
97— Jim Witte, OL
2005— Lenny Radtke, LB

NORTH DAKOTA (39)
55— Steve Myhra, G
56— Steve Myhra, G
63— Neil Reuter, T
65— Dave Lince, DE
66— Roger Bonk, LB
71— Jim LeClair, LB
Dan Martinsen, DB
72— Mike Deutsch, RB
75— Bill Deutsch, RB
79— Paul Muckenhirn, TE
80— Todd Thomas, OT
81— Milson Jones, RB
89— Cory Solberg, PK
91— Shannon Burnell, RB
93— Shannon Burnell, RB
Kevin Robson, OL
94— Mike Mooney, LB
95— Dave Hillesheim, DE
96— Juan Gomez-Tagle, PK
Mark Callahan, DL
Tim Tibesar, LB
97— Phillip Moore, RB
Jim Kleinsasser, TE
98— Jim Kleinsasser, TE
Phillip Moore, RB
99— Kelly Howe, DB
2000— Cameron Peterka, PK
01— Cameron Peterka, PK
Travis O'Neel, LB
Dan Graf, AP
03— Ben Olson, OL
Digger Anderson, LB
04— Chris Kuper, OL
Digger Anderson, LB
05— Jeff Glas, PK
Chris Kuper, OL
Digger Anderson, LB
06— Weston Dressler, WR
Adam Wolff, DL

NORTH DAKOTA ST. (35)
34— Melvin Hanson, B
46— Cliff Rothrock, C
66— Walt Odegaard, MG
67— Jim Ferge, LB
68— Jim Ferge, DT
Paul Hatchett, B
69— Paul Hatchett, HB
Joe Cichy, DB
70— Joe Cichy, DB
74— Jerry Dahl, DE
76— Rick Budde, LB
77— Lew Curry, OL
81— Wayne Schluchter, DB
82— Cliff Carmody, OG
Steve Garske, LB
83— Mike Whetstone, OG
84— Greg Hagfors, C
86— Jeff Bentrim, QB
Jim Dick, LB
87— Mike Favor, C
88— Matt Tracy, OL
Mike Favor, C
Yorrick Byers, LB
90— Phil Hansen, DL
Chris Simdorn, QB
93— Scott Fuchs, OL
T.R. McDonald, WR
95— Brad Servais, OL
97— Sean Fredricks, LB
99— Tim Strehlow, AP
2000— Lamar Gordon, RB
01— Leif Murphy, DL
Richard Lewis, KR
04— †Rob Hunt, C
06— †Jake Erickson, OL

NORTH GREENVILLE (1)
2006— Adam Bernardi, DL

NORTH PARK (2)
72— Greg Nugent, OE
90— John Love, QB

NORTH TEXAS* (6)
47— Frank Whitlow, T
51— Ray Renfro, DB
83— †Ronnie Hickman, DE
†Rayford Cooks, DL
88— †Rex Johnson, DL
90— †Mike Davis, DL

NORTHEASTERN (6)
72— Tom Rezzuti, DB
78— Dan Ross, TE
96— †Jerome Daniels, OL
2001—†L.J. McKansas, RB
03— †Liam Ezekiel, LB
04— †Liam Ezekiel, LB

NORTHEASTERN ST. (7)
69— Manuel Britto, HB
71— Roosevelt Manning, DT
74— Kevin Goodlet, DB
82— Cedric Mack, WR
94— Ricky Ceasar, DL
2000— Rod Kelly, DL
02— Micah Lomas, OL

NORTHERN ARIZ. (23)
66— Rick Ries, LB
67— Bill Hanna, DE
68— Larry Small, OG
77— Larry Friedrichs, OL
Tom Jurich, K
78— Jerry Lumpkin, LB
79— †Ed Judie, LB
82— †Pete Mandley, WR
83— †Pete Mandley, WR
†James Gee, DT
86— †Goran Lingmerth, PK
89— †Darrell Jordan, LB
93— †Terry Belden, P
95— †Rayna Stewart, DB
†Kevin O'Leary, P
†Ben Petrucci, DL
96— †Archie Amerson, RB
†Ricky Pearsall, PR
97— †Dan Finn, OL
2002—†Mark Gould, P
03— †Mark Gould, P
04— †Paul Ernster, P
06— †Alex Watson, WR

NORTHERN COLO. (27)
68— Jack O'Brien, DB
80— Todd Volkart, DT
81— Brad Wimmer, OL
82— Mark Mostek, OG
Kevin Jelden, PK
89— Vance Lechman, DB
90— Frank Wainwright, TE
92— David Oliver, OL
93— Jeff Pease, LB
94— Jeff Pease, LB
95— Tony Ramirez, OL
Tim Bowie, DB
96— Tony Ramirez, OL
Delano Washington, DB
97— Aaron Smith, DL
Dirk Johnson, DB
98— Aaron Smith, DL
Scott Zimmerman, LB
99— Corte McGuffey, QB
Jamie Heiner, LB
2000— Ryan Burkholder, OL
02— Anthony Dunn, DL
Cabel Rohloff, LB
03— †Vincent Jackson, WR
04— †Vincent Jackson, WR
†Reed Doughty, DB
05— †Reed Doughty, DB

NORTHERN ILL.* (2)
62— George Bork, B
63— George Bork, B

UNI (27)
52— Lou Bohnsack, C
60— George Asleson, G
61— Wendell Williams, G
64— Randy Schultz, FB
65— Randy Schultz, FB
67— Ray Pedersen, MG
75— Mike Timmermans, OT

85— Joe Fuller, DB
87— †Carl Boyd, RB
90— †Brian Mitchell, PK
91— †Brian Mitchell, PK
92— †Kenny Shedd, WR
†William Freeney, LB
94— †Andre Allen, LB
95— †Dedric Ward, WR
96— †Dedric Ward, WR
99— †Brad Meester, C
†Mike Furrey, WR
2000—†Eddie Berlin, WR
†Ryan Helming, QB
†Ryan Doak, DB
01— †MacKenzie Hoambrecker, PK
†Adam Vogt, LB
02— †MacKenzie Hoambrecker, PK
05— †Tanner Varner, DB
06— †Dre Dokes, DB
†Brian Wingert, PK

NORTHERN MICH. (8)
75— Daniel Stencil, OL
76— Maurice Mitchell, FL
77— Joseph Stemo, DB
82— George Works, RB
87— Jerry Woods, DB
88— Jerry Woods, DB
99— Ty Hartung, P
2000— Mark Dugas, OL

NORTHERN ST. (1)
76— Larry Kolbo, DL

NORTHWEST MO. ST. (29)
39— Marion Rogers, G
84— Steve Hansley, WR
89— Jason Agee, DB
96— Matt Uhde, DL
97— Chris Greisen, QB
98— Twan Young, DB
Aaron Crowe, LB
Chris Greisen, QB
Steve Coppinger, C
Aaron Becker, DL
99— Tony Miles, AP
David Purnell, PK
Chad Thompson, OG
2000— Andy Erpelding, OT
Tony Miles, AP/WR
Aaron Becker, DL
Brian Williams, LB
01— Seth Wand, OL
02— Seth Wand, OL
03— Jamaica Rector, WR
04— Jamaica Rector, WR
Luis Berlanga, PK
Adam Long, LB
05— Dave Tollefson, DL
06— Ben Harness, LB
Kyle Kaiser, DL
Reid Kirby, OL
Mike Peterson, OL
Thomas Smith, LB

N'WESTERN (IOWA) (1)
71— Kevin Korvor, DE

NORTHWESTERN ST. (20)
66— Al Dodd, DB
80— †Warren Griffith, C
†Joe Delaney, RB
81— †Gary Reasons, LB
82— †Gary Reasons, LB
83— †Gary Reasons, LB
84— †Arthur Berry, DT
87— †John Kulakowski, DE
91— †Andre Carron, LB
92— †Adrian Hardy, DB
†Marcus Spears, OL
93— †Marcus Spears, OL
97— †Tony Maranto, DB
98— †Jermaine Jones, DB
99— †Mike Green, DB
2000—†Terrence McGee, PR
02— †Roy Locks, DL
04— †Jamall Johnson, LB
05— †Tory Collins, DL
06— †Tory Collins, DL

NORTHWOOD (MICH.) (7)
73— Bill Chandler, DT
74— Bill Chandler, DT
98— Tyrone Nelson, OL

2004— Martell Foster, DB
Chris Wilson, DL
06— Torris Childs, RB
Charleston Hughes, LB

NORWICH (3)
79— Milt Williams, RB
84— Beau Almodobar, WR
85— Mike Norman, OL

OBERLIN (2)
45— James Boswell, B
2003— Quammie Semper, DB

OCCIDENTAL (7)
76— Rick Fry, FL
77— Rick Fry, SE
82— Dan Osborn, P
83— Ron Scott, DB
89— David Hodges, LB
90— Peter Tucker, OL
2006— Andy Collins, QB

OHIO* (2)
35— Art Lewis, T
60— Dick Grecni, C

OHIO NORTHERN (11)
95— LaVant King, WR
96— Jerry Adams, DB
98— Steve Vagedes, P
99— Jamal Robertson, RB
Kory Allen, OL
Jeremy Presar, DB
Steve Vagedes, P/WR
2000— Jamal Robertson, RB
04— Jason Trusnik, DL
05— Wes Hostetler, KR
06— Jason Trusnik, DL

OHIO WESLEYAN (8)
34— John Turley, B
51— Dale Bruce, OE
71— Steve Dutton, DE
83— Eric DiMartino, LB
90— Jeff Court, OG
Neil Ringers, DL
91— Kevin Rucker, DL
96— Craig Anderson, LB

OKLA. PANHANDLE (2)
82— Tom Rollison, DB
83— Tom Rollison, DB

OTTERBEIN (4)
82— Jim Hoyle, K
90— Ron Severance, WR
91— Ron Severance, WR
2001— Jeff Gibbs, TE

OUACHITA BAPTIST (2)
79— Ezekiel Vaughn, LB
2001— T.J. Bingham, DL

PACIFIC (4)
34— Cris Kjeldsen, G
47— Eddie LeBaron, B
48— Eddie LeBaron, B
49— Eddie LeBaron, B

PACIFIC LUTHERAN (12)
40— Marv Tommervik, B
41— Marv Tommervik, B
47— Dan D'Andrea, C
52— Ron Billings, DB
65— Marvin Peterson, C
78— John Zamberlin, LB
85— Mark Foege, PK
Tim Shannon, DL
88— Jon Kral, DL
2000— Chad Johnson, QB
02— Kyle Brown, WR
03— Casey Carlson, LB

PENN (10)
86— †Marty Peterson, OL
88— †John Zinser, OL
90— †Joe Valerio, OL
93— †Miles Macik, WR
94— †Pat Goodwillie, LB
95— †Miles Macik, WR
†Tom McGarrity, DL
96— †Mitch Marrow, DL
2001—†Jeff Hatch, OL
03— †Chris Clark, OL

PEPPERDINE (2)
47— Darwin Horn, B
55— Wixie Robinson, G

PERU ST. (4)
52— Robert Lade, OT
53— Robert Lade, T
81— Alvin Holder, RB
91— Tim Herman, DL

PIKEVILLE (1)
2005— Antwan Marsh, DB

PILLSBURY (1)
85— Calvin Addison, RB

PITTSBURG ST. (38)
61— Gary Snadon, B
70— Mike Potchard, OT
78— Brian Byers, OL
88— Jesse Wall, OL
89— John Roderique, LB
90— Ron West, WR
91— Ron West, WR
92— Ronald Moore, RB
93— Doug Bullard, OL
94— Andy Sweet, LB
Chris Brown, DB
95— Phil Schepens, OT
B.J. McGivern, LB
Chris Brown, DB
96— Bob Goltra, OL
97— Sean McNamara, OL
Brian Moorman, P
98— Ben Peterson, DE
Brian Moorman, P
99— Andrew Poling, DB
2000— Wes Baker, LB
01— Matt Howard, OL
Earl Henry, LB
Aaron McConnell, DL
02— Daniel Chappell, PK
Eric Johnson, C
Aaron McConnell, DL
03— Tyronne Armstrong, OG
Aaron McConnell, DL
04— Nathan Baker, OL
Germaine Race, RB
Chad Weeks, OL
Ryan Meredith, DL
Chad Miller, LB
05— Germaine Race, RB
Brandon Twito, TE
Chad Weeks, OL
06— Germaine Race, RB

PLYMOUTH ST. (8)
74— Robert Gibson, DB
82— Mark Barrows, LB
83— Joe Dudek, RB
84— Joe Dudek, RB
85— Joe Dudek, RB
91— Scott Allen, LB
94— Colby Compton, LB
95— Colby Compton, LB

POMONA-PITZER (1)
74— Larry Cenotto, QB

PORTLAND ST. (21)
76— June Jones, QB
77— Dave Stief, OE
79— †Stuart Gaussoin, SE
†Kurt Ijanoff, OT
80— †Neil Lomax, QB
84— Doug Mikolas, DL
88— Bary Naone, TE
Chris Crawford, QB
89— Darren Del'Andrae, QB
91— James Fuller, DB
92— John Charles, QB
93— Rick Cruz, LB
94— Sam Peoples, DB
Jesus Moreno, OT
95— Steve Papin, RB
98— †Bobby Singh, OL
2000—†Charles Dunn, RB
01— †Terry Charles, WR
05— †Joe Rubin, RB
06— †Brennan Carvalho, OL
†Adam Hayward, LB

PRAIRIE VIEW (2)
64— Otis Taylor, OE
70— Bivian Lee, DB

PRESBYTERIAN (11)
45— Andy Kavounis, G
46— Hank Caver, B
52— Joe Kirven, OE
68— Dan Eckstein, DB
71— Robert Norris, LB
78— Roy Walker, OL
79— Roy Walker, OL
83— Jimmie Turner, LB
2001— Todd Cunningham, QB
D.J. Humphries, WR
05— Marcus Brisbone, OL

PRINCETON (6)
87— †Dean Cain, DB
89— †Judd Garrett, RB
92— †Keith Elias, RB
93— †Keith Elias, RB
2001—†Taylor Northrop, PK
05— †Jay McCareins, DB

PRINCIPIA (1)
93— Matt Newton, WR

PUGET SOUND (9)
56— Robert Mitchell, G
63— Ralph Bauman, G
66— Joseph Peyton, OE
75— Bill Linnenkohl, LB
76— Dan Kuehl, DL
81— Bob Jackson, MG
82— Mike Bos, WR
83— Larry Smith, DB
87— Mike Oliphant, RB

RANDOLPH-MACON (9)
47— Albert Oley, G
57— Dave Young, G
79— Rick Eades, DL
80— Rick Eades, DL
84— Cody Dearing, QB
88— Aaron Boston, OL
96— Tim Armoska, LB
98— Chuck Davis, DL
99— Sean Eaton, WR

REDLANDS (5)
77— Randy Van Horn, OL
92— James Shields, DL
2002— Sean Lipscomb, P
Jeff Thomas, DB
03— Wil Goff, DL

RENSSELAER (5)
96— Scott Cafarelli, OL
98— Krishaun Gilmore, RB
99— Chris Swartz, DB
2004— Jon Branche, TE
05— Jon Branche, TE

RHODE ISLAND (9)
55— Charles Gibbons, T
82— †Richard Pelzer, OL
83— †Tony DeLuca, DL
84— †Brian Forster, TE
85— †Brian Forster, TE
†Tom Ehrhardt, QB
90— †Kevin Smith, DB
92— †Darren Rizzi, TE
96— †Frank Ferrara, DL

RHODES (5)
36— Henry Hammond, E
38— Gaylon Smith, B
76— Conrad Bradburn, DB
85— Jim Hever, PK
88— Larry Hayes, OL

RICHMOND (6)
84— †Eddie Martin, OL
97— †Shawn Barber, LB
†Marc Megna, DL
98— †Marc Megna, DT
†Eric King, OL
2000—†Eric Beatty, OL

RIPON (7)
57— Peter Kasson, E
75— Dick Rehbein, C
76— Dick Rehbein, OL
79— Art Peters, TE
82— Bob Wallner, OL
95— Jim Wallace, DB
2000— Nate Kok, DB

ROANOKE (1)
38— Kenneth Moore, E

ROBERT MORRIS (2)
2004—†James Noel, LB
06— †Matt Brunck, DL

ROCHESTER (7)
51— Jack Wilson, DE
52— Donald Bardell, DG
67— Dave Ragusa, LB
75— Ralph Gebhardt, DB
90— Craig Chodak, P
92— Brian Laudadio, DL
93— Geoff Long, DL

ROCKHURST (1)
41— Joe Kiernan, T

ROCKY MOUNTAIN (1)
2001— Travis Salter, DB

ROLLINS (1)
40— Charles Lingerfelt, E

ROSE-HULMAN (2)
77— Gary Ellis, DB
92— Todd Holthaus, PK

ROWAN (14)
78— Dino Hall, RB
93— Bill Fisher, DL
95— LeRoi Jones, LB
97— Terrick Grace, DB
98— Jarryn Avery, OL
99— John Gavlick, LB
Jarryn Avery, OL
Cornelius White, DL
2000— Ron Gibson, DB
01— Tony Racioppi, QB
Rob Rieck, OL
02— Gerrit Tosh, DL
04— Scott Blum, OL
05— Brian Bond, DL

SACRAMENTO ST. (9)
64— William Fuller, OT
91— Troy Mills, RB
Jim Crouch, PK
92— Jon Kirksey, DL
98— †Charles Roberts, RB
99— †Charles Roberts, RB
†Jon Osterhout, OL
2000—†Charles Roberts, RB
04— †Fred Amey, RS

SAGINAW VALLEY (10)
81— Eugene Marve, LB
84— Joe Rice, DL
90— David Cook, DB
92— Bill Schafer, TE
97— Paul Spicer, DL
Kent Kraatz, OT
98— Lamar King, DL
2000— Brian Dolph, WR
04— Todd Herremans, OL
05— John DiGiorgio, LB

ST. AMBROSE (5)
40— Nick Kerasiotis, G
51— Robert Flanagan, B
58— Robert Webb, B
87— Jerry Klosterman, DL
97— Craig Shepherd, OL

ST. AUGUSTINE'S (1)
2006— Kevin Jones, LB

ST. BONAVENTURE (2)
46— Phil Colella, B
48— Frank LoVuola, E

ST. CLOUD ST. (8)
85— Mike Lambrecht, DL
95— Randy Martin, RB
96— Randy Martin, RB
97— Mike McKinney, WR
2002— Matt Huebner, TE
Ben Nelson, WR
03— Keith Heckendorf, QB
05— Charlie Cosgrove, DL

ST. JOHN FISHER (5)
2003— Brad Keem, DL
04— Mark Robinson, RB
Will Bean, PK
Mike Fox, LB
06— Gene Lang, LB

ST. JOHN'S (MINN.) (22)
65— Pat Whalin, DB
79— Ernie England, MG

82— Rick Bell, RB
83— Chris Biggins, TE
91— Pat Mayew, QB
93— Burt Chamberlin, OL
Jim Wagner, DL
94— Jim Wagner, DL
95— Chris Palmer, WR
96— Jesse Redepenning, OL
98— Brandon Novak, LB
99— Brandon Novak, LB
Phil Barry, P
2000— Nathan Kirschner, TE
Chris Salvato, OL
02— Blake Elliott, AP/WR
Jeremy Hood, DL
Cam McCambridge, LB
03— Blake Elliott, WR
Jeremy Hood, DE
05— Damien Dumonceaux, DL
06— Nick Gunderson, DL

ST. JOHN'S (N.Y.) (1)
83— Todd Jamison, QB

ST. LAWRENCE (2)
51— Ken Spencer, LB
77— Mitch Brown, DB

ST. MARY (KAN.) (1)
86— Joe Brinson, RB

ST. MARY'S (CAL.) (7)
79— Fran McDermott, DB
80— Fran McDermott, DB
88— Jon Braff, TE
92— Mike Estrella, PK
2001—†Travis White, DL
02— †Nathan Frowsing, OL
†Weston Borba, DB

ST. MARY'S (TEX.) (1)
36— Douglas Locke, B

ST. NORBERT (8)
57— Norm Jarock, B
64— Dave Jauquet, DE
2000— Jerimiah Janssen, DL
01— Jerimiah Janssen, LB
02— Kevin O'Malley, OL
03— Joe Masciopinto, DB
Seth Schussler, TE
06— Bob Forstrom, PK

ST. OLAF (3)
53— John Gustafson, E
78— John Nahorniak, LB
80— Jon Anderson, DL

ST. THOMAS (MINN.) (12)
45— Theodore Molitor, E
48— Jack Salscheider, B
84— Neal Guggemos, DB
85— Neal Guggemos, DB
90— Gary Trettel, RB
91— Kevin DeVore, OL
94— Ryan Davis, TE
95— Ryan Davis, TE
96— Ryan Collins, TE
97— Ryan Collins, TE
2002— Sean O'Leary, DL
05— Andrew Ubbelhode, LB

SALISBURY (9)
82— Mark Lagowski, LB
84— Joe Mammano, OL
85— Robb Disbennett, QB
86— Tom Kress, DL
95— Mark Hannah, LB
2002— Beau Ridgway, OL
04— Brad DeHaven, LB
05— Brett Wehnert, OL
06— Bryon Westbrook, DB

SAM HOUSTON ST. (8)
49— Charles Williams, E
52— Don Gottlob, B
91— †Michael Bankston, DL
2001—†Jonathon Cooper, WR
†Keith Heinrich, TE
†Keith Davis, DB
04— †Lance Garner, PK
05— †Corey Roberts, TE

SAMFORD (6)
36— Norman Cooper, C
94— †Anthony Jordan, AP
2002—†Cortland Finnegan, RS
03— †Efrem Hill, WR
04— †Efrem Hill, WR
05— †Cortland Finnegan, DB

SAN DIEGO (4)
73— Bob Dulich, QB
81— Dan Herbert, DB
92— Robert Ray, P
2003—†Eric Rasmussen, QB

SAN DIEGO ST.* (6)
35— John Butler, G
66— Don Horn, QB
67— Steve Duich, OT
Haven Moses, OE
68— Fred Dryer, DE
Lloyd Edwards, B

SAN FRANCISCO (1)
42— John Sanchez, T

SAN FRAN. ST. (7)
51— Robert Williamson, OT
60— Charles Fuller, B
67— Joe Koontz, OE
76— Forest Hancock, LB
78— Frank Duncan, DB
82— Poncho James, RB
84— Jim Jones, TE

SAN JOSE ST.* (2)
38— Lloyd Thomas, E
39— LeRoy Zimmerman, B

SANTA CLARA (8)
64— Lou Pastorini, LB
71— Ronald Sani, C
79— Jim Leonard, C
80— Brian Sullivan, K
82— Gary Hoffman, OT
83— Alex Vlahos, C
Mike Rosselli, LB
85— Brent Jones, TE

SAVANNAH ST. (3)
79— Timothy Walker, DL
89— Shannon Sharpe, TE
96— Britt Henderson, DB

SEWANEE (9)
63— Martin Agnew, B
73— Mike Lumpkin, DE
77— Nino Austin, DB
79— John Hill, DB
80— Mallory Nimocs, TE
81— Greg Worsowicz, DB
86— Mark Kent, WR
90— Ray McGowan, DL
99— Antonio Crook, OL

SHAW (1)
2004— Chris Peavy, LB

SHENANDOAH (1)
2002— Gregg Anderson, DB

SHEPHERD (7)
98— James Rooths, KR
99— Damian Beane, RB
James Rooths, KR
2000— James Rooths, DB
Dalevon Smith, RB
05— Dan Peters, DB
06— Dan Peters, DB

SHIPPENSBURG (8)
53— Robert Adams, G
91— Jeff Fickes, DB
94— Doug Seidenstricker, DB
99— Jamie Ware, WR
2001— Chad Oberholzer, DL
04— John Kuhn, RB
Brent Grimes, DB
05— Brent Grimes, DB

SIENA (2)
95— †Reggie Greene, AP
97— †Reggie Greene, RB

SIMON FRASER (1)
90— Nick Mazzoli, WR

SIMPSON (9)
89— Ricky Gales, RB
96— Brent Parrott, DB
Chris Whiney, OT
97— Jeremy Whalen, DL
98— Guy Leman, RB
Clint Head, OL
2003— Mike Donnenwerth, P
Kyle Westphal, DB
04— Jason Ripke, DL

SLIPPERY ROCK (8)
74— Ed O'Reilly, RB
75— Jerry Skocik, TE
76— Chris Thull, LB
77— Bob Schrantz, TE
78— Bob Schrantz, TE
85— Jeff Williams, P
97— Dave Sabolcik, OL
98— Matt Kinsinger, DL

SONOMA ST. (3)
86— Mike Henry, LB
92— Larry Allen, OL
93— Larry Allen, OL

SOUTH CAROLINA ST. (26)
67— Tyrone Caldwell, DE
71— James Evans, LB
72— Barney Chavous, DE
73— Donnie Shell, DB
75— Harry Carson, DE
76— Robert Sims, DL
77— Ricky Anderson, RB
79— †Phillip Murphy, DL
80— †Edwin Bailey, OG
81— †Anthony Reed, FB
†Dwayne Jackson, DL
82— †Dwayne Jackson, DE
†Anthony Reed, RB
†Ralph Green, OT
†John Courtney, DT
83— †Ralph Green, OT
89— †Eric Douglas, OL
91— †Robert Porcher, DL
93— †Anthony Cook, DE
94— †Anthony Cook, DL
96— †Raleigh Roundtree, OL
97— †Chartric Darby, DL
98— †Jermaine Derricott, DB
2001—†Derek Harrison, LB
05— †Rondreikas Darby, KR
06— †Clyde Reed, OL

SOUTH DAKOTA (18)
68— John Kohler, OT
69— John Kohler, OT
71— Gene Macken, OG
72— Gary Kipling, OG
78— Bill Moats, DB
79— Benjamin Long, LB
83— Kurt Seibel, K
86— Jerry Glinsky, C
Todd Salat, DB
88— Doug VanderEsch, LB
97— Brent Petersen, DL
2000— Russel Burwell, DB
04— Brian Alderson, OL
05— Brian Alderson, OL
Wes Beschorner, QB
A.J. Schable, DL
06— Stefan Logan, AP
Christian Morton, OL

SOUTH DAKOTA ST. (17)
67— Darwin Gonnerman, HB
68— Darwin Gonnerman, FB
74— Lynn Boden, OT
77— Bill Matthews, DE
79— Charles Loewen, OL
84— Rick Wegher, RB
85— Jeff Tiefenthaler, WR
86— Jeff Tiefenthaler, WR
91— Kevin Tetzlaff, OL
92— Doug Miller, LB
93— Adam Timmerman, DL
94— Jake Hines, TE
Adam Vinatieri, P
Adam Timmerman, OL
96— Tom O'Brien, P
99— Josh Ranek, RB
2001— Josh Ranek, RB

SOUTH DAKOTA TECH (1)
73— Charles Waite, DB

SOUTH FLA.* (1)
98— †Bill Gramatica, PK

SOUTHEAST MO. ST. (8)
37— Wayne Goddard, T
94— †Doug Berg, DL
95— †Frank Russell, DB
97— †Angel Rubio, DL
2002—†Willie Ponder, WR
03— †Eugene Amano, OL
05— †David Simonhoff, P
06— †David Simonhoff, P

SOUTHEASTERN LA. (3)
70— Ronnie Hornsby, LB
83— †Bret Wright, P
85— †Willie Shepherd, DL

SOUTHEASTERN OKLA. (4)
2004— Drew Beard, QB
Kevin Burton, C
Reggie Johnson, DL
06— Rayshaun Hollings, OL

SOUTHERN U. (10)
70— Isiah Robertson, LB
72— James Wright, OG
73— Godwin Turk, LB
79— †Ken Times, DL
87— †Gerald Perry, OT
93— †Sean Wallace, DB
95— †Kendell Shello, DL
2000—†Michael Hayes, WR
03— †Lenny Williams, DB
06— †Breck Ackley, P

SOUTHERN ARK. (7)
84— Greg Stuman, LB
85— Greg Stuman, LB
97— Fred Perry, LB
98— Jason Williams, PK
2001— Eddie Key, LB
02— Nik Lewis, WR
03— Nik Lewis, AP

SOUTHERN CONN. ST. (11)
82— Mike Marshall, DB
83— Kevin Gray, OL
84— William Sixsmith, LB
86— Rick Atkinson, DB
91— Ron Lecointe, OL
92— Steve Lawrence, LB
94— Anthony Idone, DL
95— †Joe Andruzzi, OL
96— Joe Andruzzi, OL
2000— Damon Richardson, DB
02— Jacques Cesaire, DL

SOUTHERN ILL. (12)
70— Lionel Antoine, OE
71— Lionel Antoine, OE
83— †Donnell Daniel, DB
†Terry Taylor, DB
96— †Mark Gagliano, P
99— †Cornell Craig, WR
2002—†Mo Abdulqaadir, RB
03— †Alexis Moreland, DB
04— †Elmer McDaniel, OL
05— †Arkee Whitlock, RB
06— †Craig Coffin, PK
†Arkee Whitlock, AP

SOUTHERN MISS.* (4)
53— Hugh Pepper, B
56— Don Owens, T
58— Robert Yencho, E
59— Hugh McInnis, E

SOUTHERN ORE. ST. (3)
75— Dennis Webber, LB
99— Griff Yates, RB
2003— Dusty McGrorty, RB

SOUTHERN UTAH (10)
79— Lane Martino, DL
87— Jeff McComb, P
89— Randy Bostic, C
90— Randy Bostic, C
95— †Micah Deckert, TE
97— †Jimmy Brimmer, LB
99— †John Uriarte, OL
†Josh Roberts, DB
2000—†Matt Cannon, QB
†Randy Clark, OL

SOUTHWEST MINN. ST. (2)
87— James Ashley, WR
91— Wayne Hawkins, DE

SOUTHWESTERN (KAN.) (2)
82— Tom Audley, DL
84— Jackie Jenson, RB

SOUTHWESTERN OKLA. (2)
77— Louis Blanton, DB
82— Richard Lockman, LB

SPRINGFIELD (19)
68— Dick Dobbert, C
70— John Curtis, OE
76— Roy Samuelsen, MG
78— Jack Quinn, DB
79— Jack Quinn, DB
80— Steve Foster, OT
81— Jon Richardson, LB
83— Wally Case, DT
Ed Meachum, TE
85— Jim Anderson, LB
91— Fran Papasedero, DL
94— Matt Way, OL
96— Jamie McGourty, DL
98— John Cena, OL
2000— Matt Sallilia, OG
02— Greg Switaj, PK
03— Brian Dewey, OG
04— Brian Dewey, OL
06— Adam Feit, OL

STEPHEN F. AUSTIN (17)
51— James Terry, DE
79— Ronald Haynes, DL
85— James Noble, WR
86— †Darrell Harkless, DB
88— †Eric Lokey, LB
89— †David Whitmore, DB
93— †Cedric Walker, DB
95— †Joey Wylie, OL
†Lee Kirk, OL
†Damiyon Bell, DB
96— †Jeremiah Trotter, LB
97— †Mikhael Ricks, WR
†Jeremiah Trotter, LB
98— †Chad Stanley, P
99— †Ka Ron Coleman, PR
2003—†Brent Hafford, DB
05— †Keldrick Holman, DB

STILLMAN (1)
2002— James Patrick, DB

STONY BROOK (2)
87— Chuck Downey, DB
88— David Lewis, P

SUL ROSS ST. (2)
65— Tom Nelson, DE
88— Francis Jones, DB

SUSQUEHANNA (6)
51— James Hazlett, C
90— Keith Henry, DL
92— Andy Watkins, LB
96— Jeremy Ziesloft, DB
99— Antonio Nash, DB
2003— Mark Bartosic, WR

SWARTHMORE (1)
89— Marshall Happer, OL

TAMPA (5)
65— John Perry, DB
68— Ron Brown, MG
70— Leon McQuay, RB
71— Ron Mikolajczyk, OT
Sammy Gellerstedt, MG

TARLETON ST. (1)
2006— Paul Williams, PK

TENN.-MARTIN (3)
68— Julian Nunnamaker, OG
88— Emanuel McNeil, DL
91— Oscar Bunch, TE

TENNESSEE ST. (24)
67— Claude Humphrey, DT
68— Jim Marsalis, DB
69— Joe Jones, DE
70— Vernon Holland, OT
71— Cliff Brooks, DB
Joe Gilliam, QB
72— Robert Woods, OT
Waymond Bryant, LB
73— Waymond Bryant, LB
Ed Jones, DE
74— Cleveland Elam, DE
81— †Mike Jones, WR
†Malcolm Taylor, DT
82— †Walter Tate, OL
86— †Onzy Elam, LB
90— †Colin Godfrey, P
93— †Brent Alexander, DB
98— †Tyrone Butterfield, WR
99— †Lamar Carter, DL
†Avion Black, RS
†Michael Thompson, OL
2003—†Charles Anthony, RB
04— †Charles Anthony, RB
06— †D. Rodgers-Cromartie, DB

TENNESSEE TECH (15)
52— Tom Fann, OT
59— Tom Hackler, E
60— Tom Hackler, E
61— David Baxter, T
69— Larry Schreiber, HB
71— Jim Youngblood, LB
72— Jim Youngblood, LB
74— Elois Grooms, DE
76— Ed Burns, OT
89— †Ryan Weeks, PK
96— †Robert Taylor, DB
2001—†Joey Bishop, OL
†D.J. Bleisath, DL
04— †Frank Omiyale, OL
†Brandon Shelby, DB

TENN. WESLEYAN (1)
92— Derrick Scott, PK

TEXAS-ARLINGTON (5)
66— Ken Ozee, DT
67— Robert Diem, OG
Robert Willbanks, S
83— †Mark Cannon, C
84— †Bruce Collie, OL

TEX. A&M-COMMERCE (23)
38— Darrell Tully, B
53— Bruno Ashley, G
58— Sam McCord, B
59— Sam McCord, B
68— Chad Brown, OT
70— William Lewis, C
72— Curtis Wester, OG
73— Autry Beamon, DB
84— Alan Veingrad, OG
88— Kim Morton, DL
90— Terry Bagsby, DL
91— Eric Turner, DB
Dwayne Phorne, OL
92— Eric Turner, DB
Pat Williams, DB
93— Fred Woods, LB
Billy Watkins, PK
95— Kevin Mathis, DB
96— Kevin Mathis, DB
99— Antonio Wilson, LB
2003— Chris Miller, P
05— J.D. Hearn, LB
06— Darvin Peterson, DB

TEX. A&M-KINGSVILLE (61)
40— Stuart Clarkson, C
41— Stuart Clarkson, C
59— Gerald Lambert, G
60— William Crafts, T
62— Douglas Harvey, C
63— Sid Blanks, B
65— Randy Johnson, QB
66— Dwayne Nix, OE
67— Dwayne Nix, OE
68— Dwayne Nix, OE
Ray Hickl, OG
70— Dwight Harrison, DB
Margarito Guerrero, MG
71— Eldridge Small, OE
Levi Johnson, DB
72— Ernest Price, DE
74— Don Hardeman, RB
75— David Hill, TE
76— Richard Ritchie, QB
Larry Grunewald, LB
77— Larry Collins, RB
John Barefield, DE
78— Billy John, OT
79— Andy Hawkins, LB
80— Don Washington, CB
81— Durwood Roquemore, DB
82— Darrell Green, DB
83— Loyd Lewis, OG
84— Neal Lattue, PK
85— Charles Smith, C
86— Johnny Bailey, RB
Moses Horn, OG
87— Johnny Bailey, RB
Moses Horn, OG
88— Rod Mounts, OL
Johnny Bailey, RB
John Randle, DL
89— Johnny Bailey, RB
90— Keithen DeGrate, OL
91— Brian Nielsen, OL
92— Earl Dotson, OL
93— Anthony Phillips, DB
Moke Simon, DL
94— Jeff Rodgers, DL
Kevin Dogins, C
95— Jermane Mayberry, OT
Jaime Martinez, OG
Kevin Dogins, C
96— Todd Perkins, OT
97— Chris Hensley, LB
98— Cedric Johnson, DB
Cliff Clemons, OL
99— Robert Garza, C
2000— Robert Garza, C
01— Kiah Johnson, LB
02— Mike Clay, DL
Nicholas Davis, DB
03— Kevin Palmer, OL
Eddie Moten, DB
04— Deandrae Fillmore, LB
05— Deandrae Fillmore, LB

TEXAS LUTHERAN (4)
73— David Wehmeyer, RB
74— D.W. Rutledge, LB
75— Jerry Ellis, OL
2004— Holt Storrie, PK

TEXAS SOUTHERN (4)
70— Nathaniel Allen, DB
76— Freddie Dean, OL
92— †Michael Strahan, DL
2006—† Stacey Thomas, DB

TEXAS ST. (16)
53— Pence Dacus, B
63— Jerry Cole, E
64— Jerry Cole, DB
72— Bob Daigle, C
75— Bobby Kotzur, DT
82— Tim Staskus, LB
83— Tim Staskus, LB
84— †Scott Forester, C
90— †Reggie Rivers, RB
91— †Ervin Thomas, C
94— †Don Wilkerson, RB
97— †Claude Mathis, RB
2000—†C.J. Carroll, DB
01— †Clenton Ballard, DL
04— †Cory Elolf, P
05— †Fred Evans, DL

TEXAS TECH* (2)
35— Herschel Ramsey, E
45— Walter Schlinkman, B

THIEL (2)
2001— Kennard Davis, DB
05— Dave Hendricks, OL

THOMAS MORE (6)
93— Mike Flesch, OL
96— Brent Moses, OL
97— Chris Wells, LB
98— Chris Wells, LB
2000— Will Castleberry, RB
06— Mark Carlisle, LB

TIFFIN (2)
93— Brian Diliberto, RB
2003— Nate Washington, WR

TOLEDO* (1)
38— Dan Buckwick, G

TOWSON (13)
75— Dan Dullea, QB
76— Skip Chase, OE
77— Randy Bielski, DB
78— Ken Snoots, SE
82— Sean Landeta, P
83— Gary Rubeling, DB
84— Terry Brooks, OG
85— Stan Eisentooth, OL
86— David Haden, LB
93— †Tony Vinson, RB
94— †Mark Orlando, WR
99— †Jamal White, WR
2000—†Andrew Hollingsworth, DL

TRINITY (CONN.) (10)
35— Mickey Kobrosky, B
36— Mickey Kobrosky, B
55— Charles Sticka, B
59— Roger LeClerc, C
70— David Kiarsis, HB
78— Pat McNamara, FL
93— Eric Mudry, DB
94— Greg Schramm, DB
2003— Jared Carillo, OL
05— Michael Blair, DL

TRINITY (TEX.) (19)
54— Alvin Beal, B
55— Hubert Cook, C
56— Milton Robichaux, E
67— Marvin Upshaw, DT
94— James Vallerie, LB
96— John Beckwith, LB
97— Paul Morris, PK
Danny Palmer, G
98— David Coney, DL
99— David Coney, OL
Ryan Deck, LB
Mike Burton, QB
2000— John Paul Visosky, LB
01— Bill Smith, OL
02— Roy Hampton, QB
Gary Ihfe, C
Jerheme Urban, WR
Jason Leshikar, LB
03— Jarrod Smith, DL

TROY* (23)
39— Sherrill Busby, E
73— Mark King, C
74— Mark King, C
76— Perry Griggs, OE
78— Tim Tucker, LB
80— Willie Tullis, QB
84— Mitch Geier, OG
86— Freddie Thomas, DB
87— Mike Turk, QB
Freddie Thomas, DB
94— †Bob Hall, OL
95— †Bob Hall, OL
96— †Pratt Lyons, DL
†Kerry Jenkins, OL
97— †Clifford Ivory, DB
†Andy Swafford, KR
98— †Marcus Spriggs, DL
†Cleve Roberts, OL
†Al Lucas, DT
99— †Al Lucas, DT
†Michael Moore, OT
†Anthony Rabb, LB
2000—†Lawrence Tynes, PK

TRUMAN (5)
60— Dale Mills, B
65— Richard Rhodes, OT
85— Chris Hegg, QB
93— Mike Roos, DL
96— Jarrett Anderson, RB

TUFTS (6)
34— William Grinnell, E
76— Tim Whelan, RB
78— Mark Buben, DL
79— Chris Connors, QB
80— Mike Brown, OL
86— Bob Patz, DL

TULSA* (1)
34— Rudy Prochaska, C

TUSCULUM (5)
94— Matt Schults, OL
95— Eric Claridy, RB
2002— Donald Amaker, RS
03— Alan Dunn, OT
Ricardo Colclough, DB/RS

TUSKEGEE (3)
98— Che' Bryant, DB
99— Andre Dudley, DL
2002— Drayton Florence, DB

UNION (N.Y.) (14)
39— Sam Hammerstrom, B
82— Steve Bodmer, DL
83— Tim Howell, LB

84— Brian Cox, DE
85— Anthony Valente, DL
86— Rich Romer, DL
87— Rich Romer, DL
91— Greg Harrison, PK
93— Marco Lainez, LB
96— Roger Egbert, PK
2001— Joshua Stinehour, DL
03— Cliff Eisenhut, PK
05— Tom Arcidiacono, RB
06— Tom Arcidiacono, RB

UNION (TENN.) (2)
41— James Jones, B
42— James Jones, B

UPSALA (1)
64— Dick Giessuebel, LB

URSINUS (3)
96— Peter Hinckle, DB
2000— Eric Cowie, DB
01— Shearrod Duncan, RB

VALDOSTA ST. (16)
82— Mark Catano, OL
86— Jessie Tuggle, LB
89— Randy Fisher, WR
90— Deon Searcy, DB
93— Chris Hatcher, QB
94— Chris Hatcher, QB
96— Lance Funderburk, QB
97— Richard Freeman, DL/DE
2000— Dusty Bonner, QB
C.J. Lofton, TE
01— Dusty Bonner, QB
Tully Payne, C
02— C.J. Lofton, TE
04— Torrey Howard, OL
Will Rhody, PK
05— Tim Thompson, DL

VALPARAISO (6)
51— Joe Pahr, B
71— Gary Puetz, OT
72— Gary Puetz, OT
76— John Belskis, DB
85— Mike Healey, WR
99— †Eric Kenesie, DB

VILLANOVA (13)
88— †Paul Berardelli, OL
89— †Bryan Russo, OL
91— †Curtis Eller, LB
92— †Curtis Eller, LB
94— †Tyrone Frazier, LB
96— †Brian Finneran, WR
97— †Brian Finneran, WR
†Chris Boden, QB
98— †Brian Westbrook, AP/WR
2000—†Brian Westbrook, AP/RS
01— †Eamonn Allen, OL
†Brian Westbrook, RB/AP
05— †Brian Hulea, LB

VMI (4)
88— †Mark Stock, WR
95— †Thomas Haskins, RB
96— †Thomas Haskins, RB
2000—†Richard Holland, KR

VIRGINIA ST. (6)
71— Larry Brooks, DT
84— John Greene, LB
85— James Ward, DL
98— Damon Thompson, AP
99— Damon Thompson, WR
2005— P.J. Berry, KR

VIRGINIA UNION (15)
73— Herb Scott, OG
74— Herb Scott, OG
75— Anthony Leonard, DB
77— Frank Dark, DB
79— Plummer Bullock, DE
80— William Dillon, DB
81— William Dillon, DB
82— William Dillon, DB
83— Larry Curtis, DT
88— Leroy Gause, LB
91— Paul DeBerry, DB
Kevin Williams, LB
99— Ronald Hardge, DB
2001— Ralph Hunter, DB
03— Reymond Murphy, RS

WABASH (8)
76— Jimmy Parker, DB
77— David Harvey, QB
81— Pete Metzelaars, TE
88— Tim Pliske, PK
89— Mike Funk, WR
2002— Ryan Short, TE
Nate Boulais, LB
03— Blair Hammer, DT

WAGNER (10)
67— John Gloistein, OT
80— Phil Theis, OL
81— Alonzo Patterson, RB
82— Alonzo Patterson, RB
83— Selwyn Davis, OT
86— Charles Stinson, DL
87— Rich Negrin, OT
88— Terry Underwood, RB
91— Walter Lopez, PK
99— †Rick Sarille, AP

WARTBURG (7)
94— Jamey Parker, OL
Vince Penningroth, DL
95— Vince Penningroth, DL
2001— Joel Demro, OL
03— Cody Kelley, DB/WR
Vince King, DL
04— Brian McIntire, DB

WASHBURN (4)
64— Robert Hardy, DB
88— Troy Slusser, WR
2005— Fletcher Terrell, DB
06— Trey Lewis, DL

WASHINGTON-ST. LOUIS (8)
72— Shelby Jordan, LB
73— Stu Watkins, OE
74— Marion Stallings, DB
88— Paul Matthews, TE
94— Matt Gomric, LB
95— Chris Nalley, DB
96— Chris Nalley, DB
99— Tim Runnalls, DL

WASH. & JEFF. (19)
84— Ed Kusko, OL
87— A.J. Pagano, RB
91— Chris Babirad, RB
Gilbert Floyd, DB
92— Chris Babirad, RB
Todd Pivnick, OL
Kevin Pintar, OL
93— Jason Moore, OL
Shawn Prendergast, LB
94— Matt Szczypinski, DL
Mike Jones, OL
Mike Brooder, DL
95— Mike Jones, OL
96— Dan Primrose, DL
2002— Roger Snyder, RS
03— Frank Pilato, DB
04— Frank Pilato, DB
05— Aaron Krepps, WR
06— Chris Teter, OL

WASH. & LEE (6)
76— Tony Perry, OE
81— Mike Pressler, DL
83— Glenn Kirschner, OL
86— John Packett, OL
95— Robert Hall, DL
2005— Stuart Sitterson, KR

WAYNE ST. (MICH.) (2)
2006— Joique Bell, RB
David Chudzinski, PK

WAYNE ST. (NEB.) (3)
84— Herve Roussel, PK
85— Ruben Mendoza, OL
95— Brad Ottis, DL

WAYNESBURG (1)
41— Nick George, G

WEBER ST. (22)
66— Ronald McCall, DE
67— Lee White, FB
Jim Schmedding, OG
69— Carter Campbell, DE
70— Henry Reed, DE
71— David Taylor, OT
77— Dennis Duncanson, DB
78— Dennis Duncanson, DB
Randy Jordan, WR
80— †Mike Humiston, LB
89— †Peter Macon, WR
91— †Jamie Martin, QB
†Alfred Pupunu, WR
93— †Pat McNarney, TE
95— †Pokey Eckford, WR
96— †Scott Shields, DB
97— †Cameron Quayle, TE
†Scott Shields, DB/AP
98— †Scott Shields, DB
2000—†Ryan Prince, TE
04— †Brady Fosmark, DL
05— †Paul McQuistan, OL

WESLEY (11)
91— Fran Naselli, KR
95— Brandon Steinheim, RB
96— Brandon Steinheim, RB
Demetrius Stevenson, DL
97— Nate Casella, LB
99— Sean McCullin, OL
2001— Jason Visconti, QB
04— Rocky Myers, DB
05— Mario Harris, DB
06— Mario Harris, DB
Bryan Robinson, DL

WESLEYAN (CONN.) (7)
46— Bert VanderClute, G
48— Jack Geary, T
72— Robert Heller, C
73— Robert Heller, C
76— John McVicar, DL
77— John McVicar, DL
99— Matt Perceval, WR

WEST ALA. (6)
82— Charles Martin, DT
84— Andrew Fields, WR
87— Ronnie Glanton, DL
93— Matt Carman, WR
97— John Sedely, PK
2006— Mitch Warfield, PK

WEST CHESTER (11)
52— Charles Weber, DG
58— Richard Emerich, T
61— Joe Iacone, B
62— Joe Iacone, B
72— Tim Pierantozzi, QB
76— William Blystone, RB
87— Ralph Tamm, OL
88— Bill Hess, WR
92— Lee Woodall, DL
98— Kevin Ingram, WR
99— Kevin Ingram, WR

WEST GA. (9)
96— Byron Slack, TE
97— Corey Jarrells, DB
Chris Williams, OT
98— Chris Williams, OL
2000— Abed Taha, OL
01— Nate Coggins, DB
02— Marquis Floyd, DB
05— Kelvin Morris, LB
06— Odell Willis, DL

WEST LIBERTY ST. (2)
97— Greg Dailer, WR
2006— Darren Banks, DB

WEST TEX. A&M (7)
86— Stan Carraway, WR
90— Mark Bounds, P
94— Brad Bailey, WR
Brian Hurley, OL
95— Jon Mason, P
2005— Pat McCoy, OL
06— Jared Brock, LB

WEST VIRGINIA* (1)
34— Tod Goodwin, E

WEST VA. TECH (3)
82— Elliott Washington, DB
86— Calvin Wallace, DL
89— Phil Hudson, WR

WEST VA. WESLEYAN (2)
36— George Mike, T
82— Jerry Free, T

WESTERN CARO. (15)
49— Arthur Byrd, G
71— Steve Williams, DT
73— Mark Ferguson, OT
74— Jerry Gaines, SE
Steve Yates, LB
84— †Louis Cooper, DL
†Kirk Roach, PK
†Steve Kornegay, P
85— †Clyde Simmons, DL
86— †Alonzo Carmichael, TE
†Kirk Roach, PK
87— †Kirk Roach, PK
93— †Kerry Hayes, KR/WR
98— †Eric Johnson, DB
†Ken Hinsley, P

WESTERN CONN. ST. (3)
99— Greg Boucher, DL
2000— Jason Plachcinski, OT
Greg Boucher, DL

WESTERN ILL. (31)
59— Bill Larson, B
61— Leroy Jackson, B
74— John Passananti, OT
76— Scott Levenhagen, TE
Greg Lee, DB
77— Craig Phalen, DT
78— Bill Huskisson, DL
80— Mike Maher, TE
Don Greco, OG
83— †Chris Gunderson, MG
84— †Chris Gunderson, T
86— †Frank Winters, C
†Todd Auer, DL
88— †Marlin Williams, DL
93— †Rodney Harrison, DB
94— †Ross Schulte, P
97— †Aaron Stecker, RB
†Jason Grott, OL
98— †David Watson, DE
†David Bowens, DL
†James Milton, LB
99— †Edgerton Hartwell, LB
2000—†Edgerton Hartwell, LB
†Mike Scifres, P
02— †Justin Langan, PK
†R.J. Luke, TE
†Brian Caesar, DL
†Mike Scifres, P
03— †Mike O'Brien, DL
†Lee Russell, LB
04— †Justin Langan, PK

WESTERN KY. (29)
64— Dale Lindsey, LB
70— Lawrence Brame, DE
73— Mike McKoy, DB
74— John Bushong, DL
Virgil Livers, DB
75— Rick Green, LB
77— Chip Carpenter, OL
80— †Pete Walters, OG
†Tim Ford, DL
81— †Donnie Evans, DE
82— †Paul Gray, LB
83— †Paul Gray, LB
87— †James Edwards, DB
88— †Dean Tiebout, OL
†Joe Arnold, RB
95— †Brian Bixler, C
97— †Patrick Goodman, OL
98— †Patrick Goodman, C
2000—†Bobby Sippio, DB
†Melvin Wisham, LB
01— †Erik Dandy, LB
†Mel Mitchell, DB
02— †Chris Price, OL
†Sherrod Coates, LB
03— †Buster Ashley, OL
†Matt Lange, PK
†Erik Dandy, LB
04— †Buster Ashley, OL
05— †Erik Losey, OL

WESTERN MICH.* (1)
82— †Matt Meares, OL

WESTERN N.M. (4)
83— Jay Ogle, WR
88— Pat Maxwell, P
97— Anthony Gray, RB
98— Anthony Gray, RB

WESTERN ORE. (2)
2000— Brian Crawford, OL
05— Kevin Boss, TE

WESTERN ST. (12)
56— Bill Rhodes, B
78— Bill Campbell, DB
80— Justin Cross, OT
84— Jeff Guy, P
92— Reggie Alexander, WR
94— Derren Bryan, OL
96— Ben Kern, TE
Kurt Clay, DB
97— Shane Carwin, LB
2001— Josh Hotchkiss, LB
03— Chaumont Bouknight, RB
Travis Snyder, PK

WESTERN WASH. (5)
51— Norman Hash, DB
79— Patrick Locker, RB
95— Orlando Steinauer, DB
2000— Erik Totten, RS
02— Michael Koenen, P

WESTFIELD ST. (1)
2001— Josue Zamora, LB

WESTMINSTER (MO.) (6)
97— Scott Pingel, WR
98— Scott Pingel, WR
Logan Stanley, TE
Justin Peery, QB
99— Scott Pingel, WR
Justin Peery, QB

WESTMINSTER (PA.) (10)
73— Robert Pontius, DB
77— Rex Macey, FL
82— Gary DeGruttola, LB
83— Scott Higgins, DB
86— Joe Keaney, LB
88— Kevin Myers, LB
89— Joe Micchia, QB
90— Brad Tokar, RB
91— Brian DeLorenzo, DL
92— Matt Raich, LB

WHEATON (ILL.) (17)
55— Dave Burnham, B
58— Robert Bakke, T
77— Larry Wagner, LB
78— Scott Hall, QB
83— Keith Bishop, QB
95— Doug Johnston, OL
Chip Parrish, LB
96— Chip Parrish, LB
Mark Loeffler, WR
97— Chris Brown, OL
99— Chris Baughman, PK
2002— James Hoxworth, OL
03— James Hoxworth, OL
04— Brad Musso, W
05— Andrew Day, PK
06— Geoff Rowson, OL
Andy Studebaker, DL

WHITTIER (3)
38— Myron Claxton, T
62— Richard Peter, T
77— Michael Ciacci, DB

WHITWORTH (7)
52— Pete Swanson, OG
54— Larry Paradis, T
85— Wayne Ralph, WR
86— Wayne Ralph, WR
2000— Sky Blake, DL
05— Michael Allan, TE
06— Michael Allan, TE

WIDENER (21)
72— Billy Johnson, RB
73— Billy Johnson, RB
75— John Warrington, DB
76— Al Senni, OL
77— Chip Zawoiski, RB
79— Tom Deery, DB
80— Tom Deery, DB
81— Tom Deery, DB
82— Tony Stefanoni, DL
88— Dave Duffy, DL
94— O.J. McElroy, DL
Antoine Moore, DB
95— Blaise Coleman, LB
98— Bill Nourse, DL
99— Tom Eisenhower, LB
2000— Jim Jones, WR
01— Michael Coleman, WR
Jim Jones, WR
T.J. Hess, DB
02— Ryan Killian, DL
03— Thomas DeMoss, DL

WILKES (6)
73— Jeff Grandinetti, DT
93— Jason Feese, DL
97— J.J. Fadden, DL
2003— Brett Trichilo, RB
04— Brett Trichilo, RB
06— Anthony Serafin, DL

WILLAMETTE (16)
34— Loren Grannis, G
35— John Oravec, B
36— Richard Weisgerber, B
46— Marvin Goodman, E
58— William Long, C
59— Marvin Cisneros, G
64— Robert Burles, DT
65— Robert Burles, DT
69— Calvin Lee, LB
75— Gary Johnson, DL
82— Richard Milroy, DB
97— Kamell Eckroth-Bernard, DB
98— Brian Greer, OL
2004— Nate Matlock, DL
06— Brandon Bennett, OL

WILLIAM & MARY (14)
83— †Mario Shaffer, OL
86— †Michael Clemons, RB
89— †Steve Christie, P
90— †Pat Crowley, DL
93— †Craig Staub, DL
95— †Darren Sharper, DB
96— †Josh Beyer, OL
†Darren Sharper, DB
97— †Ron Harrison, DB
99— †Brett Sterba, PK
2000—†Raheem Walker, DL
02— †Dwight Beard, OL
03— †Rich Musinski, WR
04— †Lang Campbell, QB

WILLIAM JEWELL (4)
52— Al Conway, B
73— John Strada, OE
81— Guy Weber, DL
83— Mark Mundel, OL

WM. PATERSON (2)
92— Craig Paskas, DB
93— Craig Paskas, DB

WILLIAM PENN (1)
72— Bruce Polen, DB

WILLIAMS (9)
51— Charles Salmon, DG
69— Jack Maitland, HB
74— John Chandler, LB
78— Greg McAleenan, DB
90— George Rogers, DL
94— Bobby Walker, LB
95— Ethan Brooks, DL
2002— Scott Farley, SpT/DB
03— Graham Goldwasser, LB

WILMINGTON (OHIO) (6)
72— William Roll, OG
94— Jason Tincher, WR
2000— Antonio Broadnax, DB
01— Antonio Broadnax, DB
04— Brandon Tisdale, DL
06— Chad Otte, DB

WINGATE (2)
89— Jimmy Sutton, OT
2006— David Jones, DB

WINONA ST. (10)
92— Dave Ludy, AP
94— Dave Ludy, AP
97— Jamey Hutchinson, DB
2002— Kevin Curtin, RS
Deric Sieck, LB
03— Kevin Curtin, RS
Deric Sieck, LB
04— Chris Samp, WR
05— Brian Hynes, WR
06— John Tackman, LB

WINSTON-SALEM (9)
77— Cornelius Washington, DB
78— Tim Newsome, RB
84— Danny Moore, OG
87— Barry Turner, G
95— Richard Huntley, RB
96— LaTori Workman, DL
99— Thomas Washington, DL
2001— Stephon Kelly, DB
03— Brandon Hussey, RS

WIS.-EAU CLAIRE (1)
81— Roger Vann, RB

WIS.-LA CROSSE (21)
52— Ted Levanhagen, LB
72— Bryon Buelow, DB
78— Joel Williams, LB
83— Jim Byrne, DL
85— Tom Newberry, OL
88— Ted Pretasky, RB
89— Terry Strouf, OL
91— Jon Lauscher, LB
92— Norris Thomas, DB
Mike Breit, LB
93— Rick Schaaf, DL
95— Craig Kusick, QB
Erik Halverson, OL
96— Erik Halverson, OL
Mike Maslowski, LB
97— Ric Mathias, DB
99— Brock Ryan, DL
2000— Jeff Kostrewa, TE
Brian Portilia, DB
03— Andrew Mocadlo, RB
06— Steve Teeples, DB

WIS.-MILWAUKEE (1)
70— Pete Papara, LB

WIS.-PLATTEVILLE (2)
73— William Vander Velden, DE
86— Mike Hintz, DB

WIS.-RIVER FALLS (6)
80— Gerald Sonsalla, OG
82— Roland Hall, LB
87— Greg Corning, RB
95— Brian Izdepski, OT
99— Joe Green, DL
2000— Michael Snowberry, C

WIS.-STEVENS POINT (9)
77— Reed Giordana, QB
81— Chuck Braun, WR
92— Randy Simpson, DB
93— Jimmy Henderson, RB
94— Randy Simpson, LB
97— Clint Kriewalt, LB
98— Clint Kriewalt, LB
99— Andy Palzkill, DB
2003— Scott Krause, QB

WIS.-STOUT (8)
79— Joseph Bullis, DL
2000— Jeff Hazuga, DL
Kevin McCulley, P
01— Tony Beckham, DB
02— Tyrone Rhone, DB
Jamie Spielman, LB
03— Ben Knepper, OL
05— Joe Seep, DB

WIS.-SUPERIOR (3)
66— Mel Thake, DB
83— Larry Banks, MG
85— Phil Eiting, LB

WIS.-WHITEWATER (17)
75— William Barwick, OL
79— Jerry Young, WR
82— Daryl Schleim, DE
90— Reggie White, OL
96— Derrick LeVake, OL
97— Derrick LeVake, OL
2003— Chad Nimm, OL
Chad Wurth, PK
04— Trey Bell, DB
05— Justin Beaver, RB
Brady Ramseier, OL
Robb Widuch, LB
06— Justin Beaver, RB
Ryan Kleepe, DL
Max Sakellaris, OL
Jeff Schebler, PK
Derek Stanley, WR

WITTENBERG (30)
62— Donald Hunt, G
63— Bob Cherry, E
64— Chuck Green, QB
68— Jim Felts, DE
73— Steve Drongowski, OT
74— Arthur Thomas, LB
75— Robert Foster, LB
76— Dean Caven, DL
78— Dave Merritt, RB
79— Joe Govern, DL
80— Mike Dowds, DE
81— Bill Beach, DB
83— Bryant Lemon, DL
87— Eric Horstman, OL
88— Ken Bonner, OT
Eric Horstman, OL
90— Jon Warga, RB
92— Taver Johnson, LB
93— Taver Johnson, LB
Greg Brame, PK
95— Ron Cunningham, OT
Jimmy Watts, PK
96— Xan Smith, OL
97— Jonathan Farley, C
Kent Rafey, LB
Russ Fedyk, KR
98— Ken Pope, DB
99— Casey Donaldson, RB
2005— Jacob Thomas, P
06— Tristan Murray, RB

WOFFORD (21)
42— Aubrey Faust, E
47— Ken Dubard, T
49— Elbert Hammett, T
51— Jack Beeler, DB
57— Charles Bradshaw, B
61— Dan Lewis, G
70— Sterling Allen, OG
79— Keith Kinard, OL
90— David Wiley, OL
91— Tom Colter, OL
94— Brian Porzio, PK
97— †Dan Williams, OL/C
2002—†Anthony Jones, DL
†Matt Nelson, DB
03— †Eric Deutsch, OL
†Bobby Gibbs, OL
†Lee Basinger, DL
†Matt Nelson, DB
04— †Eric Deutsch, OL
†Lee Basinger, DL
05— †Katon Bethay, DL

WOOSTER (7)
79— Blake Moore, C
99— Seth Duerr, LB
2000— Seth Duerr, LB
03— Tony Sutton, RB
04— Tony Sutton, RB
Joe Kearney, DL
06— Rick Drushal, OL

WPI (3)
97— Matt Surette, TE
98— Matt Surette, TE
2003— Miguel Concepcion, RS

WORCESTER ST. (5)
92— Chris Butts, DB
93— Chris Butts, DB
94— Brian Fitzpatrick, DB
2000— Russ Watson, DL
01— Russ Watson, DL

XAVIER (OHIO) (1)
51— Tito Carinci, LB

YALE (4)
84— †John Zanieski, DL
2003—†Nate Lawrie, TE
04— †Rory Hennessey, OL
06— †Ed McCarthy, OL

YOUNGSTOWN ST. (30)
74— Don Calloway, DB
75— Don Calloway, DB
78— Ed McGlasson, OL
79— James Ferranti, OE
Jeff Lear, OT
80— Jeff Gergel, LB
81— †Paris Wicks, RB
82— †Paris Wicks, RB
88— †Jim Zdelar, OL

89— †Paul Soltis, LB
90— †Tony Bowens, DL
91— †Pat Danko, DL
92— †Dave Roberts, DB
93— †Drew Garber, OL
†Tamron Smith, RB
†Jeff Wilkins, PK
94— †Randy Smith, KR
†Leon Jones, LB
†Lester Weaver, DB
†Chris Sammarone, OL
95— †Leon Jones, LB
†Jermaine Hopkins, DL
97— †Matt Hogg, OL
†Harry Deligianis, DL
99— †Ian Dominelli, LB
2000—†Tim Johnson, LB
01— †Pat Crummey, OL
†LeVar Greene, DB
06— †Ryan Jewell, OL
†Marcus Mason, RB

NCAA Postgraduate Scholarship Winners

Following are football players who are NCAA postgraduate scholarship winners, whether or not they were able to accept the grant, plus all alternates (indicated by *) who accepted grants. The program began with the 1964 season. (Those who played in 1964 are listed as 1965 winners, those who played in 1965 as 1966 winners, etc.) To qualify, student-athletes must maintain a 3.000 grade-point average (on a 4.000 scale) during their collegiate careers, perform with distinction in varsity football and behave, on and off the field, in a manner that has brought credit to the student-athlete, his institution and intercollegiate athletics.

ABILENE CHRISTIAN
71— James Lindsey
83—* Grant Feasel
85— Daniel Remsberg
86—* James Embry
Craig Huff
90— William Clayton

ADAMS ST.
2000—Ryan Hollingshead

ADRIAN
94— Jeffrey Toner

AIR FORCE
65— Edward Fausti
67— James Hogarty
68— Kenneth Zagzebski
69—* Richard Rivers Jr.
70— Charles Longnecker
* Alfred Wurglitz
71— Ernest Jennings
Robert Parker Jr.
72— Darryl Haas
73— Mark Prill
75—* Joseph Debes
84— Jeffrey Kubiak
86— Derek Brown
88— Chad Hennings
89— David Hlatky
90— Steven Wilson
91— Christopher Howard
92— Ronald James
93— Scott Hufford
95— Preston McConnell
96— Bret Cillessen
97— Carlton Hendrix
99— Charles Gilliam
2000—Cale Bonds

UAB
97— John Rea
2000—Lee Carter

ALABAMA
69— Donald Sutton
72— John Musso Jr.
75— Randy Hall
80— Steadman Shealy
2006—DeMeco Ryans

ALABAMA ST.
92— Edward Robinson Jr.

ALBANY (N.Y.)
88—* Thomas Higgins

ALBION
81— Joel Manby
94— Michael Montico
95— Jeffrey Shooks
96— Timothy Schafer
97— Kyle Klein
98— Neil Johnson

ALBRIGHT
67—* Paul Chaiet

ALLEGHENY
65— David Wion
92— Darren Hadlock
97— Nicholas Reiser

ALMA
67— Keith Bird Jr.
79— Todd Friesner
99— Eric Brands
2000—Dustin Armstrong
07— Joshua Brehm

AMHERST
66— David Greenblatt
76— Geoffrey Miller
85— Raymond Nurme
96— Gregory Schneider

ANGELO ST.
99— Kyle Kirk
2002—Curry Dawson

APPALACHIAN ST.
78— Gill Beck
93— D.J. Campbell

ARIZONA
69— William Michael Moody
78— Jon Abbott
80— Jeffrey Whitton
88— Charles Cecil
97— Wayne Wyatt

ARIZONA ST.
78— John Harris
90— Mark Tingstad
97— Devin Kendall
98— Patrick Tillman

ARKANSAS
70— Terry Stewart
71— William Burnett
79— William Bradford Shoup
85—* Mark Lee

ARKANSAS ST.
72— John Meyer
77— Thomas Humphreys

ARKANSAS TECH
2001—Paul Peletz

ARMY
66— Samuel Champi Jr.
68— Bohdan Neswiacheny
69— James McCall Jr.
Thomas Wheelock
70— Theodore Shadid Jr.
78— Curtis Downs
81—* Stanley March
86— Donald Smith
Douglas Black
88— William Conner
90— Michael Thorson
93— Michael McElrath
95— Eric Oliver

ASHLAND
78— Daniel Bogden
88— David Biondo
90— Douglas Powell

AUBURN
66— John Cochran
69—* Roger Giffin
85— Gregg Carr
90— James Lyle IV

AUGSBURG
90— Terry Mackenthun
98— Ted Schultz

AUGUSTANA (ILL.)
69—* Jeffrey Maurus
71— Kenneth Anderson
77— Joe Thompson
86— Steven Sanders
96— Thomas King
97— Ryan Carpenter
99— Chris Meskan
2001—MacKenzie Hay
03— Todd Baldwin

AUGUSTANA (S.D.)
72— Michael Olson
75— David Zelinsky
77— James Clemens
78— Dee Donlin
Roger Goebel
90—* David Gubbrud
91— Scott Boyens
97— Mitchell Pruett

BALL ST.
67—* John Hostrawser
73— Gregory Mack
77— Arthur Yaroch
84— Richard Chitwood
88— Ronald Duncan
90— Theodore Ashburn
93— Troy Hoffer
2004—Travis Barclay

BATES
79— Christopher Howard

BAYLOR
65— Michael Kennedy
66— Edward Whiddon
94— John Eric Joe

BENEDICTINE (ILL.)
70— David Cyr
71— Thomas Danaher

BETHEL (MINN.)
2005—Matt Wassink

BOISE ST.
72— Brent McIver
76—* Glenn Sparks
79— Samuel Miller
82— Kip Bedard
92— Larry Stayner
93— David Tingstad

BOSTON COLLEGE
66—* Lawrence Marzetti
67— Michael O'Neill
69— Gary Andrachik
70— Robert Bouley
78— Richard Scudellari
87— Michael Degnan

BOSTON U.
69— Suren Donabedian Jr.
81— David Bengtson

BOWDOIN
65— Steven Ingram
67— Thomas Allen

BOWIE ST.
92— Mark Fitzgerald

BOWLING GREEN
77— Richard Preston
78— Mark Miller
91— Patrick Jackson

BRIDGEPORT
70— Terry Sparker

BRIDGEWATER (VA.)
2002—Matthew Huffman

BRIGHAM YOUNG
67— Virgil Carter
76— Orrin Olsen
77—* Stephen Miller
78— Gifford Nielsen
80— Marc Wilson
82— Daniel Plater
83— Bart Oates
84— Steve Young
85— Marvin Allen
89— Charles Cutler
94— Eric Drage
97— Chad Lewis

BROWN
65— John Kelly Jr.
70— James Lukens
74— Douglas Jost
75— William Taylor
77— Scott Nelson
78— Louis Cole
79— Robert Forster
82— Travis Holcombe
95— Rene Abdalah
2006—Nicolas Hartigan

BUCKNELL
71—* Kenneth Donahue
74— John Dailey
75— Steve Leskinen
77— Lawrence Brunt
85— David Kucera
93— David Berardinelli

BUENA VISTA
77— Steven Trost
87— Michael Habben
94— Cary Murphy

BUFFALO ST.
87— James Dunbar

BUTLER
72— George Yearsich
78— William Ginn
85— Stephen Kollias

C.W. POST
79— John Luchsinger

CALIFORNIA
66— William Krum
67— John Schmidt
68— Robert Crittenden
70— James Calkins
71— Robert Richards
83— Harvey Salem
94— Douglas Brien

UC DAVIS
76— Daniel Carmazzi
David Gellerman
77— Rolf Benirschke
79— Mark Markel
86— Robert Hagenau
90—* James Tomasin
92— Robert Kincade
Michael Shepard
93— Brian Andersen
97— Mark Grieb
99— Wesley Terrell

UC RIVERSIDE
72— Tyrone Hooks
74— Gary Van Jandegian

CAL LUTHERAN
90—* Gregory Maw

CAL POLY
69— William Creighton

CALTECH
67— William Mitchell
68— John Frazzini
74— Frank Hobbs Jr.

CANISIUS
84— Thomas Schott

CAPITAL
84—* Michael Linton

CARLETON
67— Robert Paarlberg
73— Mark Williams
83— Paul Vaaler
93— Arthur Gilliland

CARNEGIE MELLON
80— Gusty Sunseri
91— Robert O'Toole
99— Jason Funke
2000—Mike Campie

CARROLL (WIS.)
77— Stephen Thompson
95— Christopher Klippel

CARSON-NEWMAN
2001—Charlie Walker Jr.

CARTHAGE
70— William Radakovitz

CASE RESERVE
89— Christopher Nutter
91— James Meek
2006—Santo Maimone IV

CENTRAL (IOWA)
71— Vernon Den Herder
87— Scott Lindell
89— Eric Perry
92— Richard Kacmarynski
96— Rick Sanger

CENTRAL ARK.
96— Brian Barnett
2004—Landon Trusty
06— Cory Cangelosi

CENTRAL MICH.
77— John Wunderlich
80—* Michael Ball
85— Kevin Egnatuk
88— Robert Stebbins
92— Jeffrey Bender

CENTRAL MO.
99— Shane Meyer

CENTRAL WASH.
70— Danny Collins

CENTRE
69— Glenn Shearer
86— Casteel "Teel" Bruner II
88—* Robert Clark
90— James Ellington

CHADRON ST.
96— Corey Campbell

CHATTANOOGA
67— Harvey Ouzts
72—* Frank Webb
74— John McBrayer
76— Russell Gardner

CHEYNEY
76— Steven Anderson

CHICAGO
86—* Bruce Montella
89— Paul Haar
94— Frank Baker
2007—Benjamin Potts

CINCINNATI
71—* Earl Willson

CITADEL
74— Thomas Leitner
79— Kenneth Caldwell

84—* William West IV
97— Derek Beres

CLAREMONT-M-S
68— Craig Dodel
70—* Gregory Long
71— Stephen Endemano
73— Christopher Stecher
74— Samuel Reece

CLEMSON
65— James Bell Jr.
68— James Addison
73— Benjamin Anderson
79— Stephen Fuller

COAST GUARD
73— Rodney Leis
74— Leonard Kelly
81— Bruce Hensel
89—* Ty Rinoski
* Jeffery Peters
90— Richard Schachner
91— John Freda

COASTAL CARO.
2007—Anthony Franklin

COE
67— Lynn Harris

COLBY
71— Ronald Lupton
Frank Apantaku

COLGATE
73— Kenneth Nelson
80— Angelo Colosimo
89— Donald Charney

COLORADO
93— James Hansen

COLORADO COL.
69— Steven Ehrhart
72— Randy Bobier
75— Bruce Kolbezen
84— Herman Motz III
97— Ryan Egeland
98— Christopher Smith

COLORADO MINES
66— Stuart Bennett
67— Michael Greensburg
Charles Kirby
75— David Chambers

COLORADO ST.
65— Russel Mowrer
76— Mark Driscoll
87— Stephan Bartalo
88— Joseph Brookhart
93— Gregory Primus
96— Gregory Myers
99— Nathaniel Kvamme

COLORADO ST.-PUEBLO
70— Gregory Smith
73— Collon Kennedy III

COLUMBIA
72— John Sefcik
80— Mario Biaggi Jr.

CONCORDIA-M'HEAD
2005—Jordan Talge

CONNECTICUT
77—* Bernard Palmer

CORNELL
68— Ronald Kipicki
72— Thomas Albright
84— Derrick Harmon

CORNELL COLLEGE
65— Steven Miller
72— David Hilmers
73— Robert Ash
79— Brian Farrell
Thomas Zinkula
81—* Timothy Garry
83— John Ward
93— Brent Sands
94— Matthew Miller
95— Mark McDermott
99— Matthew Weiss

DARTMOUTH
66— Anthony Yezer
68— Henry Paulson Jr.

69— Randolph Wallick
71— Willie Bogan
73— Frederick Radke
74— Thomas Csatari
* Robert Funk
77— Patrick Sullivan
89— Paul Sorensen
95— O. Josh Bloom
98— Dominic Lanza

DAVIDSON
66— Stephen Smith
71— Rick Lyon
72— Robert Norris
86—* Louis Krempel
97— John Cowan Jr.

DAYTON
73— Timothy Quinn
76— Roy Gordon III
83—* Michael Pignatiello
91— Daniel Sharley
2003—Mark Kasmer

DELAWARE
86— Brian Farrell

DELAWARE VALLEY
85— Daniel Glowatski

DELTA ST.
76— William Hood

DENISON
70— Richard Trumball
73— Steven Smiljanich
76—* Dennis Thome
78— David Holcombe
86— Brian Gearinger
88— Grant Jones
92— Jonathan Fortkamp
2000—Jon Dunhan

DePAUW
68— Bruce Montgomerie
78— Mark Frazer
81— Jay True
85— Richard Bonaccorsi
86— Anthony deNicola
92— Thomas Beaulieu
2000—Tyler Kelley

DICKINSON
66— Robert Averback
71—* John West
75—* Gerald Urich

DOANE
68— John Lothrop
70— Richard Held

DRAKE
73— Joseph Worobec

DREXEL
72— Blake Lynn Ferguson

DUBUQUE
82— Timothy Finn

DUKE
68— Robert Lasky
71—* Curt Rawley

EAST CARO.
92— Keith Arnold

EAST TENN. ST.
82— Jay Patterson

EASTERN KY.
78— Steven Frommeyer

EASTERN N.M.
66— Richard James

EASTERN WASH.
98— Steven Mattson

ELIZABETH CITY ST.
73— Darnell Johnson
80— David Nickelson

ELMHURST
80— Richard Green

EMORY & HENRY
82— Thomas Browder Jr.

EMPORIA ST.
2004—Tyler Paul

EVANSVILLE
75— David Mattingly
76— Charles Uhde Jr.
79—* Neil Saunders

FERRIS ST.
79— Robert Williams
93— Monty Brown

FLORIDA
72— Carlos Alvarez
77— Darrell Carpenter
85— Garrison Rolle
87— Bret Wiechmann
90—* Cedric Smith
91— Huey Richardson
95— Michael Gilmore
97— Danny Wuerffel
99— Terrance Jackson

FLORIDA ST.
88— David Palmer
91— David Roberts
94— Kenneth Alexander
95— Derrick Brooks
98— Daryl Bush

FORDHAM
91— Eric Schweiker

FORT HAYS ST.
94— David Foster
99— Clinton Albers
2002—Casey Seyfert

FRANK. & MARSH.
69— Frank deGenova
83—* Robert Shepardson
2004—Daniel Houseman

FRESNO ST.
70—* Henry Corda
74— Dwayne Westphal
83— William Griever Jr.

FROSTBURG ST.
2000—Marty Mood

FURMAN
77— Thomas Holcomb III
82— Charles Anderson
84— Ernest Gibson
86—* David Jager
87— Stephen Squire
90— Christopher Roper
92— Paul Siffri
Eric Von Walter
96— William Phillip Jones
2007—Adnan Filipovic

GANNON
97— Patrick Rodkey

GEORGETOWN
75— James Chesley Jr.
98— Stephen Iorio
2000—Jim Gallagher

GEORGIA
68— Thomas Lawhorne Jr.
69— William Payne
71— Thomas Lyons
72— Thomas Nash Jr.
Raleigh Mixon Robinson
78— Jeffrey Lewis
80— Jeffrey Pyburn
81— Christopher Welton
84— Terrell Hoage
88— Kim Stephens
89— Richard Tardits
99— Matthew Stinchcomb
2003—Jonathan Stinchcomb

GA. SOUTHERN
2000—Voncellies Allen

GEORGIA TECH
68— William Eastman
75— James Robinson
81— Sheldon Fox
83— Ellis Gardner
86— John Ivemeyer
2003—Daniel Dyke

GETTYSBURG
70—* Herbert Ruby III
80— Richard Swartz
2003—Clifford Mason

GRAMBLING
73— Stephen Dennis

GRINNELL
72— Edward Hirsch
80—* Derek Muehrcke
2000—Troy Dougherty

GROVE CITY
95— Stephen Sems

GUST. ADOLPHUS
74— James Goodwin
81—* David Najarian
2002—Brian Bergstrom

HAMLINE
85— Kyle Aug
91— Robert Hackney

HAMPDEN-SYDNEY
78—* Wilson Newell
80— Timothy Maxa

HARVARD
68— Alan Bersin
71—* Richard Frisbie
75— Patrick McInally
76— William Emper
81— Charles Durst
85— Brian Bergstrom
87— Scott Collins

HAWAII
68— James Roberts
73—* Don Satterlee

HIRAM
68— Sherman Riemenschneider
74— Donald Brunetti

HOLY CROSS
84—* Bruce Kozerski
89— Jeffrey Wiley
91— John Lavalette

HOPE
74— Ronald Posthuma
80— Craig Groendyk
83— Kurt Brinks
85—* Scott Jecmen
98— Brandon Graham

HOUSTON
86— Gary Schoppe
87— Robert Brezina
99— Peter deGroot

IDAHO
67— Michael Lavens
Joseph McCollum Jr.
84— Boyce Bailey

IDAHO ST.
76— Richard Rodgers
92— Steven Boyenger

ILLINOIS
72— Robert Bucklin
73— Laurence McCarren Jr.
91— Curtis Lovelace
92— Michael Hopkins
93— John Wright

ILL. WESLEYAN
93— Christopher Bisaillon
97— Lon Erickson

INDIANA
73— Glenn Scolnik
79— David Abrams
81— Kevin Speer

INDIANA (PA.)
78—* John Mihota
84— Kenneth Moore

INDIANA ST.
86— Jeffrey Miller

INDIANAPOLIS
76— Rodney Pawlik

IONA
81— Neal Kurtti
82—* Paul Rupp

IOWA
69— Michael Miller
76— Robert Elliott
78— Rodney Sears
86— Larry Station Jr.
88— Michael Flagg
89— Charles Hartlieb
99— Matthew Reischl
Derek Rose

IOWA ST.
70— William Bliss

JACKSON ST.
80—* Lester Walls

JACKSONVILLE ST.
79— Dewey Barker

JAMES MADISON
79— Warren Coleman
90— Mark Kiefer

JOHN CARROLL
2006—Douglas Phillips

JOHNS HOPKINS
73— Joseph Ouslander
74— Gunter Glocker
94— Steuart Markley
95— Michael House
99— Lawrence Gulotta
2007—Brian Nickel

JUNIATA
72— Maurice Taylor
87— Robert Crossey

KANSAS
65— Ronald Oelschlager
69— David Morgan
72— Michael McCoy
73— John Schroll
78— Tom Fitch
87— Mark Henderson

KANSAS ST.
66—* Larry Anderson
83— James Gale
88— Matthew Garver

KENTUCKY
76— Thomas Ranieri
79— James Kovach
84—* Keith Martin
97— Michael Schellenberger

KENTUCKY ST.
68— James Jackson

KENYON
75— Patrick Clements

KNOX
88— Robert Monroe

LAFAYETTE
71— William Sprecher
76— Michael Kline
78— Victor Angeline III

LAMAR
73—* Richard Kubiak

LAWRENCE
68— Charles McKee
83— Christopher Matheus

LEBANON VALLEY
74—* Alan Shortell

LEHIGH
66— Robert Adelaar
68— Richard Miller
73—* Thomas Benfield
75— James Addonizio
76—* Robert Liptak
77—* Michael Yaszemski
80— David Melone

LONG BEACH ST.
84— Joseph Donohue

LA.-LAFAYETTE
71—* George Coussa

LA.-MONROE
93— Darren Rimmer
94— Robert Cobb
Michael Young

LSU
79— Robert Dugas
83— James Britt
88— Ignazio Albergamo
91— Solomon Graves
94— Chad Loup
95— Michael Blanchard
98— Chad Kessler
2006—Rudolph Niswanger

LUTHER
67— Thomas Altemeier
78—* Mark Larson
85— Larry Bonney

MARIETTA
98— Thomas Couhig

MARYLAND
78— Jonathan Claiborne

MARYVILLE (TENN.)
67— Frank Eggers II

MIT
91— Darcy Prather
92— Rodrigo Rubiano
93— Roderick Tranum
95— Corey Foster
99— Duane Stevens
2000—Nik Kozy
03— Keith Battocchi

McDANIEL
99— Thomas Lapato
2002—Jason Wingeart

McNEESE ST.
81— Daryl Burckel
86— Ross Leger

MEMPHIS
77—* James Mincey Jr.

MERCHANT MARINE
70— Robert Lavinia
76—* John Castagna

MIAMI (FLA.)
90— Robert Chudzinski
91— Michael Sullivan

MICHIGAN
67— David Fisher
74— David Gallagher
81—* John Wangler
82— Norm Betts
84— Stefan Humphries
Thomas Dixon
86— Clayton Miller
87— Kenneth Higgins
93— Christopher Hutchinson
94— Marc Milia
98— Brian Griese
2000—Rob Renes

MICHIGAN ST.
69— Allen Brenner
70— Donald Baird
94— Steven Wasylk

MICHIGAN TECH
72— Larry Ras
74— Bruce Trusock
75— Daniel Rhude

MIDDLE TENN.
73—* Edwin Zaunbrecher

MIDDLEBURY
79— Franklin Kettle

MIDLAND LUTHERAN
76— Thomas Hale

MILLERSVILLE
92— Thomas Burns III

MILLIKIN
90—* Charles Martin

MILLSAPS
67— Edward Weller
73—* Russell Gill
92— David Harrison Jr.
99— Thomas Ingram

MINNESOTA
69— Robert Stein
71— Barry Mayer
73— Douglas Kingsriter
78— Robert Weber
99— Parc Williams

MINN.-MORRIS
2007—Adam Turgeon

MINN. ST. MANKATO
70— Bernard Maczuga

MINN. ST. MOORHEAD
2000—Erik Pederson

MISSISSIPPI
66— Stanley Hindman
69— Steve Hindman
81— Kenneth Toler Jr.
86— Richard Austin
87— Jeffrey Noblin
88— Daniel Hoskins
89— Charles Walls
91— Todd Sandroni
2005—Rob Robertson

MISSISSIPPI COL.
80— Stephen Johnson
98— Joseph Fulcher
2000—Michael Brown

MISSISSIPPI ST.
69— William Nelson
73— Frank Dowsing Jr.
75— James Webb
77— William Coltharp
93— Daniel Boyd

MISSOURI
66— Thomas Lynn
67— James Whitaker
69—* Charles Weber
71— John Weisenfels
79— Christopher Garlich
82— Van Darkow
99— Jacob Stueve

MO.-ROLLA
69— Robert Nicodemus
73— Kim Colter
81— Paul Janke

MISSOURI ST.
80— Richard Suchenski
Mitchel Ware
85— Michael Armentrout
2000—Travis Brawner

MONMOUTH (ILL.)
72— Dale Brooks
90— Brent Thurness

MONTANA
75— Rock Svennungsen
79— Steven Fisher
84— Brian Salonen
91— Michael McGowan
96— David Dickenson
97— Michael Bouchee
Blaine McElmurry
98— Josh Branen
2000—Dallas Neil
01— Matt Thuesen
02— Vincent Huntsberger

MONTANA ST.
65— Gene Carlson
68— Russell Dodge
71— Jay Groepper
77— Bert Markovich
79— Jon Borchardt
James Mickelson
90— Derrick Isackson
92— Travis Annette
2003—Ryan Johnson

MORAVIAN
73— Daniel Joseph
94— Judson Frank

MOREHEAD ST.
92— James Appel

MORNINGSIDE
65— Larry White

MORRIS BROWN
83— Arthur Knight Jr.

MOUNT UNION
89— Paul Hrics
2000—Tom Bauer
01— Matt LaVerde
02— Charles Moore

MUHLENBERG
73— Edward Salo
76— Eric Butler
78— Mark Stull
81— Arthur Scavone
91— Michael Hoffman

MURRAY ST.
71— Matthew Haug
78— Edward McFarland
81—* Kris Robbins
90— Eric Crigler

NAVY
65— William Donnelly
69— William Newton
70— Daniel Pike
75—* Timothy Harden
76— Chester Moeller II
81— Theodore Dumbauld
2000—Terrence Anderson

NEBRASKA
70— Randall Reeves
71—* John Decker
72— Larry Jacobson
73— David Mason
74— Daniel Anderson
76— Thomas Heiser
77— Vince Ferragamo
78— Ted Harvey
79— James Pillen
80— Timothy Smith
81— Randy Schleusener
Jeffrey Finn
82— Eric Lindquist
85— Scott Strasburger
88— Jeffrey Jamrog
89— Mark Blazek
90— Gerald Gdowski
Jacob Young III
91— David Edeal
Patrick Tyrance Jr.
92— Patrick Engelbert
93— Michael Stigge
94— Trev Alberts
95— Robert Zatechka
96— Aaron Graham
97— Jonathan Hesse
98— Grant Wistrom
99— Joel Makovicka
2000—Tim DeBates
Brian Shaw
01— Kyle Vanden Bosch
04— Judd Davies
05— Chad Sievers
07— Dane Todd

NEB.-OMAHA
84— Kirk Hutton
Clark Toner
99— Edward Thompson

NEB. WESLEYAN
97— Justin Rice
Bren Chambers
98— Dusten Olds
Chad Wemhoff
99— Ryan Shanesy
2003—Luke Klinker
06— Scott Keller

UNLV
95— Howard McGowan

NEW HAMPSHIRE
85— Richard Leclerc

NEW MEXICO
72— Roderick Long
76— Robert Berg
79— Robert Rumbaugh
83— George Parks

NEW MEXICO ST.
76— Ralph Jackson
77—* Joseph Fox
99— David Patterson

NORTH ALA.
82—* Warren Moore

NORTH CAROLINA
75— Christopher Kupec
81— William Donnalley
83— David Drechsler
91— Kevin Donnalley

N.C. CENTRAL
91— Anthony Cooley

NORTH CAROLINA ST.
75— Justus Everett
82—* Calvin Warren Jr.

NORTH DAKOTA
79— Dale Lian
81— Douglas Moen
82— Paul Franzmeier
85— Glen Kucera
88— Kurt Otto
89— Matthew Gulseth
93— Timothy Gelinske
97— Thomas Langer
Timothy Tibesar
2003—Kelby Klosterman

NORTH DAKOTA ST.
66— James Schindler
69—* Stephen Stephens
71— Joseph Cichy
75— Paul Cichy
84— Doug Hushka
89— Charles Stock
94— Arden Beachy
98— Sean Fredricks

NORTH TEXAS
68— Ruben Draper
77— Peter Morris
2006—Nicholas Bazaldua

NORTHERN ARIZ.
78— Larry Friedrichs
2000—Jake Crissup

NORTHERN COLO.
76— Robert Bliss
77— Peter Morris
91— Thomas Langer
2000—Corte McGuffey
04— Cable Rohloff
06— Reed Doughty

UNI
81— Owen Dockter

NORTHERN MICH.
73— Guy Falkenhagen
81— Phil Kessel
86— Keith Nelsen

NORTHWEST MO. ST.
82— Robert Gregory
97— Greg Teale

NORTHWESTERN
70—* Bruce Hubbard
74— Steven Craig
77— Randolph Dean
81— Charles Kern
96— Salvatore Valenzisi
Ryan Padgett
99— Barry Gardner

NORTHWESTERN ST.
95— John Dippel
2000—William Broussard
02— Grayson Tennison

NORWICH
68— Richard Starbuck
74— Matthew Hincks

NOTRE DAME
67— Frederick Schnurr
68— James Smithberger
69— George Kunz
70— Michael Oriard
71— Lawrence DiNardo
72— Thomas Gatewood
73— Gregory Marx
74— David Casper
75— Peter Demmerle
Reggie Barnett
79— Joseph Restic
81— Thomas Gibbons
82— John Krimm Jr.
86— Gregory Dingens
89— Reginald Ho
94— Timothy Ruddy

OCCIDENTAL
66— James Wanless
67— Richard Verry
69— John St. John
78— Richard Fry
80—* Timothy Bond
89—* Curtis Page
95— Davin Lundquist

OHIO
78—* Robert Weidaw
80— Mark Geisler

OHIO NORTHERN
79— Mark Palmer
82— Larry Egbert

OHIO ST.
65— Arnold Chonko
66— Donald Unverferth
67— Ray Pryor
69— David Foley
71— Rex Kern
74— Randolph Gradishar
76— Brian Baschnagel
77— William Lukens
80— James Laughlin
84— John Frank
85— David Crecelius
86— Michael Lanese
97— Greg Bellisari
2004—Benjamin Hartsock

OKLAHOMA
72— Larry Jack Mildren Jr.
73— Joe Wylie
81— Jay Jimerson
89— Anthony Phillips
91— Michael Sawatzky
2001—Nicholas Kempenich
07— Carl Pendleton II

OKLAHOMA ST.
83—* Doug Freeman
2003—Kyle Eaton

OLIVET
75— William Ziem

OREGON
79—* Willie Blasher Jr.
91— William Musgrave
2002—Ryan Schmid

OREGON ST.
69— William Enyart
69—* Jerry Belcher

PACIFIC
72—* Byron Cosgrove
78— Brian Peets
80— Bruce Filarsky

PENN
68— Ben Mortensen
95— Michael Turner
98— John Bishop
99— David Rader
2004—Peter Veldman

PENN ST.
66— Joseph Bellas
67— John Runnells III
71— Robert Holuba
72— David Joyner
73— Bruce Bannon
74— Mark Markovich
75— John Baiorunos
79—* Charles Correal
80—* Michael Guman
81— John Walsh
84— Harry Hamilton
85— Douglas Strange
87— Brian Silverling
90— Roger Thomas Duffy
94— Craig Fayak
95— Charles Pittman
2000—Travis Forney
03— Joseph Iorio

PITTSBURGH
79— Jeff Delaney
86— Robert Schilken
89— Mark Stepnoski

POMONA-PITZER
69—* Lee Piatek
77— Scott Borg
83—* Calvin Oishi
85—* Derek Watanabe
88— Edward Irick
93— Torin Cunningham

PORTLAND ST.
79— John Urness

PRINCETON
67— Charles Peters
69— Richard Sandler
70— Keith Mauney
76— Ronald Beible
81— Mark Bailey
83— Brent Woods
86— James Petrucci
87— John Hammond
97— Marc Washington Jr.
99— Alexander Sierk

PUGET SOUND
68— Stephen Doolittle
79—* Patrick O'Loughlin
83—* Anthony Threlkeld

PURDUE
70— Michael Phipps
74— Robert Hoftiezer
75— Lawrence Burton

RANDOLPH-MACON
98— Joseph Seetoo

REDLANDS
65— Robert Jones
97— Morgan Bannister

RENSSELAER
67— Robert Darnall
69— John Contento

RHODES
71— John Churchill
79—* Philip Mischke
81— Jeffrey Lane
83—* Russell Ashford
85—* John Foropoulos
89— James Augustine
2002—Christopher Huff

RICE
81—* Lamont Jefferson
91— Donald Hollas
96— James Lamy

RICHMOND
86— Leland Melvin

RIPON
65— Phillip Steans
69— Steven Thompson
80— Thomas Klofta

ROBERT MORRIS
2005—Jonathan LeDonne

RUTGERS
90— Steven Tardy

SAGINAW VALLEY
2005—Neil Baumgartner

ST. CLOUD ST.
90— Richard Rodgers

ST. FRANCIS (PA.)
87— Christopher Tantlinger
99— Matthew Farabaugh

ST. JOHN'S (MINN.)
92— Denis McDonough
96— Christopher Palmer

ST. JOSEPH'S (IND.)
80— Michael Bettinger

ST. NORBERT
66— Michael Ryan
88— Matthew Lang

ST. PAUL'S
80— Gerald Hicks

ST. THOMAS (MINN.)
75— Mark Dienhart
97— Christopher Esterley
2000—Greg Kaiser
03— Jacob Barkley
Andrew Hilliard

SAN DIEGO
96— Douglas Popovich
2000—Michael Stadler
05— Todd Mortensen

SAN DIEGO ST.
99— Scott Auerbach

SANTA CLARA
72— Ronald Sani
77— Mark Tiernan
81—* David Alfaro
85— Alexis Vlahos
87— Patrick Sende

SEWANEE
65— Frank Stubblefield
66— Douglas Paschall
69— James Beene
71— John Popham IV
77— Dudley West
82— Gregory Worsowicz
Domenick Reina
83— Michael York
84— Michael Jordan
93— Jason Forrester
94— Frederick Cravens
96— Stephen Tudor
2003—Benjamin Tuck

SHIPPENSBURG
77— Anthony Winter

SIMPSON
71— Richard Clogg
74— Hugh Lickiss
90— Roger Grover
94— Chad Earwood

SLIPPERY ROCK
98— David Sabolcik Jr.
2000—Tim Kusniez

SOUTH CAROLINA
67— Steven Stanley Juk Jr.

SOUTH DAKOTA
79— Michael Schurrer
87— Todd Salat
93— Jason Seurer
2004—Jarrod Edelen

SOUTH DAKOTA ST.
80— Charles Loewen
81— Paul Kippley
88— Daniel Sonnek
95— Jacob Hines
2002—Joshua Ranek
04— Scott Connot

SOUTHEASTERN LA.
74— William Percy Jr.

SOUTHEASTERN OKLA.
2001—Joe Jones

SOUTHERN U.
70— Alden Roche

SOUTHERN CALIFORNIA
66— Charles Arrobio
69— Steven Sogge
70— Harry Khasigian
Steve Lehmer
74— Monte Doris
75— Patrick Haden
76— Kevin Bruce
78— Gary Bethel
80— Brad Budde
Paul McDonald
81— Gordon Adams
* Jeffrey Fisher
85— Duane Bickett
86— Anthony Colorito
* Matthew Koart
87— Jeffrey Bregel
90— John Jackson
96— Jeremy Hogue
97— Matthew Keneley

SMU
83—* Brian O'Meara
85—* Monte Goen
87— David Adamson
93— Cary Brabham

SOUTHERN MISS.
83— Richard Thompson
84— Stephen Carmody

SOUTHERN UTAH
92— Stephen McDowell

STANFORD
65—* Joe Neal
66—* Terry DeSylvia
68— John Root
71— John Sande III
72— Jackie Brown
74— Randall Poltl
75—* Keith Rowen
76— Gerald Wilson
77— Duncan McColl
81— Milton McColl
84— John Bergren
85— Scott Carpenter
86— Matthew Soderlund
87— Brian Morris
88— Douglas Robison
95— Stephen Stenstrom
96— Eric Abrams
David Walker
97— Marlon Evans

STONEHILL
93— Kevin Broderick

SUSQUEHANNA
77— Gerald Huesken
82— Daniel Distasio
2001—David Wonderlick

SWARTHMORE
72— Christopher Leinberger
83—* John Walsh

SYRACUSE
78—* Robert Avery
86— Timothy Green
94— Patrick O'Neill
95— Eric Chenoweth

TEMPLE
74— Dwight Fulton

TENNESSEE
71— Donald Denbo
Timothy Priest
77— Michael Mauck
81— Timothy Irwin
98— Peyton Manning

TENNESSEE TECH
2002—Grant Swallows

TEXAS
69— Corbin Robertson Jr.
71— Willie Zapalac Jr.
73—* Michael Bayer
74— Patrick Kelly
75— Wade Johnston
76— Robert Simmons
77— William Hamilton
97— Patrick Fitzgerald

TEXAS-ARLINGTON
69— Michael Baylor

UTEP
80— Eddie Forkerway
89— Patrick Hegarty
92— Robert Sesich

TEXAS A&M
69— Edward Hargett
71— David Elmendorf
72— Stephen Luebbehusen
88— Kip Corrington

TCU
67— John Richards
68— Eldon Gresham Jr.
73— Scott Walker
75— Terry Drennan
88— J. Clinton Hailey
2004—Nicholas Browne

TEXAS SOUTHERN
65— Leon Hardy

TEXAS ST.
82— Michael Miller

TEXAS TECH
65— James Ellis Jr.
68— John Scovell
75— Jeffrey Jobe
78—* Richard Arledge
85—* Bradford White
90— Thomas Mathiasmeier
2000—Jesse Cockrum

THOMAS MORE
98— Michael Bramlage Jr.

TOLEDO
82— Tad Wampfler
89— Kenneth Moyer
95— Chadd Dehn
97— Craig Dues
2002—Todd France
03— Christopher Tuminello

TOWSON
2003—Benjamin Whitacre

TRINITY (CONN.)
67—* Howard Wrzosek
68— Keith Miles

TRINITY (TEX.)
84—* Peter Broderick
95— Martin Thompson
98— Mark Byarlay
Jack Doran
2000—Bo Edwards

TROY
75— Mark King

TRUMAN
83— Roy Pettibone
99— Thomas Hernandez
2004—Tameem Yehyawi

TUFTS
65— Peter Smith
70— Robert Bass
79—* Don Leach
80—* James Ford
82—* Brian Gallagher
87— Robert Patz
92— Paulo Oliveira

TULSA
67—* Larry Williams
75— James Mack Lancaster II
98— Levi Gillen

TUSKEGEE
68— James Greene

UCLA
67—* Raymond Armstrong
Dallas Grider
70— Gregory Jones
74— Steven Klosterman
76— John Sciarra
77— Jeffrey Dankworth
78— John Fowler Jr.
83— Cormac Carney
84— Richard Neuheisel
86— Michael Hartmeier
90— Richard Meyer
93— Carlton Gray
96— George Kase
99— Shawn Stuart
Christian Sailer
2000—Danny Farmer

UNION (N.Y.)
88— Richard Romer

UTAH
81— James Baldwin
93— Steven Young
95— Jason Jones
2001—Kimball Christianson
05— Morgan Scalley

UTAH ST.
67— Ronnie Edwards
68— Garth Hall
70— Gary Anderson
76— Randall Stockham

VALDOSTA ST.
95— Christopher Hatcher

VALPARAISO
75—* Richard Seall

VANDERBILT
73— Barrett Sutton Jr.
75— Douglas Martin
2003—Hunter Hillenmeyer

VILLANOVA
77— David Graziano
89— Richard Spugnardi

VIRGINIA
67— Frederick Jones
83— Patrick Chester
94— Thomas Burns Jr.
96— Patrick Jeffers
98— Stephen Phelan Jr.

VMI
79— Robert Bookmiller
80— Richard Craig Jones

VIRGINIA TECH
73— Thomas Carpenito
97— Brandon Semones

WABASH
74—* Mark Nicolini
81—* Melvin Gore
83— David Broecker
87— James Herrmann
92— William Padgett
2007—Patrick Millikan

WAKE FOREST
70— Joseph Dobner
74—* Daniel Stroup
76— Thomas Fehring
78—* Michael McGlamry
83— Philip Denfeld
87— Toby Cole Jr.

WARTBURG
75— Conrad Mandsager
76— James Charles Peterson
82—* Rod Feddersen
94— Koby Kreinbring
96— Vincent Penningroth
2005—Mark Giesmann

WASHINGTON
65— William Douglas
67— Michael Ryan
72—* James Krieg
73— John Brady
77— Scott Phillips
78— Blair Bush
80— Bruce Harrell
82— Mark Jerue
83— Charles Nelson
Mark Stewart
88— David Rill
92— Edward Cunningham
97— David Janoski
2001—Marques Tuiasosopo

WASHINGTON-ST. LOUIS
94— Aaron Keen
98— Bradley Klein
2005—John Woock

WASH. & JEFF.
70— Edward Guna
82— Max Regula
91— David Conn
93— Raymond Cross Jr.
95— Michael Jones
2002—Matthew Dietz

WASH. & LEE
70— Michael Thornton
74— William Wallace Jr.
78— Jeffrey Slatcoff
79— Richard Wiles
80—* Scott Smith
81— Lonnie Nunley III
89— Michael Magoline
2003—John Melillo

WASHINGTON ST.
67— Richard Sheron
68— A. Douglas Flansburg
83— Gregory Porter
84— Patrick Lynch Jr.
85— Daniel Lynch

WAYNE ST. (MICH.)
76— Edward Skowneski Jr.
81— Phillip Emery

WEBER ST.
68— Phillip Tuckett
74—* Douglas Smith
92— David Hall
94— Deric Gurley
98— Cameron Quayle

WESLEY
2005—Rocky Myers

WESLEYAN (CONN.)
67— John Dwyer
69— Stuart Blackburn
71— James Lynch
78— John McVicar
2000—Matt Perceval

WEST TEX. A&M
75—* Ben Bentley
82— Kevin Dennis

WEST VIRGINIA
74— Ade Dillion

* Daniel Larcamp
82— Oliver Luck

WESTERN CARO.
94— Thomas Jackson III

WESTERN ILL.
89— Paul Singer
2005—Justin Langan

WESTERN KY.
72— Jimmy Barber
80— Charles DeLacey

WESTERN MICH.
68— Martin Barski
71— Jonathan Bull

WESTERN N.M.
68— Richard Mahoney

WESTERN ST.
98— Jason Eves

WESTMINSTER (PA.)
99— Brian Mihok

WHEATON (ILL.)
89— David Lauber
93— Bart Moseman
96— Pedro Arruza
99— Timothy Hardy
2006—Andrew Day

WHITTIER
76— John Getz
79— Mark Deven
87—* Timothy Younger

WIDENER
2002—Timothy Hess

WILLAMETTE
87—* Gerry Preston

WILLIAM & MARY
78— G. Kenneth Smith
80— Clarence Gaines
85— Mark Kelso

WILLIAM JEWELL
66— Charles Scrogin
70— Thomas Dunn
John Johnston

WILLIAMS
65— Jerry Jones
72— John Murray
95— Nathan Sleeper
96— Medley Gatewood

WILMINGTON (OHIO)
2007—Chad Otte

WINONA ST.
95— Nathan Gruber
2007—John Tackmann

WINSTON-SALEM
84— Eddie Sauls

WISCONSIN
66— David Fronek
80— Thomas Stauss
82—* David Mohapp
83— Mathew Vanden Boom

WIS.-LA CROSSE
97— Troy Harcey

WIS.-OSHKOSH
2000—Craig Pierstorff

WIS.-PLATTEVILLE
87— Michael Hintz

WIS.-STEVENS POINT
98— Joel Hornby
2000—Andy Palzkill

WIS.-WHITEWATER
96— Scott Hawig
2002—Peter Katz

WITTENBERG
82— William Beach
98— Kent Rafey
2004—Harold Ivery

WOOSTER
80— Edward Blake Moore
2000—Matt Mahaffey

WYOMING
74— Steven Cockreham
85— Bob Gustafson
89— Randall Welniak
96— Joseph Cummings
98— Jay Korth
Cory Wedel
2005—Trenton Franz

XAVIER (OHIO)
65— William Eastlake

YALE
66—* James Groninger
67— Howard Hilgendorf Jr.
69— Frederick Morris
71— Thomas Neville
72— David Bliss
75— John Burkus
77—* Stone Phillips
79— William Crowley
82— Richard Diana
91— Vincent Mooney
96— Matthew Siskosky

YOUNGSTOWN ST.
96— Mark Brungard

Academic All-America Hall of Fame

Since its inception in 1988, 49 former NCAA football players have been inducted into the GTE Academic All-America Hall of Fame. They were selected from among nominees by the College Sports Information Directors of America from past Academic All-Americans of the 1950s, '60s, '70s, '80s and '90s. Following are the football selections by the year selected and each player's team, position and last year played:

1988
Pete Dawkins, Army, HB, 1958
Pat Haden, Southern California, QB, 1974
Rev. Donn Moomaw, UCLA, LB, 1953
Merlin Olsen, Utah St., T, 1961

1989
Carlos Alvarez, Florida, WR, 1971
Willie Bogan, Dartmouth, DB, 1970
Steve Bramwell, Washington, DB, 1965
Joe Romig, Colorado, G, 1961
Jim Swink, TCU, B, 1956
John Wilson, Michigan St., DB, 1952

1990
Joe Theismann, Notre Dame, QB, 1970
Howard Twilley, Tulsa, TE, 1965

1991
Terry Baker, Oregon St., QB, 1962
Joe Holland, Cornell, RB, 1978
David Joyner, Penn St., OT, 1971
Brock Strom, Air Force, T, 1958

1992
Alan Ameche, Wisconsin, RB, 1954
Stephen Eisenhauer, Navy, G, 1953
Randy Gradishar, Ohio St., LB, 1973

1993
Raymond Berry, SMU, E, 1954
Dave Casper, Notre Dame, E, 1973
Jim Grabowski, Illinois, FB, 1965

1994
Richard Mayo, Air Force, QB, 1961
Lee Roy Selmon, Oklahoma, DT, 1975

1995
Pat Richter, Wisconsin, E, 1962

1996
Wade Mitchell, Georgia Tech, QB, 1956
Bob Thomas, Notre Dame, K, 1973
Byron "Whizzer" White, Colorado, HB, 1937 (honorary selection)

1997
Todd Blackledge, Penn St., QB, 1983
Tim Foley, Purdue, DB, 1970

1998
Bernie Kosar, Miami (Fla.), QB, 1984
Jack Mildren, Oklahoma, QB, 1971
Marv Levy, Coe, RB, 1949 (honorary selection)

1999
John Fowler, UCLA, LB, 1978
Chad Hennings, Air Force, DL, 1988

2000
Oliver Luck, West Virginia, QB, 1981

2001
Cris Collinsworth, Florida, WR, 1980
John R. Hall, Vanderbilt, G, 1954

2002
Richard Balzhiser, Michigan, FB, 1955

2003
Kip Corrington, Texas A&M, DB, 1987
Chris Howard, Air Force, RB, 1991
Steve Young, Brigham Young, QB, 1984

2004
Gill Beck, Appalachian St., C, 1977
Rolf Benirschke, UC Davis, K, 1976
Terry Hoage, Georgia, DB, 1983
Dave Rimington, Nebraska, C, 1982

2005
Cormac Carney, UCLA, WR, 1983

2006
Robert Burger, Notre Dame, OL, 1980
Tim Green, Syracuse, DL, 1985

2007
None

Academic All-Americans by School

Academic All-America football teams have been selected by the College Sports Information Directors of America (CoSIDA), a 2,000-member organization, since 1952. Since the program's inception, CoSIDA has bestowed Academic All-America honors on more than 14,000 student-athletes in Divisions I, II and III, and the NAIA, covering all NCAA championship sports. To be eligible, student-athletes must be regular performers and have at least a 3.200 grade-point average (on a 4.000 scale) during their college careers. University division teams (Football Bowl Subdivision and Football Championship Subdivision) are complete in this list, but college division teams (II, III, NAIA) before 1970 are missing from CoSIDA archives, with few exceptions. Following are all known first-team selections:

ABILENE CHRISTIAN
63— Jack Griggs, LB
70— Jim Lindsey, QB
74— Greg Stirman, E
76— Bill Curbo, T
77— Bill Curbo, T
87— Bill Clayton, DL
88— Bill Clayton, DL
89— Bill Clayton, DL
90— Sean Grady, WR

ADRIAN
84— Steve Dembowski, QB
94— Jay Overmyer, DB

AIR FORCE
58— Brock Strom, T
59— Rich Mayo, B
60— Rich Mayo, B
70— Ernie Jennings, E
71— Darryl Haas, LB/K
72— Bob Homburg, DE
Mark Prill, LB
73— Joe Debes, OT
74— Joe Debes, OT
78— Steve Hoog, WR
81— Mike France, LB
83— Jeff Kubiak, P
86— Chad Hennings, DL
87— Chad Hennings, DL
88— David Hlatky, OL
90— Chris Howard, RB
92— Grant Johnson, LB

AKRON
80— Andy Graham, PK

UAB
97— Johnny Rea, OL

ALABAMA
61— Tommy Brooker, E
Pat Trammell, B
64— Gaylon McCollough, C
65— Steve Sloan, QB
Dennis Homan, HB
67— Steve Davis, K
Bob Childs, LB
70— Johnny Musso, HB
71— Johnny Musso, HB
73— Randy Hall, DT
74— Randy Hall, DT
75— Danny Ridgeway, KS
79— Major Ogilvie, RB

ALABAMA A&M
89— Tracy Kendall, QB
90— Tracy Kendall, QB

ALBANY (N.Y.)
86— Thomas Higgins, OT
87— Thomas Higgins, OT
94— Andy Shein, WR
95— Rich Tallarico, OL
2000—J.T. Herfurth, OL
03— Victor Camacho, LB

ALBION
82— Bruce Drogosch, LB
86— Michael Grant, DB
90— Scott Bissell, DB
93— Eric Baxmann, LB
Jeffrey Shooks, P
94— Jeffrey Shooks, P
95— David Lefere, DB
96— David Lefere, DB

ALBRIGHT
2004—Nick Cushman, WR

ALFRED
89— Mark Szynkowski, OL

ALLEGHENY
81— Kevin Baird, P
91— Adam Lechman, OL
Darren Hadlock, LB

ALMA
86— Greg Luczak, TE
98— Rick Brands, PK
99— Dustin Armstrong, DB

AMERICAN INT'L
81— Todd Scyocurka, LB
99— Dan Grant, WR

AMHERST
2003—Paul Whiting, DB

ANGELO ST.
98— Kyle Kirk, LB

APPALACHIAN ST.
77— Gill Beck, C
92— D.J. Campbell, QB

ARIZONA
68— Mike Moody, OG
75— Jon Abbott, LB
76— Jon Abbott, T/LB
77— Jon Abbott, T/LB
79— Jeffrey Whitton, DL
87— Charles Cecil, DB
96— Wayne Wyatt, OL

ARIZONA ST.
66— Ken Dyer, OE
88— Mark Tingstad, LB
97— Patrick Tillman, LB

ARKANSAS
57— Gerald Nesbitt, FB
61— Lance Alworth, B
64— Ken Hatfield, B
65— Randy Stewart, C
Jim Lindsey, HB
Jack Brasuell, DB
68— Bob White, K
69— Bill Burnett, HB
Terry Stewart, DB
78— Brad Shoup, DB

ARK.-MONTICELLO
85— Ray Howard, OG
88— Sean Rochelle, QB

ARKANSAS ST.
59— Larry Zabrowski, OT
61— Jim McMurray, QB

ARKANSAS TECH
90— Karl Kuhn, TE
91— Karl Kuhn, TE
2000—Robert Bayer, DL
Paul Peletz, PK
01— Robert Bayer, DL

ARMY
55— Ralph Chesnauskas, E
57— James Kernan, C
Pete Dawkins, HB
58— Pete Dawkins, HB
59— Don Usry, E
65— Sam Champi, DE
67— Bud Neswiacheny, DE
69— Theodore Shadid, C
89— Michael Thorson, DB
92— Mike McElrath, DB
94— Eric Oliver, LB
2001—Brandon Perdue, DL

ASHLAND
73— Mark Gulling, DB
74— Ron Brown, LB
76— Dan Bogden, E
77— Bruce Niehm, LB
81— Mark Braun, C
91— Thomas Shiban, RB
93— Jerry Spatny, DL
96— Chad DiFranco, DB

AUBURN
57— Jimmy Phillips, E
59— Jackie Burkett, C
60— Ed Dyas, B
65— Bill Cody, LB
69— Buddy McClinton, DB
74— Bobby Davis, LB
75— Chuck Fletcher, DT
76— Chris Vacarella, RB
84— Gregg Carr, LB
94— Matt Hawkins, PK

AUGSBURG
81— Paul Elliott, DL
97— Ted Schultz, TE

AUGUSTANA (ILL.)
75— George Wesbey, T
80— Bill Dannehl, WR
84— Steve Sanders, OT
85— Steve Sanders, OT
95— Ryan Carpenter, OL
96— Ryan Carpenter, OL
97— Chris Meskan, OL
98— Chris Meskan, OL
2000—MacKenzie Hay, OL
01— Todd Baldwin, DB
02— Todd Baldwin, DB
03— Adam Guy, DB
04— Mike Clark, K

AUGUSTANA (S.D.)
72— Pat McNerney, T
73— Pat McNerney, T
74— Jim Clemens, G
75— Jim Clemens, C
77— Stan Biondi, K
86— David Gubbrud, DL
87— David Gubbrud, DL
88— David Gubbrud, LB
89— David Gubbrud, LB
96— Mitchell Pruett, TE
97— Thayne Munce, OL

AUSTIN
81— Gene Branum, PK
99— Joe Fox, OL

AUSTIN PEAY
74— Gregory Johnson, G
2005—Jordan Richardson, DL

BAKER
61— John Jacobs, B

BALDWIN-WALLACE
70— Earl Stolberg, DB
72— John Yezerski, G
78— Roger Andrachik, RB
Greg Monda, LB
81— Chuck Krajacic, OG
88— Shawn Gorman, P
91— Tom Serdinak, P
93— Adrian Allison, DL
David Coverdale, DL
94— David Coverdale, DL
2001—Matt Kish, OL
02— Matt Kish, OL
03— Joe Harbour, OL

BALL ST.
83— Rich Chitwood, C
85— Ron Duncan, TE
86— Ron Duncan, TE
87— Ron Duncan, TE
88— Ted Ashburn, OL
Greg Shackelford, DL
89— Ted Ashburn, OL
David Haugh, DB
91— Troy Hoffer, DB
92— Troy Hoffer, DB
2002—Travis Barclay, OL
03— Travis Barclay, OL

BATES
82— Neal Davidson, DB

BAYLOR
61— Ronnie Bull, RB
62— Don Trull, QB
63— Don Trull, QB
76— Cris Quinn, DE
89— Mike Welch, DB
90— Mike Welch, DB
96— Ty Atteberry, P
2005—Daniel Sepulveda, P
06— Daniel Sepulveda, P

BELOIT
90— Shane Stadler, RB

BENEDICTINE (ILL.)
2002—Patrick Ryan, DL

BENTLEY
2000—Brian Holland, DB

BETHANY (KAN.)
86— Wade Gaeddert, DB

BETHANY (W.V.)
2001—Eugene Ochap, OL

BETHEL (MINN.)
2001—Hans Bengston, DB
03— Matt Wassink, LB

BLOOMSBURG
83— Dave Pepper, DL

BOISE ST.
71— Brent McIver, IL
73— Glenn Sparks, G
78— Sam Miller, DB

BOSTON COLLEGE
77— Richard Scudellari, LB
86— Michael Degnan, DL

BOSTON U.
83— Steve Shapiro, K
85— Brad Hokin, DB
93— Andre Maksimov, OL
94— Andre Maksimov, OL

BOWDOIN
84— Mike Siegel, P
93— Michael Turmelle, DB

BOWLING GREEN
75— John Boles, DE
89— Pat Jackson, LB
90— Pat Jackson, TE

BRIDGEWATER (VA.)
2006—Jeff Highfill, QB

BRIGHAM YOUNG
73— Steve Stratton, RB
80— Scott Phillips, RB
81— Dan Plater, WR
87— Chuck Cutler, WR
88— Chuck Cutler, WR
Tim Clark, DL
89— Fred Whittingham, RB
90— Andy Boyce, WR
93— Eric Drage, WR
2000—Jared Lee, DB
01— Ryan Denney, DL

BROCKPORT ST.
97— Tom Massey, DB
98— Tom Massey, DB

BROWN
81— Travis Holcombe, OG
82— Dave Folsom, DB
86— Marty Edwards, C
87— John Cuozzo, C
2004—Nick Hartigan, RB
05— Nick Hartigan, RB

BUCKNELL
72— Douglas Nauman, T
John Ondrasik, DB

73— John Dailey, LB
74— Steve Leskinen, T
75— Larry Brunt, E
76— Larry Brunt, E
84— Rob Masonis, RB
Jim Reilly, TE
86— Mike Morrow, WR
91— David Berardinelli, WR
92— David Berardinelli, WR

BUENA VISTA
99— Ben Smith, RB
2004—Michael Irvin, LB

BUFFALO
63— Gerry Philbin, T
84— Gerry Quinlivan, LB
85— James Dunbar, C
86— James Dunbar, C
98— Dan Poulsen, DL

BUFFALO ST.
87— Clint Morano, OT

BUTLER
84— Steve Kollias, L
98— Nick Batalis, OL
Mike Goletz, DL
99— Mike Goletz, LB

C.W. POST
70— Art Canario, T
75— Frank Prochilo, RB
84— Bob Jahelka, DB
93— Jim Byrne, WR

CALIFORNIA
67— Bob Crittenden, DG
70— Robert Richards, OT
82— Harvey Salem, OT
2006—Chris Joseph, OL

UC DAVIS
72— Steve Algeo, LB
75— Dave Gellerman, LB
90— Mike Shepard, DL
98— Wes Terrell, TE

UC RIVERSIDE
71— Tyrone Hooks, HB

CALIFORNIA (PA.)
2005—Lloyd Price, LB

CAL LUTHERAN
81— John Walsh, OT

CANISIUS
82— Tom Schott, WR
83— Tom Schott, TE
86— Mike Panepinto, RB
2000—Jake Coppola, WR

CAPITAL
70— Ed Coy, E
83— Mike Linton, G
85— Kevin Sheets, WR
2002—Trevor Alexander, DL
06— Steve Leppert, OL

CARLETON
92— Scott Hanks, TE

CARNEGIE MELLON
76— Rick Lackner, LB
Dave Nackoul, E
84— Roger Roble, WR
87— Bryan Roessler, DL
Chris Haupt, LB
89— Robert O'Toole, LB
90— Frank Bellante, RB
Robert O'Toole, LB
94— Aaron Neal, TE
Merle Atkinson, DL
98— Jason Funke, DB
2005—Bryan LeBude, OL
Aaron Lewis, DB
06— Aaron Lewis, DB

CARROLL (WIS.)
76— Stephen Thompson, QB

CARSON-NEWMAN
61— David Dale, E
93— Chris Horton, OL
94— Chris Horton, OL
2000—Keith Akard, DL

CARTHAGE
61— Bob Halsey, B
77— Mark Phelps, QB

CASE RESERVE
75— John Kosko, T
82— Jim Donnelly, RB
83— Jim Donnelly, RB
84— Jim Donnelly, RB
88— Chris Hutter, TE
90— Michael Bissler, DB
95— Doug Finefrock, LB
96— Tom Mager, LB
Kenyon Meadows, DL
2000—Tim Gustafason, DL
05— Santo Maimone, DB

CENTRAL (IOWA)
79— Chris Adkins, LB
85— Scott Lindrell, LB
86— Scott Lindrell, LB
91— Rich Kacmarynski, RB
2006—Ben Bollard, DB

CENTRAL ARK.
2002—Landon Trusty, TE
03— Landon Trusty, TE
05— Cory Cangelosi, DB

CENTRAL MICH.
70— Ralph Burde, DL
74— Mike Franckowiak, QB
John Wunderlich, T
79— Mike Ball, WR
84— John DeBoer, WR
91— Jeff Bender, QB
2001—Rob Turner, WR
06— Daniel Bazuin, DL

CENTRAL MO.
97— Shane Meyer, PK

CENTRE
84— Teel Bruner, DB
85— Teel Bruner, DB
89— Bryan Ellington, DB
91— Eric Horstmeyer, WR

CHADRON ST.
73— Jerry Sutton, LB
75— Bob Lacey, KS
79— Jerry Carder, TE
95— Corey Campbell, RB
99— Casey Beran, DL
2006—Danny Woodhead, RB

CHAPMAN
96— Matt Hertzler, OL
97— Matt Hertzler, OL

CHEYNEY
75— Steve Anderson, G

CHICAGO
87— Paul Haar, OG
88— Paul Haar, OL
93— Frank Baker, RB

CINCINNATI
81— Kari Yli-Renko, OT
90— Kyle Stroh, DL
91— Kris Bjorson, TE
97— John Kobalka, DL

CITADEL
63— Vince Petno, E
76— Kenny Caldwell, LB
77— Kenny Caldwell, LB
78— Kenny Caldwell, LB
87— Thomas Frooman, RB
89— Thomas Frooman, RB

CLARION
96— Steve Witte, RB

CLEMSON
59— Lou Cordileone, T
78— Steve Fuller, QB
99— Kyle Young, OL
2000—Chad Carson, LB
Kyle Young, OL
01— Chad Carson, LB
Kyle Young, OL

COAST GUARD
70— Charles Pike, LB
71— Bruce Melnick, DB
81— Mark Butt, DB

COASTAL CARO.
2005—Josh Hoke, PK
06— Josh Hoke, PK

COE
93— Marcus Adkins, DL
2000—Timothy Vinyard, QB

COLGATE
78— Angelo Colosimo, RB
79— Angelo Colosimo, RB
85— Tom Stenglein, WR
89— Jeremy Garvey, TE
2003—John Frieser, TE

COLORADO
60— Joe Romig, G
61— Joe Romig, G
67— Kirk Tracy, OG
70— Jim Cooch, DB
73— Rick Stearns, LB
74— Rick Stearns, LB
75— Steve Young, DT
87— Eric McCarty, LB
90— Jim Hansen, OL
91— Jim Hansen, OL
92— Jim Hansen, OL
96— Ryan Olson, DL
97— Ryan Olson, DL

COLORADO COL.
96— Ryan Egeland, OL
Ryan Haygood, DL

COLORADO MINES
72— Dave Chambers, RB
83— Charles Lane, T

COLORADO ST.
55— Gary Glick, B
69— Tom French, OT
86— Steve Bartalo, RB
95— Greg Myers, DB
98— Mike Newell, OL
Nate Kvamme, LB
2002—Eric Pauly, LB

COLORADO ST.-PUEBLO
83— Dan DeRose, LB

COLUMBIA
52— Mitch Price, B
53— John Gasella, T
56— Claude Benham, B
71— John Sefcik, HB

CONCORDIA-ST. PAUL
2000—Andrew Fleischman, OL

CORNELL
77— Joseph Holland, RB
78— Joseph Holland, RB
82— Derrick Harmon, RB
83— Derrick Harmon, RB
85— Dave Van Metre, DL
2003—Kevin Rooney, DL
06— Luke Siwula, RB

CORNELL COLLEGE
72— Rob Ash, QB
Dewey Birkhofer, S
76— Joe Lauterbach, G
Tom Zinkula, DT
77— Tom Zinkula, DT
78— Tom Zinkula, DL
82— John Ward, WR
91— Bruce Feldmann, QB
92— Brent Sands, DB
93— Mark McDermott, DB
94— Mark McDermott, DB
95— Mike Tressel, DB
97— Matt Weiss, DL
98— Matt Weiss, DL

CULVER-STOCKTON
95— Mason Kaiser, DB

DARTMOUTH
70— Willie Bogan, DB
83— Michael Patsis, DB
87— Paul Sorensen, LB
88— Paul Sorensen, LB
90— Brad Preble, DB
91— Mike Bobo, WR
Tom Morrow, LB
92— Russ Torres, RB
94— David Shearer, WR
Zach Lehman, DL
97— Dominic Lanza, OL

DAVIDSON
2005—Kyle Kinsell, DL
06— Kyle Kinsell, DL

DAYTON
71— Tim Quinn, LB
72— Tim Quinn, DT
79— Scott Terry, QB
84— Greg French, K
David Kemp, LB
Jeff Slayback, L
85— Greg French, K
86— Gerry Meyer, OT
91— Brett Cuthbert, DB
Dan Rosenbaum, DB
92— Steve Lochow, DL
Dan Rosenbaum, DB
93— Steve Lochow, DL
Brad Mager, DB
94— David Overhoiser, RB
96— Josh Lemmon, OL
98— Jacob Jones, RB
99— Jimmy Lee, RB
2001—Mark Kasmer, LB
Marty McNamara, DB
02— Mark Kasmer, DB
03— Doug Jones, DB
Nick Sellett, OL
06— Brandon Cramer, DB

DEFIANCE
80— Jill Bailey, OT
Mark Bockelman, TE

DELAWARE
70— Yancey Phillips, T
71— Robert Depew, DE
72— Robert Depew, DE
2004—Ben Cross, DL

DELAWARE VALLEY
84— Dan Glowatski, WR

DELTA ST.
70— Hal Posey, RB
74— Billy Hood, E
Ricky Lewis, LB
Larry Miller, RB
75— Billy Hood, E
78— Terry Moody, DB
79— Charles Stavley, G

DENISON
75— Dennis Thome, LB
87— Grant Jones, DB
98— Jonathan Dunham, DB
99— Jonathan Dunham, DB

DePAUW
70— Jim Ceaser, LB
71— Jim Ceaser, LB
73— Neil Oslos, RB
80— Jay True, WR
85— Tony deNicola, QB
87— Michael Sherman, DB
90— Tom Beaulieu, DL
91— Tom Beaulieu, DL
Matt Nelson, LB
94— Mike Callahan, LB

DICKINSON
74— Gerald Urich, RB
79— Scott Mumma, RB

DRAKE
74— Todd Gaffney, KS
83— Tom Holt, RB
2005—Chris Daniels, DL

DREXEL
70— Lynn Ferguson, S

DUBUQUE
80— Tim Finn, RB

DUKE
66— Roger Hayes, DE
67— Bob Lasky, DT
70— Curt Rawley, DT
86— Mike Diminick, DB
87— Mike Diminick, DB
88— Mike Diminick, DB
89— Doug Key, DL
93— Travis Pearson, DL

DUQUESNE
2003—Mike Hillard, RB

EAST STROUDSBURG
84— Ernie Siegrist, TE
2004—Matt Crispell, DB

EAST TENN. ST.
71— Ken Oster, DB

EASTERN ILL.
95— Tim Carver, LB

EASTERN KY.
77— Steve Frommeyer, S

EASTERN N.M.
80— Tom Sager, DL
81— Tom Sager, DL
2003—Ty Touchstone, DB
04— Ty Touchstone, DB

EASTERN WASH.
97— Jeff Ogden, WR
Steve Mattson, DL
2002—Kyler Randall, WR
03— Kyler Randall, WR

ELON
73— John Rascoe, E
79— Bryan Burney, DB
2004—Brandon Mason, OL

EMORY & HENRY
71— Tom Wilson, LB
2000—Nathan Tuck, WR

EMPORIA ST.
79— Tom Lingg, DL
2002—Tyler Paul, RB
03— Brad Johnson, DB
Tyler Paul, RB

EVANSVILLE
74— David Mattingly, S
76— Michael Pociask, C
87— Jeffery Willman, TE
97— Sean Bennett, RB

FERRIS ST.
81— Vic Trecha, OT
92— Monty Brown, LB
2006—Michael Klobucher, LB

FINDLAY
97— Bo Hurley, QB

FLORIDA
65— Charles Casey, E
69— Carlos Alvarez, WR
71— Carlos Alvarez, WR
76— David Posey, KS
77— Wes Chandler, RB
80— Cris Collinsworth, WR
91— Brad Culpepper, DL
93— Michael Gilmore, DB
94— Terry Dean, QB
Michael Gilmore, DB
95— Danny Wuerffel, QB
96— Danny Wuerffel, QB

FLORIDA A&M
90— Irvin Clark, DL

FLORIDA ST.
72— Gary Huff, QB
79— William Jones, DB
Phil Williams, WR
80— William Jones, DB
81— Rohn Stark, P
94— Derrick Brooks, LB
96— Daryl Bush, LB
97— Daryl Bush, LB
2000—Christopher Hope, DB
01— Christopher Hope, DB

FORDHAM
90— Eric Schweiker, OL

FORT HAYS ST.
75— Greg Custer, RB
82— Ron Johnson, P
85— Paul Nelson, DL
86— Paul Nelson, DL
89— Dean Gengler, OL
2000—Adam Ryan, P
01— Casey Seyfert, DL

FORT LEWIS
72— Dee Tennison, E

FRANK. & MARSH.
77— Joe Fry, DB
78— Joe Fry, DB
2001—Mark Rowand, P

FURMAN
76— Jeff Holcomb, T

85— Brian Jager, RB
88— Kelly Fletcher, DL
89— Kelly Fletcher, DL
Chris Roper, LB
91— Eric Walter, OL
99— Stuart Rentz, RB
2000—Marion Martin, LB
06— Adnan Filipovic, OL

GANNON
2002—John Yurisinec, DB

GEORGETOWN
71— Gerry O'Dowd, HB
86— Andrew Phelan, OG

GEORGETOWN (KY.)
89— Eric Chumbley, OL
92— Bobby Wasson, PK
2001—Eddie Eviston, QB

GEORGIA
60— Francis Tarkenton, QB
65— Bob Etter, K
66— Bob Etter, K
Lynn Hughes, DB
68— Bill Stanfill, DT
71— Tom Nash, OT
Mixon Robinson, DE
77— Jeff Lewis, LB
82— Terry Hoage, DB
83— Terry Hoage, DB
92— Todd Peterson, PK
97— Matt Stinchcomb, OL
98— Matt Stinchcomb, OL
2001—Jon Stinchcomb, OL
02— Jon Stinchcomb, OL

GA. SOUTHERN
95— Rob Stockton, DB
99— Voncellies Allen, DL

GA. SOUTHWESTERN
87— Gregory Slappery, RB

GEORGIA TECH
52— Ed Gossage, T
Cecil Trainer, DE
Larry Morris, LB
55— Wade Mitchell, B
56— Allen Ecker, G
66— Jim Breland, C
W.J. Blaine, LB
Bill Eastman, DB
67— Bill Eastman, DB
80— Sheldon Fox, LB
90— Stefen Scotton, RB
99— Dan Dyke, P
2000—Dan Dyke, P
01— Dan Dyke, P
02— Dan Dyke, P

GETTYSBURG
79— Richard Swartz, LB
2002—Cliff Mason, LB

GRAMBLING
72— Floyd Harvey, RB
93— Gilad Landau, PK

GRAND VALLEY ST.
91— Mark Smith, OL
Todd Wood, DB

GRINNELL
71— Edward Hirsch, E
81— David Smiley, TE
98— Richard Wemer, WR

GROVE CITY
74— Pat McCoy, LB
89— Travis Croll, P

GUST. ADOLPHUS
80— Dave Najarian, DL
81— Dave Najarian, LB
98— Dan Duncan, OL
99— Dan Duncan, OL
2000—Brian Bergstrom, LB
01— Brian Bergstrom, LB
04— Isaac Sieling, LB

HAMLINE
73— Thomas Dufresne, E
89— Jon Voss, TE

HAMPDEN-SYDNEY
82— John Dickinson, OG

90— W.R. Jones, OL
91— David Brickhill, PK

HAMPTON
93— Tim Benson, WR

HARVARD
99— Ben Green, DB

HAWAII
97— Chris Shinnick, DB

HEIDELBERG
82— Jeff Kurtzman, DL
99— Joe Conduah, LB

HENDERSON ST.
98— Lee Daily, LB

HILLSDALE
61— James Richendollar, T
72— John Cervini, G
81— Mark Kellogg, LB
93— Jason Ahee, DB
96— Kyle Wojciechowski, OL

HOLY CROSS
83— Bruce Kozerski, T
85— Kevin Reilly, OT
87— Jeff Wiley, QB
91— Pete Dankert, DL

HOPE
73— Ronald Posthuma, T
79— Craig Groendyk, T
80— Greg Bekius, PK
82— Kurt Brinks, C
84— Scott Jecmen, DB
86— Timothy Chase, OG

HOUSTON
64— Horst Paul, E
76— Mark Mohr, DB
Kevin Rollwage, OT
77— Kevin Rollwage, OT

HUMBOLDT ST.
2006—Todd Eagle, DL

IDAHO
70— Bruce Langmeade, T

IDAHO ST.
84— Brent Koetter, DB
91— Steve Boyenger, DB
96— Trevor Bell, DB

ILLINOIS
52— Bob Lenzini, DT
64— Jim Grabowski, FB
65— Jim Grabowski, FB
66— John Wright, E
70— Jim Rucks, DE
71— Bob Bucklin, DE
80— Dan Gregus, DL
81— Dan Gregus, DL
82— Dan Gregus, DL
91— Mike Hopkins, DB
92— John Wright Jr., WR
94— Brett Larsen, P
99— Josh Whitman, TE
2000—Josh Whitman, TE

ILLINOIS COL.
80— Jay Wessler, RB
94— Warren Dodson, OL
2006—William Weller, DB

ILLINOIS ST.
76— Tony Barnes, C
80— Jeff Hembrough, DL
89— Dan Hackman, OL
95— Keith Goodnight, RB
2000—Adam Waugh, LB
01— Adam Waugh, LB

ILL. WESLEYAN
71— Keith Ihlanfeldt, DE
80— Jim Eaton, DL
Rick Hanna, DL
Mike Watson, DB
81— Mike Watson, DB
91— Chris Bisaillon, WR
92— Chris Udovich, DL
95— Jason Richards, TE
96— Lon Erickson, QB

INDIANA
67— Harry Gonso, HB
72— Glenn Scolnik, RB

80— Kevin Speer, C
94— John Hammerstein, DL
2005—Will Meyers, DB
06— Will Meyers, DB

INDIANA (PA.)
82— Kenny Moore, DB
83— Kenny Moore, DB

INDIANA ST.
71— Gary Brown, E
72— Michael Eads, E

INDIANAPOLIS
76— William Willan, E
95— Ted Munson, DL
2000—Brad Crawford, OL
03— Troy Tinsley, OL

IONA
80— Neal Kurtti, DL

IOWA
52— Bill Fenton, DE
53— Bill Fenton, DE
75— Bob Elliott, DB
85— Larry Station, LB
2001—Aaron Kampman, DL
05— Michael Elgin, OL
06— Michael Elgin, OL
Mike Klinkenborg, LB
Adam Shada, DB

IOWA ST.
52— Max Burkett, DB
82— Mark Carlson, LB
99— Dave Brcka, LB
2002—Jordan Carstens, DL

ITHACA
72— Dana Hallenbeck, LB
85— Brian Dougherty, DB
89— Peter Burns, OL
2003—Cory Coady, DL

JACKSONVILLE ST.
77— Dewey Barker, E
78— Dewey Barker, TE

JAMES MADISON
78— Warren Coleman, OT

JOHN CARROLL
83— Nick D'Angelo, LB
Jim Sferra, DL
85— Joe Burrello, LB
86— Joe Burrello, LB

JOHNS HOPKINS
77— Charles Hauck, DT
93— Michael House, DL
94— Michael House, DL
98— Chris Baugh, OL
2006—Evan Earnest, WR

JUNIATA
70— Ray Grabiak, DL
71— Ray Grabiak, DE
Maurice Taylor, IL
2004—Patrick Brown, OL
Matt Garner, DB

KALAMAZOO
92— Sean Mullendore, LB
2001—Brant Haverdink, LB

KANSAS
64— Fred Elder, T
67— Mike Sweatman, LB
68— Dave Morgan, LB
71— Mike McCoy, C
76— Tom Fitch, S
95— Darrin Simmons, P

KANSAS ST.
74— Don Lareau, LB
77— Floyd Dorsey, OG
81— Darren Gale, DB
82— Darren Gale, DB
Mark Hundley, RB
85— Troy Faunce, P
95— Kevin Lockett, WR
96— Kevin Lockett, WR
Jason Johnson, OL
2000—Jon McGraw, DB
01— Jon McGraw, DB

KENT ST.
72— Mark Reiheld, DB

91— Brad Smith, RB
2001—Brian Hallett, OL

KENTUCKY
74— Tom Ranieri, LB
78— Mark Keene, C
Jim Kovach, LB
85— Ken Pietrowiak, C
98— Jeff Zurcher, DB
2005—Taylor Begley, PK
Hayden Lane, OL
06— Hayden Lane, OL

KENYON
77— Robert Jennings, RB
85— Dan Waldeck, TE

LA VERNE
82— Scott Shier, OT

LAFAYETTE
70— William Sprecher, T
74— Mike Kline, DB
79— Ed Rogusky, RB
80— Ed Rogusky, RB
2004—Stephen Bono, OL

LAWRENCE
81— Chris Matheus, DL
Scott Reppert, RB
82— Chris Matheus, DL

LEHIGH
90— Shon Harker, DB

LEWIS & CLARK
61— Pat Clock, G
81— Dan Jones, WR

LIBERTY
98— Jarrol Everson, DL

LINFIELD
2005—Dwight Donaldson, OL

LONG BEACH ST.
83— Joe Donohue, LB

LORAS
84— John Coyle, DL
Pete Kovatisis, DB
85— John Coyle, DL
91— Mark Goedken, DL
93— Travis Michaels, LB

LA.-MONROE
70— Tom Miller, KS
74— Mike Bialas, T

LSU
59— Mickey Mangham, E
60— Charles Strange, C
61— Billy Booth, T
71— Jay Michaelson, KS
73— Tyler Lafauci, OG
Joe Winkler, DB
74— Brad Davis, RB
77— Robert Dugas, OT
84— Juan Carlos Betanzos, PK
94— Michael Blanchard, OL
97— Chad Kessler, P
2002—Rodney Reed, OL
03— Rodney Reed, OL
04— Rudy Niswanger, OL
05— Rudy Niswanger, OL

LOUISVILLE
2006—Brian Brohm, QB

LUTHER
83— Larry Bonney, DL
84— Larry Bonney, DL
89— Larry Anderson, RB
90— Joel Nerem, DL
91— Joel Nerem, DL
95— Karl Borge, DL

LYCOMING
74— Thomas Vanaskie, DB
85— Mike Kern, DL

MACALESTER
82— Lee Schaefer, OG

MANSFIELD
83— John Delate, DB

MARIETTA
83— Matt Wurtzbacher, DL

MARS HILL
92— Brent Taylor, DL

MARSHALL
98— Chad Pennington, QB
99— Chad Pennington, QB

MARYLAND
53— Bernie Faloney, B
75— Kim Hoover, DE
78— Joe Muffler, DL

MARYVILLE (TENN.)
99— Kevin Hedrick, DL

MASSACHUSETTS
99— Mike Wynne, OL

MASS.-LOWELL
85— Don Williams, RB

MIT
89— Anthony Lapes, WR
90— Darcy Prather, LB
91— Rodrigo Rubiano, DL
92— Roderick Tranum, WR
93— Corey Foster, OL
94— Corey Foster, OL
95— Scott Vollrath, P
96— Duane Stevens, DB
Brad Gray, DL
97— Duane Stevens, DB
Mike Butville, LB
Brad Gray, DL
99— Nik Kozy, DL
Angus Huang, DB
2000—Angus Huang, DB
03— Tom Kilpatrick, WR
04— Kevin Yurkewich, DL
06— Christopher Ruggiero, TE

McDANIEL
73— Chip Chaney, S
98— Tom Lapato, DB

McGILL
87— Bruno Pietrobon, WR

McNEESE ST.
78— Jim Downing, OT
79— Jim Downing, OT
90— David Easterling, DB
2000—Wes Hines, OL
02— Hadley Prince, DB

MEMPHIS
92— Pat Jansen, DL

MIAMI (FLA.)
59— Fran Curci, B
84— Bernie Kosar, QB
2002—Jonathan Vilma, LB
Matt Walters, DL

MIAMI (OHIO)
73— Andy Pederzolli, DB
2000—Brian Potter, DL

MICHIGAN
52— Dick Balzhiser, B
55— Jim Orwig, T
57— Jim Orwig, T
64— Bob Timberlake, QB
66— Dave Fisher, FB
Dick Vidmer, FB
69— Jim Mandich, OE
70— Phil Seymour, DE
71— Bruce Elliott, DB
72— Bill Hart, OG
74— Kirk Lewis, OG
75— Dan Jilek, DE
81— Norm Betts, TE
82— Stefan Humphries, OG
Robert Thompson, LB
83— Stefan Humphries, OG
85— Clay Miller, OT
86— Kenneth Higgins, WR
99— Rob Renes, DL

MICHIGAN ST.
52— John Wilson, DB
53— Don Dohoney, E
55— Buck Nystrom, G
57— Blanche Martin, HB
65— Don Bierowicz, DT
Don Japinga, DB
66— Pat Gallinagh, DT
68— Al Brenner, E/DB
69— Ron Saul, OG
Rich Saul, DE
73— John Shinsky, DT
79— Alan Davis, DB
85— Dean Altobelli, DB
86— Dean Altobelli, DB
86— Shane Bullough, LB
92— Steve Wasylk, DB
93— Steve Wasylk, DB

MICHIGAN TECH
71— Larry Ras, HB
73— Bruce Trusock, C
76— Jim Van Wagner, RB
92— Kurt Coduti, QB
2004—Joe Berger, OL

MIDWESTERN ST.
95— Corby Walker, LB

MILLERSVILLE
91— Tom Burns, OL

MILLIKIN
61— Gerald Domesick, B
75— Frank Stone, G
78— Charlie Sammis, K
79— Eric Stevens, WR
83— Marc Knowles, WR
84— Tom Kreller, RB
85— Cary Bottorff, LB
Tom Kreller, RB
90— Tim Eimermann, PK
2003—Andrew Beals, PK

MINNESOTA
56— Bob Hobert, T
60— Frank Brixius, T
68— Bob Stein, DE
70— Barry Mayer, RB
89— Brent Herbel, P
94— Justin Conzemius, DB

MINN ST. MANKATO
74— Dan Miller, C

MINN ST. MOORHEAD
88— Brad Shamla, DL
99— Adam Vossen, DL
Eric Pederson, LB

MISSISSIPPI
54— Harold Easterwood, C
59— Robert Khayat, T
Charlie Flowers, B
61— Doug Elmore, B
65— Stan Hindman, G
68— Steve Hindman, HB
69— Julius Fagan, K
74— Greg Markow, DE
77— Robert Fabris, OE
George Plasketes, DE
80— Ken Toler, WR
86— Danny Hoskins, OG
87— Danny Hoskins, OG
88— Wesley Walls, TE
89— Todd Sandroni, DB
2004—Cody Ridgeway, P
Rob Robertson, LB

MISSISSIPPI COL.
75— Anthony Saway, S
78— Steve Johnson, OT
79— Steve Johnson, OT
83— Wayne Frazier, C
97— Kyle Fulcher, LB

MISSISSIPPI ST.
53— Jackie Parker, B
56— Ron Bennett, E
72— Frank Dowsing, DB
73— Jimmy Webb, DE
76— Will Coltharp, DE
89— Stacy Russell, DB
2000—Scott Westerfield, PK

MISSOURI
62— Tom Hertz, G
66— Dan Schuppan, DE
Bill Powell, DT
68— Carl Garber, MG
70— John Weisenfels, LB
72— Greg Hill, KS
81— Van Darkow, LB
93— Matt Burgess, OL
98— Jake Stueve, TE
2003—Rob Droege, OL

MO.-ROLLA
72— Kim Colter, DB
80— Paul Janke, OG
86— Tom Reed, RB
87— Jim Pfeiffer, OT
88— Jim Pfeiffer, OL
91— Don Huff, DB
92— Don Huff, DB
94— Brian Gilmore, LB
95— Brian Gilmore, LB
96— Brian Gilmore, LB
2004—Cole Drussa, TE
05— Phil Shin, TE

MO. SOUTHERN ST.
85— Mike Testman, DB
93— Chris Tedford, OL
94— Chris Tedford, OL

MISSOURI ST.
73— Kent Stringer, QB
75— Kent Stringer, QB
78— Steve Newbold, WR

MO. WESTERN ST.
2006—Leon Douglas, DL

MONMOUTH
2002—Justin Rosato, DB

MONMOUTH (ILL.)
83— Robb Long, QB
2006—Dante Daniels, RB

MONTANA
77— Steve Fisher, DE
79— Ed Cerkovnik, DB
88— Michael McGowan, LB
89— Michael McGowan, LB
90— Michael McGowan, LB
93— Dave Dickenson, QB
95— Matt Wells, WR
96— Josh Branen, RB
Blaine McElmurry, DB
98— Justin Olsen, WR
99— Vince Huntsberger, DB
2000—Vince Huntsberger, DB
Matt Thuesen, OL
01— Vince Huntsberger, DB

MONTANA ST.
84— Dirk Nelson, P
88— Anders Larsson, PK
96— Devlan Geddes, DL
2000—Ryan Johnson, RB
01— Ryan Johnson, RB
02— Ryan Johnson, RB
Jon Montoya, DL
03— Jon Montoya, DL
05— Travis Lulay, QB

MONTCLAIR ST.
70— Bill Trimmer, DL
82— Daniel Deneher, KS

MORAVIAN
87— Jeff Pollock, WR
96— Mike Paciulli, DB

MOREHEAD ST.
74— Don Russell, KS
90— James Appel, OL
91— James Appel, OL
96— Mike Appel, OL
2003—Craig Unger, LB

MORGAN ST.
96— Willie Thompson, DL

MT. ST. JOSEPH
2004—Eric Schneider, DL

MOUNT UNION
71— Dennis Montgomery, QB
84— Rick Marabito, L
86— Scott Gindlesberger, QB
87— Paul Hrics, C
98— Darin Kershner, WR
2000—Chuck Moore, RB
01— Chuck Moore, RB
02— Matt Campbell, DL

MUHLENBERG
70— Edward Salo, G
71— Edward Salo, IL
72— Edward Salo, C
75— Keith Ordemann, LB
80— Arthur Scavone, OT
89— Joe Zeszotarski, DL
90— Mike Hoffman, DB

MURRAY ST.
76— Eddie McFarland, DB

MUSKINGUM
78— Dan Radalia, DL
79— Dan Radalia, DL

NAVY
53— Steve Eisenhauer, G
57— Tom Forrestal, QB
58— Joe Tranchini, B
69— Dan Pike, RB
80— Ted Dumbauld, LB

NEBRASKA
62— James Huge, E
63— Dennis Calridge, B
66— Marv Mueller, DB
69— Randy Reeves, DB
71— Larry Jacobson, DT
Jeff Kinney, HB
73— Frosty Anderson, E
75— Rik Bonness, C
Tom Heiser, RB
76— Vince Ferragamo, QB
Ted Harvey, DB
77— Ted Harvey, DB
78— George Andrews, DL
James Pillen, DB
79— Rod Horn, DL
Kelly Saalfeld, C
Randy Schleusener, OG
80— Jeff Finn, TE
Randy Schleusener, OG
81— Eric Lindquist, DB
David Rimington, C
Randy Theiss, OT
82— David Rimington, C
83— Scott Strasburger, DL
Rob Stuckey, DL
84— Scott Strasburger, DL
Rob Stuckey, DL
Mark Traynowicz, C
86— Dale Klein, K
Thomas Welter, OT
87— Jeffrey Jamrog, DL
Mark Blazek, DB
88— Mark Blazek, DB
John Kroeker, P
89— Gerry Gdowski, QB
Jake Young, OL
90— David Edeal, OL
Pat Tyrance, LB
Jim Wanek, OL
91— Pat Engelbert, DL
Mike Stigge, P
92— Mike Stigge, P
93— Rob Zatechka, OL
Terry Connealy, DL
Trev Alberts, LB
94— Matt Shaw, TE
Rob Zatechka, OL
Terry Connealy, DL
95— Aaron Graham, OL
96— Grant Wistrom, LB
97— Joel Mackovicka, RB
Grant Wistrom, DL
98— Joel Makovicka, RB
Chad Kelsay, DL
William Lafleur, P
99— Kyle Vanden Bosch, DL
Mike Brown, DB
2000—Kyle Vanden Bosch, DL
01— Tracey Wistrom, TE
04— Chad Sievers, LB
05— Kurt Mann, OL
Dane Todd, RB

NEB.-KEARNEY
70— John Makovicka, RB
75— Tim Brodahl, E
99— Volker Olbrich, PK
2005—Kyle Rupp, WR

NEB.-OMAHA
82— Kirk Hutton, DB
Clark Toner, LB
83— Kirk Hutton, DB
84— Jerry Kripal, QB

NEB. WESLEYAN
87— Pat Sweeney, DB
88— Pat Sweeney, DB
Mike Surls, LB

89— Scott Shaffer, RB
Scott Shipman, DB
95— Justin Rice, DL
96— Justin Rice, DL
97— Chad Wemhoff, WR
98— Ryan Shanesy, DL
2001—Grant Leach, OL
Justin Buresh, LB
05— Cody Hoegh, RB
Scott Keller, LB
06 — Kyle Elsasser, LB

NEVADA
82— David Heppe, P
2002—Erick Streelman, TE

NEW HAMPSHIRE
52— John Driscoll, T
84— Dave Morton, OL

TCNJ
2000—Curt Monday, DB

NEW MEXICO
75— Bob Johnson, S
77— Robert Rumbaugh, DT
78— Robert Rumbaugh, DL
93— Justin Hall, OL
98— Chad Smith, DB

NEW MEXICO ST.
66— Jim Bohl, B
74— Ralph Jackson, OG
75— Ralph Jackson, OG
85— Andy Weiler, KS
92— Todd Cutler, TE
Shane Hackney, OL
Tim Mauck, LB
93— Tim Mauck, LB
96— David Patterson, WR
97— David Patterson, WR
98— David Patterson, WR

NICHOLS
89— David Kane, DB

NORTH CAROLINA
64— Ken Willard, QB
85— Kevin Anthony, QB

NORTH CAROLINA ST.
60— Roman Gabriel, QB
63— Joe Scarpati, B
67— Steve Warren, OT
71— Craig John, OG
73— Justus Everett, C
Stan Fritts, RB
74— Justus Everett, C
80— Calvin Warren, P
2006—William Lee, OL

NORTH CENTRAL (ILL.)
2005—Ben Hare, DL

NORTH DAKOTA
87— Kurt Otto, QB
88— Chuck Clairmont, OL
Matt Gulseth, DB
92— Tim Gelinske, WR
Mark Ewen, LB
96— Tim Tibesar, LB
2002—Mac Schneider, OL
05— Jeff Glas, PK
06— Weston Dressler, WR
Michael Greenwood, DB

NORTH DAKOTA ST.
71— Tomm Smail, DT
93— T.R. McDonald, WR
2006—Craig Dahl, DB

NORTH PARK
83— Mike Lilgegren, DB
85— Scott Love, WR
86— Todd Love, WR
87— Todd Love, WR

NORTH TEXAS
75— Pete Morris, LB
76— Pete Morris, LB

NORTHEASTERN
85— Shawn O'Malley, LB

NORTHERN ARIZ.
89— Chris Baniszewski, WR
2003—Mark Gould, P

NORTHERN COLO.
71— Charles Putnik, OG

81— Duane Hirsch, DL
Ray Sperger, DB
82— Jim Bright, RB
89— Mike Yonkovich, DL
Tom Langer, LB
90— Tom Langer, LB
98— Corte McGuffey, QB
99— Corte McGuffey, QB
2005—Reed Doughty, DB

NORTHERN ILL.
2000—Thomas Hammock, RB
01— Thomas Hammock, RB

UNI
99— Brad Meester, OL
2006—James Lindgren, WR

NORTHERN MICH.
83— Bob Stefanski, WR
2002—Ben Laarman, LB

NORTHWEST MO. ST.
81— Robert "Chip" Gregory, LB
2004—Josh Lamberson, QB
Troy Tysdahl, LB
05— Josh Lamberson, QB

NORTHWESTERN
56— Al Viola, G
58— Andy Cvercko, T
61— Larry Onesti, C
62— Paul Flatley, B
63— George Burman, E
70— Joe Zigulich, OG
76— Randolph Dean, E
80— Jim Ford, OT
86— Michael Baum, OT
Bob Dirkes, DL
Todd Krehbiel, DB
87— Mike Baum, OL
88— Mike Baum, OL
90— Ira Adler, PK
95— Sam Valenzisi, PK
2002—Jason Wright, RB
03— Jason Wright, RB
04— Jeff Backes, DB
Luis Castillo, DL

N'WESTERN (IOWA)
83— Mark Muilenberg, RB
92— Joel Bundt, OL

NORTHWESTERN (MINN.)
2002—Jon Peterson, DB

N'WESTERN (OKLA.)
61— Stewart Arthurs, B

NORTHWESTERN ST.
92— Guy Hedrick, RB
94— John Dippel, OL

NORWICH
70— Gary Fry, RB

NOTRE DAME
52— Joe Heap, B
53— Joe Heap, B
54— Joe Heap, B
55— Don Schaefer, B
58— Bob Wetoska, E
63— Bob Lehmann, G
66— Tom Regner, OG
Jim Lynch, LB
67— Jim Smithberger, DB
68— George Kunz, OT
69— Jim Reilly, OT
70— Tom Gatewood, E
Larry DiNardo, OG
Joe Theismann, QB
71— Greg Marx, DT
Tom Gatewood, E
72— Michael Creaney, E
Greg Marx, DT
73— David Casper, E
Gary Potempa, LB
Bob Thomas, K
74— Reggie Barnett, DB
Pete Demmerle, E
77— Ken MacAfee, E
Joe Restic, S
Dave Vinson, OG
78— Joe Restic, DB
80— Bob Burger, OG
Tom Gibbons, DB
81— John Krimm, DB

85— Greg Dingens, DL
87— Ted Gradel, PK
Vince Phelan, P
92— Tim Ruddy, OL
93— Tim Ruddy, OL
2006—John Carlson, TE

OCCIDENTAL
88— Curtis Page, DL

OHIO
71— John Rousch, HB

OHIO NORTHERN
76— Jeff McFarlin, S
79— Robert Coll, WR
86— David Myers, DL
90— Chad Hummell, OL
97— Andy Roecker, OL

OHIO ST.
52— John Borton, B
54— Dick Hilinski, T
58— Bob White, B
61— Tom Perdue, E
65— Bill Ridder, MG
66— Dave Foley, OT
68— Dave Foley, OT
Mark Stier, LB
69— Bill Urbanik, DT
71— Rick Simon, OG
73— Randy Gradishar, LB
74— Brian Baschnagel, RB
75— Brian Baschnagel, RB
76— Pete Johnson, RB
Bill Lukens, OG
77— Jeff Logan, RB
80— Marcus Marek, LB
82— John Frank, TE
Joseph Smith, OT
83— John Frank, TE
84— David Crecelius, DL
Michael Lanese, WR
85— Michael Lanese, WR
89— Joseph Staysniak, OL
92— Leonard Hartman, OL
Gregory Smith, DL
95— Greg Bellisari, LB
96— Greg Bellisari, LB
99— Ahmed Plummer, DB
2003—Craig Krenzel, QB
06— Anthony Gonzalez, WR
Stan White, RB

OHIO WESLEYAN
70— Tony Heald, LB
Tom Liller, E
81— Ric Kinnan, WR
85— Kevin Connell, OG
94— Craig Anderson, LB
95— Craig Anderson, LB
96— Craig Anderson, LB

OKLAHOMA
52— Tom Catlin, C
54— Carl Allison, E
56— Jerry Tubbs, C
57— Doyle Jenning, T
58— Ross Coyle, E
62— Wayne Lee, C
63— Newt Burton, G
64— Newt Burton, G
66— Ron Shotts, HB
67— Ron Shotts, HB
68— Eddie Hinton, DB
70— Joe Wylie, RB
71— Jack Mildren, QB
72— Joe Wylie, RB
74— Randy Hughes, S
75— Dewey Selmon, LB
Lee Roy Selmon, DT
80— Jay Jimerson, DB
86— Brian Bosworth, LB

OKLA. PANHANDLE
76— Larry Johnson, G

OKLAHOMA ST.
54— Dale Meinert, G
72— Tom Wolf, OT
73— Doug Tarrant, LB
74— Tom Wolf, OT
77— Joe Avanzini, DE
2002—Kyle Eaton, OL
04— Billy Bajema, TE

OLIVET
2005—Travis Sleight, RB

OREGON
62— Steve Barnett, T
65— Tim Casey, LB
86— Mike Preacher, P
90— Bill Musgrave, QB
2000—Ryan Schmid, OL
01— Joey Harrington, QB
Ryan Schmid, OL

OREGON ST.
62— Terry Baker, B
67— Bill Enyart, FB
68— Bill Enyart, FB
93— Chad Paulson, RB

OUACHITA BAPTIST
78— David Cowling, OG

PACIFIC
78— Bruce Filarsky, OG
79— Bruce Filarsky, DL

PACIFIC LUTHERAN
82— Curt Rodin, TE

PENN
86— Rich Comizio, RB
99— Michael Germino, DL

PENN ST.
65— Joe Bellas, T
John Runnells, LB
66— John Runnells, LB
67— Rich Buzin, OT
69— Charlie Pittman, HB
Dennis Onkotz, LB
71— Dave Joyner, OT
72— Bruce Bannon, DE
73— Mark Markovich, OG
76— Chuck Benjamin, OT
78— Keith Dorney, OT
82— Todd Blackledge, QB
Harry Hamilton, DB
Scott Radicec, LB
83— Harry Hamilton, LB
84— Lance Hamilton, DB
Carmen Masciantonio, LB
85— Lance Hamilton, DB
86— John Shaffer, QB
94— Jeff Hartings, OL
Tony Pittman, DB
95— Jeff Hartings, OL
99— Travis Forney, PK
2002—Joe Iorio, OL
04— Andrew Guman, DB
05— Paul Posluszny, LB
06— Paul Posluszny, LB
Tim Shaw, DL

PITTSBURG ST.
72— Jay Sperry, RB
89— Brett Potts, DL
91— Mike Brockel, OL
92— Mike Brockel, OL
96— Brian Moorman, P
97— Brian Moorman, P
98— Ben Petersen, DL
2000—Chris Gab, LB
01— Caleb White, DL
04— Chris Beyer, OL
05— Chris Beyer, OL
Ryan Meredith, DL
06— Ryan Meredith, DL

PITTSBURGH
52— Dick Deitrick, DT
54— Lou Palatella, T
56— Joe Walton, E
58— John Guzik, G
76— Jeff Delaney, LB
80— Greg Meisner, DL
81— Rob Fada, OG
82— Rob Fada, OG
J.C. Pelusi, DL
88— Mark Stepnoski, OL
2002—Vince Crochunis, DL
03— Vince Crochunis, DL
Dan Stephens, DL
04— Vince Crochunis, DL
Dan Stephens, DL

PORTLAND ST.
72— Bill Dials, T
77— John Urness, WR
78— John Urness, WR
2000—Chris Cain, DL
05— Joey King, LB

PRINCETON
68— Dick Sandler, DT
76— Kevin Fox, OG
82— Kevin Guthrie, WR
83— Kevin Guthrie, WR
98— Alex Sierk, PK

PUGET SOUND
82— Buster Crook, DB

PURDUE
56— Len Dawson, QB
60— Jerry Beabout, T
65— Sal Ciampi, G
67— Jim Beirne, E
Lance Olssen, DT
68— Tim Foley, DB
69— Tim Foley, DB
Mike Phipps, QB
Bill Yanchar, DT
73— Bob Hoftiezer, DE
79— Ken Loushin, DL
80— Tim Seneff, DB
81— Tim Seneff, DB
89— Bruce Brineman, OL
2000—Drew Brees, QB
02— John Standeford, WR
03— John Standeford, WR

RENSSELAER
95— Alic Scott, OL
96— Dan McGovern, RB
97— Chris Cochran, DL
98— Jason Kepler, OL
99— Jason Kepler, OL
2002—Flynn Cochran, WR
03— Flynn Cochran, WR
06— Shawn Herrmann, OL

RHODE ISLAND
76— Richard Moser, RB
77— Richard Moser, RB

RHODES
90— Robert Heck, DL

RICE
52— Richard Chapman, DG
53— Richard Chapman, DG
54— Dicky Maegle, B
69— Steve Bradshaw, DG
79— LaMont Jefferson, LB
83— Brian Patterson, DB
95— Jay Lamy, DB

ROBERT MORRIS
2004—Jonathan LeDonne, LB
06— Ray Gensler, DL

ROCHESTER
82— Bob Cordaro, LB
92— Jeremy Hurd, RB
93— Jeremy Hurd, RB
2000—Brian Kowalski, LB
04— Justin Galloway, OL
05— Nicholas Zappia, OL
06— Nicholas Zappia, OL

ROSE-HULMAN
78— Rick Matovich, DL
79— Scott Lindner, DL
80— Scott Lindner, DL
Jim Novacek, P
83— Jack Grote, LB
84— Jack Grote, LB
88— Greg Kremer, LB
Shawn Ferron, PK
89— Shawn Ferron, PK
90— Ed Huonden, WR
92— Greg Hubbard, OL
93— Greg Hubbard, OL
2002—Jesse McQuiston, DB
Tim Swan, LB
05— Patrick Ludwig, OL

RUTGERS
2003—Nathan Jones, DB

SAGINAW VALLEY
93— Troy Hendrickson, PK
2003—Neil Baumgartner, LB
04— Neil Baumgartner, DL

ST. CLOUD ST.
88— Rick Rodgers, DB
89— Rick Rodgers, DB
2003—Keith Heckendorf, QB
04— Ryan Koch, WR
05— Ryan Koch, WR

ST. FRANCIS (PA.)
93— Todd Eckenroad, WR
98— Matt Farabaugh, LB
2005—Luke Palko, WR

ST. JOHN FISHER
2003—Brad Keem, DL
04— Mark Robinson, RB

ST. JOHN'S (MINN.)
72— Jim Kruzich, E
79— Terry Geraghty, DB
94— Chris Palmer, WR
Matthew Malmberg, RB
95— Chris Palmer, WR
97— Matt Emmerich, DB
2005—Jason Good, DL
Matt Hawn, LB
06— Jamie Steffensmeier, LB

ST. JOHN'S (N.Y.)
93— Anthony Russo, RB

ST. JOSEPH'S (IND.)
77— Mike Bettinger, DB
78— Mike Bettinger, DB
79— Mike Bettinger, DB
85— Ralph Laura, OT
88— Keith Woodason, OL
89— Jeff Fairchild, P

ST. NORBERT
86— Matthew Lang, LB
Karl Zacharias, P
87— Karl Zacharias, PK
Matthew Lang, LB
88— Mike Whitehouse, WR
89— Mike Whitehouse, WR
99— Mike Krueger, WR

ST. OLAF
61— Dave Hindermann, T

ST. THOMAS (MINN.)
73— Mark Dienhart, T
74— Mark Dienhart, T
77— Tom Kelly, OG
80— Doug Groebner, C
94— Curt Behrns, DB
2000—Jake Barkley, RB
01— Jake Barkley, RB
Andrew Hilliard, WR
02— Jake Barkley, RB
Andrew Hilliard, WR
04— Ben Kessler, DL
05— Ben Kessler, DL

SALVE REGINA
98— Mark DeBiasio, RB
99— Mark DeBiasio, RB

SAM HOUSTON ST.
72— Walter Anderson, KS
73— Walter Anderson, KS
93— Kevin Riley, DB

SAN DIEGO
87— Bryan Day, DB
88— Bryan Day, DB
94— Doug Popovich, DB
95— Doug Popovich, DB
96— Jeb Dougherty, DB
2004—Evan Harney, RB
05— Philip Bretsch, DB
Nick Garton, WR

SAN DIEGO ST.
98— Scott Auerbach, DB

SAN JOSE ST.
75— Tim Toews, OG

SANTA CLARA
71— Ron Sani, IL
73— Alex Damascus, RB
74— Steve Lagorio, LB
75— Mark Tiernan, LB
76— Lou Marengo, KS
Mark Tiernan, LB
80— Dave Alfaro, QB

SEWANEE
2002—Ben Tuck, PK

SHIPPENSBURG
76— Tony Winter, LB
82— Dave Butler, DL
94— Joel Yohn, PK
95— Joel Yohn, PK
2003—John Kuhn, RB
04— John Kuhn, RB

SIMPSON
98— Guy Leman, RB

SLIPPERY ROCK
2006—Mike Butterworth, OL

SOUTH CAROLINA
87— Mark Fryer, OL
88— Mark Fryer, OL
91— Joe Reeves, LB

SOUTH DAKOTA
78— Scott Pollock, QB
82— Jerus Campbell, DL
83— Jeff Sime, T
87— Dan Sonnek, RB
2002—Jarrod Edelen, P
06— Frank Leibfarth, PK

SOUTH DAKOTA ST.
74— Bob Gissler, E
75— Bill Matthews, T
77— Bill Matthews, DE
79— Tony Harris, PK
Paul Kippley, DB
2006—Cory Koenig, RB

SOUTHERN CALIFORNIA
52— Dick Nunis, DB
59— Mike McKeever, G
60— Mike McKeever, G
Marlin McKeever, E
65— Charles Arrobio, T
67— Steve Sogge, QB
68— Steve Sogge, QB
69— Harry Khasigian, OG
73— Pat Haden, QB
74— Pat Haden, QB
78— Rich Dimler, DL
79— Brad Budde, OG
Paul McDonald, QB
Keith Van Horne, T
84— Duane Bickett, LB
85— Matt Koart, DL
86— Jeffrey Bregel, OG
88— John Jackson, WR
89— John Jackson, WR
95— Jeremy Hogue, OL
Matt Keneley, DL
96— Matt Keneley, DL

SOUTHERN CONN. ST.
84— Gerald Carbonaro, OL

SOUTHERN ILL.
70— Sam Finocchio, G
88— Charles Harmke, RB
91— Dwayne Summers, DL
Jon Manley, LB

SMU
52— Dave Powell, E
53— Darrell Lafitte, G
54— Raymond Berry, E
55— David Hawk, G
57— Tom Koenig, G
58— Tom Koenig, G
62— Raymond Schoenke, T
66— John LaGrone, MG
Lynn Thornhill, OG
68— Jerry LeVias, OE
72— Cleve Whitener, LB
83— Brian O'Meara, T

SOUTHERN MISS.
92— James Singleton, DL
97— Jeremy Lindley, OL

SOUTHERN ORE.
97— Ian Reid, OL
2003—Garret Gelker, DL

SOUTHERN UTAH
88— Jim Andrus, RB
90— Steve McDowell, P

SOUTHWEST MINN. ST.
88— Bruce Saugstad, DB

SPRINGFIELD
71— Bruce Rupert, LB
84— Sean Flanders, DL
85— Sean Flanders, DL
2002—Ben Bristol, OL

STANFORD
70— John Sande, C
Terry Ewing, DB
75— Don Stevenson, RB
76— Don Stevenson, RB
77— Guy Benjamin, QB
78— Vince Mulroy, WR
Jim Stephens, OG
79— Pat Bowe, TE
Milt McColl, LB
Joe St. Geme, DB
81— John Bergren, DL
Darrin Nelson, RB
82— John Bergren, DL
83— John Bergren, DL
85— Matt Soderlund, LB
87— Brad Muster, RB
90— Ed McCaffrey, WR
91— Tommy Vardell, RB
94— Justin Armour, WR
99— Troy Walters, WR

SUL ROSS ST.
73— Archie Nexon, RB

SUSQUEHANNA
75— Gerry Huesken, T
76— Gerry Huesken, T
80— Dan Distasio, LB
99— Dave Wonderlick, OL
2000—Dave Wonderlick, OL
02— Mike Bowman, QB

SYRACUSE
60— Fred Mautino, E
71— Howard Goodman, LB
83— Tony Romano, LB
84— Tim Green, DL
85— Tim Green, DL
93— Pat O'Neill, P
99— Mark Baniewicz, OL
2003—Rich Scanlon, LB
04— Matt Tarullo, OL

TARLETON ST.
81— Ricky Bush, RB
90— Mike Loveless, OL

TENNESSEE
56— Charles Rader, T
57— Bill Johnson, G
65— Mack Gentry, DT
67— Bob Johnson, C
70— Tim Priest, DB
80— Timothy Irwin, OT
82— Mike Terry, DL
97— Peyton Manning, QB

TENN.-MARTIN
74— Randy West, E
2005—Chad McMahan, DB

TENNESSEE TECH
87— Andy Rittenhouse, DL
99— Wes Gallagher, OL

TEXAS
59— Maurice Doke, G
61— Johnny Treadwell, G
62— Johnny Treadwell, G
Pat Culpepper, B
63— Duke Carlisle, B
66— Gene Bledsoe, OT
67— Mike Perrin, DE
Corby Robertson, LB
68— Corby Robertson, LB
Scott Henderson, LB
69— Scott Henderson, LB
Bill Zapalac, DE
70— Scott Henderson, LB
Bill Zapalac, LB
72— Mike Bayer, DB
Tommy Keel, S
Steve Oxley, T
73— Tommy Keel, S
83— Doug Dawson, G
88— Lee Brockman, DL
95— Pat Fitzgerald, TE
96— Pat Fitzgerald, TE
97— Dusty Renfro, LB

UTEP
88— Pat Hegarty, QB

TEXAS A&M
56— Jack Pardee, B
71— Steve Luebbehusen, LB
76— Kevin Monk, LB
77— Kevin Monk, LB
85— Kip Corrington, DB
86— Kip Corrington, DB
87— Kip Corrington, DB
2001—Seth McKinney, OL

TEX. A&M-COMMERCE
77— Mike Hall, OT

TEX. A&M-KINGSVILLE
72— Floyd Goodwin, T
73— Johnny Jackson, E
76— Wade Whitmer, DL
77— Joe Henke, LB
Wade Whitmer, DL
78— Wade Whitmer, DL

TCU
52— Marshall Harris, T
55— Hugh Pitts, C
Jim Swink, B
56— Jim Swink, B
57— John Nikkel, E
68— Jim Ray, G
72— Scott Walker, C
74— Terry Drennan, DB
80— John McClean, DL
2002—Nick Browne, PK
03— Nick Browne, PK

TEXAS ST.
72— Jimmy Jowers, LB
73— Jimmy Jowers, LB
78— Mike Ferris, OG
79— Mike Ferris, G
Allen Kiesling, DL
81— Mike Miller, QB

TEXAS TECH
72— Jeff Jobe, E
79— Maury Buford, P
83— Chuck Alexander, DB
93— Robert King, P
99— Keith Cockrum, LB
2002—Kliff Kingsbury, QB

THOMAS MORE
97— Mike Bramlage Jr., DB

TOLEDO
83— Michael Matz, DL
95— Craig Dues, LB
2001—Todd France, PK
04— Lance Moore, WR

TOWSON
2000—Adam Overbey, WR

TRINITY (CONN.)
96— Joseph DeAngelis, OL

TRINITY (TEX.)
92— Jeff Bryan, OL
97— Mark Byarlay, RB

TRUMAN
73— Tom Roberts, T
78— Keith Driscoll, LB
79— Keith Driscoll, LB
92— K.C. Conaway, P
2001—Austin Lepper, PK
Lance Dorsey, DB
03— Tameem Yehyawi, LB

TUFTS
70— Bruce Zinsmeister, DL
81— Brian Gallagher, OG
83— Richard Guiunta, G
98— Eric Brum, DL

TULANE
71— David Hebert, DB

TULSA
64— Howard Twilley, E
65— Howard Twilley, E
74— Mack Lancaster, T
95— David Millwee, OL
96— Levi Gillen, DB
97— Levi Gillen, DB
2001—Drew McLaughlin, DL
05— Garrett Mills, TE

UCLA
52— Ed Flynn, G
Donn Moomaw, LB
53— Ira Pauly, C
54— Sam Boghosian, G
66— Ray Armstrong, E
75— John Sciarra, QB
77— John Fowler, LB
81— Cormac Carney, WR
Tim Wrightman, TE
82— Cormac Carney, WR
85— Mike Hartmeier, OG
92— Carlton Gray, DB
95— George Kase, DL
98— Shawn Stuart, OL

UNION (N.Y.)
71— Tom Anacher, LB
73— Dave Ricks, DB
87— Richard Romer, DL
93— Greg Oswitt, OL
96— Roger Egbert, PK

URSINUS
86— Chuck Odgers, DB
87— Chuck Odgers, LB

UTAH
64— Mel Carpenter, T
71— Scott Robbins, DB
73— Steve Odom, RB
76— Dick Graham, E
2003—Morgan Scalley, DB
04— Alex Smith, QB
Morgan Scalley, DB

UTAH ST.
61— Merlin Olsen, T
69— Gary Anderson, LB
74— Randy Stockham, DE
75— Randy Stockham, DE

VALDOSTA ST.
93— Chris Hatcher, QB
94— Chris Hatcher, QB

VALPARAISO
2004—Kevin Knutson, WR

VANDERBILT
58— Don Donnell, C
68— Jim Burns, DB
74— Doug Martin, E
75— Damon Regen, LB
77— Greg Martin, K
83— Phil Roach, WR
2002—Hunter Hillenmeyer, LB

VILLANOVA
86— Ron Sency, RB
88— Peter Lombardi, RB
92— Tim Matas, DL

VIRGINIA
72— Tom Kennedy, OG
75— Bob Meade, DT
92— Tom Burns, LB
93— Tom Burns, LB
95— Tiki Barber, RB
96— Tiki Barber, RB
97— Stephen Phelan, DB

VMI
78— Craig Jones, PK
79— Craig Jones, PK
84— David Twillie, OL
86— Dan Young, DL
88— Anthony McIntosh, DB

VIRGINIA TECH
67— Frank Loria, DB
72— Tommy Carpenito, LB
2001—Andre Davis, WR

WABASH
70— Roscoe Fouts, DB
71— Kendrick Shelburne, DT
82— Dave Broecker, QB

WARTBURG
75— James Charles Peterson, DB
76— Randy Groth, DB
77— Neil Mandsager, LB
90— Jerrod Staack, OL
93— Koby Kreinbring, LB
94— Vince Penningroth, DL
95— Vince Penningroth, DL
99— Paul Seberger, TE
2000—Mike Trettin, OL
01— Seth Roberson, OL
03— Mark Giesmann, P
04— Mark Giesmann, P

WASHINGTON
55— Jim Houston, E
63— Mike Briggs, T
64— Rick Redman, G
65— Steve Bramwell, DB
79— Bruce Harrell, LB
81— Mark Jerue, LB
Chuck Nelson, PK
82— Chuck Nelson, PK
86— David Rill, LB
87— David Rill, LB
91— Ed Cunningham, OL

WASHINGTON-ST. LOUIS
97— Brad Klein, LB
2004—John Woock, DB

WASH. & JEFF.
92— Raymond Cross, DL
93— Michael Jones, OL
94— Michael Jones, OL

WASH. & LEE
75— John Cocklereece, DB
78— George Ballantyne, LB
92— Evans Edwards, OL
2001—Jay Thomas, TE
02— John Melillo, OL

WASHINGTON ST.
89— Jason Hanson, PK
90— Lee Tilleman, DL
Jason Hanson, PK
91— Jason Hanson, PK

WAYNE ST. (MICH.)
71— Gary Schultz, DB
72— Walt Stasinski, DB

WAYNE ST. (NEB.)
99— Jeff Shabram, OL

WAYNESBURG
77— John Culp, RB
78— John Culp, RB
89— Andrew Barrish, OL
90— Andrew Barrish, OL
91— Karl Petrof, OL
2000—Jason Berkhimer, WR

WEBER ST.
97— Cameron Quayle, TE

WEST CHESTER
83— Eric Wentling, K
86— Gerald Desmond, K

WEST VIRGINIA
52— Paul Bischoff, E
54— Fred Wyant, B
55— Sam Huff, T
70— Kim West, K
80— Oliver Luck, QB
81— Oliver Luck, QB
83— Jeff Hostetler, QB
92— Mike Compton, OL
94— Matt Taffoni, LB
98— Eric de Groh, OL
2005—Jay Henry, LB
06— Jay Henry, LB

WESTERN CARO.
75— Mike Wade, E
76— Mike Wade, LB
84— Eddie Maddox, RB
2003—Jason Whaley, OL

WESTERN ILL.
61— Jerry Blew, G
85— Jeff McKinney, RB
91— David Fierke, OL
2004—Justin Langan, K
05— Perry Cox, OL

WESTERN KY.
71— James Barber, LB

81— Tim Ford, DL
84— Mark Fatkin, OL
85— Mark Fatkin, OG
95— Brian Bixler, OL
2002—Brian Lowder, DB

WESTERN MICH.
70— Jon Bull, OT
94— Rich Kaiser, DL
95— Rich Kaiser, DL

WESTERN ORE.
61— Francis Tresler, C

WESTERN ST.
78— Bill Campbell, DB
88— Damon Lockhart, RB

WESTERN WASH.
2000—Erik Totten, DB

WESTMINSTER (PA.)
73— Bob Clark, G
77— Scott McLuckey, LB
93— Brian Wilson, OL
98— Brian Mihok, DL
2003—Jim Chaney, OL

WHEATON (ILL.)
73— Bill Hyer, E
75— Eugene Campbell, RB
76— Eugene Campbell, RB
88— Paul Sternenberg, DL
92— Bart Moseman, DB
94— Pedro Arruza, RB
95— Jeff Brown, QB
Pedro Arruzo, RB
2003—James Hoxworth, OL

WHITTIER
86— Brent Kane, DL

WIDENER
98— Brendon Richards, LB
2001—T.J. Hess, DB
05— Doug Schlack, P

WILKES
70— Al Kenney, C
2000—Frank McCabe, TE
02— Mike Liberski, OL
03— Mike Liberski, OL
06— Bryan Vivaldo, LB

WILLAMETTE
61— Stuart Hall
2005—Tim Alton, DB

WILLIAM & MARY
74— John Gerdelman, RB
75— Ken Smith, DB
77— Ken Smith, DB
78— Robert Muscalus, TE
84— Mark Kelso, DB
88— Chris Gessner, DB
90— Jeff Nielsen, LB
93— Craig Staub, DL

WM. PATERSON
92— John Trust, RB

WILMINGTON (OHIO)
99— Kevin Otte, DB

WINGATE
2006—Frank Marino, DL

WINONA ST.
93— Nathan Gruber, DB
94— Nathan Gruber, DB
97— Travis Walch, RB
2001—Adam Lilla, WR

WISCONSIN
52— Bob Kennedy, DG
53— Alan Ameche, B
54— Alan Ameche, B
58— Jon Hobbs, B
59— Dale Hackbart, B
62— Pat Richter, E
63— Ken Bowman, C
72— Rufus Ferguson, RB
82— Kyle Borland, LB
87— Don Davey, DL
88— Don Davey, DL
89— Don Davey, DL
90— Don Davey, DL
2004—Jim Leonhard, DB

WIS.-EAU CLAIRE
74— Mark Anderson, RB
80— Mike Zeihen, DB
2001—Mike Bestul, OL
02— Mike Bestul, OL

WIS.-LA CROSSE
95— Troy Harcey, WR
96— Troy Harcey, WR

WIS.-OSHKOSH
96— Rob Stoltz, WR
97— Ryan Hinske, WR
99— Craig Pierstoff, LB
2002—Justin Schneider, DL

WIS.-PLATTEVILLE
85— Mark Hintz, DB
Mark Rae, P
86— Mike Hintz, QB
87— Mark Rae, P
2004—Chris Lee, OL

WIS.-RIVER FALLS
91— Mike Olson, LB
95— Brian Izdepski, OT
2006—Jovin Kroll, P

WIS.-STEVENS POINT
97— Joel Hornby, DL
2003—Craig Johnson, DL

WIS.-WHITEWATER
95— Scott Hawig, OL
2000—Peter Katz, DL
01— Peter Katz, DL

WITTENBERG
80— Bill Beach, DB
81— Bill Beach, DB
82— Tom Jones, OT
88— Paul Kungl, WR
90— Victor Terebuh, DB

WOFFORD
2000—Brian Bodor, DL
05— Katon Bethay, DL

WOOSTER
73— Dave Foy, LB
77— Blake Moore, C
78— Blake Moore, C
79— Blake Moore, C
80— Dale Fortner, DB
John Weisensell, OG
99— Matt Mahaffey, P
2006—Rick Drushal, OL

WYOMING
65— Bob Dinges, DE
67— George Mills, OG
73— Mike Lopiccolo, OT
84— Bob Gustafson, OT
87— Patrick Arndt, OG
94— Ryan Christopherson, RB
95— Joe Cummings, DL
96— Jay Korth, OL
Cory Wedel, PK
97— Jay Korth, OL
Cory Wedel, PK
Brian Lee, DB
98— Brian Brown, LB
2004—Trenton Franz, OL

YALE
68— Fred Morris, C
70— Tom Neville, DT
78— William Crowley, LB
81— Rich Diana, RB
Frederick Leone, DL
89— Glover Lawrence, DL
91— Scott Wagner, DB
99— Eric Johnson, WR

YOUNGSTOWN ST.
93— John Quintana, TE
98— Anthony Pannunzio, DB
2003—Scott Thiessen, DB

Bowl/All-Star Game Records

2007-08 Bowl Schedule

ALLSTATE SUGAR BOWL

New Orleans, Louisiana, January 1, 2008, 8:30 p.m.
Paul J. Hoolahan, Chief Executive Officer
The Sugar Bowl Committee
110 Veterans Memorial Boulevard, Suite 500
Metairie, Louisiana 70005
paulh@sugrbowl.gs.net
allstatesugarbowl.com
Phone: 504/828-2440 Fax: 504/828-2441
Televising Network: Fox
Facility: Louisiana Superdome
Capacity: 71,250
Title Sponsor: Allstate
Teams: Bowl Championship Series

AT&T COTTON BOWL CLASSIC

Dallas, Texas, January 1, 2008, 11:30 a.m.
Rick Baker, President
Cotton Bowl Athletic Association
Physical Address:
1300 West Mockingbird Lane, Suite 500
Dallas, Texas 75247
Mailing Address:
P.O. Box 569420
Dallas, Texas 75356
rick@attcottonbowl.com
attcottonbowl.com
Phone: 214/634-7525 Fax: 214/634-7764
Televising Network: Fox
Facility: Cotton Bowl Stadium
Capacity: 71,252
Title Sponsor: AT&T Communications
Teams: Big 12 vs. Southeastern

AUTOZONE LIBERTY BOWL

Memphis, Tennessee, December 29, 2007, 4:30 p.m.
Steve Ehrhart, Executive Director
Liberty Bowl Festival Association
3767 New Getwell Road
Memphis, Tennessee 38118
sehrhart@libertybowl.org
libertybowl.org
Phone: 901/795-7700 Fax: 901/795-7826
Televising Network: ESPN
Facility: Liberty Bowl Memorial Stadium
Capacity: 62,338
Title Sponsor: AutoZone
Teams: Southeastern vs. Conference USA

BELL HELICOPTER ARMED FORCES BOWL

Fort Worth, Texas, December 31, 2007, 12:30 p.m.
Tom Starr, Executive Director
505 Main Street, Suite 270
Fort Worth, Texas 76102
thomas.r.starr@espn.com
armedforcesbowl.com
Phone: 817/810-0012 Fax: 817/810-0252
Televising Network: ESPN
Facility: Amon G. Carter Stadium
Capacity: 44,000
Title Sponsor: Bell Helicopter
Teams: Pacific-10 vs. Mountain West

BRUT SUN BOWL

El Paso, Texas, December 31, 2007, 2 p.m.
Bernie Olivas, Executive Director
Sun Bowl Association
Los Picos Building
4150 Pinnacle Street, Suite 100
El Paso, Texas 79902
bolivas@sunbowl.org
sunbowl.org
Phone: 915/533-4416 Fax: 915/533-0661
Televising Network: CBS
Facility: Sun Bowl Stadium
Capacity: 50,426
Title Sponsor: Brut (Idelle Labs, Ltd.)
Teams: Pacific-10 vs. Big 12/Big East

CAPITAL ONE BOWL

Orlando, Florida, January 1, 2008, 1 p.m.
Steve Hogan, Executive Director
Florida Citrus Sports Association, Inc.
One Citrus Bowl Place
Orlando, Florida 32805-2451
fcsports.com
Phone: 407/423-2476 Fax: 407/425-8451
Televising Network: ABC
Facility: Florida Citrus Bowl
Capacity: 65,438
Title Sponsor: Capital One
Teams: Southeastern vs. Big Ten

CHAMPS SPORTS BOWL

Orlando, Florida, December 28, 2007, 5 p.m.
Steve Hogan, Executive Director
Florida Citrus Sports Association, Inc.
One Citrus Bowl Place
Orlando, Florida 32805-2451
fcsports.com
Phone: 407/423-2476 Fax: 407/425-8451
Televising Network: ESPN
Facility: Florida Citrus Bowl
Capacity: 65,438
Title Sponsor: Champs Sports
Teams: Atlantic Coast vs. Big Ten

CHICK-FIL-A BOWL

Atlanta, Georgia, December 31, 2007, 7:30 p.m.
Gary Stokan, President
Peach Bowl, Inc.
235 Andrew Young International Drive
Atlanta, Georgia 30303
gstokan@macoc.com
chick-fil-abowl.com
Phone: 404/586-8500 Fax: 404/586-8508
Televising Network: ESPN
Facility: Georgia Dome
Capacity: 71,250
Title Sponsor: Chick-fil-A
Teams: Southeastern vs. Atlantic Coast

EMERALD BOWL

San Francisco, California, December 28, 2007, 8:30 p.m.
Gary Cavalli, Executive Director
AT&T Park, 24 Willie Mays Plaza
San Francisco, California 94107
gcavalli@emeraldbowl.org
emeraldbowl.org
Phone: 415/972-1812
Televising Network: ESPN
Facility: AT&T Park
Capacity: 38,437
Title Sponsor: Emerald of California
Teams: Pacific-10 vs. Atlantic Coast

FEDEX ORANGE BOWL

Miami Gardens, Florida, January 3, 2008, 8 p.m.
Eric L. Poms, Chief Executive Officer
Orange Bowl Committee
703 Waterford Way, Suite 590
Miami, Florida 33126
elpoms@orangebowl.org
orangebowl.org
Phone: 305/341-4700 Fax: 305/341-4750
Televising Network: Fox
Facility: Dolphin Stadium
Capacity: 72,230
Title Sponsor: FedEx
Teams: Bowl Championship Series

GMAC BOWL

Mobile, Alabama, January 6, 2008, 8 p.m.
Frank Modarelli
GMAC Bowl
1000 Hillcrest Road, Suite 115
Mobile, Alabama 36695
frank@gmacbowl.com
gmacbowl.com
Phone: 251/635-0011 Fax: 251/635-0014
Televising Network: ESPN
Facility: Ladd-Peebles Stadium
Title Sponsor: GMAC Financial Services
Capacity: 40,646
Teams: Conference USA vs. Mid-American

GATOR BOWL CLASSIC

Jacksonville, Florida, January 1, 2008, 1 p.m.
Richard Catlett, President
One Gator Bowl Boulevard
Jacksonville, Florida 32202
rcatman@gatorbowl.com
gatorbowl.com
Phone: 904/798-1700 Fax: 904/632-2080
Televising Network: CBS
Facility: Jacksonville Municipal Stadium
Capacity: 77,000
Title Sponsor: None
Teams: Atlantic Coast vs. Big East/Big 12

GAYLORD HOTELS MUSIC CITY BOWL PRESENTED BY BRIDGESTONE

Nashville, Tennessee, December 31, 2007, 4 p.m.
Scott Ramsey, Executive Director
414 Union Street, Suite 800
Nashville, Tennessee 37219
sramsey@nashvillesports.com
musiccitybowl.com
Phone: 615/743-3130 Fax: 615/244-3540
Televising Network: ESPN
Facility: LP Field
Capacity: 67,000
Title Sponsor: Gaylord Hotels
Teams: Atlantic Coast vs. Southeastern

INSIGHT BOWL

Tempe, Arizona, December 31, 2007, 9 p.m.
John Junker, President & CEO
Insight Bowl
7135 East Camelback Road, #290
Scottsdale, Arizona 85251
jjunker@fiestabowl.org
insightbowl.org
Phone: 480/350-0900 Fax: 480/350-0916
Televising Network: NFL Network
Facility: Sun Devil Stadium
Capacity: 56,000
Title Sponsor: Insight Enterprises, Inc.
Teams: Big Ten vs. Big 12

INTERNATIONAL BOWL

Toronto, Ontario, Canada, January 5, 2008, Noon
Ken Hoffman, Executive Director
1223 Turner, Suite 300
Lansing, Mighigan 48906
loding@internationalbowl.org
internationalbowl.org
Phone: 416/619-0550 Fax: 416/619-0468
Televising Network: ESPN2
Facility: Rogers Centre
Capacity: 53,506
Title Sponsor: None
Teams: Mid-American vs. Big East

MEINEKE CAR CARE BOWL

Charlotte, North Carolina, December 29, 2007, 1 p.m.
Will Webb, Executive Director
2815 Coliseum Centre Drive, Suite 200
Charlotte, North Carolina 28217
meinekecarcarebowl.com
Phone: 704/378-4400 Fax: 704/378-4421
Television Network: ESPN
Facility: Bank of America Stadium
Capacity: 73,367
Title Sponsor: Meineke Car Care Centers
Teams: Atlantic Coast vs. Big East

MOTOR CITY BOWL

Detroit, Michigan, December 26, 2007, 7:30 p.m.
Ken Hoffman, Executive Director
Ford Field Executive Offices
2000 Brush Street, Suite 200
Detroit, Michigan 48226
director@motorcitybowl.com
motorcitybowl.com
Phone: 313/262-2010 Fax: 313/262-2009
Televising Network: ESPN
Facility: Ford Field
Capacity: 65,000
Title Sponsors: General Motors/DaimlerChrysler/Ford
Teams: Big Ten vs. Mid-American

NEW MEXICO BOWL

Albuquerque, New Mexico, December 22, 2007, 4:30 p.m.
Jeff Siembieda, Executive Director
1111 University Boulevard, SE
Albuquerque, New Mexico 87106
newmexicobowl.com
Phone: 505/925-5999 Fax: 505/925-5998
Televising Network: ESPN

Facility: University Stadium
Capacity: 37,000
Title Sponsor: None
Teams: Mountain West vs. Western Athletic

OUTBACK BOWL
Tampa, Florida, January 1, 2008, 11 a.m.
James P. McVay, President/CEO
4211 West Boy Scout Boulevard, Suite 560
Tampa, Florida 33607
jimmcvay@outbackbowl.com
outbackbowl.com
Phone: 813/874-2695 Fax: 813/873-1959
Televising Network: ESPN
Facility: Raymond James Stadium
Capacity: 65,000
Title Sponsor: Outback Steakhouse, Inc.
Teams: Big Ten vs. Southeastern

PACIFIC LIFE HOLIDAY BOWL
San Diego, California, December 27, 2007, 8 p.m.
Bruce Binkowski, Executive Director
San Diego Bowl Game Association
P.O. Box 601400
San Diego, California 92160
bink@holidaybowl.com
holidaybowl.com
Phone: 619/283-5808 Fax: 619/281-7947
Televising Network: ESPN
Facility: Qualcomm Stadium
Capacity: 70,000
Title Sponsor: Pacific Life
Teams: Pacific-10 vs. Big 12

PAPAJOHNS.COM BOWL
Birmingham, Alabama, December 22, 2007, 1 p.m.
Mark Meadows, Executive Director
2 Riverchase Office Parkway, Suite 100
Birmingham, Alabama 35244
papajohnsbowl.com
Phone: 205/733-3776 Fax: 205/733-9249
Televising Network: ESPN2
Facility: Legion Field
Capacity: 72,000
Title Sponsor: Papa John's International, Inc.
Teams: Conference USA vs. Big East

PETROSUN INDEPENDENCE BOWL
Shreveport, Louisiana, December 30, 2007, 8 p.m.
Missy Setters, Executive Director
Independence Bowl
401 Market Street, Suite 120
Shreveport, Louisiana 71101
indybowl@independencebowl.org
independencebowl.org
Phone: 318/221-0712 Fax: 318/221-7366
Televising Network: ESPN
Facility: Independence Stadium
Capacity: 50,015
Title Sponsor: PetroSun
Teams: Big 12 vs. Southeastern

PIONEER PUREVISION LAS VEGAS BOWL
Las Vegas, Nevada, December 22, 2007, 8 p.m.
Tina Kunzer-Murphy, Executive Director
1771 East Flamingo Road
Suite 216A
Las Vegas, Nevada 89119
tina.c.kunzermurphy@espn.com
lvbowl.com
Phone: 702/732-3912 Fax: 702/732-4481
Televising Network: ESPN
Facility: Sam Boyd Stadium
Capacity: 40,000
Title Sponsor: Pioneer Electronics
Teams: Mountain West vs. Pacific-10

R+L CARRIERS NEW ORLEANS BOWL
New Orleans, Louisiana, December 21, 2007, 8 p.m.
Billy Ferrante, Executive Director
New Orleans Bowl
2020 St. Charles Avenue
New Orleans, Louisiana 70130
bferrante@gnosf.org
neworleansbowl.org
Phone: 504/525-5678 Fax: 504/556-5898
Televising Network: ESPN2
Facility: Louisiana Superdome
Capacity: 68,000
Title Sponsor: R+L Carriers, Inc.
Teams: Sun Belt vs. Conference USA

ROADY'S HUMANITARIAN BOWL
Boise, Idaho, December 31, 2007, 2 p.m.
Kevin McDonald
1109 Main Street
Mezzanine B
Boise, Idaho 83702
kevin@humanitarianbowl.org
roadyshumanitarianbowl.com
Phone: 208/424-1011 Fax: 208/424-1121
Televising Network: ESPN2
Facility: Bronco Stadium
Capacity: 30,000
Title Sponsor: Roady's Truck Stops
Teams: Western Athletic vs Atlantic Coast

ROSE BOWL
Pasadena, California, January 1, 2008, 5 p.m.
Mitch Dorger, CEO
Pasadena Tournament of Roses Association
391 South Orange Grove Boulevard
Pasadena, California 91184
mdorger@rosemail.org
tournamentofroses.com
Phone: 626/449-4100 Fax: 626/449-9786
Televising Network: ABC
Facility: Rose Bowl
Capacity: 92,059
Title Sponsor: None
Teams: Bowl Championship Series

SAN DIEGO COUNTY CREDIT UNION POINSETTIA BOWL
San Diego, California, December 20, 2007, 9 p.m.
Bruce Binkowski, Executive Director
San Diego Bowl Game Association
P.O. Box 601400
San Diego, California 92160
bink@holidaybowl.com
poinsettiabowl.net
Phone: 619/285-5061 Fax: 619/281-7947
Televising Network: ESPN
Facility: Qualcomm Stadium
Capacity: 70,000
Title Sponsor: San Diego County Credit Union
Teams: Navy or At-Large vs. Mountain West

SHERATON HAWAII BOWL
Honolulu, Hawaii, December 23, 2007, 8 p.m.
Jim Donovan, Executive Director
841 Bishop Street, Suite 1628
Honolulu, Hawaii 96813
jjdonovaniii@hotmail.com
sheratonhawaiibowl.com
Phone: 808/523-3688 Fax: 808/523-3712
Television Network: ESPN
Facility: Aloha Stadium
Capacity: 50,000
Title Sponsor: Sheraton Hotels and Resorts
Teams: Western Athletic vs. Conference USA

TEXAS BOWL
Houston, Texas, December 28, 2007, 8 p.m.
Robert McNair, Chairman of the Board
Reliant Stadium
2 Reliant Park
Houston, Texas 77054-1573
texasbowl.org
Televising Network: NFL Network
Facility: Reliant Stadium
Capacity: 70,000
Title Sponsor: None
Teams: Big 12 vs. Conference USA

TOSTITOS FIESTA BOWL
Glendale, Arizona, January 1, 2008,
Time to be determined
John Junker, President
Fiesta Bowl
7135 East Camelback Road, #290
Scottsdale, Arizona 85251
jjunker@fiestabowl.org
fiestabowl.org
Phone: 480/350-0900 Fax: 480/350-0916
Televising Network: Fox
Facility: University of Phoenix Stadium
Capacity: 73,000
Title Sponsor: Tostitos (Frito-Lay)
Teams: Bowl Championship Series

VALERO ALAMO BOWL
San Antonio, Texas, December 29, 2007, 8 p.m.
Derrick Fox, President/CEO
San Antonio Bowl Association, Inc.
100 Montana Street, Suite 3D01
San Antonio, Texas 78203-1031
derrickf@alamobowl.com
alamobowl.com
Phone: 210/226-2695 Fax: 210/704-6380
Televising Network: ESPN
Facility: Alamodome
Capacity: 65,000
Title Sponsor: Valero Energy Corporation
Teams: Big Ten vs. Big 12

ALLSTATE BCS NATIONAL CHAMPIONSHIP GAME
New Orleans, Louisiana, January 7, 2008, 8 p.m.
Paul J. Hoolahan, Chief Executive Officer
The Sugar Bowl Committee
110 Veterans Memorial Blvd., Suite 500
Metairie, Louisiana 70005
paulh@sugrbowl.gs.net
bcsfootball.org
Phone: 504/828-2440 Fax: 504/828-2441
Televising Network: Fox
Facility: Louisiana Superdome
Capacity: 71,250
Teams: Bowl Championship Series

Dates and times subject to change
(All starting times listed are Eastern time)

2006-07 Bowl Results

Game-by-Game Summaries

(Note: Teams' records listed are from before the bowl game was played.)

SAN DIEGO COUNTY CREDIT UNION POINSETTIA BOWL
December 19, 2006
Qualcomm Stadium
San Diego, California

Northern Ill. .... 0 0 0 7 — 7
TCU .... 6 10 14 7 — 37
Records: Northern Ill. 7-5, TCU 10-2
Attendance: 29,709

PIONEER PUREVISION LAS VEGAS BOWL
December 21, 2006
Sam Boyd Stadium
Las Vegas, Nevada

BYU .... 0 17 7 14 — 38
Oregon .... 0 0 0 8 — 8
Records: BYU 10-2, Oregon 7-5
Attendance: 44,615

R+L CARRIERS NEW ORLEANS BOWL
December 22, 2006
Louisiana Superdome
New Orleans, Louisiana

Rice .... 7 3 0 7 — 17
Troy .... 7 14 14 0 — 35
Records: Rice 7-5, Troy 7-5
Attendance: 24,791

NEW MEXICO BOWL
December 23, 2006
University Stadium
Albuquerque, New Mexico

New Mexico .... 0 3 0 9 — 12
San Jose St. .... 0 13 7 0 — 20
Records: New Mexico 6-6, San Jose St. 8-4
Attendance: 34,111

PAPAJOHNS.COM BOWL
December 23, 2006
Legion Field
Birmingham, Alabama

South Fla. .... 14 10 0 0 — 24
East Caro. .... 7 0 0 0 — 7
Records: South Fla. 8-4, East Caro. 7-5
Attendance: 32,023

BELL HELICOPTER ARMED FORCES BOWL
December 23, 2006
Amon G. Carter Stadium
Fort Worth, Texas

Tulsa .... 0 7 0 6 — 13
Utah .... 3 6 10 6 — 25
Records: Tulsa 8-4, Utah 7-5
Attendance: 32,412

SHERATON HAWAII BOWL
December 24, 2006
Aloha Stadium
Honolulu, Hawaii

Hawaii .... 0 3 21 17 — 41
Arizona St. .... 3 7 0 14 — 24
Records: Hawaii 10-3, Arizona St. 7-5
Attendance: 43,435

MOTOR CITY BOWL
December 26, 2006
Ford Field
Detroit, Michigan

Middle Tenn. .... 0 7 0 7 — 14
Central Mich. .... 14 7 7 3 — 31
Records: Middle Tenn. 7-5, Central Mich. 9-4
Attendance: 54,113

EMERALD BOWL
December 27, 2006
AT&T Park
San Francisco, California

Florida St. .... 7 6 10 21 — 44
UCLA .... 10 10 7 0 — 27
Records: Florida St. 6-6, UCLA 7-5
Attendance: 40,331

PETROSUN INDEPENDENCE BOWL
December 28, 2006
Independence Stadium
Shreveport, Louisiana

Oklahoma St. .... 7 17 0 10 — 34
Alabama .... 7 7 3 14 — 31
Records: Oklahoma St. 6-6, Alabama 6-6
Attendance: 45,054

PACIFIC LIFE HOLIDAY BOWL
December 28, 2006
Qualcomm Stadium
San Diego, California

Texas A&M .... 7 3 0 0 — 10
California .... 7 7 14 17 — 45
Records: Texas A&M 9-3, California 9-3
Attendance: 62,395

TEXAS BOWL
December 28, 2006
Reliant Stadium
Houston, Texas

Rutgers .... 14 3 14 6 — 37
Kansas St. .... 0 10 0 0 — 10
Records: Rutgers 10-2, Kansas St. 7-5
Attendance: 52,210

GAYLORD HOTELS MUSIC CITY BOWL
December 29, 2006
LP Field
Nashville, Tennessee

Clemson .... 0 6 0 14 — 20
Kentucky .... 7 7 7 7 — 28
Records: Clemson 8-4, Kentucky 7-5
Attendance: 68,024

BRUT SUN BOWL
December 29, 2006
Sun Bowl Stadium
El Paso, Texas
Oregon St. .... 14 0 7 18 — 39
Missouri .... 7 10 14 7 — 38
Records: Oregon St. 9-4, Missouri 8-4
Attendance: 48,732

AUTOZONE LIBERTY BOWL
December 29, 2006
Liberty Bowl
Memphis, Tennessee

South Carolina .... 7 20 3 14 — 44
Houston .... 7 21 0 8 — 36
Records: South Carolina 7-5, Houston 10-3
Attendance: 56,103

INSIGHT BOWL
December 29, 2006
Sun Devil Stadium
Tempe, Arizona

Texas Tech .... 0 7 7 24 6 — 44
Minnesota .... 14 21 3 0 3 — 41
Records: Texas Tech 7-5, Minnesota 6-6
Attendance: 48,391

CHAMPS SPORTS BOWL
December 29, 2006
Florida Citrus Bowl
Orlando, Florida

Purdue .... 0 7 0 0 — 7
Maryland .... 7 14 3 0 — 24
Records: Purdue 8-5, Maryland 8-4
Attendance: 40,168

MEINEKE CAR CARE BOWL
December 30, 2006
Bank of America Stadium
Charlotte, North Carolina

Navy .... 7 14 3 0 — 24
Boston College .... 6 10 0 9 — 25
Records: Navy 9-3, Boston College 9-3
Attendance: 52,303

ALAMO BOWL
December 30, 2006
Alamodome
San Antonio, Texas

Texas .... 3 7 10 6 — 26
Iowa .... 14 0 7 3 — 24
Records: Texas 9-3, Iowa 6-6
Attendance: 65,875

CHICK-FIL-A BOWL
December 30, 2006
Georgia Dome
Atlanta, Georgia

Georgia .... 3 0 10 18 — 31
Virginia Tech .... 0 21 0 3 — 24
Records: Georgia 8-4, Virginia Tech 10-2
Attendance: 75,406

MPC COMPUTERS BOWL
December 31, 2006
Bronco Stadium
Boise, Idaho

Miami (Fla.) .... 7 7 7 0 — 21
Nevada .... 2 9 3 6 — 20
Records: Miami (Fla.) 6-6, Nevada 8-4
Attendance: 28,652

AT&T COTTON BOWL CLASSIC
January 1, 2007
Cotton Bowl Stadium
Dallas, Texas

Auburn .... 7 7 3 0 — 17
Nebraska .... 7 7 0 0 — 14
Records: Auburn 10-2, Nebraska 9-4
Attendance: 66,777

OUTBACK BOWL
January 1, 2007
Raymond James Stadium
Tampa, Florida

Tennessee .... 3 7 0 0 — 10
Penn St. .... 0 10 0 10 — 20
Records: Tennessee 9-3, Penn St. 8-4
Attendance: 65,601

TOYOTA GATOR BOWL
January 1, 2007
Alltel Stadium
Jacksonville, Florida

West Virginia .... 7 10 21 0 — 38
Georgia Tech .... 14 14 7 0 — 35
Records: West Virginia 10-2, Georgia Tech 9-4
Attendance: 67,714

CAPITAL ONE BOWL
January 1, 2007
Florida Citrus Bowl
Orlando, Florida

Wisconsin .... 10 7 0 0 — 17
Arkansas .... 7 0 0 7 — 14
Records: Wisconsin 11-1, Arkansas 10-3
Attendance: 60,774

TOSTITOS FIESTA BOWL (BCS)
January 1, 2007
University of Phoenix Stadium
Glendale, Arizona

Boise St. .... 14 7 7 7 8 — 43
Oklahoma .... 7 3 7 18 7 — 42
Records: Boise St. 12-0, Oklahoma 11-2
Attendance: 73,719

ROSE BOWL (BCS)
January 1, 2007
Rose Bowl
Pasadena, California

Southern California	3	0	16	13	—	32
Michigan	0	3	0	15	—	18

Records: Southern California 10-2, Michigan 11-1
Attendance: 93,852

FEDEX ORANGE BOWL (BCS)
January 2, 2007
Dolphin Stadium
Miami Gardens, Florida

Louisville	0	10	0	14	—	24
Wake Forest	0	3	7	3	—	13

Records: Louisville 11-1, Wake Forest 11-2
Attendance: 74,470

ALLSTATE SUGAR BOWL (BCS)
January 3, 2007
Louisiana Superdome
New Orleans, Louisiana

Notre Dame	7	7	0	0	—	14
LSU	14	7	13	7	—	41

Records: Notre Dame 10-2, LSU 10-2
Attendance: 77,781

INTERNATIONAL BOWL
January 6, 2007
Rogers Centre
Toronto, Ontario, Canada

Cincinnati	14	10	0	3	—	27
Western Mich.	0	17	0	7	—	24

Records: Cincinnati 7-5, Western Mich. 8-4
Attendance: 26,717

GMAC BOWL
January 7, 2007
Ladd-Peebles Stadium
Mobile, Alabama

Ohio	0	0	0	7	—	7
Southern Miss.	0	21	7	0	—	28

Records: Ohio 9-4, Southern Miss. 8-5
Attendance: 38,751

TOSTITOS BCS CHAMPIONSHIP GAME
January 8, 2007
University of Phoenix Stadium
Glendale, Arizona

Florida	14	20	0	7	—	41
Ohio St.	7	7	0	0	—	14

Records: Florida 12-1, Ohio St. 12-0
Attendance: 74,628

All-Time Bowl-Game Results

Major Bowl Games

ROSE BOWL

Present Site: Pasadena, California
Stadium (Capacity): Rose Bowl (91,887)
Playing Surface: Grass
Playing Sites: Tournament Park, Pasadena (1902, 1916-22); Rose Bowl, Pasadena (1923-41); Duke Stadium, Durham, N.C. (1942); Rose Bowl (since 1943)

1-1-02—Michigan 49, Stanford 0
1-1-16—Washington St. 14, Brown 0
1-1-17—Oregon 14, Penn 0
1-1-18—Mare Island 19, Camp Lewis 7
1-1-19—Great Lakes 17, Mare Island 0

1-1-20—Harvard 7, Oregon 6
1-1-21—California 28, Ohio St. 0
1-2-22—California 0, Wash. & Jeff. 0
1-1-23—Southern California 14, Penn St. 3
1-1-24—Navy 14, Washington 14

1-1-25—Notre Dame 27, Stanford 10
1-1-26—Alabama 20, Washington 19
1-1-27—Alabama 7, Stanford 7
1-2-28—Stanford 7, Pittsburgh 6
1-1-29—Georgia Tech 8, California 7

1-1-30—Southern California 47, Pittsburgh 14
1-1-31—Alabama 24, Washington St. 0
1-1-32—Southern California 21, Tulane 12
1-2-33—Southern California 35, Pittsburgh 0
1-1-34—Columbia 7, Stanford 0

1-1-35—Alabama 29, Stanford 13
1-1-36—Stanford 7, SMU 0
1-1-37—Pittsburgh 21, Washington 0
1-1-38—California 13, Alabama 0
1-2-39—Southern California 7, Duke 3

1-1-40—Southern California 14, Tennessee 0
1-1-41—Stanford 21, Nebraska 13
1-1-42—Oregon St. 20, Duke 16 (at Durham)
1-1-43—Georgia 9, UCLA 0
1-1-44—Southern California 29, Washington 0

1-1-45—Southern California 25, Tennessee 0
1-1-46—Alabama 34, Southern California 14
1-1-47—Illinois 45, UCLA 14
1-1-48—Michigan 49, Southern California 0
1-1-49—Northwestern 20, California 14

1-2-50—Ohio St. 17, California 14
1-1-51—Michigan 14, California 6
1-1-52—Illinois 40, Stanford 7
1-1-53—Southern California 7, Wisconsin 0
1-1-54—Michigan St. 28, UCLA 20

1-1-55—Ohio St. 20, Southern California 7
1-2-56—Michigan St. 17, UCLA 14
1-1-57—Iowa 35, Oregon St. 19
1-1-58—Ohio St. 10, Oregon 7
1-1-59—Iowa 38, California 12

1-1-60—Washington 44, Wisconsin 8
1-2-61—Washington 17, Minnesota 7
1-1-62—Minnesota 21, UCLA 3
1-1-63—Southern California 42, Wisconsin 37
1-1-64—Illinois 17, Washington 7

1-1-65—Michigan 34, Oregon St. 7
1-1-66—UCLA 14, Michigan St. 12
1-2-67—Purdue 14, Southern California 13
1-1-68—Southern California 14, Indiana 3
1-1-69—Ohio St. 27, Southern California 16

1-1-70—Southern California 10, Michigan 3
1-1-71—Stanford 27, Ohio St. 17
1-1-72—Stanford 13, Michigan 12
1-1-73—Southern California 42, Ohio St. 17
1-1-74—Ohio St. 42, Southern California 21

1-1-75—Southern California 18, Ohio St. 17
1-1-76—UCLA 23, Ohio St. 10
1-1-77—Southern California 14, Michigan 6
1-2-78—Washington 27, Michigan 20
1-1-79—Southern California 17, Michigan 10

1-1-80—Southern California 17, Ohio St. 16
1-1-81—Michigan 23, Washington 6
1-1-82—Washington 28, Iowa 0
1-1-83—UCLA 24, Michigan 14
1-2-84—UCLA 45, Illinois 9

1-1-85—Southern California 20, Ohio St. 17
1-1-86—UCLA 45, Iowa 28
1-1-87—Arizona St. 22, Michigan 15
1-1-88—Michigan St. 20, Southern California 17
1-2-89—Michigan 22, Southern California 14

1-1-90—Southern California 17, Michigan 10
1-1-91—Washington 46, Iowa 34
1-1-92—Washington 34, Michigan 14
1-1-93—Michigan 38, Washington 31
1-1-94—Wisconsin 21, UCLA 16

1-2-95—Penn St. 38, Oregon 20
1-1-96—Southern California 41, Northwestern 32
1-1-97—Ohio St. 20, Arizona St. 17
1-1-98—Michigan 21, Washington St. 16
1-1-99—Wisconsin 38, UCLA 31

1-1-00—Wisconsin 17, Stanford 9
1-1-01—Washington 34, Purdue 24
1-3-02—Miami (Fla.) 37, Nebraska 14
1-1-03—Oklahoma 34, Washington St. 14
1-1-04—Southern California 28, Michigan 14

1-1-05—Texas 38, Michigan 37
1-4-06—Texas 41, Southern California 38
1-1-07—Southern California 32, Michigan 18

FEDEX ORANGE BOWL

Present Site: Miami Gardens, Florida
Stadium (Capacity): Dolphin Stadium (77,823)
Playing Surface: Prescription Athletic Turf
Name Changes: Orange Bowl (1935-88); Federal Express Orange Bowl (since 1989)
Playing Sites: Miami Field Stadium (1935-37); Orange Bowl (1938-96); Joe Robbie Stadium, renamed Pro Player Stadium in 1996, renamed Dolphin Stadium in 2005 (since 1997)

1-1-35—Bucknell 26, Miami (Fla.) 0
1-1-36—Catholic 20, Mississippi 19
1-1-37—Duquesne 13, Mississippi St. 12
1-1-38—Auburn 6, Michigan St. 0
1-2-39—Tennessee 17, Oklahoma 0

1-1-40—Georgia Tech 21, Missouri 7
1-1-41—Mississippi St. 14, Georgetown 7
1-1-42—Georgia 40, TCU 26
1-1-43—Alabama 37, Boston College 21
1-1-44—LSU 19, Texas A&M 14

1-1-45—Tulsa 26, Georgia Tech 12
1-1-46—Miami (Fla.) 13, Holy Cross 6
1-1-47—Rice 8, Tennessee 0
1-1-48—Georgia Tech 20, Kansas 14
1-1-49—Texas 41, Georgia 28

1-2-50—Santa Clara 21, Kentucky 13
1-1-51—Clemson 15, Miami (Fla.) 14
1-1-52—Georgia Tech 17, Baylor 14
1-1-53—Alabama 61, Syracuse 6
1-1-54—Oklahoma 7, Maryland 0

1-1-55—Duke 34, Nebraska 7
1-2-56—Oklahoma 20, Maryland 6
1-1-57—Colorado 27, Clemson 21
1-1-58—Oklahoma 48, Duke 21
1-1-59—Oklahoma 21, Syracuse 6

1-1-60—Georgia 14, Missouri 0
1-2-61—Missouri 21, Navy 14
1-1-62—LSU 25, Colorado 7
1-1-63—Alabama 17, Oklahoma 0
1-1-64—Nebraska 13, Auburn 7

1-1-65—Texas 21, Alabama 17
1-1-66—Alabama 39, Nebraska 28
1-2-67—Florida 27, Georgia Tech 12
1-1-68—Oklahoma 26, Tennessee 24
1-1-69—Penn St. 15, Kansas 14

1-1-70—Penn St. 10, Missouri 3
1-1-71—Nebraska 17, LSU 12
1-1-72—Nebraska 38, Alabama 6
1-1-73—Nebraska 40, Notre Dame 6
1-1-74—Penn St. 16, LSU 9

1-1-75—Notre Dame 13, Alabama 11
1-1-76—Oklahoma 14, Michigan 6
1-1-77—Ohio St. 27, Colorado 10
1-2-78—Arkansas 31, Oklahoma 6
1-1-79—Oklahoma 31, Nebraska 24

1-1-80—Oklahoma 24, Florida St. 7
1-1-81—Oklahoma 18, Florida St. 17
1-1-82—Clemson 22, Nebraska 15
1-1-83—Nebraska 21, LSU 20
1-2-84—Miami (Fla.) 31, Nebraska 30

1-1-85—Washington 28, Oklahoma 17
1-1-86—Oklahoma 25, Penn St. 10
1-1-87—Oklahoma 42, Arkansas 8
1-1-88—Miami (Fla.) 20, Oklahoma 14
1-2-89—Miami (Fla.) 23, Nebraska 3

1-1-90—Notre Dame 21, Colorado 6
1-1-91—Colorado 10, Notre Dame 9
1-1-92—Miami (Fla.) 22, Nebraska 0
1-1-93—Florida St. 27, Nebraska 14
1-1-94—Florida St. 18, Nebraska 16

1-1-95—Nebraska 24, Miami (Fla.) 17
1-1-96—Florida St. 31, Notre Dame 26

12-31-96—Nebraska 41, Virginia Tech 21
1-2-98—Nebraska 42, Tennessee 17
1-2-99—Florida 31, Syracuse 10

1-1-00—Michigan 35, Alabama 34 (ot)
1-3-01—Oklahoma 13, Florida St. 2
1-2-02—Florida 56, Maryland 23
1-2-03—Southern California 38, Iowa 17
1-1-04—Miami (Fla.) 16, Florida St. 14

1-4-05—Southern California 55, Oklahoma 19
1-3-06—Penn St. 26, Florida St. 23 (3 ot)
1-2-07—Louisville 24, Wake Forest 13

ALLSTATE SUGAR BOWL

Present Site: New Orleans, Louisiana
Stadium (Capacity): Louisiana Superdome (72,500)
Playing Surface: FieldTurf
Name Changes: Sugar Bowl (1935-87); USF&G Sugar Bowl (1988-95); Nokia Sugar Bowl (1996-06); Allstate Sugar Bowl (since 2007)
Playing Sites: Tulane Stadium, New Orleans (1935-74); Louisiana Superdome (since 1975); ^Georgia Dome, Atlanta (2006)

1-1-35—Tulane 20, Temple 14
1-1-36—TCU 3, LSU 2
1-1-37—Santa Clara 21, LSU 14
1-1-38—Santa Clara 6, LSU 0
1-2-39—TCU 15, Carnegie Mellon 7

1-1-40—Texas A&M 14, Tulane 13
1-1-41—Boston College 19, Tennessee 13
1-1-42—Fordham 2, Missouri 0
1-1-43—Tennessee 14, Tulsa 7
1-1-44—Georgia Tech 20, Tulsa 18

1-1-45—Duke 29, Alabama 26
1-1-46—Oklahoma St. 33, St. Mary's (Cal.) 13
1-1-47—Georgia 20, North Carolina 10
1-1-48—Texas 27, Alabama 7
1-1-49—Oklahoma 14, North Carolina 6

1-2-50—Oklahoma 35, LSU 0
1-1-51—Kentucky 13, Oklahoma 7
1-1-52—Maryland 28, Tennessee 13
1-1-53—Georgia Tech 24, Mississippi 7
1-1-54—Georgia Tech 42, West Virginia 19

1-1-55—Navy 21, Mississippi 0
1-2-56—Georgia Tech 7, Pittsburgh 0
1-1-57—Baylor 13, Tennessee 7
1-1-58—Mississippi 39, Texas 7
1-1-59—LSU 7, Clemson 0

1-1-60—Mississippi 21, LSU 0
1-2-61—Mississippi 14, Rice 6
1-1-62—Alabama 10, Arkansas 3
1-1-63—Mississippi 17, Arkansas 13
1-1-64—Alabama 12, Mississippi 7

1-1-65—LSU 13, Syracuse 10
1-1-66—Missouri 20, Florida 18
1-2-67—Alabama 34, Nebraska 7
1-1-68—LSU 20, Wyoming 13
1-1-69—Arkansas 16, Georgia 2

1-1-70—Mississippi 27, Arkansas 22
1-1-71—Tennessee 34, Air Force 13
1-1-72—Oklahoma 40, Auburn 22
12-31-72—Oklahoma 14, Penn St. 0
12-31-73—Notre Dame 24, Alabama 23

12-31-74—Nebraska 13, Florida 10
12-31-75—Alabama 13, Penn St. 6
1-1-77—Pittsburgh 27, Georgia 3
1-2-78—Alabama 35, Ohio St. 6
1-1-79—Alabama 14, Penn St. 7

1-1-80—Alabama 24, Arkansas 9
1-1-81—Georgia 17, Notre Dame 10
1-1-82—Pittsburgh 24, Georgia 20
1-1-83—Penn St. 27, Georgia 23
1-2-84—Auburn 9, Michigan 7

1-1-85—Nebraska 28, LSU 10
1-1-86—Tennessee 35, Miami (Fla.) 7
1-1-87—Nebraska 30, LSU 15
1-1-88—Auburn 16, Syracuse 16
1-2-89—Florida St. 13, Auburn 7

1-1-90—Miami (Fla.) 33, Alabama 25
1-1-91—Tennessee 23, Virginia 22
1-1-92—Notre Dame 39, Florida 28
1-1-93—Alabama 34, Miami (Fla.) 13
1-1-94—Florida 41, West Virginia 7

1-2-95—Florida St. 23, Florida 17
12-31-95—Virginia Tech 28, Texas 10
1-2-97—Florida 52, Florida St. 20

1-1-98—Florida St. 31, Ohio St. 14
1-1-99—Ohio St. 24, Texas A&M 14

1-4-00—Florida St. 46, Virginia Tech 29
1-2-01—Miami (Fla.) 37, Florida 20
1-1-02—LSU 47, Illinois 34
1-1-03—Georgia 26, Florida St. 13
1-4-04—LSU 21, Oklahoma 14

1-3-05—Auburn 16, Virginia Tech 13
1-2-06—West Virginia 38, Georgia 35^
1-3-07—LSU 41, Notre Dame 14

AT&T COTTON BOWL CLASSIC

Present Site: Dallas, Texas
Stadium (Capacity): Cotton Bowl (71,252)
Playing Surface: Grass
Name Changes: Cotton Bowl (1937-88, 1996); Mobil Cotton Bowl (1989-95); Southwestern Bell Cotton Bowl (1997-00); SBC Cotton Bowl Classic (2001-06); AT&T Cotton Bowl Classic (since 2007)
Playing Sites: Fair Park Stadium, Dallas (1937); Cotton Bowl (since 1938)

1-1-37—TCU 16, Marquette 6
1-1-38—Rice 28, Colorado 14
1-2-39—St. Mary's (Cal.) 20, Texas Tech 13
1-1-40—Clemson 6, Boston College 3
1-1-41—Texas A&M 13, Fordham 12

1-1-42—Alabama 29, Texas A&M 21
1-1-43—Texas 14, Georgia Tech 7
1-1-44—Randolph Field 7, Texas 7
1-1-45—Oklahoma St. 34, TCU 0
1-1-46—Texas 40, Missouri 27

1-1-47—Arkansas 0, LSU 0
1-1-48—Penn St. 13, SMU 13
1-1-49—SMU 21, Oregon 13
1-2-50—Rice 27, North Carolina 13
1-1-51—Tennessee 20, Texas 14

1-1-52—Kentucky 20, TCU 7
1-1-53—Texas 16, Tennessee 0
1-1-54—Rice 28, Alabama 6
1-1-55—Georgia Tech 14, Arkansas 6
1-2-56—Mississippi 14, TCU 13

1-1-57—TCU 28, Syracuse 27
1-1-58—Navy 20, Rice 7
1-1-59—Air Force 0, TCU 0
1-1-60—Syracuse 23, Texas 14
1-2-61—Duke 7, Arkansas 6

1-1-62—Texas 12, Mississippi 7
1-1-63—LSU 13, Texas 0
1-1-64—Texas 28, Navy 6
1-1-65—Arkansas 10, Nebraska 7
1-1-66—LSU 14, Arkansas 7

12-31-66—Georgia 24, SMU 9
1-1-68—Texas A&M 20, Alabama 16
1-1-69—Texas 36, Tennessee 13
1-1-70—Texas 21, Notre Dame 17
1-1-71—Notre Dame 24, Texas 11

1-1-72—Penn St. 30, Texas 6
1-1-73—Texas 17, Alabama 13
1-1-74—Nebraska 19, Texas 3
1-1-75—Penn St. 41, Baylor 20
1-1-76—Arkansas 31, Georgia 10

1-1-77—Houston 30, Maryland 21
1-2-78—Notre Dame 38, Texas 10
1-1-79—Notre Dame 35, Houston 34
1-1-80—Houston 17, Nebraska 14
1-1-81—Alabama 30, Baylor 2

1-1-82—Texas 14, Alabama 12
1-1-83—SMU 7, Pittsburgh 3
1-2-84—Georgia 10, Texas 9
1-1-85—Boston College 45, Houston 28
1-1-86—Texas A&M 36, Auburn 16

1-1-87—Ohio St. 28, Texas A&M 12
1-1-88—Texas A&M 35, Notre Dame 10
1-2-89—UCLA 17, Arkansas 3
1-1-90—Tennessee 31, Arkansas 27
1-1-91—Miami (Fla.) 46, Texas 3

1-1-92—Florida St. 10, Texas A&M 2
1-1-93—Notre Dame 28, Texas A&M 3
1-1-94—Notre Dame 24, Texas A&M 21
1-2-95—Southern California 55, Texas Tech 14
1-1-96—Colorado 38, Oregon 6

1-1-97—BYU 19, Kansas St. 15
1-1-98—UCLA 29, Texas A&M 23
1-1-99—Texas 38, Mississippi St. 11

1-1-00—Arkansas 27, Texas 6
1-1-01—Kansas St. 35, Tennessee 21

1-1-02—Oklahoma 10, Arkansas 3
1-1-03—Texas 35, LSU 20
1-2-04—Mississippi 31, Oklahoma St. 28
1-1-05—Tennessee 38, Texas A&M 7
1-2-06—Alabama 13, Texas Tech 10

1-1-07—Auburn 17, Nebraska 14

BRUT SUN BOWL

Present Site: El Paso, Texas
Stadium (Capacity): Sun Bowl Stadium (50,426)
Playing Surface: AstroPlay
Name Changes: Sun Bowl (1936-86, 1994-95); John Hancock Sun Bowl (1987-88); John Hancock Bowl (1989-93); Norwest Bank Sun Bowl (1996); Norwest Sun Bowl (1997-99); Wells Fargo Sun Bowl (2000-03); Vitalis Sun Bowl (2004-05); Brut Sun Bowl (since 2006)
Playing Sites: Kidd Field, UTEP, El Paso (1936-62); Sun Bowl Stadium (since 1963)

1-1-36—Hardin-Simmons 14, New Mexico St. 14
1-1-37—Hardin-Simmons 34, UTEP 6
1-1-38—West Virginia 7, Texas Tech 6
1-2-39—Utah 26, New Mexico 0
1-1-40—Arizona St. 0, Catholic 0

1-1-41—Case Reserve 26, Arizona St. 13
1-1-42—Tulsa 6, Texas Tech 0
1-1-43—Second Air Force 13, Hardin-Simmons 7
1-1-44—Southwestern (Tex.) 7, New Mexico 0
1-1-45—Southwestern (Tex.) 35, U. of Mexico 0

1-1-46—New Mexico 34, Denver 24
1-1-47—Cincinnati 18, Virginia Tech 6
1-1-48—Miami (Ohio) 13, Texas Tech 12
1-1-49—West Virginia 21, UTEP 12
1-2-50—UTEP 33, Georgetown 20

1-1-51—West Tex. A&M 14, Cincinnati 13
1-1-52—Texas Tech 25, Pacific 14
1-1-53—Pacific 26, Southern Miss. 7
1-1-54—UTEP 37, Southern Miss. 14
1-1-55—UTEP 47, Florida St. 20

1-2-56—Wyoming 21, Texas Tech 14
1-1-57—George Washington 13, UTEP 0
1-1-58—Louisville 34, Drake 20
12-31-58—Wyoming 14, Hardin-Simmons 6
12-31-59—New Mexico St. 28, North Texas 8

12-31-60—New Mexico St. 20, Utah St. 13
12-30-61—Villanova 17, Wichita St. 9
12-31-62—West Tex. A&M 15, Ohio 14
12-31-63—Oregon 21, SMU 14
12-26-64—Georgia 7, Texas Tech 0

12-31-65—UTEP 13, TCU 12
12-24-66—Wyoming 28, Florida St. 20
12-30-67—UTEP 14, Mississippi 7
12-28-68—Auburn 34, Arizona 10
12-20-69—Nebraska 45, Georgia 6

12-19-70—Georgia Tech 17, Texas Tech 9
12-18-71—LSU 33, Iowa St. 15
12-30-72—North Carolina 32, Texas Tech 28
12-29-73—Missouri 34, Auburn 17
12-28-74—Mississippi St. 26, North Carolina 24

12-26-75—Pittsburgh 33, Kansas 19
1-2-77—Texas A&M 37, Florida 14
12-31-77—Stanford 24, LSU 14
12-23-78—Texas 42, Maryland 0
12-22-79—Washington 14, Texas 7

12-27-80—Nebraska 31, Mississippi St. 17
12-26-81—Oklahoma 40, Houston 14
12-25-82—North Carolina 26, Texas 10
12-24-83—Alabama 28, SMU 7
12-22-84—Maryland 28, Tennessee 27

12-28-85—Arizona 13, Georgia 13
12-25-86—Alabama 28, Washington 6
12-25-87—Oklahoma St. 35, West Virginia 33
12-24-88—Alabama 29, Army 28
12-30-89—Pittsburgh 31, Texas A&M 28

12-31-90—Michigan St. 17, Southern California 16
12-31-91—UCLA 6, Illinois 3
12-31-92—Baylor 20, Arizona 15
12-24-93—Oklahoma 41, Texas Tech 10
12-30-94—Texas 35, North Carolina 31

12-29-95—Iowa 38, Washington 18
12-31-96—Stanford 38, Michigan St. 0
12-31-97—Arizona St. 17, Iowa 7
12-31-98—TCU 28, Southern California 19

12-31-99—Oregon 24, Minnesota 20
12-29-00—Wisconsin 21, UCLA 20
12-31-01—Washington St. 33, Purdue 27
12-31-02—Purdue 34, Washington 24
12-31-03—Minnesota 31, Oregon 30
12-31-04—Arizona St. 27, Purdue 23
12-30-05—UCLA 50, Northwestern 38
12-29-06—Oregon St. 39, Missouri 38

GATOR BOWL CLASSIC

Present Site: Jacksonville, Florida
Stadium (Capacity): Jacksonville Municipal Stadium (77,000)
Playing Surface: Grass
Name Changes: Gator Bowl (1946-85, 1991); Mazda Gator Bowl (1986-90); Outback Steakhouse Gator Bowl (1992-94); Toyota Gator Bowl (1995-07); Gator Bowl Classic (since 2008)
Playing Sites: Gator Bowl (1946-93); Florida Field, Gainesville, Fla. (1994); Jacksonville Municipal Stadium, renamed Alltel Stadium in 1997, renamed Jacksonville Municipal Stadium in 2007 (since 1995)

1-1-46—Wake Forest 26, South Carolina 14
1-1-47—Oklahoma 34, North Carolina St. 13
1-1-48—Georgia 20, Maryland 20
1-1-49—Clemson 24, Missouri 23
1-2-50—Maryland 20, Missouri 7
1-1-51—Wyoming 20, Wash. & Lee 7
1-1-52—Miami (Fla.) 14, Clemson 0
1-1-53—Florida 14, Tulsa 13
1-1-54—Texas Tech 35, Auburn 13
12-31-54—Auburn 33, Baylor 13
12-31-55—Vanderbilt 25, Auburn 13
12-29-56—Georgia Tech 21, Pittsburgh 14
12-28-57—Tennessee 3, Texas A&M 0
12-27-58—Mississippi 7, Florida 3
1-2-60—Arkansas 14, Georgia Tech 7
12-31-60—Florida 13, Baylor 12
12-30-61—Penn St. 30, Georgia Tech 15
12-29-62—Florida 17, Penn St. 7
12-28-63—North Carolina 35, Air Force 0
1-2-65—Florida St. 36, Oklahoma 19
12-31-65—Georgia Tech 31, Texas Tech 21
12-31-66—Tennessee 18, Syracuse 12
12-30-67—Florida St. 17, Penn St. 17
12-28-68—Missouri 35, Alabama 10
12-27-69—Florida 14, Tennessee 13
1-2-71—Auburn 35, Mississippi 28
12-31-71—Georgia 7, North Carolina 3
12-30-72—Auburn 24, Colorado 3
12-29-73—Texas Tech 28, Tennessee 19
12-30-74—Auburn 27, Texas 3
12-29-75—Maryland 13, Florida 0
12-27-76—Notre Dame 20, Penn St. 9
12-30-77—Pittsburgh 34, Clemson 3
12-29-78—Clemson 17, Ohio St. 15
12-28-79—North Carolina 17, Michigan 15
12-29-80—Pittsburgh 37, South Carolina 9
12-28-81—North Carolina 31, Arkansas 27
12-30-82—Florida St. 31, West Virginia 12
12-30-83—Florida 14, Iowa 6
12-28-84—Oklahoma St. 21, South Carolina 14
12-30-85—Florida St. 34, Oklahoma St. 23
12-27-86—Clemson 27, Stanford 21
12-31-87—LSU 30, South Carolina 13
1-1-89—Georgia 34, Michigan St. 27
12-30-89—Clemson 27, West Virginia 7
1-1-91—Michigan 35, Mississippi 3
12-29-91—Oklahoma 48, Virginia 14
12-31-92—Florida 27, North Carolina St. 10
12-31-93—Alabama 24, North Carolina 10
12-30-94—Tennessee 45, Virginia Tech 23
1-1-96—Syracuse 41, Clemson 0
1-1-97—North Carolina 20, West Virginia 13
1-1-98—North Carolina 42, Virginia Tech 3
1-1-99—Georgia Tech 35, Notre Dame 28
1-1-00—Miami (Fla.) 28, Georgia Tech 13
1-1-01—Virginia Tech 41, Clemson 20
1-1-02—Florida St. 30, Virginia Tech 17
1-1-03—North Carolina St. 28, Notre Dame 6
1-1-04—Maryland 41, West Virginia 7
1-1-05—Florida St. 30, West Virginia 18
1-2-06—Virginia Tech 35, Louisville 24
1-1-07—West Virginia 38, Georgia Tech 35

CAPITAL ONE BOWL

Present Site: Orlando, Florida
Stadium (Capacity): Florida Citrus Bowl (65,438)
Playing Surface: Grass
Name Changes: Tangerine Bowl (1947-82); Florida Citrus Bowl (1983-93); CompUSA Florida Citrus Bowl (1994-99); OurHouse.com Florida Citrus Bowl (2000); Capital One/Florida Citrus Bowl (2001-02); Capital One Bowl (since 2003)
Playing Sites: Tangerine Bowl, Orlando (1947-72); Florida Field, Gainesville (1973); Tangerine Bowl (now Florida Citrus Bowl) (1974-82); Orlando Stadium (now Florida Citrus Bowl) (1983-85); Florida Citrus Bowl (since 1986)

1-1-47—Catawba 31, Maryville (Tenn.) 6
1-1-48—Catawba 7, Marshall 0
1-1-49—Murray St. 21, Sul Ross St. 21
1-2-50—St. Vincent 7, Emory & Henry 6
1-1-51—Charleston (W.V.) 35, Emory & Henry 14
1-1-52—Stetson 35, Arkansas St. 20
1-1-53—Tex. A&M-Commerce 33, Tennessee Tech 0
1-1-54—Arkansas St. 7, Tex. A&M-Commerce 7
1-1-55—Neb.-Omaha 7, Eastern Ky. 6
1-2-56—Juniata 6, Missouri Valley 6
1-1-57—West Tex. A&M 20, Southern Miss. 13
1-1-58—Tex. A&M-Commerce 10, Southern Miss. 9
12-27-58—Tex. A&M-Commerce 26, Missouri Valley 7
1-1-60—Middle Tenn. 21, Presbyterian 12
12-30-60—Citadel 27, Tennessee Tech 0
12-29-61—Lamar 21, Middle Tenn. 14
12-22-62—Houston 49, Miami (Ohio) 21
12-28-63—Western Ky. 27, Coast Guard 0
12-12-64—East Caro. 14, Massachusetts 13
12-11-65—East Caro. 31, Maine 0
12-10-66—Morgan St. 14, West Chester 6
12-16-67—Tenn.-Martin 25, West Chester 8
12-27-68—Richmond 49, Ohio 42
12-26-69—Toledo 56, Davidson 33
12-28-70—Toledo 40, William & Mary 12
12-28-71—Toledo 28, Richmond 3
12-29-72—Tampa 21, Kent St. 18
12-22-73—Miami (Ohio) 16, Florida 7
12-21-74—Miami (Ohio) 21, Georgia 10
12-20-75—Miami (Ohio) 20, South Carolina 7
12-18-76—Oklahoma St. 49, BYU 21
12-23-77—Florida St. 40, Texas Tech 17
12-23-78—North Carolina St. 30, Pittsburgh 17
12-22-79—LSU 34, Wake Forest 10
12-20-80—Florida 35, Maryland 20
12-19-81—Missouri 19, Southern Miss. 17
12-18-82—Auburn 33, Boston College 26
12-17-83—Tennessee 30, Maryland 23
12-22-84—Florida St. 17, Georgia 17
12-28-85—Ohio St. 10, BYU 7
1-1-87—Auburn 16, Southern California 7
1-1-88—Clemson 35, Penn St. 10
1-2-89—Clemson 13, Oklahoma 6
1-1-90—Illinois 31, Virginia 21
1-1-91—Georgia Tech 45, Nebraska 21
1-1-92—California 37, Clemson 13
1-1-93—Georgia 21, Ohio St. 14
1-1-94—Penn St. 31, Tennessee 13
1-2-95—Alabama 24, Ohio St. 17
1-1-96—Tennessee 20, Ohio St. 14
1-1-97—Tennessee 48, Northwestern 28
1-1-98—Florida 21, Penn St. 6
1-1-99—Michigan 45, Arkansas 31
1-1-00—Michigan St. 37, Florida 34
1-1-01—Michigan 31, Auburn 28
1-1-02—Tennessee 45, Michigan 17
1-1-03—Auburn 13, Penn St. 9
1-1-04—Georgia 34, Purdue 27 (ot)
1-1-05—Iowa 30, LSU 25
1-2-06—Wisconsin 24, Auburn 10
1-1-07—Wisconsin 17, Arkansas 14

Note: No classified major teams participated in games from January 1, 1947, through January 1, 1960, or in 1961 and 1963 through 1967.

AUTOZONE LIBERTY BOWL

Present Site: Memphis, Tennessee
Stadium (Capacity): Liberty Bowl Memorial Stadium (62,598)
Playing Surface: Prescription Athletic Turf
Name Changes: Liberty Bowl (1959-92); St. Jude Liberty Bowl (1993-96); AXA Liberty Bowl (1997-03); AutoZone Liberty Bowl (since 2004)
Playing Sites: Municipal Stadium, Philadelphia (1959-63); Convention Hall, Atlantic City, N.J. (1964); Liberty Bowl Memorial Stadium (since 1965)

12-19-59—Penn St. 7, Alabama 0
12-17-60—Penn St. 41, Oregon 12
12-16-61—Syracuse 15, Miami (Fla.) 14
12-15-62—Oregon St. 6, Villanova 0
12-21-63—Mississippi St. 16, North Carolina St. 12
12-19-64—Utah 32, West Virginia 6
12-18-65—Mississippi 13, Auburn 7
12-10-66—Miami (Fla.) 14, Virginia Tech 7
12-16-67—North Carolina St. 14, Georgia 7
12-14-68—Mississippi 34, Virginia Tech 17
12-13-69—Colorado 47, Alabama 33
12-12-70—Tulane 17, Colorado 3
12-20-71—Tennessee 14, Arkansas 13
12-18-72—Georgia Tech 31, Iowa St. 30
12-17-73—North Carolina St. 31, Kansas 18
12-16-74—Tennessee 7, Maryland 3
12-22-75—Southern California 20, Texas A&M 0
12-20-76—Alabama 36, UCLA 6
12-19-77—Nebraska 21, North Carolina 17
12-23-78—Missouri 20, LSU 15
12-22-79—Penn St. 9, Tulane 6
12-27-80—Purdue 28, Missouri 25
12-30-81—Ohio St. 31, Navy 28
12-29-82—Alabama 21, Illinois 15
12-29-83—Notre Dame 19, Boston College 18
12-27-84—Auburn 21, Arkansas 15
12-27-85—Baylor 21, LSU 7
12-29-86—Tennessee 21, Minnesota 14
12-29-87—Georgia 20, Arkansas 17
12-28-88—Indiana 34, South Carolina 10
12-28-89—Mississippi 42, Air Force 29
12-27-90—Air Force 23, Ohio St. 11
12-29-91—Air Force 38, Mississippi St. 15
12-31-92—Mississippi 13, Air Force 0
12-28-93—Louisville 18, Michigan St. 7
12-31-94—Illinois 30, East Caro. 0
12-30-95—East Caro. 19, Stanford 13
12-27-96—Syracuse 30, Houston 17
12-31-97—Southern Miss. 41, Pittsburgh 7
12-31-98—Tulane 41, BYU 27
12-31-99—Southern Miss. 23, Colorado St. 17
12-29-00—Colorado St. 22, Louisville 17
12-31-01—Louisville 28, BYU 10
12-31-02—TCU 17, Colorado St. 3
12-31-03—Utah 17, Southern Miss. 0
12-31-04—Louisville 44, Boise St. 40
12-31-05—Tulsa 31, Fresno St. 24
12-29-06—South Carolina 44, Houston 36

CHICK-FIL-A BOWL

Present Site: Atlanta, Georgia
Stadium (Capacity): Georgia Dome (71,990)
Name Changes: Peach Bowl (1968-96); Chick-fil-A Peach Bowl (1997-05); Chick-fil-A Bowl (since 2006)
Playing Surface: FieldTurf
Playing Sites: Grant Field, Atlanta (1968-70); Atlanta/Fulton County Stadium (1971-92); Georgia Dome (since 1993)

12-30-68—LSU 31, Florida St. 27
12-30-69—West Virginia 14, South Carolina 3
12-30-70—Arizona St. 48, North Carolina 26
12-30-71—Mississippi 41, Georgia Tech 18
12-29-72—North Carolina St. 49, West Virginia 13
12-28-73—Georgia 17, Maryland 16
12-28-74—Texas Tech 6, Vanderbilt 6
12-31-75—West Virginia 13, North Carolina St. 10
12-31-76—Kentucky 21, North Carolina 0
12-31-77—North Carolina St. 24, Iowa St. 14
12-25-78—Purdue 41, Georgia Tech 21
12-31-79—Baylor 24, Clemson 18
1-2-81—Miami (Fla.) 20, Virginia Tech 10
12-31-81—West Virginia 26, Florida 6
12-31-82—Iowa 28, Tennessee 22
12-30-83—Florida St. 28, North Carolina 3
12-31-84—Virginia 27, Purdue 24
12-31-85—Army 31, Illinois 29
12-31-86—Virginia Tech 25, North Carolina St. 24
1-2-88—Tennessee 27, Indiana 22

12-31-88—North Carolina St. 28, Iowa 23
12-30-89—Syracuse 19, Georgia 18
12-29-90—Auburn 27, Indiana 23
1-1-92—East Caro. 37, North Carolina St. 34
1-2-93—North Carolina 21, Mississippi St. 17

12-31-93—Clemson 14, Kentucky 13
1-1-95—North Carolina St. 28, Mississippi St. 24
12-30-95—Virginia 34, Georgia 27
12-28-96—LSU 10, Clemson 7
1-2-98—Auburn 21, Clemson 17

12-31-98—Georgia 35, Virginia 33
12-30-99—Mississippi St. 17, Clemson 7
12-29-00—LSU 28, Georgia Tech 14
12-31-01—North Carolina 16, Auburn 10
12-31-02—Maryland 30, Tennessee 3

1-2-04—Clemson 27, Tennessee 14
12-31-04—Miami (Fla.) 27, Florida 10
12-30-05—LSU 40, Miami (Fla.) 3
12-30-06—Georgia 31, Virginia Tech 24

TOSTITOS FIESTA BOWL

Present Site: Glendale, Arizona
Stadium (Capacity): University of Phoenix Stadium (73,000)
Playing Surface: Grass
Name Changes: Fiesta Bowl (1971-85, 1991-92); Sunkist Fiesta Bowl (1986-90); IBM OS/2 Fiesta Bowl (1993-95); Tostitos Fiesta Bowl (since 1996)
Playing Sites: Sun Devil Stadium, Tempe, Ariz. (1971-06); University of Phoenix Stadium (since 2007)

12-27-71—Arizona St. 45, Florida St. 38
12-23-72—Arizona St. 49, Missouri 35
12-21-73—Arizona St. 28, Pittsburgh 7
12-28-74—Oklahoma St. 16, BYU 6
12-26-75—Arizona St. 17, Nebraska 14

12-25-76—Oklahoma 41, Wyoming 7
12-25-77—Penn St. 42, Arizona St. 30
12-25-78—Arkansas 10, UCLA 10
12-25-79—Pittsburgh 16, Arizona 10
12-26-80—Penn St. 31, Ohio St. 19

1-1-82—Penn St. 26, Southern California 10
1-1-83—Arizona St. 32, Oklahoma 21
1-2-84—Ohio St. 28, Pittsburgh 23
1-1-85—UCLA 39, Miami (Fla.) 37
1-1-86—Michigan 27, Nebraska 23

1-2-87—Penn St. 14, Miami (Fla.) 10
1-1-88—Florida St. 31, Nebraska 28
1-2-89—Notre Dame 34, West Virginia 21
1-1-90—Florida St. 41, Nebraska 17
1-1-91—Louisville 34, Alabama 7

1-1-92—Penn St. 42, Tennessee 17
1-1-93—Syracuse 26, Colorado 22
1-1-94—Arizona 29, Miami (Fla.) 0
1-2-95—Colorado 41, Notre Dame 24
1-2-96—Nebraska 62, Florida 24

1-1-97—Penn St. 38, Texas 15
12-31-97—Kansas St. 35, Syracuse 18
1-4-99—Tennessee 23, Florida St. 16
1-2-00—Nebraska 31, Tennessee 21
1-1-01—Oregon St. 41, Notre Dame 9

1-1-02—Oregon 38, Colorado 16
1-3-03—Ohio St. 31, Miami (Fla.) 24 (2 ot)
1-2-04—Ohio St. 35, Kansas St. 28
1-1-05—Utah 35, Pittsburgh 7
1-2-06—Ohio St. 34, Notre Dame 20

1-1-07—Boise St. 43, Oklahoma 42 (ot)

PETROSUN INDEPENDENCE BOWL

Present Site: Shreveport, Louisiana
Stadium (Capacity): Independence Stadium (48,947)
Playing Surface: AstroPlay
Name Changes: Independence Bowl (1976-89, 2004-05); Poulan Independence Bowl (1990); Poulan/Weed Eater Independence Bowl (1991-97); Sanford Independence Bowl (1998-00); MainStay Independence Bowl (2001-03); PetroSun Independence Bowl (since 2006)
Playing Site: Independence Stadium (since 1976)

12-13-76—McNeese St. 20, Tulsa 16
12-17-77—Louisiana Tech 24, Louisville 14
12-16-78—East Caro. 35, Louisiana Tech 13
12-15-79—Syracuse 31, McNeese St. 7
12-13-80—Southern Miss. 16, McNeese St. 14

12-12-81—Texas A&M 33, Oklahoma St. 16
12-11-82—Wisconsin 14, Kansas St. 3
12-10-83—Air Force 9, Mississippi 3
12-15-84—Air Force 23, Virginia Tech 7
12-21-85—Minnesota 20, Clemson 13

12-20-86—Mississippi 20, Texas Tech 17
12-19-87—Washington 24, Tulane 12
12-23-88—Southern Miss. 38, UTEP 18
12-16-89—Oregon 27, Tulsa 24
12-15-90—Louisiana Tech 34, Maryland 34

12-29-91—Georgia 24, Arkansas 15
12-31-92—Wake Forest 39, Oregon 35
12-31-93—Virginia Tech 45, Indiana 20
12-28-94—Virginia 20, TCU 10
12-29-95—LSU 45, Michigan St. 26

12-31-96—Auburn 32, Army 29
12-28-97—LSU 27, Notre Dame 9
12-31-98—Mississippi 35, Texas Tech 18
12-31-99—Mississippi 27, Oklahoma 25
12-31-00—Mississippi St. 43, Texas A&M 41 (ot)

12-27-01—Alabama 14, Iowa St. 13
12-27-02—Mississippi 27, Nebraska 23
12-31-03—Arkansas 27, Missouri 14
12-28-04—Iowa St. 17, Miami (Ohio) 13
12-30-05—Missouri 38, South Carolina 31

12-28-06—Oklahoma St. 34, Alabama 31

PACIFIC LIFE HOLIDAY BOWL

Present Site: San Diego, California
Stadium (Capacity): Qualcomm Stadium (66,000)
Playing Surface: Grass
Name Changes: Holiday Bowl (1978-85, 2002); Sea World Holiday Bowl (1986-90); Thrifty Car Rental Holiday Bowl (1991-94); Plymouth Holiday Bowl (1995-97); Culligan Holiday Bowl (1998-01); Pacific Life Holiday Bowl (since 2003)
Playing Site: San Diego Jack Murphy Stadium, renamed Qualcomm Stadium in 1997 (since 1978)

12-22-78—Navy 23, BYU 16
12-21-79—Indiana 38, BYU 37
12-19-80—BYU 46, SMU 45
12-18-81—BYU 38, Washington St. 36
12-17-82—Ohio St. 47, BYU 17

12-23-83—BYU 21, Missouri 17
12-21-84—BYU 24, Michigan 17
12-22-85—Arkansas 18, Arizona St. 17
12-30-86—Iowa 39, San Diego St. 38
12-30-87—Iowa 20, Wyoming 19

12-30-88—Oklahoma St. 62, Wyoming 14
12-29-89—Penn St. 50, BYU 39
12-29-90—Texas A&M 65, BYU 14
12-30-91—BYU 13, Iowa 13
12-30-92—Hawaii 27, Illinois 17

12-30-93—Ohio St. 28, BYU 21
12-30-94—Michigan 24, Colorado St. 14
12-29-95—Kansas St. 54, Colorado St. 21
12-30-96—Colorado 33, Washington 21
12-29-97—Colorado St. 35, Missouri 24

12-30-98—Arizona 23, Nebraska 20
12-29-99—Kansas St. 24, Washington 20
12-29-00—Oregon 35, Texas 30
12-28-01—Texas 47, Washington 43
12-27-02—Kansas St. 34, Arizona St. 27

12-30-03—Washington St. 28, Texas 20
12-30-04—Texas Tech 45, California 31
12-29-05—Oklahoma 17, Oregon 14
12-28-06—California 45, Texas A&M 10

OUTBACK BOWL

Present Site: Tampa, Florida
Stadium (Capacity): Raymond James Stadium (65,500)
Playing Surface: Grass
Name Changes: Hall of Fame Bowl (1986-95); Outback Bowl (since 1996)
Playing Sites: Tampa Stadium, renamed Houlihan's Stadium in 1997 (1986-97); Tampa Community Stadium (1998); Raymond James Stadium (since 1999)

12-23-86—Boston College 27, Georgia 24
1-2-88—Michigan 28, Alabama 24
1-2-89—Syracuse 23, LSU 10
1-1-90—Auburn 31, Ohio St. 14
1-1-91—Clemson 30, Illinois 0

1-1-92—Syracuse 24, Ohio St. 17
1-1-93—Tennessee 38, Boston College 23
1-1-94—Michigan 42, North Carolina St. 7
1-2-95—Wisconsin 34, Duke 20
1-1-96—Penn St. 43, Auburn 14

1-1-97—Alabama 17, Michigan 14
1-1-98—Georgia 33, Wisconsin 6
1-1-99—Penn St. 26, Kentucky 14
1-1-00—Georgia 28, Purdue 25 (ot)
1-1-01—South Carolina 24, Ohio St. 7

1-1-02—South Carolina 31, Ohio St. 28
1-1-03—Michigan 38, Florida 30
1-1-04—Iowa 37, Florida 17
1-1-05—Georgia 24, Wisconsin 21
1-2-06—Florida 31, Iowa 24

1-1-07—Penn St. 20, Tennessee 10

INSIGHT BOWL

Present Site: Tempe, Arizona
Stadium (Capacity): Sun Devil Stadium (73,000)
Playing Surface: Grass
Name Changes: Copper Bowl (1989, 1996); Domino's Pizza Copper Bowl (1990-91); Weiser Lock Copper Bowl (1992-95); Insight.com Bowl (1997-01); Insight Bowl (since 2002)
Playing Sites: Arizona Stadium, Tucson, Ariz. (1989-99); Bank One Ballpark, Phoenix (2000-05); Sun Devil Stadium (since 2006)

12-31-89—Arizona 17, North Carolina St. 10
12-31-90—California 17, Wyoming 15
12-31-91—Indiana 24, Baylor 0
12-29-92—Washington St. 31, Utah 28
12-29-93—Kansas St. 52, Wyoming 17

12-29-94—BYU 31, Oklahoma 6
12-27-95—Texas Tech 55, Air Force 41
12-27-96—Wisconsin 38, Utah 10
12-27-97—Arizona 20, New Mexico 14
12-26-98—Missouri 34, West Virginia 31

12-31-99—Colorado 62, Boston College 28
12-28-00—Iowa St. 37, Pittsburgh 29
12-29-01—Syracuse 26, Kansas St. 3
12-26-02—Pittsburgh 38, Oregon St. 13
12-26-03—California 52, Virginia Tech 49

12-28-04—Oregon St. 38, Notre Dame 21
12-27-05—Arizona St. 45, Rutgers 40
12-29-06—Texas Tech 44, Minnesota 41 (ot)

CHAMPS SPORTS BOWL

Present Site: Orlando, Florida
Stadium (Capacity): Florida Citrus Bowl (65,438)
Playing Surface: Grass
Name Changes: Blockbuster Bowl (1990-93); Carquest Bowl (1994-97); Micron PC Bowl (1998); MicronPC.com Bowl (1999-00); Visit Florida Tangerine Bowl (2001); Mazda Tangerine Bowl (2002-03); Champs Sports Bowl (since 2004)
Note: The game was known as the Sunshine Football Classic for a short time in the 1997-98 offseason after Carquest Auto Parts dropped its sponsorship and before Micron agreed to be the title sponsor. Also, this game should not be confused with the Tangerine Bowl that became the Florida Citrus Bowl in 1982 and is now known as the Capital One Bowl.
Playing Sites: Joe Robbie Stadium, renamed Pro Player Stadium in 1996, Miami (1990-00); Florida Citrus Bowl (since 2001)

12-28-90—Florida St. 24, Penn St. 17
12-28-91—Alabama 30, Colorado 25
1-1-93—Stanford 24, Penn St. 3
1-1-94—Boston College 31, Virginia 13
1-2-95—South Carolina 24, West Virginia 21

12-30-95—North Carolina 20, Arkansas 10
12-27-96—Miami (Fla.) 31, Virginia 21
12-29-97—Georgia Tech 35, West Virginia 30
12-29-98—Miami (Fla.) 46, North Carolina St. 23
12-30-99—Illinois 63, Virginia 21

12-28-00—North Carolina St. 38, Minnesota 30
12-20-01—Pittsburgh 34, North Carolina St. 19
12-23-02—Texas Tech 55, Clemson 15
12-22-03—North Carolina St. 56, Kansas 26
12-21-04—Georgia Tech 51, Syracuse 14

12-27-05—Clemson 19, Colorado 10
12-29-06—Maryland 24, Purdue 7

PIONEER PUREVISION LAS VEGAS BOWL

Present Site: Las Vegas, Nevada
Stadium (Capacity): Sam Boyd Stadium (40,000)
Playing Surface: TurfTech
Name Changes: Las Vegas Bowl (1992-98, 2000, 2003); EA Sports Las Vegas Bowl (1999); Sega Sports Las Vegas Bowl (2001-02), Pioneer PureVision Las Vegas Bowl (since 2004)
Playing Site: Sam Boyd Stadium (since 1992)

12-18-92—Bowling Green 35, Nevada 34
12-17-93—Utah St. 42, Ball St. 33
12-15-94—UNLV 52, Central Mich. 24
12-14-95—Toledo 40, Nevada 37 (ot)
12-19-96—Nevada 18, Ball St. 15

12-20-97—Oregon 41, Air Force 13
12-19-98—North Carolina 20, San Diego St. 13
12-18-99—Utah 17, Fresno St. 16
12-21-00—UNLV 31, Arkansas 14
12-25-01—Utah 10, Southern California 6

12-25-02—UCLA 27, New Mexico 13
12-24-03—Oregon St. 55, New Mexico 14
12-23-04—Wyoming 24, UCLA 21
12-22-05—California 35, BYU 28
12-21-06—BYU 38, Oregon 8

VALERO ALAMO BOWL

Present Site: San Antonio, Texas
Stadium (Capacity): Alamodome (65,000)
Playing Surface: SportField Real Grass
Name Changes: Builders Square Alamo Bowl (1993-98); Sylvania Alamo Bowl (1999-01); Alamo Bowl (2002-03, 2006); MasterCard Alamo Bowl (2004-05); Valero Alamo Bowl (since 2007)
Playing Site: Alamodome (since 1993)

12-31-93—California 37, Iowa 3
12-31-94—Washington St. 10, Baylor 3
12-28-95—Texas A&M 22, Michigan 20
12-29-96—Iowa 27, Texas Tech 0
12-30-97—Purdue 33, Oklahoma St. 20

12-29-98—Purdue 37, Kansas St. 34
12-28-99—Penn St. 24, Texas A&M 0
12-30-00—Nebraska 66, Northwestern 17
12-29-01—Iowa 19, Texas Tech 16
12-28-02—Wisconsin 31, Colorado 28 (ot)

12-29-03—Nebraska 17, Michigan St. 3
12-29-04—Ohio St. 33, Oklahoma St. 7
12-28-05—Nebraska 32, Michigan 28
12-30-06—Texas 26, Iowa 24

ROADY'S HUMANITARIAN BOWL

Present Site: Boise, Idaho
Stadium (Capacity): Bronco Stadium (30,000)
Playing Surface: Blue AstroPlay
Name Changes: Sports Humanitarian Bowl (1997); Humanitarian Bowl (1998); Crucial.com Humanitarian Bowl (1999-03); MPC Computers Bowl (2004-06); Roady's Humanitarian Bowl (since 2007)
Playing Site: Bronco Stadium (since 1997)

12-29-97—Cincinnati 35, Utah St. 19
12-30-98—Idaho 42, Southern Miss. 35
12-30-99—Boise St. 34, Louisville 31
12-28-00—Boise St. 38, UTEP 23
12-31-01—Clemson 49, Louisiana Tech 24

12-31-02—Boise St. 34, Iowa St. 16
1-3-04—Georgia Tech 52, Tulsa 10
12-27-04—Fresno St. 37, Virginia 34 (ot)
12-28-05—Boston College 27, Boise St. 21
12-31-06—Miami (Fla.) 21, Nevada 20

MOTOR CITY BOWL

Present Site: Detroit, Michigan
Stadium (Capacity): Ford Field (65,000)
Playing Surface: FieldTurf
Playing Sites: Pontiac Silverdome (1997-01); Ford Field (since 2002)

12-26-97—Mississippi 34, Marshall 31
12-23-98—Marshall 48, Louisville 29
12-27-99—Marshall 21, BYU 3
12-27-00—Marshall 25, Cincinnati 14
12-29-01—Toledo 23, Cincinnati 16

12-26-02—Boston College 51, Toledo 25
12-26-03—Bowling Green 28, Northwestern 24
12-27-04—Connecticut 39, Toledo 10
12-26-05—Memphis 38, Akron 31
12-26-06—Central Mich. 31, Middle Tenn. 14

GAYLORD HOTELS MUSIC CITY BOWL

Presented By Bridgestone
Present Site: Nashville, Tennessee
Stadium (Capacity): LP Field (68,000)
Playing Surface: Grass
Name Changes: Music City Bowl (1998, 2000-01); HomePoint.com Music City Bowl (1999); Gaylord Hotels Music City Bowl (2002-03); Gaylord Hotels Music City Bowl Presented By Bridgestone (since 2004)
Playing Sites: Vanderbilt Stadium (1998); Adelphia Coliseum, renamed The Coliseum in 2002, renamed LP Field in 2006 (since 1999)

12-29-98—Virginia Tech 38, Alabama 7
12-29-99—Syracuse 20, Kentucky 13
12-28-00—West Virginia 49, Mississippi 38
12-28-01—Boston College 20, Georgia 16
12-30-02—Minnesota 29, Arkansas 14

12-31-03—Auburn 28, Wisconsin 14
12-31-04—Minnesota 20, Alabama 16
12-30-05—Virginia 34, Minnesota 31
12-29-06—Kentucky 28, Clemson 20

GMAC BOWL

Present Site: Mobile, Alabama
Stadium (Capacity): Ladd-Peebles Stadium (40,048)
Playing Surface: FieldTurf
Name Changes: Mobile Alabama Bowl (1999); GMAC Mobile Alabama Bowl (2000); GMAC Bowl (since 2001)
Playing Site: Ladd-Peebles Stadium (since 1999)

12-22-99—TCU 28, East Caro. 14
12-20-00—Southern Miss. 28, TCU 21
12-19-01—Marshall 64, East Caro. 61 (2 ot)
12-18-02—Marshall 38, Louisville 15
12-18-03—Miami (Ohio) 49, Louisville 28

12-22-04—Bowling Green 52, Memphis 35
12-21-05—Toledo 45, UTEP 13
1-7-07—Southern Miss. 28, Ohio 7

R+L CARRIERS NEW ORLEANS BOWL

Present Site: New Orleans, Louisiana
Stadium (Capacity): Louisiana Superdome (72,500)
Playing Surface: FieldTurf
Name Changes: New Orleans Bowl (2001-03); Wyndham New Orleans Bowl (2004-05); R+L Carriers New Orleans Bowl (since 2006)
Playing Sites: Louisiana Superdome (since 2001); ^Cajun Field, Lafayette, La. (2005)

12-18-01—Colorado St. 45, North Texas 20
12-17-02—North Texas 24, Cincinnati 19
12-16-03—Memphis 27, North Texas 17
12-14-04—Southern Miss. 31, North Texas 10
12-20-05—Southern Miss. 31, Arkansas St. 19^

12-22-06—Troy 41, Rice 17

SHERATON HAWAII BOWL

Present Site: Honolulu, Hawaii
Stadium (Capacity): Aloha Stadium (50,000)
Playing Surface: FieldTurf
Name Changes: Conagra Foods Hawaii Bowl (2002); Sheraton Hawaii Bowl (since 2003)
Playing Site: Aloha Stadium (since 2002)

12-25-02—Tulane 36, Hawaii 28
12-25-03—Hawaii 54, Houston 48 (3 ot)
12-24-04—Hawaii 59, UAB 40
12-24-05—Nevada 49, UCF 48 (ot)
12-24-06—Hawaii 41, Arizona St. 24

MEINEKE CAR CARE BOWL

Present Site: Charlotte, North Carolina
Stadium (Capacity): Bank of America Stadium (73,298)
Playing Surface: Grass
Name Changes: Continental Tire Bowl (2002-04); Meineke Car Care Bowl (since 2005)
Playing Site: Ericsson Stadium, renamed Bank of America Stadium in 2004 (since 2002)

12-28-02—Virginia 48, West Virginia 22
12-27-03—Virginia 23, Pittsburgh 16
12-30-04—Boston College 37, North Carolina 24
12-31-05—North Carolina St. 14, South Fla. 0
12-30-06—Boston College 25, Navy 24

EMERALD BOWL

Present Site: San Francisco, California
Stadium (Capacity): AT&T Park (38,437 for football)
Playing Surface: Grass
Name Changes: Diamond Walnut San Francisco Bowl (2002-03); Emerald Bowl (since 2004)
Playing Site: Pacific Bell Park, renamed SBC Park in 2004, renamed AT&T Park in 2006 (since 2002)

12-31-02—Virginia Tech 20, Air Force 13
12-31-03—Boston College 35, Colorado St. 21
12-30-04—Navy 34, New Mexico 19
12-29-05—Utah 38, Georgia Tech 10
12-27-06—Florida St. 44, UCLA 27

BELL HELICOPTER ARMED FORCES BOWL

Present Site: Fort Worth, Texas
Stadium (Capacity): Amon G. Carter Stadium (43,000)
Playing Surface: Grass
Name Changes: PlainsCapital Fort Worth Bowl (2003-04); Fort Worth Bowl (2005); Bell Helicopter Armed Forces Bowl (since 2006)
Playing Site: Amon G. Carter Stadium (since 2003)

12-23-03—Boise St. 34, TCU 31
12-23-04—Cincinnati 32, Marshall 14
12-23-05—Kansas 42, Houston 13
12-23-06—Utah 25, Tulsa 13

SAN DIEGO COUNTY CREDIT UNION POINSETTIA BOWL

Present Site: San Diego, California
Stadium (Capacity): Qualcomm Stadium (66,000)
Playing Surface: Grass
Playing Site: Qualcomm Stadium (since 2005)

12-22-05—Navy 51, Colorado St. 30
12-19-06—TCU 37, Northern Ill. 7

INTERNATIONAL BOWL

Present Site: Toronto, Ontario, Canada
Stadium (Capacity): Rogers Centre (53,506)
Playing Surface: FieldTurf
Playing Site: Rogers Centre (since 2007)

1-6-07—Cincinnati 27, Western Mich. 24

NEW MEXICO BOWL

Present Site: Albuquerque, New Mexico
Stadium (Capacity): University Stadium (38,634)
Playing Surface: Grass
Playing Site: University Stadium (since 2006)

12-23-06—San Jose St. 20, New Mexico 12

PAPAJOHNS.COM BOWL

Present Site: Birmingham, Alabama
Stadium (Capacity): Legion Field (72,000)
Playing Surface: SureTurf
Playing Site: Legion Field (since 2006)

12-23-06—South Fla. 24, East Caro. 7

TEXAS BOWL

Present Site: Houston, Texas
Stadium (Capacity): Reliant Stadium (69,500)
Playing Surface: Grass
Playing Site: Reliant Stadium (since 2006)

12-28-06—Rutgers 37, Kansas St. 10

Bowl-Game Title Sponsors

Bowl	Title Sponsor[s] (Year Began)	Bowl Name (Years)
Alamo	Builders Square (1993-98) Sylvania (1999-01) MasterCard (2002-05) Valero Energy Corp. (since 2007)	Builders Square Alamo (1993-98) Sylvania Alamo (1999-01) Alamo Bowl Presented By MasterCard (2002-03) MasterCard Alamo Bowl (2004-05) Alamo Bowl (2006) Valero Alamo (since 2007)
Armed Forces	PlainsCapital (2003-04) Bell Helicopter (since 2006)	PlainsCapital Fort Worth (2003-04) Fort Worth (2005) Bell Helicopter Armed Forces (since 2006)
Capital One	Florida Department of Citrus (1983-02) Comp USA (1994-99) OurHouse.com (2000) Capital One (since 2001)	Florida Citrus (1983-93) CompUSA Florida Citrus (1994-99) OurHouse.com Florida Citrus (2000) Capital One Florida Citrus (2001-02) Capital One (since 2003)
Champs Sports	Blockbuster Video (1990-93) Carquest Parts (1994-97) Micron PC (1998-00) Florida Tourism (2001) Mazda (2002-03) Champs Sports (since 2004)	Blockbuster (1990-93) Carquest (1994-97) Micron PC (1998) Micron PC.com (1999-00) Visit Florida Tangerine (2001) Mazda Tangerine (2002-03) Champs Sports (since 2004)
Chick-fil-A	Chick-fil-A (since 1997)	Peach (1968-96) Chick-fil-A Peach (1997-05) Chick-fil-A (since 2006)
Cotton	Mobil (1989-95) Southwestern Bell (1997-00) SBC Communications (2001-06) AT&T (since 2007)	Cotton (1937-88, 1996) Mobil Cotton (1989-95) Southwestern Bell (1997-00) SBC Cotton Bowl Classic (2001-06) AT&T Cotton Bowl Classic (since 2007)
Emerald	Diamond Walnut Growers (2002-03) Emerald of California (since 2004)	Diamond Walnut San Francisco (2002-03) Emerald (since 2004)
Fiesta	Sunkist (1986-90) IBM (1993-95) FritoLay/Tostitos (since 1996)	Fiesta (1971-85; 1991-92) Sunkist Fiesta (1986-90) IBM OS/2 Fiesta (1993-95) Tostitos Fiesta (since 1996)
Gator	Mazda (1986-91) Outback Steakhouse (1992-94) Toyota (1995-07)	Gator (1946-85) Mazda Gator (1986-91) Outback Steakhouse Gator (1992-94) Toyota Gator (1995-07) Gator Bowl Classic (since 2008)
GMAC	Mobile Alabama, Inc. (1999) GMAC Financial Services and the City of Mobile (since 2000)	Mobile Alabama (1999) GMAC Mobile Alabama (2000) GMAC (since 2001)
Hawaii	ConAgra Foods (2002) Sheraton Hotels and Resorts (since 2003)	ConAgra Foods Hawaii (2002) Sheraton Hawaii (since 2003)
Holiday	Sea World (1986-90) Thrifty Car Rental (1991-94) Plymouth (1995-97) Culligan (1998-01) Pacific Life (since 2002)	Holiday (1978-85) Sea World Holiday (1986-90) Thrifty Car Rental Holiday (1991-94) Plymouth Holiday (1995-97) Culligan Holiday (1998-01) Pacific Life Holiday (since 2002)
Humanitarian	Humanitarian Bowl Association (1997-98) Crucial Technology (1999-03) MPC Computers (2004-06) Roady's Truck Stops (since 2007)	Sports Humanitarian (1997) Humanitarian (1998) Crucial.com Humanitarian (1999-03) MPC Computers (2004-06) Roady's Humanitarian (since 2007)
Independence	Poulan (1990-97) Sanford (1998-00) MainStay Management (2001-03) PetroSun (since 2006)	Independence (1976-89, 2004-05) Poulan Independence (1990) Poulan/Weed Eater Independence (1991-97) Sanford Independence (1998-00) MainStay Independence (2001-03) PetroSun Independence (since 2006)
Insight	Domino's Pizza (1990-91) Weiser Lock (1992-95) Insight Enterprises (since 1997)	Copper (1989, 1996) Domino's Pizza Copper (1990-91) Weiser Lock Copper (1992-95) Insight.com (1997-01) Insight (since 2002)
International	None	International (since 2007)
Las Vegas	Las Vegas Convention & Visitor's Authority (1998, 2000, 2003) EA Sports (1999) Sega of America (2001-02) Pioneer Electronics (since 2004)	Las Vegas (1992-98, 2000, 2003) EA Sports Las Vegas (1999) Sega Sports Las Vegas (2001-02) Pioneer PureVision Las Vegas (since 2004)
Liberty	St. Jude (1993-96) AXA/Equitable (1997-03) AutoZone (since 2004)	Liberty (1959-92) St. Jude Liberty (1993-96) AXA Liberty (1997-03) AutoZone Liberty (since 2004)
Meineke Car Care	Continental Tires (2002-04) Meineke Car Care Centers (since 2005)	Continental Tire (2002-04) Meineke Car Care (since 2005)
Motor City	Motor City Bowl, Inc. (1997) General Motors, Daimler-Chrysler and Ford (Presenting Sponsors since 1998)	Ford Motor City (1997) Motor City (since 1998)
Music City	American General (1998) HomePoint.com (1999) Gaylord Entertainment (2002-03) Gaylord Entertainment and Bridgestone (since 2004)	Music City (1998, 2000-01) HomePoint.com Music City (1999) Gaylord Hotels Music City (2002-03) Gaylord Hotels Music City Presented by Bridgestone (since 2004)
New Mexico	None	New Mexico (since 2006)
New Orleans	Greater New Orleans Sports Foundation (2001-03) Wyndham International (2004-05) R+L Carriers (since 2006)	New Orleans (2001) Wyndham New Orleans (2004-05) R+L Carriers New Orleans (since 2006)
Orange	Federal Express (since 1989)	Orange (1935-88) Federal Express (FedEx) Orange (since 1989)
Outback	Outback Steakhouse (since 1996)	Hall of Fame (1986-95) Outback (since 1996)
Papajohns.com	Papa John's (since 2006)	Papajohns.com (since 2006)
Poinsettia	San Diego County Credit Union (since 2005)	San Diego County Credit Union Poinsettia (since 2005)
Rose	Pasadena Tournament of Roses Association (1902, since 1916) AT&T (Presenting Sponsor, 1999-02) Sony Electronics (Presenting Sponsor, 2003) Citi (Presenting Sponsor, since 2004)	Rose (since 1902) Rose Bowl Presented by AT&T (1999-02) Rose Bowl Presented By Sony (2003) Rose Bowl Presented by Citi (since 2004)
Sugar	USF&G Sugar (1988-95) Nokia Mobile Telephones (1996-06) Allstate (since 2007)	Sugar (1935-87) USF&G Sugar (1988-95) Nokia Sugar (1996-06) Allstate Sugar (2007)
Sun	John Hancock (1987-93) Norwest Corporation (1996-98) Wells Fargo (1999-03) Vitalis (since 2004) Brut/Idelle Labs (since 2006)	Sun (1936-86, 1994-95) John Hancock Sun (1987-88) John Hancock (1989-93) Norwest Bank Sun (1996) Norwest Sun (1997-98) Wells Fargo Sun (1999-03) Vitalis Sun (since 2004) Brut Sun (since 2006)
Texas	None	Texas (since 2006)

Bowl Financial Analysis, 1976-06

(Payouts are estimates.)

Year	No. Bowls	No. Teams	Total Payout	Per-Game Payout	Per-Team Payout
1976-77	11	22	$11,345,851	$515,714	$257,857
1977-78	12	24	13,323,638	1,110,303	555,152
1978-79	13	26	15,506,516	1,192,809	596,405
1979-80	15	30	17,219,624	1,324,586	662,293
1980-81	13	26	19,517,938	1,501,380	750,690
1981-82	14	28	21,791,222	1,556,516	778,258
1982-83	15	30	26,682,486	1,778,832	889,416
1983-84	15	30	32,535,788	2,169,052	1,084,256
1984-85	16	32	36,666,738	2,291,671	1,145,836
1985-86	16	32	36,995,864	2,312,242	1,156,121
1986-87	17	34	45,830,906	2,695,936	1,347,968
1987-88	17	34	48,251,516	2,838,324	1,419,162
1988-89	17	34	52,905,426	3,112,084	1,556,042
1989-90	18	36	58,208,058	3,233,781	1,616,891
1990-91	19	38	60,378,362	3,177,809	1,588,904

Year	No. Bowls	No. Teams	Total Payout	Per-Game Payout	Per-Team Payout
1991-92	18	36	63,494,554	3,527,475	1,763,738
1992-93	18	36	67,950,000	3,775,000	1,887,500
1993-94	19	38	71,006,000	3,737,158	1,868,579
1994-95	19	38	72,416,000	3,811,368	1,905,684
1995-96	18	36	101,390,000	5,632,778	2,816,389
1996-97	18	36	101,316,000	5,628,667	2,814,333
1997-98	20	40	108,750,000	5,437,500	2,718,750
1998-99	22	44	145,924,000	6,632,909	3,316,455
1999-00	23	46	146,000,000	6,373,913	3,186,957
2000-01	25	50	161,826,000	6,473,040	3,236,520
2001-02	25	50	156,900,000	6,276,000	3,138,000
2002-03	28	56	172,710,000	6,168,214	3,084,107
2003-04	28	56	202,500,000	7,232,143	3,616,071
2004-05	28	56	186,373,416	6,656,193	3,328,096
2005-06	28	56	191,500,000	7,365,385	3,682,692
2006-07	32	64	246,146,000	7,692,063	3,846,031

31 Former Major Bowl Games

(Games in which at least one team was classified major that season)

ALAMO
(San Antonio, Texas)

1-4-47—Hardin-Simmons 20, Denver 0

ALL-AMERICAN
(Called Hall of Fame Classic, 1977-85)
(Birmingham, Ala.)

12-22-77—Maryland 17, Minnesota 7
12-20-78—Texas A&M 28, Iowa St. 12
12-29-79—Missouri 24, South Carolina 14
12-27-80—Arkansas 34, Tulane 15
12-31-81—Mississippi St. 10, Kansas 0

12-31-82—Air Force 36, Vanderbilt 28
12-22-83—West Virginia 20, Kentucky 16
12-29-84—Kentucky 20, Wisconsin 19
12-31-85—Georgia Tech 17, Michigan St. 14
12-31-86—Florida St. 27, Indiana 13

12-22-87—Virginia 22, BYU 16
12-29-88—Florida 14, Illinois 10
12-28-89—Texas Tech 49, Duke 21
12-28-90—North Carolina St. 31, Southern Miss. 27

ALOHA
(Honolulu, Hawaii)

12-25-82—Washington 21, Maryland 20
12-26-83—Penn St. 13, Washington 10
12-29-84—SMU 27, Notre Dame 20
12-28-85—Alabama 24, Southern California 3
12-27-86—Arizona 30, North Carolina 21

12-25-87—UCLA 20, Florida 16
12-25-88—Washington St. 24, Houston 22
12-25-89—Michigan St. 33, Hawaii 13
12-25-90—Syracuse 28, Arizona 0
12-25-91—Georgia Tech 18, Stanford 17

12-25-92—Kansas 23, BYU 20
12-25-93—Colorado 41, Fresno St. 30
12-25-94—Boston College 12, Kansas St. 7
12-25-95—Kansas 51, UCLA 30
12-25-96—Navy 42, California 38

12-25-97—Washington 51, Michigan St. 23
12-25-98—Colorado 51, Oregon 43
12-25-99—Wake Forest 23, Arizona St. 3
12-25-00—Boston College 31, Arizona St. 17

AVIATION
(Dayton, Ohio)

12-9-61—New Mexico 28, Western Mich. 12

BACARDI
(Cuban National Sports Festival at Havana)

1-1-37—Auburn 7, Villanova 7

BLUEBONNET
(Houston, Texas)

12-19-59—Clemson 23, TCU 7
12-17-60—Alabama 3, Texas 3
12-16-61—Kansas 33, Rice 7
12-22-62—Missouri 14, Georgia Tech 10
12-21-63—Baylor 14, LSU 7

12-19-64—Tulsa 14, Mississippi 7
12-18-65—Tennessee 27, Tulsa 6
12-17-66—Texas 19, Mississippi 0
12-23-67—Colorado 31, Miami (Fla.) 21
12-31-68—SMU 28, Oklahoma 27

12-31-69—Houston 36, Auburn 7
12-31-70—Alabama 24, Oklahoma 24
12-31-71—Colorado 29, Houston 17
12-30-72—Tennessee 24, LSU 17
12-29-73—Houston 47, Tulane 7

12-23-74—Houston 31, North Carolina St. 31
12-27-75—Texas 38, Colorado 21
12-31-76—Nebraska 27, Texas Tech 24
12-31-77—Southern California 47, Texas A&M 28
12-31-78—Stanford 25, Georgia 22

12-31-79—Purdue 27, Tennessee 22
12-31-80—North Carolina 16, Texas 7
12-31-81—Michigan 33, UCLA 14
12-31-82—Arkansas 28, Florida 24
12-31-83—Oklahoma St. 24, Baylor 14

12-31-84—West Virginia 31, TCU 14
12-31-85—Air Force 24, Texas 16
12-31-86—Baylor 21, Colorado 9
12-31-87—Texas 32, Pittsburgh 27

BLUEGRASS
(Louisville, Ky.)

12-13-58—Oklahoma St. 15, Florida St. 6

CALIFORNIA
(Fresno, Calif.)

12-19-81—Toledo 27, San Jose St. 25
12-18-82—Fresno St. 29, Bowling Green 28
12-17-83—Northern Ill. 20, Cal St. Fullerton 13
12-15-84—UNLV 30, *Toledo 13
12-14-85—Fresno St. 51, Bowling Green 7

12-13-86—San Jose St. 37, Miami (Ohio) 7
12-12-87—Eastern Mich. 30, San Jose St. 27
12-10-88—Fresno St. 35, Western Mich. 30
12-9-89—Fresno St. 27, Ball St. 6
12-8-90—San Jose St. 48, Central Mich. 24

12-14-91—Bowling Green 28, Fresno St. 21

**Won by forfeit.*

CAMELLIA
(Lafayette, La.)

12-30-48—Hardin-Simmons 49, Wichita St. 12

CHERRY
(Pontiac, Mich.)

12-22-84—Army 10, Michigan St. 6
12-21-85—Maryland 35, Syracuse 18

DELTA
(Memphis, Tenn.)

1-1-48—Mississippi 13, TCU 9
1-1-49—William & Mary 20, Oklahoma St. 0

DIXIE BOWL
(Birmingham, Ala.)

1-1-48—Arkansas 21, William & Mary 19
1-1-49—Baylor 20, Wake Forest 7

DIXIE CLASSIC
(Dallas, Texas)

1-2-22—Texas A&M 22, Centre 14
1-1-25—West Va. Wesleyan 9, SMU 7
1-1-34—Arkansas 7, Centenary (La.) 7

FORT WORTH CLASSIC
(Fort Worth, Texas)

1-1-21—Centre 63, TCU 7

FREEDOM
(Anaheim, Calif.)

12-26-84—Iowa 55, Texas 17
12-30-85—Washington 20, Colorado 17
12-30-86—UCLA 31, BYU 10
12-30-87—Arizona St. 33, Air Force 28
12-29-88—BYU 20, Colorado 17

12-30-89—Washington 34, Florida 7
12-29-90—Colorado St. 32, Oregon 31
12-30-91—Tulsa 28, San Diego St. 17
12-29-92—Fresno St. 24, Southern California 7
12-30-93—Southern California 28, Utah 21

12-27-94—Utah 16, Arizona 13

GARDEN STATE
(East Rutherford, N.J.)

12-16-78—Arizona St. 34, Rutgers 18
12-15-79—Temple 28, California 17
12-14-80—Houston 35, Navy 0
12-13-81—Tennessee 28, Wisconsin 21

GOTHAM
(New York, N.Y.)

12-9-61—Baylor 24, Utah St. 9
12-15-62—Nebraska 36, Miami (Fla.) 34

GREAT LAKES
(Cleveland, Ohio)

12-6-47—Kentucky 24, Villanova 14

HARBOR
(San Diego, Calif.)

1-1-47—Montana St. 13, New Mexico 13
1-1-48—Hardin-Simmons 53, San Diego St. 0
1-1-49—Villanova 27, Nevada 7

HOUSTON
(Called galleryfurniture.com Bowl, 2000-01)
(Houston, Texas)

12-27-00—East Caro. 40, Texas Tech 27
12-28-01—Texas A&M 28, TCU 9
12-27-02—Oklahoma St. 33, Southern Miss. 23
12-30-03—Texas Tech 38, Navy 14
12-29-04—Colorado 33, UTEP 28

12-31-05—TCU 27, Iowa St. 24

LOS ANGELES CHRISTMAS FESTIVAL
(Los Angeles, Calif.)

12-25-24—Southern California 20, Missouri 7

MERCY
(Los Angeles, Calif.)

11-23-61—Fresno St. 36, Bowling Green 6

OIL
(Houston, Texas)

1-1-46—Georgia 20, Tulsa 6
1-1-47—Georgia Tech 41, St. Mary's (Cal.) 19

PASADENA BOWL
(Called Junior Rose Bowl in 1967)
(Pasadena, Calif.)

12-2-67—West Tex. A&M 35, Cal St. Northridge 13
12-6-69—San Diego St. 28, Boston U. 7
12-19-70—Long Beach St. 24, Louisville 24
12-18-71—Memphis 28, San Jose St. 9

PRESIDENTIAL CUP
(College Park, Md.)

12-9-50—Texas A&M 40, Georgia 20

RAISIN
(Fresno, Calif.)

1-1-46—Drake 13, Fresno St. 12
1-1-47—San Jose St. 20, Utah St. 0
1-1-48—Pacific 26, Wichita St. 14
1-1-49—Occidental 21, Colorado St. 20
12-31-49—San Jose St. 20, Texas Tech 13

SALAD
(Phoenix, Ariz.)

1-1-48—Nevada 13, North Texas 6
1-1-49—Drake 14, Arizona 13
1-1-50—Xavier (Ohio) 33, Arizona St. 21
1-1-51—Miami (Ohio) 34, Arizona St. 21
1-1-52—Houston 26, Dayton 21

SAN DIEGO EAST-WEST CHRISTMAS CLASSIC
(San Diego, Calif.)

12-26-21—Centre 38, Arizona 0
12-25-22—West Virginia 21, Gonzaga 13

SEATTLE
(Called Oahu Classic, 1998-2000)
(Seattle, Washington)

12-25-98—Air Force 45, Washington 25
12-29-99—Hawaii 23, Oregon St. 17
12-24-00—Georgia 37, Virginia 14
12-27-01—Georgia Tech 24, Stanford 14
12-30-02—Wake Forest 38, Oregon 17

SHRINE
(Little Rock, Ark.)

12-18-48—Hardin-Simmons 40, Ouachita Baptist 12

SILICON VALLEY FOOTBALL CLASSIC
(San Jose, Calif.)

12-31-00—Air Force 37, Fresno St. 34
12-31-01—Michigan St. 44, Fresno St. 35
12-31-02—Fresno St. 30, Georgia Tech 21
12-30-03—Fresno St. 17, UCLA 9
12-30-04—Northern Ill. 34, Troy 21

Other Major Postseason Games

There was a proliferation of postseason benefit games specially scheduled at the conclusion of the regular season during the Great Depression (principally in 1931) to raise money for relief of the unemployed in response to the President's Committee on Mobilization of Relief Resources and for other charitable causes.

The exact number of these games is unknown, but it is estimated that more than 100 college games were played nationwide during this period, often irrespective of the competing teams' records.

Most notable among these postseason games were the Tennessee-New York University game of 1931 and the Army-Navy contests of 1930 and 1931 (the two academies had severed athletics relations during 1928-31 and did not meet in regular-season play). All three games were played before huge crowds in New York City's Yankee Stadium.

Following is a list of the principal postseason benefit and charity games involving at least one major college. Not included (nor included in all-time team won-lost records) are several special feature, same-day double-header tournaments in 1931 in which four participating teams were paired to play halves or modified quarters.

Date	Site	Opposing Teams
12-6-30	New York	Colgate 7, New York U. 0
12-13-30	New York	Army 6, Navy 0
11-28-31	Kansas City	Temple 38, Missouri 6
11-28-31	Chicago	Purdue 7, Northwestern 0
11-28-31	Minneapolis	Minnesota 19, Ohio St. 7
11-28-31	Ann Arbor	Michigan 16, Wisconsin 0
11-28-31	Philadelphia	Penn St. 31, Lehigh 0
12-2-31	Chattanooga	Alabama 49, Chattanooga 0
12-3-31	Brooklyn	Manhattan 7, Rutgers 6
12-5-31	Denver	Nebraska 20, Colorado St. 7
12-5-31	Pittsburgh	Carnegie Mellon 0, Duquesne 0
12-5-31	New York	Tennessee 13, New York U. 0
12-5-31	St. Louis	St. Louis 31, Missouri 6
12-5-31	Topeka	Kansas 6, Washburn 0
12-5-31	Wichita	Kansas St. 20, Wichita St. 6
12-5-31	Columbia	Centre 9, South Carolina 7
12-5-31	Norman	Oklahoma City 6, Oklahoma 0
12-12-31	New York	Army 17, Navy 7
12-12-31	Tulsa	Oklahoma 20, Tulsa 7
1-2-33	El Paso	SMU 26, UTEP 0
12-8-34	St. Louis	SMU 7, Washington-St. Louis 0

Team-by-Team Bowl Results

All-Time Bowl-Game Records

This list includes all bowls played by a current major team, providing its opponent was classified as a major that season or it was a major team then. The list excludes games in which a home team served as a predetermined, preseason host regardless of its record and/or games scheduled before the season, thus eliminating the old Pineapple, Glass and Palm Festival. Following is the alphabetical list showing the record of each current major team in all major bowls.

Team	W	L	T
Air Force	8	8	1
Akron	0	1	0
UAB	0	1	0
Alabama	30	21	3
Arizona	5	7	1
Arizona St.	12	10	1
Arkansas	11	21	3
Arkansas St.	0	1	0
Army	2	2	0
Auburn	18	13	2
Ball St.	0	3	0
Baylor	8	8	0
Boise St.	5	2	0
Boston College	12	6	0
Bowling Green	4	3	0
BYU	8	16	1
California	8	8	1
UCF	0	1	0
Central Mich.	1	2	0
Cincinnati	4	4	0
Clemson	15	14	0
Colorado	12	15	0
Colorado St.	4	7	0
Connecticut	1	0	0
Duke	3	5	0

Team	W	L	T
East Caro.	4	4	0
Eastern Mich.	1	0	0
Florida	16	18	0
Florida St.	20	13	2
Fresno St.	9	7	0
Georgia	23	16	3
Georgia Tech	22	13	0
Hawaii	5	2	0
Houston	7	9	1
Idaho	1	0	0
Illinois	6	8	0
Indiana	3	5	0
Iowa	11	10	1
Iowa St.	2	7	0
Kansas	4	6	0
Kansas St.	6	7	0
Kent St.	0	1	0
Kentucky	6	5	0
LSU	19	18	1
Louisiana Tech	1	2	1
Louisville	6	7	1
Marshall	5	2	0
Maryland	9	10	2
Memphis	3	1	0
Miami (Fla.)	18	13	0

Team	W	L	T
Miami (Ohio)	6	3	0
Michigan	18	20	0
Michigan St.	7	10	0
Middle Tenn.	0	1	0
Minnesota	5	7	0
Mississippi	19	12	0
Mississippi St.	6	6	0
Missouri	10	14	0
Navy	6	6	1
Nebraska	22	22	0
Nevada	3	4	0
UNLV	#3	0	0
New Mexico	2	7	1
New Mexico St.	2	0	1
North Carolina	12	13	0
North Carolina St.	12	10	1
North Texas	1	5	0
Northern Ill.	2	1	0
Northwestern	1	5	0
Notre Dame	13	15	0
Ohio	0	3	0
Ohio St.	18	20	0
Oklahoma	24	15	1
Oklahoma St.	11	6	0
Oregon	7	13	0
Oregon St.	6	4	0
Penn St.	25	12	2
Pittsburgh	10	14	0
Purdue	7	7	0
Rice	4	4	0
Rutgers	1	2	0
San Diego St.	1	4	0
San Jose St.	5	3	0

Team	W	L	T
South Carolina	4	9	0
South Fla.	1	1	0
Southern California	29	16	0
SMU	4	6	1
Southern Miss.	8	7	0
Stanford	9	10	1
Syracuse	12	9	1
Temple	1	1	0
Tennessee	24	22	0
Texas	23	21	2
UTEP	5	7	0
Texas A&M	13	16	0
TCU	9	13	1
Texas Tech	9	20	1
Toledo	7	3	0
Troy	1	1	0
Tulane	4	6	0
Tulsa	5	9	0
UCLA	13	14	1
Utah	9	3	0
Utah St.	1	4	0
Vanderbilt	1	1	1
Virginia	7	9	0
Virginia Tech	7	13	0
Wake Forest	4	3	0
Washington	14	14	1
Washington St.	6	4	0
West Virginia	11	15	0
Western Mich.	0	3	0
Wisconsin	10	8	0
Wyoming	5	6	0
TOTALS	**902**	**902**	**42**

#Later lost game by forfeit. The following current Football Bowl Subdivision teams have not played in a major bowl game: Buffalo, Fla. Atlantic, Florida Int'l, La.-Lafayette and La.-Monroe.

Major Bowl Records of Non-Football Bowl Subdivision Teams

Boston U. 0-1-0; Brown 0-1-0; Bucknell 1-0-0; Cal St. Fullerton 0-1-0; Cal St. Northridge 0-1-0; Carnegie Mellon 0-1-0; Case Reserve 1-0-0; Catholic 1-0-1; Centenary (La.) 0-0-1; Centre 2-1-0; Citadel 1-0-0; Columbia 1-0-0; Davidson 0-1-0; Dayton 0-1-0; Denver 0-2-0; Drake 2-1-0; Duquesne 1-0-0; Fordham 1-1-0; George Washington 1-0-0; Georgetown 0-2-0; Gonzaga 0-1-0; Hardin-Simmons 5-2-1; Harvard 1-0-0; Holy Cross 0-1-0; Long Beach St. 0-0-1; Marquette 0-1-0; McNeese St. 1-2-0; Montana St. 0-0-1; Occidental 1-0-0; Ouachita Baptist 0-1-0; Pacific 2-1-0; Penn 0-1-0; Randolph Field 0-0-1; Richmond 1-1-0; St. Mary's (Cal.) 1-2-0; Santa Clara 3-0-0; Second Air Force 1-0-0; Southwestern (Tex.) 2-0-0; Tampa 1-0-0; Tennessee Tech 0-1-0; U. of Mexico 0-1-0; Villanova 2-2-1; Wash. & Jeff. 0-0-1; Wash. & Lee 0-1-0; West Tex. A&M 3-0-0; West Va. Wesleyan 1-0-0; Wichita St. 0-3-0; William & Mary 1-2-0; Xavier (Ohio) 1-0-0. TOTALS: 39-37-8

All-Time Bowl Appearances Leaders

(Must be classified as a major bowl game where one team was considered a major college at the time.)

Team	Appearances
Alabama	54
Tennessee	46
Texas	46
Southern California	45
Nebraska	44
Georgia	42
Oklahoma	40
Penn St.	39
LSU	38
Michigan	38
Ohio St.	38
Arkansas	35
Florida St.	35
Georgia Tech	35
Florida	34
Auburn	33
Miami (Fla.)	31
Mississippi	31
Texas Tech	30
Clemson	29
Texas A&M	29
Washington	29
Notre Dame	28
UCLA	28
Colorado	27
West Virginia	26
BYU	25
North Carolina	25
Missouri	24
Pittsburgh	24
Arizona St.	23
North Carolina St.	23
TCU	23
Iowa	22
Syracuse	22
Maryland	21
Oregon	20
Stanford	20
Virginia Tech	20
Boston College	18
Wisconsin	18
Air Force	17
California	17
Houston	17
Michigan St.	17
Oklahoma St.	17
Baylor	16
Fresno St.	16
Virginia	16

All-Time Bowl Victories Leaders

(Includes bowls where at least one team was classified a major college at the time.)

Team	Victories
Alabama	30
Southern California	29
Penn St.	25
Oklahoma	24
Tennessee	24
Georgia	23
Texas	23
Georgia Tech	22
Nebraska	22
Florida St.	20
LSU	19
Mississippi	19
Auburn	18
Miami (Fla.)	18
Michigan	18
Ohio St.	18
Florida	16
Clemson	15
Washington	14
Notre Dame	13
Texas A&M	13
UCLA	13
Arizona St.	12
Boston College	12
Colorado	12
North Carolina	12
North Carolina St.	12
Syracuse	12
Arkansas	11
Iowa	11
Oklahoma St.	11
West Virginia	11
Missouri	10
Pittsburgh	10
Wisconsin	10
Fresno St.	9
Maryland	9
Stanford	9
TCU	9
Texas Tech	9
Utah	9

Team-by-Team Major Bowl Scores With Coach of Each Bowl Team

Listed below are the 114 Football Bowl Subdivision (FBS) teams that have participated in history's 967 major bowl games (the term "major bowl" is defined above the alphabetical list of team bowl records). The teams are listed alphabetically, with each coach listed along with the bowl participated in, date played, opponent, score and team's all-time bowl-game record. After the FBS list is a group of 49 teams that played in a major bowl game or games but are no longer classified as FBS.

School/Coach	Bowl/Date	Opponent/Score
AIR FORCE		
Ben Martin	Cotton 1-1-59	TCU 0-0
Ben Martin	Gator 12-28-63	North Carolina 0-35
Ben Martin	Sugar 1-1-71	Tennessee 13-34
Ken Hatfield	Hall of Fame 12-31-82	Vanderbilt 36-28
Ken Hatfield	Independence 12-10-83	Mississippi 9-3
Fisher DeBerry	Independence 12-15-84	Virginia Tech 23-7
Fisher DeBerry	Bluebonnet 12-31-85	Texas 24-16
Fisher DeBerry	Freedom 12-30-87	Arizona St. 28-33
Fisher DeBerry	Liberty 12-28-89	Mississippi 29-42
Fisher DeBerry	Liberty 12-27-90	Ohio St. 23-11
Fisher DeBerry	Liberty 12-29-91	Mississippi St. 38-15
Fisher DeBerry	Liberty 12-31-92	Mississippi 0-13
Fisher DeBerry	Copper 12-27-95	Texas Tech 41-55
Fisher DeBerry	Las Vegas 12-20-97	Oregon 13-41
Fisher DeBerry	Oahu Classic 12-25-98	Washington 45-25
Fisher DeBerry	Silicon Valley 12-31-00	Fresno St. 37-34
Fisher DeBerry	San Francisco 12-31-02	Virginia Tech 13-20
All bowls 8-8-1		
AKRON		
J.D. Brookhart	Motor City 12-26-05	Memphis 31-38
All bowls 0-1-0		
UAB		
Watson Brown	Hawaii 12-24-04	Hawaii 40-59
All bowls 0-1-0		
ALABAMA		
Wallace Wade	Rose 1-1-26	Washington 20-19
Wallace Wade	Rose 1-1-27	Stanford 7-7
Wallace Wade	Rose 1-1-31	Washington St. 24-0
Frank Thomas	Rose 1-1-35	Stanford 29-13
Frank Thomas	Rose 1-1-38	California 0-13
Frank Thomas	Cotton 1-1-42	Texas A&M 29-21
Frank Thomas	Orange 1-1-43	Boston College 37-21
Frank Thomas	Sugar 1-1-45	Duke 26-29
Frank Thomas	Rose 1-1-46	Southern California 34-14
Harold "Red" Drew	Sugar 1-1-48	Texas 7-27
Harold "Red" Drew	Orange 1-1-53	Syracuse 61-6
Harold "Red" Drew	Cotton 1-1-54	Rice 6-28
Paul "Bear" Bryant	Liberty 12-19-59	Penn St. 0-7
Paul "Bear" Bryant	Bluebonnet 12-17-60	Texas 3-3
Paul "Bear" Bryant	Sugar 1-1-62	Arkansas 10-3
Paul "Bear" Bryant	Orange 1-1-63	Oklahoma 17-0
Paul "Bear" Bryant	Sugar 1-1-64	Mississippi 12-7
Paul "Bear" Bryant	Orange 1-1-65	Texas 17-21
Paul "Bear" Bryant	Orange 1-1-66	Nebraska 39-28
Paul "Bear" Bryant	Sugar 1-2-67	Nebraska 34-7
Paul "Bear" Bryant	Cotton 1-1-68	Texas A&M 16-20
Paul "Bear" Bryant	Gator 12-28-68	Missouri 10-35
Paul "Bear" Bryant	Liberty 12-13-69	Colorado 33-47
Paul "Bear" Bryant	Bluebonnet 12-31-70	Oklahoma 24-24
Paul "Bear" Bryant	Orange 1-1-72	Nebraska 6-38
Paul "Bear" Bryant	Cotton 1-1-73	Texas 13-17
Paul "Bear" Bryant	Sugar 12-31-73	Notre Dame 23-24
Paul "Bear" Bryant	Orange 1-1-75	Notre Dame 11-13
Paul "Bear" Bryant	Sugar 12-31-75	Penn St. 13-6
Paul "Bear" Bryant	Liberty 12-20-76	UCLA 36-6
Paul "Bear" Bryant	Sugar 1-2-78	Ohio St. 35-6
Paul "Bear" Bryant	Sugar 1-1-79	Penn St. 14-7
Paul "Bear" Bryant	Sugar 1-1-80	Arkansas 24-9
Paul "Bear" Bryant	Cotton 1-1-81	Baylor 30-2
Paul "Bear" Bryant	Cotton 1-1-82	Texas 12-14
Paul "Bear" Bryant	Liberty 12-29-82	Illinois 21-15
Ray Perkins	Sun 12-24-83	SMU 28-7
Ray Perkins	Aloha 12-28-85	Southern California 24-3

School/Coach	Bowl/Date	Opponent/Score
Ray Perkins	Sun 12-25-86	Washington 28-6
Bill Curry	Hall of Fame 1-2-88	Michigan 24-28
Bill Curry	Sun 12-24-88	Army 29-28
Bill Curry	Sugar 1-1-90	Miami (Fla.) 25-33
Gene Stallings	Fiesta 1-1-91	Louisville 7-34
Gene Stallings	Blockbuster 12-28-91	Colorado 30-25
Gene Stallings	Sugar 1-1-93	Miami (Fla.) 34-13
Gene Stallings	Gator 12-31-93	North Carolina 24-10
Gene Stallings	Florida Citrus 1-2-95	Ohio St. 24-17
Gene Stallings	Outback 1-1-97	Michigan 17-14
Mike DuBose	Music City 12-29-98	Virginia Tech 7-38
Mike DuBose	Orange 1-1-00	Michigan 34-35 (ot)
Dennis Franchione	Independence 12-27-01	Iowa St. 14-13
Mike Shula	Music City 12-31-04	Minnesota 16-20
Mike Shula	Cotton 1-2-06	Texas Tech 13-10
Joe Kines	Independence 12-28-06	Oklahoma St. 31-34

All bowls 30-21-3

ARIZONA

School/Coach	Bowl/Date	Opponent/Score
J.F. "Pop" McKale	San Diego East-West Christmas Classic 12-26-21	Centre 0-38
Miles Casteel	Salad 1-1-49	Drake 13-14
Darrell Mudra	Sun 12-28-68	Auburn 10-34
Tony Mason	Fiesta 12-25-79	Pittsburgh 10-16
Larry Smith	Sun 12-28-85	Georgia 13-13
Larry Smith	Aloha 12-27-86	North Carolina 30-21
Dick Tomey	Copper 12-31-89	North Carolina St. 17-10
Dick Tomey	Aloha 12-25-90	Syracuse 0-28
Dick Tomey	John Hancock 12-31-92	Baylor 15-20
Dick Tomey	Fiesta 1-1-94	Miami (Fla.) 29-0
Dick Tomey	Freedom 12-27-94	Utah 13-16
Dick Tomey	Insight.com 12-27-97	New Mexico 20-14
Dick Tomey	Holiday 12-30-98	Nebraska 23-20

All bowls 5-7-1

ARIZONA ST.

School/Coach	Bowl/Date	Opponent/Score
Millard "Dixie" Howell	Sun 1-1-40	Catholic 0-0
Millard "Dixie" Howell	Sun 1-1-41	Case Reserve 13-26
Ed Doherty	Salad 1-1-50	Xavier (Ohio) 21-33
Ed Doherty	Salad 1-1-51	Miami (Ohio) 21-34
Frank Kush	Peach 12-30-70	North Carolina 48-26
Frank Kush	Fiesta 12-27-71	Florida St. 45-38
Frank Kush	Fiesta 12-23-72	Missouri 49-35
Frank Kush	Fiesta 12-21-73	Pittsburgh 28-7
Frank Kush	Fiesta 12-26-75	Nebraska 17-14
Frank Kush	Fiesta 12-25-77	Penn St. 30-42
Frank Kush	Garden State 12-16-78	Rutgers 34-18
Darryl Rogers	Fiesta 1-1-83	Oklahoma 32-21
John Cooper	Holiday 12-22-85	Arkansas 17-18
John Cooper	Rose 1-1-87	Michigan 22-15
John Cooper	Freedom 12-30-87	Air Force 33-28
Bruce Snyder	Rose 1-1-97	Ohio St. 17-20
Bruce Snyder	Sun 12-31-97	Iowa 17-7
Bruce Snyder	Aloha Classic 12-25-99	Wake Forest 3-23
Bruce Snyder	Aloha Classic 12-25-00	Boston College 17-31
Dirk Koetter	Holiday 12-27-02	Kansas St. 27-34
Dirk Koetter	Sun 12-31-04	Purdue 27-23
Dirk Koetter	Insight 12-27-05	Rutgers 45-40
Dirk Koetter	Hawaii 12-24-06	Hawaii 24-41

All bowls 12-10-1

ARKANSAS

School/Coach	Bowl/Date	Opponent/Score
Fred Thomsen	Dixie Classic 1-1-34	Centenary (La.) 7-7
John Barnhill	Cotton 1-1-47	LSU 0-0
John Barnhill	Dixie 1-1-48	William & Mary 21-19
Bowden Wyatt	Cotton 1-1-55	Georgia Tech 6-14
Frank Broyles	Gator 1-2-60	Georgia Tech 14-7
Frank Broyles	Cotton 1-2-61	Duke 6-7
Frank Broyles	Sugar 1-1-62	Alabama 3-10
Frank Broyles	Sugar 1-1-63	Mississippi 13-17
Frank Broyles	Cotton 1-1-65	Nebraska 10-7
Frank Broyles	Cotton 1-1-66	LSU 7-14
Frank Broyles	Sugar 1-1-69	Georgia 16-2
Frank Broyles	Sugar 1-1-70	Mississippi 22-27
Frank Broyles	Liberty 12-20-71	Tennessee 13-14
Frank Broyles	Cotton 1-1-76	Georgia 31-10
Lou Holtz	Orange 1-2-78	Oklahoma 31-6
Lou Holtz	Fiesta 12-25-78	UCLA 10-10
Lou Holtz	Sugar 1-1-80	Alabama 9-24
Lou Holtz	Hall of Fame 12-27-80	Tulane 34-15
Lou Holtz	Gator 12-28-81	North Carolina 27-31
Lou Holtz	Bluebonnet 12-31-82	Florida 28-24
Ken Hatfield	Liberty 12-27-84	Auburn 15-21
Ken Hatfield	Holiday 12-22-85	Arizona St. 18-17
Ken Hatfield	Orange 1-1-87	Oklahoma 8-42
Ken Hatfield	Liberty 12-29-87	Georgia 17-20
Ken Hatfield	Cotton 1-2-89	UCLA 3-17
Ken Hatfield	Cotton 1-1-90	Tennessee 27-31
Jack Crowe	Independence 12-29-91	Georgia 15-24
Danny Ford	Carquest 12-30-95	North Carolina 10-20
Houston Nutt	Florida Citrus 1-1-99	Michigan 31-45
Houston Nutt	Cotton 1-1-00	Texas 27-6
Houston Nutt	Las Vegas 12-21-00	UNLV 14-31
Houston Nutt	Cotton 1-1-02	Oklahoma 3-10
Houston Nutt	Music City 12-30-02	Minnesota 14-29
Houston Nutt	Independence 12-31-03	Missouri 27-14
Houston Nutt	Capital One 1-1-07	Wisconsin 14-17

All bowls 11-21-3

ARKANSAS ST.

School/Coach	Bowl/Date	Opponent/Score
Steve Roberts	New Orleans 12-20-05	Southern Miss. 19-31

All bowls 0-1-0

ARMY

School/Coach	Bowl/Date	Opponent/Score
Jim Young	Cherry 12-22-84	Michigan St. 10-6
Jim Young	Peach 12-31-85	Illinois 31-29
Jim Young	Sun 12-24-88	Alabama 28-29
Bob Sutton	Independence 12-31-96	Auburn 29-32

All bowls 2-2-0

AUBURN

School/Coach	Bowl/Date	Opponent/Score
Jack Meagher	Bacardi, Cuba 1-1-37	Villanova 7-7
Jack Meagher	Orange 1-1-38	Michigan St. 6-0
Ralph "Shug" Jordan	Gator 1-1-54	Texas Tech 13-35
Ralph "Shug" Jordan	Gator 12-31-54	Baylor 33-13
Ralph "Shug" Jordan	Gator 12-31-55	Vanderbilt 13-25
Ralph "Shug" Jordan	Orange 1-1-64	Nebraska 7-13
Ralph "Shug" Jordan	Liberty 12-18-65	Mississippi 7-13
Ralph "Shug" Jordan	Sun 12-28-68	Arizona 34-10
Ralph "Shug" Jordan	Bluebonnet 12-31-69	Houston 7-36
Ralph "Shug" Jordan	Gator 1-2-71	Mississippi 35-28
Ralph "Shug" Jordan	Sugar 1-1-72	Oklahoma 22-40
Ralph "Shug" Jordan	Gator 12-30-72	Colorado 24-3
Ralph "Shug" Jordan	Sun 12-29-73	Missouri 17-34
Ralph "Shug" Jordan	Gator 12-30-74	Texas 27-3
Pat Dye	Tangerine 12-18-82	Boston College 33-26
Pat Dye	Sugar 1-2-84	Michigan 9-7
Pat Dye	Liberty 12-27-84	Arkansas 21-15
Pat Dye	Cotton 1-1-86	Texas A&M 16-36
Pat Dye	Florida Citrus 1-1-87	Southern California 16-7
Pat Dye	Sugar 1-1-88	Syracuse 16-16
Pat Dye	Sugar 1-2-89	Florida St. 7-13
Pat Dye	Hall of Fame 1-1-90	Ohio St. 31-24
Pat Dye	Peach 12-29-90	Indiana 27-23
Terry Bowden	Outback 1-1-96	Penn St. 14-43
Terry Bowden	Independence 12-31-96	Army 33-29
Terry Bowden	Peach 1-2-98	Clemson 21-17
Tommy Tuberville	Florida Citrus 1-1-01	Michigan 28-31
Tommy Tuberville	Peach 12-31-01	North Carolina 10-16
Tommy Tuberville	Capital One 1-1-03	Penn St. 13-9
Tommy Tuberville	Music City 12-31-03	Wisconsin 28-14
Tommy Tuberville	Sugar 1-3-05	Virginia Tech 16-13
Tommy Tuberville	Capital One 1-2-06	Wisconsin 10-24
Tommy Tuberville	Cotton 1-1-07	Nebraska 17-14

All bowls 18-13-2

BALL ST.

School/Coach	Bowl/Date	Opponent/Score
Paul Schudel	California 12-9-89	Fresno St. 6-27
Paul Schudel	Las Vegas 12-17-93	Utah St. 33-42
Bill Lynch	Las Vegas 12-19-96	Nevada 15-18

All bowls 0-3-0

BAYLOR

School/Coach	Bowl/Date	Opponent/Score
Bob Woodruff	Dixie 1-1-49	Wake Forest 20-7
George Sauer	Orange 1-1-52	Georgia Tech 14-17
George Sauer	Gator 12-31-54	Auburn 13-33
Sam Boyd	Sugar 1-1-57	Tennessee 13-7
John Bridgers	Gator 12-31-60	Florida 12-13
John Bridgers	Gotham 12-9-61	Utah St. 24-9
John Bridgers	Bluebonnet 12-21-63	LSU 14-7
Grant Teaff	Cotton 1-1-75	Penn St. 20-41
Grant Teaff	Peach 12-31-79	Clemson 24-18
Grant Teaff	Cotton 1-1-81	Alabama 2-30
Grant Teaff	Bluebonnet 12-31-83	Oklahoma St. 14-24
Grant Teaff	Liberty 12-27-85	LSU 21-7
Grant Teaff	Bluebonnet 12-31-86	Colorado 21-9
Grant Teaff	Copper 12-31-91	Indiana 0-24
Grant Teaff	John Hancock 12-31-92	Arizona 20-15
Chuck Reedy	Alamo 12-31-94	Washington St. 3-10

All bowls 8-8-0

School/Coach	Bowl/Date	Opponent/Score
BOISE ST.		
Dirk Koetter	Humanitarian 12-30-99	Louisville 34-31
Dirk Koetter	Humanitarian 12-28-00	UTEP 38-23
Dan Hawkins	Humanitarian 12-31-02	Iowa St. 34-16
Dan Hawkins	Fort Worth 12-23-03	TCU 34-31
Dan Hawkins	Liberty 12-31-04	Louisville 40-44
Dan Hawkins	MPC Computers 12-28-05	Boston College 21-27
Chris Peterson	Fiesta 1-1-07	Oklahoma 43-42 (ot)
All bowls 5-2-0		
BOSTON COLLEGE		
Frank Leahy	Cotton 1-1-40	Clemson 3-6
Frank Leahy	Sugar 1-1-41	Tennessee 19-13
Denny Myers	Orange 1-1-43	Alabama 21-37
Jack Bicknell	Tangerine 12-18-82	Auburn 26-33
Jack Bicknell	Liberty 12-29-83	Notre Dame 18-19
Jack Bicknell	Cotton 1-1-85	Houston 45-28
Jack Bicknell	Hall of Fame 12-23-86	Georgia 27-24
Tom Coughlin	Hall of Fame 1-1-93	Tennessee 23-38
Tom Coughlin	Carquest 1-1-94	Virginia 31-13
Dan Henning	Aloha 12-25-94	Kansas St. 12-7
Tom O'Brien	Insight.com 12-31-99	Colorado 28-62
Tom O'Brien	Aloha Classic 12-25-00	Arizona St. 31-17
Tom O'Brien	Music City 12-28-01	Georgia 20-16
Tom O'Brien	Motor City 12-26-02	Toledo 51-25
Tom O'Brien	San Francisco 12-31-03	Colorado St. 35-21
Tom O'Brien	Continental Tire 12-30-04	North Carolina 37-24
Tom O'Brien	MPC Computers 12-28-05	Boise St. 27-21
Frank Spaziani	Meineke Car Care 12-30-06	Navy 25-24
All bowls 12-6-0		
BOWLING GREEN		
Doyt Perry	Mercy 11-23-61	Fresno St. 6-36
Denny Stolz	California 12-18-82	Fresno St. 28-29
Denny Stolz	California 12-14-85	Fresno St. 7-51
Gary Blackney	California 12-14-91	Fresno St. 28-21
Gary Blackney	Las Vegas 12-18-92	Nevada 35-34
Gregg Brandon	Motor City 12-26-03	Northwestern 28-24
Gregg Brandon	GMAC 12-22-04	Memphis 52-35
All bowls 4-3-0		
BYU		
LaVell Edwards	Fiesta 12-28-74	Oklahoma St. 6-16
LaVell Edwards	Tangerine 12-18-76	Oklahoma St. 21-49
LaVell Edwards	Holiday 12-22-78	Navy 16-23
LaVell Edwards	Holiday 12-21-79	Indiana 37-38
LaVell Edwards	Holiday 12-19-80	SMU 46-45
LaVell Edwards	Holiday 12-18-81	Washington St. 38-36
LaVell Edwards	Holiday 12-17-82	Ohio St. 17-47
LaVell Edwards	Holiday 12-23-83	Missouri 21-17
LaVell Edwards	Holiday 12-21-84	Michigan 24-17
LaVell Edwards	Florida Citrus 12-28-85	Ohio St. 7-10
LaVell Edwards	Freedom 12-30-86	UCLA 10-31
LaVell Edwards	All-American 12-22-87	Virginia 16-22
LaVell Edwards	Freedom 12-29-88	Colorado 20-17
LaVell Edwards	Holiday 12-29-89	Penn St. 39-50
LaVell Edwards	Holiday 12-29-90	Texas A&M 14-65
LaVell Edwards	Holiday 12-30-91	Iowa 13-13
LaVell Edwards	Aloha 12-25-92	Kansas 20-23
LaVell Edwards	Holiday 12-30-93	Ohio St. 21-28
LaVell Edwards	Copper 12-29-94	Oklahoma 31-6
LaVell Edwards	Cotton 1-1-97	Kansas St. 19-15
LaVell Edwards	Liberty 12-31-98	Tulane 27-41
LaVell Edwards	Motor City 12-27-99	Marshall 3-21
Gary Crowton	Liberty 12-31-01	Louisville 10-28
Bronco Mendenhall	Las Vegas 12-22-05	California 28-35
Bronco Mendenhall	Las Vegas 12-21-06	Oregon 38-8
All bowls 8-16-1		
CALIFORNIA		
Andy Smith	Rose 1-1-21	Ohio St. 28-0
Andy Smith	Rose 1-2-22	Wash. & Jeff. 0-0
Clarence "Nibs" Price	Rose 1-1-29	Georgia Tech 7-8
Leonard "Stub" Allison	Rose 1-1-38	Alabama 13-0
Lynn "Pappy" Waldorf	Rose 1-1-49	Northwestern 14-20
Lynn "Pappy" Waldorf	Rose 1-2-50	Ohio St. 14-17
Lynn "Pappy" Waldorf	Rose 1-1-51	Michigan 6-14
Pete Elliott	Rose 1-1-59	Iowa 12-38
Roger Theder	Garden State 12-15-79	Temple 17-28
Bruce Snyder	Copper 12-31-90	Wyoming 17-15
Bruce Snyder	Florida Citrus 1-1-92	Clemson 37-13
Keith Gilbertson	Alamo 12-31-93	Iowa 37-3
Steve Mariucci	Aloha 12-25-96	Navy 38-42
Jeff Tedford	Insight 12-26-03	Virginia Tech 52-49
Jeff Tedford	Holiday 12-30-04	Texas Tech 31-45
Jeff Tedford	Las Vegas 12-22-05	BYU 35-28
Jeff Tedford	Holiday 12-28-06	Texas A&M 45-10
All bowls 8-8-1		
UCF		
George O'Leary	Hawaii 12-24-05	Nevada 48-49 (ot)
All bowls 0-1-0		
CENTRAL MICH.		
Herb Deromedi	California 12-8-90	San Jose St. 24-48
Dick Flynn	Las Vegas 12-15-94	UNLV 24-52
Jeff Quinn	Motor City 12-26-06	Middle Tenn. 31-14
All bowls 1-2-0		
CINCINNATI		
Ray Nolting	Sun 1-1-47	Virginia Tech 18-6
Sid Gillman	Sun 1-1-51	West Tex. A&M 13-14
Rick Minter	Humanitarian 12-29-97	Utah St. 35-19
Rick Minter	Motor City 12-27-00	Marshall 14-25
Rick Minter	Motor City 12-29-01	Toledo 16-23
Rick Minter	New Orleans 12-17-02	North Texas 19-24
Mark Dantonio	Fort Worth 12-23-04	Marshall 32-14
Brian Kelly	International 1-6-07	Western Mich. 27-24
All bowls 4-4-0		
CLEMSON		
Jess Neely	Cotton 1-1-40	Boston College 6-3
Frank Howard	Gator 1-1-49	Missouri 24-23
Frank Howard	Orange 1-1-51	Miami (Fla.) 15-14
Frank Howard	Gator 1-1-52	Miami (Fla.) 0-14
Frank Howard	Orange 1-1-57	Colorado 21-27
Frank Howard	Sugar 1-1-59	LSU 0-7
Frank Howard	Bluebonnet 12-19-59	TCU 23-7
Charley Pell	Gator 12-30-77	Pittsburgh 3-34
Danny Ford	Gator 12-29-78	Ohio St. 17-15
Danny Ford	Peach 12-31-79	Baylor 18-24
Danny Ford	Orange 1-1-82	Nebraska 22-15
Danny Ford	Independence 12-21-85	Minnesota 13-20
Danny Ford	Gator 12-27-86	Stanford 27-21
Danny Ford	Florida Citrus 1-1-88	Penn St. 35-10
Danny Ford	Florida Citrus 1-2-89	Oklahoma 23-6
Danny Ford	Gator 12-30-89	West Virginia 27-7
Ken Hatfield	Hall of Fame 1-1-91	Illinois 30-0
Ken Hatfield	Florida Citrus 1-1-92	California 13-37
Tommy West	Peach 12-31-93	Kentucky 14-13
Tommy West	Gator 1-1-96	Syracuse 0-41
Tommy West	Peach 12-28-96	LSU 7-10
Tommy West	Peach 1-2-98	Auburn 17-21
Tommy Bowden	Peach 12-30-99	Mississippi St. 7-17
Tommy Bowden	Gator 1-1-01	Virginia Tech 20-41
Tommy Bowden	Humanitarian 12-31-01	Louisiana Tech 49-24
Tommy Bowden	Mazda Tangerine 12-23-02	Texas Tech 15-55
Tommy Bowden	Peach 1-2-04	Tennessee 27-14
Tommy Bowden	Champs Sports 12-27-05	Colorado 19-10
Tommy Bowden	Music City 12-29-06	Kentucky 20-28
All bowls 15-14-0		
COLORADO		
Bernard "Bunnie" Oaks	Cotton 1-1-38	Rice 14-28
Dallas Ward	Orange 1-1-57	Clemson 27-21
Sonny Grandelius	Orange 1-1-62	LSU 7-25
Eddie Crowder	Bluebonnet 12-23-67	Miami (Fla.) 31-21
Eddie Crowder	Liberty 12-13-69	Alabama 47-33
Eddie Crowder	Liberty 12-12-70	Tulane 3-17
Eddie Crowder	Bluebonnet 12-31-71	Houston 29-17
Eddie Crowder	Gator 12-30-72	Auburn 3-24
Bill Mallory	Bluebonnet 12-27-75	Texas 21-38
Bill Mallory	Orange 1-1-77	Ohio St. 10-27
Bill McCartney	Freedom 12-30-85	Washington 17-20
Bill McCartney	Bluebonnet 12-31-86	Baylor 9-21
Bill McCartney	Freedom 12-29-88	BYU 17-20
Bill McCartney	Orange 1-1-90	Notre Dame 6-21
Bill McCartney	Orange 1-1-91	Notre Dame 10-9
Bill McCartney	Blockbuster 12-28-91	Alabama 25-30
Bill McCartney	Fiesta 1-1-93	Syracuse 22-26
Bill McCartney	Aloha 12-25-93	Fresno St. 41-30
Bill McCartney	Fiesta 1-2-95	Notre Dame 41-24
Rick Neuheisel	Cotton 1-1-96	Oregon 38-6
Rick Neuheisel	Holiday 12-30-96	Washington 33-21
Rick Neuheisel	Aloha Classic 12-25-98	Oregon 51-43
Gary Barnett	Insight.com 12-31-99	Boston College 62-28
Gary Barnett	Fiesta 1-1-02	Oregon 16-38
Gary Barnett	Alamo 12-28-02	Wisconsin 28-31 (ot)

School/Coach	Bowl/Date	Opponent/Score
Gary Barnett	Houston 12-29-04	UTEP 33-28
Mike Hankwitz	Champs Sports 12-27-05	Colorado 10-19
All bowls 12-15-0		
COLORADO ST.		
Bob Davis	Raisin 1-1-49	Occidental 20-21
Earle Bruce	Freedom 12-24-90	Oregon 32-31
Sonny Lubick	Holiday 12-30-94	Michigan 14-24
Sonny Lubick	Holiday 12-29-95	Kansas St. 21-54
Sonny Lubick	Holiday 12-29-97	Missouri 35-24
Sonny Lubick	Liberty 12-31-99	Southern Miss. 17-23
Sonny Lubick	Liberty 12-29-00	Louisville 22-17
Sonny Lubick	New Orleans 12-18-01	North Texas 45-20
Sonny Lubick	Liberty 12-31-02	TCU 3-17
Sonny Lubick	San Francisco 12-31-03	Boston College 21-35
Sonny Lubick	Poinsettia 12-22-05	Navy 30-51
All bowls 4-7-0		
CONNECTICUT		
Randy Edsall	Motor City 12-27-04	Toledo 39-10
All bowls 1-0-0		
DUKE		
Wallace Wade	Rose 1-2-39	Southern California 3-7
Wallace Wade	Rose 1-1-42	Oregon St. 16-20
Eddie Cameron	Sugar 1-1-45	Alabama 29-26
Bill Murray	Orange 1-1-55	Nebraska 34-7
Bill Murray	Orange 1-1-58	Oklahoma 21-48
Bill Murray	Cotton 1-2-61	Arkansas 7-6
Steve Spurrier	All-American 12-28-89	Texas Tech 21-49
Fred Goldsmith	Hall of Fame 1-2-95	Wisconsin 20-34
All bowls 3-5-0		
EAST CARO.		
Pat Dye	Independence 12-16-78	Louisiana Tech 35-13
Bill Lewis	Peach 1-1-92	North Carolina St. 37-34
Steve Logan	Liberty 12-31-94	Illinois 0-30
Steve Logan	Liberty 12-30-95	Stanford 19-13
Steve Logan	Mobile Alabama 12-22-99	TCU 14-28
Steve Logan	galleryfurniture.com 12-27-00	Texas Tech 40-27
Steve Logan	GMAC 12-19-01	Marshall 61-64 (2 ot)
Skip Holtz	Papajohns.com 12-23-06	South Fla. 7-24
All bowls 4-4-0		
EASTERN MICH.		
Jim Harkema	California 12-12-87	San Jose St. 30-27
All bowls 1-0-0		
FLORIDA		
Bob Woodruff	Gator 1-1-53	Tulsa 14-13
Bob Woodruff	Gator 12-27-58	Mississippi 3-7
Ray Graves	Gator 12-31-60	Baylor 13-12
Ray Graves	Gator 12-29-62	Penn St. 17-7
Ray Graves	Sugar 1-1-66	Missouri 18-20
Ray Graves	Orange 1-2-67	Georgia Tech 27-12
Ray Graves	Gator 12-27-69	Tennessee 14-13
Doug Dickey	Tangerine 12-22-73	Miami (Ohio) 7-16
Doug Dickey	Sugar 12-31-74	Nebraska 10-13
Doug Dickey	Gator 12-29-75	Maryland 0-13
Doug Dickey	Sun 1-2-77	Texas A&M 14-37
Charley Pell	Tangerine 12-20-80	Maryland 35-20
Charley Pell	Peach 12-31-81	West Virginia 6-26
Charley Pell	Bluebonnet 12-31-82	Arkansas 24-28
Charley Pell	Gator 12-30-83	Iowa 14-6
Galen Hall	Aloha 12-25-87	UCLA 16-20
Galen Hall	All-American 12-29-88	Illinois 14-10
Gary Darnell	Freedom 12-30-89	Washington 7-34
Steve Spurrier	Sugar 1-1-92	Notre Dame 28-39
Steve Spurrier	Gator 12-31-92	North Carolina St. 27-10
Steve Spurrier	Sugar 1-1-94	West Virginia 41-7
Steve Spurrier	Sugar 1-2-95	Florida St. 17-23
Steve Spurrier	Fiesta 1-2-96	Nebraska 24-62
Steve Spurrier	Sugar 1-2-97	Florida St. 52-20
Steve Spurrier	Florida Citrus 1-1-98	Penn St. 21-6
Steve Spurrier	Orange 1-2-99	Syracuse 31-10
Steve Spurrier	Florida Citrus 1-1-00	Michigan St. 34-37
Steve Spurrier	Sugar 1-2-01	Miami (Fla.) 20-37
Steve Spurrier	Orange 1-2-02	Maryland 56-23
Ron Zook	Outback 1-1-03	Michigan 30-38
Ron Zook	Outback 1-1-04	Iowa 17-37
Charlie Strong	Peach 12-31-04	Miami (Fla.) 10-27
Urban Meyer	Outback 1-2-06	Iowa 31-24
Urban Meyer	BCS Championship 1-8-07	Ohio St. 41-14
All bowls 16-18-0		

School/Coach	Bowl/Date	Opponent/Score
FLORIDA ST.		
Tom Nugent	Sun 1-1-55	UTEP 20-47
Tom Nugent	Bluegrass 12-13-58	Oklahoma St. 6-15
Bill Peterson	Gator 1-2-65	Oklahoma 36-19
Bill Peterson	Sun 12-24-66	Wyoming 20-28
Bill Peterson	Gator 12-30-67	Penn St. 17-17
Bill Peterson	Peach 12-30-68	LSU 27-31
Larry Jones	Fiesta 12-27-71	Arizona St. 38-45
Bobby Bowden	Tangerine 12-23-77	Texas Tech 40-17
Bobby Bowden	Orange 1-1-80	Oklahoma 7-24
Bobby Bowden	Orange 1-1-81	Oklahoma 17-18
Bobby Bowden	Gator 12-30-82	West Virginia 31-12
Bobby Bowden	Peach 12-30-83	North Carolina 28-3
Bobby Bowden	Florida Citrus 12-22-84	Georgia 17-17
Bobby Bowden	Gator 12-30-85	Oklahoma St. 34-23
Bobby Bowden	All-American 12-31-86	Indiana 27-13
Bobby Bowden	Fiesta 1-1-88	Nebraska 31-28
Bobby Bowden	Sugar 1-2-89	Auburn 13-7
Bobby Bowden	Fiesta 1-1-90	Nebraska 41-17
Bobby Bowden	Blockbuster 12-28-90	Penn St. 24-17
Bobby Bowden	Cotton 1-1-92	Texas A&M 10-2
Bobby Bowden	Orange 1-1-93	Nebraska 27-14
Bobby Bowden	Orange 1-1-94	Nebraska 18-16
Bobby Bowden	Sugar 1-2-95	Florida 23-17
Bobby Bowden	Orange 1-1-96	Notre Dame 31-26
Bobby Bowden	Sugar 1-2-97	Florida 20-52
Bobby Bowden	Sugar 1-1-98	Ohio St. 31-14
Bobby Bowden	Fiesta 1-4-99	Tennessee 16-23
Bobby Bowden	Sugar 1-4-00	Virginia Tech 46-29
Bobby Bowden	Orange 1-3-01	Oklahoma 2-13
Bobby Bowden	Gator 1-1-02	Virginia Tech 30-17
Bobby Bowden	Sugar 1-1-03	Georgia 13-26
Bobby Bowden	Orange 1-1-04	Miami (Fla.) 14-16
Bobby Bowden	Gator 1-1-05	West Virginia 30-18
Bobby Bowden	Orange 1-3-06	Penn St. 23-26 (3 ot)
Bobby Bowden	Emerald 12-27-06	UCLA 44-27
All bowls 20-13-2		
FRESNO ST.		
Alvin "Pix" Pierson	Raisin 1-1-46	Drake 12-13
Cecil Coleman	Mercy 11-23-61	Bowling Green 36-6
Jim Sweeney	California 12-18-82	Bowling Green 29-28
Jim Sweeney	California 12-14-85	Bowling Green 51-7
Jim Sweeney	California 12-10-88	Western Mich. 35-30
Jim Sweeney	California 12-9-89	Ball St. 27-6
Jim Sweeney	California 12-14-91	Bowling Green 21-28
Jim Sweeney	Freedom 12-29-92	Southern California 24-7
Jim Sweeney	Aloha 12-25-93	Colorado 30-41
Pat Hill	Las Vegas 12-18-99	Utah 16-17
Pat Hill	Silicon Valley 12-31-00	Air Force 34-37
Pat Hill	Silicon Valley 12-31-01	Michigan St. 35-44
Pat Hill	Silicon Valley 12-31-02	Georgia Tech 30-21
Pat Hill	Silicon Valley 12-30-03	UCLA 17-9
Pat Hill	MPC Computers 12-27-04	Virginia 37-34 (ot)
Pat Hill	Liberty 12-31-05	Tulsa 24-31
All bowls 9-7-0		
GEORGIA		
Wally Butts	Orange 1-1-42	TCU 40-26
Wally Butts	Rose 1-1-43	UCLA 9-0
Wally Butts	Oil 1-1-46	Tulsa 20-6
Wally Butts	Sugar 1-1-47	North Carolina 20-10
Wally Butts	Gator 1-1-48	Maryland 20-20
Wally Butts	Orange 1-1-49	Texas 28-41
Wally Butts	Presidential 12-9-50	Texas A&M 20-40
Wally Butts	Orange 1-1-60	Missouri 14-0
Vince Dooley	Sun 12-26-64	Texas Tech 7-0
Vince Dooley	Cotton 12-31-66	SMU 24-9
Vince Dooley	Liberty 12-16-67	North Carolina St. 7-14
Vince Dooley	Sugar 1-1-69	Arkansas 2-16
Vince Dooley	Sun 12-20-69	Nebraska 6-45
Vince Dooley	Gator 12-31-71	North Carolina 7-3
Vince Dooley	Peach 12-28-73	Maryland 17-16
Vince Dooley	Tangerine 12-21-74	Miami (Ohio) 10-21
Vince Dooley	Cotton 1-1-76	Arkansas 10-31
Vince Dooley	Sugar 1-1-77	Pittsburgh 3-27
Vince Dooley	Bluebonnet 12-31-78	Stanford 22-25
Vince Dooley	Sugar 1-1-81	Notre Dame 17-10
Vince Dooley	Sugar 1-1-82	Pittsburgh 20-24
Vince Dooley	Sugar 1-1-83	Penn St. 23-27
Vince Dooley	Cotton 1-2-84	Texas 10-9
Vince Dooley	Florida Citrus 12-22-84	Florida St. 17-17
Vince Dooley	Sun 12-28-85	Arizona 13-13

School/Coach	Bowl/Date	Opponent/Score
Vince Dooley	Hall of Fame 12-23-86	Boston College 24-27
Vince Dooley	Liberty 12-29-87	Arkansas 20-17
Vince Dooley	Gator 1-1-89	Michigan St. 34-27
Ray Goff	Peach 12-30-89	Syracuse 18-19
Ray Goff	Independence 12-29-91	Arkansas 24-15
Ray Goff	Florida Citrus 1-1-93	Ohio St. 21-14
Ray Goff	Peach 12-30-95	Virginia 27-34
Jim Donnan	Outback 1-1-98	Wisconsin 33-6
Jim Donnan	Peach 12-31-98	Virginia 35-33
Jim Donnan	Outback 1-1-00	Purdue 28-25 (ot)
Jim Donnan	Oahu Classic 12-24-00	Virginia 37-14
Mark Richt	Music City 12-28-01	Boston College 16-20
Mark Richt	Sugar 1-1-03	Florida St. 26-13
Mark Richt	Capital One 1-1-04	Purdue 34-27 (ot)
Mark Richt	Outback 1-1-05	Wisconsin 24-21
Mark Richt	Sugar 1-2-06	West Virginia 35-38
Mark Richt	Chick-fil-A 12-30-06	Virginia Tech 31-24
All bowls 23-16-3		
GEORGIA TECH		
Bill Alexander	Rose 1-1-29	California 8-7
Bill Alexander	Orange 1-1-40	Missouri 21-7
Bill Alexander	Cotton 1-1-43	Texas 7-14
Bill Alexander	Sugar 1-1-44	Tulsa 20-18
Bill Alexander	Orange 1-1-45	Tulsa 12-26
Bobby Dodd	Oil 1-1-47	St. Mary's (Cal.) 41-19
Bobby Dodd	Orange 1-1-48	Kansas 20-14
Bobby Dodd	Orange 1-1-52	Baylor 17-14
Bobby Dodd	Sugar 1-1-53	Mississippi 24-7
Bobby Dodd	Sugar 1-1-54	West Virginia 42-19
Bobby Dodd	Cotton 1-1-55	Arkansas 14-6
Bobby Dodd	Sugar 1-2-56	Pittsburgh 7-0
Bobby Dodd	Gator 12-29-56	Pittsburgh 21-14
Bobby Dodd	Gator 1-2-60	Arkansas 7-14
Bobby Dodd	Gator 12-30-61	Penn St. 15-30
Bobby Dodd	Bluebonnet 12-22-62	Missouri 10-14
Bobby Dodd	Gator 12-31-65	Texas Tech 31-21
Bobby Dodd	Orange 1-2-67	Florida 12-27
Bud Carson	Sun 12-19-70	Texas Tech 17-9
Bud Carson	Peach 12-30-71	Mississippi 18-41
Bill Fulcher	Liberty 12-18-72	Iowa St. 31-30
Pepper Rodgers	Peach 12-25-78	Purdue 21-41
Bill Curry	Hall of Fame 12-31-85	Michigan St. 17-14
Bobby Ross	Florida Citrus 1-1-91	Nebraska 45-21
Bobby Ross	Aloha 12-25-91	Stanford 18-17
George O'Leary	Carquest 12-29-97	West Virginia 35-30
George O'Leary	Gator 1-1-99	Notre Dame 35-28
George O'Leary	Gator 1-1-00	Miami (Fla.) 13-28
George O'Leary	Peach 12-29-00	LSU 14-28
Mac McWhorter	Seattle 12-27-01	Stanford 24-14
Chan Gailey	Silicon Valley 12-31-02	Fresno St. 21-30
Chan Gailey	Humanitarian 1-3-04	Tulsa 52-10
Chan Gailey	Champs Sports 12-21-04	Syracuse 51-14
Chan Gailey	Emerald 12-29-05	Utah 10-38
Chan Gailey	Gator 1-1-07	West Virginia 35-38
All bowls 22-13-0		
HAWAII		
Bob Wagner	Aloha 12-25-89	Michigan St. 13-33
Bob Wagner	Holiday 12-30-92	Illinois 27-17
June Jones	Oahu Classic 12-25-99	Oregon St. 23-17
June Jones	Hawaii 12-25-02	Tulane 28-36
June Jones	Hawaii 12-25-03	Houston 54-48 (3 ot)
June Jones	Hawaii 12-24-04	UAB 59-40
June Jones	Hawaii 12-24-06	Arizona St. 41-24
All bowls 5-2-0		
HOUSTON		
Clyde Lee	Salad 1-1-52	Dayton 26-21
Bill Yeoman	Tangerine 12-22-62	Miami (Ohio) 49-21
Bill Yeoman	Bluebonnet 12-31-69	Auburn 36-7
Bill Yeoman	Bluebonnet 12-31-71	Colorado 17-29
Bill Yeoman	Bluebonnet 12-29-73	Tulane 47-7
Bill Yeoman	Bluebonnet 12-23-74	North Carolina St. 31-31
Bill Yeoman	Cotton 1-1-77	Maryland 30-21
Bill Yeoman	Cotton 1-1-79	Notre Dame 34-35
Bill Yeoman	Cotton 1-1-80	Nebraska 17-14
Bill Yeoman	Garden State 12-14-80	Navy 35-0
Bill Yeoman	Sun 12-26-81	Oklahoma 14-40
Bill Yeoman	Cotton 1-1-85	Boston College 28-45
Jack Pardee	Aloha 12-25-88	Washington St. 22-24
Kim Helton	Liberty 12-27-96	Syracuse 17-30
Art Briles	Hawaii 12-25-03	Hawaii 48-54 (3 ot)
Art Briles	Fort Worth 12-23-05	Kansas 13-42
Art Briles	Liberty 12-29-06	South Carolina 36-44
All bowls 7-9-1		

School/Coach	Bowl/Date	Opponent/Score
IDAHO		
Chris Tormey	Humanitarian 12-30-98	Southern Miss. 42-35
All bowls 1-0-0		
ILLINOIS		
Ray Eliot	Rose 1-1-47	UCLA 45-14
Ray Eliot	Rose 1-1-52	Stanford 40-7
Pete Elliott	Rose 1-1-64	Washington 17-7
Mike White	Liberty 12-29-82	Alabama 15-21
Mike White	Rose 1-2-84	UCLA 9-45
Mike White	Peach 12-31-85	Army 29-31
John Mackovic	All-American 12-29-88	Florida 10-14
John Mackovic	Florida Citrus 1-1-90	Virginia 31-21
John Mackovic	Hall of Fame 1-1-91	Clemson 0-30
Lou Tepper	John Hancock 12-31-91	UCLA 3-6
Lou Tepper	Holiday 12-30-92	Hawaii 17-27
Lou Tepper	Liberty 12-31-94	East Caro. 30-0
Ron Turner	Micronpc.com 12-30-99	Virginia 63-21
Ron Turner	Sugar 1-1-02	LSU 34-47
All bowls 6-8-0		
INDIANA		
John Pont	Rose 1-1-68	Southern California 3-14
Lee Corso	Holiday 12-21-79	BYU 38-37
Bill Mallory	All-American 12-31-86	Florida St. 13-27
Bill Mallory	Peach 1-2-88	Tennessee 22-27
Bill Mallory	Liberty 12-28-88	South Carolina 34-10
Bill Mallory	Peach 12-29-90	Auburn 23-27
Bill Mallory	Copper 12-31-91	Baylor 24-0
Bill Mallory	Independence 12-31-93	Virginia Tech 20-45
All bowls 3-5-0		
IOWA		
Forest Evashevski	Rose 1-1-57	Oregon St. 35-19
Forest Evashevski	Rose 1-1-59	California 38-12
Hayden Fry	Rose 1-1-82	Washington 0-28
Hayden Fry	Peach 12-31-82	Tennessee 28-22
Hayden Fry	Gator 12-30-83	Florida 6-14
Hayden Fry	Freedom 12-26-84	Texas 55-17
Hayden Fry	Rose 1-1-86	UCLA 28-45
Hayden Fry	Holiday 12-30-86	San Diego St. 39-38
Hayden Fry	Holiday 12-30-87	Wyoming 20-19
Hayden Fry	Peach 12-31-88	North Carolina St. 23-28
Hayden Fry	Rose 1-1-91	Washington 34-46
Hayden Fry	Holiday 12-30-91	BYU 13-13
Hayden Fry	Alamo 12-31-93	California 3-37
Hayden Fry	Sun 12-29-95	Washington 38-18
Hayden Fry	Alamo 12-29-96	Texas Tech 27-0
Hayden Fry	Sun 12-31-97	Arizona St. 7-17
Kirk Ferentz	Alamo 12-29-01	Texas Tech 16-13
Kirk Ferentz	Orange 1-2-03	Southern California 17-38
Kirk Ferentz	Outback 1-1-04	Florida 37-17
Kirk Ferentz	Capital One 1-1-05	LSU 30-25
Kirk Ferentz	Outback 1-2-06	Florida 24-31
Kirk Ferentz	Alamo 12-30-06	Texas 24-26
All bowls 11-10-1		
IOWA ST.		
Johnny Majors	Sun 12-18-71	LSU 15-33
Johnny Majors	Liberty 12-18-72	Georgia Tech 30-31
Earle Bruce	Peach 12-31-77	North Carolina St. 14-24
Earle Bruce	Hall of Fame 12-20-78	Texas A&M 12-28
Dan McCarney	Insight.com 12-28-00	Pittsburgh 37-29
Dan McCarney	Independence 12-27-01	Alabama 13-14
Dan McCarney	Humanitarian 12-31-02	Boise St. 16-34
Dan McCarney	Independence 12-28-04	Miami (Ohio) 17-13
Dan McCarney	Houston 12-31-05	TCU 24-27
All bowls 2-7-0		
KANSAS		
George Sauer	Orange 1-1-48	Georgia Tech 14-20
Jack Mitchell	Bluebonnet 12-16-61	Rice 33-7
Pepper Rodgers	Orange 1-1-69	Penn St. 14-15
Don Fambrough	Liberty 12-17-73	North Carolina St. 18-31
Bud Moore	Sun 12-26-75	Pittsburgh 19-33
Don Fambrough	Hall of Fame 12-31-81	Mississippi St. 0-10
Glen Mason	Aloha 12-25-92	BYU 23-20
Glen Mason	Aloha 12-25-95	UCLA 51-30
Mark Mangino	Tangerine 12-22-03	North Carolina St. 26-56
Mark Mangino	Fort Worth 12-23-05	Houston 42-13
All bowls 4-6-0		
KANSAS ST.		
Jim Dickey	Independence 12-11-82	Wisconsin 3-14
Bill Snyder	Copper 12-29-93	Wyoming 52-17
Bill Snyder	Aloha 12-25-94	Boston College 7-12

School/Coach	Bowl/Date	Opponent/Score
Bill Snyder	Holiday 12-29-95	Colorado St. 54-21
Bill Snyder	Cotton 1-1-97	BYU 15-19
Bill Snyder	Fiesta 12-31-97	Syracuse 35-18
Bill Snyder	Alamo 12-29-98	Purdue 34-37
Bill Snyder	Holiday 12-29-99	Washington 24-20
Bill Snyder	Cotton 1-1-01	Tennessee 35-21
Bill Snyder	Insight.com 12-29-01	Syracuse 3-26
Bill Snyder	Holiday 12-27-02	Arizona St. 34-27
Bill Snyder	Fiesta 1-2-04	Ohio St. 28-35
Ron Prince	Texas 12-28-06	Rutgers 10-37

All bowls 6-7-0

KENT ST.

School/Coach	Bowl/Date	Opponent/Score
Don James	Tangerine 12-29-72	Tampa 18-21

All bowls 0-1-0

KENTUCKY

School/Coach	Bowl/Date	Opponent/Score
Paul "Bear" Bryant	Great Lakes 12-6-47	Villanova 24-14
Paul "Bear" Bryant	Orange 1-2-50	Santa Clara 13-21
Paul "Bear" Bryant	Sugar 1-1-51	Oklahoma 13-7
Paul "Bear" Bryant	Cotton 1-1-52	TCU 20-7
Fran Curci	Peach 12-31-76	North Carolina 21-0
Jerry Claiborne	Hall of Fame 12-22-83	West Virginia 16-20
Jerry Claiborne	Hall of Fame 12-29-84	Wisconsin 20-19
Bill Curry	Peach 12-31-93	Clemson 13-14
Hal Mumme	Outback 1-1-99	Penn St. 14-26
Hal Mumme	Music City 12-29-99	Syracuse 13-20
Rich Brooks	Music City 12-29-06	Clemson 28-20

All bowls 6-5-0

LSU

School/Coach	Bowl/Date	Opponent/Score
Bernie Moore	Sugar 1-1-36	TCU 2-3
Bernie Moore	Sugar 1-1-37	Santa Clara 14-21
Bernie Moore	Sugar 1-1-38	Santa Clara 0-6
Bernie Moore	Orange 1-1-44	Texas A&M 19-14
Bernie Moore	Cotton 1-1-47	Arkansas 0-0
Gaynell Tinsley	Sugar 1-2-50	Oklahoma 0-35
Paul Dietzel	Sugar 1-1-59	Clemson 7-0
Paul Dietzel	Sugar 1-1-60	Mississippi 0-21
Paul Dietzel	Orange 1-1-62	Colorado 25-7
Charlie McClendon	Cotton 1-1-63	Texas 13-0
Charlie McClendon	Bluebonnet 12-21-63	Baylor 7-14
Charlie McClendon	Sugar 1-1-65	Syracuse 13-10
Charlie McClendon	Cotton 1-1-66	Arkansas 14-7
Charlie McClendon	Sugar 1-1-68	Wyoming 20-13
Charlie McClendon	Peach 12-30-68	Florida St. 31-27
Charlie McClendon	Orange 1-1-71	Nebraska 12-17
Charlie McClendon	Sun 12-18-71	Iowa St. 33-15
Charlie McClendon	Bluebonnet 12-30-72	Tennessee 17-24
Charlie McClendon	Orange 1-1-74	Penn St. 9-16
Charlie McClendon	Sun 12-31-77	Stanford 14-24
Charlie McClendon	Liberty 12-23-78	Missouri 15-20
Charlie McClendon	Tangerine 12-22-79	Wake Forest 34-10
Jerry Stovall	Orange 1-1-83	Nebraska 20-21
Bill Arnsparger	Sugar 1-1-85	Nebraska 10-28
Bill Arnsparger	Liberty 12-27-85	Baylor 7-21
Bill Arnsparger	Sugar 1-1-87	Nebraska 15-30
Mike Archer	Gator 12-31-87	South Carolina 30-13
Mike Archer	Hall of Fame 1-2-89	Syracuse 10-23
Gerry DiNardo	Independence 12-29-95	Michigan St. 45-26
Gerry DiNardo	Peach 12-28-96	Clemson 10-7
Gerry DiNardo	Independence 12-28-97	Notre Dame 27-9
Nick Saban	Peach 12-29-00	Georgia Tech 28-14
Nick Saban	Sugar 1-1-02	Illinois 47-34
Nick Saban	Cotton 1-1-03	Texas 20-35
Nick Saban	Sugar 1-4-04	Oklahoma 21-14
Nick Saban	Capital One 1-1-05	Iowa 25-30
Les Miles	Peach 12-30-05	Miami (Fla.) 40-3
Les Miles	Sugar 1-3-07	Notre Dame 41-14

All bowls 19-18-1

LOUISIANA TECH

School/Coach	Bowl/Date	Opponent/Score
Maxie Lambright	Independence 12-17-77	Louisville 24-14
Maxie Lambright	Independence 12-16-78	East Caro. 13-35
Joe Raymond Peace	Independence 12-15-90	Maryland 34-34
Jack Bicknell III	Humanitarian 12-31-01	Clemson 24-49

All bowls 1-2-1

LOUISVILLE

School/Coach	Bowl/Date	Opponent/Score
Frank Camp	Sun 1-1-58	Drake 34-20
Lee Corso	Pasadena 12-19-70	Long Beach St. 24-24
Vince Gibson	Independence 12-17-77	Louisiana Tech 14-24
Howard Schnellenberger	Fiesta 1-1-91	Alabama 34-7
Howard Schnellenberger	Liberty 12-28-93	Michigan St. 18-7
John L. Smith	Motor City 12-23-98	Marshall 29-48
John L. Smith	Humanitarian 12-30-99	Boise St. 31-34
John L. Smith	Liberty 12-29-00	Colorado St. 17-22
John L. Smith	Liberty 12-31-01	BYU 28-10
John L. Smith	GMAC 12-18-02	Marshall 15-38
Bobby Petrino	GMAC 12-18-03	Miami (Ohio) 28-49
Bobby Petrino	Liberty 12-31-04	Boise St. 44-40
Bobby Petrino	Gator 1-2-06	Virginia Tech 24-35
Bobby Petrino	Orange 1-2-07	Wake Forest 24-13

All bowls 6-7-1

MARSHALL

School/Coach	Bowl/Date	Opponent/Score
Bob Pruett	Motor City 12-26-97	Mississippi 31-34
Bob Pruett	Motor City 12-23-98	Louisville 48-29
Bob Pruett	Motor City 12-27-99	BYU 21-3
Bob Pruett	Motor City 12-27-00	Cincinnati 25-14
Bob Pruett	GMAC 12-19-01	East Caro. 64-61 (2 ot)
Bob Pruett	GMAC 12-18-02	Louisville 38-15
Bob Pruett	Fort Worth 12-23-04	Cincinnati 14-32

All bowls 5-2-0

MARYLAND

School/Coach	Bowl/Date	Opponent/Score
Jim Tatum	Gator 1-1-48	Georgia 20-20
Jim Tatum	Gator 1-2-50	Missouri 20-7
Jim Tatum	Sugar 1-1-52	Tennessee 28-13
Jim Tatum	Orange 1-1-54	Oklahoma 0-7
Jim Tatum	Orange 1-2-56	Oklahoma 6-20
Jerry Claiborne	Peach 12-28-73	Georgia 16-17
Jerry Claiborne	Liberty 12-16-74	Tennessee 3-7
Jerry Claiborne	Gator 12-29-75	Florida 13-0
Jerry Claiborne	Cotton 1-1-77	Houston 21-30
Jerry Claiborne	Hall of Fame 12-22-77	Minnesota 17-7
Jerry Claiborne	Sun 12-23-78	Texas 0-42
Jerry Claiborne	Tangerine 12-20-80	Florida 20-35
Bobby Ross	Aloha 12-25-82	Washington 20-21
Bobby Ross	Florida Citrus 12-17-83	Tennessee 23-30
Bobby Ross	Sun 12-22-84	Tennessee 28-27
Bobby Ross	Cherry 12-21-85	Syracuse 35-18
Joe Krivak	Independence 12-15-90	Louisiana Tech 34-34
Ralph Friedgen	Orange 1-2-02	Florida 23-56
Ralph Friedgen	Peach 12-31-02	Tennessee 30-3
Ralph Friedgen	Gator 1-1-04	West Virginia 41-7
Ralph Friedgen	Champs Sports 12-29-06	Purdue 24-7

All bowls 9-10-2

MEMPHIS

School/Coach	Bowl/Date	Opponent/Score
Billy Murphy	Pasadena 12-18-71	San Jose St. 28-9
Tommy West	New Orleans 12-16-03	North Texas 27-17
Tommy West	GMAC 12-22-04	Bowling Green 35-52
Tommy West	Motor City 12-26-05	Akron 38-31

All bowls 3-1-0

MIAMI (FLA.)

School/Coach	Bowl/Date	Opponent/Score
Tom McCann	Orange 1-1-35	Bucknell 0-26
Jack Harding	Orange 1-1-46	Holy Cross 13-6
Andy Gustafson	Orange 1-1-51	Clemson 14-15
Andy Gustafson	Gator 1-1-52	Clemson 14-0
Andy Gustafson	Liberty 12-16-61	Syracuse 14-15
Andy Gustafson	Gotham 12-15-62	Nebraska 34-36
Charlie Tate	Liberty 12-10-66	Virginia Tech 14-7
Charlie Tate	Bluebonnet 12-31-67	Colorado 21-31
Howard Schnellenberger	Peach 1-2-81	Virginia Tech 20-10
Howard Schnellenberger	Orange 1-2-84	Nebraska 31-30
Jimmy Johnson	Fiesta 1-1-85	UCLA 37-39
Jimmy Johnson	Sugar 1-1-86	Tennessee 7-35
Jimmy Johnson	Fiesta 1-2-87	Penn St. 10-14
Jimmy Johnson	Orange 1-1-88	Oklahoma 20-14
Jimmy Johnson	Orange 1-2-89	Nebraska 23-3
Dennis Erickson	Sugar 1-1-90	Alabama 33-25
Dennis Erickson	Cotton 1-1-91	Texas 46-3
Dennis Erickson	Orange 1-1-92	Nebraska 22-0
Dennis Erickson	Sugar 1-1-93	Alabama 13-34
Dennis Erickson	Fiesta 1-1-94	Arizona 0-29
Dennis Erickson	Orange 1-1-95	Nebraska 17-24
Butch Davis	Carquest 12-27-96	Virginia 31-21
Butch Davis	Micron PC 12-29-98	North Carolina St. 46-23
Butch Davis	Gator 1-1-00	Georgia Tech 28-13
Butch Davis	Sugar 1-2-01	Florida 37-20
Larry Coker	Rose 1-3-02	Nebraska 37-14
Larry Coker	Fiesta 1-3-03	Ohio St. 24-31 (2 ot)
Larry Coker	Orange 1-1-04	Florida St. 16-14
Larry Coker	Peach 12-31-04	Florida 27-10
Larry Coker	Peach 12-30-05	LSU 3-40
Larry Coker	MPC Computers 12-31-06	Nevada 21-20

All bowls 18-13-0

School/Coach	Bowl/Date	Opponent/Score
MIAMI (OHIO)		
Sid Gillman	Sun 1-1-48	Texas Tech 13-12
Woody Hayes	Salad 1-1-51	Arizona St. 34-21
John Pont	Tangerine 12-22-62	Houston 21-49
Bill Mallory	Tangerine 12-22-73	Florida 16-7
Dick Crum	Tangerine 12-21-74	Georgia 21-10
Dick Crum	Tangerine 12-20-75	South Carolina 20-7
Tim Rose	California 12-13-86	San Jose St. 7-37
Terry Hoeppner	GMAC 12-18-03	Louisville 49-28
Terry Hoeppner	Independence 12-28-04	Iowa St. 13-17
All bowls 6-3-0		
MICHIGAN		
Fielding "Hurry Up" Yost	Rose 1-1-02	Stanford 49-0
H.O. "Fritz" Crisler	Rose 1-1-48	Southern California 49-0
Bennie Oosterbaan	Rose 1-1-51	California 14-6
Chalmers "Bump" Elliott	Rose 1-1-65	Oregon St. 34-7
Glenn "Bo" Schembechler	Rose 1-1-70	Southern California 3-10
Glenn "Bo" Schembechler	Rose 1-1-72	Stanford 12-13
Glenn "Bo" Schembechler	Orange 1-1-76	Oklahoma 6-14
Glenn "Bo" Schembechler	Rose 1-1-77	Southern California 6-14
Glenn "Bo" Schembechler	Rose 1-2-78	Washington 20-27
Glenn "Bo" Schembechler	Rose 1-1-79	Southern California 10-17
Glenn "Bo" Schembechler	Gator 12-28-79	North Carolina 15-17
Glenn "Bo" Schembechler	Rose 1-1-81	Washington 23-6
Glenn "Bo" Schembechler	Bluebonnet 12-31-81	UCLA 33-14
Glenn "Bo" Schembechler	Rose 1-1-83	UCLA 14-24
Glenn "Bo" Schembechler	Sugar 1-2-84	Auburn 7-9
Glenn "Bo" Schembechler	Holiday 12-21-84	BYU 17-24
Glenn "Bo" Schembechler	Fiesta 1-1-86	Nebraska 27-23
Glenn "Bo" Schembechler	Rose 1-1-87	Arizona St. 15-22
Glenn "Bo" Schembechler	Hall of Fame 1-2-88	Alabama 28-24
Glenn "Bo" Schembechler	Rose 1-2-89	Southern California 22-14
Glenn "Bo" Schembechler	Rose 1-1-90	Southern California 10-17
Gary Moeller	Gator 1-1-91	Mississippi 35-3
Gary Moeller	Rose 1-1-92	Washington 14-34
Gary Moeller	Rose 1-1-93	Washington 38-31
Gary Moeller	Hall of Fame 1-1-94	North Carolina St. 42-7
Gary Moeller	Holiday 12-30-94	Colorado St. 24-14
Lloyd Carr	Alamo 12-28-95	Texas A&M 20-22
Lloyd Carr	Outback 1-1-97	Alabama 14-17
Lloyd Carr	Rose 1-1-98	Washington St. 21-16
Lloyd Carr	Florida Citrus 1-1-99	Arkansas 45-31
Lloyd Carr	Orange 1-1-00	Alabama 35-34 (ot)
Lloyd Carr	Florida Citrus 1-1-01	Auburn 31-28
Lloyd Carr	Florida Citrus 1-1-02	Tennessee 17-45
Lloyd Carr	Outback 1-1-03	Florida 38-30
Lloyd Carr	Rose 1-1-04	Southern California 14-28
Lloyd Carr	Rose 1-1-05	Texas 37-38
Lloyd Carr	Alamo 12-28-05	Nebraska 28-32
Lloyd Carr	Rose 1-1-07	Southern California 18-32
All bowls 18-20-0		
MICHIGAN ST.		
Charlie Bachman	Orange 1-1-38	Auburn 0-6
Clarence "Biggie" Munn	Rose 1-1-54	UCLA 28-20
Duffy Daugherty	Rose 1-2-56	UCLA 17-14
Duffy Daugherty	Rose 1-1-66	UCLA 12-14
George Perles	Cherry 12-22-84	Army 6-10
George Perles	Hall of Fame 12-31-85	Georgia Tech 14-17
George Perles	Rose 1-1-88	Southern California 20-17
George Perles	Gator 1-1-89	Georgia 27-34
George Perles	Aloha 12-25-89	Hawaii 33-13
George Perles	John Hancock 12-31-90	Southern California 17-6
George Perles	Liberty 12-28-93	Louisville 7-18
Nick Saban	Independence 12-29-95	LSU 26-45
Nick Saban	Sun 12-31-96	Stanford 0-38
Nick Saban	Aloha 12-25-97	Washington 23-51
Bobby Williams	Florida Citrus 1-1-00	Florida 37-34
Bobby Williams	Silicon Valley 12-31-01	Fresno St. 44-35
John L. Smith	Alamo 12-29-03	Nebraska 3-17
All bowls 7-10-0		
MIDDLE TENN.		
Rick Stockstill	Motor City 12-26-06	Central Mich. 14-31
All bowls 0-1-0		
MINNESOTA		
Murray Warmath	Rose 1-2-61	Washington 7-17
Murray Warmath	Rose 1-1-62	UCLA 21-3
Cal Stoll	Hall of Fame 12-22-77	Maryland 7-17
John Gutekunst	Independence 12-21-85	Clemson 20-13
John Gutekunst	Liberty 12-29-86	Tennessee 14-21
Glen Mason	Sun 12-31-99	Oregon 20-24
Glen Mason	Micronpc.com 12-28-00	North Carolina St. 30-38
Glen Mason	Music City 12-30-02	Arkansas 29-14
Glen Mason	Sun 12-31-03	Oregon 31-30
Glen Mason	Music City 12-31-04	Alabama 20-16
Glen Mason	Music City 12-30-05	Virginia 31-34
Glen Mason	Insight 12-29-06	Texas Tech 41-44 (ot)
All bowls 5-7-0		
MISSISSIPPI		
Ed Walker	Orange 1-1-36	Catholic 19-20
John Vaught	Delta 1-1-48	TCU 13-9
John Vaught	Sugar 1-1-53	Georgia Tech 7-24
John Vaught	Sugar 1-1-55	Navy 0-21
John Vaught	Cotton 1-2-56	TCU 14-13
John Vaught	Sugar 1-1-58	Texas 39-7
John Vaught	Gator 12-27-58	Florida 7-3
John Vaught	Sugar 1-1-60	LSU 21-0
John Vaught	Sugar 1-2-61	Rice 14-6
John Vaught	Cotton 1-1-62	Texas 7-12
John Vaught	Sugar 1-1-63	Arkansas 17-13
John Vaught	Sugar 1-1-64	Alabama 7-12
John Vaught	Bluebonnet 12-19-64	Tulsa 7-14
John Vaught	Liberty 12-18-65	Auburn 13-7
John Vaught	Bluebonnet 12-17-66	Texas 0-19
John Vaught	Sun 12-30-67	UTEP 7-14
John Vaught	Liberty 12-14-68	Virginia Tech 34-17
John Vaught	Sugar 1-1-70	Arkansas 27-22
John Vaught	Gator 1-2-71	Auburn 28-35
Billy Kinard	Peach 12-30-71	Georgia Tech 41-18
Billy Brewer	Independence 12-10-83	Air Force 3-9
Billy Brewer	Independence 12-20-86	Texas Tech 20-17
Billy Brewer	Liberty 12-28-89	Air Force 42-29
Billy Brewer	Gator 1-1-91	Michigan 3-35
Billy Brewer	Liberty 12-31-92	Air Force 13-0
Tommy Turberville	Motor City 12-26-97	Marshall 34-31
David Cutcliffe	Independence 12-31-98	Texas Tech 35-18
David Cutcliffe	Independence 12-31-99	Oklahoma 27-25
David Cutcliffe	Music City 12-28-00	West Virginia 38-49
David Cutcliffe	Independence 12-27-02	Nebraska 27-23
David Cutcliffe	Cotton 1-2-04	Oklahoma St. 31-28
All bowls 19-12-0		
MISSISSIPPI ST.		
Ralph Sasse	Orange 1-1-37	Duquesne 12-13
Allyn McKeen	Orange 1-1-41	Georgetown 14-7
Paul Davis	Liberty 12-21-63	North Carolina St. 16-12
Bob Tyler	Sun 12-28-74	North Carolina 26-24
Emory Bellard	Sun 12-27-80	Nebraska 17-31
Emory Bellard	Hall of Fame 12-31-81	Kansas 10-0
Jackie Sherrill	Liberty 12-29-91	Air Force 15-38
Jackie Sherrill	Peach 1-2-93	North Carolina 17-21
Jackie Sherrill	Peach 1-1-95	North Carolina St. 24-28
Jackie Sherrill	Cotton 1-1-99	Texas 11-38
Jackie Sherrill	Peach 12-30-99	Clemson 17-7
Jackie Sherrill	Independence 12-31-00	Texas A&M 43-41 (ot)
All bowls 6-6-0		
MISSOURI		
Gwinn Henry	Los Angeles Christmas Festival 12-25-24	Southern California 7-20
Don Faurot	Orange 1-1-40	Georgia Tech 7-21
Don Faurot	Sugar 1-1-42	Fordham 0-2
Chauncey Simpson	Cotton 1-1-46	Texas 27-40
Don Faurot	Gator 1-1-49	Clemson 23-24
Don Faurot	Gator 1-2-50	Maryland 7-20
Dan Devine	Orange 1-1-60	Georgia 0-14
Dan Devine	Orange 1-2-61	Navy 21-14
Dan Devine	Bluebonnet 12-22-62	Georgia Tech 14-10
Dan Devine	Sugar 1-1-66	Florida 20-18
Dan Devine	Gator 12-28-68	Alabama 35-10
Dan Devine	Orange 1-1-70	Penn St. 3-10
Al Onofrio	Fiesta 12-23-72	Arizona St. 35-49
Al Onofrio	Sun 12-29-73	Auburn 34-17
Warren Powers	Liberty 12-23-78	LSU 20-15
Warren Powers	Hall of Fame 12-29-79	South Carolina 24-14
Warren Powers	Liberty 12-27-80	Purdue 25-28
Warren Powers	Tangerine 12-19-81	Southern Miss. 19-17
Warren Powers	Holiday 12-23-83	BYU 17-21
Larry Smith	Holiday 12-29-97	Colorado St. 24-35
Larry Smith	Insight.com 12-26-98	West Virginia 34-31
Gary Pinkel	Independence 12-31-03	Arkansas 14-27
Gary Pinkel	Independence 12-30-05	South Carolina 38-31
Gary Pinkel	Sun 12-29-06	Oregon St. 38-39
All bowls 10-14-0		

School/Coach	Bowl/Date	Opponent/Score
NAVY		
Bob Folwell	Rose 1-1-24	Washington 14-14
Eddie Erdelatz	Sugar 1-1-55	Mississippi 21-0
Eddie Erdelatz	Cotton 1-1-58	Rice 20-7
Wayne Hardin	Orange 1-1-61	Missouri 14-21
Wayne Hardin	Cotton 1-1-64	Texas 6-28
George Welsh	Holiday 12-22-78	BYU 23-16
George Welsh	Garden State 12-14-80	Houston 0-35
George Welsh	Liberty 12-30-81	Ohio St. 28-31
Charlie Weatherbie	Aloha 12-25-96	California 42-38
Paul Johnson	Houston 12-30-03	Texas Tech 14-38
Paul Johnson	Emerald 12-30-04	New Mexico 34-19
Paul Johnson	Poinsettia 12-22-05	Colorado St. 51-30
Paul Johnson	Meineke Car Care 12-30-06	Boston College 24-25
All bowls 6-6-1		
NEBRASKA		
Lawrence McC. "Biff" Jones	Rose 1-1-41	Stanford 13-21
Bill Glassford	Orange 1-1-55	Duke 7-34
Bob Devaney	Gotham 12-15-62	Miami (Fla.) 36-34
Bob Devaney	Orange 1-1-64	Auburn 13-7
Bob Devaney	Cotton 1-1-65	Arkansas 7-10
Bob Devaney	Orange 1-1-66	Alabama 28-39
Bob Devaney	Sugar 1-2-67	Alabama 7-34
Bob Devaney	Sun 12-20-69	Georgia 45-6
Bob Devaney	Orange 1-1-71	LSU 17-12
Bob Devaney	Orange 1-1-72	Alabama 38-6
Bob Devaney	Orange 1-1-73	Notre Dame 40-6
Tom Osborne	Cotton 1-1-74	Texas 19-3
Tom Osborne	Sugar 12-31-74	Florida 13-10
Tom Osborne	Fiesta 12-26-75	Arizona St. 14-17
Tom Osborne	Bluebonnet 12-31-76	Texas Tech 27-24
Tom Osborne	Liberty 12-19-77	North Carolina 21-17
Tom Osborne	Orange 1-1-79	Oklahoma 24-31
Tom Osborne	Cotton 1-1-80	Houston 14-17
Tom Osborne	Sun 12-27-80	Mississippi St. 31-17
Tom Osborne	Orange 1-1-82	Clemson 15-22
Tom Osborne	Orange 1-1-83	LSU 21-20
Tom Osborne	Orange 1-2-84	Miami (Fla.) 30-31
Tom Osborne	Sugar 1-1-85	LSU 28-10
Tom Osborne	Fiesta 1-1-86	Michigan 23-27
Tom Osborne	Sugar 1-1-87	LSU 30-15
Tom Osborne	Fiesta 1-1-88	Florida St. 28-31
Tom Osborne	Orange 1-2-89	Miami (Fla.) 3-23
Tom Osborne	Fiesta 1-1-90	Florida St. 17-41
Tom Osborne	Florida Citrus 1-1-91	Georgia Tech 21-45
Tom Osborne	Orange 1-1-92	Miami (Fla.) 0-22
Tom Osborne	Orange 1-1-93	Florida St. 14-27
Tom Osborne	Orange 1-1-94	Florida St. 16-18
Tom Osborne	Orange 1-1-95	Miami (Fla.) 24-17
Tom Osborne	Fiesta 1-2-96	Florida 62-24
Tom Osborne	Orange 12-31-96	Virginia Tech 41-21
Tom Osborne	Orange 1-2-98	Tennessee 42-17
Frank Solich	Holiday 12-30-98	Arizona 20-23
Frank Solich	Fiesta 1-2-00	Tennessee 31-21
Frank Solich	Alamo 12-30-00	Northwestern 66-17
Frank Solich	Rose 1-3-02	Miami (Fla.) 14-37
Frank Solich	Independence 12-27-02	Mississippi 23-27
Bo Pelini	Alamo 12-29-03	Michigan St. 17-3
Bill Callahan	Alamo 12-28-05	Michigan 32-28
Bill Callahan	Cotton 1-1-07	Auburn 14-17
All bowls 22-22-0		
NEVADA		
Joe Sheeketski	Salad 1-1-48	North Texas 13-6
Joe Sheeketski	Harbor 1-1-49	Villanova 7-27
Chris Ault	Las Vegas 12-18-92	Bowling Green 34-35
Chris Ault	Las Vegas 12-14-95	Toledo 37-40 (ot)
Jeff Tisdel	Las Vegas 12-29-96	Ball St. 18-15
Chris Ault	Hawaii 12-24-05	UCF 49-48 (ot)
Chris Ault	MPC Computers 12-31-06	Miami (Fla.) 20-21
All bowls 3-4-0		
UNLV		
Harvey Hyde	California 12-15-84	Toledo 30-13
Jeff Horton	Las Vegas 12-15-94	Central Mich. 52-24
John Robinson	Las Vegas 12-21-00	Arkansas 31-14
All bowls 3-0-0		
NEW MEXICO		
Ted Shipkey	Sun 1-2-39	Utah 0-26
Willis Barnes	Sun 1-1-44	Southwestern (Tex.) 0-7
Willis Barnes	Sun 1-1-46	Denver 34-24
Willis Barnes	Harbor 1-1-47	Montana St. 13-13
Bill Weeks	Aviation 12-9-61	Western Mich. 28-12

School/Coach	Bowl/Date	Opponent/Score
Dennis Franchione	Insight.com 12-27-97	Arizona 14-20
Rocky Long	Las Vegas 12-25-02	UCLA 13-27
Rocky Long	Las Vegas 12-24-03	Oregon St. 14-55
Rocky Long	Emerald 12-30-04	Navy 19-34
Rocky Long	New Mexico 12-23-06	San Jose St. 12-20
All bowls 2-7-1		
NEW MEXICO ST.		
Jerry Hines	Sun 1-1-36	Hardin-Simmons 14-14
Warren Woodson	Sun 12-31-59	North Texas 28-8
Warren Woodson	Sun 12-31-60	Utah St. 20-13
All bowls 2-0-1		
NORTH CAROLINA		
Carl Snavely	Sugar 1-1-47	Georgia 10-20
Carl Snavely	Sugar 1-1-49	Oklahoma 6-14
Carl Snavely	Cotton 1-2-50	Rice 13-27
Jim Hickey	Gator 12-28-63	Air Force 35-0
Bill Dooley	Peach 12-30-70	Arizona St. 26-48
Bill Dooley	Gator 12-31-71	Georgia 3-7
Bill Dooley	Sun 12-30-72	Texas Tech 32-28
Bill Dooley	Sun 12-28-74	Mississippi St. 24-26
Bill Dooley	Peach 12-31-76	Kentucky 0-21
Bill Dooley	Liberty 12-19-77	Nebraska 17-21
Dick Crum	Gator 12-28-79	Michigan 17-15
Dick Crum	Bluebonnet 12-31-80	Texas 16-7
Dick Crum	Gator 12-28-81	Arkansas 31-27
Dick Crum	Sun 12-25-82	Texas 26-10
Dick Crum	Peach 12-30-83	Florida St. 3-28
Dick Crum	Aloha 12-27-86	Arizona 21-30
Mack Brown	Peach 1-2-93	Mississippi St. 21-17
Mack Brown	Gator 12-31-93	Alabama 10-24
Mack Brown	Sun 12-30-94	Texas 31-35
Mack Brown	Carquest 12-30-95	Arkansas 20-10
Mack Brown	Gator 1-1-97	West Virginia 20-13
Carl Torbush	Gator 1-1-98	Virginia Tech 42-3
Carl Torbush	Las Vegas 12-19-98	San Diego St. 20-13
John Bunting	Peach 12-31-01	Auburn 16-10
John Bunting	Continental Tire 12-30-04	Boston College 24-37
All bowls 12-13-0		
NORTH CAROLINA ST.		
Beattie Feathers	Gator 1-1-47	Oklahoma 13-34
Earle Edwards	Liberty 12-21-63	Mississippi St. 12-16
Earle Edwards	Liberty 12-16-67	Georgia 14-7
Lou Holtz	Peach 12-29-72	West Virginia 49-13
Lou Holtz	Liberty 12-17-73	Kansas 31-18
Lou Holtz	Bluebonnet 12-23-74	Houston 31-31
Lou Holtz	Peach 12-31-75	West Virginia 10-13
Bo Rein	Peach 12-31-77	Iowa St. 24-14
Bo Rein	Tangerine 12-23-78	Pittsburgh 30-17
Dick Sheridan	Peach 12-31-86	Virginia Tech 24-25
Dick Sheridan	Peach 12-31-88	Iowa 28-23
Dick Sheridan	Copper 12-31-89	Arizona 10-17
Dick Sheridan	All-American 12-28-90	Southern Miss. 31-27
Dick Sheridan	Peach 1-1-92	East Caro. 34-37
Dick Sheridan	Gator 12-31-92	Florida 10-27
Mike O'Cain	Hall of Fame 1-1-94	Michigan 7-42
Mike O'Cain	Peach 1-1-95	Mississippi St. 28-24
Mike O'Cain	Micron PC 12-29-98	Miami (Fla.) 23-46
Chuck Amato	Micronpc.com 12-28-00	Minnesota 38-30
Chuck Amato	Tangerine 12-20-01	Pittsburgh 19-34
Chuck Amato	Gator 1-1-03	Notre Dame 28-6
Chuck Amato	Tangerine 12-22-03	Kansas 56-26
Chuck Amato	Meineke Car Care 12-31-05	South Fla. 14-0
All bowls 12-10-1		
NORTH TEXAS		
Odus Mitchell	Salad 1-1-48	Nevada 6-13
Odus Mitchell	Sun 12-31-59	New Mexico St. 8-28
Darrell Dickey	New Orleans 12-18-01	Colorado St. 20-45
Darrell Dickey	New Orleans 12-17-02	Cincinnati 24-19
Darrell Dickey	New Orleans 12-16-03	Memphis 17-27
Darrell Dickey	New Orleans 12-14-04	Southern Miss. 10-31
All bowls 1-5-0		
NORTHERN ILL.		
Bill Mallory	California 12-17-83	Cal St. Fullerton 20-13
Joe Novak	Silicon Valley 12-30-04	Troy 34-21
Joe Novak	Poinsettia 12-19-06	TCU 7-37
All bowls 2-1-0		
NORTHWESTERN		
Bob Voigts	Rose 1-1-49	California 20-14
Gary Barnett	Rose 1-1-96	Southern California 32-41
Gary Barnett	Florida Citrus 1-1-97	Tennessee 28-48

School/Coach	Bowl/Date	Opponent/Score
Randy Walker	Alamo 12-30-00	Nebraska 17-66
Randy Walker	Motor City 12-26-03	Bowling Green 24-28
Randy Walker	Sun 12-30-05	UCLA 38-50
All bowls 1-5-0		
NOTRE DAME		
Knute Rockne	Rose 1-1-25	Stanford 27-10
Ara Parseghian	Cotton 1-1-70	Texas 17-21
Ara Parseghian	Cotton 1-1-71	Texas 24-11
Ara Parseghian	Orange 1-1-73	Nebraska 6-40
Ara Parseghian	Sugar 12-31-73	Alabama 24-23
Ara Parseghian	Orange 1-1-75	Alabama 13-11
Dan Devine	Gator 12-27-76	Penn St. 20-9
Dan Devine	Cotton 1-2-78	Texas 38-10
Dan Devine	Cotton 1-1-79	Houston 35-34
Dan Devine	Sugar 1-1-81	Georgia 10-17
Gerry Faust	Liberty 12-29-83	Boston College 19-18
Gerry Faust	Aloha 12-29-84	SMU 20-27
Lou Holtz	Cotton 1-1-88	Texas A&M 10-35
Lou Holtz	Fiesta 1-2-89	West Virginia 34-21
Lou Holtz	Orange 1-1-90	Colorado 21-6
Lou Holtz	Orange 1-1-91	Colorado 9-10
Lou Holtz	Sugar 1-1-92	Florida 39-28
Lou Holtz	Cotton 1-1-93	Texas A&M 28-3
Lou Holtz	Cotton 1-1-94	Texas A&M 24-21
Lou Holtz	Fiesta 1-2-95	Colorado 24-41
Lou Holtz	Orange 1-1-96	Florida St. 26-31
Bob Davie	Independence 12-28-97	LSU 9-27
Bob Davie	Gator 1-1-99	Georgia Tech 28-35
Bob Davie	Fiesta 1-1-01	Oregon St. 9-41
Tyrone Willingham	Gator 1-1-03	North Carolina St. 6-28
Kent Baer	Insight 12-28-04	Oregon St. 21-38
Charlie Weis	Fiesta 1-2-06	Ohio St. 20-34
Charlie Weis	Sugar 1-3-07	LSU 14-41
All bowls 13-15-0		
OHIO		
Bill Hess	Sun 12-31-62	West Tex. A&M 14-15
Bill Hess	Tangerine 12-27-68	Richmond 42-49
Frank Solich	GMAC 1-7-07	Southern Miss. 7-28
All bowls 0-3-0		
OHIO ST.		
John Wilce	Rose 1-1-21	California 0-28
Wes Fesler	Rose 1-2-50	California 17-14
Woody Hayes	Rose 1-1-55	Southern California 20-7
Woody Hayes	Rose 1-1-58	Oregon 10-7
Woody Hayes	Rose 1-1-69	Southern California 27-16
Woody Hayes	Rose 1-1-71	Stanford 17-27
Woody Hayes	Rose 1-1-73	Southern California 17-42
Woody Hayes	Rose 1-1-74	Southern California 42-21
Woody Hayes	Rose 1-1-75	Southern California 17-18
Woody Hayes	Rose 1-1-76	UCLA 10-23
Woody Hayes	Orange 1-1-77	Colorado 27-10
Woody Hayes	Sugar 1-2-78	Alabama 6-35
Woody Hayes	Gator 12-29-78	Clemson 15-17
Earle Bruce	Rose 1-1-80	Southern California 16-17
Earle Bruce	Fiesta 12-26-80	Penn St. 19-31
Earle Bruce	Liberty 12-30-81	Navy 31-28
Earle Bruce	Holiday 12-17-82	BYU 47-17
Earle Bruce	Fiesta 1-2-84	Pittsburgh 28-23
Earle Bruce	Rose 1-1-85	Southern California 17-20
Earle Bruce	Florida Citrus 12-28-85	BYU 10-7
Earle Bruce	Cotton 1-1-87	Texas A&M 28-12
John Cooper	Hall of Fame 1-1-90	Auburn 14-31
John Cooper	Liberty 12-27-90	Air Force 11-23
John Cooper	Hall of Fame 1-1-92	Syracuse 17-24
John Cooper	Florida Citrus 1-1-93	Georgia 14-21
John Cooper	Holiday 12-30-93	BYU 28-21
John Cooper	Florida Citrus 1-2-95	Alabama 17-24
John Cooper	Florida Citrus 1-1-96	Tennessee 14-20
John Cooper	Rose 1-1-97	Arizona St. 20-17
John Cooper	Sugar 1-1-98	Florida St. 14-31
John Cooper	Sugar 1-1-99	Texas A&M 24-14
John Cooper	Outback 1-1-01	South Carolina 7-24
Jim Tressel	Outback 1-1-02	South Carolina 28-31
Jim Tressel	Fiesta 1-3-03	Miami (Fla.) 31-24 (2 ot)
Jim Tressel	Fiesta 1-2-04	Kansas St. 35-28
Jim Tressel	Alamo 12-29-04	Oklahoma St. 33-7
Jim Tressel	Fiesta 1-2-06	Notre Dame 34-20
Jim Tressel	BCS Championship 1-8-07	Florida 14-41
All bowls 18-20-0		

School/Coach	Bowl/Date	Opponent/Score
OKLAHOMA		
Tom Stidham	Orange 1-2-39	Tennessee 0-17
Jim Tatum	Gator 1-1-47	North Carolina St. 34-13
Bud Wilkinson	Sugar 1-1-49	North Carolina 14-6
Bud Wilkinson	Sugar 1-2-50	LSU 35-0
Bud Wilkinson	Sugar 1-1-51	Kentucky 7-13
Bud Wilkinson	Orange 1-1-54	Maryland 7-0
Bud Wilkinson	Orange 1-2-56	Maryland 20-6
Bud Wilkinson	Orange 1-1-58	Duke 48-21
Bud Wilkinson	Orange 1-1-59	Syracuse 21-6
Bud Wilkinson	Orange 1-1-63	Alabama 0-17
Gomer Jones	Gator 1-2-65	Florida St. 19-36
Chuck Fairbanks	Orange 1-1-68	Tennessee 26-24
Chuck Fairbanks	Bluebonnet 12-31-68	SMU 27-28
Chuck Fairbanks	Bluebonnet 12-31-70	Alabama 24-24
Chuck Fairbanks	Sugar 1-1-72	Auburn 40-22
Chuck Fairbanks	Sugar 12-31-72	Penn St. 14-0
Barry Switzer	Orange 1-1-76	Michigan 14-6
Barry Switzer	Fiesta 12-25-76	Wyoming 41-7
Barry Switzer	Orange 1-2-78	Arkansas 6-31
Barry Switzer	Orange 1-1-79	Nebraska 31-24
Barry Switzer	Orange 1-1-80	Florida St. 24-7
Barry Switzer	Orange 1-1-81	Florida St. 18-17
Barry Switzer	Sun 12-26-81	Houston 40-14
Barry Switzer	Fiesta 1-1-83	Arizona St. 21-32
Barry Switzer	Orange 1-1-85	Washington 17-28
Barry Switzer	Orange 1-1-86	Penn St. 25-10
Barry Switzer	Orange 1-1-87	Arkansas 42-8
Barry Switzer	Orange 1-1-88	Miami (Fla.) 14-20
Barry Switzer	Florida Citrus 1-2-89	Clemson 6-13
Gary Gibbs	Gator 12-29-91	Virginia 48-14
Gary Gibbs	John Hancock 12-24-93	Texas Tech 41-10
Gary Gibbs	Copper 12-29-94	BYU 6-31
Bob Stoops	Independence 12-31-99	Mississippi 25-27
Bob Stoops	Orange 1-3-01	Florida St. 13-2
Bob Stoops	Cotton 1-1-02	Arkansas 10-3
Bob Stoops	Rose 1-1-03	Washington St. 34-14
Bob Stoops	Sugar 1-4-04	LSU 14-21
Bob Stoops	Orange 1-4-05	Southern California 19-55
Bob Stoops	Holiday 12-29-05	Oregon 17-14
Bob Stoops	Fiesta 1-1-07	Boise St. 42-43 (ot)
All bowls 24-15-1		
OKLAHOMA ST.		
Jim Lookabaugh	Cotton 1-1-45	TCU 34-0
Jim Lookabaugh	Sugar 1-1-46	St. Mary's (Cal.) 33-13
Jim Lookabaugh	Delta 1-1-49	William & Mary 0-20
Cliff Speegle	Bluegrass 12-13-58	Florida St. 15-6
Jim Stanley	Fiesta 12-28-74	BYU 16-6
Jim Stanley	Tangerine 12-18-76	BYU 49-12
Jimmy Johnson	Independence 12-12-81	Texas A&M 16-33
Jimmy Johnson	Bluebonnet 12-31-83	Baylor 24-14
Pat Jones	Gator 12-28-84	South Carolina 21-14
Pat Jones	Gator 12-30-85	Florida St. 23-34
Pat Jones	Sun 12-25-87	West Virginia 35-33
Pat Jones	Holiday 12-30-88	Wyoming 62-14
Bob Simmons	Alamo 12-30-97	Purdue 20-33
Les Miles	Houston 12-27-02	Southern Miss. 33-23
Les Miles	Cotton 1-2-04	Mississippi 28-31
Les Miles	Alamo 12-29-04	Ohio St. 7-33
Mike Gundy	Independence 12-28-06	Alabama 34-31
All bowls 11-6-0		
OREGON		
Hugo Bezdek	Rose 1-1-17	Penn 14-0
Charles "Shy" Huntington	Rose 1-1-20	Harvard 6-7
Jim Aiken	Cotton 1-1-49	SMU 13-21
Len Casanova	Rose 1-1-58	Ohio St. 7-10
Len Casanova	Liberty 12-17-60	Penn St. 12-41
Len Casanova	Sun 12-31-63	SMU 21-14
Rich Brooks	Independence 12-16-89	Tulsa 27-24
Rich Brooks	Freedom 12-29-90	Colorado St. 31-32
Rich Brooks	Independence 12-31-92	Wake Forest 35-39
Rich Brooks	Rose 1-2-95	Penn St. 20-38
Mike Bellotti	Cotton 1-1-96	Colorado 6-38
Mike Bellotti	Las Vegas 12-20-97	Air Force 41-13
Mike Bellotti	Aloha Classic 12-25-98	Colorado 43-51
Mike Bellotti	Sun 12-31-99	Minnesota 24-20
Mike Bellotti	Holiday 12-29-00	Texas 35-30
Mike Bellotti	Fiesta 1-1-02	Colorado 38-16
Mike Bellotti	Seattle 12-30-02	Wake Forest 17-38
Mike Bellotti	Sun 12-31-03	Minnesota 30-31

School/Coach	Bowl/Date	Opponent/Score
Mike Bellotti	Holiday 12-29-05	Oklahoma 14-17
Mike Bellotti	Las Vegas 12-21-06	BYU 8-38
All bowls 7-13-0		
OREGON ST.		
Lon Stiner	Rose 1-1-42	Duke 20-16
Tommy Prothro	Rose 1-1-57	Iowa 19-35
Tommy Prothro	Liberty 12-15-62	Villanova 6-0
Tommy Prothro	Rose 1-1-65	Michigan 7-34
Dennis Erickson	Oahu Classic 12-25-99	Hawaii 17-23
Dennis Erickson	Fiesta 1-1-01	Notre Dame 41-9
Dennis Erickson	Insight 12-26-02	Pittsburgh 13-38
Mike Riley	Las Vegas 12-24-03	New Mexico 55-14
Mike Riley	Insight 12-28-04	Notre Dame 38-21
Mike Riley	Sun 12-29-06	Missouri 39-38
All bowls 6-4-0		
PENN ST.		
Hugo Bezdek	Rose 1-1-23	Southern California 3-14
Bob Higgins	Cotton 1-1-48	SMU 13-13
Charles "Rip" Engle	Liberty 12-19-59	Alabama 7-0
Charles "Rip" Engle	Liberty 12-17-60	Oregon 41-12
Charles "Rip" Engle	Gator 12-30-61	Georgia Tech 30-15
Charles "Rip" Engle	Gator 12-29-62	Florida 7-17
Joe Paterno	Gator 12-30-67	Florida St. 17-17
Joe Paterno	Orange 1-1-69	Kansas 15-14
Joe Paterno	Orange 1-1-70	Missouri 10-3
Joe Paterno	Cotton 1-1-72	Texas 30-6
Joe Paterno	Sugar 12-31-72	Oklahoma 0-14
Joe Paterno	Orange 1-1-74	LSU 16-9
Joe Paterno	Cotton 1-1-75	Baylor 41-20
Joe Paterno	Sugar 12-31-75	Alabama 6-13
Joe Paterno	Gator 12-27-76	Notre Dame 9-20
Joe Paterno	Fiesta 12-25-77	Arizona St. 42-30
Joe Paterno	Sugar 1-1-79	Alabama 7-14
Joe Paterno	Liberty 12-22-79	Tulane 9-6
Joe Paterno	Fiesta 12-26-80	Ohio St. 31-19
Joe Paterno	Fiesta 1-1-82	Southern California 26-10
Joe Paterno	Sugar 1-1-83	Georgia 27-23
Joe Paterno	Aloha 12-26-83	Washington 13-10
Joe Paterno	Orange 1-1-86	Oklahoma 10-25
Joe Paterno	Fiesta 1-2-87	Miami (Fla.) 14-10
Joe Paterno	Florida Citrus 1-1-88	Clemson 10-35
Joe Paterno	Holiday 12-29-89	BYU 50-39
Joe Paterno	Blockbuster 12-28-90	Florida St. 17-24
Joe Paterno	Fiesta 1-1-92	Tennessee 42-17
Joe Paterno	Blockbuster 1-1-93	Stanford 3-24
Joe Paterno	Florida Citrus 1-1-94	Tennessee 31-13
Joe Paterno	Rose 1-2-95	Oregon 38-20
Joe Paterno	Outback 1-1-96	Auburn 43-14
Joe Paterno	Fiesta 1-1-97	Texas 38-15
Joe Paterno	Flordia Citrus 1-1-98	Florida 6-21
Joe Paterno	Outback 1-1-99	Kentucky 26-14
Joe Paterno	Alamo 12-28-99	Texas A&M 24-0
Joe Paterno	Capital One 1-1-03	Auburn 9-13
Joe Paterno	Orange 1-3-06	Florida St. 26-23 (3 ot)
Joe Paterno	Outback 1-1-07	Tennessee 20-10
All bowls 25-12-2		
PITTSBURGH		
Jock Sutherland	Rose 1-2-28	Stanford 6-7
Jock Sutherland	Rose 1-1-30	Southern California 14-47
Jock Sutherland	Rose 1-2-33	Southern California 0-35
Jock Sutherland	Rose 1-1-37	Washington 21-0
John Michelosen	Sugar 1-2-56	Georgia Tech 0-7
John Michelosen	Gator 12-29-56	Georgia Tech 14-21
Johnny Majors	Fiesta 12-21-73	Arizona St. 7-28
Johnny Majors	Sun 12-26-75	Kansas 33-19
Johnny Majors	Sugar 1-1-77	Georgia 27-3
Jackie Sherrill	Gator 12-30-77	Clemson 34-3
Jackie Sherrill	Tangerine 12-23-78	North Carolina St. 17-30
Jackie Sherrill	Fiesta 12-25-79	Arizona 16-10
Jackie Sherrill	Gator 12-29-80	South Carolina 37-9
Jackie Sherrill	Sugar 1-1-82	Georgia 24-20
Foge Fazio	Cotton 1-1-83	SMU 3-7
Foge Fazio	Fiesta 1-2-84	Ohio St. 23-28
Mike Gottfried	Bluebonnet 12-31-87	Texas 27-32
Paul Hackett	John Hancock 12-30-89	Texas A&M 31-28
Walt Harris	Liberty 12-31-97	Southern Miss. 7-41
Walt Harris	Insight.com 12-28-00	Iowa St. 29-37
Walt Harris	Tangerine 12-20-01	North Carolina St. 34-19
Walt Harris	Insight 12-26-02	Oregon St. 38-13
Walt Harris	Continental Tire 12-27-03	Virginia 16-23
Walt Harris	Fiesta 1-1-05	Utah 7-35
All bowls 10-14-0		

School/Coach	Bowl/Date	Opponent/Score
PURDUE		
Jack Mollenkopf	Rose 1-2-67	Southern California 14-13
Jim Young	Peach 12-25-78	Georgia Tech 41-21
Jim Young	Bluebonnet 12-31-79	Tennessee 27-22
Jim Young	Liberty 12-27-80	Missouri 28-25
Leon Burtnett	Peach 12-31-84	Virginia 24-27
Joe Tiller	Alamo 12-30-97	Oklahoma St. 33-20
Joe Tiller	Alamo 12-29-98	Kansas St. 37-34
Joe Tiller	Outback 1-1-00	Georgia 25-28 (ot)
Joe Tiller	Rose 1-1-01	Washington 24-34
Joe Tiller	Sun 12-31-01	Washington St. 27-33
Joe Tiller	Sun 12-31-02	Washington 34-24
Joe Tiller	Capital One 1-1-04	Georgia 27-34 (ot)
Joe Tiller	Sun 12-31-04	Arizona St. 23-27
Joe Tiller	Champs Sports 12-29-06	Maryland 7-24
All bowls 7-7-0		
RICE		
Jimmy Kitts	Cotton 1-1-38	Colorado 28-14
Jess Neely	Orange 1-1-47	Tennessee 8-0
Jess Neely	Cotton 1-2-50	North Carolina 27-13
Jess Neely	Cotton 1-1-54	Alabama 28-6
Jess Neely	Cotton 1-1-58	Navy 7-20
Jess Neely	Sugar 1-2-61	Mississippi 6-14
Jess Neely	Bluebonnet 12-16-61	Kansas 7-33
Todd Graham	New Orleans 12-22-06	Troy 17-41
All bowls 4-4-0		
RUTGERS		
Frank Burns	Garden State 12-16-78	Arizona St. 18-34
Greg Schiano	Insight 12-27-05	Arizona St. 40-45
Greg Schiano	Texas 12-28-06	Kansas St. 37-10
All bowls 1-2-0		
SAN DIEGO ST.		
Bill Schutte	Harbor 1-1-48	Hardin-Simmons 0-53
Don Coryell	Pasadena 12-6-69	Boston U. 28-7
Denny Stolz	Holiday 12-30-86	Iowa 38-39
Al Luginbill	Freedom 12-30-91	Tulsa 17-28
Ted Tollner	Las Vegas 12-19-98	North Carolina 13-20
All bowls 1-4-0		
SAN JOSE ST.		
Bill Hubbard	Raisin 1-1-47	Utah St. 20-0
Bill Hubbard	Raisin 12-31-49	Texas Tech 20-13
Dewey King	Pasadena 12-18-71	Memphis 9-28
Jack Elway	California 12-19-81	Toledo 25-27
Claude Gilbert	California 12-31-86	Miami (Ohio) 37-7
Claude Gilbert	California 12-12-87	Eastern Mich. 27-30
Terry Shea	California 12-8-90	Central Mich. 48-24
Dick Tomey	New Mexico 12-23-06	New Mexico 20-12
All bowls 5-3-0		
SOUTH CAROLINA		
Johnny McMillan	Gator 1-1-46	Wake Forest 14-26
Paul Dietzel	Peach 12-30-69	West Virginia 3-14
Jim Carlen	Tangerine 12-20-75	Miami (Ohio) 7-20
Jim Carlen	Hall of Fame 12-29-79	Missouri 14-24
Jim Carlen	Gator 12-29-80	Pittsburgh 9-37
Joe Morrison	Gator 12-28-84	Oklahoma St. 14-21
Joe Morrison	Gator 12-31-87	LSU 13-30
Joe Morrison	Liberty 12-28-88	Indiana 10-34
Brad Scott	Carquest 1-2-95	West Virginia 24-21
Lou Holtz	Outback 1-1-01	Ohio St. 24-7
Lou Holtz	Outback 1-1-02	Ohio St. 31-28
Steve Spurrier	Independence 12-30-05	Missouri 31-38
Steve Spurrier	Liberty 12-29-06	Houston 44-36
All bowls 4-9-0		
SOUTH FLA.		
Jim Leavitt	Meineke Car Care 12-31-05	North Carolina St. 0-14
Jim Leavitt	Papajohns.com 12-23-06	East Caro. 24-7
All bowls 1-1-0		
SOUTHERN CALIFORNIA		
Elmer "Gus" Henderson	Rose 1-1-23	Penn St. 14-3
Elmer "Gus" Henderson	Los Angeles Christmas Festival 12-25-24	Missouri 20-7
Howard Jones	Rose 1-1-30	Pittsburgh 47-14
Howard Jones	Rose 1-1-32	Tulane 21-12
Howard Jones	Rose 1-2-33	Pittsburgh 35-0
Howard Jones	Rose 1-2-39	Duke 7-3
Howard Jones	Rose 1-1-40	Tennessee 14-0
Jeff Cravath	Rose 1-1-44	Washington 29-0
Jeff Cravath	Rose 1-1-45	Tennessee 25-0
Jeff Cravath	Rose 1-1-46	Alabama 14-34

School/Coach	Bowl/Date	Opponent/Score
Jeff Cravath	Rose 1-1-48	Michigan 0-49
Jess Hill	Rose 1-1-53	Wisconsin 7-0
Jess Hill	Rose 1-1-55	Ohio St. 7-20
John McKay	Rose 1-1-63	Wisconsin 42-37
John McKay	Rose 1-2-67	Purdue 13-14
John McKay	Rose 1-1-68	Indiana 14-3
John McKay	Rose 1-1-69	Ohio St. 16-27
John McKay	Rose 1-1-70	Michigan 10-3
John McKay	Rose 1-1-73	Ohio St. 42-17
John McKay	Rose 1-1-74	Ohio St. 21-42
John McKay	Rose 1-1-75	Ohio St. 18-17
John McKay	Liberty 12-22-75	Texas A&M 20-0
John Robinson	Rose 1-1-77	Michigan 14-6
John Robinson	Bluebonnet 12-31-77	Texas A&M 47-28
John Robinson	Rose 1-1-79	Michigan 17-10
John Robinson	Rose 1-1-80	Ohio St. 17-16
John Robinson	Fiesta 1-1-82	Penn St. 10-26
Ted Tollner	Rose 1-1-85	Ohio St. 20-17
Ted Tollner	Aloha 12-28-85	Alabama 3-24
Ted Tollner	Florida Citrus 1-1-87	Auburn 7-16
Larry Smith	Rose 1-1-88	Michigan St. 17-20
Larry Smith	Rose 1-2-89	Michigan 14-22
Larry Smith	Rose 1-1-90	Michigan 17-10
Larry Smith	John Hancock 12-31-90	Michigan St. 16-17
Larry Smith	Freedom 12-29-92	Fresno St. 7-24
John Robinson	Freedom 12-30-93	Utah 28-21
John Robinson	Cotton 1-2-95	Texas Tech 55-14
John Robinson	Rose 1-1-96	Northwestern 41-32
Paul Hackett	Sun 12-31-98	TCU 19-28
Pete Carroll	Las Vegas 12-25-01	Utah 6-10
Pete Carroll	Orange 1-2-03	Iowa 38-17
Pete Carroll	Rose 1-1-04	Michigan 28-14
Pete Carroll	Orange 1-4-05	Oklahoma 55-19
Pete Carroll	Rose 1-4-06	Texas 38-41
Pete Carroll	Rose 1-1-07	Michigan 32-18

All bowls 29-16-0

SMU

School/Coach	Bowl/Date	Opponent/Score
Ray Morrison	Dixie Classic 1-1-25	West Va. Wesleyan 7-9
Matty Bell	Rose 1-1-36	Stanford 0-7
Matty Bell	Cotton 1-1-48	Penn St. 13-13
Matty Bell	Cotton 1-1-49	Oregon 21-13
Hayden Fry	Sun 12-31-63	Oregon 14-21
Hayden Fry	Cotton 12-31-66	Georgia 9-24
Hayden Fry	Bluebonnet 12-31-68	Oklahoma 28-27
Ron Meyer	Holiday 12-19-80	BYU 45-46
Bobby Collins	Cotton 1-1-83	Pittsburgh 7-3
Bobby Collins	Sun 12-24-83	Alabama 7-28
Bobby Collins	Aloha 12-29-84	Notre Dame 27-20

All bowls 4-6-1

SOUTHERN MISS.

School/Coach	Bowl/Date	Opponent/Score
Thad "Pie" Vann	Sun 1-1-53	Pacific 7-26
Thad "Pie" Vann	Sun 1-1-54	UTEP 14-37
Bobby Collins	Independence 12-13-80	McNeese St. 16-14
Bobby Collins	Tangerine 12-19-81	Missouri 17-19
Curley Hallman	Independence 12-23-88	UTEP 38-18
Jeff Bower	All-American 12-28-90	North Carolina St. 27-31
Jeff Bower	Liberty 12-31-97	Pittsburgh 41-7
Jeff Bower	Humanitarian 12-30-98	Idaho 35-42
Jeff Bower	Liberty 12-31-99	Colorado St. 23-17
Jeff Bower	Mobile Alabama 12-20-00	TCU 28-21
Jeff Bower	Houston 12-27-02	Oklahoma St. 23-33
Jeff Bower	Liberty 12-31-03	Utah 0-17
Jeff Bower	New Orleans 12-14-04	North Texas 31-10
Jeff Bower	New Orleans 12-20-05	Arkansas St. 31-19
Jeff Bower	GMAC 1-7-07	Ohio 28-7

All bowls 8-7-0

STANFORD

School/Coach	Bowl/Date	Opponent/Score
Charlie Fickert	Rose 1-1-02	Michigan 0-49
Glenn "Pop" Warner	Rose 1-1-25	Notre Dame 10-27
Glenn "Pop" Warner	Rose 1-1-27	Alabama 7-7
Glenn "Pop" Warner	Rose 1-2-28	Pittsburgh 7-6
Claude "Tiny" Thornhill	Rose 1-1-34	Columbia 0-7
Claude "Tiny" Thornhill	Rose 1-1-35	Alabama 13-29
Claude "Tiny" Thornhill	Rose 1-1-36	SMU 7-0
Clark Shaughnessy	Rose 1-1-41	Nebraska 21-13
Chuck Taylor	Rose 1-1-52	Illinois 7-40
John Ralston	Rose 1-1-71	Ohio St. 27-17
John Ralston	Rose 1-1-72	Michigan 13-12
Bill Walsh	Sun 12-31-77	LSU 24-14
Bill Walsh	Bluebonnet 12-31-78	Georgia 25-22
Jack Elway	Gator 12-27-86	Clemson 21-27
Dennis Green	Aloha 12-25-91	Georgia Tech 17-18
Bill Walsh	Blockbuster 1-1-93	Penn St. 24-3
Tyrone Willingham	Liberty 12-30-95	East Caro. 13-19
Tyrone Willingham	Sun 12-31-96	Michigan St. 38-0
Tyrone Willingham	Rose 1-1-00	Wisconsin 9-17
Tyrone Willingham	Seattle 12-27-01	Georgia Tech 14-24

All bowls 9-10-1

SYRACUSE

School/Coach	Bowl/Date	Opponent/Score
Ben Schwartzwalder	Orange 1-1-53	Alabama 6-61
Ben Schwartzwalder	Cotton 1-1-57	TCU 27-28
Ben Schwartzwalder	Orange 1-1-59	Oklahoma 6-21
Ben Schwartzwalder	Cotton 1-1-60	Texas 23-14
Ben Schwartzwalder	Liberty 12-16-61	Miami (Fla.) 15-14
Ben Schwartzwalder	Sugar 1-1-65	LSU 10-13
Ben Schwartzwalder	Gator 12-31-66	Tennessee 12-18
Frank Maloney	Independence 12-15-79	McNeese St. 31-7
Dick MacPherson	Cherry 12-21-85	Maryland 18-35
Dick MacPherson	Sugar 1-1-88	Auburn 16-16
Dick MacPherson	Hall of Fame 1-2-89	LSU 23-10
Dick MacPherson	Peach 12-30-89	Georgia 19-18
Dick MacPherson	Aloha 12-25-90	Arizona 28-0
Paul Pasqualoni	Hall of Fame 1-1-92	Ohio St. 24-17
Paul Pasqualoni	Fiesta 1-1-93	Colorado 26-22
Paul Pasqualoni	Gator 1-1-96	Clemson 41-0
Paul Pasqualoni	Liberty 12-27-96	Houston 30-17
Paul Pasqualoni	Fiesta 12-31-97	Kansas St. 18-35
Paul Pasqualoni	Orange 1-2-99	Florida 10-31
Paul Pasqualoni	Music City 12-29-99	Kentucky 20-13
Paul Pasqualoni	Insight.com 12-29-01	Kansas St. 26-3
Paul Pasqualoni	Champs Sports 12-21-04	Georgia Tech 14-51

All bowls 12-9-1

TEMPLE

School/Coach	Bowl/Date	Opponent/Score
Glenn "Pop" Warner	Sugar 1-1-35	Tulane 14-20
Wayne Hardin	Garden State 12-15-79	California 28-17

All bowls 1-1-0

TENNESSEE

School/Coach	Bowl/Date	Opponent/Score
Bob Neyland	Orange 1-2-39	Oklahoma 17-0
Bob Neyland	Rose 1-1-40	Southern California 0-14
Bob Neyland	Sugar 1-1-41	Boston College 13-19
John Barnhill	Sugar 1-1-43	Tulsa 14-7
John Barnhill	Rose 1-1-45	Southern California 0-25
Bob Neyland	Orange 1-1-47	Rice 0-8
Bob Neyland	Cotton 1-1-51	Texas 20-14
Bob Neyland	Sugar 1-1-52	Maryland 13-28
Bob Neyland	Cotton 1-1-53	Texas 0-16
Bowden Wyatt	Sugar 1-1-57	Baylor 7-13
Bowden Wyatt	Gator 12-28-57	Texas A&M 3-0
Doug Dickey	Bluebonnet 12-18-65	Tulsa 27-6
Doug Dickey	Gator 12-31-66	Syracuse 18-12
Doug Dickey	Orange 1-1-68	Oklahoma 24-26
Doug Dickey	Cotton 1-1-69	Texas 13-36
Doug Dickey	Gator 12-27-69	Florida 13-14
Bill Battle	Sugar 1-1-71	Air Force 34-13
Bill Battle	Liberty 12-20-71	Arkansas 14-13
Bill Battle	Bluebonnet 12-30-72	LSU 24-17
Bill Battle	Gator 12-29-73	Texas Tech 19-28
Bill Battle	Liberty 12-16-74	Maryland 7-3
Johnny Majors	Bluebonnet 12-31-79	Purdue 22-27
Johnny Majors	Garden State 12-13-81	Wisconsin 28-21
Johnny Majors	Peach 12-31-82	Iowa 22-28
Johnny Majors	Florida Citrus 12-17-83	Maryland 30-23
Johnny Majors	Sun 12-24-84	Maryland 27-28
Johnny Majors	Sugar 1-1-86	Miami (Fla.) 35-7
Johnny Majors	Liberty 12-29-86	Minnesota 21-14
Johnny Majors	Peach 1-2-88	Indiana 27-22
Johnny Majors	Cotton 1-1-90	Arkansas 31-27
Johnny Majors	Sugar 1-1-91	Virginia 23-22
Johnny Majors	Fiesta 1-1-92	Penn St. 17-42
Phillip Fulmer	Hall of Fame 1-1-93	Boston College 38-23
Phillip Fulmer	Florida Citrus 1-1-94	Penn St. 13-31
Phillip Fulmer	Gator 12-30-94	Virginia Tech 45-23
Phillip Fulmer	Florida Citrus 1-1-96	Ohio St. 20-14
Phillip Fulmer	Florida Citrus 1-1-97	Northwestern 48-28
Phillip Fulmer	Orange 1-2-98	Nebraska 17-42
Phillip Fulmer	Fiesta 1-4-99	Florida St. 23-16
Phillip Fulmer	Fiesta 1-2-00	Nebraska 21-31
Phillip Fulmer	Cotton 1-1-01	Kansas St. 21-35
Phillip Fulmer	Florida Citrus 1-1-02	Michigan 45-17
Phillip Fulmer	Peach 12-31-02	Maryland 3-30
Phillip Fulmer	Peach 1-2-04	Clemson 14-27
Phillip Fulmer	Cotton 1-1-05	Texas A&M 38-7
Phillip Fulmer	Outback 1-1-07	Penn St. 10-20

All bowls 24-22-0

TEXAS

School/Coach	Bowl/Date	Opponent/Score
Dana Bible	Cotton 1-1-43	Georgia Tech 14-7
Dana Bible	Cotton 1-1-44	Randolph Field 7-7
Dana Bible	Cotton 1-1-46	Missouri 40-27
Blair Cherry	Sugar 1-1-48	Alabama 27-7
Blair Cherry	Orange 1-1-49	Georgia 41-28
Blair Cherry	Cotton 1-1-51	Tennessee 14-20
Ed Price	Cotton 1-1-53	Tennessee 16-0
Darrell Royal	Sugar 1-1-58	Mississippi 7-39
Darrell Royal	Cotton 1-1-60	Syracuse 14-23
Darrell Royal	Bluebonnet 12-17-60	Alabama 3-3
Darrell Royal	Cotton 1-1-62	Mississippi 12-7
Darrell Royal	Cotton 1-1-63	LSU 0-13
Darrell Royal	Cotton 1-1-64	Navy 28-6
Darrell Royal	Orange 1-1-65	Alabama 21-17
Darrell Royal	Bluebonnet 12-17-66	Mississippi 19-0
Darrell Royal	Cotton 1-1-69	Tennessee 36-13
Darrell Royal	Cotton 1-1-70	Notre Dame 21-17
Darrell Royal	Cotton 1-1-71	Notre Dame 11-24
Darrell Royal	Cotton 1-1-72	Penn St. 6-30
Darrell Royal	Cotton 1-1-73	Alabama 17-13
Darrell Royal	Cotton 1-1-74	Nebraska 3-19
Darrell Royal	Gator 12-30-74	Auburn 3-27
Darrell Royal	Bluebonnet 12-27-75	Colorado 38-21
Fred Akers	Cotton 1-2-78	Notre Dame 10-38
Fred Akers	Sun 12-23-78	Maryland 42-0
Fred Akers	Sun 12-22-79	Washington 7-14
Fred Akers	Bluebonnet 12-31-80	North Carolina 7-16
Fred Akers	Cotton 1-1-82	Alabama 14-12
Fred Akers	Sun 12-25-82	North Carolina 10-26
Fred Akers	Cotton 1-2-84	Georgia 9-10
Fred Akers	Freedom 12-26-84	Iowa 17-55
Fred Akers	Bluebonnet 12-31-85	Air Force 16-24
David McWilliams	Bluebonnet 12-31-87	Pittsburgh 32-27
David McWilliams	Cotton 1-1-91	Miami (Fla.) 3-46
John Mackovic	Sun 12-30-94	North Carolina 35-31
John Mackovic	Sugar 12-31-95	Virginia Tech 10-28
John Mackovic	Fiesta 1-1-97	Penn St. 15-38
Mack Brown	Cotton 1-1-99	Mississippi St. 38-11
Mack Brown	Cotton 1-1-00	Arkansas 6-27
Mack Brown	Holiday 12-29-00	Oregon 30-35
Mack Brown	Holiday 12-28-01	Washington 47-43
Mack Brown	Cotton 1-1-03	LSU 35-20
Mack Brown	Holiday 12-30-03	Washington St. 20-28
Mack Brown	Rose 1-1-05	Michigan 38-37
Mack Brown	Rose 1-4-06	Southern California 41-38
Mack Brown	Alamo 12-30-06	Iowa 26-24

All bowls 23-21-2

UTEP

School/Coach	Bowl/Date	Opponent/Score
Mack Saxon	Sun 1-1-37	Hardin-Simmons 6-34
Jack "Cactus Jack" Curtice	Sun 1-1-49	West Virginia 12-21
Jack "Cactus Jack" Curtice	Sun 1-2-50	Georgetown 33-20
Mike Brumbelow	Sun 1-1-54	Southern Miss. 37-14
Mike Brumbelow	Sun 1-1-55	Florida St. 47-20
Mike Brumbelow	Sun 1-1-57	George Washington 0-13
Bobby Dobbs	Sun 12-31-65	TCU 13-12
Bobby Dobbs	Sun 12-30-67	Mississippi 14-7
Bob Stull	Independence 12-23-88	Southern Miss. 18-38
Gary Nord	Humanitarian 12-28-00	Boise St. 23-38
Mike Price	Houston 12-29-04	Colorado 28-33
Mike Price	GMAC 12-21-05	Toledo 13-45

All bowls 5-7-0

TEXAS A&M

School/Coach	Bowl/Date	Opponent/Score
Dana Bible	Dixie Classic 1-2-22	Centre 22-14
Homer Norton	Sugar 1-1-40	Tulane 14-13
Homer Norton	Cotton 1-1-41	Fordham 13-12
Homer Norton	Cotton 1-1-42	Alabama 21-29
Homer Norton	Orange 1-1-44	LSU 14-19
Harry Stiteler	Presidential 12-9-50	Georgia 40-20
Paul "Bear" Bryant	Gator 12-28-57	Tennessee 0-3
Gene Stallings	Cotton 1-1-68	Alabama 20-16
Emory Bellard	Liberty 12-22-75	Southern California 0-20
Emory Bellard	Sun 1-2-77	Florida 37-14
Emory Bellard	Bluebonnet 12-31-77	Southern California 28-47
Tom Wilson	Hall of Fame 12-20-78	Iowa St. 28-12
Tom Wilson	Independence 12-12-81	Oklahoma St. 33-16
Jackie Sherrill	Cotton 1-1-86	Auburn 36-16
Jackie Sherrill	Cotton 1-1-87	Ohio St. 12-28
Jackie Sherrill	Cotton 1-1-88	Notre Dame 35-10
R.C. Slocum	John Hancock 12-30-89	Pittsburgh 28-31
R.C. Slocum	Holiday 12-29-90	BYU 65-14
R.C. Slocum	Cotton 1-1-92	Florida St. 2-10
R.C. Slocum	Cotton 1-1-93	Notre Dame 3-28
R.C. Slocum	Cotton 1-1-94	Notre Dame 21-24
R.C. Slocum	Alamo 12-28-95	Michigan 22-20
R.C. Slocum	Cotton 1-1-98	UCLA 23-29
R.C. Slocum	Sugar 1-1-99	Ohio St. 14-24
R.C. Slocum	Alamo 12-28-99	Penn St. 0-24
R.C. Slocum	Independence 12-31-00	Mississippi St. 41-43 (ot)
R.C. Slocum	Galleryfurniture.com 12-28-01	TCU 28-9
Dennis Franchione	Cotton 1-1-05	Tennessee 7-38
Dennis Franchione	Holiday 12-28-06	California 10-45

All bowls 13-16-0

TCU

School/Coach	Bowl/Date	Opponent/Score
Bill Driver	Fort Worth Classic 1-1-21	Centre 7-63
Leo "Dutch" Meyer	Sugar 1-1-36	LSU 3-2
Leo "Dutch" Meyer	Cotton 1-1-37	Marquette 16-6
Leo "Dutch" Meyer	Sugar 1-2-39	Carnegie Mellon 15-7
Leo "Dutch" Meyer	Orange 1-1-42	Georgia 26-40
Leo "Dutch" Meyer	Cotton 1-1-45	Oklahoma St. 0-34
Leo "Dutch" Meyer	Delta 1-1-48	Mississippi 9-13
Leo "Dutch" Meyer	Cotton 1-1-52	Kentucky 7-20
Abe Martin	Cotton 1-2-56	Mississippi 13-14
Abe Martin	Cotton 1-1-57	Syracuse 28-27
Abe Martin	Cotton 1-1-59	Air Force 0-0
Abe Martin	Bluebonnet 12-19-59	Clemson 7-23
Abe Martin	Sun 12-31-65	UTEP 12-13
Jim Wacker	Bluebonnet 12-31-84	West Virginia 14-31
Pat Sullivan	Independence 12-28-94	Virginia 10-20
Dennis Franchione	Sun 12-31-98	Southern California 28-19
Dennis Franchione	Mobile Alabama 12-22-99	East Caro. 28-14
Gary Patterson	Mobile Alabama 12-20-00	Southern Miss. 21-28
Gary Patterson	Galleryfurniture.com 12-28-01	Texas A&M 9-28
Gary Patterson	Liberty 12-31-02	Colorado St. 17-3
Gary Patterson	Fort Worth 12-23-03	Boise St. 31-34
Gary Patterson	Houston 12-31-05	Iowa St. 27-24
Gary Patterson	Poinsettia 12-19-06	Northern Ill. 37-7

All bowls 9-13-1

TEXAS TECH

School/Coach	Bowl/Date	Opponent/Score
Pete Cawthon	Sun 1-1-38	West Virginia 6-7
Pete Cawthon	Cotton 1-2-39	St. Mary's (Cal.) 13-20
Dell Morgan	Sun 1-1-42	Tulsa 0-6
Dell Morgan	Sun 1-1-48	Miami (Ohio) 12-13
Dell Morgan	Raisin 12-31-49	San Jose St. 13-20
DeWitt Weaver	Sun 1-1-52	Pacific 25-14
DeWitt Weaver	Gator 1-1-54	Auburn 35-13
DeWitt Weaver	Sun 1-2-56	Wyoming 14-21
J.T. King	Sun 12-26-64	Georgia 0-7
J.T. King	Gator 12-31-65	Georgia Tech 21-31
Jim Carlen	Sun 12-19-70	Georgia Tech 9-17
Jim Carlen	Sun 12-30-72	North Carolina 28-32
Jim Carlen	Gator 12-29-73	Tennessee 28-19
Jim Carlen	Peach 12-28-74	Vanderbilt 6-6
Steve Sloan	Bluebonnet 12-31-76	Nebraska 24-27
Steve Sloan	Tangerine 12-23-77	Florida St. 17-40
Spike Dykes	Independence 12-20-86	Mississippi 17-20
Spike Dykes	All-American 12-28-89	Duke 49-21
Spike Dykes	John Hancock 12-24-93	Oklahoma 10-41
Spike Dykes	Cotton 1-2-95	Southern California 14-55
Spike Dykes	Copper 12-27-95	Air Force 55-41
Spike Dykes	Alamo 12-29-96	Iowa 0-27
Spike Dykes	Independence 12-31-98	Mississippi 18-35
Mike Leach	Galleryfurniture.com 12-27-00	East Caro. 27-40
Mike Leach	Alamo 12-29-01	Iowa 13-16
Mike Leach	Mazda Tangerine 12-23-02	Clemson 55-15
Mike Leach	Houston 12-30-03	Navy 38-14
Mike Leach	Holiday 12-30-04	California 45-31
Mike Leach	Cotton 1-2-06	Alabama 10-13
Mike Leach	Insight 12-29-06	Minnesota 44-41 (ot)

All bowls 9-20-1

TOLEDO

School/Coach	Bowl/Date	Opponent/Score
Frank Lauterbur	Tangerine 12-26-69	Davidson 56-33
Frank Lauterbur	Tangerine 12-28-70	William & Mary 40-12
Jack Murphy	Tangerine 12-28-71	Richmond 28-3
Chuck Stobart	California 12-19-81	San Jose St. 27-25
Dan Simrell	California 12-15-84	UNLV 13-30
Gary Pinkel	Las Vegas 12-14-95	Nevada 40-37 (ot)
Tom Amstutz	Motor City 12-29-01	Cincinnati 23-16
Tom Amstutz	Motor City 12-26-02	Boston College 25-51
Tom Amstutz	Motor City 12-27-04	Connecticut 10-39
Tom Amstutz	GMAC 12-21-05	UTEP 45-13

All bowls 7-3-0

School/Coach	Bowl/Date	Opponent/Score
TROY		
Larry Blakeney	Silicon Valley 12-30-04	Northern Ill. 21-34
Larry Blakeney	New Orleans 12-22-06	Rice 41-17
All bowls 1-1-0		
TULANE		
Bernie Bierman	Rose 1-1-32	Southern California 12-21
Ted Cox	Sugar 1-1-35	Temple 20-14
Lowell "Red" Dawson	Sugar 1-1-40	Texas A&M 13-14
Jim Pittman	Liberty 12-12-70	Colorado 17-3
Bennie Ellender	Bluebonnet 12-29-73	Houston 7-47
Larry Smith	Liberty 12-22-79	Penn St. 6-9
Vince Gibson	Hall of Fame 12-27-80	Arkansas 15-34
Mack Brown	Independence 12-19-87	Washington 12-24
Tommy Bowden	Liberty 12-31-98	BYU 41-27
Chris Scelfo	Hawaii 12-25-02	Hawaii 36-28
All bowls 4-6-0		
TULSA		
Henry Frnka	Sun 1-1-42	Texas Tech 6-0
Henry Frnka	Sugar 1-1-43	Tennessee 7-14
Henry Frnka	Sugar 1-1-44	Georgia Tech 18-20
Henry Frnka	Orange 1-1-45	Georgia Tech 26-12
Henry Frnka	Oil 1-1-46	Georgia 6-20
J.O. "Buddy" Brothers	Gator 1-1-53	Florida 13-14
Glenn Dobbs	Bluebonnet 12-19-64	Mississippi 14-7
Glenn Dobbs	Bluebonnet 12-18-65	Tennessee 6-27
F.A. Dry	Independence 12-13-76	McNeese St. 16-20
Dave Rader	Independence 12-16-89	Oregon 24-27
Dave Rader	Freedom 12-30-91	San Diego St. 28-17
Steve Kragthorpe	Humanitarian 1-3-04	Georgia Tech 10-52
Steve Kragthorpe	Liberty 12-31-05	Fresno St. 31-24
Steve Kragthorpe	Armed Forces 12-23-06	Utah 13-25
All bowls 5-9-0		
UCLA		
Edwin "Babe" Horrell	Rose 1-1-43	Georgia 0-9
Bert LaBrucherie	Rose 1-1-47	Illinois 14-45
Henry "Red" Sanders	Rose 1-1-54	Michigan St. 20-28
Henry "Red" Sanders	Rose 1-2-56	Michigan St. 14-17
Bill Barnes	Rose 1-1-62	Minnesota 3-21
Tommy Prothro	Rose 1-1-66	Michigan St. 14-12
Dick Vermeil	Rose 1-1-76	Ohio St. 23-10
Terry Donahue	Liberty 12-20-76	Alabama 6-36
Terry Donahue	Fiesta 12-25-78	Arkansas 10-10
Terry Donahue	Bluebonnet 12-31-81	Michigan 14-33
Terry Donahue	Rose 1-1-83	Michigan 24-14
Terry Donahue	Rose 1-2-84	Illinois 45-9
Terry Donahue	Fiesta 1-1-85	Miami (Fla.) 39-37
Terry Donahue	Rose 1-1-86	Iowa 45-28
Terry Donahue	Freedom 12-30-86	BYU 31-10
Terry Donahue	Aloha 12-25-87	Florida 20-16
Terry Donahue	Cotton 1-1-89	Arkansas 17-3
Terry Donahue	John Hancock 12-31-91	Illinois 6-3
Terry Donahue	Rose 1-1-94	Wisconsin 16-21
Terry Donahue	Aloha 12-25-95	Kansas 30-51
Bob Toledo	Cotton 1-1-98	Texas A&M 29-23
Bob Toledo	Rose 1-1-99	Wisconsin 31-38
Bob Toledo	Sun 12-29-00	Wisconsin 20-21
Ed Kezirian	Las Vegas 12-25-02	New Mexico 27-13
Karl Dorrell	Silicon Valley 12-30-03	Fresno St. 9-17
Karl Dorrell	Las Vegas 12-23-04	Wyoming 21-24
Karl Dorrell	Sun 12-30-05	Northwestern 50-38
Karl Dorrell	Emerald 12-27-06	Florida St. 27-44
All bowls 13-14-1		
UTAH		
Ike Armstrong	Sun 1-2-39	New Mexico 26-0
Ray Nagel	Liberty 12-19-64	West Virginia 32-6
Ron McBride	Copper 12-29-92	Washington St. 28-31
Ron McBride	Freedom 12-30-93	Southern California 21-28
Ron McBride	Freedom 12-27-94	Arizona 16-13
Ron McBride	Copper 12-27-96	Wisconsin 10-38
Ron McBride	Las Vegas 12-18-99	Fresno St. 17-16
Ron McBride	Las Vegas 12-25-01	Southern California 10-6
Urban Meyer	Liberty 12-31-03	Southern Miss. 17-0
Urban Meyer	Fiesta 1-1-05	Pittsburgh 35-7
Kyle Whittingham	Emerald 12-29-05	Georgia Tech 38-10
Kyle Whittingham	Armed Forces 12-23-06	Tulsa 25-13
All bowls 9-3-0		
UTAH ST.		
E.L. "Dick" Romney	Raisin 1-1-47	San Jose St. 0-20
John Ralston	Sun 12-31-60	New Mexico St. 13-20
John Ralston	Gotham 12-9-61	Baylor 9-24
Charlie Weatherbie	Las Vegas 12-17-93	Ball St. 42-33
John L. Smith	Humanitarian 12-29-97	Cincinnati 19-35
All bowls 1-4-0		
VANDERBILT		
Art Guepe	Gator 12-31-55	Auburn 25-13
Steve Sloan	Peach 12-28-74	Texas Tech 6-6
George MacIntyre	Hall of Fame 12-31-82	Air Force 28-36
All bowls 1-1-1		
VIRGINIA		
George Welsh	Peach 12-31-84	Purdue 27-24
George Welsh	All-American 12-22-87	BYU 22-16
George Welsh	Florida Citrus 1-1-90	Illinois 21-31
George Welsh	Sugar 1-1-91	Tennessee 22-23
George Welsh	Gator 12-29-91	Oklahoma 14-48
George Welsh	Carquest 1-1-94	Boston College 13-31
George Welsh	Independence 12-28-94	TCU 20-10
George Welsh	Peach 12-30-95	Georgia 34-27
George Welsh	Carquest 12-27-96	Miami (Fla.) 21-31
George Welsh	Peach 12-31-98	Georgia 33-35
George Welsh	Micronpc.com 12-30-99	Illinois 21-63
George Welsh	Oahu Classic 12-24-00	Georgia 14-37
Al Groh	Continental Tire 12-28-02	West Virginia 48-22
Al Groh	Continental Tire 12-27-03	Pittsburgh 23-16
Al Groh	MPC Computers 12-27-04	Fresno St. 34-37 (ot)
Al Groh	Music City 12-30-05	Minnesota 34-31
All bowls 7-9-0		
VIRGINIA TECH		
Jimmy Kitts	Sun 1-1-47	Cincinnati 6-18
Jerry Claiborne	Liberty 12-10-66	Miami (Fla.) 7-14
Jerry Claiborne	Liberty 12-14-68	Mississippi 17-34
Bill Dooley	Peach 1-2-81	Miami (Fla.) 10-20
Bill Dooley	Independence 12-15-84	Air Force 7-23
Bill Dooley	Peach 12-31-86	North Carolina St. 25-24
Frank Beamer	Independence 12-31-93	Indiana 45-20
Frank Beamer	Gator 12-30-94	Tennessee 23-45
Frank Beamer	Sugar 12-31-95	Texas 28-10
Frank Beamer	Orange 12-31-96	Nebraska 21-41
Frank Beamer	Gator 1-1-98	North Carolina 3-42
Frank Beamer	Music City 12-28-98	Alabama 38-7
Frank Beamer	Sugar 1-4-00	Florida St. 29-46
Frank Beamer	Gator 1-1-01	Clemson 41-20
Frank Beamer	Gator 1-1-02	Florida St. 17-30
Frank Beamer	San Francisco 12-31-02	Air Force 20-13
Frank Beamer	Insight 12-26-03	California 49-52
Frank Beamer	Sugar 1-3-05	Auburn 13-16
Frank Beamer	Gator 1-2-06	Louisville 35-24
Frank Beamer	Chick-fil-A 12-30-06	Georgia 24-31
All bowls 7-13-0		
WAKE FOREST		
D.C. "Peahead" Walker	Gator 1-1-46	South Carolina 26-14
D.C. "Peahead" Walker	Dixie 1-1-49	Baylor 7-20
John Mackovic	Tangerine 12-22-79	LSU 10-34
Bill Dooley	Independence 12-31-92	Oregon 39-35
Jim Caldwell	Aloha Classic 12-25-99	Arizona St. 23-3
Jim Grobe	Seattle 12-30-02	Oregon 38-17
Jim Grobe	Orange 1-2-07	Louisville 13-24
All bowls 4-3-0		
WASHINGTON		
Enoch Bagshaw	Rose 1-1-24	Navy 14-14
Enoch Bagshaw	Rose 1-1-26	Alabama 19-20
Jimmy Phelan	Rose 1-1-37	Pittsburgh 0-21
Ralph "Pest" Welch	Rose 1-1-44	Southern California 0-29
Jim Owens	Rose 1-1-60	Wisconsin 44-8
Jim Owens	Rose 1-2-61	Minnesota 17-7
Jim Owens	Rose 1-1-64	Illinois 7-17
Don James	Rose 1-2-78	Michigan 27-20
Don James	Sun 12-22-79	Texas 14-7
Don James	Rose 1-1-81	Michigan 6-23
Don James	Rose 1-1-82	Iowa 28-0
Don James	Aloha 12-25-82	Maryland 21-20
Don James	Aloha 12-26-83	Penn St. 10-13
Don James	Orange 1-1-85	Oklahoma 28-17
Don James	Freedom 12-30-85	Colorado 20-17
Don James	Sun 12-25-86	Alabama 6-28
Don James	Independence 12-19-87	Tulane 24-12
Don James	Freedom 12-30-89	Florida 34-7
Don James	Rose 1-1-91	Iowa 46-34
Don James	Rose 1-1-92	Michigan 34-14
Don James	Rose 1-1-93	Michigan 31-38
Jim Lambright	Sun 12-29-95	Iowa 18-38
Jim Lambright	Holiday 12-30-96	Colorado 21-33

School/Coach	Bowl/Date	Opponent/Score
Jim Lambright	Aloha 12-25-97	Michigan St. 51-23
Jim Lambright	Oahu Classic 12-25-98	Air Force 25-45
Rick Neuheisel	Holiday 12-29-99	Kansas St. 20-24
Rick Neuheisel	Rose 1-1-01	Purdue 34-24
Rick Neuheisel	Holiday 12-28-01	Texas 43-47
Rick Neuheisel	Sun 12-31-02	Purdue 24-34
All bowls 14-14-1		
WASHINGTON ST.		
Bill "Lone Star" Dietz	Rose 1-1-16	Brown 14-0
Orin "Babe" Hollingbery	Rose 1-1-31	Alabama 0-24
Jim Walden	Holiday 12-18-81	BYU 36-38
Dennis Erickson	Aloha 12-25-88	Houston 24-22
Mike Price	Copper 12-29-92	Utah 31-28
Mike Price	Alamo 12-31-94	Baylor 10-3
Mike Price	Rose 1-1-98	Michigan 16-21
Mike Price	Sun 12-31-01	Purdue 33-27
Mike Price	Rose 1-1-03	Oklahoma 14-34
Bill Doba	Holiday 12-30-03	Texas 28-20
All bowls 6-4-0		
WEST VIRGINIA		
Clarence "Doc" Spears	San Diego East-West Christmas Classic 12-25-22	Gonzaga 21-13
Marshall "Little Sleepy" Glenn	Sun 1-1-38	Texas Tech 7-6
Dud DeGroot	Sun 1-1-49	UTEP 21-12
Art Lewis	Sugar 1-1-54	Georgia Tech 19-42
Gene Corum	Liberty 12-19-64	Utah 6-32
Jim Carlen	Peach 12-30-69	South Carolina 14-3
Bobby Bowden	Peach 12-29-72	North Carolina St. 13-49
Bobby Bowden	Peach 12-31-75	North Carolina St. 13-10
Don Nehlen	Peach 12-31-81	Florida 26-6
Don Nehlen	Gator 12-30-82	Florida St. 12-31
Don Nehlen	Hall of Fame 12-22-83	Kentucky 20-16
Don Nehlen	Bluebonnet 12-31-84	TCU 31-14
Don Nehlen	Sun 12-25-87	Oklahoma St. 33-35
Don Nehlen	Fiesta 1-2-89	Notre Dame 21-34
Don Nehlen	Gator 12-30-89	Clemson 7-27
Don Nehlen	Sugar 1-1-94	Florida 7-41
Don Nehlen	Carquest 1-2-95	South Carolina 21-24
Don Nehlen	Gator 1-1-97	North Carolina 13-20
Don Nehlen	Carquest 12-29-97	Georgia Tech 30-35
Don Nehlen	Insight.com 12-26-98	Missouri 31-34
Don Nehlen	Music City 12-28-00	Mississippi 49-38
Rich Rodriquez	Continental Tire 12-28-02	Virginia 22-48
Rich Rodriquez	Gator 1-1-04	Maryland 7-41
Rich Rodriguez	Gator 1-1-05	Florida St. 18-30
Rich Rodriguez	Sugar 1-2-06	Georgia 38-35
Rich Rodriguez	Gator 1-1-07	Georgia Tech 38-35
All bowls 11-15-0		
WESTERN MICH.		
Merle Schlosser	Aviation 12-9-61	New Mexico 12-28
Al Molde	California 12-10-88	Fresno St. 30-35
Bill Cubit	International 1-6-07	Cincinnati 24-27
All bowls 0-3-0		
WISCONSIN		
Ivy Williamson	Rose 1-1-53	Southern California 0-7
Milt Bruhn	Rose 1-1-60	Washington 8-44
Milt Bruhn	Rose 1-2-63	Southern California 37-42
Dave McClain	Garden State 12-13-81	Tennessee 21-28
Dave McClain	Independence 12-11-82	Kansas St. 14-3
Dave McClain	Hall of Fame 12-29-84	Kentucky 19-20
Barry Alvarez	Rose 1-1-94	UCLA 21-16
Barry Alvarez	Hall of Fame 1-2-95	Duke 34-20
Barry Alvarez	Copper 12-27-96	Utah 38-10
Barry Alvarez	Outback 1-1-98	Georgia 6-33
Barry Alvarez	Rose 1-1-99	UCLA 38-31
Barry Alvarez	Rose 1-1-00	Stanford 17-9
Barry Alvarez	Sun 12-29-00	UCLA 21-20
Barry Alvarez	Alamo 12-28-02	Colorado 31-28 (ot)
Barry Alvarez	Music City 12-31-03	Auburn 14-28
Barry Alvarez	Outback 1-1-05	Georgia 21-24
Barry Alvarez	Capital One 1-2-06	Auburn 24-10
Brett Bielema	Capital One 1-1-07	Arkansas 17-14
All bowls 10-8-0		
WYOMING		
Bowden Wyatt	Gator 1-1-51	Wash. & Lee 20-7
Phil Dickens	Sun 1-2-56	Texas Tech 21-14
Bob Devaney	Sun 12-31-58	Hardin-Simmons 14-6
Lloyd Eaton	Sun 12-24-66	Florida St. 28-20
Lloyd Eaton	Sugar 1-1-68	LSU 13-20
Fred Akers	Fiesta 12-25-76	Oklahoma 7-41
Paul Roach	Holiday 12-30-87	Iowa 19-20
Paul Roach	Holiday 12-30-88	Oklahoma St. 14-62
Paul Roach	Copper 12-31-90	California 15-17
Joe Tiller	Copper 12-29-93	Kansas St. 17-52
Joe Glenn	Las Vegas 12-23-04	UCLA 24-21
All bowls 5-6-0		

Played in Major Bowl—No Longer FBS

School/Coach	Bowl/Date	Opponent/Score
BOSTON U.		
Larry Naviaux	Pasadena 12-6-69	San Diego St. 7-28
All bowls 0-1-0		
BROWN		
Ed Robinson	Rose 1-1-16	Washington St. 0-14
All bowls 0-1-0		
BUCKNELL		
Edward "Hook" Mylin	Orange 1-1-35	Miami (Fla.) 26-0
All bowls 1-0-0		
CAL ST. FULLERTON		
Gene Murphy	California 12-17-83	Northern Ill. 13-20
All bowls 0-1-0		
CAL ST. NORTHRIDGE		
Sam Winningham	Pasadena 12-2-67	West Tex. A&M 13-35
All bowls 0-1-0		
CARNEGIE MELLON		
Bill Kern	Sugar 1-2-39	TCU 7-15
All bowls 0-1-0		
CASE RESERVE		
Bill Edwards	Sun 1-1-41	Arizona St. 26-13
All bowls 1-0-0		
CATHOLIC		
Arthur "Dutch" Bergman	Orange 1-1-36	Mississippi 20-19
Arthur "Dutch" Bergman	Sun 1-1-40	Arizona St. 0-0
All bowls 1-0-1		
CENTENARY (LA.)		
Homer Norton	Dixie Classic 1-1-34	Arkansas 7-7
All bowls 0-0-1		
CENTRE		
Charley Moran	Fort Worth Classic 1-1-21	TCU 63-7
Charley Moran	San Diego East-West Christmas Classic 12-26-21	Arizona 38-0
Charley Moran	Dixie Classic 1-2-22	Texas A&M 14-22
All bowls 2-1-0		
CITADEL		
Eddie Teague	Tangerine 12-30-60	Tennessee Tech 27-0
All bowls 1-0-0		
COLUMBIA		
Lou Little	Rose 1-1-34	Stanford 7-0
All bowls 1-0-0		
DAVIDSON		
Homer Smith	Tangerine 12-26-69	Toledo 33-56
All bowls 0-1-0		
DAYTON		
Joe Gavin	Salad 1-1-52	Houston 21-26
All bowls 0-1-0		
DENVER		
Clyde "Cac" Hubbard	Sun 1-1-46	New Mexico 24-34
Clyde "Cac" Hubbard	Alamo 1-4-47	Hardin-Simmons 0-20
All bowls 0-2-0		
DRAKE		
Vee Green	Raisin 1-1-46	Fresno St. 13-12
Al Kawal	Salad 1-1-49	Arizona 14-13
Warren Gaer	Sun 1-1-58	Louisville 20-34
All bowls 2-1-0		
DUQUESNE		
John "Little Clipper" Smith	Orange 1-1-37	Mississippi St. 13-12
All bowls 1-0-0		

School/Coach	Bowl/Date	Opponent/Score
FORDHAM		
Jim Crowley	Cotton 1-1-41	Texas A&M 12-13
Jim Crowley	Sugar 1-1-42	Missouri 2-0
All bowls 1-1-0		
GEORGE WASHINGTON		
Eugene "Bo" Sherman	Sun 1-1-57	UTEP 13-0
All bowls 1-0-0		
GEORGETOWN		
Jack Hagerty	Orange 1-1-41	Mississippi St. 7-14
Bob Margarita	Sun 1-2-50	UTEP 20-33
All bowls 0-2-0		
GONZAGA		
Charles "Gus" Dorais	San Diego East-West Christmas Classic 12-15-22	West Virginia 13-21
All bowls 0-1-0		
HARDIN-SIMMONS		
Frank Kimbrough	Sun 1-1-36	New Mexico St. 14-14
Frank Kimbrough	Sun 1-1-37	UTEP 34-6
Warren Woodson	Sun 1-1-43	Second Air Force 7-13
Warren Woodson	Alamo 1-4-47	Denver 20-6
Warren Woodson	Harbor 1-1-48	San Diego St. 53-0
Warren Woodson	Shrine 12-18-48	Ouachita Baptist 40-12
Warren Woodson	Camellia 12-30-48	Wichita St. 29-12
Sammy Baugh	Sun 12-31-58	Wyoming 6-14
All bowls 5-2-1		
HARVARD		
Robert Fisher	Rose 1-1-20	Oregon 7-6
All bowls 1-0-0		
HOLY CROSS		
John "Ox" Da Grosa	Orange 1-1-46	Miami (Fla.) 6-13
All bowls 0-1-0		
LONG BEACH ST.		
Jim Stangeland	Pasadena 12-19-70	Louisville 24-24
All bowls 0-0-1		
MARQUETTE		
Frank Murray	Cotton 1-1-37	TCU 6-16
All bowls 0-1-0		
McNEESE ST.		
Jack Doland	Independence 12-13-76	Tulsa 20-16
Ernie Duplechin	Independence 12-15-79	Syracuse 7-31
Ernie Duplechin	Independence 12-13-80	Southern Miss. 14-16
All bowls 1-2-0		
MONTANA ST.		
Clyde Carpenter	Harbor 1-1-47	New Mexico 13-13
All bowls 0-0-1		
OCCIDENTAL		
Roy Dennis	Raisin 1-1-49	Colorado St. 21-20
All bowls 1-0-0		
OUACHITA BAPTIST		
Wesley Bradshaw	Shrine 12-18-48	Hardin-Simmons 12-40
All bowls 0-1-0		
PACIFIC		
Larry Siemering	Raisin 1-1-48	Wichita St. 26-14
Ernie Jorge	Sun 1-1-52	Texas Tech 14-25
Ernie Jorge	Sun 1-1-53	Southern Miss. 26-7
All bowls 2-1-0		
PENN		
Bob Folwell	Rose 1-1-17	Oregon 0-14
All bowls 0-1-0		
RANDOLPH FIELD		
Frank Tritico	Cotton 1-1-44	Texas 7-7
All bowls 0-0-1		
RICHMOND		
Frank Jones	Tangerine 12-27-68	Ohio 49-42
Frank Jones	Tangerine 12-28-71	Toledo 3-28
All bowls 1-1-0		
ST. MARY'S (CAL.)		
Edward "Slip" Madigan	Cotton 1-2-39	Texas Tech 20-13
Jimmy Phelan	Sugar 1-1-46	Oklahoma St. 13-33
Jimmy Phelan	Oil 1-1-47	Georgia Tech 19-41
All bowls 1-2-0		
SANTA CLARA		
Lawrence "Buck" Shaw	Sugar 1-1-37	LSU 21-14
Lawrence "Buck" Shaw	Sugar 1-1-38	LSU 6-0
Len Casanova	Orange 1-2-50	Kentucky 21-13
All bowls 3-0-0		
SECOND AIR FORCE		
Red Reese	Sun 1-1-43	Hardin-Simmons 13-7
All bowls 1-0-0		
SOUTHWESTERN (TEX.)		
Randolph R.M. Medley	Sun 1-1-44	New Mexico 7-0
Randolph R.M. Medley	Sun 1-1-45	U. of Mexico 35-0
All bowls 2-0-0		
TAMPA		
Earle Bruce	Tangerine 12-29-72	Kent St. 21-18
All bowls 1-0-0		
TENNESSEE TECH		
Wilburn Tucker	Tangerine 12-30-60	Citadel 0-27
All bowls 0-1-0		
U. OF MEXICO		
Bernard A. Hoban	Sun 1-1-45	Southwestern (Tex.) 0-35
All bowls 0-1-0		
VILLANOVA		
Maurice "Clipper" Smith	Bacardi, Cuba 1-1-37	Auburn 7-7
Jordan Olivar	Great Lakes 12-6-47	Kentucky 14-24
Jordan Olivar	Harbor 1-1-49	Nevada 27-7
Alex Bell	Sun 12-30-61	Wichita St. 17-9
Alex Bell	Liberty 12-15-62	Oregon St. 0-6
All bowls 2-2-1		
WASH. & JEFF.		
Earle "Greasy" Neale	Rose 1-2-22	California 0-0
All bowls 0-0-1		
WASH. & LEE		
George Barclay	Gator 1-1-51	Wyoming 7-20
All bowls 0-1-0		
WEST TEX. A&M		
Frank Kimbrough	Sun 1-1-51	Cincinnati 14-13
Joe Kerbel	Sun 12-31-62	Ohio 15-14
Joe Kerbel	Pasadena 12-2-67	Cal St. Northridge 35-13
All bowls 3-0-0		
WEST VA. WESLEYAN		
Bob Higgins	Dixie Classic 1-1-25	SMU 9-7
All bowls 1-0-0		
WICHITA ST.		
Ralph Graham	Raisin 1-1-48	Pacific 14-26
Jim Trimble	Camellia 12-30-48	Hardin-Simmons 12-49
Hank Foldberg	Sun 12-30-61	Villanova 9-17
All bowls 0-3-0		
WILLIAM & MARY		
Rube McCray	Dixie 1-1-48	Arkansas 19-21
Rube McCray	Delta 1-1-49	Oklahoma St. 20-0
Lou Holtz	Tangerine 12-28-70	Toledo 12-40
All bowls 1-2-0		
XAVIER (OHIO)		
Ed Kluska	Salad 1-1-50	Arizona St. 33-21
All bowls 1-0-0		

Bowl Championship Series Results (1998-07)

Won-Lost Records, All BCS Games

	W-L	Pct.
LSU	3-0	1.000
Texas	2-0	1.000
Wisconsin	2-0	1.000
Auburn	1-0	1.000
Boise St.	1-0	1.000
Louisville	1-0	1.000
Oregon	1-0	1.000
Oregon St.	1-0	1.000
Penn St.	1-0	1.000
Utah	1-0	1.000
Washington	1-0	1.000
West Virginia	1-0	1.000
Ohio St.	4-1	.800
Southern California	4-1	.800
Florida	3-1	.750
Miami (Fla.)	3-1	.750
Georgia	1-1	.500
Nebraska	1-1	.500
Tennessee	1-1	.500
Oklahoma	2-3	.400
Michigan	1-3	.250
Florida St.	1-5	.167
Alabama	0-1	.000
Colorado	0-1	.000
Illinois	0-1	.000
Iowa	0-1	.000
Kansas St.	0-1	.000
Maryland	0-1	.000
Pittsburgh	0-1	.000
Purdue	0-1	.000
Stanford	0-1	.000
Syracuse	0-1	.000
Texas A&M	0-1	.000
UCLA	0-1	.000
Wake Forest	0-1	.000
Washington St.	0-1	.000
Virginia Tech	0-2	.000
Notre Dame	0-3	.000

Won-Lost Records, BCS Championship Game

	W-L	Pct.
Florida	1-0	1.000
LSU	1-0	1.000
Tennessee	1-0	1.000
Texas	1-0	1.000
Miami (Fla.)	1-1	.500
Ohio St.	1-1	.500
Southern California	1-1	.500
Florida St.	1-2	.333
Oklahoma	1-2	.333
Nebraska	0-1	.000
Virginia Tech	0-1	.000

Most BCS Games

Florida St.	6
Ohio St.	5
Oklahoma	5
Southern California	5
Florida	4
Miami (Fla.)	4
Michigan	4

Winning Percentages By Conference

	Pct. (W-L)
Mountain West	1.000 (1-0)
Western Athletic	1.000 (1-0)
Southeastern	.692 (9-4)
Pacific-10	.636 (7-4)
Big East	.556 (5-4)
Big 10	.533 (8-7)
Big 12	.417 (5-7)
Atlantic Coast	.111 (1-8)
Independents	.000 (0-3)

Major Bowl-Game Attendance

Total Yearly Attendance

Year	No. Bowls	Total Attendance	Per/Game Average
1902	1	8,000	8,000
1916	1	7,000	7,000
1917	1	26,000	26,000
1920	1	30,000	30,000
1921	2	51,000	25,500
1922	3	57,000	19,000
1923	2	48,000	24,000
1924	1	40,000	40,000
1925	3	107,000	35,667
1926	1	50,000	50,000
1927	1	57,417	57,417
1928	1	65,000	65,000
1929	1	66,604	66,604
1930	1	72,000	72,000
1931	1	60,000	60,000
1932	1	75,562	75,562
1933	1	78,874	78,874
1934	2	47,000	23,500
1935	3	111,634	37,211
1936	4	137,042	34,261
1937	6	176,396	29,399
1938	5	202,972	40,594
1939	5	224,643	44,929
1940	5	226,478	45,296
1941	5	253,735	50,747
1942	5	215,786	43,157
1943	5	240,166	48,033
1944	5	195,203	39,041
1945	5	236,279	47,256
1946	8	308,071	38,509
1947	10	304,316	30,432
1948	12	404,772	33,731
1949	13	442,531	34,041
1950	8	384,505	48,063
1951	8	392,548	49,069
1952	7	388,588	55,513
1953	6	366,299	61,050
1954	6	359,285	59,881
1955	6	357,871	59,645
1956	6	379,723	63,287
1957	6	369,162	61,527
1958	6	385,427	64,238
1959	7	392,394	56,056
1960	8	481,814	60,227
1961	9	490,113	54,457
1962	11	509,654	46,332
1963	10	481,722	48,172
1964	8	460,720	57,590
1965	8	448,541	56,068
1966	8	482,106	60,263
1967	8	521,427	**65,178
1968	9	532,113	59,124
1969	10	585,621	58,562
1970	11	649,915	59,083
1971	11	623,072	56,643
1972	12	668,031	55,669
1973	11	668,461	60,769
1974	11	631,229	57,384
1975	11	597,079	54,280
1976	11	650,881	59,171
1977	12	660,429	55,036
1978	13	730,078	56,160
1979	15	726,064	48,404
1980	15	865,236	57,682
1981	15	856,730	57,115
1982	16	871,594	54,475
1983	16	919,193	57,450
1984	16	867,319	54,207
1985	18	977,374	54,299
1986	18	975,756	54,209
1987	18	958,933	53,274
1988	18	995,830	55,324
1989	17	937,323	55,137
1990	18	1,047,772	58,210
1991	19	1,048,306	55,174
1992	18	1,049,694	58,316
1993	18	973,570	54,087
1994	19	1,036,950	54,576
1995	19	1,064,640	56,034
1996	18	1,021,466	56,748
1997	18	985,292	54,738
1998	20	1,083,244	54,162
1999	22	1,224,414	55,655
2000	23	1,241,109	53,961
2001	25	1,291,557	51,662
2002	25	1,334,808	53,392
2003	28	1,416,103	50,575
2004	28	1,458,757	52,098
2005	28	1,492,001	53,286
2006	28	1,431,218	51,115
2007	32	*1,699,637	53,114

*Record. **Record for year with more than one game played.

Bowl-by-Bowl Attendance

(Current site and stadium capacity in parentheses. For participating teams and all name changes and playing sites, refer to pages 273-277.)

ROSE BOWL

(Rose Bowl, Pasadena, Calif.; Capacity: 91,887)

Date	Attendance
1-1-02	8,000
1-1-16	7,000
1-1-17	26,000
1-1-20	30,000
1-1-21	42,000
1-2-22	40,000
1-1-23	43,000
1-1-24	40,000
1-1-25	53,000
1-1-26	50,000
1-1-27	57,417
1-2-28	65,000
1-1-29	66,604

Date	Attendance
1-1-30	72,000
1-1-31	60,000
1-1-32	75,562
1-2-33	78,874
1-1-34	35,000
1-1-35	84,474
1-1-36	84,474
1-1-37	87,196
1-1-38	90,000
1-2-39	89,452
1-1-40	92,200
1-1-41	91,500
1-1-42#	56,000
1-1-43	93,000
1-1-44	68,000
1-1-45	91,000
1-1-46	93,000
1-1-47	90,000
1-1-48	93,000
1-1-49	93,000
1-2-50	100,963
1-1-51	98,939
1-1-52	96,825
1-1-53	101,500
1-1-54	101,000
1-1-55	89,191
1-2-56	100,809
1-1-57	97,126
1-1-58	98,202
1-1-59	98,297
1-1-60	100,809
1-2-61	97,314
1-1-62	98,214
1-1-63	98,698
1-1-64	96,957
1-1-65	100,423
1-1-66	100,087
1-2-67	100,807
1-1-68	102,946
1-1-69	102,063
1-1-70	103,878
1-1-71	103,839
1-1-72	103,154
1-1-73	*106,869
1-1-74	105,267
1-1-75	106,721
1-1-76	105,464
1-1-77	106,182
1-2-78	105,312
1-1-79	105,629
1-1-80	105,526
1-1-81	104,863
1-1-82	105,611
1-1-83	104,991
1-2-84	103,217
1-1-85	102,594
1-1-86	103,292
1-1-87	103,168
1-1-88	103,847
1-2-89	101,688
1-1-90	103,450
1-1-91	101,273
1-1-92	103,566
1-1-93	94,236
1-1-94	101,237
1-2-95	102,247
1-1-96	100,102
1-1-97	100,635
1-1-98	101,219
1-1-99	93,872
1-1-00	93,731
1-1-01	94,392
1-3-02	93,781
1-1-03	86,848
1-1-04	93,849
1-1-05	93,468
1-4-06	93,986
1-1-07	93,852

**Record attendance. #Game held at Duke, Durham, N.C., due to war-time West Coast restrictions.*

FEDEX ORANGE BOWL

(Dolphin Stadium, Miami Gardens, Fla.; Capacity: 77,823)

Date	Attendance
1-1-35	5,134
1-1-36	6,568
1-1-37	9,210
1-1-38	18,972
1-2-39	32,191
1-1-40	29,278
1-1-41	29,554
1-1-42	35,786
1-1-43	25,166
1-1-44	25,203
1-1-45	23,279
1-1-46	35,709
1-1-47	36,152
1-1-48	59,578
1-1-49	60,523
1-2-50	64,816
1-1-51	65,181
1-1-52	65,839
1-1-53	66,280
1-1-54	68,640
1-1-55	68,750
1-2-56	76,561
1-1-57	73,280
1-1-58	76,561
1-1-59	75,281
1-1-60	72,186
1-2-61	72,212
1-1-62	68,150
1-1-63	72,880
1-1-64	72,647
1-1-65	72,647
1-1-66	72,214
1-2-67	72,426
1-1-68	77,993
1-1-69	77,719
1-1-70	77,282
1-1-71	80,699
1-1-72	78,151
1-1-73	80,010
1-1-74	60,477
1-1-75	71,801
1-1-76	76,799
1-1-77	65,537
1-2-78	60,987
1-1-79	66,365
1-1-80	66,714
1-1-81	71,043
1-1-82	72,748
1-1-83	68,713
1-2-84	72,549
1-1-85	56,294
1-1-86	74,178
1-1-87	52,717
1-1-88	74,760
1-2-89	79,480
1-1-90	81,190
1-1-91	77,062
1-1-92	77,747
1-1-93	57,324
1-1-94	81,536
1-1-95	*81,753
1-1-96	72,198
12-31-96	63,297
1-2-98	74,002
1-2-99	67,919
1-1-00	70,461
1-3-01	76,835
1-2-02	73,640
1-2-03	75,971
1-1-04	76,739
1-4-05	77,912
1-3-06	77,773
1-2-07	74,470

**Record attendance.*

ALLSTATE SUGAR BOWL

(Louisiana Superdome, New Orleans, La.; Capacity: 72,500)

Date	Attendance
1-1-35	22,026
1-1-36	35,000
1-1-37	41,000
1-1-38	45,000
1-2-39	50,000
1-1-40	73,000
1-1-41	73,181
1-1-42	72,000
1-1-43	70,000
1-1-44	69,000
1-1-45	72,000
1-1-46	75,000
1-1-47	73,300
1-1-48	72,000
1-1-49	82,000
1-2-50	82,470
1-1-51	82,000
1-1-52	82,000
1-1-53	82,000
1-1-54	76,000
1-1-55	82,000
1-2-56	80,175
1-1-57	81,000
1-1-58	82,000
1-1-59	82,000
1-1-60	83,000
1-2-61	82,851
1-1-62	82,910
1-1-63	82,900
1-1-64	80,785
1-1-65	65,000
1-1-66	67,421
1-2-67	82,000
1-1-68	78,963
1-1-69	82,113
1-1-70	82,500
1-1-71	78,655
1-1-72	84,031
12-31-72	80,123
12-31-73	*85,161
12-31-74	67,890
12-31-75	75,212
1-1-77	76,117
1-2-78	76,811
1-1-79	76,824
1-1-80	77,486
1-1-81	77,895
1-1-82	77,224
1-1-83	78,124
1-2-84	77,893
1-1-85	75,608
1-1-86	77,432
1-1-87	76,234
1-1-88	75,495
1-2-89	61,934
1-1-90	77,452
1-1-91	75,132
1-1-92	76,447
1-1-93	76,789
1-1-94	75,437
1-2-95	76,224
12-31-95	70,283
1-2-97	78,344
1-1-98	67,289
1-1-99	76,503
1-4-00	79,280
1-2-01	64,407
1-1-02	77,688
1-1-03	74,269
1-4-04	79,342
1-3-05	77,349
1-2-06^	74,458
1-3-07	77,781

**Record attendance. ^Game played at the Georgia Dome in Atlanta because of damage sustained to the Louisiana Superdome as a result of Hurricane Katrina.*

AT&T COTTON BOWL CLASSIC

(Cotton Bowl, Dallas, Texas; Capacity: 71,252)

Date	Attendance
1-1-37	17,000
1-1-38	37,000
1-2-39	40,000
1-1-40	20,000
1-1-41	45,500
1-1-42	38,000
1-1-43	36,000
1-1-44	15,000
1-1-45	37,000
1-1-46	45,000
1-1-47	38,000
1-1-48	43,000
1-1-49	69,000
1-2-50	75,347
1-1-51	75,349
1-1-52	75,347
1-1-53	75,504
1-1-54	75,504
1-1-55	75,504
1-2-56	75,504
1-1-57	68,000
1-1-58	75,504
1-1-59	75,504
1-1-60	75,504
1-2-61	74,000
1-1-62	75,504
1-1-63	75,504
1-1-64	75,504
1-1-65	75,504
1-1-66	76,200
12-31-66	75,400
1-1-68	75,504
1-1-69	72,000
1-1-70	73,000
1-1-71	72,000
1-1-72	72,000
1-1-73	72,000
1-1-74	67,500
1-1-75	67,500
1-1-76	74,500
1-1-77	54,500
1-2-78	*76,601
1-1-79	32,500
1-1-80	72,032
1-1-81	74,281
1-1-82	73,243
1-1-83	60,359
1-2-84	67,891
1-1-85	56,522
1-1-86	73,137
1-1-87	74,188
1-1-88	73,006
1-2-89	74,304
1-1-90	74,358
1-1-91	73,521
1-1-92	73,728
1-1-93	71,615
1-1-94	69,855
1-2-95	70,218
1-1-96	58,214
1-1-97	71,928
1-1-98	59,215
1-1-99	72,611
1-1-00	72,723
1-1-01	63,465
1-1-02	72,955
1-1-03	70,817
1-2-04	73,928
1-1-05	75,704
1-2-06	74,222
1-1-07	66,777

**Record attendance.*

BRUT SUN BOWL

(Sun Bowl Stadium, El Paso, Texas; Capacity: 50,429)

Date	Attendance
1-1-36	11,000
1-1-37	10,000
1-1-38	12,000
1-2-39	13,000
1-1-40	12,000
1-1-41	14,000
1-1-42	14,000
1-1-43	16,000
1-1-44	18,000
1-1-45	13,000
1-1-46	15,000
1-1-47	10,000
1-1-48	18,000
1-1-49	13,000
1-2-50	15,000
1-1-51	16,000
1-1-52	17,000
1-1-53	11,000
1-1-54	9,500
1-1-55	14,000
1-2-56	14,500
1-1-57	13,500
1-1-58	12,000
12-31-58	13,000
12-31-59	14,000
12-31-60	16,000
12-30-61	15,000
12-31-62	16,000
12-31-63	26,500
12-26-64	28,500
12-31-65	27,450
12-24-66	24,381
12-30-67	34,685
12-28-68	32,307
12-20-69	29,723
12-19-70	30,512
12-18-71	33,503
12-30-72	31,312
12-29-73	30,127
12-28-74	30,131
12-26-75	33,240
1-2-77	33,252
12-31-77	31,318
12-23-78	33,122
12-22-79	33,412
12-27-80	34,723
12-26-81	33,816
12-25-82	31,359
12-24-83	41,412
12-22-84	50,126
12-28-85	*52,203
12-25-86	48,722
12-25-87	43,240
12-24-88	48,719
12-30-89	44,887
12-31-90	50,562
12-31-91	42,821
12-31-92	41,622
12-24-93	43,848
12-30-94	50,612
12-29-95	49,116
12-31-96	42,721
12-31-97	49,104
12-31-98	46,612
12-31-99	48,757
12-29-00	49,093
12-31-01	47,812
12-31-02	48,917
12-31-03	49,894
12-31-04	51,288
12-30-05	50,426
12-28-06	48,732

**Record attendance.*

GATOR BOWL CLASSIC

(Jacksonville Municipal Stadium, Jacksonville, Fla.; Capacity: 77,000)

Date	Attendance
1-2-46	7,362
1-1-47	10,134
1-1-48	16,666
1-1-49	32,939
1-2-50	18,409
1-1-51	19,834
1-1-52	34,577
1-1-53	30,015
1-1-54	28,641
12-31-54	28,426
12-31-55	32,174
12-29-56	36,256
12-28-57	41,160
12-27-58	41,312
1-2-60	45,104
12-31-60	50,112
12-30-61	50,202
12-29-62	50,026
12-28-63	50,018
1-2-65	50,408
12-31-65	60,127
12-31-66	60,312
12-30-67	68,019
12-28-68	68,011
12-27-69	72,248
1-2-71	71,136
12-31-71	71,208
12-30-72	71,114
12-29-73	62,109
12-30-74	63,811
12-29-75	64,012
12-27-76	67,827
12-30-77	72,289
12-29-78	72,011
12-28-79	70,407
12-29-80	72,297
12-28-81	71,009
12-30-82	80,913
12-30-83	81,293
12-28-84	82,138
12-30-85	79,417
12-27-86	80,104
12-31-87	82,119
1-1-89	76,236
12-30-89	*82,911
1-1-91	68,927
12-29-91	62,003
12-31-92	71,233
12-31-93	67,205
12-30-94†	62,200
1-1-96	45,202
1-1-97	52,103
1-1-98	54,116
1-1-99	70,791
1-1-00	43,416
1-1-01	68,741
1-1-02	72,202
1-1-03	73,491
1-1-04	78,892
1-1-05	70,112
1-2-06	63,780
1-1-07	67,704

**Record attendance. †Played at Gainesville, Fla.*

AUTOZONE LIBERTY BOWL†

(Liberty Bowl Memorial Stadium, Memphis, Tenn.; Capacity: 62,598)

Date	Attendance
12-19-59	36,211
12-17-60	16,624
12-16-61	15,712
12-15-62	17,048
12-31-63	8,309
12-19-64	6,059
12-18-65	38,607
12-10-66	39,101
12-16-67	35,045
12-14-68	46,206
12-13-69	50,042
12-12-70	44,640
12-20-71	51,410
12-18-72	50,021
12-17-73	50,011
12-16-74	51,284
12-22-75	52,129
12-20-76	52,736
12-19-77	49,456
12-23-78	53,064
12-22-79	50,021
12-27-80	53,667
12-30-81	43,216

Date	Attendance
12-29-82	54,123
12-29-83	38,229
12-27-84	50,108
12-27-85	40,186
12-29-86	51,327
12-29-87	53,249
12-28-88	39,210
12-28-89	60,128
12-27-90	13,144
12-29-91	*61,497
12-31-92	32,107
12-28-93	21,097
12-31-94	33,280
12-30-95	47,398
12-27-96	49,163
12-31-97	50,209
12-31-98	52,192
12-31-99	54,866
12-29-00	58,302
12-31-01	58,968
12-31-02	55,207
12-31-03	55,989
12-31-04	58,355
12-31-05	54,894
12-29-06	56,103

*Record attendance. †Played at Philadelphia, 1959-63; Atlantic City, 1964; Memphis, from 1965.

CAPITAL ONE BOWL#

(Florida Citrus Bowl, Orlando, Fla.; Capacity: 65,438)

Date	Attendance
12-30-60	13,000
12-22-62	7,500
12-27-68	16,114
12-26-69	16,311
12-28-70	15,164
12-28-71	16,750
12-29-72	20,062
12-22-73@	37,234
12-21-74	20,246
12-20-75	20,247
12-18-76	37,812
12-23-77	44,502
12-23-78	31,356
12-22-79	38,666
12-20-80	52,541
12-19-81	50,045
12-18-82	51,296
12-17-83	50,183
12-22-84	51,821
12-28-85	50,920
1-1-87	51,113
1-1-88	53,152
1-2-89	53,571
1-1-90	60,016
1-1-91	72,328
1-1-92	64,192
1-1-93	65,861
1-1-94	72,456
1-2-95	71,195
1-1-96	70,797
1-1-97	63,467
1-1-98	*72,940
1-1-99	63,584
1-1-00	62,011
1-1-01	66,928
1-1-02	59,693
1-1-03	66,334
1-1-04	64,565
1-1-05	70,229
1-2-06	57,221
1-1-07	60,774

*Record attendance. #The first 14 games in the Tangerine Bowl, through 1-1-60, are not listed because no major teams were involved. The same is true for those games played in December 1961, 1963, 1964, 1965, 1966 and 1967. @ Played at Gainesville, Fla.

CHICK-FIL-A BOWL

(Georgia Dome, Atlanta, Ga.; Capacity: 71,900)

Date	Attendance
12-30-68	35,545
12-30-69	48,452
12-30-70	52,126
12-30-71	36,771
12-29-72	52,671
12-28-73	38,107
12-28-74	31,695
12-31-75	45,134
12-31-76	54,132
12-31-77	36,733
12-25-78	20,277
12-31-79	57,371
1-2-81	45,384
12-31-81	37,582
12-31-82	50,134
12-30-83	25,648
12-31-84	41,107
12-31-85	29,857
12-31-86	53,668
1-2-88	58,737
12-31-88	44,635
12-30-89	44,991
12-29-90	38,912
1-1-92	59,322
1-2-93	69,125
12-31-93	63,416
1-1-95	64,902
12-30-95	70,825
12-28-96	63,622
1-2-98	71,212
12-31-98	72,876
12-30-99	73,315
12-29-00	73,614
12-31-01	71,827
12-31-02	68,330
1-2-04	75,125
12-31-04	69,322
12-30-05	65,620
12-30-06	*75,406

*Record attendance.

TOSTITOS FIESTA BOWL†

(University of Phoenix Stadium, Glendale, Ariz.; Capacity: 73,000)

Date	Attendance
12-27-71	51,089
12-23-72	51,318
12-21-73	50,878
12-28-74	50,878
12-26-75	51,396
12-25-76	48,174
12-25-77	57,727
12-25-78	55,227
12-25-79	55,347
12-26-80	66,738
1-1-82	71,053
1-1-83	70,533
1-2-84	66,484
1-1-85	60,310
1-1-86	72,454
1-2-87	73,098
1-1-88	72,112
1-2-89	74,911
1-1-90	73,953
1-1-91	69,098
1-1-92	71,133
1-1-93	70,224
1-1-94	72,260
1-2-95	73,968
1-2-96	79,864
1-1-97	65,106
12-31-97	69,367
1-4-99	*80,470
1-2-00	71,526
1-1-01	75,428
1-1-02	74,118
1-3-03	77,502
1-2-04	73,425
1-1-05	73,519
1-2-06	76,196
1-1-07	73,719

*Record attendance. †Played at Tempe, Ariz., from 1971-06.

PETROSUN INDEPENDENCE BOWL

(Independence Stadium, Shreveport, La.; Capacity: 48,947)

Date	Attendance
12-13-76	15,542
12-17-77	18,500
12-16-78	18,200
12-15-79	27,234
12-13-80	45,000
12-12-81	47,300
12-11-82	49,503
12-10-83	41,274
12-15-84	41,000
12-21-85	42,800
12-20-86	46,369
12-19-87	41,683
12-23-88	20,242
12-16-89	30,333
12-15-90	48,325
12-29-91	46,932
12-31-92	31,337
12-31-93	33,819
12-28-94	27,242
12-29-95	48,835
12-31-96	41,366
12-28-97	*50,459
12-31-98	46,862
12-31-99	49,873
12-31-00	36.974
12-27-01	45,627
12-27-02	46,096
12-31-03	49,625
12-28-04	43,000
12-30-05	41,332
12-28-06	45,054

*Record attendance.

PACIFIC LIFE HOLIDAY BOWL

(Qualcomm Stadium, San Diego, Calif.; Capacity: 66,000)

Date	Attendance
12-28-78	52,500
12-21-79	52,200
12-19-80	50,214
12-18-81	52,419
12-17-82	52,533
12-23-83	51,480
12-21-84	61,243
12-22-85	42,324
12-30-86	59,473
12-30-87	61,892
12-30-88	60,718
12-29-89	61,113
12-29-90	61,441
12-30-91	60,646
12-30-92	44,457
12-30-93	52,108
12-30-94	59,453
12-29-95	51,051
12-30-96	54,749
12-29-97	50,761
12-30-98	65,354
12-29-99	57,118
12-29-00	63,278
12-28-01	60,548
12-27-02	58,717
12-30-03	61,102
12-30-04	*66,222
12-29-05	65,416
12-28-06	62,395

*Record attendance.

OUTBACK BOWL

(Raymond James Stadium, Tampa, Fla.; Capacity: 65,500)

Date	Attendance
12-23-86	25,368
1-2-88	60,156
1-2-89	51,112
1-1-90	52,535
1-1-91	63,154
1-1-92	57,789
1-1-93	52,056
1-1-94	52,649
1-2-95	61,384
1-1-96	65,313
1-1-97	53,161
1-1-98	56,186
1-1-99	66,005
1-1-00	54,059
1-1-01	65,229
1-1-02	*66,249
1-1-03	65,101
1-1-04	65,372
1-1-05	62,414
1-2-06	65,881
1-1-07	65,601

*Record attendance.

INSIGHT BOWL†

(Sun Devil Stadium, Tempe, Ariz.; Capacity: 73,000)

Date	Attendance
12-31-89	37,237
12-31-90	36,340
12-31-91	35,752
12-29-92	40,876
12-29-93	49,075
12-29-94	45,122
12-27-95	41,004
12-27-96	42,122
12-27-97	*49,385
12-26-98	36,147
12-31-99	35,762
12-28-00	41,813
12-29-01	40,028
12-26-02	40,533
12-26-03	42,364
12-28-04	45,917
12-27-05	43,536
12-29-06	48,391

*Record attendance. †Played at Tucson, Ariz., from 1989-99; and Phoenix from 2000-05.

CHAMPS SPORTS BOWL

(Florida Citrus Bowl, Orlando, Fla.; Capacity: 65,438)

Date	Attendance
12-28-90	*74,021
12-28-91	52,644
1-1-93	45,554
1-1-94	38,516
1-2-95	50,833
12-30-95	34,428
12-27-96	46,418
12-29-97	28,262
12-29-98	44,387
12-20-99	31,089
12-28-00	28,359
12-20-01	28,562
12-23-02	21,689
12-22-03	26,482
12-21-04	28,237
12-27-05	31,470
12-29-06	40,168

*Record attendance.

PIONEER PUREVISON LAS VEGAS BOWL

(Sam Boyd Stadium, Las Vegas, Nev.; Capacity: 40,000)

Date	Attendance
12-18-92	15,476
12-17-93	15,508
12-15-94	17,562
12-14-95	11,127
12-19-96	10,118
12-20-97	21,514
12-19-98	21,429
12-18-99	28,227
12-21-00	29,113
12-25-01	30,894
12-25-02	30,324
12-24-03	25,437
12-23-04	29,062
12-22-05	40,053
12-21-06	*44,615

*Record attendance.

VALERO ALAMO BOWL

(Alamodome, San Antonio, Texas; Capacity: 65,000)

Date	Attendance
12-31-93	45,716
12-31-94	44,106
12-28-95	64,597
12-29-96	55,677
12-30-97	55,552
12-29-98	60,780
12-28-99	65,380
12-30-00	60,028
12-29-01	65,232
12-28-02	50,690
12-29-03	56,226
12-29-04	65,265
12-28-05	62,000
12-30-06	*65,875

*Record attendance.

ROADY'S HUMANITARIAN BOWL

(Bronco Stadium, Boise, Idaho; Capacity: 30,000)

Date	Attendance
12-29-97	16,131
12-30-98	19,664
12-30-99	29,283
12-28-00	26,203
12-31-01	23,472
12-31-02	30,446
1-3-04	23,118
12-27-04	28,516
12-28-05	*30,493
12-31-06	28,652

*Record attendance.

MOTOR CITY BOWL†

(Ford Field, Detroit, Mich.; Capacity: 65,000)

Date	Attendance
12-26-97	43,340
12-23-98	32,206
12-27-99	44,863
12-27-00	52,911
12-29-01	44,164
12-26-02	51,872
12-26-03	51,286
12-27-04	52,552
12-26-05	50,616
12-26-06	*54,113

*Record attendance. †Played at Pontiac, Mich., from 1997-01.

GAYLORD HOTELS MUSIC CITY BOWL

(LP Field, Nashville, Tenn.; Capacity: 68,798)

Date	Attendance
12-29-98	41,248
12-29-99	59,221
12-28-00	47,119
12-28-01	46,125
12-30-02	39,183
12-31-03	55,109
12-31-04	66,089
12-30-05	40,519
12-29-06	*68,024

*Record attendance.

GMAC BOWL

(Ladd-Peebles Stadium, Mobile, Ala.; Capacity: 40,048)

Date	Attendance
12-22-99	34,200
12-20-00	40,300
12-19-01	40,139
12-18-02	*40,646
12-18-03	40,620
12-22-04	40,160
12-21-05	35,422
1-7-07	38,751

*Record attendance.

R+L CARRIERS NEW ORLEANS BOWL

(Louisiana Superdome, New Orleans, La.: Capacity: 72,500)

Date	Attendance
12-18-01	27,004
12-17-02	19,024
12-16-03	25,184
12-14-04	*27,253
12-20-05^	18,338
12-22-06	24,791

*Record attendance. ^Game played at Cajun Field in Lafayette, La., because of damage sustained to the Louisiana Superdome as a result of Hurricane Katrina.

SHERATON HAWAII BOWL

(Aloha Stadium, Honolulu, Hawaii; Capacity: 50,000)

Date	Attendance
12-25-02	31,535
12-25-03	29,005
12-24-04	39,662
12-24-05	26,254
12-24-06	*43,435

*Record attendance.

MEINEKE CAR CARE BOWL

(Bank of America Stadium, Charlotte, North Carolina; Capacity: 73,298)

Date	Attendance
12-28-02	*73,535
12-27-03	51,236
12-30-04	73,238
12-31-05	57,937
12-30-06	52,303

*Record attendance.

EMERALD BOWL

(AT&T Park, San Francisco, California; Capacity: 38,437)

Date	Attendance
12-31-02	25,966
12-31-03	25,621
12-30-04	30,563
12-29-05	25,742
12-27-06	*40,331

*Record attendance.

ARMED FORCES BOWL

(Amon G. Carter Stadium, Fort Worth, Texas; Capacity: 43,000)

Date	Attendance
12-23-03	*38,028
12-23-04	27,902
12-23-05	33,505
12-23-06	32,412

*Record attendance.

SAN DIEGO COUNTY CREDIT UNION POINSETTIA BOWL

(Qualcomm Stadium, San Diego, California; Capacity: 66,000)

Date	Attendance
12-22-05	*36,842
12-19-06	29,709

*Record attendance.

INTERNATIONAL BOWL

(Rogers Centre, Toronto, Ontario, Canada; Capacity: 53,506)

Date	Attendance
1-6-07	26,717

NEW MEXICO BOWL
(University Stadium, Albuquerque, New Mexico; Capacity: 38,634)

Date	Attendance
12-23-06	34,111

PAPAJOHNS.COM BOWL
(Legion Field, Birmingham, Alabama; Capacity: 72,000)

Date	Attendance
12-23-06	32,023

TEXAS BOWL
(Reliant Stadium, Houston, Texas; Capacity: 69,500)

Date	Attendance
12-28-06	52,210

BCS CHAMPIONSHIP GAME
(University of Phoenix Stadium, Glendale, Arizona; Capacity: 73,000)

Date	Attendance
1-8-07	74,628

Former Major Bowl Games

(For participating teams, refer to pages 279-280.)

ALAMO
(San Antonio, Texas)

Date	Attendance
1-4-47	3,730

ALL-AMERICAN
(Birmingham, Ala.)

Date	Attendance
12-22-77	47,000
12-20-78	41,500
12-29-79	62,785
12-27-80	30,000
12-31-81	41,672
12-31-82	75,000
12-22-83	42,000
12-29-84	47,300
12-31-85	45,000
12-31-86	30,000
12-22-87	37,000
12-29-88	48,218
12-28-89	47,750
12-28-90	44,000

(Named Hall of Fame Classic until 1986 and then discontinued after 1990 game; played at Legion Field, capacity 75,952)

ALOHA CLASSIC#
(Honolulu, Hawaii)

Date	Attendance
12-25-82	30,055
12-26-83	37,212
12-29-84	41,777
12-28-85	35,183
12-27-86	26,743
12-25-87	24,839
12-25-88	35,132
12-25-89	*50,000
12-25-90	14,185
12-25-91	34,433
12-25-92	42,933
12-25-93	44,009
12-25-94	44,862
12-25-95	41,111
12-25-96	43,380
12-25-97	44,598
12-25-98	46,451
12-25-99	40,974
12-25-00	24,397

**Record attendance. #Named Aloha Bowl before 1998.*

AVIATION
(Dayton, Ohio)

Date	Attendance
12-9-61	3,694

BACARDI
(Havana, Cuba)

Date	Attendance
1-1-37	12,000

BLUEBONNET
(Houston, Texas)

Date	Attendance
12-19-59	55,000
12-17-60	68,000
12-16-61	52,000
12-22-62	55,000
12-21-63	50,000
12-19-64	50,000
12-18-65	40,000
12-17-66	67,000
12-23-67	30,156
12-31-68	53,543
12-31-69	55,203
12-31-70	53,829
12-31-71	54,720
12-30-72	52,961
12-29-73	44,358
12-23-74	35,122
12-27-75	52,748
12-31-76	48,618
12-31-77	52,842
12-31-78	34,084
12-31-79	40,542
12-31-80	36,667
12-31-81	40,309
12-31-82	31,557
12-31-83	50,090
12-31-84	43,260
12-31-85	42,000
12-31-86	40,476
12-31-87	23,282

(Played at Rice Stadium 1959-67 and 1985, Astrodome 1968-84 and from 1986; Astrodome capacity 60,000)

BLUEGRASS
(Louisville, Ky.)

Date	Attendance
12-13-58	7,000

CALIFORNIA
(Fresno, Calif.)

Date	Attendance
12-19-81	15,565
12-18-82	30,000
12-17-83	20,464
12-15-84	21,741
12-14-85	32,554
12-13-86	10,743
12-12-87	24,000
12-10-88	31,272
12-9-89	31,610
12-8-90	25,431
12-14-91	34,825

CAMELLIA
(Lafayette, La.)

Date	Attendance
12-30-48	4,500

CHERRY
(Pontiac, Mich.)

Date	Attendance
12-22-84	70,332
12-21-85	51,858

DELTA
(Memphis, Tenn.)

Date	Attendance
1-1-48	28,120
1-1-49	15,069

DIXIE BOWL
(Birmingham, Ala.)

Date	Attendance
1-1-48	22,000
1-1-49	20,000

DIXIE CLASSIC
(Dallas, Texas)

Date	Attendance
1-2-22	12,000
1-1-25	7,000
1-1-34	12,000

FORT WORTH CLASSIC
(Fort Worth, Texas)

Date	Attendance
1-1-21	9,000

FREEDOM
(Anaheim, Calif.)

Date	Attendance
12-26-84	24,093
12-30-85	30,961
12-30-86	55,422
12-30-87	33,261
12-29-88	35,941
12-30-89	33,858
12-29-90	41,450
12-30-91	34,217
12-29-92	50,745
12-30-93	37,203
12-27-94	27,477

GARDEN STATE
(East Rutherford, N.J.)

Date	Attendance
12-16-78	33,402
12-15-79	55,493
12-14-80	41,417
12-13-81	38,782

GOTHAM
(New York, N.Y.)

Date	Attendance
12-9-61	15,123
12-15-62	6,166

GREAT LAKES
(Cleveland, Ohio)

Date	Attendance
12-6-47	14,908

HARBOR
(San Diego, Calif.)

Date	Attendance
1-1-47	7,000
1-1-48	12,000
1-1-49	20,000

HOUSTON BOWL#
(Houston, Texas)

Date	Attendance
12-27-00	33,899
12-28-01	*53,480
12-27-02	44,687
12-30-03	51,068
12-29-04	27,235
12-31-05	37,286

**Record attendance. #Named galleryfurniture.com Bowl in 2000 and 2001, and played at Reliant Astrodome. Played at Reliant Stadium from 2002 to 2005.*

LOS ANGELES CHRISTMAS FESTIVAL
(Los Angeles, Calif.)

Date	Attendance
12-25-24	47,000

MERCY
(Los Angeles, Calif.)

Date	Attendance
11-23-61	33,145

OIL
(Houston, Texas)

Date	Attendance
1-1-46	27,000
1-1-47	23,000

PASADENA
(Pasadena, Calif.)

Date	Attendance
12-2-67	28,802
12-6-69	41,276
12-19-70	20,472
12-18-71	15,244

PRESIDENTIAL CUP
(College Park, Md.)

Date	Attendance
12-9-50	12,245

RAISIN
(Fresno, Calif.)

Date	Attendance
1-1-46	10,000
1-1-47	13,000
1-1-48	13,000
1-1-49	10,000
12-31-49	9,000

SALAD
(Phoenix, Ariz.)

Date	Attendance
1-1-48	12,500
1-1-49	17,500
1-1-50	18,500
1-1-51	23,000
1-1-52	17,000

SAN DIEGO EAST-WEST CHRISTMAS CLASSIC
(San Diego, Calif.)

Date	Attendance
12-26-21	5,000
12-25-22	5,000

SEATTLE BOWL#
(Seattle, Wash.)

Date	Attendance
12-25-98	*46,451
12-25-99	40,974
12-24-00	24,187
12-27-01	30,144
12-30-02	38,241

Record attendance. #Named Oahu Classic before 2001 and played at Honolulu, Hawaii. In 2001, played at Safeco Field, Seattle, Wash. In 2002, played at Seahawks Stadium, Seattle, Wash.

SHRINE
(Little Rock, Ark.)

Date	Attendance
12-18-48	5,000

SILICON VALLEY CLASSIC
(San Jose, Calif.)

Date	Attendance
12-31-00	26,542
12-31-01	*30,456
12-31-02	10,132
12-30-03	20,126
12-30-04	21,456

**Record attendance.*

Individual Records

Only official records after 1937 are included. Prior records are included if able to be substantiated. Each team's score is in parentheses after the team name. The year listed is the actual (calendar) year the game was played; the date is included if the bowl was played twice (i.e., January and December) during one calendar year. The list also includes discontinued bowls, marked with (D). Bowls are listed by the name of the bowl at the time it was played: the first Hall of Fame Bowl (1977-85) was called the All-American Bowl in 1986-90; the second Hall of Fame Bowl (1986-95) is now called the Outback Bowl and is played in Tampa, Fla.; the Sun Bowl was called the John Hancock Bowl in 1989-93, the John Hancock Sun Bowl in 1987-88, and reverted to the Sun Bowl in 1994; the Blockbuster Bowl changed its name to the Carquest Bowl in 1993, to the Micronpc.com Bowl in 1998, to the Tangerine Bowl in 2001 and to the Champs Sports Bowl in 2004. The Copper Bowl changed its name to the Insight.com Bowl in 1997 and to the Insight Bowl in 2002. The Capital One Bowl was the former and original Tangerine Bowl from 1947-82 and was known as the Florida Citrus Bowl from 1983-02. The current Champs Sports Bowl, which was known as the Tangerine Bowl from 2001-03, is not to be confused with the current Capital One Bowl, which is the former and original Tangerine Bowl. In 2004, the San Francisco Bowl changed its name to the Emerald Bowl and the Humanitarian Bowl changed its name to the MPC Computers Bowl. In 2006, the Fort Worth Bowl changed its name to the Armed Forces Bowl. All former bowl names and sites are listed with each present bowl history. The NCAA Statistics Service thanks former staff member Steve Boda for his valuable assistance in compiling these records.

Total Offense

MOST TOTAL PLAYS
Season

83—Kyle Orton, Purdue (27) vs. Washington St. (33) (Sun, 2001) (9 rush, 74 pass, 402 yards)

MOST TOTAL YARDS

594—Ty Detmer, BYU (39) vs. Penn St. (50) (Holiday, 1989) (18 rushing yards, 576 passing yards, 67 plays)

HIGHEST AVERAGE PER PLAY
(Min. 10 Plays)

24.1—Dicky Maegle, Rice (28) vs. Alabama (6) (Cotton, 1954) (11 for 265)

MOST TOUCHDOWNS RESPONSIBLE FOR
(TDs Scored & Passed For)

6—Bobby Layne, Texas (40) vs. Missouri (27) (Cotton, 1946) (3 rush, 2 pass, 1 receiving); (D) Chuck Long, Iowa (55) vs. Texas (17) (Freedom, 1984) (6 pass)

Rushing

MOST RUSHING ATTEMPTS

46—(D) Ron Jackson, Tulsa (28) vs. San Diego St. (17) (Freedom, 1991) (211 yards)

MOST NET RUSHING YARDS

280—(D) James Gray, Texas Tech (49) vs. Duke (21) (All-American, 1989) (33 carries)

MOST NET RUSHING YARDS BY A QUARTERBACK

200—Vince Young, Texas (41) vs. Southern California (38) (Rose, 2006) (19 carries)

HIGHEST AVERAGE PER RUSH
(Min. 9 Carries)

24.1—Dicky Maegle, Rice (28) vs. Alabama (6) (Cotton, 1954) (11 for 265)

MOST NET RUSHING YARDS BY TWO RUSHERS, SAME TEAM, OVER 100 YARDS RUSHING EACH

373—Woody Green (202) & Brent McClanahan (171), Arizona St. (49) vs. Missouri (35) (Fiesta, 1972)

MOST RUSHING TOUCHDOWNS

5—Neil Snow, Michigan (49) vs. Stanford (0) (Rose, 1902) (touchdowns counted as five-point scores); Barry Sanders, Oklahoma St. (62) vs. Wyoming (14) (Holiday, 1988) (runs of 33, 2, 67, 1, 10 yards)

Passing

MOST PASS ATTEMPTS

74—Kyle Orton, Purdue (27) vs. Washington St. (33) (Sun, 2001) (completed 38)

MOST PASS COMPLETIONS

43—(D) Steve Clarkson, San Jose St. (25) vs. Toledo (27) (California, 1981) (attempted 62)

MOST CONSECUTIVE PASS COMPLETIONS

19—Mike Bobo, Georgia (33) vs. Wisconsin (6) (Outback, 1998)

MOST NET PASSING YARDS

576—Ty Detmer, BYU (39) vs. Penn St. (50) (Holiday, 1989) (42 of 59 with 2 interceptions); Byron Leftwich, Marshall (64) vs. East Caro. (61) (2 ot) (GMAC, 2001) (41 of 70 with 2 interceptions)

MOST NET PASSING YARDS, ONE QUARTER

223—Browning Nagle, Louisville (34) vs. Alabama (7) (Fiesta, 1991) (1st quarter, 9 of 16)

MOST TOUCHDOWN PASSES THROWN

6—(D) Chuck Long, Iowa (55) vs. Texas (17) (Freedom, 1984) (29 of 39 with no interceptions) (touchdown passes of 6, 11, 33, 49, 4, 15 yards)

MOST PASSES HAD INTERCEPTED

6—Bruce Lee, Arizona (10) vs. Auburn (34) (Sun, 1968) (6 of 24)

HIGHEST COMPLETION PERCENTAGE
(Min. 10 Attempts)

.929—Mike Bobo, Georgia (33) vs. Wisconsin (6) (Outback, 1998) (26 of 28 with no interceptions)

MOST YARDS PER PASS ATTEMPT
(Min. 10 Attempts)

21.3—(D) Chris McCoy, Navy (42) vs. California (38) (Aloha, 1996) (13 for 277)

MOST YARDS PER PASS COMPLETION (Min. 7 Completions)
30.8—(D) Chris McCoy, Navy (42) vs. California (38) (Aloha, 1996) (9 for 277)

Receiving

MOST PASS RECEPTIONS
20—Walker Gillette, Richmond (49) vs. Ohio (42) (Tangerine, 1968) (242 yards); (D) Norman Jordan, Vanderbilt (28) vs. Air Force (36) (Hall of Fame, 1982) (173 yards)

MOST PASS RECEIVING YARDS
308—Jason Rivers, Hawaii (41) vs. Arizona St. (24) (Hawaii, 2006) (14 receptions)

HIGHEST AVERAGE PER RECEPTION (Min. 3 Receptions)
52.3—Phil Harris, Texas (28) vs. Navy (6) (Cotton, 1964) (3 for 157); (D) Jason Anderson, Wake Forest (38) vs. Oregon (17) (Seattle, 2002) (3 for 157)

MOST TOUCHDOWNS RECEIVING
4—(D) Bob McChesney, Hardin-Simmons (49) vs. Wichita St. (12) (Camellia, 1948) (8 receptions); Fred Biletnikoff, Florida St. (36) vs. Oklahoma (19) (Gator, Jan. 2, 1965) (13 receptions); Travis LaTendresse, Utah (38) vs. Georgia Tech (10) (Emerald, 2005) (16 receptions)

Scoring

MOST POINTS SCORED
30—Barry Sanders, Oklahoma St. (62) vs. Wyoming (14) (Holiday, 1988) (5 touchdowns); (D) Sheldon Canley, San Jose St. (48) vs. Central Mich. (24) (California, 1990) (5 touchdowns); Steven Jackson, Oregon St. (55) vs. New Mexico (14) (Las Vegas, 2003) (5 touchdowns); Reggie Campbell, Navy (51) vs. Colorado St. (30) (Poinsettia, 2005) (5 touchdowns)

MOST POINTS RESPONSIBLE FOR (TDS SCORED & PASSED FOR, EXTRA POINTS, AND FGS)
40—Bobby Layne, Texas (40) vs. Missouri (27) (Cotton, 1946) (18 rushing, 12 passing, 6 receiving and 4 PATs)

MOST TOUCHDOWNS SCORED
5—Neil Snow, Michigan (49) vs. Stanford (0) (Rose, 1902) (5 rushing five-point TDs); Barry Sanders, Oklahoma St. (62) vs. Wyoming (14) (Holiday, 1988) (5 rushing); (D) Sheldon Canley, San Jose St. (48) vs. Central Mich. (24) (California, 1990) (4 rushing, 1 receiving); Steven Jackson, Oregon St. (55) vs. New Mexico (14) (Las Vegas, 2003) (4 rushing, 1 receiving); Reggie Campbell, Navy (51) vs. Colorado St. (30) (Poinsettia, 2005) (3 rushing, 2 receiving)

MOST TWO-POINT CONVERSIONS
2—Ernie Davis, Syracuse (23) vs. Texas (14) (Cotton, 1960) (2 receptions)

Kicking

MOST FIELD GOALS ATTEMPTED
6—Jess Atkinson, Maryland (23) vs. Tennessee (30) (Florida Citrus, 1983) (made 5); Kyle Bryant, Texas A&M (22) vs. Michigan (20) (Alamo, 1995) (made 5); (D) Mason Crosby, Colorado (33) vs. UTEP (28) (Houston, 2004) (made 4)

MOST FIELD GOALS MADE
5—Jess Atkinson, Maryland (23) vs. Tennessee (30) (Florida Citrus, 1983) (18, 48, 31, 22, 26 yards); Arden Czyzewski, Florida (28) vs. Notre Dame (39) (Sugar, 1992) (26, 24, 36, 37, 24 yards); Tim Rogers, Mississippi St. (24) vs. North Carolina St. (28) (Peach, Jan. 1, 1995) (37, 21, 29, 36, 30 yards); Kyle Bryant, Texas A&M (22) vs. Michigan (20) (Alamo, 1995) (27, 49, 47, 31, 37 yards); Dan Nystrom, Minnesota (29) vs. Arkansas (14) (Music City, 2002) (24, 45, 21, 22, 29 yards)

MOST EXTRA-POINT KICK ATTEMPTS
9—(D) James Weaver, Centre (63) vs. TCU (7) (Fort Worth Classic, 1921) (9 made); Bobby Luna, Alabama (61) vs. Syracuse (6) (Orange, 1953) (7 made); Layne Talbot, Texas A&M (65) vs. BYU (14) (Holiday, 1990) (9 made); Neil Rackers, Illinois (63) vs. Virginia (21) (Micronpc.com, 1999) (9 made); Josh Brown, Nebraska (66) vs. Northwestern (17) (Alamo, 2000) (9 made)

MOST EXTRA-POINT KICKS MADE
9—(D) James Weaver, Centre (63) vs. TCU (7) (Fort Worth Classic, 1921) (9 attempted); Layne Talbot, Texas A&M (65) vs. BYU (14) (Holiday, 1990) (9 attempted); Neil Rackers, Illinois (63) vs. Virginia (21) (Micronpc.com,1999) (9 attempted); Josh Brown, Nebraska (66) vs. Northwestern (17) (Alamo, 2000) (9 attempted)

MOST POINTS BY A KICKER
19—Kevin Miller, East Caro. (61) vs. Marshall (64) (2 ot) (GMAC, 2001) (4 FGs, 7 PATs)

Punting

MOST PUNTS
21—Everett Sweeney, Michigan (49) vs. Stanford (0) (Rose, 1902)

HIGHEST AVERAGE PER PUNT (Min. 5 Punts)
53.8—Mat McBriar, Hawaii (28) vs. Tulane (36) (Hawaii, 2002) (5 for 269)

Punt Returns

MOST PUNT RETURNS
9—Paddy Driscoll, Great Lakes (17) vs. Mare Island (0) (Rose, 1919) (115 yards); Buzy Rosenberg, Georgia (7) vs. North Carolina (3) (Gator, Dec. 31, 1971) (54 yards)

MOST PUNT RETURN YARDS
180—Willie Reid, Florida St. (23) vs. Penn St. (26) (3 ot) (Orange, 2006) (7 returns)

HIGHEST PUNT RETURN AVERAGE (Min. 3 Returns)
40.7—George Fleming, Washington (44) vs. Wisconsin (8) (Rose, 1960) (3 for 122)

MOST TOUCHDOWNS ON PUNT RETURNS
2—James Henry, Southern Miss. (38) vs. UTEP (18) (Independence, 1988) (65 and 45 yards)

Kickoff Returns

MOST KICKOFF RETURNS
8—Todd Howard, Michigan (17) vs. Tennessee (45) (Florida Citrus, 2002) (125 yards)

MOST KICKOFF RETURN YARDS
221—Steve Breaston, Michigan (37) vs. Texas (38) (Rose, 2005) (6 returns)

HIGHEST KICKOFF RETURN AVERAGE (Min. 2 Returns)
60.5—(D) Bob Smith, Texas A&M (40) vs. Georgia (20) (Presidential Cup, 1950) (2 for 121)

MOST TOUCHDOWNS ON KICKOFF RETURNS
1—Many players tied

Interceptions

MOST INTERCEPTIONS MADE
4—(D) Manuel Aja, Arizona St. (21) vs. Xavier (Ohio) (33) (Salad, 1950); Jim Dooley, Miami (Fla.) (14) vs. Clemson (0) (Gator, 1952)

MOST INTERCEPTION RETURN YARDAGE
148—Elmer Layden, Notre Dame (27) vs. Stanford (10) (Rose, 1925) (2 interceptions)

All-Purpose Yards

(Includes All Runs From Scrimmage, Pass Receptions and All Returns)

MOST ALL-PURPOSE PLAYS (Must Have at Least One Reception or Return)
47—(D) Ron Jackson, Tulsa (28) vs. San Diego St. (17) (Freedom, 1991) (46 rushes, 1 reception)

MOST ALL-PURPOSE YARDS GAINED (Must Have at Least One Reception or Return)
359—Sherman Williams, Alabama (24) vs. Ohio St. (17) (Florida Citrus, 1995) (166 rushing, 155 receiving, 38 kickoff returns)

Defensive Statistics

MOST TOTAL TACKLES MADE (Includes Assists)
31—Lee Roy Jordan, Alabama (17) vs. Oklahoma (0) (Orange, 1963)

MOST SOLO TACKLES
18—Rod Smith, Notre Dame (39) vs. Florida (28) (Sugar, 1992)

MOST TACKLES FOR LOSSES
6—(D) LeMarcus McDonald, TCU (9) vs. Texas A&M (28) (galleryfurniture.com, 2001)

MOST QUARTERBACK SACKS
6—Shay Muirbrook, BYU (19) vs. Kansas St. (15) (Cotton, 1997)

MOST FUMBLE RECOVERIES
2—Rod Kirby, Pittsburgh (7) vs. Arizona St. (28) (Fiesta, 1973); (D) Michael Stewart, Fresno St. (51) vs. Bowling Green (7) (California, 1985); Randall Brown, Ohio St. (17) vs. Alabama (24) (Florida Citrus, 1995); Joe Anoai, Georgia Tech (52) vs. Tulsa (10) (Humanitarian, 2004); (D) Nik Moser, Iowa St. (24) vs. TCU (27) (Houston, 2005)

MOST BLOCKED KICKS
2—Carlton Williams, Pittsburgh (7) vs. Arizona St. (28) (Fiesta, 1973) (2 PATs); Bracey Walker, North Carolina (21) vs. Mississippi St. (17) (Peach, Jan. 2, 1993) (2 punts)

MOST BLOCKED PUNTS
2—Bracey Walker, North Carolina (21) vs. Mississippi St. (17) (Peach, Jan. 2, 1993)

MOST PASSES BROKEN UP
5—Dyshod Carter, Kansas St. (34) vs. Purdue (37) (Alamo, 1998)

Team Records

Totals for each team in both-team records are in brackets after the team's score.

Total Offense

MOST TOTAL PLAYS
107—Purdue (27) vs. Washington St. (33) (Sun, 2001) (32 rush, 75 pass) (474 yards)

MOST TOTAL PLAYS, BOTH TEAMS
180—Marshall (64) [104] & East Caro. (61) [76] (2 ot) (GMAC, 2001) (1,141 yards); Hawaii (54) [91] & Houston (48) [89] (3 ot) (Hawaii, 2003) (1,158 yards)

MOST YARDS GAINED
718—Arizona St. (49) vs. Missouri (35) (Fiesta, 1972) (452 rushing, 266 passing)

MOST YARDS GAINED, BOTH TEAMS
1,211—Arizona St. (45) [679] vs, Rutgers (40) [532] (Insight, 2005) (150 plays)

HIGHEST AVERAGE GAINED PER PLAY
9.9—Hawaii (41) vs. Arizona St. (24) (Hawaii, 2006) (69 for 680)

FEWEST PLAYS
35—Tennessee (0) vs. Texas (16) (Cotton, 1953) (29 rush, 6 pass)

FEWEST PLAYS, BOTH TEAMS
105—Georgia (31) [52] & Virginia Tech (24) [53] (Chick-fil-A, 2006)

FEWEST YARDS
Minus 21—U. of Mexico (0) vs. Southwestern (Tex.) (35) (Sun, 1945) (29 rushing, -50 passing)

FEWEST YARDS, BOTH TEAMS
260—Randolph Field (7) [150] & Texas (7) [110] (Cotton, 1944)

LOWEST AVERAGE GAINED PER PLAY
0.9—Tennessee (0) vs. Texas (16) (Cotton, 1953) (35 for 32)

Rushing

MOST RUSHING ATTEMPTS
87—Oklahoma (40) vs. Auburn (22) (Sugar, Jan. 1, 1972) (439 yards)

MOST RUSHING ATTEMPTS, BOTH TEAMS
122—Mississippi St. (26) [68] & North Carolina (24) [54] (Sun, 1974) (732 yards); (D) Southern California (47) [50] & Texas A&M (28) [72] (Bluebonnet, 1977) (864 yards)

MOST NET RUSHING YARDS
524—Nebraska (62) vs. Florida (24) (Fiesta, 1996) (68 attempts)

MOST NET RUSHING YARDS, BOTH TEAMS
864—(D) Southern California (47) [378] & Texas A&M (28) [486] (Bluebonnet, 1977) (122 attempts)

HIGHEST RUSHING AVERAGE
(Min. 30 Attempts)
9.3—Texas Tech (55) vs. Air Force (41) (Copper, 1995) (39 for 361)

FEWEST RUSHING ATTEMPTS
12—(D) Vanderbilt (28) vs. Air Force (36) (Hall of Fame, 1982) (35 yards)

FEWEST RUSHING ATTEMPTS, BOTH TEAMS
50—Southern California (32) [23] & Michigan (18) [27] (Rose, 2007)

FEWEST RUSHING YARDS
Minus 61—(D) Kansas St. (7) vs. Boston College (12) (Aloha, 1994) (23 attempts)

FEWEST RUSHING YARDS, BOTH TEAMS
51—(D) Utah (16) [6] & Arizona (13) [45] (Freedom, 1994

LOWEST RUSHING AVERAGE
(Min. 20 Attempts)
Minus 2.7—(D) Kansas St. (7) vs. Boston College (12) (Aloha, 1994) (23 for -61)

RUSHING DEFENSE, FEWEST YARDS ALLOWED
Minus 61—(D) Boston College (12) vs. Kansas St. (7) (Aloha, 1994) (23 attempts)

Passing

MOST PASS ATTEMPTS
75—Purdue (27) vs. Washington St. (33) (Sun, 2001) (38 completions, 4 interceptions, 419 yards)

MOST PASS ATTEMPTS, BOTH TEAMS
116—Purdue (27) [75] & Washington St. (33) [41] (Sun, 2001) (53 completions)

MOST PASS COMPLETIONS
43—(D) San Jose St. (25) vs. Toledo (27) (California, 1981) (63 attempts, 5 interceptions, 467 yards)

MOST PASS COMPLETIONS, BOTH TEAMS
64—Texas (47) [37] & Washington (43) [27] (Holiday, 2001) (109 attempted); Texas Tech (55) [39] & Clemson (15) [25] (Tangerine, 2002) (108 attempted)

MOST PASSING YARDS
576—BYU (39) vs. Penn St. (50) (Holiday, 1989) (42 completions, 59 attempts, 2 interceptions); Marshall (64) vs. East Caro. (61) (2 ot) (GMAC, 2001) (41 completions, 70 attempts, 2 interceptions)

MOST PASSING YARDS, BOTH TEAMS
907—(D) Michigan St. (44) [376] & Fresno St. (35) [531] (Silicon Valley, 2001) (90 attempted)

MOST PASSES HAD INTERCEPTED
8—Arizona (10) vs. Auburn (34) (Sun, 1968)

MOST PASSES HAD INTERCEPTED, BOTH TEAMS
12—Auburn (34) [4] & Arizona (10) [8] (Sun, 1968)

MOST PASSES ATTEMPTED WITHOUT AN INTERCEPTION
60—Texas Tech (45) vs. California (31) (Holiday, 2004) (39 completions)

MOST PASSES ATTEMPTED WITHOUT AN INTERCEPTION, BOTH TEAMS
93—Idaho (42) [41] & Southern Miss. (35) [52] (Humanitarian, 1998) (55 completions)

HIGHEST COMPLETION PERCENTAGE
(Min. 10 Attempts)
.929—Texas (40) vs. Missouri (27) (Cotton, 1946) (13 of 14, no interceptions, 234 yards)

MOST YARDS PER ATTEMPT
(Min. 10 Attempts)
21.7—Southern California (47) vs. Pittsburgh (14) (Rose, 1930) (13 for 282)

MOST YARDS PER COMPLETION
(Min. 8 Completions)
35.2—Southern California (47) vs. Pittsburgh (14) (Rose, 1930) (8 for 282)

FEWEST PASS ATTEMPTS
2—West Virginia (14) vs. South Carolina (3) (Peach, 1969) (1 completion); (D) Army (10) vs. Michigan St. (6) (Cherry, 1984) (1 completion); Air Force (38) vs. Mississippi St. (15) (Liberty, 1991) (1 completion)

FEWEST PASS ATTEMPTS, BOTH TEAMS
9—Fordham (2) [4] & Missouri (0) [5] (Sugar, 1942)

FEWEST PASS COMPLETIONS
0—13 teams tied (see Team Record Lists)

FEWEST PASS COMPLETIONS, BOTH TEAMS
3—Arizona St. (0) [0] & Catholic (0) [3] (Sun, 1940)

FEWEST PASSING YARDS
Minus 50—U. of Mexico (0) vs. Southwestern (Tex.) (35) (Sun, 1945) (2 completions, 9 attempts, 3 interceptions)

FEWEST PASSING YARDS, BOTH TEAMS
16—Arizona St. (0) [0] & Catholic (0) [16] (Sun, 1940); Arkansas (0) [0] & LSU (0) [16] (Cotton, 1947)

LOWEST COMPLETION PERCENTAGE
.000—13 teams tied (see Team Record Lists)

FEWEST YARDS PER PASS ATTEMPT
Minus 5.6—U. of Mexico (0) vs. Southwestern (Tex.) (35) (Sun, 1945) (9 for -50)

FEWEST YARDS PER PASS COMPLETION
(Min. 1 Completion)
Minus 25.0—U. of Mexico (0) vs. Southwestern (Tex.) (35) (Sun, 1945) (2 for -50)

Scoring

MOST TOUCHDOWNS
10—Nebraska (66) vs. Northwestern (17) (Alamo, 2000) (6 rush, 4 pass)

MOST TOUCHDOWNS, BOTH TEAMS
16—Marshall (64) [9] & East Caro. (61) [7] (2 ot) (GMAC, 2001)

MOST TOUCHDOWNS RUSHING
8—(D) Centre (63) vs. TCU (7) (Fort Worth Classic, 1921)

MOST TOUCHDOWNS RUSHING, BOTH TEAMS
12—Texas Tech (55) [6] & Air Force (41) [6] (Copper, 1995)

MOST TOUCHDOWNS PASSING
6—(D) Iowa (55) vs. Texas (17) (Freedom, 1984)

MOST TOUCHDOWNS PASSING, BOTH TEAMS
9—Bowling Green (52) [5] & Memphis (35) [4] (GMAC, 2004)

MOST FIELD GOALS MADE
5—Maryland (23) vs. Tennessee (30) (Florida Citrus, 1983) (18, 48, 31, 22, 26 yards); Florida (28) vs. Notre Dame (39) (Sugar, 1992) (26, 24, 36, 37, 24 yards); Mississippi St. (24) vs. North Carolina St. (28) (Peach, Jan. 1, 1995) (37, 21, 29, 36, 30 yards); Texas A&M (22) vs. Michigan (20) (Alamo, 1995) (27, 49, 47, 31, 37 yards)

MOST FIELD GOALS MADE, BOTH TEAMS
7—Texas A&M (22) [5] & Michigan (20) [2] (Alamo, 1995); North Carolina St. (28) [2] & Mississippi St. (24) [5] (Peach, Jan. 1, 1995); Iowa (19) [4] & Texas Tech (16) [3] (Alamo, 2001)

MOST POINTS, WINNING TEAM
66—Nebraska vs. Northwestern (17) (Alamo, 2000)

MOST POINTS, LOSING TEAM
61—East Caro. vs. Marshall (64) (2 ot) (GMAC, 2001)

MOST POINTS, BOTH TEAMS
125—Marshall (64) & East Carolina (61) (2 ot) (GMAC, 2001)

LARGEST MARGIN OF VICTORY
55—Alabama (61) vs. Syracuse (6) (Orange, 1953)

FEWEST POINTS, WINNING TEAM
2—Fordham vs. Missouri (0) (Sugar, 1942)

FEWEST POINTS, LOSING TEAM
0—By many teams

FEWEST POINTS, BOTH TEAMS
0—California (0) & Wash. & Jeff. (0) (Rose, 1922); Arizona St. (0) & Catholic (0) (Sun, 1940); Arkansas (0) & LSU (0) (Cotton, 1947); Air Force (0) & TCU (0) (Cotton, 1959)

MOST POINTS IN FIRST HALF
45—Colorado (62) vs. Boston College (28) (Insight.com, 1999)

MOST POINTS IN SECOND HALF
45—Oklahoma St. (62) vs. Wyoming (14) (Holiday, 1988)

MOST POINTS IN SECOND HALF
(Including Overtime Periods)
56—Marshall (64) vs. East Caro. (61) (2 ot) (GMAC, 2001) (43 in regulation plus 13 in overtime)

MOST POINTS IN FIRST HALF, BOTH TEAMS
63—(D) Navy (42) [28] & California (38) [35] (Aloha, 1996); Bowling Green (52) [35] & Memphis (35) [28] (GMAC, 2004)

MOST POINTS IN SECOND HALF, BOTH TEAMS
64—Penn St. (50) [38] & BYU (39) [26] (Holiday, 1989); (D) Kansas (51) [34] & UCLA (30) [30] (Aloha, 1995)

MOST POINTS IN SECOND HALF, BOTH TEAMS (Including Overtime Periods)
79—Marshall (64) [56] vs. East Caro. (61) [23] (2 ot) (GMAC, 2001) (56 in regulation plus 23 in overtime)

MOST POINTS IN EACH QUARTER
1st: 28—Southern California (55) vs. Texas Tech (14) (Cotton, 1995)
2nd: 31—Nebraska (66) vs. Northwestern (17) (Alamo, 2000)
3rd: 31—(D) Iowa (55) vs. Texas (17) (Freedom, 1984)
4th: 30—Oklahoma (40) vs. Houston (14) (Sun, 1981)

MOST POINTS IN EACH QUARTER, BOTH TEAMS
1st: 34—Hawaii (59) [21] & UAB (40) [13] (Hawaii, 2004)
2nd: 45—Nebraska (66) [31] & Northwestern (17) [14] (Alamo, 2000)
3rd: 35—Oklahoma St. (62) [28] & Wyoming (14) [7] (Holiday, 1988); Kansas St. (54) [21] & Colorado St. (21) [14] (Holiday, 1995); Michigan (35) [21] & Alabama (34) [14] (Orange, 2000)
4th: 39—Memphis (38) [18] & Akron (31) [21] (Motor City, 2005)

First Downs

MOST FIRST DOWNS
36—Oklahoma (48) vs. Virginia (14) (Gator, Dec. 29, 1991) (16 rush, 18 pass, 2 penalty); Marshall (64) vs. East Caro. (61) (2 ot) (GMAC, 2001) (9 rush, 25 pass, 2 penalty)

MOST FIRST DOWNS, BOTH TEAMS
62—North Carolina St. (56) [34] vs. Kansas (26) [28] (Tangerine, 2003)

MOST FIRST DOWNS RUSHING
26—Oklahoma (40) vs. Auburn (22) (Sugar, Jan. 1, 1972); Navy (51) vs. Colorado St. (30) (Poinsettia, 2005)

MOST FIRST DOWNS RUSHING, BOTH TEAMS
36—Colorado (47) [24] & Alabama (33) [12] (Liberty, 1969); Miami (Fla.) (46) [16] & Texas (3) [20] (Cotton, 1991)

MOST FIRST DOWNS PASSING
27—BYU (39) vs. Penn St. (50) (Holiday, 1989)

MOST FIRST DOWNS PASSING, BOTH TEAMS
38—Penn St. (50) [11] & BYU (39) [27] (Holiday, 1989); Florida (31) [16] & Iowa (24) [22] (Outback, 2006)

MOST FIRST DOWNS BY PENALTY
8—West Virginia (18) vs. Florida St. (30) (Gator, 2005)

MOST FIRST DOWNS BY PENALTY, BOTH TEAMS
12—Florida St. (30) [4] & West Virginia (18) [8] (Gator, 2005)

FEWEST FIRST DOWNS
1—Alabama (29) vs. Texas A&M (21) (Cotton, 1942) (1 pass); Arkansas (0) vs. LSU (0) (Cotton, 1947) (1 rush)

FEWEST FIRST DOWNS, BOTH TEAMS
10—Randolph Field (7) [7] & Texas (7) [3] (Cotton, 1944)

FEWEST FIRST DOWNS RUSHING
0—Alabama (29) vs. Texas A&M (21) (Cotton, 1942); Navy (6) vs. Texas (28) (Cotton, 1964); Florida (18) vs. Missouri (20) (Sugar, 1966); Southern California (19) vs. TCU (28) (Sun, 1998); Purdue (7) vs. Maryland (24) (Champs Sports, 2006); Northern Ill. (7) vs. TCU (37) (Poinsettia, 2006)

FEWEST FIRST DOWNS RUSHING, BOTH TEAMS
3—Alabama (29) [0] & Texas A&M (21) [3] (Cotton, 1942)

FEWEST FIRST DOWNS PASSING
0—By 13 teams (see Team Record Lists)

FEWEST FIRST DOWNS PASSING, BOTH TEAMS
1—Alabama (10) [0] & Arkansas (3) [1] (Sugar, 1962)

Punting

MOST PUNTS
17—Duke (3) vs. Southern California (7) (Rose, 1939)

MOST PUNTS, BOTH TEAMS
28—Santa Clara (6) [14] & LSU (0) [14] (Sugar, 1938); Rice (8) [13] & Tennessee (0) [15] (Orange, 1947)

HIGHEST PUNTING AVERAGE (Min. 5 Punts)
53.9—Southern California (7) vs. Wisconsin (0) (Rose, 1953) (8 for 431)

FEWEST PUNTS
0—Oklahoma (41) vs. Wyoming (7) (Fiesta, 1976); Maryland (23) vs. Tennessee (30) (Florida Citrus, 1983); Oklahoma St. (62) vs. Wyoming (14) (Holiday, 1988); Illinois (63) vs. Virginia (21) (Micronpc.com, 1999); (D) Texas Tech (38) vs. Navy (14) (Houston, 2003); Navy (51) vs. Colorado St. (30) (Poinsettia, 2005)

LOWEST PUNTING AVERAGE (Min. 3 Punts)
17.0—Nevada (34) vs. Bowling Green (35) (Las Vegas, 1992) (4 for 68); Kentucky (14) vs. Penn St. (26) (Outback, 1999) (3 for 51)

MOST PUNTS BLOCKED BY ONE TEAM
2—LSU (25) vs. Colorado (7) (Orange, 1962); North Carolina St. (14) vs. Georgia (7) (Liberty, 1967); North Carolina (21) vs. Mississippi St. (17) (Peach, Jan. 2, 1993); Cincinnati (32) vs. Marshall (14) (Fort Worth, 2004); Iowa (30) vs. LSU (25) (Capital One, 2005)

Punt Returns

MOST PUNT RETURNS
9—Georgia (7) vs. North Carolina (3) (Gator, Dec. 31, 1971) (6.8 average)

MOST PUNT RETURN YARDS
180—Florida St. (23) vs. Penn St. (26) (3 ot) (Orange, 2006) (7 returns)

HIGHEST PUNT RETURN AVERAGE (Min. 3 Returns)
33.0—Kent St. (18) vs. Tampa (21) (Tangerine, 1972) (3 for 99)

Kickoff Returns

MOST KICKOFF RETURNS
10—Wyoming (14) vs. Oklahoma St. (62) (Holiday, 1988) (20.5 average); Florida (24) vs. Nebraska (62) (Fiesta, 1996) (26.8 average)

MOST KICKOFF RETURN YARDS
268—Florida (24) vs. Nebraska (62) (Fiesta, 1996) (10 returns)

HIGHEST KICKOFF RETURN AVERAGE (Min. 3 Returns)
42.5—Tennessee (27) vs. Maryland (28) (Sun, 1984) (4 for 170)

Fumbles

MOST FUMBLES
11—Mississippi (7) vs. Alabama (12) (Sugar, 1964) (lost 6)

MOST FUMBLES, BOTH TEAMS
17—Alabama (12) [6] & Mississippi (7) [11] (Sugar, 1964) (lost 9)

MOST FUMBLES LOST
6—By six teams (see Team Record Lists)

MOST FUMBLES LOST, BOTH TEAMS
9—Alabama (12) [3] & Mississippi (7) [6] (Sugar, 1964) (17 fumbles)

Penalties

MOST PENALTIES
21—Mississippi St. (17) vs. Clemson (7) (Peach, 1999) (188 yards)

MOST PENALTIES, BOTH TEAMS
29—McNeese St. (20) [13] & Tulsa (16) [16] (Independence, 1976) (205 yards); Florida (52) [15] & Florida St. (20) [14] (Sugar, 1997) (217 yards); Mississippi St. (17) [21] & Clemson (7) [8] (Peach, 1999) (270 yards)

MOST YARDS PENALIZED
202—Miami (Fla.) (46) vs. Texas (3) (Cotton, 1991) (16 penalties)

MOST YARDS PENALIZED, BOTH TEAMS
295—Florida St. (30) [174] & West Virginia (18) [121] (Gator, 2005)

FEWEST PENALTIES
0—By 10 teams (see Team Record Lists)

FEWEST PENALTIES, BOTH TEAMS
3—In six games (see Team Record Lists)

FEWEST YARDS PENALIZED
0—By 11 teams (see Team Record Lists)

FEWEST YARDS PENALIZED, BOTH TEAMS
10—Duquesne (13) [5] & Mississippi St. (12) [5] (Orange, 1937)

Individual Record Lists

Only official records after 1937 are included. Prior records are included if able to be substantiated. Each team's score is in parentheses after the team name. The year listed is the actual (calendar) year the game was played; the date is included if the bowl was played twice (i.e., January and December) during one calendar year. The list also includes discontinued bowls, marked with (D). Bowls are listed by the name of the bowl at the time it was played.

Total Offense

MOST PLAYS

83—Kyle Orton, Purdue (27) vs. Washington St. (33) (Sun, 2001)
82—Byron Leftwich, Marshall (64) vs. East Caro. (61) (2 ot) (GMAC, 2001)
78—Brett Basanez, Northwestern (38) vs. UCLA (50) (Sun, 2005)
74—(D) Tony Kimbrough, Western Mich. (30) vs. Fresno St. (35) (California, 1988)
70—Joel Armstrong, Rice (17) vs. Troy (41) (New Orleans, 2006)
69—Drew Brees, Purdue (25) vs. Georgia (28) (ot) (Outback, 2000)
68—Hines Ward, Georgia (27) vs. Virginia (34) (Peach, Dec. 30, 1995)
67—Casey Clausen, Tennessee (14) vs. Clemson (27) (Peach, Jan. 2, 2004)
67—Ty Detmer, BYU (39) vs. Penn St. (50) (Holiday, 1989)
65—Shane Matthews, Florida (28) vs. Notre Dame (39) (Sugar, 1992)
65—Tony Eason, Illinois (15) vs. Alabama (21) (Liberty, 1982)
65—Buster O'Brien, Richmond (49) vs. Ohio (42) (Tangerine, 1968)

MOST TOTAL YARDS

594—Ty Detmer, BYU (39) vs. Penn St. (50) (Holiday, 1989) (576 pass)
574—Colt Brennan, Hawaii (41) vs. Arizona St. (24) (Hawaii, 2006) (559 pass)
566—Byron Leftwich, Marshall (64) vs. East Caro. (61) (2 ot) (GMAC, 2001) (576 pass)
514—Sonny Cumbie, Texas Tech (45) vs. California (31) (Holiday, 2004) (520 pass)
508—(D) David Carr, Fresno St. (35) vs. Michigan St. (44) (Silicon Valley, 2001) (531 pass)
500—(D) B.J. Symons, Texas Tech (38) vs. Navy (14) (Houston, 2003) (497 pass)
498—Rudy Carpenter, Arizona St. (45) vs. Rutgers (40) (Insight, 2005) (467 pass)
495—Philip Rivers, North Carolina St. (56) vs. Kansas (26) (Tangerine, 2003) (475 pass)
486—Buster O'Brien, Richmond (49) vs. Ohio (42) (Tangerine, 1968) (447 pass)
481—(D) Chuck Long, Iowa (55) vs. Texas (17) (Freedom, 1984) (461 pass)
476—Major Applewhite, Texas (47) vs. Washington (43) (Holiday, 2001) (473 pass)
474—Trent Dilfer, Fresno St. (30) vs. Colorado (41) (Aloha, 1993) (523 pass)
469—Hines Ward, Georgia (27) vs. Virginia (34) (Peach, Dec. 30, 1995) (413 pass)
467—Vince Young, Texas (41) vs. Southern California (38) (Rose, 2006) (267 pass)
464—(D) Steve Clarkson, San Jose St. (25) vs. Toledo (27) (California, 1981) (467 pass)
457—(D) Akili Smith, Oregon (43) vs. Colorado (51) (Aloha, 1998) (456 pass)
454—John Walsh, BYU (31) vs. Oklahoma (6) (Copper, 1994) (454 pass)
448—Brett Basanez, Northwestern (38) vs. UCLA (50) (Sun, 2005) (416 pass)
446—Jim McMahon, BYU (46) vs. SMU (45) (Holiday, 1980) (446 pass)
446—(D) Whit Taylor, Vanderbilt (28) vs. Air Force (36) (Hall of Fame, 1982) (452 pass)
445—Chad Pennington, Marshall (48) vs. Louisville (29) (Motor City, 1998) (411 pass)

HIGHEST AVERAGE PER PLAY
(Minimum 10 Plays)

24.1—Dicky Maegle, Rice (28) vs. Alabama (6) (Cotton, 1954) (11 for 265)
16.5—Chad Pennington, Marshall (48) vs. Louisville (29) (Motor City, 1998) (27 for 445)
16.2—Leon Washington, Florida St. (30) vs. West Virginia (18) (Gator, 2005) (12 for 195)
14.1—Marcus Dupree, Oklahoma (21) vs. Arizona St. (32) (Fiesta, 1983) (17 for 239)
14.0—Bucky Richardson, Texas A&M (65) vs. BYU (14) (Holiday, 1990) (23 for 322)
13.2—Kordell Stewart, Colorado (41) vs. Notre Dame (24) (Fiesta, 1995) (28 for 369)
12.2—Ger Schwedes, Syracuse (23) vs. Texas (14) (Cotton, 1960) (10 for 122)
12.0—Tony Rice, Notre Dame (34) vs. West Virginia (21) (Fiesta, 1989) (24 for 288)
11.3—Rob Johnson, Southern California (55) vs. Texas Tech (14) (Cotton, 1995) (24 for 271)
11.2—(D) Dwight Ford, Southern California (47) vs. Texas A&M (28) (Bluebonnet, 1977) (14 for 157)

MOST TOUCHDOWNS RESPONSIBLE FOR (TDs SCORED & PASSED FOR)

6—(D) Chuck Long, Iowa (55) vs. Texas (17) (Freedom, 1984) (6 pass)
6—Bobby Layne, Texas (40) vs. Missouri (27) (Cotton, 1946) (3 rush, 2 pass, 1 catch)
5—Colt Brennan, Hawaii (41) vs. Arizona St. (24) (Hawaii, 2006) (5 pass)
5—Omar Haugabook, Troy (41) vs. Rice (17) (New Orleans, 2006) (1 rush, 4 pass)
5—Matt Moore, Oregon St. (39) vs. Missouri (38) (Sun, 2006) (1 rush, 4 pass)
5—Bruce Gradkowski, Toledo (45) vs. UTEP (13) (GMAC, 2005) (5 pass)
5—Matt Leinart, Southern California (55) vs. Oklahoma (19) (Orange, 2005) (5 pass)
5—Vince Young, Texas (38) vs. Michigan (37) (Rose, 2005) (4 rush, 1 pass)
5—Omar Jacobs, Bowling Green (52) vs. Memphis (35) (GMAC, 2004) (5 pass)
5—Timmy Chang, Hawaii (59) vs. UAB (40) (Hawaii, 2004) (4 pass, 1 rush)
5—Paul Pinegar, Fresno St. (37) vs. Virginia (34) (ot) (MPC Computers, 2004) (5 pass)
5—Timmy Chang, Hawaii (54) vs. Houston (48) (3 ot) (Hawaii, 2003) (5 pass)
5—Casey Clausen, Tennessee (45) vs. Michigan (17) (Florida Citrus, 2002) (3 pass, 2 rush)
5—Byron Leftwich, Marshall (64) vs. East Caro. (61) (2 ot) (GMAC, 2001) (4 pass, 1 rush)
5—Michael Bishop, Kansas St. (35) vs. Syracuse (18) (Fiesta, 1997) (4 pass, 1 rush)
5—Jeff Blake, East Caro. (37) vs. North Carolina St. (34) (Peach, 1992) (4 pass, 1 rush)
5—Peter Tom Willis, Florida St. (41) vs. Nebraska (17) (Fiesta, 1990) (5 pass)
5—(D) Sheldon Canley, San Jose St. (48) vs. Central Mich. (24) (California, 1990) (4 rush, 1 pass)
5—Johnny Rodgers, Nebraska (40) vs. Notre Dame (6) (Orange, 1973) (3 rush, 1 pass, 1 catch)
5—Buster O'Brien, Richmond (49) vs. Ohio (42) (Tangerine, 1968) (4 pass, 1 rush)
5—Steve Tensi, Florida St. (36) vs. Oklahoma (19) (Gator, Jan. 2, 1965) (5 pass)
5—Neil Snow, Michigan (49) vs. Stanford (0) (Rose, 1902) (5 rush)

Rushing

MOST RUSHING ATTEMPTS

46—(D) Ron Jackson, Tulsa (28) vs. San Diego St. (17) (Freedom, 1991) (211 yards)
43—Fred Taylor, Florida (21) vs. Penn St. (6) (Florida Citrus, 1998) (234 yards)
42—Tellis Redmon, Minnesota (30) vs. North Carolina St. (38) (Micronpc.com, 2000) (246 yards)
41—(D) Blake Ezor, Michigan St. (33) vs. Hawaii (13) (Aloha, 1989) (179 yards)
39—Terrell Fletcher, Wisconsin (34) vs. Duke (20) (Hall of Fame, 1995) (241 yards)
39—Raymont Harris, Ohio St. (28) vs. BYU (21) (Holiday, 1993) (235 yards)
39—Errict Rhett, Florida (27) vs. North Carolina St. (10) (Gator, 1992) (182 yards)
39—Charlie Wysocki, Maryland (20) vs. Florida (35) (Tangerine, 1980) (159 yards)
39—Charles White, Southern California (17) vs. Ohio St. (16) (Rose, 1980) (247 yards)
37—Cody Hull, Southern Miss. (31) vs. Arkansas St. (19) (New Orleans, 2005) (161 yards)
37—Marion Barber III, Minnesota (20) vs. Alabama (16) (Music City, 2004) (187 yards)
37—Ronnie Brown, Auburn (13) vs. Penn St. (9) (Capital One, 2003) (184 yards)
37—(D) Rodney Davis, Fresno St. (30) vs. Georgia Tech (21) (Silicon Valley, 2002) (153 yards)
37—(D) Charles Davis, Colorado (29) vs. Houston (17) (Bluebonnet, 1971) (202 yards)

MOST NET RUSHING YARDS

307—P.J. Daniels, Georgia Tech (52) vs. Tulsa (10) (Humanitarian, 2004) (31 carries)
280—(D) James Gray, Texas Tech (49) vs. Duke (21) (All-American, 1989) (33 carries)
276—(D) Curtis Dickey, Texas A&M (28) vs. Iowa St. (12) (Hall of Fame, 1978) (34 carries)
266—(D) Gaston Green, UCLA (31) vs. BYU (10) (Freedom, 1986) (33 carries)
265—Dicky Maegle, Rice (28) vs. Alabama (6) (Cotton, 1954) (11 carries)
260—Byron Hanspard, Texas Tech (55) vs. Air Force (41) (Copper, 1995) (24 carries)
254—Bob Anderson, Colorado (47) vs. Alabama (33) (Liberty, 1969) (35 carries)
254—Mike Anderson, Utah (17) vs. Fresno St. (16) (Las Vegas, 1999) (34 carries)
250—Chuck Webb, Tennessee (31) vs. Arkansas (27) (Cotton, 1990) (26 carries)
247—Charles White, Southern California (17) vs. Ohio St. (16) (Rose, 1980) (39 carries)
246—Tellis Redmon, Minnesota (30) vs. North Carolina St. (38) (Micronpc.com, 2000) (42 carries)
246—Ron Dayne, Wisconsin (38) vs. Utah (10) (Copper, 1996) (30 carries)
246—Ron Dayne, Wisconsin (38) vs. UCLA (31) (Rose, 1999) (27 carries)
241—Terrell Fletcher, Wisconsin (34) vs. Duke (20) (Hall of Fame, 1995) (39 carries)
240—Dan Alexander, Nebraska (66) vs. Northwestern (17) (Alamo, 2000) (20 carries)
239—Marcus Dupree, Oklahoma (21) vs. Arizona St. (32) (Fiesta, 1983) (17 carries)
238—DeAngelo Williams, Memphis (38) vs. Akron (31) (Motor City, 2005) (31 carries)
235—Tyrone Wheatley, Michigan (38) vs. Washington (31) (Rose, 1993) (15 carries)
235—Raymont Harris, Ohio St. (28) vs. BYU (21) (Holiday, 1993) (39 carries)
234—Jamie Morris, Michigan (28) vs. Alabama (24) (Hall of Fame, 1988) (23 carries)
234—Kevin Faulk, LSU (45) vs. Michigan St. (26) (Independence, 1995) (25 carries)
234—Fred Taylor, Florida (21) vs. Penn St. (6) (Florida Citrus, 1998) (43 carries)

MOST NET RUSHING YARDS BY A QUARTERBACK

200—Vince Young, Texas (41) vs. Southern California (38) (Rose, 2006) (19 carries)
199—Tommie Frazier, Nebraska (62) vs. Florida (24) (Fiesta, 1996) (16 carries)
192—Vince Young, Texas (38) vs. Michigan (37) (Rose, 2005) (21 carries)
180—(D) Mike Mosley, Texas A&M (28) vs. Southern California (47) (Bluebonnet, 1977) (20 carries)
164—Eddie Phillips, Texas (11) vs. Notre Dame (24) (Cotton, 1971) (23 carries)
150—Brad Smith, Missouri (38) vs. South Carolina (31) (Independence, 2005) (21 carries)
149—Jack Mildren, Oklahoma (40) vs. Auburn (22) (Sugar, 1972) (30 carries)
143—Kordell Stewart, Colorado (41) vs. Notre Dame (24) (Fiesta, 1995) (7 carries)
136—(D) Nate Sassaman, Army (10) vs. Michigan St. (6) (Cherry, 1984) (28 carries)
133—(D) Eddie Wolgast, Arizona (13) vs. Drake (14) (Salad, 1949) (22 carries) (listed in newspaper accounts as halfback but also attempted 15 passes in game)

HIGHEST AVERAGE PER RUSH
(Minimum 9 Carries)

24.1—Dicky Maegle, Rice (28) vs. Alabama (6) (Cotton, 1954) (11 for 265)
21.6—Bob Jeter, Iowa (38) vs. California (12) (Rose, 1959) (9 for 194)
16.2—Leon Washington, Florida St. (30) vs. West Virginia (18) (Gator, 2005) (12 for 195)
15.7—Tyrone Wheatley, Michigan (38) vs. Washington (31) (Rose, 1993) (15 for 235)

14.2—(D) Gary Anderson, Arkansas (34) vs. Tulane (15) (Hall of Fame, 1980) (11 for 156)
14.1—Mike Holovak, Boston College (21) vs. Alabama (37) (Orange, 1943) (10 for 141)
14.1—Marcus Dupree, Oklahoma (21) vs. Arizona St. (32) (Fiesta, 1983) (17 for 239)
13.5—James Mungro, Syracuse (20) vs. Kentucky (13) (Music City, 1999) (12 for 162)
13.4—Cortlen Johnson, Colorado (62) vs. Boston College (28) (Insight.com, 1999) (15 for 201)
12.6—Ben Barnett, Army (28) vs. Alabama (29) (John Hancock Sun, 1988) (14 for 177)
12.6—Randy Baldwin, Mississippi (42) vs. Air Force (29) (Liberty, 1989) (14 for 177)

THREE RUSHERS, SAME TEAM, GAINING MORE THAN 100 YARDS
366—Tony Dorsett (142), Elliott Walker (123) & Robert Haygood (QB) (101), Pittsburgh (33) vs. Kansas (19) (Sun, 1975)

TWO RUSHERS, SAME TEAM, GAINING MORE THAN 100 YARDS
373—Woody Green (202) & Brent McClanahan (171), Arizona St. (49) vs. Missouri (35) (Fiesta, 1972)
365—(D) George Woodard (185) & Mike Mosley (QB) (180), Texas A&M (28) vs. Southern California (47) (Bluebonnet, 1977)
365—Bob Anderson (254) & Jim Bratten (111), Colorado (47) vs. Alabama (33) (Liberty, 1969)
364—Tommie Frazier (QB) (199) & Lawrence Phillips (165), Nebraska (62) vs. Florida (24) (Fiesta, 1996)
347—Walter Packer (183) & Terry Vitrano (164), Mississippi St. (26) vs. North Carolina (24) (Sun, 1974)
343—(D) Charles White (186) & Dwight Ford (157), Southern California (47) vs. Texas A&M (28) (Bluebonnet, 1977)
330—Floyd Little (216) & Larry Csonka (114), Syracuse (12) vs. Tennessee (18) (Gator, 1966)
304—B.J. Mitchell (178) & Robert Hubbard (126), Nevada (49) vs. UCF (48) (ot) (Hawaii, 2005)
297—Chris Markey (161) & Kahlil Bell (136), UCLA (50) vs. Northwestern (38) (Sun, 2005)
297—Monroe Eley (173) & Bob Thomas (124), Arizona St. (48) vs. North Carolina (26) (Peach, 1970)
296—Leon Washington (195) & Lorenzo Booker (101), Florida St. (30) vs. West Virginia (18) (Gator, 2005)
292—Marion Barber III (187) & Laurence Maroney (105), Minnesota (20) vs. Alabama (16) (Music City, 2004)
292—Kelvin Bryant (148) & Ethan Horton (144), North Carolina (31) vs. Arkansas (27) (Gator, 1981)
291—Billy Sims (164) & J.C. Watts (QB) (127), Oklahoma (24) vs. Florida St. (7) (Orange, 1980)
288—Billy Sims (181) & Darrell Shepard (QB) (107), Oklahoma (40) vs. Houston (14) (Sun, 1981)
281—Stevie Hicks (159) & Bret Meyer (QB) (122), Iowa St. (17) vs. Miami (Ohio) (13), (Independence, 2004)
277—Danta Johnson (148) & Beau Morgan (QB) (129), Air Force (41) vs. Texas Tech (55) (Copper, 1995)
277—Willie Heston (170) & Neil Snow (107), Michigan (49) vs. Stanford (0) (Rose, 1902)
270—Anthony Brown (167) & Major Harris (QB) (103), West Virginia (33) vs. Oklahoma St. (35) (John Hancock Sun, 1987)
257—Sedrick Shaw (135) & Tavian Banks (122), Iowa (38) vs. Washington (18) (Sun, 1995)

MOST RUSHING TOUCHDOWNS
5—Barry Sanders, Oklahoma St. (62) vs. Wyoming (14) (Holiday, 1988) (runs of 33, 2, 67, 1, 10)
5—Neil Snow, Michigan (49) vs. Stanford (0) (Rose, 1902) (five-point scores)
4—Vince Young, Texas (38) vs. Michigan (37) (Rose, 2005) (runs of 20, 60, 10, 23)
4—P.J. Daniels, Georgia Tech (52) vs. Tulsa (10) (Humanitarian, 2004) (runs of 9, 1, 33, 38)
4—Steven Jackson, Oregon St. (55) vs. New Mexico (14) (Las Vegas, 2003) (runs of 3, 11, 6, 1)
4—Chris Perry, Michigan (38) vs. Florida (30) (Outback, 2003) (runs of 4, 1, 7, 12)
4—Domanick Davis, LSU (47) vs. Illinois (34) (Sugar, 2002) (runs of 4, 25, 16, 4)
4—Ron Dayne, Wisconsin (38) vs. UCLA (31) (Rose, 1999) (runs of 54, 7, 10, 22)
4—Byron Hanspard, Texas Tech (55) vs. Air Force (41) (Copper, 1995) (runs of 2, 11, 2, 29)
4—Wasean Tait, Toledo (40) vs. Nevada (37) (ot) (Las Vegas, 1995) (runs of 18, 31, 26, 3)
4—(D) Ron Jackson, Tulsa (28) vs. San Diego St. (17) (Freedom, 1991) (runs of 10, 6, 3, 4)
4—(D) Sheldon Canley, San Jose St. (48) vs. Central Mich. (24) (California, 1990) (runs of 5, 22, 59, 5)
4—(D) James Gray, Texas Tech (49) vs. Duke (21) (All-American, 1989) (runs of 2, 54, 18, 32)
4—Thurman Thomas, Oklahoma St. (35) vs. West Virginia (33) (John Hancock Sun, 1987) (runs of 5, 9, 4, 4)
4—Eric Ball, UCLA (45) vs. Iowa (28) (Rose, 1986) (runs of 30, 40, 6, 32)
4—Terry Miller, Oklahoma St. (49) vs. BYU (21) (Tangerine, 1976) (runs of 3, 78, 6, 1)
4—Sam Cunningham, Southern California (42) vs. Ohio St. (17) (Rose, 1973) (runs of 2, 1, 1, 1)
4—Woody Green, Arizona St. (49) vs. Missouri (35) (Fiesta, 1972) (runs of 2, 12, 17, 21)
4—Charles Cole, Toledo (56) vs. Davidson (33) (Tangerine, 1969) (runs of 1, 11, 16, 1)
4—(D) Gene Shannon, Houston (26) vs. Dayton (21) (Salad, 1952) (runs of 15, 19, 1, 10)

Passing

MOST PASS ATTEMPTS
74—Kyle Orton, Purdue (27) vs. Washington St. (33) (Sun, 2001)
70—Brett Basanez, Northwestern (38) vs. UCLA (50) (Sun, 2005)
70—Byron Leftwich, Marshall (64) vs. East Caro. (61) (2 ot) (GMAC, 2001)
63—(D) Trent Dilfer, Fresno St. (30) vs. Colorado (41) (Aloha, 1993)
62—(D) Steve Clarkson, San Jose St. (25) vs. Toledo (27) (California, 1981)
61—Danny O'Neil, Oregon (20) vs. Penn St. (38) (Rose, 1995)
61—(D) Sean Covey, BYU (16) vs. Virginia (22) (All-American, 1987)
60—Sonny Cumbie, Texas Tech (45) vs. California (31) (Holiday, 2004)
60—Drew Brees, Purdue (25) vs. Georgia (28) (ot) (Outback, 2000)
59—Luke Getsy, Akron (31) vs. Memphis (38) (Motor City, 2005)
59—Hines Ward, Georgia (27) vs. Virginia (34) (Peach, Dec. 30, 1995)
59—Ty Detmer, BYU (39) vs. Penn St. (50) (Holiday, 1989)

MOST PASS COMPLETIONS
43—(D) Steve Clarkson, San Jose St. (25) vs. Toledo (27) (California, 1981)
42—Ty Detmer, BYU (39) vs. Penn St. (50) (Holiday, 1989)
41—(D) B.J. Symons, Texas Tech (38) vs. Navy (14) (Houston, 2003)
41—Byron Leftwich, Marshall (64) vs. East Caro. (61) (2 ot) (GMAC, 2001)
41—Danny O'Neil, Oregon (20) vs. Penn St. (38) (Rose, 1995)
39—Sonny Cumbie, Texas Tech (45) vs. California (31) (Holiday, 2004)
39—Josh Heupel, Oklahoma (25) vs. Mississippi (27) (Independence, 1999)
39—Buster O'Brien, Richmond (49) vs. Ohio (42) (Tangerine, 1968)
38—Brett Basanez, Northwestern (38) vs. UCLA (50) (Sun, 2005)
38—Kyle Orton, Purdue (27) vs. Washington St. (33) (Sun, 2001)
38—Jack Trudeau, Illinois (29) vs. Army (31) (Peach, 1985)
38—(D) Whit Taylor, Vanderbilt (28) vs. Air Force (36) (Hall of Fame, 1982)

MOST CONSECUTIVE PASS COMPLETIONS
19—Mike Bobo, Georgia (33) vs. Wisconsin (6) (Outback, 1998)
16—Philip Rivers, North Carolina St. (56) vs. Kansas (26) (Tangerine, 2003)
11—Colt McCoy, Texas (26) vs. Iowa (24) (Alamo, 2006)
11—Joel Armstrong, Rice (17) vs. Troy (41) (New Orleans, 2006)
10—Riley Skinner, Wake Forest (13) vs. Louisville (24) (Orange, 2007)
10—Paul Smith, Tulsa (13) vs. Utah (25) (Armed Forces, 2006)
10—Danny Wimprine, Memphis (27) vs. North Texas (17) (New Orleans, 2003)
10—Danny Wuerffel, Florida (17) vs. Florida St. (23) (Sugar, Jan. 2, 1995)
10—Rick Neuheisel, UCLA (45) vs. Illinois (9) (Rose, 1984)
9—Chris Leak, Florida (41) vs. Ohio St. (14) (BCS Championship, 2007)
9—(D) Rob Johnson, Southern California (28) vs. Utah (21) (Freedom, 1993)
9—Bill Montgomery, Arkansas (16) vs. Georgia (2) (Sugar, 1969)
9—Glenn Dobbs, Tulsa (7) vs. Tennessee (14) (Sugar, 1943)
8—Erik Ainge, Tennessee (10) vs. Penn St. (20) (Outback, 2007)
8—Taylor Bennett, Georgia Tech (35) vs. West Virginia (38) (Gator, 2007)
8—Colt Brennan, Hawaii (41) vs. Arizona St. (24) (Hawaii, 2006)
8—Billy Roland, Houston (49) vs. Miami (Ohio) (21) (Tangerine, 1962)
8—Bobby Layne, Texas (40) vs. Missouri (27) (Cotton, 1946)
8—Harry Gilmer, Alabama (26) vs. Duke (29) (Sugar, 1945)

MOST NET PASSING YARDS
(Followed by Comp.-Att.-Int.)
576—Byron Leftwich, Marshall (64) vs. East Caro. (61) (2 ot) (GMAC, 2001) (41-70-2)
576—Ty Detmer, BYU (39) vs. Penn St. (50) (Holiday, 1989) (42-59-2)
559—Colt Brennan, Hawaii (41) vs. Arizona St. (24) (Hawaii, 2006) (33-42-1)
531—(D) David Carr, Fresno St. (35) vs. Michigan St. (44) (Silicon Valley, 2001) (35-56-2)
523—(D) Trent Dilfer, Fresno St. (30) vs. Colorado (41) (Aloha, 1993) (37-63-1)
520—Sonny Cumbie, Texas Tech (45) vs. California (31) (Holiday, 2004) (39-60-0)
497—(D) B.J. Symons, Texas Tech (38) vs. Navy (14) (Houston, 2003) (41-53-1)
476—Drew Bledsoe, Washington St. (31) vs. Utah (28) (Copper, 1992) (30-46-1)
475—Philip Rivers, North Carolina St. (56) vs. Kansas (26) (Tangerine, 2003) (37-45-0)
475—Timmy Chang, Hawaii (54) vs. Houston (48) (3 ot) (Hawaii, 2003) (26-42-1)
473—Major Applewhite, Texas (47) vs. Washington (43) (Holiday, 2001) (37-55-3)
467—Rudy Carpenter, Arizona St. (45) vs. Rutgers (40) (Insight, 2005) (23-35-0)
467—(D) Steve Clarkson, San Jose St. (25) vs. Toledo (27) (California, 1981) (43-62-5)
461—(D) Chuck Long, Iowa (55) vs. Texas (17) (Freedom, 1984) (29-39-0)
456—(D) Akili Smith, Oregon (43) vs. Colorado (51) (Aloha, 1998) (24-46-2)
456—Danny O'Neil, Oregon (20) vs. Penn St. (38) (Rose, 1995) (41-61-2)
455—Luke Getsy, Akron (31) vs. Memphis (38) (Motor City, 2005) (34-59-0)
454—John Walsh, BYU (31) vs. Oklahoma (6) (Copper, 1994) (31-45-0)
452—(D) Whit Taylor, Vanderbilt (28) vs. Air Force (36) (Hall of Fame, 1982) (38-51-3)
451—Browning Nagle, Louisville (34) vs. Alabama (7) (Fiesta, 1991) (20-33-1)
447—Buster O'Brien, Richmond (49) vs. Ohio (42) (Tangerine, 1968) (39-58-2)

MOST NET PASSING YARDS, ONE QUARTER
223—Browning Nagle, Louisville (34) vs. Alabama (7) (Fiesta, 1991) (1st, 9 of 16)
202—Colt Brennan, Hawaii (41) vs. Arizona St. (24) (Hawaii, 2006) (3rd, 10 of 11)
202—(D) Bret Stafford, Texas (32) vs. Pittsburgh (27) (Bluebonnet, 1987) (1st)

MOST TOUCHDOWN PASSES THROWN
6—(D) Chuck Long, Iowa (55) vs. Texas (17) (Freedom, 1984) (6, 11, 33, 49, 4, 15 yards)
5—Colt Brennan, Hawaii (41) vs. Arizona St. (24) (Hawaii, 2006) (38, 7, 36, 21, 79 yards)
5—Bruce Gradkowski, Toledo (45) vs. UTEP (13) (GMAC, 2005) (10, 33, 31, 22, 13 yards)

5—Matt Leinart, Southern California (55) vs. Oklahoma (19) (Orange, 2005) (33, 54, 5, 33, 4 yards)
5—Omar Jacobs, Bowling Green (52) vs. Memphis (35) (GMAC, 2004) (18, 36, 31, 17, 13 yards)
5—Paul Pinegar, Fresno St. (37) vs. Virginia (34) (ot) (MPC Computers, 2004) (13, 22, 22, 3, 25 yards)
5—Philip Rivers, North Carolina St. (56) vs. Kansas (26) (Tangerine, 2003) (45, 14, 3, 40, 21 yards)
5—Timmy Chang, Hawaii (54) vs. Houston (48) (3 ot) (Hawaii, 2003) (48, 7, 4, 11, 18 yards)
5—Brad Lewis, West Virginia (49) vs. Mississippi (38) (Music City, 2000) (40, 11, 35, 60, 10 yards)
5—Peter Tom Willis, Florida St. (41) vs. Nebraska (17) (Fiesta, 1990)
5—Steve Tensi, Florida St. (36) vs. Oklahoma (19) (Gator, Jan. 2, 1965)

MOST PASSES HAD INTERCEPTED
(Followed by Comp.-Att.-Int.)
6—Bruce Lee, Arizona (10) vs. Auburn (34) (Sun, 1968) (6-24-6)
5—Joel Armstrong, Rice (17) vs. Troy (41) (New Orleans, 2006) (34-54-5)
5—Wade Hill, Arkansas (15) vs. Georgia (24) (Independence, 1991) (12-31-5)
5—Kevin Murray, Texas A&M (12) vs. Ohio St. (28) (Cotton, 1987) (12-31-5)
5—Vinny Testaverde, Miami (Fla.) (10) vs. Penn St. (14) (Fiesta, 1987) (26-50-5)
5—Jeff Wickersham, LSU (10) vs. Nebraska (28) (Sugar, 1985) (20-38-5)
5—(D) Steve Clarkson, San Jose St. (25) vs. Toledo (27) (California, 1981) (43-62-5)
5—Terry McMillan, Missouri (3) vs. Penn St. (10) (Orange, 1970) (6-28-5)
5—Paul Gilbert, Georgia (6) vs. Nebraska (45) (Sun, 1969) (10-30-5)

HIGHEST COMPLETION PERCENTAGE
(Minimum 10 Attempts) (Followed by Comp.-Att.-Int.)
.929—Mike Bobo, Georgia (33) vs. Wisconsin (6) (Outback, 1998) (26-28-0)
.917—Bobby Layne, Texas (40) vs. Missouri (27) (Cotton, 1946) (11-12-0)
.900—Ken Ploen, Iowa (35) vs. Oregon St. (19) (Rose, 1957) (9-10-0)
.846—Tom Sorley, Nebraska (21) vs. North Carolina (17) (Liberty, 1977) (11-13-0)
.833—Mike Gundy, Oklahoma St. (62) vs. Wyoming (14) (Holiday, 1988) (20-24-0)
.833—Richard Todd, Alabama (13) vs. Penn St. (6) (Sugar, 1975) (10-12-0)
.822—Philip Rivers, North Carolina St. (56) vs. Kansas (26) (Tangerine, 2003) (37-45-0)
.818—Mark Farris, Texas A&M (41) vs. Mississippi St. (43) (ot) (Independence, 2000) (9-11-1)
.818—Bucky Richardson, Texas A&M (65) vs. BYU (14) (Holiday, 1990) (9-11-0)
.806—Cale Gundy, Oklahoma (48) vs. Virginia (14) (Gator, Dec. 29, 1991) (25-31-0)

MOST YARDS PER PASS ATTEMPT
(Minimum 10 Attempts)
21.3—(D) Chris McCoy, Navy (42) vs. California (38) (Aloha, 1996) (13 for 277)
19.4—Tony Rice, Notre Dame (34) vs. West Virginia (21) (Fiesta, 1989) (11 for 213)
18.7—Frank Sinkwich, Georgia (40) vs. TCU (26) (Orange, 1942) (13 for 243)
18.5—Bucky Richardson, Texas A&M (65) vs. BYU (14) (Holiday, 1990) (11 for 203)
17.3—Don Rumley, New Mexico (34) vs. Denver (24) (Sun, 1946) (12 for 207)
17.1—Chad Pennington, Marshall (48) vs. Louisville (29) (Motor City, 1998) (24 for 411)
16.7—(D) Blane Morgan, Air Force (45) vs. Washington (25) (Oahu, 1998) (16 for 267)
16.4—(D) Rob Hertel, Southern California (47) vs. Texas A&M (28) (Bluebonnet, 1977) (15 for 246)
15.4—James Street, Texas (36) vs. Tennessee (13) (Cotton, 1969) (13 for 200)
15.4—Tee Martin, Tennessee (23) vs. Florida St. (16) (Fiesta, 1999) (11 for 278)

MOST YARDS PER PASS COMPLETION
(Minimum 7 Completions)
30.8—(D) Chris McCoy, Navy (42) vs. California (38) (Aloha, 1996) (9 for 277)
30.4—Duke Carlisle, Texas (28) vs. Navy (6) (Cotton, 1964) (7 for 213)
30.4—Tony Rice, Notre Dame (34) vs. West Virginia (21) (Fiesta, 1989) (7 for 213)
28.6—James Street, Texas (36) vs. Tennessee (13) (Cotton, 1969) (7 for 200)
27.2—Chris Rix, Florida St. (30) vs. Virginia Tech (17) (Gator, 2002) (12 for 326)
27.0—Frank Sinkwich, Georgia (40) vs. TCU (26) (Orange, 1942) (9 for 243)

Receiving

MOST PASS RECEPTIONS
20—(D) Norman Jordan, Vanderbilt (28) vs. Air Force (36) (Hall of Fame, 1982) (173 yards)
20—Walker Gillette, Richmond (49) vs. Ohio (42) (Tangerine, 1968) (242 yards)
18—(D) Gerald Willhite, San Jose St. (25) vs. Toledo (27) (California, 1981) (124 yards)
16—Travis LaTendresse, Utah (38) vs. Georgia Tech (10) (Emerald, 2005) (214 yards)
16—Samie Parker, Oregon (30) vs. Minnesota (31) (Sun, 2003) (200 yards)
15—Paris Warren, Utah (35) vs. Pittsburgh (7) (Fiesta, 2005) (198 yards)
15—Denero Marriott, Marshall (64) vs. East Caro. (61) (2 ot) (GMAC, 2001) (234 yards)
15—(D) Stephone Paige, Fresno St. (29) vs. Bowling Green (28) (California, 1982) (246 yards)
14—Jason Rivers, Hawaii (41) vs. Arizona St. (24) (Hawaii, 2006) (308 yards)
14—Josh Reed, LSU (47) vs. Illinois (34) (Sugar, 2002) (239 yards)
14—Alex Van Dyke, Nevada (37) vs. Toledo (40) (ot) (Las Vegas, 1995) (176 yards)
14—J.J. Stokes, UCLA (16) vs. Wisconsin (21) (Rose, 1994) (176 yards)
14—Ron Sellers, Florida St. (17) vs. Penn St. (17) (Gator, 1967) (145 yards)

MOST PASS RECEIVING YARDS
308—Jason Rivers, Hawaii (41) vs. Arizona St. (24) (Hawaii, 2006) (14 catches)
299—(D) Rodney Wright, Fresno St. (35) vs. Michigan St. (44) (Silicon Valley, 2001) (13 catches)
270—(D) Charles Rogers, Michigan St. (44) vs. Fresno St. (35) (Silicon Valley, 2001) (10 catches)
252—Andre Rison, Michigan St. (27) vs. Georgia (34) (Gator, Jan. 1, 1989) (9 catches)
246—(D) Stephone Paige, Fresno St. (29) vs. Bowling Green (28) (California, 1982) (15 catches)
242—(D) Tony Jones, Texas (32) vs. Pittsburgh (27) (Bluebonnet, 1987) (8 catches)
242—Walker Gillette, Richmond (49) vs. Ohio (42) (Tangerine, 1968) (20 catches)
239—Josh Reed, LSU (47) vs. Illinois (34) (Sugar, 2002) (14 catches)
234—Denero Marriott, Marshall (64) vs. East Caro. (61) (2 ot) (GMAC, 2001) (15 catches)
223—Rashaun Woods, Oklahoma St. (28) vs. Mississippi (31) (Cotton, 2004) (11 catches)
222—Keyshawn Johnson, Southern California (55) vs. Texas Tech (14) (Cotton, 1995) (8 catches)
216—Keyshawn Johnson, Southern California (41) vs. Northwestern (32) (Rose, 1996) (12 catches)
214—Travis LaTendresse, Utah (38) vs. Georgia Tech (10) (Emerald, 2005) (16 catches)
212—Phillip Bobo, Washington St. (31) vs. Utah (28) (Copper, 1992) (7 catches)
210—Brandon Marshall, UCF (48) vs. Nevada (49) (ot) (Hawaii, 2005) (11 catches)
206—Darnell McDonald, Kansas St. (35) vs. Syracuse (18) (Fiesta, 1997) (7 catches)
205—Dwayne Jarrett, Southern California (32) vs. Michigan (18) (Rose, 2007) (11 catches)
201—(D) Bob McChesney, Hardin-Simmons (49) vs. Wichita St. (12) (Camellia, 1948) (8 catches)
200—Samie Parker, Oregon (30) vs. Minnesota (31) (Sun, 2003) (16 catches)

HIGHEST AVERAGE PER RECEPTION
(Minimum 3 Receptions)
52.3—(D) Jason Anderson, Wake Forest (38) vs. Oregon (17) (Seattle, 2002) (3 for 157)
52.3—Phil Harris, Texas (28) vs. Navy (6) (Cotton, 1964) (3 for 157)
49.8—Peerless Price, Tennessee (23) vs. Florida St. (16) (Fiesta, 1999) (4 for 199)
48.8—Javon Walker, Florida St. (30) vs. Virginia Tech (17) (Gator, 2002) (4 for 195)
42.0—Josh Morgan, Virginia Tech (13) vs. Auburn (16) (Sugar, 2005) (3 for 126)
39.7—Ike Hilliard, Florida (17) vs. Florida St. (23) (Sugar, Jan. 2, 1995) (3 for 119)
38.8—(D) Cory Schemm, Navy (42) vs. California (38) (Aloha, 1996) (5 for 194)
38.7—(D) Anthony Hancock, Tennessee (22) vs. Purdue (27) (Bluebonnet, 1979) (3 for 116)
36.4—Rob Turner, Indiana (34) vs. South Carolina (10) (Liberty, 1988) (5 for 182)
36.3—Clarence Cannon, Boston College (31) vs. Virginia (13) (Carquest, 1994) (3 for 109)

MOST TOUCHDOWNS RECEIVING
4—Travis LaTendresse, Utah (38) vs. Georgia Tech (10) (Emerald, 2005) (16 catches)
4—Fred Biletnikoff, Florida St. (36) vs. Oklahoma (19) (Gator, Jan. 2, 1965) (13 catches)
4—(D) Bob McChesney, Hardin-Simmons (49) vs. Wichita St. (12) (Camellia, 1948) (8 catches)
3—Brandon Marshall, UCF (48) vs. Nevada (49) (ot) (Hawaii, 2005) (11 catches)
3—Steve Smith, Southern California (55) vs. Oklahoma (19) (Orange, 2005) (7 catches)
3—Braylon Edwards, Michigan (37) vs. Texas (38) (Rose, 2005) (10 catches)
3—Jason Rivers, Hawaii (54) vs. Houston (48) (3 ot) (Hawaii, 2003) (7 catches)
3—J.R. Russell, Louisville (28) vs. Miami (Ohio) (49) (GMAC, 2003) (7 catches)
3—Plaxico Burress, Michigan St. (37) vs. Florida (34) (Florida Citrus, 2000) (13 catches)
3—Travis Taylor, Florida (34) vs. Michigan St. (37) (Florida Citrus, 2000) (11 catches)
3—David Terrell, Michigan (35) vs. Alabama (34) (ot) (Orange, 2000) (10 catches)
3—Darnell McDonald, Kansas St. (35) vs. Syracuse (18) (Fiesta, 1997) (7 catches)
3—Ike Hilliard, Florida (52) vs. Florida St. (20) (Sugar, 1997) (7 catches)
3—Keyshawn Johnson, Southern California (55) vs. Texas Tech (14) (Cotton, 1995) (8 catches)
3—(D) Ken Ealy, Central Mich. (24) vs. San Jose St. (48) (California, 1990) (7 catches)
3—Wendell Davis, LSU (30) vs. South Carolina (13) (Gator, 1987) (9 catches)
3—(D) Anthony Allen, Washington (21) vs. Maryland (20) (Aloha, 1982) (8 catches)
3—(D) Norman Jordan, Vanderbilt (28) vs. Air Force (36) (Hall of Fame, 1982) (20 catches)
3—(D) Dwayne Dixon, Florida (24) vs. Arkansas (28) (Bluebonnet, 1982) (8 catches)
3—(D) Mervyn Fernandez, San Jose St. (25) vs. Toledo (27) (California, 1981) (9 catches)
3—Clay Brown, BYU (46) vs. SMU (45) (Holiday, 1980) (5 catches)
3—Elliott Walker, Pittsburgh (34) vs. Clemson (3) (Gator, 1977) (6 catches)
3—Rhett Dawson, Florida St. (38) vs. Arizona St. (45) (Fiesta, 1971) (8 catches)
3—George Hannen, Davidson (33) vs. Toledo (56) (Tangerine, 1969)
3—Todd Snyder, Richmond (49) vs. Ohio (42) (Tangerine, 1968)

Scoring

MOST POINTS SCORED
30—Reggie Campbell, Navy (51) vs. Colorado St. (30) (Poinsettia, 2005) (5 TDs)
30—Steven Jackson, Oregon St. (55) vs. New Mexico (14) (Las Vegas, 2003) (5 TDs)
30—(D) Sheldon Canley, San Jose St. (48) vs. Central Mich. (24) (California, 1990) (5 TDs)
30—Barry Sanders, Oklahoma St. (62) vs. Wyoming (14) (Holiday, 1988) (5 TDs)
28—Bobby Layne, Texas (40) vs. Missouri (27) (Cotton, 1946) (4 TDs, 4 PATs)
25—Neil Snow, Michigan (49) vs. Stanford (0) (Rose, 1902) (5 five-point TDs)
24—Travis LaTendresse, Utah (38) vs. Georgia Tech (10) (Emerald, 2005) (4 TDs)
24—Vince Young, Texas (38) vs. Michigan (37) (Rose, 2005) (4 TDs)

24—P.J. Daniels, Georgia Tech (52) vs. Tulsa (10) (Humanitarian, 2004) (4 TDs)
24—Chris Perry, Michigan (38) vs. Florida (30) (Outback, 2003) (4 TDs)
24—Wali Lundy, Virginia (48) vs. West Virginia (22) (Continental Tire, 2002) (4 TDs)
24—Domanick Davis, LSU (47) vs. Illinois (34) (Sugar, 2002) (4 TDs)
24—Ron Dayne, Wisconsin (38) vs. UCLA (31) (Rose, 1999) (4 TDs)
24—Byron Hanspard, Texas Tech (55) vs. Air Force (41) (Copper, 1995) (4 TDs)
24—Wasean Tait, Toledo (40) vs. Nevada (37) (ot) (Las Vegas, 1995) (4 TDs)
24—(D) Ron Jackson, Tulsa (28) vs. San Diego St. (17) (Freedom, 1991) (4 TDs)
24—(D) James Gray, Texas Tech (49) vs. Duke (21) (All-American, 1989) (4 TDs)
24—Thurman Thomas, Oklahoma St. (35) vs. West Virginia (33) (John Hancock Sun, 1987) (4 TDs)
24—Eric Ball, UCLA (45) vs. Iowa (28) (Rose, 1986) (4 TDs)
24—Terry Miller, Oklahoma St. (49) vs. BYU (21) (Tangerine, 1976) (4 TDs)
24—Sam Cunningham, Southern California (42) vs. Ohio St. (17) (Rose, 1973) (4 TDs)
24—Johnny Rodgers, Nebraska (40) vs. Notre Dame (6) (Orange, 1973) (4 TDs)
24—Woody Green, Arizona St. (49) vs. Missouri (35) (Fiesta, 1972) (4 TDs)
24—Charles Cole, Toledo (56) vs. Davidson (33) (Tangerine, 1969) (4 TDs)
24—Fred Biletnikoff, Florida St. (36) vs. Oklahoma (19) (Gator, Jan. 2, 1965) (4 TDs)
24—Joe Lopasky, Houston (49) vs. Miami (Ohio) (21) (Tangerine, 1962) (4 TDs)
24—(D) Gene Shannon, Houston (26) vs. Dayton (21) (Salad, 1952) (4 TDs)
24—(D) Bob McChesney, Hardin-Simmons (49) vs. Wichita St. (12) (Camellia, 1948) (4 TDs)

MOST POINTS RESPONSIBLE FOR
(TDs Scored & Passed For, Extra Points, and FGs)

40—Bobby Layne, Texas (40) vs. Missouri (27) (Cotton, 1946) (18 rush, 12 pass, 6 receiving and 4 PATs)
36—(D) Chuck Long, Iowa (55) vs. Texas (17) (Freedom, 1984) (36 pass)
30—Colt Brennan, Hawaii (41) vs. Arizona St. (24) (Hawaii, 2006) (30 pass)
30—Omar Haugabook, Troy (41) vs. Rice (17) (New Orleans, 2006) (24 pass, 6 rush)
30—Matt Moore, Oregon St. (39) vs. Missouri (38) (Sun, 2006) (24 pass, 6 rush)
30—Reggie Campbell, Navy (51) vs. Colorado St. (30) (Poinsettia, 2005) (18 rush, 12 receiving)
30—Matt Leinart, Southern California (55) vs. Oklahoma (19) (Orange, 2005) (30 pass)
30—Vince Young, Texas (38) vs. Michigan (37) (Rose, 2005) (24 rush, 6 pass)
30—Omar Jacobs, Bowling Green (52) vs. Memphis (35) (GMAC, 2004) (30 pass)
30—Timmy Chang, Hawaii (59) vs. UAB (40) (Hawaii, 2004) (24 pass, 6 rush)
30—Paul Pinegar, Fresno St. (37) vs. Virginia (34) (ot) (MPC Computers, 2004) (30 pass)
30—Philip Rivers, North Carolina St. (56) vs. Kansas (26) (Tangerine, 2003) (30 pass)
30—Timmy Chang, Hawaii (54) vs. Houston (48) (3 ot) (Hawaii, 2003) (30 pass)
30—Steven Jackson, Oregon St. (55) vs. New Mexico (14) (Las Vegas, 2003) (24 rush, 6 receiving)
30—Byron Leftwich, Marshall (64) vs. East Caro. (61) (2 ot) (GMAC, 2001) (24 pass, 6 rush)
30—Casey Clausen, Tennessee (45) vs. Michigan (17) (Florida Citrus, 2002) (18 pass, 12 rush)
30—Michael Bishop, Kansas St. (35) vs. Syracuse (18) (Fiesta, 1997) (24 pass, 6 rush)
30—Jeff Blake, East Caro. (37) vs. North Carolina St. (34) (Peach, 1992) (24 pass, 6 rush)
30—(D) Sheldon Canley, San Jose St. (48) vs. Central Mich. (24) (California, 1990) (24 rush, 6 receiving)
30—Peter Tom Willis, Florida St. (41) vs. Nebraska (17) (Fiesta, 1990) (30 pass)
30—Barry Sanders, Oklahoma St. (62) vs. Wyoming (14) (Holiday, 1988) (30 rush)
30—Johnny Rodgers, Nebraska (40) vs. Notre Dame (6) (Orange, 1973) (18 rush, 6 pass, 6 receiving)
30—Steve Tensi, Florida St. (36) vs. Oklahoma (19) (Gator, Jan. 2, 1965) (30 pass)

MOST TOUCHDOWNS

5—Reggie Campbell, Navy (51) vs. Colorado St. (30) (Poinsettia, 2005) (3 rush, 2 catch)
5—Steven Jackson, Oregon St. (55) vs. New Mexico (14) (Las Vegas, 2003) (4 rush, 1 catch)
5—(D) Sheldon Canley, San Jose St. (48) vs. Central Mich. (24) (California, 1990) (4 rush, 1 catch)
5—Barry Sanders, Oklahoma St. (62) vs. Wyoming (14) (Holiday, 1988) (5 rush)
5—Neil Snow, Michigan (49) vs. Stanford (0) (Rose, 1902) (5 rush five-point TDs)
4—Travis LaTendresse, Utah (38) vs. Georgia Tech (10) (Emerald, 2005) (4 catch)
4—Vince Young, Texas (38) vs. Michigan (37) (Rose, 2005) (4 rush)
4—P.J. Daniels, Georgia Tech (52) vs. Tulsa (10) (Humanitarian, 2004) (4 rush)
4—Chris Perry, Michigan (38) vs. Florida (30) (Outback, 2003) (4 rush)
4—Wali Lundy, Virginia (48) vs. West Virginia (22) (Continental Tire, 2002) (2 rush, 2 catch)
4—Domanick Davis, LSU (47) vs. Illinois (34) (Sugar, 2002) (4 rush)
4—Ron Dayne, Wisconsin (38) vs. UCLA (31) (Rose, 1999) (4 rush)
4—Byron Hanspard, Texas Tech (55) vs. Air Force (41) (Copper, 1995) (4 rush)
4—Wasean Tait, Toledo (40) vs. Nevada (37) (ot) (Las Vegas, 1995) (4 rush)
4—(D) Ron Jackson, Tulsa (28) vs. San Diego St. (17) (Freedom, 1991) (4 rush)
4—(D) James Gray, Texas Tech (49) vs. Duke (21) (All-American, 1989) (4 rush)
4—Thurman Thomas, Oklahoma St. (35) vs. West Virginia (33) (John Hancock Sun, 1987) (4 rush)
4—Eric Ball, UCLA (45) vs. Iowa (28) (Rose, 1986) (4 rush)
4—Terry Miller, Oklahoma St. (49) vs. BYU (21) (Tangerine, 1976) (4 rush)
4—Sam Cunningham, Southern California (42) vs. Ohio St. (17) (Rose, 1973) (4 rush)
4—Johnny Rodgers, Nebraska (40) vs. Notre Dame (6) (Orange, 1973) (3 rush, 1 catch)
4—Woody Green, Arizona St. (49) vs. Missouri (35) (Fiesta, 1972) (4 rush)
4—Charles Cole, Toledo (56) vs. Davidson (33) (Tangerine, 1969) (4 rush)
4—Fred Biletnikoff, Florida St. (36) vs. Oklahoma (19) (Gator, Jan. 2, 1965) (4 catch)
4—Joe Lopasky, Houston (49) vs. Miami (Ohio) (21) (Tangerine, 1962) (2 rush, 1 catch, 1 punt return)
4—(D) Gene Shannon, Houston (26) vs. Dayton (21) (Salad, 1952) (4 rush)
4—(D) Bob McChesney, Hardin-Simmons (49) vs. Wichita St. (12) (Camellia, 1948) (4 catch)
4—Bobby Layne, Texas (40) vs. Missouri (27) (Cotton, 1946) (3 rush, 1 catch)
4—(D) Alvin McMillin, Centre (63) vs. TCU (7) (Fort Worth Classic, 1921) (4 rush)

MOST TWO-POINT CONVERSIONS

2—Ernie Davis, Syracuse (23) vs. Texas (14) (Cotton, 1960) (2 pass receptions)

Kicking

MOST FIELD GOALS ATTEMPTED

6—(D) Mason Crosby, Colorado (33) vs. UTEP (28) (Houston, 2004) (4 made)
6—Kyle Bryant, Texas A&M (22) vs. Michigan (20) (Alamo, 1995) (5 made)
6—Jess Atkinson, Maryland (23) vs. Tennessee (30) (Florida Citrus, 1983) (5 made)
5—Kevin Kelly, Penn St. (20) vs. Tennessee (10) (Gator, 2007) (2 made)
5—Jeremy Ito, Rutgers (37) vs. Kansas St. (10) (Texas, 2006) (3 made)
5—Jesse Ainsworth, Arizona St. (27) vs. Purdue (23) (Sun, 2004) (2 made)
5—Matt Nuzie, Connecticut (39) vs. Toledo (10) (Motor City, 2004) (4 made)
5—Billy Bennett, Georgia (26) vs. Florida St. (13) (Sugar, 2003) (4 made)
5—Dan Nystrom, Minnesota (29) vs. Arkansas (14) (Music City, 2002) (5 made)
5—Nate Kaeding, Iowa (19) vs. Texas Tech (16) (Alamo, 2001) (4 made)
5—Travis Forney, Penn St. (26) vs. Kentucky (14) (Outback, 1999) (4 made)
5—Chad Holcomb, East Caro. (19) vs. Stanford (13) (Liberty, 1995) (4 made)
5—Dan Mowrey, Florida St. (23) vs. Florida (17) (Sugar, Jan. 2, 1995) (3 made)
5—Tim Rogers, Mississippi St. (24) vs. North Carolina St. (28) (Peach, Jan. 1, 1995) (5 made)
5—Scott Bentley, Florida St. (18) vs. Nebraska (16) (Orange, 1994) (4 made)
5—Arden Czyzewski, Florida (28) vs. Notre Dame (39) (Sugar, 1992) (5 made)
5—George Hunt, Tennessee (34) vs. Air Force (13) (Sugar, 1971) (2 made)
5—Bob White, Arkansas (16) vs. Georgia (2) (Sugar, 1969) (3 made)
5—Tim Davis, Alabama (12) vs. Mississippi (7) (Sugar, 1964) (4 made)

MOST FIELD GOALS MADE

5—Dan Nystrom, Minnesota (29) vs. Arkansas (14) (Music City, 2002) (24, 45, 21, 22, 29 yards)
5—Kyle Bryant, Texas A&M (22) vs. Michigan (20) (Alamo, 1995) (27, 49, 47, 31, 37 yards)
5—Tim Rogers, Mississippi St. (24) vs. North Carolina St. (28) (Peach, Jan. 1, 1995) (37, 21, 29, 36, 30 yards)
5—Arden Czyzewski, Florida (28) vs. Notre Dame (39) (Sugar, 1992) (26, 24, 36, 37, 24 yards)
5—Jess Atkinson, Maryland (23) vs. Tennessee (30) (Florida Citrus, 1983) (18, 48, 31, 22, 26 yards)
4—Louis Sakoda, Utah (25) vs. Tulsa (13) (Armed Forces, 2006) (45, 39, 41, 34 yards)
4—Brett Jaekle, Nevada (20) vs. Miami (Fla.) (21) (MPC Computers, 2006) (33, 31, 44, 40 yards)
4—Jeremy Ito, Rutgers (40) vs. Arizona St. (45) (Insight, 2005) (25, 23, 52, 48 yards)
4—(D) Mason Crosby, Colorado (33) vs. UTEP (28) (Houston, 2004) (26, 54, 37, 20 yards)
4—Matt Nuzie, Connecticut (39) vs. Toledo (10) (Motor City, 2004) (35, 37, 25, 36 yards)
4—Mike Nugent, Ohio St. (33) vs. Oklahoma St. (7) (Alamo, 2004) (37, 35, 41, 36 yards)
4—Billy Bennett, Georgia (26) vs. Florida St. (13) (Sugar, 2003) (23, 42, 25, 35 yards)
4—(D) Luke Phillips, Oklahoma St. (33) vs. Southern Miss. (23) (Houston, 2002) (46, 52, 29, 23 yards)
4—Drew Dunning, Washington St. (33) vs. Purdue (27) (Sun, 2001) (47, 34, 30, 37 yards)
4—Nate Kaeding, Iowa (19) vs. Texas Tech (16) (Alamo, 2001) (36, 31, 46, 47 yards)
4—Kevin Miller, East Caro. (61) vs. Marshall (64) (2 ot) (GMAC, 2001) (25, 22, 32, 37 yards)
4—Travis Forney, Penn St. (26) vs. Kentucky (14) (Outback, 1999) (43, 26, 21, 25 yards)
4—Chad Holcomb, East Caro. (19) vs. Stanford (13) (Liberty, 1995) (46, 26, 41, 34 yards)
4—Kanon Parkman, Georgia (27) vs. Virginia (34) (Peach, Dec. 30, 1995) (36, 37, 20, 42 yards)
4—Scott Bentley, Florida St. (18) vs. Nebraska (16) (Orange, 1994) (34, 25, 39, 22 yards)
4—Tim Lashar, Oklahoma (25) vs. Penn St. (10) (Orange, 1986) (26, 31, 21, 22 yards)
4—(D) Todd Gregoire, Wisconsin (19) vs. Kentucky (20) (Hall of Fame, 1984) (40, 27, 20, 40 yards)
4—David Hardy, Texas A&M (33) vs. Oklahoma St. (16) (Independence, 1981) (33, 32, 50, 18 yards)
4—Paul Woodside, West Virginia (26) vs. Florida (6) (Peach, Dec. 31, 1981) (35, 42, 49, 24 yards)
4—Bob Lucchesi, Missouri (19) vs. Southern Miss. (17) (Tangerine, 1981) (45, 41, 30, 28 yards)
4—Dale Castro, Maryland (20) vs. Florida (35) (Tangerine, 1980) (35, 27, 27, 43 yards)
4—Paul Rogers, Nebraska (45) vs. Georgia (6) (Sun, 1969) (50, 32, 42, 37 yards, all in 1st quarter)
4—Tim Davis, Alabama (12) vs. Mississippi (7) (Sugar, 1964) (31, 46, 22, 48 yards)

MOST EXTRA-POINT KICK ATTEMPTS
9—Josh Brown, Nebraska (66) vs. Northwestern (17) (Alamo, 2000) (9 made)
9—Neil Rackers, Illinois (63) vs. Virginia (21) (Micronpc.com, 1999) (9 made)
9—Layne Talbot, Texas A&M (65) vs. BYU (14) (Holiday, 1990) (9 made)
9—Bobby Luna, Alabama (61) vs. Syracuse (6) (Orange, 1953) (7 made)
9—(D) James Weaver, Centre (63) vs. TCU (7) (Fort Worth Classic, 1921) (9 made)
8—Justin Ayat, Hawaii (59) vs. UAB (40) (Hawaii, 2004) (8 made)
8—Adam Kiker, North Carolina St. (56) vs. Kansas (26) (Tangerine, 2003) (8 made)
8—Jeff Chandler, Florida (56) vs. Maryland (23) (Orange, 2002) (8 made)
8—Jeremy Aldrich, Colorado (62) vs. Boston College (28) (Insight.com, 1999) (8 made)
8—Cary Blanchard, Oklahoma St. (62) vs. Wyoming (14) (Holiday, 1988) (8 made)
8—Ken Crots, Toledo (56) vs. Davidson (33) (Tangerine, 1969) (8 made)

MOST EXTRA-POINT KICKS MADE
9—Josh Brown, Nebraska (66) vs. Northwestern (17) (Alamo, 2000) (9 attempts)
9—Neil Rackers, Illinois (63) vs. Virginia (21) (Micronpc.com, 1999) (9 attempts)
9—Layne Talbot, Texas A&M (65) vs. BYU (14) (Holiday, 1990) (9 attempts)
9—(D) James Weaver, Centre (63) vs. TCU (7) (Fort Worth Classic, 1921) (9 attempts)
8—Justin Ayat, Hawaii (59) vs. UAB (40) (Hawaii, 2004) (8 attempts)
8—Adam Kiker, North Carolina St. (56) vs. Kansas (26) (Tangerine, 2003) (8 attempts)
8—Jeff Chandler, Florida (56) vs. Maryland (23) (Orange, 2002) (8 attempts)
8—Jeremy Aldrich, Colorado (62) vs. Boston College (28) (Insight.com, 1999) (8 attempts)
8—Cary Blanchard, Oklahoma St. (62) vs. Wyoming (14) (Holiday, 1988) (8 attempts)
8—Ken Crots, Toledo (56) vs. Davidson (33) (Tangerine, 1969) (8 attempts)

MOST POINTS BY A KICKER
19—Kevin Miller, East Caro. (61) vs. Marshall (64) (2 ot) (GMAC, 2001) (4 FGs, 7 PATs)
17—Dan Nystrom, Minnesota (29) vs. Arkansas (14) (Music City, 2002) (5 FGs, 2 PATs)
16—Jeremy Ito, Rutgers (40) vs. Arizona St. (45) (Insight, 2005) (4 FGs, 4 PATs)
16—Kyle Bryant, Texas A&M (22) vs. Michigan (20) (Alamo, 1995) (5 FGs, 1 PAT)
16—Tim Rogers, Mississippi St. (24) vs. North Carolina St. (28) (Peach, Jan. 1, 1995) (5 FGs, 1 PAT)
16—Arden Czyzewski, Florida (28) vs. Notre Dame (39) (Sugar, 1992) (5 FGs, 1 PAT)
15—(D) Mason Crosby, Colorado (33) vs. UTEP (28) (Houston, 2004) (4 FGs, 3 PATs)
15—Mike Nugent, Ohio St. (33) vs. Oklahoma St. (7) (Alamo, 2004) (4 FGs, 3 PATs)
15—Matt Nuzie, Connecticut (39) vs. Toledo (10) (Motor City, 2004) (4 FGs, 3 PATs)
15—Sandro Sciortino, Boston College (51) vs. Toledo (25) (Motor City, 2002) (3 FGs, 6 PATs)
15—(D) Luke Phillips, Oklahoma St. (33) vs. Southern Miss. (23) (Houston, 2002) (4 FGs, 3 PATs)
15—Drew Dunning, Washington St. (33) vs. Purdue (27) (Sun, 2001) (4 FGs, 3 PATs)
15—(D) Jeremy Aldrich, Colorado (51) vs. Oregon (43) (Aloha, 1998) (3 FGs, 6 PATs)
15—Jess Atkinson, Maryland (23) vs. Tennessee (30) (Florida Citrus, 1983) (5 FGs)
15—David Hardy, Texas A&M (33) vs. Oklahoma St. (16) (Independence, 1981) (4 FGs, 3 PATs)
15—Paul Rogers, Nebraska (45) vs. Georgia (6) (John Hancock, 1969) (4 FGs, 3 PATs)
14—Gary Cismesia, Florida St. (44) vs. UCLA (27) (Emerald, 2006) (3 FGs, 5 PATs)
14—Billy Bennett, Georgia (26) vs. Florida St. (13) (Sugar, 2003) (4 FGs, 2 PATs)
14—Jeremy Aldrich, Colorado (62) vs. Boston College (28) (Insight.com, 1999) (2 FGs, 8 PATs)
14—Cary Blanchard, Oklahoma St. (62) vs. Wyoming (14) (Holiday, 1988) (2 FGs, 8 PATs)
14—Paul Woodside, West Virginia (26) vs. Florida (6) (Peach, Dec. 31, 1981) (4 FGs, 2 PATs)

Punting

MOST PUNTS
21—Everett Sweeney, Michigan (49) vs. Stanford (0) (Rose, 1902)
16—Lem Pratt, New Mexico St. (14) vs. Hardin-Simmons (14) (Sun, 1936) (38.4 average)
14—Sammy Baugh, TCU (3) vs. LSU (2) (Sugar, 1936)
13—Hugh Keeney, Rice (8) vs. Tennessee (0) (Orange, 1947)
13—N.A. Keithley, Tulsa (6) vs. Texas Tech (0) (Sun, 1942) (37.0 average)
13—Hugh McCullough, Oklahoma (0) vs. Tennessee (17) (Orange, 1939) (40.6 average)
13—Tyler, Hardin-Simmons (14) vs. New Mexico St. (14) (Sun, 1936) (45.2 average)
13—(D) Tom Murphy, Arkansas (7) vs. Centenary (La.) (7) (Dixie Classic, 1934) (44.0 average)
12—Mitch Berger, Colorado (25) vs. Alabama (30) (Blockbuster, 1991) (41.0 average)
12—Bob Parsons, Penn St. (10) vs. Missouri (3) (Orange, 1970) (42.6 average)
12—Jim Callahan, Texas Tech (0) vs. Tulsa (6) (Sun, 1942) (43.0 average)
12—Mike Palm, Penn St. (3) vs. Southern California (14) (Rose, 1923)

HIGHEST AVERAGE PER PUNT
(Minimum 5 Punts)
53.8—Mat McBriar, Hawaii (28) vs. Tulane (36) (Hawaii, 2002) (5 for 269)
52.7—Des Koch, Southern California (7) vs. Wisconsin (0) (Rose, 1953) (7 for 369) (adjusted to current statistical rules)
52.4—Mike Sochko, Maryland (21) vs. Houston (30) (Cotton, 1977) (5 for 262)
52.3—Chris Hogue, Tennessee (17) vs. Nebraska (42) (Orange, 1998) (6 for 314)
52.0—Nick Gallery, Iowa (27) vs. Texas Tech (0) (Alamo, 1996) (5 for 260)
51.5—Sam Koch, Nebraska (32) vs. Michigan (28) (Alamo, 2005) (8 for 412)
51.5—Nick Pietsch, Colorado (51) vs. Oregon (43) (Aloha, 1998) (6 for 309)
51.0—Chris Clauss, Penn St. (10) vs. Clemson (35) (Florida Citrus, 1988) (5 for 255)
50.2—(D) Jose Arroyo, Oregon (17) vs. Wake Forest (38) (Seattle, 2002) (6 for 301)
50.2—Curtis Head, Marshall (38) vs. Louisville (15) (GMAC, 2002) (6 for 301)
50.0—Nic Schmitt, Virginia Tech (35) vs. Louisville (24) (Gator, 2006) (6 for 300)
50.0—Dana Moore, Mississippi St. (17) vs. Nebraska (31) (Sun, 1980) (5 for 250)

Punt Returns

MOST PUNT RETURNS
9—Buzy Rosenberg, Georgia (7) vs. North Carolina (3) (Gator, Dec. 31, 1971) (54 yards)
9—Paddy Driscoll, Great Lakes (17) vs. Mare Island (0) (Rose, 1919) (115 yards)
8—Thomas Lewis, Indiana (20) vs. Virginia Tech (45) (Independence, 1993) (58 yards)
7—Willie Reed, Florida St. (23) vs. Penn St. (26) (3 ot) (Orange, 2006) (180 yards)
7—Steve Breaston, Michigan (28) vs. Nebraska (32) (Alamo, 2005) (72 yards)
7—Quinton Jones, Boise St. (21) vs. Boston College (27) (MPC Computers, 2005) (151 yards)
7—Curtis Fagan, Oklahoma (10) vs. Arkansas (3) (Cotton, 2002) (20 yards)
7—Michael Waddell, North Carolina (16) vs. Auburn (10) (Peach, 2001) (66 yards)
7—Roderick Hood, Auburn (10) vs. North Carolina (16) (Peach, 2001) (26 yards)
6—Brian Bonner, TCU (37) vs. Northern Ill. (7) (Poinsettia, 2006) (89 yards)
6—Dimitrious Stanley, Ohio St. (14) vs. Tennessee (20) (Florida Citrus, 1996) (30 yards)
6—Dale Carter, Tennessee (17) vs. Penn St. (42) (Fiesta, 1992)
6—Joey Smith, Louisville (34) vs. Alabama (7) (Fiesta, 1991) (35 yards)
6—David Palmer, Alabama (30) vs. Colorado (25) (Blockbuster, 1991) (74 yards)
6—(D) Hesh Colar, San Jose St. (48) vs. Central Mich. (24) (California, 1990)
6—David Kintigh, Miami (Fla.) (10) vs. Penn St. (14) (Fiesta, 1987) (32 yards)
6—(D) Eric Metcalf, Texas (16) vs. Air Force (24) (Bluebonnet, 1985) (49 yards)
6—Vai Sikahema, BYU (7) vs. Ohio St. (10) (Florida Citrus, 1985)
6—(D) Ray Horton, Washington (21) vs. Maryland (20) (Aloha, 1982) (28 yards)
6—Bill Gribble, Washington St. (36) vs. BYU (38) (Holiday, 1981) (39 yards)
6—Johnny Rodgers, Nebraska (38) vs. Alabama (6) (Orange, 1972) (136 yards)
6—Rick Sygar, Michigan (34) vs. Oregon St. (7) (Rose, 1965) (50 yards)
6—Billy Hair, Clemson (0) vs. Miami (Fla.) (14) (Gator, 1952) (73 yards)
6—Don Zimmerman, Tulane (12) vs. Southern California (21) (Rose, 1932)

MOST PUNT RETURN YARDS
180—Willie Reid, Florida St. (23) vs. Penn St. (26) (3 ot) (Orange, 2006) (7 returns)
151—Quinton Jones, Boise St. (21) vs. Boston College (27) (MPC Computers, 2005) (7 returns)
136—Johnny Rodgers, Nebraska (38) vs. Alabama (6) (Orange, 1972) (6 returns)
122—George Fleming, Washington (44) vs. Wisconsin (8) (Rose, 1960) (3 returns)
122—Bobby Kellogg, Tulane (13) vs. Texas A&M (14) (Sugar, 1940) (5 returns)
115—Paddy Driscoll, Great Lakes (17) vs. Mare Island (0) (Rose, 1919) (9 returns)
110—James Henry, Southern Miss. (38) vs. UTEP (18) (Independence, 1988) (2 returns, touchdowns of 65 and 45 yards)
108—Freddie Milons, Alabama (34) vs. Michigan (35) (ot) (Orange, 2000) (4 returns)
106—Kevin Baugh, Penn St. (27) vs. Georgia (23) (Sugar, 1983) (5 returns)
106—Steve Holden, Arizona St. (45) vs. Florida St. (38) (Fiesta, 1971) (3 returns)

HIGHEST PUNT RETURN AVERAGE
(Minimum 3 Returns)
40.7—George Fleming, Washington (44) vs. Wisconsin (8) (Rose, 1960) (3 for 122)
35.3—Steve Holden, Arizona St. (45) vs. Florida St. (38) (Fiesta, 1971) (3 for 106)
29.6—Shawn Summers, Tennessee (45) vs. Virginia Tech (23) (Gator, 1994) (3 for 89)
27.7—Chad McCullar, Houston (48) vs. Hawaii (54) (3 ot) (Hawaii, 2003) (3 for 83)
27.0—Freddie Milons, Alabama (34) vs. Michigan (35) (ot) (Orange, 2000) (4 for 108)
25.7—Willie Reid, Florida St. (23) vs. Penn St. (26) (3 ot) (Orange, 2006) (7 for 180)
25.3—(D) Cory Rodgers, TCU (27) vs. Iowa St. (24) (Houston, 2005) (3 for 76)
24.4—Bobby Kellogg, Tulane (13) vs. Texas A&M (14) (Sugar, 1940) (5 for 122)
24.0—Roscoe Parrish, Miami (Fla.) (27) vs. Florida (10) (Peach, Dec. 31, 2004) (3 for 72)
24.0—Ryne Robinson, Miami (Ohio) (13) vs. Iowa St. (17) (Independence, 2004) (3 for 72)
24.0—Shayne Wasden, Auburn (31) vs. Ohio St. (14) (Hall of Fame, 1990) (3 for 72)

Kickoff Returns

MOST KICKOFF RETURNS
8—Todd Howard, Michigan (17) vs. Tennessee (45) (Florida Citrus, 2002) (125 yards)
7—Ramonce Taylor, Texas (38) vs. Michigan (37) (Rose, 2005) (201 yards)
7—(D) Leodis McKelvin, Troy (21) vs. Northern Ill. (34) (Silicon Valley, 2004) (143 yards)
7—Dale Carter, Tennessee (17) vs. Penn St. (42) (Fiesta, 1992) (132 yards)
7—(D) Jeff Sydner, Hawaii (13) vs. Michigan St. (33) (Aloha, 1989) (174 yards)
7—Homer Jones, BYU (37) vs. Indiana (38) (Holiday, 1979) (126 yards)
6—Grant Jones, Oklahoma St. (34) vs. Alabama (31) (Independence, 2006) (116 yards)
6—George Hill, Colorado St. (30) vs. Navy (51) (Poinsettia, 2005) (116 yards)
6—Steve Breaston, Michigan (37) vs. Texas (38) (Rose, 2005) (221 yards)
6—Marshawn Lynch, California (31) vs. Texas Tech (45) (Holiday, 2004) (115 yards)
6—John Randle, Kansas (26) vs. North Carolina St. (56) (Tangerine, 2003) (128 yards)
6—Koren Robinson, North Carolina St. (38) vs. Minnesota (30) (Micronpc.com, 2000) (151 yards)
6—Mike Rigell, BYU (27) vs. Tulane (41) (Liberty, 1998) (220 yards)
6—Dave Beazley, Northwestern (28) vs. Tennessee (48) (Florida Citrus, 1997) (137 yards)
6—(D) Deltha O'Neal, California (38) vs. Navy (42) (Aloha, 1996) (186 yards)
6—Eugene Napoleon, West Virginia (21) vs. Notre Dame (34) (Fiesta, 1989) (107 yards)
6—Tim Brown, Notre Dame (10) vs. Texas A&M (35) (Cotton, 1988) (129 yards)
6—Leroy Thompson, Penn St. (10) vs. Clemson (35) (Florida Citrus, 1988)
6—(D) Anthony Roberson, Air Force (28) vs. Arizona St. (33) (Freedom, 1987) (109 yards)

6—Casey Tiumalu, BYU (17) vs. Ohio St. (47) (Holiday, 1982) (116 yards)
6—Brian Nelson, Texas Tech (17) vs. Florida St. (40) (Tangerine, 1977) (143 yards)
6—Wally Henry, UCLA (6) vs. Alabama (36) (Liberty, 1976)
6—Steve Williams, Alabama (6) vs. Nebraska (38) (Orange, 1972)
6—Mike Fink, Missouri (35) vs. Arizona St. (49) (Fiesta, 1972) (203 yards)

MOST KICKOFF RETURN YARDS
221—Steve Breaston, Michigan (37) vs. Texas (38) (Rose, 2005) (6 returns)
220—Mike Rigell, BYU (27) vs. Tulane (41) (Liberty, 1998) (6 returns)
203—Mike Fink, Missouri (35) vs. Arizona St. (49) (Fiesta, 1972) (6 returns)
201—Ramonce Taylor, Texas (38) vs. Michigan (37) (Rose, 2005) (7 returns)
186—(D) Deltha O'Neal, California (38) vs. Navy (42) (Aloha, 1996) (6 returns)
181—Tommy Neal, Maryland (23) vs. Tennessee (30) (Florida Citrus, 1983) (5 returns)
178—Al Hoisch, UCLA (14) vs. Illinois (45) (Rose, 1947) (4 returns)
174—(D) Jeff Sydner, Hawaii (13) vs. Michigan St. (33) (Aloha, 1989) (7 returns)
169—C.J. Jones, Iowa (17) vs. Southern California (38) (Orange, 2003) (4 returns)
169—Jerome Thomas, Idaho (42) vs. Southern Miss. (35) (Humanitarian, 1998) (5 returns)

HIGHEST KICKOFF RETURN AVERAGE
(Minimum 2 Returns)
60.5—(D) Bob Smith, Texas A&M (40) vs. Georgia (20) (Presidential Cup, 1950) (2 for 121)
60.0—Jerome Pathon, Washington (21) vs. Colorado (33) (Holiday, 1996) (2 for 120)
58.0—Eddie Kennison, LSU (45) vs. Michigan St. (26) (Independence, 1995) (2 for 116)
57.5—Pete Panuska, Tennessee (27) vs. Maryland (28) (Sun, 1984) (2 for 115)
55.5—Todd Snyder, Ohio (42) vs. Richmond (49) (Tangerine, 1968) (2 for 111)
46.7—(D) Cal Beck, Utah (16) vs. Arizona (13) (Freedom, 1994) (3 for 140)
45.0—Sammy Moore, Washington St. (14) vs. Oklahoma (34) (Rose, 2003) (2 for 90)
44.5—DeAndre Wright, New Mexico (12) vs. San Jose St. (20) (New Mexico, 2006) (2 for 89)
44.5—Larry Taylor, Connecticut (39) vs. Toledo (10) (Motor City, 2004) (2 for 89)
44.5—Al Hoisch, UCLA (14) vs. Illinois (45) (Rose, 1947) (4 for 178)
43.7—Larry Key, Florida St. (40) vs. Texas Tech (17) (Tangerine, 1977) (3 for 131)

Interceptions

MOST INTERCEPTIONS MADE
4—Jim Dooley, Miami (Fla.) (14) vs. Clemson (0) (Gator, 1952)
4—(D) Manuel Aja, Arizona St. (21) vs. Xavier (Ohio) (33) (Salad, 1950)
3—T.J. Stancil, Boston College (35) vs. Colorado St. (21) (San Francisco, 2003)
3—Michael Brooks, North Carolina St. (28) vs. Iowa (23) (Peach, Dec. 31, 1988)
3—Bud Hebert, Oklahoma (24) vs. Florida St. (7) (Orange, 1980)
3—Louis Campbell, Arkansas (13) vs. Tennessee (14) (Liberty, 1971)
3—Bud McClinton, Auburn (34) vs. Arizona (10) (Sun, 1968)
3—(D) Les Derrick, Texas (19) vs. Mississippi (0) (Bluebonnet, 1966)
3—(D) Tommy Luke, Mississippi (0) vs. Texas (19) (Bluebonnet, 1966)
3—Jerry Cook, Texas (12) vs. Mississippi (7) (Cotton, 1962)
3—Ray Brown, Mississippi (39) vs. Texas (7) (Sugar, 1958)
3—Bill Paulman, Stanford (7) vs. SMU (0) (Rose, 1936)
3—Shy Huntington, Oregon (14) vs. Penn (0) (Rose, 1917)

MOST INTERCEPTION RETURN YARDAGE
148—Elmer Layden, Notre Dame (27) vs. Stanford (10) (Rose, 1925) (2 interceptions)
99—Marcus King, Missouri (38) vs. South Carolina (31) (Independence, 2005) (1 interception)
95—Marcus Washington, Colorado (38) vs. Oregon (6) (Cotton, 1996) (1 interception)
94—David Baker, Oklahoma (48) vs. Duke (21) (Orange, 1958) (1 interception)
92—Andy Avalos, Boise St. (40) vs. Louisville (44) (Liberty, 2004) (1 interception)
91—Donald Strickland, Colorado (28) vs. Wisconsin (31) (ot) (Alamo, 2002) (1 interception)
91—Don Hoover, Ohio (14) vs. West Tex. A&M (15) (Sun, 1962) (1 interception)
90—Norm Beal, Missouri (21) vs. Navy (14) (Orange, 1961) (1 interception)
90—Charlie Brembs, South Carolina (14) vs. Wake Forest (26) (Gator, 1946) (1 interception)
90—(D) G.P. Jackson, TCU (7) vs. Centre (63) (Fort Worth Classic, 1921) (1 interception)

All-Purpose Yards

(Includes All Runs From Scrimmage, Pass Receptions and All Returns)

MOST ALL-PURPOSE PLAYS
47—Tellis Redmon, Minnesota (30) vs. North Carolina St. (38) (Micronpc.com, 2000) (42 rush, 3 receptions, 2 punt returns)
47—(D) Ron Jackson, Tulsa (28) vs. San Diego St. (17) (Freedom, 1991) (46 rush, 1 reception)
46—Errict Rhett, Florida (27) vs. North Carolina St. (10) (Gator, 1992) (39 rush, 7 receptions)
42—(D) Blake Ezor, Michigan St. (33) vs. Hawaii (13) (Aloha, 1989) (41 rush, 1 reception)
41—Marion Barber III, Minnesota (20) vs. Alabama (16) (Music City, 2004) (37 rush, 4 punt returns)
41—Terrell Fletcher, Wisconsin (34) vs. Duke (20) (Hall of Fame, 1995) (39 rush, 1 reception, 1 kickoff return)
40—LaDainian Tomlinson, TCU (28) vs. East Caro. (14) (Mobile Alabama, 1999) (36 rush, 4 receptions)
39—(D) Marshall Faulk, San Diego St. (17) vs. Tulsa (28) (Freedom, 1991) (30 rush, 9 receptions)
38—Ronnie Brown, Auburn (13) vs. Penn St. (9) (Capital One, 2003) (37 rush, 1 reception)
38—(D) Rodney Davis, Fresno St. (30) vs. Georgia Tech (21) (Silicon Valley, 2002) (37 rush, 1 reception)

MOST ALL-PURPOSE YARDS GAINED
359—Sherman Williams, Alabama (24) vs. Ohio St. (17) (Florida Citrus, 1995) (166 rush, 155 receptions, 38 kickoff returns)
318—(D) Rodney Wright, Fresno St. (35) vs. Michigan St. (44) (Silicon Valley, 2001) (19 rush, 299 receptions)
315—Steve Breaston, Michigan (37) vs. Texas (38) (Rose, 2005) (15 rush, 77 receiving, 2 punt returns, 221 kickoff returns)
308—Jason Rivers, Hawaii (41) vs. Arizona St. (24) (Hawaii, 2006) (308 receiving)
307—P.J. Daniels, Georgia Tech (52) vs. Tulsa (10) (Humanitarian, 2004) (307 rush)
303—(D) Bob Smith, Texas A&M (40) vs. Georgia (20) (Presidential Cup, 1950) (160 rush, 22 receptions, 121 kickoff returns)
290—Reggie Campbell, Navy (51) vs. Colorado St. (30) (Poinsettia, 2005) (116 rushing, 89 receiving, 85 kickoff returns)
283—Andre Coleman, Kansas St. (52) vs. Wyoming (17) (Copper, 1993) (7 rush, 144 receptions, 73 punt returns, 54 kickoff returns)
279—Vincent Marshall, Houston (36) vs. South Carolina (44) (Liberty, 2006) (201 receiving, 11 punt returns, 67 kickoff returns)
279—Reggie Bush, Southern California (38) vs. Texas (41) (Rose, 2006) (82 rushing, 95 receiving, 102 kickoff returns)
279—Floyd Little, Syracuse (12) vs. Tennessee (18) (Gator, 1966) (216 rush, 16 receptions, 9 punt returns, 38 kickoff returns)
278—Byron Hanspard, Texas Tech (55) vs. Air Force (41) (Copper, 1995) (260 rush, 18 receptions)
277—Bob Anderson, Colorado (47) vs. Alabama (33) (Liberty, 1969) (254 rush, 23 kickoff returns)
276—O.J. Simpson, Southern California (16) vs. Ohio St. (27) (Rose, 1969) (171 rush, 85 receptions, 20 kickoff returns)
272—Pat Johnson, Oregon (41) vs. Air Force (13) (Las Vegas, 1997) (169 receptions, 49 punt returns, 54 kickoff returns)
270—(D) Charles Rogers, Michigan St. (44) vs. Fresno St. (35) (Silicon Valley, 2001) (270 receptions)
269—Mike Anderson, Utah (17) vs. Fresno St. (16) (Las Vegas, 1999) (254 rush, 15 receptions)
260—Ted Ginn Jr., Ohio St. (34) vs. Notre Dame (20) (Fiesta, 2006) (73 rushing, 167 receiving, 20 punt returns)
256—Terrell Fletcher, Wisconsin (34) vs. Duke (20) (Hall of Fame, 1995) (241 rush, 8 receptions, 7 kickoff returns)
256—Rondell Mealey, LSU (27) vs. Notre Dame (9) (Independence, 1997) (222 rush, 34 kickoff returns)
248—Ricky Williams, Texas (38) vs. Mississippi St. (11) (Cotton, 1999) (203 rush, 45 receptions)
247—(D) Wilford White, Arizona St. (21) vs. Miami (Ohio) (34) (Salad, 1951) (106 rush, 87 receptions, 54 kickoff returns)

Defensive Statistics

MOST TOTAL TACKLES MADE
(Includes Assists)
31—Lee Roy Jordan, Alabama (17) vs. Oklahoma (0) (Orange, 1963)
22—Bubba Brown, Clemson (17) vs. Ohio St. (15) (Gator, 1978)
22—Gordy Ceresino, Stanford (24) vs. LSU (14) (Sun, Dec. 31, 1977)
20—Vada Murray, Michigan (10) vs. Southern California (17) (Rose, 1990)
20—Carl Zander, Tennessee (27) vs. Maryland (28) (Sun, 1984)
20—(D) Gordy Ceresino, Stanford (25) vs. Georgia (22) (Bluebonnet, 1978)
19—Abdul Hodge, Iowa (24) vs. Florida (31) (Outback, 2006)
19—Cam Hall, Boise St. (40) vs. Louisville (44) (Liberty, 2004)
18—Matt Castelo, San Jose St. (20) vs. New Mexico (12) (New Mexico, 2006)
18—Maurice Lloyd, Connecticut (39) vs. Toledo (10) (Motor City, 2004)
18—Allen Stansberry, LSU (45) vs. Michigan St. (26) (Independence, 1995)
18—Ted Johnson, Colorado (41) vs. Notre Dame (24) (Fiesta, 1995)
18—Rod Smith, Notre Dame (39) vs. Florida (28) (Sugar, 1992)
18—Erick Anderson, Michigan (10) vs. Southern California (17) (Rose, 1990)
18—(D) Yepi Pauu, San Jose St. (27) vs. Eastern Mich. (30) (California, 1987)
18—Garland Rivers, Michigan (17) vs. BYU (24) (Holiday, 1984)
18—(D) Terry Hubbard, Cal St. Fullerton (13) vs. Northern Ill. (20) (California, 1983)
18—(D) Don Turner, Fresno St. (29) vs. Bowling Green (28) (California, 1982)
18—Matt Millen, Penn St. (42) vs. Arizona St. (30) (Fiesta, 1977)

MOST SOLO TACKLES
18—Rod Smith, Notre Dame (39) vs. Florida (28) (Sugar, 1992)
17—Garland Rivers, Michigan (17) vs. BYU (24) (Holiday, 1984)
15—Randy Neal, Virginia (13) vs. Boston College (31) (Carquest, 1994)
15—(D) Ken Norton Jr., UCLA (31) vs. BYU (10) (Freedom, 1986)
15—Lynn Evans, Missouri (35) vs. Arizona St. (49) (Fiesta, 1972)

MOST TACKLES FOR LOSSES
6—(D) LeMarcus McDonald, TCU (9) vs. Texas A&M (28) (galleryfurniture.com, 2001)
5—Stephen Tulloch, North Carolina St. (14) vs. South Fla. (0) (Meineke Car Care, 2005)

5—Mathias Kiwanuka, Boston College (37) vs. North Carolina (24) (Continental Tire, 2004)
5—(D) Michael Jones, Colorado (17) vs. BYU (20) (Freedom, 1988)
5—Jimmy Walker, Arkansas (10) vs. UCLA (10) (Fiesta, 1978)
4.5—Jonathan Babineaux, Iowa (30) vs. LSU (25) (Capital One, 2005)
4—Mario Williams, North Carolina St. (14) vs. South Fla. (0) (Meineke Car Care, 2005)
4—LaMarr Woodley, Michigan (37) vs. Texas (38) (Rose, 2005)
4—LeVon Pears, Southern Miss. (31) vs. North Texas (10) (New Orleans, 2004)
4—E.J. Henderson, Maryland (30) vs. Tennessee (3) (Peach, 2002)
4—Willie Blade, Mississippi St. (43) vs. Texas A&M (41) (ot) (Independence, 2000)
4—Eric Wilson, Michigan (31) vs. Auburn (28) (Florida Citrus, 2001)
4—Courtney Brown, Penn St. (26) vs. Kentucky (14) (Outback, 1999)
4—Sedrick Hodge, North Carolina (20) vs. San Diego St. (13) (Las Vegas, 1998)
4—Mike Pringley, North Carolina (20) vs. San Diego St. (13) (Las Vegas, 1998)
4—Chike Okeafor, Purdue (37) vs. Kansas St. (34) (Alamo, 1998)
4—Corey Terry, Tennessee (48) vs. Northwestern (28) (Florida Citrus, 1997)
4—(D) Clint Bruce, Navy (42) vs. California (38) (Aloha, 1996)
4—Montae Reagor, Texas Tech (0) vs. Iowa (27) (Alamo, 1996)
4—Reggie Garnett, Michigan St. (0) vs. Stanford (38) (Sun, 1996)
4—Matt Finkes, Ohio St. (14) vs. Tennessee (20) (Florida Citrus, 1996)
4—(D) Ken Norton Jr., UCLA (31) vs. BYU (10) (Freedom, 1986)
4—Reggie McKenzie, Tennessee (27) vs. Maryland (28) (Sun, 1984)

MOST QUARTERBACK SACKS
6—Shay Muirbrook, BYU (19) vs. Kansas St. (15) (Cotton, 1997)
4.5—Reggie McKenzie, Tennessee (27) vs. Maryland (28) (Sun, 1984)
4—Rusty Medearis, Miami (Fla.) (22) vs. Nebraska (0) (Orange, 1992)
4—Bobby Bell, Missouri (17) vs. BYU (21) (Holiday, 1983)
3.5—(D) Jason Berryman, Iowa St. (24) vs. TCU (27) (Houston, 2005)
3—Mike Kudla, Ohio St. (34) vs. Notre Dame (20) (Fiesta, 2006)
3—Terrence Royal, South Fla. (0) vs. North Carolina St. (14) (Meineke Car Care, 2005)
3—Stephen Tulloch, North Carolina St. (14) vs. South Fla. (0) (Meineke Car Care, 2005)
3—Alan Branch, Michigan (28) vs. Nebraska (32) (Alamo, 2005)
3—Tyler Tidwell, Navy (51) vs. Colorado St. (30) (Poinsettia, 2005)
3—Mike Alston, Toledo (45) vs. UTEP (13) (GMAC, 2005)
3—Abdul Hodge, Iowa (30) vs. LSU (25) (Capital One, 2005)
3—Jonathan Babineaux, Iowa (30) vs. LSU (25) (Capital One, 2005)
3—David Pollack, Georgia (24) vs. Wisconsin (21) (Outback, 2005)
3—Tommy Hackenbruck, Utah (35) vs. Pittsburgh (7) (Fiesta, 2005)
3—Kalimba Edwards, South Carolina (24) vs. Ohio St. (7) (Outback, 2001)
3—Chike Okeafor, Purdue (37) vs. Kansas St. (34) (Alamo, 1998)
3—Andy Katzenmoyer, Ohio St. (20) vs. Arizona St. (17) (Rose, 1997)
3—Travis Ochs, Kansas St. (15) vs. BYU (19) (Cotton, 1997)
3—Trevor Pryce, Clemson (7) vs. LSU (10) (Peach, 1996)
3—Jamie Sharper, Virginia (21) vs. Miami (Fla.) (31) (Carquest, 1996)
3—Mike Crawford, Nevada (18) vs. Ball St. (15) (Las Vegas, 1996)
3—Gabe Northern, LSU (45) vs. Michigan St. (26) (Independence, 1995)
3—James Gillyard, LSU (45) vs. Michigan St. (26) (Independence, 1995)
3—Dewayne Harris, Nebraska (24) vs. Miami (Fla.) (17) (Orange, 1995)
3—Trev Alberts, Nebraska (16) vs. Florida St. (18) (Orange, 1994)
3—(D) Alfred Williams, Colorado (17) vs. BYU (20) (Freedom, 1988)
3—(D) Jim Wahler, UCLA (31) vs. BYU (10) (Freedom, 1986)
3—James Mosley, Texas Tech (17) vs. Mississippi (20) (Independence, 1986)
3—(D) Ernie Barnes, Mississippi St. (10) vs. Kansas (0) (Hall of Fame, 1981)

FUMBLE RECOVERIES
2—(D) Nik Moser, Iowa St. (24) vs. TCU (27) (Houston, 2005)
2—Joe Anoai, Georgia Tech (52) vs. Tulsa (10) (Humanitarian, 2004)
2—Randall Brown, Ohio St. (17) vs. Alabama (24) (Florida Citrus, 1995)
2—(D) Michael Stewart, Fresno St. (51) vs. Bowling Green (7) (California, 1985)
2—Rod Kirby, Pittsburgh (7) vs. Arizona St. (28) (Fiesta, 1973)

BLOCKED KICKS
2—Bracey Walker, North Carolina (21) vs. Mississippi St. (17) (Peach, Jan. 2, 1993)
2—Carlton Williams, Pittsburgh (7) vs. Arizona St. (28) (Fiesta, 1973)

PASSES BROKEN UP
5—Dyshod Carter, Kansas St. (34) Purdue (37) (Alamo, 1998)
4—Justin Robinson, BYU (38) vs. Oregon (8) (Las Vegas, 2006)
4—Marcus Hamilton, Virginia (34) vs. Minnesota (31) (Music City, 2005)
4—Nigel Morris, Toledo (45) vs. UTEP (13) (GMAC, 2005)
4—Chris Cummings, LSU (27) vs. Notre Dame (9) (Independence, 1997)
4—Dale Carter, Tennessee (23) vs. Virginia (22) (Sugar, 1991)
4—Darryl Hardy, Tennessee (23) vs. Virginia (22) (Sugar, 1991)
4—Andre Creamer, Tennessee (35) vs. Miami (Fla.) (7) (Sugar, 1986)
4—(D) Conrad Graham, Tennessee (24) vs. LSU (17) (Bluebonnet, 1972)
3—Donte Whitner, Ohio St. (34) vs. Notre Dame (20) (Fiesta, 2006)
3—Anwar Phillips, Penn St. (26) vs. Florida St. (23) (3 ot) (Orange, 2006)
3—Fred Bennett, South Carolina (31) vs. Missouri (38) (Independence, 2005)
3—Derrick Roberson, Rutgers (40) vs. Arizona St. (45) (Insight, 2005)
3—Joe Garcia, Nevada (49) vs. UCF (48) (ot) (Hawaii, 2005)
3—DeMario Minter, Georgia (24) vs. Wisconsin (21) (Outback, 2005)
3—Aric Williams, Oregon St. (38) vs. Notre Dame (21) (Insight, 2004)
3—Anthony Madison, Alabama (16) vs. Minnesota (20) (Music City, 2004)
3—(D) Tom Hubbard, Colorado (33) vs. UTEP (28) (Houston, 2004)
3—Ashton Youboty, Ohio St. (33) vs. Oklahoma St. (7) (Alamo, 2004)
3—Harrison Smith, California (31) vs. Texas Tech (45) (Holiday, 2004)
3—Alphonso Hodge, Miami (Ohio) (13) vs. Iowa St. (17) (Independence, 2004)
3—Jazzmen Williams, Boston College (37) vs. North Carolina (24) (Continental Tire, 2004)
3—Sedrick Curry, Texas A&M (14) vs. Ohio St. (24) (Sugar, 1999)
3—Ahmed Plummer, Ohio St. (24) vs. Texas A&M (14) (Sugar, 1999)
3—(D) Damen Wheeler, Colorado (51) vs. Oregon (43) (Aloha, 1998)
3—Damion McIntosh, Kansas St. (34) vs. Purdue (37) (Alamo, 1998)
3—Kevin Hill, Idaho (42) vs. Southern Miss. (35) (Humanitarian, 1998)
3—Robert Williams, North Carolina (20) vs. West Virginia (13) (Gator, 1996)
3—Mark Tate, Penn St. (43) vs. Auburn (14) (Outback, 1996)
3—Kwame Ellis, Stanford (13) vs. East Caro. (19) (Liberty, 1995)
3—Mickey Dalton, Air Force (41) vs. Texas Tech (55) (Copper, 1995)
3—Barron Miles, Nebraska (24) vs. Miami (Fla.) (17) (Orange, 1995)
3—Percy Ellsworth, Virginia (20) vs. TCU (10) (Independence, 1994)
3—Sam McKiver, Virginia (20) vs. TCU (10) (Independence, 1994)
3—Tyrone Williams, Nebraska (16) vs. Florida St. (18) (Orange, 1994)
3—(D) John Herpin, Southern California (28) vs. Utah (21) (Freedom, 1993)
3—Demouy Williams, Washington (24) vs. Tulane (12) (Independence, 1987)

Team Record Lists

Only official records after 1937 are included. Prior records are included if able to be substantiated. Each team's score is in parentheses after the team name. Totals for each team in both-team records are in brackets after the team's score. The year listed is the actual (calendar) year the game was played; the date is included if the bowl was played twice (i.e., January and December) during one calendar year. The list also includes discontinued bowls, marked with (D). Bowls are listed by the name of the bowl at the time it was played.

Total Offense

MOST TOTAL PLAYS
107—Purdue (27) vs. Washington St. (33) (Sun, 2001) (474 yards)
104—Marshall (64) vs. East Caro. (61) (2 ot) (GMAC, 2001) (649 yards)
102—Northwestern (38) vs. UCLA (50) (Sun, 2005) (584 yards)
97—LSU (47) vs. Illinois (34) (Sugar, 2002) (595 yards)
96—Texas (20) vs. Washington St. (28) (Holiday, 2003) (327 yards)
96—North Carolina St. (10) vs. Arizona (17) (Copper, 1989) (310 yards)
95—LSU (20) vs. Texas (35) (Cotton, 2003) (441 yards)
95—Georgia (27) vs. Virginia (34) (Peach, Dec. 30, 1995) (525 yards)
95—Toledo (40) vs. Nevada (37) (ot) (Las Vegas, 1995) (561 yards)
95—North Carolina St. (28) vs. Iowa (23) (Peach, Dec. 31, 1988) (431 yards)

MOST TOTAL PLAYS, BOTH TEAMS
180—Hawaii (54) [91] & Houston (48) [89] (3 ot) (Hawaii, 2003) (1,158 yards)
180—Marshall (64) [104] & East Caro. (61) [76] (2 ot) (GMAC, 2001) (1,141 yards)
176—UCLA (50) [74] & Northwestern (38) [102] (Sun, 2005) (1,037 yards)
175—Washington St. (33) [68] & Purdue (27) [107] (Sun, 2001) (836 yards)
175—Toledo (40) [95] & Nevada (37) [80] (ot) (Las Vegas, 1995) (974 yards)
171—Auburn (34) [82] & Arizona (10) [89] (Sun, 1968) (537 yards)
169—Clemson (49) [84] vs. Louisiana Tech (24) [85] (Humanitarian, 2001) (998 yards)
169—(D) Purdue (27) [92] & Tennessee (22) [77] (Bluebonnet, 1979) (863 yards)
167—Texas (47) [85] vs. Washington (43) [82] (Holiday, 2001) (1,036 yards)
167—Idaho (42) [75] & Southern Miss. (35) [92] (Humanitarian, 1998) (900 yards)
167—(D) Fresno St. (35) [75] & Western Mich. (30) [92] (California, 1988) (943 yards)
167—Arizona St. (45) [86] & Florida St. (38) [81] (Fiesta, 1971) (863 yards)

MOST YARDS GAINED
718—Arizona St. (49) vs. Missouri (35) (Fiesta, 1972) (452 rush, 266 pass)
715—Michigan (35) vs. Mississippi (3) (Gator, Jan. 1, 1991) (324 rush, 391 pass)
698—Oklahoma St. (62) vs. Wyoming (14) (Holiday, 1988) (320 rush, 378 pass)
680—Hawaii (41) vs. Arizona St. (24) (Hawaii, 2006) (121 rush, 559 pass)
680—Texas A&M (65) vs. BYU (14) (Holiday, 1989) (356 rush, 324 pass)
679—Arizona St. (45) vs. Rutgers (40) (Insight, 2005) (212 rush, 467 pass)
659—Florida (56) vs. Maryland (23) (Orange, 2002) (203 rush, 456 pass)
655—(D) Houston (47) vs. Tulane (7) (Bluebonnet, 1973) (402 rush, 253 pass)
653—North Carolina St. (56) vs. Kansas (26) (Tangerine, 2003) (172 rush, 481 pass)
651—BYU (39) vs. Penn St. (50) (Holiday, 1989) (75 rush, 576 pass)
649—Marshall (64) vs. East Caro. (61) (2 ot) (GMAC, 2001) (73 rush, 576 pass)

MOST YARDS GAINED, BOTH TEAMS
1,211—Arizona St. (45) [679] & Rutgers (40) [532] (Insight, 2005) (150 plays)
1,183—Navy (51) [611] & Colorado St. (30) [572] (Poinsettia, 2005) (153 plays)
1,178—Nevada (49) [623] & UCF (48) [555] (ot) (Hawaii, 2005) (163 plays)
1,158—Hawaii (54) [641] & Houston (48) [517] (3 ot) (Hawaii, 2003) (180 plays)
1,143—(D) Southern California (47) [624] & Texas A&M (28) [519] (Bluebonnet, 1977) (148 plays)
1,141—Marshall (64) [649] & East Caro. (61) [492] (2 ot) (GMAC, 2001) (180 plays)
1,130—Texas (41) [556] & Southern California (38) [574] (Rose, 2006) (158 plays)
1,129—Arizona St. (49) [718] & Missouri (35) [411] (Fiesta, 1972) (134 plays)
1,120—Texas Tech (55) [606] & Air Force (41) [514] (Copper, 1995) (160 plays)
1,116—North Carolina St. (56) [653] & Kansas (26) [463] (Tangerine, 2003) (151 plays)
1,115—Penn St. (50) [464] & BYU (39) [651] (Holiday, 1989) (157 plays)
1,092—Miami (Fla.) (46) [594] & North Carolina St. (23) [498] (Micron PC, 1998) (149 plays)
1,081—California (52) [530] & Virginia Tech (49) [551] (Insight, 2003) (142 plays)
1,080—(D) Navy (42) [646] & California (38) [434] (Aloha, 1996) (147 plays)
1,079—Hawaii (59) [590] & UAB (40) [489] (Hawaii, 2004) (153 plays)
1,071—Hawaii (41) [680] & Arizona St. (24) [391] (Hawaii, 2006) (131 plays)
1,064—Texas Tech (45) [597] & California (31) [467] (Holiday, 2004) (162 plays)
1,048—Michigan (35) [715] & Mississippi (3) [333] (Gator, Jan. 1, 1991) (153 plays)
1,047—Mississippi (42) [533] & Air Force (29) [514] (Liberty, 1989) (160 plays)
1,045—Marshall (48) [611] & Louisville (29) [432] (Motor City, 1998) (144 plays)
1,039—South Carolina (44) [512] & Houston (36) [527] (Liberty, 2006) (143 plays)
1,038—Tennessee (31) [470] & Arkansas (27) [568] (Cotton, 1990) (155 plays)

HIGHEST AVERAGE GAINED PER PLAY
9.9—Hawaii (41) vs. Arizona St. (24) (Hawaii, 2006) (69 for 680)
9.6—Ohio St. (34) vs. Notre Dame (20) (Fiesta, 2006) (64 for 617)
9.6—North Carolina St. (56) vs. Kansas (26) (Tangerine, 2003) (68 for 653)
9.5—Louisville (34) vs. Alabama (7) (Fiesta, 1991) (60 for 571)
9.1—Miami (Fla.) (46) vs. North Carolina St. (23) (Micron PC, 1998) (65 for 594)
9.1—(D) Navy (42) vs. California (38) (Aloha, 1996) (71 for 646)
8.9—Florida (56) vs. Maryland (23) (Orange, 2002) (74 for 659)
8.9—Marshall (48) vs. Louisville (29) (Motor City, 1998) (69 for 613)
8.7—Oklahoma St. (62) vs. Wyoming (14) (Holiday, 1988) (80 for 698)
8.6—Missouri (38) vs. Oregon St. (39) (Sun, 2006) (65 for 561)
8.6—Virginia Tech (49) vs. California (52) (Insight, 2003) (64 for 551)
8.5—Arizona St. (45) vs. Rutgers (40) (Insight, 2005) (80 for 679)

FEWEST PLAYS
35—Tennessee (0) vs. Texas (16) (Cotton, 1953) (29 rush, 6 pass)
36—Arkansas (3) vs. UCLA (17) (Cotton, 1989) (22 rush, 14 pass)
37—TCU (0) vs. Oklahoma St. (34) (Cotton, 1945) (27 rush, 10 pass)
38—Iowa (3) vs. California (37) (Alamo, 1993) (21 rush, 17 pass)

FEWEST PLAYS, BOTH TEAMS
105—Georgia (31) [52] & Virginia Tech (24) [53] (Chick-fil-A, 2006)
107—Tennessee (17) [64] & Oklahoma (0) [43] (Orange, 1939)
107—TCU (16) [54] & Marquette (6) [53] (Cotton, 1937)

FEWEST YARDS
-21—U. of Mexico (0) vs. Southwestern (Tex.) (35) (Sun, 1945) (29 rush, -50 pass)
23—Alabama (10) vs. Missouri (35) (Gator, 1968) (-45 rush, 68 pass)
32—Tennessee (0) vs. Texas (16) (Cotton, 1953) (-14 rush, 46 pass)
38—Miami (Fla.) (0) vs. Bucknell (26) (Orange, 1935) (20 rush, 18 pass)
41—Southern California (14) vs. Alabama (34) (Rose, 1946) (6 rush, 35 pass)
42—Arkansas (3) vs. UCLA (17) (Cotton, 1989) (21 rush, 21 pass)
48—New Mexico (0) vs. Southwestern (Tex.) (7) (Sun, 1944) (38 rush, 10 pass)
50—Arkansas (3) vs. Oklahoma (10) (Cotton, 2002) (37 rush, 13 pass)
54—Arkansas (0) vs. LSU (0) (Cotton, 1947) (54 rush, 0 pass)
57—Michigan St. (0) vs. Auburn (6) (Orange, 1938) (32 rush, 25 pass)

FEWEST YARDS, BOTH TEAMS
260—Randolph Field (7) [150] & Texas (7) [110] (Cotton, 1944)
263—LSU (19) [92] & Texas A&M (14) [171] (Orange, 1944)

Rushing

MOST RUSHING ATTEMPTS
87—Oklahoma (40) vs. Auburn (22) (Sugar, Jan. 1, 1972) (439 yards)
82—Missouri (35) vs. Alabama (10) (Gator, 1968) (402 yards)
79—West Virginia (14) vs. South Carolina (3) (Peach, 1969) (356 yards)
79—Georgia Tech (31) vs. Texas Tech (21) (Gator, Dec. 31, 1965) (364 yards)
78—(D) Houston (35) vs. Navy (0) (Garden State, 1980) (405 yards)
78—Texas (16) vs. Tennessee (0) (Cotton, 1953) (296 yards)
76—Oklahoma (14) vs. Penn St. (0) (Sugar, Dec. 31, 1972) (278 yards)
74—Oklahoma (41) vs. Wyoming (7) (Fiesta, 1976) (415 yards)
74—Michigan (12) vs. Stanford (13) (Rose, 1972) (264 yards)
74—Ohio St. (20) vs. Southern California (7) (Rose, 1955) (305 yards)

MOST RUSHING ATTEMPTS, BOTH TEAMS
122—(D) Southern California (47) [50] & Texas A&M (28) [72] (Bluebonnet, 1977) (864 yards)
122—Mississippi St. (26) [68] & North Carolina (24) [54] (Sun, 1974) (732 yards)
120—Pittsburgh (33) [53] & Kansas (19) [67] (Sun, 1975) (714 yards)
117—Oklahoma (14) [65] & Michigan (6) [52] (Orange, 1976) (451 yards)
117—West Virginia (14) [79] & South Carolina (3) [38] (Peach, 1969) (420 yards)
116—Oklahoma (41) [74] & Wyoming (7) [42] (Fiesta, 1976) (568 yards)
116—Colorado (47) [70] & Alabama (33) [46] (Liberty, 1969) (628 yards)
115—Southern California (7) [47] & Wisconsin (0) [68] (Rose, 1953) (259 yards)
113—Oklahoma (40) [54] & Houston (14) [59] (Sun, 1981) (566 yards)
113—(D) Houston (35) [78] & Navy (0) [35] (Garden State, 1980) (540 yards)
113—Missouri (34) [71] & Auburn (17) [42] (Sun, 1973) (408 yards)

MOST NET RUSHING YARDS
524—Nebraska (62) vs. Florida (24) (Fiesta, 1996) (68 attempts)
486—(D) Texas A&M (28) vs. Southern California (47) (Bluebonnet, 1977) (72 attempts)
476—Nebraska (66) vs. Northwestern (17) (Alamo, 2000) (69 attempts)
473—Colorado (47) vs. Alabama (33) (Liberty, 1969) (70 attempts)
467—Navy (51) vs. Colorado St. (30) (Poinsettia, 2005) (69 attempts)
455—Mississippi St. (26) vs. North Carolina (24) (Sun, 1974) (68 attempts)
452—Arizona St. (49) vs. Missouri (35) (Fiesta, 1972) (65 attempts)
439—Oklahoma (40) vs. Auburn (22) (Sugar, Jan. 1, 1972) (87 attempts)
434—Oklahoma (41) vs. Wyoming (7) (Fiesta, 1976) (74 attempts)
431—Air Force (41) vs. Texas Tech (55) (Copper, 1995) (67 attempts)
429—Iowa (38) vs. California (12) (Rose, 1959) (55 attempts)
423—Auburn (33) vs. Baylor (13) (Gator, Dec. 31, 1954) (48 attempts)
423—(D) UCLA (31) vs. BYU (10) (Freedom, 1986) (49 attempts)
417—Oklahoma (21) vs. Arizona St. (32) (Fiesta, 1983) (63 attempts)
411—Oklahoma (24) vs. Florida St. (7) (Orange, 1980) (62 attempts)
409—Oklahoma (40) vs. Houston (14) (Sun, 1981) (54 attempts)
409—Nebraska (42) vs. Tennessee (17) (Orange, 1998) (68 attempts)
408—Missouri (27) vs. Texas (40) (Cotton, 1946)
405—(D) Houston (35) vs. Navy (0) (Garden State, 1980) (78 attempts)
402—(D) Houston (47) vs. Tulane (7) (Bluebonnet, 1973) (58 attempts)

MOST NET RUSHING YARDS, BOTH TEAMS
864—(D) Southern California (47) [378] & Texas A&M (28) [486] (Bluebonnet, 1977) (122 attempts)
792—Texas Tech (55) [361] & Air Force (41) [431] (Copper, 1995) (107 attempts)
732—Mississippi St. (26) [455] & North Carolina (24) [277] (Sun, 1974) (122 attempts)
714—Pittsburgh (33) [372] & Kansas (19) [342] (Sun, 1975) (120 attempts)
708—Nebraska (66) [476] & Northwestern (17) [232] (Alamo, 2000) (107 attempts)
701—Arizona St. (49) [453] & Missouri (35) [248] (Fiesta, 1972) (109 attempts)
681—Tennessee (31) [320] & Arkansas (27) [361] (Cotton, 1990) (110 attempts)
643—Iowa (38) [429] & California (12) [214] (Rose, 1959) (108 attempts)
628—Colorado (47) [473] & Alabama (33) [155] (Liberty, 1969) (116 attempts)
623—Nevada (49) [369] & UCF (48) [254] (ot) (Hawaii, 2005) (95 attempts)
616—Oklahoma (41) [434] & Wyoming (7) [182] (Fiesta, 1976) (116 attempts)
610—Texas (40) [202] & Missouri (27) [408] (Cotton, 1946)

HIGHEST RUSHING AVERAGE
(Minimum 30 Attempts)
9.3—Texas Tech (55) vs. Air Force (41) (Copper, 1995) (39 for 361)
8.6—(D) UCLA (31) vs. BYU (10) (Freedom, 1986) (49 for 423)
8.6—Michigan (38) vs. Washington (31) (Rose, 1993) (36 for 308)
8.4—Tennessee (31) vs. Arkansas (27) (Cotton, 1990) (38 for 320)
8.0—Texas (41) vs. Southern California (38) (Rose, 2006) (36 for 289)
8.0—Toledo (56) vs. Davidson (33) (Tangerine, 1969) (42 for 334)
7.8—Iowa (38) vs. California (12) (Rose, 1959) (55 for 429)
7.8—Northwestern (24) vs. Bowling Green (28) (Motor City, 2003) (46 for 357)
7.7—Texas Tech (28) vs. North Carolina (32) (Sun, 1972) (38 for 293)
7.7—Nebraska (62) vs. Florida (24) (Fiesta, 1996) (68 for 524)

FEWEST RUSHING ATTEMPTS
12—(D) Vanderbilt (28) vs. Air Force (36) (Hall of Fame, 1982) (35 yards)
16—Hawaii (59) vs. UAB (40) (Hawaii, 2004) (84 yards)
16—Florida (18) vs. Missouri (20) (Sugar, 1966) (-2 yards)
16—Colorado (7) vs. LSU (25) (Orange, 1962) (24 yards)
16—Oklahoma (0) vs. Tennessee (17) (Orange, 1939)
17—Florida St. (2) vs. Oklahoma (13) (Orange, 2001) (27 yards)
17—(D) Duke (21) vs. Texas Tech (49) (All-American, 1989) (67 yards)
17—Illinois (9) vs. UCLA (45) (Rose, 1984) (0 yards)
18—Texas A&M (7) vs. Tennessee (38) (Cotton, 2005) (77 yards)
18—Oregon St. (38) vs. Notre Dame (21) (Insight, 2004) (20 yards)
18—BYU (46) vs. SMU (45) (Holiday, 1980) (-2 yards)

FEWEST RUSHING ATTEMPTS, BOTH TEAMS
50—Southern California (32) [23] & Michigan (18) [27] (Rose, 2007)
51—Oregon St. (38) [18] & Notre Dame (21) [33] (Insight, 2004)
52—Hawaii (59) [16] & UAB (40) [36] (Hawaii, 2004)
53—Oklahoma (13) [36] & Florida St. (2) [17] (Orange, 2001)
54—Troy (41) [33] & Rice (17) [21] (New Orleans, 2006)
55—Texas (26) [21] & Iowa (24) [34] (Alamo, 2006)
56—Texas Tech (55) [27] & Clemson (15) [29] (Tangerine, 2002)
56—Marshall (38) [30] & Louisville (15) [26] (GMAC, 2002)
56—Mississippi (27) [33] & Oklahoma (25) [23] (Independence, 1999)
57—Georgia (31) [31] & Virginia Tech (24) [26] (Chick-fil-A, 2006)
57—Iowa (20) [36] & Wyoming (19) [21] (Holiday, 1987)
58—Rutgers (37) [37] & Kansas St. (10) [21] (Texas, 2006)
58—Texas (47) [30] & Washington (43) [28] (Holiday, 2001)
59—San Jose St. (20) [28] & New Mexico (12) [31] (New Mexico, 2006)
59—Oregon (38) [28] & Colorado (16) [31] (Fiesta, 2002)
59—Washington St. (33) [27] & Purdue (27) [32] (Sun, 2001)
59—(D) Hawaii (23) [24] & Oregon St. (17) [35] (Oahu Classic, 1999)

FEWEST RUSHING YARDS
-61—(D) Kansas St. (7) vs. Boston College (12) (Aloha, 1994) (23 attempts)
-56—Tulsa (10) vs. Georgia Tech (52) (Humanitarian, 2004) (26 attempts)
-45—Alabama (10) vs. Missouri (35) (Gator, 1968) (29 attempts)
-39—Tulsa (7) vs. Tennessee (14) (Sugar, 1943)
-30—Florida (6) vs. West Virginia (26) (Peach, Dec. 31, 1981) (34 attempts)
-28—Florida (24) vs. Nebraska (62) (Fiesta, 1996) (21 attempts)
-27—Texas (6) vs. Arkansas (27) (Cotton, 2000) (25 attempts)
-26—(D) TCU (9) vs. Texas A&M (28) (Galleryfurniture.com, 2001) (24 attempts)
-23—Southern California (19) vs. TCU (28) (Sun, 1998) (21 attempts)
-21—Florida St. (20) vs. Wyoming (28) (Sun, 1966) (31 attempts)
-20—Northern Ill. (7) vs. TCU (37) (Poinsettia, 2006) (29 attempts)
-16—BYU (3) vs. Marshall (21) (Motor City, 1999) (30 attempts)
-15—LSU (0) vs. Mississippi (20) (Sugar, 1960)
-14—Navy (6) vs. Texas (28) (Cotton, 1964) (29 attempts)
-14—Tennessee (0) vs. Texas (16) (Cotton, 1953) (29 attempts)
-12—BYU (14) vs. Texas A&M (65) (Holiday, 1990) (21 attempts)
-12—Air Force (13) vs. Tennessee (34) (Sugar, 1971)
-11—Colorado (25) vs. Alabama (30) (Blockbuster, 1991) (30 attempts)
-8—Tulane (6) vs. Penn St. (9) (Liberty, 1979) (20 attempts)
-8—Navy (14) vs. Missouri (21) (Orange, 1961) (24 attempts)
-5—Wisconsin (17) vs. Arkansas (14) (Capital One, 2007) (28 attempts)
-5—Stanford (9) vs. Wisconsin (17) (Rose, 2000) (27 attempts)

FEWEST RUSHING YARDS, BOTH TEAMS
51—(D) Utah (16) [6] & Arizona (13) [45] (Freedom, 1994)
60—Southern California (32) [48] & Michigan (18) [12] (Rose, 2007)
74—Tennessee (34) [86] & Air Force (13) [-12] (Sugar, 1971)
78—(D) Texas A&M (28) [104] & TCU (9) [-26] (galleryfurniture.com, 2001)
79—Oregon St. (38) [20] & Notre Dame (21) [59] (Insight, 2004)
81—Washington St. (10) [7] & Baylor (3) [74] (Alamo, 1994)
81—Florida St. (23) [76] & Florida (17) [5] (Sugar, Jan. 2, 1995)
83—Oklahoma (13) [56] & Florida St. (2) [27] (Orange, 2001)
88—(D) Boston College (12) [149] & Kansas St. (7) [-61] (Aloha, 1994)
93—Oklahoma (10) [56] & Arkansas (3) [37] (Cotton, 2002)
113—Georgia (31) [71] & Virginia Tech (24) [42] (Chick-fil-A, 2006)
117—Southern California (28) [68] & Michigan (14) [49] (Rose, 2004)
118—Miami (Fla.) (21) [28] & Nevada (20) [90] (MPC Computers, 2006)
118—UCLA (27) [73] & New Mexico (13) [45] (Las Vegas, 2002)
125—Pittsburgh (38) [117] & Oregon St. (13) [8] (Insight, 2002)
131—Purdue (37) [5] & Kansas St. (34) [126] (Alamo, 1998)
131—Marshall (21) [147] & BYU (3) [-16] (Motor City, 1999)
132—Texas Tech (55) [91] & Clemson (15) [41] (Tangerine, 2002)
136—Washington St. (33) [81] & Purdue (27) [55] (Sun, 2001)
137—Iowa (20) [94] & Wyoming (19) [43] (Holiday, 1987)
142—Louisville (28) [58] & BYU (10) [84] (Liberty, 2001)
143—BYU (31) [71] & Oklahoma (6) [72] (Copper, 1994)
144—Oregon St. (41) [127] & Notre Dame (9) [17] (Fiesta, 2001)

LOWEST RUSHING AVERAGE
(Minimum 20 Attempts)
-2.7—(D) Kansas St. (7) vs. Boston College (12) (Aloha, 1994) (23 for -61)
-2.2—Tulsa (10) vs. Georgia Tech (52) (Humanitarian, 2004) (26 for -56)
-1.6—Alabama (10) vs. Missouri (35) (Gator, 1968) (29 for -45)
-1.3—Florida (24) vs. Nebraska (62) (Fiesta, 1996) (21 for -28)
-1.1—Texas (6) vs. Arkansas (27) (Cotton, 2000) (25 for -27)
-1.1—Southern California (19) vs. TCU (28) (Sun, 1998) (21 for -23)
-0.9—Florida (6) vs. West Virginia (26) (Peach, Dec. 31, 1981) (32 for -30)
-0.7—Northern Ill. (7) vs. TCU (37) (Poinsettia, 2006) (29 for -20)
-0.7—Florida St. (20) vs. Wyoming (28) (Sun, 1966) (31 for -21)
-0.6—BYU (14) vs. Texas A&M (65) (Holiday, 1990) (21 for -12)
-0.5—BYU (3) vs. Marshall (21) (Motor City, 1999) (30 for -16)
-0.5—Air Force (13) vs. Tennessee (34) (Sugar, 1971) (24 for -12)
-0.5—Navy (6) vs. Texas (28) (Cotton, 1964) (29 for -14)
-0.5—Tennessee (0) vs. Texas (16) (Cotton, 1953) (29 for -14)

Passing

MOST PASS ATTEMPTS
(Followed by Comp.-Att.-Int. and Yardage)
75—Purdue (27) vs. Washington St. (33) (Sun, 2001) (38-75-4, 419 yards)
70—Northwestern (38) vs. UCLA (50) (Sun, 2005) (38-70-2, 416 yards)
70—Marshall (64) vs. East Caro. (61) (2 ot) (GMAC, 2001) (41-70-2, 576 yards)
63—(D) Fresno St. (30) vs. Colorado (41) (Aloha, 1993) (37-63-1, 523 yards)
63—(D) San Jose St. (25) vs. Toledo (27) (California, 1981) (43-63-5, 467 yards)
61—Oregon (20) vs. Penn St. (38) (Rose, 1995) (41-61-2, 456 yards)
61—(D) BYU (16) vs. Virginia (22) (All-American, 1987) (37-61-1, 394 yards)
60—Texas Tech (45) vs. California (31) (Holiday, 2004) (39-60-0, 520 yards)
60—Purdue (25) vs. Georgia (28) (ot) (Outback, 2000) (36-60-1, 378 yards)
59—Akron (31) vs. Memphis (38) (Motor City, 2005) (34-59-0, 455 yards)
59—Louisiana Tech (24) vs. Clemson (49) (Humanitarian, 2001) (401 yards)
59—Georgia (27) vs. Virginia (34) (Peach, Dec. 30, 1995) (31-59-2, 413 yards)
59—BYU (39) vs. Penn St. (50) (Holiday, 1989) (42-59-2, 576 yards)

MOST PASS ATTEMPTS, BOTH TEAMS
116—Washington St. (33) [41] & Purdue (27) [75] (Sun, 2001) (53 completed)
109—Texas (47) [55] & Washington (43) [54] (Holiday, 2001) (64 completed)
108—Texas Tech (55) [52] & Clemson (15) [56] (Tangerine, 2002) (64 completed)
102—Texas Tech (45) [60] & California (31) [42] (Holiday, 2004) (63 completed)
101—Hawaii (59) [47] & UAB (40) [54] (Hawaii, 2004) (62 completed)
96—Clemson (27) [40] & Tennessee (14) [56] (Peach, Jan. 2, 2004) (53 completed)
95—Florida (31) [40] & Iowa (24) [55] (Outback, 2006) (57 completed)
94—UCLA (50) [24] & Northwestern (38) [70] (Sun, 2005) (48 completed)
94—Mississippi St. (17) [38] & Clemson (7) [56] (Peach, 1999) (42 completed)
93—Marshall (64) [70] & East Caro. (61) [23] (2 ot) (GMAC, 2001) (52 completed)
93—Georgia (28) [33] & Purdue (25) [60] (ot) (Outback, 2000) (56 completed)
93—Idaho (42) [41] & Southern Miss. (35) [52] (Humanitarian, 1998) (55 completed)
93—Mississippi (34) [48] & Marshall (31) [45] (Motor City, 1997) (52 completed)

MOST PASS COMPLETIONS
(Followed by Comp.-Att.-Int. and Yardage)
43—(D) San Jose St. (25) vs. Toledo (27) (California, 1981) (43-63-5, 467 yards)
42—BYU (39) vs. Penn St. (50) (Holiday, 1989) (42-59-2, 576 yards)
41—(D) Texas Tech (38) vs. Navy (14) (Houston, 2003) (41-53-1, 497 yards)
41—Marshall (64) vs. East Caro. (61) (2 ot) (GMAC, 2001) (41-70-2, 576 yards)
41—Oregon (20) vs. Penn St. (38) (Rose, 1995) (41-61-2, 456 yards)
39—Texas Tech (45) vs. California (31) (Holiday, 2004) (39-60-0, 520 yards)
39—Texas Tech (55) vs. Clemson (15) (Tangerine, 2002) (39-52-1, 464 yards)
39—Oklahoma (25) vs. Mississippi (27) (Independence, 1999) (39-54-1, 390 yards)
39—Richmond (49) vs. Ohio (42) (Tangerine, 1968) (39-58-2, 447 yards)
38—Northwestern (38) vs. UCLA (50) (Sun, 2005) (38-70-2, 416 yards)
38—North Carolina St. (56) vs. Kansas (26) (Tangerine, 2003) (38-46-0, 481 yards)
38—Bowling Green (28) vs. Northwestern (24) (Motor City, 2003) (38-51-3, 386 yards)
38—Purdue (27) vs. Washington St. (33) (Sun, 2001) (38-75-4, 419 yards)
38—Illinois (29) vs. Army (31) (Peach, 1985) (38-55-2, 401 yards)
38—(D) Vanderbilt (28) vs. Air Force (36) (Hall of Fame, 1982) (38-51-3, 452 yards)
38—Florida St. (17) vs. Penn St. (17) (Gator, 1967) (38-55-4, 363 yards)

MOST PASS COMPLETIONS, BOTH TEAMS
64—Texas Tech (55) [39] & Clemson (15) [25] (Tangerine, 2002) (108 attempted)
64—Texas (47) [37] & Washington (43) [27] (Holiday, 2001) (109 attempted)
63—Texas Tech (45) [39] & California (31) [24] (Holiday, 2004) (102 attempted)
62—Hawaii (59) [31] & UAB (40) [31] (Hawaii, 2004) (101 attempted)
61—Penn St. (38) [20] & Oregon (20) [41] (Rose, 1995) (92 attempted)
59—Texas (41) [30] & Southern California (38) [29] (Rose, 2006) (81 attempted)
58—North Carolina St. (56) [38] & Kansas (26) [20] (Tangerine, 2003) (88 attempted)
57—Florida (31) [25] & Iowa (24) [32] (Outback, 2006) (95 attempted)
57—(D) Michigan St. (44) [22] & Fresno St. (35) [35] (Silicon Valley, 2001) (90 attempted)
56—Florida (56) [33] & Maryland (23) [23] (Orange, 2002) (88 attempted)
56—Georgia (28) [20] & Purdue (25) [36] (ot) (Outback, 2000) (93 attempted)
56—Richmond (49) [39] & Ohio (42) [17] (Tangerine, 1968) (91 attempted)

MOST PASSING YARDS
(Followed by Comp.-Att.-Int.)
576—Marshall (64) vs. East Caro. (61) (2 ot) (GMAC, 2001) (41-70-2)
576—BYU (39) vs. Penn St. (50) (Holiday, 1989) (42-59-2)
559—Hawaii (41) vs. Arizona St. (24) (Hawaii, 2006) (33-42-1)
531—(D) Fresno St. (35) vs. Michigan St. (44) (Silicon Valley, 2001) (35-58-2)
527—Hawaii (54) vs. Houston (48) (3 ot) (Hawaii, 2003) (29-47-1)
523—(D) Fresno St. (30) vs. Colorado (41) (Aloha, 1993) (37-63-1)
520—Texas Tech (45) vs. California (31) (Holiday, 2004) (39-60-0)
497—(D) Texas Tech (38) vs. Navy (14) (Houston, 2003) (41-53-1)
492—Washington St. (31) vs. Utah (28) (Copper, 1992) (32-48-1)
485—BYU (31) vs. Oklahoma (6) (Copper, 1994) (23-46-0)
481—North Carolina St. (56) vs. Kansas (26) (Tangerine, 2003) (38-46-0)
473—Texas (47) vs. Washington (43) (Holiday, 2001) (37-55-3)
469—(D) Iowa (55) vs. Texas (17) (Freedom, 1984) (30-40-0)
467—Arizona St. (45) vs. Rutgers (40) (Insight, 2005) (23-35-0)
467—(D) San Jose St. (25) vs. Toledo (27) (California, 1981) (43-63-5)
464—Texas Tech (55) vs. Clemson (15) (Tangerine, 2002) (39-52-1)
458—Louisville (34) vs. Alabama (7) (Fiesta, 1991) (21-39-3)
456—Florida (56) vs. Maryland (23) (Orange, 2002) (33-49-2)
456—Oregon (20) vs. Penn St. (38) (Rose, 1995) (41-61-2)
456—(D) Oregon (43) vs. Colorado (51) (Aloha, 1998) (24-46-2)
455—Akron (31) vs. Memphis (38) (Motor City, 2005) (34-59-0)
455—Florida St. (40) vs. Texas Tech (17) (Tangerine, 1977) (25-35-0)

MOST PASSING YARDS, BOTH TEAMS
907—(D) Michigan St. (44) [376] & Fresno St. (35) [531] (Silicon Valley, 2001) (90 attempted)
859—Hawaii (54) [527] & Houston (48) [332] (3 ot) (Hawaii, 2003) (81 attempted)
841—Arizona St. (45) [467] & Rutgers (40) [374] (Insight, 2005) (73 attempted)
822—Hawaii (59) [405] & UAB (40) [417] (Hawaii, 2004) (101 attempted)
808—Washington St. (31) [492] & Utah (28) [316] (Copper, 1992) (88 attempted)
792—California (52) [394] & Virginia Tech (49) [398] (Insight, 2003) (81 attempted)
791—Penn St. (50) [215] & BYU (39) [576] (Holiday, 1989) (80 attempted)
783—Texas Tech (55) [464] & Clemson (15) [319] (Tangerine, 2002) (108 attempted)
774—Florida St. (23) [325] & Florida (17) [449] (Sugar, Jan. 2, 1995) (84 attempted)
766—Texas Tech (45) [520] & California (31) [246] (Holiday, 2004) (102 attempted)
766—Texas (47) [473] & Washington (43) [293] (Holiday, 2001) (109 attempted)

750—Hawaii (41) [559] & Arizona St. (24) [191] (Hawaii, 2006) (68 attempted)
747—Marshall (48) [411] & Louisville (29) [336] (Motor City, 1998) (78 attempted)
746—LSU (47) [444] & Illinois (34) [302] (Sugar, 2002) (89 attempted)
737—Marshall (64) [576] & East Caro. (61) [161] (2 ot) (GMAC, 2001) (93 attempted)
734—Florida St. (40) [455] & Texas Tech (17) [279] (Tangerine, 1977) (63 attempted)
732—(D) Toledo (27) [265] & San Jose St. (25) [467] (California, 1981) (85 attempted)
727—Southern California (41) [391] & Northwestern (32) [336] (Rose, 1996) (83 attempted)
724—North Carolina St. (56) [481] & Kansas (26) [243] (Tangerine, 2003) (88 attempted)
715—Oregon St. (39) [356] & Missouri (38) [359] (Sun, 2006) (86 attempted)
715—South Carolina (44) [323] & Houston (36) [392] (Liberty, 2006) (69 attempted)
713—Florida (56) [456] & Maryland (23) [257] (Orange, 2002) (88 attempted)
708—Texas Tech (44) [445] & Minnesota (41) [263] (ot) (Insight, 2006) (86 attempted)
708—(D) Navy (42) [395] & California (38) [313] (Aloha, 1996) (59 attempted)

MOST PASSES HAD INTERCEPTED

8—Arizona (10) vs. Auburn (34) (Sun, 1968)
7—Illinois (15) vs. Alabama (21) (Liberty, 1982)
7—Missouri (3) vs. Penn St. (10) (Orange, 1970)
7—Texas A&M (21) vs. Alabama (29) (Cotton, 1942)
6—(D) Georgia Tech (21) vs. Fresno St. (30) (Silicon Valley, 2002)
6—Georgia (6) vs. Nebraska (45) (Sun, 1969)
6—TCU (26) vs. Georgia (40) (Orange, 1942)
6—SMU (0) vs. Stanford (7) (Rose, 1936)

MOST PASSES HAD INTERCEPTED, BOTH TEAMS

12—Auburn (34) [4] & Arizona (10) [8] (Sun, 1968)
10—Georgia (40) [6] & TCU (26) [4] (Orange, 1942)
9—Alabama (21) [2] & Illinois (15) [7] (Liberty, 1982)
8—Ohio St. (28) [3] & Texas A&M (12) [5] (Cotton, 1987)
8—Nebraska (28) [3] & LSU (10) [5] (Sugar, 1985)
8—Penn St. (10) [1] & Missouri (3) [7] (Orange, 1970)
8—Nebraska (45) [2] & Georgia (6) [6] (Sun, 1969)
8—Texas (12) [3] & Mississippi (7) [5] (Cotton, 1962)

MOST PASSES ATTEMPTED WITHOUT AN INTERCEPTION
(Followed by Comp.-Att.-Int. and Yardage)

60—Texas Tech (45) vs. California (31) (Holiday, 2004) (39-60-0, 520 yards)
59—Akron (31) vs. Memphis (38) (Motor City, 2005) (34-59-0, 455 yards)
57—(D) Western Mich. (30) vs. Fresno St. (35) (California, 1988) (24-57-0, 366 yards)
56—Tennessee (14) vs. Clemson (27) (Peach, Jan. 2, 2004) (31-56-0, 384 yards)
53—LSU (47) vs. Illinois (34) (Sugar, 2002) (31-53-0, 444 yards)
52—Southern Miss. (35) vs. Idaho (42) (Humanitarian, 1998) (31-52-0, 362 yards)
51—Nevada (37) vs. Toledo (40) (ot) (Las Vegas, 1995) (27-51-0, 330 yards)
51—Florida (34) vs. Michigan St. (37) (Florida Citrus, 2000) (25-51-0, 300 yards)

MOST PASSES ATTEMPTED WITHOUT AN INTERCEPTION, BOTH TEAMS
(Followed by Comp.-Att.-Int. and Yardage)

93—Idaho (42) [41] & Southern Miss. (35) [52] (Humanitarian, 1998) (55-93-0, 653 yards)
92—Arizona St. (27) [45] & Purdue (23) [47] (Sun, 2004) (48-92-0, 651 yards)
90—Bowling Green (35) [49] & Nevada (34) [41] (Las Vegas, 1992) (54-90-0, 597 yards)

HIGHEST COMPLETION PERCENTAGE
(Minimum 10 Attempts) (Followed by Comp.-Att.-Int. and Yardage)

.929—Texas (40) vs. Missouri (27) (Cotton, 1946) (13-14-0, 234 yards)
.900—Mississippi (13) vs. Air Force (0) (Liberty, 1992) (9-10-0, 163 yards)
.897—Georgia (33) vs. Wisconsin (6) (Outback, 1998) (26-29-0, 267 yards)
.889—Texas A&M (65) vs. BYU (14) (Holiday, 1990) (16-18-0, 324 yards)
.833—Alabama (13) vs. Penn St. (6) (Sugar, 1975) (10-12-0, 210 yards)
.828—Oklahoma St. (62) vs. Wyoming (14) (Holiday, 1988) (24-29-0, 378 yards)
.826—North Carolina St. (56) vs. Kansas (26) (Tangerine, 2003) (38-46-0, 481 yards)
.824—Nebraska (21) vs. North Carolina (17) (Liberty, 1977) (14-17-2, 161 yards)
.818—Texas A&M (41) vs. Mississippi St. (43) (ot) (Independence, 2000) (9-11-1, 133 yards)
.813—TCU (28) vs. Syracuse (27) (Cotton, 1957) (13-16-0, 202 yards)

MOST YARDS PER ATTEMPT
(Minimum 10 Attempts)

21.7—Southern California (47) vs. Pittsburgh (14) (Rose, 1930) (13 for 282)
18.8—(D) Navy (42) vs. California (38) (Aloha, 1996) (21 for 295)
18.0—Texas A&M (65) vs. BYU (14) (Holiday, 1990) (18 for 324)
17.5—Alabama (13) vs. Penn St. (6) (Sugar, 1975) (12 for 210)
17.1—Marshall (48) vs. Louisville (29) (Motor City, 1998) (24 for 411)
16.7—Texas (36) vs. Tennessee (13) (Cotton, 1969) (14 for 234)
16.7—Texas (40) vs. Missouri (27) (Cotton, 1946) (14 for 234)
16.7—(D) Air Force (45) vs. Washington (25) (Oahu Classic, 1998) (16 for 267)
15.1—West Virginia (49) vs. Mississippi (38) (Music City, 2000) (21 for 318)
14.6—Tennessee (23) vs. Florida St. (16) (Fiesta, 1999) (19 for 278)

MOST YARDS PER COMPLETION
(Minimum 8 Completions)

35.2—Southern California (47) vs. Pittsburgh (14) (Rose, 1930) (8 for 282)
29.3—Texas (36) vs. Tennessee (13) (Cotton, 1969) (8 for 234)
29.3—Texas (28) vs. Navy (6) (Cotton, 1964) (8 for 234)

FEWEST PASS ATTEMPTS

2—Air Force (38) vs. Mississippi St. (15) (Liberty, 1991) (completed 1)
2—(D) Army (10) vs. Michigan St. (6) (Cherry, 1984) (completed 1)
2—West Virginia (14) vs. South Carolina (3) (Peach, 1969) (completed 1)
3—Air Force (23) vs. Ohio St. (11) (Liberty, 1990) (completed 1)
3—Oklahoma (31) vs. Nebraska (24) (Orange, 1979) (completed 2)
3—Georgia Tech (21) vs. Pittsburgh (14) (Gator, 1956) (completed 3)
3—Georgia Tech (7) vs. Pittsburgh (0) (Sugar, 1956) (completed 0)
3—Miami (Fla.) (14) vs. Clemson (0) (Gator, 1952) (completed 2)
3—Hardin-Simmons (7) vs. Second Air Force (13) (Sun, 1943) (completed 1)
3—Catholic (20) vs. Mississippi (19) (Orange, 1936) (completed 1)

FEWEST PASS ATTEMPTS, BOTH TEAMS

9—Fordham (2) [4] & Missouri (0) [5] (Sugar, 1942)
13—Colorado (27) [9] & Clemson (21) [4] (Orange, 1957)
14—Tennessee (3) [6] & Texas A&M (0) [8] (Gator, 1957)
14—Texas (16) [8] & Tennessee (0) [6] (Cotton, 1953)
15—Utah (26) [4] & New Mexico (0) [11] (Sun, 1939)
15—LSU (7) [11] & Clemson (0) [4] (Sugar, 1959)

FEWEST PASS COMPLETIONS
(Followed by Comp.-Att.-Int.)

0—Army (28) vs. Alabama (29) (John Hancock Sun, 1988) (0-6-1)
0—Missouri (35) vs. Alabama (10) (Gator, 1968) (0-6-2)
0—(D) Missouri (14) vs. Georgia Tech (10) (Bluebonnet, 1962) (0-7-2)
0—(D) New Mexico (28) vs. Western Mich. (12) (Aviation, 1961) (0-4-0)
0—Utah St. (13) vs. New Mexico St. (20) (Sun, 1960) (0-4-0)
0—Georgia Tech (7) vs. Pittsburgh (0) (Sugar, 1956) (0-3-1)
0—Arkansas (0) vs. LSU (0) (Cotton, 1947) (0-4-1)
0—Rice (8) vs. Tennessee (0) (Orange, 1947) (0-4-2)
0—Miami (Fla.) (13) vs. Holy Cross (6) (Orange, 1946) (0-10-3)
0—Fordham (2) vs. Missouri (0) (Sugar, 1942) (0-4-0)
0—Arizona St. (0) vs. Catholic (0) (Sun, 1940) (0-7-2)
0—Tulane (13) vs. Texas A&M (14) (Sugar, 1940) (0-4-0)
0—West Virginia (7) vs. Texas Tech (6) (Sun, 1938) (0-7-0)

FEWEST PASS COMPLETIONS, BOTH TEAMS

3—Arizona St. (0) [0] & Catholic (0) [3] (Sun, 1940)
4—Penn St. (7) [2] & Alabama (0) [2] (Liberty, 1959)
4—Baylor (13) [3] & Tennessee (7) [1] (Sugar, 1957)
4—Rice (8) [0] & Tennessee (0) [4] (Orange, 1947)
5—Oklahoma (14) [3] & Michigan (6) [2] (Orange, 1976)
5—Kentucky (21) [2] & North Carolina (0) [3] (Peach, 1976)
5—Texas (16) [2] & Tennessee (0) [3] (Cotton, 1953)
5—Arkansas (0) [0] & LSU (0) [5] (Cotton, 1947)
5—Wake Forest (26) [1] & South Carolina (14) [4] (Gator, 1946)
5—Utah (26) [1] & New Mexico (0) [4] (Sun, 1939)

FEWEST PASSING YARDS
(Followed by Comp.-Att.-Int.)

-50—U. of Mexico (0) vs. Southwestern (Tex.) (35) (Sun, 1945) (2-9-3)
-2—Oklahoma (40) vs. Houston (14) (Sun, 1981) (1-5-1)
0—Army (28) vs. Alabama (29) (John Hancock Sun, 1988) (0-6-1)
0—Missouri (35) vs. Alabama (10) (Gator, 1968) (0-6-2)
0—(D) Missouri (14) vs. Georgia Tech (10) (Bluebonnet, 1962) (0-7-2)
0—(D) New Mexico (28) vs. Western Mich. (12) (Aviation, 1961) (0-4-0)
0—Utah St. (13) vs. New Mexico St. (20) (Sun, 1960) (0-4-0)
0—Georgia Tech (7) vs. Pittsburgh (0) (Sugar, 1956) (0-3-1)
0—Arkansas (0) vs. LSU (0) (Cotton, 1947) (0-4-1)
0—Rice (8) vs. Tennessee (0) (Orange, 1947) (0-4-2)
0—Miami (Fla.) (13) vs. Holy Cross (6) (Orange, 1946) (0-10-3)
0—Fordham (2) vs. Missouri (0) (Sugar, 1942) (0-4-0)
0—Tulane (13) vs. Texas A&M (14) (Sugar, 1940) (0-4-0)
0—Arizona St. (0) vs. Catholic (0) (Sun, 1940) (0-7-2)
0—West Virginia (7) vs. Texas Tech (6) (Sun, 1938) (0-7-0)
0—California (0) vs. Wash. & Jeff. (0) (Rose, 1922)
0—Oregon (6) vs. Harvard (7) (Rose, 1920)

FEWEST PASSING YARDS, BOTH TEAMS

16—Arkansas (0) [0] & LSU (0) [16] (Cotton, 1947)
16—Arizona St. (0) [0] & Catholic (0) [16] (Sun, 1940)
21—Fordham (2) [0] & Missouri (0) [21] (Sugar, 1942)
32—Rice (8) [0] & Tennessee (0) [32] (Orange, 1947)
40—Kentucky (21) [16] & North Carolina (0) [24] (Peach, 1976)
40—Baylor (13) [24] & Tennessee (7) [16] (Sugar, 1957)
52—Colorado (27) [25] & Clemson (21) [27] (Orange, 1957)
59—Miami (Fla.) (13) [0] & Holy Cross (6) [59] (Orange, 1946)
60—North Carolina (26) [10] & Texas (10) [50] (Sun, 1982)
62—Southern California (25) [45] & Tennessee (0) [17] (Rose, 1945)
68—Missouri (35) [0] & Alabama (10) [68] (Gator, 1968)
68—Penn St. (7) [41] & Alabama (0) [27] (Liberty, 1959)
74—Oklahoma (41) [23] & Wyoming (7) [51] (Fiesta, 1976)
75—Southwestern (Tex.) (7) [65] & New Mexico (0) [10] (Sun, 1944)
77—Utah (26) [18] & New Mexico (0) [59] (Sun, 1939)
78—Texas (16) [32] & Tennessee (0) [46] (Cotton, 1953)

LOWEST COMPLETION PERCENTAGE
(Followed by Comp.-Att.-Int.)

.000—Army (28) vs. Alabama (29) (John Hancock Sun, 1988) (0-6-1)
.000—Missouri (35) vs. Alabama (10) (Gator, 1968) (0-6-2)
.000—(D) Missouri (14) vs. Georgia Tech (10) (Bluebonnet, 1962) (0-7-2)
.000—(D) New Mexico (28) vs. Western Mich. (12) (Aviation, 1961) (0-4-0)
.000—Utah St. (13) vs. New Mexico St. (20) (Sun, 1960) (0-4-0)

.000—Georgia Tech (7) vs. Pittsburgh (0) (Sugar, 1956) (0-3-1)
.000—Arkansas (0) vs. LSU (0) (Cotton, 1947) (0-4-1)
.000—Rice (8) vs. Tennessee (0) (Orange, 1947) (0-4-2)
.000—Miami (Fla.) (13) vs. Holy Cross (6) (Orange, 1946) (0-10-3)
.000—Fordham (2) vs. Missouri (0) (Sugar, 1942) (0-4-0)
.000—Tulane (13) vs. Texas A&M (14) (Sugar, 1940) (0-4-0)
.000—Arizona St. (0) vs. Catholic (0) (Sun, 1940) (0-7-2)
.000—West Virginia (7) vs. Texas Tech (6) (Sun, 1938) (0-7-0)

FEWEST YARDS PER PASS ATTEMPT
-5.6—U. of Mexico (0) vs. Southwestern (Tex.) (35) (Sun, 1945) (9 for -50)
-0.4—Oklahoma (40) vs. Houston (14) (Sun, 1981) (5 for -2)
0.0—Army (28) vs. Alabama (29) (John Hancock Sun, 1988) (6 for 0)
0.0—Missouri (35) vs. Alabama (10) (Gator, 1968) (6 for 0)
0.0—(D) Missouri (14) vs. Georgia Tech (10) (Bluebonnet, 1962) (7 for 0)
0.0—(D) New Mexico (28) vs. Western Mich. (12) (Aviation, 1961) (4 for 0)
0.0—Utah St. (13) vs. New Mexico St. (20) (Sun, 1960) (4 for 0)
0.0—Georgia Tech (7) vs. Pittsburgh (0) (Sugar, 1956) (3 for 0)
0.0—Arkansas (0) vs. LSU (0) (Cotton, 1947) (4 for 0)
0.0—Rice (8) vs. Tennessee (0) (Orange, 1947) (4 for 0)
0.0—Miami (Fla.) (13) vs. Holy Cross (6) (Orange, 1946) (10 for 0)
0.0—Fordham (2) vs. Missouri (0) (Sugar, 1942) (4 for 0)
0.0—Tulane (13) vs. Texas A&M (14) (Sugar, 1940) (4 for 0)
0.0—Arizona St. (0) vs. Catholic (0) (Sun, 1940) (7 for 0)
0.0—West Virginia (7) vs. Texas Tech (6) (Sun, 1938) (7 for 0)

FEWEST YARDS PER PASS COMPLETION
(Minimum 1 completion)
-25.0—U. of Mexico (0) vs. Southwestern (Tex.) (35) (Sun, 1945) (2 for -50)
-2.0—Oklahoma (40) vs. Houston (14) (Sun, 1981) (1 for -2)
3.0—West Virginia (14) vs. South Carolina (3) (Peach, 1969) (1 for 3)
3.2—LSU (0) vs. Arkansas (0) (Cotton, 1947) (5 for 16)
3.3—North Carolina (26) vs. Texas (10) (Sun, 1982) (3 for 10)
3.3—New Mexico (0) vs. Southwestern (Tex.) (7) (Sun, 1944) (3 for 10)
4.5—Alabama (34) vs. Miami (Fla.) (13) (Sugar, 1993) (4 for 18)
4.6—Texas (14) vs. Georgia Tech (7) (Cotton, 1943) (5 for 23)
4.8—UTEP (33) vs. Georgetown (20) (Sun, 1950) (5 for 24)
5.3—Case Reserve (26) vs. Arizona St. (13) (Sun, 1941) (3 for 16)
5.3—Arkansas (3) vs. UCLA (17) (Cotton, 1989) (4 for 21)

Scoring

MOST TOUCHDOWNS
10—Nebraska (66) vs. Northwestern (17) (Alamo, 2000) (6 rush, 4 pass)
9—Marshall (64) vs. East Caro. (61) (2 ot) (GMAC, 2001) (3 rush, 4 pass, 2 interception returns)
9—Illinois (63) vs. Virginia (21) (Micronpc.com, 1999) (6 rush, 3 pass)
9—Texas A&M (65) vs. BYU (14) (Holiday, 1990) (5 rush, 4 pass)
9—Alabama (61) vs. Syracuse (6) (Orange, 1953) (4 rush, 3 pass, 1 punt return, 1 interception return)
9—(D) Centre (63) vs. TCU (7) (Fort Worth Classic, 1921) (8 rush, 1 blocked punt recovery in end zone)
8—Hawaii (59) vs. UAB (40) (Hawaii, 2004) (2 rush, 4 pass, 1 kickoff return, 1 punt return)
8—North Carolina St. (56) vs. Kansas (26) (Tangerine, 2003) (3 rush, 5 pass)
8—Florida (56) vs. Maryland (23) (Orange, 2002) (3 rush, 5 pass)
8—Colorado (62) vs. Boston College (28) (Insight.com, 1999) (5 rush, 2 interception return, 1 punt return)
8—Nebraska (62) vs. Florida (24) (Fiesta, 1996) (6 rush, 1 pass, 1 interception return)
8—Kansas St. (54) vs. Colorado St. (21) (Holiday, 1995) (4 rush, 4 pass)
8—Oklahoma St. (62) vs. Wyoming (14) (Holiday, 1988) (6 rush, 2 pass)
8—Toledo (56) vs. Davidson (33) (Tangerine, 1969) (4 rush, 3 pass, 1 fumble return)

MOST TOUCHDOWNS, BOTH TEAMS
16—Marshall (64) [9] & East Caro. (61) (2 ot) [7] (GMAC, 2001)
14—California (52) [7] & Virginia Tech (49) [7] (Insight, 2003)
13—Nevada (49) [7] & UCF (48) [6] (ot) (Hawaii, 2005)
13—Hawaii (59) [8] & UAB (40) [5] (Hawaii, 2004)
13—Hawaii (54) [7] & Houston (48) [6] (3 ot) (Hawaii, 2003)
13—Texas Tech (55) [7] & Air Force (41) [6] (Copper, 1995)
13—Richmond (49) [7] & Ohio (42) [6] (Tangerine, 1968)
12—UCLA (50) [7] & Northwestern (38) [5] (Sun, 2005)
12—Bowling Green (52) [7] & Memphis (35) [5] (GMAC, 2004)
12—LSU (47) [7] & Illinois (34) [5] (Sugar, 2002)
12—Nebraska (66) [10] & Northwestern (17) [2] (Alamo, 2000)
12—Colorado (62) [8] & Boston College (28) [4] (Insight.com, 1999)
12—Illinois (63) [9] & Virginia (21) [3] (Micronpc.com, 1999)
12—(D) Colorado (51) [6] & Oregon (43) [6] (Aloha, 1998)

MOST TOUCHDOWNS RUSHING
8—(D) Centre (63) vs. TCU (7) (Fort Worth Classic, 1921)
7—Georgia Tech (52) vs. Tulsa (10) (Humanitarian, 2004)
7—(D) Houston (47) vs. Tulane (7) (Bluebonnet, 1973)
6—Nevada (49) vs. UCF (48) (ot) (Hawaii, 2005)
6—Nebraska (66) vs. Northwestern (17) (Alamo, 2000)
6—Illinois (63) vs. Virginia (21) (Micronpc.com, 1999)
6—Nebraska (42) vs. Tennessee (17) (Orange, 1998)
6—(D) Navy (42) vs. California (38) (Aloha, 1996)
6—Nebraska (62) vs. Florida (24) (Fiesta, 1996)
6—Texas Tech (55) vs. Air Force (41) (Copper, 1995)
6—Air Force (41) vs. Texas Tech (55) (Copper, 1995)
6—Texas Tech (49) vs. Duke (21) (All-American, 1989)
6—Oklahoma St. (62) vs. Wyoming (14) (Holiday, 1988)
6—Oklahoma (42) vs. Arkansas (8) (Orange, 1987)
6—Ohio St. (47) vs. BYU (17) (Holiday, 1982)
6—Oklahoma St. (49) vs. BYU (21) (Tangerine, 1976)
6—Arizona St. (48) vs. North Carolina (26) (Peach, 1970)
6—Michigan (49) vs. Stanford (0) (Rose, 1902)

MOST TOUCHDOWNS RUSHING, BOTH TEAMS
12—Texas Tech (55) [6] & Air Force (41) [6] (Copper, 1995)
9—Texas (41) [5] & Southern California (38) [4] (Rose, 2006)
9—Nevada (49) [6] & UCF (48) [3] (ot) (Hawaii, 2005)
9—Arizona St. (48) [6] & North Carolina (26) [3] (Peach, 1970)
8—Marshall (64) [3] & East Caro. (61) [5] (2 ot) (GMAC, 2001)
8—Oklahoma St. (62) [6] & Wyoming (14) [2] (Holiday, 1988)
8—Colorado (47) [5] & Alabama (33) [3] (Liberty, 1969)
7—Georgia Tech (52) [7] & Tulsa (10) [0] (Humanitarian, 2004)
7—California (52) [5] & Virginia Tech (49) [2] (Insight, 2003)
7—Nebraska (66) [6] & Northwestern (17) [1] (Alamo, 2000)
7—Illinois (63) [6] & Virginia (21) [1] (Micronpc.com, 1999)
7—(D) Navy (42) [6] & California (38) [1] (Aloha, 1996)
7—Nebraska (62) [6] & Florida (24) [1] (Fiesta, 1996)
7—Kansas St. (54) [4] & Colorado St. (21) [3] (Holiday, 1995)
7—Oklahoma (42) [6] & Arkansas (8) [1] (Orange, 1987)
7—Oklahoma St. (35) [4] & West Virginia (33) [3] (John Hancock Sun, 1987)
7—UCLA (45) [5] & Iowa (28) [2] (Rose, 1986)
7—Oklahoma St. (49) [6] & BYU (21) [1] (Tangerine, 1976)
7—Arizona St. (49) [5] & Missouri (35) [2] (Fiesta, 1972)
7—Penn St. (41) [5] & Oregon (12) [2] (Liberty, 1960)

MOST TOUCHDOWNS PASSING
6—(D) Iowa (55) vs. Texas (17) (Freedom, 1984)
5—Hawaii (41) vs. Arizona St. (24) (Hawaii, 2006)
5—Toledo (45) vs. UTEP (13) (GMAC, 2005)
5—Southern California (55) vs. Oklahoma (19) (Orange, 2005)
5—Bowling Green (52) vs. Memphis (35) (GMAC, 2004)
5—Fresno St. (37) vs. Virginia (34) (ot) (MPC Computers, 2004)
5—North Carolina St. (56) vs. Kansas (26) (Tangerine, 2003)
5—Hawaii (54) vs. Houston (48) (3 ot) (Hawaii, 2003)
5—Texas Tech (55) vs. Clemson (15) (Tangerine, 2002)
5—Florida (56) vs. Maryland (23) (Orange, 2002)
5—Illinois (34) vs. LSU (47) (Sugar, 2002)
5—Clemson (49) vs. Louisiana Tech (24) (Humanitarian, 2001)
5—West Virginia (49) vs. Mississippi (38) (Music City, 2000)
5—Southern California (55) vs. Texas Tech (14) (Cotton, 1995)
5—Florida St. (41) vs. Nebraska (17) (Fiesta, 1990)
5—Florida St. (36) vs. Oklahoma (19) (Gator, Jan. 2, 1965)

MOST TOUCHDOWNS PASSING, BOTH TEAMS
9—Bowling Green (52) [5] & Memphis (35) [4] (GMAC, 2004)
8—LSU (47) [3] & Illinois (34) [5] (Sugar, 2002)
8—West Virginia (49) [5] & Mississippi (38) [3] (Music City, 2000)
8—(D) Iowa (55) [6] & Texas (17) [2] (Freedom, 1984)
8—Richmond (49) [4] & Ohio (42) [4] (Tangerine, 1968)
7—Hawaii (41) [5] & Arizona St. (24) [2] (Hawaii, 2006)
7—Oregon St. (39) [4] & Missouri (38) [3] (Sun, 2006)
7—South Carolina (44) [4] & Houston (36) [3] (Liberty, 2006)
7—Arizona St. (45) [4] & Rutgers (40) [3] (Insight, 2005)
7—Southern California (55) [5] & Oklahoma (19) [2] (Orange, 2005)
7—North Carolina St. (56) [5] & Kansas (26) [2] (Tangerine, 2003)
7—Hawaii (54) [5] & Houston (48) [2] (3 ot) (Hawaii, 2003)
7—(D) Michigan St. (44) [3] & Fresno St. (35) [4] (Silicon Valley, 2001)
7—Florida St. (31) [4] & Notre Dame (26) [3] (Orange, 1996)
7—East Caro. (37) [4] & North Carolina St. (34) [3] (Peach, 1992)
7—Toledo (56) [3] & Davidson (33) [4] (Tangerine, 1969)
7—Georgia (40) [4] & TCU (26) [3] (Orange, 1942)

MOST FIELD GOALS MADE
5—Minnesota (29) vs. Arkansas (14) (Music City, 2002) (24, 45, 21, 22, 29 yards)
5—Texas A&M (22) vs. Michigan (20) (Alamo, 1995) (27, 49, 47, 31, 37 yards)
5—Mississippi St. (24) vs. North Carolina St. (28) (Peach, Jan. 1, 1995) (37, 21, 29, 36, 30 yards)
5—Florida (28) vs. Notre Dame (39) (Sugar, 1992) (26, 24, 36, 37, 24 yards)
5—Maryland (23) vs. Tennessee (30) (Florida Citrus, 1983) (18, 48, 31, 22, 26 yards)
4—Utah (25) vs. Tulsa (13) (Armed Forces, 2006) (45, 39, 41, 34 yards)
4—Nevada (20) vs. Miami (Fla.) (21) (MPC Computers, 2006) (33, 31, 44, 40 yards)
4—LSU (40) vs. Miami (Fla.) (3) (Peach, 2005) (37, 47, 35, 50 yards)
4—Rutgers (40) vs. Arizona St. (45) (Insight, 2005) (25, 23, 52, 48 yards)
4—(D) Colorado (33) vs. UTEP (28) (Houston, 2004) (26, 54, 37, 20 yards)
4—Connecticut (39) vs. Toledo (10) (Motor City, 2004) (35, 37, 25, 36 yards)
4—Ohio St. (33) vs. Oklahoma St. (7) (Alamo, 2004) (37, 35, 41, 36 yards)
4—Georgia (26) vs. Florida St. (13) (Sugar, 2003) (23, 42, 25, 35 yards)
4—(D) Oklahoma St. (33) vs. Southern Miss. (23) (Houston, 2002) (46, 52, 29, 23 yards)

4—Washington St. (33) vs. Purdue (27) (Sun, 2001) (47, 34, 30, 37 yards)
4—Iowa (19) vs. Texas Tech (16) (Alamo, 2001) (36, 31, 46, 47 yards)
4—East Caro. (61) vs. Marshall (64) (2 ot) (GMAC, 2001) (25, 22, 32, 37 yards)
4—East Caro. (19) vs. Stanford (13) (Liberty, 1995) (46, 26, 41, 34 yards)
4—Oklahoma (25) vs. Penn St. (10) (Orange, 1986) (26, 31, 21, 22 yards)
4—North Carolina (26) vs. Texas (10) (Sun, 1982) (53, 47, 24, 42 yards)
4—Texas A&M (33) vs. Oklahoma St. (16) (Independence, 1981) (33, 32, 50, 18 yards)
4—West Virginia (26) vs. Florida (6) (Peach, Dec. 31, 1981) (35, 42, 49, 24 yards)
4—Missouri (19) vs. Southern Miss. (17) (Tangerine, 1981) (45, 41, 30, 28 yards)
4—Nebraska (45) vs. Georgia (6) (Sun, 1969) (50, 32, 42, 37 yards)
4—Alabama (12) vs. Mississippi (7) (Sugar, 1964) (46, 31, 34, 48 yards)

MOST FIELD GOALS MADE, BOTH TEAMS
(At Least One Field Goal by Both Teams)
7—Iowa (19) [4] & Texas Tech (16) [3] (Alamo, 2001)
7—Texas A&M (22) [5] & Michigan (20) [2] (Alamo, 1995)
7—North Carolina St. (28) [2] & Mississippi St. (24) [5] (Peach, Jan. 1, 1995)
6—Washington St. (33) [4] & Purdue (27) [2] (Sun, 2001)
6—Toledo (23) [3] & Cincinnati (16) [3] (Motor City, 2001)
6—Notre Dame (39) [1] & Florida (28) [5] (Sugar, 1992)
6—Syracuse (16) [3] & Auburn (16) [3] (Sugar, 1988)
6—Tennessee (30) [1] & Maryland (23) [5] (Florida Citrus, 1983)
5—Florida St. (44) [3] & UCLA (27) [2] (Emerald, 2006)
5—LSU (40) [4] & Miami (Fla.) (3) [1] (Peach, 2005)
5—Arizona St. (45) [1] & Rutgers (40) [4] (Insight, 2005)
5—Florida St. (30) [3] & West Virginia (18) [2] (Gator, 2005)
5—Connecticut (39) [4] & Toledo (10) [1] (Motor City, 2004)
5—Ohio St. (31) [3] & Miami (Fla.) (24) [2] (2 ot) (Fiesta, 2003)
5—Texas (47) [2] & Washington (43) [3] (Holiday, 2001)
5—Marshall (64) [1] & East Caro. (61) (2 ot) [4] (GMAC, 2001)
5—LSU (27) [2] & Notre Dame (9) [3] (Independence, 1997)
5—Penn St. (50) [3] & BYU (39) [2] (Holiday, 1989)
5—Oklahoma (25) [4] & Penn St. (10) [1] (Orange, 1986)
5—North Carolina (26) [4] & Texas (10) [1] (Sun, 1982)
5—Texas A&M (33) [4] & Oklahoma St. (16) [1] (Independence, 1981)
5—Missouri (19) [4] & Southern Miss. (17) [1] (Tangerine, 1981)
5—Penn St. (9) [3] & Tulane (6) [2] (Liberty, 1979)
5—Penn St. (30) [3] & Texas (6) [2] (Cotton, 1972)

MOST POINTS, WINNING TEAM
66—Nebraska vs. Northwestern (17) (Alamo, 2000)
65—Texas A&M vs. BYU (14) (Holiday, 1990)
64—Marshall vs. East Caro. (61) (2 ot) (GMAC, 2001)
63—Illinois vs. Virginia (21) (Micronpc.com, 1999)
62—Colorado vs. Boston College (28) (Insight.com, 1999)
62—Nebraska vs. Florida (24) (Fiesta, 1996)
62—Oklahoma St. vs. Wyoming (14) (Holiday, 1988)
61—Alabama vs. Syracuse (6) (Orange, 1953)
59—Hawaii vs. UAB (40) (Hawaii, 2004)
56—North Carolina St. vs. Kansas (26) (Tangerine, 2003)
56—Florida vs. Maryland (23) (Orange, 2002)
56—Toledo vs. Davidson (33) (Tangerine, 1969)

MOST POINTS, LOSING TEAM
61—East Caro. vs. Marshall (64) (2 ot) (GMAC, 2001)
49—Virginia Tech vs. California (52) (Insight, 2003)
48—UCF vs. Nevada (49) (ot) (Hawaii, 2005)
48—Houston vs. Hawaii (54) (3 ot) (Hawaii, 2003)
45—SMU vs. BYU (46) (Holiday, 1980)
43—Washington vs. Texas (47) (Holiday, 2001)
43—(D) Oregon vs. Colorado (51) (Aloha, 1998)
42—Ohio vs. Richmond (49) (Tangerine, 1968)
41—Texas A&M vs. Mississippi St. (43) (ot) (Independence, 2000)
41—Air Force vs. Texas Tech (55) (Copper, 1995)
40—Rutgers vs. Arizona St. (45) (Insight, 2005)
40—Boise St. vs. Louisville (44) (Liberty, 2004)
40—UAB vs. Hawaii (59) (Hawaii, 2004)

MOST POINTS, BOTH TEAMS
125—Marshall (64) & East Caro. (61) (2 ot) (GMAC, 2001)
102—Hawaii (54) & Houston (48) (3 ot) (Hawaii, 2003)
101—California (52) & Virginia Tech (49) (Insight, 2003)
99—Hawaii (59) & UAB (40) (Hawaii, 2004)
97—Nevada (49) & UCF (48) (ot) (Hawaii, 2005)
96—Texas Tech (55) & Air Force (41) (Copper, 1995)
94—(D) Colorado (51) & Oregon (43) (Aloha, 1998)
91—BYU (46) & SMU (45) (Holiday, 1980)
91—Richmond (49) & Ohio (42) (Tangerine, 1968)
90—Texas (47) & Washington (43) (Holiday, 2001)
90—Colorado (62) & Boston College (28) (Insight.com, 1999)

LARGEST MARGIN OF VICTORY
55—Alabama (61) vs. Syracuse (6) (Orange, 1953)
51—Texas A&M (65) vs. BYU (14) (Holiday, 1990)
49—Nebraska (66) vs. Northwestern (17) (Alamo, 2000)
48—Oklahoma St. (62) vs. Wyoming (14) (Holiday, 1988)
44—(D) Fresno St. (51) vs. Bowling Green (7) (California, 1985)
43—Miami (Fla.) (46) vs. Texas (3) (Cotton, 1991)
42—Georgia Tech (52) vs. Tulsa (10) (Humanitarian, 2004)
42—Illinois (63) vs. Virginia (21) (Micronpc.com, 1999)
42—Texas (42) vs. Maryland (0) (Sun, 1978)
41—Oregon St. (55) vs. New Mexico (14) (Las Vegas, 2003)
41—Syracuse (41) vs. Clemson (0) (Gator, 1996)
41—Southern California (55) vs. Texas Tech (14) (Cotton, 1995)

LARGEST DEFICIT OVERCOME TO WIN
31—Texas Tech (44) vs. Minnesota (41) (ot) (Insight, 2006) (trailed 38-7 in 3rd quarter)
30—Marshall (64) vs. East Caro. (61) (2 ot) (GMAC, 2001) (trailed 38-8 at half)
25—Georgia (28) vs. Purdue (25) (ot) (Outback, 2000) (trailed 25-0 in 2nd quarter)
24—North Carolina St. (38) vs. Minnesota (30) (Micronpc.com, 2000) (trailed 24-0 in 2nd quarter)
22—UCLA (50) vs. Northwestern (38) (Sun, 2005) (trailed 22-0 in 1st quarter)
22—BYU (46) vs. SMU (45) (Holiday, 1980) (trailed 35-13 in 3rd quarter and then trailed 45-25 with four minutes remaining in the game)
22—Notre Dame (35) vs. Houston (34) (Cotton, 1979) (trailed 34-12 in 4th quarter)
21—Missouri (38) vs. South Carolina (31) (Independence, 2005) (trailed 21-0 and 28-7 in 2nd quarter)
21—Maryland (28) vs. Tennessee (27) (Sun, 1984) (trailed 21-0 at half)
21—(D) Fresno St. (29) vs. Bowling Green (28) (California, 1982) (trailed 21-0 in 2nd quarter)
19—Texas (47) vs. Washington (43) (Holiday, 2001) (trailed 36-17 in 3rd quarter)
19—Wake Forest (39) vs. Oregon (35) (Independence, 1992) (trailed 29-10 in 3rd quarter)

FEWEST POINTS, WINNING TEAM
2—Fordham vs. Missouri (0) (Sugar, 1942)
3—Tennessee vs. Texas A&M (0) (Gator, 1957)
3—TCU vs. LSU (2) (Sugar, 1936)
6—UCLA vs. Illinois (3) (John Hancock, 1991)
6—Oregon St. vs. Villanova (0) (Liberty, 1962)
6—Tulsa vs. Texas Tech (0) (Sun, 1942)
6—Clemson vs. Boston College (3) (Cotton, 1940)
6—Auburn vs. Michigan St. (0) (Orange, 1938)
6—Santa Clara vs. LSU (0) (Sugar, 1938)

FEWEST POINTS, LOSING TEAM
0—By many teams

FEWEST POINTS, BOTH TEAMS
0—Air Force (0) & TCU (0) (Cotton, 1959)
0—Arkansas (0) & LSU (0) (Cotton, 1947)
0—Arizona St. (0) & Catholic (0) (Sun, 1940)
0—California (0) & Wash. & Jeff. (0) (Rose, 1922)

MOST POINTS SCORED IN ONE HALF
45—Colorado (62) vs. Boston College (28) (Insight.com, 1999) (1st half)
45—Oklahoma St. (62) vs. Wyoming (14) (Holiday, 1988) (2nd half)
43—Marshall (64) vs. East Caro. (61) (2 ot) (GMAC, 2001) (2nd half)
42—Georgia Tech (52) vs. Tulsa (10) (Humanitarian, 2004) (2nd half)
42—Boston College (51) vs. Toledo (25) (Motor City, 2002) (1st half)
42—Illinois (63) vs. Virginia (21) (Micronpc.com, 1999) (1st half)
42—Toledo (56) vs. Davidson (33) (Tangerine, 1969) (1st half)
40—Alabama (61) vs. Syracuse (6) (Orange, 1953) (2nd half)
38—Southern California (55) vs. Oklahoma (19) (Orange, 2005) (1st half)
38—East Caro. (61) vs. Marshall (64) (2 ot) (GMAC, 2001) (1st half)
38—Nebraska (66) vs. Northwestern (17) (Alamo, 2000) (1st half)
38—Penn St. (50) vs. BYU (39) (Holiday, 1989) (2nd half)
38—Penn St. (41) vs. Baylor (20) (Cotton, 1975) (2nd half)
38—Mississippi (41) vs. Georgia Tech (18) (Peach, 1971) (1st half)
37—(D) Michigan St. (44) vs. Fresno St. (35) (Silicon Valley, 2001) (1st half)
37—(D) Colorado (51) vs. Oregon (43) (Aloha, 1998) (1st half)
37—Texas A&M (65) vs. BYU (14) (Holiday, 1990) (1st half)

MOST POINTS SCORED IN ONE HALF, BOTH TEAMS
64—(D) Kansas (51) [34] & UCLA (30) [30] (Aloha, 1995) (2nd half)
64—Penn St. (50) [38] & BYU (39) [26] (Holiday, 1989) (2nd half)
63—Bowling Green (52) [35] & Memphis (35) [28] (GMAC, 2004) (1st half)
63—(D) Navy (42) [28] & California (38) [35] (Aloha, 1996) (1st half)
60—Boston College (51) [42] & Toledo (25) [18] (Motor City, 2002) (1st half)
58—(D) Michigan St. (44) [37] & Fresno St. (35) [21] (Silicon Valley, 2001) (1st half)
56—Marshall (64) [43] & East Caro. (61) [13] (2 ot) (GMAC, 2001) (2nd half)
55—South Carolina (44) [27] & Houston (36) [28] (Liberty, 2006) (1st half)
55—Nebraska (66) [38] & Northwestern (17) [17] (Alamo, 2000) (1st half)
54—Hawaii (59) [28] & UAB (40) [26] (Hawaii, 2004) (1st half)
54—Utah St. (42) [21] & Ball St. (33) [33] (Las Vegas, 1993) (2nd half)
53—Texas (41) [25] & Southern California (38) [28] (Rose, 2006) (2nd half)
53—Memphis (38) [25] & Akron (31) [28] (Motor City, 2005) (2nd half)
53—Texas (47) [33] & Washington (43) [20] (Holiday, 2001) (2nd half)
52—Hawaii (41) [38] & Arizona St. (24) [14] (Hawaii, 2006) (2nd half)
52—West Virginia (38) [31] & Georgia (35) [21] (Sugar, 2006) (1st half)
52—Louisville (44) [31] & Boise St. (40) [21] (Liberty, 2004) (1st half)
52—California (52) [31] & Virginia Tech (49) [21] (Insight, 2003) (2nd half)
52—Colorado (62) [45] & Boston College (28) [7] (Insight.com, 1999) (1st half)
52—Tennessee (48) [31] & Northwestern (28) [21] (Florida Citrus, 1997) (1st half)
52—Texas Tech (55) [24] & Air Force (41) [28] (Copper, 1995) (2nd half)
52—Oklahoma St. (62) [45] & Wyoming (14) [7] (Holiday, 1988) (2nd half)

MOST POINTS SCORED IN ONE QUARTER
31—Nebraska (66) vs. Northwestern (17) (Alamo, 2000) (2nd quarter)
31—(D) Iowa (55) vs. Texas (17) (Freedom, 1984) (3rd quarter)
30—Oklahoma (40) vs. Houston (14) (Sun, 1981) (4th quarter)
29—Oregon St. (41) vs. Notre Dame (9) (Fiesta, 2001) (3rd quarter)
29—Nebraska (62) vs. Florida (24) (Fiesta, 1996) (2nd quarter)
28—Boston College (55) vs. Toledo (25) (Motor City, 2002) (2nd quarter)
28—Clemson (49) vs. Louisiana Tech (24) (Humanitarian, 2001) (3rd quarter)
28—Marshall (64) vs. East Caro. (61) (ot) (GMAC, 2001) (3rd quarter)
28—West Virginia (49) vs. Mississippi (38) (Music City, 2000) (2nd quarter)
28—Illinois (63) vs. Virginia (21) (Micronpc.com, 1999) (2nd quarter)
28—Southern California (55) vs. Texas Tech (14) (Cotton, 1995) (1st quarter)
28—Oklahoma St. (62) vs. Wyoming (14) (Holiday, 1988) (3rd quarter)
28—Missouri (34) vs. Auburn (17) (Sun, 1973) (2nd quarter)
28—Mississippi (41) vs. Georgia Tech (18) (Peach, 1971) (2nd quarter)
28—Toledo (56) vs. Davidson (33) (Tangerine, 1969) (2nd quarter)
28—Houston (49) vs. Miami (Ohio) (21) (Tangerine, 1962) (2nd quarter)

MOST POINTS SCORED IN ONE QUARTER, BOTH TEAMS
45—Nebraska (66) [31] & Northwestern (17) [14] (Alamo, 2000) (2nd quarter)
43—Boston College (55) [28] & Toledo (25) [15] (Motor City, 2002) (2nd quarter)
43—(D) Navy (42) [21] & California (38) [22] (Aloha, 1996) (2nd quarter)
41—South Carolina (44) [20] & Houston (36) [21] (Liberty, 2006) (2nd quarter)
40—Arizona St. (48) [14] & North Carolina (26) [26] (Peach, 1970) (2nd quarter)
39—Memphis (38) [18] & Akron (31) [21] (Motor City, 2005) (4th quarter)
38—Missouri (34) [28] & Auburn (17) [10] (Sun, 1973) (2nd quarter)
37—Texas (47) [14] & Washington (43) [23] (Holiday, 2001) (2nd quarter)
37—(D) Kansas (51) [14] & UCLA (30) [23] (Aloha, 1995) (4th quarter)
37—Oklahoma (40) [30] & Houston (14) [7] (Sun, 1981) (4th quarter)
35—Bowling Green (52) [14] & Memphis (35) [21] (GMAC, 2004) (2nd quarter)
35—Michigan (35) [21] & Alabama (34) [14] (Orange, 2000) (3rd quarter)
35—Marshall (48) [14] & Louisville (29) [21] (Motor City, 1998) (2nd quarter)
35—Kansas St. (54) [21] & Colorado St. (21) [14] (Holiday, 1995) (3rd quarter)
35—Oklahoma St. (62) [28] & Wyoming (14) [7] (Holiday, 1988) (3rd quarter)
35—Oklahoma St. (49) [21] & BYU (21) [14] (Tangerine, 1976) (2nd quarter)
35—(D) Houston (31) [21] & North Carolina St. (31) [14] (Bluebonnet, 1974) (4th quarter)
35—Arizona St. (49) [21] & Missouri (35) [14] (Fiesta, 1972) (4th quarter)
35—Richmond (49) [21] & Ohio (42) [14] (Tangerine, 1968) (2nd quarter)

First Downs

MOST FIRST DOWNS
36—Marshall (64) vs. East Caro. (61) (2 ot) (GMAC, 2001) (9 rush, 25 pass, 2 penalty)
36—Oklahoma (48) vs. Virginia (14) (Gator, Dec. 29, 1991) (16 rush, 18 pass, 2 penalty)
35—Michigan (35) vs. Mississippi (3) (Gator, Jan. 1, 1991) (20 rush, 14 pass, 1 penalty)
35—BYU (39) vs. Penn St. (50) (Holiday, 1989) (8 rush, 27 pass, 0 penalty)
34—North Carolina St. (56) [34] vs. Kansas (26) [28] (Tangerine, 2003) (9 rush, 22 pass, 3 penalty)
34—(D) Fresno St. (30) vs. Colorado (41) (Aloha, 1993) (4 rush, 25 pass, 5 penalty)
34—Oklahoma St. (62) vs. Wyoming (14) (Holiday, 1988) (15 rush, 17 pass, 2 penalty)
34—(D) Miami (Fla.) (34) vs. Nebraska (36) (Gotham, 1962)
33—Northwestern (38) vs. UCLA (50) (Sun, 2005) (11 rush, 17 pass, 5 penalty)
33—Arizona St. (45) vs. Rutgers (40) (Insight, 2005) (11 rush, 21 pass, 1 penalty)
33—Navy (51) vs. Colorado St. (30) (Poinsettia, 2005) (26 rush, 4 pass, 3 penalty)
33—Toledo (40) vs. Nevada (37) (ot) (Las Vegas, 1995) (19 rush, 12 pass, 2 penalty)
33—Arizona St. (49) vs. Missouri (35) (Fiesta, 1972) (22 rush, 11 pass, 0 penalty)
32—Hawaii (41) vs. Arizona St. (24) (Hawaii, 2006) (5 rush, 26 pass, 1 penalty)
32—Tennessee (38) vs. Texas A&M (7) (Cotton, 2005) (17 rush, 10 pass, 5 penalty)
32—LSU (47) vs. Illinois (34) (Sugar, 2002) (7 rush, 23 pass, 2 penalty)
32—BYU (24) vs. Michigan (17) (Holiday, 1984)
32—Richmond (49) vs. Ohio (42) (Tangerine, 1968) (8 rush, 24 pass, 0 penalty)
32—Wisconsin (37) vs. Southern California (42) (Rose, 1963) (7 rush, 23 pass, 2 penalty)

MOST FIRST DOWNS, BOTH TEAMS
62—North Carolina St. (56) [34] & Kansas (26) [28] (Tangerine, 2003)
61—Penn St. (50) [26] & BYU (39) [35] (Holiday, 1989)
60—Texas (41) [30] & Southern California (38) [30] (Rose, 2006)
60—Nevada (49) [30] & UCF (48) [30] (ot) (Hawaii, 2005)
59—Navy (51) [33] & Colorado St. (30) [26] (Poinsettia, 2005)
59—Marshall (64) [36] & East Caro. (61) (2 ot) [23] (GMAC, 2001)
58—Miami (Fla.) (46) [27] & North Carolina St. (23) [31] (Micron PC, 1998)
57—UCLA (50) [24] & Northwestern (38) [33] (Sun, 2005)
57—Arizona St. (45) [33] & Rutgers (40) [24] (Insight, 2005)
57—Texas Tech (45) [30] & California (31) [27] (Holiday, 2004)
56—Toledo (40) [33] & Nevada (37) [23] (ot) (Las Vegas, 1995)
56—Mississippi (42) [30] & Air Force (29) [26] (Liberty, 1989)
55—Hawaii (54) [30] & Houston (48) [25] (3 ot) (Hawaii, 2003)
55—Michigan (35) [35] & Mississippi (3) [20] (Gator, Jan. 1, 1991)
54—Texas Tech (44) [29] & Minnesota (41) [25] (ot) (Insight, 2006)
54—West Virginia (38) [27] & Georgia (35) [27] (Sugar, 2006)
54—Hawaii (59) [23] & UAB (40) [31] (Hawaii, 2004)
54—California (52) [27] & Virginia Tech (49) [27] (Insight, 2003)
54—Boise St. (34) [28] & Louisville (31) [26] (Humanitarian, 1999)
54—UCLA (45) [29] & Iowa (28) [25] (Rose, 1986)
54—Florida St. (34) [31] & Oklahoma St. (23) [23] (Gator, 1985)

MOST FIRST DOWNS RUSHING
26—Navy (51) vs. Colorado St. (30) (Poinsettia, 2005)
26—Oklahoma (40) vs. Auburn (22) (Sugar, Jan. 1, 1972)
25—(D) Houston (26) vs. Dayton (21) (Salad, 1952)
24—Nebraska (66) vs. Northwestern (17) (Alamo, 2000)
24—Colorado (47) vs. Alabama (33) (Liberty, 1969)
23—Georgia Tech (31) vs. Texas Tech (21) (Gator, Dec. 31, 1965)
22—Nebraska (42) vs. Tennessee (17) (Orange, 1998)
22—Syracuse (30) vs. Houston (17) (Liberty, 1996)
22—(D) Arkansas (28) vs. Florida (24) (Bluebonnet, 1982)
22—Oklahoma (41) vs. Wyoming (7) (Fiesta, 1976)
22—Arizona St. (49) vs. Missouri (35) (Fiesta, 1972)
21—Nebraska (62) vs. Florida (24) (Fiesta, 1996)
21—Arkansas (27) vs. Tennessee (31) (Cotton, 1990)
21—Florida St. (7) vs. Oklahoma (24) (Orange, 1980)
21—(D) Houston (35) vs. Navy (0) (Garden State, 1980)
21—Mississippi St. (26) vs. North Carolina (24) (Sun, 1974)
21—Missouri (35) vs. Alabama (10) (Gator, 1968)

MOST FIRST DOWNS RUSHING, BOTH TEAMS
36—Miami (Fla.) (46) [16] & Texas (3) [20] (Cotton, 1991)
36—Colorado (47) [24] & Alabama (33) [12] (Liberty, 1969)
32—Navy (51) [26] & Colorado St. (30) [6] (Poinsettia, 2005)
32—Miami (Fla.) (46) [14] & North Carolina St. (23) [18] (Micron PC, 1998)
32—Texas Tech (55) [15] & Air Force (41) [17] (Copper, 1995)
32—Tennessee (31) [11] & Arkansas (27) [21] (Cotton, 1990)
32—Oklahoma (41) [22] & Wyoming (7) [10] (Fiesta, 1976)
32—Arizona St. (49) [22] & Missouri (35) [10] (Fiesta, 1972)
32—Texas (21) [19] & Notre Dame (17) [13] (Cotton, 1970)
31—Air Force (38) [18] & Mississippi St. (15) [13] (Liberty, 1991)

MOST FIRST DOWNS PASSING
27—BYU (39) vs. Penn St. (50) (Holiday, 1989)
26—Hawaii (41) vs. Arizona St. (24) (Hawaii, 2006)
25—Marshall (64) vs. East Caro. (61) (2 ot) (GMAC, 2001)
25—(D) Fresno St. (30) vs. Colorado (41) (Aloha, 1993)
24—Oregon St. (39) vs. Missouri (38) (Sun, 2006)
24—(D) Texas Tech (38) vs. Navy (14) (Houston, 2003)
24—West Virginia (31) vs. Missouri (34) (Insight.com, 1998)
24—Richmond (49) vs. Ohio (42) (Tangerine, 1968)
23—LSU (47) vs. Illinois (34) (Sugar, 2002)
23—Florida (56) vs. Maryland (23) (Orange, 2002)
23—Tennessee (48) vs. Northwestern (28) (Florida Citrus, 1997)
23—(D) San Jose St. (25) vs. Toledo (27) (California, 1981)
23—Wisconsin (37) vs. Southern California (42) (Rose, 1963)

MOST FIRST DOWNS PASSING, BOTH TEAMS
38—Florida (31) [16] & Iowa (24) [22] (Outback, 2006)
38—Penn St. (50) [11] & BYU (39) [27] (Holiday, 1989)
37—Oregon St. (39) [24] & Missouri (38) [13] (Sun, 2006)
37—Arizona St. (45) [21] & Rutgers (40) [16] (Insight, 2005)
36—Tennessee (48) [23] & Northwestern (28) [13] (Florida Citrus, 1997)
35—Texas Tech (44) [22] & Minnesota (41) [13] (ot) (Insight, 2006)
35—Hawaii (59) [17] & UAB (40) [18] (Hawaii, 2004)
35—North Carolina St. (56) [22] & Kansas (26) [13] (Tangerine, 2003)
35—California (52) [17] & Virginia Tech (49) [18] (Insight, 2003)
35—Miami (Fla.) (37) [18] & Florida (20) [17] (Sugar, 2001)
34—Hawaii (41) [26] & Arizona St. (24) [8] (Hawaii, 2006)
33—Utah (38) [21] & Georgia Tech (10) [12] (Emerald, 2005)
33—Texas Tech (45) [18] & California (31) [15] (Holiday, 2004)
33—Florida (56) [23] & Maryland (23) [10] (Orange, 2002)
33—Texas (43) [17] & Washington (43) [16] (Holiday, 2001)
33—Marshall (64) [25] & East Caro. [8] (61) (2 ot) (GMAC, 2001)

MOST FIRST DOWNS BY PENALTY
8—West Virginia (18) vs. Florida St. (30) (Gator, 2005)
6—Clemson (27) vs. Tennessee (14) (Peach, Jan. 2, 2004)
6—Florida (52) vs. Florida St. (20) (Sugar, 1997)
6—Texas (3) vs. Miami (Fla.) (46) (Cotton, 1991)
5—Wisconsin (17) vs. Arkansas (14) (Capital One, 2007)
5—Northwestern (38) vs. UCLA (50) (Sun, 2005)
5—Tennessee (38) vs. Texas A&M (7) (Cotton, 2005)
5—Iowa (27) vs. Texas Tech (0) (Alamo, 1996)
5—(D) Arizona (13) vs. Utah (16) (Freedom, 1994)
5—(D) Fresno St. (30) vs. Colorado (41) (Aloha, 1993)
5—West Virginia (21) vs. Notre Dame (34) (Fiesta, 1989)
5—(D) Washington (34) vs. Florida (7) (Freedom, 1989)
5—(D) Western Mich. (30) vs. Fresno St. (35) (California, 1988)
5—Miami (Fla.) (7) vs. Tennessee (35) (Sugar, 1986)
5—(D) Miami (Ohio) (7) vs. San Jose St. (37) (California, 1986)

MOST FIRST DOWNS BY PENALTY, BOTH TEAMS
12—Florida St. (30) [4] & West Virginia (18) [8] (Gator, 2005)
8—Tennessee (38) [5] & Texas A&M (7) [3] (Cotton, 2005)
8—Florida (52) [6] & Florida St. (20) [2] (Sugar, 1997)
8—Texas A&M (22) [4] & Michigan (20) [4] (Alamo, 1995)
8—Miami (Fla.) (46) [2] & Texas (3) [6] (Cotton, 1991)
7—Wisconsin (17) [5] & Arkansas (14) [2] (Capital One, 2007)
7—UCLA (50) [2] & Northwestern (38) [5] (Sun, 2005)

7—Clemson (27) [6] & Tennessee (14) [1] (Peach, Jan. 2, 2004)
7—Iowa (27) [5] & Texas Tech (0) [2] (Alamo, 1996)
7—(D) Washington (34) [5] & Florida (7) [2] (Freedom, 1989)
7—Tennessee (35) [2] & Miami (Fla.) (7) [5] (Sugar, 1986)
7—Tennessee (14) [3] & Arkansas (13) [4] (Liberty, 1971)

FEWEST FIRST DOWNS
1—Alabama (29) vs. Texas A&M (21) (Cotton, 1942) (passing)
1—Arkansas (0) vs. LSU (0) (Cotton, 1947) (rushing)
2—Michigan St. (0) vs. Auburn (6) (Orange, 1938) (1 rushing, 1 passing)

FEWEST FIRST DOWNS, BOTH TEAMS
10—Texas (7) [3] & Randolph Field (7) [7] (Cotton, 1944)
12—LSU (19) [4] & Texas A&M (14) [8] (Orange, 1944)

FEWEST FIRST DOWNS RUSHING
0—Purdue (7) vs. Maryland (24) (Champs Sports, 2006)
0—Northern Ill. (7) vs. TCU (37) (Poinsettia, 2006)
0—Southern California (19) vs. TCU (28) (Sun, 1998)
0—Florida (18) vs. Missouri (20) (Sugar, 1966)
0—Navy (6) vs. Texas (28) (Cotton, 1964)
0—Alabama (29) vs. Texas A&M (21) (Cotton, 1942)

FEWEST FIRST DOWNS RUSHING, BOTH TEAMS
3—Alabama (29) [0] & Texas A&M (21) [3] (Cotton, 1942)
7—Southern California (32) [4] & Michigan (18) [3] (Rose, 2007)
8—Wisconsin (17) [1] & Arkansas (14) [7] (Capital One, 2007)
8—(D) Southern California (28) [4] & Utah (21) [4] (Freedom, 1993)
9—Texas (26) [4] & Iowa (24) [5] (Alamo, 2006)
9—San Jose St. (20) [1] & New Mexico (12) [8] (New Mexico, 2006)
9—Florida St. (41) [2] & Nebraska (17) [7] (Fiesta, 1990)
9—Texas (28) [9] & Navy (6) [0] (Cotton, 1964)

FEWEST FIRST DOWNS PASSING
0—Army (28) vs. Alabama (29) (John Hancock Sun, 1988)
0—Oklahoma (40) vs. Houston (10) (Sun, 1981)
0—West Virginia (14) vs. South Carolina (3) (Peach, 1969)
0—Missouri (35) vs. Alabama (10) (Gator, 1968)
0—Virginia Tech (7) vs. Miami (Fla.) (14) (Liberty, 1966)
0—Auburn (7) vs. Mississippi (13) (Liberty, 1965)
0—Alabama (10) vs. Arkansas (3) (Sugar, 1962)
0—(D) Missouri (14) vs. Georgia Tech (10) (Bluebonnet, 1962)
0—Utah St. (13) vs. New Mexico St. (20) (Sun, 1960)
0—Arkansas (0) vs. LSU (0) (Cotton, 1947)
0—Fordham (2) vs. Missouri (0) (Sugar, 1942)
0—Arizona St. (0) vs. Catholic (0) (Sun, 1940)
0—West Virginia (7) vs. Texas Tech (6) (Sun, 1938)

FEWEST FIRST DOWNS PASSING, BOTH TEAMS
1—Alabama (10) [0] & Arkansas (3) [1] (Sugar, 1962)
4—Oklahoma (41) [1] & Wyoming (7) [3] (Fiesta, 1976)
4—Texas (16) [2] & Tennessee (0) [2] (Cotton, 1953)
4—Rice (28) [3] & Colorado (14) [1] (Cotton, 1938)

Punting

MOST PUNTS
17—Duke (3) vs. Southern California (7) (Rose, 1939)
16—Alabama (29) vs. Texas A&M (21) (Cotton, 1942)
16—New Mexico St. (14) vs. Hardin-Simmons (14) (Sun, 1936)
15—Tennessee (0) vs. Rice (8) (Orange, 1947)
14—Tulsa (7) vs. Tennessee (14) (Sugar, 1943)
14—Santa Clara (6) vs. LSU (0) (Sugar, 1938)
14—LSU (0) vs. Santa Clara (6) (Sugar, 1938)
14—TCU (3) vs. LSU (2) (Sugar, 1936)
13—Rice (8) vs. Tennessee (0) (Orange, 1947)
13—Tennessee (0) vs. Southern California (25) (Rose, 1945)
13—Oklahoma (0) vs. Tennessee (17) (Orange, 1939)
13—Catholic (20) vs. Mississippi (19) (Orange, 1936)
13—LSU (2) vs. TCU (3) (Sugar, 1936)
13—Miami (Fla.) (0) vs. Bucknell (26) (Orange, 1935)

MOST PUNTS, BOTH TEAMS
28—Rice (8) [13] & Tennessee (0) [15] (Orange, 1947)
28—Santa Clara (6) [14] & LSU (0) [14] (Sugar, 1938)
27—TCU (3) [14] & LSU (2) [13] (Sugar, 1936)
25—Tennessee (17) [12] & Oklahoma (0) [13] (Orange, 1939)
24—Catholic (20) [13] & Mississippi (19) [11] (Orange, 1936)
23—UTEP (14) [12] & Mississippi (7) [11] (Sun, 1967)
22—Auburn (6) [10] & Michigan St. (0) [12] (Orange, 1938)

HIGHEST PUNTING AVERAGE
(Minimum 5 Punts)
53.9—Southern California (7) vs. Wisconsin (0) (Rose, 1953) (8 for 431)
53.8—Hawaii (28) vs. Tulane (36) (Hawaii, 2002) (5 for 269)
52.3—Tennessee (17) vs. Nebraska (42) (Orange, 1998) (6 for 314)
52.0—Iowa (27) vs. Texas Tech (0) (Alamo, 1996) (5 for 260)
51.5—Nebraska (32) vs. Michigan (28) (Alamo, 2005) (8 for 412)
51.5—(D) Colorado (51) vs. Oregon (43) (Aloha, 1998) (6 for 309)
51.0—Penn St. (10) vs. Clemson (35) (Florida Citrus, 1988) (5 for 255)
50.2—Marshall (38) vs. Louisville (15) (GMAC, 2002) (6 for 301)
50.0—Virginia Tech (35) vs. Louisville (24) (Gator, 2006) (6 for 300)
50.0—(D) Oregon (17) vs. Wake Forest (38) (Seattle, 2002) (6 for 300)
50.0—Nevada (37) vs. Toledo (40) (ot) (Las Vegas, 1995) (5 for 250)
50.0—Mississippi St. (17) vs. Nebraska (31) (Sun, 1980) (5 for 250)

FEWEST PUNTS
0—Navy (51) vs. Colorado St. (30) (Poinsettia, 2005)
0—(D) Texas Tech (38) vs. Navy (14) (Houston, 2003)
0—Illinois (63) vs. Virginia (21) (Micronpc.com, 1999)
0—Oklahoma St. (62) vs. Wyoming (14) (Holiday, 1988)
0—Maryland (23) vs. Tennessee (30) (Florida Citrus, 1983)
0—Oklahoma (41) vs. Wyoming (7) (Fiesta, 1976)
1—Texas Tech (44) vs. Minnesota (41) (ot) (Insight, 2006)
1—California (45) vs. Texas A&M (10) (Holiday, 2006)
1—Hawaii (41) vs. Arizona St. (24) (Hawaii, 2006)
1—Ohio St. (34) vs. Notre Dame (20) (Fiesta, 2006)
1—Utah (35) vs. Pittsburgh (7) (Fiesta, 2005)
1—New Mexico (19) vs. Navy (34) (Emerald, 2004)
1—North Carolina St. (56) vs. Kansas (26) (Tangerine, 2003)
1—Virginia (48) vs. West Virginia (22) (Continental Tire, 2002)
1—Boston College (51) vs. Toledo (25) (Motor City, 2002)
1—Oklahoma (25) vs. Mississippi (27) (Independence, 1999)
1—Nebraska (62) vs. Florida (24) (Fiesta, 1996)
1—Virginia (22) vs. Tennessee (23) (Sugar, 1991)
1—BYU (39) vs. Penn St. (50) (Holiday, 1989)
1—Tennessee (30) vs. Maryland (23) (Florida Citrus, 1983)
1—Nebraska (21) vs. LSU (20) (Orange, 1983)
1—North Carolina St. (31) vs. Kansas (18) (Liberty, 1973)
1—Utah (32) vs. West Virginia (6) (Liberty, 1964)
1—(D) Miami (Fla.) (34) vs. Nebraska (36) (Gotham, 1962)
1—Georgia Tech (42) vs. West Virginia (19) (Sugar, 1954)
1—West Virginia (19) vs. Georgia Tech (42) (Sugar, 1954)
1—Missouri (23) vs. Clemson (24) (Gator, 1949)

LOWEST PUNTING AVERAGE
(Minimum 3 Punts)
17.0—Kentucky (14) vs. Penn St. (26) (Outback, 1999) (3 for 51)
17.0—Nevada (34) vs. Bowling Green (35) (Las Vegas, 1992) (4 for 68)
19.0—Cincinnati (18) vs. Virginia Tech (6) (Sun, 1947) (6 for 114)
22.0—Mississippi St. (16) vs. North Carolina St. (12) (Liberty, 1963) (3 for 66)
23.0—Bowling Green (35) vs. Nevada (34) (Las Vegas, 1992) (5 for 115)
25.5—Houston (34) vs. Notre Dame (35) (Cotton, 1979) (10 for 255)
26.0—(D) Air Force (37) vs. Fresno St. (34) (Silicon Valley, 2000) (3 for 78)
26.1—Michigan (14) vs. Alabama (17) (Outback, 1997) (7 for 183)
26.3—Oklahoma St. (34) vs. TCU (0) (Cotton, 1945) (6 for 158)
26.3—Notre Dame (35) vs. Houston (34) (Cotton, 1979) (7 for 184)
26.3—Rice (28) vs. Alabama (6) (Cotton, 1954) (8 for 210)

MOST PUNTS BLOCKED BY ONE TEAM
2—Iowa (30) vs. LSU (25) (Capital One, 2005)
2—Cincinnati (32) vs. Marshall (14) (Fort Worth, 2004)
2—North Carolina (21) vs. Mississippi St. (17) (Peach, Jan. 2, 1993)
2—North Carolina St. (14) vs. Georgia (7) (Liberty, 1967)
2—LSU (25) vs. Colorado (7) (Orange, 1962)

Punt Returns

MOST PUNT RETURNS
9—Georgia (7) vs. North Carolina (3) (Gator, Dec. 31, 1971) (6.8 average)
8—Indiana (20) vs. Virginia Tech (45) (Independence, 1993) (7.3 average)
8—Mississippi (7) vs. UTEP (14) (Sun, 1967) (9.4 average)
8—Michigan (34) vs. Oregon St. (7) (Rose, 1965) (10.6 average)
7—Florida St. (23) vs. Penn St. (26) (3 ot) (Orange, 2006) (25.7 average)
7—Michigan (28) vs. Nebraska (32) (Alamo, 2005) (10.3 average)
7—Boise St. (21) vs. Boston College (27) (MPC Computers, 2005) (21.6 average)
7—North Carolina (16) vs. Auburn (10) (Peach, 2001) (9.4 average)
7—Auburn (10) vs. North Carolina (16) (Peach, 2001) (3.7 average)
7—Oklahoma (10) vs. Arkansas (3) (Cotton, 2002) (2.9 average)
7—Stanford (38) vs. Michigan St. (0) (Sun, 1996) (13.4 average)
7—Louisville (34) vs. Alabama (7) (Fiesta, 1991) (7.3 average)
7—Southern California (14) vs. Tennessee (0) (Rose, 1940)
7—Oklahoma (0) vs. Tennessee (17) (Orange, 1939) (5.5 average)

MOST PUNT RETURN YARDS
180—Florida St. (23) vs. Penn St. (26) (3 ot) (Orange, 2006) (7 returns)
151—Boise St. (21) vs. Boston College (27) (MPC Computers, 2005) (7 returns)
136—Nebraska (38) vs. Alabama (6) (Orange, 1972) (6 returns)
128—Oklahoma (48) vs. Duke (21) (Orange, 1958)
126—Tulane (13) vs. Texas A&M (14) (Sugar, 1940) (6 returns)
124—California (37) vs. Clemson (13) (Florida Citrus, 1992) (5 returns)
124—Washington (44) vs. Wisconsin (8) (Rose, 1960) (4 returns)
108—Kansas (42) vs. Houston (13) (Fort Worth, 2005) (6 returns)
108—Alabama (34) vs. Michigan (35) (ot) (Orange, 2000) (4 returns)
108—Southern Miss. (38) vs. UTEP (18) (Independence, 1988) (2 returns)
107—Arizona St. (45) vs. Florida St. (38) (Fiesta, 1971) (5 returns)
104—Texas A&M (21) vs. Alabama (29) (Cotton, 1942) (5 returns)
100—Virginia (34) vs. Georgia (27) (Peach, Dec. 30, 1995) (4 returns)

HIGHEST PUNT RETURN AVERAGE
(Minimum 3 Returns)
33.0—Kent St. (18) vs. Tampa (21) (Tangerine, 1972) (3 for 99)
32.7—BYU (46) vs. SMU (45) (Holiday, 1980) (3 for 98)
31.0—Washington (44) vs. Wisconsin (8) (Rose, 1960) (4 for 124)
30.7—Michigan (42) vs. North Carolina St. (7) (Hall of Fame, 1994) (3 for 92)
29.7—Tennessee (45) vs. Virginia Tech (23) (Gator, 1994) (3 for 89)
29.7—Nebraska (28) vs. Florida St. (31) (Fiesta, 1988) (3 for 89)
27.7—Houston (48) vs. Hawaii (54) (3 ot) (Hawaii, 2003) (3 for 83)
27.7—Kansas St. (52) vs. Wyoming (17) (Copper, 1993) (3 for 83)
27.0—Alabama (34) vs. Michigan (35) (ot) (Orange, 2000) (4 for 108)
25.7—Florida St. (23) vs. Penn St. (26) (3 ot) (Orange, 2006) (7 for 180)
25.3—(D) TCU (27) vs. Iowa St. (24) (Houston, 2005) (3 for 76)
25.0—Virginia (34) vs. Georgia (27) (Peach, Dec. 30, 1995) (4 for 100)

Kickoff Returns

MOST KICKOFF RETURNS
10—Florida (24) vs. Nebraska (62) (Fiesta, 1996) (26.8 average)
10—Wyoming (14) vs. Oklahoma St. (62) (Holiday, 1988) (20.5 average)
9—Colorado St. (30) vs. Navy (51) (Poinsettia, 2005) (19.9 average)
9—Kansas (26) vs. North Carolina St. (56) (Tangerine, 2003) (23.3 average)
9—Maryland (23) vs. Florida (56) (Orange, 2002) (13.7 average)
9—BYU (14) vs. Texas A&M (65) (Holiday, 1990) (18.2 average)
8—Texas (38) vs. Michigan (37) (Rose, 2005) (26.8 average)
8—Boise St. (40) vs. Louisville (44) (Liberty, 2004) (23.3 average)
8—New Mexico (14) vs. Oregon St. (55) (Las Vegas, 2003) (21.9 average)
8—Michigan (17) vs. Tennessee (45) (Florida Citrus, 2002) (15.6 average)
8—Washington (43) vs. Texas (47) (Holiday, 2001) (18.0 average)
8—BYU (27) vs. Tulane (41) (Liberty, 1998) (31.0 average)
8—North Carolina St. (23) vs. Miami (Fla.) (46) (Micron PC, 1998) (18.3 average)
8—Virginia Tech (3) vs. North Carolina (42) (Gator, 1998) (19.4 average)
8—Florida St. (20) vs. Florida (52) (Sugar, 1997) (19.0 average)
8—Northwestern (32) vs. Southern California (41) (Rose, 1996) (28.1 average)
8—Nebraska (21) vs. Georgia Tech (45) (Florida Citrus, 1991) (23.6 average)
8—Notre Dame (10) vs. Texas A&M (35) (Cotton, 1988) (18.9 average)
8—Texas Tech (17) vs. Florida St. (40) (Tangerine, 1977)
8—UCLA (6) vs. Alabama (36) (Liberty, 1976) (17.6 average)
8—BYU (21) vs. Oklahoma St. (49) (Tangerine, 1976)
8—(D) Tulane (7) vs. Houston (47) (Bluebonnet, 1973) (28.1 average)
8—Missouri (35) vs. Arizona St. (49) (Fiesta, 1972) (32.3 average)
8—Arizona St. (45) vs. Florida St. (38) (Fiesta, 1971) (16.4 average)
8—Florida St. (38) vs. Arizona St. (45) (Fiesta, 1971) (23.0 average)
8—Colorado (47) vs. Alabama (33) (Liberty, 1969) (27.8 average)
8—Ohio (42) vs. Richmond (49) (Tangerine, 1968)
8—Florida St. (20) vs. UTEP (47) (Sun, 1955)
8—UCLA (14) vs. Illinois (45) (Rose, 1947) (32.4 average)

MOST KICKOFF RETURN YARDS
268—Florida (24) vs. Nebraska (62) (Fiesta, 1996) (10 returns)
259—UCLA (14) vs. Illinois (45) (Rose, 1947) (8 returns)
258—Missouri (35) vs. Arizona St. (49) (Fiesta, 1972) (8 returns)
248—BYU (27) vs. Tulane (41) (Liberty, 1998) (8 returns)
225—Northwestern (32) vs. Southern California (41) (Rose, 1996) (8 returns)
225—(D) Tulane (7) vs. Houston (47) (Bluebonnet, 1973) (8 returns)
222—Colorado (47) vs. Alabama (33) (Liberty, 1969) (8 returns)
221—Michigan (37) vs. Texas (38) (Rose, 2005) (6 returns)
214—Texas (38) vs. Michigan (37) (Rose, 2005) (8 returns)
210—Kansas (26) vs. North Carolina St. (56) (Tangerine, 2003) (9 returns)
207—(D) California (38) vs. Navy (42) (Aloha, 1996) (7 returns)
205—Wyoming (14) vs. Oklahoma (62) (Holiday, 1988) (10 returns)
204—BYU (21) vs. Oklahoma St. (49) (Tangerine, 1976) (8 returns)

HIGHEST KICKOFF RETURN AVERAGE
(Minimum 3 Returns)
42.5—Tennessee (27) vs. Maryland (28) (John Hancock, 1984) (4 for 170)
38.5—Virginia (23) vs. Pittsburgh (16) (Continental Tire, 2003) (4 for 154)
38.3—(D) Fresno St. (30) vs. Colorado (41) (Aloha, 1993) (3 for 115)
38.3—Ohio St. (28) vs. Pittsburgh (23) (Fiesta, 1984) (4 for 153)
38.2—(D) Houston (22) vs. Washington St. (24) (Aloha, 1988) (5 for 191)
37.5—LSU (45) vs. Michigan St. (26) (Independence, 1995) (4 for 150)
37.5—Notre Dame (24) vs. Alabama (23) (Sugar, 1973) (4 for 150)
37.3—Toledo (45) vs. UTEP (13) (GMAC, 2005) (3 for 112)
36.8—Ohio St. (17) vs. Syracuse (24) (Hall of Fame, 1992) (4 for 147)
36.8—Michigan (37) vs. Texas (38) (Rose, 2005) (6 for 221)
36.7—Indiana (20) vs. Virginia Tech (45) (Independence, 1993) (3 for 110)
36.2—Maryland (23) vs. Tennessee (30) (Florida Citrus, 1983) (5 for 181)
35.8—Washington (21) vs. Colorado (33) (Holiday, 1996) (5 for 179)

Fumbles

MOST FUMBLES
11—Mississippi (7) vs. Alabama (12) (Sugar, 1964) (lost 6)
9—Texas (11) vs. Notre Dame (24) (Cotton, 1971) (lost 5)
8—North Carolina St. (28) vs. Iowa (23) (Peach, Dec. 31, 1988) (lost 5)
8—(D) Houston (35) vs. Navy (0) (Garden State, 1980) (lost 3)
8—Louisville (14) vs. Louisiana Tech (24) (Independence, 1977) (lost 3)
8—North Texas (8) vs. New Mexico St. (28) (Sun, 1959) (lost 6)
8—TCU (0) vs. Air Force (0) (Cotton, 1959) (lost 3)
8—Colorado (27) vs. Clemson (21) (Orange, 1957) (lost 3)

MOST FUMBLES, BOTH TEAMS
17—Alabama (12) [6] & Mississippi (7) [11] (Sugar, 1964) (lost 9)
14—Louisiana Tech (24) [6] & Louisville (14) [8] (Independence, 1977) (lost 6)
14—Tennessee (34) [7] & Air Force (13) [7] (Sugar, 1971) (lost 7)
13—TCU (0) [8] & Air Force (0) [5] (Cotton, 1959) (lost 6)
12—North Carolina St. (28) [8] & Iowa (23) [4] (Peach, Dec. 31, 1988) (lost 8)
12—(D) Houston (35) [8] & Navy (0) [4] (Garden State, 1980) (lost 6)
12—New Mexico St. (28) [4] & North Texas (8) [8] (Sun, 1959) (lost 8)
11—(D) Toledo (27) [7] & San Jose St. (25) [4] (California, 1981) (lost 3)
11—Oklahoma (41) [6] & Wyoming (7) [5] (Fiesta, 1976)

MOST FUMBLES LOST
6—Tulsa (10) vs. Georgia Tech (52) (Humanitarian, 2004) (7 fumbles)
6—Texas A&M (2) vs. Florida St. (10) (Cotton, 1992) (6 fumbles)
6—East Caro. (31) vs. Maine (0) (Tangerine, 1965) (6 fumbles)
6—Mississippi (7) vs. Alabama (12) (Sugar, 1964) (11 fumbles)
6—North Texas (8) vs. New Mexico St. (28) (Sun, 1959) (8 fumbles)
6—(D) Arizona St. (21) vs. Xavier (Ohio) (33) (Salad, 1950) (7 fumbles)
5—Southern Miss. (35) vs. Idaho (42) (Humanitarian, 1998) (6 fumbles)
5—UCLA (16) vs. Wisconsin (21) (Rose, 1994) (5 fumbles)
5—North Carolina St. (28) vs. Iowa (23) (Peach, Dec. 31, 1988) (8 fumbles)
5—(D) North Carolina (21) vs. Arizona (30) (Aloha, 1986) (5 fumbles)
5—(D) Bowling Green (7) vs. Fresno St. (51) (California, 1985) (6 fumbles)
5—(D) Georgia (22) vs. Stanford (25) (Bluebonnet, 1978) (6 fumbles)
5—(D) Texas A&M (28) vs. Southern California (47) (Bluebonnet, 1977) (7 fumbles)
5—Auburn (27) vs. Texas (3) (Gator, 1974) (7 fumbles)
5—Texas (11) vs. Notre Dame (24) (Cotton, 1971) (9 fumbles)
5—Georgia (2) vs. Arkansas (16) (Sugar, 1969) (7 fumbles)
5—(D) Utah St. (9) vs. Baylor (24) (Gotham, 1961) (5 fumbles)
5—Rice (7) vs. Navy (20) (Cotton, 1958) (5 fumbles)
5—Auburn (13) vs. Vanderbilt (25) (Gator, 1955) (5 fumbles)
5—Oklahoma (7) vs. Kentucky (13) (Sugar, 1951)
5—Missouri (7) vs. Maryland (20) (Gator, 1950) (7 fumbles)
5—Texas A&M (21) vs. Alabama (29) (Cotton, 1942) (6 fumbles)

MOST FUMBLES LOST, BOTH TEAMS
9—Alabama (12) [3] & Mississippi (7) [6] (Sugar, 1964) (17 fumbles)
8—Idaho (42) [3] & Southern Miss. (35) [5] (Humanitarian, 1998) (9 fumbles)
8—North Carolina St. (28) [5] & Iowa (23) [3] (Peach, Dec. 31, 1988) (12 fumbles)
8—New Mexico St. (28) [2] & North Texas (8) [6] (Sun, 1959) (12 fumbles)
8—Navy (20) [3] & Rice (7) [5] (Cotton, 1958) (10 fumbles)
7—Georgia Tech (52) [1] & Tulsa (10) [6] (Humanitarian, 2004) (8 fumbles)
7—Florida St. (10) [1] & Texas A&M (2) [6] (Cotton, 1992) (7 fumbles)
7—Texas A&M (37) [3] & Florida (14) [4] (Sun, Jan. 2, 1977) (8 fumbles)
7—Arizona St. (28) [3] & Pittsburgh (7) [4] (Fiesta, 1973) (9 fumbles)
7—Tennessee (34) [3] & Air Force (13) [4] (Sugar, 1971) (14 fumbles)
7—Michigan St. (28) [4] & UCLA (20) [3] (Rose, 1954) (8 fumbles)

Penalties

MOST PENALTIES
21—Mississippi St. (17) vs. Clemson (7) (Peach, 1999) (188 yards)
20—(D) Fresno St. (35) vs. Western Mich. (30) (California, 1988) (166 yards)
19—Oregon (41) vs. Air Force (13) (Las Vegas, 1997) (166 yards)
18—Oregon St. (41) vs. Notre Dame (9) (Fiesta, 2001) (174 yards)
18—Alabama (34) vs. Michigan (35) (ot) (Orange, 2000) (132 yards)
18—Washington St. (31) vs. Utah (28) (Copper, 1992) (136 yards)
17—Florida St. (30) vs. West Virginia (18) (Gator, 2005) (174 yards)
16—Miami (Fla.) (46) vs. Texas (3) (Cotton, 1991) (202 yards)
16—Tulsa (16) vs. McNeese St. (20) (Independence, 1976) (100 yards)
16—Tennessee (17) vs. Oklahoma (0) (Orange, 1939) (130 yards)

MOST PENALTIES, BOTH TEAMS
29—Mississippi St. (17) [21] & Clemson (7) [8] (Peach, 1999) (270 yards)
29—Florida (52) [15] & Florida St. (20) [14] (Sugar, 1997) (217 yards)
29—McNeese St. (20) [13] & Tulsa (16) [16] (Independence, 1976) (205 yards)
28—Florida St. (30) [17] & West Virginia (18) [11] (Gator, 2005) (295 yards)
28—Michigan (35) [10] & Alabama (34) [18] (ot) (Orange, 2000) (247 yards)
28—(D) Fresno St. (35) [20] & Western Mich. (30) [8] (California, 1988) (231 yards)
27—Marshall (48) [14] & Louisville (29) [13] (Motor City, 1998) (232 yards)
26—Oregon (41) [19] & Air Force (13) [7] (Las Vegas, 1997) (223 yards)
26—Tennessee (35) [11] & Miami (Fla.) (7) [15] (Sugar, 1986) (245 yards)
25—Oregon St. (41) [18] & Notre Dame (9) [7] (Fiesta, 2001) (216 yards)
25—Washington St. (31) [18] & Utah (28) [7] (Copper, 1992) (191 yards)
25—Tennessee (17) [16] & Oklahoma (0) [9] (Orange, 1939) (221 yards)

MOST YARDS PENALIZED
202—Miami (Fla.) (46) vs. Texas (3) (Cotton, 1991) (16 penalties)
188—Mississippi St. (17) vs. Clemson (7) (Peach, 1999) (21 penalties)
174—Florida St. (30) vs. West Virginia (18) (Gator, 2005) (17 penalties)
174—Oregon St. (41) vs. Notre Dame (9) (Fiesta, 2001) (18 penalties)
166—Oregon (41) vs. Air Force (13) (Las Vegas, 1997) (19 penalties)
166—(D) Fresno St. (35) vs. Western Mich. (30) (California, 1988) (20 penalties)
164—Illinois (30) vs. East Caro. (0) (Liberty, 1994) (15 penalties)

163—(D) San Jose St. (37) vs. Miami (Ohio) (7) (California, 1986) (14 penalties)
153—Purdue (25) vs. Georgia (28) (ot) (Outback, 2000) (14 penalties)
151—Utah (17) vs. Fresno St. (16) (Las Vegas, 1999) (15 penalties)
150—Utah St. (42) vs. Ball St. (33) (Las Vegas, 1993) (15 penalties)
150—Oklahoma (48) vs. Duke (21) (Orange, 1958) (12 penalties)

MOST YARDS PENALIZED, BOTH TEAMS
295—Florida St. (30) [174] & West Virginia (18) [121] (Gator, 2005)
270—Mississippi St. (17) [188] & Clemson (7) [82] (Peach, 1999)
270—Miami (Fla.) (46) [202] & Texas (3) [68] (Cotton, 1991)
264—(D) San Jose St. (37) [163] & Miami (Ohio) (7) [101] (California, 1986)
247—Michigan (35) [115] & Alabama (34) [132] (ot) (Orange, 2000)
245—Tennessee (35) [125] & Miami (Fla.) (7) [120] (Sugar, 1986)
242—(D) Michigan (33) [148] & UCLA (14) [94] (Bluebonnet, 1981)
232—Marshall (48) [123] & Louisville (29) [109] (Motor City, 1998)
231—(D) Fresno St. (35) [166] & Western Mich. (30) [65] (California, 1988)
226—(D) Hawaii (23) [88] & Oregon St. (17) [138] (Oahu Classic, 1999)

FEWEST PENALTIES
0—Northern Ill. (7) vs. TCU (37) (Poinsettia, 2006)
0—SMU (7) vs. Alabama (28) (Sun, 1983)
0—Louisiana Tech (13) vs. East Caro. (35) (Independence, 1978)
0—Texas (17) vs. Alabama (13) (Cotton, 1973)
0—Air Force (13) vs. Tennessee (34) (Sugar, 1971)
0—(D) Rice (7) vs. Kansas (33) (Bluebonnet, 1961)
0—Pittsburgh (14) vs. Georgia Tech (21) (Gator, 1956)
0—Clemson (0) vs. Miami (Fla.) (14) (Gator, 1952)
0—Texas (7) vs. Randolph Field (7) (Cotton, 1944)
0—Alabama (20) vs. Washington (19) (Rose, 1926)

FEWEST PENALTIES, BOTH TEAMS
3—Oregon St. (39) [2] & Missouri (38) [1] (Sun, 2006)
3—Alabama (28) [3] & SMU (7) [0] (Sun, 1983)
3—Penn St. (30) [2] & Texas (6) [1] (Cotton, 1972)
3—Texas (21) [1] & Notre Dame (17) [2] (Cotton, 1970)
3—Penn St. (15) [1] & Kansas (14) [2] (Orange, 1969)
3—(D) Kansas (33) [3] & Rice (7) [0] (Bluebonnet, 1961)

FEWEST YARDS PENALIZED
0— Northern Ill. (7) vs. TCU (37) (Poinsettia, 2006)
0—North Texas (10) vs. Southern Miss. (31) (New Orleans, 2004)
0—SMU (7) vs. Alabama (28) (Sun, 1983)
0—Louisiana Tech (13) vs. East Caro. (35) (Independence, 1978)
0—Texas (17) vs. Alabama (13) (Cotton, 1973)
0—Air Force (13) vs. Tennessee (34) (Sugar, 1971)
0—(D) Rice (7) vs. Kansas (33) (Bluebonnet, 1961)
0—Pittsburgh (14) vs. Georgia Tech (21) (Gator, 1956)
0—Clemson (0) vs. Miami (Fla.) (14) (Gator, 1952)
0—Texas (7) vs. Randolph Field (7) (Cotton, 1944)
0—Alabama (20) vs. Washington (19) (Rose, 1926)

FEWEST YARDS PENALIZED, BOTH TEAMS
10—Duquesne (13) [5] & Mississippi St. (12) [5] (Orange, 1937)
15—Texas (21) [5] & Notre Dame (17) [10] (Cotton, 1970)
15—(D) Kansas (33) [15] vs. Rice (7) [0] (Bluebonnet, 1961)

Miscellaneous Records

SCORELESS TIES#
1959—Air Force 0, TCU 0 (Cotton)
1947—Arkansas 0, LSU 0 (Cotton)
1940—Arizona St. 0, Catholic 0 (Sun)
1922—California 0, Wash. & Jeff. 0 (Rose)

TIE GAMES#
(Not Scoreless)
1991—BYU 13, Iowa 13 (Holiday)
1990—Louisiana Tech 34, Maryland 34 (Independence)
1988—Auburn 16, Syracuse 16 (Sugar)
1985—Arizona 13, Georgia 13 (Sun)
1984—Florida St. 17, Georgia 17 (Florida Citrus)
1978—Arkansas 10, UCLA 10 (Fiesta)
1977—(D) Maryland 17, Minnesota 17 (Hall of Fame)
1974—Texas Tech 6, Vanderbilt 6 (Peach)
1974—(D) Houston 31, North Carolina St. 31 (Bluebonnet)
1970—(D) Alabama 24, Oklahoma 24 (Bluebonnet)
1970—(D) Long Beach St. 24, Louisville 24 (Pasadena)
1967—Florida St. 17, Penn St. 17 (Gator)
1960—(D) Alabama 3, Texas 3 (Bluebonnet)
1948—Georgia 20, Maryland 20 (Gator)
1948—Penn St. 13, SMU 13 (Cotton)
1947—(D) Montana St. 13, New Mexico 13 (Harbor)
1944—Randolph Field 7, Texas 7 (Cotton)
1937—(D) Auburn 7, Villanova 7 (Bacardi)
1936—Hardin-Simmons 14, New Mexico St. 14 (Sun)
1934—(D) Arkansas 7, Centenary (La.) 7 (Dixie Classic)
1927—Alabama 7, Stanford 7 (Rose)
1924—Navy 14, Washington 14 (Rose)

OVERTIME GAMES#
1995—Toledo (40) vs. Nevada (37) (Las Vegas) (1 ot)
2000—Georgia (28) vs. Purdue (25) (Outback) (1 ot)
2000—Michigan (35) vs. Alabama (34) (Orange) (1 ot)
2000—Mississippi St. (43) vs. Texas A&M (41) (Independence) (1 ot)
2001—Marshall (64) vs. East Caro. (61) (GMAC) (2 ot)
2002—Wisconsin (31) vs. Colorado (28) (Alamo) (1 ot)
2003—Ohio St. (31) vs. Miami (Fla.) (24) (Fiesta) (2 ot)
2003—Hawaii (54) vs. Houston (48) (Hawaii) (3 ot)
2004—Georgia (34) vs. Purdue (27) (Capital One) (1 ot)
2004—Fresno St. (37) vs. Virginia (34) (MPC Computers) (1 ot)
2005—Nevada (49) vs. UCF (48) (Hawaii) (1 ot)
2006—Penn St. (26) vs. Florida St. (23) (Orange) (3 ot)
2006—Texas Tech (44) vs. Minnesota (41) (Insight) (1 ot)
2007—Boise St. (43) vs. Oklahoma (42) (Fiesta) (1 ot)

#Beginning in 1995-96, tied bowl games were allowed to use a tiebreaker system.

Longest Plays

Only official records after 1937 are included. Prior records are included if able to be substantiated. Each team's score is in parentheses after the team name. Totals for each team in both-team records are in brackets after the team's score. The year listed is the actual (calendar) year the game was played; the date is included if the bowl was played twice (i.e., January and December) during one calendar year. The list also includes discontinued bowls, marked with (D). Bowls are listed by the name of the bowl at the time it was played.

LONGEST RUNS FROM SCRIMMAGE

Yds.	Player, Team (Score) vs. Opponent (Score)	Bowl, Year
99*	Terry Baker (QB), Oregon St. (6) vs. Villanova (0)	Liberty, 1962
95*#	Dicky Maegle, Rice (28) vs. Alabama (6)	Cotton, 1954
94*(D)	Dwight Ford, Southern California (47) vs. Texas A&M (28)	Bluebonnet, 1977
94*	Larry Smith, Florida (27) vs. Georgia Tech (12)	Orange, 1967
94*	Hascall Henshaw, Arizona St. (13) vs. Case Reserve (26)	Sun, 1941

*#Famous bench-tackle play; Maegle tackled on Alabama 40-yard line by Tommy Lewis, awarded touchdown. *Scored touchdown on play.*

LONGEST PASS PLAYS

Yds.	Players, Team (Score) vs. Opponent (Score)	Bowl, Year
95*	Ronnie Fletcher to Ben Hart, Oklahoma (19) vs. Florida St. (36)	Gator, Jan. 2, 1965
93*(D)	Stan Heath to Tommy Kalminir, Nevada (13) vs. North Texas (6)	Salad, 1948
91*(D)	Mark Barsotti to Stephen Shelley, Fresno St. (27) vs. Ball St. (6)	California, 1989
89*	Pete Gonzalez to Jake Hoffart, Pittsburgh (7) vs. Southern Miss. (41)	Liberty, 1997
88*	Michael Bishop to Darnell McDonald, Kansas St. (34) vs. Purdue (37)	Alamo, 1998
88*	Dave Schnell to Rob Turner, Indiana (34) vs. South Carolina (10)	Liberty, 1988
87*(D)	Mike Thomas to L.C. Stevens, North Carolina (20) vs. Arkansas (10)	Carquest, Dec. 30, 1995
87*	Drew Bledsoe to Phillip Bobo, Washington St. (31) vs. Utah (28)	Copper, 1992
87*	Randy Wright to Tim Stracka, Wisconsin (14) vs. Kansas St. (3)	Independence, 1982
87*	Ger Schwedes to Ernie Davis, Syracuse (23) vs. Texas (14)	Cotton, 1960

Yds.	Players, Team (Score) vs. Opponent (Score)	Bowl, Year
86*	Brad Otton to Keyshawn Johnson, Southern California (55) vs. Texas Tech (14)	Cotton, 1995

**Scored touchdown on play.*

LONGEST FIELD GOALS

Yds.	Player, Team (Score) vs. Opponent (Score)	Bowl, Year
62	Tony Franklin, Texas A&M (37) vs. Florida (14)	Sun, Jan. 2, 1977
56	Greg Cox, Miami (Fla.) (20) vs. Oklahoma (14)	Orange, 1988
55(D)	Russell Erxleben, Texas (38) vs. Colorado (21)	Bluebonnet, 1975
54(D)	Mason Crosby, Colorado (33) vs. UTEP (28)	Houston, 2004
54	Carlos Huerta, Miami (Fla.) (22) vs. Nebraska (0)	Orange, 1992
54	Quin Rodriguez, Southern California (16) vs. Michigan St. (17)	John Hancock, 1990
54	Luis Zendejas, Arizona St. (32) vs. Oklahoma (21)	Fiesta, 1983

LONGEST PUNTS

Yds.	Player, Team (Score) vs. Opponent (Score)	Bowl, Year
84$	Kyle Rote, SMU (21) vs. Oregon (13)	Cotton, 1949
82	Ike Pickle, Mississippi St. (12) vs. Duquesne (13)	Orange, 1937
80	Elmer Layden, Notre Dame (27) vs. Stanford (10)	Rose, 1925
79$	Doak Walker, SMU (21) vs. Oregon (13)	Cotton, 1949
78	Chris Hogue, Tennessee (17) vs. Nebraska (42)	Orange, 1998
78	Glenn Dobbs, Tulsa (7) vs. Tennessee (14)	Sugar, 1943
77	Mike Sochko, Maryland (21) vs. Houston (30)	Cotton, 1977
74(D)	Bryce Benekos, UTEP (28) vs. Colorado (33)	Houston, 2004
74	Bill Bradley, Texas (36) vs. Tennessee (13)	Cotton, 1969
73	Sean Reali, Syracuse (41) vs. Clemson (0)	Gator, 1996

$Quick kick.

LONGEST PUNT RETURNS

Yds.	Player, Team (Score) vs. Opponent (Score)	Bowl, Year
92*	Quinton Jones, Boise St. (21) vs. Boston College (27)	MPC Computers, 2005
88*	Ben Kelly, Colorado (62) vs. Boston College (28)	Insight.com, 1999
87*	Willie Reid, Florida St. (23) vs. Penn St. (26) (3 ot)	Orange, 2006
86*	Javier Arenas, Alabama (31) vs. Oklahoma St. (34)	Independence, 2006
86*	Aramis Dandoy, Southern California (7) vs. Ohio St. (20)	Rose, 1955
85*	Brian Murph, Kansas (42) vs. Houston (13)	Fort Worth, 2005
85*	Darran Hall, Colorado St. (35) vs. Missouri (24)	Holiday, 1997
83*	Vai Sikahema, BYU (46) vs. SMU (45)	Holiday, 1980
82*	Marcus Wall, North Carolina (31) vs. Texas (35)	Sun, 1994
82	Willie Drewrey, West Virginia (12) vs. Florida St. (31)	Gator, 1982
80*(D)	Gary Anderson, Arkansas (34) vs. Tulane (15)	Hall of Fame, 1980
80*	Cecil Ingram, Alabama (61) vs. Syracuse (6)	Orange, 1953

**Scored touchdown on play.*

LONGEST KICKOFF RETURNS

Yds.	Player, Team (Score) vs. Opponent (Score)	Bowl, Year
100*	C.J. Jones, Iowa (17) vs. Southern California (38)	Orange, 2003
100*(D)	Deltha O'Neal, California (38) vs. Navy (42)	Aloha, 1996
100*	Derrick Mason, Michigan St. (26) vs. LSU (45)	Independence, 1995
100*	Kirby Dar Dar, Syracuse (26) vs. Colorado (22)	Fiesta, 1993
100*	Pete Panuska, Tennessee (27) vs. Maryland (28)	Sun, 1984
100*	Dave Lowery, BYU (21) vs. Oklahoma St. (49)	Tangerine, 1976
100*	Mike Fink, Missouri (35) vs. Arizona St. (49)	Fiesta, 1972
100*(D)	Bob Smith, Texas A&M (40) vs. Georgia (20)	Presidential Cup, 1950
100*!	Al Hoisch, UCLA (14) vs. Illinois (45)	Rose, 1947

**Scored touchdown on play. !Rose Bowl records carry as 103-yard return.*

LONGEST INTERCEPTION RETURNS

Yds.	Player, Team (Score) vs. Opponent (Score)	Bowl, Year
99*	Marcus King, Missouri (38) vs. South Carolina (31)	Independence, 2005
95*	Marcus Washington, Colorado (38) vs. Oregon (6)	Cotton, 1996
94*	David Baker, Oklahoma (48) vs. Duke (21)	Orange, 1958
92*	Andy Avalos, Boise St. (40) vs. Louisville (44)	Liberty, 2004
91*	Donald Strickland, Colorado (28) vs. Wisconsin (31)	Alamo, 2002
91*	Don Hoover, Ohio (14) vs. West Tex. A&M (15)	Sun, 1962
90*	Norm Beal, Missouri (21) vs. Navy (14)	Orange, 1961
90*	Charlie Brembs, South Carolina (14) vs. Wake Forest (26)	Gator, 1946
90*(D)	G.P. Jackson, TCU (7) vs. Centre (63)	Fort Worth Classic, 1921

**Scored touchdown on play.*

LONGEST MISCELLANEOUS RETURNS

Yds.	Player, Team (Score) vs. Opponent (Score)	Bowl, Year
98	Greg Mather, Navy (14) vs. Missouri (21) (Int. Lat.)	Orange, 1961
89(D)	Charlie Owens, TCU (9) vs. Texas A&M (28) (Fumble return)	galleryfurniture.com, 2001
80	Antonio Banks, Virginia Tech (45) vs. Indiana (20) (Blocked field goal return)	Independence, 1993
79	Tremain Mack, Miami (Fla.) (31) vs. Virginia (21) (Fumble return)	Carquest, 1996
78	Devin Hester, Miami (Fla.) (27) vs. Florida (10) (Blocked field goal return)	Peach, Dec. 31, 2004
75	Payton Williams, Fresno St. (16) vs. Utah (17) (Blocked field goal return)	Las Vegas, 1999
74	Morgan Scalley, Utah (17) vs. Southern Miss. (0) (Fumble return)	Liberty, 2003
73	Dick Carpenter, Oklahoma (48) vs. Duke (21) (Int. Lat.)	Orange, 1958
70	Carlos Posey, Missouri (34) vs. West Virginia (31) (Blocked punt return)	Insight.com, 1998
65	Steve Manstedt, Nebraska (19) vs. Texas (3) (Fumble return)	Cotton, 1974

Bowl Championship Series Individual Record Lists (1999-07)

Only games played since the formation of the Bowl Championship Series are included. For the All Bowls records, only official records after 1937 are included. Prior records are included if able to be substantiated. Each team's score is in parentheses after the team name. The year listed is the actual (calendar) year the game was played; the date is included if the bowl was played twice (i.e., January and December) during one calendar year. The list also includes discontinued bowls, marked with (D). Bowls are listed by the name of the bowl at the time it was played.

Total Offense

MOST TOTAL YARDS

467—Vince Young, Texas (41) vs. Southern California (38) (Rose, 2006) (267 pass, 200 rush)
444—Rohan Davey, LSU (47) vs. Illinois (34) (Sugar, 2002) (444 pass)
408—Troy Smith, Ohio St. (34) vs. Notre Dame (20) (Fiesta, 2006) (342 pass, 66 rush)
396—Alex Smith, Utah (35) vs. Pittsburgh (7) (Fiesta, 2005) (328 pass, 68 rush)
387—J.D. Booty, Southern California (32) vs. Michigan (18) (Rose, 2007) (391 pass, -4 rush)
372—Vince Young, Texas (38) vs. Michigan (37) (Rose, 2005) (192 rush, 180 pass)

MOST TOTAL YARDS, CHAMPIONSHIP GAME

467—Vince Young, Texas (41) vs. Southern California (38) (Rose, 2006) (267 pass, 200 rush)
362—Ken Dorsey, Miami (Fla.) (37) vs. Nebraska (14) (Rose, 2002) (362 pass)
322—Michael Vick, Virginia Tech (29) vs. Florida St. (46) (Sugar, 2000) (225 pass, 97 rush)
321—Matt Leinart, Southern California (55) vs. Oklahoma (19) (Orange, 2005) (332 pass, -11 rush)
297—Tee Martin, Tennessee (23) vs. Florida St. (16) (Fiesta, 1999) (278 pass, 19 rush)

MOST TOTAL YARDS, ALL BOWLS

594—Ty Detmer, BYU (39) vs. Penn St. (50) (Holiday, 1989) (576 pass, 18 rush)

MOST TOUCHDOWNS RESPONSIBLE FOR (TDs SCORED AND PASSED FOR)

5—Vince Young, Texas (38) vs. Michigan (37) (Rose, 2005) (4 rush, 1 pass)
5—Matt Leinart, Southern California (55) vs. Oklahoma (19) (Orange, 2005) (5 pass)

MOST TOUCHDOWNS RESPONSIBLE FOR, CHAMPIONSHIP GAME
5—Matt Leinart, Southern California (55) vs. Oklahoma (19) (Orange, 2005) (5 pass)

MOST TOUCHDOWNS RESPONSIBLE FOR, ALL BOWLS
6—(D) Chuck Long, Iowa (55) vs. Texas (17) (Freedom, 1984) (6 pass)
6—Bobby Layne, Texas (40) vs. Missouri (27) (Cotton, 1946) (3 rush, 2 pass, 1 catch)

Rushing

MOST RUSHING ATTEMPTS
34—Ron Dayne, Wisconsin (17) vs. Stanford (9) (Rose, 2000) (200 yards)
30—Quentin Griffin, Oklahoma (34) vs. Washington St. (14) (Rose, 2003) (144 yards)
28—Domanick Davis, LSU (47) vs. Illinois (34) (Sugar, 2002) (129 yards)
27—Ron Dayne, Wisconsin (38) vs. UCLA (31) (Rose, 1999) (246 yards)
26—Steve Slaton, West Virginia (38) vs. Georgia (35) (Sugar, 2006) (204 yards)
26—Austin Scott, Penn St. (26) vs. Florida St. (23) (3 ot) (Orange, 2006) (110 yards)

MOST RUSHING ATTEMPTS, CHAMPIONSHIP GAME
25—Adrian Peterson, Oklahoma (19) vs. Southern California (55) (Orange, 2005) (82 yards)
23—Maurice Clarett, Ohio St. (31) vs. Miami (Fla.) (24) (2 ot) (Fiesta, 2003) (47 yards)
22—Eric Crouch, Nebraska (14) vs. Miami (Fla.) (37) (Rose, 2002) (114 yards)
20—LenDale White, Southern California (38) vs. Texas (41) (Rose, 2006) (124 yards)
20—Willis McGahee, Miami (Fla.) (24) vs. Ohio St. (31) (2 ot) (Fiesta, 2003) (67 yards)
20—Clinton Portis, Miami (Fla.) (37) vs. Nebraska (14) (Rose, 2002) (104 yards)

MOST RUSHING ATTEMPTS, ALL BOWLS
46—(D) Ron Jackson, Tulsa (28) vs. San Diego St. (17) (Freedom, 1991) (211 yards)

MOST NET RUSHING YARDS
246—Ron Dayne, Wisconsin (38) vs. UCLA (31) (Rose, 1999) (27 attempts)
204—Steve Slaton, West Virginia (38) vs. Georgia (35) (Sugar, 2006) (26 attempts)
200—Vince Young, Texas (41) vs. Southern California (38) (Rose, 2006) (19 attempts)
200—Ron Dayne, Wisconsin (17) vs. Stanford (9) (Rose, 2000) (34 attempts)
192—Vince Young, Texas (38) vs. Michigan (37) (Rose, 2005) (21 attempts)

MOST RUSHING YARDS, CHAMPIONSHIP GAME
200—Vince Young, Texas (41) vs. Southern California (38) (Rose, 2006) (19 attempts)
124—LenDale White, Southern California (38) vs. Texas (41) (Rose, 2006) (20 attempts)
118—LenDale White, Southern California (55) vs. Oklahoma (19) (Orange, 2005) (15 attempts)
117—Justin Vincent, LSU (21) vs. Oklahoma (14) (Sugar, 2004) (16 attempts)
114—Eric Crouch, Nebraska (14) vs. Miami (Fla.) (37) (Rose, 2002) (22 attempts)

MOST RUSHING YARDS, ALL BOWLS
307—P.J. Daniels, Georgia Tech (52) vs. Tulsa (10) (Humanitarian, 2004) (31 carries)

MOST RUSHING YARDS BY A QUARTERBACK
200—Vince Young, Texas (41) vs. Southern California (38) (Rose, 2006) (19 attempts)
192—Vince Young, Texas (38) vs. Michigan (37) (Rose, 2005) (21 attempts)
114—Eric Crouch, Nebraska (14) vs. Miami (Fla.) (37) (Rose, 2002) (22 attempts)
97—Michael Vick, Virginia Tech (29) vs. Florida St. (46) (Sugar, 2000) (23 attempts)
81—Craig Krenzel, Ohio St. (31) vs. Miami (Fla.) (24) (2 ot) (Fiesta, 2003) (19 attempts)

MOST RUSHING YARDS BY A QUARTERBACK, CHAMPIONSHIP GAME
200—Vince Young, Texas (41) vs. Southern California (38) (Rose, 2006) (19 attempts)
114—Eric Crouch, Nebraska (14) vs. Miami (Fla.) (37) (Rose, 2002) (22 attempts)
97—Michael Vick, Virginia Tech (29) vs. Florida St. (46) (Sugar, 2000) (23 attempts)
81—Craig Krenzel, Ohio St. (31) vs. Miami (Fla.) (24) (2 ot) (Fiesta, 2003) (19 attempts)

MOST RUSHING YARDS BY A QUARTERBACK, ALL BOWLS
200—Vince Young, Texas (41) vs. Southern California (38) (Rose, 2006) (19 attempts)

MOST RUSHING YARDS PER ATTEMPT
(Minimum 15 Attempts)
10.53—Vince Young, Texas (41) vs. Southern California (38) (Rose, 2006) (19 for 200)
9.31—Ernest Graham, Florida (56) vs. Maryland (23) (Orange, 2002) (16 for 149)
9.14—Vince Young, Texas (38) vs. Michigan (37) (Rose, 2005) (21 for 192)
9.11—Ron Dayne, Wisconsin (38) vs. UCLA (31) (Rose, 1999) (27 for 246)
9.07—Ernest Graham, Florida (20) vs. Miami (Fla.) (37) (Sugar, 2001) (15 for 136)

MOST RUSHING YARDS PER ATTEMPT, CHAMPIONSHIP GAME
(Minimum 15 Attempts)
10.53—Vince Young, Texas (41) vs. Southern California (38) (Rose, 2006) (19 for 200)
7.87—LenDale White, Southern California (55) vs. Oklahoma (19) (Orange, 2005) (15 for 118)
7.31—Justin Vincent, LSU (21) vs. Oklahoma (14) (Sugar, 2004) (16 for 117)
6.20—LenDale White, Southern California (38) vs. Texas (41) (Rose, 2006) (20 for 124)
5.53—Travis Minor, Florida St. (16) vs. Tennessee (23) (Fiesta, 1999) (15 for 83)

MOST RUSHING YARDS PER ATTEMPT, ALL BOWLS
(Minimum 15 Attempts)
15.67—Tyrone Wheatley, Michigan (38) vs. Washington (31) (Rose, 1993) (15 for 235)

MOST RUSHING TOUCHDOWNS
4—Vince Young, Texas (38) vs. Michigan (37) (Rose, 2005)
4—Domanick Davis, LSU (47) vs. Illinois (34) (Sugar, 2002)
4—Ron Dayne, Wisconsin (38) vs. UCLA (31) (Rose, 1999)
3—Vince Young, Texas (41) vs. Southern California (38) (Rose, 2006)
3—LenDale White, Southern California (38) vs. Texas (41) (Rose, 2006)
3—Darius Walker, Notre Dame (20) vs. Ohio St. (34) (Fiesta, 2006)
3—Steve Slaton, West Virginia (38) vs. Georgia (35) (Sugar, 2006)
3—Shaun Alexander, Alabama (34) vs. Michigan (35) (ot) (Orange, 2000)

MOST RUSHING TOUCHDOWNS, CHAMPIONSHIP GAME
3—Vince Young, Texas (41) vs. Southern California (38) (Rose, 2006)
3—LenDale White, Southern California (38) vs. Texas (41) (Rose, 2006)
2—LenDale White, Southern California (55) vs. Oklahoma (19) (Orange, 2005)
2—Kejuan Jones, Oklahoma (14) vs. LSU (21) (Sugar, 2004)
2—Craig Krenzel, Ohio St. (31) vs. Miami (Fla.) (24) (2 ot) (Fiesta, 2003)
2—Maurice Clarett, Ohio St. (31) vs. Miami (Fla.) (24) (2 ot) (Fiesta, 2003)
2—Andre Kendrick, Virginia Tech (29) vs. Florida St. (46) (Sugar, 2000)

MOST RUSHING TOUCHDOWNS, ALL BOWLS
5—Barry Sanders, Oklahoma St. (62) vs. Wyoming (14) (Holiday, 1988)
5—Neil Snow, Michigan (49) vs. Stanford (0) (Rose, 1902) (five-point scores)

Passing

MOST PASS ATTEMPTS
53—Rohan Davey, LSU (47) vs. Illinois (34) (Sugar, 2002) (31 completions)
52—Eli Roberson, Kansas St. (28) vs. Ohio St. (35) (Fiesta, 2004) (20 completions)
52—Chris Weinke, Florida St. (2) vs. Oklahoma (13) (Orange, 2001) (25 completions)
46—John Navarre, Michigan (14) vs. Southern California (28) (Rose, 2004) (27 completions)
46—Tom Brady, Michigan (35) vs. Alabama (34) (ot) (Orange, 2000) (34 completions)

MOST PASS ATTEMPTS, CHAMPIONSHIP GAME
52—Chris Weinke, Florida St. (2) vs. Oklahoma (13) (Orange, 2001) (25 completions)
43—Ken Dorsey, Miami (Fla.) (24) vs. Ohio St. (31) (2 ot) (Fiesta, 2003) (28 completions)
40—Vince Young, Texas (41) vs. Southern California (38) (Rose, 2006) (30 completions)
40—Matt Leinart, Southern California (38) vs. Texas (41) (Rose, 2006) (29 completions)
39—Josh Heupel, Oklahoma (13) vs. Florida St. (2) (Orange, 2001) (25 completions)

MOST PASS ATTEMPTS, ALL BOWLS
74—Kyle Orton, Purdue (27) vs. Washington St. (33) (Sun, 2001) (38 completions)

MOST PASS COMPLETIONS
34—Tom Brady, Michigan (35) vs. Alabama (34) (ot) (Orange, 2000) (46 attempts)
31—Rohan Davey, LSU (47) vs. Illinois (34) (Sugar, 2002) (53 attempts)
30—Vince Young, Texas (41) vs. Southern California (38) (Rose, 2006) (40 attempts)
29—Matt Leinart, Southern California (38) vs. Texas (41) (Rose, 2006) (40 attempts)
29—Brady Quinn, Notre Dame (20) vs. Ohio St. (34) (Fiesta, 2006) (45 attempts)
29—Alex Smith, Utah (35) vs. Pittsburgh (7) (Fiesta, 2005) (37 attempts)

MOST PASS COMPLETIONS, CHAMPIONSHIP GAME
30—Vince Young, Texas (41) vs. Southern California (38) (Rose, 2006) (40 attempts)
29—Matt Leinart, Southern California (38) vs. Texas (41) (Rose, 2006) (40 attempts)
28—Ken Dorsey, Miami (Fla.) (24) vs. Ohio St. (31) (2 ot) (Fiesta, 2003) (43 attempts)
25—Chris Leak, Florida (41) vs. Ohio St. (14) (BCS, 2007) (36 attempts)
25—Chris Weinke, Florida St. (2) vs. Oklahoma (13) (Orange, 2001) (52 attempts)
25—Josh Heupel, Oklahoma (13) vs. Florida St. (2) (Orange, 2001) (39 attempts)

MOST PASS COMPLETIONS, ALL BOWLS
43—(D) Steve Clarkson, San Jose St. (25) vs. Toledo (27) (California, 1981) (62 attempts)

MOST PASSING YARDS
444—Rohan Davey, LSU (47) vs. Illinois (34) (Sugar, 2002) (31 of 53)
391—J.D. Booty, Southern California (32) vs. Michigan (18) (Rose, 2007) (27 of 45)
369—Tom Brady, Michigan (35) vs. Alabama (34) (ot) (Orange, 2000) (34 of 46)
365—Matt Leinart, Southern California (38) vs. Texas (41) (Rose, 2006) (29 of 40)
362—Ken Dorsey, Miami (Fla.) (37) vs. Nebraska (14) (Rose, 2002) (22 of 35)
350—Joey Harrington, Oregon (38) vs. Colorado (16) (Fiesta, 2002) (28 of 42)

MOST PASSING YARDS, CHAMPIONSHIP GAME
365—Matt Leinart, Southern California (38) vs. Texas (41) (Rose, 2006) (29 of 40)
362—Ken Dorsey, Miami (Fla.) (37) vs. Nebraska (14) (Rose, 2002) (22 of 35)
332—Matt Leinart, Southern California (55) vs. Oklahoma (19) (Orange, 2005) (18 of 35)
329—Chris Weinke, Florida St. (46) vs. Virginia Tech (29) (Sugar, 2000) (20 of 34)
296—Ken Dorsey, Miami (Fla.) (24) vs. Ohio St. (31) (2 ot) (Fiesta, 2003) (28 of 43)

MOST PASSING YARDS, ALL BOWLS
576—Byron Leftwich, Marshall (64) vs. East Caro. (61) (2 ot) (GMAC, 2001) (41 of 70)
576—Ty Detmer, BYU (39) vs. Penn St. (50) (Holiday, 1989) (42 of 59)

MOST PASSES WITHOUT AN INTERCEPTION
53—Rohan Davey, LSU (47) vs. Illinois (34) (Sugar, 2002)

MOST PASSES WITHOUT AN INTERCEPTION, CHAMPIONSHIP GAME
40—Vince Young, Texas (41) vs. Southern California (38) (Rose, 2006)

MOST TOUCHDOWN PASSES
5—Matt Leinart, Southern California (55) vs. Oklahoma (19) (Orange, 2005)
4—J.D. Booty, Southern California (32) vs. Michigan (18) (Rose, 2007)
4—Alex Smith, Utah (35) vs. Pittsburgh (7) (Fiesta, 2005)
4—Chad Henne, Michigan (37) vs. Texas (38) (Rose, 2005)
4—Craig Krenzel, Ohio St. (35) vs. Kansas St. (28) (Fiesta, 2004)
4—Kurt Kittner, Illinois (34) vs. LSU (47) (Sugar, 2002)

4—Rex Grossman, Florida (56) vs. Maryland (23) (Orange, 2002)
4—Joey Harrington, Oregon (38) vs. Colorado (16) (Fiesta, 2002)
4—Tom Brady, Michigan (35) vs. Alabama (34) (ot) (Orange, 2000)
4—Chris Weinke, Florida St. (46) vs. Virginia Tech (29) (Sugar, 2000)

MOST TOUCHDOWN PASSES, CHAMPIONSHIP GAME
5—Matt Leinart, Southern California (55) vs. Oklahoma (19) (Orange, 2005)
4—Chris Weinke, Florida St. (46) vs. Virginia Tech (29) (Sugar, 2000)
3—Ken Dorsey, Miami (Fla.) (37) vs. Nebraska (14) (Rose, 2002)
2—Jason White, Oklahoma (19) vs. Southern California (55) (Orange, 2005)
2—Ken Dorsey, Miami (Fla.) (24) vs. Ohio St. (31) (2 ot) (Fiesta, 2003)
2—Tee Martin, Tennessee (23) vs. Florida St. (16) (Fiesta, 1999)

MOST TOUCHDOWN PASSES, ALL BOWLS
6—(D) Chuck Long, Iowa (55) vs. Texas (17) (Freedom, 1984)

HIGHEST COMPLETION PERCENTAGE
(Minimum 20 Attempts)
.784—Alex Smith, Utah Utah (35) vs. Pittsburgh (7) (Fiesta, 2005) (29 of 37)
.750—Vince Young, Texas (41) vs. Southern California (38) (Rose, 2006) (30 of 40)
.739—Tom Brady, Michigan (35) vs. Alabama (34) (ot) (Orange, 2000) (34 of 46)
.727—Marques Tuiasosopo, Washington (34) vs. Purdue (24) (Rose, 2001) (16 of 22)
.725—Matt Leinart, Southern California (38) vs. Texas (41) (Rose, 2006) (29 of 40)

HIGHEST COMPLETION PERCENTAGE, CHAMPIONSHIP GAME
(Minimum 20 Attempts)
.750—Vince Young, Texas (41) vs. Southern California (38) (Rose, 2006) (30 of 40)
.725—Matt Leinart, Southern California (38) vs. Texas (41) (Rose, 2006) (29 of 40)
.694—Chris Leak, Florida (41) vs. Ohio St. (14) (BCS, 2007) (25 of 36)
.667—Jason White, Oklahoma (19) vs. Southern California (55) (Orange, 2005) (24 of 36)
.651—Ken Dorsey, Miami (Fla.) (24) vs. Ohio St. (31) (2 ot) (Fiesta, 2003) (28 of 43)
.641—Josh Heupel, Oklahoma (13) vs. Florida St. (2) (Orange, 2001) (25 of 39)

HIGHEST COMPLETION PERCENTAGE, ALL BOWLS
(Minimum 20 Attempts)
.929—Mike Bobo, Georgia (33) vs. Wisconsin (6) (Outback, 1998) (26 of 28)

Receiving

MOST RECEPTIONS
15—Paris Warren, Utah (35) vs. Pittsburgh (7) (Fiesta, 2005) (198 yards)
14—Josh Reed, LSU (47) vs. Illinois (34) (Sugar, 2002) (239 yards)
11—Dwayne Jarrett, Southern California (32) vs. Michigan (18) (Rose, 2007) (205 yards)
11—Kellen Winslow Jr., Miami (Fla.) (24) vs. Ohio St. (31) (2 ot) (Fiesta, 2003) (122 yards)
11—David Boston, Ohio St. (24) vs. Texas A&M (14) (Sugar, 1999) (105 yards)
10—Harry Douglas, Louisville (24) vs. Wake Forest (13) (Orange, 2007) (165 yards)
10—David Thomas, Texas (41) vs. Southern California (38) (Rose, 2006) (88 yards)
10—Dwayne Jarrett, Southern California (38) vs. Texas (41) (Rose, 2006) (121 yards)
10—Braylon Edwards, Michigan (37) vs. Texas (38) (Rose, 2005) (109 yards)
10—Braylon Edwards, Michigan (14) vs. Southern California (28) (Rose, 2004) (107 yards)
10—Daniel Graham, Colorado (16) vs. Oregon (38) (Fiesta, 2002) (89 yards)
10—Taylor Jacobs, Florida (56) vs. Maryland (23) (Orange, 2002) (170 yards)
10—David Terrell, Michigan (35) vs. Alabama (34) (ot) (Orange, 2000) (150 yards)

MOST RECEPTIONS, CHAMPIONSHIP GAME
11—Kellen Winslow Jr., Miami (Fla.) (24) vs. Ohio St. (31) (2 ot) (Fiesta, 2003) (122 yards)
10—David Thomas, Texas (41) vs. Southern California (38) (Rose, 2006) (88 yards)
10—Dwayne Jarrett, Southern California (38) vs. Texas (41) (Rose, 2006) (121 yards)
9—Percy Harvin, Florida (41) vs. Ohio St. (14) (BCS, 2007) (60 yards)
7—Steve Smith, Southern California (55) vs. Oklahoma (19) (Orange, 2005) (113 yards)
7—Travis Wilson, Oklahoma (19) vs. Southern California (55) (Orange, 2005) (59 yards)
7—Andre Johnson, Miami (Fla.) (37) vs. Nebraska (14) (Rose, 2002) (199 yards)
7—Atrews Bell, Florida St. (2) vs. Oklahoma (13) (Orange, 2001) (137 yards)

MOST RECEPTIONS, ALL BOWLS
20—(D) Norman Jordan, Vanderbilt (28) vs. Air Force (36) (Hall of Fame, 1982) (173 yards)
20—Walker Gillette, Richmond (49) vs. Ohio (42) (Tangerine, 1968) (242 yards)

MOST RECEIVING YARDS
239—Josh Reed, LSU (47) vs. Illinois (34) (Sugar, 2002) (14 catches)
205—Dwayne Jarrett, Southern California (32) vs. Michigan (18) (Rose, 2007) (11 catches)
199—Andre Johnson, Miami (Fla.) (37) vs. Nebraska (14) (Rose, 2002) (7 catches)
199—Peerless Price, Tennessee (23) vs. Florida St. (16) (Fiesta, 1999) (4 catches)
198—Paris Warren, Utah (35) vs. Pittsburgh (7) (Fiesta, 2005) (15 catches)
178—Walter Young, Illinois (34) vs. LSU (47) (Sugar, 2002) (6 catches)

MOST RECEIVING YARDS, CHAMPIONSHIP GAME
199—Andre Johnson, Miami (Fla.) (37) vs. Nebraska (14) (Rose, 2002) (7 catches)
199—Peerless Price, Tennessee (23) vs. Florida St. (16) (Fiesta, 1999) (4 catches)
163—Peter Warrick, Florida St. (46) vs. Virginia Tech (29) (Sugar, 2000) (6 catches)
137—Atrews Bell, Florida St. (2) vs. Oklahoma (13) (Orange, 2001) (7 catches)
135—Ron Dugans, Florida St. (16) vs. Tennessee (23) (Fiesta, 1999) (6 catches)

MOST RECEIVING YARDS, ALL BOWLS
308—Jason Rivers, Hawaii (41) vs. Arizona St. (24) (Hawaii, 2006) (14 catches)

MOST TOUCHDOWNS RECEIVING
3—Steve Smith, Southern California (55) vs. Oklahoma (19) (Orange, 2005)
3—Braylon Edwards, Michigan (37) vs. Texas (38) (Rose, 2005)
3—David Terrell, Michigan (35) vs. Alabama (34) (ot) (Orange, 2000)
2—20 times

MOST TOUCHDOWNS RECEIVING, CHAMPIONSHIP GAME
3—Steve Smith, Southern California (55) vs. Oklahoma (19) (Orange, 2005)
2—Travis Wilson, Oklahoma (19) vs. Southern California (55) (Orange, 2005)
2—Andre Johnson, Miami (Fla.) (37) vs. Nebraska (14) (Rose, 2002)
2—Ron Dugans, Florida St. (46) vs. Virginia Tech (29) (Sugar, 2000)
2—Peter Warrick, Florida St. (46) vs. Virginia Tech (29) (Sugar, 2000)

MOST TOUCHDOWNS RECEIVING, ALL BOWLS
4—Travis LaTendresse, Utah (38) vs. Georgia Tech (10) (Emerald, 2005)
4—Fred Biletnikoff, Florida St. (36) vs. Oklahoma (19) (Gator, 1965)
4—(D) Bob McChesney, Hardin-Simmons (49) vs. Wichita St. (12) (Camellia, 1948)

HIGHEST AVERAGE PER RECEPTION
(Minimum 3 Receptions)
49.8—Peerless Price, Tennessee (23) vs. Florida St. (16) (Fiesta, 1999) (4 for 199)
42.0—Josh Morgan, Virginia Tech (13) vs. Auburn (16) (Sugar, 2005) (3 for 126)
34.0—Durell Price, UCLA (31) vs. Wisconsin (38) (Rose, 1999) (3 for 102)

HIGHEST AVERAGE PER RECEPTION, CHAMPIONSHIP GAME
(Minimum 3 Receptions)
49.8—Peerless Price, Tennessee (23) vs. Florida St. (16) (Fiesta, 1999) (4 for 199)

HIGHEST AVERAGE PER RECEPTION, ALL BOWLS
(Minimum 3 Receptions)
52.3—(D) Jason Anderson, Wake Forest (38) vs. Oregon (17) (Seattle, 2002) (3 for 157)
52.3—Phil Harris, Texas (28) vs. Navy (6) (Cotton, 1964) (3 for 157)

All-Purpose Yards

MOST ALL-PURPOSE YARDS
315—Steve Breaston, Michigan (37) vs. Texas (38) (Rose, 2005) (221 kickoff return, 77 receiving, 15 rush, 2 punt return)
279—Reggie Bush, Southern California (38) vs. Texas (41) (Rose, 2006) (102 kickoff return, 95 receiving, 82 rushing)
260—Ted Ginn Jr., Ohio St. (34) vs. Notre Dame (20) (Fiesta, 2006) (167 receiving, 73 rushing, 20 punt return)
246—Ron Dayne, Wisconsin (38) vs. UCLA (31) (Rose, 1999) (246 rush)
242—Peerless Price, Tennessee (23) vs. Florida St. (16) (Fiesta, 1999) (199 receiving, 43 punt return)

MOST ALL-PURPOSE YARDS, CHAMPIONSHIP GAME
279—Reggie Bush, Southern California (38) vs. Texas (41) (Rose, 2006) (102 kickoff return, 95 receiving, 82 rushing)
242—Peerless Price, Tennessee (23) vs. Florida St. (16) (Fiesta, 1999) (199 receiving, 43 punt return)
226—Andre Johnson, Miami (Fla.) (37) vs. Nebraska (14) (Rose, 2002) (199 receiving, 27 kickoff return)
220—Peter Warrick, Florida St. (46) vs. Virginia Tech (29) (Sugar, 2000) (163 receiving, 57 punt return)
149—Reggie Bush, Southern California (55) vs. Oklahoma (19) (Orange, 2005) (75 rush, 31 receiving, 36 kickoff return, 7 punt return)

MOST ALL-PURPOSE YARDS, ALL BOWLS
359—Sherman Williams, Alabama (24) vs. Ohio St. (17) (Florida Citrus, 1995) (166 rush, 155 receptions, 38 kickoff returns)

Scoring

MOST POINTS SCORED
24—Vince Young, Texas (38) vs. Michigan (37) (Rose, 2005) (4 TDs)
24—Domanick Davis, LSU (47) vs. Illinois (34) (Sugar, 2002) (4 TDs)
24—Ron Dayne, Wisconsin (38) vs. UCLA (31) (Rose, 1999) (4 TDs)
20—Vince Young, Texas (41) vs. Southern California (38) (Rose, 2006) (3 TDs, 1 2-pt. conversion)
20—Peter Warrick, Florida St. (46) vs. Virginia Tech (29) (Sugar, 2000) (3 TDs, 1 2-pt. conversion)

MOST POINTS SCORED, CHAMPIONSHIP GAME
20—Vince Young, Texas (41) vs. Southern California (38) (Rose, 2006) (3 TDs, 1 2-pt. conversion)
20—Peter Warrick, Florida St. (46) vs. Virginia Tech (29) (Sugar, 2000) (3 TDs, 1 2-pt. conversion)
18—LenDale White, Southern California (38) vs. Texas (41) (Rose, 2006) (3 TDs)
18—Steve Smith, Southern California (55) vs. Oklahoma (19) (Orange, 2005) (3 TDs)
13—Ryan Killeen, Southern California (55) vs. Oklahoma (19) (Orange, 2005) (2 FGs, 7 PATs)

MOST POINTS SCORED, ALL BOWLS
30—Reggie Campbell, Navy (51) vs. Colorado St. (30) (Poinsettia, 2005) (5 TDs)
30—Steven Jackson, Oregon St. (55) vs. New Mexico (14) (Las Vegas, 2003) (5 TDs)
30—(D) Sheldon Canley, San Jose St. (48) vs. Central Mich. (24) (California, 1990) (5 TDs)
30—Barry Sanders, Oklahoma St. (62) vs. Wyoming (14) (Holiday, 1988) (5 TDs)

Kicking

MOST POINTS SCORED BY A KICKER
14—Billy Bennett, Georgia (26) vs. Florida St. (13) (Sugar, 2003) (4 FGs, 2 PATs)

MOST POINTS SCORED BY A KICKER, CHAMPIONSHIP GAME
13—Ryan Killeen, Southern California (55) vs. Oklahoma (19) (Orange, 2005) (2 FGs, 7 PATs)

MOST POINTS SCORED BY A KICKER, ALL BOWLS
19—Kevin Miller, East Caro. (61) vs. Marshall (64) (2 ot) (GMAC, 2001) (4 FGs, 7 PATs)

MOST FIELD GOALS ATTEMPTED
5—Billy Bennett, Georgia (26) vs. Florida St. (13) (Sugar, 2003) (4 made)

MOST FIELD GOALS ATTEMPTED, CHAMPIONSHIP GAME
3—David Pino, Texas (41) vs. Southern California (38) (Rose, 2006) (2 made)
3—Tim Duncan, Oklahoma (13) vs. Florida St. (2) (Orange, 2001) (2 made)

MOST FIELD GOALS ATTEMPTED, ALL BOWLS
6—3 times

MOST FIELD GOALS MADE
4—Billy Bennett, Georgia (26) vs. Florida St. (13) (Sugar, 2003)
3—Garrett Rivas, Michigan (37) vs. Texas (38) (Rose, 2005)
3—John Vaughn, Auburn (16) vs. Virginia Tech (13) (Sugar, 2005)
3—John Peattie, Miami (Fla.) (16) vs. Florida St. (14) (Orange, 2004)
3—Todd Sievers, Miami (Fla.) (37) vs. Florida (20) (Sugar, 2001)

MOST FIELD GOALS MADE, CHAMPIONSHIP GAME
2—Chris Hetland, Florida (41) vs. Ohio St. (14) (BCS, 2007)
2—David Pino, Texas (41) vs. Southern California (38) (Rose, 2006)
2—Ryan Killeen, Southern California (55) vs. Oklahoma (19) (Orange, 2005)
2—Tim Duncan, Oklahoma (13) vs. Florida St. (2) (Orange, 2001)

MOST FIELD GOALS MADE, ALL BOWLS
5—5 times

MOST EXTRA-POINT KICK ATTEMPTS
8—Jeff Chandler, Florida (56) vs. Maryland (23) (Orange, 2002) (8 made)

MOST EXTRA-POINT KICK ATTEMPTS, CHAMPIONSHIP GAME
7—Ryan Killeen, Southern California (55) vs. Oklahoma (19) (Orange, 2005) (7 made)

MOST EXTRA-POINT KICK ATTEMPTS, ALL BOWLS
9—5 players

MOST EXTRA-POINT KICKS MADE
8—Jeff Chandler, Florida (56) vs. Maryland (23) (Orange, 2002) (8 attempts)

MOST EXTRA-POINT KICKS MADE, CHAMPIONSHIP GAME
7—Ryan Killeen, Southern California (55) vs. Oklahoma (19) (Orange, 2005) (7 attempts)

MOST EXTRA-POINT KICKS MADE, ALL BOWLS
9—4 players

Punting

MOST PUNTS
11—Jeremy Kapinos, Penn St. (26) vs. Florida St. (23) (3 ot) (Orange, 2006)

MOST PUNTS, CHAMPIONSHIP GAME
10—Keith Cottrell, Florida St. (2) vs. Oklahoma (13) (Orange, 2001)

MOST PUNTS, ALL BOWLS
21—Everett Sweeney, Michigan (49) vs. Stanford (0) (Rose, 1902)

HIGHEST AVERAGE PER PUNT
(Minimum 3 Punts)
48.25—Jonathan Kilgo, Georgia (26) vs. Florida St. (13) (Sugar, 2003) (4 for 193)

HIGHEST AVERAGE PER PUNT, CHAMPIONSHIP GAME
(Minimum 3 Punts)
47.67—Andy Groom, Ohio St. (31) vs. Miami (Fla.) (24) (Fiesta, 2003) (6 for 286)

HIGHEST AVERAGE PER PUNT, ALL BOWLS
(Minimum 5 Punts)
53.8—Mat McBriar, Hawaii (28) vs. Tulane (36) (Hawaii, 2002) (5 for 269)

Punt Returns

MOST PUNT RETURNS
7—Willie Reid, Florida St. (23) vs. Penn St. (26) (3 ot) (Orange, 2006) (180 yards)
4—Brandon James, Florida (41) vs. Ohio St. (14) (BCS, 2007) (28 yards)
4—Reggie Smith, Oklahoma (42) vs. Boise St. (43) (ot) (Fiesta, 2007) (27 yards)
4—Desmond Reed, Southern California (32) vs. Michigan (18) (Rose, 2007) (14 yards)
4—Antonio Perkins, Oklahoma (34) vs. Washington St. (14) (Rose, 2003) (90 yards)
4—Leon Washington, Florida St. (13) vs. Georgia (26) (Sugar, 2003) (68 yards)
4—Phillip Buchanon, Miami (Fla.) (37) vs. Nebraska (14) (Rose, 2002) (37 yards)
4—Freddie Milons, Alabama (34) vs. Michigan (35) (ot) (Orange, 2000) (108 yards)
4—Ike Charlton, Virginia Tech (29) vs. Florida St. (46) (Sugar, 2000) (88 yards)

MOST PUNT RETURNS, CHAMPIONSHIP GAME
4—Brandon James, Florida (41) vs. Ohio St. (14) (BCS, 2007) (28 yards)
4—Phillip Buchanon, Miami (Fla.) (37) vs. Nebraska (14) (Rose, 2002) (37 yards)
4—Ike Charlton, Virginia Tech (29) vs. Florida St. (46) (Sugar, 2000) (88 yards)

MOST PUNT RETURNS, ALL BOWLS
9—Buzy Rosenberg, Georgia (7) vs. North Carolina (3) (Gator, Dec. 31, 1971) (54 yards)
9—Paddy Driscoll, Great Lakes (17) vs. Mare Island (0) (Rose, 1919) (115 yards)

MOST PUNT RETURN YARDS
180—Willie Reid, Florida St. (23) vs. Penn St. (26) (3 ot) (Orange, 2006) (7 returns)
108—Freddie Milons, Alabama (34) vs. Michigan (35) (ot) (Orange, 2000) (4 returns)
90—Antonio Perkins, Oklahoma (34) vs. Washington St. (14) (Rose, 2003) (4 returns)
88—Ike Charlton, Virginia Tech (29) vs. Florida St. (46) (Sugar, 2000) (4 returns)
85—DeJuan Groce, Nebraska (14) vs. Miami (Fla.) (37) (Rose, 2002) (3 returns)

MOST PUNT RETURN YARDS, CHAMPIONSHIP GAME
88—Ike Charlton, Virginia Tech (29) vs. Florida St. (46) (Sugar, 2000) (4 returns)
85—DeJuan Groce, Nebraska (14) vs. Miami (Fla.) (37) (Rose, 2002) (3 returns)
57—Peter Warrick, Florida St. (46) vs. Virginia Tech (29) (Sugar, 2000) (2 returns)
43—Peerless Price, Tennessee (23) vs. Florida St. (16) (Fiesta, 1999) (3 returns)
37—Phillip Buchanon, Miami (Fla.) (37) vs. Nebraska (14) (Rose, 2002) (4 returns)

MOST PUNT RETURN YARDS, ALL BOWLS
180—Willie Reid, Florida St. (23) vs. Penn St. (26) (3 ot) (Orange, 2006) (7 returns)

HIGHEST PUNT RETURN AVERAGE
(Minimum 3 Returns)
28.33—DeJuan Groce, Nebraska (14) vs. Miami (Fla.) (37) (Rose, 2002) (3 for 85)

HIGHEST PUNT RETURN AVERAGE, CHAMPIONSHIP GAME
(Minimum 3 Returns)
28.33—DeJuan Groce, Nebraska (14) vs. Miami (Fla.) (37) (Rose, 2002) (3 for 85)

HIGHEST PUNT RETURN AVERAGE, ALL BOWLS
(Minimum 3 Returns)
40.67—George Fleming, Washington (44) vs. Wisconsin (8) (Rose, 1960) (3 for 122)

PUNT RETURNS FOR TOUCHDOWNS
87—Willie Reid, Florida St. (23) vs. Penn St. (26) (3 ot) (Orange, 2006) (2nd quarter)
71—DeJuan Groce, Nebraska (14) vs. Miami (Fla.) (37) (Rose, 2002) (4th quarter)
62—Freddie Milons, Alabama (34) vs. Michigan (35) (ot) (Orange, 2000) (3rd quarter)
60—Bobby Newcombe, Nebraska (31) vs. Tennessee (21) (Fiesta, 2000) (1st quarter)
59—Peter Warrick, Florida St. (46) vs. Virginia Tech (29) (Sugar, 2000) (2nd quarter)
51—Antonio Perkins, Oklahoma (34) vs. Washington St. (14) (Rose, 2003) (2nd quarter)
45—Terrell Roberts, Oregon St. (41) vs. Notre Dame (9) (Fiesta, 2001) (3rd quarter)
*16—Kevin Griffin, Ohio St. (24) vs. Texas A&M (14) (Sugar, 1999) (1st quarter)
*7—John Hollins, Ohio St. (35) vs. Kansas St. (28) (Fiesta, 2004) (1st quarter)
*6—Jeff Chaney, Florida St. (46) vs. Virginia Tech (29) (Sugar, 2000) (1st quarter)

**Return of a blocked punt.*

Kickoff Returns

MOST KICKOFF RETURNS
7—Ramonce Taylor, Texas (38) vs. Michigan (37) (Rose, 2005) (201 yards)
6—Steve Breaston, Michigan (37) vs. Texas (38) (Rose, 2005) (221 yards)
5—Reggie Bush, Southern California (38) vs. Texas (41) (Rose, 2006) (102 yards)
5—Rich Parson, Maryland (23) vs. Florida (56) (Orange, 2002) (74 yards)
5—Josh Davis, Nebraska (14) vs. Miami (Fla.) (37) (Rose, 2002) (119 yards)
5—Sirr Parker, Texas A&M (14) vs. Ohio St. (24) (Sugar, 1999) (71 yards)

MOST KICKOFF RETURNS, CHAMPIONSHIP GAME
5—Reggie Bush, Southern California (38) vs. Texas (41) (Rose, 2006) (102 yards)
5—Josh Davis, Nebraska (14) vs. Miami (Fla.) (37) (Rose, 2002) (119 yards)
3—Mark Bradley, Oklahoma (19) vs. Southern California (55) (Orange, 2005) (70 yards)
3—Travis Wilson, Oklahoma (19) vs. Southern California (55) (Orange, 2005) (51 yards)

MOST KICKOFF RETURNS, ALL BOWLS
8—Todd Howard, Michigan (17) vs. Tennessee (45) (Florida Citrus, 2002) (125 yards)

MOST KICKOFF RETURN YARDS
221—Steve Breaston, Michigan (37) vs. Texas (38) (Rose, 2005) (6 returns)
201—Ramonce Taylor, Texas (38) vs. Michigan (37) (Rose, 2005) (7 returns)
169—C.J. Jones, Iowa (17) vs. Southern California (38) (Orange, 2003) (4 returns)
119—Josh Davis, Nebraska (14) vs. Miami (Fla.) (37) (Rose, 2002) (5 returns)
102—Reggie Bush, Southern California (38) vs. Texas (41) (Rose, 2006) (5 returns)

MOST KICKOFF RETURN YARDS, CHAMPIONSHIP GAME
119—Josh Davis, Nebraska (14) vs. Miami (Fla.) (37) (Rose, 2002) (5 returns)
102—Reggie Bush, Southern California (38) vs. Texas (41) (Rose, 2006) (5 returns)

93—Ted Ginn Jr., Ohio St. (14) vs. Florida (41) (BCS, 2007) (1 return)
75—Andre Kendrick, Virginia Tech (29) vs. Florida St. (46) (Sugar, 2000) (2 returns)
70—Mark Bradley, Oklahoma (19) vs. Southern California (55) (Orange, 2005) (3 returns)
51—Travis Wilson, Oklahoma (19) vs. Southern California (55) (Orange, 2005) (3 returns)

MOST KICKOFF RETURN YARDS, ALL BOWLS
221—Steve Breaston, Michigan (37) vs. Texas (38) (Rose, 2005) (6 returns)

HIGHEST KICKOFF RETURN AVERAGE (Minimum 3 Returns)
42.25—C.J. Jones, Iowa (17) vs. Southern California (38) (Orange, 2003) (4 for 169)

HIGHEST KICKOFF RETURN AVERAGE, CHAMPIONSHIP GAME (Minimum 3 Returns)
23.80—Josh Davis, Nebraska (14) vs. Miami (Fla.) (37) (Rose, 2002) (5 for 119)

HIGHEST KICKOFF RETURN AVERAGE, ALL BOWLS (Minimum 3 Returns)
46.67—(D) Cal Beck, Utah (16) vs. Arizona (13) (Freedom, 1994) (3 for 140)

KICKOFF RETURNS FOR TOUCHDOWNS
100—C.J. Jones, Iowa (17) vs. Southern California (38) (Orange, 2003) (opening kickoff)
93—Ted Ginn Jr., Ohio St. (14) vs. Florida (41) (BCS, 2007) (opening kickoff)
89—Sammy Moore, Washington St. (14) vs. Oklahoma (34) (Rose, 2003) (4th quarter)

Defensive Statistics

MOST TOTAL TACKLES
17—Rufus Alexander, Oklahoma (43) vs. Boise St. (42) (ot) (Fiesta, 2007) (14 solos, 3 assists)
15—James Laurinaitis, Ohio St. (14) vs. Florida (41) (BCS, 2007) (10 solos, 5 assists)
15—Marcus Freeman, Ohio St. (14) vs. Florida (41) (BCS, 2007) (9 solos, 6 assists)
15—Jonathan Abbate, Wake Forest (13) vs. Louisville (24) (Orange, 2007) (4 solos, 11 assists)
14—Travis Carroll, Florida (20) vs. Miami (Fla.) (37) (Sugar, 2001) (8 solos, 6 assists)
14—Sharcus Steen, Stanford (9) vs. Wisconsin (17) (Rose, 2000) (11 solos, 3 assists)
14—Dat Nguyen, Texas A&M (14) vs. Ohio St. (24) (Sugar, 1999) (13 solos, 1 assist)

MOST SOLO TACKLES
14—Rufus Alexander, Oklahoma (43) vs. Boise St. (42) (ot) (Fiesta, 2007)
13—Dat Nguyen, Texas A&M (14) vs. Ohio St. (24) (Sugar, 1999)

MOST TACKLES FOR LOSS
4—Brian Cushing, Southern California (32) vs. Michigan (18) (Rose, 2007)
4—LaMarr Woodley, Michigan (37) vs. Texas (38) (Rose, 2005)

MOST QUARTERBACKS SACKS
3—Derrick Harvey, Florida (41) vs. Ohio St. (14) (BCS, 2007)
3—Brian Cushing, Southern California (32) vs. Michigan (18) (Rose, 2007)
3—Mike Kudla, Ohio St. (34) vs. Notre Dame (20) (Fiesta, 2006)
3—Tommy Hackenbruck, Utah (35) vs. Pittsburgh (7) (Fiesta, 2005)

MOST PASSES BROKEN UP
3—Jonathan Zenon, LSU (41) vs. Notre Dame (14) (Sugar, 2007)
3—William Gay, Louisville (24) vs. Wake Forest (13) (Orange, 2007)
3—Donte Whitner, Ohio St. (34) vs. Notre Dame (20) (Fiesta, 2006)
3—Anwar Phillips, Penn St. (26) vs. Florida St. (23) (3 ot) (Orange, 2006)
3—Sedrick Curry, Texas A&M (14) vs. Ohio St. (24) (Sugar, 1999)
3—Ahmed Plummer, Ohio St. (24) vs. Texas A&M (14) (Sugar, 1999)

INTERCEPTIONS RETURNED FOR TOUCHDOWNS
71—Bruce Thornton, Georgia (26) vs. Florida St. (13) (Sugar, 2003)
54—Dwayne Goodrich, Tennessee (23) vs. Florida St. (16) (Fiesta, 1999)
47—James Lewis, Miami (Fla.) (37) vs. Nebraska (14) (Rose, 2002)
46—Jamar Fletcher, Wisconsin (38) vs. UCLA (31) (Rose, 1999)
33—Marcus Walker, Oklahoma (42) vs. Boise St. (43) (ot) (Fiesta, 2007)
27—Marty Tadman, Boise St. (43) vs. Oklahoma (42) (ot) (Fiesta, 2007)
20—Marcus Spears, LSU (21) vs. Oklahoma (14) (Sugar, 2004)

FUMBLES RETURNED FOR TOUCHDOWNS
None

Bowl Championship Series Team Record Lists (1999-07)

Only games played since the formation of the Bowl Championship Series are included. For the All Bowls records, only official records after 1937 are included. Prior records are included if able to be substantiated. Each team's score is in parentheses after the team name. Totals for each team in both-team records are in brackets after the team's score. The year listed is the actual (calendar) year the game was played; the date is included if the bowl was played twice (i.e., January and December) during one calendar year. The list also includes discontinued bowls, marked with (D). Bowls are listed by the name of the bowl at the time it was played.

Total Offense

MOST TOTAL PLAYS
97—LSU (47) vs. Illinois (34) (Sugar, 2002)
87—Penn St. (26) vs. Florida St. (23) (3 ot) (Orange, 2006)
84—Michigan (14) vs. Southern California (28) (Rose, 2004)
84—Kansas St. (28) vs. Ohio St. (35) (Fiesta, 2004)
83—Miami (Fla.) (37) vs. Florida (20) (Sugar, 2001)

MOST TOTAL PLAYS, CHAMPIONSHIP GAME
82—Texas (41) vs. Southern California (38) (Rose, 2006)
81—Virginia Tech (29) vs. Florida St. (46) (Sugar, 2000)
80—Florida (41) vs. Ohio St. (14) (BCS, 2007)
77—Miami (Fla.) (24) vs. Ohio St. (31) (2 ot) (Fiesta, 2003)
76—Oklahoma (19) vs. Southern California (55) (Orange, 2005)
75—Oklahoma (13) vs. Florida St. (2) (Orange, 2001)

MOST TOTAL PLAYS, ALL BOWLS
107—Purdue (27) vs. Washington St. (33) (Sun, 2001)

MOST TOTAL PLAYS, BOTH TEAMS
158—Texas (41) [82] & Southern California (38) [76] (Rose, 2006)
156—Penn St. (26) [87] & Florida St. (23) [69] (3 ot) (Orange, 2006)
154—LSU (47) [97] & Illinois (34) [57] (Sugar, 2002)
154—Miami (Fla.) (37) [83] & Florida (20) [71] (Sugar, 2001)
153—Florida (56) [74] & Maryland (23) [79] (Orange, 2002)

MOST TOTAL PLAYS, BOTH TEAMS, CHAMPIONSHIP GAME
158—Texas (41) [82] & Southern California (38) [76] (Rose, 2006)
150—Miami (Fla.) (24) [77] & Ohio St. (31) [73] (2 ot) (Fiesta, 2003)
144—Oklahoma (13) [75] & Florida St. (2) [69] (Orange, 2001)
139—Oklahoma (19) [76] & Southern California (55) [63] (Orange, 2005)
138—Virginia Tech (29) [81] & Florida St. (46) [57] (Sugar, 2000)

MOST TOTAL PLAYS, BOTH TEAMS, ALL BOWLS
180—Hawaii (54) [91] & Houston (48) [89] (3 ot) (Hawaii, 2003)
180—Marshall (64) [104] & East Caro. (61) [76] (2 ot) (GMAC, 2001)

MOST TOTAL YARDS
659—Florida (56) vs. Maryland (23) (Orange, 2002) (203 rush, 456 pass)
628—LSU (47) vs. Illinois (34) (Sugar, 2002) (184 rush, 444 pass)
617—Ohio St. (34) vs. Notre Dame (20) (Fiesta, 2006) (275 rush, 342 pass)
577—LSU (41) vs. Notre Dame (14) (Sugar, 2007) (245 rush, 332 pass)
574—Southern California (38) vs. Texas (41) (Rose, 2006) (209 rush, 365 pass)
556—Texas (41) vs. Southern California (38) (Rose, 2006) (289 rush, 267 pass)

MOST TOTAL YARDS, CHAMPIONSHIP GAME
574—Southern California (38) vs. Texas (41) (Rose, 2006) (209 rush, 365 pass)
556—Texas (41) vs. Southern California (38) (Rose, 2006) (289 rush, 267 pass)
525—Southern California (55) vs. Oklahoma (19) (Orange, 2005) (193 rush, 332 pass)
503—Virginia Tech (29) vs. Florida St. (46) (Sugar, 2000) (278 rush, 225 pass)
472—Miami (Fla.) (37) vs. Nebraska (14) (Rose, 2002) (362 pass, 110 rush)

MOST TOTAL YARDS, ALL BOWLS
718—Arizona St. (49) vs. Missouri (35) (Fiesta, 1972) (452 rush, 266 pass)

MOST TOTAL YARDS, BOTH TEAMS
1,130—Texas (41) [556] & Southern California (38) [574] (Rose, 2006)
1,035—Wisconsin (38) [497] & UCLA (31) [538] (Rose, 1999)
1,019—Florida (56) [659] & Maryland (23) [360] (Orange, 2002)
1,017—LSU (47) [628] & Illinois (34) [389] (Sugar, 2002)
1,003—West Virginia (38) [502] & Georgia (35) [501] (Sugar, 2006)

MOST TOTAL YARDS, BOTH TEAMS, CHAMPIONSHIP GAME
1,130—Texas (41) [556] & Southern California (38) [574] (Rose, 2006)
897—Southern California (55) [525] & Oklahoma (19) [372] (Orange, 2005)
862—Florida St. (46) [359] & Virginia Tech (29) [503] (Sugar, 2000)
731—Miami (Fla.) (37) [472] & Nebraska (14) [259] (Rose, 2002)
645—Tennessee (23) [392] & Florida St. (16) [253] (Fiesta, 1999)

MOST TOTAL YARDS, BOTH TEAMS, ALL BOWLS
1,211—Arizona St. (45) [679] & Rutgers (40) [532] (Insight, 2005)

MOST YARDS GAINED PER PLAY
9.64—Ohio St. (34) vs. Notre Dame (20) (Fiesta, 2006) (64 for 617)
8.91—Florida (56) vs. Maryland (23) (Orange, 2002) (74 for 659)
8.33—Southern California (55) vs. Oklahoma (19) (Orange, 2005) (63 for 525)
8.21—Georgia (35) vs. West Virginia (38) (Sugar, 2006) (61 for 501)
8.13—LSU (41) vs. Notre Dame (14) (Sugar, 2007) (71 for 577)
7.74—Miami (Fla.) (37) vs. Nebraska (14) (Rose, 2002) (61 for 372)

MOST YARDS GAINED PER PLAY, CHAMPIONSHIP GAME
8.33—Southern California (55) vs. Oklahoma (19) (Orange, 2005) (63 for 525)
7.74—Miami (Fla.) (37) vs. Nebraska (14) (Rose, 2002) (61 for 372)
7.32—Texas (41) vs. Southern California (38) (Rose, 2006) (76 for 556)
7.00—Southern California (38) vs. Texas (41) (Rose, 2006) (82 for 574)
6.30—Florida St. (46) vs. Virginia Tech (29) (Sugar, 2000) (57 for 359)

MOST YARDS GAINED PER PLAY, ALL BOWLS
9.86—Hawaii (41) vs. Arizona St. (24) (Hawaii, 2006) (69 for 680)

FEWEST TOTAL YARDS
82—Ohio St. (14) vs. Florida (41) (BCS, 2007) (47 rush, 35 pass)
154—Oklahoma (14) vs. LSU (21) (Sugar, 2004) (52 rush, 102 pass)
155—Notre Dame (9) vs. Oregon St. (41) (Fiesta, 2001) (17 rush, 138 pass)
206—Florida St. (14) vs. Miami (Fla.) (16) (Orange, 2004) (110 rush, 96 pass)
243—Washington St. (14) vs. Oklahoma (34) (Rose, 2003) (4 rush, 239 pass)
253—Florida St. (16) vs. Tennessee (23) (Fiesta, 1999) (108 rush, 145 pass)

FEWEST TOTAL YARDS, CHAMPIONSHIP GAME
82—Ohio St. (14) vs. Florida (41) (BCS, 2007) (47 rush, 35 pass)
154—Oklahoma (14) vs. LSU (21) (Sugar, 2004) (52 rush, 102 pass)
253—Florida St. (16) vs. Tennessee (23) (Fiesta, 1999) (108 rush, 145 pass)
259—Nebraska (14) vs. Miami (Fla.) (37) (Rose, 2002) (197 rush, 62 pass)
267—Ohio St. (31) vs. Miami (Fla.) (24) (2 ot) (Fiesta, 2003) (145 rush, 122 pass)
270—Oklahoma (13) vs. Florida St. (2) (Orange, 2001) (56 rush, 214 pass)

FEWEST TOTAL YARDS, ALL BOWLS
-21—U. of Mexico (0) vs. Southwestern (Tex.) (35) (Sun, 1945) (29 rush, -50 pass)

FEWEST TOTAL YARDS, BOTH TEAMS
452—Florida (41) [370] & Ohio St. (14) [82] (BCS, 2007)
466—LSU (21) [312] & Oklahoma (14) [154] (Sugar, 2004)
538—Georgia (26) [276] & Florida St. (13) [262] (Sugar, 2003)
571—Oklahoma (13) [270] & Florida St. (2) [301] (Orange, 2001)
581—Miami (Fla.) (16) [375] & Florida St. (14) [206] (Orange, 2004)
590—Wisconsin (17) [331] & Stanford (9) [259] (Rose, 2000)

FEWEST TOTAL YARDS, BOTH TEAMS, CHAMPIONSHIP GAME
452—Florida (41) [370] & Ohio St. (14) [82] (BCS, 2007)
466—LSU (21) [312] & Oklahoma (14) [154] (Sugar, 2004)

FEWEST TOTAL YARDS, BOTH TEAMS, ALL BOWLS
260—Randolph Field (7) [150] & Texas (7) [110] (Cotton, 1944)

Rushing

MOST RUSHING ATTEMPTS
63—West Virginia (38) vs. Georgia (35) (Sugar, 2006) (382 yards)
55—Nebraska (31) vs. Tennessee (21) (Fiesta, 2000) (323 yards)
53—Wisconsin (17) vs. Stanford (9) (Rose, 2000) (226 yards)
52—Ohio St. (31) vs. Miami (Fla.) (24) (2 ot) (Fiesta, 2003) (145 yards)
52—Washington (34) vs. Purdue (24) (Rose, 2001) (268 yards)
52—Virginia Tech (29) vs. Florida St. (46) (Sugar, 2000) (278 yards)

MOST RUSHING ATTEMPTS, CHAMPIONSHIP GAME
52—Ohio St. (31) vs. Miami (Fla.) (24) (2 ot) (Fiesta, 2003) (145 yards)
52—Virginia Tech (29) vs. Florida St. (46) (Sugar, 2000) (278 yards)
49—Nebraska (14) vs. Miami (Fla.) (37) (Rose, 2002) (197 yards)
45—Tennessee (23) vs. Florida St. (16) (Fiesta, 1999) (114 yards)
43—Florida (41) vs. Ohio St. (14) (BCS, 2007) (156 yards)
41—Southern California (38) vs. Texas (41) (Rose, 2006) (209 yards)
41—Florida St. (16) vs. Tennessee (23) (Fiesta, 1999) (108 yards)

MOST RUSHING ATTEMPTS, ALL BOWLS
87—Oklahoma (40) vs. Auburn (22) (Sugar, Jan. 1, 1972) (439 yards)

MOST RUSHING ATTEMPTS, BOTH TEAMS
91—West Virginia (38) [63] & Georgia (35) [28] (Sugar, 2006)
86—Wisconsin (38) [48] & UCLA (31) [38] (Rose, 1999)
86—Tennessee (23) [45] & Florida St. (16) [41] (Fiesta, 1999)
85—Ohio St. (31) [52] & Miami (Fla.) (24) [33] (2 ot) (Fiesta, 2003)
81—Nebraska (31) [55] & Tennessee (21) [26] (Fiesta, 2000)

MOST RUSHING ATTEMPTS, BOTH TEAMS, CHAMPIONSHIP GAME
86—Tennessee (23) [45] & Florida St. (16) [41] (Fiesta, 1999)
85—Ohio St. (31) [52] & Miami (Fla.) (24) [33] (2 ot) (Fiesta, 2003)
77—Texas (41) [36] & Southern California (38) [41] (Rose, 2006)
75—Miami (Fla.) (37) [26] & Nebraska (14) [49] (Rose, 2002)
75—Florida St. (46) [23] & Virginia Tech (29) [52] (Sugar, 2000)

MOST RUSHING ATTEMPTS, BOTH TEAMS, ALL BOWLS
122—(D) Southern California (47) [50] & Texas A&M (28) [72] (Bluebonnet, 1977) (864 yards)
122—Mississippi St. (26) [68] & North Carolina (24) [54] (Sun, 1974) (732 yards)

MOST RUSHING YARDS
382—West Virginia (38) vs. Georgia (35) (Sugar, 2006) (63 attempts)
343—Wisconsin (38) vs. UCLA (31) (Rose, 1999) (48 attempts)
323—Nebraska (31) vs. Tennessee (21) (Fiesta, 2000) (55 attempts)
289—Texas (41) vs. Southern California (38) (Rose, 2006) (36 attempts)
278—Virginia Tech (29) vs. Florida St. (46) (Sugar, 2000) (52 attempts)

MOST RUSHING YARDS, CHAMPIONSHIP GAME
289—Texas (41) vs. Southern California (38) (Rose, 2006) (36 attempts)
278—Virginia Tech (29) vs. Florida St. (46) (Sugar, 2000) (52 attempts)
209—Southern California (38) vs. Texas (41) (Rose, 2006) (41 attempts)
197—Nebraska (14) vs. Miami (Fla.) (37) (Rose, 2002) (49 attempts)
193—Southern California (55) vs. Oklahoma (19) (Orange, 2005) (28 attempts)

MOST RUSHING YARDS, ALL BOWLS
524—Nebraska (62) vs. Florida (24) (Fiesta, 1996) (68 attempts)

MOST RUSHING YARDS, BOTH TEAMS
606—West Virginia (38) [382] & Georgia (35) [224] (Sugar, 2006)
498—Texas (41) [289] & Southern California (38) [209] (Rose, 2006)
463—Wisconsin (38) [343] & UCLA (31) [120] (Rose, 1999)
389—Texas (38) [264] & Michigan (37) [125] (Rose, 2005)
388—LSU (41) [143] & Notre Dame (14) [245] (Sugar, 2007)
367—Nebraska (31) [323] & Tennessee (21) [44] (Fiesta, 2000)

MOST RUSHING YARDS, BOTH TEAMS, CHAMPIONSHIP GAME
498—Texas (41) [289] & Southern California (38) [209] (Rose, 2006)
321—Southern California (55) [193] & Oklahoma (19) [128] (Orange, 2005)
308—Florida St. (46) [30] & Virginia Tech (29) [278] (Sugar, 2000)
307—Miami (Fla.) (37) [110] & Nebraska (14) [197] (Rose, 2002)
222—Tennessee (23) [114] & Florida St. (16) [108] (Fiesta, 1999)

MOST RUSHING YARDS, BOTH TEAMS, ALL BOWLS
864—(D) Southern California (47) [378] & Texas A&M (28) [486] (Bluebonnet, 1977)

MOST RUSHING YARDS PER ATTEMPT
8.12—Florida (56) vs. Maryland (23) (Orange, 2002) (25 for 203)
8.03—Texas (41) vs. Southern California (38) (Rose, 2006) (36 for 289)
8.00—Georgia (35) vs. West Virginia (38) (Sugar, 2006) (28 for 224)
7.15—Wisconsin (38) vs. UCLA (31) (Rose, 1999) (48 for 343)
7.00—Florida (20) vs. Miami (Fla.) (37) (Sugar, 2001) (20 for 140)

MOST RUSHING YARDS PER ATTEMPT, CHAMPIONSHIP GAME
8.03—Texas (41) vs. Southern California (38) (Rose, 2006) (36 for 289)
6.89—Southern California (55) vs. Oklahoma (19) (Orange, 2005) (28 for 193)
5.35—Virginia Tech (29) vs. Florida St. (46) (Sugar, 2000) (52 for 278)
5.10—Southern California (38) vs. Texas (41) (Rose, 2006) (41 for 209)
4.23—Miami (Fla.) (37) vs. Nebraska (14) (Rose, 2002) (26 for 110)

MOST RUSHING YARDS PER ATTEMPT, ALL BOWLS
9.3—Texas Tech (55) vs. Air Force (41) (Copper, 1995) (39 for 361)

FEWEST RUSHING ATTEMPTS
17—Florida St. (2) vs. Oklahoma (13) (Orange, 2001) (27 yards)
20—Florida (20) vs. Miami (Fla.) (37) (Sugar, 2001) (140 yards)
21—Washington St. (14) vs. Oklahoma (34) (Rose, 2003) (4 yards)
21—Illinois (34) vs. LSU (47) (Sugar, 2002) (87 yards)
22—Virginia Tech (13) vs. Auburn (16) (Sugar, 2005) (76 yards)
22—Iowa (17) vs. Southern California (38) (Orange, 2003) (119 yards)

FEWEST RUSHING ATTEMPTS, CHAMPIONSHIP GAME
17—Florida St. (2) vs. Oklahoma (13) (Orange, 2001) (27 yards)
23—Ohio St. (14) vs. Florida (41) (BCS, 2007) (47 yards)
23—Florida St. (46) vs. Virginia Tech (29) (Sugar, 2000) (30 yards)
26—Miami (Fla.) (37) vs. Nebraska (14) (Rose, 2002) (110 yards)
28—Southern California (55) vs. Oklahoma (19) (Orange, 2005) (193 yards)
33—Oklahoma (14) vs. LSU (21) (Sugar, 2004) (52 yards)
33—Miami (Fla.) (24) vs. Ohio St. (31) (2 ot) (Fiesta, 2003) (65 yards)

FEWEST RUSHING ATTEMPTS, ALL BOWLS
12—(D) Vanderbilt (28) vs. Air Force (36) (Hall of Fame, 1982) (35 yards)

FEWEST RUSHING ATTEMPTS, BOTH TEAMS
50—Southern California (32) [23] & Michigan (18) [27] (Rose, 2007)
53—Oklahoma (13) [36] & Florida St. (2) [17] (Orange, 2001)
59—Oregon (38) [28] & Colorado (16) [31] (Fiesta, 2002)
60—Michigan (35) [23] & Alabama (34) [37] (ot) (Orange, 2000)
61—Utah (35) [31] & Pittsburgh (7) [30] (Fiesta, 2005)
63—Southern California (28) [25] & Michigan (14) [38] (Rose, 2004)
63—Miami (Fla.) (37) [43] & Florida (20) [20] (Sugar, 2001)

FEWEST RUSHING ATTEMPTS, BOTH TEAMS, CHAMPIONSHIP GAME
53—Oklahoma (13) [36] & Florida St. (2) [17] (Orange, 2001)

FEWEST RUSHING ATTEMPTS, BOTH TEAMS, ALL BOWLS
50—Southern California (32) [23] & Michigan (18) [27] (Rose, 2007)

FEWEST RUSHING YARDS
-5—Stanford (9) vs. Wisconsin (17) (Rose, 2000) (27 attempts)
4—Washington St. (14) vs. Oklahoma (34) (Rose, 2003) (21 attempts)
12—Michigan (18) vs. Southern California (32) (Rose, 2007) (27 attempts)
17—Pittsburgh (7) vs. Utah (35) (Fiesta, 2005) (30 attempts)
17—Notre Dame (9) vs. Oregon St. (41) (Fiesta, 2001) (37 attempts)
26—Florida St. (23) vs. Penn St. (26) (3 ot) (Orange, 2006) (26 attempts)

FEWEST RUSHING YARDS, CHAMPIONSHIP GAME
27—Florida St. (2) vs. Oklahoma (13) (Orange, 2001) (17 attempts)
30—Florida St. (46) vs. Virginia Tech (29) (Sugar, 2000) (23 attempts)
47—Ohio St. (14) vs. Florida (41) (BCS, 2007) (23 attempts)
52—Oklahoma (14) vs. LSU (21) (Sugar, 2004) (33 attempts)
56—Oklahoma (13) vs. Florida St. (2) (Orange, 2001) (36 attempts)
65—Miami (Fla.) (24) vs. Ohio St. (31) (2 ot) (Fiesta, 2003) (33 attempts)

FEWEST RUSHING YARDS, ALL BOWLS
-61—(D) Kansas St. (7) vs. Boston College (12) (Aloha, 1994) (23 attempts)

FEWEST RUSHING YARDS, BOTH TEAMS
60—Southern California (32) [48] & Michigan (18) [12] (Rose, 2007)
83—Oklahoma (13) [56] & Florida St. (2) [27] (Orange, 2001)
117—Southern California (28) [68] & Michigan (14) [49] (Rose, 2004)
144—Oregon St. (41) [127] & Notre Dame (9) [17] (Fiesta, 2001)
150—Oklahoma (34) [146] & Washington St. (14) [4] (Rose, 2003)
156—Utah (35) [139] & Pittsburgh (7) [17] (Fiesta, 2005)

FEWEST RUSHING YARDS, BOTH TEAMS, CHAMPIONSHIP GAME
83—Oklahoma (13) [56] & Florida St. (2) [27] (Orange, 2001)

FEWEST RUSHING YARDS, BOTH TEAMS, ALL BOWLS
51—(D) Utah (16) [6] & Arizona (13) [45] (Freedom, 1994)

Passing

MOST PASS ATTEMPTS
53—LSU (47) vs. Illinois (34) (Sugar, 2002) (31 completions)
52—Kansas St. (28) vs. Ohio St. (35) (Fiesta, 2004) (20 completions)
52—Florida St. (2) vs. Oklahoma (13) (Orange, 2001) (25 completions)
51—Florida (20) vs. Miami (Fla.) (37) (Sugar, 2001) (24 completions)
49—Florida (56) vs. Maryland (23) (Orange, 2002) (33 completions)

MOST PASS ATTEMPTS, CHAMPIONSHIP GAME
52—Florida St. (2) vs. Oklahoma (13) (Orange, 2001) (25 completions)
44—Miami (Fla.) (24) vs. Ohio St. (31) (2 ot) (Fiesta, 2003) (29 completions)
41—Southern California (38) vs. Texas (41) (Rose, 2006) (29 completions)
40—Texas (41) vs. Southern California (38) (Rose, 2006) (30 completions)
39—Oklahoma (13) vs. Florida St. (2) (Orange, 2001) (25 completions)

MOST PASS ATTEMPTS, ALL BOWLS
75—Purdue (27) vs. Washington St. (33) (Sun, 2001) (38 completions)

MOST PASS ATTEMPTS, BOTH TEAMS
91—Miami (Fla.) (37) [40] & Florida (20) [51] (Sugar, 2001)
91—Oklahoma (13) [39] & Florida St. (2) [52] (Orange, 2001)
89—Oregon (38) [42] & Colorado (16) [47] (Fiesta, 2002)
89—LSU (47) [53] & Illinois (34) [36] (Sugar, 2002)
88—Florida (56) [49] & Maryland (23) [39] (Orange, 2002)

MOST PASS ATTEMPTS, BOTH TEAMS, CHAMPIONSHIP GAME
91—Oklahoma (13) [39] & Florida St. (2) [52] (Orange, 2001)
81—Texas (41) [40] & Southern California (38) [41] (Rose, 2006)
71—Southern California (55) [35] & Oklahoma (19) [36] (Orange, 2005)
65—Ohio St. (31) [21] & Miami (Fla.) (24) [44] (2 ot) (Fiesta, 2003)
63—Florida St. (46) [34] & Virginia Tech (29) [29] (Sugar, 2000)

MOST PASS ATTEMPTS, BOTH TEAMS, ALL BOWLS
116—Washington St. (33) [41] & Purdue (27) [75] (Sun, 2001)

MOST COMPLETIONS
35—Michigan (35) vs. Alabama (34 (ot) (Orange, 2000) (47 attempts)
33—Florida (56) vs. Maryland (23) (Orange, 2002) (49 attempts)
31—LSU (47) vs. Illinois (34) (Sugar, 2002) (53 attempts)
30—Texas (41) vs. Southern California (38) (Rose, 2006) (40 attempts)
29—Southern California (38) vs. Texas (41) (Rose, 2006) (41 attempts)
29—Notre Dame (20) vs. Ohio St. (34) (Fiesta, 2006) (45 attempts)
29—Utah (35) vs. Pittsburgh (7) (Fiesta, 2005) (37 attempts)
29—Miami (Fla.) (24) vs. Ohio St. (31) (2 ot) (Fiesta, 2003) (44 attempts)

MOST COMPLETIONS, CHAMPIONSHIP GAME
30—Texas (41) vs. Southern California (38) (Rose, 2006) (40 attempts)
29—Southern California (38) vs. Texas (41) (Rose, 2006) (41 attempts)
29—Miami (Fla.) (24) vs. Ohio St. (31) (2 ot) (Fiesta, 2003) (44 attempts)
26—Florida (41) vs. Ohio St. (14) (BCS, 2007) (37 attempts)
25—Oklahoma (13) vs. Florida St. (2) (Orange, 2001) (39 attempts)
25—Florida St. (2) vs. Oklahoma (13) (Orange, 2001) (52 attempts)

MOST COMPLETIONS, ALL BOWLS
43—(D) San Jose St. (25) vs. Toledo (27) (California, 1981) (63 attempts)

MOST COMPLETIONS, BOTH TEAMS
59—Texas (41) [30] & Southern California (38) [29] (Rose, 2006)
56—Florida (56) [33] & Maryland (23) [23] (Orange, 2002)
53—Southern California (32) [27] & Michigan (18) [26] (Rose, 2007)
52—Oregon (38) [28] & Colorado (16) [24] (Fiesta, 2002)
51—Utah (35) [29] & Pittsburgh (7) [22] (Fiesta, 2005)
51—Southern California (28) [24] & Michigan (14) [27] (Rose, 2004)

MOST COMPLETIONS, BOTH TEAMS, CHAMPIONSHIP GAME
59—Texas (41) [30] & Southern California (38) [29] (Rose, 2006)
50—Oklahoma (13) [25] & Florida St. (2) [25] (Orange, 2001)
42—Southern California (55) [18] & Oklahoma (19) [24] (Orange, 2005)
36—Ohio St. (31) [7] & Miami (Fla.) (24) [29] (2 ot) (Fiesta, 2003)
35—Florida St. (46) [20] & Virginia Tech (29) [15] (Sugar, 2000)

MOST COMPLETIONS, BOTH TEAMS, ALL BOWLS
64—Texas Tech (55) [39] & Clemson (15) [25] (Tangerine, 2002)
64—Texas (47) [37] & Washington (43) [27] (Holiday, 2001)

MOST PASSING YARDS
456—Florida (56) vs. Maryland (23) (Orange, 2002) (33 completions)
444—LSU (47) vs. Illinois (34) (Sugar, 2002) (31 completions)
418—UCLA (31) vs. Wisconsin (38) (Rose, 1999) (21 completions)
391—Southern California (32) vs. Michigan (18) (Rose, 2007) (27 completions)
369—Michigan (35) vs. Alabama (34) (ot) (Orange, 2000) (35 completions)
365—Southern California (38) vs. Texas (41) (Rose, 2006) (29 completions)

MOST PASSING YARDS, CHAMPIONSHIP GAME
365—Southern California (38) vs. Texas (41) (Rose, 2006) (29 completions)
362—Miami (Fla.) (37) vs. Nebraska (14) (Rose, 2002) (22 completions)
332—Southern California (55) vs. Oklahoma (19) (Orange, 2005) (18 completions)
329—Florida St. (46) vs. Virginia Tech (29) (Sugar, 2000) (20 completions)
304—Miami (Fla.) (24) vs. Ohio St. (31) (2 ot) (Fiesta, 2003) (29 completions)

MOST PASSING YARDS, ALL BOWLS
576—Marshall (64) vs. East Caro. (61) (2 ot) (GMAC, 2001) (41 completions)
576—BYU (39) vs. Penn St. (50) (Holiday, 1989) (42 completions)

MOST PASSING YARDS, BOTH TEAMS
746—LSU (47) [444] & Illinois (34) [302] (Sugar, 2002)
713—Florida (56) [456] & Maryland (23) [257] (Orange, 2002)
700—Southern California (32) [391] & Michigan (18) [309] (Rose, 2007)
632—Texas (41) [267] & Southern California (38) [365] (Rose, 2006)
629—Oregon (38) [350] & Colorado (16) [279] (Fiesta, 2002)
628—Ohio St. (34) [342] & Notre Dame (20) [286] (Fiesta, 2006)

MOST PASSING YARDS, BOTH TEAMS, CHAMPIONSHIP GAME
632—Texas (41) [267] & Southern California (38) [365] (Rose, 2006)
576—Southern California (55) [332] & Oklahoma (19) [244] (Orange, 2005)
554—Florida St. (46) [329] & Virginia Tech (29) [225] (Sugar, 2000)
488—Oklahoma (13) [214] & Florida St. (2) [274] (Orange, 2001)
426—Ohio St. (31) [122] & Miami (Fla.) (24) [304] (2 ot) (Fiesta, 2003)

MOST PASSING YARDS, BOTH TEAMS, ALL BOWLS
907—(D) Michigan St. (44) [376] & Fresno St. (35) [531] (Silicon Valley, 2001)

MOST PASSES HAD INTERCEPTED
3—Oklahoma (42) vs. Boise St. (43) (ot) (Fiesta, 2007)
3—Oklahoma (19) vs. Southern California (55) (Orange, 2005)
3—Colorado (16) vs. Oregon (38) (Fiesta, 2002)
3—Florida (20) vs. Miami (Fla.) (37) (Sugar, 2001)
2—17 times

MOST PASSES HAD INTERCEPTED, CHAMPIONSHIP GAME
3—Oklahoma (19) vs. Southern California (55) (Orange, 2005)
2—7 times

MOST PASSES HAD INTERCEPTED, ALL BOWLS
8—Arizona (10) vs. Auburn (34) (Sun, 1968)

MOST PASSES HAD INTERCEPTED, BOTH TEAMS
5—Miami (Fla.) (37) [2] & Florida (20) [3] (Sugar, 2001)
4—Boise St. (43) [1] & Oklahoma (42) [3] (ot) (Fiesta, 2007)
4—LSU (21) [2] & Oklahoma (14) [2] (Sugar, 2004)
4—Ohio St. (31) [2] & Miami (Fla.) (24) [2] (2 ot) (Fiesta, 2003)
4—Oregon (38) [1] & Colorado (16) [3] (Fiesta, 2002)
4—Tennessee (23) [2] & Florida St. (16) [2] (Fiesta, 1999)

MOST PASSES HAD INTERCEPTED, BOTH TEAMS, CHAMPIONSHIP GAME
4—LSU (21) [2] & Oklahoma (14) [2] (Sugar, 2004)
4—Ohio St. (31) [2] & Miami (Fla.) (24) [2] (2 ot) (Fiesta, 2003)
4—Tennessee (23) [2] & Florida St. (16) [2] (Fiesta, 1999)
3—Oklahoma (13) [1] & Florida St. (2) [2] (Orange, 2001)

MOST PASSES HAD INTERCEPTED, BOTH TEAMS, ALL BOWLS
12—Auburn (34) [4] & Arizona (10) [8] (Sun, 1968)

FEWEST PASS ATTEMPTS
14—Ohio St. (14) vs. Florida (41) (BCS, 2007) (4 completions)
14—West Virginia (38) vs. Georgia (35) (Sugar, 2006) (11 completions)
14—Wisconsin (17) vs. Stanford (9) (Rose, 2000) (7 completions)
15—Georgia (26) vs. Florida St. (13) (Sugar, 2003) (10 completions)
15—Nebraska (14) vs. Miami (Fla.) (37) (Rose, 2002) (5 completions)
15—Nebraska (31) vs. Tennessee (21) (Fiesta, 2000) (9 completions)
16—Auburn (16) vs. Virginia Tech (13) (Sugar, 2005) (11 completions)

FEWEST PASS ATTEMPTS, CHAMPIONSHIP GAME
14—Ohio St. (14) vs. Florida (41) (BCS, 2007) (4 completions)
15—Nebraska (14) vs. Miami (Fla.) (37) (Rose, 2002) (5 completions)
19—Tennessee (23) vs. Florida St. (16) (Fiesta, 1999) (11 completions)
21—Ohio St. (31) vs. Miami (Fla.) (24) (2 ot) (Fiesta, 2003) (7 completions)
22—Florida St. (16) vs. Tennessee (23) (Fiesta, 1999) (9 completions)
24—LSU (21) vs. Oklahoma (14) (Sugar, 2004) (14 completions)

FEWEST PASS ATTEMPTS, ALL BOWLS
2—Air Force (38) vs. Mississippi St. (15) (Liberty, 1991) (1 completion)
2—(D) Army (10) vs. Michigan St. (6) (Cherry, 1984) (1 completion)
2—West Virginia (14) vs. South Carolina (3) (Peach, 1969) (1 completion)

FEWEST PASS ATTEMPTS, BOTH TEAMS
41—Georgia (26) [15] & Florida St. (13) [26] (Sugar, 2003)
41—Tennessee (23) [19] & Florida St. (16) [22] (Fiesta, 1999)
47—West Virginia (38) [14] & Georgia (35) [33] (Sugar, 2006)
48—Miami (Fla.) (16) [29] & Florida St. (14) [19] (Orange, 2004)
49—Wisconsin (17) [14] & Stanford (9) [35] (Rose, 2000)

FEWEST PASS ATTEMPTS, BOTH TEAMS, CHAMPIONSHIP GAME
41—Tennessee (23) [19] & Florida St. (16) [22] (Fiesta, 1999)

FEWEST PASS ATTEMPTS, BOTH TEAMS, ALL BOWLS
9—Fordham (2) [4] & Missouri (0) [5] (Sugar, 1942)

FEWEST COMPLETIONS
4—Ohio St. (14) vs. Florida (41) (BCS, 2007) (14 attempts)
5—Nebraska (14) vs. Miami (Fla.) (37) (Rose, 2002) (15 attempts)
6—Florida St. (14) vs. Miami (Fla.) (16) (Orange, 2004) (19 attempts)
7—Ohio St. (31) vs. Miami (Fla.) (24) (2 ot) (Fiesta, 2003) (21 attempts)
7—Wisconsin (17) vs. Stanford (9) (Rose, 2000) (14 attempts)
9—Nebraska (31) vs. Tennessee (21) (Fiesta, 2000) (15 attempts)
9—Wisconsin (38) vs. UCLA (31) (Rose, 1999) (17 attempts)
9—Florida St. (16) vs. Tennessee (23) (Fiesta, 1999) (22 attempts)

FEWEST COMPLETIONS, CHAMPIONSHIP GAME
4—Ohio St. (14) vs. Florida (41) (BCS, 2007) (14 attempts)
5—Nebraska (14) vs. Miami (Fla.) (37) (Rose, 2002) (15 attempts)
7—Ohio St. (31) vs. Miami (Fla.) (24) (2 ot) (Fiesta, 2003) (21 attempts)
9—Florida St. (16) vs. Tennessee (23) (Fiesta, 1999) (22 attempts)
11—Tennessee (23) vs. Florida St. (16) (Fiesta, 1999) (19 attempts)
13—Oklahoma (14) vs. LSU (21) (Sugar, 2004) (37 attempts)

FEWEST COMPLETIONS, ALL BOWLS
0—13 times

FEWEST COMPLETIONS, BOTH TEAMS
20—Miami (Fla.) (16) [14] & Florida St. (14) [6] (Orange, 2004)
20—Tennessee (23) [11] & Florida St. (16) [9] (Fiesta, 1999)
23—Georgia (26) [10] & Florida St. (13) [13] (Sugar, 2003)
25—Wisconsin (17) [7] & Stanford (9) [18] (Rose, 2000)
27—LSU (21) [14] & Oklahoma (14) [13] (Sugar, 2004)
27—Miami (Fla.) (37) [22] & Nebraska (14) [5] (Rose, 2002)

FEWEST COMPLETIONS, BOTH TEAMS, CHAMPIONSHIP GAME
20—Tennessee (23) [11] & Florida St. (16) [9] (Fiesta, 1999)

FEWEST COMPLETIONS, BOTH TEAMS, ALL BOWLS
3—Arizona St. (0) [0] & Catholic (0) [3] (Sun, 1940)

FEWEST PASSING YARDS
35—Ohio St. (14) vs. Florida (41) (BCS, 2007) (4 completions)
62—Nebraska (14) vs. Miami (Fla.) (37) (Rose, 2002) (5 completions)
96—Florida St. (14) vs. Miami (Fla.) (16) (Orange, 2004) (6 completions)
102—Oklahoma (14) vs. LSU (21) (Sugar, 2004) (13 completions)
105—Wisconsin (17) vs. Stanford (9) (Rose, 2000) (7 completions)
120—West Virginia (38) vs. Georgia (35) (Sugar, 2006) (11 completions)

FEWEST PASSING YARDS, CHAMPIONSHIP GAME
35—Ohio St. (14) vs. Florida (41) (BCS, 2007) (4 completions)
62—Nebraska (14) vs. Miami (Fla.) (37) (Rose, 2002) (5 completions)
102—Oklahoma (14) vs. LSU (21) (Sugar, 2004) (13 completions)
122—Ohio St. (31) vs. Miami (Fla.) (24) (2 ot) (Fiesta, 2003) (7 completions)
145—Florida St. (16) vs. Tennessee (23) (Fiesta, 1999) (9 completions)
153—LSU (21) vs. Oklahoma (14) (Sugar, 2004) (14 completions)

FEWEST PASSING YARDS, ALL BOWLS
-50—U. of Mexico (0) vs. Southwestern (Tex.) (35) (Sun, 1945) (2 completions)

FEWEST PASSING YARDS, BOTH TEAMS
249—Florida (41) [214] vs. Ohio St. (14) [35] (BCS, 2007)
253—Miami (Fla.) (16) [157] & Florida St. (14) [96] (Orange, 2004)
255—LSU (21) [153] & Oklahoma (14) [102] (Sugar, 2004)
272—Georgia (26) [125] & Florida St. (13) [147] (Sugar, 2003)
369—Wisconsin (17) [105] & Stanford (9) [264] (Rose, 2000)
397—West Virginia (38) [120] & Georgia (35) [277] (Sugar, 2006)

FEWEST PASSING YARDS, BOTH TEAMS, CHAMPIONSHIP GAME
249—Florida (41) [214] vs. Ohio St. (14) [35] (BCS, 2007)
255—LSU (21) [153] & Oklahoma (14) [102] (Sugar, 2004)

FEWEST PASSING YARDS, BOTH TEAMS, ALL BOWLS
16—Arkansas (0) [0] & LSU (0) [16] (Cotton, 1947)
16—Arizona St. (0) [0] & Catholic (0) [16] (Sun, 1940)

Scoring

MOST POINTS
56—Florida vs. Maryland (23) (Orange, 2002)
55—Southern California vs. Oklahoma (19) (Orange, 2005)
47—LSU vs. Illinois (34) (Sugar, 2002)
46—Florida St. vs. Virginia Tech (29) (Sugar, 2000)
43—Boise St. vs. Oklahoma (42) (ot) (Fiesta, 2007)
42—Oklahoma vs. Boise St. (43) (ot) (Fiesta, 2007)
41—Texas vs. Southern California (38) (Rose, 2006)
41—Oregon St. vs. Notre Dame (9) (Fiesta, 2001)

MOST POINTS, CHAMPIONSHIP GAME
55—Southern California vs. Oklahoma (19) (Orange, 2005)
46—Florida St. vs. Virginia Tech (29) (Sugar, 2000)
41—Florida vs. Ohio St. (14) (BCS, 2007)
41—Texas vs. Southern California (38) (Rose, 2006)
38—Southern California vs. Texas (41) (Rose, 2006)
37—Miami (Fla.) vs. Nebraska (14) (Rose, 2002)

MOST POINTS, ALL BOWLS
66—Nebraska vs. Northwestern (17) (Alamo, 2000)

MOST POINTS, BOTH TEAMS
85—Boise St. (43) & Oklahoma (42) (ot) (Fiesta, 2007)
81—LSU (47) & Illinois (34) (Sugar, 2002)
79—Texas (41) & Southern California (38) (Rose, 2006)
79—Florida (56) & Maryland (23) (Orange, 2002)
75—Texas (38) & Michigan (37) (Rose, 2005)
75—Florida St. (46) & Virginia Tech (29) (Sugar, 2000)

MOST POINTS, BOTH TEAMS, CHAMPIONSHIP GAME
79—Texas (41) & Southern California (38) (Rose, 2006)
75—Florida St. (46) & Virginia Tech (29) (Sugar, 2000)
74—Southern California (55) & Oklahoma (19) (Orange, 2005)
55—Florida (41) & Ohio St. (14) (BCS, 2007)
55—Ohio St. (31) & Miami (Fla.) (24) (2 ot) (Fiesta, 2003)
51—Miami (Fla.) (37) & Nebraska (14) (Rose, 2002)

MOST POINTS, BOTH TEAMS, ALL BOWLS
125—Marshall (64) & East Caro. (61) (2 ot) (GMAC, 2001)

MOST POINTS IN A HALF
38—Southern California (55) vs. Oklahoma (19) (Orange, 2005) (1st half)

MOST POINTS IN A HALF, CHAMPIONSHIP GAME
38—Southern California (55) vs. Oklahoma (19) (Orange, 2005) (1st half)

MOST POINTS IN A HALF, ALL BOWLS
45—Colorado (62) vs. Boston College (28) (Insight.com, 1999) (1st half)
45—Oklahoma St. (62) vs. Wyoming (14) (Holiday, 1988) (2nd half)

MOST POINTS IN A HALF, BOTH TEAMS
53—Texas (41) [25] & Southern California (38) [28] (Rose, 2006) (2nd half)

MOST POINTS IN A HALF, BOTH TEAMS, CHAMPIONSHIP GAME
53—Texas (41) [25] & Southern California (38) [28] (Rose, 2006) (2nd half)

MOST POINTS IN A HALF, BOTH TEAMS, ALL BOWLS
64—(D) Kansas (51) [34] & UCLA (30) [30] (Aloha, 1995) (2nd half)
64—Penn St. (50) [38] & BYU (39) [26] (Holiday, 1989) (2nd half)

MOST POINTS IN A QUARTER
29—Oregon St. (41) vs. Notre Dame (9) (Fiesta, 2001) (3rd quarter)

MOST POINTS IN A QUARTER, CHAMPIONSHIP GAME
27—Miami (Fla.) (37) vs. Nebraska (14) (Rose, 2002) (2nd quarter)

MOST POINTS IN A QUARTER, ALL BOWLS
31—Nebraska (66) vs. Northwestern (17) (Alamo, 2000) (2nd quarter)
31—(D) Iowa (55) vs. Texas (17) (Freedom, 1984) (3rd quarter)

MOST POINTS IN A QUARTER, BOTH TEAMS
35—Michigan (35) [21] & Alabama (34) [14] (Orange, 2000) (3rd quarter)

MOST POINTS IN A QUARTER, BOTH TEAMS, CHAMPIONSHIP GAME
32—Texas (41) [18] & Southern California (38) [14] (Rose, 2006) (4th quarter)

MOST POINTS IN A QUARTER, BOTH TEAMS, ALL BOWLS
45—Nebraska (66) [31] & Northwestern (17) [14] (Alamo, 2000) (2nd quarter)

MOST POINTS BY A LOSING TEAM
42—Oklahoma vs. Boise St. (43) (ot) (Fiesta, 2007)
38—Southern California vs. Texas (41) (Rose, 2006)

MOST POINTS BY A LOSING TEAM, CHAMPIONSHIP GAME
38—Southern California vs. Texas (41) (Rose, 2006)

MOST POINTS BY A LOSING TEAM, ALL BOWLS
61—East Caro. vs. Marshall (64) (2 ot) (GMAC, 2001)

MOST TOUCHDOWNS SCORED
8—Florida (56) vs. Maryland (23) (Orange, 2002) (3 rush, 5 pass)

MOST TOUCHDOWNS SCORED, CHAMPIONSHIP GAME
7—Southern California (55) vs. Oklahoma (19) (Orange, 2005) (2 rush, 5 pass)

MOST TOUCHDOWNS SCORED, ALL BOWLS
10—Nebraska (66) vs. Northwestern (17) (Alamo, 2000) (6 rush, 4 pass)

MOST TOUCHDOWNS, BOTH TEAMS
12—LSU (47) [7] & Illinois (34) [5] (Sugar, 2002)

MOST TOUCHDOWNS, BOTH TEAMS, CHAMPIONSHIP GAME
10—Texas (41) [5] & Southern California (38) [5] (Rose, 2006)
10—Florida St. (46) [6] & Virginia Tech (29) [4] (Sugar, 2000)

MOST TOUCHDOWNS, BOTH TEAMS, ALL BOWLS
16—Marshall (64) [9] & East Caro. (61) (2 ot) [7] (GMAC, 2001)

MOST RUSHING TOUCHDOWNS
5—Texas (41) vs. Southern California (38) (Rose, 2006)
4—Southern California (38) vs. Texas (41) (Rose, 2006)
4—West Virginia (38) vs. Georgia (35) (Sugar, 2006)
4—Texas (38) vs. Michigan (37) (Rose, 2005)
4—Kansas St. (28) vs. Ohio St. (35) (Fiesta, 2004)
4—Ohio St. (31) vs. Miami (Fla.) (24) (2 ot) (Fiesta, 2003)
4—Southern California (38) vs. Iowa (17) (Orange, 2003)
4—LSU (47) vs. Illinois (34) (Sugar, 2002)
4—Wisconsin (38) vs. UCLA (31) (Rose, 1999)

MOST RUSHING TOUCHDOWNS, CHAMPIONSHIP GAME
5—Texas (41) vs. Southern California (38) (Rose, 2006)
4—Southern California (38) vs. Texas (41) (Rose, 2006)
4—Ohio St. (31) vs. Miami (Fla.) (24) (2 ot) (Fiesta, 2003)
3—Florida (41) vs. Ohio St. (14) (BCS, 2007)
3—Virginia Tech (29) vs. Florida St. (46) (Sugar, 2000)
2—Southern California (55) vs. Oklahoma (19) (Orange, 2005)
2—LSU (21) vs. Oklahoma (14) (Sugar, 2004)
2—Oklahoma (14) vs. LSU (21) (Sugar, 2004)
2—Florida St. (16) vs. Tennessee (23) (Fiesta, 1999)

MOST RUSHING TOUCHDOWNS, ALL BOWLS
8—(D) Centre (63) vs. TCU (7) (Fort Worth Classic, 1921)

MOST RUSHING TOUCHDOWNS, BOTH TEAMS
9—Texas (41) [5] & Southern California (38) [4] (Rose, 2006)
6—West Virginia (38) [4] & Georgia (35) [2] (Sugar, 2006)
5—Ohio St. (34) [2] & Notre Dame (20) [3] (Fiesta, 2006)
5—Ohio St. (31) [4] & Miami (Fla.) (24) [1] (2 ot) (Fiesta, 2003)
5—Florida (56) [3] & Maryland (23) [2] (Orange, 2002)
5—Wisconsin (38) [4] & UCLA (31) [1] (Rose, 1999)

MOST RUSHING TOUCHDOWNS, BOTH TEAMS, CHAMPIONSHIP GAME
9—Texas (41) [5] & Southern California (38) [4] (Rose, 2006)
5—Ohio St. (31) [4] & Miami (Fla.) (24) [1] (2 ot) (Fiesta, 2003)
4—Florida (41) [3] & Ohio St. (14) [1] (BCS, 2007)
4—LSU (21) [2] & Oklahoma (14) [2] (Sugar, 2004)
3—Florida St. (46) [0] & Virginia Tech (29) [3] (Sugar, 2000)

MOST RUSHING TOUCHDOWNS, BOTH TEAMS, ALL BOWLS
12—Texas Tech (55) [6] & Air Force (41) [6] (Copper, 1995)

MOST TOUCHDOWN PASSES
5—Southern California (55) vs. Oklahoma (19) (Orange, 2005)
5—Florida (56) vs. Maryland (23) (Orange, 2002)
5—Illinois (34) vs. LSU (47) (Sugar, 2002)
4—9 times

MOST TOUCHDOWN PASSES, CHAMPIONSHIP GAME
5—Southern California (55) vs. Oklahoma (19) (Orange, 2005)
4—Florida St. (46) vs. Virginia Tech (29) (Sugar, 2000)
3—Miami (Fla.) (37) vs. Nebraska (14) (Rose, 2002)

MOST TOUCHDOWN PASSES, ALL BOWLS
6—(D) Iowa (55) vs. Texas (17) (Freedom, 1984)

MOST TOUCHDOWN PASSES, BOTH TEAMS
8—LSU (47) [3] & Illinois (34) [5] (Sugar, 2002)
7—Southern California (55) [5] & Oklahoma (19) [2] (Orange, 2005)
6—Southern California (32) [4] & Michigan (18) [2] (Rose, 2007)
6—Boise St. (43) [4] & Oklahoma (42) [2] (ot) (Fiesta, 2007)
6—Florida (56) [5] & Maryland (23) [1] (Orange, 2002)

MOST TOUCHDOWN PASSES, BOTH TEAMS, CHAMPIONSHIP GAME
7—Southern California (55) [5] & Oklahoma (19) [2] (Orange, 2005)
5—Florida St. (46) [4] & Virginia Tech (29) [1] (Sugar, 2000)
3—Miami (Fla.) (37) [3] & Nebraska (14) [0] (Rose, 2002)

MOST TOUCHDOWN PASSES, BOTH TEAMS, ALL BOWLS
9—Bowling Green (52) [5] & Memphis (35) [4] (GMAC, 2004)

FEWEST POINTS
2—Florida St. vs. Oklahoma (13) (Orange, 2001)
7—Pittsburgh vs. Utah (35) (Fiesta, 2005)
9—Notre Dame vs. Oregon St. (41) (Fiesta, 2001)
9—Stanford vs. Wisconsin (17) (Rose, 2000)
10—Syracuse vs. Florida (31) (Orange, 1999)

FEWEST POINTS, CHAMPIONSHIP GAME
2—Florida St. vs. Oklahoma (13) (Orange, 2001)
13—Oklahoma vs. Florida St. (2) (Orange, 2001)
14—Ohio St. vs. Florida (41) (BCS, 2007)
14—Oklahoma vs. LSU (21) (Sugar, 2004)
14—Nebraska vs. Miami (Fla.) (37) (Rose, 2002)
16—Florida St. vs. Tennessee (23) (Fiesta, 1999)

FEWEST POINTS, ALL BOWLS
0—By Many Teams

FEWEST POINTS, BOTH TEAMS
15—Oklahoma (13) & Florida St. (2) (Orange, 2001)
26—Wisconsin (17) & Stanford (9) (Rose, 2000)
29—Auburn (16) & Virginia Tech (13) (Sugar, 2005)
30—Miami (Fla.) (16) & Florida St. (14) (Orange, 2004)
35—LSU (21) & Oklahoma (14) (Sugar, 2004)

FEWEST POINTS, BOTH TEAMS, CHAMPIONSHIP GAME
15—Oklahoma (13) & Florida St. (2) (Orange, 2001)

FEWEST POINTS, BOTH TEAMS, ALL BOWLS
0—4 times

SAFETIES
Penn St. (26) vs. Florida St. (23) (3 ot) (Orange, 2006)
Oklahoma (19) vs. Southern California (55) (Orange, 2005)
Florida St. (2) vs. Oklahoma (13) (Orange, 2001)

First Downs

MOST FIRST DOWNS
32—LSU (47) vs. Illinois (34) (Sugar, 2002)

MOST FIRST DOWNS, CHAMPIONSHIP GAME
30—Texas (41) vs. Southern California (38) (Rose, 2006)
30—Southern California (38) vs. Texas (41) (Rose, 2006)

MOST FIRST DOWNS, ALL BOWLS
36—Marshall (64) vs. East Caro. (61) (2 ot) (GMAC, 2001)
36—Oklahoma (48) vs. Virginia (14) (Gator, Dec. 29, 1991)

MOST FIRST DOWNS, BOTH TEAMS
60—Texas (41) [30] & Southern California (38) [30] (Rose, 2006)

MOST FIRST DOWNS, BOTH TEAMS, CHAMPIONSHIP GAME
60—Texas (41) [30] & Southern California (38) [30] (Rose, 2006)

MOST FIRST DOWNS, BOTH TEAMS, ALL BOWLS
62—North Carolina St. (56) [34] & Kansas (26) [28] (Tangerine, 2003)

MOST FIRST DOWNS RUSHING
16—LSU (41) vs. Notre Dame (14) (Sugar, 2007)
15—Texas (41) vs. Southern California (38) (Rose, 2006)

MOST FIRST DOWNS RUSHING, CHAMPIONSHIP GAME
15—Texas (41) vs. Southern California (38) (Rose, 2006)

MOST FIRST DOWNS RUSHING, ALL BOWLS
26—Navy (51) vs. Colorado St. (30) (Poinsettia, 2005)
26—Oklahoma (40) vs. Auburn (22) (Sugar, Jan. 1, 1972)

MOST FIRST DOWNS PASSING
23—LSU (47) vs. Illinois (34) (Sugar, 2002)
23—Florida (56) vs. Maryland (23) (Orange, 2002)

MOST FIRST DOWNS PASSING, CHAMPIONSHIP GAME
15—Southern California (38) vs. Texas (41) (Rose, 2006)

MOST FIRST DOWNS PASSING, ALL BOWLS
27—BYU (39) vs. Penn St. (50) (Holiday, 1989)

MOST FIRST DOWNS BY PENALTY
4—Oklahoma (42) vs. Boise St. (43) (ot) (Fiesta, 2007)
4—Tennessee (23) vs. Florida St. (16) (Fiesta, 1999)

MOST FIRST DOWNS BY PENALTY, CHAMPIONSHIP GAME
4—Tennessee (23) vs. Florida St. (16) (Fiesta, 1999)

MOST FIRST DOWNS BY PENALTY, ALL BOWLS
8—West Virginia (18) vs. Florida St. (30) (Gator, 2005)

Scoring Drives

LONGEST SCORING DRIVE BY YARDS
99—Nebraska (31) vs. Tennessee (21) (Fiesta, 2000) (10 plays, TD)

LONGEST SCORING DRIVE BY YARDS, CHAMPIONSHIP GAME
92—Oklahoma (19) vs. Southern California (55) (Orange, 2005) (12 plays, TD)

LONGEST SCORING DRIVE BY PLAYS
16—Michigan (14) vs. Southern California (28) (Rose, 2004) (76 yards, TD)
16—Purdue (24) vs. Washington (34) (Rose, 2001) (90 yards, TD)

LONGEST SCORING DRIVE BY PLAYS, CHAMPIONSHIP GAME
13—Oklahoma (19) vs. Southern California (55) (Orange, 2005) (68 yards, FG)

LONGEST SCORING DRIVE BY TIME
8:10—Purdue (24) vs. Washington (34) (Rose, 2001) (90 yards in 16 plays, TD)

LONGEST SCORING DRIVE BY TIME, CHAMPIONSHIP GAME
6:07—Oklahoma (19) vs. Southern California (55) (Orange, 2005) (68 yards in 13 plays, FG)

Time Of Possession

MOST TIME OF POSSESSION
40:48—Florida (41) vs. Ohio St. (14) (BCS, 2007)
39:16—LSU (47) vs. Illinois (34) (Sugar, 2002)

MOST TIME OF POSSESSION, CHAMPIONSHIP GAME
40:48—Florida (41) vs. Ohio St. (14) (BCS, 2007)
36:33—Oklahoma (13) vs. Florida St. (2) (Orange, 2001)

Turnovers

MOST TURNOVERS
5—Oklahoma (19) vs. Southern California (55) (Orange, 2005)
5—Miami (Fla.) (24) vs. Ohio St. (31) (2 ot) (Fiesta, 2003)

MOST TURNOVERS, CHAMPIONSHIP GAME
5—Oklahoma (19) vs. Southern California (55) (Orange, 2005)
5—Miami (Fla.) (24) vs. Ohio St. (31) (2 ot) (Fiesta, 2003)

MOST TURNOVERS, BOTH TEAMS
7—Ohio St. (31) [2] & Miami (Fla.) (24) [5] (2 ot) (Fiesta, 2003)
7—Tennessee (23) [3] & Florida St. (16) [4] (Fiesta, 1999)

MOST TURNOVERS, BOTH TEAMS, CHAMPIONSHIP GAME
7—Ohio St. (31) [2] & Miami (Fla.) (24) [5] (2 ot) (Fiesta, 2003)
7—Tennessee (23) [3] & Florida St. (16) [4] (Fiesta, 1999)

MOST FUMBLES
4—Texas (41) vs. Southern California (38) (Rose, 2006) (1 lost)
4—Georgia (35) vs. West Virginia (38) (Sugar, 2006) (3 lost)
4—Nebraska (14) vs. Miami (Fla.) (37) (Rose, 2002) (2 lost)
4—Florida St. (16) vs. Tennessee (23) (Fiesta, 1999) (1 lost)

MOST FUMBLES, CHAMPIONSHIP GAME
4—Texas (41) vs. Southern California (38) (Rose, 2006) (1 lost)
4—Nebraska (14) vs. Miami (Fla.) (37) (Rose, 2002) (2 lost)
4—Florida St. (16) vs. Tennessee (23) (Fiesta, 1999) (1 lost)

MOST FUMBLES, ALL BOWLS
11—Mississippi (7) vs. Alabama (12) (Sugar, 1964) (6 lost)

MOST FUMBLES, BOTH TEAMS
7—Tennessee (23) [3] & Florida St. (16) [4] (Fiesta, 1999)

MOST FUMBLES, BOTH TEAMS, CHAMPIONSHIP GAME
7—Tennessee (23) [3] & Florida St. (16) [4] (Fiesta, 1999)

MOST FUMBLES, BOTH TEAMS, ALL BOWLS
17—Alabama (12) [6] & Mississippi (7) [11] (Sugar, 1964) (9 lost)

MOST FUMBLES LOST
3—Georgia (35) vs. West Virginia (38) (Sugar, 2006)
3—Virginia Tech (29) vs. Florida St. (46) (Sugar, 2000)
3—Syracuse (10) vs. Florida (31) (Orange, 1999)

MOST FUMBLES LOST, CHAMPIONSHIP GAME
3—Virginia Tech (29) vs. Florida St. (46) (Sugar, 2000)

MOST FUMBLES LOST, ALL BOWLS
6—6 times

MOST FUMBLES LOST, BOTH TEAMS
4—Louisville (24) [2] & Wake Forest (13) [2] (Orange, 2007)
3—Boise St. (43) [2] vs. Oklahoma (42) [1] (ot) (Fiesta, 2007)
3—West Virginia (38) [0] & Georgia (35) [3] (Sugar, 2006)
3—Ohio St. (31) [0] & Miami (Fla.) (24) [3] (2 ot) (Fiesta, 2003)
3—Florida St. (46) [0] & Virginia Tech (29) [3] (Sugar, 2000)
3—Tennessee (23) [2] & Florida St. (16) [1] (Fiesta, 1999)
3—Florida (31) [0] & Syracuse (10) [3] (Orange, 1999)

MOST FUMBLES LOST, BOTH TEAMS, CHAMPIONSHIP GAME
3—Ohio St. (31) [0] & Miami (Fla.) (24) [3] (2 ot) (Fiesta, 2003)
3—Florida St. (46) [0] & Virginia Tech (29) [3] (Sugar, 2000)
3—Tennessee (23) [2] & Florida St. (16) [1] (Fiesta, 1999)

MOST FUMBLES LOST, BOTH TEAMS, ALL BOWLS
9—Alabama (12) [3] & Mississippi (7) [6] (Sugar, 1964)

MOST PASSES HAD INTERCEPTED
3—Boise St. (43) vs. Oklahoma (42) (ot) (Fiesta, 2007)
3—Oklahoma (19) vs. Southern California (55) (Orange, 2005)
3—Colorado (16) vs. Oregon (38) (Fiesta, 2002)
3—Florida (20) vs. Miami (Fla.) (37) (Sugar, 2001)

MOST PASSES HAD INTERCEPTED, CHAMPIONSHIP GAME
3—Oklahoma (19) vs. Southern California (55) (Orange, 2005)

MOST PASSES HAD INTERCEPTED, ALL BOWLS
8—Arizona (10) vs. Auburn (34) (Sun, 1968)

MOST PASSES HAD INTERCEPTED, BOTH TEAMS
5—Miami (Fla.) (37) [2] & Florida (20) [3] (Sugar, 2001)

MOST PASSES HAD INTERCEPTED, BOTH TEAMS, CHAMPIONSHIP GAME
4—LSU (21) [2] & Oklahoma (14) [2] (Sugar, 2004)
4—Ohio St. (31) [2] & Miami (Fla.) (24) [2] (Fiesta, 2003)
4—Tennessee (23) [2] & Florida St. (16) [2] (Fiesta, 1999)

MOST PASSES HAD INTERCEPTED, BOTH TEAMS, ALL BOWLS
12—Auburn (34) [4] & Arizona (10) [8] (Sun, 1968)

Punts

MOST PUNTS
11—Penn St. (26) vs. Florida St. (23) (3 ot) (Orange, 2006)

MOST PUNTS, CHAMPIONSHIP GAME
10—Florida St. (2) vs. Oklahoma (13) (Orange, 2001)

MOST PUNTS, ALL BOWLS
17—Duke (3) vs. Southern California (7) (Rose, 1939)

MOST PUNTS, BOTH TEAMS
20—Penn St. (26) [11] & Florida St. (23) [9] (3 ot) (Orange, 2006)

MOST PUNTS, BOTH TEAMS, CHAMPIONSHIP GAME
18—Oklahoma (13) [8] & Florida St. (2) [10] (Orange, 2001)

MOST PUNTS, BOTH TEAMS, ALL BOWLS
28—Rice (8) [13] & Tennessee (0) [15] (Orange, 1947)
28—Santa Clara (6) [14] & LSU (0) [14] (Sugar, 1938)

FEWEST PUNTS
1—Ohio St. (34) vs. Notre Dame (20) (Fiesta, 2006)
1—Utah (35) vs. Pittsburgh (7) (Fiesta, 2005)

FEWEST PUNTS, CHAMPIONSHIP GAME
2—Texas (41) vs. Southern California (38) (Rose, 2006)
2—Southern California (38) vs. Texas (41) (Rose, 2006)
4—Florida (41) vs. Ohio St. (14) (BCS, 2007)
4—Southern California (55) vs. Oklahoma (19) (Orange, 2005)
4—Oklahoma (19) vs. Southern California (55) (Orange, 2005)
4—Miami (Fla.) (24) vs. Ohio St. (31) (2 ot) (Fiesta, 2003)
4—Miami (Fla.) (37) vs. Nebraska (14) (Rose, 2002)

FEWEST PUNTS, ALL BOWLS
0—6 times

FEWEST PUNTS, BOTH TEAMS
4—Texas (41) [2] & Southern California (38) [2] (Rose, 2006)

FEWEST PUNTS, BOTH TEAMS, CHAMPIONSHIP GAME
4—Texas (41) [2] & Southern California (38) [2] (Rose, 2006)

Punt Returns

MOST PUNT RETURN YARDS
180—Florida St. (23) vs. Penn St. (26) (3 ot) (Orange, 2006) (7 returns)

MOST PUNT RETURN YARDS, CHAMPIONSHIP GAME
88—Tennessee (23) vs. Florida St. (16) (Fiesta, 1999) (4 returns)

MOST PUNT RETURN YARDS, ALL BOWLS
180—Florida St. (23) vs. Penn St. (26) (3 ot) (Orange, 2006) (7 returns)

Kickoff Returns

MOST KICKOFF RETURN YARDS
221—Michigan (37) vs. Texas (38) (Rose, 2005) (6 returns)

MOST KICKOFF RETURN YARDS, CHAMPIONSHIP GAME
193—Ohio St. (14) vs. Florida (41) (BCS, 2007) (6 returns)
139—Oklahoma (19) vs. Southern California (55) (Orange, 2005) (7 returns)

MOST KICKOFF RETURN YARDS, ALL BOWLS
268—Florida (24) vs. Nebraska (62) (Fiesta, 1996) (10 returns)

Penalties

MOST PENALTIES
18—Oregon St. (41) vs. Notre Dame (9) (Fiesta, 2001)
18—Alabama (34) vs. Michigan (35) (ot) (Orange, 2000)

MOST PENALTIES, CHAMPIONSHIP GAME
12—Miami (Fla.) (37) vs. Nebraska (14) (Rose, 2002)
12—Florida St. (16) vs. Tennessee (23) (Fiesta, 1999)

MOST PENALTIES, ALL BOWLS
21—Mississippi St. (17) vs. Clemson (7) (Peach, 1999)

MOST PENALTIES, BOTH TEAMS
28—Michigan (35) [10] & Alabama (34) [18] (ot) (Orange, 2000)

MOST PENALTIES, BOTH TEAMS, CHAMPIONSHIP GAME
21—Tennessee (23) [9] & Florida St. (16) [12] (Fiesta, 1999)

MOST PENALTIES, BOTH TEAMS, ALL BOWLS
29—Mississippi St. (17) [21] & Clemson (7) [8] (Peach, 1999)
29—Florida (52) [15] & Florida St. (20) [14] (Sugar, 1997)
29—McNeese St. (20) [13] & Tulsa (16) [16] (Independence, 1976)

MOST YARDS PENALIZED
174—Oregon St. (41) vs. Notre Dame (9) (Fiesta, 2001) (18 penalties)

MOST YARDS PENALIZED, CHAMPIONSHIP GAME
110—Florida St. (16) vs. Tennessee (23) (Fiesta, 1999) (12 penalties)

MOST YARDS PENALIZED, ALL BOWLS
202—Miami (Fla.) (46) vs. Texas (3) (Cotton, 1991) (16 penalties)

MOST YARDS PENALIZED, BOTH TEAMS
247—Michigan (35) [115] & Alabama (34) [132] (ot) (Orange, 2000)

MOST YARDS PENALIZED, BOTH TEAMS, CHAMPIONSHIP GAME
165—Tennessee (23) [55] & Florida St. (16) [110] (Fiesta, 1999)

MOST YARDS PENALIZED, BOTH TEAMS, ALL BOWLS
295—Florida St. (30) [174] & West Virginia (18) [121] (Gator, 2005)

Attendance

HIGHEST ATTENDANCE
94,392—Washington (34) vs. Purdue (Rose, 2001)

HIGHEST ORANGE BOWL ATTENDANCE (BCS GAMES ONLY)
77,912—Southern California (55) vs. Oklahoma (19), 2005

HIGHEST SUGAR BOWL ATTENDANCE (BCS GAMES ONLY)
79,342—LSU (21) vs. Oklahoma (14), 2004

HIGHEST FIESTA BOWL ATTENDANCE (BCS GAMES ONLY)
80,470—Tennessee (23) vs. Florida St. (16), 1999

HIGHEST BCS CHAMPIONSHIP GAME ATTENDANCE
74,628—Florida (41) vs. Ohio St. (14), 2007

Bowl Championship Series Longest Plays (1999-07)

Only games played since the formation of the Bowl Championship Series are included. For the All Bowls records, only official records after 1937 are included. Prior records are included if able to be substantiated. Each team's score is in parentheses after the team name. The year listed is the actual (calendar) year the game was played; the date is included if the bowl was played twice (i.e., January and December) during one calendar year. The list also includes discontinued bowls, marked with (D). Bowls are listed by the name of the bowl at the time it was played.

LONGEST RUNS FROM SCRIMMAGE
68*—Ted Ginn Jr., Ohio St. (34) vs. Notre Dame (20) (Fiesta, 2006)
64—Justin Vincent, LSU (21) vs. Oklahoma (14) (Sugar, 2004)
64—Ron Dayne, Wisconsin (17) vs. Stanford (9) (Rose, 2000)
60*—Antonio Pittman, Ohio St. (34) vs. Notre Dame (20) (Fiesta, 2006)
60*—Vince Young, Texas (38) vs. Michigan (37) (Rose, 2005)

**Scored touchdown on play.*

LONGEST RUNS FROM SCRIMMAGE, CHAMPIONSHIP GAME
64—Justin Vincent, LSU (21) vs. Oklahoma (14) (Sugar, 2004)
45—Vince Young, Texas (41) vs. Southern California (38) (Rose, 2006)
45—Reggie Bush, Southern California (55) vs. Oklahoma (19) (Orange, 2005)
39—LenDale White, Southern California (55) vs. Oklahoma (19) (Orange, 2005)
39*—Clinton Portis, Miami (Fla.) (37) vs. Nebraska (14) (Rose, 2002)

**Scored touchdown on play.*

LONGEST RUN FROM SCRIMMAGE, ALL BOWLS
99*—Terry Baker, Oregon St. (6) vs. Villanova (0) (Liberty, 1962)

**Scored touchdown on play.*

LONGEST PASS PLAYS FROM SCRIMMAGE
85*—Troy Smith to Santonio Holmes, Ohio St. (34) vs. Notre Dame (20) (Fiesta, 2006)
80*—Brian Randall to Josh Morgan, Virginia Tech (13) vs. Auburn (16) (Sugar, 2005)
79*—Joey Harrington to Samie Parker, Oregon (38) vs. Colorado (16) (Fiesta, 2002)
79*—Tee Martin to Peerless Price, Tennessee (23) vs. Florida St. (16) (Fiesta, 1999)
64*—Shaun Hill to Jafar Williams, Maryland (23) vs. Florida (56) (Orange, 2002)
64*—Chris Weinke to Peter Warrick, Florida St. (46) vs. Virginia Tech (29) (Sugar, 2000)

**Scored touchdown on play.*

LONGEST PASS PLAYS FROM SCRIMMAGE, CHAMPIONSHIP GAME
79*—Tee Martin to Peerless Price, Tennessee (23) vs. Florida St. (16) (Fiesta, 1999)
64*—Chris Weinke to Peter Warrick, Florida St. (46) vs. Virginia Tech (29) (Sugar, 2000)
63*—Chris Weinke to Ron Dugans, Florida St. (46) vs. Virginia Tech (29) (Sugar, 2000)
54*—Matt Leinart to Dwayne Jarrett, Southern California (55) vs. Oklahoma (19) (Orange, 2005)
49*—Michael Vick to Andre Davis, Virginia Tech (29) vs. Florida St. (46) (Sugar, 2000)

**Scored touchdown on play.*

LONGEST PASS PLAY FROM SCRIMMAGE, ALL BOWLS
95*—Ronnie Fletcher to Ben Hart, Oklahoma (19) vs. Florida St. (36) (Gator, Jan. 2, 1965)

**Scored touchdown on play.*

LONGEST FIELD GOAL
51—Jon Peattie, Miami (Fla.) (16) vs. Florida St. (14) (Orange, 2004)
51—Jeff Chandler, Florida (20) vs. Miami (Fla.) (37) (Sugar, 2001)

LONGEST FIELD GOAL, CHAMPIONSHIP GAME
46—David Pino, Texas (41) vs. Southern California (38) (Rose, 2006)

LONGEST FIELD GOAL, ALL BOWLS
62—Tony Franklin, Texas A&M (37) vs. Florida (14) (Sun, Jan. 2, 1977)

LONGEST PUNT
60—Brooks Barnard, Maryland (23) vs. Florida (56) (Orange, 2002)

LONGEST PUNT, CHAMPIONSHIP GAME
59—Eric Wilber, Florida (41) vs. Ohio St. (14) (BCS, 2007)
59—Blake Ferguson, Oklahoma (14) vs. LSU (21) (Sugar, 2004)

LONGEST PUNT, ALL BOWLS
84$—Kyle Rote, SMU (21) vs. Oregon (13) (Cotton, 1949)

$Quick kick.

Bowl Coaching Records

All-Time Bowl Appearances

(Ranked by Most Bowl Games Coached)

Coach (Teams Taken to Bowl)	G	W-L-T	#Pct.
*Joe Paterno, Penn St.	33	22-10-1	.682
*Bobby Bowden, West Virginia, Florida St.	30	20-9-1	.683
Paul "Bear" Bryant, Alabama, Texas A&M, Kentucky	29	15-12-2	.552
Tom Osborne, Nebraska	25	12-13-0	.480
Lou Holtz, William & Mary, North Carolina St., Arkansas, Notre Dame, South Carolina	22	12-8-2	.591
LaVell Edwards, BYU	22	7-14-1	.341
Vince Dooley, Georgia	20	8-10-2	.450
John Vaught, Mississippi	18	10-8-0	.556
Hayden Fry, SMU, Iowa	17	7-9-1	.441
Bo Schembechler, Michigan	17	5-12-0	.294
Johnny Majors, Iowa St., Pittsburgh, Tennessee	16	9-7-0	.563
Darrell Royal, Texas	16	8-7-1	.531
Don James, Kent St., Washington	15	10-5-0	.667
*Mack Brown, Tulane, North Carolina, Texas	15	9-6-0	.600
George Welsh, Navy, Virginia	15	5-10-0	.333
Jackie Sherrill, Pittsburgh, Texas A&M, Mississippi St.	14	8-6-0	.571
*Phillip Fulmer, Tennessee	14	7-7-0	.500
*Steve Spurrier, Duke, Florida, South Carolina	14	7-7-0	.500
*Frank Beamer, Virginia Tech	14	6-8-0	.429
John Cooper, Arizona St., Ohio St.	14	5-9-0	.357
Bobby Dodd, Georgia Tech	13	9-4-0	.692
Terry Donahue, UCLA	13	8-4-1	.654
Barry Switzer, Oklahoma	13	8-5-0	.615
Charlie McClendon, LSU	13	7-6-0	.538
Don Nehlen, West Virginia	13	4-9-0	.308
Earle Bruce, Ohio St., Colorado St.	12	7-5-0	.583
Fisher DeBerry, Air Force	12	6-6-0	.500
Woody Hayes, Miami (Ohio), Ohio St.	12	6-6-0	.500
*Lloyd Carr, Michigan	12	5-7-0	.417
Shug Jordan, Auburn	12	5-7-0	.417

Active coach. #Ties computed as half won and half lost.

All-Time Bowl Victories

Coach	Wins	Record	Coach	Wins	Record
*Joe Paterno	22	22-10-1	Barry Switzer	8	8-5-0
*Bobby Bowden	20	20-9-1	Jackie Sherrill	8	8-6-0
Paul "Bear" Bryant	15	15-12-2	Darrell Royal	8	8-7-1
Lou Holtz	12	12-8-2	Vince Dooley	8	8-10-2
Tom Osborne	12	12-13-0	Pat Dye	7	7-2-1
Don James	10	10-5-0	Bob Devaney	7	7-3-0
John Vaught	10	10-8-0	Dan Devine	7	7-3-0
Bobby Dodd	9	9-4-0	Earle Bruce	7	7-5-0
*Mack Brown	9	9-6-0	Charlie McClendon	7	7-6-0
Johnny Majors	9	9-7-0	*Phillip Fulmer	7	7-7-0
John Robinson	8	8-1-0	*Steve Spurrier	7	7-7-0
Barry Alvarez	8	8-3-0	Hayden Fry	7	7-9-1
Terry Donahue	8	8-4-1	LaVell Edwards	7	7-14-1

Active coach.

All-Time Bowl Winning Percentage

(Minimum 11 Games)

Coach, Last Team Coached	G	W-L-T	#Pct.
Barry Alvarez, Wisconsin	11	8-3-0	.727
Bobby Dodd, Georgia Tech	13	9-4-0	.692
*Bobby Bowden, Florida St.	30	20-9-1	.683
*Joe Paterno, Penn St.	33	22-10-1	.682
Don James, Washington	15	10-5-0	.667
Terry Donahue, UCLA	13	8-4-1	.654
Barry Switzer, Oklahoma	13	8-5-0	.615
*Mack Brown, Texas	15	9-6-0	.600
Lou Holtz, South Carolina	22	12-8-2	.591
Bill Yeoman, Houston	11	6-4-1	.591
Earle Bruce, Colorado St.	12	7-5-0	.583
Jackie Sherrill, Mississippi St.	14	8-6-0	.571
Johnny Majors, Tennessee	16	9-7-0	.563
John Vaught, Mississippi	18	10-8-0	.556
Paul "Bear" Bryant, Alabama	29	15-12-2	.552
Bill Snyder, Kansas St.	11	6-5-0	.545
Charlie McClendon, LSU	13	7-6-0	.538
Darrell Royal, Texas	16	8-7-1	.531
*Phillip Fulmer, Tennessee	14	7-7-0	.500
*Steve Spurrier, South Carolina	14	7-7-0	.500
Fisher DeBerry, Air Force	12	6-6-0	.500
Woody Hayes, Ohio St.	12	6-6-0	.500
Tom Osborne, Nebraska	25	12-13-0	.480
Vince Dooley, Georgia	20	8-10-2	.450
Hayden Fry, Iowa	17	7-9-1	.441
*Frank Beamer, Virginia Tech	14	6-8-0	.429
*Lloyd Carr, Michigan	12	5-7-0	.417
Shug Jordan, Auburn	12	5-7-0	.417
John Cooper, Ohio St.	14	5-9-0	.357
LaVell Edwards, BYU	22	7-14-1	.341
George Welsh, Virginia	15	5-10-0	.333
Don Nehlen, West Virginia	13	4-9-0	.308
Bo Schembechler, Michigan	17	5-12-0	.294
Jerry Claiborne, Kentucky	11	3-8-0	.273
R.C. Slocum, Texas A&M	11	3-8-0	.273

Active coach. #Ties computed as half won and half lost.

All-Time Bowl Coaching History

A total of 524 coaches have head-coached in history's 967 major bowl games (the term "major bowl" is defined above the alphabetical list of team bowl records). Below is an alphabetical list of all 524 bowl coaches, with their alma mater and year, their birth date, and their game-by-game bowl records, with name and date of each bowl, opponent, final score (own score first) and opposing coach (in parentheses). A handful coached service teams or colleges never in the major category but are included because they coached against a major team in a major bowl.

Coach/School	Bowl/Date	Opponent/Score (Coach)
JIM AIKEN, 0-1-0	(Wash. & Jeff. '22)	Born 5-26-1899
Oregon	Cotton 1-1-49	SMU 12-21 (Matty Bell)
FRED AKERS, 2-8-0	(Arkansas '60)	Born 3-17-38
Wyoming	Fiesta 12-19-76	Oklahoma 7-41 (Barry Switzer)
Texas	Cotton 1-2-78	Notre Dame 10-38 (Dan Devine)
Texas	Sun 12-23-78	Maryland 42-0 (Jerry Claiborne)
Texas	Sun 12-22-79	Washington 7-14 (Don James)
Texas	Bluebonnet 12-31-80	North Carolina 7-16 (Dick Crum)
Texas	Cotton 1-1-82	Alabama 14-12 (Paul "Bear" Bryant)
Texas	Sun 12-25-82	North Carolina 10-26 (Dick Crum)
Texas	Cotton 1-2-84	Georgia 9-10 (Vince Dooley)
Texas	Freedom 12-26-84	Iowa 17-55 (Hayden Fry)
Texas	Bluebonnet 12-31-85	Air Force 16-24 (Fisher DeBerry)
BILL ALEXANDER, 3-2-0	(Georgia Tech '12)	Born 6-6-1889
Georgia Tech	Rose 1-1-29	California 8-7 (Clarence "Nibs" Price)
Georgia Tech	Orange 1-1-40	Missouri 21-7 (Don Faurot)
Georgia Tech	Cotton 1-1-43	Texas 7-14 (Dana Bible)
Georgia Tech	Sugar 1-1-44	Tulsa 20-18 (Henry Frnka)
Georgia Tech	Orange 1-1-45	Tulsa 12-26 (Henry Frnka)
LEONARD "STUB" ALLISON, 1-0-0	(Carleton '17)	Born 1892
California	Rose 1-1-38	Alabama 13-0 (Frank Thomas)
BARRY ALVAREZ, 8-3-0	(Nebraska '69)	Born 12-30-46
Wisconsin	Rose 1-1-94	UCLA 21-16 (Terry Donahue)
Wisconsin	Hall of Fame 1-2-95	Duke 34-20 (Fred Goldsmith)
Wisconsin	Copper 12-27-96	Utah 38-10 (Ron McBride)
Wisconsin	Outback 1-1-98	Georgia 6-33 (Jim Donnan)
Wisconsin	Rose 1-1-99	UCLA 38-31 (Bob Toledo)
Wisconsin	Rose 1-1-00	Stanford 17-9 (Tyrone Willingham)
Wisconsin	Sun 12-29-00	UCLA 21-20 (Bob Toledo)
Wisconsin	Alamo 12-28-02	Colorado 31-28 (ot) (Gary Barnett)
Wisconsin	Music City 12-31-03	Auburn 14-28 (Tommy Tuberville)
Wisconsin	Outback 1-1-05	Georgia 21-24 (Mark Richt)
Wisconsin	Capital One 1-2-06	Auburn 24-10 (Tommy Tuberville)
CHUCK AMATO, 4-1-0	(North Carolina St. '69)	Born 6-26-46
North Carolina St.	Micronpc.com 12-28-00	Minnesota 38-30 (Glen Mason)
North Carolina St.	Tangerine 12-20-01	Pittsburgh 19-34 (Walt Harris)
North Carolina St.	Gator 1-1-03	Notre Dame 28-6 (Tyrone Willingham)
North Carolina St.	Tangerine 12-22-03	Kansas 56-26 (Mark Mangino)
North Carolina St.	Meineke Care Care 12-31-05	South Fla. 14-0 (Jim Leavitt)
TOM AMSTUTZ, 2-2-0	(Toledo '77)	Born 8-30-55
Toledo	Motor City 12-29-01	Cincinnati 23-16 (Rick Minter)
Toledo	Motor City 12-26-02	Boston College 25-51 (Tom O'Brien)
Toledo	Motor City 12-27-04	Connecticut 10-39 (Randy Edsall)
Toledo	GMAC 12-21-05	UTEP 45-13 (Mike Price)
MIKE ARCHER, 1-1-0	[Miami (Fla.) '75]	Born 7-26-53
LSU	Gator 12-31-87	South Carolina 30-13 (Joe Morrison)
LSU	Hall of Fame 1-2-89	Syracuse 10-23 (Dick MacPherson)

Coach/School	Bowl/Date	Opponent/Score (Coach)
IKE ARMSTRONG, 1-0-0 (Drake '23) Born 6-8-1895		
Utah	Sun 1-2-39	New Mexico 16-0 (Ted Shipkey)
BILL ARNSPARGER, 0-3-0 [Miami (Ohio) '50] Born 12-16-26		
LSU	Sugar 1-1-85	Nebraska 10-28 (Tom Osborne)
LSU	Liberty 12-27-85	Baylor 7-21 (Grant Teaff)
LSU	Sugar 1-1-87	Nebraska 15-30 (Tom Osborne)
CHRIS AULT, 1-3-0 (Nevada '68) Born 11-8-47		
Nevada	Las Vegas 12-18-92	Bowling Green 34-35 (Gary Blackney)
Nevada	Las Vegas 12-14-95	Toledo 37-40 (ot) (Gary Pinkel)
Nevada	Hawaii 12-24-05	UCF 49-48 (ot) (George O'Leary)
Nevada	MPC Computers 12-31-06	Miami (Fla.) 20-21 (Larry Coker)
CHARLEY BACHMAN, 0-1-0 (Notre Dame '17) Born 12-1-92		
Michigan St.	Orange 1-1-38	Auburn 0-6 (Jack Meagher)
KENT BAER, 0-1-0 (Utah St. '73) Born 5-2-51		
Notre Dame	Insight 12-28-04	Oregon St. 21-38 (Mike Riley)
ENOCH BAGSHAW, 0-1-1 (Washington '08) Born 1884		
Washington	Rose 1-1-24	Navy 14-14 (Bob Folwell)
Washington	Rose 1-1-26	Alabama 19-20 (Wallace Wade)
GEORGE BARCLAY, 1-1-0 (North Carolina '35) Born 5-14-11		
Wash. & Lee	Gator 1-1-51	Wyoming 7-20 (Bowden Wyatt)
BILL BARNES, 0-1-0 (Tennessee '41) Born 10-20-17		
UCLA	Rose 1-1-62	Minnesota 3-21 (Murray Warmath)
WILLIS BARNES, 1-1-1 (Nebraska) Born 10-22-1900		
New Mexico	Sun 1-1-44	Southwestern (Tex.) 0-7 (R. M. Medley)
New Mexico	Sun 1-1-46	Denver 34-24 (Clyde "Cac" Hubbard)
New Mexico	Harbor 1-1-47	Montana St. 13-13 (Clyde Carpenter)
GARY BARNETT, 2-4-0 (Missouri '69) Born 5-23-46		
Northwestern	Rose 1-1-96	Southern California 32-41 (John Robinson)
Northwestern	Fla. Citrus 1-1-97	Tennessee 28-48 (Phillip Fulmer)
Colorado	Insight.com 12-31-99	Boston College 62-28 (Tom O'Brien)
Colorado	Fiesta 1-1-02	Oregon 16-38 (Mike Bellotti)
Colorado	Alamo 12-28-02	Wisconsin 28-31 (ot) (Barry Alvarez)
Colorado	Houston 12-29-04	UTEP 33-28 (Mike Price)
JOHN BARNHILL, 2-1-1 (Tennessee '28) Born 2-21-03		
Tennessee	Sugar 1-1-43	Tulsa 14-7 (Henry Frnka)
Tennessee	Rose 1-1-45	Southern California 0-25 (Jeff Cravath)
Arkansas	Cotton 1-1-47	LSU 0-0 (Bernie Moore)
Arkansas	Dixie 1-1-48	William & Mary 21-19 (Rube McCray)
BILL BATTLE, 4-1-0 (Alabama '63) Born 12-8-41		
Tennessee	Sugar 1-1-71	Air Force 34-13 (Ben Martin)
Tennessee	Liberty 12-20-71	Arkansas 14-13 (Frank Broyles)
Tennessee	Bluebonnet 12-30-72	LSU 24-17 (Charlie McClendon)
Tennessee	Gator 12-29-73	Texas Tech 19-28 (Jim Carlen)
Tennessee	Liberty 12-16-74	Maryland 7-3 (Jerry Claiborne)
SAMMY BAUGH, 0-1-0 (TCU '37) Born 3-17-14		
Hardin-Simmons	Sun 12-31-58	Wyoming 6-14 (Bob Devaney)
FRANK BEAMER, 6-8-0 (Virginia Tech '69) Born 10-18-46		
Virginia Tech	Independence 12-31-93	Indiana 45-20 (Bill Mallory)
Virginia Tech	Gator 12-30-94	Tennessee 23-45 (Phillip Fulmer)
Virginia Tech	Sugar 12-31-95	Texas 28-10 (John Mackovic)
Virginia Tech	Orange 12-31-96	Nebraska 21-41 (Tom Osborne)
Virginia Tech	Gator 1-1-98	North Carolina 3-42 (Carl Torbush)
Virginia Tech	Music City 12-29-98	Alabama 38-7 (Mike DuBose)
Virginia Tech	Sugar 1-4-00	Florida St. 29-46 (Bobby Bowden)
Virginia Tech	Gator 1-1-01	Clemson 41-20 (Tommy Bowden)
Virginia Tech	Gator 1-1-02	Florida St. 17-30 (Bobby Bowden)
Virginia Tech	San Francisco 12-31-02	Air Force 20-13 (Fisher DeBerry)
Virginia Tech	Insight 12-26-03	California 49-52 (Jeff Tedford)
Virginia Tech	Sugar 1-3-05	Auburn 13-16 (Tommy Tuberville)
Virginia Tech	Gator 1-2-06	Louisville 35-24 (Bobby Petrino)
Virginia Tech	Chick-fil-A 12-30-06	Georgia 24-31 (Mark Richt)
ALEX BELL, 1-1-0 (Villanova '38) Born 8-12-15		
Villanova	Sun 12-20-61	Wichita St. 17-9 (Hank Foldberg)
Villanova	Liberty 12-15-62	Oregon St. 0-6 (Tommy Prothro)
MATTY BELL, 1-1-1 (Centre '20) Born 2-22-1899		
SMU	Rose 1-1-36	Stanford 0-7 (Claude "Tiny" Thornhill)
SMU	Cotton 1-1-48	Penn St. 13-13 (Bob Higgins)
SMU	Cotton 1-1-49	Oregon 21-13 (Jim Aiken)
EMORY BELLARD, 2-3-0 (Texas St. '49) Born 12-17-27		
Texas A&M	Liberty 12-22-75	Southern California 0-20 (John McKay)
Texas A&M	Sun 1-2-77	Florida 37-14 (Doug Dickey)
Texas A&M	Bluebonnet 12-31-77	Southern California 28-47 (John Robinson)
Mississippi St.	Sun 12-27-80	Nebraska 17-31 (Tom Osborne)
Mississippi St.	Hall of Fame 12-31-81	Kansas 10-0 (Don Fambrough)
MIKE BELLOTTI, 4-6-0 (UC Davis '73) Born 12-21-50		
Oregon	Cotton 1-1-96	Colorado 6-38 (Rick Neuheisel)
Oregon	Las Vegas 12-20-97	Air Force 41-13 (Fisher DeBerry)
Oregon	Aloha Classic 12-25-98	Colorado 43-51 (Rick Neuheisel)
Oregon	Sun 12-31-99	Minnesota 24-20 (Glen Mason)
Oregon	Holiday 12-29-00	Texas 35-30 (Mack Brown)
Oregon	Fiesta 1-1-02	Colorado 38-16 (Gary Barnett)
Oregon	Seattle 12-30-02	Wake Forest 17-38 (Jim Grobe)
Oregon	Sun 12-31-03	Minnesota 30-31 (Glen Mason)
Oregon	Holiday 12-29-05	Oklahoma 14-17 (Bob Stoops)
Oregon	Las Vegas 12-21-06	BYU 8-38 (Bronco Mendenhall)
ARTHUR "DUTCH" BERGMAN, 1-0-1 (Notre Dame '20) Born 2-23-1895		
Catholic	Orange 1-1-36	Mississippi 20-19 (Ed Walker)
Catholic	Sun 1-1-40	Arizona St. 0-0 (Millard "Dixie" Howell)
HUGO BEZDEK, 1-1-0 (Chicago '06) Born 4-1-1884		
Oregon	Rose 1-1-17	Penn 14-0 (Bob Folwell)
Penn St.	Rose 1-1-23	Southern California 3-14 (Elmer "Gus" Henderson)
DANA X. BIBLE, 3-0-1 (Carson-Newman '12) Born 10-8-1891		
Texas A&M	Dixie Classic 1-2-22	Centre 22-14 (Charley Moran)
Texas	Cotton 1-1-43	Georgia Tech 14-7 (Bill Alexander)
Texas	Cotton 1-1-44	Randolph Field 7-7 (Frank Tritico)
Texas	Cotton 1-1-46	Missouri 40-27 (Chauncey Simpson)
JACK BICKNELL, 2-2-0 (Montclair St. '60) Born 2-20-38		
Boston College	Tangerine 12-18-82	Auburn 26-33 (Pat Dye)
Boston College	Liberty 12-29-83	Notre Dame 18-19 (Gerry Faust)
Boston College	Cotton 1-1-85	Houston 45-28 (Bill Yeoman)
Boston College	Hall of Fame 12-23-86	Georgia 27-24 (Vince Dooley)
JACK BICKNELL III, 0-1-0 (Boston College '84) Born 11-17-63		
Louisiana Tech	Humanitarian 12-31-01	Clemson 24-49 (Tommy Bowden)
BRETT BIELEMA, 1-0-0 (Iowa '92) Born 1-13-70		
Wisconsin	Capital One 1-1-07	Arkansas 17-14 (Houston Nutt)
BERNIE BIERMAN, 0-1-0 (Minnesota '16) Born 3-11-1894		
Tulane	Rose 1-1-32	Southern California 12-21 (Howard Jones)
GARY BLACKNEY, 2-0-0 (Connecticut '67) Born 12-10-55		
Bowling Green	California 12-14-91	Fresno St. 28-21 (Jim Sweeney)
Bowling Green	Las Vegas 12-18-92	Nevada 35-34 (Chris Ault)
LARRY BLAKENEY, 1-1-0 (Auburn '70) Born 9-21-47		
Troy	Silicon Valley 12-30-04	Northern Ill. 21-34 (Joe Novak)
Troy	New Orleans 12-22-06	Rice 41-17 (Todd Graham)
BOBBY BOWDEN, 20-9-1 (Samford '53) Born 11-8-29		
West Virginia	Peach 12-29-72	North Carolina St. 13-49 (Lou Holtz)
West Virginia	Peach 12-31-75	North Carolina St. 13-10 (Lou Holtz)
Florida St.	Tangerine 12-23-77	Texas Tech 40-17 (Steve Sloan)
Florida St.	Orange 1-1-80	Oklahoma 7-24 (Barry Switzer)
Florida St.	Orange 1-1-81	Oklahoma 17-18 (Barry Switzer)
Florida St.	Gator 12-30-82	West Virginia 31-12 (Don Nehlen)
Florida St.	Peach 12-30-83	North Carolina 28-3 (Dick Crum)
Florida St.	Fla. Citrus 12-22-84	Georgia 17-17 (Vince Dooley)
Florida St.	Gator 12-30-85	Oklahoma St. 34-23 (Pat Jones)
Florida St.	All-American 12-31-86	Indiana 27-13 (Bill Mallory)
Florida St.	Fiesta 1-1-88	Nebraska 31-28 (Tom Osborne)
Florida St.	Sugar 1-2-89	Auburn 13-7 (Pat Dye)
Florida St.	Fiesta 1-1-90	Nebraska 41-17 (Tom Osborne)
Florida St.	Blockbuster 12-28-90	Penn St. 24-17 (Joe Paterno)
Florida St.	Cotton 1-1-92	Texas A&M 10-2 (R.C. Slocum)
Florida St.	Orange 1-1-93	Nebraska 27-14 (Tom Osborne)
Florida St.	Orange 1-1-94	Nebraska 18-16 (Tom Osborne)
Florida St.	Sugar 1-2-95	Florida 23-17 (Steve Spurrier)
Florida St.	Orange 1-1-96	Notre Dame 31-26 (Lou Holtz)
Florida St.	Sugar 1-2-97	Florida 20-52 (Steve Spurrier)
Florida St.	Sugar 1-1-98	Ohio St. 31-14 (John Cooper)
Florida St.	Fiesta 1-4-99	Tennessee 16-23 (Phillip Fulmer)
Florida St.	Sugar 1-4-00	Virginia Tech 46-29 (Frank Beamer)
Florida St.	Orange 1-3-01	Oklahoma 2-13 (Bob Stoops)
Florida St.	Gator 1-1-02	Virginia Tech 30-17 (Frank Beamer)
Florida St.	Sugar 1-1-03	Georgia 13-26 (Mark Richt)
Florida St.	Orange 1-1-04	Miami (Fla.) 14-16 (Larry Coker)
Florida St.	Gator 1-1-05	West Virginia 30-18 (Rich Rodriguez)
Florida St.	Orange 1-3-06	Penn St. 23-26 (3 ot) (Joe Paterno)
Florida St.	Emerald 12-27-06	UCLA 44-27 (Karl Dorrell)
TERRY BOWDEN, 2-1-0 (West Virginia '78) Born 2-24-56		
Auburn	Outback 1-1-96	Penn St. 14-43 (Joe Paterno)
Auburn	Independence 12-31-96	Army 32-29 (Bob Sutton)
Auburn	Peach 1-2-98	Clemson 21-17 (Tommy West)
TOMMY BOWDEN, 4-3-0 (West Virginia '77) Born 7-10-54		
Clemson	Peach 12-30-99	Mississippi St. 7-17 (Jackie Sherrill)
Clemson	Gator 1-1-01	Virginia Tech 20-41 (Frank Beamer)
Clemson	Humanitarian 12-31-01	Louisiana Tech 49-24 (Jack Bicknell III)
Clemson	Tangerine 12-23-02	Texas Tech 15-55 (Mike Leach)
Clemson	Peach 1-2-04	Tennessee 27-14 (Phillip Fulmer)
Clemson	Champs Sports 12-27-05	Colorado 19-10 (Mike Hankwitz)
Clemson	Music City 12-29-06	Kentucky 20-28 (Rich Brooks)
JEFF BOWER, 6-4-0 (Southern Miss. '76) Born 5-28-53		
Southern Miss.	All-American 12-28-90	North Carolina St. 27-31 (Dick Sheridan)
Southern Miss.	Liberty 12-31-97	Pittsburgh 41-7 (Walt Harris)
Southern Miss.	Humanitarian 12-30-98	Idaho 35-42 (Chris Tormey)
Southern Miss.	Liberty 12-31-99	Colorado St. 23-17 (Sonny Lubick)
Southern Miss.	Mobile Alabama 12-20-00	TCU 28-21 (Gary Patterson)
Southern Miss.	Houston 12-27-02	Oklahoma St. 23-33 (Les Miles)

Coach/School	Bowl/Date	Opponent/Score (Coach)
Southern Miss.	Liberty 12-31-03	Utah 0-17 (Urban Meyer)
Southern Miss.	New Orleans 12-14-04	North Texas 31-10 (Darrell Dickey)
Southern Miss.	New Orleans 12-20-05	Arkansas St. 31-19 (Steve Roberts)
Southern Miss.	GMAC 1-7-07	Ohio 28-7 (Frank Solich)
SAM BOYD, 1-0-0 (Baylor '38) Born 8-12-15		
Baylor	Sugar 1-1-57	Tennessee 13-7 (Bowden Wyatt)
WESLEY BRADSHAW, 0-1-0 (Baylor '23) Born 11-26-1898		
Ouachita Baptist	Shrine 12-18-48	Hardin-Simmons 12-40 (Warren Woodson)
GREGG BRANDON, 2-0-0 (Northern Colo. '78) Born 2-29-56		
Bowling Green	Motor City 12-26-03	Northwestern 28-24 (Randy Walker)
Bowling Green	GMAC 12-22-04	Memphis 52-35 (Tommy West)
BILLY BREWER, 3-2-0 (Mississippi '61) Born 10-8-35		
Mississippi	Independence 12-10-83	Air Force 3-9 (Ken Hatfield)
Mississippi	Independence 12-20-86	Texas Tech 20-17 (Spike Dykes)
Mississippi	All-American 12-29-89	Air Force 42-29 (Fisher DeBerry)
Mississippi	Gator 1-1-91	Michigan 3-35 (Gary Moeller)
Mississippi	Liberty 12-31-92	Air Force 13-0 (Fisher DeBerry)
JOHN BRIDGERS, 2-1-0 (Auburn '47) Born 1-13-22		
Baylor	Gator 12-31-60	Florida 12-13 (Ray Graves)
Baylor	Gotham 12-9-61	Utah St. 24-9 (John Ralston)
Baylor	Bluebonnet 12-21-63	LSU 14-7 (Charlie McClendon)
ART BRILES, 0-3-0 (Texas Tech '79) Born 12-3-55		
Houston	Hawaii 12-25-03	Hawaii 48-54 (3 ot) (June Jones)
Houston	Fort Worth 12-23-05	Kansas 13-42 (Mark Mangino)
Houston	Liberty 12-29-06	South Carolina 36-44 (Steve Spurrier)
J.D. BROOKHART, 0-1-0 (Colorado St. '88) Born 10-17-64		
Akron	Motor City 12-26-05	Memphis 31-38 (Tommy West)
RICH BROOKS, 2-3-0 (Oregon St. '63) Born 8-20-41		
Oregon	Independence 12-16-89	Tulsa 27-24 (Dave Rader)
Oregon	Freedom 12-29-90	Colorado St. 31-32 (Earle Bruce)
Oregon	Independence 12-31-92	Wake Forest 35-39 (Bill Dooley)
Oregon	Rose 1-2-95	Penn St. 20-38 (Joe Paterno)
Kentucky	Music City 12-29-06	Clemson 28-20 (Tommy Bowden)
J.O. "BUDDY" BROTHERS, 0-1-0 (Texas Tech '31) Born 5-29-09		
Tulsa	Gator 1-1-53	Florida 13-14 (Bob Woodruff)
MACK BROWN, 9-6-0 (Florida St. '74) Born 8-27-51		
Tulane	Independence 12-19-87	Washington 12-24 (Don James)
North Carolina	Peach 1-2-93	Mississippi St. 21-17 (Jackie Sherrill)
North Carolina	Gator 12-31-93	Alabama 10-24 (Gene Stallings)
North Carolina	Sun 12-30-94	Texas 31-35 (John Mackovic)
North Carolina	Carquest 12-30-95	Arkansas 20-10 (Danny Ford)
North Carolina	Gator 1-1-97	West Virginia 20-13 (Don Nehlen)
Texas	Cotton 1-1-99	Mississippi St. 38-11 (Jackie Sherrill)
Texas	Cotton 1-1-00	Arkansas 6-27 (Houston Nutt)
Texas	Holiday 12-29-00	Oregon 30-35 (Mike Bellotti)
Texas	Holiday 12-28-01	Washington 47-43 (Rick Neuheisel)
Texas	Cotton 1-1-03	LSU 35-20 (Nick Saban)
Texas	Holiday 12-30-03	Washington St. 20-28 (Bill Doba)
Texas	Rose 1-1-05	Michigan 38-37 (Lloyd Carr)
Texas	Rose 1-4-06	Southern California 41-38 (Pete Carroll)
Texas	Alamo 12-30-06	Iowa 26-24 (Kirk Ferentz)
WATSON BROWN, 0-1-0 (Vanderbilt '72) Born 4-19-50		
UAB	Hawaii 12-24-04	Hawaii 40-59 (June Jones)
FRANK BROYLES, 4-6-0 (Georgia Tech '47) Born 12-26-24		
Arkansas	Gator 1-2-60	Duke 6-7 (Bill Murray)
Arkansas	Cotton 1-2-61	Duke 6-7 (Bill Murray)
Arkansas	Sugar 1-1-62	Alabama 3-10 (Paul "Bear" Bryant)
Arkansas	Sugar 1-1-63	Mississippi 13-17 (John Vaught)
Arkansas	Cotton 1-1-65	Nebraska 10-7 (Bob Devaney)
Arkansas	Cotton 1-1-66	LSU 7-14 (Charlie McClendon)
Arkansas	Sugar 1-1-69	Georgia 16-2 (Vince Dooley)
Arkansas	Sugar 1-1-70	Mississippi 22-27 (John Vaught)
Arkansas	Liberty 12-20-71	Tennessee 13-14 (Bill Battle)
Arkansas	Cotton 1-1-76	Georgia 31-10 (Vince Dooley)
EARLE BRUCE, 7-5-0 (Ohio St. '53) Born 3-8-31		
Tampa	Tangerine 12-29-72	Kent St. 21-18 (Don James)
Iowa St.	Peach 12-31-77	North Carolina St. 14-24 (Bo Rein)
Iowa St.	Hall of Fame 12-20-78	Texas A&M 12-28 (Tom Wilson)
Ohio St.	Rose 1-1-80	Southern California 16-17 (John Robinson)
Ohio St.	Fiesta 12-26-80	Penn St. 19-31 (Joe Paterno)
Ohio St.	Liberty 12-30-81	Navy 31-28 (George Welsh)
Ohio St.	Holiday 12-17-82	BYU 47-17 (LaVell Edwards)
Ohio St.	Fiesta 1-2-84	Pittsburgh 28-23 (Foge Fazio)
Ohio St.	Rose 1-1-85	Southern California 17-20 (Ted Tollner)
Ohio St.	Fla. Citrus 12-28-85	BYU 10-7 (LaVell Edwards)
Ohio St.	Cotton 1-1-87	Texas A&M 28-12 (Jackie Sherrill)
Colorado St.	Freedom 12-29-90	Oregon 32-31 (Rich Brooks)
MILT BRUHN, 0-2-0 (Minnesota '35) Born 7-28-12		
Wisconsin	Rose 1-1-60	Washington 8-44 (Jim Owens)
Wisconsin	Rose 1-2-63	Southern California 37-42 (John McKay)

Coach/School	Bowl/Date	Opponent/Score (Coach)
MIKE BRUMBELOW, 2-1-0 (TCU '30) Born 7-13-06		
UTEP	Sun 1-1-54	Southern Miss. 37-14 (Thad "Pie" Vann)
UTEP	Sun 1-1-55	Florida St. 47-20 (Tom Nugent)
UTEP	Sun 1-1-57	George Washington 0-13 (Eugene "Bo" Sherman)
PAUL "BEAR" BRYANT, 15-12-2 (Alabama '36) Born 9-11-13		
Kentucky	Great Lakes 12-6-47	Villanova 24-14 (Jordan Oliver)
Kentucky	Orange 1-2-50	Santa Clara 13-21 (Len Casanova)
Kentucky	Sugar 1-1-51	Oklahoma 13-7 (Bud Wilkinson)
Kentucky	Cotton 1-1-52	TCU 20-7 (Leo "Dutch" Meyer)
Texas A&M	Gator 12-28-57	Tennessee 0-3 (Bowden Wyatt)
Alabama	Liberty 12-19-59	Penn St. 0-7 (Charles "Rip" Engle)
Alabama	Bluebonnet 12-17-60	Texas 3-3 (Darrell Royal)
Alabama	Sugar 1-1-62	Arkansas 10-3 (Frank Broyles)
Alabama	Orange 1-1-63	Oklahoma 17-0 (Bud Wilkinson)
Alabama	Sugar 1-1-64	Mississippi 12-7 (John Vaught)
Alabama	Orange 1-1-65	Texas 17-21 (Darrell Royal)
Alabama	Orange 1-1-66	Nebraska 39-28 (Bob Devaney)
Alabama	Sugar 1-2-67	Nebraska 34-7 (Bob Devaney)
Alabama	Cotton 1-1-68	Texas A&M 16-20 (Gene Stallings)
Alabama	Gator 12-28-68	Missouri 10-35 (Dan Devine)
Alabama	Liberty 12-13-69	Colorado 33-47 (Eddie Crowder)
Alabama	Bluebonnet 12-31-70	Oklahoma 24-24 (Chuck Fairbanks)
Alabama	Orange 1-1-72	Nebraska 6-38 (Bob Devaney)
Alabama	Cotton 1-1-73	Texas 13-17 (Darrell Royal)
Alabama	Sugar 12-31-73	Notre Dame 23-24 (Ara Parseghian)
Alabama	Orange 1-1-75	Notre Dame 11-13 (Ara Parseghian)
Alabama	Sugar 12-31-75	Penn St. 13-6 (Joe Paterno)
Alabama	Liberty 12-20-76	UCLA 36-6 (Terry Donahue)
Alabama	Sugar 1-2-78	Ohio St. 35-6 (Woody Hayes)
Alabama	Sugar 1-1-79	Penn St. 14-7 (Joe Paterno)
Alabama	Sugar 1-1-80	Arkansas 24-9 (Lou Holtz)
Alabama	Cotton 1-1-81	Baylor 30-2 (Grant Teaff)
Alabama	Cotton 1-1-82	Texas 12-14 (Fred Akers)
Alabama	Liberty 12-29-82	Illinois 21-15 (Mike White)
JOHN BUNTING, 1-1-0 (North Carolina '72) Born 7-15-50		
North Carolina	Peach 12-31-01	Auburn 16-10 (Tommy Tuberville)
North Carolina	Continental Tire 12-30-04	Boston College 24-37 (Tom O'Brien)
FRANK BURNS, 0-1-0 (Rutgers '49) Born 3-16-28		
Rutgers	Garden State 12-16-78	Arizona St. 18-34 (Frank Kush)
LEON BURTNETT, 0-1-0 [Southwestern (Kan.) '65] Born 5-30-43		
Purdue	Peach 12-31-84	Virginia 24-27 (George Welsh)
WALLY BUTTS, 5-2-1 (Mercer '28) Born 2-7-05		
Georgia	Orange 1-1-42	TCU 40-26 (Leo "Dutch" Meyer)
Georgia	Rose 1-1-43	UCLA 9-0 (Edwin "Babe" Horrell)
Georgia	Oil 1-1-46	Tulsa 20-6 (Henry Frnka)
Georgia	Sugar 1-1-47	North Carolina 20-10 (Carl Snavely)
Georgia	Gator 1-1-48	Maryland 20-20 (Jim Tatum)
Georgia	Orange 1-1-49	Texas 28-41 (Blair Cherry)
Georgia	Presidential Cup 12-9-50	Texas A&M 20-40 (Harry Stiteler)
Georgia	Orange 1-1-60	Missouri 14-0 (Dan Devine)
JIM CALDWELL, 1-0-0 (Iowa '77) Born 1-16-55		
Wake Forest	Aloha Classic 12-25-99	Arizona St. 23-3 (Bruce Snyder)
BILL CALLAHAN, 1-1-0 [Benedictine (Ill.) '78] Born 7-31-56		
Nebraska	Alamo 12-28-05	Michigan 32-28 (Lloyd Carr)
Nebraska	Cotton 1-1-07	Auburn 14-17 (Tommy Tuberville)
EDDIE CAMERON, 1-0-0 (Wash. & Lee '24) Born 4-22-02		
Duke	Sugar 1-1-45	Alabama 29-26 (Frank Thomas)
FRANK CAMP, 1-0-0 (Transylvania '30) Born 12-23-05		
Louisville	Sun 1-1-58	Drake 34-20 (Warren Gaer)
JIM CARLEN, 2-5-1 (Georgia Tech '55) Born 7-11-33		
West Virginia	Peach 12-30-69	South Carolina 14-3 (Paul Dietzel)
Texas Tech	Sun 12-19-70	Georgia Tech 9-17 (Bud Carson)
Texas Tech	Sun 12-30-72	North Carolina 28-32 (Bill Dooley)
Texas Tech	Gator 12-29-73	Tennessee 28-19 (Bill Battle)
Texas Tech	Peach 12-28-74	Vanderbilt 6-6 (Steve Sloan)
South Carolina	Tangerine 12-20-75	Miami (Ohio) 7-20 (Dick Crum)
South Carolina	Hall of Fame 12-29-79	Missouri 14-24 (Warren Powers)
South Carolina	Gator 12-29-80	Pittsburgh 8-37 (Jackie Sherrill)
CLYDE CARPENTER, 0-0-1 (Montana '32) Born 4-17-08		
Montana St.	Harbor 1-1-47	New Mexico 13-13 (Willis Barnes)
LLOYD CARR, 5-7-0 (Northern Mich. '68) Born 7-30-45		
Michigan	Alamo 12-28-95	Texas A&M 20-22 (R.C. Slocum)
Michigan	Outback 1-1-97	Alabama 14-17 (Gene Stallings)
Michigan	Rose 1-1-98	Washington St. 21-16 (Mike Price)
Michigan	Florida Citrus 1-1-99	Arkansas 45-31 (Houston Nutt)
Michigan	Orange 1-1-00	Alabama 35-34 (ot) (Mike DuBose)
Michigan	Fla. Citrus 1-1-01	Auburn 31-28 (Tommy Tuberville)
Michigan	Fla. Citrus 1-1-02	Tennessee 17-45 (Phillip Fulmer)
Michigan	Outback 1-1-03	Florida 38-30 (Ron Zook)
Michigan	Rose 1-1-04	Southern California 14-28 (Pete Carroll)
Michigan	Rose 1-1-05	Texas 37-38 (Mack Brown)
Michigan	Alamo 12-28-05	Nebraska 28-32 (Bill Callahan)
Michigan	Rose 1-1-07	Southern California 18-32 (Pete Carroll)

Coach/School	Bowl/Date	Opponent/Score (Coach)
PETE CARROLL, 4-2-0 (Pacific '73) Born 9-15-51		
Southern California..	Las Vegas 12-25-01	Utah 6-10 (Ron McBride)
Southern California..	Orange 1-2-03	Iowa 38-17 (Kirk Ferentz)
Southern California..	Rose 1-1-04	Michigan 28-14 (Lloyd Carr)
Southern California..	Orange 1-4-05	Oklahoma 55-19 (Bob Stoops)
Southern California..	Rose 1-4-06	Texas 38-41 (Mack Brown)
Southern California..	Rose 1-1-07	Michigan 32-18 (Lloyd Carr)
BUD CARSON, 1-1-0 (North Carolina '52) Born 4-28-30		
Georgia Tech.........	Sun 12-19-70	Texas Tech 17-9 (Jim Carlen)
Georgia Tech.........	Peach 12-30-71	Mississippi 18-41 (Billy Kinard)
LEN CASANOVA, 2-2-0 (Santa Clara '27) Born 6-12-05		
Santa Clara	Orange 1-2-50	Kentucky 21-13 (Paul "Bear" Bryant)
Oregon	Rose 1-1-58	Ohio St. 7-10 (Woody Hayes)
Oregon	Liberty 12-17-60	Penn St. 12-41 (Charles "Rip" Engle)
Oregon	Sun 12-31-63	SMU 21-14 (Hayden Fry)
MILES CASTEEL, 0-1-0 (Kalamazoo '25) Born 12-30-1896		
Arizona	Salad 1-1-49	Drake 13-14 (Al Kawal)
PETE CAWTHON, 0-2-0 [Southwestern (Tex.) '20] Born 8-24-1898		
Texas Tech.............	Sun 1-1-38	West Virginia 6-7 (Marshall "Little Sleepy" Glenn)
Texas Tech.............	Cotton 1-2-39	St. Mary's (Cal.) 13-20 (Edward "Slip" Madigan)
BLAIR CHERRY, 2-1-0 (TCU '24) Born 9-7-01		
Texas	Sugar 1-1-48	Alabama 27-7 (Harold "Red" Drew)
Texas	Orange 1-1-49	Georgia 41-28 (Wally Butts)
Texas	Cotton 1-1-51	Tennessee 14-20 (Bob Neyland)
JERRY CLAIBORNE, 3-8-0 (Kentucky '50) Born 8-26-28		
Virginia Tech...........	Liberty 12-10-66	Miami (Fla.) 7-14 (Charlie Tate)
Virginia Tech...........	Liberty 12-14-68	Mississippi 17-34 (John Vaught)
Maryland................	Peach 12-28-73	Georgia 16-17 (Vince Dooley)
Maryland................	Liberty 12-16-74	Tennessee 3-7 (Bill Battle)
Maryland................	Gator 12-29-75	Florida 13-0 (Doug Dickey)
Maryland................	Cotton 1-1-77	Houston 21-30 (Bill Yeoman)
Maryland................	Hall of Fame 12-22-77	Minnesota 17-7 (Cal Stoll)
Maryland................	Sun 12-23-78	Texas 0-42 (Fred Akers)
Maryland................	Tangerine 12-20-80	Florida 20-35 (Charley Pell)
Kentucky.................	Hall of Fame 12-22-83	West Virginia 16-20 (Don Nehlen)
Kentucky.................	Hall of Fame 12-29-84	Wisconsin 20-19 (Dave McClain)
LARRY COKER, 4-2-0 (Northeastern '70) Born 6-23-48		
Miami (Fla.)	Rose 1-3-02	Nebraska 37-14 (Frank Solich)
Miami (Fla.)	Fiesta 1-3-02	Ohio St. 24-31 (2 ot) (Jim Tressel)
Miami (Fla.)	Orange 1-1-04	Florida St. 16-14 (Bobby Bowden)
Miami (Fla.)	Peach 12-31-04	Florida 27-10 (Charlie Strong)
Miami (Fla.)	Peach 12-30-05	LSU 3-40 (Les Miles)
Miami (Fla.)	MPC Computers 12-31-06	Nevada 21-20 (Chris Ault)
CECIL COLEMAN, 1-0-0 (Arizona St. '50) Born 4-12-26		
Fresno St.	Mercy 11-23-61	Bowling Green 36-6 (Doyt Perry)
BOBBY COLLINS, 3-2-0 (Mississippi St. '55) Born 10-25-33		
Southern Miss.	Independence 12-13-70	McNeese St. 16-14 (Ernie Duplechin)
Southern Miss.	Tangerine 12-19-81	Missouri 17-19 (Warren Powers)
SMU	Cotton 1-1-83	Pittsburgh 7-3 (Foge Fazio)
SMU	Sun 12-24-83	Alabama 7-28 (Ray Perkins)
SMU	Aloha 12-29-84	Notre Dame 27-20 (Gerry Faust)
JOHN COOPER, 5-9-0 (Iowa St. '62) Born 7-2-37		
Arizona St.	Holiday 12-22-85	Arkansas 17-18 (Ken Hatfield)
Arizona St.	Rose 1-1-87	Michigan 22-15 (Glenn "Bo" Schembechler)
Arizona St.	Freedom 12-30-87	Air Force 33-28 (Fisher DeBerry)
Ohio St.	Hall of Fame 1-1-90	Auburn 14-31 (Pat Dye)
Ohio St.	Liberty 12-27-90	Air Force 11-23 (Fisher DeBerry)
Ohio St.	Hall of Fame 1-1-92	Syracuse 17-24 (Paul Pasqualoni)
Ohio St.	Fla. Citrus 1-1-93	Georgia 14-21 (Ray Goff)
Ohio St.	Holiday 12-30-93	BYU 28-21 (LaVell Edwards)
Ohio St.	Fla. Citrus 1-2-95	Alabama 17-24 (Gene Stallings)
Ohio St.	Fla. Citrus 1-1-96	Tennessee 14-20 (Phillip Fulmer)
Ohio St.	Rose 1-1-97	Arizona St. 20-17 (Bruce Snyder)
Ohio St.	Sugar 1-1-98	Florida St. 14-31 (Bobby Bowden)
Ohio St.	Sugar 1-1-99	Texas A&M 24-14 (R.C. Slocum)
Ohio St.	Outback 1-1-01	South Carolina 7-24 (Lou Holtz)
LEE CORSO, 1-0-1 (Florida St. '57) Born 8-7-35		
Louisville................	Pasadena 12-19-70	Long Beach St. 24-24 (Jim Stangeland)
Indiana..................	Holiday 12-21-79	BYU 38-37 (LaVell Edwards)
GENE CORUM, 0-1-0 (West Virginia '48) Born 5-29-21		
West Virginia..........	Liberty 12-19-64	Utah 6-32 (Ray Nagel)
DON CORYELL, 1-0-0 (Washington '50) Born 10-17-24		
San Diego St.	Pasadena 12-6-69	Boston U. 28-7 (Larry Naviaux)
TOM COUGHLIN, 1-1-0 (Syracuse '68) Born 8-31-46		
Boston College........	Hall of Fame 1-1-93	Tennessee 23-38 (Phillip Fulmer)
Boston College........	Carquest 1-1-94	Virginia 31-13 (George Welsh)
TED COX, 1-0-0 (Minnesota '26) Born 6-30-03		
Tulane	Sugar 1-1-35	Temple 20-14 (Glenn "Pop" Warner)

Coach/School	Bowl/Date	Opponent/Score (Coach)
JEFF CRAVATH, 2-2-0 (Southern California '27) Born 2-5-05		
Southern California..	Rose 1-1-44	Washington 29-0 (Ralph "Pest" Welch)
Southern California..	Rose 1-1-45	Tennessee 25-0 (John Barnhill)
Southern California..	Rose 1-1-46	Alabama 14-34 (Frank Thomas)
Southern California..	Rose 1-1-48	Michigan 0-49 (H.O. "Fritz" Crisler)
H.O. "FRITZ" CRISLER, 1-0-0 (Chicago '22) Born 1-2-1899		
Michigan	Rose 1-1-48	Southern California 49-0 (Jeff Cravath)
EDDIE CROWDER, 3-2-0 (Oklahoma '55) Born 8-26-31		
Colorado	Bluebonnet 12-23-67	Miami (Fla.) 31-21 (Charlie Tate)
Colorado	Liberty 12-13-69	Alabama 47-33 (Paul "Bear" Bryant)
Colorado	Liberty 12-12-70	Tulane 3-17 (Jim Pittman)
Colorado	Bluebonnet 12-31-71	Houston 29-17 (Bill Yeoman)
Colorado	Gator 12-20-72	Auburn 3-24 (Ralph "Shug" Jordan)
JACK CROWE, 0-1-0 (UAB '70) Born 4-6-48		
Arkansas	Independence 12-29-91	Georgia 15-24 (Ray Goff)
JIM CROWLEY, 1-1-0 (Notre Dame '25) Born 9-10-02		
Fordham................	Cotton 1-1-41	Texas A&M 12-13 (Homer Norton)
Fordham................	Sugar 1-1-42	Missouri 2-0 (Don Faurot)
GARY CROWTON, 0-1-0 (BYU '83) Born 6-14-57		
BYU	Liberty 12-31-01	Louisville 10-28 (John L. Smith)
DICK CRUM, 6-2-0 (Mount Union '57) Born 4-29-34		
Miami (Ohio)..........	Tangerine 12-21-74	Georgia 21-10 (Vince Dooley)
Miami (Ohio)..........	Tangerine 12-20-75	South Carolina 20-7 (Jim Carlen)
North Carolina........	Gator 12-28-79	Michigan 17-15 (Glenn "Bo" Schembechler)
North Carolina........	Bluebonnet 12-31-80	Texas 16-7 (Fred Akers)
North Carolina........	Gator 12-28-81	Arkansas 31-27 (Lou Holtz)
North Carolina........	Sun 12-25-82	Texas 26-10 (Fred Akers)
North Carolina........	Peach 12-30-83	Florida St. 3-28 (Bobby Bowden)
North Carolina........	Aloha 12-27-86	Arizona 21-30 (Larry Smith)
BILL CUBIT, 0-1-0 (Delaware '75) Born 10-14-53		
Western Mich.	International 1-6-07	Cincinnati 24-27 (Brian Kelly)
FRAN CURCI, 1-0-0 [Miami (Fla.) '60] Born 6-11-38		
Kentucky................	Peach 12-31-76	North Carolina 21-0 (Bill Dooley)
BILL CURRY, 2-3-0 (Georgia Tech '65) Born 10-21-42		
Georgia Tech..........	Hall of Fame 12-31-85	Michigan St. 17-14 (George Perles)
Alabama	Hall of Fame 1-2-88	Michigan 24-28 (Glenn "Bo" Schembechler)
Alabama	Sun 12-24-88	Army 29-28 (Jim Young)
Alabama	Sugar 1-1-90	Miami (Fla.) 25-33 (Dennis Erickson)
Kentucky................	Peach 12-31-93	Clemson 13-14 (Tommy West)
JACK "CACTUS JACK" CURTICE, 1-1-0 (Transylvania '30) Born 5-24-07		
UTEP	Sun 1-1-49	West Virginia 12-21 (Dud DeGroot)
UTEP	Sun 1-2-50	Georgetown 33-20 (Bob Margarita)
DAVID CUTCLIFFE, 4-1-0 (Alabama '76) Born 9-16-54		
Mississippi	Independence 12-31-98	Texas Tech 35-18 (Spike Dykes)
Mississippi	Independence 12-31-99	Oklahoma 27-25 (Bob Stoops)
Mississippi	Music City 12-28-00	West Virginia 38-49 (Don Nehlen)
Mississippi	Independence 12-27-02	Nebraska 27-23 (Frank Solich)
Mississippi	Cotton 1-2-04	Oklahoma St. 31-28 (Les Miles)
JOHN "OX" Da GROSA, 0-1-0 (Colgate '26) Born 2-17-02		
Holy Cross.............	Orange 1-1-46	Miami (Fla.) 6-13 (Jack Harding)
MARK DANTONIO, 1-0-0 (South Carolina '79) Born 3-9-56		
Cincinnati	Fort Worth 12-23-04	Marshall 32-14 (Bob Pruett)
GARY DARNELL, 0-1-0 (Oklahoma St. '71) Born 10-15-48		
Florida....................	Freedom 12-29-89	Washington 7-34 (Don James)
DUFFY DAUGHERTY, 1-1-0 (Syracuse '40) Born 9-8-15		
Michigan St.	Rose 1-2-56	UCLA 17-14 (Henry "Red" Sanders)
Michigan St.	Rose 1-1-66	UCLA 12-14 (Tommy Prothro)
BOB DAVIE, 0-3-0 (Youngstown St. '76) Born 9-30-54		
Notre Dame...........	Independence 12-28-97	LSU 9-27 (Gerry DiNardo)
Notre Dame...........	Gator 1-1-99	Georgia Tech 28-35 (George O'Leary)
Notre Dame...........	Fiesta 1-1-01	Oregon St. 9-41 (Dennis Erickson)
BOB DAVIS, 0-1-0 (Utah '30) Born 2-13-08		
Colorado St.	Raisin 1-1-49	Occidental 20-21 (Roy Dennis)
BUTCH DAVIS, 4-0-0 (Arkansas '74) Born 11-17-51		
Miami (Fla.)	Carquest 12-27-96	Virginia 31-21 (George Welsh)
Miami (Fla.)	Micron PC 12-29-98	North Carolina St. 46-23 (Mike O'Cain)
Miami (Fla.)	Gator 1-1-00	Georgia Tech 28-13 (George O'Leary)
Miami (Fla.)	Sugar 1-2-01	Florida 37-20 (Steve Spurrier)
PAUL DAVIS, 1-0-0 (Mississippi '47) Born 2-3-22		
Mississippi St.	Liberty 12-21-63	North Carolina St. 16-12 (Earle Edwards)
LOWELL "RED" DAWSON, 0-1-0 (Tulane '30) Born 12-26-06		
Tulane	Sugar 1-1-40	Texas A&M 13-14 (Homer Norton)
FISHER DeBERRY, 6-6-0 (Wofford '60) Born 9-9-38		
Air Force	Independence 12-15-84	Virginia Tech 23-7 (Bill Dooley)
Air Force	Bluebonnet 12-31-85	Texas 24-16 (Fred Akers)
Air Force	Freedom 12-30-87	Arizona St. 28-33 (John Cooper)

Coach/School	Bowl/Date	Opponent/Score (Coach)
Air Force	Liberty 12-29-89	Mississippi 29-42 (Billy Brewer)
Air Force	Liberty 12-27-90	Ohio St. 23-11 (John Cooper)
Air Force	Liberty 12-29-91	Mississippi St. 38-15 (Jackie Sherrill)
Air Force	Liberty 12-31-92	Mississippi 0-13 (Billy Brewer)
Air Force	Copper 12-27-95	Texas Tech 41-55 (Spike Dykes)
Air Force	Las Vegas 12-20-97	Oregon 13-41 (Mike Bellotti)
Air Force	Oahu Classic 12-25-98	Washington 45-25 (Jim Lambright)
Air Force	Silicon Valley 12-31-00	Fresno St. 37-34 (Pat Hill)
Air Force	San Francisco 12-31-02	Virginia Tech 13-20 (Frank Beamer)

DUD DeGROOT, 1-0-0 (Stanford '24) Born 11-20-1895

West Virginia	Sun 1-1-49	UTEP 21-12 (Jack "Cactus Jack" Curtice)

ROY DENNIS, 1-0-0 (Occidental '33) Born 5-13-05

Occidental	Raisin 1-1-49	Colorado St. 21-20 (Bob Davis)

HERB DEROMEDI, 0-1-0 (Michigan '60) Born 5-26-39

Central Mich.	California 12-8-90	San Jose St. 24-48 (Terry Shea)

BOB DEVANEY, 7-3-0 (Alma '39) Born 4-2-15

Wyoming	Sun 12-31-58	Hardin-Simmons 14-6 (Sammy Baugh)
Nebraska	Gotham 12-15-62	Miami (Fla.) 36-34 (Andy Gustafson)
Nebraska	Orange 1-1-64	Auburn 13-7 (Ralph "Shug" Jordan)
Nebraska	Cotton 1-1-65	Arkansas 7-10 (Frank Broyles)
Nebraska	Orange 1-1-66	Alabama 28-39 (Paul "Bear" Bryant)
Nebraska	Sugar 1-2-67	Alabama 7-34 (Paul "Bear" Bryant)
Nebraska	Sun 12-20-69	Georgia 45-6 (Vince Dooley)
Nebraska	Orange 1-1-71	LSU 17-12 (Charlie McClendon)
Nebraska	Orange 1-1-72	Alabama 38-6 (Paul "Bear" Bryant)
Nebraska	Orange 1-1-73	Notre Dame 40-6 (Ara Parseghian)

DAN DEVINE, 7-3-0 (Minn. Duluth '48) Born 12-23-24

Missouri	Orange 1-1-60	Georgia 0-14 (Wally Butts)
Missouri	Orange 1-2-61	Navy 21-14 (Wayne Hardin)
Missouri	Bluebonnet 12-22-62	Georgia Tech 14-10 (Bobby Dodd)
Missouri	Sugar 1-1-66	Florida 20-18 (Ray Graves)
Missouri	Gator 12-28-68	Alabama 35-10 (Paul "Bear" Bryant)
Missouri	Orange 1-1-70	Penn St. 3-10 (Joe Paterno)
Notre Dame	Gator 12-27-76	Penn St. 20-9 (Joe Paterno)
Notre Dame	Cotton 1-2-78	Texas 38-10 (Fred Akers)
Notre Dame	Cotton 1-1-79	Houston 35-34 (Bill Yeoman)
Notre Dame	Sugar 1-1-81	Georgia 10-17 (Vince Dooley)

PHIL DICKENS, 1-0-0 (Tennessee '37) Born 6-29-14

Wyoming	Sun 1-2-56	Texas Tech 21-14 (DeWitt Weaver)

DARRELL DICKEY, 1-3-0 (Kansas St. '84) Born 12-6-59

North Texas	New Orleans 12-18-01	Colorado St. 20-45 (Sonny Lubick)
North Texas	New Orleans 12-17-02	Cincinnati 24-19 (Rick Minter)
North Texas	New Orleans 12-16-03	Memphis 17-27 (Tommy West)
North Texas	New Orleans 12-14-04	Southern Miss. 10-31 (Jeff Bower)

DOUG DICKEY, 2-7-0 (Florida '54) Born 6-24-32

Tennessee	Bluebonnet 12-18-65	Tulsa 27-6 (Glenn Dobbs)
Tennessee	Gator 12-31-66	Syracuse 18-12 (Ben Schwartzwalder)
Tennessee	Orange 1-1-68	Oklahoma 24-26 (Chuck Fairbanks)
Tennessee	Cotton 1-1-69	Texas 13-35 (Darrell Royal)
Tennessee	Gator 12-27-69	Florida 13-14 (Ray Graves)
Florida	Tangerine 12-22-73	Miami (Ohio) 7-16 (Bill Mallory)
Florida	Sugar 12-31-74	Nebraska 10-13 (Tom Osborne)
Florida	Gator 12-29-75	Maryland 0-13 (Jerry Claiborne)
Florida	Sun 1-2-77	Texas A&M 14-37 (Emory Bellard)

JIM DICKEY, 0-1-0 (Houston '56) Born 3-22-34

Kansas St.	Independence 12-11-82	Wisconsin 3-14 (Dave McClain)

BILL "LONE STAR" DIETZ, 1-0-0 (Carlisle '12) Born 8-15-1885

Washington St.	Rose 1-1-16	Brown 14-0 (Ed Robinson)

PAUL DIETZEL, 2-2-0 [Miami (Ohio) '48] Born 9-5-24

LSU	Sugar 1-1-59	Clemson 7-0 (Frank Howard)
LSU	Sugar 1-1-60	Mississippi 0-21 (John Vaught)
LSU	Orange 1-1-62	Colorado 25-7 (Sonny Grandelius)
South Carolina	Peach 12-20-69	West Virginia 3-14 (Jim Carlen)

GERRY DiNARDO, 3-0-0 (Notre Dame '75) Born 11-10-52

LSU	Independence 12-29-95	Michigan St. 45-26 (Nick Saban)
LSU	Peach 12-28-96	Clemson 10-7 (Tommy West)
LSU	Independence 12-28-97	Notre Dame 27-9 (Bob Davie)

BILL DOBA, 1-0-0 (Ball St. '62) Born 9-7-40

Washington St.	Holiday 12-30-03	Texas 28-20 (Mack Brown)

BOBBY DOBBS, 2-0-0 (Army '46) Born 10-13-22

UTEP	Sun 12-31-65	TCU 13-12 (Abe Martin)
UTEP	Sun 12-30-67	Mississippi 14-7 (John Vaught)

GLENN DOBBS, 1-1-0 (Tulsa '43) Born 7-12-20

Tulsa	Bluebonnet 12-19-64	Mississippi 14-7 (John Vaught)
Tulsa	Bluebonnet 12-18-65	Tennessee 6-27 (Doug Dickey)

BOBBY DODD, 9-4-0 (Tennessee '31) Born 11-11-08

Georgia Tech	Oil 1-1-47	St. Mary's (Cal.) 41-19 (Jimmy Phelan)
Georgia Tech	Orange 1-1-48	Kansas 20-14 (George Sauer)
Georgia Tech	Orange 1-1-52	Baylor 17-14 (George Sauer)
Georgia Tech	Sugar 1-1-53	Mississippi 24-7 (John Vaught)
Georgia Tech	Sugar 1-1-54	West Virginia 42-19 (Art Lewis)
Georgia Tech	Cotton 1-1-55	Arkansas 14-6 (Bowden Wyatt)

Coach/School	Bowl/Date	Opponent/Score (Coach)
Georgia Tech	Sugar 1-2-56	Pittsburgh 7-0 (John Michelosen)
Georgia Tech	Gator 12-29-56	Pittsburgh 21-14 (John Michelosen)
Georgia Tech	Gator 1-2-60	Arkansas 7-14 (Frank Broyles)
Georgia Tech	Gator 12-30-61	Penn St. 15-30 (Charles "Rip" Engle)
Georgia Tech	Bluebonnet 12-22-62	Missouri 10-14 (Dan Devine)
Georgia Tech	Gator 12-31-65	Texas Tech 31-21 (J.T. King)
Georgia Tech	Orange 1-2-67	Florida 12-27 (Ray Graves)

ED DOHERTY, 0-2-0 (Boston College '44) Born 7-25-18

Arizona St.	Salad 1-1-50	Xavier (Ohio) 21-33 (Ed Kluska)
Arizona St.	Salad 1-1-51	Miami (Ohio) 21-34 (Woody Hayes)

JACK DOLAND, 1-0-0 (Tulane '50) Born 3-3-28

McNeese St.	Independence 12-13-76	Tulsa 20-16 (F.A. Dry)

TERRY DONAHUE, 8-4-1 (UCLA '67) Born 6-24-44

UCLA	Liberty 12-30-76	Alabama 6-36 (Paul "Bear" Bryant)
UCLA	Fiesta 12-25-78	Arkansas 10-10 (Lou Holtz)
UCLA	Bluebonnet 12-31-81	Michigan 14-33 (Glenn "Bo" Schembechler)
UCLA	Rose 1-1-83	Michigan 24-14 (Glenn "Bo" Schembechler)
UCLA	Rose 1-2-84	Illinois 45-9 (Mike White)
UCLA	Fiesta 1-1-85	Miami (Fla.) 39-37 (Jimmy Johnson)
UCLA	Rose 1-1-86	Iowa 45-28 (Hayden Fry)
UCLA	Freedom 12-30-86	BYU 31-10 (LaVell Edwards)
UCLA	Aloha 12-25-87	Florida 20-16 (Galen Hall)
UCLA	Cotton 1-2-89	Arkansas 17-3 (Ken Hatfield)
UCLA	John Hancock 12-31-91	Illinois 6-3 (Lou Tepper)
UCLA	Rose 1-1-94	Wisconsin 16-21 (Barry Alvarez)
UCLA	Aloha 12-25-95	Kansas 30-51 (Glen Mason)

JIM DONNAN, 4-0-0 (North Carolina St. '68) Born 1-29-45

Georgia	Outback 1-1-98	Wisconsin 33-6 (Barry Alvarez)
Georgia	Peach 12-31-98	Virginia 35-33 (George Welsh)
Georgia	Outback 1-1-00	Purdue 28-25 (ot) (Joe Tiller)
Georgia	Oahu Classic 12-24-00	Virginia 37-14 (George Welsh)

BILL DOOLEY, 3-7-0 (Mississippi St. '56) Born 5-19-34

North Carolina	Peach 12-30-70	Arizona St. 26-48 (Frank Kush)
North Carolina	Gator 12-31-71	Georgia 3-7 (Vince Dooley)
North Carolina	Sun 12-30-72	Texas Tech 32-28 (Jim Carlen)
North Carolina	Sun 12-28-74	Mississippi St. 24-26 (Bob Tyler)
North Carolina	Peach 12-31-76	Kentucky 0-21 (Fran Curci)
North Carolina	Liberty 12-19-77	Nebraska 17-21 (Tom Osborne)
Virginia Tech	Peach 1-2-81	Miami (Fla.) 10-20 (Howard Schnellenberger)
Virginia Tech	Independence 12-15-84	Air Force 7-23 (Fisher DeBerry)
Virginia Tech	Peach 12-31-86	North Carolina St. 25-24 (Dick Sheridan)
Wake Forest	Independence 12-31-92	Oregon 39-35 (Rich Brooks)

VINCE DOOLEY, 8-10-2 (Auburn '54) Born 9-4-32

Georgia	Sun 12-26-64	Texas Tech 7-0 (J.T. King)
Georgia	Cotton 12-31-66	SMU 24-9 (Hayden Fry)
Georgia	Liberty 12-16-67	North Carolina St. 7-14 (Earle Edwards)
Georgia	Sugar 1-1-69	Arkansas 2-16 (Frank Broyles)
Georgia	Sun 12-20-69	Nebraska 6-45 (Bob Devaney)
Georgia	Gator 12-31-71	North Carolina 7-3 (Bill Dooley)
Georgia	Peach 12-28-73	Maryland 17-16 (Jerry Claiborne)
Georgia	Tangerine 12-21-74	Miami (Ohio) 10-21 (Dick Crum)
Georgia	Cotton 1-1-76	Arkansas 10-31 (Frank Broyles)
Georgia	Sugar 1-1-77	Pittsburgh 3-27 (Johnny Majors)
Georgia	Bluebonnet 12-31-78	Stanford 22-25 (Bill Walsh)
Georgia	Sugar 1-1-81	Notre Dame 17-10 (Dan Devine)
Georgia	Sugar 1-1-82	Pittsburgh 20-24 (Jackie Sherrill)
Georgia	Sugar 1-1-83	Penn St. 23-27 (Joe Paterno)
Georgia	Cotton 1-2-84	Texas 10-9 (Fred Akers)
Georgia	Fla. Citrus 12-22-84	Florida St. 17-17 (Bobby Bowden)
Georgia	Sun 12-28-85	Arizona 13-13 (Larry Smith)
Georgia	Hall of Fame 12-23-86	Boston College 24-27 (Jack Bicknell)
Georgia	Liberty 12-29-87	Arkansas 20-17 (Ken Hatfield)
Georgia	Gator 1-1-89	Michigan St. 34-27 (George Perles)

CHARLES "GUS" DORAIS, 0-1-0 (Notre Dame '14) Born 7-21-1891

Gonzaga	San Diego East-West Christmas Classic 12-25-22	West Virginia 13-21 (Clarence "Doc" Spears)

KARL DORRELL, 1-3-0 (UCLA '87) Born 12-18-63

UCLA	Silicon Valley 12-30-03	Fresno St. 9-17 (Pat Hill)
UCLA	Las Vegas 12-23-04	Wyoming 21-24 (Joe Glenn)
UCLA	Sun 12-30-05	Northwestern 50-38 (Randy Walker)
UCLA	Emerald 12-27-06	Florida St. 27-44 (Bobby Bowden)

HAROLD "RED" DREW, 1-2-0 (Bates '16) Born 11-9-1894

Alabama	Sugar 1-1-48	Texas 7-27 (Blair Cherry)
Alabama	Orange 1-1-53	Syracuse 61-6 (Ben Schwartzwalder)
Alabama	Cotton 1-1-54	Rice 6-28 (Jess Neely)

BILL DRIVER, 0-1-0 (Missouri '09) Born 11-7-1883

TCU	Fort Worth Classic 1-1-21	Centre 7-63 (Charley Moran)

F.A. DRY, 0-1-0 (Oklahoma St. '53) Born 9-2-31

Tulsa	Independence 12-13-76	McNeese St. 16-20 (Jack Doland)

Coach/School	Bowl/Date	Opponent/Score (Coach)
MIKE DUBOSE, 0-2-0 (Alabama '74) Born 1-5-53		
Alabama	Music City 12-29-98	Virginia Tech 7-38 (Frank Beamer)
Alabama	Orange 1-1-00	Michigan 34-35 (ot) (Lloyd Carr)
ERNIE DUPLECHIN, 0-2-0 (Louisiana Col. '55) Born 7-19-32		
McNeese St.	Independence 12-15-79	Syracuse 7-31 (Frank Maloney)
McNeese St.	Independence 12-13-80	Southern Miss. 14-16 (Bobby Collins)
PAT DYE, 7-2-1 (Georgia '62) Born 11-6-39		
East Caro.	Independence 12-16-78	Louisiana Tech 35-13 (Maxie Lambright)
Auburn	Tangerine 12-18-82	Boston College 33-26 (Jack Bicknell)
Auburn	Sugar 1-2-84	Michigan 9-7 (Glenn "Bo" Schembechler)
Auburn	Liberty 12-27-84	Arkansas 21-15 (Ken Hatfield)
Auburn	Cotton 1-1-86	Texas A&M 16-36 (Jackie Sherrill)
Auburn	Fla. Citrus 1-1-87	Southern California 16-7 (Ted Tollner)
Auburn	Sugar 1-1-88	Syracuse 16-16 (Dick MacPherson)
Auburn	Sugar 1-2-89	Florida St. 7-13 (Bobby Bowden)
Auburn	Hall of Fame 1-1-90	Ohio St. 31-14 (John Cooper)
Auburn	Peach 12-29-90	Indiana 27-23 (Bill Mallory)
SPIKE DYKES, 2-5-0 (Stephen F. Austin '59) Born 4-15-38		
Texas Tech	Independence 12-20-86	Mississippi 17-20 (Billy Brewer)
Texas Tech	All-American 12-28-89	Duke 49-21 (Steve Spurrier)
Texas Tech	John Hancock 12-24-93	Oklahoma 10-41 (Gary Gibbs)
Texas Tech	Cotton 1-2-95	Southern California 14-55 (John Robinson)
Texas Tech	Copper 12-27-95	Air Force 55-41 (Fisher DeBerry)
Texas Tech	Alamo 12-29-96	Iowa 0-27 (Hayden Fry)
Texas Tech	Independence 12-31-98	Mississippi 18-35 (David Cutcliffe)
LLOYD EATON, 1-1-0 (Black Hills St. '40) Born 3-23-18		
Wyoming	Sun 12-24-66	Florida St. 28-20 (Bill Peterson)
Wyoming	Sugar 1-1-68	LSU 13-20 (Charlie McClendon)
RANDY EDSALL, 1-0-0 (Syracuse '80) Born 8-27-58		
Connecticut	Motor City 12-27-04	Toledo 39-10 (Tom Amstutz)
BILL EDWARDS, 1-0-0 (Wittenberg '31) Born 6-21-05		
Case Reserve	Sun 1-1-41	Arizona St. 26-13 (Millard "Dixie" Howell)
EARLE EDWARDS, 1-1-0 (Penn St. '31) Born 11-10-08		
North Carolina St.	Liberty 12-21-63	Mississippi St. 12-16 (Paul Davis)
North Carolina St.	Liberty 12-16-67	Georgia 14-7 (Vince Dooley)
LaVELL EDWARDS, 7-14-1 (Utah St. '52) Born 10-11-30		
BYU	Fiesta 12-28-74	Oklahoma St. 6-16 (Jim Stanley)
BYU	Tangerine 12-18-76	Oklahoma St. 21-49 (Jim Stanley)
BYU	Holiday 12-22-78	Navy 16-23 (George Welsh)
BYU	Holiday 12-21-79	Indiana 37-38 (Lee Corso)
BYU	Holiday 12-19-80	SMU 46-45 (Ron Meyer)
BYU	Holiday 12-18-81	Washington St. 38-36 (Jim Walden)
BYU	Holiday 12-17-82	Ohio St. 17-47 (Earle Bruce)
BYU	Holiday 12-23-83	Missouri 21-17 (Warren Powers)
BYU	Holiday 12-21-84	Michigan 24-17 (Glenn "Bo" Schembechler)
BYU	Fla. Citrus 12-28-85	Ohio St. 7-10 (Earle Bruce)
BYU	Freedom 12-30-86	UCLA 10-31 (Terry Donahue)
BYU	All-American 12-22-87	Virginia 16-22 (George Welsh)
BYU	Freedom 12-29-88	Colorado 20-17 (Bill McCartney)
BYU	Holiday 12-29-89	Penn St. 39-50 (Joe Paterno)
BYU	Holiday 12-29-90	Texas A&M 14-65 (R.C. Slocum)
BYU	Holiday 12-30-91	Iowa 13-13 (Hayden Fry)
BYU	Aloha 12-25-92	Kansas 20-23 (Glen Mason)
BYU	Holiday 12-30-93	Ohio St. 21-28 (John Cooper)
BYU	Copper 12-29-94	Oklahoma 31-6 (Gary Gibbs)
BYU	Cotton 1-1-97	Kansas St. 19-15 (Bill Snyder)
BYU	Liberty 12-31-98	Tulane 27-41 (Chris Scelfo)
BYU	Motor City 12-27-99	Marshall 3-21 (Bob Pruett)
RAY ELIOT, 2-0-0 (Illinois '32) Born 6-13-05		
Illinois	Rose 1-1-47	UCLA 45-14 (Bert LaBrucherie)
Illinois	Rose 1-1-52	Stanford 40-7 (Chuck Taylor)
BENNIE ELLENDER, 0-1-0 (Tulane '48) Born 3-2-25		
Tulane	Bluebonnet 12-29-73	Houston 7-47 (Bill Yeoman)
CHALMERS "BUMP" ELLIOTT, 1-0-0 (Michigan '48) Born 1-30-25		
Michigan	Rose 1-1-65	Oregon St. 34-7 (Tommy Prothro)
PETE ELLIOTT, 1-1-0 (Michigan '49) Born 9-29-26		
California	Rose 1-1-59	Iowa 12-38 (Forest Evashevski)
Illinois	Rose 1-1-64	Washington 17-7 (Jim Owens)
JACK ELWAY, 0-2-0 (Washington St. '53) Born 5-30-31		
San Jose St.	California 12-19-81	Toledo 25-27 (Chuck Stobart)
Stanford	Gator 12-27-86	Clemson 21-27 (Danny Ford)
CHARLES "RIP" ENGLE, 3-1-0 (McDaniel '30) Born 3-26-06		
Penn St.	Liberty 12-19-53	Alabama 7-0 (Paul "Bear" Bryant)
Penn St.	Liberty 12-17-60	Oregon 41-12 (Len Casanova)
Penn St.	Gator 12-30-61	Georgia Tech 30-15 (Bobby Dodd)
Penn St.	Gator 12-29-62	Florida 7-17 (Ray Graves)
EDDIE ERDELATZ, 2-0-0 (St. Mary's (Cal.) '36) Born 4-21-13		
Navy	Sugar 1-1-55	Mississippi 21-0 (John Vaught)
Navy	Cotton 1-1-58	Rice 20-7 (Jess Neely)

Coach/School	Bowl/Date	Opponent/Score (Coach)
DENNIS ERICKSON, 5-5-0 (Montana St. '70) Born 3-24-47		
Washington St.	Aloha 12-25-88	Houston 24-22 (Jack Pardee)
Miami (Fla.)	Sugar 1-1-90	Alabama 33-25 (Bill Curry)
Miami (Fla.)	Cotton 1-1-91	Texas 46-3 (David McWilliams)
Miami (Fla.)	Orange 1-1-92	Nebraska 22-0 (Tom Osborne)
Miami (Fla.)	Sugar 1-1-93	Alabama 13-34 (Gene Stallings)
Miami (Fla.)	Fiesta 1-1-94	Arizona 0-24 (Dick Tomey)
Miami (Fla.)	Orange 1-1-95	Nebraska 17-24 (Tom Osborne)
Oregon St.	Oahu Classic 12-25-99	Hawaii 17-23 (June Jones)
Oregon St.	Fiesta 1-1-01	Notre Dame 41-9 (Bob Davie)
Oregon St.	Insight 12-26-02	Pittsburgh 13-38 (Walt Harris)
FOREST EVASHEVSKI, 2-0-0 (Michigan '41) Born 2-19-18		
Iowa	Rose 1-1-57	Oregon St. 35-19 (Tommy Prothro)
Iowa	Rose 1-1-59	California 38-12 (Pete Elliott)
CHUCK FAIRBANKS, 3-1-1 (Michigan St. '55) Born 6-10-33		
Oklahoma	Orange 1-1-68	Tennessee 26-24 (Doug Dickey)
Oklahoma	Bluebonnet 12-31-68	SMU 27-28 (Hayden Fry)
Oklahoma	Bluebonnet 12-31-70	Alabama 24-24 (Paul "Bear" Bryant)
Oklahoma	Sugar 1-1-72	Auburn 40-22 (Ralph "Shug" Jordan)
Oklahoma	Sugar 12-31-72	Penn St. 14-0 (Joe Paterno)
DON FAMBROUGH, 0-2-0 (Kansas '48) Born 10-19-22		
Kansas	Liberty 12-17-73	North Carolina St. 18-31 (Lou Holtz)
Kansas	Hall of Fame 12-31-81	Mississippi St. 0-10 (Emory Bellard)
DON FAUROT, 0-4-0 (Missouri '25) Born 6-23-02		
Missouri	Orange 1-1-40	Georgia Tech 7-21 (Bill Alexander)
Missouri	Sugar 1-1-42	Fordham 0-2 (Jim Crowley)
Missouri	Gator 1-1-49	Clemson 23-24 (Frank Howard)
Missouri	Gator 1-2-50	Maryland 7-21 (Jim Tatum)
GERRY FAUST, 1-1-0 (Dayton '58) Born 5-21-35		
Notre Dame	Liberty 12-29-83	Boston College 19-18 (Jack Bicknell)
Notre Dame	Aloha 12-29-84	SMU 20-27 (Bobby Collins)
FOGE FAZIO, 0-2-0 (Pittsburgh '60) Born 2-28-39		
Pittsburgh	Cotton 1-1-83	SMU 3-7 (Bobby Collins)
Pittsburgh	Fiesta 1-2-84	Ohio St. 23-28 (Earle Bruce)
BEATTIE FEATHERS, 0-1-0 (Tennessee '34) Born 6-1-12		
North Carolina St.	Gator 1-1-47	Oklahoma 13-34 (Jim Tatum)
KIRK FERENTZ, 3-3-0 (Connecticut '78) Born 8-1-55		
Iowa	Alamo 12-29-01	Texas Tech 19-16 (Mike Leach)
Iowa	Orange 1-2-03	Southern California 17-38 (Pete Carroll)
Iowa	Outback 1-1-04	Florida 37-17 (Ron Zook)
Iowa	Capital One 1-1-05	LSU 30-25 (Nick Saban)
Iowa	Outback 1-2-06	Florida 24-31 (Urban Meyer)
Iowa	Alamo 12-30-06	Texas 24-26 (Mack Brown)
WES FESLER, 1-0-0 (Ohio St. '32) Born 6-29-08		
Ohio St.	Rose 1-2-50	California 17-14 (Lynn "Pappy" Waldorf)
CHARLIE FICKERT, 0-1-0 (Stanford '98) Born 2-23-1873		
Stanford	Rose 1-1-02	Michigan 0-49 (Fielding "Hurry Up" Yost)
ROBERT FISHER, 1-0-0 (Harvard '12) Born 12-3-1888		
Harvard	Rose 1-1-20	Oregon 7-6 (Charles "Shy" Huntington)
DICK FLYNN, 0-1-0 (Michigan St. '65) Born 7-17-43		
Central Mich.	Las Vegas 12-15-94	UNLV 24-52 (Jeff Horton)
HANK FOLDBERG, 0-1-0 (Army '48) Born 3-12-23		
Wichita St.	Sun 12-30-61	Villanova 9-17 (Alex Bell)
BOB FOLWELL, 0-1-1 (Penn '08) Born 1885		
Penn	Rose 1-1-17	Oregon 0-14 (Hugo Bezdek)
Navy	Rose 1-1-24	Washington 14-14 (Enoch Bagshaw)
DANNY FORD, 6-3-0 (Alabama '70) Born 4-2-48		
Clemson	Gator 12-29-78	Ohio St. 17-15 (Woody Hayes)
Clemson	Peach 12-31-79	Baylor 18-24 (Grant Teaff)
Clemson	Orange 1-1-82	Nebraska 22-15 (Tom Osborne)
Clemson	Independence 12-21-85	Minnesota 13-20 (John Gutekunst)
Clemson	Gator 12-27-86	Stanford 27-21 (Jack Elway)
Clemson	Fla. Citrus 1-1-88	Penn St. 35-10 (Joe Paterno)
Clemson	Fla. Citrus 1-2-89	Oklahoma 23-6 (Barry Switzer)
Clemson	Gator 12-30-89	West Virginia 27-7 (Don Nehlen)
Arkansas	Carquest 12-30-95	North Carolina 10-20 (Mack Brown)
DENNIS FRANCHIONE, 3-3-0 (Pittsburg St. '73) Born 3-28-51		
New Mexico	Insight.com 12-27-97	Arizona 14-20 (Dick Tomey)
TCU	Sun 12-31-98	Southern California 28-19 (Paul Hackett)
TCU	Mobile Alabama 12-22-99	East Caro. 28-14 (Steve Logan)
Alabama	Independence 12-27-01	Iowa St. 14-13 (Dan McCarney)
Texas A&M	Cotton 1-1-05	Tennessee 7-38 (Phillip Fulmer)
Texas A&M	Holiday 12-28-06	California 10-45 (Jeff Tedford)
RALPH FRIEDGEN, 3-1-0 (Maryland '69) Born 4-4-47		
Maryland	Orange 1-2-02	Florida 23-56 (Steve Spurrier)
Maryland	Peach 12-31-02	Tennessee 30-3 (Phillip Fulmer)
Maryland	Gator 1-1-04	West Virginia 41-7 (Rich Rodriquez)
Maryland	Champs Sports 12-29-06	Purdue 24-7 (Joe Tiller)

Coach/School	Bowl/Date	Opponent/Score (Coach)
HENRY FRNKA, 2-3-0 (Austin '26) Born 3-16-03		
Tulsa	Sun 1-1-42	Texas Tech 6-0 (Dell Morgan)
Tulsa	Sugar 1-1-43	Tennessee 7-14 (John Barnhill)
Tulsa	Sugar 1-1-44	Georgia Tech 18-20 (Bill Alexander)
Tulsa	Orange 1-1-45	Georgia Tech 26-12 (Bill Alexander)
Tulsa	Oil 1-1-46	Georgia 6-20 (Wally Butts)
HAYDEN FRY, 7-9-1 (Baylor '51) Born 2-28-29		
SMU	Sun 12-31-63	Oregon 13-21 (Len Casanova)
SMU	Cotton 12-31-66	Georgia 9-24 (Vince Dooley)
SMU	Bluebonnet 12-31-68	Oklahoma 28-27 (Chuck Fairbanks)
Iowa	Rose 1-1-82	Washington 0-28 (Don James)
Iowa	Peach 12-31-82	Tennessee 28-22 (Johnny Majors)
Iowa	Gator 12-30-83	Florida 6-14 (Charley Pell)
Iowa	Freedom 12-26-84	Texas 55-17 (Fred Akers)
Iowa	Rose 1-1-86	UCLA 28-45 (Terry Donahue)
Iowa	Holiday 12-30-86	San Diego St. 39-38 (Denny Stolz)
Iowa	Holiday 12-30-87	Wyoming 20-19 (Paul Roach)
Iowa	Peach 12-31-88	North Carolina St. 23-29 (Dick Sheridan)
Iowa	Rose 1-1-91	Washington 34-46 (Don James)
Iowa	Holiday 12-30-91	BYU 13-13 (LaVell Edwards)
Iowa	Alamo 12-31-93	California 3-37 (Keith Gilbertson)
Iowa	Sun 12-29-95	Washington 38-18 (Jim Lambright)
Iowa	Alamo 12-29-96	Texas Tech 27-0 (Spike Dykes)
Iowa	Sun 12-31-97	Arizona St. 7-17 (Bruce Snyder)
BILL FULCHER, 1-0-0 (Georgia Tech '57) Born 2-9-34		
Georgia Tech	Liberty 12-18-72	Iowa St. 31-30 (Johnny Majors)
PHILLIP FULMER, 7-7-0 (Tennessee '72) Born 9-1-50		
Tennessee	Hall of Fame 1-1-93	Boston College 38-23 (Tom Coughlin)
Tennessee	Fla. Citrus 1-1-94	Penn St. 13-31 (Joe Paterno)
Tennessee	Gator 12-30-94	Virginia Tech 45-23 (Frank Beamer)
Tennessee	Fla. Citrus 1-1-96	Ohio St. 20-14 (John Cooper)
Tennessee	Fla. Citrus 1-1-97	Northwestern 48-28 (Gary Barnett)
Tennessee	Orange 1-2-98	Nebraska 17-42 (Tom Osborne)
Tennessee	Fiesta 1-4-99	Florida St. 23-16 (Bobby Bowden)
Tennessee	Fiesta 1-2-00	Nebraska 21-31 (Frank Solich)
Tennessee	Cotton 1-1-01	Kansas St. 21-35 (Bill Snyder)
Tennessee	Fla. Citrus 1-1-02	Michigan 45-17 (Lloyd Carr)
Tennessee	Peach 12-31-02	Maryland 3-30 (Ralph Friedgen)
Tennessee	Peach 1-2-04	Clemson 14-27 (Tommy Bowden)
Tennessee	Cotton 1-1-05	Texas A&M 38-7 (Dennis Franchione)
Tennessee	Outback 1-1-07	Penn St. 10-20 (Joe Paterno)
WARREN GAER, 0-1-0 (Drake '35) Born 2-7-12		
Drake	Sun 1-1-58	Louisville 20-34 (Frank Camp)
CHAN GAILEY, 2-3-0 (Florida '74) Born 1-5-52		
Georgia Tech	Silicon Valley 12-31-02	Fresno St. 21-30 (Pat Hill)
Georgia Tech	Humanitarian 1-3-04	Tulsa 52-10 (Steve Kragthorpe)
Georgia Tech	Champs Sports 12-21-04	Syracuse 51-14 (Paul Pasqualoni)
Georgia Tech	Emerald 12-29-05	Utah 10-38 (Kyle Whittingham)
Georgia Tech	Gator 1-1-07	West Virginia 35-38 (Rich Rodriguez)
JOE GAVIN, 0-1-0 (Notre Dame '31) Born 3-20-08		
Dayton	Salad 1-1-52	Houston 21-26 (Clyde Lee)
GARY GIBBS, 2-1-0 (Oklahoma '75) Born 8-13-52		
Oklahoma	Gator 12-29-91	Virginia 48-14 (George Welsh)
Oklahoma	John Hancock 12-24-93	Texas Tech 41-10 (Spike Dykes)
Oklahoma	Copper 12-29-94	BYU 6-31 (LaVell Edwards)
VINCE GIBSON, 0-2-0 (Florida St. '55) Born 3-27-33		
Louisville	Independence 12-17-77	Louisiana Tech 14-24 (Maxie Lambright)
Tulane	Hall of Fame 12-27-80	Arkansas 15-34 (Lou Holtz)
CLAUDE GILBERT, 1-1-0 (San Jose St. '59) Born 7-10-32		
San Jose St.	California 12-13-86	Miami (Ohio) 37-7 (Tim Rose)
San Jose St.	California 12-12-87	Eastern Mich. 27-30 (Jim Harkema)
KEITH GILBERTSON, 1-0-0 (Central Wash. '71) Born 5-15-48		
California	Alamo 12-31-93	Iowa 37-3 (Hayden Fry)
SID GILLMAN, 1-1-0 (Ohio St. '34) Born 10-26-11		
Miami (Ohio)	Sun 1-1-48	Texas Tech 13-12 (Dell Morgan)
Cincinnati	Sun 1-1-51	West Tex. A&M 13-14 (Frank Kimbrough)
BILL GLASSFORD, 0-1-0 (Pittsburgh '37) Born 3-8-14		
Nebraska	Orange 1-1-55	Duke 7-34 (Bill Murray)
JOE GLENN, 1-0-0 (South Dakota '71) Born 3-7-49		
Wyoming	Las Vegas 12-23-04	UCLA 24-21 (Karl Dorrell)
MARSHALL "LITTLE SLEEPY" GLENN, 1-0-0 (West Virginia '31) Born 4-22-08		
West Virginia	Sun 1-1-38	Texas Tech 7-6 (Pete Cawthon)
RAY GOFF, 2-2-0 (Georgia '78) Born 7-10-55		
Georgia	Peach 12-30-89	Syracuse 18-19 (Dick MacPherson)
Georgia	Independence 12-29-91	Arkansas 24-15 (Jack Crowe)
Georgia	Fla. Citrus 1-1-93	Ohio St. 21-14 (John Cooper)
Georgia	Peach 12-30-95	Virginia 27-34 (George Welsh)
FRED GOLDSMITH, 0-1-0 (Florida '67) Born 3-3-44		
Duke	Hall of Fame 1-2-95	Wisconsin 20-34 (Barry Alvarez)
MIKE GOTTFRIED, 0-1-0 (Morehead St. '66) Born 12-17-44		
Pittsburgh	Bluebonnet 12-31-87	Texas 27-32 (David McWilliams)
RALPH GRAHAM, 0-1-0 (Kansas St. '34) Born 8-16-10		
Wichita St.	Raisin 1-1-48	Pacific 14-26 (Larry Siemering)
TODD GRAHAM, 0-1-0 (East Central '87) Born 12-5-64		
Rice	New Orleans 12-22-06	Troy 17-41 (Larry Blakeney)
SONNY GRANDELIUS, 0-1-0 (Michigan St. '51) Born 4-16-29		
Colorado	Orange 1-1-62	LSU 7-25 (Paul Dietzel)
RAY GRAVES, 4-1-0 (Tennessee '43) Born 12-31-18		
Florida	Gator 12-31-60	Baylor 13-12 (John Bridgers)
Florida	Gator 12-29-62	Penn St. 17-7 (Charles "Rip" Engle)
Florida	Sugar 1-1-66	Missouri 18-20 (Dan Devine)
Florida	Orange 1-2-67	Georgia Tech 27-12 (Bobby Dodd)
Florida	Gator 12-27-69	Tennessee 14-13 (Doug Dickey)
DENNIS GREEN, 0-1-0 (Iowa '71) Born 2-17-49		
Stanford	Aloha 12-25-91	Georgia Tech 17-18 (Bobby Ross)
VEE GREEN, 1-0-0 (Illinois '24) Born 10-9-1900		
Drake	Raisin 1-1-46	Fresno St. 13-12 (Alvin "Pix" Pierson)
JIM GROBE, 1-1-0 (Virginia '75) Born 2-17-52		
Wake Forest	Seattle 12-30-02	Oregon 38-17 (Mike Bellotti)
Wake Forest	Orange 1-2-07	Louisville 13-24 (Bobby Petrino)
AL GROH, 3-1-0 (Virginia '67) Born 7-13-44		
Virginia	Continental Tire 12-28-02	West Virginia 48-22 (Rich Rodriguez)
Virginia	Continental Tire 12-27-03	Pittsburgh 23-16 (Walt Harris)
Virginia	MPC Computers 12-27-04	Fresno St. 34-37 (ot) (Pat Hill)
Virginia	Music City 12-30-05	Minnesota 34-31 (Glen Mason)
ART GUEPE, 1-0-0 (Marquette '37) Born 1-28-15		
Vanderbilt	Gator 12-31-55	Auburn 25-13 (Ralph "Shug" Jordan)
MIKE GUNDY, 1-0-0 (Oklahoma St. '89) Born 8-12-67		
Oklahoma St.	Independence 12-28-06	Alabama 34-31 (Joe Kines)
ANDY GUSTAFSON, 1-3-0 (Pittsburgh '26) Born 4-3-03		
Miami (Fla.)	Orange 1-1-51	Clemson 14-15 (Frank Howard)
Miami (Fla.)	Gator 1-1-52	Clemson 14-0 (Frank Howard)
Miami (Fla.)	Liberty 12-16-61	Syracuse 14-15 (Ben Schwartzwalder)
Miami (Fla.)	Gotham 12-15-62	Nebraska 34-36 (Bob Devaney)
JOHN GUTEKUNST, 1-1-0 (Duke '66) Born 4-13-44		
Minnesota	Independence 12-21-85	Clemson 20-13 (Danny Ford)
Minnesota	Liberty 12-29-86	Tennessee 14-21 (Johnny Majors)
PAUL HACKETT, 1-1-0 (UC Davis '69) Born 6-5-47		
Pittsburgh	John Hancock 12-30-89	Texas A&M 31-28 (R.C. Slocum)
Southern California	Sun 12-31-98	TCU 19-28 (Dennis Franchione)
JACK HAGERTY, 0-1-0 (Georgetown '26) Born 7-3-03		
Georgetown	Orange 1-1-41	Mississippi St. 7-14 (Alvin McKeen)
GALEN HALL, 1-1-0 (Penn St. '62) Born 8-14-40		
Florida	Aloha 12-25-87	UCLA 16-20 (Terry Donahue)
Florida	All-American 12-29-88	Illinois 14-10 (John Mackovic)
CURLEY HALLMAN, 1-0-0 (Texas A&M '70) Born 9-3-47		
Southern Miss.	Independence 12-23-88	UTEP 38-18 (Bob Stull)
MIKE HANKWITZ, 0-1-0 (Michigan '70) Born 12-14-47		
Colorado	Champs Sports 12-27-05	Clemson 10-19 (Tommy Bowden)
WAYNE HARDIN, 1-2-0 (Pacific '50) Born 3-23-27		
Navy	Orange 1-2-61	Missouri 14-21 (Dan Devine)
Navy	Cotton 1-1-64	Texas 6-28 (Darrell Royal)
Temple	Garden State 12-15-79	California 28-17 (Roger Theder)
JACK HARDING, 1-0-0 (Pittsburgh '26) Born 1-5-1898		
Miami (Fla.)	Orange 1-1-48	Holy Cross 13-6 (John "Ox" Da Grosa)
JIM HARKEMA, 1-0-0 (Kalamazoo '64) Born 6-25-42		
Eastern Mich.	California 12-12-87	San Jose St. 30-27 (Claude Gilbert)
WALT HARRIS, 2-4-0 (Pacific '68) Born 11-9-46		
Pittsburgh	Liberty 12-31-97	Southern Miss. 7-41 (Jeff Bower)
Pittsburgh	Insight.com 12-28-00	Iowa St. 29-37 (Dan McCarney)
Pittsburgh	Tangerine 12-20-01	North Carolina St. 34-19 (Chuck Amato)
Pittsburgh	Insight 12-26-02	Oregon St. 38-13 (Dennis Erickson)
Pittsburgh	Continental Tire 12-27-03	Virginia 16-23 (Al Groh)
Pittsburgh	Fiesta 1-1-05	Utah 7-35 (Urban Meyer)
KEN HATFIELD, 4-6-0 (Arkansas '65) Born 6-8-43		
Air Force	Hall of Fame 12-31-82	Vanderbilt 36-28 (George MacIntyre)
Air Force	Independence 12-10-83	Mississippi 9-3 (Billy Brewer)
Arkansas	Liberty 12-27-84	Auburn 15-21 (Pat Dye)
Arkansas	Holiday 12-22-85	Arizona St. 18-17 (John Cooper)
Arkansas	Orange 1-1-87	Oklahoma 8-42 (Barry Switzer)
Arkansas	Liberty 12-29-87	Georgia 17-20 (Vince Dooley)
Arkansas	Cotton 1-2-89	UCLA 3-17 (Terry Donahue)
Arkansas	Cotton 1-1-90	Tennessee 27-31 (Johnny Majors)
Clemson	Hall of Fame 1-1-91	Illinois 30-0 (John Mackovic)
Clemson	Fla. Citrus 1-1-92	California 13-37 (Bruce Snyder)

Coach/School	Bowl/Date	Opponent/Score (Coach)
DAN HAWKINS, 2-2-0 (UC Davis '84) Born 11-10-60		
Boise St.	Humanitarian 12-31-02	Iowa St. 34-16 (Dan McCarney)
Boise St.	Fort Worth 12-23-03	TCU 34-31 (Gary Patterson)
Boise St.	Liberty 12-31-04	Louisville 40-44 (Bobby Petrino)
Boise St.	MPC Computers 12-28-05	Boston College 21-27 (Tom O'Brien)
WOODY HAYES, 6-6-0 (Denison '35) Born 2-14-13		
Miami (Ohio)	Salad 1-1-51	Arizona St. 34-21 (Ed Doherty)
Ohio St.	Rose 1-1-55	Southern California 20-7 (Jess Hill)
Ohio St.	Rose 1-1-58	Oregon 10-7 (Len Casanova)
Ohio St.	Rose 1-1-69	Southern California 27-16 (John McKay)
Ohio St.	Rose 1-1-71	Stanford 17-27 (John Ralston)
Ohio St.	Rose 1-1-73	Southern California 17-42 (John McKay)
Ohio St.	Rose 1-1-74	Southern California 42-21 (John McKay)
Ohio St.	Rose 1-1-75	Southern California 17-18 (John McKay)
Ohio St.	Rose 1-1-76	UCLA 10-23 (Dick Vermeil)
Ohio St.	Orange 1-1-77	Colorado 27-10 (Bill Mallory)
Ohio St.	Sugar 1-2-78	Alabama 6-35 (Paul "Bear" Bryant)
Ohio St.	Gator 12-29-78	Clemson 15-17 (Danny Ford)
KIM HELTON, 0-1-0 (Florida '70) Born 7-28-48		
Houston	Liberty 12-27-96	Syracuse 17-30 (Paul Pasqualoni)
ELMER "GUS" HENDERSON, 2-0-0 (Oberlin '12) Born 3-10-1889		
Southern California	Rose 1-1-23	Penn St. 14-3 (Hugo Bezdek)
Southern California	L.A. Christmas Festival 12-25-24	Missouri 20-7 (Gwinn Henry)
DAN HENNING, 1-0-0 (William & Mary '64) Born 7-21-42		
Boston College	Aloha 12-25-94	Kansas St. 12-7 (Bill Snyder)
GWINN HENRY, 0-1-0 (Howard Payne '17) Born 8-5-1887		
Missouri	L.A. Christmas Festival 12-25-24	Southern California 7-20 (Elmer "Gus" Henderson)
BILL HESS, 0-2-0 (Ohio '47) Born 2-5-23		
Ohio	Sun 12-31-62	West Tex. A&M 14-15 (Joe Kerbel)
Ohio	Tangerine 12-27-68	Richmond 42-49 (Frank Jones)
JIM HICKEY, 1-0-0 (William & Mary '42) Born 1-22-20		
North Carolina	Gator 12-28-63	Air Force 35-0 (Ben Martin)
BOB HIGGINS, 1-0-1 (Penn St. '20) Born 12-24-1893		
West Va. Wesleyan	Dixie Classic 1-1-25	SMU 9-7 (Ray Morrison)
Penn St.	Cotton 1-1-48	SMU 13-13 (Matty Bell)
JESS HILL, 1-1-0 (Southern California '30) Born 1-20-07		
Southern California	Rose 1-1-53	Wisconsin 7-0 (Ivy Williamson)
Southern California	Rose 1-1-55	Ohio St. 7-20 (Woody Hayes)
PAT HILL, 3-4-0 (UC Riverside '73) Born 12-17-51		
Fresno St.	Las Vegas 12-18-99	Utah 16-17 (Ron McBride)
Fresno St.	Silicon Valley 12-31-00	Air Force 34-37 (Fisher DeBerry)
Fresno St.	Silicon Valley 12-31-01	Michigan St. 35-44 (Bobby Williams)
Fresno St.	Silicon Valley 12-31-02	Georgia Tech 30-21 (Chan Gailey)
Fresno St.	Silicon Valley 12-30-03	UCLA 17-9 (Karl Dorrell)
Fresno St.	MPC Computers 12-27-04	Virginia 37-34 (ot) (Al Groh)
Fresno St.	Liberty 12-31-05	Tulsa 24-31 (Steve Kragthorpe)
JERRY HINES, 0-0-1 (New Mexico St. '26) Born 10-11-03		
New Mexico St.	Sun 1-1-36	Hardin-Simmons 14-14 (Frank Kimbrough)
BERNARD A. HOBAN, 0-1-0 (Dartmouth '12) Born 4-21-1890		
U. of Mexico	Sun 1-1-45	Southwestern (Tex.) 0-35 (Randolph R.M. Medley)
TERRY HOEPPNER, 1-1-0 (Franklin '69) Born 8-19-47		
Miami (Ohio)	GMAC 12-18-03	Louisville 49-28 (Bobby Petrino)
Miami (Ohio)	Independence 12-28-04	Iowa St. 13-17 (Dan McCarney)
ORIN "BABE" HOLLINGBERY, 0-1-0 (No college) Born 7-15-1893		
Washington St.	Rose 1-1-31	Alabama 0-24 (Wallace Wade)
LOU HOLTZ, 12-8-2 (Kent St. '59) Born 1-6-37		
William & Mary	Tangerine 12-28-70	Toledo 12-40 (Frank Lauterbur)
North Carolina St.	Peach 12-29-72	West Virginia 49-13 (Bobby Bowden)
North Carolina St.	Liberty 12-17-73	Kansas 31-18 (Don Fambrough)
North Carolina St.	Bluebonnet 12-23-74	Houston 31-31 (Bill Yeoman)
North Carolina St.	Peach 12-31-75	West Virginia 10-13 (Bobby Bowden)
Arkansas	Orange 1-2-78	Oklahoma 31-6 (Barry Switzer)
Arkansas	Fiesta 12-25-78	UCLA 10-10 (Terry Donahue)
Arkansas	Sugar 1-1-80	Alabama 9-24 (Paul "Bear" Bryant)
Arkansas	Hall of Fame 12-27-80	Tulane 34-15 (Vince Gibson)
Arkansas	Gator 12-28-81	North Carolina 27-31 (Dick Crum)
Arkansas	Bluebonnet 12-31-82	Florida 28-24 (Charley Pell)
Notre Dame	Cotton 1-1-88	Texas A&M 10-35 (Jackie Sherrill)
Notre Dame	Fiesta 1-2-89	West Virginia 34-21 (Don Nehlen)
Notre Dame	Orange 1-1-90	Colorado 21-6 (Bill McCartney)
Notre Dame	Orange 1-1-91	Colorado 9-10 (Bill McCartney)
Notre Dame	Sugar 1-1-92	Florida 39-28 (Steve Spurrier)
Notre Dame	Cotton 1-1-93	Texas A&M 28-3 (R.C. Slocum)
Notre Dame	Cotton 1-1-94	Texas A&M 24-21 (R.C. Slocum)
Notre Dame	Fiesta 1-2-95	Colorado 24-41 (Bill McCartney)
Notre Dame	Orange 1-1-96	Florida St. 26-31 (Bobby Bowden)
South Carolina	Outback 1-1-01	Ohio St. 24-7 (John Cooper)
South Carolina	Outback 1-1-02	Ohio St. 31-28 (Jim Tressel)

Coach/School	Bowl/Date	Opponent/Score (Coach)
SKIP HOLTZ, 0-1-0 (Notre Dame '86) Born 3-12-64		
East Caro.	Papajohns.com 12-23-06	South Fla. 7-24 (Jim Leavitt)
EDWIN "BABE" HORRELL, 0-1-0 (California '26) Born 9-29-02		
UCLA	Rose 1-1-43	Georgia 0-9 (Wally Butts)
JEFF HORTON, 1-0-0 (Nevada '81) Born 7-13-57		
UNLV	Las Vegas 12-15-94	Central Mich. 52-24 (Dick Flynn)
FRANK HOWARD, 3-3-0 (Alabama '31) Born 3-25-09		
Clemson	Gator 1-1-49	Missouri 24-23 (Don Faurot)
Clemson	Orange 1-1-51	Miami (Fla.) 15-14 (Andy Gustafson)
Clemson	Gator 1-1-52	Miami (Fla.) 0-14 (Andy Gustafson)
Clemson	Orange 1-1-57	Colorado 21-27 (Dallas Ward)
Clemson	Sugar 1-1-59	LSU 0-7 (Paul Dietzel)
Clemson	Bluebonnet 12-19-59	TCU 23-7 (Abe Martin)
MILLARD "DIXIE" HOWELL, 0-1-1 (Alabama '35) Born 11-24-12		
Arizona St.	Sun 1-1-40	Catholic 0-0 (Arthur "Dutch" Bergman)
Arizona St.	Sun 1-1-41	Case Reserve 13-26 (Bill Edwards)
BILL HUBBARD, 2-0-0 (Stanford '30) Born 2-5-07		
San Jose St.	Raisin 1-1-47	Utah St. 20-0 (E.L. "Dick" Romney)
San Jose St.	Raisin 12-31-49	Texas Tech 20-13 (Dell Morgan)
CLYDE "CAC" HUBBARD, 0-2-0 (Oregon St. '21) Born 9-13-1897		
Denver	Sun 1-1-46	New Mexico 24-34 (Willis Barnes)
Denver	Alamo 1-4-47	Hardin-Simmons 0-20 (Warren Woodson)
CHARLES "SHY" HUNTINGTON, 0-1-0 (Oregon) Born 7-7-1891		
Oregon	Rose 1-1-20	Harvard 6-7 (Robert Fisher)
HARVEY HYDE, 1-0-0 (Redlands '62) Born 7-13-39		
UNLV	California 12-15-84	Toledo 30-13 (Dan Simrell)
DON JAMES, 10-5-0 [Miami (Fla.) '54] Born 12-31-32		
Kent St.	Tangerine 12-29-72	Tampa 18-21 (Earle Bruce)
Washington	Rose 1-2-78	Michigan 27-20 (Glenn "Bo" Schembechler)
Washington	Sun 12-22-79	Texas 14-7 (Fred Akers)
Washington	Rose 1-1-81	Michigan 6-23 (Glenn "Bo" Schembechler)
Washington	Rose 1-1-82	Iowa 28-0 (Hayden Fry)
Washington	Aloha 12-25-82	Maryland 21-20 (Bobby Ross)
Washington	Aloha 12-26-83	Penn St. 10-13 (Joe Paterno)
Washington	Orange 1-1-85	Oklahoma 28-17 (Barry Switzer)
Washington	Freedom 12-30-85	Colorado 20-17 (Bill McCartney)
Washington	Sun 12-25-86	Alabama 6-28 (Ray Perkins)
Washington	Independence 12-18-87	Tulane 24-12 (Mack Brown)
Washington	Freedom 12-29-89	Florida 34-7 (Gary Darnell)
Washington	Rose 1-1-91	Iowa 46-34 (Hayden Fry)
Washington	Rose 1-1-92	Michigan 34-14 (Gary Moeller)
Washington	Rose 1-1-93	Michigan 31-38 (Gary Moeller)
JIMMY JOHNSON, 3-4-0 (Arkansas '65) Born 7-16-43		
Oklahoma St.	Independence 12-12-81	Texas A&M 16-33 (Tom Wilson)
Oklahoma St.	Bluebonnet 12-31-83	Baylor 24-14 (Grant Teaff)
Miami (Fla.)	Fiesta 1-1-85	UCLA 37-39 (Terry Donahue)
Miami (Fla.)	Sugar 1-1-86	Tennessee 7-35 (Johnny Majors)
Miami (Fla.)	Fiesta 1-2-87	Penn St. 10-14 (Joe Paterno)
Miami (Fla.)	Orange 1-1-88	Oklahoma 20-14 (Barry Switzer)
Miami (Fla.)	Orange 1-2-89	Nebraska 23-3 (Tom Osborne)
PAUL JOHNSON, 2-2-0 (Western Caro. '79) Born 8-20-59		
Navy	Houston 12-30-03	Texas Tech 14-38 (Mike Leach)
Navy	Emerald 12-30-04	New Mexico 34-19 (Rocky Long)
Navy	Poinsettia 12-22-05	Colorado St. 51-30 (Sonny Lubick)
Navy	Meineke Car Care 12-30-06	Boston College 24-25 (Frank Spaziani)
FRANK JONES, 1-1-0 (North Carolina '48) Born 8-30-21		
Richmond	Tangerine 12-27-68	Ohio 49-42 (Bill Hess)
Richmond	Tangerine 12-28-71	Toledo 3-28 (John Murphy)
GOMER JONES, 0-1-0 (Ohio St. '36) Born 2-26-14		
Oklahoma	Gator 1-2-65	Florida St. 19-36 (Bill Peterson)
HOWARD JONES, 5-0-0 (Yale '08) Born 8-23-1885		
Southern California	Rose 1-1-30	Pittsburgh 47-14 (Jock Sutherland)
Southern California	Rose 1-1-32	Tulane 21-12 (Bernie Bierman)
Southern California	Rose 1-2-33	Pittsburgh 35-0 (Jock Sutherland)
Southern California	Rose 1-2-39	Duke 7-3 (Wallace Wade)
Southern California	Rose 1-1-40	Tennessee 14-0 (Bob Neyland)
JUNE JONES, 4-1-0 (Portland St. '77) Born 2-14-53		
Hawaii	Oahu Classic 12-25-99	Oregon St. 23-17 (Dennis Erickson)
Hawaii	Hawaii 12-25-02	Tulane 28-36 (Chris Scelfo)
Hawaii	Hawaii 12-25-03	Houston 54-48 (3 ot) (Art Briles)
Hawaii	Hawaii 12-24-04	UAB 59-40 (Watson Brown)
Hawaii	Hawaii 12-24-06	Arizona St. 41-24 (Dirk Koetter)
LARRY JONES, 0-1-0 (LSU '54) Born 12-18-33		
Florida St.	Fiesta 12-27-71	Arizona St. 38-45 (Frank Kush)
LAWRENCE McC. "BIFF" JONES, 0-1-0 (Army '17) Born 10-8-95		
Nebraska	Rose 1-1-41	Stanford 13-21 (Clark Shaughnessy)

Coach/School	Bowl/Date	Opponent/Score (Coach)
PAT JONES, 3-1-0 (Arkansas '69) Born 11-4-47		
Oklahoma St.	Gator 12-28-84	South Carolina 21-14 (Joe Morrison)
Oklahoma St.	Gator 12-30-85	Florida St. 23-34 (Bobby Bowden)
Oklahoma St.	Sun 12-25-87	West Virginia 35-33 (Don Nehlen)
Oklahoma St.	Holiday 12-30-88	Wyoming 62-14 (Paul Roach)
RALPH "SHUG" JORDAN, 5-7-0 (Auburn '32) Born 9-25-10		
Auburn	Gator 1-1-54	Texas Tech 13-35 (DeWitt Weaver)
Auburn	Gator 12-31-54	Baylor 33-13 (George Sauer)
Auburn	Gator 12-31-55	Vanderbilt 13-25 (Art Gueppe)
Auburn	Orange 1-1-64	Nebraska 7-13 (Bob Devaney)
Auburn	Liberty 12-18-65	Mississippi 7-13 (John Vaught)
Auburn	Sun 12-28-68	Arizona 34-10 (Darrell Mudra)
Auburn	Bluebonnet 12-31-69	Houston 7-36 (Bill Yeoman)
Auburn	Gator 1-2-71	Mississippi 35-28 (John Vaught)
Auburn	Sugar 1-1-72	Oklahoma 22-40 (Chuck Fairbanks)
Auburn	Gator 12-30-72	Colorado 24-3 (Eddie Crowder)
Auburn	Sun 12-29-73	Missouri 17-34 (Al Onofrio)
Auburn	Gator 12-30-74	Texas 27-3 (Darrell Royal)
ERNIE JORGE, 1-1-0 [St. Mary's (Cal.) '36] Born 10-7-14		
Pacific	Sun 1-1-52	Texas Tech 14-25 (DeWitt Weaver)
Pacific	Sun 1-1-53	Southern Miss. 26-7 (Thad "Pie" Vann)
AL KAWAL, 1-0-0 (Northwestern '35) Born 7-4-12		
Drake	Salad 1-1-49	Arizona 14-13 (Miles Casteel)
BRIAN KELLY, 0-1-0 (Assumption '83) Born 10-25-62		
Cincinnati	International 1-6-07	Western Mich. 27-24 (Bill Cubit)
JOE KERBEL, 2-0-0 (Oklahoma '47) Born 5-3-21		
West Tex. A&M	Sun 12-21-62	Ohio 15-14 (Bill Hess)
West Tex. A&M	Pasadena 12-2-67	Cal St. Northridge 35-13 (Sam Winningham)
BILL KERN, 0-1-0 (Pittsburgh '28) Born 9-2-06		
Carnegie Mellon	Sugar 1-2-39	TCU 7-15 (Leo "Dutch" Meyer)
ED KEZIRIAN, 1-0-0 (UCLA '75) Born 8-4-52		
UCLA	Las Vegas 12-25-02	New Mexico 27-13 (Rocky Long)
FRANK KIMBROUGH, 2-0-1 (Hardin-Simmons '26) Born 6-24-04		
Hardin-Simmons	Sun 1-1-36	New Mexico St. 14-14 (Jerry Hines)
Hardin-Simmons	Sun 1-1-37	UTEP 34-6 (Max Saxon)
West Tex. A&M	Sun 1-1-51	Cincinnati 14-13 (Sid Gillman)
BILLY KINARD, 1-0-0 (Mississippi '56) Born 12-16-33		
Mississippi	Peach 12-30-71	Georgia Tech 41-18 (Bud Carson)
JOE KINES, 0-1-0 (Jacksonville St. '67) Born 7-13-44		
Alabama	Independence 12-28-06	Oklahoma St. 31-34 (Mike Gundy)
DEWEY KING, 0-1-0 (North Dakota '50) Born 10-1-25		
San Jose St.	Pasadena 12-18-71	Memphis 9-28 (Billy Murphy)
J.T. KING, 0-2-0 (Texas '38) Born 10-22-12		
Texas Tech	Sun 12-26-64	Georgia 0-7 (Vince Dooley)
Texas Tech	Gator 12-31-65	Georgia Tech 21-31 (Bobby Dodd)
JIMMY KITTS, 1-1-0 (SMU) Born 6-14-1900		
Rice	Cotton 1-1-38	Colorado 28-14 (Bernard "Bunnie" Oakes)
Virginia Tech	Sun 1-1-47	Cincinnati 6-18 (Ray Nolting)
ED KLUSKA, 1-0-0 [Xavier (Ohio) '40] Born 5-21-18		
Xavier (Ohio)	Salad 1-1-50	Arizona St. 33-21 (Ed Doherty)
DIRK KOETTER, 4-2-0 (Idaho St. '81) Born 2-5-59		
Boise St.	Humanitarian 12-30-99	Louisville 34-31 (John L. Smith)
Boise St.	Humanitarian 12-28-00	UTEP 38-23 (Gary Nord)
Arizona St.	Holiday 12-27-02	Kansas St. 27-34 (Bill Snyder)
Arizona St.	Sun 12-31-04	Purdue 27-23 (Joe Tiller)
Arizona St.	Insight 12-27-05	Rutgers 45-40 (Greg Schiano)
Arizona St.	Hawaii 12-24-06	Hawaii 24-41 (June Jones)
STEVE KRAGTHORPE, 1-2-0 (West Tex. A&M '88) Born 4-28-65		
Tulsa	Humanitarian 1-3-04	Georgia Tech 10-52 (Chan Gailey)
Tulsa	Liberty 12-31-05	Fresno St. 38-31 (Pat Hill)
Tulsa	Armed Forces 12-23-06	Utah 13-25 (Kyle Whittingham)
JOE KRIVAK, 0-0-1 (Syracuse '57) Born 3-20-35		
Maryland	Independence 12-15-90	Louisiana Tech 34-34 (Joe Raymond Peace)
FRANK KUSH, 6-1-0 (Michigan St. '53) Born 1-20-29		
Arizona St.	Peach 12-30-70	North Carolina 48-26 (Bill Dooley)
Arizona St.	Fiesta 12-27-71	Florida St. 45-38 (Larry Jones)
Arizona St.	Fiesta 12-23-72	Missouri 49-35 (Al Onofrio)
Arizona St.	Fiesta 12-21-73	Pittsburgh 28-7 (Johnny Majors)
Arizona St.	Fiesta 12-26-75	Nebraska 17-14 (Tom Osborne)
Arizona St.	Fiesta 12-25-77	Penn St. 30-42 (Joe Paterno)
Arizona St.	Garden State 12-16-78	Rutgers 34-18 (Frank Burns)
BERT LaBRUCHERIE, 0-1-0 (UCLA '29) Born 1-19-05		
UCLA	Rose 1-1-47	Illinois 14-45 (Ray Eliot)
JIM LAMBRIGHT, 1-3-0 (Washington '65) Born 4-26-42		
Washington	Sun 12-29-95	Iowa 18-38 (Hayden Fry)
Washington	Holiday 12-30-96	Colorado 21-33 (Rick Neuheisel)

Coach/School	Bowl/Date	Opponent/Score (Coach)
Washington	Aloha 12-25-97	Michigan St. 51-23 (Nick Saban)
Washington	Oahu Classic 12-25-98	Air Force 25-45 (Fisher DeBerry)
MAXIE LAMBRIGHT, 1-1-0 (Southern Miss. '49) Born 6-3-24		
Louisiana Tech	Independence 12-17-77	Louisville 24-14 (Vince Gibson)
Louisiana Tech	Independence 12-16-78	East Caro. 13-35 (Pat Dye)
FRANK LAUTERBUR, 2-0-0 (Mount Union '49) Born 8-8-25		
Toledo	Tangerine 12-26-69	Davidson 56-33 (Homer Smith)
Toledo	Tangerine 12-28-70	William & Mary 40-12 (Lou Holtz)
MIKE LEACH, 4-3-0 (BYU '83) Born 3-9-61		
Texas Tech	Galleryfurniture.com 12-27-00	East Caro. 27-40 (Steve Logan)
Texas Tech	Alamo 12-29-01	Iowa 16-19 (Kirk Ferentz)
Texas Tech	Tangerine 12-23-02	Clemson 55-15 (Tommy Bowden)
Texas Tech	Houston 12-30-03	Navy 38-14 (Paul Johnson)
Texas Tech	Holiday 12-30-04	California 45-31 (Jeff Tedford)
Texas Tech	Cotton 1-2-06	Alabama 10-13 (Mike Shula)
Texas Tech	Insight 12-29-06	Minnesota 44-41 (ot) (Glen Mason)
FRANK LEAHY, 1-1-0 (Notre Dame '31) Born 8-27-08		
Boston College	Cotton 1-1-40	Clemson 3-6 (Jess Neely)
Boston College	Sugar 1-1-41	Tennessee 19-13 (Bob Neyland)
JIM LEAVITT, 1-1-0 (Missouri '78) Born 12-5-56		
South Fla.	Meineke Car Care 12-31-05	North Carolina St. 0-14 (Chuck Amato)
South Fla.	Papajohns.com 12-23-06	East Caro. 24-7 (Skip Holtz)
CLYDE LEE, 1-0-0 [Centenary (La.) '32] Born 2-11-08		
Houston	Salad 1-1-52	Dayton 26-21 (Joe Gavin)
ART LEWIS, 0-1-0 (Ohio '36) Born 2-18-11		
West Virginia	Sugar 1-1-54	Georgia Tech 19-42 (Bobby Dodd)
BILL LEWIS, 1-0-0 (East Stroudsburg '63) Born 8-5-41		
East Caro.	Peach 1-1-92	North Carolina St. 37-34 (Dick Sheridan)
LOU LITTLE, 1-0-0 (Penn '20) Born 12-6-1893		
Columbia	Rose 1-1-34	Stanford 7-0 (Claude "Tiny" Thornhill)
STEVE LOGAN, 2-3-0 (Tulsa '75) Born 2-3-53		
East Caro.	Liberty 12-31-94	Illinois 0-30 (Lou Tepper)
East Caro.	Liberty 12-30-95	Stanford 19-13 (Tyrone Willingham)
East Caro.	Mobile Alabama 12-22-99	TCU 14-28 (Dennis Franchione)
East Caro.	Galleryfurniture.com 12-27-00	Texas Tech 40-27 (Mike Leach)
East Caro.	GMAC 12-19-01	Marshall 61-64 (2 ot) (Bob Pruett)
ROCKY LONG, 0-4-0 (New Mexico '74) Born 1-27-50		
New Mexico	Las Vegas 12-25-02	UCLA 13-27 (Ed Kezirian)
New Mexico	Las Vegas 12-24-03	Oregon St. 14-55 (Mike Riley)
New Mexico	Emerald 12-30-04	Navy 19-34 (Paul Johnson)
New Mexico	New Mexico 12-23-06	San Jose St. 12-20 (Dick Tomey)
JIM LOOKABAUGH, 2-1-0 (Oklahoma St. '25) Born 6-15-02		
Oklahoma St.	Cotton 1-1-45	TCU 34-0 (Leo "Dutch" Meyer)
Oklahoma St.	Sugar 1-1-46	St. Mary's (Cal.) 33-13 (Jimmy Phelan)
Oklahoma St.	Delta 1-1-49	William & Mary 0-20 (Rube McCray)
SONNY LUBICK, 3-6-0 (Western Mont. '60) Born 3-12-37		
Colorado St.	Holiday 12-30-94	Michigan 14-24 (Gary Moeller)
Colorado St.	Holiday 12-29-95	Kansas St. 21-54 (Bill Snyder)
Colorado St.	Holiday 12-29-97	Missouri 35-24 (Larry Smith)
Colorado St.	Liberty 12-31-99	Southern Miss. 17-23 (Jeff Bower)
Colorado St.	Liberty 12-29-00	Louisville 22-17 (John L. Smith)
Colorado St.	New Orleans 12-18-01	North Texas 45-20 (Darrell Dickey)
Colorado St.	Liberty 12-31-02	TCU 3-17 (Gary Patterson)
Colorado St.	San Francisco 12-31-03	Boston College 21-35 (Tom O'Brien)
Colorado St.	Poinsettia 12-22-05	Navy 30-51 (Paul Johnson)
AL LUGINBILL, 0-1-0 (Cal Poly Pomona '67) Born 11-3-46		
San Diego St.	Freedom 12-30-91	Tulsa 17-28 (Dave Rader)
BILL LYNCH, 0-1-0 (Butler '77) Born 6-12-54		
Ball St.	Las Vegas 12-19-96	Nevada 15-18 (Jeff Tisdel)
GEORGE MacINTYRE, 0-1-0 [Miami (Fla.) '61] Born 4-30-39		
Vanderbilt	Hall of Fame 12-31-82	Air Force 28-36 (Ken Hatfield)
JOHN MACKOVIC, 2-5-0 (Wake Forest '65) Born 10-1-43		
Wake Forest	Tangerine 12-22-79	LSU 10-34 (Charlie McClendon)
Illinois	All-American 12-29-88	Florida 10-14 (Galen Hall)
Illinois	Fla. Citrus 1-1-90	Virginia 31-21 (George Welsh)
Illinois	Hall of Fame 1-1-91	Clemson 0-30 (Ken Hatfield)
Texas	Sun 12-30-94	North Carolina 35-31 (Mack Brown)
Texas	Sugar 12-31-95	Virginia Tech 10-28 (Frank Beamer)
Texas	Fiesta 1-1-97	Penn St. 15-38 (Joe Paterno)
DICK MacPHERSON, 3-1-1 (Springfield '58) Born 11-4-30		
Syracuse	Cherry 12-21-85	Maryland 18-35 (Bobby Ross)
Syracuse	Sugar 1-1-88	Auburn 16-16 (Pat Dye)
Syracuse	Hall of Fame 1-2-89	LSU 23-10 (Mike Archer)
Syracuse	Peach 12-30-89	Georgia 19-18 (Ray Goff)
Syracuse	Aloha 12-25-90	Arizona 28-0 (Dick Tomey)
EDWARD "SLIP" MADIGAN, 1-0-0 (Notre Dame '20) Born 11-18-1895		
St. Mary's (Cal.)	Cotton 1-2-39	Texas Tech 20-13 (Pete Cawthon)

Coach/School	Bowl/Date	Opponent/Score (Coach)
JOHNNY MAJORS, 9-7-0 (Tennessee '57) Born 5-21-35		
Iowa St.	Sun 12-18-71	LSU 15-33 (Charlie McClendon)
Iowa St.	Liberty 12-18-72	Georgia Tech 30-31 (Bill Fulcher)
Pittsburgh	Fiesta 12-21-73	Arizona St. 7-28 (Frank Kush)
Pittsburgh	Sun 12-26-75	Kansas 33-19 (Bud Moore)
Pittsburgh	Sugar 1-1-77	Georgia 27-3 (Vince Dooley)
Tennessee	Bluebonnet 12-31-79	Purdue 22-27 (Jim Young)
Tennessee	Garden State 12-13-81	Wisconsin 28-21 (Dave McClain)
Tennessee	Peach 12-31-82	Iowa 22-28 (Hayden Fry)
Tennessee	Fla. Citrus 12-17-83	Maryland 30-23 (Bobby Ross)
Tennessee	Sun 12-24-84	Maryland 27-28 (Bobby Ross)
Tennessee	Sugar 1-1-86	Miami (Fla.) 35-7 (Jimmy Johnson)
Tennessee	Liberty 12-29-86	Minnesota 21-14 (John Gutekunst)
Tennessee	Peach 1-2-88	Indiana 27-22 (Bill Mallory)
Tennessee	Cotton 1-1-90	Arkansas 31-27 (Ken Hatfield)
Tennessee	Sugar 1-1-91	Virginia 23-22 (George Welsh)
Tennessee	Fiesta 1-1-92	Penn St. 17-42 (Joe Paterno)
BILL MALLORY, 4-6-0 [Miami (Ohio) '57] Born 5-30-35		
Miami (Ohio)	Tangerine 12-22-73	Florida 16-7 (Doug Dickey)
Colorado	Bluebonnet 12-27-75	Texas 21-38 (Darrell Royal)
Colorado	Orange 1-1-77	Ohio St. 10-27 (Woody Hayes)
Northern Ill.	California 12-17-83	Cal St. Fullerton 20-13 (Gene Murphy)
Indiana	All-American 12-31-86	Florida St. 13-27 (Bobby Bowden)
Indiana	Peach 1-2-88	Tennessee 22-27 (Johnny Majors)
Indiana	Liberty 12-28-88	South Carolina 34-10 (Joe Morrison)
Indiana	Peach 12-29-90	Auburn 23-27 (Pat Dye)
Indiana	Copper 12-31-91	Baylor 24-0 (Grant Teaff)
Indiana	Independence 12-31-93	Virginia Tech 20-45 (Frank Beamer)
FRANK MALONEY, 1-0-0 (Michigan '62) Born 9-26-40		
Syracuse	Independence 12-15-79	McNeese St. 31-7 (Ernie Duplechin)
MARK MANGINO, 1-1-0 (Youngstown St. '86) Born 8-26-56		
Kansas	Tangerine 12-22-03	North Carolina St. 26-56 (Chuck Amato)
Kansas	Fort Worth 12-23-05	Houston 42-13 (Art Briles)
BOB MARGARITA, 0-1-0 (Brown '44) Born 11-3-20		
Georgetown	Sun 1-2-50	UTEP 20-33 (Jack "Cactus Jack" Curtice)
STEVE MARIUCCI, 0-1-0 (Northern Mich. '77) Born 11-4-55		
California	Aloha 12-25-96	Navy 38-42 (Charlie Weatherbie)
ABE MARTIN, 1-3-1 (TCU '32) Born 10-8-08		
TCU	Cotton 1-2-56	Mississippi 13-14 (John Vaught)
TCU	Cotton 1-1-57	Syracuse 28-27 (Ben Schwartzwalder)
TCU	Cotton 1-1-59	Air Force 0-0 (Ben Martin)
TCU	Bluebonnet 12-19-59	Clemson 7-23 (Frank Howard)
TCU	Sun 12-31-65	UTEP 12-13 (Bobby Dobbs)
BEN MARTIN, 0-2-1 (Navy '46) Born 6-28-21		
Air Force	Cotton 1-1-59	TCU 0-0 (Abe Martin)
Air Force	Gator 12-28-63	North Carolina 0-35 (Jim Hickey)
Air Force	Sugar 1-1-71	Tennessee 13-34 (Bill Battle)
GLEN MASON, 5-3-0 (Ohio St. '72) Born 4-9-50		
Kansas	Aloha 12-25-92	BYU 23-20 (LaVell Edwards)
Kansas	Aloha 12-25-95	UCLA 51-30 (Terry Donahue)
Minnesota	Sun 12-31-99	Oregon 20-24 (Mike Bellotti)
Minnesota	Music City 12-30-02	Arkansas 29-14 (Houston Nutt)
Minnesota	Sun 12-31-03	Oregon 31-30 (Mike Bellotti)
Minnesota	Music City 12-31-04	Alabama 20-16 (Mike Shula)
Minnesota	Music City 12-30-05	Virginia 31-34 (Al Groh)
Minnesota	Insight 12-29-06	Texas Tech 41-44 (ot) (Mike Leach)
TONY MASON, 0-1-0 (Clarion '50) Born 3-2-30		
Arizona	Fiesta 12-25-79	Pittsburgh 10-16 (Jackie Sherrill)
RON McBRIDE, 3-3-0 (San Jose St. '63) Born 10-14-39		
Utah	Copper 12-29-92	Washington St. 28-31 (Mike Price)
Utah	Freedom 12-30-93	Southern California 21-28 (John Robinson)
Utah	Freedom 12-27-94	Arizona 16-13 (Dick Tomey)
Utah	Copper 12-27-96	Wisconsin 10-38 (Barry Alvarez)
Utah	Las Vegas 12-18-99	Fresno St. 17-16 (Pat Hill)
Utah	Las Vegas 12-25-01	Southern California 10-6 (Pete Carroll)
TOM McCANN, 0-1-0 (Illinois '24) Born 11-7-1898		
Miami (Fla.)	Orange 1-1-35	Bucknell 0-26 (Edward "Hook" Mylin)
DAN McCARNEY, 2-3-0 (Iowa '75) Born 7–28-53		
Iowa St.	Insight.com 12-28-00	Pittsburgh 37-29 (Walt Harris)
Iowa St.	Independence 12-27-01	Alabama 13-14 (Dennis Franchione)
Iowa St.	Humanitarian 12-31-02	Boise St. 16-34 (Dan Hawkins)
Iowa St.	Independence 12-28-04	Miami (Ohio) 17-13 (Terry Hoeppner)
Iowa St.	Houston 12-31-05	TCU 24-27 (Gary Patterson)
BILL McCARTNEY, 3-6-0 (Missouri '62) Born 8-22-40		
Colorado	Freedom 12-30-85	Washington 17-20 (Don James)
Colorado	Bluebonnet 12-31-86	Baylor 9-21 (Grant Teaff)
Colorado	Freedom 12-29-88	BYU 17-20 (LaVell Edwards)
Colorado	Orange 1-1-90	Notre Dame 6-21 (Lou Holtz)
Colorado	Orange 1-1-91	Notre Dame 10-9 (Lou Holtz)
Colorado	Blockbuster 12-28-91	Alabama 25-30 (Gene Stallings)
Colorado	Fiesta 1-1-93	Syracuse 22-26 (Paul Pasqualoni)
Colorado	Aloha 12-25-93	Fresno St. 41-30 (Jim Sweeney)
Colorado	Fiesta 1-2-95	Notre Dame 41-24 (Lou Holtz)

Coach/School	Bowl/Date	Opponent/Score (Coach)
DAVE McCLAIN, 1-2-0 (Bowling Green '60) Born 1-28-38		
Wisconsin	Garden State 12-13-81	Tennessee 21-28 (Johnny Majors)
Wisconsin	Independence 12-11-82	Kansas St. 14-3 (Jim Dickey)
Wisconsin	Hall of Fame 12-29-84	Kentucky 19-20 (Jerry Claiborne)
CHARLIE McCLENDON, 7-6-0 (Kentucky '50) Born 10-17-22		
LSU	Cotton 1-1-63	Texas 13-0 (Darrell Royal)
LSU	Bluebonnet 12-21-63	Baylor 7-14 (John Bridgers)
LSU	Sugar 1-1-65	Syracuse 13-10 (Ben Schwartzwalder)
LSU	Cotton 1-1-66	Arkansas 14-7 (Frank Broyles)
LSU	Sugar 1-1-68	Wyoming 20-13 (Lloyd Eaton)
LSU	Peach 12-30-68	Florida St. 31-27 (Bill Peterson)
LSU	Orange 1-1-71	Nebraska 12-17 (Bob Devaney)
LSU	Sun 12-18-71	Iowa St. 33-15 (Johnny Majors)
LSU	Bluebonnet 12-30-72	Tennessee 17-24 (Bill Battle)
LSU	Orange 1-1-74	Penn St. 9-16 (Joe Paterno)
LSU	Sun 12-31-77	Stanford 14-24 (Bill Walsh)
LSU	Liberty 12-23-78	Missouri 15-20 (Warren Powers)
LSU	Tangerine 12-22-79	Wake Forest 34-10 (John Mackovic)
RUBE McCRAY, 1-1-0 (Ky. Wesleyan '30) Born 6-13-05		
William & Mary	Dixie 1-1-48	Arkansas 19-21 (John Barnhill)
William & Mary	Delta 1-1-49	Oklahoma St. 20-0 (Jim Lookabaugh)
J.F. "POP" McKALE, 0-1-0 (Albion '10) Born 6-12-1887		
Arizona	San Diego East-West Christmas Classic 12-26-21	Centre 0-38 (Charley Moran)
JOHN McKAY, 6-3-0 (Oregon St. '50) Born 7-5-23		
Southern California	Rose 1-2-63	Wisconsin 42-37 (Milt Bruhn)
Southern California	Rose 1-2-67	Purdue 13-14 (Jack Mollenkopf)
Southern California	Rose 1-1-68	Indiana 14-3 (John Pont)
Southern California	Rose 1-1-69	Ohio St. 16-27 (Woody Hayes)
Southern California	Rose 1-1-70	Michigan 10-3 (Glenn "Bo" Schembechler)
Southern California	Rose 1-1-73	Ohio St. 42-17 (Woody Hayes)
Southern California	Rose 1-1-74	Ohio St. 21-42 (Woody Hayes)
Southern California	Rose 1-1-75	Ohio St. 18-17 (Woody Hayes)
Southern California	Liberty 12-22-75	Texas A&M 20-0 (Emory Bellard)
ALLYN McKEEN, 1-0-0 (Tennessee '29) Born 1-26-05		
Mississippi St.	Orange 1-1-41	Georgetown 14-7 (Jack Hagerty)
JOHNNIE McMILLAN, 0-1-0 (South Carolina '41) Born 1-27-19		
South Carolina	Gator 1-1-46	Wake Forest 14-26 (D.C. "Peahead" Walker)
MAC McWHORTER, 1-0-0 (Georgia '73) Born 6-17-50		
Georgia Tech	Seattle 12-27-01	Stanford 24-14 (Tyrone Willingham)
DAVID McWILLIAMS, 1-1-0 (Texas '64) Born 4-18-42		
Texas	Bluebonnet 12-31-87	Pittsburgh 32-27 (Mike Gottfried)
Texas	Cotton 1-1-91	Miami (Fla.) 3-46 (Dennis Erickson)
JACK MEAGHER, 1-0-1 (Notre Dame '17) Born 7-4-1894		
Auburn	Bacardi, Cuba 1-1-37	Villanova 7-7 (Maurice "Clipper" Smith)
Auburn	Orange 1-1-38	Michigan St. 6-0 (Charlie Bachman)
RANDOLPH R.M. MEDLEY, 2-0-0 (Mo. Wesleyan '21) Born 9-22-1898		
Southwestern (Tex.)	Sun 1-1-44	New Mexico 7-0 (Willis Barnes)
Southwestern (Tex.)	Sun 1-1-45	U. of Mexico 35-0 (Bernard A. Hoban)
BRONCO MENDENHALL, 1-1-0 (Oregon St. '88) Born 2-21-66		
BYU	Las Vegas 12-22-05	California 28-35 (Jeff Tedford)
BYU	Las Vegas 12-21-06	Oregon 38-8 (Mike Bellotti)
LEO "DUTCH" MEYER, 3-4-0 (TCU '22) Born 1-15-1898		
TCU	Sugar 1-1-36	LSU 3-2 (Bernie Moore)
TCU	Cotton 1-1-37	Marquette 16-6 (Frank Murray)
TCU	Sugar 1-2-39	Carnegie Mellon 15-7 (Bill Kern)
TCU	Orange 1-1-42	Georgia 26-40 (Wally Butts)
TCU	Cotton 1-1-45	Oklahoma St. 0-34 (Jim Lookabaugh)
TCU	Delta 1-1-48	Mississippi 9-13 (John Vaught)
TCU	Cotton 1-1-52	Kentucky 7-20 (Paul "Bear" Bryant)
RON MEYER, 0-1-0 (Purdue '63) Born 2-17-41		
SMU	Holiday 12-19-80	BYU 45-46 (LaVell Edwards)
URBAN MEYER, 4-0-0 (Cincinnati '86) Born 7-10-64		
Utah	Liberty 12-31-03	Southern Miss. 17-0 (Jeff Bower)
Utah	Fiesta 1-1-05	Pittsburgh 35-7 (Walt Harris)
Florida	Outback 1-2-06	Iowa 31-24 (Kirk Ferentz)
Florida	BCS Championship 1-8-07	Ohio St. 41-14 (Jim Tressel)
JOHN MICHELOSEN, 0-2-0 (Pittsburgh '38) Born 2-13-16		
Pittsburgh	Sugar 1-2-56	Georgia Tech 0-7 (Bobby Dodd)
Pittsburgh	Gator 12-29-56	Georgia Tech 14-21 (Bobby Dodd)
LES MILES, 3-2-0 (Michigan '76) Born 11-10-53		
Oklahoma St.	Houston 12-27-02	Southern Miss. 33-23 (Jeff Bower)
Oklahoma St.	Cotton 1-2-04	Mississippi 28-31 (David Cutcliffe)
Oklahoma St.	Alamo 12-29-04	Ohio St. 7-33 (Jim Tressel)
LSU	Peach 12-30-05	Miami (Fla.) 40-3 (Larry Coker)
LSU	Sugar 1-3-07	Notre Dame 41-14 (Charlie Weis)

Coach/School	Bowl/Date	Opponent/Score (Coach)
RICK MINTER, 1-3-0 (Henderson St. '77) Born 10-4-54		
Cincinnati	Humanitarian 12-29-97	Utah St. 35-19 (John L. Smith)
Cincinnati	Motor City 12-27-00	Marshall 14-25 (Bob Pruett)
Cincinnati	Motor City 12-29-01	Toledo 16-23 (Tom Anstutz)
Cincinnati	New Orleans 12-17-02	North Texas 19-24 (Darrell Dickey)
JACK MITCHELL, 1-0-0 (Oklahoma '49) Born 12-3-24		
Kansas	Bluebonnet 12-16-61	Rice 33-7 (Jess Neely)
ODUS MITCHELL, 0-2-0 (West Tex. A&M '25) Born 6-29-1899		
North Texas	Salad 1-1-48	Nevada 6-13 (Joe Sheeketski)
North Texas	Sun 12-31-59	New Mexico St. 8-28 (Warren Woodson)
GARY MOELLER, 4-1-0 (Ohio St. '63) Born 1-26-41		
Michigan	Gator 1-1-91	Mississippi 35-3 (Billy Brewer)
Michigan	Rose 1-1-92	Washington 14-34 (Don James)
Michigan	Rose 1-1-93	Washington 38-31 (Don James)
Michigan	Hall of Fame 1-1-94	North Carolina St. 42-7 (Mike O'Cain)
Michigan	Holiday 12-30-94	Colorado St. 24-14 (Sonny Lubick)
AL MOLDE, 0-1-0 (Gust. Adolphus '66) Born 11-15-43		
Western Mich.	California 12-10-88	Fresno St. 30-35 (Jim Sweeney)
JACK MOLLENKOPF, 1-0-0 (Bowling Green '31) Born 11-24-05		
Purdue	Rose 1-2-67	Southern California 14-13 (John McKay)
BERNIE MOORE, 1-3-1 (Carson-Newman '17) Born 4-30-1895		
LSU	Sugar 1-1-36	TCU 2-3 (Leo "Dutch" Meyer)
LSU	Sugar 1-1-37	Santa Clara 14-21 (Lawrence "Buck" Shaw)
LSU	Sugar 1-1-38	Santa Clara 0-6 (Lawrence "Buck" Shaw)
LSU	Orange 1-1-44	Texas A&M 19-14 (Homer Norton)
LSU	Cotton 1-1-47	Arkansas 0-0 (John Barnhill)
BUD MOORE, 0-1-0 (Alabama '61) Born 10-16-39		
Kansas	Sun 12-26-75	Pittsburgh 19-33 (Johnny Majors)
CHARLEY MORAN, 2-1-0 (Tennessee '98) Born 2-22-1878		
Centre	Fort Worth Classic 1-1-21	TCU 63-7 (Bill Driver)
Centre	San Diego East-West Christmas Classic 12-26-21	Arizona 38-0 (J.F. "Pop" McKale)
Centre	Dixie Classic 1-2-22	Texas A&M 14-22 (Dana Bible)
DELL MORGAN, 0-3-0 (Austin '25) Born 2-14-02		
Texas Tech	Sun 1-1-42	Tulsa 0-6 (Henry Frnka)
Texas Tech	Sun 1-1-48	Miami (Ohio) 12-13 (Sid Gillman)
Texas Tech	Raisin 12-31-49	San Jose St. 13-20 (Bill Hubbard)
JOE MORRISON, 0-3-0 (Cincinnati '59) Born 8-21-37		
South Carolina	Gator 12-28-84	Oklahoma St. 14-21 (Pat Jones)
South Carolina	Gator 12-31-87	LSU 13-30 (Mike Archer)
South Carolina	Liberty 12-28-88	Indiana 10-34 (Bill Mallory)
RAY MORRISON, 0-1-0 (Vanderbilt '12) Born 2-28-1885		
SMU	Dixie Classic 1-1-25	West Va. Wesleyan 7-9 (Bob Higgins)
DARRELL MUDRA, 0-1-0 (Peru St. '51) Born 1-4-29		
Arizona	Sun 12-28-68	Auburn 10-34 (Ralph "Shug" Jordan)
HAL MUMME, 0-2-0 (Tarleton St. '75) Born 3-29-52		
Kentucky	Outback 1-1-99	Penn St. 14-26 (Joe Paterno)
Kentucky	Music City 12-29-99	Syracuse 13-20 (Paul Pasqualoni)
CLARENCE "BIGGIE" MUNN, 1-0-0 (Minnesota '32) Born 9-11-08		
Michigan St.	Rose 1-1-54	UCLA 28-20 (Henry "Red" Sanders)
BILLY MURPHY, 1-0-0 (Mississippi St. '47) Born 1-13-21		
Memphis	Pasadena 12-18-71	San Jose St. 28-9 (Dewey King)
GENE MURPHY, 0-1-0 (North Dakota '62) Born 8-6-39		
Cal St. Fullerton	California 12-17-83	Northern Ill. 13-20 (Bill Mallory)
JACK MURPHY, 1-0-0 (Heidelberg '54) Born 8-6-32		
Toledo	Tangerine 12-28-71	Richmond 28-3 (Frank Jones)
BILL MURRAY, 2-1-0 (Duke '31) Born 9-9-08		
Duke	Orange 1-1-55	Nebraska 34-7 (Bill Glassford)
Duke	Orange 1-1-58	Oklahoma 21-48 (Bud Wilkinson)
Duke	Cotton 1-2-61	Arkansas 7-6 (Frank Broyles)
FRANK MURRAY, 0-1-0 (Tufts '08) Born 2-12-85		
Marquette	Cotton 1-1-37	TCU 6-16 (Leo "Dutch" Meyer)
DENNY MYERS, 0-1-0 (Iowa '30) Born 11-10-05		
Boston College	Orange 1-1-43	Alabama 21-37 (Frank Thomas)
EDWARD "HOOK" MYLIN, 1-0-0 (Frank. & Marsh.) Born 10-23-1897		
Bucknell	Orange 1-1-35	Miami (Fla.) 26-0 (Tom McCann)
RAY NAGEL, 1-0-0 (UCLA '50) Born 5-18-27		
Utah	Liberty 12-19-64	West Virginia 32-6 (Gene Corum)
LARRY NAVIAUX, 0-1-0 (Nebraska '59) Born 12-17-36		
Boston U.	Pasadena 12-6-69	San Diego St. 7-28 (Don Coryell)
EARLE "GREASY" NEALE, 0-0-1 (West Va. Wesleyan '14) Born 11-5-1891		
Wash. & Jeff.	Rose 1-2-22	California 0-0 (Andy Smith)

Coach/School	Bowl/Date	Opponent/Score (Coach)
JESS NEELY, 4-3-0 (Vanderbilt '23) Born 1-4-1898		
Clemson	Cotton 1-1-40	Boston College 6-3 (Frank Leahy)
Rice	Orange 1-1-47	Tennessee 8-0 (Bob Neyland)
Rice	Cotton 1-2-50	North Carolina 27-13 (Carl Snavely)
Rice	Cotton 1-1-54	Alabama 28-6 (Harold "Red" Drew)
Rice	Cotton 1-1-58	Navy 7-20 (Eddie Erdelatz)
Rice	Sugar 1-2-61	Mississippi 6-14 (John Vaught)
Rice	Bluebonnet 12-16-61	Kansas 7-33 (Jack Mitchell)
DON NEHLEN, 4-9-0 (Bowling Green '58) Born 1-1-36		
West Virginia	Peach 12-31-81	Florida 26-6 (Charley Pell)
West Virginia	Gator 12-30-82	Florida St. 12-31 (Bobby Bowden)
West Virginia	Hall of Fame 12-22-83	Kentucky 20-16 (Jerry Claiborne)
West Virginia	Bluebonnet 12-31-84	TCU 31-14 (Jim Wacker)
West Virginia	Sun 12-25-87	Oklahoma St. 33-35 (Pat Jones)
West Virginia	Fiesta 1-2-89	Notre Dame 21-34 (Lou Holtz)
West Virginia	Gator 12-30-89	Clemson 7-27 (Danny Ford)
West Virginia	Sugar 1-1-94	Florida 7-41 (Steve Spurrier)
West Virginia	Carquest 1-2-95	South Carolina 21-24 (Brad Scott)
West Virginia	Gator 1-1-97	North Carolina 13-20 (Mack Brown)
West Virginia	Carquest 12-29-97	Georgia Tech 30-35 (George O'Leary)
West Virginia	Insight.com 12-26-98	Missouri 31-34 (Larry Smith)
West Virginia	Music City 12-28-00	Mississippi 49-38 (David Cutcliffe)
RICK NEUHEISEL, 4-3-0 (UCLA '84) Born 2-7-61		
Colorado	Cotton 1-1-96	Oregon 38-6 (Mike Bellotti)
Colorado	Holiday 12-30-96	Washington 33-21 (Jim Lambright)
Colorado	Aloha Classic 12-25-98	Oregon 51-43 (Mike Bellotti)
Washington	Holiday 12-29-99	Kansas St. 20-24 (Bill Snyder)
Washington	Rose 1-1-01	Purdue 34-24 (Joe Tiller)
Washington	Holiday 12-28-01	Texas 43-47 (Mack Brown)
Washington	Sun 12-31-02	Purdue 24-34 (Joe Tiller)
BOB NEYLAND, 2-5-0 (Army '16) Born 2-17-1892		
Tennessee	Orange 1-2-39	Oklahoma 17-0 (Tom Stidham)
Tennessee	Rose 1-1-40	Southern California 0-14 (Howard Jones)
Tennessee	Sugar 1-1-41	Boston College 13-19 (Frank Leahy)
Tennessee	Orange 1-1-47	Rice 0-8 (Jess Neely)
Tennessee	Cotton 1-1-51	Texas 20-14 (Blair Cherry)
Tennessee	Sugar 1-1-52	Maryland 13-28 (Jim Tatum)
Tennessee	Cotton 1-1-53	Texas 0-16 (Ed Price)
RAY NOLTING, 1-0-0 (Cincinnati '36) Born 11-8-13		
Cincinnati	Sun 1-1-47	Virginia Tech 18-6 (Jimmy Kitts)
HOMER NORTON, 2-2-1 (Birmingham So. '16) Born 12-30-1896		
Centenary (La.)	Dixie Classic 1-1-34	Arkansas 7-7 (Fred Thomsen)
Texas A&M	Sugar 1-1-40	Tulane 14-13 (Lowell "Red" Dawson)
Texas A&M	Cotton 1-1-41	Fordham 13-12 (Jim Crowley)
Texas A&M	Cotton 1-1-42	Alabama 21-29 (Frank Thomas)
Texas A&M	Orange 1-1-44	LSU 14-19 (Bernie Moore)
JOE NOVAK, 1-1-0 [Miami (Ohio) '67] Born 4-19-45		
Northern Ill.	Silicon Valley 12-30-04	Troy 34-21 (Larry Blakeney)
Northern Ill.	Poinsettia 12-19-06	TCU 7-37 (Gary Patterson)
TOM NUGENT, 0-2-0 (Ithaca '36) Born 2-24-16		
Florida St.	Sun 1-1-55	UTEP 20-47 (Mike Brumbelow)
Florida St.	Bluegrass 12-13-58	Oklahoma St. 6-15 (Cliff Speegle)
HOUSTON NUTT, 2-5-0 (Oklahoma St. '81) Born 10-14-57		
Arkansas	Fla. Citrus 1-1-99	Michigan 31-45 (Lloyd Carr)
Arkansas	Cotton 1-1-00	Texas 27-6 (Mack Brown)
Arkansas	Las Vegas 12-21-00	UNLV 14-31 (John Robinson)
Arkansas	Cotton 1-1-02	Oklahoma 3-10 (Bob Stoops)
Arkansas	Music City 12-30-02	Minnesota 14-29 (Glen Mason)
Arkansas	Independence 12-31-03	Missouri 27-14 (Gary Pinkel)
Arkansas	Capital One 1-1-07	Wisconsin 14-17 (Brett Bielema)
TOM O'BRIEN, 6-1-0 (Navy '71) Born 10-5-48		
Boston College	Insight.com 12-31-99	Colorado 28-62 (Gary Barnett)
Boston College	Aloha Classic 12-25-00	Arizona St. 31-17 (Bruce Snyder)
Boston College	Music City 12-28-01	Georgia 20-16 (Mark Richt)
Boston College	Motor City 12-26-02	Toledo 51-25 (Tom Anstutz)
Boston College	San Francisco 12-31-03	Colorado St. 35-21 (Sonny Lubick)
Boston College	Continental Tire 12-30-04	North Carolina 37-24 (John Bunting)
Boston College	MPC Computers 12-28-05	Boise St. 27-21 (Dan Hawkins)
MIKE O'CAIN, 1-2-0 (Clemson '77) Born 7-20-54		
North Carolina St.	Hall of Fame 1-1-94	Michigan 7-42 (Gary Moeller)
North Carolina St.	Peach 1-1-95	Mississippi St. 28-24 (Jackie Sherrill)
North Carolina St.	Micron PC 12-29-98	Miami (Fla.) 23-46 (Butch Davis)
GEORGE O'LEARY, 2-3-0 (New Hampshire '68) Born 8-17-46		
Georgia Tech	Carquest 12-29-97	West Virginia 35-30 (Don Nehlen)
Georgia Tech	Gator 1-1-99	Notre Dame 35-28 (Bob Davie)
Georgia Tech	Gator 1-1-00	Miami (Fla.) 13-28 (Butch Davis)
Georgia Tech	Peach 12-29-00	LSU 14-28 (Nick Saban)
UCF	Hawaii 12-24-05	Nevada 48-49 (ot) (Chris Ault)
BERNARD "BUNNIE" OAKES, 0-1-0 (Illinois '24) Born 9-15-1898		
Colorado	Cotton 1-1-38	Rice 14-28 (Jimmy Kitts)
JORDAN OLIVAR, 1-1-0 (Villanova '38) Born 1-30-15		
Villanova	Great Lakes 12-6-47	Kentucky 14-24 (Paul "Bear" Bryant)
Villanova	Harbor 1-1-49	Nevada 27-7 (Joe Sheeketski)

Coach/School	Bowl/Date	Opponent/Score (Coach)
AL ONOFRIO, 1-1-0 (Arizona St. '43) Born 3-15-21		
Missouri	Fiesta 12-23-72	Arizona St. 35-49 (Frank Kush)
Missouri	Sun 12-29-73	Auburn 34-17 (Ralph "Shug" Jordan)
BENNIE OOSTERBAAN, 1-0-0 (Michigan '28) Born 2-24-06		
Michigan	Rose 1-1-51	California 14-6 (Lynn "Pappy" Waldorf)
TOM OSBORNE, 12-13-0 (Hastings '59) Born 2-23-37		
Nebraska	Cotton 1-1-74	Texas 19-3 (Darrell Royal)
Nebraska	Sugar 12-31-74	Florida 13-10 (Doug Dickey)
Nebraska	Fiesta 12-26-75	Arizona St. 14-17 (Frank Kush)
Nebraska	Bluebonnet 12-31-76	Texas Tech 27-24 (Steve Sloan)
Nebraska	Liberty 12-19-77	North Carolina 21-17 (Bill Dooley)
Nebraska	Orange 1-1-79	Oklahoma 24-31 (Barry Switzer)
Nebraska	Cotton 1-1-80	Houston 14-17 (Bill Yeoman)
Nebraska	Sun 12-27-80	Mississippi St. 31-17 (Emory Bellard)
Nebraska	Orange 1-1-82	Clemson 15-22 (Danny Ford)
Nebraska	Orange 1-1-83	LSU 21-20 (Jerry Stovall)
Nebraska	Orange 1-2-84	Miami (Fla.) 30-31 (Howard Schnellenberger)
Nebraska	Sugar 1-1-85	LSU 28-10 (Bill Arnsparger)
Nebraska	Fiesta 1-1-86	Michigan 23-27 (Glenn "Bo" Schembechler)
Nebraska	Sugar 1-1-87	LSU 30-15 (Bill Arnsparger)
Nebraska	Fiesta 1-1-88	Florida St. 28-31 (Bobby Bowden)
Nebraska	Orange 1-2-89	Miami (Fla.) 3-23 (Jimmy Johnson)
Nebraska	Fiesta 1-1-90	Florida St. 17-41 (Bobby Bowden)
Nebraska	Fla. Citrus 1-1-91	Georgia Tech 21-45 (Bobby Ross)
Nebraska	Orange 1-1-92	Miami (Fla.) 0-22 (Dennis Erickson)
Nebraska	Orange 1-1-93	Florida St. 14-27 (Bobby Bowden)
Nebraska	Orange 1-1-94	Florida St. 16-18 (Bobby Bowden)
Nebraska	Orange 1-1-95	Miami (Fla.) 24-17 (Dennis Erickson)
Nebraska	Fiesta 1-2-96	Florida 62-24 (Steve Spurrier)
Nebraska	Orange 12-31-96	Virginia Tech 41-21 (Frank Beamer)
Nebraska	Orange 1-2-98	Tennessee 42-17 (Phillip Fulmer)
JIM OWENS, 2-1-0 (Oklahoma '50) Born 3-6-27		
Washington	Rose 1-1-60	Wisconsin 44-8 (Milt Bruhn)
Washington	Rose 1-2-61	Minnesota 17-7 (Murray Warmath)
Washington	Rose 1-1-64	Illinois 7-17 (Pete Elliott)
JACK PARDEE, 0-1-0 (Texas A&M '57) Born 4-9-36		
Houston	Aloha 12-25-88	Washington St. 22-24 (Dennis Erickson)
ARA PARSEGHIAN, 3-2-0 [Miami (Ohio) '49] Born 5-21-23		
Notre Dame	Cotton 1-1-70	Texas 17-21 (Darrell Royal)
Notre Dame	Cotton 1-1-71	Texas 24-11 (Darrell Royal)
Notre Dame	Orange 1-1-73	Nebraska 6-40 (Bob Devaney)
Notre Dame	Sugar 12-31-73	Alabama 24-23 (Paul "Bear" Bryant)
Notre Dame	Orange 1-1-75	Alabama 13-11 (Paul "Bear" Bryant)
PAUL PASQUALONI, 6-3-0 (Penn St. '72) Born 8-16-49		
Syracuse	Hall of Fame 1-1-92	Ohio St. 24-17 (John Cooper)
Syracuse	Fiesta 1-1-93	Colorado 26-22 (Bill McCartney)
Syracuse	Gator 1-1-96	Clemson 41-0 (Tommy West)
Syracuse	Liberty 12-27-96	Houston 30-17 (Kim Helton)
Syracuse	Fiesta 12-31-97	Kansas St. 18-35 (Bill Snyder)
Syracuse	Orange 1-2-99	Florida 10-31 (Steve Spurrier)
Syracuse	Music City 12-29-99	Kentucky 20-13 (Hal Mumme)
Syracuse	Insight.com 12-29-01	Kansas St. 26-3 (Bill Snyder)
Syracuse	Champs Sports 12-21-04	Syracuse 14-51 (Chan Gailey)
JOE PATERNO, 22-10-1 (Brown '50) Born 12-21-26		
Penn St.	Gator 12-30-67	Florida St. 17-17 (Bill Peterson)
Penn St.	Orange 1-1-69	Kansas 15-14 (Pepper Rodgers)
Penn St.	Orange 1-1-70	Missouri 10-3 (Dan Devine)
Penn St.	Cotton 1-1-72	Texas 30-6 (Darrell Royal)
Penn St.	Sugar 12-31-72	Oklahoma 0-14 (Chuck Fairbanks)
Penn St.	Orange 1-1-74	LSU 16-9 (Charlie McClendon)
Penn St.	Cotton 1-1-75	Baylor 41-20 (Grant Teaff)
Penn St.	Sugar 12-31-75	Alabama 6-13 (Paul "Bear" Bryant)
Penn St.	Gator 12-27-76	Notre Dame 9-20 (Dan Devine)
Penn St.	Fiesta 12-25-77	Arizona St. 42-30 (Frank Kush)
Penn St.	Sugar 1-1-79	Alabama 7-14 (Paul "Bear" Bryant)
Penn St.	Liberty 12-22-79	Tulane 9-6 (Larry Smith)
Penn St.	Fiesta 12-26-80	Ohio St. 31-19 (Earle Bruce)
Penn St.	Fiesta 1-1-82	Southern California 26-10 (John Robinson)
Penn St.	Sugar 1-1-83	Georgia 27-23 (Vince Dooley)
Penn St.	Aloha 12-26-83	Washington 13-10 (Don James)
Penn St.	Orange 1-1-86	Oklahoma 10-25 (Barry Switzer)
Penn St.	Fiesta 1-1-87	Miami (Fla.) 14-10 (Jimmy Johnson)
Penn St.	Fla. Citrus 1-1-88	Clemson 10-35 (Danny Ford)
Penn St.	Holiday 12-29-89	BYU 50-39 (LaVell Edwards)
Penn St.	Blockbuster 12-28-90	Florida St. 17-24 (Bobby Bowden)
Penn St.	Fiesta 1-1-92	Tennessee 42-17 (Johnny Majors)
Penn St.	Blockbuster 1-1-93	Stanford 3-24 (Bill Walsh)
Penn St.	Fla. Citrus 1-1-94	Tennessee 31-13 (Phillip Fulmer)
Penn St.	Rose 1-2-95	Oregon 38-20 (Rich Brooks)
Penn St.	Outback 1-1-96	Auburn 43-14 (Terry Bowden)
Penn St.	Fiesta 1-1-97	Texas 38-15 (John Mackovic)
Penn St.	Alamo 12-28-99	Texas A&M 24-0 (R.C. Slocum)
Penn St.	Fla. Citrus 1-1-98	Florida 6-21 (Steve Spurrier)
Penn St.	Outback 1-1-99	Kentucky 26-14 (Hal Mumme)
Penn St.	Alamo 12-28-99	Texas A&M 24-0 (R.C. Slocum)
Penn St.	Capital One 1-1-03	Auburn 9-13 (Tommy Tuberville)
Penn St.	Orange 1-3-06	Florida St. 26-23 (3 ot) (Bobby Bowden)
Penn St.	Outback 1-1-07	Tennessee 20-10 (Phillip Fulmer)
GARY PATTERSON, 3-3-0 (Kansas St. '83) Born 2-13-60		
TCU	Mobile Alabama 12-20-00	Southern Miss. 21-28 (Jeff Bower)
TCU	galleryfurniture.com 12-28-01	Texas A&M 9-28 (R.C. Slocum)
TCU	Liberty 12-31-02	Colorado St. 17-3 (Sonny Lubick)
TCU	Fort Worth 12-23-03	Boise St. 31-34 (Dan Hawkins)
TCU	Houston 12-31-05	Iowa St. 27-24 (Dan McCarney)
TCU	Poinsettia 12-19-06	Northern Ill. 37-7 (Joe Novak)
JOE RAYMOND PEACE, 0-0-1 (Louisiana Tech '68) Born 6-5-45		
Louisiana Tech	Independence 12-15-90	Maryland 34-34 (Joe Krivak)
CHARLEY PELL, 2-3-0 (Alabama '64) Born 2-27-41		
Clemson	Gator 12-30-77	Pittsburgh 3-34 (Jackie Sherrill)
Florida	Tangerine 12-20-80	Maryland 35-20 (Jerry Claiborne)
Florida	Peach 12-31-81	West Virginia 6-26 (Don Nehlen)
Florida	Bluebonnet 12-31-82	Arkansas 24-28 (Lou Holtz)
Florida	Gator 12-30-83	Iowa 14-6 (Hayden Fry)
RAY PERKINS, 3-0-0 (Alabama '67) Born 11-6-41		
Alabama	Sun 12-24-83	SMU 28-7 (Bobby Collins)
Alabama	Aloha 12-28-85	Southern California 24-3 (Ted Tollner)
Alabama	Sun 12-26-86	Washington 28-6 (Don James)
GEORGE PERLES, 3-4-0 (Michigan St. '60) Born 7-16-34		
Michigan St.	Cherry 12-22-84	Army 6-10 (Jim Young)
Michigan St.	Hall of Fame 12-31-85	Georgia Tech 14-17 (Bill Curry)
Michigan St.	Rose 1-1-88	Southern California 20-17 (Larry Smith)
Michigan St.	Gator 1-1-89	Georgia 27-34 (Vince Dooley)
Michigan St.	Aloha 12-25-89	Hawaii 33-13 (Bob Wagner)
Michigan St.	John Hancock 12-31-90	Southern California 17-16 (Larry Smith)
Michigan St.	Liberty 12-28-93	Louisville 7-18 (Howard Schnellenberger)
DOYT PERRY, 0-1-0 (Bowling Green '32) Born 1-6-10		
Bowling Green	Mercy 11-23-61	Fresno St. 6-36 (Cecil Coleman)
BILL PETERSON, 1-2-1 (Ohio Northern '46) Born 5-14-20		
Florida St.	Gator 1-2-65	Oklahoma 36-19 (Gomer Jones)
Florida St.	Sun 12-24-66	Wyoming 20-28 (Lloyd Eaton)
Florida St.	Gator 12-30-67	Penn St. 17-17 (Joe Paterno)
Florida St.	Peach 12-30-68	LSU 27-31 (Charlie McClendon)
CHRIS PETERSON, 1-0-0 (UC Davis '88) Born 10-13-65		
Boise St.	Fiesta 1-1-07	Oklahoma 43-42 (ot) (Bob Stoops)
BOBBY PETRINO, 2-2-0 [Carroll (Mont.) '83] Born 3-10-61		
Louisville	GMAC 12-18-03	Miami (Ohio) 28-49 (Terry Hoeppner)
Louisville	Liberty 12-31-04	Boise St. 44-40 (Dan Hawkins)
Louisville	Gator 1-2-06	Virginia Tech 24-35 (Frank Beamer)
Louisville	Orange 1-2-07	Wake Forest 24-13 (Jim Grobe)
JIMMY PHELAN, 0-3-0 (Notre Dame '19) Born 12-5-1892		
Washington	Rose 1-1-37	Pittsburgh 0-21 (Jock Sutherland)
St. Mary's (Cal.)	Sugar 1-1-46	Oklahoma St. 12-33 (Jim Lookabaugh)
St. Mary's (Cal.)	Oil 1-1-47	Georgia Tech 19-41 (Bobby Dodd)
ALVIN "PIX" PIERSON, 0-1-0 (Nevada '22) Born 7-25-1898		
Fresno St.	Raisin 1-1-46	Drake 12-13 (Vee Green)
GARY PINKEL, 2-2-0 (Kent St. '75) Born 4-27-52		
Toledo	Las Vegas 12-14-95	Nevada 40-37 (ot) (Chris Ault)
Missouri	Independence 12-31-03	Arkansas 14-27 (Houston Nutt)
Missouri	Independence 12-30-05	South Carolina 38-31 (Steve Spurrier)
Missouri	Sun 12-29-06	Oregon St. 38-39 (Mike Riley)
JIM PITTMAN, 1-0-0 (Mississippi St. '50) Born 8-28-25		
Tulane	Liberty 12-12-70	Colorado 17-3 (Eddie Crowder)
JOHN PONT, 0-2-0 [Miami (Ohio) '52] Born 11-13-27		
Miami (Ohio)	Tangerine 12-22-52	Houston 21-49 (Bill Yeoman)
Indiana	Rose 1-1-68	Southern California 3-14 (John McKay)
WARREN POWERS, 3-2-0 (Nebraska '63) Born 2-19-41		
Missouri	Liberty 12-23-78	LSU 20-15 (Charlie McClendon)
Missouri	Hall of Fame 12-29-79	South Carolina 24-14 (Jim Carlen)
Missouri	Liberty 12-27-80	Purdue 25-28 (Jim Young)
Missouri	Tangerine 12-19-81	Southern Miss. 19-17 (Bobby Collins)
Missouri	Holiday 12-23-83	BYU 17-21 (LaVell Edwards)
CLARENCE "NIBS" PRICE, 0-1-0 (California '14) Born 1889		
California	Rose 1-1-29	Georgia Tech 7-8 (Bill Alexander)
ED PRICE, 1-0-0 (Texas '33) Born 1-12-09		
Texas	Cotton 1-1-53	Tennessee 16-0 (Bob Neyland)
MIKE PRICE, 3-4-0 (Puget Sound '69) Born 4-6-46		
Washington St.	Copper 12-29-92	Utah 31-28 (Ron McBride)
Washington St.	Alamo 12-31-94	Baylor 10-3 (Chuck Reedy)
Washington St.	Rose 1-1-98	Michigan 16-21 (Lloyd Carr)
Washington St.	Sun 12-31-01	Purdue 33-27 (Joe Tiller)
Washington St.	Rose 1-1-03	Oklahoma 14-34 (Bob Stoops)
UTEP	Houston 12-29-04	Colorado 28-33 (Gary Barnett)
UTEP	GMAC 12-21-05	Toledo 13-45 (Tom Amstutz)

Coach/School	Bowl/Date	Opponent/Score (Coach)
RON PRINCE, 0-1-0 (Appalachian St. '92) Born 9-10-69		
Kansas St.	Texas 12-28-06	Rutgers 10-37 (Greg Schiano)
TOMMY PROTHRO, 2-2-0 (Duke '42) Born 7-20-20		
Oregon St.	Rose 1-1-57	Iowa 19-35 (Forest Evashevski)
Oregon St.	Liberty 12-15-62	Villanova 6-0 (Alex Bell)
Oregon St.	Rose 1-1-65	Michigan 7-34 (Chalmers "Bump" Elliott)
UCLA	Rose 1-1-66	Michigan St. 14-12 (Duffy Daugherty)
BOB PRUETT, 5-2-0 (Marshall '65) Born 6-30-43		
Marshall	Motor City 12-26-97	Mississippi 31-34 (Tommy Tuberville)
Marshall	Motor City 12-23-98	Louisville 48-29 (John L. Smith)
Marshall	Motor City 12-27-99	BYU 21-3 (LaVell Edwards)
Marshall	Motor City 12-27-00	Cincinnati 25-14 (Rick Minter)
Marshall	GMAC 12-19-01	East Caro. 64-61 (2 ot) (Steve Logan)
Marshall	GMAC 12-18-02	Louisville 38-15 (John L. Smith)
Marshall	Fort Worth 12-23-04	Cincinnati 14-32 (Mark Dantonio)
JEFF QUINN, 1-0-0 (Elmhurst '85) Born 9-26-62		
Central Mich.	Motor City 12-26-06	Middle Tenn. 31-14 (Rick Stockstill)
DAVE RADER, 1-1-0 (Tulsa '80) Born 3-9-57		
Tulsa	Independence 12-16-89	Oregon 24-27 (Rich Brooks)
Tulsa	Freedom 12-30-91	San Diego St. 28-17 (Al Luginbill)
JOHN RALSTON, 2-2-0 (California '54) Born 4-25-27		
Utah St.	Sun 12-31-60	New Mexico St. 13-20 (Warren Woodson)
Utah St.	Gotham 12-9-61	Baylor 9-24 (John Bridgers)
Stanford	Rose 1-1-71	Ohio St. 27-17 (Woody Hayes)
Stanford	Rose 1-1-72	Michigan 13-12 (Glenn "Bo" Schembechler)
CHUCK REEDY, 0-1-0 (Appalachian St. '71) Born 5-31-49		
Baylor	Alamo 12-31-94	Washington St. 3-10 (Mike Price)
RED REESE, 1-0-0 (Washington St. '25) Born 3-2-1899		
Second Air Force	Sun 1-1-43	Hardin-Simmons 13-7 (Warren Woodson)
BO REIN, 2-0-0 (Ohio St. '68) Born 7-20-45		
North Carolina St.	Peach 12-31-77	Iowa St. 24-14 (Earle Bruce)
North Carolina St.	Tangerine 12-23-78	Pittsburgh 30-17 (Jackie Sherrill)
MARK RICHT, 4-2-0 [Miami (Fla.) '82] Born 2-18-60		
Georgia	Music City 12-28-01	Boston College 16-20 (Tom O'Brien)
Georgia	Sugar 1-1-03	Florida St. 26-13 (Bobby Bowden)
Georgia	Capital One 1-1-04	Purdue 34-27 (ot) (Joe Tiller)
Georgia	Outback 1-1-05	Wisconsin 24-21 (Barry Alvarez)
Georgia	Sugar 1-2-06	West Virginia 35-38 (Rich Rodriguez)
Georgia	Chick-fil-A 12-30-06	Virginia Tech 31-24 (Frank Beamer)
MIKE RILEY, 3-0-0 (Alabama '75) Born 7-6-53		
Oregon St.	Las Vegas 12-24-03	New Mexico 55-14 (Rocky Long)
Oregon St.	Insight 12-28-04	Notre Dame 38-21 (Kent Baer)
Oregon St.	Sun 12-29-06	Missouri 39-38 (Gary Pinkel)
PAUL ROACH, 0-3-0 (Black Hills St. '52) Born 10-24-27		
Wyoming	Holiday 12-30-87	Iowa 19-20 (Hayden Fry)
Wyoming	Holiday 12-30-88	Oklahoma St. 14-62 (Pat Jones)
Wyoming	Copper 12-31-90	California 15-17 (Bruce Snyder)
STEVE ROBERTS, 0-1-0 (Ouachita Baptist '87) Born 10-13-64		
Arkansas St.	New Orleans 12-20-05	Southern Miss. 19-31 (Jeff Bower)
ED ROBINSON, 0-1-0 (Brown '96) Born 10-15-73		
Brown	Rose 1-1-16	Washington St. 0-14 (Bill "Lone Star"Dietz)
JOHN ROBINSON, 8-1-0 (Oregon '58) Born 7-25-35		
Southern California	Rose 1-1-77	Michigan 14-6 (Glenn "Bo" Schembechler)
Southern California	Bluebonnet 12-31-77	Texas A&M 47-28 (Emory Bellard)
Southern California	Rose 1-1-79	Michigan 17-10 (Glenn "Bo" Schembechler)
Southern California	Rose 1-1-80	Ohio St. 17-16 (Earle Bruce)
Southern California	Fiesta 1-1-82	Penn St. 10-26 (Joe Paterno)
Southern California	Freedom 12-30-93	Utah 28-21 (Ron McBride)
Southern California	Cotton 1-2-95	Texas Tech 55-14 (Spike Dykes)
Southern California	Rose 1-1-96	Northwestern 41-32 (Gary Barnett)
UNLV	Las Vegas 12-21-00	Arkansas 31-14 (Houston Nutt)
KNUTE ROCKNE, 1-0-0 (Notre Dame '14) Born 3-4-1888		
Notre Dame	Rose 1-1-25	Stanford 27-10 (Glenn "Pop" Warner)
PEPPER RODGERS, 0-2-0 (Georgia Tech '55) Born 10-8-31		
Kansas	Orange 1-1-69	Penn St. 14-15 (Joe Paterno)
Georgia Tech	Peach 12-25-78	Purdue 21-41 (Jim Young)
RICH RODRIGUEZ, 2-3-0 (West Virginia '86) Born 5-24-63		
West Virginia	Continental Tire 12-28-02	Virginia 22-48 (Al Groh)
West Virginia	Gator 1-1-04	Maryland 7-41 (Ralph Friedgen)
West Virginia	Gator 1-1-05	Florida St. 18-30 (Bobby Bowden)
West Virginia	Sugar 1-2-06	Georgia 38-35 (Mark Richt)
West Virginia	Gator 1-1-07	Georgia Tech 38-35 (Chan Gailey)
DARRYL ROGERS, 1-0-0 (Fresno St. '57) Born 5-28-34		
Arizona St.	Fiesta 1-1-83	Oklahoma 32-21 (Barry Switzer)

Coach/School	Bowl/Date	Opponent/Score (Coach)
E.L. "DICK" ROMNEY, 0-1-0 (Utah '17) Born 2-12-1895		
Utah St.	Raisin 1-1-47	San Jose St. 0-20 (Bill Hubbard)
TIM ROSE, 0-1-0 [Xavier (Ohio) '62] Born 10-14-41		
Miami (Ohio)	California 12-13-86	San Jose St. 7-37 (Claude Gilbert)
BOBBY ROSS, 4-2-0 (VMI '59) Born 12-23-36		
Maryland	Aloha 12-25-82	Washington 20-21 (Don James)
Maryland	Fla. Citrus 12-17-83	Tennessee 23-30 (Johnny Majors)
Maryland	Sun 12-22-84	Tennessee 28-27 (Johnny Majors)
Maryland	Cherry 12-21-85	Syracuse 35-18 (Dick MacPherson)
Georgia Tech	Fla. Citrus 1-1-91	Nebraska 45-21 (Tom Osborne)
Georgia Tech	Aloha 12-25-91	Stanford 18-17 (Dennis Green)
DARRELL ROYAL, 8-7-1 (Oklahoma '50) Born 7-6-24		
Texas	Sugar 1-1-58	Mississippi 7-39 (John Vaught)
Texas	Cotton 1-1-60	Syracuse 14-23 (Ben Schwartzwalder)
Texas	Bluebonnet 12-17-60	Alabama 3-3 (Paul "Bear" Bryant)
Texas	Cotton 1-1-62	Mississippi 12-7 (John Vaught)
Texas	Cotton 1-1-63	LSU 0-13 (Charlie McClendon)
Texas	Cotton 1-1-64	Navy 28-6 (Wayne Hardin)
Texas	Orange 1-1-65	Alabama 21-17 (Paul "Bear" Bryant)
Texas	Bluebonnet 12-17-66	Mississippi 19-0 (John Vaught)
Texas	Cotton 1-1-69	Tennessee 36-13 (Doug Dickey)
Texas	Cotton 1-1-70	Notre Dame 21-17 (Ara Parseghian)
Texas	Cotton 1-1-71	Notre Dame 11-24 (Ara Parseghian)
Texas	Cotton 1-1-72	Penn St. 6-30 (Joe Paterno)
Texas	Cotton 1-1-73	Alabama 17-13 (Paul "Bear" Bryant)
Texas	Cotton 1-1-74	Nebraska 3-19 (Tom Osborne)
Texas	Gator 12-30-74	Auburn 3-27 (Ralph "Shug" Jordan)
Texas	Bluebonnet 12-27-75	Colorado 38-21 (Bill Mallory)
NICK SABAN, 3-5-0 (Kent St. '73) Born 10-31-51		
Michigan St.	Independence 12-29-95	LSU 26-45 (Gerry DiNardo)
Michigan St.	Sun 12-31-96	Stanford 0-38 (Tyrone Willingham)
Michigan St.	Aloha 12-25-97	Washington 23-51 (Jim Lambright)
LSU	Peach 12-29-00	Georgia Tech 28-14 (George O'Leary)
LSU	Sugar 1-1-02	Illinois 47-34 (Ron Turner)
LSU	Cotton 1-1-03	Texas 20-35 (Mack Brown)
LSU	Sugar 1-4-04	Oklahoma 21-14 (Bob Stoops)
LSU	Capital One 1-1-05	Iowa 25-30 (Kirk Ferentz)
HENRY "RED" SANDERS, 0-2-0 (Vanderbilt '27) Born 3-7-05		
UCLA	Rose 1-1-54	Michigan St. 20-28 (Clarence "Biggie" Munn)
UCLA	Rose 1-2-56	Michigan St. 14-17 (Duffy Daugherty)
RALPH SASSE, 0-1-0 (Army '10) Born 7-19-89		
Mississippi St.	Orange 1-1-37	Duquesne 12-13 (John Smith)
GEORGE SAUER, 0-3-0 (Nebraska '34) Born 12-11-10		
Kansas	Orange 1-1-48	Georgia Tech 14-20 (Bobby Dodd)
Baylor	Orange 1-1-52	Georgia Tech 14-17 (Bobby Dodd)
Baylor	Gator 12-31-54	Auburn 13-33 (Ralph "Shug" Jordan)
MACK SAXON, 0-1-0 (Texas) Born 1901		
UTEP	Sun 1-1-37	Hardin-Simmons 6-34 (Frank Kimbrough)
CHRIS SCELFO, 2-0-0 (La.-Monroe '85) Born 9-30-63		
Tulane	Liberty 12-31-98	BYU 41-27 (LaVell Edwards)
Tulane	Hawaii 12-25-02	Hawaii 36-28 (June Jones)
GLENN "BO" SCHEMBECHLER, 5-12-0 [Miami (Ohio) '51] Born 4-1-29		
Michigan	Rose 1-1-70	Southern California 3-10 (John McKay)
Michigan	Rose 1-1-72	Stanford 12-13 (John Ralston)
Michigan	Orange 1-1-76	Oklahoma 6-14 (Barry Switzer)
Michigan	Rose 1-1-77	Southern California 6-14 (John Robinson)
Michigan	Rose 1-2-78	Washington 20-27 (Don James)
Michigan	Rose 1-1-79	Southern California 10-17 (John Robinson)
Michigan	Gator 12-28-79	North Carolina 15-17 (Dick Crum)
Michigan	Rose 1-1-81	Washington 23-6 (Don James)
Michigan	Bluebonnet 12-31-81	UCLA 33-14 (Terry Donahue)
Michigan	Rose 1-1-83	UCLA 14-24 (Terry Donahue)
Michigan	Sugar 1-2-84	Auburn 7-9 (Pat Dye)
Michigan	Holiday 12-21-84	BYU 17-24 (LaVell Edwards)
Michigan	Fiesta 1-1-86	Nebraska 27-23 (Tom Osborne)
Michigan	Rose 1-1-87	Arizona St. 15-22 (John Cooper)
Michigan	Hall of Fame 1-2-88	Alabama 28-24 (Bill Curry)
Michigan	Rose 1-2-89	Southern California 22-14 (Larry Smith)
Michigan	Rose 1-1-90	Southern California 10-17 (Larry Smith)
GREG SCHIANO, 1-1-0 (Bucknell '88) Born 6-1-66		
Rutgers	Insight 12-27-05	Arizona St. 40-45 (Dirk Koetter)
Rutgers	Texas 12-28-06	Kansas St. 37-10 (Ron Prince)
MERLE SCHLOSSER, 0-1-0 (Illinois '50) Born 10-14-27		
Western Mich.	Aviation 12-9-61	New Mexico 12-28 (Bill Weeks)
HOWARD SCHNELLENBERGER, 4-0-0 (Kentucky '56) Born 3-16-34		
Miami (Fla.)	Peach 1-2-81	Virginia Tech 20-10 (Bill Dooley)
Miami (Fla.)	Orange 1-2-84	Nebraska 31-30 (Tom Osborne)
Louisville	Fiesta 1-1-91	Alabama 34-7 (Gene Stallings)
Louisville	Liberty 12-28-93	Michigan St. 18-7 (George Perles)

Coach/School	Bowl/Date	Opponent/Score (Coach)
PAUL SCHUDEL, 0-2-0 [Miami (Ohio) '66] Born 7-2-44		
Ball St.	California 12-9-89	Fresno St. 6-27 (Jim Sweeney)
Ball St.	Las Vegas 12-17-93	Utah St. 33-42 (Charlie Weatherbie)
BILL SCHUTTE, 0-1-0 (Idaho '33) Born 5-7-10		
San Diego St.	Harbor 1-1-48	Hardin-Simmons 0-53 (Warren Woodson)
BEN SCHWARTZWALDER, 2-5-0 (West Virginia '35) Born 6-2-09		
Syracuse	Orange 1-1-53	Alabama 6-61 (Harold "Red" Drew)
Syracuse	Cotton 1-1-57	TCU 27-28 (Abe Martin)
Syracuse	Orange 1-1-59	Oklahoma 6-21 (Bud Wilkinson)
Syracuse	Cotton 1-1-60	Texas 23-14 (Darrell Royal)
Syracuse	Liberty 12-16-61	Miami (Fla.) 15-14 (Andy Gustafson)
Syracuse	Sugar 1-1-65	LSU 10-13 (Charlie McClendon)
Syracuse	Gator 12-31-66	Tennessee 12-18 (Doug Dickey)
BRAD SCOTT, 1-0-0 (Mo.-Rolla '76) Born 9-30-54		
South Carolina	Carquest 1-2-95	West Virginia 24-21 (Don Nehlen)
CLARK SHAUGHNESSY, 1-0-0 (Minnesota '14) Born 3-6-1892		
Stanford	Rose 1-1-41	Nebraska 21-13 (Lawrence McC. "Biff" Jones)
LAWRENCE "BUCK" SHAW, 2-0-0 (Notre Dame '22) Born 3-28-99		
Santa Clara	Sugar 1-1-37	LSU 21-14 (Bernie Moore)
Santa Clara	Sugar 1-1-38	LSU 6-0 (Bernie Moore)
TERRY SHEA, 1-0-0 (Oregon '68) Born 6-12-46		
San Jose St.	California 12-8-90	Central Mich. 48-24 (Herb Deromedi)
JOE SHEEKETSKI, 1-1-0 (Notre Dame '33) Born 4-15-09		
Nevada	Salad 1-1-48	North Texas 13-6 (Odus Mitchell)
Nevada	Harbor 1-1-49	Villanova 7-27 (Jordan Olivar)
DICK SHERIDAN, 2-4-0 (South Carolina '64) Born 8-9-41		
North Carolina St.	Peach 12-31-86	Virginia Tech 24-25 (Bill Dooley)
North Carolina St.	Peach 12-31-88	Iowa 28-23 (Hayden Fry)
North Carolina St.	Copper 12-31-89	Arizona 10-17 (Dick Tomey)
North Carolina St.	All-American 12-28-90	Southern Miss. 31-27 (Jeff Bower)
North Carolina St.	Peach 1-1-92	East Caro. 34-37 (Bill Lewis)
North Carolina St.	Gator 12-31-92	Florida 10-27 (Steve Spurrier)
EUGENE "BO" SHERMAN, 1-0-0 (Henderson St. '30) Born 7-5-08		
George Washington	Sun 1-1-57	UTEP 13-0 (Mike Brumbelow)
JACKIE SHERRILL, 8-6-0 (Alabama '66) Born 11-28-43		
Pittsburgh	Gator 12-30-77	Clemson 34-3 (Charley Pell)
Pittsburgh	Tangerine 12-23-78	North Carolina St. 17-30 (Bo Rein)
Pittsburgh	Fiesta 12-25-79	Arizona 16-10 (Tony Mason)
Pittsburgh	Gator 12-29-80	South Carolina 37-9 (Jim Carlen)
Pittsburgh	Sugar 1-1-82	Georgia 24-20 (Vince Dooley)
Texas A&M	Cotton 1-1-86	Auburn 36-16 (Pat Dye)
Texas A&M	Cotton 1-1-87	Ohio St. 12-28 (Earle Bruce)
Texas A&M	Cotton 1-1-88	Notre Dame 35-10 (Lou Holtz)
Mississippi St.	Liberty 12-29-91	Air Force 15-38 (Fisher DeBerry)
Mississippi St.	Peach 1-2-93	North Carolina 17-21 (Mack Brown)
Mississippi St.	Peach 1-1-95	North Carolina St. 24-28 (Mike O'Cain)
Mississippi St.	Cotton 1-1-99	Texas 11-38 (Mack Brown)
Mississippi St.	Peach 12-30-99	Clemson 17-7 (Tommy Bowden)
Mississippi St.	Independence 12-31-00	Texas A&M 43-41 (ot) (R.C. Slocum)
TED SHIPKEY, 0-1-0 (Stanford '27) Born 9-28-04		
New Mexico	Sun 1-2-39	Utah 0-28 (Ike Armstrong)
MIKE SHULA, 1-1-0 (Alabama '86) Born 6-3-65		
Alabama	Music City 12-31-04	Minnesota 16-20 (Glenn Mason)
Alabama	Cotton 1-2-06	Texas Tech 13-10 (Mike Leach)
LARRY SIEMERING, 1-0-0 (San Francisco '35) Born 11-24-10		
Pacific	Raisin 1-1-48	Wichita St. 26-14 (Ralph Graham)
BOB SIMMONS, 0-1-0 (Bowling Green '71) Born 6-13-48		
Oklahoma St.	Alamo 12-30-97	Purdue 20-33 (Joe Tiller)
CHAUNCEY SIMPSON, 0-1-0 (Missouri '25) Born 12-21-02		
Missouri	Cotton 1-1-46	Texas 27-40 (Dana Bible)
DAN SIMRELL, 0-1-0 (Toledo '65) Born 4-9-43		
Toledo	California 12-15-84	UNLV 13-30 (Harvey Hyde)
STEVE SLOAN, 0-2-1 (Alabama '66) Born 8-19-44		
Vanderbilt	Peach 12-28-74	Texas Tech 6-6 (Jim Carlen)
Texas Tech	Bluebonnet 12-31-76	Nebraska 24-27 (Tom Osborne)
Texas Tech	Tangerine 12-23-77	Florida St. 17-40 (Bobby Bowden)
R.C. SLOCUM, 3-8-0 (McNeese St. '67) Born 11-7-44		
Texas A&M	John Hancock 12-30-89	Pittsburgh 28-31 (Paul Hackett)
Texas A&M	Holiday 12-29-90	BYU 65-14 (LaVell Edwards)
Texas A&M	Cotton 1-1-92	Florida St. 2-10 (Bobby Bowden)
Texas A&M	Cotton 1-1-93	Notre Dame 3-28 (Lou Holtz)
Texas A&M	Cotton 1-1-94	Notre Dame 21-24 (Lou Holtz)
Texas A&M	Alamo 12-28-95	Michigan 22-20 (Lloyd Carr)
Texas A&M	Cotton 1-1-98	UCLA 23-29 (Bob Toledo)
Texas A&M	Sugar 1-1-99	Ohio St. 14-24 (John Cooper)
Texas A&M	Alamo 12-28-99	Penn St. 0-24 (Joe Paterno)
Texas A&M	Independence 12-31-00	Mississippi St. 41-43 (ot) (Jackie Sherrill)
Texas A&M	galleryfurniture.com 12-28-01	TCU 28-9 (Gary Patterson)

Coach/School	Bowl/Date	Opponent/Score (Coach)
ANDY SMITH, 1-0-1 (Penn '06) Born 9-10-1883		
California	Rose 1-1-21	Ohio St. 28-0 (John Wilce)
California	Rose 1-2-22	Wash. & Jeff. 0-0 (Earle "Greasy" Neale)
HOMER SMITH, 0-1-0 (Princeton '54) Born 10-9-31		
Davidson	Tangerine 12-26-69	Toledo 33-56 (Frank Lauterbur)
JOHN L. SMITH, 1-6-0 (Weber St. '71) Born 11-5-48		
Utah St.	Humanitarian 12-29-97	Cincinnati 19-35 (Rick Minter)
Louisville	Motor City 12-23-98	Marshall 29-48 (Bob Pruett)
Louisville	Humanitarian 12-30-99	Boise St. 31-34 (Dirk Koetter)
Louisville	Liberty 12-29-00	Colorado St. 17-22 (Sonny Lubick)
Louisville	Liberty 12-31-01	BYU 28-10 (Gary Crowton)
Louisville	GMAC 12-18-02	Marshall 15-38 (Bob Pruett)
Michigan St.	Alamo 12-29-03	Nebraska 3-17 (Frank Solich)
JOHN "LITTLE CLIPPER" SMITH, 1-0-0 (Notre Dame '29) Born 12-12-04		
Duquesne	Orange 1-1-37	Mississippi St. 13-12 (Ralph Sasse)
LARRY SMITH, 3-6-1 (Bowling Green '62) Born 9-12-39		
Tulane	Liberty 12-22-79	Penn St. 6-9 (Joe Paterno)
Arizona	Sun 12-28-85	Georgia 13-13 (Vince Dooley)
Arizona	Aloha 12-27-86	North Carolina 30-21 (Dick Crum)
Southern California	Rose 1-1-88	Michigan St. 17-20 (George Perles)
Southern California	Rose 1-2-89	Michigan 14-22 (Glenn "Bo" Schembechler)
Southern California	Rose 1-1-90	Michigan 17-10 (Glenn "Bo" Schembechler)
Southern California	John Hancock 12-31-90	Michigan St. 16-17 (George Perles)
Southern California	Freedom 12-29-92	Fresno St. 7-24 (Jim Sweeney)
Missouri	Holiday 12-29-97	Colorado St. 24-35 (Sonny Lubick)
Missouri	Insight.com 12-26-98	West Virginia 34-31 (Don Nehlen)
MAURICE "CLIPPER" SMITH, 0-0-1 (Notre Dame '21) Born 10-15-1898		
Villanova	Bacardi, Cuba 1-1-37	Auburn 7-7 (Jack Meagher)
CARL SNAVELY, 0-3-0 (Lebanon Valley '15) Born 7-30-1894		
North Carolina	Sugar 1-1-47	Georgia 10-20 (Wally Butts)
North Carolina	Sugar 1-1-49	Oklahoma 6-14 (Bud Wilkinson)
North Carolina	Cotton 1-2-50	Rice 13-27 (Jess Neely)
BILL SNYDER, 6-5-0 (William Jewell '63) Born 10-7-41		
Kansas St.	Copper 12-29-93	Wyoming 52-17 (Joe Tiller)
Kansas St.	Aloha 12-25-94	Boston College 7-12 (Dan Henning)
Kansas St.	Holiday 12-29-95	Colorado St. 54-21 (Sonny Lubick)
Kansas St.	Cotton 1-1-97	BYU 15-19 (LaVell Edwards)
Kansas St.	Fiesta 12-31-97	Syracuse 35-18 (Paul Pasqualoni)
Kansas St.	Alamo 12-29-98	Purdue 34-37 (Joe Tiller)
Kansas St.	Holiday 12-29-99	Washington 24-20 (Rick Neuheisel)
Kansas St.	Cotton 1-1-01	Tennessee 35-21 (Phillip Fulmer)
Kansas St.	Insight.com 12-29-01	Syracuse 3-26 (Paul Pasqualoni)
Kansas St.	Holiday 12-27-02	Arizona St. 34-27 (Dirk Koetter)
Kansas St.	Fiesta 1-2-04	Ohio St. 28-35 (Jim Tressel)
BRUCE SNYDER, 3-3-0 (Oregon '62) Born 3-14-40		
California	Copper 12-31-90	Wyoming 17-15 (Paul Roach)
California	Fla. Citrus 1-1-92	Clemson 37-13 (Ken Hatfield)
Arizona St.	Rose 1-1-97	Ohio St. 17-20 (John Cooper)
Arizona St.	Sun 12-31-97	Iowa 17-7 (Hayden Fry)
Arizona St.	Aloha Classic 12-25-99	Wake Forest 3-23 (Jim Caldwell)
Arizona St.	Aloha Classic 12-25-00	Boston College 17-31 (Tom O'Brien)
FRANK SOLICH, 2-4-0 (Nebraska '66) Born 9-8-44		
Nebraska	Holiday 12-30-98	Arizona 20-23 (Dick Tomey)
Nebraska	Fiesta 1-2-00	Tennessee 31-21 (Phillip Fulmer)
Nebraska	Alamo 12-30-00	Northwestern 66-17 (Randy Walker)
Nebraska	Rose 1-3-02	Miami (Fla.) 14-37 (Larry Coker)
Nebraska	Independence 12-27-02	Mississippi 23-27 (David Cutcliffe)
Ohio	GMAC 1-7-07	Southern Miss. 7-28 (Jeff Bower)
FRANK SPAZIANI, 1-0-0 (Penn St. '69) Born 4-1-47		
Boston College	Meineke Car Care 12-30-06	Navy 25-24 (Paul Johnson)
CLARENCE "DOC" SPEARS, 1-0-0 (Dartmouth '16) Born 7-24-1894		
West Virginia	San Diego East-West Christmas Classic 12-25-22	Gonzaga 21-13 (Charles "Gus" Dorais)
CLIFF SPEEGLE, 1-0-0 (Oklahoma '41) Born 11-4-17		
Oklahoma St.	Bluegrass 12-13-58	Florida St. 15-6 (Tom Nugent)
STEVE SPURRIER, 7-7-0 (Florida '67) Born 4-20-45		
Duke	All-American 12-28-89	Texas Tech 21-49 (Spike Dykes)
Florida	Sugar 1-1-92	Notre Dame 28-39 (Lou Holtz)
Florida	Gator 12-31-92	North Carolina St. 27-10 (Dick Sheridan)
Florida	Sugar 1-1-94	West Virginia 41-7 (Don Nehlen)
Florida	Sugar 1-2-95	Florida St. 17-23 (Bobby Bowden)
Florida	Fiesta 1-2-96	Nebraska 24-62 (Tom Osborne)
Florida	Sugar 1-2-97	Florida St. 52-20 (Bobby Bowden)
Florida	Fla. Citrus 1-1-98	Penn St. 21-6 (Joe Paterno)
Florida	Orange 1-2-99	Syracuse 31-10 (Paul Pasqualoni)
Florida	Fla. Citrus 1-1-00	Michigan St. 34-37 (Bobby Williams)
Florida	Sugar 1-2-01	Miami (Fla.) 20-37 (Butch Davis)
Florida	Orange 1-2-02	Maryland 56-23 (Ralph Friedgen)
South Carolina	Independence 12-30-05	Missouri 31-38 (Gary Pinkel)
South Carolina	Liberty 12-29-06	Houston 44-36 (Art Briles)

Coach/School	Bowl/Date	Opponent/Score (Coach)
GENE STALLINGS, 6-1-0 (Texas A&M '57) Born 3-2-35		
Texas A&M	Cotton 1-1-68	Alabama 20-16 (Paul "Bear" Bryant)
Alabama	Fiesta 1-1-91	Louisville 7-34 (Howard Schnellenberger)
Alabama	Blockbuster 12-28-91	Colorado 30-25 (Bill McCartney)
Alabama	Sugar 1-1-93	Miami (Fla.) 34-13 (Dennis Erickson)
Alabama	Gator 12-31-93	North Carolina 24-10 (Mack Brown)
Alabama	Fla. Citrus 1-2-95	Ohio St. 24-17 (John Cooper)
Alabama	Outback 1-1-97	Michigan 17-14 (Lloyd Carr)
JIM STANGELAND, 0-0-1 (Arizona St. '48) Born 12-21-21		
Long Beach St.	Pasadena 12-19-70	Louisville 24-24 (Lee Corso)
JIM STANLEY, 2-0-0 (Texas A&M '59) Born 5-22-35		
Oklahoma St.	Fiesta 12-28-74	BYU 16-6 (LaVell Edwards)
Oklahoma St.	Tangerine 12-18-76	BYU 49-12 (LaVell Edwards)
TOM STIDHAM, 0-1-0 (Haskell '27) Born 3-27-04		
Oklahoma	Orange 1-2-39	Tennessee 0-17 (Bob Neyland)
LON STINER, 1-0-0 (Nebraska '27) Born 6-20-03		
Oregon St.	Rose 1-1-42	Duke 20-16 (Wallace Wade)
HARRY STITELER, 1-0-0 (Texas A&M '31) Born 9-17-09		
Texas A&M	Presidential Cup 12-9-50	Georgia 40-20 (Wally Butts)
CHUCK STOBART, 1-0-0 (Ohio '59) Born 10-27-34		
Toledo	California 12-19-81	San Jose St. 27-25 (Jack Elway)
RICK STOCKSTILL, 0-1-0 (Florida St. '82) Born 12-23-57		
Middle Tenn.	Motor City 12-26-06	Central Mich. 14-31 (Jeff Quinn)
CAL STOLL, 0-1-0 (Minnesota '50) Born 12-12-23		
Minnesota	Hall of Fame 12-22-77	Maryland 7-17 (Jerry Claiborne)
DENNY STOLZ, 0-3-0 (Alma '55) Born 9-12-34		
Bowling Green	California 12-18-82	Fresno St. 28-29 (Jim Sweeney)
Bowling Green	California 12-14-85	Fresno St. 7-51 (Jim Sweeney)
San Diego St.	Holiday 12-30-86	Iowa 38-39 (Hayden Fry)
BOB STOOPS, 4-4-0 (Iowa '83) Born 9-6-60		
Oklahoma	Independence 12-31-99	Mississippi 25-27 (David Cutcliffe)
Oklahoma	Orange 1-3-01	Florida St. 13-2 (Bobby Bowden)
Oklahoma	Cotton 1-1-02	Arkansas 10-3 (Houston Nutt)
Oklahoma	Rose 1-1-03	Washington St. 34-14 (Mike Price)
Oklahoma	Sugar 1-4-04	LSU 14-21 (Nick Saban)
Oklahoma	Orange 1-4-05	Southern California 19-55 (Pete Carroll)
Oklahoma	Holiday 12-29-05	Oregon 17-14 (Mike Bellotti)
Oklahoma	Fiesta 1-1-07	Boise St. 42-43 (ot) (Chris Peterson)
JERRY STOVALL, 0-1-0 (LSU '63) Born 4-30-41		
LSU	Orange 1-1-83	Nebraska 20-21 (Tom Osborne)
CHARLIE STRONG, 0-1-0 (Central Ark. '82) Born 8-2-60		
Florida	Peach 12-31-04	Miami (Fla.) 10-27 (Larry Coker)
BOB STULL, 0-1-0 (Kansas St. '68) Born 11-21-45		
UTEP	Independence 12-23-88	Southern Miss. 18-38 (Curley Hallman)
PAT SULLIVAN, 0-1-0 (Auburn '72) Born 1-18-50		
TCU	Independence 12-28-94	Virginia 10-20 (George Welsh)
JOCK SUTHERLAND, 1-3-0 (Pittsburgh '18) Born 3-21-1889		
Pittsburgh	Rose 1-1-28	Stanford 6-7 (Glenn "Pop" Warner)
Pittsburgh	Rose 1-1-30	Southern California 14-47 (Howard Jones)
Pittsburgh	Rose 1-2-33	Southern California 0-35 (Howard Jones)
Pittsburgh	Rose 1-1-37	Washington 21-0 (Jimmy Phelan)
BOB SUTTON, 0-1-0 (Eastern Mich. '74) Born 1-28-51		
Army	Independence 12-31-96	Auburn 29-32 (Terry Bowden)
JIM SWEENEY, 5-2-0 (Portland '51) Born 9-1-29		
Fresno St.	California 12-18-82	Bowling Green 29-28 (Denny Stolz)
Fresno St.	California 12-14-85	Bowling Green 51-7 (Denny Stolz)
Fresno St.	California 12-10-88	Western Mich. 35-30 (Al Molde)
Fresno St.	California 12-9-89	Ball St. 27-8 (Paul Schudel)
Fresno St.	California 12-13-91	Bowling Green 21-28 (Gary Blackney)
Fresno St.	Freedom 12-29-92	Southern California 24-7 (Larry Smith)
Fresno St.	Aloha 12-25-93	Colorado 30-41 (Bill McCartney)
BARRY SWITZER, 8-5-0 (Arkansas '60) Born 10-5-37		
Oklahoma	Orange 1-1-76	Michigan 14-6 (Glenn "Bo" Schembechler)
Oklahoma	Fiesta 12-25-76	Wyoming 41-7 (Fred Akers)
Oklahoma	Orange 1-2-78	Arkansas 6-31 (Lou Holtz)
Oklahoma	Orange 1-1-79	Nebraska 31-24 (Tom Osborne)
Oklahoma	Orange 1-1-80	Florida St. 24-7 (Bobby Bowden)
Oklahoma	Orange 1-1-81	Florida St. 18-17 (Bobby Bowden)
Oklahoma	Sun 12-26-81	Houston 40-14 (Bill Yeoman)
Oklahoma	Fiesta 1-1-83	Arizona St. 21-32 (Darryl Rogers)
Oklahoma	Orange 1-1-85	Washington 17-28 (Don James)
Oklahoma	Orange 1-1-86	Penn St. 25-10 (Joe Paterno)
Oklahoma	Orange 1-1-87	Arkansas 42-8 (Ken Hatfield)
Oklahoma	Orange 1-1-88	Miami (Fla.) 14-20 (Jimmy Johnson)
Oklahoma	Fla. Citrus 1-2-89	Clemson 6-13 (Danny Ford)
CHARLIE TATE, 1-1-0 (Florida '42) Born 2-20-21		
Miami (Fla.)	Liberty 12-10-66	Virginia Tech 14-7 (Jerry Claiborne)
Miami (Fla.)	Bluebonnet 12-23-67	Colorado 21-31 (Eddie Crowder)

Coach/School	Bowl/Date	Opponent/Score (Coach)
JIM TATUM, 3-2-1 (North Carolina '35) Born 7-22-13		
Oklahoma	Gator 1-1-47	North Carolina St. 34-13 (Beattie Feathers)
Maryland	Gator 1-1-48	Georgia 20-20 (Wally Butts)
Maryland	Gator 1-2-50	Missouri 20-7 (Don Faurot)
Maryland	Sugar 1-1-52	Tennessee 28-13 (Bob Neyland)
Maryland	Orange 1-1-54	Oklahoma 0-7 (Bud Wilkinson)
Maryland	Orange 1-2-56	Oklahoma 6-20 (Bud Wilkinson)
CHUCK TAYLOR, 0-1-0 (Stanford '43) Born 1-24-20		
Stanford	Rose 1-1-52	Illinois 7-40 (Ray Eliot)
GRANT TEAFF, 4-4-0 (McMurry '56) Born 11-12-33		
Baylor	Cotton 1-1-75	Penn St. 20-41 (Joe Paterno)
Baylor	Peach 12-31-79	Clemson 24-18 (Danny Ford)
Baylor	Cotton 1-1-81	Alabama 2-30 (Paul "Bear" Bryant)
Baylor	Bluebonnet 12-31-83	Oklahoma St. 14-24 (Jimmy Johnson)
Baylor	Liberty 12-27-85	LSU 21-7 (Bill Arnsparger)
Baylor	Bluebonnet 12-31-86	Colorado 21-9 (Bill McCartney)
Baylor	Copper 12-31-91	Indiana 0-24 (Bill Mallory)
Baylor	John Hancock 12-31-92	Arizona 20-15 (Dick Tomey)
EDDIE TEAGUE, 1-0-0 (North Carolina '44) Born 12-14-21		
Citadel	Tangerine 12-30-60	Tennessee Tech 27-0 (Wilburn Tucker)
JEFF TEDFORD, 3-1-0 (Fresno St. '83) Born 8-15-61		
California	Insight 12-26-03	Virginia Tech 52-49 (Frank Beamer)
California	Holiday 12-30-04	Texas Tech 31-45 (Mike Leach)
California	Las Vegas 12-22-05	BYU 35-28 (Bronco Mendenhall)
California	Holiday 12-28-06	Texas A&M 45-10 (Dennis Franchione)
LOU TEPPER, 1-2-0 (Rutgers '67) Born 7-21-45		
Illinois	John Hancock 12-31-91	UCLA 3-6 (Terry Donahue)
Illinois	Holiday 12-30-92	Hawaii 17-27 (Bob Wagner)
Illinois	Liberty 12-31-94	East Caro. 30-0 (Steve Logan)
ROBERT THEDER, 0-1-0 (Western Mich. '63) Born 9-22-39		
California	Garden State 12-15-79	Temple 17-28 (Wayne Hardin)
FRANK THOMAS, 4-2-0 (Notre Dame '23) Born 11-14-1898		
Alabama	Rose 1-1-35	Stanford 29-13 (Claude "Tiny" Thornhill)
Alabama	Rose 1-1-38	California 0-13 (Leonard "Stub" Allison)
Alabama	Cotton 1-1-42	Texas A&M 29-21 (Homer Norton)
Alabama	Orange 1-1-43	Boston College 37-21 (Denny Myers)
Alabama	Sugar 1-1-45	Duke 26-29 (Eddie Cameron)
Alabama	Rose 1-1-46	Southern California 34-14 (Jeff Cravath)
FRED THOMSEN, 0-0-1 (Nebraska '25) Born 4-25-1897		
Arkansas	Dixie Classic 1-1-34	Centenary (La.) 7-7 (Homer Norton)
CLAUDE "TINY" THORNHILL, 1-2-0 (Pittsburgh '17) Born 4-14-1893		
Stanford	Rose 1-1-34	Columbia 0-7 (Lou Little)
Stanford	Rose 1-1-35	Alabama 13-29 (Frank Thomas)
Stanford	Rose 1-1-36	SMU 7-0 (Matty Bell)
JOE TILLER, 3-7-0 (Montana St. '64) Born 12-7-42		
Wyoming	Copper 12-29-93	Kansas St. 17-52 (Bill Snyder)
Purdue	Alamo 12-30-97	Oklahoma St. 33-20 (Bob Simmons)
Purdue	Alamo 12-29-98	Kansas St. 37-34 (Bill Snyder)
Purdue	Outback 1-1-00	Georgia 25-28 (ot) (Jim Donnan)
Purdue	Rose 1-1-01	Washington 24-34 (Rick Neuheisel)
Purdue	Sun 12-31-01	Washington St. 27-33 (Mike Price)
Purdue	Sun 12-31-02	Washington 34-24 (Rick Neuheisel)
Purdue	Capital One 1-1-04	Georgia 27-34 (ot) (Mark Richt)
Purdue	Sun 12-31-04	Arizona St. 23-27 (Dirk Koetter)
Purdue	Champs Sports 12-29-06	Maryland 7-24 (Ralph Friedgen)
GAYNELL TINSLEY, 0-1-0 (LSU '37) Born 2-1-15		
LSU	Sugar 1-2-50	Oklahoma 0-35 (Bud Wilkinson)
JEFF TISDEL, 1-0-0 (Nevada '77) Born 1-10-56		
Nevada	Las Vegas 12-19-96	Ball St. 18-15 (Bill Lynch)
BOB TOLEDO, 1-2-0 (San Fran. St. '68) Born 3-4-46		
UCLA	Cotton 1-1-98	Texas A&M 29-23 (R.C. Slocum)
UCLA	Rose 1-1-99	Wisconsin 31-38 (Barry Alvarez)
UCLA	Sun 12-29-00	Wisconsin 20-21 (Barry Alvarez)
TED TOLLNER, 1-3-0 (Cal Poly '62) Born 5-29-40		
Southern California	Rose 1-1-85	Ohio St. 20-17 (Earle Bruce)
Southern California	Aloha 12-28-85	Alabama 3-24 (Ray Perkins)
Southern California	Fla. Citrus 1-1-87	Auburn 7-16 (Pat Dye)
San Diego St.	Las Vegas 12-19-98	North Carolina 13-20 (Carl Torbush)
DICK TOMEY, 5-3-0 (DePauw '61) Born 6-20-38		
Arizona	Copper 12-30-89	North Carolina St. 17-10 (Dick Sheridan)
Arizona	Aloha 12-28-90	Syracuse 0-28 (Dick MacPherson)
Arizona	John Hancock 12-31-92	Baylor 15-20 (Grant Teaff)
Arizona	Fiesta 1-1-94	Miami (Fla.) 29-0 (Dennis Erickson)
Arizona	Freedom 12-27-94	Utah 13-16 (Ron McBride)
Arizona	Insight.com 12-27-97	New Mexico 20-14 (Dennis Franchione)
Arizona	Holiday 12-30-98	Nebraska 23-20 (Frank Solich)
San Jose St.	New Mexico 12-23-06	New Mexico 20-12 (Rocky Long)
CARL TORBUSH, 2-0-0 (Carson-Newman '74) Born 10-11-51		
North Carolina	Gator 1-1-98	Virginia Tech 42-3 (Frank Beamer)
North Carolina	Las Vegas 12-19-98	San Diego St. 20-13 (Ted Tollner)

Coach/School	Bowl/Date	Opponent/Score (Coach)
CHRIS TORMEY, 1-0-0 (Idaho '78) Born 5-1-55		
Idaho	Humanitarian 12-30-98	Southern Miss. 42-35 (Jeff Bower)
JIM TRESSEL, 4-2-0 (Baldwin-Wallace '75) Born 12-5-52		
Ohio St.	Outback 1-1-02	South Carolina 28-31 (Lou Holtz)
Ohio St.	Fiesta 1-3-03	Miami (Fla.) 31-24 (2 ot) (Larry Coker)
Ohio St.	Fiesta 1-2-04	Kansas St. 35-28 (Bill Snyder)
Ohio St.	Alamo 12-29-04	Oklahoma St. 33-7 (Les Miles)
Ohio St.	Fiesta 1-2-06	Notre Dame 34-20 (Charlie Weis)
Ohio St.	BCS Championship 1-8-07	Florida 14-41 (Urban Meyer)
JIM TRIMBLE, 0-1-0 (Indiana '42) Born 5-29-18		
Wichita St.	Camellia 12-30-48	Hardin-Simmons 12-49 (Warren Woodson)
FRANK TRITICO, 0-0-1 (La.-Lafayette '34) Born 3-25-09		
Randolph Field	Cotton 1-1-44	Texas 7-7 (Dana Bible)
TOMMY TUBERVILLE, 6-3-0 (Southern Ark. '76) Born 9-18-54		
Mississippi	Motor City 12-26-97	Marshall 34-31 (Bob Pruett)
Mississippi	Independence 12-31-98	Texas Tech 35-18 (Spike Dykes)
Auburn	Fla. Citrus 1-1-01	Michigan 28-31 (Lloyd Carr)
Auburn	Peach 12-31-01	North Carolina 10-16 (John Bunting)
Auburn	Capital One 1-1-03	Penn St. 13-9 (Joe Paterno)
Auburn	Music City 12-31-03	Wisconsin 28-14 (Barry Alvarez)
Auburn	Sugar 1-3-05	Virginia Tech 16-13 (Frank Beamer)
Auburn	Capital One 1-2-06	Wisconsin 10-24 (Barry Alvarez)
Auburn	Cotton 1-1-07	Nebraska 17-14 (Bill Callahan)
WILBURN TUCKER, 0-1-0 (Tennessee Tech '43) Born 8-11-20		
Tennessee Tech	Tangerine 12-30-60	Citadel 0-27 (Eddie Teague)
RON TURNER, 1-1-0 (Pacific '77) Born 12-5-53		
Illinois	Micronpc.com 12-30-99	Virginia 63-21 (George Welsh)
Illinois	Sugar 1-1-02	LSU 34-47 (Nick Saban)
BOB TYLER, 1-0-0 (Mississippi '58) Born 7-4-32		
Mississippi St.	Sun 12-28-74	North Carolina 26-24 (Bill Dooley)
THAD "PIE" VANN, 0-2-0 (Mississippi '28) Born 9-22-07		
Southern Miss.	Sun 1-1-53	Pacific 7-26 (Ernie Jorge)
Southern Miss.	Sun 1-1-54	UTEP 14-37 (Mike Brumbelow)
JOHN VAUGHT, 10-8-0 (TCU '33) Born 5-6-08		
Mississippi	Delta 1-1-48	TCU 13-9 (Leo "Dutch" Meyer)
Mississippi	Sugar 1-1-53	Georgia Tech 7-24 (Bobby Dodd)
Mississippi	Sugar 1-1-55	Navy 0-21 (Eddie Erdelatz)
Mississippi	Cotton 1-2-56	TCU 14-13 (Abe Martin)
Mississippi	Sugar 1-1-58	Texas 39-7 (Darrell Royal)
Mississippi	Gator 12-27-58	Florida 7-3 (Bob Woodruff)
Mississippi	Sugar 1-1-60	LSU 21-0 (Paul Dietzel)
Mississippi	Sugar 1-2-61	Rice 14-6 (Jess Neely)
Mississippi	Cotton 1-1-62	Texas 7-12 (Darrell Royal)
Mississippi	Sugar 1-1-63	Arkansas 17-13 (Frank Broyles)
Mississippi	Sugar 1-1-64	Alabama 7-12 (Paul "Bear" Bryant)
Mississippi	Bluebonnet 12-19-64	Tulsa 7-14 (Glenn Dobbs)
Mississippi	Liberty 12-18-65	Auburn 13-7 (Ralph "Shug" Jordan)
Mississippi	Bluebonnet 12-17-66	Texas 0-19 (Darrell Royal)
Mississippi	Sun 12-30-67	UTEP 7-14 (Bobby Dobbs)
Mississippi	Liberty 12-14-68	Virginia Tech 34-17 (Jerry Claiborne)
Mississippi	Sugar 1-1-70	Arkansas 27-22 (Frank Broyles)
Mississippi	Gator 1-2-71	Auburn 28-35 (Ralph "Shug" Jordan)
DICK VERMEIL, 1-0-0 (San Jose St. '58) Born 10-30-36		
UCLA	Rose 1-1-76	Ohio St. 23-10 (Woody Hayes)
BOB VOIGTS, 1-0-0 (Northwestern '39) Born 3-29-16		
Northwestern	Rose 1-1-49	California 20-14 (Lynn "Pappy" Waldorf)
JIM WACKER, 0-1-0 (Valparaiso '60) Born 4-28-37		
TCU	Bluebonnet 12-31-84	West Virginia 14-31 (Don Nehlen)
WALLACE WADE, 2-2-1 (Brown '17) Born 6-15-1892		
Alabama	Rose 1-1-26	Washington 20-19 (Enoch Bagshaw)
Alabama	Rose 1-1-27	Stanford 7-7 (Glenn "Pop" Warner)
Alabama	Rose 1-1-31	Washington St. 24-0 (Orin "Babe" Hollingbery)
Duke	Rose 1-2-39	Southern California 3-7 (Howard Jones)
Duke	Rose 1-1-42	Oregon St. 16-20 (Lon Stiner)
BOB WAGNER, 1-1-0 (Wittenberg '69) Born 5-16-47		
Hawaii	Aloha 12-25-89	Michigan St. 13-33 (George Perles)
Hawaii	Holiday 12-30-92	Illinois 27-17 (Lou Tepper)
JIM WALDEN, 0-1-0 (Wyoming '60) Born 4-10-38		
Washington St.	Holiday 12-18-81	BYU 36-38 (LaVell Edwards)
LYNN "PAPPY" WALDORF, 0-3-0 (Syracuse '25) Born 10-3-02		
California	Rose 1-1-49	Northwestern 14-20 (Bob Voigts)
California	Rose 1-2-50	Ohio St. 14-17 (Wes Fesler)
California	Rose 1-1-51	Michigan 6-14 (Bennie Oosterbaan)
D.C. "PEAHEAD" WALKER, 1-1-0 (Samford '22) Born 2-17-1900		
Wake Forest	Gator 1-1-46	South Carolina 26-14 (Johnnie McMillan)
Wake Forest	Dixie 1-1-49	Baylor 7-20 (Bob Woodruff)
ED WALKER, 0-1-0 (Stanford '27) Born 3-25-01		
Mississippi	Orange 1-1-36	Catholic 19-20 (Arthur "Dutch" Bergman)
RANDY WALKER, 0-3-0 (Miami (Ohio) '76) Born 5-29-54		
Northwestern	Alamo 12-20-00	Nebraska 17-66 (Frank Solich)
Northwestern	Motor City 12-26-03	Bowling Green 24-28 (Gregg Brandon)
Northwestern	Sun 12-30-05	UCLA 38-50 (Karl Dorrell)
BILL WALSH, 3-0-0 (San Jose St. '54) Born 11-30-31		
Stanford	Sun 12-31-77	LSU 24-14 (Charlie McClendon)
Stanford	Bluebonnet 12-31-78	Georgia 25-22 (Vince Dooley)
Stanford	Blockbuster 1-1-93	Penn St. 24-3 (Joe Paterno)
DALLAS WARD, 1-0-0 (Oregon St. '27) Born 8-11-06		
Colorado	Orange 1-1-57	Clemson 27-21 (Frank Howard)
MURRAY WARMATH, 1-1-0 (Tennessee '35) Born 12-26-13		
Minnesota	Rose 1-2-61	Washington 7-17 (Jim Owens)
Minnesota	Rose 1-1-62	UCLA 21-3 (Bill Barnes)
GLENN "POP" WARNER, 1-2-1 (Cornell '95) Born 4-5-1871		
Stanford	Rose 1-1-25	Notre Dame 10-27 (Knute Rockne)
Stanford	Rose 1-1-27	Alabama 7-7 (Wallace Wade)
Stanford	Rose 1-2-28	Pittsburgh 7-6 (Jock Sutherland)
Temple	Sugar 1-1-35	Tulane 14-20 (Ted Cox)
CHARLIE WEATHERBIE, 2-0-0 (Oklahoma St. '77) Born 1-17-55		
Utah St.	Las Vegas 12-17-93	Ball St. 42-33 (Paul Schudel)
Navy	Aloha 12-25-96	California 42-38 (Steve Mariucci)
DeWITT WEAVER, 2-1-0 (Tennessee '37) Born 5-11-12		
Texas Tech	Sun 1-1-52	Pacific 25-14 (Ernie Jorge)
Texas Tech	Gator 1-1-54	Auburn 35-13 (Ralph "Shug" Jordan)
Texas Tech	Sun 1-2-56	Wyoming 14-21 (Phil Dickens)
BILL WEEKS, 1-0-0 (Iowa St. '51) Born 10-20-29		
New Mexico	Aviation 12-9-61	Western Mich. 28-12 (Merle Schlosser)
CHARLIE WEIS, 0-2-0 (Notre Dame '78) Born 3-30-56		
Notre Dame	Fiesta 1-2-06	Ohio St. 20-34 (Jim Tressel)
Notre Dame	Sugar 1-3-07	LSU 14-41 (Les Miles)
RALPH "PEST" WELCH, 0-1-0 (Purdue '30) Born 8-11-07		
Washington	Rose 1-1-44	Southern California 0-29 (Jeff Cravath)
GEORGE WELSH, 5-10-0 (Navy '56) Born 8-26-33		
Navy	Holiday 12-22-78	BYU 23-16 (LaVell Edwards)
Navy	Garden State 12-14-80	Houston 0-35 (Bill Yeoman)
Navy	Liberty 12-30-81	Ohio St. 28-31 (Earle Bruce)
Virginia	Peach 12-31-84	Purdue 27-24 (Leon Burtnett)
Virginia	All-American 12-22-87	BYU 22-16 (LaVell Edwards)
Virginia	Fla. Citrus 1-1-90	Illinois 21-31 (John Mackovic)
Virginia	Sugar 1-1-91	Tennessee 22-23 (Johnny Majors)
Virginia	Gator 12-29-91	Oklahoma 14-48 (Gary Gibbs)
Virginia	Carquest 1-1-94	Boston College 13-31 (Tom Coughlin)
Virginia	Independence 12-28-94	TCU 20-10 (Pat Sullivan)
Virginia	Peach 12-30-95	Georgia 34-27 (Ray Goff)
Virginia	Carquest 12-27-96	Miami (Fla.) 21-31 (Butch Davis)
Virginia	Peach 12-31-98	Georgia 33-35 (Jim Donnan)
Virginia	Micronpc.com 12-30-99	Illinois 21-63 (Ron Turner)
Virginia	Oahu Classic 12-24-00	Georgia 14-37 (Jim Donnan)
TOMMY WEST, 3-4-0 (Tennessee '75) Born 7-31-54		
Clemson	Peach 12-31-93	Kentucky 14-13 (Bill Curry)
Clemson	Gator 1-1-96	Syracuse 0-41 (Paul Pasqualoni)
Clemson	Peach 12-28-96	LSU 7-10 (Gerry DiNardo)
Clemson	Peach 1-2-98	Auburn 17-21 (Terry Bowden)
Memphis	New Orleans 12-16-03	North Texas 27-17 (Darrell Dickey)
Memphis	GMAC 12-22-04	Bowling Green 35-52 (Gregg Brandon)
Memphis	Motor City 12-26-05	Akron 38-31 (J.D. Brookhart)
MIKE WHITE, 0-3-0 (California '58) Born 1-3-36		
Illinois	Liberty 12-29-82	Alabama 15-21 (Paul "Bear" Bryant)
Illinois	Rose 1-2-84	UCLA 9-45 (Terry Donahue)
Illinois	Peach 12-31-85	Army 29-31 (Jim Young)
KYLE WHITTINGHAM, 2-0-0 (BYU '84) Born 11-21-59		
Utah	Emerald 12-29-05	Georgia Tech 38-10 (Chan Gailey)
Utah	Armed Forces 12-23-06	Tulsa 25-13 (Steve Kragthorpe)
JOHN WILCE, 0-1-0 (Wisconsin '10) Born 5-12-88		
Ohio St.	Rose 1-1-21	California 0-28 (Andy Smith)
BUD WILKINSON, 6-2-0 (Minnesota '37) Born 4-12-16		
Oklahoma	Sugar 1-1-49	North Carolina 14-6 (Carl Snavely)
Oklahoma	Sugar 1-2-50	LSU 35-0 (Gaynell Tinsley)
Oklahoma	Sugar 1-1-51	Kentucky 7-13 (Paul "Bear" Bryant)
Oklahoma	Orange 1-1-54	Maryland 7-0 (Jim Tatum)
Oklahoma	Orange 1-2-56	Maryland 20-6 (Jim Tatum)
Oklahoma	Orange 1-1-58	Duke 48-21 (Bill Murray)
Oklahoma	Orange 1-1-59	Syracuse 21-6 (Ben Schwartzwalder)
Oklahoma	Orange 1-1-63	Alabama 0-17 (Paul "Bear" Bryant)
BOBBY WILLIAMS, 2-0-0 (Purdue '82) Born 11-21-58		
Michigan St.	Fla. Citrus 1-1-00	Florida 37-34 (Steve Spurrier)
Michigan St.	Silicon Valley 12-31-01	Fresno St. 44-35 (Pat Hill)

Coach/School	Bowl/Date	Opponent/Score (Coach)
IVY WILLIAMSON, 0-1-0 (Michigan '33)		Born 2-4-11
Wisconsin	Rose 1-1-53	Southern California 0-7 (Jess Hill)
TYRONE WILLINGHAM, 1-4-0 (Michigan St. '77)		Born 12-30-53
Stanford	Liberty 12-30-95	East Caro. 13-19 (Steve Logan)
Stanford	Sun 12-31-96	Michigan St. 38-0 (Nick Saban)
Stanford	Rose 1-1-00	Wisconsin 9-17 (Barry Alvarez)
Stanford	Seattle 12-27-01	Georgia Tech 14-24 (Mac McWhorter)
Notre Dame	Gator 1-1-03	North Carolina St. 6-28 (Chuck Amato)
TOM WILSON, 2-0-0 (Texas Tech '66)		Born 2-24-44
Texas A&M	Hall of Fame 12-20-78	Iowa St. 28-12 (Earle Bruce)
Texas A&M	Independence 12-12-81	Oklahoma St. 33-16 (Jimmy Johnson)
SAM WINNINGHAM, 0-1-0 (Colorado '50)		Born 10-11-26
Cal St. Northridge	Pasadena 12-2-67	West Tex. A&M 13-35 (Joe Kerbel)
BOB WOODRUFF, 2-1-0 (Tennessee '39)		Born 3-14-16
Baylor	Dixie 1-1-49	Wake Forest 20-7 (D.C. "Peahead" Walker)
Florida	Gator 1-1-53	Tulsa 14-13 (J.O. "Buddy" Brothers)
Florida	Gator 12-27-58	Mississippi 3-7 (John Vaught)
WARREN WOODSON, 6-1-0 (Baylor '24)		Born 2-24-03
Hardin-Simmons	Sun 1-1-43	Second Air Force 7-13 (Red Reese)
Hardin-Simmons	Alamo 1-4-47	Denver 20-6 (Clyde "Cac" Hubbard)
Hardin-Simmons	Harbor 1-1-48	San Diego St. 53-0 (Bill Schutte)
Hardin-Simmons	Shrine 12-18-48	Ouachita Baptist 40-12 (Wesley Bradshaw)
Hardin-Simmons	Camellia 12-30-48	Wichita St. 49-12 (Jim Trimble)
New Mexico St.	Sun 12-31-59	North Texas 28-8 (Odus Mitchell)
New Mexico St.	Sun 12-31-60	Utah St. 20-13 (John Ralston)
BOWDEN WYATT, 2-2-0 (Tennessee '39)		Born 11-3-17
Wyoming	Gator 1-1-51	Wash. & Lee 20-7 (George Barclay)
Arkansas	Cotton 1-1-55	Georgia Tech 6-14 (Bobby Dodd)
Tennessee	Sugar 1-1-57	Baylor 7-13 (Sam Boyd)
Tennessee	Gator 12-26-57	Texas A&M 3-0 (Paul "Bear" Bryant)
BILL YEOMAN, 6-4-1 (Army '50)		Born 12-26-27
Houston	Tangerine 12-22-62	Miami (Ohio) 49-21 (John Pont)
Houston	Bluebonnet 12-31-69	Auburn 36-7 (Ralph "Shug" Jordan)
Houston	Bluebonnet 12-31-71	Colorado 17-29 (Eddie Crowder)
Houston	Bluebonnet 12-29-73	Tulane 47-7 (Bennie Ellender)
Houston	Bluebonnet 12-23-74	North Carolina St. 31-31 (Lou Holtz)
Houston	Cotton 1-1-77	Maryland 30-21 (Jerry Claiborne)
Houston	Cotton 1-1-79	Notre Dame 34-35 (Dan Devine)
Houston	Cotton 1-1-80	Nebraska 17-14 (Tom Osborne)
Houston	Garden State 12-14-80	Navy 35-0 (George Welsh)
Houston	Sun 12-26-81	Oklahoma 14-40 (Barry Switzer)
Houston	Cotton 1-1-85	Boston College 28-45 (Jack Bicknell)
FIELDING "HURRY UP" YOST, 1-0-0 (Lafayette '97)		Born 4-30-1871
Michigan	Rose 1-1-02	Stanford 49-0 (Charlie Fickert)
JIM YOUNG, 5-1-0 (Bowling Green '57)		Born 4-21-35
Purdue	Peach 12-25-78	Georgia Tech 41-21 (Pepper Rodgers)
Purdue	Bluebonnet 12-31-79	Tennessee 27-22 (Johnny Majors)
Purdue	Liberty 12-27-80	Missouri 28-25 (Warren Powers)
Army	Cherry 12-22-84	Michigan St. 10-6 (George Perles)
Army	Peach 12-31-85	Illinois 31-29 (Mike White)
Army	Sun 12-24-88	Alabama 28-29 (Bill Curry)
RON ZOOK, 0-2-0 [Miami (Ohio) '76]		Born 4-28-54
Florida	Outback 1-1-03	Michigan 30-38 (Lloyd Carr)
Florida	Outback 1-1-04	Iowa 17-37 (Kirk Ferentz)

Coaches Who Have Taken More Than One Team to a Bowl Game

FIVE TEAMS (1)
Lou Holtz: William & Mary, North Carolina St., Arkansas, Notre Dame & South Carolina

FOUR TEAMS (4)
Earle Bruce: Tampa, Iowa St., Ohio St. & Colorado St.
*Dennis Franchione: New Mexico, TCU, Alabama & Texas A&M
Bill Mallory: Miami (Ohio), Colorado, Northern Ill. & Indiana
Larry Smith: Tulane, Arizona, Southern California & Missouri

THREE TEAMS (14)
*Mack Brown: Tulane, North Carolina & Texas
Bear Bryant: Kentucky, Texas A&M & Alabama
Jim Carlen: West Virginia, Texas Tech & South Carolina
Jerry Claiborne: Virginia Tech, Maryland & Kentucky
Bill Curry: Georgia Tech, Alabama & Kentucky

Bill Dooley: North Carolina, Virginia Tech & Wake Forest
*Dennis Erickson: Washington St., Miami (Fla.) & Oregon St.
Ken Hatfield: Air Force, Arkansas & Clemson
John Mackovic: Wake Forest, Illinois & Texas
Johnny Majors: Iowa St., Pittsburgh & Tennessee

Jackie Sherrill: Pittsburgh, Texas A&M & Mississippi St.
John L. Smith: Utah St., Louisville & Michigan St.
*Steve Spurrier: Duke, Florida & South Carolina
Bowden Wyatt: Wyoming, Arkansas & Tennessee

TWO TEAMS (71)
Fred Akers: Wyoming & Texas
Gary Barnett: Northwestern & Colorado
John Barnhill: Tennessee & Arkansas
Emory Bellard: Texas A&M & Mississippi St.
Hugo Bezdek: Oregon & Penn St.

Dana X. Bible: Texas A&M & Texas
*Bobby Bowden: West Virginia & Florida St.
*Rich Brooks: Oregon & Kentucky
Len Casanova: Santa Clara & Oregon
Bobby Collins: Southern Miss. & SMU

John Cooper: Arizona St. & Ohio St.
Lee Corso: Louisville & Indiana
Dick Crum: Miami (Ohio) & North Carolina
Bob Devaney: Wyoming & Nebraska
Dan Devine: Missouri & Notre Dame

Doug Dickey: Tennessee & Florida
Paul Dietzel: LSU & South Carolina
Pat Dye: East Caro. & Auburn
Pete Elliott: California & Illinois
Jack Elway: San Jose St. & Stanford

Bob Folwell: Penn & Navy
Danny Ford: Clemson & Arkansas
Hayden Fry: SMU & Iowa
Vince Gibson: Louisville & Tulane
Sid Gillman: Miami (Ohio) & Cincinnati

Paul Hackett: Pittsburgh & Southern California
Wayne Hardin: Navy & Temple
Woody Hayes: Miami (Ohio) & Ohio St.
Bob Higgins: West Va. Wesleyan & Penn St.
Don James: Kent St. & Washington

Jimmy Johnson: Oklahoma St. & Miami (Fla.)
Frank Kimbrough: Hardin-Simmons & West Tex. A&M
Jimmy Kitts: Rice & Virginia Tech
Dirk Koetter: Boise St. & Arizona St.
Glen Mason: Kansas & Minnesota

*Urban Meyer: Utah & Florida
*Les Miles: Oklahoma St. & LSU
Jess Neely: Clemson & Rice
Rick Neuheisel: Colorado & Washington
Homer Norton: Centenary (La.) & Texas A&M

*George O'Leary: Georgia Tech & UCF
Charley Pell: Clemson & Florida
Jimmy Phelan: Washington & St. Mary's (Cal.)
*Gary Pinkel: Toledo & Missouri
John Pont: Miami (Ohio) & Indiana

*Mike Price: Washington St. & UTEP
Tommy Prothro: Oregon St. & UCLA
John Ralston: Utah St. & Stanford
John Robinson: Southern California & UNLV
Pepper Rodgers: Kansas & Georgia Tech

Bobby Ross: Maryland & Georgia Tech
*Nick Saban: Michigan St. & LSU
George Sauer: Kansas & Baylor
*Howard Schnellenberger: Miami (Fla.) & Louisville
Steve Sloan: Vanderbilt & Texas Tech

Bruce Snyder: California & Arizona St.
*Frank Solich: Nebraska & Ohio
Gene Stallings: Texas A&M & Alabama
Denny Stolz: Bowling Green & San Diego St.
Jim Tatum: Oklahoma & Maryland

*Joe Tiller: Wyoming & Purdue
Ted Tollner: Southern California & San Diego St.
*Tommy Tuberville: Mississippi & Auburn
Wallace Wade: Alabama & Duke
Pop Warner: Stanford & Temple

*Charlie Weatherbie: Utah St. & Navy
George Welsh: Navy & Virginia
*Tommy West: Clemson & Memphis
Bob Woodruff: Baylor & Florida
Warren Woodson: Hardin-Simmons & New Mexico St.

Jim Young: Purdue & Army

**Active coach.*

Coaches With the Most Years Taking One College to a Bowl Game

Coach, Team Taken	Bowls	Consecutive Years
*Joe Paterno, Penn St.	33	13 (1971-83)
*Bobby Bowden, Florida St.	28	25 (1982-2006)
Tom Osborne, Nebraska	25	25 (1973-97)
Bear Bryant, Alabama	24	24 (1959-82)
LaVell Edwards, BYU	22	17 (1978-94)
Vince Dooley, Georgia	20	9 (1980-88)
John Vaught, Mississippi	18	14 (1957-70)
Bo Schembechler, Michigan	17	15 (1975-89)
Darrell Royal, Texas	16	8 (1968-75)
*Frank Beamer, Virginia Tech	14	14 (1993-2006)
Hayden Fry, Iowa	14	8 (1981-88)
*Phillip Fulmer, Tennessee	14	13 (1992-2004)
Don James, Washington	14	9 (1979-87)
Bobby Dodd, Georgia Tech	13	6 (1951-56)
Terry Donahue, UCLA	13	8 (1981-88)
Charlie McClendon, LSU	13	4 (1970-73)
Don Nehlen, West Virginia	13	4 (1981-84)
Barry Switzer, Oklahoma	13	8 (1975-82)
*Lloyd Carr, Michigan	12	12 (1995-2006)
Fisher DeBerry, Air Force	12	4 (1989-92)
Ralph Jordan, Auburn	12	7 (1968-74)
George Welsh, Virginia	12	4 (1993-96)
Barry Alvarez, Wisconsin	11	5 (1996-2000)
John Cooper, Ohio St.	11	10 (1990-99)
Woody Hayes, Ohio St.	11	7 (1972-78)
Johnny Majors, Tennessee	11	7 (1981-87)
R.C. Slocum, Texas A&M	11	5 (1989-94)
Bill Snyder, Kansas St.	11	11 (1993-2003)
*Steve Spurrier, Florida	11	11 (1992-2002)
Bill Yeoman, Houston	11	4 (1978-81)
*Mike Bellotti, Oregon	10	7 (1997-2003)
*Jeff Bower, Southern Miss.	10	5 (2002-06)
Frank Broyles, Arkansas	10	4 (1959-62)
Fred Akers, Texas	9	9 (1977-85)
*Mack Brown, Texas	9	9 (1998-2006)
Bob Devaney, Nebraska	9	5 (1962-66)
Pat Dye, Auburn	9	9 (1982-90)
Lou Holtz, Notre Dame	9	9 (1987-95)
*Sonny Lubick, Colorado St.	9	5 (1999-2003)
Bill McCartney, Colorado	9	7 (1988-94)
John McKay, Southern California	9	4 (1966-69; 1972-75)
Paul Pasqualoni, Syracuse	9	5 (1995-99)
*Joe Tiller, Purdue	9	8 (1997-2004)
Earle Bruce, Ohio St.	8	8 (1979-86)
Wally Butts, Georgia	8	4 (1945-48)
Danny Ford, Clemson	8	5 (1985-89)
John Robinson, Southern California	8	4 (1976-79)
Grant Teaff, Baylor	8	2 (1979-80; 1985-86; 1991-92)
Bud Wilkinson, Oklahoma	8	3 (1948-50)

**Active coach.*

Coaches Who Have Coached in a Bowl Game and Also Coached a Team in the NCAA Basketball Tournament

Coach, School	Bowl	NCAA Tournament
Clarence "Nibs" Price, California	Rose 1-1-29	NCAA 1946
E.L. "Dick" Romney, Utah St.	Raisin 1-1-47	NCAA 1939

Conference Bowl Records

All-Time Football Bowl Subdivision Won-Lost Records

(Through 2006-07 Bowls, Using 2006 Conference Alignments)

ATLANTIC COAST CONFERENCE

School	Bowls	W-L-T	Pct.	Last Appearance
Atlantic				
Boston College	18	12-6-0	.667	2006 Meineke Car Care
Clemson	29	15-14-0	.517	2006 Music City
Florida St.	35	20-13-2	.600	2006 Emerald
Maryland	21	9-10-2	.476	2006 Champs Sports
North Carolina St.	23	12-10-1	.544	2005 Meineke Car Care
Wake Forest	7	4-3-0	.571	2007 Orange
Coastal				
Duke	8	3-5-0	.375	1995 Hall of Fame
Georgia Tech	35	22-13-0	.629	2007 Gator
Miami (Fla.)	31	18-13-0	.581	2006 MPC Computers
North Carolina	25	12-13-0	.480	2004 Continental Tire
Virginia	16	7-9-0	.438	2005 Music City
Virginia Tech	20	7-13-0	.350	2006 Chick-fil-A
Current Members	**268**	**141-122-5**	**.535**	

BIG EAST CONFERENCE

School	Bowls	W-L-T	Pct.	Last Appearance
Connecticut	1	1-0-0	1.000	2004 Motor City
Cincinnati	8	4-4-0	.500	2007 International
Louisville	14	6-7-1	.464	2007 Orange
Pittsburgh	24	10-14-0	.417	2005 Fiesta
Rutgers	3	1-2-0	.333	2006 Texas
South Fla.	2	1-1-0	.500	2006 Papajohns.com
Syracuse	22	12-9-1	.568	2004 Champs Sports
West Virginia	26	11-15-0	.423	2007 Gator
Current Members	**100**	**46-52-2**	**.470**	

BIG TEN CONFERENCE

School	Bowls	W-L-T	Pct.	Last Appearance
Illinois	14	6-8-0	.429	2002 Sugar
Indiana	8	3-5-0	.375	1993 Independence
Iowa	22	11-10-1	.523	2006 Alamo
Michigan	38	18-20-0	.474	2007 Rose
Michigan St.	17	7-10-0	.412	2003 Alamo
Minnesota	12	5-7-0	.417	2006 Insight
Northwestern	6	1-5-0	.167	2005 Sun
Ohio St.	38	18-20-0	.474	2007 BCS Championship
Penn St.	39	25-12-2	.667	2007 Outback
Purdue	14	7-7-0	.500	2006 Champs Sports
Wisconsin	18	10-8-0	.556	2007 Capital One
Current Members	**226**	**111-112-3**	**.498**	

BIG 12 CONFERENCE

School	Bowls	W-L-T	Pct.	Last Appearance
North				
Colorado	27	12-15-0	.444	2005 Champs Sports
Iowa St.	9	2-7-0	.222	2005 Houston
Kansas	10	4-6-0	.400	2005 Fort Worth
Kansas St.	13	6-7-0	.462	2006 Texas
Missouri	23	10-13-0	.435	2006 Sun
Nebraska	44	22-22-0	.500	2007 Cotton
South				
Baylor	16	8-8-0	.500	1994 Alamo
Oklahoma	40	24-15-1	.613	2007 Fiesta
Oklahoma St.	17	11-6-0	.647	2006 Independence
Texas	46	23-21-2	.522	2006 Alamo
Texas A&M	29	13-16-0	.448	2006 Holiday
Texas Tech	30	9-20-1	.317	2006 Insight
Current Members	**304**	**144-156-4**	**.480**	

CONFERENCE USA

School	Bowls	W-L-T	Pct.	Last Appearance
East				
UAB	1	0-1-0	.000	2004 Hawaii
UCF	1	0-1-0	.000	2005 Hawaii
East Caro.	8	4-4-0	.500	2006 Papajohns.com
Marshall	7	5-2-0	.714	2004 Fort Worth
Memphis	4	3-1-0	.750	2005 Motor City
Southern Miss.	15	8-7-0	.533	2007 GMAC

School	Bowls	W-L-T	Pct.	Last Appearance
West				
Houston	17	7-9-1	.441	2006 Liberty
Rice	8	4-4-0	.500	2006 New Orleans
SMU	11	4-6-1	.409	1984 Aloha
UTEP	12	5-7-0	.417	2005 GMAC
Tulane	10	4-6-0	.400	2002 Hawaii
Tulsa	14	5-9-0	.357	2006 Armed Forces
Current Members	**108**	**49-57-2**	**.463**	

MID-AMERICAN CONFERENCE

School	Bowls	W-L-T	Pct.	Last Appearance
East				
Akron	1	0-1-0	.000	2005 Motor City
Bowling Green	7	4-3-0	.571	2004 GMAC
Buffalo	0	0-0-0	.000	Has never appeared
Kent St.	1	0-1-0	.000	1972 Tangerine
Miami (Ohio)	9	6-3-0	.667	2004 Independence
Ohio	3	0-3-0	.000	2007 GMAC
West				
Ball St.	3	0-3-0	.000	1996 Las Vegas
Central Mich.	3	1-2-0	.333	2006 Motor City
Eastern Mich.	1	1-0-0	1.000	1987 California
Northern Ill.	3	2-1-0	.667	2006 Poinsettia
Toledo	10	7-3-0	.700	2005 GMAC
Western Mich.	3	0-3-0	.000	2007 International
Current Members	**44**	**21-23-0**	**.477**	

MOUNTAIN WEST CONFERENCE

School	Bowls	W-L-T	Pct.	Last Appearance
Air Force	17	8-8-1	.500	2002 San Francisco
BYU	25	8-16-1	.340	2006 Las Vegas
Colorado St.	11	4-7-0	.364	2005 Poinsettia
UNLV	3	3-0-0	1.000	2000 Las Vegas
New Mexico	10	2-7-1	.250	2006 New Mexico
San Diego St.	5	1-4-0	.200	1998 Las Vegas
TCU	23	9-13-1	.413	2006 Poinsettia
Utah	12	9-3-0	.750	2006 Armed Forces
Wyoming	11	5-6-0	.455	2004 Las Vegas
Current Members	**117**	**49-64-4**	**.436**	

PACIFIC-10 CONFERENCE

School	Bowls	W-L-T	Pct.	Last Appearance
Arizona	13	5-7-1	.423	1998 Holiday
Arizona St.	23	12-10-1	.543	2006 Hawaii
California	17	8-8-1	.500	2006 Holiday
Oregon	20	7-13-0	.350	2006 Las Vegas
Oregon St.	10	6-4-0	.600	2006 Sun
Southern California	44	28-16-0	.636	2007 Rose
Stanford	20	9-10-1	.475	2001 Seattle
UCLA	28	13-14-1	.482	2006 Emerald
Washington	29	14-14-1	.500	2002 Sun
Washington St.	10	6-4-0	.600	2003 Holiday
Current Members	**214**	**108-100-6**	**.519**	

SOUTHEASTERN CONFERENCE

School	Bowls	W-L-T	Pct.	Last Appearance
Eastern				
Florida	34	16-18-0	.471	2007 BCS Championship
Georgia	42	23-16-3	.583	2006 Chick-fil-A
Kentucky	11	6-5-0	.545	2006 Music City
South Carolina	13	4-9-0	.308	2006 Liberty
Tennessee	46	24-22-0	.522	2007 Outback
Vanderbilt	3	1-1-1	.500	1982 Hall of Fame
Western				
Alabama	54	30-21-3	.583	2006 Independence
Arkansas	35	11-21-3	.357	2007 Capital One
Auburn	33	18-13-2	.576	2007 Cotton
LSU	38	19-18-1	.513	2007 Sugar
Mississippi	31	19-12-0	.613	2004 Cotton
Mississippi St.	12	6-6-0	.500	2000 Independence
Current Members	**352**	**177-162-13**	**.521**	

SUN BELT CONFERENCE

School	Bowls	W-L-T	Pct.	Last Appearance
Arkansas St.	1	0-1-0	.000	2005 New Orleans
Fla. Atlantic	0	0-0-0	.000	Has never appeared
Florida Int'l	0	0-0-0	.000	Has never appeared
La.-Lafayette	0	0-0-0	.000	Has never appeared
La.-Monroe	0	0-0-0	.000	Has never appeared
Middle Tenn.	1	0-1-0	.000	2006 Motor City
North Texas	6	1-5-0	.167	2004 New Orleans
Troy	2	1-1-0	.500	2006 New Orleans
Current Members	**10**	**2-8-0**	**.200**	

WESTERN ATHLETIC CONFERENCE

School	Bowls	W-L-T	Pct.	Last Appearance
Boise St.	7	5-2-0	.714	2007 Fiesta
Fresno St.	16	9-7-0	.563	2005 Liberty
Hawaii	7	5-2-0	.714	2006 Hawaii
Idaho	1	1-0-0	1.000	1998 Humanitarian
Louisiana Tech	4	1-2-1	.375	2001 Humanitarian
Nevada	7	3-4-0	.429	2006 MPC Computers
New Mexico St.	3	2-0-1	.833	1960 Sun
San Jose St.	8	5-3-0	.625	2006 New Mexico
Utah St.	5	1-4-0	.200	1997 Humanitarian
Current Members	**58**	**32-24-2**	**.569**	

INDEPENDENTS

School	Bowls	W-L-T	Pct.	Last Appearance
Army	4	2-2-0	.500	1996 Independence
Navy	13	6-6-1	.500	2006 Meineke Car Care
Notre Dame	28	13-15-0	.464	2007 Sugar
Temple	2	1-1-0	.500	1979 Garden State
Current Members	**47**	**22-24-1**	**.479**	

Award Winners in Bowl Games

Most Valuable Players in Major Bowls

Bowls that are played twice in the same calendar year (i.e., January and December) are listed in chronological order.

ALAMO BOWL

Year	Player, Team, Position
1993	Dave Barr, California, quarterback (offense)
	Jerrott Willard, California, linebacker (defense)
	Larry Blue, Iowa, defensive tackle (sportsmanship award)
1994	Chad Davis, Washington St., quarterback (offense)
	Ron Childs, Washington St., linebacker (defense)
	Adrian Robinson, Baylor, defensive back (sportsmanship award)
1995	Kyle Bryant, Texas A&M, kicker (offense)
	Keith Mitchell, Texas A&M, linebacker (defense)
	Jarrett Irons, Michigan, linebacker (sportsmanship award)
1996	Sedrick Shaw, Iowa, running back (offense)
	James DeVries, Iowa, defensive lineman (defense)
	Shane Dunn, Texas Tech (sportsmanship award)
1997	Billy Dicken, Purdue, quarterback (offense)
	Adrian Beasley, Purdue, safety (defense)
	Kevin Williams, Oklahoma St., cornerback (sportsmanship award)
1998	Drew Brees, Purdue, quarterback (offense)
	Rosevelt Colvin, Purdue, defensive end (defense)
	Jarrod Cooper, Kansas St., free safety (sportsmanship award)
1999	Rashard Casey, Penn St., quarterback (offense)
	LaVar Arrington, Penn St., linebacker (defense)
2000	Dan Alexander, running back, Nebraska (offense)
	Kyle Vanden Bosch, defensive line, Nebraska (defense)
2001	Aaron Greving, running back, Iowa (offense)
	Derrick Pickens, defensive line, Iowa (defense)
2002	Brooks Bollinger, Wisconsin, quarterback (offense)
	Jeff Mack, Wisconsin, linebacker (defense)
	Zac Colvin, Colorado, wide receiver (sportsmanship award)
2003	Jammal Lord, Nebraska, quarterback (offense)
	Trevor Johnson, Nebraska, defensive end (defense)
	Joe Tate, Michigan St., offensive guard (sportsmanship award)
2004	Ted Ginn, Ohio St., wide receiver (offense)
	Simon Fraser, Ohio St., defensive end (defense)
	Donovan Woods, Oklahoma St., quarterback (sportsmanship award)
2005	Cory Ross, Nebraska, running back (offense)
	Leon Hall, Michigan, cornerback (defense)
	Steve Breaston, Michigan, wide receiver (sportsmanship award)
2006	Colt McCoy, Texas, quarterback (offense)
	Aaron Ross, Texas, cornerback (defense)
	Mike Elgin, Iowa, offensive line (sportsmanship award)

ARMED FORCES BOWL

(Formerly Fort Worth Bowl, 2003-05)

Year Player, Team, Position
2003 T.J. Acree, Boise St., wide receiver
2004 Gino Guidugli, Cincinnati, quarterback
2005 Jason Swanson, Kansas, quarterback
Kevin Kolb, Houston, quarterback
2006 Louie Sakoda, Utah, kicker
Paul Smith, Tulsa, quarterback

CAPITAL ONE BOWL

(Formerly Tangerine Bowl, 1947-82; Florida Citrus Bowl, 1983-93; CompUSA Florida Citrus Bowl, 1994-99; OurHouse.com Florida Citrus Bowl, 2000; Capital One/Florida Citrus Bowl, 2001-02)

Year Player, Team, Position
1949 Dale McDaniels, Murray St.
Ted Scown, Sul Ross St.
1950 Don Henigan, St. Vincent
Chick Davis, Emory & Henry
1951 Pete Anania, Charleston (W.V.)
Charles Hubbard, Charleston (W.V.)
1952 Bill Johnson, Stetson
Dave Laude, Stetson
1953 Marvin Brown, Tex. A&M-Commerce
1954 Billy Ray Norris, Tex. A&M-Commerce
Bobby Spann, Arkansas St.
1955 Bill Englehardt, Neb.-Omaha
1956 Pat Tarquinio, Juniata
1957 Ron Mills, West Tex. A&M
1958 Garry Berry, Tex. A&M-Commerce
Neal Hinson, Tex. A&M-Commerce
1958 Sam McCord, Tex. A&M-Commerce
1960 Bucky Pitts, Middle Tenn.
Bob Waters, Presbyterian
Jerry Nettles, Citadel
1961 Win Herbert, Lamar
1962 Joe Lopasky, Houston
Billy Roland, Houston
1963 Sharon Miller, Western Ky.
1964 Bill Cline, East Caro.
Jerry Whelchel, Massachusetts
1965 Dave Alexander, East Caro.
1966 Willie Lanier, Morgan St.
1967 Errol Hook, Tenn.-Martin
Gordon Lambert, Tenn.-Martin
1968 Buster O'Brien, Richmond, back
Walker Gillette, Richmond, lineman
1969 Chuck Ealy, Toledo, back
Dan Crockett, Toledo, lineman
1970 Chuck Ealy, Toledo, back
Vince Hubler, William & Mary, lineman
1971 Chuck Ealy, Toledo, back
Mel Long, Toledo, lineman
1972 Freddie Solomon, Tampa, back
Jack Lambert, Kent St., lineman
1973 Chuck Varner, Miami (Ohio), back
Brad Cousino, Miami (Ohio), lineman
1974 Sherman Smith, Miami (Ohio), back
Brad Cousino, Miami (Ohio), lineman (tie)
John Roudebush, Miami (Ohio), lineman (tie)
1975 Rob Carpenter, Miami (Ohio), back
Jeff Kelly, Miami (Ohio), lineman
1976 Terry Miller, Oklahoma St., back
Phillip Dokes, Oklahoma St., lineman

Most Valuable Player (1977-Present)
1977 Jimmy Jordan, Florida St., quarterback
1978 Ted Brown, North Carolina St., running back
1979 David Woodley, LSU, quarterback
1980 Cris Collinsworth, Florida, wide receiver
1981 Jeff Gaylord, Missouri, linebacker
1982 Randy Campbell, Auburn, quarterback
1983 Johnnie Jones, Tennessee, running back
1984 James Jackson, Georgia, quarterback
1985 Larry Kolic, Ohio St., middle guard
1987 Aundray Bruce, Auburn, linebacker
1988 Rodney Williams, Clemson, quarterback
1989 Terry Allen, Clemson, tailback
1990 Jeff George, Illinois, quarterback
1991 Shawn Jones, Georgia Tech, quarterback
1992 Mike Pawlawski, California, quarterback
1993 Garrison Hearst, Georgia, running back
1994 Bobby Engram, Penn St., wide receiver (overall)
Charlie Garner, Tennessee, tailback (offense)
Lee Rubin, Penn St., free safety (defense)
Raymond Austin, Tennessee, strong safety (defense)
1995 Sherman Williams, Alabama, running back (overall)

Year Player, Team, Position
Joey Galloway, Ohio St., wide receiver (offense)
Dameian Jeffries, Alabama, defensive end (defense)
Matt Finkes, Ohio St., defensive end (defense)
1996 Jay Graham, Tennessee, running back (overall)
Rickey Dudley, Ohio St., tight end (offense)
Leonard Little, Tennessee, defensive end (defense)
Matt Finkes, Ohio St., defensive end (defense)
1997 Peyton Manning, Tennessee, quarterback (overall)
Brian Musso, Northwestern, wide receiver (offense)
Tyrone Hines, Tennessee, linebacker (defense)
Mike Nelson, Northwestern, linebacker (defense)
1998 Fred Taylor, Florida, tailback (overall)
Fred Weary, Florida, cornerback (defense)
Chris Eberly, Penn St., tailback (offense)
Brandon Short, Penn St., linebacker (defense)
1999 Anthony Thomas, Michigan, running back
Sam Sword, Michigan, linebacker (defense)
2000 Plaxico Burress, Michigan St., wide receiver (overall)
Travis Taylor, Florida, wide receiver (offense)
Julien Peterson, Michigan St. (defense)
Andra Davis, Florida (defense)
2001 Anthony Thomas, Michigan, running back (overall)
Ben Leard, Auburn, quarterback (offense)
Javar Mills, Auburn, defensive end (defense)
Eric Wilson, Michigan, defensive line (defense)
2002 Casey Clausen, Tennessee, quarterback (overall)
B.J. Askew, Michigan, running back (offense)
John Henderson, Tennessee, defensive line (defense)
Larry Foote, Michigan, linebacker (defense)
2003 Ronnie Brown, Auburn, running back (overall)
Michael Robinson, Penn St., quarterback (offense)
Dontarrious Thomas, Auburn, linebacker (defense)
Anthony Adams, Penn St., defensive tackle (defense)
2004 David Greene, Georgia, quarterback
2005 Drew Tate, Iowa, quarterback
2006 Brian Calhoun, Wisconsin, running back
2007 John Stocco, Wisconsin, quarterback

CHAMPS SPORTS BOWL

(Formerly Blockbuster Bowl, 1990-93; Carquest Bowl, 1994-97; Micron PC Bowl, 1998; MicronPC.com Bowl, 1999-00; Visit Florida Tangerine Bowl, 2001; Mazda Tangerine Bowl, 2002-03)

Year Player, Team, Position
1990 Amp Lee, Florida St., running back
1991 David Palmer, Alabama, wide receiver
1992 Darrien Gordon, Stanford, cornerback
1993 Glenn Foley, Boston College, quarterback
1995 Leon Johnson, North Carolina, running back
1996 Tremain Mack, Miami (Fla.), strong safety
1997 Joe Hamilton, Georgia Tech, quarterback
1998 Scott Covington, Miami (Fla.), quarterback
1999 Kurt Kittner, Illinois, quarterback
2000 Philip Rivers, North Carolina St., quarterback
2001 Antonio Bryant, Pittsburgh, wide receiver (overall)
Phillip Rivers, North Carolina St., quarterback (offense)
Lewis Moore, Pittsburgh, linebacker (defense)
Terrance Martin, North Carolina St., defensive line (defense)
Dantonio Burnett, North Carolina St., linebacker (defense)
2002 Kliff Kingsbury, Texas Tech, quarterback (Player of Game)
Kliff Kingsbury, Texas Tech, quarterback (MVP Offense)
Derrick Hamilton, Clemson, wide receiver (MVP Offense)
John Saldi, Texas Tech, linebacker (MVP Defense)
John Leake, Clemson, linebacker (MVP Defense)
2003 Philip Rivers, North Carolina St., quarterback
2004 Reggie Ball, Georgia Tech, quarterback
2005 James Davis, Clemson, running back
2006 Sam Hollenbach, Maryland, quarterback

CHICK-FIL-A BOWL

(Formerly Peach Bowl, 1968-05)

Year Player, Team, Position
1968 Mike Hillman, LSU (offense)
Buddy Millican, Florida St. (defense)
1969 Ed Williams, West Virginia (offense)
Carl Crennel, West Virginia (defense)
1970 Monroe Eley, Arizona St. (offense)
Junior Ah You, Arizona St. (defense)

Year Player, Team, Position
1971 Norris Weese, Mississippi (offense)
Crowell Armstrong, Mississippi (defense)
1972 Dave Buckey, North Carolina St. (offense)
George Bell, North Carolina St. (defense)
1973 Louis Carter, Maryland (offense)
Sylvester Boler, Georgia (defense)
1974 Larry Isaac, Texas Tech (offense)
Dennis Harrison, Vanderbilt (defense)
1975 Dan Kendra, West Virginia (offense)
Ray Marshall, West Virginia (defense)
1976 Rod Stewart, Kentucky (offense)
Mike Martin, Kentucky (defense)
1977 Johnny Evans, North Carolina St. (offense)
Richard Carter, North Carolina St. (defense)
1978 Mark Herrmann, Purdue (offense)
Calvin Clark, Purdue (defense)
1979 Mike Brannan, Baylor (offense)
Andrew Melontree, Baylor (defense)
1980 Jim Kelly, Miami (Fla.) (offense)
Jim Burt, Miami (Fla.) (defense)
1981 Mickey Walczak, West Virginia (offense)
Don Stemple, West Virginia (defense)
1982 Chuck Long, Iowa (offense)
Clay Uhlenhake, Iowa (defense)
1983 Eric Thomas, Florida St. (offense)
Alphonso Carreker, Florida St. (defense)
1984 Howard Petty, Virginia (offense)
Ray Daly, Virginia (defense)
1985 Rob Healy, Army (offense)
Peel Chronister, Army (defense)
1986 Erik Kramer, North Carolina St. (offense)
Derrick Taylor, North Carolina St. (defense)
1987 Reggie Cobb, Tennessee (offense)
Van Waiters, Indiana (defense)
1988 Shane Montgomery, North Carolina St. (offense)
Michael Brooks, North Carolina St. (defense)
1989 Michael Owens, Syracuse (offense)
Rodney Hampton, Georgia (offense)
Terry Wooden, Syracuse (defense)
Morris Lewis, Georgia (defense)
1990 Stan White, Auburn (offense)
Vaughn Dunbar, Indiana (offense)
Darrel Crawford, Auburn (defense)
Mike Dumas, Indiana (defense)
1991 Jeff Blake, East Caro. (offense)
Terry Jordan, North Carolina St. (offense)
Robert Jones, East Caro. (defense)
Billy Ray Haynes, North Carolina St. (defense)
1993 Natrone Means, North Carolina, running back (offense)
Greg Plump, Mississippi St., quarterback (offense)
Bracey Walker, North Carolina, strong safety (defense)
Marc Woodard, Mississippi St., linebacker (defense)
1993 Emory Smith, Clemson, fullback (offense)
Pookie Jones, Kentucky, quarterback (offense)
Brentson Buckner, Clemson, tackle (defense)
Zane Beehn, Kentucky, end (defense)
1995 Treymayne Stephens, North Carolina St., running back
1995 Tiki Barber, Virginia, running back (offense)
Hines Ward, Georgia, quarterback (offense)
Skeet Jones, Virginia, linebacker (defense)
Whit Marshall, Georgia, linebacker (defense)
1996 Herb Tyler, LSU, quarterback (offense)
Raymond Priester, Clemson, running back (offense)
Anthony McFarland, LSU, defensive lineman (defense)
Trevor Pryce, Clemson, defensive lineman (defense)
1998 Dameyune Craig, Auburn, quarterback
Takeo Spikes, Auburn, linebacker
Raymond Priester, Clemson, running back
Rahim Abdullah, Clemson, linebacker
1999 Brian Wofford, Clemson, wide receiver
Chad Carson, Clemson, linebacker
Robert Bean, Mississippi St., cornerback
2000 Rohan Davey, LSU, quarterback
Bradie James, LSU, linebacker
2001 Ronald Curry, North Carolina, quarterback (offense)
Ryan Sims, North Carolina, defensive line (defense)
2002 Scott McBrien, Maryland, quarterback (offense)
E.J. Henderson, Maryland, linebacker (defense)
2004 Chad Jasmin, Clemson, running back (offense)
LeRoy Hill, Clemson, linebacker (defense)
2004 Roscoe Parrish, Miami (Fla.), wide receiver
Devin Hester, Miami (Fla.), defensive back

Year Player, Team, Position
2005 Matt Flynn, LSU, quarterback, (offense)
Melvin Oliver, LSU, defensive end (defense)
2006 Matthew Stafford, Georgia, quarterback (offense)
Tony Taylor, Georgia, linebacker (defense)

COTTON BOWL

Year Player, Team, Position
1937 Ki Aldrich, TCU, center
Sammy Baugh, TCU, quarterback
L.D. Meyer, TCU, end
1938 Ernie Lain, Rice, back
Byron "Whizzer" White, Colorado, quarterback
1939 Jerry Dowd, St. Mary's (Tex.), center
Elmer Tarbox, Texas Tech, back
1940 Banks McFadden, Clemson, back
1941 Charles Henke, Texas A&M, guard
John Kimbrough, Texas A&M, fullback
Chip Routt, Texas A&M, tackle
Lou De Filippo, Fordham, center
Joe Ungerer, Fordham, tackle
1942 Martin Ruby, Texas A&M, tackle
Jimmy Nelson, Alabama, halfback
Holt Rast, Alabama, end
Don Whitmire, Alabama, tackle
1943 Jack Freeman, Texas, guard
Roy McKay, Texas, fullback
Stanley Mauldin, Texas, tackle
Harvey Hardy, Georgia Tech, guard
Jack Marshall, Georgia Tech, end
1944 Joe Parker, Texas, end
Martin Ruby, Randolph Field, tackle
Glenn Dobbs, Randolph Field, quarterback
1945 Neil Armstrong, Oklahoma St., end
Bob Fenimore, Oklahoma St., back
Ralph Foster, Oklahoma St., tackle
1946 Hub Bechtol, Texas, end
Bobby Layne, Texas, back
Jim Kekeris, Missouri, tackle
1947 Alton Baldwin, Arkansas, end
Y.A. Tittle, LSU, quarterback
1948 Doak Walker, SMU, back
Steve Suhey, Penn St., guard
1949 Kyle Rote, SMU, back
Doak Walker, SMU, back
Brad Ecklund, Oregon, center
Norm Van Brocklin, Oregon, quarterback
1950 Billy Burkhalter, Rice, halfback
Joe Watson, Rice, center
James "Froggie" Williams, Rice, end
1951 Bud McFadin, Texas, guard
Andy Kozar, Tennessee, fullback
Hank Lauricella, Tennessee, halfback
Horace "Bud" Sherrod, Tennessee, defensive end
1952 Keith Flowers, TCU, fullback
Emery Clark, Kentucky, halfback
Ray Correll, Kentucky, guard
Vito "Babe" Parilli, Kentucky, quarterback
1953 Richard Ochoa, Texas, fullback
Harley Sewell, Texas, guard
Bob Griesbach, Tennessee, linebacker
1954 Richard Chapman, Rice, tackle
Dan Hart, Rice, end
Dicky Maegle, Rice, halfback
1955 Bud Brooks, Arkansas, guard
George Humphreys, Georgia Tech, fullback
1956 Buddy Alliston, Mississippi, guard
Eagle Day, Mississippi, quarterback
1957 Norman Hamilton, TCU, tackle
Jim Brown, Syracuse, halfback
1958 Tom Forrestal, Navy, quarterback
Tony Stremic, Navy, guard
1959 Jack Spikes, TCU, fullback
Dave Phillips, Air Force, tackle
1960 Maurice Doke, Texas, guard
Ernie Davis, Syracuse, halfback
1961 Lance Alworth, Arkansas, halfback
Dwight Bumgarner, Duke, tackle
1962 Mike Cotten, Texas, quarterback
Bob Moser, Texas, end
1963 Johnny Treadwell, Texas, guard
Lynn Amedee, LSU, quarterback
1964 Scott Appleton, Texas, tackle
Duke Carlisle, Texas, quarterback
1965 Ronnie Caveness, Arkansas, linebacker
Fred Marshall, Arkansas, quarterback
1966 Joe Labruzzo, LSU, tailback
David McCormick, LSU, tackle
1966 Kent Lawrence, Georgia, tailback
George Patton, Georgia, tackle

Year Player, Team, Position
1968 Grady Allen, Texas A&M, defensive end
Edd Hargett, Texas A&M, quarterback
Bill Hobbs, Texas A&M, linebacker
1969 Tom Campbell, Texas, linebacker
Charles "Cotton" Speyrer, Texas, wide receiver
James Street, Texas, quarterback
1970 Steve Worster, Texas, fullback
Bob Olson, Notre Dame, linebacker
1971 Eddie Phillips, Texas, quarterback
Clarence Ellis, Notre Dame, cornerback
1972 Bruce Bannon, Penn St., defensive end
Lydell Mitchell, Penn St., running back
1973 Randy Braband, Texas, linebacker
Alan Lowry, Texas, quarterback
1974 Wade Johnston, Texas, linebacker
Tony Davis, Nebraska, tailback
1975 Ken Quesenberry, Baylor, safety
Tom Shuman, Penn St., quarterback
1976 Ike Forte, Arkansas, running back
Hal McAfee, Arkansas, linebacker
1977 Alois Blackwell, Houston, running back
Mark Mohr, Houston, cornerback
1978 Vagas Ferguson, Notre Dame, running back
Bob Golic, Notre Dame, linebacker
1979 David Hodge, Houston, linebacker
Joe Montana, Notre Dame, quarterback
1980 Terry Elston, Houston, quarterback
David Hodge, Houston, linebacker
1981 Warren Lyles, Alabama, nose guard
Major Ogilvie, Alabama, running back
1982 Robert Brewer, Texas, quarterback
Robbie Jones, Alabama, linebacker
1983 Wes Hopkins, SMU, strong safety
Lance McIlhenny, SMU, quarterback
1984 Jeff Leiding, Texas, linebacker
John Lastinger, Georgia, quarterback
1985 Bill Romanowski, Boston College, linebacker
Steve Strachan, Boston College, fullback
1986 Domingo Bryant, Texas A&M, strong safety
Bo Jackson, Auburn, tailback
1987 Chris Spielman, Ohio St., linebacker
Roger Vick, Texas A&M, fullback
1988 Adam Bob, Texas A&M, linebacker
Bucky Richardson, Texas A&M, quarterback
1989 LaSalle Harper, Arkansas, linebacker
Troy Aikman, UCLA, quarterback
1990 Carl Pickens, Tennessee, free safety
Chuck Webb, Tennessee, tailback
1991 Craig Erickson, Miami (Fla.), quarterback
Russell Maryland, Miami (Fla.), defensive lineman
1992 Sean Jackson, Florida St., running back
Chris Crooms, Texas A&M, safety
1993 Rick Mirer, Notre Dame, quarterback
Devon McDonald, Notre Dame, defensive end
1994 Lee Becton, Notre Dame, running back
Antonio Shorter, Texas A&M, linebacker
1995 Keyshawn Johnson, Southern California, wide receiver
John Herpin, Southern California, cornerback
1996 Herchell Troutman, Colorado, running back
Marcus Washington, Colorado, defensive back
1997 Steve Sarkisian, BYU, quarterback
Kevin Lockett, Kansas St., wide receiver
Shay Muirbrook, BYU, linebacker
1998 Cade McNown, UCLA, quarterback
Dat Nguyen, Texas A&M, linebacker
1999 Ricky Williams, Texas, running back
Aaron Babino, Texas, linebacker
2000 Cedric Cobbs, Arkansas, running back
D.J. Cooper, Arkansas, linebacker
2001 Jonathan Beasley, Kansas St., quarterback
Chris Johnson, Kansas St., defensive end
2002 Quentin Griffin, Oklahoma, running back
Roy Williams, Oklahoma, defensive back
2003 Roy Williams, Texas, wide receiver (offense)
Cory Redding, Texas, defensive line (defense)
2004 Eli Manning, Mississippi, quarterback (offense)
Josh Cooper, Mississippi, defensive line (defense)
2005 Rick Clausen, Tennessee, quarterback (offense)
Justin Harrell, Tennessee, defensive line (defense)
2006 Brodie Croyle, Alabama, quarterback (offense)
DeMeco Ryans, Alabama, linebacker (defense)
2007 Courtney Taylor, Auburn, wide receiver (offense)
Will Herring, Auburn, linebacker (defense)

EMERALD BOWL
(Formerly San Francisco Bowl, 2002-03)

Year Player, Team, Position
2002 Bryan Randall, Virginia Tech, quarterback (offense)
Anthony Schlegel, Air Force, linebacker (defense)
2003 Derrick Knight, Boston College, running back (offense)
T.J. Stancil, Boston College, defensive back (defense)
2004 Aaron Polanco, Navy, quarterback (offense)
Vaughn Kelly, Navy, defensive back (defense)
2005 Travis LaTendresse, Utah, wide receiver (offense)
Eric Weddle, Utah, cornerback (defense)
2006 Lorenzo Booker, Florida St., wide receiver (offense)
Tony Carter, Florida St., cornerback (defense)

FIESTA BOWL

Year Player, Team, Position
1971 Gary Huff, Florida St., quarterback
Junior Ah You, Arizona St., defensive end
1972 Woody Green, Arizona St., halfback
Mike Fink, Missouri, defensive back
1973 Greg Hudson, Arizona St., split end
Mike Haynes, Arizona St., cornerback
1974 Kenny Walker, Oklahoma St., running back
Phillip Dokes, Oklahoma St., defensive tackle
1975 John Jefferson, Arizona St., split end
Larry Gordon, Arizona St., linebacker
1976 Thomas Lott, Oklahoma, quarterback
Terry Peters, Oklahoma, cornerback
1977 Matt Millen, Penn St., linebacker
Dennis Sproul, Arizona St., quarterback (sportsmanship award)
1978 James Owens, UCLA, running back
Jimmy Walker, Arkansas, defensive tackle
Kenny Easley, UCLA, safety (sportsmanship award)
1979 Mark Schubert, Pittsburgh, kicker
Dave Liggins, Arizona, safety
Dan Fidler, Pittsburgh, offensive guard (sportsmanship award)
1980 Curt Warner, Penn St., running back
Frank Case, Penn St., defensive end (sportsmanship award)
1982 Curt Warner, Penn St., running back
Leo Wisniewski, Penn St., nose tackle
George Achica, Southern California, nose guard (sportsmanship award)
1983 Marcus Dupree, Oklahoma, running back
Jim Jeffcoat, Arizona St., defensive lineman
Paul Ferrer, Oklahoma, center (sportsmanship award)
1984 John Congemi, Pittsburgh, quarterback
Rowland Tatum, Ohio St., linebacker (sportsmanship award)
1985 Gaston Green, UCLA, tailback
James Washington, UCLA, defensive back
Bruce Fleming, Miami (Fla.), linebacker (sportsmanship award)
1986 Jamie Morris, Michigan, running back
Mark Messner, Michigan, defensive tackle
Mike Mallory, Michigan, linebacker (sportsmanship award)
1987 D.J. Dozier, Penn St., running back
Shane Conlan, Penn St., linebacker
Paul O'Connor, Miami (Fla.), offensive guard (sportsmanship award)
1988 Danny McManus, Florida St., quarterback
Neil Smith, Nebraska, defensive lineman
Steve Forch, Nebraska, linebacker (sportsmanship award)
1989 Tony Rice, Notre Dame, quarterback
Frank Stams, Notre Dame, defensive end
Chris Parker, West Virginia, defensive lineman (sportsmanship award)
1990 Peter Tom Willis, Florida St., quarterback
Odell Haggins, Florida St., nose guard
Jake Young, Nebraska, center (sportsmanship award)
1991 Browning Nagle, Louisville, quarterback
Ray Buchanan, Louisville, free safety
1992 O.J. McDuffie, Penn St., wide receiver
Reggie Givens, Penn St., outside linebacker
1993 Marvin Graves, Syracuse, quarterback
Kevin Mitchell, Syracuse, nose guard
1994 Chuck Levy, Arizona, running back
Tedy Bruschi, Arizona, defensive end
Paul White, Miami (Fla.), cornerback (sportsmanship award)
1995 Kordell Stewart, Colorado, quarterback
Shannon Clavelle, Colorado, defensive tackle
Oliver Gibson, Notre Dame, nose guard (sportsmanship award)

Year Player, Team, Position
1996 Tommie Frazier, Nebraska, quarterback
Michael Booker, Nebraska, cornerback
Danny Wuerffel, Florida, quarterback (sportsmanship award)
1997 Curtis Enis, Penn St., tailback
Brandon Noble, Penn St., defensive tackle
Ryan Fiebiger, Texas, center (sportsmanship award)
1998 Michael Bishop, Kansas St., quarterback
Travis Ochs, Kansas St., linebacker
Jason Walters, Syracuse, end (sportsmanship)
1999 Peerless Price, Tennessee, wide receiver
Dwayne Goodrich, Tennessee, cornerback
Ross Brannon, Florida St., offensive tackle (sportsmanship)
2000 Eric Crouch, Nebraska, quarterback
Mike Brown, Nebraska, defensive back (defense)
2001 Jonathan Smith, Oregon St., quarterback
Darnell Robinson, Oregon St., linebacker
2002 Joey Harrington, Oregon, quarterback
Steve Smith, Oregon, defensive back
2003 Craig Krenzel, Ohio St., quarterback
Mike Doss, Ohio St., defensive back
2004 Craig Krenzel, Ohio St., quarterback
A.J. Hawk, Ohio St., linebacker
2005 Alex Smith, Utah, quarterback (co-offense)
Paris Warren, Utah, wide receiver (co-offense)
Steve Fifita, Utah, nose guard (defense)
2006 Troy Smith, Ohio St., quarterback (offense)
A.J. Hawk, Ohio St., linebacker (defense)
2007 Jared Zabransky, Boise St., quarterback (offense)
Marty Tadman, Boise St., safety (defense)

GATOR BOWL

Year Player, Team, Position
1946 Nick Sacrinty, Wake Forest
1947 Joe Golding, Oklahoma
1948 Lu Gambino, Maryland
1949 Bobby Gage, Clemson
1950 Bob Ward, Maryland
1951 Eddie Talboom, Wyoming
1952 Jim Dooley, Miami (Fla.)
1953 Marv Matuszak, Tulsa
John Hall, Florida
1954 Vince Dooley, Auburn
Bobby Cavazos, Texas Tech
1954 Billy Hooper, Baylor
Joe Childress, Auburn
1955 Joe Childress, Auburn
Don Orr, Vanderbilt
1956 Corny Salvaterra, Pittsburgh
Wade Mitchell, Georgia Tech
1957 John David Crow, Texas A&M
Bobby Gordon, Tennessee
1958 Dave Hudson, Florida
Bobby Franklin, Mississippi
1960 Maxie Baughan, Georgia Tech
Jim Mooty, Arkansas
1960 Bobby Ply, Baylor
Larry Libertore, Florida
1961 Joe Auer, Georgia Tech
Galen Hall, Penn St.
1962 Dave Robinson, Penn St.
Tom Shannon, Florida
1963 David Sicks, Air Force
Ken Willard, North Carolina
1965 Carl McAdams, Oklahoma
Fred Biletnikoff, Florida St.
Steve Tensi, Florida
1965 Donny Anderson, Texas Tech
Lenny Snow, Georgia Tech
1966 Floyd Little, Syracuse
Dewey Warren, Tennessee
1967 Tom Sherman, Penn St.
Kim Hammond, Florida St.
1968 Mike Hall, Alabama
Terry McMillan, Missouri
1969 Curt Watson, Tennessee
Mike Kelley, Florida
1971 Archie Manning, Mississippi
Pat Sullivan, Auburn
1971 James Webster, North Carolina
Jimmy Poulos, Georgia
1972 Mark Cooney, Colorado
Wade Whatley, Auburn
1973 Haskell Stanback, Tennessee
Joe Barnes, Texas Tech
1974 Earl Campbell, Texas
Phil Gargis, Auburn

Year Player, Team, Position
1975 Sammy Green, Florida
Steve Atkins, Maryland
1976 Jim Cefalo, Penn St.
Al Hunter, Notre Dame
1977 Jerry Butler, Clemson
Matt Cavanaugh, Pittsburgh
1978 Art Schlichter, Ohio St.
Steve Fuller, Clemson
1979 John Wangler, Michigan
Anthony Carter, Michigan
Matt Kupec, North Carolina
Amos Lawrence, North Carolina
1980 George Rogers, South Carolina
Rick Trocano, Pittsburgh
1981 Gary Anderson, Arkansas
Kelvin Bryant, North Carolina
Ethan Horton, North Carolina
1982 Paul Woodside, West Virginia
Greg Allen, Florida St.
1983 Owen Gill, Iowa
Tony Lilly, Florida
1984 Mike Hold, South Carolina
Thurman Thomas, Oklahoma St.
1985 Thurman Thomas, Oklahoma St.
Chip Ferguson, Florida St.
1986 Brad Muster, Stanford
Rodney Williams, Clemson
1987 Harold Green, South Carolina
Wendell Davis, LSU
1989 Andre Rison, Michigan St.
Wayne Johnson, Georgia
1989 Mike Fox, West Virginia
Levon Kirkland, Clemson
1991 Tyrone Ashley, Mississippi
Michigan offensive line: Tom Dohring, Matt Elliott, Steve Everitt, Dean Dingman, Greg Skrepenak
1991 Cale Gundy, Oklahoma
Tyrone Lewis, Virginia
1992 Errict Rhett, Florida
Reggie Lawrence, North Carolina St.
1993 Brian Burgdorf, Alabama
Corey Holliday, North Carolina
1994 James Stewart, Tennessee
Dwayne Thomas, Virginia Tech
1996 Donovan McNabb, Syracuse, quarterback
Peter Ford, Clemson, cornerback
1997 Oscar Davenport, North Carolina, quarterback
David Saunders, West Virginia, wide receiver
1998 Chris Keldorf, North Carolina, quarterback
Al Clark, Virginia Tech, quarterback
1999 Dez White, Georgia Tech, wide receiver
Joe Hamilton, Georgia Tech, running back
Autry Denson, Notre Dame, running back
2000 Nate Webster, Miami (Fla.), linebacker
2001 Michael Vick, Virginia Tech, quarterback
2002 Javon Walker, Florida St., wide receiver
2003 Phillip Rivers, North Carolina St., quarterback
2004 Scott McBrien, Maryland, quarterback
2005 Leon Washington, Florida St., running back
2006 Cedric Humes, Virginia Tech, running back
Hunter Cantwell, Louisville, quarterback
2007 Patrick White, West Virginia, quarterback
Calvin Johnson, Georgia Tech, wide receiver

GMAC BOWL

(Formerly Mobile Alabama Bowl, 1999; GMAC Mobile Alabama Bowl, 2000)

Year Player, Team, Position
1999 Casey Printers, TCU, quarterback
2000 LaDainian Tomlinson, TCU, running back (overall)
LeRoy Handy, Southern Miss., wide receiver (offense)
Leo Barnes, Southern Miss., defensive back (defense)
2001 Byron Leftwich, Marshall, quarterback
2002 Byron Leftwich, Marshall, quarterback
2003 Ben Roethlisberger, Miami (Ohio), quarterback (overall)
Martin Nance, Miami (Ohio), wide receiver (offense)
Matt Pusateri, Miami (Ohio), defensive back (defense)
Jared Parseghian, Miami (Ohio), kicker (special teams)
2004 Omar Jacobs, Bowling Green, quarterback
2005 Bruce Gradkowski, quarterback, Toledo (overall)
Trinity Dawson, running back, Toledo (offense)
Mike Alston, linebacker, Toledo (defense)
Steve Odom, wide receiver, Toledo (special teams)

Year Player, Team, Position
2007 Jeremy Young, Southern Miss., quarterback (offense)
James Delany, Southern Miss., linebacker (defense)
Britt Barefoot, Southern Miss., kicker (special teams)

HAWAII BOWL

Year Player, Team, Position
2002 Lynaris Elpheage, Tulane, cornerback
2003 Timmy Chang, Hawaii, quarterback (Hawaii MVP)
Jackie Battle, Houston, running back (Houston MVP)
2004 Timmy Chang, Hawaii, quarterback (Hawaii co-MVP)
Chad Owens, Hawaii, wide receiver (Hawaii co-MVP)
Darrell Hackney, UAB, quarterback (UAB MVP)
2005 B.J. Mitchell, Nevada, running back (Nevada MVP)
Brandon Marshall, UCF, wide receiver (UCF MVP)
2006 Colt Brennan, Hawaii, quarterback (Hawaii co-MVP)
Jason Rivers, Hawaii, wide receiver (Hawaii co-MVP)
Ryan Torain, Arizona St., running back (Arizona St. MVP)

HOLIDAY BOWL

Year Player, Team, Position
1978 Phil McConkey, Navy, wide receiver
1979 Marc Wilson, BYU, quarterback
Tim Wilbur, Indiana, cornerback
1980 Jim McMahon, BYU, quarterback
Craig James, SMU, running back
1981 Jim McMahon, BYU, quarterback
Kyle Whittingham, BYU, linebacker
1982 Tim Spencer, Ohio St., running back
Garcia Lane, Ohio St., cornerback
1983 Steve Young, BYU, quarterback
Bobby Bell, Missouri, defensive end
1984 Robbie Bosco, BYU, quarterback
Leon White, BYU, linebacker
1985 Bobby Joe Edmonds, Arkansas, running back
Greg Battle, Arizona St., linebacker
1986 Todd Santos, San Diego St., quarterback (co-offensive)
Mark Vlasic, Iowa, quarterback (co-offensive)
Richard Brown, San Diego St., linebacker
1987 Craig Burnett, Wyoming, quarterback
Anthony Wright, Iowa, cornerback
1988 Barry Sanders, Oklahoma St., running back
Sim Drain, Oklahoma St., linebacker
1989 Blair Thomas, Penn St., running back
Ty Detmer, BYU, quarterback
1990 Bucky Richardson, Texas A&M, quarterback
William Thomas, Texas A&M, linebacker
1991 Ty Detmer, BYU, quarterback
Josh Arnold, BYU, defensive back (co-defensive)
Carlos James, Iowa, defensive back (co-defensive)
1992 Michael Carter, Hawaii, quarterback
Junior Tagoai, Hawaii, defensive tackle
1993 John Walsh, BYU, quarterback (co-offensive)
Raymont Harris, Ohio St., running back (co-offensive)
Lorenzo Styles, Ohio St., linebacker
1994 Todd Collins, Michigan, quarterback (co-offensive)
Anthoney Hill, Colorado St., quarterback (co-offensive)
Matt Dyson, Michigan, linebacker
1995 Brian Kavanagh, Kansas St., quarterback (offense)
Mario Smith, Kansas St., defensive back (defense)
1996 Koy Detmer, Colorado, quarterback (offense)
Nick Ziegler, Colorado, defensive end (defense)
1997 Moses Moreno, Colorado St., quarterback
Darran Hall, Colorado St., wide receiver
1998 Keith Smith, Arizona, quarterback
Chris McAlister, Arizona, cornerback
1999 Jonathan Beasley, Kansas St., quarterback
Darren Howard, Kansas St., linebacker
2000 Joey Harrington, Oregon, quarterback
2001 Major Applewhite, Texas, quarterback (co-offensive)
Willie Hurst, Washington, tailback (co-offensive)
Derrick Johnson, Texas, linebacker (defensive)
2002 Ell Roberson, Kansas St., quarterback (offense)
Terrell Suggs, Arizona St., defensive end (defense)
2003 Sammy Moore, Washington St., wide receiver (offense)
Kyle Basler, Washington St., punter (defense)

Year Player, Team, Position
2004 Sonny Cumbie, Texas Tech, quarterback (offense)
Vincent Meeks, Texas Tech, defensive back (defense)
2005 Rhett Bomar, Oklahoma, quarterback (offense)
Anthony Trucks, Oregon, safety (co-defensive)
C.J. Ah You, Oklahoma, defensive end (co-defensive)
2006 Nate Longshore, California, quarterback (co-offensive)
Marshawn Lynch, California, running back (co-offensive)
Desmond Bishop, California, linebacker (defensive)

HUMANITARIAN BOWL
(Formerly Sports Humanitarian Bowl, 1997; Humanitarian Bowl, 1998-03; MPC Computers Bowl, 2004-06)

Year Player, Team, Position
1997 Steve Smith, Utah St., wide receiver
Chad Plummer, Cincinnati, quarterback
1998 Lee Roberts, Southern Miss., quarterback
John Walsh, Idaho, quarterback
1999 Brock Forsey, Boise St., running back
Chris Redman, Louisville, quarterback
2000 Bart Hendricks, Boise St., quarterback
Chris Porter, UTEP, running back
2001 Woodrow Dantzler, Clemson, quarterback
2002 Bobby Hammer, Boise St., defensive lineman
2003 P.J. Daniels, Georgia Tech, running back
2004 Paul Pinegar, Fresno St., quarterback
2005 Matthew Ryan, Boston College, quarterback (Boston College MVP)
Jared Zabransky, Boise St., quarterback (Boise St. MVP)
2006 Kirby Freeman, Miami (Fla.), quarterback [Miami (Fla.) MVP]
Jeff Rowe, Nevada, quarterback (Nevada MVP)

INDEPENDENCE BOWL

Year Player, Team, Position
1976 Terry McFarland, McNeese St., quarterback
Terry Clark, Tulsa, cornerback
1977 Keith Thibodeaux, Louisiana Tech, quarterback
Otis Wilson, Louisville, linebacker
1978 Theodore Sutton, East Caro., fullback
Zack Valentine, East Caro., defensive end
1979 Joe Morris, Syracuse, running back
Clay Carroll, McNeese St., defensive tackle
1980 Stephan Starring, McNeese St., quarterback
Jerald Baylis, Southern Miss., nose guard
1981 Gary Kubiak, Texas A&M, quarterback
Mike Green, Oklahoma St., linebacker
1982 Randy Wright, Wisconsin, quarterback
Tim Krumrie, Wisconsin, nose guard
1983 Marty Louthan, Air Force, quarterback
Andre Townsend, Mississippi, defensive tackle
1984 Bart Weiss, Air Force, quarterback
Scott Thomas, Air Force, safety
1985 Rickey Foggie, Minnesota, quarterback
Bruce Holmes, Minnesota, linebacker
1986 Mark Young, Mississippi, quarterback
James Mosley, Texas Tech, defensive end
1987 Chris Chandler, Washington, quarterback
David Rill, Washington, linebacker
1988 James Henry, Southern Miss., punt returner/cornerback
1989 Bill Musgrave, Oregon, quarterback
Chris Oldham, Oregon, defensive back
1990 Mike Richardson, Louisiana Tech, running back
Lorenzo Baker, Louisiana Tech, linebacker
1991 Andre Hastings, Georgia, flanker
Torrey Evans, Georgia, linebacker
1992 Todd Dixon, Wake Forest, split end
1993 Maurice DeShazo, Virginia Tech, quarterback
Antonio Banks, Virginia Tech, safety
1994 Mike Groh, Virginia, quarterback
Mike Frederick, Virginia, defensive end
1995 Kevin Faulk, LSU, running back
Gabe Northern, LSU, defensive end
1996 Dameyune Craig, Auburn, quarterback
Takeo Spikes, Auburn, linebacker
Ben Kotwica, Army, linebacker
1997 Rondell Mealey, LSU, running back
Arnold Miller, LSU, defensive end
1998 Romaro Miller, Mississippi, quarterback
1999 Tim Strickland, Mississippi, cornerback
2000 Ja'Mar Toombs, Texas A&M, running back
Willie Blade, Mississippi St., defensive tackle

Year Player, Team, Position
2001 Seneca Wallace, Iowa St., quarterback
Waine Bacon, Alabama, safety (co-defense)
Matt Word, Iowa St., linebacker (co-defense)
2002 Eli Manning, Mississippi, quarterback (offense)
Chris Kelsay, Nebraska, defensive end (defense)
2003 Cedric Cobbs, Arkansas, running back (offense)
Caleb Miller, Arkansas, linebacker (defense)
2004 Bret Meyer, Iowa St., quarterback (offense)
Nik Moser, Iowa St., defensive back (defense)
2005 Brad Smith, Missouri, quarterback (offense)
Marcus King, Missouri, cornerback (defense)
2006 Dantrell Savage, Oklahoma St., tailback (offense)
Jeremy Nethon, Oklahoma St., linebacker (defense)

INSIGHT BOWL
(Formerly Copper Bowl, 1989-96; Insight.com Bowl, 1997-01)

Year Player, Team, Position
1989 Shane Montgomery, North Carolina St., quarterback
Scott Geyer, Arizona, defensive back
1990 Mike Pawlawski, California, quarterback
Robert Midgett, Wyoming, linebacker
1991 Vaughn Dunbar, Indiana, tailback
Mark Hagen, Indiana, linebacker
1992 Drew Bledsoe, Washington St., quarterback (overall)
Phillip Bobo, Washington St., wide receiver (offense)
Kareem Leary, Utah, defensive back (defense)
1993 Andre Coleman, Kansas St., wide receiver (offense)
Kenny McEntyre, Kansas St., cornerback (defense)
1994 John Walsh, BYU, quarterback (overall)
Jamal Willis, BYU, running back (offense)
Broderick Simpson, Oklahoma, linebacker (defense)
1995 Byron Hanspard, Texas Tech, running back (overall)
Zebbie Lethridge, Texas Tech, quarterback (offense)
Mickey Dalton, Air Force, cornerback (defense)
1996 Ron Dayne, Wisconsin, running back
1997 Kelvin Eafon, Arizona, running back
1998 Julian Jones, Missouri, free safety
1999 Cortlen Johnson, Colorado, running back
2000 Sage Rosenfels, Iowa St., quarterback (offense)
Reggie Hayward, Iowa St., defensive end (defense)
2001 James Mungro, Syracuse, running back
2002 Brandon Miree, Pittsburgh, running back (offense)
Claude Harriott, Pittsburgh, defensive lineman (defense)
Derek Anderson, Oregon St., quarterback (sportsmanship)
2003 Aaron Rodgers, California, quarterback (offense)
Ryan Gutierrez, California, defensive back (defense)
2004 Derek Anderson, Oregon St., quarterback (offense)
Trent Bray, Oregon St., linebacker (defense)
2005 Rudy Carpenter, Arizona St., quarterback (offense)
Jamar Williams, Arizona St., linebacker (defense)
Ryan Neill, Rutgers, defensive end (sportsmanship)
2006 Graham Harrell, Texas Tech, quarterback (offense)
Antonio Huffman, Texas Tech, cornerback (defense)

LAS VEGAS BOWL

Year Player, Team, Position
1992 Chris Vargas, Nevada, quarterback
1993 Anthony Calvillo, Utah St., quarterback
Mike Neu, Ball St., quarterback
1994 Henry Bailey, UNLV, running back
1995 Wasean Tait, Toledo, running back
Alex Van Dyke, Nevada, wide receiver
1996 Brad Maynard, Ball St., punter
Mike Crawford, Nevada, linebacker
1997 Pat Johnson, Oregon, wide receiver
Bryce Fisher, Air Force, defensive tackle
1998 Joe Tuipala, San Diego St., linebacker
Ronald Curry, North Carolina, quarterback
1999 Mike Anderson, Utah, running back
2000 Jason Thomas, UNLV, quarterback
Boo Williams, Arkansas, wide receiver
2001 Dameon Hunter, Utah, running back
Troy Polamalu, Southern California, safety
2002 Craig Bragg, UCLA, wide receiver
2003 Steven Jackson, Oregon St., running back
2004 Corey Bramlet, Wyoming, quarterback
2005 Marshawn Lynch, California, running back
2006 Jonny Harline, BYU, wide reciever

LIBERTY BOWL

Year Player, Team, Position
1959 Jay Huffman, Penn St.
1960 Dick Hoak, Penn St.
1961 Ernie Davis, Syracuse
1962 Terry Baker, Oregon St.
1963 Ode Burrell, Mississippi St.
1964 Ernest Adler, Utah
1965 Tom Bryan, Auburn
1966 Jimmy Cox, Miami (Fla.)
1967 Jim Donnan, North Carolina St.
1968 Steve Hindman, Mississippi
1969 Bob Anderson, Colorado
1970 Dave Abercrombie, Tulane
1971 Joe Ferguson, Arkansas
1972 Jim Stevens, Georgia Tech
1973 Stan Fritts, North Carolina St.
1974 Randy White, Maryland
1975 Ricky Bell, Southern California
1976 Barry Krauss, Alabama
1977 Matt Kupec, North Carolina
1978 James Wilder, Missouri
1979 Roch Hontas, Tulane
1980 Mark Herrmann, Purdue
1981 Eddie Meyers, Navy
1982 Jeremiah Castille, Alabama
1983 Doug Flutie, Boston College
1984 Bo Jackson, Auburn
1985 Cody Carlson, Baylor
1986 Jeff Francis, Tennessee
1987 Greg Thomas, Arkansas
1988 Dave Schnell, Indiana
1989 Randy Baldwin, Mississippi
1990 Rob Perez, Air Force
1991 Rob Perez, Air Force
1992 Cassius Ware, Mississippi
1993 Jeff Brohm, Louisville
1994 Johnny Johnson, Illinois
1995 Kwame Ellis, Stanford, cornerback
1996 Malcolm Thomas, Syracuse, running back
1997 Sherrod Gideon, Southern Miss., wide receiver
1998 Shaun King, Tulane, quarterback
1999 Adalius Thomas, Southern Miss., defensive end
2000 Cecil Sapp, Colorado St., running back
2001 David Ragone, Louisville, quarterback
2002 LaTarence Dunbar, TCU, wide receiver (offense)
Jason Goss, TCU, defensive back (defense)
2003 Brandon Warfield, Utah, running back (offense)
Lewis Powell, Utah, defensive line (defense)
2004 Stefan LeFors, Louisville, quarterback
2005 Paul Smith, Tulsa, quarterback
2006 Blake Mitchell, South Carolina, quarterback

MEINEKE CAR CARE BOWL
(Formerly Continental Tire Bowl, 2002-04)

Year Player, Team, Position
2002 Wali Lundy, Virginia, running back
2003 Matt Schaub, Virginia, quarterback
2004 Paul Peterson, Boston College, quarterback
2005 Stephen Tulloch, North Carolina St., linebacker
2006 Jolonn Dunbar, Boston College, linebacker

MOTOR CITY BOWL

Year Player, Team, Position
1997 Deuce McCallister, Mississippi, running back
B.J. Cohen, Marshall, defensive end
1998 Chad Pennington, Marshall, quarterback
1999 Doug Chapman, Marshall, running back
2000 Byron Leftwich, Marshall, quarterback
Michael Owens, Marshall, roverback
2001 Chester Taylor, Toledo, running back
David Gardner, Toledo, defensive line
2002 Brian St. Pierre, Boston College, quarterback
2003 Jason Wright, Northwestern, running back (co-MVP)
Josh Harris, Bowling Green, quarterback (co-MVP)
2004 Dan Orlovsky, Connecticut, quarterback
2005 DeAngelo Williams, Memphis, running back
2006 Dan LeFevour, Central Mich., quarterback

MUSIC CITY BOWL

Year Player, Team, Position
1998 Corey Moore, Virginia Tech, defensive end
1999 James Mungro, Syracuse, running back
2000 Brad Lewis, West Virginia, quarterback
2001 William Green, Boston College, running back
2002 Dan Nystrom, Minnesota, place kicker
2003 Jason Campbell, Auburn, quarterback

Year Player, Team, Position
2004 Marion Barber III, Minnesota, running back
2005 Marques Hagans, Virginia, quarterback
2006 Andre' Woodson, Kentucky, quarterback

NEW ORLEANS BOWL

Year Player, Team, Position
2001 Justin Gallimore, Colorado St., defensive back
2002 Kevin Galbreath, North Texas, running back
2003 Danny Wimprine, Memphis, quarterback
2004 Michael Boley, Southern Miss., linebacker
2005 Shawn Nelson, Southern Miss., wide receiver
2006 Omar Haugabook, Troy, quarterback

ORANGE BOWL

Year Player, Team, Position
1965 Joe Namath, Alabama, quarterback
1966 Steve Sloan, Alabama, quarterback
1967 Larry Smith, Florida, tailback
1968 Bob Warmack, Oklahoma, quarterback
1969 Donnie Shanklin, Kansas, halfback
1970 Chuck Burkhart, Penn St., quarterback
Mike Reid, Penn St., defensive tackle
1971 Jerry Tagge, Nebraska, quarterback
Willie Harper, Nebraska, defensive end
1972 Jerry Tagge, Nebraska, quarterback
Rich Glover, Nebraska, defensive guard
1973 Johnny Rodgers, Nebraska, wingback
Rich Glover, Nebraska, defensive guard
1974 Tom Shuman, Penn St., quarterback
Randy Crowder, Penn St., defensive tackle
1975 Wayne Bullock, Notre Dame, fullback
Leroy Cook, Alabama, defensive end
1976 Steve Davis, Oklahoma, quarterback
Lee Roy Selmon, Oklahoma, defensive tackle
1977 Rod Gerald, Ohio St., quarterback
Tom Cousineau, Ohio St., linebacker
1978 Roland Sales, Arkansas, running back
Reggie Freeman, Arkansas, nose guard
1979 Billy Sims, Oklahoma, running back
Reggie Kinlaw, Oklahoma, nose guard
1980 J.C. Watts, Oklahoma, quarterback
Bud Hebert, Oklahoma, free safety
1981 J.C. Watts, Oklahoma, quarterback
Jarvis Coursey, Florida St., defensive end
1982 Homer Jordan, Clemson, quarterback
Jeff Davis, Clemson, linebacker
1983 Turner Gill, Nebraska, quarterback
Dave Rimington, Nebraska, center
1984 Bernie Kosar, Miami (Fla.), quarterback
Jack Fernandez, Miami (Fla.), linebacker
1985 Jacque Robinson, Washington, tailback
Ron Holmes, Washington, defensive tackle
1986 Sonny Brown, Oklahoma, defensive back
Tim Lashar, Oklahoma, kicker
1987 Dante Jones, Oklahoma, linebacker
Spencer Tillman, Oklahoma, halfback
1988 Bernard Clark, Miami (Fla.), linebacker
Darrell Reed, Oklahoma, defensive end
1989 Steve Walsh, Miami (Fla.), quarterback
Charles Fryar, Nebraska, cornerback
1990 Raghib Ismail, Notre Dame, tailback/wide receiver
Darian Hagan, Colorado, quarterback
1991 Charles Johnson, Colorado, quarterback
Chris Zorich, Notre Dame, nose guard
1992 Larry Jones, Miami (Fla.), running back
Tyrone Leggett, Nebraska, cornerback
1993 Charlie Ward, Florida St., quarterback
Corey Dixon, Nebraska, split end
1994 Tommie Frazier, Nebraska, quarterback
Charlie Ward, Florida St., quarterback
1995 Tommie Frazier, Nebraska, quarterback
Chris T. Jones, Miami (Fla.), cornerback
1996 Andre Cooper, Florida St., wide receiver
Derrick Mayes, Notre Dame, wide receiver
1997 Damon Benning, Nebraska, running back
Ken Oxendine, Virginia Tech, running back
1998 Ahman Green, Nebraska, running back
1999 Travis Taylor, Florida, wide receiver
2000 David Terrell, Michigan, wide receiver
2001 Torrance Marshall, Oklahoma, linebacker
2002 Taylor Jacobs, Florida, wide receiver
2003 Carson Palmer, Southern California, quarterback
2004 Jarrett Payton, Miami (Fla.), running back
2005 Matt Leinart, Southern California, quarterback
2006 Willie Reid, Florida St., wide receiver
2007 Brian Brohm, Louisville, quarterback

OUTBACK BOWL
(Formerly Hall of Fame Bowl, 1986-95)

Year Player, Team, Position
1986 Shawn Halloran, Boston College, quarterback
James Jackson, Georgia, quarterback
1988 Jamie Morris, Michigan, tailback
Bobby Humphrey, Alabama, tailback
1989 Robert Drummond, Syracuse, running back
1990 Reggie Slack, Auburn, quarterback
Derek Isaman, Ohio St., linebacker
1991 DeChane Cameron, Clemson, quarterback
1992 Marvin Graves, Syracuse, quarterback
1993 Heath Shuler, Tennessee, quarterback
1994 Tyrone Wheatley, Michigan, running back
1995 Terrell Fletcher, Wisconsin, running back
1996 Bobby Engram, Penn St., wide receiver
1997 Dwayne Rudd, Alabama, linebacker
1998 Mike Bobo, Georgia, quarterback
1999 Courtney Brown, Penn St., defensive end
2000 Drew Brees, Purdue, quarterback
2001 Ryan Brewer, South Carolina, wide receiver
2002 Phil Petty, South Carolina, quarterback
2003 Chris Perry, Michigan, running back
2004 Fred Russell, Iowa, running back
2005 David Pollack, Georgia, defensive end
2006 Dallas Baker, Florida, wide receiver
2007 Tony Hunt, Penn St., running back

POINSETTIA BOWL

Year Player, Team, Position
2005 Reggie Campbell, Navy, running back (offense)
Tyler Tidwell, Navy, linebacker (defense)
2006 Jeff Ballard, TCU, quarterback (offense)
Tommy Blake, TCU, defensive end (defense)

ROSE BOWL

Year Player, Team, Position
1902 Neil Snow, Michigan, fullback
1916 Carl Dietz, Washington St., fullback
1917 John Beckett, Oregon, tackle
1918 Hollis Huntington, Mare Island, fullback
1919 George Halas, Great Lakes, end
1920 Edward Casey, Harvard, halfback
1921 Harold "Brick" Muller, California, end
1922 Russell Stein, Wash. & Jeff., tackle
1923 Leo Calland, Southern California, guard
1924 Ira McKee, Navy, quarterback
1925 Elmer Layden, Notre Dame, fullback
Ernie Nevers, Stanford, fullback
1926 Johnny Mack Brown, Alabama, halfback
George Wilson, Washington, halfback
1927 Fred Pickhard, Alabama, tackle
1928 Clifford Hoffman, Stanford, fullback
1929 Benjamin Lom, California, halfback
1930 Russell Saunders, Southern California, quarterback
1931 John "Monk" Campbell, Alabama, quarterback
1932 Ernie Pinckert, Southern California, halfback
1933 Homer Griffith, Southern California, quarterback
1934 Cliff Montgomery, Columbia, quarterback
1935 Millard "Dixie" Howell, Alabama, halfback
1936 James "Monk" Moscrip, Stanford, end
Keith Topping, Stanford, end
1937 William Daddio, Pittsburgh, end
1938 Victor Bottari, California, halfback
1939 Doyle Nave, Southern California, quarterback
Alvin Krueger, Southern California, end
1940 Ambrose Schindler, Southern California, quarterback
1941 Peter Kmetovic, Stanford, halfback
1942 Donald Durdan, Oregon St., halfback
1943 Charles Trippi, Georgia, halfback
1944 Norman Verry, Southern California, guard
1945 James Hardy, Southern California, quarterback
1946 Harry Gilmer, Alabama, halfback
1947 Claude "Buddy" Young, Illinois, halfback
Julius Rykovich, Illinois, halfback
1948 Robert Chappius, Michigan, halfback
1949 Frank Aschenbrenner, Northwestern, halfback
1950 Fred Morrison, Ohio St., fullback
1951 Donald Dufek, Michigan, fullback
1952 William Tate, Illinois, halfback
1953 Rudy Bukich, Southern California, quarterback
1954 Billy Wells, Michigan St., halfback
1955 Dave Leggett, Ohio St., quarterback
1956 Walter Kowalczyk, Michigan St., halfback
1957 Kenneth Ploen, Iowa, quarterback
1958 Jack Crabtree, Oregon, quarterback
1959 Bob Jeter, Iowa, halfback

Year Player, Team, Position
1960 Bob Schloredt, Washington, quarterback
George Fleming, Washington, halfback
1961 Bob Schloredt, Washington, quarterback
1962 Sandy Stephens, Minnesota, quarterback
1963 Pete Beathard, Southern California, quarterback
Ron VanderKelen, Wisconsin, quarterback
1964 Jim Grabowski, Illinois, fullback
1965 Mel Anthony, Michigan, fullback
1966 Bob Stiles, UCLA, defensive back
1967 John Charles, Purdue, halfback
1968 O.J. Simpson, Southern California, tailback
1969 Rex Kern, Ohio St., quarterback
1970 Bob Chandler, Southern California, flanker
1971 Jim Plunkett, Stanford, quarterback
1972 Don Bunce, Stanford, quarterback
1973 Sam Cunningham, Southern California, fullback
1974 Cornelius Greene, Ohio St., quarterback
1975 Pat Haden, Southern California, quarterback
John McKay Jr., Southern California, split end
1976 John Sciarra, UCLA, quarterback
1977 Vince Evans, Southern California, quarterback
1978 Warren Moon, Washington, quarterback
1979 Charles White, Southern California, tailback
Rick Leach, Michigan, quarterback
1980 Charles White, Southern California, tailback
1981 Butch Woolfolk, Michigan, running back
1982 Jacque Robinson, Washington, running back
1983 Don Rogers, UCLA, free safety
Tom Ramsey, UCLA, quarterback
1984 Rick Neuheisel, UCLA, quarterback
1985 Tim Green, Southern California, quarterback
Jack Del Rio, Southern California, linebacker
1986 Eric Ball, UCLA, tailback
1987 Jeff Van Raaphorst, Arizona St., quarterback
1988 Percy Snow, Michigan St., linebacker
1989 Leroy Hoard, Michigan, fullback
1990 Ricky Ervins, Southern California, tailback
1991 Mark Brunell, Washington, quarterback
1992 Steve Emtman, Washington, defensive tackle
Billy Joe Hobert, Washington, quarterback
1993 Tyrone Wheatley, Michigan, running back
1994 Brent Moss, Wisconsin, tailback
1995 Danny O'Neil, Oregon, quarterback
Ki-Jana Carter, Penn St., running back
1996 Keyshawn Johnson, Southern California, wide receiver
1997 Joe Germaine, Ohio St., quarterback
1998 Brian Griese, Michigan, quarterback
1999 Ron Dayne, Wisconsin, running back
2000 Ron Dayne, Wisconsin, running back
2001 Marques Tuiasosopo, Washington, quarterback
2002 Ken Dorsey, Miami (Fla.), quarterback
Andre Johnson, Miami (Fla.), wide receiver
2003 Nate Hybl, Oklahoma, quarterback
2004 Matt Leinart, Southern California, quarterback
2005 Vince Young, Texas, quarterback
2006 Vince Young, Texas, quarterback
2007 Dwayne Jarrett, Southern California, wide receiver
Brian Cushing, Southern California, linebacker

SUGAR BOWL
Miller-Digby Memorial Trophy

Year Player, Team, Position
1948 Bobby Layne, Texas, quarterback
1949 Jack Mitchell, Oklahoma, quarterback
1950 Leon Heath, Oklahoma, fullback
1951 Walt Yowarsky, Kentucky, tackle
1952 Ed Modzelewski, Maryland, fullback
1953 Leon Hardemann, Georgia Tech, halfback
1954 "Pepper" Rodgers, Georgia Tech, quarterback
1955 Joe Gattuso, Navy, fullback
1956 Franklin Brooks, Georgia Tech, guard
1957 Del Shofner, Baylor, halfback
1958 Raymond Brown, Mississippi, quarterback
1959 Billy Cannon, LSU, halfback
1960 Bobby Franklin, Mississippi, quarterback
1961 Jake Gibbs, Mississippi, quarterback
1962 Mike Fracchia, Alabama, fullback
1963 Glynn Griffing, Mississippi, quarterback
1964 Tim Davis, Alabama, kicker
1965 Doug Moreau, LSU, flanker
1966 Steve Spurrier, Florida, quarterback
1967 Kenny Stabler, Alabama, quarterback
1968 Glenn Smith, LSU, halfback
1969 Chuck Dicus, Arkansas, flanker
1970 Archie Manning, Mississippi, quarterback
1971 Bobby Scott, Tennessee, quarterback
1972 Jack Mildren, Oklahoma, quarterback

Year Player, Team, Position
1972 Tinker Owens, Oklahoma, flanker
1973 Tom Clements, Notre Dame, quarterback
1974 Tony Davis, Nebraska, fullback
1975 Richard Todd, Alabama, quarterback
1977 Matt Cavanaugh, Pittsburgh, quarterback
1978 Jeff Rutledge, Alabama, quarterback
1979 Barry Krauss, Alabama, linebacker
1980 Major Ogilvie, Alabama, running back
1981 Herschel Walker, Georgia, running back
1982 Dan Marino, Pittsburgh, quarterback
1983 Todd Blackledge, Penn St., quarterback
1984 Bo Jackson, Auburn, running back
1985 Craig Sundberg, Nebraska, quarterback
1986 Daryl Dickey, Tennessee, quarterback
1987 Steve Taylor, Nebraska, quarterback
1988 Don McPherson, Syracuse, quarterback
1989 Sammie Smith, Florida St., running back
1990 Craig Erickson, Miami (Fla.), quarterback
1991 Andy Kelly, Tennessee, quarterback
1992 Jerome Bettis, Notre Dame, fullback
1993 Derrick Lassic, Alabama, running back
1994 Errict Rhett, Florida, running back
1995 Warrick Dunn, Florida St., running back
1995 Bryan Still, Virginia Tech, wide receiver
1997 Danny Wuerffel, Florida, quarterback
1998 E.G. Green, Florida St., wide receiver
1999 David Boston, Ohio St., wide receiver
2000 Peter Warrick, Florida St., wide receiver
2001 Ken Dorsey, Miami (Fla.), quarterback
2002 Rohan Davey, LSU, quarterback
2003 Musa Smith, Georgia, running back
2004 Justin Vincent, LSU, running back
2005 Jason Campbell, Auburn, quarterback
2006 Sean Slaton, West Virginia, running back
2007 JaMarcus Russell, LSU, quarterback

SUN BOWL
(Named John Hancock Bowl, 1989-93)

C.M. Hendricks Most Valuable Player Trophy (1954-Present)

Jimmy Rogers Jr. Most Valuable Lineman Trophy (1961-Present)

John Folmer Most Valuable Special Teams Trophy (1994-Present)

Year Player, Team, Position
1950 Harvey Gabriel, UTEP, halfback
1951 Bill Cross, West Tex. A&M, end
1952 Junior Arteburn, Texas Tech, quarterback
1953 Tom McCormick, Pacific, halfback
1954 Dick Shinaut, UTEP, quarterback
1955 Jesse Whittenton, UTEP, quarterback
1956 Jim Crawford, Wyoming, halfback
1957 Claude Austin, George Washington
1958 Leonard Kucewski, Wyoming, guard
1959 Charley Johnson, New Mexico St., quarterback
1960 Charley Johnson, New Mexico St., quarterback
1961 Billy Joe, Villanova, fullback
Richie Ross, Villanova, guard
1962 Jerry Logan, West Tex. A&M, halfback
Don Hoovler, Ohio, guard
1963 Bob Berry, Oregon, quarterback
John Hughes, SMU, guard
1964 Preston Ridlehuber, Georgia, quarterback
Jim Wilson, Georgia, tackle
1965 Billy Stevens, UTEP, quarterback
Ronny Nixon, TCU, tackle
1966 Jim Kiick, Wyoming, tailback
Jerry Durling, Wyoming, middle guard
1967 Billy Stevens, UTEP, quarterback
Fred Carr, UTEP, linebacker
1968 Buddy McClintock, Auburn, defensive back
David Campbell, Auburn, tackle
1969 Paul Rogers, Nebraska, halfback
Jerry Murtaugh, Nebraska, linebacker
1970 Rock Perdoni, Georgia Tech, defensive tackle
Bill Flowers, Georgia Tech, linebacker
1971 Bert Jones, LSU, quarterback
Matt Blair, Iowa St., linebacker
1972 George Smith, Texas Tech, halfback
Ecomet Burley, Texas Tech, defensive tackle
1973 Ray Bybee, Missouri, fullback
John Kelsey, Missouri, tight end
1974 Terry Vitrano, Mississippi St., fullback
Jimmy Webb, Mississippi St., defensive tackle
1975 Robert Haygood, Pittsburgh, quarterback
Al Romano, Pittsburgh, middle guard
1977 Tony Franklin, Texas A&M, kicker
Edgar Fields, Texas A&M, defensive tackle

Year Player, Team, Position
1977 Charles Alexander, LSU, tailback
Gordy Ceresino, Stanford, linebacker
1978 Johnny "Ham" Jones, Texas, running back
Dwight Jefferson, Texas, defensive end
1979 Paul Skansi, Washington, flanker
Doug Martin, Washington, defensive tackle
1980 Jeff Quinn, Nebraska, quarterback
Jimmy Williams, Nebraska, defensive end
1981 Darrell Shepard, Oklahoma, quarterback
Rick Bryan, Oklahoma, defensive tackle
1982 Ethan Horton, North Carolina, tailback
Ronnie Mullins, Texas, defensive end
1983 Walter Lewis, Alabama, quarterback
Wes Neighbors, Alabama, center
1984 Rick Badanjek, Maryland, fullback
Carl Zander, Tennessee, linebacker
1985 Max Zendejas, Arizona, kicker
Peter Anderson, Georgia, center
1986 Cornelius Bennett, Alabama, defensive end
Steve Alvord, Washington, middle guard
1987 Thurman Thomas, Oklahoma St., running back
Darnell Warren, West Virginia, linebacker
1988 David Smith, Alabama, quarterback
Derrick Thomas, Alabama, linebacker
1989 Alex Van Pelt, Pittsburgh, quarterback
Anthony Williams, Texas A&M, linebacker
1990 Courtney Hawkins, Michigan St., wide receiver
Craig Hartsuyker, Southern California, linebacker
1991 Arnold Ale, UCLA, inside linebacker
Jimmy Rogers Jr., Illinois, lineman
1992 Melvin Bonner, Baylor, flanker
1993 Jerald Moore, Oklahoma, running back
1994 Priest Holmes, Texas, running back
Blake Brockermeyer, Texas, offensive lineman
Marcus Wall, North Carolina, wide receiver
1995 Sedrick Shaw, Iowa, running back
Jared DeVries, Iowa, defensive tackle
Brion Hurley, Iowa, kicker
1996 Troy Walters, Stanford, flanker
Kailee Wong, Stanford, defensive end
Chad Hutchinson, Stanford, quarterback
1997 Mike Martin, Arizona St., running back
1998 Basil Mitchell, TCU, tailback
London Dunlap, TCU, defensive end
Adam Abrams, Southern California, placekicker
1999 Billy Cockerham, Minnesota, quarterback
Dyron Russ, Minnesota, tackle
Ryan Rindels, Minnesota, punter
2000 Freddie Mitchell, UCLA, wide receiver
Oscar Cabrera, UCLA, offensive lineman
Michael Bennett, Wisconsin, running back
2001 Lamont Thompson, Washington St., safety
Akin Ayodele, Purdue, defensive end
Drew Dunning, Washington St., placekicker
2002 Kyle Orton, Purdue, quarterback
Shaun Phillips, Purdue, defensive end
Anthony Chambers, Purdue, wide receiver
2003 Samie Parker, Oregon, wide receiver
2004 Sam Keller, Arizona St., quarterback
Brandon Villarreal, Purdue, defensive tackle
Dave Brytus, Purdue, punter
2005 Chris Markey, UCLA, running back (co-MVP)
Kahlil Bell, UCLA, running back (co-MVP)
Kevin Mims, Northwestern, defensive end (lineman)
Brandon Breazell, UCLA, wide receiver (special teams)
2006 Matt Moore, Oregon St., quarterback (MVP)
Xzavie Jackson, Missouri, defensive end (lineman)
Jeff Wolfert, Missouri, placekicker (special teams)

TEXAS BOWL

Year Player, Team, Position
2006 Ray Rice, Rutgers, running back

Most Valuable Players in Former Major Bowls

ALL-AMERICAN BOWL
(Birmingham, Ala.; Known as Hall of Fame Classic, 1977-85)

Year Player, Team, Position
1977 Chuck White, Maryland, split end
Charles Johnson, Maryland, defensive tackle
1978 Curtis Dickey, Texas A&M, running back
1979 Phil Bradley, Missouri, quarterback
1980 Gary Anderson, Arkansas, running back
Billy Ray Smith, Arkansas, linebacker
1981 John Bond, Mississippi St., quarterback
Johnie Cooks, Mississippi St., linebacker
1982 Whit Taylor, Vanderbilt, quarterback
Carl Dieudonne, Air Force, defensive end
1983 Jeff Hostetler, West Virginia, quarterback
1984 Mark Logan, Kentucky, running back
Todd Gregoire, Wisconsin, placekicker
1985 Mark Ingram, Michigan St., wide receiver
1986 Sammie Smith, Florida St., running back
1987 Scott Secules, Virginia, quarterback
1988 Emmitt Smith, Florida, running back
1989 Jerry Gray, Texas Tech, running back
1990 Brett Favre, Southern Miss., quarterback

ALOHA CLASSIC
(Honolulu, Hawaii; Named Aloha Bowl, 1982-97)

Year Player, Team, Position
1982 Offense—Tim Cowan, Washington, quarterback
Defense—Tony Caldwell, Washington, linebacker
1983 Offense—Danny Greene, Washington, wide receiver
Defense—George Reynolds, Penn St., punter
1984 Offense—Jeff Atkins, SMU, running back
Defense—Jerry Ball, SMU, nose guard
1985 Offense—Gene Jelks, Alabama, running back
Defense—Cornelius Bennett, Alabama, linebacker
1986 Offense—Alfred Jenkins, Arizona, quarterback
Defense—Chuck Cecil, Arizona, safety
1987 Troy Aikman, UCLA, quarterback
Emmitt Smith, Florida, running back
1988 David Dacus, Houston quarterback
Victor Wood, Washington St., wide receiver
1989 Blake Ezor, Michigan St., tailback
Chris Roscoe, Hawaii, wide receiver
1990 Todd Burden, Arizona, cornerback
Marvin Graves, Syracuse, quarterback
1991 Tommy Vardell, Stanford, running back
Shawn Jones, Georgia Tech, quarterback
1992 Tom Young, BYU, quarterback
Dana Stubblefield, Kansas, defensive tackle
1993 Rashaan Salaam, Colorado, tailback
Trent Dilfer, Fresno St., quarterback
1994 David Green, Boston College, running back (offensive)
Mike Mamula, Boston College, defensive end (defense)
Joe Gordon, Kansas St., cornerback
1995 Mark Williams, Kansas, quarterback
Karim Abdul-Jabbar, UCLA, running back
1996 Chris McCoy, Navy, quarterback
Pat Barnes, California, quarterback
1997 Rashaan Shehee, Washington, running back
1998 Mike Moschetti, Colorado, quarterback
Akili Smith, Oregon, quarterback
1999 Ben Sankey, Wake Forest, quarterback
2000 Tim Hasselbeck, Boston College, quarterback

AVIATION BOWL
(Dayton, Ohio)

Year Player, Team, Position
1961 Bobby Santiago, New Mexico, running back
Chuck Cummings, New Mexico, guard

BLUEBONNET BOWL
(Houston, Texas)

Year Player, Team, Position
1959 Lowndes Shingles, Clemson
Bob Lilly, TCU
1960 James Saxton, Texas
Lee Roy Jordan, Alabama
1961 Ken Coleman, Kansas
Elvin Basham, Kansas
1962 Bill Tobin, Missouri
Conrad Hitchler, Missouri
1963 Don Trull, Baylor
James Ingram, Baylor
1964 Jerry Rhome, Tulsa
Willy Townes, Tulsa
1965 Dewey Warren, Tennessee
Frank Emanuel, Tennessee
1966 Chris Gilbert, Texas
Fred Edwards, Texas
1967 Bob Anderson, Colorado
Ted Hendricks, Miami (Fla.)
1968 Joe Pearce, Oklahoma
Rufus Cormier, SMU
1969 Jim Strong, Houston
Jerry Drones, Houston

Year Player, Team, Position
1970 Greg Pruitt, Oklahoma
Jeff Rouzie, Alabama
1971 Charlie Davis, Colorado
Butch Brezina, Houston
1972 Condredge Holloway, Tennessee
Carl Johnson, Tennessee
1973 D.C. Nobles, Houston
Deryl McGallion, Houston
1974 John Housmann, Houston
Mack Mitchell, Houston
1975 Earl Campbell, Texas
Tim Campbell, Texas
1976 Chuck Malito, Nebraska
Rodney Allison, Texas Tech
1977 Rob Hertel, Southern California
Walt Underwood, Southern California
1978 Steve Dils, Stanford
Gordy Ceresino, Stanford
1979 Mark Herrmann, Purdue
Roland James, Tennessee
1980 Amos Lawrence, North Carolina
Steve Streater, North Carolina
1981 Butch Woolfolk, Michigan
Ben Needham, Michigan
1982 Gary Anderson, Arkansas
Dwayne Dixon, Florida
1983 Rusty Hilger, Oklahoma St.
Alfred Anderson, Baylor
1984 Willie Drewrey, West Virginia
1985 Pat Evans, Air Force
James McKinney, Texas
1986 Ray Berry, Baylor
Mark Hatcher, Colorado
1987 Tony Jones, Texas
Zeke Gadson, Pittsburgh

BLUEGRASS BOWL
(Louisville, Ky.)

Year Player, Team, Position
1958 Forrest Campbell, Oklahoma St.

CALIFORNIA RAISIN BOWL
(Beginning in 1992, Mid-American Conference and Big West Conference winners met in Las Vegas Bowl)

Year Player, Team, Position
1981 Arnold Smiley, Toledo, running back
Marlin Russell, Toledo, linebacker
1982 Chip Otten, Bowling Green, tailback
Jac Tomasello, Bowling Green, defensive back
1983 Lou Wicks, Northern Ill., fullback
James Pruitt, Cal St. Fullerton, wide receiver
1984 Randall Cunningham, UNLV, quarterback
Steve Morgan, Toledo, tailback
1985 Mike Mancini, Fresno St., punter
Greg Meehan, Bowling Green, flanker
1986 Mike Perez, San Jose St., quarterback
Andrew Marlatt, Miami (Ohio), defensive tackle
1987 Gary Patton, Eastern Mich., tailback
Mike Perez, San Jose St., quarterback
1988 Darrell Rosette, Fresno St., running back
Tony Kimbrough, Western Mich., quarterback
1989 Ron Cox, Fresno St., linebacker
Sean Jones, Ball St., wide receiver
1990 Sheldon Canley, San Jose St., tailback
Ken Ealy, Central Mich., wide receiver
1991 Mark Szlachcic, Bowling Green, wide receiver
Mark Barsotti, Fresno St., quarterback

CHERRY BOWL
(Pontiac, Mich.)

Year Player, Team, Position
1984 Nate Sassaman, Army
1985 Stan Gelbaugh, Maryland
Scott Shankweiler, Maryland

DELTA BOWL
(Memphis, Tenn.)

Year Player, Team, Position
1948 Charlie Conerly, Mississippi

FREEDOM BOWL
(Anaheim, Calif.)

Year Player, Team, Position
1984 Chuck Long, Iowa, quarterback
William Harris, Texas, tight end
1985 Chris Chandler, Washington, quarterback
Barry Helton, Colorado, punter
1986 Gaston Green, UCLA, tailback
Shane Shumway, BYU, defensive back
1987 Daniel Ford, Arizona St., quarterback
Chad Hennings, Air Force, defensive tackle
1988 Ty Detmer, BYU, quarterback
Eric Bieniemy, Colorado, halfback
1989 Cary Conklin, Washington, quarterback
Huey Richardson, Florida, linebacker
1990 Todd Yert, Colorado St., running back
Bill Musgrave, Oregon, quarterback
1991 Marshall Faulk, San Diego St., running back
Ron Jackson, Tulsa, running back
1992 Lorenzo Neal, Fresno St., fullback
Estrus Crayton, Southern California, tailback
1993 Johnnie Morton, Southern California, wide receiver
Henry Lusk, Utah, wide receiver
1994 Tedy Bruschi, Arizona, defensive end
Cal Beck, Utah, kick returner

GARDEN STATE BOWL
(East Rutherford, N.J.)

Year Player, Team, Position
1978 John Mistler, Arizona St.
1979 Mark Bright, Temple
1980 Terald Clark, Houston
1981 Steve Alatorre, Tennessee
Anthony Hancock, Tennessee
Randy Wright, Wisconsin

GOTHAM BOWL
(New York, N.Y.)

Year Player, Team, Position
1961 Don Trull, Baylor
1962 Willie Ross, Nebraska
George Mira, Miami (Fla.)

HARBOR BOWL
(San Diego, Calif.)

Year Player, Team, Position
1947 Bryan Brock, New Mexico
Bill Nelson, Montana St.

HOUSTON BOWL
(Houston, Texas: Named galleryfurniture.com Bowl in 2000 and 2001)

Year Player, Team, Position
2001 Byron Jones, Texas A&M, defensive back (overall)
Joe Weber, Texas A&M, running back (offense)
2002 Rashaun Woods, Oklahoma St., wide receiver (overall/offense)
2003 B.J. Symons, Texas Tech, quarterback (overall/offense)
2004 Joel Klatt, Colorado, quarterback (offense)
Tom Hubbard, Colorado, defensive back (defense)
2005 Todd Blythe, Iowa St., wide receiver (offense)
Jason Berryman, Iowa St., defensive end (defense)

MERCY BOWL
(Los Angeles, Calif.)

Year Player, Team, Position
1961 Beau Carter, Fresno St.

PASADENA BOWL
(Pasadena, Calif.; Named Junior Rose Bowl in 1967)

Year Player, Team, Position
1967 Eugene "Mercury" Morris, West Tex. A&M
Albie Owens, West Tex. A&M
1969 John Featherstone, San Diego St.
1970 Leon Burns, Long Beach St.
Paul Mattingly, Louisville
1971 Tom Carlsen, Memphis
Dornell Harris, Memphis

PRESIDENTIAL CUP
(College Park, Md.)

Year Player, Team, Position
1950 Bob Smith, Texas A&M
Zippy Morocco, Georgia

SALAD BOWL
(Phoenix, Ariz.)

Year Player, Team, Position
1950 Bob McQuade, Xavier
Wilford White, Arizona St.
1951 Jim Bailey, Miami (Ohio)
1952 Gene Shannon, Houston

SEATTLE BOWL
(Seattle, Wash.; Known as Oahu Classic, 1998-2000)

Year Player, Team, Position
1998 Blane Morgan, Air Force, quarterback
1999 Avion Weaver, Hawaii, running back
2000 Terrance Edwards, Georgia, wide receiver
2001 George Godsey, Georgia Tech, quarterback
2002 James MacPherson, Wake Forest, quarterback

SILICON VALLEY CLASSIC
(San Jose, Calif.)

Year Player, Team, Position
2001 Nick Myers, Michigan St., defensive end
Charles Rogers, Michigan St., wide receiver
2002 Rodney Davis, Fresno St., running back
2003 Rodney Davis, Fresno St., running back
2004 DeWhitt Betterson, Troy, running back (offense)
Lionel Hickenbottom, Northern Ill., defensive back (defense)
Dustin Utschig, Northern Ill. (special teams)

Heisman Trophy Winners in Bowl Games

YEAR-BY-YEAR BOWL RESULTS FOR HEISMAN WINNERS
(Includes bowl games immediately after awarding of Heisman Trophy)

Of the 71 winners of the 72 Heisman Trophies (Archie Griffin won twice), 47 played in bowl games after they received their prize. Of those 47 players, only 22 were on the winning team in the bowl.

Houston's Andre Ware is the only Heisman recipient to miss a bowl date since 1969. The Cougars were on probation during the 1989 season and were ineligible for selection to a bowl. Before that lapse, Oklahoma's Steve Owens in 1969 was the last Heisman awardee not to participate in a bowl game.

Only three of the first 22 Heisman Trophy winners played in bowl games after receiving the award—TCU's Davey O'Brien in 1938, Georgia's Frank Sinkwich in 1942 and SMU's Doak Walker in 1948.

Year	Heisman Winner, Team, Position	Bowl (Opponent, Result)
1935	Jay Berwanger, Chicago, HB	Did not play in bowl
1936	Larry Kelley, Yale, E	Did not play in bowl
1937	Clint Frank, Yale, HB	Did not play in bowl
1938	Davey O'Brien, TCU, QB	Sugar (Carnegie Mellon, W 15-7)
1939	Nile Kinnick, Iowa, HB	Did not play in bowl
1940	Tom Harmon, Michigan, HB	Did not play in bowl
1941	Bruce Smith, Minnesota, HB	Did not play in bowl
1942	Frank Sinkwich, Georgia, HB	Rose (UCLA, W 9-0)
1943	Angelo Bertelli, Notre Dame, QB	Did not play in bowl
1944	Les Horvath, Ohio St., QB	Did not play in bowl

Year	Heisman Winner, Team, Position	Bowl (Opponent, Result)
1945	Doc Blanchard, Army, FB	Did not play in bowl
1946	Glenn Davis, Army, HB	Did not play in bowl
1947	Johnny Lujack, Notre Dame, QB	Did not play in bowl
1948	Doak Walker, SMU, HB	Cotton (Oregon, W 21-13)
1949	Leon Hart, Notre Dame, E	Did not play in bowl
1950	Vic Janowicz, Ohio St., HB	Did not play in bowl
1951	Dick Kazmeier, Princeton, HB	Did not play in bowl
1952	Billy Vessels, Oklahoma, HB	Did not play in bowl
1953	John Lattner, Notre Dame, HB	Did not play in bowl
1954	Alan Ameche, Wisconsin, FB	Did not play in bowl
1955	Howard Cassady, Ohio St., HB	Did not play in bowl
1956	Paul Hornung, Notre Dame, QB	Did not play in bowl
1957	John David Crow, Texas A&M, HB	Gator (Tennessee, L 3-0)
1958	Pete Dawkins, Army, HB	Did not play in bowl
1959	Billy Cannon, LSU, HB	Sugar (Mississippi, L 21-0)
1960	Joe Bellino, Navy, HB	Orange (Missouri, L 21-14)
1961	Ernie Davis, Syracuse, HB	Liberty [Miami (Fla.), W 15-14]
1962	Terry Baker, Oregon St., QB	Liberty (Villanova, W 6-0)
1963	Roger Staubach, Navy, QB	Cotton (Texas, L 28-6)
1964	John Huarte, Notre Dame, QB	Did not play in bowl
1965	Mike Garrett, Southern California, HB	Did not play in bowl
1966	Steve Spurrier, Florida, QB	Orange (Georgia Tech, W 27-12)
1967	Gary Beban, UCLA, QB	Did not play in bowl
1968	O.J. Simpson, Southern California, HB	Rose (Ohio St., L 27-16)
1969	Steve Owens, Oklahoma, HB	Did not play in bowl
1970	Jim Plunkett, Stanford, QB	Rose (Ohio St., W 27-17)
1971	Pat Sullivan, Auburn, QB	Sugar (Oklahoma, L 40-22)
1972	Johnny Rodgers, Nebraska, FL	Orange (Notre Dame, W 40-6)
1973	John Cappelletti, Penn St., HB	Orange (LSU, W 16-9)
1974	Archie Griffin, Ohio St., HB	Rose (Southern California, L 18-17)
1975	Archie Griffin, Ohio St., HB	Rose (UCLA, L 23-10)
1976	Tony Dorsett, Pittsburgh, HB	Sugar (Georgia, W 27-3)
1977	Earl Campbell, Texas, HB	Cotton (Notre Dame, L 38-10)
1978	Billy Sims, Oklahoma, HB	Orange (Nebraska, W 31-24)
1979	Charles White, Southern California, HB	Rose (Ohio St., W 17-16)
1980	George Rogers, South Carolina, HB	Gator (Pittsburgh, L 37-9)
1981	Marcus Allen, Southern California, HB	Fiesta (Penn St., L 26-10)
1982	Herschel Walker, Georgia, HB	Sugar (Penn St., L 27-23)
1983	Mike Rozier, Nebraska, HB	Orange [Miami (Fla.), L 31-30]
1984	Doug Flutie, Boston College, QB	Cotton (Houston, W 45-28)
1985	Bo Jackson, Auburn, HB	Cotton (Texas A&M, L 36-16)
1986	Vinny Testaverde, Miami (Fla.), QB	Fiesta (Penn St., L 14-10)
1987	Tim Brown, Notre Dame, WR	Cotton (Texas A&M, L 35-10)
1988	Barry Sanders, Oklahoma St., RB	Holiday (Wyoming, W 62-14)
1989	Andre Ware, Houston, QB	Did not play in bowl
1990	Ty Detmer, BYU, QB	Holiday (Texas A&M, L 65-14)
1991	Desmond Howard, Michigan, WR	Rose (Washington, L 34-14)
1992	Gino Torretta, Miami (Fla.), QB	Sugar (Alabama, L 34-13)
1993	Charlie Ward, Florida St., QB	Orange (Nebraska, W 18-16)
1994	Rashaan Salaam, Colorado, RB	Fiesta (Notre Dame, W 41-24)
1995	Eddie George, Ohio St., RB	Fla. Citrus (Tennessee, L 20-14)
1996	Danny Wuerffel, Florida, QB	Sugar (Florida St., W 52-20)
1997	Charles Woodson, Michigan, CB	Rose (Washington St., W 21-16)
1998	Ricky Williams, Texas, RB	Cotton (Mississippi St., W 38-11)
1999	Ron Dayne, Wisconsin, RB	Rose (Stanford, W 17-9)
2000	Chris Weinke, Florida St., QB	Orange (Oklahoma, L 13-2)
2001	Eric Crouch, Nebraska, QB	Rose [Miami (Fla.), L 37-14]
2002	Carson Palmer, Southern California, QB	Orange (Iowa, W 38-17)
2003	Jason White, Oklahoma, QB	Sugar (LSU, L 21-14)
2004	Matt Leinart, Southern California, QB	Orange (Oklahoma, W 55-19)
2005	Reggie Bush, Southern California, RB	Rose (Texas, L 41-38)
2006	Troy Smith, Ohio St., QB	BCS Championship (Florida, L 41-14)

BOWLS FOR HEISMAN WINNERS

Bowl	Heisman Winner Year	Heisman Winners
Rose	1942, 1968, 1970, 1974, 1975, 1979, 1991, 1997, 1999, 2001, 2005	11
Orange	1960, 1966, 1972, 1973, 1978, 1983, 1993, 2000, 2002, 2004	10
Sugar	1938, 1959, 1971, 1976, 1982, 1992, 1996, 2003	8
Cotton	1948, 1963, 1977, 1984, 1985, 1987, 1998	7
Fiesta	1981, 1986, 1994	3
Gator	1957, 1980	2
Holiday	1988, 1990	2
Liberty	1961, 1962	2
Fla. Citrus	1995	1
BCS Championship	2006	1

HEISMAN TROPHY WINNERS WHO WERE BOWL-GAME MVPs

Heisman Winner, Team (Year Won)	Bowl, Year Played
Doak Walker, SMU (1948)	Cotton, 1948
Doak Walker, SMU (1948)	Cotton, 1949
John David Crow, Texas A&M (1957)	Gator, 1957
Billy Cannon, LSU (1959)	Sugar, 1959
Ernie Davis, Syracuse (1961)	Cotton, 1960
Ernie Davis, Syracuse (1961)	Liberty, 1961
Terry Baker, Oregon St. (1962)	Liberty, 1962
Steve Spurrier, Florida (1966)	Sugar, 1966
O.J. Simpson, Southern California (1968)	Rose, 1968
Jim Plunkett, Stanford (1970)	Rose, 1971
Pat Sullivan, Auburn (1971)	Gator, 1971
Johnny Rodgers, Nebraska (1972)	Orange, 1973
Earl Campbell, Texas (1977)	Gator, 1974
Earl Campbell, Texas (1977)	Bluebonnet, 1975*
Billy Sims, Oklahoma (1978)	Orange, 1979
Charles White, Southern California (1979)	Rose, 1979
Charles White, Southern California (1979)	Rose, 1980
George Rogers, South Carolina (1980)	Gator, 1980
Herschel Walker, Georgia (1982)	Sugar, 1981
Doug Flutie, Boston College (1984)	Liberty, 1983
Bo Jackson, Auburn (1985)	Sugar, 1984
Bo Jackson, Auburn (1985)	Liberty, 1984
Bo Jackson, Auburn (1985)	Cotton, 1986
Barry Sanders, Oklahoma St. (1988)	Holiday, 1988
Ty Detmer, BYU (1990)	Freedom, 1988*
Ty Detmer, BYU (1990)	Holiday, 1989
Ty Detmer, BYU (1990)	Holiday, 1991
Charlie Ward, Florida St. (1993)	Orange, 1994
Danny Wuerffel, Florida (1996)	Sugar, 1997
Ricky Williams, Texas (1998)	Cotton, 1999
Ron Dayne, Wisconsin (1999)	Rose, 1999
Ron Dayne, Wisconsin (1999)	Rose, 2000
Carson Palmer, Southern California (2002)	Orange, 2003
Matt Leinart, Southern California (2004)	Rose, 2004
Matt Leinart, Southern California (2004)	Orange, 2005

**Discontinued bowl.*

Bowls and Polls

Associated Press No. 1 Teams Defeated in Bowl Games

Date	Bowl	Teams Involved	Score	New No. 1
1-1-51	Sugar	No. 7 Kentucky beat No. 1 Oklahoma	13-7	Same
1-1-52	Sugar	No. 3 Maryland beat No. 1 Tennessee	28-13	Same
1-1-54	Orange	No. 4 Oklahoma beat No. 1 Maryland	7-0	Same
1-1-61	Rose	No. 6 Washington beat No. 1 Minnesota	17-7	Same
1-1-65	Orange	No. 5 Texas beat No. 1 Alabama	21-17	Same
1-1-66	Rose	No. 5 UCLA beat No. 1 Michigan St.	14-12	Alabama
1-1-71	Cotton	No. 6 Notre Dame beat No. 1 Texas	24-11	Nebraska
12-31-73	Sugar	No. 3 Notre Dame beat No. 1 Alabama	24-23	Notre Dame
1-1-76	Rose	No. 11 UCLA beat No. 1 Ohio St.	23-10	Oklahoma
1-2-78	Cotton	No. 5 Notre Dame beat No. 1 Texas	38-10	Notre Dame
1-1-79	Sugar	No. 2 Alabama beat No. 1 Penn St.	14-7	Alabama
1-1-80	Rose	No. 3 Southern California beat No. 1 Ohio St.	17-16	Alabama
1-1-83	Sugar	No. 2 Penn St. beat No. 1 Georgia	27-23	Penn St.
1-2-84	Orange	No. 5 Miami (Fla.) beat No. 1 Nebraska	31-30	Miami (Fla.)
1-1-86	Orange	No. 3 Oklahoma beat No. 1 Penn St.	25-10	Oklahoma
1-2-87	Fiesta	No. 2 Penn St. beat No. 1 Miami (Fla.)	14-10	Penn St.
1-1-88	Orange	No. 2 Miami (Fla.) beat No. 1 Oklahoma	20-14	Miami (Fla.)
1-1-90	Orange	No. 4 Notre Dame beat No. 1 Colorado	21-6	Miami (Fla.)
1-1-93	Sugar	No. 2 Alabama beat No. 1 Miami (Fla.)	34-13	Alabama
1-2-97	Sugar	No. 3 Florida beat No. 1 Florida St.	52-20	Florida
1-3-03	Fiesta	No. 2 Ohio St. beat No. 1 Miami (Fla.)	31-24	Ohio St. (2 ot)
1-4-06	Rose	No. 2 Texas beat No. 1 Southern California	41-38	Texas
1-8-07	BCS	No. 2 Florida beat No. 1 Ohio St.	41-14	Florida

Associated Press No. 1 Vs. No. 2 in Bowl Games

Date	Bowl	Teams, Score
1-1-63	Rose	No. 1 Southern California 42, No. 2 Wisconsin 37
1-1-64	Cotton	No. 1 Texas 28, No. 2 Navy 6
1-1-69	Rose	No. 1 Ohio St. 27, No. 2 Southern California 16
1-1-72	Orange	No. 1 Nebraska 38, No. 2 Alabama 6
1-1-79	Sugar	No. 2 Alabama 14, No. 1 Penn St. 7
1-1-83	Sugar	No. 2 Penn St. 27, No. 1 Georgia 23
1-2-87	Fiesta	No. 2 Penn St. 14, No. 1 Miami (Fla.) 10
1-1-88	Orange	No. 2 Miami (Fla.) 20, No. 1 Oklahoma 14
1-1-93	Sugar*	No. 2 Alabama 34, No. 1 Miami (Fla.) 13
1-1-94	Orange*	No. 1 Florida St. 18, No. 2 Nebraska 16
1-2-96	Fiesta*	No. 1 Nebraska 62, No. 2 Florida 24
1-4-99	Fiesta#	No. 1 Tennessee 23, No. 2 Florida St. 16
1-4-00	Sugar#	No. 1 Florida St. 46, No. 2 Virginia Tech 29
1-3-03	Fiesta#	No. 2 Ohio St. 31, No. 1 Miami (Fla.) 24 (2 ot)
1-4-05	Orange#	No. 1 Southern California 55, No. 2 Oklahoma 19
1-4-06	Rose#	No. 2 Texas 41, No. 1 Southern California 38
1-8-07	BCS#	No. 2 Florida 41, No. 1 Ohio St. 14

**Bowl alliance matched the No. 1 and No. 2 teams. #Bowl Championship Series matched the No. 1 and No. 2 teams.*

Bowl Games and the National Championship

(How the bowl games determined the national champion from 1965 to present. Year listed is the football season before the bowl games.)

Note: The national champion was selected before the bowl games as follows: Associated Press (1936-64 and 1966-67); United Press International (1950-73); Football Writers Association of America (1954); and National Football Foundation and Hall of Fame (1959-70).

1965 The Associated Press (AP) selected Alabama as national champion after it defeated Nebraska, 39-28, in the Orange Bowl January 1, 1966.

1968 AP selected Ohio State as national champion after it defeated Southern California, 27-16, in the Rose Bowl January 1, 1969.

1969 AP selected Texas as national champion after it defeated Notre Dame, 21-17, in the Cotton Bowl January 1, 1970.

1970 AP selected Nebraska as national champion after it defeated LSU, 17-12, in the Orange Bowl January 1, 1971.

1971 AP selected Nebraska as national champion after it defeated Alabama, 38-6, in the Orange Bowl January 1, 1972.

1972 AP selected Southern California as national champion after it defeated Ohio State, 42-17, in the Rose Bowl January 1, 1973.

1973 AP selected Notre Dame as national champion after it defeated Alabama, 24-23, in the Sugar Bowl December 31, 1973.

Beginning in 1974, all four of the national polls waited until after the bowl-game results before selecting a national champion. The following list shows how the bowl games figured in the final national championship polls for AP and UPI:

1974 First year of the agreement between the American Football Coaches Association (AFCA) and the UPI Board of Coaches to declare any teams on NCAA probation ineligible for the poll. AP—Oklahoma (11-0-0) did not participate in a bowl game because of NCAA probation. UPI—Southern California (10-1-1) defeated Ohio State, 18-17, in the Rose Bowl January 1, 1975.

1975 AP and UPI both selected Oklahoma (11-1-0). Coach Barry Switzer's Sooners defeated Michigan, 14-6, in the Orange Bowl January 1, 1976. Ohio State had led the AP poll for nine consecutive weeks until a 23-10 loss to UCLA in the Rose Bowl on January 1, 1976. Oklahoma had led the AP poll for the first four weeks of the year.

1976 AP and UPI both selected Tony Dorsett-led Pittsburgh (12-0-0). Pittsburgh whipped Georgia, 27-3, in the Sugar Bowl January 1, 1977. Pittsburgh took over the No. 1 position from Michigan in the ninth week of the season en route to an undefeated year.

1977 AP and UPI were in agreement again, picking Notre Dame as national titlist. The Irish crushed previously undefeated and top-ranked Texas, 38-10, in the Cotton Bowl January 2, 1978. Notre Dame was the sixth team to be ranked No. 1 during the 1977 season in the AP poll.

1978 This was the last time until the 1991 season that the two polls split on a national champion, with AP selecting Alabama (11-1-0) and UPI going for Southern California (12-1-0). Alabama, ranked No. 2 in the AP poll, upset No. 1 Penn State, 14-7, in the Sugar Bowl January 1, 1979. Alabama had been ranked No. 1 in the first two weeks of the season until a 24-14 loss to Southern California.

1979 Unbeaten Alabama (12-0-0) was the unanimous choice of both polls. Bear Bryant's Tide whipped Arkansas easily, 24-9, in the Sugar Bowl January 1, 1980, to claim the title.

1980 Georgia made it three No. 1's in a row for the Southeastern Conference with an undefeated season (12-0-0) to take the top spot in both polls. Vince Dooley's Bulldogs downed Notre Dame, 17-10, behind freshman phenom Herschel Walker in the Sugar Bowl January 1, 1981.

1981 Both polls selected unbeaten Clemson (12-0-0). The Tigers gave coach Danny Ford the first Clemson national football championship with a 22-15 victory over Nebraska in the Orange Bowl January 1, 1982. Clemson did not take over the AP No. 1 slot until the next-to-last poll of the year.

1982 AP and UPI both selected Penn State (11-1-0). The Nittany Lions were No. 2 in the AP poll but knocked off No. 1 Georgia, 27-23, in the Sugar Bowl January 1, 1983. Georgia had led the AP poll for the final five weeks of the season.

1983 AP and UPI had no choice but to select Miami (Florida) as the unanimous champion after the No. 2 Hurricanes downed No. 1 Nebraska, 31-30, in the Orange Bowl January 2, 1984. Many observers felt this may have been the most exciting Orange Bowl ever played as the Cornhuskers failed on a two-point conversion attempt with 48 seconds remaining. Nebraska had led the AP poll since the first week of the season.

1984 Unknown and a victim of the Mountain time zone, BYU (13-0-0) overcame many obstacles to ascend to No. 1 in both polls. Coach LaVell Edwards' Cougars downed Michigan, 24-17, in the Holiday Bowl December 21, 1984. BYU took over the top spot in the AP poll with three weeks left in the season after four other teams came and went as the top-rated team.

1985 Oklahoma (11-1-0) returned as the unanimous choice of both polls. Barry Switzer's Sooners knocked off top-rated Penn State, 25-10, in the Orange Bowl January 1, 1986, to claim the national title.

1986 Penn State (12-0-0) had to battle top-rated Miami (Florida) in the Fiesta Bowl to take the top slot in both polls. Joe Paterno's No. 2 Nittany Lions upset the Hurricanes, 14-10, January 2, 1987, to claim the championship. Miami (Florida) had been ranked No. 1 for the final 10 weeks of the season.

1987 Miami (Florida) (12-0-0) bounced back to a similar scenario as Jimmy Johnson's Hurricanes played underdog and finished ranked first in both polls. The No. 2 Hurricanes beat No. 1-ranked Oklahoma, 20-14, in the Orange Bowl January 1, 1988. The Sooners had been the top-rated AP team for 13 of the season's 15 polls.

1988 Notre Dame (12-0-0) finished as the top team in both polls and gave the Fiesta Bowl its second national title game in three seasons. Lou Holtz's Irish whipped West Virginia, 34-21, January 2, 1989, to claim their eighth AP title. Notre Dame took over the top spot in the poll from UCLA in the ninth week of the season.

1989 Miami (Florida) (11-1-0) claimed its second national title in three years in both polls. The Hurricanes downed Alabama, 33-25, in the Sugar Bowl January 1, 1990, while No. 1-ranked Colorado lost to Notre Dame, 21-6, in the Orange Bowl to clear the way. Notre Dame led the AP poll for 12 of the 15 weeks.

1990 Colorado (11-1-0) and Georgia Tech (11-0-1) split the polls for the first time since 1978 with the Buffs taking the AP vote and the Jackets the UPI. Colorado bounced back from a disappointing 1989 title march to edge Notre Dame, 10-9, in the Orange Bowl January 1, 1991. Georgia Tech had little trouble with Nebraska, 45-21, in the Florida Citrus Bowl January 1, 1991, to finish as Division I-A's only undefeated team.

1991 Miami (Florida) (12-0-0) and Washington (12-0-0) kept Division I-A playoff talk alive with a split in the national polls for the second consecutive year. The Hurricanes took the AP vote, while the Huskies took both the USA Today/CNN and UPI polls. If either had stumbled in a bowl, then the other would have been a unanimous selection. However, Washington drubbed Michigan, 34-14, in the Rose Bowl, and Miami (Florida) had little trouble shutting out Nebraska, 22-0, in the Orange Bowl later that evening.

1992 No. 2 Alabama (13-0-0) turned in a magnificent performance in the Sugar Bowl by upsetting No. 1 Miami (Florida), 34-13, in a game dominated by the Crimson Tide. It marked the first year of the bowl coalition, and the bowlmeisters managed to match the top two teams for the national championship. It also marked the 17th time that a No. 1 team in the AP poll was knocked off in a bowl game since 1951. Alabama was named No. 1 in all polls after the January 1, 1993, matchup.

1993 No. 1 Florida State downed No. 2 Nebraska, 18-16, in the Orange Bowl to become a unanimous national champion. Notre Dame, winner over Texas A&M (24-21) in the Cotton Bowl, wanted to claim the title after beating the Seminoles in the regular season. But a late-season loss to Boston College cost the Irish in the polls. Florida State was No. 1 in all polls after the bowls.

1994 No. 1 Nebraska halted a seven-game bowl losing streak by posting a come-from-behind victory, 24-17, over Miami (Florida) in the Orange Bowl to cap a perfect 13-0 season with the national title. No. 2 Penn State, also undefeated at 12-0, downed Oregon, 38-20, in the Rose Bowl but had to settle for second place in the polls. Nebraska was No. 1 in all polls after the bowls.

1995 Another unanimous year for undefeated and No. 1 Nebraska. The Cornhuskers posted back-to-back national titles with a convincing 62-24 victory over No. 2 Florida in the bowl alliance's Fiesta Bowl matchup.

1996 No. 3 Florida took the national crown in all polls after meeting and beating No. 1 Florida State, 52-20, in the bowl alliance matchup in the Sugar Bowl. Just a month earlier, the Seminoles had knocked off No. 1 Florida and the Gators returned the favor. No. 2 Arizona State was defeated, 20-17, by Ohio State in the non-alliance Rose Bowl and dropped out of national championship consideration.

1997 In the last year before the bowl alliance would include the Rose Bowl, the two top-ranked teams—Michigan and Nebraska—never met for the title. Michigan, the final No. 1 in the Associated Press media poll, defeated Washington State, 21-16, in the Rose Bowl, while Nebraska, No. 1 in the final USA Today/ESPN coaches' poll, rolled over Tennessee, 42-17, in the Orange Bowl. Both teams were rewarded with a piece of the national title. It was the fourth time in the 1990s that the national champion was either shared or unclear.

1998 In the first year of the Bowl Championship Series (BCS), the No. 1 and No. 2 teams (Tennessee and Florida State, respectively) met for the title in the Fiesta. The BCS rankings were a compilation of the Associated Press, USA Today/ESPN, Seattle Times, New York Times and Sagarin polls, and schedule strength, to arrive at the top two teams. Tennessee defeated Florida State, 23-16, and was a unanimous No. 1 in all polls.

1999 In the second year of the BCS, No. 1 Florida State met No. 2 Virginia Tech in the Sugar Bowl. Florida State downed the Hokies, 46-29, to capture the title. The Seminoles, ranked No. 1 all year, went wire-to-wire in most polls for its second national prize in the 1990s.

2000 The third year of the BCS again matched the No. 1 and No. 2 teams (Oklahoma and Florida State, respectively), this time in the Orange Bowl. Oklahoma used team speed and a stingy defense to down the Seminoles, 13-2, holding Heisman Trophy winner Chirs Weinke without a touchdown. The Sooners were a unanimous pick in all polls.

2001 In the fourth year of the BCS, Miami (Florida) became the only undefeated team in the country (12-0) and claimed the mythical title by defeating Nebraska, 37-14, in the Rose Bowl. Miami was ranked No. 1 in the AP poll but Nebraska, No. 4 in the poll, was selected for the championship game over No. 2 Oregon. Heisman Trophy winner Eric Crouch was a member of the losing Cornhusker squad, while coach Larry Coker led Miami to the title in his first season as a head coach.

2002 The fifth year of the BCS ratings matched the No. 1 and No. 2 teams [Miami (Florida) and Ohio State] in the Fiesta Bowl and it turned out to be one of the most exciting college football bowls/poll championships. No. 2 Ohio State prevailed 31-24 after two overtime periods over No. 1 Miami (Florida), a team that had been ranked No. 1 since the first week of the season. Jim Tressel coached the Buckeyes to their first title since 1968 in only his second year at the helm. He also had four Division I-AA national titles at Youngstown State.

2003 The sixth year of the BCS brought nothing but questions as the No. 1 and No. 2 teams in both major polls failed to meet in the title game. Southern California and LSU were No. 1 and No. 2, respectively, in both polls (media and coaches'), but No. 3 Oklahoma held onto its No. 1 spot in the BCS final ratings despite being trounced in the Big 12 Conference championship game. The BCS matched Oklahoma and No. 2 LSU in the Sugar Bowl for the BCS title, while No. 1 Southern California played in the Rose Bowl against Michigan. LSU beat Oklahoma, 21-14, to claim the BCS title and the No. 1 slot in the USA Today/ESPN poll, but Southern California downed Michigan, 28-14, to secure its No. 1 ranking in the Associated Press final poll. That meant another split national championship and grumbling began again for a better system to determine a clear-cut national titlist.

2004 In the seventh year of the BCS, five teams – Auburn, Boise State, Oklahoma, Southern California and Utah – finished the regular season undefeated. Southern California and Oklahoma ended the season ranked No. 1 and No. 2, respectively, in the BCS standings and in both polls, earning spots in the BCS national championship game, this time the Orange Bowl. Southern California won, 55-19, to take the national championship outright and secure its second straight season with at least a portion of the title.

2005 In the eighth year of the BCS, only two teams – Southern California and Texas – finished the regular season undefeated. Southern California and Texas ended the season ranked No. 1 and No. 2, respectively, in the BCS standings and in both polls, earning spots in the BCS national championship game. Texas rallied and scored with 18 seconds left to beat Southern California, 41-38, in the Rose Bowl to take the national championship outright.

2006 In the ninth year of the BCS, just two teams – Boise State and Ohio State – again finished the regular season with perfect records. However, it was Florida that was second in both the BCS standings and the polls, earning the Gators a trip to meet Ohio State in the BCS national championship game. Florida swamped the Buckeyes in the newly-formed BCS National Championship Game, 41-14, to take the national title.

Bowl Results of Teams Ranked in The Associated Press Poll

The bowls and national polls have been perpetually linked since 1936, when The Associated Press introduced its weekly college football poll. The final AP poll was released at the end of the regular season until 1965, when bowl results were included for one year, dropped for two more and then added again in 1968 until the present. This is a list of the key bowl games as they related to the AP poll since 1936 (with pertinent references made to other polls where applicable).

(Key to polls: AP, Associated Press; UPI, United Press International; FW, Football Writers; NFF, National Football Foundation and Hall of Fame; USA/CNN, USA Today/Cable News Network; USA/NFF, USA Today/National Football Foundation and Hall of Fame; UPI/NFF, United Press International/National Football Foundation and Hall of Fame.)

1936 SUGAR—No. 6 Santa Clara beat No. 2 LSU, 21-14; ROSE—No. 3 Pittsburgh beat No. 5 Washington, 21-0; ORANGE—No. 14 Duquesne beat unranked Mississippi St., 13-12; COTTON—No. 16 TCU beat No. 20 Marquette, 16-6. (Minnesota selected No. 1 but did not play in a bowl)

1937 ROSE—No. 2 California beat No. 4 Alabama, 13-0; SUGAR—No. 9 Santa Clara beat No. 8 LSU, 6-0; COTTON—No. 18 Rice beat No. 17 Colorado, 28-14. (Pittsburgh selected No. 1 but did not play in a bowl)

1938 SUGAR—No. 1 TCU beat No. 6 Carnegie Mellon, 15-7; ORANGE—No. 2 Tennessee beat No. 4 Oklahoma, 17-0; ROSE—No. 7 Southern California beat No. 3 Duke, 7-3; COTTON—Unranked St. Mary's (Cal.) beat No. 11 Texas Tech, 20-13. (TCU selected No. 1)

1939 SUGAR—No. 1 Texas A&M beat No. 5 Tulane, 14-13; ROSE—No. 3 Southern California beat No. 2 Tennessee, 14-0; ORANGE—No. 16 Georgia Tech beat No. 6 Missouri, 21-7; COTTON—No. 12 Clemson beat No. 11 Boston College, 6-3. (Texas A&M selected No. 1)

1940 ROSE—No. 2 Stanford beat No. 7 Nebraska, 21-13; SUGAR—No. 5 Boston College beat No. 4 Tennessee, 19-13; COTTON—No. 6 Texas A&M beat No. 12 Fordham, 13-12; ORANGE—No. 9 Mississippi St. beat No. 13 Georgetown, 14-7. (Minnesota selected No. 1 but did not play in a bowl)

1941 ROSE—No. 12 Oregon St. beat No. 2 Duke, 20-16 (played at Durham, N.C., because of World War II); SUGAR—No. 6 Fordham beat No. 7 Missouri, 2-0; COTTON—No. 20 Alabama beat No. 9 Texas A&M, 29-21; ORANGE—No. 14 Georgia beat unranked TCU, 40-26. (Minnesota selected No. 1 but did not play in a bowl)

1942 ROSE—No. 2 Georgia beat No. 13 UCLA, 9-0; SUGAR—No. 7 Tennessee beat No. 4 Tulsa, 14-7; COTTON—No. 11 Texas beat No. 5 Georgia Tech, 14-7; ORANGE—No. 10 Alabama beat No. 8 Boston College, 37-21. (Ohio St. selected No. 1 but did not play in a bowl)

1943 ROSE—Unranked Southern California beat No. 12 Washington, 29-0; COTTON—No. 14 Texas tied unranked Randolph Field, 7-7; SUGAR—No. 13 Georgia Tech beat No. 15 Tulsa, 20-18. (Notre Dame selected No. 1 but did not play in a bowl)

1944 ROSE—No. 7 Southern California beat No. 12 Tennessee, 25-0; ORANGE—Unranked Tulsa beat No. 13 Georgia Tech, 26-12; No. 3 Randolph Field beat No. 20 Second Air Force, 13-6, in a battle of military powers. (Army selected No. 1 but did not play in a bowl)

1945 ROSE—No. 2 Alabama beat No. 11 Southern California, 34-14; COTTON—No. 10 Texas beat unranked Missouri, 40-27; ORANGE—Unranked Miami (Fla.) beat No. 16 Holy Cross, 13-6; SUGAR—No. 5 Oklahoma St. beat No. 7 St. Mary's (Cal.), 33-13. (Army selected No. 1 but did not play in a bowl)

1946 COTTON—No. 8 LSU tied No. 16 Arkansas, 0-0; ROSE—No. 5 Illinois beat No. 4 UCLA, 45-14; SUGAR—No. 3 Georgia beat No. 9 North Carolina, 20-10; ORANGE—No. 10 Rice beat No. 7 Tennessee, 8-0. (Notre Dame selected No. 1 but did not play in a bowl)

1947 ORANGE—No. 10 Georgia Tech beat No. 12 Kansas, 20-14; ROSE—No. 2 Michigan beat No. 8 Southern California, 49-0; SUGAR—No. 5 Texas beat No. 6 Alabama, 27-7; COTTON—No. 3 SMU tied No. 4 Penn St., 13-13. (Notre Dame selected No. 1 but did not play in a bowl; Michigan also declared champion in vote after Rose Bowl victory but AP kept Notre Dame as vote of record)

1948 ROSE—No. 7 Northwestern beat No. 4 California, 20-14; COTTON—No. 10 SMU beat No. 9 Oregon, 21-13; SUGAR—No. 5 Oklahoma beat No. 3 North Carolina, 14-6; ORANGE—Unranked Texas beat No. 8 Georgia, 41-28. (Michigan selected No. 1 but did not play in a bowl)

1949 ORANGE—No. 15 Santa Clara beat No. 11 Kentucky, 21-13; COTTON—No. 5 Rice beat No. 16 North Carolina, 27-13; ROSE—No. 6 Ohio St. beat No. 3 California, 17-14; SUGAR—No. 2 Oklahoma beat No. 9 LSU, 35-0. (Notre Dame selected No. 1 but did not play in a bowl)

1950 ROSE—No. 9 Michigan beat No. 5 California, 14-6; SUGAR—No. 7 Kentucky beat No. 1 Oklahoma, 13-7; ORANGE—No. 10 Clemson beat No. 15 Miami (Fla.), 15-14; COTTON—No. 4 Tennessee beat No. 3 Texas, 20-14. (Oklahoma selected No. 1 in vote before losing in Sugar Bowl)

1951 COTTON—No. 15 Kentucky beat No. 11 TCU, 20-7; ORANGE—No. 5 Georgia Tech beat No. 9 Baylor, 17-14; ROSE—No. 4 Illinois beat No. 7 Stanford, 40-7; SUGAR—No. 3 Maryland beat No. 1 Tennessee, 28-13. (Tennessee selected No. 1 in vote before losing in Sugar Bowl)

1952 ROSE—No. 5 Southern California beat No. 11 Wisconsin, 7-0; SUGAR—No. 2 Georgia Tech beat No. 7 Mississippi, 24-7; ORANGE—No. 9 Alabama beat No. 14 Syracuse, 61-6; COTTON—No. 10 Texas beat No. 8 Tennessee, 16-0. (Michigan St. selected No. 1 but did not play in a bowl)

1953 SUGAR—No. 8 Georgia Tech beat No. 10 West Virginia, 42-19; ORANGE—No. 4 Oklahoma beat No. 1 Maryland, 7-0; COTTON—No. 5 Rice beat No. 13

Alabama, 28-6; ROSE—No. 3 Michigan St. beat No. 5 UCLA, 28-20. (Maryland selected No. 1 before losing in Orange Bowl)

1954 ROSE—No. 1 Ohio St. beat No. 17 Southern California, 20-7; ORANGE—No. 14 Duke beat unranked Nebraska, 34-7; SUGAR—No. 5 Navy beat No. 6 Mississippi, 21-0; COTTON—Unranked Georgia Tech beat No. 10 Arkansas, 14-6. (Ohio St. remained No. 1 but UCLA named in UPI and FW polls)

1955 GATOR—Unranked Vanderbilt beat No. 8 Auburn, 25-13; ROSE—No. 2 Michigan St. beat No. 4 UCLA, 17-14; ORANGE—No. 1 Oklahoma beat No. 3 Maryland, 20-6; COTTON—No. 10 Mississippi beat No. 6 TCU, 14-13; SUGAR—No. 7 Georgia Tech beat No. 11 Pittsburgh, 7-0. (Oklahoma remained No. 1)

1956 SUGAR—No. 11 Baylor beat No. 2 Tennessee, 13-7; ORANGE—No. 20 Colorado beat No. 19 Clemson, 27-21; GATOR—No. 4 Georgia Tech beat No. 13 Pittsburgh, 21-14; ROSE—No. 3 Iowa beat No. 10 Oregon St., 35-19; COTTON—No. 14 TCU beat No. 8 Syracuse, 28-27. (Oklahoma selected No. 1 but did not play in a bowl)

1957 GATOR—No. 13 Tennessee beat No. 9 Texas A&M, 3-0; ROSE—No. 2 Ohio St. beat unranked Oregon, 10-7; COTTON—No. 5 Navy beat No. 8 Rice, 20-7; ORANGE—No. 4 Oklahoma beat No. 16 Duke, 48-21; SUGAR—No. 7 Mississippi beat No. 11 Texas, 39-7. (Auburn selected No. 1 but did not play in a bowl; Ohio St. selected No. 1 in both UPI and FW polls)

1958 SUGAR—No. 1 LSU beat No. 12 Clemson, 7-0; COTTON—No. 6 Air Force tied No. 10 TCU, 0-0; ROSE—No. 2 Iowa beat No. 16 California, 38-12; ORANGE—No. 5 Oklahoma beat No. 9 Syracuse, 21-6. (LSU remained No. 1 in AP and UPI but Iowa selected in FW poll)

1959 COTTON—No. 1 Syracuse beat No. 4 Texas, 23-14; ROSE—No. 8 Washington beat No. 6 Wisconsin, 44-8; ORANGE—No. 5 Georgia beat No. 18 Missouri, 14-0; SUGAR—No. 2 Mississippi beat No. 3 LSU, 21-0; BLUEBONNET—No. 11 Clemson beat No. 7 TCU, 23-7; LIBERTY—No. 12 Penn St. beat No. 10 Alabama, 7-0; GATOR—No. 9 Arkansas beat unranked Georgia Tech, 14-7. (Syracuse selected No. 1 by all four polls)

1960 ROSE—No. 6 Washington beat No. 1 Minnesota, 17-7; COTTON—No. 10 Duke beat No. 7 Arkansas, 7-6; SUGAR—No. 2 Mississippi beat unranked Rice, 14-6; ORANGE—No. 5 Missouri beat No. 4 Navy, 21-14; BLUEBONNET—No. 9 Alabama tied unranked Texas, 3-3. (Minnesota selected No. 1 by AP, UPI and NFF before losing in Rose Bowl; Mississippi named No. 1 in FW poll)

1961 COTTON—No. 3 Texas beat No. 5 Mississippi, 12-7; SUGAR—No. 1 Alabama beat No. 9 Arkansas, 10-3; ORANGE—No. 4 LSU beat No. 7 Colorado, 25-7; GOTHAM—Unranked Baylor beat No. 10 Utah St., 24-9; ROSE—No. 6 Minnesota beat No. 16 UCLA, 21-3. (Alabama selected No. 1 in AP, UPI and NFF, but Ohio St. picked by FW poll)

1962 ROSE—No. 1 Southern California beat No. 2 Wisconsin, 42-37; SUGAR—No. 3 Mississippi beat No. 6 Arkansas, 17-13; COTTON—No. 7 LSU beat No. 4 Texas, 13-0; GATOR—Unranked Florida beat No. 9 Penn St., 17-7; ORANGE—No. 5 Alabama beat No. 8 Oklahoma, 17-0. (Southern California selected No. 1 by all four polls)

1963 COTTON—No. 1 Texas beat No. 2 Navy, 28-6; ORANGE—No. 6 Nebraska beat No. 5 Auburn, 13-7; ROSE—No. 3 Illinois beat unranked Washington, 17-7; SUGAR—No. 8 Alabama beat No. 7 Mississippi, 12-7. (Texas selected No. 1 by all four polls)

1964 ORANGE—No. 5 Texas beat No. 1 Alabama, 21-17; ROSE—No. 4 Michigan beat No. 8 Oregon St., 34-7; COTTON—No. 2 Arkansas beat No. 6 Nebraska, 10-7; SUGAR—No. 7 LSU beat unranked Syracuse, 13-10. (Alabama selected No. 1 by AP and UPI before losing in the Orange Bowl, while Arkansas No. 1 in FW poll and Notre Dame No. 1 in NFF poll)

1965 ***(First year final poll taken after bowl games)*** ROSE—No. 5 UCLA beat No. 1 Michigan St., 14-12; COTTON—Unranked LSU beat No. 2 Arkansas, 14-7; SUGAR—No. 6 Missouri beat unranked Florida, 20-18; ORANGE—No. 4 Alabama beat No. 3 Nebraska, 39-28; BLUEBONNET—No. 7 Tennessee beat unranked Tulsa, 27-6; GATOR—Unranked Georgia Tech beat No. 10 Texas Tech, 31-21. (Alabama selected No. 1 in final poll but Michigan St. named by UPI and NFF polls and tied with Alabama in FW poll)

1966 ***(Returned to final poll taken before bowls)*** SUGAR—No. 3 Alabama beat No. 6 Nebraska, 34-7; ROSE—No. 7 Purdue beat unranked Southern California, 14-13; COTTON—No. 4 Georgia beat No. 10 SMU, 24-9; ORANGE—Unranked Florida beat No. 8 Georgia Tech, 27-12; LIBERTY—No. 9 Miami (Fla.) beat unranked Virginia Tech, 14-7. (Notre Dame selected No. 1 by AP, UPI and FW polls and tied with Michigan St. in NFF poll; neither team played in a bowl game and they tied in a regular-season game)

1967 ROSE—No. 1 Southern California beat No. 4 Indiana, 14-3; SUGAR—Unranked LSU beat No. 6 Wyoming, 20-13; ORANGE—No. 3 Oklahoma beat No. 2 Tennessee, 26-24; COTTON—Unranked Texas A&M beat No. 8 Alabama, 20-16; GATOR—No. 10 Penn St. tied unranked Florida St., 17-17. (Southern California selected No. 1 in all four polls)

1968 ***(Returned to final poll taken after bowl games)*** ROSE—No. 1 Ohio St. beat No. 2 Southern California, 27-16; SUGAR—No. 9 Arkansas beat No. 4 Georgia, 16-2; ORANGE—No. 3 Penn St. beat No. 6 Kansas, 15-14; COTTON—No. 5 Texas beat No. 8 Tennessee, 36-13; BLUEBONNET—No. 20 SMU beat No. 10 Oklahoma, 28-27; GATOR—No. 16 Missouri beat No. 12 Alabama, 35-10. (Ohio St. remained No. 1)

1969 COTTON—No. 1 Texas beat No. 9 Notre Dame, 21-17; SUGAR—No. 13 Mississippi beat No. 3 Arkansas, 27-22; ORANGE—No. 2 Penn St. beat No. 6 Missouri, 10-3; ROSE—No. 5 Southern California beat No. 7 Michigan, 10-3. (Texas remained No. 1)

1970 COTTON—No. 6 Notre Dame beat No. 1 Texas, 24-11; ROSE—No. 12 Stanford beat No. 2 Ohio St., 27-17; SUGAR—No. 5 Tennessee beat No. 11 Air Force, 34-13; ORANGE—No. 3 Nebraska beat No. 8 LSU, 17-12; PEACH—No. 9 Arizona St. beat unranked North Carolina, 48-26. (Nebraska selected No. 1 in AP and FW polls while Texas was No. 1 in UPI and tied with Ohio St. in NFF poll)

1971 ORANGE—No. 1 Nebraska beat No. 2 Alabama, 38-6; SUGAR—No. 3 Oklahoma beat No. 5 Auburn, 40-22; ROSE—No. 16 Stanford beat No. 4 Michigan, 13-12; GATOR—No. 6 Georgia beat unranked North Carolina, 7-3; COTTON—No. 10 Penn St. beat No. 12 Texas, 30-6; FIESTA—No. 8 Arizona St. beat unranked Florida St., 45-38; BLUEBONNET—No. 7 Colorado beat No. 15 Houston, 29-17. (Nebraska remained No. 1 in all four polls)

1972 ROSE—No. 1 Southern California beat No. 3 Ohio St., 42-17; COTTON—No. 7 Texas beat No. 4 Alabama, 17-13; SUGAR—No. 2 Oklahoma beat No. 5 Penn St., 14-0; ORANGE—No. 9 Nebraska beat No. 12 Notre Dame, 40-6; GATOR—No. 6 Auburn beat No. 13 Colorado, 24-3; BLUEBONNET—No. 11 Tennessee beat No. 10 LSU, 24-17. (Southern California remained No. 1 in all four polls)

1973 SUGAR—No. 3 Notre Dame beat No. 1 Alabama, 24-23; ROSE—No. 4 Ohio St. beat No. 7 Southern California, 42-21; ORANGE—No. 6 Penn St. beat No. 13 LSU, 16-9; COTTON—No. 12 Nebraska beat No. 8 Texas, 19-3; FIESTA—No. 10 Arizona St. beat unranked Pittsburgh, 28-7; BLUEBONNET—No. 14 Houston beat No. 17 Tulane, 47-7. (Notre Dame selected No. 1 in AP, FW and NFF polls, Alabama named No. 1 by UPI. No. 2 Oklahoma was on probation and could not go to a bowl game)

1974 ROSE—No. 5 Southern California beat No. 3 Ohio St., 18-17; ORANGE—No. 9 Notre Dame beat No. 2 Alabama, 13-11; GATOR—No. 6 Auburn beat No. 11 Texas, 27-3; COTTON—No. 7 Penn St. beat No. 12 Baylor, 41-20; SUGAR—No. 8 Nebraska beat No. 18 Florida, 13-10; LIBERTY—Unranked Tennessee beat No. 10 Maryland, 7-3. (Oklahoma selected No. 1 in AP poll despite being on probation and not able to participate in bowl game; Southern California named No. 1 by UPI, FW and NFF polls)

1975 ROSE—No. 11 UCLA beat No. 1 Ohio St., 23-10; ORANGE—No. 3 Oklahoma beat No. 5 Michigan, 14-6; LIBERTY—No. 17 Southern California beat No. 2 Texas A&M, 20-0; SUGAR—No. 4 Alabama beat No. 8 Penn St., 13-6; FIESTA—No. 7 Arizona St. beat No. 6 Nebraska, 17-14; COTTON—No. 18 Arkansas beat No. 12 Georgia, 31-10; BLUEBONNET—No. 9 Texas beat No. 10 Colorado, 38-21. (Oklahoma selected No. 1 in all four polls)

1976 SUGAR—No. 1 Pittsburgh beat No. 5 Georgia, 27-3; ROSE—No. 3 Southern California beat No. 2 Michigan, 14-6; COTTON—No. 6 Houston beat No. 4 Maryland, 30-21; LIBERTY—No. 16 Alabama beat No. 7 UCLA, 36-6; ORANGE—No. 11 Ohio St. beat No. 12 Colorado, 27-10; FIESTA—No. 8 Oklahoma beat unranked Wyoming, 41-7; SUN—No. 10 Texas A&M beat unranked Florida, 37-14; BLUEBONNET—No. 13 Nebraska beat No. 9 Texas Tech, 27-24. (Pittsburgh remained No. 1 in all four polls)

1977 COTTON—No. 5 Notre Dame beat No. 1 Texas, 38-10; ORANGE—No. 6 Arkansas beat No. 2 Oklahoma, 31-6; SUGAR—No. 3 Alabama beat No. 9 Ohio St., 35-6; ROSE—No. 13 Washington beat No. 4 Michigan, 27-20; FIESTA—No. 8 Penn St. beat No. 15 Arizona St., 42-30; GATOR—No. 10 Pittsburgh beat No. 11 Clemson, 34-3. (Notre Dame selected No. 1 in all four polls)

1978 SUGAR—No. 2 Alabama beat No. 1 Penn St., 14-7; ROSE—No. 3 Southern California beat No. 5 Michigan, 17-10; ORANGE—No. 4 Oklahoma beat No. 6 Nebraska, 31-24; COTTON—No. 10 Notre Dame beat No. 9 Houston, 35-34; GATOR—No. 7 Clemson beat No. 20 Ohio St., 17-15; FIESTA—No. 8 Arkansas tied No. 15 UCLA, 10-10. (Alabama selected No. 1 in AP, FW and NFF polls, while Southern California named in UPI)

1979 ROSE—No. 3 Southern California beat No. 1 Ohio St., 17-16; SUGAR—No. 2 Alabama beat No. 6 Arkansas, 24-9; ORANGE—No. 5 Oklahoma beat No. 4 Florida St., 24-7; COTTON—No. 8 Houston beat No. 7 Nebraska, 17-14; SUN—No. 13 Washington beat No. 11 Texas, 14-7; FIESTA—No. 10 Pittsburgh beat unranked Arizona, 16-10. (Alabama selected No. 1 in all four polls)

1980 SUGAR—No. 1 Georgia beat No. 7 Notre Dame, 17-10; ORANGE—No. 4 Oklahoma beat No. 2 Florida St., 18-17; ROSE—No. 5 Michigan beat No. 16 Washington, 23-6; COTTON—No. 9 Alabama beat No. 6 Baylor, 30-2; GATOR—No. 3 Pittsburgh beat No. 18 South Carolina, 37-9; SUN—No. 8 Nebraska beat No. 17 Mississippi St., 31-17; FIESTA—No. 10 Penn St. beat No. 11 Ohio St., 31-19; BLUEBONNET—No. 13 North Carolina beat unranked Texas, 16-7. (Georgia remained No. 1 in all four polls)

1981 ORANGE—No. 1 Clemson beat No. 4 Nebraska, 22-15; SUGAR—No. 10 Pittsburgh beat No. 2 Georgia, 24-20; COTTON—No. 6 Texas beat No. 3 Alabama, 14-12; GATOR—No. 11 North Carolina beat unranked Arkansas, 31-27; ROSE—No. 12 Washington beat No. 13 Iowa, 28-0; FIESTA—No. 7 Penn St. beat No. 8 Southern California, 26-10. (Clemson remained No. 1 in all four polls)

1982 SUGAR—No. 2 Penn St. beat No. 1 Georgia, 27-23; ORANGE—No. 3 Nebraska beat No. 13 LSU, 21-20; COTTON—No. 4 SMU beat No. 6 Pittsburgh, 7-3; ROSE—No. 5 UCLA beat No. 19 Michigan, 24-14; ALOHA—No. 9 Washington beat No. 16 Maryland, 21-20; FIESTA—No. 11 Arizona St. beat No. 12 Oklahoma, 32-21; BLUEBONNET—No. 14 Arkansas beat unranked Florida, 28-24. (Penn St. selected No. 1 in all four polls)

1983 ORANGE—No. 5 Miami (Fla.) beat No. 1 Nebraska, 31-30; COTTON—No. 7 Georgia beat No. 2 Texas, 10-9; SUGAR—No. 3 Auburn beat No. 8 Michigan, 9-7; ROSE—Unranked UCLA beat No. 4 Illinois, 45-9; HOLIDAY—No. 9 BYU beat unranked Missouri, 21-17; GATOR—No. 11 Florida beat No. 10 Iowa, 14-6; FIESTA—No. 14 Ohio St. beat No. 15 Pittsburgh, 28-23. [Miami (Fla.) selected No. 1 in all four polls]

1984 HOLIDAY—No. 1 BYU beat unranked Michigan, 24-17; ORANGE—No. 4 Washington beat No. 2 Oklahoma, 28-17; SUGAR—No. 5 Nebraska beat No. 11 LSU, 28-10; ROSE—No. 18 Southern California beat No. 6 Ohio St., 20-17; COTTON—No. 8 Boston College beat unranked Houston, 45-28; GATOR—No. 9 Oklahoma St. beat No. 7 South Carolina, 21-14; ALOHA—No. 10 SMU beat No. 17 Notre Dame, 27-20. (BYU remained No. 1 in all four polls)

1985 ORANGE—No. 3 Oklahoma beat No. 1 Penn St., 25-10; SUGAR—No. 8 Tennessee beat No. 2 Miami (Fla.), 35-7; ROSE—No. 13 UCLA beat No. 4 Iowa, 45-28; COTTON—No. 11 Texas A&M beat No. 16 Auburn, 36-16; FIESTA—No. 5

Michigan beat No. 7 Nebraska, 27-23; BLUEBONNET—No. 10 Air Force beat unranked Texas, 24-16. (Oklahoma selected No. 1 in all four polls)

1986 FIESTA—No. 2 Penn St. beat No. 1 Miami (Fla.), 14-10; ORANGE—No. 3 Oklahoma beat No. 9 Arkansas, 42-8; ROSE—No. 7 Arizona St. beat No. 4 Michigan, 22-15; SUGAR—No. 6 Nebraska beat No. 5 LSU, 30-15; COTTON—No. 11 Ohio St. beat No. 8 Texas A&M, 28-12; CITRUS—No. 10 Auburn beat unranked Southern California, 16-7; SUN—No. 13 Alabama beat No. 12 Washington, 28-6. (Penn St. selected No. 1 in all four polls)

1987 ORANGE—No. 2 Miami (Fla.) beat No. 1 Oklahoma, 20-14; FIESTA—No. 3 Florida St. beat No. 5 Nebraska, 31-28; SUGAR—No. 4 Syracuse tied No. 6 Auburn, 16-16; ROSE—No. 8 Michigan St. beat No. 16 Southern California, 20-17; COTTON—No. 13 Texas A&M beat No. 12 Notre Dame, 35-10; GATOR—No. 7 LSU beat No. 9 South Carolina, 30-13; ALOHA—No. 10 UCLA beat unranked Florida, 20-16. [Miami (Fla.) selected No. 1 in all four polls]

1988 FIESTA—No. 1 Notre Dame beat No. 3 West Virginia, 34-21; ORANGE—No. 2 Miami (Fla.) beat No. 6 Nebraska, 23-3; SUGAR—No. 4 Florida St. beat No. 7 Auburn, 13-7; ROSE—No. 11 Michigan beat No. 5 Southern California, 22-14; COTTON—No. 9 UCLA beat No. 8 Arkansas, 17-3; CITRUS—No. 13 Clemson beat No. 10 Oklahoma, 13-6. (Notre Dame selected No. 1 in all four polls)

1989 ORANGE—No. 4 Notre Dame beat No. 1 Colorado, 21-6; SUGAR—No. 2 Miami (Fla.) beat No. 7 Alabama, 33-25; ROSE—No. 12 Southern California beat No. 3 Michigan, 17-10; COTTON—No. 8 Tennessee beat No. 10 Arkansas, 31-27; FIESTA—No. 5 Florida St. beat No. 6 Nebraska, 41-17; HALL OF FAME—No. 9 Auburn beat No. 21 Ohio St., 31-14; CITRUS—No. 11 Illinois beat No. 15 Virginia, 31-21. [Miami (Fla.) selected No. 1 in all four polls]

1990 ORANGE—No. 1 Colorado beat No. 5 Notre Dame, 10-9; CITRUS—No. 2 Georgia Tech beat No. 19 Nebraska, 45-21; COTTON—No. 4 Miami (Fla.) beat No. 3 Texas, 46-3; BLOCKBUSTER—No. 6 Florida St. beat No. 7 Penn St., 24-17; ROSE—No. 8 Washington beat No. 17 Iowa, 46-34; GATOR—No. 12 Michigan beat No. 15 Mississippi, 35-3; SUGAR—No. 10 Tennessee beat unranked Virginia, 23-22. (Colorado selected No. 1 in AP, FW and NFF polls, but Georgia Tech picked in UPI poll)

1991 ORANGE—No. 1 Miami (Fla.) beat No. 11 Nebraska, 22-0; ROSE—No. 2 Washington beat No. 4 Michigan, 34-14; COTTON—No. 5 Florida St. beat No. 9 Texas A&M, 10-3; BLOCKBUSTER—No. 8 Alabama beat No. 15 Colorado, 30-25; SUGAR—No. 18 Notre Dame beat No. 3 Florida, 39-28; FIESTA—No. 6 Penn St. beat No. 10 Tennessee, 42-17; CITRUS—No. 14 California beat No. 13 Clemson, 37-13; PEACH—No. 12 East Caro. beat No. 21 North Carolina St., 37-34; HOLIDAY—No. 7 Iowa tied unranked BYU, 13-13. [Miami (Fla.) selected No. 1 in AP poll, while Washington named in USA/CNN, NFF and FW polls]

1992 SUGAR—No. 2 Alabama beat No. 1 Miami (Fla.), 34-13; GATOR—No. 14 Florida beat No. 12 North Carolina St., 27-10; COTTON—No. 5 Notre Dame beat No. 4 Texas A&M, 28-3; HALL OF FAME—No. 17 Tennessee beat No. 16 Boston College, 38-23; CITRUS—No. 8 Georgia beat No. 15 Ohio St., 21-14; ROSE—No. 7 Michigan beat No. 9 Washington, 38-31; ORANGE—No. 3 Florida St. beat No. 11 Nebraska, 27-14; FIESTA—No. 6 Syracuse beat No. 10 Colorado, 26-22; BLOCKBUSTER—No. 13 Stanford beat No. 21 Penn St., 24-3; PEACH—No. 19 North Carolina beat No. 24 Mississippi St., 21-17; COPPER—No. 18 Washington St. beat unranked Utah, 31-28. (Alabama selected No. 1 in all four polls)

1993 ORANGE—No. 1 Florida St. beat No. 2 Nebraska, 18-16; SUGAR—No. 8 Florida beat No. 3 West Virginia, 41-7; ROSE—No. 9 Wisconsin beat No. 14 UCLA, 21-16; COTTON—No. 4 Notre Dame beat No. 7 Texas A&M, 24-21; CARQUEST—No. 15 Boston College beat unranked Virginia, 31-13; FIESTA—No. 16 Arizona beat No. 10 Miami (Fla.), 29-0; FLORIDA CITRUS—No. 13 Penn St. beat No. 6 Tennessee, 31-13; HALL OF FAME—No. 23 Michigan beat unranked North Carolina St., 42-7; GATOR—No. 18 Alabama beat No. 12 North Carolina, 24-10; PEACH—No. 24 Clemson beat unranked Kentucky, 14-13; INDEPENDENCE—No. 22 Virginia Tech beat unranked Indiana, 45-20; HOLIDAY—No. 11 Ohio St. beat unranked BYU, 28-21; COPPER—No. 20 Kansas St. beat unranked Wyoming, 52-17; LIBERTY—No. 25 Louisville beat unranked Michigan St., 18-7; ALOHA—No. 17 Colorado beat No. 25 Fresno St., 41-30; JOHN HANCOCK—No. 19 Oklahoma beat unranked Texas Tech, 41-10. (Florida St. selected in all four major polls—AP, FW, USA/CNN and USA/NFF)

1994 ORANGE—No. 1 Nebraska beat No. 3 Miami (Fla.), 24-17; ROSE—No. 2 Penn St. beat No. 12 Oregon, 38-20; FIESTA—No. 4 Colorado beat unranked Notre Dame, 41-24; SUGAR—No. 7 Florida St. beat No. 5 Florida, 23-17; FLORIDA CITRUS—No. 6 Alabama beat No. 13 Ohio St., 24-17; FREEDOM—No. 14 Utah beat No. 15 Arizona, 16-13; ALOHA—Unranked Boston College beat No. 11 Kansas St., 12-7; HOLIDAY—No. 20 Michigan beat No. 10 Colorado St., 24-14; PEACH—No. 23 North Carolina St. beat No. 16 Mississippi St., 28-24; INDEPENDENCE—No. 18 Virginia beat unranked TCU, 20-10; SUN—Unranked Texas beat No. 19 North Carolina, 35-31; GATOR—Unranked Tennessee beat No. 17 Virginia Tech, 45-23. (Nebraska selected in all four major polls—AP, UPI, USA/CNN and FW)

1995 FIESTA—No. 1 Nebraska beat No. 2 Florida, 62-24; ROSE—No. 17 Southern California beat No. 3 Northwestern, 41-32; FLORIDA CITRUS—No. 4 Tennessee beat No. 4 Ohio St., 20-14; ORANGE—No. 8 Florida St. beat No. 6 Notre Dame, 31-26; COTTON—No. 7 Colorado beat No. 12 Oregon, 38-6; SUGAR—No. 13 Virginia Tech beat No. 9 Texas, 28-10; HOLIDAY—No. 10 Kansas St. beat unranked Colorado St., 54-21; ALOHA—No. 11 Kansas beat unranked UCLA, 51-30; ALAMO—No. 19 Texas A&M beat No. 14 Michigan, 22-20; OUTBACK—No. 15 Penn St. beat No. 16 Auburn, 43-14; PEACH—No. 18 Virginia beat unranked Georgia, 34-27. (Nebraska selected in all four major polls—AP, UPI, USA/CNN and FW)

1996 SUGAR—No. 3 Florida beat No. 1 Florida St., 52-20; FIESTA—No. 7 Penn St. beat No. 20 Texas, 38-15; ROSE—No. 4 Ohio St. beat No. 2 Arizona St., 20-17; COTTON—No. 5 BYU beat No. 14 Kansas St., 19-15; FLORIDA CITRUS—No. 9 Tennessee beat No. 11 Northwestern, 48-28; GATOR—No. 12 North Carolina beat No. 25 West Virginia, 20-13; OUTBACK—No. 16 Alabama beat No. 15 Michigan, 17-14; ORANGE—No. 6 Nebraska beat No. 10 Virginia Tech, 41-21; INDEPENDENCE—Unranked Auburn beat No. 24 Army, 32-29; SUN—Unranked Stanford beat unranked Michigan St., 38-0; HOLIDAY—No. 8 Colorado beat No. 13 Washington, 33-21; ALAMO—No. 21 Iowa beat unranked Texas Tech, 27-0; PEACH—No. 17 LSU beat unranked Clemson, 10-7; COPPER—Unranked Wisconsin beat unranked Utah, 38-10; CARQUEST—No. 19 Miami (Fla.) beat unranked Virginia, 31-21; LIBERTY—No. 23 Syracuse beat unranked Houston, 30-17; ALOHA—Unranked Navy beat unranked California, 42-38; LAS VEGAS—Unranked Nevada beat unranked Ball St., 18-15. (Florida selected in all four major polls—AP, USA/CNN, FW and NFF/HOF)

1997 ROSE—No. 1 Michigan beat No. 9 Washington St., 21-16; ORANGE—No. 2 Nebraska beat No. 7 Tennessee, 42-17; SUGAR—No. 3 Florida St. beat No. 12 Ohio St., 31-14; FIESTA—No. 8 Kansas St. beat No. 21 Syracuse, 35-18; COTTON—No. 5 UCLA beat No. 20 Texas A&M, 29-23; FLORIDA CITRUS—No. 4 Florida beat No. 16 Penn St., 21-6; ALAMO—No. 15 Purdue beat No. 24 Oklahoma St., 33-20; GATOR—No. 6 North Carolina beat unranked Virginia Tech, 42-3; HOLIDAY—No. 17 Colorado St. beat No. 23 Missouri, 35-24; PEACH—No. 11 Auburn beat unranked Clemson, 21-17; LAS VEGAS—Unranked Oregon beat unranked Air Force, 41-13; ALOHA—No. 18 Washington beat unranked Michigan St., 51-23; MOTOR CITY—No. 22 Mississippi beat unranked Marshall, 34-31; INSIGHT.COM—Unranked Arizona beat unranked New Mexico, 20-14; INDEPENDENCE—No. 13 LSU beat unranked Notre Dame, 27-9; CARQUEST—No. 25 Georgia Tech beat unranked West Virginia, 35-30; HUMANITARIAN—Unranked Cincinnati beat unranked Utah St., 35-19; SUN—No. 14 Arizona St. beat unranked Iowa, 17-7; LIBERTY—No. 19 Southern Miss. beat unranked Pittsburgh, 41-7; OUTBACK—No. 10 Georgia beat unranked Wisconsin, 33-6. (Michigan selected by AP [media], FW and NFF/HOF, while Nebraska was picked by the USA/ESPN [coaches])

1998 FIESTA—No. 1 Tennessee beat No. 2 Florida St., 23-16; SUGAR—No. 3 Ohio St. beat No. 8 Texas A&M, 24-14; ROSE—No. 9 Wisconsin beat No. 6 UCLA, 38-31; ORANGE—No. 7 Florida beat No. 18 Syracuse, 31-10; HOLIDAY—No. 5 Arizona beat No. 14 Nebraska, 23-20; FLORIDA CITRUS—No. 15 Michigan beat No. 11 Arkansas, 45-31; GATOR—No. 12 Georgia Tech beat No. 17 Notre Dame, 35-28; COTTON—No. 20 Texas beat No. 25 Mississippi St., 38-11; PEACH—No. 19 Georgia beat No. 13 Virginia, 35-33; LIBERTY—No. 10 Tulane beat unranked BYU, 41-27; OUTBACK—No. 22 Penn St. beat unranked Kentucky, 26-14; MICRON PC—No. 24 Miami (Fla.) beat unranked North Carolina St., 46-23; OAHU CLASSIC—No. 16 Air Force beat unranked Washington, 45-25; ALOHA CLASSIC—Unranked Colorado beat No. 21 Oregon, 51-43; INSIGHT.COM—No. 23 Missouri beat unranked West Virginia, 34-31; LAS VEGAS—Unranked North Carolina beat unranked San Diego St., 20-13; MOTOR CITY—Unranked Marshall beat unranked Louisville, 48-29; MUSIC CITY—Unranked Virginia Tech beat unranked Alabama, 38-7; HUMANITARIAN—Unranked Idaho beat unranked Southern Miss., 42-35; SUN—Unranked TCU beat unranked Southern California, 28-19; INDEPENDENCE—Unranked Mississippi beat unranked Texas Tech, 35-18. (Tennessee, No. 1 in the BCS poll, defeated No. 2 Florida St., 23-16, in the Fiesta Bowl and was named champion in all four major polls—AP [media], USA/ESPN [coaches], FW and NFF/HOF)

1999 SUGAR—No. 1 Florida St. beat No. 2 Virginia Tech, 46-29; FIESTA—No. 3 Nebraska beat No. 6 Tennessee, 31-21; ROSE—No. 4 Wisconsin beat No. 22 Stanford, 17-9; ORANGE—No. 8 Michigan beat No. 5 Alabama, 35-34 in overtime; HOLIDAY—No. 7 Kansas St. beat unranked Washington, 24-20; FLORIDA CITRUS—No. 9 Michigan St. beat No. 10 Florida, 37-34; MOTOR CITY—No. 11 Marshall beat unranked BYU, 21-3; SUN—Unranked Oregon beat No. 12 Minnesota, 24-20; ALAMO—No. 13 Penn St. beat No. 18 Texas A&M, 24-0; COTTON—No. 24 Arkansas beat No. 14 Texas, 27-6; PEACH—No. 15 Mississippi St. beat unranked Clemson, 17-7; LIBERTY—No. 16 Southern Miss. beat unranked Colorado St., 23-17; GATOR—No. 23 Miami (Fla.) beat No. 17 Georgia Tech, 28-13; OUTBACK—No. 21 Georgia beat No. 19 Purdue, 28-25 in overtime; INSIGHT.COM—Unranked Colorado beat No. 25 Boston College, 62-28; LAS VEGAS—Unranked Utah beat unranked Fresno St., 17-16; MOBILE ALABAMA—Unranked TCU beat unranked East Caro., 28-14; ALOHA CLASSIC—Unranked Wake Forest beat unranked Arizona St., 23-3; OAHU CLASSIC—Unranked Hawaii beat unranked Oregon St., 23-17; MUSIC CITY—Unranked Syracuse beat unranked Kentucky, 20-13; HUMANITARIAN—Unranked Boise St. beat unranked Louisville, 34-31; MICRONPC.COM—Unranked Illinois beat unranked Virginia, 63-21; INDEPENDENCE—Unranked Mississippi beat unranked Oklahoma, 27-25. (BCS No. 1 Florida St. beat BCS No. 2 Virginia Tech, 46-29, in the Sugar Bowl and was selected champion in all four major polls—AP [media], USA/ESPN [coaches], FW and NFF/HOF)

2000 ORANGE—No. 1 Oklahoma beat No. 3 Florida St., 13-2; SUGAR—No. 2 Miami (Fla.) beat No. 7 Florida, 37-20; FIESTA—No. 5 Oregon St. beat No. 10 Notre Dame, 41-9; ROSE—No. 4 Washington beat No. 14 Purdue, 34-24; FLORIDA CITRUS—No. 17 Michigan beat No. 20 Auburn, 31-28; GATOR—No. 6 Virginia Tech beat No. 16 Clemson, 41-20; OUTBACK—Unranked South Carolina beat No. 19 Ohio St., 24-7; COTTON—No. 11 Kansas St. beat No. 21 Tennessee, 35-21; INDEPENDENCE–Unranked Mississippi St. beat unranked Texas A&M, 43-41, in overtime; ALAMO—No. 9 Nebraska beat No. 18 Northwestern, 66-17; HOLIDAY—No. 8 Oregon beat No. 12 Texas, 35-30; LIBERTY—No. 23 Colorado St. beat No. 22 Louisville, 22-17; PEACH—Unranked LSU beat No. 15 Georgia Tech, 28-14; OAHU CLASSIC—No. 24 Georgia beat unranked Virginia, 37-14; MOBILE ALABAMA—Unranked Southern Miss. beat No. 13 TCU, 28-21. (BCS No. 1 Oklahoma beat BCS No. 2 Florida St., 13-2, in the Orange Bowl and was selected champion in all four major polls—AP [media], USA/ESPN [coaches], FW and NFF/HOF)

2001 ROSE—No. 1 Miami (Fla.) beat No. 4 Nebraska, 37-14; FIESTA—No. 2 Oregon beat No. 3 Colorado, 38-16; ORANGE—No. 5 Florida beat No. 6 Maryland, 56-23; SUGAR—No. 12 LSU beat No. 7 Illinois, 47-34; FLORIDA CITRUS—No. 8 Tennessee beat No. 17 Michigan, 45-17; GATOR—No. 24 Florida St. beat No. 15 Virginia Tech, 30-17; OUTBACK—No. 14 South Carolina beat No. 22 Ohio St., 31-28; COTTON—No. 10 Oklahoma beat unranked Arkansas, 10-3; PEACH—Unranked North Carolina beat unranked Auburn, 16-10; LIBERTY—No. 23 Louisville beat No. 19 BYU, 28-10; SILICON VALLEY—Unranked Michigan St. beat No. 20 Fresno St., 44-35; SUN—No. 13 Washington St. beat unranked Purdue, 33-

27; INSIGHT.COM—No. 18 Syracuse beat unranked Kansas St., 26-3; MOTOR CITY—No. 25 Toledo beat unranked Cincinnati, 23-16; HOLIDAY—No. 9 Texas beat No. 21 Washington, 47-43; MUSIC CITY—Unranked Boston College beat No. 16 Georgia, 20-16; SEATTLE—Unranked Georgia Tech beat No. 11 Stanford, 24-14. [BCS No. 1 Miami (Fla.) beat BCS No. 2 Nebraska, 37-14, in the Rose Bowl and was selected champion in all four major polls—AP (media), USA/ESPN (coaches), FW and NFF/HOF].

2002 FIESTA—No. 2 Ohio St. beat No. 1 Miami (Fla.), 31-24 in two overtimes; ORANGE—No. 5 Southern California beat No. 3 Iowa, 38-17; ROSE—No. 8 Oklahoma beat No. 7 Washington St., 34-14; SUGAR—No. 4 Georgia beat No. 16 Florida St., 26-13; CAPITAL ONE—No. 19 Auburn beat No. 10 Penn St., 13-9; GATOR—No. 17 North Carolina St. beat No. 11 Notre Dame, 28-6. [BCS No. 2 Ohio St. beat BCS No. 1 Miami (Fla.), 31-24 in two overtimes, in the Fiesta Bowl and was selected champion in all four major polls—AP (media), USA/ESPN (coaches), FW and NFF/HOF].

2003 SUGAR—No. 2 LSU beat No. 3 Oklahoma, 21-14; FIESTA—No. 7 Ohio St. beat No. 8 Kansas St., 35-28; ORANGE—No. 10 Miami (Fla.) beat No. 9 Florida St., 16-14; ROSE—No. 1 Southern California beat No. 4 Michigan, 28-14; PEACH—Unranked Clemson beat No. 6 Tennessee, 27-14; COTTON—No. 16 Mississippi beat No. 21 Oklahoma St., 31-28; CAPITAL ONE—No. 11 Georgia beat No. 12 Purdue, 34-27 in overtime; OUTBACK—No. 13 Iowa beat No. 17 Florida, 37-17; HOLIDAY—No. 15 Washington St. beat No. 5 Texas, 28-20. (BCS No. 2 LSU beat BCS No. 1 Oklahoma, 21-14, in the Sugar Bowl and was selected champion in two of the four major polls—USA/ESPN and NFF/HOF. BCS No. 3 Southern California beat BCS No. 4 Michigan, 28-14, in the Rose Bowl and was selected champion in the other two major polls—AP and FW).

2004 ORANGE—No. 1 Southern California beat No. 2 Oklahoma, 55-19; SUGAR—No. 3 Auburn beat No. 9 Virginia Tech, 16-13; ROSE—No. 5 Texas beat No. 12 Michigan, 38-37; FIESTA—No. 6 Utah beat No. 20 Pittsburgh, 35-7; HOLIDAY—No. 21 Texas Tech beat No. 4 California, 45-31; OUTBACK—No. 7 Georgia beat No. 16 Wisconsin, 24-21; LIBERTY—No. 8 Louisville beat No. 10 Boise St., 44-40; CAPITAL ONE—No. 13 Iowa beat No. 11 LSU, 30-25; PEACH—No. 14 Miami (Fla.) beat No. 19 Florida, 27-10; GATOR—No. 15 Florida St. beat No. 23 West Virginia, 30-18; COTTON—No. 17 Tennessee beat No. 25 Texas A&M, 38-7; MPC COMPUTERS—Unranked Fresno St. beat No. 18 Virginia, 37-34 in overtime; ALAMO—No. 22 Ohio St. beat unranked Oklahoma St., 33-7; SUN—No. 24 Arizona St. beat unranked Purdue, 27-23. (BCS No. 1 Southern California beat BCS No. 2 Oklahoma, 55-19, in the Orange Bowl and was selected champion in all four major polls—AP [media], USA/ESPN [coaches], FW and NFF/HOF).

2005 ROSE—No. 2 Texas beat No. 1 Southern California, 41-38; ORANGE—No. 3 Penn St. beat No. 22 Florida St., 26-23 in three overtimes; FIESTA—No. 4 Ohio St. beat No. 5 Notre Dame, 34-20; HOLIDAY—Unranked Oklahoma beat No. 6 Oregon, 17-14; CAPITAL ONE—No. 21 Wisconsin beat No. 7 Auburn, 24-10; SUGAR—No. 11 West Virginia beat No. 8 Georgia, 38-35; PEACH—No. 10 LSU beat No. 9 Miami (Fla.), 40-3; GATOR—No. 12 Virginia Tech beat No. 15 Louisville, 35-24; COTTON—No. 13 Alabama beat No. 18 Texas Tech, 13-10; HOUSTON—No. 14 TCU beat unranked Iowa St., 27-24; OUTBACK—No. 16 Florida beat No. 25 Iowa, 31-24; SUN—No. 17 UCLA beat unranked Northwestern, 50-38; MPC COMPUTERS—No. 19 Boston College beat unranked Boise St., 27-21; ALAMO—Unranked Nebraska beat No. 20 Michigan, 32-28; CHAMPS SPORTS—No. 23 Clemson beat unranked Colorado, 19-10; EMERALD—Unranked Utah beat No. 24 Georgia Tech, 38-10. (BCS No. 2 Texas beat BCS No. 1 Southern California, 41-38, in the Rose Bowl and was selected champion in all four major polls—AP [media], USA/ESPN [coaches], FW and NFF/HOF).

2006 BCS—No. 2 Florida beat No. 1 Ohio St., 41-14; SUGAR—No. 3 LSU beat No. 17 Notre Dame, 41-14; ROSE—No. 4 Southern California beat No. 8 Michigan, 32-18; FIESTA—No. 5 Boise St. beat No. 11 Oklahoma, 43-42 (ot); ORANGE—No. 6 Louisville beat No. 18 Wake Forest, 24-13; CAPITAL ONE—No. 7 Wisconsin beat No. 15 Arkansas, 17-14; COTTON—No. 9 Auburn beat unranked Nebraska, 17-14; GATOR—No. 10 West Virginia beat unranked Georgia Tech, 38-35; TEXAS—No. 12 Rutgers beat unranked Kanasas St., 37-10; ALAMO—No. 13 Texas beat unranked Iowa, 26-24; HOLIDAY—No. 14 California beat unranked Texas A&M, 45-10; LAS VEGAS—No. 16 BYU beat unranked Oregon, 38-8; CHICK-FIL-A—No. 23 Georgia beat No. 19 Virginia Tech, 31-24; MEINEKE CAR CARE—No. 20 Boston College beat unranked Navy, 25-24; SUN—No. 21 Oregon St. beat unranked Missouri, 39-38; POINSETTIA—No. 22 TCU beat unranked Northern Ill., 37-7; OUTBACK—No. 24 Penn St. beat No. 25 Tennessee, 20-10. (BCS No. 2 Florida beat BCS No. 1 Ohio St., 41-14, in the BCS National Championship Game and was selected champion in all four major polls—AP [media], USA/ESPN [coaches], FW and NFF/HOF).

Most Consecutive Bowl-Game Victories

(Bowls do not have to be in consecutive years; year listed is calendar year in which bowl was played)

College	Victories (Years)
Florida St.	11 (1985-86-88-89-90-91-92-93-94-95-96)
Southern California	9 (1923-24-30-32-33-39-40-44-45)
Georgia Tech	8 (1947-48-52-53-54-55-56-56)
UCLA	8 (1983-84-85-86-86-87-89-91)
Boston College	7 (2000-01-02-03-04-05-06)
Syracuse	7 (1989-89-90-92-93-96-96)
Alabama	6 (1975-76-78-79-80-81)
Colorado	6 (1993-95-96-97-98-99)
Nebraska	6 (1969-71-72-73-74-74)
Southern California	6 (1975-75-77-77-79-80)
Utah	6 (1999-2001-03-05-05-06)
Alabama	5 (1991-93-93-95-97)
Arizona St.	5 (1970-71-72-73-75)
Clemson	5 (1986-88-89-89-91)
Fresno St.	5 (1961-82-85-88-89)
Georgia Tech	5 (1985-91-91-97-99)
LSU	5 (1995-96-97-2000-02)
Marshall	5 (1998-99-2000-01-02)
Miami (Fla.)	5 (1988-89-90-91-92)
Miami (Fla.)	5 (1996-98-2000-01-02)
Mississippi	5 (1956-58-58-60-61)
North Carolina	5 (1995-97-98-98-2001)
Notre Dame	5 (1973-75-76-78-79)
Penn St.	5 (1979-80-81-82-83)
Tennessee	5 (1986-86-88-90-91)
Texas	5 (1964-65-66-69-70)
30 teams with	4 (Most recent; Ohio St. – 2003-04-05-06)

Most Consecutive Seasons With Bowl-Game Victories

11 Florida St.—85 Gator, Oklahoma St. 34-23; 86 All-American, Indiana 27-13; 87 Fiesta, Nebraska 31-28; 88 Sugar, Auburn 13-7; 89 Fiesta, Nebraska 41-17; 90 Blockbuster, Penn St. 24-17; 92 Cotton, Texas A&M 10-2; 93 Orange, Nebraska 27-14; 94 Orange, Nebraska 18-16; 95 Sugar, Florida 23-17; 96 Orange, Notre Dame 31-26. Coach: Bobby Bowden.

7 UCLA—83 Rose, Michigan 24-14; 84 Rose, Illinois 45-9; 85 Fiesta, Miami (Fla.) 39-37; 86 Rose, Iowa 45-28; 86 Freedom, BYU 31-10; 87 Aloha, Florida 20-16; 89 Cotton, Arkansas, 17-3. Coach: Terry Donahue.

7 Boston College—00 Aloha Classic, Arizona St. 31-17; 01 Music City, Georgia 20-16; 02 Motor City, Toledo 51-25; 03 San Francisco, Colorado St. 35-21; 04 Continental Tire, North Carolina 37-24; 05 MPC Computers, Boise St. 27-21; 06 Meineke Car Care, Navy 25-24. Coach: Tom O'Brien first six, Frank Spaziani last one.

6 Georgia Tech—52 Orange, Baylor 17-14; 53 Sugar, Mississippi 24-7; 54 Sugar, West Virginia 42-19; 55 Cotton, Arkansas 14-6; 56 Sugar, Pittsburgh 7-0; 56 Gator, Pittsburgh 21-14. Coach: Bobby Dodd.

6 Nebraska—69 Sun, Georgia 45-6; 71 Orange, LSU 17-12; 72 Orange, Alabama 38-6; 73 Orange, Notre Dame 40-6; 74 Cotton, Texas 19-3; 74 Sugar, Florida 13-10. Coaches: Bob Devaney first four games, Tom Osborne last two.

6 Alabama—75 Sugar, Penn St. 13-6; 76 Liberty, UCLA 36-6; 78 Sugar, Ohio St. 35-6; 79 Sugar, Penn St. 14-7; 80 Sugar, Arkansas 24-9; 81 Cotton, Baylor 30-2. Coach: Paul "Bear" Bryant.

6 Southern California—75 Rose, Ohio St. 18-17; 75 Liberty, Texas A&M 20-0; 77 Rose, Michigan 14-6; 77 Bluebonnet, Texas A&M 47-28; 79 Rose, Michigan 17-10; 80 Rose, Ohio St. 17-16. Coaches: John McKay first two games, John Robinson last four.

Active Consecutive Appearances in Bowl Games

(Must have appeared in 2006-07 bowls)

Team	Appearances	Team	Appearances
Michigan	32	Georgia Tech	10
Florida St.	25	Louisville	9
Florida	16	Miami (Fla.)	9
Virginia Tech	14	Oklahoma	9
Georgia	10	Texas	9

Undefeated, Untied Team Matchups in Bowl Games

Bowl	Date	Winner (Record Going In, Coach)	Loser (Record Going In, Coach)
Rose	1-1-21	California 28 (8-0, Andy Smith)	Ohio St. 0 (7-0, John Wilce)
Rose	1-2-22	0-0 tie: California (9-0, Andy Smith); Wash. & Jeff. (10-0, Earle "Greasy" Neale)	
Rose	1-1-27	7-7 tie: Alabama (9-0, Wallace Wade); Stanford (10-0, Glenn "Pop" Warner)	
Rose	1-1-31	Alabama 24 (9-0, Wallace Wade)	Washington St. 0 (9-0, Orin "Babe" Hollingbery)
Orange	1-2-39	Tennessee 17 (10-0, Bob Neyland)	Oklahoma 0 (10-0, Tom Stidham)
Sugar	1-1-41	Boston College 19 (10-0, Frank Leahy)	Tennessee 13 (10-0, Bob Neyland)
Sugar	1-1-52	Maryland 28 (9-0, Jim Tatum)	Tennessee 13 (10-0, Bob Neyland)
Orange	1-2-56	Oklahoma 20 (10-0, Bud Wilkinson)	Maryland 6 (10-0, Jim Tatum)
Orange	1-1-72	Nebraska 38 (12-0, Bob Devaney)	Alabama 6 (11-0, Paul "Bear" Bryant)
Sugar	12-31-73	Notre Dame 24 (10-0, Ara Parseghian)	Alabama 23 (11-0, Paul "Bear" Bryant)
Fiesta	1-2-87	Penn St. 14 (11-0, Joe Paterno)	Miami (Fla.) 10 (11-0, Jimmy Johnson)
Orange	1-1-88	Miami (Fla.) 20 (11-0, Jimmy Johnson)	Oklahoma 14 (11-0, Barry Switzer)
Fiesta	1-2-89	Notre Dame 34 (11-0, Lou Holtz)	West Virginia 21 (11-0, Don Nehlen)
Sugar	1-1-93	Alabama 34 (12-0, Gene Stallings)	Miami (Fla.) 13 (11-0, Dennis Erickson)
Fiesta	1-2-96	Nebraska 62 (11-0, Tom Osborne)	Florida 24 (12-0, Steve Spurrier)
Sugar	1-4-00	Florida St. 46 (11-0, Bobby Bowden)	Virginia Tech 29 (11-0, Frank Beamer)
Fiesta	1-3-03	Ohio St. 31 (13-0, Jim Tressel)	Miami (Fla.) 24 (2 ot) (12-0, Larry Coker)
Orange	1-4-05	Southern California 55 (12-0, Pete Carroll)	Oklahoma 19 (12-0, Bob Stoops)
Rose	1-4-06	Texas 41 (12-0, Mack Brown)	Southern California 38 (12-0, Pete Carroll)

Undefeated Team Matchups in Bowl Games

(Both teams were undefeated but one or both was tied one or more times)

Bowl	Date	Winner (Record Going In, Coach)	Loser (Record Going In, Coach)
Rose	1-1-25	Notre Dame 27 (9-0, Knute Rockne)	Stanford 10 (7-0-1, Glenn "Pop" Warner)
Rose	1-1-26	Alabama 20 (9-0, Wallace Wade)	Washington 19 (10-0-1, Enoch Bagshaw)
Rose	1-2-33	Southern California 35 (9-0, Howard Jones)	Pittsburgh 0 (8-0-2, Jock Sutherland)
Rose	1-1-35	Alabama 29 (9-0, Frank Thomas)	Stanford 13 (9-0-1, Claude "Tiny" Thornhill)
Rose	1-1-38	California 13 (9-0-1, Leonard "Stub" Allison)	Alabama 0 (9-0, Frank Thomas)
Rose	1-1-40	Southern California 14 (7-0-2, Howard Jones)	Tennessee 0 (10-0, Bob Neyland)
Sugar	1-1-40	Texas A&M 14 (10-0, Homer Norton)	Tulane 13 (8-0-1, Lowell "Red" Dawson)
Rose	1-1-45	Southern California 25 (7-0-2, Jeff Cravath)	Tennessee 0 (7-0-1, John Barnhill)
Cotton	1-1-48	13-13 tie: Penn St. (9-0, Bob Higgins); SMU (9-0-1, Matty Bell)	
Orange	1-1-51	Clemson 15 (8-0-1, Frank Howard)	Miami (Fla.) 14 (9-0-1, Andy Gustafson)
Sugar	1-1-53	Georgia Tech 24 (11-0, Bobby Dodd)	Mississippi 7 (8-0-2, John Vaught)
Rose	1-1-69	Ohio St. 27 (9-0, Woody Hayes)	Southern California 16 (9-0-1, John McKay)
Rose	1-1-80	Southern California 17 (10-0-1, John Robinson)	Ohio St. 16 (11-0, Earle Bruce)
California	12-14-85	Fresno St. 51 (10-0-1, Jim Sweeney)	Bowling Green 7 (11-0, Denny Stolz)

Bowl Rematches of Regular-Season Opponents

Date	Regular Season	Date	Bowl-Game Rematch
10-9-43	Texas A&M 28, LSU 13	1-1-44	(Orange) LSU 19, Texas A&M 14
11-22-45	South Carolina 13, Wake Forest 13	1-1-46	(Gator) Wake Forest 26, South Carolina 14
10-6-56	Iowa 14, Oregon St. 13	1-1-57	(Rose) Iowa 35, Oregon St. 19
10-31-59	LSU 7, Mississippi 3	1-1-60	(Sugar) Mississippi 21, LSU 0
9-18-65	Michigan St. 13, UCLA 3	1-1-66	(Rose) UCLA 14, Michigan St. 12
10-4-75	Ohio St. 41, UCLA 20	1-1-76	(Rose) UCLA 23, Ohio St. 10
11-11-78	Nebraska 17, Oklahoma 14	1-1-79	(Orange) Oklahoma 31, Nebraska 24
9-25-82	UCLA 31, Michigan 27	1-1-83	(Rose) UCLA 24, Michigan 14
9-7-87	Michigan St. 27, Southern California 13	1-1-88	(Rose) Michigan St. 20, Southern California 17
11-26-94	Florida 31, Florida St. 31	1-2-95	(Sugar) Florida St. 23, Florida 17
9-23-95	Toledo 49, Nevada 35	12-14-95	(Las Vegas) Toledo 40, Nevada 37 (ot)
11-30-96	Florida St. 24, Florida 21	1-2-97	(Sugar) Florida 52, Florida St. 20
11-15-97	Notre Dame 24, LSU 6	12-28-97	(Independence) LSU 27, Notre Dame 9

Bowl-Game Facts

The Bowl/Basketball Connection

Twelve times in history, a football bowl winner also won the NCAA Division I men's basketball championship during the same academic year. They are as follows:

Year	School	Bowl	Date of Bowl
2006-07	Florida	BCS Championship	1-8-07
2005-06	Florida	Outback	1-2-06
1999-00	Michigan St.	Florida Citrus	1-1-00
1992-93	North Carolina	Peach	1-2-93
1988-89	Michigan	Rose	1-2-89
1981-82	North Carolina	Gator	12-28-81
1973-74	North Carolina St.	Liberty	12-17-73
1965-66	UTEP	Sun	12-31-65
1950-51	Kentucky	Sugar	1-1-51
1947-48	Kentucky	Great Lakes	12-6-47
1945-46	Oklahoma St.	Sugar	1-1-46
1944-45	Oklahoma St.	Cotton	1-1-45

One-Time Wonders

Nine current Football Bowl Subdivision teams have played in only one bowl game in their football history, and three of those have posted victories. The one-time bowlers (listed alphabetically) are as follows:

School	Date	Bowl	Opponent (Score)
Akron	12-26-05	Motor City	Memphis (L, 38-31)
UAB	12-24-04	Hawaii	Hawaii (L, 59-40)
Arkansas St.	12-20-05	New Orleans	Southern Miss. (L, 31-19)
UCF	12-24-05	Hawaii	Nevada (L, 49-48 [ot])
Connecticut	12-27-04	Motor City	Toledo (W, 39-10)
Eastern Mich.	12-12-87	California	San Jose St. (W, 30-27)
Idaho	12-30-98	Humanitarian	Southern Miss. (W, 42-35)
Kent St.	12-29-72	Tangerine	Tampa (L, 21-18)
Middle Tenn.	12-26-06	Motor City	Central Mich. (L, 31-14)

Year-by-Year Bowl Facts

(A note about bowl-game dates: Traditionally, bowl games have been played on January 1, but as more bowl games joined the holiday lineup, schedule adjustments were made whereby some bowl games are now played as early as mid-December. In the interest of avoiding confusion, all years referred to in bowl records are the actual calendar year in which the bowl game was played.)

1917 Coach Hugo Bezdek led the first of three teams to the Rose Bowl from 1917 to 1923. His Oregon team beat Penn, 14-0, in 1917; his Mare Island squad defeated Camp Lewis, 19-7, in 1918; and his Penn State team lost to Southern California, 14-3, in 1923. In his 1923 trip with the Nittany Lions, Bezdek almost came to blows with Southern California coach Elmer "Gloomy Gus" Henderson because Penn State did not arrive for the game until an hour after the scheduled kickoff time. Henderson accused Bezdek of not taking the field until the hot California sun had gone down to give his winterized Easterners an advantage.

1919 George Halas (yes, "Papa Bear") was the player of the game for Great Lakes Naval Training Station in Chicago as the Sailors shut out Mare Island, 17-0, in another of the wartime Rose Bowls.

1923 The first Rose Bowl game actually played in the stadium in Pasadena saw Southern California defeat Penn State, 14-3.

1926 Johnny Mack Brown, one of Hollywood's most famous movie cowboys, also was one of college football's most exciting players at Alabama. He was selected player of the game for the Rose Bowl in the Crimson Tide's 20-19 victory over Washington.

1927 The Rose Bowl becomes the first coast-to-coast radio broadcast of a sporting event.

1929 The Rose Bowl game became one of the most famous in bowl history because of California player Roy Riegels' now-legendary wrong-way run. Early in the second quarter, with each team just changing possessions, Georgia Tech was on its own 20. Tech halfback Stumpy Thompson broke for a seven-yard run, fumbled, and Riegels picked up the ball, momentarily headed for the Tech goal, then reversed his field and started running the wrong way. Teammate Benny Lom tried to stop him and finally did on the California one-yard line, where the dazed Riegels was pounced on by a group of Tech tacklers. Lom went back to punt on the next play and the kick was blocked out of the end zone for a safety, which decided the contest, eventually won by Georgia Tech, 8-7.

1938 The first Orange Bowl played in Miami's new stadium, which seated 22,000 at the time, saw Auburn edge Michigan State, 6-0. Also, in the second annual Cotton Bowl, Colorado's do-it-all standout Byron "Whizzer" White, the Rhodes Scholar and future U.S. Supreme Court justice, passed for one score and returned a pass interception for another, but the Buffs lost to Rice, 28-14.

1941 On December 6, 1941, Hawaii defeated Willamette, 20-6, but a second Rainbows' postseason game, scheduled with San Jose State for the next week, was cancelled after the attack on Pearl Harbor.

1942 You would think a team making only one first down and gaining only 75 yards to its opponent's 309 yards could not come out of a game a 29-21 victor, but it happened in the Cotton Bowl as Alabama downed Texas A&M. The Tide intercepted seven of A&M's 42 passes and recovered five Aggie fumbles. Also, the Rose Bowl was moved for one year to Durham, N.C., because of wartime considerations that precluded large gatherings on the West Coast, and Oregon State downed Duke, 20-16.

1946 The first and only bowl game decided after time expired was the Orange Bowl when Miami (Florida) downed Holy Cross, 13-6. Time expired as Miami halfback Al Hudson returned an 89-yard intercepted pass for the deciding score.

1949 A Pacific Coast team had never been allowed to play in a major bowl other than the Rose Bowl, but the conference leadership let Oregon play in the Cotton Bowl against SMU. Doak Walker and Kyle Rote led SMU to a 20-13 victory over the Ducks and quarterback Norm Van Brocklin. John McKay, later the head coach at Southern California, also was on the Oregon roster.

1953 The Rose, Cotton, Sugar and Orange Bowls were televised nationally for the first time.

1954 Dicky Maegle of Rice may be the best-remembered bowl player, not because of his 265 yards rushing and three touchdowns vs. Alabama in 1954, but because of what happened on a 95-yard scoring run. Alabama's Tommy Lewis became infamous by coming off the bench to tackle Maegle in the Cotton Bowl, won by Rice, 28-6.

1960 In one of those pupil-vs.-teacher battles, former Georgia Tech player and assistant coach Frank Broyles led his Arkansas Razorbacks to a 14-7 Gator Bowl victory over his former coach, Bobby Dodd, and the Yellow Jackets.

1962 Oregon State quarterback Terry Baker turned in the longest run in bowl history with a 99-yard scamper to down Villanova, 6-0, in the Liberty Bowl. Baker, an outstanding athlete, became the only Heisman Trophy winner to play in an NCAA Final Four basketball game later that academic year (1963).

1964 Utah and West Virginia became the first teams to play a major bowl game indoors when they met in the Atlantic City Convention Hall. Utah won the Liberty Bowl, 32-6, beneath the bright indoor lights.

1965 The first Orange Bowl played under the lights in Miami saw Texas stun national champion Alabama and quarterback Joe Namath, 21-17.

1968 It was the student beating the teacher in the Cotton Bowl as Texas A&M head coach Gene Stallings saw his Aggies hold on for a 20-16 victory over Alabama and legendary head coach Paul "Bear" Bryant. Stallings had played (at Texas A&M) and coached (at Alabama) under Bryant. The "Bear" met Stallings at midfield after the contest and lifted the 6-foot-3 Aggie coach up in admiration. Also, the Astro-Bluebonnet Bowl (also known as the Bluebonnet Bowl) became the first bowl game to be played in a domed stadium as the Astrodome served as the site of the December 31, 1968, game between SMU (28) and Oklahoma (27).

1970 Three of the four legendary Four Horsemen of Notre Dame came to Dallas to watch the Fighting Irish drop a 21-17 Cotton Bowl game to Texas. The only other time Notre Dame had played in a bowl game was the 1925 Rose Bowl, when the Four Horsemen led the Irish to a 27-10 victory over Stanford.

1971 Notre Dame snapped the second-longest winning streak going into a bowl game by halting Texas' 30-game string, 24-11, in the Cotton Bowl. In 1951, Kentucky had stopped Oklahoma's 31-game streak in the Sugar Bowl, 13-7.

1976 Archie Griffin started his fourth straight Rose Bowl for Ohio State (1973-76), totaling 412 yards on 79 carries in the four games. The Buckeyes, under legendary head coach Woody Hayes, won only the 1974 contest, but Griffin is the only player to win two Heisman Trophies (1974-75).

1989 Texas Tech's James Gray set a college bowl record with 280 yards rushing (broken by Georgia Tech's P.J. Daniels with 307 yards in the 2004 Humanitarian Bowl) in the All-American Bowl against Duke. BYU's Ty Detmer set the bowl passing mark with 576 yards (tied by Marshall's Byron Leftwich in the 2001 GMAC Bowl) versus Penn State in the Holiday Bowl.

Special Regular- and Postseason Games

Postseason Games

UNSANCTIONED OR OTHER BOWLS

The following bowl and/or postseason games were unsanctioned by the NCAA or otherwise had no team classified as major college at the time of the bowl. Most are postseason games; in many cases, complete dates and/or statistics are not available and the scores are listed only to provide a historical reference. Attendance of the game, if known, is listed in parentheses after the score.

ALL-SPORTS BOWL
(Oklahoma City, Okla.)
12-9-61—Okla. Panhandle 28, Langston 14 (8,000)
12-8-62—Neb.-Omaha 34, East Central 21 (2,500)
12-7-63—Northeastern St. 59, Slippery Rock 12
12-5-64—Sul Ross St. 21, East Central 13

ALUMINUM BOWL (NAIA TITLE GAME)
(Little Rock, Ark.)
12-22-56—Montana St. 0, St. Joseph's (Ind.) 0

ANGEL BOWL
(Los Angeles, Calif.)
12-28-46—Florida A&M 6, Wiley 6 (12,000)

AZALEA BOWL
(Orlando, Fla.)
1-1-46—Knoxville 18, Florida Normal 0 (4,000)

AZALEA CLASSIC
(Mobile, Ala.)
12-4-71—Jackson St. 40, Alabama A&M 21
12-7-74—Bethune-Cookman 19, Langston 3 (1,000)

AZTEC BOWL
(Mexico)
12-50—Whittier 27, Mexico All-Stars 14 (at Mexico City)
12-53—Mexico City 45, Eastern N.M. 26 (at Mexico City)
12-97—Division III All-Stars 42, Mexico Collegians 41 (12,000) (at Toluca)
12-12-98—Division III All-Stars 40, Mexico Collegians 13 (18,000) (at Monterrey)
12-99—Division III All-Stars 44, Mexico Collegians 13 (12,000) (at Mexico City)
12-00—Division III All-Stars 27, Mexico Collegians 26 (8,000) (at Merida)
12-15-01—Division III All-Stars 37, Mexico Collegians 5 (10,000) (at Saltillo)
12-02—Division III All-Stars 15, Mexico Collegians 9 (6,000) (at Torreon)

12-13-03—Mexico Collegians 34, Division III All-Stars 31 (8,000) (at Cancun)
12-11-04—Division III All-Stars 23, Mexico Collegians 3 (8,000) (at Cancun)
12-17-05—Division III All-Stars 53, Mexico Collegians 15 (13,000) (at Toluca)
12-16-06—Division III All-Stars 28, Mexico Collegians 7 (16,000) (at Aguascalientes)

BEAN BOWL
(Scottsbluff, Neb.)
11-24-49—Idaho St. 20, Chadron St. 2
11-23-50—Doane 14, Northern Colo. 6

BEAVER BOWL
(Corry, Pa.)
11-15-58—Slippery Rock 6, Edinboro 0 (3,000)

BICENTENNIAL BOWL
(Little Rock, Ark.)
11-29-75—Henderson St. 27, East Central 14 (2,000)

BICENTENNIAL BOWL
(Richmond, Va.)
12-11-76—South Carolina St. 26, Norfolk St. 10 (7,500)

BOOT HILL BOWL
(Dodge City, Kan.)
12-70—Cameron 13, N.M. Highlands 12
12-4-71—Dakota St. 23, Northwestern Okla. 20 (2,000)
12-2-72—William Penn 17, Emporia St. 14 (2,000)
12-1-73—Millikin 51, Bethany (Kan.) 7 (1,600)
11-30-74—Washburn 21, Millikin 7 (2,500)
11-22-75—Buena Vista 24, St. Mary's (Kan.) 21 (2,700)
11-20-76—Benedictine 29, Washburn 14 (3,000)
11-19-77—Mo. Western St. 35, Benedictine 30 (1,000)
11-18-78—Chadron St. 30, Baker (Kan.) 19 (3,000)
11-17-79—Pittsburg St. 43, Peru St. 14 (2,800)
11-21-80—Cameron 34, Adams St. 16

BOTANY BOWL
11-24-55—Neb.-Kearney 34, Northern St. 13

BOY'S RANCH BOWL
(Abilene, Texas)
12-13-47—Missouri Valley 20, McMurry 13 (2,500)

BURLEY BOWL
(Johnson City, Tenn.)
1-1-46—High Point 7, Milligan 7 (3,500)
11-28-46—Southeastern La. 21, Milligan 13 (7,500)
11-27-47—West Chester 20, Carson-Newman 6 (10,000)
11-25-48—West Chester 7, Appalachian St. 2 (12,000)
11-24-49—Emory & Henry 32, Hanover 0 (12,000)
11-23-50—Emory & Henry 26, Appalachian St. 6 (12,000)
11-22-51—Charleston (W.V.) 27, Lebanon Valley 20 (9,000)
11-27-52—East Tenn. St. 34, Emory & Henry 16
11-26-53—East Tenn. St. 48, Emory & Henry 12
11-25-54—Appalachian St. 28, East Tenn. St. 13
11-24-55—East Tenn. St. 7, Appalachian St. 0
11-22-56—Memphis 32, East Tenn. St. 12

CAJUN BOWL
12-47—McNeese St. 0, Southern Ark. 0

CATTLE BOWL
(Fort Worth, Texas)
1-1-47—Ark.-Pine Bluff 7, Lane 0 (1,000)
1-1-48—Samuel Huston 7, Philander Smith 0 (800)

CEMENT BOWL
(Allentown, Pa.)
12-8-62—West Chester 46, Hofstra 12

CHARITY BOWL
(Los Angeles, Calif.)
12-25-37—Fresno St. 27, Central Ark. 26 (5,000)

CHRISTMAS BOWL
(Natchitoches, La.)
12-6-58—Northwestern St. 18, Sam Houston St. 11
12-5-59—Delta St. 19, East Central 0

CIGAR BOWL
(Tampa, Fla.)
1-1-47—Delaware 21, Rollins 7 (9,500)
1-1-48—Missouri Valley 26, West Chester 7 (10,000)
1-1-49—Missouri Valley 13, St. Thomas (Minn.) 13 (11,000)
1-2-50—Florida St. 19, Wofford 6 (14,000)
1-1-51—Wis.-La Crosse 47, Valparaiso 14 (12,000)
12-29-51—Brooke Army Medical 20, Camp LeJeune Marines 0 (7,500) (see Cigar Bowl in Service Games)
12-13-52—Tampa 21, Lenoir-Rhyne 12 (7,500)
1-1-54—Missouri Valley 12, Wis.-La Crosse 12 (5,000)
12-17-54—Tampa 21, Charleston (W.V.) 0

CITRACADO BOWL
(see Citracado Bowl in Service Games)

COCONUT BOWL
(Miami, Fla.)
1-1-42—Florida Normal 0, Miami All-Stars 0 (9,000)
1-1-46—Bethune-Cookman 32, Albany St. (Ga.) 0 (5,000)
1-1-47—Bethune-Cookman 13, Columbia (S.C.) Sporting Club 0 (5,000)

CORN BOWL
(Bloomington, Ill.)
11-27-47—Southern Ill. 21, North Central (Ill.) 0 (5,500)
11-25-48—Ill. Wesleyan 6, Eastern Ill. 0 (8,500)
11-24-49—Western Ill. 13, Wheaton (Ill.) 0 (4,567)
11-23-50—Mo.-Rolla 7, Illinois St. 6 (2,500)
11-22-51—Lewis 21, William Jewell 12 (2,000)
11-26-53—Western Ill. 32, Iowa Wesleyan 0
11-24-55—Luther 24, Western Ill. 20 (3,100)

COSMOPOLITAN BOWL
(Alexandria, La.)
12-51—McNeese St. 13, Louisiana Col. 6

COTTON-TOBACCO BOWL
(Greensboro, N.C.)
1-1-46—Johnson C. Smith 18, Allen 6
1-1-47—Norfolk St. 0, Richmond 0 (10,000)

COWBOY BOWL
(Lawton, Okla.)
12-11-71—Howard Payne 16, Cameron 13
12-9-72—Harding 30, Langston 27

DOLL AND TOY CHARITY GAME
(Gulfport, Miss.)
12-3-37—Southern Miss. 7, Appalachian St. 0 (2,000)

EASTERN BOWL
(Allentown, Pa.)
12-14-63—East Caro. 27, Northeastern 6 (2,700)

ELKS BOWL
1-2-54—Charleston (W.V.) 12, East Caro. 0 (4,500) (at Greenville, N.C.)
12-11-54—Newberry 20, Appalachian St. 13 (at Raleigh, N.C.)

FISH BOWL
(Corpus Christi, Texas)
11-48—Southwestern (Tex.) 7, Corpus Christi 0

FISH BOWL
(Norfolk, Va.)
12-4-48—Hampton 20, Central St. (Ohio) 19

FLOWER BOWL
(Jacksonville, Fla.)
1-1-42—Johnson C. Smith 13, Lane 0 (4,500)
1-1-43—N.C. A&T 14, Southern U. 6 (2,000)
1-1-44—Allen 33, Winston-Salem 0 (2,000)
1-1-45—Texas College 18, N.C. A&T 0 (5,000)
1-1-46—Grambling 19, Lane 6 (6,000)
1-1-47—Delaware St. 7, Florida Normal 6 (3,000)
1-1-48—Bethune-Cookman 6, Lane 0 (3,000)

FRUIT BOWL
(San Francisco, Calif.)
12-14-47—Central St. (Ohio) 26, Prairie View 0 (9,000)
12-5-48—Southern U. 30, San Fran. St. 0 (5,000)

GATE CITY BOWL
(Atlanta, Ga.)
12-21-74—Tuskegee 15, Norfolk St. 14 (6,252)

GLASS BOWL
(Toledo, Ohio)
12-7-46—Toledo 21, Bates 12 (12,000)
12-6-47—Toledo 20, New Hampshire 14 (13,500)
12-4-48—Toledo 27, Oklahoma City 14 (8,500)
12-3-49—Cincinnati 33, Toledo 13

GOLD BOWL
(Richmond, Va.)
12-3-77—South Carolina St. 10, Winston-Salem 7 (14,000)
12-2-78—Virginia Union 21, N.C. A&T 6 (7,500)
12-1-79—South Carolina St. 39, Norfolk St. 7 (8,000)
12-6-80—N.C. A&T 37, N.C. Central 0 (3,374)

GOLDEN ISLES BOWL
(Brunswick, Ga.)
12-1-62—McNeese St. 21, Samford 14

GRAPE BOWL
(Lodi, Calif.)
12-13-47—Pacific 35, Utah St. 21 (12,000)
12-11-48—Hardin-Simmons 35, Pacific 35 (10,000)

GREAT LAKES BOWL
(Cleveland, Ohio)
12-5-48—John Carroll 14, Canisius 13 (18,000)

GREAT SOUTHWEST BOWL
(Grand Prairie, Texas)
12-31-60—Tex. A&M-Kingsville 45, Arkansas Tech 14 (3,900)

HOLIDAY BOWL
(St. Petersburg, Fla.)
12-21-57—Pittsburg St. 27, Hillsdale 26
12-20-58—Northeastern St. 19, Northern Ariz. 13
12-19-59—Tex. A&M-Kingsville 20, Lenoir-Rhyne 7 (9,500)
12-10-60—Lenoir-Rhyne 15, Humboldt St. 14 (also served as NAIA national title game)

HOOSIER BOWL
(See Turkey Bowl)

INTERNATIONAL BOWL
12-52—Tex. A&M-Kingsville 49, Hereico Colegio Military 0

IODINE BOWL
(Charleston, S.C.)
12-3-49—Johnson C. Smith 20, Allen 12
12-9-50—Allen 20, Bethune-Cookman 0 (1,000)
12-1-51—Allen 33, Morris College 14 (3,000)
12-5-53—Allen 33, Paul Quinn 6

KICKAPOO BOWL
(Wichita Falls, Texas)
12-5-47—Midwestern St. 39, Central Ark. 20 (5,000)

LIONS BOWL
(Ruston, La.)
12-46—Grambling 69, Miss. Industrial 12
12-5-47—Grambling 47, Bethune-Cookman 6
12-49—Grambling 21, Texas College 18
12-2-50—Bishop 35, Grambling 0
12-1-51—Grambling 52, Bishop 0 (at Shreveport, La.)
12-6-52—Grambling 27, Alcorn St. 13 (at Monroe, La.)

LIONS BOWL
(Salisbury, N.C.)
12-13-52—Clarion 13, East Caro. 6 (3,000)

MERCY BOWL II
(Anaheim, Calif.)
12-11-71—Cal St. Fullerton 17, Fresno St. 14 (16,854)

MIRZA SHRINE BOWL
(Pittsburg, Kan.)
12-1-50—Central Mo. 32, Pittsburg St. 21

MISSOURI-KANSAS BOWL
(Kansas City, Mo.)
12-4-48—Emporia St. 34, Missouri St. 20

MOILA SHRINE CLASSIC
(St. Joseph, Mo.)
11-24-79—Mo. Western St. 72, William Jewell 44 (1,600)
11-22-80—Truman 17, Pittsburg St. 14 (500)

NATIONAL CLASSIC
(Greensboro, N.C.)
12-4-54—N.C. Central 19, Tennessee St. 6

NEW YEAR'S CLASSIC
(Honolulu, Hawaii)
1-1-34—Santa Clara 26, Hawaii 7
1-1-35—Hawaii 14, California 0 (later called Poi Bowl)

OIL BOWL
(Houston, Texas)
1-1-44—La.-Lafayette 24, Ark.-Monticello 7 (12,000)

OLEANDER BOWL
(Galveston, Texas)
1-2-50—McMurry 19, Missouri Valley 13 (7,500)

OLYMPIAN BOWL
(see Pythian Bowl)

OPTIMIST BOWL
(Houston, Texas)
12-21-46—North Texas 14, Pacific 13 (5,000)

ORANGE BLOSSOM CLASSIC
(Miami, Fla.)
12-2-33—Florida A&M 9, Howard 6
12-13-34—Florida A&M 13, Virginia St. 12
12-12-35—Kentucky St. 19, Florida A&M 10

12-5-36—Prairie View 25, Florida A&M 0
12-9-37—Florida A&M 25, Hampton 20
12-8-38—Florida A&M 9, Kentucky St. 7
12-9-39—Florida A&M 42, Wiley 0
12-7-40—Central St. (Ohio) 0, Florida A&M 0
12-6-41—Florida A&M 15, Tuskegee 7
12-12-42—Florida A&M 12, Texas College 6
12-4-43—Hampton 39, Florida A&M 0
12-9-44—Virginia St. 19, Florida A&M 6
12-8-45—Wiley 32, Florida A&M 6
12-7-46—Lincoln (Pa.) 20, Florida A&M 0 (at Tampa)
12-6-47—Florida A&M 7, Hampton 0
12-4-48—Virginia Union 10, Florida A&M 6 (16,000)
12-10-49—N.C. A&T 20, Florida A&M 14
12-2-50—Central St. (Ohio) 13, Florida A&M 6
12-1-51—Florida A&M 67, N.C. Central 6
12-6-52—Florida A&M 29, Virginia St. 7
12-5-53—Prairie View 33, Florida A&M 27
12-4-54—Florida A&M 67, Md.-East. Shore 19
12-3-55—Grambling 28, Florida A&M 21
12-1-56—Tennessee St. 41, Florida A&M 39
12-14-57—Florida A&M 27, Md.-East. Shore 21
12-13-58—Prairie View 26, Florida A&M 8
12-5-59—Florida A&M 28, Prairie View 7
12-10-60—Florida A&M 40, Langston 26
12-9-61—Florida A&M 14, Jackson St. 8 (47,791)
12-8-62—Jackson St. 22, Florida A&M 6
12-14-63—Morgan St. 30, Florida A&M 7
12-5-64—Florida A&M 42, Grambling 15
12-4-65—Morgan St. 36, Florida A&M 7
12-3-66—Florida A&M 43, Alabama A&M 26
12-2-67—Grambling 28, Florida A&M 25
12-7-68—Alcorn St. 36, Florida A&M 9 (37,398)
12-6-69—Florida A&M 23, Grambling 19 (36,784) (at Tallahassee, Fla.)
12-12-70—Jacksonville St. 21, Florida A&M 7 (31,184)
12-11-71—Florida A&M 27, Kentucky St. 9 (26,161)
12-2-72—Florida A&M 41, Md.-East. Shore 21 (21,606)
12-8-73—Florida A&M 23, South Carolina St. 12 (18,996)
12-7-74—Florida A&M 17, Howard 13 (20,166)
12-6-75—Florida A&M 40, Kentucky St. 13 (27,875)
12-4-76—Florida A&M 26, Central St. (Ohio) 21 (18,000)
12-3-77—Florida A&M 37, Delaware St. 15 (29,493)
12-2-78—Florida A&M 31, Grambling 7

ORCHID BOWL
(Mexico City, Mexico)
1-1-42—Louisiana Col. 10, U. of Mexico 0 (8,000)
12-28-46—Mississippi Col. 43, U. of Mexico 7 (7,500)

PALM FESTIVAL
(Miami, Fla.)
1-2-33—Miami (Fla.) 7, Manhattan 0 (6,000)
1-1-34—Duquesne 33, Miami (Fla.) 7 (3,500) (forerunner to Orange Bowl)

PALMETTO SHRINE
(Columbia, S.C.)
12-10-55—Lenoir-Rhyne 14, Newberry 13 (6,000)

PAPER BOWL
(Pensacola, Fla.)
12-18-48—Jacksonville St. 19, Troy 0
12-16-49—Jacksonville St. 12, West Ala. 7 (3,000)
12-2-50—Pensacola Alumni Cardinals 7, Jacksonville St. 6 (3,600)

PEACH BLOSSOM CLASSIC
(Atlanta, Ga.)
12-9-39—Morris Brown 13, Virginia St. 7
12-6-40—Morris Brown 28, Kentucky St. 6 (1,500)
12-6-41—Morris Brown 7, N.C. Central 6 (6,000) (at Columbus, Ga.)
12-4-42—Morris Brown 20, Lane 0 (3,000) (at Columbus, Ga.)

PEACH BOWL
(Macon, Ga.)
12-13-46—Tenn. Wesleyan 14, Ga. Military 13 (5,000)
12-6-47—Virginia St. 48, Morris Brown 0
12-3-49—Morris Brown 33, Texas College 28 (at Atlanta, Ga.)

PEANUT BOWL
(Dothan, Ala.)
12-21-68—Ouachita Baptist 39, West Ala. 6

PEAR BOWL
(Medford, Ore.)
11-28-46—Southern Ore. St. 13, Central Wash. 8 (3,000) (at Ashland, Ore.)
11-27-47—Pacific Lutheran 27, Southern Ore. St. 21
11-25-48—Col. of Idaho 27, Southern Ore. St. 20 (2,500)
11-24-49—Pacific (Ore.) 33, UC Davis 15 (4,000)
11-23-50—Lewis & Clark 61, San Fran. St. 7 (4,000)
11-24-51—Pacific (Ore.) 25, UC Davis 7 (4,000)

PECAN BOWL
(Orangeburg, S.C.)
12-7-46—South Carolina St. 13, Johnson C. Smith 6
12-13-47—South Carolina St. 7, Allen 0 (3,000)

PELICAN BOWL
(New Orleans, La.)
12-2-72—Grambling 56, N.C. Central 6 (22,500) (at Durham, N.C.)
12-7-74—Grambling 28, South Carolina St. 7 (30,120)
12-27-75—Southern U. 15, South Carolina St. 12 (6,748)

PENINSULA BOWL
(Charleston, S.C.)
12-2-50—Allen 47, South Carolina St. 13 (7,500)

PHILLIPS FIELD BOWL
(Tampa, Fla.)
12-8-51—Tampa 7, Brandeis 0

PIEDMONT TOBACCO BOWL
(Fayetteville, N.C.)
12-7-46—Allen 40, Fayetteville St. 6 (900)

PINEAPPLE BOWL
(Honolulu, Hawaii)
1-1-40—Oregon St. 39, Hawaii 6 (formerly called Poi Bowl)
1-1-41—Fresno St. 3, Hawaii 0
1-1-47—Hawaii 19, Utah 16 (25,000)
1-1-48—Hawaii 33, Redlands 32 (12,000)
1-1-49—Oregon St. 47, Hawaii 27 (15,000)
1-2-50—Stanford 74, Hawaii 20
1-1-51—Hawaii 28, Denver 27
1-1-52—San Diego St. 34, Hawaii 13

POI BOWL
(Honolulu, Hawaii)
1-1-36—Southern California 38, Hawaii 6
1-2-37—Hawaii 18, Honolulu All-Stars 12
1-1-38—Washington 53, Hawaii 13 (13,500)
1-2-39—UCLA 32, Hawaii 7 (later called Pineapple Bowl)

POULTRY BOWL
(Gainesville, Ga.)
12-8-73—Stephen F. Austin 31, Gardner-Webb 10 (2,500)
12-7-74—Guilford 7, William Penn 7 (1,000) (at Greensboro, N.C.) (Guilford awarded win on 10-8 edge in first downs)

PRAIRIE VIEW BOWL
(Also called Bayou City Bowl)
(Houston, Texas)
1-1-29—Atlanta 7, Prairie View 0
1-1-30—Fisk 20, Prairie View 0
1-1-31—Tuskegee 19, Prairie View 7
1-1-32—Prairie View 27, Alabama St. 2
1-1-33—Prairie View 14, Tuskegee 0
1-1-34—Prairie View 20, Langston 7
1-1-35—Tuskegee 15, Prairie View 6
1-1-36—Wiley 7, Prairie View 6
1-1-37—Tuskegee 6, Prairie View 0 (3,000)
1-1-38—Prairie View 27, Florida A&M 14
1-2-39—Prairie View 34, Tuskegee 0
1-1-40—Prairie View 7, Xavier (La.) 6
1-1-41—Prairie View 7, Alabama St. 6
1-1-42—Kentucky St. 19, Prairie View 13
1-1-43—Langston 18, Prairie View 13
1-1-44—Prairie View 6, Wiley 0 (5,000)
1-1-45—Wiley 26, Prairie View 0 (4,000)
1-1-46—Prairie View 12, Tuskegee 0 (10,000)
1-1-47—Prairie View 14, Lincoln (Mo.) 0 (1,500) (called Houston Bowl)
1-1-48—Texas Southern 13, Prairie View 0
1-1-49—Central St. (Ohio) 6, Prairie View 0 (9,000)
1-2-50—Prairie View 27, Fisk 6 (4,718)
1-1-51—Prairie View 6, Bishop 0
1-1-52—Prairie View 27, Ark.-Pine Bluff 26
1-1-53—Texas Southern 13, Prairie View 12 (13,000)
1-1-54—Prairie View 33, Texas Southern 8
1-1-55—Prairie View 14, Texas Southern 12 (10,000)
1-2-56—Prairie View 59, Fisk 0 (7,500)
1-1-57—Prairie View 27, Texas Southern 6
1-1-58—Prairie View 6, Texas Southern 6 (3,500)
1-1-59—Prairie View 34, Langston 8
1-1-60—Prairie View 47, Wiley 10 (1,200)
12-31-60—Prairie View 19, Ark.-Pine Bluff 8 (1,400)
12-1-62—Prairie View 37, Central St. (Ohio) 16

PRETZEL BOWL
(Reading, Pa.)
11-24-51—West Chester 32, Albright 9 (7,500)

PYTHIAN BOWL
(Salisbury, N.C.)
11-26-49—Appalachian St. 21, Catawba 7
12-9-50—West Liberty St. 28, Appalachian St. 26
12-8-51—Lenoir-Rhyne 13, California (Pa.) 7 (4,500)

REFRIGERATOR BOWL
(Evansville, Ind.)
12-4-48—Evansville 13, Missouri Valley 7 (7,500)
12-3-49—Evansville 22, Hillsdale 7
12-2-50—Abilene Christian 13, Gust. Adolphus 7 (8,000)
12-2-51—Arkansas St. 46, Camp Breckinridge 12 (10,000)
12-7-52—Western Ky. 34, Arkansas St. 19 (9,500)
12-6-53—Sam Houston St. 14, Col. of Idaho 12 (7,500)
12-5-54—Delaware 19, Kent St. 7 (4,500)
12-4-55—Jacksonville St. 12, Rhode Island 10 (7,000)
12-1-56—Sam Houston St. 27, Middle Tenn. 13 (3,000)

RICE BOWL
(Stuggart, Ark.)
12-57—Arkansas Tech 19, Ark.-Monticello 7
12-58—Louisiana Col. 39, Arkansas Tech 12
12-2-60—East Central 25, Henderson St. 7

ROCKET BOWL
(Huntsville, Ala.)
11-19-60—Maryville (Tenn.) 19, Millsaps 0

SAN JACINTO SHRINE BOWL
(Pasadena, Texas)
12-4-76—Abilene Christian 22, Harding 12 (8,000)

SHARE BOWL
(Knoxville, Tenn.)
12-11-71—Carson-Newman 54, Fairmont St. 3 (1,200)

SHRIMP BOWL
(Galveston, Texas)
12-27-52—Sam Houston St. 41, Northeastern St. 20 (3,500)

SHRINE BOWL
(Ardmore, Okla.)
12-9-72—Southwestern Okla. 28, Angelo St. 6

SILVER BOWL
(Mexico City, Mexico)
12-20-47—Mexico All-Stars 24, Randolph Field 19
12-11-48—Pacific Fleet 33, Mexico All-Stars 26
12-17-49—Trinity (Tex.) 52, Mexico 6

SMOKY MOUNTAIN BOWL
(Bristol, Tenn.)
11-24-49—West Liberty St. 20, Western Caro. 0 (1,000)

SPACE CITY BOWL
(Huntsville, Ala.)
11-24-66—Jacksonville St. 41, Ark.-Monticello 30
12-9-67—Samford 20, Ark.-Monticello 7

STEEL BOWL
(Birmingham, Ala.)
1-1-41—Morris Brown 19, Central St. (Ohio) 3 (8,000)
1-1-42—Southern College All-Stars 26, Nashville Pros 13
1-1-52—Bethune-Cookman 27, Texas College 13 (1,500)

SUGAR CUP CLASSIC
(New Orleans, La.)
11-28-64—Grambling 42, Bishop 6

TEXHOMA BOWL
(Denison, Texas)
12-10-48—Ouachita Baptist 7, Southeastern Okla. 0
11-25-49—Austin (Tex.) 27, East Central 6

TEXTILE BOWL
(Spartanburg, S.C.)
11-30-74—Wofford 20, South Carolina St. 0 (3,000)

TOBACCO BOWL
(Lexington, Ky.)
12-14-46—Muhlenberg 26, St. Bonaventure 25 (3,000)

TROPICAL BOWL
12-18-51—Morris Brown 21, Alcorn St. 0
12-13-52—Bethune-Cookman 54, Albany St. (Ga.) 0
12-12-53—Virginia Union 13, Bethune-Cookman 0

TURKEY BOWL
11-28-46—Evansville 19, Northern Ill. 7 (12,000) (also called Hoosier Bowl)

VULCAN BOWL
(Birmingham, Ala.)
1-1-42—Langston 13, Morris Brown 0 (7,000)
1-1-43—Texas College 13, Tuskegee 10 (6,000)
1-1-44—Tuskegee 12, Clark (Ga.) 7 (6,000)
1-1-45—Tennessee St. 13, Tuskegee 0 (5,000)
1-1-46—Tennessee St. 33, Texas College 6 (9,000)
1-1-47—Tennessee St. 32, Louisville Municipal 0 (4,000)
1-2-48—Central St. (Ohio) 27, Grambling 21 (8,000)
1-1-49—Kentucky St. 23, N.C. A&T 13 (5,000)

WEST VIRGINIA BOWL
(Clarksburg, W.V.)
12-60—Fairmont St. 13, Salem Int'l 7
11-61—West Va. Wesleyan 12, Salem Int'l 0

WILL ROGERS BOWL
(Oklahoma City, Okla.)
1-1-47—Pepperdine 38, Neb. Wesleyan 13 (800)

YAM BOWL
(Dallas, Texas)
12-25-46—Texas Southern 64, Tuskegee 7 (5,000)
12-25-47—Southern U. 46, Fort Valley St. 0 (1,200)

SERVICE GAMES

AIRBORNE BOWL
12-15-57—101st Airborne 20, 82nd Airborne 14
12-5-59—Fort Campbell 26, Fort Bragg 7

ARAB BOWL
(Oran, Africa)
1-1-44—Army 10, Navy 7 (15,000)

ARMY ALL-STAR GAMES
8-30-42—Washington Redskins 26, Western Army All-Stars 7 (at Los Angeles, Calif.)
9-6-42—Western Army All-Stars 16, Chicago Cardinals 10 (at Denver, Colo.)
9-9-42—Western Army All-Stars 12, Detroit Lions 0 (at Detroit, Mich.)
9-12-42—Eastern Army All-Stars 16, New York Giants 0 (at New York, N.Y.)
9-13-42—Green Bay Packers 36, Western Army All-Stars 21 (at Milwaukee, Wis.)
9-16-42—Eastern Army All-Stars 13, Brooklyn Dodgers 7 (at Baltimore, Md.)
9-19-42—New York Giants 10, Western Army All-Stars 7 (at New York, N.Y.)
9-20-42—Chicago Bears 14, Eastern Army All-Stars 7 (at Boston, Mass.)

ARMY PACIFIC OLYMPICS
(Osaka, Japan)
1-13-46—11th Airborne Angels 27, Clark Field 6
1-27-46—11th Airborne Angels 18, Honolulu All-Stars 0

ARMY-NAVY BENEFIT BOWL
(Tallahassee, Fla.)
12-20-52—Parris Island 49, Fort Benning 0

ATOM BOWL
(Nagasaki, Japan)
12-45—Nishahaya Tigers 14, Bertelli's Bears 13 (2,000)

BAMBINO BOWL
(Bari, Italy)
11-23-44—Technical School 13, Playboys 0 (5,000)

BAMBOO BOWL
(Manila, Philippines)
1-1-46—Clark Field Acpacs 14, Leyte Base 12 (40,000)
1-1-47—Manila Raiders 13, Scofield Barracks 6 (12,000)
12-47—Ryukgus Command Sea Horses 21, Hawaiian Mid-Pacific Commandos 0
1-1-50—All-Navy Guam 19, Clark Air Force Base 7

BLUEBONNET BOWL
(Houston, Texas)
12-25-46—Texas Southern 49, Camp Hood 0

CHERRY BOWL
(Yokohama, Japan)
1-1-52—Camp Drake 26, Yoksuka Naval Base 12

CHIGGER BOWL
(Dutch Guiana)
1-1-45—Army Air Base Bonecrushers 6, Army Airway Rams 0 (1,200)

CHINA BOWL
(Shanghai)
1-27-46—Navy All-Stars 12, Army All-Stars 0
1-1-47—11th Airborne 12, Army-Navy All-Stars 6
1-1-48—Marines (Guam) 45, China All-Stars 0

CIGAR BOWL
12-29-51—Brooke Army Medical 20, Camp LeJeune 0 (7,500)

CITRICADO BOWL
12-56—San Diego Marines 25, UC Santa Barb. 14

COCONUT BOWL
(New Guinea)
1-6-45—Bulldogs 18, Crimson Tide 7 (3,000)

COFFEE BOWL
(London, England)
3-19-44—United States 18, Canada 0

CONCH BOWL
(Key West, Fla.)
11-24-57—Keesler Air Force Base 27, Maxwell Air Force Base 7
11-28-58—Keesler Air Force Base 14, Maxwell Air Force Base 8

COSMOPOLITAN BOWL
(Alexandria, La.)
12-50—Camp Polk 26, Louisiana Col. 7
12-52—Louisiana Col. 14, Alexander Air Base 0

ELECTRONICS BOWL
(Biloxi, Miss.)
12-9-51—Keesler Air Force Base 13, Camp LeJeune 0
12-53—Eglin Air Force Base 19, Keesler Air Force Base 8
12-54—Shaw Air Force Base 20, Keesler Air Force Base 19

EUROPEAN "ORANGE BOWL"
(Heidelberg, Germany)
12-7-46—1st Division Artillery 27, 60th Infantry 13

EUROPEAN "ROSE BOWL"
(Augsburg, Germany)
12-7-46—9th Division 20, 16th Infantry 7 (3,000)

EUROPEAN "SUGAR BOWL"
(Nuremberg, Germany)
12-7-46—Grafenwohr Military 0, 39th Infantry 0

G. I. BOWL
(London, England)
11-12-44—Army G.I.'s 20, Navy Bluejackets 0 (60,000)

ICE BOWL
(Fairbanks, Alaska)
1-1-49—Ladd Air Force Base 0, University of Alaska 0 (500)
1-2-50—University of Alaska 3, Ladd Air Force Base 0
1-1-51—University of Alaska 0, Ladd Air Force Base 0
12-30-52—Ladd Air Force Base 47, University of Alaska 0

IRANIAN BOWL
(Teheran, Iran)
12-12-44—Camp Amirabad 20, Camp Khorramsahr 0 (9,000)

JUNGLE BOWL
(Southwest Pacific)
1-1-45—American All-Stars 49, Marines 0 (6,400)

LILY BOWL
(Hamilton, Bermuda)
1-3-43—Army 19, Navy 18
1-1-44—Navy 19, Army 0
1-7-45—Navy 39, Army 6 (11,000)
1-5-47—Army 7, Navy 7 (9,000)
1-1-48—Air Force 12, Navy 12
1-1-49—Navy All-Stars 25, Kindley Fliers 6

MARINE BOWL
(Pritchard Field, Southwest Pacific)
12-24-44—4th Marines 0, 29th Marines 0 (7,000)

MISSILE BOWL
(Orlando, Fla.)
12-3-60—Quantico Marines 36, Pensacola Air Force Base 6
12-9-61—Fort Eustis 25, Quantico Marines 24
12-15-62—Fort Campbell 14, Lackland Air Force Base 10
12-14-63—Quantico Marines 13, San Diego Marines 10
12-5-64—Fort Benning 9, Fort Eustis 3

PALMETTO SHRINE
(Charleston, S.C.)
1-1-55—Fort Jackson 26, Shaw Air Force Base 21

PARC DES PRINCES BOWL
(Paris, France)
12-19-44—9th Air Force 6, 1st General Hospital 0 (20,000)

POI BOWL
(Honolulu, Hawaii)
(Pacific Ocean Areas Service Championship)
1-8-45—Navy 14, Army Air Force 0 (29,000)

POINSETTIA BOWL
(San Diego, Calif.)
12-20-52—Bolling Air Force Base 35, San Diego NTC 14
12-19-53—Fort Ord 55, Quantico Marines 19
12-19-54—Fort Sill 27, Bolling Air Force Base 6
12-17-55—Fort Ord 35, Pensacola NAS 13

POTATO BOWL
(Belfast, Ireland)
1-1-44—Galloping Gaels 0, Wolverines 0

RICE BOWL
(Tokyo, Japan)
1-1-46—11th Airborne Angels 25, 41st Division 12 (15,000)
12-46—Yokota Air Base 13, 1st AD 8 (7,000)
1-1-48—Korea All-Stars 19, Japan All-Stars 13
1-1-49—Army Ground Forces 13, Air Force 7 (20,000)
1-1-50—Air Force All-Stars 18, Army All-Stars 14
1-1-53—Camp Drake 25, Yokosuka Naval Base 6
1-1-54—Camp Fisher 19, Nagoya Air Base 13
1-1-55—Air Force 21, Marines 14
12-31-55—Air Force 33, Army 14 (40,000)
12-30-56—Army 21, Air Force 6
12-7-57—Johnson Air Base Vanguards 6, Marine Corps Sukiran Streaks 0
12-20-58—Air Force 20, Army 0

RIVIERA BOWL
(Marseille, France)
1-1-45—Railway Shop Battalion Unit 37, Army All-Stars 0 (18,000)

SALAD BOWL
(Phoenix, Ariz.)
1-1-53—San Diego Navy 81, 101st Airborne 20
1-1-54—Fort Ord 67, Great Lakes 12

SATELLITE BOWL
(Cocoa, Fla.)
12-29-57—Fort Carson 12, Fort Dix 6

SHRIMP BOWL
(Galveston, Texas)
1-1-55—Fort Ord 36, Fort Hood 0
12-18-55—Fort Hood 33, Little Creek 13
12-8-56—Bolling Air Force Base 29, Fort Hood 14
12-15-57—Bolling Air Force Base 28, San Diego Marines 7
12-14-58—Eglin Air Force Base 15, Brooke Medics 7
12-13-59—Quantico Marines 90, McClellan Air Force Base 0

SHURI BOWL
12-58—Air Force 60, Marine Corps 0

SPAGHETTI BOWL
(Florence, Italy)
1-1-45—5th Army 20, 12th Air Force 0 (20,000)
1-1-53—Salzburg Army 12, Wiesbaden AFC 7 (at Leghorn, Italy)

SUKIYAKI BOWL
12-56—Air Force 29, Marines 7

TEA BOWL
(London, England)
2-13-44—Canada 16, United States 6 (30,000)
12-31-44—Air Service Command Warriors 13, 8th Air Force Shuttle Raiders 0 (12,000)

TREASURY BOWL
(New York, N.Y.)
12-16-44—Randolph Field 13, 2nd Air Force 6 (8,356)

TYPHOON BOWL
12-56—Army 13, Marines 0

VALOR BOWL
(Chattanooga, Tenn.)
12-7-57—Hamilton Air Force Base 12, Quantico Marines 6

POSTSEASON BOWL INVOLVING NON-FOOTBALL BOWL SUBDIVISION TEAMS

HERITAGE BOWL
Site: Atlanta, Ga.
Stadium (Capacity): Georgia Dome (71,228)
Name Changes: Alamo Heritage Bowl (1991); Heritage Bowl (1993-94, 96-99); Jim Walters Heritage Bowl (1995)
Playing Surface: AstroTurf

Playing Sites: Joe Robbie Stadium, Miami (1991); Bragg Memorial Stadium, Tallahassee (1993); Georgia Dome, Atlanta (1994-99)

Date	Score (Attendance)
12-21-91	Alabama St. 36, N.C. A&T 13 (7,724)
1-2-93	Grambling 45, Florida A&M 15 (11,273)
1-1-94	Southern U. 11, South Carolina St. 0 (36,128)
12-30-94	South Carolina St. 31, Grambling 27 (22,179)
12-29-95	Southern U. 30, Florida A&M 25 (25,164)
12-31-96	Howard 27, Southern U. 24 (18,126)
12-27-97	Southern U. 34, South Carolina St. 28 (32,629)
12-26-98	Southern U. 28, Bethune-Cookman 2 (32,955)
12-18-99	Hampton 24, Southern U. 3 (29,561)

MINERAL WATER BOWL
Site: Excelsior Springs, Mo.
Stadium (Capacity): Tiger Stadium (3,000)
Playing Surface: SprinTurf
Playing Sites: Roosevelt Field (1954-75, 2000-03); Tiger Stadium (since 2004)

Date	Score (Attendance)
11-25-54	Hastings 20, Col. of Emporia 14 (4,000)
11-24-55	Missouri Valley 31, Hastings 7
11-22-56	St. Benedict's 14, Northeastern St. 13 (2,000)
11-30-57	William Jewell 33, Hastings 14 (2,000)
11-22-58	Lincoln (Mo.) 21, Emporia St. 0 (2,500)
11-28-59	Col. of Emporia 21, Austin (Tex.) 20 (3,000)
11-26-60	Hillsdale 17, UNI 6 (6,000)
11-25-61	Truman 22, Parsons 8 (8,000)
11-24-62	Adams St. 23, Northern Ill. 20
11-30-63	Northern Ill. 21, Missouri St. 14
11-28-64	North Dakota St. 14, Western St. 13 (4,500)
11-27-65	North Dakota 37, Northern Ill. 20
11-26-66	Adams St. 14, Missouri St. 8 (5,500)
11-25-67	Doane 14, William Jewell 14 (6,500)
11-30-68	Doane 10, Central Mo. 0 (6,000)
11-29-69	St. John's (Minn.) 21, Simpson 0 (5,000)
11-28-70	Franklin 40, Wayne St. (Neb.) 12 (2,500)
12-4-71	Bethany (Kan.) 17, Missouri Valley 14 (2,500)
11-18-72	Ottawa 27, Friends 20 (4,500)
11-73	William Jewell 20, St. Mary's (Kan.) 9
11-23-74	Midland 32, Friends 6 (1,500)
11-22-75	Mo. Western St. 44, Graceland (Ia.) 0 (3,300)
1976-91	Game not played
1992-99	Junior-college bowl
12-2-00	Winona St. 43, Mo. Western 41 (3 ot) (2,300)
12-1-01	Central Mo. 48, Minn. Duluth 17 (3,592)
12-7-02	Emporia St. 34, Winona St. 27 (ot) (3,022)
12-6-03	Mo. Western St. 24, Concordia-St. Paul 14 (2,500)
12-4-04	Washburn 36, Northern St. 33 (3,674)
12-3-05	Mo. Western St. 35, Concordia-St. Paul 23 (2,250)
12-2-06	Pittsburg St. 35, Bemidji St. 27 (3,022)

NCAA-CERTIFIED ALL-STAR GAMES

EAST-WEST SHRINE CLASSIC
Present Site: Houston
Stadium (Capacity): Reliant Stadium (71,500)
Playing Surface: Grass
Playing Sites: Ewing Field, San Francisco (1925); Kezar Stadium, San Francisco (1927-41); Sugar Bowl, New Orleans (1942); Kezar Stadium, San Francisco (1943-66); Candlestick Park, San Francisco (1967-68); Stanford Stadium, Palo Alto (1969); Oakland Coliseum (1971); Candlestick Park, San Francisco (1971-73); Stanford Stadium, Palo Alto (1974-00); SBC Park, San Francisco (2001-05); Alamodome, San Antonio (2006); Reliant Stadium, Houston (since 2007)

Date	Score (Attendance)
12-26-25	West 7-0 (20,000)
1-1-27	West 7-3 (15,000)
12-26-27	West 16-6 (27,500)
12-29-28	East 20-0 (55,000)
1-1-30	East 19-7 (58,000)
12-27-30	West 3-0 (40,000)
1-1-32	East 6-0 (45,000)
1-2-33	West 21-13 (45,000)
1-1-34	West 12-0 (35,000)
1-1-35	West 19-13 (52,000)
1-1-36	East 19-3 (55,000)
1-1-37	East 3-0 (38,000)
1-1-38	Tie 0-0 (55,000)
1-2-39	West 14-0 (60,000)
1-1-40	West 28-11 (50,000)
1-1-41	West 20-14 (60,000)
1-3-42	Tie 6-6 (35,000)
1-1-43	East 13-12 (57,000)
1-1-44	Tie 13-13 (55,000)
1-1-45	West 13-7 (60,000)
1-1-46	Tie 7-7 (60,000)
1-1-47	West 13-9 (60,000)
1-1-48	East 40-9 (60,000)
1-1-49	East 14-12 (59,000)
12-31-49	East 28-6 (60,000)
12-30-50	West 16-7 (60,000)
12-29-51	East 15-14 (60,000)
12-27-52	East 21-20 (60,000)
1-2-54	West 31-7 (60,000)
1-1-55	East 13-12 (60,000)
12-31-55	East 29-6 (60,000)
12-29-56	West 7-6 (60,000)
12-28-57	West 27-13 (60,000)
12-27-58	East 26-14 (60,000)
1-2-60	West 21-14 (60,000)
12-31-60	East 7-0 (60,000)
12-30-61	West 21-8 (60,000)
12-29-62	East 25-19 (60,000)
12-28-63	Tie 6-6 (60,000)
1-2-65	West 11-7 (60,000)
12-31-65	West 22-7 (47,000)
12-31-66	East 45-22 (46,000)
12-30-67	East 16-14 (29,000)
12-28-68	West 18-7 (29,000)
12-27-69	West 15-0 (70,000)
1-2-71	West 17-13 (50,000)
12-31-71	West 17-13 (35,000)
12-30-72	East 9-3 (37,000)
12-29-73	East 35-7 (30,000)
12-28-74	East 16-14 (35,000)
1-3-76	West 21-14 (75,000)
1-2-77	West 30-14 (45,000)
12-31-77	West 23-3 (65,000)
1-6-79	East 56-17 (72,000)
1-5-80	West 20-10 (75,000)
1-10-81	East 21-3 (76,000)
1-9-82	West 20-13 (75,000)
1-15-83	East 26-25 (72,999)
1-7-84	East 27-19 (77,000)
1-5-85	West 21-10 (72,000)
1-11-86	East 18-7 (77,000)
1-10-87	West 24-21 (74,000)
1-16-88	West 16-13 (62,000)
1-15-89	East 24-6 (76,000)
1-21-90	West 22-21 (78,000)
1-26-91	West 24-21 (72,000)
1-19-92	West 14-6 (83,000)
1-24-93	East 31-17 (84,000)
1-15-94	West 29-28 (60,000)
1-14-95	West 30-28 (35,079)
1-13-96	West 34-18 (68,500)
1-11-97	East 17-13 (62,500)
1-10-98	West 24-7 (32,500)
1-16-99	East 20-10 (50,000)
1-15-00	East 35-21 (65,246)
1-14-01	West 20-10 (31,549)
1-12-02	West 21-13 (25,035)
1-11-03	East 20-17
1-10-04	West 28-7 (25,602)
1-15-05	East 45-27 (25,518)
1-21-06	West 35-31 (18,533)
1-20-07	West 21-3 (23,554)

Series record: West won 44, East 33, 5 ties.

HULA BOWL
Present Site: Honolulu, Hawaii
Stadium (Capacity): Aloha Stadium (50,000)
Playing Surface: Grass
Format: From 1947 through 1950, the College All-Stars played the Hawaii All-Stars. Beginning in 1951, the Hawaiian team was augmented by players from the National Football League. This format, however, was changed to an all-collegiate contest—first between the East and West, then between North and South (in 1963), and then back to East and West in 1974 and 1995-96. In 1994, the format went to a collection of collegiate all-stars versus a collection of Hawaiian former collegiate players. In 1997, it reverted back to North-South. In 2005, it returned to an East-West format. Teams are broken down into players from the western United States (team named Kai, Hawaiian for ocean) against eastern United States (team named Aina, Hawaiian for land)
Playing Sites: Honolulu Stadium (1960-74); Aloha Stadium (1975-97, since 2006); War Memorial (1998-05)

Date	Score (Attendance)
1-10-60	East 34-8 (23,000)
1-8-61	East 14-7 (17,017)
1-7-62	Tie 7-7 (20,598)
1-6-63	North 20-13 (20,000)
1-4-64	North 20-13 (18,177)
1-9-65	South 16-14 (22,100)
1-8-66	North 27-26 (25,000)
1-7-67	North 28-27 (23,500)
1-6-68	North 50-6 (21,000)
1-4-69	North 13-7 (23,000)
1-10-70	South 35-13 (25,000)
1-9-71	North 42-32 (23,500)
1-8-72	North 24-7 (23,000)
1-6-73	South 17-3 (23,000)
1-5-74	East 24-14 (23,000)
1-4-75	East 34-25 (22,000)
1-10-76	East 16-0 (45,458)
1-8-77	West 20-17 (45,579)
1-7-78	West 42-22 (48,197)
1-6-79	East 29-24 (49,132)
1-5-80	East 17-10 (47,096)
1-10-81	West 24-17 (39,010)
1-9-82	West 26-23 (43,002)
1-15-83	East 30-14 (39,456)
1-7-84	West 21-16 (34,216)
1-5-85	East 34-14 (30,767)
1-11-86	West 23-10 (29,564)
1-10-87	West 16-14 (17,775)
1-16-88	West 20-18 (26,737)
1-7-89	East 21-10 (25,000)
1-13-90	West 21-13 (28,742)
1-19-91	East 23-10 (21,926)
1-11-92	West 27-20 (23,112)
1-16-93	West 13-10 (25,479)
1-22-94	College All-Stars 28-15 (33,947)
1-22-95	East 20-9 (19,074)
1-21-96	East 17-10 (25,112)
1-19-97	South 26, North 13 (24,725)
1-18-98	South 20, North 19 (20,079)
1-24-99	South 34, North 14 (23,719)
12-22-99	Tie 28-28 (23,719)
1-20-01	North 31, South 23 (23,719)
2-2-02	South 45, North 28 (24,000)
2-1-03	South 27, North 24
1-17-04	South 26, North 7
1-22-05	East 20, West 13
1-21-06	East 10, West 7
1-14-07	East 18, West 10 (8,000)

Series records: North-South (1963-73, 97-04)—North won 9, South 9, 1 tie; East-West (1960-62, 1974-93, 1995-96 and 2005-07)—East won 16, West 11, 1 tie; College All-Stars vs. Hawaiian All-Stars (1994)—College All-Stars won 1, Hawaiian All-Stars 0.

LAS VEGAS ALL-AMERICAN CLASSIC (Known as Paradise Bowl, 2002-03)
Present Site: Las Vegas, Nev.
Stadium (Capacity): Sam Boyd (40,000)
Playing Surface: TurfTech
Playing Sites: Hansen Stadium, St. George, Utah (2002-03); Sam Boyd Stadium, Las Vegas (since 2004)

Date	Score
2-2-02	West 33, Utah -Colorado 30 (2 ot)
1-25-03	Midwest 36, West 31
1-17-04	West 14, East 7
1-22-05	West 21, East 16
1-14-06	East 41, West 3
1-15-07	No game played

Series record: East-West (2004-06): West won 2, East 1.

MAGNOLIA GRIDIRON CLASSIC
Present Site: Jackson, Miss.
Stadium (Capacity): Mississippi Veterans Memorial (60,492)
Playing Surface: Grass
Format: One team is comprised primarily of Football Bowl Subdivision (FBS) seniors from schools that did not qualify for or had already played in bowl games. The other team is comprised primarily of players from the Football Championship Subdivision (FCS).

Date	Score (Attendance)
12-24-05	White (FBS) 17, Red (FCS) 9 (100)
12-23-06	Green (FBS) 32, Red (FCS) 14 (1,500)

SENIOR BOWL

Played at Ladd-Peebles Stadium in Mobile, Ala., since 1951 under the auspices of the National Football League. North and South teams are composed of senior players who have used all of their collegiate eligibility. In 1991, the teams switched from North and South to AFC and NFC; in 1994, the teams switched back to North and South.

Date	Score (Attendance)
1-7-50	South 22, North 13 (at Jacksonville, Fla.)
1-6-51	South 19, North 18
1-5-52	North 20, South 6
1-3-53	North 28, South 13
1-9-54	North 20, South 14
1-8-55	South 12, North 6
1-7-56	South 12, North 2
1-5-57	South 21, North 7
1-11-58	North 15, South 13
1-3-59	South 21, North 12
1-9-60	North 26, South 7 (40,119)
1-7-61	South 33, North 26
1-6-62	South 42, North 7
1-5-63	South 33, North 27
1-4-64	South 28, North 21 (37,094)
1-9-65	Tie 7-7 (40,605)
1-8-66	South 27, North 18
1-7-67	North 35, South 13
1-6-68	South 34, North 21
1-11-69	North 27, South 16
1-10-70	Tie 37-37
1-9-71	North 31, South 13 (40,646)
1-8-72	North 26, South 21 (40,646)
1-6-73	South 33, North 30 (40,646)
1-12-74	North 16, South 13 (40,646)
1-11-75	Tie 17-17 (40,646)
1-10-76	North 42, South 35 (40,646)
1-9-77	North 27, South 24 (40,646)
1-7-78	Tie 17-17 (40,646)
1-13-79	South 41, North 21 (40,100)
1-12-80	North 57, South 3 (40,646)
1-17-81	North 23, South 10 (40,102)
1-16-82	South 27, North 10 (39,410)
1-22-83	North 14, South 6 (37,511)
1-14-84	South 21, North 20 (38,254)
1-12-85	South 23, North 7 (33,500)
1-18-86	North 31, South 17 (40,646)
1-17-87	South 42, North 38
1-23-88	North 21, South 7
1-21-89	South 13, North 12 (39,742)
1-20-90	North 41, South 0 (42,400)
1-19-91	AFC 38, NFC 28 (37,500)
1-18-92	AFC 13, NFC 10 (37,100)
1-16-93	NFC 21, AFC 6 (37,124)
1-22-94	South 35, North 32 (39,200)
1-21-95	South 14, North 7 (40,007)
1-20-96	North 25, South 10 (40,700)
1-18-97	North 35, South 14 (40,646)
1-17-98	South 31, North 8 (40,820)
1-23-99	South 31, North 21 (41,000)
1-22-00	North 24, South 21 (40,646)
1-21-01	South 21, North 16 (40,646)
1-19-02	South 41, North 26 (40,646)
1-18-03	North 17, South 0 (40,646)
1-24-04	South 28, North 10 (40,646)
1-29-05	North 23, South 13 (40,646)
1-28-06	North 31, South 14 (40,646)
1-27-07	North 27, South 0 (40,646)

Series records: North-South (1950-90 and 1994 to present)—South won 26, North 25, 4 ties; AFC-NFC (1991-93)—AFC won 2, NFC 1.

TEXAS VS. THE NATION®

Present Site: El Paso, Texas
Stadium (Capacity): Sun Bowl Stadium (50,426)
Playing Surface: AstroPlay
Format: The Texas team is comprised of players who have high school or collegiate ties to the state, are natives of the state, and a few regional or special circumstance exceptions. The Nation roster is a squad of top-rated seniors from the rest of the country.

Date	Score (Attendance)
2-2-07	The Nation 24, Texas 20 (21,528)

DISCONTINUED ALL-STAR FOOTBALL GAMES

Many of these games were identified without complete information such as scores, teams, sites or dates. Please send any updates or additional information to: NCAA Statistics Service, P.O. Box 6222, Indianapolis, Indiana 46206-6222.

ALL-AMERICAN BOWL (1969-77) (Tampa, Fla.)

Date	Score (Attendance)
1-4-69	North 21, South 15 (16,380)
1-3-70	South 24, North 23 (17,642)
1-10-71	North 39, South 2 (12,000)
1-9-72	North 27, South 8 (20,137)
1-7-73	North 10, South 6 (23,416)
1-6-74	North 28, South 7 (24,536)
1-5-75	South 28, North 22 (19,246)
1-10-76	North 21, South 14 (15,321)
1-2-77	North 21, South 20 (14,207)

AMERICAN COLLEGE ALL-STAR GAME (1948) (Los Angeles, Calif.)

Date	Score
12-18-48	American All-Stars 43, Canadian All-Stars 0
12-26-48	American All-Stars 14, Hawaiian All-Stars 0

BLACK COLLEGE ALL-STAR BOWL (1979-82)

Date	Score (Location, Attendance)
1-7-79	East 25, West 20 (at New Orleans, La.)
1-5-80	West 27, East 21 (ot) (at New Orleans, La.)
1-17-81	West 19, East 10 (at Jackson, Miss.) (7,500)
1-16-82	West 7, East 0 (at Jackson, Miss.)

BLUE-GRAY ALL-STAR CLASSIC

Playing Sites: Cramton Bowl, Montgomery, Ala. (1939-01); Movie Gallery Veterans Stadium, Troy, Ala. (2003)

Date	Score (Attendance)
1-2-39	Blue 7-0 (8,000)
12-30-39	Gray 33-20 (10,000)
12-28-40	Blue 14-12 (14,000)
12-27-41	Gray 16-0 (15,571)
12-26-42	Gray 24-0 (16,000)
1943	No Game
12-30-44	Gray 24-7 (16,000)
12-29-45	Blue 26-0 (20,000)
12-28-46	Gray 20-13 (22,500)
12-27-47	Gray 33-6 (22,500)
12-25-48	Blue 19-13 (15,000)
12-31-49	Gray 27-13 (21,500)
12-30-50	Gray 31-6 (21,000)
12-29-51	Gray 20-14 (22,000)
12-27-52	Gray 28-7 (22,000)
12-26-53	Gray 40-20 (18,500)
12-25-54	Blue 14-7 (18,000)
12-31-55	Gray 20-19 (19,000)
12-29-56	Blue 14-0 (21,000)
12-28-57	Gray 21-20 (16,000)
12-27-58	Blue 16-0 (16,000)
12-26-59	Blue 20-8 (20,000)
12-31-60	Blue 35-7 (18,000)
12-30-61	Gray 9-7 (18,000)
12-29-62	Blue 10-6 (20,000)
12-28-63	Gray 21-14 (20,000)
12-26-64	Blue 10-6 (16,000)
12-25-65	Gray 23-19 (18,000)
12-24-66	Blue 14-9 (18,000)
12-30-67	Blue 22-16 (23,350)
12-28-68	Gray 28-7 (18,000)
12-27-69	Tie 6-6 (21,500)
12-28-70	Gray 38-7 (23,000)
12-28-71	Gray 9-0 (24,000)
12-27-72	Gray 27-15 (20,000)
12-18-73	Blue 20-14 (21,000)
12-17-74	Blue 29-24 (12,000)
12-19-75	Blue 14-13 (10,000)
12-24-76	Gray 31-10 (16,000)
12-30-77	Blue 20-16 (5,000)
12-29-78	Gray 28-24 (18,380)
12-25-79	Blue 22-13 (18,312)
12-25-80	Blue 24-23 (25,000)
12-25-81	Blue 21-9 (19,000)
12-25-82	Gray 20-10 (21,000)
12-25-83	Gray 17-13 (2,000)
12-25-84	Gray 33-6 (24,080)
12-25-85	Blue 27-20 (18,500)
12-25-86	Blue 31-7 (18,500)
12-25-87	Gray 12-10 (20,300)
12-25-88	Blue 22-21 (20,000)
12-25-89	Gray 28-10 (16,000)
12-25-90	Blue 17-14 (17,500)
12-25-91	Gray 20-12 (21,000)
12-25-92	Gray 27-17 (20,500)
12-25-93	Gray 17-10 (18,500)
12-25-94	Blue 38-27 (23,500)
12-25-95	Blue 26-7 (18,500)
12-25-96	Blue 44-34 (17,000)
12-25-97	Gray 31-24 (25,214)
12-25-98	Gray 31-24 (17,500)
12-25-99	Tie 22-22 (15,531)
12-25-00	Gray 40-37 (18,000)
12-25-01	Blue 28-10 (18,000)
12-25-02	No game played
12-25-03	Blue 31-24 (10,252)
12-25-04	No game played
12-25-05	No game played

Series record: Gray won 33, Blue 29, 2 ties.

CAMP FOOTBALL FOUNDATION BOWL (1974)

CANADIAN-AMERICAN BOWL (1978-79) (Tampa, Fla.)

Date	Score (Attendance)
1-8-78	U.S. All-Stars 22, Canadian All-Stars 7 (11,328)
1-6-79	U.S. All-Stars 34, Canadian All-Stars 14 (11,033)

CHALLENGE BOWL (1978-79) (Seattle, Wash.)

Date	Score (Attendance)
1-14-78	Pacific-8 27, Big Ten 20 (20,578)
1-13-79	Pacific-10 36, Big Eight 23 (23,961)

CHICAGO COLLEGE ALL-STAR FOOTBALL GAME (1934-76)

An all-star team composed of the top senior collegiate players met the National Football League champions (1933-66) or the Super Bowl champions (1967-75) from the previous season, beginning in 1934. The only time the all-stars did not play the league champions was in 1935. All games except 1943 and 1944 were played at Soldier Field, Chicago, Ill. The 1943 and 1944 games were played at Dyche Stadium, Evanston, Ill.

Date	Score (Attendance)
8-31-34	(Tie) Chicago Bears 0-0 (79,432)
8-29-35	Chicago Bears 5, All-Stars 0 (77,450)
9-2-36	(Tie) Detroit 7-7 (76,000)
9-1-37	All-Stars 6, Green Bay 0 (84,560)
8-31-38	All-Stars 28, Washington 16 (74,250)
8-30-39	New York Giants 9, All-Stars 0 (81,456)
8-29-40	Green Bay 45, All-Stars 28 (84,567)
8-28-41	Chicago Bears 37, All-Stars 13 (98,203)
8-28-42	Chicago Bears 21, All-Stars 0 (101,100)
8-25-43	All-Stars 27, Washington 7 (48,471)
8-30-44	Chicago Bears 24, All-Stars 21 (48,769)
8-30-45	Green Bay 19, All-Stars 7 (92,753)
8-23-46	All-Stars 16, Los Angeles 0 (97,380)
8-22-47	All-Stars 16, Chicago Bears 0 (105,840)
8-20-48	Chicago Cardinals 28, All-Stars 0 (101,220)
8-12-49	Philadelphia 38, All-Stars 0 (93,780)
8-11-50	All-Stars 17, Philadelphia 7 (88,885)
8-17-51	Cleveland 33, All-Stars 0 (92,180)
8-15-52	Los Angeles 10, All-Stars 7 (88,316)
8-14-53	Detroit 24, All-Stars 10 (93,818)
8-13-54	Detroit 31, All-Stars 6 (93,470)
8-12-55	All-Stars 30, Cleveland 27 (75,000)
8-10-56	Cleveland 26, All-Stars 0 (75,000)
8-9-57	New York Giants 22, All-Stars 12 (75,000)
8-15-58	All-Stars 35, Detroit 19 (70,000)
8-14-59	Baltimore 29, All-Stars 0 (70,000)
8-12-60	Baltimore 32, All-Stars 7 (70,000)
8-4-61	Philadelphia 28, All-Stars 14 (66,000)
8-3-62	Green Bay 42, All-Stars 20 (65,000)
8-2-63	All-Stars 20, Green Bay 17 (65,000)
8-7-64	Chicago Bears 28, All-Stars 17 (65,000)
8-6-65	Cleveland 24, All-Stars 16 (68,000)
8-5-66	Green Bay 38, All-Stars 0 (72,000)
8-4-67	Green Bay 27, All-Stars 0 (70,934)
8-2-68	Green Bay 34, All-Stars 17 (69,917)

Date	Score (Attendance)
8-1-69	New York Jets 26, All-Stars 24 (74,208)
7-31-70	Kansas City 24, All-Stars 3 (69,940)
7-30-71	Baltimore 24, All-Stars 17 (52,289)
7-28-72	Dallas 20, All-Stars 7 (54,162)
7-27-73	Miami 14, All-Stars 3 (54,103)
1974	No game played
8-1-75	Pittsburgh 21, All-Stars 14 (54,103)
7-23-76	*Pittsburgh 24, All-Stars 0 (52,895)

Game was not completed due to thunderstorms.

CHRISTIAN BOWL (1955)
(Murfreesboro, Tenn.)

Date	Score (Attendance)
12-26-55	East 21, West 10 (4,000)

COACHES ALL-AMERICAN GAME (1961-76)
at Buffalo, N.Y.

Date	Score (Attendance)
6-23-61	West 30, East 20 (12,913)
6-29-62	East 13, West 8 (22,759)
6-29-63	West 22, East 21 (20,840)
6-27-64	East 18, West 15 (21,112)
6-26-65	East 34, West 14 (25,501)

at Atlanta, Ga.

Date	Score (Attendance)
7-9-66	West 24, East 7 (38,236)
7-9-67	East 12, West 9 (29,145)
6-28-68	West 34, East 20 (21,120)
6-28-69	West 14, East 10 (17,008)

at Lubbock, Texas

Date	Score (Attendance)
6-28-70	East 34, West 27 (42,150)
6-26-71	West 33, East 28 (43,320)
6-24-72	East 42, West 20 (42,314)
6-23-73	West 20, East 6 (43,272)
6-22-74	West 36, East 6 (42,368)
6-21-75	East 23, West 21 (36,108)
6-19-76	West 35, East 17 (36,504)

COPPER BOWL (1958-60)
(Tempe, Ariz.)

Date	Score (Attendance)
12-20-58	Southwest All-Stars 22, National All-Stars 13 (12,000)
12-26-59	National All-Stars 21, Southwest All-Stars 6 (16,000)
12-31-60	National All-Stars 27, Southwest All-Stars 8 (8,000)

CRUSADE BOWL (1963)
(Baltimore, Md.)

Date	Score (Attendance)
1-6-63	East 38, West 10 (2,400)

DALLAS ALL-STAR GAME (1936-39)
(Dallas, Texas)

Date	Score
9-7-36	Southwest All-Stars 7, Chicago Bears 6
9-6-37	Southwest All-Stars 6, Chicago Bears 0
9-5-38	Southwest All-Stars 13, Washington Redskins 7
9-4-39	Green Bay Packers 31, Southwest All-Stars 20

DIXIE CLASSIC (1928-31)
(Dallas, Texas)

Date	Score (Attendance)
12-29-28	Southwest Conference 14, Small Texas Schools 6
1-1-29	Big Six Conference 14, Southwest Conference 6 (10,000)
1-1-30	Midwest 25, Southwest Conference 12 (15,000)
1-1-31	Southwest Conference 18, Midwest 0 (14,000)

EAST-WEST BLACK ALL-STAR GAME (1971)
(Houston, Texas)

Date	Score (Attendance)
12-11-71	East 19, West 10 (5,156)

EAST-WEST COLLEGE ALL-STAR GAME (1932)
(Demonstrated at Tenth Olympiad, Los Angeles, Calif.; East team composed of players from Harvard, Princeton and Yale, West team composed of players from California, Southern California and Stanford)

Date	Score (Attendance)
8-8-32	West 7, East 6 (50,000)

EPSON IVY BOWL (1989-90)
(Yokohama, Japan)

Date	Score (Attendance)
12-1989	Ivy League Seniors 49, Japan Collegiate All-Stars 17
12-25-90	Ivy League Seniors 47, Japan Collegiate All-Stars 10

FREEDOM BOWL ALL-STAR CLASSIC (1984-86)
(Atlanta, Ga. and Washington, D.C.)
Southwestern Athletic Conference vs. Mid-Eastern Athletic Conference.

Date	Score (Attendance)
1-14-84	SWAC 36, MEAC 22 (16,097)
1-12-85	SWAC 14, MEAC 0 (18,352)
1-11-86	SWAC 16, MEAC 14 (10,200)
12-20-86	MEAC 12, SWAC 7 (8,962)

FREEDOM BOWL ALL-STAR CLASSIC (1990)
(Houston, Texas)

Date	Score
1-13-90	North 14, South 13

FREEDOM CLASSIC (1976)

Date	Score (Attendance)
1976	West 12, East 9 (6,654)

JAPAN BOWL
(Yokohama, Japan)

Date	Score (Attendance)
1-18-76	West 27-18 (68,000)
1-16-77	West 21-10 (58,000)
1-15-78	East 26-10 (32,500)
1-14-79	East 33-14 (55,000)
1-13-80	West 28-17 (27,000)
1-17-81	West 25-13 (30,000)
1-16-82	West 28-17 (28,000)
1-23-83	West 30-21 (30,000)
1-15-84	West 26-21 (26,000)
1-13-85	West 28-14 (30,000)
1-11-86	East 31-14 (30,000)
1-11-87	West 24-17 (30,000)
1-10-88	West 17-3 (30,000)
1-15-89	East 30-7 (29,000)
1-13-90	East 24-10 (27,000)
1-12-91	West 20-14 (30,000)
1-11-92	East 14-13 (50,000)
1-9-93	East 27-13 (46,000)

LOS ANGELES ALL-STAR GAME (1948)
(Los Angeles, Calif.)

Date	Score
1-18-48	West 34, East 20

MARTIN LUTHER KING ALL-AMERICA CLASSIC (1990-91)
(Division I-A vs. all other divisions)

Date	Score (Attendance)
1-15-90	All Div. All-Stars 35, I-A All-Stars 24 (350) (at San Jose, Calif.)
1-14-91	I-A All-Stars 21, All Div. All-Stars 14 (6,272) (at St. Petersburg, Fla.)

NEW YORK ALL-STAR GAME
(New York, N.Y.)

Date	Teams, Score
1936	New York Giants 12, All-Stars 2
1937	New York Giants 14, All-Stars 7
1938	New York Giants 6, All-Stars 0
1939	New York Giants 10, All-Stars 0
1940	All-Stars 16, New York Giants 6
1941	New York Giants 23, All-Stars 3
9-12-42	Eastern Army All-Stars 16, New York Giants 0 (see Army All-Star Games)
1947	New York Giants 21, All-Stars 0
1949	All-Stars 28, New York Giants 13

NORTH-SOUTH ALL-STAR SHRINE GAME (1930-34, 39-48, 1948-73, 1976)

Date	Score (Attendance)
1-1-30	North 21, South 12 (20,000) (at Atlanta, Ga.) (Southern Conference All-Star Game)
12-28-30	South 7, North 0 (2,000) (at New York, N.Y.)
12-10-32	South 7, North 6 (500) (at Baltimore, Md.)
12-24-33	North 3, South 0 (5,000) (at New York, N.Y.)
1-1-34	North 7, South 0 (12,000) (at Knoxville, Tenn.) (Southeastern Conference All-Star Game)

at Birmingham, Ala.

Date	Score (Attendance)
1-39	North 7, South 0
12-39	South 33, North 20
12-40	North 14, South 12
12-41	South 16, North 0
12-42	South 24, North 0
1-44	South 24, North 7
1-45	North 26, South 0
1-46	South 20, North 13
1-47	South 33, North 6
1-48	North 19, South 13

at Miami, Fla.

Date	Score (Attendance)
12-25-48	South 24, North 14 (33,056)
12-25-49	North 20, South 14 (37,378)
12-25-50	South 14, North 9 (39,132)
12-25-51	South 35, North 7 (39,995)
12-25-52	North 21, South 21 (42,866)
12-25-53	South 20, North 0 (44,715)
12-25-54	South 20, North 17 (37,847)
12-26-55	South 20, North 7 (42,179)
12-26-56	North 17, South 7 (39,181)
12-25-57	North 23, South 20 (28,303)
12-27-58	South 49, North 20 (35,519)
12-26-59	North 27, South 17 (35,185)
12-26-60	North 41, South 14 (26,146)
12-25-61	South 35, North 16 (18,892)
12-22-62	South 15, North 14 (16,952)
12-21-63	South 23, North 14 (19,120)
12-25-64	North 37, South 30 (29,124)
12-25-65	South 21, North 14 (25,640)
12-26-66	North 27, South 14 (28,569)
12-25-67	North 24, South 0 (17,400)
12-25-68	North 3, South 0 (18,063)
12-25-69	North 31, South 10 (23,527)
12-25-70	North 28, South 7 (15,402)
12-27-71	South 7, North 6 (18,640)
12-25-72	North 17, South 10 (18,013)
12-25-73	South 27, North 6 (10,672)

at Pontiac, Mich.

Date	Score (Attendance)
12-17-76	South 24, North 0 (41,627)

OHIO SHRINE BOWL (1972-76)
(Columbus, Ohio)

Date	Score
12-9-72	East 20, West 7
12-1-73	East 8, West 6
12-7-74	East 27, West 6
1975	West 17, East 7
12-4-76	East 24, West 8 (played elsewhere)

OLYMPIA GOLD BOWL (1982)
(San Diego, Calif.)

Date	Score (Attendance)
1-16-82	National All-Stars 30, American All-Stars 21 (22,316)

OLYMPIC GAME (1933)
(Chicago, Ill.)

Date	Score (Attendance)
8-24-33	East 13, West 7 (50,000)

OPTIMIST ALL-AMERICA BOWL (1958-62)
(Tucson, Ariz.)

Date	Score (Attendance)
1-4-58	College All-Stars 56, Tucson Cowboys 28
1-3-59	Major-College 14, Small-College 12 (10,000)
1-2-60	Major College 53, Small-College 0 (14,500)
12-26-60	Major-College 25, Small-College 12
12-30-61	Major-College 31, Small-College 0 (14,000)
12-29-62	Small-College 14, Major-College 13

POTATO BOWL (1967)
(Bakersfield, Calif.)

Date	Score (Attendance)
12-23-67	North 23, South 7 (5,600)

ROCKY MOUNTAIN CONFERENCE-NORTH CENTRAL CONFERENCE GAME (1930)
(Elks Charity Bowl)
(Denver, Colo.)

Date	Score
1-1-30	North Central 13, Rocky Mountain 6

SALAD BOWL ALL-STAR GAME (1955)
(Phoenix, Ariz.)

Date	Score (Attendance)
1-1-55	Skyline Conference 20, Border Conference 13 (8,000)
12-31-55	Border Conference 13, Skyline Conference 10

SHERIDAN BLACK ALL-STAR GAME (1979-82)
(See Black College All-Star Bowl)

SMOKE BOWL (1941)
(Richmond, Va.)

Date	Score (Attendance)
1-1-41	Norfolk All-Stars 16, Richmond All-Stars 2 (5,000)

SOUTHWEST CHALLENGE BOWL (1963-64)
(Corpus Christi, Texas)

Date	Score (Attendance)
1-5-63	National 33, Southwest 13
1-4-64	National 66, Southwest 14 (10,200)

U.S. BOWL (1962)
(Washington, D. C.)
(Teams were composed of players selected in the recent NFL draft)

Date	Score
1-7-62	West 33, East 19

THE VILLAGES GRIDIRON CLASSIC
Playing Sites: Florida Citrus Bowl, Orlando (1999-03); The Villages Polo Stadium, Lady Lake, Fla. (2004-05)

The Villages Gridiron Classic was known as the Rotary Gridiron Classic for the first five years. The format changed from a Team Florida vs. Team USA to a North vs. South format in 2004.

Date	Score (Attendance)
1-16-99	Team Florida 17, Team USA 9 (29,725)
1-15-00	Team USA 21, Team Florida 14 (21,298)
1-13-01	Team Florida 10, Team USA 0 (25,000)
1-19-02	Team Florida 42, Team USA 13 (20,344)
1-25-03	Team USA 20, Team Florida 17 (9,375)
1-31-04	North 35, South 31 (12,312)
1-15-05	South 24, North 21 (12,635)

Series records: Team Florida-Team USA (1999-03)—Team Florida won 3, Team USA 2; North-South (2004-05)**—North won 1, South 1.

FORMER SPECIAL PRESEASON GAMES PLAYED IN USA

BCA CLASSIC
Sponsor: Black Coaches' Association
Playing Sites: Spartan Stadium, East Lansing, Mich. (1998); Royal-Memorial Stadium, Austin, Texas (1999); LaVell Edwards Stadium, Provo, Utah (2001); Memorial/Osborne Stadium, Lincoln, Neb. (2002); Arrowhead Stadium, Kansas City, Mo. (2003); FedEx Field, Landover, Md. (2004)

Date	Score (Attendance)
8-29-98	Colorado St. 23, Michigan St. 16 (68,624)
8-28-99	North Carolina St. 23, Texas 20 (82,252)
8-27-00	Game cancelled because of weather
8-25-01	BYU 70, Tulane 35 (49,008)
8-24-02	Nebraska 48, Arizona St. 10 (77,779)
8-23-03	Kansas St. 42, California 28 (50,823)
8-28-04	Southern California 24, Virginia Tech 13 (91,665)

EDDIE ROBINSON CLASSIC
Playing Sites: Ohio Stadium, Columbus, Ohio (1997); Memorial Stadium (now Memorial/Osborne Stadium), Lincoln, Neb. (1998); Notre Dame Stadium, South Bend, Ind. (1999); Arrowhead Stadium, Kansas City, Mo. (2000, 2002); Camp Randall Stadium, Madison, Wis. (2001)

Date	Score (Attendance)
8-28-97	Ohio St. 24, Wyoming 10 (89,112)
8-29-98	Nebraska 56, Louisiana Tech 27 (76,021)
8-28-99	Notre Dame 48, Kansas 13 (80,012)
8-26-00	Kansas St. 27, Iowa 7 (77,148)
8-25-01	Wisconsin 26, Virginia 17 (76,740)
8-24-02	Florida St. 38, Iowa St. 31 (55,132)

KICKOFF CLASSIC
Sponsor: National Association of Collegiate Directors of Athletics (NACDA).
Playing Site: Giants Stadium (1983-02)

Date	Score (Attendance)
8-29-83	Nebraska 44, Penn St. 6 (71,123)
8-27-84	Miami (Fla.) 20, Auburn 18 (51,131)
8-29-85	BYU 28, Boston College 14 (51,227)
8-27-86	Alabama 16, Ohio St. 10 (68,296)
8-30-87	Tennessee 23, Iowa 22 (54,681)
8-27-88	Nebraska 23, Texas A&M 14 (58,172)
8-31-89	Notre Dame 36, Virginia 13 (77,323)
8-31-90	Southern California 34, Syracuse 16 (57,293)
8-28-91	Penn St. 34, Georgia Tech 22 (77,409)
8-29-92	North Carolina St. 24, Iowa 14 (46,251)
8-28-93	Florida St. 42, Kansas 0 (51,734)
8-28-94	Nebraska 31, West Virginia 0 (58,233)
8-27-95	Ohio St. 38, Boston College 6 (62,711)
8-25-96	Penn St. 24, Southern California 7 (77,716)
8-24-97	Syracuse 34, Wisconsin 0 (51,185)
8-31-98	Florida St. 23, Texas A&M 14 (59,232)
8-29-99	Miami (Fla.) 23, Ohio St. 12 (73,037)
8-27-00	Southern California 29, Penn St. 5 (78,902)
8-26-01	Georgia Tech 13, Syracuse 7 (41,517)
8-31-02	Notre Dame 22, Maryland 0 (72,903)

PIGSKIN CLASSIC
Playing Sites: Anaheim Stadium (now Angel Stadium of Anaheim), Anaheim, Calif. (1990-94); Michigan Stadium, Ann Arbor, Michigan (1995); Cougar Stadium (now LaVell Edwards Stadium), Provo, Utah (1996); Soldier Field, Chicago (1997); L.A. Memorial Coliseum, Los Angeles, Calif. (1998); Beaver Stadium, State College, Pa. (1999); Alltel Stadium, Jacksonville, Fla. (2000); Memorial/Osborne Stadium, Lincoln, Neb. (2001); Ohio Stadium, Columbus, Ohio (2002)

Date	Score (Attendance)
8-26-90	Colorado 31, Tennessee 31 (33,458)
8-29-91	Florida St. 44, BYU 28 (38,363)
8-26-92	Texas A&M 10, Stanford 7 (35,240)
8-29-93	North Carolina 31, Southern California 9 (49,309)
8-29-94	Ohio St. 34, Fresno St. 10 (28,513)
8-26-95	Michigan 18, Virginia 17 (101,444)
8-24-96	BYU 41, Texas A&M 37 (55,229)
8-23-97	Northwestern 24, Oklahoma 0 (36,804)
8-30-98	Southern California 27, Purdue 17 (56,623)
8-28-99	Penn St. 41, Arizona 7 (97,168)
8-26-00	Florida St. 29, BYU 3 (54,260)
8-25-01	Nebraska 21, TCU 7 (77,473)
8-24-02	Ohio St. 45, Texas Tech 21 (100,037)

HISPANIC COLLEGE FUND CLASSIC
Sponsor: Transamerica
Playing Sites: Jones Stadium, Lubbock, Texas (2000); Memorial Stadium, Norman, Okla. (2001); Lane Stadium, Blacksburg, Va. (2002)

Date	Score (Attendance)
8-26-00	Texas Tech 24, New Mexico 3 (42,238)
8-25-01	Oklahoma 41, North Carolina 27 (75,423)
8-25-02	Virginia Tech 63, Arkansas St. 7 (54,016)

JIM THORPE CLASSIC
Sponsor: Jim Thorpe Association
Playing Sites: Folsom Field, Boulder, Colo. (2001); Scott/Harrison Field, Charlottesville, Va. (2002)

Date	Score (Attendance)
8-26-01	Fresno St. 24, Colorado 22 (47,762)
8-22-02	Colorado St. 35, Virginia 29 (57,120)

JOHN THOMPSON FOUNDATION CHALLENGE CLASSIC
Sponsor: John Thompson Foundation
Playing Sites: Papa John's Cardinal Stadium, Louisville, Ky. (2001); Camp Randall Stadium, Madison, Wis. (2002)

Date	Score (Attendance)
8-23-01	Louisville 45, New Mexico St. 24 (38,129)
8-23-02	Wisconsin 23, Fresno St. 21 (75,136)

BCA BOWL
Playing Site: Carter-Finley Stadium, Raleigh, N.C. (2002)

Date	Score (Attendance)
8-24-02	North Carolina St. 34, New Mexico 24 (47,018)

CONFERENCE CHAMPIONSHIP GAMES

ATLANTIC COAST CONFERENCE CHAMPIONSHIP
Present Site: Jacksonville, Fla.
Stadium (Capacity): Jacksonville Municipal Stadium (77,000)
Playing Surface: Grass
Playing Site: Alltel Stadium (now Jacksonville Municipal Stadium), Jacksonville, Fla. (since 2005)

Date	Score (Attendance)
12-3-05	Florida St. (Atlantic Div.) 27, Virginia Tech (Coastal Div.) 22 (72,749)
12-2-06	Wake Forest (Atlantic Div.) 9, Georgia Tech (Coastal Div.) 6 (62,850)

BIG 12 CONFERENCE CHAMPIONSHIP
Present Site: San Antonio, Texas
Stadium (Capacity): Alamodome (65,000)
Playing Surface: Grass
Playing Sites: Trans World Dome (now Edward Jones Dome), St. Louis, Mo. (1996; 1998); Alamodome, San Antonio, Texas (1997; 1999); Arrowhead Stadium, Kansas City, Mo. (2000; 2003-04; 2006); Texas Stadium, Irving, Texas (2001); Reliant Stadium, Houston, Texas (2002; 2005)

Date	Score (Attendance)
12-7-96	Texas (South Div.) 37, Nebraska (North Div.) 27 (63,109)
12-6-97	Nebraska (North Div.) 54, Texas A&M (South Div.) 15 (64,824)
12-5-98	Texas A&M (South Div.) 36, Kansas St. (North Div.) 33 (60,789)
12-4-99	Nebraska (North Div.) 22, Texas (South Div.) 6 (65,035)
12-2-00	Oklahoma (South Div.) 27, Kansas St. (North Div.) 24 (79,655)
12-1-01	Colorado (North Div.) 39, Texas (South Div.) 37 (65,675)
12-7-02	Oklahoma (South Div.) 29, Colorado (North Div.) 7 (63,332)
12-6-03	Kansas St. (North Div.) 35, Oklahoma (South Div.) 7 (79,451)
12-4-04	Oklahoma (South Div.) 42, Colorado (North Div.) 3 (62,130)
12-3-05	Texas (South Div.) 70, Colorado (North Div.) 3 (71,107)
12-2-06	Oklahoma (South Div.) 21, Nebraska (North Div.) 7 (80,031)

CONFERENCE USA CHAMPIONSHIP
Present Site: Team with highest conference winning percentage
Stadium (Capacity): To be determined
Playing Surface: To be determined
Playing Site: Florida Citrus Bowl, Orlando (2005); Robertson Stadium, Houston (2006)

Date	Score (Attendance)
12-3-05	Tulsa (West Div.) 44, UCF (East Div.) 27 (51,978)
12-1-06	Houston (West Div.) 34, Southern Miss. (East Div.) 20 (31,818)

MID-AMERICAN CONFERENCE CHAMPIONSHIP
Present Site: Detroit, Mich.
Stadium (Capacity): Ford Field (65,000)
Playing Surface: FieldTurf
Playing Sites: Marshall University Stadium, Huntington, W.Va. (1997-00, 02); Glass Bowl, Toledo, Ohio (2001); Doyt Perry Stadium, Bowling Green, Ohio (2003); Ford Field, Detroit, Mich. (since 2004)

Date	Score (Attendance)
12-5-97	Marshall (East Div.) 34, Toledo (West Div.) 14 (28,021)
12-4-98	Marshall (East Div.) 23, Toledo (West Div.) 17 (28,085)
12-3-99	Marshall (East Div.) 34, Western Mich. (West Div.) 30 (28,069)
12-1-00	Marshall (East Div.) 19, Western Mich. (West Div.) 14 (24,816)
11-30-01	Toledo (West Div.) 41, Marshall (East Div.) 36 (20,025)
12-07-02	Marshall (East Div.) 49, Toledo (West Div.) 45 (24,582)
12-4-03	Miami (Ohio) (East Div.) 49, Bowling Green (West Div.) 27 (24,833)
12-2-04	Toledo (West Div.) 35, Miami (Ohio) (East Div.) 27 (22,138)
12-1-05	Akron (East Div.) 31, Northern Ill. (West Div.) 30 (12,051)
11-31-06	Central Mich. (West Div.) 31, Ohio (East Div.) 10 (25,483)

SOUTHEASTERN CONFERENCE CHAMPIONSHIP
Present Site: Atlanta, Ga.
Stadium (Capacity): Georgia Dome (71,250)
Playing Surface: FieldTurf
Playing Sites: Legion Field, Birmingham, Ala. (1992-93); Georgia Dome, Atlanta (since 1994)

Date	Score (Attendance)
12-5-92	Alabama (Western Div.) 28, Florida (Eastern Div.) 21 (83,091)
12-4-93	Florida (Eastern Div.) 28, Alabama (Western Div.) 13 (76,345)
12-3-94	Florida (Eastern Div.) 24, Alabama (Western Div.) 23 (74,751)

Date	Score (Attendance)
12-2-95	Florida (Eastern Div.) 34, Arkansas (Western Div.) 3 (71,325)
12-7-96	Florida (Eastern Div.) 45, Alabama (Western Div.) 30 (74,132)
12-6-97	Tennessee (Eastern Div.) 30, Auburn (Western Div.) 29 (74,896)
12-5-98	Tennessee (Eastern Div.) 24, Mississippi St. (Western Div.) 14 (74,795)
12-4-99	Alabama (Western Div.) 34, Florida (Eastern Div.) 7 (74,309)
12-2-00	Florida (Eastern Div.) 28, Auburn (Western Div.) 6 (73,427)
12-8-01	LSU (Western Div.) 31, Tennessee (Eastern Div.) 20 (74,843)
12-7-02	Georgia (Eastern Div.) 30, Arkansas (Western Div.) 3 (75,835)
12-6-03	LSU (Western Div.) 34, Georgia (Eastern Div.) 13 (74,913)
12-4-04	Auburn (Western Div.) 38, Tennessee (Eastern Div.) 28 (74,892)
12-3-05	Georgia (Eastern Div.) 34, LSU (Western Div.) 14 (73,717)
12-2-06	Florida (Eastern Div.) 38, Arkansas (Western Div.) 28 (73,374)

WESTERN ATHLETIC CONFERENCE CHAMPIONSHIP

Site: Las Vegas, Nev.
Stadium (Capacity): Sam Boyd (32,000)
Playing Surface: Monsanto Turf
Playing Site: Sam Boyd Stadium (1996-98)

Date	Score (Attendance)
12-7-96	BYU (Mountain Div.) 28, Wyoming (Pacific Div.) 25 (41,238)
12-6-97	Colorado St. (Pacific Div.) 41, New Mexico (Mountain Div.) 13 (12,706)
12-5-98	Air Force (Pacific Div.) 20, BYU (Mountain Div.) 13 (32,745)

REGULAR-SEASON GAMES PLAYED IN FOREIGN COUNTRIES

TOKYO, JAPAN

(Called Mirage Bowl 1976-85, Coca-Cola Classic from 1986. Played at Tokyo Olympic Memorial Stadium 1976-87, Tokyo Dome from 1988-93.)

Date	Score (Attendance)
9-4-76	Grambling 42, Morgan St. 16 (50,000)
12-11-77	Grambling 35, Temple 32 (50,000)
12-10-78	Temple 28, Boston College 24 (55,000)
11-24-79	Notre Dame 40, Miami (Fla.) 15 (62,574)
11-30-80	UCLA 34, Oregon St. 3 (86,000)
11-28-81	Air Force 21, San Diego St. 16 (80,000)
11-27-82	Clemson 21, Wake Forest 17 (64,700)
11-26-83	SMU 34, Houston 12 (70,000)
11-17-84	Army 45, Montana 31 (60,000)
11-30-85	Southern California 20, Oregon 6 (65,000)
11-30-86	Stanford 29, Arizona 24 (55,000)
11-28-87	California 17, Washington St. 17 (45,000)
12-3-88	Oklahoma St. 45, Texas Tech 42 (56,000)
12-4-89	Syracuse 24, Louisville 13 (50,000)
12-2-90	Houston 62, Arizona St. 45 (50,000)
11-30-91	Clemson 33, Duke 21 (50,000)
12-6-92	Nebraska 38, Kansas St. 24 (50,000)
12-5-93	Wisconsin 41, Michigan St. 20 (51,500)

MELBOURNE, AUSTRALIA

Date	Score (Attendance)
12-6-85	Wyoming 24, UTEP 21 (22,000)*
12-4-87	BYU 30, Colorado St. 26 (76,652)†

**Played at V.F.L. Park. †Played at Princes Park.*

YOKOHAMA, JAPAN

Date	Score (Attendance)
12-2-78	BYU 28, UNLV 24 (27,500)

OSAKA, JAPAN

Date	Score (Attendance)
9-3-78	Utah St. 10, Idaho St. 0 (15,000)

HAVANA, CUBA
(Played at Almandares Park)

Date	Score (Attendance)
12-25-07	LSU 56, Havana University 0 (10,000)

DUBLIN, IRELAND

#Called Emerald Isle Classic. Played at Lansdowne Road Stadium. ¢Played at Croke Park.

Date	Score (Attendance)
11-19-88	Boston College 38, Army 24 (45,525)#
12-2-89	Pittsburgh 46, Rutgers 29 (19,800)#
11-2-96	Notre Dame 54, Navy 27 (38,651)¢

LONDON, ENGLAND

Date	Score (Attendance)
10-16-88	Richmond 20, Boston U. 17 (6,000)

MILAN, ITALY

(Played at The Arena.)

Date	Score (Attendance)
10-28-89	Villanova 28, Rhode Island 25 (5,000)

LIMERICK, IRELAND

(Wild Geese Classic. Played at Limerick Gaelic Grounds.)

Date	Score (Attendance)
11-16-91	Holy Cross 24, Fordham 19 (17,411)

FRANKFURT, GERMANY

(Played at Wald Stadium.)

Date	Score (Attendance)
9-19-92	Heidelberg 7, Otterbein 7 (4,351)

GALWAY, IRELAND

(Called Christopher Columbus Classic.)

Date	Score (Attendance)
11-29-92	Bowdoin 7, Tufts 6 (2,500)

HAMILTON, BERMUDA

(Played at Bermuda National Soccer Stadium.)

Date	Score (Attendance)
11-20-93	Georgetown 17, Wash. & Lee 14 (3,218)
11-19-94	Davidson 28, Sewanee 14 (2,000)
10-28-95	Fordham 17, Holy Cross 10 (2,436)

EXHIBITION GAMES

(Games involving an active NCAA member versus an exhibition opponent played in the United States. Not counted as a regular-season game.)

ORLANDO, FLORIDA

(Played at Citrus Bowl)

Date	Score (Attendance)
10-3-92	UCF 42, Moscow Bears 6 (5,412)

EXHIBITION GAMES PLAYED IN FOREIGN COUNTRIES

(Games involving an active NCAA member versus a team from another country. Not counted as a regular-season game.)

KYOTO, JAPAN

(Played at Nishi Kyogoku Stadium)

Date	Score (Attendance)
3-29-97	Harvard 42, Kyoto 35 (16,000)

COLLEGE FOOTBALL TROPHY GAMES

Following is a list of the current college football trophy games. The games are listed alphabetically by the trophy-object name. The date refers to the season the trophy was first exchanged and is not necessarily the start of competition between the participants. A game involving interdivision teams is listed in the higher-division classification.

FOOTBALL BOWL SUBDIVISION

Trophy	Date	Colleges
Anniversary Award	1985	Bowling Green-Kent St.
Apple Cup	1962	Washington-Washington St.
Axe	1933	California-Stanford
Band Drum	1935	Kansas-Missouri
Battle for the Bell	1997	Marshall-Ohio
Bayou Bucket	1974	Houston-Rice
Beehive Boot	1971	BYU, Utah, Utah St., Southern Utah, Weber St.
Bell	1927	Missouri-Nebraska
Bell Clapper	1931	Oklahoma-Oklahoma St.
Big Game	1979	Arizona-Arizona St.
Black Diamond Trophy	1997	Virginia Tech-West Virginia
Blue Key Victory Bell	1940	Ball St.-Indiana St.
Brass Spittoon	1950	Indiana-Michigan St.
Brass Spittoon	1981	New Mexico St.-UTEP
Bronze Boot	1968	Colorado St.-Wyoming
Cannon	1943	Illinois-Purdue
Commander in Chief's	1972	Air Force, Army, Navy
Commonwealth Cup	1996	Virginia-Virginia Tech
Cy-Hawk	1977	Iowa-Iowa St.
Floyd of Rosedale	1935	Iowa-Minnesota
Foy-O.D.K.	1948	Alabama-Auburn
Fremont Cannon	1970	Nevada-UNLV
Golden Boot	1996	LSU-Arkansas
Golden Egg	1927	Mississippi-Mississippi St.
Golden Hat	1941	Oklahoma-Texas
Governor's Cup	1969	Kansas-Kansas St.
Governor's Cup	1958	Florida-Florida St.
Governor's Cup	1983	Colorado-Colorado St.
Governor's Cup	1994	Louisville-Kentucky
Governor's Cup	1995	Georgia-Georgia Tech
Governor's Flag*	1953	Arizona-Arizona St.
Governor's Victory Bell	1993	Minnesota-Penn St.
Illibuck	1925	Illinois-Ohio St.
Iron Bowl	1983	Alabama-Auburn
Jefferson-Epps Trophy	1995	Florida St.-Virginia
Keg of Nails	1950	Cincinnati-Louisville
Kit Carson Rifle	1938	Arizona-New Mexico
Land Grant Trophy	1993	Michigan St.-Penn St.
Little Brown Jug	1909	Michigan-Minnesota
Mayors' Cup	1998	Rice-SMU
Megaphone	1949	Michigan St.-Notre Dame
Old Oaken Bucket	1925	Indiana-Purdue
Old Wagon Wheel	1948	BYU-Utah St.
Paniolo Trophy	1979	Hawaii-Wyoming
Paul Bunyan Axe	1948	Minnesota-Wisconsin
Paul Bunyan-Governor of Michigan	1953	Michigan-Michigan St.
Peace Pipe	1929	Missouri-Oklahoma
Peace Pipe	1955	Miami (Ohio)-Western Mich.
Peace Pipe	1980	Bowling Green-Toledo
Ram-Falcon	1980	Air Force-Colorado St.
Sabine Shoe	1937	Lamar—La.-Lafayette
Schwartzwalder Trophy	1993	Syracuse-West Virginia
Shillelagh	1952	Notre Dame-Southern California

Trophy	Date	Colleges
Shillelagh	1958	Notre Dame-Purdue
Silver Spade/Brass Spittoon	1955	New Mexico St.-UTEP
Steel Tire	1976	Akron-Youngstown St.
Telephone	1960	Iowa St.-Missouri
Territorial Cup	1899	Arizona-Arizona St.
Textile Bowl	1981	Clemson-North Carolina St.
Tomahawk	1945	Illinois-Northwestern
Victory Bell	1942	Southern California-UCLA
Victory Bell	1948	Cincinnati-Miami (Ohio)
Victory Bell	1948	Duke-North Carolina
Wagon Wheel	1946	Akron-Kent St.
Williams Trophy	1998	Rice-Tulsa

**Changed to Big Game Trophy in 1979.*

FOOTBALL CHAMPIONSHIP SUBDIVISION

Trophy	Date	Colleges
Battle for the Paddle	1998	Nicholls St.-Texas St.
Bill Knight	1986	Massachusetts-New Hampshire
Brice-Colwell Musket	1946	Maine-New Hampshire
Chief Caddo	1962	Northwestern St.-Stephen F. Austin
Gem State	1978	Boise St., Idaho, Idaho St.
Governor's	1979	Central Conn. St.-Southern Conn. St.
Governor's Cup	1972	Brown-Rhode Island
Governor's Cup	1975	Dartmouth-Princeton
Governor's Cup	1984	Eastern Wash.-Idaho
Grizzly-Bobcat Painting	1984	Montana-Montana St.
Harvey—Shin-A-Ninny Totem Pole	1961	Middle Tenn.-Tennessee Tech
Little Brown Stein	1938	Idaho-Montana
Mare's	1987	Murray St.–Tenn.-Martin
Ol' Mountain Jug	1976	Appalachian St.-Western Caro.
Ol' School Bell	1988	Jacksonville St.-Troy
Ram—Crusader Cup	1951	Fordham-Holy Cross
Red Belt	1978	Murray St.-Western Ky.
Ron Rogerson Memorial	1988	Maine-Rhode Island
Sergeant York	2007	Austin Peay, Tenn.-Martin, Tennessee St., Tennessee Tech
Silver Shako	1976	Citadel-VMI
Team of Game's MVP	1960	Lafayette-Lehigh
Top Dog	1971	Butler-Indianapolis
Victory Carriage	1960	UC Davis-Sacramento St.

NON-NCAA MEMBERS

Trophy	Date	Colleges
Home Stake-Gold Mine	1950	Black Hills St.-South Dak. Tech
Paint Bucket	1961	Jamestown-Valley City St.

Coaching Records

All-Divisions Coaching Records

Winningest Coaches All-Time

BY PERCENTAGE

This list includes all coaches with at least 10 seasons at four-year colleges (regardless of division or association). Bowl and playoff games included.

Coach (Alma Mater) (Colleges Coached, Tenure)	Years	Won	Lost	Tied	Pct.†
1. *Larry Kehres (Mount Union 1971) (Mount Union 1986-06)	21	246	20	3	.920
2. Knute Rockne (Notre Dame 1914) (Notre Dame 1918-30)	13	105	12	5	.881
3. Frank Leahy (Notre Dame 1931) (Boston College 1939-40, Notre Dame 41-43, 46-53)	13	107	13	9	.864
4. Bob Reade (Cornell College 1954) [Augustana (Ill.) 1979-94]	16	146	23	1	.862
5. Doyt Perry (Bowling Green 1932) (Bowling Green 1955-64)	10	77	11	5	.855
6. Dick Farley (Boston U. 1968) (Williams 1987-03)	17	114	19	3	.849
7. George Woodruff (Yale 1889) (Penn 1892-01, Illinois 1903, Carlisle 1905)	12	142	25	2	.846
8. Alonzo S. Jake Gaither (Knoxville 1927) (Florida A&M 1945-69)	25	204	36	4	.844
9. Dave Maurer (Denison 1954) (Wittenberg 1969-83)	15	129	23	3	.842
10. Paul Hoerneman (Heidelberg 1938) (Heidelberg 1946-59)	14	102	18	4	.839
11. Barry Switzer (Arkansas 1960) (Oklahoma 1973-88)	16	157	29	4	.837
12. Tom Osborne (Hastings 1959) (Nebraska 1973-97)	25	255	49	3	.836
13. Don Coryell (Washington 1950) (Whittier 1957-59, San Diego St. 61-72)	15	127	24	3	.834
14. Percy Haughton (Harvard 1899) (Cornell 1899-00, Harvard 1908-16, Columbia 1923-24)	13	96	17	6	.832
15. Bob Neyland (Army 1916) (Tennessee 1926-34, 36-40, 46-52)	21	173	31	12	.829
16. Fielding Yost (West Virginia 1895) (Ohio Wesleyan 1897, Nebraska 1898, Kansas 1899, Stanford 1900, Michigan 1901-23, 25-26)	29	196	36	12	.828
17. Bud Wilkinson (Minnesota 1937) (Oklahoma 1947-63)	17	145	29	4	.826
18. *Chuck Broyles (Pittsburg St. 1970) (Pittsburg St. 1990-06)	17	174	36	2	.825
19. Jay Locey (Oregon St. 1978) (Linfield 1996-05)	10	84	18	0	.824
20. Chuck Klausing (Slippery Rock 1948) [Indiana (Pa.) 1964-69, Carnegie Mellon 1976-85]	16	123	26	2	.821
21. Henry A. Kean (Fisk 1920) (Kentucky St. 1931-42, Tennessee St. 1944-54)	23	165	33	9	.819
22. *Mike Kelly (Manchester 1970) (Dayton 1981-06)	26	235	53	1	.815
23. *Joe Fincham (Ohio 1988) (Wittenberg 1996-06)	11	100	23	0	.813
24. Jock Sutherland (Pittsburgh 1918) (Lafayette 1919-23; Pittsburgh 1924-38)	20	144	28	14	.812
25. Ron Schipper (Hope 1952) [Central (Iowa) 1961-96]	36	287	67	3	.808
26. *Chris Creighton (Kenyon 1991) (Ottawa 1997-00; Wabash 2001-06)	10	84	20	0	.808
27. Bob Devaney (Alma 1939) (Wyoming 1957-61, Nebraska 1962-72)	16	136	30	7	.806
28. *Ken Sparks (Carson-Newman 1968) (Carson-Newman 1980-06)	27	259	62	2	.805
29. Frank Thomas (Notre Dame 1923) (Chattanooga 1925-28, Alabama 1931-42, 44-46)	19	141	33	9	.795
30. Harold Burry [Westminster (Pa.) 1935] [Westminster (Pa.) 1952-71]	20	127	31	5	.794
31. Ad Rutschman (Linfield 1954) (Linfield 1968-91)	24	183	48	3	.788
32. Henry Williams (Yale 1891) (Army 1891, Minnesota 1900-21)	23	141	34	12	.786
33. Pete Schmidt (Alma 1970) (Albion 1983-96)	14	104	27	4	.785
34. Jim Sochor (San Fran. St. 1960) (UC Davis 1970-88)	19	156	41	5	.785
35. William M. Bill Edwards (Wittenberg 1931) (Case Tech 1934-40, Vanderbilt 1949-52, Wittenberg 1955-68)	25	176	46	8	.783
36. *John Gagliardi (Colorado Col. 1949) [Carroll (Mont.) 1949-52, St. John's (Minn.) 1953-06]	58	443	120	11	.781
37. Gil Dobie (Minnesota 1902) (North Dakota St. 1906-07, Washington 1908-16, Navy 1917-19, Cornell 1920-35, Boston College 1936-38)	33	180	45	15	.781
38. Bear Bryant (Alabama 1936) (Maryland 1945, Kentucky 1946-53, Texas A&M 1954-57, Alabama 1958-82)	38	323	85	17	.780
39. Fred Folsom (Dartmouth 1895) (Colorado 1895-99, 01-02, Dartmouth 1903-06, Colorado 1908-15)	19	106	28	6	.779
40. *Jimmie Keeling (Howard Payne 1958) (Hardin-Simmons 1990-06)	17	143	41	0	.777
41. *David Bennett (Presbyterian 1984) (Catawba 1995-01, Coastal Caro. 2003-06)	11	97	28	0	.776
42. Bo Schembechler [Miami (Ohio) 1951] [Miami (Ohio) 1963-68, Michigan 1969-89]	27	234	65	8	.775
43. Roger Harring (Wis.-La Crosse 1958) (Wis.-La Crosse 1969-99)	31	261	75	7	.771
44. *Phillip Fulmer (Tennessee 1972) (Tennessee 1992-06)	15	137	41	0	.770
45. Fritz Crisler (Chicago 1922) (Minnesota 1930-31, Princeton 1932-37, Michigan 1938-47)	18	116	32	9	.768
46. Charley Moran (Tennessee 1898) (Texas A&M 1909-14, Centre 1919-23, Bucknell 1924-26, Catawba 1930-33)	18	122	33	12	.766
47. *Mike Swider [Wheaton (Ill.) 1977] [Wheaton (Ill.) 1996-06]	11	88	27	0	.765
Wallace Wade (Brown 1917) (Alabama 1923-30, Duke 1931-41, 46-50)	24	171	49	10	.765
49. Frank Kush (Michigan St. 1953) (Arizona St. 1958-79)	22	176	54	1	.764
50. *Bill Zwaan (Delaware 1979) (Widener 1997-02, West Chester 2003-06)	10	90	28	0	.763

**Active coach. †Ties computed as half won and half lost.*

BY VICTORIES

This list includes all coaches with at least 10 seasons at four-year colleges (regardless of division or association). Bowl and playoff games included.

Coach (Alma Mater) (Colleges Coached, Tenure)	Years	Won	Lost	Tied	Pct.†
1. *John Gagliardi (Colorado Col. 1949) [Carroll (Mont.) 1949-52, St. John's (Minn.) 1953-06]	58	443	120	11	.781
2. Eddie Robinson (Leland 1941) (Grambling 1941-42, 45-97)	55	408	165	15	.707
3. *Bobby Bowden (Samford 1953) (Samford 1959-62, West Virginia 1970-75, Florida St. 1976-06)	41	366	113	4	.762
4. *Joe Paterno (Brown 1950) (Penn St. 1966-06)	41	363	121	3	.748
5. Bear Bryant (Alabama 1936) (Maryland 1945, Kentucky 1946-53, Texas A&M 1954-57, Alabama 1958-82)	38	323	85	17	.780
6. Pop Warner (Cornell 1895) (Georgia 1895-96, Cornell 1897-98, Carlisle 1899-03, Cornell 1904-06, Carlisle 1907-14, Pittsburgh 1915-23, Stanford 1924-32, Temple 1933-38)	44	319	106	32	.733
7. Amos Alonzo Stagg (Yale 1890) (Springfield 1890-91, Chicago 1892-32, Pacific 1933-46)	57	314	199	35	.605
8. Roy Kidd (Eastern Ky. 1954) (Eastern Ky. 1964-02)	39	313	124	8	.712
9. Frosty Westering (Neb.-Omaha 1952) (Parsons 1962-63, Lea 1966-71, Pacific Lutheran 1972-03)	40	305	96	7	.756
10. Tubby Raymond (Michigan 1950) (Delaware 1966-01)	36	300	119	3	.714
11. Ron Schipper (Hope 1952) [Central (Iowa) 1961-96]	36	287	67	3	.808
12. Roger Harring (Wis.-La Crosse 1958) (Wis.-La Crosse 1969-99)	31	261	75	7	.771
13. *Ken Sparks (Carson-Newman 1968) (Carson-Newman 1980-06)	27	259	62	2	.805

Coach (Alma Mater) (Colleges Coached, Tenure)	Years	Won	Lost	Tied	Pct.†
14. LaVell Edwards (Utah St. 1952) (Brigham Young 1972-00)	29	257	101	3	.716
15. Tom Osborne (Hastings 1959) (Nebraska 1973-97)	25	255	49	3	.836
Jim Malosky (Minnesota 1951) (Minn. Duluth 1958-97)	40	255	125	13	.665
17. *Frank Girardi (West Chester 1961) (Lycoming 1972-06)	35	254	90	5	.735
18. Lou Holtz (Kent St. 1959) (William & Mary 1969-71, North Carolina St. 1972-75, Arkansas 1977-83, Minnesota 1984-85, Notre Dame 1986-96, South Carolina 1999-04)	33	249	132	7	.651
19. *Larry Kehres (Mount Union 1971) (Mount Union 1986-06)	21	246	20	3	.920
20. Woody Hayes (Denison 1935) [Denison 1946-48, Miami (Ohio) 1949-50, Ohio St. 1951-78]	33	238	72	10	.759
21. Billy Joe (Villanova 1963) [Cheyney 1972-78, Central St. (Ohio) 1981-93, Florida A&M 1994-04]	31	237	108	4	.685
22. *Mike Kelly (Manchester 1970) (Dayton 1981-06)	26	235	53	1	.815
#John A. Merritt (Kentucky St. 1950) (Jackson St. 1952-62, Tennessee St. 1963-83)	32	235	70	12	.760
24. Bo Schembechler [Miami (Ohio) 1951] [Miami (Ohio) 1963-68, Michigan 1969-89]	27	234	65	8	.775
25. Arnett W. Mumford (Wilberforce 1924) (Jarvis Christian 1924-26, Bishop 1927-29, Texas Col. 1931-35, Southern U. 1936-42, 44-61)	36	233	85	23	.717
26. Hayden Fry (Baylor 1951) (SMU 1962-72, North Texas 1973-78, Iowa 1979-98)	37	232	178	10	.564
27. Fred T. Long (Millikin 1918) (Paul Quinn 1921-22, Wiley 1923-47, Prairie View 1948, Texas Col. 1949-55, Wiley 1956-65)	45	227	151	31	.593
28. Gene Carpenter (Huron 1963) (Adams St. 1968, Millersville 1970-00)	32	219	89	6	.707
@Ron Harms (Valparaiso 1959) [Concordia (Neb.) 1964-69, Adams St. 1970-73, Tex. A&M-Kingsville 1979-99]	31	219	112	4	.660
30. Ron Randleman (William Penn 1964) (William Penn 1969-75, Pittsburg St. 1976-81, Sam Houston St. 1982-04)	36	218	167	6	.565
31. Jim Christopherson (Concordia-M'head 1960) (Concordia-M'head 1969-00)	32	217	102	7	.676
Fred Martinelli (Otterbein 1951) (Ashland 1959-93)	35	217	119	12	.641
*Bob Ford (Springfield 1959) [St. Lawrence 1965-68, Albany (N.Y.) 1973-06]	38	217	158	1	.578
34. *Willard Bailey (Norfolk St. 1962) (Virginia Union 1971-83, Norfolk St. 1984-92, Virginia Union 1995-03, St. Paul's 2005-06)	33	216	126	7	.629
35. Bill Manlove (Temple 1958) (Widener 1969-91, Delaware Valley 1992-95, La Salle 1997-01)	33	215	111	1	.659
36. Peter Mazzaferro (Centre 1954) (Waynesburg 1959-62, Curry 1963, Bridgewater St. 1968-86, 88-04)	41	209	157	11	.569
37. Jess Neely (Vanderbilt 1924) (Rhodes 1924-27, Clemson 1931-39, Rice 1940-66)	40	207	176	19	.539
38. Jim Butterfield (Maine 1953) (Ithaca 1967-93)	27	206	71	1	.743
*Dennis Douds (Slippery Rock 1963) (East Stroudsburg 1974-06)	33	206	134	3	.605
40. Bud Elliott (Baker 1953) [Southwestern (Kan.) 1964-68, Washburn 1969-70, Emporia St. 1971-73, Texas-Arlington 1974-83, Northwest Mo. St. 1988-93, Eastern N.M. 1994-04]	37	205	179	9	.533
41. Alonzo S. Jake Gaither (Knoxville 1927) (Florida A&M 1945-69)	25	204	36	4	.844
42. Warren Woodson (Baylor 1924) [Conway St. 1935-40, Hardin-Simmons 1941-42, 46-51, Arizona 1952-56, New Mexico St. 1958-67, Trinity (Tex.) 1972-73]	31	203	95	14	.673
Cleveland L. Abbott (South Dakota St. 1916) (Tuskegee 1923-54)	32	203	96	28	.664
44. Don Nehlen (Bowling Green 1958) (Bowling Green 1968-76, West Virginia 1980-00)	30	202	128	8	.609
45. Vince Dooley (Auburn 1954) (Georgia 1964-88)	25	201	77	10	.715
Eddie Anderson (Notre Dame 1922) (Loras 1922-24, DePaul 1925-31, Holy Cross 1933-38, Iowa 1939-42, 46-49, Holy Cross 1950-64)	39	201	128	15	.606
Keith W. Piper (Baldwin-Wallace 1948) (Denison 1954-92)	39	201	141	18	.583
48. Darrell Mudra (Peru St. 1951) (Adams St. 1959-62, North Dakota St. 1963-65, Arizona 1967-68, Western Ill. 1969-73, Florida St. 1974-75, Eastern Ill. 1978-82, UNI 1983-87)	26	200	81	4	.709
Jim Sweeney (Portland 1951) (Montana St. 1963-67, Washington St. 1968-75, Fresno St. 1976-77, 80-96)	32	200	154	4	.564
50. Frank Cignetti [Indiana (Pa.) 1960] [West Virginia 1976-79, Indiana (Pa.) 1986-05]	24	198	78	1	.717
Dana X. Bible (Carson-Newman 1912) (Mississippi Col. 1913-15, LSU 1916, Texas A&M 1917,17-28, Nebraska 1929-36, Texas 1937-46)	33	198	72	23	.715
*Frank Beamer (Virginia Tech 1969) (Murray St. 1981-86, Virginia Tech 1987-06)	26	198	105	4	.651

**Active coach. †Ties computed as half won and half lost. #Tennessee State's participation in 1981 and 1982 FCS championships (1-2 record) vacated by action of the NCAA Committee on Infractions. @Texas A&M-Kingsville's participation in the 1996, 1997 and 1998 Division II championships (2-3 record) vacated by action of the NCAA Committee on Infractions.*

Winningest Active Coaches

BY PERCENTAGE

This list includes all coaches with at least five seasons at four-year colleges (regardless of division or association). Bowl and playoff games included.

Coach, College	Years	Won	Lost	Tied	Pct.†
1. Larry Kehres, Mount Union	21	246	20	3	.920
2. Chris Hatcher, Ga. Southern	7	76	12	0	.864
3. Jim Purtill, St. Norbert	8	74	12	0	.860
4. Pete Carroll, Southern California	6	65	12	0	.844
5. Urban Meyer, Florida	6	61	12	0	.836
6. Chuck Broyles, Pittsburg St.	17	174	36	2	.825
7. Bob Stoops, Oklahoma	8	86	19	0	.819
8. Mike Kelly, Dayton	26	235	53	1	.815
9. Joe Fincham, Wittenberg	11	100	23	0	.813
10. Chris Creighton, Wabash	10	84	20	0	.808
11. Ken Sparks, Carson-Newman	27	259	62	2	.805
12. Bryan Collins, C.W. Post	9	80	20	0	.800
13. Jay Accorsi, Rowan	5	47	12	0	.797
14. Mark Richt, Georgia	6	61	17	0	.782
15. John Gagliardi, St. John's (Minn.)	58	443	120	11	.781
16. Jimmie Keeling, Hardin-Simmons	17	143	41	0	.777
17. David Bennett, Coastal Caro.	11	97	28	0	.776
18. Phillip Fulmer, Tennessee	15	137	41	0	.770
19. Mike Swider, Wheaton (Ill.)	11	88	27	0	.765
20. Bill Zwaan, West Chester	10	90	28	0	.763
21. Bobby Bowden, Florida St.	41	366	113	4	.762
22. Lloyd Carr, Michigan	12	113	36	0	.758
23. Steve Spurrier, South Carolina	17	157	50	2	.756
24. Al Bagnoli, Penn	25	190	63	0	.751
25. Pete Fredenburg, Mary Hardin-Baylor	9	75	25	0	.750

†Ties computed as half won and half lost.

BY VICTORIES

This list includes all coaches with at least five seasons at four-year colleges (regardless of division or association). Bowl and playoff games included.

Coach, College	Years	Won	Lost	Tied	Pct.†
1. John Gagliardi, St. John's (Minn.)	58	443	120	11	.781
2. Bobby Bowden, Florida St.	41	366	113	4	.762
3. Joe Paterno, Penn St.	41	363	121	3	.748
4. Ken Sparks, Carson-Newman	27	259	62	2	.805
5. Frank Girardi, Lycoming	35	254	90	5	.735
6. Larry Kehres, Mount Union	21	246	20	3	.920
7. Mike Kelly, Dayton	26	235	53	1	.815
8. Bob Ford, Albany (N.Y.)	38	217	158	1	.578
9. Willard Bailey, St. Paul's	33	216	126	7	.629
10. Dennis Douds, East Stroudsburg	33	206	134	3	.605
11. Frank Beamer, Virginia Tech	26	198	105	4	.651
12. Jim Tressel, Ohio St.	21	197	71	2	.733
13. Joe Taylor, Hampton	24	191	71	4	.726
Mel Tjeerdsma, Northwest Mo. St.	23	191	75	4	.715
15. Al Bagnoli, Penn	25	190	63	0	.751
16. Chris Ault, Nevada	22	185	78	1	.703
17. Jerry Moore, Appalachian St.	25	181	116	2	.609

	Coach, College	Years	Won	Lost	Tied	Pct.†
18.	Dennis Franchione, Texas A&M	24	180	96	2	.651
19.	Walt Hameline, Wagner	26	179	93	2	.657
	Mack Brown, Texas	23	179	96	1	.650
	Eric Hamilton, TCNJ	30	179	115	6	.607
22.	Joe Glenn, Wyoming	22	178	86	1	.674
	Jimmye Laycock, William & Mary	27	178	127	2	.583
24.	Rob Ash, Montana St.	27	176	99	5	.638
25.	Andy Talley, Villanova	27	175	112	2	.609

†Ties computed as half won and half lost.

Matchups of Coaches Each With 200 Victories

Date	Coaches, Teams (Victories Going In)	Winner (Score)
11-11-1961	Arnett Mumford, Southern U. (232)	
	Fred Long, Wiley (215)	Wiley (21-19)
1-1-1978	Bear Bryant, Alabama (272)	Alabama (35-6)
Sugar Bowl	Woody Hayes, Ohio St. (231)	
10-11-1980	Eddie Robinson, Grambling (284)	Grambling (52-27)
	John Merritt, Tennessee St. (200)	
10-10-1981	Eddie Robinson, Grambling (294)	
	John Merritt, Tennessee St. (209)	Tennessee St. (14-10)
10-9-1982	Eddie Robinson, Grambling (301)	
	John Merritt, Tennessee St. (218)	Tennessee St. (22-8)
10-8-1983	Eddie Robinson, Grambling (308)	Tie (7-7)
	John Merritt, Tennessee St. (228)	
11-28-1987	John Gagliardi, St. John's (Minn.) (251)	
	Ron Schipper, Central (Iowa) (202)	Central (Iowa) (13-3)
11-25-1989	John Gagliardi, St. John's (Minn.) (268)	St. John's (Minn.) (27-24)
	Ron Schipper, Central (Iowa) (224)	
12-28-1990	Joe Paterno, Penn St. (229)	
Blockbuster Bowl	Bobby Bowden, Florida St. (204)	Florida St. (24-17)
11-27-1993	John Gagliardi, St. John's (Minn.) (305)	St. John's (Minn.) (47-25)
	Roger Harring, Wis.-La Crosse (210)	
1-1-1994	Bobby Bowden, Florida St. (238)	Florida St. (18-16)
Orange Bowl	Tom Osborne, Nebraska (206)	
9-17-1994	Joe Paterno, Penn St. (258)	Penn St. (61-21)
	Hayden Fry, Iowa (202)	
10-21-1995	Joe Paterno, Penn St. (273)	Penn St. (41-27)
	Hayden Fry, Iowa (210)	
1-1-1996	Bobby Bowden, Florida St. (258)	Florida St. (31-26)
Orange Bowl	Lou Holtz, Notre Dame (208)	
10-19-1996	Joe Paterno, Penn St. (284)	
	Hayden Fry, Iowa (217)	Iowa (21-20)
11-17-1996	Jim Malosky, Minn. Duluth (250)	Minn. Duluth (17-3)
	Roger Harring, Wis.-La Crosse (241)	
11-30-1996	John Gagliardi, St. John's (Minn.) (336)	
	Roger Harring, Wis.-La Crosse (242)	Wis.-La Crosse (37-30)
12-4-1999	John Gagliardi, St. John's (Minn.) (364)	
	Frosty Westering, Pacific Lutheran (274)	Pacific Lutheran (19-9)
8-26-2000	Bobby Bowden, Florida St. (304)	Florida St. (29-3)
	LaVell Edwards, Brigham Young (251)	
11-25-2000	John Gagliardi, St. John's (Minn.) (374)	St. John's (Minn.) (28-21) (ot)
	Frosty Westering, Pacific Lutheran (286)	
12-1-2001	John Gagliardi, St. John's (Minn.) (387)	St. John's (Minn.) (31-6)
	Frosty Westering, Pacific Lutheran (294)	
12-20-2003	John Gagliardi, St. John's (Minn.) (413)	St. John's (Minn.) (24-6)
	Larry Kehres, Mount Union (205)	
10-2-2004	Billy Joe, Florida A&M (235)	Florida A&M (35-10)
	Willard Bailey, Virginia Union (212)	
1-3-2006	Bobby Bowden, Florida St. (359)	
Orange Bowl	Joe Paterno, Penn St. (353)	Penn St. (26-23) (3 ot)

Coaches With 200 or More Victories at One College

(Bowl and Playoff Games Included)

Coach (College, Tenure)	Years	Won	Lost	Tied	Pct.#
*John Gagliardi, St. John's (Minn.) (1953–)	†54	419	114	10	.781
Eddie Robinson, Grambling (1941-42, 45-97)	†55	408	165	15	.707
*Joe Paterno, Penn St. (1966–)	41	363	121	3	.748
Roy Kidd, Eastern Ky. (1964-2002)	†39	315	123	8	.715
Tubby Raymond, Delaware (1966-2001)	†36	300	119	3	.714
*Bobby Bowden, Florida St. (1976–)	31	293	81	4	.780
Ron Schipper, Central (Iowa) (1961-96)	†36	287	67	3	.808
Frosty Westering, Pacific Lutheran (1972-2003)	†32	261	70	4	.785
Roger Harring, Wis.-La Crosse (1969-99)	†31	261	75	7	.771
*Ken Sparks, Carson-Newman (1980–)	†27	259	62	2	.805
LaVell Edwards, Brigham Young (1972-2000)	29	257	101	3	.716
Tom Osborne, Nebraska (1973-97)	25	255	49	3	.836
Jim Malosky, Minn. Duluth (1958-97)	†40	255	125	13	.665
*Frank Girardi, Lycoming (1972–)	†35	254	90	5	.735
*Larry Kehres, Mount Union (1986–)	†21	246	20	3	.920
Amos Alonzo Stagg, Chicago (1892-1932)	41	244	111	27	.674
*Mike Kelly, Dayton (1981–)	†26	235	53	1	.815
Bear Bryant, Alabama (1958-82)	25	232	46	9	.824
Fred Martinelli, Ashland (1959-93)	†35	217	119	12	.641
Jim Butterfield, Ithaca (1967-93)	†27	206	71	1	.743
*Dennis Douds, East Stroudsburg (1974–)	†33	206	134	3	.605
Woody Hayes, Ohio St. (1951-78)	28	205	61	10	.761
Jake Gaither, Florida A&M (1945-69)	†25	203	36	4	.844
Vince Dooley, Georgia (1964-88)	25	201	77	10	.715

*†Zero to nine years in FBS. *Active coach. #Ties computed as half won and half lost.*

Football Bowl Subdivision (FBS) Coaching Records

Winningest Active Coaches

BY PERCENTAGE

(Minimum five years as FBS head coach; record at four-year colleges only.)

	Coach, College	Years	Won	Lost	Tied	Pct.†
1.	Pete Carroll, Southern California	6	65	12	0	.844
2.	Urban Meyer, Florida	6	61	12	0	.836
3.	Bob Stoops, Oklahoma	8	86	19	0	.819
4.	Mark Richt, Georgia	6	61	17	0	.782
5.	Phillip Fulmer, Tennessee	15	137	41	0	.770
6.	Bobby Bowden, Florida St.	41	366	113	4	.762
7.	Lloyd Carr, Michigan	12	113	36	0	.758
8.	Steve Spurrier, South Carolina	17	157	50	2	.756
9.	Joe Paterno, Penn St.	41	363	121	3	.748
10.	Paul Johnson, Navy	10	99	35	0	.739
11.	Dan Hawkins, Colorado	11	94	33	1	.738
12.	Jim Tressel, Ohio St.	21	197	71	2	.733
13.	Gary Patterson, TCU	7	54	20	0	.730
14.	Butch Davis, North Carolina	6	51	20	0	.718
15.	Chris Ault, Nevada	22	185	78	1	.703
16.	Dennis Erickson, Arizona St.	18	149	64	1	.699
17.	Frank Solich, Ohio	8	71	31	0	.696
18.	Nick Saban, Alabama	11	91	42	1	.683
19.	Jeff Tedford, California	5	43	20	0	.683
20.	Ralph Friedgen, Maryland	6	50	24	0	.676
21.	Les Miles, LSU	6	50	25	0	.667
22.	Tom Amstutz, Toledo	6	49	25	0	.662
23.	Tommy Tuberville, Auburn	12	96	49	0	.662
24.	Larry Blakeney, Troy	16	127	65	1	.661
25.	Frank Beamer, Virginia Tech	26	198	105	4	.652
26.	Dennis Franchione, Texas A&M	24	180	96	2	.651
27.	Mack Brown, Texas	23	179	96	1	.650
28.	Tommy Bowden, Clemson	10	78	42	0	.650
29.	Mike Leach, Texas Tech	7	56	33	0	.629
30.	Tom O'Brien, North Carolina St.	10	75	45	0	.625
31.	Jim Leavitt, South Fla.	10	70	43	0	.619
32.	Mike Bellotti, Oregon	17	118	73	2	.617
33.	Chan Gailey, Georgia Tech	8	61	38	0	.616
34.	June Jones, Hawaii	8	64	40	0	.615
35.	Rich Rodriguez, West Virginia	14	95	60	2	.611

Fewer than five years as FBS head coach (must have at least five years at four-year college, includes record at all four-year colleges):

Coach, College	Years	Won	Lost	Tied	Pct.†
Brian Kelly, Cincinnati	16	138	51	2	.728
Joe Glenn, Wyoming	22	178	86	1	.674
Bill Cubit, Western Mich.	7	49	27	1	.643

†Ties computed as half won and half lost.

BY VICTORIES

(Minimum five years as FBS head coach; record at four-year colleges only.)

Coach, College	Years	Won	Lost	Tied	Pct.†
1. Bobby Bowden, Florida St.	41	366	113	4	.762
2. Joe Paterno, Penn St.	41	363	121	3	.748
3. Frank Beamer, Virginia Tech	26	198	105	4	.651
4. Jim Tressel, Ohio St.	21	197	71	2	.733
5. Chris Ault, Nevada	22	185	78	1	.703
6. Dennis Franchione, Texas A&M	24	180	96	2	.651
7. Mack Brown, Texas	23	179	96	1	.650
8. Dick Tomey, San Jose St.	26	170	122	7	.580
9. Steve Spurrier, South Carolina	17	157	50	2	.756
10. Mike Price, UTEP	25	150	137	0	.523
11. Dennis Erickson, Arizona St.	18	149	64	1	.699
12. Phillip Fulmer, Tennessee	15	137	41	0	.770
13. Howard Schnellenberger, Fla. Atlantic	22	133	114	3	.538
14. Larry Blakeney, Troy	16	127	65	1	.661
15. Sonny Lubick, Colorado St.	18	126	84	0	.600
16. Mike Bellotti, Oregon	17	118	73	2	.617
17. Joe Tiller, Purdue	16	114	79	1	.590
18. Lloyd Carr, Michigan	12	113	36	0	.758
19. Jeff Bower, Southern Miss.	17	112	77	1	.592
20. Gary Pinkel, Missouri	16	110	72	3	.603
21. Rich Brooks, Kentucky	22	108	139	4	.438
22. Houston Nutt, Arkansas	14	102	67	0	.604
23. Hal Mumme, New Mexico St.	16	101	84	1	.546
24. Paul Johnson, Navy	10	99	35	0	.739
25. Tommy Tuberville, Auburn	12	96	49	0	.662
26. Rich Rodriguez, West Virginia	14	95	60	2	.611
27. Dan Hawkins, Colorado	11	94	33	1	.738
28. Nick Saban, Alabama	11	91	42	1	.683
29. Bob Stoops, Oklahoma	8	86	19	0	.819
30. Bill Lynch, Indiana	14	81	67	3	.546
31. Tommy Bowden, Clemson	10	78	42	0	.650
Bob Toledo, Tulane	13	78	68	0	.534
33. Pat Hill, Fresno St.	10	76	51	0	.598
34. Tom O'Brien, North Carolina St.	10	76	45	0	.628
35. Steve Roberts, Arkansas St.	13	75	67	1	.528
Bobby Johnson, Vanderbilt	13	75	79	0	.487

Fewer than five years as FBS head coach (must have at least five years at four-year college, includes record at all four-year colleges):

Coach, College	Years	Won	Lost	Tied	Pct.†
Joe Glenn, Wyoming	22	178	86	1	.674
Brian Kelly, Cincinnati	16	138	51	2	.728
Bill Cubit, Western Mich.	7	49	27	1	.643

†Ties computed as half won and half lost.

Winningest Coaches All-Time

BY PERCENTAGE

Minimum 10 years as head coach at FBS institutions; record at four-year colleges only; bowl games included; ties computed as half won, half lost. Active coaches indicated by (*). College Football Hall of Fame members indicated by (†).

Coach (Alma Mater) (Colleges Coached, Tenure)	Years	Won	Lost	Tied	Pct.
1. Knute Rockne (Notre Dame 1914)† (Notre Dame 1918-30)	13	105	12	5	.881
2. Frank Leahy (Notre Dame 1931)† (Boston College 1939-40; Notre Dame 41-43, 46-53)	13	107	13	9	.864
3. George Woodruff (Yale 1889)† (Penn 1892-1901; Illinois 03; Carlisle 05)	12	142	25	2	.846
4. Barry Switzer (Arkansas 1960)† (Oklahoma 1973-88)	16	157	29	4	.837
5. Tom Osborne (Hastings 1959)† (Nebraska 1973-97)	25	255	49	3	.836
6. Percy Haughton (Harvard 1899)† (Cornell 1899-1900; Harvard 08-16; Columbia 23-24)	13	96	17	6	.832
7. Bob Neyland (Army 1916)† (Tennessee 1926-34, 36-40, 46-52)	21	173	31	12	.829
8. Fielding Yost (West Virginia 1895)† (Ohio Wesleyan 1897; Nebraska 98; Kansas 99; Stanford 1900; Michigan 01-23, 25-26)	29	196	36	12	.828
9. Bud Wilkinson (Minnesota 1937)† (Oklahoma 1947-63)	17	145	29	4	.826
10. Jock Sutherland (Pittsburgh 1918)† (Lafayette 1919-23; Pittsburgh 24-38)	20	144	28	14	.812
11. Bob Devaney (Alma 1939)† (Wyoming 1957-61; Nebraska 62-72)	16	136	30	7	.806
12. Frank Thomas (Notre Dame 1923)† (Chattanooga 1925-28; Alabama 31-42, 44-46)	19	141	33	9	.795
13. Henry Williams (Yale 1891)† (Army 1891; Minnesota 1900-21)	23	141	34	12	.786
14. Gil Dobie (Minnesota 1902)† (North Dakota St. 1906-07; Washington 08-16; Navy 17-19; Cornell 20-35; Boston College 36-38)	33	180	45	15	.781
15. Bear Bryant (Alabama 1936)† (Maryland 1945; Kentucky 46-53; Texas A&M 54-57; Alabama 58-82)	38	323	85	17	.780
16. Fred Folsom (Dartmouth 1895) (Colorado 1895-99, 1901-02; Dartmouth 03-06; Colorado 08-15)	19	106	28	6	.779
17. Bo Schembechler [Miami (Ohio) 1951]† [Miami (Ohio) 1963-68; Michigan 69-89]	27	234	65	8	.775
18.*Phillip Fulmer (Tennessee 1972) (Tennessee 1992—)	15	137	41	0	.770
19. Fritz Crisler (Chicago 1922)† (Minnesota 1930-31; Princeton 32-37; Michigan 38-47)	18	116	32	9	.768
20. Wallace Wade (Brown 1917)† (Alabama 1923-30; Duke 31-41, 46-50)	24	171	49	10	.765
21. Frank Kush (Michigan St. 1953)† (Arizona St. 1958-79)	22	176	54	1	.764
22. Dan McGugin (Michigan 1904)† (Vanderbilt 1904-17, 19-34)	30	197	55	19	.762
23.*Bobby Bowden (Samford 1953)√† (Samford 1959-62; West Virginia 70-75; Florida St. 76—)	41	366	113	4	.762
24. Jimmy Crowley (Notre Dame 1925)# (Michigan St. 1929-32; Fordham 33-41)	13	78	21	10	.761
25. Andy Smith (Penn St., Penn 1905)† (Penn 1909-12; Purdue 13-15; California 16-25)	17	116	32	13	.761
26. Woody Hayes (Denison 1935)† [Denison 1946-48; Miami (Ohio) 49-50; Ohio St. 51-78]	33	238	72	10	.759
27. Red Blaik [Miami (Ohio) 1918; Army 1920]† (Dartmouth 1934-40; Army 41-58)	25	166	48	14	.759
28. *Lloyd Carr (Northern Mich. 1968) (Michigan 1995—)	12	113	36	0	.758
29.*Steve Spurrier (Florida 1967)# (Duke 1987-89; Florida 90-2001; South Carolina 05—)	17	157	50	2	.756
30. Darrell Royal (Oklahoma 1950)† (Mississippi St. 1954-55; Washington 56; Texas 57-76)	23	184	60	5	.749
31. John McKay (Oregon 1950)† (Southern California 1960-75)	16	127	40	8	.749
32.*Joe Paterno (Brown 1950)† (Penn St. 1966—)	41	363	121	3	.748
33. John Vaught (TCU 1933)† (Mississippi 1947-70, 73)	25	190	61	12	.745
34. Dan Devine (Minn. Duluth 1948)† (Arizona St. 1955-57; Missouri 58-70; Notre Dame 75-80)	22	172	57	9	.742
35. Gus Henderson (Oberlin 1912) (Southern California 1919-24; Tulsa 25-35; Occidental 40-42)	20	126	42	7	.740
36. Ara Parseghian [Miami (Ohio) 1949]† [Miami (Ohio) 1951-55; Northwestern 56-63; Notre Dame 64-74]	24	170	58	6	.739
37. Elmer Layden (Notre Dame 1925)# (Loras 1925-26; Duquesne 27-33; Notre Dame 34-40)	16	103	34	11	.733
38. Pop Warner (Cornell 1895)† (Georgia 1895-96; Cornell 97-98; Carlisle 99-1903; Cornell 04-06; Carlisle 07-14; Pittsburgh 15-23; Stanford 24-32; Temple 33-38)	44	319	106	32	.733
39. Howard Jones (Yale 1908)† (Syracuse 1908; Yale 09; Ohio St. 10; Yale 13; Iowa 16-23; Duke 24; Southern California 25-40)	29	194	64	21	.733
40. Jim Tatum (North Carolina 1935)† (North Carolina 1942; Oklahoma 46; Maryland 47-55; North Carolina 56-58)	14	100	35	7	.729
41. Francis Schmidt (Nebraska 1914)† (Tulsa 1919-21; Arkansas 22-28; TCU 29-33; Ohio St. 34-40; Idaho 41-42)	24	159	56	11	.728
42. Tad Jones (Yale 1908)† (Syracuse 1909-10; Yale 16-17, 20-27)	12	69	24	6	.727
43. Frank Cavanaugh (Dartmouth 1897)† (Cincinnati 1898; Holy Cross 1903-05; Dartmouth 11-16; Boston College 19-26; Neb.-Omaha 19; Fordham 27-32)	25	148	50	18	.727
44. Bill Roper (Princeton 1903)† (VMI 1903-04; Princeton 06-08; Missouri 09; Princeton 10-11; Swarthmore 15-16; Princeton 19-30)	22	112	37	19	.723

Coach (Alma Mater) (Colleges Coached, Tenure)	Years	Won	Lost	Tied	Pct.
45. R.C. Slocum (McNeese St. 1967) (Texas A&M 1989-2002)	14	123	47	2	.721
46. Doc Kennedy (Kansas & Penn 1903) (Kansas 1904-10; Haskell 11-16)	13	85	31	7	.720
47. LaVell Edwards (Utah St. 1952)† (Brigham Young 1972-2000)	29	257	101	3	.716
48. Vince Dooley (Auburn 1954)† (Georgia 1964-88)	25	201	77	10	.715
49. Dana X. Bible (Carson-Newman 1912)† (Mississippi Col. 1913-15; LSU 16; Texas A&M 17, 19-28; Nebraska 29-36; Texas 37-46)	33	198	72	23	.715
50. Bobby Dodd (Tennessee 1931)† (Georgia Tech 1945-66)	22	165	64	8	.713

#Member of College Football Hall of Fame as a player. √Includes games forfeited, team and/or individual statistics abrogated, and coaching records changed by action of the NCAA Committee on Infractions.

BY VICTORIES

Minimum 10 years as head coach at FBS institutions; record at four-year colleges only; bowl games included; ties computed as half won, half lost. After each coach's name is his alma mater, year graduated, total years coached, won-lost record and percentage, tenure at each college coached, and won-lost record there. Active coaches are denoted by an asterisk (*).

(Minimum 170 Victories)

1\. 366 *Bobby Bowden (Born 11-8-1929 Birmingham, Ala.)
Samford 1953 (√41: 366-113-4 .762)
Samford 1959-62 (31-6-0); West Virginia 70-75 (√42-26-0); Florida St. 76-2006 (293-81-4)

2\. 363 *Joe Paterno (Born 12-21-1926 Brooklyn, N.Y.)
Brown 1951 (41: 363-121-3 .748)
Penn St. 1966-2006 (363-121-3)

3\. 323 Bear Bryant (Born 9-11-1913 Moro Bottoms, Ark.; Died 1-26-1983)
Alabama 1936 (38: 323-85-17 .780)
Maryland 1945 (6-2-1); Kentucky 46-53 (60-23-5); Texas A&M 54-57 (25-14-2); Alabama 58-82 (232-46-9)

4\. 319 Pop Warner (Born 4-5-1871 Springville, N.Y.; Died 9-7-1954)
Cornell 1895 (44: 319-106-32 .733)
Georgia 1895-96 (7-4-0); Cornell 97-98, 1904-06 (36-13-3); Carlisle 1899-1903, 07-14 (114-42-8); Pittsburgh 15-23 (60-12-4); Stanford 24-32 (71-17-8); Temple 33-38 (31-18-9)

5\. 314 Amos Alonzo Stagg (Born 8-16-1862 West Orange, N.J.; Died 3-17-1965)
Yale 1888 (57: 314-199-35 .605)
Springfield 1890-91 (10-11-1); Chicago 92-1932 (244-111-27); Pacific 33-46 (60-77-7)

6\. 257 LaVell Edwards (Born 10-11-1930 Provo, Utah)
Utah St. 1952 (29: 257-101-3 .716)
Brigham Young 1972-2000 (257-101-3)

7\. 255 Tom Osborne (Born 2-23-1937 Hastings, Neb.)
Hastings 1959 (25: 255-49-3 .836)
Nebraska 1973-97 (255-49-3)

8\. 249 Lou Holtz (Born 1-6-1937 Follansbee, W.Va.)
Kent St. 1959 (32: 249-132-7 .651)
William & Mary 1969-71 (13-20-0); North Carolina St. 72-75 (33-12-3); Arkansas 77-83 (60-21-2); Minnesota 84-85 (10-12-0); Notre Dame 86-96 (100-30-2); South Carolina 99-2004 (33-37-0)

9\. 238 Woody Hayes (Born 2-13-1914 Clifton, Ohio; Died 3-12-1987)
Denison 1935 (33: 238-72-10 .759)
Denison 1946-48 (19-6-0); Miami (Ohio) 49-50 (14-5-0); Ohio St. 51-78 (205-61-10)

10\. 234 Bo Schembechler (Born 9-1-1929 Barberton, Ohio; Died 11-17-2006)
Miami (Ohio) 1951 (27: 234-65-8 .775)
Miami (Ohio) 1963-68 (40-17-3); Michigan 69-89 (194-48-5)

11\. 232 Hayden Fry (Born 2-28-1929 Odessa, Tex.)
Baylor 1951 (√37: 232-178-10 .564)
SMU 1962-72 (49-66-1); North Texas 73-78 (√40-23-3); Iowa 79-98 (142-89-6)

12\. 207 Jess Neely (Born 1-4-1898 Smyrna, Tenn.; Died 4-9-1983)
Vanderbilt 1924 (40: 207-176-19 .539)
Rhodes 1924-27 (20-17-2); Clemson 31-39 (43-35-7); Rice 40-66 (144-124-10)

13\. 203 Warren Woodson (Born 2-24-1903 Fort Worth, Texas; Died 2-22-1998)
Baylor 1924 (31: 203-95-14 .673)
Central Ark. 1935-39 (40-8-3); Hardin-Simmons 41-42, 46-51 (58-24-6); Arizona 52-56 (26-22-2); New Mexico St. 58-67 (63-36-3); Trinity (Tex.) 72-73 (16-5-0)

14\. 202 Don Nehlen (Born 1-1-1936 Canton, Ohio)
Bowling Green 1958 (30: 202-128-8 .609)
Bowling Green 1968-76 (53-35-4); West Virginia 80-2000 (149-93-4)

15\. 201 Vince Dooley (Born 9-4-1932 Mobile, Ala.)
Auburn 1954 (25: 201-77-10 .715)
Georgia 1964-88 (201-77-10)

201 Eddie Anderson (Born 11-13-1900 Mason City, Iowa; Died 4-26-1974)
Notre Dame 1922 (39: 201-128-15 .606)
Loras 1922-24 (16-6-2); DePaul 25-31 (21-22-3); Holy Cross 33-38, 50-64 (129-67-8); Iowa 39-42, 46-49 (35-33-2)

17\. 200 Jim Sweeney (Born 9-1-1929 Butte, Mont.)
Portland 1951 (32: 200-154-4 .564)
Montana St. 1963-67 (31-20-0); Washington St. 68-75 (26-59-1); Fresno St. 76-77, 80-96 (143-75-3)

18\. 198 Dana X. Bible (Born 10-8-1891 Jefferson City, Tenn.; Died 1-19-1980)
Carson-Newman 1912 (33: 198-72-23 .715)
Mississippi Col. 1913-15 (12-7-2); LSU 16 (1-0-2); Texas A&M 17, 19-28 (72-19-9); Nebraska 29-36 (50-15-7); Texas 37-46 (63-31-3)

198 *Frank Beamer (Born 4-18-1946 Mt. Airy, N.C.)
Virginia Tech 1969 (26: 198-105-4 .651)
Murray St. 1981-86 (42-23-2); Virginia Tech 1987-2006 (156-82-2)

20\. 197 Dan McGugin (Born 7-29-1879 Tingley, Iowa; Died 1-19-1936)
Michigan 1904 (30: 197-55-19 .762)
Vanderbilt 1904-17, 19-34 (197-55-19)

21\. 196 Fielding Yost (Born 4-30-1871 Fairview, W.Va.; Died 8-20-1946)
West Virginia 1895 (29: 196-36-12 .828)
Ohio Wesleyan 1897 (7-1-1); Nebraska 98 (7-4-0); Kansas 99 (10-0-0); Stanford 1900 (7-2-1); Michigan 01-23, 25-26 (165-29-10)

22\. 194 Howard Jones (Born 8-23-1885 Excello, Ohio; Died 7-27-1941)
Yale 1908 (29: 194-64-21 .733)
Syracuse 1908 (6-3-1); Yale 09, 13 (15-2-3); Ohio St. 10 (6-1-3); Iowa 16-23 (42-17-1); Duke 24 (4-5-0); Southern California 25-40 (121-36-13)

23\. 192 John Cooper (Born 7-2-1937 Powell, Tenn.)
Iowa St. 1962 (24: 192-84-6 .691)
Tulsa 1977-84 (56-32-0); Arizona St. 85-87 (25-9-2); Ohio St. 88-2000 (112-43-4)

24\. 190 John Vaught (Born 5-6-1908 Olney, Texas)
TCU 1933 (25: 190-61-12 .745)
Mississippi 1947-70, 73 (190-61-12)

25\. 189 George Welsh (Born 8-26-1933 Coaldale, Pa.)
Navy 1960 (28: 189-132-4 .588)
Navy 1973-81 (55-46-1); Virginia 82-2000 (134-86-3)

26\. 185 John Heisman (Born 10-23-1869 Cleveland, Ohio; Died 10-3-1936)
Brown 1890 (36: 185-70-18 .711)
Oberlin 1892, 94 (11-3-1); Akron 93 (5-2-0); Auburn 95-99 (12-4-2); Clemson 1900-03 (19-3-2); Georgia Tech 04-19 (102-29-6); Penn 20-22 (16-10-2); Wash. & Jeff. 23 (6-1-1); Rice 24-27 (14-18-3)

185 Johnny Majors (Born 5-21-1935 Lynchburg, Tenn.)
Tennessee 1957 (29: 185-137-10 .572)
Iowa St. 1968-72 (24-30-1); Pittsburgh 73-76, 93-96 (45-45-1); Tennessee 77-92 (116-62-8)

28\. 184 Darrell Royal (Born 7-6-1924 Hollis, Okla.)
Oklahoma 1950 (23: 184-60-5 .749)
Mississippi St. 1954-55 (12-8-0); Washington 56 (5-5-0); Texas 57-76 (167-47-5)

29\. 180 Gil Dobie (Born 1-31-1879 Hastings, Minn.; Died 12-24-1948)
Minnesota 1902 (33: 180-45-15 .781)
North Dakota St. 1906-07 (7-0-0); Washington 08-16 (58-0-3); Navy 17-19 (17-3-0); Cornell 20-35 (82-36-7); Boston College 36-38 (16-6-5)

180 *Dennis Franchione (Born 3-28-1951 Girard, Kan.)
Pittsburg St. 1973 (24: 180-96-2 .651)
Southwestern (Kan.) 1981-82 (14-4-2); Pittsburg St. 85-89 (53-6-0); Texas St. 90-91 (13-9-0); New Mexico 92-97 (33-36-0); TCU 98-2000 (25-11-0); Alabama 01-02 (17-8-0); Texas A&M 03-06 (25-22-0)

180 Carl Snavely (Born 7-30-1894 Omaha, Neb.; Died 7-12-1975)
Lebanon Valley 1915 (32: 180-96-16 .644)
Bucknell 1927-33 (42-16-8); North Carolina 34-35, 45-52 (59-35-5); Cornell 36-44 (46-26-3); Washington-St. Louis 53-58 (33-19-0)

180 Jackie Sherrill (Born 11-28-1943 Duncan, Okla.)
Alabama 1966 (26: 180-120-4 .599)
Washington St. 1976 (3-8-0); Pittsburgh 77-81 (50-9-1); Texas A&M 82-88 (52-28-1); Mississippi St. 91-2003 (75-75-2)

33\. 179 Mack Brown (Born 8-27-1951 Cookeville, Tenn.)
Florida St. 1974 (23: 179-96-1 .650)
Appalachian St. 1983 (6-5); Tulane 85-87 (11-23); North Carolina 88-97 (69-46-1); Texas 98-2006 (93-22)

179 Jerry Claiborne (Born 8-26-1928 Hopkinsville, Ky.; Died 9-24-2000)
Kentucky 1950 (28: 179-122-8 .592)
Virginia Tech 1961-70 (61-39-2); Maryland 72-81 (77-37-3); Kentucky 82-89 (41-46-3)

35\. 178 Ben Schwartzwalder (Born 6-2-1909 Point Pleasant, W.Va.; Died 4-28-1993)
West Virginia 1933 (28: 178-96-3 .648)
Muhlenberg 1946-48 (25-5-0); Syracuse 49-73 (153-91-3)

36\. 176 Frank Kush (Born 1-20-1929 Windber, Pa.)
Michigan St. 1953 (22: 176-54-1 .764)
Arizona St. 1958-79 (176-54-1)

176 Don James (Born 12-31-1932 Massillon, Ohio)
Miami (Fla.) 1954 (22: 176-78-3 .691)
Kent St. 1971-74 (25-19-1); Washington 75-92 (151-59-2)

176 Ralph Jordan (Born 9-25-1910 Selma, Ala.; Died 7-17-1980)
Auburn 1932 (√25: 176-83-6 .675)
Auburn 1951-75 (√176-83-6)

39\. 174 Pappy Waldorf (Born 10-3-1902 Clifton Springs, N.Y.; Died 8-15-1981)
Syracuse 1925 (31: 174-100-22 .625)
Oklahoma City 1925-27 (17-11-3); Oklahoma St. 29-33 (34-10-7); Kansas St. 34 (7-2-1); Northwestern 35-46 (49-45-7); California 47-56 (67-32-4)

40. 173 Bob Neyland (Born 2-17-1892 Greenville, Texas; Died 3-28-1962)
Army 1916 (21: 173-31-12 .829)
Tennessee 1926-34, 36-40, 46-52 (173-31-12)

41. 172 Dan Devine (Born 12-23-1924 Augusta, Wis.; Died 5-9-2002)
Minn. Duluth 1948 (22: 172-57-9 .742)
Arizona St. 1955-57 (27-3-1); Missouri 58-70 (92-38-7);
Notre Dame 75-80 (53-16-1)

42. 171 Wallace Wade (Born 6-15-1892 Trenton, Tenn.; Died 10-7-1986)
Brown 1917 (24: 171-49-10 .765)
Alabama 1923-30 (61-13-3); Duke 31-41, 46-50 (110-36-7)

43. 170 Ara Parseghian (Born 5-21-1923 Akron, Ohio)
Miami (Ohio) 1949 (24: 170-58-6 .739)
Miami (Ohio) 1951-55 (39-6-1); Northwestern 56-63 (36-35-1);
Notre Dame 64-74 (95-17-4)

170 Grant Teaff (Born 11-12-1933 Hermleigh, Texas)
McMurry 1956 (30: 170-151-8 .529)
McMurry 1960-65 (23-35-2); Angelo St. 69-71 (19-11-0); Baylor 72-92 (128-105-6)

√ *Includes games forfeited, team and/or individual statistics abrogated, and coaching records changed by action of the NCAA Committee on Infractions.*

Best Career Starts by Wins

(Head coaches with at least half their seasons at a major college at the time and minimum five years coached)

1 SEASON

Coach, Team	Season	W	L	T	Pct.
George Woodruff, Penn	1892	15	1	0	.938
Walter Camp, Yale	1888	13	0	0	1.000
Larry Coker, Miami (Fla.)	2001	12	0	0	1.000
Bill Battle, Tennessee	1970	11	1	0	.917
Gary Blackney, Bowling Green	1991	11	1	0	.917
John Robinson, Southern California	1976	11	1	0	.917
Dick Crum, Miami (Ohio)	1974	10	0	1	.955
Barry Switzer, Oklahoma	1973	10	0	1	.955
Chuck Fairbanks, Oklahoma	1967	10	1	0	.909
Larry Siemering, Pacific	1947	10	1	0	.909
Dwight Wallace, Ball St.	1978	10	1	0	.909
Mike Archer, LSU	1987	10	1	1	.875

5 SEASONS

Coach, Team	Seasons	W	L	T	Pct.
Walter Camp, Yale, Stanford	1888-92	69	2	2	.959
George Woodruff, Penn	1892-96	67	5	0	.931
Bob Pruett, Marshall	1996-2000	58	9	0	.866
*Bob Stoops, Oklahoma	1999-2003	55	11	0	.833
*Pete Carroll, Southern California	2001-05	54	10	0	.844
Larry Coker, Miami (Fla.)	2001-05	53	9	0	.855
*Mark Richt, Georgia	2001-05	52	13	0	.800
Barry Switzer, Oklahoma	1973-77	51	5	2	.896
John Robinson, Southern California	1976-80	50	8	2	.850
R.C. Slocum, Texas A&M	1989-93	49	12	1	.798
*Lloyd Carr, Michigan	1995-99	49	13	0	.790
*Frank Solich, Nebraska	1998-2002	49	16	0	.754

10 SEASONS

Coach, Team	Seasons	W	L	T	Pct.
George Woodruff, Penn	1892-1901	124	15	2	.887
*Paul Johnson, Ga. Southern, Navy	1997-2006	99	35	0	.739
Barry Switzer, Oklahoma	1973-82	98	17	3	.843
Tom Osborne, Nebraska	1973-82	96	24	2	.795
*Phillip Fulmer, Tennessee	1992-2001	95	20	0	.826
*Lloyd Carr, Michigan	1995-2004	95	28	0	.772
Amos Alonzo Stagg, Springfield, Chicago	1890-99	95	34	9	.721
Bud Wilkinson, Oklahoma	1947-56	94	8	3	.910
*Joe Paterno, Penn St.	1966-75	94	18	1	.836
R.C. Slocum, Texas A&M	1989-98	94	28	2	.766
*Dan Hawkins, Willamette, Boise St.	1993-97, 2001-05	93	22	1	.806
*Steve Spurrier, Duke, Florida	1987-96	93	27	2	.770

15 SEASONS

Coach, Team(s)	Seasons	W	L	T	Pct.
Barry Switzer, Oklahoma	1973-87	148	26	4	.843
Tom Osborne, Nebraska	1973-87	147	34	2	.809
*Steve Spurrier, Duke, Florida	1987-2001	142	40	2	.777
*Joe Paterno, Penn St.	1966-80	141	31	1	.818
LaVell Edwards, Brigham Young	1972-86	137	45	1	.751
*Phil Fulmer, Tennessee	1992-2006	137	41	0	.770
Amos Alonzo Stagg, Springfield, Chicago	1890-1904	136	48	14	.722
Dennis Erickson, Idaho, Wyoming, Washington St., Miami (Fla.), Oregon St.	1982-94, 99-2000	131	46	1	.739
Bud Wilkinson, Oklahoma	1947-61	129	24	4	.834
Bob Neyland, Tennessee	1926-34, 36-40, 46	128	16	8	.868
Bob Devaney, Wyoming, Nebraska	1957-71	127	28	6	.807
Bill Snyder, Kansas St.	1989-2003	127	55	1	.697

20 SEASONS

Coach, Team(s)	Seasons	W	L	T	Pct.
Tom Osborne, Nebraska	1973-92	195	46	3	.805
*Joe Paterno, Penn St.	1966-85	187	44	2	.807
LaVell Edwards, Brigham Young	1972-91	183	62	3	.744
Bo Schembechler, Miami (Ohio), Michigan	1963-82	171	45	6	.784
Bob Neyland, Tennessee	1926-34, 36-40, 46-51	165	29	11	.832
Frank Kush, Arizona St.	1958-77	164	49	1	.769
Amos Alonzo Stagg, Springfield, Chicago	1890-1909	163	51	18	.741
Darrell Royal, Mississippi St., Washington, Texas	1954-73	161	49	4	.762
Vince Dooley, Georgia	1964-83	161	60	7	.721
Johnny Vaught, Mississippi	1947-66	157	44	10	.768
Pop Warner, Georgia, Cornell, Carlisle	1895-1914	157	59	11	.716
John Cooper, Tulsa, Arizona St., Ohio St.	1977-96	157	70	6	.687

25 SEASONS

Coach, Team(s)	Seasons	W	L	T	Pct.
Tom Osborne, Nebraska	1973-97	255	49	3	.836
*Joe Paterno, Penn St.	1966-90	229	60	3	.789
LaVell Edwards, Brigham Young	1972-96	228	81	3	.736
Bo Schembechler, Miami (Ohio), Michigan	1963-87	215	61	7	.772
*Bobby Bowden, Samford, West Virginia, Florida St.	1959-62, 70-90	205	74	3	.732
Vince Dooley, Georgia	1964-88	201	77	10	.715
Lou Holtz, William & Mary, North Carolina St., Arkansas, Minnesota, Notre Dame	1969-94	199	89	7	.686
Bear Bryant, Maryland, Kentucky, Texas A&M, Alabama	1945-69	193	61	15	.745
Pop Warner, Georgia, Cornell, Carlisle, Pittsburgh	1895-1919	193	62	12	.745
Johnny Vaught, Mississippi	1947-70, 73	190	61	12	.745

30 SEASONS

Coach, Team(s)	Seasons	W	L	T	Pct.
*Joe Paterno, Penn St.	1966-95	278	72	3	.792
*Bobby Bowden, Samford, West Virginia, Florida St.	1959-62, 70-95	259	81	4	.759
Bear Bryant, Maryland, Kentucky, Texas A&M, Alabama	1945-74	242	71	16	.760
Lou Holtz, William & Mary, North Carolina St., Arkansas, Minnesota, Notre Dame, South Carolina	1969-96, 99-2001	233	113	7	.670
Pop Warner, Georgia, Cornell, Carlisle, Pittsburgh, Stanford	1895-1924	224	72	16	.744
Woody Hayes, Denison, Miami (Ohio), Ohio St.	1946-75	213	63	8	.764
Amos Alonzo Stagg, Springfield, Chicago	1890-1919	204	76	20	.713
Dan McGugin, Vanderbilt	1904-17, 19-34	197	55	19	.762
Warren Woodson, Central Ark., Hardin-Simmons, Arizona, New Mexico St., Trinity (Tex.)	1935-42, 46-56, 58-67, 72	195	92	14	.671
Hayden Fry, SMU, North Texas, Iowa	1962-91	189	140	9	.572

35 SEASONS

Coach, Team(s)	Seasons	W	L	T	Pct.
*Joe Paterno, Penn St.	1966-2000	322	90	3	.780
*Bobby Bowden, Samford, West Virginia, Florida St.	1959-62, 70-2000	315	87	4	.781
Bear Bryant, Maryland, Kentucky, Texas A&M, Alabama	1945-79	296	77	16	.781
Pop Warner, Georgia, Cornell, Carlisle, Pittsburgh, Stanford	1895-1929	266	81	19	.753
Amos Alonzo Stagg, Springfield, Chicago	1890-1924	230	84	23	.717
Hayden Fry, SMU, North Texas, Iowa	1962-96	222	165	10	.572
John Heisman, Oberlin, Akron, Auburn, Clemson, Georgia Tech, Penn, Wash. & Jeff., Rice	1892-1926	183	64	16	.726

40 SEASONS

Coach, Team(s)	Seasons	W	L	T	Pct.
*Bobby Bowden, Samford, West Virginia, Florida St.	1959-62, 70-2005	359	107	4	.768
*Joe Paterno, Penn St.	1966-2005	354	117	3	.750
Pop Warner, Georgia, Cornell, Carlisle, Pittsburgh, Stanford, Temple	1895-1934	300	92	25	.749

Coach, Team(s)	Seasons	W	L	T	Pct.
Amos Alonzo Stagg, Springfield, Chicago	1890-1929	248	108	24	.684
Jess Neely, Rhodes, Clemson, Rice	1924-27, 31-66	207	176	19	.539

41 SEASONS

Coach, Team(s)	Seasons	W	L	T	Pct.
*Bobby Bowden, Samford, West Virginia, Florida St.	1959-62, 70-2006	366	113	4	.762
*Joe Paterno, Penn St.	1966-2006	363	121	3	.748
Pop Warner, Georgia, Cornell, Carlisle, Pittsburgh, Stanford, Temple	1895-1935	307	95	25	.748
Amos Alonzo Stagg, Springfield, Chicago	1890-1930	249	113	26	.675

42 SEASONS

Coach, Team(s)	Seasons	W	L	T	Pct.
Pop Warner, Georgia, Cornell, Carlisle, Pittsburgh, Stanford, Temple	1895-1936	313	98	27	.745
Amos Alonzo Stagg, Springfield, Chicago	1890-1931	251	118	27	.668

43 SEASONS

Coach, Team(s)	Seasons	W	L	T	Pct.
Pop Warner, Georgia, Cornell, Carlisle, Pittsburgh, Stanford, Temple	1895-1937	316	100	31	.742
Amos Alonzo Stagg, Springfield, Chicago	1890-1932	254	122	28	.663

44 SEASONS

Coach, Team(s)	Seasons	W	L	T	Pct.
Pop Warner, Georgia, Cornell, Carlisle, Pittsburgh, Stanford, Temple	1895-1938	319	106	32	.733
Amos Alonzo Stagg, Springfield, Chicago, Pacific	1890-1933	259	127	28	.659

**Active coach.*

Best Career Starts by Percentage

(Head coaches with at least half their seasons at a major college at the time and minimum five years coached)

1 SEASON

Coach, Team	Season	W	L	T	Pct.
Larry Coker, Miami (Fla.)	2001	12	0	0	1.000
Dan McGugin, Vanderbilt	1904	9	0	0	1.000
Bennie Oosterbaan, Michigan	1948	9	0	0	1.000
Carroll Widdoes, Ohio St.	1944	9	0	0	1.000
Galen Hall, Florida	1984	8	0	0	1.000
William Dietz, Washington St.	1915	7	0	0	1.000
John Heisman, Oberlin	1892	7	0	0	1.000
Dick Crum, Miami (Ohio)	1974	10	0	1	.955
Barry Switzer, Oklahoma	1973	10	0	1	.955
Aldo Donelli, Duquesne	1939	8	0	1	.944
Francis Schmidt, Tulsa	1919	8	0	1	.944

5 SEASONS

Coach, Team(s)	Seasons	W	L	T	Pct.
Gil Dobie, North Dakota St., Washington	1906-10	26	0	1	.981
Walter Camp, Yale, Stanford	1888-92	69	2	2	.959
George Woodruff, Penn	1892-96	67	5	0	.931
Bob Neyland, Tennessee	1926-30	43	2	3	.927
Knute Rockne, Notre Dame	1918-22	39	3	3	.900
Barry Switzer, Oklahoma	1973-77	51	5	2	.896
Elmer Henderson, Southern California	1919-23	36	5	0	.878
Bud Wilkinson, Oklahoma	1947-51	46	6	1	.877
Henry Williams, Army, Minnesota	1891, 1900-03	47	4	6	.877
Frank Leahy, Boston College, Notre Dame	1939-43	44	5	3	.875

10 SEASONS

Coach, Team(s)	Seasons	W	L	T	Pct.
Gil Dobie, North Dakota St., Washington	1906-15	59	0	2	.984
Bud Wilkinson, Oklahoma	1947-56	94	8	3	.910
Fielding Yost, Ohio Wesleyan, Nebraska, Kansas, Stanford, Michigan	1897-1906	90	9	3	.897
Knute Rockne, Notre Dame	1918-27	81	8	5	.888
George Woodruff, Penn	1892-1901	124	15	2	.887
Percy Haughton, Cornell, Harvard	1899-1900, 08-15	81	9	5	.879
Frank Leahy, Boston College, Notre Dame	1939-43, 46-50	84	9	6	.879
Bob Neyland, Tennessee	1926-34, 36	82	9	7	.872
Henry Williams, Army, Minnesota	1891, 1900-08	79	10	8	.856
Barry Switzer, Oklahoma	1973-82	98	17	3	.843

15 SEASONS

Coach, Team(s)	Seasons	W	L	T	Pct.
Gil Dobie, North Dakota St., Washington, Navy, Cornell	1906-20	88	5	3	.932
Bob Neyland, Tennessee	1926-34, 36-40, 46	128	16	8	.868
Fielding Yost, Ohio Wesleyan, Nebraska, Kansas, Stanford, Michigan	1897-1911	114	14	9	.858
Barry Switzer, Oklahoma	1973-87	148	26	4	.843
Henry Williams, Army, Minnesota	1891, 1900-13	106	17	9	.837
Bud Wilkinson, Oklahoma	1947-61	129	24	4	.834
Fred Folsom, Colorado, Dartmouth	1895-99, 1901-06, 08-11	89	17	5	.824
*Joe Paterno, Penn St.	1966-80	141	31	1	.818
Elmer Henderson, Southern California, Tulsa	1919-33	107	24	3	.810
Tom Osborne, Nebraska	1973-87	147	34	2	.809

20 SEASONS

Coach, Team(s)	Seasons	W	L	T	Pct.
Gil Dobie, North Dakota St., Washington, Navy, Cornell	1906-25	122	11	3	.908
Henry Williams, Army, Minnesota	1891, 1900-18	133	22	11	.834
Bob Neyland, Tennessee	1926-34, 36-40, 46-51	165	29	11	.832
Fielding Yost, Ohio Wesleyan, Nebraska, Kansas, Stanford, Michigan	1897-1916	142	25	10	.831
Jock Sutherland, Lafayette, Pittsburgh	1919-38	144	28	14	.812
*Joe Paterno, Penn St.	1966-85	187	44	2	.807
Tom Osborne, Nebraska	1973-92	195	46	3	.805
Wallace Wade, Alabama, Duke	1923-41, 46	150	37	6	.793
Bo Schembechler, Miami (Ohio), Michigan	1963-82	171	45	6	.784
Dan McGugin, Vanderbilt	1904-17, 19-24	131	33	12	.778

25 SEASONS

Coach, Team(s)	Seasons	W	L	T	Pct.
Gil Dobie, North Dakota St., Washington, Navy, Cornell	1906-30	146	22	8	.852
Tom Osborne, Nebraska	1973-97	255	49	3	.836
Fielding Yost, Ohio Wesleyan, Nebraska, Kansas, Stanford, Michigan	1897-1921	168	34	11	.815
*Joe Paterno, Penn St.	1966-90	229	60	3	.789
Dan McGugin, Vanderbilt	1904-17, 19-29	168	42	14	.781
Bo Schembechler, Miami (Ohio), Michigan	1963-87	215	61	7	.772
Red Blaik, Dartmouth, Army	1934-58	166	48	14	.759
John Heisman, Oberlin, Akron, Auburn, Clemson, Georgia Tech	1892-1916	127	37	11	.757
Howard Jones, Syracuse, Yale, Ohio St., Iowa, Duke, Southern California	1908-10, 13, 16-36	170	54	15	.755
Woody Hayes, Denison, Miami (Ohio), Ohio St.	1946-70	167	54	7	.748

30 SEASONS

Coach, Team(s)	Seasons	W	L	T	Pct.
Gil Dobie, North Dakota St., Washington, Navy, Cornell	1906-35	164	39	10	.793
*Joe Paterno, Penn St.	1966-95	278	72	3	.792
Woody Hayes, Denison, Miami (Ohio), Ohio St.	1946-75	213	63	8	.764
Dan McGugin, Vanderbilt	1904-17, 19-34	197	55	19	.762
Bear Bryant, Maryland, Kentucky, Texas A&M, Alabama	1945-74	242	71	16	.760
*Bobby Bowden, Samford, West Virginia, Florida St.	1959-62, 70-95	259	81	4	.759
John Heisman, Oberlin, Akron, Auburn, Clemson, Georgia Tech, Penn	1892-1921	159	48	13	.752
Pop Warner, Georgia, Cornell, Carlisle, Pittsburgh, Stanford	1895-1924	224	72	16	.744
Amos Alonzo Stagg, Springfield, Chicago	1890-1919	204	76	20	.713
Dana X. Bible, Mississippi Col., LSU, Texas A&M, Nebraska, Texas	1913-17, 19-43	175	67	23	.704

35 SEASONS

Coach, Team(s)	Seasons	W	L	T	Pct.
*Bobby Bowden, Samford, West Virginia, Florida St.	1959-62, 70-2000	315	87	4	.781
Bear Bryant, Maryland, Kentucky, Texas A&M, Alabama	1945-79	296	77	16	.781
*Joe Paterno, Penn St.	1966-2000	322	90	3	.780
Pop Warner, Georgia, Cornell, Carlisle, Pittsburgh, Stanford	1895-1929	266	81	19	.753
John Heisman, Oberlin, Akron, Auburn, Clemson, Georgia Tech, Penn, Wash. & Jeff., Rice	1892-1926	183	64	16	.726
Amos Alonzo Stagg, Springfield, Chicago	1890-1924	230	84	23	.717
Hayden Fry, SMU, North Texas, Iowa	1962-96	222	165	10	.572

40 SEASONS

Coach, Team(s)	Seasons	W	L	T	Pct.
*Bobby Bowden, Samford, West Virginia, Florida St.	1959-62, 70-2005	359	107	4	.768
*Joe Paterno, Penn St.	1966-2005	354	117	3	.750
Pop Warner, Georgia, Cornell, Carlisle, Pittsburgh, Stanford, Temple	1895-1934	300	92	25	.749
Amos Alonzo Stagg, Springfield, Chicago	1890-1929	248	108	24	.684
Jess Neely, Rhodes, Clemson, Rice	1924-27, 31-66	207	176	19	.539

41 SEASONS

Coach, Team(s)	Seasons	W	L	T	Pct.
*Bobby Bowden, Samford, West Virginia, Florida St.	1959-62, 70-2006	366	113	4	.762
*Joe Paterno, Penn St.	1966-2006	363	121	3	.748
Pop Warner, Georgia, Cornell, Carlisle, Pittsburgh, Stanford, Temple	1895-1935	307	95	25	.748
Amos Alonzo Stagg, Springfield, Chicago	1890-1930	249	113	26	.675

42 SEASONS

Coach, Team(s)	Seasons	W	L	T	Pct.
Pop Warner, Georgia, Cornell, Carlisle, Pittsburgh, Stanford, Temple	1895-1936	313	98	27	.745
Amos Alonzo Stagg, Springfield, Chicago	1890-1931	251	118	27	.668

43 SEASONS

Coach, Team(s)	Seasons	W	L	T	Pct.
Pop Warner, Georgia, Cornell, Carlisle, Pittsburgh, Stanford, Temple	1895-1937	316	100	31	.742
Amos Alonzo Stagg, Springfield, Chicago	1890-1932	254	122	28	.663

44 SEASONS

Coach, Team(s)	Seasons	W	L	T	Pct.
Pop Warner, Georgia, Cornell, Carlisle, Pittsburgh, Stanford, Temple	1895-1938	319	106	32	.733
Amos Alonzo Stagg, Springfield, Chicago, Pacific	1890-1933	259	127	28	.659

*Active coach.

Coaches to Reach 200 and 300 Victories

(Must have five years or 50 victories at a school that was classified as a major college at the time)

200 VICTORIES

	WHEN MILESTONE REACHED		
Coach (Date Reached Milestone)	Age in Yrs.-Days	Career Game (Record)	Career Yr.-Game
Eddie Anderson (11-14-1964)	64-1	342nd (200-127-15)	39-8
*Bobby Bowden (10-27-1990)	60-353	279th (200-76-3)	25-7
Bear Bryant (9-10-1971)	57-364	282nd (200-66-16)	27-1
Vince Dooley (11-26-1988)	56-84	286th (200-76-10)	25-11
LaVell Edwards (9-24-1994)	64-348	277th (200-74-3)	23-4
Hayden Fry (11-20-1993)	64-265	361st (200-152-9)	32-11
Woody Hayes (11-2-1974)	61-261	268th (200-60-8)	29-8
Lou Holtz (9-9-1995)	58-243	297th (200-90-7)	26-2
Jess Neely (9-26-1964)	66-265	373rd (200-155-18)	38-1
Don Nehlen (11-11-2000)	64-314	355th (200-127-8)	30-9
Tom Osborne (10-7-1993)	56-224	249th (200-46-3)	21-5
*Joe Paterno (9-5-1987)	60-258	246th (200-44-2)	22-1
Bo Schembechler (10-4-1986)	57-33	262nd (200-55-7)	24-4
Amos Alonzo Stagg (10-11-1919)	57-56	294th (200-74-20)	30-1
Jim Sweeney (11-2-1996)	67-62	355th (200-151-4)	32-8
Pop Warner (9-24-1921)	50-172	276th (200-62-14)	28-1
Warren Woodson (10-13-1973)	70-231	307th (200-93-14)	31-6

*Active coach.

300 VICTORIES

	WHEN MILESTONE REACHED		
Coach (Date Reached Milestone)	Age in Yrs.-Days	Career Game (Record)	Career Yr.-Game
*Joe Paterno (9-12-1998)	71-266	380th (300-77-3)	32-2
*Bobby Bowden (10-23-1999)	69-349	389th (300-85-4)	34-8
Bear Bryant (10-3-1980)	67-22	393rd (300-77-16)	36-4
Amos Alonzo Stagg (11-6-1943)	81-82	507th (300-173-34)	54-7
Pop Warner (11-24-1934)	63-233	415th (300-91-24)	41-8

*Active coach.

EDDIE ROBINSON
A Coach For The Ages

Because Grambling is not an FBS member, most football historians agree that Grambling's Eddie Robinson not be listed in the major college coaches' section. But there is no denying that the Tigers' former head coach belongs in any mention of great collegiate coaches.

Robinson, who retired after the 1997 season and died April 3, 2007, compiled one of the most impressive coaching legacies in collegiate history. He is one of only two college football coaches (see John Gagliardi on the next page) with more than 400 victories (408) and he coached in more games (588) than any other coach in the 135 years of college football.

Robinson spent all 55 seasons of his illustrious career at Grambling (he coached two years during World War II at Grambling High School).

Here is a breakdown of the milestone victories in his career:

Victory No.	(Date Reached Milestone)	Age in Yrs.-Days	Career Game (Record)	Career Yr.-Game
100th	(11-9-1957)	38-270	146th (100-39-7)	15-6
200th	(10-16-1971)	52-246	285th (200-74-11)	29-6
300th	(9-25-1982)	63-225	411th (300-98-13)	40-3
400th	(10-7-1995)	76-237	560th (400-145-15)	53-5

COACHING RECORDS

JOHN GAGLIARDI
A Coach For The Ages

John Gagliardi is probably not as well known as Eddie Robinson, but his accomplishments are no less remarkable. Both coaches are known as great teachers, men whose lives touched many young college student-athletes and molded them into responsible adults.

Gagliardi became the winningest coach in college football history in 2003 by passing Robinson and heads into this season with 443 career wins.

Fifty-four of Gagliardi's seasons have been at St. John's University in Collegeville, Minnesota. Gagliardi's biggest strength is his ability to relate to his players and get them to play hard even though they receive no scholarships based on athletics ability. In fact, his basic philosophy is boiled down to "Winning With Nos." That is:

* No spring practices;
* No scholarships;
* No compulsory weightlifting program;
* No calling him "coach"— players call him John;
* No long practices — an hour and a half or less; and
* No tackling in practice — players wear shorts or sweats.

Gagliardi began his remarkable career in 1949 at Carroll College (Montana), where he coached for four seasons before assuming the St. John's head position in 1953. He is now coaching in his seventh decade and seems fit enough to continue well into the new century. He passed the legendary Amos Alonzo Stagg in coaching longevity at 58 years last season.

His career includes 28 Minnesota Intercollegiate Athletic Conference titles and four national championships (1963, 1965, 1976 and 2003).

Victory No.	(Date Reached Milestone)	Age in Yrs.-Days	Career Game (Record)	Career Yr.-Game
100th	(10-9-1965)	38-343	135th (100-32-3)	17-5
200th	(10-11-1980)	53-345	274th (200-67-7)	32-5
300th	(10-16-1993)	66-350	405th (300-95-10)	45-6
400th	(12-7-2002)	76-38	524th (400-113-11)	54-13

Other Coaching Milestones

(Must have five years or 50 victories at a school that was classified as a major college at the time)

YOUNGEST COACHES TO REACH 100 VICTORIES

Coach	Age in Yrs.-Days
George Woodruff	35-261
Elmer Layden	37-175
Fielding Yost	37-191
Pop Warner	37-235
Amos Alonzo Stagg	38-51
Don Faurot	39-131
Matty Bell	39-256
Dana X. Bible	40-44
Andy Smith	40-71
Bennie Owen	40-72
Dan McGugin	40-78
Hugo Bezdek	40-120
Terry Bowden	40-280

YOUNGEST COACHES TO REACH 200 VICTORIES

Coach	Age in Yrs.-Days
Pop Warner	50-172
Vince Dooley	56-84
Tom Osborne	56-224
Bo Schembechler	57-33
Amos Alonzo Stagg	57-56
Bear Bryant	57-364
Lou Holtz	58-243

YOUNGEST COACHES TO REACH 300 VICTORIES

Coach	Age in Yrs.-Days
Pop Warner	63-233
Bear Bryant	67-22
*Bobby Bowden	69-349
*Joe Paterno	71-266
Amos Alonzo Stagg	81-82

**Active coach.*

FEWEST GAMES TO REACH 100 VICTORIES

Coach	Career Game (Record at Time)
Gil Dobie	108 (100-5-3)
George Woodruff	109 (100-9-0)
Bud Wilkinson	111 (100-8-3)
Fielding Yost	114 (100-10-4)
Knute Rockne	117 (100-12-5)
Bob Neyland	120 (100-12-8)
Frank Leahy	121 (100-13-8)
*Joe Paterno	122 (100-21-1)
Barry Switzer	122 (100-18-4)
Henry Williams	122 (100-13-9)
*Phillip Fulmer	123 (100-23-0)
Fred Folsom	126 (100-20-6)
Gus Henderson	126 (100-23-3)
Tom Osborne	126 (100-24-2)
Frank Thomas	128 (100-21-7)
Wallace Wade	129 (100-24-5)
Bo Schembechler	130 (100-24-6)
Bobby Dodd	131 (100-28-3)
*Steve Spurrier	131 (100-29-2)
Frank Kush	131 (100-30-1)
Charley Moran	131 (100-24-7)
*Lloyd Carr	132 (100-32-0)
Dan McGugin	132 (100-25-7)
R.C. Slocum	132 (100-30-2)
Jock Sutherland	132 (100-22-10)

**Active coach.*

FEWEST GAMES TO REACH 200 VICTORIES

Coach	Career Game (Record at Time)
*Joe Paterno	246 (200-44-2)
Tom Osborne	249 (200-46-3)
Bo Schembechler	262 (200-55-7)
Woody Hayes	268 (200-60-8)
Pop Warner	276 (200-62-14)
LaVell Edwards	277 (200-74-3)
*Bobby Bowden	279 (200-76-3)
Bear Bryant	282 (200-66-16)
Vince Dooley	286 (200-76-10)
Amos Alonzo Stagg	294 (200-74-20)

**Active coach.*

FEWEST GAMES TO REACH 300 VICTORIES

Coach	Career Game (Record at Time)
*Joe Paterno	380 (300-77-3)
*Bobby Bowden	389 (300-85-4)
Bear Bryant	393 (300-77-16)
Pop Warner	415 (300-91-24)
Amos Alonzo Stagg	507 (300-173-34)

*Active coach.

All-Time Division I Coaching Longevity Records

(Minimum 10 Head-Coaching Seasons in Division I; Bowl Games Included)

MOST GAMES

Games	Coach, School(s) and Years
548	Amos Alonzo Stagg, Springfield 1890-91, Chicago 92-1932, Pacific 33-46
487	*Joe Paterno, Penn St. 1966-2006
483	*Bobby Bowden, Samford 1959-62, West Virginia 70-75, Florida St. 76-2006
457	Pop Warner, Georgia 1895-96, Cornell 97-98 & 1904-06, Carlisle 1899-1903 & 07-14, Pittsburgh 15-23, Stanford 24-32, Temple 33-38
425	Bear Bryant, Maryland 1945, Kentucky 46-53, Texas A&M 54-57, Alabama 58-82
420	Hayden Fry, SMU 1962-72, North Texas 73-78, Iowa 79-98
402	Jess Neely, Rhodes 1924-27, Clemson 31-39, Rice 40-66
388	Lou Holtz, William & Mary 1969-71, North Carolina St. 72-75, Arkansas 77-83, Minnesota 84-85, Notre Dame 86-96, South Carolina 99-2004
361	LaVell Edwards, Brigham Young 1972-2000
358	Jim Sweeney, Montana St. 1963-67, Washington St. 68-75, Fresno St. 76-77 & 80-96
344	Eddie Anderson, Loras 1922-24, DePaul 25-31, Holy Cross 33-38 & 50-64, Iowa 39-42 & 46-49
338	Don Nehlen, Bowling Green 1968-76, West Virginia 80-2000
332	Johnny Majors, Iowa St. 1968-72, Pittsburgh 73-76 & 93-96, Tennessee 77-92
329	Grant Teaff, McMurry 1960-65, Angelo St. 69-71, Baylor 72-92
325	George Welsh, Navy 1973-81, Virginia 82-2000
320	Woody Hayes, Denison 1946-48, Miami (Ohio) 49-50, Ohio St. 51-78
318	Ray Morrison, SMU 1915-16 & 22-34, Vanderbilt 18 & 35-39, Temple 40-48, Austin 49-52
312	Ken Hatfield, Air Force 1979-83, Arkansas 84-89, Clemson 90-93, Rice 94-2005
312	Warren Woodson, Central Ark. 1935-39, Hardin-Simmons 41-42 & 46-51, Arizona 52-56, New Mexico St. 58-67, Trinity (Tex.) 72-73
309	Jerry Claiborne, Virginia Tech 1961-70, Maryland 72-81, Kentucky 82-89
307	*Frank Beamer, Murray St. 1981-86, Virginia Tech 87-2006
307	Tom Osborne, Nebraska 1973-97
307	Bo Schembechler, Miami (Ohio) 1963-68, Michigan 69-89
304	Jackie Sherrill, Washington St. 1976, Pittsburgh 77-81, Texas A&M 82-88, Mississippi St. 91-2003
301	Bill Mallory, Miami (Ohio) 1969-73, Colorado 74-78, Northern Ill. 80-83, Indiana 84-96
299	Ossie Solem, Luther 1920, Drake 21-31, Iowa 32-36, Syracuse 37-42 & 44-45, Springfield 46-57
299	*Dick Tomey, Hawaii 1977-86, Arizona 87-2000, San Jose St. 05-06

*Active coach.

MOST YEARS

Years	Coach, School(s) and Years
57	Amos Alonzo Stagg, Springfield 1890-91, Chicago 92-1932, Pacific 33-46
44	Pop Warner, Georgia 1895-96, Cornell 97-98 & 1904-06, Carlisle 99-1903 & 07-14, Pittsburgh 15-23, Stanford 24-32, Temple 33-38
41	*Bobby Bowden, Samford 1959-62, West Virginia 70-75, Florida St. 76-2006
41	*Joe Paterno, Penn St. 1966-2006
40	Jess Neely, Rhodes 1924-27, Clemson 31-39, Rice 40-66
39	Eddie Anderson, Loras 1922-24, DePaul 25-31, Holy Cross 33-38 & 50-54, Iowa 39-42 & 46-49
38	Bear Bryant, Maryland 1945, Kentucky 46-53, Texas A&M 54-57, Alabama 58-82
37	Hayden Fry, SMU 1962-72, North Texas 73-78, Iowa 79-98
37	Ossie Solem, Luther 1920, Drake 21-31, Iowa 32-36, Syracuse 37-45, Springfield 46-57
36	John Heisman, Oberlin 1892 & 94, Akron 93, Auburn 95-99, Clemson 1900-03, Georgia Tech 04-19, Penn 20-22, Wash. & Jeff. 23, Rice 24-27
34	Tuss McLaughry, Westminster (Pa.) 1916, 18 & 21, Amherst 22-25, Brown 26-40, Dartmouth 41-54
34	Ray Morrison, SMU 1915-16 & 22-34, Vanderbilt 18 & 35-39, Temple 40-48, Austin 49-52
33	Dana X. Bible, Mississippi Col. 1913-15, LSU 16, Texas A&M 17 & 19-28, Nebraska 29-36, Texas 37-46
33	Gil Dobie, North Dakota St. 1906-07, Washington 08-16, Navy 17-19, Cornell 20-35, Boston College 36-38
33	Woody Hayes, Denison 1946-48, Miami (Ohio) 49-50, Ohio St. 51-78
33	Lou Holtz, William & Mary 1969-71, North Carolina St. 72-75, Arkansas 77-83, Minnesota 84-85, Notre Dame 86-96, South Carolina 99-2004
33	Lou Little, Georgetown 1924-29, Columbia 30-56
32	Clark Shaughnessy, Tulane 1915-20 & 22-26, Loyola (Ill.) 27-32, Chicago 33-39, Stanford 40-41, Maryland 42 & 46, Pittsburgh 43-45, Hawaii 65
32	Carl Snavely, Bucknell 1927-33, North Carolina 34-35 & 45-52, Cornell 36-44, Washington-St. Louis 53-58
32	William Spaulding, Western Mich. 1907-21, Minnesota 22-24, UCLA 25-38
32	Jim Sweeney, Montana St. 1963-67, Washington St. 68-75, Fresno St. 76-77 & 80-96
31	Pappy Waldorf, Oklahoma City 1925-27, Oklahoma St. 29-33, Kansas St. 34, Northwestern 35-46, California 47-56
31	Warren Woodson, Central Ark. 1935-39, Hardin-Simmons 41-42 & 46-51, Arizona 52-56, New Mexico St. 58-67, Trinity (Tex.) 72-73
30	Bob Blackman, Denver 1953-54, Dartmouth 55-70, Illinois 71-76, Cornell 77-82
30	Frank Dobson, Georgia 1909, Clemson 10-12, Richmond 13-17 & 19-33, South Carolina 18, Maryland 35-39
30	Harvey Harman, Haverford 1922-29, Sewanee 30, Penn 31-37, Rutgers 38-55
30	Frank Howard, Clemson 1940-69
30	Dan McGugin, Vanderbilt 1904-17 & 19-34
30	Grant Teaff, McMurry 1960-65, Angelo St. 69-71, Baylor 72-92

*Active coach.

MOST SCHOOLS

Schools	Coach, Schools and Years
8	John Heisman, Oberlin 1892 & 94, Akron 93, Auburn 95-99, Clemson 1900-03, Georgia Tech 04-19, Penn 20-22, Wash. & Jeff. 23, Rice 24-27
8	Lou Saban, Case Reserve 1950-52, Northwestern 55, Western Ill. 57-59, Maryland 66, Miami (Fla.) 77-78, Army 79, UCF 83-84, Chowan 2001-02
7	*Dennis Franchione, Southwestern (Kan.) 1981-82, Pittsburg St. 85-89, Texas St. 90-91, New Mexico 92-97, TCU 98-2000, Alabama 01-02, Texas A&M 03-06
7	Chuck Mills, Pomona-Pitzer 1959-61, Indiana (Pa.) 62-63, Merchant Marine 64, Utah St. 67-72, Wake Forest 73-77, Southern Ore. St. 80-88, Coast Guard 97
7	Darrell Mudra, Adams St. 1959-62, North Dakota St. 63-65, Arizona 67-68, Western Ill. 69-73, Florida St. 74-75, Eastern Ill. 78-82, UNI 83-87
7	Clark Shaughnessy, Tulane 1915-20 & 22-26, Loyola (Ill.) 27-32, Chicago 33-39, Stanford 40-41, Maryland 42 & 46, Pittsburgh 43-45, Hawaii 65
7	Clarence Spears, Dartmouth 1917-20, West Virginia 21-24, Minnesota 25-29, Oregon 30-31, Wisconsin 32-35, Toledo 36-42, Maryland 43-44
6	*Watson Brown, Austin Peay 1979-80, Cincinnati 83, Rice 84-85, Vanderbilt 86-90, UAB 95-2006, Tennessee Tech 2007
6	Frank Cavanaugh, Cincinnati 1898, Holy Cross 1903-05, Dartmouth 11-16, Boston College 19-26, Neb.-Omaha 19, Fordham 27-32
6	*Dennis Erickson, Idaho 1982-85 & 2006, Wyoming 86, Washington St. 87-88, Miami (Fla.) 89-94, Oregon St. 99-2002, Arizona St. 2007
6	Lou Holtz, William & Mary 1969-71, North Carolina St. 72-75, Arkansas 77-83, Minnesota 84-85, Notre Dame 86-96, South Carolina 99-2004
6	Howard Jones, Syracuse 1908, Yale 09 & 13, Ohio St. 10, Iowa 16-23, Duke 24, Southern California 25-40
6	Pop Warner, Georgia 1895-96, Cornell 97-98 & 1904-06, Carlisle 1899-1903 & 07-14, Pittsburgh 15-23, Stanford 24-32, Temple 33-38
5	Matty Bell, Haskell 1920-21, Carroll (Wis.) 22, TCU 23-28, Texas A&M 29-33, SMU 35-41 & 45-49
5	Dana X. Bible, Mississippi Col. 1913-15, LSU 16, Texas A&M 17 & 19-28, Nebraska 29-36, Texas 37-46
5	Earle Bruce, Tampa 1972, Iowa St. 73-78, Ohio St. 79-87, UNI 88, Colorado St. 89-92
5	Jack Curtice, West Tex. A&M 1940-41, UTEP 46-49, Utah 50-57, Stanford 58-61, UC Santa Barb. 62-69
5	Dudley DeGroot, UC Santa Barb. 1926-28, San Jose St. 32-39, Rochester 40-43, West Virginia 48-49, New Mexico 50-52
5	Gil Dobie, North Dakota St. 1906-07, Washington 08-16, Navy 17-19, Cornell 20-35, Boston College 36-38
5	Frank Dobson, Georgia 1909, Clemson 10-12, Richmond 13-17 & 19-33, South Carolina 18, Maryland 35-39
5	Ed Doherty, Arizona St. 1947-50, Rhode Island 51, Arizona 57-58, Xavier (Ohio) 59-61, Holy Cross 71-75
5	Red Drew, Trinity (Conn.) 1921-23, Birmingham So. 24-27, Chattanooga 29-30, Mississippi 46, Alabama 47-54
5	Stuart Holcomb, Findlay 1932-35, Muskingum 36-40, Wash. & Jeff. 41, Miami (Ohio) 42-43, Purdue 47-55
5	Al Molde, Sioux Falls 1971-72, Minn.-Morris 73-79, Central Mo. 80-82, Eastern Ill. 83-86, Western Mich. 87-96
5	Darryl Rogers, Cal St. East Bay 1965, Fresno St. 66-72, San Jose St. 73-75, Michigan St. 76-79, Arizona St. 80-84

Schools	Coach, Schools and Years
5	John Rowland, Henderson St. 1925-30, Ouachita Baptist 31, Citadel 40-42, Oklahoma City 46-47, George Washington 48-51
5	Francis Schmidt, Tulsa 1919-21, Arkansas 22-28, TCU 29-33, Ohio St. 34-40, Idaho 41-42
5	Clipper Smith, Gonzaga 1925-28, Santa Clara 29-35, Villanova 36-42, San Francisco 46, Lafayette 49-51
5	Ossie Solem, Luther 1920, Drake 21-31, Iowa 32-36, Syracuse 37-45, Springfield 46-57
5	Skip Stahley, Delaware 1934, Brown 41-43, George Washington 46-47, Toledo 48-49, Idaho 54-60
5	Jim Wacker, Texas Lutheran 1971-75, North Dakota St. 76-78, Texas St. 79-82, TCU 83-91, Minnesota 92-96
5	Pappy Waldorf, Oklahoma City 1925-27, Oklahoma St. 29-33, Kansas St. 34, Northwestern 35-46, California 47-56
5	Warren Woodson, Central Ark. 1935-39, Hardin-Simmons 41-42, Arizona 52-56, New Mexico St. 58-67, Trinity (Tex.) 72-73
5	Fielding Yost, Ohio Wesleyan 1897, Nebraska 98, Kansas 99, Stanford 1900, Michigan 01-23 & 25-26

**Active coach.*

MOST YEARS COACHED AT ONE COLLEGE

Coach, College (Years)	Years	School W-L-T	Overall W-L-T
*Joe Paterno, Penn St. (1966-2006)	41 #	363-121-3	363-121-3
Amos Alonzo Stagg, Chicago (1892-1932)	41	244-111-27	314-199-35
*Bobby Bowden, Florida St. (1976-2006)	31	293-81-4	366-113-4
Frank Howard, Clemson (1940-69)	30 #	165-118-12	165-118-12
Dan McGugin, Vanderbilt (1904-17, 19-34)	30 #	197-55-19	197-55-19
LaVell Edwards, Brigham Young (1972-2000)	29 #	257-101-3	257-101-3
Robert Zuppke, Illinois (1913-41)	29 #	131-81-13	131-81-13
Woody Hayes, Ohio St. (1951-78)	28	205-61-10	238-72-10
Lou Little, Columbia (1930-56)	27	110-116-10	151-128-13
Jess Neely, Rice (1940-66)	27	144-124-10	207-176-19
William Alexander, Georgia Tech (1920-44)	25 #	134-95-15	134-95-15
Ike Armstrong, Utah (1925-49)	25 #	140-55-15	140-55-15
Bear Bryant, Alabama (1958-82)	25	232-46-9	323-85-17
Vince Dooley, Georgia (1964-88)	25 #	201-77-10	201-77-10
Ralph Jordan, Auburn (1951-75)	25 #	176-83-6	176-83-6
Tom Osborne, Nebraska (1973-97)	25 #	255-49-3	255-49-3
Ben Schwartzwalder, Syracuse (1949-73)	25	153-91-3	178-96-3
John Vaught, Mississippi (1947-70, 73)	25 #	190-61-12	190-61-12
Bill Yeoman, Houston (1962-86)	25 #	160-108-8	160-108-8
Fielding Yost, Michigan (1901-23, 25-26)	25	165-29-10	196-36-12
Edward Robinson, Brown (1898-1901, 04-07, 10-25)	24	140-82-12	157-88-13
Frank Camp, Louisville (1946-68)	23 #	118-96-2	118-96-2
Fisher DeBerry, Air Force (1984-2006)	23 #	169-109-1	169-109-1
*Chris Ault, Nevada (1976-92, 94-95, 2004-06)	22 #	185-78-1	185-78-1
Wally Butts, Georgia (1939-60)	22 #	140-86-9	140-86-9
Bobby Dodd, Georgia Tech (1945-66)	22 #	165-64-8	165-64-8
Frank Kush, Arizona St. (1958-79)	22 #	176-54-1	176-54-1
Bennie Owen, Oklahoma (1905-26)	22	122-54-16	155-60-19
Henry Williams, Minnesota (1900-21)	22	140-33-11	141-34-12

**Active coach. #Never coached at any other college.*

Active Coaching Longevity Records

(Minimum Five Years as an FBS Head Coach; Includes Bowl Games)

MOST GAMES

Games	Coach, School(s) and Years
487	Joe Paterno, Penn St., 1966-2006
483	Bobby Bowden, Samford 1959-62, West Virginia 70-75, Florida St. 76-2006
307	Frank Beamer, Murray St. 1981-86, Virginia Tech 87-2006
299	Dick Tomey, Hawaii 1977-86, Arizona 87-2000, San Jose St. 05-06
287	Mike Price, Weber St. 1981-88, Washington St. 89-2002, UTEP 04-06

MOST YEARS

Years	Coach, School(s) and Years
41	Bobby Bowden, Samford 1959-62, West Virginia 70-75, Florida St. 76-2006
41	Joe Paterno, Penn St. 1966-2006
26	Frank Beamer, Murray St. 1981-86, Virginia Tech 87-2006
26	Dick Tomey, Hawaii 1977-86, Arizona 87-2000, San Jose St. 05-06
25	Mike Price, Weber St. 1981-88, Washington St. 89-2002, UTEP 04-06

MOST YEARS AT CURRENT SCHOOL

Years	Coach, School and Years
41	Joe Paterno, Penn St. 1966-2006
31	Bobby Bowden, Florida St. 1976-2006
22	Chris Ault, Nevada 1976-92, 94-95, 2004-06

MOST SCHOOLS

Schools	Coach, Schools and Years
7	Dennis Franchione, Southwestern (Kan.) 1981-82, Pittsburg St. 85-89, Texas St. 90-91, New Mexico 92-97, TCU 98-2000, Alabama 01-02, Texas A&M 03-06
6	Watson Brown, Austin Peay 1979-80, Cincinnati 83, Rice 84-85, Vanderbilt 86-90, UAB 95-2006, Tennessee Tech 2007
6	Dennis Erickson, Idaho 82-85 & 2006, Wyoming 86, Washington St. 87-88, Miami (Fla.) 89-94, Oregon St. 99-2002, Arizona St. 2007
5	Hal Mumme, Iowa Wesleyan 1989-91, Valdosta St. 92-96, Kentucky 97-2000, Southeastern La. 03-04, New Mexico St. 05-06
4	Mack Brown, Appalachian St. 1983, Tulane 85-87, North Carolina 88-97, Texas 98-2006
4	Bill Lynch, Butler 1985-89, Ball St. 95-2002, DePauw 04, Indiana 07
4	Howard Schnellenberger, Miami (Fla.) 1979-83, Louisville 85-94, Oklahoma 95, Fla. Atlantic 2001-06

Major-College Brother vs. Brother Coaching Matchups

(Thanks to Tex Noel of Bedford, Indiana)
(Each brother's victories in parentheses)

Mack Brown, Tulane (2), vs. Watson, Vanderbilt (0), 1986-87
Vince Dooley, Georgia (1), vs. Bill, North Carolina (0), 1971 Gator Bowl
Bump Elliott, Michigan (6), vs. Pete, Illinois (1), 1960-66
Howard Jones, Yale 1909 and Iowa 1922 (2), vs. Tad, Syracuse 1909 and Yale 1922 (0)
E. Lowell "Dick" Romney, Utah St. (3) vs. G. "Ott", Montana St. (0), 1922, 1925 and 1927

E. Lowell "Dick" Romney, Utah St. (5) vs. G. "Ott", Brigham Young (0), 1932-36
Pop Warner, Cornell (0) vs. Bill, Colgate (0) (tie), 1906

Annual FBS Head-Coaching Changes

Year	Changes	Teams	Pct.
1947	27	125	.216
1948	24	121	.198
1949	22	114	.193
1950	23	119	.193
1951	23	115	.200
1952	15	113	.133
1953	18	111	.162
1954	14	103	.136
1955	23	103	.223
1956	19	105	.181
1957	22	108	.204
1958	18	109	.165
1959	18	110	.164
1960	18	114	.158
1961	11	112	.098
1962	20	119	.168
1963	12	118	.102
1964	14	116	.121
1965	16	114	.140
1966	16	116	.138
1967	21	114	.184
1968	14	114	.123
1969	22	118	.186
1970	13	118	.110
1971	27	119	.227
1972	17	121	.140
1973	36	126	†.286
1974	28	128	.219
1975	18	134	.134
1976	23	137	.168
1977	27	144	.188
1978	27	139	.194

Year	Changes	Teams	Pct.
1979	26	139	.187
1980	27	139	.194
1981	17	137	.123
1982	17	97	.175
1983	22	105	.210
1984	16	105	.152
1985	15	105	.143
1986	22	105	.210
1987	24	104	.231
1988	9	104	.087
1989	19	106	.179
1990	20	106	.189
1991	16	106	.151
1992	16	107	.150
1993	15	106	.142
1994	15	107	.140
1995	21	108	.194
1996	9	111	*.081
1997	24	112	.214
1998	14	112	.125
1999	20	114	.175
2000	14	114	.123
2001	24	115	.209
2002	13	117	.111
2003	18	117	.154
2004	14	117	.120
2005	24	119	.202
2006	11	119	.092
2007	23	119	.193

*Record low. †Record high.

Records of FBS First-Year Head Coaches

(Coaches with no previous head-coaching experience at a four-year college.)

							Teams' Previous Season Record				
Year	No.	Won	Lost	Tied	Pct.	Bowl Record	Won	Lost	Tied	Pct.	Bowl Record
1948	14	56	68	7	.454	0-1	76	52	8	.588	2-1
1949	8	26	49	3	.353	0-1	35	41	4	.463	0-0
1950	10	37	56	4	.402	0-0	49	42	6	.536	2-0
1951	13	60	67	4	.473	1-2	39	88	7	.317	1-1
1952	8	31	42	3	.428	0-0	38	40	0	.487	0-0
1953	8	29	45	5	.399	0-0	48	28	7	.620	1-2
1954	8	31	43	4	.423	0-0	40	33	7	.543	1-0
1955	9	36	50	4	.422	0-1	36	52	1	.410	0-0
1956	14	47	80	11	.380	1-0	61	68	6	.474	0-1
1957	9	32	50	6	.398	0-0	44	42	2	.511	0-0
1958	7	26	44	0	.371	0-0	37	31	2	.543	0-0
1959	8	34	43	2	.443	0-0	41	35	2	.538	0-1
1960	14	54	80	5	.406	1-0	57	78	2	.423	0-0
1961	8	26	50	0	.342	0-0	38	38	2	.500	0-0
1962	12	40	74	4	.356	2-0	52	66	2	.442	1-1
1963	8	23	49	6	.333	0-0	32	46	1	.411	0-1
1964	12	45	67	7	.408	1-1	42	71	4	.376	0-0
1965	8	28	47	2	.377	0-0	36	42	1	.462	0-0
1966	10	46	50	3	.480	0-0	38	56	5	.409	0-0
1967	18	58	114	5	.342	1-0	60	116	4	.344	0-1
1968	6	19	40	1	.325	0-0	20	38	2	.350	0-0
1969	15	49	90	1	.353	0-0	62	85	3	.423	0-1
1970	10	45	61	1	.425	1-0	46	54	0	.460	0-2
1971	12	57	72	0	.442	1-1	64	61	0	.512	0-1
1972	11	57	64	1	.471	1-0	53	64	2	.454	1-0
1973	14	84	63	8	.568	1-0	83	71	2	.538	3-0
1974	17	63	116	5	.356	1-0	78	105	1	.427	1-0
1975	10	38	72	0	.345	0-1	43	67	0	.391	0-0
1976	15	57	109	2	.345	3-1	72	91	5	.443	3-1
1977	14	55	94	5	.373	1-0	66	88	3	.430	0-2
1978	16	68	104	3	.397	0-0	77	96	3	.446	0-1
1979	11	53	66	3	.447	0-0	66	57	1	.536	2-2
1980	12	54	75	2	.420	0-0	60	68	3	.469	1-0
1981	6	25	40	0	.385	0-0	31	35	1	.470	0-1
1982	10	51	59	1	.464	0-1	58	57	2	.504	2-2
1983	12	51	82	2	.385	1-0	60	73	1	.451	1-1
1984	7	47	28	1	*.625	2-1	45	35	1	.562	3-0
1985	5	19	37	0	.339	0-0	20	32	4	.393	0-0
1986	12	53	81	0	.396	0-1	56	76	3	.426	1-1
1987	9	51	49	3	.510	1-1	52	50	1	.510	0-2
1988	4	25	20	0	.556	1-0	22	23	1	.489	1-1
1989	7	32	49	1	.396	0-2	39	43	0	.476	1-2
1990	9	46	42	2	.522	1-1	41	48	1	.461	0-1
1991	10	38	72	1	.347	1-0	46	64	2	.420	0-2
1992	4	15	20	1	.431	0-0	32	14	0	.696	1-1
1993	8	29	58	2	.337	0-1	41	51	1	.446	2-2
1994	7	30	40	2	.431	2-1	40	39	0	.506	1-0
1995	10	57	56	2	.504	1-2	45	65	3	.412	2-1
1996	6	27	42	0	.391	1-1	29	38	1	.434	0-1
1997	11	47	79	0	.373	0-1	56	70	0	.444	1-1
1998	9	44	59	0	.427	0-2	52	52	0	.500	1-2
1999	8	40	51	0	.440	1-1	34	55	0	.382	0-0
2000	8	39	54	0	.419	1-2	41	49	0	.456	0-0
2001	12	72	67	0	.518	2-2	68	68	0	.500	2-0
2002	6	27	47	0	.365	0-1	24	43	0	.358	1-0
2003	9	60	56	0	.517	2-3	60	52	0	.536	1-2
2004	10	44	69	0	.389	1-1	47	75	0	.385	1-0
2005	11	51	73	0	.411	1-2	57	62	0	.479	1-6
2006	9	56	57	0	.496	2-3	42	63	0	.400	1-3

*Record percentage for first-year coaches. 1984 coaches and their records, with bowl game indicated by an asterisk (*): Pat Jones, Oklahoma St. (*10-2-0); Galen Hall, Florida (8-0-0, took over from Charley Pell after three games); Bill Arnsparger, LSU (8-*3-1); Fisher DeBerry, Air Force (*8-4-0); Dick Anderson, Rutgers (7-3-0); Mike Sheppard, Long Beach St. (4-7-0); Ron Chismar, Wichita St. (2-9-0).

Most Victories by FBS First-Year Head Coaches

Coach, College, Year	W	L	T
Chris Petersen, Boise St., 2006	*13	0	0
Larry Coker, Miami (Fla.), 2001	*12	0	0
Bret Bielema, Wisconsin, 2006	*12	1	0
Gary Blackney, Bowling Green, 1991	*11	1	0
John Robinson, Southern California, 1976	*11	1	0
Bill Battle, Tennessee, 1970	*11	1	0
Gregg Brandon, Bowling Green, 2003	*11	3	0
Dick Crum, Miami (Ohio), 1974	*10	0	1
Barry Switzer, Oklahoma, 1973	10	0	1
John Jenkins, Houston, 1990	10	1	0
Dwight Wallace, Ball St., 1978	10	1	0
Chuck Fairbanks, Oklahoma, 1967	*10	1	0
Mike Archer, LSU, 1987	*10	1	1
Ralph Friedgen, Maryland, 2001	10	2	0
Tom Amstutz, Toledo, 2001	*10	2	0
Rick Neuheisel, Colorado, 1995	*10	2	0
Paul Pasqualoni, Syracuse, 1992	*10	2	0
Curley Hallman, Southern Miss., 1988	*10	2	0
Pat Jones, Oklahoma St., 1984	*10	2	0
Earle Bruce, Tampa, 1972	*10	2	0
Billy Kinard, Mississippi, 1971	*10	2	0
Bill Doba, Washington St., 2003	*10	3	0

*Bowl game victory included.

Only first-year coaches to win a national championship: Bennie Oosterbaan, Michigan, 1948 (9-0-0); Larry Coker, Miami (Fla.), 2001 (12-0-0).

Football Championship Subdivision (FCS) Coaching Records

Winningest Active Coaches

(Minimum five years as FBS and/or FCS head coach; record at four-year colleges only.)

BY PERCENTAGE

	Coach, College	Years	Won	Lost	Tied	Pct.†
1.	Mike Kelly, Dayton	26	235	53	1	.815
2.	Al Bagnoli, Penn	25	190	63	0	.751
3.	K.C. Keeler, Delaware	14	129	43	1	.749
4.	Joe Taylor, Hampton	24	191	71	4	.726
5.	Pete Lembo, Elon	6	49	20	0	.710
6.	Pete Richardson, Southern U.	19	155	63	1	.710
7.	Buddy Pough, South Carolina St.	5	40	17	0	.702
8.	Bobby Lamb, Furman	5	43	19	0	.694
9.	Mark Farley, UNI	6	51	24	0	.680
10.	Don Brown, Massachusetts	10	78	37	0	.678
11.	Dick Biddle, Colgate	11	88	42	0	.677
12.	Walt Hameline, Wagner	26	179	93	2	.657
13.	Anthony Jones, Alabama A&M	8	59	31	0	.656
14.	Alvin Wyatt Sr., Bethune-Cookman	10	72	39	0	.649
15.	Rob Ash, Montana St.	27	176	99	5	.638
16.	Kevin Higgins, Citadel	9	65	38	1	.630
17.	Jerry Kill, Southern Ill.	13	92	55	0	.626
18.	Jack Siedlecki, Yale	19	111	66	2	.626
19.	Joe Walton, Robert Morris	13	82	49	1	.625
20.	Jon Heacock, Youngstown St.	6	43	27	0	.614
21.	Andy Talley, Villanova	27	175	112	2	.609
22.	Jerry Moore, Appalachian St.	25	181	116	2	.609
23.	Phil Estes, Brown	9	54	35	0	.607
24.	Kevin Callahan, Monmouth	14	85	56	0	.603
25.	Don Patterson, Western Ill.	8	55	37	0	.598

Fewer than five years as FBS and/or FCS head coach (includes record at all four-year colleges):

Coach, College	Years	Won	Lost	Tied	Pct.†
Chris Hatcher, Ga. Southern	7	76	12	0	.864
David Bennett, Coastal Caro.	11	97	28	0	.776
Charles Priore, Stony Brook	7	44	15	0	.746
Rocky Hager, Northeastern	13	103	46	1	.690
Rick Comegy, Jackson St.	15	113	56	0	.669
Jerry Schmitt, Duquesne	7	42	27	0	.609
Todd Whitten, Sam Houston St.	8	54	35	0	.607
John Zamberlin, Idaho St.	10	63	41	0	.606

†Ties computed as half won and half lost. Includes bowl and playoff games.

BY VICTORIES

(Minimum five years as FBS or FCS head coach; record at four-year colleges only.)

	Coach, College	Years	Won	Lost	Tied	Pct.†
1.	Mike Kelly, Dayton	26	235	53	1	.815
2.	Bob Ford, Albany (N.Y.)	38	217	158	1	.578
3.	Joe Taylor, Hampton	24	191	71	4	.726
4.	Al Bagnoli, Penn	25	190	63	0	.751
5.	Jerry Moore, Appalachian St.	25	181	116	2	.609
6.	Walt Hameline, Wagner	26	179	93	2	.657
7.	Jimmye Laycock, William & Mary	27	178	127	2	.583
8.	Rob Ash, Montana St.	27	176	99	5	.638
9.	Andy Talley, Villanova	27	175	112	2	.609
10.	Pete Richardson, Southern U.	19	155	63	1	.710
11.	Mike Ayers, Wofford	22	134	110	2	.549
12.	K.C. Keeler, Delaware	14	129	43	1	.749
13.	Bob Spoo, Eastern Ill.	19	119	98	1	.548
14.	Tim Murphy, Harvard	20	112	94	1	.543
15.	Jack Siedlecki, Yale	19	111	66	2	.626
16.	Matt Ballard, Morehead St.	19	108	91	1	.543
17.	Ron McBride, Weber St.	15	98	75	0	.566
18.	Terry Allen, Missouri St.	14	97	68	0	.588
19.	Steve Patton, Gardner-Webb	14	95	65	1	.593
20.	Watson Brown, Tennessee Tech	22	94	151	1	.384
21.	Jerry Kill, Southern Ill.	13	92	55	0	.626
22.	Dick Biddle, Colgate	11	88	42	0	.677
23.	Gordy Combs, Towson	15	86	73	0	.541
24.	Kevin Callahan, Monmouth	14	85	56	0	.603
	Jim Reid, VMI	16	85	92	3	.481

Fewer than five years as FBS and/or FCS head coach (includes record at all four-year colleges):

Coach, College	Years	Won	Lost	Tied	Pct.†
Rick Comegy, Jackson St.	15	113	56	0	.669
Rocky Hager, Northeastern	13	103	46	1	.690
David Bennett, Coastal Caro.	11	97	28	0	.776
Chris Hatcher, Ga. Southern	7	76	12	0	.864
John Zamberlin, Idaho St.	10	63	41	0	.606
Todd Whitten, Sam Houston St.	8	54	35	0	.607
Charles Priore, Stony Brook	7	44	15	0	.746
Jerry Schmitt, Duquesne	7	42	27	0	.609

†Ties computed as half won and half lost. Includes bowl and playoff games.

Winningest Coaches All-Time

(Minimum 10 years as head coach at FCS institutions; record at four-year colleges only; bowl and playoff games included)

BY PERCENTAGE

	Coach (Alma Mater) (Colleges Coached, Tenure)	Years	Won	Lost	Tied	Pct.†
1.	*Mike Kelly (Manchester 1970) (Dayton 1981-2006)	26	235	53	1	.815
2.	Greg Gattuso (Penn St. 1983) (Duquesne 1993-2004)	12	97	32	0	.752
3.	*Al Bagnoli (Central Conn. St. 1975) [Union (N.Y.) 1982-91, Penn 92-2006]	25	190	63	0	.751
4.	*Jim Tressel (Baldwin-Wallace 1975) (Youngstown St. 1986-2000, Ohio St. 01-06)	21	197	71	2	.733
5.	*Joe Taylor (Western Ill. 1972) (Howard 1983, Virginia Union 84-91, Hampton 92-2006)	24	191	72	4	.723
6.	Tubby Raymond (Michigan 1950) (Delaware 1966-2001)	36	300	119	3	.714
7.	Roy Kidd (Eastern Ky. 1954) (Eastern Ky. 1964-2002)	39	313	124	8	.712
8.	W.C. Gorden (Tennessee St. 1952) (Jackson St. 1976-91)	16	119	47	5	.711
9.	*Pete Richardson (Dayton 1968) (Winston-Salem 1988-92, Southern U. 93-2006)	19	155	63	1	.710
10.	Eddie Robinson (Leland 1941) (Grambling 1941-42, 45-97)	55	408	165	15	.707
11.	*Chris Ault (Nevada 1968) (Nevada 1976-92, 94-95, 2004-06)	22	185	78	1	.703
12.	Billy Joe (Villanova 1963) [Cheyney 1972-78, Central St. (Ohio) 81-93, Florida A&M 94-2004]	31	237	108	4	.685
13.	*Dick Biddle (Duke 1971) (Colgate 1996-2006)	11	88	42	0	.677
14.	Mark Whipple (Brown 1979) (New Haven 1988-93, Brown 94-97, Massachusetts 98-2003)	16	120	60	0	.667
15.	*Walt Hameline (Brockport St. 1975) (Wagner 1981-2006)	26	179	93	2	.657
16.	Joe Gardi (Maryland 1960) (Hofstra 1990-2005)	16	119	62	2	.656
17.	Bill Hayes (N.C. Central 1965) (Winston-Salem 1976-87, N.C. A&T 88-2002)	27	196	103	2	.654
18.	Alvin Wyatt Sr. (Bethune-Cookman 1970) (Bethune-Cookman 1997-2006)	10	72	39	0	.649
19.	*Rob Ash (Cornell College 1973) (Juniata 1980-88, Drake 89-2006, Montana St. 2007)	27	176	99	5	.638
20.	Marino Casem [Xavier (La.) 1956] (Alabama St. 1963, Alcorn St. 64-85, Southern U. 87-88, 92)	26	159	93	8	.627

*†Ties computed as half won, half lost. *Active coach.*

BY VICTORIES

	Coach (Alma Mater) (Colleges Coached, Tenure)	Years	Won	Lost	Tied	Pct.†
1.	Eddie Robinson (Leland 1941) (Grambling 1941-42, 45-97)	55	408	165	15	.707
2.	Roy Kidd (Eastern Ky. 1954) (Eastern Ky. 1964-2002)	39	313	124	8	.712
3.	Tubby Raymond (Michigan 1950) (Delaware 1966-2001)	36	300	119	3	.714
4.	Billy Joe (Villanova 1963) (Cheyney 1972-78, Central St. (Ohio) 81-93, Florida A&M 94-2004)	31	237	108	4	.685
5.	*Mike Kelly (Manchester 1970) (Dayton 1981-2006)	26	235	53	1	.815
6.	Ron Randleman (William Penn 1964) (William Penn 1969-75, Pittsburg St. 76-81, Sam Houston St. 82-2004)	36	218	167	6	.565

	Coach (Alma Mater) (Colleges Coached, Tenure)	Years	Won	Lost	Tied	Pct.†
7.	*Jim Tressel (Baldwin-Wallace 1975) (Youngstown St. 1986-2000, Ohio St. 01-06)	21	197	71	2	.733
8.	Bill Hayes (N.C. Central 1965) (Winston-Salem 1976-87, N.C. A&T 1988-02)	27	196	103	2	.654
9.	*Joe Taylor (Western Ill. 1972) (Howard 1983, Virginia Union 84-91, Hampton 92-2006)	24	191	72	4	.723
10.	*Al Bagnoli (Central Conn. St. 1975) [Union (N.Y.) 1982-91, Penn 92-2006]	25	190	63	0	.751
11.	*Chris Ault (Nevada 1968) (Nevada 1976-92, 94-95, 2004-06)	22	185	78	1	.703
12.	*Jerry Moore (Baylor 1961) (North Texas 1979-80, Texas Tech 81-85, Appalachian St. 1989-2006)	25	181	116	2	.609
13.	*Walt Hameline (Brockport St. 1975) (Wagner 1981-2006)	26	179	93	2	.657
	Carmen Cozza [Miami (Ohio) 1952] (Yale 1965-96)	32	179	119	5	.599
15.	*Jimmye Laycock (William & Mary 1970) (William & Mary 1980-2006)	27	178	127	2	.583
16.	*Rob Ash (Cornell College 1973) (Juniata 1980-88, Drake 89-2006, Montana St. 2007)	27	176	99	5	.638
17.	*Andy Talley (Southern Conn. St. 1967) (St. Lawrence 1979-83, Villanova 85-2006)	27	175	112	2	.609
18.	Bill Bowes (Penn St. 1965) (New Hampshire 1972-98)	27	169	112	5	.600
19.	Marino Casem [Xavier (La.) 1956] (Alabama St. 1963, Alcorn St. 64-85, Southern U. 87-88, 92)	26	159	93	8	.627
20.	*Pete Richardson (Dayton 1968) (Winston-Salem 1988-92, Southern U. 93-2006)	19	155	63	1	.710

*†Ties computed as half won, half lost. *Active coach.*

Annual FCS Head-Coaching Changes

(From the 1982 reorganization of the division for parallel comparisons)

Year	Changes	Teams	Pct.
1982	7	92	.076
1983	17	84	.202
1984	14	87	.161
1985	11	87	.126
1986	18	86	.209
1987	13	87	.149
1988	12	88	.136
1989	21	89	†.236
1990	16	89	.180
1991	6	87	*.069
1992	14	89	.157
1993	13	#115	.113
1994	17	116	.147
1995	11	119	.092
1996	11	116	.095
1997	20	118	.169
1998	14	119	.118
1999	17	122	.139
2000	24	122	.197
2001	12	123	.098
2002	14	122	.115
2003	17	122	.139
2004	18	122	.148
2005	11	117	.094
2006	20	115	.174
2007	16	118	.136

**Record low. †Record high. #Twenty-seven teams switched from Divisions II & III to FCS.*

FCS Championship Coaches

All coaches who have coached teams in the FCS championship playoffs since 1978 are listed here with their playoff record, alma mater and year graduated, team, year coached, opponent, and score.

Dan Allen (1-2) (Hanover 1978)
Boston U. 1993 UNI 27-21 (2 ot)
Boston U. 1993 Idaho 14-21
Boston U. 1994 Eastern Ky. 23-30

Pokey Allen (3-1) (Utah 1965)
Boise St. 1994 North Texas 42-20
Boise St. 1994 Appalachian St. 17-14
Boise St. 1994 Marshall 28-24
Boise St. 1994 Youngstown St. 14-28

Terry Allen (6-7) (UNI 1979)
UNI 1990 Boise St. 3-20
UNI 1991 Weber St. 38-21
UNI 1991 Marshall 13-41
UNI 1992 Eastern Wash. 17-14
UNI 1992 McNeese St. 29-7
UNI 1992 Youngstown St. 7-19
UNI 1993 Boston U. 21-27 (2 ot)
UNI 1994 Montana 20-23
UNI 1995 Murray St. 35-34
UNI 1995 Marshall 24-41
UNI 1996 Eastern Ill. 21-14
UNI 1996 William & Mary 38-35
UNI 1996 Marshall 14-31

Dave Arnold (3-0) (Drake 1967)
Montana St. 1984 Arkansas St. 31-24
Montana St. 1984 Rhode Island 32-20
Montana St. 1984* Louisiana Tech 19-6

Dave Arslanian (0-1) (Weber St. 1972)
Weber St. 1991 UNI 21-38

Chris Ault (9-7) (Nevada 1968)
Nevada 1978 Massachusetts 21-44
Nevada 1979 Eastern Ky. 30-33
Nevada 1983 Idaho St. 27-20
Nevada 1983 North Texas 20-17 (ot)
Nevada 1983 Southern Ill. 7-23
Nevada 1985 Arkansas St. 24-23
Nevada 1985 Furman 12-35
Nevada 1986 Idaho 27-7
Nevada 1986 Tennessee St. 33-6
Nevada 1986 Ga. Southern 38-48
Nevada 1990 La.-Monroe 27-14
Nevada 1990 Furman 42-35 (3 ot)
Nevada 1990 Boise St. 59-52 (3 ot)
Nevada 1990 Ga. Southern 13-36
Nevada 1991 McNeese St. 22-16
Nevada 1991 Youngstown St. 28-30

Stephen Axman (0-1) (C.W. Post 1969)
Northern Ariz. 1996 Furman 31-42

Mike Ayers (2-1) (Georgetown [Ky.] 1974)
Wofford 2003 N.C. A&T 31-10
Wofford 2003 Western Ky. 34-17
Wofford 2003 Delaware 9-24

David Bailiff (2-1) (Texas St. 1981)
Texas St. 2005 Ga. Southern 50-35
Texas St. 2005 Cal Poly 14-7
Texas St. 2005 UNI 37-40 (ot)

Randy Ball (3-4) (Truman 1973)
Western Ill. 1991 Marshall 17-20 (ot)
Western Ill. 1996 Murray St. 6-34
Western Ill. 1997 Jackson St. 31-24
Western Ill. 1997 McNeese St. 12-14
Western Ill. 1998 Montana 52-9
Western Ill. 1998 Florida A&M 24-21
Western Ill. 1998 Ga. Southern 14-42

Darren Barbier (0-1) (Nicholls St. 1982)
Nicholls St. 1996 Montana 3-48

Frank Beamer (0-1) (Virginia Tech 1969)
Murray St. 1986 Eastern Ill. 21-28

David Bennett (0-1) (Presbyterian 1984)
Coastal Caro. 2006 Appalachian St. 28-45

Todd Berry (2-2) (Tulsa 1983)
Illinois St. 1998 Northwestern St. 28-48
Illinois St. 1999 Colgate 56-13
Illinois St. 1999 Hofstra 37-20
Illinois St. 1999 Ga. Southern 17-28

Dick Biddle (3-5) (Duke 1971)
Colgate 1997 Villanova 28-49
Colgate 1998 Ga. Southern 28-49
Colgate 1999 Illinois St. 13-56
Colgate 2003 Massachusetts 19-7
Colgate 2003 Western Ill. 28-27
Colgate 2003 Fla. Atlantic 36-24
Colgate 2003 Delaware 0-40
Colgate 2005 New Hampshire 21-55

Larry Blakeney (5-7) (Auburn 1970)
Troy 1993 Stephen F. Austin 42-20
Troy 1993 McNeese St. 35-28
Troy 1993 Marshall 21-24
Troy 1994 James Madison 26-45
Troy 1995 Ga. Southern 21-24
Troy 1996 Florida A&M 29-25
Troy 1996 Murray St. 31-3
Troy 1996 Montana 7-70
Troy 1998 Florida A&M 17-27
Troy 1999 James Madison 27-7
Troy 1999 Florida A&M 10-17
Troy 2000 Appalachian St. 30-33

Terry Bowden (2-2) (West Virginia 1978)
Samford 1991 New Hampshire 29-13
Samford 1991 James Madison 24-21
Samford 1991 Youngstown St. 0-10
Samford 1992 Delaware 21-56

Bill Bowes (0-2) (Penn St. 1965)
New Hampshire 1991 Samford 13-29
New Hampshire 1994 Appalachian St. 10-17 (ot)

Jesse Branch (1-2) (Arkansas 1964)
Missouri St. 1989 Maine 38-35
Missouri St. 1989 Stephen F. Austin 25-55
Missouri St. 1990 Idaho 35-41

Billy Brewer (1-1) (Mississippi 1961)
Louisiana Tech 1982 South Carolina St. 38-3
Louisiana Tech 1982 Delaware 0-17

Don Brown (3-2) (Norwich 1977)
Northeastern 2002 Fordham 24-29
Massachusetts 2006 Lafayette 35-14
Massachusetts 2006 New Hampshire 24-17
Massachusetts 2006 Montana 19-17
Massachusetts 2006 Appalachian St. 17-28

James Carson (0-3) (Jackson St. 1963)
Jackson St. 1995 Marshall 8-38
Jackson St. 1996 William & Mary 6-45
Jackson St. 1997 Western Ill. 24-31

Rick Carter (0-1) (Earlham 1965)
Holy Cross 1983 Western Caro. 21-28

Marino Casem (0-1) [Xavier (La.) 1956]
Alcorn St. 1984 Louisiana Tech 21-44

Mike Cavan (1-1) (Georgia 1972)
East Tenn. St. 1996 Villanova 35-29
East Tenn. St. 1996 Montana 14-44

George Chaump (4-2) (Bloomsburg 1958)
Marshall 1987 James Madison 41-12
Marshall 1987 Weber St. 51-23
Marshall 1987 Appalachian St. 24-10
Marshall 1987 La.-Monroe 42-43
Marshall 1988 North Texas 7-0
Marshall 1988 Furman 9-13

David Clawson (2-2) (Williams 1989)
Fordham 2002 Northeastern 29-24

Fordham .... 2002 Villanova 10-24
Richmond .... 2005 Hampton 38-10
Richmond .... 2005 Furman 20-24

L.C. Cole (0-2) (Nebraska 1980)
Tennessee St. .... 1998 Appalachian St. 31-45
Tennessee St. .... 1999 N.C. A&T 10-24

Pat Collins (4-0) (Louisiana Tech 1963)
La.-Monroe .... 1987 North Texas 30-9
La.-Monroe .... 1987 Eastern Ky. 33-32
La.-Monroe .... 1987 UNI 44-41 (ot)
La.-Monroe .... 1987* Marshall 43-42

Archie Cooley Jr. (0-1) (Jackson St. 1962)
Mississippi Val. ...... 1984 Louisiana Tech 19-66

Jack Cosgrove (2-2) (Maine 1978)
Maine .... 2001 McNeese St. 14-10
Maine .... 2001 UNI 28-56
Maine .... 2002 Appalachian St. 14-13
Maine .... 2002 Ga. Southern 7-31

Bruce Craddock (0-1) (Truman 1966)
Western Ill. .... 1988 Western Ky. 32-35

Jim Criner (3-1) (Cal Poly Pomona 1961)
Boise St. .... 1980 Grambling 14-9
Boise St. .... 1980* Eastern Ky. 31-29
Boise St. .... 1981 Jackson St. 19-7
Boise St. .... 1981 Eastern Ky. 17-23

Jack Crowe (0-2) (UAB 1970)
Jacksonville St. .... 2003 Western Ky. 7-45
Jacksonville St. .... 2004 Furman 7-49

Bill Davis (2-2) (Johnson C. Smith 1965)
South Carolina St. .. 1981 Tennessee St. 26-25
South Carolina St. .. 1981 Idaho St. 12-41
South Carolina St. .. 1982 Furman 17-0
South Carolina St. .. 1982 Louisiana Tech 3-38

Rey Dempsey (3-0) (Geneva 1958)
Southern Ill. .... 1983 Indiana St. 23-7
Southern Ill. .... 1983 Nevada 23-7
Southern Ill. .... 1983* Western Caro. 43-7

Mick Dennehy (3-4) (Montana 1973)
Montana .... 1996 Nicholls St. 48-3
Montana .... 1996 East Tenn. St. 44-14
Montana .... 1996 Troy 70-7
Montana .... 1996 Marshall 29-49
Montana .... 1997 McNeese St. 14-19
Montana .... 1998 Western Ill. 9-52
Montana .... 1999 Youngstown St. 27-30

Jim Dennison (0-1) (Wooster 1960)
Akron .... 1985 Rhode Island 27-35

Jim Donnan (15-4) (North Carolina St. 1967)
Marshall .... 1991 Western Ill. 20-17 (ot)
Marshall .... 1991 UNI 41-13
Marshall .... 1991 Eastern Ky. 14-7
Marshall .... 1991 Youngstown St. 17-25
Marshall .... 1992 Eastern Ky. 44-0
Marshall .... 1992 Middle Tenn. 35-21
Marshall .... 1992 Delaware 28-7
Marshall .... 1992* Youngstown St. 31-28
Marshall .... 1993 Howard 28-14
Marshall .... 1993 Delaware 34-31
Marshall .... 1993 Troy 24-21
Marshall .... 1993 Youngstown St. 5-17
Marshall .... 1994 Middle Tenn. 49-14
Marshall .... 1994 James Madison 28-21 (ot)
Marshall .... 1994 Boise St. 24-28
Marshall .... 1995 Jackson St. 38-8
Marshall .... 1995 UNI 41-24
Marshall .... 1995 McNeese St. 25-13
Marshall .... 1995 Montana 20-22

Boots Donnelly (6-7) (Middle Tenn. 1965)
Middle Tenn. .... 1984 Eastern Ky. 27-10
Middle Tenn. .... 1984 Indiana St. 42-41 (3 ot)
Middle Tenn. .... 1984 Louisiana Tech 13-21
Middle Tenn. .... 1985 Ga. Southern 21-28
Middle Tenn. .... 1989 Appalachian St. 24-21
Middle Tenn. .... 1989 Ga. Southern 3-45
Middle Tenn. .... 1990 Jackson St. 28-7
Middle Tenn. .... 1990 Boise St. 13-20
Middle Tenn. .... 1991 Sam Houston St. 20-19 (ot)
Middle Tenn. .... 1991 Eastern Ky. 13-23
Middle Tenn. .... 1992 Appalachian St. 35-10
Middle Tenn. .... 1992 Marshall 21-35
Middle Tenn. .... 1994 Marshall 14-49

Larry Donovan (0-1) (Nebraska 1964)
Montana .... 1982 Idaho 7-21

Fred Dunlap (1-2) (Colgate 1950)
Colgate .... 1982 Boston U. 21-7
Colgate .... 1982 Delaware 13-20
Colgate .... 1983 Western Caro. 23-24

Rich Ellerson (1-1) (Hawaii 1977)
Cal Poly .... 2005 Montana 35-21
Cal Poly .... 2005 Texas St. 7-14

Dave Elson (1-2) (Butler 1994)
Western Ky. .... 2003 Jacksonville St. 45-7
Western Ky. .... 2003 Wofford 17-34
Western Ky. .... 2004 Sam Houston St. 24-54

Dennis Erickson (1-2) (Montana St. 1970)
Idaho .... 1982 Montana 21-7
Idaho .... 1982 Eastern Ky. 30-38
Idaho .... 1985 Eastern Wash. 38-42

Mark Farley (6-3) (UNI 1986)
UNI .... 2001 Eastern Ill. 49-43
UNI .... 2001 Maine 56-28
UNI .... 2001 Montana 0-38
UNI .... 2003 Montana St. 35-14
UNI .... 2003 Delaware 7-37
UNI .... 2005 Eastern Wash. 41-38
UNI .... 2005 New Hampshire 24-21
UNI .... 2005 Texas St. 40-37 (ot)
UNI .... 2005 Appalachian St. 16-21

Mo Forte (0-1) (Minnesota 1971)
N.C. A&T .... 1986 Ga. Southern 21-52

Joe Gardi (2-5) (Maryland 1960)
Hofstra .... 1995 Delaware 17-38
Hofstra .... 1997 Delaware 14-24
Hofstra .... 1999 Lehigh 27-15
Hofstra .... 1999 Illinois St. 20-37
Hofstra .... 2000 Furman 31-24
Hofstra .... 2000 Ga. Southern 20-48
Hofstra .... 2001 Lehigh 24-27 (ot)

Keith Gilbertson (2-3) (Central Wash. 1971)
Idaho .... 1986 Nevada 7-27
Idaho .... 1987 Weber St. 30-59
Idaho .... 1988 Montana 38-19
Idaho .... 1988 Northwestern St. 38-30
Idaho .... 1988 Furman 7-38

Joe Glenn (8-2) (South Dakota 1971)
Montana .... 2000 Eastern Ill. 45-13
Montana .... 2000 Richmond 34-20
Montana .... 2000 Appalachian St. 19-16 (ot)
Montana .... 2000 Ga. Southern 25-27
Montana .... 2001 Northwestern St. 28-19
Montana .... 2001 Sam Houston St. 49-24
Montana .... 2001 UNI 38-0
Montana .... 2001* Furman 13-6
Montana .... 2002 Northwestern St. 45-14
Montana .... 2002 McNeese St. 20-24

Sam Goodwin (3-3) (Henderson St. 1966)
Northwestern St. .... 1988 Boise St. 22-13
Northwestern St. .... 1988 Idaho 30-38
Northwestern St. .... 1997 Eastern Wash. 10-40
Northwestern St. .... 1998 Illinois St. 48-28
Northwestern St. .... 1998 Appalachian St. 31-20
Northwestern St. .... 1998 Massachusetts 31-41

W.C. Gorden (0-9) (Tennessee St. 1952)
Jackson St. .... 1978 Florida A&M 10-15
Jackson St. .... 1981 Boise St. 7-19
Jackson St. .... 1982 Eastern Ill. 13-16 (ot)
Jackson St. .... 1985 Ga. Southern 0-27
Jackson St. .... 1986 Tennessee St. 23-32
Jackson St. .... 1987 Arkansas St. 32-35
Jackson St. .... 1988 Stephen F. Austin 0-24
Jackson St. .... 1989 Montana 7-48
Jackson St. .... 1990 Middle Tenn. 7-28

Mike Gottfried (0-1) (Morehead St. 1966)
Murray St. .... 1979 Lehigh 9-28

Lynn Graves (%3-1) (Stephen F. Austin 1965)
Stephen F. Austin .... 1989% Grambling 59-56
Stephen F. Austin .... 1989% Missouri St. 55-25
Stephen F. Austin .... 1989% Furman 21-19
Stephen F. Austin .... 1989% Ga. Southern 34-37

Bob Griffin (2-3) (Southern Conn. St. 1963)
Rhode Island .... 1981 Idaho St. 0-51
Rhode Island .... 1984 Richmond 23-17
Rhode Island .... 1984 Montana St. 20-32
Rhode Island .... 1985 Akron 35-27
Rhode Island .... 1985 Furman 15-59

Skip Hall (2-2) (Concordia-M'head 1966)
Boise St. .... 1988 Northwestern St. 13-22
Boise St. .... 1990 UNI 20-3
Boise St. .... 1990 Middle Tenn. 20-13
Boise St. .... 1990 Nevada 52-59 (3 ot)

Jack Harbaugh (6-3) (Bowling Green 1961)
Western Ky. .... 1997 Eastern Ky. 42-14
Western Ky. .... 1997 Eastern Wash. 21-38
Western Ky. .... 2000 Florida A&M 27-0
Western Ky. .... 2000 Appalachian St. 14-17
Western Ky. .... 2001 Furman 20-24
Western Ky. .... 2002 Murray St. 59-20
Western Ky. .... 2002 Western Ill. 31-28
Western Ky. .... 2002 Ga. Southern 31-28
Western Ky. .... 2002* McNeese St. 34-14

Bobby Hauck (5-4) (Montana 1988)
Montana .... 2003 Western Ill. 40-43 (2 ot)
Montana .... 2004 Northwestern St. 56-7
Montana .... 2004 New Hampshire 47-17
Montana .... 2004 Sam Houston St. 34-13
Montana .... 2004 James Madison 21-31
Montana .... 2005 Cal Poly 21-35
Montana .... 2006 McNeese St. 31-6
Montana .... 2006 Southern Ill. 20-3
Montana .... 2006 Massachusetts 17-24

Bill Hayes (1-2) (N.C. Central 1964)
N.C. A&T .... 1992 Citadel 0-44
N.C. A&T .... 1999 Tennessee St. 24-10
N.C. A&T .... 1999 Youngstown St. 3-41

Jon Heacock (2-1) (Muskingum 1983)
Youngstown St. ...... 2006 James Madison 35-31
Youngstown St. ...... 2006 Illinois St. 28-21
Youngstown St. ...... 2006 Appalachian St. 24-49

Jim Hess (1-1) (Southeastern Okla. 1959)
Stephen F. Austin .... 1988 Jackson St. 24-0
Stephen F. Austin .... 1988 Ga. Southern 6-27

Kevin Higgins (2-3) (West Chester 1979)
Lehigh .... 1998 Richmond 24-33
Lehigh .... 1998 Massachusetts 21-27
Lehigh .... 1999 Hofstra 15-27
Lehigh .... 2000 Western Ill. 37-7
Lehigh .... 2000 Delaware 22-47

Skip Holtz (1-1) (Notre Dame 1986)
Connecticut .... 1998 Hampton 42-34
Connecticut .... 1998 Ga. Southern 30-52

Rudy Hubbard (2-0) (Ohio St. 1968)
Florida A&M .... 1978 Jackson St. 15-10
Florida A&M .... 1978* Massachusetts 35-28

Mark Hutson (0-1) (Oklahoma 1989)
Eastern Ill. .... 2006 Illinois St. 13-24

Sonny Jackson (1-1) (Nicholls St. 1963)
Nicholls St. .... 1986 Appalachian St. 28-26
Nicholls St. .... 1986 Ga. Southern 31-55

Billy Joe (3-6) (Villanova 1963)
Florida A&M .... 1996 Troy 25-29
Florida A&M .... 1997 Ga. Southern 37-52
Florida A&M .... 1998 Troy 27-17
Florida A&M .... 1998 Western Ill. 21-24
Florida A&M .... 1999 Appalachian St. 44-29
Florida A&M .... 1999 Troy 17-10
Florida A&M .... 1999 Youngstown St. 24-27
Florida A&M .... 2000 Western Ky. 0-27
Florida A&M .... 2001 Ga. Southern 35-60

Bobby Johnson (4-4) (Clemson 1973)
Furman .... 1996 Northern Ariz. 42-31
Furman .... 1996 Marshall 0-54
Furman .... 1999 Massachusetts 23-30 (ot)
Furman .... 2000 Hofstra 24-31
Furman .... 2001 Western Ky. 24-20
Furman .... 2001 Lehigh 34-17
Furman .... 2001 Ga. Southern 24-17
Furman .... 2001 Montana 6-13

Denver Johnson (1-1) (Tulsa 1981)
Illinois St. .... 2006 Eastern Ill. 24-13
Illinois St. .... 2006 Youngstown St. 21-28

Paul Johnson (14-3) (Western Caro. 1979)
Ga. Southern .... 1997 Florida A&M 52-37
Ga. Southern .... 1997 Delaware 7-16
Ga. Southern .... 1998 Colgate 49-28
Ga. Southern .... 1998 Connecticut 52-30
Ga. Southern .... 1998 Western Ill. 42-14
Ga. Southern .... 1998 Massachusetts 43-55
Ga. Southern .... 1999 Northern Ariz. 72-29
Ga. Southern .... 1999 Massachusetts 38-21
Ga. Southern .... 1999 Illinois St. 28-17
Ga. Southern .... 1999* Youngstown St. 59-24

Ga. Southern.......... 2000 McNeese St. 42-17
Ga. Southern.......... 2000 Hofstra 48-20
Ga. Southern.......... 2000 Delaware 27-18
Ga. Southern.......... 2000* Montana 27-25
Ga. Southern.......... 2001 Florida A&M 60-35

Ga. Southern.......... 2001 Appalachian St. 38-24
Ga. Southern.......... 2001 Furman 17-24

Cardell Jones (0-2) (Alcorn St. 1965)
Alcorn St. .... 1992 La.-Monroe 27-78
Alcorn St. .... 1994 Youngstown St. 20-63

Bobby Keasler (8-7) (La.-Monroe 1970)
McNeese St. .... 1991 Nevada 16-22
McNeese St. .... 1992 Idaho 23-20
McNeese St. .... 1992 UNI 7-29
McNeese St. .... 1993 William & Mary 34-28
McNeese St. .... 1993 Troy 28-35

McNeese St. .... 1994 Idaho 38-21
McNeese St. .... 1994 Montana 28-30
McNeese St. .... 1995 Idaho 33-3
McNeese St. .... 1995 Delaware 52-18
McNeese St. .... 1995 Marshall 13-25

McNeese St. .... 1997 Montana 19-14
McNeese St. .... 1997 Western Ill. 14-12
McNeese St. .... 1997 Delaware 23-21
McNeese St. .... 1997 Youngstown St. 9-10
McNeese St. .... 1998 Massachusetts 19-21

K.C. Keeler (5-1) (Delaware 1981)
Delaware .... 2003 Southern Ill. 48-7
Delaware .... 2003 UNI 37-7
Delaware .... 2003 Wofford 24-9
Delaware .... 2003* Colgate 40-0
Delaware .... 2004 Lafayette 28-14

Delaware .... 2004 William & Mary 38-44 (2 ot)

Roy Kidd (16-15) (Eastern Ky. 1954)
Eastern Ky. .... 1979 Nevada 33-30
Eastern Ky. .... 1979* Lehigh 30-7
Eastern Ky. .... 1980 Lehigh 23-20
Eastern Ky. .... 1980 Boise St. 29-31
Eastern Ky. .... 1981 Delaware 35-28

Eastern Ky. .... 1981 Boise St. 23-17
Eastern Ky. .... 1981 Idaho St. 23-34
Eastern Ky. .... 1982 Idaho St. 38-30
Eastern Ky. .... 1982 Tennessee St. 13-7
Eastern Ky. .... 1982* Delaware 17-14

Eastern Ky. .... 1983 Boston U. 20-24
Eastern Ky. .... 1984 Middle Tenn. 10-27
Eastern Ky. .... 1986 Furman 23-10
Eastern Ky. .... 1986 Eastern Ill. 24-22
Eastern Ky. .... 1986 Arkansas St. 10-24

Eastern Ky. .... 1987 Western Ky. 40-17
Eastern Ky. .... 1987 La.-Monroe 32-33
Eastern Ky. .... 1988 Massachusetts 28-17
Eastern Ky. .... 1988 Western Ky. 41-24
Eastern Ky. .... 1988 Ga. Southern 17-21

Eastern Ky. .... 1989 Youngstown St. 24-28
Eastern Ky. .... 1990 Furman 17-45
Eastern Ky. .... 1991 Appalachian St. 14-3
Eastern Ky. .... 1991 Middle Tenn. 23-13
Eastern Ky. .... 1991 Marshall 7-14

Eastern Ky. .... 1992 Marshall 0-44
Eastern Ky. .... 1993 Ga. Southern 12-14
Eastern Ky. .... 1994 Boston U. 30-23
Eastern Ky. .... 1994 Youngstown St. 15-18
Eastern Ky. .... 1995 Montana 0-48

Eastern Ky. .... 1997 Western Ky. 14-42

Jerry Kill (2-4) [Southwestern (Kan.) 1983]
Southern Ill. .... 2003 Delaware 7-48
Southern Ill. .... 2004 Eastern Wash. 31-35
Southern Ill. .... 2005 Eastern Ill. 21-6
Southern Ill. .... 2005 Appalachian St. 24-38
Southern Ill. .... 2006 Tenn.-Martin 36-30

Southern Ill. .... 2006 Montana 3-20

Jim Koetter (0-1) (Idaho St. 1961)
Idaho St. .... 1983 Nevada 20-27

Dave Kragthorpe (3-0) (Utah St. 1955)
Idaho St. .... 1981 Rhode Island 51-0
Idaho St. .... 1981 South Carolina St. 41-12
Idaho St. .... 1981* Eastern Ky. 34-23

Mike Kramer (3-4) (Idaho 1977)
Eastern Wash. .... 1997 Northwestern St. 40-10
Eastern Wash. .... 1997 Western Ky. 38-21
Eastern Wash. .... 1997 Youngstown St. 14-25
Montana St. .... 2002 McNeese St. 14-21
Montana St. .... 2003 UNI 14-35
Montana St. .... 2006 Furman 31-13
Montana St. .... 2006 Appalachian St. 28-45

Larry Lacewell (6-4) (Ark.-Monticello 1959)
Arkansas St. .... 1984 Chattanooga 37-10
Arkansas St. .... 1984 Montana St. 14-31
Arkansas St. .... 1985 Grambling 10-7
Arkansas St. .... 1985 Nevada 23-24
Arkansas St. .... 1986 Sam Houston St. 48-7

Arkansas St. .... 1986 Delaware 55-14
Arkansas St. .... 1986 Eastern Ky. 24-10
Arkansas St. .... 1986 Ga. Southern 21-48
Arkansas St. .... 1987 Jackson St. 35-32
Arkansas St. .... 1987 UNI 28-49

Bobby Lamb (3-4) (Furman 1987)
Furman .... 2002 Villanova 38-45
Furman .... 2004 Jacksonville St. 49-7
Furman .... 2004 James Madison 13-14
Furman .... 2005 Nicholls St. 14-12
Furman .... 2005 Richmond 24-20

Furman .... 2005 Appalachian St. 23-29
Furman .... 2006 Montana St. 13-31

Jimmye Laycock (4-7) (William & Mary 1970)
William & Mary...... 1986 Delaware 17-51
William & Mary...... 1989 Furman 10-24
William & Mary...... 1990 Massachusetts 38-0
William & Mary...... 1990 UCF 38-52
William & Mary...... 1993 McNeese St. 28-34

William & Mary...... 1996 Jackson St. 45-6
William & Mary...... 1996 UNI 35-38
William & Mary...... 2001 Appalachian St. 27-40
William & Mary...... 2004 Hampton 42-35
William & Mary...... 2004 Delaware 44-38 (2 ot)

William & Mary...... 2004 James Madison 34-48

Pete Lembo (1-2) (Georgetown 1992)
Lehigh.................... 2001 Hofstra 27-24 (ot)
Lehigh.................... 2001 Furman 17-34
Lehigh.................... 2004 James Madison 14-13

Tom Lichtenberg (0-1) (Louisville 1962)
Maine..................... 1989 Missouri St. 35-38

Mickey Matthews (4-2) (West Tex. A&M 1986)
James Madison....... 1999 Troy 7-27
James Madison....... 2004 Lehigh 14-13
James Madison....... 2004 Furman 14-13
James Madison....... 2004 William & Mary 48-34
James Madison....... 2004* Montana 31-21

James Madison....... 2006 Youngstown St. 31-35

Sean McDonnell (3-3) (New Hampshire 1978)
New Hampshire ..... 2004 Ga. Southern 27-23
New Hampshire ..... 2004 Montana 17-47
New Hampshire ..... 2005 Colgate 55-21
New Hampshire ..... 2005 UNI 21-24
New Hampshire ..... 2006 Hampton 41-38

New Hampshire ..... 2006 Massachusetts 17-24

Gene McDowell (2-2) (Florida St. 1963)
UCF........................ 1990 Youngstown St. 20-17
UCF........................ 1990 William & Mary 52-38
UCF........................ 1990 Ga. Southern 7-44
UCF........................ 1993 Youngstown St. 30-56

John Merritt (†1-2) (Kentucky St. 1950)
Tennessee St. .... 1981† South Carolina St. 25-26 (ot)
Tennessee St. .... 1982† Eastern Ill. 20-19
Tennessee St. .... 1982† Eastern Ky. 7-13

Al Molde (1-2) (Gust. Adolphus 1966)
Eastern Ill. .... 1983 Indiana St. 13-16 (2 ot)
Eastern Ill. .... 1986 Murray St. 28-21
Eastern Ill. .... 1986 Eastern Ky. 22-24

Jerry Moore (14-10) (Baylor 1961)
Appalachian St. ..... 1989 Middle Tenn. 21-24
Appalachian St. ..... 1991 Eastern Ky. 3-14
Appalachian St. ..... 1992 Middle Tenn. 10-35
Appalachian St. ..... 1994 New Hampshire 17-10 (ot)
Appalachian St. ..... 1994 Boise St. 14-17

Appalachian St. ..... 1995 James Madison 31-24
Appalachian St. ..... 1995 Stephen F. Austin 17-27
Appalachian St. ..... 1998 Tennessee St. 45-31
Appalachian St. ..... 1998 Northwestern St. 20-31
Appalachian St. ..... 1999 Florida A&M 29-44

Appalachian St. ..... 2000 Troy 33-30
Appalachian St. ..... 2000 Western Ky. 17-14
Appalachian St. ..... 2000 Montana 16-19 (ot)
Appalachian St. ..... 2001 William & Mary 40-27
Appalachian St. ..... 2001 Ga. Southern 24-38

Appalachian St. ..... 2002 Maine 13-14
Appalachian St. ..... 2005 Lafayette 34-23
Appalachian St. ..... 2005 Southern Ill. 38-24
Appalachian St. ..... 2005 Furman 29-23
Appalachian St. ..... 2005* UNI 21-16

Appalachian St. ..... 2006 Coastal Caro. 45-28
Appalachian St. ..... 2006 Montana St. 38-17
Appalachian St. ..... 2006 Youngstown St. 49-24
Appalachian St. ..... 2006* Massachusetts 28-17

Darrell Mudra (4-3) (Peru St. 1951)
Eastern Ill. .... 1982 Jackson St. 16-13 (ot)
Eastern Ill. .... 1982 Tennessee St. 19-20
UNI .... 1985 Eastern Wash. 17-14
UNI .... 1985 Ga. Southern 33-40
UNI .... 1987 Youngstown St. 31-28

UNI .... 1987 Arkansas St. 49-28
UNI .... 1987 La.-Monroe 41-44 (ot)

Tim Murphy (0-1) (Springfield 1978)
Maine.................... 1987 Ga. Southern 28-31 (ot)

Corky Nelson (0-3) (Texas St. 1964)
North Texas............ 1983 Nevada 17-20 (ot)
North Texas............ 1987 La.-Monroe 9-30
North Texas............ 1988 Marshall 0-7

Buddy Nix (0-1) (West Ala. 1961)
Chattanooga .... 1984 Arkansas St. 10-37

Houston Nutt (1-2) (Oklahoma St. 1981)
Murray St. .... 1995 UNI 34-35
Murray St. .... 1996 Western Ill. 34-6
Murray St. .... 1996 Troy 3-31

Joe Pannunzio (0-1) (Colorado-St. Pueblo 1982)
Murray St. .... 2002 Western Ky. 20-59

Don Patterson (2-3) (Army 1973)
Western Ill. .... 2000 Lehigh 7-37
Western Ill. .... 2002 Eastern Ill. 48-9
Western Ill. .... 2002 Western Ky. 28-31
Western Ill. .... 2003 Montana 43-40 (2 ot)
Western Ill. .... 2003 Colgate 27-28

John Pearce (2-2) (Tex. A&M-Commerce 1970)
Stephen F. Austin .... 1993 Troy 20-42
Stephen F. Austin .... 1995 Eastern Ill. 34-29
Stephen F. Austin .... 1995 Appalachian St. 27-17
Stephen F. Austin .... 1995 Montana 14-70

Bob Pickett (1-1) (Maine 1959)
Massachusetts......... 1978 Nevada 44-21
Massachusetts......... 1978 Florida A&M 28-35

Mike Price (1-1) (Puget Sound 1969)
Weber St. .... 1987 Idaho 59-30
Weber St. .... 1987 Marshall 23-51

Bob Pruett (4-0) (Marshall 1965)
Marshall................ 1996 Delaware 59-14
Marshall................ 1996 Furman 54-0
Marshall................ 1996 UNI 31-14
Marshall................ 1996* Montana 49-29

Joe Purzycki (0-1) (Delaware 1971)
James Madison....... 1987 Marshall 12-41

Dennis Raetz (1-2) (Nebraska 1968)
Indiana St. .... 1983 Eastern Ill. 16-13 (2 ot)
Indiana St. .... 1983 Southern Ill. 7-23
Indiana St. .... 1984 Middle Tenn. 41-42 (3 ot)

Ron Randleman (3-4) (William Penn 1964)
Sam Houston St. .... 1986 Arkansas St. 7-48
Sam Houston St. .... 1991 Middle Tenn. 19-20 (ot)
Sam Houston St. .... 2001 Northern Ariz. 34-31
Sam Houston St. .... 2001 Montana 24-49
Sam Houston St. .... 2004 Western Ky. 54-24

Sam Houston St. .... 2004 Eastern Wash. 35-34
Sam Houston St. .... 2004 Montana 13-34

Tubby Raymond (11-11) (Michigan 1950)
Delaware .... 1981 Eastern Ky. 28-35
Delaware .... 1982 Colgate 20-13
Delaware .... 1982 Louisiana Tech 17-0
Delaware .... 1982 Eastern Ky. 14-17
Delaware .... 1986 William & Mary 51-17

Delaware .... 1986 Arkansas St. 14-55
Delaware .... 1988 Furman 7-21
Delaware .... 1991 James Madison 35-42 (2 ot)
Delaware .... 1992 Samford 56-21
Delaware .... 1992 La.-Monroe 41-18

Delaware .... 1992 Marshall 7-28
Delaware .... 1993 Montana 49-48
Delaware .... 1993 Marshall 31-34
Delaware .... 1995 Hofstra 38-17
Delaware .... 1995 McNeese St. 18-52

Delaware .... 1996 Marshall 14-59
Delaware .... 1997 Hofstra 24-14

Delaware .... 1997 Ga. Southern 16-7
Delaware .... 1997 McNeese St. 21-23
Delaware .... 2000 Portland St. 49-14
Delaware .... 2000 Lehigh 47-22
Delaware .... 2000 Ga. Southern 18-27

Don Read (8-4) (Sacramento St. 1959)
Montana .... 1988 Idaho 19-38
Montana .... 1989 Jackson St. 48-7
Montana .... 1989 Eastern Ill. 25-19
Montana .... 1989 Ga. Southern 15-45
Montana .... 1993 Delaware 48-49
Montana .... 1994 UNI 23-20
Montana .... 1994 McNeese St. 30-28
Montana .... 1994 Youngstown St. 9-28
Montana .... 1995 Eastern Ky. 48-0
Montana .... 1995 Ga. Southern 45-0
Montana .... 1995 Stephen F. Austin 70-14
Montana .... 1995* Marshall 22-20

Jim Reid (1-4) (Maine 1973)
Massachusetts......... 1988 Eastern Ky. 17-28
Massachusetts......... 1990 William & Mary 0-38
Richmond .... 1998 Lehigh 23-24
Richmond .... 2000 Youngstown St. 10-3
Richmond .... 2000 Montana 20-34

Dave Roberts (2-5) (Western Caro. 1968)
Western Ky. .... 1987 Eastern Ky. 17-40
Western Ky. .... 1988 Western Ill. 35-32
Western Ky. .... 1988 Eastern Ky. 24-41
La.-Monroe .... 1990 Nevada 14-27
La.-Monroe .... 1992 Alcorn St. 78-27
La.-Monroe .... 1992 Delaware 18-41
La.-Monroe .... 1993 Idaho 31-34

Steve Roberts (0-1) (Ouachita Baptist 1987)
Northwestern St. .... 2001 Montana 19-28

Eddie Robinson (0-3) (Leland 1941)
Grambling.............. 1980 Boise St. 9-14
Grambling.............. 1985 Arkansas St. 7-10
Grambling.............. 1989 Stephen F. Austin 56-59

Erk Russell (16-2) (Auburn 1949)
Ga. Southern.......... 1985 Jackson St. 27-0
Ga. Southern.......... 1985 Middle Tenn. 28-21
Ga. Southern.......... 1985 UNI 40-33
Ga. Southern.......... 1985* Furman 44-42
Ga. Southern.......... 1986 N.C. A&T 52-21
Ga. Southern.......... 1986 Nicholls St. 55-31
Ga. Southern.......... 1986 Nevada 48-38
Ga. Southern.......... 1986* Arkansas St. 48-21
Ga. Southern.......... 1987 Maine 31-28 (ot)
Ga. Southern.......... 1987 Appalachian St. 0-19
Ga. Southern.......... 1988 Citadel 38-20
Ga. Southern.......... 1988 Stephen F. Austin 27-6
Ga. Southern.......... 1988 Eastern Ky. 21-17
Ga. Southern.......... 1988 Furman 12-17
Ga. Southern.......... 1989 Villanova 52-36
Ga. Southern.......... 1989 Middle Tenn. 45-3
Ga. Southern.......... 1989 Montana 45-15
Ga. Southern.......... 1989* Stephen F. Austin 37-34

Jimmy Satterfield (7-3) (South Carolina 1962)
Furman .... 1986 Eastern Ky. 10-23
Furman .... 1988 Delaware 21-7
Furman .... 1988 Marshall 13-9
Furman .... 1988 Idaho 38-7
Furman .... 1988* Ga. Southern 17-12
Furman .... 1989 William & Mary 24-10
Furman .... 1989 Youngstown St. 42-23
Furman .... 1989 Stephen F. Austin 19-21
Furman .... 1990 Eastern Ky. 45-17
Furman .... 1990 Nevada 35-42 (3 ot)

Rip Scherer (2-2) (William & Mary 1974)
James Madison....... 1991 Delaware 42-35 (2 ot)
James Madison....... 1991 Samford 21-24
James Madison....... 1994 Troy 45-26
James Madison....... 1994 Marshall 21-28 (ot)

Howard Schnellenberger (2-1) (Kentucky 1956)
Fla. Atlantic .... 2003 Bethune-Cookman 32-24
Fla. Atlantic .... 2003 Northern Ariz. 48-25
Fla. Atlantic .... 2003 Colgate 24-36

Mike Sewak (2-3) (Virginia 1981)
Ga. Southern.......... 2002 Bethune-Cookman 34-0
Ga. Southern.......... 2002 Maine 31-7
Ga. Southern.......... 2002 Western Ky. 28-31
Ga. Southern.......... 2004 New Hampshire 23-27
Ga. Southern.......... 2005 Texas St. 35-50

Dal Shealy (1-2) (Carson-Newman 1960)
Richmond .... 1984 Boston U. 35-33
Richmond .... 1984 Rhode Island 17-23
Richmond .... 1987 Appalachian St. 3-20

Dick Sheridan (3-3) (South Carolina 1964)
Furman .... 1982 South Carolina St. 0-17
Furman .... 1983 Boston U. 35-16
Furman .... 1983 Western Caro. 7-14
Furman .... 1985 Rhode Island 59-15
Furman .... 1985 Nevada 35-12
Furman .... 1985 Ga. Southern 42-44

Matt Simon (0-1) (Eastern N.M. 1976)
North Texas........... 1994 Boise St. 20-24

Jason Simpson (0-1) (Southern Miss. 1995)
Tenn.-Martin .... 2006 Southern Ill. 30-36

George Small (0-1) (N.C. A&T 1979)
N.C. A&T.............. 2003 Wofford 10-31

John L. Smith (3-5) (Weber St. 1971)
Idaho .... 1989 Eastern Ill. 21-38
Idaho .... 1990 Missouri St. 41-35
Idaho .... 1990 Ga. Southern 27-28
Idaho .... 1992 McNeese St. 20-23
Idaho .... 1993 La.-Monroe 34-31
Idaho .... 1993 Boston U. 21-14
Idaho .... 1993 Youngstown St. 16-35
Idaho .... 1994 McNeese St. 21-38

Jerome Souers (^1-3) (Oregon 1983)
Northern Ariz. .... 1999^ Ga. Southern 29-72
Northern Ariz. .... 2001 Sam Houston St. 31-34
Northern Ariz. .... 2003 McNeese St. 35-3
Northern Ariz. .... 2003 Fla. Atlantic 25-48

Bob Spoo (1-7) (Purdue 1960)
Eastern Ill. .... 1989 Idaho 38-21
Eastern Ill. .... 1989 Montana 19-25
Eastern Ill. .... 1995 Stephen F. Austin 29-34
Eastern Ill. .... 1996 UNI 14-21
Eastern Ill. .... 2000 Montana 13-45
Eastern Ill. .... 2001 UNI 43-49
Eastern Ill. .... 2002 Western Ill. 9-48
Eastern Ill. .... 2005 Southern Ill. 6-21

Scott Stoker (0-2) (Northwestern St. 1991)
Northwestern St. .... 2002 Montana 14-45
Northwestern St. .... 2004 Montana 7-56

Tim Stowers (6-2) (Auburn 1979)
Ga. Southern.......... 1990 Citadel 31-0
Ga. Southern.......... 1990 Idaho 28-27
Ga. Southern.......... 1990 UCF 44-7
Ga. Southern.......... 1990* Nevada 36-13
Ga. Southern.......... 1993 Eastern Ky. 14-12
Ga. Southern.......... 1993 Youngstown St. 14-34
Ga. Southern.......... 1995 Troy 24-21
Ga. Southern.......... 1995 Montana 0-45

Charlie Taaffe (1-3) (Siena 1973)
Citadel.................. 1988 Ga. Southern 20-38
Citadel.................. 1990 Ga. Southern 0-31
Citadel.................. 1992 N.C. A&T 44-0
Citadel.................. 1992 Youngstown St. 17-42

Andy Talley (3-6) (Southern Conn. St. 1967)
Villanova............... 1989 Ga. Southern 36-52
Villanova............... 1991 Youngstown St. 16-17
Villanova............... 1992 Youngstown St. 20-23
Villanova............... 1996 East Tenn. St. 29-35
Villanova............... 1997 Colgate 49-28
Villanova............... 1997 Youngstown St. 34-37
Villanova............... 2002 Furman 45-38
Villanova............... 2002 Fordham 24-10
Villanova............... 2002 McNeese St. 28-39

Tommy Tate (3-4) (McNeese St. 1979)
McNeese St. .... 2000 Ga. Southern 17-42
McNeese St. .... 2001 Maine 10-14
McNeese St. .... 2002 Montana St. 21-14
McNeese St. .... 2002 Montana 24-20
McNeese St. .... 2002 Villanova 39-28
McNeese St. .... 2002 Western Ky. 14-34
McNeese St. .... 2003 Northern Ariz. 3-35

Frank Tavani (0-3) (Lebanon Valley 1975)
Lafayette................ 2004 Delaware 14-28
Lafayette................ 2005 Appalachian St. 23-34
Lafayette................ 2006 Massachusetts 14-35

Joe Taylor (0-5) (Western Ill. 1972)
Hampton .... 1997 Youngstown St. 13-28
Hampton .... 1998 Connecticut 34-42
Hampton .... 2004 William & Mary 35-42
Hampton .... 2005 Richmond 10-38
Hampton .... 2006 New Hampshire 38-41

Rick Taylor (1-3) (Gettysburg 1964)
Boston U. .... 1982 Colgate 7-21
Boston U. .... 1983 Eastern Ky. 24-20
Boston U. .... 1983 Furman 16-35
Boston U. .... 1984 Richmond 33-35

Bill Thomas (1-1) (Tennessee St. 1971)
Tennessee St. .... 1986 Jackson St. 32-23
Tennessee St. .... 1986 Nevada 6-33

Jay Thomas (0-1) (Southern Miss. 1988)
Nicholls St. .... 2005 Furman 12-14

Chris Tormey (0-1) (Idaho 1978)
Idaho .... 1995 McNeese St. 3-33

Jim Tressel (23-6) (Baldwin-Wallace 1975)
Youngstown St. ...... 1987 UNI 28-31
Youngstown St. ...... 1989 Eastern Ky. 28-24
Youngstown St. ...... 1989 Furman 23-42
Youngstown St. ...... 1990 UCF 17-20
Youngstown St. ...... 1991 Villanova 17-16
Youngstown St. ...... 1991 Nevada 30-28
Youngstown St. ...... 1991 Samford 10-0
Youngstown St. ...... 1991* Marshall 25-17
Youngstown St. ...... 1992 Villanova 23-20
Youngstown St. ...... 1992 Citadel 42-17
Youngstown St. ...... 1992 UNI 19-7
Youngstown St. ...... 1992 Marshall 28-31
Youngstown St. ...... 1993 UCF 56-30
Youngstown St. ...... 1993 Ga. Southern 34-14
Youngstown St. ...... 1993 Idaho 35-16
Youngstown St. ...... 1993* Marshall 17-5
Youngstown St. ...... 1994 Alcorn St. 63-20
Youngstown St. ...... 1994 Eastern Ky. 18-15
Youngstown St. ...... 1994 Montana 28-9
Youngstown St. ...... 1994* Boise St. 28-14
Youngstown St. ...... 1997 Hampton 28-13
Youngstown St. ...... 1997 Villanova 37-34
Youngstown St. ...... 1997 Eastern Wash. 25-14
Youngstown St. ...... 1997* McNeese St. 10-9
Youngstown St. ...... 1999 Montana 30-27
Youngstown St. ...... 1999 N.C. A&T 41-3
Youngstown St. ...... 1999 Florida A&M 27-24
Youngstown St. ...... 1999 Ga. Southern 24-59
Youngstown St. ...... 2000 Richmond 3-10

Matt Viator (0-1) (McNeese St. 1986)
McNeese St. .... 2006 Montana 6-31

Tim Walsh (0-1) (UC Riverside 1977)
Portland St. .... 2000 Delaware 14-49

Bob Waters (3-1) (Presbyterian 1960)
Western Caro. ...... 1983 Colgate 24-23
Western Caro. ...... 1983 Holy Cross 28-21
Western Caro. ...... 1983 Furman 14-7
Western Caro. ...... 1983 Southern Ill. 7-43

Mark Whipple (5-2) (Brown 1979)
Massachusetts......... 1998 McNeese St. 21-19
Massachusetts......... 1998 Lehigh 27-21
Massachusetts......... 1998 Northwestern St. 41-31
Massachusetts......... 1998* Ga. Southern 55-43
Massachusetts......... 1999 Furman 30-23 (ot)
Massachusetts......... 1999 Ga. Southern 21-38
Massachusetts......... 2003 Colgate 7-19

John Whitehead (1-2) (East Stroudsburg 1950)
Lehigh .... 1979 Murray St. 28-9
Lehigh .... 1979 Eastern Ky. 7-30
Lehigh .... 1980 Eastern Ky. 20-23

A.L. Williams (3-1) (Louisiana Tech 1957)
Louisiana Tech .... 1984 Mississippi Val. 66-19
Louisiana Tech .... 1984 Alcorn St. 44-21
Louisiana Tech .... 1984 Middle Tenn. 21-13
Louisiana Tech .... 1984 Montana St. 6-19

Steve Wilson (0-1) (Howard 1979)
Howard .... 1993 Marshall 14-28

Alex Wood (0-1) (Iowa 1979)
James Madison....... 1995 Appalachian St. 24-31

Sparky Woods (2-2) (Carson-Newman 1976)
Appalachian St. ..... 1986 Nicholls St. 26-28
Appalachian St. ..... 1987 Richmond 20-3
Appalachian St. ..... 1987 Ga. Southern 19-0
Appalachian St. ..... 1987 Marshall 10-24

Paul Wulff (1-2) (Washington St. 1990)
Eastern Wash. .... 2004 Southern Ill. 35-31
Eastern Wash. .... 2004 Sam Houston St. 34-35
Eastern Wash. .... 2005 UNI 38-41

Alvin Wyatt (0-2) (Bethune-Cookman 1970)
Bethune-Cookman ... 2002 Ga. Southern 0-34
Bethune-Cookman ... 2003 Fla. Atlantic 24-32

Dick Zornes (1-2) (Eastern Wash. 1968)
Eastern Wash. .... 1985 Idaho 42-38
Eastern Wash. .... 1985 UNI 14-17
Eastern Wash. .... 1992 UNI 14-17

**National championship. †Tennessee State's participation vacated by action of the NCAA Committee on Infractions. %Stephen F. Austin's participation vacated by action of the NCAA Committee on Infractions. ^Northern Arizona's participation vacated by action of the NCAA Committee on Infractions.*

Coaching Honors

FBS Coach-of-the-Year Award

(Selected by the American Football Coaches Association [AFCA] and the Football Writers Association of America [FWAA])

AFCA

1935 Lynn Waldorf, Northwestern
1936 Dick Harlow, Harvard
1937 Edward Mylin, Lafayette
1938 Bill Kern, Carnegie Mellon
1939 Eddie Anderson, Iowa

1940 Clark Shaughnessy, Stanford
1941 Frank Leahy, Notre Dame
1942 Bill Alexander, Georgia Tech
1943 Amos Alonzo Stagg, Pacific
1944 Carroll Widdoes, Ohio St.

1945 Bo McMillin, Indiana
1946 Red Blaik, Army
1947 Fritz Crisler, Michigan
1948 Bennie Oosterbaan, Michigan
1949 Bud Wilkinson, Oklahoma

1950 Charlie Caldwell, Princeton
1951 Chuck Taylor, Stanford
1952 Biggie Munn, Michigan St.
1953 Jim Tatum, Maryland
1954 Red Sanders, UCLA

1955 Duffy Daugherty, Michigan St.
1956 Bowden Wyatt, Tennessee
1957 Woody Hayes, Ohio St.
1958 Paul Dietzel, LSU
1959 Ben Schwartzwalder, Syracuse

1960 Murray Warmath, Minnesota
1961 Bear Bryant, Alabama
1962 John McKay, Southern California
1963 Darrell Royal, Texas
1964 Frank Broyles, Arkansas, and Ara Parseghian, Notre Dame

1965 Tommy Prothro, UCLA
1966 Tom Cahill, Army
1967 John Pont, Indiana
1968 Joe Paterno, Penn St.
1969 Bo Schembechler, Michigan

1970 Charlie McClendon, LSU, and Darrell Royal, Texas
1971 Bear Bryant, Alabama
1972 John McKay, Southern California
1973 Bear Bryant, Alabama
1974 Grant Teaff, Baylor

1975 Frank Kush, Arizona St.
1976 Johnny Majors, Pittsburgh
1977 Don James, Washington
1978 Joe Paterno, Penn St.
1979 Earle Bruce, Ohio St.

1980 Vince Dooley, Georgia
1981 Danny Ford, Clemson
1982 Joe Paterno, Penn St.
1983 Ken Hatfield, Air Force
1984 LaVell Edwards, Brigham Young

1985 Fisher DeBerry, Air Force
1986 Joe Paterno, Penn St.
1987 Dick MacPherson, Syracuse
1988 Don Nehlen, West Virginia
1989 Bill McCartney, Colorado

1990 Bobby Ross, Georgia Tech
1991 Bill Lewis, East Carolina
1992 Gene Stallings, Alabama
1993 Barry Alvarez, Wisconsin
1994 Tom Osborne, Nebraska

1995 Gary Barnett, Northwestern
1996 Bruce Snyder, Arizona St.
1997 Lloyd Carr, Michigan
1998 Phillip Fulmer, Tennessee
1999 Frank Beamer, Virginia Tech

2000 Bob Stoops, Oklahoma
2001 Larry Coker, Miami (Fla.) & Ralph Friedgen, Maryland
2002 Jim Tressel, Ohio St.
2003 Pete Carroll, Southern California
2004 Tommy Tuberville, Auburn

2005 Joe Paterno, Penn St.
2006 Jim Grobe, Wake Forest

EDDIE ROBINSON COACH OF THE YEAR (FWAA)

1957 Woody Hayes, Ohio St.
1958 Paul Dietzel, LSU
1959 Ben Schwartzwalder, Syracuse
1960 Murray Warmath, Minnesota
1961 Darrell Royal, Texas

1962 John McKay, Southern California
1963 Darrell Royal, Texas
1964 Ara Parseghian, Notre Dame
1965 Duffy Daugherty, Michigan St.
1966 Tom Cahill, Army

1967 John Pont, Indiana
1968 Woody Hayes, Ohio St.
1969 Bo Schembechler, Michigan
1970 Alex Agase, Northwestern
1971 Bob Devaney, Nebraska

1972 John McKay, Southern California
1973 Johnny Majors, Pittsburgh
1974 Grant Teaff, Baylor
1975 Woody Hayes, Ohio St.
1976 Johnny Majors, Pittsburgh

1977 Lou Holtz, Arkansas
1978 Joe Paterno, Penn St.
1979 Earle Bruce, Ohio St.
1980 Vince Dooley, Georgia
1981 Danny Ford, Clemson

1982 Joe Paterno, Penn St.
1983 Howard Schnellenberger, Miami (Fla.)
1984 LaVell Edwards, Brigham Young
1985 Fisher DeBerry, Air Force
1986 Joe Paterno, Penn St.

1987 Dick MacPherson, Syracuse
1988 Lou Holtz, Notre Dame
1989 Bill McCartney, Colorado
1990 Bobby Ross, Georgia Tech
1991 Don James, Washington

1992 Gene Stallings, Alabama
1993 Terry Bowden, Auburn
1994 Rich Brooks, Oregon
1995 Gary Barnett, Northwestern
1996 Bruce Snyder, Arizona St.

1997 Mike Price, Washington St.
1998 Phillip Fulmer, Tennessee
1999 Frank Beamer, Virginia Tech
2000 Bob Stoops, Oklahoma
2001 Ralph Friedgen, Maryland

2002 Jim Tressel, Ohio St.
2003 Nick Saban, LSU
2004 Urban Meyer, Utah
2005 Charlie Weis, Notre Dame
2006 Greg Schiano, Rutgers

FCS Coach-of-the-Year Award

(Selected by the American Football Coaches Association)

1983 Rey Dempsey, Southern Ill.
1984 Dave Arnold, Montana St.
1985 Dick Sheridan, Furman
1986 Erk Russell, Ga. Southern
1987 Mark Duffner, Holy Cross

1988 Jimmy Satterfield, Furman
1989 Erk Russell, Ga. Southern
1990 Tim Stowers, Ga. Southern
1991 Mark Duffner, Holy Cross
1992 Charlie Taafe, Citadel

1993 Dan Allen, Boston U.
1994 Jim Tressel, Youngstown St.
1995 Don Read, Montana
1996 Ray Tellier, Columbia
1997 Andy Talley, Villanova

1998 Mark Whipple, Massachusetts
1999 Paul Johnson, Ga. Southern
2000 Paul Johnson, Ga. Southern
2001 Bobby Johnson, Furman
2002 Jack Harbaugh, Western Ky.

2003 Dick Biddle, Colgate
2004 Mickey Matthews, James Madison
2005 Jerry Moore, Appalachian St.
2006 Jerry Moore, Appalachian St.

OTHER 2006 COACHING AWARDS

THE ESPN/HOME DEPOT COACH OF THE YEAR – Greg Schiano, Rutgers (Presented by The Home Depot to the nation's top coach)

BEAR BRYANT COACH OF THE YEAR – Chris Petersen, Boise St. (Presented by the National Sportscasters and Sportswriters Association)

WALTER CAMP COACH OF THE YEAR – Greg Schiano, Rutgers (Presented by the Walter Camp Foundation)

ASSOCIATED PRESS COACH OF THE YEAR – Jim Grobe, Wake Forest (Presented by The Associated Press member newspapers, TV and radio stations)

BOBBY DODD COACH OF THE YEAR – Jim Grobe, Wake Forest (Presented by the Bobby Dodd Coach of the Year Foundation, Atlanta, Georgia)

GEORGE MUNGER COACH OF THE YEAR – Greg Schiano, Rutgers (Presented annually by the Maxwell Football Club. The award is named for former University of Pennsylvania coach George Munger. His devotion to ethics in athletics, and his commitment to education is the standard for which all college coaches should strive.)

THE SPORTING NEWS COACH OF THE YEAR – Jim Grobe, Wake Forest

THE WOODY HAYES TROPHY – Jim Tressel, Ohio St.

SCHUTT SPORTS COACH OF THE YEAR – Greg Schiano, Rutgers (Presented by equipment manufacturer Schutt Sports and announced by American Football Monthly magazine)

SCHUTT SPORTS COACH OF THE YEAR (FCS) – Jerry Moore, Appalachian St. (Presented by equipment manufacturer Schutt Sports and announced by American Football Monthly magazine)

AFCA ASSISTANT COACH OF THE YEAR (FBS) – John Chavis, Tennessee, Associate Head Coach, Defensive Coordinator and Linebackers Coach (Presented by the American Football Coaches Association)

AFCA ASSISTANT COACH OF THE YEAR (FCS) – Sam Eddy, Youngstown St., Assistant Head Coach and Running Backs Coach (Presented by the American Football Coaches Association)

FRANK BROYLES AWARD (Top FBS Assistant Coach Award) – Bud Foster, Virginia Tech, Defensive Coordinator (Presented by Former Arkansas head coach Frank Broyles)

EDDIE ROBINSON COACH OF THE YEAR (FCS) – Jerry Moore, Appalachian St. (Presented by The Sports Network)

FOOTBALL GAZETTE COACH OF THE YEAR (FCS) – Craig Bohl, North Dakota St. (Presented by the weekly Football Gazette)

Added and Discontinued Programs

Nationally Prominent Teams That Permanently Dropped Football

Listed alphabetically at right are the all-time records of teams formerly classified as major college that permanently discontinued football. Also included are those teams that, retroactively, are considered to have been major college (before the advent of official classification in 1937) by virtue of their schedules (i.e., at least half of their games versus other major-college opponents). All schools listed were considered to have been major college or classified in either Division I-A or I-AA for a minimum of 10 consecutive seasons.

Team	Inclusive Seasons	Years	Won	Lost	Tied	Pct.†
Boston U.	1884-1997	78	315	371	28	.461
Cal St. Fullerton	1970-1992	23	107	150	3	.417
Canisius	1918-2002	13	42	72	5	.374
Carlisle Indian School	1893-1917	25	167	88	13	.647
Centenary (La.)	1894-1947	36	148	100	21	.589
Creighton	1900-1942	43	183	139	27	.563
Denver	1885-1960	73	273	262	40	.510
Detroit	1896-1964	64	305	200	25	.599
East Tenn. St.	1920-2003	80	342	398	27	.463
George Washington	1890-1966	58	209	240	34	.468
Gonzaga	1892-1941	39	130	99	20	.562
Haskell Institute	1896-1938	43	199	166	18	.543
Lamar	1951-1989	39	171	225	9	.433
Long Beach St.	1955-1991	37	199	183	4	.521
Manhattan	1923-1942	20	77	75	11	.506
Marquette	1892-1960	68	273	220	38	.550
New York U.	1873-1952	66	201	231	32	.468
Pacific	1919-1995	77	346	397	23	.467
St. John's (N.Y.)	1884-2002	25	148	108	1	.578
St. Louis	1899-1949	49	235	179	33	.563
St. Mary's (Cal.)	1892-2003	32	172	148	3	.537
St. Peter's	1971-1987, 1989-2006	35	82	219	1	.273
San Francisco	*1924-1951; 1965-1971	38	133	169	20	.444
Siena	1965-2003	17	34	123	0	.217
Texas-Arlington	1959-1985	27	129	150	2	.463
Wichita St.	1897-1986	89	375	402	47	.484
Xavier (Ohio)	1900-1973	61	302	223	21	.572

*†Ties computed as half won and half lost. *Discontinued football during 1952 after having been classified major college. Resumed at the Division II level during 1959-71, when it was discontinued again.*

Added or Resumed Programs Since 1968

NCAA Member Colleges

1968 (4)
Boise St.; *Chicago; New Jersey City (dropped 2002); UNLV.

1969 (2)
*Adelphi (dropped 1972); Towson.

1970 (6)
Cal St. Fullerton (dropped 1993); *Fordham; *Georgetown; Plattsburgh St. (dropped 1979); Plymouth St.; *St. Mary's (Cal.) (dropped 2003).

1971 (6)
Boston St. (dropped 1982); Dist. Columbia (dropped 1974, resumed 1978, dropped 1990); Federal City (dropped 1975); *New England Col. (dropped 1973); Rochester Inst. (dropped 1978); St. Peter's (suspended after one game 1984, resumed 1985, dropped 1988, resumed 1989, dropped 2006).

1972 (6)
Kean; *Lake Forest; Nicholls St.; Salisbury; *San Diego; Wm. Paterson.

1973 (7)
Albany St. (N.Y.); *Benedictine (Ill.); Bowie St.; James Madison; New Haven (dropped 2003); NYIT (dropped 1984); Seton Hall (dropped 1982).

1974 (2)
FDU-Florham; Framingham St.

1975 (2)
*Brooklyn (dropped 1991); *Canisius (dropped 2002).

1976 (1)
Oswego St. (dropped 1977).

1977 (2)
*Catholic; *Minn. St. Mankato.

1978 (7)
*Buffalo; *Dist. Columbia (dropped 1990); Iona; Marist; Pace; *St. Francis (Pa.); *St. John's (N.Y.) (dropped 2002).

1979 (2)
UCF; *Duquesne.

1980 (5)
*Loras; Mass.-Lowell; *Miles (dropped 1989, resumed 1990); Ramapo (dropped 1993); *Sonoma St. (dropped 1997).

1981 (4)
Buffalo St.; Mercyhurst; *West Ga.; Western New Eng.

1982 (2)
Valdosta St.; Westfield St.

1983 (2)
*Ky. Wesleyan; Stony Brook.

1984 (3)
Fitchburg St.; *Ga. Southern; *Samford.

1985 (6)
Ferrum; MacMurray; Maritime (N.Y.) (dropped 1986, resumed 1987, dropped 1989, resumed 2006); *St. Peter's (dropped 1988, resumed 1989, dropped 2006); *Villanova; Worcester St.

1986 (4)
*UC Santa Barb. (dropped 1992); Menlo; *Quincy; Wesley.

1987 (5)
*Aurora; *Drake; *Gallaudet (dropped 1994, resumed 2001, dropped 2003, resumed 2007); *Maritime (N.Y.) (dropped 1989, resumed 2006); St. John Fisher.

1988 (7)
Assumption; Bentley; Mass.-Boston (dropped 2000); Mass.-Dartmouth; *MIT (last team was in 1901); Siena (dropped 2003); Stonehill.

1989 (4)
*Gannon; Methodist; *St. Peter's (dropped 2006); *SMU.

1990 (3)
*Hardin-Simmons; *Miles; Thomas More.

1991 (3)
UAB; Charleston So.; Sacred Heart.

1992 (1)
*West Tex. A&M.

1993 (3)
*King's (Pa.); Monmouth; Salve Regina.

1994 (2)
Chapman; Robert Morris.

1996 (3)
Fairfield (dropped 2002); Merrimack; Westminster (Mo.).

1997 (3)
Hartwick; *La Salle; South Fla.

1998 (1)
Jacksonville.

1999 (3)
Bryant; St. Anselm; Wis. Lutheran.

2000 (4)
East Tex. Baptist; Greensboro; Mary Hardin-Baylor; Shenandoah.

2001 (7)
Averett; Chris. Newport; Fla. Atlantic; *Gallaudet (dropped 2003, resumed 2007); Rockford; Stillman; Utica.

2002 (2)
Florida Int'l; *St. Augustine's (dropped 1966).

2003 (4)
*Charleston (W.V.) (dropped 1957); Coastal Caro.; Shaw; *Southeastern La. (dropped 1986).

2005 (2)
Becker; St. Paul's (dropped 1988).

2006 (2)
LaGrange; *Maritime (N.Y.) (dropped 1989).

2007 (3)
*Birmingham-So. (dropped 1940); *Gallaudet (dropped 2003); *UNC Pembroke (dropped 1951).

**Previously dropped football.*

Non-NCAA Senior Colleges

1968 (2)
#Mo. Southern St.; #Southwest Minn. St.

1970 (1)
#Mo. Western St.

1971 (3)
#Concordia-St. Paul; #Gardner-Webb; #Grand Valley St.

1972 (5)
#Dr. Martin Luther; #Mars Hill; Northwestern (Minn.); Pillsbury; #Western Conn. St.

1973 (2)
#Liberty; #Mass. Maritime.

1974 (3)
#*N.M. Highlands; Northeastern Ill. (dropped 1988); #Saginaw Valley.

1976 (2)
#Maranatha Baptist; #Mesa St.

1977 (2)
Evangel; Olivet Nazarene.

1978 (3)
*Baptist Christian (dropped 1983); *St. Ambrose; *Yankton (dropped 1984).

1979 (2)
Fort Lauderdale (dropped 1982); Lubbock Christian (dropped 1983).

1980 (1)
Mid-America Nazarene.

1983 (2)
Ga. Southwestern (dropped 1989); #Loras.

1984 (3)
St. Paul Bible; #Southwest Baptist; *Union (Ky.).

1985 (4)
*Cumberland (Ky.); *Lambuth; *Tenn. Wesleyan; #Tiffin.

1986 (4)
*St. Francis (Ill.); Trinity Bible (N.D.); Urbana; #Wingate.

1987 (1)
#Greenville.

1988 (5)
Campbellsville; Mary; #Midwestern St.; Trinity (Ill.); *Western Mont.

1990 (3)
*Cumberland; Lindenwood; #Mt. St. Joseph (Ohio).

1991 (3)
Clinch Valley; #Lees-McRae (dropped 1994); #*Tusculum.

1993 (6)
#Ark.-Pine Bluff; *Bethel (Tenn.); #Chowan; Malone; St. Xavier (Ill.); Sue Bennett.

1996 (1)
*McKendree.

1998 (1)
#*Texas Lutheran.

2000 (3)
#Mount Ida; *Northern Mont. (dropped 1972); *Paul Quinn (dropped 1961).

2001 (4)
#Louisiana Col. (dropped 1969); #Minn.-Crookston; Southwestern Assemblies of God; Va.-Wise.

2002 (1)
Edward Waters.

2003 (1)
#North Greenville.

2005 (4)
#Central St. (Ohio); Concordia (Ala.); Seton Hill; Shorter.

2006 (2)
*Brevard (dropped 1952); Morrisville St.

2007 (3)
Faulkner; Marian (Ind.); *St. Vincent (dropped 1963).

**Previously dropped football. #Now NCAA member.*

Discontinued Programs Since 1950

(Includes NCAA member colleges and nonmember colleges; also colleges that closed or merged with other institutions.)

Before 1950, the following institutions had a major-college football program when it was discontinued and the year discontinued is in parentheses: Carlisle Indian School (1918); Centenary (La.) (1948); Creighton (1943); Gonzaga (1942); Haskell Institute (1939); Manhattan (1943).

1950 (9)
Alliance; Canisius (resumed 1975; dropped 2002); Huntington; Oklahoma City; *Portland; Rio Grande; Rollins; *St. Louis (I-A); Steubenville.

1951 (39)
Arkansas Col.; Atlantic Christian; Canterbury; Catholic (resumed 1977); CCNY; Corpus Christi (resumed 1954, dropped 1967); Daniel Baker; Detroit Tech; *Duquesne (resumed 1979) (I-AA); East Tex. Baptist (resumed 2000); Gannon (resumed 1989); *Georgetown (resumed 1970) (I-AA); Glassboro St. (resumed 1964—name changed to Rowan in 1992); Hartwick; High Point; LeMoyne-Owen; Lowell Textile; Lycoming (resumed 1954); McKendree (resumed 1996); Milligan; Mt. St. Mary's (Md.); Nevada (resumed 1952); New Bedford Textile; New England Col. (resumed 1971, dropped 1973); Niagara; UNC Pembroke (resumed 2007); Northern Idaho; Panzer; St. Mary's (Cal.) (resumed 1970, dropped 2003); St. Michael's (N.M.); Shurtleff (resumed 1953, dropped 1954); Southern Idaho; Southwestern (Tenn.) (resumed 1952—name changed to Rhodes in 1986); Southwestern (Tex.); Tillotson; Tusculum (resumed 1991); Washington (Md.); West Va. Wesleyan (resumed 1953); William Penn (resumed 1953).

1952 (14)
Aquinas; Brevard (resumed 2007); Clarkson; Erskine; Louisville Municipal; *Loyola Marymount; Nebraska Central; Rider; Samuel Huston; *San Francisco (resumed 1959, dropped 1972); Shaw (resumed 1953, dropped 1979); St. Bonaventure; St. Martin's; Teikyo Westmar (resumed 1953).

1953 (10)
Arnold; Aurora; Bethel (Tenn.) (resumed 1993); Cedarville; Champlain; Davis & Elkins (resumed 1955, dropped 1962); Georgetown (Ky.) (resumed 1955); *New York U. (I-A); *Santa Clara (resumed 1959, dropped 1993); Union (Tenn.).

1954 (8)
Adelphi (resumed 1969, dropped 1972); Case Tech (resumed 1955); Quincy (resumed 1986); St. Francis (Pa.) (resumed 1978); St. Michael's (Vt.); Shurtleff; *Wash. & Lee (resumed 1955); York (Neb.).

1955 (2)
*Fordham (resumed 1970) (I-AA); St. Mary's (Minn.).

1956 (4)
Brooklyn (resumed 1975, dropped 1991); Hendrix (resumed 1957, dropped 1961); William Carey; Wisconsin Extension.

1957 (4)
Charleston (W.V.) (resumed 2003); Lewis; Midwestern (Iowa) (resumed 1966); Stetson.

1959 (2)
Florida N&I; West Ga. (resumed 1981).

1960 (5)
Brandeis; Leland; Loras (resumed 1980); St. Ambrose (resumed 1978); Xavier (La.).

1961 (9)
*Denver (I-A); Hawaii (resumed 1962); Hendrix; Lincoln (Pa.); *Marquette (I-A); Paul Quinn (resumed 2000); Scranton; Texas College; Tougaloo.

1962 (5)
Azusa Pacific (resumed 1965); Davis & Elkins; San Diego (resumed 1972); Southern Cal Col.; Westminster (Utah) (resumed 1965, dropped 1979).

1963 (3)
Benedictine (Ill.) (resumed 1973); *Hardin-Simmons (resumed 1990); St. Vincent (resumed 2007).

1964 (2)
King's (Pa.) (resumed 1993); Paine.

1965 (7)
Claflin; *Detroit (I-A); Dillard; Miss. Industrial; Morris; Philander Smith; Rust.

1966 (1)
St. Augustine's (resumed 2002).

1967 (6)
Benedict; Corpus Christi; *George Washington (I-A); Jarvis Christian; Ozarks; South Caro. Trade.

1968 (2)
Edward Waters (resumed 2002); Frederick.

1969 (6)
Allen; Case Tech and Western Reserve merged to form Case Reserve; George Fox; Louisiana Col. (resumed 2001); UC San Diego; Wiley.

1971 (5)
Bradley; *Buffalo (resumed 1978); Hiram Scott; Lake Forest (resumed 1972); Parsons.

1972 (8)
Adelphi; UC Santa Barb. (resumed 1986, dropped 1992); Haverford; North Dak.-Ellendale; Northern Mont. (resumed 2000); Northwood (Tex.); San Francisco (I-A); Sonoma St. (resumed 1980, dropped 1997).

1973 (2)
New England Col.; N.M. Highlands (resumed 1974).

1974 (6)
Col. of Emporia; Dist. Columbia (resumed 1978, dropped 1990); Drexel; Ill.-Chicago; Samford (resumed 1984) (I-AA); *Xavier (Ohio) (I-A).

1975 (6)
Baptist Christian (resumed 1978, dropped 1983); Bridgeport; Federal City; *Tampa; Vermont; Wis.-Milwaukee.

1976 (3)
UC Riverside; Minn. St. Mankato (resumed 1977); Northland.

1977 (4)
Caltech; Oswego St.; Whitman; Yankton (resumed 1978, dropped 1984).

1978 (3)
Cal St. L.A.; Col. of Idaho; Rochester Inst.

1979 (5)
Miles (resumed 1980, dropped 1989, resumed 1990); Mont. St.-Billings; Plattsburgh St.; Shaw (resumed 2003); Westminster (Utah).

1980 (3)
Alliant Int'l; Gallaudet (resumed 1987); Md.-East. Shore.

1981 (2)
Bluefield St.; *Villanova (resumed 1985) (I-AA).

1982 (4)
Boston St.; Fort Lauderdale; Milton; Seton Hall.

1983 (3)
Baptist Christian; Cal Poly Pomona; Lubbock Christian.

1984 (5)
Fisk; NYIT; St. Peter's (suspended after one game, resumed 1985, dropped 1988, resumed 1989, dropped 2006) (I-AA); So. Dak.-Springfield; Yankton.

1985 (1)
Colorado St.-Pueblo.

1986 (4)
Drake (resumed 1987) (I-AA); Maritime (N.Y.) (resumed 1987, dropped 1989, resumed 2006); Southeastern La. (resumed 2003) (I-AA); *Texas-Arlington (I-A).

1987 (4)
Bishop; *SMU (resumed 1989) (I-A); Western Mont. (resumed 1988); *Wichita St. (I-A).

1988 (4)
Northeastern Ill.; St. Paul's (resumed 2005); St. Peter's (resumed 1989, dropped 2006); Texas Lutheran (resumed 1998).

1989 (3)
Ga. Southwestern; Maritime (N.Y.) (resumed 2006); Miles (resumed 1990).

1990 (2)
*Lamar (I-A); Lincoln (Mo.) (resumed 1999).

1991 (3)
Brooklyn; Tarkio; West Tex. A&M (resumed 1992).

1992 (3)
*Long Beach St. (I-A); Pacific (Ore.); St. Mary of the Plains.

1993 (5)
*Cal St. Fullerton (I-A); Cameron; Ramapo; Santa Clara; Wis.-Superior.

1994 (5)
Cal St. East Bay; Gallaudet (resumed 2001); Lees-McRae; Oregon Tech; Upsala.

1995 (1)
San Fran. St.

1996 (1)
*Pacific (I-A).

1997 (3)
Cal St. Chico; Central St. (Ohio) (resumed 2005); Sonoma St.

1998 (2)
Boston U. (I-AA); Evansville (I-AA).

2000 (3)
Mass.-Boston; Morningside; Swarthmore.

2001 (1)
Cal St. Northridge (I-AA).

2002 (6)
Canisius (I-AA); Fairfield (I-AA); Mass.-Lowell; Morris Brown; New Jersey City; St. John's (N.Y.) (I-AA).

2003 (5)
East Tenn. St. (I-AA); Gallaudet (resumed 2007); New Haven; St. Mary's (Cal.) (I-AA); Siena (I-AA).

2005 (2)
Si Tanka, Allen.

2006 (2)
Mansfield; St. Peter's.

**Classified major college previous year.*

***Note:** In parentheses is classification at the time the institution discontinued the football program. Before 1978, major-college programs are identified as I-A.*

Championship Results

Division I Championship

2006 Title Game Summary

Mountaineers Execute Game Plan Perfectly in Repeat Win: Appalachian State stuck with its offensive game plan of feeding the ball to tailback Kevin Richardson and relying on the legs and arm of freshman quarterback Armanti Edwards against a stingy Massachusetts defense in the Division I Football Championship final.

The Mountaineers duo proved to be too much for Massachusetts, which had not allowed any points in the second half during the playoffs, as Appalachian State took the title, 28-17, in front of 22,808 fans December 15 in Chattanooga, Tennessee.

Richardson ran for four touchdowns and set a Football Championship Subdivision record with 30 rushing scores on the season. Edwards, who surpassed 2,000 yards passing and 1,000 rushing this season, hurt the Minutemen with 146 yards passing and 81 yards on the ground.

"It was no mystery coming in," said Massachusetts coach Don Brown. "We knew we had our hands full. We got them in third-and-longs and Edwards hurt us with his legs, which we knew he could."

Richardson, who totaled 179 yards rushing, consistently found running room despite playing with a shoulder injury. He said the adrenaline of trying to win Appalachian State's second straight national championship helped take his mind off the soreness.

"It always feels good coming from nothing and working hard enough to be successful," Richardson told the Chattanooga Times-Free Press. "I couldn't worry about the pain, because this was a once-in-a-lifetime opportunity."

The Mountaineers became the first program to win consecutive Football Championship Subdivision titles since Georgia Southern in 1999 and 2000.

Most of the 22,808 in attendance — the largest gathering for a title game since Finley Stadium started hosting the event in 1997 — were rooting for Appalachian State. The institution's campus is located in Boone, North Carolina, which is within driving distance of Chattanooga.

"It almost was like playing at home," said Appalachian State coach Jerry Moore, whose team went 14-1, with the lone loss coming at North Carolina State, 23-10.

Massachusetts, which trailed, 14-7, at the half, tied the game on a 17-yard touchdown pass from Liam Coen to Brad Listorti with 4:22 remaining in the third quarter.

Richardson's third scoring run gave Appalachian State a 21-14 advantage with 13:22 remaining in the game.

Minutemen kicker Matt Koepplin pulled his team to within four points with a field goal at the 8:46 mark.

Appalachian State then put the game in the hands of Richardson. The Mountaineers chewed 6:46 off the clock, thanks to giving the ball to Richardson 10 times. He capped the 80-yard drive with a 2-yard touchdown run with 1:51 remaining.

"Our offensive linemen did a great job," Richardson said. "We just came out and finished our game."

Appalachian State defensive back Corey Lynch intercepted Coen on Massachusetts' final drive. The Minutemen ended their season 13-2.

"We pride ourselves on the physical yards, and Appalachian State just made more physical yards than we did," Brown said.

The Mountaineers rushed for 285 yards compared to 151 for Massachusetts, which was seeking its first national crown since 1998.

FINLEY STADIUM/DAVENPORT FIELD, CHATTANOOGA, TENNESSEE; DECEMBER 15

(Note: The time listed at the beginning of each scoring play is the time remaining in the quarter. Listed after the scoring play or conversion are the number of plays, yards and time elapsed on the scoring drive.)

Score by Quarters	**1**	**2**	**3**	**4**	**Final**
Appalachian St. (Record: 14-1)	7	7	0	14	28
Massachusetts (Record: 13-2)	7	0	7	3	17

FIRST QUARTER

11:49 Massachusetts—Matt Lawrence 1 run (Chris Koepplin kick), 8-80 3:11, Appalachian St. 0 - Massachusetts 7

1:15 Appalachian St.—Kevin Richardson 45 run (Julian Rauch kick), 4-70 1:27, Appalachian St. 7 - Massachusetts 7

SECOND QUARTER

0:49 Appalachian St.—Richardson 6 run (Rauch kick), 11-78 4:19, Appalachian St. 14 - Massachusetts 7

THIRD QUARTER

4:22 Massachusetts—Brad Listorti 17 pass from Liam Coen (Koepplin kick), 11-81 4:25, Appalachian St. 14 - Massachusetts 14

FOURTH QUARTER

13:22 Appalachian St.—Richardson 4 run (Rauch kick), 13-71 5:50, Appalachian St. 21 - Massachusetts 14

8:46 Massachusetts—Koepplin 42 field goal, 10-55 4:31, Appalachian St. 21 - Massachusetts 17

1:51 Appalachian St.—Richardson 2 run (Rauch kick), 14-80 6:46, Appalachian St. 28 - Massachusetts 17

	Appalachian St.	**Massachusetts**
FIRST DOWNS	24	19
RUSHES-YARDS (NET)	53-285	32-151
PASSING YDS (NET)	146	221
Passes Att-Comp-Int	19-12-1	33-20-2
TOTAL OFFENSE PLAYS-YARDS	72-431	65-372
Fumble Returns-Yards	0-0	0-0
Punt Returns-Yards	3-36	1-2
Kickoff Returns-Yards	4-79	0-0
Interception Returns-Yards	2-23	1-0
Punts (Number-Avg.)	4-31.5	4-44.8
Fumbles-Lost	0-0	0-0
Penalties-Yards	3-15	2-25
Possession Time	33:10	26:50
Third-Down Conversions	7 of 14	5 of 12
Fourth-Down Conversions	2 of 2	1 of 1
Red-Zone Scores-Chances	3-3	2-2
Sacks By: Number-Yards	1-4	1-7

INDIVIDUAL STATISTICS

Rushing—Appalachian St.: Richardson 30-179; Armanti Edwards 15-81; Devon Moore 6-29; Team 2-minus 4. Massachusetts: Steve Baylark 24-133; Lawrence 2-13; Mike Omar 1-8; Rasheed Rancher 1-3; Coen 2-minus 2; Tim Washington 2-minus 4.

Passing—Appalachian St.: Edwards 12-19-1-146. Massachusetts: Coen 20-33-2-221.

Receiving—Appalachian St.: Dexter Jackson 3-44; William Mayfield 3-44; T.J. Courman 3-25; Josh Johnson 1-15; Richardson 1-14; Daniel Bettis 1-4. Massachusetts: Listorti 5-78; J.J. Moore 4-61; Brandon London 4-31; Baylark 3-24; Lawrence 2-14; Washington 1-7; Rancher 1-6.

Sacks (UA-A)—Appalachian St.: Marques Murrell 0-1; Omarr Byrom 0-1. Massachusetts: Brandon Collier 1-0.

Tackles (UA-A)—Appalachian St.: Jeremy Wiggins 7-1; Corey Lynch 7-0; Pierre Banks 5-1; Jerome Touchstone 5-0; Monte Smith 3-1; Murrell 3-1; Cam Speer 3-0; Justin Woazeah 3-0; Byrom 2-1; Jacque Roman 2-0; Gary Tharrington 1-1; Daniel Orlebar 1-0; Mike King 1-0. Massachusetts: Charles Walker 9-2; Jason Hatchell 8-0; James Ihedigbo 6-0; Sean Smalls 5-0; David Burris 5-0; Brad Anderson 2-2; Tracy Belton 3-0; Michael Meggett 3-0; Brandon Smith 3-0; George Byrd 2-1; Jason Leonard 2-0; Domenique Milton 2-0; Brandon Freeman 2-0; Darrlyn Fenner 1-0; E.J. Barthel 1-0; Brian Ellis 1-0; Michael Hanson 1-0; Darnel DeLaire 1-0; Alex Miller 1-0; Courtney Robinson 1-0; Coen 1-0; Collier 1-0; Eric Dickson 0-1; London 0-1; John Hatchell 0-1.

Interceptions—Appalachian St.: Lynch 1-17; Smith 1-6. Massachusetts: Ihedigbo 1-0.

Fumbles—Appalachian St.: None. Massachusetts: None.
Stadium: Finley Stadium/Davenport Field
Attendance: 22,808
Kickoff time: 8:10 p.m. **End of Game:** 11:07 p.m. **Total elapsed time:** 2:57
Officials—Referee: J. Sullivan; Umpire: J. Shaw; Linesman: T. Stapleton; Line Judge: D. Schinderle; Back Judge: R. Quinlan; Field Judge: R. Townsend; Side Judge: K. Rockwell; Scorer: L. Trent.
Temperature: 49 **Wind:** NW 1 **Weather:** Clear

NCAA Division I Football Championship History

1978 At the 72nd NCAA Convention (January 1978) in Atlanta, Ga., the membership voted to establish the Division I-AA Football Championship and a statistics program for the division. The format for the first I-AA championship, held in Wichita Falls, Texas, was a single-elimination, four-team tournament. Florida A&M defeated Massachusetts, 35-28, in the title game. The game was televised by ABC.

1981 The championship expanded to include eight teams in a single-elimination tournament.

1982 The championship expanded to include 12 teams. Eight teams played first-round games at campus sites, and the top four teams, seeded by the Division I-AA Football Committee, received byes.

1986 The championship field expanded to its current format of 16 teams with each team playing a first-round game.

1987 Louisiana-Monroe defeated Marshall, 43-42, in the closest game in championship history.

1989 A then-record 25,725 fans watched Georgia Southern down Stephen F. Austin, 37-34, in the championship game at Allen E. Paulson Stadium in Statesboro, Ga.

1990 Georgia Southern won its fourth I-AA championship, adding to its titles in 1985, 1986 and 1989.

1991 Youngstown State won its first national championship with a 25-17 victory over Marshall. Penguin head coach Jim Tressel joined his father, Lee, as the only father-son combination to win NCAA football titles. Lee Tressel won the 1978 Division III championship at Baldwin-Wallace.

1992 A then-record crowd of 31,304 in Huntington, W.Va., saw Marshall return the favor with a 31-28 win over Youngstown State for its first I-AA title.

1993 The I-AA championship provided for a maximum field of 16 teams. Six member conferences (Big Sky, Gateway, Ohio Valley, Southern, Southland and Yankee) were granted automatic qualification for their respective winners. Youngstown State won its second I-AA title with a 17-5 victory over Marshall before a crowd of 29,218 in Huntington, W.Va.

1994 Youngstown State won its third national title in four years with a 28-14 victory over Boise State.

1995 Montana won its first Division I-AA title before a championship record crowd of 32,106 in Huntington, W.Va.

1996 Marshall, making its fifth visit to the championship game since 1991, won its second Division I-AA title with a 49-29 victory over defending champion Montana before 30,052 in Huntington, W.Va.

1997 Youngstown State won its fourth national title in the 1990s with a 10-9 victory over McNeese State in Chattanooga, Tenn.

1999 Georgia Southern closed out the century with another national title, posting a 59-24 victory over Youngstown State. The Eagles won their fifth title, surpassing Youngstown State's four championships and taking over the division lead in crowns.

2000 Georgia Southern rallied past Montana, 27-25, to claim back-to-back titles for the third time in its Division I-AA history.

2001 Montana won a defensive duel with Furman, 13-6, to claim its second title.

2002 Western Kentucky won its first Division I-AA championship with a 34-14 victory over McNeese State, which lost in the final for the second time (1997 in 10-9 loss to Youngstown State). Coach Jack Harbaugh, father of former Chicago Bears' and Indianapolis Colts' quarterback Jim Harbaugh, won his first NCAA title.

2003 Delaware won its first NCAA crown since winning the 1979 Division II championship. The Blue Hens outscored their opponents by a combined margin of 149-23 and posted the first championship-game shutout with a 40-0 blanking of previously unbeaten Colgate. It was the first NCAA title for head coach and former Delaware linebacker K.C. Keeler, who had five second-place finishes at Division III Rowan.

2004 James Madison was the second straight champion to come out of the Atlantic 10 Conference after defeating Montana, 31-21. The 2003 champion was Delaware. The Dukes also made history on its way to the championship game, becoming the first team to advance to the title contest with three straight wins on the road. James Madison won preliminary-round games at Lehigh, Furman and William and Mary.

2005 Appalachian State made it championship number eight for the Southern Conference as the Mountaineers rallied from a 16-7 halftime deficit to defeat the University of Northern Iowa, 21-16. The two teams played in front of a crowd of 19,219.

2006 Division I-AA is now known as the Football Championship Subdivision (FCS) and Division I-A is now the Football Bowl Subdivision (FBS). Since the NCAA does not sponsor a championship for the FBS, the tournament to determine an FCS winner is now called the Division I Football Championship. Appalachian State became the first repeat champion since Georgia Southern in 1999 and 2000. The Mountaineers scored two fourth-quarter touchdowns to break a 14-14 tie and take a 28-17 victory in front of a crowd of 22,808, the highest attendance in the championship's 10-year run in Chattanooga.

Division I All-Time Championship Results

Year	Champion	Coach	Score	Runner-Up	Site	Attendance
1978	Florida A&M	Rudy Hubbard	35-28	Massachusetts	Wichita Falls, Texas	13,604
1979	Eastern Ky.	Roy Kidd	30-7	Lehigh	Orlando, Fla.	5,200
1980	Boise St.	Jim Criner	31-29	Eastern Ky.	Sacramento, Calif.	8,157
1981	Idaho St.	Dave Kragthorpe	34-23	Eastern Ky.	Wichita Falls, Texas	11,002
1982	Eastern Ky.	Roy Kidd	17-14	Delaware	Wichita Falls, Texas	11,257
1983	Southern Ill.	Rey Dempsey	43-7	Western Caro.	Charleston, S.C.	15,950
1984	Montana St.	Dave Arnold	19-6	Louisiana Tech	Charleston, S.C.	9,125
1985	Ga. Southern	Erk Russell	44-42	Furman	Tacoma, Wash.	5,306
1986	Ga. Southern	Erk Russell	48-21	Arkansas St.	Tacoma, Wash.	4,419
1987	La.-Monroe	Pat Collins	43-42	Marshall	Pocatello, Idaho	11,513
1988	Furman	Jimmy Satterfield	17-12	Ga. Southern	Pocatello, Idaho	11,500
1989	Ga. Southern	Erk Russell	37-34	*Stephen F. Austin	Statesboro, Ga.	25,725
1990	Ga. Southern	Tim Stowers	36-13	Nevada	Statesboro, Ga.	23,204
1991	Youngstown St.	Jim Tressel	25-17	Marshall	Statesboro, Ga.	12,667
1992	Marshall	Jim Donnan	31-28	Youngstown St.	Huntington, W.Va.	31,304
1993	Youngstown St.	Jim Tressel	17-5	Marshall	Huntington, W.Va.	29,218
1994	Youngstown St.	Jim Tressel	28-14	Boise St.	Huntington, W.Va.	27,674
1995	Montana	Don Read	22-20	Marshall	Huntington, W.Va.	32,106
1996	Marshall	Bob Pruett	49-29	Montana	Huntington, W.Va.	30,052
1997	Youngstown St.	Jim Tressel	10-9	McNeese St.	Chattanooga, Tenn.	14,771
1998	Massachusetts	Mark Whipple	55-43	Ga. Southern	Chattanooga, Tenn.	17,501
1999	Ga. Southern	Paul Johnson	59-24	Youngstown St.	Chattanooga, Tenn.	20,052
2000	Ga. Southern	Paul Johnson	27-25	Montana	Chattanooga, Tenn.	17,156
2001	Montana	Joe Glenn	13-6	Furman	Chattanooga, Tenn.	12,698
2002	Western Ky.	Jack Harbaugh	34-14	McNeese St.	Chattanooga, Tenn.	12,360
2003	Delaware	K.C. Keeler	40-0	Colgate	Chattanooga, Tenn.	14,281
2004	James Madison	Mickey Matthews	31-21	Montana	Chattanooga, Tenn.	15,599
2005	Appalachian St.	Jerry Moore	21-16	UNI	Chattanooga, Tenn.	19,219
2006	Appalachian St.	Jerry Moore	28-17	Massachusetts	Chattanooga, Tenn.	22,808

**Stephen F. Austin's participation in 1989 Division I championship vacated.*

2006 Division I Championship Results

FIRST ROUND
Appalachian St. 45, Coastal Caro. 28
Montana St. 31, Furman 13
Illinois St. 24, Eastern Ill. 13
Youngstown St. 35, James Madison 31
Massachusetts 35, Lafayette 14
New Hampshire 41, Hampton 38
Southern Ill. 36, Tenn.-Martin 30
Montana 31, McNeese St. 6

QUARTERFINALS
Appalachian St. 38, Montana St. 17
Youngstown St. 28, Illinois St. 21
Massachusetts 24, New Hampshire 17
Montana 20, Southern Ill. 3

SEMIFINALS
Appalachian St. 49, Youngstown St. 24
Massachusetts 19, Montana 17

CHAMPIONSHIP
Appalachian St. 28, Massachusetts 17

Individual Records

GAME

NET YARDS RUSHING
333—Adrian Peterson, Ga. Southern (38) vs. Massachusetts (21), 12-4-99.

RUSHES ATTEMPTED
46—Tamron Smith, Youngstown St. (10) vs. Samford (0), 12-14-91.

TOUCHDOWNS BY RUSHING
6—Sean Sanders, Weber St. (59) vs. Idaho (30), 11-28-87.

NET YARDS PASSING
517—Todd Hammel, Stephen F. Austin (59) vs. Grambling (56), 11-25-89.

PASSES ATTEMPTED
82—Steve McNair, Alcorn St. (20) vs. Youngstown St. (63), 11-25-94.

PASSES COMPLETED
52—Steve McNair, Alcorn St. (20) vs. Youngstown St. (63), 11-25-94.

PASSES HAD INTERCEPTED
7—Jeff Gilbert, Western Caro. (7) vs. Southern Ill. (43), 12-17-83.

TOUCHDOWN PASSES
6—Mike Smith, UNI (41) vs. La.-Monroe (44), 12-12-87; Clemente Gordon, Grambling (56) vs. Stephen F. Austin (59), 11-25-89.

COMPLETION PERCENTAGE
(Min. 15 Attempts)
.882—Jeff Ryan, Youngstown St. (41) vs. N.C. A&T (3), 12-4-99 (15 of 17).

NET YARDS RUSHING AND PASSING
539—Todd Hammel, Stephen F. Austin (59) vs. Grambling (56), 11-25-89 (22 rushing, 517 passing).

RUSHING AND PASSING PLAYS
91—Steve McNair, Alcorn St. (20) vs. Youngstown St. (63), 11-25-94 (9 rushing, 82 passing).

PUNTING AVERAGE
(Min. 3 Punts)
54.5—Jay Heibel, Lehigh (22) vs. Delaware (47), 12-2-2000 (4 for 218).

PUNTS
14—Fred McRae, Jackson St. (0) vs. Stephen F. Austin (24), 11-26-88.

RECEPTIONS
18—Brian Forster, Rhode Island (23) vs. Richmond (17), 12-1-84.

NET YARDS RECEIVING
288—Randy Moss, Marshall (59) vs. Delaware (14), 11-30-96 (8 catches).

TOUCHDOWN RECEPTIONS
4—Tony DiMaggio, Rhode Island (35) vs. Akron (27), 11-30-85; Randy Moss, Marshall (49) vs. Montana (29), 12-21-96.

INTERCEPTIONS
4—Greg Shipp, Southern Ill. (43) vs. Western Caro. (7), 12-17-83.

YARDS GAINED ON INTERCEPTION RETURNS
117—Kevin Sullivan, Massachusetts (44) vs. Nevada (21), 12-9-78.

YARDS GAINED ON PUNT RETURNS
121—Darren Sharper, William & Mary (45) vs. Jackson St. (6), 11-30-96.

YARDS GAINED ON KICKOFF RETURNS
232—Mike Cadore, Eastern Ky. (32) vs. La.-Monroe (33), 12-5-87, 6 returns, 1 for 99-yard TD.

POINTS
36—Sean Sanders, Weber St. (59) vs. Idaho (30), 11-28-87.

TOUCHDOWNS
6—Sean Sanders, Weber St. (59) vs. Idaho (30), 11-28-87.

EXTRA POINTS
10—Andy Larson, Montana (70) vs. Stephen F. Austin (14), 12-9-95.

FIELD GOALS
5—Matt Fordyce, Fordham (29) vs. Northeastern (24), 11-30-2002; Justin Langan, Western Ill. (43) vs. Montana St. (40) (2 ot), 11-29-2003.

TOURNAMENT

NET YARDS RUSHING
897—Adrian Peterson, Ga. Southern, 1999 (134 vs. Northern Ariz., 333 vs. Massachusetts, 183 vs. Illinois St., 247 vs. Youngstown St.)

RUSHES ATTEMPTED
123—Ray Whalen, Nevada, 1990 (21 vs. La.-Monroe, 34 vs. Furman, 44 vs. Boise St., 24 vs. Ga. Southern).

NET YARDS PASSING
1,500—Dave Dickenson, Montana, 1995 (441 vs. Eastern Ky., 408 vs. Ga. Southern, 370 vs. Stephen F. Austin, 281 vs. Marshall).

PASSES ATTEMPTED
177—Jeff Gilbert, Western Caro., 1983 (47 vs. Colgate, 52 vs. Holy Cross, 45 vs. Furman, 33 vs. Southern Ill.); Brian Ah Yat, Montana, 1996 (48 vs. Nicholls St., 34 vs. East Tenn. St., 40 vs. Troy, 55 vs. Marshall).

PASSES COMPLETED
122—Dave Dickenson, Montana, 1995 (31 vs. Eastern Ky., 37 vs. Ga. Southern, 25 vs. Stephen F. Austin, 29 vs. Marshall).

PASSES HAD INTERCEPTED
11—Todd Hammel, Stephen F. Austin, 1989 (0 vs. Grambling, 4 vs. Missouri St., 2 vs. Furman, 5 vs. Ga. Southern).

TOUCHDOWN PASSES
14—Todd Hammel, Stephen F. Austin, 1989 (5 vs. Grambling, 4 vs. Missouri St., 2 vs. Furman, 3 vs. Ga. Southern).

COMPLETION PERCENTAGE
(Min. 40 Completions)
.769—Giovanni Carmazzi, Hofstra, 1999, 50 of 65 (22-30 vs. Lehigh, 28-35 vs. Illinois St.)

RECEPTIONS
41—Joe Douglass, Montana, 1996 (10 vs. Nicholls St., 10 vs. East Tenn. St., 8 vs. Troy, 13 vs. Marshall).

NET YARDS RECEIVING
636—Randy Moss, Marshall, 1996 (288 vs. Delaware, 82 vs. Furman, 46 vs. UNI, 220 vs. Montana).

TOUCHDOWN RECEPTIONS
10—Randy Moss, Marshall, 1996 (3 vs. Delaware, 2 vs. Furman, 1 vs. UNI, 4 vs. Montana).

POINTS
74—Adrian Peterson, Ga. Southern, 1999 (6 vs. Northern Ariz., 32 vs. Massachusetts, 18 vs. Illinois St., 18 vs. Youngstown St.).

TOUCHDOWNS
12—Adrian Peterson, Ga. Southern, 1999 (1 vs. Northern Ariz., 5 vs. Massachusetts, 3 vs. Illinois St., 3 vs. Youngstown St.).

LONGEST PLAYS

RUSH
90—Henry Fields, McNeese St. (38) vs. Idaho (21), 11-26-94, TD.

PASS (INCLUDING RUN)
90—Paul Singer 22 pass to Derek Swanson and 68 fumble recovery advancement by Steve Williams, Western Ill. (32) vs. Western Ky. (35), 11-26-88.

FIELD GOAL
56—Tony Zendejas, Nevada (27) vs. Idaho St. (20), 11-26-83.

PUNT
88—Mike Cassidy, Rhode Island (20) vs. Montana St. (32), 12-8-84.

PUNT RETURN
86—Antonio Veals, Western Ky. (59) vs. Murray St. (20), 11-30-2002, TD.

KICKOFF RETURN
100—Chris Fontenette, McNeese St. (7) vs. UNI (29), 12-5-92, TD.

INTERCEPTION RETURN
100—Melvin Cunningham, Marshall (28) vs. James Madison (21) (ot), 12-3-94, TD; Paul Williams, Delaware (38) vs. Hofstra (17), 11-25-95, TD.

FUMBLE RETURN
95—Randy Smith, Youngstown St. (63) vs. Alcorn St. (20), 11-25-94, TD.

Team Records

GAME

FIRST DOWNS
41—Montana (45) vs. Ga. Southern (0), 12-2-95.

FIRST DOWNS BY RUSHING
26—La.-Monroe (78) vs. Alcorn St. (27), 11-28-92.

FIRST DOWNS BY PASSING
29—Alcorn St. (20) vs. Youngstown St. (63), 11-25-94.

NET YARDS RUSHING
638—Ga. Southern (59) vs. Youngstown St. (24), 12-18-99 (59 rushes).

RUSHES ATTEMPTED
81—Youngstown St. (10) vs. Samford (0), 12-14-91.

NET YARDS PASSING
537—Montana (30) vs. McNeese St. (28), 12-3-94.

PASSES ATTEMPTED
90—Rhode Island (15) vs. Furman (59), 12-7-85.

PASSES COMPLETED
52—Alcorn St. (20) vs. Youngstown St. (63), 11-25-94.

PASSES HAD INTERCEPTED
7—Western Caro. (7) vs. Southern Ill. (43), 12-17-83; Rhode Island (15) vs. Furman (59), 12-7-85; Weber St. (23) vs. Marshall (51), 12-5-87.

COMPLETION PERCENTAGE
(Min. 20 Attempts)
.850—Illinois St. (37) vs. Hofstra (20), 12-4-99(34 of 40).

NET YARDS RUSHING AND PASSING
742—La.-Monroe (78) vs. Alcorn St. (27), 11-28-92 (502 rushing, 240 passing).

RUSHING AND PASSING PLAYS
114—Nevada (42) vs. Furman (35) (3 ot), 12-1-90 (47 rushing, 67 passing).

PUNTING AVERAGE
(Min. 4 Punts)
54.5—Lehigh (22) vs. Delaware (47), 12-2-2000 (4 for 218).

PUNTS
14—Jackson St. (0) vs. Stephen F. Austin (24), 11-26-88.

PUNTS BLOCKED
2—Florida A&M (35) vs. Massachusetts (28), 12-16-78; Boise St. (14) vs. Grambling (9), 12-13-80.

YARDS GAINED ON PUNT RETURNS
128—William & Mary (45) vs. Jackson St. (6), 11-30-96.

YARDS GAINED ON KICKOFF RETURNS
244—Hampton (35) vs. William & Mary (42), 11-27-2004.

YARDS GAINED ON INTERCEPTION RETURNS
164—Marshall (51) vs. Weber St. (23), 12-5-87.

YARDS PENALIZED
172—Tennessee St. (32) vs. Jackson St. (23), 11-29-86.

FUMBLES LOST
7—Jackson St. (8) vs. Marshall (38), 11-25-95.

POINTS
78—La.-Monroe vs. Alcorn St. (27), 11-28-92.

TOURNAMENT

FIRST DOWNS
125—Montana, 1995 (25 vs. Eastern Ky., 41 vs. Ga. Southern, 38 vs. Stephen F. Austin, 21 vs. Marshall).

NET YARDS RUSHING
2,030—Ga. Southern, 1999 (559 vs. Northern Ariz., 470 vs. Massachusetts, 363 vs. Illinois St., 638 vs. Youngstown St.).

NET YARDS PASSING
1,703—Montana, 1996 (447 vs. Nicholls St., 467 vs. East Tenn. St., 454 vs. Troy, 335 vs. Marshall).

NET YARDS RUSHING AND PASSING
2,253—Ga. Southern, 1999 (659 vs. Northern Ariz., 500 vs. Massachusetts, 439 vs. Illinois St., 655 vs. Youngstown St.).

PASSES ATTEMPTED
197—Montana, 1996 (53 vs. Nicholls St., 44 vs. East Tenn. St., 45 vs. Troy, 55 vs. Marshall).

PASSES COMPLETED
137—Montana, 1995 (35 vs. Eastern Ky., 42 vs. Ga. Southern, 31 vs. Stephen F. Austin, 29 vs. Marshall).

PASSES HAD INTERCEPTED
11—Stephen F. Austin, 1989 (0 vs. Grambling, 4 vs. Missouri St., 2 vs. Furman, 5 vs. Ga. Southern).

PUNTS
29—UNI, 1992 (11 vs. Eastern Wash., 10 vs. McNeese St., 8 vs. Youngstown St.).

YARDS PENALIZED
350—Ga. Southern, 1986 (106 vs. N.C. A&T, 104 vs. Nicholls St., 75 vs. Nevada, 65 vs. Arkansas St.).

FUMBLES LOST
10—Appalachian St., 2005 (2 vs. Lafayette, 3 vs. Southern Ill., 3 vs. Furman, 2 vs. UNI).

POINTS
203—Ga. Southern, 1986 (52 vs. N.C. A&T, 55 vs. Nicholls St., 48 vs. Nevada, 48 vs. Arkansas St.).

Championship Game Records

INDIVIDUAL

NET YARDS RUSHING
247—Adrian Peterson, Ga. Southern (59) vs. Youngstown St. (24), 1999 (25 rushes).

RUSHES ATTEMPTED
35—Marcel Shipp, Massachusetts (55) vs. Ga. Southern (43), 1998 (244 yards).

TOUCHDOWNS BY RUSHING
4—John Bagwell, Furman (42) vs. Ga. Southern (44), 1985; Kevin Richardson, Appalachian St. (28) vs. Massachusetts (17), 2006.

NET YARDS PASSING
474—Tony Peterson, Marshall (42) vs. La.-Monroe (43), 1987 (28 of 54).

PASSES ATTEMPTED
57—Kelly Bradley, Montana St. (19) vs. Louisiana Tech (6), 1984 (32 completions).

PASSES COMPLETED
36—Brian Ah Yat, Montana (29) vs. Marshall (49), 1996 (55 attempts).

PASSES HAD INTERCEPTED
7—Jeff Gilbert, Western Caro. (7) vs. Southern Ill. (43), 1983.

TOUCHDOWN PASSES
4—Tracy Ham, Ga. Southern (44) vs. Furman (42), 1985; Tony Peterson, Marshall (42) vs. La.-Monroe (43), 1987; Eric Kresser, Marshall (49) vs. Montana (29), 1996.

COMPLETION PERCENTAGE
(Min. 8 Attempts)
.875—Mark Brungard, Youngstown St. (17) vs. Marshall (5), 1993 (7 of 8).

NET YARDS RUSHING AND PASSING
509—Tracy Ham, Ga. Southern (44) vs. Furman (42), 1985 (90 rushing, 419 passing; 56 plays).

RUSHING AND PASSING PLAYS
67—Brian Ah Yat, Montana (29) vs. Marshall (49), 1996 (12 rush, 55 pass; 301 yards).

PUNTING AVERAGE
(Min. 3 Punts)
51.0—Andrew Maclay, Massachusetts (55) vs. Ga. Southern (43), 1998 (4 for 204).

PUNTS
10—Rick Titus, Delaware (14) vs. Eastern Ky. (17), 1982 (41.6 average).

RECEPTIONS
13—Joe Douglass, Montana (29) vs. Marshall (49), 1996 (117 yards).

RECEIVING YARDS
220—Randy Moss, Marshall (49) vs. Montana (29), 1996 (9 catches).

TOUCHDOWN RECEPTIONS
4—Randy Moss, Marshall (49) vs. Montana (29), 1996 (9 catches for 220 yards).

INTERCEPTIONS
4—Greg Shipp, Southern Ill. (43) vs. Western Caro. (7), 1983.

YARDS GAINED ON INTERCEPTION RETURNS
58—Chris Cook, Boise St. (14) vs. Youngstown St. (28), 1994 (1 interception).

YARDS GAINED ON PUNT RETURNS
99—Anthony Williams, Ga. Southern (59) vs. Youngstown St. (24), 1999 (6 returns).

YARDS GAINED ON KICKOFF RETURNS
213—Andre Coleman, Youngstown St. (24) vs. Ga. Southern (59), 1999 (9 returns).

POINTS
24—John Bagwell, Furman (42) vs. Ga. Southern (44), 1985; Randy Moss, Marshall (49) vs. Montana (29), 1996; Kevin Richardson, Appalachian St. (28) vs. Massachusetts (17), 2006.

TOUCHDOWNS
4—John Bagwell, Furman (42) vs. Ga. Southern (44), 1985; Randy Moss, Marshall (49) vs. Montana (29), 1996; Kevin Richardson, Appalachian St. (28) vs. Massachusetts (17), 2006.

EXTRA POINTS
8—Chris Chambers, Ga. Southern (59) vs. Youngstown St. (24), 1999.

FIELD GOALS
4—Tim Foley, Ga. Southern (48) vs. Arkansas St. (21), 1986.

LONGEST PLAYS

RUSH
73—Mark Myers, Ga. Southern (27) vs. Montana (25), 2000.

PASS COMPLETION
79—Tracy Ham to Ricky Harris, Ga. Southern (48) vs. Arkansas St. (21), 1986.

FIELD GOAL
55—David Cool, Ga. Southern (12) vs. Furman (17), 1988.

PUNT
72—Rick Titus, Delaware (14) vs. Eastern Ky. (17), 1982.

TEAM

FIRST DOWNS
32—James Madison (31) vs. Montana (21), 2004 (20 rushing, 10 passing, 2 by penalty).

FIRST DOWNS BY RUSHING
23—Ga. Southern (59) vs. Youngstown St. (24), 1999.

FIRST DOWNS BY PASSING
19—Marshall (42) vs. La.-Monroe (43), 1987.

FIRST DOWNS BY PENALTY
3—Eastern Ky. (23) vs. Idaho St. (34), 1981; Furman (42) vs. Ga. Southern (44), 1985; La.-Monroe (43) vs. Marshall (42), 1987; Montana (29) vs. Marshall (49), 1996.

NET YARDS RUSHING
638—Ga. Southern (59) vs. Youngstown St. (24), 1999 (59 rushes).

RUSHES ATTEMPTED
76—Florida A&M (35) vs. Massachusetts (28), 1978 (470 yards).

NET YARDS PASSING
474—Marshall (42) vs. La.-Monroe (43), 1987 (28 of 54).

PASSES ATTEMPTED
57—Montana St. (19) vs. Louisiana Tech (6), 1984 (32 completions).

PASSES COMPLETED
36—Montana (29) vs. Marshall (49), 1996 (55 attempts).

COMPLETION PERCENTAGE
(Min. 10 Attempts)
.760—Southern Ill. (43) vs. Western Caro. (7), 1983 (19 of 25).

PASSES HAD INTERCEPTED
7—Western Caro. (7) vs. Southern Ill. (43), 1983.

NET YARDS RUSHING AND PASSING
655—Ga. Southern (59) vs. Youngstown St. (24), 1999 (638 rushing, 17 passing; 63 plays).

RUSHING AND PASSING PLAYS
90—Montana (29) vs. Marshall (49), 1996 (35 rushing, 55 passing; 430 yards).

PUNTING AVERAGE
(Min. 3 Punts)
51.0—Massachusetts (55) vs. Ga. Southern (43), 1998 (4 for 204).

PUNTS
10—Delaware (14) vs. Eastern Ky. (17), 1982 (41.6 average).

YARDS GAINED ON PUNT RETURNS
99—Ga. Southern (59) vs. Youngstown St. (24), 1999 (7 returns).

YARDS GAINED ON KICKOFF RETURNS
229—Western Caro. (7) vs. Southern Ill. (43), 1983 (8 returns).

YARDS GAINED ON INTERCEPTION RETURNS
70—Marshall (31) vs. Youngstown St. (28), 1992 (2 interceptions).

YARDS PENALIZED
162—Idaho St. (34) vs. Eastern Ky. (23), 1981 (12 penalties).

FUMBLES
6—Ga. Southern (43) vs. Massachusetts (55), 1998 (6 lost).

FUMBLES LOST
6—Ga. Southern (43) vs. Massachusetts (55), 1998 (6 fumbles).

POINTS
59—Ga. Southern vs. Youngstown St. (24), 1999.

ATTENDANCE
32,106—Marshall University Stadium, Huntington, W.Va., 1995.

Won-Lost Records in Tournament Play

Team (Years Participated)	Yrs.	Won	Lost	Pct.	1st	2nd
Akron (1985)	1	0	1	.000	0	0
Alcorn St. (1984-92-94)	3	0	3	.000	0	0
Appalachian St. (1986-87-89-91-92-94-95-98-99-2000-01-02-05-06)	14	16	12	.571	2	0
Arkansas St. (1984-85-86-87)	4	6	4	.600	0	1
Bethune-Cookman (2002-03)	2	0	2	.000	0	0
Boise St. (1980-81-88-90-94)	5	8	4	.667	1	1
Boston U. (1982-83-84-93-94)	5	2	5	.286	0	0
Cal Poly (2005)	1	1	1	.500	0	0
UCF (1990-93)	2	2	2	.500	0	0
Chattanooga (1984)	1	0	1	.000	0	0
Citadel (1988-90-92)	3	1	3	.250	0	0
Coastal Caro. (2006)	1	0	1	.000	0	0
Colgate (1982-83-97-98-99-2003-05)	7	4	7	.364	0	1
Connecticut (1998)	1	1	1	.500	0	0
Delaware (1981-82-86-88-91-92-93-95-96-97-2000-03-04)	13	16	12	.571	1	1
East Tenn. St. (1996)	1	1	1	.500	0	0
Eastern Ill. (1982-83-86-89-95-96-2000-01-02-05-06)	11	3	11	.214	0	0
Eastern Ky. (1979-80-81-82-83-84-86-87-88-89-90-91-92-93-94-95-97)	17	16	15	.516	2	2
Eastern Wash. (1985-92-97-2004-05)	5	4	5	.444	0	0
Florida A&M (1978-96-97-98-99-2000-01)	7	5	6	.455	1	0
Fla. Atlantic (2003)	1	2	1	.667	0	0
Fordham (2002)	1	1	1	.500	0	0
Furman (1982-83-85-86-88-89-90-96-99-2000-01-02-04-05-06)	15	17	14	.548	1	2
Ga. Southern (1985-86-87-88-89-90-93-95-97-98-99-2000-01-02-04-05)	16	38	10	.792	6	2
Grambling (1980-85-89)	3	0	3	.000	0	0
Hampton (1997-98-2004-05-06)	5	0	5	.000	0	0
Hofstra (1995-97-99-2000-01)	5	2	5	.286	0	0
Holy Cross (1983)	1	0	1	.000	0	0
Howard (1993)	1	0	1	.000	0	0
Idaho (1982-85-86-87-88-89-90-92-93-94-95)	11	6	11	.353	0	0
Idaho St. (1981-83)	2	3	1	.750	1	0
Illinois St. (1998-99-2006)	3	3	3	.500	0	0
Indiana St. (1983-84)	2	1	2	.333	0	0
Jackson St. (1978-81-82-85-86-87-88-89-90-95-96-97)	12	0	12	.000	0	0
Jacksonville St. (2003-04)	2	0	2	.000	0	0
James Madison (1987-91-94-95-99-2004-06)	7	6	6	.500	1	0
Lafayette (2004-05-06)	3	0	3	.000	0	0
Lehigh (1979-80-98-99-2000-01-04)	7	4	7	.364	0	1
La.-Monroe (1987-90-92-93)	4	5	3	.625	1	0
Louisiana Tech (1982-84)	2	4	2	.667	0	1
Maine (1987-89-2001-02)	4	2	4	.333	0	0
Marshall (1987-88-91-92-93-94-95-96)	8	23	6	.793	2	4
Massachusetts (1978-88-90-98-99-2003-06)	7	9	6	.600	1	2
McNeese St. (1991-92-93-94-95-97-98-2000-01-02-03-06)	12	11	12	.478	0	2
Middle Tenn. (1984-85-89-90-91-92-94)	7	6	7	.462	0	0
Mississippi Val. (1984)	1	0	1	.000	0	0
Missouri St. (1989-90)	2	1	2	.333	0	0
Montana (1982-88-89-93-94-95-96-97-98-99-2000-01-02-03-04-05-06)	17	24	15	.615	2	3
Montana St. (1984-2002-03-06)	4	4	3	.571	1	0
Murray St. (1979-86-95-96-2002)	5	1	5	.167	0	0
Nevada (1978-79-83-85-86-90-91)	7	9	7	.563	0	1
New Hampshire (1991-94-2004-05-06)	5	3	5	.375	0	0
Nicholls St. (1986-96-2005)	3	1	3	.250	0	0
N.C. A&T (1986-92-99-2003)	4	1	4	.200	0	0
North Texas (1983-87-88-94)	4	0	4	.000	0	0
Northeastern (2002)	1	0	1	.000	0	0
Northern Ariz.# (1996-2001-03)	3	1	3	.250	0	0
UNI (1985-87-90-91-92-93-94-95-96-2001-03-05)	12	15	12	.556	0	1
Northwestern St. (1988-97-98-2001-02-04)	6	3	6	.333	0	0
Portland St. (2000)	1	0	1	.000	0	0
Rhode Island (1981-84-85)	3	2	3	.400	0	0
Richmond (1984-87-98-2000-05)	5	3	5	.375	0	0
Sam Houston St. (1986-91-2001-04)	4	3	4	.429	0	0
Samford (1991-92)	2	2	2	.500	0	0
South Carolina St. (1981-82)	2	2	2	.500	0	0
Southern Ill. (1983-2003-04-05-06)	5	5	4	.556	1	0
Stephen F. Austin¢ (1988-93-95)	3	3	3	.500	0	0
Tenn.-Martin (2006)	1	0	1	.000	0	0
Tennessee St.* (1986-98-99)	3	1	3	.250	0	0
Texas St. (2005)	1	2	1	.667	0	0
Troy (1993-94-95-96-98-99-2000)	7	5	7	.417	0	0
Villanova (1989-91-92-96-97-2002)	6	3	6	.333	0	0
Weber St. (1987-91)	2	1	2	.333	0	0
Western Caro. (1983)	1	3	1	.750	0	1
Western Ill. (1988-91-96-97-98-2000-02-03)	8	5	8	.385	0	0
Western Ky. (1987-88-97-2000-01-02-03-04)	8	8	7	.533	1	0
William & Mary (1986-89-90-93-96-2001-04)	7	4	7	.364	0	0
Wofford (2003)	1	2	1	.667	0	0
Youngstown St. (1987-89-90-91-92-93-94-97-99-2000-06)	11	25	7	.781	4	2

#Northern Arizona's competition in the 1999 Division I-AA championship was vacated by action of the NCAA Committee on Infractions (record was 0-1).
¢Stephen F. Austin's competition in the 1989 Division I-AA championship was vacated by action of the NCAA Committee on Infractions (record was 3-1).
**Tennessee State's competition in the 1981 and 1982 Division I-AA championships was vacated by action of the NCAA Committee on Infractions (record was 1-2).*

Year-by-Year Division I Championship Results

Year (Number of Teams)	Coach	Record	Result
1978 (4)			
Florida A&M	Rudy Hubbard	2-0	Champion
Massachusetts	Bob Pickett	1-1	Second
Jackson St.	W.C. Gorden	0-1	Lost 1st Round
Nevada	Chris Ault	0-1	Lost 1st Round
1979 (4)			
Eastern Ky.	Roy Kidd	2-0	Champion
Lehigh	John Whitehead	1-1	Second
Murray St.	Mike Gottfried	0-1	Lost 1st Round
Nevada	Chris Ault	0-1	Lost 1st Round
1980 (4)			
Boise St.	Jim Criner	2-0	Champion
Eastern Ky.	Roy Kidd	1-1	Second
Grambling	Eddie Robinson	0-1	Lost 1st Round
Lehigh	John Whitehead	0-1	Lost 1st Round
1981 (8)			
Idaho St.	Dave Kragthorpe	3-0	Champion
Eastern Ky.	Roy Kidd	2-1	Second
Boise St.	Jim Criner	1-1	Semifinalist
South Carolina St.	Bill Davis	1-1	Semifinalist
Delaware	Tubby Raymond	0-1	Lost 1st Round
Jackson St.	W.C. Gorden	0-1	Lost 1st Round
Rhode Island	Bob Griffin	0-1	Lost 1st Round
*Tennessee St.	John Merritt	0-1	Vacated
1982 (12)			
Eastern Ky.	Roy Kidd	3-0	Champion
Delaware	Tubby Raymond	2-1	Second
Louisiana Tech	Billy Brewer	1-1	Semifinalist
*Tennessee St.	John Merritt	1-1	Vacated
Colgate	Fred Dunlap	1-1	Quarterfinalist
Eastern Ill.	Darrell Mudra	1-1	Quarterfinalist
Idaho	Dennis Erickson	1-1	Quarterfinalist
South Carolina St.	Bill Davis	1-1	Quarterfinalist
Boston U.	Rick Taylor	0-1	Lost 1st Round
Furman	Dick Sheridan	0-1	Lost 1st Round
Jackson St.	W.C. Gorden	0-1	Lost 1st Round
Montana	Larry Donovan	0-1	Lost 1st Round
1983 (12)			
Southern Ill.	Rey Dempsey	3-0	Champion
Western Caro.	Bob Waters	3-1	Second
Furman	Dick Sheridan	1-1	Semifinalist
Nevada	Chris Ault	2-1	Semifinalist
Boston U.	Rick Taylor	1-1	Quarterfinalist
Holy Cross	Rick Carter	0-1	Quarterfinalist
Indiana St.	Dennis Raetz	1-1	Quarterfinalist
North Texas	Corky Nelson	0-1	Quarterfinalist
Colgate	Fred Dunlap	0-1	Lost 1st Round
Eastern Ill.	Al Molde	0-1	Lost 1st Round
Eastern Ky.	Roy Kidd	0-1	Lost 1st Round
Idaho St.	Jim Koetter	0-1	Lost 1st Round
1984 (12)			
Montana St.	Dave Arnold	3-0	Champion
Louisiana Tech	A.L. Williams	3-1	Second
Middle Tenn.	James Donnelly	2-1	Semifinalist
Rhode Island	Bob Griffin	1-1	Semifinalist
Alcorn St.	Marino Casem	0-1	Quarterfinalist
Arkansas St.	Larry Lacewell	1-1	Quarterfinalist
Indiana St.	Dennis Raetz	0-1	Quarterfinalist
Richmond	Dal Shealy	1-1	Quarterfinalist
Boston U.	Rick Taylor	0-1	Lost 1st Round
Chattanooga	Buddy Nix	0-1	Lost 1st Round
Eastern Ky.	Roy Kidd	0-1	Lost 1st Round
Mississippi Val.	Archie Cooley Jr.	0-1	Lost 1st Round
1985 (12)			
Ga. Southern	Erk Russell	4-0	Champion
Furman	Dick Sheridan	2-1	Second
Nevada	Chris Ault	1-1	Semifinalist
UNI	Darrell Mudra	1-1	Semifinalist
Arkansas St.	Larry Lacewell	1-1	Quarterfinalist
Eastern Wash.	Dick Zornes	1-1	Quarterfinalist
Middle Tenn.	James Donnelly	0-1	Quarterfinalist
Rhode Island	Bob Griffin	1-1	Quarterfinalist
Akron	Jim Dennison	0-1	Lost 1st Round
Grambling	Eddie Robinson	0-1	Lost 1st Round
Idaho	Dennis Erickson	0-1	Lost 1st Round
Jackson St.	W.C. Gorden	0-1	Lost 1st Round

Year (Number of Teams)	Coach	Record	Result
1986 (16)			
Ga. Southern	Erk Russell	4-0	Champion
Arkansas St.	Larry Lacewell	3-1	Second
Eastern Ky.	Roy Kidd	2-1	Semifinalist
Nevada	Chris Ault	2-1	Semifinalist
Delaware	Tubby Raymond	1-1	Quarterfinalist
Eastern Ill.	Al Molde	1-1	Quarterfinalist
Nicholls St.	Sonny Jackson	1-1	Quarterfinalist
Tennessee St.	William Thomas	1-1	Quarterfinalist
Appalachian St.	Sparky Woods	0-1	Lost 1st Round
Furman	Jimmy Satterfield	0-1	Lost 1st Round
Idaho	Keith Gilbertson	0-1	Lost 1st Round
Jackson St.	W.C. Gorden	0-1	Lost 1st Round
Murray St.	Frank Beamer	0-1	Lost 1st Round
N.C. A&T	Maurice Forte	0-1	Lost 1st Round
Sam Houston St.	Ron Randleman	0-1	Lost 1st Round
William & Mary	Jimmye Laycock	0-1	Lost 1st Round
1987 (16)			
La.-Monroe	Pat Collins	4-0	Champion
Marshall	George Chaump	3-1	Second
Appalachian St.	Sparky Woods	2-1	Semifinalist
UNI	Darrell Mudra	2-1	Semifinalist
Arkansas St.	Larry Lacewell	1-1	Quarterfinalist
Eastern Ky.	Roy Kidd	1-1	Quarterfinalist
Ga. Southern	Erk Russell	1-1	Quarterfinalist
Weber St.	Mike Price	1-1	Quarterfinalist
Idaho	Keith Gilbertson	0-1	Lost 1st Round
Jackson St.	W.C. Gorden	0-1	Lost 1st Round
James Madison	Joe Purzycki	0-1	Lost 1st Round
Maine	Tim Murphy	0-1	Lost 1st Round
North Texas	Corky Nelson	0-1	Lost 1st Round
Richmond	Dal Shealy	0-1	Lost 1st Round
Western Ky.	Dave Roberts	0-1	Lost 1st Round
Youngstown St.	Jim Tressel	0-1	Lost 1st Round
1988 (16)			
Furman	Jimmy Satterfield	4-0	Champion
Ga. Southern	Erk Russell	3-1	Second
Eastern Ky.	Roy Kidd	2-1	Semifinalist
Idaho	Keith Gilbertson	2-1	Semifinalist
Marshall	George Chaump	1-1	Quarterfinalist
Northwestern St.	Sam Goodwin	1-1	Quarterfinalist
Stephen F. Austin	Jim Hess	1-1	Quarterfinalist
Western Ky.	Dave Roberts	1-1	Quarterfinalist
Boise St.	Skip Hall	0-1	Lost 1st Round
Citadel	Charlie Taaffe	0-1	Lost 1st Round
Delaware	Tubby Raymond	0-1	Lost 1st Round
Jackson St.	W.C. Gorden	0-1	Lost 1st Round
Massachusetts	Jim Reid	0-1	Lost 1st Round
Montana	Don Read	0-1	Lost 1st Round
North Texas	Corky Nelson	0-1	Lost 1st Round
Western Ill.	Bruce Craddock	0-1	Lost 1st Round
1989 (16)			
Ga. Southern	Erk Russell	4-0	Champion
*Stephen F. Austin	Lynn Graves	3-1	Vacated
Furman	Jimmy Satterfield	2-1	Semifinalist
Montana	Don Read	2-1	Semifinalist
Eastern Ill.	Bob Spoo	1-1	Quarterfinalist
Middle Tenn.	James Donnelly	1-1	Quarterfinalist
Missouri St.	Jesse Branch	1-1	Quarterfinalist
Youngstown St.	Jim Tressel	1-1	Quarterfinalist
Appalachian St.	Jerry Moore	0-1	Lost 1st Round
Eastern Ky.	Roy Kidd	0-1	Lost 1st Round
Grambling	Eddie Robinson	0-1	Lost 1st Round
Idaho	John L. Smith	0-1	Lost 1st Round
Jackson St.	W.C. Gorden	0-1	Lost 1st Round
Maine	Tom Lichtenberg	0-1	Lost 1st Round
Villanova	Andy Talley	0-1	Lost 1st Round
William & Mary	Jimmye Laycock	0-1	Lost 1st Round
1990 (16)			
Ga. Southern	Tim Stowers	4-0	Champion
Nevada	Chris Ault	3-1	Second
Boise St.	Skip Hall	2-1	Semifinalist
UCF	Gene McDowell	2-1	Semifinalist
Furman	Jimmy Satterfield	1-1	Quarterfinalist
Idaho	John L. Smith	1-1	Quarterfinalist
Middle Tenn.	James Donnelly	1-1	Quarterfinalist
William & Mary	Jimmye Laycock	1-1	Quarterfinalist
Citadel	Charlie Taaffe	0-1	Lost 1st Round
Eastern Ky.	Roy Kidd	0-1	Lost 1st Round
Jackson St.	W.C. Gorden	0-1	Lost 1st Round
La.-Monroe	Dave Roberts	0-1	Lost 1st Round

Year (Number of Teams)	Coach	Record	Result
Massachusetts	Jim Reid	0-1	Lost 1st Round
Missouri St.	Jesse Branch	0-1	Lost 1st Round
UNI	Terry Allen	0-1	Lost 1st Round
Youngstown St.	Jim Tressel	0-1	Lost 1st Round
1991 (16)			
Youngstown St.	Jim Tressel	4-0	Champion
Marshall	Jim Donnan	3-1	Second
Eastern Ky.	Roy Kidd	2-1	Semifinalist
Samford	Terry Bowden	2-1	Semifinalist
James Madison	Rip Scherer	1-1	Quarterfinalist
Middle Tenn.	James Donnelly	1-1	Quarterfinalist
Nevada	Chris Ault	1-1	Quarterfinalist
UNI	Terry Allen	1-1	Quarterfinalist
Appalachian St.	Jerry Moore	0-1	Lost 1st Round
Delaware	Tubby Raymond	0-1	Lost 1st Round
McNeese St.	Bobby Keasler	0-1	Lost 1st Round
New Hampshire	Bill Bowes	0-1	Lost 1st Round
Sam Houston St.	Ron Randleman	0-1	Lost 1st Round
Villanova	Andy Talley	0-1	Lost 1st Round
Weber St.	Dave Arslanian	0-1	Lost 1st Round
Western Ill.	Randy Ball	0-1	Lost 1st Round
1992 (16)			
Marshall	Jim Donnan	4-0	Champion
Youngstown St.	Jim Tressel	3-1	Second
Delaware	Tubby Raymond	2-1	Semifinalist
UNI	Terry Allen	2-1	Semifinalist
Citadel	Charlie Taaffe	1-1	Quarterfinalist
La.-Monroe	Dave Roberts	1-1	Quarterfinalist
McNeese St.	Bobby Keasler	1-1	Quarterfinalist
Middle Tenn.	James Donnelly	1-1	Quarterfinalist
Alcorn St.	Cardell Jones	0-1	Lost 1st Round
Appalachian St.	Jerry Moore	0-1	Lost 1st Round
Eastern Ky.	Roy Kidd	0-1	Lost 1st Round
Eastern Wash.	Dick Zornes	0-1	Lost 1st Round
Idaho	John L. Smith	0-1	Lost 1st Round
N.C. A&T	Bill Hayes	0-1	Lost 1st Round
Samford	Terry Bowden	0-1	Lost 1st Round
Villanova	Andy Talley	0-1	Lost 1st Round
1993 (16)			
Youngstown St.	Jim Tressel	4-0	Champion
Marshall	Jim Donnan	3-1	Second
Idaho	John L. Smith	2-1	Semifinalist
Troy	Larry Blakeney	2-1	Semifinalist
Boston U.	Dan Allen	1-1	Quarterfinalist
Delaware	Tubby Raymond	1-1	Quarterfinalist
Ga. Southern	Tim Stowers	1-1	Quarterfinalist
McNeese St.	Bobby Keasler	1-1	Quarterfinalist
UCF	Gene McDowell	0-1	Lost 1st Round
Eastern Ky.	Roy Kidd	0-1	Lost 1st Round
Howard	Steve Wilson	0-1	Lost 1st Round
La.-Monroe	Dave Roberts	0-1	Lost 1st Round
Montana	Don Read	0-1	Lost 1st Round
UNI	Terry Allen	0-1	Lost 1st Round
Stephen F. Austin	John Pearce	0-1	Lost 1st Round
William & Mary	Jimmye Laycock	0-1	Lost 1st Round
1994 (16)			
Youngstown St.	Jim Tressel	4-0	Champion
Boise St.	Pokey Allen	3-1	Second
Marshall	Jim Donnan	2-1	Semifinalist
Montana	Don Read	2-1	Semifinalist
Appalachian St.	Jerry Moore	1-1	Quarterfinalist
Eastern Ky.	Roy Kidd	1-1	Quarterfinalist
James Madison	Rip Scherer	1-1	Quarterfinalist
McNeese St.	Bobby Keasler	1-1	Quarterfinalist
Alcorn St.	Cardell Jones	0-1	Lost 1st Round
Boston U.	Dan Allen	0-1	Lost 1st Round
Idaho	John L. Smith	0-1	Lost 1st Round
Middle Tenn.	James Donnelly	0-1	Lost 1st Round
New Hampshire	Bill Bowes	0-1	Lost 1st Round
North Texas	Matt Simon	0-1	Lost 1st Round
UNI	Terry Allen	0-1	Lost 1st Round
Troy	Larry Blakeney	0-1	Lost 1st Round
1995 (16)			
Montana	Don Read	4-0	Champion
Marshall	Jim Donnan	3-1	Second
McNeese St.	Bobby Keasler	2-1	Semifinalist
Stephen F. Austin	John Pearce	2-1	Semifinalist
Appalachian St.	Jerry Moore	1-1	Quarterfinalist
Delaware	Tubby Raymond	1-1	Quarterfinalist
Ga. Southern	Tim Stowers	1-1	Quarterfinalist
UNI	Terry Allen	1-1	Quarterfinalist

Year (Number of Teams)	Coach	Record	Result
Eastern Ill.	Bob Spoo	0-1	Lost 1st Round
Eastern Ky.	Roy Kidd	0-1	Lost 1st Round
Hofstra	Joe Gardi	0-1	Lost 1st Round
Idaho	Chris Tormey	0-1	Lost 1st Round
Jackson St.	James Carson	0-1	Lost 1st Round
James Madison	Alex Wood	0-1	Lost 1st Round
Murray St.	Houston Nutt	0-1	Lost 1st Round
Troy	Larry Blakeney	0-1	Lost 1st Round
1996 (16)			
Marshall	Bob Pruett	4-0	Champion
Montana	Mick Dennehy	3-1	Second
UNI	Terry Allen	2-1	Semifinalist
Troy	Larry Blakeney	2-1	Semifinalist
East Tenn. St.	Mike Cavan	1-1	Quarterfinalist
Furman	Bobby Johnson	1-1	Quarterfinalist
Murray St.	Houston Nutt	1-1	Quarterfinalist
William & Mary	Jimmye Laycock	1-1	Quarterfinalist
Delaware	Tubby Raymond	0-1	Lost 1st Round
Eastern Ill.	Bob Spoo	0-1	Lost 1st Round
Florida A&M	Billy Joe	0-1	Lost 1st Round
Jackson St.	James Carson	0-1	Lost 1st Round
Nicholls St.	Darren Barbier	0-1	Lost 1st Round
Northern Ariz.	Stephen Axman	0-1	Lost 1st Round
Villanova	Andy Talley	0-1	Lost 1st Round
Western Ill.	Randy Ball	0-1	Lost 1st Round
1997 (16)			
Youngstown St.	Jim Tressel	4-0	Champion
McNeese St.	Bobby Keasler	3-1	Second
Delaware	Tubby Raymond	2-1	Semifinalist
Eastern Wash.	Mike Kramer	2-1	Semifinalist
Ga. Southern	Paul Johnson	1-1	Quarterfinalist
Villanova	Andy Talley	1-1	Quarterfinalist
Western Ill.	Randy Ball	1-1	Quarterfinalist
Western Ky.	Jack Harbaugh	1-1	Quarterfinalist
Colgate	Dick Biddle	0-1	Lost 1st Round
Eastern Ky.	Roy Kidd	0-1	Lost 1st Round
Florida A&M	Billy Joe	0-1	Lost 1st Round
Hampton	Joe Taylor	0-1	Lost 1st Round
Hofstra	Joe Gardi	0-1	Lost 1st Round
Jackson St.	James Carson	0-1	Lost 1st Round
Montana	Mick Dennehy	0-1	Lost 1st Round
Northwestern St.	Sam Goodwin	0-1	Lost 1st Round
1998 (16)			
Massachusetts	Mark Whipple	4-0	Champion
Ga. Southern	Paul Johnson	3-1	Second
Northwestern St.	Sam Goodwin	2-1	Semifinalist
Western Ill.	Randy Ball	2-1	Semifinalist
Appalachian St.	Jerry Moore	1-1	Quarterfinalist
Connecticut	Skip Holtz	1-1	Quarterfinalist
Florida A&M	Billy Joe	1-1	Quarterfinalist
Lehigh	Kevin Higgins	1-1	Quarterfinalist
Colgate	Dick Biddle	0-1	Lost 1st Round
Hampton	Joe Taylor	0-1	Lost 1st Round
Illinois St.	Todd Berry	0-1	Lost 1st Round
McNeese St.	Bobby Keasler	0-1	Lost 1st Round
Montana	Mick Dennehy	0-1	Lost 1st Round
Richmond	Jim Reid	0-1	Lost 1st Round
Tennessee St.	L.C. Cole	0-1	Lost 1st Round
Troy	Larry Blakeney	0-1	Lost 1st Round
1999 (16)			
Ga. Southern	Paul Johnson	4-0	Champion
Youngstown St.	Jim Tressel	3-1	Second
Florida A&M	Billy Joe	2-1	Semifinalist
Illinois St.	Todd Berry	2-1	Semifinalist
Hofstra	Joe Gardi	1-1	Quarterfinalist
Massachusetts	Mark Whipple	1-1	Quarterfinalist
N.C. A&T	Bill Hayes	1-1	Quarterfinalist
Troy	Larry Blakeney	1-1	Quarterfinalist
Appalachian St.	Jerry Moore	0-1	Lost 1st Round
Colgate	Dick Biddle	0-1	Lost 1st Round
Furman	Bobby Johnson	0-1	Lost 1st Round
James Madison	Mickey Matthews	0-1	Lost 1st Round
Lehigh	Kevin Higgins	0-1	Lost 1st Round
Montana	Mick Dennehy	0-1	Lost 1st Round
*Northern Ariz.	Jerome Souers	0-1	Vacated
Tennessee St.	L.C. Cole	0-1	Lost 1st Round
2000 (16)			
Ga. Southern	Paul Johnson	4-0	Champion
Montana	Joe Glenn	3-1	Second
Appalachian St.	Jerry Moore	2-1	Semifinalist

Year (Number of Teams)	Coach	Record	Result
Delaware	Tubby Raymond	2-1	Semifinalist
Hofstra	Joe Gardi	1-1	Quarterfinalist
Lehigh	Kevin Higgins	1-1	Quarterfinalist
Richmond	Jim Reid	1-1	Quarterfinalist
Western Ky.	Jack Harbaugh	1-1	Quarterfinalist
Eastern Ill.	Bob Spoo	0-1	Lost 1st Round
Florida A&M	Billy Joe	0-1	Lost 1st Round
Furman	Bobby Johnson	0-1	Lost 1st Round
McNeese St.	Tommy Tate	0-1	Lost 1st Round
Portland St.	Tim Walsh	0-1	Lost 1st Round
Troy	Larry Blakeney	0-1	Lost 1st Round
Western Ill.	Don Patterson	0-1	Lost 1st Round
Youngstown St.	Jim Tressel	0-1	Lost 1st Round
2001 (16)			
Montana	Joe Glenn	4-0	Champion
Furman	Bobby Johnson	3-1	Second
UNI	Mark Farley	2-1	Semifinalist
Ga. Southern	Paul Johnson	2-1	Semifinalist
Appalachian St.	Jerry Moore	1-1	Quarterfinalist
Lehigh	Pete Lembo	1-1	Quarterfinalist
Maine	Jack Cosgrove	1-1	Quarterfinalist
Sam Houston St.	Ron Randleman	1-1	Quarterfinalist
Eastern Ill.	Bob Spoo	0-1	Lost 1st Round
Florida A&M	Billy Joe	0-1	Lost 1st Round
Hofstra	Joe Gardi	0-1	Lost 1st Round
McNeese St.	Tommy Tate	0-1	Lost 1st Round
Northern Ariz.	Jerome Souers	0-1	Lost 1st Round
Northwestern St.	Steve Roberts	0-1	Lost 1st Round
Western Ky.	Jack Harbaugh	0-1	Lost 1st Round
William & Mary	Jimmye Laycock	0-1	Lost 1st Round
2002 (16)			
Western Ky.	Jack Harbaugh	4-0	Champion
McNeese St.	Tommy Tate	3-1	Second
Ga. Southern	Mike Sewak	2-1	Semifinalist
Villanova	Andy Talley	2-1	Semifinalist
Fordham	David Clawson	1-1	Quarterfinalist
Maine	Jack Cosgrove	1-1	Quarterfinalist
Montana	Joe Glenn	1-1	Quarterfinalist
Western Ill.	Don Patterson	1-1	Quarterfinalist
Appalachian St.	Jerry Moore	0-1	Lost 1st Round
Bethune-Cookman	Alvin Wyatt	0-1	Lost 1st Round
Eastern Ill.	Bob Spoo	0-1	Lost 1st Round
Furman	Bobby Lamb	0-1	Lost 1st Round
Montana St.	Mike Kramer	0-1	Lost 1st Round
Murray St.	Joe Pannunzio	0-1	Lost 1st Round
Northeastern	Don Brown	0-1	Lost 1st Round
Northwestern St.	Scott Stoker	0-1	Lost 1st Round
2003 (16)			
Delaware	K.C. Keeler	4-0	Champion
Colgate	Dick Biddle	3-1	Second
Fla. Atlantic	Howard Schnellenberger	2-1	Semifinalist
Wofford	Mike Ayers	2-1	Semifinalist
Northern Ariz.	Jerome Souers	1-1	Quarterfinalist
UNI	Mark Farley	1-1	Quarterfinalist
Western Ill.	Don Patterson	1-1	Quarterfinalist
Western Ky.	David Elson	1-1	Quarterfinalist
Bethune-Cookman	Alvin Wyatt Sr.	0-1	Lost 1st Round
Jacksonville St.	Jack Crowe	0-1	Lost 1st Round
Massachusetts	Mark Whipple	0-1	Lost 1st Round
McNeese St.	Tommy Tate	0-1	Lost 1st Round
Montana	Bobby Hauck	0-1	Lost 1st Round
Montana St.	Mike Kramer	0-1	Lost 1st Round
N.C. A&T	Bill Hayes	0-1	Lost 1st Round
Southern Ill.	Jerry Kill	0-1	Lost 1st Round
2004 (16)			
James Madison	Mickey Matthews	4-0	Champion
Montana	Bobby Hauck	3-1	Second
Sam Houston St.	Ron Randleman	2-1	Semifinalist
William & Mary	Jimmye Laycock	2-1	Semifinalist
Delaware	K.C. Keeler	1-1	Quarterfinalist
Eastern Wash.	Paul Wulff	1-1	Quarterfinalist
Furman	Bobby Lamb	1-1	Quarterfinalist
New Hampshire	Sean McDonnell	1-1	Quarterfinalist
Ga. Southern	Mike Sewak	0-1	Lost 1st Round
Hampton	Joe Taylor	0-1	Lost 1st Round
Jacksonville St.	Jack Crowe	0-1	Lost 1st Round
Lafayette	Frank Tavani	0-1	Lost 1st Round
Lehigh	Pete Lembo	0-1	Lost 1st Round
Northwestern St.	Steve Stoker	0-1	Lost 1st Round
Southern Ill.	Jerry Kill	0-1	Lost 1st Round
Western Ky.	David Elson	0-1	Lost 1st Round
2005 (16)			
Appalachian St.	Jerry Moore	4-0	Champion
UNI	Mark Farley	3-1	Second
Furman	Bobby Lamb	2-1	Semifinalist
Texas St.	David Bailiff	2-1	Semifinalist
Cal Poly	Rich Ellerson	1-1	Quarterfinalist
New Hampshire	Sean McDonnell	1-1	Quarterfinalist
Richmond	Dave Clawson	1-1	Quarterfinalist
Southern Ill.	Jerry Kill	1-1	Quarterfinalist
Colgate	Dick Biddle	0-1	Lost 1st Round
Eastern Ill.	Bob Spoo	0-1	Lost 1st Round
Eastern Wash.	Paul Wulff	0-1	Lost 1st Round
Ga. Southern	Mike Sewak	0-1	Lost 1st Round
Hampton	Joe Taylor	0-1	Lost 1st Round
Lafayette	Frank Tavani	0-1	Lost 1st Round
Montana	Bobby Hauck	0-1	Lost 1st Round
Nicholls St.	Jay Thomas	0-1	Lost 1st Round
2006 (16)			
Appalachian St.	Jerry Moore	4-0	Champion
Massachusetts	Dan Brown	3-1	Second
Montana	Bobby Hauck	2-1	Semifinalist
Youngstown St.	Jon Heacock	2-1	Semifinalist
Illinois St.	Denver Johnson	1-1	Quarterfinalist
Montana St.	Mike Kramer	1-1	Quarterfinalist
New Hampshire	Sean McDonnell	1-1	Quarterfinalist
Southern Ill.	Jerry Kill	1-1	Quarterfinalist
Coastal Caro.	David Bennett	0-1	Lost 1st Round
Eastern Ill.	Bob Spoo	0-1	Lost 1st Round
Furman	Bobby Lamb	0-1	Lost 1st Round
Hampton	Joe Taylor	0-1	Lost 1st Round
James Madison	Mickey Matthews	0-1	Lost 1st Round
Lafayette	Frank Tavani	0-1	Lost 1st Round
McNeese St.	Matt Viator	0-1	Lost 1st Round
Tenn.-Martin	Jason Simpson	0-1	Lost 1st Round

**Competition in championship vacated by action of the NCAA Committee on Infractions.*

Division I Championship Record of Each College by Coach

(79 Colleges; 1978-06)

	Yrs	Won	Lost	CH	2D
AKRON					
Jim Dennison (Wooster '60) 85	1	0	1	0	0
ALCORN ST.					
Marino Casem [Xavier (La.) '56] 84	1	0	1	0	0
Cardell Jones (Alcorn St. '65) 92, 94	2	0	2	0	0
TOTAL	3	0	3	0	0
APPALACHIAN ST.					
Sparky Woods (Carson-Newman '76) 86, 87	2	2	2	0	0
Jerry Moore (Baylor '61) 89, 91, 92, 94, 95, 98, 99, 00, 01, 02, 05-CH, 06-CH	12	14	10	2	0
TOTAL	14	16	12	2	0
ARKANSAS ST.					
Larry Lacewell (Ark.-Monticello '59) 84, 85, 86-2D, 87	4	6	4	0	1
BETHUNE-COOKMAN					
Alvin Wyatt (Bethune-Cookman '70) 02, 03	2	0	2	0	0
BOISE ST.					
Jim Criner (Cal Poly Pomona '61) 80-CH, 81	2	3	1	1	0
Skip Hall (Concordia-M'head '66) 88, 90	2	2	2	0	0
Pokey Allen (Utah '65) 94-2D	1	3	1	0	1
TOTAL	5	8	4	1	1
BOSTON U.					
Rick Taylor (Gettysburg '64) 82, 83, 84	3	1	3	0	0
Dan Allen (Hanover '78) 93, 94	2	1	2	0	0
TOTAL	5	2	5	0	0
CAL POLY					
Rich Ellerson (Hawaii '77) 05	1	1	1	0	0
UCF					
Gene McDowell (Florida St. '63) 90, 93	2	2	2	0	0
CHATTANOOGA					
Buddy Nix (West Ala. '61) 84	1	0	1	0	0
CITADEL					
Charlie Taaffe (Siena '73) 88, 90, 92	3	1	3	0	0

	Yrs	Won	Lost	CH	2D
COASTAL CARO.					
David Bennett (Presbyterian '84) 06	1	0	1	0	0
COLGATE					
Fred Dunlap (Colgate '50) 82, 83	2	1	2	0	0
Dick Biddle (Duke '71) 97, 98, 99, 03-2D, 05	5	3	5	0	1
TOTAL	7	4	7	0	1
CONNECTICUT					
Skip Holtz (Notre Dame '86) 98	1	1	1	0	0
DELAWARE					
Harold "Tubby" Raymond (Michigan '50) 81, 82-2D, 86, 88, 91, 92, 93, 95, 96, 97,00	11	11	11	0	1
K.C. Keeler (Delaware '81) 03-CH, 04	2	5	1	1	0
TOTAL	13	16	12	1	1
EAST TENN. ST.					
Mike Cavan (Georgia '72) 96	1	1	1	0	0
EASTERN ILL.					
Darrell Mudra (Peru St. '51) 82	1	1	1	0	0
Al Molde (Gust. Adolphus '66) 83, 86	2	1	2	0	0
Bob Spoo (Purdue '60) 89, 95, 96, 00, 01, 02, 05	7	1	7	0	0
Mark Hutson (Oklahoma '89) 06	1	0	1	0	0
TOTAL	11	3	11	0	0
EASTERN KY.					
Roy Kidd (Eastern Ky. '54) 79-CH, 80-2D, 81-2D, 82-CH, 83, 84, 86, 87, 88, 89, 90, 91, 92, 93, 94, 95, 97	17	16	15	2	2
EASTERN WASH.					
Dick Zornes (Eastern Wash. '68) 85, 92	2	1	2	0	0
Mike Kramer (Idaho '77) 97	1	2	1	0	0
Paul Wulff (Washington St. '90) 04, 05	2	1	2	0	0
TOTAL	5	4	5	0	0
FLORIDA A&M					
Rudy Hubbard (Ohio St. '68) 78-CH	1	2	0	1	0
Billy Joe (Villanova '63) 96, 97, 98, 99, 00, 01	6	3	6	0	0
TOTAL	7	5	6	1	0
FLA. ATLANTIC					
Howard Schnellenberger (Alabama '56) 03	1	2	1	0	0
FORDHAM					
David Clawson (Williams '89) 02	1	1	1	0	0
FURMAN					
Dick Sheridan (South Carolina '64) 82, 83, 85-2D	3	3	3	0	1
Jimmy Satterfield (South Carolina '62) 86, 88-CH, 89, 90	4	7	3	1	0
Bobby Johnson (Clemson '73) 96, 99, 00, 01-2D	4	4	4	0	1
Bobby Lamb (Furman '87) 02, 04, 05, 06	4	3	4	0	0
TOTAL	15	17	14	1	2
GA. SOUTHERN					
Erk Russell (Auburn '49) 85-CH, 86-CH, 87, 88-2D, 89-CH	5	16	2	3	1
Tim Stowers (Auburn '79) 90-CH, 93, 95	3	6	2	1	0
Paul Johnson (Western Caro. '74) 97, 98-2D, 99-CH, 00-CH, 01	5	14	3	2	1
Mike Sewak (Virginia '81) 02, 04, 05	3	2	3	0	0
TOTAL	16	38	10	6	2
GRAMBLING					
Eddie Robinson (Leland '41) 80, 85, 89	3	0	3	0	0
HAMPTON					
Joe Taylor (Western Ill. '72) 97, 98, 04, 05, 06	5	0	5	0	0
HOFSTRA					
Joe Gardi (Maryland '60) 95, 97, 99, 00, 01	5	2	5	0	0
HOLY CROSS					
Rick Carter (Earlham '65) 83	1	0	1	0	0
HOWARD					
Steve Wilson (Howard '79) 93	1	0	1	0	0
IDAHO					
Dennis Erickson (Montana St. '70) 82, 85	2	1	2	0	0
Keith Gilbertson (Central Wash. '71) 86, 87, 88	3	2	3	0	0
John L. Smith (Weber St. '71) 89, 90, 92, 93, 94	5	3	5	0	0
Chris Tormey (Idaho '78) 95	1	0	1	0	0
TOTAL	11	6	11	0	0
IDAHO ST.					
Dave Kragthorpe (Utah St. '55) 81-CH	1	3	0	1	0
Jim Koetter (Idaho St. '61) 83	1	0	1	0	0
TOTAL	2	3	1	1	0
ILLINOIS ST.					
Todd Berry (Tulsa '83) 98, 99	2	2	2	0	0
Denver Johnson (Tulsa '81) 06	1	1	1	0	0
TOTAL	3	3	3	0	0
INDIANA ST.					
Dennis Raetz (Nebraska '68) 83, 84	2	1	2	0	0
JACKSON ST.					
W.C. Gorden (Tennessee St. '52) 78, 81, 82, 85, 86, 87, 88, 89, 90	9	0	9	0	0
James Carson (Jackson St. '63) 95, 96, 97	3	0	3	0	0
TOTAL	12	0	12	0	0
JACKSONVILLE ST.					
Jack Crowe (UAB '70) 03, 04	2	0	2	0	0
JAMES MADISON					
Joe Purzycki (Delaware '71) 87	1	0	1	0	0
Rip Scherer (William & Mary '74) 91, 94	2	2	2	0	0
Alex Wood (Iowa '79) 95	1	0	1	0	0
Mickey Matthews (West Tex. A&M '76) 99, 04-CH, 06	3	4	2	1	0
TOTAL	7	6	6	1	0
LAFAYETTE					
Frank Tavani (Lebanon Valley '75) 04, 05, 06	3	0	3	0	0
LEHIGH					
John Whitehead (East Stroudsburg '50) 79-2D, 80	2	1	2	0	1
Kevin Higgins (West Chester '77) 98, 99, 00	3	2	3	0	0
Pete Lembo (Georgetown '92) 01, 04	2	1	2	0	0
TOTAL	7	4	7	0	1
LA.-MONROE					
Pat Collins (Louisiana Tech '63) 87-CH	1	4	0	1	0
Dave Roberts (Western Caro. '68) 90, 92, 93	3	1	3	0	0
TOTAL	4	5	3	1	0
LOUISIANA TECH					
Billy Brewer (Mississippi '61) 82	1	1	1	0	0
A.L. Williams (Louisiana Tech '57) 84-2D	1	3	1	0	1
TOTAL	2	4	2	0	1
MAINE					
Tim Murphy (Springfield '78) 87	1	0	1	0	0
Tom Lichtenberg (Louisville '62) 89	1	0	1	0	0
Jack Cosgrove (Maine '78) 01, 02	2	2	2	0	0
TOTAL	4	2	4	0	0
MARSHALL					
George Chaump (Bloomsburg '58) 87-2D, 88	2	4	2	0	1
Jim Donnan (North Carolina St. '67) 91-2D, 92-CH, 93-2D, 94, 95-2D	5	15	4	1	3
Bob Pruett (Marshall '65) 96-CH	1	4	0	1	0
TOTAL	8	23	6	2	4
MASSACHUSETTS					
Bob Pickett (Maine '59) 78-2D	1	1	1	0	1
Jim Reid (Maine '73) 88, 90	2	0	2	0	0
Mark Whipple (Brown '79) 98-CH, 99, 03	3	5	2	1	0
Dan Brown (Norwich '77) 06-2D	1	3	1	0	1
TOTAL	7	9	6	1	2
McNEESE ST.					
Bobby Keasler (La.-Monroe '70) 91, 92, 93, 94, 95, 97-2D, 98	7	8	7	0	1
Tommy Tate (McNeese St. '79) 00, 01, 02-2D, 03	4	3	4	0	1
Matt Viator (McNeese St. '86) 06	1	0	1	0	0
TOTAL	12	11	12	0	2
MIDDLE TENN.					
James "Boots" Donnelly (Middle Tenn. '65) 84, 85, 89, 90, 91, 92, 94	7	6	7	0	0
MISSISSIPPI VAL.					
Archie Cooley Jr. (Jackson St. '62) 84	1	0	1	0	0
MISSOURI ST.					
Jesse Branch (Arkansas '64) 89, 90	2	1	2	0	0
MONTANA					
Larry Donovan (Nebraska '64) 82	1	0	1	0	0
Don Read (Sacramento St. '59) 88, 89, 93, 94, 95-CH	5	8	4	1	0
Mick Dennehy (Montana '73) 96-2D, 97, 98, 99	4	3	4	0	1
Joe Glenn (South Dakota '71) 00-2D, 01-CH, 02	3	8	2	1	1
Bobby Hauck (Montana '88) 03, 04-2D, 05, 06	4	5	4	0	1
TOTAL	17	24	15	2	3

	Yrs	Won	Lost	CH	2D
MONTANA ST.					
Dave Arnold (Drake '67) 84-CH	1	3	0	1	0
Mike Kramer (Idaho '77) 02, 03, 06	3	1	3	0	0
TOTAL	4	4	3	1	0
MURRAY ST.					
Mike Gottfried (Morehead St. '66) 79	1	0	1	0	0
Frank Beamer (Virginia Tech '69) 86	1	0	1	0	0
Houston Nutt (Oklahoma St. '81) 95, 96	2	1	2	0	0
Joe Pannunzio (Colorado St.-Pueblo '82) 02	1	0	1	0	0
TOTAL	5	1	5	0	0
NEVADA					
Chris Ault (Nevada '68) 78, 79, 83, 85, 86, 90-2D, 91	7	9	7	0	1
NEW HAMPSHIRE					
Bill Bowes (Penn St. '65) 91, 94	2	0	2	0	0
Sean McDonnell (New Hampshire '78) 04, 05, 06	3	3	3	0	0
TOTAL	5	3	5	0	0
NICHOLLS ST.					
Sonny Jackson (Nicholls St. '63) 86	1	1	1	0	0
Darren Barbier (Nicholls St. '82) 96	1	0	1	0	0
Jay Thomas (Southern Miss. '88) 05	1	0	1	0	0
TOTAL	3	1	3	0	0
N.C. A&T					
Maurice "Mo" Forte (Minnesota '71) 86	1	0	1	0	0
Bill Hayes (N.C. Central '64) 92, 99, 03	3	1	3	0	0
TOTAL	4	1	4	0	0
NORTH TEXAS					
Corky Nelson (Texas St. '64) 83, 87, 88	3	0	3	0	0
Matt Simon (Eastern N.M. '76) 94	1	0	1	0	0
TOTAL	4	0	4	0	0
NORTHEASTERN					
Don Brown (Norwich '77) 02	1	0	1	0	0
NORTHERN ARIZ. #					
Stephen Axman (C.W. Post '69) 96	1	0	1	0	0
Jerome Souers (Oregon '83) 99, 01, 03	3	1	3	0	0
TOTAL	4	1	4	0	0
UNI					
Darrell Mudra (Peru St. '51) 85, 87	2	3	2	0	0
Terry Allen (UNI '79) 90, 91, 92, 93, 94, 95, 96	7	6	7	0	0
Mark Farley (UNI '86) 01, 03, 05-2D	3	6	3	0	1
TOTAL	12	15	12	0	1
NORTHWESTERN ST.					
Sam Goodwin (Henderson St. '66) 88, 97, 98	3	3	3	0	0
Steve Roberts (Ouachita Baptist '87) 01	1	0	1	0	0
Scott Stoker (Northwestern St. '91) 02, 04	2	0	2	0	0
TOTAL	6	3	6	0	0
PORTLAND ST.					
Tim Walsh (UC Riverside '77) 00	1	0	1	0	0
RHODE ISLAND					
Bob Griffin (Southern Conn. St. '63) 81, 84, 85	3	2	3	0	0
RICHMOND					
Dal Shealy (Carson-Newman '60) 84, 87	2	1	2	0	0
Jim Reid (Maine '73) 98, 00	2	1	2	0	0
Dave Clawson (Williams '89) 05	1	1	1	0	0
TOTAL	5	3	5	0	0
SAM HOUSTON ST.					
Ron Randleman (William Penn '64) 86, 91, 01, 04	4	3	4	0	0
SAMFORD					
Terry Bowden (West Virginia '78) 91, 92	2	2	2	0	0
SOUTH CAROLINA ST.					
Bill Davis (Johnson C. Smith '65) 81, 82	2	2	2	0	0
SOUTHERN ILL.					
Rey Dempsey (Geneva '58) 83-CH	1	3	0	1	0
Jerry Kill [Southwestern (Kan.) '82] 03, 04, 05, 06	4	2	4	0	0
TOTAL	5	5	4	1	0
STEPHEN F. AUSTIN¢					
Jim Hess (Southeastern Okla. '59) 88	1	1	1	0	0
Lynn Graves (Stephen F. Austin '65) 89-2D	1	3	1	0	1
John Pearce (Tex. A&M-Kingsville '70) 93, 95	2	2	2	0	0
TOTAL	4	6	4	0	1
TENN.-MARTIN					
Jason Simpson (Southern Miss. '95) 06	1	0	1	0	0

	Yrs	Won	Lost	CH	2D
TENNESSEE ST.*					
John Merritt (Kentucky St. '50) 81, 82	2	1	2	0	0
Bill Thomas (Tennessee St. '71) 86	1	1	1	0	0
L.C. Cole (Nebraska '80) 98, 99	2	0	2	0	0
TOTAL	5	2	5	0	0
TEXAS ST.					
David Bailiff (Texas St. '81) 05	1	2	1	0	0
TROY					
Larry Blakeney (Auburn '70) 93, 94, 95, 96, 98, 99, 00	7	5	7	0	0
VILLANOVA					
Andy Talley (Southern Conn. St. '67) 89, 91, 92, 96, 97, 02	6	3	6	0	0
WEBER ST.					
Mike Price (Puget Sound '69) 87	1	1	1	0	0
Dave Arslanian (Weber St. '72) 91	1	0	1	0	0
TOTAL	2	1	2	0	0
WESTERN CARO.					
Bob Waters (Presbyterian '60) 83-2D	1	3	1	0	1
WESTERN ILL.					
Bruce Craddock (Truman '66) 88	1	0	1	0	0
Randy Ball (Truman '73) 91, 96, 97, 98	4	3	4	0	0
Don Patterson (Army '73) 00, 02, 03	3	2	3	0	0
TOTAL	8	5	8	0	0
WESTERN KY.					
Dave Roberts (Western Caro. '68) 87, 88	2	1	2	0	0
Jack Harbaugh (Bowling Green '61) 97, 00, 01, 02-CH	4	6	3	1	0
Dave Elson (Butler '94) 03, 04	2	1	2	0	0
TOTAL	8	8	7	1	0
WILLIAM & MARY					
Jimmye Laycock (William & Mary '70) 86, 89, 90, 93, 96, 01, 04	7	4	7	0	0
WOFFORD					
Mike Ayers [Georgetown (Ky.) '74] 03	1	2	1	0	0
YOUNGSTOWN ST.					
Jim Tressel (Baldwin-Wallace '75) 87, 89, 90, 91-CH, 92-2D, 93-CH, 94-CH, 97-CH, 99-2D, 00	10	23	6	4	2
Jon Heacock (Muskingum '83) 06	1	2	1	0	0
TOTAL	11	25	7	4	2

*#Northern Arizona's competition in the 1999 Division I-AA championship was vacated by action of the NCAA Committee on Infractions (record was 0-1). *Tennessee State's competition in the 1981 and 1982 Division I-AA championships was vacated by action of the NCAA Committee on Infractions (record was 1-2). ¢Stephen F. Austin's competition in the 1989 Division I-AA championship was vacated by action of the NCAA Committee on Infractions (record was 3-1).*

Division I Championship Team Leaders

MOST APPEARANCES

Eastern Ky.	17
Montana	17
Ga. Southern	16
Furman	15
Appalachian St.	14
Delaware	13
Jackson St.	12
McNeese St.	12
UNI	12
Eastern Ill.	11
Idaho#	11
Youngstown St.	11

MOST VICTORIES

Ga. Southern	38
Youngstown St.	25
Montana	24
Marshall#	23
Furman	17
Appalachian St.	16
Delaware	16
Eastern Ky.	16
UNI	15
McNeese St.	11

MOST CONSECUTIVE APPEARANCES

14	Montana	1993-present
10	Eastern Ky.	1986-95
7	UNI	1990-96

6	Eastern Ky.	1979-84
6	Florida A&M	1996-01
6	Ga. Southern	1997-02
6	Ga. Southern	1985-90
6	Idaho#	1985-90
6	Jackson St.	1985-90
6	Marshall#	1991-96
6	Youngstown St.	1989-94

HIGHEST WINNING PERCENTAGE
(Min. 10 Games Played)

Marshall#	23-6	.793
Ga. Southern	38-10	.792
Youngstown St.	25-7	.781
Boise St.#	8-4	.667
Montana	24-15	.615
Massachusetts	9-6	.600
Arkansas St.#	6-4	.600
Stephen F. Austin	6-4	.600
Appalachian St.	16-12	.571
Delaware	16-12	.571
Nevada#	9-7	.563
Furman	17-14	.548

#No longer a FCS member.

Division I Championship Attendance History

Year	Teams	G	Total Attend.	Avg. PG
1978	4	3	34,630	11,543
1979	4	3	20,300	6,767
1980	4	3	36,957	12,319
1981	8	7	81,455	11,636
1982	12	11	106,801	9,709
1983	12	11	103,631	9,421
1984	12	11	122,142	11,104
1985	12	11	86,996	7,909
1986	16	15	153,832	10,255
1987	16	15	133,956	8,930
1988	16	15	146,782	9,785
1989	16	15	145,198	9,680
1990	16	15	180,027	12,002
1991	16	15	169,605	11,307
1992	16	15	199,450	13,297
1993	16	15	178,884	11,926
1994	16	15	209,761	13,984
1995	16	15	209,367	13,958
1996	16	15	178,768	11,918
1997	16	15	152,219	10,418
1998	16	15	146,084	9,739
1999	16	15	178,742	11,916
2000	16	15	163,764	10,918
2001	16	15	166,707	11,114
2002	16	15	124,835	8,322
2003	16	15	151,411	10,094
2004	16	15	154,558	10,304
2005	16	15	153,132	10,209
2006	16	15	202,351	13,490

1978

First Round (12/9):	Site	Attendance
Florida A&M 15, Jackson St. 10	Jackson, Miss.	7,000
Massachusetts 44, Nevada 21	Reno, Nev.	14,026
Championship (12/16):		
Florida A&M 35, Massachusetts 28	Wichita Falls, Tex.	13,604

1979

First Round (12/8):	Site	Attendance
Lehigh 28, Murray St. 9	Murray, Ky.	10,000
Eastern Ky. 33, Nevada 30 (2 ot)	Richmond, Ky.	5,100
Championship (12/15):		
Eastern Ky. 30, Lehigh 7	Orlando, Fla.	5,200

1980

First Round (12/13):	Site	Attendance
Eastern Ky. 23, Lehigh 20	Bethlehem, Pa.	11,500
Boise St. 14, Grambling 9	Boise, Id.	17,300
Championship (12/20):		
Boise St. 31, Eastern Ky. 29	Sacramento, Cal.	8,157

1981

First Round (12/5):	Site	Attendance
Eastern Ky. 35, Delaware 28	Richmond, Ky.	8,100
Boise St. 19, Jackson St. 7	Jackson, Miss.	11,500
Idaho St. 51, Rhode Island 0	Pocatello, Id.	12,153
South Carolina St. 26, Tennessee St. 25 (ot)	Orangeburg, S.C.	6,224
Semifinals (12/12):	**Site**	**Attendance**
Eastern Ky. 23, Boise St. 17	Boise, Id.	20,176
Idaho St. 41, South Carolina St. 12	Pocatello, Id.	12,300
Championship (12/19):		
Idaho St. 34, Eastern Ky. 23	Wichita Falls, Tex.	11,002

1982

First Round (11/27):	Site	Attendance
Idaho 21, Montana 7	Moscow, Id.	8,000
Eastern Ill. 16, Jackson St. 13 (ot)	Charleston, Ill.	5,000
South Carolina St. 17, Furman 0	Greenville, S.C.	13,865
Colgate 21, Boston U. 7	Hamilton, N.Y.	5,000
Quarterfinals (12/4):		
Eastern Ky. 38, Idaho 30	Richmond, Ky.	10,893
Tennessee St. 20, Eastern Ill. 19	Nashville, Tenn.	8,000
Louisiana Tech 38, South Carolina St. 3	Ruston, La.	13,000
Delaware 20, Colgate 13	Newark, Del.	11,448
Semifinals (12/11):		
Eastern Ky. 13, Tennessee St. 7	Richmond, Ky.	7,338
Delaware 17, Louisiana Tech 0	Ruston, La.	13,000
Championship (12/18):		
Eastern Ky. 17, Delaware 14	Wichita Falls, Tex.	11,257

1983

First Round (11/27):	Site	Attendance
Indiana St. 16, Eastern Ill. 13 (2 ot)	Terre Haute, Ind.	6,222
Nevada 27, Idaho St. 20	Pocatello, Id.	10,333
Western Caro. 24, Colgate 23	Cullowhee, N.C.	6,500
Boston U. 24, Eastern Ky. 20	Richmond, Ky.	4,800
Quarterfinals (12/3):		
Southern Ill. 23, Indiana St. 7	Carbondale, Ill.	8,000
Nevada 20, North Texas 17 (ot)	Reno, Nev.	7,878
Western Caro. 28, Holy Cross 21	Worcester, Mass.	10,814
Furman 35, Boston U. 16	Greenville, S.C.	7,600
Semifinals (12/10):		
Southern Ill. 23, Nevada 7	Carbondale, Ill.	12,500
Western Caro. 14, Furman 7	Greenville, S.C.	13,034
Championship (12/17):		
Southern Ill. 43, Western Caro. 7	Charleston, S.C.	15,950

1984

First Round (11/24):	Site	Attendance
Louisiana Tech 66, Mississippi Val. 19	Ruston, La.	17,500
Middle Tenn. 27, Eastern Ky. 10	Richmond, Ky.	4,800
Richmond 35, Boston U. 33	Richmond, Va.	11,236
Arkansas St. 37, Chattanooga 10	Jonesboro, Ark.	10,872
Quarterfinals (12/1):		
Louisiana Tech 44, Alcorn St. 21	Jackson, Miss.	16,204
Middle Tenn. 42, Indiana St. 41 (3 ot)	Terre Haute, Ind.	6,225
Rhode Island 23, Richmond 17	Kingston, R.I.	10,446
Montana St. 31, Arkansas St. 14	Bozeman, Mont.	12,037
Semifinals (12/8):		
Louisiana Tech 21, Middle Tenn. 13	Murfreesboro, Tenn.	11,000
Montana St. 32, Rhode Island 20	Bozeman, Mont.	12,697
Championship (12/15):		
Montana St. 19, Louisiana Tech 6	Charleston, S.C.	9,125

1985

First Round (11/30):	Site	Attendance
Ga. Southern 27, Jackson St. 0	Statesboro, Ga.	4,128
Eastern Wash. 42, Idaho 38	Moscow, Id.	6,500
Rhode Island 35, Akron 27	Kingston, R.I.	7,317
Arkansas St. 10, Grambling 7	Jonesboro, Ark.	5,730
Quarterfinals (12/7):		
Ga. Southern 28, Middle Tenn. 21	Murfreesboro, Tenn.	9,500
UNI 17, Eastern Wash. 14	Cedar Falls, Ia.	6,220
Furman 59, Rhode Island 15	Greenville, S.C.	9,454
Nevada 24, Arkansas St. 23	Reno, Nev.	10,241
Semifinals (12/14):		
Ga. Southern 40, UNI 33	Cedar Falls, Ia.	12,300
Furman 35, Nevada 12	Greenville, S.C.	10,300
Championship (12/21):		
Ga. Southern 44, Furman 42	Tacoma, Wash.	5,306

1986

First Round (11/29):	Site	Attendance
Nevada 27, Idaho 7	Reno, Nev.	13,715
Tennessee St. 32, Jackson St. 23	Jackson, Miss.	24,000
Ga. Southern 52, N.C. A&T 21	Statesboro, Ga.	7,767
Nicholls St. 28, Appalachian St. 26	Boone, N.C.	6,250
Arkansas St. 48, Sam Houston St. 7	Jonesboro, Ark.	4,500
Delaware 51, William & Mary 17	Williamsburg, Va.	6,340
Eastern Ill. 28, Murray St. 21	Charleston, Ill.	9,500
Eastern Ky. 23, Furman 10	Greenville, S.C.	8,000
Quarterfinals (12/6):		
Nevada 33, Tennessee St. 6	Reno, Nev.	13,102
Ga. Southern 55, Nicholls St. 31	Statesboro, Ga.	9,121
Arkansas St. 55, Delaware 14	Newark, Del.	12,018
Eastern Ky. 24, Eastern Ill. 22	Charleston, Ill.	9,500
Semifinals (12/13):		
Ga. Southern 48, Nevada 38	Reno. Nev.	15,100
Arkansas St. 24, Eastern Ky. 10	Jonesboro, Ark.	10,500

Championship (12/20):	**Site**	**Attendance**
Ga. Southern 48, Arkansas St. 21	Tacoma, Wash.	4,419

1987

First Round (11/28):	**Site**	**Attendance**
Appalachian St. 20, Richmond 3	Boone, N.C.	4,138
Ga. Southern 31, Maine 28 (ot)	Statesboro, Ga.	9,440
Weber St. 59, Idaho 30	Moscow, Id.	4,900
Marshall 41, James Madison 12	Huntington, W.Va.	15,584
La.-Monroe 30, North Texas 9	Monroe, La.	9,500
Eastern Ky. 40, Western Ky. 17	Richmond, Ky.	4,050
UNI 31, Youngstown St. 28	Cedar Falls, Ia.	3,887
Arkansas St. 35, Jackson St. 32	Jackson, Miss.	7,500
Quarterfinals (12/5):		
Appalachian St. 19, Ga. Southern 0	Boone, N.C.	9,229
Marshall 51, Weber St. 23	Huntington, W.Va.	13,197
La.-Monroe 33, Eastern Ky. 32	Monroe, La.	10,475
UNI 49, Arkansas St. 28	Cedar Falls, Ia.	6,100
Semifinals (12/12):		
Marshall 24, Appalachian St. 10	Boone, N.C.	10,000
La.-Monroe 44, UNI 41 (2 ot)	Monroe, La.	14,443
Championship (12/19):		
La.-Monroe 43, Marshall 42	Pocatello, Id.	11,513

1988

First Round (11/26):	**Site**	**Attendance**
Idaho 38, Montana 19	Moscow, Id.	5,500
Northwestern St. 22, Boise St. 13	Boise, Id.	10,537
Furman 21, Delaware 7	Greenville, S.C.	7,487
Marshall 7, North Texas 0	Huntington, W.Va.	15,086
Ga. Southern 38, Citadel 20	Statesboro, Ga.	11,011
Stephen F. Austin 24, Jackson St. 0	Nacogdoches, Tex.	5,384
Western Ky. 35, Western Ill. 32	Macomb, Ill.	6,000
Eastern Ky. 28, Massachusetts 17	Richmond, Ky.	4,600
Quarterfinals (12/3):		
Idaho 38, Northwestern St. 30	Moscow, Id.	6,800
Furman 13, Marshall 9	Huntington, W.Va.	16,820
Ga. Southern 27, Stephen F. Austin 6	Statesboro, Ga.	12,289
Eastern Ky. 41, Western Ky. 24	Richmnond, Ky.	8,100
Semifinals (12/10):	**Site**	**Attendance**
Furman 38, Idaho 7	Greenville, S.C.	11,645
Ga. Southern 21, Eastern Ky. 17	Statesboro, Ga.	14,023
Championship (12/17):		
Furman 17, Ga. Southern 12	Pocatello, Id.	11,500

1989

First Round (11/25):	**Site**	**Attendance**
Ga. Southern 52, Villanova 36	Statesboro, Ga.	10,161
Middle Tenn. 24, Appalachian St. 21	Murfreesboro, Tenn.	5,000
Eastern Ill. 38, Idaho 21	Moscow, Id.	6,025
Montana 48, Jackson St. 7	Missoula, Mont.	11,854
Furman 24, William & Mary 10	Greenville, S.C.	8,642
Youngstown St. 28, Eastern Ky. 24	Richmond, Ky.	3,898
Stephen F. Austin 59, Grambling 56	Nacogdoches, Tex.	7,106
Missouri St. 38, Maine 35	Springfield, Mo.	7,270
Quarterfinals (12/2):		
Ga. Southern 45, Middle Tenn. 3	Statesboro, Ga.	11,272
Montana 25, Eastern Ill. 19	Missoula, Mont.	12,285
Furman 42, Youngstown St. 23	Greenville, S.C.	8,033
Stephen F. Austin 55, Missouri St. 25	Nacogdoches, Tex.	10,491
Semifinals (12/9):		
Ga. Southern 45, Montana 15	Statesboro, Ga.	10,421
Stephen F. Austin 21, Furman 19	Greenville, S.C.	7,015
Championship (12/16):		
Ga. Southern 37, Stephen F. Austin 34	Statesboro, Ga.	25,725

1990

First Round (11/24):	**Site**	**Attendance**
Middle Tenn. 28, Jackson St. 7	Murfreesboro, Tenn.	7,000
Boise St. 20, UNI 3	Boise, Id.	11,691
Nevada 27, La.-Monroe 14	Reno, Nev.	11,008
Furman 45, Eastern Ky. 17	Richmond, Ky.	4,528
UCF 20, Youngstown St. 17	Youngstown, Ohio	5,000
William & Mary 38, Massachusetts 0	Williamsburg, Va.	5,000
Ga. Southern 31, Citadel 0	Statesboro, Ga.	11,881
Idaho 41, Missouri St. 35	Springfield, Mo.	8,750
Quarterfinals (12/1):		
Boise St. 20, Middle Tenn. 13	Boise, Id.	15,849
Nevada 42, Furman 35 (3 ot)	Reno, Nev.	11,519
UCF 52, William & Mary 38	Orlando, Fla.	20,067
Ga. Southern 28, Idaho 27	Statesboro, Ga.	11,571
Semifinals (12/8):		
Nevada 59, Boise St. 52 (3 ot)	Reno, Nev.	19,776
Ga. Southern 44, UCF 7	Statesboro, Ga.	13,183
Championship (12/15):		
Ga. Southern 36, Nevada 13	Statesboro, Ga.	23,204

1991

First Round (11/30):	**Site**	**Attendance**
Nevada 22, McNeese St. 16	Reno, Nev.	15,000
Youngstown St. 17, Villanova 16	Youngstown, Ohio	9,556
James Madison 42, Delaware 35 (2 ot)	Newark, Del.	14,905
Samford 29, New Hampshire 13	Durham, N.H.	6,034
Eastern Ky. 14, Appalachian St. 3	Richmond, Ky.	2,750
Middle Tenn. 20, Sam Houston St. 19 (ot)	Murfreesboro, Tenn.	2,000
UNI 38, Weber St. 21	Cedar Falls, Ia.	8,723
Marshall 20, Western Ill. 17 (ot)	Huntington, W.Va.	16,840
Quarterfinals (12/7):		
Youngstown St. 30, Nevada 28	Reno, Nev.	13,476
Samford 24, James Madison 21	Harrisonburg, Va.	9,028
Eastern Ky. 23, Middle Tenn. 13	Richmond, Ky.	3,650
Marshall 41, UNI 13	Huntington, W.Va.	16,889
Semifinals (12/14):		
Youngstown St. 10, Samford 0	Youngstown, Ohio	17,003
Marshall 14, Eastern Ky. 7	Huntington, W.Va.	21,084
Championship (12/21):		
Youngstown St. 25, Marshall 17	Statesboro, Ga.	12,667

1992

First Round (11/28):	**Site**	**Attendance**
La.-Monroe 78, Alcorn St. 27	Monroe, La.	14,416
Delaware 56, Samford 21	Newark, Del.	11,364
Middle Tenn. 35, Appalachian St. 10	Murfreesboro, Tenn.	4,000
Marshall 44, Eastern Ky. 0	Huntington, W.Va.	16,598
Citadel 44, N.C. A&T 0	Charleston, S.C.	12,300
Youngstown St. 23, Villanova 20	Youngstown, Ohio	9,465
UNI 17, Eastern Wash. 14	Cedar Falls, Ia.	13,149
McNeese St. 23, Idaho 20	Moscow, Id.	6,000
Quarterfinals (12/5):		
Delaware 41, La.-Monroe 18	Monroe, La.	10,172
Marshall 35, Middle Tenn. 21	Huntington, W.Va.	14,011
Youngstown St. 42, Citadel 17	Charleston, S.C.	12,300
UNI 29, McNeese St. 7	Cedar Falls, Ia.	13,375
Semifinals (12/12):		
Marshall 28, Delaware 7	Huntington, W.Va.	16,323
Youngstown St. 19, UNI 7	Cedar Falls, Ia.	14,682
Championship (12/19):		
Marshall 31, Youngstown St. 28	Huntington, W.Va.	31,304

1993

First Round (11/27):	**Site**	**Attendance**
Ga. Southern 14, Eastern Ky. 12	Statesboro, Ga.	7,278
Youngstown St. 56, UCF 30	Youngstown, Ohio	7,408
Boston U. 27, UNI 21 (2 ot)	Boston, Mass.	6,882
Idaho 34, La.-Monroe 31	Monroe, La.	5,500
Delaware 49, Montana 48	Missoula, Mont.	11,271
Marshall 28, Howard 14	Huntington, W.Va.	13,554
McNeese St. 34, William & Mary 28	Lake Charles, La.	17,167
Troy 42, Stephen F. Austin 20	Troy, Ala.	4,500
Quarterfinals (12/4):		
Youngstown St. 34, Ga. Southern 14	Youngstown, Ohio	9,503
Idaho 21, Boston U. 14	Moscow, Id.	8,800
Marshall 34, Delaware 31	Huntington, W.Va.	13,687
Troy 35, McNeese St. 28	Lake Charles, La.	20,000
Semifinals (12/11):		
Youngstown St. 35, Idaho 16	Youngstown, Ohio	9,644
Marshall 24, Troy 21	Huntington, W.Va.	14,472
Championship (12/18):		
Youngstown St. 17, Marshall 5	Huntington, W.Va.	29,218

1994

First Round (11/26):	**Site**	**Attendance**
Youngstown St. 63, Alcorn St. 20	Youngstown, Ohio	17,795
Eastern Ky. 30, Boston U. 23	Richmond, Ky.	4,111
McNeese St. 38, Idaho 21	Lake Charles, La.	16,000
Montana 23, UNI 20	Missoula, Mont.	7,958
Marshall 49, Middle Tenn. St. 14	Huntington, W.Va.	17,349
James Madison 45, Troy 26	Harrisonburg, Va.	5,200
Boise St. 24, North Texas 20	Boise, Id.	14,706
Appalachian St. 17, New Hampshire 10 (ot)	Durham, N.H.	7,329
Quarterfinals (12/3):		
Youngstown St. 18, Eastern Ky. 15	Youngstown, Ohio	16,023
Montana 30, McNeese St. 28	Missoula, Mont.	8,419
Marshall 28, James Madison 21 (ot)	Huntington, W.Va.	16,494
Boise St. 17, Appalachian St. 14	Boise, Id.	15,302
Semifinals (12/10):		
Youngstown St. 28, Montana 9	Youngstown, Ohio	15,333
Boise St. 28, Marshall 24	Boise, Id.	20,068
Championship (12/17):		
Youngstown St. 28, Boise St. 14	Huntington, W.Va.	27,674

1995

First Round (11/25):	**Site**	**Attendance**
McNeese St. 33, Idaho 3	Lake Charles, La.	15,736
Delaware 38, Hofstra 17	Newark, Del.	13,295
UNI 35, Murray St. 34	Murray, Ky.	7,635
Marshall 38, Jackson St. 8	Huntington, W.Va.	13,035
Appalachian St. 31, James Madison 24	Boone, N.C.	9,467
Stephen F. Austin 34, Eastern Ill. 29	Nacogdoches, Tex.	3,552
Ga. Southern 24, Troy 21	Troy, Ala.	6,000
Montana 48, Eastern Ky. 0	Missoula, Mont.	13,830

	Site	Attendance
Quarterfinals (12/2):		
McNeese St. 52, Delaware 18	Lake Charles, La.	17,239
Marshall 41, UNI 24	Huntington, W.Va.	14,472
Stephen F. Austin 27, Appalachian St. 17	Boone, N.C.	8,941
Montana 45, Ga. Southern 0	Missoula, Mont.	18,518
Semifinals (12/9):		
Marshall 25, McNeese St. 13	Lake Charles, La.	18,018
Montana 70, Stephen F. Austin 14	Missoula, Mont.	18,523
Championship (12/16):		
Montana 22, Marshall 20	Huntington, W.Va.	32,106

1996

First Round (11/30):	Site	Attendance
Montana 48, Nicholls St. 3	Missoula, Mont.	13,438
East Tenn. St. 35, Villanova 29	Johnson City, Tenn.	4,939
Troy 29, Florida A&M 25	Troy, Ala.	10,200
Murray St. 34, Western Ill. 6	Murray, Ky.	2,753
Marshall 59, Delaware 14	Huntington, W.Va.	15,429
Furman 42, Northern Ariz. 31	Flagstaff, Ariz.	8,700
UNI 21, Eastern Ill. 14	Cedar Falls, Ia.	10,402
William & Mary 45, Jackson St. 6	Williamsburg, Va.	4,057
Quarterfinals (12/7):		
Montana 44, East Tenn. St. 14	Missoula, Mont.	15,025
Troy 31, Murray St. 3	Troy, Ala.	6,100
Marshall 54, Furman 0	Huntington, W.Va.	14,096
UNI 38, William & Mary 35	Cedar Falls, Ia.	10,796
Semifinals (12/14):		
Montana 70, Troy 7	Missoula, Mont.	18,367
Marshall 31, UNI 14	Huntington, W.Va.	14,414
Championship (12/21):		
Marshall 49, Montana 29	Huntington, W.Va.	30,052

1997

First Round (11/29):	Site	Attendance
Villanova 49, Colgate 28	Villanova, Pa.	8,875
Youngstown St. 28, Hampton 13	Youngstown, Ohio	12,431
Western Ky. 42, Eastern Ky. 14	Bowling Green, Ky.	9,000
Eastern Wash. 40, Northwestern St. 10	Cheney, Wash.	6,384
Delaware 24, Hofstra 14	Newark, Del.	14,075
Ga. Southern 52, Florida A&M 37	Statesboro, Ga.	10,409
McNeese St. 19, Montana 14	Lake Charles, La.	13,681
Western Ill. 31, Jackson St. 24	Macomb, Ill.	8,980
Quarterfinals (12/6):	Site	Attendance
Youngstown St. 37, Villanova 34	Villanova, Pa.	7,591
Eastern Wash. 38, Western Ky. 21	Cheney, Wash.	6,829
Delaware 16, Ga. Southern 7	Newark, Del.	11,203
McNeese St. 14, Western Ill. 12	Macomb, Ill.	5,000
Semifinals (12/13):		
Youngstown St. 25, Eastern Wash. 14	Cheney, Wash.	8,529
McNeese St. 23, Delaware 21	Newark, Del.	14,461
Championship (12/20):		
Youngstown St. 10, McNeese St. 9	Chattanooga, Tenn.	14,771

1998

First Round (11/28):	Site	Attendance
Ga. Southern 49, Colgate 28	Statesboro, Ga.	7,676
Connecticut 42, Hampton 34	Storrs, Conn.	6,193
Florida A&M 27, Troy 17	Tallahassee, Fla.	16,509
Western Ill. 52, Montana 9	Macomb, Ill.	3,614
Lehigh 24, Richmond 23	Richmond, Va.	10,254
Massachusetts 21, McNeese St. 19	Lake Charles, La.	11,349
Appalachian St. 45, Tennessee St. 31	Boone, N.C.	3,885
Northwestern St. 48, Illinois St. 28	Natchitoches, La.	8,118
Quarterfinals (12/5):		
Ga. Southern 52, Connecticut 30	Statesboro, Ga.	9,096
Western Ill. 24, Florida A&M 21 (12/4)	Macomb, Ill.	7,400
Massachusetts 27, Lehigh 21	Amherst, Mass.	12,108
Northwestern St. 31, Appalachian St. 20	Natchitoches, La.	10,817
Semifinals (12/12):		
Ga. Southern 42, Western Ill. 14	Statesboro, Ga.	11,140
Massachusetts 41, Northwestern St. 31	Natchitoches, La.	10,424
Championship (12/19):		
Massachusetts 55, Ga. Southern 43	Chattanooga, Tenn.	17,501

1999

First Round (11/27):	Site	Attendance
N.C. A&T 24, Tennessee St. 10	Nashville, Tenn.	10,736
Youngstown St. 30, Montana 27	Missoula, Mont.	17,261
Troy 27, James Madison 7	Troy, Ala.	17,102
Florida A&M 44, Appalachian St. 29	Boone, N.C.	6,837
Hofstra 27, Lehigh 15	Hempstead, N.Y.	6,770
Illinois St. 56, Colgate 13	Normal, Ill.	7,133
Massachusetts 30, Furman 23 (ot)	Greenville, S.C.	7,215
Ga. Southern 72, Northern Ariz. 29	Statesboro, Ga.	7,140
Quarterfinals (12/4):		
Youngstown St. 41, N.C. A&T 3	Youngstown, Ohio	16,955
Illinois St. 37, Hofstra 20	Hempstead, N.Y.	5,586
Florida A&M 17, Troy 10	Troy, Ala.	12,689
Ga. Southern 38, Massachusetts 21	Statesboro, Ga.	13,121
Semifinals (12/11):	Site	Attendance
Youngstown St. 27, Florida A&M 24	Youngstown, Ohio	17,846
Ga. Southern 28, Illinois St. 17	Statesboro, Ga.	12,299
Championship (12/20):		
Ga. Southern 59, Youngstown St. 24	Chattanooga, Tenn.	20,052

2000

First Round (11/25):	Site	Attendance
Montana 45, Eastern Ill. 13	Missoula, Mont.	16,212
Richmond 10, Youngstown St. 3	Richmond, Va.	5,484
Western Ky. 27, Florida A&M 0	Bowling Green, Ky.	3,200
Appalachian St. 33, Troy 30	Troy, Ala.	17,589
Ga. Southern 42, McNeese St. 17	Statesboro, Ga.	5,350
Hofstra 31, Furman 24	Greenville, S.C.	4,214
Lehigh 37, Western Ill. 7	Macomb, Ill.	3,204
Delaware 49, Portland St. 14	Newark, Del.	12,945
Quarterfinals (12/2):		
Montana 34, Richmond 20	Missoula, Mont.	17,345
Appalachian St. 17, Western Ky. 14	Boone, N.C.	5,100
Ga. Southern 48, Hofstra 20	Statesboro, Ga.	7,139
Delaware 47, Lehigh 22	Newark, Del.	16,390
Semifinals (12/9):		
Montana 19, Appalachian St. 16 (ot)	Missoula, Mont.	17,401
Ga. Southern 27, Delaware 18	Newark, Del.	15,035
Championship (12/16):		
Ga. Southern 27, Montana 25	Chattanooga, Tenn.	17,156

2001

First Round (12/1):	Site	Attendance
Montana 28, Northwestern St. 19	Missoula, Mont.	17,289
Sam Houston St. 34, Northern Ariz. 31	Huntsville, Tex.	8,143
Maine 14, McNeese St. 10	Lake Charles, La.	12,450
UNI 49, Eastern Ill. 43	Charleston, Ill.	6,824
Ga. Southern 60, Florida A&M 35	Statesboro, Ga.	9,884
Appalachian St. 40, William & Mary 27	Boone, N.C.	5,279
Lehigh 27, Hofstra 24 (ot)	Bethlehem, Pa.	10,131
Furman 24, Western Ky. 20	Greenville, S.C.	6,143
Quarterfinals (12/8):		
Montana 49, Sam Houston St. 24	Missoula, Mont.	18,125
UNI 56, Maine 28	Cedar Falls, Ia.	9,525
Ga. Southern 38, Appalachian St. 24	Statesboro, Ga.	9,352
Furman 34, Lehigh 17	Greenville, S.C.	10,189
Semifinals (12/15):	Site	Attendance
Montana 38, UNI 0	Missoula, Mont.	18,848
Furman 24, Ga. Southern 17	Statesboro, Ga.	11,827
Championship (12/21):		
Montana 13, Furman 6	Chattanooga, Tenn.	12,698

2002

First Round (11/30):	Site	Attendance
McNeese St. 21, Montana St. 14	Lake Charles, La.	16,211
Montana 45, Northwestern St. .14	Missoula, Mont.	15,758
Villanova 45, Furman 38	Villanova, Pa.	3,031
Fordham 29, Northeastern 24	Boston, Mass.	6,848
Ga. Southern 34, Bethune-Cookman 0	Statesboro, Ga.	7,395
Maine 14, Appalachian St. 13	Boone, N.C.	4,311
Western Ky. 59, Murray St. 20	Bowling Green, Ky.	3,300
Western Ill. 48, Eastern Ill. 9	Macomb, Ill.	2,429
Quarterfinals (12/7):		
McNeese St. 24, Montana 20	Lake Charles, La.	15,758
Villanova 24, Fordham 10	Villanova, Pa.	4,351
Ga. Southern 31, Maine 7	Statesboro, Ga.	6,708
Western Ky. 31, Western Ill. 28	Macomb, Ill.	3,285
Semifinals (12/14):		
McNeese St. 39, Villanova 28	Lake Charles, La.	16,517
Western Ky. 31, Ga. Southern 28	Statesboro, Ga.	6,573
Championship (12/20):		
Western Ky. 34, McNeese St. 14	Chattanooga, Tenn.	12,360

2003

First Round (11/29):	Site	Attendance
Northern Ariz. 35, McNeese St. 3	Lake Charles, La.	14,300
Fla. Atlantic 32, Bethune-Cookman 24	Daytona Beach, Fla.	8,468
Colgate 19, Massachusetts 7	Hamilton, N.Y.	4,197
Western Ill. 43, Montana 40 (2 ot)	Missoula, Mont.	10,165
Wofford 31, N.C. A&T 10	Spartanburg, S.C.	10,500
Western Ky. 45, Jacksonville St. 7	Bowling Green, Ky.	3,573
Delaware 48, Southern Ill. 7	Newark, Del.	14,572
UNI 35, Montana St. 14	Cedar Falls, Ia.	10,165
Quarterfinals (12/6):		
Fla. Atlantic 48, Northern Ariz. 25	Flagstaff, Ariz.	9,314
Colgate 28, Western Ill. 27	Hamilton, N.Y.	5,287
Wofford 34, Western Ky. 17	Spartanburg, S.C.	7,500
Delaware 37, UNI 7	Newark, Del.	11,881
Semifinals (12/13):		
Colgate 36, Fla. Atlantic 24	Boca Raton, Fla.	12,857
Delaware 24, Wofford 9	Newark, Del.	14,351

Championship (12/19):	Site	Attendance
Delaware 40, Colgate 0	Chattanooga, Tenn.	14,281

2004

First Round (11/27):	Site	Attendance
Eastern Wash. 35, Southern Ill. 31	Carbondale, Ill.	7,062
Sam Houston St. 54, Western Ky. 24	Huntsville, Tex.	3,767
Montana 56, Northwestern St. 7	Missoula, Mont.	15,507
New Hampshire 27, Ga. Southern 23	Statesboro, Ga.	5,541
William & Mary 42, Hampton 35	Williamsburg, Va.	7,144
Delaware 28, Lafayette 14	Newark, Del.	13,757
James Madison 14, Lehigh 13	Bethlehem, Pa.	5,568
Furman 49, Jacksonville St. 7	Greenville, S.C.	4,892
Quarterfinals (12/4):		
Sam Houston St. 35, Eastern Wash. 34	Cheney, Wash.	6,817
Montana 47, New Hampshire 17	Missoula, Mont.	20,055
William & Mary 44, Delaware 38 (2 ot)	Williamsburg, Va.	8,715
James Madison 14, Furman 13	Greenville, S.C.	6,260
Semifinals (12/11):		
Montana 34, Sam Houston St. 13	Missoula, Mont.	22,583
James Madison 48, William & Mary 34	Williamsburg, Va.	11,291
Championship (12/17):		
James Madison 31, Montana 21	Chattanooga, Tenn.	15,599

2005

First Round (11/26):	Site	Attendance
New Hampshire 55, Colgate 21	Durham, N.H.	7,708
UNI 41, Eastern Wash. 38	Cedar Falls, Ia.	7,746
Cal Poly 35, Montana 21	Missoula, Mont.	16,162
Texas St. 50, Ga. Southern 35	San Marcos, Tex.	10,000
Richmond 38, Hampton 10	Hampton, Va.	5,343
Furman 14, Nicholls St. 12	Greenville, S.C.	4,125
Southern Ill. 21, Eastern Ill. 6	Charleston, Ill.	2,896
Appalachian St. 34, Lafayette 23	Boone, N.C.	6,327

Quarterfinals (12/3):	Site	Attendance
UNI 24, New Hampshire 21	Durham, N.H.	8,448
Texas St. 14, Cal Poly 7	San Marcos, Tex.	15,411
Furman 24, Richmond 20	Richmond, Va.	6,603
Appalachian St. 38, Southern Ill. 24	Boone, N.C.	11,108
Semifinals:		
UNI 40, Texas St. 37 (ot) (12/9)	San Marcos, Tex.	15,712
Appalachian St. 29, Furman 23 (12/10)	Boone, N.C.	15,307
Championship (12/16):		
Appalachian St. 21, UNI 16	Chattanooga, Tenn.	19,219

2006

First Round (11/25):	Site	Attendance
Appalachian St. 45, Coastal Caro. 28	Boone, N.C.	16,223
Montana St. 31, Furman 13	Bozeman, Mont.	9,427
Illinois St. 24, Eastern Ill. 13	Charleston, Ill.	4,400
Youngstown St. 35, James Madison 31	Youngstown, Ohio	11,627
Massachusetts 35, Lafayette 14	Amherst, Mass.	5,388
New Hampshire 41, Hampton 38	Hampton, Va.	3,401
Southern Ill. 36, Tenn.-Martin 30	Carbondale, Ill.	5,694
Montana 31, McNeese St. 6	Missoula, Mont.	20,077
Quarterfinals (12/2):		
Appalachian St. 38, Montana St. 17	Boone, N.C.	15,116
Youngstown St. 28, Illinois St. 21	Youngstown, Ohio	10,813
Massachusetts 24, New Hampshire 17	Amherst, Mass.	17,000
Montana 20, Southern Ill. 3	Missoula, Mont.	18,883
Semifinals:		
Appalachian St. 49, Youngstown St. 24 (12/9)	Boone, N.C.	18,040
Massachusetts 19, Montana 17 (12/8)	Missoula, Mont.	23,454
Championship (12/15):		
Appalachian St. 28, Massachusetts 17	Chattanooga, Tenn.	22,808

Attendance Records

All-Time College Football Attendance

(Includes all divisions and non-NCAA teams)

Year	No. Teams	G	Total Attendance	P/G Avg.	Yearly Total Att.	Change Percent
1948	685	—	19,134,159	—	—	—
1949	682	—	19,651,995	—	Up 517,836	+2.71
1950	674	—	18,961,688	—	Dn 690,307	-3.51
1951	635	—	17,480,533	—	Dn 1,481,155	-7.81
1952	625	—	17,288,062	—	Dn 192,471	-1.10
1953	618	—	16,681,731	—	Dn 606,331	-3.51
1954	614	—	17,048,603	—	Up 366,872	+2.20
1955	621	—	17,266,556	—	Up 217,953	+1.28
1956	618	—	18,031,805	—	Up 765,249	+4.43
1957	618	2,586	18,290,724	7,073	Up 258,919	+1.44
1958	618	2,673	19,280,709	7,213	Up 989,985	+5.41
1959	623	2,695	19,615,344	7,278	Up 334,635	+1.74
1960	620	2,711	20,403,409	7,526	Up 788,065	+4.02
1961	616	2,697	20,677,604	7,667	Up 274,195	+1.34
1962	610	2,679	21,227,162	7,924	Up 549,558	+2.66
1963	616	2,686	22,237,094	8,279	Up 1,009,932	+4.76
1964	622	2,745	23,354,477	8,508	Up 1,117,383	+5.02
1965	616	2,749	24,682,572	8,979	Up 1,328,095	+5.69
1966	616	2,768	25,275,899	9,131	Up 593,327	+2.40
1967	610	2,764	26,430,639	9,562	Up 1,154,740	+4.57
1968	612	2,786	27,025,846	9,701	Up 595,207	+2.25
1969	615	2,820	27,626,160	9,797	Up 600,314	+2.22
1970	617	2,895	29,465,604	10,178	Up 1,839,444	+6.66
1971	618	2,955	30,455,442	10,306	Up 989,838	+3.36
1972	620	2,997	30,828,802	10,287	Up 373,360	+1.23
1973	630	3,062	31,282,540	10,216	Up 453,738	+1.47
1974	634	3,101	31,234,855	10,073	Dn 47,685	-0.15
1975	634	3,089	31,687,847	10,258	Up 452,992	+1.45
1976	637	3,108	32,012,008	10,299	Up 324,161	+1.02
1977	638	3,145	32,905,178	10,463	Up 893,170	+2.79

Beginning in 1978, attendance includes NCAA teams only.

All-Time NCAA Attendance

Annual Total NCAA Attendance

(Includes Only NCAA Teams, All Divisions)

Year	No. Teams	G	Total Attendance	P/G Avg.	Yearly Total Att.	Change Percent
1978	484	2,422	32,369,730	13,365	—	—
1979	478	2,381	32,874,755	13,807	Up 505,025	+1.56
1980	485	2,451	33,707,772	13,753	Up 833,017	+2.53
1981	497	2,505	34,230,471	13,665	Up 522,699	+1.55
1982	510	2,569	35,176,195	13,693	Up 945,724	+2.76
1983	505	2,557	34,817,264	13,616	Dn 358,931	-1.02
1984	501	2,542	35,211,076	13,852	Up 393,812	+1.13
1985	509	2,599	34,951,548	13,448	Dn 259,528	-0.74
1986	510	2,605	35,030,902	13,448	Up 79,354	+0.23
1987	507	2,589	35,007,541	13,522	Dn 23,361	-0.07
1988	524	2,644	34,323,842	12,982	Dn 683,699	-1.95
1989	524	2,630	35,116,188	13,352	Up 792,346	+2.31
1990	533	2,704	35,329,946	13,066	Up 213,758	+0.61
1991	548	2,776	35,528,220	12,798	Up 198,274	+0.56
1992	552	2,824	35,225,431	12,474	Dn 302,789	-0.85
1993	560	2,888	34,870,634	12,074	Dn 354,797	-1.01
1994	568	2,907	36,459,896	12,542	Up 1,591,352	+4.56
1995	565	2,923	35,637,784	12,192	Dn 822,112	-2.25
1996	566	2,925	36,083,053	12,336	Up 445,269	+1.25
1997	581	2,998	36,857,849	12,294	Up 774,796	+2.15
1998	595	3,044	37,491,078	12,316	Up 633,229	+1.72
1999	601	3,137	39,482,657	12,586	Up 1,991,477	+5.31
2000	606	3,122	39,059,225	12,511	Dn 423,432	-1.07
2001	608	3,193	40,480,823	12,678	Up 1,421,598	+3.64
2002	*617	3,395	44,556,215	13,124	Up 4,075,392	+10.07
2003	*617	3,401	46,144,539	13,568	Up 1,588,324	+3.56
2004	612	3,266	43,105,548	13,198	Dn 3,038,991	-6.59
2005	615	3,304	43,486,574	13,162	Up 381,026	+0.88
2006	615	3,392	*47,909,313	*14,124	*Up 4,422,739	*+10.17

**Record.*

Annual Football Bowl Subdivision (FBS) Attendance

Year	Teams	G	Attendance	Avg.
1976	137	796	23,917,522	30,047
1977	144	799	24,613,285	30,805
1978	139	772	25,017,915	32,407
1979	139	774	25,862,801	33,414
1980	139	776	26,499,022	34,148
1981	137	768	26,588,688	34,621
1982	97	567	24,771,855	43,689
1983	105	602	25,381,761	42,162
1984	105	606	25,783,807	42,548
1985	105	605	25,434,412	42,040
1986	105	611	25,692,095	42,049
1987	104	607	25,471,744	41,963
1988	104	605	25,079,490	41,454
1989	106	603	25,307,915	41,970
1990	106	615	25,513,098	41,485
1991	106	610	25,646,067	42,043
1992	107	617	25,402,046	41,170
1993	106	613	25,305,438	41,281
1994	107	614	25,590,190	41,678
1995	108	623	25,836,469	41,471
1996	111	644	26,620,942	41,337
1997	112	655	27,565,959	42,085
1998	112	651	27,674,217	42,510
1999	114	666	29,032,973	43,593
2000	114	661	28,839,284	43,630
2001	115	688	30,298,574	44,039
2002	117	775	34,384,264	44,367
2003	117	772	35,085,646	45,447
2004	118	711	32,495,401	45,704
2005	117	709	32,641,526	46,039
2006	119	796	*36,814,468	*46,249

**Record.*

Annual Football Championship Subdivision (FCS) Attendance

Year	Teams	G	Attendance	Avg.
1978	38	201	2,032,766	10,113
1979	39	211	2,073,890	9,829
1980	46	251	2,617,932	10,430
1981	50	270	2,950,156	10,927
1982	92	483	5,655,519	*11,709
1983	84	450	4,879,709	10,844
1984	87	465	5,061,480	10,885
1985	87	471	5,143,077	10,919
1986	86	456	5,044,992	11,064
1987	87	460	5,129,250	11,151
1988	88	465	4,801,637	10,326
1989	89	471	5,278,520	11,020
1990	87	473	5,328,477	11,265
1991	89	490	5,386,425	10,993
1992	88	485	5,057,955	10,429
1993	115	623	5,356,873	8,599
1994	117	643	*6,193,989	9,633
1995	119	647	5,660,329	8,749
1996	116	629	5,255,033	8,355
1997	118	642	5,212,048	8,118
1998	119	631	5,555,862	8,805
1999	122	661	5,949,345	9,001
2000	122	664	5,722,107	8,618
2001	123	649	5,375,851	8,283
2002	123	700	5,525,250	7,893
2003	121	699	6,070,116	8,684
2004	119	658	5,650,727	8,588
2005	116	638	5,436,122	8,521
2006	116	642	5,723,876	8,916

**Record.*

Annual Division II Attendance

Year	Teams	G	Attendance	Avg.
1978	103	518	2,871,683	*5,544
1979	105	526	2,775,569	5,277
1980	111	546	2,584,765	4,734
1981	121	589	2,726,537	4,629
1982	126	618	2,745,964	4,443

Year	Teams	G	Attendance	Avg.
1983	122	611	2,705,892	4,429
1984	114	568	2,413,947	4,250
1985	114	569	2,475,325	4,350
1986	111	551	2,404,852	4,365
1987	107	541	2,424,041	4,481
1988	117	580	2,570,964	4,493
1989	116	579	2,572,496	4,428
1990	120	580	2,472,811	4,263
1991	128	622	2,490,929	4,005
1992	129	643	2,733,094	4,251
1993	142	718	2,572,053	3,582
1994	142	704	2,791,074	3,965
1995	138	705	2,459,792	3,489
1996	139	701	2,514,241	3,587
1997	142	710	2,349,442	3,309
1998	149	747	2,443,660	3,271
1999	147	749	2,504,118	3,343
2000	149	739	2,512,290	3,400
2001	145	752	2,648,761	3,522
2002	149	783	2,647,038	3,381
2003	150	786	2,835,856	3,608
2004	148	768	2,851,498	3,713
2005	147	778	2,989,274	3,842
2006	143	776	*3,005,214	3,873

*Record.

Annual Division III Attendance

Year	Teams	G	Attendance	Avg.
1978	204	931	*2,447,366	*2,629
1979	195	870	2,162,495	2,486
1980	189	878	2,006,053	2,285
1981	189	878	1,965,090	2,238
1982	195	901	2,002,857	2,223
1983	194	894	1,849,902	2,069
1984	195	903	1,951,842	2,162
1985	203	954	1,898,734	1,990
1986	208	987	1,888,963	1,914
1987	209	981	1,982,506	2,021
1988	215	994	1,871,751	1,883
1989	213	977	1,957,257	1,948
1990	220	1,036	2,015,560	1,946
1991	225	1,054	2,004,799	1,902
1992	228	1,079	2,032,336	1,884
1993	197	934	1,636,270	1,752
1994	202	946	1,884,643	1,992
1995	200	948	1,681,194	1,773
1996	200	951	1,692,837	1,780
1997	209	991	1,730,400	1,746
1998	215	1,015	1,817,339	1,790
1999	218	1,061	1,996,221	1,881
2000	221	1,058	1,985,544	1,877
2001	225	1,104	2,157,637	1,954
2002	228	1,137	1,999,663	1,759
2003	229	1,144	2,152,921	1,882
2004	227	1,129	2,107,855	1,867
2005	227	1,135	2,088,019	1,840
2006	229	1,141	2,099,746	1,840

*Record.

Annual Conference Attendance Leaders

(Based on per-game average; minimum 20 games)

FBS

Year	Conference	Teams	Attendance	P/G Avg.
1978	Big Ten	10	3,668,926	61,149
1979	Big Ten	10	3,865,170	63,363
1980	Big Ten	10	3,781,232	64,089
1981	Big Ten	10	3,818,728	63,645
1982	Big Ten	10	3,935,722	66,707
1983	Big Ten	10	3,710,931	67,471
1984	Big Ten	10	3,943,802	67,997
1985	Big Ten	10	4,015,693	66,928
1986	Big Ten	10	4,006,845	65,686
1987	Big Ten	10	3,990,524	65,418
1988	Southeastern	10	3,912,241	63,101
1989	Southeastern	10	4,123,005	65,445
1990	Southeastern	10	4,215,400	63,870
1991	Southeastern	10	4,063,190	66,610
1992	Southeastern	12	4,844,014	63,737
1993	Big Ten	11	4,320,397	63,535
1994	Big Ten	11	4,452,839	66,460
1995	Big Ten	11	4,592,499	67,537
1996	Big Ten	11	4,321,276	67,520
1997	Big Ten	11	4,744,211	67,774
1998	Southeastern	12	5,059,534	69,309
1999	Southeastern	12	5,500,664	70,521
2000	Southeastern	12	5,143,777	72,448
2001	Southeastern	12	5,554,028	73,079
2002	Southeastern	12	6,085,156	73,315
2003	Southeastern	12	6,146,890	74,059
2004	Southeastern	12	5,719,678	74,282
2005	Southeastern	12	5,593,429	74,579
2006	Southeastern	12	*6,586,408	*75,706

*Record.

FCS

Year	Conference	Teams	Attendance	P/G Avg.
1978	Southwestern Athletic	5	483,159	17,895
1979	Southwestern Athletic	6	513,768	16,055
1980	Southwestern Athletic	7	611,234	16,085
1981	Southwestern Athletic	7	662,221	18,921
1982	Southwestern Athletic	7	634,505	18,129
1983	Southwestern Athletic	8	709,160	16,117
1984	Southwestern Athletic	8	702,186	17,555
1985	Southwestern Athletic	8	790,296	17,961
1986	Southwestern Athletic	8	621,584	16,357
1987	Southwestern Athletic	8	697,534	16,608
1988	Southwestern Athletic	8	541,127	14,240
1989	Southwestern Athletic	8	796,844	18,110
1990	Southwestern Athletic	7	828,169	20,704
1991	Southwestern Athletic	8	856,491	18,223
1992	Southwestern Athletic	8	873,772	20,804
1993	Southwestern Athletic	8	772,714	18,398
1994	Southwestern Athletic	8	*958,508	*23,378
1995	Southwestern Athletic	8	628,702	16,545
1996	Southwestern Athletic	8	600,798	15,405
1997	Southwestern Athletic	8	567,929	15,776
1998	Southwestern Athletic	9	516,042	13,580
1999	Southwestern Athletic	10	781,226	15,318
2000	Southwestern Athletic	10	506,076	11,502
2001	Southwestern Athletic	10	583,599	12,417
2002	Southwestern Athletic	10	459,911	10,950
2003	Southwestern Athletic	10	579,976	12,083
2004	Southwestern Athletic	10	521,986	11,600
2005	Southern	8	512,370	11,138
2006	Southwestern Athletic	10	824,740	15,561

*Record.

Division II

Year	Conference	Teams	Attendance	P/G Avg.
1978	Mid-Continent	6	237,458	9,133
1979	Mid-Continent	6	313,790	9,509
1980	Southern Intercollegiate	12	356,744	7,280
1981	Lone Star	8	340,876	7,575
1982	Lone Star	8	348,780	8,507
1983	Lone Star	8	296,350	7,228
1984	Central Intercollegiate	12	418,075	6,743
1985	Central Intercollegiate	12	378,160	6,099
1986	Central Intercollegiate	12	380,172	6,670
1987	Lone Star	6	208,709	6,325
1988	Central Intercollegiate	12	343,070	6,473
1989	Lone Star	8	249,570	5,942
1990	Southern Intercollegiate	9	264,741	6,967
1991	Central Intercollegiate	11	349,962	6,603
1992	Southern Intercollegiate	9	344,504	7,489
1993	Southern Intercollegiate	9	342,446	8,352
1994	Southern Intercollegiate	9	*456,289	*10,140
1995	Southern Intercollegiate	10	321,751	6,846
1996	Southern Intercollegiate	10	310,491	6,750
1997	Southern Intercollegiate	10	314,975	6,562
1998	Southern Intercollegiate	11	399,277	7,005
1999	Southern Intercollegiate	10	305,640	6,946
2000	Southern Intercollegiate	8	288,807	7,405

Year	Conference	Teams	Attendance	P/G Avg.
2001	Southern Intercollegiate	8	220,869	7,125
2002	North Central	9	307,688	5,594
2003	Southern Intercollegiate	9	254,321	6,521
2004	Southern Intercollegiate	9	289,352	6,889
2005	Southern Intercollegiate	10	292,627	6,361
2006	Southern Intercollegiate	10	388,552	7,770

**Record.*

Division III

Year	Conference	Teams	Attendance	P/G Avg.
1979	Great Lakes	6	90,531	3,482
1980	Great Lakes	7	113,307	3,333
1981	Ohio Athletic	14	*196,640	2,979
1982	New Jersey State	7	98,502	2,985
1983	Heartland	7	121,825	3,384
1984	Heartland	7	107,500	2,986
1985	Ohio Athletic	9	125,074	2,719
1986	Heartland	7	91,793	2,550
1987	Heartland	6	84,815	3,029
1988	Heartland	5	82,966	2,963
1989	Old Dominion	5	70,676	2,945
1990	Old Dominion	6	86,238	2,974
1991	Old Dominion	6	101,774	3,283
1992	Old Dominion	6	100,132	3,338
1993	Old Dominion	6	96,526	3,218
1994	Old Dominion	6	111,334	*3,976
1995	Old Dominion	6	105,819	3,527
1996	Old Dominion	6	90,277	3,113
1997	Old Dominion	6	92,810	3,094
1998	Old Dominion	6	112,329	3,744
1999	Old Dominion	7	103,435	2,955
2000	Old Dominion	7	115,054	3,486
2001	Old Dominion	7	108,487	3,014
2002	Ohio Athletic	10	149,453	2,768
2003	Ohio Athletic	10	163,948	3,093
2004	Old Dominion	7	89,388	2,883
2005	Minnesota Intercollegiate	9	129,785	3,018
2006	Minnesota Intercollegiate	9	148,203	3,222

**Record. Note: 1978 figures not available.*

Annual FBS Conference Attendance

(Since 1978)

ATLANTIC COAST CONFERENCE

Season	Teams	Games	Attendance	P/G	Change in P/G (Percent)
1978	7	39	1,475,410	37,831	Up 3.88
1979	7	40	1,620,776	40,519	Up 7.11
1980	7	41	1,590,495	38,793	Dn 4.26
1981	7	40	1,589,152	39,729	Up 2.41
1982	7	41	1,706,451	41,621	Up 4.76
1983	8	49	2,087,800	42,608	Up 3.71
1984	8	46	1,998,274	43,441	Up 1.96
1985	8	48	2,029,574	42,283	Dn 2.67
1986	8	45	1,848,949	41,088	Dn 2.83
1987	8	47	1,970,198	41,919	Up 2.02
1988	8	47	1,911,949	40,680	Dn 2.96
1989	8	49	2,010,317	41,027	Up 0.85
1990	8	47	1,988,781	42,314	Up 3.14
1991	8	51	2,257,413	44,263	Up 4.61
1992	9	53	2,332,674	44,013	Dn 0.56
1993	9	54	2,379,045	44,056	Up 0.10
1994	9	51	2,248,700	44,092	Up 0.08
1995	9	51	2,329,868	45,684	Up 3.61
1996	9	50	2,203,849	44,077	Dn 3.52
1997	9	52	2,333,784	44,880	Up 1.82
1998	9	51	2,330,879	45,704	Up 1.84
1999	9	51	2,298,711	45,073	Dn 1.38
2000	9	54	2,653,816	49,145	Up 9.03
2001	9	56	2,784,520	49,724	Up 1.18
2002	9	58	2,957,611	50,993	Up 2.55
2003	9	58	3,012,392	51,938	Up 1.85
2004	11	66	3,678,508	55,735	Up 7.31
2005	12	72	3,761,402	52,242	Dn 6.27
2006	12	85	4,499,567	52,936	Up 1.33

BIG EAST CONFERENCE

Season	Teams	Games	Attendance	P/G	Change in P/G (Percent)
1991	8	47	1,788,611	38,056	Dn 7.00
1992	8	48	1,847,269	38,485	Up 1.13
1993	8	47	1,787,843	38,039	Dn 1.16
1994	8	46	1,902,096	41,350	Up 8.70
1995	8	44	1,679,043	38,160	Dn 7.71
1996	8	47	1,825,870	38,848	Up 1.80
1997	8	46	1,657,056	36,023	Dn 7.27
1998	8	48	1,914,957	39,895	Up 10.75
1999	8	46	1,837,478	39,945	Up 0.13
2000	8	49	2,030,230	41,433	Up 3.73
2001	8	49	1,927,280	39,332	Dn 5.07
2002	8	53	2,315,608	43,691	Up 11.08
2003	8	51	2,390,358	46,870	Up 7.28
2004	7	41	1,549,992	37,805	Dn 19.34
2005	8	46	1,812,406	39,400	Up 4.22
2006	8	52	2,030,211	39,043	Dn 0.91

BIG TEN CONFERENCE

Season	Teams	Games	Attendance	P/G	Change in P/G (Percent)
1978	10	60	3,668,926	61,149	Up 2.87
1979	10	61	3,865,170	63,363	Up 3.62
1980	10	59	3,781,232	64,089	Up 1.15
1981	10	60	3,818,728	63,645	Dn 0.69
1982	10	59	3,935,722	66,707	Up 4.81
1983	10	55	3,710,931	67,471	Up 1.15
1984	10	58	3,943,802	67,997	Up 0.78
1985	10	60	4,015,693	66,928	Dn 1.57
1986	10	61	4,006,845	65,686	Dn 1.86
1987	10	61	3,990,524	65,418	Dn 0.41
1988	10	59	3,714,231	62,953	Dn 3.77
1989	10	59	3,492,647	59,197	Dn 5.97
1990	10	60	3,533,504	58,892	Dn 0.52
1991	10	61	3,674,654	60,240	Up 2.29
1992	10	60	3,600,410	60,007	Dn 0.39
1993	11	68	4,320,397	63,535	Up 5.88
1994	11	67	4,452,839	66,460	Up 4.60
1995	11	68	4,592,499	67,537	Up 1.62
1996	11	64	4,321,276	67,520	Dn 0.03
1997	11	70	4,744,211	67,774	Up 0.38
1998	11	65	4,354,383	66,991	Dn 1.16
1999	11	70	4,701,095	67,159	Up 0.25
2000	11	67	4,591,153	68,525	Up 2.03
2001	11	66	4,622,376	70,036	Up 2.21
2002	11	78	5,455,105	69,937	Dn 0.14
2003	11	75	5,264,867	70,198	Up 0.37
2004	11	66	4,591,722	69,572	Dn 0.89
2005	11	69	5,007,067	72,566	Up 4.30
2006	11	75	5,223,202	69,643	Dn 4.03

BIG 12 CONFERENCE

Season	Teams	Games	Attendance	P/G	Change in P/G (Percent)
1996	12	69	3,549,474	51,442	Up 3.39
1997	12	71	3,640,692	51,277	Dn 0.32
1998	12	71	3,661,740	51,574	Up 0.58
1999	12	72	3,904,491	54,229	Up 5.15
2000	12	74	3,995,338	53,991	Dn 0.44
2001	12	76	4,215,088	55,462	Up 2.72
2002	12	79	4,358,818	55,175	Dn 0.52
2003	12	81	4,565,288	56,362	Up 2.15
2004	12	72	4,126,492	57,312	Up 1.69
2005	12	72	4,204,574	58,397	Up 1.89
2006	12	83	4,894,337	58,968	Up 0.98

CONFERENCE USA

Season	Teams	Games	Attendance	P/G	Change in P/G (Percent)
1996	6	33	825,899	25,027	Up 12.87
1997	7	38	963,239	25,348	Up 1.28
1998	8	44	1,239,052	28,160	Up 11.09
1999	9	52	1,476,223	28,389	Up 0.81
2000	9	49	1,388,331	28,333	Dn 0.20
2001	10	53	1,432,512	27,029	Dn 4.60
2002	10	61	1,627,131	26,674	Dn 1.31
2003	11	67	2,167,173	32,346	Up 21.26
2004	11	58	1,644,833	28,359	Dn 12.33
2005	12	66	1,685,809	25,543	Dn 9.93
2006	12	72	1,918,457	26,645	Up 4.31

MID-AMERICAN CONFERENCE

Season	Teams	Games	Attendance	P/G	Change in P/G (Percent)
1978	10	51	722,026	14,157	Up 14.36
1979	10	52	696,784	13,400	Dn 5.35
1980	10	51	714,415	14,008	Up 4.54
1981	10	53	804,158	15,173	Up 8.32
1982@	10	51	980,087	19,217	Up 26.65
1983	10	51	884,888	17,351	Dn 9.71
1984	10	53	918,133	17,323	Dn 0.16
1985	10	49	719,024	14,674	Dn 15.29
1986	9	47	679,866	14,465	Dn 1.42
1987	9	45	652,285	14,495	Up 0.21
1988	9	46	765,563	16,643	Up 14.82
1989	9	44	689,698	15,675	Dn 5.82
1990	9	45	744,368	16,542	Up 5.53
1991	9	45	608,485	13,522	Dn 18.26
1992	10	49	704,233	14,372	Up 5.97
1993	10	51	726,847	14,252	Dn 0.83
1994	10	51	754,296	14,790	Up 3.77
1995	10	50	748,138	14,963	Up 1.17
1996	10	50	787,035	15,741	Up 5.18
1997	12	63	1,130,939	17,951	Up 14.04
1998	12	61	1,022,567	16,763	Dn 6.62
1999	13	67	1,195,463	17,843	Up 5.32
2000	13	67	1,080,812	16,132	Dn 9.59
2001	13	66	1,171,999	17,758	Up 10.08
2002	14	81	1,420,525	17,537	Dn 1.24
2003	14	84	1,496,906	17,820	Up 1.61
2004	14	71	1,270,813	17,899	Up 0.44
2005	12	58	840,377	14,489	Dn 19.05
2006	12	62	1,097,147	17,696	Up 22.13

@Mid-American and Missouri Valley divided between FBS and FCS.

MOUNTAIN WEST CONFERENCE
(Members came from Western Athletic Conference)

Season	Teams	Games	Attendance	P/G	Change in P/G (Percent)
1999	8	43	1,489,527	34,640	Up 3.12
2000	8	44	1,419,326	32,257	Dn 6.88
2001	8	45	1,432,365	31,830	Dn 1.32
2002	8	46	1,604,755	34,886	Up 9.60
2003	8	49	1,607,660	32,809	Dn 5.95
2004	8	46	1,619,810	35,213	Up 7.33
2005	9	48	1,693,216	35,275	Up 0.18
2006	9	54	1,769,390	32,766	Dn 7.11

PACIFIC-10 CONFERENCE

Season	Teams	Games	Attendance	P/G	Change in P/G (Percent)
1978	10	57	2,632,755	46,189	Up 5.56
1979	10	59	2,741,656	46,469	Up 0.61
1980	10	58	2,777,146	47,882	Up 3.04
1981	10	59	2,772,237	46,987	Dn 1.87
1982	10	59	2,745,676	46,537	Dn 0.96
1983	10	58	2,740,406	47,248	Up 1.53
1984	10	63	2,976,655	47,248	No Change
1985	10	56	2,665,356	47,596	Up 0.74
1986	10	59	2,856,910	48,422	Up 1.74
1987	10	57	2,866,723	50,293	Up 3.86
1988	10	60	3,058,637	50,977	Up 1.36
1989	10	60	3,006,176	50,103	Dn 1.71
1990	10	58	2,872,173	49,520	Dn 1.16
1991	10	59	2,851,991	48,339	Dn 2.38
1992	10	60	2,825,401	47,090	Dn 2.58
1993	10	57	2,731,361	47,919	Up 1.76
1994	10	59	2,785,373	47,210	Dn 1.48
1995	10	57	2,680,510	47,026	Dn 0.39
1996	10	58	2,761,006	47,604	Up 1.23
1997	10	60	2,891,522	48,192	Up 1.24
1998	10	60	3,024,262	50,404	Up 4.59
1999	10	59	2,857,994	48,441	Dn 3.89
2000	10	61	2,987,809	48,980	Up 1.11
2001	10	58	2,784,069	48,001	Dn 2.00
2002	10	66	3,299,852	49,998	Up 4.16
2003	10	62	3,199,732	51,609	Up 3.22
2004	10	58	3,229,666	55,684	Up 7.90
2005	10	60	3,448,759	57,479	Up 3.22
2006	10	64	3,604,124	56,314	Dn 2.03

SOUTHEASTERN CONFERENCE

Season	Teams	Games	Attendance	P/G	Change in P/G (Percent)
1978	10	61	3,464,112	56,789	Up 2.62
1979	10	59	3,376,833	57,234	Up 0.78
1980	10	66	3,951,104	59,865	Up 4.60
1981	10	61	3,846,492	63,057	Up 5.33
1982	10	66	4,206,507	63,735	Up 1.08
1983	10	65	4,214,702	64,842	Up 1.74
1984	10	63	4,007,351	63,609	Dn 1.90
1985	10	63	4,017,104	63,764	Up 0.24
1986	10	69	4,351,832	63,070	Dn 1.09
1987	10	64	4,117,046	64,329	Up 2.00
1988	10	62	3,912,241	63,101	Dn 1.91
1989	10	63	4,123,005	65,445	Up 3.71
1990	10	66	4,215,400	63,870	Dn 2.41
1991	10	61	4,063,190	66,610	Up 4.29
1992	12	76	4,844,014	63,737	Dn 4.31
1993	12	78	4,897,564	62,789	Dn 1.49
1994	12	77	4,891,615	63,527	Up 1.18
1995	12	76	4,827,834	63,524	Dn 0.01
1996	12	76	4,932,802	64,905	Up 2.17
1997	12	76	5,005,126	65,857	Up 1.47
1998	12	73	5,059,534	69,309	Up 5.24
1999	12	78	5,500,664	70,521	Up 1.75
2000	12	71	5,143,777	72,448	Up 2.73
2001	12	76	5,554,028	73,079	Up 0.87
2002	12	83	6,085,156	73,315	Up 0.32
2003	12	83	6,146,890	74,059	Up 1.01
2004	12	77	5,719,678	74,282	Up 0.30
2005	12	75	5,593,429	74,579	Up 0.40
2006	12	87	6,586,408	75,706	Up 1.51

SUN BELT CONFERENCE

Season	Teams	Games	Attendance	P/G	Change in P/G (Percent)
2001	7	34	454,829	13,377	— —
2002	7	38	498,801	13,126	Dn 1.88
2003	8	42	602,763	14,352	Up 9.34
2004	9	42	758,249	18,054	Up 25.79
2005	6	31	523,315	16,881	Dn 6.50
2006	6	42	718,075	17,097	Up 1.28

WESTERN ATHLETIC CONFERENCE

Season	Teams	Games	Attendance	P/G	Change in P/G (Percent)
1978	7	37	906,518	24,500	Dn 1.84
1979	8	47	1,349,156	28,705	Up 17.16
1980	9	51	1,354,492	26,559	Dn 5.41
1981	9	51	1,443,515	28,304	Up 6.57
1982	9	53	1,605,684	30,296	Up 7.04
1983	9	52	1,567,062	30,136	Dn 0.53
1984	9	55	1,741,793	31,669	Up 5.09
1985	9	55	1,744,123	31,711	Up 0.13
1986	9	51	1,748,857	34,291	Up 8.14
1987	9	54	1,927,572	35,696	Up 4.10
1988	9	54	1,795,735	33,254	Dn 6.84
1989	9	55	1,844,999	33,545	Up 0.88
1990	9	55	1,784,807	32,451	Dn 3.26
1991	9	55	1,883,861	34,252	Up 5.55
1992	10	60	2,111,587	35,193	Up 2.85
1993	10	61	2,109,441	34,581	Dn 1.74
1994	10	61	2,090,620	34,272	Dn 0.89
1995	10	63	1,987,860	31,553	Dn 7.93
1996	16	91	2,615,219	28,739	Dn 8.92
1997	16	92	2,758,817	29,987	Up 4.34
1998	16	91	2,594,194	28,508	Dn 4.93
1999	8	45	1,207,602	26,836	Dn 5.87
2000	9	51	1,403,284	27,515	Up 2.53
2001	10	49	1,212,887	24,753	Dn 10.04
2002	10	58	1,453,406	25,059	Up 1.24
2003	10	59	1,455,837	24,675	Dn 1.53
2004	10	58	1,422,684	24,529	Dn 0.59
2005	9	51	1,101,350	21,595	Dn 11.96
2006	9	55	1,264,695	22,994	Up 6.48

ALL-TIME ATTENDANCE OTHER CONFERENCES
(Conferences that either discontinued or changed names)

BIG EIGHT CONFERENCE
(All members went into Big 12 Conference after 1995 season)

Season	Teams	Games	Attendance	P/G	Change in P/G (Percent)
1978	8	48	2,549,553	53,116	Dn 1.45
1979	8	46	2,457,633	53,427	Up 0.59
1980	8	49	2,629,195	53,657	Up 0.43
1981	8	50	2,559,480	51,190	Dn 4.60
1982	8	48	2,377,389	49,529	Dn 3.24

Season	Teams	Games	Attendance	P/G	Change in P/G (Percent)
1983	8	49	2,398,184	48,943	Dn 1.18
1984	8	45	2,247,010	49,934	Up 2.02
1985	8	54	2,504,509	46,380	Dn 7.12
1986	8	49	2,242,082	45,757	Dn 1.34
1987	8	49	2,182,199	44,535	Dn 2.67
1988	8	49	2,184,333	44,578	Up 0.10
1989	8	49	2,362,465	48,214	Up 8.16
1990	8	49	2,257,825	46,078	Dn 4.43
1991	8	49	2,308,238	47,107	Up 2.23
1992	8	47	2,247,907	47,828	Up 1.53
1993	8	48	2,126,247	44,297	Dn 7.38
1994	8	46	2,194,545	47,708	Up 7.70
1995	8	50	2,414,804	48,296	Up 1.23

BIG WEST CONFERENCE
(Discontinued sponsorship of football after 2000 season)

Season	Teams	Games	Attendance	P/G	Change in P/G (Percent)
1988	8	38	570,533	15,014	Up 2.58
1989	8	37	528,921	14,295	Dn 4.79
1990	8	41	650,800	15,873	Up 11.04
1991	8	37	570,332	15,414	Dn 2.89
1992	7	36	515,291	14,314	Dn 7.14
1993	10	48	778,224	16,213	Up 13.27
1994	10	49	705,539	14,399	Dn 11.19
1995	10	51	793,452	15,558	Up 8.05
1996	6	34	554,684	16,314	Up 4.86
1997	6	32	584,020	18,251	Up 11.87
1998	7	37	631,791	17,075	Dn 6.44
1999	7	35	669,254	19,122	Up 11.99
2000	6	29	504,238	17,388	Dn 9.07

IVY GROUP
(Went into FCS after 1981 season)

Season	Teams	Games	Attendance	P/G	Change in P/G (Percent)
1978	8	40	547,395	13,685	Up 4.87
1979	8	40	534,597	13,365	Dn 2.34
1980	8	43	514,433	11,964	Dn 10.48
1981	8	41	564,059	13,758	Up 14.99

MISSOURI VALLEY CONFERENCE
(Discontinued sponsorship of football after 1985 season)

Season	Teams	Games	Attendance	P/G	Change in P/G (Percent)
1978	7	39	523,565	13,425	Up 5.83
1979	7	37	481,706	13,019	Dn 3.02
1980	7	35	473,462	13,527	Up 3.90
1981	8	43	575,174	13,376	Dn 1.12
1982	8	40	594,515	14,863	Up 11.12
1983	7	37	412,412	11,146	Dn 23.63
1984	7	37	427,112	11,544	Up 3.57
1985	5	26	308,137	11,851	Up 2.66

PACIFIC COAST CONFERENCE
(Became Big West Conference after 1987 season)

Season	Teams	Games	Attendance	P/G	Change in P/G (Percent)
1978	6	29	279,772	9,647	Dn 3.81
1979	6	25	322,305	12,892	Up 33.64
1980	6	28	353,022	12,608	Dn 2.20
1981	6	27	360,005	13,334	Up 5.76
1982	7	34	487,638	14,342	Up 7.56
1983	7	35	500,380	14,297	Dn 0.31
1984	8	39	597,420	15,318	Up 5.52
1985	8	40	654,045	16,351	Up 6.74
1986	8	42	753,466	17,940	Up 9.72
1987	8	41	600,129	14,637	Dn 18.41

SOUTHERN CONFERENCE
(Went into FCS after 1981 season)

Season	Teams	Games	Attendance	P/G	Change in P/G (Percent)
1978	7	34	372,009	10,941	Up 11.20
1979	8	47	478,107	10,172	Dn 7.03
1980	8	40	484,727	12,118	Up 19.13
1981	8	42	459,576	10,942	Dn 9.70

SOUTHLAND CONFERENCE
(Went into FCS after 1981 season)

Season	Teams	Games	Attendance	P/G	Change in P/G (Percent)
1978	6	37	467,915	12,646	Dn 13.67
1979	6	31	491,917	15,868	Up 25.48
1980	6	32	452,311	14,135	Dn 10.92
1981	6	30	427,106	14,237	Up 0.72

SOUTHWEST CONFERENCE
(Discontinued after 1995 season; teams went to Big 12 and Western Athletic Conferences)

Season	Teams	Games	Attendance	P/G	Change in P/G (Percent)
1978	9	45	2,033,212	45,182	Up 15.46
1979	9	52	2,301,148	44,253	Dn 2.06
1980	9	54	2,263,881	41,924	Dn 5.26
1981	9	54	2,232,757	41,347	Dn 1.38
1982	9	52	2,226,009	42,808	Up 3.53
1983	9	56	2,292,540	40,938	Dn 4.37
1984	9	53	2,177,507	41,085	Up 0.36
1985	9	51	2,077,717	40,740	Dn 0.84
1986	9	53	2,006,663	37,862	Dn 7.06
1987	8	48	1,859,454	38,739	Up 2.32
1988	8	46	1,774,120	38,568	Dn 0.44
1989	9	51	1,914,608	37,541	Dn 2.66
1990	9	53	2,087,248	39,382	Up 4.90
1991	9	50	2,062,309	41,246	Up 4.73
1992	8	47	1,697,152	36,110	Dn 12.45
1993	8	45	1,587,652	35,281	Dn 2.30
1994	8	43	1,588,955	36,952	Up 4.74
1995	8	43	1,653,888	38,463	Up 4.09

Annual FCS Conference Attendance

(Since 1978)

ATLANTIC 10 CONFERENCE
(Formerly Yankee Conference)

Season	Teams	Games	Attendance	P/G	Change in P/G (Percent)
1978	6	32	207,502	6,484	Dn 9.81
1979	6	29	197,293	6,803	Up 4.92
1980	6	32	211,822	6,619	Dn 2.70
1981	6	29	233,680	8,058	Up 21.74
1982	6	32	254,789	7,962	Dn 1.19
1983	6	30	218,186	7,273	Dn 8.65
1984	6	31	284,709	9,184	Up 26.28
1985	6	36	257,170	7,144	Dn 22.21
1986	8	44	486,299	11,052	Up 54.70
1987	8	43	408,170	9,492	Dn 14.12
1988	9	47	447,641	9,524	Up 0.34
1989	9	48	460,683	9,598	Up 0.78
1990	9	49	423,459	8,642	Dn 9.96
1991	9	48	431,522	8,990	Up 4.03
1992	9	53	461,366	8,705	Dn 3.17
1993	12	67	550,245	8,213	Dn 7.09
1994	12	67	630,847	9,416	Up 14.65
1995	12	66	578,742	8,769	Dn 6.87
1996	12	64	526,442	8,226	Dn 6.19
1997	12	65	486,798	7,489	Dn 8.96
1998	11	59	533,945	9,050	Up 20.84
1999	11	61	563,885	9,244	Up 2.14
2000	10	58	512,307	8,833	Dn 4.45
2001	11	57	433,699	7,609	Dn 13.86
2002	11	67	488,814	7,296	Dn 4.11
2003	11	66	535,253	8,110	Up 11.16
2004	12	67	533,692	7,966	Dn 1.78
2005	12	68	578,820	8,512	Up 6.85
2006	12	66	607,108	9,199	Up 8.07

BIG SKY CONFERENCE

Season	Teams	Games	Attendance	P/G	Change in P/G (Percent)
1978	7	36	393,274	10,924	Up 4.16
1979	8	47	463,920	9,871	Dn 7.70
1980	8	45	520,250	11,561	Up 17.12
1981	8	47	538,920	11,466	Dn 0.82
1982	8	43	463,393	10,777	Dn 6.01
1983	8	44	474,167	10,777	No change
1984	8	47	475,645	10,120	Dn 6.10
1985	8	48	481,015	10,021	Dn 0.98
1986	8	46	469,368	10,204	Up 1.83
1987	9	52	537,300	10,333	Up 1.26
1988	9	50	513,467	10,269	Dn 0.62
1989	9	52	550,975	10,596	Up 3.18
1990	9	50	531,060	10,621	Up 0.24
1991	9	56	623,326	11,131	Up 4.80
1992	8	46	437,592	9,513	Dn 14.54
1993	8	48	460,613	9,596	Up 0.87
1994	8	47	530,089	11,278	Up 17.53
1995	8	46	530,022	11,522	Up 2.16
1996	8	44	360,082	8,184	Dn 28.97
1997	8	47	385,728	8,207	Up 0.03

Season	Teams	Games	Attendance	P/G	Change in P/G (Percent)
1998	9	49	398,690	8,137	Dn 0.85
1999	9	50	492,618	9,852	Up 21.08
2000	9	51	420,423	8,244	Dn 16.32
2001	8	46	414,964	9,021	Up 9.43
2002	8	47	452,885	9,636	Up 6.82
2003	8	49	495,861	10,120	Up 5.02
2004	8	51	520,179	10,200	Up 0.79
2005	8	44	475,752	10,813	Up 6.01
2006	8	46	492,774	10,712	Dn 0.93

BIG SOUTH CONFERENCE

Season	Teams	Games	Attendance	P/G	Change in P/G (Percent)
2003	5	29	136,101	4,693	— —
2004	5	28	157,612	5,629	Up 19.94
2005	5	31	141,981	4,580	Dn 18.64
2006	5	28	191,476	6,838	Up 49.30

GATEWAY FOOTBALL CONFERENCE

Season	Teams	Games	Attendance	P/G	Change in P/G (Percent)
1985	6	35	281,632	8,047	Up 8.01
1986	7	37	351,972	9,513	Up 16.03
1987	7	36	315,318	8,759	Dn 7.93
1988	7	36	332,800	9,244	Up 5.54
1989	7	40	315,633	7,891	Dn 14.64
1990	7	36	313,409	8,706	Up 10.33
1991	7	38	332,482	8,750	Up 0.51
1992	7	40	345,823	8,646	Dn 1.19
1993	7	36	285,921	7,942	Dn 8.14
1994	7	40	293,437	7,336	Dn 7.63
1995	7	41	317,344	7,740	Up 5.51
1996	6	33	294,724	8,931	Up 15.39
1997	7	41	399,221	9,737	Up 9.02
1998	7	39	366,029	9,385	Dn 3.62
1999	7	39	392,203	10,056	Up 7.15
2000	7	40	385,483	9,637	Dn 4.17
2001	8	44	436,217	9,914	Up 2.87
2002	8	49	458,622	9,360	Dn 5.59
2003	8	50	509,725	10,195	Up 8.92
2004	8	46	453,748	9,864	Dn 3.25
2005	8	46	463,944	10,086	Up 2.25
2006	8	47	498,885	10,615	Up 5.24

GREAT WEST FOOTBALL CONFERENCE

Season	Teams	Games	Attendance	P/G	Change in P/G (Percent)
2005	2	10	54,811	5,481	—
2006	2	10	65,479	6,548	Up 19.47

IVY GROUP

Season	Teams	Games	Attendance	P/G	Change in P/G (Percent)
1982	8	44	602,857	13,701	Dn 0.41
1983	8	43	653,263	15,192	Up 10.88
1984	8	39	591,562	15,168	Dn 0.16
1985	8	41	562,184	13,712	Dn 9.60
1986	8	43	543,983	12,651	Dn 7.74
1987	8	42	602,480	14,345	Up 13.39
1988	8	42	513,674	12,230	Dn 14.74
1989	8	43	557,872	12,974	Up 6.08
1990	8	41	471,245	11,494	Dn 11.41
1991	8	39	466,928	11,973	Up 4.17
1992	8	40	401,980	10,050	Dn 16.06
1993	8	42	420,915	10,022	Dn 0.28
1994	8	42	445,900	10,617	Up 5.94
1995	8	42	396,539	9,441	Dn 11.08
1996	8	40	413,112	10,328	Up 9.40
1997	8	39	284,650	7,299	Dn 29.33
1998	8	40	445,801	11,145	Up 52.69
1999	8	44	516,589	11,741	Up 5.35
2000	8	40	456,317	11,408	Dn 2.84
2001	8	38	410,268	10,797	Dn 5.36
2002	8	41	387,600	9,454	Dn 12.44
2003	8	42	431,729	10,279	Up 8.73
2004	8	40	393,993	9,850	Dn 4.17
2005	8	40	384,250	9,606	Dn 2.48
2006	8	42	410,042	9,763	Up 1.63

METRO ATLANTIC ATHLETIC CONFERENCE

Season	Teams	Games	Attendance	P/G	Change in P/G (Percent)
1993	6	29	34,483	1,189	Up 13.02
1994	7	35	41,364	1,182	Dn 0.59
1995	8	37	51,549	1,393	Up 17.85
1996	9	41	57,742	1,408	Up 1.08
1997	9	46	69,249	1,505	Up 6.89
1998	9	44	75,134	1,708	Up 13.49
1999	9	46	96,105	2,089	Up 22.31
2000	8	39	73,227	1,878	Dn 10.10
2001	8	38	76,874	2,023	Up 7.72
2002	9	46	88,361	1,921	Dn 5.04
2003	6	33	62,007	1,879	Dn 2.19
2004	5	22	41,443	1,884	Up 0.27
2005	5	26	51,356	1,975	Up 4.83
2006	5	25	41,946	1,678	Dn 15.04

MID-EASTERN ATHLETIC CONFERENCE

Season	Teams	Games	Attendance	P/G	Change in P/G (Percent)
1978	4	19	141,234	7,433	Dn 2.96
1979	4	24	131,942	5,498	Dn 26.03
1980	6	29	308,530	10,639	Up 93.51
1981	6	35	357,982	10,228	Dn 3.86
1982	6	35	358,315	10,238	Up 0.10
1983	6	34	335,664	9,872	Dn 3.57
1984	5	27	209,612	7,763	Dn 21.36
1985	5	23	263,687	11,465	Up 47.69
1986	6	32	270,405	8,450	Dn 32.29
1987	6	30	354,899	11,830	Up 40.00
1988	7	39	466,030	11,948	Up 1.00
1989	7	41	521,529	12,720	Up 6.45
1990	7	36	475,909	13,220	Up 3.93
1991	7	40	578,412	14,460	Up 9.38
1992	7	38	450,962	11,867	Dn 17.93
1993	7	40	440,012	11,000	Dn 7.31
1994	7	40	556,159	13,904	Up 26.40
1995	8	37	350,770	9,480	Dn 31.82
1996	8	41	445,672	10,870	Up 14.66
1997	9	42	427,794	10,186	Dn 6.29
1998	9	41	466,929	11,389	Up 11.81
1999	9	41	479,754	11,701	Up 2.74
2000	9	40	424,796	10,620	Dn 9.24
2001	9	41	431,278	10,519	Dn 0.95
2002	9	49	453,947	9,264	Dn 11.93
2003	9	39	388,800	9,969	Up 7.61
2004	9	45	469,089	10,424	Up 4.56
2005	9	43	428,584	9,967	Dn 4.38
2006	9	50	599,871	11,997	Up 20.37

NORTHEAST CONFERENCE

Season	Teams	Games	Attendance	P/G	Change in P/G (Percent)
1996	5	27	40,800	1,511	Dn 10.70
1997	5	24	37,014	1,542	Up 2.05
1998	5	24	36,189	1,508	Dn 2.20
1999	8	37	70,411	1,903	Up 26.19
2000	9	47	70,750	1,505	Dn 20.91
2001	9	41	71,428	1,742	Up 15.75
2002	8	41	84,272	2,055	Up 17.97
2003	8	37	89,255	2,412	Up 17.37
2004	8	43	95,004	2,209	Dn 8.42
2005	8	40	94,899	2,372	Up 7.38
2006	8	42	113,680	2,707	Up 14.12

OHIO VALLEY CONFERENCE

Season	Teams	Games	Attendance	P/G	Change in P/G (Percent)
1978	7	37	355,893	9,619	Dn 8.47
1979	7	36	349,165	9,699	Up 0.83
1980	8	45	470,001	10,444	Up 7.68
1981	9	47	428,182	9,110	Dn 12.77
1982	8	43	367,591	8,549	Dn 6.16
1983	8	44	356,124	8,094	Dn 5.32
1984	8	45	377,991	8,400	Up 3.78
1985	8	44	420,016	9,546	Up 13.64
1986	8	44	379,014	8,614	Dn 9.76
1987	7	35	277,978	7,942	Dn 7.80
1988	7	38	302,609	7,963	Up 0.26
1989	7	34	296,739	8,728	Up 9.61
1990	7	40	465,183	11,630	Up 33.25
1991	8	42	316,755	7,542	Dn 35.15
1992	9	49	395,264	8,067	Up 8.83
1993	9	49	294,714	6,015	Dn 25.44
1994	9	49	354,903	7,243	Up 20.42
1995	9	50	373,967	7,479	Up 3.26
1996	9	49	363,860	7,426	Dn 0.71
1997	8	42	265,345	6,318	Dn 14.92
1998	8	42	365,046	8,692	Up 37.58
1999	8	42	346,085	8,240	Dn 5.20

Season	Teams	Games	Attendance	P/G	Change in P/G (Percent)
2000	8	41	308,925	7,535	Dn 8.56
2001	7	36	247,651	6,879	Dn 8.71
2002	7	38	261,071	6,870	Dn 0.13
2003	9	48	343,855	7,164	Up 4.28
2004	9	44	325,894	7,407	Up 3.39
2005	9	47	342,599	7,289	Dn 1.59
2006	9	46	322,634	7,014	Dn 3.77

PATRIOT LEAGUE

Season	Teams	Games	Attendance	P/G	Change in P/G (Percent)
1990	6	30	223,893	7,463	Up 3.15
1991	6	32	231,155	7,224	Dn 3.20
1992	6	31	202,187	6,522	Dn 9.72
1993	6	29	165,581	5,710	Dn 12.45
1994	6	32	198,274	6,196	Up 8.51
1995	6	29	157,625	5,435	Dn 12.28
1996	6	32	185,275	5,790	Up 6.53
1997	7	38	175,992	4,631	Dn 20.02
1998	7	40	239,275	5,982	Up 29.17
1999	7	39	194,058	4,976	Dn 16.82
2000	7	36	214,731	5,965	Up 19.88
2001	8	39	220,294	5,649	Dn 5.30
2002	8	45	234,475	5,211	Dn 7.75
2003	8	49	277,167	5,656	Up 8.54
2004	7	40	214,518	5,363	Dn 5.18
2005	7	40	223,538	5,588	Up 4.20
2006	7	39	206,134	5,285	Dn 5.42

PIONEER FOOTBALL LEAGUE

Season	Teams	Games	Attendance	P/G	Change in P/G (Percent)
1993	6	32	94,995	2,969	Dn 16.15
1994	6	32	129,678	4,052	Up 36.48
1995	6	32	115,148	3,598	Dn 11.20
1996	6	31	117,406	3,787	Up 5.25
1997	6	30	109,234	3,641	Dn 3.86
1998	5	27	103,882	3,847	Dn 6.65
1999	5	28	116,840	4,173	Up 8.47
2000	5	27	125,886	4,662	Up 11.72
2001	9	45	146,710	3,260	Dn 30.07
2002	9	50	166,582	3,332	Up 2.21
2003	9	54	210,949	3,906	Up 17.23
2004	9	52	164,693	3,167	Dn 18.92
2005	9	47	152,780	3,251	Up 2.65
2006	8	44	150,502	3,421	Up 5.23

SOUTHERN CONFERENCE

Season	Teams	Games	Attendance	P/G	Change in P/G (Percent)
1982	8	42	451,214	10,743	Dn 1.82
1983	9	47	442,328	9,411	Dn 12.40
1984	9	49	497,040	10,144	Up 7.79
1985	9	49	501,420	10,233	Up 0.88
1986	9	47	484,589	10,310	Up 0.75
1987	8	47	516,773	10,995	Up 6.64
1988	8	43	479,649	11,155	Up 1.46
1989	8	44	495,918	11,271	Up 1.04
1990	8	44	504,248	11,415	Up 1.28
1991	8	46	574,059	12,480	Up 9.33
1992	9	55	700,613	12,738	Up 2.07
1993	9	51	617,620	12,110	Dn 4.93
1994	9	53	667,283	12,590	Up 3.96
1995	9	47	532,530	11,330	Dn 10.01
1996	9	51	578,350	11,340	Up 0.09
1997	9	52	491,680	9,455	Dn 16.62
1998	9	50	483,003	9,660	Up 2.17
1999	9	49	514,800	10,506	Up 8.76
2000	9	52	545,732	10,495	Dn 0.10
2001	9	51	496,364	9,733	Dn 7.26
2002	9	53	520,455	9,820	Up 0.89
2003	9	54	563,433	10,434	Up 6.25
2004	8	45	448,341	9,963	Dn 4.51
2005	8	46	512,370	11,138	Up 11.79
2006	8	48	605,819	12,621	Up 13.31

SOUTHLAND CONFERENCE

Season	Teams	Games	Attendance	P/G	Change in P/G (Percent)
1982	6	31	438,147	14,134	Up 0.63
1983	7	35	469,010	13,400	Dn 5.19
1984	7	38	458,259	12,059	Dn 10.01
1985	7	35	408,960	11,685	Dn 3.10
1986	6	30	395,515	13,184	Up 12.83
1987	7	35	412,898	11,797	Dn 10.52
1988	7	40	441,301	11,033	Dn 6.48
1989	7	38	423,772	11,152	Up 1.08
1990	7	38	436,110	11,477	Up 2.91
1991	8	41	392,513	9,573	Dn 16.59
1992	8	45	429,971	9,555	Dn 0.19
1993	8	43	403,508	9,384	Dn 1.79
1994	7	43	435,078	10,118	Up 7.82
1995	6	33	316,426	9,589	Dn 5.23
1996	8	46	411,357	8,943	Dn 6.74
1997	8	46	388,593	8,448	Dn 5.54
1998	8	44	460,335	10,462	Up 23.84
1999	8	44	406,336	9,235	Dn 11.73
2000	8	40	399,925	9,998	Up 8.26
2001	7	36	330,689	9,186	Dn 8.12
2002	7	41	394,810	9,630	Up 4.83
2003	6	33	331,628	10,049	Up 4.35
2004	6	35	323,644	9,247	Dn 7.98
2005	6	32	304,578	9,518	Up 2.93
2006	7	39	338,616	8,682	Dn 8.78

SOUTHWESTERN ATHLETIC CONFERENCE

Season	Teams	Games	Attendance	P/G	Change in P/G (Percent)
1978	5	27	483,159	17,895	Dn 5.30
1979	6	32	513,768	16,055	Dn 10.28
1980	7	38	611,234	16,085	Up 0.19
1981	7	35	662,221	18,921	Up 17.63
1982	7	35	634,505	18,129	Dn 4.19
1983	8	44	709,160	16,117	Dn 11.10
1984	8	40	702,186	17,555	Up 8.92
1985	8	44	790,296	17,961	Up 2.31
1986	8	38	621,584	16,357	Dn 8.93
1987	8	42	697,534	16,608	Up 1.53
1988	8	38	541,127	14,240	Dn 14.26
1989	8	44	796,844	18,110	Up 27.18
1990	7	40	828,169	20,704	Up 14.32
1991	8	47	856,491	18,223	Dn 11.98
1992	8	42	873,772	20,804	Up 14.16
1993	8	42	772,714	18,398	Dn 11.57
1994	8	41	958,508	23,378	Up 27.07
1995	8	38	628,702	16,545	Dn 29.23
1996	8	39	600,798	15,405	Dn 6.35
1997	8	36	567,929	15,776	Up 2.41
1998	9	38	516,042	13,580	Dn 13.92
1999	10	51	781,226	15,318	Up 12.80
2000	10	44	506,076	11,502	Dn 24.91
2001	10	47	583,599	12,417	Up 7.96
2002	10	42	459,911	10,950	Dn 11.81
2003	10	48	579,976	12,083	Up 10.35
2004	10	45	521,986	11,600	Dn 4.00
2005	10	46	484,248	10,527	Dn 9.25
2006	10	53	824,740	15,561	Up 47.82

ALL-TIME ATTENDANCE OTHER CONFERENCES
(Conferences that either discontinued or changed names)

AMERICAN WEST CONFERENCE

Season	Teams	Games	Attendance	P/G	Change in P/G (Percent)
1994	4	20	82,986	4,149	Dn 8.77
1995	4	23	97,798	4,252	Up 2.48

COLONIAL ATHLETIC ASSOCIATION

Season	Teams	Games	Attendance	P/G	Change in P/G (Percent)
1986	5	24	241,192	10,050	Up 23.97
1987	6	29	241,831	8,339	Dn 17.02
1988	6	31	195,686	6,312	Dn 24.31
1989	5	26	196,767	7,568	Up 19.90

GULF STAR CONFERENCE
(Teams went to Southland Conference)

Season	Teams	Games	Attendance	P/G	Change in P/G (Percent)
1984	4	20	149,516	7,476	Dn 9.23
1985	4	22	166,046	7,548	Up 0.96
1986	5	25	211,094	8,444	Up 11.87

MID-CONTINENT CONFERENCE

(Discontinued after 1984 season; Four members went to Gateway)

Season	Teams	Games	Attendance	P/G	Change in P/G (Percent)
1981	3	17	140,506	8,265	Up 4.74
1982	4	23	191,975	8,347	Up 0.99
1983	4	21	167,219	7,963	Dn 4.60
1984	4	24	175,181	7,299	Dn 8.34

Largest Regular-Season Crowds

Largest Regular-Season Crowds*

Attendance	Date	Home	Visitor
112,118	11-24-03	Michigan 35,	Ohio St. 21
111,794	11-6-99	Michigan 37,	Northwestern 3
111,726	9-13-03	Michigan 38,	Notre Dame 0
111,609	10-30-04	Michigan 27,	Michigan St. 20
111,591	11-19-05	Michigan 21,	Ohio St. 25
111,575	11-20-99	Michigan 24,	Ohio St. 17
111,571	11-24-01	Michigan 20,	Ohio St. 26
111,542	11-2-02	Michigan 49,	Michigan St. 3
111,523	9-4-99	Michigan 26,	Notre Dame 22
111,518	10-9-04	Michigan 38,	Minnesota 35
111,514	10-21-00	Michigan 14,	Michigan St. 0
111,502	10-12-02	Michigan 27,	Penn St. 24 (ot)
111,496	10-26-02	Michigan 9,	Iowa 34
111,491	8-31-02	Michigan 31,	Washington 29
111,428	9-25-04	Michigan 27,	Iowa 30
111,386	9-10-05	Michigan 10,	Notre Dame 17
111,349	10-25-03	Michigan 31,	Purdue 3
111,349	10-7-06	Michigan 31,	Michigan St. 13
111,347	11-13-04	Michigan 41,	Northwestern 10
111,341	9-30-00	Michigan 13,	Wisconsin 10
111,249	10-15-05	Michigan 27,	Penn St. 25
111,238	9-26-98	Michigan 29,	Michigan St. 17
111,217	11-14-98	Michigan 27,	Wisconsin 10
111,117	10-8-05	Michigan 20,	Minnesota 23
111,058	9-23-06	Michigan 27,	Wisconsin 13

**In the 59 seasons official national attendance records have been maintained.*

2006 Top 10 Regular-Season Crowds

Attendance	Home	Visitor	Date	Site
111,349	Michigan 31,	Michigan St. 13	10-7	Ann Arbor, Mich.
111,058	Michigan 27,	Wisconsin 13	9-23	Ann Arbor, Mich.
110,923	Michigan 20,	Iowa 6	10-21	Ann Arbor, Mich.
110,007	Penn St. 10,	Michigan 17	10-14	State College, Pa.
109,668	Michigan 27,	Vanderbilt 7	9-2	Ann Arbor, Mich.
109,359	Michigan 34,	Ball St. 26	11-4	Ann Arbor, Mich.
109,114	Michigan 17,	Northwestern 3	10-28	Ann Arbor, Mich.
108,837	Penn St. 33,	Northwestern 7	9-30	State College, Pa.
108,712	Michigan 41,	Central Mich. 17	9-9	Ann Arbor, Mich.
108,607	Penn St. 17,	Michigan St. 13	11-18	State College, Pa.

Pre-1948 Regular-Season Crowds in Excess of 100,000

Attendance	Date	Site	Opponents, Score
120,000*	11-26-27	Soldier Field, Chicago	Notre Dame 7, Southern California 6
120,000*	10-13-28	Soldier Field, Chicago	Notre Dame 7, Navy 0
112,912	11-16-29	Soldier Field, Chicago	Notre Dame 13, Southern California 12
110,000*	11-27-26	Soldier Field, Chicago	Army 21, Navy 21
110,000*	11-29-30	Soldier Field, Chicago	Notre Dame 7, Army 6
104,953	12-6-47	Los Angeles	Notre Dame 38, Southern California 7

**Estimated attendance; others are audited figures.*

Additional Records

Highest Average Attendance Per Home Game: 111,175, Michigan, 1999 (667,049 in 6)

Highest Total Home Attendance: 857,911, Penn St., 2002 (8 games); (7-game total: 776,429, Michigan, 2003)

Highest Total Attendance, Home and Away: 1,263,815, Ohio St., 2003 (13 games); (11-game total: 1,044,370, Michigan, 1997)

Highest Bowl Single-Game Attendance: 106,869, 1973 Rose Bowl (Southern California 42, Ohio St. 17)

Most Consecutive Home Sellout Crowds: 282, Nebraska (current, from Nov. 3, 1962)

Most Consecutive 100,000-Plus Crowds: 194, Michigan (current, from Nov. 8, 1975)

2006 Attendance

Football Bowl Subdivision

Rank, School	Games	Attendance	Average
1. Michigan	7	770,183	110,026
2. Penn St.	7	752,972	107,567
3. Tennessee	7	740,521	105,789
4. Ohio St.	7	735,674	105,096
5. Georgia	7	649,222	92,746
6. LSU	8	737,696	92,212
7. Alabama	8	737,104	92,138
8. Southern California	6	548,880	91,480
9. Florida	7	632,866	90,409
10. Texas	7	619,534	88,505
11. Auburn	8	680,506	85,063
12. Nebraska	7	595,309	85,044
13. Oklahoma	6	507,366	84,561
14. Clemson	7	580,942	82,992
15. Wisconsin	7	569,576	81,368
16. Notre Dame	7	565,565	80,795
17. Florida St.	8	644,256	80,532
18. Texas A&M	7	531,894	75,985
19. South Carolina	7	529,412	75,630
20. Arkansas	6	443,368	73,895
21. Michigan St.	7	495,731	70,819
22. Iowa	7	494,095	70,585
23. Virginia Tech	8	529,864	66,233
24. UCLA	7	454,683	64,955
25. California	7	450,223	64,318
26. Brigham Young	6	363,146	60,524
27. West Virginia	7	411,408	58,773
28. Oregon	6	350,267	58,378
29. Virginia	6	346,389	57,732
30. Washington	6	344,897	57,483
31. Kentucky	7	401,307	57,330
32. North Carolina St.	7	395,779	56,540
33. Missouri	7	391,424	55,918
34. Arizona	7	390,589	55,798
35. Purdue	7	388,198	55,457
36. Arizona St.	6	327,369	54,562
37. Mississippi	7	376,604	53,801
38. Minnesota	6	313,239	52,207
39. Texas Tech	6	305,243	50,874
40. Georgia Tech	7	354,321	50,617
41. Maryland	7	345,752	49,393
42. North Carolina	7	342,000	48,857
43. Kansas St.	8	373,547	46,693
44. Iowa St.	7	323,197	46,171
45. Colorado	6	276,286	46,048
46. Kansas	7	308,961	44,137
47. Illinois	7	304,118	43,445
48. Pittsburgh	7	303,138	43,305
49. Utah	6	259,675	43,279
50. UTEP	6	254,662	42,444
51. Miami (Fla.)	7	293,359	41,908
52. Stanford	5	208,710	41,742
53. Mississippi St.	7	290,688	41,527
54. Louisville	6	248,891	41,482
55. Rutgers	6	246,675	41,113
56. Oklahoma St.	6	245,726	40,954
57. Oregon St.	7	285,808	40,830
58. Connecticut	7	272,576	38,939
59. Boston College	7	271,903	38,843
60. Fresno St.	6	231,307	38,551
61. Air Force	6	228,206	38,034
62. Syracuse	6	223,577	37,263
63. East Caro.	6	223,006	37,168
64. Baylor	7	259,559	37,080
65. Hawaii	8	292,708	36,589
66. Vanderbilt	6	209,168	34,861
67. Washington St.	7	242,698	34,671
68. Navy	5	166,375	33,275

Rank, School	Games	Attendance	Average
69. Indiana	7	231,443	33,063
70. Wake Forest	6	195,091	32,515
71. Memphis	7	227,077	32,440
72. TCU	6	191,557	31,926
73. UCF	7	220,980	31,569
74. Army	5	153,469	30,694
75. Boise St.	6	182,718	30,453
76. South Fla.	6	181,333	30,222
77. San Diego St.	6	175,364	29,227
78. Southern Miss.	6	173,963	28,994
79. New Mexico	7	200,431	28,633
80. Northwestern	6	167,973	27,996
81. Marshall	5	130,155	26,031
82. Colorado St.	5	120,916	24,183
83. UAB	6	138,835	23,139
84. Middle Tenn.	5	110,185	22,037
85. Houston	8	175,277	21,910
86. Central Mich.	5	107,817	21,563
87. Tulsa	6	128,186	21,364
88. Troy	5	104,048	20,810
89. Northern Ill.	6	124,623	20,771
90. Cincinnati	7	142,613	20,373
91. Toledo	6	121,863	20,311
92. Duke	7	137,061	19,580
93. UNLV	6	115,442	19,240
94. Wyoming	6	114,653	19,109
95. Arkansas St.	5	95,344	19,069
96. Tulane	5	94,710	18,942
97. San Jose St.	7	131,978	18,854
98. Western Mich.	5	93,124	18,625
99. La.-Monroe	5	111,564	18,594
100. New Mexico St.	7	123,172	17,596
101. Kent St.	5	85,018	17,004
102. Bowling Green	4	67,335	16,834
103. Nevada	6	100,367	16,728
104. Ohio	5	83,622	16,724
105. Buffalo	5	82,084	16,417
106. Akron	5	80,658	16,132
107. Temple	4	63,241	15,810
108. North Texas	5	78,249	15,650
109. SMU	6	92,565	15,428
110. Miami (Ohio)	5	76,219	15,244
111. Florida Int'l	5	75,552	15,110
112. Ball St.	6	90,367	15,061
113. Rice	4	59,041	14,760
114. Eastern Mich.	4	58,934	14,734
115. Louisiana Tech	5	72,928	14,586
116. Idaho	5	72,717	14,543
117. La.-Lafayette	6	87,096	14,516
118. Utah St.	5	56,800	11,360
119. Fla. Atlantic	5	46,382	9,276

FBS Conferences

Rank, Conference	Teams	Total Games	2006 Attendance	Average	Change In Avg. from 2005
1. Southeastern	12	87	*6,586,408	*75,706	1,127
2. Big Ten	11	75	5,223,202	69,643	-2,923
3. Big 12	12	83	*4,894,337	*58,968	571
4. Pacific-10	10	64	*3,604,124	56,314	-1,165
5. Atlantic Coast	12	85	*4,499,567	52,936	694
6. Independents	4	23	1,090,444	47,411	6,542
7. Big East	8	52	2,030,211	39,043	-357
8. Mountain West	9	54	*1,769,390	32,766	-2,509
9. Conference USA	12	72	1,918,457	26,645	1,102
10. Western Athletic	9	55	1,264,695	22,994	1,399
11. Mid-American	12	62	1,097,147	17,696	3,207
12. Sun Belt	6	42	718,075	17,097	216

**Conference record.*

Football Championship Subdivision

Rank, School	Games	Attendance	Average
1. Montana	9	203,403	22,600
2. Delaware	7	152,773	21,825
3. Appalachian St.	9	184,911	20,546
4. Jackson St.	5	101,572	20,314
5. Yale	5	92,809	18,562
6. Southern U.	5	82,265	16,453
7. Florida A&M	4	63,663	15,916
8. Ga. Southern	7	109,281	15,612
9. Harvard	5	77,742	15,548
10. Youngstown St.	8	121,269	15,159
11. James Madison	5	75,664	15,133
12. Citadel	5	72,996	14,599
13. South Carolina St.	4	58,374	14,594
14. Alcorn St.	3	39,955	13,318
15. Grambling	3	39,686	13,229
16. Texas St.	6	77,314	12,886
17. Illinois St.	5	64,021	12,804
18. Montana St.	7	89,309	12,758
19. Tennessee St.	5	62,849	12,570
20. Furman	6	74,649	12,442
21. Princeton	5	61,100	12,220
22. Penn	5	60,104	12,021
23. Norfolk St.	7	83,871	11,982
24. Massachusetts	8	93,301	11,663
25. N.C. A&T	5	57,979	11,596
26. Alabama St.	4	44,879	11,220
27. Liberty	6	66,765	11,128
28. UNI	6	66,721	11,120
29. McNeese St.	6	65,293	10,882
30. Western Ill.	5	53,506	10,701
31. William & Mary	5	53,225	10,645
32. Jacksonville St.	4	41,775	10,444
33. Hampton	6	60,578	10,096
34. Missouri St.	6	60,270	10,045
35. Alabama A&M	5	49,631	9,926
36. Eastern Ky.	5	48,800	9,760
37. Southern Ill.	7	66,556	9,508
38. Sam Houston St.	5	47,347	9,469
39. Lehigh	6	54,962	9,160
40. Northwestern St.	5	45,303	9,061
41. Western Ky.	6	54,306	9,051
42. Western Caro.	5	44,026	8,805
43. Villanova	5	41,819	8,364
44. Lafayette	5	41,682	8,336
45. Wofford	6	50,002	8,334
46. New Hampshire	5	40,706	8,141
47. Coastal Caro.	6	48,805	8,134
48. Ark.-Pine Bluff	5	40,069	8,014
49. Cal Poly	5	39,369	7,874
50. VMI	4	30,929	7,732
51. Stephen F. Austin	6	46,115	7,686
52. Chattanooga	4	29,928	7,482
53. Morgan St.	4	29,833	7,458
54. Idaho St.	5	37,176	7,435
55. Portland St.	4	29,182	7,296
56. Richmond	6	43,580	7,263
57. Bethune-Cookman	6	43,132	7,189
58. Eastern Wash.	5	35,580	7,116
59. Southeast Mo. St.	5	34,247	6,849
60. Elon	6	40,026	6,671
61. Mississippi Val.	5	33,333	6,667
62. Northern Ariz.	5	33,042	6,608
63. Brown	5	32,585	6,517

Rank, School	Games	Attendance	Average
64. Eastern Ill.	6	38,690	6,448
65. Weber St.	6	35,976	5,996
66. Southeastern La.	5	29,805	5,961
67. Sacramento St.	5	29,106	5,821
68. Holy Cross	5	28,710	5,742
69. Texas Southern	4	22,705	5,676
70. Dartmouth	5	27,983	5,597
71. Prairie View	5	26,643	5,329
72. Samford	6	31,921	5,320
73. Southern Utah	5	26,110	5,222
74. Maine	5	26,039	5,208
75. Hofstra	4	20,402	5,101
76. Tennessee Tech	5	25,174	5,035
77. Cornell	6	30,045	5,008
78. Columbia	6	27,674	4,612
79. Morehead St.	5	22,999	4,600
80. Towson	6	27,551	4,592
81. Nicholls St.	6	27,439	4,573
82. Bucknell	6	27,406	4,568
83. Stony Brook	4	17,343	4,336
84. Drake	7	30,199	4,314
85. San Diego	6	25,849	4,308
86. Gardner-Webb	6	25,162	4,194
87. Dayton	5	20,680	4,136
88. Tenn.-Martin	5	20,590	4,118
89. Howard	5	20,284	4,057
90. Austin Peay	5	19,764	3,953
91. Savannah St.	5	19,448	3,890
92. Fordham	6	22,337	3,723
93. Murray St.	5	18,588	3,718
94. Delaware St.	5	17,514	3,503
95. Colgate	6	20,957	3,493
96. Davidson	5	17,328	3,466
97. Charleston So.	6	19,815	3,303
98. Northeastern	4	13,022	3,256
99. Wagner	5	16,111	3,222
100. Rhode Island	6	19,026	3,171
101. Central Conn. St.	4	12,598	3,150
102. Albany (N.Y.)	5	15,577	3,115
103. Indiana St.	4	12,236	3,059
104. Monmouth	7	20,836	2,977
105. Jacksonville	4	9,983	2,496
106. Robert Morris	5	12,022	2,404
107. Sacred Heart	6	13,026	2,171
108. Marist	6	12,754	2,126
109. Georgetown	5	10,080	2,016
110. Butler	7	13,753	1,965
111. Valparaiso	5	9,711	1,942
112. Duquesne	5	9,216	1,843
113. La Salle	5	8,995	1,799
114. Iona	5	7,740	1,548
115. St. Francis (Pa.)	6	6,167	1,028
116. St. Peter's	4	3,241	810
2006 Reclassifying Teams			
North Dakota St.	5	81,886	16,377
Central Ark.	5	49,771	9,954
South Dakota St.	4	38,608	9,652
UC Davis	5	35,165	7,033
Winston-Salem	4	29,680	7,420
Northern Colo.	6	28,857	4,810

FCS Conferences

Rank, Conference	Teams	Total Games	2006 Attendance	Average	Change In Avg. from 2005
1. Southwestern	10	53	824,740	15,561	5,034
2. Southern	8	48	605,819	12,621	1,483
3. Mid-Eastern	9	50	*599,871	11,997	2,030
4. Big Sky	8	46	492,774	10,712	-101
5. Gateway	8	47	498,885	*10,615	529
6. Ivy	8	42	410,042	9,763	157
7. Atlantic 10	12	66	607,108	9,199	687
8. Southland #	7	39	338,616	8,682	-836
9. Ohio Valley	9	46	322,634	7,014	-275
10. Big South	5	28	*191,476	*6,838	2,258
11. Great West	2	10	*65,479	*6,548	1,067
12. Patriot	7	39	206,134	5,285	-303
13. Independents #	3	10	39,212	3,921	-1,138
14. Pioneer #	8	44	150,502	3,421	170
15. Northeast	8	42	*113,680	*2,707	335
16. Metro Atlantic	5	25	41,946	1,678	-297

**Conference record. #Different lineups in 2005.*

Division II

Rank, School	Games	Attendance	Average
1. Fort Valley St.	3	41,047	13,682
2. Tuskegee	5	55,979	11,195
3. West Tex. A&M	7	74,461	10,637
4. North Ala.	6	60,548	10,091
5. Grand Valley St.	8	72,651	9,081
6. Abilene Christian	5	45,005	9,001
7. North Dakota	6	52,963	8,827
8. Albany St. (Ga.)	4	34,683	8,670
9. Pittsburg St.	6	50,375	8,395
10. Morehouse	5	41,361	8,272
11. South Dakota	6	48,326	8,054
12. Miles	5	39,855	7,971
13. N.C. Central	6	47,186	7,864
14. Clark Atlanta	6	42,993	7,165
15. Central Mo.	6	41,942	6,990
16. Northwest Mo. St.	8	52,578	6,572
17. Tex. A&M-Kingsville	5	32,400	6,480
18. Northeastern St.	5	31,039	6,207
19. Washburn	5	30,889	6,177
20. Midwestern St.	7	42,377	6,053
21. Delta St.	6	36,301	6,050
22. West Ala.	6	34,701	5,783
23. Lane	5	28,274	5,654
24. Elizabeth City St.	5	27,840	5,568
25. Tarleton St.	4	22,163	5,540
26. Benedict	5	27,655	5,531
27. Arkansas Tech	5	27,336	5,467
28. Emporia St.	5	27,299	5,459
29. Valdosta St.	5	26,199	5,239
30. Neb.-Omaha	6	31,256	5,209
31. Lenoir-Rhyne	5	25,803	5,160
32. Johnson C. Smith	4	20,026	5,006
33. St. Paul's	5	22,912	4,582
34. Angelo St.	6	26,149	4,358
35. Virginia Union	5	21,611	4,322
36. Henderson St.	5	21,537	4,307
37. Mo. Southern St.	6	25,803	4,300
38. Southern Ark.	5	21,485	4,297
39. Millersville	6	25,149	4,191
40. Presbyterian	5	20,556	4,111
41. Stillman	5	20,514	4,102
42. Eastern N.M.	5	20,193	4,038
43. East Stroudsburg	6	24,196	4,032
44. Bloomsburg	6	23,815	3,969
45. St. Cloud St.	6	23,613	3,935
46. Mo. Western St.	5	19,594	3,918
47. Ferris St.	5	19,572	3,914

Rank, School	Games	Attendance	Average
48. Shepherd	7	27,327	3,903
49. Shaw	3	11,596	3,865
50. Shippensburg	6	22,863	3,810
51. California (Pa.)	6	22,800	3,800
52. Indiana (Pa.)	5	18,959	3,791
53. Slippery Rock	5	18,900	3,780
54. Chadron St.	5	18,600	3,720
55. Catawba	5	18,069	3,613
56. Augustana (S.D.)	5	17,909	3,581
57. Ashland	5	17,810	3,562
58. Southeastern Okla.	5	17,563	3,512
59. Bryant	7	24,384	3,483
60. Fayetteville St.	5	17,332	3,466
61. Kutztown	5	17,325	3,465
62. Livingstone	5	17,278	3,455
63. East Central	5	17,200	3,440
64. Kentucky St.	5	17,198	3,439
65. Harding	5	17,104	3,420
66. Carson-Newman	5	16,935	3,387
67. Minn. Duluth	5	16,804	3,360
68. Bowie St.	5	16,565	3,313
69. Central Okla.	7	23,064	3,294
70. Newberry	9	29,295	3,255
71. Clarion	5	16,252	3,250
72. West Chester	5	16,200	3,240
73. Humboldt St.	5	15,875	3,175
74. West Ga.	5	15,847	3,169
75. Minn. St. Mankato	6	18,891	3,148
76. Central Wash.	4	12,567	3,141
77. Ouachita Baptist	4	12,150	3,037
78. Northern St.	5	15,087	3,017
79. North Greenville	7	21,043	3,006
80. Saginaw Valley	5	15,001	3,000
81. Indianapolis	6	17,979	2,996
82. Mars Hill	5	14,960	2,992
83. Neb.-Kearney	5	14,189	2,837
84. Truman	5	14,014	2,802
85. Tex. A&M-Commerce	5	13,986	2,797
86. Northern Mich.	5	13,905	2,781
87. Charleston (W.V.)	5	13,848	2,769
88. Southwestern Okla.	5	13,800	2,760
89. Ark.-Monticello	4	10,827	2,706
90. Winona St.	5	13,464	2,692
91. Edinboro	6	16,060	2,676
92. St. Augustine's	5	13,337	2,667
93. Wingate	6	15,516	2,586
94. Western Ore.	4	10,300	2,575
95. Tusculum	5	12,816	2,563
96. Fort Hays St.	6	15,088	2,514
97. Southwest Baptist	5	12,435	2,487
98. Virginia St.	4	9,844	2,461
99. Bentley	6	14,320	2,386
100. Mo.-Rolla	5	11,900	2,380
101. Michigan Tech	5	11,793	2,358
102. Glenville St.	4	9,309	2,327
103. West Liberty St.	6	13,925	2,320
104. Mansfield	5	11,592	2,318
105. Wayne St. (Mich.)	6	13,758	2,293
106. Cheyney	5	10,784	2,156
107. Lock Haven	5	10,547	2,109
108. Merrimack	5	10,320	2,064
109. Northwood (Mich.)	6	11,920	1,986
110. C.W. Post	5	9,295	1,859
111. Assumption	4	7,163	1,790
112. Western Wash.	6	10,540	1,756
113. Southwest Minn. St.	6	10,519	1,753
114. Adams St.	5	8,685	1,737
115. Minn. St. Moorhead	5	8,636	1,727
116. Colorado Mines	6	10,355	1,725
117. Hillsdale	5	8,380	1,676
118. St. Joseph's (Ind.)	3	5,017	1,672
119. Mercyhurst	5	8,301	1,660
120. Concordia-St. Paul	4	6,605	1,651
121. Southern Conn. St.	5	7,542	1,508
122. Western N.M.	6	9,033	1,505
123. Wayne St. (Neb.)	6	9,007	1,501
124. Stonehill	5	7,472	1,494
125. Mesa St.	5	7,162	1,432
126. Pace	5	7,018	1,403
127. Bemidji St.	5	6,944	1,388
128. N.M. Highlands	6	7,781	1,296
129. Concord	5	5,850	1,170
130. Fort Lewis	4	4,406	1,101
131. Findlay	5	5,494	1,098
132. West Virginia St.	6	6,439	1,073
133. American Int'l	4	4,180	1,045
134. Lincoln (Mo.)	5	5,000	1,000
West Va. Wesleyan	5	5,000	1,000
136. Okla. Panhandle	5	4,809	961
137. St. Anselm	5	4,750	950
138. Gannon	5	4,739	947
139. Fairmont St.	5	4,196	839
140. Western St.	4	3,303	825
141. Upper Iowa	5	3,100	620
142. Tiffin	6	3,279	546
143. Minn.-Crookston	3	1,399	466

Division II Conferences

Rank, Conference	Teams	Total Games	2006 Attendance	Average	Change In Avg. from 2005
1. Southern Intercollegiate	10	50	388,522	7,770	1,409
2. Mid-America Intercollegiate #	10	58	312,578	5,389	-137
3. Lone Star	13	71	379,400	5,344	-504
4. Gulf South #	11	56	284,035	5,072	121
5. North Central #	9	50	232,869	4,657	-835
6. Central Intercollegiate #	11	54	241,337	4,469	-226
7. South Atlantic	8	45	153,950	3,421	191
8. Pennsylvania State Athletic	14	76	255,442	3,361	112
9. Great Lakes Intercollegiate	13	71	221,303	3,117	-234
10. Independents #	4	21	52,027	2,477	1,037
11. West Virginia Intercollegiate #	8	43	85,894	1,998	341
12. Rocky Mountain #	9	47	91,018	1,937	-411
13. Northeast-10	10	51	96,444	1,891	195
14. Northern Sun #	9	49	79,507	1,623	-178
15. Great Lakes Football #	4	19	25,196	1,326	-305

 # Different lineups in 2005.

Division III

Rank, School	Games	Attendance	Average
1. St. John's (Minn.)	6	51,284	8,547
2. Wabash	5	27,237	5,447
3. Wis.-Whitewater	9	40,087	4,454
4. Wartburg	5	21,716	4,343
5. Trinity (Conn.)	4	17,101	4,275
6. Williams	4	16,881	4,220
7. Luther	4	16,655	4,163
8. Mississippi Col.	5	20,542	4,108
9. Baldwin-Wallace	5	20,390	4,078
10. Emory & Henry	6	24,357	4,059
11. Mount Union	8	30,183	3,772
12. Concordia-M'head	4	14,991	3,747
13. Bethel (Minn.)	5	18,420	3,684
14. Chris. Newport	6	21,917	3,652
15. Amherst	4	14,000	3,500
16. Cortland St.	6	20,722	3,453
17. Loras	5	17,196	3,439
18. St. Olaf	5	17,124	3,424
19. Wooster	5	17,095	3,419
20. Hampden-Sydney	5	17,090	3,418
21. Hardin-Simmons	6	20,016	3,336
22. Gust. Adolphus	4	12,682	3,170
23. Wilmington (Ohio)	4	11,947	2,986
24. Louisiana Col.	4	11,789	2,947
25. Wash. & Lee	5	14,650	2,930
26. Linfield	5	14,405	2,881
27. Sul Ross St.	5	14,401	2,880
28. Gettysburg	5	14,273	2,854
29. St. Thomas (Minn.)	6	17,050	2,841
30. Wheaton (Ill.)	6	16,756	2,792
31. Maryville (Tenn.)	5	13,944	2,788
32. Anderson (Ind.)	4	11,000	2,750
33. Wis.-La Crosse	4	10,973	2,743
34. Tufts	4	10,965	2,741
35. Alfred	6	16,434	2,739
36. TCNJ	4	10,871	2,717
37. Wis.-Eau Claire	5	13,500	2,700
38. Franklin	6	15,950	2,658
39. Grove City	6	15,920	2,653
40. Rowan	6	15,829	2,638
41. Elmhurst	5	13,125	2,625
42. Wittenberg	4	10,411	2,602
43. Mary Hardin-Baylor	7	18,104	2,586
44. Merchant Marine	6	15,125	2,520
45. Howard Payne	4	9,925	2,481
46. McDaniel	6	14,712	2,452
47. Wis.-Stevens Point	3	7,316	2,438
48. Adrian	5	12,000	2,400
49. Chapman	4	9,500	2,375
50. Otterbein	5	11,849	2,369
51. East Tex. Baptist	4	9,455	2,363
52. Defiance	5	11,813	2,362
53. Whitworth	7	16,460	2,351
54. Wesley	10	23,513	2,351
55. Wis.-Stout	6	14,051	2,341
56. Wash. & Jeff.	6	14,014	2,335
57. Albright	6	13,994	2,332
58. Susquehanna	5	11,600	2,320
59. Muhlenberg	5	11,552	2,310
60. Wesleyan (Conn.)	4	9,225	2,306
61. Capital	7	16,099	2,299
62. Thomas More	5	11,486	2,297
63. Coe	5	11,359	2,271
64. FDU-Florham	6	13,613	2,268
65. Widener	6	13,500	2,250
66. Texas Lutheran	6	13,474	2,245
67. LaGrange	5	11,100	2,220
68. Hope	5	11,051	2,210
69. Norwich	5	11,000	2,200
70. Rochester	5	10,795	2,159
71. Huntingdon	4	8,609	2,152
72. Rose-Hulman	5	10,750	2,150
73. Coast Guard	6	12,675	2,112
74. Delaware Valley	5	10,500	2,100
Knox	5	10,500	2,100
76. Lycoming	4	8,349	2,087
77. Bridgewater (Va.)	5	10,365	2,073
78. Puget Sound	5	10,310	2,062
79. Wilkes	6	12,277	2,046
80. Muskingum	5	10,174	2,034
81. Mt. St. Joseph	5	10,168	2,033
82. St. John Fisher	7	14,189	2,027
83. Rensselaer	4	8,055	2,013
84. Shenandoah	5	9,981	1,996
85. Ferrum	4	7,984	1,996
86. Sewanee	5	9,791	1,958
87. Pacific Lutheran	5	9,600	1,920
88. Monmouth (Ill.)	5	9,580	1,916
89. Wis.-Oshkosh	4	7,521	1,880
90. Ohio Northern	5	9,327	1,865
91. Juniata	5	9,300	1,860
92. Ohio Wesleyan	5	9,297	1,859
93. Millsaps	7	12,942	1,848
94. King's (Pa.)	5	9,150	1,830
95. Willamette	4	7,310	1,827
96. Moravian	5	9,066	1,813
97. Western New Eng.	5	9,023	1,804
98. Wis.-Platteville	5	8,926	1,785
99. Alma	5	8,889	1,777
100. John Carroll	5	8,843	1,769
101. Montclair St.	4	7,072	1,768
102. Central (Iowa)	6	10,600	1,766
103. McMurry	4	7,000	1,750
104. Denison	5	8,650	1,730
105. Hamilton	4	6,887	1,721
106. Thiel	5	8,563	1,712
107. Middlebury	4	6,805	1,701
108. Averett	5	8,475	1,695
109. Wm. Paterson	5	8,400	1,680
110. Washington-St. Louis	5	8,396	1,679
111. Salisbury	5	8,379	1,675
112. Waynesburg	6	9,950	1,658
113. Lebanon Valley	5	8,266	1,653
114. Colby	4	6,533	1,633
115. North Central (Ill.)	5	8,150	1,630
116. Dubuque	5	8,092	1,618
117. Carroll (Wis.)	5	7,921	1,584
Hanover	5	7,921	1,584
119. Union (N.Y.)	5	7,916	1,583
120. Trinity (Tex.)	6	9,300	1,550
121. Dickinson	5	7,700	1,540
122. Rhodes	6	9,202	1,533
123. Albion	5	7,640	1,528
124. Catholic	5	7,601	1,520
125. Mass.-Dartmouth	4	6,050	1,513
126. Kean	5	7,557	1,511
127. Cal Lutheran	5	7,550	1,510
128. Lawrence	5	7,545	1,509
129. DePauw	4	6,000	1,500
130. Redlands	5	7,486	1,497
131. Olivet	5	7,318	1,463
132. Curry	5	7,303	1,460
133. Ill. Wesleyan	5	7,280	1,456
134. Guilford	4	5,800	1,450
135. Simpson	5	7,200	1,440
136. Frank. & Marsh.	5	7,199	1,440
137. St. Norbert	5	7,187	1,437
138. Allegheny	4	5,644	1,411
139. Kenyon	4	5,550	1,387
140. Carnegie Mellon	6	8,315	1,385
141. Springfield	8	10,948	1,368
142. Westminster (Pa.)	5	6,702	1,340
143. Buena Vista	5	6,700	1,340
144. Bethany (W.V.)	4	5,340	1,335
145. Frostburg St.	6	7,900	1,317
146. Ursinus	5	6,577	1,315
147. Case Reserve	6	7,852	1,308
148. Plymouth St.	4	5,178	1,294
149. Marietta	5	6,277	1,255
150. Westfield St.	4	4,998	1,250
151. Beloit	5	6,241	1,248
152. Augustana (Ill.)	5	6,196	1,239
153. Ithaca	5	6,152	1,230
154. N.C. Wesleyan	5	6,130	1,226
155. Benedictine (Ill.)	5	6,083	1,216
156. Illinois Col.	5	6,072	1,214
157. Chicago	4	4,785	1,196
158. Claremont-M-S	5	5,977	1,195
159. St. Lawrence	6	7,056	1,176
160. Bates	4	4,684	1,171
Fitchburg St.	4	4,684	1,171
162. Manchester	5	5,850	1,170

Rank, School	Games	Attendance	Average
163. Hartwick	5	5,848	1,169
164. Hamline	6	6,884	1,147
165. Western Conn. St.	5	5,614	1,122
166. Neb. Wesleyan	5	5,550	1,110
167. Randolph-Macon	5	5,429	1,086
168. Carthage	5	5,425	1,085
169. Utica	5	5,423	1,085
170. Wis.-River Falls	4	4,311	1,077
171. Mass. Maritime	4	4,276	1,069
172. Colorado Col.	6	6,249	1,041
173. Hobart	4	4,106	1,026
174. Bowdoin	4	4,099	1,025
175. WPI	6	6,139	1,023
176. Occidental	5	5,050	1,010
177. Greensboro	5	5,042	1,008
178. Endicott	5	4,959	992
179. Carleton	5	4,955	991
180. Husson	5	4,937	987
181. Westminster (Mo.)	4	3,900	975
182. North Park	5	4,800	960
183. Eureka	5	4,778	955
184. Lewis & Clark	4	3,805	951
185. Bridgewater St.	5	4,750	950
186. Nichols	5	4,685	937
187. Augsburg	4	3,594	898
188. Johns Hopkins	5	4,450	890
189. Mount Ida	4	3,550	887
190. Kalamazoo	4	3,500	875
191. La Verne	4	3,455	863
192. Austin	5	4,200	840
193. Concordia (Ill.)	4	3,300	825
194. Heidelberg	4	3,242	811
195. Salve Regina	5	4,042	808

Rank, School	Games	Attendance	Average
196. Lake Forest	5	4,034	807
197. Brockport St.	5	4,025	805
198. Methodist	6	4,682	780
199. Framingham St.	4	3,100	775
Greenville	4	3,100	775
201. Lakeland	5	3,850	770
202. Pomona-Pitzer	4	2,987	746
203. Cornell College	5	3,700	740
204. Aurora	5	3,503	701
205. Earlham	5	3,403	680
206. Rockford	4	2,636	659
207. Millikin	5	3,199	639
208. Buffalo St.	4	2,533	633
209. Oberlin	5	2,995	599
210. MacMurray	5	2,958	591
211. Worcester St.	5	2,941	588
212. Whittier	5	2,935	587
213. MIT	5	2,874	574
214. Wis. Lutheran	7	3,679	525
215. Grinnell	6	3,055	509
216. Centre	5	2,525	505
217. Hiram	5	2,403	481
218. Menlo	6	2,881	480
219. Bluffton	5	2,350	470
220. Ripon	5	2,240	448
221. Concordia (Wis.)	6	2,631	438
222. Maranatha Baptist	4	1,709	427
223. Martin Luther	4	1,600	400
224. Becker	3	1,034	344
225. Maine Maritime	4	1,275	318
226. Maritime (N.Y.)	3	740	247
227. Macalester	5	1,200	240
228. Principia	3	650	217
229. Blackburn	4	809	202

Division III Conferences

Rank, Conference	Teams	Total Games	2006 Attendance	Average	Change In Avg. from 2005
1. Minnesota Intercollegiate	9	46	148,203	3,222	204
2. American Southwest #	9	46	126,142	2,742	312
3. Wisconsin Intercollegiate	8	40	106,685	2,667	293
4. Old Dominion Athletic	7	35	85,292	2,437	-76
5. New England Small College #	10	40	97,180	2,430	146
6. Ohio Athletic	10	53	128,331	2,421	-259
7. Iowa Intercollegiate	9	45	103,218	2,294	183
8. Middle Atlantic	11	58	119,615	2,062	-111
9. North Coast	10	47	92,685	1,972	190
10. New Jersey Athletic #	8	40	78,803	1,970	213
11. Presidents' Athletic	7	37	71,975	1,945	104
12. USA South	8	41	78,155	1,906	-276
13. Heartland Collegiate Athletic #	8	40	75,802	1,895	279
14. Centennial	7	36	66,463	1,846	-28
15. Northwest #	7	36	64,771	1,799	-579
16. Atlantic Central #	4	27	46,227	1,712	174
17. Empire 8	7	41	69,994	1,707	-189
18. Liberty League #	7	36	59,192	1,644	-43
19. College Conf. of Illinois & Wisconsin	8	41	64,931	1,584	-138
20. Michigan Intercollegiate	7	36	54,077	1,502	-742
21. Southern Collegiate Athletic #	7	38	53,960	1,420	-459
22. University Athletic	4	21	29,348	1,398	-173
23. Midwest Intercollegiate	10	51	64,375	1,262	-10
24. Independents #	10	44	52,469	1,192	183
25. New England Football #	16	75	84,057	1,121	193
26. Southern California Intercollegiate	7	33	35,440	1,074	10
27. Illini-Badger	8	39	30,203	774	94
28. Upper Midwest	6	24	11,541	481	-162

 # Different lineups in 2005.

Division Totals

	Teams	Total Games or Sessions	2006 Attendance	2006 Average	Change In Total	Change In Avg. from 2005
Home Attendance, Division I FBS	119	745	34,142,038	45,828	3,571,123	200
FBS Neutral-Site Attendance		19	972,791	51,200	302,815	-4,631
FBS Bowl Game Attendance		32	1,699,639	53,114	298,914	1,235
NCAA DIVISION I FBS TOTALS	**119**	**796**	***36,814,468**	***46,249**	**4,172,942**	**210**
Home Attendance, Division I FCS	116	622	5,000,273	8,039	250,119	340
FCS Neutral-Site Attendance		19	700,795	36,884	35,063	3,597
FCS Championship Game		1	22,808	22,808	2,572	2,572
NCAA DIVISION I FCS TOTALS	**116**	**642**	**5,723,876**	**8,916**	**287,754**	**395**
NCAA DIVISION I TOTALS	**235**	**1,438**	**42,538,344**	**29,582**	**4,460,696**	**1,314**
Home Attendance, NCAA Division II	143	750	2,809,938	3,747	1,237	7
Division II Neutral-Site Attendance		25	187,839	7,514	14,103	832
Division II Championship Game		1	7,437	7,437	600	600
NCAA DIVISION II TOTALS	**143**	**776**	***3,005,214**	**3,873**	**15,940**	**31**
Home Attendance, NCAA Division III	229	1,129	2,083,303	1,845	14,572	0
Division III Neutral-Site Attendance		11	10,392	945	-4,277	-183
Division III Championship Game		1	6,051	6,051	1,432	1,432
NCAA DIVISION III TOTALS	**229**	**1,141**	**2,099,746**	**1,840**	**11,727**	**0**
Home Attendance, Reclassifying Teams	8	37	266,009	7,189	-65,624	-348
NATIONAL TOTALS FOR 2006	**615**	**3,392**	***47,909,313**	***14,124**	**4,422,739**	**962**

** Record.*

NOTE: *The total attendance for the Division I FCS tournament (15 games) was 202,351 for an average of 13,490, the Division II tournament (23 games) was 119,341 for an average of 5,189 and the Division III tournament (31 games) was 67,740 for an average of 2,185.*

Annual Team Attendance Leaders

Annual Leading FBS Teams in Per-Game Home Attendance

Year/Teams	G	Attendance	Avg.
1949			
Michigan	6	563,363	93,894
Ohio St.	5	382,146	76,429
SMU	8	484,000	60,500
1950			
Michigan	6	493,924	82,321
Ohio St.	5	368,021	73,604
SMU	5	309,000	61,800
1951			
Ohio St.	6	455,737	75,956
Michigan	6	445,635	74,273
Illinois	4	237,035	59,259
1952			
Ohio St.	6	453,911	75,652
Michigan	6	395,907	65,985
Texas	#5	311,160	62,232
1953			
Ohio St.	5	397,998	79,600
Southern California	6	413,617	68,936
Michigan	6	353,860	58,977
1954			
Ohio St.	6	479,840	79,973
Michigan	6	409,454	68,242
UCLA	5	318,371	63,674
1955			
Michigan	7	544,838	77,834
Ohio St.	7	493,178	70,454
Southern California	7	467,085	66,726
1956			
Ohio St.	6	494,575	82,429
Michigan	7	566,145	80,878
Minnesota	6	375,407	62,568
1957			
Michigan	6	504,954	84,159
Ohio St.	6	484,118	80,686
Minnesota	5	319,942	63,988
1958			
Ohio St.	6	499,352	82,225
Michigan	6	405,115	67,519
LSU	5	296,576	59,315
1959			
Ohio St.	6	495,536	82,589
Michigan	6	456,385	76,064
LSU	7	408,727	58,390
1960			
Ohio St.	5	413,583	82,717
Michigan St.	4	274,367	68,592
Michigan	6	374,682	62,447
1961			
Ohio St.	5	414,712	82,942
Michigan	7	514,924	73,561
LSU	6	381,409	63,651
1962			
Ohio St.	6	497,644	82,941
Michigan St.	4	272,568	68,142
LSU	6	397,701	66,284
1963			
Ohio St.	5	416,023	83,205
LSU	6	396,846	66,141
Michigan St.	5	326,597	65,319
1964			
Ohio St.	7	583,740	83,391
Michigan St.	4	284,933	71,233
Michigan	6	388,829	64,805
1965			
Ohio St.	5	416,282	83,256
Michigan	6	480,487	80,081
Michigan St.	5	346,296	69,259
1966			
Ohio St.	6	488,399	81,400
Michigan St.	6	426,750	71,125
Michigan	6	413,599	68,933
1967			
Ohio St.	5	383,502	76,700
Michigan	6	447,289	74,548
Michigan St.	6	411,916	68,653
1968			
Ohio St.	6	482,564	80,427
Southern California	5	354,945	70,989
Michigan St.	6	414,177	69,030
1969			
Ohio St.	5	431,175	86,235
Michigan	6	428,780	71,463
Michigan St.	5	352,123	70,425
1970			
Ohio St.	5	432,451	86,490
Michigan	6	476,164	79,361
Purdue	5	340,090	68,018
1971			
Ohio St.	6	506,699	84,450
Michigan	7	564,376	80,625
Wisconsin	6	408,885	68,148
1972			
Michigan	6	513,398	85,566
Ohio St.	6	509,420	84,903
Nebraska	6	456,859	76,143
1973			
Ohio St.	6	523,369	87,228
Michigan	7	595,171	85,024
Nebraska	6	456,726	76,121
1974			
Michigan	6	562,105	93,684
Ohio St.	6	525,314	87,552
Nebraska	7	534,388	76,341
1975			
Michigan	7	689,146	98,449
Ohio St.	6	527,141	87,856
Nebraska	7	533,368	76,195
1976			
Michigan	7	722,113	103,159
Ohio St.	6	526,216	87,702
Tennessee	7	564,922	80,703
1977			
Michigan	7	729,418	104,203
Ohio St.	6	525,535	87,589
Tennessee	7	582,979	83,283
1978			
Michigan	6	629,690	104,948
Ohio St.	7	614,881	87,840
Tennessee	†8	627,381	78,422
1979			
Michigan	7	730,315	104,331
Ohio St.	7	611,794	87,399
Tennessee	6	512,139	85,357
1980			
Michigan	6	625,750	104,292
Tennessee	†8	709,193	88,649
Ohio St.	7	615,476	87,925

Year/Teams	G	Attendance	Avg.
1981			
Michigan	6	632,990	105,498
Tennessee	6	558,996	93,166
Ohio St.	6	521,760	86,960
1982			
Michigan	6	631,743	105,291
Tennessee	6	561,102	93,517
Ohio St.	7	623,152	89,022
1983			
Michigan	6	626,916	104,486
Ohio St.	6	534,110	89,018
Tennessee	†8	679,420	84,928
1984			
Michigan	7	726,734	103,819
Tennessee	7	654,602	93,515
Ohio St.	6	536,691	89,449
1985			
Michigan	6	633,530	105,588
Tennessee	7	658,690	94,099
Ohio St.	6	535,284	89,214
1986			
Michigan	6	631,261	105,210
Tennessee	7	643,317	91,902
Ohio St.	6	536,210	89,368
1987			
Michigan	7	731,281	104,469
Tennessee	‡8	705,434	88,179
Ohio St.	6	511,772	85,295
1988			
Michigan	6	628,807	104,801
Tennessee	6	551,677	91,946
Ohio St.	6	516,972	86,162
1989			
Michigan	6	632,136	105,356
Tennessee	6	563,502	93,917
Ohio St.	6	511,812	85,302
1990			
Michigan	6	627,046	104,508
Tennessee	7	666,540	95,220
Ohio St.	6	536,297	89,383
1991			
Michigan	6	632,024	105,337
Tennessee	6	578,389	96,398
Penn St.	6	575,077	95,846
1992			
Michigan	6	635,201	105,867
Tennessee	6	575,544	95,924
Penn St.	6	569,195	94,866
1993			
Michigan	7	739,620	105,660
Tennessee	7	667,280	95,326
Penn St.	6	564,190	94,032
1994			
Michigan	6	637,300	106,217
Penn St.	6	577,731	96,289
Tennessee	6	573,821	95,637
1995			
Michigan	7	726,368	103,767
Tennessee	7	662,857	94,694
Penn St.	6	561,546	93,591
1996			
Michigan	6	635,589	105,932
Tennessee	6	632,509	105,418
Penn St.	6	577,001	96,167
1997			
Tennessee	6	639,227	106,538
Michigan	7	745,139	106,448
Penn St.	6	582,517	97,086
1998			
Michigan	6	665,787	110,965
Tennessee	6	641,484	106,914
Penn St.	6	579,190	96,532
1999			
Michigan	6	667,049	*111,175
Tennessee	7	747,870	106,839
Penn St.	7	675,503	96,500
2000			
Michigan	6	664,930	110,822
Tennessee	6	645,567	107,595
Ohio St.	6	586,542	97,757
2001			
Michigan	6	659,447	109,908
Penn St.	6	645,457	107,576
Tennessee	6	641,059	106,843
2002			
Michigan	7	774,033	110,576
Penn St.	8	*857,911	107,239
Tennessee	7	746,936	106,705
2003			
Michigan	7	776,429	110,918
Penn St.	7	739,403	105,629
Tennessee	7	735,269	105,038
2004			
Michigan	6	666,149	111,025
Tennessee	7	746,507	106,644
Ohio St.	6	629,257	104,876
2005			
Michigan	7	776,405	110,915
Tennessee	6	645,558	107,593
Ohio St.	7	735,120	105,017
2006			
Michigan	7	770,183	110,026
Penn St.	7	752,972	107,567
Tennessee	7	740,521	105,789

**Record. #Includes neutral-site game (Oklahoma) at Dallas counted as a home game (75,500). †Includes neutral-site game at Memphis counted as a home game. Attendance: 1978 (40,879), 1980 (50,003), 1983 (20,135). ‡Includes neutral-site game at East Rutherford (54,681).*

Annual Leading FCS Teams in Per-Game Home Attendance

(Min. 5 home games)

Year	Team	Avg.
1978	Southern U.	28,333
1979	Grambling	29,900
1980	Southern U.	29,708
1981	Grambling	30,835
1982	Southern U.	32,265
1983	Jackson St.	29,117
1984	Jackson St.	29,215
1985	Yale	29,347
1986	Jackson St.	25,177
1987	Jackson St.	32,734
1988	Jackson St.	26,500
1989	Jackson St.	32,269
1990	Grambling	30,152
1991	Grambling	27,181
1992	Southern U.	28,906
1993	Jackson St.	28,917
1994	Alcorn St.	26,203
1995	Jackson St.	34,849
1996	Alcorn St.	21,536
1997	Jackson St.	*38,873
1998	South Fla.	27,143
1999	Jackson St.	28,933
2000	Southern U.	27,190
2001	Jackson St.	29,067
2002	Jackson St.	23,691
2003	Yale	23,578
2004	Florida A&M	25,609
2005	Montana	22,479
2006	Montana	22,600

**Record.*

Annual Leading Division II Teams in Per-Game Home Attendance

(Min. 5 home games)

Year	Team	Avg.
1958	Southern Miss.	11,998
1959	Southern Miss.	13,964
1960	Florida A&M	12,083
1961	Akron	12,988
1962	Mississippi Col.	13,125
1963	San Diego St.	14,200
1964	Southern U.	12,633
1965	San Diego St.	15,227
1966	San Diego St.	15,972
1967	San Diego St.	*41,030
1968	San Diego St.	36,969
1969	Grambling	27,680
1970	Tampa	24,204
1971	Grambling	29,341
1972	Grambling	22,663
1973	Morgan St.	22,371
1974	Southern U.	33,563
1975	Texas Southern	22,800
1976	Southern U.	25,864
1977	Florida A&M	21,376
1978	Delaware	18,981
1979	Delaware	19,644
1980	Alabama A&M	15,820
1981	Norfolk St.	19,750
1982	Norfolk St.	16,183
1983	Norfolk St.	15,417
1984	Norfolk St.	18,500
1985	Norfolk St.	18,430
1986	Norfolk St.	13,836
1987	North Dakota St.	14,120
1988	UCF	21,905
1989	North Dakota St.	16,833
1990	Norfolk St.	14,904
1991	Norfolk St.	16,779
1992	Norfolk St.	14,196
1993	Norfolk St.	15,346
1994	Clark Atlanta	20,223
1995	Norfolk St.	16,593
1996	Norfolk St.	15,676
1997	North Dakota St.	12,512
1998	Tuskegee	13,269
1999	Tuskegee	13,336
2000	North Dakota St.	12,723
2001	Tuskegee	12,957
2002	Tuskegee	11,851
2003	North Dakota St.	11,567
2004	North Dakota St.	13,269
2005	West Tex. A&M	13,089
2006	Tuskegee	11,195

**Record.*

Annual Leading Division III Teams in Per-Game Home Attendance

(Min. 5 home games)

Year	Team	Avg.
1974	Albany St. (Ga.)	9,380
1975	Wittenberg	7,000
1976	Morehouse	11,600
1977	Dayton	10,315
1978	Dayton	9,827
1979	UCF	11,240
1980	UCF	10,450
1981	Dayton	10,025
1982	Dayton	7,906
1983	Dayton	6,542
1984	Dayton	8,332
1985	Villanova	11,740
1986	Villanova	*11,883
1987	Trinity (Conn.)	6,254
1988	St. John's (Minn.)	5,788
1989	Dayton	5,962
1990	Dayton	6,185
1991	Dayton	7,657
1992	Dayton	6,098
1993	St. John's (Minn.)	6,655
1994	Hampden-Sydney	6,614
1995	St. John's (Minn.)	6,574
1996	St. John's (Minn.)	6,834
1997	Emory & Henry	5,853
1998	St. John's (Minn.)	6,562
1999	Mount Union	5,743
2000	Emory & Henry	6,263
2001	St. John's (Minn.)	6,674
2002	St. John's (Minn.)	5,717
2003	St. John's (Minn.)	6,496
2004	St. John's (Minn.)	7,819
2005	St. John's (Minn.)	7,925
2006	St. John's (Minn.)	8,547

**Record.*

2006 Statistical Leaders

2006 Bowl Subdivision (FBS) Individual Leaders

Rushing

Rank, Player	Pos	Cl.	G	Att.	Net	TD	Avg.	Yds/Gm
1. Garrett Wolfe, Northern Ill.	RB	SR	13	309	1,928	18	6.24	148.31
2. Ian Johnson, Boise St.	RB	SO	12	276	1,714	25	6.21	142.83
3. Ray Rice, Rutgers	RB	SO	13	335	1,794	20	5.36	138.00
4. Steve Slaton, West Virginia	RB	SO	13	248	1,744	16	7.03	134.15
5. Ahmad Bradshaw, Marshall	RB	JR	12	249	1,523	19	6.12	126.92
6. Dwayne Wright, Fresno St.	RB	JR	12	261	1,462	11	5.60	121.83
7. Jon Cornish, Kansas	RB	SR	12	250	1,457	8	5.83	121.42
8. P.J. Hill, Wisconsin	RB	FR	13	311	1,569	15	5.05	120.69
9. Michael Hart, Michigan	RB	JR	13	318	1,562	14	4.91	120.15
10. Darren McFadden, Arkansas	TB	SO	14	284	1,647	14	5.80	117.64
11. Damion Fletcher, Southern Miss.	RB	FR	13	276	1,388	11	5.03	106.77
12. Tony Hunt, Penn St.	RB	SR	13	277	1,386	11	5.00	106.62
13. Tashard Choice, Georgia Tech	RB	JR	14	297	1,473	12	4.96	105.21
14. Marshawn Lynch, California	RB	JR	13	223	1,356	11	6.08	104.31
15. Kevin Smith, UCF	RB	SO	9	206	934	7	4.53	103.78
16. Patrick White, West Virginia	QB	SO	12	165	1,219	18	7.39	101.58
17. Calvin Dawson, La.-Monroe	RB	JR	12	213	1,210	11	5.68	100.83
18. Yvenson Bernard, Oregon St.	RB	JR	13	296	1,307	12	4.42	100.54
19. Tyrell Fenroy, La.-Lafayette	RB	SO	12	223	1,193	10	5.35	99.42
20. Amir Pinnix, Minnesota	RB	JR	13	252	1,272	10	5.05	97.85
21. Darius Walker, Notre Dame	RB	JR	13	255	1,267	7	4.97	97.46
22. Matt Forte, Tulane	RB	JR	9	163	859	8	5.27	95.44
23. Rodney Ferguson, New Mexico	RB	SO	13	252	1,234	7	4.90	94.92
24. Antonio Pittman, Ohio St.	RB	JR	13	242	1,233	14	5.10	94.85
25. Branden Ore, Virginia Tech	RB	SO	12	241	1,137	16	4.72	94.75
26. Ryan Torain, Arizona St.	RB	JR	13	223	1,229	7	5.51	94.54
27. Jalen Parmele, Toledo	RB	JR	12	207	1,131	8	5.46	94.25
28. James Davis, Clemson	RB	SO	13	203	1,187	17	5.85	91.31
29. Mark Bonds, Western Mich.	RB	JR	12	252	1,082	7	4.29	90.17
30. Reggie Arnold, Arkansas St.	RB	FR	12	209	1,076	4	5.15	89.67
31. Kalvin McRae, Ohio	RB	JR	14	258	1,252	15	4.85	89.43
32. Chris Markey, UCLA	RB	JR	13	227	1,107	2	4.88	85.15
33. Quinton Smith, Rice	RB	SR	13	211	1,096	10	5.19	84.31
34. Felix Jones, Arkansas	TB	SO	14	154	1,168	6	7.58	83.43
35. Tyrell Sutton, Northwestern	RB	SO	12	189	1,000	5	5.29	83.33
35. BenJarvus Green-Ellis, Mississippi	RB	JR	12	234	1,000	7	4.27	83.33
37. Dennis Kennedy, Akron	RB	SO	11	226	914	9	4.04	83.09
38. Robert Hubbard, Nevada	RB	SR	12	209	996	6	4.77	83.00
39. Tony Temple, Missouri	RB	JR	13	193	1,063	7	5.51	81.77
40. LaRod Stephens-Howlin, Pittsburgh	RB	SO	11	178	893	9	5.02	81.18
40. Kenny Irons, Auburn	RB	SR	11	198	893	4	4.51	81.18
42. Curtis Brown, Brigham Young	RB	SR	13	201	1,010	7	5.02	77.69
43. Yonus Davis, San Jose St.	RB	JR	13	163	1,007	6	6.18	77.46
44. Nate Ilaoa, Hawaii	RB	SR	13	131	990	13	7.56	76.15
45. Joseph Doss, Memphis	RB	JR	12	224	910	7	4.06	75.83
46. Jonathan Stewart, Oregon	RB	SO	13	183	981	10	5.36	75.46
47. Donald Brown II, Connecticut	RB	FR	12	161	896	7	5.57	74.67
48. Dantrell Savage, Oklahoma St.	RB	JR	11	126	820	8	6.51	74.55
49. Tim Brown, Temple	RB	SR	10	182	731	2	4.02	73.10
50. Eugene Jarvis, Kent St.	RB	SO	11	185	798	3	4.31	72.55
51. Jackie Battle, Houston	RB	SR	13	184	943	15	5.13	72.54
52. C.J. Spiller, Clemson	RB	FR	13	129	938	10	7.27	72.15
53. Shannon Woods, Texas Tech	RB	SO	13	152	926	10	6.09	71.23
54. Patrick Jackson, Louisiana Tech	RB	SO	12	170	854	7	5.02	71.17
55. Brandon Jackson, Nebraska	RB	JR	14	188	989	8	5.26	70.64
56. Jason Snelling, Virginia	RB	SR	11	183	772	7	4.22	70.18
57. Chris Bullock, Bowling Green	RB	FR	11	160	769	4	4.81	69.91
58. Jamaal Charles, Texas	RB	SO	12	156	831	7	5.33	69.25
59. Cory Boyd, South Carolina	RB	JR	12	164	823	8	5.02	68.58
60. Anthony Alridge, Houston	RB	JR	14	95	959	8	10.09	68.50
61. Eugene Gross, Middle Tenn.	RB	SR	13	202	882	11	4.37	67.85
62. Kenny Cattouse, Troy	RB	JR	12	168	810	4	4.82	67.50
63. Terry Caulley, Connecticut	RB	SR	10	120	674	3	5.62	67.40
64. Lonta Hobbs, TCU	RB	SR	10	145	665	7	4.59	66.50
65. Kolby Smith, Louisville	RB	SR	13	154	862	7	5.60	66.31
66. Adam Ballard, Navy	RB	JR	12	154	792	3	5.14	66.00
67. Ronnie McGill, North Carolina	RB	SR	12	192	790	7	4.11	65.83
68. Chad Hall, Air Force	RB	JR	12	155	784	5	5.06	65.33
69. Mike Goodson, Texas A&M	RB	FR	13	127	847	4	6.67	65.15
70. Courtney Tennial, Tulsa	RB	JR	13	171	845	14	4.94	65.00
71. Albert Young, Iowa	RB	JR	12	178	779	7	4.38	64.92
71. Hugh Charles, Colorado	RB	JR	12	139	779	1	5.60	64.92
73. Ken Darby, Alabama	RB	SR	13	210	835	0	3.98	64.23
74. Atiyyah Henderson, San Diego St.	RB	FR	12	174	764	1	4.39	63.67
75. Allen Patrick, Oklahoma	RB	JR	12	169	761	4	4.50	63.42

Rank, Player	Pos	Cl.	G	Att.	Net	TD	Avg.	Yds/Gm
76. LaMarcus Coker, Tennessee	RB	FR	11	108	696	5	6.44	63.27
77. Charles Pierre, Fla. Atlantic	RB	SO	12	207	756	5	3.65	63.00
78. Pierre Thomas, Illinois	RB	SR	12	131	755	5	5.76	62.92
79. Lance Ball, Maryland	RB	JR	13	174	815	8	4.68	62.69
80. Javarris James, Miami (Fla.)	RB	FR	13	175	802	4	4.58	61.69
81. Aaron Brown, TCU	RB	SO	13	154	801	9	5.20	61.62
82. Kregg Lumpkin, Georgia	RB	JR	13	162	798	6	4.93	61.38
83. L.V. Whitworth, Boston College	RB	JR	13	174	791	4	4.55	60.85
84. Jamario Thomas, North Texas	RB	JR	11	181	668	2	3.69	60.73
85. Julian Edelman, Kent St.	QB	SO	11	169	658	7	3.89	59.82
86. Delone Carter, Syracuse	RB	FR	12	156	713	4	4.57	59.42
87. Marcus Cross, Utah St.	RB	JR	11	176	650	3	3.69	59.09
88. Ontario Sneed, Central Mich.	RB	SO	13	135	764	4	5.66	58.77
89. James Starks, Buffalo	QB	FR	12	175	704	6	4.02	58.67
90. Chris Nickson, Vanderbilt	QB	SO	12	146	694	9	4.75	57.83
91. Toney Baker, North Carolina St.	RB	SO	12	157	688	6	4.38	57.33
92. Chauncey Washington, Southern California	RB	JR	13	157	744	9	4.74	57.23
93. Keon Lattimore, Maryland	RB	JR	13	160	743	3	4.64	57.15
94. Bernard Jackson, Colorado	QB	JR	12	155	677	7	4.37	56.42
95. Jorvorskie Lane, Texas A&M	RB	SO	13	166	725	19	4.37	55.77
96. Kory Sheets, Purdue	RB	SO	14	158	780	11	4.94	55.71
97. Anthony Dixon, Mississippi St.	RB	FR	12	169	668	9	3.95	55.67
98. Dwight Tardy, Washington St.	RB	SO	12	145	667	4	4.60	55.58
99. Louis Rankin, Washington	RB	JR	12	142	666	4	4.69	55.50
100. Wynel Seldon, Wyoming	RB	SO	11	156	610	1	3.91	55.45

Passing Efficiency

(Minimum 15 Attempts Per Game)

Rank, Player	Pos	Cl.	G	Att	Comp	CPct	Int	IPct	Yds	Yds/Att	TD	TDPct	Rating
1. Colt Brennan, Hawaii	QB	JR	14	559	406	72.63	12	2.15	5,549	9.93	58	10.38	186.0
2. John Beck, Brigham Young	QB	SR	12	417	289	69.30	8	1.92	3,885	9.32	32	7.67	169.1
3. JaMarcus Russell, LSU	QB	JR	13	342	232	67.84	8	2.34	3,129	9.15	28	8.19	167.0
4. Tyler Palko, Pittsburgh	QB	SR	12	322	220	68.32	9	2.80	2,871	8.92	25	7.76	163.2
5. Kevin Kolb, Houston	QB	SR	14	432	292	67.59	4	0.93	3,809	8.82	30	6.94	162.7
6. Jared Zabransky, Boise St.	QB	SR	13	288	191	66.32	8	2.78	2,587	8.98	23	7.99	162.6
7. Troy Smith, Ohio St.	QB	SR	13	311	203	65.27	6	1.93	2,542	8.17	30	9.65	161.9
8. Colt McCoy, Texas	QB	FR	13	318	217	68.24	7	2.20	2,570	8.08	29	9.12	161.8
9. Brian Brohm, Louisville	QB	JR	11	313	199	63.58	5	1.60	3,049	9.74	16	5.11	159.1
10. Justin Willis, SMU	QB	FR	11	270	182	67.41	6	2.22	2,047	7.58	26	9.63	158.4
11. Adam Tafralis, San Jose St.	QB	JR	13	276	181	65.58	7	2.54	2,284	8.28	21	7.61	155.1
12. Chase Holbrook, New Mexico St.	QB	SO	12	567	397	70.02	9	1.59	4,619	8.15	34	6.00	155.1
13. Andre Woodson, Kentucky	QB	JR	13	419	264	63.01	7	1.67	3,515	8.39	31	7.40	154.5
14. Erik Ainge, Tennessee	QB	JR	12	348	233	66.95	9	2.59	2,989	8.59	19	5.46	151.9
15. Jordan Palmer, UTEP	QB	SR	12	429	282	65.73	14	3.26	3,595	8.38	26	6.06	149.6
16. Bobby Reid, Oklahoma St.	QB	SO	13	267	148	55.43	11	4.12	2,266	8.49	24	8.99	148.1
17. Nate Davis, Ball St.	QB	FR	12	244	150	61.48	8	3.28	1,975	8.09	18	7.38	147.3
18. Brady Quinn, Notre Dame	QB	SR	13	467	289	61.88	7	1.50	3,426	7.34	37	7.92	146.7
19. Dan LeFevour, Central Mich.	QB	FR	14	388	247	63.66	10	2.58	3,031	7.81	26	6.70	146.2
20. Zac Taylor, Nebraska	QB	SR	14	391	233	59.59	8	2.05	3,197	8.18	26	6.65	146.1
21. Graham Harrell, Texas Tech	QB	SO	13	616	412	66.88	11	1.79	4,555	7.39	38	6.17	145.8
22. Chase Daniel, Missouri	QB	SO	13	452	287	63.50	10	2.21	3,527	7.80	28	6.19	145.1
23. Chris Leak, Florida	QB	SR	14	365	232	63.56	13	3.56	2,942	8.06	23	6.30	144.9
24. John David Booty, Southern California	QB	JR	13	436	269	61.70	9	2.06	3,347	7.68	29	6.65	144.0
25. John Stocco, Wisconsin	QB	SR	11	268	158	58.96	6	2.24	2,185	8.15	17	6.34	143.9
26. Chad Henne, Michigan	QB	JR	13	328	203	61.89	8	2.44	2,508	7.65	22	6.71	143.4
27. Paul Thompson, Oklahoma	QB	SR	14	336	204	60.71	11	3.27	2,667	7.94	22	6.55	142.4
28. Nate Longshore, California	QB	SO	13	377	227	60.21	13	3.45	3,021	8.01	24	6.37	141.6
29. Paul Smith, Tulsa	QB	JR	13	350	233	66.57	9	2.57	2,727	7.79	15	4.29	141.0
30. Bryan Cupito, Minnesota	QB	SR	13	359	214	59.61	9	2.51	2,819	7.85	22	6.13	140.8
31. Jeff Rowe, Nevada	QB	SR	12	266	172	64.66	8	3.01	1,907	7.17	17	6.39	140.0
32. Matt Moore, Oregon St.	QB	SR	14	378	229	60.58	7	1.85	3,022	7.99	18	4.76	139.7
33. Riley Skinner, Wake Forest	QB	FR	14	260	171	65.77	5	1.92	2,051	7.89	9	3.46	139.6
34. Matt Grothe, South Fla.	QB	FR	13	317	202	63.72	14	4.42	2,576	8.13	15	4.73	138.8
35. Brandon Cox, Auburn	QB	JR	13	271	163	60.15	9	3.32	2,198	8.11	14	5.17	138.7
36. Jeff Ballard, TCU	QB	SR	13	307	190	61.89	5	1.63	2,394	7.80	13	4.23	138.1
37. Will Proctor, Clemson	QB	SR	13	304	183	60.20	11	3.62	2,353	7.74	16	5.26	135.3
38. Stephen McGee, Texas A&M	QB	SO	13	313	194	61.98	2	0.64	2,295	7.33	12	3.83	134.9
39. Rudy Carpenter, Arizona St.	QB	SO	13	332	184	55.42	14	4.22	2,523	7.60	23	6.93	133.7
40. Brett Ratliff, Utah	QB	SR	13	391	228	58.31	9	2.30	2,796	7.15	23	5.88	133.2
41. Alex Brink, Washington St.	QB	JR	12	396	241	60.86	10	2.53	2,899	7.32	19	4.80	133.1
42. Sam Hollenbach, Maryland	QB	SR	13	328	203	61.89	11	3.35	2,371	7.23	15	4.57	131.0
43. Drew Tate, Iowa	QB	SR	11	352	207	58.81	13	3.69	2,623	7.45	18	5.11	130.9
44. Shawn Bell, Baylor	QB	SR	9	383	241	62.92	10	2.61	2,582	6.74	19	4.96	130.7
45. Curtis Painter, Purdue	QB	SO	14	530	315	59.43	19	3.58	3,985	7.52	22	4.15	129.1
46. Matt Ryan, Boston College	QB	JR	12	426	263	61.74	10	2.35	2,942	6.91	15	3.52	126.7
47. John Parker Wilson, Alabama	QB	SO	13	379	216	56.99	10	2.64	2,707	7.14	17	4.49	126.5
48. Lester Ricard, Tulane	QB	SR	12	400	229	57.25	10	2.50	2,795	6.99	18	4.50	125.8
49. Martin Hankins, Memphis	QB	JR	12	377	226	59.95	13	3.45	2,550	6.76	18	4.77	125.6
50. Phil Horvath, Northern Ill.	QB	SR	11	269	157	58.36	9	3.35	1,932	7.18	11	4.09	125.5

Rank, Player	Pos	Cl.	G	Att	Comp	CPct	Int	IPct	Yds	Yds/Att	TD	TDPct	Rating
51. Drew Stanton, Michigan St.	QB	SR	11	269	164	60.97	10	3.72	1,807	6.72	12	4.46	124.7
52. Julian Edelman, Kent St.	QB	SO	11	242	134	55.37	11	4.55	1,859	7.68	10	4.13	124.4
53. Mike Kokal, Miami (Ohio)	QB	JR	11	355	208	58.59	8	2.25	2,419	6.81	14	3.94	124.3
54. Caleb Hanie, Colorado St.	QB	JR	12	342	209	61.11	12	3.51	2,427	7.10	11	3.22	124.3
55. Dustin Grutza, Cincinnati	QB	SO	12	225	137	60.89	13	5.78	1,632	7.25	9	4.00	123.5
56. Kerry Meier, Kansas	QB	FR	9	184	104	56.52	10	5.43	1,193	6.48	13	7.07	123.4
57. Adam DiMichele, Temple	QB	SO	11	220	135	61.36	12	5.45	1,518	6.90	10	4.55	123.4
58. Bernard Morris, Marshall	QB	JR	11	188	116	61.70	12	6.38	1,346	7.16	8	4.26	123.1
59. Chris Nickson, Vanderbilt	QB	SO	12	292	160	54.79	13	4.45	2,085	7.14	15	5.14	122.8
60. James Pinkney, East Caro.	QB	SR	13	397	232	58.44	10	2.52	2,783	7.01	12	3.02	122.3
61. Sean Glennon, Virginia Tech	QB	SO	13	302	170	56.29	11	3.64	2,191	7.25	11	3.64	122.0
62. Omar Haugabook, Troy	QB	JR	13	393	241	61.32	17	4.33	2,401	6.11	21	5.34	121.6
63. Chris Williams, UAB	QB	SR	10	168	95	56.55	7	4.17	1,112	6.62	9	5.36	121.5
64. Kyle Wright, Miami (Fla.)	QB	JR	10	250	152	60.80	7	2.80	1,655	6.62	8	3.20	121.4
65. Luke Getsy, Akron	QB	SR	12	380	199	52.37	11	2.89	2,662	7.01	18	4.74	121.1
66. Anthony Turner, Bowling Green	QB	SO	10	252	144	57.14	5	1.98	1,596	6.33	11	4.37	120.8
67. Dennis Dixon, Oregon	QB	JR	12	322	197	61.18	14	4.35	2,143	6.66	12	3.73	120.7
68. Mike Teel, Rutgers	QB	SO	13	296	164	55.41	13	4.39	2,135	7.21	12	4.05	120.6
69. Chris Nelson, New Mexico	QB	SR	10	216	112	51.85	6	2.78	1,435	6.64	12	5.56	120.4
70. Clint Marks, Middle Tenn.	QB	SR	13	283	171	60.42	9	3.18	1,917	6.77	8	2.83	120.3
71. Jeremy Young, Southern Miss.	QB	JR	14	281	161	57.30	6	2.14	1,769	6.30	12	4.27	120.0
72. Karsten Sween, Wyoming	QB	FR	9	212	128	60.38	8	3.77	1,304	6.15	9	4.25	118.5
73. Kellen Lewis, Indiana	QB	FR	11	346	190	54.91	7	2.02	2,221	6.42	14	4.05	118.1
74. Drew Weatherford, Florida St.	QB	SO	12	318	177	55.66	11	3.46	2,154	6.77	12	3.77	118.1
75. Ryan Cubit, Western Mich.	QB	SR	11	365	224	61.37	13	3.56	2,138	5.86	16	4.38	117.9
76. Bret Meyer, Iowa St.	QB	JR	12	374	211	56.42	12	3.21	2,546	6.81	12	3.21	117.8
77. Steven Moffett, UCF	QB	SR	10	215	119	55.35	5	2.33	1,385	6.44	8	3.72	117.1
78. Joe Dailey, North Carolina	QB	JR	10	195	112	57.44	10	5.13	1,316	6.75	7	3.59	115.7
79. Perry Patterson, Syracuse	QB	SR	12	300	158	52.67	4	1.33	1,865	6.22	12	4.00	115.4
80. Kinsmon Lancaster, La.-Monroe	QB	SO	12	250	142	56.80	14	5.60	1,789	7.16	7	2.80	115.0
81. Willie Tuitama, Arizona	QB	SO	10	211	118	55.92	6	2.84	1,335	6.33	7	3.32	114.3
82. Patrick Cowan, UCLA	QB	SO	12	276	145	52.54	9	3.26	1,782	6.46	11	3.99	113.4
83. Rusty Smith, Fla. Atlantic	QB	FR	12	194	108	55.67	8	4.12	1,285	6.62	6	3.09	113.3
84. Zac Champion, Louisiana Tech	QB	JR	13	364	190	52.20	18	4.95	2,466	6.77	14	3.85	111.9
85. Anthony Morelli, Penn St.	QB	JR	13	386	208	53.89	8	2.07	2,424	6.28	11	2.85	111.9
86. Matthew Stafford, Georgia	QB	FR	13	256	135	52.73	13	5.08	1,749	6.83	7	2.73	109.0
87. Reggie Ball, Georgia Tech	QB	SR	13	304	135	44.41	14	4.61	1,820	5.99	20	6.58	107.2
88. Thaddeus Lewis, Duke	QB	FR	12	340	180	52.94	16	4.71	2,134	6.28	11	3.24	106.9
89. Tom Brandstater, Fresno St.	QB	SO	11	268	146	54.48	14	5.22	1,490	5.56	13	4.85	106.7
90. Andy Schmitt, Eastern Mich.	QB	FR	9	213	131	61.50	6	2.82	1,182	5.55	2	.94	105.6
91. Jameel Sewell, Virginia	QB	FR	11	247	143	57.89	6	2.43	1,342	5.43	5	2.02	105.4
92. Steven Wichman, Idaho	QB	SR	12	319	155	48.59	14	4.39	2,158	6.76	8	2.51	104.9
93. Rocky Hinds, UNLV	QB	SO	12	359	194	54.04	13	3.62	2,148	5.98	8	2.23	104.4
94. Corey Leonard, Arkansas St.	QB	FR	12	222	109	49.10	8	3.60	1,321	5.95	8	3.60	103.8
95. Josh Freeman, Kansas St.	QB	FR	11	270	140	51.85	15	5.56	1,780	6.59	6	2.22	103.5
96. Jerry Babb, La.-Lafayette	QB	SR	12	262	140	53.44	14	5.34	1,535	5.86	9	3.44	103.3
97. Bernard Jackson, Colorado	QB	JR	12	219	108	49.32	7	3.20	1,298	5.93	7	3.20	103.3
98. Daniel Evans, North Carolina St.	QB	SO	12	307	163	53.09	11	3.58	1,843	6.00	6	1.95	102.8
99. Austen Everson, Ohio	QB	SR	13	253	137	54.15	8	3.16	1,356	5.36	7	2.77	102.0
100. Brent Schaeffer, Mississippi	QB	JR	12	244	115	47.13	10	4.10	1,442	5.91	9	3.69	100.7

Total Offense

				Rush				Pass		Total		Yds/	Yds/
Rank, Player	Pos.	Cl.	G	Att	Gain	Loss	Net	Att	Yds	Plays	Yds	Pl	Gm
1. Colt Brennan, Hawaii	QB	JR	14	86	504	138	366	559	5,549	645	5,915	9.17	422.5
2. Chase Holbrook, New Mexico St.	QB	SO	12	80	153	231	-78	567	4,619	647	4,541	7.02	378.4
3. Graham Harrell, Texas Tech	QB	SO	13	33	40	118	-78	616	4,555	649	4,477	6.90	344.4
4. John Beck, Brigham Young	QB	SR	12	50	123	131	-8	417	3,885	467	3,877	8.30	323.1
5. Chase Daniel, Missouri	QB	SO	13	147	598	219	379	452	3,527	599	3,906	6.52	300.5
6. Jordan Palmer, UTEP	QB	SR	12	47	100	186	-86	429	3,595	476	3,509	7.37	292.4
7. Curtis Painter, Purdue	QB	SO	14	76	288	181	107	530	3,985	606	4,092	6.75	292.3
8. Kevin Kolb, Houston	QB	SR	14	111	397	243	154	432	3,809	543	3,963	7.30	283.1
9. Brian Brohm, Louisville	QB	JR	11	47	163	118	45	313	3,049	360	3,094	8.59	281.3
10. Shawn Bell, Baylor	QB	SR	9	27	33	170	-137	383	2,582	410	2,445	5.96	271.7
11. Brady Quinn, Notre Dame	QB	SR	13	82	304	233	71	467	3,426	549	3,497	6.37	269.0
12. Andre Woodson, Kentucky	QB	JR	13	70	135	272	-137	419	3,515	489	3,378	6.91	259.8
13. Dan LeFevour, Central Mich.	QB	FR	14	132	735	214	521	388	3,031	520	3,552	6.83	253.7
14. John David Booty, Southern California	QB	JR	13	33	50	103	-53	436	3,347	469	3,294	7.02	253.4
15. JaMarcus Russell, LSU	QB	JR	13	52	282	140	142	342	3,129	394	3,271	8.30	251.6
16. Drew Tate, Iowa	QB	SR	11	49	205	81	124	352	2,623	401	2,747	6.85	249.7
17. Matt Grothe, South Fla.	QB	FR	13	178	802	180	622	317	2,576	495	3,198	6.46	246.0
18. Tyler Palko, Pittsburgh	QB	SR	12	66	238	161	77	322	2,871	388	2,948	7.60	245.7
19. Mike Kokal, Miami (Ohio)	QB	JR	11	136	526	249	277	355	2,419	491	2,696	5.49	245.1
20. Alex Brink, Washington St.	QB	JR	12	78	220	212	8	396	2,899	474	2,907	6.13	242.3
21. Kellen Lewis, Indiana	QB	FR	11	124	638	197	441	346	2,221	470	2,662	5.66	242.0
22. Matt Ryan, Boston College	QB	JR	12	52	128	182	-54	426	2,942	478	2,888	6.04	240.7
23. Erik Ainge, Tennessee	QB	JR	12	26	14	116	-102	348	2,989	374	2,887	7.72	240.6
24. Patrick White, West Virginia	QB	SO	12	165	1,298	79	1,219	179	1,655	344	2,874	8.35	239.5
25. Brett Ratliff, Utah	QB	SR	13	97	451	195	256	391	2,796	488	3,052	6.25	234.8
26. Paul Smith, Tulsa	QB	JR	13	101	391	103	288	350	2,727	451	3,015	6.69	231.9
27. Chris Nickson, Vanderbilt	QB	SO	12	146	897	203	694	292	2,085	438	2,779	6.34	231.6
28. James Pinkney, East Caro.	QB	SR	13	105	418	202	216	397	2,783	502	2,999	5.97	230.7

Rank, Player	Pos.	Cl.	G	Rush Att	Rush Gain	Rush Loss	Rush Net	Pass Att	Pass Yds	Total Plays	Total Yds	Yds/Pl	Yds/Gm
29. Julian Edelman, Kent St.	QB	SO	11	169	868	210	658	242	1,859	411	2,517	6.12	228.8
30. Nate Longshore, California	QB	SO	13	28	48	95	-47	377	3,021	405	2,974	7.34	228.8
31. Stephen McGee, Texas A&M	QB	SO	13	146	831	165	666	313	2,295	459	2,961	6.45	227.8
32. Bret Meyer, Iowa St.	QB	JR	12	137	439	262	177	374	2,546	511	2,723	5.33	226.9
33. Zac Taylor, Nebraska	QB	SR	14	60	154	186	-32	391	3,197	451	3,165	7.02	226.1
34. Lester Ricard, Tulane	QB	SR	12	60	131	243	-112	400	2,795	460	2,683	5.83	223.6
35. Justin Willis, SMU	QB	FR	11	132	591	237	354	270	2,047	402	2,401	5.97	218.3
36. Jeff Ballard, TCU	QB	SR	13	110	533	110	423	307	2,394	417	2,817	6.76	216.7
37. Dennis Dixon, Oregon	QB	JR	12	94	511	69	442	322	2,143	416	2,585	6.21	215.4
38. Matt Moore, Oregon St.	QB	SR	14	77	214	225	-11	378	3,022	455	3,011	6.62	215.1
39. John Parker Wilson, Alabama	QB	SO	13	82	290	207	83	379	2,707	461	2,790	6.05	214.6
40. Jared Zabransky, Boise St.	QB	SR	13	98	363	166	197	288	2,587	386	2,784	7.21	214.2
41. Bobby Reid, Oklahoma St.	QB	SO	13	119	652	152	500	267	2,266	386	2,766	7.17	212.8
42. Chris Leak, Florida	QB	SR	14	77	238	208	30	365	2,942	442	2,972	6.72	212.3
43. Bryan Cupito, Minnesota	QB	SR	13	37	60	129	-69	359	2,819	396	2,750	6.94	211.5
44. Martin Hankins, Memphis	QB	JR	12	33	73	85	-12	377	2,550	410	2,538	6.19	211.5
45. Troy Smith, Ohio St.	QB	SR	13	72	332	128	204	311	2,542	383	2,746	7.17	211.2
46. Colt McCoy, Texas	QB	FR	13	68	289	119	170	318	2,570	386	2,740	7.10	210.8
47. Luke Getsy, Akron	QB	SR	12	58	134	276	-142	380	2,662	438	2,520	5.75	210.0
48. Omar Haugabook, Troy	QB	JR	13	140	554	241	313	393	2,401	533	2,714	5.09	208.8
49. Anthony Turner, Bowling Green	QB	SO	10	141	598	118	480	252	1,596	393	2,076	5.28	207.6
50. Caleb Hanie, Colorado St.	QB	JR	12	108	351	296	55	342	2,427	450	2,482	5.52	206.8
51. Drew Stanton, Michigan St.	QB	SR	11	110	599	154	445	269	1,807	379	2,252	5.94	204.7
52. Paul Thompson, Oklahoma	QB	SR	14	71	275	124	151	336	2,667	407	2,818	6.92	201.3
53. Rudy Carpenter, Arizona St.	QB	SO	13	84	296	227	69	332	2,523	416	2,592	6.23	199.4
54. Zac Champion, Louisiana Tech	QB	JR	13	68	311	223	88	364	2,466	432	2,554	5.91	196.5
55. Adam Tafralis, San Jose St.	QB	JR	13	89	363	133	230	276	2,284	365	2,514	6.89	193.4
56. John Stocco, Wisconsin	QB	SR	11	48	94	173	-79	268	2,185	316	2,106	6.66	191.5
57. Ryan Cubit, Western Mich.	QB	SR	11	34	57	117	-60	365	2,138	399	2,078	5.21	188.9
58. Will Proctor, Clemson	QB	SR	13	61	201	116	85	304	2,353	365	2,438	6.68	187.5
59. Chad Henne, Michigan	QB	JR	13	47	88	171	-83	328	2,508	375	2,425	6.47	186.5
60. Sam Hollenbach, Maryland	QB	SR	13	51	144	129	15	328	2,371	379	2,386	6.30	183.5
61. Steven Wichman, Idaho	QB	SR	12	52	178	145	33	319	2,158	371	2,191	5.91	182.6
62. Andy Schmitt, Eastern Mich.	QB	FR	9	107	540	79	461	213	1,182	320	1,643	5.13	182.6
63. Anthony Morelli, Penn St.	QB	JR	13	39	94	182	-88	386	2,424	425	2,336	5.50	179.7
64. Drew Weatherford, Florida St.	QB	SO	12	57	119	133	-14	318	2,154	375	2,140	5.71	178.3
65. Kinsmon Lancaster, La.-Monroe	QB	SO	12	111	464	131	333	250	1,789	361	2,122	5.88	176.8
66. Jeff Rowe, Nevada	QB	SR	12	93	414	207	207	266	1,907	359	2,114	5.89	176.2
67. Rocky Hinds, UNLV	QB	SO	12	49	142	191	-49	359	2,148	408	2,099	5.14	174.9
68. Isiah Williams, Illinois	QB	FR	12	154	770	194	576	261	1,489	415	2,065	4.98	172.1
69. Thaddeus Lewis, Duke	QB	FR	12	99	190	264	-74	340	2,134	439	2,060	4.69	171.7
70. Kerry Meier, Kansas	QB	FR	9	99	447	103	344	184	1,193	283	1,537	5.43	170.8
71. Reggie Ball, Georgia Tech	QB	SR	13	122	561	207	354	304	1,820	426	2,174	5.10	167.2
72. Phil Horvath, Northern Ill.	QB	SR	11	31	29	138	-109	269	1,932	300	1,823	6.08	165.7
73. Bernard Jackson, Colorado	QB	JR	12	155	884	207	677	219	1,298	374	1,975	5.28	164.6
74. Kyle Wright, Miami (Fla.)	QB	JR	10	49	140	161	-21	250	1,655	299	1,634	5.46	163.4
75. Sean Glennon, Virginia Tech	QB	SO	13	63	142	223	-81	302	2,191	365	2,110	5.78	162.3
76. Nate Davis, Ball St.	QB	FR	12	29	72	120	-48	244	1,975	273	1,927	7.06	160.6
77. Mike Teel, Rutgers	QB	SO	13	13	11	61	-50	296	2,135	309	2,085	6.75	160.4
78. Josh Freeman, Kansas St.	QB	FR	11	54	163	184	-21	270	1,780	324	1,759	5.43	159.9
79. Jerry Babb, La.-Lafayette	QB	SR	12	104	475	115	360	262	1,535	366	1,895	5.18	157.9
80. Patrick Cowan, UCLA	QB	SO	12	54	228	120	108	276	1,782	330	1,890	5.73	157.5
81. Dustin Grutza, Cincinnati	QB	SO	12	85	405	159	246	225	1,632	310	1,878	6.06	156.5
82. Josh Padrick, Florida Int'l	QB	SR	12	57	76	222	-146	388	2,014	445	1,868	4.20	155.7
83. Brandon Cox, Auburn	QB	JR	13	51	40	217	-177	271	2,198	322	2,021	6.28	155.5
84. Daniel Evans, North Carolina St.	QB	SO	12	37	87	100	-13	307	1,843	344	1,830	5.32	152.5
85. Bernard Morris, Marshall	QB	JR	11	82	451	127	324	188	1,346	270	1,670	6.19	151.8
86. Shaun Carney, Air Force	QB	JR	12	188	764	146	618	137	1,192	325	1,810	5.57	150.8
87. Matthew Stafford, Georgia	QB	FR	13	47	274	83	191	256	1,749	303	1,940	6.40	149.2
88. Garrett Wolfe, Northern Ill.	RB	SR	13	309	2,039	111	1,928	0	0	309	1,928	6.24	148.3
89. Clint Marks, Middle Tenn.	QB	SR	13	52	137	183	-46	283	1,917	335	1,871	5.59	143.9
90. Tom Brandstater, Fresno St.	QB	SO	11	32	149	63	86	268	1,490	300	1,576	5.25	143.3
91. Ian Johnson, Boise St.	RB	SO	12	276	1,755	41	1,714	0	0	276	1,714	6.21	142.8
92. Jeremy Young, Southern Miss.	QB	JR	14	81	354	130	224	281	1,769	362	1,993	5.51	142.4
93. Riley Skinner, Wake Forest	QB	FR	14	52	116	187	-71	260	2,051	312	1,980	6.35	141.4
94. Perry Patterson, Syracuse	QB	SR	12	82	188	362	-174	300	1,865	382	1,691	4.43	140.9
95. Jameel Sewell, Virginia	QB	FR	11	95	408	208	200	247	1,342	342	1,542	4.51	140.2
96. Ray Rice, Rutgers	RB	SO	13	335	1,831	37	1,794	1	0	336	1,794	5.34	138.0
97. Steven Moffett, UCF	QB	SR	10	31	82	89	-7	215	1,385	246	1,378	5.60	137.8
98. Joe Dailey, North Carolina	QB	JR	10	50	184	123	61	195	1,316	245	1,377	5.62	137.7
99. Corey Leonard, Arkansas St.	QB	FR	12	116	554	223	331	222	1,321	338	1,652	4.89	137.7
100. Chris Nelson, New Mexico	QB	SR	10	40	93	155	-62	216	1,435	256	1,373	5.36	137.3

Passing Yards Per Game

Rank, Player	Pos.	Cl.	G	Att	Comp	Int	CPct	Comp/ Gm	Yds/ Att	Yds/ Comp	TD	Yds	Yds/ Gm
1. Colt Brennan, Hawaii	QB	JR	14	559	406	12	72.63	29.0	9.93	13.67	58	5,549	396.3
2. Chase Holbrook, New Mexico St.	QB	SO	12	567	397	9	70.02	33.0	8.15	11.63	34	4,619	384.9
3. Graham Harrell, Texas Tech	QB	SO	13	616	412	11	66.88	31.6	7.39	11.06	38	4,555	350.3
4. John Beck, Brigham Young	QB	SR	12	417	289	8	69.30	24.0	9.32	13.44	32	3,885	323.7
5. Jordan Palmer, UTEP	QB	SR	12	429	282	14	65.73	23.5	8.38	12.75	26	3,595	299.5
6. Shawn Bell, Baylor	QB	SR	9	383	241	10	62.92	26.7	6.74	10.71	19	2,582	286.8
7. Curtis Painter, Purdue	QB	SO	14	530	315	19	59.43	22.5	7.52	12.65	22	3,985	284.6
8. Brian Brohm, Louisville	QB	JR	11	313	199	5	63.58	18.0	9.74	15.32	16	3,049	277.1
9. Kevin Kolb, Houston	QB	SR	14	432	292	4	67.59	20.8	8.82	13.04	30	3,809	272.0
10. Chase Daniel, Missouri	QB	SO	13	452	287	10	63.50	22.0	7.80	12.29	28	3,527	271.3
11. Andre Woodson, Kentucky	QB	JR	13	419	264	7	63.01	20.3	8.39	13.31	31	3,515	270.3
12. Brady Quinn, Notre Dame	QB	SR	13	467	289	7	61.88	22.2	7.34	11.85	37	3,426	263.5
13. John David Booty, Southern California	QB	JR	13	436	269	9	61.70	20.6	7.68	12.44	29	3,347	257.4
14. Erik Ainge, Tennessee	QB	JR	12	348	233	9	66.95	19.4	8.59	12.83	19	2,989	249.0
15. Matt Ryan, Boston College	QB	JR	12	426	263	10	61.74	21.9	6.91	11.19	15	2,942	245.1
16. Alex Brink, Washington St.	QB	JR	12	396	241	10	60.86	20.0	7.32	12.03	19	2,899	241.5
17. JaMarcus Russell, LSU	QB	JR	13	342	232	8	67.84	17.8	9.15	13.49	28	3,129	240.6
18. Tyler Palko, Pittsburgh	QB	SR	12	322	220	9	68.32	18.3	8.92	13.05	25	2,871	239.2
19. Drew Tate, Iowa	QB	SR	11	352	207	13	58.81	18.8	7.45	12.67	18	2,623	238.4
20. Lester Ricard, Tulane	QB	SR	12	400	229	10	57.25	19.0	6.99	12.21	18	2,795	232.9
21. Nate Longshore, California	QB	SO	13	377	227	13	60.21	17.4	8.01	13.31	24	3,021	232.3
22. Zac Taylor, Nebraska	QB	SR	14	391	233	8	59.59	16.6	8.18	13.72	26	3,197	228.3
23. Luke Getsy, Akron	QB	SR	12	380	199	11	52.37	16.5	7.01	13.38	18	2,662	221.8
24. Mike Kokal, Miami (Ohio)	QB	JR	11	355	208	8	58.59	18.9	6.81	11.63	14	2,419	219.9
25. Bryan Cupito, Minnesota	QB	SR	13	359	214	9	59.61	16.4	7.85	13.17	22	2,819	216.8
26. Dan LeFevour, Central Mich.	QB	FR	14	388	247	10	63.66	17.6	7.81	12.27	26	3,031	216.5
27. Matt Moore, Oregon St.	QB	SR	14	378	229	7	60.58	16.3	7.99	13.20	18	3,022	215.8
28. Brett Ratliff, Utah	QB	SR	13	391	228	9	58.31	17.5	7.15	12.26	23	2,796	215.0
29. James Pinkney, East Caro.	QB	SR	13	397	232	10	58.44	17.8	7.01	12.00	12	2,783	214.0
30. Martin Hankins, Memphis	QB	JR	12	377	226	13	59.95	18.8	6.76	11.28	18	2,550	212.5
31. Bret Meyer, Iowa St.	QB	JR	12	374	211	12	56.42	17.5	6.81	12.07	12	2,546	212.1
32. Chris Leak, Florida	QB	SR	14	365	232	13	63.56	16.5	8.06	12.68	23	2,942	210.1
33. Paul Smith, Tulsa	QB	JR	13	350	233	9	66.57	17.9	7.79	11.70	15	2,727	209.7
34. John Parker Wilson, Alabama	QB	SO	13	379	216	10	56.99	16.6	7.14	12.53	17	2,707	208.2
35. Caleb Hanie, Colorado St.	QB	JR	12	342	209	12	61.11	17.4	7.10	11.61	11	2,427	202.2
36. Kellen Lewis, Indiana	QB	FR	11	346	190	7	54.91	17.2	6.42	11.69	14	2,221	201.9
37. Jared Zabransky, Boise St.	QB	SR	13	288	191	8	66.32	14.6	8.98	13.54	23	2,587	199.0
38. John Stocco, Wisconsin	QB	SR	11	268	158	6	58.96	14.3	8.15	13.83	17	2,185	198.6
39. Matt Grothe, South Fla.	QB	FR	13	317	202	14	63.72	15.5	8.13	12.75	15	2,576	198.1
40. Colt McCoy, Texas	QB	FR	13	318	217	7	68.24	16.6	8.08	11.84	29	2,570	197.6
41. Troy Smith, Ohio St.	QB	SR	13	311	203	6	65.27	15.6	8.17	12.52	30	2,542	195.5
42. Ryan Cubit, Western Mich.	QB	SR	11	365	224	13	61.37	20.3	5.86	9.54	16	2,138	194.3
43. Rudy Carpenter, Arizona St.	QB	SO	13	332	184	14	55.42	14.1	7.60	13.71	23	2,523	194.0
44. Chad Henne, Michigan	QB	JR	13	328	203	8	61.89	15.6	7.65	12.35	22	2,508	192.9
45. Paul Thompson, Oklahoma	QB	SR	14	336	204	11	60.71	14.5	7.94	13.07	22	2,667	190.5
46. Zac Champion, Louisiana Tech	QB	JR	13	364	190	18	52.20	14.6	6.77	12.98	14	2,466	189.6
47. Anthony Morelli, Penn St.	QB	JR	13	386	208	8	53.89	16.0	6.28	11.65	11	2,424	186.4
48. Justin Willis, SMU	QB	FR	11	270	182	6	67.41	16.5	7.58	11.25	26	2,047	186.0
49. Omar Haugabook, Troy	QB	JR	13	393	241	17	61.32	18.5	6.11	9.96	21	2,401	184.6
50. Jeff Ballard, TCU	QB	SR	13	307	190	5	61.89	14.6	7.80	12.60	13	2,394	184.1
51. Sam Hollenbach, Maryland	QB	SR	13	328	203	11	61.89	15.6	7.23	11.68	15	2,371	182.3
52. Will Proctor, Clemson	QB	SR	13	304	183	11	60.20	14.0	7.74	12.86	16	2,353	181.0
53. Steven Wichman, Idaho	QB	SR	12	319	155	14	48.59	12.9	6.76	13.92	8	2,158	179.8
54. Drew Weatherford, Florida St.	QB	SO	12	318	177	11	55.66	14.7	6.77	12.17	12	2,154	179.5
55. Rocky Hinds, UNLV	QB	SO	12	359	194	13	54.04	16.1	5.98	11.07	8	2,148	179.0
56. Dennis Dixon, Oregon	QB	JR	12	322	197	14	61.18	16.4	6.66	10.88	12	2,143	178.5
57. Thaddeus Lewis, Duke	QB	FR	12	340	180	16	52.94	15.0	6.28	11.86	11	2,134	177.8
58. Stephen McGee, Texas A&M	QB	SO	13	313	194	2	61.98	14.9	7.33	11.83	12	2,295	176.5
59. Adam Tafralis, San Jose St.	QB	JR	13	276	181	7	65.58	13.9	8.28	12.62	21	2,284	175.6
60. Phil Horvath, Northern Ill.	QB	SR	11	269	157	9	58.36	14.2	7.18	12.31	11	1,932	175.6
61. Bobby Reid, Oklahoma St.	QB	SO	13	267	148	11	55.43	11.3	8.49	15.31	24	2,266	174.3
62. Chris Nickson, Vanderbilt	QB	SO	12	292	160	13	54.79	13.3	7.14	13.03	15	2,085	173.7
63. Brandon Cox, Auburn	QB	JR	13	271	163	9	60.15	12.5	8.11	13.48	14	2,198	169.0
64. Julian Edelman, Kent St.	QB	SO	11	242	134	11	55.37	12.1	7.68	13.87	10	1,859	169.0
65. Sean Glennon, Virginia Tech	QB	SO	13	302	170	11	56.29	13.0	7.25	12.89	11	2,191	168.5
66. Josh Padrick, Florida Int'l	QB	SR	12	388	213	14	54.90	17.7	5.19	9.46	5	2,014	167.8
67. Kyle Wright, Miami (Fla.)	QB	JR	10	250	152	7	60.80	15.2	6.62	10.89	8	1,655	165.5
68. Nate Davis, Ball St.	QB	FR	12	244	150	8	61.48	12.5	8.09	13.17	18	1,975	164.5
69. Drew Stanton, Michigan St.	QB	SR	11	269	164	10	60.97	14.9	6.72	11.02	12	1,807	164.2
70. Mike Teel, Rutgers	QB	SO	13	296	164	13	55.41	12.6	7.21	13.02	12	2,135	164.2
71. Josh Freeman, Kansas St.	QB	FR	11	270	140	15	51.85	12.7	6.59	12.71	6	1,780	161.8
72. Anthony Turner, Bowling Green	QB	SO	10	252	144	5	57.14	14.4	6.33	11.08	11	1,596	159.6
73. Jeff Rowe, Nevada	QB	SR	12	266	172	8	64.66	14.3	7.17	11.09	17	1,907	158.9
74. Perry Patterson, Syracuse	QB	SR	12	300	158	4	52.67	13.1	6.22	11.80	12	1,865	155.4
75. Daniel Evans, North Carolina St.	QB	SO	12	307	163	11	53.09	13.5	6.00	11.31	6	1,843	153.5
76. Kinsmon Lancaster, La.-Monroe	QB	SO	12	250	142	14	56.80	11.8	7.16	12.60	7	1,789	149.0
77. Patrick Cowan, UCLA	QB	SO	12	276	145	9	52.54	12.0	6.46	12.29	11	1,782	148.5
78. Clint Marks, Middle Tenn.	QB	SR	13	283	171	9	60.42	13.1	6.77	11.21	8	1,917	147.4
79. Riley Skinner, Wake Forest	QB	FR	14	260	171	5	65.77	12.2	7.89	11.99	9	2,051	146.5
80. Karsten Sween, Wyoming	QB	FR	9	212	128	8	60.38	14.2	6.15	10.19	9	1,304	144.8

Rank, Player	Pos.	Cl.	G	Att	Comp	Int	CPct	Comp/ Gm	Yds/ Att	Yds/ Comp	TD	Yds	Yds/ Gm
81. Chris Nelson, New Mexico	QB	SR	10	216	112	6	51.85	11.2	6.64	12.81	12	1,435	143.5
82. Reggie Ball, Georgia Tech	QB	SR	13	304	135	14	44.41	10.3	5.99	13.48	20	1,820	140.0
83. Steven Moffett, UCF	QB	SR	10	215	119	5	55.35	11.9	6.44	11.64	8	1,385	138.5
84. Adam DiMichele, Temple	QB	SO	11	220	135	12	61.36	12.2	6.90	11.24	10	1,518	138.0
85. Patrick White, West Virginia	QB	SO	12	179	118	7	65.92	9.8	9.25	14.03	13	1,655	137.9
86. Dustin Grutza, Cincinnati	QB	SO	12	225	137	13	60.89	11.4	7.25	11.91	9	1,632	136.0
87. Tom Brandstater, Fresno St.	QB	SO	11	268	146	14	54.48	13.2	5.56	10.21	13	1,490	135.4
88. Matthew Stafford, Georgia	QB	FR	13	256	135	13	52.73	10.3	6.83	12.96	7	1,749	134.5
89. Willie Tuitama, Arizona	QB	SO	10	211	118	6	55.92	11.8	6.33	11.31	7	1,335	133.5
90. Kerry Meier, Kansas	QB	FR	9	184	104	10	56.52	11.5	6.48	11.47	13	1,193	132.5
91. Joe Dailey, North Carolina	QB	JR	10	195	112	10	57.44	11.2	6.75	11.75	7	1,316	131.6
92. Andy Schmitt, Eastern Mich.	QB	FR	9	213	131	6	61.50	14.5	5.55	9.02	2	1,182	131.3
93. Jerry Babb, La.-Lafayette	QB	SR	12	262	140	14	53.44	11.6	5.86	10.96	9	1,535	127.9
94. Jeremy Young, Southern Miss.	QB	JR	14	281	161	6	57.30	11.5	6.30	10.99	12	1,769	126.3
95. Isiah Williams, Illinois	QB	FR	12	261	103	9	39.46	8.5	5.70	14.46	9	1,489	124.0
96. Bernard Morris, Marshall	QB	JR	11	188	116	12	61.70	10.5	7.16	11.60	8	1,346	122.3
97. Jameel Sewell, Virginia	QB	FR	11	247	143	6	57.89	13.0	5.43	9.38	5	1,342	122.0
98. Brent Schaeffer, Mississippi	QB	JR	12	244	115	10	47.13	9.5	5.91	12.54	9	1,442	120.1
99. Kyle Israel, UCF	QB	JR	12	166	108	5	65.06	9.0	8.55	13.15	6	1,420	118.3
100. Chris Williams, UAB	QB	SR	10	168	95	7	56.55	9.5	6.62	11.71	9	1,112	111.2

Total Passing Yards

Rank, Player	Pos.	Cl.	G	Att	Comp	Int	CPct	Comp/ Gm	Yds/ Att	Yds/ Comp	TD	Yds
1. Colt Brennan, Hawaii	QB	JR	14	559	406	12	72.63	29.0	9.93	13.67	58	5,549
2. Chase Holbrook, New Mexico St.	QB	SO	12	567	397	9	70.02	33.0	8.15	11.63	34	4,619
3. Graham Harrell, Texas Tech	QB	SO	13	616	412	11	66.88	31.6	7.39	11.06	38	4,555
4. Curtis Painter, Purdue	QB	SO	14	530	315	19	59.43	22.5	7.52	12.65	22	3,985
5. John Beck, Brigham Young	QB	SR	12	417	289	8	69.30	24.0	9.32	13.44	32	3,885
6. Kevin Kolb, Houston	QB	SR	14	432	292	4	67.59	20.8	8.82	13.04	30	3,809
7. Jordan Palmer, UTEP	QB	SR	12	429	282	14	65.73	23.5	8.38	12.75	26	3,595
8. Chase Daniel, Missouri	QB	SO	13	452	287	10	63.50	22.0	7.80	12.29	28	3,527
9. Andre Woodson, Kentucky	QB	JR	13	419	264	7	63.01	20.3	8.39	13.31	31	3,515
10. Brady Quinn, Notre Dame	QB	SR	13	467	289	7	61.88	22.2	7.34	11.85	37	3,426
11. John David Booty, Southern California	QB	JR	13	436	269	9	61.70	20.6	7.68	12.44	29	3,347
12. Zac Taylor, Nebraska	QB	SR	14	391	233	8	59.59	16.6	8.18	13.72	26	3,197
13. JaMarcus Russell, LSU	QB	JR	13	342	232	8	67.84	17.8	9.15	13.49	28	3,129
14. Brian Brohm, Louisville	QB	JR	11	313	199	5	63.58	18.0	9.74	15.32	16	3,049
15. Dan LeFevour, Central Mich.	QB	FR	14	388	247	10	63.66	17.6	7.81	12.27	26	3,031
16. Matt Moore, Oregon St.	QB	SR	14	378	229	7	60.58	16.3	7.99	13.20	18	3,022
17. Nate Longshore, California	QB	SO	13	377	227	13	60.21	17.4	8.01	13.31	24	3,021
18. Erik Ainge, Tennessee	QB	JR	12	348	233	9	66.95	19.4	8.59	12.83	19	2,989
19. Matt Ryan, Boston College	QB	JR	12	426	263	10	61.74	21.9	6.91	11.19	15	2,942
19. Chris Leak, Florida	QB	SR	14	365	232	13	63.56	16.5	8.06	12.68	23	2,942
21. Alex Brink, Washington St.	QB	JR	12	396	241	10	60.86	20.0	7.32	12.03	19	2,899
22. Tyler Palko, Pittsburgh	QB	SR	12	322	220	9	68.32	18.3	8.92	13.05	25	2,871
23. Bryan Cupito, Minnesota	QB	SR	13	359	214	9	59.61	16.4	7.85	13.17	22	2,819
24. Brett Ratliff, Utah	QB	SR	13	391	228	9	58.31	17.5	7.15	12.26	23	2,796
25. Lester Ricard, Tulane	QB	SR	12	400	229	10	57.25	19.0	6.99	12.21	18	2,795
26. James Pinkney, East Caro.	QB	SR	13	397	232	10	58.44	17.8	7.01	12.00	12	2,783
27. Paul Smith, Tulsa	QB	JR	13	350	233	9	66.57	17.9	7.79	11.70	15	2,727
28. John Parker Wilson, Alabama	QB	SO	13	379	216	10	56.99	16.6	7.14	12.53	17	2,707
29. Paul Thompson, Oklahoma	QB	SR	14	336	204	11	60.71	14.5	7.94	13.07	22	2,667
30. Luke Getsy, Akron	QB	SR	12	380	199	11	52.37	16.5	7.01	13.38	18	2,662
31. Drew Tate, Iowa	QB	SR	11	352	207	13	58.81	18.8	7.45	12.67	18	2,623
32. Jared Zabransky, Boise St.	QB	SR	13	288	191	8	66.32	14.6	8.98	13.54	23	2,587
33. Shawn Bell, Baylor	QB	SR	9	383	241	10	62.92	26.7	6.74	10.71	19	2,582
34. Matt Grothe, South Fla.	QB	FR	13	317	202	14	63.72	15.5	8.13	12.75	15	2,576
35. Colt McCoy, Texas	QB	FR	13	318	217	7	68.24	16.6	8.08	11.84	29	2,570
36. Martin Hankins, Memphis	QB	JR	12	377	226	13	59.95	18.8	6.76	11.28	18	2,550
37. Bret Meyer, Iowa St.	QB	JR	12	374	211	12	56.42	17.5	6.81	12.07	12	2,546
38. Troy Smith, Ohio St.	QB	SR	13	311	203	6	65.27	15.6	8.17	12.52	30	2,542
39. Rudy Carpenter, Arizona St.	QB	SO	13	332	184	14	55.42	14.1	7.60	13.71	23	2,523
40. Chad Henne, Michigan	QB	JR	13	328	203	8	61.89	15.6	7.65	12.35	22	2,508
41. Zac Champion, Louisiana Tech	QB	JR	13	364	190	18	52.20	14.6	6.77	12.98	14	2,466
42. Caleb Hanie, Colorado St.	QB	JR	12	342	209	12	61.11	17.4	7.10	11.61	11	2,427
43. Anthony Morelli, Penn St.	QB	JR	13	386	208	8	53.89	16.0	6.28	11.65	11	2,424
44. Mike Kokal, Miami (Ohio)	QB	JR	11	355	208	8	58.59	18.9	6.81	11.63	14	2,419
45. Omar Haugabook, Troy	QB	JR	13	393	241	17	61.32	18.5	6.11	9.96	21	2,401
46. Jeff Ballard, TCU	QB	SR	13	307	190	5	61.89	14.6	7.80	12.60	13	2,394
47. Sam Hollenbach, Maryland	QB	SR	13	328	203	11	61.89	15.6	7.23	11.68	15	2,371
48. Will Proctor, Clemson	QB	SR	13	304	183	11	60.20	14.0	7.74	12.86	16	2,353
49. Stephen McGee, Texas A&M	QB	SO	13	313	194	2	61.98	14.9	7.33	11.83	12	2,295
50. Adam Tafralis, San Jose St.	QB	JR	13	276	181	7	65.58	13.9	8.28	12.62	21	2,284
51. Bobby Reid, Oklahoma St.	QB	SO	13	267	148	11	55.43	11.3	8.49	15.31	24	2,266
52. Kellen Lewis, Indiana	QB	FR	11	346	190	7	54.91	17.2	6.42	11.69	14	2,221
53. Brandon Cox, Auburn	QB	JR	13	271	163	9	60.15	12.5	8.11	13.48	14	2,198
54. Sean Glennon, Virginia Tech	QB	SO	13	302	170	11	56.29	13.0	7.25	12.89	11	2,191
55. John Stocco, Wisconsin	QB	SR	11	268	158	6	58.96	14.3	8.15	13.83	17	2,185
56. Steven Wichman, Idaho	QB	SR	12	319	155	14	48.59	12.9	6.76	13.92	8	2,158
57. Drew Weatherford, Florida St.	QB	SO	12	318	177	11	55.66	14.7	6.77	12.17	12	2,154

Rank, Player	Pos.	Cl.	G	Att	Comp	Int	CPct	Comp/ Gm	Yds/ Att	Yds/ Comp	TD	Yds
58. Rocky Hinds, UNLV	QB	SO	12	359	194	13	54.04	16.1	5.98	11.07	8	2,148
59. Dennis Dixon, Oregon	QB	JR	12	322	197	14	61.18	16.4	6.66	10.88	12	2,143
60. Ryan Cubit, Western Mich.	QB	SR	11	365	224	13	61.37	20.3	5.86	9.54	16	2,138
61. Mike Teel, Rutgers	QB	SO	13	296	164	13	55.41	12.6	7.21	13.02	12	2,135
62. Thaddeus Lewis, Duke	QB	FR	12	340	180	16	52.94	15.0	6.28	11.86	11	2,134
63. Chris Nickson, Vanderbilt	QB	SO	12	292	160	13	54.79	13.3	7.14	13.03	15	2,085
64. Riley Skinner, Wake Forest	QB	FR	14	260	171	5	65.77	12.2	7.89	11.99	9	2,051
65. Justin Willis, SMU	QB	FR	11	270	182	6	67.41	16.5	7.58	11.25	26	2,047
66. Josh Padrick, Florida Int'l	QB	SR	12	388	213	14	54.90	17.7	5.19	9.46	5	2,014
67. Nate Davis, Ball St.	QB	FR	12	244	150	8	61.48	12.5	8.09	13.17	18	1,975
68. Phil Horvath, Northern Ill.	QB	SR	11	269	157	9	58.36	14.2	7.18	12.31	11	1,932
69. Clint Marks, Middle Tenn.	QB	SR	13	283	171	9	60.42	13.1	6.77	11.21	8	1,917
70. Jeff Rowe, Nevada	QB	SR	12	266	172	8	64.66	14.3	7.17	11.09	17	1,907
71. Perry Patterson, Syracuse	QB	SR	12	300	158	4	52.67	13.1	6.22	11.80	12	1,865
72. Julian Edelman, Kent St.	QB	SO	11	242	134	11	55.37	12.1	7.68	13.87	10	1,859
73. Daniel Evans, North Carolina St.	QB	SO	12	307	163	11	53.09	13.5	6.00	11.31	6	1,843
74. Reggie Ball, Georgia Tech	QB	SR	13	304	135	14	44.41	10.3	5.99	13.48	20	1,820
75. Drew Stanton, Michigan St.	QB	SR	11	269	164	10	60.97	14.9	6.72	11.02	12	1,807
76. Kinsmon Lancaster, La.-Monroe	QB	SO	12	250	142	14	56.80	11.8	7.16	12.60	7	1,789
77. Patrick Cowan, UCLA	QB	SO	12	276	145	9	52.54	12.0	6.46	12.29	11	1,782
78. Josh Freeman, Kansas St.	QB	FR	11	270	140	15	51.85	12.7	6.59	12.71	6	1,780
79. Jeremy Young, Southern Miss.	QB	JR	14	281	161	6	57.30	11.5	6.30	10.99	12	1,769
80. Matthew Stafford, Georgia	QB	FR	13	256	135	13	52.73	10.3	6.83	12.96	7	1,749
81. Patrick White, West Virginia	QB	SO	12	179	118	7	65.92	9.8	9.25	14.03	13	1,655
81. Kyle Wright, Miami (Fla.)	QB	JR	10	250	152	7	60.80	15.2	6.62	10.89	8	1,655
83. Dustin Grutza, Cincinnati	QB	SO	12	225	137	13	60.89	11.4	7.25	11.91	9	1,632
84. Anthony Turner, Bowling Green	QB	SO	10	252	144	5	57.14	14.4	6.33	11.08	11	1,596
85. Jerry Babb, La.-Lafayette	QB	SR	12	262	140	14	53.44	11.6	5.86	10.96	9	1,535
86. Adam DiMichele, Temple	QB	SO	11	220	135	12	61.36	12.2	6.90	11.24	10	1,518
87. Tom Brandstater, Fresno St.	QB	SO	11	268	146	14	54.48	13.2	5.56	10.21	13	1,490
88. Isiah Williams, Illinois	QB	FR	12	261	103	9	39.46	8.5	5.70	14.46	9	1,489
89. Brent Schaeffer, Mississippi	QB	JR	12	244	115	10	47.13	9.5	5.91	12.54	9	1,442
90. Chris Nelson, New Mexico	QB	SR	10	216	112	6	51.85	11.2	6.64	12.81	12	1,435
91. Kyle Israel, UCF	QB	JR	12	166	108	5	65.06	9.0	8.55	13.15	6	1,420
92. Steven Moffett, UCF	QB	SR	10	215	119	5	55.35	11.9	6.44	11.64	8	1,385
93. Austen Everson, Ohio	QB	SR	13	253	137	8	54.15	10.5	5.36	9.90	7	1,356
94. Bernard Morris, Marshall	QB	JR	11	188	116	12	61.70	10.5	7.16	11.60	8	1,346
95. Jameel Sewell, Virginia	QB	FR	11	247	143	6	57.89	13.0	5.43	9.38	5	1,342
96. Willie Tuitama, Arizona	QB	SO	10	211	118	6	55.92	11.8	6.33	11.31	7	1,335
97. Corey Leonard, Arkansas St.	QB	FR	12	222	109	8	49.10	9.0	5.95	12.12	8	1,321
98. Syvelle Newton, South Carolina	QB	SR	13	162	95	7	58.64	7.3	8.12	13.85	12	1,316
98. Joe Dailey, North Carolina	QB	JR	10	195	112	10	57.44	11.2	6.75	11.75	7	1,316
100. Karsten Sween, Wyoming	QB	FR	9	212	128	8	60.38	14.2	6.15	10.19	9	1,304

Pass Completions Per Game

Rank, Player	Pos	Cl.	G	Att	Comp	Int	CPct	Yds	Yds/ Att	Yds/ Comp	TD	Comp/ Gm
1. Chase Holbrook, New Mexico St.	QB	SO	12	567	397	9	70.02	4,619	8.15	11.63	34	33.08
2. Graham Harrell, Texas Tech	QB	SO	13	616	412	11	66.88	4,555	7.39	11.06	38	31.69
3. Colt Brennan, Hawaii	QB	JR	14	559	406	12	72.63	5,549	9.93	13.67	58	29.00
4. Shawn Bell, Baylor	QB	SR	9	383	241	10	62.92	2,582	6.74	10.71	19	26.78
5. John Beck, Brigham Young	QB	SR	12	417	289	8	69.30	3,885	9.32	13.44	32	24.08
6. Jordan Palmer, UTEP	QB	SR	12	429	282	14	65.73	3,595	8.38	12.75	26	23.50
7. Curtis Painter, Purdue	QB	SO	14	530	315	19	59.43	3,985	7.52	12.65	22	22.50
8. Brady Quinn, Notre Dame	QB	SR	13	467	289	7	61.88	3,426	7.34	11.85	37	22.23
9. Chase Daniel, Missouri	QB	SO	13	452	287	10	63.50	3,527	7.80	12.29	28	22.08
10. Matt Ryan, Boston College	QB	JR	12	426	263	10	61.74	2,942	6.91	11.19	15	21.92
11. Kevin Kolb, Houston	QB	SR	14	432	292	4	67.59	3,809	8.82	13.04	30	20.86
12. John David Booty, Southern California	QB	JR	13	436	269	9	61.70	3,347	7.68	12.44	29	20.69
13. Ryan Cubit, Western Mich.	QB	SR	11	365	224	13	61.37	2,138	5.86	9.54	16	20.36
14. Andre Woodson, Kentucky	QB	JR	13	419	264	7	63.01	3,515	8.39	13.31	31	20.31
15. Alex Brink, Washington St.	QB	JR	12	396	241	10	60.86	2,899	7.32	12.03	19	20.08
16. Erik Ainge, Tennessee	QB	JR	12	348	233	9	66.95	2,989	8.59	12.83	19	19.42
17. Lester Ricard, Tulane	QB	SR	12	400	229	10	57.25	2,795	6.99	12.21	18	19.08
18. Mike Kokal, Miami (Ohio)	QB	JR	11	355	208	8	58.59	2,419	6.81	11.63	14	18.91
19. Martin Hankins, Memphis	QB	JR	12	377	226	13	59.95	2,550	6.76	11.28	18	18.83
20. Drew Tate, Iowa	QB	SR	11	352	207	13	58.81	2,623	7.45	12.67	18	18.82
21. Omar Haugabook, Troy	QB	JR	13	393	241	17	61.32	2,401	6.11	9.96	21	18.54
22. Tyler Palko, Pittsburgh	QB	SR	12	322	220	9	68.32	2,871	8.92	13.05	25	18.33
23. Brian Brohm, Louisville	QB	JR	11	313	199	5	63.58	3,049	9.74	15.32	16	18.09
24. Paul Smith, Tulsa	QB	JR	13	350	233	9	66.57	2,727	7.79	11.70	15	17.92
25. JaMarcus Russell, LSU	QB	JR	13	342	232	8	67.84	3,129	9.15	13.49	28	17.85
25. James Pinkney, East Caro.	QB	SR	13	397	232	10	58.44	2,783	7.01	12.00	12	17.85
27. Josh Padrick, Florida Int'l	QB	SR	12	388	213	14	54.90	2,014	5.19	9.46	5	17.75
28. Dan LeFevour, Central Mich.	QB	FR	14	388	247	10	63.66	3,031	7.81	12.27	26	17.64
29. Bret Meyer, Iowa St.	QB	JR	12	374	211	12	56.42	2,546	6.81	12.07	12	17.58
30. Brett Ratliff, Utah	QB	SR	13	391	228	9	58.31	2,796	7.15	12.26	23	17.54
31. Nate Longshore, California	QB	SO	13	377	227	13	60.21	3,021	8.01	13.31	24	17.46
32. Caleb Hanie, Colorado St.	QB	JR	12	342	209	12	61.11	2,427	7.10	11.61	11	17.42
33. Kellen Lewis, Indiana	QB	FR	11	346	190	7	54.91	2,221	6.42	11.69	14	17.27

Rank, Player	Pos	Cl.	G	Att	Comp	Int	CPct	Yds	Yds/ Att	Yds/ Comp	TD	Comp/ Gm
34. Colt McCoy, Texas	QB	FR	13	318	217	7	68.24	2,570	8.08	11.84	29	16.69
35. Zac Taylor, Nebraska	QB	SR	14	391	233	8	59.59	3,197	8.18	13.72	26	16.64
36. John Parker Wilson, Alabama	QB	SO	13	379	216	10	56.99	2,707	7.14	12.53	17	16.62
37. Luke Getsy, Akron	QB	SR	12	380	199	11	52.37	2,662	7.01	13.38	18	16.58
38. Chris Leak, Florida	QB	SR	14	365	232	13	63.56	2,942	8.06	12.68	23	16.57
39. Justin Willis, SMU	QB	FR	11	270	182	6	67.41	2,047	7.58	11.25	26	16.55
40. Bryan Cupito, Minnesota	QB	SR	13	359	214	9	59.61	2,819	7.85	13.17	22	16.46
41. Dennis Dixon, Oregon	QB	JR	12	322	197	14	61.18	2,143	6.66	10.88	12	16.42
42. Matt Moore, Oregon St.	QB	SR	14	378	229	7	60.58	3,022	7.99	13.20	18	16.36
43. Rocky Hinds, UNLV	QB	SO	12	359	194	13	54.04	2,148	5.98	11.07	8	16.17
44. Anthony Morelli, Penn St.	QB	JR	13	386	208	8	53.89	2,424	6.28	11.65	11	16.00
45. Troy Smith, Ohio St.	QB	SR	13	311	203	6	65.27	2,542	8.17	12.52	30	15.62
45. Chad Henne, Michigan	QB	JR	13	328	203	8	61.89	2,508	7.65	12.35	22	15.62
45. Sam Hollenbach, Maryland	QB	SR	13	328	203	11	61.89	2,371	7.23	11.68	15	15.62
48. Matt Grothe, South Fla.	QB	FR	13	317	202	14	63.72	2,576	8.13	12.75	15	15.54
49. Kyle Wright, Miami (Fla.)	QB	JR	10	250	152	7	60.80	1,655	6.62	10.89	8	15.20
50. Thaddeus Lewis, Duke	QB	FR	12	340	180	16	52.94	2,134	6.28	11.86	11	15.00
51. Stephen McGee, Texas A&M	QB	SO	13	313	194	2	61.98	2,295	7.33	11.83	12	14.92
52. Drew Stanton, Michigan St.	QB	SR	11	269	164	10	60.97	1,807	6.72	11.02	12	14.91
53. Drew Weatherford, Florida St.	QB	SO	12	318	177	11	55.66	2,154	6.77	12.17	12	14.75
54. Jared Zabransky, Boise St.	QB	SR	13	288	191	8	66.32	2,587	8.98	13.54	23	14.69
55. Jeff Ballard, TCU	QB	SR	13	307	190	5	61.89	2,394	7.80	12.60	13	14.62
55. Zac Champion, Louisiana Tech	QB	JR	13	364	190	18	52.20	2,466	6.77	12.98	14	14.62
57. Paul Thompson, Oklahoma	QB	SR	14	336	204	11	60.71	2,667	7.94	13.07	22	14.57
58. Andy Schmitt, Eastern Mich.	QB	FR	9	213	131	6	61.50	1,182	5.55	9.02	2	14.56
59. Anthony Turner, Bowling Green	QB	SO	10	252	144	5	57.14	1,596	6.33	11.08	11	14.40
60. John Stocco, Wisconsin	QB	SR	11	268	158	6	58.96	2,185	8.15	13.83	17	14.36
61. Jeff Rowe, Nevada	QB	SR	12	266	172	8	64.66	1,907	7.17	11.09	17	14.33
62. Phil Horvath, Northern Ill.	QB	SR	11	269	157	9	58.36	1,932	7.18	12.31	11	14.27
63. Karsten Sween, Wyoming	QB	FR	9	212	128	8	60.38	1,304	6.15	10.19	9	14.22
64. Rudy Carpenter, Arizona St.	QB	SO	13	332	184	14	55.42	2,523	7.60	13.71	23	14.15
65. Will Proctor, Clemson	QB	SR	13	304	183	11	60.20	2,353	7.74	12.86	16	14.08
66. Adam Tafralis, San Jose St.	QB	JR	13	276	181	7	65.58	2,284	8.28	12.62	21	13.92
67. Daniel Evans, North Carolina St.	QB	SO	12	307	163	11	53.09	1,843	6.00	11.31	6	13.58
68. Chris Nickson, Vanderbilt	QB	SO	12	292	160	13	54.79	2,085	7.14	13.03	15	13.33
69. Tom Brandstater, Fresno St.	QB	SO	11	268	146	14	54.48	1,490	5.56	10.21	13	13.27
70. Perry Patterson, Syracuse	QB	SR	12	300	158	4	52.67	1,865	6.22	11.80	12	13.17
71. Clint Marks, Middle Tenn.	QB	SR	13	283	171	9	60.42	1,917	6.77	11.21	8	13.15
72. Sean Glennon, Virginia Tech	QB	SO	13	302	170	11	56.29	2,191	7.25	12.89	11	13.08
73. Jameel Sewell, Virginia	QB	FR	11	247	143	6	57.89	1,342	5.43	9.38	5	13.00
74. Steven Wichman, Idaho	QB	SR	12	319	155	14	48.59	2,158	6.76	13.92	8	12.92
75. Josh Freeman, Kansas St.	QB	FR	11	270	140	15	51.85	1,780	6.59	12.71	6	12.73
76. Mike Teel, Rutgers	QB	SO	13	296	164	13	55.41	2,135	7.21	13.02	12	12.62
77. Brandon Cox, Auburn	QB	JR	13	271	163	9	60.15	2,198	8.11	13.48	14	12.54
78. Nate Davis, Ball St.	QB	FR	12	244	150	8	61.48	1,975	8.09	13.17	18	12.50
79. Adam DiMichele, Temple	QB	SO	11	220	135	12	61.36	1,518	6.90	11.24	10	12.27
80. Riley Skinner, Wake Forest	QB	FR	14	260	171	5	65.77	2,051	7.89	11.99	9	12.21
81. Julian Edelman, Kent St.	QB	SO	11	242	134	11	55.37	1,859	7.68	13.87	10	12.18
82. Patrick Cowan, UCLA	QB	SO	12	276	145	9	52.54	1,782	6.46	12.29	11	12.08
83. Steven Moffett, UCF	QB	SR	10	215	119	5	55.35	1,385	6.44	11.64	8	11.90
84. Kinsmon Lancaster, La.-Monroe	QB	SO	12	250	142	14	56.80	1,789	7.16	12.60	7	11.83
85. Willie Tuitama, Arizona	QB	SO	10	211	118	6	55.92	1,335	6.33	11.31	7	11.80
86. Jerry Babb, La.-Lafayette	QB	SR	12	262	140	14	53.44	1,535	5.86	10.96	9	11.67
87. Kerry Meier, Kansas	QB	FR	9	184	104	10	56.52	1,193	6.48	11.47	13	11.56
88. Jeremy Young, Southern Miss.	QB	JR	14	281	161	6	57.30	1,769	6.30	10.99	12	11.50
89. Dustin Grutza, Cincinnati	QB	SO	12	225	137	13	60.89	1,632	7.25	11.91	9	11.42
90. Bobby Reid, Oklahoma St.	QB	SO	13	267	148	11	55.43	2,266	8.49	15.31	24	11.38
91. Aaron Opelt, Toledo	QB	FR	9	188	102	5	54.26	875	4.65	8.58	6	11.33
92. Chris Nelson, New Mexico	QB	SR	10	216	112	6	51.85	1,435	6.64	12.81	12	11.20
92. Joe Dailey, North Carolina	QB	JR	10	195	112	10	57.44	1,316	6.75	11.75	7	11.20
94. David Pevoto, Army	QB	JR	10	193	106	14	54.92	1,012	5.24	9.55	6	10.60
95. Bernard Morris, Marshall	QB	JR	11	188	116	12	61.70	1,346	7.16	11.60	8	10.55
96. Austen Everson, Ohio	QB	SR	13	253	137	8	54.15	1,356	5.36	9.90	7	10.54
97. Matthew Stafford, Georgia	QB	FR	13	256	135	13	52.73	1,749	6.83	12.96	7	10.38
97. Reggie Ball, Georgia Tech	QB	SR	13	304	135	14	44.41	1,820	5.99	13.48	20	10.38
99. Patrick White, West Virginia	QB	SO	12	179	118	7	65.92	1,655	9.25	14.03	13	9.83
100. Brent Schaeffer, Mississippi	QB	JR	12	244	115	10	47.13	1,442	5.91	12.54	9	9.58

Receptions Per Game

Rank, Player	Pos	Cl.	G	Rec	Yds	TD	Rec/ Gm	Yds/ Rec	Yds/ Gm
1. Chris Williams, New Mexico St.	WR	SO	12	92	1,415	12	7.67	15.38	117.92
2. Ryne Robinson, Miami (Ohio)	WR	SR	12	91	1,178	8	7.58	12.95	98.17
3. Mike Walker, UCF	WR	SR	12	90	1,178	7	7.50	13.09	98.17
4. Robert Johnson, Texas Tech	WR	SR	12	89	871	11	7.42	9.79	72.58
5. Jarett Dillard, Rice	WR	SO	13	91	1,247	21	7.00	13.70	95.92
5. Joel Filani, Texas Tech	WR	SR	13	91	1,300	13	7.00	14.29	100.00
7. Davone Bess, Hawaii	WR	SO	14	96	1,220	15	6.86	12.71	87.14
8. Earl Bennett, Vanderbilt	WR	SO	12	82	1,146	6	6.83	13.98	95.50
8. Johnnie Lee Higgins Jr., UTEP	WR	SR	12	82	1,319	13	6.83	16.09	109.92
10. Chandler Williams, Florida Int'l	WR	SR	10	67	664	1	6.70	9.91	66.40
11. Dorien Bryant, Purdue	WR	JR	14	87	1,068	6	6.21	12.28	76.29
12. Eric Deslauriers, Eastern Mich.	WR	SR	12	74	898	5	6.17	12.14	74.83
13. Jeff Samardzija, Notre Dame	WR	SR	13	78	1,017	12	6.00	13.04	78.23
14. Keenan Burton, Kentucky	WR	JR	13	77	1,036	12	5.92	13.45	79.69
15. A.J. Harris, New Mexico St.	WR	SO	12	71	789	7	5.92	11.11	65.75
16. Dwayne Jarrett, Southern California	WR	JR	12	70	1,015	12	5.83	14.50	84.58
17. Shannon Woods, Texas Tech	RB	SO	13	75	572	2	5.77	7.63	44.00
18. Vincent Marshall, Houston	WR	SR	14	80	979	8	5.71	12.24	69.93
19. Jaison Williams, Oregon	WR	SO	12	68	984	6	5.67	14.47	82.00
20. Aundrae Allison, East Caro.	WR	SR	11	62	708	4	5.64	11.42	64.36
21. Casey Flair, UNLV	WR	SO	12	67	816	4	5.58	12.18	68.00
22. Sidney Rice, South Carolina	WR	SO	13	72	1,090	10	5.54	15.14	83.85
23. Corey Partridge, Bowling Green	WR	SO	10	55	658	3	5.50	11.96	65.80
24. Steve Smith, Southern California	WR	SR	13	71	1,083	9	5.46	15.25	83.31
24. Robert Meachem, Tennessee	WR	JR	13	71	1,298	11	5.46	18.28	99.85
26. Calvin Johnson, Georgia Tech	WR	JR	14	76	1,202	15	5.43	15.82	85.86
27. Harry Douglas, Louisville	WR	JR	13	70	1,265	6	5.38	18.07	97.31
27. James Jones, San Jose St.	WR	SR	13	70	893	10	5.38	12.76	68.69
29. Kerry Reed, Michigan St.	WR	SR	12	64	775	5	5.33	12.11	64.58
30. Sammie Stroughter, Oregon St.	WR	JR	14	74	1,293	5	5.29	17.47	92.36
31. Gary Banks, Troy	WR	JR	13	68	603	8	5.23	8.87	46.38
32. Bryan Anderson, Central Mich.	WR	FR	14	73	867	5	5.21	11.88	61.93
33. Johnny Quinn, North Texas	WR	SR	11	57	633	4	5.18	11.11	57.55
34. DJ Hall, Alabama	WR	JR	12	62	1,056	5	5.17	17.03	88.00
35. Nate Ilaoa, Hawaii	RB	SR	13	67	837	5	5.15	12.49	64.38
35. Rhema McKnight, Notre Dame	WR	SR	13	67	907	15	5.15	13.54	69.77
37. Jason Rivers, Hawaii	WR	JR	14	72	1,178	10	5.14	16.36	84.14
38. James Hardy, Indiana	WR	SO	10	51	722	10	5.10	14.16	72.20
39. Chansi Stuckey, Clemson	WR	SR	10	50	700	3	5.00	14.00	70.00
40. Dwayne Bowe, LSU	WR	SR	13	65	990	12	5.00	15.23	76.15
41. Michael Ford, Wyoming	WR	JR	12	60	674	4	5.00	11.23	56.17
41. Michael Bumpus, Washington St.	WR	JR	12	60	558	1	5.00	9.30	46.50
43. Travis Brown, New Mexico	WR	JR	13	64	867	4	4.92	13.55	66.69
44. Dominique Zeigler, Baylor	WR	SR	11	54	741	3	4.91	13.72	67.36
45. Johnny Walker, Colorado St.	WR	JR	12	58	586	0	4.83	10.10	48.83
46. Curtis Brown, Brigham Young	RB	SR	13	62	566	3	4.77	9.13	43.54
47. Derek Kinder, Pittsburgh	WR	JR	12	57	847	6	4.75	14.86	70.58
48. Samuel Smith, Florida Int'l	TE	SR	10	47	458	2	4.70	9.74	45.80
49. Travis Beckum, Wisconsin	TE	SO	13	61	903	5	4.69	14.80	69.46
49. Jamarko Simmons, Western Mich.	RB	SO	13	61	668	2	4.69	10.95	51.38
51. Craig Davis, LSU	WR	SR	12	56	836	4	4.67	14.93	69.67
52. Derrek Richards, Utah	WR	JR	13	60	717	6	4.62	11.95	55.15
52. Adarius Bowman, Oklahoma St.	WR	JR	13	60	1,181	12	4.62	19.68	90.85
54. Syndric Steptoe, Arizona	WR	SR	12	55	568	2	4.58	10.33	47.33
54. Ryan Wolfe, UNLV	WR	FR	12	55	911	5	4.58	16.56	75.92
56. Ted Ginn Jr., Ohio St.	WR	JR	13	59	781	9	4.54	13.24	60.08
56. Logan Payne, Minnesota	WR	SR	13	59	804	9	4.54	13.63	61.85
56. Early Doucet, LSU	WR	JR	13	59	772	8	4.54	13.08	59.38
56. DeSean Jackson, California	WR	SO	13	59	1,060	9	4.54	17.97	81.54
60. Chris Hopkins, Toledo	TE	SR	12	54	565	7	4.50	10.46	47.08
61. Mario Urrutia, Louisville	WR	SO	13	58	973	6	4.46	16.78	74.85
61. Steve Breaston, Michigan	WR	SR	13	58	670	2	4.46	11.55	51.54
61. Idris Moss, Tulsa	WR	SR	13	58	803	1	4.46	13.84	61.77
61. Chase Coffman, Missouri	TE	SO	13	58	638	9	4.46	11.00	49.08
61. Jonny Harline, Brigham Young	TE	SR	13	58	935	12	4.46	16.12	71.92
66. Malcolm Kelly, Oklahoma	WR	SO	14	62	993	10	4.43	16.02	70.93
67. Derek Dubois, New Mexico St.	WR	SO	12	53	800	7	4.42	15.09	66.67
67. Trent Shelton, Baylor	WR	SR	12	53	802	8	4.42	15.13	66.83
69. Matt rannon, Michigan St.	WR	SR	10	44	518	3	4.40	11.77	51.80
70. Britt Davis, Northern Ill.	WR	SO	13	57	731	3	4.38	12.82	56.23
71. William Franklin, Missouri	WR	JR	11	48	829	6	4.36	17.27	75.36
72. Kevin Ogletree, Virginia	WR	SO	12	52	582	4	4.33	11.19	48.50
72. Jeremy Trimble, Army	WR	JR	12	52	534	2	4.33	10.27	44.50
72. Dante Love, Ball St.	WR	SO	12	52	735	4	4.33	14.13	61.25
75. Caleb Spencer, Nevada	WR	SR	13	56	570	2	4.31	10.18	43.85
75. Darius Walker, Notre Dame	RB	JR	13	56	391	1	4.31	6.98	30.08
77. Dallas Baker, Florida	WR	SR	14	60	920	10	4.29	15.33	65.71
78. Matt Spaeth, Minnesota	TE	SR	11	47	564	4	4.27	12.00	51.27
78. Brian Hernandez, Utah	WR	JR	11	47	424	1	4.27	9.02	38.55
78. John Carlson, Notre Dame	TE	SR	11	47	634	4	4.27	13.49	57.64

Rank, Player	Pos	Cl.	G	Rec	Yds	TD	Rec/ Gm	Yds/ Rec	Yds/ Gm
81. Damarcus Davis, Tulane	WR	SR	12	51	607	4	4.25	11.90	50.58
82. Sonny Shackelford, Washington	WR	SR	12	50	666	7	4.17	13.32	55.50
82. Nick Cleaver, New Mexico St.	TE	JR	12	50	684	4	4.17	13.68	57.00
82. Michael Thomas, Arizona	WR	SO	12	50	597	2	4.17	11.94	49.75
85. Courtney Taylor, Auburn	WR	SR	13	54	704	2	4.15	13.04	54.15
86. Greg Orton, Purdue	WR	SO	14	58	790	5	4.14	13.62	56.43
87. Jason Hill, Washington St.	WR	SR	10	41	600	7	4.10	14.63	60.00
88. Trumaine Riley, Eastern Mich.	WR	SR	11	45	364	0	4.09	8.09	33.09
89. Brandon Gibson, Washington St.	WR	SO	12	49	731	4	4.08	14.92	60.92
90. Marcus Smith, New Mexico	WR	JR	13	53	859	9	4.08	16.21	66.08
90. Martin Rucker, Missouri	TE	JR	13	53	511	5	4.08	9.64	39.31
92. Andre Caldwell, Florida	WR	JR	14	57	577	6	4.07	10.12	41.21
92. Donnie Avery, Houston	WR	JR	14	57	852	5	4.07	14.95	60.86
94. Dustin Keller, Purdue	TE	JR	14	56	771	4	4.00	13.77	55.07
95. Preston Brown, Tulane	WR	SR	11	44	467	2	4.00	10.61	42.45
96. Quentily Harmon, TCU	WR	SR	13	52	791	3	4.00	15.21	60.85
97. Damon Morton, Colorado St.	WR	JR	12	48	722	4	4.00	15.04	60.17
98. John Broussard, San Jose St.	WR	SR	13	52	844	7	4.00	16.23	64.92
98. Ontario Sneed, Central Mich.	RB	SO	13	52	415	7	4.00	7.98	31.92
100. Keith Brown, Alabama	WR	JR	11	44	590	3	4.00	13.41	53.64

Receiving Yards Per Game

Rank, Player	Pos	Cl.	G	Rec	Yds	TD	Rec/ Gm	Yds/ Rec	Yds/ Gm
1. Chris Williams, New Mexico St.	WR	SO	12	92	1,415	12	7.67	15.38	117.92
2. Johnnie Lee Higgins Jr., UTEP	WR	SR	12	82	1,319	13	6.83	16.09	109.92
3. Joel Filani, Texas Tech	WR	SR	13	91	1,300	13	7.00	14.29	100.00
4. Robert Meachem, Tennessee	WR	JR	13	71	1,298	11	5.46	18.28	99.85
5. Ryne Robinson, Miami (Ohio)	WR	SR	12	91	1,178	8	7.58	12.95	98.17
5. Mike Walker, UCF	WR	SR	12	90	1,178	7	7.50	13.09	98.17
7. Harry Douglas, Louisville	WR	JR	13	70	1,265	6	5.38	18.07	97.31
8. Jarett Dillard, Rice	WR	SO	13	91	1,247	21	7.00	13.70	95.92
9. Earl Bennett, Vanderbilt	WR	SO	12	82	1,146	6	6.83	13.98	95.50
10. Sammie Stroughter, Oregon St.	WR	JR	14	74	1,293	5	5.29	17.47	92.36
11. Adarius Bowman, Oklahoma St.	WR	JR	13	60	1,181	12	4.62	19.68	90.85
12. DJ Hall, Alabama	WR	JR	12	62	1,056	5	5.17	17.03	88.00
13. Davone Bess, Hawaii	WR	SO	14	96	1,220	15	6.86	12.71	87.14
14. Calvin Johnson, Georgia Tech	WR	JR	14	76	1,202	15	5.43	15.82	85.86
15. Dwayne Jarrett, Southern California	WR	JR	12	70	1,015	12	5.83	14.50	84.58
16. Jason Rivers, Hawaii	WR	JR	14	72	1,178	10	5.14	16.36	84.14
17. Sidney Rice, South Carolina	WR	SO	13	72	1,090	10	5.54	15.14	83.85
18. Steve Smith, Southern California	WR	SR	13	71	1,083	9	5.46	15.25	83.31
19. Jaison Williams, Oregon	WR	SO	12	68	984	6	5.67	14.47	82.00
20. DeSean Jackson, California	WR	SO	13	59	1,060	9	4.54	17.97	81.54
21. Keenan Burton, Kentucky	WR	JR	13	77	1,036	12	5.92	13.45	79.69
22. Jeff Samardzija, Notre Dame	WR	SR	13	78	1,017	12	6.00	13.04	78.23
23. Dorien Bryant, Purdue	WR	JR	14	87	1,068	6	6.21	12.28	76.29
24. David Harvey, Akron	WR	FR	12	43	914	10	3.58	21.26	76.17
25. Dwayne Bowe, LSU	WR	SR	13	65	990	12	5.00	15.23	76.15
26. Ryan Wolfe, UNLV	WR	FR	12	55	911	5	4.58	16.56	75.92
27. William Franklin, Missouri	WR	JR	11	48	829	6	4.36	17.27	75.36
28. Mario Urrutia, Louisville	WR	SO	13	58	973	6	4.46	16.78	74.85
29. Eric Deslauriers, Eastern Mich.	WR	SR	12	74	898	5	6.17	12.14	74.83
30. Robert Johnson, Texas Tech	WR	SR	12	89	871	11	7.42	9.79	72.58
31. James Hardy, Indiana	WR	SO	10	51	722	10	5.10	14.16	72.20
32. Jonny Harline, Brigham Young	TE	SR	13	58	935	12	4.46	16.12	71.92
33. Malcolm Kelly, Oklahoma	WR	SO	14	62	993	10	4.43	16.02	70.93
34. Tony Burks, Mississippi St.	WR	JR	12	35	850	5	2.92	24.29	70.83
35. Derek Kinder, Pittsburgh	WR	JR	12	57	847	6	4.75	14.86	70.58
36. Mario Manningham, Michigan	WR	SO	10	38	703	9	3.80	18.50	70.30
37. Chansi Stuckey, Clemson	WR	SR	10	50	700	3	5.00	14.00	70.00
38. Vincent Marshall, Houston	WR	SR	14	80	979	8	5.71	12.24	69.93
39. Rhema McKnight, Notre Dame	WR	SR	13	67	907	15	5.15	13.54	69.77
40. Craig Davis, LSU	WR	SR	12	56	836	4	4.67	14.93	69.67
41. Travis Beckum, Wisconsin	TE	SO	13	61	903	5	4.69	14.80	69.46
42. Marcus Monk, Arkansas	WR	JR	14	50	962	11	3.57	19.24	68.71
43. James Jones, San Jose St.	WR	SR	13	70	893	10	5.38	12.76	68.69
44. Casey Flair, UNLV	WR	SO	12	67	816	4	5.58	12.18	68.00
45. Kenny McKinley, South Carolina	WR	SO	13	51	880	5	3.92	17.25	67.69
46. Dominique Zeigler, Baylor	WR	SR	11	54	741	3	4.91	13.72	67.36
47. Najah Pruden, Kent St.	WR	SR	12	39	808	6	3.25	20.72	67.33
48. Trent Shelton, Baylor	WR	SR	12	53	802	8	4.42	15.13	66.83
49. Travis Brown, New Mexico	WR	JR	13	64	867	4	4.92	13.55	66.69
50. Derek Dubois, New Mexico St.	WR	SO	12	53	800	7	4.42	15.09	66.67
51. Chandler Williams, Florida Int'l	WR	SR	10	67	664	1	6.70	9.91	66.40
52. LaGregory Sapp, La.-Monroe	WR	SO	12	43	796	3	3.58	18.51	66.33
53. Marcus Smith, New Mexico	WR	JR	13	53	859	9	4.08	16.21	66.08
54. Corey Partridge, Bowling Green	WR	SO	10	55	658	3	5.50	11.96	65.80
55. A.J. Harris, New Mexico St.	WR	SO	12	71	789	7	5.92	11.11	65.75
56. Dallas Baker, Florida	WR	SR	14	60	920	10	4.29	15.33	65.71
57. John Broussard, San Jose St.	WR	SR	13	52	844	7	4.00	16.23	64.92

Rank, Player	Pos	Cl.	G	Rec	Yds	TD	Rec/ Gm	Yds/ Rec	Yds/ Gm
58. Kerry Reed, Michigan St.	WR	SR	12	64	775	5	5.33	12.11	64.58
59. Nate Ilaoa, Hawaii	RB	SR	13	67	837	5	5.15	12.49	64.38
60. Aundrae Allison, East Caro.	WR	SR	11	62	708	4	5.64	11.42	64.36
61. Dicky Lyons, Kentucky	WR	SO	13	50	822	9	3.85	16.44	63.23
62. Bryan Anderson, Central Mich.	WR	FR	14	73	867	5	5.21	11.88	61.93
63. Logan Payne, Minnesota	WR	SR	13	59	804	9	4.54	13.63	61.85
64. Idris Moss, Tulsa	WR	SR	13	58	803	1	4.46	13.84	61.77
65. Darius Hill, Ball St.	TE	JR	12	42	741	10	3.50	17.64	61.75
66. Limas Sweed, Texas	WR	JR	13	46	801	12	3.54	17.41	61.62
67. Dante Love, Ball St.	WR	SO	12	52	735	4	4.33	14.13	61.25
68. Brandon Gibson, Washington St.	WR	SO	12	49	731	4	4.08	14.92	60.92
69. Donnie Avery, Houston	WR	JR	14	57	852	5	4.07	14.95	60.86
70. Quentily Harmon, TCU	WR	SR	13	52	791	3	4.00	15.21	60.85
71. Jabari Arthur, Akron	WR	JR	12	45	730	4	3.75	16.22	60.83
72. Andy Brodell, Iowa	WR	SO	12	39	724	5	3.25	18.56	60.33
73. Damon Morton, Colorado St.	WR	JR	12	48	722	4	4.00	15.04	60.17
74. Ted Ginn Jr., Ohio St.	WR	JR	13	59	781	9	4.54	13.24	60.08
75. Hakeem Nicks, North Carolina	WR	FR	11	39	660	4	3.55	16.92	60.00
75. Jason Hill, Washington St.	WR	SR	10	41	600	7	4.10	14.63	60.00
77. Willie Edwards, UAB	WR	JR	12	39	719	2	3.25	18.44	59.92
78. Early Doucet, LSU	WR	JR	13	59	772	8	4.54	13.08	59.38
79. Eron Riley, Duke	WR	SO	11	32	643	3	2.91	20.09	58.45
80. Damien Linson, Central Mich.	WR	SR	14	55	812	5	3.93	14.76	58.00
81. John Carlson, Notre Dame	TE	SR	11	47	634	4	4.27	13.49	57.64
82. Johnny Quinn, North Texas	WR	SR	11	57	633	4	5.18	11.11	57.55
83. Terry Moss, Ball St.	WR	SR	12	27	685	8	2.25	25.37	57.08
84. Nick Cleaver, New Mexico St.	TE	JR	12	50	684	4	4.17	13.68	57.00
84. Cody Slate, Marshall	TE	FR	12	43	684	6	3.58	15.91	57.00
86. Duke Calhoun, Memphis	WR	FR	12	42	681	6	3.50	16.21	56.75
87. Anthony Gonzalez, Ohio St.	SE	JR	13	51	734	8	3.92	14.39	56.46
88. Greg Orton, Purdue	WR	SO	14	58	790	5	4.14	13.62	56.43
89. Britt Davis, Northern Ill.	WR	SO	13	57	731	3	4.38	12.82	56.23
90. Michael Ford, Wyoming	WR	JR	12	60	674	4	5.00	11.23	56.17
91. Sonny Shackelford, Washington	WR	SR	12	50	666	7	4.17	13.32	55.50
92. Derrek Richards, Utah	WR	JR	13	60	717	6	4.62	11.95	55.15
93. Dustin Keller, Purdue	TE	JR	14	56	771	4	4.00	13.77	55.07
94. Oderick Turner, Pittsburgh	WR	FR	12	44	660	8	3.67	15.00	55.00
95. Lavelle Hawkins, California	WR	JR	13	46	705	5	3.54	15.33	54.23
96. Courtney Taylor, Auburn	WR	SR	13	54	704	2	4.15	13.04	54.15
97. Todd Blythe, Iowa St.	WR	JR	9	34	484	8	3.78	14.24	53.78
98. Keith Brown, Alabama	WR	JR	11	44	590	3	4.00	13.41	53.64
99. Darrius Heyward-Bey, Maryland	WR	FR	13	45	694	5	3.46	15.42	53.38
100. Jayson Swain, Tennessee	WR	SR	13	49	688	6	3.77	14.04	52.92

Total Receiving Yards

Rank, Player	Pos	Cl.	G	Rec	Yds	TD	Rec/ Gm	Yds/ Rec	Yds/ Gm
1. Chris Williams, New Mexico St.	WR	SO	12	92	1,415	12	7.67	15.38	117.92
2. Johnnie Lee Higgins Jr., UTEP	WR	SR	12	82	1,319	13	6.83	16.09	109.92
3. Joel Filani, Texas Tech	WR	SR	13	91	1,300	13	7.00	14.29	100.00
4. Robert Meachem, Tennessee	WR	JR	13	71	1,298	11	5.46	18.28	99.85
5. Sammie Stroughter, Oregon St.	WR	JR	14	74	1,293	5	5.29	17.47	92.36
6. Harry Douglas, Louisville	WR	JR	13	70	1,265	6	5.38	18.07	97.31
7. Jarett Dillard, Rice	WR	SO	13	91	1,247	21	7.00	13.70	95.92
8. Davone Bess, Hawaii	WR	SO	14	96	1,220	15	6.86	12.71	87.14
9. Calvin Johnson, Georgia Tech	WR	JR	14	76	1,202	15	5.43	15.82	85.86
10. Adarius Bowman, Oklahoma St.	WR	JR	13	60	1,181	12	4.62	19.68	90.85
11. Ryne Robinson, Miami (Ohio)	WR	SR	12	91	1,178	8	7.58	12.95	98.17
11. Mike Walker, UCF	WR	SR	12	90	1,178	7	7.50	13.09	98.17
11. Jason Rivers, Hawaii	WR	JR	14	72	1,178	10	5.14	16.36	84.14
14. Earl Bennett, Vanderbilt	WR	SO	12	82	1,146	6	6.83	13.98	95.50
15. Sidney Rice, South Carolina	WR	SO	13	72	1,090	10	5.54	15.14	83.85
16. Steve Smith, Southern California	WR	SR	13	71	1,083	9	5.46	15.25	83.31
17. Dorien Bryant, Purdue	WR	JR	14	87	1,068	6	6.21	12.28	76.29
18. DeSean Jackson, California	WR	SO	13	59	1,060	9	4.54	17.97	81.54
19. DJ Hall, Alabama	WR	JR	12	62	1,056	5	5.17	17.03	88.00
20. Keenan Burton, Kentucky	WR	JR	13	77	1,036	12	5.92	13.45	79.69
21. Jeff Samardzija, Notre Dame	WR	SR	13	78	1,017	12	6.00	13.04	78.23
22. Dwayne Jarrett, Southern California	WR	JR	12	70	1,015	12	5.83	14.50	84.58
23. Malcolm Kelly, Oklahoma	WR	SO	14	62	993	10	4.43	16.02	70.93
24. Dwayne Bowe, LSU	WR	SR	13	65	990	12	5.00	15.23	76.15
25. Jaison Williams, Oregon	WR	SO	12	68	984	6	5.67	14.47	82.00
26. Vincent Marshall, Houston	WR	SR	14	80	979	8	5.71	12.24	69.93
27. Mario Urrutia, Louisville	WR	SO	13	58	973	6	4.46	16.78	74.85
28. Marcus Monk, Arkansas	WR	JR	14	50	962	11	3.57	19.24	68.71
29. Jonny Harline, Brigham Young	TE	SR	13	58	935	12	4.46	16.12	71.92
30. Dallas Baker, Florida	WR	SR	14	60	920	10	4.29	15.33	65.71
31. David Harvey, Akron	WR	FR	12	43	914	10	3.58	21.26	76.17
32. Ryan Wolfe, UNLV	WR	FR	12	55	911	5	4.58	16.56	75.92
33. Rhema McKnight, Notre Dame	WR	SR	13	67	907	15	5.15	13.54	69.77

Rank, Player	Pos	Cl.	G	Rec	Yds	TD	Rec/ Gm	Yds/ Rec	Yds/ Gm
34. Travis Beckum, Wisconsin	TE	SO	13	61	903	5	4.69	14.80	69.46
35. Eric Deslauriers, Eastern Mich.	WR	SR	12	74	898	5	6.17	12.14	74.83
36. James Jones, San Jose St.	WR	SR	13	70	893	10	5.38	12.76	68.69
37. Kenny McKinley, South Carolina	WR	SO	13	51	880	5	3.92	17.25	67.69
38. Robert Johnson, Texas Tech	WR	SR	12	89	871	11	7.42	9.79	72.58
39. Bryan Anderson, Central Mich.	WR	FR	14	73	867	5	5.21	11.88	61.93
39. Travis Brown, New Mexico	WR	JR	13	64	867	4	4.92	13.55	66.69
41. Marcus Smith, New Mexico	WR	JR	13	53	859	9	4.08	16.21	66.08
42. Donnie Avery, Houston	WR	JR	14	57	852	5	4.07	14.95	60.86
43. Tony Burks, Mississippi St.	WR	JR	12	35	850	5	2.92	24.29	70.83
44. Derek Kinder, Pittsburgh	WR	JR	12	57	847	6	4.75	14.86	70.58
45. John Broussard, San Jose St.	WR	SR	13	52	844	7	4.00	16.23	64.92
46. Nate Ilaoa, Hawaii	RB	SR	13	67	837	5	5.15	12.49	64.38
47. Craig Davis, LSU	WR	SR	12	56	836	4	4.67	14.93	69.67
48. William Franklin, Missouri	WR	JR	11	48	829	6	4.36	17.27	75.36
49. Dicky Lyons, Kentucky	WR	SO	13	50	822	9	3.85	16.44	63.23
50. Casey Flair, UNLV	WR	SO	12	67	816	4	5.58	12.18	68.00
51. Damien Linson, Central Mich.	WR	SR	14	55	812	5	3.93	14.76	58.00
52. Najah Pruden, Kent St.	WR	SR	12	39	808	6	3.25	20.72	67.33
53. Logan Payne, Minnesota	WR	SR	13	59	804	9	4.54	13.63	61.85
54. Idris Moss, Tulsa	WR	SR	13	58	803	1	4.46	13.84	61.77
55. Trent Shelton, Baylor	WR	SR	12	53	802	8	4.42	15.13	66.83
56. Limas Sweed, Texas	WR	JR	13	46	801	12	3.54	17.41	61.62
57. Derek Dubois, New Mexico St.	WR	SO	12	53	800	7	4.42	15.09	66.67
58. LaGregory Sapp, La.-Monroe	WR	SO	12	43	796	3	3.58	18.51	66.33
59. Quentily Harmon, TCU	WR	SR	13	52	791	3	4.00	15.21	60.85
60. Greg Orton, Purdue	WR	SO	14	58	790	5	4.14	13.62	56.43
61. A.J. Harris, New Mexico St.	WR	SO	12	71	789	7	5.92	11.11	65.75
62. Ted Ginn Jr., Ohio St.	WR	JR	13	59	781	9	4.54	13.24	60.08
63. Kerry Reed, Michigan St.	WR	SR	12	64	775	5	5.33	12.11	64.58
64. Early Doucet, LSU	WR	JR	13	59	772	8	4.54	13.08	59.38
65. Dustin Keller, Purdue	TE	JR	14	56	771	4	4.00	13.77	55.07
66. Darius Hill, Ball St.	TE	JR	12	42	741	10	3.50	17.64	61.75
66. Dominique Zeigler, Baylor	WR	SR	11	54	741	3	4.91	13.72	67.36
68. Dante Love, Ball St.	WR	SO	12	52	735	4	4.33	14.13	61.25
69. Anthony Gonzalez, Ohio St.	SE	JR	13	51	734	8	3.92	14.39	56.46
70. Britt Davis, Northern Ill.	WR	SO	13	57	731	3	4.38	12.82	56.23
70. Brandon Gibson, Washington St.	WR	SO	12	49	731	4	4.08	14.92	60.92
72. Jabari Arthur, Akron	WR	JR	12	45	730	4	3.75	16.22	60.83
73. Ross Dickerson, Hawaii	WR	SR	14	54	726	7	3.86	13.44	51.86
74. Andy Brodell, Iowa	WR	SO	12	39	724	5	3.25	18.56	60.33
75. James Hardy, Indiana	WR	SO	10	51	722	10	5.10	14.16	72.20
75. Damon Morton, Colorado St.	WR	JR	12	48	722	4	4.00	15.04	60.17
77. Willie Edwards, UAB	WR	JR	12	39	719	2	3.25	18.44	59.92
78. Derrek Richards, Utah	WR	JR	13	60	717	6	4.62	11.95	55.15
79. Aundrae Allison, East Caro.	WR	SR	11	62	708	4	5.64	11.42	64.36
80. Lavelle Hawkins, California	WR	JR	13	46	705	5	3.54	15.33	54.23
81. Courtney Taylor, Auburn	WR	SR	13	54	704	2	4.15	13.04	54.15
82. Mario Manningham, Michigan	WR	SO	10	38	703	9	3.80	18.50	70.30
83. Chansi Stuckey, Clemson	WR	SR	10	50	700	3	5.00	14.00	70.00
84. Darrius Heyward-Bey, Maryland	WR	FR	13	45	694	5	3.46	15.42	53.38
85. Ian Sample, Hawaii	WR	SR	14	54	690	10	3.86	12.78	49.29
86. Jayson Swain, Tennessee	WR	SR	13	49	688	6	3.77	14.04	52.92
87. Terry Moss, Ball St.	WR	SR	12	27	685	8	2.25	25.37	57.08
88. Chris Davis, Florida St.	WR	SR	13	49	684	4	3.77	13.96	52.62
88. Cody Slate, Marshall	TE	FR	12	43	684	6	3.58	15.91	57.00
88. Nick Cleaver, New Mexico St.	TE	JR	12	50	684	4	4.17	13.68	57.00
91. Duke Calhoun, Memphis	WR	FR	12	42	681	6	3.50	16.21	56.75
92. Derrick Stewart, Cincinnati	WR	FR	13	33	675	5	2.54	20.45	51.92
93. Michael Ford, Wyoming	WR	JR	12	60	674	4	5.00	11.23	56.17
94. Jeron Harvey, Houston	WR	SR	14	41	671	4	2.93	16.37	47.93
95. Steve Breaston, Michigan	WR	SR	13	58	670	2	4.46	11.55	51.54
96. Jamarko Simmons, Western Mich.	RB	SO	13	61	668	2	4.69	10.95	51.38
97. Sonny Shackelford, Washington	WR	SR	12	50	666	7	4.17	13.32	55.50
98. Chandler Williams, Florida Int'l	WR	SR	10	67	664	1	6.70	9.91	66.40
99. Hakeem Nicks, North Carolina	WR	FR	11	39	660	4	3.55	16.92	60.00
99. Oderick Turner, Pittsburgh	WR	FR	12	44	660	8	3.67	15.00	55.00

Interceptions

Rank, Player	Pos	Cl.	G	Int	Yds	TD	Int/Gm
1. Stanley Franks, Idaho	DB	JR	12	9	220	1	.75
2. Dwight Lowery, San Jose St.	DB	JR	13	9	111	0	.69
3. Daymeion Hughes, California	DB	SR	13	8	113	2	.62
4. Aqib Talib, Kansas	DB	SO	10	6	82	0	.60
5. John Talley, Duke	DB	SR	12	7	150	1	.58
5. Quintin Demps, UTEP	DB	JR	12	7	61	0	.58
7. Ryan Smith, Florida	DB	JR	14	8	44	0	.57
8. DeJuan Tribble, Boston College	DB	JR	13	7	108	3	.54
8. Eric Weddle, Utah	DB	SR	13	7	80	2	.54
8. Tony Taylor, Georgia	LB	SR	13	7	97	1	.54
8. Trae Williams, South Fla.	DB	JR	13	7	8	0	.54
12. Lionell Singleton, Florida Int'l	DB	JR	10	5	59	0	.50
12. Josh Thompson, La.-Monroe	DB	SO	12	6	80	0	.50
14. William Gay, Louisville	DB	SR	13	6	70	0	.46
14. Aaron Ross, Texas	DB	SR	13	6	7	0	.46
14. Joe Garcia, Nevada	DB	SR	13	6	76	1	.46
14. Korey Hall, Boise St.	LB	SR	13	6	108	0	.46
14. Anthony Scirrotto, Penn St.	DB	SO	13	6	122	0	.46
14. Simeon Castille, Alabama	DB	JR	13	6	71	0	.46
14. Tra Battle, Georgia	DB	SR	13	6	154	1	.46
14. Marty Tadman, Boise St.	DB	JR	13	6	176	2	.46
22. Marcus Hamilton, Virginia	DB	SR	11	5	101	0	.45
23. Reggie Nelson, Florida	DB	JR	14	6	70	1	.43

STATISTICAL LEADERS

Rank, Player	Pos	Cl.	G	Int	Yds	TD	Int/Gm
24. Greg James, La.-Monroe	DB	FR	12	5	36	0	.42
24. Kareen Taylor, North Carolina	DB	SR	12	5	96	0	.42
24. Terrence Wheatley, Colorado	DB	SR	12	5	26	0	.42
24. Eric Frampton, Washington St.	DB	SR	12	5	50	1	.42
24. Mike Newton, Buffalo	DB	FR	12	5	108	0	.42
24. Londen Fryar, Western Mich.	DB	SO	12	5	123	1	.42
24. Joe Hudson, Miami (Ohio)	LB	SO	12	5	48	0	.42
24. Will Meyers, Indiana	DB	SR	12	5	74	0	.42
32. Kenny Phillips, Miami (Fla.)	DB	SO	10	4	5	0	.40
33. Damon Nickson, Middle Tenn.	DB	JR	13	5	31	1	.38
33. James Laurinaitis, Ohio St.	LB	SO	13	5	56	0	.38
33. Will Gulley, Houston	DB	SR	13	5	43	0	.38
33. Jonathan Hefney, Tennessee	DB	JR	13	5	75	0	.38
33. Jairus Byrd, Oregon	DB	FR	13	5	30	0	.38
33. Quinton Andrews, West Virginia	DB	FR	13	5	67	0	.38
39. Darius Butler, Connecticut	DB	JR	11	4	37	0	.36
39. Louis Delmas, Western Mich.	DB	SO	11	4	52	0	.36
39. Lionel Mitchell, Alabama	DB	JR	11	4	131	1	.36
42. Josh Gattis, Wake Forest	DB	SR	14	5	0	0	.36
42. Sabby Piscitelli, Oregon St.	DB	SR	14	5	35	0	.36
44. Corey Small, Fla. Atlantic	DB	SO	12	4	32	1	.33
44. Kevin Payne, La.-Monroe	DB	SR	12	4	50	0	.33
44. Khayyam Burns, Arkansas St.	DB	JR	12	4	116	1	.33
44. Taheem Acevedo, Fla. Atlantic	DB	JR	12	4	21	0	.33
44. C.J.Wilson, Baylor	DB	SR	12	4	98	1	.33
44. Sha'reff Rashad, UCF	DB	SO	12	4	65	0	.33
44. David Skehan, Tulane	DB	JR	12	4	41	1	.33
44. Brandon McDonald, Memphis	DB	SR	12	4	83	0	.33
44. LeVance Richmond, Southern Miss.	DB	JR	12	4	69	0	.33
44. Dorsey Golston, Wyoming	DB	SR	12	4	45	0	.33
44. Derek Pegues, Mississippi St.	DB	SO	12	4	95	2	.33
44. Michael Klyce, Arizona	DB	JR	9	3	64	0	.33
44. Scott White, Washington	LB	SR	12	4	54	0	.33
44. Reggie Corner, Akron	DB	SR	12	4	38	0	.33
44. Kenny Lewis, Bowling Green	DB	SO	12	4	13	0	.33
44. Barry Church, Toledo	DB	FR	12	4	127	2	.33
44. E.J. Biggers, Western Mich.	DB	SO	12	4	6	0	.33
44. Andre Kirkland, Kent St.	DB	SR	12	4	15	0	.33
44. Jack Williams, Kent St.	DB	JR	12	4	44	1	.33
44. Tracy Porter, Indiana	DB	JR	12	4	53	0	.33
44. Nick Hawthrone, Nevada	DB	SR	12	4	87	1	.33
44. Courtney Bryan, New Mexico St.	DB	SR	12	4	35	1	.33
44. Damon Jenkins, Fresno St.	DB	JR	9	3	70	1	.33
44. Joe Fields, Syracuse	DB	JR	12	4	6	0	.33
44. Danny Lansanah, Connecticut	LB	JR	12	4	64	1	.33
44. Jamie Silva, Boston College	DB	JR	12	4	0	0	.33
70. Djay Jones, Georgia Tech	DB	JR	13	4	29	1	.31
70. Victor Harris, Virginia Tech	DB	SO	13	4	75	1	.31
70. Roger Williams, Florida St.	DB	JR	13	4	45	0	.31
70. Dominic Ross, Cincinnati	DB	SR	13	4	14	0	.31
70. Courtney Greene, Rutgers	DB	SO	13	4	26	0	.31
70. Mike Richardson, Notre Dame	DB	SR	13	4	21	0	.31
70. Michael Griffin, Texas	DB	SR	13	4	41	0	.31
70. Bobby Blackshire, Tulsa	DB	SR	13	4	26	0	.31
70. Pierre Parker, East Caro.	DB	SR	13	4	5	0	.31
70. Kasey Ross, East Caro.	DB	SR	13	4	128	2	.31
70. Justin Robinson, Brigham Young	DB	SR	13	4	69	1	.31
70. DeAndre Wright, New Mexico	DB	SO	13	4	22	0	.31
70. Christopher Owens, San Jose St.	DB	SO	13	4	72	0	.31
70. Marcus McClinton, Kentucky	DB	SO	13	4	13	0	.31
70. Jonathan Zenon, LSU	DB	JR	13	4	81	2	.31
70. Craig Steltz, LSU	DB	JR	13	4	111	0	.31
70. Jonathan Wade, Tennessee	DB	SR	13	4	59	0	.31
70. Patrick Chung, Oregon	DB	SO	13	4	38	0	.31
70. Trey Brown, UCLA	DB	JR	13	4	38	0	.31
70. Pacino Horne, Central Mich.	DB	SR	13	4	49	0	.31
70. Marvin White, TCU	DB	SR	13	4	45	0	.31
70. Dominique Barber, Minnesota	FS	JR	13	4	57	1	.31
70. Malcolm Jenkins, Ohio St.	DB	SO	13	4	99	1	.31
93. Donny Baker, San Diego St.	DB	SR	10	3	24	0	.30
93. Dwain Crawford, Baylor	DB	SO	10	3	15	0	.30
95. Riley Swanson, Wake Forest	DB	SR	14	4	32	0	.29
95. Caleb Hendrix, Southern Miss.	DB	SR	14	4	8	0	.29
95. Nic Harris, Oklahoma	DB	SO	14	4	11	0	.29
95. Andrew Shanle, Nebraska	DB	SR	14	4	19	0	.29
95. T.J. Wright, Ohio	DB	SR	14	4	33	0	.29
95. Reggie Lewis, Florida	DB	SR	14	4	35	0	.29

Punting

(Minimum 3.6 Punts Per Game)

Rank, Player	Pos	Cl.	G	Punts	Yds	Avg	Punts/ Gm
1. Daniel Sepulveda, Baylor	P	SR	12	66	3,068	46.48	5.50
2. Chris Miller, Ball St.	P	JR	12	57	2,637	46.26	4.75
3. Kody Bliss, Auburn	P	SR	13	47	2,149	45.72	3.62
4. Durant Brooks, Georgia Tech	P	JR	14	79	3,596	45.52	5.64
5. Geoffrey Price, Notre Dame	P	SR	12	50	2,272	45.44	4.17
6. Kip Facer, UNLV	P	SR	12	46	2,078	45.17	3.83
7. Britton Colquitt, Tennessee	P	SO	12	46	2,066	44.91	3.83
8. Matt Fodge, Oklahoma St.	P	SO	13	50	2,244	44.88	3.85
9. Kyle Stringer, Boise St.	P	SR	13	47	2,097	44.62	3.62
10. Justin Brantly, Texas A&M	P	SO	13	50	2,215	44.30	3.85
11. Joe Radigan, Rutgers	P	SR	13	56	2,467	44.05	4.31
12. Nick Folk, Arizona	K/P	SR	12	74	3,259	44.04	6.17
13. Louie Sakoda, Utah	K/P	SO	13	59	2,598	44.03	4.54
14. Waylon Prather, San Jose St.	P	JR	13	63	2,771	43.98	4.85
15. Thomas Morstead, SMU	K/P	SO	12	50	2,191	43.82	4.17
16. Matt DiLallo, Colorado	P	FR	12	47	2,056	43.74	3.92
17. Jim Kaylor, Colorado St.	P	JR	12	63	2,754	43.71	5.25
18. Ryan Dougherty, East Caro.	P	SR	13	51	2,226	43.65	3.92
19. Brandon Fields, Michigan St.	P	SR	12	57	2,469	43.32	4.75
20. Sean Douglas, Washington	P	SR	12	72	3,110	43.19	6.00
21. Billy Vinnedge, Wyoming	P	JR	12	61	2,634	43.18	5.08
22. Adam Podlesh, Maryland	P	SR	13	56	2,400	42.86	4.31
23. Andrew Larson, California	P	JR	13	49	2,087	42.59	3.77
24. Aaron Perez, UCLA	P	SO	13	62	2,639	42.56	4.77
25. Chris Beckman, Tulane	P	SR	12	52	2,207	42.44	4.33
26. Eric Wilbur, Florida	P	SR	13	53	2,244	42.34	4.08
27. Nic Schmitt, Virginia Tech	K/P	SR	13	61	2,575	42.21	4.69
28. Owen Tolson, Army	P	JR	12	49	2,067	42.18	4.08
29. Johnny Ayers, Boston College	P	JR	13	59	2,483	42.08	4.54
30. Tim Reyer, Kansas St.	P	JR	13	61	2,566	42.07	4.69
31. Adam Graessle, Pittsburgh	P	SR	12	49	2,059	42.02	4.08
32. Tony Mikulec, Central Mich.	P	JR	14	63	2,644	41.97	4.50
33. Brendan Carney, Syracuse	P	SR	12	72	3,021	41.96	6.00
34. Jeremy Kapinos, Penn St.	P	SR	13	61	2,555	41.89	4.69
35. Kenneth DeBauche, Wisconsin	P	JR	13	59	2,468	41.83	4.54
36. Brian Monroe, Miami (Fla.)	P	SR	12	58	2,419	41.71	4.83
37. Brett Kern, Toledo	P	JR	12	60	2,502	41.70	5.00
38. Zoltan Mesko, Michigan	P	SO	13	50	2,079	41.58	3.85
39. Jonathon Johnson, Arizona St.	P	JR	13	54	2,241	41.50	4.15
40. Darryl Blunt, Washington St.	P	SO	11	53	2,192	41.36	4.82
41. Cole Chason, Clemson	P	SR	13	50	2,064	41.28	3.85
42. Kyle Loomis, Oregon St.	P	FR	14	62	2,558	41.26	4.43
43. Sam Swank, Wake Forest	K/P	SO	14	70	2,887	41.24	5.00
44. Mike Brandtner, Iowa St.	P	FR	12	56	2,309	41.23	4.67
45. David Wooldridge, North Carolina	K/P	SR	11	62	2,548	41.10	5.64
46. Jacob Richardson, Miami (Ohio)	P	SO	12	58	2,383	41.09	4.83
47. Michael Hughes, San Diego St.	K/P	JR	10	48	1,971	41.06	4.80
48. Colby Smith, Middle Tenn.	P	SR	13	69	2,830	41.01	5.31
49. Michael Cohen, Oklahoma	P	JR	13	51	2,091	41.00	3.92
50. Graham Gano, Florida St.	K/P	SO	13	67	2,736	40.84	5.15
51. Greg Johnson, Texas	P	SR	12	46	1,877	40.80	3.83
52. Truman Spencer, North Texas	P	SO	10	52	2,118	40.73	5.20
53. A.J. Trapasso, Ohio St.	K/P	JR	13	49	1,990	40.61	3.77
54. Kevin Payne, La.-Monroe	DB/P	SR	12	45	1,826	40.58	3.75
55. Tyson Beattie, Indiana	P	SR	12	64	2,592	40.50	5.33
56. Justin Kucek, Minnesota	P	SO	13	56	2,257	40.30	4.31
57. Jordan Scott, New Mexico	P	JR	13	70	2,815	40.21	5.38
58. Chris Pavasaris, Connecticut	P	JR	12	71	2,845	40.07	5.92
59. Zach Johnson, Eastern Mich.	K/P	SO	12	65	2,603	40.05	5.42
60. Jason Wright, Troy	P	SR	13	59	2,359	39.98	4.54
61. Parker Mullins, UAB	P	SR	12	58	2,314	39.90	4.83
62. Matt Lasher, Ohio	K/P	SR	14	77	3,055	39.68	5.50
63. Jay Ottovegio, Stanford	P	JR	12	61	2,417	39.62	5.08
64. Aaron Horne, UCF	P	SR	12	44	1,742	39.59	3.67
65. Adam Crossett, Missouri	K/P	JR	13	47	1,852	39.40	3.62
66. T.J. Conley, Idaho	P	SO	12	67	2,640	39.40	5.58
67. Gordon Ely-Kelso, Georgia	P	SR	13	51	2,007	39.35	3.92
68. Dan Titchener, Nebraska	P	SO	14	66	2,592	39.27	4.71
69. Kyle Tucker, Kansas	P	JR	12	58	2,276	39.24	4.83
70. Tim Masthay, Kentucky	P	SO	13	50	1,959	39.18	3.85
71. Zacary Whited, Nevada	P	JR	11	40	1,564	39.10	3.64
72. Brit Framel, La.-Lafayette	P	SR	12	54	2,110	39.07	4.50
73. John Deraney, North Carolina St.	K/P	SR	12	76	2,968	39.05	6.33
74. Rob Park, Mississippi	P	SO	12	58	2,256	38.90	4.83
75. Jared Scruggs, Rice	P	SR	13	63	2,444	38.79	4.85

Rank, Player	Pos	Cl.	G	Punts	Yds	Avg	Punts/ Gm
76. Brian Steel, Cincinnati	P	JR	13	70	2,715	38.79	5.38
77. John Stec, Akron	P	FR	12	60	2,318	38.63	5.00
78. Britt Barefoot, Southern Miss.	P	SO	14	52	2,007	38.60	3.71
79. Jake Brownell, Temple	P	FR	12	78	3,004	38.51	6.50
80. Chris Keagle, Louisiana Tech	P	SO	13	66	2,534	38.39	5.08
81. Chris Gould, Virginia	K/P	JR	12	56	2,148	38.36	4.67
82. Greg Woidneck, Southern California	P	SO	13	48	1,838	38.29	3.69
83. Jim Laney, Western Mich.	P	JR	13	62	2,369	38.21	4.77
84. Blake McAdams, Mississippi St.	P	SO	12	68	2,598	38.21	5.67
85. P.J. Fitzgerald, Alabama	P	FR	13	57	2,176	38.18	4.38
86. Jacob Skinner, Arkansas	P	SR	14	61	2,327	38.15	4.36
87. Brett Shrable, Arkansas St.	P	SO	12	52	1,983	38.13	4.33
88. Greg Veteto, Navy	P	JR	11	41	1,563	38.12	3.73
89. Andy Dittbenner, Northern Ill.	P	SO	10	55	2,085	37.91	5.50
90. Ben Woods, Buffalo	P	JR	12	67	2,539	37.90	5.58
91. Leon Jackson III, Utah St.	QB/P	JR	12	74	2,791	37.72	6.17
92. Andy Fenstermaker, Iowa	P	SR	13	55	2,073	37.69	4.23
93. Alex Feinberg, Duke	K/P	JR	12	63	2,366	37.56	5.25
94. Brett Upson, Vanderbilt	K/P	FR	12	52	1,945	37.40	4.33
95. Mike O'Neill, Fla. Atlantic	P	JR	12	60	2,233	37.22	5.00
96. Slade Larscheid, Northwestern	K/P	SR	12	65	2,417	37.18	5.42
97. Kyle Yelton, Illinois	P	FR	12	50	1,837	36.74	4.17
98. Ryan Hotchkiss, UTEP	P	SR	12	50	1,813	36.26	4.17
99. Alonso Rojas, Bowling Green	P	FR	12	56	1,996	35.64	4.67
100. Chris Cook, Florida Int'l	P	FR	11	54	1,909	35.35	4.91

Punt Returns

(Minimum 1.2 Returns Per Game)

Rank, Player	Pos	Cl.	G	Ret	Yds	TD	Yds/ Ret	Ret/ Gm
1. DeSean Jackson, California	WR	SO	13	25	455	4	18.20	1.92
2. Jeremy Trimble, Army	WR	JR	12	18	325	2	18.06	1.50
3. Sammie Stroughter, Oregon St.	WR	JR	14	30	470	3	15.67	2.14
4. Ean Randolph, South Fla.	WR	SR	13	25	370	1	14.80	1.92
5. Yamon Figurs, Kansas St.	WR	SR	12	22	323	2	14.68	1.83
6. Mikey Henderson, Georgia	WR	JR	11	25	367	2	14.68	2.27
7. Chris Garrett, Ohio	WR	FR	14	26	378	1	14.54	1.86
8. Joe Chapple, Western Mich.	WR	SR	13	16	230	0	14.38	1.23
9. DeAngelo Wilson, Nevada	DB	SO	13	16	228	0	14.25	1.23
10. Derek Pegues, Mississippi St.	DB	SO	12	25	350	1	14.00	2.08
11. Frantz Simeon, Fla. Atlantic	WR	SO	12	15	201	0	13.40	1.25
12. Eddie Royal, Virginia Tech	WR	JR	13	23	304	1	13.22	1.77
13. Syndric Steptoe, Arizona	WR	SR	12	20	261	1	13.05	1.67
14. Perrish Cox, Oklahoma St.	DB	FR	12	24	308	0	12.83	2.00
15. Larry Taylor, Connecticut	RB	JR	10	20	255	1	12.75	2.00
16. Brian Bonner, TCU	DB	JR	13	24	305	0	12.71	1.85
17. Jonathan Hefney, Tennessee	DB	JR	13	17	206	0	12.12	1.31
18. Derrick Williams, Penn St.	WR	SO	13	25	301	1	12.04	1.92
19. Dominic Jones, Minnesota	SS	SO	13	19	218	0	11.47	1.46
20. Steve Breaston, Michigan	WR	SR	13	29	332	1	11.45	2.23
21. Leodis McKelvin, Troy	DB	JR	13	28	314	1	11.21	2.15
22. Marshay Green, Mississippi	RB	FR	12	20	224	1	11.20	1.67
23. Marquis Wilson, Utah	WR	SO	13	22	246	0	11.18	1.69
24. Nathan Meikle, Brigham Young	WR	SR	12	29	324	0	11.17	2.42
25. Ted Ginn Jr., Ohio St.	WR	JR	13	24	266	1	11.08	1.85
26. Brandon James, Florida	RB	FR	13	33	363	1	11.00	2.54
26. Jonathan Lamb, Kansas	DB	SR	11	15	165	0	11.00	1.36
28. Vaughn Rivers, West Virginia	DB	JR	13	18	195	1	10.83	1.38
29. Aaron Ross, Texas	DB	SR	13	23	240	1	10.43	1.77
30. Queito Teasley, Baylor	WR	SO	9	11	114	0	10.36	1.22
31. Lionell Singleton, Florida Int'l	DB	JR	10	14	140	0	10.00	1.40
32. Ryne Robinson, Miami (Ohio)	WR	SR	12	18	175	1	9.72	1.50
33. Damon Morton, Colorado St.	WR	JR	12	21	204	1	9.71	1.75
34. Brandon Tate, North Carolina	WR	SO	12	20	194	1	9.70	1.67
35. Mike Brown, Virginia	DB	SO	11	14	134	0	9.57	1.27
36. Derrick Stewart, Cincinnati	WR	FR	13	25	231	0	9.24	1.92
37. Javier Arenas, Alabama	DB	FR	13	31	286	2	9.23	2.38
38. Danny Amendola, Texas Tech	WR	JR	13	41	377	0	9.20	3.15
39. Willie Idlette, Wake Forest	WR	SR	14	22	202	0	9.18	1.57
40. Tom Zbikowski, Notre Dame	DB	SR	12	16	144	1	9.00	1.33
41. Marty Tadman, Boise St.	DB	JR	13	16	143	0	8.94	1.23
42. Kenny McKinley, South Carolina	WR	SO	13	17	151	0	8.88	1.31
43. Brandon King, Rice	DB	SO	10	13	115	0	8.85	1.30
44. DeJuan Tribble, Boston College	DB	JR	13	27	236	0	8.74	2.08
45. Fred Smith, Tulane	WR	JR	12	22	191	0	8.68	1.83
46. Darrelle Revis, Pittsburgh	DB	JR	12	22	190	1	8.64	1.83
47. Chris Davis, Florida St.	WR	SR	13	26	224	0	8.62	2.00
48. Darrell Blackman, North Carolina St.	WR	JR	11	24	206	1	8.58	2.18
49. Corey Partridge, Bowling Green	WR	SO	10	14	120	0	8.57	1.40
50. Jasper Faulk, Southern Miss.	DB	SR	14	23	197	0	8.57	1.64
51. Hoost Marsh, Wyoming	WR	JR	12	24	205	0	8.54	2.00
52. Terrence Nunn, Nebraska	WR	JR	14	18	153	0	8.50	1.29
53. Danny Oquendo, Maryland	WR	SO	13	26	218	0	8.38	2.00
54. Jon Drager, Kent St.	RB	JR	10	12	100	0	8.33	1.20
55. Blake Warren, SMU	WR	SR	12	21	174	0	8.29	1.75
56. Bruce Johnson, Miami (Fla.)	DB	SO	11	23	186	0	8.09	2.09
57. Trumaine Riley, Eastern Mich.	WR	SR	11	21	169	0	8.05	1.91
58. Thomas Wilson, New Mexico	WR	SR	13	20	158	0	7.90	1.54
59. Idris Moss, Tulsa	WR	SR	13	25	197	0	7.88	1.92
60. Reggie Smith, Oklahoma	DB	SO	14	37	287	1	7.76	2.64
61. Marcus Brock, TCU	WR	SR	11	14	107	0	7.64	1.27
62. Carl Sims, Baylor	WR	SO	9	15	114	0	7.60	1.67
63. Vincent Marshall, Houston	WR	SR	14	20	148	0	7.40	1.43
64. Chad Schroeder, Texas A&M	WR	SR	13	19	140	0	7.37	1.46
65. Clifton Smith, Fresno St.	RB	JR	10	19	139	0	7.32	1.90
66. Jason Tomlinson, Navy	WR	SR	13	18	116	0	6.44	1.38
67. Royce Adams, Purdue	DB	FR	14	22	141	0	6.41	1.57
68. Marlon Wood, Washington	WR	JR	12	35	214	0	6.11	2.92
69. Leon Wright, Duke	CB	FR	11	15	91	0	6.07	1.36
70. Myron Newberry, Hawaii	DB	JR	13	22	130	0	5.91	1.69
71. B.J. Hill, Ball St.	RB	SO	12	23	134	0	5.83	1.92
72. Zach Hampton, Wisconsin	DB	SR	13	31	178	0	5.74	2.38
73. Damien Linson, Central Mich.	WR	SR	14	24	135	0	5.63	1.71
74. Robert Dunn, Auburn	WR	SO	12	22	120	0	5.45	1.83
75. Desmond Reed, Southern California	RB	JR	12	20	109	0	5.45	1.67
76. Stephone Robinson, Colorado	DB	JR	12	15	76	0	5.07	1.25
77. Ibrahim Halsey, Illinois	RB	SR	12	23	116	0	5.04	1.92
78. Terry Love, Michigan St.	WR	JR	12	18	88	0	4.89	1.50
79. Kevin Jones, Arkansas St.	WR	SO	12	15	63	0	4.20	1.25
80. Steve Odom, Toledo	WR	SR	12	19	70	0	3.68	1.58
81. Wes Williams, Idaho	WR	SO	9	15	53	0	3.53	1.67

Kickoff Returns

(Minimum 1.2 Returns Per Game)

Rank, Player	Pos	Cl.	G	Ret	Yds	TD	Yds/ Ret	Ret/ Gm
1. Marcus Thigpen, Indiana	RB	SO	12	24	723	3	30.13	2.00
2. David Harvey, Akron	WR	FR	12	17	510	0	30.00	1.42
3. Lionell Singleton, Florida Int'l	DB	JR	10	12	354	1	29.50	1.20
4. Darrell Blackman, North Carolina St.	WR	JR	11	19	549	1	28.89	1.73
5. Damon Nickson, Middle Tenn.	DB	JR	13	21	605	2	28.81	1.62
6. Jonathan Stewart, Oregon	RB	SO	13	23	646	0	28.09	1.77
7. Jeff Smith, Boston College	RB	FR	13	23	645	1	28.04	1.77
8. Brandon West, Western Mich.	RB	FR	13	22	615	0	27.95	1.69
9. Lowell Robinson, Pittsburgh	WR	JR	12	26	725	1	27.88	2.17
10. Kerry Franks, Texas A&M	WR	JR	13	16	443	1	27.69	1.23
11. Josh Wilson, Maryland	DB	SR	13	31	847	1	27.32	2.38
12. Cedric Peerman, Virginia	RB	SO	12	19	519	0	27.32	1.58
13. Grant Jones, Oklahoma St.	DB	SR	13	21	572	1	27.24	1.62
14. Darius Reynaud, West Virginia	WR	JR	13	30	813	1	27.10	2.31
15. C.J. Gable, Southern California	RB	FR	13	16	432	0	27.00	1.23
15. Tristan Davis, Auburn	DB	SO	12	28	756	0	27.00	2.33
17. JaJuan Spillman, Louisville	WR	FR	12	17	450	1	26.47	1.42
18. Marcus Herford, Kansas	WR	SO	11	29	757	0	26.10	2.64
19. Naaman Roosevelt, Buffalo	QB	FR	12	28	724	1	25.86	2.33
20. Dominick Goodman, Cincinnati	WR	SO	13	21	541	0	25.76	1.62
21. Syndric Steptoe, Arizona	WR	SR	12	16	409	0	25.56	1.33
22. Jabari Marshall, Duke	WR	SO	12	38	953	0	25.08	3.17
23. Ross Dickerson, Hawaii	WR	SR	14	26	650	1	25.00	1.86
23. Dwayne Sanders, Nevada	WR	FR	11	22	550	0	25.00	2.00
25. Keenan Burton, Kentucky	WR	JR	13	31	765	1	24.68	2.38
26. Michael Grandberry, Memphis	WR	SO	12	21	517	0	24.62	1.75
27. Dominic Jones, Minnesota	SS	SO	13	32	786	1	24.56	2.46
28. David Grimes, Notre Dame	WR	SO	12	21	514	0	24.48	1.75
29. Ted Ginn Jr., Ohio St.	WR	JR	13	18	440	1	24.44	1.38
30. A.J. Wallace, Penn St.	DB	FR	13	16	388	0	24.25	1.23
31. Patrick Jackson, Louisiana Tech	RB	SO	12	29	702	1	24.21	2.42
32. Felix Jones, Arkansas	TB	SO	14	23	554	1	24.09	1.64
33. Terry Moss, Ball St.	WR	SR	12	23	551	0	23.96	1.92
34. Eric Wright, UNLV	DB	JR	9	18	430	0	23.89	2.00
35. Perrish Cox, Oklahoma St.	DB	FR	12	25	595	1	23.80	2.08
36. Brandon Tate, North Carolina	WR	SO	12	38	902	2	23.74	3.17
37. Mikail Baker, Baylor	WR	SO	12	22	522	0	23.73	1.83
38. Derek Pegues, Mississippi St.	DB	SO	12	29	687	0	23.69	2.42
39. Marculus Elliott, UAB	RB	SR	12	27	638	0	23.63	2.25
40. Leodis McKelvin, Troy	DB	JR	13	27	634	0	23.48	2.08
41. Eric Fraser, Central Mich.	DB	FR	14	25	584	0	23.36	1.79
42. Mico McSwain, Mississippi	RB	SO	11	14	322	0	23.00	1.27
43. Chris Johnson, East Caro.	RB	JR	12	21	482	1	22.95	1.75

Rank, Player	Pos	Cl.	G	Ret	Yds	TD	Yds/ Ret	Ret/ Gm
44. Jamaal Evans, Georgia Tech	RB	FR	11	20	456	0	22.80	1.82
45. Queito Teasley, Baylor	WR	SO	9	15	341	0	22.73	1.67
46. Eddie Royal, Virginia Tech	WR	JR	13	19	431	0	22.68	1.46
47. Michael Ray Garvin, Florida St.	DB	SO	13	16	362	0	22.63	1.23
48. Brice McCain, Utah	DB	SO	13	18	404	0	22.44	1.38
49. Coye Francies, Oregon St.	DB	JR	14	22	493	0	22.41	1.57
50. Anthony Alridge, Houston	RB	JR	14	27	603	0	22.33	1.93
51. Kevin Marion, Wake Forest	WR	JR	12	22	490	0	22.27	1.83
52. Steve Breaston, Michigan	WR	SR	13	21	467	0	22.24	1.62
53. Kory Sheets, Purdue	RB	SO	14	19	422	0	22.21	1.36
54. Corey Anderson, Army	WR	JR	12	23	509	0	22.13	1.92
55. Asher Allen, Georgia	DB	FR	13	19	420	0	22.11	1.46
56. Chastin West, Fresno St.	WR	FR	12	24	527	1	21.96	2.00
57. Brandon Thompkins, Arkansas St.	WR	FR	12	25	548	0	21.92	2.08
58. Richard Davis, Toledo	RB	SO	12	32	701	0	21.91	2.67
59. Trumaine Riley, Eastern Mich.	WR	SR	11	31	678	0	21.87	2.82
60. Jason Harper, Temple	RB	FR	12	18	393	0	21.83	1.50
61. Jason Evans, Stanford	RB	JR	12	16	349	0	21.81	1.33
62. Bruce Johnson, Miami (Fla.)	DB	SO	11	15	326	0	21.73	1.36
63. Milan Moses, Iowa St.	WR	JR	9	15	325	0	21.67	1.67
64. Kris Bartels, Fla. Atlantic	DB	JR	12	16	345	0	21.56	1.33
65. Donald Massey, TCU	WR	JR	13	16	342	0	21.38	1.23
66. Curtis Brinkley, Syracuse	RB	SO	12	21	448	0	21.33	1.75
67. Brandon Sumrall, Southern Miss.	DB	SO	14	19	401	0	21.11	1.36
68. Sherrick McManis, Northwestern	DB	FR	11	28	588	0	21.00	2.55
68. Idris Moss, Tulsa	WR	SR	13	18	378	0	21.00	1.38
68. Reggie Campbell, Navy	RB	JR	13	17	357	0	21.00	1.31
71. Kevin Robinson, Utah St.	WR	JR	12	31	641	0	20.68	2.58
72. Curtis Francis, UCF	RB	JR	12	21	434	0	20.67	1.75
73. Willie Foster, Rutgers	WR	SR	13	18	370	0	20.56	1.38
74. Damon Morton, Colorado St.	WR	JR	12	18	368	0	20.44	1.50
75. Jeremiah Johnson, Oregon	RB	SO	13	16	327	0	20.44	1.23
76. Demond Williams, Michigan St.	DB	SR	12	34	690	0	20.29	2.83
77. Quinton Jones, Boise St.	DB	SR	12	24	483	0	20.13	2.00
78. Chubb Small, Marshall	RB	SO	12	18	361	0	20.06	1.50
79. Evan Robertson, North Texas	RB	FR	12	16	320	0	20.00	1.33
80. Anton McDuffie, Army	DB	JR	11	15	298	0	19.87	1.36
81. Deon Wallace, La.-Lafayette	RB	FR	10	20	395	0	19.75	2.00
82. Dorien Bryant, Purdue	WR	JR	14	25	490	0	19.60	1.79
82. Andre Bratton, Miami (Ohio)	RB	FR	12	15	294	0	19.60	1.25
84. Fred Smith, Tulane	WR	JR	12	25	487	0	19.48	2.08
85. Earl Goldsmith, Missouri	RB	SO	10	13	253	0	19.46	1.30
86. Chris Douglas, Rice	RB	FR	10	15	290	0	19.33	1.50
87. Alex Washington, Vanderbilt	WR	FR	12	19	364	0	19.16	1.58
88. Javier Arenas, Alabama	DB	FR	13	18	344	0	19.11	1.38
89. Zach Muzzy, North Texas	WR	SR	12	19	359	0	18.89	1.58
90. Marcus Perez, Northern Ill.	WR	SO	12	17	321	0	18.88	1.42
91. Roy Lewis, Washington	DB	JR	12	18	339	0	18.83	1.50
92. Jarvis Minton, Wisconsin	WR	JR	10	15	282	0	18.80	1.50
93. Shawn Bayes, Kent St.	WR	SO	12	22	413	0	18.77	1.83
94. Marcus Smith, New Mexico	WR	JR	13	18	335	0	18.61	1.38
95. Raymond Fry, Idaho	WR	FR	11	26	475	0	18.27	2.36
96. Brandon James, Florida	RB	FR	13	21	383	0	18.24	1.62
97. Britt Davis, Northern Ill.	WR	SO	13	18	321	0	17.83	1.38
98. Daunte Owens, Florida Int'l	RB	FR	9	12	212	0	17.67	1.33
99. Stephone Robinson, Colorado	DB	JR	12	15	261	0	17.40	1.25
100. Shannon Woods, Texas Tech	RB	SO	13	18	310	0	17.22	1.38

Field Goals

Rank, Player	Pos	Cl.	G	FGA	FGM	Pct.	FG/ Gm
1. Justin Medlock, UCLA	K	SR	13	32	28	.875	2.15
2. Jeremy Ito, Rutgers	K	JR	13	29	22	.759	1.69
2. Kevin Kelly, Penn St.	K	SO	13	34	22	.647	1.69
4. Sam Swank, Wake Forest	K	SO	14	31	23	.742	1.64
5. Arthur Carmody, Louisville	K	JR	13	25	21	.840	1.62
6. Mason Crosby, Colorado	K	SR	12	28	19	.679	1.58
7. Alexis Serna, Oregon St.	K	JR	14	29	22	.759	1.57
8. Michael Torres, UCF	K	JR	11	24	17	.708	1.55
9. Dan Ennis, Maryland	K	SR	13	25	20	.800	1.54
9. Chris Nendick, Northern Ill.	K	JR	13	27	20	.741	1.54
9. John Vaughn, Auburn	K	SR	13	24	20	.833	1.54
12. Kenny Byrd, New Mexico	K	SR	13	23	19	.826	1.46
13. Brian Jackson, Ball St.	K	SR	12	19	17	.895	1.42
14. Robert Lee, East Caro.	K	SR	10	23	14	.609	1.40
15. Brandon Pace, Virginia Tech	K	SR	13	19	18	.947	1.38
15. James Wilhoit, Tennessee	K	SR	13	22	18	.818	1.38
15. Jeff Wolfert, Missouri	K	SO	13	20	18	.900	1.38
15. Kevin Lovell, Cincinnati	K	SR	13	23	18	.783	1.38
19. Denis Hopovac, North Texas	K	SR	11	21	15	.714	1.36
20. Garrett Hartley, Oklahoma	K	JR	14	20	19	.950	1.36
21. Patrick Shadle, Syracuse	K	SO	12	18	16	.889	1.33
21. Reagan Schneider, UTEP	K	SR	12	20	16	.800	1.33
21. Andrew Wellock, Eastern Mich.	K	SR	12	23	16	.696	1.33
24. Pat McAfee, West Virginia	K	SO	13	22	17	.773	1.31
24. Jeff Snodgrass, Kansas St.	K	SR	13	24	17	.708	1.31
24. Nate Meyer, Western Mich.	K	SR	13	24	17	.708	1.31
24. Garrett Rivas, Michigan	K	SR	13	20	17	.850	1.31
28. Brett Swenson, Michigan St.	K	FR	12	19	15	.789	1.25
28. Alex Trlica, Texas Tech	K	JR	12	21	15	.714	1.25
28. Jason Reda, Illinois	K	JR	12	19	15	.789	1.25
28. Nick Folk, Arizona	K	SR	12	20	15	.750	1.25
28. Paul Martinez, Oregon	K	SR	12	22	15	.682	1.25
33. Ryan Succop, South Carolina	K	SO	13	20	16	.800	1.23
33. Louie Sakoda, Utah	K	SO	13	20	16	.800	1.23
35. Josh Arauco, Arkansas St.	K	FR	10	16	12	.750	1.20
35. Matt Reagan, Memphis	K	FR	10	17	12	.706	1.20
37. Jamie Christensen, Alabama	K	JR	11	17	13	.765	1.18
38. Cole Wilson, La.-Monroe	K	JR	12	15	14	.933	1.17
38. Joshua Shene, Mississippi	K	FR	12	17	14	.824	1.17
40. Jad Dean, Clemson	K	SR	13	22	15	.682	1.15
40. Taylor Mehlhaff, Wisconsin	K	JR	13	20	15	.750	1.15
40. Tom Schneider, California	K	JR	13	20	15	.750	1.15
40. Mario Danelo, Southern California	K	JR	13	16	15	.938	1.15
44. Darren McCaleb, Southern Miss.	K	SR	14	24	16	.667	1.14
45. Kyle Schlicher, Iowa	K	SR	12	20	13	.650	1.08
45. Thomas Morstead, SMU	K	SO	12	18	13	.722	1.08
45. Scott Webb, Kansas	K	JR	12	18	13	.722	1.08
48. Gary Cismesia, Florida St.	K	JR	13	20	14	.700	1.08
48. Jesse Ainsworth, Arizona St.	K	SR	13	19	14	.737	1.08
48. Jared McLaughlin, Brigham Young	K	SR	13	18	14	.778	1.08
48. Ben Bell, Houston	K	SO	13	18	14	.778	1.08
52. John Deraney, North Carolina St.	K	SR	12	16	12	.750	1.00
52. Anthony Montgomery, Boise St.	K	SR	13	14	13	.929	1.00
52. Austin Miller, Army	K	SR	12	17	12	.706	1.00
52. Layne Neumann, Texas A&M	K	SR	12	15	12	.800	1.00
52. Tino Amancio, Idaho	K	SO	12	17	12	.706	1.00
52. Austin Starr, Indiana	K	SO	12	15	12	.800	1.00
52. Conor Lee, Pittsburgh	K	SO	12	14	12	.857	1.00
52. Lones Seiber, Kentucky	K	FR	11	19	11	.579	1.00
60. Matt Lasher, Ohio	K	SR	14	18	13	.722	.93
60. Dan Kelly, Hawaii	K	SO	14	17	13	.765	.93
62. Jon Peattie, Miami (Fla.)	K	SR	13	19	12	.632	.92
62. Chris Manfredini, TCU	K	JR	13	14	12	.857	.92
64. Drew Edmiston, La.-Lafayette	K	SO	12	14	11	.786	.92
64. Ryan Havens, Baylor	K	SR	12	14	11	.786	.92
64. Clint Stitser, Fresno St.	K	JR	12	16	11	.688	.92
64. Chris Gould, Virginia	K	JR	12	19	11	.579	.92
68. Travis Bell, Georgia Tech	K	JR	14	18	12	.667	.86
68. Rick Albreski, Central Mich.	K	SO	14	20	12	.600	.86
70. Greg Whibbs, Troy	K	JR	13	19	11	.579	.85
70. Jarod Tracy, Tulsa	K	JR	13	12	11	.917	.85
72. Connor Barth, North Carolina	K	JR	12	10	10	1.000	.83
72. Trevor Cook, Miami (Ohio)	K	FR	12	13	10	.769	.83
72. Jason Ricks, Oklahoma St.	K	SO	12	12	10	.833	.83
72. Aric Goodman, Wyoming	K	FR	12	16	10	.625	.83
72. Michael Braunstein, Washington	K	JR	12	12	10	.833	.83
77. Warley Leroy, Fla. Atlantic	K	SO	11	14	9	.643	.82
78. Sergio Aguayo, UNLV	K	JR	10	16	8	.500	.80
79. Loren Langley, Washington St.	K	JR	9	13	7	.538	.78
80. Zach Sasser, Air Force	K	SR	12	14	9	.643	.75
80. Ross Thevenot, Tulane	K	FR	12	15	9	.600	.75
80. Swayze Waters, UAB	K	SO	12	12	9	.750	.75
83. Jared Strubeck, San Jose St.	K	SO	13	12	9	.750	.69
83. Peter LoCoco, TCU	K	SR	13	12	9	.750	.69
85. Joel Howells, Northwestern	K	SR	12	12	8	.667	.67
85. Adam Tanalski, Buffalo	K	SR	9	7	6	.857	.67
85. Clark Fangmeier, Rice	K	FR	12	11	8	.727	.67
85. Matt Harmon, Navy	K	SO	12	11	8	.727	.67
85. Bret Culbertson, Iowa St.	K	JR	12	11	8	.727	.67
85. Garrett Palmer, San Diego St.	K	JR	12	14	8	.571	.67
85. Jason Smith, Colorado St.	K	SO	12	15	8	.533	.67
85. Bryan Hahnfeldt, Vanderbilt	K	SO	12	17	8	.471	.67
85. Danny Horwedel, Louisiana Tech	K	JR	12	12	8	.667	.67
85. Aaron Zagory, Stanford	K	JR	12	13	8	.615	.67
95. Ryan Ohliger, Boston College	K	JR	11	11	7	.636	.64
95. Jason Giannini, Minnesota	K	SO	11	12	7	.583	.64
97. Colby Smith, Middle Tenn.	P/K	SR	13	13	8	.615	.62
97. Carl Gioia, Notre Dame	K	SR	13	13	8	.615	.62
97. Brett Jaekle, Nevada	K	SO	13	11	8	.727	.62
97. Colt David, LSU	K	SO	13	13	8	.615	.62
97. Aaron Pettrey, Ohio St.	K	SO	13	11	8	.727	.62

All-Purpose Running

Rank, Player	Pos	Cl.	G	Rush	Rec	PR	KOR	Yards	Yds/ Gm	Plays	Yds/Pl
1. Garrett Wolfe, Northern Ill.	RB	SR	13	1,928	249	0	0	2,177	167.46	337	6.46
2. Steve Slaton, West Virginia	RB	SO	13	1,744	360	0	0	2,104	161.85	275	7.65
3. Johnnie Lee Higgins Jr., UTEP	WR	SR	12	-2	1,319	281	275	1,873	156.08	113	16.58
4. Chris Williams, New Mexico St.	WR	SO	12	53	1,415	92	301	1,861	155.08	116	16.04
5. Ian Johnson, Boise St.	RB	SO	12	1,714	55	0	0	1,769	147.42	284	6.23
6. Darren McFadden, Arkansas	TB	SO	14	1,647	149	0	262	2,058	147.00	305	6.75
7. Patrick Jackson, Louisiana Tech	RB	SO	12	854	181	0	702	1,737	144.75	221	7.86
8. Curtis Brown, Brigham Young	RB	SR	13	1,010	566	0	288	1,864	143.38	276	6.75
9. Keenan Burton, Kentucky	WR	JR	13	-7	1,036	51	765	1,845	141.92	113	16.33
10. Nate Ilaoa, Hawaii	RB	SR	13	990	837	0	0	1,827	140.54	198	9.23
11. Ray Rice, Rutgers	RB	SO	13	1,794	30	0	0	1,824	140.31	339	5.38
12. Dwayne Wright, Fresno St.	RB	JR	12	1,462	221	0	0	1,683	140.25	290	5.80
13. Shannon Woods, Texas Tech	RB	SO	13	926	572	0	310	1,808	139.08	245	7.38
14. Ahmad Bradshaw, Marshall	RB	JR	12	1,523	129	6	0	1,658	138.17	267	6.21
15. Jon Cornish, Kansas	RB	SR	12	1,457	194	0	0	1,651	137.58	274	6.03
16. Marshawn Lynch, California	RB	JR	13	1,356	328	0	101	1,785	137.31	262	6.81
17. Jonathan Stewart, Oregon	RB	SO	13	981	144	0	646	1,771	136.23	226	7.84
18. Calvin Dawson, La.-Monroe	RB	JR	12	1,210	155	0	268	1,633	136.08	246	6.64
19. P.J. Hill, Wisconsin	RB	FR	13	1,569	197	0	0	1,766	135.85	329	5.37
20. Matt Forte, Tulane	RB	JR	9	859	360	0	0	1,219	135.44	192	6.35
21. Anthony Alridge, Houston	RB	JR	14	959	274	0	603	1,836	131.14	141	13.02
22. Felix Jones, Arkansas	TB	SO	14	1,168	107	0	554	1,829	130.64	192	9.53
23. Michael Hart, Michigan	RB	JR	13	1,562	125	0	0	1,687	129.77	335	5.04
24. Darius Walker, Notre Dame	RB	JR	13	1,267	391	0	0	1,658	127.54	311	5.33
25. Tony Hunt, Penn St.	RB	SR	13	1,386	259	0	0	1,645	126.54	304	5.41
26. Sammie Stroughter, Oregon St.	WR	JR	14	-22	1,293	470	0	1,741	124.36	108	16.12
27. Quinton Smith, Rice	RB	SR	13	1,096	410	0	102	1,608	123.69	258	6.23
28. Dorien Bryant, Purdue	WR	JR	14	150	1,068	0	490	1,708	122.00	131	13.04
29. Yvenson Bernard, Oregon St.	RB	JR	13	1,307	276	0	0	1,583	121.77	339	4.67
30. Kevin Smith, UCF	RB	SO	9	934	158	0	0	1,092	121.33	229	4.77
31. DeSean Jackson, California	WR	SO	13	19	1,060	455	38	1,572	120.92	91	17.27
32. David Harvey, Akron	WR	FR	12	7	914	8	510	1,439	119.92	69	20.86
33. Darius Reynaud, West Virginia	WR	JR	13	221	520	0	813	1,554	119.54	83	18.72
34. Steve Breaston, Michigan	WR	SR	13	79	670	332	467	1,548	119.08	118	13.12
35. Damion Fletcher, Southern Miss.	RB	FR	13	1,388	142	0	0	1,530	117.69	294	5.20
36. Rodney Ferguson, New Mexico	RB	SO	13	1,234	291	0	0	1,525	117.31	280	5.45
37. Ted Ginn Jr., Ohio St.	WR	JR	13	17	781	266	440	1,504	115.69	104	14.46
38. Tyrell Fenroy, La.-Lafayette	RB	SO	12	1,193	176	0	0	1,369	114.08	238	5.75
39. Ryne Robinson, Miami (Ohio)	WR	SR	12	11	1,178	175	0	1,364	113.67	112	12.18
40. Branden Ore, Virginia Tech	RB	SO	12	1,137	214	0	0	1,351	112.58	259	5.22
41. Tashard Choice, Georgia Tech	RB	JR	14	1,473	98	0	0	1,571	112.21	309	5.08
42. Kevin Robinson, Utah St.	WR	JR	12	35	582	74	641	1,332	111.00	87	15.31
43. Idris Moss, Tulsa	WR	SR	13	63	803	197	378	1,441	110.85	115	12.53
44. Trumaine Riley, Eastern Mich.	WR	SR	11	5	364	169	678	1,216	110.55	101	12.04
45. Ryan Torain, Arizona St.	RB	JR	13	1,229	205	0	0	1,434	110.31	241	5.95
46. Kalvin McRae, Ohio	RB	JR	14	1,252	280	0	0	1,532	109.43	287	5.34
47. Damon Morton, Colorado St.	WR	JR	12	17	722	204	368	1,311	109.25	95	13.80
48. C.J. Spiller, Clemson	RB	FR	13	938	210	33	234	1,415	108.85	172	8.23
49. Naaman Roosevelt, Buffalo	QB	FR	12	9	429	144	724	1,306	108.83	75	17.41
50. Jalen Parmele, Toledo	RB	JR	12	1,131	128	0	46	1,305	108.75	226	5.77
51. Amir Pinnix, Minnesota	RB	JR	13	1,272	138	0	0	1,410	108.46	268	5.26
52. Aaron Brown, TCU	RB	SO	13	801	455	0	145	1,401	107.77	193	7.26
53. Cory Boyd, South Carolina	RB	JR	12	823	406	0	64	1,293	107.75	203	6.37
54. Marcus Thigpen, Indiana	RB	SO	12	387	180	0	723	1,290	107.50	140	9.21
55. Syndric Steptoe, Arizona	WR	SR	12	34	568	261	409	1,272	106.00	98	12.98
56. Chris Markey, UCLA	RB	JR	13	1,107	261	9	0	1,377	105.92	264	5.22
57. Tyrell Sutton, Northwestern	RB	SO	12	1,000	261	0	8	1,269	105.75	230	5.52
58. Darrell Blackman, North Carolina St.	WR	JR	11	47	358	206	549	1,160	105.45	82	14.15
59. LaRod Stephens-Howlin, Pittsburgh	RB	SO	11	893	231	0	31	1,155	105.00	198	5.83
59. Robert Hubbard, Nevada	RB	SR	12	996	243	0	21	1,260	105.00	234	5.38
61. Reggie Campbell, Navy	RB	JR	13	706	244	55	357	1,362	104.77	131	10.40
62. Antonio Pittman, Ohio St.	RB	JR	13	1,233	127	0	0	1,360	104.62	256	5.31
63. Brandon Jackson, Nebraska	RB	JR	14	989	313	0	157	1,459	104.21	230	6.34
64. Mark Bonds, Western Mich.	RB	JR	12	1,082	164	0	0	1,246	103.83	278	4.48
65. DJ Hall, Alabama	WR	JR	12	48	1,056	0	139	1,243	103.58	75	16.57
66. Brandon West, Western Mich.	RB	FR	13	633	96	0	615	1,344	103.38	169	7.95
67. Terry Moss, Ball St.	WR	SR	12	0	685	0	551	1,236	103.00	50	24.72
68. Joel Filani, Texas Tech	WR	SR	13	34	1,300	0	0	1,334	102.62	95	14.04
69. Harry Douglas, Louisville	WR	JR	13	49	1,265	16	3	1,333	102.54	81	16.46
70. Robert Meachem, Tennessee	WR	JR	13	3	1,298	12	16	1,329	102.23	77	17.26
71. Kory Sheets, Purdue	RB	SO	14	780	213	8	422	1,423	101.64	206	6.91
72. Patrick White, West Virginia	QB	SO	12	1,219	0	0	0	1,219	101.58	165	7.39
73. Dennis Kennedy, Akron	RB	SO	11	914	193	0	0	1,107	100.64	265	4.18
74. James Davis, Clemson	RB	SO	13	1,187	115	0	0	1,302	100.15	209	6.23
75. Ross Dickerson, Hawaii	WR	SR	14	13	726	0	650	1,389	99.21	84	16.54
76. Earl Bennett, Vanderbilt	WR	SO	12	11	1,146	33	0	1,190	99.17	95	12.53
77. Brandon Tate, North Carolina	WR	SO	12	20	72	194	902	1,188	99.00	66	18.00
78. Jarett Dillard, Rice	WR	SO	13	5	1,247	0	33	1,285	98.85	94	13.67
79. Mike Walker, UCF	WR	SR	12	0	1,178	0	0	1,178	98.17	90	13.09
80. Vincent Marshall, Houston	WR	SR	14	59	979	148	184	1,370	97.86	114	12.02

Rank, Player	Pos	Cl.	G	Rush	Rec	PR	KOR	Yards	Yds/ Gm	Plays	Yds/Pl
81. Donald Brown II, Connecticut	RB	FR	12	896	66	0	210	1,172	97.67	183	6.40
82. Tim Brown, Temple	RB	SR	10	731	218	20	0	969	96.90	219	4.42
83. Eddie Royal, Virginia Tech	WR	JR	13	24	497	304	431	1,256	96.62	78	16.10
84. Jason Snelling, Virginia	RB	SR	11	772	282	0	0	1,054	95.82	212	4.97
85. Richard Davis, Toledo	RB	SO	12	282	160	0	701	1,143	95.25	140	8.16
86. LaMarcus Coker, Tennessee	RB	FR	11	696	168	0	180	1,044	94.91	130	8.03
87. Derek Pegues, Mississippi St.	DB	SO	12	0	0	350	687	1,132	94.33	58	19.52
88. Marcus Smith, New Mexico	WR	JR	13	22	859	0	335	1,216	93.54	78	15.59
89. Davone Bess, Hawaii	WR	SO	14	0	1,220	83	0	1,303	93.07	101	12.90
90. Joseph Doss, Memphis	RB	JR	12	910	205	0	0	1,115	92.92	249	4.48
91. Curtis Brinkley, Syracuse	RB	SO	12	571	91	0	448	1,110	92.50	170	6.53
92. Jeremiah Johnson, Oregon	RB	SO	13	644	100	127	327	1,198	92.15	149	8.04
93. Reggie Arnold, Arkansas St.	RB	FR	12	1,076	16	0	0	1,092	91.00	213	5.13
94. Adarius Bowman, Oklahoma St.	WR	JR	13	1	1,181	0	0	1,182	90.92	61	19.38
95. Ontario Sneed, Central Mich.	RB	SO	13	764	415	0	0	1,179	90.69	187	6.30
96. Marlon Lucky, Nebraska	RB	SO	14	728	383	0	153	1,264	90.29	181	6.98
97. Yonus Davis, San Jose St.	RB	JR	13	1,007	86	0	69	1,162	89.38	175	6.64
98. Eugene Jarvis, Kent St.	RB	SO	11	798	126	42	10	976	88.73	210	4.65
99. Kenny Irons, Auburn	RB	SR	11	893	78	0	0	971	88.27	208	4.67
100. Pierre Thomas, Illinois	RB	SR	12	755	79	0	223	1,057	88.08	150	7.05

Scoring

Rank, Player	Pos	Cl.	G	TD	OKM	OKA	FGM	FGA	Pts	Pts/Gm
1. Ian Johnson, Boise St.	RB	SO	12	25	0	0	0	0	152	12.67
2. Ahmad Bradshaw, Marshall	RB	JR	12	21	0	0	0	0	126	10.50
3. Jarett Dillard, Rice	WR	SO	13	21	0	0	0	0	126	9.69
4. Arthur Carmody, Louisville	K	JR	13	0	60	60	21	25	123	9.46
5. Ray Rice, Rutgers	RB	SO	13	20	0	0	0	0	120	9.23
6. Patrick White, West Virginia	QB	SO	12	18	0	0	0	0	108	9.00
7. Garrett Wolfe, Northern Ill.	RB	SR	13	19	0	0	0	0	116	8.92
8. Jorvorskie Lane, Texas A&M	RB	SO	13	19	0	0	0	0	114	8.77
9. Pat McAfee, West Virginia	K	SO	13	0	62	62	17	22	113	8.69
9. Justin Medlock, UCLA	K	SR	13	0	29	29	28	32	113	8.69
11. Branden Ore, Virginia Tech	RB	SO	12	17	0	0	0	0	102	8.50
12. Steve Slaton, West Virginia	RB	SO	13	18	0	0	0	0	108	8.31
12. Nate Ilaoa, Hawaii	RB	SR	13	18	0	0	0	0	108	8.31
14. Jeremy Ito, Rutgers	K	JR	13	0	41	42	22	29	107	8.23
15. Alex Trlica, Texas Tech	K	JR	12	0	51	51	15	21	96	8.00
16. Alexis Serna, Oregon St.	K	JR	14	0	45	45	22	29	111	7.93
17. James Davis, Clemson	RB	SO	13	17	0	0	0	0	102	7.85
18. Anthony Montgomery, Boise St.	K	SR	13	0	61	63	13	14	100	7.69
18. Jared McLaughlin, Brigham Young	K	SR	13	0	58	62	14	18	100	7.69
20. Jeff Wolfert, Missouri	K	SO	13	0	45	45	18	20	99	7.62
21. Garrett Hartley, Oklahoma	K	JR	14	0	49	50	19	20	106	7.57
22. Brian Jackson, Ball St.	K	SR	12	0	37	38	17	19	90	7.50
22. Johnnie Lee Higgins Jr., UTEP	WR	SR	12	15	0	0	0	0	90	7.50
24. Tom Schneider, California	K	JR	13	0	52	52	15	20	97	7.46
25. P.J. Hill, Wisconsin	RB	FR	13	16	0	0	0	0	96	7.38
25. Kevin Kelly, Penn St.	K	SO	13	0	30	30	22	34	96	7.38
25. James Wilhoit, Tennessee	K	SR	13	0	42	43	18	22	96	7.38
25. Courtney Tennial, Tulsa	RB	JR	13	16	0	0	0	0	96	7.38
29. Paul Martinez, Oregon	K	SR	12	1	37	39	15	22	88	7.33
30. Chris Nendick, Northern Ill.	K	JR	13	0	35	36	20	27	95	7.31
31. Sam Swank, Wake Forest	K	SO	14	0	33	33	23	31	102	7.29
32. John Vaughn, Auburn	K	SR	13	0	34	34	20	24	94	7.23
33. Garrett Rivas, Michigan	K	SR	13	0	42	44	17	20	93	7.15
33. Ben Bell, Houston	K	SO	13	0	51	53	14	18	93	7.15
35. Dan Ennis, Maryland	K	SR	13	0	32	32	20	25	92	7.08
35. Brandon Pace, Virginia Tech	K	SR	13	0	38	40	18	19	92	7.08
35. Taylor Mehlhaff, Wisconsin	K	JR	13	0	47	47	15	20	92	7.08
38. Jad Dean, Clemson	K	SR	13	0	46	49	15	22	91	7.00
38. Kalvin McRae, Ohio	RB	JR	14	16	0	0	0	0	98	7.00
38. Darren McFadden, Arkansas	TB	SO	14	16	0	0	0	0	98	7.00
38. Louie Sakoda, Utah	K	SO	13	0	43	43	16	20	91	7.00
42. Marshawn Lynch, California	RB	JR	13	15	0	0	0	0	90	6.92
42. Jackie Battle, Houston	RB	SR	13	15	0	0	0	0	90	6.92
42. Rhema McKnight, Notre Dame	WR	SR	13	15	0	0	0	0	90	6.92
45. Conor Lee, Pittsburgh	K	SO	12	0	47	47	12	14	83	6.92
46. Michael Torres, UCF	K	JR	11	0	25	25	17	24	76	6.91
47. Mario Danelo, Southern California	K	JR	13	0	44	48	15	16	89	6.85
48. Reagan Schneider, UTEP	K	SR	12	0	34	37	16	20	82	6.83
49. Kenny Byrd, New Mexico	K	SR	13	0	31	31	19	23	88	6.77
50. Matt Forte, Tulane	RB	JR	9	10	0	0	0	0	60	6.67
51. Anthony Allen, Louisville	RB	FR	13	14	0	0	0	0	86	6.62
51. Michael Hart, Michigan	RB	JR	13	14	0	0	0	0	86	6.62
53. Davone Bess, Hawaii	WR	SO	14	15	0	0	0	0	92	6.57
54. Ryan Succop, South Carolina	K	SO	13	0	37	39	16	20	85	6.54
55. Brett Swenson, Michigan St.	K	FR	12	0	33	33	15	19	78	6.50
56. Antonio Pittman, Ohio St.	RB	JR	13	14	0	0	0	0	84	6.46
56. Jesse Ainsworth, Arizona St.	K	SR	13	0	42	42	14	19	84	6.46
56. Nate Meyer, Western Mich.	K	SR	13	0	33	34	17	24	84	6.46

Rank, Player	Pos	Cl.	G	TD	OKM	OKA	FGM	FGA	Pts	Pts/Gm
56. Tony Hunt, Penn St.	RB	SR	13	14	0	0	0	0	84	6.46
60. Calvin Johnson, Georgia Tech	WR	JR	14	15	0	0	0	0	90	6.43
60. Darren McCaleb, Southern Miss.	K	SR	14	0	42	42	16	24	90	6.43
62. Jason Ricks, Oklahoma St.	K	SO	12	0	47	49	10	12	77	6.42
63. Robert Lee, East Caro.	K	SR	10	0	22	22	14	23	64	6.40
64. Jeff Snodgrass, Kansas St.	K	SR	13	0	32	32	17	24	83	6.38
65. Mason Crosby, Colorado	K	SR	12	0	19	19	19	28	76	6.33
65. Scott Webb, Kansas	K	JR	12	0	37	39	13	18	76	6.33
67. Kevin Lovell, Cincinnati	K	SR	13	0	28	28	18	23	82	6.31
68. Gary Cismesia, Florida St.	K	JR	13	0	39	40	14	20	81	6.23
69. Yvenson Bernard, Oregon St.	RB	JR	13	13	0	0	0	0	80	6.15
70. Dan Kelly, Hawaii	K	SO	14	0	47	50	13	17	86	6.14
71. Matt Reagan, Memphis	K	FR	10	0	25	26	12	17	61	6.10
72. Thomas Morstead, SMU	K	SO	12	0	34	35	13	18	73	6.08
73. Aaron Pettrey, Ohio St.	K	SO	13	0	55	58	8	11	79	6.08
74. Greg Carr, Florida St.	WR	SO	12	12	0	0	0	0	72	6.00
74. James Hardy, Indiana	WR	SO	10	10	0	0	0	0	60	6.00
74. Rick Albreski, Central Mich.	K	SO	14	0	48	51	12	20	84	6.00
74. DeSean Jackson, California	WR	SO	13	13	0	0	0	0	78	6.00
74. Jeff Samardzija, Notre Dame	WR	SR	13	13	0	0	0	0	78	6.00
74. Joel Filani, Texas Tech	WR	SR	13	13	0	0	0	0	78	6.00
74. Chris Williams, New Mexico St.	WR	SO	12	12	0	0	0	0	72	6.00
74. Dwayne Wright, Fresno St.	RB	JR	12	12	0	0	0	0	72	6.00
74. Keenan Burton, Kentucky	WR	JR	13	13	0	0	0	0	78	6.00
74. Lones Seiber, Kentucky	K	FR	11	0	33	34	11	19	66	6.00
74. Dwayne Jarrett, Southern California	WR	JR	12	12	0	0	0	0	72	6.00
85. Kyle Schlicher, Iowa	K	SR	12	0	32	33	13	20	71	5.92
86. Jarod Tracy, Tulsa	K	JR	13	0	43	45	11	12	76	5.85
87. Patrick Shadle, Syracuse	K	SO	12	0	21	21	16	18	69	5.75
88. Colt David, LSU	K	SO	13	0	50	51	8	13	74	5.69
88. Quinton Smith, Rice	RB	SR	13	12	0	0	0	0	74	5.69
90. Jason Reda, Illinois	K	JR	12	0	23	23	15	19	68	5.67
90. Robert Johnson, Texas Tech	WR	SR	12	11	0	0	0	0	68	5.67
92. Travis Bell, Georgia Tech	K	JR	14	0	43	43	12	18	79	5.64
93. Carl Gioia, Notre Dame	K	SR	13	0	49	54	8	13	73	5.62
94. Nick Folk, Arizona	K	SR	12	0	22	22	15	20	67	5.58
95. Kory Sheets, Purdue	RB	SO	14	13	0	0	0	0	78	5.57
96. C.J. Spiller, Clemson	RB	FR	13	12	0	0	0	0	72	5.54
96. Shannon Woods, Texas Tech	RB	SO	13	12	0	0	0	0	72	5.54
96. Limas Sweed, Texas	WR	JR	13	12	0	0	0	0	72	5.54
96. Adarius Bowman, Oklahoma St.	WR	JR	13	12	0	0	0	0	72	5.54
96. Chris Manfredini, TCU	K	JR	13	0	36	41	12	14	72	5.54
96. Jonny Harline, Brigham Young	TE	SR	13	12	0	0	0	0	72	5.54
96. Dwayne Bowe, LSU	WR	SR	13	12	0	0	0	0	72	5.54

Points Responsible For

Rank, Player	Pos	Cl.	G	Passing Conv	Passing TD	Pts Scored	Total PRF	PRF/Gm
1. Colt Brennan, Hawaii	QB	JR	14	3	58	34	388	27.71
2. Chase Holbrook, New Mexico St.	QB	SO	12	1	34	26	232	19.33
3. John Beck, Brigham Young	QB	SR	12	0	32	36	228	19.00
4. Graham Harrell, Texas Tech	QB	SO	13	1	38	12	242	18.62
5. Brady Quinn, Notre Dame	QB	SR	13	0	37	12	234	18.00
6. Justin Willis, SMU	QB	FR	11	1	26	22	180	16.36
7. Patrick White, West Virginia	QB	SO	12	0	13	108	186	15.50
8. Andre Woodson, Kentucky	QB	JR	13	0	31	6	192	14.77
8. Chase Daniel, Missouri	QB	SO	13	0	28	24	192	14.77
10. Kevin Kolb, Houston	QB	SR	14	0	30	24	204	14.57
11. Dan LeFevour, Central Mich.	QB	FR	14	1	26	44	202	14.43
12. Troy Smith, Ohio St.	QB	SR	13	0	30	6	186	14.31
12. Colt McCoy, Texas	QB	FR	13	0	29	12	186	14.31
14. John David Booty, Southern California	QB	JR	13	0	29	6	180	13.85
15. Jared Zabransky, Boise St.	QB	SR	13	1	23	38	178	13.69
16. Tyler Palko, Pittsburgh	QB	SR	12	0	25	12	162	13.50
16. Jordan Palmer, UTEP	QB	SR	12	0	26	6	162	13.50
18. JaMarcus Russell, LSU	QB	JR	13	0	28	6	174	13.38
18. Bobby Reid, Oklahoma St.	QB	SO	13	0	24	30	174	13.38
20. Shawn Bell, Baylor	QB	SR	9	0	19	6	120	13.33
21. Ian Johnson, Boise St.	RB	SO	12	0	0	152	152	12.67
21. Kerry Meier, Kansas	QB	FR	9	1	13	34	114	12.67
23. Nate Longshore, California	QB	SO	13	0	24	18	162	12.46
24. Omar Haugabook, Troy	QB	JR	13	0	21	30	156	12.00
24. Curtis Painter, Purdue	QB	SO	14	0	22	36	168	12.00
24. Chris Nickson, Vanderbilt	QB	SO	12	0	15	54	144	12.00
27. Zac Taylor, Nebraska	QB	SR	14	1	26	8	166	11.86
28. Matt Grothe, South Fla.	QB	FR	13	1	15	56	148	11.38
28. Brett Ratliff, Utah	QB	SR	13	1	23	8	148	11.38
30. Alex Brink, Washington St.	QB	JR	12	1	19	20	136	11.33
31. Chris Leak, Florida	QB	SR	14	0	23	18	156	11.14
32. Paul Thompson, Oklahoma	QB	SR	14	1	22	20	154	11.00
33. Rudy Carpenter, Arizona St.	QB	SO	13	0	23	0	138	10.62

Rank, Player	Pos	Cl.	G	Passing Conv	Passing TD	Pts Scored	Total PRF	PRF/Gm
33. Paul Smith, Tulsa	QB	JR	13	0	15	48	138	10.62
33. Adam Tafralis, San Jose St.	QB	JR	13	0	21	12	138	10.62
36. Jeff Rowe, Nevada	QB	SR	12	0	17	24	126	10.50
36. Ahmad Bradshaw, Marshall	RB	JR	12	0	0	126	126	10.50
38. Chad Henne, Michigan	QB	JR	13	1	22	2	136	10.46
39. Kellen Lewis, Indiana	QB	FR	11	0	14	30	114	10.36
40. Reggie Ball, Georgia Tech	QB	SR	13	0	20	12	132	10.15
40. Bryan Cupito, Minnesota	QB	SR	13	0	22	0	132	10.15
42. Anthony Turner, Bowling Green	QB	SO	10	1	11	32	100	10.00
42. Erik Ainge, Tennessee	QB	JR	12	0	19	6	120	10.00
42. Shaun Carney, Air Force	QB	JR	12	0	12	48	120	10.00
45. Matt Moore, Oregon St.	QB	SR	14	0	18	30	138	9.86
46. Matt Ryan, Boston College	QB	JR	12	1	15	26	118	9.83
46. Martin Hankins, Memphis	QB	JR	12	1	18	8	118	9.83
48. John Stocco, Wisconsin	QB	SR	11	0	17	6	108	9.82
48. Drew Tate, Iowa	QB	SR	11	0	18	0	108	9.82
50. Jeff Ballard, TCU	QB	SR	13	0	13	48	126	9.69
50. Jarett Dillard, Rice	WR	SO	13	0	0	126	126	9.69
52. Mike Kokal, Miami (Ohio)	QB	JR	11	1	14	20	106	9.64
53. Luke Getsy, Akron	QB	SR	12	1	18	4	114	9.50
54. Arthur Carmody, Louisville	K	JR	13	0	0	123	123	9.46
55. Drew Stanton, Michigan St.	QB	SR	11	0	12	30	102	9.27
55. Julian Edelman, Kent St.	QB	SO	11	0	10	42	102	9.27
57. Ray Rice, Rutgers	RB	SO	13	0	0	120	120	9.23
58. Bret Meyer, Iowa St.	QB	JR	12	0	12	38	110	9.17
59. Ryan Cubit, Western Mich.	QB	SR	11	1	16	2	100	9.09
60. Nate Davis, Ball St.	QB	FR	12	0	18	0	108	9.00
60. Lester Ricard, Tulane	QB	SR	12	0	18	0	108	9.00
62. Garrett Wolfe, Northern Ill.	RB	SR	13	0	0	116	116	8.92
63. Jorvorskie Lane, Texas A&M	RB	SO	13	0	0	114	114	8.77
64. Brian Brohm, Louisville	QB	JR	11	0	16	0	96	8.73
65. Pat McAfee, West Virginia	K	SO	13	0	0	113	113	8.69
65. Justin Medlock, UCLA	K	SR	13	0	0	113	113	8.69
67. Branden Ore, Virginia Tech	RB	SO	12	0	0	102	102	8.50
68. Will Proctor, Clemson	QB	SR	13	2	16	10	110	8.46
68. Stephen McGee, Texas A&M	QB	SO	13	3	12	32	110	8.46
70. Steve Slaton, West Virginia	RB	SO	13	0	0	108	108	8.31
70. Nate Ilaoa, Hawaii	RB	SR	13	0	0	108	108	8.31
72. Darren McFadden, Arkansas	TB	SO	14	0	3	98	116	8.29
73. Jeremy Ito, Rutgers	K	JR	13	0	0	107	107	8.23
74. Kaipo-Noa Kaheaku-Enhada, Navy	QB	SO	11	0	5	60	90	8.18
75. Alex Trlica, Texas Tech	K	JR	12	0	0	96	96	8.00
76. Alexis Serna, Oregon St.	K	JR	14	0	0	111	111	7.93
77. Sam Hollenbach, Maryland	QB	SR	13	0	15	12	102	7.85
77. James Davis, Clemson	RB	SO	13	0	0	102	102	7.85
77. John Parker Wilson, Alabama	QB	SO	13	0	17	0	102	7.85
80. Jerry Babb, La.-Lafayette	QB	SR	12	1	9	38	94	7.83
81. Chris Nelson, New Mexico	QB	SR	10	0	12	6	78	7.80
82. Anthony Montgomery, Boise St.	K	SR	13	0	0	100	100	7.69
82. Jared McLaughlin, Brigham Young	K	SR	13	0	0	100	100	7.69
84. Brian Jackson, Ball St.	K	SR	12	1	0	90	92	7.67
85. Tom Brandstater, Fresno St.	QB	SO	11	0	13	6	84	7.64
86. Jeff Wolfert, Missouri	K	SO	13	0	0	99	99	7.62
87. Garrett Hartley, Oklahoma	K	JR	14	0	0	106	106	7.57
88. Caleb Hanie, Colorado St.	QB	JR	12	0	11	24	90	7.50
88. Johnnie Lee Higgins Jr., UTEP	WR	SR	12	0	0	90	90	7.50
90. Tom Schneider, California	K	JR	13	0	0	97	97	7.46
91. Chris Williams, UAB	QB	SR	10	0	9	20	74	7.40
92. P.J. Hill, Wisconsin	RB	FR	13	0	0	96	96	7.38
92. Syvelle Newton, South Carolina	QB	SR	13	0	12	24	96	7.38
92. James Wilhoit, Tennessee	K	SR	13	0	0	96	96	7.38
92. Kevin Kelly, Penn St.	K	SO	13	0	0	96	96	7.38
92. Courtney Tennial, Tulsa	RB	JR	13	0	0	96	96	7.38
92. James Pinkney, East Caro.	QB	SR	13	0	12	24	96	7.38
98. Paul Martinez, Oregon	K	SR	12	0	0	88	88	7.33
98. Karsten Sween, Wyoming	QB	FR	9	0	9	12	66	7.33
100. Chris Nendick, Northern Ill.	K	JR	13	0	0	95	95	7.31

Total Tackles

Rank, Player	Pos	Cl.	G	Solo	Ast	Total	TT/Gm
1. Alvin Bowen, Iowa St.	LB	JR	12	95	60	155	12.92
2. Matthew Castelo, San Jose St.	LB	JR	13	81	84	165	12.69
3. J Leman, Illinois	LB	JR	12	75	77	152	12.67
4. H.B. Blades, Pittsburgh	LB	SR	12	86	61	147	12.25
5. Keyonvis Bouie, Florida Int'l	LB	SR	10	69	51	120	12.00
6. Patrick Willis, Mississippi	LB	SR	12	87	50	137	11.42
7. David Vobora, Idaho	LB	JR	12	84	50	134	11.17
8. Tyrone McKenzie, Iowa St.	LB	SO	12	59	70	129	10.75
9. Troy Collavo, UTEP	LB	SR	12	47	78	125	10.42
10. Drew Fowler, Air Force	LB	JR	12	47	76	123	10.25
11. Jordon Dizon, Colorado	LB	JR	12	64	57	121	10.08
12. Mike Klinkenborg, Iowa	LB	JR	13	56	73	129	9.92
13. Vince Hall, Virginia Tech	LB	JR	13	63	65	128	9.85
14. Desmond Bishop, California	LB	SR	13	65	61	126	9.69
15. Kelvin Smith, Syracuse	LB	SR	12	58	57	115	9.58
16. Daniel Holtzclaw, Eastern Mich.	LB	SO	12	39	75	114	9.50
16. Michael Okwo, Stanford	LB	SR	10	57	38	95	9.50
18. Wesley Woodyard, Kentucky	LB	JR	13	80	42	122	9.38
19. Terrel White, Bowling Green	LB	SR	10	40	53	93	9.30
20. Tim McCarthy, Northern Ill.	LB	SO	12	38	73	111	9.25
21. Ryan Henegan, Connecticut	LB	JR	10	50	42	92	9.20
22. Jeff Bublavi, Buffalo	LB	SR	12	59	51	110	9.17
23. Joe Martin, San Diego St.	LB	SR	12	59	50	109	9.08

Rank, Player	Pos	Cl.	G	Solo	Ast	Total	TT/Gm
23. Joe Sturdivant, SMU	DB	SR	12	80	29	109	9.08
25. Brian Raines, Rice	LB	SO	13	85	33	118	9.08
26. Thomas Keith, Central Mich.	LB	JR	14	64	63	127	9.07
27. Michael Richardson, Eastern Mich.	LB	SR	12	49	59	108	9.00
28. Paul Posluszny, Penn St.	LB	SR	13	69	47	116	8.92
28. Dustin Utschig, Northern Ill.	DB	SR	13	66	50	116	8.92
30. James Laurinaitis, Ohio St.	LB	SO	13	53	62	115	8.85
31. Erin Henderson, Maryland	LB	SO	13	58	56	114	8.77
31. Quincy Black, New Mexico	DB	SR	13	57	57	114	8.77
33. C.J. Wallace, Washington	DB	SR	12	62	43	105	8.75
34. Dan Connor, Penn St.	LB	JR	13	70	43	113	8.69
35. Andre Kirkland, Kent St.	DB	SR	12	63	41	104	8.67
35. Curtis Keyes, Marshall	DB	SR	12	56	48	104	8.67
35. Cason Shrode, Army	LB	SR	12	51	53	104	8.67
38. Jon Abbate, Wake Forest	LB	JR	14	49	71	120	8.57
39. Korey Hall, Boise St.	LB	SR	13	57	54	111	8.54
40. Patrick Lowery, North Carolina St.	LB	SR	12	45	57	102	8.50
40. Quinton Culberson, Mississippi St.	LB	SR	12	52	50	102	8.50
40. Steve Tate, Utah	DB	JR	12	58	44	102	8.50
43. Wesley Jefferson, Maryland	LB	JR	13	51	59	110	8.46
44. Rufus Alexander, Oklahoma	LB	SR	14	75	43	118	8.43
45. Clint Session, Pittsburgh	LB	SR	12	67	34	101	8.42
46. Buster Davis, Florida St.	LB	SR	13	57	52	109	8.38
46. Rob Caldwell, Navy	LB	SR	13	49	60	109	8.38
48. Jolonn Dunbar, Boston College	LB	JR	11	50	42	92	8.36
48. Joe Jiannoni, Utah	LB	JR	11	48	44	92	8.36
50. Darran Matthews, Eastern Mich.	LB	JR	12	41	59	100	8.33
50. Eric Frampton, Washington St.	DB	SR	12	55	45	100	8.33
52. Danny Lansanah, Connecticut	LB	JR	12	45	54	99	8.25
52. Tim McManigal, New Mexico St.	LB	SR	12	30	69	99	8.25
52. Jon Banks, Iowa St.	DB	JR	12	58	41	99	8.25
55. Jasper Brinkley, South Carolina	LB	JR	13	85	22	107	8.23
55. Cameron Jensen, Brigham Young	LB	SR	13	57	50	107	8.23
55. Marcus Bacon, Missouri	LB	SR	13	44	63	107	8.23
58. Alexander Bostic III, Florida Int'l	LB	SR	12	55	43	98	8.17
58. Kevin Payne, La.-Monroe	DB	SR	12	75	23	98	8.17
60. Brandon Archer, Kansas St.	LB	SR	13	57	49	106	8.15
61. Adam Leonard, Hawaii	LB	SO	14	62	52	114	8.14
62. Blair Phillips, Oregon	LB	SR	13	56	49	105	8.08
63. Mike Sherels, Minnesota	LB	JR	13	67	37	104	8.00
63. Barrett Scruggs, Army	LB	SR	12	53	43	96	8.00
63. Matt Couch, Marshall	LB	SR	12	36	60	96	8.00
63. Marvin Mitchell, Tennessee	LB	SR	13	75	29	104	8.00
63. Ollice Ervin, Buffalo	LB	JR	12	44	52	96	8.00
63. Joe Hudson, Miami (Ohio)	LB	SO	12	54	42	96	8.00
69. Doug Kress, Central Mich.	LB	SR	14	47	64	111	7.93
70. Mike Pagnotta, Colorado St.	DB	SO	9	46	25	71	7.89
71. Michael Tauiliili, Duke	LB	SO	12	32	62	94	7.83
71. Otis Wiley, Michigan St.	DB	SO	12	62	32	94	7.83
71. Rory Johnson, Mississippi	LB	FR	12	47	47	94	7.83
74. Christopher Vedder, San Jose St.	DB	SR	13	55	46	101	7.77
75. Jonathan Goff, Vanderbilt	LB	JR	12	67	26	93	7.75
76. Edmond Miles, Iowa	LB	SR	13	57	43	100	7.69
76. Maurice Crum, Notre Dame	LB	JR	13	47	53	100	7.69
76. Damaja Jones, San Jose St.	LB	SR	13	50	50	100	7.69
79. Zach Diles, Kansas St.	LB	SR	13	53	46	99	7.62
80. Clayton Mullins, Miami (Ohio)	LB	SO	12	45	46	91	7.58
81. Nelson Coleman, Tulsa	LB	JR	13	43	55	98	7.54
81. Chinedum Ndukwe, Notre Dame	DB	SR	13	58	40	98	7.54
83. Joey Card, Miami (Ohio)	DB	SR	12	56	34	90	7.50
83. Klint Kubiak, Colorado St.	DB	SO	12	49	41	90	7.50
83. Mike Rivera, Kansas	LB	SO	12	48	42	90	7.50
83. Scott White, Washington	LB	SR	12	45	45	90	7.50
83. Trevor Hooper, Stanford	DB	SR	12	45	45	90	7.50
83. Erik Keys, Ball St.	DB	SR	12	46	44	90	7.50
89. Ramon Guzman, Buffalo	LB	SR	9	38	29	67	7.44
90. Gerald McRath, Southern Miss.	LB	SO	14	54	50	104	7.43
91. Jeramy Edwards, Duke	LB	SR	12	49	40	89	7.42
91. Spencer Larsen, Arizona	LB	JR	12	63	26	89	7.42
91. Chris May, Eastern Mich.	DB	FR	12	42	47	89	7.42
91. Jacob Wyatt, Eastern Mich.	DB	SO	12	47	42	89	7.42
95. David Harris, Michigan	LB	SR	13	73	23	96	7.38
95. Keenan Blalark, Northern Ill.	LB	SR	13	30	66	96	7.38
95. Tony Taylor, Georgia	LB	SR	13	65	31	96	7.38
95. Jonathan Hefney, Tennessee	DB	JR	13	68	28	96	7.38
99. Kareem Byrom, Buffalo	DB	JR	12	49	39	88	7.33
99. Russell Allen, San Diego St.	LB	SO	12	49	39	88	7.33
99. Rakine Toomes, San Jose St.	DB	SR	12	42	46	88	7.33
99. John Mackey, Akron	DB	JR	12	52	36	88	7.33

Solo Tackles

Rank, Player	Pos	Cl.	G	Solo	ST/Gm
1. Alvin Bowen, Iowa St.	LB	JR	12	95	7.92
2. Patrick Willis, Mississippi	LB	SR	12	87	7.25
3. H.B. Blades, Pittsburgh	LB	SR	12	86	7.17
4. David Vobora, Idaho	LB	JR	12	84	7.00
5. Keyonvis Bouie, Florida Int'l	LB	SR	10	69	6.90
6. Joe Sturdivant, SMU	DB	SR	12	80	6.67
7. Jasper Brinkley, South Carolina	LB	JR	13	85	6.54
7. Brian Raines, Rice	LB	SO	13	85	6.54
9. Kevin Payne, La.-Monroe	DB	SR	12	75	6.25
9. J Leman, Illinois	LB	JR	12	75	6.25
11. Matthew Castelo, San Jose St.	LB	JR	13	81	6.23
12. Wesley Woodyard, Kentucky	LB	JR	13	80	6.15
13. Brannon Condren, Troy	DB	SR	13	76	5.85
14. Marvin Mitchell, Tennessee	LB	SR	13	75	5.77
15. Michael Okwo, Stanford	LB	SR	10	57	5.70
16. David Harris, Michigan	LB	SR	13	73	5.62
17. Clint Session, Pittsburgh	LB	SR	12	67	5.58
17. Jonathan Goff, Vanderbilt	LB	JR	12	67	5.58
19. Stephen Nicholas, South Fla.	LB	SR	13	71	5.46
20. Dan Connor, Penn St.	LB	JR	13	70	5.38
21. Rufus Alexander, Oklahoma	LB	SR	14	75	5.36
22. Jordon Dizon, Colorado	LB	JR	12	64	5.33
23. Paul Posluszny, Penn St.	LB	SR	13	69	5.31
24. Andre Kirkland, Kent St.	DB	SR	12	63	5.25
24. Spencer Larsen, Arizona	LB	JR	12	63	5.25
26. Jonathan Hefney, Tennessee	DB	JR	13	68	5.23
27. Otis Wiley, Michigan St.	DB	SO	12	62	5.17
27. C.J. Wallace, Washington	DB	SR	12	62	5.17
29. Mike Sherels, Minnesota	LB	JR	13	67	5.15
30. Mike Pagnotta, Colorado St.	DB	SO	9	46	5.11
31. Israel Route, Tulane	DB	SR	11	56	5.09
32. Dominic Jones, Minnesota	SS	SO	13	66	5.08
32. Dustin Utschig, Northern Ill.	DB	SR	13	66	5.08
34. Ryan Henegan, Connecticut	LB	JR	10	50	5.00
34. Desmond Bishop, California	LB	SR	13	65	5.00
34. Reggie Carrington, SMU	LB	JR	12	60	5.00
34. Tony Taylor, Georgia	LB	SR	13	65	5.00
38. Anthony Spencer, Purdue	DL	SR	14	69	4.93
39. Chris Horton, UCLA	DB	JR	13	64	4.92
40. Jeff Bublavi, Buffalo	LB	SR	12	59	4.92
40. Joe Martin, San Diego St.	LB	SR	12	59	4.92
40. Tyrone McKenzie, Iowa St.	LB	SO	12	59	4.92
43. Vince Hall, Virginia Tech	LB	JR	13	63	4.85
43. Michael Griffin, Texas	DB	SR	13	63	4.85
45. Kelvin Smith, Syracuse	LB	SR	12	58	4.83
45. Jon Banks, Iowa St.	DB	JR	12	58	4.83
45. Steve Tate, Utah	DB	JR	12	58	4.83
48. Andray Downs, Rice	DB	SR	13	62	4.77
49. Terrell Vinson, Purdue	DB	JR	12	57	4.75
50. Charles Godfrey, Iowa	DB	JR	13	61	4.69
51. Durell Mapp, North Carolina	LB	JR	12	56	4.67
51. Curtis Keyes, Marshall	DB	SR	12	56	4.67
51. Joey Card, Miami (Ohio)	DB	SR	12	56	4.67
54. Ben Moffitt, South Fla.	LB	JR	13	60	4.62
54. Dennis Keyes, UCLA	DB	JR	13	60	4.62
54. Andre Sexton, Oklahoma St.	DB	FR	13	60	4.62
57. Alexander Bostic III, Florida Int'l	LB	SR	12	55	4.58
57. David Skehan, Tulane	DB	JR	12	55	4.58
57. Eric Frampton, Washington St.	DB	SR	12	55	4.58
57. Andre Jones, Akron	DB	SO	12	55	4.58
61. Thomas Keith, Central Mich.	LB	JR	14	64	4.57
62. Jolonn Dunbar, Boston College	LB	JR	11	50	4.55
63. Joe Hudson, Miami (Ohio)	LB	SO	12	54	4.50
63. Clinton Snyder, Stanford	LB	SO	12	54	4.50
65. Erin Henderson, Maryland	LB	SO	13	58	4.46
65. Josh Barrett, Arizona St.	DB	JR	13	58	4.46
65. Marvin White, TCU	DB	SR	13	58	4.46
65. Chinedum Ndukwe, Notre Dame	DB	SR	13	58	4.46
69. Larry Edwards, North Carolina	LB	SR	9	40	4.44
70. Adam Leonard, Hawaii	LB	SO	14	62	4.43
71. Will Meyers, Indiana	DB	SR	12	53	4.42
71. Jerod Mayo, Tennessee	LB	SO	12	53	4.42
71. Barrett Scruggs, Army	LB	SR	12	53	4.42
71. Kendric Hawkins, Buffalo	DB	FR	12	53	4.42
75. Michael Hamlin, Clemson	DB	SO	10	44	4.40
76. Buster Davis, Florida St.	LB	SR	13	57	4.38
76. Quincy Black, New Mexico	DB	SR	13	57	4.38
76. Brandon Archer, Kansas St.	LB	SR	13	57	4.38

Rank, Player	Pos	Cl.	G	Solo	ST/Gm
76. Cameron Jensen, Brigham Young	LB	SR	13	57	4.38
76. Korey Hall, Boise St.	LB	SR	13	57	4.38
76. Edmond Miles, Iowa	LB	SR	13	57	4.38
76. Braxton Kelley, Kentucky	LB	SO	13	57	4.38
83. Ryan Babb, Troy	LB	SR	11	48	4.36
83. Joe Jiannoni, Utah	LB	JR	11	48	4.36
85. John Mackey, Akron	DB	JR	12	52	4.33
85. Brett Sturm, San Diego St.	DB	SR	12	52	4.33
85. Quinton Culberson, Mississippi St.	LB	SR	12	52	4.33
88. Duane Coleman, Clemson	DB	SR	13	56	4.31
88. Mike Klinkenborg, Iowa	LB	JR	13	56	4.31
88. Blair Phillips, Oregon	LB	SR	13	56	4.31
88. Miguel Merrick, Iowa	DB	SR	13	56	4.31
92. Kareen Taylor, North Carolina	DB	SR	12	51	4.25
92. Jeremy Burnett, South Fla.	DB	SR	12	51	4.25
92. Cason Shrode, Army	LB	SR	12	51	4.25
92. Tracy Porter, Indiana	DB	JR	12	51	4.25
92. Jon Beason, Miami (Fla.)	LB	JR	12	51	4.25
97. Mark Zalewski, Wisconsin	LB	SR	13	55	4.23
97. Ameer Ismail, Western Mich.	LB	SR	13	55	4.23
97. Christopher Vedder, San Jose St.	DB	SR	13	55	4.23
97. Sam Olajubutu, Arkansas	LB	SR	13	55	4.23

Pass Sacks

Rank, Player	Pos	Cl.	G	Solo	Ast	Yds	Total	PS/Gm
1. Ameer Ismail, Western Mich.	LB	SR	13	16	2	111	17	1.31
2. Abraham Wright, Colorado	DL	SR	12	12	0	95	12	1.00
3. Jamaal Anderson, Arkansas	DL	JR	14	12	3	95	13.5	.96
4. Gaines Adams, Clemson	DL	SR	13	12	1	79	12.5	.96
4. Justin Hickman, UCLA	DL	SR	13	12	1	97	12.5	.96
4. Bruce Davis, UCLA	DL	JR	13	12	1	75	12.5	.96
7. Albert McClellan, Marshall	DL	SO	12	10	3	80	11.5	.96
8. LaMarr Woodley, Michigan	DL	SR	13	12	0	119	12	.92
9. Mkristo Bruce, Washington St.	DL	SR	12	11	0	66	11	.92
10. Erik Walden, Middle Tenn.	DL	JR	13	11	1	83	11.5	.88
10. Ian Campbell, Kansas St.	DL	SO	13	11	1	67	11.5	.88
10. Larry English, Northern Ill.	DL	SO	13	11	1	77	11.5	.88
13. Justin Rogers, SMU	DL	SR	11	9	1	85	9.5	.86
14. Kareem Brown, Miami (Fla.)	DL	SR	13	10	2	51	11	.85
15. Calais Campbell, Miami (Fla.)	DL	SO	13	10	1	59	10.5	.81
15. Victor Abiamiri, Notre Dame	DL	SR	13	9	3	73	10.5	.81
15. Dan Bazuin, Central Mich.	DL	SR	13	10	1	65	10.5	.81
18. Jameel McClain, Syracuse	DL	JR	12	9	1	51	9.5	.79
18. Victor DeGrate, Oklahoma St.	DL	SR	12	9	1	51	9.5	.79
20. Derrick Harvey, Florida	DL	SO	14	10	2	89	11	.79
21. William Van DeSteeg, Minnesota	DE	SO	13	10	0	50	10	.77
22. Anthony Spencer, Purdue	DL	SR	14	10	1	70	10.5	.75
22. Trevor Scott, Buffalo	DL	JR	12	8	2	62	9	.75
22. Kevin Hogan, Kent St.	DL	FR	10	6	3	31	7.5	.75
22. Devon Parks, Bowling Green	DL	SR	12	9	0	58	9	.75
26. Charles Johnson, Georgia	DL	JR	13	8	3	53	9.5	.73
26. Quentin Groves, Auburn	DL	JR	13	9	1	62	9.5	.73
26. J.J. Milan, Nevada	DL	SR	13	9	1	56	9.5	.73
29. Dorian Smith, Oregon St.	DL	JR	12	8	1	68	8.5	.71
29. Shawn Moorehead, Iowa St.	DL	SR	12	8	1	41	8.5	.71
31. Cory Muse, SMU	DL	JR	10	6	2	58	7	.70
32. Malik Jackson, Louisville	LB	JR	13	9	0	59	9	.69
32. Darius Sanders, Oregon	DL	SR	13	9	0	64	9	.69
34. Melila Purcell, Hawaii	DL	SR	14	9	1	39	9.5	.68
35. Quinn Pitcock, Ohio St.	DL	SR	12	8	0	42	8	.67
35. Xzavie Jackson, Missouri	DL	SR	12	8	0	51	8	.67
37. Vernon Gholston, Ohio St.	DL	JR	13	8	1	73	8.5	.65
37. Tim Crowder, Texas	DL	SR	13	8	1	60	8.5	.65
37. Andrew Browning, Boise St.	DL	SR	13	7	3	49	8.5	.65
40. Philip Wheeler, Georgia Tech	LB	JR	14	9	0	68	9	.64
41. Alexander Bostic III, Florida Int'l	LB	SR	12	7	1	54	7.5	.63
41. Lance Broadus, Washington St.	DL	JR	12	7	1	39	7.5	.63
41. Titus Brown, Mississippi St.	DL	JR	12	7	1	54	7.5	.63
44. Amobi Okoye, Louisville	DL	SR	13	7	2	32	8	.62
44. Nathan Peterson, Oklahoma St.	DL	JR	13	7	2	67	8	.62
44. Courtney Gordon, Rice	DL	SR	13	8	0	55	8	.62
44. Tyson Jackson, LSU	DL	JR	13	6	4	39	8	.62
44. Zach Davidson, Western Mich.	DL	SO	13	7	2	60	8	.62
44. Jay Alford, Penn St.	DL	SR	13	7	2	43	8	.62
44. Jamaal Westerman, Rutgers	DL	SO	13	7	2	56	8	.62
44. Ramel Meekins, Rutgers	DL	SR	13	8	0	46	8	.62
52. Martrel Brown, North Carolina St.	DL	JR	12	7	0	64	7	.58
52. Mike Alston, Toledo	LB	SR	12	6	2	55	7	.58
52. Curtis Gatewood, Vanderbilt	DL	JR	12	6	2	48	7	.58
52. Leger Douzable, UCF	DL	JR	12	6	2	61	7	.58
52. Brent Curvey, Iowa St.	DL	SR	12	6	2	46	7	.58
52. Antwan Applewhite, San Diego St.	DL	JR	12	6	2	52	7	.58
58. Kevin Akins, Boston College	LB	SO	13	7	1	54	7.5	.58
58. Stephen Nicholas, South Fla.	LB	SR	13	7	1	57	7.5	.58
58. Chris Harrington, Texas A&M	DL	JR	13	7	1	58	7.5	.58
58. Antwain Robinson, Arkansas	DL	SO	13	7	1	54	7.5	.58
58. Jarvis Moss, Florida	DL	JR	13	7	1	60	7.5	.58
63. Chris McKillop, Pittsburgh	DL	JR	10	5	1	37	5.5	.55
63. Craig Rusch, Northern Ill.	DL	SO	10	5	1	26	5.5	.55
65. Larry McSwain, UAB	DL	SR	11	6	0	49	6	.55

Rank, Player	Pos	Cl.	G	Solo	Ast	Yds	Total	PS/Gm
66. Diyral Briggs, Bowling Green	DL	SO	12	6	1	45	6.5	.54
66. Michael Heard, Mississippi St.	DL	SR	12	6	1	35	6.5	.54
68. Eric Wicks, West Virginia	DB	SR	13	7	0	42	7	.54
68. Tommy Blake, TCU	DL	JR	13	6	2	50	7	.54
68. Derek Landri, Notre Dame	DL	SR	13	5	4	53	7	.54
68. David Mahoney, Navy	LB	SR	13	7	0	46	7	.54
68. Ezra Butler, Nevada	LB	JR	13	5	4	55	7	.54
68. Casper Brinkley, South Carolina	LB	JR	13	6	2	42	7	.54
68. Eric Norwood, South Carolina	DL	FR	13	5	4	67	7	.54
68. Dallas Sartz, Southern California	LB	SR	13	7	0	44	7	.54
68. Tim Shaw, Penn St.	LB	SR	13	7	0	48	7	.54
77. Jameson Hartke, Ohio	DL	SO	14	7	1	54	7.5	.54
77. Phillip Hunt, Houston	DL	SO	14	7	1	39	7.5	.54
79. Antwan Barnes, Florida Int'l	LB	SR	12	6	0	51	6	.50
79. Rodney Hardeway, La.-Lafayette	DL	JR	12	6	0	26	6	.50
79. Adam Carriker, Nebraska	DL	SR	14	7	0	45	7	.50
79. Jeremy Geathers, UNLV	DL	SO	11	4	3	43	5.5	.50
79. Colt Brooks, Boise St.	LB	SR	13	6	1	27	6.5	.50
79. Greyson Gunheim, Washington	DL	JR	12	6	0	37	6	.50
79. Mitch King, Iowa	DL	SO	11	3	5	35	5.5	.50
79. Brian Mattison, Iowa	DL	JR	13	6	1	57	6.5	.50
79. Chris Robinson, South Fla.	LB	FR	13	6	1	56	6.5	.50
88. Trevor Anderson, Cincinnati	DL	SO	13	5	2	32	6	.46
88. Deandre Levy, Wisconsin	LB	SO	13	5	2	38	6	.46
88. Rondell Biggs, Michigan	DL	SR	13	6	0	32	6	.46
88. Shawn Crable, Michigan	LB	SR	13	6	0	43	6	.46
88. Eric Foster, Rutgers	DL	JR	13	4	4	44	6	.46
88. John Chan, Navy	DL	SR	13	5	2	46	6	.46
88. Robert Latu, Tulsa	DL	SR	13	6	0	34	6	.46
88. Dexter Davis, Arizona St.	DL	FR	13	6	0	35	6	.46
96. Jeffrey Fitzgerald, Virginia	DL	FR	12	5	1	38	5.5	.46
96. Joe Clermond, Pittsburgh	DL	JR	12	5	1	25	5.5	.46
96. Daniel Muir, Kent St.	DB	SR	12	4	3	33	5.5	.46
96. Brion Stokes, Akron	LB	JR	12	5	1	26	5.5	.46
96. Allen Cray, South Fla.	DL	JR	12	5	1	31	5.5	.46

Tackles for Loss

Rank, Player	Pos	Cl.	G	Solo	Ast	Yds	Total	TFL/Gm
1. Ameer Ismail, Western Mich.	LB	SR	13	23	5	133	25.5	1.96
2. Anthony Spencer, Purdue	DL	SR	14	25	3	110	26.5	1.89
3. Antwan Barnes, Florida Int'l	LB	SR	12	19	7	87	22.5	1.88
4. Keyonvis Bouie, Florida Int'l	LB	SR	10	14	8	56	18	1.80
5. Jason Jones, EasternMich.	DL	JR	11	18	1	71	18.5	1.68
6. Albert McClellan, Marshall	DL	SO	12	17	6	101	20	1.67
7. Alexander Bostic III, Florida Int'l	LB	SR	12	17	4	81	19	1.58
7. J Leman, Illinois	LB	JR	12	16	6	65	19	1.58
9. Calais Campbell, Miami (Fla.)	DL	SO	13	19	3	75	20.5	1.58
10. Justin Hickman, UCLA	DL	SR	13	17	4	117	19	1.46
10. Charles Johnson, Georgia	DL	JR	13	17	4	87	19	1.46
12. Jamaal Anderson, Arkansas	DL	JR	14	16	8	106	20	1.43
13. Mike Alston, Toledo	LB	SR	12	14	6	85	17	1.42
14. Lawrence Timmons, Florida St.	LB	JR	13	13	10	71	18	1.38
15. Joe Clermond, Pittsburgh	DL	JR	12	14	5	40	16.5	1.38
15. Adrian Haywood, SMU	DL	SR	12	14	5	71	16.5	1.38
17. Justin Rogers, SMU	DL	SR	11	13	4	95	15	1.36
18. Bruce Davis, UCLA	DL	JR	13	17	1	104	17.5	1.35
18. Ezra Butler, Nevada	LB	JR	13	14	7	84	17.5	1.35
20. Mkristo Bruce, Washington St.	DL	SR	12	14	4	77	16	1.33
21. Ian Campbell, Kansas St.	DL	SO	13	16	2	82	17	1.31
22. David Vobora, Idaho	LB	JR	12	13	5	63	15.5	1.29
22. Cameron Craig, Army	DL	SR	12	13	5	57	15.5	1.29
24. Gaines Adams, Clemson	DL	SR	13	16	1	88	16.5	1.27
24. Tommy Blake, TCU	DL	JR	13	13	7	83	16.5	1.27
24. LaMarr Woodley, Michigan	DL	SR	13	15	3	131	16.5	1.27
27. Matt Muncy, Ohio	LB	SR	14	10	14	54	17	1.21
28. Jameel McClain, Syracuse	DL	JR	12	12	5	61	14.5	1.21
28. Titus Brown, Mississippi St.	DL	JR	12	12	5	75	14.5	1.21
30. Geno Hayes, Florida St.	LB	SO	10	9	6	62	12	1.20
31. Stephen Nicholas, South Fla.	LB	SR	13	15	1	76	15.5	1.19
31. Malik Jackson, Louisville	LB	JR	13	15	1	72	15.5	1.19
31. Derek Landri, Notre Dame	DL	SR	13	12	7	80	15.5	1.19
34. Codey Lowe, Duke	LB	SR	12	11	6	66	14	1.17
34. James McClinton, Kansas	DL	JR	12	10	8	57	14	1.17
34. Abraham Wright, Colorado	DL	SR	12	13	2	99	14	1.17
37. George Selvie, South Fla.	DL	FR	13	14	2	52	15	1.15
37. Dan Bazuin, Central Mich.	DL	SR	13	12	6	74	15	1.15
37. Desmond Bishop, California	LB	SR	13	12	6	43	15	1.15
37. Victor Abiamiri, Notre Dame	DL	SR	13	12	6	88	15	1.15
37. Courtney Gordon, Rice	DL	SR	13	15	0	74	15	1.15
37. Antwain Robinson, Arkansas	DL	SO	13	13	4	80	15	1.15
37. Larry English, Northern Ill.	DL	SO	13	14	2	92	15	1.15

Rank, Player	Pos	Cl.	G	Solo	Ast	Yds	Total	TFL/Gm
37. David Harris, Michigan	LB	SR	13	14	2	48	15	1.15
37. Vernon Gholston, Ohio St.	DL	JR	13	12	6	86	15	1.15
46. Craig Rusch, Northern Ill.	DL	SO	10	8	7	38	11.5	1.15
46. Terrel White, Bowling Green	LB	SR	10	9	5	53	11.5	1.15
48. Deljuan Robinson, Mississippi St.	DL	SR	11	11	3	45	12.5	1.14
49. Andre Kirkland, Kent St.	DB	SR	12	11	5	30	13.5	1.13
49. Trevor Scott, Buffalo	DL	JR	12	12	3	75	13.5	1.13
51. J.K. Sabb, Middle Tenn.	LB	SR	13	13	3	69	14.5	1.12
51. Erik Walden, Middle Tenn.	DL	JR	13	13	3	90	14.5	1.12
51. Kevin McCullough, Cincinnati	LB	SR	13	10	9	36	14.5	1.12
51. William Van DeSteeg, Minnesota	DE	SO	13	13	3	59	14.5	1.12
51. Jay Alford, Penn St.	DL	SR	13	13	3	58	14.5	1.12
56. Melila Purcell, Hawaii	DL	SR	14	14	3	47	15.5	1.11
56. Martavius Prince, Southern Miss.	DL	JR	14	14	3	49	15.5	1.11
58. Kevin Hogan, Kent St.	DL	FR	10	9	4	39	11	1.10
59. Mitch King, Iowa	DL	SO	11	8	8	49	12	1.09
60. Brion Stokes, Akron	LB	JR	12	11	4	45	13	1.08
60. Xzavie Jackson, Missouri	DL	SR	12	12	2	65	13	1.08
62. Eric Foster, Rutgers	DL	JR	13	10	8	66	14	1.08
62. Rashad Bobino, Texas	LB	SO	13	13	2	46	14	1.08
62. Jasper Brinkley, South Carolina	LB	JR	13	13	2	31	14	1.08
62. Tim Crowder, Texas	DL	SR	13	13	2	75	14	1.08
62. J.J. Milan, Nevada	DL	SR	13	12	4	72	14	1.08
67. Cliff Avril, Purdue	LB	JR	14	13	4	65	15	1.07
68. Cory Muse, SMU	DL	JR	10	9	3	63	10.5	1.05
69. Patrick Bailey, Duke	LB	JR	12	9	7	48	12.5	1.04
69. Jerod Mayo, Tennessee	LB	SO	12	11	3	51	12.5	1.04
69. Brent Curvey, Iowa St.	DL	SR	12	11	3	57	12.5	1.04
69. Chris Norwell, Illinois	DL	JR	12	9	7	49	12.5	1.04
73. Everette Brown, Florida St.	DL	FR	13	10	7	45	13.5	1.04
73. Brian Cushing, Southern California	LB	SO	13	11	5	52	13.5	1.04
73. Christian Taylor, UCLA	LB	JR	13	11	5	52	13.5	1.04
73. Marque Fountain, Oklahoma St.	DL	JR	13	12	3	63	13.5	1.04
73. Jamaal Westerman, Rutgers	DL	SO	13	11	5	66	13.5	1.04
78. Philip Wheeler, Georgia Tech	LB	JR	14	14	1	80	14.5	1.04
78. Jay Moore, Nebraska	DL	SR	14	12	5	70	14.5	1.04
78. Derrick Doggett, Oregon St.	LB	JR	14	14	1	78	14.5	1.04
81. Franklin Lloyd, Troy	DL	SR	13	11	4	35	13	1.00
81. Adam Carriker, Nebraska	DL	SR	14	12	4	61	14	1.00
81. Shawn Moorehead, Iowa St.	DL	SR	12	11	2	46	12	1.00
81. Greyson Gunheim, Washington	DL	JR	12	10	4	55	12	1.00
81. Stevon Moss, Kent St.	LB	SO	12	8	8	47	12	1.00
81. Landon Cohen, Ohio	DL	JR	14	11	6	44	14	1.00
81. Quinn Pitcock, Ohio St.	DL	SR	12	11	2	49	12	1.00
81. Ramel Meekins, Rutgers	DL	SR	13	11	4	60	13	1.00
81. Trevor Anderson, Cincinnati	DL	SO	13	10	6	50	13	1.00
81. Clint Session, Pittsburgh	LB	SR	12	10	4	33	12	1.00
81. Jeramy Edwards, Duke	LB	SR	12	10	4	36	12	1.00
92. Derrick Harvey, Florida	DL	SO	14	12	3	95	13.5	.96
93. Kareem Brown, Miami (Fla.)	DL	SR	13	11	3	51	12.5	.96
93. Jonathan Casillas, Wisconsin	LB	SO	13	10	5	38	12.5	.96
93. Brian Raines, Rice	LB	SO	13	12	1	52	12.5	.96
93. Casper Brinkley, South Carolina	LB	JR	13	10	5	72	12.5	.96
93. Amobi Okoye, Louisville	DL	SR	13	11	3	55	12.5	.96
98. Josh Pinnick, Fla. Atlantic	DL	JR	12	10	3	46	11.5	.96
98. Devon Parks, Bowling Green	DL	SR	12	10	3	61	11.5	.96
98. Victor DeGrate, Oklahoma St.	DL	SR	12	11	1	55	11.5	.96
98. Patrick Willis, Mississippi	LB	SR	12	10	3	44	11.5	.96
98. Cortlan Booker, Ball St.	DL	SR	12	9	5	49	11.5	.96
98. Donta Moore, Connecticut	LB	JR	12	8	7	41	11.5	.96

Passes Defended

Rank, Player	Pos	Cl.	G	PBU	Int.	Passes Def.	PD/Gm
1. Aqib Talib, Kansas	DB	SO	10	22	6	28	2.80
2. Aaron Ross, Texas	DB	SR	13	16	6	22	1.69
3. Brandon Flowers, Virginia Tech	DB	SO	13	18	3	21	1.62
4. Lionell Singleton, Florida Int'l	DB	JR	10	11	5	16	1.60
5. Courtney Bryan, New Mexico St.	DB	SR	12	15	4	19	1.58
6. T.J. Wright, Ohio	DB	SR	14	18	4	22	1.57
7. Daymeion Hughes, California	DB	SR	13	11	8	19	1.46
8. William Gay, Louisville	DB	SR	13	12	6	18	1.38
8. Leon Hall, Michigan	DB	SR	13	15	3	18	1.38
8. Mike Mickens, Cincinnati	DB	SO	13	15	3	18	1.38
11. Stanley Franks, Idaho	DB	JR	12	7	9	16	1.33
12. Jonathan Wade, Tennessee	DB	SR	13	13	4	17	1.31
13. Riley Swanson, Wake Forest	DB	SR	14	14	4	18	1.29
14. John Talley, Duke	DB	SR	12	8	7	15	1.25
15. Jonathan Zenon, LSU	DB	JR	13	12	4	16	1.23
15. Chevis Jackson, LSU	DB	JR	13	14	2	16	1.23
15. Dwight Lowery, San Jose St.	DB	JR	13	7	9	16	1.23
18. Mark Parson, Ohio	DB	SO	14	16	1	17	1.21
18. Caleb Hendrix, Southern Miss.	DB	SR	14	13	4	17	1.21
20. Donny Baker, San Diego St.	DB	SR	10	9	3	12	1.20
21. Israel Route, Tulane	DB	SR	11	12	1	13	1.18
22. Sha'reff Rashad, UCF	DB	SO	12	10	4	14	1.17
23. Glenn Sharpe, Miami (Fla.)	DB	JR	13	13	2	15	1.15
24. Ryan Smith, Florida	DB	JR	14	8	8	16	1.14
24. Chris Houston, Arkansas	DB	JR	14	13	3	16	1.14
26. Joey Card, Miami (Ohio)	DB	SR	12	11	2	13	1.08
26. Eric Frampton, Washington St.	DB	SR	12	8	5	13	1.08
26. Davanzo Tate, Akron	DB	JR	12	13	0	13	1.08
29. Trae Williams, South Fla.	DB	JR	13	7	7	14	1.08
29. Joe Garcia, Nevada	DB	SR	13	8	6	14	1.08
29. DeAndre Wright, New Mexico	DB	SO	13	10	4	14	1.08
29. Trevard Lindley, Kentucky	DB	FR	13	12	2	14	1.08
29. David Irons, Auburn	DB	SR	13	12	2	14	1.08

Rank, Player	Pos	Cl.	G	PBU	Int.	Passes Def.	PD/Gm
29. Terrell Thomas, Southern California	DB	JR	13	12	2	14	1.08
29. Anthony Scirrotto, Penn St.	DB	SO	13	8	6	14	1.08
36. Jahi Word-Daniels, Georgia Tech	DB	SO	14	13	2	15	1.07
36. Sabby Piscitelli, Oregon St.	DB	SR	14	10	5	15	1.07
36. Jasper Faulk, Southern Miss.	DB	SR	14	13	2	15	1.07
39. Corey Small, Fla. Atlantic	DB	SO	12	8	4	12	1.00
39. Josh Wilson, Maryland	DB	SR	13	12	1	13	1.00
39. Quintin Demps, UTEP	DB	JR	12	5	7	12	1.00
39. James Johnson, Marshall	DB	SO	12	10	2	12	1.00
39. Kasey Ross, East Caro.	DB	SR	13	9	4	13	1.00
39. Eric Wright, UNLV	DB	JR	9	8	1	9	1.00
39. Glover Quin, New Mexico	DB	SO	13	13	0	13	1.00
39. Fred Bennett, South Carolina	DB	SR	13	11	2	13	1.00
39. Dashon Goldson, Washington	DB	SR	11	10	1	11	1.00
39. Trey Brown, UCLA	DB	JR	13	9	4	13	1.00
39. Reggie Corner, Akron	DB	SR	12	8	4	12	1.00
39. Terrence Wheatley, Colorado	DB	SR	12	7	5	12	1.00
39. Alan Ball, Illinois	DB	SR	12	11	1	12	1.00
39. Tracy Porter, Indiana	DB	JR	12	8	4	12	1.00
39. Demond Williams, Michigan St.	DB	SR	12	10	2	12	1.00
39. Tony Davis, Penn St.	DB	SO	13	13	0	13	1.00
39. Jack Ikegwuonu, Wisconsin	DB	SO	13	11	2	13	1.00
39. Darius Butler, Connecticut	DB	JR	11	7	4	11	1.00
39. Randy Phillips, Miami (Fla.)	DB	SO	11	10	1	11	1.00
58. Josh Gattis, Wake Forest	DB	SR	14	8	5	13	.93
58. Willie Gaston, Houston	DB	SR	14	12	1	13	.93
58. Matterral Richardson, Arkansas	DB	JR	14	12	1	13	.93
61. Kenny Scott, Georgia Tech	DB	SR	13	10	2	12	.92
61. Miguel Merrick, Iowa	DB	SR	13	9	3	12	.92
61. Tra Battle, Georgia	DB	SR	13	6	6	12	.92
61. Jairus Byrd, Oregon	DB	FR	13	7	5	12	.92
61. DeJuan Tribble, Boston College	DB	JR	13	5	7	12	.92
61. Simeon Castille, Alabama	DB	JR	13	6	6	12	.92
61. Michael Griffin, Texas	DB	SR	13	8	4	12	.92
68. Khayyam Burns, Arkansas St.	DB	JR	12	7	4	11	.92
68. Andre Kirkland, Kent St.	DB	SR	12	7	4	11	.92
68. Alex Bernard, New Mexico St.	DB	JR	12	9	2	11	.92
68. Gavin Smart, Louisville	DB	SR	12	8	3	11	.92
68. Kevin Sanders, UAB	DB	SO	12	8	3	11	.92
73. Damon Jenkins, Fresno St.	DB	JR	9	5	3	8	.89
74. Cortney Grixby, Nebraska	DB	JR	14	11	1	12	.86
74. Nic Harris, Oklahoma	DB	SO	14	8	4	12	.86
74. Marcus Walker, Oklahoma	DB	JR	14	9	3	12	.86
77. Reggie Doucet, Middle Tenn.	DB	SR	13	8	3	11	.85
77. Mike Jenkins, South Fla.	DB	JR	13	10	1	11	.85
79. Greg James, La.-Monroe	DB	FR	12	5	5	10	.83
79. Jordan Peterson, Texas A&M	DB	FR	12	8	2	10	.83
79. C.J. Wilson, Baylor	DB	SR	12	6	4	10	.83
79. Ben Criddle, Brigham Young	DB	JR	12	8	2	10	.83
79. David Heard, Mississippi St.	DB	SR	12	8	2	10	.83
79. Walter Thurmond III, Oregon	DB	FR	12	9	1	10	.83
79. Antoine Cason, Arizona	DB	JR	12	7	3	10	.83
79. Tyron Brackenridge, Washington St.	DB	SR	12	7	3	10	.83
79. Barry Church, Toledo	DB	FR	12	6	4	10	.83
79. Trey Lewis, Ball St.	DB	JR	12	10	0	10	.83
79. Londen Fryar, Western Mich.	DB	SO	12	5	5	10	.83
79. Otis Wiley, Michigan St.	DB	SO	12	10	0	10	.83
79. Josh Thompson, La.-Monroe	DB	SO	12	4	6	10	.83
92. Marcus Hamilton, Virginia	DB	SR	11	4	5	9	.82
92. Louis Delmas, Western Mich.	DB	SO	11	5	4	9	.82
94. Brandon King, Rice	DB	SO	10	6	2	8	.80
95. Alphonso Smith, Wake Forest	DB	SO	14	8	3	11	.79
95. Reggie Nelson, Florida	DB	JR	14	5	6	11	.79
95. Reggie Smith, Oklahoma	DB	SO	14	8	3	11	.79
95. Andrew Shanle, Nebraska	DB	SR	14	7	4	11	.79
99. Antonio Lewis, West Virginia	DB	JR	13	8	2	10	.77
99. Eric Wicks, West Virginia	DB	SR	13	7	3	10	.77
99. Marcus McClinton, Kentucky	DB	SO	13	6	4	10	.77
99. Justin Robinson, Brigham Young	DB	SR	13	6	4	10	.77
99. Antonio Huffman, Texas Tech	DB	SR	13	8	2	10	.77
99. Nick Graham, Tulsa	DB	SR	13	9	1	10	.77
99. Travis Williams, East Caro.	DB	JR	13	8	2	10	.77
99. Will Gulley, Houston	DB	SR	13	5	5	10	.77
99. Nick Sanders, TCU	DB	FR	13	7	3	10	.77
99. Paul Oliver, Georgia	DB	JR	13	7	3	10	.77
99. Charles Johnson, Georgia	DL	JR	13	10	0	10	.77

Forced Fumbles

Rank, Player	Pos	Cl.	G	FF	FF/Gm
1. Clint Session, Pittsburgh	LB	SR	12	5	.42
1. Jack Williams, Kent St.	DB	JR	12	5	.42
1. Jeramie Johnson, Mississippi St.	DB	SR	12	5	.42
4. Ramel Meekins, Rutgers	DL	SR	13	5	.38
4. Brian Raines, Rice	LB	SO	13	5	.38
4. Marcus McClinton, Kentucky	DB	SO	13	5	.38
4. Wesley Woodyard, Kentucky	LB	JR	13	5	.38
8. Israel Route, Tulane	DB	SR	11	4	.36
9. Anthony Spencer, Purdue	DL	SR	14	5	.36
10. George Hall, Purdue	LB	SR	12	4	.33
10. Tyrone McKenzie, Iowa St.	LB	SO	12	4	.33
10. Shavar Greer, Marshall	DL	SR	12	4	.33
10. Albert McClellan, Marshall	DL	SO	12	4	.33
10. Rakine Toomes, San Jose St.	DB	SR	12	4	.33
10. Myron Pryor, Kentucky	DL	SO	12	4	.33
10. Greg Hardy, Mississippi	DL	FR	12	4	.33
10. David Herron Jr., Michigan St.	LB	SR	12	4	.33
10. Theo Horrocks, Vanderbilt	DL	JR	12	4	.33
10. Andre Kirkland, Kent St.	DB	SR	12	4	.33
10. Kareem Byrom, Buffalo	DB	JR	12	4	.33
21. Sean Mosley, Middle Tenn.	DL	JR	13	4	.31
21. Michael Griffin, Texas	DB	SR	13	4	.31
21. Matthew Castelo, San Jose St.	LB	JR	13	4	.31
21. Chris Robinson, South Fla.	LB	FR	13	4	.31
21. Dan Bazuin, Central Mich.	DL	SR	13	4	.31
21. Larry English, Northern Ill.	DL	SO	13	4	.31
21. Jarvis Moss, Florida	DL	JR	13	4	.31
21. Zack Follett, California	LB	SO	13	4	.31
21. LaMarr Woodley, Michigan	DL	SR	13	4	.31
21. Brian Mattison, Iowa	DL	JR	13	4	.31
31. Chris McKillop, Pittsburgh	DL	JR	10	3	.30
32. Coye Francies, Oregon St.	DB	JR	14	4	.29
32. Melila Purcell, Hawaii	DL	SR	14	4	.29
32. Rufus Alexander, Oklahoma	LB	SR	14	4	.29
35. Ryan Babb, Troy	LB	SR	11	3	.27
35. Jeremy Geathers, UNLV	DL	SO	11	3	.27
37. Jonathan Harris, Middle Tenn.	DB	SR	12	3	.25
37. Alexander Bostic III, Florida Int'l	LB	SR	12	3	.25
37. Josh Alexander, La.-Monroe	LB	SR	12	3	.25
37. Michael Johnson, Georgia Tech	DL	SO	12	3	.25
37. Josh Thompson, La.-Monroe	DB	SO	12	3	.25
37. Rodney Hardeway, La.-Lafayette	DL	JR	12	3	.25
37. James Black, Florida Int'l	LB	SR	12	3	.25
37. James McClinton, Kansas	DL	JR	12	3	.25
37. Paul Como, Kansas	DL	SR	12	3	.25
37. Joe Sturdivant, SMU	DB	SR	12	3	.25
37. Andrew Sendejo, Rice	DB	FR	12	3	.25
37. Jonathan Bailes, San Diego St.	DL	SR	12	3	.25
37. Steve Tate, Utah	DB	JR	12	3	.25
37. Uche Anyanwu, Nevada	DB	SO	12	3	.25
37. Curtis Gatewood, Vanderbilt	DL	JR	12	3	.25
37. Rory Johnson, Mississippi	LB	FR	12	3	.25
37. Clinton Snyder, Stanford	LB	SO	12	3	.25
37. Greyson Gunheim, Washington	DL	JR	12	3	.25
37. Daniel Howell, Washington	LB	JR	12	3	.25
37. Andre Jones, Akron	DB	SO	12	3	.25
37. Usama Young, Kent St.	DB	SR	12	3	.25
37. Justin Harrison, Illinois	DB	JR	12	3	.25
37. Deante Battle, Northwestern	DB	JR	12	3	.25
37. Terrell Lemon, Syracuse	DB	SR	12	3	.25
61. Erik Walden, Middle Tenn.	DL	JR	13	3	.23
61. Erin Henderson, Maryland	LB	SO	13	3	.23
61. Calais Campbell, Miami (Fla.)	DL	SO	13	3	.23
61. George Selvie, South Fla.	DL	FR	13	3	.23
61. Reed Williams, West Virginia	LB	SO	13	3	.23
61. Dan Connor, Penn St.	LB	JR	13	3	.23
61. Shawn Crable, Michigan	LB	SR	13	3	.23
61. OJ Swift, New Mexico	DB	JR	13	3	.23
61. Damaja Jones, San Jose St.	LB	SR	13	3	.23
61. Quin Harris, Louisiana Tech	LB	SO	13	3	.23
61. Quentin Groves, Auburn	DL	JR	13	3	.23
61. Danny McCray, LSU	DB	FR	13	3	.23
61. Charles Johnson, Georgia	DL	JR	13	3	.23
61. Dexter Davis, Arizona St.	DL	FR	13	3	.23
61. Dennis Keyes, UCLA	DB	JR	13	3	.23
61. Bruce Davis, UCLA	DL	JR	13	3	.23
61. Rob Caldwell, Navy	LB	SR	13	3	.23
61. Ryan McBean, Oklahoma St.	DL	SR	13	3	.23
61. Jake Ratliff, Texas Tech	DL	SO	13	3	.23
61. Aaron Ross, Texas	DB	SR	13	3	.23
61. Tim Crowder, Texas	DL	SR	13	3	.23
61. Andre Sexton, Oklahoma St.	DB	FR	13	3	.23
61. Keith Rivers, Southern California	LB	JR	13	3	.23
61. Zach Davidson, Western Mich.	DL	SO	13	3	.23
61. Mario Reese, Minnesota	LB	SR	13	3	.23

Rank, Player	Pos	Cl.	G	FF	FF/Gm
61. James Laurinaitis, Ohio St.	LB	SO	13	3	.23
61. Lamar Myles, Louisville	LB	SO	13	3	.23
61. Xavier Adibi, Virginia Tech	LB	JR	13	3	.23
89. Duan Bracey, Eastern Mich.	DB/WR	JR	9	2	.22
89. Brandon Crawford, Ball St.	DE	FR	9	2	.22
91. Daniel Drayton, Oregon St.	DB	JR	14	3	.21
91. Jacob Patek, Hawaii	DB	JR	14	3	.21
91. Brandon Sumrall, Southern Miss.	DB	SO	14	3	.21
91. Bo Ruud, Nebraska	LB	JR	14	3	.21
95. Lawrence Wilson, Ohio St.	DL	SO	10	2	.20
95. Gabe Long, Utah	DL	JR	10	2	.20
95. B.J. Steed, UAB	LB	SO	10	2	.20
95. Evander Hood, Missouri	DL	SO	10	2	.20
95. Wesley Smith, Memphis	DB	SR	10	2	.20
95. Kendall Briscoe, New Mexico	DL	FR	10	2	.20
95. Jon Radford, Colorado St.	LB	SR	10	2	.20
95. Michael Okwo, Stanford	LB	SR	10	2	.20

2006 Bowl Subdivision (FBS) Team Statistics

Rushing Offense

Rank, Team	G	Att	Net	Avg.	TD	Yds/Gm	W	L	T
1. Navy	13	764	4,251	5.56	39	327.00	9	4	0
2. West Virginia	13	590	3,939	6.68	48	303.00	11	2	0
3. Air Force	12	660	2,753	4.17	22	229.42	4	8	0
4. Arkansas	14	539	3,199	5.94	26	228.50	10	4	0
5. Clemson	13	495	2,832	5.72	31	217.85	8	5	0
6. Boise St.	13	551	2,784	5.05	39	214.15	13	0	0
7. Oklahoma St.	13	522	2,704	5.18	28	208.00	7	6	0
8. Texas A&M	13	540	2,689	4.98	32	206.85	9	4	0
9. TCU	13	557	2,530	4.54	28	194.62	11	2	0
10. Illinois	12	434	2,266	5.22	15	188.83	2	10	0
11. La.-Lafayette	12	478	2,261	4.73	20	188.42	6	6	0
12. Louisville	13	483	2,409	4.99	35	185.31	12	1	0
13. Connecticut	12	486	2,195	4.52	18	182.92	4	8	0
14. Oregon	13	472	2,364	5.01	26	181.85	7	6	0
15. Rutgers	13	496	2,342	4.72	28	180.15	11	2	0
16. Fresno St.	12	430	2,160	5.02	15	180.00	4	8	0
17. Oklahoma	14	557	2,480	4.45	25	177.14	11	3	0
18. Bowling Green	12	505	2,120	4.20	19	176.67	4	8	0
19. Kansas	12	438	2,117	4.83	20	176.42	6	6	0
20. San Jose St.	13	489	2,283	4.67	19	175.62	9	4	0
21. Michigan	13	535	2,282	4.27	21	175.54	11	2	0
22. Colorado	12	461	2,075	4.50	12	172.92	2	10	0
23. Nebraska	14	554	2,387	4.31	27	170.50	9	5	0
24. Nevada	13	511	2,212	4.33	26	170.15	8	5	0
25. Southern Miss.	14	535	2,378	4.44	23	169.86	9	5	0
26. Ohio St.	13	480	2,208	4.60	25	169.85	12	1	0
27. Arizona St.	13	497	2,206	4.44	17	169.69	7	6	0
28. Houston	14	490	2,356	4.81	29	168.29	10	4	0
29. Arkansas St.	12	507	2,012	3.97	12	167.67	6	6	0
30. Marshall	12	406	2,005	4.94	23	167.08	5	7	0
31. LSU	13	450	2,155	4.79	25	165.77	11	2	0
32. Northern Ill.	13	443	2,142	4.84	20	164.77	7	6	0
33. California	13	427	2,116	4.96	21	162.77	10	3	0
34. Texas	13	483	2,114	4.38	24	162.62	10	3	0
35. Georgia Tech	14	526	2,274	4.32	17	162.43	9	5	0
36. Tulsa	13	484	2,107	4.35	30	162.08	8	5	0
37. Wisconsin	13	536	2,102	3.92	24	161.69	12	1	0
38. Florida	14	476	2,240	4.71	24	160.00	13	1	0
39. Kent St.	12	486	1,901	3.91	17	158.42	6	6	0
40. Toledo	12	470	1,875	3.99	21	156.25	5	7	0
41. La.-Monroe	12	445	1,864	4.19	19	155.33	4	8	0
42. Minnesota	13	467	2,007	4.30	25	154.38	6	7	0
43. Penn St.	13	457	1,950	4.27	16	150.00	9	4	0
44. Wake Forest	14	542	2,099	3.87	19	149.93	11	3	0
45. Vanderbilt	12	385	1,795	4.66	18	149.58	4	8	0
46. Missouri	13	457	1,943	4.25	16	149.46	8	5	0
47. Auburn	13	470	1,927	4.10	21	148.23	11	2	0
48. Ohio	14	525	2,067	3.94	22	147.64	9	5	0
49. South Carolina	13	414	1,876	4.53	19	144.31	8	5	0
50. South Fla.	13	485	1,874	3.86	22	144.15	9	4	0
51. Iowa	13	432	1,865	4.32	16	143.46	6	7	0
52. Northwestern	12	422	1,705	4.04	16	142.08	4	8	0
53. Brigham Young	13	437	1,845	4.22	27	141.92	11	2	0
54. Utah	13	451	1,826	4.05	14	140.46	8	5	0
55. UCF	12	442	1,673	3.79	11	139.42	4	8	0
56. Western Mich.	13	471	1,751	3.72	10	134.69	8	5	0
57. Cincinnati	13	513	1,737	3.39	11	133.62	8	5	0
58. Wyoming	12	441	1,588	3.60	12	132.33	6	6	0
59. Middle Tenn.	13	474	1,705	3.60	24	131.15	7	6	0
60. Rice	13	438	1,703	3.89	15	131.00	7	6	0
61. Maryland	13	450	1,693	3.76	14	130.23	9	4	0
62. Louisiana Tech	13	415	1,692	4.08	13	130.15	3	10	0
63. UCLA	13	436	1,687	3.87	11	129.77	7	6	0
64. Central Mich.	14	422	1,811	4.29	21	129.36	10	4	0
65. Michigan St.	12	387	1,550	4.01	15	129.17	4	8	0
66. Troy	13	436	1,671	3.83	15	128.54	8	5	0
67. Washington St.	12	392	1,540	3.93	12	128.33	6	6	0
68. Southern California	13	416	1,664	4.00	18	128.00	11	2	0
69. Washington	12	402	1,535	3.82	12	127.92	5	7	0
70. Army	12	417	1,531	3.67	16	127.58	3	9	0
71. Georgia	13	426	1,656	3.89	21	127.38	9	4	0
72. Notre Dame	13	423	1,634	3.86	14	125.69	10	3	0
73. UAB	12	432	1,507	3.49	14	125.58	3	9	0
74. Mississippi	12	422	1,504	3.56	11	125.33	4	8	0
75. SMU	12	404	1,503	3.72	7	125.25	6	6	0
76. Purdue	14	400	1,738	4.35	23	124.14	8	6	0
77. Alabama	13	455	1,600	3.52	10	123.08	6	7	0
78. Pittsburgh	12	380	1,476	3.88	15	123.00	6	6	0
79. North Carolina St.	12	374	1,436	3.84	11	119.67	3	9	0
80. San Diego St.	12	422	1,430	3.39	10	119.17	3	9	0
81. Oregon St.	14	474	1,655	3.49	20	118.21	10	4	0
82. Hawaii	14	298	1,651	5.54	22	117.93	11	3	0
83. North Texas	12	437	1,404	3.21	5	117.00	3	9	0
84. Miami (Fla.)	13	431	1,508	3.50	14	116.00	7	6	0
85. East Caro.	13	450	1,502	3.34	16	115.54	7	6	0
86. Kansas St.	13	372	1,497	4.02	16	115.15	7	6	0
87. Utah St.	12	430	1,377	3.20	6	114.75	1	11	0
88. Idaho	12	399	1,370	3.43	14	114.17	4	8	0
89. Indiana	12	392	1,366	3.48	13	113.83	5	7	0
90. Virginia Tech	13	455	1,474	3.24	22	113.38	10	3	0
91. North Carolina	12	382	1,360	3.56	12	113.33	3	9	0
92. Boston College	13	437	1,469	3.36	20	113.00	10	3	0
93. Memphis	12	372	1,340	3.60	12	111.67	2	10	0
94. New Mexico	13	433	1,444	3.33	10	111.08	6	7	0
95. Fla. Atlantic	12	452	1,314	2.91	9	109.50	5	7	0
96. Tennessee	13	382	1,404	3.68	17	108.00	9	4	0
97. Syracuse	12	420	1,283	3.05	8	106.92	4	8	0
98. Eastern Mich.	12	374	1,269	3.39	10	105.75	1	11	0
99. Iowa St.	12	401	1,221	3.04	16	101.75	4	8	0
100. Virginia	12	364	1,199	3.29	12	99.92	5	7	0
101. Kentucky	13	411	1,282	3.12	12	98.62	8	5	0
102. Duke	12	412	1,179	2.86	10	98.25	0	12	0
103. Florida St.	13	363	1,255	3.46	17	96.54	7	6	0
104. Mississippi St.	12	394	1,142	2.90	14	95.17	3	9	0
105. Tulane	12	353	1,106	3.13	10	92.17	4	8	0
106. Ball St.	12	366	1,103	3.01	10	91.92	5	7	0
107. Buffalo	12	380	1,082	2.85	15	90.17	2	10	0
108. UNLV	12	345	1,074	3.11	11	89.50	2	10	0
109. Miami (Ohio)	12	386	1,040	2.69	11	86.67	2	10	0
110. Arizona	12	379	1,010	2.66	11	84.17	6	6	0
111. Akron	12	365	1,005	2.75	13	83.75	5	7	0
112. Texas Tech	13	220	1,019	4.63	13	78.38	8	5	0
113. Colorado St.	12	372	918	2.47	10	76.50	4	8	0
114. New Mexico St.	12	323	910	2.82	16	75.83	4	8	0
115. Stanford	12	367	781	2.13	3	65.08	1	11	0
116. UTEP	12	288	691	2.40	8	57.58	5	7	0
117. Florida Int'l	12	299	682	2.28	5	56.83	0	12	0
118. Temple	12	345	644	1.87	4	53.67	1	11	0
119. Baylor	12	235	482	2.05	9	40.17	4	8	0

Passing Offense

Rank, Team	G	Att	Comp	Int	Pct.	Yds	Yds/ Att	TD	Yds/ Gm	IPct	Yds/ Cmp	W	L	T
1. Hawaii	14	615	444	12	72.20	6,178	10.05	62	441.3	1.95	13.91	11	3	0
2. New Mexico St.	12	607	421	12	69.36	4,792	7.89	34	399.3	1.98	11.38	4	8	0
3. Texas Tech	13	655	438	11	66.87	4,803	7.33	39	369.5	1.68	10.97	8	5	0
4. Brigham Young	13	452	311	9	68.81	4,206	9.31	33	323.5	1.99	13.52	11	2	0
5. UTEP	12	447	290	17	64.88	3,754	8.40	29	312.8	3.80	12.94	5	7	0
6. Purdue	14	541	322	20	59.52	4,082	7.55	24	291.6	3.70	12.68	8	6	0
7. Louisville	13	384	245	7	63.80	3,770	9.82	22	290.0	1.82	15.39	12	1	0
8. Houston	14	445	300	5	67.42	3,889	8.74	30	277.8	1.12	12.96	10	4	0
9. Kentucky	13	436	273	7	62.61	3,597	8.25	31	276.7	1.61	13.18	8	5	0
10. Missouri	13	465	291	11	62.58	3,590	7.72	29	276.2	2.37	12.34	8	5	0
11. Baylor	12	510	307	17	60.20	3,300	6.47	24	275.0	3.33	10.75	4	8	0
12. Tennessee	13	415	265	11	63.86	3,438	8.28	24	264.5	2.65	12.97	9	4	0
13. Notre Dame	13	471	290	7	61.57	3,433	7.29	37	264.1	1.49	11.84	10	3	0
14. Southern California	13	447	273	11	61.07	3,430	7.67	30	263.8	2.46	12.56	11	2	0
15. Washington St.	12	430	260	12	60.47	3,117	7.25	23	259.8	2.79	11.99	6	6	0
16. Ball St.	12	373	232	11	62.20	3,112	8.34	27	259.3	2.95	13.41	5	7	0
17. California	13	413	245	14	59.32	3,292	7.97	25	253.2	3.39	13.44	10	3	0
18. LSU	13	368	245	9	66.58	3,272	8.89	30	251.7	2.45	13.36	11	2	0
19. South Carolina	13	389	243	13	62.47	3,259	8.38	24	250.7	3.34	13.41	8	5	0
20. Pittsburgh	12	332	228	9	68.67	2,991	9.01	28	249.3	2.71	13.12	6	6	0
21. Tulane	12	440	245	12	55.68	2,958	6.72	18	246.5	2.73	12.07	4	8	0
22. Central Mich.	14	447	280	11	62.64	3,443	7.70	28	245.9	2.46	12.30	10	4	0
23. Nebraska	14	411	244	8	59.37	3,417	8.31	32	244.1	1.95	14.00	9	5	0
24. Oregon St.	14	425	259	9	60.94	3,393	7.98	20	242.4	2.12	13.10	10	4	0
25. Boston College	13	459	285	11	62.09	3,135	6.83	16	241.2	2.40	11.00	10	3	0
26. Oregon	13	486	288	18	59.26	3,133	6.45	18	241.0	3.70	10.88	7	6	0
27. Iowa	13	423	248	19	58.63	3,118	7.37	21	239.8	4.49	12.57	6	7	0
28. Florida	14	399	255	14	63.91	3,305	8.28	29	236.1	3.51	12.96	13	1	0
29. Florida St.	13	439	239	16	54.44	3,039	6.92	19	233.8	3.64	12.72	7	6	0
30. UCF	12	381	227	10	59.58	2,805	7.36	14	233.8	2.62	12.36	4	8	0
31. East Caro.	13	430	248	11	57.67	3,024	7.03	13	232.6	2.56	12.19	7	6	0
32. Miami (Ohio)	12	420	241	11	57.38	2,779	6.62	15	231.6	2.62	11.53	2	10	0
33. Texas	13	371	244	9	65.77	2,975	8.02	31	228.8	2.43	12.19	10	3	0
34. Utah	13	411	238	12	57.91	2,963	7.21	25	227.9	2.92	12.45	8	5	0
35. Michigan St.	12	417	248	13	59.47	2,731	6.55	18	227.6	3.12	11.01	4	8	0
36. UNLV	12	441	242	17	54.88	2,728	6.19	16	227.3	3.85	11.27	2	10	0
37. Akron	12	384	202	11	52.60	2,720	7.08	18	226.7	2.86	13.47	5	7	0
38. Tulsa	13	365	243	9	66.58	2,944	8.07	16	226.5	2.47	12.12	8	5	0
39. Memphis	12	394	234	14	59.39	2,695	6.84	21	224.6	3.55	11.52	2	10	0
40. Indiana	12	430	232	12	53.95	2,665	6.20	16	222.1	2.79	11.49	5	7	0
41. Minnesota	13	373	218	11	58.45	2,874	7.71	22	221.1	2.95	13.18	6	7	0
42. Colorado St.	12	363	221	13	60.88	2,617	7.21	13	218.1	3.58	11.84	4	8	0
43. South Fla.	13	356	226	15	63.48	2,827	7.94	16	217.5	4.21	12.51	9	4	0
44. Iowa St.	12	378	213	12	56.35	2,593	6.86	12	216.1	3.17	12.17	4	8	0
45. Ohio St.	13	340	221	6	65.00	2,791	8.21	31	214.7	1.76	12.63	12	1	0
46. Louisiana Tech	13	413	214	19	51.82	2,787	6.75	17	214.4	4.60	13.02	3	10	0
47. Rice	13	435	248	14	57.01	2,783	6.40	29	214.1	3.22	11.22	7	6	0
48. TCU	13	352	216	6	61.36	2,780	7.90	15	213.8	1.70	12.87	11	2	0
49. Alabama	13	393	224	10	57.00	2,767	7.04	18	212.8	2.54	12.35	6	7	0
50. Wisconsin	13	331	195	9	58.91	2,749	8.31	21	211.5	2.72	14.10	12	1	0
51. Cincinnati	13	345	207	17	60.00	2,689	7.79	17	206.8	4.93	12.99	8	5	0
52. Boise St.	13	306	204	9	66.67	2,684	8.77	25	206.5	2.94	13.16	13	0	0
53. New Mexico	13	390	204	9	52.31	2,676	6.86	18	205.8	2.31	13.12	6	7	0
54. Oklahoma St.	13	321	174	11	54.21	2,623	8.17	27	201.8	3.43	15.07	7	6	0
55. Vanderbilt	12	337	187	14	55.49	2,417	7.17	16	201.4	4.15	12.93	4	8	0
56. UCLA	13	400	224	14	56.00	2,604	6.51	16	200.3	3.50	11.63	7	6	0
57. Kansas St.	13	415	214	20	51.57	2,601	6.27	10	200.1	4.82	12.15	7	6	0
58. Penn St.	13	424	226	9	53.30	2,599	6.13	12	199.9	2.12	11.50	9	4	0
59. Northern Ill.	13	386	217	15	56.22	2,580	6.68	16	198.5	3.89	11.89	7	6	0
60. Kansas	12	363	203	19	55.92	2,372	6.53	19	197.7	5.23	11.68	6	6	0
61. Arizona St.	13	349	190	14	54.44	2,569	7.36	23	197.6	4.01	13.52	7	6	0
62. Miami (Fla.)	13	360	213	15	59.17	2,567	7.13	16	197.5	4.17	12.05	7	6	0
63. Idaho	12	346	168	16	48.55	2,353	6.80	8	196.1	4.62	14.01	4	8	0
64. Michigan	13	331	206	8	62.24	2,538	7.67	22	195.2	2.42	12.32	11	2	0
65. SMU	12	316	203	10	64.24	2,331	7.38	29	194.3	3.16	11.48	6	6	0
66. Washington	12	373	179	16	47.99	2,326	6.24	19	193.8	4.29	12.99	5	7	0
67. Clemson	13	327	198	11	60.55	2,510	7.68	18	193.1	3.36	12.68	8	5	0
68. La.-Monroe	12	313	179	15	57.19	2,310	7.38	10	192.5	4.79	12.91	4	8	0
69. Mississippi St.	12	360	171	16	47.50	2,300	6.39	10	191.7	4.44	13.45	3	9	0
70. Oklahoma	14	340	205	11	60.29	2,682	7.89	22	191.6	3.24	13.08	11	3	0
71. Troy	13	408	252	18	61.76	2,488	6.10	22	191.4	4.41	9.87	8	5	0
72. Texas A&M	13	330	202	4	61.21	2,477	7.51	13	190.5	1.21	12.26	9	4	0
73. Fla. Atlantic	12	352	189	14	53.69	2,254	6.40	11	187.8	3.98	11.93	5	7	0
74. Nevada	13	342	216	12	63.16	2,436	7.12	23	187.4	3.51	11.28	8	5	0
75. Marshall	12	295	180	16	61.02	2,247	7.62	16	187.3	5.42	12.48	5	7	0
76. Duke	12	358	189	17	52.79	2,222	6.21	12	185.2	4.75	11.76	0	12	0
77. Western Mich.	13	408	252	13	61.76	2,403	5.89	20	184.8	3.19	9.54	8	5	0
78. UAB	12	304	177	12	58.22	2,214	7.28	12	184.5	3.95	12.51	3	9	0
79. Georgia	13	342	184	16	53.80	2,397	7.01	12	184.4	4.68	13.03	9	4	0
80. Maryland	13	335	204	12	60.90	2,380	7.10	16	183.1	3.58	11.67	9	4	0

Rank, Team	G	Att	Comp	Int	Pct.	Yds	Yds/ Att	TD	Yds/ Gm	IPct	Yds/ Cmp	W	L	T
81. North Carolina St.	12	379	196	16	51.72	2,188	5.77	10	182.3	4.22	11.16	3	9	0
82. Virginia Tech	13	322	181	12	56.21	2,363	7.34	13	181.8	3.73	13.06	10	3	0
83. San Jose St.	13	294	187	8	63.61	2,361	8.03	23	181.6	2.72	12.63	9	4	0
84. North Carolina	12	333	169	18	50.75	2,156	6.47	11	179.7	5.41	12.76	3	9	0
85. Wyoming	12	346	210	13	60.69	2,148	6.21	17	179.0	3.76	10.23	6	6	0
86. Buffalo	12	354	200	13	56.50	2,136	6.03	9	178.0	3.67	10.68	2	10	0
87. Florida Int'l	12	408	220	15	53.92	2,115	5.18	5	176.3	3.68	9.61	0	12	0
88. Auburn	13	282	171	10	60.64	2,245	7.96	14	172.7	3.55	13.13	11	2	0
89. Toledo	12	386	215	11	55.70	2,048	5.31	13	170.7	2.85	9.53	5	7	0
90. Eastern Mich.	12	370	217	16	58.65	2,046	5.53	7	170.5	4.32	9.43	1	11	0
91. Georgia Tech	14	369	174	16	47.15	2,375	6.44	25	169.6	4.34	13.65	9	5	0
92. Bowling Green	12	347	195	11	56.20	2,029	5.85	12	169.1	3.17	10.41	4	8	0
93. Northwestern	12	332	188	17	56.63	2,028	6.11	8	169.0	5.12	10.79	4	8	0
94. Arizona	12	356	191	14	53.65	2,024	5.69	9	168.7	3.93	10.60	6	6	0
95. Stanford	12	316	167	11	52.85	2,002	6.34	10	166.8	3.48	11.99	1	11	0
96. Rutgers	13	298	165	13	55.37	2,144	7.19	12	164.9	4.36	12.99	11	2	0
97. Kent St.	12	267	143	12	53.56	1,958	7.33	10	163.2	4.49	13.69	6	6	0
98. Temple	12	308	184	15	59.74	1,944	6.31	13	162.0	4.87	10.57	1	11	0
99. Southern Miss.	14	353	198	7	56.09	2,257	6.39	14	161.2	1.98	11.40	9	5	0
100. West Virginia	13	233	149	8	63.95	2,059	8.84	15	158.4	3.43	13.82	11	2	0
101. Fresno St.	12	322	178	15	55.28	1,898	5.89	16	158.2	4.66	10.66	4	8	0
102. Virginia	12	345	203	11	58.84	1,887	5.47	8	157.3	3.19	9.30	5	7	0
103. Syracuse	12	311	161	5	51.77	1,885	6.06	13	157.1	1.61	11.71	4	8	0
104. Wake Forest	14	287	188	6	65.51	2,199	7.66	11	157.1	2.09	11.70	11	3	0
105. Illinois	12	332	140	14	42.17	1,878	5.66	11	156.5	4.22	13.41	2	10	0
106. Middle Tenn.	13	313	181	11	57.83	2,007	6.41	9	154.4	3.51	11.09	7	6	0
107. San Diego St.	12	294	171	17	58.16	1,804	6.14	8	150.3	5.78	10.55	3	9	0
108. Arkansas	14	302	154	18	50.99	2,093	6.93	23	149.5	5.96	13.59	10	4	0
109. Arkansas St.	12	300	144	15	48.00	1,735	5.78	8	144.6	5.00	12.05	6	6	0
110. Connecticut	12	313	161	12	51.44	1,692	5.41	14	141.0	3.83	10.51	4	8	0
111. Utah St.	12	298	155	14	52.01	1,676	5.62	9	139.7	4.70	10.81	1	11	0
112. Mississippi	12	280	134	10	47.86	1,633	5.83	9	136.1	3.57	12.19	4	8	0
113. Army	12	293	163	24	55.63	1,601	5.46	10	133.4	8.19	9.82	3	9	0
114. La.-Lafayette	12	276	142	14	51.45	1,550	5.62	9	129.2	5.07	10.92	6	6	0
115. Ohio	14	331	180	15	54.38	1,806	5.46	9	129.0	4.53	10.03	9	5	0
116. Colorado	12	254	119	8	46.85	1,422	5.60	7	118.5	3.15	11.95	2	10	0
117. North Texas	12	253	136	19	53.75	1,382	5.46	9	115.2	7.51	10.16	3	9	0
118. Air Force	12	146	84	4	57.53	1,215	8.32	12	101.3	2.74	14.46	4	8	0
119. Navy	13	112	51	4	45.54	728	6.50	7	56.0	3.57	14.27	9	4	0

Passing Efficiency

Rank, Team	G	Att	Comp	Pct	Int	IPct	Yds	Yds/Att	TD	TD Pct	Rating	W	L	T
1. Hawaii	14	615	444	72.20	12	1.95	6,178	10.05	62	10.08	185.95	11	3	0
2. Brigham Young	13	452	311	68.81	9	1.99	4,206	9.31	33	7.30	167.08	11	2	0
3. Pittsburgh	12	332	228	68.67	9	2.71	2,991	9.01	28	8.43	166.79	6	6	0
4. LSU	13	368	245	66.58	9	2.45	3,272	8.89	30	8.15	163.30	11	2	0
5. Louisville	13	384	245	63.80	7	1.82	3,770	9.82	22	5.73	161.53	12	1	0
6. Boise St.	13	306	204	66.67	9	2.94	2,684	8.77	25	8.17	161.46	13	0	0
7. Houston	14	445	300	67.42	5	1.12	3,889	8.74	30	6.74	160.81	10	4	0
8. Ohio St.	13	340	221	65.00	6	1.76	2,791	8.21	31	9.12	160.51	12	1	0
9. Texas	13	371	244	65.77	9	2.43	2,975	8.02	31	8.36	155.88	10	3	0
10. West Virginia	13	233	149	63.95	8	3.43	2,059	8.84	15	6.44	152.51	11	2	0
11. Kentucky	13	436	273	62.61	7	1.61	3,597	8.25	31	7.11	152.15	8	5	0
12. San Jose St.	13	294	187	63.61	8	2.72	2,361	8.03	23	7.82	151.43	9	4	0
13. Nebraska	14	411	244	59.37	8	1.95	3,417	8.31	32	7.79	151.04	9	5	0
14. Florida	14	399	255	63.91	14	3.51	3,305	8.28	29	7.27	150.45	13	1	0
15. Ball St.	12	373	232	62.20	11	2.95	3,112	8.34	27	7.24	150.27	5	7	0
16. New Mexico St.	12	607	421	69.36	12	1.98	4,792	7.89	34	5.60	150.24	4	8	0
17. SMU	12	316	203	64.24	10	3.16	2,331	7.38	29	9.18	150.12	6	6	0
18. UTEP	12	447	290	64.88	17	3.80	3,754	8.40	29	6.49	149.25	5	7	0
19. Air Force	12	146	84	57.53	4	2.74	1,215	8.32	12	8.22	149.05	4	8	0
20. Tennessee	13	415	265	63.86	11	2.65	3,438	8.28	24	5.78	147.27	9	4	0
21. South Carolina	13	389	243	62.47	13	3.34	3,259	8.38	24	6.17	146.55	8	5	0
22. Notre Dame	13	471	290	61.57	7	1.49	3,433	7.29	37	7.86	145.78	10	3	0
23. Texas Tech	13	655	438	66.87	11	1.68	4,803	7.33	39	5.95	144.79	8	5	0
24. Wisconsin	13	331	195	58.91	9	2.72	2,749	8.31	21	6.34	144.16	12	1	0
25. Tulsa	13	365	243	66.58	9	2.47	2,944	8.07	16	4.38	143.89	8	5	0
26. Oklahoma St.	13	321	174	54.21	11	3.43	2,623	8.17	27	8.41	143.74	7	6	0
27. Michigan	13	331	206	62.24	8	2.42	2,538	7.67	22	6.65	143.71	11	2	0
28. Missouri	13	465	291	62.58	11	2.37	3,590	7.72	29	6.24	143.30	8	5	0
29. Central Mich.	14	447	280	62.64	11	2.46	3,443	7.70	28	6.26	143.05	10	4	0
30. Southern California	13	447	273	61.07	11	2.46	3,430	7.67	30	6.71	142.78	11	2	0
31. Oklahoma	14	340	205	60.29	11	3.24	2,682	7.89	22	6.47	141.44	11	3	0
32. California	13	413	245	59.32	14	3.39	3,292	7.97	25	6.05	139.45	10	3	0
33. Oregon St.	14	425	259	60.94	9	2.12	3,393	7.98	20	4.71	139.26	10	4	0
34. TCU	13	352	216	61.36	6	1.70	2,780	7.90	15	4.26	138.39	11	2	0
35. Wake Forest	14	287	188	65.51	6	2.09	2,199	7.66	11	3.83	138.33	11	3	0
36. Nevada	13	342	216	63.16	12	3.51	2,436	7.12	23	6.73	138.21	8	5	0
37. Auburn	13	282	171	60.64	10	3.55	2,245	7.96	14	4.96	136.76	11	2	0
38. Minnesota	13	373	218	58.45	11	2.95	2,874	7.71	22	5.90	136.69	6	7	0

Rank, Team	G	Att	Comp	Pct	Int	IPct	Yds	Yds/Att	TD	TD Pct	Rating	W	L	T
39. South Fla.	13	356	226	63.48	15	4.21	2,827	7.94	16	4.49	136.61	9	4	0
40. Clemson	13	327	198	60.55	11	3.36	2,510	7.68	18	5.50	136.51	8	5	0
41. Texas A&M	13	330	202	61.21	4	1.21	2,477	7.51	13	3.94	134.83	9	4	0
42. Washington St.	12	430	260	60.47	12	2.79	3,117	7.25	23	5.35	133.46	6	6	0
43. Utah	13	411	238	57.91	12	2.92	2,963	7.21	25	6.08	132.69	8	5	0
44. Marshall	12	295	180	61.02	16	5.42	2,247	7.62	16	5.42	132.03	5	7	0
45. Cincinnati	13	345	207	60.00	17	4.93	2,689	7.79	17	4.93	131.88	8	5	0
46. Purdue	14	541	322	59.52	20	3.70	4,082	7.55	24	4.44	130.13	8	6	0
47. Arizona St.	13	349	190	54.44	14	4.01	2,569	7.36	23	6.59	129.96	7	6	0
48. Maryland	13	335	204	60.90	12	3.58	2,380	7.10	16	4.78	129.17	9	4	0
49. UCF	12	381	227	59.58	10	2.62	2,805	7.36	14	3.67	128.32	4	8	0
50. Iowa	13	423	248	58.63	19	4.49	3,118	7.37	21	4.96	127.92	6	7	0
51. Memphis	12	394	234	59.39	14	3.55	2,695	6.84	21	5.33	127.34	2	10	0
52. Rice	13	435	248	57.01	14	3.22	2,783	6.40	29	6.67	126.30	7	6	0
53. Boston College	13	459	285	62.09	11	2.40	3,135	6.83	16	3.49	126.18	10	3	0
54. Alabama	13	393	224	57.00	10	2.54	2,767	7.04	18	4.58	126.17	6	7	0
55. Colorado St.	12	363	221	60.88	13	3.58	2,617	7.21	13	3.58	126.11	4	8	0
56. Miami (Fla.)	13	360	213	59.17	15	4.17	2,567	7.13	16	4.44	125.43	7	6	0
57. UAB	12	304	177	58.22	12	3.95	2,214	7.28	12	3.95	124.51	3	9	0
58. Virginia Tech	13	322	181	56.21	12	3.73	2,363	7.34	13	4.04	123.71	10	3	0
59. Baylor	12	510	307	60.20	17	3.33	3,300	6.47	24	4.71	123.42	4	8	0
60. Vanderbilt	12	337	187	55.49	14	4.15	2,417	7.17	16	4.75	123.10	4	8	0
61. Michigan St.	12	417	248	59.47	13	3.12	2,731	6.55	18	4.32	122.52	4	8	0
62. Arkansas	14	302	154	50.99	18	5.96	2,093	6.93	23	7.62	122.43	10	4	0
63. Troy	13	408	252	61.76	18	4.41	2,488	6.10	22	5.39	121.99	8	5	0
64. Akron	12	384	202	52.60	11	2.86	2,720	7.08	18	4.69	121.84	5	7	0
65. East Caro.	13	430	248	57.67	11	2.56	3,024	7.03	13	3.02	121.63	7	6	0
66. Wyoming	12	346	210	60.69	13	3.76	2,148	6.21	17	4.91	121.55	6	6	0
67. Western Mich.	13	408	252	61.76	13	3.19	2,403	5.89	20	4.90	121.08	8	5	0
68. New Mexico	13	390	204	52.31	9	2.31	2,676	6.86	18	4.62	120.55	6	7	0
69. Rutgers	13	298	165	55.37	13	4.36	2,144	7.19	12	4.03	120.40	11	2	0
70. Tulane	12	440	245	55.68	12	2.73	2,958	6.72	18	4.09	120.22	4	8	0
71. La.-Monroe	12	313	179	57.19	15	4.79	2,310	7.38	10	3.19	120.15	4	8	0
72. Florida St.	13	439	239	54.44	16	3.64	3,039	6.92	19	4.33	119.54	7	6	0
73. Miami (Ohio)	12	420	241	57.38	11	2.62	2,779	6.62	15	3.57	119.53	2	10	0
74. Southern Miss.	14	353	198	56.09	7	1.98	2,257	6.39	14	3.97	118.93	9	5	0
75. Kent St.	12	267	143	53.56	12	4.49	1,958	7.33	10	3.75	118.57	6	6	0
76. Oregon	13	486	288	59.26	18	3.70	3,133	6.45	18	3.70	118.27	7	6	0
77. Northern Ill.	13	386	217	56.22	15	3.89	2,580	6.68	16	4.15	118.25	7	6	0
78. Iowa St.	12	378	213	56.35	12	3.17	2,593	6.86	12	3.17	118.05	4	8	0
79. Kansas	12	363	203	55.92	19	5.23	2,372	6.53	19	5.23	117.59	6	6	0
80. Temple	12	308	184	59.74	15	4.87	1,944	6.31	13	4.22	116.91	1	11	0
81. UCLA	13	400	224	56.00	14	3.50	2,604	6.51	16	4.00	116.88	7	6	0
82. Georgia Tech	14	369	174	47.15	16	4.34	2,375	6.44	25	6.78	114.95	9	5	0
83. Georgia	13	342	184	53.80	16	4.68	2,397	7.01	12	3.51	114.90	9	4	0
84. Middle Tenn.	13	313	181	57.83	11	3.51	2,007	6.41	9	2.88	114.12	7	6	0
85. Navy	13	112	51	45.54	4	3.57	728	6.50	7	6.25	113.58	9	4	0
86. Syracuse	12	311	161	51.77	5	1.61	1,885	6.06	13	4.18	113.29	4	8	0
87. Louisiana Tech	13	413	214	51.82	19	4.60	2,787	6.75	17	4.12	112.87	3	10	0
88. Indiana	12	430	232	53.95	12	2.79	2,665	6.20	16	3.72	112.76	5	7	0
89. Fresno St.	12	322	178	55.28	15	4.66	1,898	5.89	16	4.97	111.89	4	8	0
90. UNLV	12	441	242	54.88	17	3.85	2,728	6.19	16	3.63	111.12	2	10	0
91. Bowling Green	12	347	195	56.20	11	3.17	2,029	5.85	12	3.46	110.39	4	8	0
92. Penn St.	13	424	226	53.30	9	2.12	2,599	6.13	12	2.83	109.88	9	4	0
93. Fla. Atlantic	12	352	189	53.69	14	3.98	2,254	6.40	11	3.13	109.85	5	7	0
94. Stanford	12	316	167	52.85	11	3.48	2,002	6.34	10	3.16	109.50	1	11	0
95. Washington	12	373	179	47.99	16	4.29	2,326	6.24	19	5.09	108.61	5	7	0
96. Buffalo	12	354	200	56.50	13	3.67	2,136	6.03	9	2.54	108.23	2	10	0
97. San Diego St.	12	294	171	58.16	17	5.78	1,804	6.14	8	2.72	107.16	3	9	0
98. Duke	12	358	189	52.79	17	4.75	2,222	6.21	12	3.35	106.50	0	12	0
99. Virginia	12	345	203	58.84	11	3.19	1,887	5.47	8	2.32	106.02	5	7	0
100. Toledo	12	386	215	55.70	11	2.85	2,048	5.31	13	3.37	105.68	5	7	0
101. Northwestern	12	332	188	56.63	17	5.12	2,028	6.11	8	2.41	105.62	4	8	0
102. North Carolina	12	333	169	50.75	18	5.41	2,156	6.47	11	3.30	105.28	3	9	0
103. Idaho	12	346	168	48.55	16	4.62	2,353	6.80	8	2.31	104.11	4	8	0
104. Connecticut	12	313	161	51.44	12	3.83	1,692	5.41	14	4.47	103.90	4	8	0
105. Eastern Mich.	12	370	217	58.65	16	4.32	2,046	5.53	7	1.89	102.64	1	11	0
106. Kansas St.	13	415	214	51.57	20	4.82	2,601	6.27	10	2.41	102.56	7	6	0
107. Arizona	12	356	191	53.65	14	3.93	2,024	5.69	9	2.53	101.93	6	6	0
108. Mississippi St.	12	360	171	47.50	16	4.44	2,300	6.39	10	2.78	101.44	3	9	0
109. North Carolina St.	12	379	196	51.72	16	4.22	2,188	5.77	10	2.64	100.46	3	9	0
110. Mississippi	12	280	134	47.86	10	3.57	1,633	5.83	9	3.21	100.35	4	8	0
111. Ohio	14	331	180	54.38	15	4.53	1,806	5.46	9	2.72	100.14	9	5	0
112. Utah St.	12	298	155	52.01	14	4.70	1,676	5.62	9	3.02	99.81	1	11	0
113. La.-Lafayette	12	276	142	51.45	14	5.07	1,550	5.62	9	3.26	99.19	6	6	0
114. Colorado	12	254	119	46.85	8	3.15	1,422	5.60	7	2.76	96.72	2	10	0
115. North Texas	12	253	136	53.75	19	7.51	1,382	5.46	9	3.56	96.40	3	9	0
116. Army	12	293	163	55.63	24	8.19	1,601	5.46	10	3.41	96.38	3	9	0
117. Arkansas St.	12	300	144	48.00	15	5.00	1,735	5.78	8	2.67	95.38	6	6	0
118. Florida Int'l	12	408	220	53.92	15	3.68	2,115	5.18	5	1.23	94.14	0	12	0
119. Illinois	12	332	140	42.17	14	4.22	1,878	5.66	11	3.31	92.22	2	10	0

Total Offense

Rank, Team	G	Pl	Yds	Avg	TD	Yds/Gm	W	L	T
1. Hawaii	14	913	7,829	8.58	89	559.21	11	3	0
2. Louisville	13	867	6,179	7.13	61	475.31	12	1	0
3. New Mexico St.	12	930	5,702	6.13	53	475.17	4	8	0
4. Brigham Young	13	889	6,051	6.81	63	465.46	11	2	0
5. West Virginia	13	823	5,998	7.29	65	461.38	11	2	0
6. Texas Tech	13	875	5,822	6.65	54	447.85	8	5	0
7. Houston	14	935	6,245	6.68	60	446.07	10	4	0
8. Missouri	13	922	5,533	6.00	48	425.62	8	5	0
9. Oregon	13	958	5,497	5.74	48	422.85	7	6	0
10. Boise St.	13	857	5,468	6.38	68	420.62	13	0	0
11. LSU	13	818	5,427	6.63	59	417.46	11	2	0
12. California	13	840	5,408	6.44	54	416.00	10	3	0
13. Purdue	14	941	5,820	6.18	48	415.71	8	6	0
14. Nebraska	14	965	5,804	6.01	59	414.57	9	5	0
15. Clemson	13	822	5,342	6.50	55	410.92	8	5	0
16. Oklahoma St.	13	843	5,327	6.32	61	409.77	7	6	0
17. TCU	13	909	5,310	5.84	46	408.46	11	2	0
18. Texas A&M	13	870	5,166	5.94	46	397.38	9	4	0
19. Florida	14	875	5,545	6.34	57	396.07	13	1	0
20. South Carolina	13	803	5,135	6.39	43	395.00	8	5	0
21. Southern California	13	863	5,094	5.90	50	391.85	11	2	0
22. Texas	13	854	5,089	5.96	63	391.46	10	3	0
23. Notre Dame	13	894	5,067	5.67	55	389.77	10	3	0
24. Tulsa	13	849	5,051	5.95	47	388.54	8	5	0
25. Washington St.	12	822	4,657	5.67	38	388.08	6	6	0
26. Ohio St.	13	820	4,999	6.10	61	384.54	12	1	0
27. Iowa	13	855	4,983	5.83	38	383.31	6	7	0
28. Navy	13	876	4,979	5.68	48	383.00	9	4	0
29. Arkansas	14	841	5,292	6.29	55	378.00	10	4	0
30. Minnesota	13	840	4,881	5.81	50	375.46	6	7	0
31. Kentucky	13	847	4,879	5.76	45	375.31	8	5	0
32. Central Mich.	14	869	5,254	6.05	55	375.29	10	4	0
33. Kansas	12	801	4,489	5.60	44	374.08	6	6	0
34. UCF	12	823	4,478	5.44	26	373.17	4	8	0
35. Wisconsin	13	867	4,851	5.60	48	373.15	12	1	0
36. Tennessee	13	797	4,842	6.08	44	372.46	9	4	0
37. Pittsburgh	12	712	4,467	6.27	49	372.25	6	6	0
38. Michigan	13	866	4,820	5.57	47	370.77	11	2	0
39. UTEP	12	735	4,445	6.05	41	370.42	5	7	0
40. Oklahoma	14	897	5,162	5.75	52	368.71	11	3	0
41. Utah	13	862	4,789	5.56	45	368.38	8	5	0
42. Arizona St.	13	846	4,775	5.64	44	367.31	7	6	0
43. Northern Ill.	13	829	4,722	5.70	39	363.23	7	6	0
44. South Fla.	13	841	4,701	5.59	40	361.62	9	4	0
45. Oregon St.	14	899	5,048	5.62	46	360.57	10	4	0
46. Nevada	13	853	4,648	5.45	53	357.54	8	5	0
47. San Jose St.	13	783	4,644	5.93	43	357.23	9	4	0
48. Michigan St.	12	804	4,281	5.32	37	356.75	4	8	0
49. Marshall	12	701	4,252	6.07	43	354.33	5	7	0
50. Boston College	13	896	4,604	5.14	42	354.15	10	3	0
51. Ball St.	12	739	4,215	5.70	39	351.25	5	7	0
52. Vanderbilt	12	722	4,212	5.83	35	351.00	4	8	0
53. Penn St.	13	881	4,549	5.16	32	349.92	9	4	0
54. East Caro.	13	880	4,526	5.14	33	348.15	7	6	0
55. La.-Monroe	12	758	4,174	5.51	32	347.83	4	8	0
56. Bowling Green	12	852	4,149	4.87	32	345.75	4	8	0
57. Illinois	12	766	4,144	5.41	27	345.33	2	10	0
58. Rice	13	873	4,486	5.14	45	345.08	7	6	0
58. Rutgers	13	794	4,486	5.65	46	345.08	11	2	0
60. Louisiana Tech	13	828	4,479	5.41	31	344.54	3	10	0
61. Cincinnati	13	858	4,426	5.16	31	340.46	8	5	0
62. Tulane	12	793	4,064	5.12	29	338.67	4	8	0
63. Fresno St.	12	752	4,058	5.40	35	338.17	4	8	0
64. Memphis	12	766	4,035	5.27	34	336.25	2	10	0
65. Alabama	13	848	4,367	5.15	34	335.92	6	7	0
66. Indiana	12	822	4,031	4.90	35	335.92	5	7	0
67. Georgia Tech	14	895	4,649	5.19	45	332.07	9	5	0
68. Southern Miss.	14	888	4,635	5.22	44	331.07	9	5	0
69. Air Force	12	806	3,968	4.92	36	330.67	4	8	0
70. Florida St.	13	802	4,294	5.35	42	330.31	7	6	0
71. UCLA	13	836	4,291	5.13	31	330.08	7	6	0
72. Toledo	12	856	3,923	4.58	37	326.92	5	7	0
73. Connecticut	12	799	3,887	4.86	34	323.92	4	8	0
74. Washington	12	775	3,861	4.98	33	321.75	5	7	0
75. Kent St.	12	753	3,859	5.12	30	321.58	6	6	0
76. Auburn	13	752	4,172	5.55	37	320.92	11	2	0
77. Troy	13	844	4,159	4.93	38	319.92	8	5	0
78. Western Mich.	13	879	4,154	4.73	35	319.54	8	5	0
79. SMU	12	720	3,834	5.33	41	319.50	6	6	0
80. Miami (Ohio)	12	806	3,819	4.74	27	318.25	2	10	0
81. Iowa St.	12	779	3,814	4.90	29	317.83	4	8	0
82. La.-Lafayette	12	754	3,811	5.05	31	317.58	6	6	0
83. New Mexico	13	823	4,120	5.01	32	316.92	6	7	0
84. UNLV	12	786	3,802	4.84	30	316.83	2	10	0
85. Kansas St.	13	787	4,098	5.21	35	315.23	7	6	0
86. Baylor	12	745	3,782	5.08	36	315.17	4	8	0
87. Miami (Fla.)	13	791	4,075	5.15	31	313.46	7	6	0
88. Maryland	13	785	4,073	5.19	32	313.31	9	4	0
89. Arkansas St.	12	807	3,747	4.64	21	312.25	6	6	0
90. Georgia	13	768	4,053	5.28	40	311.77	9	4	0
91. Wyoming	12	787	3,736	4.75	32	311.33	6	6	0
92. Northwestern	12	754	3,733	4.95	25	311.08	4	8	0
93. Akron	12	749	3,725	4.97	32	310.42	5	7	0
94. Idaho	12	745	3,723	5.00	24	310.25	4	8	0
95. UAB	12	736	3,721	5.06	28	310.08	3	9	0
96. Wake Forest	14	829	4,298	5.18	33	307.00	11	3	0
97. North Carolina St.	12	753	3,624	4.81	25	302.00	3	9	0
98. Fla. Atlantic	12	804	3,568	4.44	22	297.33	5	7	0
99. Virginia Tech	13	777	3,837	4.94	40	295.15	10	3	0
100. Colorado St.	12	735	3,535	4.81	26	294.58	4	8	0
101. North Carolina	12	715	3,516	4.92	27	293.00	3	9	0
102. Colorado	12	715	3,497	4.89	20	291.42	2	10	0
103. Mississippi St.	12	754	3,442	4.56	29	286.83	3	9	0
104. Middle Tenn.	13	787	3,712	4.72	39	285.54	7	6	0
105. Duke	12	770	3,401	4.42	24	283.42	0	12	0
106. Ohio	14	856	3,873	4.52	34	276.64	9	5	0
107. Eastern Mich.	12	744	3,315	4.46	17	276.25	1	11	0
108. San Diego St.	12	716	3,234	4.52	21	269.50	3	9	0
109. Buffalo	12	734	3,218	4.38	28	268.17	2	10	0
110. Syracuse	12	731	3,168	4.33	23	264.00	4	8	0
111. Mississippi	12	702	3,137	4.47	21	261.42	4	8	0
112. Army	12	710	3,132	4.41	28	261.00	3	9	0
113. Virginia	12	709	3,086	4.35	21	257.17	5	7	0
114. Utah St.	12	728	3,053	4.19	18	254.42	1	11	0
115. Arizona	12	735	3,034	4.13	22	252.83	6	6	0
116. Florida Int'l	12	707	2,797	3.96	15	233.08	0	12	0
117. North Texas	12	690	2,786	4.04	15	232.17	3	9	0
118. Stanford	12	683	2,783	4.07	15	231.92	1	11	0
119. Temple	12	653	2,588	3.96	18	215.67	1	11	0

Scoring Offense

Rank, Team	G	Pts.	Avg.	TD	Kxp	Oxp	Dkxp	Doxp	FG	Saf	W	L	T
1. Hawaii	14	656	46.86	89	75	3	0	0	13	1	11	3	0
2. Boise St.	13	516	39.69	68	61	3	0	1	13	0	13	0	0
3. West Virginia	13	505	38.85	65	62	1	0	0	17	0	11	2	0
4. Louisville	13	491	37.77	61	60	1	0	0	21	0	12	1	0
5. Brigham Young	13	478	36.77	63	58	0	0	0	14	0	11	2	0
6. Texas	13	467	35.92	63	60	0	0	0	9	1	10	3	0
7. Oklahoma St.	13	458	35.23	61	57	1	0	0	11	0	7	6	0
8. Ohio St.	13	450	34.62	61	57	0	0	0	9	0	12	1	0
9. LSU	13	438	33.69	59	57	0	0	0	9	0	11	2	0
10. Houston	14	462	33.00	60	55	1	0	0	15	0	10	4	0
11. California	13	427	32.85	54	52	2	0	0	15	1	10	3	0
12. Clemson	13	425	32.69	55	46	2	0	0	15	0	8	5	0
13. Texas Tech	13	422	32.46	54	51	1	0	0	15	0	8	5	0
14. Pittsburgh	12	381	31.75	49	47	0	0	0	12	2	6	6	0
15. New Mexico St.	12	374	31.17	53	42	1	0	0	4	0	4	8	0
16. Notre Dame	13	403	31.00	55	49	0	0	0	8	0	10	3	0
17. Nebraska	14	428	30.57	59	55	1	0	0	5	1	9	5	0

Rank, Team	G	Pts.	Avg.	TD	Kxp	Oxp	Dkxp	Doxp	FG	Saf	W	L	T
18. Southern California	13	396	30.46	50	44	1	0	0	16	1	11	2	0
19. Oklahoma	14	424	30.29	52	49	1	0	0	19	2	11	3	0
20. Missouri	13	391	30.08	48	45	0	0	0	18	2	8	5	0
20. Nevada	13	391	30.08	53	47	0	0	0	8	1	8	5	0
22. Rutgers	13	387	29.77	46	41	2	0	0	22	0	11	2	0
23. Central Mich.	14	416	29.71	55	48	1	0	0	12	0	10	4	0
23. Florida	14	416	29.71	57	50	1	0	0	6	2	13	1	0
25. Oregon	13	383	29.46	48	43	2	0	0	16	0	7	6	0
26. Michigan	13	380	29.23	47	43	2	0	0	17	0	11	2	0
26. Wisconsin	13	380	29.23	48	47	0	0	0	15	0	12	1	0
26. TCU	13	380	29.23	46	41	0	0	0	21	0	11	2	0
29. Kansas	12	348	29.00	44	37	2	0	0	13	2	6	6	0
30. Minnesota	13	376	28.92	50	47	0	0	1	9	0	6	7	0
31. Arkansas	14	404	28.86	55	50	1	0	0	6	2	10	4	0
32. Navy	13	367	28.23	48	47	0	0	0	10	1	9	4	0
33. Utah	13	363	27.92	45	43	1	0	0	16	0	8	5	0
34. Tennessee	13	362	27.85	44	42	0	0	0	18	1	9	4	0
34. Texas A&M	13	362	27.85	46	36	4	0	0	14	0	9	4	0
36. Oregon St.	14	389	27.79	46	45	1	0	0	22	0	10	4	0
37. Tulsa	13	360	27.69	47	45	0	0	0	11	0	8	5	0
38. UTEP	12	328	27.33	41	34	0	0	0	16	0	5	7	0
39. Ball St.	12	326	27.17	39	37	1	0	0	17	1	5	7	0
40. SMU	12	325	27.08	41	36	2	0	0	13	0	6	6	0
41. Rice	13	350	26.92	45	38	1	0	0	12	2	7	6	0
42. Arizona St.	13	348	26.77	44	42	0	0	0	14	0	7	6	0
43. Kentucky	13	347	26.69	45	42	0	0	0	11	1	8	5	0
44. South Carolina	13	346	26.62	43	40	0	0	0	16	0	8	5	0
45. Florida St.	13	345	26.54	42	39	2	2	0	14	2	7	6	0
46. Boston College	13	338	26.00	42	35	1	0	0	15	2	10	3	0
46. Purdue	14	364	26.00	48	47	0	0	0	9	1	8	6	0
48. Marshall	12	311	25.92	43	36	1	0	0	5	0	5	7	0
49. Virginia Tech	13	336	25.85	40	38	0	0	0	18	2	10	3	0
50. Northern Ill.	13	331	25.46	39	35	1	0	0	20	0	7	6	0
51. Southern Miss.	14	356	25.43	44	42	0	0	0	16	1	9	5	0
52. Michigan St.	12	302	25.17	37	33	0	0	0	15	1	4	8	0
53. Georgia	13	327	25.15	40	33	2	0	0	16	1	9	4	0
54. Georgia Tech	14	349	24.93	45	43	0	0	0	12	0	9	5	0
55. San Jose St.	13	324	24.92	43	37	1	0	0	9	0	9	4	0
56. Auburn	13	322	24.77	37	34	2	0	0	20	1	11	2	0
57. Washington St.	12	295	24.58	38	33	1	0	0	10	1	6	6	0
58. Iowa	13	310	23.85	38	37	0	0	0	15	0	6	7	0
59. Baylor	12	283	23.58	36	32	0	0	0	11	1	4	8	0
60. Memphis	12	281	23.42	34	30	1	0	0	15	0	2	10	0
60. Toledo	12	281	23.42	37	30	3	0	0	7	1	5	7	0
62. Air Force	12	279	23.25	36	32	1	0	0	9	1	4	8	0
63. Indiana	12	277	23.08	35	29	0	0	0	12	1	5	7	0
64. Fresno St.	12	276	23.00	35	31	0	0	0	11	1	4	8	0
64. Western Mich.	13	299	23.00	35	33	1	0	0	18	0	8	5	0
64. South Fla.	13	299	23.00	40	34	1	0	0	7	1	9	4	0
64. UCLA	13	299	23.00	31	29	0	0	0	28	0	7	6	0
68. Alabama	13	298	22.92	34	29	0	0	0	21	1	6	7	0
69. Kansas St.	13	296	22.77	35	33	1	0	0	17	0	7	6	0
69. Middle Tenn.	13	296	22.77	39	38	0	0	0	8	0	7	6	0
69. Troy	13	296	22.77	38	35	0	0	0	11	0	8	5	0
72. Penn St.	13	290	22.31	32	30	0	0	0	22	1	9	4	0
73. Vanderbilt	12	264	22.00	35	27	0	0	0	9	0	4	8	0
74. Maryland	13	284	21.85	32	32	0	0	0	20	0	9	4	0
74. New Mexico	13	284	21.85	32	31	0	0	0	19	2	6	7	0
76. La.-Monroe	12	262	21.83	32	25	0	0	0	15	0	4	8	0
76. Washington	12	262	21.83	33	32	1	0	0	10	0	5	7	0
78. Wake Forest	14	302	21.57	33	33	0	0	0	23	1	11	3	0
79. East Caro.	13	280	21.54	33	31	0	0	0	17	0	7	6	0
80. Wyoming	12	258	21.50	32	30	0	0	0	12	0	6	6	0
81. Connecticut	12	257	21.42	34	28	2	0	0	7	0	4	8	0
82. Cincinnati	13	274	21.08	31	28	2	0	0	18	1	8	5	0
83. La.-Lafayette	12	248	20.67	31	27	1	0	0	11	0	6	6	0
84. UNLV	12	238	19.83	30	20	4	0	0	10	0	2	10	0
85. Ohio	14	276	19.71	34	29	1	0	0	13	1	9	5	0
86. Akron	12	236	19.67	32	22	2	0	0	6	0	5	7	0
87. Miami (Fla.)	13	255	19.62	31	31	0	0	0	12	1	7	6	0
88. Illinois	12	235	19.58	27	24	1	0	0	15	1	2	10	0
89. Bowling Green	12	234	19.50	32	28	1	0	0	4	0	4	8	0
90. UCF	12	232	19.33	26	25	0	0	0	17	0	4	8	0
90. Army	12	232	19.33	28	26	1	0	0	12	0	3	9	0
92. Iowa St.	12	226	18.83	29	24	1	0	0	8	1	4	8	0
93. UAB	12	225	18.75	28	22	1	0	0	11	0	3	9	0
94. Tulane	12	224	18.67	29	23	0	0	0	9	0	4	8	0
95. Louisiana Tech	13	242	18.62	31	30	0	1	0	8	0	3	10	0
96. Miami (Ohio)	12	222	18.50	27	22	1	0	0	12	0	2	10	0
97. Mississippi St.	12	221	18.42	29	27	1	0	0	6	0	3	9	0
98. Buffalo	12	220	18.33	28	23	1	0	0	9	0	2	10	0
99. North Carolina	12	216	18.00	27	24	0	0	0	10	0	3	9	0
100. Kent St.	12	214	17.83	30	26	0	0	0	2	1	6	6	0

Rank, Team	G	Pts.	Avg.	TD	Kxp	Oxp	Dkxp	Doxp	FG	Saf	W	L	T
101. North Carolina St.	12	210	17.50	25	22	0	0	0	12	1	3	9	0
102. Syracuse	12	209	17.42	23	21	1	0	0	16	0	4	8	0
103. Idaho	12	203	16.92	24	23	0	0	0	12	0	4	8	0
104. Colorado St.	12	202	16.83	26	22	0	0	0	8	0	4	8	0
105. Arizona	12	199	16.58	22	22	0	0	0	15	0	6	6	0
106. Northwestern	12	198	16.50	25	24	0	0	0	8	0	4	8	0
107. Colorado	12	196	16.33	20	19	0	0	0	19	0	2	10	0
108. Mississippi	12	188	15.67	21	20	0	0	0	14	0	4	8	0
109. Arkansas St.	12	182	15.17	21	16	1	0	0	12	1	6	6	0
110. Fla. Atlantic	12	181	15.08	22	18	1	0	0	9	1	5	7	0
110. Virginia	12	181	15.08	21	19	0	0	0	12	0	5	7	0
112. Duke	12	179	14.92	24	15	2	0	0	4	2	0	12	0
113. San Diego St.	12	170	14.17	21	20	0	0	0	8	0	3	9	0
114. Eastern Mich.	12	167	13.92	17	15	0	0	1	16	0	1	11	0
115. North Texas	12	154	12.83	15	13	1	0	0	15	2	3	9	0
116. Temple	12	131	10.92	18	12	1	0	0	3	0	1	11	0
117. Utah St.	12	130	10.83	18	14	1	0	0	2	0	1	11	0
118. Stanford	12	127	10.58	15	13	0	0	0	8	0	1	11	0
119. Florida Int'l	12	115	9.58	15	10	0	0	0	5	0	0	12	0

Rushing Defense

Rank, Team	G	Att	Net	Avg.	TD	Yds/Gm	W	L	T
1. Michigan	13	301	564	1.87	5	43.4	11	2	0
2. TCU	13	367	791	2.16	8	60.8	11	2	0
3. Texas	13	345	795	2.30	8	61.2	10	3	0
4. Miami (Fla.)	13	391	882	2.26	12	67.8	7	6	0
5. Florida	14	370	1,015	2.74	8	72.5	13	1	0
6. Western Mich.	13	380	989	2.60	11	76.1	8	5	0
7. Penn St.	13	400	1,137	2.84	8	87.5	9	4	0
8. Boise St.	13	361	1,158	3.21	7	89.1	13	0	0
9. UCLA	13	419	1,184	2.83	9	91.1	7	6	0
9. Southern California	13	399	1,184	2.97	6	91.1	11	2	0
11. Virginia Tech	13	429	1,186	2.76	7	91.2	10	3	0
12. Florida St.	13	421	1,203	2.86	11	92.5	7	6	0
13. West Virginia	13	407	1,213	2.98	12	93.3	11	2	0
14. LSU	13	400	1,262	3.16	7	97.1	11	2	0
15. Ohio St.	13	384	1,278	3.33	9	98.3	12	1	0
16. Oklahoma	14	424	1,382	3.26	10	98.7	11	3	0
17. Rutgers	13	447	1,313	2.94	10	101.0	11	2	0
18. Clemson	13	463	1,340	2.89	13	103.1	8	5	0
19. Louisville	13	403	1,362	3.38	12	104.8	12	1	0
20. Georgia Tech	14	445	1,467	3.30	13	104.8	9	5	0
21. Wake Forest	14	475	1,481	3.12	11	105.8	11	3	0
22. Utah	13	449	1,384	3.08	11	106.5	8	5	0
23. Wyoming	12	404	1,279	3.17	16	106.6	6	6	0
24. SMU	12	403	1,290	3.20	16	107.5	6	6	0
25. Cincinnati	13	380	1,398	3.68	13	107.5	8	5	0
26. Boston College	13	402	1,403	3.49	12	107.9	10	3	0
27. Georgia	13	433	1,407	3.25	15	108.2	9	4	0
28. Kansas	12	373	1,308	3.51	13	109.0	6	6	0
29. Oregon St.	14	444	1,542	3.47	19	110.1	10	4	0
30. Colorado	12	410	1,349	3.29	12	112.4	2	10	0
31. Brigham Young	13	408	1,483	3.63	10	114.1	11	2	0
32. Washington St.	12	400	1,369	3.42	14	114.1	6	6	0
33. Arkansas	14	461	1,604	3.48	10	114.6	10	4	0
34. Wisconsin	13	388	1,492	3.85	9	114.8	12	1	0
35. South Fla.	13	460	1,498	3.26	9	115.2	9	4	0
36. Mississippi St.	12	404	1,385	3.43	16	115.4	3	9	0
37. Nebraska	14	436	1,632	3.74	14	116.6	9	5	0
38. Navy	13	416	1,517	3.65	14	116.7	9	4	0
39. Arizona St.	13	422	1,520	3.60	9	116.9	7	6	0
40. New Mexico	13	442	1,535	3.47	11	118.1	6	7	0
41. Virginia	12	430	1,432	3.33	12	119.3	5	7	0
42. Arizona	12	369	1,436	3.89	10	119.7	6	6	0
43. Middle Tenn.	13	431	1,563	3.63	17	120.2	7	6	0
44. Northern Ill.	13	441	1,585	3.59	14	121.9	7	6	0
45. Auburn	13	434	1,614	3.72	8	124.2	11	2	0
46. Alabama	13	409	1,620	3.96	12	124.6	6	7	0
47. California	13	430	1,630	3.79	11	125.4	10	3	0
48. Central Mich.	14	506	1,771	3.50	18	126.5	10	4	0
49. La.-Lafayette	12	391	1,523	3.90	20	126.9	6	6	0
50. Southern Miss.	14	456	1,789	3.92	19	127.8	9	5	0
51. Illinois	12	462	1,535	3.32	19	127.9	2	10	0
52. Nevada	13	413	1,671	4.05	15	128.5	8	5	0
53. Troy	13	458	1,684	3.68	18	129.5	8	5	0
54. Ohio	14	455	1,828	4.02	16	130.6	9	5	0
55. Texas A&M	13	399	1,717	4.30	20	132.1	9	4	0
56. Michigan St.	12	416	1,594	3.83	8	132.8	4	8	0
57. Iowa	13	480	1,737	3.62	14	133.6	6	7	0
58. Missouri	13	465	1,749	3.76	11	134.5	8	5	0
59. Hawaii	14	485	1,905	3.93	13	136.1	11	3	0
60. Akron	12	485	1,635	3.37	18	136.3	5	7	0
61. Notre Dame	13	468	1,779	3.80	11	136.8	10	3	0
62. Tulsa	13	422	1,789	4.24	16	137.6	8	5	0
63. Toledo	12	428	1,655	3.87	17	137.9	5	7	0
64. Kent St.	12	454	1,668	3.67	19	139.0	6	6	0
65. Marshall	12	406	1,671	4.12	22	139.3	5	7	0
66. Washington	12	419	1,675	4.00	16	139.6	5	7	0
67. Fresno St.	12	404	1,689	4.18	18	140.8	4	8	0
68. Air Force	12	415	1,695	4.08	15	141.3	4	8	0
69. Houston	14	479	2,008	4.19	18	143.4	10	4	0
70. Bowling Green	12	420	1,731	4.12	23	144.3	4	8	0
71. East Caro.	13	476	1,887	3.96	17	145.2	7	6	0
72. Oklahoma St.	13	473	1,907	4.03	17	146.7	7	6	0
72. Tennessee	13	469	1,907	4.07	12	146.7	9	4	0
74. UAB	12	409	1,761	4.31	15	146.8	3	9	0
75. South Carolina	13	469	1,909	4.07	14	146.8	8	5	0
76. San Jose St.	13	472	1,929	4.09	15	148.4	9	4	0
77. Arkansas St.	12	393	1,782	4.53	18	148.5	6	6	0
78. Kansas St.	13	473	1,932	4.08	15	148.6	7	6	0
78. Oregon	13	452	1,932	4.27	21	148.6	7	6	0
80. Colorado St.	12	438	1,789	4.08	21	149.1	4	8	0
81. UCF	12	400	1,791	4.48	16	149.3	4	8	0
82. North Texas	12	465	1,792	3.85	19	149.3	3	9	0
83. Tulane	12	428	1,794	4.19	23	149.5	4	8	0
84. La.-Monroe	12	424	1,805	4.26	18	150.4	4	8	0
85. North Carolina St.	12	481	1,806	3.75	16	150.5	3	9	0
86. Texas Tech	13	511	1,964	3.84	17	151.1	8	5	0
87. UTEP	12	439	1,829	4.17	26	152.4	5	7	0
88. Florida Int'l	12	505	1,839	3.64	15	153.3	0	12	0
89. Iowa St.	12	404	1,845	4.57	19	153.8	4	8	0
90. New Mexico St.	12	414	1,871	4.52	18	155.9	4	8	0
91. Vanderbilt	12	453	1,872	4.13	15	156.0	4	8	0
92. Minnesota	13	485	2,056	4.24	19	158.2	6	7	0
93. Northwestern	12	445	1,900	4.27	21	158.3	4	8	0
94. Mississippi	12	459	1,907	4.15	14	158.9	4	8	0
95. UNLV	12	477	1,937	4.06	23	161.4	2	10	0
96. Maryland	13	461	2,118	4.59	16	162.9	9	4	0
97. Fla. Atlantic	12	397	1,960	4.94	15	163.3	5	7	0
98. Idaho	12	408	1,980	4.85	28	165.0	4	8	0
99. Duke	12	441	2,016	4.57	21	168.0	0	12	0
100. North Carolina	12	464	2,073	4.47	29	172.8	3	9	0
101. Miami (Ohio)	12	437	2,081	4.76	20	173.4	2	10	0
102. Indiana	12	453	2,089	4.61	22	174.1	5	7	0
103. Ball St.	12	426	2,108	4.95	16	175.7	5	7	0
104. Memphis	12	478	2,136	4.47	20	178.0	2	10	0
105. Connecticut	12	479	2,155	4.50	20	179.6	4	8	0
106. San Diego St.	12	488	2,161	4.43	14	180.1	3	9	0
107. Pittsburgh	12	477	2,175	4.56	17	181.3	6	6	0
108. Kentucky	13	476	2,398	5.04	24	184.5	8	5	0
109. Buffalo	12	473	2,218	4.69	35	184.8	2	10	0
110. Syracuse	12	467	2,221	4.76	20	185.1	4	8	0
111. Utah St.	12	443	2,235	5.05	22	186.3	1	11	0
112. Rice	13	463	2,442	5.27	19	187.8	7	6	0
113. Baylor	12	461	2,293	4.97	19	191.1	4	8	0
114. Purdue	14	542	2,677	4.94	23	191.2	8	6	0
115. Army	12	499	2,387	4.78	24	198.9	3	9	0
116. Eastern Mich.	12	501	2,416	4.82	21	201.3	1	11	0
117. Stanford	12	519	2,526	4.87	26	210.5	1	11	0
118. Louisiana Tech	13	515	2,930	5.69	38	225.4	3	10	0
119. Temple	12	490	2,923	5.97	41	243.6	1	11	0

Pass Defense

Rank, Team	G	Att	Comp	Pct	Yds/Cmp	Int	IPct	Yds	Yds/Att	TD	Yds/Gm	CM	W	L	T
1. Virginia Tech	13	314	161	51.27	10.35	17	5.41	1,667	5.31	6	128.23	1	10	3	0
2. Wisconsin	13	387	185	47.80	9.72	15	3.88	1,798	4.65	6	138.31	0	12	1	0
3. LSU	13	364	172	47.25	11.01	16	4.40	1,894	5.20	11	145.69	0	11	2	0
4. Florida Int'l	12	297	168	56.57	10.55	11	3.70	1,772	5.97	18	147.67	0	0	12	0
5. Georgia	13	342	182	53.22	10.71	19	5.56	1,950	5.70	11	150.00	1	9	4	0
6. Rutgers	13	312	162	51.92	12.14	15	4.81	1,966	6.30	8	151.23	1	11	2	0
7. Army	12	268	167	62.31	11.21	4	1.49	1,872	6.99	16	156.00	0	3	9	0
8. Wyoming	12	319	166	52.04	11.30	11	3.45	1,876	5.88	10	156.33	3	6	6	0
9. Miami (Ohio)	12	275	163	59.27	11.66	14	5.09	1,900	6.91	14	158.33	0	2	10	0
10. Kent St.	12	326	171	52.45	11.15	16	4.91	1,907	5.85	8	158.92	2	6	6	0
11. Tulsa	13	345	188	54.49	11.01	8	2.32	2,070	6.00	14	159.23	0	8	5	0
12. Arkansas St.	12	277	158	57.04	12.22	19	6.86	1,931	6.97	14	160.92	0	6	6	0
13. North Carolina St.	12	269	138	51.30	14.49	7	2.60	2,000	7.43	12	166.67	0	3	9	0
14. Auburn	13	339	185	54.57	11.82	10	2.95	2,186	6.45	13	168.15	0	11	2	0
15. Virginia	12	291	171	58.76	11.94	10	3.44	2,042	7.02	10	170.17	0	5	7	0
16. Fla. Atlantic	12	305	163	53.44	12.57	18	5.90	2,049	6.72	16	170.75	0	5	7	0
17. San Diego St.	12	295	175	59.32	11.77	9	3.05	2,060	6.98	22	171.67	0	3	9	0
18. Ohio	14	415	217	52.29	11.12	13	3.13	2,412	5.81	14	172.29	0	9	5	0
19. Alabama	13	331	184	55.59	12.23	16	4.83	2,250	6.80	15	173.08	2	6	7	0
20. Oregon	13	362	199	54.97	11.33	15	4.14	2,255	6.23	17	173.46	0	7	6	0
21. TCU	13	386	207	53.63	10.93	16	4.15	2,263	5.86	9	174.08	0	11	2	0
22. Bowling Green	12	294	188	63.95	11.12	12	4.08	2,091	7.11	15	174.25	0	4	8	0
23. Stanford	12	325	196	60.31	10.84	7	2.15	2,124	6.54	14	177.00	0	1	11	0
24. Clemson	13	385	214	55.58	10.79	14	3.64	2,310	6.00	9	177.69	1	8	5	0
25. Connecticut	12	279	158	56.63	13.56	12	4.30	2,142	7.68	15	178.50	0	4	8	0
26. Southern Miss.	14	393	206	52.42	12.25	17	4.33	2,524	6.42	14	180.29	0	9	5	0
27. Tennessee	13	331	190	57.40	12.37	16	4.83	2,351	7.10	16	180.85	1	9	4	0
28. Colorado St.	12	312	180	57.69	12.08	7	2.24	2,175	6.97	11	181.25	0	4	8	0
29. Pittsburgh	12	341	215	63.05	10.15	11	3.23	2,182	6.40	17	181.83	2	6	6	0
30. Ohio St.	13	415	242	58.31	9.79	21	5.06	2,368	5.71	10	182.15	1	12	1	0
31. Illinois	12	335	186	55.52	11.76	10	2.99	2,187	6.53	11	182.25	0	2	10	0
32. Texas Tech	13	365	213	58.36	11.13	11	3.01	2,371	6.50	19	182.38	0	8	5	0
33. Florida	14	458	244	53.28	10.50	21	4.59	2,561	5.59	10	182.93	0	13	1	0
34. South Fla.	13	389	199	51.16	11.97	15	3.86	2,382	6.12	11	183.23	0	9	4	0
35. East Caro.	13	376	222	59.04	10.78	16	4.26	2,394	6.37	17	184.15	0	7	6	0
36. Arkansas	14	433	215	49.65	12.05	16	3.70	2,591	5.98	20	185.07	0	10	4	0
37. Missouri	13	400	231	57.75	10.45	13	3.25	2,414	6.04	19	185.69	0	8	5	0
38. Akron	12	336	186	55.36	12.01	7	2.08	2,234	6.65	13	186.17	0	5	7	0
39. Eastern Mich.	12	319	203	63.64	11.05	7	2.19	2,244	7.03	20	187.00	1	1	11	0
40. Miami (Fla.)	13	362	193	53.31	12.64	12	3.31	2,440	6.74	9	187.69	0	7	6	0
41. Oklahoma	14	434	225	51.84	11.72	18	4.15	2,638	6.08	15	188.43	0	11	3	0
42. North Texas	12	317	202	63.72	11.23	6	1.89	2,269	7.16	18	189.08	0	3	9	0
43. South Carolina	13	313	170	54.31	14.53	14	4.47	2,470	7.89	13	190.00	0	8	5	0
44. Texas A&M	13	368	203	55.16	12.20	11	2.99	2,477	6.73	14	190.54	0	9	4	0
45. Boise St.	13	397	227	57.18	11.16	20	5.04	2,534	6.38	17	194.92	2	13	0	0
46. Mississippi	12	340	203	59.71	11.53	3	.88	2,340	6.88	18	195.00	1	4	8	0
47. Toledo	12	341	193	56.60	12.13	11	3.23	2,342	6.87	19	195.17	0	5	7	0
48. North Carolina	12	306	190	62.09	12.35	7	2.29	2,346	7.67	14	195.50	1	3	9	0
49. Georgia Tech	14	461	238	51.63	11.52	13	2.82	2,741	5.95	11	195.79	1	9	5	0
50. La.-Monroe	12	360	214	59.44	11.00	19	5.28	2,353	6.54	15	196.08	0	4	8	0
51. Vanderbilt	12	293	176	60.07	13.39	14	4.78	2,357	8.04	18	196.42	1	4	8	0
52. Nevada	13	364	217	59.62	11.80	20	5.49	2,560	7.03	15	196.92	0	8	5	0
53. Kansas St.	13	384	224	58.33	11.43	10	2.60	2,561	6.67	18	197.00	0	7	6	0
53. Penn St.	13	440	244	55.45	10.50	13	2.95	2,561	5.82	10	197.00	0	9	4	0
55. Maryland	13	366	215	58.74	11.95	8	2.19	2,570	7.02	14	197.69	0	9	4	0
56. Florida St.	13	414	227	54.83	11.36	12	2.90	2,578	6.23	17	198.31	1	7	6	0
57. Western Mich.	13	382	226	59.16	11.46	24	6.28	2,591	6.78	14	199.31	0	8	5	0
58. Cincinnati	13	419	219	52.27	11.97	14	3.34	2,621	6.26	14	201.62	1	8	5	0
59. Boston College	13	450	270	60.00	9.77	21	4.67	2,638	5.86	11	202.92	0	10	3	0
60. Notre Dame	13	339	187	55.16	14.14	11	3.24	2,644	7.80	24	203.38	0	10	3	0
61. Northwestern	12	341	210	61.58	11.67	11	3.23	2,450	7.18	14	204.17	0	4	8	0
61. La.-Lafayette	12	324	200	61.73	12.25	6	1.85	2,450	7.56	16	204.17	0	6	6	0
63. Middle Tenn.	13	372	214	57.53	12.41	14	3.76	2,656	7.14	18	204.31	0	7	6	0
64. Southern California	13	436	238	54.59	11.18	11	2.52	2,662	6.11	13	204.77	0	11	2	0
65. Brigham Young	13	445	245	55.06	10.88	18	4.04	2,666	5.99	12	205.08	1	11	2	0
66. Buffalo	12	275	184	66.91	13.41	10	3.64	2,467	8.97	21	205.58	2	2	10	0
67. Mississippi St.	12	309	179	57.93	13.80	12	3.88	2,471	8.00	18	205.92	0	3	9	0
68. San Jose St.	13	390	240	61.54	11.17	16	4.10	2,680	6.87	18	206.15	1	9	4	0
69. Arizona	12	358	221	61.73	11.22	13	3.63	2,479	6.92	14	206.58	0	6	6	0
70. Houston	14	404	232	57.43	12.55	12	2.97	2,912	7.21	21	208.00	1	10	4	0
71. Temple	12	307	181	58.96	13.85	9	2.93	2,506	8.16	22	208.83	0	1	11	0
72. Iowa	13	423	241	56.97	11.34	14	3.31	2,732	6.46	20	210.15	0	6	7	0
73. Arizona St.	13	389	212	54.50	12.93	15	3.86	2,742	7.05	28	210.92	0	7	6	0
74. UAB	12	317	200	63.09	12.75	12	3.79	2,550	8.04	19	212.50	1	3	9	0
75. Air Force	12	303	202	66.67	12.68	9	2.97	2,561	8.45	20	213.42	0	4	8	0
76. Syracuse	12	348	226	64.94	11.38	17	4.89	2,571	7.39	17	214.25	0	4	8	0
77. Troy	13	421	244	57.96	11.45	16	3.80	2,793	6.63	17	214.85	0	8	5	0
78. Central Mich.	14	486	302	62.14	9.97	16	3.29	3,011	6.20	23	215.07	0	10	4	0
79. Nebraska	14	446	238	53.36	12.66	12	2.69	3,014	6.76	17	215.29	1	9	5	0
80. Louisville	13	414	208	50.24	13.48	12	2.90	2,804	6.77	12	215.69	2	12	1	0

Rank, Team	G	Att	Comp	Pct	Yds/Cmp	Int	IPct	Yds	Yds/Att	TD	Yds/Gm	CM	W	L	T
80. Utah	13	366	221	60.38	12.69	17	4.64	2,804	7.66	19	215.69	1	8	5	0
82. Wake Forest	14	446	255	57.17	11.90	22	4.93	3,034	6.80	12	216.71	0	11	3	0
83. Baylor	12	364	210	57.69	12.40	16	4.40	2,605	7.16	24	217.08	1	4	8	0
84. Oklahoma St.	13	372	226	60.75	12.50	10	2.69	2,826	7.60	20	217.38	2	7	6	0
85. Navy	13	394	243	61.68	11.69	12	3.05	2,840	7.21	19	218.46	0	9	4	0
86. Fresno St.	12	365	233	63.84	11.44	5	1.37	2,666	7.30	26	222.17	0	4	8	0
87. UCLA	13	421	236	56.06	12.31	13	3.09	2,904	6.90	18	223.38	1	7	6	0
88. Oregon St.	14	430	233	54.19	13.44	17	3.95	3,132	7.28	17	223.71	0	10	4	0
89. Michigan	13	488	262	53.69	11.16	12	2.46	2,924	5.99	19	224.92	0	11	2	0
90. UNLV	12	315	211	66.98	12.85	9	2.86	2,711	8.61	21	225.92	0	2	10	0
91. Rice	13	358	202	56.42	14.58	11	3.07	2,946	8.23	32	226.62	0	7	6	0
92. Duke	12	343	206	60.06	13.24	10	2.92	2,728	7.95	27	227.33	0	0	12	0
93. Indiana	12	318	196	61.64	13.97	13	4.09	2,739	8.61	29	228.25	0	5	7	0
94. Colorado	12	390	261	66.92	10.51	12	3.08	2,742	7.03	22	228.50	0	2	10	0
95. Idaho	12	356	223	62.64	12.35	16	4.49	2,753	7.73	26	229.42	0	4	8	0
96. Memphis	12	307	200	65.15	13.84	10	3.26	2,768	9.02	24	230.67	0	2	10	0
97. Michigan St.	12	355	206	58.03	13.45	8	2.25	2,771	7.81	32	230.92	0	4	8	0
98. New Mexico St.	12	332	195	58.73	14.37	14	4.22	2,802	8.44	28	233.50	3	4	8	0
99. Texas	13	410	239	58.29	12.85	13	3.17	3,071	7.49	21	236.23	0	10	3	0
100. New Mexico	13	427	256	59.95	12.05	14	3.28	3,086	7.23	28	237.38	1	6	7	0
101. Iowa St.	12	374	271	72.46	10.56	6	1.60	2,862	7.65	26	238.50	1	4	8	0
102. Washington	12	388	238	61.34	12.11	10	2.58	2,882	7.43	15	240.17	1	5	7	0
103. California	13	421	237	56.29	13.21	21	4.99	3,131	7.44	17	240.85	0	10	3	0
104. Purdue	14	455	279	61.32	12.10	11	2.42	3,377	7.42	20	241.21	3	8	6	0
105. Hawaii	14	446	244	54.71	13.87	14	3.14	3,384	7.59	29	241.71	0	11	3	0
106. UTEP	12	396	256	64.65	11.37	15	3.79	2,910	7.35	18	242.50	2	5	7	0
107. Northern Ill.	13	411	265	64.48	11.91	7	1.70	3,156	7.68	22	242.77	1	7	6	0
108. Washington St.	12	383	214	55.87	13.63	16	4.18	2,917	7.62	15	243.08	0	6	6	0
109. West Virginia	13	425	244	57.41	12.96	16	3.76	3,163	7.44	17	243.31	1	11	2	0
110. SMU	12	418	268	64.11	11.01	11	2.63	2,950	7.06	19	245.83	0	6	6	0
111. UCF	12	392	244	62.24	12.24	10	2.55	2,986	7.62	22	248.83	0	4	8	0
112. Utah St.	12	314	202	64.33	14.84	6	1.91	2,997	9.54	33	249.75	0	1	11	0
113. Tulane	12	386	247	63.99	12.15	8	2.07	3,002	7.78	23	250.17	1	4	8	0
114. Marshall	12	398	254	63.82	11.89	12	3.02	3,020	7.59	20	251.67	1	5	7	0
115. Ball St.	12	394	251	63.71	12.33	9	2.28	3,094	7.85	19	257.83	1	5	7	0
116. Louisiana Tech	13	366	225	61.48	14.90	10	2.73	3,352	9.16	31	257.85	0	3	10	0
117. Minnesota	13	434	270	62.21	12.91	17	3.92	3,487	8.03	24	268.23	0	6	7	0
118. Kentucky	13	406	235	57.88	14.88	14	3.45	3,496	8.61	24	268.92	1	8	5	0
119. Kansas	12	470	248	52.77	13.02	12	2.55	3,229	6.87	22	269.08	3	6	6	0

Pass Efficiency Defense

Rank, Team	G	Att	Comp	Pct	Int	IPct	Yds	Yds/Att	TD	TD Pct	Rating	W	L	T
1. Wisconsin	13	387	185	47.80	15	3.88	1,798	4.65	6	1.55	84.19	12	1	0
2. Virginia Tech	13	314	161	51.27	17	5.41	1,667	5.31	6	1.91	91.37	10	3	0
3. LSU	13	364	172	47.25	16	4.40	1,894	5.20	11	3.02	92.19	11	2	0
4. Florida	14	458	244	53.28	21	4.59	2,561	5.59	10	2.18	98.31	13	1	0
5. Kent St.	12	326	171	52.45	16	4.91	1,907	5.85	8	2.45	99.92	6	6	0
6. Georgia	13	342	182	53.22	19	5.56	1,950	5.70	11	3.22	100.60	9	4	0
7. TCU	13	386	207	53.63	16	4.15	2,263	5.86	9	2.33	102.25	11	2	0
8. Rutgers	13	312	162	51.92	15	4.81	1,966	6.30	8	2.56	103.68	11	2	0
9. Georgia Tech	14	461	238	51.63	13	2.82	2,741	5.95	11	2.39	103.78	9	5	0
10. Ohio St.	13	415	242	58.31	21	5.06	2,368	5.71	10	2.41	104.06	12	1	0
11. South Fla.	13	389	199	51.16	15	3.86	2,382	6.12	11	2.83	104.26	9	4	0
12. Wyoming	12	319	166	52.04	11	3.45	1,876	5.88	10	3.13	104.85	6	6	0
13. Oklahoma	14	434	225	51.84	18	4.15	2,638	6.08	15	3.46	105.97	11	3	0
14. Penn St.	13	440	244	55.45	13	2.95	2,561	5.82	10	2.27	105.98	9	4	0
15. Ohio	14	415	217	52.29	13	3.13	2,412	5.81	14	3.37	105.99	9	5	0
16. Brigham Young	13	445	245	55.06	18	4.04	2,666	5.99	12	2.70	106.23	11	2	0
17. Clemson	13	385	214	55.58	14	3.64	2,310	6.00	9	2.34	106.44	8	5	0
18. Arkansas	14	433	215	49.65	16	3.70	2,591	5.98	20	4.62	107.82	10	4	0
19. Boston College	13	450	270	60.00	21	4.67	2,638	5.86	11	2.44	107.98	10	3	0
20. Cincinnati	13	419	219	52.27	14	3.34	2,621	6.26	14	3.34	109.19	8	5	0
21. Southern Miss.	14	393	206	52.42	17	4.33	2,524	6.42	14	3.56	109.45	9	5	0
22. Southern California	13	436	238	54.59	11	2.52	2,662	6.11	13	2.98	110.68	11	2	0
23. Louisville	13	414	208	50.24	12	2.90	2,804	6.77	12	2.90	110.86	12	1	0
24. Miami (Fla.)	13	362	193	53.31	12	3.31	2,440	6.74	9	2.49	111.49	7	6	0
25. Michigan	13	488	262	53.69	12	2.46	2,924	5.99	19	3.89	111.96	11	2	0
26. Wake Forest	14	446	255	57.17	22	4.93	3,034	6.80	12	2.69	113.36	11	3	0
27. Tulsa	13	345	188	54.49	8	2.32	2,070	6.00	14	4.06	113.65	8	5	0
28. Oregon	13	362	199	54.97	15	4.14	2,255	6.23	17	4.70	114.54	7	6	0
29. Florida St.	13	414	227	54.83	12	2.90	2,578	6.23	17	4.11	114.86	7	6	0
30. Boise St.	13	397	227	57.18	20	5.04	2,534	6.38	17	4.28	114.87	13	0	0
31. Illinois	12	335	186	55.52	10	2.99	2,187	6.53	11	3.28	115.20	2	10	0
32. Fla. Atlantic	12	305	163	53.44	18	5.90	2,049	6.72	16	5.25	115.34	5	7	0
33. Auburn	13	339	185	54.57	10	2.95	2,186	6.45	13	3.83	115.52	11	2	0
34. Western Mich.	13	382	226	59.16	24	6.28	2,591	6.78	14	3.66	115.70	8	5	0
35. Nebraska	14	446	238	53.36	12	2.69	3,014	6.76	17	3.81	117.36	9	5	0
36. La.-Monroe	12	360	214	59.44	19	5.28	2,353	6.54	15	4.17	117.50	4	8	0
37. Missouri	13	400	231	57.75	13	3.25	2,414	6.04	19	4.75	117.67	8	5	0
38. Alabama	13	331	184	55.59	16	4.83	2,250	6.80	15	4.53	117.99	6	7	0

Rank, Team	G	Att	Comp	Pct	Int	IPct	Yds	Yds/Att	TD	TD Pct	Rating	W	L	T
39. Texas A&M	13	368	203	55.16	11	2.99	2,477	6.73	14	3.80	118.32	9	4	0
40. Arkansas St.	12	277	158	57.04	19	6.86	1,931	6.97	14	5.05	118.52	6	6	0
41. East Caro.	13	376	222	59.04	16	4.26	2,394	6.37	17	4.52	118.89	7	6	0
42. Florida Int'l	12	297	168	56.57	11	3.70	1,772	5.97	18	6.06	119.31	0	12	0
43. Troy	13	421	244	57.96	16	3.80	2,793	6.63	17	4.04	119.45	8	5	0
44. Akron	12	336	186	55.36	7	2.08	2,234	6.65	13	3.87	119.85	5	7	0
45. Iowa	13	423	241	56.97	14	3.31	2,732	6.46	20	4.73	120.24	6	7	0
46. Oregon St.	14	430	233	54.19	17	3.95	3,132	7.28	17	3.95	120.52	10	4	0
47. Kansas	12	470	248	52.77	12	2.55	3,229	6.87	22	4.68	120.85	6	6	0
48. Nevada	13	364	217	59.62	20	5.49	2,560	7.03	15	4.12	121.29	8	5	0
49. UCLA	13	421	236	56.06	13	3.09	2,904	6.90	18	4.28	121.98	7	6	0
50. California	13	421	237	56.29	21	4.99	3,131	7.44	17	4.04	122.12	10	3	0
51. Virginia	12	291	171	58.76	10	3.44	2,042	7.02	10	3.44	122.21	5	7	0
52. Central Mich.	14	486	302	62.14	16	3.29	3,011	6.20	23	4.73	123.17	10	4	0
53. North Carolina St.	12	269	138	51.30	7	2.60	2,000	7.43	12	4.46	123.27	3	9	0
54. Tennessee	13	331	190	57.40	16	4.83	2,351	7.10	16	4.83	123.35	9	4	0
55. Colorado St.	12	312	180	57.69	7	2.24	2,175	6.97	11	3.53	123.41	4	8	0
56. Miami (Ohio)	12	275	163	59.27	14	5.09	1,900	6.91	14	5.09	123.95	2	10	0
57. Texas Tech	13	365	213	58.36	11	3.01	2,371	6.50	19	5.21	124.12	8	5	0
58. Washington St.	12	383	214	55.87	16	4.18	2,917	7.62	15	3.92	124.45	6	6	0
59. Kansas St.	13	384	224	58.33	10	2.60	2,561	6.67	18	4.69	124.58	7	6	0
60. Stanford	12	325	196	60.31	7	2.15	2,124	6.54	14	4.31	125.10	1	11	0
61. South Carolina	13	313	170	54.31	14	4.47	2,470	7.89	13	4.15	125.35	8	5	0
62. Arizona	12	358	221	61.73	13	3.63	2,479	6.92	14	3.91	125.51	6	6	0
63. West Virginia	13	425	244	57.41	16	3.76	3,163	7.44	17	4.00	125.59	11	2	0
64. Middle Tenn.	13	372	214	57.53	14	3.76	2,656	7.14	18	4.84	125.92	7	6	0
65. Maryland	13	366	215	58.74	8	2.19	2,570	7.02	14	3.83	125.93	9	4	0
66. Toledo	12	341	193	56.60	11	3.23	2,342	6.87	19	5.57	126.23	5	7	0
67. San Jose St.	13	390	240	61.54	16	4.10	2,680	6.87	18	4.62	126.25	9	4	0
68. Pittsburgh	12	341	215	63.05	11	3.23	2,182	6.40	17	4.99	126.75	6	6	0
69. Northwestern	12	341	210	61.58	11	3.23	2,450	7.18	14	4.11	129.05	4	8	0
70. Houston	14	404	232	57.43	12	2.97	2,912	7.21	21	5.20	129.16	10	4	0
71. Arizona St.	13	389	212	54.50	15	3.86	2,742	7.05	28	7.20	129.75	7	6	0
72. Connecticut	12	279	158	56.63	12	4.30	2,142	7.68	15	5.38	130.23	4	8	0
73. Baylor	12	364	210	57.69	16	4.40	2,605	7.16	24	6.59	130.78	4	8	0
74. Washington	12	388	238	61.34	10	2.58	2,882	7.43	15	3.87	131.30	5	7	0
75. Texas	13	410	239	58.29	13	3.17	3,071	7.49	21	5.12	131.78	10	3	0
76. Navy	13	394	243	61.68	12	3.05	2,840	7.21	19	4.82	132.07	9	4	0
77. Bowling Green	12	294	188	63.95	12	4.08	2,091	7.11	15	5.10	132.32	4	8	0
78. Utah	13	366	221	60.38	17	4.64	2,804	7.66	19	5.19	132.60	8	5	0
79. SMU	12	418	268	64.11	11	2.63	2,950	7.06	19	4.55	133.12	6	6	0
80. Mississippi	12	340	203	59.71	3	0.88	2,340	6.88	18	5.29	133.22	4	8	0
81. Purdue	14	455	279	61.32	11	2.42	3,377	7.42	20	4.40	133.31	8	6	0
81. Syracuse	12	348	226	64.94	17	4.89	2,571	7.39	17	4.89	133.31	4	8	0
83. Hawaii	14	446	244	54.71	14	3.14	3,384	7.59	29	6.50	133.61	11	3	0
84. UTEP	12	396	256	64.65	15	3.79	2,910	7.35	18	4.55	133.75	5	7	0
85. New Mexico	13	427	256	59.95	14	3.28	3,086	7.23	28	6.56	135.79	6	7	0
86. San Diego St.	12	295	175	59.32	9	3.05	2,060	6.98	22	7.46	136.47	3	9	0
87. Mississippi St.	12	309	179	57.93	12	3.88	2,471	8.00	18	5.83	136.53	3	9	0
88. Oklahoma St.	13	372	226	60.75	10	2.69	2,826	7.60	20	5.38	136.98	7	6	0
89. North Carolina	12	306	190	62.09	7	2.29	2,346	7.67	14	4.58	137.02	3	9	0
90. Notre Dame	13	339	187	55.16	11	3.24	2,644	7.80	24	7.08	137.59	10	3	0
91. Army	12	268	167	62.31	4	1.49	1,872	6.99	16	5.97	137.69	3	9	0
92. La.-Lafayette	12	324	200	61.73	6	1.85	2,450	7.56	16	4.94	137.81	6	6	0
93. Marshall	12	398	254	63.82	12	3.02	3,020	7.59	20	5.03	138.09	5	7	0
94. Vanderbilt	12	293	176	60.07	14	4.78	2,357	8.04	18	6.14	138.39	4	8	0
95. Colorado	12	390	261	66.92	12	3.08	2,742	7.03	22	5.64	138.42	2	10	0
96. North Texas	12	317	202	63.72	6	1.89	2,269	7.16	18	5.68	138.78	3	9	0
97. Eastern Mich.	12	319	203	63.64	7	2.19	2,244	7.03	20	6.27	138.99	1	11	0
98. UCF	12	392	244	62.24	10	2.55	2,986	7.62	22	5.61	139.60	4	8	0
99. Minnesota	13	434	270	62.21	17	3.92	3,487	8.03	24	5.53	140.11	6	7	0
100. Ball St.	12	394	251	63.71	9	2.28	3,094	7.85	19	4.82	141.01	5	7	0
101. Idaho	12	356	223	62.64	16	4.49	2,753	7.73	26	7.30	142.67	4	8	0
102. Kentucky	13	406	235	57.88	14	3.45	3,496	8.61	24	5.91	142.84	8	5	0
103. UAB	12	317	200	63.09	12	3.79	2,550	8.04	19	5.99	142.88	3	9	0
104. Northern Ill.	13	411	265	64.48	7	1.70	3,156	7.68	22	5.35	143.26	7	6	0
105. Tulane	12	386	247	63.99	8	2.07	3,002	7.78	23	5.96	144.85	4	8	0
106. Temple	12	307	181	58.96	9	2.93	2,506	8.16	22	7.17	145.35	1	11	0
107. Fresno St.	12	365	233	63.84	5	1.37	2,666	7.30	26	7.12	145.92	4	8	0
108. Duke	12	343	206	60.06	10	2.92	2,728	7.95	27	7.87	147.05	0	12	0
109. Michigan St.	12	355	206	58.03	8	2.25	2,771	7.81	32	9.01	148.81	4	8	0
110. Rice	13	358	202	56.42	11	3.07	2,946	8.23	32	8.94	148.88	7	6	0
111. New Mexico St.	12	332	195	58.73	14	4.22	2,802	8.44	28	8.43	148.99	4	8	0
112. Air Force	12	303	202	66.67	9	2.97	2,561	8.45	20	6.60	153.54	4	8	0
113. UNLV	12	315	211	66.98	9	2.86	2,711	8.61	21	6.67	155.58	2	10	0
114. Indiana	12	318	196	61.64	13	4.09	2,739	8.61	29	9.12	155.87	5	7	0
115. Iowa St.	12	374	271	72.46	6	1.60	2,862	7.65	26	6.95	156.51	4	8	0
116. Memphis	12	307	200	65.15	10	3.26	2,768	9.02	24	7.82	160.12	2	10	0
117. Buffalo	12	275	184	66.91	10	3.64	2,467	8.97	21	7.64	160.18	2	10	0
118. Louisiana Tech	13	366	225	61.48	10	2.73	3,352	9.16	31	8.47	160.92	3	10	0
119. Utah St.	12	314	202	64.33	6	1.91	2,997	9.54	33	10.51	175.33	1	11	0

Total Defense

Rank, Team	G	Plays	Yds	Avg	TD	Yds/Gm	W	L	T
1. Virginia Tech	13	743	2,853	3.84	14	219.46	10	3	0
2. TCU	13	753	3,054	4.06	19	234.92	11	2	0
3. LSU	13	764	3,156	4.13	20	242.77	11	2	0
4. Rutgers	13	759	3,279	4.32	22	252.23	11	2	0
5. Wisconsin	13	775	3,290	4.25	18	253.08	12	1	0
6. Florida	14	828	3,576	4.32	23	255.43	13	1	0
7. Miami (Fla.)	13	753	3,322	4.41	22	255.54	7	6	0
8. Georgia	13	775	3,357	4.33	28	258.23	9	4	0
9. Wyoming	12	723	3,155	4.36	32	262.92	6	6	0
10. Michigan	13	789	3,488	4.42	25	268.31	11	2	0
11. Western Mich.	13	762	3,580	4.70	31	275.38	8	5	0
12. Ohio St.	13	799	3,646	4.56	19	280.46	12	1	0
13. Clemson	13	848	3,650	4.30	25	280.77	8	5	0
14. Boise St.	13	758	3,692	4.87	30	284.00	13	0	0
15. Penn St.	13	840	3,698	4.40	21	284.46	9	4	0
16. Oklahoma	14	858	4,020	4.69	29	287.14	11	3	0
17. Virginia	12	721	3,474	4.82	27	289.50	5	7	0
18. Florida St.	13	835	3,781	4.53	31	290.85	7	6	0
19. Auburn	13	773	3,800	4.92	22	292.31	11	2	0
20. Southern California	13	835	3,846	4.61	21	295.85	11	2	0
21. Tulsa	13	767	3,859	5.03	30	296.85	8	5	0
22. Texas	13	755	3,866	5.12	31	297.38	10	3	0
23. Alabama	13	740	3,870	5.23	30	297.69	6	7	0
24. Kent St.	12	780	3,575	4.58	28	297.92	6	6	0
25. South Fla.	13	849	3,880	4.57	25	298.46	9	4	0
26. Arkansas	14	894	4,195	4.69	32	299.64	10	4	0
27. Georgia Tech	14	906	4,208	4.64	29	300.57	9	5	0
28. Florida Int'l	12	802	3,611	4.50	39	300.92	0	12	0
29. Ohio	14	870	4,240	4.87	33	302.86	9	5	0
30. Southern Miss.	14	849	4,313	5.08	35	308.07	9	5	0
31. Cincinnati	13	799	4,019	5.03	30	309.15	8	5	0
32. Arkansas St.	12	670	3,713	5.54	35	309.42	6	6	0
33. Illinois	12	797	3,722	4.67	38	310.17	2	10	0
34. Boston College	13	852	4,041	4.74	23	310.85	10	3	0
35. UCLA	13	840	4,088	4.87	31	314.46	7	6	0
36. North Carolina St.	12	750	3,806	5.07	29	317.17	3	9	0
37. Bowling Green	12	714	3,822	5.35	46	318.50	4	8	0
38. Brigham Young	13	853	4,149	4.86	23	319.15	11	2	0
39. Missouri	13	865	4,163	4.81	32	320.23	8	5	0
40. Louisville	13	817	4,166	5.10	26	320.46	12	1	0
41. Mississippi St.	12	713	3,856	5.41	39	321.33	3	9	0
42. Oregon	13	814	4,187	5.14	42	322.08	7	6	0
43. Utah	13	815	4,188	5.14	33	322.15	8	5	0
44. Akron	12	821	3,869	4.71	34	322.42	5	7	0
45. Wake Forest	14	921	4,515	4.90	25	322.50	11	3	0
46. Texas A&M	13	767	4,194	5.47	34	322.62	9	4	0
47. Middle Tenn.	13	803	4,219	5.25	39	324.54	7	6	0
48. Nevada	13	777	4,231	5.45	33	325.46	8	5	0
49. Arizona	12	727	3,915	5.39	28	326.25	6	6	0
50. Tennessee	13	800	4,258	5.32	31	327.54	9	4	0
51. Arizona St.	13	811	4,262	5.26	41	327.85	7	6	0
52. East Caro.	13	852	4,281	5.02	35	329.31	7	6	0
53. Colorado St.	12	750	3,964	5.29	33	330.33	4	8	0
54. La.-Lafayette	12	715	3,973	5.56	38	331.08	6	6	0
55. Miami (Ohio)	12	712	3,981	5.59	37	331.75	2	10	0
56. Nebraska	14	882	4,646	5.27	32	331.86	9	5	0
57. Toledo	12	769	3,997	5.20	42	333.08	5	7	0
58. Texas Tech	13	876	4,335	4.95	39	333.46	8	5	0
59. Oregon St.	14	874	4,674	5.35	38	333.86	10	4	0
60. Fla. Atlantic	12	702	4,009	5.71	37	334.08	5	7	0
61. Navy	13	810	4,357	5.38	33	335.15	9	4	0
62. West Virginia	13	832	4,376	5.26	33	336.62	11	2	0
63. South Carolina	13	782	4,379	5.60	29	336.85	8	5	0
64. North Texas	12	782	4,061	5.19	40	338.42	3	9	0
65. Notre Dame	13	807	4,423	5.48	40	340.23	10	3	0
66. Colorado	12	800	4,091	5.11	34	340.92	2	10	0
67. Central Mich.	14	992	4,782	4.82	42	341.57	10	4	0
68. Iowa	13	903	4,469	4.95	34	343.77	6	7	0
69. Troy	13	879	4,477	5.09	36	344.38	8	5	0
70. Kansas St.	13	857	4,493	5.24	38	345.62	7	6	0
71. La.-Monroe	12	784	4,158	5.30	34	346.50	4	8	0
72. Houston	14	883	4,920	5.57	40	351.43	10	4	0
73. San Diego St.	12	783	4,221	5.39	41	351.75	3	9	0
74. Vanderbilt	12	746	4,229	5.67	34	352.42	4	8	0
75. SMU	12	821	4,240	5.16	38	353.33	6	6	0
76. Mississippi	12	799	4,247	5.32	33	353.92	4	8	0
77. San Jose St.	13	862	4,609	5.35	34	354.54	9	4	0
78. Air Force	12	718	4,256	5.93	40	354.67	4	8	0
79. Army	12	767	4,259	5.55	45	354.92	3	9	0
80. New Mexico	13	869	4,621	5.32	40	355.46	6	7	0
81. Washington St.	12	783	4,286	5.47	32	357.17	6	6	0
82. Connecticut	12	758	4,297	5.67	39	358.08	4	8	0
83. UAB	12	726	4,311	5.94	37	359.25	3	9	0
84. Maryland	13	827	4,688	5.67	35	360.62	9	4	0
85. Northwestern	12	786	4,350	5.53	39	362.50	4	8	0
86. Fresno St.	12	769	4,355	5.66	48	362.92	4	8	0
87. Pittsburgh	12	818	4,357	5.33	34	363.08	6	6	0
88. Michigan St.	12	771	4,365	5.66	43	363.75	4	8	0
89. Oklahoma St.	13	845	4,733	5.60	41	364.08	7	6	0
90. Northern Ill.	13	852	4,741	5.56	36	364.69	7	6	0
91. California	13	851	4,761	5.59	30	366.23	10	3	0
92. North Carolina	12	770	4,419	5.74	47	368.25	3	9	0
93. Hawaii	14	931	5,289	5.68	43	377.79	11	3	0
94. Kansas	12	843	4,537	5.38	38	378.08	6	6	0
95. Washington	12	807	4,557	5.65	34	379.75	5	7	0
96. UNLV	12	792	4,648	5.87	49	387.33	2	10	0
97. Stanford	12	844	4,650	5.51	46	387.50	1	11	0
98. Eastern Mich.	12	820	4,660	5.68	42	388.33	1	11	0
99. New Mexico St.	12	746	4,673	6.26	50	389.42	4	8	0
100. Buffalo	12	748	4,685	6.26	58	390.42	2	10	0
101. Marshall	12	804	4,691	5.83	43	390.92	5	7	0
102. Iowa St.	12	778	4,707	6.05	47	392.25	4	8	0
103. Idaho	12	764	4,733	6.20	57	394.42	4	8	0
104. UTEP	12	835	4,739	5.68	46	394.92	5	7	0
105. Duke	12	784	4,744	6.05	54	395.33	0	12	0
106. UCF	12	792	4,777	6.03	42	398.08	4	8	0
107. Syracuse	12	815	4,792	5.88	37	399.33	4	8	0
108. Tulane	12	814	4,796	5.89	51	399.67	4	8	0
109. Indiana	12	771	4,828	6.26	54	402.33	5	7	0
110. Baylor	12	825	4,898	5.94	51	408.17	4	8	0
111. Memphis	12	785	4,904	6.25	47	408.67	2	10	0
112. Rice	13	821	5,388	6.56	54	414.46	7	6	0
113. Minnesota	13	919	5,543	6.03	45	426.38	6	7	0
114. Purdue	14	997	6,054	6.07	45	432.43	8	6	0
115. Ball St.	12	820	5,202	6.34	38	433.50	5	7	0
116. Utah St.	12	757	5,232	6.91	62	436.00	1	11	0
117. Temple	12	797	5,429	6.81	65	452.42	1	11	0
118. Kentucky	13	882	5,894	6.68	50	453.38	8	5	0
119. Louisiana Tech	13	881	6,282	7.13	73	483.23	3	10	0

Scoring Defense

Rank, Team	G	TD	Kxp	Oxp	Dkxp	Doxp	FG	Saf	Pts	Pts/Gm	W	L	T
1. Virginia Tech	13	14	13	1	0	0	14	1	143	11.0	10	3	0
2. Wisconsin	13	18	17	0	0	1	10	0	157	12.1	12	1	0
3. TCU	13	19	19	0	0	0	9	0	160	12.3	11	2	0
4. LSU	13	20	18	0	0	0	8	1	164	12.6	11	2	0
5. Ohio St.	13	19	17	1	0	0	11	0	166	12.8	12	1	0
6. Florida	14	23	19	0	0	0	10	1	189	13.5	13	1	0
7. Auburn	13	22	19	0	0	0	10	0	181	13.9	11	2	0
8. Rutgers	13	22	17	2	0	0	11	0	186	14.3	11	2	0
9. Penn St.	13	21	19	0	0	0	14	0	187	14.4	9	4	0
10. Brigham Young	13	23	19	2	0	0	10	0	191	14.7	11	2	0
11. Southern California	13	21	19	1	0	0	16	1	197	15.2	11	2	0
12. Wake Forest	14	25	23	0	0	0	14	0	215	15.4	11	3	0
13. Miami (Fla.)	13	22	20	0	0	0	15	2	201	15.5	7	6	0
14. Boston College	13	23	22	0	0	0	14	1	204	15.7	10	3	0
15. Michigan	13	25	22	0	0	0	11	1	207	15.9	11	2	0
16. Clemson	13	25	23	1	1	0	11	0	210	16.2	8	5	0
17. Louisville	13	26	22	2	0	0	10	0	212	16.3	12	1	0

Rank, Team	G	TD	Kxp	Oxp	Dkxp	Doxp	FG	Saf	Pts	Pts/Gm	W	L	T
18. South Fla.	13	25	20	0	0	0	16	1	220	16.9	9	4	0
19. Oklahoma	14	29	28	1	0	0	12	1	242	17.3	11	3	0
20. Boise St.	13	30	24	2	0	0	7	0	229	17.6	13	0	0
20. Georgia	13	28	24	1	0	0	11	1	229	17.6	9	4	0
22. Virginia	12	27	26	0	0	0	8	1	214	17.8	5	7	0
23. Ohio	14	33	31	0	0	0	8	0	253	18.1	9	5	0
24. Arkansas	14	32	28	0	0	0	12	0	256	18.3	10	4	0
24. Nebraska	14	32	26	1	0	0	12	0	256	18.3	9	5	0
26. Texas	13	31	28	0	0	0	8	0	238	18.3	10	3	0
27. Georgia Tech	14	29	27	1	0	0	18	0	257	18.4	9	5	0
28. Southern Miss.	14	35	30	0	0	0	6	1	260	18.6	9	5	0
29. South Carolina	13	29	27	1	0	0	12	2	243	18.7	8	5	0
30. Nevada	13	33	33	0	0	0	6	0	249	19.2	8	5	0
31. Alabama	13	30	27	2	0	0	13	0	250	19.2	6	7	0
32. California	13	30	29	0	0	0	14	0	251	19.3	10	3	0
33. Missouri	13	32	29	2	0	0	9	1	254	19.5	8	5	0
33. Tennessee	13	31	27	1	0	0	13	0	254	19.5	9	4	0
35. Arizona	12	28	28	0	0	0	13	0	235	19.6	6	6	0
36. Cincinnati	13	30	27	1	0	0	14	2	255	19.6	8	5	0
37. Florida St.	13	31	26	1	0	0	14	1	258	19.8	7	6	0
37. Utah	13	33	25	1	0	0	11	0	258	19.8	8	5	0
39. UCLA	13	31	27	1	0	0	14	1	259	19.9	7	6	0
39. Western Mich.	13	31	28	0	0	0	15	0	259	19.9	8	5	0
41. Navy	13	33	27	0	0	0	12	0	261	20.1	9	4	0
42. Kent St.	12	28	24	2	0	0	15	0	241	20.1	6	6	0
43. Tulsa	13	30	24	2	0	0	18	0	262	20.2	8	5	0
44. Texas A&M	13	34	32	0	0	0	9	2	267	20.5	9	4	0
45. Iowa	13	34	32	0	0	0	11	0	269	20.7	6	7	0
46. East Caro.	13	35	31	0	0	0	9	1	270	20.8	7	6	0
46. San Jose St.	13	34	29	1	0	0	11	1	270	20.8	9	4	0
48. Northern Ill.	13	36	30	1	0	0	9	0	275	21.2	7	6	0
49. West Virginia	13	33	29	2	0	0	17	0	282	21.7	11	2	0
50. North Carolina St.	12	29	26	0	0	0	20	1	262	21.8	3	9	0
51. Maryland	13	35	32	0	0	0	14	0	284	21.8	9	4	0
52. Colorado St.	12	33	32	0	0	0	11	0	263	21.9	4	8	0
53. Wyoming	12	32	27	3	0	0	13	0	264	22.0	6	6	0
54. Oregon St.	14	38	32	2	0	0	15	1	311	22.2	10	4	0
55. Troy	13	36	33	1	0	0	12	1	289	22.2	8	5	0
56. Colorado	12	34	31	0	0	0	10	1	267	22.3	2	10	0
56. La.-Monroe	12	34	32	0	0	0	9	2	267	22.3	4	8	0
58. Central Mich.	14	42	37	1	0	0	7	0	312	22.3	10	4	0
59. Akron	12	34	32	0	0	0	11	1	271	22.6	5	7	0
60. Pittsburgh	12	34	29	3	0	0	11	1	274	22.8	6	6	0
61. Mississippi	12	33	30	1	0	0	15	0	275	22.9	4	8	0
62. Washington St.	12	32	29	0	0	0	18	1	277	23.1	6	6	0
63. Middle Tenn.	13	39	38	0	0	0	10	0	302	23.2	7	6	0
64. Houston	14	40	34	2	0	0	17	0	329	23.5	10	4	0
65. Vanderbilt	12	34	28	2	0	0	16	0	284	23.7	4	8	0
66. Kansas St.	13	38	36	0	0	0	15	0	309	23.8	7	6	0
67. Notre Dame	13	40	34	0	0	0	12	0	310	23.8	10	3	0
68. New Mexico	13	40	37	1	0	0	11	0	312	24.0	6	7	0
69. Hawaii	14	43	37	1	0	1	12	1	337	24.1	11	3	0
70. Arkansas St.	12	35	32	0	0	0	15	1	289	24.1	6	6	0
71. SMU	12	38	36	0	0	0	10	0	294	24.5	6	6	0
72. Syracuse	12	37	37	0	0	0	12	0	295	24.6	4	8	0
73. La.-Lafayette	12	38	36	0	0	0	10	1	296	24.7	6	6	0
74. UAB	12	37	29	1	0	0	14	1	297	24.8	3	9	0
75. Fla. Atlantic	12	37	35	0	0	0	14	0	299	24.9	5	7	0
76. Arizona St.	13	41	41	0	0	0	13	0	326	25.1	7	6	0
76. Texas Tech	13	39	35	0	0	0	19	0	326	25.1	8	5	0
78. Air Force	12	40	32	0	0	0	10	0	302	25.2	4	8	0
79. Miami (Ohio)	12	37	30	2	0	0	16	0	304	25.3	2	10	0
79. North Texas	12	40	34	0	0	0	10	0	304	25.3	3	9	0
81. Kansas	12	38	25	3	0	0	15	1	306	25.5	6	6	0
82. Oklahoma St.	13	41	35	2	0	0	16	0	333	25.6	7	6	0
83. Ball St.	12	38	31	1	0	0	16	0	309	25.8	5	7	0
83. Mississippi St.	12	39	33	0	0	0	14	0	309	25.8	3	9	0
85. Washington	12	34	28	2	0	0	25	0	311	25.9	5	7	0
86. Minnesota	13	45	39	0	0	0	9	1	338	26.0	6	7	0
87. Florida Int'l	12	39	36	1	0	0	13	1	313	26.1	0	12	0
88. Northwestern	12	39	36	0	0	0	14	1	314	26.2	4	8	0
89. Oregon	13	42	39	0	0	0	18	0	345	26.5	7	6	0
90. Purdue	14	45	38	3	0	0	20	0	374	26.7	8	6	0
91. Illinois	12	38	37	0	0	0	18	1	321	26.8	2	10	0
92. Eastern Mich.	12	42	38	1	0	0	10	0	322	26.8	1	11	0
93. Connecticut	12	39	39	0	0	0	17	0	324	27.0	4	8	0
94. San Diego St.	12	41	37	0	0	0	14	0	325	27.1	3	9	0
95. Toledo	12	42	36	2	0	1	12	1	332	27.7	5	7	0
96. Army	12	45	40	0	0	0	7	2	335	27.9	3	9	0
97. Fresno St.	12	48	39	0	0	0	4	0	339	28.3	4	8	0
98. Bowling Green	12	46	43	0	0	0	7	0	340	28.3	4	8	0
99. Kentucky	13	50	40	1	0	0	9	0	369	28.4	8	5	0
100. Michigan St.	12	43	39	0	0	0	14	1	341	28.4	4	8	0

Rank, Team	G	TD	Kxp	Oxp	Dkxp	Doxp	FG	Saf	Pts	Pts/Gm	W	L	T
101. UCF	12	42	35	0	0	0	18	2	345	28.8	4	8	0
102. Marshall	12	43	39	2	0	0	16	1	351	29.3	5	7	0
103. Memphis	12	47	44	0	0	0	13	0	365	30.4	2	10	0
104. North Carolina	12	47	43	1	0	0	13	0	366	30.5	3	9	0
105. Iowa St.	12	47	42	2	0	0	13	1	369	30.8	4	8	0
105. New Mexico St.	12	50	37	3	1	0	8	0	369	30.8	4	8	0
107. UTEP	12	46	41	3	0	0	16	2	375	31.3	5	7	0
108. Stanford	12	46	45	0	0	0	18	1	377	31.4	1	11	0
109. UNLV	12	49	44	1	0	0	14	0	382	31.8	2	10	0
110. Baylor	12	51	48	1	0	0	11	1	391	32.6	4	8	0
111. Indiana	12	54	49	0	0	0	7	0	394	32.8	5	7	0
112. Rice	13	54	49	1	0	0	19	0	432	33.2	7	6	0
113. Tulane	12	51	48	2	0	0	14	0	400	33.3	4	8	0
114. Duke	12	54	50	0	1	0	10	0	406	33.8	0	12	0
115. Idaho	12	57	54	0	0	0	7	0	417	34.8	4	8	0
116. Buffalo	12	58	52	2	0	0	9	0	431	35.9	2	10	0
117. Utah St.	12	62	61	0	0	0	9	1	462	38.5	1	11	0
118. Temple	12	65	61	0	0	0	15	0	496	41.3	1	11	0
119. Louisiana Tech	13	73	68	0	0	0	12	0	542	41.7	3	10	0

Net Punting

Rank, Team	G	Punts	Yds	Avg	Ret	RetYds	TB	NetAvg	W	L	T
1. Utah	13	59	2,598	44.03	19	45	5	41.58	8	5	0
2. Georgia Tech	14	79	3,596	45.52	33	164	11	40.66	9	5	0
3. Baylor	12	68	3,111	45.75	31	298	8	39.01	4	8	0
4. Auburn	13	47	2,149	45.72	18	177	8	38.55	11	2	0
5. Texas Tech	13	44	1,943	44.16	21	136	6	38.34	8	5	0
6. New Mexico St.	12	33	1,340	40.61	7	55	1	38.33	4	8	0
7. Ball St.	12	60	2,703	45.05	26	186	11	38.28	5	7	0
8. California	13	49	2,087	42.59	19	132	4	38.27	10	3	0
9. Wake	14	70	2,887	41.24	14	70	7	38.24	11	3	0
10. Eastern Mich.	12	70	2,784	39.77	12	37	4	38.10	1	11	0
11. Notre Dame	13	51	2,309	45.27	21	242	7	37.78	10	3	0
12. Florida	14	55	2,244	40.80	19	71	5	37.69	13	1	0
13. Tennessee	13	47	2,102	44.72	24	254	4	37.62	9	4	0
14. Miami (Fla.)	13	68	2,781	40.90	18	124	5	37.60	7	6	0
15. Texas	13	53	2,112	39.85	21	100	1	37.58	10	3	0
16. Pittsburgh	12	52	2,163	41.60	23	191	1	37.54	6	6	0
17. Wisconsin	13	59	2,468	41.83	31	177	4	37.47	12	1	0
18. Boston College	13	60	2,483	41.38	22	156	4	37.45	10	3	0
19. Central Mich.	14	63	2,644	41.97	23	149	7	37.38	10	4	0
20. Ohio	14	78	3,075	39.42	18	65	5	37.31	9	5	0
21. Syracuse	12	72	3,021	41.96	24	199	7	37.25	4	8	0
22. Arizona St.	13	55	2,276	41.38	20	148	4	37.24	7	6	0
23. Michigan St.	12	58	2,469	42.57	23	192	6	37.19	4	8	0
24. Nebraska	14	68	2,660	39.12	18	73	3	37.16	9	5	0
25. Texas A&M	13	52	2,286	43.96	25	242	6	37.00	9	4	0
26. North Texas	12	60	2,439	40.65	33	160	3	36.98	3	9	0
27. SMU	12	51	2,191	42.96	22	226	4	36.96	6	6	0
28. San Jose St.	13	64	2,797	43.70	26	236	10	36.89	9	4	0
29. West Virginia	13	35	1,449	41.40	17	160	0	36.83	11	2	0
30. Oklahoma	14	62	2,460	39.68	20	83	5	36.73	11	3	0
31. Colorado	12	56	2,353	42.02	32	299	0	36.68	2	10	0
32. Clemson	13	51	2,106	41.29	18	136	5	36.67	8	5	0
33. Boise St.	13	48	2,097	43.69	22	220	6	36.60	13	0	0
34. Ohio St.	13	49	1,990	40.61	15	119	4	36.55	12	1	0
35. Army	12	49	2,067	42.18	23	178	5	36.51	3	9	0
36. Troy	13	61	2,386	39.11	20	100	3	36.49	8	5	0
37. Penn St.	13	62	2,585	41.69	24	107	11	36.42	9	4	0
38. Arizona	12	77	3,361	43.65	31	364	10	36.32	6	6	0
39. UNLV	12	47	2,111	44.91	23	364	2	36.32	2	10	0
40. Toledo	12	63	2,589	41.10	15	204	5	36.27	5	7	0
41. Brigham Young	13	41	1,636	39.90	15	131	1	36.22	11	2	0
42. UCLA	13	63	2,639	41.89	29	227	7	36.06	7	6	0
43. South Carolina	13	30	1,267	42.23	14	187	0	36.00	8	5	0
44. Rutgers	13	56	2,467	44.05	26	352	5	35.98	11	2	0
45. Virginia Tech	13	62	2,582	41.65	26	212	7	35.97	10	3	0
46. Iowa	13	56	2,107	37.63	14	33	3	35.96	6	7	0
47. Maryland	13	56	2,400	42.86	18	250	7	35.89	9	4	0
48. Memphis	12	43	1,817	42.26	14	156	6	35.84	2	10	0
49. Iowa St.	12	56	2,309	41.23	27	218	5	35.55	4	8	0
50. Purdue	14	57	2,329	40.86	21	167	7	35.47	8	6	0
51. Kansas St.	13	63	2,566	40.73	25	213	6	35.44	7	6	0
52. Stanford	12	68	2,640	38.82	31	214	1	35.38	1	11	0
53. East Caro.	13	52	2,226	42.81	22	271	6	35.29	7	6	0
54. Florida St.	13	69	2,772	40.17	19	221	6	35.23	7	6	0
55. Colorado St.	12	65	2,760	42.46	31	311	8	35.22	4	8	0
56. Middle Tenn.	13	70	2,830	40.43	31	250	6	35.14	7	6	0
57. Michigan	13	64	2,542	39.72	27	187	6	34.92	11	2	0
58. Idaho	12	71	2,798	39.41	35	304	1	34.85	4	8	0
59. North Carolina St.	12	76	2,968	39.05	29	181	7	34.83	3	9	0
60. Virginia	12	81	3,165	39.07	35	225	6	34.81	5	7	0

Rank, Team	G	Punts	Yds	Avg	Ret	RetYds	TB	NetAvg	W	L	T
61. New Mexico	13	71	2,815	39.65	23	269	4	34.73	6	7	0
62. Washington St.	12	58	2,300	39.66	29	257	2	34.53	6	6	0
63. Alabama	13	57	2,176	38.18	26	190	1	34.49	6	7	0
64. Wyoming	12	63	2,634	41.81	30	322	7	34.48	6	6	0
65. Kansas	12	59	2,276	38.58	18	123	6	34.46	6	6	0
66. Tulane	12	63	2,602	41.30	37	392	2	34.44	4	8	0
67. Kentucky	13	56	2,104	37.57	22	80	5	34.36	8	5	0
68. Hawaii	14	17	646	38.00	8	62	0	34.35	11	3	0
69. North Carolina	12	66	2,630	39.85	31	244	6	34.33	3	9	0
70. Oklahoma St.	13	52	2,264	43.54	28	402	4	34.27	7	6	0
71. Mississippi	12	59	2,275	38.56	32	216	2	34.22	4	8	0
72. Indiana	12	66	2,615	39.62	31	297	3	34.21	5	7	0
73. Miami (Ohio)	12	59	2,383	40.39	27	250	6	34.12	2	10	0
74. Minnesota	13	57	2,257	39.60	29	235	4	34.07	6	7	0
75. Connecticut	12	74	2,845	38.45	30	191	7	33.97	4	8	0
76. Washington	12	74	3,120	42.16	22	328	14	33.95	5	7	0
77. Oregon St.	14	62	2,558	41.26	26	295	8	33.92	10	4	0
78. Southern Miss.	14	53	2,030	38.30	26	213	1	33.91	9	5	0
79. Rice	13	66	2,527	38.29	19	197	5	33.79	7	6	0
80. UCF	12	46	1,742	37.87	17	129	3	33.76	4	8	0
81. UTEP	12	51	1,813	35.55	21	73	1	33.73	5	7	0
82. Arkansas St.	12	53	2,015	38.02	21	168	3	33.72	6	6	0
83. Southern California	13	49	1,838	37.51	18	146	2	33.71	11	2	0
84. Marshall	12	40	1,520	38.00	12	94	4	33.65	5	7	0
85. Cincinnati	13	73	2,816	38.58	23	226	7	33.56	8	5	0
86. Vanderbilt	12	54	1,945	36.02	16	95	2	33.52	4	8	0
87. Louisville	13	46	1,775	38.59	19	135	5	33.48	12	1	0
88. Air Force	12	41	1,655	40.37	15	144	7	33.44	4	8	0
89. UAB	12	59	2,314	39.22	19	203	7	33.41	3	9	0
90. Oregon	13	38	1,495	39.34	15	168	3	33.34	7	6	0
91. Tulsa	13	48	1,835	38.23	21	175	3	33.33	8	5	0
92. Fla. Atlantic	12	64	2,399	37.48	27	229	2	33.28	5	7	0
93. Georgia	13	53	2,009	37.91	20	186	3	33.26	9	4	0
94. Louisiana Tech	13	71	2,711	38.18	27	257	5	33.15	3	10	0
95. LSU	13	40	1,642	41.05	15	178	7	33.10	11	2	0
96. San Diego St.	12	65	2,592	39.88	30	308	7	32.98	3	9	0
97. Northern Ill.	13	55	2,085	37.91	22	234	2	32.93	7	6	0
98. Navy	13	46	1,647	35.80	19	122	1	32.72	9	4	0
99. TCU	13	57	2,094	36.74	27	176	3	32.60	11	2	0
100. Arkansas	14	63	2,327	36.94	19	156	6	32.56	10	4	0
101. La.-Monroe	12	50	2,010	40.20	19	229	8	32.42	4	8	0
102. La.-Lafayette	12	55	2,111	38.38	28	270	3	32.38	6	6	0
103. Nevada	13	54	2,046	37.89	25	202	5	32.30	8	5	0
104. Missouri	13	48	1,852	38.58	17	188	6	32.17	8	5	0
105. Akron	12	65	2,386	36.71	31	260	2	32.09	5	7	0
106. Utah St.	12	81	2,976	36.74	42	318	3	32.07	1	11	0
107. Mississippi St.	12	68	2,598	38.21	43	422	1	31.71	3	9	0
108. Buffalo	12	74	2,693	36.39	38	320	3	31.26	2	10	0
109. Northwestern	12	67	2,417	36.07	30	250	5	30.85	4	8	0
110. Temple	12	80	3,033	37.91	42	492	4	30.76	1	11	0
111. Western Mich.	13	68	2,549	37.49	27	307	8	30.62	8	5	0
112. Duke	12	68	2,485	36.54	37	396	1	30.43	0	12	0
113. South Fla.	13	59	2,139	36.25	22	307	3	30.03	9	4	0
114. Houston	14	41	1,552	37.85	25	281	2	30.02	10	4	0
115. Fresno St.	12	63	2,321	36.84	21	331	5	30.00	4	8	0
116. Kent St.	12	64	2,133	33.33	17	142	4	29.86	6	6	0
117. Illinois	12	67	2,338	34.90	22	251	6	29.36	2	10	0
118. Bowling Green	12	60	1,987	33.12	16	225	5	27.70	4	8	0
119. Florida Int'l	12	83	2,890	34.82	34	514	6	27.18	0	12	0

Punt Returns

Rank, Team	G	Ret	Yds	TD	Avg	W	L	T
1. Kentucky	13	18	368	1	20.44	8	5	0
2. UTEP	12	13	260	2	20.00	5	7	0
3. Army	12	18	325	2	18.06	3	9	0
4. California	13	27	466	4	17.26	10	3	0
5. New Mexico St.	12	6	92	0	15.33	4	8	0
6. Oregon St.	14	32	480	3	15.00	10	4	0
7. Georgia	13	34	505	3	14.85	9	4	0
8. UCF	12	18	257	1	14.28	4	8	0
9. Nevada	13	22	299	0	13.59	8	5	0
10. Western Mich.	13	18	244	0	13.56	8	5	0
11. Kansas	12	24	324	2	13.50	6	6	0
12. Northern Ill.	13	22	291	2	13.23	7	6	0
13. Mississippi St.	12	27	355	1	13.15	3	9	0
14. South Fla.	13	34	446	1	13.12	9	4	0
15. Ohio	14	37	485	1	13.11	9	5	0
16. Kansas St.	13	30	391	3	13.03	7	6	0
17. Air Force	12	11	143	1	13.00	4	8	0
18. Fla. Atlantic	12	16	207	0	12.94	5	7	0
19. Texas	13	28	362	3	12.93	10	3	0
20. Brigham Young	13	31	399	1	12.87	11	2	0
21. Buffalo	12	15	192	1	12.80	2	10	0
22. Florida Int'l	12	21	268	2	12.76	0	12	0
23. Virginia Tech	13	28	353	1	12.61	10	3	0
24. Indiana	12	18	226	1	12.56	5	7	0
25. Arizona	12	21	260	1	12.38	6	6	0
26. Connecticut	12	22	264	1	12.00	4	8	0
27. Oklahoma St.	13	34	404	0	11.88	7	6	0
28. Marshall	12	15	176	1	11.73	5	7	0
29. Oregon	13	35	400	1	11.43	7	6	0
30. Tennessee	13	21	239	1	11.38	9	4	0
31. Mississippi	12	20	224	1	11.20	4	8	0
32. Troy	13	29	322	1	11.10	8	5	0
33. Wake Forest	14	33	366	1	11.09	11	3	0
34. Minnesota	13	20	219	0	10.95	6	7	0
35. Michigan	13	33	357	1	10.82	11	2	0
36. Iowa St.	12	20	213	1	10.65	4	8	0
37. San Jose St.	13	17	179	1	10.53	9	4	0
38. TCU	13	40	417	0	10.43	11	2	0
39. Memphis	12	15	155	0	10.33	2	10	0
40. Penn St.	13	36	369	1	10.25	9	4	0
41. Colorado St.	12	34	347	2	10.21	4	8	0
42. Ohio St.	13	30	306	1	10.20	12	1	0

Rank, Team	G	Ret	Yds	TD	Avg	W	L	T
43. Florida	14	49	499	1	10.18	13	1	0
44. North Carolina	12	21	212	1	10.10	3	9	0
44. UNLV	12	21	212	2	10.10	2	10	0
46. Miami (Ohio)	12	22	222	1	10.09	2	10	0
47. Iowa	13	29	292	0	10.07	6	7	0
48. Rutgers	13	19	187	2	9.84	11	2	0
49. Southern Miss.	14	26	242	1	9.31	9	5	0
50. Boston College	13	29	267	0	9.21	10	3	0
51. Alabama	13	34	308	2	9.06	6	7	0
52. Florida St.	13	35	317	1	9.06	7	6	0
53. East Caro.	13	18	162	0	9.00	7	6	0
53. Wyoming	12	27	243	0	9.00	6	6	0
53. West Virginia	13	26	234	1	9.00	11	2	0
56. Texas Tech	13	42	377	0	8.98	8	5	0
57. Tulane	12	22	191	0	8.68	4	8	0
58. Utah	13	36	312	0	8.67	8	5	0
59. Navy	13	20	171	0	8.55	9	4	0
60. Pittsburgh	12	26	222	1	8.54	6	6	0
61. LSU	13	31	264	1	8.52	11	2	0
62. Maryland	13	28	238	0	8.50	9	4	0
63. Arizona St.	13	35	296	0	8.46	7	6	0
64. UCLA	13	22	186	1	8.45	7	6	0
65. Boise St.	13	34	286	0	8.41	13	0	0
66. Middle Tenn.	13	17	142	0	8.35	7	6	0
67. Virginia	12	33	272	0	8.24	5	7	0
68. Fresno St.	12	29	238	1	8.21	4	8	0
69. Nebraska	14	36	294	0	8.17	9	5	0
70. North Carolina St.	12	28	225	1	8.04	3	9	0
71. Hawaii	14	29	233	0	8.03	11	3	0
72. Texas A&M	13	22	175	0	7.95	9	4	0
73. Michigan St.	12	20	158	2	7.90	4	8	0
74. Oklahoma	14	38	299	1	7.87	11	3	0
75. SMU	12	23	180	0	7.83	6	6	0
76. South Carolina	13	19	147	0	7.74	8	5	0
77. Eastern Mich.	12	22	170	0	7.73	1	11	0
78. Syracuse	12	21	161	0	7.67	4	8	0
79. Houston	14	21	160	0	7.62	10	4	0
80. Baylor	12	30	228	0	7.60	4	8	0
81. Clemson	13	27	204	1	7.56	8	5	0
82. Northwestern	12	13	98	1	7.54	4	8	0
83. Missouri	13	25	187	0	7.48	8	5	0
84. Georgia Tech	14	45	336	0	7.47	9	5	0
85. La.-Lafayette	12	18	134	1	7.44	6	6	0
86. Cincinnati	13	34	251	0	7.38	8	5	0
87. North Texas	12	19	140	1	7.37	3	9	0
88. Notre Dame	13	23	169	1	7.35	10	3	0
89. Bowling Green	12	18	132	0	7.33	4	8	0
90. Arkansas	14	33	239	0	7.24	10	4	0
91. Miami (Fla.)	13	39	281	0	7.21	7	6	0
92. Rice	13	28	201	0	7.18	7	6	0
93. Tulsa	13	29	206	0	7.10	8	5	0
94. Kent St.	12	20	142	0	7.10	6	6	0
95. Louisville	13	39	265	1	6.79	12	1	0
96. Wisconsin	13	36	237	1	6.58	12	1	0
97. Washington	12	37	242	1	6.54	5	7	0
98. New Mexico	13	28	179	0	6.39	6	7	0
99. Purdue	14	24	149	0	6.21	8	6	0
100. Southern California	13	21	130	0	6.19	11	2	0
101. San Diego St.	12	17	98	0	5.76	3	9	0
102. Ball St.	12	24	138	1	5.75	5	7	0
103. Stanford	12	13	73	0	5.62	1	11	0
104. Colorado	12	22	123	0	5.59	2	10	0
105. Washington St.	12	17	93	0	5.47	6	6	0
106. Auburn	13	28	153	1	5.46	11	2	0
107. Central Mich.	14	27	144	0	5.33	10	4	0
108. Utah St.	12	14	74	0	5.29	1	11	0
109. Idaho	12	21	109	0	5.19	4	8	0
110. Duke	12	21	107	0	5.10	0	12	0
111. Illinois	12	23	116	0	5.04	2	10	0
112. Louisiana Tech	13	23	115	0	5.00	3	10	0
113. Toledo	12	20	98	0	4.90	5	7	0
114. Vanderbilt	12	22	104	0	4.73	4	8	0
115. UAB	12	16	73	0	4.56	3	9	0
116. La.-Monroe	12	18	82	0	4.56	4	8	0
117. Arkansas St.	12	18	68	0	3.78	6	6	0
118. Akron	12	17	59	0	3.47	5	7	0
119. Temple	12	11	35	0	3.18	1	11	0

Kickoff Returns

Rank, Team	G	Ret	Yds	TD	Avg	W	L	T
1. Kansas St.	13	36	977	3	27.14	7	6	0
2. Arizona St.	13	33	872	1	26.42	7	6	0
3. Texas A&M	13	25	652	1	26.08	9	4	0
4. Auburn	13	36	934	0	25.94	11	2	0
5. Boston College	13	35	906	1	25.89	10	3	0
6. Clemson	13	26	660	1	25.38	8	5	0
7. Arkansas	14	37	921	2	24.89	10	4	0
8. Oklahoma St.	13	50	1,231	2	24.62	7	6	0
9. Pittsburgh	12	43	1,038	1	24.14	6	6	0
10. Kentucky	13	43	1,033	1	24.02	8	5	0
11. Virginia	12	39	933	0	23.92	5	7	0
12. West Virginia	13	50	1,192	1	23.84	11	2	0
13. Arizona	12	22	524	0	23.82	6	6	0
14. Nevada	13	33	783	0	23.73	8	5	0
15. Duke	12	55	1,281	0	23.29	0	12	0
16. Southern California	13	28	650	1	23.21	11	2	0
17. Texas	13	26	603	0	23.19	10	3	0
18. Middle Tenn.	13	46	1,061	2	23.07	7	6	0
19. Oregon	13	49	1,129	0	23.04	7	6	0
20. Minnesota	13	38	873	1	22.97	6	7	0
21. SMU	12	44	1,010	1	22.95	6	6	0
22. Baylor	12	45	1,027	0	22.82	4	8	0
23. Oklahoma	14	37	844	1	22.81	11	3	0
24. Mississippi	12	43	976	0	22.70	4	8	0
25. Oregon St.	14	41	926	1	22.59	10	4	0
26. Maryland	13	47	1,050	1	22.34	9	4	0
27. Western Mich.	13	33	737	0	22.33	8	5	0
28. Indiana	12	47	1,043	3	22.19	5	7	0
29. North Carolina	12	50	1,106	2	22.12	3	9	0
30. Cincinnati	13	36	788	0	21.89	8	5	0
31. Utah	13	31	676	0	21.81	8	5	0
32. UAB	12	43	937	0	21.79	3	9	0
33. Louisiana Tech	13	71	1,541	1	21.70	3	10	0
34. Ohio St.	13	30	651	1	21.70	12	1	0
35. North Carolina St.	12	41	886	1	21.61	3	9	0
36. Temple	12	64	1,381	1	21.58	1	11	0
37. Kansas	12	45	971	0	21.58	6	6	0
38. UCLA	13	30	647	0	21.57	7	6	0
39. Notre Dame	13	45	965	0	21.44	10	3	0
40. Houston	14	50	1,072	0	21.44	10	4	0
41. Buffalo	12	45	961	1	21.36	2	10	0
42. Akron	12	41	872	0	21.27	5	7	0
43. Penn St.	13	32	678	1	21.19	9	4	0
44. Georgia	13	41	868	1	21.17	9	4	0
45. Memphis	12	47	993	0	21.13	2	10	0
46. Florida Int'l	12	40	841	1	21.03	0	12	0
47. TCU	13	29	607	0	20.93	11	2	0
48. Virginia Tech	13	29	606	0	20.90	10	3	0
49. Ohio	14	35	726	0	20.74	9	5	0
50. UNLV	12	51	1,055	0	20.69	2	10	0
51. Mississippi St.	12	39	801	0	20.54	3	9	0
52. California	13	29	595	0	20.52	10	3	0
53. New Mexico	13	45	923	0	20.51	6	7	0
54. Eastern Mich.	12	40	819	0	20.48	1	11	0
55. Connecticut	12	48	982	0	20.46	4	8	0
56. Brigham Young	13	28	571	0	20.39	11	2	0
57. Louisville	13	32	651	1	20.34	12	1	0
58. Marshall	12	44	892	0	20.27	5	7	0
59. LSU	13	19	384	1	20.21	11	2	0
60. Miami (Ohio)	12	43	869	0	20.21	2	10	0
61. Toledo	12	40	808	0	20.20	5	7	0
62. Boise St.	13	33	661	0	20.03	13	0	0
63. Wake Forest	14	35	701	0	20.03	11	3	0
64. La.-Monroe	12	36	721	0	20.03	4	8	0
65. Miami (Fla.)	13	31	618	0	19.94	7	6	0
66. Fresno St.	12	48	954	1	19.88	4	8	0
67. Hawaii	14	46	909	1	19.76	11	3	0
68. Rutgers	13	32	630	0	19.69	11	2	0
69. East Caro.	13	36	708	1	19.67	7	6	0
70. Tulsa	13	36	706	0	19.61	8	5	0
71. Troy	13	47	919	0	19.55	8	5	0
72. Illinois	12	41	801	0	19.54	2	10	0
73. New Mexico St.	12	33	642	0	19.45	4	8	0
74. Georgia Tech	14	42	815	0	19.40	9	5	0
75. Ball St.	12	45	871	0	19.36	5	7	0
76. UCF	12	43	831	0	19.33	4	8	0
77. Washington	12	41	792	0	19.32	5	7	0
78. Army	12	57	1,099	0	19.28	3	9	0
79. Michigan	13	32	616	0	19.25	11	2	0
80. Southern Miss.	14	44	845	0	19.20	9	5	0
81. South Carolina	13	38	728	0	19.16	8	5	0
82. Arkansas St.	12	51	977	0	19.16	6	6	0
83. Rice	13	58	1,096	0	18.90	7	6	0
84. Fla. Atlantic	12	46	868	0	18.87	5	7	0
85. Central Mich.	14	47	883	1	18.79	10	4	0

Rank, Team	G	Ret	Yds	TD	Avg	W	L	T
86. Kent St.	12	35	656	0	18.74	6	6	0
87. Purdue	14	52	974	0	18.73	8	6	0
88. La.-Lafayette	12	43	805	0	18.72	6	6	0
89. Florida St.	13	35	653	0	18.66	7	6	0
90. UTEP	12	45	835	1	18.56	5	7	0
91. Michigan St.	12	45	834	0	18.53	4	8	0
92. Iowa St.	12	40	737	0	18.43	4	8	0
93. Utah St.	12	52	958	0	18.42	1	11	0
94. Wyoming	12	37	679	0	18.35	6	6	0
95. Colorado	12	32	583	0	18.22	2	10	0
96. Alabama	13	31	564	0	18.19	6	7	0
97. North Texas	12	44	797	0	18.11	3	9	0
98. Colorado St.	12	28	507	0	18.11	4	8	0
99. Northwestern	12	38	684	0	18.00	4	8	0
100. Syracuse	12	41	737	0	17.98	4	8	0
101. Stanford	12	48	859	0	17.90	1	11	0
102. Vanderbilt	12	41	732	0	17.85	4	8	0
103. Idaho	12	53	944	0	17.81	4	8	0
104. San Jose St.	13	31	552	0	17.81	9	4	0
105. Air Force	12	34	605	0	17.79	4	8	0
106. Iowa	13	28	498	0	17.79	6	7	0
107. South Fla.	13	36	633	0	17.58	9	4	0
108. Bowling Green	12	46	808	0	17.57	4	8	0
109. Washington St.	12	31	543	0	17.52	6	6	0
110. Florida	14	26	455	0	17.50	13	1	0
110. San Diego St.	12	48	840	0	17.50	3	9	0
112. Nebraska	14	28	488	0	17.43	9	5	0
113. Tulane	12	49	853	0	17.41	4	8	0
114. Northern Ill.	13	42	728	0	17.33	7	6	0
115. Missouri	13	24	410	0	17.08	8	5	0
116. Navy	13	30	488	0	16.27	9	4	0
117. Tennessee	13	37	594	0	16.05	9	4	0
118. Texas Tech	13	37	587	0	15.86	8	5	0
119. Wisconsin	13	27	405	0	15.00	12	1	0

Turnover Margin

		Gained			Lost						
Rank, Team	G	Fum	Int	Total	Fum	Int	Total	TM/Gm	W	L	T
1. Minnesota	13	15	17	32	3	11	14	1.38	6	7	0
2. Boston College	13	16	21	37	11	11	22	1.15	10	3	0
2. Kentucky	13	18	14	32	10	7	17	1.15	8	5	0
4. Brigham Young	13	9	18	27	4	9	13	1.08	11	2	0
4. Michigan	13	14	12	26	4	8	12	1.08	11	2	0
6. Wake Forest	14	9	22	31	12	6	18	.93	11	3	0
7. Nevada	13	17	20	37	13	12	25	.92	8	5	0
7. Western Mich.	13	10	24	34	9	13	22	.92	8	5	0
9. Syracuse	12	11	17	28	12	5	17	.92	4	8	0
10. Boise St.	13	11	20	31	11	9	20	.85	13	0	0
10. Rutgers	13	16	15	31	7	13	20	.85	11	2	0
12. La.-Monroe	12	15	19	34	9	15	24	.83	4	8	0
13. Ohio St.	13	6	21	27	12	6	18	.69	12	1	0
13. Texas	13	19	13	32	14	9	23	.69	10	3	0
13. Texas A&M	13	11	11	22	9	4	13	.69	9	4	0
13. San Jose St.	13	14	16	30	13	8	21	.69	9	4	0
17. Colorado	12	12	12	24	8	8	16	.67	2	10	0
17. Air Force	12	13	9	22	10	4	14	.67	4	8	0
17. Pittsburgh	12	15	11	26	9	9	18	.67	6	6	0
20. Houston	14	13	12	25	11	5	16	.64	10	4	0
21. Rice	13	18	11	29	7	14	21	.62	7	6	0
21. Utah	13	11	17	28	8	12	20	.62	8	5	0
23. Arizona	12	13	13	26	5	14	19	.58	6	6	0
24. Oregon St.	14	16	17	33	16	9	25	.57	10	4	0
25. Alabama	13	11	16	27	10	10	20	.54	6	7	0
25. West Virginia	13	8	16	24	9	8	17	.54	11	2	0
25. TCU	13	10	16	26	13	6	19	.54	11	2	0
28. Central Mich.	14	13	16	29	11	11	22	.50	10	4	0
28. Washington St.	12	14	16	30	12	12	24	.50	6	6	0
30. California	13	7	21	28	8	14	22	.46	10	3	0
30. Middle Tenn.	13	13	14	27	10	11	21	.46	7	6	0
32. Southern Miss.	14	8	17	25	12	7	19	.43	9	5	0
33. UAB	12	14	12	26	9	12	21	.42	3	9	0
34. Auburn	13	15	10	25	10	10	20	.38	11	2	0
34. Oklahoma St.	13	16	10	26	10	11	21	.38	7	6	0
34. Notre Dame	13	8	11	19	7	7	14	.38	10	3	0
37. Florida	14	8	21	29	10	14	24	.36	13	1	0
38. UCLA	13	14	13	27	9	14	23	.31	7	6	0
38. East Caro.	13	11	16	27	12	11	23	.31	7	6	0
38. Southern California	13	11	11	22	7	11	18	.31	11	2	0
38. Virginia Tech	13	10	17	27	11	12	23	.31	10	3	0
42. Kent St.	12	12	16	28	13	12	25	.25	6	6	0
43. Georgia Tech	14	12	13	25	6	16	22	.21	9	5	0
44. Fla. Atlantic	12	8	18	26	10	14	24	.17	5	7	0
44. Virginia	12	7	10	17	4	11	15	.17	5	7	0
46. Clemson	13	16	14	30	17	11	28	.15	8	5	0
46. Missouri	13	15	13	28	15	11	26	.15	8	5	0
46. New Mexico	13	11	14	25	14	9	23	.15	6	7	0
46. Northern Ill.	13	14	7	21	4	15	19	.15	7	6	0
46. Louisville	13	13	12	25	16	7	23	.15	12	1	0
51. Akron	12	14	7	21	9	11	20	.08	5	7	0
51. Bowling Green	12	7	12	19	7	11	18	.08	4	8	0
51. SMU	12	12	11	23	12	10	22	.08	6	6	0
51. Ball St.	12	9	9	18	6	11	17	.08	5	7	0
55. Penn St.	13	12	13	25	15	9	24	.08	9	4	0
55. Navy	13	12	12	24	19	4	23	.08	9	4	0
57. Hawaii	14	15	14	29	16	12	28	.07	11	3	0
58. LSU	13	5	16	21	12	9	21	.00	11	2	0
58. Wisconsin	13	10	15	25	16	9	25	.00	12	1	0
58. UTEP	12	10	15	25	8	17	25	.00	5	7	0

Rank, Team	G	Gained Fum	Gained Int	Gained Total	Lost Fum	Lost Int	Lost Total	TM/Gm	W	L	T
58. Texas Tech	13	13	11	24	13	11	24	.00	8	5	0
58. Nebraska	14	13	12	25	17	8	25	.00	9	5	0
58. Memphis	12	10	10	20	6	14	20	.00	2	10	0
58. Tennessee	13	4	16	20	9	11	20	.00	9	4	0
58. Miami (Ohio)	12	8	14	22	11	11	22	.00	2	10	0
66. Oklahoma	14	14	18	32	22	11	33	-.07	11	3	0
66. Purdue	14	17	11	28	9	20	29	-.07	8	6	0
68. Arizona St.	13	9	15	24	11	14	25	-.08	7	6	0
68. Georgia	13	11	19	30	15	16	31	-.08	9	4	0
70. Connecticut	12	8	12	20	9	12	21	-.08	4	8	0
70. Michigan St.	12	12	8	20	8	13	21	-.08	4	8	0
70. Idaho	12	9	16	25	10	16	26	-.08	4	8	0
73. South Carolina	13	7	14	21	10	13	23	-.15	8	5	0
74. Vanderbilt	12	12	14	26	14	14	28	-.17	4	8	0
75. Miami (Fla.)	13	9	12	21	9	15	24	-.23	7	6	0
76. Mississippi	12	10	3	13	6	10	16	-.25	4	8	0
76. Toledo	12	7	11	18	10	11	21	-.25	5	7	0
78. Arkansas	14	5	16	21	7	18	25	-.29	10	4	0
78. Ohio	14	12	13	25	14	15	29	-.29	9	5	0
80. Kansas St.	13	16	10	26	10	20	30	-.31	7	6	0
80. South Fla.	13	10	15	25	14	15	29	-.31	9	4	0
82. Arkansas St.	12	7	19	26	15	15	30	-.33	6	6	0
82. Indiana	12	9	13	22	14	12	26	-.33	5	7	0
82. Wyoming	12	10	11	21	12	13	25	-.33	6	6	0
82. Buffalo	12	10	10	20	11	13	24	-.33	2	10	0
86. Tulsa	13	6	8	14	10	9	19	-.38	8	5	0
87. Iowa St.	12	9	6	15	8	12	20	-.42	4	8	0
87. Kansas	12	16	12	28	14	19	33	-.42	6	6	0
87. Mississippi St.	12	8	12	20	9	16	25	-.42	3	9	0
90. Cincinnati	13	9	14	23	12	17	29	-.46	8	5	0
90. Maryland	13	9	8	17	11	12	23	-.46	9	4	0
90. Troy	13	9	16	25	13	18	31	-.46	8	5	0
93. Fresno St.	12	9	5	14	5	15	20	-.50	4	8	0
93. Utah St.	12	13	6	19	11	14	25	-.50	1	11	0
93. La.-Lafayette	12	10	6	16	8	14	22	-.50	6	6	0
93. Eastern Mich.	12	8	7	15	5	16	21	-.50	1	11	0
97. Baylor	12	11	16	27	17	17	34	-.58	4	8	0
97. Colorado St.	12	5	7	12	6	13	19	-.58	4	8	0
97. UCF	12	2	10	12	9	10	19	-.58	4	8	0
97. San Diego St.	12	9	9	18	8	17	25	-.58	3	9	0
97. Northwestern	12	11	11	22	12	17	29	-.58	4	8	0
102. Florida St.	13	7	12	19	11	16	27	-.62	7	6	0
102. Louisiana Tech	13	19	10	29	18	19	37	-.62	3	10	0
104. Duke	12	13	10	23	14	17	31	-.67	0	12	0
104. Washington	12	4	10	14	6	16	22	-.67	5	7	0
106. Florida Int'l	12	6	11	17	11	15	26	-.75	0	12	0
106. Temple	12	8	9	17	11	15	26	-.75	1	11	0
106. Marshall	12	10	12	22	15	16	31	-.75	5	7	0
109. Oregon	13	7	15	22	14	18	32	-.77	7	6	0
110. New Mexico St.	12	10	14	24	22	12	34	-.83	4	8	0
111. Iowa	13	6	14	20	12	19	31	-.85	6	7	0
112. North Carolina	12	10	7	17	10	18	28	-.92	3	9	0
112. UNLV	12	9	9	18	12	17	29	-.92	2	10	0
112. North Carolina St.	12	5	7	12	7	16	23	-.92	3	9	0
112. Tulane	12	6	8	14	13	12	25	-.92	4	8	0
112. Stanford	12	8	7	15	15	11	26	-.92	1	11	0
117. Illinois	12	10	10	20	21	14	35	-1.25	2	10	0
117. North Texas	12	8	6	14	10	19	29	-1.25	3	9	0
119. Army	12	15	4	19	13	24	37	-1.50	3	9	0

Fumbles Recovered

Rank, Team	No.
1. Louisiana Tech	19
1. Texas	19
3. Kentucky	18
3. Rice	18
5. Nevada	17
5. Purdue	17
7. Boston College	16
7. Clemson	16
7. Kansas	16
7. Kansas St.	16
7. Oklahoma St.	16
7. Oregon St.	16
7. Rutgers	16
14. Army	15
14. Auburn	15
14. Hawaii	15
14. La.-Monroe	15
14. Minnesota	15
14. Missouri	15
14. Pittsburgh	15
21. Akron	14
21. UAB	14
21. Michigan	14
21. Northern Ill.	14
21. Oklahoma	14
21. San Jose St.	14
21. UCLA	14
21. Washington St.	14
29. Air Force	13
29. Arizona	13
29. Central Mich.	13
29. Duke	13
29. Houston	13
29. Louisville	13
29. Middle Tenn.	13

Rank, Team	No.
29. Nebraska	13
29. Texas Tech	13
29. Utah St.	13
39. Colorado	12
39. Georgia Tech	12
39. Kent St.	12
39. Michigan St.	12
39. Navy	12
39. Ohio	12
39. Penn St.	12
39. SMU	12
39. Vanderbilt	12
48. Alabama	11
48. Baylor	11
48. Boise St.	11
48. East Caro.	11
48. Georgia	11
48. New Mexico	11
48. Northwestern	11
48. Southern California	11
48. Syracuse	11
48. Texas A&M	11
48. Utah	11
59. Buffalo	10
59. Illinois	10
59. La.-Lafayette	10
59. Marshall	10
59. Memphis	10
59. Mississippi	10
59. New Mexico St.	10
59. North Carolina	10
59. South Fla.	10
59. UTEP	10
59. TCU	10
59. Virginia Tech	10
59. Western Mich.	10
59. Wisconsin	10
59. Wyoming	10
74. Arizona St.	9
74. Ball St.	9
74. Brigham Young	9
74. Cincinnati	9
74. Fresno St.	9
74. Idaho	9
74. Indiana	9
74. Iowa St.	9
74. Maryland	9
74. Miami (Fla.)	9
74. UNLV	9
74. San Diego St.	9
74. Troy	9
74. Wake Forest	9
88. Connecticut	8
88. Eastern Mich.	8
88. Florida	8
88. Fla. Atlantic	8
88. Miami (Ohio)	8
88. Mississippi St.	8
88. North Texas	8
88. Notre Dame	8
88. Southern Miss.	8
88. Stanford	8
88. Temple	8
88. West Virginia	8
100. Arkansas St.	7
100. Bowling Green	7
100. California	7
100. Florida St.	7
100. Oregon	7
100. South Carolina	7
100. Toledo	7
100. Virginia	7
108. Florida Int'l	6
108. Iowa	6
108. Ohio St.	6
108. Tulane	6
108. Tulsa	6
113. Arkansas	5
113. Colorado St.	5
113. LSU	5
113. North Carolina St.	5
117. Tennessee	4
117. Washington	4
119. UCF	2

Rank, Team	No.
60. Mississippi St.	12
60. Navy	12
60. Nebraska	12
74. Florida Int'l	11
74. Northwestern	11
74. Notre Dame	11
74. Pittsburgh	11
74. Purdue	11
74. Rice	11
74. Southern California	11
74. SMU	11
74. Texas A&M	11
74. Texas Tech	11
74. Toledo	11
74. Wyoming	11
86. Auburn	10
86. Buffalo	10
86. UCF	10
86. Duke	10
86. Illinois	10
86. Kansas St.	10
86. Louisiana Tech	10
86. Memphis	10
86. Oklahoma St.	10
86. Virginia	10
86. Washington	10
97. Air Force	9
97. Ball St.	9
97. UNLV	9
97. San Diego St.	9
97. Temple	9
102. Maryland	8
102. Michigan St.	8
102. Tulane	8
102. Tulsa	8
106. Akron	7
106. Colorado St.	7
106. Eastern Mich.	7
106. North Carolina	7
106. North Carolina St.	7
106. Northern Ill.	7
106. Stanford	7
113. Iowa St.	6
113. La.-Lafayette	6
113. North Texas	6
113. Utah St.	6
117. Fresno St.	5
118. Army	4
119. Mississippi	3

Passes Intercepted

Rank, Team	No.
1. Western Mich.	24
2. Wake Forest	22
3. Boston College	21
3. California	21
3. Florida	21
3. Ohio St.	21
7. Boise St.	20
7. Nevada	20
9. Arkansas St.	19
9. Georgia	19
9. La.-Monroe	19
12. Brigham Young	18
12. Fla. Atlantic	18
12. Oklahoma	18
15. Minnesota	17
15. Oregon St.	17
15. Southern Miss.	17
15. Syracuse	17
15. Utah	17
15. Virginia Tech	17
21. Alabama	16
21. Arkansas	16
21. Baylor	16
21. Central Mich.	16
21. East Caro.	16
21. Idaho	16
21. Kent St.	16
21. LSU	16
21. San Jose St.	16
21. Tennessee	16
21. TCU	16
21. Troy	16
21. Washington St.	16
21. West Virginia	16
35. Arizona St.	15
35. Oregon	15
35. Rutgers	15
35. South Fla.	15
35. UTEP	15
35. Wisconsin	15
41. Cincinnati	14
41. Clemson	14
41. Hawaii	14
41. Iowa	14
41. Kentucky	14
41. Miami (Ohio)	14
41. Middle Tenn.	14
41. New Mexico	14
41. New Mexico St.	14
41. South Carolina	14
41. Vanderbilt	14
52. Arizona	13
52. Georgia Tech	13
52. Indiana	13
52. Missouri	13
52. Ohio	13
52. Penn St.	13
52. Texas	13
52. UCLA	13
60. UAB	12
60. Bowling Green	12
60. Colorado	12
60. Connecticut	12
60. Florida St.	12
60. Houston	12
60. Kansas	12
60. Louisville	12
60. Marshall	12
60. Miami (Fla.)	12
60. Michigan	12

Turnovers Gained

Rank, Team	No.
1. Boston College	37
1. Nevada	37
3. La.-Monroe	34
3. Western Mich.	34
5. Oregon St.	33
6. Kentucky	32
6. Minnesota	32
6. Oklahoma	32
6. Texas	32
10. Boise St.	31
10. Rutgers	31
10. Wake Forest	31
13. Clemson	30
13. Georgia	30
13. San Jose St.	30
13. Washington St.	30
17. Central Mich.	29
17. Florida	29
17. Hawaii	29
17. Louisiana Tech	29
17. Rice	29
22. California	28
22. Kansas	28
22. Kent St.	28
22. Missouri	28
22. Purdue	28
22. Syracuse	28
22. Utah	28
29. Alabama	27
29. Baylor	27
29. Brigham Young	27
29. East Caro.	27
29. Middle Tenn.	27
29. Ohio St.	27
29. UCLA	27
29. Virginia Tech	27
37. UAB	26
37. Arizona	26
37. Arkansas St.	26
37. Fla. Atlantic	26
37. Kansas St.	26
37. Michigan	26
37. Oklahoma St.	26
37. Pittsburgh	26
37. TCU	26
37. Vanderbilt	26
47. Auburn	25
47. Georgia Tech	25
47. Houston	25
47. Idaho	25
47. Louisville	25
47. Nebraska	25
47. New Mexico	25
47. Ohio	25
47. Penn St.	25
47. South Fla.	25
47. Southern Miss.	25
47. UTEP	25
47. Troy	25
47. Wisconsin	25
61. Arizona St.	24
61. Colorado	24
61. Navy	24
61. New Mexico St.	24
61. Texas Tech	24
61. West Virginia	24
67. Cincinnati	23
67. Duke	23
67. SMU	23
70. Air Force	22
70. Indiana	22
70. Marshall	22
70. Miami (Ohio)	22
70. Northwestern	22
70. Oregon	22
70. Southern California	22
70. Texas A&M	22
78. Akron	21
78. Arkansas	21
78. LSU	21
78. Miami (Fla.)	21
78. Northern Ill.	21
78. South Carolina	21
78. Wyoming	21
85. Buffalo	20
85. Connecticut	20
85. Illinois	20
85. Iowa	20
85. Memphis	20
85. Michigan St.	20
85. Mississippi St.	20
85. Tennessee	20
93. Army	19
93. Bowling Green	19
93. Florida St.	19
93. Notre Dame	19
93. Utah St.	19
98. Ball St.	18
98. UNLV	18
98. San Diego St.	18
98. Toledo	18
102. Florida Int'l	17
102. Maryland	17
102. North Carolina	17
102. Temple	17

Rank, Team	No.
102. Virginia	17
107. La.-Lafayette	16
108. Eastern Mich.	15
108. Iowa St.	15
108. Stanford	15
111. Fresno St.	14
111. North Texas	14
111. Tulane	14
111. Tulsa	14
111. Washington	14
116. Mississippi	13
117. UCF	12
117. Colorado St.	12
117. North Carolina St.	12

Fumbles Lost

Rank, Team	No.
1. Minnesota	3
2. Brigham Young	4
2. Michigan	4
2. Northern Ill.	4
2. Virginia	4
6. Arizona	5
6. Eastern Mich.	5
6. Fresno St.	5
9. Ball St.	6
9. Colorado St.	6
9. Georgia Tech	6
9. Memphis	6
9. Mississippi	6
9. Washington	6
15. Arkansas	7
15. Bowling Green	7
15. North Carolina St.	7
15. Notre Dame	7
15. Rice	7
15. Rutgers	7
15. Southern California	7
22. California	8
22. Colorado	8
22. Iowa St.	8
22. La.-Lafayette	8
22. Michigan St.	8
22. San Diego St.	8
22. UTEP	8
22. Utah	8
30. Akron	9
30. UAB	9
30. UCF	9
30. Connecticut	9
30. La.-Monroe	9
30. Miami (Fla.)	9
30. Mississippi St.	9
30. Pittsburgh	9
30. Purdue	9
30. Tennessee	9
30. Texas A&M	9
30. UCLA	9
30. West Virginia	9
30. Western Mich.	9
44. Air Force	10
44. Alabama	10
44. Auburn	10
44. Florida	10
44. Fla. Atlantic	10
44. Idaho	10
44. Kansas St.	10
44. Kentucky	10
44. Middle Tenn.	10
44. North Carolina	10
44. North Texas	10
44. Oklahoma St.	10
44. South Carolina	10
44. Tulsa	10
44. Toledo	10
59. Arizona St.	11
59. Boise St.	11
59. Boston College	11
59. Buffalo	11
59. Central Mich.	11
59. Florida Int'l	11
59. Florida St.	11
59. Houston	11
59. Maryland	11
59. Miami (Ohio)	11
59. Temple	11
59. Utah St.	11
59. Virginia Tech	11
72. Cincinnati	12
72. East Caro.	12
72. Iowa	12
72. LSU	12
72. UNLV	12
72. Northwestern	12
72. Ohio St.	12
72. SMU	12
72. Southern Miss.	12
72. Syracuse	12
72. Wake Forest	12
72. Washington St.	12
72. Wyoming	12
85. Army	13
85. Kent St.	13
85. Nevada	13
85. San Jose St.	13
85. TCU	13
85. Texas Tech	13
85. Troy	13
85. Tulane	13
93. Duke	14
93. Indiana	14
93. Kansas	14
93. New Mexico	14
93. Ohio	14
93. Oregon	14
93. South Fla.	14
93. Texas	14
93. Vanderbilt	14
102. Arkansas St.	15
102. Georgia	15
102. Marshall	15
102. Missouri	15
102. Penn St.	15
102. Stanford	15
108. Hawaii	16
108. Louisville	16
108. Oregon St.	16
108. Wisconsin	16
112. Baylor	17
112. Clemson	17
112. Nebraska	17
115. Louisiana Tech	18
116. Navy	19
117. Illinois	21
118. New Mexico St.	22
118. Oklahoma	22

Passes Had Intercepted

Rank, Team	No.
1. Air Force	4
1. Navy	4
1. Texas A&M	4
4. Houston	5
4. Syracuse	5
6. Ohio St.	6
6. TCU	6
6. Wake Forest	6
9. Kentucky	7
9. Louisville	7
9. Notre Dame	7
9. Southern Miss.	7
13. Colorado	8
13. Michigan	8
13. Nebraska	8
13. San Jose St.	8
13. West Virginia	8
18. Boise St.	9
18. Brigham Young	9
18. LSU	9
18. New Mexico	9
18. Oregon St.	9
18. Penn St.	9
18. Pittsburgh	9
18. Texas	9
18. Tulsa	9
18. Wisconsin	9
28. Alabama	10
28. Auburn	10
28. UCF	10
28. Mississippi	10
28. SMU	10
33. Akron	11
33. Ball St.	11
33. Boston College	11
33. Bowling Green	11
33. Central Mich.	11
33. Clemson	11
33. East Caro.	11
33. Miami (Ohio)	11
33. Middle Tenn.	11
33. Minnesota	11
33. Missouri	11
33. Oklahoma	11
33. Oklahoma St.	11
33. Southern California	11
33. Stanford	11
33. Tennessee	11
33. Texas Tech	11
33. Toledo	11
33. Virginia	11
52. UAB	12
52. Connecticut	12
52. Hawaii	12
52. Indiana	12
52. Iowa St.	12
52. Kent St.	12
52. Maryland	12
52. Nevada	12
52. New Mexico St.	12
52. Tulane	12
52. Utah	12
52. Virginia Tech	12
52. Washington St.	12
65. Buffalo	13
65. Colorado St.	13
65. Michigan St.	13
65. Rutgers	13
65. South Carolina	13
65. Western Mich.	13
65. Wyoming	13
72. Arizona	14
72. Arizona St.	14
72. California	14
72. Florida	14
72. Fla. Atlantic	14
72. Illinois	14
72. La.-Lafayette	14
72. Memphis	14
72. Rice	14
72. UCLA	14
72. Utah St.	14
72. Vanderbilt	14
84. Arkansas St.	15
84. Florida Int'l	15
84. Fresno St.	15
84. La.-Monroe	15
84. Miami (Fla.)	15
84. Northern Ill.	15
84. Ohio	15
84. South Fla.	15
84. Temple	15
93. Eastern Mich.	16
93. Florida St.	16
93. Georgia	16
93. Georgia Tech	16
93. Idaho	16
93. Marshall	16
93. Mississippi St.	16
93. North Carolina St.	16
93. Washington	16
102. Baylor	17
102. Cincinnati	17
102. Duke	17
102. UNLV	17
102. Northwestern	17
102. San Diego St.	17
102. UTEP	17
109. Arkansas	18
109. North Carolina	18
109. Oregon	18
109. Troy	18
113. Iowa	19
113. Kansas	19
113. Louisiana Tech	19
113. North Texas	19
117. Kansas St.	20
117. Purdue	20
119. Army	24

Turnovers Lost

Rank, Team	No.
1. Michigan	12
2. Brigham Young	13
2. Texas A&M	13
4. Air Force	14
4. Minnesota	14
4. Notre Dame	14
7. Virginia	15
8. Colorado	16
8. Houston	16
8. Mississippi	16
11. Ball St.	17
11. Kentucky	17
11. Syracuse	17
11. West Virginia	17
15. Bowling Green	18
15. Ohio St.	18
15. Pittsburgh	18
15. Southern California	18
15. Wake Forest	18
20. Arizona	19
20. UCF	19
20. Colorado St.	19
20. Northern Ill.	19
20. Southern Miss.	19
20. TCU	19
20. Tulsa	19
27. Akron	20
27. Alabama	20
27. Auburn	20
27. Boise St.	20
27. Fresno St.	20
27. Iowa St.	20
27. Memphis	20
27. Rutgers	20
27. Tennessee	20
27. Utah	20
37. UAB	21
37. Connecticut	21
37. Eastern Mich.	21
37. LSU	21
37. Michigan St.	21
37. Middle Tenn.	21
37. Oklahoma St.	21
37. Rice	21
37. San Jose St.	21

Rank, Team	No.
37. Toledo	21
47. Boston College	22
47. California	22
47. Central Mich.	22
47. Georgia Tech	22
47. La.-Lafayette	22
47. Miami (Ohio)	22
47. SMU	22
47. Washington	22
47. Western Mich.	22
56. East Caro.	23
56. Louisville	23
56. Maryland	23
56. Navy	23
56. New Mexico	23
56. North Carolina St.	23
56. South Carolina	23
56. Texas	23
56. UCLA	23
56. Virginia Tech	23
66. Buffalo	24
66. Florida	24
66. Fla. Atlantic	24
66. La.-Monroe	24
66. Miami (Fla.)	24
66. Penn St.	24
66. Texas Tech	24
66. Washington St.	24
74. Arizona St.	25
74. Arkansas	25
74. Kent St.	25
74. Mississippi St.	25
74. Nebraska	25
74. Nevada	25
74. Oregon St.	25
74. San Diego St.	25
74. UTEP	25
74. Tulane	25
74. Utah St.	25
74. Wisconsin	25
74. Wyoming	25
87. Florida Int'l	26
87. Idaho	26
87. Indiana	26
87. Missouri	26
87. Stanford	26
87. Temple	26
93. Florida St.	27
94. Clemson	28
94. Hawaii	28
94. North Carolina	28
94. Vanderbilt	28
98. Cincinnati	29
98. UNLV	29
98. North Texas	29
98. Northwestern	29
98. Ohio	29
98. Purdue	29
98. South Fla.	29
105. Arkansas St.	30
105. Kansas St.	30
107. Duke	31
107. Georgia	31
107. Iowa	31
107. Marshall	31
107. Troy	31
112. Oregon	32
113. Kansas	33
113. Oklahoma	33
115. Baylor	34
115. New Mexico St.	34
117. Illinois	35
118. Army	37
118. Louisiana Tech	37

Fewest Penalties Per Game

Rank, Team	G	Pen	Pen/Gm	W	L	T
1. Northwestern	12	39	3.25	4	8	0
2. Air Force	12	47	3.92	4	8	0
3. Navy	13	52	4.00	9	4	0
3. Vanderbilt	12	48	4.00	4	8	0
5. Clemson	13	54	4.15	8	5	0
6. Nevada	13	55	4.23	8	5	0
7. Maryland	13	56	4.31	9	4	0
8. Memphis	12	52	4.33	2	10	0
8. Army	12	52	4.33	3	9	0
10. Penn St.	13	58	4.46	9	4	0
11. Virginia	12	54	4.50	5	7	0
12. East Caro.	13	59	4.54	7	6	0
12. Missouri	13	59	4.54	8	5	0
14. UCF	12	55	4.58	4	8	0
15. Rutgers	13	60	4.62	11	2	0
16. Iowa St.	12	56	4.67	4	8	0
17. Wisconsin	13	61	4.69	12	1	0
18. Colorado St.	12	57	4.75	4	8	0
19. Michigan	13	62	4.77	11	2	0
19. Ohio St.	13	62	4.77	12	1	0
19. Northern Ill.	13	62	4.77	7	6	0
22. Wake Forest	14	67	4.79	11	3	0
23. San Jose St.	13	63	4.85	9	4	0
24. Illinois	12	59	4.92	2	10	0
24. Indiana	12	59	4.92	5	7	0
24. Mississippi	12	59	4.92	4	8	0
27. Tennessee	13	64	4.92	9	4	0
28. Oklahoma	14	69	4.93	11	3	0
29. Ball St.	12	60	5.00	5	7	0
29. Stanford	12	60	5.00	1	11	0
29. Washington	12	60	5.00	5	7	0
29. New Mexico	13	65	5.00	6	7	0
29. Iowa	13	65	5.00	6	7	0
29. Louisville	13	65	5.00	12	1	0
35. Tulsa	13	66	5.08	8	5	0
36. Fresno St.	12	61	5.08	4	8	0
37. Louisiana Tech	13	68	5.23	3	10	0
37. Minnesota	13	68	5.23	6	7	0
39. Colorado	12	63	5.25	2	10	0
40. Nebraska	14	74	5.29	9	5	0
40. Purdue	14	74	5.29	8	6	0
42. Southern Miss.	14	75	5.36	9	5	0
43. Connecticut	12	65	5.42	4	8	0
43. Washington St.	12	65	5.42	6	6	0
43. Utah St.	12	65	5.42	1	11	0
46. California	13	71	5.46	10	3	0
47. Bowling Green	12	66	5.50	4	8	0
47. Mississippi St.	12	66	5.50	3	9	0
49. Auburn	13	72	5.54	11	2	0
49. Middle Tenn.	13	72	5.54	7	6	0
49. Texas	13	72	5.54	10	3	0
52. Kansas	12	67	5.58	6	6	0
53. Pittsburgh	12	68	5.67	6	6	0
53. Wyoming	12	68	5.67	6	6	0
55. Oklahoma St.	13	74	5.69	7	6	0
56. Arizona	12	69	5.75	6	6	0
56. Miami (Ohio)	12	69	5.75	2	10	0
56. Arkansas St.	12	69	5.75	6	6	0
59. Rice	13	75	5.77	7	6	0
60. Buffalo	12	70	5.83	2	10	0
60. La.-Lafayette	12	70	5.83	6	6	0
60. Fla. Atlantic	12	70	5.83	5	7	0
63. Boise St.	13	76	5.85	13	0	0
64. San Diego St.	12	71	5.92	3	9	0
64. Syracuse	12	71	5.92	4	8	0
66. Texas A&M	13	77	5.92	9	4	0
66. Virginia Tech	13	77	5.92	10	3	0
68. Arkansas	14	83	5.93	10	4	0
68. Central Mich.	14	83	5.93	10	4	0
70. Alabama	13	78	6.00	6	7	0
70. Duke	12	72	6.00	0	12	0
70. Boston College	13	78	6.00	10	3	0
70. Tulane	12	72	6.00	4	8	0
70. Georgia	13	78	6.00	9	4	0
75. Troy	13	79	6.08	8	5	0
76. North Carolina	12	73	6.08	3	9	0
76. UNLV	12	73	6.08	2	10	0
76. UTEP	12	73	6.08	5	7	0
79. Georgia Tech	14	86	6.14	9	5	0
80. Kentucky	13	80	6.15	8	5	0
81. Southern California	13	81	6.23	11	2	0
81. Utah	13	81	6.23	8	5	0
83. Temple	12	75	6.25	1	11	0
84. Oregon St.	14	88	6.29	10	4	0
85. North Texas	12	76	6.33	3	9	0
86. UCLA	13	83	6.38	7	6	0
86. LSU	13	83	6.38	11	2	0
88. Baylor	12	77	6.42	4	8	0
89. Western Mich.	13	84	6.46	8	5	0
90. SMU	12	78	6.50	6	6	0
91. Ohio	14	92	6.57	9	5	0
92. Marshall	12	79	6.58	5	7	0
93. South Carolina	13	86	6.62	8	5	0
94. Notre Dame	13	87	6.69	10	3	0
95. Michigan St.	12	81	6.75	4	8	0
96. Cincinnati	13	88	6.77	8	5	0
96. Miami (Fla.)	13	88	6.77	7	6	0
98. Houston	14	95	6.79	10	4	0
99. Kent St.	12	82	6.83	6	6	0
100. Florida St.	13	89	6.85	7	6	0
100. West Virginia	13	89	6.85	11	2	0
100. Kansas St.	13	89	6.85	7	6	0
103. Toledo	12	83	6.92	5	7	0
104. La.-Monroe	12	85	7.08	4	8	0
105. TCU	13	93	7.15	11	2	0
106. North Carolina St.	12	86	7.17	3	9	0
107. Brigham Young	13	94	7.23	11	2	0
108. Florida Int'l	12	87	7.25	0	12	0
109. Eastern Mich.	12	88	7.33	1	11	0
109. Idaho	12	88	7.33	4	8	0
109. New Mexico St.	12	88	7.33	4	8	0
112. Hawaii	14	103	7.36	11	3	0
113. Texas Tech	13	96	7.38	8	5	0
114. Oregon	13	98	7.54	7	6	0
115. UAB	12	94	7.83	3	9	0
116. Arizona St.	13	103	7.92	7	6	0
117. South Fla.	13	104	8.00	9	4	0
118. Florida	14	116	8.29	13	1	0
119. Akron	12	111	9.25	5	7	0

Fewest Yards Penalized Per Game

Rank, Team	G	Penalty Yds	Yds/Gm	W	L	T
1. Northwestern	12	336	28.00	4	8	0
2. Virginia	12	391	32.58	5	7	0
3. Vanderbilt	12	399	33.25	4	8	0
4. Nevada	13	437	33.62	8	5	0
4. Penn St.	13	437	33.62	9	4	0
6. Navy	13	438	33.69	9	4	0
7. Air Force	12	408	34.00	4	8	0
8. Stanford	12	428	35.67	1	11	0
9. Iowa St.	12	429	35.75	4	8	0
10. Clemson	13	471	36.23	8	5	0
11. Missouri	13	480	36.92	8	5	0
12. Maryland	13	483	37.15	9	4	0
13. Oklahoma	14	521	37.21	11	3	0
14. Army	12	447	37.25	3	9	0
15. Wisconsin	13	485	37.31	12	1	0
16. Memphis	12	448	37.33	2	10	0
17. Rutgers	13	487	37.46	11	2	0
18. Tennessee	13	490	37.69	9	4	0
19. San Jose St.	13	491	37.77	9	4	0
20. Illinois	12	460	38.33	2	10	0
21. Mississippi	12	464	38.67	4	8	0
22. Colorado St.	12	467	38.92	4	8	0
23. Purdue	14	548	39.14	8	6	0
24. East Caro.	13	511	39.31	7	6	0
25. Fresno St.	12	474	39.50	4	8	0
26. Northern Ill.	13	521	40.08	7	6	0
27. UCF	12	484	40.33	4	8	0
28. New Mexico	13	544	41.85	6	7	0
29. Southern Miss.	14	589	42.07	9	5	0
30. Indiana	12	505	42.08	5	7	0
31. Washington	12	508	42.33	5	7	0
32. Middle Tenn.	13	552	42.46	7	6	0
33. Connecticut	12	511	42.58	4	8	0
34. Rice	13	557	42.85	7	6	0
34. Alabama	13	557	42.85	6	7	0
36. Ohio St.	13	564	43.38	12	1	0
37. Boston College	13	566	43.54	10	3	0
38. Michigan	13	570	43.85	11	2	0
38. Minnesota	13	570	43.85	6	7	0
40. Nebraska	14	614	43.86	9	5	0
41. Pittsburgh	12	527	43.92	6	6	0
42. Tulsa	13	572	44.00	8	5	0
43. Wake Forest	14	619	44.21	11	3	0
44. Iowa	13	581	44.69	6	7	0
45. Louisville	13	582	44.77	12	1	0
46. Ball St.	12	548	45.67	5	7	0
47. Auburn	13	595	45.77	11	2	0
48. Wyoming	12	550	45.83	6	6	0
49. La.-Lafayette	12	553	46.08	6	6	0
50. Kansas	12	554	46.17	6	6	0
51. Buffalo	12	555	46.25	2	10	0
52. Colorado	12	559	46.58	2	10	0
52. Temple	12	559	46.58	1	11	0
54. Syracuse	12	562	46.83	4	8	0
55. Georgia	13	611	47.00	9	4	0
55. Duke	12	564	47.00	0	12	0
57. Louisiana Tech	13	612	47.08	3	10	0
58. Utah St.	12	565	47.08	1	11	0
59. Oklahoma St.	13	614	47.23	7	6	0
60. Washington St.	12	568	47.33	6	6	0
61. California	13	620	47.69	10	3	0
62. Tulane	12	574	47.83	4	8	0
63. Texas A&M	13	623	47.92	9	4	0
64. Arizona	12	578	48.17	6	6	0
64. Bowling Green	12	578	48.17	4	8	0
66. Boise St.	13	648	49.85	13	0	0
67. Southern California	13	652	50.15	11	2	0
68. Central Mich.	14	703	50.21	10	4	0
69. LSU	13	657	50.54	11	2	0
70. Arkansas St.	12	609	50.75	6	6	0
71. Texas	13	661	50.85	10	3	0
72. Georgia Tech	14	713	50.93	9	5	0
73. Virginia Tech	13	664	51.08	10	3	0
74. North Texas	12	619	51.58	3	9	0
75. San Diego St.	12	620	51.67	3	9	0
76. Mississippi St.	12	623	51.92	3	9	0
77. South Carolina	13	678	52.15	8	5	0
78. Fla. Atlantic	12	632	52.67	5	7	0
79. North Carolina	12	633	52.75	3	9	0
80. Kentucky	13	687	52.85	8	5	0
81. Notre Dame	13	695	53.46	10	3	0
82. SMU	12	642	53.50	6	6	0
83. La.-Monroe	12	643	53.58	4	8	0
84. Florida St.	13	697	53.62	7	6	0
85. Arkansas	14	754	53.86	10	4	0
86. UTEP	12	651	54.25	5	7	0
87. Miami (Ohio)	12	656	54.67	2	10	0
88. Marshall	12	668	55.67	5	7	0
89. Western Mich.	13	724	55.69	8	5	0
90. Michigan St.	12	672	56.00	4	8	0
91. Baylor	12	678	56.50	4	8	0
92. UNLV	12	685	57.08	2	10	0
93. Utah	13	744	57.23	8	5	0
94. Ohio	14	804	57.43	9	5	0
95. Kansas St.	13	747	57.46	7	6	0
96. Troy	13	750	57.69	8	5	0
97. Kent St.	12	696	58.00	6	6	0
97. North Carolina St.	12	696	58.00	3	9	0
99. Houston	14	813	58.07	10	4	0
100. Cincinnati	13	755	58.08	8	5	0
101. UAB	12	702	58.50	3	9	0
102. Eastern Mich.	12	709	59.08	1	11	0
103. Brigham Young	13	769	59.15	11	2	0
104. Oregon St.	14	837	59.79	10	4	0
105. Oregon	13	780	60.00	7	6	0
106. UCLA	13	781	60.08	7	6	0
107. TCU	13	788	60.62	11	2	0
108. Miami (Fla.)	13	805	61.92	7	6	0
109. Florida	14	888	63.43	13	1	0
110. Florida Int'l	12	769	64.08	0	12	0
111. Arizona St.	13	835	64.23	7	6	0
112. Texas Tech	13	844	64.92	8	5	0
113. Hawaii	14	929	66.36	11	3	0
114. West Virginia	13	867	66.69	11	2	0
115. Toledo	12	801	66.75	5	7	0
116. South Fla.	13	916	70.46	9	4	0
117. New Mexico St.	12	885	73.75	4	8	0
118. Akron	12	888	74.00	5	7	0
119. Idaho	12	921	76.75	4	8	0

Punt Return Yardage Defense

Rank, Team	Ret	Return Yds	Yds/Ret	W	L	T
1. Iowa	14	33	2.36	6	7	0
2. Utah	19	45	2.37	8	5	0
3. Eastern Mich.	12	37	3.08	1	11	0
4. UTEP	21	73	3.48	5	7	0
5. Ohio	18	65	3.61	9	5	0
6. Kentucky	22	80	3.64	8	5	0
7. Florida	19	71	3.74	13	1	0
8. Nebraska	18	73	4.06	9	5	0
9. Oklahoma	20	83	4.15	11	3	0
10. Penn St.	24	107	4.46	9	4	0
11. Texas	21	100	4.76	10	3	0
12. North Texas	33	160	4.85	3	9	0
13. Georgia Tech	33	164	4.97	9	5	0
14. Troy	20	100	5.00	8	5	0
14. Wake Forest	14	70	5.00	11	3	0
16. Wisconsin	31	177	5.71	12	1	0
17. Vanderbilt	16	95	5.94	4	8	0
18. North Carolina St.	29	181	6.24	3	9	0
19. Connecticut	30	191	6.37	4	8	0
20. Navy	19	122	6.42	9	4	0
21. Virginia	35	225	6.43	5	7	0
22. Texas Tech	21	136	6.48	8	5	0
23. Central Mich.	23	149	6.48	10	4	0
24. TCU	27	176	6.52	11	2	0
25. Mississippi	32	216	6.75	4	8	0
26. Kansas	18	123	6.83	6	6	0
27. Miami (Fla.)	18	124	6.89	7	6	0
28. Stanford	31	214	6.90	1	11	0
29. Michigan	27	187	6.93	11	2	0
30. California	19	132	6.95	10	3	0
31. Boston College	22	156	7.09	10	3	0
32. Louisville	19	135	7.11	12	1	0
33. Ball St.	26	186	7.15	5	7	0
34. Alabama	26	190	7.31	6	7	0
35. Arizona St.	20	148	7.40	7	6	0
36. Clemson	18	136	7.56	8	5	0
37. Utah St.	42	318	7.57	1	11	0
38. UCF	17	129	7.59	4	8	0
39. Army	23	178	7.74	3	9	0
40. Hawaii	8	62	7.75	11	3	0

Rank, Team	Ret	Return Yds	Yds/Ret	W	L	T
41. UCLA	29	227	7.83	7	6	0
42. Marshall	12	94	7.83	5	7	0
43. New Mexico St.	7	55	7.86	4	8	0
44. North Carolina	31	244	7.87	3	9	0
45. Ohio St.	15	119	7.93	12	1	0
46. Purdue	21	167	7.95	8	6	0
47. Arkansas St.	21	168	8.00	6	6	0
48. Middle Tenn.	31	250	8.06	7	6	0
49. Iowa St.	27	218	8.07	4	8	0
50. Nevada	25	202	8.08	8	5	0
51. Minnesota	29	235	8.10	6	7	0
52. Southern California	18	146	8.11	11	2	0
53. Virginia Tech	26	212	8.15	10	3	0
54. Southern Miss.	26	213	8.19	9	5	0
55. Arkansas	19	156	8.21	10	4	0
56. Syracuse	24	199	8.29	4	8	0
57. Pittsburgh	23	191	8.30	6	6	0
58. Northwestern	30	250	8.33	4	8	0
58. Tulsa	21	175	8.33	8	5	0
60. Michigan St.	23	192	8.35	4	8	0
61. Kent St.	17	142	8.35	6	6	0
62. Akron	31	260	8.39	5	7	0
63. Buffalo	38	320	8.42	2	10	0
64. Fla. Atlantic	27	229	8.48	5	7	0
65. Kansas St.	25	213	8.52	7	6	0
66. Idaho	35	304	8.69	4	8	0
67. Brigham Young	15	131	8.73	11	2	0
68. Washington St.	29	257	8.86	6	6	0
69. San Jose St.	26	236	9.08	9	4	0
70. Miami (Ohio)	27	250	9.26	2	10	0
71. Georgia	20	186	9.30	9	4	0
72. Colorado	32	299	9.34	2	10	0
73. West Virginia	17	160	9.41	11	2	0
74. Louisiana Tech	27	257	9.52	3	10	0
75. Indiana	31	297	9.58	5	7	0
76. Air Force	15	144	9.60	4	8	0
77. Baylor	31	298	9.61	4	8	0
78. La.-Lafayette	28	270	9.64	6	6	0
79. Texas A&M	25	242	9.68	9	4	0
80. Mississippi St.	43	422	9.81	3	9	0
81. Cincinnati	23	226	9.83	8	5	0
82. Auburn	18	177	9.83	11	2	0
83. Boise St.	22	220	10.00	13	0	0
84. Colorado St.	31	311	10.03	4	8	0
85. San Diego St.	30	308	10.27	3	9	0
86. SMU	22	226	10.27	6	6	0
87. Rice	19	197	10.37	7	6	0
88. Tennessee	24	254	10.58	9	4	0
89. Tulane	37	392	10.59	4	8	0
90. Northern Ill.	22	234	10.64	7	6	0
91. UAB	19	203	10.68	3	9	0
92. Duke	37	396	10.70	0	12	0
93. Wyoming	30	322	10.73	6	6	0
94. Missouri	17	188	11.06	8	5	0
95. Memphis	14	156	11.14	2	10	0
96. Oregon	15	168	11.20	7	6	0
97. Houston	25	281	11.24	10	4	0
98. Oregon St.	26	295	11.35	10	4	0
99. Western Mich.	27	307	11.37	8	5	0
100. Illinois	22	251	11.41	2	10	0
101. Notre Dame	21	242	11.52	10	3	0
102. Florida St.	19	221	11.63	7	6	0
103. New Mexico	23	269	11.70	6	7	0
104. Temple	42	492	11.71	1	11	0
105. Arizona	31	364	11.74	6	6	0
106. LSU	15	178	11.87	11	2	0
107. La.-Monroe	19	229	12.05	4	8	0
108. East Caro.	22	271	12.32	7	6	0
109. South Carolina	14	187	13.36	8	5	0
110. Rutgers	26	352	13.54	11	2	0
111. Toledo	15	204	13.60	5	7	0
112. Maryland	18	250	13.89	9	4	0
113. South Fla.	22	307	13.95	9	4	0
114. Bowling Green	16	225	14.06	4	8	0
115. Oklahoma St.	28	402	14.36	7	6	0
116. Washington	22	328	14.91	5	7	0
117. Florida Int'l	34	514	15.12	0	12	0
118. Fresno St.	21	331	15.76	4	8	0
119. UNLV	23	364	15.83	2	10	0

Kickoff Return Yardage Defense

Rank, Team	Ret	Return Yds	Yds/Ret	W	L	T
1. Air Force	37	494	13.35	4	8	0
2. Purdue	49	717	14.63	8	6	0
3. Ohio	39	579	14.85	9	5	0
4. Tulsa	53	827	15.60	8	5	0
5. Army	40	634	15.85	3	9	0
6. Western Mich.	35	560	16.00	8	5	0
7. Marshall	42	706	16.81	5	7	0
8. Houston	60	1,025	17.08	10	4	0
9. West Virginia	62	1,060	17.10	11	2	0
10. Boston College	57	975	17.11	10	3	0
11. Toledo	47	811	17.26	5	7	0
12. San Jose St.	45	783	17.40	9	4	0
13. Oklahoma	49	853	17.41	11	3	0
14. North Carolina	28	489	17.46	3	9	0
15. Middle Tenn.	48	848	17.67	7	6	0
16. Nebraska	61	1,096	17.97	9	5	0
17. Central Mich.	64	1,154	18.03	10	4	0
18. Kansas St.	35	635	18.14	7	6	0
19. Minnesota	41	746	18.20	6	7	0
20. Texas A&M	46	838	18.22	9	4	0
21. Auburn	13	237	18.23	11	2	0
22. Boise St.	70	1,282	18.31	13	0	0
23. Penn St.	37	679	18.35	9	4	0
24. Kentucky	49	902	18.41	8	5	0
25. Ohio St.	42	774	18.43	12	1	0
26. Connecticut	44	818	18.59	4	8	0
27. TCU	56	1,051	18.77	11	2	0
28. Tennessee	35	657	18.77	9	4	0
29. Southern California	37	695	18.78	11	2	0
30. Duke	24	452	18.83	0	12	0
31. UNLV	37	702	18.97	2	10	0
32. Troy	40	761	19.03	8	5	0
33. East Caro.	42	800	19.05	7	6	0
34. Syracuse	30	573	19.10	4	8	0
35. Indiana	37	707	19.11	5	7	0
36. Alabama	56	1,080	19.29	6	7	0
37. Brigham Young	59	1,139	19.31	11	2	0
38. Washington	32	619	19.34	5	7	0
39. Florida	61	1,181	19.36	13	1	0
40. SMU	43	837	19.47	6	6	0
41. Texas	51	994	19.49	10	3	0
42. Iowa St.	30	588	19.60	4	8	0
43. Arizona	14	276	19.71	6	6	0
44. Vanderbilt	45	889	19.76	4	8	0
45. Utah	41	811	19.78	8	5	0
46. Nevada	34	674	19.82	8	5	0
47. Colorado St.	26	516	19.85	4	8	0
48. LSU	51	1,013	19.86	11	2	0
49. Rice	50	996	19.92	7	6	0
50. Notre Dame	59	1,177	19.95	10	3	0
51. Cincinnati	44	878	19.95	8	5	0
52. New Mexico	23	459	19.96	6	7	0
53. Akron	39	779	19.97	5	7	0
54. Northwestern	28	563	20.11	4	8	0
55. Miami (Fla.)	33	664	20.12	7	6	0
56. South Fla.	41	825	20.12	9	4	0
57. Maryland	47	951	20.23	9	4	0
58. North Texas	29	588	20.28	3	9	0
59. South Carolina	43	874	20.33	8	5	0
60. Louisville	70	1,424	20.34	12	1	0
61. New Mexico St.	56	1,141	20.38	4	8	0
62. Pittsburgh	41	837	20.41	6	6	0
63. UCLA	47	961	20.45	7	6	0
64. Navy	53	1,088	20.53	9	4	0
65. Oregon St.	44	905	20.57	10	4	0
66. Wyoming	35	721	20.60	6	6	0
67. Mississippi St.	33	682	20.67	3	9	0
68. Wisconsin	32	663	20.72	12	1	0
69. Arkansas St.	39	813	20.85	6	6	0
70. Temple	27	564	20.89	1	11	0
71. Stanford	19	400	21.05	1	11	0
72. Michigan St.	40	843	21.08	4	8	0
73. Missouri	52	1,097	21.10	8	5	0
74. Oregon	49	1,037	21.16	7	6	0
75. UCF	47	995	21.17	4	8	0
76. Oklahoma St.	48	1,017	21.19	7	6	0
77. Miami (Ohio)	38	806	21.21	2	10	0
78. San Diego St.	29	616	21.24	3	9	0
78. Virginia Tech	29	616	21.24	10	3	0
80. Louisiana Tech	40	853	21.33	3	10	0

Rank, Team	Ret	Return Yds	Yds/Ret	W	L	T
81. Utah St.	30	640	21.33	1	11	0
82. Eastern Mich.	23	491	21.35	1	11	0
83. Arkansas	48	1,026	21.38	10	4	0
84. Northern Ill.	36	771	21.42	7	6	0
85. Ball St.	44	945	21.48	5	7	0
86. Buffalo	34	732	21.53	2	10	0
87. Colorado	18	392	21.78	2	10	0
88. Hawaii	66	1,439	21.80	11	3	0
89. Georgia	50	1,093	21.86	9	4	0
90. Texas Tech	36	788	21.89	8	5	0
91. Memphis	51	1,119	21.94	2	10	0
92. Michigan	60	1,318	21.97	11	2	0
93. La.-Lafayette	44	970	22.05	6	6	0
94. Rutgers	47	1,037	22.06	11	2	0
95. Illinois	31	684	22.06	2	10	0
96. Kent St.	23	510	22.17	6	6	0
96. Wake Forest	46	1,020	22.17	11	3	0
98. Fresno St.	31	692	22.32	4	8	0
99. UAB	30	671	22.37	3	9	0
100. California	45	1,007	22.38	10	3	0
101. Mississippi	26	583	22.42	4	8	0
102. Virginia	21	474	22.57	5	7	0
103. Florida Int'l	22	497	22.59	0	12	0
104. UTEP	49	1,107	22.59	5	7	0
105. La.-Monroe	43	973	22.63	4	8	0
106. Arizona St.	30	685	22.83	7	6	0
107. Iowa	42	964	22.95	6	7	0
108. Baylor	31	716	23.10	4	8	0
109. Tulane	40	926	23.15	4	8	0
110. Idaho	35	819	23.40	4	8	0
111. Washington St.	45	1,060	23.56	6	6	0
112. Bowling Green	40	946	23.65	4	8	0
113. Clemson	57	1,363	23.91	8	5	0
114. Southern Miss.	43	1,041	24.21	9	5	0
115. Florida St.	43	1,051	24.44	7	6	0
116. North Carolina St.	29	711	24.52	3	9	0
117. Fla. Atlantic	40	994	24.85	5	7	0
118. Kansas	32	814	25.44	6	6	0
119. Georgia Tech	50	1,349	26.98	9	5	0

Third-Down Efficiency Offense

Rank, Team	Att	Conv	Pct.
1. Hawaii	133	77	57.89
2. Brigham Young	168	94	55.95
3. Air Force	174	95	54.60
4. Texas A&M	177	89	50.28
5. West Virginia	153	76	49.67
6. Ohio St.	159	78	49.06
7. Missouri	190	92	48.42
8. LSU	145	70	48.28
9. Tennessee	162	78	48.15
10. Oregon	181	87	48.07
11. Navy	173	83	47.98
12. South Carolina	151	72	47.68
13. Purdue	191	90	47.12
14. Louisville	160	74	46.25
15. Southern California	178	82	46.07
16. Tulsa	161	74	45.96
17. Nebraska	199	90	45.23
18. Marshall	144	65	45.14
19. TCU	179	80	44.69
20. Utah	187	83	44.39
21. Florida	167	74	44.31
21. Oklahoma St.	167	74	44.31
23. Houston	174	76	43.68
24. Boise St.	154	67	43.51
25. Arkansas St.	176	76	43.18
25. UCF	176	76	43.18
27. East Caro.	186	80	43.01
28. Nevada	157	67	42.68
29. California	163	69	42.33
30. Michigan St.	173	73	42.20
31. Clemson	162	68	41.98
32. Arkansas	167	70	41.92
33. New Mexico St.	175	73	41.71
34. Texas	156	65	41.67
35. Alabama	185	77	41.62
36. Southern Miss.	181	75	41.44
37. Wisconsin	169	70	41.42
38. Bowling Green	186	76	40.86
39. Memphis	164	67	40.85
40. Cincinnati	196	80	40.82
41. Colorado St.	177	72	40.68
42. Iowa	160	65	40.63
43. Rutgers	170	69	40.59
44. Pittsburgh	143	58	40.56
45. Auburn	156	63	40.38
46. Oklahoma	177	71	40.11
47. Michigan	180	72	40.00
47. Middle Tenn.	175	70	40.00
47. SMU	155	62	40.00
50. Tulane	173	69	39.88
50. San Jose St.	163	65	39.88
52. Central Mich.	177	70	39.55
52. Notre Dame	177	70	39.55
54. Toledo	193	76	39.38
55. La.-Monroe	155	61	39.35
56. Georgia	159	62	38.99
57. Iowa St.	158	61	38.61
58. Boston College	184	71	38.59
58. New Mexico	184	71	38.59
60. Baylor	165	63	38.18
61. Western Mich.	198	75	37.88
62. Arizona St.	169	64	37.87
63. Georgia Tech	196	74	37.76
64. Penn St.	186	70	37.63
65. South Fla.	165	62	37.58
65. Fresno St.	157	59	37.58
67. Army	155	58	37.42
68. Rice	182	68	37.36
68. Fla. Atlantic	174	65	37.36
70. Washington St.	166	62	37.35
71. Kentucky	170	63	37.06
72. Texas Tech	149	55	36.91
73. Minnesota	166	61	36.75
74. Maryland	158	58	36.71
75. UTEP	150	55	36.67
76. Oregon St.	175	64	36.57
77. Kansas	167	61	36.53
78. Syracuse	173	63	36.42
79. Northern Ill.	177	64	36.16
80. Illinois	169	61	36.09
81. UCLA	183	66	36.07
82. Virginia Tech	173	62	35.84
83. Mississippi St.	162	58	35.80
84. Northwestern	160	57	35.63
85. Wake Forest	171	60	35.09
86. Connecticut	180	63	35.00
87. Louisiana Tech	169	59	34.91
88. Troy	178	62	34.83
89. Kansas St.	176	61	34.66
90. Ohio	194	67	34.54
91. Miami (Fla.)	168	58	34.52
92. North Carolina	155	53	34.19
93. San Diego St.	162	55	33.95
94. Florida St.	177	60	33.90
95. La.-Lafayette	160	54	33.75
96. Washington	172	58	33.72
97. Indiana	167	56	33.53
98. Colorado	159	53	33.33
99. Vanderbilt	149	49	32.89
100. Ball St.	153	50	32.68
101. Kent St.	151	49	32.45
102. North Carolina St.	170	55	32.35
103. Buffalo	155	50	32.26
104. UAB	149	48	32.21
105. Wyoming	168	54	32.14
106. Idaho	157	50	31.85
107. UNLV	161	51	31.68
108. Miami (Ohio)	169	53	31.36
109. Arizona	173	53	30.64
110. Virginia	167	51	30.54
111. Stanford	149	45	30.20
112. Duke	166	50	30.12
113. Eastern Mich.	163	49	30.06
114. Mississippi	150	44	29.33
115. North Texas	159	46	28.93
116. Utah St.	161	46	28.57
117. Akron	157	44	28.03
118. Temple	155	38	24.52
119. Florida Int'l	166	39	23.49

Fourth-Down Efficiency Offense

Rank, Team	Att	Conv	Pct.
1. Boise St.	21	17	80.95
2. Auburn	14	11	78.57
3. LSU	17	13	76.47
4. Southern California	28	20	71.43
5. Oklahoma St.	20	14	70.00
6. Colorado St.	16	11	68.75
6. Texas	16	11	68.75
8. Western Mich.	25	17	68.00
9. Troy	24	16	66.67
9. North Texas	21	14	66.67
9. Wyoming	21	14	66.67
9. Arizona	15	10	66.67
9. Army	15	10	66.67
9. Louisville	12	8	66.67
9. Michigan	12	8	66.67
9. Iowa	9	6	66.67
9. Wake Forest	6	4	66.67
18. Minnesota	28	18	64.29
18. Georgia	14	9	64.29
18. North Carolina	14	9	64.29
21. Memphis	22	14	63.64
21. Ohio St.	11	7	63.64
21. Oklahoma	11	7	63.64
24. Navy	19	12	63.16
25. Tulsa	21	13	61.90
26. Nebraska	23	14	60.87
27. Clemson	10	6	60.00
28. La.-Lafayette	32	19	59.38
29. New Mexico St.	44	26	59.09
30. Rice	17	10	58.82
31. California	12	7	58.33
32. Houston	33	19	57.58
32. Notre Dame	33	19	57.58
34. South Fla.	23	13	56.52
35. Texas A&M	16	9	56.25
36. Akron	27	15	55.56
36. UAB	18	10	55.56
36. East Caro.	18	10	55.56
36. West Virginia	9	5	55.56
40. Oregon St.	20	11	55.00
40. Vanderbilt	20	11	55.00
42. UNLV	33	18	54.55
42. Fla. Atlantic	22	12	54.55
42. Air Force	22	12	54.55
42. Brigham Young	11	6	54.55
42. Rutgers	11	6	54.55
42. Tennessee	11	6	54.55
48. Alabama	13	7	53.85
48. New Mexico	13	7	53.85
50. Maryland	15	8	53.33
50. San Jose St.	15	8	53.33
52. Missouri	17	9	52.94
52. San Diego St.	17	9	52.94
52. Pittsburgh	17	9	52.94
55. Toledo	36	19	52.78
56. Connecticut	19	10	52.63
56. Northern Ill.	19	10	52.63
58. Nevada	21	11	52.38
59. Kentucky	22	11	50.00
59. Florida	18	9	50.00
59. North Carolina St.	14	7	50.00
59. Georgia Tech	12	6	50.00
59. Kansas	12	6	50.00
59. Idaho	10	5	50.00
65. Bowling Green	33	16	48.48
66. Texas Tech	23	11	47.83
67. Central Mich.	17	8	47.06
68. Cincinnati	13	6	46.15
68. Middle Tenn.	13	6	46.15
68. Ohio	13	6	46.15
71. Iowa St.	24	11	45.83
72. Florida St.	11	5	45.45
72. TCU	11	5	45.45
74. South Carolina	20	9	45.00
74. Washington St.	20	9	45.00
74. Washington	20	9	45.00
77. Ball St.	18	8	44.44
77. Illinois	9	4	44.44
79. Fresno St.	16	7	43.75
80. Kansas St.	23	10	43.48
80. Mississippi	23	10	43.48
82. Oregon	26	11	42.31
83. Utah	19	8	42.11
84. UCF	24	10	41.67
85. Miami (Ohio)	29	12	41.38
86. Kent St.	22	9	40.91
87. Hawaii	20	8	40.00
87. Eastern Mich.	15	6	40.00
87. Marshall	10	4	40.00
90. SMU	13	5	38.46
91. Baylor	11	4	36.36
91. UCLA	11	4	36.36
93. Arizona St.	20	7	35.00
93. La.-Monroe	20	7	35.00
95. Indiana	23	8	34.78
96. Duke	24	8	33.33
96. Boston College	21	7	33.33
96. Penn St.	18	6	33.33
96. Utah St.	18	6	33.33
96. Southern Miss.	18	6	33.33
96. Stanford	18	6	33.33
96. Buffalo	15	5	33.33
96. Wisconsin	15	5	33.33
96. Mississippi St.	15	5	33.33
96. Virginia	9	3	33.33
106. Michigan St.	16	5	31.25
107. Arkansas	13	4	30.77
108. Purdue	17	5	29.41
109. Florida Int'l	24	7	29.17
110. Tulane	14	4	28.57
111. Syracuse	11	3	27.27
111. Virginia Tech	11	3	27.27
113. Miami (Fla.)	8	2	25.00
114. Arkansas St.	17	4	23.53
115. UTEP	13	3	23.08
116. Louisiana Tech	15	3	20.00
117. Northwestern	11	2	18.18
118. Temple	23	4	17.39
119. Colorado	13	2	15.38

Third-Down Efficiency Defense

Rank, Team	Att	Conv	Pct.
1. Virginia Tech	185	50	27.03
2. Georgia	164	45	27.44
3. New Mexico St.	128	36	28.13
4. Wisconsin	181	51	28.18
5. UCLA	176	50	28.41
6. Texas A&M	153	44	28.76
7. Michigan	182	53	29.12
8. Rutgers	183	55	30.05
9. Southern Miss.	179	54	30.17
10. Oklahoma	192	58	30.21
11. Louisville	180	55	30.56
12. Miami (Fla.)	170	52	30.59
13. TCU	173	53	30.64
14. Western Mich.	170	53	31.18
15. Georgia Tech	208	66	31.73
16. LSU	182	58	31.87
17. Florida St.	191	61	31.94
18. Penn St.	190	61	32.11
19. California	167	54	32.34
20. Virginia	170	55	32.35
21. Fla. Atlantic	145	47	32.41
22. Arkansas	188	61	32.45
23. Boise St.	166	54	32.53
24. Oregon St.	178	58	32.58
25. Brigham Young	177	58	32.77
26. Florida	186	61	32.80
27. Nebraska	192	63	32.81
28. Ohio St.	176	58	32.95
29. North Carolina St.	166	55	33.13
29. Connecticut	160	53	33.13
31. Ohio	186	62	33.33
32. Cincinnati	179	60	33.52
33. Kent St.	170	57	33.53
34. Alabama	161	54	33.54
35. Washington	169	57	33.73
36. Notre Dame	160	55	34.38
37. Wake Forest	185	64	34.59
37. Toledo	159	55	34.59

STATISTICAL LEADERS

Rank, Team	Att	Conv	Pct.
39. Wyoming	170	59	34.71
40. La.-Lafayette	152	53	34.87
41. Boston College	186	65	34.95
42. Oregon	177	62	35.03
43. Nevada	157	56	35.67
44. Akron	184	66	35.87
45. Michigan St.	160	58	36.25
46. Clemson	190	69	36.32
47. Texas	170	62	36.47
48. Middle Tenn.	159	58	36.48
49. Mississippi St.	148	54	36.49
50. Kansas St.	185	68	36.76
51. Arizona St.	174	64	36.78
52. South Carolina	163	60	36.81
53. Tulsa	170	63	37.06
54. South Fla.	191	71	37.17
55. East Caro.	172	64	37.21
56. Oklahoma St.	179	67	37.43
57. Buffalo	136	51	37.50
58. Colorado St.	156	59	37.82
59. Arkansas St.	137	52	37.96
60. La.-Monroe	155	59	38.06
61. Utah	176	67	38.07
62. Troy	186	71	38.17
63. Ball St.	165	63	38.18
64. Auburn	166	64	38.55
65. Arizona	153	59	38.56
66. Missouri	181	70	38.67
67. Washington St.	168	65	38.69
68. Southern California	191	74	38.74
69. Temple	139	54	38.85
70. Central Mich.	199	78	39.20
70. San Jose St.	176	69	39.20
72. Florida Int'l	173	68	39.31
73. Hawaii	183	72	39.34
74. Purdue	190	76	40.00
74. Illinois	180	72	40.00
76. Kansas	186	75	40.32
77. Army	151	61	40.40
78. Rice	160	65	40.63
79. Vanderbilt	150	61	40.67
80. Bowling Green	145	59	40.69
81. Texas Tech	179	73	40.78
82. Iowa	191	78	40.84
83. Northwestern	159	65	40.88
84. Northern Ill.	176	72	40.91
85. Tennessee	170	70	41.18
86. Pittsburgh	177	73	41.24
86. West Virginia	177	73	41.24
88. Miami (Ohio)	159	66	41.51
89. Navy	168	70	41.67
90. UNLV	153	64	41.83
91. Eastern Mich.	160	67	41.88
92. Indiana	155	65	41.94
93. UAB	148	63	42.57
94. Baylor	162	69	42.59
94. Mississippi	162	69	42.59
96. Maryland	180	77	42.78
97. North Carolina	153	66	43.14
98. New Mexico	189	82	43.39
99. UTEP	164	72	43.90
100. Duke	157	69	43.95
101. North Texas	165	73	44.24
102. San Diego St.	164	73	44.51
103. Idaho	143	64	44.76
104. Syracuse	162	73	45.06
105. Iowa St.	157	71	45.22
106. Tulane	161	73	45.34
107. SMU	173	79	45.66
108. Fresno St.	164	75	45.73
109. Kentucky	157	73	46.50
110. Houston	193	90	46.63
111. Marshall	162	76	46.91
112. Utah St.	146	69	47.26
113. Colorado	178	85	47.75
114. UCF	165	79	47.88
115. Stanford	163	79	48.47
116. Minnesota	168	82	48.81
117. Memphis	153	75	49.02
118. Louisiana Tech	159	78	49.06
119. Air Force	141	79	56.03

Fourth-Down Efficiency Defense

Rank, Team	Att	Conv	Pct.
1. Arizona	10	1	10.00
2. North Carolina St.	6	1	16.67
3. Wisconsin	20	4	20.00
4. Florida St.	14	3	21.43
5. Cincinnati	18	4	22.22
6. Kansas	16	4	25.00
7. Tulane	19	5	26.32
8. Arkansas	18	5	27.78
8. SMU	18	5	27.78
8. Ohio	18	5	27.78
11. Virginia Tech	10	3	30.00
12. Louisville	22	7	31.82
13. Hawaii	24	8	33.33
13. Boston College	18	6	33.33
13. Florida	18	6	33.33
16. Houston	22	8	36.36
16. New Mexico	22	8	36.36
16. Minnesota	22	8	36.36
19. Notre Dame	19	7	36.84
19. Southern California	19	7	36.84
21. Kentucky	24	9	37.50
21. Marshall	16	6	37.50
23. Missouri	21	8	38.10
24. Miami (Fla.)	13	5	38.46
24. Syracuse	13	5	38.46
26. Clemson	23	9	39.13
26. Nebraska	23	9	39.13
28. Navy	25	10	40.00
28. LSU	20	8	40.00
28. Michigan	20	8	40.00
28. UNLV	15	6	40.00
28. Rutgers	15	6	40.00
33. Texas	12	5	41.67
33. Vanderbilt	12	5	41.67
35. Auburn	19	8	42.11
36. Maryland	14	6	42.86
37. Northern Ill.	16	7	43.75
38. New Mexico St.	25	11	44.00
39. Florida Int'l	18	8	44.44
39. TCU	18	8	44.44
41. Ball St.	20	9	45.00
41. Eastern Mich.	20	9	45.00
43. Nevada	22	10	45.45
43. Oklahoma	22	10	45.45
43. Baylor	11	5	45.45
43. Miami (Ohio)	11	5	45.45
47. Brigham Young	24	11	45.83
48. Tennessee	13	6	46.15
49. Duke	15	7	46.67
49. Georgia	15	7	46.67
51. South Fla.	19	9	47.37
52. La.-Monroe	23	11	47.83
52. Penn St.	23	11	47.83
54. Kent St.	25	12	48.00
54. Pittsburgh	25	12	48.00
56. Middle Tenn.	22	11	50.00
56. North Texas	20	10	50.00
56. San Diego St.	20	10	50.00
56. Army	18	9	50.00
56. Stanford	16	8	50.00
56. Arkansas St.	14	7	50.00
56. Fresno St.	14	7	50.00
56. Colorado St.	14	7	50.00
56. Arizona St.	12	6	50.00
56. UAB	10	5	50.00
56. Idaho	10	5	50.00
67. Akron	29	15	51.72
68. UCLA	27	14	51.85
68. San Jose St.	27	14	51.85
70. Purdue	25	13	52.00
71. Boise St.	19	10	52.63
71. UTEP	19	10	52.63
73. Buffalo	17	9	52.94
73. Colorado	17	9	52.94
75. UCF	15	8	53.33
76. Northwestern	13	7	53.85
76. Troy	13	7	53.85
78. Oregon St.	22	12	54.55
79. Southern Miss.	31	17	54.84
80. Fla. Atlantic	20	11	55.00

Rank, Team	Att	Conv	Pct.
80. La.-Lafayette	20	11	55.00
80. Washington St.	20	11	55.00
80. West Virginia	20	11	55.00
84. Wyoming	18	10	55.56
85. California	25	14	56.00
86. Rice	16	9	56.25
87. Central Mich.	23	13	56.52
88. Bowling Green	14	8	57.14
88. Mississippi	14	8	57.14
88. Texas Tech	14	8	57.14
88. Air Force	14	8	57.14
92. Iowa	19	11	57.89
92. Western Mich.	19	11	57.89
92. Wake Forest	19	11	57.89
92. Washington	19	11	57.89
96. Alabama	17	10	58.82
96. Ohio St.	17	10	58.82
98. Toledo	22	13	59.09
99. Kansas St.	25	15	60.00
99. Georgia Tech	15	9	60.00
101. Temple	21	13	61.90
102. Illinois	8	5	62.50
103. Oregon	19	12	63.16
103. Utah St.	19	12	63.16
105. Mississippi St.	11	7	63.64
106. Texas A&M	17	11	64.71
107. South Carolina	27	18	66.67
107. Connecticut	15	10	66.67
107. Michigan St.	15	10	66.67
107. Iowa St.	12	8	66.67
107. Memphis	12	8	66.67
107. North Carolina	6	4	66.67
113. Oklahoma St.	16	11	68.75
114. Louisiana Tech	17	12	70.59
115. Virginia	14	10	71.43
116. Utah	11	8	72.73
117. Tulsa	15	11	73.33
118. East Caro.	24	19	79.17
119. Indiana	5	4	80.00

Tackles for Loss

Rank, Team	G	Solo	Ast	Yds	Total	TFL/Gm
1. Florida Int'l	12	75	46	341	98.0	8.17
2. Florida St.	13	75	61	440	105.5	8.12
3. Middle Tenn.	13	90	30	436	105.0	8.08
4. Kent St.	12	69	54	332	96.0	8.00
5. UCLA	13	89	28	441	103.0	7.92
5. Rutgers	13	81	44	403	103.0	7.92
7. Miami (Fla.)	13	86	30	380	101.0	7.77
8. Oklahoma St.	13	87	26	401	100.0	7.69
9. Oregon St.	14	97	20	528	107.0	7.64
10. TCU	13	79	40	450	99.0	7.62
11. Ohio	14	71	64	381	103.0	7.36
12. SMU	12	69	34	378	86.0	7.17
13. Michigan	13	86	14	440	93.0	7.15
13. Ohio St.	13	78	30	390	93.0	7.15
15. Texas	13	82	21	442	92.5	7.12
16. Boston College	13	75	34	356	92.0	7.08
16. Clemson	13	83	18	391	92.0	7.08
18. Kansas St.	13	83	16	355	91.0	7.00
18. Troy	13	80	22	402	91.0	7.00
18. Louisville	13	81	20	425	91.0	7.00
21. Arkansas	14	73	48	466	97.0	6.93
22. South Carolina	13	80	20	375	90.0	6.92
22. Western Mich.	13	73	34	449	90.0	6.92
24. Connecticut	12	54	56	289	82.0	6.83
25. Tennessee	13	84	8	290	88.0	6.77
26. Illinois	12	60	42	271	81.0	6.75
27. Southern California	13	73	28	362	87.0	6.69
28. Duke	12	52	56	286	80.0	6.67
28. Washington St.	12	64	32	312	80.0	6.67
30. Cincinnati	13	66	40	367	86.0	6.62
30. South Fla.	13	78	16	395	86.0	6.62
32. Utah	13	66	38	293	85.0	6.54
33. Buffalo	12	61	34	315	78.0	6.50
33. Mississippi St.	12	57	42	288	78.0	6.50
35. Rice	13	80	8	372	84.0	6.46
36. Ball St.	12	61	32	248	77.0	6.42
37. Oklahoma	14	68	43	357	89.5	6.39
38. Pittsburgh	12	67	18	232	76.0	6.33
38. Virginia	12	63	26	304	76.0	6.33
40. Auburn	13	68	28	321	82.0	6.31
41. Georgia Tech	14	75	26	410	88.0	6.29
41. Nebraska	14	73	30	386	88.0	6.29
43. Washington	12	57	36	303	75.0	6.25
44. Arizona St.	13	74	13	310	80.5	6.19
45. Akron	12	54	40	247	74.0	6.17
46. Missouri	13	54	52	354	80.0	6.15
47. UAB	12	60	27	276	73.5	6.13
48. Georgia	13	64	30	315	79.0	6.08
48. North Carolina St.	12	57	32	326	73.0	6.08
50. Southern Miss.	14	74	22	320	85.0	6.07
51. Notre Dame	13	63	30	355	78.0	6.00
52. Kansas	12	53	36	292	71.0	5.92
52. Nevada	13	62	30	347	77.0	5.92
52. Tulane	12	46	50	265	71.0	5.92
55. Purdue	14	76	12	331	82.0	5.86
56. Idaho	12	58	24	246	70.0	5.83
57. Virginia Tech	13	59	32	329	75.0	5.77
58. Bowling Green	12	50	38	308	69.0	5.75
59. Vanderbilt	12	65	6	297	68.0	5.67
60. Florida	14	69	20	351	79.0	5.64
61. Eastern Mich.	12	53	28	227	67.0	5.58
62. Penn St.	13	64	16	364	72.0	5.54
63. Wake Forest	14	65	24	309	77.0	5.50
63. Wyoming	12	51	30	299	66.0	5.50
65. Colorado	12	54	23	266	65.5	5.46
65. Navy	13	54	34	297	71.0	5.46
65. Wisconsin	13	58	26	275	71.0	5.46
68. Central Mich.	14	59	34	323	76.0	5.43
69. Colorado St.	12	54	22	272	65.0	5.42
69. Syracuse	12	51	28	268	65.0	5.42
71. California	13	48	44	244	70.0	5.38
71. Northern Ill.	13	57	26	277	70.0	5.38
73. Marshall	12	50	28	278	64.0	5.33
74. LSU	13	48	42	310	69.0	5.31
75. Brigham Young	13	58	21	267	68.5	5.27
76. Indiana	12	51	24	203	63.0	5.25
76. Toledo	12	46	34	233	63.0	5.25
78. Iowa	13	51	34	243	68.0	5.23
79. UCF	12	51	22	274	62.0	5.17
79. Temple	12	52	20	207	62.0	5.17
81. Boise St.	13	53	28	283	67.0	5.15
81. Texas Tech	13	54	26	253	67.0	5.15
81. Oregon	13	59	16	308	67.0	5.15
84. Hawaii	14	61	22	293	72.0	5.14
85. Fla. Atlantic	12	46	30	207	61.0	5.08
85. New Mexico	13	53	26	300	66.0	5.08
85. Michigan St.	12	48	26	255	61.0	5.08
88. Kentucky	13	56	18	246	65.0	5.00
88. West Virginia	13	56	18	289	65.0	5.00
90. Fresno St.	12	41	36	225	59.0	4.92
90. Miami (Ohio)	12	50	18	265	59.0	4.92
92. UTEP	12	42	33	201	58.5	4.88
93. San Jose St.	13	54	18	220	63.0	4.85
94. Houston	14	42	50	221	67.0	4.79
94. UNLV	12	44	27	197	57.5	4.79
96. Iowa St.	12	48	18	206	57.0	4.75
96. North Texas	12	43	28	181	57.0	4.75
96. San Diego St.	12	53	8	201	57.0	4.75
99. East Caro.	13	50	22	195	61.0	4.69
100. Maryland	13	44	32	204	60.0	4.62
101. Arkansas St.	12	47	16	214	55.0	4.58
101. New Mexico St.	12	34	42	192	55.0	4.58
103. Mississippi	12	41	24	172	53.0	4.42
103. Utah St.	12	37	32	199	53.0	4.42
103. La.-Lafayette	12	44	18	220	53.0	4.42
106. Minnesota	13	47	18	237	56.0	4.31
107. Baylor	12	41	21	175	51.5	4.29
108. Alabama	13	42	26	202	55.0	4.23
108. Texas A&M	13	38	34	238	55.0	4.23
110. Arizona	12	41	18	197	50.0	4.17
110. Army	12	41	18	170	50.0	4.17
110. Northwestern	12	44	12	203	50.0	4.17
113. Tulsa	13	40	28	208	54.0	4.15
114. La.-Monroe	12	43	10	198	48.0	4.00
115. Stanford	12	36	20	181	46.0	3.83
115. Air Force	12	37	18	186	46.0	3.83
117. Memphis	12	33	22	167	44.0	3.67
117. North Carolina	12	42	4	218	44.0	3.67
119. Louisiana Tech	13	24	38	132	43.0	3.31

Fewest Tackles for Loss Allowed

Rank, Team	G	Solo	Ast	Yds	Total	TFL/Gm
1. Purdue	14	46	8	232	50.0	3.57
2. Hawaii	14	46	10	201	51.0	3.64
3. Texas Tech	13	39	18	201	48.0	3.69
4. Rutgers	13	43	18	139	52.0	4.00
4. TCU	13	43	18	167	52.0	4.00
6. Clemson	13	44	18	187	53.0	4.08
6. Minnesota	13	41	24	182	53.0	4.08
8. Brigham Young	13	41	26	210	54.0	4.15
8. Iowa	13	49	10	190	54.0	4.15
10. Ohio St.	13	45	20	231	55.0	4.23
10. Oklahoma St.	13	42	26	201	55.0	4.23
12. Louisville	13	44	26	209	57.0	4.38
13. Memphis	12	40	26	198	53.0	4.42
14. California	13	43	30	219	58.0	4.46
14. Oregon	13	52	12	191	58.0	4.46
16. Fresno St.	12	41	26	209	54.0	4.50
16. Pittsburgh	12	44	20	231	54.0	4.50
18. Southern California	13	48	22	215	59.0	4.54
19. Utah	13	43	34	209	60.0	4.62
20. LSU	13	43	36	234	61.0	4.69
20. Tulsa	13	46	30	187	61.0	4.69
22. Arkansas	14	57	18	224	66.0	4.71
23. South Carolina	13	51	22	246	62.0	4.77
24. Marshall	12	44	27	200	57.5	4.79
24. Southern Miss.	14	53	28	254	67.0	4.79
26. Navy	13	51	24	217	63.0	4.85
27. Houston	14	50	36	315	68.0	4.86
28. Georgia	13	55	18	234	64.0	4.92
28. Michigan	13	61	6	234	64.0	4.92
28. Notre Dame	13	51	26	301	64.0	4.92
28. Tennessee	13	58	12	251	64.0	4.92
32. UCF	12	46	28	184	60.0	5.00
32. La.-Lafayette	12	41	38	189	60.0	5.00
34. Florida	14	62	18	284	71.0	5.07
35. Illinois	12	43	36	271	61.0	5.08
35. La.-Monroe	12	52	18	256	61.0	5.08
37. Oklahoma	14	58	28	235	72.0	5.14
38. Idaho	12	50	24	245	62.0	5.17
38. North Carolina St.	12	53	18	250	62.0	5.17
38. Air Force	12	54	16	192	62.0	5.17
41. Oregon St.	14	59	28	299	73.0	5.21
42. Boise St.	13	53	30	273	68.0	5.23
43. Washington	12	47	32	254	63.0	5.25
44. Alabama	13	58	22	304	69.0	5.31
44. Kansas St.	13	64	10	279	69.0	5.31
46. Texas	13	63	13	263	69.5	5.35
47. Nebraska	14	66	18	296	75.0	5.36
48. Maryland	13	54	32	226	70.0	5.38
49. Georgia Tech	14	68	15	307	75.5	5.39
50. UTEP	12	43	44	275	65.0	5.42
50. Utah St.	12	51	28	214	65.0	5.42
52. Bowling Green	12	54	26	219	67.0	5.58
53. UCLA	13	62	22	281	73.0	5.62
53. Missouri	13	48	50	306	73.0	5.62
55. Arkansas St.	12	56	24	307	68.0	5.67
55. Mississippi St.	12	56	24	297	68.0	5.67
55. Mississippi	12	47	42	301	68.0	5.67
55. Tulane	12	57	22	339	68.0	5.67
59. Texas A&M	13	53	42	248	74.0	5.69
59. Wisconsin	13	65	18	306	74.0	5.69
61. Iowa St.	12	62	14	323	69.0	5.75
62. Auburn	13	57	36	314	75.0	5.77
62. Nevada	13	65	20	328	75.0	5.77
64. Baylor	12	62	16	415	70.0	5.83
64. UNLV	12	58	24	336	70.0	5.83
64. Colorado	12	53	34	291	70.0	5.83
67. Florida St.	13	56	40	289	76.0	5.85
67. San Jose St.	13	60	32	286	76.0	5.85
69. Boston College	13	64	25	315	76.5	5.88
70. Arizona St.	13	67	20	337	77.0	5.92
70. South Fla.	13	67	20	253	77.0	5.92
70. San Diego St.	12	60	22	235	71.0	5.92
73. UAB	12	52	40	335	72.0	6.00
73. Army	12	61	22	276	72.0	6.00
73. West Virginia	13	59	38	246	78.0	6.00
73. Louisiana Tech	13	57	42	345	78.0	6.00
77. New Mexico St.	12	53	40	281	73.0	6.08
77. Virginia Tech	13	56	46	319	79.0	6.08
77. Northwestern	12	59	28	282	73.0	6.08
80. Western Mich.	13	59	41	303	79.5	6.12
81. Central Mich.	14	65	42	376	86.0	6.14
82. Troy	13	67	26	324	80.0	6.15
83. Eastern Mich.	12	62	24	298	74.0	6.17
83. Toledo	12	56	36	335	74.0	6.17
83. Indiana	12	62	24	307	74.0	6.17
86. Kentucky	13	76	10	373	81.0	6.23
87. Virginia	12	59	32	337	75.0	6.25
87. Washington St.	12	58	34	298	75.0	6.25
89. Ohio	14	62	54	329	89.0	6.36
90. Ball St.	12	55	44	341	77.0	6.42
90. North Carolina	12	70	14	289	77.0	6.42
90. SMU	12	63	28	344	77.0	6.42
93. Miami (Fla.)	13	70	28	363	84.0	6.46
93. Middle Tenn.	13	72	24	317	84.0	6.46
95. Fla. Atlantic	12	69	18	294	78.0	6.50
95. Kansas	12	62	32	258	78.0	6.50
95. Vanderbilt	12	73	10	276	78.0	6.50
98. Cincinnati	13	68	34	307	85.0	6.54
99. Michigan St.	12	67	24	363	79.0	6.58
99. Wyoming	12	64	30	319	79.0	6.58
101. New Mexico	13	68	36	353	86.0	6.62
102. Northern Ill.	13	72	30	351	87.0	6.69
103. Florida Int'l	12	68	28	324	82.0	6.83
104. Colorado St.	12	60	46	360	83.0	6.92
104. Connecticut	12	60	46	315	83.0	6.92
106. Buffalo	12	65	38	334	84.0	7.00
106. Rice	13	82	18	402	91.0	7.00
108. Penn St.	13	76	34	377	93.0	7.15
109. Akron	12	70	34	373	87.0	7.25
109. Syracuse	12	67	40	442	87.0	7.25
111. Arizona	12	73	30	411	88.0	7.33
111. Stanford	12	73	30	444	88.0	7.33
113. East Caro.	13	85	24	380	97.0	7.46
114. Wake Forest	14	79	54	434	106.0	7.57
115. North Texas	12	62	60	363	92.0	7.67
116. Duke	12	75	36	413	93.0	7.75
117. Kent St.	12	70	54	373	97.0	8.08
117. Miami (Ohio)	12	80	34	400	97.0	8.08
119. Temple	12	80	38	507	99.0	8.25

Pass Sacks

Rank, Team	G	Yds	Total	PS/Gm
1. Western Mich.	13	327	46.0	3.54
2. Louisville	13	280	45.0	3.46
3. Oregon St.	14	342	47.0	3.36
4. Michigan	13	325	42.0	3.23
5. Rutgers	13	259	41.0	3.15
6. UCLA	13	270	40.0	3.08
6. Kansas St.	13	227	40.0	3.08
6. Penn St.	13	279	40.0	3.08
6. LSU	13	239	40.0	3.08
10. Texas	13	306	39.0	3.00
10. Washington St.	12	211	36.0	3.00
12. Miami (Fla.)	13	249	38.0	2.92
12. Oklahoma St.	13	250	38.0	2.92
12. Ohio St.	13	278	38.0	2.92
15. Nevada	13	232	37.0	2.85
15. TCU	13	276	37.0	2.85
15. South Fla.	13	257	37.0	2.85
15. Troy	13	230	37.0	2.85
19. Syracuse	12	207	34.0	2.83
20. Clemson	13	233	36.0	2.77
20. Middle Tenn.	13	247	36.0	2.77
22. Arizona St.	13	210	35.0	2.69
22. Missouri	13	215	35.0	2.69
22. Southern California	13	229	35.0	2.69
25. Arkansas	14	262	37.0	2.64
26. Kansas	12	208	31.0	2.58
26. SMU	12	244	31.0	2.58
28. Boise St.	13	189	33.0	2.54
28. South Carolina	13	204	33.0	2.54
28. Georgia	13	213	33.0	2.54
31. Georgia Tech	14	276	35.0	2.50
31. Kent St.	12	176	30.0	2.50
31. Virginia	12	203	30.0	2.50
34. Rice	13	235	32.0	2.46
35. Florida	14	258	34.0	2.43
36. Marshall	12	189	29.0	2.42
36. Wyoming	12	193	29.0	2.42
38. Cincinnati	13	209	31.0	2.38
38. West Virginia	13	216	31.0	2.38
38. Notre Dame	13	230	31.0	2.38

Rank, Team	G	Yds	Total	PS/Gm
41. Bowling Green	12	193	28.0	2.33
41. Fresno St.	12	150	28.0	2.33
43. Oregon	13	210	30.0	2.31
43. Texas Tech	13	162	30.0	2.31
43. Virginia Tech	13	218	30.0	2.31
46. Nebraska	14	238	32.0	2.29
46. Wake Forest	14	196	32.0	2.29
48. Colorado St.	12	161	27.0	2.25
48. Washington	12	171	27.0	2.25
50. Auburn	13	190	29.0	2.23
50. New Mexico	13	202	29.0	2.23
50. Wisconsin	13	175	29.0	2.23
50. Navy	13	181	29.0	2.23
50. Northern Ill.	13	183	29.0	2.23
50. Boston College	13	179	29.0	2.23
56. Central Mich.	14	223	31.0	2.21
56. Purdue	14	190	31.0	2.21
58. La.-Lafayette	12	154	26.0	2.17
58. Vanderbilt	12	198	26.0	2.17
60. Buffalo	12	171	25.0	2.08
60. UCF	12	183	25.0	2.08
60. Colorado	12	172	25.0	2.08
60. Kentucky	13	157	27.0	2.08
60. North Carolina St.	12	193	25.0	2.08
65. Hawaii	14	184	29.0	2.07
66. California	13	136	26.0	2.00
66. Iowa St.	12	142	24.0	2.00
66. Florida St.	13	200	26.0	2.00
66. Utah	13	181	26.0	2.00
66. North Carolina	12	162	24.0	2.00
66. Florida Int'l	12	158	24.0	2.00
72. Minnesota	13	140	25.0	1.92
72. Northwestern	12	127	23.0	1.92
74. Oklahoma	14	203	26.0	1.86
75. Brigham Young	13	175	24.0	1.85
76. UAB	12	146	22.0	1.83
76. Connecticut	12	151	22.0	1.83
76. Toledo	12	152	22.0	1.83
76. UTEP	12	122	22.0	1.83
76. Mississippi St.	12	143	22.0	1.83
81. Southern Miss.	14	157	25.0	1.79
82. Illinois	12	140	21.0	1.75
82. UNLV	12	121	21.0	1.75
82. Pittsburgh	12	106	21.0	1.75
85. Ball St.	12	113	20.0	1.67
85. Miami (Ohio)	12	153	20.0	1.67
87. Houston	14	138	23.0	1.64
87. Ohio	14	170	23.0	1.64
89. Iowa	13	143	21.0	1.62
90. Fla. Atlantic	12	130	19.0	1.58
90. Tulane	12	134	19.0	1.58
90. Air Force	12	112	19.0	1.58
90. La.-Monroe	12	126	19.0	1.58
94. Maryland	13	99	20.0	1.54
94. Texas A&M	13	136	20.0	1.54
94. Tulsa	13	139	20.0	1.54
97. Akron	12	85	17.0	1.42
97. Eastern Mich.	12	98	17.0	1.42
97. Memphis	12	108	17.0	1.42
97. Idaho	12	102	17.0	1.42
101. East Caro.	13	99	18.0	1.38
101. San Jose St.	13	103	18.0	1.38
103. Michigan St.	12	135	16.0	1.33
103. North Texas	12	96	16.0	1.33
105. Tennessee	13	122	17.0	1.31
106. Arizona	12	99	15.0	1.25
106. Mississippi	12	69	15.0	1.25
106. San Diego St.	12	114	15.0	1.25
106. Temple	12	99	15.0	1.25
106. New Mexico St.	12	94	15.0	1.25
111. Duke	12	99	14.0	1.17
111. Stanford	12	111	14.0	1.17
111. Indiana	12	68	14.0	1.17
114. Arkansas St.	12	103	13.0	1.08
115. Alabama	13	100	13.0	1.00
116. Baylor	12	83	11.0	.92
116. Utah St.	12	89	11.0	.92
116. Army	12	68	11.0	.92
119. Louisiana Tech	13	52	8.0	.62

Fewest Pass Sacks Allowed

Rank, Team	G	Yds	Total	PS/Gm
1. Rutgers	13	62	8	.62
2. Arkansas	14	70	9	.64
3. Fresno St.	12	75	12	1.00
3. California	13	84	13	1.00
5. La.-Monroe	12	83	13	1.08
6. Clemson	13	100	15	1.15
6. Utah	13	121	15	1.15
6. West Virginia	13	82	15	1.15
6. TCU	13	82	15	1.15
10. Memphis	12	86	14	1.17
11. Oklahoma	14	111	17	1.21
12. Oregon	13	85	16	1.23
12. Tulsa	13	82	16	1.23
14. Brigham Young	13	111	17	1.31
14. Western Mich.	13	135	17	1.31
14. Southern California	13	109	17	1.31
14. Georgia	13	121	17	1.31
18. Southern Miss.	14	112	19	1.36
19. Minnesota	13	100	18	1.38
19. San Jose St.	13	103	18	1.38
19. Oklahoma St.	13	120	18	1.38
22. Ohio	14	145	20	1.43
22. Purdue	14	157	20	1.43
24. LSU	13	146	19	1.46
24. Tennessee	13	134	19	1.46
24. Texas A&M	13	112	19	1.46
24. Texas	13	136	19	1.46
24. Texas Tech	13	134	19	1.46
24. Missouri	13	163	19	1.46
24. Ohio St.	13	146	19	1.46
31. Boise St.	13	142	20	1.54
31. Maryland	13	121	20	1.54
31. Louisville	13	121	20	1.54
34. Georgia Tech	14	178	22	1.57
35. Marshall	12	109	19	1.58
35. North Carolina St.	12	119	19	1.58
35. Air Force	12	93	19	1.58
35. Utah St.	12	117	19	1.58
35. Washington	12	122	19	1.58
35. Vanderbilt	12	112	19	1.58
41. UCLA	13	151	21	1.62
42. Florida	14	166	23	1.64
43. Bowling Green	12	106	20	1.67
43. Army	12	140	20	1.67
45. Navy	13	130	22	1.69
46. North Texas	12	180	21	1.75
47. Boston College	13	177	23	1.77
47. Penn St.	13	194	23	1.77
47. Iowa	13	124	23	1.77
50. UCF	12	125	22	1.83
50. North Carolina	12	157	22	1.83
52. Michigan	13	159	24	1.85
52. South Carolina	13	149	24	1.85
54. Wake Forest	14	177	26	1.86
55. Idaho	12	146	23	1.92
55. Pittsburgh	12	163	23	1.92
55. Northern Ill.	13	194	25	1.92
55. UNLV	12	204	23	1.92
59. Florida St.	13	135	26	2.00
59. Hawaii	14	148	28	2.00
59. Miami (Fla.)	13	215	26	2.00
62. Central Mich.	14	204	29	2.07
63. Fla. Atlantic	12	182	25	2.08
63. UTEP	12	186	25	2.08
63. La.-Lafayette	12	118	25	2.08
63. South Fla.	13	144	27	2.08
63. San Diego St.	12	143	25	2.08
68. Nebraska	14	206	30	2.14
69. Alabama	13	204	28	2.15
69. Nevada	13	177	28	2.15
69. Kansas St.	13	199	28	2.15
69. Middle Tenn.	13	169	28	2.15
73. Eastern Mich.	12	157	26	2.17
73. Indiana	12	189	26	2.17
73. Kansas	12	138	26	2.17
73. Northwestern	12	162	26	2.17
77. East Caro.	13	209	29	2.23
77. Troy	13	219	29	2.23
77. Virginia Tech	13	219	29	2.23
80. Wisconsin	13	219	30	2.31

Rank, Team	G	Yds	Total	PS/Gm
81. UAB	12	227	28	2.33
81. Ball St.	12	210	28	2.33
81. Michigan St.	12	202	28	2.33
84. Houston	14	218	33	2.36
85. Notre Dame	13	216	31	2.38
86. Mississippi St.	12	207	29	2.42
86. Washington St.	12	181	29	2.42
86. Mississippi	12	193	29	2.42
86. Tulane	12	227	29	2.42
90. Louisiana Tech	13	246	32	2.46
91. Colorado	12	172	30	2.50
91. Toledo	12	199	30	2.50
91. Illinois	12	205	30	2.50
91. Oregon St.	14	222	35	2.50
95. Cincinnati	13	192	33	2.54
96. Akron	12	242	31	2.58
96. Arizona	12	249	31	2.58
96. Connecticut	12	184	31	2.58
99. Auburn	13	194	34	2.62
100. Florida Int'l	12	221	32	2.67
100. SMU	12	225	32	2.67
100. Kent St.	12	216	32	2.67
103. Rice	13	266	35	2.69
104. Virginia	12	219	33	2.75
105. Arizona St.	13	219	37	2.85
106. Arkansas St.	12	246	36	3.00
106. Baylor	12	320	36	3.00
106. Kentucky	13	274	39	3.00
109. Iowa St.	12	244	38	3.17
110. New Mexico	13	252	43	3.31
111. New Mexico St.	12	207	40	3.33
111. Wyoming	12	217	40	3.33
113. Colorado St.	12	283	41	3.42
114. Buffalo	12	222	42	3.50
115. Duke	12	254	43	3.58
116. Syracuse	12	345	45	3.75
117. Temple	12	364	48	4.00
118. Miami (Ohio)	12	268	49	4.08
119. Stanford	12	359	50	4.17

2006 Championship Subdivision (FCS) Individual Leaders

Rushing

Rank, Player	Pos	Cl.	G	Att.	Net	TD	Avg.	Yds/Gm
1. Justise Hairston, Central Conn. St.	RB	SR	11	277	1,847	20	6.67	167.91
1. Marcus Mason, Youngstown St.	RB	SR	12	302	1,847	23	6.12	153.92
3. Scott Phaydavong, Drake	RB	JR	11	277	1,613	10	5.82	146.64
4. Arkee Whitlock, Southern Ill.	RB	SR	13	317	1,828	25	5.77	140.62
5. Mike McLeod, Yale	RB	SO	10	297	1,364	19	4.59	136.40
6. Pierre Rembert, Illinois St.	RB	SR	13	355	1,743	16	4.91	134.08
7. D.D. Terry, Sam Houston St.	RB	SR	10	215	1,328	15	6.18	132.80
8. Steve Baylark, Massachusetts	RB	SR	15	338	1,960	15	5.80	130.67
9. Herb Donaldson, Western Ill.	RB	SO	11	233	1,417	18	6.08	128.82
10. Donald Chapman, Tenn.-Martin	RB	JR	11	269	1,412	15	5.25	128.36
11. Chris Fletcher, Austin Peay	RB	JR	11	255	1,401	16	5.49	127.36
12. Clifton Dawson, Harvard	RB	SR	10	237	1,213	20	5.12	121.30
13. Todd Harris, St. Francis (Pa.)	RB	SR	11	275	1,330	11	4.84	120.91
14. Deshawn Baker, South Carolina St.	RB	SR	11	204	1,289	9	6.32	117.18
15. Jordan Scott, Colgate	RB	SO	11	290	1,234	12	4.26	112.18
16. Javarris Williams, Tennessee St.	RB	SO	11	245	1,233	11	5.03	112.09
17. Emmanuel Marc, Delaware St.	RB	SR	11	187	1,230	12	6.58	111.82
18. Kevin Richardson, Appalachian St.	RB	JR	15	302	1,676	30	5.55	111.73
19. Jerry Brant, Jacksonville	RB	SR	10	204	1,110	7	5.44	111.00
20. Eldra Buckley, Chattanooga	RB	SR	11	215	1,204	7	5.60	109.45
21. Eugene Holloman, James Madison	RB	JR	10	191	1,084	8	5.68	108.40
22. Vincent Webb, Eastern Ill.	RB	SR	13	264	1,405	7	5.32	108.08
23. Joe Sandberg, Penn	RB	SR	10	210	1,042	13	4.96	104.20
24. Treyvn Smith, Weber St.	RB	SO	11	205	1,129	8	5.51	102.64
25. Josh Barnett, Idaho St.	RB	JR	11	200	1,117	6	5.59	101.55
26. James Noble, Cal Poly	RB	SO	10	196	1,009	7	5.15	100.90
27. Corey Lewis, UNI	RB	SO	9	134	894	10	6.67	99.33
28. Jay Peck, Alabama St.	RB	JR	11	249	1,086	8	4.36	98.73
29. Clay Green, Jacksonville St.	RB	SR	11	242	1,083	15	4.48	98.45
30. Jonathan Hurt, Lafayette	RB	SR	12	229	1,165	15	5.09	97.08
31. Maurice Murray, Northeastern	RB	JR	11	216	1,061	11	4.91	96.45
32. Alonzo Coleman, Hampton	RB	SR	11	158	1,052	12	6.66	95.64
33. Martell Mallet, Ark.-Pine Bluff	RB	JR	12	235	1,121	14	4.77	93.42
34. Sean Mizzer, VMI	RB	SR	11	209	1,022	9	4.89	92.91
35. Rashad Jennings, Liberty	RB	SO	11	179	1,020	10	5.70	92.73
36. Alex Henderson, Northern Ariz.	RB	FR	11	189	1,016	5	5.38	92.36
37. Darius Fudge, Western Caro.	RB	SR	11	229	1,001	4	4.37	91.00
38. Lerron Moore, Western Ky.	RB	SR	10	195	891	9	4.57	89.10
39. Luke Siwula, Cornell	RB	JR	10	202	885	4	4.38	88.50
40. Tony West, Indiana St.	RB	JR	9	160	791	5	4.94	87.89
41. Elijah Brooks, William & Mary	RB	SR	11	183	931	8	5.09	84.64
42. JT Rogan, San Diego	RB	SO	12	190	1,002	14	5.27	83.50
43. Jabari McGee, Morehead St.	RB	SR	11	170	907	7	5.34	82.45
44. Marques Thompson, Lehigh	RB	SR	11	181	904	6	4.99	82.18
45. Joe Casey, Rhode Island	RB	SO	11	191	874	6	4.58	79.45
46. Lamar Lewis, Ga. Southern	RB	JR	10	149	782	7	5.25	78.20
47. Cedrick Gipson, Furman	RB	JR	12	190	938	4	4.94	78.17
48. Tim Hightower, Richmond	RB	JR	11	177	850	5	4.80	77.27

Rank, Player	Pos	Cl.	G	Att.	Net	TD	Avg.	Yds/Gm
49. Jonathon Hubbard, Davidson	RB	SR	10	189	769	13	4.07	76.90
50. Armanti Edwards, Appalachian St.	QB	FR	15	188	1,153	15	6.13	76.87
51. Arel Gordon, Maine	WR	SR	11	172	843	5	4.90	76.64
52. Chris Covington, Ga. Southern	RB	SO	11	164	824	8	5.02	74.91
53. Byron Lawrence, Northwestern St.	RB	SO	11	187	821	4	4.39	74.64
54. Tory Cooper, Citadel	RB	JR	11	160	807	8	5.04	73.36
55. Mark Dunn, Eastern Ky.	RB	JR	11	166	802	9	4.83	72.91
56. Chad Simpson, Morgan St.	RB	JR	11	147	795	9	5.41	72.27
57. Michael Ferguson, N.C. A&T	RB	SO	9	141	631	4	4.48	70.11
58. Dane Samuels, Iona	RB	JR	10	158	698	4	4.42	69.80
59. William Ford, South Carolina St.	RB	SO	11	112	752	10	6.71	68.36
60. Jason Butler, Wagner	RB	JR	11	156	735	4	4.71	66.82
60. Stan Zwinggi, Texas St.	RB	SO	11	131	735	3	5.61	66.82
62. Kevious Johnson, Wofford	RB	JR	11	115	730	6	6.35	66.36
63. Kendall Addison, Southern U.	RB	JR	11	111	720	7	6.49	65.45
64. Aaron Mason, Montana St.	RB	FR	10	153	645	9	4.22	64.50
65. Louie Runnels, Stephen F. Austin	RB	JR	11	145	709	6	4.89	64.45
66. Vernardus Cooper, Alcorn St.	RB	JR	11	152	698	6	4.59	63.45
66. Johey Hargrett, Mississippi Val.	RB	SO	11	164	698	5	4.26	63.45
68. David Sinisi, Monmouth	RB	FR	12	171	754	13	4.41	62.83
69. Anthony Ash, Tennessee Tech	RB	SR	11	150	689	5	4.59	62.64
70. Jay Lucas, Southeastern La.	RB	SO	11	134	684	6	5.10	62.18
71. Kevin Beverly, Hampton	RB	JR	12	134	746	12	5.57	62.17
72. Ta'Mar Scott, Alabama A&M	RB	SR	12	154	740	9	4.81	61.67
73. Zach Terrell, Liberty	QB	SO	11	144	673	13	4.67	61.18
74. Conte Cuttino, Stony Brook	RB	FR	11	140	672	3	4.80	61.09
75. Marcus Allen, Albany (N.Y.)	RB	SR	11	125	667	3	5.34	60.64
76. Jamie Leonard, McNeese St.	RB	JR	10	102	605	5	5.93	60.50
77. Josh Johnson, San Diego	QB	JR	12	107	720	11	6.73	60.00
78. Darian Williams, UNI	RB	JR	11	108	653	5	6.05	59.36
78. Tim Holloman, Southeast Mo. St.	RB	SO	11	121	653	6	5.40	59.36
80. Jerome Felton, Furman	RB	JR	12	162	707	23	4.36	58.92
81. Willie Cashmore, Drake	RB	JR	11	106	645	18	6.08	58.64
82. Josh DeStefano, Bucknell	RB	JR	11	118	643	3	5.45	58.45
83. Mike Kielt, Holy Cross	RB	SO	9	108	524	6	4.85	58.22
84. Jason Payne, Sacred Heart	RB	JR	11	110	621	4	5.65	56.45
85. Jeremy McCullough, Duquesne	RB	SR	10	149	564	2	3.79	56.40
86. Akinbounle Oyalowo, Brown	RB	SR	9	126	498	6	3.95	55.33
87. Tyler Thigpen, Coastal Caro.	QB	SR	12	113	656	5	5.81	54.67
87. Norris Smith, Eastern Ill.	RB	SO	12	135	656	6	4.86	54.67
89. Arnell Fontenot, Prairie View	RB	JR	9	113	483	3	4.27	53.67
90. Johnny Sanchez, Southern Utah	RB	JR	11	103	589	4	5.72	53.55
91. Nic Luke, Alabama A&M	RB	SR	12	137	640	3	4.67	53.33
92. Monte' Anthony, Norfolk St.	RB	SR	11	144	586	8	4.07	53.27
93. Michael Hobbs, Wofford	RB	JR	11	122	579	9	4.75	52.64
94. Kareem Huggins, Hofstra	RB	JR	11	136	572	4	4.21	52.00
95. Josh Vaughan, Richmond	RB	SO	11	91	569	5	6.25	51.73
96. John Popper, Valparaiso	RB	FR	11	139	567	2	4.08	51.55
97. Jordan E. Davis, Columbia	RB	SO	10	155	507	0	3.27	50.70
98. Antoine Rutherford, Howard	RB	SR	10	115	504	4	4.38	50.40
99. Abdulan Kuuan, Grambling	RB	SR	11	140	551	6	3.94	50.09
100. Terrance Gass, Holy Cross	RB	SO	9	107	450	4	4.21	50.00

Passing Efficiency

(Minimum 15 Attempts Per Game)

Rank, Player	Pos	Cl.	G	Att	Comp	CPct	Int	IPct	Yds	Yds/Att	TD	TDPct	Rating
1. Josh Johnson, San Diego	QB	JR	12	371	246	66.31	5	1.35	3,320	8.95	34	9.16	169.0
2. Jason Murrietta, Northern Ariz.	QB	SR	11	329	214	65.05	5	1.52	2,827	8.59	34	10.33	168.3
3. Tyler Thigpen, Coastal Caro.	QB	SR	12	339	217	64.01	11	3.24	3,296	9.72	29	8.55	167.4
4. Chris Wallace, Ark.-Pine Bluff	QB	SR	12	210	129	61.43	9	4.29	2,023	9.63	20	9.52	165.2
5. Justin Rascati, James Madison	QB	SR	12	231	153	66.23	6	2.60	2,045	8.85	20	8.66	164.0
6. Liam Coen, Massachusetts	QB	JR	15	334	217	64.97	10	2.99	3,016	9.03	26	7.78	160.5
7. Nick Hill, Southern Ill.	QB	JR	13	196	121	61.73	4	2.04	1,721	8.78	15	7.65	156.7
8. Princeton Shepherd, Hampton	QB	SR	11	222	150	67.57	4	1.80	1,750	7.88	17	7.66	155.5
9. Collin Drafts, Charleston So.	QB	SR	11	319	223	69.91	14	4.39	2,665	8.35	21	6.58	153.0
10. Ricky Santos, New Hampshire	QB	JR	13	432	293	67.82	7	1.62	3,125	7.23	29	6.71	147.5
11. Eric Sanders, UNI	QB	JR	11	249	169	67.87	7	2.81	1,934	7.77	15	6.02	147.4
12. Sean Schaefer, Towson	QB	SO	10	380	260	68.42	9	2.37	3,033	7.98	19	5.00	147.2
13. Scott Knapp, Duquesne	QB	SO	10	351	209	59.54	13	3.70	2,853	8.13	28	7.98	146.7
14. Kevin Hoyng, Dayton	QB	SR	10	221	131	59.28	8	3.62	2,052	9.29	11	4.98	146.5
15. Jimmy Oliver, Jackson St.	QB	JR	11	221	138	62.44	12	5.43	1,906	8.62	14	6.33	144.9
16. Sedale Threatt, Lehigh	QB	JR	11	246	151	61.38	5	2.03	2,008	8.16	14	5.69	144.7
17. Albert Chester II, Florida A&M	QB	JR	10	264	164	62.12	5	1.89	1,986	7.52	18	6.82	144.0
18. Josh Dudash, Stony Brook	QB	JR	11	285	179	62.81	4	1.40	2,231	7.83	15	5.26	143.1
19. Luke Drone, Illinois St.	QB	JR	13	349	203	58.17	13	3.72	2,961	8.48	21	6.02	141.8
20. Dominic Randolph, Holy Cross	QB	SO	9	299	184	61.54	6	2.01	2,237	7.48	19	6.35	141.3
21. Armanti Edwards, Appalachian St.	QB	FR	15	274	167	60.95	10	3.65	2,251	8.22	15	5.47	140.7
22. Matt Bassuener, Georgetown	QB	SR	10	209	144	68.90	8	3.83	1,359	6.50	15	7.18	139.5
23. Brian Boland, Monmouth	QB	SR	12	305	197	64.59	9	2.95	2,353	7.71	14	4.59	138.6
24. Justin Haddix, Western Ky.	QB	SR	11	279	171	61.29	9	3.23	2,186	7.84	14	5.02	137.2
25. Stephen McGrath, Marist	QB	JR	11	239	151	63.18	10	4.18	2,014	8.43	8	3.35	136.6

Rank, Player	Pos	Cl.	G	Att	Comp	CPct	Int	IPct	Yds	Yds/Att	TD	TDPct	Rating
26. Sawyer Smith, Portland St.	QB	SR	9	188	100	53.19	8	4.26	1,491	7.93	14	7.45	135.9
27. Eric Cwalinski, Robert Morris	QB	SO	11	270	157	58.15	14	5.19	2,066	7.65	19	7.04	135.3
28. Vashon Winton, Delaware St.	QB	SO	10	168	99	58.93	2	1.19	1,171	6.97	10	5.95	134.7
29. Steve LaFalce, Western Ill.	QB	SR	11	279	176	63.08	9	3.23	2,121	7.60	11	3.94	133.5
30. Mike Saraceno, Colgate	QB	JR	11	259	151	58.30	9	3.47	2,048	7.91	11	4.25	131.8
31. Jeff Terrell, Princeton	QB	SR	10	331	195	58.91	11	3.32	2,445	7.39	17	5.14	131.3
32. Antonio Hefner, Tennessee St.	QB	SO	9	199	109	54.77	11	5.53	1,668	8.38	9	4.52	129.1
33. Joe Flacco, Delaware	QB	JR	11	417	264	63.31	10	2.40	2,783	6.67	18	4.32	128.8
34. Brad Maurer, Lafayette	QB	SR	12	307	181	58.96	10	3.26	2,239	7.29	13	4.23	127.7
35. Ryan Alexander, Davidson	QB	JR	10	377	215	57.03	10	2.65	2,581	6.85	21	5.57	127.6
36. Marvin Burroughs, Villanova	QB	SR	11	283	171	60.42	9	3.18	2,123	7.50	9	3.18	127.6
37. Michael Potts, William & Mary	QB	JR	9	216	124	57.41	7	3.24	1,559	7.22	10	4.63	126.8
38. Brock Smith, Liberty	QB	SO	11	186	107	57.53	5	2.69	1,376	7.40	7	3.76	126.7
39. Josh Swogger, Montana	QB	SR	13	358	195	54.47	12	3.35	2,685	7.50	17	4.75	126.4
40. Wes Pope, Elon	QB	JR	11	375	228	60.80	12	3.20	2,572	6.86	16	4.27	126.1
41. Duran Lawson, Citadel	QB	JR	11	325	203	62.46	11	3.38	2,138	6.58	14	4.31	125.2
42. Eric Ward, Richmond	QB	FR	10	221	132	59.73	6	2.71	1,424	6.44	11	4.98	124.8
43. Chris Walker, Alcorn St.	QB	SO	9	170	83	48.82	4	2.35	1,233	7.25	10	5.88	124.5
44. Brandon Landers, Grambling	QB	SO	11	293	150	51.19	11	3.75	2,138	7.30	17	5.80	124.1
45. Tom Zetts, Youngstown St.	QB	JR	14	301	171	56.81	11	3.65	2,086	6.93	14	4.65	123.1
46. Mark Cunningham, Austin Peay	QB	JR	11	326	197	60.43	13	3.99	2,236	6.86	12	3.68	122.2
47. Mike Fritz, Dartmouth	QB	SR	10	263	162	61.60	10	3.80	1,838	6.99	7	2.66	121.5
48. Anthony Doria, St. Francis (Pa.)	QB	SR	11	286	151	52.80	6	2.10	1,871	6.54	15	5.24	120.9
49. Derrick Fourroux, McNeese St.	QB	FR	12	217	118	54.38	7	3.23	1,490	6.87	10	4.61	120.8
50. Kelcy Luke, Alabama A&M	QB	JR	12	301	174	57.81	8	2.66	1,818	6.04	16	5.32	120.8
51. Devin Campbell, Gardner-Webb	QB	SO	11	311	174	55.95	17	5.47	2,215	7.12	15	4.82	120.8
52. Bradley George, Texas St.	QB	FR	10	233	124	53.22	10	4.29	1,676	7.19	11	4.72	120.6
53. Joseph DiGiacomo, Brown	QB	SR	10	301	168	55.81	15	4.98	2,161	7.18	13	4.32	120.4
54. Renaldo Gray, Furman	QB	JR	10	168	95	56.55	3	1.79	1,184	7.05	4	2.38	120.0
55. Matt Hardin, Jacksonville St.	QB	JR	11	233	127	54.51	10	4.29	1,728	7.42	8	3.43	119.6
56. Brian Yost, Morehead St.	QB	JR	11	286	170	59.44	12	4.20	1,891	6.61	11	3.85	119.3
57. Tino Edgecombe, Texas Southern	QB	JR	10	192	110	57.29	10	5.21	1,292	6.73	9	4.69	118.9
58. Nathan Ford, Cornell	QB	SO	10	202	112	55.45	9	4.46	1,417	7.01	8	3.96	118.5
59. Chris Pizzotti, Harvard	QB	JR	9	142	70	49.30	5	3.52	1,051	7.40	6	4.23	118.4
60. Anton Clarkson, Hofstra	QB	SR	10	287	160	55.75	3	1.05	1,881	6.55	8	2.79	117.9
61. Ron Whitcomb, Maine	QB	SR	11	240	151	62.92	8	3.33	1,398	5.83	9	3.75	117.6
62. Danny Southall, Stephen F. Austin	QB	JR	11	294	169	57.48	4	1.36	1,877	6.38	8	2.72	117.4
63. Chris Horton, Jacksonville	QB	JR	10	268	125	46.64	10	3.73	1,899	7.09	15	5.60	117.2
64. Casey Hansen, Norfolk St.	QB	JR	11	283	148	52.30	16	5.65	2,166	7.65	10	3.53	116.9
65. Jack Rolovich, Montana St.	QB	JR	11	228	113	49.56	10	4.39	1,674	7.34	10	4.39	116.9
66. Matt Gutierrez, Idaho St.	QB	SR	11	342	187	54.68	14	4.09	2,237	6.54	16	4.68	116.9
67. Josh Greco, Eastern Ky.	QB	JR	11	267	150	56.18	13	4.87	1,834	6.87	10	3.75	116.5
68. Matt Brennan, Cal Poly	QB	SO	11	169	76	44.97	7	4.14	1,208	7.15	10	5.92	116.3
69. Robert Irvin, Penn	QB	SO	10	312	174	55.77	12	3.85	2,128	6.82	10	3.21	115.9
70. Cleveland McCoy, South Carolina St.	QB	JR	11	183	94	51.37	9	4.92	1,224	6.69	10	5.46	115.7
71. Reilly Murphy, Indiana St.	QB	JR	9	261	143	54.79	8	3.07	1,747	6.69	8	3.07	115.0
72. Wes Marshall, Southern Utah	QB	JR	11	323	183	56.66	14	4.33	1,942	6.01	16	4.95	114.8
73. Tyler Arciaga, Sacred Heart	QB	SR	11	368	211	57.34	14	3.80	2,076	5.64	19	5.16	114.2
74. Lee Sweeney, Tennessee Tech	QB	FR	11	356	189	53.09	17	4.78	2,292	6.44	17	4.78	113.4
75. Marcel Marquez, Sacramento St.	QB	JR	11	270	142	52.59	15	5.56	1,910	7.07	10	3.70	113.1
76. Cole Stinson, Eastern Ill.	QB	JR	12	224	122	54.46	11	4.91	1,349	6.02	12	5.36	112.9
77. Matt Polhemus, Yale	QB	JR	10	208	109	52.40	6	2.88	1,437	6.91	5	2.40	112.6
78. Chris Hanson, La Salle	QB	SO	10	163	98	60.12	10	6.13	973	5.97	7	4.29	112.2
79. Travis Clark, Ga. Southern	QB	SO	11	283	147	51.94	4	1.41	1,808	6.39	8	2.83	112.1
80. Craig Hormann, Columbia	QB	JR	10	329	189	57.45	6	1.82	2,008	6.10	7	2.13	112.1
81. Brett Hicks, Sam Houston St.	QB	JR	11	270	145	53.70	11	4.07	1,786	6.61	8	2.96	110.9
82. Ryan Doerffler, Valparaiso	QB	JR	11	306	148	48.37	13	4.25	2,050	6.70	13	4.25	110.2
83. Scott Bonnono, St. Peter's	QB	JR	10	431	241	55.92	13	3.02	2,470	5.73	15	3.48	109.5
84. Zac Barnard, Murray St.	QB	FR	11	277	156	56.32	11	3.97	1,583	5.71	11	3.97	109.5
85. Seth Babin, Southeastern La.	QB	SR	10	225	138	61.33	6	2.67	1,117	4.96	8	3.56	109.4
86. Dustin Croick, Iona	QB	JR	9	236	135	57.20	9	3.81	1,474	6.25	5	2.12	109.0
87. Matt Nichols, Eastern Wash.	QB	FR	11	259	143	55.21	17	6.56	1,749	6.75	8	3.09	109.0
88. Aries Nelson, Mississippi Val.	QB	SR	11	250	120	48.00	10	4.00	1,606	6.42	10	4.00	107.2
89. Matt Lopez, Chattanooga	QB	SR	9	172	86	50.00	8	4.65	1,043	6.06	8	4.65	107.0
90. Jefferson Adcock, Samford	QB	SR	11	169	91	53.85	7	4.14	915	5.41	5	2.96	100.8
91. Roch Charpentier, Northwestern St.	QB	SO	10	160	80	50.00	4	2.50	837	5.23	5	3.13	99.3
92. T.J. Brown, Butler	QB	JR	10	313	158	50.48	8	2.56	1,572	5.02	10	3.19	98.1
93. Daniel Bocanegra, Albany (N.Y.)	QB	SO	11	175	90	51.43	7	4.00	932	5.33	5	2.86	97.6
94. Kevin Ballatore, Southeast Mo. St.	QB	SR	11	211	102	48.34	6	2.84	1,105	5.24	7	3.32	97.6
95. Garrett Williams, Savannah St.	QB	SO	11	225	111	49.33	14	6.22	1,264	5.62	8	3.56	95.8
96. Matt Abbey, Wagner	QB	SO	11	307	150	48.86	12	3.91	1,618	5.27	9	2.93	95.0
97. John Skelton, Fordham	QB	FR	9	167	74	44.31	8	4.79	960	5.75	6	3.59	94.9
98. Wayne Campbell, N.C. A&T	QB	FR	11	230	100	43.48	17	7.39	1,094	4.76	9	3.91	81.6

Total Offense

Rank, Player	Pos.	Cl.	G	Rush Att	Rush Gain	Rush Loss	Rush Net	Pass Att	Pass Yds	Total Plays	Total Yds	Yds/Pl	Yds/Gm
1. Josh Johnson, San Diego	QB	JR	12	107	828	108	720	371	3,320	478	4,040	8.45	336.7
2. Tyler Thigpen, Coastal Caro.	QB	SR	12	113	780	124	656	339	3,296	452	3,952	8.74	329.3
3. Sean Schaefer, Towson	QB	SO	10	61	152	212	-60	380	3,033	441	2,973	6.74	297.3

Rank, Player	Pos.	Cl.	G	Rush Att	Rush Gain	Rush Loss	Net	Pass Att	Pass Yds	Total Plays	Total Yds	Yds/ Pl	Yds/ Gm
4. Collin Drafts, Charleston So.	QB	SR	11	130	654	141	513	319	2,665	449	3,178	7.08	288.9
5. Scott Knapp, Duquesne	QB	SO	10	40	95	139	-44	351	2,853	391	2,809	7.18	280.9
6. Ryan Alexander, Davidson	QB	JR	10	54	261	76	185	377	2,581	431	2,766	6.42	276.6
7. Jeff Terrell, Princeton	QB	SR	10	106	417	145	272	331	2,445	437	2,717	6.22	271.7
8. Ricky Santos, New Hampshire	QB	JR	13	149	608	230	378	432	3,125	581	3,503	6.03	269.5
9. Jason Murrietta, Northern Ariz.	QB	SR	11	83	288	243	45	329	2,827	412	2,872	6.97	261.1
10. Dominic Randolph, Holy Cross	QB	SO	9	49	208	119	89	299	2,237	348	2,326	6.68	258.4
11. Joe Flacco, Delaware	QB	JR	11	83	225	171	54	417	2,783	500	2,837	5.67	257.9
12. Wes Pope, Elon	QB	JR	11	86	202	167	35	375	2,572	461	2,607	5.66	237.0
13. Scott Bonnono, St. Peter's	QB	JR	10	53	93	215	-122	431	2,470	484	2,348	4.85	234.8
14. Luke Drone, Illinois St.	QB	JR	13	57	173	123	50	349	2,961	406	3,011	7.42	231.6
15. Albert Chester II, Florida A&M	QB	JR	10	89	404	84	320	264	1,986	353	2,306	6.53	230.6
16. Armanti Edwards, Appalachian St.	QB	FR	15	188	1,258	105	1,153	274	2,251	462	3,404	7.37	226.9
17. Mike Fritz, Dartmouth	QB	SR	10	101	578	168	410	263	1,838	364	2,248	6.18	224.8
18. Jimmy Oliver, Jackson St.	QB	JR	11	110	673	127	546	221	1,906	331	2,452	7.41	222.9
19. Joseph DiGiacomo, Brown	QB	SR	10	75	268	201	67	301	2,161	376	2,228	5.93	222.8
20. Marvin Burroughs, Villanova	QB	SR	11	116	532	206	326	283	2,123	399	2,449	6.14	222.6
21. Duran Lawson, Citadel	QB	JR	11	112	455	157	298	325	2,138	437	2,436	5.57	221.5
22. Kevin Hoyng, Dayton	QB	SR	10	113	419	273	146	221	2,052	334	2,198	6.58	219.8
23. Brian Boland, Monmouth	QB	SR	12	99	407	154	253	305	2,353	404	2,606	6.45	217.2
24. Mike Saraceno, Colgate	QB	JR	11	86	420	96	324	259	2,048	345	2,372	6.88	215.6
25. Chris Horton, Jacksonville	QB	JR	10	68	368	128	240	268	1,899	336	2,139	6.37	213.9
26. Justin Rascati, James Madison	QB	SR	12	114	589	71	518	231	2,045	345	2,563	7.43	213.6
27. Reilly Murphy, Indiana St.	QB	JR	9	73	272	105	167	261	1,747	334	1,914	5.73	212.7
28. Brad Maurer, Lafayette	QB	SR	12	94	440	145	295	307	2,239	401	2,534	6.32	211.2
29. Sedale Threatt, Lehigh	QB	JR	11	117	478	168	310	246	2,008	363	2,318	6.39	210.7
30. Wes Marshall, Southern Utah	QB	JR	11	119	531	165	366	323	1,942	442	2,308	5.22	209.8
31. Josh Swogger, Montana	QB	SR	13	89	298	257	41	358	2,685	447	2,726	6.10	209.7
32. Danny Southall, Stephen F. Austin	QB	JR	11	109	560	142	418	294	1,877	403	2,295	5.69	208.6
33. Robert Irvin, Penn	QB	SO	10	14	5	58	-53	312	2,128	326	2,075	6.37	207.5
34. Lee Sweeney, Tennessee Tech	QB	FR	11	44	104	129	-25	356	2,292	400	2,267	5.67	206.1
35. Brandon Landers, Grambling	QB	SO	11	64	278	161	117	293	2,138	357	2,255	6.32	205.0
36. Antonio Hefner, Tennessee St.	QB	SO	9	79	341	169	172	199	1,668	278	1,840	6.62	204.4
37. Josh Dudash, Stony Brook	QB	JR	11	45	96	82	14	285	2,231	330	2,245	6.80	204.1
38. Stephen McGrath, Marist	QB	JR	11	84	342	127	215	239	2,014	323	2,229	6.90	202.6
39. Craig Hormann, Columbia	QB	JR	10	43	98	91	7	329	2,008	372	2,015	5.42	201.5
40. Justin Haddix, Western Ky.	QB	SR	11	57	151	126	25	279	2,186	336	2,211	6.58	201.0
41. Matt Gutierrez, Idaho St.	QB	SR	11	66	128	162	-34	342	2,237	408	2,203	5.40	200.3
42. Steve LaFalce, Western Ill.	QB	SR	11	54	171	113	58	279	2,121	333	2,179	6.54	198.1
43. Liam Coen, Massachusetts	QB	JR	15	32	62	124	-62	334	3,016	366	2,954	8.07	196.9
44. Mark Cunningham, Austin Peay	QB	JR	11	45	80	160	-80	326	2,236	371	2,156	5.81	196.0
45. Devin Campbell, Gardner-Webb	QB	SO	11	54	107	171	-64	311	2,215	365	2,151	5.89	195.5
46. Eric Sanders, UNI	QB	JR	11	74	369	158	211	249	1,934	323	2,145	6.64	195.0
47. Brian Yost, Morehead St.	QB	JR	11	119	465	225	240	286	1,891	405	2,131	5.26	193.7
48. Kelcy Luke, Alabama A&M	QB	JR	12	114	591	166	425	301	1,818	415	2,243	5.40	186.9
49. Matt Polhemus, Yale	QB	JR	10	74	516	92	424	208	1,437	282	1,861	6.60	186.1
50. Casey Hansen, Norfolk St.	QB	JR	11	48	91	219	-128	283	2,166	331	2,038	6.16	185.3
51. Chris Wallace, Ark.-Pine Bluff	QB	SR	12	72	354	175	179	210	2,023	282	2,202	7.81	183.5
52. Marcel Marquez, Sacramento St.	QB	JR	11	110	338	249	89	270	1,910	380	1,999	5.26	181.7
53. Anton Clarkson, Hofstra	QB	SR	10	76	150	216	-66	287	1,881	363	1,815	5.00	181.5
54. Ryan Doerffler, Valparaiso	QB	JR	11	56	99	164	-65	306	2,050	362	1,985	5.48	180.5
55. Aries Nelson, Mississippi Val.	QB	SR	11	89	559	192	367	250	1,606	339	1,973	5.82	179.4
56. Bradley George, Texas St.	QB	FR	10	45	180	76	104	233	1,676	278	1,780	6.40	178.0
57. Nathan Ford, Cornell	QB	SO	10	103	479	134	345	202	1,417	305	1,762	5.78	176.2
58. Tyler Arciaga, Sacred Heart	QB	SR	11	38	41	192	-151	368	2,076	406	1,925	4.74	175.0
59. Princeton Shepherd, Hampton	QB	SR	11	65	278	122	156	222	1,750	287	1,906	6.64	173.3
60. Tom Zetts, Youngstown St.	QB	JR	14	82	440	106	334	301	2,086	383	2,420	6.32	172.9
61. Eric Cwalinski, Robert Morris	QB	SO	11	58	58	226	-168	270	2,066	328	1,898	5.79	172.5
62. Michael Potts, William & Mary	QB	JR	9	14	12	41	-29	216	1,559	230	1,530	6.65	170.0
63. Matt Nichols, Eastern Wash.	QB	FR	11	49	245	130	115	259	1,749	308	1,864	6.05	169.5
64. Josh Greco, Eastern Ky.	QB	JR	11	51	144	118	26	267	1,834	318	1,860	5.85	169.1
65. Anthony Doria, St. Francis (Pa.)	QB	SR	11	30	45	68	-23	286	1,871	316	1,848	5.85	168.0
66. Justise Hairston, Central Conn. St.	RB	SR	11	277	1,877	30	1,847	1	0	278	1,847	6.64	167.9
67. Matt Bassuener, Georgetown	QB	SR	10	98	434	122	312	209	1,359	307	1,671	5.44	167.1
68. Travis Clark, Ga. Southern	QB	SO	11	28	91	73	18	283	1,808	311	1,826	5.87	166.0
69. Nick Hill, Southern Ill.	QB	JR	13	91	494	112	382	196	1,721	287	2,103	7.33	161.8
70. Sawyer Smith, Portland St.	QB	SR	9	28	64	104	-40	188	1,491	216	1,451	6.72	161.2
71. Ron Whitcomb, Maine	QB	SR	11	162	552	191	361	240	1,398	402	1,759	4.38	159.9
72. Brett Hicks, Sam Houston St.	QB	JR	11	26	36	82	-46	270	1,786	296	1,740	5.88	158.2
73. Matt Hardin, Jacksonville St.	QB	JR	11	43	119	121	-2	233	1,728	276	1,726	6.25	156.9
74. Derrick Fourroux, McNeese St.	QB	FR	12	123	495	118	377	217	1,490	340	1,867	5.49	155.6
75. Eric Ward, Richmond	QB	FR	10	57	220	90	130	221	1,424	278	1,554	5.59	155.4
76. Marcus Mason, Youngstown St.	RB	SR	12	302	1,882	35	1,847	0	0	302	1,847	6.12	153.9
77. Dustin Croick, Iona	QB	JR	9	64	104	197	-93	236	1,474	300	1,381	4.60	153.4
78. Chris Walker, Alcorn St.	QB	SO	9	36	189	51	138	170	1,233	206	1,371	6.66	152.3
79. Cleveland McCoy, South Carolina St.	QB	JR	11	113	636	216	420	183	1,224	296	1,644	5.55	149.5
80. T.J. Brown, Butler	QB	JR	10	60	116	201	-85	313	1,572	373	1,487	3.99	148.7
81. Scott Phaydavong, Drake	RB	JR	11	277	1,698	85	1,613	0	0	277	1,613	5.82	146.6
82. Jack Rolovich, Montana St.	QB	JR	11	36	68	130	-62	228	1,674	264	1,612	6.11	146.5
83. Matt Abbey, Wagner	QB	SO	11	33	77	106	-29	307	1,618	340	1,589	4.67	144.5
84. Jimmie Russell, Bethune-Cookman	QB	JR	11	112	598	171	427	160	1,139	272	1,566	5.76	142.4
85. Matt Brennan, Cal Poly	QB	SO	11	118	471	127	344	169	1,208	287	1,552	5.41	141.1

Rank, Player	Pos.	Cl.	G	Rush Att	Rush Gain	Rush Loss	Rush Net	Pass Att	Pass Yds	Total Plays	Total Yds	Yds/Pl	Yds/Gm
86. Arkee Whitlock, Southern Ill.	RB	SR	13	317	1,884	56	1,828	0	0	317	1,828	5.77	140.6
87. Vashon Winton, Delaware St.	QB	SO	10	64	348	114	234	168	1,171	232	1,405	6.06	140.5
88. Derek Cassidy, Rhode Island	QB	SO	10	158	586	269	317	122	1,060	280	1,377	4.92	137.7
89. Mike McLeod, Yale	RB	SO	10	297	1,431	67	1,364	0	0	297	1,364	4.59	136.4
90. Tino Edgecombe, Texas Southern	QB	JR	10	40	150	97	53	192	1,292	232	1,345	5.80	134.5
91. Pierre Rembert, Illinois St.	RB	SR	13	355	1,813	70	1,743	0	0	355	1,743	4.91	134.1
92. D.D. Terry, Sam Houston St.	RB	SR	10	215	1,365	37	1,328	0	0	215	1,328	6.18	132.8
93. Steve Baylark, Massachusetts	RB	SR	15	338	2,023	63	1,960	0	0	338	1,960	5.80	130.7
94. Zac Barnard, Murray St.	QB	FR	11	34	25	172	-147	277	1,583	311	1,436	4.62	130.5
95. Herb Donaldson, Western Ill.	RB	SO	11	233	1,437	20	1,417	0	0	233	1,417	6.08	128.8
96. Donald Chapman, Tenn.-Martin	RB	JR	11	269	1,463	51	1,412	0	0	269	1,412	5.25	128.4
97. Brock Smith, Liberty	QB	SO	11	30	100	65	35	186	1,376	216	1,411	6.53	128.3
98. Chris Fletcher, Austin Peay	RB	JR	11	255	1,441	40	1,401	1	0	256	1,401	5.47	127.4
99. Renaldo Gray, Furman	QB	JR	10	63	180	110	70	168	1,184	231	1,254	5.43	125.4
100. Jarod Rucker, Bethune-Cookman	QB	JR	10	73	338	194	144	137	1,091	210	1,235	5.88	123.5

Passing Yards Per Game

Rank, Player	Pos.	Cl.	G	Att	Comp	Int	CPct	Comp/Gm	Yds/Att	Yds/Comp	TD	Yds	Yds/Gm
1. Sean Schaefer, Towson	QB	SO	10	380	260	9	68.42	26.0	7.98	11.67	19	3,033	303.3
2. Scott Knapp, Duquesne	QB	SO	10	351	209	13	59.54	20.9	8.13	13.65	28	2,853	285.3
3. Josh Johnson, San Diego	QB	JR	12	371	246	5	66.31	20.5	8.95	13.50	34	3,320	276.6
4. Tyler Thigpen, Coastal Caro.	QB	SR	12	339	217	11	64.01	18.0	9.72	15.19	29	3,296	274.6
5. Ryan Alexander, Davidson	QB	JR	10	377	215	10	57.03	21.5	6.85	12.00	21	2,581	258.1
6. Jason Murrietta, Northern Ariz.	QB	SR	11	329	214	5	65.05	19.4	8.59	13.21	34	2,827	257.0
7. Joe Flacco, Delaware	QB	JR	11	417	264	10	63.31	24.0	6.67	10.54	18	2,783	253.0
8. Dominic Randolph, Holy Cross	QB	SO	9	299	184	6	61.54	20.4	7.48	12.16	19	2,237	248.5
9. Scott Bonnono, St. Peter's	QB	JR	10	431	241	13	55.92	24.1	5.73	10.25	15	2,470	247.0
10. Jeff Terrell, Princeton	QB	SR	10	331	195	11	58.91	19.5	7.39	12.54	17	2,445	244.5
11. Collin Drafts, Charleston So.	QB	SR	11	319	223	14	69.91	20.2	8.35	11.95	21	2,665	242.2
12. Ricky Santos, New Hampshire	QB	JR	13	432	293	7	67.82	22.5	7.23	10.67	29	3,125	240.3
13. Wes Pope, Elon	QB	JR	11	375	228	12	60.80	20.7	6.86	11.28	16	2,572	233.8
14. Luke Drone, Illinois St.	QB	JR	13	349	203	13	58.17	15.6	8.48	14.59	21	2,961	227.7
15. Joseph DiGiacomo, Brown	QB	SR	10	301	168	15	55.81	16.8	7.18	12.86	13	2,161	216.1
16. Robert Irvin, Penn	QB	SO	10	312	174	12	55.77	17.4	6.82	12.23	10	2,128	212.8
17. Lee Sweeney, Tennessee Tech	QB	FR	11	356	189	17	53.09	17.1	6.44	12.13	17	2,292	208.3
18. Josh Swogger, Montana	QB	SR	13	358	195	12	54.47	15.0	7.50	13.77	17	2,685	206.5
19. Kevin Hoyng, Dayton	QB	SR	10	221	131	8	59.28	13.1	9.29	15.66	11	2,052	205.2
20. Matt Gutierrez, Idaho St.	QB	SR	11	342	187	14	54.68	17.0	6.54	11.96	16	2,237	203.3
21. Mark Cunningham, Austin Peay	QB	JR	11	326	197	13	60.43	17.9	6.86	11.35	12	2,236	203.2
22. Josh Dudash, Stony Brook	QB	JR	11	285	179	4	62.81	16.2	7.83	12.46	15	2,231	202.8
23. Devin Campbell, Gardner-Webb	QB	SO	11	311	174	17	55.95	15.8	7.12	12.73	15	2,215	201.3
24. Liam Coen, Massachusetts	QB	JR	15	334	217	10	64.97	14.4	9.03	13.90	26	3,016	201.0
25. Craig Hormann, Columbia	QB	JR	10	329	189	6	57.45	18.9	6.10	10.62	7	2,008	200.8
26. Justin Haddix, Western Ky.	QB	SR	11	279	171	9	61.29	15.5	7.84	12.78	14	2,186	198.7
27. Albert Chester II, Florida A&M	QB	JR	10	264	164	5	62.12	16.4	7.52	12.11	18	1,986	198.6
28. Casey Hansen, Norfolk St.	QB	JR	11	283	148	16	52.30	13.4	7.65	14.64	10	2,166	196.9
29. Brian Boland, Monmouth	QB	SR	12	305	197	9	64.59	16.4	7.71	11.94	14	2,353	196.0
30. Brandon Landers, Grambling	QB	SO	11	293	150	11	51.19	13.6	7.30	14.25	17	2,138	194.3
30. Duran Lawson, Citadel	QB	JR	11	325	203	11	62.46	18.4	6.58	10.53	14	2,138	194.3
32. Reilly Murphy, Indiana St.	QB	JR	9	261	143	8	54.79	15.8	6.69	12.22	8	1,747	194.1
33. Marvin Burroughs, Villanova	QB	SR	11	283	171	9	60.42	15.5	7.50	12.42	9	2,123	193.0
34. Steve LaFalce, Western Ill.	QB	SR	11	279	176	9	63.08	16.0	7.60	12.05	11	2,121	192.8
35. Chris Horton, Jacksonville	QB	JR	10	268	125	10	46.64	12.5	7.09	15.19	15	1,899	189.9
36. Tyler Arciaga, Sacred Heart	QB	SR	11	368	211	14	57.34	19.1	5.64	9.84	19	2,076	188.7
37. Anton Clarkson, Hofstra	QB	SR	10	287	160	3	55.75	16.0	6.55	11.76	8	1,881	188.1
38. Eric Cwalinski, Robert Morris	QB	SO	11	270	157	14	58.15	14.2	7.65	13.16	19	2,066	187.8
39. Brad Maurer, Lafayette	QB	SR	12	307	181	10	58.96	15.0	7.29	12.37	13	2,239	186.5
40. Ryan Doerffler, Valparaiso	QB	JR	11	306	148	13	48.37	13.4	6.70	13.85	13	2,050	186.3
41. Mike Saraceno, Colgate	QB	JR	11	259	151	9	58.30	13.7	7.91	13.56	11	2,048	186.1
42. Antonio Hefner, Tennessee St.	QB	SO	9	199	109	11	54.77	12.1	8.38	15.30	9	1,668	185.3
43. Mike Fritz, Dartmouth	QB	SR	10	263	162	10	61.60	16.2	6.99	11.35	7	1,838	183.8
44. Stephe McGrath, Marist	QB	JR	11	239	151	10	63.18	13.7	8.43	13.34	8	2,014	183.0
45. Sedale Threatt, Lehigh	QB	JR	11	246	151	5	61.38	13.7	8.16	13.30	14	2,008	182.5
46. Wes Marshall, Southern Utah	QB	JR	11	323	183	14	56.66	16.6	6.01	10.61	16	1,942	176.5
47. Eric Sanders, UNI	QB	JR	11	249	169	7	67.87	15.3	7.77	11.44	15	1,934	175.8
48. Marcel Marquez, Sacramento St.	QB	JR	11	270	142	15	52.59	12.9	7.07	13.45	10	1,910	173.6
49. Jimmy Oliver, Jackson St.	QB	JR	11	221	138	12	62.44	12.5	8.62	13.81	14	1,906	173.2
50. Michael Potts, William & Mary	QB	JR	9	216	124	7	57.41	13.7	7.22	12.57	10	1,559	173.2
51. Brian Yost, Morehead St.	QB	JR	11	286	170	12	59.44	15.4	6.61	11.12	11	1,891	171.9
52. Danny Southall, Stephen F. Austin	QB	JR	11	294	169	4	57.48	15.3	6.38	11.11	8	1,877	170.6
53. Justin Rascati, James Madison	QB	SR	12	231	153	6	66.23	12.7	8.85	13.37	20	2,045	170.4
54. Anthony Doria, St. Francis (Pa.)	QB	SR	11	286	151	6	52.80	13.7	6.54	12.39	15	1,871	170.0
55. Chris Wallace, Ark.-Pine Bluff	QB	SR	12	210	129	9	61.43	10.7	9.63	15.68	20	2,023	168.5
56. Bradley George, Texas St.	QB	FR	10	233	124	10	53.22	12.4	7.19	13.52	11	1,676	167.6
57. Josh Greco, Eastern Ky.	QB	JR	11	267	150	13	56.18	13.6	6.87	12.23	10	1,834	166.7
58. Sawyer Smith, Portland St.	QB	SR	9	188	100	8	53.19	11.1	7.93	14.91	14	1,491	165.6
59. Travis Clark, Ga. Southern	QB	SO	11	283	147	4	51.94	13.3	6.39	12.30	8	1,808	164.3
60. Dustin Croick, Iona	QB	JR	9	236	135	9	57.20	15.0	6.25	10.92	5	1,474	163.7
61. Brett Hicks, Sam Houston St.	QB	JR	11	270	145	11	53.70	13.1	6.61	12.32	8	1,786	162.3
62. Princeton Shepherd, Hampton	QB	SR	11	222	150	4	67.57	13.6	7.88	11.67	17	1,750	159.0

Rank, Player	Pos.	Cl.	G	Att	Comp	Int	CPct	Comp/ Gm	Yds/ Att	Yds/ Comp	TD	Yds	Yds/ Gm
63. Matt Nichols, Eastern Wash.	QB	FR	11	259	143	17	55.21	13.0	6.75	12.23	8	1,749	159.0
64. T.J. Brown, Butler	QB	JR	10	313	158	8	50.48	15.8	5.02	9.95	10	1,572	157.2
65. Matt Hardin, Jacksonville St.	QB	JR	11	233	127	10	54.51	11.5	7.42	13.61	8	1,728	157.0
66. Jack Rolovich, Montana St.	QB	JR	11	228	113	10	49.56	10.2	7.34	14.81	10	1,674	152.1
67. Kelcy Luke, Alabama A&M	QB	JR	12	301	174	8	57.81	14.5	6.04	10.45	16	1,818	151.5
68. Armanti Edwards, Appalachian St.	QB	FR	15	274	167	10	60.95	11.1	8.22	13.48	15	2,251	150.0
69. Tom Zetts, Youngstown St.	QB	JR	14	301	171	11	56.81	12.2	6.93	12.20	14	2,086	149.0
70. Matt Abbey, Wagner	QB	SO	11	307	150	12	48.86	13.6	5.27	10.79	9	1,618	147.0
71. Aries Nelson, Mississippi Val.	QB	SR	11	250	120	10	48.00	10.9	6.42	13.38	10	1,606	146.0
72. Zac Barnard, Murray St.	QB	FR	11	277	156	11	56.32	14.1	5.71	10.15	11	1,583	143.9
73. Matt Polhemus, Yale	QB	JR	10	208	109	6	52.40	10.9	6.91	13.18	5	1,437	143.7
74. Eric Ward, Richmond	QB	FR	10	221	132	6	59.73	13.2	6.44	10.79	11	1,424	142.4
75. Nathan Ford, Cornell	QB	SO	10	202	112	9	55.45	11.2	7.01	12.65	8	1,417	141.7
76. Chris Walker, Alcorn St.	QB	SO	9	170	83	4	48.82	9.2	7.25	14.86	10	1,233	137.0
77. Matt Bassuener, Georgetown	QB	SR	10	209	144	8	68.90	14.4	6.50	9.44	15	1,359	135.9
78. Nick Hill, Southern Ill.	QB	JR	13	196	121	4	61.73	9.3	8.78	14.22	15	1,721	132.3
79. Tino Edgecombe, Texas Southern	QB	JR	10	192	110	10	57.29	11.0	6.73	11.75	9	1,292	129.2
80. Ron Whitcomb, Maine	QB	SR	11	240	151	8	62.92	13.7	5.83	9.26	9	1,398	127.0
81. Brock Smith, Liberty	QB	SO	11	186	107	5	57.53	9.7	7.40	12.86	7	1,376	125.0
82. Derrick Fourroux, McNeese St.	QB	FR	12	217	118	7	54.38	9.8	6.87	12.63	10	1,490	124.1
83. Renaldo Gray, Furman	QB	JR	10	168	95	3	56.55	9.5	7.05	12.46	4	1,184	118.4
84. Vashon Winton, Delaware St.	QB	SO	10	168	99	2	58.93	9.9	6.97	11.83	10	1,171	117.1
85. Chris Pizzotti, Harvard	QB	JR	9	142	70	5	49.30	7.7	7.40	15.01	6	1,051	116.7
86. Matt Lopez, Chattanooga	QB	SR	9	172	86	8	50.00	9.5	6.06	12.13	8	1,043	115.8
87. Garrett Williams, Savannah St.	QB	SO	11	225	111	14	49.33	10.0	5.62	11.39	8	1,264	114.9
88. Cole Stinson, Eastern Ill.	QB	JR	12	224	122	11	54.46	10.1	6.02	11.06	12	1,349	112.4
89. Seth Babin, Southeastern La.	QB	SR	10	225	138	6	61.33	13.8	4.96	8.09	8	1,117	111.7
90. Cleveland McCoy, South Carolina St.	QB	JR	11	183	94	9	51.37	8.5	6.69	13.02	10	1,224	111.2
91. Matt Brennan, Cal Poly	QB	SO	11	169	76	7	44.97	6.9	7.15	15.89	10	1,208	109.8
92. Jarod Rucker, Bethune-Cookman	QB	JR	10	137	79	2	57.66	7.9	7.96	13.81	11	1,091	109.1
93. John Skelton, Fordham	QB	FR	9	167	74	8	44.31	8.2	5.75	12.97	6	960	106.6
94. Derek Cassidy, Rhode Island	QB	SO	10	122	60	8	49.18	6.0	8.69	17.67	6	1,060	106.0
95. Jimmie Russell, Bethune-Cookman	QB	JR	11	160	88	3	55.00	8.0	7.12	12.94	9	1,139	103.5
96. Kevin Ballatore, Southeast Mo. St.	QB	SR	11	211	102	6	48.34	9.2	5.24	10.83	7	1,105	100.4
97. Wayne Campbell, N.C. A&T	QB	FR	11	230	100	17	43.48	9.0	4.76	10.94	9	1,094	99.4
98. Chris Hanson, La Salle	QB	SO	10	163	98	10	60.12	9.8	5.97	9.93	7	973	97.3
99. Mario Melton, Morgan St.	QB	SO	10	148	70	9	47.30	7.0	6.24	13.20	5	924	92.4
100. Ryan Holmes, Central Conn. St.	QB	JR	11	105	59	3	56.19	5.3	9.14	16.27	5	960	87.2

Total Passing Yards

Rank, Player	Pos.	Cl.	G	Att	Comp	Int	CPct	Comp/ Gm	Yds/ Att	Yds/ Comp	TD	Yds
1. Josh Johnson, San Diego	QB	JR	12	371	246	5	66.31	20.5	8.95	13.50	34	3,320
2. Tyler Thigpen, Coastal Caro.	QB	SR	12	339	217	11	64.01	18.0	9.72	15.19	29	3,296
3. Ricky Santos, New Hampshire	QB	JR	13	432	293	7	67.82	22.5	7.23	10.67	29	3,125
4. Sean Schaefer, Towson	QB	SO	10	380	260	9	68.42	26.0	7.98	11.67	19	3,033
5. Liam Coen, Massachusetts	QB	JR	15	334	217	10	64.97	14.4	9.03	13.90	26	3,016
6. Luke Drone, Illinois St.	QB	JR	13	349	203	13	58.17	15.6	8.48	14.59	21	2,961
7. Scott Knapp, Duquesne	QB	SO	10	351	209	13	59.54	20.9	8.13	13.65	28	2,853
8. Jason Murrietta, Northern Ariz.	QB	SR	11	329	214	5	65.05	19.4	8.59	13.21	34	2,827
9. Joe Flacco, Delaware	QB	JR	11	417	264	10	63.31	24.0	6.67	10.54	18	2,783
10. Josh Swogger, Montana	QB	SR	13	358	195	12	54.47	15.0	7.50	13.77	17	2,685
11. Collin Drafts, Charleston So.	QB	SR	11	319	223	14	69.91	20.2	8.35	11.95	21	2,665
12. Ryan Alexander, Davidson	QB	JR	10	377	215	10	57.03	21.5	6.85	12.00	21	2,581
13. Wes Pope, Elon	QB	JR	11	375	228	12	60.80	20.7	6.86	11.28	16	2,572
14. Scott Bonnono, St. Peter's	QB	JR	10	431	241	13	55.92	24.1	5.73	10.25	15	2,470
15. Jeff Terrell, Princeton	QB	SR	10	331	195	11	58.91	19.5	7.39	12.54	17	2,445
16. Brian Boland, Monmouth	QB	SR	12	305	197	9	64.59	16.4	7.71	11.94	14	2,353
17. Lee Sweeney, Tennessee Tech	QB	FR	11	356	189	17	53.09	17.1	6.44	12.13	17	2,292
18. Armanti Edwards, Appalachian St.	QB	FR	15	274	167	10	60.95	11.1	8.22	13.48	15	2,251
19. Brad Maurer, Lafayette	QB	SR	12	307	181	10	58.96	15.0	7.29	12.37	13	2,239
20. Matt Gutierrez, Idaho St.	QB	SR	11	342	187	14	54.68	17.0	6.54	11.96	16	2,237
20. Dominic Randolph, Holy Cross	QB	SO	9	299	184	6	61.54	20.4	7.48	12.16	19	2,237
22. Mark Cunningham, Austin Peay	QB	JR	11	326	197	13	60.43	17.9	6.86	11.35	12	2,236
23. Josh Dudash, Stony Brook	QB	JR	11	285	179	4	62.81	16.2	7.83	12.46	15	2,231
24. Devin Campbell, Gardner-Webb	QB	SO	11	311	174	17	55.95	15.8	7.12	12.73	15	2,215
25. Justin Haddix, Western Ky.	QB	SR	11	279	171	9	61.29	15.5	7.84	12.78	14	2,186
26. Casey Hansen, Norfolk St.	QB	JR	11	283	148	16	52.30	13.4	7.65	14.64	10	2,166
27. Joseph DiGiacomo, Brown	QB	SR	10	301	168	15	55.81	16.8	7.18	12.86	13	2,161
28. Brandon Landers, Grambling	QB	SO	11	293	150	11	51.19	13.6	7.30	14.25	17	2,138
28. Duran Lawson, Citadel	QB	JR	11	325	203	11	62.46	18.4	6.58	10.53	14	2,138
30. Robert Irvin, Penn	QB	SO	10	312	174	12	55.77	17.4	6.82	12.23	10	2,128
31. Marvin Burroughs, Villanova	QB	SR	11	283	171	9	60.42	15.5	7.50	12.42	9	2,123
32. Steve LaFalce, Western Ill.	QB	SR	11	279	176	9	63.08	16.0	7.60	12.05	11	2,121
33. Tom Zetts, Youngstown St.	QB	JR	14	301	171	11	56.81	12.2	6.93	12.20	14	2,086
34. Tyler Arciaga, Sacred Heart	QB	SR	11	368	211	14	57.34	19.1	5.64	9.84	19	2,076
35. Eric Cwalinski, Robert Morris	QB	SO	11	270	157	14	58.15	14.2	7.65	13.16	19	2,066
36. Kevin Hoyng, Dayton	QB	SR	10	221	131	8	59.28	13.1	9.29	15.66	11	2,052
37. Ryan Doerffler, Valparaiso	QB	JR	11	306	148	13	48.37	13.4	6.70	13.85	13	2,050
38. Mike Saraceno, Colgate	QB	JR	11	259	151	9	58.30	13.7	7.91	13.56	11	2,048

Rank, Player	Pos.	Cl.	G	Att	Comp	Int	CPct	Comp/ Gm	Yds/ Att	Yds/ Comp	TD	Yds
39. Justin Rascati, James Madison	QB	SR	12	231	153	6	66.23	12.7	8.85	13.37	20	2,045
40. Chris Wallace, Ark.-Pine Bluff	QB	SR	12	210	129	9	61.43	10.7	9.63	15.68	20	2,023
41. Stephen McGrath, Marist	QB	JR	11	239	151	10	63.18	13.7	8.43	13.34	8	2,014
42. Sedale Threatt, Lehigh	QB	JR	11	246	151	5	61.38	13.7	8.16	13.30	14	2,008
42. Craig Hormann, Columbia	QB	JR	10	329	189	6	57.45	18.9	6.10	10.62	7	2,008
44. Albert Chester II, Florida A&M	QB	JR	10	264	164	5	62.12	16.4	7.52	12.11	18	1,986
45. Wes Marshall, Southern Utah	QB	JR	11	323	183	14	56.66	16.6	6.01	10.61	16	1,942
46. Eric Sanders, UNI	QB	JR	11	249	169	7	67.87	15.3	7.77	11.44	15	1,934
47. Marcel Marquez, Sacramento St.	QB	JR	11	270	142	15	52.59	12.9	7.07	13.45	10	1,910
48. Jimmy Oliver, Jackson St.	QB	JR	11	221	138	12	62.44	12.5	8.62	13.81	14	1,906
49. Chris Horton, Jacksonville	QB	JR	10	268	125	10	46.64	12.5	7.09	15.19	15	1,899
50. Brian Yost, Morehead St.	QB	JR	11	286	170	12	59.44	15.4	6.61	11.12	11	1,891
51. Anton Clarkson, Hofstra	QB	SR	10	287	160	3	55.75	16.0	6.55	11.76	8	1,881
52. Danny Southall, Stephen F. Austin	QB	JR	11	294	169	4	57.48	15.3	6.38	11.11	8	1,877
53. Anthony Doria, St. Francis (Pa.)	QB	SR	11	286	151	6	52.80	13.7	6.54	12.39	15	1,871
54. Mike Fritz, Dartmouth	QB	SR	10	263	162	10	61.60	16.2	6.99	11.35	7	1,838
55. Josh Greco, Eastern Ky.	QB	JR	11	267	150	13	56.18	13.6	6.87	12.23	10	1,834
56. Kelcy Luke, Alabama A&M	QB	JR	12	301	174	8	57.81	14.5	6.04	10.45	16	1,818
57. Travis Clark, Ga. Southern	QB	SO	11	283	147	4	51.94	13.3	6.39	12.30	8	1,808
58. Brett Hicks, Sam Houston St.	QB	JR	11	270	145	11	53.70	13.1	6.61	12.32	8	1,786
59. Princeton Shepherd, Hampton	QB	SR	11	222	150	4	67.57	13.6	7.88	11.67	17	1,750
60. Matt Nichols, Eastern Wash.	QB	FR	11	259	143	17	55.21	13.0	6.75	12.23	8	1,749
61. Reilly Murphy, Indiana St.	QB	JR	9	261	143	8	54.79	15.8	6.69	12.22	8	1,747
62. Matt Hardin, Jacksonville St.	QB	JR	11	233	127	10	54.51	11.5	7.42	13.61	8	1,728
63. Nick Hill, Southern Ill.	QB	JR	13	196	121	4	61.73	9.3	8.78	14.22	15	1,721
64. Bradley George, Texas St.	QB	FR	10	233	124	10	53.22	12.4	7.19	13.52	11	1,676
65. Jack Rolovich, Montana St.	QB	JR	11	228	113	10	49.56	10.2	7.34	14.81	10	1,674
66. Antonio Hefner, Tennessee St.	QB	SO	9	199	109	11	54.77	12.1	8.38	15.30	9	1,668
67. Matt Abbey, Wagner	QB	SO	11	307	150	12	48.86	13.6	5.27	10.79	9	1,618
68. Aries Nelson, Mississippi Val.	QB	SR	11	250	120	10	48.00	10.9	6.42	13.38	10	1,606
69. Zac Barnard, Murray St.	QB	FR	11	277	156	11	56.32	14.1	5.71	10.15	11	1,583
70. T.J. Brown, Butler	QB	JR	10	313	158	8	50.48	15.8	5.02	9.95	10	1,572
71. Michael Potts, William & Mary	QB	JR	9	216	124	7	57.41	13.7	7.22	12.57	10	1,559
72. Sawyer Smith, Portland St.	QB	SR	9	188	100	8	53.19	11.1	7.93	14.91	14	1,491
73. Derrick Fourroux, McNeese St.	QB	FR	12	217	118	7	54.38	9.8	6.87	12.63	10	1,490
74. Dustin Croick, Iona	QB	JR	9	236	135	9	57.20	15.0	6.25	10.92	5	1,474
75. Matt Polhemus, Yale	QB	JR	10	208	109	6	52.40	10.9	6.91	13.18	5	1,437
76. Eric Ward, Richmond	QB	FR	10	221	132	6	59.73	13.2	6.44	10.79	11	1,424
77. Nathan Ford, Cornell	QB	SO	10	202	112	9	55.45	11.2	7.01	12.65	8	1,417
78. Ron Whitcomb, Maine	QB	SR	11	240	151	8	62.92	13.7	5.83	9.26	9	1,398
79. Brock Smith, Liberty	QB	SO	11	186	107	5	57.53	9.7	7.40	12.86	7	1,376
80. Matt Bassuener, Georgetown	QB	SR	10	209	144	8	68.90	14.4	6.50	9.44	15	1,359
81. Cole Stinson, Eastern Ill.	QB	JR	12	224	122	11	54.46	10.1	6.02	11.06	12	1,349
82. Tino Edgecombe, Texas Southern	QB	JR	10	192	110	10	57.29	11.0	6.73	11.75	9	1,292
83. Garrett Williams, Savannah St.	QB	SO	11	225	111	14	49.33	10.0	5.62	11.39	8	1,264
84. Chris Walker, Alcorn St.	QB	SO	9	170	83	4	48.82	9.2	7.25	14.86	10	1,233
85. Cleveland McCoy, South Carolina St.	QB	JR	11	183	94	9	51.37	8.5	6.69	13.02	10	1,224
86. Matt Brennan, Cal Poly	QB	SO	11	169	76	7	44.97	6.9	7.15	15.89	10	1,208
87. Renaldo Gray, Furman	QB	JR	10	168	95	3	56.55	9.5	7.05	12.46	4	1,184
88. Vashon Winton, Delaware St.	QB	SO	10	168	99	2	58.93	9.9	6.97	11.83	10	1,171
89. Jimmie Russell, Bethune-Cookman	QB	JR	11	160	88	3	55.00	8.0	7.12	12.94	9	1,139
90. Seth Babin, Southeastern La.	QB	SR	10	225	138	6	61.33	13.8	4.96	8.09	8	1,117
91. Kevin Ballatore, Southeast Mo. St.	QB	SR	11	211	102	6	48.34	9.2	5.24	10.83	7	1,105
92. Wayne Campbell, N.C. A&T	QB	FR	11	230	100	17	43.48	9.0	4.76	10.94	9	1,094
93. Jarod Rucker, Bethune-Cookman	QB	JR	10	137	79	2	57.66	7.9	7.96	13.81	11	1,091
94. Derek Cassidy, Rhode Island	QB	SO	10	122	60	8	49.18	6.0	8.69	17.67	6	1,060
95. Chris Pizzotti, Harvard	QB	JR	9	142	70	5	49.30	7.7	7.40	15.01	6	1,051
96. Matt Lopez, Chattanooga	QB	SR	9	172	86	8	50.00	9.5	6.06	12.13	8	1,043
97. Chris Hanson, La Salle	QB	SO	10	163	98	10	60.12	9.8	5.97	9.93	7	973
98. John Skelton, Fordham	QB	FR	9	167	74	8	44.31	8.2	5.75	12.97	6	960
98. Ryan Holmes, Central Conn. St.	QB	JR	11	105	59	3	56.19	5.3	9.14	16.27	5	960
100. Daniel Bocanegra, Albany (N.Y.)	QB	SO	11	175	90	7	51.43	8.1	5.33	10.36	5	932

Pass Completions Per Game

Rank, Player	Pos	Cl.	G	Att	Comp	Int	CPct	Yds	Yds/ Att	Yds/ Comp	TD	Comp/ Gm
1. Sean Schaefer, Towson	QB	SO	10	380	260	9	68.42	3,033	7.98	11.67	19	26.00
2. Scott Bonnono, St. Peter's	QB	JR	10	431	241	13	55.92	2,470	5.73	10.25	15	24.10
3. Joe Flacco, Delaware	QB	JR	11	417	264	10	63.31	2,783	6.67	10.54	18	24.00
4. Ricky Santos, New Hampshire	QB	JR	13	432	293	7	67.82	3,125	7.23	10.67	29	22.54
5. Ryan Alexander, Davidson	QB	JR	10	377	215	10	57.03	2,581	6.85	12.00	21	21.50
6. Scott Knapp, Duquesne	QB	SO	10	351	209	13	59.54	2,853	8.13	13.65	28	20.90
7. Wes Pope, Elon	QB	JR	11	375	228	12	60.80	2,572	6.86	11.28	16	20.73
8. Josh Johnson, San Diego	QB	JR	12	371	246	5	66.31	3,320	8.95	13.50	34	20.50
9. Dominic Randolph, Holy Cross	QB	SO	9	299	184	6	61.54	2,237	7.48	12.16	19	20.44
10. Collin Drafts, Charleston So.	QB	SR	11	319	223	14	69.91	2,665	8.35	11.95	21	20.27
11. Jeff Terrell, Princeton	QB	SR	10	331	195	11	58.91	2,445	7.39	12.54	17	19.50
12. Jason Murrietta, Northern Ariz.	QB	SR	11	329	214	5	65.05	2,827	8.59	13.21	34	19.45
13. Tyler Arciaga, Sacred Heart	QB	SR	11	368	211	14	57.34	2,076	5.64	9.84	19	19.18
14. Craig Hormann, Columbia	QB	JR	10	329	189	6	57.45	2,008	6.10	10.62	7	18.90
15. Duran Lawson, Citadel	QB	JR	11	325	203	11	62.46	2,138	6.58	10.53	14	18.45

Rank, Player	Pos	Cl.	G	Att	Comp	Int	CPct	Yds	Yds/ Att	Yds/ Comp	TD	Comp/ Gm
16. Tyler Thigpen, Coastal Caro.	QB	SR	12	339	217	11	64.01	3,296	9.72	15.19	29	18.08
17. Mark Cunningham, Austin Peay	QB	JR	11	326	197	13	60.43	2,236	6.86	11.35	12	17.91
18. Robert Irvin, Penn	QB	SO	10	312	174	12	55.77	2,128	6.82	12.23	10	17.40
19. Lee Sweeney, Tennessee Tech	QB	FR	11	356	189	17	53.09	2,292	6.44	12.13	17	17.18
20. Matt Gutierrez, Idaho St.	QB	SR	11	342	187	14	54.68	2,237	6.54	11.96	16	17.00
21. Joseph DiGiacomo, Brown	QB	SR	10	301	168	15	55.81	2,161	7.18	12.86	13	16.80
22. Wes Marshall, Southern Utah	QB	JR	11	323	183	14	56.66	1,942	6.01	10.61	16	16.64
23. Brian Boland, Monmouth	QB	SR	12	305	197	9	64.59	2,353	7.71	11.94	14	16.42
24. Albert Chester II, Florida A&M	QB	JR	10	264	164	5	62.12	1,986	7.52	12.11	18	16.40
25. Josh Dudash, Stony Brook	QB	JR	11	285	179	4	62.81	2,231	7.83	12.46	15	16.27
26. Mike Fritz, Dartmouth	QB	SR	10	263	162	10	61.60	1,838	6.99	11.35	7	16.20
27. Steve LaFalce, Western Ill.	QB	SR	11	279	176	9	63.08	2,121	7.60	12.05	11	16.00
27. Anton Clarkson, Hofstra	QB	SR	10	287	160	3	55.75	1,881	6.55	11.76	8	16.00
29. Reilly Murphy, Indiana St.	QB	JR	9	261	143	8	54.79	1,747	6.69	12.22	8	15.89
30. Devin Campbell, Gardner-Webb	QB	SO	11	311	174	17	55.95	2,215	7.12	12.73	15	15.82
31. T.J. Brown, Butler	QB	JR	10	313	158	8	50.48	1,572	5.02	9.95	10	15.80
32. Luke Drone, Illinois St.	QB	JR	13	349	203	13	58.17	2,961	8.48	14.59	21	15.62
33. Justin Haddix, Western Ky.	QB	SR	11	279	171	9	61.29	2,186	7.84	12.78	14	15.55
33. Marvin Burroughs, Villanova	QB	SR	11	283	171	9	60.42	2,123	7.50	12.42	9	15.55
35. Brian Yost, Morehead St.	QB	JR	11	286	170	12	59.44	1,891	6.61	11.12	11	15.45
36. Danny Southall, Stephen F. Austin	QB	JR	11	294	169	4	57.48	1,877	6.38	11.11	8	15.36
36. Eric Sanders, UNI	QB	JR	11	249	169	7	67.87	1,934	7.77	11.44	15	15.36
38. Brad Maurer, Lafayette	QB	SR	12	307	181	10	58.96	2,239	7.29	12.37	13	15.08
39. Josh Swogger, Montana	QB	SR	13	358	195	12	54.47	2,685	7.50	13.77	17	15.00
39. Dustin Croick, Iona	QB	JR	9	236	135	9	57.20	1,474	6.25	10.92	5	15.00
41. Kelcy Luke, Alabama A&M	QB	JR	12	301	174	8	57.81	1,818	6.04	10.45	16	14.50
42. Liam Coen, Massachusetts	QB	JR	15	334	217	10	64.97	3,016	9.03	13.90	26	14.47
43. Matt Bassuener, Georgetown	QB	SR	10	209	144	8	68.90	1,359	6.50	9.44	15	14.40
44. Eric Cwalinski, Robert Morris	QB	SO	11	270	157	14	58.15	2,066	7.65	13.16	19	14.27
45. Zac Barnard, Murray St.	QB	FR	11	277	156	11	56.32	1,583	5.71	10.15	11	14.18
46. Seth Babin, Southeastern La.	QB	SR	10	225	138	6	61.33	1,117	4.96	8.09	8	13.80
47. Michael Potts, William & Mary	QB	JR	9	216	124	7	57.41	1,559	7.22	12.57	10	13.78
48. Anthony Doria, St. Francis (Pa.)	QB	SR	11	286	151	6	52.80	1,871	6.54	12.39	15	13.73
48. Ron Whitcomb, Maine	QB	SR	11	240	151	8	62.92	1,398	5.83	9.26	9	13.73
48. Stephen McGrath, Marist	QB	JR	11	239	151	10	63.18	2,014	8.43	13.34	8	13.73
48. Mike Saraceno, Colgate	QB	JR	11	259	151	9	58.30	2,048	7.91	13.56	11	13.73
48. Sedale Threatt, Lehigh	QB	JR	11	246	151	5	61.38	2,008	8.16	13.30	14	13.73
53. Matt Abbey, Wagner	QB	SO	11	307	150	12	48.86	1,618	5.27	10.79	9	13.64
53. Josh Greco, Eastern Ky.	QB	JR	11	267	150	13	56.18	1,834	6.87	12.23	10	13.64
53. Brandon Landers, Grambling	QB	SO	11	293	150	11	51.19	2,138	7.30	14.25	17	13.64
53. Princeton Shepherd, Hampton	QB	SR	11	222	150	4	67.57	1,750	7.88	11.67	17	13.64
57. Ryan Doerffler, Valparaiso	QB	JR	11	306	148	13	48.37	2,050	6.70	13.85	13	13.45
57. Casey Hansen, Norfolk St.	QB	JR	11	283	148	16	52.30	2,166	7.65	14.64	10	13.45
59. Travis Clark, Ga. Southern	QB	SO	11	283	147	4	51.94	1,808	6.39	12.30	8	13.36
60. Eric Ward, Richmond	QB	FR	10	221	132	6	59.73	1,424	6.44	10.79	11	13.20
61. Brett Hicks, Sam Houston St.	QB	JR	11	270	145	11	53.70	1,786	6.61	12.32	8	13.18
62. Kevin Hoyng, Dayton	QB	SR	10	221	131	8	59.28	2,052	9.29	15.66	11	13.10
63. Matt Nichols, Eastern Wash.	QB	FR	11	259	143	17	55.21	1,749	6.75	12.23	8	13.00
64. Marcel Marquez, Sacramento St.	QB	JR	11	270	142	15	52.59	1,910	7.07	13.45	10	12.91
65. Justin Rascati, James Madison	QB	SR	12	231	153	6	66.23	2,045	8.85	13.37	20	12.75
66. Jimmy Oliver, Jackson St.	QB	JR	11	221	138	12	62.44	1,906	8.62	13.81	14	12.55
67. Chris Horton, Jacksonville	QB	JR	10	268	125	10	46.64	1,899	7.09	15.19	15	12.50
68. Bradley George, Texas St.	QB	FR	10	233	124	10	53.22	1,676	7.19	13.52	11	12.40
69. Tom Zetts, Youngstown St.	QB	JR	14	301	171	11	56.81	2,086	6.93	12.20	14	12.21
70. Antonio Hefner, Tennessee St.	QB	SO	9	199	109	11	54.77	1,668	8.38	15.30	9	12.11
71. Matt Hardin, Jacksonville St.	QB	JR	11	233	127	10	54.51	1,728	7.42	13.61	8	11.55
72. Nathan Ford, Cornell	QB	SO	10	202	112	9	55.45	1,417	7.01	12.65	8	11.20
73. Armanti Edwards, Appalachian St.	QB	FR	15	274	167	10	60.95	2,251	8.22	13.48	15	11.13
74. Sawyer Smith, Portland St.	QB	SR	9	188	100	8	53.19	1,491	7.93	14.91	14	11.11
75. Tino Edgecombe, Texas Southern	QB	JR	10	192	110	10	57.29	1,292	6.73	11.75	9	11.00
76. Aries Nelson, Mississippi Val.	QB	SR	11	250	120	10	48.00	1,606	6.42	13.38	10	10.91
77. Matt Polhemus, Yale	QB	JR	10	208	109	6	52.40	1,437	6.91	13.18	5	10.90
78. Chris Wallace, Ark.-Pine Bluff	QB	SR	12	210	129	9	61.43	2,023	9.63	15.68	20	10.75
79. Jack Rolovich, Montana St.	QB	JR	11	228	113	10	49.56	1,674	7.34	14.81	10	10.27
80. Cole Stinson, Eastern Ill.	QB	JR	12	224	122	11	54.46	1,349	6.02	11.06	12	10.17
81. Garrett Williams, Savannah St.	QB	SO	11	225	111	14	49.33	1,264	5.62	11.39	8	10.09
82. Vashon Winton, Delaware St.	QB	SO	10	168	99	2	58.93	1,171	6.97	11.83	10	9.90
83. Derrick Fourroux, McNeese St.	QB	FR	12	217	118	7	54.38	1,490	6.87	12.63	10	9.83
84. Chris Hanson, La Salle	QB	SO	10	163	98	10	60.12	973	5.97	9.93	7	9.80
85. Brock Smith, Liberty	QB	SO	11	186	107	5	57.53	1,376	7.40	12.86	7	9.73
86. Matt Lopez, Chattanooga	QB	SR	9	172	86	8	50.00	1,043	6.06	12.13	8	9.56
87. Renaldo Gray, Furman	QB	JR	10	168	95	3	56.55	1,184	7.05	12.46	4	9.50
88. Nick Hill, Southern Ill.	QB	JR	13	196	121	4	61.73	1,721	8.78	14.22	15	9.31
89. Kevin Ballatore, Southeast Mo. St.	QB	SR	11	211	102	6	48.34	1,105	5.24	10.83	7	9.27
90. Chris Walker, Alcorn St.	QB	SO	9	170	83	4	48.82	1,233	7.25	14.86	10	9.22
91. Wayne Campbell, N.C. A&T	QB	FR	11	230	100	17	43.48	1,094	4.76	10.94	9	9.09
92. Cleveland McCoy, South Carolina St.	QB	JR	11	183	94	9	51.37	1,224	6.69	13.02	10	8.55
93. Antonio Miller, Chattanooga	QB	JR	11	161	91	5	56.52	739	4.59	8.12	4	8.27
93. Jefferson Adcock, Samford	QB	SR	11	169	91	7	53.85	915	5.41	10.05	5	8.27
95. John Skelton, Fordham	QB	FR	9	167	74	8	44.31	960	5.75	12.97	6	8.22
96. Daniel Bocanegra, Albany (N.Y.)	QB	SO	11	175	90	7	51.43	932	5.33	10.36	5	8.18
97. Roch Charpentier, Northwestern St.	QB	SO	10	160	80	4	50.00	837	5.23	10.46	5	8.00
97. Jimmie Russell, Bethune-Cookman	QB	JR	11	160	88	3	55.00	1,139	7.12	12.94	9	8.00
99. Jarod Rucker, Bethune-Cookman	QB	JR	10	137	79	2	57.66	1,091	7.96	13.81	11	7.90
100. Chris Pizzotti, Harvard	QB	JR	9	142	70	5	49.30	1,051	7.40	15.01	6	7.78

Receptions Per Game

Rank, Player	Pos	Cl.	G	Rec	Yds	TD	Rec/ Gm	Yds/ Rec	Yds/ Gm
1. Maurice Price, Charleston So.	WR	JR	11	103	985	10	9.36	9.56	89.55
2. Alex Watson, Northern Ariz.	WR	JR	11	82	1,017	15	7.45	12.40	92.45
3. Jaleel Kindell, St. Peter's	WR	SO	10	74	855	3	7.40	11.55	85.50
4. David Ball, New Hampshire	WR	SR	13	93	1,114	13	7.15	11.98	85.69
5. Lou Russo, La Salle	WR	SR	10	70	744	5	7.00	10.63	74.40
6. Lanis Frederick, Austin Peay	WR	SO	11	77	1,101	7	7.00	14.30	100.09
7. Terrell Hudgins, Elon	WR	FR	10	69	1,027	8	6.90	14.88	102.70
8. Michael Mayers, Elon	WR	JR	11	73	866	3	6.64	11.86	78.73
9. Ryan Maher, Holy Cross	WR	JR	11	69	797	6	6.27	11.55	72.45
9. Eric Weems, Bethune-Cookman	WR	SR	11	69	918	9	6.27	13.30	83.45
11. Eric Yancey, Towson	WR	SR	11	68	826	10	6.18	12.15	75.09
12. Bruce Hocker, Duquesne	WR	JR	10	61	1,070	16	6.10	17.54	107.00
12. Dan Spriggs, Duquesne	WR	SR	10	61	778	4	6.10	12.75	77.80
14. Adam San Miguel, Monmouth	WR	SR	12	73	872	6	6.08	11.95	72.67
15. Brett Dioguardi, Davidson	WR	SR	10	59	859	6	5.90	14.56	85.90
16. Ben Patrick, Delaware	TE	SR	11	64	639	6	5.82	9.98	58.09
16. Duvaughn Flagler, Gardner-Webb	WR	JR	11	64	740	7	5.82	11.56	67.27
18. Aaron Love, Delaware	WR	SO	10	58	740	4	5.80	12.76	74.00
19. Curtis Hamilton, Western Ky.	WR	JR	9	52	841	10	5.78	16.17	93.44
19. Nate Miller, Butler	WR	JR	9	52	551	5	5.78	10.60	61.22
21. Arel Gordon, Maine	WR	SR	11	63	535	3	5.73	8.49	48.64
21. Michael Caputo, St. Francis (Pa.)	WR	SR	11	63	857	8	5.73	13.60	77.91
21. Roosevelt Kiser, Florida A&M	WR	SR	11	63	647	5	5.73	10.27	58.82
24. Ryan Fuselier, Dartmouth	WR	SR	10	57	711	3	5.70	12.47	71.10
25. Emanuel Hassell, Chattanooga	WR	SR	11	62	468	1	5.64	7.55	42.55
26. Brendan Circle, Princeton	WR	JR	10	56	835	7	5.60	14.91	83.50
27. Shaine Smith, Hofstra	WR	SR	11	60	951	9	5.45	15.85	86.45
27. Michael Hines, Western Caro.	WR	JR	11	60	461	5	5.45	7.68	41.91
29. Arman Shields, Richmond	WR	JR	10	54	643	5	5.40	11.91	64.30
30. Keith LeVan, New Hampshire	RB	JR	13	70	672	5	5.38	9.60	51.69
31. Carl Berman, Indiana St.	WR	SR	11	59	783	5	5.36	13.27	71.18
32. Marco Thomas, Western Ill.	WR	SR	11	58	738	4	5.27	12.72	67.09
33. John Bond, St. Peter's	WR	JR	9	47	528	6	5.22	11.23	58.67
34. Clyde Edwards, Grambling	WR	JR	11	56	789	11	5.09	14.09	71.73
35. Jerome Simpson, Coastal Caro.	WR	JR	12	61	1,077	16	5.08	17.66	89.75
36. Micheal Jefferson, Montana St.	WR	SR	13	66	1,023	9	5.08	15.50	78.69
37. Shaheer McBride, Delaware St.	WR	JR	11	55	852	11	5.00	15.49	77.45
37. Gerard Landry, Southern U.	WR	JR	11	55	727	5	5.00	13.22	66.09
37. Steve Ogden, Valparaiso	WR	SO	11	55	1,048	8	5.00	19.05	95.27
40. Marquay McDaniel, Hampton	WR	SR	12	59	786	14	4.92	13.32	65.50
41. Chris Turner, Wagner	WR	SR	11	54	658	8	4.91	12.19	59.82
41. Joey Hew Len, Southern Utah	WR	SR	11	54	575	8	4.91	10.65	52.27
43. Sam Logan, Indiana St.	WR	SR	10	49	535	4	4.90	10.92	53.50
43. Nick Ruhe, Dayton	WR	SR	10	49	977	3	4.90	19.94	97.70
45. Onrea Jones, Hampton	WR	SR	12	57	679	5	4.75	11.91	56.58
46. Charles Sullivan, Hofstra	WR	JR	11	52	526	1	4.73	10.12	47.82
46. Wes Doyle, San Diego	WR	JR	11	52	909	11	4.73	17.48	82.64
48. Braden Lepisto, Penn	WR	JR	10	47	625	2	4.70	13.30	62.50
48. Carlton McFadgen, Dayton	WR	SR	10	47	845	5	4.70	17.98	84.50
50. Ben Hannula, San Diego	WR	SO	12	56	549	4	4.67	9.80	45.75
51. Larry Shipp, Tennessee Tech	WR	JR	11	51	799	8	4.64	15.67	72.64
52. Beaux Jones, Davidson	WR	JR	10	46	570	5	4.60	12.39	57.00
53. Marcus Lee, Towson	WR	SO	11	50	546	1	4.55	10.92	49.64
53. Dwayne Eley, Stony Brook	WR	SO	11	50	670	4	4.55	13.40	60.91
53. Kyle Barber, Eastern Ky.	WR	JR	11	50	462	1	4.55	9.24	42.00
56. Paul Raymond, Brown	WR	JR	10	45	654	4	4.50	14.53	65.40
56. Lonnie Hill, Brown	WR	SR	10	45	707	5	4.50	15.71	70.70
58. Demetrius Harrison, Towson	WR	JR	11	49	650	4	4.45	13.27	59.09
58. Jeff Moore, Samford	WR	JR	11	49	668	5	4.45	13.63	60.73
58. Willie Hayward, Florida A&M	WR	JR	11	49	674	5	4.45	13.76	61.27
61. Austin Knowlin, Columbia	WR	FR	10	44	553	4	4.40	12.57	55.30
61. Ryan Hubbard, Davidson	WR	JR	10	44	542	5	4.40	12.32	54.20
63. Tony Davis, Eastern Wash.	WR	FR	11	48	541	2	4.36	11.27	49.18
63. Austin Gaines, Gardner-Webb	WR	SR	11	48	690	3	4.36	14.38	62.73
63. Brent Craft, Georgetown	WR	JR	11	48	447	2	4.36	9.31	40.64
63. Henry Tolbert, Grambling	WR	SR	11	48	730	4	4.36	15.21	66.36
63. Rod Harper, Murray St.	WR	SO	11	48	573	8	4.36	11.94	52.09
68. Matt Carre, Penn	RB	SR	10	43	697	3	4.30	16.21	69.70
69. Freddie Young, Samford	WR	SR	11	47	393	1	4.27	8.36	35.73
69. Crawford Kilpatrick, Southeastern La.	WR	FR	11	47	391	3	4.27	8.32	35.55
71. William Mayfield, Appalachian St.	WR	SR	15	64	1,129	5	4.27	17.64	75.27
72. Donell Wheaton, Montana St.	WR	SR	13	55	757	4	4.23	13.76	58.23
73. Chandler Henley, Yale	WR	SR	10	42	578	2	4.20	13.76	57.80
73. Bernie Cevis, La Salle	WR	JR	10	42	539	5	4.20	12.83	53.90
75. Thomas Harrison, Holy Cross	WR	JR	11	46	569	4	4.18	12.37	51.73
76. Joe Ort, Lafayette	WR	SR	12	50	814	3	4.17	16.28	67.83
77. Jonathan Summers, Bethune-Cookman	WR	SR	9	37	458	4	4.11	12.38	50.89
78. Zac Canty, Cornell	WR	SO	10	41	499	3	4.10	12.17	49.90
78. Brian Brigham, Princeton	WR	SR	10	41	520	2	4.10	12.68	52.00
80. Kory Alston, Gardner-Webb	WR	SR	11	45	487	4	4.09	10.82	44.27

Rank, Player	Pos	Cl.	G	Rec	Yds	TD	Rec/ Gm	Yds/ Rec	Yds/ Gm
81. Marky Filipe, Weber St.	RB	SR	11	44	459	2	4.00	10.43	41.73
82. Carl Sims, Western Ill.	WR	SO	10	40	521	2	4.00	13.03	52.10
83. Ryan Bagley, Montana	WR	JR	14	55	725	4	3.93	13.18	51.79
84. Eric Allen, Montana	WR	JR	13	51	801	5	3.92	15.71	61.62
85. Steven Whitehead, McNeese St.	RB	JR	12	47	596	3	3.92	12.68	49.67
86. Tyrone Timmons, Mississippi Val.	WR	SR	11	43	615	7	3.91	14.30	55.91
87. Tyrell Williams, Stephen F. Austin	WR	JR	10	39	342	2	3.90	8.77	34.20
88. Nick DeGasperis, Columbia	WR	SR	9	35	462	0	3.89	13.20	51.33
89. Justin Stepp, Furman	WR	SR	12	46	599	1	3.83	13.02	49.92
90. Kervin Michaud, Delaware	WR	SO	11	42	387	2	3.82	9.21	35.18
90. Mark Williams, Savannah St.	WR	FR	11	42	522	4	3.82	12.43	47.45
90. Ramses Barden, Cal Poly	WR	SO	11	42	824	5	3.82	19.62	74.91
90. Curtis Walls, N.C. A&T	WR	JR	11	42	477	1	3.82	11.36	43.36
90. James Callaham, Norfolk St.	WR	SR	11	42	572	1	3.82	13.62	52.00
95. Tremayne Kirkland, Portland St.	WR	SR	10	38	533	7	3.80	14.03	53.30
96. T.J. Peterson, Youngstown St.	WR	SR	14	53	767	7	3.79	14.47	54.79
97. Micah Rucker, Eastern Ill.	WR	JR	13	49	966	13	3.77	19.71	74.31
98. L.C. Baker, James Madison	WR	JR	12	45	624	8	3.75	13.87	52.00
98. Kevin Francis, Alabama A&M	WR	SR	12	45	439	3	3.75	9.76	36.58
100. Joseph Nicholas, William & Mary	WR	JR	11	41	597	8	3.73	14.56	54.27
100. Johnny Gray, UNI	WR	SO	11	41	607	5	3.73	14.80	55.18

Receiving Yards Per Game

Rank, Player	Pos	Cl.	G	Rec	Yds	TD	Rec/ Gm	Yds/ Rec	Yds/ Gm
1. Bruce Hocker, Duquesne	WR	JR	10	61	1,070	16	6.10	17.54	107.00
2. Terrell Hudgins, Elon	WR	FR	10	69	1,027	8	6.90	14.88	102.70
3. Lanis Frederick, Austin Peay	WR	SO	11	77	1,101	7	7.00	14.30	100.09
4. Nick Ruhe, Dayton	WR	SR	10	49	977	3	4.90	19.94	97.70
5. Steve Ogden, Valparaiso	WR	SO	11	55	1,048	8	5.00	19.05	95.27
6. Curtis Hamilton, Western Ky.	WR	JR	9	52	841	10	5.78	16.17	93.44
7. Alex Watson, Northern Ariz.	WR	JR	11	82	1,017	15	7.45	12.40	92.45
8. Jerome Simpson, Coastal Caro.	WR	JR	12	61	1,077	16	5.08	17.66	89.75
9. Maurice Price, Charleston So.	WR	JR	11	103	985	10	9.36	9.56	89.55
10. Shaine Smith, Hofstra	WR	SR	11	60	951	9	5.45	15.85	86.45
11. Brett Dioguardi, Davidson	WR	SR	10	59	859	6	5.90	14.56	85.90
12. David Ball, New Hampshire	WR	SR	13	93	1,114	13	7.15	11.98	85.69
13. Jaleel Kindell, St. Peter's	WR	SO	10	74	855	3	7.40	11.55	85.50
14. Carlton McFadgen, Dayton	WR	SR	10	47	845	5	4.70	17.98	84.50
15. Brendan Circle, Princeton	WR	JR	10	56	835	7	5.60	14.91	83.50
16. Eric Weems, Bethune-Cookman	WR	SR	11	69	918	9	6.27	13.30	83.45
17. Wes Doyle, San Diego	WR	JR	11	52	909	11	4.73	17.48	82.64
18. Michael Mayers, Elon	WR	JR	11	73	866	3	6.64	11.86	78.73
19. Micheal Jefferson, Montana St.	WR	SR	13	66	1,023	9	5.08	15.50	78.69
20. Michael Caputo, St. Francis (Pa.)	WR	SR	11	63	857	8	5.73	13.60	77.91
21. Dan Spriggs, Duquesne	WR	SR	10	61	778	4	6.10	12.75	77.80
22. Shaheer McBride, Delaware St.	WR	JR	11	55	852	11	5.00	15.49	77.45
23. William Mayfield, Appalachian St.	WR	SR	15	64	1,129	5	4.27	17.64	75.27
24. Jason Jones, Ark.-Pine Bluff	WR	JR	12	37	903	13	3.08	24.41	75.25
25. Eric Yancey, Towson	WR	SR	11	68	826	10	6.18	12.15	75.09
26. Ramses Barden, Cal Poly	WR	SO	11	42	824	5	3.82	19.62	74.91
27. Lou Russo, La Salle	WR	SR	10	70	744	5	7.00	10.63	74.40
28. Micah Rucker, Eastern Ill.	WR	JR	13	49	966	13	3.77	19.71	74.31
29. Aaron Love, Delaware	WR	SO	10	58	740	4	5.80	12.76	74.00
30. Adam San Miguel, Monmouth	WR	SR	12	73	872	6	6.08	11.95	72.67
31. Larry Shipp, Tennessee Tech	WR	JR	11	51	799	8	4.64	15.67	72.64
32. Ryan Maher, Holy Cross	WR	JR	11	69	797	6	6.27	11.55	72.45
33. Clyde Edwards, Grambling	WR	JR	11	56	789	11	5.09	14.09	71.73
34. Carl Berman, Indiana St.	WR	SR	11	59	783	5	5.36	13.27	71.18
35. Ryan Fuselier, Dartmouth	WR	SR	10	57	711	3	5.70	12.47	71.10
36. Lonnie Hill, Brown	WR	SR	10	45	707	5	4.50	15.71	70.70
37. Matt Carre, Penn	RB	SR	10	43	697	3	4.30	16.21	69.70
38. Akilah Lacey, Idaho St.	WR	SR	11	37	753	10	3.36	20.35	68.45
39. Joe Ort, Lafayette	WR	SR	12	50	814	3	4.17	16.28	67.83
40. Duvaughn Flagler, Gardner-Webb	WR	JR	11	64	740	7	5.82	11.56	67.27
41. Marco Thomas, Western Ill.	WR	SR	11	58	738	4	5.27	12.72	67.09
42. Henry Tolbert, Grambling	WR	SR	11	48	730	4	4.36	15.21	66.36
43. Gerard Landry, Southern U.	WR	JR	11	55	727	5	5.00	13.22	66.09
44. Marquay McDaniel, Hampton	WR	SR	12	59	786	14	4.92	13.32	65.50
45. Paul Raymond, Brown	WR	JR	10	45	654	4	4.50	14.53	65.40
46. John Matthews, San Diego	WR	SO	10	32	649	7	3.20	20.28	64.90
47. Arman Shields, Richmond	WR	JR	10	54	643	5	5.40	11.91	64.30
48. Corey Mazza, Harvard	WR	SR	10	36	635	8	3.60	17.64	63.50
49. Austin Gaines, Gardner-Webb	WR	SR	11	48	690	3	4.36	14.38	62.73
50. Braden Lepisto, Penn	WR	JR	10	47	625	2	4.70	13.30	62.50
51. Skyler Moore, Northern Ariz.	WR	SO	11	39	687	9	3.55	17.62	62.45
52. Jason Barnes, Sacramento St.	WR	SR	10	28	623	2	2.80	22.25	62.30
53. Eric Allen, Montana	WR	JR	13	51	801	5	3.92	15.71	61.62
54. Willie Hayward, Florida A&M	WR	JR	11	49	674	5	4.45	13.76	61.27
55. Nate Miller, Butler	WR	JR	9	52	551	5	5.78	10.60	61.22

Rank, Player	Pos	Cl.	G	Rec	Yds	TD	Rec/ Gm	Yds/ Rec	Yds/ Gm
56. Dwayne Eley, Stony Brook	WR	SO	11	50	670	4	4.55	13.40	60.91
57. Pierre Jackson, Illinois St.	WR	SR	13	46	790	6	3.54	17.17	60.77
58. Jeff Moore, Samford	WR	JR	11	49	668	5	4.45	13.63	60.73
59. Chris Turner, Wagner	WR	SR	11	54	658	8	4.91	12.19	59.82
60. Kendrick Ballantyne, Northeastern	TE	SR	11	39	655	7	3.55	16.79	59.55
60. Prince Prempeh, Marist	WR	SR	11	32	655	2	2.91	20.47	59.55
62. Geavon Tribble, Jacksonville	WR	SO	10	30	594	4	3.00	19.80	59.40
63. Demetrius Harrison, Towson	WR	JR	11	49	650	4	4.45	13.27	59.09
64. Roosevelt Kiser, Florida A&M	WR	SR	11	63	647	5	5.73	10.27	58.82
65. John Bond, St. Peter's	WR	JR	9	47	528	6	5.22	11.23	58.67
66. Donell Wheaton, Montana St.	WR	SR	13	55	757	4	4.23	13.76	58.23
67. Ben Patrick, Delaware	TE	SR	11	64	639	6	5.82	9.98	58.09
67. Emery Sammons, Norfolk St.	WR	SR	11	35	639	3	3.18	18.26	58.09
69. Chandler Henley, Yale	WR	SR	10	42	578	2	4.20	13.76	57.80
70. Michael Johnson, Chattanooga	WR	SR	11	39	631	8	3.55	16.18	57.36
71. Beaux Jones, Davidson	WR	JR	10	46	570	5	4.60	12.39	57.00
72. Onrea Jones, Hampton	WR	SR	12	57	679	5	4.75	11.91	56.58
73. Tyrone Timmons, Mississippi Val.	WR	SR	11	43	615	7	3.91	14.30	55.91
74. Brandon Perry, Sam Houston St.	WR	SR	11	33	614	3	3.00	18.61	55.82
75. Brandon London, Massachusetts	WR	SR	14	50	781	9	3.57	15.62	55.79
76. Patrick Bugg, Eastern Ky.	TE	SR	11	37	611	7	3.36	16.51	55.55
77. Rodrick Wolfe, Morgan St.	WR	JR	9	29	498	6	3.22	17.17	55.33
78. Austin Knowlin, Columbia	WR	FR	10	44	553	4	4.40	12.57	55.30
79. Johnny Gray, UNI	WR	SO	11	41	607	5	3.73	14.80	55.18
80. Brandon Turner, Liberty	WR	JR	11	39	604	3	3.55	15.49	54.91
81. T.J. Peterson, Youngstown St.	WR	SR	14	53	767	7	3.79	14.47	54.79
82. Dominique Edison, Stephen F. Austin	WR	SO	10	30	543	5	3.00	18.10	54.30
83. Joseph Nicholas, William & Mary	WR	JR	11	41	597	8	3.73	14.56	54.27
84. Ryan Hubbard, Davidson	WR	JR	10	44	542	5	4.40	12.32	54.20
85. Frank Trovato, Lehigh	WR	SR	11	39	594	4	3.55	15.23	54.00
85. Lynell Suggs, Stony Brook	WR	SO	11	38	594	7	3.45	15.63	54.00
87. Bernie Cevis, La Salle	WR	JR	10	42	539	5	4.20	12.83	53.90
88. Sam Logan, Indiana St.	WR	SR	10	49	535	4	4.90	10.92	53.50
89. Tremayne Kirkland, Portland St.	WR	SR	10	38	533	7	3.80	14.03	53.30
90. Clarence Cotton, Mississippi Val.	WR	JR	11	30	577	4	2.73	19.23	52.45
91. Joey Hew Len, Southern Utah	WR	SR	11	54	575	8	4.91	10.65	52.27
92. Carl Sims, Western Ill.	WR	SO	10	40	521	2	4.00	13.03	52.10
93. Rod Harper, Murray St.	WR	SO	11	48	573	8	4.36	11.94	52.09
94. L.C. Baker, James Madison	WR	JR	12	45	624	8	3.75	13.87	52.00
94. James Callaham, Norfolk St.	WR	SR	11	42	572	1	3.82	13.62	52.00
94. Brian Brigham, Princeton	WR	SR	10	41	520	2	4.10	12.68	52.00
97. Ryan Bagley, Montana	WR	JR	14	55	725	4	3.93	13.18	51.79
98. Thomas Harrison, Holy Cross	WR	JR	11	46	569	4	4.18	12.37	51.73
99. Keith LeVan, New Hampshire	RB	JR	13	70	672	5	5.38	9.60	51.69
100. Taurean Rhetta, Jacksonville St.	WR	JR	11	30	568	4	2.73	18.93	51.64

Total Receiving Yards

Rank, Player	Pos	Cl.	G	Rec	Yds	TD	Rec/ Gm	Yds/ Rec	Yds/ Gm
1. William Mayfield, Appalachian St.	WR	SR	15	64	1,129	5	4.27	17.64	75.27
2. David Ball, New Hampshire	WR	SR	13	93	1,114	13	7.15	11.98	85.69
3. Lanis Frederick, Austin Peay	WR	SO	11	77	1,101	7	7.00	14.30	100.09
4. Jerome Simpson, Coastal Caro.	WR	JR	12	61	1,077	16	5.08	17.66	89.75
5. Bruce Hocker, Duquesne	WR	JR	10	61	1,070	16	6.10	17.54	107.00
6. Steve Ogden, Valparaiso	WR	SO	11	55	1,048	8	5.00	19.05	95.27
7. Terrell Hudgins, Elon	WR	FR	10	69	1,027	8	6.90	14.88	102.70
8. Micheal Jefferson, Montana St.	WR	SR	13	66	1,023	9	5.08	15.50	78.69
9. Alex Watson, Northern Ariz.	WR	JR	11	82	1,017	15	7.45	12.40	92.45
10. Maurice Price, Charleston So.	WR	JR	11	103	985	10	9.36	9.56	89.55
11. Nick Ruhe, Dayton	WR	SR	10	49	977	3	4.90	19.94	97.70
12. Micah Rucker, Eastern Ill.	WR	JR	13	49	966	13	3.77	19.71	74.31
13. Shaine Smith, Hofstra	WR	SR	11	60	951	9	5.45	15.85	86.45
14. Eric Weems, Bethune-Cookman	WR	SR	11	69	918	9	6.27	13.30	83.45
15. Wes Doyle, San Diego	WR	JR	11	52	909	11	4.73	17.48	82.64
16. Jason Jones, Ark.-Pine Bluff	WR	JR	12	37	903	13	3.08	24.41	75.25
17. Adam San Miguel, Monmouth	WR	SR	12	73	872	6	6.08	11.95	72.67
18. Michael Mayers, Elon	WR	JR	11	73	866	3	6.64	11.86	78.73
19. Brett Dioguardi, Davidson	WR	SR	10	59	859	6	5.90	14.56	85.90
20. Michael Caputo, St. Francis (Pa.)	WR	SR	11	63	857	8	5.73	13.60	77.91
21. Jaleel Kindell, St. Peter's	WR	SO	10	74	855	3	7.40	11.55	85.50
22. Shaheer McBride, Delaware St.	WR	JR	11	55	852	11	5.00	15.49	77.45
23. Carlton McFadgen, Dayton	WR	SR	10	47	845	5	4.70	17.98	84.50
24. Curtis Hamilton, Western Ky.	WR	JR	9	52	841	10	5.78	16.17	93.44
25. Brendan Circle, Princeton	WR	JR	10	56	835	7	5.60	14.91	83.50
26. Eric Yancey, Towson	WR	SR	11	68	826	10	6.18	12.15	75.09
27. Ramses Barden, Cal Poly	WR	SO	11	42	824	5	3.82	19.62	74.91
28. Joe Ort, Lafayette	WR	SR	12	50	814	3	4.17	16.28	67.83
29. Eric Allen, Montana	WR	JR	13	51	801	5	3.92	15.71	61.62
30. Larry Shipp, Tennessee Tech	WR	JR	11	51	799	8	4.64	15.67	72.64
31. Ryan Maher, Holy Cross	WR	JR	11	69	797	6	6.27	11.55	72.45
32. Pierre Jackson, Illinois St.	WR	SR	13	46	790	6	3.54	17.17	60.77

Rank, Player	Pos	Cl.	G	Rec	Yds	TD	Rec/ Gm	Yds/ Rec	Yds/ Gm
33. Clyde Edwards, Grambling	WR	JR	11	56	789	11	5.09	14.09	71.73
34. Marquay McDaniel, Hampton	WR	SR	12	59	786	14	4.92	13.32	65.50
35. Carl Berman, Indiana St.	WR	SR	11	59	783	5	5.36	13.27	71.18
36. Brandon London, Massachusetts	WR	SR	14	50	781	9	3.57	15.62	55.79
37. Dan Spriggs, Duquesne	WR	SR	10	61	778	4	6.10	12.75	77.80
38. T.J. Peterson, Youngstown St.	WR	SR	14	53	767	7	3.79	14.47	54.79
39. Donell Wheaton, Montana St.	WR	SR	13	55	757	4	4.23	13.76	58.23
40. Akilah Lacey, Idaho St.	WR	SR	11	37	753	10	3.36	20.35	68.45
41. Lou Russo, La Salle	WR	SR	10	70	744	5	7.00	10.63	74.40
42. Aaron Love, Delaware	WR	SO	10	58	740	4	5.80	12.76	74.00
42. Duvaughn Flagler, Gardner-Webb	WR	JR	11	64	740	7	5.82	11.56	67.27
44. Marco Thomas, Western Ill.	WR	SR	11	58	738	4	5.27	12.72	67.09
45. Henry Tolbert, Grambling	WR	SR	11	48	730	4	4.36	15.21	66.36
46. Gerard Landry, Southern U.	WR	JR	11	55	727	5	5.00	13.22	66.09
47. Ryan Bagley, Montana	WR	JR	14	55	725	4	3.93	13.18	51.79
48. Ryan Fuselier, Dartmouth	WR	SR	10	57	711	3	5.70	12.47	71.10
49. Lonnie Hill, Brown	WR	SR	10	45	707	5	4.50	15.71	70.70
50. Matt Carre, Penn	RB	SR	10	43	697	3	4.30	16.21	69.70
51. Austin Gaines, Gardner-Webb	WR	SR	11	48	690	3	4.36	14.38	62.73
52. Skyler Moore, Northern Ariz.	WR	SO	11	39	687	9	3.55	17.62	62.45
53. Onrea Jones, Hampton	WR	SR	12	57	679	5	4.75	11.91	56.58
54. Willie Hayward, Florida A&M	WR	JR	11	49	674	5	4.45	13.76	61.27
55. Keith LeVan, New Hampshire	RB	JR	13	70	672	5	5.38	9.60	51.69
56. Dwayne Eley, Stony Brook	WR	SO	11	50	670	4	4.55	13.40	60.91
57. Jeff Moore, Samford	WR	JR	11	49	668	5	4.45	13.63	60.73
58. Chris Turner, Wagner	WR	SR	11	54	658	8	4.91	12.19	59.82
59. Kendrick Ballantyne, Northeastern	TE	SR	11	39	655	7	3.55	16.79	59.55
59. Prince Prempeh, Marist	WR	SR	11	32	655	2	2.91	20.47	59.55
61. Paul Raymond, Brown	WR	JR	10	45	654	4	4.50	14.53	65.40
62. Demetrius Harrison, Towson	WR	JR	11	49	650	4	4.45	13.27	59.09
63. John Matthews, San Diego	WR	SO	10	32	649	7	3.20	20.28	64.90
64. Roosevelt Kiser, Florida A&M	WR	SR	11	63	647	5	5.73	10.27	58.82
65. Arman Shields, Richmond	WR	JR	10	54	643	5	5.40	11.91	64.30
66. Craig Chambers, Montana	WR	JR	13	41	641	8	3.15	15.63	49.31
67. Ben Patrick, Delaware	TE	SR	11	64	639	6	5.82	9.98	58.09
67. Emery Sammons, Norfolk St.	WR	SR	11	35	639	3	3.18	18.26	58.09
69. Corey Mazza, Harvard	WR	SR	10	36	635	8	3.60	17.64	63.50
70. Michael Johnson, Chattanooga	WR	SR	11	39	631	8	3.55	16.18	57.36
71. Braden Lepisto, Penn	WR	JR	10	47	625	2	4.70	13.30	62.50
72. L.C. Baker, James Madison	WR	JR	12	45	624	8	3.75	13.87	52.00
73. Jason Barnes, Sacramento St.	WR	SR	10	28	623	2	2.80	22.25	62.30
74. Tyrone Timmons, Mississippi Val.	WR	SR	11	43	615	7	3.91	14.30	55.91
75. Brandon Perry, Sam Houston St.	WR	SR	11	33	614	3	3.00	18.61	55.82
76. Patrick Bugg, Eastern Ky.	TE	SR	11	37	611	7	3.36	16.51	55.55
77. Johnny Gray, UNI	WR	SO	11	41	607	5	3.73	14.80	55.18
78. Brad Listorti, Massachusetts	TE	JR	15	38	604	3	2.53	15.89	40.27
78. Brandon Turner, Liberty	WR	JR	11	39	604	3	3.55	15.49	54.91
80. Justin Stepp, Furman	WR	SR	12	46	599	1	3.83	13.02	49.92
81. Joseph Nicholas, William & Mary	WR	JR	11	41	597	8	3.73	14.56	54.27
82. Steven Whitehead, McNeese St.	RB	JR	12	47	596	3	3.92	12.68	49.67
83. J.J. Moore, Massachusetts	WR	JR	15	46	594	4	3.07	12.91	39.60
83. Geavon Tribble, Jacksonville	WR	SO	10	30	594	4	3.00	19.80	59.40
83. Lynell Suggs, Stony Brook	WR	SO	11	38	594	7	3.45	15.63	54.00
83. Frank Trovato, Lehigh	WR	SR	11	39	594	4	3.55	15.23	54.00
87. Chandler Henley, Yale	WR	SR	10	42	578	2	4.20	13.76	57.80
88. Clarence Cotton, Mississippi Val.	WR	JR	11	30	577	4	2.73	19.23	52.45
89. Joey Hew Len, Southern Utah	WR	SR	11	54	575	8	4.91	10.65	52.27
90. Rod Harper, Murray St.	WR	SO	11	48	573	8	4.36	11.94	52.09
91. James Callaham, Norfolk St.	WR	SR	11	42	572	1	3.82	13.62	52.00
92. Beaux Jones, Davidson	WR	JR	10	46	570	5	4.60	12.39	57.00
93. Thomas Harrison, Holy Cross	WR	JR	11	46	569	4	4.18	12.37	51.73
94. Taurean Rhetta, Jacksonville St.	WR	JR	11	30	568	4	2.73	18.93	51.64
95. Erik Burke, Colgate	WR	JR	11	38	565	1	3.45	14.87	51.36
96. Andre Roberts, Citadel	WR	FR	11	35	557	5	3.18	15.91	50.64
97. Austin Knowlin, Columbia	WR	FR	10	44	553	4	4.40	12.57	55.30
98. Nate Miller, Butler	WR	JR	9	52	551	5	5.78	10.60	61.22
99. Ben Hannula, San Diego	WR	SO	12	56	549	4	4.67	9.80	45.75
100. Marcus Lee, Towson	WR	SO	11	50	546	1	4.55	10.92	49.64

Interceptions

Rank, Player	Pos	Cl.	G	Int	Yds	TD	Int/Gm
1. Dre Dokes, UNI	DB	SR	11	7	116	1	.64
2. Brent Webber, Sacramento St.	DB	JR	10	6	23	0	.60
3. Chris Parsons, UNI	DB	JR	11	6	34	0	.55
3. Dominique Rodgers, Tennessee St.	DB	JR	11	6	70	0	.55
3. Jean-Pierre Marshall, Mississippi Val.	DB	JR	11	6	2	0	.55
3. Bobbie Williams, Bethune-Cookman	DB	JR	11	6	25	0	.55
7. Andy Shalbrack, Columbia	DB	FR	10	5	62	0	.50
7. Steward Franks, Ark.-Pine Bluff	DB	SO	12	6	96	0	.50
7. Frank Moore, Alabama A&M	DB	SO	12	6	50	0	.50
10. Mike Niklos, Robert Morris	DB	SR	11	5	23	0	.45
10. Ken Chicoine, Cal Poly	DB	SR	11	5	35	0	.45
10. Andy Green, Drake	DB	SO	11	5	131	1	.45
10. Stacey Thomas, Texas Southern	DB	SR	11	5	105	1	.45
10. Walter Musgrove, Texas St.	DB	SR	11	5	3	0	.45
10. Jarmaul George, Southern U.	DB	JR	11	5	5	0	.45
10. Brandon Jackson, Ga. Southern	DB	SO	11	5	17	0	.45
17. David Jiles, Monmouth	DB	SR	12	5	88	1	.42
17. Travarous Bain, Hampton	DB	SR	12	5	65	0	.42
17. Patrick O'Neill, San Diego	DB	SO	12	5	46	0	.42
20. Dewitt Myers, Coastal Caro.	DB	SR	10	4	33	0	.40
20. Steven Williams, Harvard	DB	JR	10	4	15	0	.40
20. Kevin Kelleher, Princeton	DB	JR	10	4	44	0	.40

STATISTICAL LEADERS

Rank, Player	Pos	Cl.	G	Int	Yds	TD	Int/Gm
20. Patrick FitzGerald, Davidson	DB	JR	10	4	0	0	.40
20. Reggie Dorsainvil, Iona	DB	JR	10	4	39	0	.40
20. Bobby Abare, Yale	LB	SO	10	4	78	2	.40
20. Steven Santoro, Yale	DB	SO	10	4	67	0	.40
27. Corey Lynch, Appalachian St.	DB	JR	13	5	101	0	.38
28. Raji El-Amin, Rhode Island	DB	JR	11	4	33	0	.36
28. Raquan Pride, Rhode Island	DB	SR	11	4	61	0	.36
28. Odell Jackson, Portland St.	DB	SR	11	4	40	0	.36
28. Andrew Harris, Richmond	DB	JR	11	4	18	0	.36
28. Drew Mack, Towson	DB	SO	11	4	87	1	.36
28. Micheal Dorsey, Portland St.	DB	JR	11	4	120	0	.36
28. Dominic Dixon, Portland St.	DB	SR	11	4	58	0	.36
28. Jonathan Carmon, Charleston So.	DB	JR	11	4	24	0	.36
28. David Hyland, Morehead St.	DB	SO	11	4	42	0	.36
28. Alex Davis, Butler	LB	JR	11	4	21	0	.36
28. Carlton Brown, Jackson St.	DB	SR	11	4	38	0	.36
28. C.L. Grogan, Northwestern St.	DB	JR	11	4	0	0	.36
28. Chris Bland, Elon	DB	JR	11	4	124	1	.36
28. Quintez Smith, Chattanooga	DB	JR	11	4	111	1	.36
28. Maurice Smith, Tennessee Tech	DB	SO	11	4	21	0	.36
28. Jason Beach, Florida A&M	DB	JR	11	4	88	0	.36
28. Mike Radon, Missouri St.	DB	SR	11	4	94	1	.36
28. Alfred Phillips, Wagner	DB	JR	11	4	80	1	.36
28. Jon Wilson, Sacred Heart	DB	SR	11	4	20	0	.36
28. Ernest Moore, Lehigh	DB	JR	11	4	35	0	.36
28. Stephen Collage, Bucknell	DB	JR	11	4	125	0	.36
49. Kyle Campbell, Delaware	DB	SR	9	3	15	0	.33
49. Scott Horcher, Dayton	DB	FR	9	3	7	0	.33
49. Brandon Cramer, Dayton	DB	JR	9	3	87	1	.33
49. Jamelle Juneau, McNeese St.	DB	JR	12	4	96	0	.33
49. Jeremy Blocker, Furman	DB	SR	12	4	48	0	.33
49. Quinton Teal, Coastal Caro.	DB	SR	12	4	3	0	.33
49. Derius Swinton, Hampton	DB	SR	12	4	98	1	.33
49. Terrell Whitehead, Norfolk St.	DB	FR	9	3	58	0	.33
49. Jeremy Wiggins, Appalachian St.	DB	SR	15	5	60	0	.33
49. Seymour Loftman, Eastern Ill.	DB	SO	12	4	44	0	.33
49. Matt Mullenax, Brown	DB	JR	9	3	1	0	.33
60. Tom Nelson, Illinois St.	DB	SO	13	4	63	0	.31
61. Michael Beach, Montana St.	DB	JR	10	3	71	1	.30
61. Myles Williams, Southern U.	DL	SO	10	3	90	1	.30
61. Jason Fobbs, Prairie View	DB	SO	10	3	38	0	.30
61. Josh Adams, Northwestern St.	DB	FR	10	3	19	0	.30
61. Craig Agee, Jacksonville St.	DB	SR	10	3	17	1	.30
61. Zach Denton, Eastern Ky.	DB	SO	10	3	54	0	.30
61. LaQuinn Ellerbe, South Carolina St.	DB	SO	10	3	16	0	.30
61. Michael Williams, Bethune-Cookman	DB	SO	10	3	0	0	.30
61. Kyle Postell, Duquesne	DB	SR	10	3	32	0	.30
61. Aaron Strader, Duquesne	DB	SO	10	3	100	1	.30
61. Tim Strickland, Princeton	DB	SR	10	3	47	0	.30
61. J.J. Artis, Princeton	DB	SR	10	3	0	0	.30
61. Tyson Maugle, Penn	DB	SO	10	3	34	0	.30
61. Colin Nash, Cornell	DB	JR	10	3	27	0	.30
61. Marcosus LeBlanc, Montana St.	DB	SR	10	3	1	0	.30
61. Rashad Barksdale, Albany (N.Y.)	DB	SR	10	3	3	0	.30
61. Randy Samuel, Cal Poly	DB	SR	10	3	0	0	.30
61. Ryan Schmidtz, Butler	DB	SO	10	3	27	0	.30
61. Torian Johnson, Lafayette	DB	SR	10	3	27	0	.30
61. Ty Sparrow, Weber St.	DB	SR	10	3	68	0	.30
61. Philip Ashley, Charleston So.	DB	FR	10	3	31	0	.30
82. Torrey Thomas, Montana	DB	JR	14	4	92	1	.29
82. Jason Perry, Youngstown St.	DB	SR	14	4	141	2	.29
82. Codera Jackson, Youngstown St.	DB	SR	14	4	48	0	.29
85. David Horton, Richmond	DB	FR	11	3	20	1	.27
85. Stephen Howell, Richmond	DB	JR	11	3	4	0	.27
85. James Kazil, Robert Morris	DB	JR	11	3	62	0	.27
85. Matt Hill, Monmouth	DB	SR	11	3	47	0	.27
85. Casey Gough, Holy Cross	DB	SR	11	3	0	0	.27
85. Marcus Taylor, Fordham	LB	SR	11	3	27	0	.27
85. Cody Williams, Colgate	DB	JR	11	3	51	0	.27
85. Mario E. Brown, Gardner-Webb	LB	SO	11	3	34	0	.27
85. Jamaal Walton, VMI	DB	SR	11	3	0	0	.27
85. Christian Kelly, VMI	DB	FR	11	3	0	0	.27
85. C.J. Hirschman, Charleston So.	DB	JR	11	3	32	0	.27
85. Poul Collins, Drake	DB	JR	11	3	28	0	.27
85. Nick Ross, Drake	LB	SR	11	3	23	0	.27
85. DeShaun Lewis, Alcorn St.	DB	JR	11	3	89	1	.27
85. Corey McLaurin, Alcorn St.	DB	SO	11	3	68	0	.27
85. Chris Dupuy, Alabama St.	LB	SR	11	3	24	0	.27
85. Keldrick Holman, Stephen F. Austin	DB	SR	11	3	83	0	.27
85. Kevin Adleman, Wofford	LB	SR	11	3	89	1	.27
85. Mitchell Dukes, Western Caro.	DB	SR	11	3	46	2	.27
85. Terrione Benefield, Ga. Southern	LB	FR	11	3	14	0	.27
85. Aaron Strong, Tennessee St.	DB	SR	11	3	16	0	.27
85. Nikkeda Rutland, Tennessee St.	DB	SR	11	3	10	0	.27
85. Brandon Gathof, Eastern Ky.	DB	SO	11	3	46	0	.27
85. Rickey Jackson, Howard	DB	JR	11	3	42	0	.27
85. Travis Watters, Western Ky.	DB	SO	11	3	38	0	.27
85. Milo Otis, Stony Brook	LB	SO	11	3	23	0	.27
85. Jeff Hodges, Sacred Heart	DB	SO	11	3	21	0	.27
85. Charles Manigo, Portland St.	DB	SR	11	3	39	0	.27
85. Jeff Wheeler, Northern Ariz.	DB	SR	11	3	70	2	.27
85. Kurt Karstens, Northern Ariz.	DB	SO	11	3	21	0	.27
85. D.J. Clark, Idaho St.	DB	SO	11	3	63	1	.27

Punting

(Minimum 3.6 Punts Per Game)

Rank, Player	Pos	Cl.	G	Punts	Yds	Avg	Punts/ Gm
1. Breck Ackley, Southern U.	K/P	SR	11	49	2,228	45.47	4.45
2. David Simonhoff, Southeast Mo. St.	P	SR	11	59	2,644	44.81	5.36
3. Benjamin Dato, Fordham	K/P	JR	11	58	2,587	44.60	5.27
4. Rhian Madrid, Northern Ariz.	P	SR	10	43	1,909	44.40	4.30
5. Colin McDonough, Princeton	K/P	SR	9	34	1,483	43.62	3.78
6. Dan Zeidman, Idaho St.	P	JR	11	53	2,310	43.58	4.82
7. Michael Hanna, Gardner-Webb	P	SO	11	46	2,000	43.48	4.18
8. Mitch Lively, Sacramento St.	K/P	SR	11	62	2,694	43.45	5.64
9. Chris MacDonald, Texas St.	P	JR	11	46	1,996	43.39	4.18
10. Nathan Stokes, Missouri St.	K/P	JR	11	54	2,310	42.78	4.91
11. Brandon Lane, Elon	P	SO	9	35	1,485	42.43	3.89
12. Ryan Donckers, Eastern Wash.	P	SR	11	62	2,627	42.37	5.64
13. Chris Hicks, Samford	P	SR	11	60	2,530	42.17	5.45
14. Dan Carpenter, Montana	K/P	JR	14	62	2,595	41.85	4.43
15. Tim Mayse, Western Caro.	K/P	SR	11	50	2,082	41.64	4.55
16. Nick Coromelas, Cal Poly	K/P	SR	11	44	1,828	41.55	4.00
17. Wesley Taylor, Florida A&M	K/P	JR	11	43	1,774	41.26	3.91
18. Andrew Levers, Portland St.	P	SR	11	58	2,392	41.24	5.27
19. Zach Walden, Jacksonville St.	P	JR	11	57	2,349	41.21	5.18
20. Chris Tommie, Wofford	K/P	SO	10	37	1,522	41.14	3.70
21. Dan Jordan, Ga. Southern	P	JR	11	62	2,540	40.97	5.64
22. Mason Webb, Morehead St.	P	SO	11	48	1,965	40.94	4.36
23. Andrew Bergeron, Ark.-Pine Bluff	P	JR	12	56	2,278	40.68	4.67
24. Phil Azarik, Bucknell	K/P	SO	11	57	2,309	40.51	5.18
25. Steve Morgan, Brown	P	JR	10	36	1,458	40.50	3.60
26. Adam Peters, VMI	P	SR	11	53	2,136	40.30	4.82
27. Mike Snoy, Weber St.	P	FR	11	63	2,537	40.27	5.73
28. Jason Sutton, Colgate	P	SR	11	57	2,283	40.05	5.18
29. Derek Marks, Sacred Heart	K/P	SO	11	57	2,271	39.84	5.18
30. Curtis Parks, Sam Houston St.	P	SR	11	42	1,673	39.83	3.82
31. Anthony Johnson, Alabama St.	K/P	SR	11	63	2,505	39.76	5.73
32. Jon Mahan, Tennessee Tech	P	SR	11	63	2,498	39.65	5.73
33. Blake Bercegeay, McNeese St.	K/P	SO	12	51	2,009	39.39	4.25
34. Mark Kaspar, Citadel	P	SO	11	53	2,083	39.30	4.82
35. Jim Hall, Southeastern La.	P	SR	11	55	2,160	39.27	5.00
36. Tim Wright, Murray St.	P	SR	11	53	2,079	39.23	4.82
37. Jon Rocholl, Columbia	P	SO	10	55	2,151	39.11	5.50
38. Scott Ravanesi, Southern Ill.	K/P	FR	12	45	1,759	39.09	3.75
39. Stephon Solomon, Texas Southern	P	FR	11	49	1,904	38.86	4.45
40. Marshall Burton, Northwestern St.	K/P	JR	11	58	2,253	38.84	5.27
41. Chris Lynch, Albany (N.Y.)	P	SO	11	45	1,745	38.78	4.09
42. Bryan Giannecchini, Rhode Island	K/P	JR	11	47	1,821	38.74	4.27
43. Cyrus Maddox, Davidson	P	SR	10	45	1,738	38.62	4.50
44. Zach Ugarte, Villanova	K/P	FR	11	44	1,695	38.52	4.00
45. Antonio Gomez, Norfolk St.	K/P	SR	11	41	1,573	38.37	3.73
46. Piotr Czech, Wagner	K/P	JR	11	67	2,565	38.28	6.09
47. Ben Beasley, Liberty	K/P	SR	11	48	1,827	38.06	4.36
48. Tim Buckley, Alcorn St.	QB/P	FR	11	52	1,975	37.98	4.73
49. Chris Johansen, Indiana St.	P	SO	11	55	2,084	37.89	5.00
50. Bill Shears, Towson	P	FR	11	40	1,515	37.88	3.64
51. Jason Leo, Lehigh	P	SO	11	40	1,514	37.85	3.64
52. Tyler Bolton, Montana St.	WR/P	SO	10	36	1,362	37.83	3.60
53. Lee Woodson, N.C. A&T	P	SO	11	60	2,263	37.72	5.45
54. Eric Hernandez, Prairie View	P	SR	9	47	1,771	37.68	5.22
55. Brandon Wubs, Drake	K/P	FR	11	48	1,796	37.42	4.36
56. Sean Comeaux, Nicholls St.	P	JR	11	44	1,644	37.36	4.00
57. Joe Bishop, Youngstown St.	P	SR	14	59	2,203	37.34	4.21
58. Christopher MacGriff, Georgetown	K/P	JR	10	37	1,380	37.30	3.70
59. Nick Maxwell, Cornell	P	SO	8	44	1,638	37.23	5.50
60. Ryan Gooch, Stephen F. Austin	P	JR	11	50	1,858	37.16	4.55
61. Stuart Kenworthy, Delaware	P	SO	11	46	1,709	37.15	4.18
62. Matt Schindel, Harvard	K/P	JR	10	46	1,705	37.07	4.60
63. Phil Buchanan, Butler	K/P	SR	11	78	2,882	36.95	7.09
64. Benton Kuszmaul, Eastern Ky.	P	JR	11	48	1,767	36.81	4.36
65. Kash Kiefer, Maine	P	SO	11	43	1,580	36.74	3.91
66. Sean McGinty, Stony Brook	P	SR	11	61	2,206	36.16	5.55
67. Zach Yates, Eastern Ill.	K/P	SO	13	59	2,128	36.07	4.54

Rank, Player	Pos	Cl.	G	Punts	Yds	Avg	Punts/ Gm
68. Anthony Melillo, Penn	P	JR	10	55	1,982	36.04	5.50
69. Blair Pritchard, William & Mary	K/P	SR	11	47	1,691	35.98	4.27
70. Matt Henry, New Hampshire	P	SR	13	51	1,832	35.92	3.92
71. Ryan McManaway, Holy Cross	P	SR	11	43	1,543	35.88	3.91
72. Joseph Recktenwald, Jacksonville	P	FR	10	47	1,686	35.87	4.70
73. Jared White, Northeastern	P	SR	11	49	1,757	35.86	4.45
74. Bradley Rowe, Marist	K/P	JR	11	51	1,823	35.75	4.64
75. David Kovalcik, Duquesne	P	JR	10	43	1,534	35.67	4.30
76. Jordan Ortiz, Southern Utah	K/P	FR	9	36	1,282	35.61	4.00
77. Tom Mante, Yale	K/P	FR	10	40	1,422	35.55	4.00
78. Chris Lofrese, Iona	K/P	SR	10	56	1,987	35.48	5.60
79. Brian Scullin, Dartmouth	QB/P	SO	10	49	1,734	35.39	4.90
80. Anthony Perlozzo, La Salle	K/P	SO	10	55	1,936	35.20	5.50
81. Rashan Cylar, Alabama A&M	K/P	FR	12	49	1,707	34.84	4.08
82. Josh Brite, Delaware St.	P	JR	11	54	1,880	34.81	4.91
83. Chris Rose, Central Conn. St.	WR/P	SR	11	44	1,531	34.80	4.00
84. Zack Girlarski, Mississippi Val.	K/P	FR	11	51	1,753	34.37	4.64
85. Ross Coffee, Austin Peay	K/P	SO	11	52	1,752	33.69	4.73
86. Adam Ivey, Tenn.-Martin	P	SO	11	47	1,583	33.68	4.27
87. Michael Walser, Robert Morris	K/P	SO	11	52	1,751	33.67	4.73
88. Mitch Secrest, Valparaiso	P	FR	11	54	1,789	33.13	4.91
89. Jeremy Johnson, Savannah St.	P	JR	11	58	1,863	32.12	5.27

Punt Returns

(Minimum 1.2 Returns Per Game)

Rank, Player	Pos	Cl.	G	Ret	Yds	TD	Yds/ Ret	Ret/ Gm
1. Derrick Harris, Sam Houston St.	DB	SR	11	15	366	2	24.40	1.36
2. Nate Hughes, Alcorn St.	WR	SR	11	22	460	2	20.91	2.00
3. Eric Weems, Bethune-Cookman	WR	SR	11	19	331	1	17.42	1.73
4. Steven Whitehead, McNeese St.	RB	JR	12	21	353	1	16.81	1.75
5. Eric Davis, Missouri St.	WR	SO	11	15	246	2	16.40	1.36
6. Anthony Bey, St. Peter's	DB	FR	10	15	228	1	15.20	1.50
7. Craig Turner, Southern Ill.	DB	JR	13	23	343	1	14.91	1.77
8. Tuff Harris, Montana	DB	SR	14	46	667	2	14.50	3.29
9. Shaun Adair, Lafayette	WR	SO	12	16	231	0	14.44	1.33
10. L.C. Baker, James Madison	WR	JR	12	19	259	0	13.63	1.58
11. C.J. Hirschman, Charleston So.	DB	JR	11	19	258	1	13.58	1.73
12. Frank Trovato, Lehigh	WR	SR	11	22	283	1	12.86	2.00
13. Jaymar Johnson, Jackson St.	WR	SR	11	19	241	1	12.68	1.73
14. Dexter Jackson, Appalachian St.	WR	JR	15	30	369	2	12.30	2.00
15. Nolan Applegate, Bucknell	DB	SO	11	23	281	0	12.22	2.09
16. Larue Burley, Southern Utah	WR	SR	11	20	242	1	12.10	1.82
17. Dedrick Poole, Ark.-Pine Bluff	WR	SR	11	14	168	0	12.00	1.27
18. Stephen Tedesco, Sacred Heart	WR	FR	11	14	165	0	11.79	1.27
19. Brandon Hudson, Delaware St.	DB	FR	11	19	221	1	11.63	1.73
20. Wynton Jackson, Liberty	WR	JR	11	26	298	0	11.46	2.36
21. Nick Ruhe, Dayton	WR	SR	10	19	214	0	11.26	1.90
22. Greg Ambrogi, Penn	DB	JR	10	25	276	1	11.04	2.50
23. Andre Roberts, Citadel	WR	FR	11	18	193	0	10.72	1.64
24. Jeff Moore, Samford	WR	JR	11	14	146	1	10.43	1.27
25. Jayson Foster, Ga. Southern	WR	JR	11	24	250	1	10.42	2.18
26. Matt Fanning, Holy Cross	WR	SR	11	20	207	0	10.35	1.82
27. Bryan Walters, Cornell	WR	FR	8	27	274	0	10.15	3.38
28. Jason Perry, Youngstown St.	DB	SR	14	19	191	1	10.05	1.36
29. Clarence Cotton, Mississippi Val.	WR	JR	11	19	189	0	9.95	1.73
30. Roosevelt Kiser, Florida A&M	WR	SR	11	17	169	0	9.94	1.55
31. Kory Alston, Gardner-Webb	WR	SR	11	19	186	1	9.79	1.73
32. Justin Stepp, Furman	WR	SR	12	26	248	0	9.54	2.17
33. Craig Agee, Jacksonville St.	DB	SR	10	18	166	0	9.22	1.80
34. Lamir Whetstone, Maine	DB	SO	11	15	137	0	9.13	1.36
35. Nate Conner, Jacksonville	WR	JR	10	24	218	0	9.08	2.40
36. Jessie Burtojn, Tenn.-Martin	WR	JR	12	22	198	0	9.00	1.83
37. Alfred Phillips, Wagner	DB	JR	11	27	234	0	8.67	2.45
38. Dan Spriggs, Duquesne	WR	SR	10	30	257	0	8.57	3.00
39. Marquay McDaniel, Hampton	WR	SR	12	28	239	0	8.54	2.33
40. Rashad Barksdale, Albany (N.Y.)	DB	SR	10	26	221	0	8.50	2.60
41. Ken Chicoine, Cal Poly	DB	SR	11	26	220	0	8.46	2.36
42. Michael Coe, Alabama St.	DB	SR	11	21	176	0	8.38	1.91
43. Kory Austin, Montana St.	DB	JR	13	20	166	0	8.30	1.54
44. Eric Yancey, Towson	WR	SR	11	22	182	0	8.27	2.00
45. Justise Hairston, Central Conn. St.	RB	SR	11	15	123	0	8.20	1.36
46. Johnny Gray, UNI	WR	SO	11	19	155	0	8.16	1.73
47. J.J. Moore, Massachusetts	WR	JR	15	30	244	0	8.13	2.00
48. Adam San Miguel, Monmouth	WR	SR	12	32	257	0	8.03	2.67
49. Ken Stivers, San Diego	WR	SO	12	23	175	0	7.61	1.92
50. Derek Cox, William & Mary	WR	SO	11	17	129	0	7.59	1.55
51. Nick Feldman, Morehead St.	WR	JR	11	24	181	1	7.54	2.18
52. Steven Williams, Harvard	DB	JR	10	16	117	0	7.31	1.60
53. Mario Hines, Robert Morris	WR	JR	10	28	203	1	7.25	2.80
54. Brendan Ferrigno, Portland St.	WR	SR	11	25	179	0	7.16	2.27
55. Brian Shields, Princeton	WR	SR	10	25	169	0	6.76	2.50
56. Greg Asplint, Iona	WR	SR	9	23	154	0	6.70	2.56
57. Brandon Markey, Brown	RB	SR	9	12	79	0	6.58	1.33
58. Jason Horton, Illinois St.	WR	JR	13	16	104	0	6.50	1.23
59. Jai Wilson, Morgan St.	WR	JR	10	22	140	0	6.36	2.20
60. Dominic Henry, South Carolina St.	WR	SO	10	12	76	0	6.33	1.20
61. Dwayne Eley, Stony Brook	WR	SO	11	20	125	0	6.25	1.82
62. Larry Duncan, Howard	WR	SR	10	12	72	0	6.00	1.20
62. Nick Rhodes, Stephen F. Austin	WR	JR	11	18	108	0	6.00	1.64
62. Morris Crosby, Texas St.	WR	SO	10	13	78	0	6.00	1.30
65. Brian Tandy, Georgetown	DB	SR	10	17	100	0	5.88	1.70
66. Tad Crawford, Columbia	DB	SR	10	15	85	0	5.67	1.50
67. Collin McGann, Butler	DB	SR	10	12	65	0	5.42	1.20
68. Salim Koroma, Villanova	WR	SO	11	15	66	0	4.40	1.36
69. Zach Brower, Drake	WR	SO	10	17	71	0	4.18	1.70
70. Adam Kesler, Eastern Ill.	WR	SO	10	24	99	0	4.13	2.40
71. Andrew Moore, Colgate	DB	SR	10	13	52	0	4.00	1.30
72. J.C. Brown, Western Caro.	WR	SR	11	22	87	0	3.95	2.00
73. Philip Galligan, Dartmouth	WR	SO	10	12	33	0	2.75	1.20

Kickoff Returns

(Minimum 1.2 Returns Per Game)

Rank, Player	Pos	Cl.	G	Ret	Yds	TD	Yds/ Ret	Ret/ Gm
1. Ulysses Banks, Alabama A&M	RB	FR	10	13	454	2	34.92	1.30
2. Kevin Teel, Hampton	WR	SO	11	23	718	1	31.22	2.09
3. Dane Samuels, Iona	RB	JR	10	16	439	0	27.44	1.60
4. Kadafi Tunsil, Delaware St.	DB	SR	11	15	408	0	27.20	1.36
5. Dedrick Poole, Ark.-Pine Bluff	WR	SR	11	23	621	0	27.00	2.09
6. Kenny Mitchell, Georgetown	WR	SO	11	41	1,075	0	26.22	3.73
7. Jessie Burtojn, Tenn.-Martin	WR	JR	12	20	524	2	26.20	1.67
8. Rashaad Woodard, Delaware	DB	SR	10	21	548	0	26.10	2.10
9. William Ford, South Carolina St.	RB	SO	11	20	517	1	25.85	1.82
10. Michael Mayers, Elon	WR	JR	11	16	408	0	25.50	1.45
11. Davin Walker, Eastern Ky.	WR	SO	11	28	712	1	25.43	2.55
12. Mike Wall, Albany (N.Y.)	WR	JR	11	14	349	1	24.93	1.27
13. Steven Santoro, Yale	DB	SO	10	18	443	1	24.61	1.80
14. Bryan Walters, Cornell	WR	FR	8	22	540	1	24.55	2.75
15. Mario Hines, Robert Morris	WR	JR	10	20	490	0	24.50	2.00
16. Clay Green, Jacksonville St.	RB	SR	11	18	439	0	24.39	1.64
17. Larue Burley, Southern Utah	WR	SR	11	24	580	0	24.17	2.18
18. Steven Whitehead, McNeese St.	RB	JR	12	19	455	0	23.95	1.58
19. Raji El-Amin, Rhode Island	DB	JR	11	36	860	0	23.89	3.27
20. Anthony Huntly, Savannah St.	WR	SO	11	25	588	1	23.52	2.27
21. Keantwon Gray, Grambling	K	SR	11	21	492	1	23.43	1.91
22. Erick Fitzpatrick, Morehead St.	RB	SO	11	24	559	0	23.29	2.18
23. Courtney Robinson, Massachusetts	DB	SO	15	21	489	0	23.29	1.40
24. Andre Taylor, Sacramento St.	WR	SR	11	15	349	0	23.27	1.36
25. Desmond Foster, Alabama St.	DB	SR	11	15	348	1	23.20	1.36
26. Derrick Parrott, Murray St.	DB	JR	9	16	370	0	23.13	1.78
27. Arkee Whitlock, Southern Ill.	RB	SR	13	19	439	0	23.11	1.46
28. William Middleton, Furman	DB	SO	12	25	577	1	23.08	2.08
29. Evin Jones, Sacred Heart	RB	SO	11	18	413	1	22.94	1.64
29. Eric Davis, Missouri St.	WR	SO	11	18	413	0	22.94	1.64
31. L.D. Briscoe, Jackson St.	RB	FR	10	14	321	0	22.93	1.40
32. Roosevelt Kiser, Florida A&M	WR	SR	11	33	753	0	22.82	3.00
33. Kirk Konert, Davidson	WR	SO	10	27	616	0	22.81	2.70
34. David Caldwell, William & Mary	DB	FR	11	16	365	0	22.81	1.45
35. Rob Schulte, Montana	WR	SO	13	26	580	0	22.31	2.00
36. Isiejah Allen, Fordham	DB	FR	11	25	557	1	22.28	2.27
37. Chad Kackert, New Hampshire	RB	FR	13	19	423	0	22.26	1.46
38. Tom Nelson, Illinois St.	DB	SO	13	20	445	0	22.25	1.54
38. Kyle Postell, Duquesne	DB	SR	10	12	267	0	22.25	1.20
40. Stan Zwinggi, Texas St.	RB	SO	11	14	311	0	22.21	1.27
41. Chad Simpson, Morgan St.	RB	JR	11	14	310	0	22.14	1.27
42. Mike Malone, Western Caro.	RB	JR	11	30	663	0	22.10	2.73
43. Larry Shipp, Tennessee Tech	WR	JR	11	17	375	0	22.06	1.55
44. Brandon Markey, Brown	RB	SR	9	24	528	1	22.00	2.67
45. Cord Parks, Northeastern	DB	SO	11	20	439	0	21.95	1.82
46. Derrick Harris, Sam Houston St.	DB	SR	11	26	570	0	21.92	2.36
47. Craig Turner, Southern Ill.	DB	JR	13	20	437	0	21.85	1.54
48. Anthony Bey, St. Peter's	DB	FR	10	18	393	0	21.83	1.80
49. Geoff Bean, Colgate	DB	SR	11	25	545	0	21.80	2.27
50. Josh Pastore, Lehigh	RB	SO	11	27	588	0	21.78	2.45
51. Kervin Michaud, Delaware	WR	SO	11	17	368	0	21.65	1.55
52. Rashad Etheridge, Western Ky.	DB	FR	11	19	410	0	21.58	1.73
53. Duvaughn Flagler, Gardner-Webb	WR	JR	11	20	431	0	21.55	1.82
54. Jason Payne, Sacred Heart	RB	JR	11	17	366	0	21.53	1.55
55. Charlie Spiller, Alcorn St.	WR	SR	11	19	406	0	21.37	1.73

Rank, Player	Pos	Cl.	G	Ret	Yds	TD	Yds/ Ret	Ret/ Gm
56. Marquice Maynard, Ga. Southern	RB	JR	11	14	298	0	21.29	1.27
57. Corey Council, Bethune-Cookman	WR	SO	11	31	659	0	21.26	2.82
58. Chris Miller, Northwestern St.	WR	JR	10	13	275	0	21.15	1.30
59. Geavon Tribble, Jacksonville	WR	SO	10	12	253	0	21.08	1.20
60. Albert Turner, Southern U.	WR	JR	10	25	527	0	21.08	2.50
61. Casey Gough, Holy Cross	DB	SR	11	30	632	0	21.07	2.73
62. Salim Koroma, Villanova	WR	SO	11	28	589	0	21.04	2.55
63. Jonte Coven, Fordham	RB	JR	10	13	272	0	20.92	1.30
64. Rashad Howard, Norfolk St.	WR	JR	10	25	522	0	20.88	2.50
65. Anthony Weeden, Prairie View	RB	FR	9	12	249	0	20.75	1.33
66. Arman Shields, Richmond	WR	JR	10	12	248	0	20.67	1.20
67. Quinten Ponius, Eastern Ill.	DB	SO	13	16	329	0	20.56	1.23
68. David Morgan, Colgate	WR	SO	11	15	308	0	20.53	1.36
69. Greg Skidmore, Northwestern St.	RB	SR	11	19	382	0	20.11	1.73
70. Nick Ruhe, Dayton	WR	SR	10	24	482	0	20.08	2.40
71. Jerome Brooks, Stephen F. Austin	RB	SR	11	14	281	0	20.07	1.27
72. Jarrett Morrow, Tennessee St.	WR	SR	11	15	301	0	20.07	1.36
73. James Hill, Appalachian St.	WR	SO	15	20	401	0	20.05	1.33
74. J.J. Yates, N.C. A&T	CB	JR	11	24	481	0	20.04	2.18
75. Jared Colmer, St. Francis (Pa.)	WR	FR	10	14	279	0	19.93	1.40
76. Nate Conner, Jacksonville	WR	JR	10	32	630	0	19.69	3.20
77. Philip Galligan, Dartmouth	WR	SO	10	21	413	0	19.67	2.10
78. Elton Peterson, Southeast Mo. St.	RB	SR	10	18	353	0	19.61	1.80
79. T.J. Clegg, Elon	RB	JR	10	18	352	0	19.56	1.80
80. Sam Shepherd, Penn	WR	SO	9	11	215	0	19.55	1.22
81. Tory Cooper, Citadel	RB	JR	11	17	332	0	19.53	1.55
82. Kevin Frederick, Marist	WR	SR	11	17	331	0	19.47	1.55
83. J.J. Cox Jr., Stony Brook	WR	JR	11	17	329	0	19.35	1.55
84. Jason Davis, Bucknell	RB	FR	10	17	328	0	19.29	1.70
85. Alfred Phillips, Wagner	DB	JR	11	24	458	0	19.08	2.18
86. Tim Watson, Lafayette	RB	SO	11	22	418	0	19.00	2.00
87. Eric Frazier, La Salle	WR	FR	10	22	417	0	18.95	2.20
88. Peter Ploszek, Princeton	RB	SO	10	13	245	0	18.85	1.30
89. Tim Maypray, VMI	WR	FR	10	17	320	0	18.82	1.70
90. Leonard Moore, Howard	WR	JR	11	22	412	0	18.73	2.00
91. Ken Cornist, Idaho St.	RB	SO	11	16	298	0	18.63	1.45
91. Zack Zimmer, Butler	DB	JR	10	16	298	0	18.63	1.60
93. Carl Berman, Indiana St.	WR	SR	11	37	689	0	18.62	3.36
94. Daniel Davis, Texas Southern	WR	JR	11	18	331	0	18.39	1.64
95. Emanuel Hassell, Chattanooga	WR	SR	11	20	367	0	18.35	1.82
96. Bryant Burch, Charleston So.	WR	SR	11	16	292	0	18.25	1.45
96. Milan Williams, Dartmouth	DB	SO	10	20	365	0	18.25	2.00
96. Neil Sherlock, Harvard	WR	SR	10	20	365	0	18.25	2.00
99. Del Ben, Savannah St.	WR	JR	10	19	346	0	18.21	1.90
100. Tyler Putnam, Drake	WR	SR	10	13	236	0	18.15	1.30

Field Goals

Rank, Player	Pos	Cl.	G	FGA	FGM	Pct.	FG/ Gm
1. Dan Carpenter, Montana	K	JR	14	30	24	.800	1.71
2. Rob Zarrilli, Hofstra	K	JR	11	21	18	.857	1.64
2. Robert Weeks, Northwestern St.	K	SO	11	24	18	.750	1.64
4. Brian Wingert, UNI	K	SR	11	23	17	.739	1.55
5. Blake Bercegeay, McNeese St.	K	SO	12	20	18	.900	1.50
6. Brett Bergstrom, Eastern Wash.	DL/K	SR	11	18	15	.833	1.36
7. Andrew Paterini, Hampton	K	SR	12	21	16	.762	1.33
8. Eric Azorr, Portland St.	K	SR	11	21	14	.667	1.27
8. Wesley Taylor, Florida A&M	K	JR	11	22	14	.636	1.27
10. Alan Kimball, Yale	K	JR	10	19	12	.632	1.20
10. Chris Lofrese, Iona	K	SR	10	14	12	.857	1.20
12. Robbie Dehaze, Northern Ariz.	K	JR	11	17	13	.765	1.18
12. Jason Fralicker, Albany (N.Y.)	K	JR	11	19	13	.684	1.18
12. Chris James, Western Ky.	K	JR	11	17	13	.765	1.18
12. Cory Long, Stephen F. Austin	K	SO	11	19	13	.684	1.18
12. Gavin Hallford, Jacksonville St.	K	SO	11	22	13	.591	1.18
17. Craig Coffin, Southern Ill.	K	SR	13	16	15	.938	1.15
18. Mark Troyan, Duquesne	K	SO	9	17	10	.588	1.11
19. Brad Smith, Davidson	K	SR	10	12	11	.917	1.10
20. Jason Leo, Lehigh	P/K	SO	11	18	12	.667	1.09
20. Shannon Fleming, Samford	K	JR	11	14	12	.857	1.09
20. Nick Coromelas, Cal Poly	K	SR	11	18	12	.667	1.09
20. Andrew Wilcox, Elon	K	SO	11	18	12	.667	1.09
24. Chris Koepplin, Massachusetts	K	JR	15	23	16	.696	1.07
25. Jon Rocholl, Columbia	P/K	SO	10	16	10	.625	1.00
26. Jeff Hastings, Montana St.	K	SR	13	15	12	.800	.92
26. Zach Yates, Eastern Ill.	K	SO	13	16	12	.750	.92
28. David Rabil, James Madison	K	SR	12	13	11	.846	.92
29. Andrew Howard, Richmond	K	FR	11	13	10	.769	.91
29. Blake Vandiver, Citadel	K	SR	11	16	10	.625	.91
29. Eric Benson, Tennessee St.	P/K	SO	11	14	10	.714	.91
29. Conor Foley, Weber St.	K	SO	11	19	10	.526	.91
29. Barrett Way, VMI	K	JR	11	12	10	.833	.91
34. Hunter Smith, Gardner-Webb	K	SR	10	11	9	.818	.90
34. Peter Zell, Cornell	K	JR	10	14	9	.643	.90
34. Conner Louden, Princeton	P/K	SO	10	16	9	.563	.90
34. Jordan Quiroz, Butler	K	SO	10	13	9	.692	.90
34. Taylor Long, Eastern Ky.	K	SO	10	17	9	.529	.90
39. Fred Weingart, Monmouth	K	JR	9	15	8	.533	.89
40. Brian Palmer, Youngstown St.	K	SO	14	15	12	.800	.86
41. Kevin Mazur, Illinois St.	K	SO	13	19	11	.579	.85
42. Josh Hoke, Coastal Caro.	K	SR	12	17	10	.588	.83
42. Taylor Brown, Tenn.-Martin	K	SR	12	16	10	.625	.83
44. Juan Gamboa, Sacramento St.	K	SO	11	12	9	.750	.82
44. Jonathan Williams, Alcorn St.	K	FR	11	14	9	.643	.82
44. Anthony Johnson, Alabama St.	K	SR	11	14	9	.643	.82
44. Nathan Stokes, Missouri St.	K	JR	11	14	9	.643	.82
44. Will Carney, Bucknell	K	SO	11	16	9	.563	.82
44. Micah Clukey, Fordham	K	SR	11	16	9	.563	.82
44. Piotr Czech, Wagner	K	JR	11	15	9	.600	.82
51. Steve Morgan, Brown	P/K	JR	10	12	8	.667	.80
51. Matt Schindel, Harvard	K	JR	10	14	8	.571	.80
53. Andy Kempler, Dartmouth	K	JR	9	13	7	.538	.78
54. Eric Perri, Jackson St.	K	FR	8	8	6	.750	.75
54. Hutch Parker, San Diego	K	JR	12	10	9	.900	.75
56. Zach Hobby, Delaware	K	SO	11	14	8	.571	.73
56. Josh Brite, Delaware St.	P/K	JR	11	12	8	.667	.73
56. Ross Coffee, Austin Peay	K	SO	11	12	8	.667	.73
56. Logan Reese, Drake	K	SO	11	13	8	.615	.73
56. Breck Ackley, Southern U.	K	SR	11	13	8	.615	.73
61. Devin McNeill, Maine	K	FR	10	11	7	.636	.70
61. Kyle Hooper, Indiana St.	K	SR	10	11	7	.636	.70
63. Julian Rauch, Appalachian St.	K	JR	15	14	10	.714	.67
64. Blair Pritchard, William & Mary	K	SR	11	12	7	.583	.64
64. Alex Romero, Nicholls St.	K	JR	11	10	7	.700	.64
64. Nick Robinson, Wofford	K	SR	11	12	7	.583	.64
64. Michael Gaston, South Carolina St.	K	SR	11	10	7	.700	.64
64. Antonio Gomez, Norfolk St.	K	SR	11	12	7	.583	.64
64. Taylor Rowan, Western Ill.	K	SO	11	13	7	.538	.64
70. Mat Johnson, Northeastern	K	FR	10	10	6	.600	.60
70. Esteban Lopez, Chattanooga	K	SR	10	11	6	.545	.60
70. Donovan Curry, Jacksonville	K	FR	10	11	6	.545	.60
73. Scott Beckler, Furman	K	JR	12	13	7	.538	.58
73. John Heflin, Ark.-Pine Bluff	K	JR	12	14	7	.500	.58
75. Dan Zeidman, Idaho St.	P/K	JR	11	8	6	.750	.55
75. Jesus Cortez, Bethune-Cookman	K	SR	11	9	6	.667	.55
75. Nick Ellis, Charleston So.	K	JR	11	9	6	.667	.55
75. Mike DeSantis, Holy Cross	K	SR	11	11	6	.545	.55
75. Dennis Wiehberg, Howard	K	FR	11	10	6	.600	.55
75. Tim Manuel, Grambling	P/K	JR	11	10	6	.600	.55
75. Jonathan Parsons, Western Caro.	K	SO	11	10	6	.600	.55
82. Joe Marcoux, Villanova	K	SO	10	11	5	.455	.50
82. Rick Ziska, Lafayette	K	SR	12	10	6	.600	.50
82. Jacob Thomas, St. Peter's	K	FR	10	9	5	.556	.50
85. Tom Manning, New Hampshire	K	FR	13	9	6	.667	.46
86. Colin Gallagher, Rhode Island	K	SR	11	12	5	.417	.45
86. Bradley Rowe, Marist	K	JR	11	7	5	.714	.45
86. D'Javan Conway, Texas Southern	K	JR	11	8	5	.625	.45
86. Mike Krieg, Valparaiso	K	FR	11	8	5	.625	.45
86. Zack Girlarski, Mississippi Val.	K	FR	11	7	5	.714	.45
86. Rhonnie Skeete, Morgan St.	K	SO	11	10	5	.500	.45
92. Zacry Kolegue, Liberty	K	JR	10	8	4	.500	.40
93. Ben Beasley, Liberty	K	SR	11	8	4	.500	.36
93. Nathan DiLorenzo, Robert Morris	K	SR	11	8	4	.500	.36
93. Gary Crass, Murray St.	K	SR	11	5	4	.800	.36
93. Adam Sciulli, St. Francis (Pa.)	K	JR	11	6	4	.667	.36
97. Jeremy Licea, Alabama A&M	K	FR	12	7	4	.571	.33
97. Eric Hernandez, Prairie View	P/K	SR	9	9	3	.333	.33
99. Eric Bjonerud, Georgetown	K	JR	10	4	3	.750	.30
99. Collin Schermann, Southeast Mo. St.	K	SO	10	7	3	.429	.30
99. Braden Lepisto, Penn	WR/K	JR	10	4	3	.750	.30

All-Purpose Running

Rank, Player	Pos	Cl.	G	Rush	Rec	PR	KOR	Yards	Yds/ Gm	Plays	Yds/Pl
1. Justise Hairston, Central Conn. St.	RB	SR	11	1,847	58	123	170	2,198	199.82	305	7.21
2. Arkee Whitlock, Southern Ill.	RB	SR	13	1,828	63	0	439	2,330	179.23	342	6.81
3. Chris Fletcher, Austin Peay	RB	JR	11	1,401	200	0	241	1,842	167.45	291	6.33
4. Nick Ruhe, Dayton	WR	SR	10	0	977	214	482	1,673	167.30	92	18.18
5. Marcus Mason, Youngstown St.	RB	SR	12	1,847	79	0	0	1,926	160.50	309	6.23
6. Clifton Dawson, Harvard	RB	SR	10	1,213	239	0	116	1,568	156.80	263	5.96
7. D.D. Terry, Sam Houston St.	RB	SR	10	1,328	237	0	0	1,565	156.50	237	6.60
8. Clay Green, Jacksonville St.	RB	SR	11	1,083	109	81	439	1,712	155.64	285	6.01
9. Scott Phaydavong, Drake	RB	JR	11	1,613	87	0	0	1,700	154.55	285	5.96
10. Mike McLeod, Yale	RB	SO	10	1,364	132	0	0	1,496	149.60	305	4.90
11. Roosevelt Kiser, Florida A&M	WR	SR	11	55	647	169	753	1,624	147.64	119	13.65
12. Pierre Rembert, Illinois St.	RB	SR	13	1,743	90	0	76	1,909	146.85	374	5.10
13. Steve Baylark, Massachusetts	RB	SR	15	1,960	237	0	0	2,197	146.47	361	6.09
14. Dedrick Poole, Ark.-Pine Bluff	WR	SR	11	240	517	168	621	1,546	140.55	100	15.46
15. Carl Berman, Indiana St.	WR	SR	11	46	783	16	689	1,534	139.45	115	13.34
16. Herb Donaldson, Western Ill.	RB	SO	11	1,417	116	0	0	1,533	139.36	247	6.21
17. JT Rogan, San Diego	RB	SO	12	1,002	313	0	347	1,662	138.50	230	7.23
18. Todd Harris, St. Francis (Pa.)	RB	SR	11	1,330	87	0	102	1,519	138.09	294	5.17
19. Dane Samuels, Iona	RB	JR	10	698	197	0	439	1,334	133.40	204	6.54
20. Donald Chapman, Tenn.-Martin	RB	JR	11	1,412	37	0	0	1,449	131.73	277	5.23
21. Tory Cooper, Citadel	RB	JR	11	807	247	62	332	1,448	131.64	223	6.49
22. Javarris Williams, Tennessee St.	RB	SO	11	1,233	210	0	0	1,443	131.18	258	5.59
23. Kevin Richardson, Appalachian St.	RB	JR	15	1,676	285	0	0	1,961	130.73	332	5.91
24. Erick Fitzpatrick, Morehead St.	RB	SO	11	381	459	34	559	1,433	130.27	119	12.04
25. Steven Whitehead, McNeese St.	RB	JR	12	156	596	353	455	1,560	130.00	111	14.05
26. Jordan Scott, Colgate	RB	SO	11	1,234	176	0	0	1,410	128.18	309	4.56
27. Eric Weems, Bethune-Cookman	WR	SR	11	145	918	331	14	1,408	128.00	117	12.03
28. Nate Conner, Jacksonville	WR	JR	10	-2	433	218	630	1,279	127.90	86	14.87
29. Michael Mayers, Elon	WR	JR	11	131	866	0	408	1,405	127.73	109	12.89
30. Alex Henderson, Northern Ariz.	RB	FR	11	1,016	215	0	158	1,389	126.27	207	6.71
31. Arel Gordon, Maine	WR	SR	11	843	535	0	0	1,378	125.27	235	5.86
32. Emmanuel Marc, Delaware St.	RB	SR	11	1,230	129	0	0	1,359	123.55	204	6.66
33. Joe Sandberg, Penn	RB	SR	10	1,042	189	0	0	1,231	123.10	232	5.31
34. Deshawn Baker, South Carolina St.	RB	SR	11	1,289	63	0	0	1,352	122.91	211	6.41
35. Vincent Webb, Eastern Ill.	RB	SR	13	1,405	183	0	0	1,588	122.15	288	5.51
36. Eldra Buckley, Chattanooga	RB	SR	11	1,204	139	0	0	1,343	122.09	233	5.76
37. Jonathan Hurt, Lafayette	RB	SR	12	1,165	299	0	0	1,464	122.00	257	5.70
38. Kenny Mitchell, Georgetown	WR	SO	11	53	212	0	1,075	1,340	121.82	69	19.42
39. William Ford, South Carolina St.	RB	SO	11	752	66	0	517	1,335	121.36	137	9.74
40. Eugene Holloman, James Madison	RB	JR	10	1,084	122	0	0	1,206	120.60	202	5.97
41. James Noble, Cal Poly	RB	SO	10	1,009	0	0	195	1,204	120.40	207	5.82
42. Jerry Brant, Jacksonville	RB	SR	10	1,110	91	0	0	1,201	120.10	213	5.64
43. Sean Mizzer, VMI	RB	SR	11	1,022	121	12	147	1,302	118.36	233	5.59
44. Corey Lewis, UNI	RB	SO	9	894	167	0	0	1,061	117.89	153	6.93
45. Jayson Foster, Ga. Southern	WR	JR	11	346	368	250	323	1,287	117.00	112	11.49
46. Jay Peck, Alabama St.	RB	JR	11	1,086	146	0	54	1,286	116.91	264	4.87
47. Josh Barnett, Idaho St.	RB	JR	11	1,117	149	0	0	1,266	115.09	221	5.73
48. Eric Yancey, Towson	WR	SR	11	0	826	182	252	1,260	114.55	104	12.12
49. Treyvn Smith, Weber St.	RB	SO	11	1,129	75	0	42	1,246	113.27	213	5.85
50. Micheal Jefferson, Montana St.	WR	SR	13	129	1,023	0	298	1,450	111.54	96	15.10
51. Lanis Frederick, Austin Peay	WR	SO	11	2	1,101	62	48	1,213	110.27	90	13.48
52. Martell Mallet, Ark.-Pine Bluff	RB	JR	12	1,121	180	0	20	1,321	110.08	255	5.18
53. Alex Watson, Northern Ariz.	WR	JR	11	2	1,017	88	103	1,210	110.00	103	11.75
54. Stan Zwinggi, Texas St.	RB	SO	11	735	159	0	311	1,205	109.55	157	7.68
55. Duvaughn Flagler, Gardner-Webb	WR	JR	11	14	740	0	431	1,185	107.73	85	13.94
56. Larry Shipp, Tennessee Tech	WR	JR	11	6	799	0	375	1,180	107.27	73	16.16
57. Bruce Hocker, Duquesne	WR	JR	10	0	1,070	0	0	1,070	107.00	61	17.54
58. Bryan Walters, Cornell	WR	FR	8	0	33	274	540	847	105.88	52	16.29
59. Tony West, Indiana St.	RB	JR	9	791	149	0	10	950	105.56	178	5.34
60. Jason Payne, Sacred Heart	RB	JR	11	621	174	0	366	1,161	105.55	151	7.69
61. Mario Hines, Robert Morris	WR	JR	10	21	341	203	490	1,055	105.50	74	14.26
62. Jason Butler, Wagner	RB	JR	11	735	203	1	221	1,160	105.45	185	6.27
63. Wynton Jackson, Liberty	WR	JR	11	19	519	298	323	1,159	105.36	85	13.64
64. DeQuese May, Villanova	RB	SR	11	538	479	0	141	1,158	105.27	148	7.82
65. Terrell Hudgins, Elon	WR	FR	10	21	1,027	0	0	1,048	104.80	70	14.97
66. Darius Fudge, Western Caro.	RB	SR	11	1,001	151	0	0	1,152	104.73	242	4.76
67. Maurice Murray, Northeastern	RB	JR	11	1,061	83	0	0	1,144	104.00	219	5.22
67. Kevious Johnson, Wofford	RB	JR	11	730	108	0	306	1,144	104.00	134	8.54
69. Nate Hughes, Alcorn St.	WR	SR	11	62	371	460	248	1,141	103.73	83	13.75
70. Dan Spriggs, Duquesne	WR	SR	10	0	778	257	0	1,035	103.50	91	11.37
71. Emery Sammons, Norfolk St.	WR	SR	11	2	639	223	272	1,136	103.27	63	18.03
72. Curtis Hamilton, Western Ky.	WR	JR	9	5	841	20	63	929	103.22	59	15.75
73. Luke Siwula, Cornell	RB	JR	10	885	141	0	0	1,026	102.60	213	4.82
74. Lerron Moore, Western Ky.	RB	SR	10	891	129	0	0	1,020	102.00	210	4.86
75. Elijah Brooks, William & Mary	RB	SR	11	931	163	0	27	1,121	101.91	208	5.39
76. Tim Hightower, Richmond	RB	JR	11	850	269	0	0	1,119	101.73	211	5.30
77. Chad Simpson, Morgan St.	RB	JR	11	795	13	0	310	1,118	101.64	167	6.69
78. Johnny Gray, UNI	WR	SO	11	106	607	155	245	1,113	101.18	81	13.74
79. Marques Thompson, Lehigh	RB	SR	11	904	196	0	0	1,100	100.00	199	5.53
80. Adam San Miguel, Monmouth	WR	SR	12	63	872	257	0	1,192	99.33	116	10.28

Rank, Player	Pos	Cl.	G	Rush	Rec	PR	KOR	Yards	Yds/ Gm	Plays	Yds/Pl
81. Ryan Maher, Holy Cross	WR	JR	11	78	797	19	198	1,092	99.27	97	11.26
82. Alonzo Coleman, Hampton	RB	SR	11	1,052	28	0	0	1,080	98.18	161	6.71
83. Rashad Jennings, Liberty	RB	SO	11	1,020	56	0	0	1,076	97.82	185	5.82
84. Jabari McGee, Morehead St.	RB	SR	11	907	162	0	0	1,069	97.18	189	5.66
85. Larue Burley, Southern Utah	WR	SR	11	9	230	242	580	1,061	96.45	64	16.58
86. Jessie Burtojn, Tenn.-Martin	WR	JR	12	63	367	198	524	1,152	96.00	68	16.94
87. Mark Dunn, Eastern Ky.	RB	JR	11	802	252	0	0	1,054	95.82	187	5.64
88. Kareem Huggins, Hofstra	RB	JR	11	572	79	162	235	1,048	95.27	176	5.95
88. Steve Ogden, Valparaiso	WR	SO	11	0	1,048	0	0	1,048	95.27	55	19.05
90. Jason Jones, Ark.-Pine Bluff	WR	JR	12	0	903	0	240	1,143	95.25	49	23.33
91. Brandon Markey, Brown	RB	SR	9	210	34	79	528	851	94.56	101	8.43
92. Raji El-Amin, Rhode Island	DB	JR	11	0	0	137	860	1,030	93.64	53	19.43
93. Cedrick Gipson, Furman	RB	JR	12	938	182	0	0	1,120	93.33	204	5.49
94. Lamar Lewis, Ga. Southern	RB	JR	10	782	136	0	0	918	91.80	167	5.50
95. Eric Davis, Missouri St.	WR	SO	11	17	332	246	413	1,008	91.64	71	14.20
96. Carlton McFadgen, Dayton	WR	SR	10	46	845	0	23	914	91.40	56	16.32
97. Maurice Price, Charleston So.	WR	JR	11	15	985	0	0	1,000	90.91	107	9.35
98. Chad Kackert, New Hampshire	RB	FR	13	584	166	0	423	1,173	90.23	148	7.93
99. Kervin Michaud, Delaware	WR	SO	11	234	387	0	368	989	89.91	115	8.60
100. Arman Shields, Richmond	WR	JR	10	1	643	0	248	892	89.20	68	13.12

Scoring

Rank, Player	Pos	Cl.	G	TD	OKM	OKA	FGM	FGA	Pts	Pts/Gm
1. Clifton Dawson, Harvard	RB	SR	10	22	0	0	0	0	132	13.20
2. Kevin Richardson, Appalachian St.	RB	JR	15	31	0	0	0	0	186	12.40
3. Mike McLeod, Yale	RB	SO	10	20	0	0	0	0	120	12.00
4. Jerome Felton, Furman	RB	JR	12	23	0	0	0	0	140	11.67
5. Arkee Whitlock, Southern Ill.	RB	SR	13	25	0	0	0	0	150	11.54
6. Marcus Mason, Youngstown St.	RB	SR	12	23	0	0	0	0	138	11.50
7. Justise Hairston, Central Conn. St.	RB	SR	11	20	0	0	0	0	120	10.91
8. Herb Donaldson, Western Ill.	RB	SO	11	18	0	0	0	0	108	9.82
8. Chris Fletcher, Austin Peay	RB	JR	11	18	0	0	0	0	108	9.82
8. Willie Cashmore, Drake	RB	JR	11	18	0	0	0	0	108	9.82
11. D.D. Terry, Sam Houston St.	RB	SR	10	16	0	0	0	0	98	9.80
12. Bruce Hocker, Duquesne	WR	JR	10	16	0	0	0	0	96	9.60
13. Clay Green, Jacksonville St.	RB	SR	11	16	0	0	0	0	96	8.73
14. Jonathan Hurt, Lafayette	RB	SR	12	17	0	0	0	0	102	8.50
14. JT Rogan, San Diego	RB	SO	12	17	0	0	0	0	102	8.50
16. Joe Sandberg, Penn	RB	SR	10	14	0	0	0	0	84	8.40
17. Donald Chapman, Tenn.-Martin	RB	JR	11	15	0	0	0	0	92	8.36
18. Alex Watson, Northern Ariz.	WR	JR	11	15	0	0	0	0	90	8.18
19. Brian Wingert, UNI	K	SR	11	0	38	39	17	23	89	8.09
20. Dan Carpenter, Montana	K	JR	14	0	41	44	24	30	113	8.07
21. Jerome Simpson, Coastal Caro.	WR	JR	12	16	0	0	0	0	96	8.00
21. Andrew Paterini, Hampton	K	SR	12	0	48	52	16	21	96	8.00
23. Pierre Rembert, Illinois St.	RB	SR	13	17	0	0	0	0	102	7.85
24. Jonathon Hubbard, Davidson	RB	SR	10	13	0	0	0	0	78	7.80
25. Craig Coffin, Southern Ill.	K	SR	13	0	55	55	15	16	100	7.69
26. Marquay McDaniel, Hampton	WR	SR	12	15	0	0	0	0	90	7.50
26. Martell Mallet, Ark.-Pine Bluff	RB	JR	12	15	0	0	0	0	90	7.50
28. Robbie Dehaze, Northern Ariz.	K	JR	11	0	43	44	13	17	82	7.45
28. Jordan Scott, Colgate	RB	SO	11	13	0	0	0	0	82	7.45
30. Blake Bercegeay, McNeese St.	K	SO	12	0	33	36	18	20	87	7.25
31. Steve Baylark, Massachusetts	RB	SR	15	18	0	0	0	0	108	7.20
32. Zach Terrell, Liberty	QB	SO	11	13	0	0	0	0	78	7.09
33. David Sinisi, Monmouth	RB	FR	12	14	0	0	0	0	84	7.00
34. David Rabil, James Madison	K	SR	12	0	50	51	11	13	83	6.92
35. Mark Troyan, Duquesne	K	SO	9	0	31	33	10	17	61	6.78
36. Corey Lewis, UNI	RB	SO	9	10	0	0	0	0	60	6.67
36. Curtis Hamilton, Western Ky.	WR	JR	9	10	0	0	0	0	60	6.67
36. Josh Johnson, San Diego	QB	JR	12	12	0	0	0	0	80	6.67
36. Julian Rauch, Appalachian St.	K	JR	15	0	70	71	10	14	100	6.67
40. Gavin Hallford, Jacksonville St.	K	SO	11	0	34	35	13	22	73	6.64
41. Chris Koepplin, Massachusetts	K	JR	15	0	51	52	16	23	99	6.60
41. Derek Cassidy, Rhode Island	QB	SO	10	11	0	0	0	0	66	6.60
43. Josh Hoke, Coastal Caro.	K	SR	12	0	49	50	10	17	79	6.58
44. Emmanuel Marc, Delaware St.	RB	SR	11	12	0	0	0	0	72	6.55
44. Alonzo Coleman, Hampton	RB	SR	11	12	0	0	0	0	72	6.55
44. Javarris Williams, Tennessee St.	RB	SO	11	12	0	0	0	0	72	6.55
47. Alan Kimball, Yale	K	JR	10	0	29	31	12	19	65	6.50
47. Kevin Beverly, Hampton	RB	JR	12	13	0	0	0	0	78	6.50
47. Jason Jones, Ark.-Pine Bluff	WR	JR	12	13	0	0	0	0	78	6.50
50. Brad Smith, Davidson	K	SR	10	0	30	32	11	12	63	6.30
51. Jason Leo, Lehigh	P/K	SO	11	0	33	34	12	18	69	6.27
51. Robert Weeks, Northwestern St.	K	SO	11	0	15	17	18	24	69	6.27
51. Wesley Taylor, Florida A&M	K	JR	11	0	27	29	14	22	69	6.27
54. Rob Zarrilli, Hofstra	K	JR	11	0	14	16	18	21	68	6.18
55. Brian Palmer, Youngstown St.	K	SO	14	0	50	54	12	15	86	6.14
56. Eric Azorr, Portland St.	K	SR	11	0	25	27	14	21	67	6.09
57. David Ball, New Hampshire	WR	SR	13	13	0	0	0	0	78	6.00
57. Todd Harris, St. Francis (Pa.)	RB	SR	11	11	0	0	0	0	66	6.00

Rank, Player	Pos	Cl.	G	TD	OKM	OKA	FGM	FGA	Pts	Pts/Gm
57. Wes Doyle, San Diego	WR	JR	11	11	0	0	0	0	66	6.00
57. Eric Haw, Jackson St.	RB	SO	10	10	0	0	0	0	60	6.00
57. Clyde Edwards, Grambling	WR	JR	11	11	0	0	0	0	66	6.00
57. Armanti Edwards, Appalachian St.	QB	FR	15	15	0	0	0	0	90	6.00
57. Micah Rucker, Eastern Ill.	WR	JR	13	13	0	0	0	0	78	6.00
57. William Ford, South Carolina St.	RB	SO	11	11	0	0	0	0	66	6.00
57. Deshawn Baker, South Carolina St.	RB	SR	11	11	0	0	0	0	66	6.00
57. Shaheer McBride, Delaware St.	WR	JR	11	11	0	0	0	0	66	6.00
57. Chris James, Western Ky.	K	JR	11	0	27	27	13	17	66	6.00
57. Matt Dickin, Villanova	RB	JR	11	11	0	0	0	0	66	6.00
57. Brett Bergstrom, Eastern Wash.	DL/K	SR	11	0	21	22	15	18	66	6.00
57. Aaron Mason, Montana St.	RB	FR	10	10	0	0	0	0	60	6.00
57. Maurice Murray, Northeastern	RB	JR	11	11	0	0	0	0	66	6.00
72. Kevin Mazur, Illinois St.	K	SO	13	0	44	47	11	19	77	5.92
73. Andrew Wilcox, Elon	K	SO	11	0	29	30	12	18	65	5.91
74. Andrew Howard, Richmond	K	FR	11	0	34	34	10	13	64	5.82
74. Jason Fralicker, Albany (N.Y.)	K	JR	11	0	25	25	13	19	64	5.82
76. Taylor Rowan, Western Ill.	K	SO	11	0	42	42	7	13	63	5.73
77. Cory Long, Stephen F. Austin	K	SO	11	0	23	23	13	19	62	5.64
78. Lerron Moore, Western Ky.	RB	SR	10	9	0	0	0	0	56	5.60
79. Nick Robinson, Wofford	K	SR	11	0	40	41	7	12	61	5.55
79. Nick Coromelas, Cal Poly	K	SR	11	0	25	27	12	18	61	5.55
81. Ricky Santos, New Hampshire	QB	JR	13	12	0	0	0	0	72	5.54
82. Matt Schindel, Harvard	K	JR	10	0	31	33	8	14	55	5.50
82. Taylor Brown, Tenn.-Martin	K	SR	12	0	36	37	10	16	66	5.50
84. Eric Yancey, Towson	WR	SR	11	10	0	0	0	0	60	5.45
84. Akilah Lacey, Idaho St.	WR	SR	11	10	0	0	0	0	60	5.45
84. Maurice Price, Charleston So.	WR	JR	11	10	0	0	0	0	60	5.45
84. Jabari McGee, Morehead St.	RB	SR	11	10	0	0	0	0	60	5.45
84. Scott Phaydavong, Drake	RB	JR	11	10	0	0	0	0	60	5.45
84. Tory Cooper, Citadel	RB	JR	11	10	0	0	0	0	60	5.45
84. Daryl Jones, Norfolk St.	RB	JR	11	10	0	0	0	0	60	5.45
84. Eric Weems, Bethune-Cookman	WR	SR	11	10	0	0	0	0	60	5.45
84. Sean Mizzer, VMI	RB	SR	11	10	0	0	0	0	60	5.45
84. Rashad Jennings, Liberty	RB	SO	11	10	0	0	0	0	60	5.45
94. Eugene Holloman, James Madison	RB	JR	10	9	0	0	0	0	54	5.40
94. Nuru Goodrum, Citadel	RB	SR	10	9	0	0	0	0	54	5.40
94. Taylor Long, Eastern Ky.	K	SO	10	0	27	28	9	17	54	5.40
97. Zach Hobby, Delaware	K	SO	11	0	35	37	8	14	59	5.36
97. Logan Reese, Drake	K	SO	11	0	35	40	8	13	59	5.36
97. Josh Brite, Delaware St.	P/K	JR	11	0	35	39	8	12	59	5.36
100. Zach Yates, Eastern Ill.	K	SO	13	0	33	38	12	16	69	5.31

Points Responsible For

Rank, Player	Pos	Cl.	G	Passing Conv	Passing TD	Pts Scored	Total PRF	PRF/Gm
1. Josh Johnson, San Diego	QB	JR	12	4	34	80	292	24.33
2. Jason Murrietta, Northern Ariz.	QB	SR	11	2	34	10	218	19.82
3. Ricky Santos, New Hampshire	QB	JR	13	0	29	72	246	18.92
4. Scott Knapp, Duquesne	QB	SO	10	0	28	6	174	17.40
5. Tyler Thigpen, Coastal Caro.	QB	SR	12	1	29	32	208	17.33
6. Collin Drafts, Charleston So.	QB	SR	11	1	21	44	172	15.64
7. Albert Chester II, Florida A&M	QB	JR	10	2	18	28	140	14.00
8. Dominic Randolph, Holy Cross	QB	SO	9	1	19	8	124	13.78
9. Clifton Dawson, Harvard	RB	SR	10	0	0	132	132	13.20
10. Sean Schaefer, Towson	QB	SO	10	1	19	14	130	13.00
10. Jeff Terrell, Princeton	QB	SR	10	1	17	26	130	13.00
12. Kelcy Luke, Alabama A&M	QB	JR	12	2	16	54	154	12.83
13. Ryan Alexander, Davidson	QB	JR	10	0	21	0	126	12.60
14. Joe Flacco, Delaware	QB	JR	11	0	18	30	138	12.55
15. Justin Rascati, James Madison	QB	SR	12	0	20	30	150	12.50
16. Kevin Richardson, Appalachian St.	RB	JR	15	0	0	186	186	12.40
17. Sedale Threatt, Lehigh	QB	JR	11	1	14	50	136	12.36
18. Matt Gutierrez, Idaho St.	QB	SR	11	0	16	36	132	12.00
18. Armanti Edwards, Appalachian St.	QB	FR	15	0	15	90	180	12.00
18. Mike McLeod, Yale	RB	SO	10	0	0	120	120	12.00
21. Jerome Felton, Furman	RB	JR	12	0	0	140	140	11.67
21. Chris Wallace, Ark.-Pine Bluff	QB	SR	12	2	20	16	140	11.67
23. Luke Drone, Illinois St.	QB	JR	13	0	21	24	150	11.54
23. Arkee Whitlock, Southern Ill.	RB	SR	13	0	0	150	150	11.54
25. Marcus Mason, Youngstown St.	RB	SR	12	0	0	138	138	11.50
26. Tyler Arciaga, Sacred Heart	QB	SR	11	1	19	8	124	11.27
26. Wes Pope, Elon	QB	JR	11	1	16	26	124	11.27
28. Brandon Landers, Grambling	QB	SO	11	2	17	16	122	11.09
29. Justise Hairston, Central Conn. St.	RB	SR	11	0	0	120	120	10.91
29. Eric Cwalinski, Robert Morris	QB	SO	11	0	19	6	120	10.91
31. Liam Coen, Massachusetts	QB	JR	15	0	26	0	156	10.40
32. Princeton Shepherd, Hampton	QB	SR	11	0	17	12	114	10.36
32. Wes Marshall, Southern Utah	QB	JR	11	0	16	18	114	10.36
32. Jimmy Oliver, Jackson St.	QB	JR	11	0	14	30	114	10.36
35. Derek Cassidy, Rhode Island	QB	SO	10	0	6	66	102	10.20

Rank, Player	Pos	Cl.	G	Passing Conv	Passing TD	Pts Scored	Total PRF	PRF/Gm
35. Vashon Winton, Delaware St.	QB	SO	10	0	10	42	102	10.20
35. Chris Horton, Jacksonville	QB	JR	10	0	15	12	102	10.20
38. Nick Hill, Southern Ill.	QB	JR	13	1	15	38	130	10.00
39. Herb Donaldson, Western Ill.	RB	SO	11	0	0	108	108	9.82
39. Willie Cashmore, Drake	RB	JR	11	0	0	108	108	9.82
39. Chris Fletcher, Austin Peay	RB	JR	11	0	0	108	108	9.82
42. Joseph DiGiacomo, Brown	QB	SR	10	0	13	20	98	9.80
42. D.D. Terry, Sam Houston St.	RB	SR	10	0	0	98	98	9.80
44. Antonio Hefner, Tennessee St.	QB	SO	9	1	9	32	88	9.78
45. Mike Saraceno, Colgate	QB	JR	11	1	11	38	106	9.64
45. Eric Sanders, UNI	QB	JR	11	1	15	14	106	9.64
47. Bruce Hocker, Duquesne	WR	JR	10	0	0	96	96	9.60
48. JT Rogan, San Diego	RB	SO	12	0	2	102	114	9.50
49. Matt Bassuener, Georgetown	QB	SR	10	1	15	2	94	9.40
50. Sawyer Smith, Portland St.	QB	SR	9	0	14	0	84	9.33
50. Brad Maurer, Lafayette	QB	SR	12	1	13	32	112	9.33
50. Reilly Murphy, Indiana St.	QB	JR	9	0	8	36	84	9.33
53. Anthony Doria, St. Francis (Pa.)	QB	SR	11	0	15	12	102	9.27
53. Lee Sweeney, Tennessee Tech	QB	FR	11	0	17	0	102	9.27
55. Chris Walker, Alcorn St.	QB	SO	9	1	10	20	82	9.11
56. Justin Haddix, Western Ky.	QB	SR	11	1	14	14	100	9.09
57. Joe Sandberg, Penn	RB	SR	10	0	1	84	90	9.00
57. Scott Bonnono, St. Peter's	QB	JR	10	0	15	0	90	9.00
59. Devin Campbell, Gardner-Webb	QB	SO	11	0	15	6	96	8.73
59. Steve LaFalce, Western Ill.	QB	SR	11	0	11	30	96	8.73
59. Clay Green, Jacksonville St.	RB	SR	11	0	0	96	96	8.73
62. Marvin Burroughs, Villanova	QB	SR	11	1	9	38	94	8.55
63. Jonathan Hurt, Lafayette	RB	SR	12	0	0	102	102	8.50
63. Brian Boland, Monmouth	QB	SR	12	0	14	18	102	8.50
65. Nathan Ford, Cornell	QB	SO	10	0	8	36	84	8.40
66. Donald Chapman, Tenn.-Martin	RB	JR	11	0	0	92	92	8.36
66. Duran Lawson, Citadel	QB	JR	11	0	14	8	92	8.36
68. Tom Zetts, Youngstown St.	QB	JR	14	2	14	28	116	8.29
69. Ron Whitcomb, Maine	QB	SR	11	0	9	36	90	8.18
69. Alex Watson, Northern Ariz.	WR	JR	11	0	0	90	90	8.18
69. Josh Dudash, Stony Brook	QB	JR	11	0	15	0	90	8.18
69. Cleveland McCoy, South Carolina St.	QB	JR	11	0	10	30	90	8.18
73. Brian Wingert, UNI	K	SR	11	0	0	89	89	8.09
74. Dan Carpenter, Montana	K	JR	14	0	0	113	113	8.07
75. Jerome Simpson, Coastal Caro.	WR	JR	12	0	0	96	96	8.00
75. Andrew Paterini, Hampton	K	SR	12	0	0	96	96	8.00
77. Josh Swogger, Montana	QB	SR	13	0	17	0	102	7.85
77. Pierre Rembert, Illinois St.	RB	SR	13	0	0	102	102	7.85
79. Eric Ward, Richmond	QB	FR	10	0	11	12	78	7.80
79. Jonathon Hubbard, Davidson	RB	SR	10	0	0	78	78	7.80
79. Jarod Rucker, Bethune-Cookman	QB	JR	10	0	11	12	78	7.80
82. Craig Coffin, Southern Ill.	K	SR	13	0	0	100	100	7.69
83. Josh Collier, Wofford	QB	JR	11	0	5	54	84	7.64
83. Danny Southall, Stephen F. Austin	QB	JR	11	0	8	36	84	7.64
85. Kevin Hoyng, Dayton	QB	SR	10	1	11	8	76	7.60
86. Marquay McDaniel, Hampton	WR	SR	12	0	0	90	90	7.50
86. Derrick Fourroux, McNeese St.	QB	FR	12	0	10	30	90	7.50
86. Martell Mallet, Ark.-Pine Bluff	RB	JR	12	0	0	90	90	7.50
89. Robbie Dehaze, Northern Ariz.	K	JR	11	0	0	82	82	7.45
89. Jordan Scott, Colgate	RB	SO	11	0	0	82	82	7.45
91. Michael Potts, William & Mary	QB	JR	9	0	10	6	66	7.33
92. Marcel Marquez, Sacramento St.	QB	JR	11	2	10	16	80	7.27
93. Blake Bercegeay, McNeese St.	K	SO	12	0	0	87	87	7.25
94. Steve Baylark, Massachusetts	RB	SR	15	0	0	108	108	7.20
94. Robert Irvin, Penn	QB	SO	10	0	10	12	72	7.20
96. Zach Terrell, Liberty	QB	SO	11	0	0	78	78	7.09
96. Aries Nelson, Mississippi Val.	QB	SR	11	0	10	18	78	7.09
96. Ryan Doerffler, Valparaiso	QB	JR	11	0	13	0	78	7.09
99. David Sinisi, Monmouth	RB	FR	12	0	0	84	84	7.00
99. Cole Stinson, Eastern Ill.	QB	JR	12	0	12	12	84	7.00

Total Tackles

Rank, Player	Pos	Cl.	G	Solo	Ast	Total	TT/Gm
1. Mike Gallihugh, Colgate	LB	JR	11	84	56	140	12.73
2. Cameron Siskowic, Illinois St.	LB	SR	13	75	79	154	11.85
3. Akeem Jordan, James Madison	LB	SR	12	69	71	140	11.67
4. Jada Ross, Charleston So.	LB	JR	11	51	76	127	11.55
4. Chad Nkang, Elon	LB	SR	11	52	75	127	11.55
6. Jerome Gordon, St. Peter's	LB	FR	10	54	61	115	11.50
7. Nathan Williams, Murray St.	LB	JR	9	55	45	100	11.11
8. Zachary DeOssie, Brown	LB	SR	10	68	42	110	11.00
8. Kyle Shotwell, Cal Poly	LB	SR	11	61	60	121	11.00
10. Cyrus Mulitalo, Sacramento St.	LB	SO	11	56	64	120	10.91
11. Pago Togafau, Idaho St.	LB	SR	11	44	72	116	10.55
11. Marcus Taylor, Fordham	LB	SR	11	52	64	116	10.55
13. Kye Stewart, Illinois St.	LB	JR	12	57	69	126	10.50
14. Rolando Garcia, Sacred Heart	LB	SR	11	57	58	115	10.45
15. Stacey Thomas, Texas Southern	DB	SR	11	46	68	114	10.36
15. Trent Newton, Savannah St.	LB	SO	11	54	60	114	10.36
17. Gian Villante, Hofstra	LB	JR	9	34	58	92	10.22
18. Joe Anastasio, Penn	LB	JR	10	49	53	102	10.20
19. Tad Crawford, Columbia	DB	SR	10	39	62	101	10.10
19. Brian Kelly, Dayton	LB	SR	10	37	64	101	10.10
21. Mario E. Brown, Gardner-Webb	LB	SO	11	53	57	110	10.00
21. Andrew Jones, Furman	LB	JR	12	47	73	120	10.00
21. Jerome Bennett, Western Ill.	LB	JR	10	47	53	100	10.00
24. Dan Adams, Holy Cross	LB	SR	11	69	40	109	9.91
24. Andy Romans, Lafayette	LB	SO	11	57	52	109	9.91
26. Adam Goloboski, Richmond	LB	SR	11	56	52	108	9.82
26. Chris Dupuy, Alabama St.	LB	SR	11	73	35	108	9.82

Rank, Player	Pos	Cl.	G	Solo	Ast	Total	TT/Gm
26. Adam Casper, Southeast Mo. St.	LB	JR	11	63	45	108	9.82
29. Donald Thomas, Eastern Ill.	LB	JR	13	49	78	127	9.77
30. Scooter Archie, Indiana St.	DB	JR	11	40	67	107	9.73
31. Jamar Leath, Coastal Caro.	LB	SR	12	47	69	116	9.67
32. Tyler DeBry, Weber St.	LB	SR	11	34	72	106	9.64
32. J.R. Webber, Murray St.	DB	SR	11	71	35	106	9.64
34. Justin Cottrell, Dartmouth	LB	JR	10	44	51	95	9.50
35. Adam Hayward, Portland St.	LB	SR	11	56	48	104	9.45
35. Jonathan Corto, Sacred Heart	LB	SR	11	54	50	104	9.45
37. Allyn Bacchus, Villanova	DB	SR	11	62	41	103	9.36
37. Colin Disch, Albany (N.Y.)	LB	JR	11	47	56	103	9.36
39. Bobby Daly, Montana St.	LB	SO	13	53	68	121	9.31
40. John Mohring, Ga. Southern	LB	SR	10	61	32	93	9.30
41. Dorian Petersen, Bucknell	LB	SR	11	63	38	101	9.18
42. Johnny Baldwin, Alabama A&M	LB	SR	12	54	56	110	9.17
43. Tristan Burge, Eastern Ill.	DB	SR	13	48	70	118	9.08
44. Jason Hatchell, Massachusetts	LB	JR	15	59	75	134	8.93
45. Justin Durant, Hampton	LB	SR	11	65	33	98	8.91
46. Ein Williams, Wagner	LB	SR	10	28	61	89	8.90
46. Ian Wilson, Dartmouth	DB	JR	10	48	41	89	8.90
46. Vernon Wilder, Florida A&M	LB	JR	10	32	57	89	8.90
49. Luke Bonus, Hofstra	LB	FR	11	37	60	97	8.82
50. Charles Walker, Massachusetts	LB	SR	15	37	94	131	8.73
51. Tyler Knight, Mississippi Val.	LB	SR	11	44	52	96	8.73
52. Rafael Price, Indiana St.	DB	JR	11	47	48	95	8.64
52. Andy Jones, Indiana St.	LB	SR	11	39	56	95	8.64
52. Joshua Lawson, Citadel	DB	JR	11	44	51	95	8.64
55. Joe Gibalski, Dartmouth	LB	SR	10	39	47	86	8.60
56. KeiAndre Hepburn, Delaware	LB	SR	11	59	35	94	8.55
56. Dan Smith, Marist	LB	JR	11	35	59	94	8.55
58. Jordan Manning, Towson	LB	SO	11	57	36	93	8.45
58. Jimmy Adams, Drake	LB	SR	11	60	33	93	8.45
58. Darius Leak, Morgan St.	LB	SR	11	43	50	93	8.45
58. Corey Weaver, Elon	LB	SO	11	42	51	93	8.45
62. Andre Lewis, Western Ky.	LB	JR	9	36	40	76	8.44
63. Jason Williams, Western Ill.	LB	SO	11	41	51	92	8.36
63. Damian Perkins, Stephen F. Austin	LB	SO	11	34	58	92	8.36
63. Chadd Oliphant, Sam Houston St.	DB	SR	11	40	52	92	8.36
66. Josh Mitchell, Charleston So.	LB	JR	9	22	53	75	8.33
67. Husain Karim, New Hampshire	LB	JR	13	50	58	108	8.31
68. Eric Schultz, Harvard	LB	SO	10	42	41	83	8.30
69. D.J. Robinson, Portland St.	LB	SR	11	43	48	91	8.27
69. Mike Marzotto, Butler	LB	JR	11	45	46	91	8.27
69. Timothy Lockett, Howard	LB	SR	11	50	41	91	8.27
72. Brandin Jordan, Southern Ill.	LB	FR	13	41	66	107	8.23
73. Brian Bradford, Towson	LB	JR	9	56	18	74	8.22
74. Eric Brewer, Brown	LB	JR	10	39	43	82	8.20
74. Drew Quinn, Columbia	LB	SO	10	41	41	82	8.20
76. Michael Evans, Missouri St.	LB	SR	11	30	60	90	8.18
77. Niall Campbell, Illinois St.	LB	SR	13	54	52	106	8.15
78. Ronnie McCullough, Bethune-Cookman	LB	JR	9	33	40	73	8.11
79. Isaiah Dottin-Carter, James Madison	LB	SR	10	24	57	81	8.10
80. Christopher Paulus, Georgetown	LB	SR	11	36	53	89	8.09
80. Freddie Parish IV, Stephen F. Austin	DB	SR	11	31	58	89	8.09
82. Brad Anderson, Massachusetts	LB	SR	14	42	70	112	8.00
82. Andrew Rowell, Citadel	LB	JR	11	40	48	88	8.00
82. Justin Bass, Ark.-Pine Bluff	LB	SR	12	31	65	96	8.00
82. Adam Brekke, Columbia	LB	SR	10	38	42	80	8.00
86. Marty Hutchinson, Youngstown St.	LB	SR	14	57	54	111	7.93
87. Mike Pavelko, Gardner-Webb	LB	SO	11	33	54	87	7.91
87. Marion Rumph, Western Ky.	DB	JR	11	35	52	87	7.91
89. Lee Robinson, Alcorn St.	LB	SO	10	45	34	79	7.90
90. Jon Wilson, Sacred Heart	DB	SR	11	45	41	86	7.82
90. Bryan Brand, Wagner	LB	JR	11	36	50	86	7.82
92. Atelea Raass, Idaho St.	LB	SR	11	38	47	85	7.73
92. Sam Nana-Sinkham, Bucknell	LB	FR	11	51	34	85	7.73
92. Shelton Gaffney, Western Caro.	LB	SR	11	43	42	85	7.73
92. Daniel Becker, Austin Peay	LB	FR	11	42	43	85	7.73
92. Keldrick Holman, Stephen F. Austin	DB	SR	11	33	52	85	7.73
92. Aaron Williams, Tennessee Tech	LB	FR	11	27	58	85	7.73
92. Matt Hill, Monmouth	DB	SR	11	51	34	85	7.73
99. Chris Stimmel, Central Conn. St.	LB	JR	11	42	42	84	7.64
99. Huck Correia, Marist	DB	SR	11	37	47	84	7.64
99. Jeremy Castillo, Texas St.	LB	SR	11	35	49	84	7.64
99. Maguell Davis, Norfolk St.	LB	JR	11	35	49	84	7.64
99. Fu'ad Khaleel, Western Ill.	DB	SR	11	36	48	84	7.64

Solo Tackles

Rank, Player	Pos	Cl.	G	Solo	ST/Gm
1. Mike Gallihugh, Colgate	LB	JR	11	84	7.64
2. Zachary DeOssie, Brown	LB	SR	10	68	6.80
3. Chris Dupuy, Alabama St.	LB	SR	11	73	6.64
4. J.R. Webber, Murray St.	DB	SR	11	71	6.45
5. Dan Adams, Holy Cross	LB	SR	11	69	6.27
6. Brian Bradford, Towson	LB	JR	9	56	6.22
7. Nathan Williams, Murray St.	LB	JR	9	55	6.11
8. John Mohring, Ga. Southern	LB	SR	10	61	6.10
9. Justin Durant, Hampton	LB	SR	11	65	5.91
10. Cameron Siskowic, Illinois St.	LB	SR	13	75	5.77
11. Akeem Jordan, James Madison	LB	SR	12	69	5.75
12. Dorian Petersen, Bucknell	LB	SR	11	63	5.73
12. Adam Casper, Southeast Mo. St.	LB	JR	11	63	5.73
14. Allyn Bacchus, Villanova	DB	SR	11	62	5.64
15. Rodney Shepherd, Samford	LB	SO	11	61	5.55
15. Kyle Shotwell, Cal Poly	LB	SR	11	61	5.55
17. Jimmy Adams, Drake	LB	SR	11	60	5.45
18. Jerome Gordon, St. Peter's	LB	FR	10	54	5.40
19. KeiAndre Hepburn, Delaware	LB	SR	11	59	5.36
20. Jordan Manning, Towson	LB	SO	11	57	5.18
20. Rolando Garcia, Sacred Heart	LB	SR	11	57	5.18
20. Andy Romans, Lafayette	LB	SO	11	57	5.18
23. Adam Goloboski, Richmond	LB	SR	11	56	5.09
23. Cyrus Mulitalo, Sacramento St.	LB	SO	11	56	5.09
23. Adam Hayward, Portland St.	LB	SR	11	56	5.09
26. Jonathan Corto, Sacred Heart	LB	SR	11	54	4.91
26. Trent Newton, Savannah St.	LB	SO	11	54	4.91
28. Joe Anastasio, Penn	LB	JR	10	49	4.90
29. Mario E. Brown, Gardner-Webb	LB	SO	11	53	4.82
30. Ian Wilson, Dartmouth	DB	JR	10	48	4.80
31. Kye Stewart, Illinois St.	LB	JR	12	57	4.75
32. Marcus Taylor, Fordham	LB	SR	11	52	4.73
32. Chad Nkang, Elon	LB	SR	11	52	4.73
34. Jerome Bennett, Western Ill.	LB	JR	10	47	4.70
35. John Clements, New Hampshire	DB	SO	12	56	4.67
36. Jada Ross, Charleston So.	LB	JR	11	51	4.64
36. Matt Hill, Monmouth	DB	SR	11	51	4.64
36. Sam Nana-Sinkham, Bucknell	LB	FR	11	51	4.64
39. Larry Abare, Yale	DB	SO	10	46	4.60
39. Bobby Abare, Yale	LB	SO	10	46	4.60
41. Kenny Scott, Towson	DB	JR	11	50	4.55
41. Timothy Lockett, Howard	LB	SR	11	50	4.55
43. Johnny Baldwin, Alabama A&M	LB	SR	12	54	4.50
43. Lee Robinson, Alcorn St.	LB	SO	10	45	4.50
43. Aaron Woods, Jacksonville	DB	JR	8	36	4.50
46. Dave Schratz, UNI	LB	SR	11	49	4.45
46. Chris Johnson, Chattanooga	LB	JR	11	49	4.45
48. Kyle Campbell, Delaware	DB	SR	9	40	4.44
49. Markeseo Jackson, Tenn.-Martin	LB	SR	12	53	4.42
50. Brigham Farrand, Bucknell	LB	FR	10	44	4.40
50. Justin Cottrell, Dartmouth	LB	JR	10	44	4.40
52. Mizraim Farley, Rhode Island	LB	SR	11	48	4.36
52. Jason Beach, Florida A&M	DB	JR	11	48	4.36
54. Jose Yearwood, Brown	DB	JR	10	43	4.30
55. Erik Johnson, Delaware	LB	SO	11	47	4.27
55. Rafael Price, Indiana St.	DB	JR	11	47	4.27
55. Nick Ross, Drake	LB	SR	11	47	4.27
55. Virgil Gray, Rhode Island	DB	SR	11	47	4.27
55. Colin Disch, Albany (N.Y.)	LB	JR	11	47	4.27
60. Eric Schultz, Harvard	LB	SO	10	42	4.20
61. Ryan Slater, Bucknell	LB	JR	11	46	4.18
61. Taylor Lanigan, Murray St.	LB	FR	11	46	4.18
61. Stacey Thomas, Texas Southern	DB	SR	11	46	4.18
64. Allen Nelson, McNeese St.	LB	SO	12	50	4.17
65. Niall Campbell, Illinois St.	LB	SR	13	54	4.15
66. Drew Quinn, Columbia	LB	SO	10	41	4.10
66. Gus Krimm, Cornell	DB	SO	10	41	4.10
68. Larry Brantley, Rhode Island	LB	JR	11	45	4.09
68. D.J. Senter, Southern Utah	DB	SO	11	45	4.09
68. Mike Marzotto, Butler	LB	JR	11	45	4.09
68. Chris Parsons, UNI	DB	JR	11	45	4.09
68. Jon Wilson, Sacred Heart	DB	SR	11	45	4.09
68. Farod Muhammad, Central Conn. St.	DB	SR	11	45	4.09
74. Bobby Daly, Montana St.	LB	SO	13	53	4.08
75. Marty Hutchinson, Youngstown St.	LB	SR	14	57	4.07
76. Raji El-Amin, Rhode Island	DB	JR	11	44	4.00
76. Chris Barry, Yale	LB	SR	10	40	4.00
76. Seth Harrell, Southeast Mo. St.	LB	SR	11	44	4.00
76. Robert Takeno, Southern Utah	LB	FR	10	40	4.00
76. LaVar Porter, Southern Utah	LB	JR	11	44	4.00
76. Kit Hartsfield, Austin Peay	LB	FR	11	44	4.00
76. Brett Mazzaro, Morehead St.	LB	JR	11	44	4.00
76. John Hoppe, Dayton	LB	SR	10	40	4.00
76. Tyler Knight, Mississippi Val.	LB	SR	11	44	4.00
76. Joshua Lawson, Citadel	DB	JR	11	44	4.00

Rank, Player	Pos	Cl.	G	Solo	ST/Gm
76. Jay McCurty, Samford	DB	JR	11	44	4.00
76. Scott Williams, Penn	DB	SR	10	40	4.00
76. Andre Lewis, Western Ky.	LB	JR	9	36	4.00
76. Pago Togafau, Idaho St.	LB	SR	11	44	4.00
90. Jason Hatchell, Massachusetts	LB	JR	15	59	3.93
91. Jamar Leath, Coastal Caro.	LB	SR	12	47	3.92
91. Andrew Jones, Furman	LB	JR	12	47	3.92
91. Anthony Addonizio, Monmouth	LB	SR	12	47	3.92
94. John Wormuth, Maine	LB	JR	11	43	3.91
94. Jason Vanatta, Austin Peay	DB	SO	11	43	3.91
94. Shelton Gaffney, Western Caro.	LB	SR	11	43	3.91
94. George Summers, Jacksonville St.	LB	SR	11	43	3.91
94. Darius Leak, Morgan St.	LB	SR	11	43	3.91
94. Bobbie Williams, Bethune-Cookman	DB	JR	11	43	3.91
94. D.J. Robinson, Portland St.	LB	SR	11	43	3.91
94. Terrance Calloway, Idaho St.	DB	JR	11	43	3.91

Pass Sacks

Rank, Player	Pos	Cl.	G	Solo	Ast	Yds	Total	PS/Gm
1. Edgar Jones, Southeast Mo. St.	DL	JR	10	11	2	88	12	1.20
2. Christopher Traylor, Alabama A&M	DL	JR	9	9	1	79	9.5	1.06
3. Matt King, Maine	DL	SR	11	9	5	86	11.5	1.05
3. Chris Hunsaker, Northern Ariz.	LB	SR	11	9	5	81	11.5	1.05
5. Bryan Smith, McNeese St.	DL	JR	12	12	1	85	12.5	1.04
6. Ray Gensler, Robert Morris	DL	SR	11	8	6	89	11	1.00
7. Endor Cooper, Howard	LB	SO	9	8	1	62	8.5	.94
8. Kevin Winston, James Madison	DL	SR	12	11	0	74	11	.92
9. Marques Murrell, Appalachian St.	DL	SR	15	10	6	90	13	.87
10. Adam Hayward, Portland St.	LB	SR	11	9	1	71	9.5	.86
10. Rudolph Hardie, Howard	DL	SR	11	8	3	64	9.5	.86
10. Vincent Davis, Texas Southern	LB	SR	11	9	1	45	9.5	.86
13. Jon Johnson, Prairie View	DL	SR	9	7	1	46	7.5	.83
14. Kroy Biermann, Montana	DL	JR	14	8	7	63	11.5	.82
15. Mykol Gardiner, Duquesne	DL	FR	8	6	1	43	6.5	.81
16. Travis Decker, Duquesne	DL	JR	10	7	2	60	8	.80
16. Jermaine McGhee, Prairie View	DL	SR	10	6	4	43	8	.80
18. Darren Schmidt, Columbia	DL	SR	10	7	1	62	7.5	.75
18. Lee Robinson, Alcorn St.	LB	SO	10	6	3	64	7.5	.75
18. Niel Andrews, Davidson	LB	SR	10	7	1	44	7.5	.75
21. Kevin Jennings, Drake	DL	SR	11	8	0	57	8	.73
22. Brian Johnston, Gardner-Webb	DL	JR	11	7	1	47	7.5	.68
22. Kyle Horne, Wofford	LB	SR	11	7	1	39	7.5	.68
24. Chuck Suppon, James Madison	DL	SR	12	7	2	57	8	.67
24. Kendall Langford, Hampton	DL	JR	12	6	4	57	8	.67
26. Desmond Bryant, Harvard	DL	JR	10	5	3	15	6.5	.65
27. Mike DeVito, Maine	DL	SR	11	5	4	36	7	.64
27. Mark Butler, Alcorn St.	DL	JR	11	6	2	60	7	.64
27. Kyle Shotwell, Cal Poly	LB	SR	11	7	0	48	7	.64
27. Ryan Shotwell, Cal Poly	DL	FR	11	5	4	54	7	.64
27. Chris Marzotto, Butler	DL	JR	11	6	2	48	7	.64
27. Terrell Floyd, Morgan St.	DL	JR	11	7	0	51	7	.64
27. Mark Huygens, UNI	DL	SO	11	6	2	34	7	.64
34. Michael Berg, Harvard	DL	SR	9	5	1	40	5.5	.61
35. Sonny McCracken, Harvard	DB	SO	10	5	2	26	6	.60
35. Brad Bagdis, Harvard	DL	JR	10	5	2	65	6	.60
37. Thomas Massey, Hofstra	DL	JR	11	4	5	49	6.5	.59
37. Rodney Hughes, Bethune-Cookman	DL	JR	11	4	5	40	6.5	.59
37. Pate Moleni, Weber St.	DL	SO	11	5	3	30	6.5	.59
40. Eric Bakhtiari, San Diego	DL	JR	12	7	0	47	7	.58
41. David Burris, Massachusetts	DL	JR	15	6	5	54	8.5	.57
42. Rio Stotler, Weber St.	DL	SO	10	5	1	39	5.5	.55
42. Jim Walter, Davidson	DL	SR	10	4	3	24	5.5	.55
44. Adrian Tracy, William & Mary	DL	FR	11	5	2	41	6	.55
44. James Gonsoulin, Wofford	DL	SR	11	5	2	40	6	.55
44. Vincent Lands, Southern U.	LB	JR	11	6	0	46	6	.55
44. Andre Coleman, Albany (N.Y.)	DL	SR	11	5	2	40	6	.55
44. Dennis Justiniani, Charleston So.	DL	JR	11	4	4	22	6	.55
44. Mike Brannon, Sacramento St.	DL	SO	11	6	0	36	6	.55
44. D.J. Robinson, Portland St.	LB	SR	11	5	2	43	6	.55
51. Lorenzo Wims, Southern Ill.	DL	SR	13	7	0	52	7	.54
52. Isaiah Dottin-Carter, James Madison	LB	SR	10	5	0	37	5	.50
52. Levi Erickson, Southern Utah	LB	SR	11	4	3	46	5.5	.50
52. Justen Peek, Cal Poly	LB	SR	11	3	5	38	5.5	.50
52. Ronald Green, Mississippi Val.	DL	SO	10	3	4	28	5	.50
52. John Archie, Jackson St.	LB	SR	11	4	3	47	5.5	.50
52. Gary Tharrington, Appalachian St.	DL	FR	15	5	5	60	7.5	.50
52. Robert Armstrong, Morgan St.	DL	FR	10	5	0	28	5	.50
52. Ryan Esdale, Duquesne	DL	SR	10	4	2	35	5	.50
52. Ryan Blessing, Cornell	LB	JR	10	5	0	33	5	.50
52. Terry Dunn, Central Conn. St.	DL	SR	11	5	1	41	5.5	.50
52. Alex Buzbee, Georgetown	DL	SR	11	5	1	33	5.5	.50
52. Greg Peach, Eastern Wash.	DL	SO	11	4	3	25	5.5	.50
52. John Baranowski, James Madison	DL	JR	12	5	2	31	6	.50
65. Dustin Dlouhy, Montana	DL	SR	14	5	3	37	6.5	.46
66. Mike Murphy, Montana	DL	SR	13	5	2	33	6	.46
66. Pierre Walters, Eastern Ill.	DL	SO	13	6	0	41	6	.46
68. Akeem Jordan, James Madison	LB	SR	12	5	1	29	5.5	.46

Rank, Player	Pos	Cl.	G	Solo	Ast	Yds	Total	PS/Gm
69. Mario E. Brown, Gardner-Webb	LB	SO	11	5	0	26	5	.45
69. Chris White, Cal Poly	DL	SR	11	4	2	35	5	.45
69. Kyle Sand, Morehead St.	DL	JR	11	5	0	38	5	.45
69. Martin Jackson, Alcorn St.	DL	SR	11	5	0	34	5	.45
69. Jerrell Guyton, Morgan St.	LB	SO	11	5	0	37	5	.45
69. Wakeem Goode, Hampton	LB	SO	11	5	0	47	5	.45
69. Colyn Haugh, Robert Morris	DL	SR	11	4	2	33	5	.45
69. Chris Nielsen, Holy Cross	LB	SR	11	4	2	27	5	.45
77. Matt Curtis, Harvard	DL	SO	10	2	5	31	4.5	.45
77. Barron Pullum, Mississippi Val.	DL	SR	10	4	1	23	4.5	.45
77. Kyle Council, Iona	DB	SR	10	3	3	30	4.5	.45
80. Jason Vincent, Chattanooga	LB	JR	9	3	2	29	4	.44
81. Reyshawn Bobo, Montana St.	LB	JR	13	5	1	35	5.5	.42
81. James Terry, Youngstown St.	LB	JR	13	4	3	17	5.5	.42
83. Keith Bloom, Lafayette	DL	SR	12	4	2	17	5	.42
83. Brian Sweeney, Monmouth	DL	SR	12	5	0	35	5	.42
85. Patrick McCrossan, Maine	DL	JR	11	3	3	24	4.5	.41
85. Adam Torosian, Cal Poly	DL	JR	11	4	1	24	4.5	.41
85. Daniel Brooks, Jackson St.	LB	JR	11	3	3	18	4.5	.41
85. Branden Daniel, Ga. Southern	DL	SO	11	4	1	20	4.5	.41
85. Steve Tennin, Samford	DL	SR	11	4	1	8	4.5	.41
85. Chris Wash, Missouri St.	DL	SR	11	3	3	37	4.5	.41
85. Jordan Lacy, UNI	DL	JR	11	4	1	30	4.5	.41
85. Mark Sheehan, Albany (N.Y.)	DL	JR	11	4	1	30	4.5	.41
85. Jay Edwards, Fordham	DL	SR	11	3	3	38	4.5	.41
85. Jonathan Corto, Sacred Heart	LB	SR	11	4	1	33	4.5	.41
85. Matt Brunck, Robert Morris	LB	SR	11	3	3	38	4.5	.41
85. Jamil Young, Northeastern	LB	SR	11	4	1	27	4.5	.41
97. Ken Sussman, Hofstra	DL	JR	10	3	2	24	4	.40
97. Timothy Knicky, Stephen F. Austin	DL	FR	10	4	0	20	4	.40
97. Omarr Byrom, Appalachian St.	DL	SR	15	4	4	36	6	.40
97. Matt Wolfman, Marist	DL	JR	10	3	2	30	4	.40
97. Brandt Hollander, Yale	DL	JR	10	4	0	30	4	.40
97. Rob McGuire, Central Conn. St.	LB	SR	10	3	2	20	4	.40
97. James Henderson, Sacramento St.	DL	JR	10	4	0	20	4	.40
97. Daren Stone, Maine	DB	SR	10	4	0	39	4	.40

Tackles for Loss

Rank, Player	Pos	Cl.	G	Solo	Ast	Yds	Total	TFL/Gm
1. Chris Hunsaker, Northern Ariz.	LB	SR	11	17	8	101	21	1.91
1. Kyle Shotwell, Cal Poly	LB	SR	11	16	10	80	21	1.91
3. Rudolph Hardie, Howard	DL	SR	11	16	8	87	20	1.82
4. Edgar Jones, Southeast Mo. St.	DL	JR	10	15	6	103	18	1.80
5. Michael Berg, Harvard	DL	SR	9	14	4	68	16	1.78
6. Eric Bakhtiari, San Diego	DL	JR	12	18	6	97	21	1.75
7. Matt King, Maine	DL	SR	11	15	8	104	19	1.73
7. Mark Butler, Alcorn St.	DL	JR	11	14	10	98	19	1.73
9. Bryan Smith, McNeese St.	DL	JR	12	18	4	102	20	1.67
10. Ken Sussman, Hofstra	DL	JR	10	12	9	57	16.5	1.65
10. Darren Schmidt, Columbia	DL	SR	10	13	7	89	16.5	1.65
12. Vincent Lands, Southern U.	LB	JR	11	14	8	94	18	1.64
13. Dannel Shepard, Florida A&M	LB	JR	9	12	5	55	14.5	1.61
14. Ray Gensler, Robert Morris	DL	SR	11	12	11	106	17.5	1.59
15. Adam Hayward, Portland St.	LB	SR	11	13	7	81	16.5	1.50
15. Chad Nkang, Elon	LB	SR	11	13	7	56	16.5	1.50
15. Vincent Davis, Texas Southern	LB	SR	11	14	5	64	16.5	1.50
18. Adrian Tracy, William & Mary	DL	FR	11	13	5	68	15.5	1.41
18. John Archie, Jackson St.	LB	SR	11	12	7	73	15.5	1.41
20. John Mohring, Ga. Southern	LB	SR	10	12	4	31	14	1.40
21. Akeem Jordan, James Madison	LB	SR	12	15	3	56	16.5	1.38
22. Dennis Justiniani, Charleston So.	DL	JR	11	12	6	44	15	1.36
22. Cory Terzis, Fordham	DL	SR	11	12	6	48	15	1.36
24. Jermaine McGhee, Prairie View	DL	SR	10	9	9	72	13.5	1.35
25. Kevin Winston, James Madison	DL	SR	12	15	2	84	16	1.33
26. Kendall Langford, Hampton	DL	JR	12	11	9	79	15.5	1.29
27. Christopher Traylor, Alabama A&M	DL	JR	9	10	3	82	11.5	1.28
27. Jon Johnson, Prairie View	DL	SR	9	8	7	56	11.5	1.28
29. Leland Jones, Alabama St.	LB	SO	10	11	3	43	12.5	1.25
29. Lee Robinson, Alcorn St.	LB	SO	10	10	5	80	12.5	1.25
31. Lorenzo Wims, Southern Ill.	DL	SR	13	12	8	74	16	1.23
32. Matt Brunck, Robert Morris	LB	SR	11	8	11	72	13.5	1.23
32. Chris Dupuy, Alabama St.	LB	SR	11	10	7	54	13.5	1.23
32. Terrell Floyd, Morgan St.	DL	JR	11	11	5	66	13.5	1.23
35. Endor Cooper, Howard	LB	SO	9	7	8	65	11	1.22
36. Brad Bagdis, Harvard	DL	JR	10	8	8	77	12	1.20
36. Travis Decker, Duquesne	DL	JR	10	10	4	74	12	1.20
38. Alex Buzbee, Georgetown	DL	SR	11	9	8	53	13	1.18
38. Brian Conway, Drake	LB	SR	11	12	2	39	13	1.18
38. Justin Durant, Hampton	LB	SR	11	10	6	48	13	1.18
38. Andre Coleman, Albany (N.Y.)	DL	SR	11	10	6	64	13	1.18
42. Marques Murrell, Appalachian St.	DL	SR	15	14	7	101	17.5	1.17
42. James Wilson, Citadel	DL	SR	9	10	1	47	10.5	1.17

Rank, Player	Pos	Cl.	G	Solo	Ast	Yds	Total	TFL/Gm
44. Jay Edwards, Fordham	DL	SR	11	10	5	69	12.5	1.14
44. Chris Marzotto, Butler	DL	JR	11	11	3	59	12.5	1.14
44. Geoffrey Woods, Tennessee Tech	DL	JR	11	9	7	36	12.5	1.14
44. Dan Adams, Holy Cross	LB	SR	11	10	5	26	12.5	1.14
44. Martin Jackson, Alcorn St.	DL	SR	11	11	3	53	12.5	1.14
49. Kyle Sprenkle, Lafayette	DL	JR	12	11	5	46	13.5	1.13
50. Bryan Adams, Villanova	LB	SR	11	11	2	46	12	1.09
50. Kyle Sand, Morehead St.	DL	JR	11	10	4	54	12	1.09
50. LeMarcus Rowell, Jacksonville St.	LB	SR	11	12	0	46	12	1.09
50. Marcus Taylor, Fordham	LB	SR	11	9	6	57	12	1.09
54. David Burris, Massachusetts	DL	JR	15	11	10	69	16	1.07
54. Gary Tharrington, Appalachian St.	DL	FR	15	13	6	79	16	1.07
56. Mykol Gardiner, Duquesne	DL	FR	8	8	1	47	8.5	1.06
56. Brian Winn, La Salle	LB	FR	8	6	5	33	8.5	1.06
58. Mike Greene, Georgetown	LB	JR	10	9	3	25	10.5	1.05
58. Zachary DeOssie, Brown	LB	SR	10	8	5	32	10.5	1.05
58. Joe Anastasio, Penn	LB	JR	10	8	5	30	10.5	1.05
61. Cyrus Mulitalo, Sacramento St.	LB	SO	11	10	3	57	11.5	1.05
61. Jada Ross, Charleston So.	LB	JR	11	7	9	37	11.5	1.05
61. Jerrell Guyton, Morgan St.	LB	SO	11	9	5	44	11.5	1.05
61. Aaron Williams, Tennessee Tech	LB	FR	11	7	9	42	11.5	1.05
61. Tyler Knight, Mississippi Val.	LB	SR	11	9	5	49	11.5	1.05
61. Damian Perkins, Stephen F. Austin	LB	SO	11	8	7	44	11.5	1.05
61. Kyle Hunt, Southeast Mo. St.	DL	SR	11	9	5	37	11.5	1.05
61. D.J. Robinson, Portland St.	LB	SR	11	9	5	57	11.5	1.05
61. Pate Moleni, Weber St.	DL	SO	11	9	5	44	11.5	1.05
70. Adam Goloboski, Richmond	LB	SR	11	9	4	26	11	1.00
70. Trent Newton, Savannah St.	LB	SO	11	5	12	37	11	1.00
70. Bud Crawford, Davidson	LB	JR	10	8	4	51	10	1.00
70. Andrew Jones, Furman	LB	JR	12	10	4	26	12	1.00
70. Taurean Charles, Bethune-Cookman	LB	SR	11	9	4	41	11	1.00
70. Ryan Esdale, Duquesne	DL	SR	10	8	4	45	10	1.00
70. Brian Fairbanks, Penn	DL	SR	10	7	6	26	10	1.00
70. Jonathan Corto, Sacred Heart	LB	SR	11	7	8	42	11	1.00
70. Colin Disch, Albany (N.Y.)	LB	JR	11	8	6	23	11	1.00
70. Kroy Biermann, Montana	DL	JR	14	8	12	74	14	1.00
70. Mike Brannon, Sacramento St.	DL	SO	11	9	4	44	11	1.00
81. Bobby Daly, Montana St.	LB	SO	13	8	9	38	12.5	.96
82. Nate Wilson, Tenn.-Martin	DL	FR	12	11	1	34	11.5	.96
83. Mike DeVito, Maine	DL	SR	11	7	7	44	10.5	.95
83. Chris White, Cal Poly	DL	SR	11	8	5	50	10.5	.95
83. Kevin Jennings, Drake	DL	SR	11	9	3	61	10.5	.95
83. Alden Blizzard, Hampton	DL	SR	11	9	3	42	10.5	.95
83. Rodney Hughes, Bethune-Cookman	DL	JR	11	7	7	54	10.5	.95
83. Jason Williams, Western Ill.	LB	SO	11	8	5	47	10.5	.95
89. Eric Schultz, Harvard	LB	SO	10	6	7	32	9.5	.95
89. Ken Woodard, Jackson St.	LB	SR	10	8	3	31	9.5	.95
89. Niel Andrews, Davidson	LB	SR	10	8	3	46	9.5	.95
92. Chandre' Ward, Prairie View	LB	SR	9	6	5	33	8.5	.94
93. Jeff Koval, Youngstown St.	LB	SR	14	10	6	43	13	.93
94. Brandin Jordan, Southern Ill.	LB	FR	13	7	10	35	12	.92
94. Pierre Walters, Eastern Ill.	DL	SO	13	9	6	66	12	.92
96. Kye Stewart, Illinois St.	LB	JR	12	8	6	32	11	.92
96. Justin Bass, Ark.-Pine Bluff	LB	SR	12	9	4	31	11	.92
98. Thomas Massey, Hofstra	DL	JR	11	7	6	60	10	.91
98. Mario E. Brown, Gardner-Webb	LB	SO	11	8	4	38	10	.91
98. Mike Gallihugh, Colgate	LB	JR	11	8	4	44	10	.91
98. Josh Hackett, Austin Peay	LB	JR	11	7	6	38	10	.91
98. Kyle Horne, Wofford	LB	SR	11	8	4	44	10	.91
98. Jeff Rommes, Robert Morris	LB	SR	11	6	8	35	10	.91
98. Tom Pandolf, Albany (N.Y.)	DL	SO	11	8	4	40	10	.91
98. Eric Rakus, Lehigh	DL	SR	11	7	6	20	10	.91
98. Sherman Logan, Richmond	DL	JR	11	7	6	35	10	.91
98. Tyson Butler, Sacramento St.	LB	SR	11	7	6	34	10	.91
98. Jordan Manning, Towson	LB	SO	11	10	0	18	10	.91

Passes Defended

Rank, Player	Pos	Cl.	G	PBU	Int.	Passes Def.	PD/Gm
1. Tim Strickland, Princeton	DB	SR	10	14	3	17	1.70
2. Tyson Maugle, Penn	DB	SO	10	13	3	16	1.60
2. Kedron Dunn, Texas Southern	DB	SR	10	14	2	16	1.60
4. David Hyland, Morehead St.	DB	SO	11	11	4	15	1.36
5. Andre Fuller, Montana St.	DB	JR	13	15	2	17	1.31
6. Steven Williams, Harvard	DB	JR	10	9	4	13	1.30
6. Greg Ambrogi, Penn	DB	JR	10	11	2	13	1.30
6. Robson Noel, Jacksonville	DB	SO	10	12	1	13	1.30
9. Michael Coe, Alabama St.	DB	SR	11	12	2	14	1.27
10. Colin Nash, Cornell	DB	JR	10	9	3	12	1.20
11. Raji El-Amin, Rhode Island	DB	JR	11	9	4	13	1.18
11. David Horton, Richmond	DB	FR	11	10	3	13	1.18
11. Drew Mack, Towson	DB	SO	11	9	4	13	1.18
11. Odell Jackson, Portland St.	DB	SR	11	9	4	13	1.18
11. Dominique Rodgers, Tennessee St.	DB	JR	11	7	6	13	1.18
11. James Monds, Bethune-Cookman	DB	JR	11	11	2	13	1.18
11. Dre Dokes, UNI	DB	SR	11	6	7	13	1.18
18. Jahmar Reynolds, St. Peter's	DB	JR	10	11	0	11	1.10
18. Patrick FitzGerald, Davidson	DB	JR	10	7	4	11	1.10
18. Ronnie Jackson, Chattanooga	DB	JR	10	10	1	11	1.10
18. Josh Adams, Northwestern St.	DB	FR	10	8	3	11	1.10
22. Travis Watters, Western Ky.	DB	SO	11	9	3	12	1.09
22. Quintez Smith, Chattanooga	DB	JR	11	8	4	12	1.09
22. Josh Harris, Morehead St.	DB	SO	11	11	1	12	1.09
22. Andy Green, Drake	DB	SO	11	7	5	12	1.09
22. C.L. Grogan, Northwestern St.	DB	JR	11	8	4	12	1.09
22. Derrick Huff, Eastern Ky.	DB	JR	11	11	1	12	1.09

Rank, Player	Pos	Cl.	G	PBU	Int.	Passes Def.	PD/Gm
28. Quinton Teal, Coastal Caro.	DB	SR	12	9	4	13	1.08
29. Kory Austin, Montana St.	DB	JR	13	12	2	14	1.08
29. Tom Nelson, Illinois St.	DB	SO	13	10	4	14	1.08
31. Jason Perry, Youngstown St.	DB	SR	14	11	4	15	1.07
32. Rashaad Woodard, Delaware	DB	SR	10	10	0	10	1.00
32. Virgil Gray, Rhode Island	DB	SR	11	9	2	11	1.00
32. Josh Brisco, San Diego	DB	SR	12	10	2	12	1.00
32. Stacey Thomas, Texas Southern	DB	SR	11	6	5	11	1.00
32. Jason Fobbs, Prairie View	DB	SO	10	7	3	10	1.00
32. Jean-Pierre Marshall, Mississippi Val.	DB	JR	11	5	6	11	1.00
32. Carlton Brown, Jackson St.	DB	SR	11	7	4	11	1.00
32. Jimmy Toussaint, Alabama St.	DB	JR	11	9	2	11	1.00
32. Russ Washington, Northwestern St.	DB	SR	11	9	2	11	1.00
32. J.J. Yates, N.C. A&T	CB	JR	11	10	1	11	1.00
32. Kofi Amoah, Delaware St.	DB	SR	11	10	1	11	1.00
32. Mike Niklos, Robert Morris	DB	SR	11	6	5	11	1.00
32. Ryan Chrobak, Albany (N.Y.)	DB	SR	10	9	1	10	1.00
45. David Jiles, Monmouth	DB	SR	12	6	5	11	.92
45. Jeremy Blocker, Furman	DB	SR	12	7	4	11	.92
45. Calvin Bannister, Hampton	DB	SR	12	8	3	11	.92
45. Travarous Bain, Hampton	DB	SR	12	6	5	11	.92
45. Patrick O'Neill, San Diego	DB	SO	12	6	5	11	.92
45. Kalvin Moore, Ark.-Pine Bluff	DB	SR	12	8	3	11	.92
51. Derek Cox, William & Mary	DB	SO	11	9	1	10	.91
51. Hassan Stewart, Stony Brook	DB	SR	11	9	1	10	.91
51. Matthew Palermo, Bucknell	LB	SR	11	8	2	10	.91
51. Casey Gough, Holy Cross	DB	SR	11	7	3	10	.91
51. Mark Restelli, Cal Poly	LB	SO	11	9	1	10	.91
51. Jarmaul George, Southern U.	DB	JR	11	5	5	10	.91
51. Walter Musgrove, Texas St.	DB	SR	11	5	5	10	.91
51. Maurice Smith, Tennessee Tech	DB	SO	11	6	4	10	.91
59. Anthony Melvin, Idaho St.	DB	JR	10	9	0	9	.90
59. Ryan Tully, Harvard	LB	SR	10	7	2	9	.90
59. J.J. Artis, Princeton	DB	SR	10	6	3	9	.90
59. Randy Samuel, Cal Poly	DB	SR	10	6	3	9	.90
59. Michael Hill, Duquesne	DB	SR	10	7	2	9	.90
59. Reggie Dorsainvil, Iona	DB	JR	10	5	4	9	.90
59. Andy Shalbrack, Columbia	DB	FR	10	4	5	9	.90
66. James Temple, Illinois St.	DB	SR	13	8	3	11	.85
66. Corey Lynch, Appalachian St.	DB	JR	13	6	5	11	.85
68. D.J. Clark, Idaho St.	DB	SO	11	6	3	9	.82
68. Kevis Buckley, Austin Peay	DB	FR	11	7	2	9	.82
68. Orthel Edwards, Mississippi Val.	DB	SR	11	8	1	9	.82
68. DeShaun Lewis, Alcorn St.	DB	JR	11	6	3	9	.82
68. Scorpio Babers, Sam Houston St.	DB	SR	11	8	1	9	.82
68. Karlos Sullivan, Elon	DB	FR	11	7	2	9	.82
68. Brandon Jackson, Ga. Southern	DB	SO	11	4	5	9	.82
68. Andre Twine, Norfolk St.	DB	JR	11	8	1	9	.82
68. Alfred Phillips, Wagner	DB	JR	11	5	4	9	.82
68. Micheal Dorsey, Portland St.	DB	JR	11	5	4	9	.82
68. Jeff Wheeler, Northern Ariz.	DB	SR	11	6	3	9	.82
68. Anthony Wilson, Central Conn. St.	DB	SO	11	8	1	9	.82
68. Jon Wilson, Sacred Heart	DB	SR	11	5	4	9	.82
68. Matt Hill, Monmouth	DB	SR	11	6	3	9	.82
68. Julian Ahye, Lehigh	DB	JR	11	9	0	9	.82
83. Michael Beach, Montana St.	DB	JR	10	5	3	8	.80
83. Roderick Clark, Jacksonville	DB	FR	10	7	1	8	.80
83. Myles Williams, Southern U.	DL	SO	10	5	3	8	.80
83. Justin Woazeah, Appalachian St.	DB	JR	15	10	2	12	.80
83. Thomas Claiborn, Howard	DB	SR	10	7	1	8	.80
83. Steven Santoro, Yale	DB	SO	10	4	4	8	.80
83. Paul Rice, Yale	DB	FR	10	7	1	8	.80
83. Aaron Strader, Duquesne	DB	SO	10	5	3	8	.80
83. Kyle Postell, Duquesne	DB	SR	10	5	3	8	.80
83. Terrance Long, St. Francis (Pa.)	DB	SO	10	7	1	8	.80
93. Gregory Clark, Florida A&M	DB	JR	9	5	2	7	.78
93. Filmon Dawkins, Wofford	DB	SO	9	6	1	7	.78
95. Brandon Bruner, Southern Ill.	DB	SR	13	8	2	10	.77
95. Terrance Sanders, Eastern Ill.	DB	SR	13	7	3	10	.77
97. Frank Moore, Alabama A&M	DB	SO	12	3	6	9	.75
97. Steward Franks, Ark.-Pine Bluff	DB	SO	12	3	6	9	.75
99. Jerome Touchstone, Appalachian St.	DB	JR	15	9	2	11	.73
100. Raquan Pride, Rhode Island	DB	SR	11	4	4	8	.73
100. Christopher Wilson, Mississippi Val.	DB	SR	11	7	1	8	.73
100. Corey McLaurin, Alcorn St.	DB	SO	11	5	3	8	.73
100. Derrick Harris, Sam Houston St.	DB	SR	11	6	2	8	.73
100. Jermaine Boggan, Nicholls St.	DB	JR	11	6	2	8	.73
100. Chris Bland, Elon	DB	JR	11	4	4	8	.73
100. Aaron Strong, Tennessee St.	DB	SR	11	5	3	8	.73
100. Bobbie Williams, Bethune-Cookman	DB	JR	11	2	6	8	.73
100. Blake Boyd, Western Ky.	LB	FR	11	6	2	8	.73
100. Mike Radon, Missouri St.	DB	SR	11	4	4	8	.73
100. Chris Parsons, UNI	DB	JR	11	2	6	8	.73
100. Derrick Brown, Southern Utah	DB	JR	11	6	2	8	.73
100. Anthony Randolph, Cal Poly	DB	SR	11	8	0	8	.73
100. Courtney Brown, Cal Poly	DB	SR	11	7	1	8	.73
100. Ken Chicoine, Cal Poly	DB	SR	11	3	5	8	.73
100. Brett Mazzaro, Morehead St.	LB	JR	11	7	1	8	.73
100. Poul Collins, Drake	DB	JR	11	5	3	8	.73
100. Tyler Marley, Drake	DB	JR	11	7	1	8	.73
100. Ernie Greywacz, Central Conn. St.	DL	SO	11	8	0	8	.73
100. Sam Orah, Fordham	DB	JR	11	7	1	8	.73
100. Cody Williams, Colgate	DB	JR	11	5	3	8	.73
100. David Frisbey, Bucknell	DB	SR	11	7	1	8	.73
100. Mario E. Brown, Gardner-Webb	LB	SO	11	5	3	8	.73
100. E.L. Estes, Liberty	DB	SR	11	6	2	8	.73

Forced Fumbles

Rank, Player	Pos	Cl.	G	FF	FF/Gm
1. Jerome Bennett, Western Ill.	LB	JR	10	5	.50
2. Jeremy Castillo, Texas St.	LB	SR	11	5	.45
3. Brigham Walker, Princeton	WR	SR	10	4	.40
3. Lamar Herron, Texas Southern	WR	JR	10	4	.40
3. Marques Murrell, Appalachian St.	DL	SR	15	6	.40
6. Marcus Taylor, Fordham	LB	SR	11	4	.36
6. Antonio Johnson, N.C. A&T	DL	JR	11	4	.36
6. D.J. Senter, Southern Utah	DB	SO	11	4	.36
6. Tamar Butler, Murray St.	LB	FR	11	4	.36
10. Thomas Davis, Wagner	DL	JR	9	3	.33
10. Dominique Clark, Savannah St.	DL	JR	9	3	.33
12. Andrew Moore, Colgate	DB	SR	10	3	.30
12. Patrick Kimener, Penn	DB	JR	10	3	.30
12. Britton Ertman, Penn	DB	SO	10	3	.30
12. Calen Hunt, Drake	LB	FR	10	3	.30
12. Bud Crawford, Davidson	LB	JR	10	3	.30
12. Jerome Gordon, St. Peter's	LB	FR	10	3	.30
12. Steven Santoro, Yale	DB	SO	10	3	.30
19. Matt King, Maine	DL	SR	11	3	.27
19. Adam Goloboski, Richmond	LB	SR	11	3	.27
19. Kenny Scott, Towson	DB	JR	11	3	.27
19. Michael Pigram, William & Mary	LB	SO	11	3	.27
19. Terrance Calloway, Idaho St.	DB	JR	11	3	.27
19. Adrian Adderley, Wagner	DL	SO	11	3	.27
19. Kevin Adleman, Wofford	LB	SR	11	3	.27
19. Chad Nkang, Elon	LB	SR	11	3	.27
19. Trevar Broughton, Citadel	DL	JR	11	3	.27
19. Kofi Nkrumah, Morgan St.	LB	SR	11	3	.27
19. Jerrell Guyton, Morgan St.	LB	SO	11	3	.27
19. Rudolph Hardie, Howard	DL	SR	11	3	.27
19. Timothy Lockett, Howard	LB	SR	11	3	.27
19. Josh Balloon, Bethune-Cookman	LB	JR	11	3	.27
19. Jason Williams, Western Ill.	LB	SO	11	3	.27
19. Jeff Rommes, Robert Morris	LB	SR	11	3	.27
19. Okeba Rollinson, Charleston So.	DB	SO	11	3	.27
19. Manny Rojas, Liberty	LB	SR	11	3	.27
19. Ryan Shotwell, Cal Poly	DL	FR	11	3	.27
19. Jimmy Adams, Drake	LB	SR	11	3	.27
19. Dale Murzyn, Butler	DB	JR	11	3	.27
19. Tyler Knight, Mississippi Val.	LB	SR	11	3	.27
19. Martin Jackson, Alcorn St.	DL	SR	11	3	.27
19. Will Roach, Murray St.	LB	FR	11	3	.27
19. Patrick Reed, South Carolina St.	LB	SR	11	3	.27
19. Adam Hayward, Portland St.	LB	SR	11	3	.27
45. James Ihedigbo, Massachusetts	DB	SR	15	4	.27
46. Tony LeZotte, James Madison	DB	JR	12	3	.25
46. Markeseo Jackson, Tenn.-Martin	LB	SR	12	3	.25
46. Aaron Woods, Jacksonville	DB	JR	8	2	.25
46. John Keith, Ark.-Pine Bluff	DB	SO	12	3	.25
46. Johnny Baldwin, Alabama A&M	LB	SR	12	3	.25
46. Allen Nelson, McNeese St.	LB	SO	12	3	.25
46. Kevin Winston, James Madison	DL	SR	12	3	.25
46. Mykol Gardiner, Duquesne	DL	FR	8	2	.25
54. Cameron Siskowic, Illinois St.	LB	SR	13	3	.23
54. Pierre Walters, Eastern Ill.	DL	SO	13	3	.23
54. James Terry, Youngstown St.	LB	JR	13	3	.23
57. Gian Villante, Hofstra	LB	JR	9	2	.22
57. Mike Berry, Texas Southern	DL	SR	9	2	.22
57. Chandre' Ward, Prairie View	LB	SR	9	2	.22
57. Christopher Traylor, Alabama A&M	DL	JR	9	2	.22
57. Morgan Lobelo, La Salle	DL	SR	9	2	.22
57. Michael Berg, Harvard	DL	SR	9	2	.22
57. Bryan Jarrett, Eastern Wash.	DB	JR	9	2	.22
64. John Hatchell, Massachusetts	DL	SR	14	3	.21
64. Dustin Dlouhy, Montana	DL	SR	14	3	.21

Rank, Player	Pos	Cl.	G	FF	FF/Gm
64. Kroy Biermann, Montana	DL	JR	14	3	.21
67. Kevin Allen, William & Mary	DB	SO	10	2	.20
67. Michael Hill, Duquesne	DB	SR	10	2	.20
67. Travis Decker, Duquesne	DL	JR	10	2	.20
67. Val Ford, Prairie View	DB	SO	10	2	.20
67. Jermaine McGhee, Prairie View	DL	SR	10	2	.20
67. Ronald Green, Mississippi Val.	DL	SO	10	2	.20
67. Lee Robinson, Alcorn St.	LB	SO	10	2	.20
67. Leland Jones, Alabama St.	LB	SO	10	2	.20
67. Shane Richburg, Sam Houston St.	LB	SO	10	2	.20
67. Jairus Jarvis, Nicholls St.	WR	SO	10	2	.20
67. Pierre Banks, Appalachian St.	LB	JR	15	3	.20
67. Jamel Trott, Delaware St.	DB	SR	10	2	.20
67. Akeem Green, Delaware St.	DB	JR	10	2	.20
67. Dwayne Johnson, St. Peter's	DL	SR	10	2	.20
67. Anthony Bey, St. Peter's	DB	FR	10	2	.20
67. Kyle Council, Iona	DB	SR	10	2	.20
67. John Hoppe, Dayton	LB	SR	10	2	.20
67. Jim Walter, Davidson	DL	SR	10	2	.20
67. Eric Halberstadt, Duquesne	LB	SO	10	2	.20
67. Andrew Dete, Dartmouth	LB	SO	10	2	.20
67. Drew Quinn, Columbia	LB	SO	10	2	.20
67. Brian Tandy, Georgetown	DB	SR	10	2	.20
67. JoJo Smith, Columbia	DB	JR	10	2	.20
90. Luke Bonus, Hofstra	LB	FR	11	2	.18
90. Kyle Arrington, Hofstra	DB	JR	11	2	.18
90. Jamil Young, Northeastern	LB	SR	11	2	.18
90. Chad Hunter, Lafayette	DB	SR	11	2	.18
90. Casey Gough, Holy Cross	DB	SR	11	2	.18
90. Dorian Petersen, Bucknell	LB	SR	11	2	.18
90. Ryan Slater, Bucknell	LB	JR	11	2	.18
90. Matthew Palermo, Bucknell	LB	SR	11	2	.18
90. Brian Johnston, Gardner-Webb	DL	JR	11	2	.18
90. Marcus Brown, VMI	DB	JR	11	2	.18
90. Tyler Turner, Liberty	DL	SR	11	2	.18
90. Jeff Wheeler, Northern Ariz.	DB	SR	11	2	.18
90. Andrew Rowell, Citadel	LB	JR	11	2	.18
90. Jacques Williams, Tennessee Tech	LB	JR	11	2	.18
90. Nikkeda Rutland, Tennessee St.	DB	SR	11	2	.18
90. Kendall Magana, Southeast Mo. St.	DB	SO	11	2	.18
90. T.C. Myers, Samford	DB	SR	11	2	.18
90. Keyon Brooks, South Carolina St.	DL	SO	11	2	.18
90. David Erby, South Carolina St.	LB	FR	11	2	.18

Rank, Player	Pos	Cl.	G	FF	FF/Gm
90. Brandon Colbert, N.C. A&T	LB	SO	11	2	.18
90. Darius Leak, Morgan St.	LB	SR	11	2	.18
90. Richie Richards, Stony Brook	DB	SR	11	2	.18
90. Jimmy Judd, Southern Utah	DL	SR	11	2	.18
90. Kyle Shotwell, Cal Poly	LB	SR	11	2	.18
90. Mike Marzotto, Butler	LB	JR	11	2	.18
90. Chauncey Brown, Ark.-Pine Bluff	DL	SR	11	2	.18
90. Glen Bell, Southern U.	DB	SO	11	2	.18
90. John Archie, Jackson St.	LB	SR	11	2	.18
90. David Hicks, Grambling	LB	SR	11	2	.18
90. Zaire Wilborn, Grambling	DB	JR	11	2	.18
90. Damian Perkins, Stephen F. Austin	LB	SO	11	2	.18
90. Keldrick Holman, Stephen F. Austin	DB	SR	11	2	.18
90. Marquis Rogers, Southeastern La.	DL	SR	11	2	.18
90. Jay Skidmore, Southeastern La.	LB	SR	11	2	.18
90. Brennen Harris, Southeastern La.	LB	JR	11	2	.18
90. Isaiah Greenhouse, Northwestern St.	LB	FR	11	2	.18
90. Levon Bailey, Nicholls St.	LB	SR	11	2	.18
90. Dustin Gisclair, Nicholls St.	LB	SR	11	2	.18
90. Seth Goldwire, Wofford	LB	SO	11	2	.18
90. Curt Williams, Tennessee Tech	RB	JR	11	2	.18
90. Maurice Smith, Tennessee Tech	DB	SO	11	2	.18
90. Steve Young, Sacred Heart	DB	SO	11	2	.18
90. Jon Wilson, Sacred Heart	DB	SR	11	2	.18
90. Matt Brunck, Robert Morris	LB	SR	11	2	.18
90. James Kazil, Robert Morris	DB	JR	11	2	.18
90. Devon C. Douglas, Central Conn. St.	DL	SR	11	2	.18
90. Ernie Greywacz, Central Conn. St.	DL	SO	11	2	.18
90. Mark Sheehan, Albany (N.Y.)	DL	JR	11	2	.18
90. Colin Disch, Albany (N.Y.)	LB	JR	11	2	.18
90. Tyrone Kelly, Delaware St.	DB	SR	11	2	.18
90. Travis Roland, Bethune-Cookman	DB	JR	11	2	.18
90. Huck Correia, Marist	DB	SR	11	2	.18
90. Jowan Thornton, Wagner	DL	JR	11	2	.18
90. Bryan Brand, Wagner	LB	JR	11	2	.18
90. Chevar Rankins, Stony Brook	OL	FR	11	2	.18
90. Clint Knickrehm, Idaho St.	RB	FR	11	2	.18
90. Greg Peach, Eastern Wash.	DL	SO	11	2	.18
90. Adam Macomber, Eastern Wash.	DB	SO	11	2	.18
90. Adrian Tracy, William & Mary	DL	FR	11	2	.18
90. Jason Vega, Northeastern	LB	SO	11	2	.18
90. Bruno Dorismond, Maine	DL	JR	11	2	.18

2006 Championship Subdivision (FCS) Team Statistics

Rushing Offense

Rank, Team	G	Att	Net	Avg.	TD	Yds/Gm	W	L	T
1. Central Conn. St.	11	563	3,134	5.57	42	284.91	8	3	0
2. Wofford	11	571	2,899	5.08	32	263.55	7	4	0
3. South Carolina St.	11	498	2,663	5.35	27	242.09	7	4	0
4. Appalachian St.	15	664	3,619	5.45	48	241.27	14	1	0
5. Bucknell	11	539	2,587	4.80	24	235.18	6	5	0
6. Nicholls St.	11	544	2,573	4.73	18	233.91	4	7	0
7. Southern Ill.	13	573	3,035	5.30	37	233.46	9	4	0
8. Drake	11	495	2,545	5.14	31	231.36	9	2	0
9. Youngstown St.	14	581	3,132	5.39	38	223.71	11	3	0
10. UNI	11	443	2,412	5.44	22	219.27	7	4	0
11. James Madison	12	493	2,620	5.31	26	218.33	9	3	0
12. Tenn.-Martin	12	507	2,619	5.17	23	218.25	9	3	0
13. VMI	11	511	2,273	4.45	16	206.64	1	10	0
14. San Diego	12	438	2,411	5.50	32	200.92	11	1	0
15. Yale	10	429	2,008	4.68	23	200.80	8	2	0
16. Rhode Island	11	573	2,113	3.69	20	192.09	4	7	0
17. Delaware St.	11	366	2,104	5.75	25	191.27	8	3	0
18. Eastern Ill.	13	514	2,437	4.74	15	187.46	8	5	0
19. Liberty	11	432	2,035	4.71	23	185.00	6	5	0
20. Howard	11	465	2,033	4.37	10	184.82	5	6	0
21. Ga. Southern	11	422	2,015	4.77	20	183.18	3	8	0
22. Cal Poly	11	475	2,011	4.23	18	182.82	7	4	0
23. Coastal Caro.	12	434	2,188	5.04	23	182.33	9	3	0
24. Cornell	10	452	1,821	4.03	14	182.10	5	5	0
25. Western Ill.	11	423	1,994	4.71	30	181.27	5	6	0
26. Prairie View	10	408	1,797	4.40	15	179.70	3	7	0
27. Massachusetts	15	555	2,675	4.82	24	178.33	13	2	0
28. Chattanooga	11	394	1,954	4.96	13	177.64	3	8	0
29. Morehead St.	11	431	1,934	4.49	18	175.82	2	9	0
30. Hampton	12	421	2,101	4.99	28	175.08	10	2	0
31. Alabama A&M	12	472	2,084	4.42	22	173.67	9	3	0
32. Illinois St.	13	520	2,206	4.24	26	169.69	9	4	0
33. Jacksonville St.	11	430	1,865	4.34	23	169.55	6	5	0
33. St. Francis (Pa.)	11	398	1,865	4.69	15	169.55	3	8	0
33. Maine	11	456	1,865	4.09	17	169.55	6	5	0
36. McNeese St.	12	462	2,033	4.40	17	169.42	7	5	0
37. Furman	12	508	2,020	3.98	30	168.33	8	4	0
38. Albany (N.Y.)	11	450	1,836	4.08	15	166.91	7	4	0
39. Colgate	11	438	1,820	4.16	22	165.45	4	7	0
40. Jacksonville	10	390	1,647	4.22	11	164.70	4	6	0
41. Lafayette	12	434	1,973	4.55	29	164.42	6	6	0
42. Richmond	11	382	1,794	4.70	13	163.09	6	5	0
43. Western Ky.	11	417	1,764	4.23	16	160.36	6	5	0
44. Harvard	10	381	1,603	4.21	21	160.30	7	3	0
45. Morgan St.	11	403	1,743	4.33	16	158.45	5	6	0
46. Citadel	11	430	1,732	4.03	20	157.45	5	6	0
47. Jackson St.	10	416	1,717	4.13	23	156.09	5	5	0
48. New Hampshire	13	489	2,018	4.13	31	155.23	9	4	0
49. Stephen F. Austin	11	394	1,699	4.31	14	154.45	4	7	0
50. Lehigh	11	441	1,688	3.83	21	153.45	6	5	0
51. Monmouth	12	465	1,834	3.94	23	152.83	10	2	0
52. Northwestern St.	11	439	1,664	3.79	9	151.27	4	7	0
53. Texas St.	11	351	1,653	4.71	13	150.27	5	6	0
54. Austin Peay	11	382	1,650	4.32	18	150.00	3	8	0
55. Tennessee St.	11	417	1,648	3.95	21	149.82	6	5	0
56. Alabama St.	11	429	1,629	3.80	14	148.09	5	6	0
57. Northeastern	11	396	1,621	4.09	18	147.36	5	6	0

Rank, Team	G	Att	Net	Avg.	TD	Yds/Gm	W	L	T
58. Indiana St.	11	378	1,617	4.28	15	147.00	1	10	0
59. Sam Houston St.	11	334	1,605	4.81	20	145.91	6	5	0
60. Villanova	11	388	1,576	4.06	24	143.27	6	5	0
61. Southern Utah	11	342	1,560	4.56	12	141.82	3	8	0
62. Montana	14	524	1,951	3.72	21	139.36	12	2	0
63. Northern Ariz.	11	390	1,517	3.89	11	137.91	6	5	0
63. Southeast Mo. St.	11	389	1,517	3.90	19	137.91	4	7	0
65. Eastern Ky.	11	361	1,481	4.10	14	134.64	6	5	0
66. Florida A&M	11	357	1,473	4.13	12	133.91	7	4	0
67. Bethune-Cookman	11	369	1,469	3.98	20	133.55	5	6	0
68. Mississippi Val.	11	400	1,467	3.67	15	133.36	6	5	0
69. Ark.-Pine Bluff	12	393	1,589	4.04	21	132.42	8	4	0
70. Princeton	10	375	1,294	3.45	12	129.40	9	1	0
71. William & Mary	11	326	1,392	4.27	11	126.55	3	8	0
72. Fordham	11	402	1,382	3.44	8	125.64	3	8	0
73. Idaho St.	11	356	1,358	3.81	13	123.45	2	9	0
74. Penn	10	304	1,229	4.04	16	122.90	5	5	0
75. Wagner	11	326	1,351	4.14	10	122.82	4	7	0
76. Davidson	10	308	1,219	3.96	16	121.90	6	4	0
77. Weber St.	11	358	1,339	3.74	11	121.73	4	7	0
78. Dayton	10	408	1,213	2.97	19	121.30	4	6	0
79. Stony Brook	11	351	1,333	3.80	13	121.18	5	6	0
80. Alcorn St.	10	339	1,332	3.93	14	121.09	6	4	0
81. Brown	10	344	1,183	3.44	15	118.30	3	7	0
82. Southern U.	11	382	1,299	3.40	18	118.09	5	6	0
83. Georgetown	11	352	1,266	3.60	3	115.09	2	9	0
84. Holy Cross	11	344	1,241	3.61	12	112.82	7	4	0
85. Tennessee Tech	11	368	1,224	3.33	7	111.27	4	7	0
86. Eastern Wash.	11	366	1,192	3.26	10	108.36	3	8	0
87. Portland St.	11	383	1,191	3.11	9	108.27	7	4	0
88. Marist	11	368	1,185	3.22	18	107.73	4	7	0
89. Iona	10	376	1,076	2.86	7	107.60	3	7	0
90. Valparaiso	11	358	1,170	3.27	15	106.36	3	8	0
91. Norfolk St.	11	374	1,145	3.06	20	104.09	4	7	0
92. Delaware	11	345	1,140	3.30	20	103.64	5	6	0
93. Dartmouth	10	310	1,033	3.33	11	103.30	2	8	0
94. Western Caro.	11	335	1,135	3.39	6	103.18	2	9	0
95. Southeastern La.	11	313	1,133	3.62	9	103.00	2	9	0
96. Charleston So.	11	312	1,129	3.62	14	102.64	9	2	0
97. La Salle	10	385	1,026	2.66	6	102.60	3	7	0
98. Missouri St.	11	355	1,110	3.13	8	100.91	2	9	0
99. Samford	11	307	1,094	3.56	8	99.45	3	8	0
100. Gardner-Webb	11	324	1,069	3.30	13	97.18	6	5	0
101. Grambling	11	333	1,060	3.18	12	96.36	3	8	0
102. Murray St.	11	341	1,048	3.07	7	95.27	1	10	0
103. Savannah St.	11	336	1,047	3.12	5	95.18	2	9	0
104. Montana St.	13	390	1,230	3.15	13	94.62	8	5	0
105. N.C. A&T	11	370	1,033	2.79	8	93.91	0	11	0
106. Duquesne	10	284	939	3.31	7	93.90	7	3	0
107. Texas Southern	11	320	1,015	3.17	9	92.27	3	8	0
108. Robert Morris	11	403	993	2.46	9	90.27	7	4	0
109. Elon	11	290	935	3.22	9	85.00	5	6	0
110. Towson	11	327	927	2.83	11	84.27	7	4	0
111. Sacred Heart	11	250	874	3.50	6	79.45	2	9	0
112. Hofstra	11	325	759	2.34	7	69.00	2	9	0
113. Columbia	10	264	678	2.57	4	67.80	5	5	0
114. Sacramento St.	11	346	703	2.03	10	63.91	4	7	0
115. Butler	11	278	521	1.87	5	47.36	3	8	0
116. St. Peter's	10	202	379	1.88	2	37.90	2	8	0

Passing Offense

Rank, Team	G	Att	Comp	Int	Pct.	Yds	Yds/ Att	TD	Yds/ Gm	IPct	Yds/ Cmp	W	L	T
1. San Diego	12	391	260	5	66.50	3,520	9.00	36	293.3	1.28	13.54	11	1	0
2. Duquesne	10	357	212	13	59.38	2,877	8.06	28	287.7	3.64	13.57	7	3	0
3. Towson	11	409	275	11	67.24	3,161	7.73	19	287.4	2.69	11.49	7	4	0
4. Coastal Caro.	12	353	223	11	63.17	3,429	9.71	30	285.8	3.12	15.38	9	3	0
5. Holy Cross	11	421	259	7	61.52	2,987	7.10	25	271.5	1.66	11.53	7	4	0
6. Northern Ariz.	11	340	222	6	65.29	2,939	8.64	34	267.2	1.76	13.24	6	5	0
7. Davidson	10	381	216	10	56.69	2,617	6.87	21	261.7	2.62	12.12	6	4	0
8. Charleston So.	11	348	239	16	68.68	2,863	8.23	23	260.3	4.60	11.98	9	2	0
9. Delaware	11	420	264	10	62.86	2,783	6.63	18	253.0	2.38	10.54	5	6	0
10. Grambling	11	367	197	11	53.68	2,771	7.55	24	251.9	3.00	14.07	3	8	0
11. St. Peter's	10	433	242	13	55.89	2,480	5.73	15	248.0	3.00	10.25	2	8	0
12. Dayton	10	272	152	11	55.88	2,472	9.09	12	247.2	4.04	16.26	4	6	0
13. Elon	11	387	238	12	61.50	2,707	6.99	18	246.1	3.10	11.37	5	6	0
14. Princeton	10	336	197	12	58.63	2,458	7.32	17	245.8	3.57	12.48	9	1	0
15. New Hampshire	13	441	301	7	68.25	3,190	7.23	29	245.4	1.59	10.60	9	4	0
16. Gardner-Webb	11	378	218	21	57.67	2,655	7.02	19	241.4	5.56	12.18	6	5	0
17. Penn	10	359	194	12	54.04	2,309	6.43	11	230.9	3.34	11.90	5	5	0
18. Illinois St.	13	351	203	14	57.83	2,961	8.44	21	227.8	3.99	14.59	9	4	0
19. Brown	10	327	178	16	54.43	2,276	6.96	13	227.6	4.89	12.79	3	7	0
20. Montana	14	429	237	13	55.24	3,181	7.41	19	227.2	3.03	13.42	12	2	0
21. Stony Brook	11	327	200	5	61.16	2,489	7.61	17	226.3	1.53	12.45	5	6	0
22. Montana St.	13	410	224	19	54.63	2,940	7.17	17	226.2	4.63	13.13	8	5	0
23. Eastern Ky.	11	336	191	15	56.85	2,418	7.20	14	219.8	4.46	12.66	6	5	0
24. Florida A&M	11	325	195	8	60.00	2,352	7.24	20	213.8	2.46	12.06	7	4	0
25. Indiana St.	11	386	206	9	53.37	2,346	6.08	14	213.3	2.33	11.39	1	10	0
26. William & Mary	11	360	196	10	54.44	2,334	6.48	16	212.2	2.78	11.91	3	8	0
27. Idaho St.	11	358	195	14	54.47	2,320	6.48	17	210.9	3.91	11.90	2	9	0
28. Harvard	10	290	152	12	52.41	2,102	7.25	13	210.2	4.14	13.83	7	3	0
29. Tennessee Tech	11	362	190	17	52.49	2,305	6.37	17	209.5	4.70	12.13	4	7	0
30. Austin Peay	11	329	199	13	60.49	2,293	6.97	13	208.5	3.95	11.52	3	8	0
31. Massachusetts	15	343	222	11	64.72	3,082	8.99	26	205.5	3.21	13.88	13	2	0
32. Western Ky.	11	285	175	9	61.40	2,248	7.89	15	204.4	3.16	12.85	6	5	0
33. Bethune-Cookman	11	297	167	5	56.23	2,230	7.51	20	202.7	1.68	13.35	5	6	0
34. Eastern Wash.	11	345	184	19	53.33	2,221	6.44	13	201.9	5.51	12.07	3	8	0
35. Columbia	10	338	191	6	56.51	2,019	5.97	7	201.9	1.78	10.57	5	5	0
36. Marist	11	273	166	12	60.81	2,215	8.11	9	201.4	4.40	13.34	4	7	0
36. Texas St.	11	320	170	15	53.13	2,215	6.92	16	201.4	4.69	13.03	5	6	0
38. Monmouth	12	317	203	10	64.04	2,409	7.60	14	200.8	3.15	11.87	10	2	0
39. Western Ill.	11	287	180	9	62.72	2,201	7.67	13	200.1	3.14	12.23	5	6	0
40. Sam Houston St.	11	338	187	14	55.33	2,191	6.48	12	199.2	4.14	11.72	6	5	0
41. Valparaiso	11	331	159	13	48.04	2,185	6.60	13	198.6	3.93	13.74	3	8	0
42. Norfolk St.	11	285	148	16	51.93	2,166	7.60	10	196.9	5.61	14.64	4	7	0
43. Citadel	11	330	207	11	62.73	2,163	6.55	14	196.6	3.33	10.45	5	6	0
44. Dartmouth	10	291	179	12	61.51	1,962	6.74	7	196.2	4.12	10.96	2	8	0
45. Villanova	11	284	172	9	60.56	2,140	7.54	9	194.5	3.17	12.44	6	5	0

Rank, Team	G	Att	Comp	Int	Pct.	Yds	Yds/ Att	TD	Yds/ Gm	IPct	Yds/ Cmp	W	L	T
46. Hofstra	11	345	184	4	53.33	2,119	6.14	11	192.6	1.16	11.52	2	9	0
47. Jacksonville	10	277	128	11	46.21	1,916	6.92	15	191.6	3.97	14.97	4	6	0
48. Colgate	11	271	154	10	56.83	2,105	7.77	11	191.4	3.69	13.67	4	7	0
48. Missouri St.	11	313	176	10	56.23	2,105	6.73	10	191.4	3.19	11.96	2	9	0
48. Robert Morris	11	282	161	16	57.09	2,105	7.46	19	191.4	5.67	13.07	7	4	0
51. Ark.-Pine Bluff	12	244	142	10	58.20	2,292	9.39	24	191.0	4.10	16.14	8	4	0
52. Iona	10	297	168	12	56.57	1,903	6.41	7	190.3	4.04	11.33	3	7	0
53. Murray St.	11	356	205	14	57.58	2,088	5.87	16	189.8	3.93	10.19	1	10	0
54. Southern U.	11	313	188	19	60.06	2,086	6.66	16	189.6	6.07	11.10	5	6	0
55. UNI	11	255	172	7	67.45	2,079	8.15	17	189.0	2.75	12.09	7	4	0
56. Lehigh	11	256	157	6	61.33	2,077	8.11	14	188.8	2.34	13.23	6	5	0
57. Sacred Heart	11	372	211	14	56.72	2,076	5.58	19	188.7	3.76	9.84	2	9	0
58. Richmond	11	312	187	10	59.94	2,066	6.62	17	187.8	3.21	11.05	6	5	0
59. Southeastern La.	11	392	250	10	63.78	2,064	5.27	14	187.6	2.55	8.26	2	9	0
60. Lafayette	12	307	181	10	58.96	2,239	7.29	13	186.6	3.26	12.37	6	6	0
61. Tennessee St.	11	250	140	13	56.00	2,004	8.02	9	182.2	5.20	14.31	6	5	0
62. La Salle	10	276	153	18	55.43	1,812	6.57	14	181.2	6.52	11.84	3	7	0
63. Sacramento St.	11	292	150	19	51.37	1,977	6.77	10	179.7	6.51	13.18	4	7	0
64. Southern Utah	11	333	187	15	56.16	1,976	5.93	16	179.6	4.50	10.57	3	8	0
65. Portland St.	11	267	141	12	52.81	1,969	7.37	18	179.0	4.49	13.96	7	4	0
66. Texas Southern	11	319	164	22	51.41	1,966	6.16	14	178.7	6.90	11.99	3	8	0
67. Georgetown	11	318	207	15	65.09	1,948	6.13	19	177.1	4.72	9.41	2	9	0
68. Hampton	12	291	187	5	64.26	2,122	7.29	20	176.8	1.72	11.35	10	2	0
69. Ga. Southern	11	311	160	6	51.45	1,944	6.25	8	176.7	1.93	12.15	3	8	0
70. Appalachian St.	15	342	201	14	58.77	2,646	7.74	18	176.4	4.09	13.16	14	1	0
71. Northwestern St.	11	326	170	11	52.15	1,931	5.92	10	175.5	3.37	11.36	4	7	0
71. St. Francis (Pa.)	11	293	155	7	52.90	1,931	6.59	16	175.5	2.39	12.46	3	8	0
73. Jackson St.	10	234	139	13	59.40	1,917	8.19	14	174.3	5.56	13.79	5	5	0
74. Drake	11	264	129	11	48.86	1,914	7.25	7	174.0	4.17	14.84	9	2	0
75. Furman	12	287	165	6	57.49	2,075	7.23	8	172.9	2.09	12.58	8	4	0
76. Alcorn St.	10	279	134	12	48.03	1,902	6.82	14	172.9	4.30	14.19	6	4	0
77. James Madison	12	237	157	6	66.24	2,074	8.75	20	172.8	2.53	13.21	9	3	0
78. Weber St.	11	302	164	15	54.30	1,896	6.28	12	172.4	4.97	11.56	4	7	0
79. Stephen F. Austin	11	300	172	5	57.33	1,895	6.32	8	172.3	1.67	11.02	4	7	0
80. Morehead St.	11	288	170	12	59.03	1,891	6.57	11	171.9	4.17	11.12	2	9	0
81. Butler	11	372	190	11	51.08	1,887	5.07	11	171.5	2.96	9.93	3	8	0
82. Mississippi Val.	11	283	137	14	48.41	1,839	6.50	12	167.2	4.95	13.42	6	5	0
83. Eastern Ill.	13	315	175	18	55.56	2,135	6.78	22	164.2	5.71	12.20	8	5	0
84. Chattanooga	11	335	178	13	53.13	1,788	5.34	12	162.5	3.88	10.04	3	8	0
85. Samford	11	351	185	16	52.71	1,786	5.09	10	162.4	4.56	9.65	3	8	0
86. Jacksonville St.	11	237	129	10	54.43	1,743	7.35	8	158.5	4.22	13.51	6	5	0
87. Youngstown St.	14	317	181	12	57.10	2,211	6.97	17	157.9	3.79	12.22	11	3	0
88. Cornell	10	226	124	10	54.87	1,556	6.88	8	155.6	4.42	12.55	5	5	0
89. Alabama A&M	12	306	176	8	57.52	1,862	6.08	16	155.2	2.61	10.58	9	3	0
90. McNeese St.	12	262	140	10	53.44	1,844	7.04	15	153.7	3.82	13.17	7	5	0
91. Northeastern	11	234	134	11	57.26	1,685	7.20	8	153.2	4.70	12.57	5	6	0
92. Western Caro.	11	298	157	6	52.68	1,677	5.63	9	152.5	2.01	10.68	2	9	0
93. Wagner	11	327	156	12	47.71	1,671	5.11	10	151.9	3.67	10.71	4	7	0
94. Yale	10	210	109	6	51.90	1,437	6.84	5	143.7	2.86	13.18	8	2	0
95. Liberty	11	211	122	5	57.82	1,565	7.42	7	142.3	2.37	12.83	6	5	0
96. Southern Ill.	13	206	125	4	60.68	1,806	8.77	17	138.9	1.94	14.45	9	4	0
97. Fordham	11	260	113	12	43.46	1,482	5.70	9	134.7	4.62	13.12	3	8	0
98. Maine	11	249	155	8	62.25	1,421	5.71	9	129.2	3.21	9.17	6	5	0
99. Delaware St.	11	214	121	4	56.54	1,420	6.64	12	129.1	1.87	11.74	8	3	0
100. South Carolina St.	11	193	101	9	52.33	1,349	6.99	11	122.6	4.66	13.36	7	4	0
101. N.C. A&T	11	283	128	19	45.23	1,342	4.74	9	122.0	6.71	10.48	0	11	0
102. Morgan St.	11	230	116	10	50.43	1,295	5.63	9	117.7	4.35	11.16	5	6	0
103. Cal Poly	11	174	78	7	44.83	1,285	7.39	10	116.8	4.02	16.47	7	4	0
104. Savannah St.	11	245	115	14	46.94	1,281	5.23	8	116.5	5.71	11.14	2	9	0
105. Rhode Island	11	157	74	12	47.13	1,276	8.13	8	116.0	7.64	17.24	4	7	0
105. Southeast Mo. St.	11	252	122	10	48.41	1,276	5.06	8	116.0	3.97	10.46	4	7	0
107. Alabama St.	11	217	95	11	43.78	1,268	5.84	8	115.3	5.07	13.35	5	6	0
108. Howard	11	257	120	13	46.69	1,255	4.88	12	114.1	5.06	10.46	5	6	0
109. Tenn.-Martin	12	220	112	9	50.91	1,281	5.82	9	106.8	4.09	11.44	9	3	0
110. Albany (N.Y.)	11	227	115	8	50.66	1,170	5.15	6	106.4	3.52	10.17	7	4	0
111. VMI	11	145	74	3	51.03	1,132	7.81	8	102.9	2.07	15.30	1	10	0
112. Central Conn. St.	11	131	70	4	53.44	1,121	8.56	7	101.9	3.05	16.01	8	3	0
113. Bucknell	11	139	55	6	39.57	889	6.40	4	80.8	4.32	16.16	6	5	0
114. Wofford	11	111	60	6	54.05	784	7.06	5	71.3	5.41	13.07	7	4	0
115. Prairie View	10	209	77	8	36.84	701	3.35	5	70.1	3.83	9.10	3	7	0
116. Nicholls St.	11	95	39	7	41.05	635	6.68	5	57.7	7.37	16.28	4	7	0

Passing Efficiency

Rank, Team	G	Att	Comp	Pct	Int	IPct	Yds	Yds/Att	TD	TD Pct	Rating	W	L	T
1. San Diego	12	391	260	66.50	5	1.28	3,520	9.00	36	9.21	169.95	11	1	0
2. Northern Ariz.	11	340	222	65.29	6	1.76	2,939	8.64	34	10.00	167.38	6	5	0
3. Coastal Caro.	12	353	223	63.17	11	3.12	3,429	9.71	30	8.50	166.61	9	3	0
4. James Madison	12	237	157	66.24	6	2.53	2,074	8.75	20	8.44	162.49	9	3	0
5. Ark.-Pine Bluff	12	244	142	58.20	10	4.10	2,292	9.39	24	9.84	161.37	8	4	0
6. Massachusetts	15	343	222	64.72	11	3.21	3,082	8.99	26	7.58	158.78	13	2	0
7. Southern Ill.	13	206	125	60.68	4	1.94	1,806	8.77	17	8.25	157.69	9	4	0

Rank, Team	G	Att	Comp	Pct	Int	IPct	Yds	Yds/Att	TD	TD Pct	Rating	W	L	T
8. UNI	11	255	172	67.45	7	2.75	2,079	8.15	17	6.67	152.49	7	4	0
9. Charleston So.	11	348	239	68.68	16	4.60	2,863	8.23	23	6.61	150.42	9	2	0
10. New Hampshire	13	441	301	68.25	7	1.59	3,190	7.23	29	6.58	147.59	9	4	0
11. Duquesne	10	357	212	59.38	13	3.64	2,877	8.06	28	7.84	145.69	7	3	0
12. Hampton	12	291	187	64.26	5	1.72	2,122	7.29	20	6.87	144.80	10	2	0
13. Lehigh	11	256	157	61.33	6	2.34	2,077	8.11	14	5.47	142.81	6	5	0
14. Towson	11	409	275	67.24	11	2.69	3,161	7.73	19	4.65	142.07	7	4	0
15. Illinois St.	13	351	203	57.83	14	3.99	2,961	8.44	21	5.98	140.43	9	4	0
16. Stony Brook	11	327	200	61.16	5	1.53	2,489	7.61	17	5.20	139.24	5	6	0
17. Dayton	10	272	152	55.88	11	4.04	2,472	9.09	12	4.41	138.71	4	6	0
17. Western Ky.	11	285	175	61.40	9	3.16	2,248	7.89	15	5.26	138.71	6	5	0
19. Bethune-Cookman	11	297	167	56.23	5	1.68	2,230	7.51	20	6.73	138.13	5	6	0
20. Holy Cross	11	421	259	61.52	7	1.66	2,987	7.10	25	5.94	137.37	7	4	0
21. Jackson St.	10	234	139	59.40	13	5.56	1,917	8.19	14	5.98	136.85	5	5	0
22. Central Conn. St.	11	131	70	53.44	4	3.05	1,121	8.56	7	5.34	136.81	8	3	0
23. Florida A&M	11	325	195	60.00	8	2.46	2,352	7.24	20	6.15	136.17	7	4	0
24. Monmouth	12	317	203	64.04	10	3.15	2,409	7.60	14	4.42	136.10	10	2	0
25. Western Ill.	11	287	180	62.72	9	3.14	2,201	7.67	13	4.53	135.80	5	6	0
26. Appalachian St.	15	342	201	58.77	14	4.09	2,646	7.74	18	5.26	132.97	14	1	0
27. Grambling	11	367	197	53.68	11	3.00	2,771	7.55	24	6.54	132.71	3	8	0
28. Marist	11	273	166	60.81	12	4.40	2,215	8.11	9	3.30	131.04	4	7	0
29. Robert Morris	11	282	161	57.09	16	5.67	2,105	7.46	19	6.74	130.69	7	4	0
30. VMI	11	145	74	51.03	3	2.07	1,132	7.81	8	5.52	130.65	1	10	0
31. Princeton	10	336	197	58.63	12	3.57	2,458	7.32	17	5.06	129.60	9	1	0
32. Elon	11	387	238	61.50	12	3.10	2,707	6.99	18	4.65	129.40	5	6	0
33. Colgate	11	271	154	56.83	10	3.69	2,105	7.77	11	4.06	128.06	4	7	0
34. Villanova	11	284	172	60.56	9	3.17	2,140	7.54	9	3.17	128.02	6	5	0
35. Portland St.	11	267	141	52.81	12	4.49	1,969	7.37	18	6.74	128.00	7	4	0
36. Delaware	11	420	264	62.86	10	2.38	2,783	6.63	18	4.29	127.94	5	6	0
37. Lafayette	12	307	181	58.96	10	3.26	2,239	7.29	13	4.23	127.72	6	6	0
38. Davidson	10	381	216	56.69	10	2.62	2,617	6.87	21	5.51	127.34	6	4	0
39. Richmond	11	312	187	59.94	10	3.21	2,066	6.62	17	5.45	127.09	6	5	0
40. Delaware St.	11	214	121	56.54	4	1.87	1,420	6.64	12	5.61	127.00	8	3	0
41. Georgetown	11	318	207	65.09	15	4.72	1,948	6.13	19	5.97	126.84	2	9	0
42. Liberty	11	211	122	57.82	5	2.37	1,565	7.42	7	3.32	126.31	6	5	0
43. Montana	14	429	237	55.24	13	3.03	3,181	7.41	19	4.43	126.04	12	2	0
44. Youngstown St.	14	317	181	57.10	12	3.79	2,211	6.97	17	5.36	125.81	11	3	0
45. Citadel	11	330	207	62.73	11	3.33	2,163	6.55	14	4.24	125.09	5	6	0
46. Tennessee St.	11	250	140	56.00	13	5.20	2,004	8.02	9	3.60	124.81	6	5	0
47. Austin Peay	11	329	199	60.49	13	3.95	2,293	6.97	13	3.95	124.18	3	8	0
48. Eastern Ill.	13	315	175	55.56	18	5.71	2,135	6.78	22	6.98	124.15	8	5	0
49. McNeese St.	12	262	140	53.44	10	3.82	1,844	7.04	15	5.73	123.78	7	5	0
50. Furman	12	287	165	57.49	6	2.09	2,075	7.23	8	2.79	123.25	8	4	0
51. Gardner-Webb	11	378	218	57.67	21	5.56	2,655	7.02	19	5.03	122.18	6	5	0
52. Eastern Ky.	11	336	191	56.85	15	4.46	2,418	7.20	14	4.17	122.07	6	5	0
53. St. Francis (Pa.)	11	293	155	52.90	7	2.39	1,931	6.59	16	5.46	121.50	3	8	0
54. Southern U.	11	313	188	60.06	19	6.07	2,086	6.66	16	5.11	120.81	5	6	0
55. Alabama A&M	12	306	176	57.52	8	2.61	1,862	6.08	16	5.23	120.64	9	3	0
56. South Carolina St.	11	193	101	52.33	9	4.66	1,349	6.99	11	5.70	120.49	7	4	0
57. Harvard	10	290	152	52.41	12	4.14	2,102	7.25	13	4.48	119.80	7	3	0
58. Northeastern	11	234	134	57.26	11	4.70	1,685	7.20	8	3.42	119.67	5	6	0
59. Montana St.	13	410	224	54.63	19	4.63	2,940	7.17	17	4.15	119.25	8	5	0
60. Jacksonville St.	11	237	129	54.43	10	4.22	1,743	7.35	8	3.38	118.88	6	5	0
61. Morehead St.	11	288	170	59.03	12	4.17	1,891	6.57	11	3.82	118.43	2	9	0
62. Texas St.	11	320	170	53.13	15	4.69	2,215	6.92	16	5.00	118.37	5	6	0
63. William & Mary	11	360	196	54.44	10	2.78	2,334	6.48	16	4.44	117.97	3	8	0
64. Dartmouth	10	291	179	61.51	12	4.12	1,962	6.74	7	2.41	117.83	2	8	0
65. Cal Poly	11	174	78	44.83	7	4.02	1,285	7.39	10	5.75	117.75	7	4	0
66. Wofford	11	111	60	54.05	6	5.41	784	7.06	5	4.50	117.48	7	4	0
67. Rhode Island	11	157	74	47.13	12	7.64	1,276	8.13	8	5.10	116.90	4	7	0
68. Missouri St.	11	313	176	56.23	10	3.19	2,105	6.73	10	3.19	116.85	2	9	0
69. Idaho St.	11	358	195	54.47	14	3.91	2,320	6.48	17	4.75	116.78	2	9	0
70. Brown	10	327	178	54.43	16	4.89	2,276	6.96	13	3.98	116.20	3	7	0
71. Norfolk St.	11	285	148	51.93	16	5.61	2,166	7.60	10	3.51	116.09	4	7	0
72. Stephen F. Austin	11	300	172	57.33	5	1.67	1,895	6.32	8	2.67	115.83	4	7	0
73. Maine	11	249	155	62.25	8	3.21	1,421	5.71	9	3.61	115.64	6	5	0
74. Cornell	10	226	124	54.87	10	4.42	1,556	6.88	8	3.54	115.57	5	5	0
75. Southeastern La.	11	392	250	63.78	10	2.55	2,064	5.27	14	3.57	114.71	2	9	0
76. La Salle	10	276	153	55.43	18	6.52	1,812	6.57	14	5.07	114.24	3	7	0
77. Jacksonville	10	277	128	46.21	11	3.97	1,916	6.92	15	5.42	114.23	4	6	0
78. Murray St.	11	356	205	57.58	14	3.93	2,088	5.87	16	4.49	113.83	1	10	0
79. Alcorn St.	10	279	134	48.03	12	4.30	1,902	6.82	14	5.02	113.22	6	4	0
80. Sam Houston St.	11	338	187	55.33	14	4.14	2,191	6.48	12	3.55	113.18	6	5	0
81. Hofstra	11	345	184	53.33	4	1.16	2,119	6.14	11	3.19	113.10	2	9	0
82. Sacred Heart	11	372	211	56.72	14	3.76	2,076	5.58	19	5.11	112.91	2	9	0
83. Southern Utah	11	333	187	56.16	15	4.50	1,976	5.93	16	4.80	112.89	3	8	0
84. Tennessee Tech	11	362	190	52.49	17	4.70	2,305	6.37	17	4.70	112.09	4	7	0
85. Indiana St.	11	386	206	53.37	9	2.33	2,346	6.08	14	3.63	111.76	1	10	0
86. Yale	10	210	109	51.90	6	2.86	1,437	6.84	5	2.38	111.52	8	2	0
87. Penn	10	359	194	54.04	12	3.34	2,309	6.43	11	3.06	111.45	5	5	0
88. Drake	11	264	129	48.86	11	4.17	1,914	7.25	7	2.65	110.22	9	2	0
88. Weber St.	11	302	164	54.30	15	4.97	1,896	6.28	12	3.97	110.22	4	7	0
90. Iona	10	297	168	56.57	12	4.04	1,903	6.41	7	2.36	110.12	3	7	0

Rank, Team	G	Att	Comp	Pct	Int	IPct	Yds	Yds/Att	TD	TD Pct	Rating	W	L	T
91. Columbia	10	338	191	56.51	6	1.78	2,019	5.97	7	2.07	109.96	5	5	0
92. St. Peter's	10	433	242	55.89	13	3.00	2,480	5.73	15	3.46	109.44	2	8	0
93. Eastern Wash.	11	345	184	53.33	19	5.51	2,221	6.44	13	3.77	108.80	3	8	0
94. Valparaiso	11	331	159	48.04	13	3.93	2,185	6.60	13	3.93	108.56	3	8	0
95. Ga. Southern	11	311	160	51.45	6	1.93	1,944	6.25	8	2.57	108.54	3	8	0
96. Mississippi Val.	11	283	137	48.41	14	4.95	1,839	6.50	12	4.24	107.08	6	5	0
97. Sacramento St.	11	292	150	51.37	19	6.51	1,977	6.77	10	3.42	106.56	4	7	0
98. Western Caro.	11	298	157	52.68	6	2.01	1,677	5.63	9	3.02	105.91	2	9	0
99. Northwestern St.	11	326	170	52.15	11	3.37	1,931	5.92	10	3.07	105.23	4	7	0
100. Tenn.-Martin	12	220	112	50.91	9	4.09	1,281	5.82	9	4.09	105.13	9	3	0
101. Texas Southern	11	319	164	51.41	22	6.90	1,966	6.16	14	4.39	103.86	3	8	0
102. Chattanooga	11	335	178	53.13	13	3.88	1,788	5.34	12	3.58	101.99	3	8	0
103. Morgan St.	11	230	116	50.43	10	4.35	1,295	5.63	9	3.91	101.91	5	6	0
104. Nicholls St.	11	95	39	41.05	7	7.37	635	6.68	5	5.26	99.88	4	7	0
105. Butler	11	372	190	51.08	11	2.96	1,887	5.07	11	2.96	97.55	3	8	0
106. Samford	11	351	185	52.71	16	4.56	1,786	5.09	10	2.85	95.73	3	8	0
107. Albany (N.Y.)	11	227	115	50.66	8	3.52	1,170	5.15	6	2.64	95.67	7	4	0
108. Alabama St.	11	217	95	43.78	11	5.07	1,268	5.84	8	3.69	94.91	5	6	0
109. Bucknell	11	139	55	39.57	6	4.32	889	6.40	4	2.88	94.19	6	5	0
110. Fordham	11	260	113	43.46	12	4.62	1,482	5.70	9	3.46	93.57	3	8	0
111. Southeast Mo. St.	11	252	122	48.41	10	3.97	1,276	5.06	8	3.17	93.47	4	7	0
112. Wagner	11	327	156	47.71	12	3.67	1,671	5.11	10	3.06	93.38	4	7	0
113. Howard	11	257	120	46.69	13	5.06	1,255	4.88	12	4.67	93.01	5	6	0
114. Savannah St.	11	245	115	46.94	14	5.71	1,281	5.23	8	3.27	90.17	2	9	0
115. N.C. A&T	11	283	128	45.23	19	6.71	1,342	4.74	9	3.18	82.10	0	11	0
116. Prairie View	10	209	77	36.84	8	3.83	701	3.35	5	2.39	65.21	3	7	0

Total Offense

Rank, Team	G	Pl	Yds	Avg	TD	Yds/Gm	W	L	T
1. San Diego	12	829	5,931	7.15	71	494.25	11	1	0
2. Coastal Caro.	12	787	5,617	7.14	54	468.08	9	3	0
3. Appalachian St.	15	1,006	6,265	6.23	71	417.67	14	1	0
4. UNI	11	698	4,491	6.43	41	408.27	7	4	0
5. Drake	11	759	4,459	5.87	40	405.36	9	2	0
6. Northern Ariz.	11	730	4,456	6.10	48	405.09	6	5	0
7. New Hampshire	13	930	5,208	5.60	63	400.62	9	4	0
8. Illinois St.	13	871	5,167	5.93	50	397.46	9	4	0
9. James Madison	12	730	4,694	6.43	51	391.17	9	3	0
10. Central Conn. St.	11	694	4,255	6.13	51	386.82	8	3	0
11. Holy Cross	11	765	4,228	5.53	37	384.36	7	4	0
12. Massachusetts	15	898	5,757	6.41	52	383.80	13	2	0
13. Davidson	10	689	3,836	5.57	38	383.60	6	4	0
14. Youngstown St.	14	898	5,343	5.95	58	381.64	11	3	0
15. Duquesne	10	641	3,816	5.95	37	381.60	7	3	0
16. Western Ill.	11	710	4,195	5.91	45	381.36	5	6	0
17. Princeton	10	711	3,752	5.28	29	375.20	9	1	0
18. Southern Ill.	13	779	4,841	6.21	57	372.38	9	4	0
19. Towson	11	736	4,088	5.55	31	371.64	7	4	0
20. Harvard	10	671	3,705	5.52	35	370.50	7	3	0
21. Dayton	10	680	3,685	5.42	35	368.50	4	6	0
22. Montana	14	953	5,132	5.39	45	366.57	12	2	0
23. South Carolina St.	11	691	4,012	5.81	40	364.73	7	4	0
23. Western Ky.	11	702	4,012	5.72	31	364.73	6	5	0
25. Charleston So.	11	660	3,992	6.05	41	362.91	9	2	0
26. Indiana St.	11	764	3,963	5.19	31	360.27	1	10	0
27. Ga. Southern	11	733	3,959	5.40	30	359.91	3	8	0
28. Austin Peay	11	711	3,943	5.55	32	358.45	3	8	0
29. Colgate	11	709	3,925	5.54	34	356.82	4	7	0
30. Delaware	11	765	3,923	5.13	38	356.64	5	6	0
31. Jacksonville	10	667	3,563	5.34	27	356.30	4	6	0
32. Eastern Ky.	11	697	3,899	5.59	30	354.45	6	5	0
33. Citadel	11	760	3,895	5.13	34	354.09	5	6	0
34. Penn	10	663	3,538	5.34	30	353.80	5	5	0
35. Monmouth	12	782	4,243	5.43	38	353.58	10	2	0
36. Hampton	12	712	4,223	5.93	52	351.92	10	2	0
37. Eastern Ill.	13	829	4,572	5.52	38	351.69	8	5	0
38. Texas St.	11	671	3,868	5.76	30	351.64	5	6	0
39. Lafayette	12	741	4,212	5.68	43	351.00	6	6	0
40. Richmond	11	694	3,860	5.56	34	350.91	6	5	0
41. Grambling	11	700	3,831	5.47	40	348.27	3	8	0
42. Florida A&M	11	682	3,825	5.61	33	347.73	7	4	0
42. Morehead St.	11	719	3,825	5.32	30	347.73	2	9	0
44. Stony Brook	11	678	3,822	5.64	33	347.45	5	6	0
45. Brown	10	671	3,459	5.15	29	345.90	3	7	0
46. St. Francis (Pa.)	11	691	3,796	5.49	31	345.09	3	8	0
46. Sam Houston St.	11	672	3,796	5.65	37	345.09	6	5	0
48. Yale	10	639	3,445	5.39	32	344.50	8	2	0
49. Lehigh	11	697	3,765	5.40	38	342.27	6	5	0
50. Furman	12	795	4,095	5.15	39	341.25	8	4	0
51. Chattanooga	11	729	3,742	5.13	26	340.18	3	8	0
52. William & Mary	11	686	3,726	5.43	27	338.73	3	8	0
53. Gardner-Webb	11	702	3,724	5.30	35	338.55	6	5	0
54. Villanova	11	672	3,716	5.53	33	337.82	6	5	0
55. Cornell	10	678	3,377	4.98	23	337.70	5	5	0
56. Bethune-Cookman	11	666	3,699	5.55	43	336.27	5	6	0
57. Wofford	11	682	3,683	5.40	44	334.82	7	4	0
58. Idaho St.	11	714	3,678	5.15	32	334.36	2	9	0
59. Tennessee St.	11	667	3,652	5.48	30	332.00	6	5	0
60. Elon	11	677	3,642	5.38	31	331.09	5	6	0
61. Jackson St.	10	650	3,634	5.59	42	330.36	5	5	0
62. Alabama A&M	12	778	3,946	5.07	40	328.83	9	3	0
63. Jacksonville St.	11	667	3,608	5.41	35	328.00	6	5	0
64. Liberty	11	643	3,600	5.60	34	327.27	6	5	0
65. Northwestern St.	11	765	3,595	4.70	19	326.82	4	7	0
66. Stephen F. Austin	11	694	3,594	5.18	23	326.73	4	7	0
67. Tenn.-Martin	12	727	3,900	5.36	38	325.00	9	3	0
68. Ark.-Pine Bluff	12	637	3,881	6.09	45	323.42	8	4	0
69. McNeese St.	12	724	3,877	5.35	36	323.08	7	5	0
70. Southern Utah	11	675	3,536	5.24	30	321.45	3	8	0
71. Tennessee Tech	11	730	3,529	4.83	24	320.82	4	7	0
72. Montana St.	13	800	4,170	5.21	32	320.77	8	5	0
73. Delaware St.	11	580	3,524	6.08	44	320.36	8	3	0
74. Bucknell	11	678	3,476	5.13	28	316.00	6	5	0
75. Eastern Wash.	11	711	3,413	4.80	24	310.27	3	8	0
76. VMI	11	656	3,405	5.19	25	309.55	1	10	0
77. Marist	11	641	3,400	5.30	27	309.09	4	7	0
78. Rhode Island	11	730	3,389	4.64	29	308.09	4	7	0
79. Southern U.	11	695	3,385	4.87	36	307.73	5	6	0
80. Valparaiso	11	689	3,355	4.87	28	305.00	3	8	0
81. Norfolk St.	11	659	3,311	5.02	33	301.00	4	7	0
82. Mississippi Val.	11	683	3,306	4.84	27	300.55	6	5	0
82. Northeastern	11	630	3,306	5.25	26	300.55	5	6	0
84. Cal Poly	11	649	3,296	5.08	30	299.64	7	4	0
85. Dartmouth	10	601	2,995	4.98	18	299.50	2	8	0
86. Howard	11	722	3,288	4.55	23	298.91	5	6	0
87. Maine	11	705	3,286	4.66	28	298.73	6	5	0
88. Iona	10	673	2,979	4.43	15	297.90	3	7	0
89. Weber St.	11	660	3,235	4.90	25	294.09	4	7	0
90. Alcorn St.	10	618	3,234	5.23	34	294.00	6	4	0
91. Missouri St.	11	668	3,215	4.81	24	292.27	2	9	0
92. Georgetown	11	670	3,214	4.80	22	292.18	2	9	0
93. Nicholls St.	11	639	3,208	5.02	24	291.64	4	7	0
94. Southeastern La.	11	705	3,197	4.53	23	290.64	2	9	0
95. Portland St.	11	650	3,160	4.86	29	287.27	7	4	0
96. St. Peter's	10	635	2,859	4.50	21	285.90	2	8	0
97. Murray St.	11	697	3,136	4.50	26	285.09	1	10	0
98. La Salle	10	661	2,838	4.29	20	283.80	3	7	0
99. Robert Morris	11	685	3,098	4.52	32	281.64	7	4	0
100. Morgan St.	11	633	3,038	4.80	26	276.18	5	6	0
101. Wagner	11	653	3,022	4.63	22	274.73	4	7	0
102. Albany (N.Y.)	11	677	3,006	4.44	26	273.27	7	4	0
103. Texas Southern	11	639	2,981	4.67	27	271.00	3	8	0
104. Columbia	10	602	2,697	4.48	17	269.70	5	5	0
105. Sacred Heart	11	622	2,950	4.74	27	268.18	2	9	0
106. Alabama St.	11	646	2,897	4.48	26	263.36	5	6	0
107. Samford	11	658	2,880	4.38	19	261.82	3	8	0

Rank, Team	G	Pl	Yds	Avg	TD	Yds/Gm	W	L	T
108. Hofstra	11	670	2,878	4.30	19	261.64	2	9	0
109. Fordham	11	662	2,864	4.33	19	260.36	3	8	0
110. Western Caro.	11	633	2,812	4.44	20	255.64	2	9	0
111. Southeast Mo. St.	11	641	2,793	4.36	28	253.91	4	7	0
112. Prairie View	10	617	2,498	4.05	22	249.80	3	7	0
113. Sacramento St.	11	638	2,680	4.20	20	243.64	4	7	0
114. Butler	11	650	2,408	3.70	18	218.91	3	8	0
115. N.C. A&T	11	653	2,375	3.64	17	215.91	0	11	0
116. Savannah St.	11	581	2,328	4.01	17	211.64	2	9	0

Scoring Offense

Rank, Team	G	Pts.	Avg.	TD	Kxp	Oxp	Dkxp	Doxp	FG	Saf	W	L	T
1. San Diego	12	514	42.83	71	51	4	1	0	9	0	11	1	0
2. New Hampshire	13	459	35.31	63	57	0	0	0	8	0	9	4	0
3. Appalachian St.	15	528	35.20	71	70	0	0	0	10	1	14	1	0
4. Southern Ill.	13	448	34.46	57	55	2	1	0	15	0	9	4	0
5. Northern Ariz.	11	378	34.36	48	43	3	0	0	13	1	6	5	0
6. Coastal Caro.	12	411	34.25	54	49	2	1	0	10	1	9	3	0
7. Hampton	12	410	34.17	52	48	0	0	0	16	1	10	2	0
8. Central Conn. St.	11	363	33.00	51	44	2	0	0	3	0	8	3	0
9. James Madison	12	389	32.42	51	50	0	0	0	11	0	9	3	0
10. Youngstown St.	14	440	31.43	58	50	2	0	0	12	1	11	3	0
11. UNI	11	341	31.00	41	39	1	0	0	18	0	7	4	0
12. Delaware St.	11	335	30.45	44	39	0	0	0	10	1	8	3	0
13. Western Ill.	11	333	30.27	45	42	0	0	0	7	0	5	6	0
14. Wofford	11	329	29.91	44	42	0	0	0	7	1	7	4	0
15. Davidson	10	295	29.50	38	30	2	0	0	11	0	6	4	0
16. Illinois St.	13	377	29.00	50	44	0	0	0	11	0	9	4	0
17. Bethune-Cookman	11	314	28.55	43	38	0	0	0	6	0	5	6	0
18. Duquesne	10	285	28.50	37	33	0	0	0	10	0	7	3	0
19. Jackson St.	10	312	31.20	42	28	7	0	0	6	0	5	5	0
20. Ark.-Pine Bluff	12	333	27.75	45	36	3	0	0	7	0	8	4	0
21. Drake	11	303	27.55	40	35	0	0	0	8	2	9	2	0
22. Massachusetts	15	413	27.53	52	51	0	0	0	16	1	13	2	0
23. Montana	14	385	27.50	45	41	0	0	0	24	1	12	2	0
24. Charleston So.	11	300	27.27	41	34	1	0	0	6	0	9	2	0
25. Lehigh	11	299	27.18	38	33	1	0	0	12	0	6	5	0
26. South Carolina St.	11	298	27.09	40	37	0	0	0	7	0	7	4	0
27. Grambling	11	295	26.82	40	29	3	1	0	6	0	3	8	0
28. Harvard	10	267	26.70	35	31	1	0	0	8	0	7	3	0
29. Lafayette	12	316	26.33	43	38	1	0	0	6	0	6	6	0
30. Delaware	11	289	26.27	38	35	1	0	0	8	0	5	6	0
31. Jacksonville St.	11	285	25.91	35	34	0	0	0	13	1	6	5	0
32. Yale	10	257	25.70	32	29	0	0	0	12	0	8	2	0
33. McNeese St.	12	303	25.25	36	33	0	0	0	18	0	7	5	0
34. Southern U.	11	276	25.09	36	32	0	0	0	8	2	5	6	0
35. Dayton	10	250	25.00	35	23	3	0	0	3	1	4	6	0
35. Holy Cross	11	275	25.00	37	33	1	0	0	6	0	7	4	0
37. Tenn.-Martin	12	298	24.83	38	36	1	0	0	10	1	9	3	0
38. Florida A&M	11	273	24.82	33	27	2	0	0	14	1	7	4	0
39. Richmond	11	272	24.73	34	34	0	0	0	10	2	6	5	0
40. Furman	12	295	24.58	39	34	1	0	0	7	2	8	4	0
41. Gardner-Webb	11	270	24.55	35	33	0	0	0	9	0	6	5	0
42. Citadel	11	264	24.00	34	28	1	0	0	10	0	5	6	0
43. Alcorn St.	10	263	26.30	34	26	1	0	0	9	2	6	4	0
43. Sam Houston St.	11	263	23.91	37	25	2	0	0	4	0	6	5	0
45. Monmouth	12	286	23.83	38	29	1	0	0	9	0	10	2	0
46. Alabama A&M	12	285	23.75	40	25	4	0	0	4	0	9	3	0
47. Liberty	11	259	23.55	34	29	0	0	0	8	1	6	5	0
48. Western Ky.	11	258	23.45	31	27	2	0	0	13	1	6	5	0
49. Princeton	10	233	23.30	29	25	1	0	0	10	1	9	1	0
50. Idaho St.	11	255	23.18	32	28	0	0	0	11	1	2	9	0
51. Elon	11	253	23.00	31	29	1	0	0	12	0	5	6	0
52. Eastern Ill.	13	297	22.85	38	33	0	0	0	12	0	8	5	0
53. Norfolk St.	11	251	22.82	33	25	1	0	0	8	1	4	7	0
54. Penn	10	228	22.80	30	25	0	0	0	7	1	5	5	0
55. Cal Poly	11	248	22.55	30	26	2	0	0	12	1	7	4	0
56. Brown	10	225	22.50	29	25	1	0	0	8	0	3	7	0
57. Villanova	11	247	22.45	33	30	1	0	0	5	1	6	5	0
58. Colgate	11	246	22.36	34	21	3	0	0	5	0	4	7	0
59. Austin Peay	11	245	22.27	32	27	1	0	0	8	0	3	8	0
59. Portland St.	11	245	22.27	29	25	1	0	0	14	1	7	4	0
61. Texas St.	11	244	22.18	30	28	0	0	0	12	0	5	6	0
62. Stony Brook	11	242	22.00	33	25	1	1	0	5	0	5	6	0
63. Tennessee St.	11	241	21.91	30	23	2	0	0	10	2	6	5	0
64. Eastern Ky.	11	238	21.64	30	27	1	0	0	9	1	6	5	0
65. Indiana St.	11	236	21.45	31	26	0	0	0	8	0	1	10	0
65. Towson	11	236	21.45	31	25	1	0	0	7	1	7	4	0
67. Ga. Southern	11	235	21.36	30	20	4	0	0	9	0	3	8	0
68. Robert Morris	11	234	21.27	32	30	0	0	0	4	0	7	4	0
69. St. Francis (Pa.)	11	227	20.64	31	29	0	0	0	4	0	3	8	0
70. Jacksonville	10	206	20.60	27	24	1	0	0	6	0	4	6	0
71. Albany (N.Y.)	11	224	20.36	26	25	0	0	0	13	2	7	4	0
72. Bucknell	11	222	20.18	28	27	0	0	0	9	0	6	5	0
73. Montana St.	13	261	20.08	32	25	3	0	0	12	1	8	5	0

Rank, Team	G	Pts.	Avg.	TD	Kxp	Oxp	Dkxp	Doxp	FG	Saf	W	L	T
74. Morehead St.	11	218	19.82	30	27	1	0	0	3	0	2	9	0
75. Maine	11	217	19.73	28	26	0	0	0	7	1	6	5	0
76. Southern Utah	11	215	19.55	30	27	0	0	0	2	1	3	8	0
77. Eastern Wash.	11	214	19.45	24	23	0	0	0	15	1	3	8	0
77. Rhode Island	11	214	19.45	29	25	0	0	0	5	0	4	7	0
79. Valparaiso	11	212	19.27	28	27	0	0	0	5	1	3	8	0
80. William & Mary	11	209	19.00	27	26	0	0	0	7	0	3	8	0
81. Cornell	10	189	18.90	23	22	0	0	0	9	1	5	5	0
82. Stephen F. Austin	11	204	18.55	23	23	0	0	0	13	2	4	7	0
83. Southeast Mo. St.	11	203	18.45	28	24	1	0	0	3	0	4	7	0
83. Texas Southern	11	203	18.45	27	18	2	0	0	5	2	3	8	0
85. Chattanooga	11	201	18.27	26	25	1	0	0	6	0	3	8	0
85. Weber St.	11	201	18.27	25	19	0	0	0	10	1	4	7	0
87. Marist	11	200	18.18	27	23	0	0	0	5	0	4	7	0
87. Northeastern	11	200	18.18	26	24	1	0	0	6	0	5	6	0
89. Alabama St.	11	199	18.09	26	16	0	0	0	9	0	5	6	0
89. Mississippi Val.	11	199	18.09	27	18	2	0	0	5	0	6	5	0
89. VMI	11	199	18.09	25	17	1	0	0	10	0	1	10	0
89. Morgan St.	11	199	18.09	26	20	0	0	0	5	4	5	6	0
93. Murray St.	11	195	17.73	26	25	1	0	0	4	0	1	10	0
94. Missouri St.	11	194	17.64	24	23	0	0	0	9	0	2	9	0
95. Tennessee Tech	11	192	17.45	24	18	0	0	0	10	0	4	7	0
96. Nicholls St.	11	189	17.18	24	24	0	0	0	7	0	4	7	0
96. Sacred Heart	11	189	17.18	27	19	1	0	0	2	0	2	9	0
98. Northwestern St.	11	187	17.00	19	15	1	0	0	18	1	4	7	0
99. Hofstra	11	185	16.82	19	15	1	0	0	18	0	2	9	0
100. Southeastern La.	11	181	16.45	23	14	3	0	0	7	1	2	9	0
101. Howard	11	180	16.36	23	19	0	0	0	7	1	5	6	0
101. Wagner	11	180	16.36	22	21	0	0	0	9	0	4	7	0
103. Prairie View	10	156	15.60	22	11	2	0	0	3	0	3	7	0
104. St. Peter's	10	154	15.40	21	13	0	0	0	5	0	2	8	0
105. Sacramento St.	11	168	15.27	20	17	2	0	0	9	0	4	7	0
106. Samford	11	166	15.09	19	16	0	0	0	12	0	3	8	0
107. Columbia	10	150	15.00	17	15	0	0	0	11	0	5	5	0
108. Georgetown	11	164	14.91	22	18	1	0	0	4	0	2	9	0
109. Dartmouth	10	147	14.70	18	16	1	0	0	7	0	2	8	0
109. Iona	10	147	14.70	15	13	2	1	0	12	1	3	7	0
111. La Salle	10	146	14.60	20	14	2	0	0	2	1	3	7	0
112. Western Caro.	11	159	14.45	20	17	1	0	0	6	1	2	9	0
113. Fordham	11	158	14.36	19	15	1	0	0	9	0	3	8	0
114. Butler	11	156	14.18	18	17	0	0	0	9	2	3	8	0
115. N.C. A&T	11	114	10.36	17	12	0	0	0	0	0	0	11	0
116. Savannah St.	11	108	9.82	17	4	1	0	0	0	0	2	9	0

Rushing Defense

Rank, Team	G	Att	Net	Avg.	TD	Yds/Gm	W	L	T
1. Maine	11	335	703	2.10	9	63.9	6	5	0
2. Harvard	10	329	665	2.02	14	66.5	7	3	0
3. Iona	10	271	669	2.47	6	66.9	3	7	0
4. James Madison	12	417	1,018	2.44	17	84.8	9	3	0
5. Albany (N.Y.)	11	414	992	2.40	6	90.2	7	4	0
6. Robert Morris	11	383	1,098	2.87	7	99.8	7	4	0
7. Jackson St.	10	332	1,103	3.32	15	100.3	5	5	0
8. Monmouth	12	354	1,208	3.41	11	100.7	10	2	0
9. Montana	14	469	1,495	3.19	11	106.8	12	2	0
10. San Diego	12	370	1,287	3.48	11	107.3	11	1	0
11. Appalachian St.	15	530	1,625	3.07	9	108.3	14	1	0
12. Charleston So.	11	393	1,197	3.05	12	108.8	9	2	0
13. Portland St.	11	365	1,232	3.38	13	112.0	7	4	0
14. Weber St.	11	403	1,238	3.07	15	112.5	4	7	0
15. Tenn.-Martin	12	409	1,355	3.31	13	112.9	9	3	0
16. Massachusetts	15	492	1,706	3.47	16	113.7	13	2	0
17. Alabama A&M	12	384	1,366	3.56	14	113.8	9	3	0
18. Jacksonville St.	11	378	1,263	3.34	11	114.8	6	5	0
19. Cal Poly	11	385	1,268	3.29	7	115.3	7	4	0
20. Mississippi Val.	11	356	1,274	3.58	17	115.8	6	5	0
21. Richmond	11	399	1,275	3.20	13	115.9	6	5	0
22. Morgan St.	11	379	1,287	3.40	12	117.0	5	6	0
23. Villanova	11	372	1,291	3.47	14	117.4	6	5	0
24. Prairie View	10	342	1,187	3.47	12	118.7	3	7	0
25. Northwestern St.	11	313	1,319	4.21	9	119.9	4	7	0
26. Montana St.	13	484	1,560	3.22	18	120.0	8	5	0
27. Sacramento St.	11	388	1,342	3.46	16	122.0	4	7	0
28. South Carolina St.	11	394	1,343	3.41	11	122.1	7	4	0
29. Alabama St.	11	341	1,352	3.96	10	122.9	5	6	0
30. Eastern Ill.	13	406	1,601	3.94	18	123.2	8	5	0
31. Idaho St.	11	377	1,373	3.64	17	124.8	2	9	0
32. Princeton	10	322	1,249	3.88	15	124.9	9	1	0
33. Furman	12	396	1,503	3.80	17	125.3	8	4	0
34. Brown	10	352	1,253	3.56	12	125.3	3	7	0
35. La Salle	10	313	1,260	4.03	16	126.0	3	7	0
36. Duquesne	10	333	1,262	3.79	9	126.2	7	3	0
37. Northern Ariz.	11	355	1,393	3.92	12	126.6	6	5	0
38. Yale	10	340	1,272	3.74	12	127.2	8	2	0
39. Central Conn. St.	11	386	1,408	3.65	6	128.0	8	3	0
40. Liberty	11	381	1,426	3.74	12	129.6	6	5	0
41. Butler	11	380	1,440	3.79	18	130.9	3	8	0
42. Drake	11	344	1,468	4.27	13	133.5	9	2	0
43. Southern Ill.	13	490	1,742	3.56	19	134.0	9	4	0
44. Hofstra	11	407	1,476	3.63	17	134.2	2	9	0
45. Davidson	10	345	1,345	3.90	15	134.5	6	4	0
46. Cornell	10	352	1,350	3.84	19	135.0	5	5	0
47. Hampton	12	442	1,627	3.68	8	135.6	10	2	0
48. Tennessee St.	11	383	1,505	3.93	15	136.8	6	5	0
49. Penn	10	381	1,378	3.62	9	137.8	5	5	0
50. Bethune-Cookman	11	392	1,516	3.87	13	137.8	5	6	0
51. Howard	11	416	1,518	3.65	19	138.0	5	6	0
52. UNI	11	380	1,519	4.00	18	138.1	7	4	0
53. Lafayette	12	435	1,671	3.84	16	139.3	6	6	0
54. Wofford	11	383	1,542	4.03	14	140.2	7	4	0
55. Delaware St.	11	427	1,549	3.63	15	140.8	8	3	0
56. Stephen F. Austin	11	368	1,555	4.23	14	141.4	4	7	0
57. Eastern Ky.	11	391	1,590	4.07	15	144.5	6	5	0
58. Morehead St.	11	356	1,591	4.47	18	144.6	2	9	0
59. Wagner	11	416	1,592	3.83	15	144.7	4	7	0
60. Towson	11	339	1,613	4.76	11	146.6	7	4	0
61. Alcorn St.	10	439	1,614	3.68	18	146.7	6	4	0
62. Northeastern	11	394	1,620	4.11	16	147.3	5	6	0
63. Citadel	11	355	1,625	4.58	24	147.7	5	6	0
64. Fordham	11	437	1,629	3.73	12	148.1	3	8	0
65. Illinois St.	13	452	1,931	4.27	14	148.5	9	4	0
66. Marist	11	384	1,642	4.28	22	149.3	4	7	0
67. Lehigh	11	420	1,653	3.94	17	150.3	6	5	0
68. Sam Houston St.	11	454	1,670	3.68	13	151.8	6	5	0
69. Ga. Southern	11	407	1,673	4.11	11	152.1	3	8	0
70. Colgate	11	431	1,674	3.88	19	152.2	4	7	0
70. Nicholls St.	11	412	1,674	4.06	13	152.2	4	7	0
72. Columbia	10	399	1,539	3.86	12	153.9	5	5	0
73. Dayton	10	355	1,550	4.37	14	155.0	4	6	0

Rank, Team	G	Att	Net	Avg.	TD	Yds/Gm	W	L	T
73. Texas St.	11	388	1,705	4.39	12	155.0	5	6	0
75. Southern U.	11	453	1,726	3.81	20	156.9	5	6	0
76. Elon	11	445	1,728	3.88	19	157.1	5	6	0
77. New Hampshire	13	481	2,055	4.27	24	158.1	9	4	0
78. Texas Southern	11	414	1,739	4.20	23	158.1	3	8	0
79. Holy Cross	11	395	1,753	4.44	21	159.4	7	4	0
80. Georgetown	11	444	1,760	3.96	25	160.0	2	9	0
81. Valparaiso	11	406	1,792	4.41	27	162.9	3	8	0
82. Jacksonville	10	332	1,644	4.95	18	164.4	4	6	0
83. Ark.-Pine Bluff	12	428	1,973	4.61	18	164.4	8	4	0
84. Chattanooga	11	409	1,809	4.42	23	164.5	3	8	0
85. Stony Brook	11	405	1,833	4.53	23	166.6	5	6	0
86. Sacred Heart	11	441	1,837	4.17	20	167.0	2	9	0
87. Southeast Mo. St.	11	399	1,850	4.64	21	168.2	4	7	0
88. Grambling	11	424	1,863	4.39	21	169.4	3	8	0
89. Youngstown St.	14	498	2,378	4.78	24	169.9	11	3	0
90. Samford	11	433	1,876	4.33	16	170.5	3	8	0
91. Western Ky.	11	399	1,878	4.71	23	170.7	6	5	0
92. McNeese St.	12	475	2,054	4.32	17	171.2	7	5	0
93. Western Ill.	11	419	1,895	4.52	23	172.3	5	6	0
94. Dartmouth	10	387	1,725	4.46	20	172.5	2	8	0
95. Southern Utah	11	432	1,903	4.41	17	173.0	3	8	0
96. Tennessee Tech	11	391	1,904	4.87	21	173.1	4	7	0
97. Bucknell	11	400	2,028	5.07	19	184.4	6	5	0
98. Austin Peay	11	446	2,036	4.57	19	185.1	3	8	0
99. Eastern Wash.	11	420	2,044	4.87	19	185.8	3	8	0
100. Norfolk St.	11	442	2,057	4.65	17	187.0	4	7	0
101. William & Mary	11	446	2,059	4.62	19	187.2	3	8	0
102. Missouri St.	11	457	2,096	4.59	23	190.5	2	9	0
103. Southeastern La.	11	423	2,122	5.02	26	192.9	2	9	0
104. Delaware	11	409	2,147	5.25	18	195.2	5	6	0
105. Coastal Caro.	12	490	2,354	4.80	26	196.2	9	3	0
106. St. Peter's	10	406	2,024	4.99	30	202.4	2	8	0
107. Savannah St.	11	453	2,241	4.95	30	203.7	2	9	0
108. Gardner-Webb	11	445	2,256	5.07	21	205.1	6	5	0
109. Western Caro.	11	448	2,292	5.12	27	208.4	2	9	0
110. St. Francis (Pa.)	11	378	2,319	6.13	28	210.8	3	8	0
111. VMI	11	397	2,364	5.95	34	214.9	1	10	0
112. Florida A&M	11	421	2,374	5.64	30	215.8	7	4	0
113. Rhode Island	11	442	2,376	5.38	26	216.0	4	7	0
114. Murray St.	11	480	2,550	5.31	26	231.8	1	10	0
115. N.C A&T	11	463	2,891	6.24	42	262.8	0	11	0
116. Indiana St.	11	549	3,315	6.04	43	301.4	1	10	0

Pass Defense

Rank, Team	G	Att	Comp	Pct	Yds/Cmp	Int	IPct	Yds	Yds/Att	TD	Yds/Gm	CM	W	L	T
1. Robert Morris	11	267	121	45.32	11.69	13	4.87	1,414	5.30	7	128.55	0	7	4	0
2. Cal Poly	11	261	125	47.89	11.70	12	4.60	1,463	5.61	12	133.00	1	7	4	0
3. Hampton	12	313	151	48.24	10.80	16	5.11	1,631	5.21	15	135.92	0	10	2	0
4. Southern U.	11	249	130	52.21	11.82	14	5.62	1,537	6.17	12	139.73	0	5	6	0
5. La Salle	10	234	101	43.16	13.96	5	2.14	1,410	6.03	11	141.00	0	3	7	0
6. Florida A&M	11	253	121	47.83	12.85	10	3.95	1,555	6.15	11	141.36	1	7	4	0
7. Tenn.-Martin	12	329	157	47.72	10.90	13	3.95	1,711	5.20	8	142.58	1	9	3	0
8. Howard	11	262	138	52.67	11.49	9	3.44	1,585	6.05	9	144.09	0	5	6	0
9. Prairie View	10	213	116	54.46	12.70	9	4.23	1,473	6.92	11	147.30	1	3	7	0
10. Nicholls St.	11	272	153	56.25	10.71	8	2.94	1,638	6.02	13	148.91	0	4	7	0
11. Columbia	10	246	146	59.35	10.25	15	6.10	1,497	6.09	8	149.70	0	5	5	0
12. Albany (N.Y.)	11	298	158	53.02	10.49	12	4.03	1,657	5.56	9	150.64	0	7	4	0
13. Duquesne	10	266	136	51.13	11.13	12	4.51	1,514	5.69	11	151.40	0	7	3	0
14. Richmond	11	261	156	59.77	10.78	12	4.60	1,681	6.44	10	152.82	0	6	5	0
15. Coastal Caro.	12	277	146	52.71	12.58	19	6.86	1,836	6.63	11	153.00	0	9	3	0
16. Western Ky.	11	273	144	52.75	11.70	6	2.20	1,685	6.17	7	153.18	0	6	5	0
17. Mississippi Val.	11	268	123	45.90	13.71	10	3.73	1,686	6.29	12	153.27	1	6	5	0
18. Samford	11	245	148	60.41	11.47	9	3.67	1,698	6.93	13	154.36	0	3	8	0
19. Alabama St.	11	251	135	53.78	12.62	10	3.98	1,704	6.79	17	154.91	0	5	6	0
20. Jacksonville St.	11	290	141	48.62	12.12	11	3.79	1,709	5.89	11	155.36	0	6	5	0
21. Bethune-Cookman	11	267	139	52.06	12.60	14	5.24	1,751	6.56	20	159.18	1	5	6	0
22. Rhode Island	11	261	143	54.79	12.26	11	4.21	1,753	6.72	15	159.36	0	4	7	0
23. Montana	14	394	208	52.79	10.74	19	4.82	2,234	5.67	12	159.57	2	12	2	0
24. Delaware St.	11	277	153	55.23	11.55	10	3.61	1,767	6.38	9	160.64	0	8	3	0
25. San Diego	12	340	166	48.82	11.70	16	4.71	1,942	5.71	10	161.83	0	11	1	0
26. Monmouth	12	345	169	48.99	11.51	16	4.64	1,946	5.64	8	162.17	1	10	2	0
27. Tennessee Tech	11	278	145	52.16	12.39	7	2.52	1,796	6.46	15	163.27	1	4	7	0
28. Norfolk St.	11	214	112	52.34	16.04	5	2.34	1,797	8.40	18	163.36	1	4	7	0
29. Eastern Ky.	11	266	150	56.39	12.05	11	4.14	1,808	6.80	14	164.36	0	6	5	0
30. Iona	10	303	161	53.14	10.26	14	4.62	1,652	5.45	12	165.20	0	3	7	0
31. Maine	11	302	170	56.29	10.74	9	2.98	1,826	6.05	9	166.00	0	6	5	0
32. Massachusetts	15	426	246	57.75	10.14	11	2.58	2,494	5.85	8	166.27	0	13	2	0
33. McNeese St.	12	304	175	57.57	11.42	13	4.28	1,998	6.57	17	166.50	1	7	5	0
34. South Carolina St.	11	263	145	55.13	12.74	13	4.94	1,848	7.03	13	168.00	0	7	4	0
35. Appalachian St.	15	423	216	51.06	11.71	16	3.78	2,529	5.98	15	168.60	0	14	1	0
36. Alabama A&M	12	288	133	46.18	15.32	15	5.21	2,037	7.07	15	169.75	1	9	3	0
37. Colgate	11	269	140	52.04	13.40	6	2.23	1,876	6.97	11	170.55	0	4	7	0
38. Furman	12	305	175	57.38	11.70	9	2.95	2,048	6.71	9	170.67	1	8	4	0
39. Grambling	11	267	159	59.55	11.93	7	2.62	1,897	7.10	13	172.45	0	3	8	0
40. N.C. A&T	11	219	136	62.10	13.99	4	1.83	1,902	8.68	19	172.91	0	0	11	0
41. Western Caro.	11	248	153	61.69	12.44	14	5.65	1,904	7.68	14	173.09	0	2	9	0
42. Austin Peay	11	289	165	57.09	11.58	6	2.08	1,910	6.61	14	173.64	0	3	8	0
43. Savannah St.	11	226	128	56.64	14.93	6	2.65	1,911	8.46	18	173.73	0	2	9	0
44. Jackson St.	10	285	131	45.96	14.62	14	4.91	1,915	6.72	17	174.09	3	5	5	0
45. New Hampshire	13	353	215	60.91	10.56	11	3.12	2,270	6.43	17	174.62	1	9	4	0
46. Holy Cross	11	297	155	52.19	12.49	11	3.70	1,936	6.52	8	176.00	0	7	4	0
47. Liberty	11	283	163	57.60	11.90	8	2.83	1,940	6.86	9	176.36	0	6	5	0
48. Lehigh	11	289	150	51.90	12.97	13	4.50	1,945	6.73	12	176.82	0	6	5	0
49. Hofstra	11	275	169	61.45	11.53	5	1.82	1,949	7.09	14	177.18	2	2	9	0
49. Stony Brook	11	297	191	64.31	10.20	11	3.70	1,949	6.56	12	177.18	0	5	6	0
51. Alcorn St.	10	282	167	59.22	11.77	10	3.55	1,966	6.97	14	178.73	2	6	4	0
52. Northwestern St.	11	315	164	52.06	12.04	12	3.81	1,974	6.27	17	179.45	0	4	7	0
53. St. Francis (Pa.)	11	251	150	59.76	13.21	7	2.79	1,982	7.90	22	180.18	0	3	8	0
54. Southern Utah	11	278	159	57.19	12.50	7	2.52	1,988	7.15	18	180.73	1	3	8	0
55. Wagner	11	283	167	59.01	11.93	7	2.47	1,993	7.04	15	181.18	1	4	7	0

Rank, Team	G	Att	Comp	Pct	Yds/Cmp	Int	IPct	Yds	Yds/Att	TD	Yds/Gm	CM	W	L	T
56. Western Ill.	11	275	163	59.27	12.39	10	3.64	2,020	7.35	12	183.64	0	5	6	0
57. Eastern Wash.	11	265	162	61.13	12.54	14	5.28	2,032	7.67	16	184.73	0	3	8	0
58. Valparaiso	11	268	152	56.72	13.38	6	2.24	2,033	7.59	18	184.82	1	3	8	0
59. Princeton	10	289	144	49.83	12.86	14	4.84	1,852	6.41	9	185.20	0	9	1	0
60. Weber St.	11	294	162	55.10	12.68	9	3.06	2,054	6.99	16	186.73	0	4	7	0
61. Montana St.	13	388	203	52.32	11.96	14	3.61	2,428	6.26	15	186.77	2	8	5	0
62. Morgan St.	11	280	159	56.79	12.93	8	2.86	2,056	7.34	17	186.91	0	5	6	0
62. Tennessee St.	11	307	174	56.68	11.82	13	4.23	2,056	6.70	15	186.91	3	6	5	0
64. Ga. Southern	11	272	146	53.68	14.15	14	5.15	2,066	7.60	18	187.82	0	3	8	0
65. Illinois St.	13	361	205	56.79	11.92	17	4.71	2,443	6.77	15	187.92	2	9	4	0
66. Portland St.	11	357	192	53.78	10.88	19	5.32	2,088	5.85	8	189.82	0	7	4	0
67. Youngstown St.	14	390	223	57.18	11.96	15	3.85	2,668	6.84	16	190.57	0	11	3	0
68. Southern Ill.	13	365	213	58.36	11.67	7	1.92	2,486	6.81	11	191.23	1	9	4	0
69. Cornell	10	257	136	52.92	14.19	8	3.11	1,930	7.51	7	193.00	1	5	5	0
70. Stephen F. Austin	11	302	190	62.91	11.21	7	2.32	2,129	7.05	13	193.55	2	4	7	0
71. Towson	11	340	198	58.24	10.81	10	2.94	2,140	6.29	17	194.55	0	7	4	0
72. Drake	11	358	194	54.19	11.09	18	5.03	2,151	6.01	8	195.55	0	9	2	0
73. James Madison	12	332	213	64.16	11.02	6	1.81	2,347	7.07	8	195.58	1	9	3	0
74. Lafayette	12	327	190	58.10	12.36	10	3.06	2,348	7.18	19	195.67	0	6	6	0
75. Missouri St.	11	279	173	62.01	12.50	9	3.23	2,162	7.75	14	196.55	0	2	9	0
76. Dartmouth	10	265	171	64.53	11.54	3	1.13	1,973	7.45	12	197.30	2	2	8	0
77. Marist	11	322	201	62.42	10.81	6	1.86	2,172	6.75	17	197.45	2	4	7	0
78. St. Peter's	10	244	148	60.66	13.38	3	1.23	1,980	8.11	14	198.00	2	2	8	0
79. Southeastern La.	11	292	173	59.25	12.60	7	2.40	2,179	7.46	18	198.09	0	2	9	0
80. Murray St.	11	258	142	55.04	15.38	13	5.04	2,184	8.47	23	198.55	0	1	10	0
81. Sacred Heart	11	291	183	62.89	12.01	9	3.09	2,198	7.55	18	199.82	0	2	9	0
82. Wofford	11	321	190	59.19	11.68	16	4.98	2,220	6.92	12	201.82	1	7	4	0
83. Indiana St.	11	245	156	63.67	14.25	5	2.04	2,223	9.07	16	202.09	0	1	10	0
84. Texas St.	11	305	167	54.75	13.32	10	3.28	2,224	7.29	17	202.18	0	5	6	0
85. Sam Houston St.	11	308	180	58.44	12.36	8	2.60	2,225	7.22	20	202.27	0	6	5	0
86. Delaware	11	291	174	59.79	12.80	11	3.78	2,228	7.66	16	202.55	0	5	6	0
86. Texas Southern	11	305	167	54.75	13.34	17	5.57	2,228	7.30	17	202.55	0	3	8	0
88. Ark.-Pine Bluff	12	345	189	54.78	12.91	13	3.77	2,440	7.07	19	203.33	2	8	4	0
89. Fordham	11	286	174	60.84	12.88	15	5.24	2,241	7.84	22	203.73	0	3	8	0
90. UNI	11	304	177	58.22	12.67	15	4.93	2,242	7.38	14	203.82	0	7	4	0
91. Gardner-Webb	11	301	192	63.79	11.88	7	2.33	2,281	7.58	15	207.36	1	6	5	0
92. William & Mary	11	275	175	63.64	13.05	8	2.91	2,284	8.31	16	207.64	1	3	8	0
93. Southeast Mo. St.	11	341	192	56.30	11.92	12	3.52	2,288	6.71	15	208.00	0	4	7	0
94. Georgetown	11	266	165	62.03	13.90	6	2.26	2,293	8.62	11	208.45	0	2	9	0
95. Central Conn. St.	11	363	203	55.92	11.34	10	2.75	2,302	6.34	18	209.27	1	8	3	0
96. Northeastern	11	307	206	67.10	11.18	6	1.95	2,303	7.50	19	209.36	0	5	6	0
97. Eastern Ill.	13	412	251	60.92	10.91	17	4.13	2,738	6.65	14	210.62	0	8	5	0
98. Elon	11	313	191	61.02	12.17	17	5.43	2,325	7.43	9	211.36	2	5	6	0
99. Citadel	11	303	178	58.75	13.10	5	1.65	2,332	7.70	17	212.00	0	5	6	0
100. Brown	10	289	188	65.05	11.34	7	2.42	2,131	7.37	15	213.10	0	3	7	0
101. Chattanooga	11	289	174	60.21	13.57	11	3.81	2,361	8.17	14	214.64	1	3	8	0
102. Bucknell	11	327	186	56.88	12.77	10	3.06	2,375	7.26	16	215.91	0	6	5	0
103. Dayton	10	286	167	58.39	13.02	14	4.90	2,174	7.60	21	217.40	2	4	6	0
104. Davidson	10	314	174	55.41	12.83	10	3.18	2,232	7.11	12	223.20	1	6	4	0
105. VMI	11	286	190	66.43	12.96	10	3.50	2,463	8.61	18	223.91	0	1	10	0
106. Penn	10	338	181	53.55	12.41	11	3.25	2,247	6.65	13	224.70	1	5	5	0
107. Charleston So.	11	330	207	62.73	12.06	18	5.45	2,496	7.56	12	226.91	0	9	2	0
108. Harvard	10	343	185	53.94	12.32	12	3.50	2,280	6.65	9	228.00	0	7	3	0
109. Sacramento St.	11	337	190	56.38	13.48	15	4.45	2,562	7.60	19	232.91	0	4	7	0
110. Yale	10	307	191	62.21	12.23	14	4.56	2,335	7.61	14	233.50	2	8	2	0
111. Jacksonville	10	335	197	58.81	11.89	5	1.49	2,342	6.99	21	234.20	0	4	6	0
112. Morehead St.	11	315	158	50.16	16.63	7	2.22	2,627	8.34	25	238.82	1	2	9	0
113. Butler	11	327	195	59.63	13.66	10	3.06	2,664	8.15	24	242.18	1	3	8	0
114. Northern Ariz.	11	327	171	52.29	16.22	9	2.75	2,774	8.48	25	252.18	2	6	5	0
115. Villanova	11	363	231	63.64	12.29	4	1.10	2,840	7.82	19	258.18	0	6	5	0
116. Idaho St.	11	365	221	60.55	12.90	7	1.92	2,851	7.81	20	259.18	0	2	9	0

Pass Efficiency Defense

Rank, Team	G	Att	Comp	Pct	Int	IPct	Yds	Yds/Att	TD	TD Pct	Rating	W	L	T
1. Robert Morris	11	267	121	45.32	13	4.87	1,414	5.30	7	2.62	88.70	7	4	0
2. Tenn.-Martin	12	329	157	47.72	13	3.95	1,711	5.20	8	2.43	91.51	9	3	0
3. Monmouth	12	345	169	48.99	16	4.64	1,946	5.64	8	2.32	94.76	10	2	0
4. San Diego	12	340	166	48.82	16	4.71	1,942	5.71	10	2.94	97.07	11	1	0
5. Hampton	12	313	151	48.24	16	5.11	1,631	5.21	15	4.79	97.56	10	2	0
6. Portland St.	11	357	192	53.78	19	5.32	2,088	5.85	8	2.24	99.68	7	4	0
7. Montana	14	394	208	52.79	19	4.82	2,234	5.67	12	3.05	100.83	12	2	0
8. Cal Poly	11	261	125	47.89	12	4.60	1,463	5.61	12	4.60	100.96	7	4	0
9. Albany (N.Y.)	11	298	158	53.02	12	4.03	1,657	5.56	9	3.02	101.62	7	4	0
10. Drake	11	358	194	54.19	18	5.03	2,151	6.01	8	2.23	101.99	9	2	0
11. Iona	10	303	161	53.14	14	4.62	1,652	5.45	12	3.96	102.73	3	7	0
12. Jacksonville St.	11	290	141	48.62	11	3.79	1,709	5.89	11	3.79	103.03	6	5	0
13. Duquesne	10	266	136	51.13	12	4.51	1,514	5.69	11	4.14	103.53	7	3	0
14. Princeton	10	289	144	49.83	14	4.84	1,852	6.41	9	3.11	104.22	9	1	0
15. La Salle	10	234	101	43.16	5	2.14	1,410	6.03	11	4.70	105.05	3	7	0
16. Appalachian St.	15	423	216	51.06	16	3.78	2,529	5.98	15	3.55	105.46	14	1	0
17. Florida A&M	11	253	121	47.83	10	3.95	1,555	6.15	11	4.35	105.87	7	4	0
18. Mississippi Val.	11	268	123	45.90	10	3.73	1,686	6.29	12	4.48	106.06	6	5	0

Rank, Team	G	Att	Comp	Pct	Int	IPct	Yds	Yds/Att	TD	TD Pct	Rating	W	L	T
19. Coastal Caro.	12	277	146	52.71	19	6.86	1,836	6.63	11	3.97	107.76	9	3	0
20. Massachusetts	15	426	246	57.75	11	2.58	2,494	5.85	8	1.88	107.91	13	2	0
21. Howard	11	262	138	52.67	9	3.44	1,585	6.05	9	3.44	107.98	5	6	0
22. Holy Cross	11	297	155	52.19	11	3.70	1,936	6.52	8	2.69	108.44	7	4	0
23. Western Ky.	11	273	144	52.75	6	2.20	1,685	6.17	7	2.56	108.61	6	5	0
24. Southern U.	11	249	130	52.21	14	5.62	1,537	6.17	12	4.82	108.71	5	6	0
25. Columbia	10	246	146	59.35	15	6.10	1,497	6.09	8	3.25	108.95	5	5	0
26. Montana St.	13	388	203	52.32	14	3.61	2,428	6.26	15	3.87	110.41	8	5	0
27. Maine	11	302	170	56.29	9	2.98	1,826	6.05	9	2.98	110.96	6	5	0
28. Harvard	10	343	185	53.94	12	3.50	2,280	6.65	9	2.62	111.40	7	3	0
29. Delaware St.	11	277	153	55.23	10	3.61	1,767	6.38	9	3.25	112.29	8	3	0
30. Jackson St.	10	285	131	45.96	14	4.91	1,915	6.72	17	5.96	112.30	5	5	0
31. Alabama A&M	12	288	133	46.18	15	5.21	2,037	7.07	15	5.21	112.38	9	3	0
32. Lehigh	11	289	150	51.90	13	4.50	1,945	6.73	12	4.15	113.14	6	5	0
33. Northwestern St.	11	315	164	52.06	12	3.81	1,974	6.27	17	5.40	114.93	4	7	0
34. Penn	10	338	181	53.55	11	3.25	2,247	6.65	13	3.85	115.63	5	5	0
35. Nicholls St.	11	272	153	56.25	8	2.94	1,638	6.02	13	4.78	116.78	4	7	0
36. Richmond	11	261	156	59.77	12	4.60	1,681	6.44	10	3.83	117.35	6	5	0
37. Furman	12	305	175	57.38	9	2.95	2,048	6.71	9	2.95	117.64	8	4	0
38. Illinois St.	13	361	205	56.79	17	4.71	2,443	6.77	15	4.16	117.94	9	4	0
39. Cornell	10	257	136	52.92	8	3.11	1,930	7.51	7	2.72	118.74	5	5	0
40. Tennessee Tech	11	278	145	52.16	7	2.52	1,796	6.46	15	5.40	119.24	4	7	0
41. Colgate	11	269	140	52.04	6	2.23	1,876	6.97	11	4.09	119.61	4	7	0
42. Wofford	11	321	190	59.19	16	4.98	2,220	6.92	12	3.74	119.66	7	4	0
43. Eastern Ill.	13	412	251	60.92	17	4.13	2,738	6.65	14	3.40	119.68	8	5	0
44. Central Conn. St.	11	363	203	55.92	10	2.75	2,302	6.34	18	4.96	120.02	8	3	0
44. Liberty	11	283	163	57.60	8	2.83	1,940	6.86	9	3.18	120.02	6	5	0
46. Southeast Mo. St.	11	341	192	56.30	12	3.52	2,288	6.71	15	4.40	120.14	4	7	0
47. Youngstown St.	14	390	223	57.18	15	3.85	2,668	6.84	16	4.10	120.51	11	3	0
48. South Carolina St.	11	263	145	55.13	13	4.94	1,848	7.03	13	4.94	120.55	7	4	0
49. Tennessee St.	11	307	174	56.68	13	4.23	2,056	6.70	15	4.89	120.61	6	5	0
50. Prairie View	10	213	116	54.46	9	4.23	1,473	6.92	11	5.16	121.18	3	7	0
51. Davidson	10	314	174	55.41	10	3.18	2,232	7.11	12	3.82	121.35	6	4	0
52. Bethune-Cookman	11	267	139	52.06	14	5.24	1,751	6.56	20	7.49	121.42	5	6	0
53. Towson	11	340	198	58.24	10	2.94	2,140	6.29	17	5.00	121.69	7	4	0
54. Southern Ill.	13	365	213	58.36	7	1.92	2,486	6.81	11	3.01	121.72	9	4	0
55. Rhode Island	11	261	143	54.79	11	4.21	1,753	6.72	15	5.75	121.75	4	7	0
56. Elon	11	313	191	61.02	17	5.43	2,325	7.43	9	2.88	122.02	5	6	0
57. Eastern Ky.	11	266	150	56.39	11	4.14	1,808	6.80	14	5.26	122.59	6	5	0
58. McNeese St.	12	304	175	57.57	13	4.28	1,998	6.57	17	5.59	122.71	7	5	0
59. Texas Southern	11	305	167	54.75	17	5.57	2,228	7.30	17	5.57	123.41	3	8	0
60. Austin Peay	11	289	165	57.09	6	2.08	1,910	6.61	14	4.84	124.45	3	8	0
61. New Hampshire	13	353	215	60.91	11	3.12	2,270	6.43	17	4.82	124.58	9	4	0
62. Ark.-Pine Bluff	12	345	189	54.78	13	3.77	2,440	7.07	19	5.51	124.85	8	4	0
63. Alabama St.	11	251	135	53.78	10	3.98	1,704	6.79	17	6.77	125.21	5	6	0
64. Stony Brook	11	297	191	64.31	11	3.70	1,949	6.56	12	4.04	125.35	5	6	0
65. UNI	11	304	177	58.22	15	4.93	2,242	7.38	14	4.61	125.48	7	4	0
66. Weber St.	11	294	162	55.10	9	3.06	2,054	6.99	16	5.44	125.62	4	7	0
67. Alcorn St.	10	282	167	59.22	10	3.55	1,966	6.97	14	4.96	127.05	6	4	0
68. Charleston So.	11	330	207	62.73	18	5.45	2,496	7.56	12	3.64	127.33	9	2	0
69. Texas St.	11	305	167	54.75	10	3.28	2,224	7.29	17	5.57	127.89	5	6	0
70. James Madison	12	332	213	64.16	6	1.81	2,347	7.07	8	2.41	127.92	9	3	0
71. Bucknell	11	327	186	56.88	10	3.06	2,375	7.26	16	4.89	127.94	6	5	0
72. Western Ill.	11	275	163	59.27	10	3.64	2,020	7.35	12	4.36	128.13	5	6	0
73. Samford	11	245	148	60.41	9	3.67	1,698	6.93	13	5.31	128.78	3	8	0
74. Ga. Southern	11	272	146	53.68	14	5.15	2,066	7.60	18	6.62	129.05	3	8	0
75. Sacramento St.	11	337	190	56.38	15	4.45	2,562	7.60	19	5.64	129.96	4	7	0
76. Grambling	11	267	159	59.55	7	2.62	1,897	7.10	13	4.87	130.10	3	8	0
77. Wagner	11	283	167	59.01	7	2.47	1,993	7.04	15	5.30	130.70	4	7	0
78. Lafayette	12	327	190	58.10	10	3.06	2,348	7.18	19	5.81	131.47	6	6	0
79. Stephen F. Austin	11	302	190	62.91	7	2.32	2,129	7.05	13	4.30	131.69	4	7	0
80. Yale	10	307	191	62.21	14	4.56	2,335	7.61	14	4.56	132.02	8	2	0
81. Marist	11	322	201	62.42	6	1.86	2,172	6.75	17	5.28	132.76	4	7	0
82. Morgan St.	11	280	159	56.79	8	2.86	2,056	7.34	17	6.07	132.80	5	6	0
83. Western Caro.	11	248	153	61.69	14	5.65	1,904	7.68	14	5.65	133.53	2	9	0
84. Southern Utah	11	278	159	57.19	7	2.52	1,988	7.15	18	6.47	133.60	3	8	0
85. Hofstra	11	275	169	61.45	5	1.82	1,949	7.09	14	5.09	134.20	2	9	0
86. Delaware	11	291	174	59.79	11	3.78	2,228	7.66	16	5.50	134.70	5	6	0
87. Eastern Wash.	11	265	162	61.13	14	5.28	2,032	7.67	16	6.04	134.87	3	8	0
88. Jacksonville	10	335	197	58.81	5	1.49	2,342	6.99	21	6.27	135.23	4	6	0
89. Sam Houston St.	11	308	180	58.44	8	2.60	2,225	7.22	20	6.49	135.32	6	5	0
90. Dayton	10	286	167	58.39	14	4.90	2,174	7.60	21	7.34	136.69	4	6	0
91. Missouri St.	11	279	173	62.01	9	3.23	2,162	7.75	14	5.02	137.20	2	9	0
91. Chattanooga	11	289	174	60.21	11	3.81	2,361	8.17	14	4.84	137.20	3	8	0
93. Southeastern La.	11	292	173	59.25	7	2.40	2,179	7.46	18	6.16	137.43	2	9	0
94. Valparaiso	11	268	152	56.72	6	2.24	2,033	7.59	18	6.72	138.11	3	8	0
95. Citadel	11	303	178	58.75	5	1.65	2,332	7.70	17	5.61	138.56	5	6	0
96. Gardner-Webb	11	301	192	63.79	7	2.33	2,281	7.58	15	4.98	139.25	6	5	0
97. Brown	10	289	188	65.05	7	2.42	2,131	7.37	15	5.19	139.32	3	7	0
98. Dartmouth	10	265	171	64.53	3	1.13	1,973	7.45	12	4.53	139.72	2	8	0
99. Idaho St.	11	365	221	60.55	7	1.92	2,851	7.81	20	5.48	140.36	2	9	0
100. Sacred Heart	11	291	183	62.89	9	3.09	2,198	7.55	18	6.19	140.57	2	9	0

Rank, Team	G	Att	Comp	Pct	Int	IPct	Yds	Yds/Att	TD	TD Pct	Rating	W	L	T
101. Fordham	11	286	174	60.84	15	5.24	2,241	7.84	22	7.69	141.51	3	8	0
102. Morehead St.	11	315	158	50.16	7	2.22	2,627	8.34	25	7.94	142.00	2	9	0
103. Northern Ariz.	11	327	171	52.29	9	2.75	2,774	8.48	25	7.65	143.28	6	5	0
104. Georgetown	11	266	165	62.03	6	2.26	2,293	8.62	11	4.14	143.55	2	9	0
105. Villanova	11	363	231	63.64	4	1.10	2,840	7.82	19	5.23	144.39	6	5	0
106. St. Peter's	10	244	148	60.66	3	1.23	1,980	8.11	14	5.74	145.34	2	8	0
107. Murray St.	11	258	142	55.04	13	5.04	2,184	8.47	23	8.91	145.45	1	10	0
108. Norfolk St.	11	214	112	52.34	5	2.34	1,797	8.40	18	8.41	145.92	4	7	0
109. Butler	11	327	195	59.63	10	3.06	2,664	8.15	24	7.34	146.14	3	8	0
110. Northeastern	11	307	206	67.10	6	1.95	2,303	7.50	19	6.19	146.63	5	6	0
111. William & Mary	11	275	175	63.64	8	2.91	2,284	8.31	16	5.82	146.75	3	8	0
112. Savannah St.	11	226	128	56.64	6	2.65	1,911	8.46	18	7.96	148.60	2	9	0
113. St. Francis (Pa.)	11	251	150	59.76	7	2.79	1,982	7.90	22	8.76	149.48	3	8	0
114. VMI	11	286	190	66.43	10	3.50	2,463	8.61	18	6.29	152.52	1	10	0
115. Indiana St.	11	245	156	63.67	5	2.04	2,223	9.07	16	6.53	157.39	1	10	0
116. N.C. A&T	11	219	136	62.10	4	1.83	1,902	8.68	19	8.68	160.03	0	11	0

Total Defense

Rank, Team	G	Plays	Yds	Avg	TD	Yds/Gm	W	L	T
1. Robert Morris	11	650	2,512	3.86	19	228.36	7	4	0
2. Maine	11	637	2,529	3.97	18	229.91	6	5	0
3. Iona	10	574	2,321	4.04	24	232.10	3	7	0
4. Albany (N.Y.)	11	712	2,649	3.72	18	240.82	7	4	0
5. Cal Poly	11	646	2,731	4.23	20	248.27	7	4	0
6. Tenn.-Martin	12	738	3,066	4.15	22	255.50	9	3	0
7. Monmouth	12	699	3,154	4.51	21	262.83	10	2	0
8. Prairie View	10	555	2,660	4.79	25	266.00	3	7	0
9. Montana	14	863	3,729	4.32	25	266.36	12	2	0
10. La Salle	10	547	2,670	4.88	33	267.00	3	7	0
11. Richmond	11	660	2,956	4.48	26	268.73	6	5	0
12. San Diego	12	710	3,229	4.55	22	269.08	11	1	0
13. Mississippi Val.	11	624	2,960	4.74	34	269.09	6	5	0
14. Jacksonville St.	11	668	2,972	4.45	25	270.18	6	5	0
15. Hampton	12	755	3,258	4.32	23	271.50	10	2	0
16. Jackson St.	10	617	3,018	4.89	36	274.36	5	5	0
17. Appalachian St.	15	953	4,154	4.36	27	276.93	14	1	0
18. Duquesne	10	599	2,776	4.63	20	277.60	7	3	0
19. Alabama St.	11	592	3,056	5.16	31	277.82	5	6	0
20. Massachusetts	15	918	4,200	4.58	26	280.00	13	2	0
21. James Madison	12	749	3,365	4.49	25	280.42	9	3	0
22. Howard	11	678	3,103	4.58	31	282.09	5	6	0
23. Alabama A&M	12	672	3,403	5.06	30	283.58	9	3	0
24. South Carolina St.	11	657	3,191	4.86	25	290.09	7	4	0
25. Harvard	10	672	2,945	4.38	24	294.50	7	3	0
26. Furman	12	701	3,551	5.07	32	295.92	8	4	0
27. Southern U.	11	702	3,263	4.65	37	296.64	5	6	0
28. Bethune-Cookman	11	659	3,267	4.96	34	297.00	5	6	0
29. Weber St.	11	697	3,292	4.72	34	299.27	4	7	0
30. Northwestern St.	11	628	3,293	5.24	29	299.36	4	7	0
31. Nicholls St.	11	684	3,312	4.84	27	301.09	4	7	0
32. Delaware St.	11	704	3,316	4.71	25	301.45	8	3	0
33. Portland St.	11	722	3,320	4.60	24	301.82	7	4	0
34. Columbia	10	645	3,036	4.71	21	303.60	5	5	0
35. Morgan St.	11	659	3,343	5.07	30	303.91	5	6	0
36. Liberty	11	664	3,366	5.07	22	306.00	6	5	0
37. Montana St.	13	872	3,988	4.57	34	306.77	8	5	0
38. Eastern Ky.	11	657	3,398	5.17	30	308.91	6	5	0
39. Princeton	10	611	3,101	5.08	24	310.10	9	1	0
40. Hofstra	11	682	3,425	5.02	32	311.36	2	9	0
41. Colgate	11	700	3,550	5.07	30	322.73	4	7	0
42. Tennessee St.	11	690	3,561	5.16	31	323.73	6	5	0
43. Western Ky.	11	672	3,563	5.30	34	323.91	6	5	0
44. Samford	11	678	3,574	5.27	32	324.91	3	8	0
45. Southern Ill.	13	855	4,228	4.95	32	325.23	9	4	0
46. Alcorn St.	10	721	3,580	4.97	35	325.45	6	4	0
47. Wagner	11	699	3,585	5.13	31	325.91	4	7	0
48. Lehigh	11	709	3,598	5.07	29	327.09	6	5	0
49. Cornell	10	609	3,280	5.39	29	328.00	5	5	0
50. Drake	11	702	3,619	5.16	22	329.00	9	2	0
51. New Hampshire	13	834	4,325	5.19	42	332.69	9	4	0
52. Eastern Ill.	13	818	4,339	5.30	37	333.77	8	5	0
53. Stephen F. Austin	11	670	3,684	5.50	28	334.91	4	7	0
54. Lafayette	12	762	4,019	5.27	36	334.92	6	6	0
55. Holy Cross	11	692	3,689	5.33	31	335.36	7	4	0
56. Charleston So.	11	723	3,693	5.11	26	335.73	9	2	0
57. Tennessee Tech	11	669	3,700	5.53	40	336.36	4	7	0
58. Illinois St.	13	813	4,374	5.38	32	336.46	9	4	0
59. Central Conn. St.	11	749	3,710	4.95	25	337.27	8	3	0
60. McNeese St.	12	779	4,052	5.20	35	337.67	7	5	0
61. Brown	10	641	3,384	5.28	31	338.40	3	7	0
62. Ga. Southern	11	679	3,739	5.51	33	339.91	3	8	0
63. Towson	11	679	3,753	5.53	30	341.18	7	4	0
64. Grambling	11	691	3,760	5.44	39	341.82	3	8	0
65. UNI	11	684	3,761	5.50	33	341.91	7	4	0
66. Wofford	11	704	3,762	5.34	27	342.00	7	4	0
67. Stony Brook	11	702	3,782	5.39	38	343.82	5	6	0
68. Marist	11	706	3,814	5.40	40	346.73	4	7	0
69. Valparaiso	11	674	3,825	5.68	51	347.73	3	8	0
70. Coastal Caro.	12	767	4,190	5.46	39	349.17	9	3	0
71. Norfolk St.	11	656	3,854	5.88	37	350.36	4	7	0
72. Fordham	11	723	3,870	5.35	36	351.82	3	8	0
73. Southern Utah	11	710	3,891	5.48	35	353.73	3	8	0
74. Sam Houston St.	11	762	3,895	5.11	37	354.09	6	5	0
75. Sacramento St.	11	725	3,904	5.38	36	354.91	4	7	0
76. Western Ill.	11	694	3,915	5.64	36	355.91	5	6	0
77. Northeastern	11	701	3,923	5.60	37	356.64	5	6	0
78. Florida A&M	11	674	3,929	5.83	45	357.18	7	4	0
78. Texas St.	11	693	3,929	5.67	32	357.18	5	6	0
80. Davidson	10	659	3,577	5.43	30	357.70	6	4	0
81. Austin Peay	11	735	3,946	5.37	35	358.73	3	8	0
82. Citadel	11	658	3,957	6.01	43	359.73	5	6	0
83. Youngstown St.	14	888	5,046	5.68	42	360.43	11	3	0
84. Texas Southern	11	719	3,967	5.52	44	360.64	3	8	0
85. Yale	10	647	3,607	5.57	27	360.70	8	2	0
86. Penn	10	719	3,625	5.04	23	362.50	5	5	0
87. Sacred Heart	11	732	4,035	5.51	40	366.82	2	9	0
88. Ark.-Pine Bluff	12	773	4,413	5.71	39	367.75	8	4	0
89. Georgetown	11	710	4,053	5.71	37	368.45	2	9	0
89. Elon	11	758	4,053	5.35	31	368.45	5	6	0
91. Dartmouth	10	652	3,698	5.67	32	369.80	2	8	0
92. Eastern Wash.	11	685	4,076	5.95	38	370.55	3	8	0
93. Dayton	10	641	3,724	5.81	36	372.40	4	6	0
94. Butler	11	707	4,104	5.80	45	373.09	3	8	0
95. Rhode Island	11	703	4,129	5.87	44	375.36	4	7	0
96. Villanova	11	735	4,131	5.62	35	375.55	6	5	0
97. Southeast Mo. St.	11	740	4,138	5.59	40	376.18	4	7	0
98. Savannah St.	11	679	4,152	6.11	53	377.45	2	9	0
99. Northern Ariz.	11	682	4,167	6.11	38	378.82	6	5	0
100. Chattanooga	11	698	4,170	5.97	40	379.09	3	8	0
101. Western Caro.	11	696	4,196	6.03	42	381.45	2	9	0
102. Morehead St.	11	671	4,218	6.29	43	383.45	2	9	0
103. Idaho St.	11	742	4,224	5.69	41	384.00	2	9	0
104. Missouri St.	11	736	4,258	5.79	40	387.09	2	9	0
105. St. Francis (Pa.)	11	629	4,301	6.84	54	391.00	3	8	0
105. Southeastern La.	11	715	4,301	6.02	46	391.00	2	9	0
107. William & Mary	11	721	4,343	6.02	35	394.82	3	8	0
108. Delaware	11	700	4,375	6.25	37	397.73	5	6	0
109. Jacksonville	10	667	3,986	5.98	43	398.60	4	6	0
110. Bucknell	11	727	4,403	6.06	35	400.27	6	5	0
111. St. Peter's	10	650	4,004	6.16	47	400.40	2	8	0
112. Gardner-Webb	11	746	4,537	6.08	42	412.45	6	5	0
113. Murray St.	11	738	4,734	6.41	51	430.36	1	10	0
114. N.C. A&T	11	682	4,793	7.03	66	435.73	0	11	0
115. VMI	11	683	4,827	7.07	58	438.82	1	10	0
116. Indiana St.	11	794	5,538	6.97	63	503.45	1	10	0

Scoring Defense

Rank, Team	G	TD	Kxp	Oxp	Dkxp	Doxp	FG	Saf	Pts	Pts/Gm	W	L	T
1. Monmouth	12	21	9	1	0	0	5	0	152	12.7	10	2	0
2. San Diego	12	22	15	1	0	0	2	0	155	12.9	11	1	0
3. Albany (N.Y.)	11	18	11	0	0	0	8	0	143	13.0	7	4	0
4. Maine	11	18	13	0	0	0	7	1	144	13.1	6	5	0
5. Massachusetts	15	26	23	0	0	0	7	0	200	13.3	13	2	0
6. Hampton	12	23	18	0	0	0	6	0	174	14.5	10	2	0
7. Robert Morris	11	19	15	1	0	0	10	0	161	14.6	7	4	0
8. Cal Poly	11	20	17	2	0	0	7	0	162	14.7	7	4	0
9. Appalachian St.	15	27	25	1	0	0	10	2	223	14.9	14	1	0
10. Drake	11	22	19	0	0	0	5	1	168	15.3	9	2	0
11. Duquesne	10	20	20	0	0	0	5	0	155	15.5	7	3	0
12. Liberty	11	22	19	0	0	0	7	0	172	15.6	6	5	0
13. Tenn.-Martin	12	22	19	1	0	0	11	1	188	15.7	9	3	0
14. Montana	14	25	22	2	0	0	15	2	225	16.1	12	2	0
15. Columbia	10	21	20	0	0	0	5	1	163	16.3	5	5	0
16. James Madison	12	25	22	1	0	0	9	0	201	16.8	9	3	0
17. Iona	10	24	19	0	0	0	3	1	174	17.4	3	7	0
18. Central Conn. St.	11	25	15	1	0	0	7	2	192	17.5	8	3	0
18. Delaware St.	11	25	21	0	0	0	7	0	192	17.5	8	3	0
20. Jacksonville St.	11	25	25	0	0	0	6	0	193	17.5	6	5	0
21. Princeton	10	24	20	0	0	0	5	0	179	17.9	9	1	0
22. Charleston So.	11	26	20	1	0	0	7	0	199	18.1	9	2	0
22. Richmond	11	26	25	0	0	0	6	0	199	18.1	6	5	0
24. Portland St.	11	24	23	0	0	0	11	1	202	18.4	7	4	0
25. South Carolina St.	11	25	20	0	0	0	10	2	204	18.5	7	4	0
26. Alabama A&M	12	30	20	2	0	0	8	0	228	19.0	9	3	0
27. Penn	10	23	21	1	0	0	10	0	191	19.1	5	5	0
28. Harvard	10	24	20	1	0	0	8	1	192	19.2	7	3	0
29. Wofford	11	27	25	1	0	0	8	0	213	19.4	7	4	0
30. Southern Ill.	13	32	26	1	0	0	12	0	256	19.7	9	4	0
31. Prairie View	10	25	19	2	0	0	9	0	200	20.0	3	7	0
32. Illinois St.	13	32	27	2	0	0	13	0	262	20.2	9	4	0
33. Lehigh	11	29	25	0	0	0	7	1	222	20.2	6	5	0
34. Alabama St.	11	31	27	0	1	0	4	0	227	20.6	5	6	0
35. Nicholls St.	11	27	24	0	0	0	14	0	228	20.7	4	7	0
36. Yale	10	27	18	2	0	0	8	0	208	20.8	8	2	0
37. Stephen F. Austin	11	28	23	3	0	0	11	1	232	21.1	4	7	0
38. Eastern Ill.	13	37	30	1	0	0	7	0	275	21.2	8	5	0
39. Wagner	11	31	25	2	0	0	6	0	233	21.2	4	7	0
40. Furman	12	32	30	1	1	0	9	1	255	21.3	8	4	0
41. Holy Cross	11	31	27	2	0	0	6	0	235	21.4	7	4	0
42. Howard	11	31	24	0	0	0	9	0	237	21.5	5	6	0
42. Towson	11	30	28	0	0	0	9	1	237	21.5	7	4	0
44. Cornell	10	29	24	2	0	0	5	0	217	21.7	5	5	0
45. Eastern Ky.	11	30	28	0	0	0	10	1	240	21.8	6	5	0
46. Montana St.	13	34	29	2	0	0	15	2	286	22.0	8	5	0
46. Morgan St.	11	30	26	0	0	0	10	3	242	22.0	5	6	0
46. Tennessee St.	11	31	20	3	0	0	10	0	242	22.0	6	5	0
49. Colgate	11	30	30	0	0	0	11	0	243	22.1	4	7	0
50. Mississippi Val.	11	34	22	2	0	0	5	0	245	22.3	6	5	0
51. Hofstra	11	32	23	2	0	0	9	0	246	22.4	2	9	0
52. Lafayette	12	36	33	0	0	0	7	0	270	22.5	6	6	0
53. Texas St.	11	32	31	0	0	0	7	2	248	22.5	5	6	0
54. McNeese St.	12	35	26	1	0	0	11	0	271	22.6	7	5	0
55. Bethune-Cookman	11	34	25	1	0	0	6	0	249	22.6	5	6	0
55. Northwestern St.	11	29	25	1	0	0	16	0	249	22.6	4	7	0
55. UNI	11	33	31	0	1	0	6	0	249	22.6	7	4	0
58. Samford	11	32	29	0	0	0	9	1	250	22.7	3	8	0
59. Davidson	10	30	23	2	0	0	7	0	228	22.8	6	4	0
60. Youngstown St.	14	42	41	0	0	0	10	0	323	23.1	11	3	0
61. Elon	11	31	27	2	0	0	13	0	256	23.3	5	6	0
62. Alcorn St.	10	35	27	3	0	0	5	1	260	23.6	6	4	0
62. Ga. Southern	11	33	30	1	0	0	10	0	260	23.6	3	8	0
64. Western Ky.	11	34	32	0	0	0	9	0	263	23.9	6	5	0
65. New Hampshire	13	42	38	2	0	0	6	0	312	24.0	9	4	0
66. Weber St.	11	34	29	1	0	0	10	0	265	24.1	4	7	0
67. Brown	10	31	28	0	0	0	9	0	241	24.1	3	7	0
68. Bucknell	11	35	32	0	0	0	8	1	268	24.4	6	5	0
69. Austin Peay	11	35	34	0	0	0	9	0	271	24.6	3	8	0
70. Coastal Caro.	12	39	33	0	0	0	10	0	297	24.8	9	3	0
71. Jackson St.	10	36	27	4	0	0	6	2	273	24.8	5	5	0
71. Villanova	11	35	31	0	0	0	10	1	273	24.8	6	5	0
73. Southern Utah	11	35	31	1	0	0	11	0	276	25.1	3	8	0
74. Western Ill.	11	36	32	1	0	0	9	0	277	25.2	5	6	0
75. Stony Brook	11	38	35	0	0	0	5	0	278	25.3	5	6	0
76. Dartmouth	10	32	26	3	0	0	10	0	254	25.4	2	8	0
77. Ark.-Pine Bluff	12	39	27	4	0	0	12	0	305	25.4	8	4	0
78. Southern U.	11	37	31	0	0	0	9	0	280	25.5	5	6	0
79. La Salle	10	33	29	1	0	0	8	1	255	25.5	3	7	0
80. Grambling	11	39	29	0	0	0	6	0	281	25.5	3	8	0

Rank, Team	G	TD	Kxp	Oxp	Dkxp	Doxp	FG	Saf	Pts	Pts/Gm	W	L	T
81. William & Mary	11	35	32	1	0	0	13	0	283	25.7	3	8	0
82. Dayton	10	36	31	2	0	0	2	1	259	25.9	4	6	0
83. Delaware	11	37	36	0	0	0	9	0	285	25.9	5	6	0
83. Sam Houston St.	11	37	36	0	0	0	9	0	285	25.9	6	5	0
85. Georgetown	11	37	35	0	0	0	10	0	287	26.1	2	9	0
86. Sacramento St.	11	36	34	1	0	0	12	0	288	26.2	4	7	0
87. Fordham	11	36	31	0	0	0	14	0	289	26.3	3	8	0
87. Norfolk St.	11	37	28	1	0	0	11	2	289	26.3	4	7	0
89. Northeastern	11	37	37	0	0	0	9	2	290	26.4	5	6	0
90. Marist	11	40	26	2	0	0	7	0	291	26.5	4	7	0
91. Eastern Wash.	11	38	33	1	0	0	11	0	296	26.9	3	8	0
91. Tennessee Tech	11	40	36	1	0	0	6	0	296	26.9	4	7	0
91. Northern Ariz.	11	38	34	2	0	0	10	0	296	26.9	6	5	0
94. Sacred Heart	11	40	37	0	1	0	7	0	300	27.3	2	9	0
95. Chattanooga	11	40	33	1	0	0	9	1	304	27.6	3	8	0
96. Southeast Mo. St.	11	40	37	0	0	0	10	0	307	27.9	4	7	0
97. Missouri St.	11	40	38	0	0	0	10	0	308	28.0	2	9	0
98. Citadel	11	43	42	0	0	0	4	1	314	28.5	5	6	0
99. Western Caro.	11	42	38	1	0	0	8	0	316	28.7	2	9	0
100. Morehead St.	11	43	33	2	0	0	9	0	322	29.3	2	9	0
101. Florida A&M	11	45	39	1	0	0	4	2	327	29.7	7	4	0
102. Texas Southern	11	44	38	1	0	0	7	2	329	29.9	3	8	0
102. Gardner-Webb	11	42	35	2	0	0	12	1	329	29.9	6	5	0
104. Idaho St.	11	41	32	0	0	0	16	2	330	30.0	2	9	0
105. Butler	11	45	40	2	0	0	5	1	331	30.1	3	8	0
106. Rhode Island	11	44	44	0	0	0	8	0	332	30.2	4	7	0
107. Southeastern La.	11	46	45	0	0	0	10	0	351	31.9	2	9	0
108. Jacksonville	10	43	41	0	0	0	8	0	323	32.3	4	6	0
109. Valparaiso	11	51	42	1	0	0	8	2	378	34.4	3	8	0
110. Savannah St.	11	53	49	0	0	0	4	0	379	34.5	2	9	0
111. St. Peter's	10	47	42	3	1	0	5	0	347	34.7	2	8	0
112. Murray St.	11	51	45	1	0	0	9	3	386	35.1	1	10	0
113. St. Francis (Pa.)	11	54	49	1	1	0	7	0	398	36.2	3	8	0
114. VMI	11	58	53	0	0	0	10	1	433	39.4	1	10	0
115. N.C. A&T	11	66	59	0	0	0	6	1	475	43.2	0	11	0
116. Indiana St.	11	63	59	0	0	0	18	1	493	44.8	1	10	0

Net Punting

Rank, Team	G	Punts	Yds	Avg	Ret	RetYds	TB	NetAvg	W	L	T
1. Northern Ariz.	11	49	2,109	43.04	15	194	0	39.08	6	5	0
2. Southern U.	11	50	2,230	44.60	27	276	3	37.88	5	6	0
3. Montana	14	67	2,783	41.54	32	173	4	37.76	12	2	0
4. Idaho St.	11	54	2,310	42.78	24	145	7	37.50	2	9	0
5. Sacred Heart	11	57	2,271	39.84	25	123	2	36.98	2	9	0
6. Princeton	10	45	1,828	40.62	18	162	2	36.13	9	1	0
7. Wofford	11	46	1,891	41.11	24	214	1	36.02	7	4	0
8. Brown	10	36	1,458	40.50	16	88	4	35.83	3	7	0
9. Cal Poly	11	58	2,350	40.52	29	277	0	35.74	7	4	0
10. Massachusetts	15	53	2,168	40.91	20	149	7	35.45	13	2	0
11. Morehead St.	11	48	1,965	40.94	17	144	6	35.44	2	9	0
12. Fordham	11	58	2,587	44.60	30	416	6	35.36	3	8	0
13. Southern Ill.	13	45	1,759	39.09	22	128	2	35.36	9	4	0
14. Youngstown St.	14	60	2,222	37.03	21	96	1	35.10	11	3	0
15. Samford	11	61	2,551	41.82	31	314	5	35.03	3	8	0
16. Tennessee Tech	11	64	2,500	39.06	31	183	4	34.95	4	7	0
17. Appalachian St.	15	56	2,075	37.05	18	66	3	34.80	14	1	0
18. Gardner-Webb	11	48	2,078	43.29	23	311	5	34.73	6	5	0
19. Yale	10	40	1,422	35.55	11	37	0	34.63	8	2	0
20. Jacksonville St.	11	59	2,376	40.27	18	278	3	34.54	6	5	0
21. Drake	11	48	1,796	37.42	14	41	5	34.48	9	2	0
22. Elon	11	50	2,030	40.60	26	209	5	34.42	5	6	0
23. Delaware	11	46	1,709	37.15	12	88	2	34.37	5	6	0
24. Southeast Mo. St.	11	71	2,901	40.86	39	343	6	34.34	4	7	0
25. Southeastern La.	11	56	2,165	38.66	23	257	0	34.07	2	9	0
26. Holy Cross	11	44	1,575	35.80	13	36	2	34.07	7	4	0
27. Chattanooga	11	63	2,352	37.33	24	86	6	34.06	3	8	0
28. Eastern Wash.	11	63	2,641	41.92	29	398	5	34.02	3	8	0
29. Portland St.	11	59	2,422	41.05	36	343	4	33.88	7	4	0
30. Sacramento St.	11	65	2,708	41.66	40	454	3	33.75	4	7	0
31. Bucknell	11	57	2,309	40.51	26	246	7	33.74	6	5	0
32. Citadel	11	54	2,083	38.57	33	203	3	33.70	5	6	0
33. Weber St.	11	63	2,537	40.27	31	285	7	33.52	4	7	0
34. Dayton	10	49	1,719	35.08	21	82	0	33.41	4	6	0
35. Ga. Southern	11	62	2,540	40.97	28	255	11	33.31	3	8	0
36. James Madison	12	43	1,588	36.93	17	97	3	33.28	9	3	0
37. Northwestern St.	11	59	2,253	38.19	26	194	5	33.20	4	7	0
38. Alabama St.	11	64	2,505	39.14	29	262	6	33.17	5	6	0
39. Georgetown	11	51	1,888	37.02	25	178	1	33.14	2	9	0
40. Stephen F. Austin	11	52	1,926	37.04	16	205	0	33.10	4	7	0
41. Hampton	12	44	1,671	37.98	14	140	4	32.98	10	2	0
42. Lafayette	12	52	1,933	37.17	21	119	5	32.96	6	6	0
43. Cornell	10	51	1,907	37.39	28	186	2	32.96	5	5	0

Rank, Team	G	Punts	Yds	Avg	Ret	RetYds	TB	NetAvg	W	L	T
44. Duquesne	10	44	1,551	35.25	18	85	1	32.86	7	3	0
45. Columbia	10	55	2,151	39.11	31	248	5	32.78	5	5	0
46. Wagner	11	67	2,565	38.28	23	209	8	32.78	4	7	0
47. Ark.-Pine Bluff	12	57	2,324	40.77	25	338	6	32.74	8	4	0
48. Penn	10	55	1,982	36.04	24	122	3	32.73	5	5	0
49. Illinois St.	13	43	1,711	39.79	14	127	9	32.65	9	4	0
50. Florida A&M	11	45	1,774	39.42	16	226	4	32.62	7	4	0
51. Harvard	10	50	1,838	36.76	16	133	4	32.50	7	3	0
52. Missouri St.	11	57	2,310	40.53	32	383	4	32.40	2	9	0
53. Alcorn St.	10	53	1,988	37.51	19	122	8	32.19	6	4	0
54. Texas Southern	11	56	2,071	36.98	21	196	4	32.05	3	8	0
55. William & Mary	11	49	1,727	35.24	18	97	3	32.04	3	8	0
56. Eastern Ky.	11	50	1,767	35.34	22	134	2	31.86	6	5	0
57. San Diego	12	28	967	34.54	8	38	2	31.75	11	1	0
58. Norfolk St.	11	43	1,574	36.60	25	169	2	31.74	4	7	0
59. McNeese St.	12	53	2,011	37.94	29	289	2	31.74	7	5	0
60. Montana St.	13	75	2,598	34.64	30	200	1	31.71	8	5	0
61. Butler	11	78	2,882	36.95	32	390	1	31.69	3	8	0
62. Prairie View	10	60	2,156	35.93	24	196	3	31.67	3	7	0
63. Hofstra	11	70	2,518	35.97	32	242	3	31.66	2	9	0
64. Dartmouth	10	50	1,744	34.88	20	122	2	31.64	2	8	0
65. Rhode Island	11	49	1,835	37.45	22	285	0	31.63	4	7	0
66. Monmouth	12	50	1,774	35.48	24	196	0	31.56	10	2	0
67. Bethune-Cookman	11	42	1,417	33.74	8	52	2	31.55	5	6	0
68. Davidson	10	45	1,738	38.62	24	281	2	31.49	6	4	0
69. Lehigh	11	41	1,514	36.93	20	203	1	31.49	6	5	0
70. Murray St.	11	64	2,346	36.66	24	231	5	31.48	1	10	0
71. Albany (N.Y.)	11	57	2,129	37.35	16	178	8	31.42	7	4	0
72. Western Caro.	11	58	2,335	40.26	29	396	6	31.36	2	9	0
73. Colgate	11	57	2,283	40.05	28	376	6	31.35	4	7	0
74. Sam Houston St.	11	45	1,693	37.62	17	245	2	31.29	6	5	0
75. Indiana St.	11	55	2,084	37.89	27	315	3	31.07	1	10	0
76. Delaware St.	11	54	1,880	34.81	20	144	3	31.04	8	3	0
77. Alabama A&M	12	50	1,707	34.14	7	38	6	30.98	9	3	0
78. Charleston So.	11	42	1,493	35.55	19	94	5	30.93	9	2	0
79. Eastern Ill.	13	61	2,138	35.05	25	192	3	30.92	8	5	0
80. Grambling	11	38	1,529	40.24	22	327	2	30.58	3	8	0
81. Furman	12	46	1,584	34.43	17	141	2	30.50	8	4	0
82. Western Ill.	11	30	1,132	37.73	10	119	5	30.43	5	6	0
83. Coastal Caro.	12	32	1,058	33.06	11	85	0	30.41	9	3	0
84. New Hampshire	13	57	1,926	33.79	13	139	3	30.30	9	4	0
85. UNI	11	34	1,329	39.09	13	201	5	30.24	7	4	0
86. Southern Utah	11	54	1,917	35.50	22	225	3	30.22	3	8	0
87. Maine	11	51	1,769	34.69	15	70	8	30.18	6	5	0
88. Tennessee St.	11	40	1,359	33.98	16	134	1	30.13	6	5	0
89. Richmond	11	44	1,458	33.14	14	93	2	30.11	6	5	0
90. Jackson St.	10	39	1,472	37.74	20	245	3	29.92	5	5	0
91. Nicholls St.	11	44	1,644	37.36	22	248	4	29.91	4	7	0
92. Central Conn. St.	11	45	1,531	34.02	18	168	1	29.84	8	3	0
93. Liberty	11	48	1,827	38.06	27	276	6	29.81	6	5	0
94. Mississippi Val.	11	65	2,110	32.46	23	165	1	29.62	6	5	0
95. Stony Brook	11	62	2,206	35.58	30	293	4	29.56	5	6	0
96. Howard	11	60	1,965	32.75	21	174	1	29.52	5	6	0
97. Texas St.	11	48	2,021	42.10	23	466	7	29.48	5	6	0
98. Villanova	11	45	1,695	37.67	25	312	3	29.40	6	5	0
99. Iona	10	60	1,982	33.03	19	183	2	29.32	3	7	0
100. Jacksonville	10	61	2,110	34.59	19	238	5	29.05	4	6	0
101. Robert Morris	11	55	1,751	31.84	27	144	1	28.85	7	4	0
102. Northeastern	11	51	1,757	34.45	19	214	4	28.69	5	6	0
103. Marist	11	52	1,823	35.06	25	293	2	28.65	4	7	0
104. Austin Peay	11	53	1,752	33.06	22	185	4	28.06	3	8	0
105. Savannah St.	11	59	1,863	31.58	26	219	0	27.86	2	9	0
106. N.C. A&T	11	63	2,299	36.49	32	415	7	27.68	0	11	0
107. Tenn.-Martin	12	55	1,757	31.95	27	204	2	27.51	9	3	0
108. Valparaiso	11	58	1,856	32.00	29	273	0	27.29	3	8	0
109. Towson	11	43	1,515	35.23	26	266	4	27.19	7	4	0
110. La Salle	10	56	1,936	34.57	28	380	2	27.07	3	7	0
111. Morgan St.	11	54	1,760	32.59	28	259	3	26.69	5	6	0
112. VMI	11	55	2,165	39.36	34	626	4	26.53	1	10	0
113. South Carolina St.	11	40	1,226	30.65	12	158	1	26.20	7	4	0
114. Western Ky.	11	41	1,455	35.49	16	389	2	25.02	6	5	0
115. St. Peter's	10	53	1,563	29.49	26	279	3	23.09	2	8	0
116. St. Francis (Pa.)	11	51	1,492	29.25	28	342	0	22.55	3	8	0

Punt Returns

Rank, Team	G	Ret	Yds	TD	Avg	W	L	T
1. Norfolk St.	11	23	476	2	20.70	4	7	0
2. Sam Houston St.	11	19	376	3	19.79	6	5	0
3. Alcorn St.	10	26	502	3	19.31	6	4	0
4. Wofford	11	10	175	2	17.50	7	4	0
5. Missouri St.	11	18	288	3	16.00	2	9	0
6. McNeese St.	12	23	361	1	15.70	7	5	0
7. Delaware St.	11	26	403	4	15.50	8	3	0
8. Bethune-Cookman	11	25	384	1	15.36	5	6	0
9. St. Peter's	10	16	232	1	14.50	2	8	0
10. Charleston So.	11	21	291	2	13.86	9	2	0
11. Southern Ill.	13	28	372	2	13.29	9	4	0
12. Lehigh	11	24	315	1	13.13	6	5	0

Rank, Team	G	Ret	Yds	TD	Avg	W	L	T
13. Montana	14	57	733	2	12.86	12	2	0
14. James Madison	12	22	276	0	12.55	9	3	0
15. Dayton	10	20	247	1	12.35	4	6	0
16. Western Ill.	11	11	135	1	12.27	5	6	0
17. Bucknell	11	23	281	0	12.22	6	5	0
18. Southern Utah	11	23	274	2	11.91	3	8	0
19. Tenn.-Martin	12	33	382	1	11.58	9	3	0
20. Lafayette	12	21	241	0	11.48	6	6	0
21. Sacred Heart	11	18	204	1	11.33	2	9	0
22. Liberty	11	28	315	0	11.25	6	5	0
23. Jackson St.	10	23	256	1	11.13	5	5	0
23. Richmond	11	23	256	1	11.13	6	5	0
25. Weber St.	11	38	415	1	10.92	4	7	0
26. Rhode Island	11	15	159	1	10.60	4	7	0
27. Elon	11	17	179	0	10.53	5	6	0
28. Hofstra	11	19	199	0	10.47	2	9	0
29. Ga. Southern	11	24	250	1	10.42	3	8	0
30. Appalachian St.	15	37	373	2	10.08	14	1	0
31. Eastern Ky.	11	26	258	0	9.92	6	5	0
32. Penn	10	27	267	1	9.89	5	5	0
33. Marist	11	18	177	0	9.83	4	7	0
34. Furman	12	27	263	0	9.74	8	4	0
35. Northwestern St.	11	19	184	0	9.68	4	7	0
36. Mississippi Val.	11	22	212	0	9.64	6	5	0
37. Idaho St.	11	24	230	0	9.58	2	9	0
38. Ark.-Pine Bluff	12	21	201	0	9.57	8	4	0
39. Samford	11	25	238	1	9.52	3	8	0
40. Gardner-Webb	11	20	188	1	9.40	6	5	0
41. Florida A&M	11	18	169	0	9.39	7	4	0
42. Texas Southern	11	14	131	0	9.36	3	8	0
43. Colgate	11	26	238	0	9.15	4	7	0
44. Citadel	11	31	282	0	9.10	5	6	0
45. Fordham	11	14	127	0	9.07	3	8	0
46. Cornell	10	32	290	0	9.06	5	5	0
47. New Hampshire	13	33	299	1	9.06	9	4	0
48. Maine	11	23	207	1	9.00	6	5	0
49. Holy Cross	11	25	224	0	8.96	7	4	0
50. Jacksonville St.	11	35	310	1	8.86	6	5	0
51. Montana St.	13	40	354	0	8.85	8	5	0
52. Morehead St.	11	26	228	1	8.77	2	9	0
53. Wagner	11	30	261	0	8.70	4	7	0
54. Duquesne	10	34	295	0	8.68	7	3	0
55. Massachusetts	15	33	284	0	8.61	13	2	0
56. Alabama St.	11	25	215	0	8.60	5	6	0
57. Towson	11	23	196	0	8.52	7	4	0
58. Albany (N.Y.)	11	36	306	0	8.50	7	4	0
58. Delaware	11	12	102	0	8.50	5	6	0
60. Prairie View	10	17	144	1	8.47	3	7	0
61. Jacksonville	10	28	237	0	8.46	4	6	0
62. South Carolina St.	11	13	110	1	8.46	7	4	0
63. Central Conn. St.	11	21	176	1	8.38	8	3	0
64. Hampton	12	32	267	0	8.34	10	2	0
65. Cal Poly	11	33	269	0	8.15	7	4	0
66. UNI	11	21	171	0	8.14	7	4	0
67. Indiana St.	11	8	65	1	8.13	1	10	0
68. Eastern Wash.	11	17	137	1	8.06	3	8	0
69. Monmouth	12	33	265	0	8.03	10	2	0
70. Valparaiso	11	24	190	0	7.92	3	8	0
71. Yale	10	8	63	0	7.88	8	2	0
72. Tennessee St.	11	13	101	0	7.77	6	5	0
73. Youngstown St.	14	24	186	1	7.75	11	3	0
74. Sacramento St.	11	14	108	0	7.71	4	7	0
75. Stony Brook	11	22	168	0	7.64	5	6	0
76. Brown	10	16	122	0	7.63	3	7	0
77. Northern Ariz.	11	29	221	0	7.62	6	5	0
78. Alabama A&M	12	20	152	0	7.60	9	3	0
78. Savannah St.	11	15	114	0	7.60	2	9	0
80. Southern U.	11	25	188	0	7.52	5	6	0
81. Western Ky.	11	14	105	0	7.50	6	5	0
82. San Diego	12	33	244	0	7.39	11	1	0
83. William & Mary	11	18	133	0	7.39	3	8	0
84. Nicholls St.	11	21	149	0	7.10	4	7	0
85. Portland St.	11	27	189	0	7.00	7	4	0
86. Morgan St.	11	30	208	0	6.93	5	6	0
87. Robert Morris	11	29	200	1	6.90	7	4	0
88. Iona	10	28	192	0	6.86	3	7	0
89. Grambling	11	12	82	0	6.83	3	8	0
90. Austin Peay	11	10	67	0	6.70	3	8	0
90. Northeastern	11	10	67	0	6.70	5	6	0
92. Illinois St.	13	18	120	0	6.67	9	4	0
93. Villanova	11	17	111	0	6.53	6	5	0
94. Princeton	10	26	169	0	6.50	9	1	0
95. Howard	11	22	141	0	6.41	5	6	0
96. Southeastern La.	11	14	84	0	6.00	2	9	0
96. Stephen F. Austin	11	18	108	0	6.00	4	7	0
98. Harvard	10	25	149	0	5.96	7	3	0
99. Columbia	10	16	93	0	5.81	5	5	0
100. VMI	11	8	46	0	5.75	1	10	0
101. Chattanooga	11	25	142	0	5.68	3	8	0
102. Georgetown	11	23	128	0	5.57	2	9	0
103. N.C. A&T	11	13	72	0	5.54	0	11	0
104. Western Caro.	11	24	132	1	5.50	2	9	0
105. Murray St.	11	13	69	1	5.31	1	10	0
106. Butler	11	19	98	1	5.16	3	8	0
107. St. Francis (Pa.)	11	13	67	0	5.15	3	8	0
108. Drake	11	24	121	0	5.04	9	2	0
109. La Salle	10	17	81	0	4.76	3	7	0
110. Davidson	10	18	83	0	4.61	6	4	0
111. Coastal Caro.	12	13	58	1	4.46	9	3	0
112. Southeast Mo. St.	11	20	89	0	4.45	4	7	0
113. Tennessee Tech	11	16	67	0	4.19	4	7	0
114. Texas St.	11	18	74	0	4.11	5	6	0
115. Eastern Ill.	13	30	122	0	4.07	8	5	0
116. Dartmouth	10	16	50	0	3.13	2	8	0

Kickoff Returns

Rank, Team	G	Ret	Yds	TD	Avg	W	L	T
1. James Madison	12	32	867	1	27.09	9	3	0
2. Alabama A&M	12	39	1,037	2	26.59	9	3	0
3. Liberty	11	32	818	3	25.56	6	5	0
4. Hampton	12	36	910	1	25.28	10	2	0
5. Georgetown	11	52	1,263	0	24.29	2	9	0
6. Iona	10	32	765	0	23.91	3	7	0
7. Ark.-Pine Bluff	12	51	1,182	0	23.18	8	4	0
8. Delaware	11	42	972	0	23.14	5	6	0
9. Eastern Ky.	11	42	960	1	22.86	6	5	0
10. Northern Ariz.	11	35	790	1	22.57	6	5	0
11. Tennessee St.	11	39	880	0	22.56	6	5	0
12. Delaware St.	11	29	652	0	22.48	8	3	0
13. Western Ky.	11	36	808	0	22.44	6	5	0
14. Ga. Southern	11	37	830	0	22.43	3	8	0
15. Southern Utah	11	36	807	0	22.42	3	8	0
16. San Diego	12	27	604	1	22.37	11	1	0
17. Morehead St.	11	49	1,096	0	22.37	2	9	0
18. UNI	11	38	840	1	22.11	7	4	0
19. Weber St.	11	41	900	1	21.95	4	7	0
20. Tenn.-Martin	12	31	677	2	21.84	9	3	0
21. Illinois St.	13	40	866	0	21.65	9	4	0
22. Davidson	10	34	728	0	21.41	6	4	0
23. Massachusetts	15	36	770	0	21.39	13	2	0
24. Brown	10	42	894	1	21.29	3	7	0
25. Holy Cross	11	39	830	0	21.28	7	4	0
26. Stephen F. Austin	11	35	744	0	21.26	4	7	0
27. Portland St.	11	28	593	1	21.18	7	4	0
28. Elon	11	47	994	0	21.15	5	6	0
29. Penn	10	31	655	1	21.13	5	5	0
30. New Hampshire	13	49	1,035	1	21.12	9	4	0
31. Yale	10	38	801	1	21.08	8	2	0
32. Montana	14	43	904	0	21.02	12	2	0
33. Florida A&M	11	52	1,091	0	20.98	7	4	0
34. South Carolina St.	11	35	730	1	20.86	7	4	0
35. Lehigh	11	37	770	0	20.81	6	5	0
36. Furman	12	39	807	1	20.69	8	4	0
37. Colgate	11	44	904	0	20.55	4	7	0
38. Southern Ill.	13	48	986	0	20.54	9	4	0
39. Fordham	11	54	1,109	1	20.54	3	8	0
40. Western Caro.	11	45	923	1	20.51	2	9	0
41. Harvard	10	33	674	1	20.42	7	3	0
42. Alabama St.	11	32	651	1	20.34	5	6	0
43. Missouri St.	11	37	749	0	20.24	2	9	0
44. Wofford	11	37	745	1	20.14	7	4	0
45. Jacksonville St.	11	33	662	0	20.06	6	5	0
46. Northeastern	11	37	739	0	19.97	5	6	0
47. Cornell	10	38	758	1	19.95	5	5	0
48. Norfolk St.	11	40	794	0	19.85	4	7	0
49. Bethune-Cookman	11	42	830	0	19.76	5	6	0
50. Savannah St.	11	52	1,027	1	19.75	2	9	0
51. Albany (N.Y.)	11	30	592	1	19.73	7	4	0
52. Sacramento St.	11	37	730	0	19.73	4	7	0
53. Chattanooga	11	44	866	0	19.68	3	8	0
54. Rhode Island	11	53	1,042	0	19.66	4	7	0
55. Lafayette	12	49	961	1	19.61	6	6	0
56. Robert Morris	11	30	587	0	19.57	7	4	0
57. Southeast Mo. St.	11	42	820	0	19.52	4	7	0
58. Cal Poly	11	30	584	0	19.47	7	4	0

Rank, Team	G	Ret	Yds	TD	Avg	W	L	T
59. Wagner	11	37	719	1	19.43	4	7	0
60. Maine	11	27	522	1	19.33	6	5	0
61. Villanova	11	42	806	0	19.19	6	5	0
62. Eastern Wash.	11	41	786	0	19.17	3	8	0
63. Drake	11	25	478	0	19.12	9	2	0
64. William & Mary	11	41	782	0	19.07	3	8	0
65. Southern U.	11	42	800	0	19.05	5	6	0
66. Texas St.	11	35	664	0	18.97	5	6	0
67. Jacksonville	10	51	966	0	18.94	4	6	0
68. Sam Houston St.	11	42	794	0	18.90	6	5	0
69. McNeese St.	12	43	809	0	18.81	7	5	0
70. Tennessee Tech	11	42	789	0	18.79	4	7	0
71. Northwestern St.	11	37	695	0	18.78	4	7	0
72. Grambling	11	47	882	1	18.77	3	8	0
73. Alcorn St.	10	38	712	0	18.74	6	4	0
74. Prairie View	10	30	560	0	18.67	3	7	0
74. Sacred Heart	11	48	896	1	18.67	2	9	0
76. Howard	11	41	764	0	18.63	5	6	0
77. Eastern Ill.	13	40	738	0	18.45	8	5	0
78. Gardner-Webb	11	47	867	0	18.45	6	5	0
79. Princeton	10	36	664	0	18.44	9	1	0
80. Idaho St.	11	48	884	0	18.42	2	9	0
81. Southeastern La.	11	49	900	0	18.37	2	9	0
82. Morgan St.	11	43	786	0	18.28	5	6	0
83. Valparaiso	11	61	1,114	0	18.26	3	8	0
84. Dartmouth	10	47	856	0	18.21	2	8	0
85. Youngstown St.	14	40	720	0	18.00	11	3	0
86. VMI	11	50	898	0	17.96	1	10	0
87. Western Ill.	11	33	591	0	17.91	5	6	0
88. Montana St.	13	36	642	0	17.83	8	5	0
89. La Salle	10	42	748	0	17.81	3	7	0
90. Murray St.	11	51	906	0	17.76	1	10	0
91. Coastal Caro.	12	45	789	0	17.53	9	3	0
92. Bucknell	11	46	804	0	17.48	6	5	0
93. Dayton	10	36	627	0	17.42	4	6	0
94. Stony Brook	11	40	695	0	17.38	5	6	0
95. Hofstra	11	36	616	0	17.11	2	9	0
96. St. Peter's	10	54	922	0	17.07	2	8	0
97. Citadel	11	37	629	0	17.00	5	6	0
98. Towson	11	39	662	0	16.97	7	4	0
99. Austin Peay	11	39	661	1	16.95	3	8	0
100. Samford	11	36	609	0	16.92	3	8	0
101. Appalachian St.	15	35	590	0	16.86	14	1	0
102. Richmond	11	24	404	0	16.83	6	5	0
103. Jackson St.	10	37	622	0	16.81	5	5	0
104. Charleston So.	11	30	503	0	16.77	9	2	0
105. Texas Southern	11	48	803	0	16.73	3	8	0
106. St. Francis (Pa.)	11	58	969	0	16.71	3	8	0
107. Indiana St.	11	60	997	0	16.62	1	10	0
108. N.C. A&T	11	61	1,011	0	16.57	0	11	0
109. Butler	11	49	803	0	16.39	3	8	0
110. Nicholls St.	11	37	605	0	16.35	4	7	0
111. Duquesne	10	26	413	0	15.88	7	3	0
112. Central Conn. St.	11	33	516	0	15.64	8	3	0
113. Monmouth	12	26	404	0	15.54	10	2	0
114. Marist	11	48	743	0	15.48	4	7	0
115. Columbia	10	30	422	0	14.07	5	5	0
116. Mississippi Val.	11	40	558	0	13.95	6	5	0

Turnover Margin

Rank, Team	G	Gained Fum	Gained Int	Gained Total	Lost Fum	Lost Int	Lost Total	TM/Gm	W	L	T
1. Wofford	11	15	16	31	4	6	10	1.91	7	4	0
2. Delaware St.	11	17	10	27	7	4	11	1.45	8	3	0
3. South Carolina St.	11	16	13	29	5	9	14	1.36	7	4	0
4. Yale	10	9	14	23	6	6	12	1.10	8	2	0
5. Drake	11	10	18	28	5	11	16	1.09	9	2	0
6. Central Conn. St.	11	14	10	24	9	4	13	1.00	8	3	0
6. McNeese St.	12	18	13	31	9	10	19	1.00	7	5	0
6. San Diego	12	4	16	20	3	5	8	1.00	11	1	0
6. Columbia	10	9	15	24	8	6	14	1.00	5	5	0
10. Eastern Ill.	13	19	17	36	6	18	24	.92	8	5	0
11. Ga. Southern	11	9	14	23	7	6	13	.91	3	8	0
12. Hampton	12	10	16	26	11	5	16	.83	10	2	0
13. Portland St.	11	12	19	31	10	12	22	.82	7	4	0
14. Youngstown St.	14	13	15	28	6	12	18	.71	11	3	0
15. New Hampshire	13	12	11	23	7	7	14	.69	9	4	0
16. Alabama A&M	12	11	15	26	10	8	18	.67	9	3	0
17. Butler	11	12	10	22	4	11	15	.64	3	8	0
17. UNI	11	7	15	22	8	7	15	.64	7	4	0
19. Prairie View	10	18	9	27	13	8	21	.60	3	7	0
20. Alabama St.	11	15	10	25	8	11	19	.55	5	6	0
20. Charleston So.	11	8	18	26	4	16	20	.55	9	2	0
20. Elon	11	6	17	23	5	12	17	.55	5	6	0
20. William & Mary	11	10	8	18	2	10	12	.55	3	8	0
20. Stony Brook	11	10	11	21	10	5	15	.55	5	6	0
20. Stephen F. Austin	11	10	7	17	6	5	11	.55	4	7	0
20. Southeast Mo. St.	11	10	12	22	6	10	16	.55	4	7	0
20. Liberty	11	6	8	14	3	5	8	.55	6	5	0
20. Lehigh	11	7	13	20	8	6	14	.55	6	5	0
29. Duquesne	10	14	12	26	8	13	21	.50	7	3	0
29. Montana	14	11	19	30	10	13	23	.50	12	2	0
29. Monmouth	12	11	16	27	11	10	21	.50	10	2	0
32. Bucknell	11	9	10	19	8	6	14	.45	6	5	0
32. Jacksonville St.	11	9	11	20	5	10	15	.45	6	5	0
34. Illinois St.	13	6	17	23	4	14	18	.38	9	4	0
35. Holy Cross	11	7	11	18	7	7	14	.36	7	4	0
35. Western Ill.	11	9	10	19	6	9	15	.36	5	6	0
35. VMI	11	10	10	20	13	3	16	.36	1	10	0
38. Ark.-Pine Bluff	12	13	13	26	12	10	22	.33	8	4	0
39. Davidson	10	12	10	22	9	10	19	.30	6	4	0
39. Harvard	10	11	12	23	8	12	20	.30	7	3	0
41. Hofstra	11	11	5	16	9	4	13	.27	2	9	0
41. Northeastern	11	11	6	17	3	11	14	.27	5	6	0
41. Maine	11	10	9	19	8	8	16	.27	6	5	0
41. Northern Ariz.	11	6	9	15	6	6	12	.27	6	5	0
45. Massachusetts	15	13	11	24	9	11	20	.27	13	2	0
46. James Madison	12	7	6	13	4	6	10	.25	9	3	0
47. Penn	10	9	11	20	6	12	18	.20	5	5	0

Rank, Team	G	Gained Fum	Gained Int	Gained Total	Lost Fum	Lost Int	Lost Total	TM/Gm	W	L	T
48. Cal Poly	11	9	12	21	12	7	19	.18	7	4	0
48. Eastern Wash.	11	12	14	26	5	19	24	.18	3	8	0
48. Western Caro.	11	2	14	16	8	6	14	.18	2	9	0
48. Mississippi Val.	11	11	10	21	5	14	19	.18	6	5	0
48. Delaware	11	9	11	20	8	10	18	.18	5	6	0
53. Southern Ill.	13	6	7	13	7	4	11	.15	9	4	0
54. Alcorn St.	10	15	10	25	12	12	24	.09	6	4	0
54. Missouri St.	11	10	9	19	8	10	18	.09	2	9	0
54. Southeastern La.	11	14	7	21	10	10	20	.09	2	9	0
54. Morgan St.	11	14	8	22	11	10	21	.09	5	6	0
54. Fordham	11	11	15	26	13	12	25	.09	3	8	0
59. Tenn.-Martin	12	11	13	24	14	9	23	.08	9	3	0
60. Albany (N.Y.)	11	9	12	21	13	8	21	.00	7	4	0
60. Northwestern St.	11	13	12	25	14	11	25	.00	4	7	0
60. Princeton	10	4	14	18	6	12	18	.00	9	1	0
60. Furman	12	9	9	18	12	6	18	.00	8	4	0
60. Dayton	10	6	14	20	9	11	20	.00	4	6	0
65. Appalachian St.	15	13	16	29	16	14	30	-.07	14	1	0
66. Colgate	11	11	6	17	8	10	18	-.09	4	7	0
66. Wagner	11	12	7	19	8	12	20	-.09	4	7	0
68. Montana St.	13	11	14	25	8	19	27	-.15	8	5	0
69. Weber St.	11	9	9	18	5	15	20	-.18	4	7	0
70. Bethune-Cookman	11	9	14	23	21	5	26	-.27	5	6	0
70. Murray St.	11	8	13	21	10	14	24	-.27	1	10	0
70. Grambling	11	15	7	22	14	11	25	-.27	3	8	0
70. Sam Houston St.	11	14	8	22	11	14	25	-.27	6	5	0
70. Tennessee St.	11	7	13	20	10	13	23	-.27	6	5	0
70. Chattanooga	11	7	11	18	8	13	21	-.27	3	8	0
70. Villanova	11	11	4	15	9	9	18	-.27	6	5	0
70. Texas St.	11	12	10	22	10	15	25	-.27	5	6	0
78. Coastal Caro.	12	3	19	22	15	11	26	-.33	9	3	0
78. Lafayette	12	6	10	16	10	10	20	-.33	6	6	0
80. Marist	11	8	6	14	6	12	18	-.36	4	7	0
80. Richmond	11	6	12	18	12	10	22	-.36	6	5	0
80. Western Ky.	11	8	6	14	9	9	18	-.36	6	5	0
80. Towson	11	9	10	19	12	11	23	-.36	7	4	0
84. Cornell	10	3	8	11	5	10	15	-.40	5	5	0
85. Sacramento St.	11	5	15	20	6	19	25	-.45	4	7	0
85. Citadel	11	9	5	14	8	11	19	-.45	5	6	0
85. Southern Utah	11	11	7	18	8	15	23	-.45	3	8	0
88. Iona	10	5	14	19	12	12	24	-.50	3	7	0
88. Jacksonville	10	8	5	13	7	11	18	-.50	4	6	0
90. Austin Peay	11	9	6	15	8	13	21	-.55	3	8	0
90. Indiana St.	11	11	5	16	13	9	22	-.55	1	10	0
92. Dartmouth	10	10	3	13	7	12	19	-.60	2	8	0
93. Eastern Ky.	11	6	11	17	9	15	24	-.64	6	5	0
93. Southern U.	11	12	14	26	14	19	33	-.64	5	6	0
93. Rhode Island	11	5	11	16	11	12	23	-.64	4	7	0
96. St. Peter's	10	16	3	19	13	13	26	-.70	2	8	0
97. Florida A&M	11	5	10	15	15	8	23	-.73	7	4	0
97. Howard	11	10	9	19	14	13	27	-.73	5	6	0
97. St. Francis (Pa.)	11	5	7	12	13	7	20	-.73	3	8	0
97. Sacred Heart	11	4	9	13	7	14	21	-.73	2	9	0
97. Robert Morris	11	12	13	25	17	16	33	-.73	7	4	0
102. Jackson St.	10	4	14	18	14	13	27	-.82	5	5	0
102. Norfolk St.	11	8	5	13	6	16	22	-.82	4	7	0
102. Savannah St.	11	14	6	20	15	14	29	-.82	2	9	0
105. Morehead St.	11	5	7	12	10	12	22	-.91	2	9	0
106. Samford	11	8	9	17	12	16	28	-1.00	3	8	0
106. Texas Southern	11	12	17	29	18	22	40	-1.00	3	8	0
108. Idaho St.	11	5	7	12	10	14	24	-1.09	2	9	0
108. Valparaiso	11	5	6	11	10	13	23	-1.09	3	8	0
110. La Salle	10	10	5	15	8	18	26	-1.10	3	7	0
111. Nicholls St.	11	12	8	20	26	7	33	-1.18	4	7	0
111. Gardner-Webb	11	14	7	21	13	21	34	-1.18	6	5	0
113. N.C. A&T	11	10	4	14	9	19	28	-1.27	0	11	0
113. Tennessee Tech	11	9	7	16	13	17	30	-1.27	4	7	0
115. Brown	10	1	7	8	6	16	22	-1.40	3	7	0
116. Georgetown	11	6	6	12	13	15	28	-1.45	2	9	0

Fumbles Recovered

Rank, Team	No.
1. Eastern Ill.	19
2. McNeese St.	18
2. Prairie View	18
4. Delaware St.	17
5. St. Peter's	16
5. South Carolina St.	16
7. Alabama St.	15
7. Alcorn St.	15
7. Grambling	15
7. Wofford	15
11. Central Conn. St.	14
11. Duquesne	14
11. Gardner-Webb	14
11. Morgan St.	14
11. Sam Houston St.	14
11. Savannah St.	14
11. Southeastern La.	14
18. Appalachian St.	13
18. Ark.-Pine Bluff	13
18. Massachusetts	13
18. Northwestern St.	13
18. Youngstown St.	13
23. Butler	12
23. Davidson	12
23. Eastern Wash.	12
23. New Hampshire	12
23. Nicholls St.	12
23. Portland St.	12
23. Robert Morris	12
23. Southern U.	12
23. Texas Southern	12
23. Texas St.	12
23. Wagner	12
34. Alabama A&M	11
34. Colgate	11
34. Fordham	11
34. Harvard	11
34. Hofstra	11
34. Indiana St.	11
34. Mississippi Val.	11
34. Monmouth	11
34. Montana	11
34. Montana St.	11
34. Northeastern	11
34. Southern Utah	11
34. Tenn.-Martin	11
34. Villanova	11
48. Dartmouth	10
48. Drake	10
48. Hampton	10
48. Howard	10
48. La Salle	10
48. Maine	10
48. Missouri St.	10
48. N.C. A&T	10
48. Southeast Mo. St.	10
48. Stephen F. Austin	10
48. Stony Brook	10

Rank, Team	No.
48. VMI	10
48. William & Mary	10
61. Albany (N.Y.)	9
61. Austin Peay	9
61. Bethune-Cookman	9
61. Bucknell	9
61. Cal Poly	9
61. Citadel	9
61. Columbia	9
61. Delaware	9
61. Furman	9
61. Ga. Southern	9
61. Jacksonville St.	9
61. Penn	9
61. Tennessee Tech	9
61. Towson	9
61. Weber St.	9
61. Western Ill.	9
61. Yale	9
78. Charleston So.	8
78. Jacksonville	8
78. Marist	8
78. Murray St.	8
78. Norfolk St.	8
78. Samford	8
78. Western Ky.	8
85. Chattanooga	7
85. Holy Cross	7
85. James Madison	7
85. Lehigh	7
85. UNI	7
85. Tennessee St.	7
91. Dayton	6
91. Eastern Ky.	6
91. Elon	6
91. Georgetown	6
91. Illinois St.	6
91. Lafayette	6
91. Liberty	6
91. Northern Ariz.	6
91. Richmond	6
91. Southern Ill.	6
101. Florida A&M	5
101. Idaho St.	5
101. Iona	5
101. Morehead St.	5
101. Rhode Island	5
101. Sacramento St.	5
101. St. Francis (Pa.)	5
101. Valparaiso	5
109. Jackson St.	4
109. Princeton	4
109. Sacred Heart	4
109. San Diego	4
113. Coastal Caro.	3
113. Cornell	3
115. Western Caro.	2
116. Brown	1

Rank, Team	No.
32. McNeese St.	13
32. Murray St.	13
32. Robert Morris	13
32. South Carolina St.	13
32. Tenn.-Martin	13
32. Tennessee St.	13
40. Albany (N.Y.)	12
40. Cal Poly	12
40. Duquesne	12
40. Harvard	12
40. Northwestern St.	12
40. Richmond	12
40. Southeast Mo. St.	12
47. Chattanooga	11
47. Delaware	11
47. Eastern Ky.	11
47. Holy Cross	11
47. Jacksonville St.	11
47. Massachusetts	11
47. New Hampshire	11
47. Penn	11
47. Rhode Island	11
47. Stony Brook	11
57. Alabama St.	10
57. Alcorn St.	10
57. Bucknell	10
57. Butler	10
57. Central Conn. St.	10
57. Davidson	10
57. Delaware St.	10
57. Florida A&M	10
57. Lafayette	10
57. Mississippi Val.	10
57. Texas St.	10
57. Towson	10
57. VMI	10
57. Western Ill.	10
71. Furman	9
71. Howard	9
71. Maine	9
71. Missouri St.	9
71. Northern Ariz.	9

Rank, Team	No.
71. Prairie View	9
71. Sacred Heart	9
71. Samford	9
71. Weber St.	9
80. Cornell	8
80. Liberty	8
80. Morgan St.	8
80. Nicholls St.	8
80. Sam Houston St.	8
80. William & Mary	8
86. Brown	7
86. Gardner-Webb	7
86. Grambling	7
86. Idaho St.	7
86. Morehead St.	7
86. St. Francis (Pa.)	7
86. Southeastern La.	7
86. Southern Ill.	7
86. Southern Utah	7
86. Stephen F. Austin	7
86. Tennessee Tech	7
86. Wagner	7
98. Austin Peay	6
98. Colgate	6
98. Georgetown	6
98. James Madison	6
98. Marist	6
98. Northeastern	6
98. Savannah St.	6
98. Valparaiso	6
98. Western Ky.	6
107. Citadel	5
107. Hofstra	5
107. Indiana St.	5
107. Jacksonville	5
107. La Salle	5
107. Norfolk St.	5
113. N.C. A&T	4
113. Villanova	4
115. Dartmouth	3
115. St. Peter's	3

Passes Intercepted

Rank, Team	No.
1. Coastal Caro.	19
1. Montana	19
1. Portland St.	19
4. Charleston So.	18
4. Drake	18
6. Eastern Ill.	17
6. Elon	17
6. Illinois St.	17
6. Texas Southern	17
10. Appalachian St.	16
10. Hampton	16
10. Monmouth	16
10. San Diego	16
10. Wofford	16
15. Alabama A&M	15
15. Columbia	15
15. Fordham	15

Rank, Team	No.
15. UNI	15
15. Sacramento St.	15
15. Youngstown St.	15
21. Bethune-Cookman	14
21. Dayton	14
21. Eastern Wash.	14
21. Ga. Southern	14
21. Iona	14
21. Jackson St.	14
21. Montana St.	14
21. Princeton	14
21. Southern U.	14
21. Western Caro.	14
21. Yale	14
32. Ark.-Pine Bluff	13
32. Lehigh	13

Turnovers Gained

Rank, Team	No.
1. Eastern Ill.	36
2. McNeese St.	31
2. Portland St.	31
2. Wofford	31
5. Montana	30
6. Appalachian St.	29
6. South Carolina St.	29
6. Texas Southern	29
9. Drake	28
9. Youngstown St.	28
11. Delaware St.	27
11. Monmouth	27
11. Prairie View	27
14. Alabama A&M	26
14. Ark.-Pine Bluff	26
14. Charleston So.	26
14. Duquesne	26
14. Eastern Wash.	26
14. Fordham	26
14. Hampton	26
14. Southern U.	26
22. Alabama St.	25
22. Alcorn St.	25
22. Montana St.	25
22. Northwestern St.	25
22. Robert Morris	25
27. Central Conn. St.	24
27. Columbia	24
27. Massachusetts	24
27. Tenn.-Martin	24
31. Bethune-Cookman	23
31. Elon	23
31. Ga. Southern	23
31. Harvard	23
31. Illinois St.	23

Rank, Team	No.
31. New Hampshire	23
31. Yale	23
38. Butler	22
38. Coastal Caro.	22
38. Davidson	22
38. Grambling	22
38. Morgan St.	22
38. UNI	22
38. Sam Houston St.	22
38. Southeast Mo. St.	22
38. Texas St.	22
47. Albany (N.Y.)	21
47. Cal Poly	21
47. Gardner-Webb	21
47. Mississippi Val.	21
47. Murray St.	21
47. Southeastern La.	21
47. Stony Brook	21
54. Dayton	20
54. Delaware	20
54. Jacksonville St.	20
54. Lehigh	20
54. Nicholls St.	20
54. Penn	20
54. Sacramento St.	20
54. San Diego	20
54. Savannah St.	20
54. Tennessee St.	20
54. VMI	20
65. Bucknell	19
65. Howard	19
65. Iona	19
65. Maine	19
65. Missouri St.	19
65. St. Peter's	19

Rank, Team	No.
65. Towson	19
65. Wagner	19
65. Western Ill.	19
74. Chattanooga	18
74. Furman	18
74. Holy Cross	18
74. Jackson St.	18
74. Princeton	18
74. Richmond	18
74. Southern Utah	18
74. Weber St.	18
74. William & Mary	18
83. Colgate	17
83. Eastern Ky.	17
83. Northeastern	17
83. Samford	17
83. Stephen F. Austin	17
88. Hofstra	16
88. Indiana St.	16
88. Lafayette	16
88. Rhode Island	16
88. Tennessee Tech	16
88. Western Caro.	16
94. Austin Peay	15
94. Florida A&M	15
94. La Salle	15
94. Northern Ariz.	15
94. Villanova	15
99. Citadel	14
99. Liberty	14
99. Marist	14
99. N.C. A&T	14
99. Western Ky.	14
104. Dartmouth	13
104. Jacksonville	13
104. James Madison	13
104. Norfolk St.	13
104. Sacred Heart	13
104. Southern Ill.	13
110. Georgetown	12
110. Idaho St.	12
110. Morehead St.	12
110. St. Francis (Pa.)	12
114. Cornell	11
114. Valparaiso	11
116. Brown	8

Rank, Team	No.
103. Tenn.-Martin	14
109. Coastal Caro.	15
109. Florida A&M	15
109. Savannah St.	15
112. Appalachian St.	16
113. Robert Morris	17
114. Texas Southern	18
115. Bethune-Cookman	21
116. Nicholls St.	26

Fumbles Lost

Rank, Team	No.
1. William & Mary	2
2. Liberty	3
2. Northeastern	3
2. San Diego	3
5. Butler	4
5. Charleston So.	4
5. Illinois St.	4
5. James Madison	4
5. Wofford	4
10. Cornell	5
10. Drake	5
10. Eastern Wash.	5
10. Elon	5
10. Jacksonville St.	5
10. Mississippi Val.	5
10. South Carolina St.	5
10. Weber St.	5
18. Brown	6
18. Eastern Ill.	6
18. Marist	6
18. Norfolk St.	6
18. Northern Ariz.	6
18. Penn	6
18. Princeton	6
18. Sacramento St.	6
18. Southeast Mo. St.	6
18. Stephen F. Austin	6
18. Western Ill.	6
18. Yale	6
18. Youngstown St.	6
31. Dartmouth	7
31. Delaware St.	7
31. Ga. Southern	7
31. Holy Cross	7
31. Jacksonville	7
31. New Hampshire	7
31. Sacred Heart	7
31. Southern Ill.	7
39. Alabama St.	8
39. Austin Peay	8
39. Bucknell	8
39. Chattanooga	8
39. Citadel	8
39. Colgate	8
39. Columbia	8
39. Delaware	8
39. Duquesne	8
39. Harvard	8
39. La Salle	8
39. Lehigh	8
39. Maine	8
39. Missouri St.	8
39. Montana St.	8
39. UNI	8
39. Southern Utah	8
39. Wagner	8
39. Western Caro.	8
58. Central Conn. St.	9
58. Davidson	9
58. Dayton	9
58. Eastern Ky.	9
58. Hofstra	9
58. Massachusetts	9
58. McNeese St.	9
58. N.C. A&T	9
58. Villanova	9
58. Western Ky.	9
68. Alabama A&M	10
68. Idaho St.	10
68. Lafayette	10
68. Montana	10
68. Morehead St.	10
68. Murray St.	10
68. Portland St.	10
68. Southeastern La.	10
68. Stony Brook	10
68. Tennessee St.	10
68. Texas St.	10
68. Valparaiso	10
80. Hampton	11
80. Monmouth	11
80. Morgan St.	11
80. Rhode Island	11
80. Sam Houston St.	11
85. Alcorn St.	12
85. Ark.-Pine Bluff	12
85. Cal Poly	12
85. Furman	12
85. Iona	12
85. Richmond	12
85. Samford	12
85. Towson	12
93. Albany (N.Y.)	13
93. Fordham	13
93. Gardner-Webb	13
93. Georgetown	13
93. Indiana St.	13
93. Prairie View	13
93. St. Francis (Pa.)	13
93. St. Peter's	13
93. Tennessee Tech	13
93. VMI	13
103. Grambling	14
103. Howard	14
103. Jackson St.	14
103. Northwestern St.	14
103. Southern U.	14

Passes Had Intercepted

Rank, Team	No.
1. VMI	3
2. Central Conn. St.	4
2. Delaware St.	4
2. Hofstra	4
2. Southern Ill.	4
6. Bethune-Cookman	5
6. Hampton	5
6. Liberty	5
6. San Diego	5
6. Stephen F. Austin	5
6. Stony Brook	5
12. Bucknell	6
12. Columbia	6
12. Furman	6
12. Ga. Southern	6
12. James Madison	6
12. Lehigh	6
12. Northern Ariz.	6
12. Western Caro.	6
12. Wofford	6
12. Yale	6
22. Cal Poly	7
22. Holy Cross	7
22. New Hampshire	7
22. Nicholls St.	7
22. UNI	7
22. St. Francis (Pa.)	7
28. Alabama A&M	8
28. Albany (N.Y.)	8
28. Florida A&M	8
28. Maine	8
28. Prairie View	8
33. Indiana St.	9
33. South Carolina St.	9
33. Tenn.-Martin	9
33. Villanova	9
33. Western Ill.	9
33. Western Ky.	9
39. Ark.-Pine Bluff	10
39. Colgate	10
39. Cornell	10
39. Davidson	10
39. Delaware	10
39. Jacksonville St.	10
39. Lafayette	10
39. McNeese St.	10
39. Missouri St.	10
39. Monmouth	10
39. Morgan St.	10
39. Richmond	10
39. Southeast Mo. St.	10
39. Southeastern La.	10
39. William & Mary	10
54. Alabama St.	11
54. Butler	11
54. Citadel	11
54. Coastal Caro.	11
54. Dayton	11
54. Drake	11
54. Grambling	11
54. Jacksonville	11
54. Massachusetts	11
54. Northeastern	11
54. Northwestern St.	11
54. Towson	11
66. Alcorn St.	12
66. Dartmouth	12
66. Elon	12
66. Fordham	12
66. Harvard	12
66. Iona	12
66. Marist	12
66. Morehead St.	12
66. Penn	12
66. Portland St.	12
66. Princeton	12
66. Rhode Island	12
66. Wagner	12
66. Youngstown St.	12
80. Austin Peay	13
80. Chattanooga	13
80. Duquesne	13
80. Howard	13
80. Jackson St.	13
80. Montana	13
80. St. Peter's	13
80. Tennessee St.	13
80. Valparaiso	13
89. Appalachian St.	14
89. Idaho St.	14
89. Illinois St.	14
89. Mississippi Val.	14
89. Murray St.	14
89. Sacred Heart	14
89. Sam Houston St.	14
89. Savannah St.	14
97. Eastern Ky.	15
97. Georgetown	15
97. Southern Utah	15
97. Texas St.	15
97. Weber St.	15
102. Brown	16
102. Charleston So.	16
102. Norfolk St.	16
102. Robert Morris	16
102. Samford	16
107. Tennessee Tech	17
108. Eastern Ill.	18
108. La Salle	18
110. Eastern Wash.	19
110. Montana St.	19
110. N.C. A&T	19
110. Sacramento St.	19
110. Southern U.	19
115. Gardner-Webb	21
116. Texas Southern	22

Turnovers Lost

Rank, Team	No.
1. Liberty	8
1. San Diego	8
3. James Madison	10
3. Wofford	10
5. Delaware St.	11
5. Southern Ill.	11
5. Stephen F. Austin	11
8. Northern Ariz.	12
8. William & Mary	12
8. Yale	12
11. Central Conn. St.	13
11. Ga. Southern	13
11. Hofstra	13

Rank, Team	No.
14. Bucknell	14
14. Columbia	14
14. Holy Cross	14
14. Lehigh	14
14. New Hampshire	14
14. Northeastern	14
14. South Carolina St.	14
14. Western Caro.	14
22. Butler	15
22. Cornell	15
22. Jacksonville St.	15
22. UNI	15
22. Stony Brook	15
22. Western Ill.	15
28. Drake	16
28. Hampton	16
28. Maine	16
28. Southeast Mo. St.	16
28. VMI	16
33. Elon	17
34. Alabama A&M	18
34. Colgate	18
34. Delaware	18
34. Furman	18
34. Illinois St.	18
34. Jacksonville	18
34. Marist	18
34. Missouri St.	18
34. Penn	18
34. Princeton	18
34. Villanova	18
34. Western Ky.	18
34. Youngstown St.	18
47. Alabama St.	19
47. Cal Poly	19
47. Citadel	19
47. Dartmouth	19
47. Davidson	19
47. McNeese St.	19
47. Mississippi Val.	19
54. Charleston So.	20
54. Dayton	20
54. Harvard	20
54. Lafayette	20
54. Massachusetts	20
54. St. Francis (Pa.)	20
54. Southeastern La.	20
54. Wagner	20
54. Weber St.	20
63. Albany (N.Y.)	21
63. Austin Peay	21
63. Chattanooga	21
63. Duquesne	21
63. Monmouth	21
63. Morgan St.	21
63. Prairie View	21
63. Sacred Heart	21
71. Ark.-Pine Bluff	22
71. Brown	22
71. Indiana St.	22
71. Morehead St.	22
71. Norfolk St.	22
71. Portland St.	22
71. Richmond	22
78. Florida A&M	23
78. Montana	23
78. Rhode Island	23
78. Southern Utah	23
78. Tenn.-Martin	23
78. Tennessee St.	23
78. Towson	23
78. Valparaiso	23
86. Alcorn St.	24
86. Eastern Ill.	24
86. Eastern Ky.	24
86. Eastern Wash.	24
86. Idaho St.	24
86. Iona	24
86. Murray St.	24
93. Fordham	25
93. Grambling	25
93. Northwestern St.	25
93. Sacramento St.	25
93. Sam Houston St.	25
93. Texas St.	25
99. Bethune-Cookman	26
99. Coastal Caro.	26
99. La Salle	26
99. St. Peter's	26
103. Howard	27
103. Jackson St.	27
103. Montana St.	27
106. Georgetown	28
106. N.C. A&T	28
106. Samford	28
109. Savannah St.	29
110. Appalachian St.	30
110. Tennessee Tech	30
112. Nicholls St.	33
112. Robert Morris	33
112. Southern U.	33
115. Gardner-Webb	34
116. Texas Southern	40

Fewest Penalties Per Game

Rank, Team	G	Pen	Pen/Gm	W	L	T
1. Dayton	10	30	3.00	4	6	0
2. Wofford	11	41	3.73	7	4	0
3. Delaware	11	43	3.91	5	6	0
4. Bucknell	11	45	4.09	6	5	0
4. William & Mary	11	45	4.09	3	8	0
6. Davidson	10	42	4.20	6	4	0
7. Citadel	11	47	4.27	5	6	0
8. Villanova	11	48	4.36	6	5	0
9. Lafayette	12	53	4.42	6	6	0
10. VMI	11	49	4.45	1	10	0
11. Wagner	11	50	4.55	4	7	0
12. Dartmouth	10	46	4.60	2	8	0
13. Austin Peay	11	51	4.64	3	8	0
13. Missouri St.	11	51	4.64	2	9	0
13. Butler	11	51	4.64	3	8	0
13. Marist	11	51	4.64	4	7	0
17. Illinois St.	13	61	4.69	9	4	0
18. Furman	12	57	4.75	8	4	0
19. Richmond	11	54	4.91	6	5	0
19. Elon	11	54	4.91	5	6	0
21. Robert Morris	11	55	5.00	7	4	0
22. New Hampshire	13	66	5.08	9	4	0
23. Penn	10	51	5.10	5	5	0
24. Southern Ill.	13	68	5.23	9	4	0
25. Murray St.	11	58	5.27	1	10	0
25. Valparaiso	11	58	5.27	3	8	0
25. Western Ill.	11	58	5.27	5	6	0
28. Brown	10	53	5.30	3	7	0
28. Columbia	10	53	5.30	5	5	0
30. Hofstra	11	59	5.36	2	9	0
31. Monmouth	12	65	5.42	10	2	0
32. Youngstown St.	14	76	5.43	11	3	0
33. Central Conn. St.	11	60	5.45	8	3	0
33. Tennessee Tech	11	60	5.45	4	7	0
33. Holy Cross	11	60	5.45	7	4	0
33. Rhode Island	11	60	5.45	4	7	0
37. Eastern Ill.	13	71	5.46	8	5	0
38. Yale	10	55	5.50	8	2	0
39. Georgetown	11	62	5.64	2	9	0
39. Towson	11	62	5.64	7	4	0
39. Northeastern	11	62	5.64	5	6	0
39. Sam Houston St.	11	62	5.64	6	5	0
43. James Madison	12	68	5.67	9	3	0
44. Indiana St.	11	63	5.73	1	10	0
44. Western Ky.	11	63	5.73	6	5	0
46. Princeton	10	58	5.80	9	1	0
47. Cal Poly	11	64	5.82	7	4	0
48. Colgate	11	65	5.91	4	7	0
49. San Diego	12	71	5.92	11	1	0
50. Drake	11	66	6.00	9	2	0
50. La Salle	10	60	6.00	3	7	0
50. Southeastern La.	11	66	6.00	2	9	0
50. Western Caro.	11	66	6.00	2	9	0
50. St. Peter's	10	60	6.00	2	8	0
50. Morehead St.	11	66	6.00	2	9	0
56. Nicholls St.	11	67	6.09	4	7	0
56. Sacred Heart	11	67	6.09	2	9	0
56. Chattanooga	11	67	6.09	3	8	0
59. Lehigh	11	68	6.18	6	5	0
59. Stony Brook	11	68	6.18	5	6	0
59. Samford	11	68	6.18	3	8	0
59. Gardner-Webb	11	68	6.18	6	5	0
63. Cornell	10	63	6.30	5	5	0
64. Coastal Caro.	12	76	6.33	9	3	0
64. Massachusetts	15	95	6.33	13	2	0
66. Jacksonville St.	11	70	6.36	6	5	0
66. Maine	11	70	6.36	6	5	0
66. Liberty	11	70	6.36	6	5	0
69. Jacksonville	10	64	6.40	4	6	0
70. Eastern Wash.	11	71	6.45	3	8	0
70. Ga. Southern	11	71	6.45	3	8	0
70. Stephen F. Austin	11	71	6.45	4	7	0
73. Southeast Mo. St.	11	72	6.55	4	7	0
74. Montana	14	92	6.57	12	2	0
75. Appalachian St.	15	99	6.60	14	1	0
76. Harvard	10	67	6.70	7	3	0
76. Prairie View	10	67	6.70	3	7	0
78. Ark.-Pine Bluff	12	81	6.75	8	4	0
79. Charleston So.	11	75	6.82	9	2	0
79. St. Francis (Pa.)	11	75	6.82	3	8	0
81. UNI	11	76	6.91	7	4	0
82. Tenn.-Martin	12	83	6.92	9	3	0
83. Howard	11	77	7.00	5	6	0
83. N.C. A&T	11	77	7.00	0	11	0
83. Idaho St.	11	77	7.00	2	9	0
86. Southern U.	11	78	7.09	5	6	0
87. Weber St.	11	79	7.18	4	7	0
88. Alabama St.	11	81	7.36	5	6	0
88. Fordham	11	81	7.36	3	8	0
90. Savannah St.	11	83	7.55	2	9	0
91. Albany (N.Y.)	11	84	7.64	7	4	0
92. Portland St.	11	85	7.73	7	4	0
93. Alabama A&M	12	93	7.75	9	3	0
94. Montana St.	13	101	7.77	8	5	0
95. Northern Ariz.	11	87	7.91	6	5	0
95. Southern Utah	11	87	7.91	3	8	0
97. Texas St.	11	89	8.09	5	6	0
98. Alcorn St.	10	81	8.10	6	4	0
99. Iona	10	82	8.20	3	7	0
100. Florida A&M	11	91	8.27	7	4	0
101. Mississippi Val.	11	92	8.36	6	5	0
102. Sacramento St.	11	94	8.55	4	7	0
102. Tennessee St.	11	94	8.55	6	5	0
104. Duquesne	10	87	8.70	7	3	0
105. South Carolina St.	11	96	8.73	7	4	0
106. Morgan St.	11	97	8.82	5	6	0
107. Eastern Ky.	11	98	8.91	6	5	0
108. Hampton	12	109	9.08	10	2	0

Rank, Team	G	Pen	Pen/Gm	W	L	T
109. Norfolk St.	11	101	9.18	4	7	0
110. Jackson St.	10	93	9.30	5	5	0
111. Delaware St.	11	103	9.36	8	3	0
112. Northwestern St.	11	104	9.45	4	7	0
112. Texas Southern	11	104	9.45	3	8	0
114. Bethune-Cookman	11	108	9.82	5	6	0
115. Grambling	11	110	10.00	3	8	0
116. McNeese St.	12	121	10.08	7	5	0

Fewest Yards Penalized Per Game

Rank, Team	G	Penalty Yds	Yds/Gm	W	L	T
1. Dayton	10	303	30.30	4	6	0
2. Citadel	11	342	31.09	5	6	0
3. Wofford	11	351	31.91	7	4	0
4. Bucknell	11	356	32.36	6	5	0
5. Davidson	10	326	32.60	6	4	0
6. New Hampshire	13	448	34.46	9	4	0
7. Delaware	11	391	35.55	5	6	0
8. VMI	11	397	36.09	1	10	0
9. William & Mary	11	400	36.36	3	8	0
10. Richmond	11	426	38.73	6	5	0
11. Elon	11	427	38.82	5	6	0
12. Western Ill.	11	431	39.18	5	6	0
13. Lafayette	12	472	39.33	6	6	0
14. Dartmouth	10	398	39.80	2	8	0
15. Villanova	11	439	39.91	6	5	0
16. Furman	12	479	39.92	8	4	0
17. Butler	11	444	40.36	3	8	0
18. Rhode Island	11	447	40.64	4	7	0
19. Illinois St.	13	533	41.00	9	4	0
20. Murray St.	11	471	42.82	1	10	0
21. Valparaiso	11	475	43.18	3	8	0
22. Georgetown	11	477	43.36	2	9	0
23. Wagner	11	478	43.45	4	7	0
24. Marist	11	479	43.55	4	7	0
25. Penn	10	444	44.40	5	5	0
26. Youngstown St.	14	634	45.29	11	3	0
27. Missouri St.	11	502	45.64	2	9	0
27. Robert Morris	11	502	45.64	7	4	0
29. Western Ky.	11	503	45.73	6	5	0
30. Austin Peay	11	508	46.18	3	8	0
31. Cal Poly	11	510	46.36	7	4	0
32. Tennessee Tech	11	512	46.55	4	7	0
33. Brown	10	468	46.80	3	7	0
34. James Madison	12	562	46.83	9	3	0
35. Columbia	10	471	47.10	5	5	0
36. Southern Ill.	13	613	47.15	9	4	0
37. Central Conn. St.	11	519	47.18	8	3	0
37. Western Caro.	11	519	47.18	2	9	0
39. Holy Cross	11	520	47.27	7	4	0
40. St. Peter's	10	474	47.40	2	8	0
41. Towson	11	525	47.73	7	4	0
42. Princeton	10	481	48.10	9	1	0
43. Drake	11	530	48.18	9	2	0
44. Indiana St.	11	532	48.36	1	10	0
45. La Salle	10	485	48.50	3	7	0
46. Sam Houston St.	11	534	48.55	6	5	0
47. Yale	10	488	48.80	8	2	0
48. Hofstra	11	537	48.82	2	9	0
49. Lehigh	11	553	50.27	6	5	0
50. Monmouth	12	609	50.75	10	2	0
51. Eastern Ill.	13	660	50.77	8	5	0
52. Nicholls St.	11	569	51.73	4	7	0
53. San Diego	12	626	52.17	11	1	0
54. Harvard	10	525	52.50	7	3	0
55. Cornell	10	533	53.30	5	5	0
56. Samford	11	587	53.36	3	8	0
57. Stony Brook	11	591	53.73	5	6	0
58. Coastal Caro.	12	651	54.25	9	3	0
59. Chattanooga	11	597	54.27	3	8	0
60. Colgate	11	600	54.55	4	7	0
61. Northeastern	11	609	55.36	5	6	0
62. Eastern Wash.	11	610	55.45	3	8	0
63. Ga. Southern	11	615	55.91	3	8	0
64. Southeastern La.	11	617	56.09	2	9	0
65. Massachusetts	15	842	56.13	13	2	0
66. Southeast Mo. St.	11	618	56.18	4	7	0
67. Jacksonville	10	567	56.70	4	6	0
68. Jacksonville St.	11	624	56.73	6	5	0
69. Gardner-Webb	11	626	56.91	6	5	0
69. Southern U.	11	626	56.91	5	6	0
71. St. Francis (Pa.)	11	633	57.55	3	8	0
71. Stephen F. Austin	11	633	57.55	4	7	0
73. Alabama St.	11	636	57.82	5	6	0
73. Morehead St.	11	636	57.82	2	9	0
73. Sacred Heart	11	636	57.82	2	9	0
76. N.C. A&T	11	642	58.36	0	11	0
77. Liberty	11	648	58.91	6	5	0
78. Charleston So.	11	649	59.00	9	2	0
78. Weber St.	11	649	59.00	4	7	0
80. Maine	11	652	59.27	6	5	0
81. UNI	11	669	60.82	7	4	0
82. Idaho St.	11	672	61.09	2	9	0
83. Appalachian St.	15	918	61.20	14	1	0
84. Prairie View	10	623	62.30	3	7	0
85. Tennessee St.	11	698	63.45	6	5	0
86. Alabama A&M	12	762	63.50	9	3	0
87. Albany (N.Y.)	11	700	63.64	7	4	0
88. Montana St.	13	839	64.54	8	5	0
89. Tenn.-Martin	12	782	65.17	9	3	0
90. Eastern Ky.	11	718	65.27	6	5	0
91. Northern Ariz.	11	719	65.36	6	5	0
92. Fordham	11	726	66.00	3	8	0
93. Howard	11	730	66.36	5	6	0
94. Montana	14	932	66.57	12	2	0
95. Portland St.	11	741	67.36	7	4	0
96. Savannah St.	11	745	67.73	2	9	0
97. Sacramento St.	11	751	68.27	4	7	0
98. Ark.-Pine Bluff	12	840	70.00	8	4	0
99. Mississippi Val.	11	771	70.09	6	5	0
100. Southern Utah	11	781	71.00	3	8	0
101. Hampton	12	858	71.50	10	2	0
102. Northwestern St.	11	794	72.18	4	7	0
103. Texas St.	11	807	73.36	5	6	0
104. Alcorn St.	10	742	74.20	6	4	0
105. Texas Southern	11	846	76.91	3	8	0
106. South Carolina St.	11	853	77.55	7	4	0
107. Norfolk St.	11	860	78.18	4	7	0
108. Iona	10	784	78.40	3	7	0
109. Bethune-Cookman	11	873	79.36	5	6	0
110. Grambling	11	877	79.73	3	8	0
111. Duquesne	10	808	80.80	7	3	0
112. Florida A&M	11	902	82.00	7	4	0
113. Delaware St.	11	936	85.09	8	3	0
114. McNeese St.	12	1,032	86.00	7	5	0
115. Morgan St.	11	971	88.27	5	6	0
116. Jackson St.	10	1,068	106.80	5	5	0

Punt Return Yardage Defense

Rank, Team	Ret	Return Yds	Yds/Ret	W	L	T
1. Holy Cross	13	36	2.77	7	4	0
2. Drake	14	41	2.93	9	2	0
3. Yale	11	37	3.36	8	2	0
4. Chattanooga	24	86	3.58	3	8	0
5. Appalachian St.	18	66	3.67	14	1	0
6. Dayton	21	82	3.90	4	6	0
7. Youngstown St.	21	96	4.57	11	3	0
8. Maine	15	70	4.67	6	5	0
9. Duquesne	18	85	4.72	7	3	0
10. San Diego	8	38	4.75	11	1	0
11. Sacred Heart	25	123	4.92	2	9	0
12. Charleston So.	19	94	4.95	9	2	0
13. Penn	24	122	5.08	5	5	0
14. Robert Morris	27	144	5.33	7	4	0
15. William & Mary	18	97	5.39	3	8	0
16. Montana	32	173	5.41	12	2	0
17. Alabama A&M	7	38	5.43	9	3	0
18. Brown	16	88	5.50	3	7	0
19. Lafayette	21	119	5.67	6	6	0
20. James Madison	17	97	5.71	9	3	0
21. Southern Ill.	22	128	5.82	9	4	0
22. Tennessee Tech	31	183	5.90	4	7	0
23. Idaho St.	24	145	6.04	2	9	0
24. Eastern Ky.	22	134	6.09	6	5	0
25. Dartmouth	20	122	6.10	2	8	0
26. Citadel	33	203	6.15	5	6	0
27. Alcorn St.	19	122	6.42	6	4	0
28. Bethune-Cookman	8	52	6.50	5	6	0
29. Cornell	28	186	6.64	5	5	0
29. Richmond	14	93	6.64	6	5	0
31. Montana St.	30	200	6.67	8	5	0
32. Norfolk St.	25	169	6.76	4	7	0
33. Georgetown	25	178	7.12	2	9	0

Rank, Team	Ret	Return Yds	Yds/Ret	W	L	T
34. Mississippi Val.	23	165	7.17	6	5	0
35. Delaware St.	20	144	7.20	8	3	0
36. Delaware	12	88	7.33	5	6	0
37. Massachusetts	20	149	7.45	13	2	0
38. Northwestern St.	26	194	7.46	4	7	0
39. Tenn.-Martin	27	204	7.56	9	3	0
40. Hofstra	32	242	7.56	2	9	0
41. Eastern Ill.	25	192	7.68	8	5	0
42. Coastal Caro.	11	85	7.73	9	3	0
43. Columbia	31	248	8.00	5	5	0
44. Elon	26	209	8.04	5	6	0
45. Monmouth	24	196	8.17	10	2	0
45. Prairie View	24	196	8.17	3	7	0
47. Howard	21	174	8.29	5	6	0
48. Furman	17	141	8.29	8	4	0
49. Harvard	16	133	8.31	7	3	0
50. Tennessee St.	16	134	8.38	6	5	0
51. Austin Peay	22	185	8.41	3	8	0
52. Savannah St.	26	219	8.42	2	9	0
53. Morehead St.	17	144	8.47	2	9	0
54. Southeast Mo. St.	39	343	8.79	4	7	0
55. Wofford	24	214	8.92	7	4	0
56. Princeton	18	162	9.00	9	1	0
57. Alabama St.	29	262	9.03	5	6	0
58. Illinois St.	14	127	9.07	9	4	0
59. Wagner	23	209	9.09	4	7	0
60. Ga. Southern	28	255	9.11	3	8	0
61. Weber St.	31	285	9.19	4	7	0
62. Morgan St.	28	259	9.25	5	6	0
63. Central Conn. St.	18	168	9.33	8	3	0
63. Texas Southern	21	196	9.33	3	8	0
65. Valparaiso	29	273	9.41	3	8	0
66. Bucknell	26	246	9.46	6	5	0
67. Portland St.	36	343	9.53	7	4	0
68. Cal Poly	29	277	9.55	7	4	0
69. Murray St.	24	231	9.63	1	10	0
70. Iona	19	183	9.63	3	7	0
71. Stony Brook	30	293	9.77	5	6	0
72. McNeese St.	29	289	9.97	7	5	0
73. Hampton	14	140	10.00	10	2	0
74. Samford	31	314	10.13	3	8	0
75. Lehigh	20	203	10.15	6	5	0
76. Liberty	27	276	10.22	6	5	0
76. Southern U.	27	276	10.22	5	6	0
78. Southern Utah	22	225	10.23	3	8	0
79. Towson	26	266	10.23	7	4	0
80. New Hampshire	13	139	10.69	9	4	0
81. St. Peter's	26	279	10.73	2	8	0
82. Albany (N.Y.)	16	178	11.13	7	4	0
83. Southeastern La.	23	257	11.17	2	9	0
84. Northeastern	19	214	11.26	5	6	0
85. Nicholls St.	22	248	11.27	4	7	0
86. Sacramento St.	40	454	11.35	4	7	0
87. Indiana St.	27	315	11.67	1	10	0
88. Davidson	24	281	11.71	6	4	0
89. Marist	25	293	11.72	4	7	0
90. Western Ill.	10	119	11.90	5	6	0
91. Missouri St.	32	383	11.97	2	9	0
92. Butler	32	390	12.19	3	8	0
93. St. Francis (Pa.)	28	342	12.21	3	8	0
94. Jackson St.	20	245	12.25	5	5	0
95. Villanova	25	312	12.48	6	5	0
96. Jacksonville	19	238	12.53	4	6	0
97. Stephen F. Austin	16	205	12.81	4	7	0
98. Northern Ariz.	15	194	12.93	6	5	0
99. Rhode Island	22	285	12.95	4	7	0
100. N.C. A&T	32	415	12.97	0	11	0
101. South Carolina St.	12	158	13.17	7	4	0
102. Colgate	28	376	13.43	4	7	0
103. Ark.-Pine Bluff	25	338	13.52	8	4	0
104. Gardner-Webb	23	311	13.52	6	5	0
105. La Salle	28	380	13.57	3	7	0
106. Western Caro.	29	396	13.66	2	9	0
107. Eastern Wash.	29	398	13.72	3	8	0
108. Fordham	30	416	13.87	3	8	0
109. Florida A&M	16	226	14.13	7	4	0
110. Sam Houston St.	17	245	14.41	6	5	0
111. Grambling	22	327	14.86	3	8	0
112. Jacksonville St.	18	278	15.44	6	5	0
113. UNI	13	201	15.46	7	4	0
114. VMI	34	626	18.41	1	10	0
115. Texas St.	23	466	20.26	5	6	0
116. Western Ky.	16	389	24.31	6	5	0

Kickoff Return Yardage Defense

Rank, Team	Ret	Return Yds	Yds/Ret	W	L	T
1. South Carolina St.	52	703	13.52	7	4	0
2. Alcorn St.	47	664	14.13	6	4	0
3. Western Ill.	31	439	14.16	5	6	0
4. Stony Brook	41	589	14.37	5	6	0
5. Albany (N.Y.)	34	514	15.12	7	4	0
6. Maine	37	560	15.14	6	5	0
7. Alabama St.	29	445	15.34	5	6	0
8. Robert Morris	37	568	15.35	7	4	0
9. Bucknell	40	644	16.10	6	5	0
10. Cal Poly	37	597	16.14	7	4	0
11. William & Mary	36	593	16.47	3	8	0
12. Monmouth	46	759	16.50	10	2	0
13. San Diego	78	1,301	16.68	11	1	0
14. Indiana St.	40	669	16.73	1	10	0
15. Delaware St.	55	936	17.02	8	3	0
16. Dartmouth	30	511	17.03	2	8	0
17. Montana St.	47	803	17.09	8	5	0
18. Eastern Ill.	50	867	17.34	8	5	0
19. Hofstra	26	452	17.38	2	9	0
20. Elon	43	749	17.42	5	6	0
21. Sacred Heart	36	629	17.47	2	9	0
22. Cornell	35	625	17.86	5	5	0
23. Austin Peay	39	699	17.92	3	8	0
24. Central Conn. St.	51	920	18.04	8	3	0
25. Idaho St.	32	578	18.06	2	9	0
26. Western Caro.	25	454	18.16	2	9	0
27. Princeton	42	763	18.17	9	1	0
28. Morgan St.	33	600	18.18	5	6	0
29. Samford	29	529	18.24	3	8	0
30. Lehigh	52	952	18.31	6	5	0
31. Wagner	31	568	18.32	4	7	0
32. Prairie View	27	495	18.33	3	7	0
33. Tenn.-Martin	49	902	18.41	9	3	0
34. Duquesne	49	908	18.53	7	3	0
35. Sam Houston St.	37	686	18.54	6	5	0
36. Stephen F. Austin	45	836	18.58	4	7	0
37. Penn	42	782	18.62	5	5	0
38. Davidson	42	785	18.69	6	4	0
39. Savannah St.	25	468	18.72	2	9	0
40. Youngstown St.	68	1,274	18.74	11	3	0
41. Montana	62	1,164	18.77	12	2	0
42. Massachusetts	67	1,260	18.81	13	2	0
43. Norfolk St.	38	717	18.87	4	7	0
44. Citadel	41	775	18.90	5	6	0
45. Holy Cross	46	876	19.04	7	4	0
46. Southern U.	43	820	19.07	5	6	0
47. Eastern Wash.	29	556	19.17	3	8	0
48. Harvard	42	806	19.19	7	3	0
49. Jackson St.	48	924	19.25	5	5	0
50. Southern Ill.	51	983	19.27	9	4	0
51. Illinois St.	54	1,042	19.30	9	4	0
52. Southeastern La.	31	606	19.55	2	9	0
53. Jacksonville St.	51	1,001	19.63	6	5	0
54. Hampton	63	1,243	19.73	10	2	0
55. Weber St.	38	750	19.74	4	7	0
56. Drake	48	953	19.85	9	2	0
57. Dayton	35	696	19.89	4	6	0
58. Tennessee St.	34	679	19.97	6	5	0
59. Richmond	39	781	20.03	6	5	0
60. Gardner-Webb	38	764	20.11	6	5	0
61. Coastal Caro.	52	1,047	20.13	9	3	0
62. McNeese St.	47	948	20.17	7	5	0
63. Nicholls St.	28	565	20.18	4	7	0
64. Texas St.	40	808	20.20	5	6	0
65. Portland St.	44	889	20.20	7	4	0
66. St. Francis (Pa.)	32	647	20.22	3	8	0
67. Northeastern	36	728	20.22	5	6	0
68. Valparaiso	35	708	20.23	3	8	0
69. Bethune-Cookman	42	852	20.29	5	6	0
70. Texas Southern	32	650	20.31	3	8	0
71. Charleston So.	45	919	20.42	9	2	0
71. Colgate	45	919	20.42	4	7	0
73. New Hampshire	73	1,495	20.48	9	4	0
74. Southern Utah	36	745	20.69	3	8	0
75. Rhode Island	37	767	20.73	4	7	0
76. Iona	32	664	20.75	3	7	0
77. Appalachian St.	53	1,100	20.75	14	1	0
78. Liberty	40	831	20.78	6	5	0
79. Yale	43	896	20.84	8	2	0
80. Florida A&M	45	938	20.84	7	4	0

Rank, Team	Ret	Return Yds	Yds/Ret	W	L	T
81. UNI	28	584	20.86	7	4	0
82. Lafayette	57	1,190	20.88	6	6	0
83. Northern Ariz.	21	439	20.90	6	5	0
84. Delaware	42	879	20.93	5	6	0
85. Eastern Ky.	42	881	20.98	6	5	0
86. VMI	40	840	21.00	1	10	0
87. James Madison	48	1,009	21.02	9	3	0
88. Furman	47	1,000	21.28	8	4	0
89. Georgetown	28	597	21.32	2	9	0
90. Chattanooga	30	650	21.67	3	8	0
91. Howard	35	763	21.80	5	6	0
92. Jacksonville	31	676	21.81	4	6	0
93. Ark.-Pine Bluff	45	985	21.89	8	4	0
94. Tennessee Tech	32	706	22.06	4	7	0
95. Butler	32	707	22.09	3	8	0
96. Villanova	33	731	22.15	6	5	0
97. Morehead St.	33	732	22.18	2	9	0
98. Mississippi Val.	29	646	22.28	6	5	0
99. Sacramento St.	27	606	22.44	4	7	0
100. Alabama A&M	44	996	22.64	9	3	0
101. Marist	40	906	22.65	4	7	0
102. Brown	39	888	22.77	3	7	0
103. Columbia	31	706	22.77	5	5	0
104. Western Ky.	37	843	22.78	6	5	0
105. Fordham	25	573	22.92	3	8	0
106. Murray St.	38	871	22.92	1	10	0
107. La Salle	30	689	22.97	3	7	0
108. Towson	33	764	23.15	7	4	0
109. Wofford	31	719	23.19	7	4	0
110. Ga. Southern	40	929	23.23	3	8	0
111. Missouri St.	28	659	23.54	2	9	0
112. Northwestern St.	40	944	23.60	4	7	0
113. Grambling	36	853	23.69	3	8	0
114. Southeast Mo. St.	23	575	25.00	4	7	0
115. St. Peter's	28	701	25.04	2	8	0
116. N.C. A&T	22	651	29.59	0	11	0

Third-Down Efficiency Offense

Rank, Team	Att	Conv	Pct.
1. San Diego	156	91	58.33
2. Western Ill.	137	71	51.82
3. Bethune-Cookman	138	71	51.45
4. Illinois St.	178	89	50.00
5. Charleston So.	134	66	49.25
6. Coastal Caro.	153	75	49.02
7. UNI	129	63	48.84
8. New Hampshire	185	89	48.11
9. Western Ky.	142	68	47.89
10. Liberty	139	66	47.48
11. Youngstown St.	179	84	46.93
12. Furman	158	74	46.84
13. Southern Ill.	139	65	46.76
14. Holy Cross	147	68	46.26
15. Tennessee St.	131	60	45.80
16. James Madison	143	65	45.45
17. Richmond	139	63	45.32
18. Yale	132	59	44.70
19. Drake	146	65	44.52
20. Monmouth	171	76	44.44
21. Northern Ariz.	142	62	43.66
22. Appalachian St.	188	82	43.62
23. Delaware	156	68	43.59
24. Florida A&M	141	61	43.26
25. Davidson	137	59	43.07
26. St. Francis (Pa.)	142	61	42.96
27. Duquesne	138	59	42.75
27. Hampton	138	59	42.75
29. Eastern Ky.	144	60	41.67
30. Brown	135	56	41.48
30. Texas St.	135	56	41.48
32. Towson	145	60	41.38
33. Maine	158	65	41.14
34. Wofford	149	61	40.94
35. Villanova	132	54	40.91
36. Lehigh	135	55	40.74
37. Bucknell	150	61	40.67
37. Elon	150	61	40.67
39. Georgetown	144	57	39.58
40. Rhode Island	165	65	39.39
41. Jackson St.	117	46	39.32
42. Citadel	158	62	39.24
43. Alabama A&M	153	60	39.22
44. Grambling	136	53	38.97
45. Indiana St.	154	60	38.96
46. Massachusetts	172	67	38.95
47. Marist	131	51	38.93
48. Nicholls St.	134	52	38.81
49. Ark.-Pine Bluff	132	51	38.64
50. Gardner-Webb	107	41	38.32
51. Harvard	141	54	38.30
52. Mississippi Val.	144	55	38.19
53. La Salle	131	50	38.17
53. Norfolk St.	131	50	38.17
55. Robert Morris	152	58	38.16
56. Southern Utah	139	53	38.13
57. McNeese St.	147	56	38.10
58. Central Conn. St.	142	54	38.03
59. Eastern Ill.	166	63	37.95
60. Austin Peay	141	53	37.59
61. Valparaiso	149	56	37.58
62. Sam Houston St.	136	51	37.50
63. Howard	158	59	37.34
64. Dartmouth	134	50	37.31
65. Tenn.-Martin	161	60	37.27
66. Montana	202	75	37.13
67. Sacramento St.	152	56	36.84
68. St. Peter's	147	54	36.73
69. Dayton	131	48	36.64
69. South Carolina St.	131	48	36.64
71. Stony Brook	142	51	35.92
72. Morehead St.	148	53	35.81
72. William & Mary	148	53	35.81
74. Lafayette	137	49	35.77
75. Iona	151	54	35.76
76. Southern U.	135	48	35.56
77. Cornell	147	52	35.37
78. Colgate	148	52	35.14
79. Princeton	137	48	35.04
80. Columbia	143	50	34.97
80. Penn	143	50	34.97
82. Sacred Heart	135	47	34.81
83. Albany (N.Y.)	141	49	34.75
84. Idaho St.	151	52	34.44
85. Jacksonville	128	44	34.38
86. Stephen F. Austin	137	47	34.31
87. Southeastern La.	155	53	34.19
88. Northeastern	138	47	34.06
89. Missouri St.	144	48	33.33
90. Jacksonville St.	145	48	33.10
91. Northwestern St.	167	55	32.93
92. Tennessee Tech	152	50	32.89
92. Alabama St.	149	49	32.89
94. VMI	138	45	32.61
95. Murray St.	152	49	32.24
96. Cal Poly	140	45	32.14
97. Eastern Wash.	156	49	31.41
98. Texas Southern	131	41	31.30
99. Western Caro.	144	45	31.25
100. Chattanooga	157	49	31.21
101. Morgan St.	135	42	31.11
102. Fordham	151	46	30.46
103. Ga. Southern	158	48	30.38
104. N.C. A&T	139	42	30.22
105. Southeast Mo. St.	143	43	30.07
106. Delaware St.	117	34	29.06
107. Portland St.	148	43	29.05
108. Samford	142	40	28.17
109. Savannah St.	134	37	27.61
110. Montana St.	175	48	27.43
111. Hofstra	156	42	26.92
112. Wagner	132	35	26.52
113. Weber St.	142	37	26.06
114. Alcorn St.	128	33	25.78
115. Prairie View	141	36	25.53
116. Butler	156	38	24.36

Fourth-Down Efficiency Offense

Rank, Team	Att	Conv	Pct.
1. Youngstown St.	11	10	90.91
2. Ark.-Pine Bluff	8	7	87.50
3. Florida A&M	6	5	83.33
4. Delaware	18	14	77.78
5. Harvard	18	13	72.22
6. Jackson St.	14	10	71.43
6. Liberty	7	5	71.43

Rank, Team	Att	Conv	Pct.
8. Bethune-Cookman	10	7	70.00
9. Central Conn. St.	26	18	69.23
10. Northwestern St.	18	12	66.67
10. Southern Ill.	12	8	66.67
10. Delaware St.	9	6	66.67
13. Lafayette	17	11	64.71
14. Cal Poly	14	9	64.29
15. Massachusetts	19	12	63.16
16. Davidson	16	10	62.50
16. Lehigh	16	10	62.50
18. Chattanooga	21	13	61.90
19. Jacksonville St.	13	8	61.54
20. Appalachian St.	25	15	60.00
20. Citadel	20	12	60.00
20. Charleston So.	10	6	60.00
20. Yale	10	6	60.00
24. New Hampshire	22	13	59.09
25. Alcorn St.	19	11	57.89
26. Rhode Island	26	15	57.69
27. Tenn.-Martin	21	12	57.14
28. Brown	23	13	56.52
29. Samford	16	9	56.25
29. Southern Utah	16	9	56.25
31. William & Mary	25	14	56.00
32. Northeastern	18	10	55.56
32. VMI	18	10	55.56
32. Princeton	18	10	55.56
35. Coastal Caro.	20	11	55.00
36. Alabama A&M	31	17	54.84
37. Dartmouth	15	8	53.33
38. Illinois St.	17	9	52.94
39. James Madison	19	10	52.63
39. Montana	19	10	52.63
41. Colgate	25	13	52.00
42. Georgetown	24	12	50.00
42. San Diego	22	11	50.00
42. Austin Peay	18	9	50.00
42. Monmouth	16	8	50.00
42. Weber St.	16	8	50.00
42. Richmond	16	8	50.00
42. Sacramento St.	12	6	50.00
42. Duquesne	10	5	50.00
42. Northern Ariz.	10	5	50.00
51. Towson	23	11	47.83
52. Furman	17	8	47.06
52. Jacksonville	17	8	47.06
54. Grambling	30	14	46.67
54. Stephen F. Austin	15	7	46.67
56. Albany (N.Y.)	13	6	46.15
56. Portland St.	13	6	46.15
56. McNeese St.	13	6	46.15
56. Hofstra	13	6	46.15
60. St. Francis (Pa.)	20	9	45.00
61. Dayton	18	8	44.44
62. Southeast Mo. St.	16	7	43.75
62. Elon	16	7	43.75
64. Cornell	23	10	43.48
65. Ga. Southern	21	9	42.86
65. Hampton	14	6	42.86
65. Nicholls St.	14	6	42.86
68. Prairie View	26	11	42.31
68. Wofford	26	11	42.31
70. Eastern Ky.	12	5	41.67
71. Sam Houston St.	17	7	41.18
71. Villanova	17	7	41.18
73. Indiana St.	22	9	40.91
73. Missouri St.	22	9	40.91
75. South Carolina St.	25	10	40.00
75. Eastern Wash.	15	6	40.00
75. Iona	15	6	40.00
75. Western Ill.	15	6	40.00
75. Western Ky.	10	4	40.00
80. Drake	18	7	38.89
80. Valparaiso	18	7	38.89
82. Maine	26	10	38.46
82. Bucknell	13	5	38.46
82. Eastern Ill.	13	5	38.46
82. Wagner	13	5	38.46
86. Fordham	21	8	38.10
87. Montana St.	24	9	37.50
87. Norfolk St.	16	6	37.50
87. Sacred Heart	16	6	37.50
87. Tennessee Tech	16	6	37.50
87. Penn	16	6	37.50
87. UNI	8	3	37.50
93. Butler	19	7	36.84
93. Robert Morris	19	7	36.84
95. Marist	17	6	35.29
95. Texas Southern	17	6	35.29
95. N.C. A&T	17	6	35.29
98. Morehead St.	24	8	33.33
98. Howard	15	5	33.33
98. Mississippi Val.	9	3	33.33
101. Alabama St.	13	4	30.77
102. Stony Brook	17	5	29.41
103. Idaho St.	21	6	28.57
103. Columbia	14	4	28.57
105. Holy Cross	18	5	27.78
106. Murray St.	23	6	26.09
106. Western Caro.	23	6	26.09
108. Savannah St.	28	7	25.00
109. St. Peter's	25	6	24.00
110. La Salle	17	4	23.53
111. Tennessee St.	13	3	23.08
112. Morgan St.	22	5	22.73
113. Southeastern La.	21	4	19.05
114. Gardner-Webb	6	1	16.67
115. Southern U.	14	2	14.29
116. Texas St.	9	0	0.00

Third-Down Efficiency Defense

Rank, Team	Att	Conv	Pct.
1. Robert Morris	146	37	25.34
2. Northwestern St.	125	34	27.20
3. Princeton	128	35	27.34
4. Montana	196	55	28.06
4. Portland St.	139	39	28.06
6. Jacksonville St.	146	41	28.08
7. Alabama St.	120	35	29.17
8. Appalachian St.	219	65	29.68
9. Cal Poly	151	46	30.46
10. Duquesne	133	41	30.83
11. Hampton	165	51	30.91
12. Northern Ariz.	142	45	31.69
13. Southern U.	141	45	31.91
14. Albany (N.Y.)	166	53	31.93
15. Tennessee Tech	136	44	32.35
16. Alabama A&M	141	46	32.62
17. Tenn.-Martin	165	54	32.73
18. Texas Southern	125	41	32.80
19. Towson	131	43	32.82
20. Stephen F. Austin	130	43	33.08
21. Howard	145	48	33.10
22. Harvard	148	49	33.11
23. San Diego	155	52	33.55
24. Drake	146	49	33.56
25. Prairie View	119	40	33.61
26. Massachusetts	202	68	33.66
27. Cornell	127	43	33.86
28. Penn	147	50	34.01
29. Iona	135	46	34.07
30. Monmouth	167	57	34.13
31. Maine	149	51	34.23
32. Montana St.	191	67	35.08
33. New Hampshire	179	63	35.20
34. Hofstra	150	53	35.33
35. Alcorn St.	143	51	35.66
36. Jackson St.	137	49	35.77
37. Wofford	145	52	35.86
38. Youngstown St.	170	61	35.88
39. Florida A&M	128	46	35.94
40. Austin Peay	150	54	36.00
41. Liberty	136	49	36.03
42. Mississippi Val.	127	46	36.22
43. Central Conn. St.	160	58	36.25
44. Texas St.	137	50	36.50
45. Citadel	142	52	36.62
45. Fordham	142	52	36.62
47. Colgate	152	56	36.84
48. La Salle	111	41	36.94
49. Eastern Ky.	138	51	36.96
50. Grambling	142	53	37.32
51. Rhode Island	139	52	37.41
52. Brown	138	52	37.68
53. Jacksonville	122	46	37.70

Rank, Team	Att	Conv	Pct.
54. Bucknell	143	54	37.76
55. Columbia	135	51	37.78
56. Weber St.	153	58	37.91
57. Idaho St.	163	62	38.04
58. Southeastern La.	134	51	38.06
59. Ga. Southern	151	58	38.41
60. Bethune-Cookman	140	54	38.57
60. Valparaiso	140	54	38.57
60. Morgan St.	140	54	38.57
63. Dayton	131	51	38.93
64. Furman	151	59	39.07
65. Holy Cross	148	58	39.19
66. Coastal Caro.	153	60	39.22
67. Nicholls St.	140	55	39.29
68. Richmond	147	58	39.46
68. Samford	147	58	39.46
70. Delaware St.	153	61	39.87
71. Eastern Wash.	140	56	40.00
71. Western Caro.	135	54	40.00
73. South Carolina St.	147	59	40.14
74. Norfolk St.	132	53	40.15
75. James Madison	159	64	40.25
76. Sacramento St.	154	62	40.26
77. Davidson	136	55	40.44
78. Lafayette	153	62	40.52
79. Chattanooga	148	60	40.54
80. Sam Houston St.	160	66	41.25
81. Lehigh	147	61	41.50
82. Stony Brook	141	59	41.84
83. Villanova	150	63	42.00
84. St. Peter's	121	51	42.15
85. Morehead St.	149	63	42.28
86. Southern Ill.	182	77	42.31
87. Ark.-Pine Bluff	158	67	42.41
88. Wagner	141	60	42.55
89. Missouri St.	155	66	42.58
90. Southeast Mo. St.	157	67	42.68
91. McNeese St.	154	66	42.86
92. Gardner-Webb	121	52	42.98
93. St. Francis (Pa.)	116	50	43.10
94. Eastern Ill.	169	73	43.20
95. Illinois St.	171	74	43.27
96. UNI	131	57	43.51
97. Yale	126	55	43.65
98. Charleston So.	153	67	43.79
99. Georgetown	141	62	43.97
100. Butler	138	61	44.20
101. Dartmouth	135	60	44.44
102. Elon	158	71	44.94
103. Western Ky.	135	61	45.19
104. Southern Utah	143	65	45.45
105. Delaware	138	63	45.65
106. Sacred Heart	147	68	46.26
107. William & Mary	134	63	47.01
108. Murray St.	138	65	47.10
109. Savannah St.	125	59	47.20
110. Tennessee St.	145	69	47.59
111. N.C. A&T	114	56	49.12
112. Marist	149	74	49.66
113. Northeastern	142	71	50.00
114. Western Ill.	143	74	51.75
115. Indiana St.	139	75	53.96
116. VMI	132	79	59.85

Fourth-Down Efficiency Defense

Rank, Team	Att	Conv	Pct.
1. Eastern Ky.	17	3	17.65
2. Tenn.-Martin	22	4	18.18
3. Iona	18	4	22.22
4. Portland St.	23	6	26.09
5. Maine	19	5	26.32
6. Howard	18	5	27.78
7. Robert Morris	14	4	28.57
8. Grambling	20	6	30.00
9. Towson	23	7	30.43
10. Jackson St.	13	4	30.77
11. Montana St.	16	5	31.25
12. Monmouth	19	6	31.58
13. Appalachian St.	28	9	32.14
14. Butler	21	7	33.33
14. Bethune-Cookman	15	5	33.33

Rank, Team	Att	Conv	Pct.
14. Jacksonville St.	15	5	33.33
14. Valparaiso	15	5	33.33
14. Tennessee Tech	12	4	33.33
19. Ga. Southern	17	6	35.29
20. Lafayette	14	5	35.71
20. Wagner	14	5	35.71
22. San Diego	22	8	36.36
22. Eastern Wash.	11	4	36.36
22. Northwestern St.	11	4	36.36
25. Alabama St.	19	7	36.84
25. Marist	19	7	36.84
27. Delaware St.	16	6	37.50
27. Texas St.	16	6	37.50
29. Prairie View	13	5	38.46
30. Penn	23	9	39.13
31. Harvard	20	8	40.00
31. Duquesne	15	6	40.00
31. Cal Poly	10	4	40.00
31. Norfolk St.	10	4	40.00
35. Youngstown St.	27	11	40.74
36. Eastern Ill.	17	7	41.18
37. Central Conn. St.	24	10	41.67
38. Yale	19	8	42.11
38. Elon	19	8	42.11
38. Ark.-Pine Bluff	19	8	42.11
41. Illinois St.	21	9	42.86
41. Princeton	21	9	42.86
41. Liberty	21	9	42.86
41. Georgetown	14	6	42.86
41. Jacksonville	14	6	42.86
41. James Madison	14	6	42.86
47. Sam Houston St.	23	10	43.48
48. Cornell	16	7	43.75
48. South Carolina St.	16	7	43.75
50. Wofford	25	11	44.00
51. Drake	18	8	44.44
51. Western Ill.	18	8	44.44
53. Albany (N.Y.)	20	9	45.00
53. Charleston So.	20	9	45.00
55. Dayton	11	5	45.45
56. Southern Ill.	24	11	45.83
57. Southern Utah	13	6	46.15
58. Rhode Island	28	13	46.43
59. McNeese St.	15	7	46.67
60. Massachusetts	21	10	47.62
60. Savannah St.	21	10	47.62
62. Citadel	22	11	50.00
62. Montana	20	10	50.00
62. Dartmouth	18	9	50.00
62. Florida A&M	18	9	50.00
62. Fordham	16	8	50.00
62. Indiana St.	14	7	50.00
62. Murray St.	12	6	50.00
69. Furman	29	15	51.72
70. New Hampshire	27	14	51.85
71. Coastal Caro.	23	12	52.17
72. Delaware	21	11	52.38
72. Southeast Mo. St.	21	11	52.38
72. Nicholls St.	21	11	52.38
75. Hofstra	19	10	52.63
75. Northern Ariz.	19	10	52.63
77. Davidson	17	9	52.94
77. Idaho St.	17	9	52.94
79. Columbia	15	8	53.33
79. Tennessee St.	15	8	53.33
81. Austin Peay	26	14	53.85
81. Villanova	26	14	53.85
81. UNI	13	7	53.85
84. Texas Southern	24	13	54.17
85. Alabama A&M	20	11	55.00
85. Southern U.	20	11	55.00
87. Sacramento St.	18	10	55.56
87. Hampton	18	10	55.56
89. Lehigh	21	12	57.14
89. St. Francis (Pa.)	14	8	57.14
89. Weber St.	14	8	57.14
89. Western Ky.	14	8	57.14
93. Morehead St.	19	11	57.89
94. N.C. A&T	17	10	58.82
94. St. Peter's	17	10	58.82
94. Richmond	17	10	58.82
97. Alcorn St.	22	13	59.09
98. La Salle	10	6	60.00

Rank, Team	Att	Conv	Pct.
99. Stony Brook	13	8	61.54
99. Morgan St.	13	8	61.54
101. Bucknell	24	15	62.50
102. Colgate	19	12	63.16
103. Brown	14	9	64.29
103. Stephen F. Austin	14	9	64.29
105. Southeastern La.	20	13	65.00
106. Northeastern	12	8	66.67
106. Samford	12	8	66.67
108. Sacred Heart	16	11	68.75
109. Gardner-Webb	13	9	69.23
110. Chattanooga	10	7	70.00
111. Holy Cross	18	13	72.22
112. Mississippi Val.	11	8	72.73
112. VMI	11	8	72.73
114. Western Caro.	15	11	73.33
115. William & Mary	9	7	77.78
116. Missouri St.	9	8	88.89

Tackles for Loss

Rank, Team	G	Solo	Ast	Yds	Total	TFL/Gm
1. Harvard	10	66	55	377	93.5	9.35
2. Hampton	12	76	53	420	102.5	8.54
3. Alcorn St.	11	69	48	425	93.0	8.45
4. Southern U.	11	54	66	333	87.0	7.91
5. Cal Poly	11	60	48	364	84.0	7.64
5. Maine	11	64	40	363	84.0	7.64
5. Norfolk St.	11	64	40	361	84.0	7.64
8. Albany (N.Y.)	11	66	34	314	83.0	7.55
8. Robert Morris	11	52	62	410	83.0	7.55
10. Bethune-Cookman	11	60	43	305	81.5	7.41
11. Fordham	11	62	38	306	81.0	7.36
12. Tennessee Tech	11	51	56	281	79.0	7.18
13. James Madison	12	75	22	409	86.0	7.17
14. Howard	11	58	40	332	78.0	7.09
15. Penn	10	52	36	255	70.0	7.00
15. Portland St.	11	57	40	312	77.0	7.00
17. San Diego	12	66	34	335	83.0	6.92
18. Alabama St.	11	60	32	286	76.0	6.91
18. Elon	11	54	44	301	76.0	6.91
20. Southern Ill.	13	64	50	385	89.0	6.85
21. Central Conn. St.	11	55	40	310	75.0	6.82
21. Jackson St.	11	55	40	328	75.0	6.82
23. Prairie View	10	43	50	297	68.0	6.80
24. Sacramento St.	11	62	24	280	74.0	6.73
24. Weber St.	11	50	48	262	74.0	6.73
26. Duquesne	10	52	30	296	67.0	6.70
27. Charleston So.	11	48	50	269	73.0	6.64
27. Hofstra	11	52	42	282	73.0	6.64
29. Richmond	11	54	36	252	72.0	6.55
30. Morgan St.	11	57	29	273	71.5	6.50
31. Columbia	10	47	34	257	64.0	6.40
32. Montana St.	13	60	44	300	82.0	6.31
33. Grambling	11	44	48	266	68.0	6.18
33. Texas Southern	11	50	36	264	68.0	6.18
33. Mississippi Val.	11	46	44	254	68.0	6.18
33. South Carolina St.	11	49	38	229	68.0	6.18
33. Murray St.	11	54	28	273	68.0	6.18
38. Alabama A&M	12	52	44	349	74.0	6.17
39. Southeastern La.	11	53	28	227	67.0	6.09
40. McNeese St.	12	62	22	369	73.0	6.08
41. Butler	11	50	32	260	66.0	6.00
41. Villanova	11	53	26	254	66.0	6.00
41. Lafayette	12	57	30	262	72.0	6.00
44. Appalachian St.	15	68	40	368	88.0	5.87
45. Ga. Southern	11	50	29	196	64.5	5.86
45. Youngstown St.	14	62	40	278	82.0	5.86
45. Wofford	11	46	37	284	64.5	5.86
48. Sacred Heart	11	39	50	197	64.0	5.82
49. Tennessee St.	11	50	27	258	63.5	5.77
50. Tenn.-Martin	12	57	24	252	69.0	5.75
51. Wagner	11	40	46	224	63.0	5.73
52. Texas St.	11	41	42	243	62.0	5.64
53. Monmouth	12	51	32	272	67.0	5.58
54. Jacksonville St.	11	51	20	256	61.0	5.55
55. Davidson	10	41	28	243	55.0	5.50
56. Massachusetts	15	60	44	373	82.0	5.47
57. Marist	11	37	46	226	60.0	5.45
57. Southeast Mo. St.	11	47	26	248	60.0	5.45
59. Iona	10	33	42	242	54.0	5.40
60. Eastern Ky.	11	45	28	231	59.0	5.36
60. Idaho St.	11	39	40	281	59.0	5.36
60. Florida A&M	11	47	24	223	59.0	5.36
63. Coastal Caro.	12	44	40	218	64.0	5.33
64. Northern Ariz.	11	40	36	254	58.0	5.27
65. Delaware St.	11	40	34	192	57.0	5.18
65. Eastern Wash.	11	36	42	177	57.0	5.18
65. Stephen F. Austin	11	40	34	189	57.0	5.18
68. Montana	14	40	64	303	72.0	5.14
69. Brown	10	42	18	222	51.0	5.10
69. Cornell	10	43	16	214	51.0	5.10
71. Sam Houston St.	11	36	40	142	56.0	5.09
72. Georgetown	11	39	32	175	55.0	5.00
72. Morehead St.	11	45	20	201	55.0	5.00
74. Furman	12	46	26	222	59.0	4.92
74. Ark.-Pine Bluff	12	39	40	204	59.0	4.92
76. Chattanooga	11	35	38	204	54.0	4.91
76. Drake	11	42	24	236	54.0	4.91
78. Citadel	11	32	42	199	53.0	4.82
78. Valparaiso	11	39	28	171	53.0	4.82
78. Holy Cross	11	44	18	162	53.0	4.82
81. Yale	10	43	10	196	48.0	4.80
82. Illinois St.	13	48	28	195	62.0	4.77
82. Missouri St.	11	37	31	185	52.5	4.77
84. Liberty	11	39	26	234	52.0	4.73
84. Towson	11	49	6	152	52.0	4.73
84. St. Francis (Pa.)	11	38	28	196	52.0	4.73
87. Dayton	10	39	16	153	47.0	4.70
88. Rhode Island	11	41	20	152	51.0	4.64
88. William & Mary	11	39	24	183	51.0	4.64
90. New Hampshire	13	52	16	226	60.0	4.62
91. La Salle	10	32	28	163	46.0	4.60
92. Western Ill.	11	32	37	196	50.5	4.59
93. Delaware	11	32	36	155	50.0	4.55
93. Lehigh	11	40	20	203	50.0	4.55
93. Western Caro.	11	33	34	137	50.0	4.55
93. Samford	11	46	8	174	50.0	4.55
97. St. Peter's	10	29	32	169	45.0	4.50
98. Austin Peay	11	31	36	148	49.0	4.45
98. Savannah St.	11	29	40	210	49.0	4.45
98. Colgate	11	38	22	245	49.0	4.45
98. Northwestern St.	11	37	24	205	49.0	4.45
98. UNI	11	42	14	172	49.0	4.45
103. Eastern Ill.	13	37	40	222	57.0	4.38
104. Nicholls St.	11	30	34	182	47.0	4.27
105. Dartmouth	10	32	20	169	42.0	4.20
106. Indiana St.	11	29	34	188	46.0	4.18
106. Southern Utah	11	36	20	211	46.0	4.18
108. Princeton	10	25	32	151	41.0	4.10
109. N.C. A&T	11	30	26	128	43.0	3.91
109. Stony Brook	11	36	14	147	43.0	3.91
111. Jacksonville	10	26	24	150	38.0	3.80
112. Western Ky.	11	27	23	148	38.5	3.50
113. Northeastern	11	31	12	158	37.0	3.36
114. Gardner-Webb	11	26	20	166	36.0	3.27
115. Bucknell	11	25	14	114	32.0	2.91
116. VMI	11	18	26	109	31.0	2.82

Fewest Tackles for Loss Allowed

Rank, Team	G	Solo	Ast	Yds	Total	TFL/Gm
1. Davidson	10	26	12	109	32.0	3.20
2. Massachusetts	15	39	30	189	54.0	3.60
3. Eastern Ill.	13	29	37	155	47.5	3.65
4. James Madison	12	35	18	118	44.0	3.67
5. UNI	11	34	14	196	41.0	3.73
6. Cornell	10	33	12	213	39.0	3.90
7. Albany (N.Y.)	11	28	30	140	43.0	3.91
8. Youngstown St.	14	34	42	185	55.0	3.93
9. San Diego	12	36	24	174	48.0	4.00
10. Tenn.-Martin	12	40	18	210	49.0	4.08
11. Delaware	11	40	10	192	45.0	4.09
12. McNeese St.	12	41	18	181	50.0	4.17
13. Richmond	11	33	26	162	46.0	4.18
14. Delaware St.	11	31	32	153	47.0	4.27
14. Western Ill.	11	32	30	177	47.0	4.27
14. Sam Houston St.	11	34	26	158	47.0	4.27
17. Western Ky.	11	41	14	179	48.0	4.36
17. Gardner-Webb	11	37	22	218	48.0	4.36
19. Southern Ill.	13	45	27	192	58.5	4.50
20. Liberty	11	36	28	158	50.0	4.55
20. Northeastern	11	38	24	227	50.0	4.55
20. Texas St.	11	29	42	173	50.0	4.55
23. Lehigh	11	43	16	226	51.0	4.64

Rank, Team	G	Solo	Ast	Yds	Total	TFL/Gm
23. William & Mary	11	38	26	212	51.0	4.64
25. Furman	12	42	28	223	56.0	4.67
26. Appalachian St.	15	48	46	248	71.0	4.73
26. Indiana St.	11	37	30	214	52.0	4.73
26. Austin Peay	11	36	32	220	52.0	4.73
29. Coastal Caro.	12	37	40	194	57.0	4.75
29. Lafayette	12	40	34	228	57.0	4.75
31. Georgetown	11	36	34	182	53.0	4.82
31. St. Francis (Pa.)	11	32	42	128	53.0	4.82
33. Ga. Southern	11	43	21	183	53.5	4.86
34. Charleston So.	11	37	34	223	54.0	4.91
34. Cal Poly	11	42	24	187	54.0	4.91
36. Central Conn. St.	11	32	45	186	54.5	4.95
37. N.C. A&T	11	37	36	240	55.0	5.00
37. Chattanooga	11	39	32	180	55.0	5.00
37. Yale	10	39	22	163	50.0	5.00
37. Western Caro.	11	43	24	223	55.0	5.00
37. Stony Brook	11	39	32	179	55.0	5.00
42. Wagner	11	34	44	205	56.0	5.09
42. Elon	11	43	26	205	56.0	5.09
44. Brown	10	34	34	225	51.0	5.10
45. Dartmouth	10	42	20	220	52.0	5.20
46. Holy Cross	11	46	25	262	58.5	5.32
47. Jacksonville St.	11	38	42	244	59.0	5.36
47. Southern Utah	11	48	22	243	59.0	5.36
47. Stephen F. Austin	11	37	44	229	59.0	5.36
50. Harvard	10	40	28	205	54.0	5.40
50. Penn	10	40	28	219	54.0	5.40
52. Monmouth	12	50	30	245	65.0	5.42
53. Hofstra	11	41	38	267	60.0	5.45
53. Samford	11	57	6	208	60.0	5.45
55. Illinois St.	13	54	36	250	72.0	5.54
56. Alcorn St.	11	44	34	246	61.0	5.55
56. Portland St.	11	43	36	214	61.0	5.55
56. Nicholls St.	11	46	30	176	61.0	5.55
56. Florida A&M	11	44	34	230	61.0	5.55
60. Columbia	10	44	24	217	56.0	5.60
60. Jacksonville	10	48	16	260	56.0	5.60
62. Hampton	12	52	33	270	68.5	5.71
63. Bucknell	11	54	18	210	63.0	5.73
63. Howard	11	34	58	188	63.0	5.73
63. Drake	11	52	22	213	63.0	5.73
63. VMI	11	50	26	220	63.0	5.73
67. Mississippi Val.	11	46	36	278	64.0	5.82
67. Norfolk St.	11	51	26	288	64.0	5.82
67. Sacred Heart	11	46	36	304	64.0	5.82
70. Duquesne	10	40	38	234	59.0	5.90
71. Northwestern St.	11	45	40	238	65.0	5.91
72. Citadel	11	45	42	228	66.0	6.00
72. Idaho St.	11	53	26	228	66.0	6.00
72. Villanova	11	52	28	277	66.0	6.00
72. Valparaiso	11	46	40	241	66.0	6.00
72. Southeastern La.	11	55	22	228	66.0	6.00
77. Montana St.	13	59	40	355	79.0	6.08
78. Marist	11	46	42	215	67.0	6.09
78. Texas Southern	11	46	42	299	67.0	6.09
80. Alabama A&M	12	47	54	266	74.0	6.17
81. Towson	11	59	18	301	68.0	6.18
82. Colgate	11	57	24	217	69.0	6.27
82. Morehead St.	11	58	22	290	69.0	6.27
84. Princeton	10	42	42	237	63.0	6.30
84. St. Peter's	10	42	42	287	63.0	6.30
86. Eastern Wash.	11	55	30	269	70.0	6.36
86. Fordham	11	55	30	280	70.0	6.36
88. New Hampshire	13	72	22	329	83.0	6.38
89. Eastern Ky.	11	49	44	260	71.0	6.45
89. Tennessee St.	11	58	26	279	71.0	6.45
89. Jackson St.	11	49	44	259	71.0	6.45
89. Southern U.	11	52	38	281	71.0	6.45
93. Grambling	11	54	36	346	72.0	6.55
93. Southeast Mo. St.	11	61	22	219	72.0	6.55
93. Weber St.	11	57	30	352	72.0	6.55
93. Tennessee Tech	11	50	44	339	72.0	6.55
97. Butler	11	60	28	280	74.0	6.73
97. Wofford	11	58	32	226	74.0	6.73
97. Missouri St.	11	46	56	277	74.0	6.73
100. Montana	14	64	62	390	95.0	6.79
101. Maine	11	61	28	298	75.0	6.82
102. Sacramento St.	11	51	52	350	77.0	7.00
103. Alabama St.	11	54	48	336	78.0	7.09
103. South Carolina St.	11	66	24	282	78.0	7.09
105. Ark.-Pine Bluff	12	57	58	371	86.0	7.17
106. Murray St.	11	64	30	300	79.0	7.18
107. Bethune-Cookman	11	58	46	384	81.0	7.36
107. Savannah St.	11	53	56	298	81.0	7.36
107. Northern Ariz.	11	59	44	360	81.0	7.36
110. Prairie View	10	54	40	233	74.0	7.40
111. Dayton	10	59	32	348	75.0	7.50
112. La Salle	10	60	34	367	77.0	7.70
113. Morgan St.	11	65	42	315	86.0	7.82
114. Robert Morris	11	70	40	361	90.0	8.18
115. Iona	10	62	50	352	87.0	8.70
116. Rhode Island	11	86	40	388	106.0	9.64

Pass Sacks

Rank, Team	G	Yds	Total	PS/Gm
1. Harvard	10	263	42.0	4.20
2. James Madison	12	319	48.0	4.00
3. Maine	11	247	38.0	3.45
4. Cal Poly	11	260	37.0	3.36
5. Alabama A&M	12	263	39.0	3.25
6. Prairie View	10	185	31.0	3.10
7. Alcorn St.	11	236	34.0	3.09
7. Robert Morris	11	244	34.0	3.09
9. Wofford	11	201	32.0	2.91
10. Duquesne	10	208	29.0	2.90
11. Hampton	12	237	34.0	2.83
12. Howard	11	213	31.0	2.82
13. Southern Ill.	13	244	36.0	2.77
14. Bethune-Cookman	11	177	30.0	2.73
14. Morgan St.	11	176	30.0	2.73
14. Portland St.	11	204	30.0	2.73
17. Central Conn. St.	11	179	29.0	2.64
18. Massachusetts	15	239	39.0	2.60
19. Albany (N.Y.)	11	188	28.0	2.55
19. Northern Ariz.	11	183	28.0	2.55
19. Norfolk St.	11	198	28.0	2.55
22. Montana	14	196	35.0	2.50
23. Appalachian St.	15	252	37.0	2.47
24. Montana St.	13	189	32.0	2.46
25. Weber St.	11	145	27.0	2.45
26. South Carolina St.	11	136	26.0	2.36
27. Penn	10	159	23.0	2.30
28. McNeese St.	12	210	27.0	2.25
29. Davidson	10	139	22.0	2.20
30. Charleston So.	11	139	24.0	2.18
31. Jackson St.	11	171	23.0	2.09
31. Southeast Mo. St.	11	146	23.0	2.09
31. Texas Southern	11	137	23.0	2.09
34. Butler	11	125	22.0	2.00
34. San Diego	12	175	24.0	2.00
34. Mississippi Val.	11	111	22.0	2.00
34. Hofstra	11	152	22.0	2.00
34. Cornell	10	122	20.0	2.00
34. Columbia	10	127	20.0	2.00
34. Colgate	11	144	22.0	2.00
34. Sacramento St.	11	135	22.0	2.00
42. Idaho St.	11	176	21.0	1.91
42. Villanova	11	125	21.0	1.91
42. Texas St.	11	144	21.0	1.91
45. Lafayette	12	137	22.0	1.83
46. Fordham	11	137	20.0	1.82
46. Elon	11	156	20.0	1.82
46. Tennessee St.	11	143	20.0	1.82
46. Southern U.	11	125	20.0	1.82
46. UNI	11	115	20.0	1.82
46. Liberty	11	158	20.0	1.82
52. Monmouth	12	148	21.0	1.75
52. Tenn.-Martin	12	123	21.0	1.75
54. Alabama St.	11	126	19.0	1.73
54. Southeastern La.	11	101	19.0	1.73
54. Chattanooga	11	111	19.0	1.73
54. Western Ill.	11	123	19.0	1.73
54. Samford	11	99	19.0	1.73
54. Richmond	11	100	19.0	1.73
60. Youngstown St.	14	122	24.0	1.71
61. Iona	10	112	17.0	1.70
61. Yale	10	108	17.0	1.70
63. Eastern Wash.	11	109	18.0	1.64
63. Northeastern	11	119	18.0	1.64
63. Stephen F. Austin	11	107	18.0	1.64
63. Morehead St.	11	115	18.0	1.64
63. Wagner	11	101	18.0	1.64
68. Brown	10	102	16.0	1.60
69. Georgetown	11	87	17.0	1.55
69. Marist	11	113	17.0	1.55

Rank, Team	G	Yds	Total	PS/Gm
69. William & Mary	11	104	17.0	1.55
69. Murray St.	11	153	17.0	1.55
73. Dartmouth	10	97	15.0	1.50
74. New Hampshire	13	124	19.0	1.46
75. Drake	11	115	16.0	1.45
75. Eastern Ky.	11	120	16.0	1.45
75. Nicholls St.	11	115	16.0	1.45
75. Southern Utah	11	116	16.0	1.45
75. Jacksonville St.	11	129	16.0	1.45
80. Coastal Caro.	12	102	17.0	1.42
81. La Salle	10	85	14.0	1.40
82. Illinois St.	13	107	18.0	1.38
83. Grambling	11	112	15.0	1.36
83. Lehigh	11	118	15.0	1.36
83. St. Francis (Pa.)	11	90	15.0	1.36
83. Tennessee Tech	11	111	15.0	1.36
83. Missouri St.	11	108	15.0	1.36
83. Sacred Heart	11	100	15.0	1.36
83. Northwestern St.	11	93	15.0	1.36
83. Gardner-Webb	11	90	15.0	1.36
91. Indiana St.	11	96	14.0	1.27
92. Dayton	10	82	12.0	1.20
92. Jacksonville	10	92	12.0	1.20
92. St. Peter's	10	99	12.0	1.20
95. Citadel	11	89	13.0	1.18
95. Delaware	11	77	13.0	1.18
95. Holy Cross	11	76	13.0	1.18
95. Western Ky.	11	92	13.0	1.18
95. Towson	11	69	13.0	1.18
95. Delaware St.	11	83	13.0	1.18
101. Furman	12	109	14.0	1.17
102. Eastern Ill.	13	106	15.0	1.15
103. Princeton	10	67	11.0	1.10
104. Rhode Island	11	43	12.0	1.09
104. Valparaiso	11	85	12.0	1.09
106. Florida A&M	11	96	11.0	1.00
106. Savannah St.	11	75	11.0	1.00
106. Ga. Southern	11	61	11.0	1.00
109. Ark.-Pine Bluff	12	67	11.0	.92
110. Bucknell	11	51	9.0	.82
110. N.C. A&T	11	55	9.0	.82
110. Stony Brook	11	50	9.0	.82
113. Sam Houston St.	11	50	8.0	.73
114. VMI	11	56	7.0	.64
115. Austin Peay	11	40	6.0	.55
116. Western Caro.	11	22	4.0	.36

Fewest Pass Sacks Allowed

Rank, Team	G	Yds	Total	PS/Gm
1. Ga. Southern	11	49	6	.55
2. Central Conn. St.	11	46	8	.73
3. Eastern Ill.	13	83	10	.77
4. Albany (N.Y.)	11	57	9	.82
4. Wofford	11	60	9	.82
4. Chattanooga	11	58	9	.82
7. Sam Houston St.	11	76	10	.91
8. Youngstown St.	14	99	13	.93
9. Cal Poly	11	78	11	1.00
9. Nicholls St.	11	50	11	1.00
9. Penn	10	65	10	1.00
9. Delaware St.	11	69	11	1.00
9. Liberty	11	58	11	1.00
14. Massachusetts	15	105	16	1.07
15. Coastal Caro.	12	99	13	1.08
16. Jackson St.	11	39	12	1.09
16. Samford	11	108	12	1.09
18. Furman	12	96	14	1.17
18. Tenn.-Martin	12	94	14	1.17
18. James Madison	12	52	14	1.17
21. Drake	11	86	13	1.18
21. Wagner	11	101	13	1.18
21. St. Francis (Pa.)	11	55	13	1.18
21. Richmond	11	94	13	1.18
21. Indiana St.	11	114	13	1.18
21. Georgetown	11	82	13	1.18
27. Appalachian St.	15	118	18	1.20
27. Davidson	10	71	12	1.20
29. Southern Ill.	13	87	16	1.23
30. San Diego	12	83	15	1.25
31. Colgate	11	89	14	1.27
32. Yale	10	74	13	1.30
33. McNeese St.	12	93	16	1.33
34. Texas St.	11	88	15	1.36
35. Illinois St.	13	98	18	1.38
36. Jacksonville	10	97	14	1.40
37. Monmouth	12	127	17	1.42
38. Western Caro.	11	119	16	1.45
39. Bucknell	11	100	17	1.55
39. Florida A&M	11	109	17	1.55
39. VMI	11	107	17	1.55
39. Northeastern	11	136	17	1.55
43. Alabama A&M	12	100	19	1.58
43. Lafayette	12	119	19	1.58
45. Columbia	10	93	16	1.60
45. Harvard	10	111	16	1.60
47. Alcorn St.	11	98	18	1.64
47. William & Mary	11	121	18	1.64
47. Western Ill.	11	106	18	1.64
47. Southeast Mo. St.	11	102	18	1.64
51. Cornell	10	132	17	1.70
51. Princeton	10	105	17	1.70
51. Duquesne	10	117	17	1.70
54. Lehigh	11	148	19	1.73
54. Marist	11	86	19	1.73
54. South Carolina St.	11	133	19	1.73
54. Gardner-Webb	11	133	19	1.73
54. Western Ky.	11	117	19	1.73
54. Stony Brook	11	79	19	1.73
60. Eastern Ky.	11	119	20	1.82
60. Tennessee St.	11	163	20	1.82
60. Howard	11	100	20	1.82
60. Jacksonville St.	11	137	20	1.82
64. Morgan St.	11	139	21	1.91
64. Southern Utah	11	144	21	1.91
64. Southern U.	11	150	21	1.91
64. Northwestern St.	11	141	21	1.91
64. N.C. A&T	11	170	21	1.91
64. UNI	11	144	21	1.91
70. Austin Peay	11	157	22	2.00
70. Texas Southern	11	172	22	2.00
70. Tennessee Tech	11	144	22	2.00
70. Stephen F. Austin	11	144	22	2.00
70. Missouri St.	11	158	22	2.00
70. Prairie View	10	103	20	2.00
70. Maine	11	147	22	2.00
70. Hampton	12	130	24	2.00
70. Charleston So.	11	148	22	2.00
79. Delaware	11	141	23	2.09
80. Citadel	11	142	24	2.18
80. Valparaiso	11	151	24	2.18
82. Butler	11	177	25	2.27
82. Savannah St.	11	162	25	2.27
82. Elon	11	139	25	2.27
82. Villanova	11	177	25	2.27
82. Portland St.	11	144	25	2.27
82. Morehead St.	11	158	25	2.27
82. Idaho St.	11	143	25	2.27
89. Alabama St.	11	188	26	2.36
89. Southeastern La.	11	132	26	2.36
89. Holy Cross	11	188	26	2.36
89. Eastern Wash.	11	168	26	2.36
93. Montana St.	13	197	31	2.38
94. Dartmouth	10	166	24	2.40
95. Murray St.	11	184	27	2.45
95. Sacred Heart	11	187	27	2.45
97. Brown	10	171	25	2.50
98. Sacramento St.	11	208	28	2.55
98. Grambling	11	195	28	2.55
100. New Hampshire	13	206	35	2.69
101. St. Peter's	10	186	27	2.70
102. La Salle	10	187	28	2.80
103. Fordham	11	190	31	2.82
103. Norfolk St.	11	219	31	2.82
103. Mississippi Val.	11	181	31	2.82
106. Bethune-Cookman	11	252	33	3.00
106. Rhode Island	11	187	33	3.00
106. Ark.-Pine Bluff	12	232	36	3.00
106. Hofstra	11	186	33	3.00
106. Robert Morris	11	208	33	3.00
111. Towson	11	218	34	3.09
112. Dayton	10	230	31	3.10
113. Northern Ariz.	11	232	36	3.27
114. Iona	10	213	33	3.30
115. Weber St.	11	271	37	3.36
116. Montana	14	290	49	3.50

Conference Standings and Champions

2006 Conference Standings

(Full-season records include postseason play; ties in standings broken by full-season records unless otherwise noted.)

Football Bowl Subdivision

ATLANTIC COAST CONFERENCE

Team	Conference W	L	Pct.	Full Season W	L	Pct.
Atlantic						
Wake Forest	6	2	.750	11	3	.786
Boston College	5	3	.625	10	3	.769
Maryland	5	3	.625	9	4	.692
Clemson	5	3	.625	8	5	.615
Florida St.	3	5	.375	7	6	.538
North Carolina St.	2	6	.250	3	9	.250
Coastal						
Georgia Tech	7	1	.875	9	5	.643
Virginia Tech	6	2	.750	10	3	.769
Virginia	4	4	.500	5	7	.417
Miami (Fla.)	3	5	.375	7	6	.538
North Carolina	2	6	.250	3	9	.250
Duke	0	8	.000	0	12	.000

ACC Championship Game: Wake Forest 9, Georgia Tech 6, December 2 at Jacksonville, Fla.

Bowl Games (4-4): Wake Forest (0-1), lost to Louisville, 24-13, in Orange Bowl; Boston College (1-0), defeated Navy, 25-14, in Meineke Car Care Bowl; Clemson (0-1), lost to Kentucky, 28-20, in Music City Bowl; Maryland (1-0), defeated Purdue, 24-7, in Champs Sports Bowl; Florida St. (1-0), defeated UCLA, 44-27, in Emerald Bowl; Georgia Tech (0-1), lost to West Virginia, 38-35, in Gator Bowl; Virginia Tech (0-1), lost to Georgia, 31-24, in Chick-fil-A Bowl; Miami (Fla.) (1-0), defeated Nevada, 21-20, in MPC Computers Bowl.

BIG EAST CONFERENCE

Team	Conference W	L	Pct.	Full Season W	L	Pct.
Louisville	6	1	.857	12	1	.923
West Virginia	5	2	.714	11	2	.846
Rutgers	5	2	.714	11	2	.846
South Fla.	4	3	.571	9	4	.692
Cincinnati	4	3	.571	8	5	.615
Pittsburgh	2	5	.286	6	6	.500
Connecticut	1	6	.143	4	8	.333
Syracuse	1	6	.143	4	8	.333

Bowl Games (5-0): Louisville (1-0), defeated Wake Forest, 24-13, in Orange Bowl; West Virginia (1-0), defeated Georgia Tech, 38-35, in Gator Bowl; Rutgers (1-0), defeated Kansas St., 37-10, in Texas Bowl; South Fla. (1-0), defeated East Caro., 24-7, in Papajohns.com Bowl; Cincinnati (1-0), defeated Western Mich., 27-24, in International Bowl.

BIG TEN CONFERENCE

Team	Conference W	L	Pct.	Full Season W	L	Pct.
Ohio St.	8	0	1.000	12	1	.923
Wisconsin	7	1	.875	12	1	.923
Michigan	7	1	.875	11	2	.846
Penn St.	5	3	.625	9	4	.692
Purdue	5	3	.625	8	6	.571
Minnesota	3	5	.375	6	7	.462
Indiana	3	5	.375	5	7	.417
Iowa	2	6	.250	6	7	.462
Northwestern	2	6	.250	4	8	.333
Michigan St.	1	7	.125	4	8	.333
Illinois	1	7	.125	2	10	.167

Bowl Games (2-5): Ohio St. (0-1), lost to Florida, 41-14, in BCS National Championship Game; Wisconsin (1-0), defeated Arkansas, 17-14, in Capital One Bowl; Michigan (0-1), lost to Southern California, 32-18, in Rose Bowl; Penn St. (1-0), defeated Tennessee, 20-10, in Outback Bowl; Purdue (0-1), lost to Maryland, 24-7, in Champs Sports Bowl; Minnesota (0-1), lost to Texas Tech, 44-41 (ot), in Insight Bowl; Iowa (0-1), lost to Texas, 26-24, in Alamo Bowl.

BIG 12 CONFERENCE

Team	Conference W	L	Pct.	Full Season W	L	Pct.
North						
Nebraska	6	2	.750	9	5	.643
Missouri	4	4	.500	8	5	.615
Kansas St.	4	4	.500	7	6	.538
Kansas	3	5	.375	6	6	.500
Colorado	2	6	.250	2	10	.167
Iowa St.	1	7	.125	4	8	.333
South						
Oklahoma	7	1	.875	11	3	.786
Texas	6	2	.750	10	3	.769
Texas A&M	5	3	.625	9	4	.692
Texas Tech	4	4	.500	8	5	.615
Oklahoma St.	3	5	.375	7	6	.538
Baylor	3	5	.375	4	8	.333

Big 12 Championship Game: Oklahoma 21, Nebraska 7, December 2, at Kansas City, Mo.

Bowl Games (3-5): Nebraska (0-1), lost to Auburn, 17-14, in Cotton Bowl Classic; Missouri (0-1), lost to Oregon St., 39-38, in Sun Bowl; Kansas St. (0-1), lost to Rutgers, 37-10, in Texas Bowl; Oklahoma (0-1), lost to Boise St., 43-42 (ot), in Fiesta Bowl; Texas (1-0), defeated Iowa, 26-24, in Alamo Bowl; Texas A&M (0-1), lost to California, 45-10, in Holiday Bowl; Texas Tech (1-0), defeated Minnesota, 44-41 (ot), in Insight Bowl; Oklahoma St. (1-0), defeated Alabama, 34-31, in Independence Bowl.

CONFERENCE USA

Team	Conference W	L	Pct.	Full Season W	L	Pct.
East						
Southern Miss.	6	2	.750	9	5	.643
East Caro.	5	3	.625	7	6	.538
Marshall	4	4	.500	5	7	.417
UCF	3	5	.375	4	8	.333
UAB	2	6	.250	3	9	.250
Memphis	1	7	.125	2	10	.167
West						
Houston	7	1	.875	10	4	.714
Rice	6	2	.750	7	6	.538
Tulsa	5	3	.625	8	5	.615
SMU	4	4	.500	6	6	.500
UTEP	3	5	.375	5	7	.417
Tulane	2	6	.250	4	8	.333

Conference USA Championship Game: Houston 34, Southern Miss. 20, December 1, at Houston, Texas.

Bowl Games (1-4): Southern Miss. (1-0), defeated Ohio, 28-7, in GMAC Bowl; East Caro. (0-1), lost to South Fla., 24-7, in Papajohns.com Bowl; Houston (0-1), lost to South Carolina, 44-36, in Liberty Bowl; Rice (0-1), lost to Troy, 41-17, in New Orleans Bowl; Tulsa (0-1), lost to Utah, 25-13, in Armed Forces Bowl.

MID-AMERICAN CONFERENCE

Team	Conference W	L	Pct.	Full Season W	L	Pct.
East						
Ohio	7	1	.875	9	5	.643
Kent St.	5	3	.625	6	6	.500
Akron	3	5	.375	5	7	.417
Bowling Green	3	5	.375	4	8	.333
Miami (Ohio)	2	6	.250	2	10	.167
Buffalo	1	7	.125	2	10	.167
West						
Central Mich.	7	1	.875	10	4	.714
Western Mich.	6	2	.750	8	5	.615
Northern Ill.	5	3	.625	7	6	.538
Ball St.	5	3	.625	5	7	.417
Toledo	3	5	.375	5	7	.417
Eastern Mich.	1	7	.125	1	11	.083

MAC Championship Game: Central Mich. 31, Ohio 10, November 31, at Detroit, Mich.

Bowl Games (1-3): Ohio (0-1), lost to Southern Miss., 28-7, in GMAC Bowl; Central Mich. (1-0), defeated Middle Tenn., 31-14, in Motor City Bowl; Western Mich. (0-1), lost to Cincinnati, 27-24, in International Bowl; Northern Ill. (0-1), lost to TCU, 37-7, in Poinsettia Bowl.

MOUNTAIN WEST CONFERENCE

Team	Conference W	L	Pct.	Full Season W	L	Pct.
BYU	8	0	1.000	11	2	.846
TCU	6	2	.750	11	2	.846
Utah	5	3	.625	8	5	.615
Wyoming	5	3	.625	6	6	.500
New Mexico	4	4	.500	6	7	.462
Air Force	3	5	.375	4	8	.333
San Diego St.	3	5	.375	3	9	.250
Colorado St.	1	7	.125	4	8	.333
UNLV	1	7	.125	2	10	.167

Bowl Games (3-1): BYU (1-0), defeated Oregon, 38-8, in Las Vegas Bowl; TCU (1-0), defeated Northern Ill., 37-7, in Poinsettia Bowl; Utah (1-0), defeated Tulsa, 25-13, in Armed Forces Bowl; New Mexico (0-1), lost to San Jose St., 20-12, in New Mexico Bowl.

PACIFIC-10 CONFERENCE

Team	Conference W	L	Pct.	Full Season W	L	Pct.
Southern California	7	2	.778	11	2	.846
California	7	2	.778	10	3	.769
Oregon St.	6	3	.667	10	4	.714
UCLA	5	4	.556	7	6	.538
Oregon	4	5	.444	7	6	.538
Arizona St.	4	5	.444	7	6	.538
Arizona	4	5	.444	6	6	.500
Washington St.	4	5	.444	6	6	.500
Washington	3	6	.333	5	7	.417
Stanford	1	8	.111	1	11	.083

Bowl Games (3-3): Southern California (1-0), defeated Michigan, 32-18, in Rose Bowl; California (1-0), defeated Texas A&M, 45-10, in Holiday Bowl; Oregon St. (1-0), defeated Missouri, 39-38, in Sun Bowl; UCLA (0-1), lost to Florida St., 44-27, in Emerald Bowl; Oregon (0-1), lost to BYU, 38-8, in Las Vegas Bowl; Arizona St. (0-1), lost to Hawaii, 41-24, in Hawaii Bowl.

SOUTHEASTERN CONFERENCE

Team	Conference W	L	Pct.	Full Season W	L	Pct.
East						
Florida	7	1	.875	13	1	.929
Tennessee	5	3	.625	9	4	.692
Georgia	4	4	.500	9	4	.692
Kentucky	4	4	.500	8	5	.615
South Carolina	3	5	.375	8	5	.615
Vanderbilt	1	7	.125	4	8	.333
West						
Arkansas	7	1	.875	10	4	.714
LSU	6	2	.750	11	2	.846
Auburn	6	2	.750	11	2	.846
Alabama	2	6	.250	6	7	.462
Mississippi	2	6	.250	4	8	.333
Mississippi St.	1	7	.125	3	9	.250

SEC Championship Game: Florida 38, Arkansas 28, December 2, at Atlanta, Ga.

Bowl Games (5-4): Florida (0-1), defeated Ohio St., 41-14, in BCS National Championship Game; Tennessee (0-1), lost to Penn St., 20-10, in Outback Bowl; Georgia (1-0), defeated Virginia Tech, 31-24, in Chick-fil-A Bowl; Kentucky (1-0), defeated Clemson, 28-20, in Music City Bowl; South Carolina (1-0), defeated Houston, 44-36, in Liberty Bowl; Arkansas (0-1), lost to Wisconsin, 17-14, in Capital One Bowl; LSU (1-0), defeated Notre Dame, 41-14, in Sugar Bowl; Auburn (1-0), defeated Nebraska, 17-14, in Cotton Bowl Classic; Alabama (0-1), lost to Oklahoma St., 34-31, in Independence Bowl.

SUN BELT CONFERENCE

Team	Conference W	L	Pct.	Full Season W	L	Pct.
Troy	6	1	.857	8	5	.615
Middle Tenn.	6	1	.857	7	6	.538
Arkansas St.	4	3	.571	6	6	.500
Fla. Atlantic	4	3	.571	5	7	.417
La.-Lafayette	3	4	.429	6	6	.500
La.-Monroe	3	4	.429	4	8	.333
North Texas	2	5	.286	3	9	.250
Florida Int'l	0	7	.000	0	12	.000

Bowl Games (1-1): Troy (1-0), defeated Rice, 41-17, in New Orleans Bowl; Middle Tenn. (0-1), lost to Central Mich., 31-14, in Motor City Bowl.

WESTERN ATHLETIC CONFERENCE

	Conference			Full Season		
Team	**W**	**L**	**Pct.**	**W**	**L**	**Pct.**
Boise St.	8	0	1.000	13	0	1.000
Hawaii	7	1	.875	11	3	.786
San Jose St.	5	3	.625	9	4	.692
Nevada	5	3	.625	8	5	.615
Fresno St.	4	4	.500	4	8	.333
Idaho	3	5	.375	4	8	.333
New Mexico St.	2	6	.250	4	8	.333
Louisiana Tech	1	7	.125	3	10	.231
Utah St.	1	7	.125	1	11	.083

Bowl Games (3-1): Boise St. (1-0), defeated Oklahoma, 43-42 (ot), in Fiesta Bowl; Hawaii (1-0), defeated Arizona St., 41-24, in Hawaii Bowl; San Jose St. (1-0), defeated New Mexico, 20-12, in New Mexico Bowl; Nevada (0-1), lost to Miami (Fla.), 21-20, in MPC Computers Bowl.

INDEPENDENTS

	Full Season		
Team	**W**	**L**	**Pct.**
Notre Dame	10	3	.769
Navy	9	4	.692
Army	3	9	.250
Temple	1	11	.083

Bowl Games (0-2): Notre Dame (0-1), lost to LSU, 41-14, in Sugar Bowl; Navy (0-1), lost to Boston College, 25-24, in Meineke Car Care Bowl.

Football Championship Subdivision

ATLANTIC 10 CONFERENCE

	Conference			Full Season		
Team	**W**	**L**	**Pct.**	**W**	**L**	**Pct.**
North						
Massachusetts	8	0	1.000	13	2	.867
New Hampshire	5	3	.625	9	4	.692
Maine	5	3	.625	6	5	.545
Northeastern	4	4	.500	5	6	.455
Rhode Island	2	6	.250	4	7	.364
Hofstra	1	7	.125	2	9	.182
South						
James Madison	7	1	.875	9	3	.750
Villanova	5	3	.625	6	5	.545
Towson	4	4	.500	7	4	.636
Richmond	3	5	.375	6	5	.545
Delaware	3	5	.375	5	6	.455
William & Mary	1	7	.125	3	8	.273

NCAA Division I Championship (4-3): New Hampshire (1-1, defeated Hampton, 41-38, in first round; lost to Massachusetts, 24-17, in quarterfinals); Massachusetts (3-1, defeated Lafayette, 35-14, in first round; defeated New Hampshire, 24-17, in quarterfinals; defeated Montana, 19-17, in semifinals; lost to Appalachian St., 28-17, in championship game); James Madison (0-1, lost to Youngstown St., 35-31, in first round).

BIG SKY CONFERENCE

	Conference			Full Season		
Team	**W**	**L**	**Pct.**	**W**	**L**	**Pct.**
Montana	8	0	1.000	12	2	.857
Montana St.	6	2	.750	7	4	.636
Portland St.	6	2	.750	8	5	.615
Northern Ariz.	5	3	.625	6	5	.545
Sacramento St.	4	4	.500	4	7	.364
Weber St.	3	5	.375	4	7	.364
Eastern Wash.	3	5	.375	3	8	.273
Idaho St.	1	7	.125	2	9	.182
Northern Colo.*	0	8	.000	1	10	.091

**First year as member of Big Sky.*

NCAA Division I Championship (3-2): Montana (2-1, defeated McNeese St., 31-6, in first round; defeated Southern Ill., 20-3, in quarterfinals; lost to Massachusetts, 19-17, in semifinals); Montana St. (1-1, defeated Furman, 31-13, in first round; lost to Appalachian St., 38-17, in quarterfinals).

BIG SOUTH CONFERENCE

	Conference			Full Season		
Team	**W**	**L**	**Pct.**	**W**	**L**	**Pct.**
Coastal Caro.	4	0	1.000	9	3	.750
Charleston So.	2	2	.500	9	2	.818
Gardner-Webb	2	2	.500	6	5	.545
Liberty	2	2	.500	6	5	.545
VMI	0	4	.000	1	10	.091

NCAA Division I Championship (0-1): Coastal Caro. (0-1, lost to Appalachian St., 45-28, in first round).

GATEWAY FOOTBALL CONFERENCE

	Conference			Full Season		
Team	**W**	**L**	**Pct.**	**W**	**L**	**Pct.**
Youngstown St.	6	1	.857	11	3	.786
Illinois St.	5	2	.714	9	4	.692
UNI	5	2	.714	7	4	.636
Southern Ill.	4	3	.571	9	4	.692
Western Ky.	4	3	.571	6	5	.545
Western Ill.	2	5	.286	5	6	.455
Missouri St.	1	6	.143	2	9	.182
Indiana St.	1	6	.143	1	10	.091

NCAA Division I Championship (4-3): Youngstown St. (2-1, defeated James Madison, 35-31, in first round; defeated Illinois St., 28-21, in quarterfinals; lost to Appalachian St., 49-24, in semifinals); Illinois St. (1-1, defeated Eastern Ill., 24-13, in first round; lost to Youngstown St., 28-21, in quarterfinals); Southern Ill. (1-1, defeated Tenn.-Martin, 36-30, in first round; lost to Montana, 20-3, in quarterfinals).

GREAT WEST FOOTBALL CONFERENCE

	Conference			Full Season		
Team	**W**	**L**	**Pct.**	**W**	**L**	**Pct.**
North Dakota St.	4	0	1.000	10	1	.909
South Dakota St.	3	1	.750	7	4	.636
Cal Poly	2	2	.500	7	4	.636
UC Davis	1	3	.250	6	5	.545
Southern Utah	0	4	.000	3	8	.273

IVY GROUP

	Conference			Full Season		
Team	**W**	**L**	**Pct.**	**W**	**L**	**Pct.**
Princeton	6	1	.857	9	1	.900
Yale	6	1	.857	8	2	.800
Harvard	4	3	.571	7	3	.700
Cornell	3	4	.429	5	5	.500
Penn	3	4	.429	5	5	.500
Brown	2	5	.286	3	7	.300
Columbia	2	5	.286	2	8	.200
Dartmouth	2	5	.286	2	8	.200

METRO ATLANTIC ATHLETIC CONFERENCE

	Conference			Full Season		
Team	**W**	**L**	**Pct.**	**W**	**L**	**Pct.**
Duquesne	3	1	.750	7	3	.700
Marist	3	1	.750	4	7	.364
Iona	2	2	.500	3	7	.300
St. Peter's	1	2	.333	2	7	.222
La Salle	0	3	.000	2	7	.222

MID-EASTERN ATHLETIC CONFERENCE

	Conference			Full Season		
Team	**W**	**L**	**Pct.**	**W**	**L**	**Pct.**
Hampton	7	1	.875	10	2	.833
Delaware St.	6	2	.750	8	3	.727
South Carolina St.	6	2	.750	7	4	.636
Florida A&M	5	3	.625	7	4	.636
Howard	4	4	.500	5	6	.455
Morgan St.	4	4	.500	5	6	.455
Bethune-Cookman	3	5	.375	5	6	.455
Norfolk St.	1	7	.125	4	7	.364
N.C. A&T	0	8	.000	0	11	.000

NCAA Division I Championship (0-1): Hampton (0-1, lost to New Hampshire, 41-38, in first round).

NORTHEAST CONFERENCE

	Conference			Full Season		
Team	**W**	**L**	**Pct.**	**W**	**L**	**Pct.**
Monmouth	6	1	.857	10	2	.833
Albany (N.Y.)	5	2	.714	7	4	.636
Robert Morris	5	2	.714	7	4	.636
Stony Brook	5	2	.714	5	6	.455
Central Conn. St.	4	3	.571	8	3	.727
St. Francis (Pa.)	2	5	.286	3	8	.273
Sacred Heart	1	6	.143	2	9	.182
Wagner	0	7	.000	4	7	.364

Gridiron Classic: San Diego 27, Monmouth 7, December 2, at West Long Branch, N.J.

OHIO VALLEY CONFERENCE

	Conference			Full Season		
Team	**W**	**L**	**Pct.**	**W**	**L**	**Pct.**
Eastern Ill.	7	1	.875	8	5	.615
Tenn.-Martin	6	1	.857	9	3	.750
Tennessee St.	5	2	.714	6	5	.545
Eastern Ky.	5	3	.625	6	5	.545
Jacksonville St.	5	3	.625	6	5	.545
Tennessee Tech	4	4	.500	4	7	.364
Southeast Mo. St.	2	6	.250	4	7	.364
Samford	1	7	.145	3	8	.273
Murray St.	0	8	.000	1	10	.091

NCAA Division I Championship (0-2): Eastern Ill. (0-1, lost to Illinois St., 24-13, in first round); Tenn.-Martin (0-1, lost to Southern Ill., 36-30, in first round).

PATRIOT LEAGUE

	Conference			Full Season		
Team	**W**	**L**	**Pct.**	**W**	**L**	**Pct.**
Lafayette*	5	1	.833	6	6	.500
Lehigh	5	1	.833	6	5	.545
Holy Cross	4	2	.667	7	4	.636
Bucknell	3	3	.500	6	5	.545
Colgate	3	3	.500	4	7	.364
Fordham	1	5	.167	3	8	.375
Georgetown	0	6	.000	2	9	.182

**Received Patriot League's automatic bid to the Division I playoffs by virtue of regular-season win vs. Lehigh.*

NCAA Division I Championship (0-1): Lafayette (0-1, lost to Massachusetts, 35-14, in first round).

PIONEER FOOTBALL LEAGUE

	Conference			Full Season		
Team	**W**	**L**	**Pct.**	**W**	**L**	**Pct.**
San Diego	7	0	1.000	11	1	.917
Drake	6	1	.857	9	2	.818
Davidson	5	2	.714	6	4	.600
Jacksonville	4	3	.571	4	6	.400
Butler	2	5	.714	3	8	.273
Morehead St.	2	5	.714	2	9	.182
Dayton	1	6	.143	3	8	.273
Valparaiso	1	6	.143	3	8	.273

Gridiron Classic: San Diego 27, Monmouth 7, December 2, at West Long Branch, N.J.

SOUTHERN CONFERENCE

	Conference			Full Season		
Team	**W**	**L**	**Pct.**	**W**	**L**	**Pct.**
Appalachian St.	7	0	1.000	14	1	.933
Furman	6	1	.857	8	4	.667
Wofford	5	2	.714	7	4	.636
Citadel	4	3	.571	5	6	.455
Elon	2	5	.286	5	6	.455
Chattanooga	2	5	.286	3	8	.273
Ga. Southern	2	5	.286	3	8	.273
Western Caro.	0	7	.000	2	9	.182

NCAA Division I Championship (4-1): Appalachian St. (4-0, defeated Coastal Caro., 45-28, in first round; defeated Montana St., 38-17, in quarterfinals; defeated Youngstown St., 49-24, in semifinals; defeated Massachusetts, 28-17, in championship game); Furman (0-1, lost to Montana St., 31-13, in first round).

SOUTHLAND CONFERENCE

	Conference			Full Season		
Team	**W**	**L**	**Pct.**	**W**	**L**	**Pct.**
McNeese St.	5	1	.833	7	5	.583
Sam Houston St.	4	2	.667	6	5	.545
Stephen F. Austin	4	2	.667	4	7	.364

Team	Conference W	L	Pct.	Full Season W	L	Pct.
Texas St.	3	3	.500	5	6	.455
Nicholls St.	2	4	.333	4	7	.364
Northwestern St.	2	4	.333	4	7	.364
Southeastern La.	1	5	.167	2	9	.182

NCAA Division I Championship (0-1): McNeese St. (0-1, lost to Montana, 31-6, in first round).

SOUTHWESTERN ATHLETIC CONFERENCE

Team	Conference W	L	Pct.	Full Season W	L	Pct.
Eastern Division						
Alabama A&M	6	3	.667	9	3	.750
Alcorn St.	5	4	.556	6	5	.545
Mississippi Val.	5	4	.556	6	5	.545
Jackson St.	5	4	.556	6	5	.545
Alabama St.	5	4	.556	5	6	.455
Western Division						
Ark.-Pine Bluff	7	2	.778	8	4	.667
Southern U.	4	5	.444	5	6	.455
Texas Southern	3	6	.333	3	8	.273
Grambling	3	6	.333	3	8	.273
Prairie View	2	7	.222	3	7	.300

SWAC Championship Game: Alabama A&M 22, Ark.-Pine Bluff 13, December 16, at Birmingham, Ala.

INDEPENDENTS

Team	Full Season W	L	Pct.
*Austin Peay	3	8	.273
Savannah St.	2	9	.182

**Became independent for 2006 season.*

Major-College Alignment History

(Originally called major-college, now Football Bowl Subdivision)

Team	Years Major
Air Force	1957-present
Akron	1987-present
Alabama	1937-40, 46-present
UAB	1996-present
Alcorn St.	1977
Appalachian St.	1974-81
Arizona	1939-40, 46-present
Arizona St.	1946-48, 50-54, 56-present
Arkansas	1937-40, 46-present
Arkansas St.	1975-81, 92-present
Army	1937-40, 46-present
Auburn	1937-40, 46-present
Ball St.	1975-81, 83-present
Baylor	1937-40, 46-present
Boise St.	1996-present
Boston College	1939-40, 46-present
Boston U.	1939-40, 47-65
Bowling Green	1961-81, 83-present
BYU	1938-40, 46-present
Brown	1937-40, 46-81
Bucknell	1938-40, 46-47
Buffalo	1962-70, 99-present
California	1937-40, 46-present
Cal St. Fullerton	1976-92
Carnegie Tech	1937-40
Case Reserve	1948
Centenary	1938-47
UCF	1996-present
Central Mich.	1975-present
Chattanooga	1946-48, 50, 77-81
Chicago	1937-39
Cincinnati	1946, 48-81, 83-present
Citadel	1939, 46-52, 59-81
Clemson	1937-40, 46-present
Colgate	1937-40, 46-81
Colorado	1937-40, 46-present
Colorado Col.	1946-47
Colorado St.	1940, 46-present
Columbia	1938-40, 46-81
Connecticut	2002-present
Cornell	1937-40, 46-81
Creighton	1939-42
Dartmouth	1937-40, 46-81
Davidson	1937-40, 46-53, 67-76
Dayton	1956-76
Denver	1940-60
Detroit	1939-64
Drake	1939-40, 46-58, 73-80
Duke	1937-40, 46-present
Duquesne	1937-40, 47-50
East Caro.	1966-present
East Tenn. St.	1978-81
Eastern Mich.	1976-81, 83-present
Florida	1937-40, 46-present
Fla. Atlantic	2006-present
Florida Int'l	2006-present
Florida St.	1955-present
Fordham	1937-40, 46-54
Fresno St.	1973-present
Furman	1946-53, 55-57, 65, 73-81
Georgetown	1937-40, 46-50
George Washington	1939-66
Georgia	1937-40, 46-present
Georgia Tech	1937-40, 46-present
Gonzaga	1938-41
Grambling	1977
Hardin-Simmons	1946-48, 50-62
Harvard	1937-40, 46-81
Haskell	1937-38
Hawaii	1974-present
Holy Cross	1938-40, 46-81
Houston	1949-present
Idaho	1938-40, 46-67, 69-77, 97-present
Illinois	1937-40, 46-present
Illinois St.	1976-81
Indiana	1937-40, 46-present
Indiana St.	1976-81
Iowa	1937-40, 46-present
Iowa St.	1937-40, 46-present
Jackson St.	1977
Kansas	1937-40, 46-present
Kansas St.	1937-40, 46-present
Kent St.	1962-81, 83-present
Kentucky	1937, 40-present
Lafayette	1938-40, 46-50
Lamar	1974-81
Lehigh	1938-40, 46-47
Long Beach St.	1973-91
La.-Lafayette	1974-present
La.-Monroe	1975-81, 94-present
LSU	1937-40, 46-present
Louisiana Tech	1975-81, 89-present
Louisville	1951, 62-present
Loyola Marymount	1950-51
Loyola (Ill.)	1940
Manhattan	1937-42
Marquette	1937-60
Marshall	1962-81, 98-present
Maryland	1937, 40, 46-present
McNeese St.	1975-81
Memphis	1960-present
Merchant Marine	1946-47
Miami (Fla.)	1946-present
Miami (Ohio)	1948-49, 61-81, 83-present
Michigan	1937-40, 46-present
Michigan St.	1937-40, 46-present
Middle Tenn.	1999-present
Minnesota	1937-40, 46-present
Mississippi	1937-40, 46-present
Mississippi St.	1937-40, 46-present
Missouri	1937-40, 46-present
Montana	1939-40, 46-62
Montana St.	1946-48
Navy	1937-40, 46-present
Nebraska	1937-40, 46-present
UNLV	1978-present
Nevada	1946-50, 92-present
New Hampshire	1940
New Mexico	1940, 46-present
New Mexico St.	1946-47, 52-53, 59-present
New York U.	1937-48, 51-52
North Carolina	1937-40, 46-present
North Carolina St.	1940, 46-present
North Texas	1957-81, 95-present
Northern Ariz.	1946-47
Northern Colo.	1946-47
Northern Ill.	1969-81, 83-present
Northwestern	1937-40, 46-present
Northwestern St.	1976-77
Notre Dame	1937-40, 46-present
Ohio	1948, 61-81, 83-present
Ohio St.	1937-40, 46-present
Oklahoma	1937-40, 46-present
Oklahoma St.	1939-40, 46-present
Oregon	1937-40, 46-present
Oregon St.	1937-40, 46-present
Pacific	1950-60, 62-63, 66, 69-95
Penn	1937-40, 46-81
Penn St.	1938-40, 46-present
Pittsburgh	1937-40, 46-present
Portland	1946-48
Princeton	1937-40, 46-81
Purdue	1937-40, 46-present
Rice	1937-40, 46-present
Richmond	1940, 46-81
Rutgers	1946-present
St. Louis	1940-49
St. Mary's (Cal.)	1937-40, 46-50
San Diego St.	1969-present
San Francisco	1940-51
San Jose St.	1939-40, 50-present
Santa Clara	1937-42, 46-52
Sewanee	1937
South Carolina	1939-40, 46-present
South Fla.	2001-present
Southern California	1937-40, 46-present
Southern Ill.	1973-81
SMU	1937-40, 46-86, 89-present
Southern Miss.	1960, 63-present
Southern U.	1977
Stanford	1937-40, 46-present
Syracuse	1937-40, 46-present
Tampa	1973-74
Temple	1938-40, 46-53, 71-present
Tennessee	1937-40, 46-present
Tennessee St.	1977-80
Texas	1937-40, 46-present
Texas-Arlington	1972-81
Texas A&M	1937-40, 46-present
TCU	1937-40, 46-present
UTEP	1940, 46-present
Texas Southern	1977
Texas Tech	1937-40, 46-present

Team	Years Major
Toledo	1962-present
Trinity (Tex.)	1960
Troy	2002-present
Tulane	1937-40, 46-present
Tulsa	1937-40, 46-present
UCLA	1937-40, 46-present
Utah	1938-40, 46-present
Utah St.	1939-40, 46-present
Vanderbilt	1937-40, 46-present
Villanova	1939-40, 46-80

Team	Years Major
Virginia	1940, 46-present
VMI	1939-40, 46-81
Virginia Tech	1940, 46-present
Wake Forest	1939-40, 46-present
Washington	1937-40, 46-present
Wash. & Lee	1940, 46-53
Washington-St. Louis	1937-40
Washington St.	1937-40, 46-present
West Tex. A&M	1946-47, 51-53, 58-80

Team	Years Major
West Virginia	1939-40, 46-present
Western Caro.	1977-81
Western Mich.	1962-present
Wichita St.	1946-86
William & Mary	1940, 46-81
Wisconsin	1937-40, 46-present
Wyoming	1940, 46-present
Xavier (Ohio)	1960-73
Yale	1937-40, 46-81

All-Time Conference Champions

Football Bowl Subdivision

ATLANTIC COAST CONFERENCE

Founded: In 1953 when charter members all left the Southern Conference to form the ACC. **Charter members** (7): Clemson, Duke, Maryland, North Carolina, North Carolina St., South Carolina and Wake Forest. **Admitted later** (6): Virginia (1953), Georgia Tech (1978), Florida St. (1992), Miami (Fla.) (2004), Virginia Tech (2004) and Boston College (2005). **Withdrew later** (1): South Carolina (1971). **Current members** (12): Boston College, Clemson, Duke, Florida St., Georgia Tech, Maryland, Miami (Fla.), North Carolina, North Carolina St., Virginia, Virginia Tech and Wake Forest.

Year	Champion (Record)
1953	Duke (4-0) & Maryland (3-0)
1954	Duke (4-0)
1955	Maryland (4-0) & Duke (4-0)
1956	Clemson (4-0-1)
1957	North Carolina St. (5-0-1)
1958	Clemson (5-1)
1959	Clemson (6-1)
1960	Duke (5-1)
1961	Duke (5-1)
1962	Duke (6-0)
1963	North Carolina (6-1) & North Carolina St. (6-1)
1964	North Carolina St. (5-2)
1965	Clemson (5-2) & North Carolina St. (5-2)
1966	Clemson (6-1)
1967	Clemson (6-0)
1968	North Carolina St. (6-1)
1969	South Carolina (6-0)
1970	Wake Forest (5-1)
1971	North Carolina (6-0)
1972	North Carolina (6-0)
1973	North Carolina St. (6-0)
1974	Maryland (6-0)
1975	Maryland (5-0)
1976	Maryland (5-0)
1977	North Carolina (5-0-1)
1978	Clemson (6-0)
1979	North Carolina St. (5-1)
1980	North Carolina (6-0)
1981	Clemson (6-0)
1982	Clemson (6-0)
1983	Maryland (5-0)
1984	Maryland (5-0)
1985	Maryland (6-0)
1986	Clemson (5-1-1)
1987	Clemson (6-1)
1988	Clemson (6-1)
1989	Virginia (6-1) & Duke (6-1)
1990	Georgia Tech (6-0-1)
1991	Clemson (6-0-1)
1992	Florida St. (8-0)
1993	Florida St. (8-0)
1994	Florida St. (8-0)
1995	Virginia (7-1) & Florida St. (7-1)
1996	Florida St. (8-0)
1997	Florida St. (8-0)
1998	Florida St. (7-1) & Georgia Tech (7-1)
1999	Florida St. (8-0)
2000	Florida St. (8-0)
2001	Maryland (7-1)
2002	Florida St. (7-1)
2003	Florida St. (7-1)
2004	Virginia Tech (7-1)

Year	Regular Season Champion (Record)
2005	Florida St.* & Boston College (Atlantic, 5-3) Virginia Tech (Coastal, 7-1)
2006	Wake Forest (Atlantic, 6-2) Georgia Tech (Coastal, 7-1)

**Won tiebreaker to represent division in ACC championship game.*

In 2005, the Atlantic Coast began a championship game to determine the league's representative in the Bowl Championship Series (BCS) bowls. Following are the results of the Atlantic Division Champion (A) vs. the Coastal Division Champion (C):

2005 Florida St. (A) 27, Virginia Tech (C) 22
2006 Wake Forest (A) 9, Georgia Tech (C) 6

BIG EAST CONFERENCE

Founded: In 1991 when eight charter members all went from independent status to form the Big East. **Charter members** (8): Boston College, Miami (Fla.), Pittsburgh, Rutgers (football only), Syracuse, Temple (football only), Virginia Tech (football only) and West Virginia (football only). **Admitted later** (4): Connecticut (2004), Cincinnati (2005), Louisville (2005) and South Fla. (2005). **Withdrew later** (4): Miami (Fla.) (2003), Virginia Tech (2003), Boston College (2004) and Temple (2004). **Current members** (8): Cincinnati, Connecticut, Louisville, Pittsburgh, Rutgers, South Fla., Syracuse and West Virginia. Note: In 1991 and 1992, the team ranked highest in the USA Today/CNN coaches poll was declared champion. Beginning in 1993, the champion was decided by a seven-game round-robin schedule.

Year	Champion (Record)
1991	Miami (Fla.) (2-0, No. 1) & Syracuse (5-0, No. 16)
1992	Miami (Fla.) (4-0, No. 1)
1993	West Virginia (7-0)
1994	Miami (Fla.) (7-0)
1995	Virginia Tech (6-1) & Miami (Fla.) (6-1)
1996	Virginia Tech (6-1), Miami (Fla.) (6-1) & Syracuse (6-1)
1997	Syracuse (6-1)
1998	Syracuse (6-1)
1999	Virginia Tech (7-0)
2000	Miami (Fla.) (7-0)
2001	Miami (Fla.) (7-0)
2002	Miami (Fla.) (7-0)
2003	Miami (Fla.) (6-1) & West Virginia (6-1)
2004	Pittsburgh (4-2), Boston College (4-2), Syracuse (4-2) & West Virginia (4-2)
2005	West Virginia (7-0)
2006	Louisville (6-1)

BIG TEN CONFERENCE

Founded: In 1895 as the Intercollegiate Conference of Faculty Representatives, better known as the Western Conference. **Charter members** (7): Chicago, Illinois, Michigan, Minnesota, Northwestern, Purdue and Wisconsin. **Admitted later** (5): Indiana (1899), Iowa (1899), Ohio St. (1912), Michigan St. (1950) and Penn St. (1993). **Withdrew later** (2): Michigan (1907, rejoined in 1917) and Chicago (1940). **Note:** Iowa belonged to both the Missouri Valley and Western Conferences from 1907 to 1910. Unofficially called the Big Ten from 1912 until after 1939, then Big Nine from 1940 until Michigan St. began conference play in 1953. Formally renamed **Big Ten** in 1984. **Current members** (11): Illinois, Indiana, Iowa, Michigan, Michigan St., Minnesota, Northwestern, Ohio St., Penn St., Purdue and Wisconsin.

Year	Champion (Record)
1896	Wisconsin (2-0-1)
1897	Wisconsin (3-0)
1898	Michigan (3-0)
1899	Chicago (4-0)
1900	Iowa (3-0-1) & Minnesota (3-0-1)
1901	Michigan (4-0) & Wisconsin (2-0)
1902	Michigan (5-0)
1903	Michigan (3-0-1), Minnesota (3-0-1) & Northwestern (1-0-2)
1904	Minnesota (3-0) & Michigan (2-0)
1905	Chicago (7-0)
1906	Wisconsin (3-0), Minnesota (2-0) & Michigan (1-0)
1907	Chicago (4-0)
1908	Chicago (5-0)
1909	Minnesota (3-0)
1910	Illinois (4-0) & Minnesota (2-0)
1911	Minnesota (3-0-1)
1912	Wisconsin (6-0)
1913	Chicago (7-0)
1914	Illinois (6-0)
1915	Minnesota (3-0-1) & Illinois (3-0-2)
1916	Ohio St. (4-0)
1917	Ohio St. (4-0)
1918	Illinois (4-0), Michigan (2-0) & Purdue (1-0)
1919	Illinois (6-1)
1920	Ohio St. (5-0)
1921	Iowa (5-0)
1922	Iowa (5-0) & Michigan (4-0)
1923	Illinois (5-0) & Michigan (4-0)
1924	Chicago (3-0-3)
1925	Michigan (5-1)
1926	Michigan (5-0) & Northwestern (5-0)
1927	Illinois (5-0)
1928	Illinois (4-1)
1929	Purdue (5-0)
1930	Michigan (5-0) & Northwestern (5-0)
1931	Purdue (5-1), Michigan (5-1) & Northwestern (5-1)
1932	Michigan (6-0)
1933	Michigan (5-0-1)
1934	Minnesota (5-0)
1935	Minnesota (5-0) & Ohio St. (5-0)
1936	Northwestern (6-0)
1937	Minnesota (5-0)
1938	Minnesota (4-1)
1939	Ohio St. (5-1)
1940	Minnesota (6-0)
1941	Minnesota (5-0)
1942	Ohio St. (5-1)
1943	Purdue (6-0) & Michigan (6-0)
1944	Ohio St. (6-0)
1945	Indiana (5-0-1)
1946	Illinois (6-1)
1947	Michigan (6-0)
1948	Michigan (6-0)
1949	Ohio St. (4-1-1) & Michigan (4-1-1)
1950	Michigan (4-1-1)
1951	Illinois (5-0-1)
1952	Wisconsin (4-1-1) & Purdue (4-1-1)
1953	Michigan St. (5-1) & Illinois (5-1)
1954	Ohio St. (7-0)

Year Champion (Record)
1955 Ohio St. (6-0)
1956 Iowa (5-1)
1957 Ohio St. (7-0)
1958 Iowa (5-1)
1959 Wisconsin (5-2)
1960 Minnesota (5-1) & Iowa (5-1)
1961 Ohio St. (6-0)
1962 Wisconsin (6-1)
1963 Illinois (5-1-1)
1964 Michigan (6-1)
1965 Michigan St. (7-0)
1966 Michigan St. (7-0)
1967 Indiana (6-1), Purdue (6-1) & Minnesota (6-1)
1968 Ohio St. (7-0)
1969 Ohio St. (6-1) & Michigan (6-1)
1970 Ohio St. (7-0)
1971 Michigan (8-0)
1972 Ohio St. (8-0) & Michigan (7-1)
1973 Ohio St. (7-0-1) & Michigan (7-0-1)
1974 Ohio St. (7-1) & Michigan (7-1)
1975 Ohio St. (8-0)
1976 Michigan (7-1) & Ohio St. (7-1)
1977 Michigan (7-1) & Ohio St. (7-1)
1978 Michigan (7-1) & Michigan St. (7-1)
1979 Ohio St. (8-0)
1980 Michigan (8-0)
1981 Iowa (6-2) & Ohio St. (6-2)
1982 Michigan (8-1)
1983 Illinois (9-0)
1984 Ohio St. (7-2)
1985 Iowa (7-1)
1986 Michigan (7-1) & Ohio St. (7-1)
1987 Michigan St. (7-0-1)
1988 Michigan (7-0-1)
1989 Michigan (8-0)
1990 Iowa (6-2), Michigan (6-2), Michigan St. (6-2) & Illinois (6-2)
1991 Michigan (8-0)
1992 Michigan (6-0-2)
1993 Ohio St. (6-1-1) & Wisconsin (6-1-1)
1994 Penn St. (8-0)
1995 Northwestern (8-0)
1996 Ohio St. (7-1) & Northwestern (7-1)
1997 Michigan (8-0)
1998 Ohio St. (7-1), Wisconsin (7-1) & Michigan (7-1)
1999 Wisconsin (7-1)
2000 Michigan (6-2), Northwestern (6-2) & Purdue (6-2)
2001 Illinois (7-1)
2002 Iowa (8-0) & Ohio St. (8-0)
2003 Michigan (7-1)
2004 Iowa (7-1) & Michigan (7-1)
2005 Penn St. (7-1) & Ohio St. (7-1)
2006 Ohio St. (8-0)

BIG 12 CONFERENCE

Founded: In 1996 when 12 charter members combined eight members of Big Eight Conference with four former Southwest Conference members. **Charter members** (12): Baylor, Colorado, Iowa St., Kansas, Kansas St., Missouri, Nebraska, Oklahoma, Oklahoma St., Texas, Texas A&M and Texas Tech. **Current members** (12): Baylor, Colorado, Iowa St., Kansas, Kansas St., Missouri, Nebraska, Oklahoma, Oklahoma St., Texas, Texas A&M and Texas Tech.

Year Regular Season Champion (Record)
1996 Nebraska (North, 8-0)
Texas (South, 6-2)
1997 Nebraska (North, 8-0)
Texas A&M (South, 6-2)
1998 Kansas St. (North, 8-0)
Texas A&M (South, 7-1)
1999 Nebraska* & Kansas St. (North, 7-1)
Texas (South, 6-2)
2000 Kansas St.* & Nebraska (North, 6-2)
Oklahoma (South, 8-0)
2001 Colorado* & Nebraska (North, 7-1)
Texas (South, 7-1)
2002 Colorado (North, 7-1)
Oklahoma* & Texas (South, 6-2)
2003 Kansas St. (North, 6-2)
Oklahoma (South, 8-0)
2004 Colorado* & Iowa St. (North, 4-4)
Oklahoma (South, 8-0)
2005 Colorado (South, 5-3)
Texas (South, 8-0)
2006 Nebraska (North, 6-2)
Oklahoma (South, 7-1)

**Won tiebreaker to represent division in Big 12 championship game.*

In 1996, the Big 12 began a championship game to determine the league's representative in the BCS bowls. Following are the results of the North Division Champion (N) vs. the South Division Champion (S):

1996 Texas (S) 37, Nebraska (N) 27
1997 Nebraska (N) 54, Texas A&M (S) 15
1998 Texas A&M (S) 36, Kansas St. (N) 33 (2 ot)
1999 Nebraska (N) 22, Texas (S) 6
2000 Oklahoma (S) 27, Kansas St. (N) 24
2001 Colorado (N) 39, Texas (S) 37
2002 Oklahoma (S) 29, Colorado (N) 7
2003 Kansas St. (N) 35, Oklahoma (S) 7
2004 Oklahoma (S) 42, Colorado (N) 3
2005 Texas (S) 70, Colorado (N) 3
2006 Oklahoma (S) 21, Nebraska (N) 7

CONFERENCE USA

Founded: In 1996 when five charter members went from independent status and one former Southwest Conference member combined to form Conference USA. **Charter members** (6): Cincinnati, Houston, Louisville, Memphis, Southern Miss. and Tulane. **Admitted later** (11): East Caro. (1997), Army (1998), UAB (1999), TCU (2001), South Fla. (2003), UCF (2005), Marshall (2005), Rice (2005), SMU (2005), UTEP (2005) and Tulsa (2005). **Withdrew later** (5): Army (2004), Cincinnati (2004), Louisville (2004), South Fla. (2004) and TCU (2004). **Current members** (12): UAB, UCF, East Caro., Houston, Marshall, Memphis, Rice, SMU, Southern Miss., Tulane, Tulsa and UTEP.

Year Champion (Record)
1996 Houston (4-1) & Southern Miss. (4-1)
1997 Southern Miss. (6-0)
1998 Tulane (6-0)
1999 Southern Miss. (6-0)
2000 Louisville (6-1)
2001 Louisville (6-1)
2002 Cincinnati (6-2) & TCU (6-2)
2003 Southern Miss. (8-0)
2004 Louisville (8-0)

Year Regular Season Champion (Record)
2005 UCF (East, 7-1)
Tulsa (West, 6-2)
2006 Southern Miss. (East, 6-2)
Houston (West, 7-1)

In 2005, Conference USA began a championship game to determine a league champion. Following are the results of the East Division Champion (E) vs. the West Division Champion (W):

2005 Tulsa (W) 44, UCF (E) 27
2006 Houston (W) 34, Southern Miss. (E) 20

MID-AMERICAN CONFERENCE

Founded: In 1946. **Charter members** (6): Butler, Cincinnati, Miami (Ohio), Ohio, Western Mich. and Western Reserve (now Case Reserve). **Admitted later** (14): Kent St. (1951), Toledo (1951), Bowling Green (1952), Marshall (1954 and 1997), Central Mich. (1972), Eastern Mich. (1972), Ball St. (1973), Northern Ill. (1973 and 1997), Akron (1992), Buffalo (1999), UCF (2002) and Temple (2007). **Withdrew later** (7): Butler (1950), Cincinnati (1953), Case Reserve (1955), Marshall (1969 and 2004), Northern Ill. (1986) and UCF (2004). **Current members** (13): Akron, Ball St., Bowling Green, Buffalo, Central Mich., Eastern Mich., Kent St., Miami (Ohio), Northern Ill., Ohio, Temple, Toledo and Western Mich.

Year Champion (Record)
1947 Cincinnati (3-1)
1948 Miami (Ohio) (4-0)
1949 Cincinnati (4-0)
1950 Miami (Ohio) (4-0)
1951 Cincinnati (3-0)
1952 Cincinnati (3-0)
1953 Ohio (5-0-1)
1954 Miami (Ohio) (4-0)
1955 Miami (Ohio) (5-0)
1956 Bowling Green (5-0-1)
1957 Miami (Ohio) (5-0)
1958 Miami (Ohio) (5-0)
1959 Bowling Green (6-0)
1960 Ohio (6-0)
1961 Bowling Green (5-1)
1962 Bowling Green (5-0-1)
1963 Ohio (5-1)
1964 Bowling Green (5-1)
1965 Bowling Green (5-1) & Miami (Ohio) (5-1)
1966 Miami (Ohio) (5-1) & Western Mich. (5-1)
1967 Toledo (5-1) & Ohio (5-1)
1968 Ohio (6-0)
1969 Toledo (5-0)
1970 Toledo (5-0)
1971 Toledo (5-0)
1972 Kent St. (4-1)
1973 Miami (Ohio) (5-0)
1974 Miami (Ohio) (5-0)
1975 Miami (Ohio) (6-0)
1976 Ball St. (4-1)
1977 Miami (Ohio) (5-0)
1978 Ball St. (8-0)
1979 Central Mich. (8-0-1)
1980 Central Mich. (7-2)
1981 Toledo (8-1)
1982 Bowling Green (7-2)
1983 Northern Ill. (8-1)
1984 Toledo (7-1-1)
1985 Bowling Green (9-0)
1986 Miami (Ohio) (6-2)
1987 Eastern Mich. (7-1)
1988 Western Mich. (7-1)
1989 Ball St. (6-1-1)
1990 Central Mich. (7-1)
1991 Bowling Green (8-0)
1992 Bowling Green (8-0)
1993 Ball St. (7-0-1)
1994 Central Mich. (8-1)
1995 Toledo (7-0-1)
1996 Ball St. (7-1)

Year Regular Season Champion (Record)
1997 Marshall (East, 7-1)
Toledo (West, 7-1)
1998 Marshall* & Miami (Ohio) (East, 7-1)
Toledo (West, 6-2)
1999 Marshall (East, 8-0)
Western Mich. (West, 6-2)
2000 Marshall* & Akron (East, 5-1)
Western Mich.* & Toledo (West, 4-1)
2001 Marshall (East, 6-0)
Toledo*, Northern Ill. & Ball St. (West, 4-1)
2002 Marshall (East, 7-1)
Toledo* & Northern Ill. (West, 7-1)
2003 Miami (Ohio) (East, 8-0)
Bowling Green (West, 7-1)
2004 Miami (Ohio) (East, 7-1)
Toledo* & Northern Ill. (West, 7-1)
2005 Akron*, Miami (Ohio) & Bowling Green (East, 5-3)
Northern Ill.* & Toledo (West, 6-2)
2006 Ohio (East, 7-1)
Central Mich. (West, 7-1)

**Won tiebreaker to represent division in MAC championship game.*

Since 1997, the MAC has conducted a championship game between the East and West division champion to determine a league champion. Following are the results of the East Division champion (E) vs. the West Division champion (W):

1997 Marshall (E) 34, Toledo (W) 14
1998 Marshall (E) 23, Toledo (W) 17
1999 Marshall (E) 34, Western Mich. (W) 30
2000 Marshall (E) 19, Western Mich. (W) 14
2001 Toledo (W) 41, Marshall (E) 36
2002 Marshall (E) 49, Toledo (W) 45
2003 Miami (Ohio) (E) 49, Bowling Green (W) 27
2004 Toledo (W) 35, Miami (Ohio) (E) 27
2005 Akron (E) 31, Northern Ill. (W) 30
2006 Central Mich. (W) 31, Ohio (E) 10

MOUNTAIN WEST CONFERENCE

Founded: In 1999. **Charter members** (8): Air Force, BYU, Colorado St., UNLV, New Mexico, San Diego St., Utah and Wyoming. All left the Western Athletic Conference after two years of 16-team league. **Admitted later** (1): TCU (2005). **Current members** (9): Air Force, BYU, Colorado St., UNLV, New Mexico, San Diego St., TCU, Utah and Wyoming.

Year Champion (Record)
1999 BYU (5-2), Colorado St. (5-2) & Utah (5-2)
2000 Colorado St. (6-1)
2001 BYU (7-0)
2002 Colorado St. (6-1)
2003 Utah (6-1)
2004 Utah (7-0)
2005 TCU (8-0)
2006 BYU (8-0)

PACIFIC-10 CONFERENCE

Founded: In 1915 as the **Pacific Coast Conference** by group of four charter members. **Charter members** (4): California, Oregon, Oregon St. and Washington. **Admitted later** (6): Washington St. (1917), Stanford (1918), Idaho (1922), Southern California (1922), Montana (1924) and UCLA (1928). **Withdrew later** (2): Montana (1950) and Idaho (1958).

The Pacific Coast Conference dissolved in 1959 and the Athletic Association of Western Universities was founded with five charter members. **Charter members** (5): California, Southern California, Stanford, UCLA and Washington. **Admitted later** (5): Washington St. (1962), Oregon (1964), Oregon St. (1964), Arizona (1978) and Arizona St. (1978). Conference renamed **Pacific-8** in 1968 and **Pacific-10** in 1978. **Current members** (10): Arizona, Arizona St., California, Oregon, Oregon St., Southern California, Stanford, UCLA, Washington and Washington St.

Year	Champion (Record)
1916	Washington (3-0-1)
1917	Washington (3-0)
1918	California (3-0)
1919	Oregon (2-1) & Washington (2-1)
1920	California (3-0)
1921	California (5-0)
1922	California (3-0)
1923	California (5-0)
1924	Stanford (3-0-1)
1925	Washington (5-0)
1926	Stanford (4-0)
1927	Southern California (4-0-1) & Stanford (4-0-1)
1928	Southern California (4-0-1)
1929	Southern California (6-1)
1930	Washington St. (6-0)
1931	Southern California (7-0)
1932	Southern California (6-0)
1933	Oregon (4-1) & Stanford (4-1)
1934	Stanford (5-0)
1935	California (4-1), Stanford (4-1) & UCLA (4-1)
1936	Washington (6-0-1)
1937	California (6-0-1)
1938	Southern California (6-1) & California (6-1)
1939	Southern California (5-0-2) & UCLA (5-0-3)
1940	Stanford (7-0)
1941	Oregon St. (7-2)
1942	UCLA (6-1)
1943	Southern California (4-0)
1944	Southern California (3-0-2)
1945	Southern California (6-0)
1946	UCLA (7-0)
1947	Southern California (6-0)
1948	California (6-0) & Oregon (6-0)
1949	California (7-0)
1950	California (5-0-1)
1951	Stanford (6-1)
1952	Southern California (6-0)
1953	UCLA (6-1)
1954	UCLA (6-0)
1955	UCLA (6-0)
1956	Oregon St. (6-1-1)
1957	Oregon (6-2) & Oregon St. (6-2)
1958	California (6-1)
1959	Washington (3-1), Southern California (3-1) & UCLA (3-1)
1960	Washington (4-0)
1961	UCLA (3-1)
1962	Southern California (4-0)
1963	Washington (4-1)
1964	Oregon St. (3-1) & Southern California (3-1)
1965	UCLA (4-0)
1966	Southern California (4-1)
1967	Southern California (6-1)
1968	Southern California (6-0)
1969	Southern California (6-0)
1970	Stanford (6-1)
1971	Stanford (6-1)
1972	Southern California (7-0)
1973	Southern California (7-0)
1974	Southern California (6-0-1)
1975	UCLA (6-1) & California (6-1)
1976	Southern California (7-0)
1977	Washington (6-1)
1978	Southern California (6-1)
1979	Southern California (6-0-1)
1980	Washington (6-1)
1981	Washington (6-2)
1982	UCLA (5-1-1)
1983	UCLA (6-1-1)
1984	Southern California (7-1)
1985	UCLA (6-2)
1986	Arizona St. (5-1-1)
1987	Southern California (7-1) & UCLA (7-1)
1988	Southern California (8-0)
1989	Southern California (6-0-1)
1990	Washington (7-1)
1991	Washington (8-0)
1992	Stanford (6-2) & Washington (6-2)
1993	UCLA (6-2), Arizona (6-2) & Southern California (6-2)
1994	Oregon (7-1)
1995	Southern California (6-1-1) & Washington (6-1-1)
1996	Arizona St. (8-0)
1997	Washington St. (7-1) & UCLA (7-1)
1998	UCLA (8-0)
1999	Stanford (7-1)
2000	Oregon (7-1), Oregon St. (7-1) & Washington (7-1)
2001	Oregon (7-1)
2002	Southern California (7-1) & Washington St. (7-1)
2003	Southern California (7-1)
2004	Southern California (8-0)
2005	Southern California (8-0)
2006	California (7-2) & Southern California (7-2)

SOUTHEASTERN CONFERENCE

Founded: In 1933 when charter members all left the **Southern Conference** to become the SEC. **Charter members** (13): Alabama, Auburn, Florida, Georgia, Georgia Tech, Kentucky, LSU, Mississippi, Mississippi St., Sewanee, Tennessee, Tulane and Vanderbilt. **Admitted later** (2): Arkansas (1992) and South Carolina (1992). **Withdrew later** (3): Sewanee (1940), Georgia Tech (1964) and Tulane (1966). **Current members** (12): Alabama, Arkansas, Auburn, Florida, Georgia, Kentucky, LSU, Mississippi, Mississippi St., South Carolina, Tennessee and Vanderbilt.

Year	Champion (Record)
1933	Alabama (5-0-1)
1934	Tulane (8-0) & Alabama (7-0)
1935	LSU (5-0)
1936	LSU (6-0)
1937	Alabama (6-0)
1938	Tennessee (7-0)
1939	Tennessee (6-0), Georgia Tech (6-0) & Tulane (5-0)
1940	Tennessee (5-0)
1941	Mississippi St. (4-0-1)
1942	Georgia (6-1)
1943	Georgia Tech (4-0)
1944	Georgia Tech (4-0)
1945	Alabama (6-0)
1946	Georgia (5-0) & Tennessee (5-0)
1947	Mississippi (6-1)
1948	Georgia (6-0)
1949	Tulane (5-1)
1950	Kentucky (5-1)
1951	Georgia Tech (7-0) & Tennessee (5-0)
1952	Georgia (6-0)
1953	Alabama (4-0-3)
1954	Mississippi (5-1)
1955	Mississippi (5-1)
1956	Tennessee (6-0)
1957	Auburn (7-0)
1958	LSU (6-0)
1959	Georgia (7-0)
1960	Mississippi (5-0-1)
1961	Alabama (7-0) & LSU (6-0)
1962	Mississippi (6-0)
1963	Mississippi (5-0-1)
1964	Alabama (8-0)
1965	Alabama (6-1-1)
1966	Alabama (6-0) & Georgia (6-0)
1967	Tennessee (6-0)
1968	Georgia (5-0-1)
1969	Tennessee (5-1)
1970	LSU (5-0)
1971	Alabama (7-0)
1972	Alabama (7-1)
1973	Alabama (8-0)
1974	Alabama (6-0)
1975	Alabama (6-0)
1976	Georgia (5-1) & Kentucky (5-1)
1977	Alabama (7-0) & Kentucky (6-0)
1978	Alabama (6-0)
1979	Alabama (6-0)
1980	Georgia (6-0)
1981	Georgia (6-0) & Alabama (6-0)
1982	Georgia (6-0)
1983	Auburn (6-0)
1984	Florida (5-0-1)#
1985	Tennessee (5-1)*
1986	LSU (5-1)
1987	Auburn (5-0-1)
1988	Auburn (6-1) & LSU (6-1)
1989	Alabama (6-1), Tennessee (6-1) & Auburn (6-1)
1990	Tennessee (5-1-1)*
1991	Florida (7-0)

Year	Regular Season Champion (Record)
1992	Florida^ & Georgia (Eastern, 6-2) Alabama (Western, 8-0)
1993	Florida (Eastern, 7-1)* Alabama# (Western, 8-0)
1994	Florida (Eastern, 7-1) Alabama (Western, 8-0)
1995	Florida (Eastern, 8-0) Arkansas (Western, 6-2)
1996	Florida (Eastern, 8-0) Alabama^ & LSU (Western, 6-2)
1997	Tennessee (Eastern, 7-1) Auburn^ & LSU (Western, 6-2)
1998	Tennessee (Eastern, 8-0) Mississippi St.^ & Arkansas (Western, 6-2)
1999	Florida (Eastern, 7-1) Alabama (Western, 7-1)
2000	Florida (Eastern, 7-1) Auburn (Western, 6-2)
2001	Tennessee (Eastern, 7-1) LSU^ & Auburn (Western, 5-3)
2002	Georgia (Eastern, 7-1) Arkansas^, Auburn & LSU (Western, 5-3)
2003	Georgia^, Florida & Tennessee (Eastern, 6-2) LSU^ & Mississippi (Western, 7-1)
2004	Tennessee (Eastern, 7-1) Auburn (Western, 8-0)
2005	Georgia (Eastern, 6-2) LSU^ & Auburn (Western, 7-1)
2006	Florida (East, 7-1) Arkansas (West, 7-1)

*#Title vacated. *Ineligible for title (probation): Florida (5-1) in 1985, Florida (6-1) in 1990 and Auburn (8-0) in 1993. ^Won tiebreaker to represent division in SEC championship game.*

Since 1992, the SEC has conducted a championship game to determine the league's representative in the BCS bowls. Following are the results of the Western Division champion (W) vs. the Eastern Division champion (E):

Year	Result
1992	Alabama (W) 28, Florida (E) 21
1993	Florida (E) 28, Alabama (W) 13
1994	Florida (E) 24, Alabama (W) 23
1995	Florida (E) 34, Arkansas (W) 3
1996	Florida (E) 45, Alabama (W) 30
1997	Tennessee (E) 30, Auburn (W) 29
1998	Tennessee (E) 24, Mississippi St. (W) 14
1999	Alabama (W) 34, Florida (E) 7
2000	Florida (E) 28, Auburn (W) 6
2001	LSU (W) 31, Tennessee (E) 20
2002	Georgia (E) 30, Arkansas (W) 3
2003	LSU (W) 34, Georgia (E) 13
2004	Auburn (W) 38, Tennessee (E) 28
2005	Georgia 34 (E), LSU (W) 14
2006	Florida (E) 38, Arkansas (W) 28

SUN BELT CONFERENCE

Founded: In 2001 when four former members of the Big West Conference combined with three former Football Bowl Subdivision independents. **Charter members** (7): Arkansas St. (from Big West), Idaho (from Big West), La.-Lafayette (independent), La.-Monroe (independent), Middle Tenn. (independent), New Mexico St. (from Big West), North Texas (from Big West). **Admitted later** (4): Utah St. (from independent, 2003), Troy (from independent, 2004), Fla. Atlantic (2005) and Florida Int'l (2005). **Withdrew later** (3): Idaho (2004), New Mexico St. (2004) and Utah St. (2004). **Current members** (8): Arkansas St., Fla. Atlantic, Florida Int'l, La.-Lafayette, La.-Monroe, Middle Tenn., North Texas and Troy.

Year	Champion (Record)
2001	North Texas (5-1) & Middle Tenn. (5-1)
2002	North Texas (6-0)
2003	North Texas (7-0)
2004	North Texas (7-0)
2005	Arkansas St. (5-2), La.-Lafayette (5-2) & La.-Monroe (5-2)
2006	Middle Tenn. (6-1) & Troy (6-1)

WESTERN ATHLETIC CONFERENCE

Founded: In 1962 when charter members left the Skyline and Border Conferences to form the WAC. In 1996, three former Southwest Conference members joined two former Big West members and one former independent team to form a 16-team league, the largest conference alignment ever in the Football Bowl Subdivision. The league was divided into Mountain and Pacific divisions. In 1999, eight members split off to form the Mountain West Conference. **Charter members** (6): Arizona (from Border), Arizona St. (from Border), BYU (from Skyline), New Mexico (from Skyline), Utah (from Skyline) and Wyoming (from Skyline). **Admitted later** (18): Colorado St. (1968), UTEP (1968), San Diego St. (1978), Hawaii (1979), Air Force (1980), Fresno St. (1992), UNLV (1996), Rice (1996), San Jose St. (1996), SMU (1996), TCU (1996), Tulsa (1996), Nevada (2000), Boise St. (2001), Louisiana Tech (2001), Idaho (2005), New Mexico St. (2005) and Utah St. (2005). **Withdrew later** (15): Arizona (1978), Arizona St. (1978), Air Force (1999), BYU (1999), Colorado St. (1999), UNLV (1999), New Mexico (1999), San Diego St. (1999), Utah (1999), Wyoming (1999), TCU (2000), Rice (2004), SMU (2004), UTEP (2004) and Tulsa (2004). **Current members** (9): Boise St., Fresno St., Hawaii, Idaho, Louisiana Tech, Nevada, New Mexico St., San Jose St. and Utah St.

Year	Champion (Record)
1962	New Mexico (2-1-1)
1963	New Mexico (3-1)
1964	Arizona (3-1), Utah (3-1) & New Mexico (3-1)
1965	BYU (4-1)
1966	Wyoming (5-0)
1967	Wyoming (5-0)
1968	Wyoming (6-1)
1969	Arizona St. (6-1)
1970	Arizona St. (7-0)
1971	Arizona St. (7-0)
1972	Arizona St. (5-1)
1973	Arizona (6-1) & Arizona St. (6-1)
1974	BYU (6-0-1)
1975	Arizona St. (7-0)
1976	BYU (6-1) & Wyoming (6-1)
1977	Arizona St. (6-1) & BYU (6-1)
1978	BYU (5-1)
1979	BYU (7-0)
1980	BYU (6-1)
1981	BYU (7-1)
1982	BYU (7-1)
1983	BYU (7-0)
1984	BYU (8-0)
1985	Air Force (7-1) & BYU (7-1)
1986	San Diego St. (7-1)
1987	Wyoming (8-0)
1988	Wyoming (8-0)
1989	BYU (7-1)
1990	BYU (7-1)
1991	BYU (7-0-1)
1992	Hawaii (6-2), Fresno St. (6-2) & BYU (6-2)
1993	Wyoming (6-2), Fresno St. (6-2) & BYU (6-2)
1994	Colorado St. (7-1)
1995	Colorado St. (6-2), Air Force (6-2), Utah (6-2) & BYU (6-2)

Year	Regular Season Champion (Record)
1996	BYU (Mountain, 8-0) Wyoming (Pacific, 7-1)
1997	New Mexico (Mountain, 6-2) Colorado St. (Pacific, 7-1)
1998	Air Force (Mountain, 7-1) BYU (Pacific, 7-1)

Year	Champion (Record)
1999	Fresno St. (5-2), Hawaii (5-2) & TCU (5-2)
2000	TCU (7-1) & UTEP (7-1)
2001	Louisiana Tech (7-1)
2002	Boise St. (8-0)
2003	Boise St. (8-0)
2004	Boise St. (8-0)
2005	Boise St. (7-1) & Nevada (7-1)
2006	Boise St. (8-0)

From 1996 to 1998, the WAC conducted a championship game to determine a league champion. Following are the results of the Mountain Division Champion (M) vs. the Pacific Division Champion (P):

1996	BYU (M) 28, Wyoming (P) 25
1997	Colorado St. (P) 41, New Mexico (M) 13
1998	Air Force (M) 20, BYU (P) 13

Football Championship Subdivision

BIG SKY CONFERENCE

Founded: In 1963 when six charter members—Gonzaga, Idaho, Idaho St., Montana, Montana St. and Weber St.—banded together to form the Big Sky. **Admitted later** (8): Boise St. (1970), Northern Ariz. (1970), Nevada (1979, replacing charter member Gonzaga), Eastern Wash. (1987), Cal St. Northridge (1996), Sacramento St. (1996), Portland St. (1996) and Northern Colo. (2006). **Withdrew later** (5): Gonzaga (1979), Nevada (1992), Boise St. (1996), Idaho (1996) and Cal St. Northridge (2001, dropped football). **Current members** (9): Eastern Wash., Idaho St., Montana, Montana St., Northern Ariz., Northern Colo., Portland St., Sacramento St. and Weber St.

Year	Champion (Record)
1963	Idaho St. (3-1)
1964	Montana St. (3-0)
1965	Idaho (3-1) & Weber St. (3-1)
1966	Montana St. (4-0)
1967	Montana St. (4-0)
1968	Idaho (3-1), Montana St. (3-1) & Weber St. (3-1)
1969	Montana (4-0)#
1970	Montana (5-0)
1971	Idaho (4-1)
1972	Montana St. (5-1)
1973	Boise St. (6-0)#
1974	Boise St. (6-0)#
1975	Boise St. (5-0-1)#
1976	Montana St. (6-0)#
1977	Boise St. (6-0)
1978	Northern Ariz. (6-0)
1979	Montana St. (6-1)
1980	Boise St. (6-1)
1981	Idaho St. (6-1)*
1982	Montana (5-2)*
1983	Nevada (6-1)*
1984	Montana St. (6-1)*
1985	Idaho (6-1)*
1986	Nevada (7-0)*
1987	Idaho (7-1)*
1988	Idaho (7-1)*
1989	Idaho (8-0)*
1990	Nevada (7-1)*
1991	Nevada (8-0)*
1992	Eastern Wash. (6-1)* & Idaho (6-1)*
1993	Montana (7-0)*
1994	Boise St. (6-1)*
1995	Montana (6-1)*
1996	Montana (7-0)*
1997	Eastern Wash. (7-1)*
1998	Montana (6-2)*
1999	Montana (7-1)*
2000	Montana (8-0)*
2001	Montana (7-0)*
2002	Idaho St. (5-2), Montana (5-2)* & Montana St. (5-2)*
2003	Montana (5-2)*, Montana St. (5-2)* & Northern Ariz. (5-2)*
2004	Eastern Wash. (6-1)* & Montana (6-1)*
2005	Eastern Wash. (5-2)*, Montana (5-2)* & Montana St. (5-2)
2006	Montana (8-0)*

#Participated in NCAA Division II Championship.
**Participated in NCAA Division I Championship.*

BIG SOUTH CONFERENCE

Founded: In 1983 as an all-sports conference. Football was added as the conference's 18th championship sport in 2002. Three former Football Championship Subdivision independents and one school moving from Division II joined to play football. **Charter members** (4): Charleston So., Elon, Gardner-Webb (from Division II) and Liberty. **Admitted later** (2): Coastal Caro. (restarted program, 2003) and VMI (from Southern Conference, 2003). **Withdrew later** (1): Elon (2003). **Current members** (5): Charleston So., Coastal Caro., Gardner-Webb, Liberty and VMI.

Year	Champion (Record)
2002	Gardner-Webb (3-0)
2003	Gardner-Webb (4-0)
2004	Coastal Caro. (4-0)
2005	Charleston So. (3-1) & Coastal Caro. (3-1)
2006	Coastal Caro. (4-0)*

**Participated in NCAA Division I Championship.*

COLONIAL ATHLETIC ASSOCIATION

Founded: In 1985 as an all-sports conference. Football was added as the conference's 22nd championship sport in 2007. Twelve institutions that competed in football in the Atlantic 10 Conference moved to the CAA after the Atlantic 10 discontinued sponsorship of the sport. **Charter members** (12): Delaware, Hofstra, James Madison, Maine, Massachusetts, New Hampshire, Northeastern, Rhode Island, Richmond, Towson, Villanova and William & Mary.

GATEWAY FOOTBALL CONFERENCE

Founded: In 1982 as a women's athletics organization by 10 Midwestern universities. Six members started as a football conference in 1985. **Charter members** (6): (Football) Eastern Ill., Illinois St., Missouri St., UNI, Southern Ill. and Western Ill. Four members—Eastern Ill., Missouri St., UNI and Western Ill.—were members of the Mid-Continent Conference for football. **Admitted later** (3): Indiana St. (1986), Youngstown St. (1997) and Western Ky. (2001). **Withdrew later** (2): Eastern Ill. (1996) and Western Ky. (2007). **Current members** (7): Illinois St., Indiana St., Missouri St., UNI, Southern Ill., Western Ill. and Youngstown St.

Year	Champion (Record)
1985	UNI (5-0)*
1986	Eastern Ill. (5-1)*
1987	UNI (6-0)*
1988	Western Ill. (6-0)*
1989	Missouri St. (5-1)*
1990	UNI (5-1)*
1991	UNI (5-1)*
1992	UNI (5-1)*
1993	UNI (5-1)*
1994	UNI (6-0)*
1995	Eastern Ill. (5-1)* & UNI (5-1)*
1996	UNI (5-0)*
1997	Western Ill. (6-0)*
1998	Western Ill. (5-1)*
1999	Illinois St. (6-0)*
2000	Western Ill. (5-1)*
2001	UNI (6-1)*
2002	Western Ill. (6-1)* & Western Ky. (6-1)*
2003	UNI (6-1)* & Southern Ill. (6-1)*
2004	Southern Ill. (7-0)*
2005	UNI (5-2)*, Southern Ill. (5-2)* & Youngstown St. (5-2)
2006	Youngstown St. (6-1)*

**Participated in NCAA Division I Championship.*

GREAT WEST FOOTBALL CONFERENCE

Founded: In 2004 by a group of six charter members. **Charter members** (6): UC Davis, Cal Poly, North Dakota St., Northern Colo., South Dakota St. and Southern Utah. **Withdrew later** (1): Northern Colo. (2005). **Current members** (5): UC Davis, Cal Poly, North Dakota St., South Dakota St. and Southern Utah.

Year	Champion (Record)
2004	Cal Poly (4-1)
2005	UC Davis (4-1) & Cal Poly (4-1)*
2006	North Dakota St. (4-0)

**Participated in NCAA Division I Championship.*

IVY GROUP

Founded: In 1956 by a group of eight charter members. **Charter members** (8): Brown, Columbia, Cornell, Dartmouth, Harvard, Penn, Princeton and Yale. **Current members** (8): Brown, Columbia, Cornell, Dartmouth, Harvard, Penn, Princeton and Yale.

Year	Champion (Record)
1956	Yale (7-0)
1957	Princeton (6-1)
1958	Dartmouth (6-1)
1959	Penn (6-1)
1960	Yale (7-0)
1961	Columbia (6-1) & Harvard (6-1)
1962	Dartmouth (7-0)
1963	Dartmouth (5-2) & Princeton (5-2)
1964	Princeton (7-0)
1965	Dartmouth (7-0)
1966	Dartmouth (6-1), Harvard (6-1) & Princeton (6-1)
1967	Yale (7-0)
1968	Harvard (6-0-1) & Yale (6-0-1)
1969	Dartmouth (6-1), Yale (6-1) & Princeton (6-1)
1970	Dartmouth (7-0)

Year	Champion (Record)
1971	Cornell (6-1) & Dartmouth (6-1)
1972	Dartmouth (5-1-1)
1973	Dartmouth (6-1)
1974	Harvard (6-1) & Yale (6-1)
1975	Harvard (6-1)
1976	Brown (6-1) & Yale (6-1)
1977	Yale (6-1)
1978	Dartmouth (6-1)
1979	Yale (6-1)
1980	Yale (6-1)
1981	Yale (6-1) & Dartmouth (6-1)
1982	Harvard (5-2), Penn (5-2) & Dartmouth (5-2)
1983	Harvard (5-1-1) & Penn (5-1-1)
1984	Penn (7-0)
1985	Penn (6-1)
1986	Penn (7-0)
1987	Harvard (6-1)
1988	Penn (6-1) & Cornell (6-1)
1989	Princeton (6-1) & Yale (6-1)
1990	Cornell (6-1) & Dartmouth (6-1)
1991	Dartmouth (6-0-1)
1992	Dartmouth (6-1) & Princeton (6-1)
1993	Penn (7-0)
1994	Penn (7-0)
1995	Princeton (5-1-1)
1996	Dartmouth (7-0)
1997	Harvard (7-0)
1998	Penn (6-1)
1999	Brown (6-1) & Yale (6-1)
2000	Penn (6-1)
2001	Harvard (7-0)
2002	Penn (7-0)
2003	Penn (7-0)
2004	Harvard (7-0)
2005	Brown (6-1)
2006	Princeton (6-1) & Yale (6-1)

METRO ATLANTIC ATHLETIC CONFERENCE

Founded: In 1980 by six charter members — Army, Fairfield, Fordham, Iona, Manhattan and St. Peter's. Competition followed one year in men's cross country and men's soccer. Canisius and Siena both joined the conference in 1989. Football was added in 1993, with Georgetown and St. John's (N.Y.) as associate members of the conference. **Charter members** (6): Canisius, Georgetown, Iona, St. John's (N.Y.), St. Peter's and Siena. **Admitted later** (4): Duquesne (as associate member in 1994), Marist (1994), Fairfield (1996) and La Salle (as associate member in 1999). **Withdrew later** (6): St. John's (N.Y.) (1998 and 2003, dropped football), Georgetown (1999), Canisius (2003, dropped football), Fairfield (2003, dropped football), Siena (2004, dropped football) and St. Peter's (2007, dropped football). **Readmitted** (1): St. John's (N.Y.) (2002). **Current members** (4): Duquesne, Iona, La Salle and Marist.

Year	Champion (Record)
1993	Iona (5-0)
1994	Marist (6-1) & St. John's (N.Y.) (6-1)
1995	Duquesne (7-0)
1996	Duquesne (8-0)
1997	Georgetown (7-0)
1998	Fairfield (6-1) & Georgetown (6-1)
1999	Duquesne (6-1)
2000	Duquesne (7-0)
2001	Duquesne (6-0)
2002	Duquesne (8-0)
2003	Duquesne (5-0)
2004	Duquesne (4-0)
2005	Duquesne (4-0)
2006	Duquesne (3-1) & Marist (3-1)

MID-EASTERN ATHLETIC CONFERENCE

Founded: In 1970 with first playing season in 1971 by six charter members. **Charter members** (6): Delaware St., Howard, Morgan St., N.C. A&T, N.C. Central and South Carolina St. **Admitted later** (5): Bethune-Cookman (1979), Florida A&M (1979), Hampton (1996), Norfolk St. (1997) and Savannah St. (2001). **Withdrew later** (4): Morgan St. (1979), N.C. Central (1979), Florida A&M (1984 and 2003) and Savannah St. (2003). **Readmitted** (2): Morgan St. (1984) and Florida A&M (1986 and 2005). **Current members** (9): Bethune-Cookman, Delaware St., Florida A&M, Hampton, Howard, Morgan St., Norfolk St., N.C. A&T and South Carolina St.

Year	Champion (Record)
1971	Morgan St. (5-0-1)
1972	N.C. Central (5-1)
1973	N.C. Central (5-1)
1974	South Carolina St. (5-1)
1975	South Carolina St. (5-1)
1976	South Carolina St. (5-1)
1977	South Carolina St. (6-0)
1978	South Carolina St. (5-0-1)
1979	Morgan St. (5-0)#
1980	South Carolina St. (5-0)
1981	South Carolina St. (5-0)*
1982	South Carolina St. (4-1)*
1983	South Carolina St. (4-0)
1984	Bethune-Cookman (4-0)
1985	Delaware St. (4-0)
1986	N.C. A&T (4-1)*
1987	Howard (5-0)
1988	Bethune-Cookman (4-2), Florida A&M (4-2) & Delaware St. (4-2)
1989	Delaware St. (5-1)
1990	Florida A&M (6-0)
1991	N.C. A&T (5-1)√
1992	N.C. A&T (5-1)*
1993	Howard (6-0)*
1994	South Carolina St. (6-0)√
1995	Florida A&M (6-0)√
1996	Florida A&M (7-0)*
1997	Hampton (7-0)*
1998	Florida A&M (7-1)* & Hampton (7-1)*
1999	N.C. A&T (8-0)*
2000	Florida A&M (7-1)*
2001	Florida A&M (7-1)*
2002	Bethune-Cookman (7-1)*
2003	N.C. A&T (6-1)*
2004	Hampton (6-1)* & South Carolina St. (6-1)
2005	Hampton (8-0)*
2006	Hampton (7-1)*

*#Participated in NCAA Division II Championship. *Participated in NCAA Division I Championship. √Participated in Heritage Bowl.*

NORTHEAST CONFERENCE

Founded: In 1996 when five charter members all went from independent status to form the Northeast Conference. **Charter members** (5): Central Conn. St., Monmouth, Robert Morris, St. Francis (Pa.) and Wagner. **Admitted later** (4): Sacred Heart (1998), Albany (N.Y.) (1999), Stony Brook (1999) and St. John's (N.Y.) (2000). **Withdrew later** (2): St. John's (N.Y.) (2002) and Stony Brook (2007). **Current members** (7): Albany (N.Y.), Central Conn. St., Monmouth, Robert Morris, Sacred Heart, St. Francis (Pa.) and Wagner.

Year	Champion (Record)
1996	Robert Morris (3-1) & Monmouth (3-1)
1997	Robert Morris (4-0)
1998	Monmouth (4-1) & Robert Morris (4-1)
1999	Robert Morris (7-0)
2000	Robert Morris (8-0)
2001	Sacred Heart (8-0)
2002	Albany (N.Y.) (6-1)
2003	Monmouth (6-1) & Albany (N.Y.) (6-1)
2004	Monmouth (6-1) & Central Conn. St. (6-1)
2005	Central Conn. St. (5-2) & Stony Brook (5-2)
2006	Monmouth (6-1)

OHIO VALLEY CONFERENCE

Founded: In 1948 by six charter members, five of which withdrew from the Kentucky Intercollegiate Athletic Conference (Eastern Ky., Louisville, Morehead St., Murray St. and Western Ky.), plus Evansville. **Charter members** (6): Eastern Ky., Evansville, Louisville, Morehead St., Murray St. and Western Ky. **Admitted later** (13): Marshall (1949), Tennessee Tech (1949), Middle Tenn. (1952), East Tenn. St. (1957), Austin Peay (1962), Akron (1979), Youngstown St. (1980), Tennessee St. (1988), Southeast Mo. St. (1991), Tenn.-Martin (1992), Eastern Ill. (1996), Jacksonville St. (2003) and Samford (2003). **Readmitted** (2): Western Ky. (1999) and Austin Peay (2007). **Withdrew later** (10): Louisville (1949), Evansville (1952), Marshall (1952), East Tenn. St. (1979), Western Ky. (1982 and 2000), Akron (1987), Youngstown St. (1988), Morehead St. (1996), Austin Peay (1997) and Middle Tenn. (1998). **Current members** (10): Austin Peay, Eastern Ill., Eastern Ky., Jacksonville St., Murray St., Samford, Southeast Mo. St., Tenn.-Martin, Tennessee St. and Tennessee Tech.

Team	Champion (Record)
1948	Murray St. (3-1)
1949	Evansville (3-1)
1950	Murray St. (5-0-1)
1951	Murray St. (5-1)
1952	Tennessee St. (4-1) & Western Ky. (4-1)
1953	Tennessee Tech (5-0)
1954	Eastern Ky. (5-0)
1955	Tennessee Tech (5-0)
1956	Middle Tenn. (5-0)
1957	Middle Tenn. (5-0)
1958	Middle Tenn. (5-1) & Tennessee Tech (5-1)
1959	Middle Tenn. (5-0-1) & Tennessee Tech (5-0-1)
1960	Tennessee Tech (6-0)
1961	Tennessee Tech (6-0)
1962	East Tenn. St. (4-2)
1963	Western Ky. (7-0)
1964	Middle Tenn. (6-1)#
1965	Middle Tenn. (7-0)
1966	Morehead St. (6-1)
1967	Eastern Ky. (5-0-2)#
1968	Eastern Ky. (7-0)
1969	East Tenn. St. (6-0-1)#
1970	Western Ky. (5-1-1)
1971	Western Ky. (5-2)
1972	Tennessee Tech (7-0)#
1973	Western Ky. (7-0)#
1974	Eastern Ky. (6-1)
1975	Tennessee Tech (6-1) & Western Ky. (6-1)#
1976	Eastern Ky. (6-1)#
1977	Austin Peay (6-1)
1978	Western Ky. (6-0)
1979	Murray St. (6-0)*
1980	Western Ky. (6-1)
1981	Eastern Ky. (8-0)*
1982	Eastern Ky. (7-0)*
1983	Eastern Ky. (6-1)*
1984	Eastern Ky. (6-1)*
1985	Middle Tenn. (7-0)*
1986	Murray St. (5-2)
1987	Eastern Ky. (5-1)* & Youngstown St. (5-1)
1988	Eastern Ky. (6-0)*
1989	Middle Tenn. (6-0)*
1990	Eastern Ky. (5-1)* & Middle Tenn. (5-1)*
1991	Eastern Ky. (7-0)*
1992	Middle Tenn. (8-0)*
1993	Eastern Ky. (8-0)*
1994	Eastern Ky. (8-0)*
1995	Murray St. (8-0)*
1996	Murray St. (8-0)*
1997	Eastern Ky. (7-0)*
1998	Tennessee St. (6-1)*
1999	Tennessee St. (7-0)*
2000	Western Ky. (7-0)*
2001	Eastern Ill. (6-0)*
2002	Eastern Ill. (5-1)* & Murray St. (5-1)*
2003	Jacksonville St. (7-1)*
2004	Jacksonville St. (7-1)*
2005	Eastern Ill. (8-0)*
2006	Eastern Ill. (7-1)* & Tenn.-Martin (6-1)*

*#Participated in NCAA Division II Championship. *Participated in NCAA Division I Championship.*

PATRIOT LEAGUE

Founded: In 1984 originally as the Colonial League with six charter members. **Charter members** (6): Bucknell, Colgate, Davidson, Holy Cross, Lafayette and Lehigh. **Admitted later** (3): Fordham (1990), Towson (1997) and Georgetown (2001). **Withdrew later** (2): Davidson (1989) and Towson (2003). **Current members** (7): Bucknell, Colgate, Fordham, Georgetown, Holy Cross, Lafayette and Lehigh.

Year	Champion (Record)
1986	Holy Cross (4-0)
1987	Holy Cross (4-0)
1988	Lafayette (5-0)
1989	Holy Cross (4-0)
1990	Holy Cross (5-0)
1991	Holy Cross (5-0)
1992	Lafayette (5-0)
1993	Lehigh (4-1)
1994	Lafayette (5-0)
1995	Lehigh (5-0)
1996	Bucknell (4-1)
1997	Colgate (6-0)*
1998	Lehigh (6-0)*
1999	Colgate (5-1)* & Lehigh (5-1)*
2000	Lehigh (6-0)*
2001	Lehigh (7-0)*
2002	Colgate (6-1) & Fordham (6-1)*

Year Champion (Record)
2003 Colgate (7-0)*
2004 Lafayette (5-1)* & Lehigh (5-1)*
2005 Colgate (5-1)* & Lafayette (5-1)*
2006 Colgate (5-1), Lafayette (5-1)* & Lehigh (5-1)

**Participated in NCAA Division I Championship.*

PIONEER FOOTBALL LEAGUE

Founded: Started in 1993 with Division I-AA charter members Butler, Dayton, Drake, Evansville, San Diego and Valparaiso. **Admitted later** (4): Austin Peay (2001), Davidson (2001), Jacksonville (2001) and Morehead St. (2001). **Withdrew later** (2): Evansville (1997, dropped football) and Austin Peay (2005). **Current members** (8): Butler, Davidson, Dayton, Drake, Jacksonville, Morehead St., San Diego and Valparaiso.

Year Champion (Record)
1993 Dayton (5-0)
1994 Butler (4-1) & Dayton (4-1)
1995 Drake (5-0)
1996 Dayton (5-0)
1997 Dayton (5-0)
1998 Drake (4-0)
1999 Dayton (4-0)
2000 Dayton (3-1), Drake (3-1) & Valparaiso (3-1)

Year Regular Season Champion (Record)
2001 Dayton (North, 4-0)
Jacksonville (South, 3-0)
2002 Dayton (North, 4-0)
Morehead St. (South, 3-0)
2003 Valparaiso* & San Diego (North, 3-1)
Morehead St. (South, 3-0)
2004 Drake (North, 4-0)
Morehead St.* & Jacksonville (South, 2-1)
2005 San Diego (North, 4-0)
Morehead St. (South, 3-0)

Year Champion (Record)
2006 San Diego (7-0)

**Won tiebreaker to represent division in PFL championship game.*

From 2001 to 2005, the PFL conducted a championship game between the North and South division champion to determine a league champion. Following are the results of the North Division champion (N) vs. the South Division champion (S):

2001 Dayton (N) 46, Jacksonville (S) 14
2002 Dayton (N) 28, Morehead St. (S) 0
2003 Valparaiso (N) 54, Morehead St. (S) 42
2004 Drake (N) 20, Morehead St. (S) 17
2005 San Diego (N) 47, Morehead St. (S) 40

SOUTHERN CONFERENCE

Founded: In 1921 by 14 institutions to form the Southern Intercollegiate Conference. Roots for the conference can actually be traced back to 1894 when several football-playing schools formed a confederation known as the Southeastern Intercollegiate Athletic Association. **Charter members** (14): Alabama, Auburn, Clemson, Georgia, Georgia Tech, Kentucky, Maryland, Mississippi St., North Carolina, North Carolina St., Tennessee, Virginia, Virginia Tech and Wash. & Lee. **Admitted later** (18): Florida (1922), LSU (1922), Mississippi (1922), South Carolina (1922), Tulane (1922), Vanderbilt (1922), VMI (1924), Citadel (1936), Furman (1936), West Virginia (1951), Appalachian St. (1971), Marshall (1976), Chattanooga (1976), Western Caro. (1976), East Tenn. St. (1978), Ga. Southern (1992), Wofford (1997) and Elon (2003). **Withdrew later:** Since 1922, membership has changed drastically, with a total of 39 schools having been affiliated with the league, including 11 of the 12 schools currently comprising the Southeastern Conference and nine of the 12 schools currently comprising the Atlantic Coast Conference. **Current members** (8): Appalachian St., Chattanooga, Citadel, Elon, Furman, Ga. Southern, Western Caro. and Wofford.

Year Champion (Record√)
1922 Georgia Tech
1923 Vanderbilt
1924 Alabama
1925 Alabama
1926 Alabama
1927 Georgia Tech
1928 Georgia Tech
1929 Tulane
1930 Alabama & Tulane
1931 Tulane
1932 Auburn & Tennessee
1933 Duke (4-0)
1934 Wash. & Lee (4-0)
1935 Duke (5-0)
1936 Duke (7-0)
1937 Maryland (2-0)
1938 Duke (5-0)
1939 Clemson (4-0)
1940 Clemson (4-0)
1941 Duke (5-0)
1942 William & Mary (4-0)
1943 Duke (4-0)
1944 Duke (4-0)
1945 Duke (4-0)
1946 North Carolina (4-0-1)
1947 William & Mary (7-1)
1948 Clemson (5-0)
1949 North Carolina (5-0)
1950 Wash. & Lee (6-0)
1951 Maryland (5-0) & VMI (5-0)
1952 Duke (5-0)
1953 West Virginia (4-0)
1954 West Virginia (3-0)
1955 West Virginia (4-0)
1956 West Virginia (5-0)
1957 VMI (6-0)
1958 West Virginia (4-0)
1959 VMI (6-0-1)
1960 VMI (4-1)
1961 Citadel (5-1)
1962 VMI (6-0)
1963 Virginia Tech (5-0)
1964 West Virginia (5-0)
1965 West Virginia (4-0)
1966 East Caro. (4-1-1) & William & Mary (4-1-1)
1967 West Virginia (4-0-1)
1968 Richmond (6-0)
1969 Davidson (5-1) & Richmond (5-1)
1970 William & Mary (3-1)
1971 Richmond (5-1)
1972 East Caro. (7-0)
1973 East Caro. (7-0)
1974 VMI (5-1)
1975 Richmond (5-1)
1976 East Caro. (4-1)
1977 Chattanooga (4-1) & VMI (4-1)
1978 Chattanooga (4-1) & Furman (4-1)
1979 Chattanooga (5-1)
1980 Furman (7-0)
1981 Furman (5-2)
1982 Furman (6-1)*
1983 Furman (6-0-1)*
1984 Chattanooga (5-1)*
1985 Furman (6-0)*
1986 Appalachian St. (6-0-1)*
1987 Appalachian St. (7-0)*
1988 Furman (6-1)* & Marshall (6-1)*
1989 Furman (7-0)*
1990 Furman (6-1)*
1991 Appalachian St. (6-1)*
1992 Citadel (6-1)*
1993 Ga. Southern (7-1)*
1994 Marshall (7-1)*
1995 Appalachian St. (8-0)*
1996 Marshall (8-0)*
1997 Ga. Southern (7-1)*
1998 Ga. Southern (8-0)*
1999 Appalachian St. (7-1)*, Furman (7-1)* &
Ga. Southern (7-1)*
2000 Ga. Southern (7-1)*
2001 Furman (7-1)* & Ga. Southern (7-1)*
2002 Ga. Southern (7-1)*
2003 Wofford (8-0)*
2004 Furman (6-1)* & Ga. Southern (6-1)*
2005 Appalachian St. (6-1)*
2006 Appalachian St. (7-0)*

**Participated in NCAA Division I Championship. √No records available until 1933.*

SOUTHLAND CONFERENCE

Founded: In 1963 by a group of five institutions. **Charter members** (5): Abilene Christian, Arkansas St., Lamar, Texas-Arlington and Trinity (Tex.). **Admitted later** (14): La.-Lafayette (1971), Louisiana Tech (1971), La.-Monroe (1972), McNeese St. (1972), North Texas (1982), Northwestern St. (1987), Sam Houston St. (1987), Texas St. (1987), Stephen F. Austin (1987), Nicholls St. (1992), Jacksonville St. (1996), Troy (1996), Southeastern La. (2005) and Central Ark. (2006). **Withdrew later** (11): Trinity (Tex.) (1972), Abilene Christian (1973), La.-Lafayette (1982), Texas-Arlington (1986, dropped football), Arkansas St. (1987), Lamar (1987), Louisiana Tech (1987), North Texas (1995), La.-Monroe (1996), Troy (2000) and Jacksonville St. (2003). **Current members** (8): Central Ark., McNeese St., Nicholls St., Northwestern St., Sam Houston St., Southeastern La., Stephen F. Austin and Texas St.

Year Champion (Record)
1964 Lamar (3-0-1)
1965 Lamar (3-1)
1966 Texas-Arlington (3-1)
1967 Texas-Arlington (4-0)
1968 Arkansas St. (3-0-1)
1969 Arkansas St. (4-0)
1970 Arkansas St. (4-0)
1971 Louisiana Tech (4-1)
1972 Louisiana Tech (5-0)
1973 Louisiana Tech (5-0)
1974 Louisiana Tech (5-0)
1975 Arkansas St. (5-0)
1976 La.-Lafayette (4-1) & McNeese St. (4-1)
1977 Louisiana Tech (4-0-1)
1978 Louisiana Tech (4-1)
1979 McNeese St. (5-0)
1980 McNeese St. (5-0)
1981 Texas-Arlington (4-1)
1982 Louisiana Tech (5-0)*
1983 La.-Monroe (5-1) & North Texas (5-1)*
1984 Louisiana Tech (5-1)*
1985 Arkansas St. (5-1)*
1986 Arkansas St. (5-0)*
1987 La.-Monroe (6-0)*
1988 Northwestern St. (6-0)*
1989 Stephen F. Austin (5-0-1)*
1990 La.-Monroe (5-1)*
1991 McNeese St. (4-1-2)*
1992 La.-Monroe (7-0)*
1993 McNeese St. (7-0)*
1994 North Texas (5-0-1)*
1995 McNeese St. (5-0)*
1996 Troy (5-1)*
1997 McNeese St. (6-1)* & Northwestern St. (6-1)*
1998 Northwestern St. (6-1)*
1999 Stephen F. Austin (6-1) & Troy (6-1)*
2000 Troy (6-1)*
2001 McNeese St. (5-1)* & Sam Houston St. (5-1)*
2002 McNeese St. (6-0)*
2003 McNeese St. (5-0)*
2004 Northwestern St. (4-1)* & Sam Houston St. (4-1)*
2005 Nicholls St. (5-1)* & Texas St. (5-1)*
2006 McNeese St. (5-1)*

**Participated in NCAA Division I Championship.*

SOUTHWESTERN ATHLETIC CONFERENCE

Founded: In 1920 by a group of six institutions. **Charter members** (6): Bishop, Paul Quinn, Prairie View, Sam Houston College, Texas College and Wiley. **Admitted later** (11): Langston (1931), Southern U. (1934), Arkansas AM&N (1936), Texas Southern (1954), Grambling (1958), Jackson St. (1958), Alcorn St. (1962), Mississippi Val. (1968), Alabama St. (1982), Ark.-Pine Bluff (1998), Alabama A&M (1999) and Morris Brown (2001). **Withdrew later** (9): Paul Quinn (1929), Bishop (1956), Langston (1957), Sam Houston College (1959), Texas College (1961), Wiley (1968), Arkansas AM&N (1970), Prairie View (1990, dropped program, readmitted 1991) and Morris Brown (2002). **Current members** (10): Alabama A&M, Alabama St., Alcorn St., Ark.-Pine Bluff, Grambling, Jackson St., Mississippi Val., Prairie View, Southern U. and Texas Southern.

Year Champion (Record√)
1921 Wiley
1922 Paul Quinn
1923 Wiley
1924 Paul Quinn
1925 Bishop
1926 Sam Houston College
1927 Wiley
1928 Wiley
1929 Wiley
1930 Wiley
1931 Prairie View
1932 Wiley
1933 Langston & Prairie View
1934 Texas College
1935 Texas College
1936 Texas College & Langston

Year	Champion (Record√)
1937	Southern U. & Langston
1938	Southern U. & Langston
1939	Langston
1940	Southern U. & Langston
1941	No champion
1942	Texas College
1943	No champion
1944	Langston (5-1), Texas College (5-1) & Wiley (5-1)
1945	Wiley (6-0)
1946	Southern U. (5-1)
1947	Southern U. (7-0)
1948	Southern U. (7-0)
1949	Langston (6-0-1) & Southern U. (6-0-1)
1950	Southern U. (7-0)
1951	Prairie View (6-1)
1952	Prairie View (6-0)
1953	Prairie View (6-0)
1954	Prairie View (6-0)
1955	Southern U. (6-1)
1956	Langston (5-1) & Texas Southern (5-1)
1957	Wiley (6-0)
1958	Prairie View (5-0)
1959	Southern U. (7-0)
1960	Grambling (6-1), Prairie View (6-1) & Southern U. (6-1)
1961	Jackson St. (6-1)
1962	Jackson St. (6-1)
1963	Prairie View (7-0)
1964	Prairie View (7-0)
1965	Grambling (6-1)
1966	Arkansas AM&N (4-2-1), Grambling (4-2-1), Southern U. (4-2-1) & Texas Southern (4-2-1)
1967	Grambling (6-1)

Year	Champion (Record√)
1968	Alcorn St. (6-1), Grambling (6-1) & Texas Southern (6-1)
1969	Alcorn St. (6-0-1)
1970	Alcorn St. (6-0)
1971	Grambling (5-1)
1972	Grambling (5-1) & Jackson St. (5-1)
1973	Grambling (5-1) & Jackson St. (5-1)
1974	Alcorn St. (5-1) & Grambling (5-1)
1975	Grambling (4-2) & Southern U. (4-2)
1976	Alcorn St. (5-1)
1977	Grambling (6-0)
1978	Grambling (5-0-1)
1979	Alcorn St. (5-1) & Grambling (5-1)
1980	Grambling (5-1)* & Jackson St. (5-1)
1981	Jackson St. (5-1)*
1982	Jackson St. (6-0)*
1983	Grambling (6-0-1)
1984	Alcorn St. (7-0)*
1985	Grambling (6-1)* & Jackson St. (6-1)*
1986	Jackson St. (7-0)*
1987	Jackson St. (7-0)*
1988	Jackson St. (7-0)*
1989	Jackson St. (7-0)*
1990	Jackson St. (5-1)*
1991	Alabama St. (6-0-1)#
1992	Alcorn St. (7-0)*
1993	Southern U. (7-0)#
1994	Alcorn St. (6-1)* & Grambling (6-1)#
1995	Jackson St. (7-0)*
1996	Jackson St. (6-1)*
1997	Southern U. (8-0)#
1998	Southern U. (8-0)#
1999	Jackson St. (Eastern, 7-2) Southern U. (Western, 9-0)#

Year	Regular Season Champion (Record)
2000	Alabama A&M^ & Alabama St. (Eastern, 5-2) Grambling (Western, 6-1)
2001	Alabama St. (Eastern, 6-1) Grambling (Western, 6-1)
2002	Alabama A&M (Eastern, 6-1) Grambling (Western, 6-1)
2003	Alabama St.^ & Alcorn St. (Eastern, 5-2) Southern U. (Western, 6-1)
2004	Alabama St. (Eastern, 6-1) Southern U. (Western, 6-1)
2005	Alabama A&M (Eastern, 7-2) Grambling (Western, 9-0)
2006	Alabama A&M (Eastern, 6-3) Ark.-Pine Bluff (Western, 7-2)

*√No records available until 1944. *Participated in NCAA Division I Championship. #Participated in Heritage Bowl. ^Won tiebreaker to represent division in SWAC championship game.*

Since 1999, the SWAC has conducted a championship game between the East and West division champion to determine a league champion. Following are the results of the East Division champion (E) vs. the West Division champion (W):

Year	Result
1999	Southern U. (W) 31, Jackson St. (E) 30
2000	Grambling (W) 14, Alabama A&M (E) 6
2001	Grambling (W) 38, Alabama St. (E) 31
2002	Grambling (W) 31, Alabama A&M (E) 19
2003	Southern U. (W) 20, Alabama St. (E) 9
2004	Alabama St. (E) 40, Southern U. (W) 35
2005	Grambling (W) 45, Alabama A&M (E) 6
2006	Alabama A&M (E) 22, Ark.-Pine Bluff (W) 13

Discontinued Conferences

Football Bowl Subdivision (FBS)

BIG EIGHT CONFERENCE

Founded: Originally founded in 1907 as the Missouri Valley Intercollegiate Athletic Association. Charter members were Iowa, Kansas, Missouri, Nebraska and Washington-St. Louis. Six schools were admitted later: Drake (1908), Iowa St. (1908), Kansas St. (1913), Grinnell (1919), Oklahoma (1920) and Oklahoma St. (1925). Iowa withdrew in 1911. The Big Six Conference was founded in 1928 when charter members left the MVIAA. Iowa St., Kansas, Kansas St., Missouri, Nebraska and Oklahoma were joined by Colorado (1948) (conference then known as Big Seven) and Oklahoma St. (1958) (conference then known as Big Eight until 1996). All eight members of the Big Eight joined four former Southwest Conference members (Baylor, Texas, Texas A&M and Texas Tech) to form the Big 12 Conference in 1996.

Year	Champion (Record)
1907	Iowa (1-0) & Nebraska (1-0)
1908	Kansas (4-0)
1909	Missouri (4-0-1)
1910	Nebraska (2-0)
1911	Iowa St. (2-0-1) & Nebraska (2-0-1)
1912	Iowa St. (2-0) & Nebraska (2-0)
1913	Missouri (4-0) & Nebraska (3-0)
1914	Nebraska (3-0)
1915	Nebraska (4-0)
1916	Nebraska (3-1)
1917	Nebraska (2-0)
1918	No Champion—War
1919	Missouri (4-0-1)
1920	Oklahoma (4-0-1)
1921	Nebraska (3-0)
1922	Nebraska (5-0)
1923	Nebraska (3-0-2)
1924	Missouri (5-1)
1925	Missouri (5-1)

Year	Champion (Record)
1926	Oklahoma St. (3-0-1)
1927	Missouri (5-1)
1928	Nebraska (4-0)
1929	Nebraska (3-0-2)
1930	Kansas (4-1)
1931	Nebraska (5-0)
1932	Nebraska (5-0)
1933	Nebraska (5-0)
1934	Kansas St. (5-0)
1935	Nebraska (4-0-1)
1936	Nebraska (5-0)
1937	Nebraska (3-0-2)
1938	Oklahoma (5-0)
1939	Missouri (5-0)
1940	Nebraska (5-0)
1941	Missouri (5-0)
1942	Missouri (4-0-1)
1943	Oklahoma (5-0)
1944	Oklahoma (4-0-1)
1945	Missouri (5-0)
1946	Oklahoma (4-1) & Kansas (4-1)
1947	Kansas (4-0-1) & Oklahoma (4-0-1)
1948	Oklahoma (5-0)
1949	Oklahoma (5-0)
1950	Oklahoma (6-0)
1951	Oklahoma (6-0)
1952	Oklahoma (5-0-1)
1953	Oklahoma (6-0)
1954	Oklahoma (6-0)
1955	Oklahoma (6-0)
1956	Oklahoma (6-0)
1957	Oklahoma (6-0)
1958	Oklahoma (6-0)
1959	Oklahoma (5-1)
1960	Missouri (7-0)
1961	Colorado (7-0)
1962	Oklahoma (7-0)
1963	Nebraska (7-0)
1964	Nebraska (6-1)
1965	Nebraska (7-0)
1966	Nebraska (6-1)

Year	Champion (Record)
1967	Oklahoma (7-0)
1968	Kansas (6-1) & Oklahoma (6-1)
1969	Missouri (6-1) & Nebraska (6-1)
1970	Nebraska (7-0)
1971	Nebraska (7-0)
1972	Nebraska (5-1-1)*
1973	Oklahoma (7-0)
1974	Oklahoma (7-0)
1975	Nebraska (6-1) & Oklahoma (6-1)
1976	Colorado (5-2), Oklahoma (5-2) & Oklahoma St. (5-2)
1977	Oklahoma (7-0)
1978	Nebraska (6-1) & Oklahoma (6-1)
1979	Oklahoma (7-0)
1980	Oklahoma (7-0)
1981	Nebraska (7-0)
1982	Nebraska (7-0)
1983	Nebraska (7-0)
1984	Oklahoma (6-1) & Nebraska (6-1)
1985	Oklahoma (7-0)
1986	Oklahoma (7-0)
1987	Oklahoma (7-0)
1988	Nebraska (7-0)
1989	Colorado (7-0)
1990	Colorado (7-0)
1991	Colorado (6-0-1) & Nebraska (6-0-1)
1992	Nebraska (6-1)
1993	Nebraska (7-0)
1994	Nebraska (7-0)
1995	Nebraska (7-0)

**Oklahoma (5-1-1) forfeited title.*

BIG WEST CONFERENCE

Founded: In 1969 as the Pacific Coast Athletic Association. Charter members were UC Santa Barb., Cal St. L.A., Fresno St., Long Beach St., Pacific, San Diego St. and San Jose St. Twelve schools were admitted later: Cal St. Fullerton (1974), Utah St. (1977), UNLV (1982), New Mexico St. (1983), Nevada (1992), Arkansas St. (1993, readmitted 1998), La.-

Lafayette (1993), Louisiana Tech (1993), Northern Ill. (1993), Boise St. (1996), Idaho (1996) and North Texas (1996). The following schools withdrew, in chronological order: UC Santa Barb. (1972), Cal St. L.A. (1974), San Diego St. (1976), Fresno St. (1991), Long Beach St. (1991, dropped football), Cal St. Fullerton (1992, dropped football), Arkansas St. (1996, readmitted 1998), La.-Lafayette (1996), Louisiana Tech (1996), UNLV (1996), Northern Ill. (1996), Pacific (1996, dropped football) and San Jose St. (1996). The conference was renamed the Big West Conference in 1988. In 2001, Arkansas St., Idaho, New Mexico St. and North Texas joined La.-Lafayette, La.-Monroe and Middle Tenn. for the inaugural season of football in the Sun Belt Conference. Boise St. became a member of the Western Athletic Conference and Utah St. became an FBS independent.

Year	Champion (Record)
1969	San Diego St. (6-0)
1970	Long Beach St. (5-1) & San Diego St. (5-1)
1971	Long Beach St. (5-1)
1972	San Diego St. (4-0)
1973	San Diego St. (3-0-1)
1974	San Diego St. (4-0)
1975	San Jose St. (5-0)
1976	San Jose St. (4-0)
1977	Fresno St. (4-0)
1978	San Jose St. (4-1) & Utah St. (4-1)
1979	Utah St. (5-0)
1980	Long Beach St. (5-0)
1981	San Jose St. (5-0)
1982	Fresno St. (6-0)
1983	Cal St. Fullerton (5-1)
1984	Cal St. Fullerton (6-1)#
1985	Fresno St. (7-0)
1986	San Jose St. (7-0)
1987	San Jose St. (7-0)
1988	Fresno St. (7-0)
1989	Fresno St. (7-0)
1990	San Jose St. (7-0)
1991	Fresno St. (6-1) & San Jose St. (6-1)
1992	Nevada (5-1)
1993	La.-Lafayette (5-1) & Utah St. (5-1)
1994	La.-Lafayette (5-1), Nevada (5-1) & UNLV (5-1)
1995	Nevada (6-0)
1996	Nevada (4-1) & Utah St. (4-1)
1997	Utah St. (4-1) & Nevada (4-1)
1998	Idaho (4-1)
1999	Boise St. (5-1)
2000	Boise St. (5-0)

#UNLV forfeited title.

BORDER INTERCOLLEGIATE ATHLETIC ASSOCIATION

Founded: In 1931 as Border Intercollegiate Athletic Association. Charter members were Arizona, Arizona St. Teachers' (Flagstaff) (now Northern Ariz.), Arizona St. Teachers' (Tempe) (now Arizona St.), New Mexico and New Mexico A&M (now New Mexico St.). Texas Tech was admitted in 1932, Texas Mines (now UTEP) was admitted in 1935, and Hardin-Simmons and West Texas St. Teachers' (now West Tex. A&M) were admitted in 1941.

Year	Champion (Record)
1931	Arizona St. (3-1)
1932	Texas Tech (2-0)*
1933	Texas Tech (1-0)*
1934	Texas Tech (1-0)*
1935	Arizona (4-0)
1936	Arizona (3-0-1)
1937	Texas Tech (3-0)
1938	New Mexico St. (4-1)**
	New Mexico (4-2)**
1939	Arizona St. (4-0)
1940	Arizona St. (3-0-1)
1941	Arizona (5-0)
1942	Hardin-Simmons (3-0-1)
	Texas Tech (3-0-1)
1943	No full conference program
1944	Texas Tech (2-0)
1945	Arizona (1-0)
1946	Hardin-Simmons (6-0)
1947	Texas Tech (4-0)

**Texas Tech has been listed by some as conference champion for the years 1932, 1933 and 1934, but conference rules forbade an official conference championship. This was due to the fact that the conference covered such a large area that games between all members were not practical.*

***Texas Tech won its two conference games in 1938 but did not win the official championship since it did not meet the conference three-game requirement. Its victory over New Mexico did not count toward the championship, permitting New Mexico to share championship honors with New Mexico St.*

MISSOURI VALLEY CONFERENCE

Founded: Originally founded as the Missouri Valley Intercollegiate Athletic Association. Several charter members left in 1928 to form the Big Six Conference, which became the Big Eight later. But Drake, Grinnell, Oklahoma A&M (now Oklahoma St.) and Washington-St. Louis continued the MVIAA. Creighton joined in 1928, Butler in 1932, Tulsa and Washburn in 1935, St. Louis in 1937, Wichita St. in 1947, Bradley and Detroit in 1949, Houston in 1951, Cincinnati and North Texas in 1957, Louisville in 1964, Memphis in 1968, and West Tex. A&M in 1972.

Year	Champion
1928	Drake
1929	Drake
1930	Drake & Oklahoma St.
1931	Drake
1932	Oklahoma St.
1933	Drake & Oklahoma St.
1934	Washington-St. Louis
1935	Washington-St. Louis & Tulsa
1936	Tulsa & Creighton
1937	Tulsa
1938	Tulsa
1939	Washington-St. Louis
1940	Tulsa
1941	Tulsa
1942	Tulsa
1943	Tulsa
1944	Oklahoma St.
1945	Oklahoma St.
1946	Tulsa
1947	Tulsa
1948	Oklahoma St.
1949	Detroit
1950	Tulsa
1951	Tulsa
1952	Houston
1953	Oklahoma St. & Detroit
1954	Wichita St.
1955	Wichita St. & Detroit
1956	Houston
1957	Houston
1958	North Texas
1959	North Texas & Houston
1960	Wichita St.
1961	Wichita St.
1962	Tulsa
1963	Cincinnati & Wichita St.
1964	Cincinnati
1965	Tulsa
1966	North Texas & Tulsa
1967	North Texas
1968	Memphis
1969	Memphis
1970	Louisville
1971	Memphis
1972	Louisville, West Tex. A&M & Drake
1973	North Texas
1974	Tulsa
1975	Tulsa
1976	Tulsa & New Mexico St.
1977	West Tex. A&M
1978	New Mexico St.
1979	West Tex. A&M
1980	Tulsa
1981	Drake & Tulsa
1982	Tulsa
1983	Tulsa
1984	Tulsa
1985	Tulsa

OLD ROCKY MOUNTAIN CONFERENCE

(Mountain States Athletic Conference and Big Seven Conference)

Founded: This conference predates every conference except the Big Ten and consisted of BYU (1922), Colorado (1900), Colorado Agricultural College (now Colorado St.) (1900), Colorado St. College (1900), Denver (1900), Utah (1902), Utah St. (1902) and Wyoming (1905). Before 1938, these schools were part of the Rocky Mountain Conference, other members of which, at that time, were Colorado College, Colorado Mines, Greeley St. Teachers' (now Northern Colo.), Montana St. (1917) and Western St. Teachers' (now Western St.) (1925). A split took place in 1938, when the Mountain States Athletic Conference or "Big Seven" was formed. The name Rocky Mountain Conference was retained by the last six schools after 1938. Some members went into the Western Athletic Conference when the RMC was dissolved in 1962.

Year	Champion
1900	Colorado College
1901	Colorado
1902	Colorado
1903	Colorado
1904	Colorado Mines
1905	Colorado Mines
1906	Colorado Mines
1907	Colorado Mines
1908	Denver
1909	Denver
1910	Colorado
1911	Colorado
1912	Colorado Mines
1913	Colorado
1914	Colorado Mines
1915	Colorado Aggies
1916	Colorado Aggies
1917	Denver
1918	Colorado Mines
1919	Colorado Aggies
1920	Colorado Aggies
1921	Utah St.
1922	Utah
1923	Colorado
1924	Colorado
1925	Colorado Aggies
1926	Utah
1927	Colorado Aggies
1928	Utah
1929	Utah
1930	Utah
1931	Utah
1932	Utah
1933	Utah, Denver* & Colorado St.*
1934	Colorado, Northern Colo. & Colorado St.*
1935	Colorado & Utah St.*
1936	Utah St.
1937	Colorado
1938	Utah (4-0-2)
1939	Colorado (5-1-0)
1940	Utah (5-1-0)
1941	Utah (4-0-2)
1942	Colorado & Utah (5-1-0)
1943	Colorado (2-0-0)
1944	Colorado (2-0-0)
1945	Denver (4-1-0)
1946	Utah St. & Denver (4-1-1)
1947	Utah (6-0-0)
1948	Utah
1949	Wyoming
1950	Wyoming
1951	Utah
1952	Utah
1953	Utah
1954	Denver
1955	Colorado St.
1956	Wyoming
1957	Utah
1958	Wyoming
1959	Wyoming
1960	Wyoming & Utah St.
1961	Wyoming & Utah St.

**In final ratings, according to conference rules, tie games were not counted in awarding championships. Thus, teams marked with * shared the championship because one or more ties were not counted in their conference records.*

SOUTHLAND CONFERENCE

(Football Bowl Subdivision only 1975-79, now Football Championship Subdivision conference)

SOUTHWEST CONFERENCE

Founded: In 1914 as the Southwest Athletic Conference with charter members Arkansas, Baylor, Oklahoma, Oklahoma St., Rice, Southwestern (Tex.), Texas and Texas A&M. Five teams were added: SMU (1918), Phillips (1920), TCU (1923), Texas Tech (1960) and Houston (1976). Five withdrew: Southwestern (Tex.) (1917), Oklahoma (1920), Phillips (1921), Oklahoma St. (1925)

and Arkansas (1992). Of the eight members in the final (1995) season, four (Baylor, Texas, Texas A&M and Texas Tech) joined with eight members of the Big Eight Conference to form the Big 12 Conference in 1996. The other members in 1996: Houston (to Conference USA), Rice (to Western Athletic Conference), SMU (to Western Athletic Conference) and TCU (to Western Athletic Conference).

Year	Champion (Record)
1914	No champion
1915	Oklahoma (3-0)*
1916	No champion
1917	Texas A&M (2-0)
1918	No champion
1919	Texas A&M (4-0)
1920	Texas (5-0)
1921	Texas A&M (3-0-2)
1922	Baylor (5-0)
1923	SMU (5-0)
1924	Baylor (4-0-1)
1925	Texas A&M (4-1)
1926	SMU (5-0)
1927	Texas A&M (4-0-1)
1928	Texas (5-1)
1929	TCU (4-0-1)
1930	Texas (4-1)
1931	SMU (5-0-1)
1932	TCU (6-0)
1933	No champion*
1934	Rice (5-1)
1935	SMU (6-0)
1936	Arkansas (5-1)
1937	Rice (4-1-1)
1938	TCU (6-0)
1939	Texas A&M (6-0)
1940	Texas A&M (5-1)
1941	Texas A&M (5-1)
1942	Texas (5-1)
1943	Texas (5-0)
1944	TCU (3-1-1)
1945	Texas (5-1)
1946	Rice (5-1) & Arkansas (5-1)
1947	SMU (5-0-1)
1948	SMU (5-0-1)
1949	Rice (6-0)
1950	Texas (6-0)
1951	TCU (5-1)
1952	Texas (6-0)
1953	Rice (5-1) & Texas (5-1)
1954	Arkansas (5-1)
1955	TCU (5-1)
1956	Texas A&M (6-0)
1957	Rice (5-1)
1958	TCU (5-1)
1959	Texas (5-1), TCU (5-1) & Arkansas (5-1)
1960	Arkansas (6-1)
1961	Texas (6-1) & Arkansas (6-1)
1962	Texas (6-0-1)
1963	Texas (7-0)
1964	Arkansas (7-0)
1965	Arkansas (7-0)
1966	SMU (6-1)
1967	Texas A&M (6-1)
1968	Texas (6-1) & Arkansas (6-1)
1969	Texas (7-0)
1970	Texas (7-0)
1971	Texas (6-1)
1972	Texas (7-0)
1973	Texas (7-0)
1974	Baylor (6-1)
1975	Arkansas (6-1), Texas A&M (6-1) & Texas (6-1)
1976	Houston (7-1) & Texas Tech (7-1)
1977	Texas (8-0)
1978	Houston (7-1)
1979	Houston (7-1) & Arkansas (7-1)
1980	Baylor (8-0)
1981	SMU (7-1)¢
1982	SMU (7-0-1)
1983	Texas (8-0)
1984	SMU (6-2) & Houston (6-2)
1985	Texas A&M (7-1)
1986	Texas A&M (7-1)
1987	Texas A&M (6-1)
1988	Arkansas (7-0)
1989	Arkansas (7-1)
1990	Texas (8-0)
1991	Texas A&M (8-0)
1992	Texas A&M (7-0)
1993	Texas A&M (7-0)
1994	Baylor (4-3), Rice (4-3), Texas (4-3), TCU (4-3) & Texas Tech (4-3)*
1995	Texas (7-0)

**Forfeited title: Baylor (3-0) in 1915, Arkansas (4-1) in 1933 and Texas A&M (6-0-1) in 1994 on probation. ¢SMU on probation; did not forfeit championship.*

Football Championship Subdivision (FCS)

AMERICAN WEST CONFERENCE

Founded: Started FCS play in 1993 with charter members Cal St. Northridge, Sacramento St. and Southern Utah. Other members were UC Davis and Cal Poly (both Division II members at the time). Cal Poly became an FCS member in 1994, and UC Davis withdrew in 1994. Last-year members were Cal Poly (became independent), Cal St. Northridge (to Big Sky Conference), Sacramento St. (to Big Sky Conference) and Southern Utah (became independent).

Year	Champion (Record)
1993	Southern Utah (3-1) & UC Davis (3-1)#
1994	Cal Poly (3-0)
1995	Sacramento St. (3-0)

ATLANTIC 10 CONFERENCE

Founded: In 1947 as the Yankee Conference by six institutions from the old New England College Conference. **Charter members** (6): Connecticut, Maine, Massachusetts, New Hampshire, Rhode Island and Vermont. **Admitted later** (10): Boston U. (1971), Holy Cross (1971), Delaware (1983), Richmond (1984), Villanova (1985), James Madison (1993), Northeastern (1993) William & Mary (1993), Hofstra (2001) and Towson (2004). **Withdrew later** (4): Holy Cross (1972), Vermont (1974, dropped football), Boston U. (1997, dropped football) and Connecticut (2000). Last-year members were Delaware, Hofstra, James Madison, Maine, Massachusetts, New Hampshire, Northeastern, Rhode Island, Richmond, Towson, Villanova and William & Mary.

Year	Champion (Record)
1947	New Hampshire (4-0)
1948	New Hampshire (3-1)
1949	Connecticut (2-0-1) & Maine (2-0-1)
1950	New Hampshire (4-0)
1951	Maine (3-0-1)
1952	Connecticut (3-1), Maine (3-1) & Rhode Island (3-1)
1953	New Hampshire (3-1) & Rhode Island (3-1)
1954	New Hampshire (4-0)
1955	Rhode Island (4-0-1)
1956	Connecticut (3-0-1)
1957	Connecticut (3-0-1) & Rhode Island (3-0-1)
1958	Connecticut (4-0)
1959	Connecticut (4-0)
1960	Connecticut (3-1) & Massachusetts (3-1)
1961	Maine (5-0)
1962	New Hampshire (4-0-1)
1963	Massachusetts (5-0)
1964	Massachusetts (5-0)
1965	Maine (5-0)
1966	Massachusetts (5-0)
1967	Massachusetts (5-0)
1968	Connecticut (4-1) & New Hampshire (4-1)
1969	Massachusetts (5-0)
1970	Connecticut (4-0-1)
1971	Connecticut (3-1-1) & Massachusetts (3-1-1)
1972	Massachusetts (5-0)
1973	Connecticut (5-0-1)
1974	Maine (4-2) & Massachusetts (4-2)
1975	New Hampshire (5-0)
1976	New Hampshire (4-1)
1977	Massachusetts (5-0)
1978	Massachusetts (5-0)*
1979	Boston U. (4-1) & Massachusetts (4-1)
1980	Boston U. (5-0)
1981	Massachusetts (4-1) & Rhode Island (4-1)*
1982	Boston U. (3-2)*, Connecticut (3-2), Maine (3-2) and Massachusetts (3-2)
1983	Boston U. (4-1)* & Connecticut (4-1)
1984	Boston U. (4-1)* & Rhode Island (4-1)*
1985	Rhode Island (5-0)*
1986	Connecticut (5-2), Delaware (5-2)* & Massachusetts (5-2)
1987	Maine (6-1)* & Richmond (6-1)*
1988	Delaware (6-2)* & Massachusetts (6-2)*
1989	Connecticut (6-2), Maine (6-2)* & Villanova (6-2)*
1990	Massachusetts (7-1)*
1991	Delaware (7-1)*, New Hampshire (7-1)* & Villanova (7-1)*
1992	Delaware (7-1)*
1993	Boston U. (9-0)*
1994	New Hampshire (8-0)*
1995	Delaware (8-0)*
1996	William & Mary (7-1)*
1997	Villanova (8-0)*
1998	Richmond (7-1)*
1999	James Madison (7-1)* & Massachusetts (7-1)*
2000	Delaware (7-1)* & Richmond (7-1)*
2001	Hofstra (7-2)*, Maine (7-2)*, Villanova (7-2) & William & Mary (7-2)*
2002	Maine (7-2)* & Northeastern (7-2)*
2003	Delaware (8-1)* & Massachusetts (8-1)*
2004	Delaware (7-1)*, James Madison (7-1)* & William & Mary (7-1)*
2005	New Hampshire (7-1)* & Richmond (7-1)*
2006	Massachusetts (8-0)*

**Participated in NCAA Division I Championship.*

Division II

EASTERN COLLEGIATE FOOTBALL CONFERENCE

Year	Champion
1993	Bentley
1994	Bentley
1995	Stonehill
1996	Salve Regina
1997	Albany (N.Y.)
1998	Albany (N.Y.)
1999	American Int'l
2000	American Int'l

GREAT NORTHWEST ATHLETIC CONFERENCE

(Formerly Columbia Football Association)

Year	Champion
1999	Western Wash.
2000	Central Wash. & Western Wash.
2001	Western Wash.
2002	Central Wash.
2003	Western Wash.
2004	Central Wash.
2005	Central Wash.

MIDWEST INTERCOLLEGIATE FOOTBALL CONFERENCE

Year	Champion
1990	Grand Valley St.
1991	Butler
1992	Ferris St., Butler, Grand Valley St. & Hillsdale
1993	Ferris St.
1994	Ferris St.
1995	Ferris St.
1996	Ferris St.
1997	Grand Valley St. & Ashland
1998	Grand Valley St.

NORTHERN CALIFORNIA ATHLETIC CONFERENCE

(Far Western Football Conference from 1929-81)

Year	Champion
1925	St. Mary's (Cal.)
1926	St. Mary's (Cal.)
1927	St. Mary's (Cal.)
1928	St. Mary's (Cal.)
1929	UC Davis
1930	Fresno St.
1931	None
1932	Nevada & San Jose St.
1933	Nevada
1934	Fresno St. & San Jose St.
1935	Fresno St.
1936	Pacific
1937	Fresno St.
1938	Pacific
1939	Nevada

Year	Champion
1940	Pacific
1941	Pacific
1942	Pacific
1943-46	None
1947	UC Davis & Southern Ore.
1948	Cal St. Chico & Southern Ore.
1949	UC Davis
1950	San Fran. St.
1951	UC Davis
1952	Humboldt St.
1953	Cal St. Chico
1954	San Fran. St.
1955	Cal St. Chico
1956	UC Davis, Humboldt St. & San Fran. St.
1957	San Fran. St.
1958	San Fran. St.
1959	San Fran. St.
1960	Humboldt St.
1961	Humboldt St. & San Fran. St.
1962	San Fran. St.
1963	UC Davis, San Fran. St. & Humboldt St.
1964	Sacramento St.
1965	San Fran. St.
1966	Sacramento St.
1967	San Fran. St.
1968	Humboldt St.
1969	Cal St. East Bay
1970	Cal St. Chico
1971	UC Davis & Cal St. Chico
1972	UC Davis
1973	UC Davis & Cal St. Chico
1974	UC Davis
1975	UC Davis
1976	UC Davis
1977	UC Davis
1978	UC Davis
1979	UC Davis
1980	UC Davis
1981	UC Davis & Cal St. East Bay
1982	UC Davis
1983	UC Davis
1984	UC Davis
1985	UC Davis
1986	UC Davis
1987	UC Davis
1988	UC Davis
1989	UC Davis
1990	UC Davis
1991	Sonoma St.
1992	UC Davis
1993	Cal St. Chico
1994	Humboldt St. & Cal St. Chico
1995	Humboldt St.
1996	Cal St. Chico

Division III

ASSOCIATION OF MIDEAST COLLEGES

Members (4): Thomas More, Bluffton, Wilmington (Ohio) and Mt. St. Joseph

Year	Champion
1991	Thomas More (3-0)
1992	Thomas More (3-0)
1993	Thomas More (3-0)
1994	Bluffton & Thomas More (2-1)
1995	Thomas More (3-0)

FREEDOM FOOTBALL CONFERENCE

Year	Champion
1992	WPI (5-0)
1993	WPI (5-0)
1994	Merchant Marine (5-0) & Plymouth St. (6-0)
1995	Plymouth St. (7-0)
1996	Coast Guard (5-1) & Springfield (5-1)
1997	Coast Guard (6-0)
1998	Springfield (6-0)
1999	Western Conn. St. (6-0)
2000	Springfield (6-0)
2001	Plymouth St. (5-1) & Western Conn. St. (5-1)*
2002	Springfield (6-0)
2003	Springfield (6-0)

**Received conference's automatic bid to the Division III playoffs.*

INDEPENDENT COLLEGE ATHLETIC CONFERENCE

Year	Champion
1970-73	Champion unknown
1974	Ithaca
1975	Ithaca
1976	Alfred
1977	Champion unknown
1978	Ithaca
1979	Ithaca
1980	Ithaca
1981	Alfred
1982	St. Lawrence
1983	St. Lawrence
1984	Ithaca
1985	Ithaca
1986	Ithaca
1987	Ithaca

2006 Results

2006 Results for All Divisions

Listed alphabetically in this section are 2006 results for all football-playing NCAA member institutions. The division designation for each school is indicated to the right of the school location.

The coach listed is for the 2006 season for historical purposes. The record is for all years as a head coach at four-year colleges.

Key: ■–home game, *–neutral site.

ABILENE CHRISTIAN

Abilene, TX 79699 II

Coach: Chris Thomsen, TCU 1993
Record: 2 Years, 12-9-0

2006 RESULTS (8-3)

24 Central Okla. ■ 18
51 Southeastern Okla. 14
31 Southwestern Okla. ■ 0
21 Eastern N.M. 0
45 Northeastern St. 20
35 Angelo St. ■ 7
49 West Tex. A&M 33
36 Tarleton St. ■ 37
41 Tex. A&M-Kingsville 38
30 Midwestern St. ■ 46
27 West Tex. A&M 30

Nickname: Wildcats
Colors: Purple & White
Stadium: Shotwell
Capacity: 15,000; Year Built: 1959
AD: Jared Mosley
SID: Lance Fleming

ADAMS ST.

Alamosa, CO 81102....................................II

Coach: Wayne McGinn, Adams St. 1981
Record: 9 Years, 45-53-0

2006 RESULTS (6-5)

37 Dixie St. ■ 7
11 West Tex. A&M 31
26 Colorado Mines 7
34 N.M. Highlands ■ 17
10 Western N.M. 25
14 Fort Lewis ■ 17
7 Neb.-Kearney 31
21 Mesa St. ■ 13
28 Western St. * 10
55 Okla. Panhandle 7
28 Chadron St. ■ 44

Nickname: Grizzlies
Colors: Green & White
Stadium: Rex Field
Capacity: 2,800; Year Built: 1949
AD: Larry Mortensen
SID: Chris Day

ADRIAN

Adrian, MI 49221 III

Coach: Jim Lyall, Michigan 1974
Record: 17 Years, 76-83-1

2006 RESULTS (5-5)

0 Defiance ■ 10
17 Bluffton ■ 6
24 Westminster (Pa.) 27
35 Kalamazoo ■ 14
10 Olivet 13
42 Tri-State ■ 10
20 Hope 28
33 Wis. Lutheran 13
31 Albion ■ 26
28 Alma 45

Nickname: Bulldogs
Colors: Gold & Black
Stadium: Multisport Performance
Capacity: 2,500; Year Built: 2006
AD: Michael Duffy
SID: Nate Jorgensen

AIR FORCE

USAF Academy, CO 80840-5001............FBS

Coach: Fisher DeBerry, Wofford 1960
Record: 23 Years, 169-109-1

2006 RESULTS (4-8)

30 Tennessee 31
31 Wyoming 24
24 New Mexico ■ 7
17 Navy ■ 24
24 Colorado St. ■ 21
12 San Diego St. 19
14 Brigham Young ■ 33
43 Army 7
17 Notre Dame ■ 39
14 Utah ■ 17
39 UNLV 42
14 TCU 38

Nickname: Falcons
Colors: Blue & Silver
Stadium: Falcon
Capacity: 46,692; Year Built: 1962
AD: Hans J. Mueh
SID: Troy Garnhart

AKRON

Akron, OH 44325....................................FBS

Coach: J.D. Brookhart, Colorado St. 1988
Record: 3 Years, 18-18-0

2006 RESULTS (5-7)

16 Penn St. 34
20 North Carolina St. 17
21 Central Mich. 24
33 North Texas ■ 13
15 Kent St. 37
14 Cincinnati 20
24 Miami (Ohio) ■ 13
20 Toledo 35
35 Bowling Green ■ 28
31 Buffalo ■ 16
7 Ohio 17
0 Western Mich. ■ 17

Nickname: Zips
Colors: Blue & Gold
Stadium: Rubber Bowl
Capacity: 31,000; Year Built: 1940
AD: Mack Rhoades
SID: Shawn Nestor

ALABAMA

Tuscaloosa, AL 35487 ....FBS

Coach: Mike Shula, Alabama 1986
Record: 4 Years, 26-23-0

2006 RESULTS (6-7)

25 Hawaii ■ 17
13 Vanderbilt ■ 10
41 La.-Monroe ■ 7
23 Arkansas 24
13 Florida 28
30 Duke ■ 14
26 Mississippi ■ 23
13 Tennessee 16
38 Florida Int'l ■ 3
16 Mississippi St. ■ 24
14 LSU 28
15 Auburn ■ 22
31 Oklahoma St. * 34

Nickname: Crimson Tide
Colors: Crimson & White
Stadium: Bryant-Denny
Capacity: 92,138; Year Built: 1929
AD: Mal Moore
SID: Doug Walker
Note: Joe Kines (Jacksonville St. 1967) was the head coach for the Independence Bowl vs. Oklahoma St. and is officially charged with the loss.

UAB

Birmingham, AL 35294-0110 ....FBS

Coach: Watson Brown, Vanderbilt 1973
Record: 22 Years, 94-151-1

2006 RESULTS (3-9)

17 Oklahoma 24
17 East Caro. ■ 12
0 Georgia 34
10 Mississippi St. ■ 16
21 Troy ■ 3
35 Memphis ■ 29
33 Rice 34
24 Marshall ■ 31
9 SMU 22
17 UTEP ■ 36
20 Southern Miss. 25
22 UCF 31

Nickname: Blazers
Colors: Forest Green & Old Gold
Stadium: Legion Field
Capacity: 83,091; Year Built: 1927
AD: Brian Mackin
SID: Norm Reilly

ALABAMA A&M

Normal, AL 35762....................................FCS

Coach: Anthony Jones, Wichita St. 1984
Record: 8 Years, 59-31-0

2006 RESULTS (9-3)

27 Tennessee St. 20
30 Grambling ■ 27
20 Mississippi Val. 23
19 Texas Southern 14
28 Southern U. ■ 21
21 Stillman ■ 14
21 Ark.-Pine Bluff 23
21 Alabama St. * 13
34 Jackson St. 21
35 Alcorn St. ■ 26
7 Prairie View ■ 13
22 Ark.-Pine Bluff * 13

Nickname: Bulldogs
Colors: Maroon & White
Stadium: Louis Crews
Capacity: 21,000; Year Built: 1996
AD: Betty Kelly Austin
SID: Thomas Galbraith

ALABAMA ST.

Montgomery, AL 36101-0271..................FCS

Coach: Charles Coe, Kansas St. 1971
Record: 4 Years, 29-18-0

2006 RESULTS (5-6)

0 Troy 38
9 Texas Southern ■ 10
31 Ark.-Pine Bluff ■ 13
33 Alcorn St. 28
20 Southern U. 38
13 Jackson St. * 19
10 Prairie View 7
13 Alabama A&M * 21
35 Grambling 16
25 Mississippi Val. ■ 20
10 Tuskegee ■ 17

Nickname: Hornets
Colors: Black & Old Gold

Stadium: Cramton Bowl
Capacity: 21,600; Year Built: 1922
AD: Ron Dickerson Sr.
SID: A.A. Moore

ALBANY (N.Y.)

Albany, NY 12222 ....FCS

Coach: Bob Ford, Springfield 1959
Record: 38 Years, 217-158-1

2006 RESULTS (7-4)

17 Lehigh 16
7 Fordham ■ 9
17 Delaware 10
19 Central Conn. St. ■ 14
21 Cornell 23
21 Stony Brook 33
24 Sacred Heart 13
48 St. Francis (Pa.) ■ 0
34 Wagner ■ 0
16 Robert Morris 6
0 Monmouth ■ 19

Nickname: Great Danes
Colors: Purple & Gold
Stadium: University Field
Capacity: 5,000; Year Built: 1967
AD: Lee McElroy
SID: Brian DePasquale

ALBANY ST. (GA.)

Albany, GA 31705 II

Coach: Mike White, Albany St. (Ga.) 1990
Record: 7 Years, 51-25-0

2006 RESULTS (7-4)

0 N.C. Central 20
16 Valdosta St. ■ 20
21 Kentucky St. 7
14 Stillman ■ 7
10 Benedict 3
14 Miles ■ 0
24 Clark Atlanta ■ 13
10 Tuskegee 17
16 Morehouse 6
21 Fort Valley St. 3
28 Newberry 34

Nickname: Golden Rams
Colors: Blue & Gold
Stadium: Hugh Mills Memorial
Capacity: 11,000; Year Built: 1957
AD: Joshua Murfree Jr.
SID: Edythe Y. Bradley

ALBION

Albion, MI 49224......................................III

Coach: Craig Rundle, Albion 1974
Record: 21 Years, 122-80-1

2006 RESULTS (5-5)

31 Butler ■ 10
7 Wheaton (Ill.) 29
24 Thiel 20
21 Hope 24
38 Wis. Lutheran ■ 7
17 Olivet ■ 20
35 Alma 45
21 Kalamazoo ■ 13
26 Adrian 31
30 Tri-State ■ 28

Nickname: Britons
Colors: Purple & Gold
Stadium: Sprankle-Sprandel
Capacity: 4,244; Year Built: 1976
AD: Lisa Roschek
SID: Bobby Lee

ALBRIGHT

Reading, PA 19612-5234 III

Coach: E.J. Sandusky, Penn St. 1992
Record: 10 Years, 50-52-0

2006 RESULTS (2-8)

13 Ursinus ■ 32
21 Susquehanna ■ 24
14 King's (Pa.) 38
48 Juniata ■ 14
12 Widener 33
13 Delaware Valley ■ 21
35 FDU-Florham 39
6 Wilkes ■ 30
42 Lycoming 35
33 Lebanon Valley ■ 55

Nickname: Lions
Colors: Red & White
Stadium: Eugene L. Shirk
Capacity: 5,000; Year Built: 1925
AD: Stephen George
SID: Jeff Feiler

ALCORN ST.

Alcorn State, MS 39096-7500 ....FCS

Coach: Johnny Thomas, Alcorn St. 1978
Record: 9 Years, 46-53-0

2006 RESULTS (6-5)

6 La.-Monroe 24
14 Ark.-Pine Bluff 42
28 Alabama St. ■ 33
23 Morehouse * 6
17 Prairie View 14
45 Texas Southern ■ 23
26 Southern U. ■ 10
25 Mississippi Val. 28
26 Alabama A&M 35
32 Jackson St. * 31
21 Grambling 14

Nickname: Braves
Colors: Purple & Gold
Stadium: Jack Spinks
Capacity: 22,500; Year Built: 1992
AD: Wiley Jones
SID: LaToya Shields

ALFRED

Alfred, NY 14802 III

Coach: David Murray, Springfield 1981
Record: 17 Years, 96-77-1

2006 RESULTS (8-3)

14 Thiel ■ 0
17 St. Lawrence 14
34 Springfield 41
48 Norwich ■ 13
41 Hartwick 21
24 Utica 3
24 Husson 7
14 Hobart ■ 21
28 Ithaca ■ 17
13 St. John Fisher ■ 41
40 Rochester ■ 34

Nickname: Saxons
Colors: Purple & Gold
Stadium: Merrill Field
Capacity: 5,000; Year Built: 1926
AD: James M. Moretti
SID: Mark Whitehouse

ALLEGHENY

Meadville, PA 16335.................................III

Coach: Mark Matlak, Allegheny 1978
Record: 5 Years, 26-25-0

2006 RESULTS (6-4)

35 Westminster (Pa.) 10
10 Wash. & Jeff. 22
52 Hiram ■ 7
23 Denison 6
27 Wabash 41
49 Kenyon ■ 38
21 Wooster 27
30 Ohio Wesleyan ■ 13
21 Wittenberg 39
35 Oberlin ■ 14

Nickname: Gators
Colors: Blue & Gold
Stadium: Frank B. Fuhrer Field
Capacity: 3,500; Year Built: 1948
AD: Betsy Mitchell
SID: Bill Salyer

ALMA

Alma, MI 48801...III

Coach: Jim Cole, Alma 1974
Record: 16 Years, 93-61-0

2006 RESULTS (6-4)

31 Cornell College ■ 32
33 Wis.-Eau Claire ■ 30
24 Wittenberg 42
58 Tri-State 36
43 Hope ■ 49
42 Wis. Lutheran 0
45 Albion ■ 35
24 Olivet 28
37 Kalamazoo 35
45 Adrian ■ 28

Nickname: Scots
Colors: Maroon & Cream
Stadium: Bahlke Field
Capacity: 4,000; Year Built: 1986
AD: Ellen Curtis
SID: To be named

AMERICAN INT'L

Springfield, MA 01109-3189......................II

Coach: Art Wilkins, Bucknell 1972
Record: 13 Years, 79-55-0

2006 RESULTS (6-4)

34 St. Anselm 10
20 Bryant ■ 7
21 Bentley ■ 18
12 Southern Conn. St. 20
13 Merrimack 37
21 Assumption 14
7 Pace ■ 0
13 C.W. Post 22
28 Stonehill ■ 6
10 Bentley 14

Nickname: Yellow Jackets
Colors: Gold, White & Black
Stadium: John Homer Miller Field
Capacity: 5,000; Year Built: 1964
AD: Richard F. Bedard
SID: Greg Royce

AMHERST

Amherst, MA 01002-5000.........................III

Coach: E.J. Mills, Dayton 1988
Record: 10 Years, 57-23-0

2006 RESULTS (5-3)

31 Bates ■ 6
20 Bowdoin 7
3 Middlebury 7
38 Colby ■ 3
23 Wesleyan (Conn.) 0
24 Tufts ■ 6
0 Trinity (Conn.) 24
7 Williams ■ 37

Nickname: Lord Jeffs
Colors: Purple & White
Stadium: Pratt Field
Capacity: 8,000; Year Built: 1891
AD: Suzanne R. Coffey
SID: Tanner Lipsett

ANDERSON (IND.)

Anderson, IN 46012-3495..........................III

Coach: Jeff Judge, Iowa St. 1987
Record: 4 Years, 19-21-0

2006 RESULTS (2-8)

17 Taylor (Ind.) ■ 10
13 DePauw 25
24 Earlham 32
14 Mt. St. Joseph 36
24 Franklin ■ 38
13 Defiance 45
11 Bluffton ■ 26
14 Rose-Hulman 38
3 Hanover 27
19 Manchester ■ 16

Nickname: Ravens
Colors: Orange & Black
Stadium: Macholtz
Capacity: 4,300
AD: Michael Zapolski
SID: Justin Bates

ANGELO ST.

San Angelo, TX 76909 II

Coach: Dale Carr, Colorado St. 1987
Record: 2 Years, 12-10-0

2006 RESULTS (3-7)

9 Western St. ■ 8
6 East Central ■ 20
24 Central Okla. 30
17 Midwestern St. 41
17 Eastern N.M. ■ 7
7 Abilene Christian 35
9 Tex. A&M-Commerce ■ 17
10 West Tex. A&M ■ 26
10 Tarleton St. 41
38 Tex. A&M-Kingsville ■ 20

Nickname: Rams
Colors: Blue & Gold
Stadium: San Angelo
Capacity: 17,500; Year Built: 1962
AD: Kathleen Brasfield
SID: M.L. Stark Hinkle

APPALACHIAN ST.

Boone, NC 28608.................................FCS

Coach: Jerry Moore, Baylor 1961
Record: 25 Years, 181-116-2

2006 RESULTS (14-1)

10 North Carolina St. 23
21 James Madison ■ 10
41 Mars Hill ■ 0
41 Gardner-Webb 6
45 Elon ■ 21
56 Chattanooga 21
14 Wofford ■ 7
27 Ga. Southern 20
40 Furman ■ 7
42 Citadel ■ 13
31 Western Caro. 9
45 Coastal Caro. ■ 28
38 Montana St. ■ 17
49 Youngstown St. ■ 24
28 Massachusetts * 17

Nickname: Mountaineers
Colors: Black & Gold
Stadium: Kidd Brewer
Capacity: 16,650; Year Built: 1962
AD: Charles Cobb
SID: Mike Flynn

ARIZONA

Tucson, AZ 85721-0096..........................FBS

Coach: Mike Stoops, Iowa 1986
Record: 3 Years, 12-22-0

2006 RESULTS (6-6)

16 Brigham Young ■ 13
3 LSU 45
28 Stephen F. Austin ■ 10
3 Southern California ■ 20
10 Washington ■ 21
7 UCLA 27
20 Stanford 7
10 Oregon St. ■ 17
27 Washington St. 17
24 California ■ 20
37 Oregon 10
14 Arizona St. ■ 28

Nickname: Wildcats
Colors: Cardinal & Navy
Stadium: Arizona
Capacity: 57,400; Year Built: 1928
AD: Jim Livengood
SID: Tom Duddleston Jr.

ARIZONA ST.

Tempe, AZ 85287-2505 ....FBS

Coach: Dirk Koetter, Idaho St. 1981
Record: 9 Years, 66-44-0

2006 RESULTS (7-6)

35 Northern Ariz. ■ 14
52 Nevada ■ 21
21 Colorado 3
21 California 49
13 Oregon ■ 48
21 Southern California 28
38 Stanford ■ 3
26 Washington 23
10 Oregon St. 44
47 Washington St. ■ 14
12 UCLA ■ 24
28 Arizona 14
24 Hawaii 41

Nickname: Sun Devils
Colors: Maroon & Gold
Stadium: Sun Devil
Capacity: 73,656; Year Built: 1959
AD: Lisa Love
SID: Mark Brand

ARKANSAS

Fayetteville, AR 72701 ....FBS

Coach: Houston Nutt, Oklahoma St. 1981
Record: 14 Years, 102-67-0

2006 RESULTS (10-4)

14 Southern California ■ 50
20 Utah St. ■ 0
21 Vanderbilt 19
24 Alabama ■ 23
27 Auburn 10
63 Southeast Mo. St. ■ 7
38 Mississippi ■ 3
44 La.-Monroe * 10
26 South Carolina 20
31 Tennessee ■ 14
28 Mississippi St. 14
26 LSU * 31
28 Florida * 38
14 Wisconsin * 17

Nickname: Razorbacks
Colors: Cardinal & White
Stadium: Razorback
Capacity: 72,000; Year Built: 1938
AD: J. Frank Broyles
SID: Kevin Trainor

ARK.-MONTICELLO

Monticello, AR 71656.................................II

Coach: Gwaine Mathews, Delta St. 1988
Record: 2 Years, 2-20-0

2006 RESULTS (1-10)

15 Southern Ark. 18
3 Sam Houston St. 41
27 Ouachita Baptist ■ 6
21 Harding 29
3 Northwestern St. 20
17 Henderson St. ■ 33
7 North Ala. 47
14 West Ga. ■ 20
14 West Ala. ■ 37
3 Valdosta St. 51
0 Delta St. 53

Nickname: Boll Weevils
Colors: Kelly Green & White
Stadium: Convoy Leslie-Cotton Boll
Capacity: 4,500; Year Built: 1934
AD: Alvy Early
SID: Paul Smith

ARK.-PINE BLUFF

Pine Bluff, AR 71601 ....FCS

Coach: Mo Forte, Minnesota 1969
Record: 14 Years, 58-92-1

2006 RESULTS (8-4)

0 Mississippi Val. * 10
42 Alcorn St. ■ 14
13 Alabama St. 31
16 Southern Ill. ■ 48
35 Tuskegee * 19
33 Grambling * 28
23 Alabama A&M ■ 21
43 Jackson St. ■ 40
28 Prairie View 21
45 Southern U. 20
42 Texas Southern ■ 31
13 Alabama A&M * 22

Nickname: Golden Lions
Colors: Black & Gold
Stadium: Golden Lion
Capacity: 12,500; Year Built: 2000
AD: Craig Curry
SID: Carl Whimper

ARKANSAS ST.

State University, AR 72467.......................FBS

Coach: Steve Roberts, Ouachita Baptist 1987
Record: 13 Years, 75-67-1

2006 RESULTS (6-6)

14 Army ■ 6
7 Oklahoma St. * 35
9 SMU 55
31 Florida Int'l 6
10 La.-Monroe ■ 6
26 Memphis 23
29 North Texas ■ 10
0 Fla. Atlantic 29
0 Auburn 27
10 Middle Tenn. ■ 38
33 Troy 26
13 La.-Lafayette 28

Nickname: Indians
Colors: Scarlet & Black
Stadium: Indian
Capacity: 30,406; Year Built: 1974
AD: Dean Lee
SID: Jerry Scott

ARKANSAS TECH

Russellville, AR 72801-2222........................II

Coach: Steve Mullins, Ark.-Monticello 1980
Record: 10 Years, 66-41-0

2006 RESULTS (7-3)

33 Northeastern St. ■ 32
33 Texas Col. 21
28 West Ga. ■ 21
14 Valdosta St. 51
14 North Ala. 38
13 Delta St. ■..31
7 Henderson St. ■..6
55 Ouachita Baptist 35
36 Southern Ark. 29
26 Harding ■..3

Nickname: Wonder Boys
Colors: Green & Gold
Stadium: Buerkle Field
Capacity: 6,000
AD: Steve Mullins
SID: Ben Greenberg

ARMY

West Point, NY 10996-2101...................FBS

Coach: Bobby Ross, VMI 1959
Record: 18 Years, 103-101-2

2006 RESULTS (3-9)

6 Arkansas St. 14
17 Kent St. ■...14
24 Texas A&M * 28
27 Baylor 20
14 Rice ■...48
62 VMI ■..7
7 Connecticut..21
17 TCU ■..31
28 Tulane 42
7 Air Force ■...43
9 Notre Dame 41
14 Navy * 26

Nickname: Black Knights/Cadets
Colors: Black, Gold & Gray
Stadium: Michie
Capacity: 38,115; Year Built: 1924
AD: Kevin Anderson
SID: Bob Beretta

ASHLAND

Ashland, OH 44805...................................II

Coach: Lee Owens, Bluffton 1977
Record: 12 Years, 58-75-0

2006 RESULTS (4-6)

16 Saginaw Valley ■..27
24 Grand Valley St. 30
30 Hillsdale ■ 24
19 Northwood (Mich.)..33
24 Mercyhurst ■...21
24 Northern Mich. 17
7 Ferris St. ■ 38
0 Findlay ■ 7
17 Wayne St. (Mich.)...33
45 Gannon 14

Nickname: Eagles
Colors: Purple & Gold
Stadium: Community
Capacity: 5,700; Year Built: 1963
AD: Bill Goldring
SID: Al King

ASSUMPTION

Worcester, MA 01609 II

Coach: Cory Bailey, Fordham 1998
Record: 3 Years, 9-20-0

2006 RESULTS (4-6)

7 C.W. Post...28
16 Stonehill 3
26 St. Anselm ■...23
21 Bryant 45
14 Bentley ■...10
24 Southern Conn. St. 26
14 American Int'l ■..21
12 Merrimack 34
0 Nicholls St. 44
19 Pace ■...0

Nickname: Greyhounds
Colors: Blue, White, & Grey
Stadium: Multi-Sport
Capacity: 1,200; Year Built: 2005
AD: Ted Paulauskas
SID: Steve Morris

AUBURN

Auburn, AL 36849-5113.........................FBS

Coach: Tommy Tuberville, Southern Ark. 1976
Record: 12 Years, 96-49-0

2006 RESULTS (11-2)

40 Washington St. ■ 14
34 Mississippi St. 0
7 LSU ■...3
38 Buffalo ■...7
24 South Carolina 17
10 Arkansas ■..27
27 Florida ■..17
38 Tulane ■ 13
23 Mississippi...17
27 Arkansas St. ■ 0
15 Georgia ■..37
22 Alabama 15
17 Nebraska * 14

Nickname: Tigers
Colors: Burnt Orange & Navy Blue
Stadium: Jordan-Hare
Capacity: 87,451; Year Built: 1939
AD: Jay Jacobs
SID: Kirk Sampson

AUGSBURG

Minneapolis, MN 55454 III

Coach: Frank Haege, Wis.-Stout 1992
Record: 2 Years, 2-18-0

2006 RESULTS (1-9)

24 Northwestern (Minn.)......................................31
0 St. John's (Minn.) ■ 60
17 St. Olaf 68
28 Concordia-M'head ■ 34
14 Wartburg ■...38
21 St. Thomas (Minn.) 47
7 Carleton ■...37
27 Gust. Adolphus 41
21 Bethel (Minn.) 48
28 Hamline * 17

Nickname: Auggies
Colors: Maroon & Gray
Stadium: Edor Nelson Field
Capacity: 2,000; Year Built: 1984
AD: Paul Grauer
SID: Don Stoner

AUGUSTANA (ILL.)

Rock Island, IL 61201-2296........................III

Coach: Jim Barnes, Augustana (Ill.) 1981
Record: 12 Years, 92-31-0

2006 RESULTS (7-3)

53 MacMurray 7
7 Baldwin-Wallace ■ 17
7 Wis.-Platteville...24
24 Ill. Wesleyan ■ 7
28 Elmhurst..14
17 Wheaton (Ill.) ■ 14
28 Carthage ■ 14
0 North Central (Ill.) 27
31 North Park ■ 0
34 Millikin 23

Nickname: Vikings
Colors: Gold & Blue
Stadium: Ericson Field
Capacity: 3,200; Year Built: 1938
AD: Charles J. Gordon
SID: Dave Wrath

AUGUSTANA (S.D.)

Sioux Falls, SD 57197 II

Coach: Brad Salem, Augustana (S.D.) 1992
Record: 2 Years, 11-11-0

2006 RESULTS (5-6)

27 Northern St. ■ 17
35 Concordia-St. Paul..16
21 Minn. St. Mankato ■ 16
28 Neb.-Omaha 59
21 North Dakota ■ 24
35 Minn. Duluth 7
27 St. Cloud St. ■ 23
14 South Dakota 38
28 Central Wash. ■ 34
6 Western Wash. 10
13 Central Ark. 37

Nickname: Vikings
Colors: Navy & Yellow
Stadium: Howard Wood
Capacity: 10,000; Year Built: 1957
AD: Bill Gross
SID: Kevin Ludwig

AURORA

Aurora, IL 60506.......................................III

Coach: Rich Duncan, Bethany (W.V.) 1990
Record: 2 Years, 10-10-0

2006 RESULTS (5-5)

6 Rockford ■ 16
0 Coe 45
27 MacMurray 13
7 Greenville...14
13 Concordia (Wis.) ■ 42
15 Benedictine (Ill.) ■ 7
42 Concordia (Ill.) 7
29 Eureka ■ 14
25 Lakeland ■ 20
7 Valparaiso...20

Nickname: Spartans
Colors: Royal Blue & White
Stadium: Aurora Field
Capacity: 1,750
AD: Mark Walsh
SID: Brian Kipley

AUSTIN

Sherman, TX 75090-4440..........................III

Coach: Ronnie Gage, North Texas 1976
Record: 1 Year, 4-6-0

2006 RESULTS (4-6)

0 Texas Lutheran 45
0 McMurry ■..23
17 Kalamazoo ■ 14
7 Southwestern Assemblies of God 0
7 Trinity (Tex.) 34
7 Rhodes ■ 21
11 Millsaps ■ 26
44 Sewanee 20
14 DePauw 24
34 Centre ■ 28

Nickname: Kangaroos
Colors: Crimson & Gold

Stadium: Jerry Apple
Capacity: 2,500; Year Built: 2000
AD: Timothy P. Millerick
SID: Jeff Kelly

AUSTIN PEAY

Clarksville, TN 37044-4576 ....FCS

Coach: Carroll McCray, Gardner-Webb 1983
Record: 4 Years, 11-33-0

2006 RESULTS (3-8)

13 Southeast Mo. St. ■ 38
28 Cumberland (Tenn.)....................21
10 Samford 17
23 Dayton 28
10 Tenn.-Martin ■....................20
14 Mo.-Rolla....................21
26 Cumberland (Ky.) ■ 27
49 Charleston (W.V.) ■....................10
35 North Greenville ■....................44
23 Morehead St. 21
14 Western Ky. 24

Nickname: Governors
Colors: Red & White
Stadium: Governors
Capacity: 10,000; Year Built: 1946
AD: Dave Loos
SID: Brad Kirtley

AVERETT

Danville, KY 24541 III

Coach: Mike Dunlevy, Otterbein 1987
Record: 5 Years, 27-21-0

2006 RESULTS (7-3)

7 Mount Union ■....................64
17 Wesley 38
54 Guilford ■....................34
21 Ferrum ■....................14
28 Methodist....................25
24 N.C. Wesleyan 20
62 Greensboro ■....................21
18 Shenandoah....................0
31 Chris. Newport....................41
58 Maryville (Tenn.) ■....................44

Nickname: Cougars
Colors: Navy & Gold
Stadium: Cougar Den
Capacity: 3,000; Year Built: 2000
AD: Charles S. Harris
SID: Sam Ferguson

BALDWIN-WALLACE

Berea, OH 44017 III

Coach: John Snell, Baldwin-Wallace 1987
Record: 5 Years, 35-17-0

2006 RESULTS (7-3)

17 Augustana (Ill.)....................7
31 Marietta 37
14 Wilmington (Ohio) 0
24 John Carroll ■ 8
36 Heidelberg ■....................10
30 Muskingum....................3
0 Mount Union ■....................14
13 Ohio Northern ■ 7
42 Otterbein....................31
7 Capital ■ 19

Nickname: Yellow Jackets
Colors: Brown & Gold
Stadium: George Finnie
Capacity: 8,100; Year Built: 1971
AD: Stephen Bankson
SID: Kevin Ruple

BALL ST.

Muncie, IN 47306....................FBS

Coach: Brady Hoke, Ball St. 1982
Record: 4 Years, 15-31-0

2006 RESULTS (5-7)

38 Eastern Mich. ■ 20
23 Indiana ■....................24
28 Purdue....................38
24 North Dakota St. ■ 29
28 Northern Ill. ■....................40
55 Buffalo 25
7 Central Mich....................18
27 Western Mich. ■ 41
20 Miami (Ohio)....................17
26 Michigan....................34
20 Toledo....................17
30 Kent St. ■....................6

Nickname: Cardinals
Colors: Cardinal & White
Stadium: Ball State
Capacity: 22,500; Year Built: 1967
AD: Thomas J. Collins
SID: Joe Hernandez

BATES

Lewiston, ME 04240 III

Coach: Mark Harriman, Springfield 1980
Record: 9 Years, 17-55-0

2006 RESULTS (1-7)

6 Amherst....................31
12 Tufts 21
7 Williams ■ 27
14 Wesleyan (Conn.) ■....................17
7 Middlebury....................31
7 Colby ■ 10
14 Bowdoin....................23
20 Hamilton ■ 6

Nickname: Bobcats
Colors: Garnet
Stadium: Garcelon Field
Capacity: 3,000; Year Built: 1900
AD: Dana Mulholland
SID: Andy Walter

BAYLOR

Waco, TX 76798-7096 ....FBS

Coach: Guy Morriss, TCU 1973
Record: 6 Years, 24-45-0

2006 RESULTS (4-8)

7 TCU ■....................17
47 Northwestern St. ■....................10
15 Washington St. * 17
20 Army ■....................27
17 Kansas St. ■....................3
34 Colorado....................31
31 Texas 63
36 Kansas ■....................35
21 Texas A&M ■....................31
21 Texas Tech 55
24 Oklahoma St. 66
10 Oklahoma ■....................36

Nickname: Bears
Colors: Green & Gold
Stadium: Floyd Casey
Capacity: 50,000; Year Built: 1950
AD: Ian McCaw
SID: Nick Joos

BECKER

Leicester, MA 01524....................III

Coach: Mel Mills, Louisville 1992
Record: 1 Year, 0-9-0

2006 RESULTS (0-9)

10 Utica ■ 20
14 Maine Maritime 33
16 WPI 52
21 Mount Ida ■....................33
6 Rensselaer 56
22 Hartwick....................40
16 Maritime (N.Y.)....................29
3 Husson ■ 28
0 Bryant 42

Nickname: Hawks
Colors: Royal Blue, White & Black
Stadium: Alumni Field at WPI
Capacity: 2,800; Year Built: 1916
AD: Frank Millerick/Craig Barnett
SID: Bettiann Michalik

BELOIT

Beloit, WI 53511-5595....................III

Coach: Chris Brann, West Va. Wesleyan 1991
Record: 6 Years, 10-50-0

2006 RESULTS (1-9)

10 Macalester ■....................0
0 Carroll (Wis.)....................29
0 Monmouth (Ill.) ■ 31
22 Knox ■....................32
0 Lake Forest 23
7 Ripon 41
20 Illinois Col. ■....................30
7 Lawrence....................13
7 St. Norbert ■....................37
22 Grinnell....................39

Nickname: Buccaneers
Colors: Navy Blue & Gold
Stadium: Strong
Capacity: 3,500; Year Built: 1934
AD: Kim Chandler
SID: Keith E. Domke

BEMIDJI ST.

Bemidji, MN 56601-2699 II

Coach: Jeff Tesch, Minn. St. Moorhead 1978
Record: 11 Years, 71-47-0

2006 RESULTS (9-3)

7 Minn. Duluth ■ 23
30 Minot St. 9
21 Minn. St. Moorhead....................9
56 Minn.-Crookston ■ 7
25 Northern St.....................22
21 Mary ■....................27
40 Wayne St. (Neb.) 37
28 Winona St. ■ 7
23 Southwest Minn. St. ■....................15
27 Concordia-St. Paul *....................7
44 Upper Iowa * 20
27 Pittsburg St. *....................35

Nickname: Beavers
Colors: Kelly Green & White
Stadium: Chet Anderson
Capacity: 5,000; Year Built: 1940
AD: Rick Goeb
SID: Andy Bartlett

BENEDICT

Columbia, SC 29204 II

Coach: John Hendrick, Pittsburgh 1981
Record: 4 Years, 18-25-0

2006 RESULTS (3-7)

24 Morehouse ■....................25
21 Savannah St. 7
27 Clark Atlanta 18
14 Tuskegee 41
0 Lenoir-Rhyne ■....................17
3 Albany St. (Ga.) ■ 10

13 Kentucky St. ■ 5
10 Fort Valley St. 16
7 Stillman ■ 12
12 Lane 17

Nickname: Tigers
Colors: Purple & Gold
Stadium: Charles W. Johnson
Capacity: 11,026; Year Built: 2006
AD: Willie Washington
SID: Derrick A. Johnson

BENEDICTINE (ILL.)

Lisle, IL 60532-0900 III

Coach: Jon Cooper, North Park 1972
Record: 2 Years, 7-13-0

2006 RESULTS (4-6)

0 Elmhurst 34
22 North Park ■ 7
0 North Central (Ill.) ■ 38
34 Concordia (Ill.) ■ 12
0 Lakeland 14
13 Greenville ■ 20
7 Aurora 15
35 Eureka ■ 7
12 MacMurray 8
0 Concordia (Wis.) 28

Nickname: Eagles
Colors: Red & White
Stadium: Sports Complex at Benedictine
Capacity: 3,000; Year Built: 2004
AD: Dave Swanson
SID: Tony Hamilton

BENTLEY

Waltham, MA 02154-4705 II

Coach: Peter Yetten, Boston U. 1971
Record: 19 Years, 139-51-1

2006 RESULTS (6-5)

9 East Stroudsburg 7
13 Southern Conn. St. ■ 19
18 American Int'l 21
24 Merrimack ■ 21
10 Assumption 14
21 Pace ■ 6
7 C.W. Post 14
13 Stonehill ■ 7
14 St. Anselm 6
15 Bryant ■ 36
14 American Int'l ■ 10

Nickname: Falcons
Colors: Blue & Gold
Stadium: Bentley College
Capacity: 4,800; Year Built: 1990
AD: Robert DeFelice
SID: Dick Lipe

BETHANY (W.V.)

Bethany, WV 26032-0417 III

Coach: Tim Weaver, Davidson 1990
Record: 1 Year, 4-6-0

2006 RESULTS (4-6)

20 Muskingum 45
42 Hiram ■ 7
34 Ohio Wesleyan 28
7 Thiel ■ 49
34 Grove City ■ 28
15 Waynesburg 41
13 Westminster (Pa.) 49
21 Thomas More 17
6 Carnegie Mellon 44
0 Wash. & Jeff. ■ 54

Nickname: Bison
Colors: Kelly Green & White
Stadium: Bethany Field
Capacity: 1,000; Year Built: 1938
AD: Kosmas Mouratidis
SID: Brian Rose

BETHEL (MINN.)

St. Paul, MN 55112-6999 III

Coach: Steve Johnson, Bethel (Minn.) 1980
Record: 18 Years, 120-62-1

2006 RESULTS (9-2)

13 Buena Vista ■ 0
23 Simpson 17
21 Concordia-M'head ■ 7
14 Carleton 17
17 St. Thomas (Minn.) ■ 7
40 Gust. Adolphus 0
35 St. Olaf ■ 29
35 Hamline 0
48 Augsburg ■ 21
28 St. John's (Minn.) 13
21 Wis.-La Crosse 28

Nickname: Royals
Colors: Blue & Gold
Stadium: Royal
Capacity: 3,500; Year Built: 1996
AD: Robert Bjorklund
SID: Dan Berglund

BETHUNE-COOKMAN

Daytona Beach, FL 32114-3099 ..... FCS

Coach: Alvin Wyatt Sr., Bethune-Cookman 1970
Record: 10 Years, 72-39-0

2006 RESULTS (5-6)

29 Southern U. * 30
55 Savannah St. ■ 6
45 South Carolina St. 21
22 Norfolk St. ■ 21
14 Morgan St. 28
31 Delaware St. ■ 33
10 Winston-Salem ■ 6
70 N.C. A&T ■ 7
17 Hampton 34
0 Howard ■ 28
21 Florida A&M * 35

Nickname: Wildcats
Colors: Maroon & Gold
Stadium: Municipal Stadium/Larry Kelly Field
Capacity: 10,000; Year Built: 1988
AD: Lynn W. Thompson
SID: Bryan J. Harvey

BIRMINGHAM-SO.
(Reclassifying to FCS)

Birmingham, AL 35254 ..... FCS

Coach: Joey Jones, Alabama 1984
(First year as head coach)

Resuming program in 2007,
previously dropped in 1940

Nickname: Panthers
Colors: Black, Gold & White
Stadium: Regions Park
Capacity: 10,800; Year Built: 1988
AD: Joe Dean Jr.
SID: Fred Sington

BLACKBURN

Carlinville, IL 62626 III

Coach: Roger VanDeZande, Oregon St. 1982
Record: 3 Years, 4-19-0

2006 RESULTS (3-7)

3 Concordia (Ill.) 13
13 Greenville 44
7 Martin Luther ■ 34
51 Principia 0
14 Crown (Minn.) 6
0 Westminster (Mo.) ■ 26
0 Rockford ■ 61
7 Maranatha Baptist 34
21 Martin Luther * 17
6 MacMurray ■ 34

Nickname: Battlin' Beavers
Colors: Scarlet & Black
Stadium: The Beaver Dome
Capacity: 1,500; Year Built: 1989
AD: Curtis Campbell
SID: Tom Emery

BLOOMSBURG

Bloomsburg, PA 17815 II

Coach: Danny Hale, West Chester 1968
Record: 19 Years, 158-54-1

2006 RESULTS (12-2)

3 James Madison 14
24 California (Pa.) ■ 19
28 Edinboro 10
24 Clarion ■ 10
35 Shippensburg 14
30 West Chester ■ 27
41 Kutztown ■ 14
31 Mansfield 7
28 Millersville 16
45 East Stroudsburg ■ 37
35 Cheyney 6
21 West Chester ■ 20
24 Shepherd 21
3 Northwest Mo. St. 33

Nickname: Huskies
Colors: Maroon & Gold
Stadium: Robert B. Redman
Capacity: 5,000; Year Built: 1974
AD: Mary Gardner
SID: Tom McGuire

BLUFFTON

Bluffton, OH 45817-2104 III

Coach: Greg Brooks, Ohio 1977
Record: 4 Years, 13-27-0

2006 RESULTS (3-7)

6 Centre 21
6 Adrian 17
17 Kalamazoo ■ 14
7 Franklin 31
14 Manchester ■ 9
12 Rose-Hulman ■ 21
26 Anderson (Ind.) 11
6 Hanover ■ 7
0 Mt. St. Joseph 17
6 Defiance ■ 20

Nickname: Beavers
Colors: Royal Purple & White
Stadium: Salzman
Capacity: 3,000; Year Built: 1993
AD: Phill Talavinia
SID: Bill Hanefeld Jr.

BOISE ST.

Boise, ID 83725-1020 ..... FBS

Coach: Chris Petersen, UC Davis 1988
Record: 1 Year, 13-0-0

2006 RESULTS (13-0)

45 Sacramento St. ■ 0
42 Oregon St. ■ 14
17 Wyoming 10
41 Hawaii ■ 34
36 Utah 3
55 Louisiana Tech ■ 14
40 New Mexico St. 28
42 Idaho 26
45 Fresno St. ■ 21
23 San Jose St. 20

49 Utah St. ■ 10
38 Nevada 7
43 Oklahoma * 42

Nickname: Broncos
Colors: Blue & Orange
Stadium: Bronco
Capacity: 30,000; Year Built: 1970
AD: Gene Bleymaier
SID: Max Corbet

BOSTON COLLEGE

Chestnut Hill, MA 02467-3861 ....FBS

Coach: Tom O'Brien, Navy 1971
Record: 10 Years, 75-45-0

2006 RESULTS (10-3)

31 Central Mich..24
34 Clemson ■ 33
30 Brigham Young ■ 23
15 North Carolina St..17
22 Maine ■..0
22 Virginia Tech ■..3
24 Florida St..19
41 Buffalo ■..0
14 Wake Forest..21
28 Duke ■..7
38 Maryland ■..16
14 Miami (Fla.)..17
25 Navy * 24

Nickname: Eagles
Colors: Maroon & Gold
Stadium: Alumni
Capacity: 44,500; Year Built: 1957
AD: Gene DeFilippo
SID: Chris Cameron
Note: Frank Spaziani (Penn St. 1969) was the head coach for the Meineke Car Care Bowl vs. Navy and is officially credited with the win.

BOWDOIN

Brunswick, ME 04011 III

Coach: Dave Caputi, Middlebury 1981
Record: 7 Years, 12-44-0

2006 RESULTS (2-6)

0 Williams..27
7 Amherst ■ 20
6 Tufts ■..16
0 Hamilton 12
0 Trinity (Conn.) ■ 34
0 Wesleyan (Conn.)..18
23 Bates ■ 14
13 Colby..10

Nickname: Polar Bears
Colors: White
Stadium: Whittier Field
Capacity: 6,000; Year Built: 1896
AD: Jeffrey H. Ward
SID: Jim Caton

BOWIE ST.

Bowie, MD 20715-9465 II

Coach: Mike Lynn, Morgan St. 1990
Record: 3 Years, 18-14-0

2006 RESULTS (5-5)

38 West Virginia St. ■..0
14 Johnson C. Smith 13
20 Morgan St..28
3 Livingstone *..7
13 N.C. Central ■..35
17 Shaw 14
12 Elizabeth City St. ■..16
24 St. Paul's 0
7 Virginia Union ■..9
16 Virginia St. ■..7

Nickname: Bulldogs
Colors: Black & Gold
Stadium: Bulldog
Capacity: 2,964; Year Built: 1992
AD: Derek Carter
SID: Gregory C. Goings

BOWLING GREEN

Bowling Green, OH 43403......................FBS

Coach: Gregg Brandon, Northern Colo. 1978
Record: 4 Years, 30-19-0

2006 RESULTS (4-8)

14 Wisconsin * 35
48 Buffalo ■..40
33 Florida Int'l 28
3 Kent St. ■..38
21 Ohio..9
7 Ohio St. 35
24 Eastern Mich. ■ 21
14 Central Mich..31
14 Temple..28
28 Akron..35
7 Miami (Ohio) ■ 9
21 Toledo..31

Nickname: Falcons
Colors: Orange & Brown
Stadium: Doyt Perry
Capacity: 23,724; Year Built: 1966
AD: Greg Christopher
SID: J.D. Campbell

BRIDGEWATER (VA.)

Bridgewater, VA 22812-1599 III

Coach: Michael Clark, Cincinnati 1980
Record: 12 Years, 83-50-1

2006 RESULTS (8-2)

41 McDaniel..0
30 Shenandoah ■..0
30 Ferrum..27
58 LaGrange ■ 21
31 Hampden-Sydney ■ 13
28 Guilford..33
17 Emory & Henry ■..21
27 Wash. & Lee ■..8
35 Randolph-Macon..24
20 Catholic 13

Nickname: Eagles
Colors: Cardinal & Vegas Gold
Stadium: Jopson Field
Capacity: 3,500; Year Built: 1971
AD: Curtis L. Kendall
SID: Steve Cox

BRIDGEWATER ST.

Bridgewater, MA 02325-9998 III

Coach: Chuck Denune, Heidelberg 1998
Record: 2 Years, 17-3-0

2006 RESULTS (8-2)

7 Mass.-Dartmouth ■..15
28 Salve Regina 14
28 Maine Maritime..21
15 Fitchburg St. ■..7
46 Framingham St..17
17 Coast Guard ■..21
28 Westfield St. ■..13
41 Worcester St..20
34 Mass. Maritime ■ 19
41 Coast Guard..22

Nickname: Bears
Colors: Crimson & White
Stadium: Ed Swenson Field
Capacity: 2,000; Year Built: 1974
AD: John C. Harper
SID: Michael Holbrook

BYU

Provo, UT 84602....................................FBS

Coach: Bronco Mendenhall, Oregon St. 1988
Record: 2 Years, 17-8-0

2006 RESULTS (11-2)

13 Arizona..16
49 Tulsa ■..24
23 Boston College..30
38 Utah St. ■ 0
31 TCU 17
47 San Diego St. ■..17
52 UNLV ■ 7
33 Air Force 14
24 Colorado St. 3
55 Wyoming ■..7
42 New Mexico ■ 17
33 Utah..31
38 Oregon * 8

Nickname: Cougars
Colors: Dark Blue & White
Stadium: LaVell Edwards
Capacity: 64,045; Year Built: 1964
AD: Tom Holmoe
SID: Jeff Reynolds

BROCKPORT ST.

Brockport, NY 14420-2989 III

Coach: Rocco Salomone, Brockport St. 1988
Record: 12 Years, 76-46-1

2006 RESULTS (4-6)

21 Salisbury 3
10 Cortland St. 17
22 Frostburg St. 0
7 Ithaca ■ 26
20 St. John Fisher ■ 27
3 Springfield..27
17 Wesley..48
16 Morrisville St. ■ 0
18 Apprentice ■ 31
48 Buffalo St. ■ 0

Nickname: Golden Eagles
Colors: Green & Gold
Stadium: Special Olympics
Capacity: 10,000; Year Built: 1979
AD: Linda J. Case
SID: Kelly Vergin

BROWN

Providence, RI 02912 ....FCS

Coach: Phil Estes, New Hampshire 1981
Record: 9 Years, 54-35-0

2006 RESULTS (3-7)

34 Georgetown ■..21
21 Harvard ■..38
21 Rhode Island..28
30 Holy Cross..35
3 Princeton 17
28 Cornell ■..7
30 Penn 27
24 Yale ■..27
13 Dartmouth..19
21 Columbia ■..22

Nickname: Bears
Colors: Brown, Red & White
Stadium: Brown
Capacity: 20,000; Year Built: 1925
AD: Michael Goldberger
SID: Christopher Humm

BRYANT

Smithfield, RI 02917-1284 II

Coach: Marty Fine, Western N.M. 1984
Record: 5 Years, 29-22-0

2006 RESULTS (8-3)

49 Southern Conn. St. ■..20
7 American Int'l 20
34 Merrimack ■ 7
45 Assumption ■ 21
31 Pace 17
21 C.W. Post ■..24
35 Stonehill 14
41 St. Anselm ■..0
36 Bentley 15
42 Becker ■ 0
29 West Chester ■ 31

Nickname: Bulldogs
Colors: Black, Gold & White
Stadium: Bulldog
Capacity: 4,400; Year Built: 1999
AD: Bill Smith
SID: Jason Sullivan

BUCKNELL

Lewisburg, PA 17837 ....FCS

Coach: Tim Landis, Randolph-Macon 1986
Record: 14 Years, 73-77-1

2006 RESULTS (6-5)

31	Duquesne ■	28
0	Lafayette ■	31
20	Cornell ■	5
21	Richmond	48
48	Marist	19
24	Penn ■	34
17	Georgetown	7
7	Lehigh	38
13	Fordham ■	3
10	Holy Cross	27
31	Colgate ■	28

Nickname: Bison
Colors: Orange & Blue
Stadium: Christy Mathewson
Capacity: 13,100; Year Built: 1924
AD: John P. Hardt
SID: Jon Terry

BUENA VISTA

Storm Lake, IA 50588-9990 III

Coach: Jay Anderson, Drake 1995
Record: 1 Year, 4-6-0

2006 RESULTS (4-6)

0	Bethel (Minn.)	13
3	Central (Iowa) ■	24
17	Coe	41
16	Cornell College	0
15	Simpson ■	14
30	Luther ■	27
20	Loras	10
13	Wartburg ■	20
25	Dubuque	27
17	Waldorf ■	20

Nickname: Beavers
Colors: Navy Blue & Gold
Stadium: J. Leslie Rollins
Capacity: 3,500; Year Built: 1980
AD: Jan Travis
SID: Nick Huber

BUFFALO

Buffalo, NY 14260 ....FBS

Coach: Turner Gill, North Texas 1990
Record: 1 Year, 2-10-0

2006 RESULTS (2-10)

9	Temple ■	3
40	Bowling Green	48
13	Northern Ill.	31
7	Auburn	38
25	Ball St. ■	55
31	Miami (Ohio) ■	38
7	Ohio	42
0	Boston College	41
41	Kent St. ■	14
16	Akron	31
3	Wisconsin	35
28	Central Mich. ■	55

Nickname: Bulls
Colors: Royal Blue & White
Stadium: UB Stadium
Capacity: 29,013; Year Built: 1993
AD: Warde Manuel
SID: Paul Vecchio

BUFFALO ST.

Buffalo, NY 14222-1095 III

Coach: Paul Shaffner, Ithaca 1982
Record: 7 Years, 28-43-0

2006 RESULTS (3-7)

34	Morrisville St. ■	6
7	Ithaca	45
20	Cortland St. ■	38
30	Kean	50
14	Montclair St. ■	22
7	Rowan *	35
20	Wm. Paterson	27
24	Western Conn. St. ■	21
34	TCNJ	33
0	Brockport St.	48

Nickname: Bengals
Colors: Orange & Black
Stadium: Coyer Field
Capacity: 3,000; Year Built: 1964
AD: Jerry S. Boyes
SID: Jeff Ventura

BUTLER

Indianapolis, IN 46208-3485 ....FCS

Coach: Jeff Voris, DePauw 1989
Record: 6 Years, 18-42-0

2006 RESULTS (3-8)

10	Albion	31
30	Hanover ■	20
14	Robert Morris ■	35
7	Jacksonville ■	31
23	Dayton ■	20
3	San Diego	56
0	Drake ■	29
32	Valparaiso ■	10
20	Mo.-Rolla	35
7	Morehead St. ■	14
10	Davidson	50

Nickname: Bulldogs
Colors: Blue & White
Stadium: Butler Bowl
Capacity: 2,500; Year Built: 1927
AD: Barry Collier
SID: Jim McGrath

C.W. POST

Brookville, NY 11548 II

Coach: Bryan Collins, St. John's (N.Y.) 1987
Record: 9 Years, 80-20-0

2006 RESULTS (7-3)

28	Assumption ■	7
28	Pace ■	7
0	Shepherd	24
24	Stonehill	20
34	St. Anselm ■	0
24	Bryant	21
14	Bentley ■	7
28	Southern Conn. St.	34
22	American Int'l ■	13
10	Merrimack	13

Nickname: Pioneers
Colors: Green & Gold
Stadium: Hickox Field
Capacity: 5,000; Year Built: 1966
AD: Bryan Collins
SID: Tom Emberley

CALIFORNIA

Berkeley, CA 94720 ....FBS

Coach: Jeff Tedford, Fresno St. 1983
Record: 5 Years, 43-20-0

2006 RESULTS (10-3)

18	Tennessee	35
42	Minnesota ■	17
42	Portland St. ■	16
49	Arizona St. ■	21
41	Oregon St.	13
45	Oregon ■	24
21	Washington St.	3
31	Washington ■	24
38	UCLA ■	24
20	Arizona	24
9	Southern California	23
26	Stanford ■	17
45	Texas A&M *	10

Nickname: Golden Bears
Colors: Blue & Gold
Stadium: Memorial
Capacity: 67,537; Year Built: 1923
AD: Sandy Barbour
SID: Kevin Klintworth

UC DAVIS

Davis, CA 95616-8674 ....FCS

Coach: Bob Biggs, UC Davis 1973
Record: 14 Years, 114-48-1

2006 RESULTS (6-5)

38	Northern Colo.	7
13	TCU	46
45	Montana St.	0
24	Youngstown St.	38
17	Cal Poly	23
33	Central Ark. ■	13
27	Southern Utah ■	7
21	South Dakota St.	22
24	North Dakota St. ■	28
30	Sacramento St. ■	16
37	San Diego ■	27

Nickname: Aggies
Colors: Yale Blue & Gold
Stadium: Aggie Stadium
Capacity: 10,000; Year Built: 2007
AD: Greg Warzecka
SID: Mike Robles

CALIFORNIA (PA.)

California, PA 15419 II

Coach: John Luckhardt, Purdue 1968
Record: 22 Years, 169-58-2

2006 RESULTS (8-3)

26	Fairmont St. ■	9
19	Bloomsburg	24
43	Cheyney ■	8
34	East Stroudsburg	41
51	Lock Haven ■	7
10	Edinboro	0
24	Slippery Rock ■	14
41	Millersville ■	0
35	Shippensburg	20
41	Clarion	14
17	Indiana (Pa.) ■	21

Nickname: Vulcans
Colors: Red & Black
Stadium: Hepner-Bailey Field at Adamson Stadium
Capacity: 5,000; Year Built: 1970
AD: Thomas G. Pucci
SID: Tom Byrnes

CAL LUTHERAN

Thousand Oaks, CA 91360-2787...............III

Coach: Scott Squires, Pacific Lutheran 1988
Record: 11 Years, 55-44-0

2006 RESULTS (6-3)

17	Pacific Lutheran	14
26	Willamette ■	16
55	La Verne ■	12
35	Whittier	10
27	Claremont-M-S	30
34	Chapman ■	14
27	Occidental ■	28
27	Pomona-Pitzer ■	24
20	Redlands	24

Nickname: Kingsmen
Colors: Violet & Gold

Stadium: Mt. Clef
Capacity: 2,000; Year Built: 1962
AD: Daniel E. Kuntz
SID: Scott Flanders

CAL POLY

San Luis Obispo, CA 93407....................FCS

Coach: Rich Ellerson, Hawaii 1977
Record: 7 Years, 45-34-0

2006 RESULTS (7-4)

44 Fort Lewis ■ 0
17 Weber St. 0
17 Sacramento St. 10
7 San Jose St. 17
18 Southern Utah ■ 14
23 UC Davis ■ 17
28 South Dakota St. ■ 29
16 San Diego St. 14
9 Montana 10
14 North Dakota St. 51
55 Savannah St. ■ 0

Nickname: Mustangs
Colors: Green & Gold
Stadium: Alex G. Spanos
Capacity: 11,750; Year Built: 1935
AD: Alison Cone
SID: Eric Burdick

CAPITAL

Columbus, OH 43209 III

Coach: Jim Collins, Wittenberg 1987
Record: 13 Years, 62-74-0

2006 RESULTS (11-2)

57 Wittenberg ■ 7
43 Wilmington (Ohio) ■ 0
65 Heidelberg 7
52 Marietta ■ 10
24 John Carroll 21
17 Ohio Northern 10
26 Otterbein ■ 0
12 Mount Union 38
52 Muskingum ■ 14
19 Baldwin-Wallace 7
32 Wittenberg ■ 14
41 North Central (Ill.) ■ 13
14 Mount Union 17

Nickname: Crusaders
Colors: Purple & White
Stadium: Bernlohr
Capacity: 3,000; Year Built: 2001
AD: Roger Welsh
SID: Leonard Reich

CARLETON

Northfield, MN 55057................................III

Coach: Kurt Ramler, St. John's (Minn.) 1997
Record: 1 Year, 4-6-0

2006 RESULTS (4-6)

50 Minn.-Morris 14
52 Macalester ■ 0
17 Bethel (Minn.) ■ 14
19 St. John's (Minn.) 29
10 St. Thomas (Minn.) 14
11 Hamline ■ 16
37 Augsburg 7
20 Concordia-M'head ■ 25
15 St. Olaf 48
10 Gust. Adolphus ■ 14

Nickname: Knights
Colors: Maize & Blue
Stadium: Laird
Capacity: 7,500; Year Built: 1926
AD: Leon Lunder
SID: Eric Sieger

CARNEGIE MELLON

Pittsburgh, PA 15213-3890 III

Coach: Rich Lackner, Carnegie Mellon 1979
Record: 21 Years, 148-60-2

2006 RESULTS (11-1)

27 Hiram 6
28 Grove City 0
33 Westminster (Pa.) ■ 6
34 Frank. & Marsh. ■ 14
50 Colorado Col. ■ 26
20 Case Reserve 10
27 Chicago ■ 0
10 Washington-St. Louis 7
44 Bethany (W.V.) ■ 6
14 Thiel 7
21 Millsaps ■ 0
0 Wesley 37

Nickname: Tartans
Colors: Cardinal, White & Grey
Stadium: Gesling
Capacity: 3,500; Year Built: 1990
AD: Susan Bassett
SID: Mark Fisher

CARROLL (WIS.)

Waukesha, WI 53186-5593 III

Coach: Henny Hiemenz, Ithaca 1999
Record: 1 Year, 4-6-0

2006 RESULTS (4-6)

6 Carthage ■ 10
29 Beloit ■ 0
49 Grinnell 14
7 Monmouth (Ill.) 38
14 Ripon ■ 21
16 Illinois Col. 21
0 St. Norbert 41
24 Knox ■ 20
37 Lawrence ■ 6
14 Lake Forest 21

Nickname: Pioneers
Colors: Orange & White
Stadium: Van Male Field
Capacity: 4,200; Year Built: 1976
AD: Kris Jacobsen
SID: Rick Mobley

CARSON-NEWMAN

Jefferson City, TN 37760 II

Coach: Ken Sparks, Carson-Newman 1968
Record: 27 Years, 259-62-2

2006 RESULTS (8-3)

44 Webber Int'l ■ 0
41 Shaw ■ 7
24 St. Augustine's 14
27 Virginia St. 21
18 Newberry 32
10 Mars Hill ■ 7
22 Catawba 24
21 Lenoir-Rhyne ■ 3
7 Presbyterian 28
52 Wingate ■ 14
23 Tusculum 3

Nickname: Eagles
Colors: Orange & Blue
Stadium: Burke-Tarr
Capacity: 5,200; Year Built: 2005
AD: David W. Barger
SID: Michael Baur

CARTHAGE

Kenosha, WI 53140.................................III

Coach: Tim Rucks, Carthage 1983
Record: 17 Years, 71-88-4

2006 RESULTS (6-4)

10 Carroll (Wis.) 6
21 Lakeland 14
31 Whittier ■ 2
13 Elmhurst ■ 20
31 Ill. Wesleyan 28
52 North Park ■ 7
14 Augustana (Ill.) 28
16 Millikin ■ 7
3 Wheaton (Ill.) ■ 52
24 North Central (Ill.) 34

Nickname: Red Men
Colors: Red, White & Black
Stadium: Art Keller Field
Capacity: 1,681; Year Built: 1965
AD: Robert R. Bonn
SID: Steve Marovich

CASE RESERVE

Cleveland, OH 44106 III

Coach: Greg Debeljak, John Carroll 1988
Record: 3 Years, 13-17-0

2006 RESULTS (5-5)

29 Oberlin ■ 23
27 Denison 14
43 Kenyon ■ 13
7 Wooster 21
7 Ursinus ■ 16
10 Carnegie Mellon ■ 20
6 Washington-St. Louis 13
10 Chicago ■ 9
33 Grove City 40
27 Wash. & Lee ■ 9

Nickname: Spartans
Colors: Blue, Gray & White
Stadium: E.L. Finnigan Field
Capacity: 3,000; Year Built: 1968
AD: David L. Diles
SID: Creg Jantz

CATAWBA

Salisbury, NC 28144-2488 II

Coach: Chip Hester, Guilford 1992
Record: 5 Years, 36-18-0

2006 RESULTS (6-4)

21 Winston-Salem ■ 7
35 Livingstone 6
31 Virginia St. ■ 13
7 Mars Hill 25
14 Newberry 21
24 Carson-Newman ■ 22
20 Tusculum ■ 21
8 Wingate 24
21 Presbyterian ■ 14
32 Lenoir-Rhyne 24

Nickname: Catawba Indians
Colors: Blue & White
Stadium: Shuford
Capacity: 4,500; Year Built: 1926
AD: Dennis Davidson
SID: Jim Lewis

CATHOLIC

Washington, DC 20064.............................III

Coach: David Dunn, San Diego 1989
Record: 2 Years, 3-15-0

2006 RESULTS (3-7)

17 Shenandoah 6
34 Ohio Wesleyan ■ 33
13 McDaniel ■ 14
14 Randolph-Macon 7
0 Wash. & Lee ■ 28
14 La Salle ■ 27
21 Hampden-Sydney 41
27 Emory & Henry 31

18 Guilford 41
13 Bridgewater (Va.) ■ 20

Nickname: Cardinals
Colors: Cardinal Red & Black
Stadium: Cardinal
Capacity: 3,500; Year Built: 1985
AD: Mike Allen
SID: Barbara Jonas

CENTRAL (IOWA)

Pella, IA 50219 III

Coach: Jeff Martin, Central (Iowa) 1990
Record: 3 Years, 25-7-0

2006 RESULTS (10-1)

17 St. Thomas (Minn.) 7
24 Hope ■ 13
24 Buena Vista 3
13 Wartburg ■ 7
19 Luther 13
40 Dubuque ■ 14
34 Cornell College 7
44 Loras ■ 7
31 Coe 28
23 Simpson ■ 0
13 St. John's (Minn.) ■ 21

Nickname: Dutch
Colors: Red & White
Stadium: A.N. Kuyper
Capacity: 5,000; Year Built: 1977
AD: Al Dorenkamp
SID: Larry Happel

CENTRAL ARK.

(Reclassifying to FCS)

Conway, AR 72035-0001 II

Coach: Clint Conque, Nicholls St. 1983
Record: 7 Years, 52-29-0

2006 RESULTS (8-3)

39 Henderson St. * 6
3 Illinois St. 18
16 Missouri St. ■ 14
37 Stephen F. Austin 35
24 South Dakota ■ 0
7 South Dakota St. 20
13 UC Davis 33
38 Sam Houston St. 30
55 Southern Ark. ■ 21
37 Augustana (S.D.) ■ 13
34 Ga. Southern 31

Nickname: Bears
Colors: Purple & Gray
Stadium: Estes
Capacity: 8,500; Year Built: 1939
AD: Bradley Teague
SID: Steve East

CENTRAL CONN. ST.

New Britain, CT 06050-4010 ....FCS

Coach: Jeff McInerney, Slippery Rock 1982
Record: 1 Year, 8-3-0

2006 RESULTS (8-3)

34 Marist ■ 6
17 Ga. Southern 13
29 Southern Conn. St. 26
14 Albany (N.Y.) 19
73 St. Peter's 13
62 St. Francis (Pa.) ■ 21
17 Robert Morris 23
27 Wagner ■ 6
13 Monmouth 19
42 Sacred Heart 14
35 Stony Brook ■ 32

Nickname: Blue Devils
Colors: Blue & White
Stadium: Arute Field
Capacity: 3,000; Year Built: 2001
AD: Charles Jones Jr.
SID: Thomas Pincince

UCF

Orlando, FL 32816-3555 ....FBS

Coach: George O'Leary, New Hampshire 1969
Record: 11 Years, 64-57-0

2006 RESULTS (4-8)

35 Villanova ■ 16
0 Florida 42
17 South Fla. ■ 24
14 Southern Miss. ■ 19
23 Marshall 22
7 Pittsburgh ■ 52
29 Rice ■ 40
31 Houston 51
10 East Caro. ■ 23
26 Memphis 24
9 Tulane 10
31 UAB ■ 22

Nickname: Golden Knights
Colors: Black & Gold
Stadium: Florida Citrus
Capacity: 65,438; Year Built: 1936
AD: Keith R. Tribble
SID: Jason Baum

CENTRAL MICH.

Mount Pleasant, MI 48859-0001 ....FBS

Coach: Brian Kelly, Assumption 1983
Record: 16 Years, 138-51-2

2006 RESULTS (10-4)

24 Boston College ■ 31
17 Michigan 41
24 Akron ■ 21
24 Eastern Mich. 17
36 Kentucky 45
42 Toledo 20
18 Ball St. ■ 7
31 Bowling Green ■ 14
42 Temple 26
31 Western Mich. ■ 7
10 Northern Ill. 31
55 Buffalo 28
31 Ohio * 10
31 Middle Tenn. * 14

Nickname: Chippewas
Colors: Maroon & Gold
Stadium: Kelly-Shorts
Capacity: 30,199; Year Built: 1972
AD: David W. Heeke Jr.
SID: Don Helinski

Note: Jeff Quinn (Elmhurst 1984) was the head coach for the Motor City Bowl vs. Middle Tenn. and is officially credited with the win.

CENTRAL MO.

Warrensburg, MO 64093 II

Coach: Willie Fritz, Pittsburg St. 1983
Record: 10 Years, 75-36-0

2006 RESULTS (5-6)

78 Lincoln (Mo.) 0
52 Dakota St. ■ 0
10 Washburn ■ 14
21 Truman 24
37 Fort Hays St. 14
20 Mo. Western St. ■ 30
49 Southwest Baptist ■ 24
26 Mo. Southern St. 31
14 Northwest Mo. St. ■ 31
48 Emporia St. ■ 21
30 Pittsburg St. 35

Nickname: Mules
Colors: Cardinal & Black
Stadium: Audrey J. Walton
Capacity: 10,000; Year Built: 1995
AD: Jerry M. Hughes
SID: Rob McCutcheon

CENTRAL OKLA.

Edmond, OK 73034 II

Coach: Chuck Langston, Oklahoma 1995
Record: 4 Years, 25-18-0

2006 RESULTS (5-6)

29 Mo. Western St. ■ 32
18 Abilene Christian 24
30 Angelo St. ■ 24
19 Eastern N.M. 16
10 Tex. A&M-Commerce ■ 3
37 East Central ■ 0
31 Northwestern Okla. ■ 26
7 Southeastern Okla. ■ 9
22 Southwestern Okla. 25
7 West Tex. A&M ■ 38
23 Northeastern St. 26

Nickname: Bronchos
Colors: Bronze & Blue
Stadium: Wantland
Capacity: 10,000; Year Built: 1965
AD: Bill Farley
SID: Mike Kirk

CENTRAL WASH.

Ellensburg, WA 98926 II

Coach: John Zamberlin, Pacific Lutheran 1979
Record: 10 Years, 63-41-0

2006 RESULTS (6-5)

14 North Dakota ■ 28
20 Humboldt St. 0
21 Eastern Wash. 14
25 Minn. Duluth 31
24 St. Cloud St. ■ 14
7 South Dakota 10
28 Western Ore. ■ 21
42 Western Wash. * 28
34 Augustana (S.D.) 28
17 Minn. St. Mankato ■ 33
14 Neb.-Omaha 48

Nickname: Wildcats
Colors: Crimson & Black
Stadium: Tomlinson
Capacity: 4,000; Year Built: 1941
AD: Jack Bishop
SID: Jonathan Gordon

CENTRE

Danville, KY 40422-1394 III

Coach: Andy Frye, Muskingum 1981
Record: 9 Years, 52-38-0

2006 RESULTS (5-5)

21 Bluffton ■ 6
17 Maryville (Tenn.) 14
10 Rhodes 20
15 Wash. & Lee ■ 24
14 Sewanee ■ 0
12 Millsaps 38
10 Trinity (Tex.) ■ 17
28 DePauw ■ 24
41 LaGrange 10
28 Austin 34

Nickname: Colonels
Colors: Gold & White
Stadium: Farris
Capacity: 2,500; Year Built: 1925
AD: Brian E. Chafin
SID: Mike Pritchard

CHADRON ST.

Chadron, NE 69337-2690 II

Coach: Bill O'Boyle, Western Ill. 1987
Record: 2 Years, 16-7-0

2006 RESULTS (12-1)

21 Mary....................................3
35 Montana St..............................24
38 Wayne St. (Neb.).........................14
57 Colorado Mines ■.........................0
40 N.M. Highlands..........................20
35 Western N.M. ■...........................7
40 Fort Lewis..............................27
31 Neb.-Kearney ■...........................12
27 Mesa St.................................19
47 Western St. ■............................0
44 Adams St................................28
43 West Tex. A&M ■.........................17
21 Northwest Mo. St........................28

Nickname: Eagles
Colors: Cardinal & White
Stadium: Elliott Field
Capacity: 4,000; Year Built: 1930
AD: Bradley Roy Smith
SID: Con Marshall

CHAPMAN

Orange, CA 92866....................................III

Coach: Bob Owens, La Verne 1971
Record: 8 Years, 24-48-0

2006 RESULTS (4-5)

24 Menlo...................................27
42 Pacific Lutheran ■.......................25
13 Redlands.................................7
21 Claremont-M-S...........................28
0 Whittier.................................17
14 Cal Lutheran............................34
21 Pomona-Pitzer ■.........................14
21 Occidental ■............................41
35 La Verne ■..............................12

Nickname: Panthers
Colors: Cardinal & Gray
Stadium: Ernie Chapman
Capacity: 3,000
AD: David Currey
SID: Doug Aiken

CHARLESTON (W.V.)

Charleston, WV 25304 II

Coach: Tony DeMeo, Iona 1971
Record: 18 Years, 90-88-2

2006 RESULTS (5-6)

24 Findlay ■...............................25
30 Seton Hill ■............................25
7 Elizabeth City St........................12
0 Glenville St.............................35
19 West Va. Wesleyan.......................17
42 West Virginia St. ■.....................29
28 Concord.................................18
0 Shepherd ■...............................17
13 Fairmont St. ■..........................27
10 Austin Peay.............................49
21 West Liberty St.........................13

Nickname: Golden Eagles
Colors: Maroon & Gold
Stadium: University of Charleston
Capacity: 18,600; Year Built: 1964
AD: Tom Nozica
SID: Jim Workman

CHARLESTON SO.

Charleston, SC 29423-8087....................FCS

Coach: Jay Mills, Western Wash. 1984
Record: 6 Years, 24-40-0

2006 RESULTS (9-2)

21 Presbyterian............................13
38 Citadel.................................35
20 Wingate ■...............................17
20 North Greenville ■......................10
38 Savannah St.............................13
47 Edward Waters ■..........................0
27 VMI ■...................................22
24 Georgetown ■............................10
28 Gardner-Webb ■..........................14
20 Liberty.................................34
17 Coastal Caro............................31

Nickname: Buccaneers
Colors: Navy & Old Gold
Stadium: CSU Stadium
Capacity: 3,000; Year Built: 1970
AD: Hank Small
SID: Blake Freeland

CHATTANOOGA

Chattanooga, TN 37403-2598 ....FCS

Coach: Rodney Allison, Texas Tech 1980
Record: 4 Years, 14-31-0

2006 RESULTS (3-8)

31 Tennessee Tech...........................7
14 Memphis.................................33
21 Western Ky..............................28
27 Ga. Southern ■..........................26
21 Citadel.................................24
21 Appalachian St. ■.......................56
17 Western Caro............................14
22 Furman..................................28
17 Elon ■..................................20
10 Jacksonville St. ■......................13
0 Wofford..................................55

Nickname: Mocs
Colors: Navy Blue & Old Gold
Stadium: Finley
Capacity: 20,668; Year Built: 1997
AD: Rick Hart
SID: Jeff Romero

CHEYNEY

Cheyney, PA 19319-0200...........................II

Coach: Tim Newsom, West Virginia 1992
Record: 2 Years, 3-19-0

2006 RESULTS (1-10)

20 Clark Atlanta...........................23
6 Indiana (Pa.) ■..........................33
8 California (Pa.).........................43
6 Edinboro ■...............................28
12 West Chester............................53
18 Clarion.................................21
26 Mansfield ■..............................6
7 East Stroudsburg.........................48
6 Kutztown ■...............................28
12 Millersville............................48
6 Bloomsburg ■.............................35

Nickname: Wolves
Colors: Blue & White
Stadium: O'Shield-Stevenson
Capacity: 3,500
AD: Patric Simon
SID: Lenn Margolis

CHICAGO

Chicago, IL 60637......................................III

Coach: Dick Maloney, Mass.-Boston 1974
Record: 13 Years, 65-54-0

2006 RESULTS (4-5)

55 Concordia (Ill.) ■.......................0
10 Elmhurst................................23
34 Macalester...............................7
6 DePauw ■.................................31
7 Washington-St. Louis ■...................26
0 Carnegie Mellon..........................27
9 Case Reserve.............................10
28 Northwestern (Minn.) ■..................20
44 Eureka..................................12

Nickname: Maroons
Colors: Maroon & White
Stadium: Stagg Field
Capacity: 1,500; Year Built: 1969
AD: Thomas Weingartner
SID: Dave Hilbert

CHOWAN

Murfreesboro, NC 27855 II

Coach: Lorick Atkinson, Gardner-Webb 1989
Record: 2 Years, 2-18-0

2006 RESULTS (0-10)

0 Western Caro.............................42
20 Union (Ky.) ■...........................23
7 Methodist................................31
7 Tiffin ■.................................25
25 Southern Va.............................28
5 Brevard ■................................10
6 North Greenville.........................52
0 Webber Int'l ■...........................28
3 Wesley...................................37
0 Newport News.............................37

Nickname: Hawks
Colors: Columbia Blue & White
Stadium: James G. Garrison
Capacity: 3,500
AD: Dennis E. Helsel
SID: Meredith Long

CHRIS. NEWPORT

Newport News, VA 23606-2998 III

Coach: Matt Kelchner, Susquehanna 1982
Record: 6 Years, 42-22-0

2006 RESULTS (8-3)

8 Rowan....................................32
15 Mary Hardin-Baylor ■....................10
23 Salisbury...............................17
17 Shenandoah...............................3
28 Greensboro ■.............................0
48 Maryville (Tenn.).......................31
21 Methodist ■..............................0
34 N.C. Wesleyan...........................46
41 Averett ■...............................31
55 Ferrum ■.................................7
23 Wash. & Jeff. ■.........................27

Nickname: Captains
Colors: Blue & Silver
Stadium: POMOCO
Capacity: 3,100; Year Built: 2001
AD: C.J. Woollum
SID: Francis Tommasino

CINCINNATI

Cincinnati, OH 45221-0021 ....FBS

Coach: Mark Dantonio, South Carolina 1979
Record: 3 Years, 18-17-0

2006 RESULTS (8-5)

31 Eastern Ky. ■............................0
15 Pittsburgh ■............................33
7 Ohio St..................................37
13 Virginia Tech...........................29
24 Miami (Ohio) ■..........................10
20 Akron ■.................................14
17 Louisville..............................23
23 South Fla. ■.............................6
17 Syracuse ■...............................3
24 West Virginia...........................42
30 Rutgers ■...............................11
26 Connecticut.............................23
27 Western Mich. *.........................24

Nickname: Bearcats
Colors: Red & Black
Stadium: Nippert
Capacity: 35,000; Year Built: 1916
AD: Michael J. Thomas
SID: Tom Hathaway

Note: Brian Kelly (see Central Mich.) was named head coach before the International Bowl vs. Western Mich. and is officially credited with the win.

CITADEL

Charleston, SC 29409-6150....................FCS

Coach: Kevin Higgins, West Chester 1977
Record: 9 Years, 65-38-1

2006 RESULTS (5-6)

3 Texas A&M 35
35 Charleston So. ■....38
6 Pittsburgh....51
24 Chattanooga ■....21
20 Wofford....28
17 Furman....23
30 Western Caro. ■....27
24 Ga. Southern ■....21
13 Appalachian St.....42
48 VMI ■....21
44 Elon....7

Nickname: Bulldogs
Colors: Blue & White
Stadium: Johnson Hagood
Capacity: 21,000; Year Built: 1948
AD: Les Robinson
SID: Kevin Rhodes

CLAREMONT-M-S

Claremont, CA 91711-6400 III

Coach: Rick Candaele, Albertson 1969
Record: 15 Years, 62-73-0

2006 RESULTS (4-5)

34 Kenyon ■....10
0 Puget Sound....21
13 Occidental....42
28 Chapman ■....21
30 Cal Lutheran ■....27
9 Redlands....21
28 Whittier ■....25
14 La Verne ■....21
14 Pomona-Pitzer....31

Nickname: Stags
Colors: Maroon, Gold & White
Stadium: Zinda Field
Capacity: 3,000; Year Built: 1955
AD: Michael L. Sutton
SID: Kelly Beck

CLARION

Clarion, PA 16214......................................II

Coach: Jay Foster, Plymouth St. 1985
Record: 1 Year, 1-10-0

2006 RESULTS (1-10)

13 Tiffin....21
10 Kutztown....27
21 West Chester ■....49
10 Bloomsburg....24
7 Slippery Rock ■....31
21 Cheyney ■....18
7 Indiana (Pa.)....33
0 Edinboro ■....13
7 Lock Haven....14
14 California (Pa.) ■....41
10 Shippensburg....35

Nickname: Golden Eagles
Colors: Blue & Gold
Stadium: Memorial Field
Capacity: 5,000; Year Built: 1965
AD: David Katis
SID: Rich Herman

CLARK ATLANTA

Atlanta, GA 30314 II

Coach: Ted Bahhur, Kent St. 1992
Record: 2 Years, 8-13-0

2006 RESULTS (5-5)

8 Fort Valley St. ■....9
23 Cheyney ■....20
18 Benedict ■....27
15 Lane....23
9 Kentucky St.....22
43 George Mason (Club) ■....0
13 Albany St. (Ga.)....24
32 Morehouse ■....25
10 Tuskegee ■....6
6 Miles....0

Nickname: Panthers
Colors: Red, Black & Grey
Stadium: Panther
Capacity: 6,000; Year Built: 1995
AD: Brenda Edmond
SID: Lawanda Pearson

CLEMSON

Clemson, SC 29634 ....FBS

Coach: Tommy Bowden, West Virginia 1977
Record: 10 Years, 78-42-0

2006 RESULTS (8-5)

54 Fla. Atlantic ■....6
33 Boston College....34
27 Florida St.....20
52 North Carolina ■....7
51 Louisiana Tech ■....0
27 Wake Forest....17
63 Temple *....9
31 Georgia Tech ■....7
7 Virginia Tech....24
12 Maryland ■....13
20 North Carolina St. ■....14
28 South Carolina ■....31
20 Kentucky *....28

Nickname: Tigers
Colors: Burnt Orange & Northwest Purple
Stadium: Memorial
Capacity: 81,473; Year Built: 1942
AD: Terry Don Phillips
SID: Tim Bourret

COAST GUARD

New London, CT 06320-4195 III

Coach: Bill George, Ithaca 1980
Record: 8 Years, 22-54-0

2006 RESULTS (8-3)

7 Merchant Marine....21
35 Plymouth St. ■....7
35 Westfield St.....21
41 Mass. Maritime ■....0
31 Fitchburg St.....30
21 Bridgewater St.....17
17 Worcester St. ■....10
3 Maine Maritime....0
42 Framingham St. ■....21
28 Curry ■....34
22 Bridgewater St. ■....41

Nickname: Bears
Colors: Blue & White
Stadium: Cadet Memorial Field
Capacity: 4,500; Year Built: 1932
AD: Raymond Cieplik
SID: Jason Southard

COASTAL CARO.

Conway, SC 29528-6054.......................FCS

Coach: David Bennett, Presbyterian 1984
Record: 11 Years, 97-28-0

2006 RESULTS (9-3)

20 Elon ■....23
41 Wofford....38
21 Ga. Southern....38
33 South Carolina St. ■....14
31 Winston-Salem....12
29 Furman ■....27
31 VMI....27
28 Liberty ■....26
66 Savannah St. ■....6
52 Gardner-Webb....24
31 Charleston So. ■....17
28 Appalachian St.....45

Nickname: Chanticleers
Colors: Coastal Green, Bronze & Black
Stadium: Brooks
Capacity: 7,312; Year Built: 2003
AD: Warren Koegel
SID: John A. Martin

COE

Cedar Rapids, IA 52402-5092....................III

Coach: Erik Raeburn, Mount Union 1994
Record: 7 Years, 50-23-0

2006 RESULTS (7-3)

34 Ill. Wesleyan....21
45 Aurora ■....0
16 Luther....10
41 Buena Vista ■....17
30 Loras ■....32
37 Dubuque....23
12 Simpson....3
7 Wartburg ■....10
28 Central (Iowa) ■....31
31 Cornell College....14

Nickname: Kohawks
Colors: Crimson & Gold
Stadium: Clark Field
Capacity: 2,200; Year Built: 1989
AD: John Chandler
SID: Ryan Workman

COLBY

Waterville, ME 04901-8849 III

Coach: Edward Mestieri, Springfield 1976
Record: 3 Years, 15-9-0

2006 RESULTS (2-6)

10 Trinity (Conn.)....27
0 Middlebury ■....23
24 Wesleyan (Conn.) ■....21
3 Amherst....38
0 Hamilton ■....6
10 Bates....7
0 Tufts....7
10 Bowdoin ■....13

Nickname: Mules
Colors: Blue & Gray
Stadium: Seaverns Field
Capacity: 2,000; Year Built: 1950
AD: Marcella K. Zalot
SID: Bill Sodoma

COLGATE

Hamilton, NY 13346-1304......................FCS

Coach: Dick Biddle, Duke 1971
Record: 11 Years, 88-42-0

2006 RESULTS (4-7)

7 Massachusetts....28
28 Dartmouth ■....7
12 Monmouth ■....17
31 Georgetown ■....14
26 Princeton ■....27
14 Cornell....38
46 Fordham....3

10 Lafayette ■ 27
15 Lehigh 23
29 Holy Cross ■ 28
28 Bucknell 31

Nickname: Raiders
Colors: Maroon, Gray & White
Stadium: Andy Kerr
Capacity: 10,221; Year Built: 1937
AD: David T. Roach
SID: Bob Cornell

COLORADO

Boulder, CO 80309 ....FBS

Coach: Dan Hawkins, UC Davis 1984
Record: 11 Years, 94-33-1

2006 RESULTS (2-10)

10 Montana St. ■ 19
10 Colorado St. * 14
3 Arizona St. ■ 21
13 Georgia 14
13 Missouri 28
31 Baylor ■ 34
30 Texas Tech ■ 6
3 Oklahoma 24
15 Kansas 20
21 Kansas St. ■ 34
33 Iowa St. ■ 16
14 Nebraska 37

Nickname: Buffaloes
Colors: Silver, Black & Gold
Stadium: Folsom
Capacity: 53,750; Year Built: 1924
AD: Mike R. Bohn
SID: David Plati

COLORADO COL.

Colorado Springs, CO 80903 III

Coach: Bob Bodor, Denison 1988
Record: 4 Years, 11-27-0

2006 RESULTS (5-5)

34 Pomona-Pitzer 27
34 Occidental 48
46 Lewis & Clark ■ 3
26 Carnegie Mellon 50
56 Macalester ■ 35
14 Huntingdon ■ 21
10 Rhodes 28
25 Puget Sound ■ 28
34 Rockford ■ 23
28 Southwestern Assemblies of God ■ 6

Nickname: Tigers
Colors: Black & Gold
Stadium: Washburn Field
Capacity: 2,000; Year Built: 1898
AD: Julie Soriero
SID: Dave Moross

COLORADO MINES

Golden, CO 80401 II

Coach: Bob Stitt, Doane 1986
Record: 7 Years, 44-34-0

2006 RESULTS (4-7)

21 Washburn 41
31 Fort Hays St. ■ 24
7 Adams St. ■ 26
0 Chadron St. 57
69 Okla. Panhandle ■ 0
16 N.M. Highlands ■ 19
10 Western N.M. 6
34 Fort Lewis ■ 41
20 Neb.-Kearney 14
22 Mesa St. ■ 28
13 Western St. 21

Nickname: Orediggers
Colors: Silver & Blue
Stadium: Brooks Field
Capacity: 4,000; Year Built: 1922
AD: Thomas E. Spicer
SID: Gregory Murphy

COLORADO ST.

Fort Collins, CO 80523-6011 ....FBS

Coach: Sonny Lubick, Western Mont. 1960
Record: 18 Years, 126-84-0

2006 RESULTS (4-8)

30 Weber St. ■ 6
14 Colorado * 10
10 Nevada 28
35 Fresno St. 23
28 UNLV ■ 7
21 Air Force 24
0 Wyoming 24
19 New Mexico ■ 20
3 Brigham Young ■ 24
22 Utah 35
14 TCU ■ 45
6 San Diego St. 17

Nickname: Rams
Colors: Green & Gold
Stadium: Hughes
Capacity: 34,400; Year Built: 1968
AD: Paul Kowalczyk
SID: Gary Ozzello

COLUMBIA

New York, NY 10027 ....FCS

Coach: Norries Wilson, Minnesota 1989
Record: 1 Year, 5-5-0

2006 RESULTS (5-5)

37 Fordham ■ 7
23 Georgetown ■ 21
6 Princeton ■ 19
24 Iona ■ 0
0 Penn 16
7 Dartmouth ■ 20
3 Yale 21
7 Harvard 24
21 Cornell ■ 14
22 Brown 21

Nickname: Lions
Colors: Columbia Blue & White
Stadium: Lawrence A. Wien
Capacity: 17,000; Year Built: 1984
AD: M. Dianne Murphy
SID: Todd Kennedy

CONCORD

Athens, WV 24712 II

Coach: Greg Quick, Baldwin-Wallace 1978
Record: 14 Years, 47-92-0

2006 RESULTS (3-8)

13 Wingate 35
12 Tiffin ■ 32
13 Fairmont St. ■ 10
27 West Liberty St. ■ 23
10 West Va. Wesleyan 7
18 Charleston (W.V.) ■ 28
13 West Virginia St. 22
0 Shepherd 42
0 Glenville St. ■ 19
0 Delaware St. 62
25 North Greenville 28

Nickname: Mountain Lions
Colors: Maroon & Gray
Stadium: Callaghan
Capacity: 5,000
AD: Greg Quick
SID: Ernie Horn

CONCORDIA (ILL.)

River Forest, IL 60305-1499 III

Coach: Lonnie Pries, Concordia (Ill.) 1993
Record: 1 Year, 2-8-0

2006 RESULTS (2-8)

13 Blackburn ■ 3
0 Chicago 55
0 Rose-Hulman 56
12 Benedictine (Ill.) 34
41 Eureka ■ 12
41 MacMurray 46
20 Concordia (Wis.) 31
7 Aurora ■ 42
0 Lakeland ■ 34
7 Greenville 45

Nickname: Cougars
Colors: Maroon & Gold
Stadium: Concordia
Capacity: 1,500; Year Built: 2000
AD: Pete Gnan
SID: Jim Egan

CONCORDIA (WIS.)

Mequon, WI 53097-2402 III

Coach: Jeff Gabrielsen, Ripon 1980
Record: 17 Years, 111-54-0

2006 RESULTS (10-1)

30 Simpson ■ 16
30 North Central (Ill.) 24
39 Wis. Lutheran 0
56 Eureka 0
47 MacMurray ■ 7
42 Aurora 13
31 Concordia (Ill.) ■ 20
30 Lakeland 18
14 Greenville ■ 7
28 Benedictine (Ill.) ■ 0
6 North Central (Ill.) ■ (at Wis. Lutheran) 35

Nickname: Falcons
Colors: Royal Blue & White
Stadium: Century
Capacity: 2,500
AD: Robert M. Barnhill
SID: Rick Riehl

CONCORDIA-M'HEAD

Moorhead, MN 56562-3597 III

Coach: Terry Horan, Concordia-M'head 1989
Record: 6 Years, 44-20-0

2006 RESULTS (4-6)

7 Minn. St. Moorhead 28
7 Bethel (Minn.) 21
12 St. John's (Minn.) ■ 14
34 Augsburg 28
21 Hamline 3
14 St. Olaf ■ 49
15 St. Thomas (Minn.) ■ 21
25 Carleton 20
0 Gust. Adolphus ■ 7
41 Minn.-Morris * 21

Nickname: Cobbers
Colors: Maroon & Gold
Stadium: Jake Christiansen
Capacity: 7,500; Year Built: 1966
AD: Larry Papenfuss
SID: Jim Cella

CONCORDIA-ST. PAUL

St. Paul, MN 55104 II

Coach: Mark Mauer, Nebraska 1982
Record: 3 Years, 21-13-0

2006 RESULTS (5-6)

7 North Dakota St. 66
16 Augustana (S.D.) ■ 35

28 Northern St. ■ 20
22 Mary 19
17 Winona St. ■ 24
21 Southwest Minn. St. ■ 23
18 Minn. St. Moorhead 20
41 Upper Iowa 14
27 Wayne St. (Neb.) 24
7 Bemidji St. * 27
49 Minn.-Crookston * 0

Nickname: Golden Bears
Colors: Navy Blue & Vegas Gold
Stadium: James S. Griffin
Capacity: 6,000; Year Built: 1970
AD: Thomas Rubbelke
SID: Jen Foley

CONNECTICUT

Storrs, CT 06269 .....FBS

Coach: Randy Edsall, Syracuse 1980
Record: 8 Years, 41-51-0

2006 RESULTS (4-8)

52 Rhode Island ■ 7
13 Wake Forest ■ 24
14 Indiana 7
17 Navy ■ 41
16 South Fla. 38
21 Army ■ 7
11 West Virginia ■ 37
13 Rutgers 24
46 Pittsburgh ■ 45
14 Syracuse 20
23 Cincinnati ■ 26
17 Louisville 48

Nickname: Huskies, UConn
Colors: National Flag Blue & White
Stadium: Rentschler Field
Capacity: 40,000; Year Built: 2003
AD: Jeffrey A. Hathaway
SID: Leigh Torbin

CORNELL

Ithaca, NY 14853 .....FCS

Coach: Jim Knowles, Cornell 1987
Record: 3 Years, 15-15-0

2006 RESULTS (5-5)

5 Bucknell 20
9 Yale ■ 21
23 Albany (N.Y.) ■ 21
23 Harvard 33
38 Colgate ■ 14
7 Brown 28
14 Princeton ■ 7
28 Dartmouth ■ 25
14 Columbia 21
28 Penn ■ 27

Nickname: Big Red
Colors: Carnelian Red & White
Stadium: Schoellkopf
Capacity: 25,597; Year Built: 1915
AD: J. Andrew Noel
SID: Jeremy Hartigan

CORNELL COLLEGE

Mt. Vernon, IA 52314-1098 III

Coach: Matt Dillon, Cornell College 1981
Record: 1 Year, 2-8-0

2006 RESULTS (2-8)

30 Northwestern (Minn.) ■ 14
32 Alma 31
14 Dubuque 32
7 Simpson ■ 34
0 Buena Vista ■ 16
14 Loras 21
7 Central (Iowa) ■ 34
6 Luther 37
7 Wartburg 41
14 Coe ■ 31

Nickname: Rams
Colors: Purple & White
Stadium: Ash Park Field
Capacity: 2,500; Year Built: 1922
AD: Tina Hill
SID: Darren Miller

CORTLAND ST.

Cortland, NY 13045 III

Coach: Dan MacNeill, Cortland St. 1979
Record: 10 Years, 61-41-0

2006 RESULTS (9-2)

52 Morrisville St. 14
17 Brockport St. ■ 10
38 Buffalo St. 20
30 Wm. Paterson ■ 14
24 Kean ■ 14
49 Western Conn. St. 21
41 Montclair St. 3
26 TCNJ ■ 14
7 Rowan 14
23 Ithaca ■ 20
7 Rensselaer ■ 26

Nickname: Red Dragons
Colors: Red & White
Stadium: Cortland Stadium Complex
Capacity: 6,500; Year Built: 2002
AD: Joan Sitterly
SID: Fran Elia

CURRY

Milton, MA 02186 III

Coach: Skip Bandini, Mass. Maritime 1981
Record: 1 Year, 11-1-0

2006 RESULTS (11-1)

10 Worcester St. 7
21 Fitchburg St. ■ 0
27 Westfield St. ■ 0
19 Western New Eng. ■ 10
35 Salve Regina 0
49 MIT ■ 13
35 Endicott 14
40 Plymouth St. 26
37 Nichols ■ 13
43 Mass.-Dartmouth 34
34 Coast Guard 28
14 Springfield 42

Nickname: Colonels
Colors: Purple & White
Stadium: D. Forbes Will Field
Capacity: 1,500; Year Built: 1965
AD: Vincent Eruzione
SID: Ken Golner

DARTMOUTH

Hanover, NH 03755 .....FCS

Coach: Buddy Teevens, Dartmouth 1979
Record: 17 Years, 64-115-2

2006 RESULTS (2-8)

7 Colgate 28
14 New Hampshire ■ 56
10 Penn 17
14 Yale ■ 26
21 Holy Cross ■ 24
20 Columbia 7
0 Harvard ■ 28
25 Cornell 28
19 Brown ■ 13
17 Princeton 27

Nickname: Big Green
Colors: Dartmouth Green & White
Stadium: Memorial Field
Capacity: 17,000; Year Built: 1923
AD: Jo Ann Harper
SID: Kathy Phillips

DAVIDSON

Davidson, NC 28035 .....FCS

Coach: Tripp Merritt, Charlotte 1990
Record: 2 Years, 10-10-0

2006 RESULTS (6-4)

19 VMI 20
16 Wingate ■ 22
24 Lenoir-Rhyne 14
21 San Diego ■ 50
38 Jacksonville ■ 3
27 Morehead St. 24
37 Dayton ■ 36
48 Valparaiso 14
15 Drake 35
50 Butler ■ 10

Nickname: Wildcats
Colors: Red & Black
Stadium: Smith Field at Richardson Stadium
Capacity: 4,000; Year Built: 1924
AD: James E. Murphy III
SID: Rick Bender

DAYTON

Dayton, OH 45469 .....FCS

Coach: Mike Kelly, Manchester 1970
Record: 26 Years, 235-53-1

2006 RESULTS (4-6)

21 Robert Morris ■ 14
35 Wittenberg 28
28 Austin Peay ■ 23
20 Butler 23
15 Morehead St. ■ 22
21 Jacksonville 28
36 Davidson 37
9 Drake ■ 21
51 Valparaiso ■ 7
14 San Diego 56

Nickname: Flyers
Colors: Red & Blue
Stadium: Welcome
Capacity: 11,000; Year Built: 1949
AD: Ted Kissell
SID: Doug Hauschild

DEFIANCE

Defiance, OH 43512 III

Coach: Robert Taylor, Albion 1995
Record: 4 Years, 18-22-0

2006 RESULTS (7-3)

13 Otterbein ■ 25
10 Adrian 0
17 Tri-State ■ 10
19 Manchester 7
13 Rose-Hulman 10
45 Anderson (Ind.) ■ 13
20 Hanover 10
6 Mt. St. Joseph ■ 20
0 Franklin ■ 21
20 Bluffton 6

Nickname: Yellow Jackets
Colors: Purple & Gold
Stadium: Justin F. Coressel
Capacity: 4,176; Year Built: 1994
AD: Dick Kaiser
SID: Nate Jorgensen

DELAWARE

Newark, DE 19716 ....FCS

Coach: K.C. Keeler, Delaware 1981
Record: 14 Years, 129-43-1

2006 RESULTS (5-6)

30 West Chester ■ 7
10 Albany (N.Y.) ■ 17
24 Rhode Island 17
49 New Hampshire ■ 52
24 Northeastern 27
10 Hofstra ■ 6
28 Richmond 24
35 Towson ■ 49
24 James Madison 44
28 William & Mary ■ 14
27 Villanova ■ 28

Nickname: Fightin' Blue Hens
Colors: Blue & Gold
Stadium: Delaware
Capacity: 22,000; Year Built: 1952
AD: Edgar N. Johnson
SID: Scott Selheimer

DELAWARE ST.

Dover, DE 19901 ....FCS

Coach: Al Lavan, Colorado St. 1968
Record: 3 Years, 19-14-0

2006 RESULTS (8-3)

34 Florida A&M * 14
63 St. Francis (Pa.) ■ 28
3 Northwestern St. 23
14 Hampton ■ 29
33 Bethune-Cookman 31
37 N.C. A&T ■ 21
29 Morgan St. 7
10 South Carolina St. ■ 9
62 Concord ■ 0
33 Norfolk St. 10
17 Howard 20

Nickname: Hornets
Colors: Red & Columbia Blue
Stadium: Alumni Field
Capacity: 5,000; Year Built: 1957
AD: Chuck Bell
SID: Dennis Jones

DELAWARE VALLEY

Doylestown, PA 18901-2699 III

Coach: Jim Clements, Widener 1996
Record: 1 Year, 8-3-0

2006 RESULTS (8-3)

19 FDU-Florham 7
7 Wilkes 14
17 Lycoming ■ 16
19 Lebanon Valley 18
39 Moravian ■ 0
21 Albright 13
10 Susquehanna ■ 17
10 King's (Pa.) 0
21 Juniata ■ 0
16 Widener 0
9 Salisbury ■ 15

Nickname: Aggies
Colors: Green & Gold
Stadium: James Work
Capacity: 4,000; Year Built: 1978
AD: Frank Wolfgang
SID: Matthew Levy

DELTA ST.

Cleveland, MS 38733 II

Coach: Rick Rhoades, Central Mo. 1970
Record: 11 Years, 78-48-1

2006 RESULTS (12-3)

61 West Va. Tech ■ 0
17 Stephen F. Austin 14
13 Henderson St. 16
34 Ouachita Baptist ■ 6
22 Southern Ark. 0
31 Arkansas Tech 13
35 Valdosta St. ■ 28
10 North Ala. ■ 17
21 West Ga. 7
41 West Ala. ■ 14
53 Ark.-Monticello ■ 0
17 Elizabeth City St. 10
24 N.C. Central 17
27 North Ala. 10
30 Grand Valley St. 49

Nickname: Statesmen
Colors: Forest Green & White
Stadium: Travis E. Parker Field
Capacity: 8,000; Year Built: 1970
AD: Jeremy McClain
SID: Matt Jones

DENISON

Granville, OH 43023 III

Coach: Nick Fletcher, Johns Hopkins 1976
Record: 12 Years, 50-69-0

2006 RESULTS (3-7)

14 Randolph-Macon 20
14 Case Reserve ■ 27
14 Gettysburg 31
6 Allegheny ■ 23
7 Oberlin 18
10 Ohio Wesleyan ■ 35
42 Hiram 7
41 Kenyon ■ 35
14 Wabash ■ 41
21 Earlham 16

Nickname: Big Red
Colors: Red & White
Stadium: Deeds Field-Piper Stadium
Capacity: 3,000; Year Built: 1922
AD: Larry Scheiderer
SID: Craig Hicks

DePAUW

Greencastle, IN 46135 III

Coach: Matt Walker, DePauw 1999
Record: 1 Year, 6-4-0

2006 RESULTS (6-4)

25 Anderson (Ind.) ■ 13
23 Hope ■ 14
15 Trinity (Tex.) 26
31 Chicago 6
31 Sewanee ■ 24
27 Rhodes 6
7 Millsaps 31
24 Centre 28
24 Austin ■ 14
20 Wabash 23

Nickname: Tigers
Colors: Old Gold & Black
Stadium: Blackstock
Capacity: 4,000; Year Built: 1941
AD: Page Cotton Jr.
SID: Bill Wagner

DICKINSON

Carlisle, PA 17013 III

Coach: Darwin Breaux, West Chester 1977
Record: 14 Years, 87-56-1

2006 RESULTS (8-3)

14 Juniata ■ 0
28 Hobart 31
20 Merchant Marine ■ 7
21 Johns Hopkins 13
24 Muhlenberg ■ 14
24 McDaniel 17
28 Frank. & Marsh. ■ 14
22 Hampden-Sydney 21
30 Gettysburg ■ 14
24 Ursinus 31
21 Wesley 49

Nickname: Red Devils
Colors: Red & White
Stadium: Biddle Field
Capacity: 2,577; Year Built: 1909
AD: Leslie J. Poolman
SID: Charlie McGuire

DRAKE

Des Moines, IA 50311-4505 ....FCS

Coach: Rob Ash, Cornell College 1973
Record: 27 Years, 176-99-5

2006 RESULTS (9-2)

7 UNI ■ 48
40 Upper Iowa ■ 7
35 Wis.-Platteville ■ 7
21 Valparaiso 7
33 Morehead St. ■ 7
35 Waldorf ■ 3
29 Butler 0
0 San Diego ■ 37
21 Dayton 9
35 Davidson ■ 15
47 Jacksonville 28

Nickname: Bulldogs
Colors: Blue & White
Stadium: Drake
Capacity: 18,000; Year Built: 1925
AD: Sandy Hatfield Clubb
SID: Mike Mahon

DUBUQUE

Dubuque, IA 52001 III

Coach: Vince Brautigam, Iowa Wesleyan 1988
Record: 17 Years, 80-95-0

2006 RESULTS (6-4)

20 Wis.-Platteville ■ 34
48 Wis. Lutheran 7
32 Cornell College ■ 14
20 Loras 23
51 Luther 34
23 Coe ■ 37
14 Central (Iowa) 40
20 Simpson ■ 9
27 Buena Vista ■ 25
17 Wartburg 14

Nickname: Spartans
Colors: Blue & White
Stadium: Chalmers Field
Capacity: 2,800; Year Built: 1942
AD: Dan Runkle
SID: Paul Misner

DUKE

Durham, NC 27708-0555 ....FBS

Coach: Ted Roof, Georgia Tech 1987
Record: 3 Years, 3-31-0

2006 RESULTS (0-12)

0 Richmond ■ 13
13 Wake Forest 14
0 Virginia Tech 36
0 Virginia ■ 37
14 Alabama 30
24 Florida St. ■ 51
15 Miami (Fla.) ■ 20
28 Vanderbilt ■ 45
13 Navy ■ 38
7 Boston College 28
21 Georgia Tech 49
44 North Carolina ■ 45

Nickname: Blue Devils
Colors: Royal Blue & White
Stadium: Wallace Wade
Capacity: 33,941; Year Built: 1929
AD: Joe Alleva
SID: Art Chase

DUQUESNE

Pittsburgh, PA 15282 ....FCS

Coach: Jerry Schmitt, Westminster (Pa.) 1982
Record: 7 Years, 42-27-0

2006 RESULTS (7-3)

28 Bucknell......31
27 Robert Morris......7
41 St. Francis (Pa.) ■......10
24 Sacred Heart ■......21
19 West Liberty St. ■......21
20 Fordham......17
35 St. Peter's......21
40 Marist ■......10
13 Iona ■......17
38 La Salle......0

Nickname: Dukes
Colors: Red & Blue
Stadium: Arthur J. Rooney Field
Capacity: 4,500; Year Built: 1993
AD: Greg Amodio
SID: Dave Saba

EARLHAM

Richmond, IN 47374 III

Coach: Gerry Keesling, Earlham 1982
Record: 3 Years, 8-22-0

2006 RESULTS (3-7)

17 Rose-Hulman......24
49 Manchester......35
32 Anderson (Ind.) ■......24
15 Wabash ■......48
14 Wittenberg......28
31 Oberlin ■......41
30 Kenyon......33
24 Hiram ■......16
31 Wooster......38
16 Denison ■......21

Nickname: Quakers
Colors: Maroon & White
Stadium: M.O. Ross Field
Capacity: 1,500; Year Built: 1975
AD: Frank Carr
SID: Don Tincher

EAST CARO.

Greenville, NC 27858-4353 ....FBS

Coach: Skip Holtz, Notre Dame 1986
Record: 7 Years, 46-35-0

2006 RESULTS (7-6)

23 Navy......28
12 UAB......17
35 Memphis ■......20
10 West Virginia ■......27
31 Virginia ■......21
10 Tulsa ■......31
38 SMU ■......21
20 Southern Miss.......17
23 UCF......10
33 Marshall ■......20
17 Rice......18
21 North Carolina St.......16
7 South Fla. *......24

Nickname: Pirates
Colors: Purple & Gold
Stadium: Dowdy-Ficklen
Capacity: 43,000; Year Built: 1963
AD: Terry Holland
SID: Tom McClellan

EAST CENTRAL

Ada, OK 74820..II

Coach: Kurt Nichols, Jacksonville St. 1986
Record: 1 Year, 2-8-0

2006 RESULTS (2-8)

12 Pittsburg St. ■......52
20 Angelo St.......6
15 Eastern N.M. ■......24
14 Midwestern St.......63
29 Northeastern St. ■......40
0 Central Okla.......37
34 Tex. A&M-Kingsville ■......37
10 Tex. A&M-Commerce......3
28 Southwestern Okla. ■......38
6 Southeastern Okla.......42

Nickname: Tigers
Colors: Orange & Black
Stadium: Norris Field
Capacity: 5,000
AD: Brian DeAngelis
SID: Brian Johnson

EAST STROUDSBURG

East Stroudsburg, PA 18301..........................II

Coach: Dennis Douds, Slippery Rock 1963
Record: 33 Years, 206-134-3

2006 RESULTS (7-4)

7 Bentley ■......9
45 Lock Haven ■......14
20 Indiana (Pa.)......35
41 California (Pa.) ■......34
61 Mansfield......7
30 Millersville......19
12 Edinboro......0
48 Cheyney ■......7
28 West Chester ■......49
37 Bloomsburg......45
56 Kutztown ■......16

Nickname: Warriors
Colors: Red & Black
Stadium: Eiler-Martin
Capacity: 6,000; Year Built: 1969
AD: Thomas Gioglio
SID: Ryan Yanoshak

EAST TEX. BAPTIST

Marshall, TX 75670-1498 III

Coach: Ralph Harris, Sul Ross St.
Record: 7 Years, 35-37-0

2006 RESULTS (3-7)

0 Trinity (Tex.)......41
14 Ouachita Baptist ■......47
17 Howard Payne......24
16 Sul Ross St. ■......17
28 Texas Lutheran......31
41 McMurry ■......24
17 Hardin-Simmons......56
32 Louisiana Col. *......29
35 Mississippi Col.......30
28 Mary Hardin-Baylor ■......33

Nickname: Tigers
Colors: Navy & Gold
Stadium: Ornelas
Capacity: 3,000; Year Built: 2000
AD: Kent Reeves
SID: David Weaver

EASTERN ILL.

Charleston, IL 61920-3099 ....FCS

Coach: Mark Hutson, Oklahoma 1989
Record: 1 Year, 8-5-0

2006 RESULTS (8-5)

17 Illinois......42
31 Indiana St. ■......21
30 Illinois St.......44
24 Samford......13
9 Hawaii......44
21 Southeast Mo. St. ■......0
28 Eastern Ky.......21
20 Murray St. ■......10
9 Tenn.-Martin......15
29 Tennessee St. ■......3
38 Tennessee Tech......14
28 Jacksonville St. ■......24
13 Illinois St. ■......24

Nickname: Panthers
Colors: Blue & Gray
Stadium: O'Brien
Capacity: 10,000; Year Built: 1970
AD: Richard A. McDuffie
SID: Rich Moser

EASTERN KY.

Richmond, KY 40475-3101 ....FCS

Coach: Danny Hope, Eastern Ky. 1981
Record: 4 Years, 26-19-0

2006 RESULTS (6-5)

0 Cincinnati......31
26 Western Ky. ■......21
17 Western Caro.......20
14 Tennessee Tech......27
0 Jacksonville St. ■......28
31 Samford......12
21 Eastern Ill. ■......28
27 Southeast Mo. St.......21
51 Murray St. ■......21
31 Tenn.-Martin......28
20 Tennessee St. ■......3

Nickname: Colonels
Colors: Maroon & White
Stadium: Roy Kidd
Capacity: 20,000; Year Built: 1969
AD: Mark S. Sandy
SID: Michael Clark

EASTERN MICH.

Ypsilanti, MI 48197.................................FBS

Coach: Jeff Genyk, Bowling Green 1982
Record: 3 Years, 9-25-0

2006 RESULTS (1-11)

20 Ball St.......38
20 Michigan St.......52
6 Northwestern......14
17 Central Mich. ■......24
14 La.-Lafayette......33
21 Bowling Green......24
17 Toledo ■......13
15 Western Mich.......18
10 Ohio ■......16
21 Navy *......49
6 Kent St.......14
0 Northern Ill. ■......27

Nickname: Eagles
Colors: Green & White
Stadium: Rynearson
Capacity: 30,200; Year Built: 1969
AD: Derrick L. Gragg
SID: Jim Streeter

EASTERN N.M.

Portales, NM 88130..II

Coach: Mark Ribaudo, Arizona 1988
Record: 2 Years, 8-13-0

2006 RESULTS (3-7)

7 Northeastern St.......42
24 East Central......15
16 Central Okla. ■......19
0 Abilene Christian ■......21
7 Angelo St.......17

14 West Tex. A&M ■ 21
0 Tarleton St. 48
37 Tex. A&M-Kingsville ■ 14
19 Midwestern St. 29
63 Okla. Panhandle ■ 14

Nickname: Greyhounds
Colors: Green & Silver
Stadium: Greyhound
Capacity: 6,100; Year Built: 1969
AD: Michael Maguire
SID: Robert McKinney

EASTERN WASH.

Cheney, WA 99004 ....FCS

Coach: Paul Wulff, Washington St. 1990
Record: 7 Years, 44-36-0

2006 RESULTS (3-8)

17 Oregon St. 56
3 West Virginia 52
14 Central Wash. ■ 21
19 Montana St. 10
20 Sacramento St. ■ 21
17 Montana ■ 33
34 Northern Colo. 0
0 Portland St. 34
36 Northern Ariz. ■ 44
14 Weber St. 19
40 Idaho St. ■ 6

Nickname: Eagles
Colors: Red & White
Stadium: Woodward Field
Capacity: 8,600; Year Built: 1967
AD: Michael Westfall
SID: Dave Cook

EDINBORO

Edinboro, PA 16444-0001 II

Coach: Scott Browning, Ohio St. 1981
Record: 1 Year, 6-5-0

2006 RESULTS (6-5)

28 West Chester 14
54 St. Anselm ■ 0
10 Bloomsburg ■ 28
28 Cheyney 6
20 Indiana (Pa.) ■ 23
0 California (Pa.) ■ 10
0 East Stroudsburg ■ 12
13 Clarion 0
21 Slippery Rock 24
54 Shippensburg ■ 30
51 Lock Haven 25

Nickname: Fighting Scots
Colors: Red & White
Stadium: Sox Harrison
Capacity: 6,000; Year Built: 1965
AD: Bruce R. Baumgartner
SID: Bob Shreve

ELIZABETH CITY ST.

Elizabeth City, NC 27909 II

Coach: Waverly Tillar, Virginia Union 1975
Record: 4 Years, 16-26-0

2006 RESULTS (9-3)

26 Livingstone 0
12 Charleston (W.V.) ■ 7
43 Fayetteville St. ■ 31
33 Newberry 49
49 St. Augustine's 0
27 Virginia St. ■ 0
16 Bowie St. 12
36 Shaw ■ 0
7 St. Paul's 3
29 Virginia Union ■ 21
14 N.C. Central * 17
10 Delta St. ■ 17

Nickname: Vikings
Colors: Royal Blue & White
Stadium: Roebuck
Capacity: 5,000; Year Built: 1983
AD: Thurlis J. Little Jr.
SID: April J. Emory

ELMHURST

Elmhurst, IL 60126-3296 III

Coach: Tom Journell, Wittenberg 1987
Record: 3 Years, 16-14-0

2006 RESULTS (6-4)

34 Benedictine (Ill.) ■ 0
23 Chicago ■ 10
33 Olivet 16
20 Carthage 13
14 Augustana (Ill.) ■ 28
16 North Central (Ill.) 30
25 Ill. Wesleyan ■ 13
0 Wheaton (Ill.) 34
17 Millikin ■ 22
24 North Park 7

Nickname: Bluejays
Colors: Blue & White
Stadium: Langhorst Field
Capacity: 2,500; Year Built: 1920
AD: Paul Krohn
SID: Kevin Juday

ELON

Elon, NC 27244-2010 ....FCS

Coach: Pete Lembo, Georgetown 1992
Record: 6 Years, 49-20-0

2006 RESULTS (5-6)

23 Coastal Caro. 20
17 Towson ■ 24
28 Presbyterian ■ 0
21 Appalachian St. 45
37 Western Caro. ■ 19
21 Ga. Southern 28
21 Wofford ■ 35
20 Chattanooga 17
13 Furman ■ 24
45 N.C. A&T 0
7 Citadel ■ 44

Nickname: Phoenix
Colors: Maroon & Gold
Stadium: Rhodes
Capacity: 11,250; Year Built: 2001
AD: Dave Blank
SID: Matt Eviston

EMORY & HENRY

Emory, VA 24327-0947 III

Coach: Don Montgomery, Mount Union 1977
Record: 2 Years, 7-13-0

2006 RESULTS (6-4)

20 Marietta ■ 28
24 N.C. Wesleyan ■ 21
16 Apprentice 7
8 Methodist ■ 16
21 Hampden-Sydney 24
28 Randolph-Macon ■ 7
21 Bridgewater (Va.) 17
31 Catholic ■ 27
6 Wash. & Lee 24
27 Guilford ■ 23

Nickname: Wasps
Colors: Blue & Gold
Stadium: Fullerton Field
Capacity: 5,500; Year Built: 1926
AD: Robert J. Johnson
SID: Nathan Graybeal

EMPORIA ST.

Emporia, KS 66801-5087 II

Coach: David Wiemers, Washburn 1990
Record: 6 Years, 35-32-0

2006 RESULTS (3-8)

69 Okla. Panhandle 6
18 Winona St. ■ 21
48 Fort Hays St. ■ 10
35 Southwest Baptist 31
57 Pittsburg St. ■ 59
17 Northwest Mo. St. 49
13 Truman ■ 14
12 Mo. Western St. 24
6 Washburn 37
21 Central Mo. 48
33 Mo. Southern St. ■ 34

Nickname: Hornets
Colors: Old Gold & Black
Stadium: Jones Field at Welch Stadium
Capacity: 7,000; Year Built: 1937
AD: Kent Weiser
SID: Donald Weast

ENDICOTT

Beverly, MA 01915 III

Coach: J.B. Wells, Trinity (Conn.) 1991
Record: 4 Years, 23-16-0

2006 RESULTS (6-4)

28 Hartwick 30
7 Rensselaer ■ 27
34 Mass. Maritime 0
40 Salve Regina ■ 7
7 Nichols 3
24 Plymouth St. ■ 7
14 Curry ■ 35
0 Western New Eng. 3
28 Mass.-Dartmouth ■ 0
21 MIT 16

Nickname: Gulls
Colors: Blue, Kelly Green & White
Stadium: Endicott
Capacity: 2,200; Year Built: 2003
AD: Larry R. Hiser
SID: Mike DePlacido

EUREKA

Eureka, IL 61530-1500 III

Coach: Dan Sullivan, Loras 1997
Record: 2 Years, 1-18-0

2006 RESULTS (0-10)

0 Knox 23
6 North Park 34
0 Concordia (Wis.) ■ 56
12 Concordia (Ill.) 41
6 Lakeland ■ 45
20 Greenville ■ 26
7 Benedictine (Ill.) 35
14 Aurora 29
30 MacMurray ■ 48
12 Chicago ■ 44

Nickname: Red Devils
Colors: Maroon & Gold
Stadium: McKinzie
Capacity: 2,500; Year Built: 1930
AD: Sandy Schuster
SID: Brian Sullivan

FDU-FLORHAM

Madison, NJ 07940 III

Coach: Rich Mosca, West Liberty St. 1972
Record: 5 Years, 13-37-0

2006 RESULTS (2-8)

7 Delaware Valley ■ 19
14 TCNJ ■ 20

16 Wilkes ■ 30
14 Lycoming 23
19 Lebanon Valley ■ 29
14 Moravian 28
39 Albright ■ 35
21 Susquehanna 16
17 King's (Pa.) ■ 21
31 Juniata 39

Nickname: Devils
Colors: Cardinal & Navy
Stadium: Robert T. Shields
Capacity: 4,000; Year Built: 1973
AD: William T. Klika
SID: Jim Henry

FAIRMONT ST.

Fairmont, WV 26554 II

Coach: Rusty Elliott, Fairmont St. 1979
Record: 5 Years, 20-31-0

2006 RESULTS (4-7)

9 California (Pa.) 26
7 North Greenville 28
10 Concord 13
14 West Virginia St. ■ 0
0 Shepherd 20
14 Glenville St. 16
20 West Liberty St. ■ 27
27 Charleston (W.V.) 13
11 St. Joseph's (Ind.) ■ 19
20 West Va. Wesleyan ■ 3
30 Webber Int'l ■ 13

Nickname: Falcons
Colors: Maroon, White & Fairmont Gold
Stadium: Duvall-Rosier Field
Capacity: 5,000; Year Built: 1929
AD: David Scott Gines
SID: Jim Brinkman

FAYETTEVILLE ST.

Fayetteville, NC 28301-4298 II

Coach: Kenny Phillips, East Caro. 1987
Record: 7 Years, 44-32-0

2006 RESULTS (3-7)

0 Wingate 19
25 Virginia Union 12
6 Presbyterian ■ 7
31 Elizabeth City St. 43
21 St. Paul's ■ 24
30 Virginia St. 3
6 N.C. Central ■ 49
7 Johnson C. Smith 10
3 St. Augustine's ■ 15
34 Livingstone ■ 16

Nickname: Broncos
Colors: Royal Blue & Lily White
Stadium: Jeralds Ath. Complex
Capacity: 6,200; Year Built: 1940
AD: Edward McLean/Major Boyd
SID: Marion Crowe Jr.

FERRIS ST.

Big Rapids, MI 49307-2295 II

Coach: Jeff Pierce, Ferris St. 1979
Record: 12 Years, 77-55-0

2006 RESULTS (8-3)

31 Kentucky St. 13
28 Mercyhurst 7
26 Saginaw Valley ■ 23
27 Hillsdale 29
42 Northern Mich. 24
7 Michigan Tech ■ 41
35 Gannon ■ 14
38 Ashland 7
6 Grand Valley St. ■ 28
17 Northwood (Mich.) 14
21 Wayne St. (Mich.) ■ 17

Nickname: Bulldogs
Colors: Crimson & Gold
Stadium: Top Taggart Field
Capacity: 6,200; Year Built: 1957
AD: Tom Kirinovic
SID: Joe Gorby

FERRUM

Ferrum, VA 24088 III

Coach: Dave Davis, Elon 1971
Record: 13 Years, 66-60-0

2006 RESULTS (2-7)

35 Guilford 49
27 Bridgewater (Va.) ■ 30
42 Shenandoah ■ 0
14 Averett 21
14 Maryville (Tenn.) ■ 20
14 Methodist 24
35 Greensboro 23
14 N.C. Wesleyan ■ 55
7 Chris. Newport 55

Nickname: Panthers
Colors: Black & Gold
Stadium: W.B. Adams
Capacity: 5,500; Year Built: 1970
AD: Abe Naff
SID: Gary Holden

FINDLAY

Findlay, OH 45840 II

Coach: Dan Simrell, Toledo 1966
Record: 15 Years, 80-83-2

2006 RESULTS (2-9)

25 Charleston (W.V.) 24
0 Grand Valley St. ■ 13
6 Northwood (Mich.) 29
3 Wayne St. (Mich.) ■ 24
16 Indianapolis 34
14 Saginaw Valley ■ 31
7 Mercyhurst 24
17 Gannon ■ 20
7 Ashland 0
7 Hillsdale 10
15 Michigan Tech ■ 33

Nickname: Oilers
Colors: Orange & Black
Stadium: Donnell
Capacity: 7,500; Year Built: 1928
AD: Steven Rackley
SID: David Buck

FITCHBURG ST.

Fitchburg, MA 01420-2697 III

Coach: Patrick Haverty, Worcester St. 1991
Record: 5 Years, 30-20-0

2006 RESULTS (4-5)

0 Curry 21
33 Mass.-Dartmouth 26
30 Framingham St. ■ 6
7 Bridgewater St. 15
30 Coast Guard ■ 31
7 Worcester St. ■ 21
33 Mass. Maritime 0
7 Westfield St. ■ 6
13 Maine Maritime 21

Nickname: Falcons
Colors: Green, Gold & White
Stadium: Robert Elliot
Capacity: 1,000; Year Built: 1984
AD: Sue E. Lauder
SID: Rusty Eggen

FLORIDA

Gainesville, FL 32611 ....FBS

Coach: Urban Meyer, Cincinnati 1986
Record: 6 Years, 61-12-0

2006 RESULTS (13-1)

34 Southern Miss. ■ 7
42 UCF ■ 0
21 Tennessee 20
26 Kentucky ■ 7
28 Alabama ■ 13
23 LSU ■ 10
17 Auburn 27
21 Georgia * 14
25 Vanderbilt 19
17 South Carolina ■ 16
62 Western Caro. ■ 0
21 Florida St. 14
38 Arkansas * 28
41 Ohio St. * 14

Nickname: Gators
Colors: Orange & Blue
Stadium: Florida Field
Capacity: 88,548; Year Built: 1929
AD: Jeremy N. Foley
SID: Steve McClain

FLORIDA A&M

Tallahassee, FL 32307 ....FCS

Coach: Rubin Carter, Miami (Fla.) 1975
Record: 2 Years, 13-9-0

2006 RESULTS (7-4)

14 Delaware St. * 34
10 Miami (Fla.) 51
31 Howard 23
25 Winston-Salem ■ 21
25 Tennessee St. * 22
21 South Carolina St. ■ 28
36 Norfolk St. 33
24 Morgan St. ■ 23
45 N.C. A&T 12
7 Hampton ■ 59
35 Bethune-Cookman * 21

Nickname: Rattlers
Colors: Orange & Green
Stadium: Bragg Memorial
Capacity: 25,500; Year Built: 1957
AD: Nelson E. Townsend
SID: Ronnie Johnson

FLA. ATLANTIC

Boca Raton, FL 33431-0991 ....FBS

Coach: Howard Schnellenberger, Kentucky 1956
Record: 22 Years, 133-114-3

2006 RESULTS (5-7)

6 Clemson 54
0 Kansas St. 45
8 Oklahoma St. 48
6 South Carolina 45
21 La.-Monroe 19
32 Southern Utah ■ 7
0 La.-Lafayette ■ 6
29 Arkansas St. ■ 0
14 Middle Tenn. 35
17 Troy ■ 24
17 North Texas 16
31 Florida Int'l * 0

Nickname: Owls
Colors: Blue & Red
Stadium: Lockhart
Capacity: 20,540; Year Built: 1998
AD: Craig W. Angelos
SID: Katrina McCormack

FLORIDA INT'L

Miami, FL 33199 .... FBS

Coach: Don Strock, Virginia Tech 1973
Record: 5 Years, 15-41-0

2006 RESULTS (0-12)

6 Middle Tenn. 7
20 South Fla. 21
28 Bowling Green ■ 33
10 Maryland 14
6 Arkansas St. ■ 31
22 North Texas 25
0 Miami (Fla.) 35
3 Alabama 38
0 La.-Monroe ■ 35
7 La.-Lafayette ■ 17
0 Fla. Atlantic * 31
13 Troy ■ 26

Nickname: Golden Panthers
Colors: Blue & Gold
Stadium: FIU
Capacity: 17,000; Year Built: 1995
AD: Peter Garcia
SID: Rich Kelch

FLORIDA ST.

Tallahassee, FL 32306 .... FBS

Coach: Bobby Bowden, Samford 1953
Record: 41 Years, 366-113-4

2006 RESULTS (7-6)

13 Miami (Fla.) 10
24 Troy ■ 17
20 Clemson ■ 27
55 Rice ■ 7
20 North Carolina St. 24
51 Duke 24
19 Boston College ■ 24
24 Maryland 27
33 Virginia ■ 0
0 Wake Forest ■ 30
28 Western Mich. ■ 20
14 Florida ■ 21
44 UCLA * 27

Nickname: Seminoles
Colors: Garnet & Gold
Stadium: Bobby Bowden Field at Doak S. Campbell Stadium
Capacity: 82,300; Year Built: 1950
AD: David R. Hart Jr.
SID: Jeff Purinton

FORDHAM

Bronx, NY 10458-5155 .... FCS

Coach: Tom Masella, Wagner 1981
Record: 5 Years, 20-34-0

2006 RESULTS (3-8)

9 Monmouth ■ 23
9 Albany (N.Y.) 7
7 Columbia 37
21 Holy Cross 28
17 Duquesne ■ 20
13 Marist ■ 9
3 Colgate ■ 46
3 Bucknell 13
24 Lafayette ■ 31
14 Lehigh 45
38 Georgetown ■ 30

Nickname: Rams
Colors: Maroon & White
Stadium: Jack Coffey Field
Capacity: 7,000; Year Built: 1930
AD: Francis X. McLaughlin
SID: Joe DiBari

FORT HAYS ST.

Hays, KS 67601 II

Coach: Kevin Verdugo, Colorado St. 1991
Record: 2 Years, 3-18-0

2006 RESULTS (1-10)

14 Tex. A&M-Commerce ■ 17
24 Colorado Mines 31
10 Emporia St. 48
7 Washburn ■ 37
14 Central Mo. ■ 37
21 Southwest Baptist 39
28 Pittsburg St. ■ 35
0 Northwest Mo. St. 59
10 Mo. Southern St. ■ 0
10 Mo. Western St. 24
15 Truman ■ 40

Nickname: Tigers
Colors: Black & Gold
Stadium: Lewis Field
Capacity: 6,362; Year Built: 1936
AD: Curtis Hammeke
SID: Ryan Prickett

FORT LEWIS

Durango, CO 81301-3999 II

Coach: Ed Rifilato, Idaho 1998
Record: 5 Years, 27-26-0

2006 RESULTS (7-4)

23 Western N.M. 7
0 Cal Poly 44
12 Idaho St. 48
21 Neb.-Kearney ■ 16
35 Mesa St. 20
35 Western St. ■ 14
17 Adams St. 14
27 Chadron St. ■ 40
41 Colorado Mines 34
25 N.M. Highlands ■ 28
24 Dixie St. 14

Nickname: Skyhawks
Colors: Navy Blue, Light Blue & Gold
Stadium: Ray Dennison Memorial
Capacity: 4,000; Year Built: 1958
AD: Kent Stanley
SID: Andrew Beardsley

FORT VALLEY ST.

Fort Valley, GA 31030 II

Coach: Deondri Clark, Florida St. 1993
Record: 4 Years, 26-17-0

2006 RESULTS (4-7)

9 Clark Atlanta 8
24 Morehouse ■ 14
3 Valdosta St. 31
7 Miles 15
20 Tuskegee * 34
19 Howard 34
11 Stillman 34
16 Benedict ■ 10
41 Lane 27
3 Albany St. (Ga.) ■ 21
16 Kentucky St. 19

Nickname: Wildcats
Colors: Royal Blue & Old Gold
Stadium: Wildcat
Capacity: 7,500; Year Built: 1957
AD: Gwendolyn Reeves
SID: Russell Boone Jr.

FRAMINGHAM ST.

Framingham, MA 01701-9101 III

Coach: Mark Sullivan, Massachusetts 1985
Record: 5 Years, 4-41-0

2006 RESULTS (1-8)

12 Nichols 31
14 MIT ■ 21
6 Fitchburg St. 30
14 Worcester St. ■ 26
17 Bridgewater St. ■ 46
0 Westfield St. 33
24 Maine Maritime ■ 40
14 Mass. Maritime 6
21 Coast Guard 42

Nickname: Rams
Colors: Black & Gold
Stadium: Maple Street Field
Capacity: 1,500; Year Built: 1900
AD: Thomas M. Kelley
SID: Kathy Lynch

FRANKLIN

Franklin, IN 46131 III

Coach: Mike Leonard, Hanover 1984
Record: 4 Years, 21-19-0

2006 RESULTS (9-1)

38 Ohio Wesleyan ■ 23
45 Wabash ■ 38
31 Tri-State 28
31 Bluffton ■ 7
38 Anderson (Ind.) 24
14 Mt. St. Joseph ■ 21
28 Rose-Hulman ■ 11
31 Manchester 15
21 Defiance 0
35 Hanover ■ 10

Nickname: Grizzlies
Colors: Navy & Old Gold
Stadium: Stewart "Red" Faught
Capacity: 2,000; Year Built: 1999
AD: Kerry N. Prather
SID: Kevin Elixman

FRANK. & MARSH.

Lancaster, PA 17604-3003 III

Coach: John Troxell, Lafayette 1994
Record: 1 Year, 3-7-0

2006 RESULTS (3-7)

21 Wash. & Lee ■ 7
13 Kean ■ 21
14 Carnegie Mellon 34
24 Muhlenberg 10
7 Johns Hopkins ■ 14
21 Union (N.Y.) 28
14 Dickinson 28
31 McDaniel ■ 7
10 Ursinus ■ 42
30 Gettysburg 38

Nickname: Diplomats
Colors: Blue & White
Stadium: Sponaugle-Williamson Field
Capacity: 4,000; Year Built: 1920
AD: Timothy D. Downes
SID: Steve Peed

FRESNO ST.

Fresno, CA 93740-0048 .... FBS

Coach: Pat Hill, UC Riverside 1973
Record: 10 Years, 76-51-0

2006 RESULTS (4-8)

28 Nevada ■ 19
24 Oregon ■ 31
20 Washington 21
23 Colorado St. ■ 35
12 Utah St. 13
37 Hawaii ■ 68
6 LSU 38
21 Boise St. 45
23 New Mexico St. ■ 18
34 Idaho ■ 0
34 Louisiana Tech 27
14 San Jose St. 24

Nickname: Bulldogs
Colors: Red & Blue

Stadium: Bulldog
Capacity: 41,031; Year Built: 1980
AD: Thomas C. Boeh
SID: Steve Weakland

FROSTBURG ST.

Frostburg, MD 21532-1099 III

Coach: Rubin Stevenson, Salisbury 1984
Record: 7 Years, 29-40-0

2006 RESULTS (2-7)

10 Apprentice ■ 20
7 Randolph-Macon ■ 10
0 Brockport St. ■ 22
7 Wesley ■ 32
7 Thomas More ■ 13
7 Union (Ky.) 3
14 Westminster (Pa.) ■ 6
7 Waynesburg 21
15 Salisbury * 42

Nickname: Bobcats
Colors: Red, White & Black
Stadium: Bobcat
Capacity: 4,000; Year Built: 1974
AD: Ralph L. Brewer
SID: Noah Becker

FURMAN

Greenville, SC 29613 ....FCS

Coach: Bobby Lamb, Furman 1987
Record: 5 Years, 43-19-0

2006 RESULTS (8-4)

17 Jacksonville St. ■ 13
24 West Ga. ■ 7
42 North Carolina 45
42 Western Caro. ■ 7
35 Wofford 21
27 Coastal Caro. 29
23 Citadel ■ 17
28 Chattanooga ■ 22
7 Appalachian St. 40
24 Elon 13
13 Ga. Southern ■ 10
13 Montana St. 31

Nickname: Paladins
Colors: Purple & White
Stadium: Paladin
Capacity: 16,000; Year Built: 1981
AD: Gary Clark
SID: Hunter Reid

GALLAUDET

Washington, DC 20002........................III

Coach: Ed Hottle, Frostburg St. 1999
First year as head coach

Resuming varsity program in 2007
dropped to club status in 2004

Nickname: Bison
Colors: Buff & Blue
Stadium: Hotchkiss Field
Capacity: 1,500
AD: James DeStefano
SID: Oscar Ocuto

GANNON

Erie, PA 16541-0001 II

Coach: Bill Elias, Massachusetts 1977
Record: 8 Years, 32-50-0

2006 RESULTS (1-10)

7 Hillsdale ■ 35
10 Saginaw Valley 26
14 Indianapolis ■ 49
14 Mercyhurst 35
3 Tiffin 15
3 Wayne St. (Mich.) ■ 30
14 Ferris St. 35
20 Findlay 17
13 Michigan Tech ■ 14
21 Northern Mich. 48
14 Ashland ■ 45

Nickname: Golden Knights
Colors: Maroon & Gold
Stadium: Gannon University Field
Capacity: 2,500; Year Built: 2001
AD: Bill Elias
SID: Dan Teliski

GARDNER-WEBB

Boiling Springs, NC 28017 ....FCS

Coach: Steve Patton, Furman 1977
Record: 13 Years, 87-54-0

2006 RESULTS (6-5)

49 Jacksonville 14
30 Tennessee Tech ■ 26
9 Tenn.-Martin 35
6 Appalachian St. ■ 41
28 Southeastern La. 21
31 Glenville St. ■ 23
27 Liberty 24
35 VMI ■ 31
14 Charleston So. 28
24 Coastal Caro. ■ 52
17 Wofford ■ 34

Nickname: Runnin' Bulldogs
Colors: Scarlet, White & Black
Stadium: Spangler
Capacity: 7,200; Year Built: 1969
AD: Chuck Burch
SID: Marc Rabb

GEORGETOWN

Washington, DC 20057-1121 ....FCS

Coach: Kevin Kelly, Springfield 1982
Record: 1 Year, 2-9-0

2006 RESULTS (2-9)

13 Holy Cross ■ 26
7 Stony Brook ■ 0
21 Brown 34
21 Columbia 23
14 Colgate 31
3 Lehigh ■ 28
7 Bucknell ■ 17
10 Charleston So. 24
24 Marist ■ 21
14 Lafayette 45
30 Fordham 38

Nickname: Hoyas
Colors: Blue & Gray
Stadium: Multi-Sport Field
Capacity: 2,500; Year Built: 2005
AD: Bernard Muir
SID: Mex Carey

GEORGIA

Athens, GA 30602-1661 ....FBS

Coach: Mark Richt, Miami (Fla.) 1982
Record: 6 Years, 61-17-0

2006 RESULTS (9-4)

48 Western Ky. ■ 12
18 South Carolina 0
34 UAB ■ 0
14 Colorado ■ 13
14 Mississippi 9
33 Tennessee ■ 51
22 Vanderbilt ■ 24
27 Mississippi St. ■ 24
14 Florida * 21
20 Kentucky 24
37 Auburn 15
15 Georgia Tech ■ 12
31 Virginia Tech * 24

Nickname: Bulldogs
Colors: Red & Black
Stadium: Sanford
Capacity: 92,746; Year Built: 1929
AD: Damon Evans
SID: Claude Felton

GA. SOUTHERN

Statesboro, GA 30460-8086 ....FCS

Coach: Brian VanGorder, Wayne St. (Mich.) 1991
Record: 4 Years, 18-26-0

2006 RESULTS (3-8)

13 Central Conn. St. ■ 17
38 Coastal Caro. ■ 21
26 Chattanooga 27
24 Western Caro. 14
14 North Dakota St. ■ 34
28 Elon ■ 21
20 Appalachian St. ■ 27
21 Citadel 24
10 Wofford ■ 28
10 Furman 13
31 Central Ark. ■ 34

Nickname: Eagles
Colors: Blue & White
Stadium: Allen E. Paulson
Capacity: 18,000; Year Built: 1984
AD: Samuel Q. Baker
SID: Patrick Osterman

GEORGIA TECH

Atlanta, GA 30332-0455........................FBS

Coach: Chan Gailey, Florida 1974
Record: 8 Years, 61-38-0

2006 RESULTS (9-5)

10 Notre Dame ■ 14
38 Samford ■ 6
35 Troy ■ 20
24 Virginia ■ 7
38 Virginia Tech 27
27 Maryland ■ 23
7 Clemson 31
30 Miami (Fla.) ■ 23
31 North Carolina St. 23
7 North Carolina 0
49 Duke ■ 21
12 Georgia 15
6 Wake Forest * 9
35 West Virginia * 38

Nickname: Yellow Jackets
Colors: Old Gold & White
Stadium: Bobby Dodd Stadium/Grant Field
Capacity: 55,000; Year Built: 1913
AD: Dan Radakovich
SID: Allison George

GETTYSBURG

Gettysburg, PA 17325-1668 III

Coach: Barry H. Streeter, Lebanon Valley 1971
Record: 28 Years, 141-137-5

2006 RESULTS (5-5)

12 Lebanon Valley 13
28 Hampden-Sydney ■ 20
42 Rochester 54
31 Denison ■ 14
14 McDaniel 17
23 Johns Hopkins ■ 18
27 Ursinus ■ 18
14 Muhlenberg 54
14 Dickinson 30
38 Frank. & Marsh. ■ 30

Nickname: Bullets
Colors: Orange & Blue
Stadium: Shirk Field at Musselman
Capacity: 6,176; Year Built: 1965
AD: David Wright
SID: To be named

GLENVILLE ST.

Glenville, WV 26351 II

Coach: Alan Fiddler, Glenville St. 1987
Record: 3 Years, 19-14-0

2006 RESULTS (5-6)

20 Johnson C. Smith ■ 23
7 Liberty 31
35 Charleston (W.V.) ■ 0
6 Shepherd 23
21 Ky. Wesleyan 13
16 Fairmont St. ■ 14
23 Gardner-Webb 31
10 West Liberty St. 38
19 Concord 0
21 West Virginia St. ■ 23
39 West Va. Wesleyan 14

Nickname: Pioneers
Colors: Royal Blue & White
Stadium: I.L. and Sue Morris
Capacity: 5,000; Year Built: 1977
AD: Steven Harold
SID: Dwaine Osborne

GRAMBLING

Grambling, LA 71245 ....FCS

Coach: Melvin Spears, Alcorn St. 1983
Record: 3 Years, 20-14-0

2006 RESULTS (3-8)

26 Hampton * 27
27 Alabama A&M 30
22 Houston 42
53 Prairie View * 7
28 Mississippi Val. 25
28 Ark.-Pine Bluff * 33
36 Jackson St. ■ 7
28 Texas Southern 33
16 Alabama St. ■ 35
17 Southern U. * 21
14 Alcorn St. ■ 21

Nickname: Tigers
Colors: Black & Gold
Stadium: Robinson
Capacity: 19,600; Year Built: 1983
AD: Troy A. Mathieu
SID: Ryan McGinty

GRAND VALLEY ST.

Allendale, MI 49401 II

Coach: Chuck Martin, Millikin 1990
Record: 3 Years, 38-3-0

2006 RESULTS (15-0)

13 Findlay 0
30 Ashland ■ 24
31 St. Joseph's (Ind.) 6
41 Michigan Tech ■ 20
36 Wayne St. (Mich.) 13
49 Mercyhurst ■ 17
33 Indianapolis 7
45 Northwood (Mich.) ■ 7
28 Ferris St. 6
49 Saginaw Valley ■ 35
47 Northern Mich. 17
35 South Dakota ■ 17
30 North Dakota ■ 20
49 Delta St. ■ 30
17 Northwest Mo. St. * 14

Nickname: Lakers
Colors: Blue, Black & White
Stadium: Arend D. Lubbers
Capacity: 8,550; Year Built: 1979
AD: Tim W. Selgo
SID: Tim Nott

GREENSBORO

Greensboro, NC 27401-1875.......III

Coach: Neal Mitchell, Washington-St. Louis 1992
Record: 5 Years, 13-37-0

2006 RESULTS (3-7)

13 Mars Hill ■ 38
39 Maryville (Tenn.) ■ 36
17 Southern Va. ■ 16
30 Guilford 36
0 Chris. Newport 28
10 Shenandoah ■ 36
21 Averett 62
23 Ferrum ■ 35
17 Methodist 13
20 N.C. Wesleyan 42

Nickname: The Pride
Colors: Green, White & Silver
Stadium: Jamieson
Capacity: 10,000
AD: Kim A. Strable
SID: Bob Lowe

GREENVILLE

Greenville, IL 62246 III

Coach: Eric Hehman, Taylor (Ind.) 1994
Record: 2 Years, 10-10-0

2006 RESULTS (6-4)

44 Blackburn ■ 13
0 Taylor (Ind.) 13
13 Lakeland 28
14 Aurora ■ 7
20 Benedictine (Ill.) 13
26 Eureka 20
34 MacMurray ■ 20
7 Concordia (Wis.) 14
45 Concordia (Ill.) ■ 7
14 Washington-St. Louis 17

Nickname: Panthers
Colors: Orange & Black
Stadium: Francis Field
Capacity: 2,000; Year Built: 1987
AD: Doug Faulkner
SID: B.J. Schneck

GRINNELL

Grinnell, IA 50112 III

Coach: Greg Wallace, Missouri Valley 1970
Record: 19 Years, 67-112-1

2006 RESULTS (2-8)

31 Kenyon ■ 57
13 St. Norbert 63
14 Carroll (Wis.) ■ 49
18 Lawrence 45
31 Monmouth (Ill.) ■ 51
35 Knox ■ 34
14 Lake Forest 21
13 Illinois Col. ■ 33
14 Ripon 55
39 Beloit ■ 22

Nickname: Pioneers
Colors: Scarlet & Black
Stadium: Rosenbloom Field
Capacity: 1,750; Year Built: 1911
AD: Greg Wallace
SID: To be named

GROVE CITY

Grove City, PA 16127-2104 III

Coach: Chris Smith, Grove City 1972
Record: 23 Years, 88-130-2

2006 RESULTS (3-7)

0 Carnegie Mellon ■ 28
20 Thomas More ■ 21
18 Waynesburg 29
21 Westminster (Pa.) ■ 20
28 Bethany (W.V.) 34
0 Thiel ■ 20
18 Wash. & Jeff. 52
21 Rochester ■ 38
40 Case Reserve ■ 33
14 Merchant Marine 6

Nickname: Wolverines
Colors: Crimson & White
Stadium: Robert E. Thorn Field
Capacity: 3,500; Year Built: 1981
AD: Donald L. Lyle
SID: R.A. Briggs

GUILFORD

Greensboro, NC 27410-4173.......III

Coach: Kevin Kiesel, Gettysburg 1981
Record: 14 Years, 75-67-1

2006 RESULTS (6-4)

49 Ferrum ■ 35
27 Methodist 11
34 Averett 54
43 Hampden-Sydney 46
36 Greensboro ■ 30
33 Bridgewater (Va.) ■ 28
12 Wash. & Lee 34
14 Randolph-Macon 6
41 Catholic ■ 18
23 Emory & Henry 27

Nickname: Quakers
Colors: Crimson & Gray
Stadium: Armfield Athletic
Capacity: 2,000; Year Built: 1960
AD: Marion Kirby
SID: Dave Walters

GUST. ADOLPHUS

Saint Peter, MN 56082-1498.......III

Coach: Jay Schoenebeck, Gust. Adolphus 1980
Record: 13 Years, 63-67-0

2006 RESULTS (6-4)

35 Willamette 7
7 St. Thomas (Minn.) ■ 21
20 Hamline 8
13 St. Olaf ■ 41
0 Bethel (Minn.) ■ 40
7 St. John's (Minn.) 34
51 Macalester 0
41 Augsburg ■ 27
7 Concordia-M'head 0
14 Carleton 10

Nickname: Golden Gusties
Colors: Black & Gold
Stadium: Hollingsworth Field
Capacity: 3,500; Year Built: 2007
AD: Alan Molde
SID: Tim Kennedy

HAMILTON

Clinton, NY 13323 III

Coach: Steve Stetson, Dartmouth 1973
Record: 17 Years, 78-81-4

2006 RESULTS (2-6)

0 Tufts 17
0 Wesleyan (Conn.) 7
0 Trinity (Conn.) ■ 13
12 Bowdoin ■ 0
6 Colby 0
0 Williams ■ 15
0 Middlebury ■ 10
6 Bates 20

Nickname: Continentals
Colors: Buff & Blue
Stadium: Steuben Field
Capacity: 2,500
AD: Susan Viscomi
SID: Jim Taylor

HAMLINE

St. Paul, MN 55104 III

Coach: Paul Miller, Minn.-Morris 1973
Record: 7 Years, 26-44-0

2006 RESULTS (3-7)
38 Mayville St. ■ 7
6 St. Olaf 31
8 Gust. Adolphus ■ 20
35 Macalester ■ 7
3 Concordia-M'head ■ 21
16 Carleton 11
7 St. John's (Minn.) 56
0 Bethel (Minn.) ■ 35
7 St. Thomas (Minn.) ■ 35
17 Augsburg * 28

Nickname: Pipers
Colors: Burgundy & Gray
Stadium: Klas Center
Capacity: 2,000; Year Built: 2004
AD: Dan O'Brien
SID: Troy Mallat

HAMPDEN-SYDNEY
Hampden-Sydney, VA 23943 III

Coach: Marty Favret, Catholic 1984
Record: 7 Years, 46-24-0

2006 RESULTS (4-6)
35 Sewanee 42
20 Gettysburg 28
46 Guilford ■ 43
13 Bridgewater (Va.) 31
24 Emory & Henry ■ 21
6 Wash. & Lee 28
41 Catholic ■ 21
21 Dickinson ■ 22
10 Johns Hopkins 24
46 Randolph-Macon ■ 21

Nickname: Tigers
Colors: Garnet & Gray
Stadium: Hundley
Capacity: 2,400; Year Built: 1964
AD: Joseph E. Bush
SID: Bryan Hicks

HAMPTON
Hampton, VA 23668 ....FCS

Coach: Joe Taylor, Western Ill. 1972
Record: 24 Years, 191-73-4

2006 RESULTS (10-2)
27 Grambling * 26
46 Howard ■ 7
48 N.C. A&T ■ 14
26 Morgan St. * 7
29 Delaware St. 14
42 Central St. (Ohio) * 12
42 Norfolk St. ■ 13
6 South Carolina St. 13
13 Winston-Salem ■ 3
34 Bethune-Cookman ■ 17
59 Florida A&M 7
38 New Hampshire ■ 41

Nickname: Pirates
Colors: Royal Blue & White
Stadium: Armstrong Field
Capacity: 17,000; Year Built: 1928
AD: Joseph Taylor
SID: Jamar Ross

HANOVER
Hanover, IN 47243-0108 III

Coach: Wayne Perry, DePauw 1972
Record: 25 Years, 172-81-2

2006 RESULTS (4-6)
23 Thomas More 25
20 Butler 30
0 Wash. & Jeff. ■ 35
41 Rose-Hulman ■ 8
0 Mt. St. Joseph ■ 24
32 Manchester 14
10 Defiance ■ 20
7 Bluffton 6
27 Anderson (Ind.) ■ 3
10 Franklin 35

Nickname: Panthers
Colors: Red & Blue
Stadium: L.S. Ayres Field
Capacity: 4,000; Year Built: 1973
AD: Lynn Hall
SID: Carter Cloyd

HARDIN-SIMMONS
Abilene, TX 79698 III

Coach: Jimmie Keeling, Howard Payne 1958
Record: 17 Years, 143-41-0

2006 RESULTS (8-2)
49 Wis.-Stevens Point ■ 17
21 Linfield ■ 6
48 Mississippi Col. ■ 28
16 Mary Hardin-Baylor 28
56 East Tex. Baptist ■ 17
42 Howard Payne 23
56 Sul Ross St. ■ 14
35 Texas Lutheran 7
42 McMurry ■ 13
21 Mary Hardin-Baylor 33

Nickname: Cowboys
Colors: Purple & Gold
Stadium: Shelton
Capacity: 4,000; Year Built: 1993
AD: John Neese
SID: Chad Grubbs

HARDING
Searcy, AR 72149-2281 II

Coach: Randy Tribble, Harding 1977
Record: 13 Years, 72-62-1

2006 RESULTS (6-4)
42 Southwest Baptist 30
27 Mo. Southern St. ■ 30
14 North Ala. 41
29 Ark.-Monticello ■ 21
24 West Ala. ■ 16
34 West Ga. 16
17 Southern Ark. ■ 6
34 Henderson St. ■ 28
3 Arkansas Tech 26
20 Ouachita Baptist 34

Nickname: Bisons
Colors: Black & Gold
Stadium: First Security
Capacity: 6,000; Year Built: 1999
AD: Greg Harnden
SID: Scott Goode

HARTWICK
Oneonta, NY 13820-4020 III

Coach: Mark Carr, New Hampshire 1990
Record: 5 Years, 19-29-0

2006 RESULTS (4-6)
30 Endicott ■ 28
14 Ithaca 44
19 Husson 20
16 St. John Fisher 57
21 Alfred ■ 41
40 Becker ■ 22
20 Mount Ida 21
42 Norwich ■ 20
20 Springfield 44
35 Utica ■ 17

Nickname: Hawks
Colors: Royal Blue & White
Stadium: All-Weather Field
Capacity: 1,200; Year Built: 1985
AD: Debra P. Warren
SID: Dave Caspole

HARVARD
Cambridge, MA 02138 ....FCS

Coach: Tim Murphy, Springfield 1978
Record: 20 Years, 112-94-1

2006 RESULTS (7-3)
31 Holy Cross ■ 14
38 Brown 21
35 Lehigh 33
33 Cornell ■ 23
24 Lafayette ■ 7
28 Princeton 31
28 Dartmouth 0
24 Columbia ■ 7
13 Penn 22
13 Yale ■ 34

Nickname: Crimson
Colors: Crimson, Black & White
Stadium: Harvard
Capacity: 30,898; Year Built: 1903
AD: Robert L. Scalise
SID: Chuck Sullivan

HAWAII
Honolulu, HI 96822-2370 ....FBS

Coach: June Jones, Portland St. 1977
Record: 8 Years, 64-40-0

2006 RESULTS (11-3)
17 Alabama 25
42 UNLV ■ 13
34 Boise St. 41
44 Eastern Ill. ■ 9
41 Nevada ■ 34
68 Fresno St. 37
49 New Mexico St. 30
68 Idaho ■ 10
63 Utah St. 10
61 Louisiana Tech ■ 17
54 San Jose St. ■ 17
42 Purdue ■ 35
32 Oregon St. ■ 35
41 Arizona St. ■ 24

Nickname: Rainbow Warriors
Colors: Green, Black, Silver & White
Stadium: Aloha
Capacity: 50,000; Year Built: 1975
AD: Herman R. Frazier
SID: Lois Manin

HEIDELBERG
Tiffin, OH 44883-2462 III

Coach: Brian Cochran, John Carroll 1990
Record: 4 Years, 1-39-0

2006 RESULTS (0-10)
34 Oberlin 48
7 John Carroll 42
7 Capital ■ 65
0 Mount Union 58
10 Baldwin-Wallace 36
6 Otterbein ■ 34
14 Wilmington (Ohio) ■ 21
17 Marietta 32
3 Ohio Northern ■ 47
12 Muskingum 28

Nickname: Berg
Colors: Red, Orange & Black
Stadium: Frost-Kalnow
Capacity: 7,500; Year Built: 1941
AD: Jerry McDonald
SID: Morgan Hawley

HENDERSON ST.
Arkadelphia, AR 71999-0001 II

Coach: Scott Maxfield, Louisiana Tech 1984
Record: 2 Years, 11-11-0

2006 RESULTS (8-3)

6 Central Ark. * 39
31 Pikeville 9
16 Delta St. ■ 13
31 West Ala. 10
16 West Ga. ■ 9
33 Ark.-Monticello 17
6 Arkansas Tech 7
71 Paul Quinn ■ 19
28 Harding 34
48 Ouachita Baptist ■ 28
24 Southern Ark. ■ 6

Nickname: Reddies
Colors: Red & Gray
Stadium: Carpenter-Haygood
Capacity: 9,600; Year Built: 1968
AD: Sam Goodwin
SID: Troy Mitchell

HILLSDALE

Hillsdale, MI 49242-1298 II

Coach: Keith Otterbein, Hillsdale 1979
Record: 14 Years, 82-72-3

2006 RESULTS (5-6)

35 Gannon 7
24 Northern Mich. ■ 31
24 Ashland 30
29 Ferris St. ■ 27
12 Michigan Tech 14
14 Indianapolis ■ 13
26 Wayne St. (Mich.) 41
40 Mercyhurst ■ 21
14 Tiffin 24
10 Findlay ■ 7
30 Saginaw Valley 46

Nickname: Chargers
Colors: Royal Blue & White
Stadium: Frank "Muddy" Waters Field
Capacity: 8,500; Year Built: 1973
AD: Michael J. Kovalchik
SID: Brad Monastiere

HIRAM

Hiram, OH 44234-0067 III

Coach: Mike Lazusky, Shippensburg 1994
Record: 3 Years, 1-29-0

2006 RESULTS (0-10)

6 Carnegie Mellon ■ 27
7 Bethany (W.V.) 42
7 Allegheny 52
14 Oberlin ■ 28
34 Kenyon 69
0 Wooster ■ 52
7 Denison ■ 42
16 Earlham 24
0 Ohio Wesleyan 58
0 Wittenberg ■ 35

Nickname: Terriers
Colors: Blue & Red
Stadium: Charles Henry Field
Capacity: 2,000; Year Built: 1961
AD: Thomas E. Mulligan
SID: Jeff Hoedt

HOBART

Geneva, NY 14456 III

Coach: Mike Cragg, Slippery Rock 1983
Record: 12 Years, 81-39-0

2006 RESULTS (8-2)

31 Dickinson ■ 28
31 Wm. Paterson 27
24 Rensselaer 17
19 WPI ■ 14
30 Merchant Marine 19
27 St. Lawrence 7
21 Alfred 14
14 Union (N.Y.) ■ 31
31 Rochester ■ 21
18 Rowan 20

Nickname: Statesmen
Colors: Royal Purple & Orange
Stadium: Boswell Field
Capacity: 4,500; Year Built: 1975
AD: Michael J. Hanna
SID: Ken DeBolt

HOFSTRA

Hempstead, NY 11549 ....FCS

Coach: Dave Cohen, C.W. Post 1988
Record: 1 Year, 2-9-0

2006 RESULTS (2-9)

17 Stony Brook 8
31 Marshall 54
30 Towson ■ 33
16 William & Mary 14
16 Villanova ■ 20
6 Delaware 10
10 Maine 21
6 New Hampshire 10
13 Rhode Island ■ 20
24 Northeastern ■ 34
16 Massachusetts 22

Nickname: Pride
Colors: Gold, White & Blue
Stadium: James M. Shuart
Capacity: 15,000; Year Built: 1963
AD: Jack W. Hayes
SID: Jim Sheehan

HOLY CROSS

Worcester, MA 01610-2395 ....FCS

Coach: Tom Gilmore, Penn 1986
Record: 3 Years, 16-17-0

2006 RESULTS (7-4)

26 Georgetown 13
14 Northeastern ■ 24
14 Harvard 31
27 Marist 0
28 Fordham ■ 21
35 Brown ■ 30
24 Dartmouth 21
38 Lafayette 28
14 Lehigh ■ 28
27 Bucknell ■ 10
28 Colgate 29

Nickname: Crusaders
Colors: Royal Purple
Stadium: Fitton Field
Capacity: 23,500; Year Built: 1924
AD: Richard M. Regan Jr.
SID: Charles Bare

HOPE

Holland, MI 49422-9000 III

Coach: Dean Kreps, Monmouth (Ill.) 1984
Record: 12 Years, 67-49-0

2006 RESULTS (7-4)

13 Central (Iowa) 24
14 DePauw 23
21 Wheaton (Ill.) ■ 35
24 Albion ■ 21
49 Alma 43
45 Kalamazoo ■ 7
28 Adrian ■ 20
21 Tri-State 7
16 Olivet 8
26 Wis. Lutheran ■ 7
0 Mount Union 49

Nickname: Flying Dutchmen
Colors: Orange & Blue
Stadium: Holland Municipal
Capacity: 5,322; Year Built: 1979
AD: Raymond E. Smith
SID: Tom Renner

HOUSTON

Houston, TX 77204 ....FBS

Coach: Art Briles, Texas Tech 1979
Record: 4 Years, 26-24-0

2006 RESULTS (10-4)

31 Rice 30
45 Tulane ■ 7
42 Grambling ■ 22
34 Oklahoma St. ■ 25
13 Miami (Fla.) 14
28 La.-Lafayette ■ 31
27 Southern Miss. 31
34 UTEP ■ 17
51 UCF ■ 31
27 Tulsa ■ 10
37 SMU 27
23 Memphis 20
34 Southern Miss. ■ 20
36 South Carolina * 44

Nickname: Cougars
Colors: Scarlet & White with Navy Trim
Stadium: John O'Quinn/Robertson
Capacity: 31,784; Year Built: 1942
AD: Dave Maggard
SID: Chris Burkhalter

HOWARD

Washington, DC 20059 ....FCS

Coach: Rayford Petty, Elon 1979
Record: 5 Years, 25-30-0

2006 RESULTS (5-6)

7 Hampton 46
23 Florida A&M ■ 31
7 Rutgers 56
34 Fort Valley St. ■ 19
0 Winston-Salem 12
12 Morgan St. ■ 18
26 N.C. A&T 0
13 Norfolk St. ■ 10
10 South Carolina St. 28
28 Bethune-Cookman 0
20 Delaware St. ■ 17

Nickname: Bison
Colors: Blue, White & Red
Stadium: Greene
Capacity: 8,890; Year Built: 1986
AD: Dwight F. Datcher
SID: Edward Hill

HOWARD PAYNE

Brownwood, TX 76801 III

Coach: Mike Redwine, Mid-America Nazarene 1987
Record: 12 Years, 65-60-2

2006 RESULTS (5-5)

7 Southern Nazarene 0
24 East Tex. Baptist ■ 17
16 Paul Quinn 9
56 Sul Ross St. 60
23 Texas Lutheran ■ 28
21 McMurry 25
23 Hardin-Simmons ■ 42
47 Louisiana Col. 45
30 Mississippi Col. ■ 15
7 Mary Hardin-Baylor 55

Nickname: Yellow Jackets
Colors: Navy Blue & Old Gold
Stadium: Gordon Wood
Capacity: 7,600; Year Built: 1962
AD: Mike Jones
SID: Abram Choate

HUMBOLDT ST.

Arcata, CA 95521-8299 II

Coach: Doug Adkins, Central Wash. 1970
Record: 7 Years, 31-43-0

2006 RESULTS (9-1)

28 Western Wash. ■ 23
0 Central Wash. ■ 20
48 Dixie St. 28
30 Southern Ore. ■ 13
29 Western Ore. 21
31 Azusa Pacific 24
45 Dixie St. ■ 7
55 Texas Col. 21
35 Southern Ore. 17
23 Western Ore. ■ 20

Nickname: Lumberjacks
Colors: Green & Gold
Stadium: Redwood Bowl
Capacity: 7,000; Year Built: 1946
AD: Dan Collen
SID: Dan Pambianco

HUNTINGDON

Montgomery, AL 36106 III

Coach: Mike Turk, Troy 1987
Record: 3 Years, 17-11-0

2006 RESULTS (6-4)

12 Ithaca 31
44 Sewanee ■ 24
35 Millsaps 34
21 Rhodes 7
17 Wesley ■ 38
13 Trinity (Tex.) ■ 24
21 Colorado Col. 14
9 Thomas More 20
35 LaGrange ■ 0
42 Southwestern Assemblies of God 17

Nickname: Hawks
Colors: Scarlet Red, White & Pearl Gray
Stadium: W. James Samford Jr.
Capacity: 2,500; Year Built: 2004
AD: Hugh Phillips
SID: Tim Lutz

HUSSON

Bangor, ME 04401 III

Coach: Gabby Price, Maine 1973
Record: 4 Years, 11-23-0

2006 RESULTS (6-4)

14 Pace 27
21 Utica ■ 7
14 Norwich 13
20 Hartwick ■ 19
12 Mount Ida 13
16 Springfield ■ 43
27 Maritime (N.Y.) 19
7 Alfred ■ 24
17 La Salle ■ 7
28 Becker 3

Nickname: Eagles
Colors: Green, White & Gold
Stadium: John Winkin Sports Complex
Capacity: 3,000; Year Built: 2003
AD: Jonathan Price
SID: Warren Caruso

IDAHO

Moscow, ID 83844-2302 ....FBS

Coach: Dennis Erickson, Montana St. 1969
Record: 18 Years, 149-64-1

2006 RESULTS (4-8)

17 Michigan St. 27
10 Washington St. 56
27 Idaho St. ■ 24
0 Oregon St. 38
41 Utah St. 21
28 New Mexico St. ■ 20
24 Louisiana Tech 14
26 Boise St. ■ 42
10 Hawaii 68
7 Nevada ■ 45
0 Fresno St. 34
13 San Jose St. ■ 28

Nickname: Vandals
Colors: Silver & Gold
Stadium: Kibbie Dome
Capacity: 16,000; Year Built: 1975
AD: Robert Spear
SID: Becky Paull

IDAHO ST.

Pocatello, ID 83209-8173 ....FCS

Coach: Larry Lewis, Boise St. 1981
Record: 8 Years, 39-50-0

2006 RESULTS (2-9)

10 UNLV 54
48 Fort Lewis ■ 12
24 Idaho 27
27 Northern Ariz. ■ 33
41 Northern Colo. 13
13 Portland St. 34
35 Montana St. ■ 42
10 Montana 23
14 Sacramento St. ■ 22
6 Eastern Wash. 40
27 Weber St. ■ 30

Nickname: Bengals
Colors: Orange & Black
Stadium: Holt Arena
Capacity: 12,000; Year Built: 1970
AD: Paul A. Bubb
SID: Frank Mercogliano

ILLINOIS

Champaign, IL 61820 ....FBS

Coach: Ron Zook, Miami (Ohio) 1976
Record: 5 Years, 27-33-0

2006 RESULTS (2-10)

42 Eastern Ill. ■ 17
0 Rutgers 33
21 Syracuse ■ 31
7 Iowa ■ 24
23 Michigan St. 20
32 Indiana ■ 34
17 Ohio ■ 20
12 Penn St. 26
24 Wisconsin 30
10 Ohio St. ■ 17
31 Purdue ■ 42
16 Northwestern 27

Nickname: Fighting Illini
Colors: Orange & Blue
Stadium: Memorial
Capacity: 69,249; Year Built: 1923
AD: Ronald E. Guenther
SID: Kent Brown

ILLINOIS COL.

Jacksonville, IL 62650-2299 III

Coach: Aaron Keen, Washington-St. Louis 1995
Record: 4 Years, 19-21-0

2006 RESULTS (6-4)

20 Millikin ■ 24
34 Knox ■ 13
14 Lake Forest 11
21 Ripon 31
21 Lawrence ■ 20
21 Carroll (Wis.) ■ 16
30 Beloit 20
33 Grinnell 13
7 Monmouth (Ill.) ■ 17
0 St. Norbert 49

Nickname: Blueboys
Colors: Blue & White
Stadium: England Field
Capacity: 2,500; Year Built: 1960
AD: Gale F. Vaughn
SID: James T. Murphy

ILLINOIS ST.

Normal, IL 61790-2660 ....FCS

Coach: Denver Johnson, Tulsa 1981
Record: 10 Years, 62-51-0

2006 RESULTS (9-4)

23 Kansas St. 24
18 Central Ark. ■ 3
44 Eastern Ill. ■ 30
35 Murray St. 14
28 Western Ky. 27
37 Southern Ill. ■ 10
27 Western Ill. 14
13 Youngstown St. ■ 27
38 Missouri St. ■ 14
42 Indiana St. 20
27 UNI 38
24 Eastern Ill. 13
21 Youngstown St. 28

Nickname: Redbirds
Colors: Red & White
Stadium: Hancock
Capacity: 15,000; Year Built: 1967
AD: Sheahon Zenger
SID: Todd Kober

ILL. WESLEYAN

Bloomington, IL 61702-2900 III

Coach: Norm Eash, Ill. Wesleyan 1975
Record: 20 Years, 119-70-1

2006 RESULTS (3-7)

21 Coe ■ 34
21 Olivet ■ 6
7 Mt. St. Joseph 28
7 Augustana (Ill.) 24
28 Carthage ■ 31
12 Millikin 6
13 Elmhurst 25
44 North Park ■ 0
21 North Central (Ill.) ■ 47
14 Wheaton (Ill.) 49

Nickname: Titans
Colors: Green & White
Stadium: Illinois Wesleyan
Capacity: 3,500; Year Built: 1893
AD: Dennis Bridges
SID: Stew Salowitz

INDIANA

Bloomington, IN 47408-1590 ....FBS

Coach: Terry Hoeppner, Franklin 1969
Record: 8 Years, 57-39-0

2006 RESULTS (5-7)

39 Western Mich. ■ 20
24 Ball St. 23
28 Southern Ill. ■ 35
7 Connecticut ■ 14
17 Wisconsin ■ 52
34 Illinois 32
31 Iowa ■ 28
3 Ohio St. 44
46 Michigan St. ■ 21
26 Minnesota 63
3 Michigan ■ 34
19 Purdue 28

Nickname: Hoosiers
Colors: Cream & Crimson
Stadium: Memorial
Capacity: 52,354; Year Built: 1960
AD: Richard I. Greenspan
SID: Pete Rhoda

INDIANA (PA.)

Indiana, PA 15705-1077 II

Coach: Lou Tepper, Rutgers 1967
Record: 13 Years, 73-59-2

2006 RESULTS (8-2)

33 Cheyney 6
35 East Stroudsburg ■ 20
14 Millersville 17
23 Edinboro 20
23 Lock Haven ■ 14
33 Clarion ■ 7
20 Shippensburg 16
42 Mansfield ■ 6
17 Slippery Rock ■ 21
21 California (Pa.) 17

Nickname: Crimson Hawks
Colors: Crimson & Gray
Stadium: George P. Miller
Capacity: 6,500; Year Built: 1962
AD: Frank J. Condino
SID: Mike Hoffman

INDIANA ST.

Terre Haute, IN 47809 ....FCS

Coach: Lou West, Cincinnati 1977
Record: 2 Years, 1-21-0

2006 RESULTS (1-10)

35 Purdue 60
21 Eastern Ill. 31
40 Murray St. ■ 59
14 Northern Ill. 48
3 Southern Ill. 55
17 Youngstown St. 55
14 UNI ■ 34
28 Missouri St. ■ 22
3 Western Ky. 41
41 Western Ill. 46
20 Illinois St. ■ 42

Nickname: Sycamores
Colors: Royal Blue & White
Stadium: Memorial
Capacity: 12,764; Year Built: 1970
AD: Ron Prettyman
SID: Ace Hunt

INDIANAPOLIS

Indianapolis, IN 46227-3697 II

Coach: Joe Polizzi, Hillsdale 1976
Record: 13 Years, 69-71-1

2006 RESULTS (6-5)

20 Northern Mich. 27
34 Michigan Tech ■ 31
49 Gannon 14
35 St. Joseph's (Ind.) ■ 22
34 Findlay ■ 16
13 Hillsdale 14
7 Grand Valley St. ■ 33
39 Wayne St. (Mich.) 14
16 Saginaw Valley 23
45 Mercyhurst ■ 19
0 Northwood (Mich.) ■ 23

Nickname: Greyhounds
Colors: Crimson & Grey
Stadium: Key
Capacity: 5,500; Year Built: 1971
AD: Sue Willey
SID: Mitchell Wigness

IONA

New Rochelle, NY 10801 ....FCS

Coach: Fred Mariani, St. Joseph's (Ind.) 1974
Record: 9 Years, 36-56-0

2006 RESULTS (3-7)

7 Montclair St. ■ 21
3 Wagner 7
16 Sacred Heart 27
20 Western Conn. St. ■ 21
24 Stonehill ■ 7
0 Columbia 24
28 La Salle ■ 0
17 Duquesne 13
15 St. Peter's ■ 30
17 Marist 24

Nickname: Gaels
Colors: Maroon & Gold
Stadium: Mazzella Field
Capacity: 1,200; Year Built: 1989
AD: Patrick Lyons
SID: Mike Laprey

IOWA

Iowa City, IA 52242 ....FBS

Coach: Kirk Ferentz, Connecticut 1978
Record: 11 Years, 67-64-0

2006 RESULTS (6-7)

41 Montana ■ 7
20 Syracuse 13
27 Iowa St. ■ 17
24 Illinois 7
17 Ohio St. ■ 38
47 Purdue ■ 17
28 Indiana 31
6 Michigan 20
24 Northern Ill. ■ 14
7 Northwestern ■ 21
21 Wisconsin ■ 24
24 Minnesota 34
24 Texas * 26

Nickname: Hawkeyes
Colors: Black & Gold
Stadium: Kinnick
Capacity: 70,397; Year Built: 1929
AD: Gary Barta
SID: Phil Haddy

IOWA ST.

Ames, IA 50011 ....FBS

Coach: Dan McCarney, Iowa 1975
Record: 12 Years, 56-85-0

2006 RESULTS (4-8)

45 Toledo ■ 43
16 UNLV ■ 10
17 Iowa 27
14 Texas 37
28 UNI ■ 27
14 Nebraska ■ 28
9 Oklahoma 34
26 Texas Tech ■ 42
10 Kansas St. 31
10 Kansas ■ 41
16 Colorado 33
21 Missouri ■ 16

Nickname: Cyclones
Colors: Cardinal & Gold
Stadium: Jack Trice
Capacity: 55,000; Year Built: 1975
AD: Jamie Pollard
SID: Tom Kroeschell

ITHACA

Ithaca, NY 14850 III

Coach: Michael Welch, Ithaca 1973
Record: 13 Years, 104-37-0

2006 RESULTS (7-3)

31 Huntingdon ■ 12
45 Buffalo St. ■ 7
44 Hartwick ■ 14
10 St. John Fisher 34
26 Brockport St. 7
44 Norwich 7
33 Utica ■ 7
24 Springfield ■ 7
17 Alfred 28
20 Cortland St. 23

Nickname: Bombers
Colors: Blue & Gold
Stadium: Jim Butterfield
Capacity: 5,000; Year Built: 1958
AD: Ken Kutler
SID: Mike Warwick

JACKSON ST.

Jackson, MS 39217 ....FCS

Coach: Rick Comegy, Millersville 1976
Record: 15 Years, 114-56-0

2006 RESULTS (6-5)

44 Paul Quinn ■ 20
30 Tennessee St. * 31
29 Mississippi Val. ■ 24
29 Texas Southern 5
19 Alabama St. * 13
31 Southern U. ■ 28
7 Grambling 36
40 Ark.-Pine Bluff 43
21 Alabama A&M ■ 34
31 Prairie View ■ 7
31 Alcorn St. * 32

Nickname: Tigers
Colors: Royal Blue & White
Stadium: Mississippi Memorial
Capacity: 62,512; Year Built: 1949
AD: Robert L. Braddy Sr.
SID: Wesley Peterson

JACKSONVILLE

Jacksonville, FL 32211-3394 ....FCS

Coach: Steve Gilbert, West Chester 1979
Record: 18 Years, 76-102-0

2006 RESULTS (4-6)

14 Gardner-Webb ■ 49
13 Southeastern La. 41
31 Butler 7
34 Valparaiso 17
3 Davidson 38
28 Dayton ■ 21
28 Morehead St. 24
6 North Greenville 41
21 San Diego ■ 38
28 Drake ■ 47

Nickname: Dolphins
Colors: Green & White
Stadium: Milne Field
Capacity: 5,000; Year Built: 1997
AD: C. Alan Verlander
SID: Joel Lamp

JACKSONVILLE ST.

Jacksonville, AL 36265-1602 ....FCS

Coach: Jack Crowe, UAB 1970
Record: 12 Years, 57-64-0

2006 RESULTS (6-5)

13 Furman 17
38 Southeast Mo. St. ■ 7
14 Tenn.-Martin 24
28 Eastern Ky. 0
49 Murray St. ■ 17
3 Mississippi St. 35
31 Tennessee St. ■ 38
17 Tennessee Tech 10

13 Chattanooga 10
55 Samford ■ 7
24 Eastern Ill. 28

Nickname: Gamecocks
Colors: Red & White
Stadium: Paul Snow
Capacity: 15,000; Year Built: 1947
AD: Jim Fuller
SID: Greg Seitz

JAMES MADISON

Harrisonburg, VA 22807 ....FCS

Coach: Mickey Matthews, West Tex. A&M 1976
Record: 8 Years, 56-40-0

2006 RESULTS (9-3)

14 Bloomsburg ■ 3
10 Appalachian St. 21
52 Northeastern ■ 14
45 VMI 7
35 Rhode Island ■ 23
42 New Hampshire 23
31 William & Mary ■ 17
27 Richmond 10
44 Delaware ■ 24
20 Villanova 21
38 Towson 3
31 Youngstown St. 35

Nickname: Dukes
Colors: Purple & Gold
Stadium: Bridgeforth
Capacity: 15,000; Year Built: 1974
AD: Jeffrey T. Bourne
SID: Gary Michael

JOHN CARROLL

University Heights, OH 44118-4581 III

Coach: Regis Scafe, Case Reserve 1971
Record: 13 Years, 74-60-0

2006 RESULTS (5-5)

22 Wooster 30
42 Heidelberg ■ 7
9 Ohio Northern ■ 23
8 Baldwin-Wallace 24
21 Capital ■ 24
20 Marietta 7
38 Muskingum 0
35 Wilmington (Ohio) ■ 0
14 Mount Union 31
14 Otterbein ■ 0

Nickname: Blue Streaks
Colors: Blue & Gold
Stadium: Don Shula Stadium at Wasmer Field
Capacity: 5,000; Year Built: 2003
AD: Laurie Massa
SID: Chris Wenzler

JOHNS HOPKINS

Baltimore, MD 21218-2684 III

Coach: Jim Margraff, Johns Hopkins 1982
Record: 17 Years, 107-63-3

2006 RESULTS (5-5)

10 Rochester ■ 20
21 Randolph-Macon 14
20 St. Lawrence 21
13 Dickinson ■ 21
14 Frank. & Marsh. 7
18 Gettysburg 23
10 Muhlenberg ■ 7
7 Ursinus 17
24 Hampden-Sydney ■ 10
48 McDaniel ■ 7

Nickname: Blue Jays
Colors: Columbia Blue & Black
Stadium: Homewood Field
Capacity: 8,500; Year Built: 1906
AD: Thomas P. Calder
SID: Ernie Larossa

JOHNSON C. SMITH

Charlotte, NC 28216 II

Coach: Daryl McNeill, South Carolina St. 1982
Record: 6 Years, 27-36-0

2006 RESULTS (7-4)

19 Edward Waters * 14
23 Glenville St. 20
13 Bowie St. ■ 14
40 Virginia Union 37
13 St. Paul's 7
19 Livingstone 0
9 St. Augustine's ■ 15
10 Fayetteville St. ■ 7
27 Savannah St. ■ 6
7 N.C. Central 52
7 Tuskegee * 17

Nickname: Golden Bulls
Colors: Gold & Blue
Stadium: Irwin Belk Complex/Memorial
Capacity: 4,500/26,000; Year Built: 2003/1990
AD: Stephen W. Joyner
SID: Kristene Kelly

JUNIATA

Huntingdon, PA 16652 III

Coach: Darrell Alt, Frostburg St. 1996
Record: 3 Years, 3-27-0

2006 RESULTS (2-8)

0 Dickinson 14
15 Lycoming ■ 20
14 Lebanon Valley 26
14 Moravian ■ 33
14 Albright 48
34 Susquehanna ■ 9
7 King's (Pa.) 23
13 Widener ■ 35
0 Delaware Valley 21
39 FDU-Florham ■ 31

Nickname: Eagles
Colors: Yale Blue & Old Gold
Stadium: Chuck Knox
Capacity: 3,000; Year Built: 1988
AD: Lawrence R. Bock
SID: Joel Cookson

KALAMAZOO

Kalamazoo, MI 49006-3295 III

Coach: Terrance Brooks, Towson 1991
Record: 2 Years, 6-13-0

2006 RESULTS (2-7)

14 Austin 17
14 Bluffton 17
14 Adrian 35
33 Tri-State ■ 30
7 Hope 45
31 Wis. Lutheran ■ 19
13 Albion 21
35 Alma ■ 37
24 Olivet ■ 43

Nickname: Hornets
Colors: Orange & Black
Stadium: Angell Field
Capacity: 3,000; Year Built: 1946
AD: Timon Corwin
SID: Steve Wideen

KANSAS

Lawrence, KS 66045-8881 ....FBS

Coach: Mark Mangino, Youngstown St. 1987
Record: 5 Years, 25-35-0

2006 RESULTS (6-6)

49 Northwestern St. ■ 18
21 La.-Monroe ■ 19
31 Toledo 37
13 South Fla. ■ 7
32 Nebraska 39
18 Texas A&M ■ 21
32 Oklahoma St. ■ 42
35 Baylor 36
20 Colorado ■ 15
41 Iowa St. 10
39 Kansas St. ■ 20
17 Missouri 42

Nickname: Jayhawks
Colors: Crimson & Blue
Stadium: Memorial
Capacity: 50,071; Year Built: 1921
AD: Lew Perkins
SID: Mason Logan

KANSAS ST.

Manhattan, KS 66502-3355 ....FBS

Coach: Ron Prince, Appalachian St. 1992
Record: 1 Year, 7-6-0

2006 RESULTS (7-6)

24 Illinois St. ■ 23
45 Fla. Atlantic ■ 0
23 Marshall ■ 7
6 Louisville ■ 24
3 Baylor 17
31 Oklahoma St. ■ 27
3 Nebraska ■ 21
21 Missouri 41
31 Iowa St. ■ 10
34 Colorado 21
45 Texas ■ 42
20 Kansas 39
10 Rutgers * 37

Nickname: Wildcats
Colors: Purple & White
Stadium: Bill Snyder Family
Capacity: 50,000; Year Built: 1968
AD: Tim Weiser
SID: Garry Bowman

KEAN

Union, NJ 07083 III

Coach: Dan Garrett, Montclair St. 1997
Record: 1 Year, 7-4-0

2006 RESULTS (7-4)

19 Merchant Marine 29
21 Frank. & Marsh. 13
37 Morrisville St. 7
50 Buffalo St. ■ 30
14 Cortland St. 24
19 Montclair St. ■ 13
12 Rowan 16
20 Wm. Paterson ■ 17
34 Western Conn. St. ■ 6
10 TCNJ 14
37 King's (Pa.) ■ 0

Nickname: Cougars
Colors: Blue & White
Stadium: Kean Alumni
Capacity: 5,300; Year Built: 1998
AD: Glenn Hedden
SID: Karyn Pinter

KENT ST.

Kent, OH 44242-0001 ....FBS

Coach: Doug Martin, Kentucky 1985
Record: 3 Years, 12-22-0

2006 RESULTS (6-6)

0 Minnesota ■ 44
14 Army 17
16 Miami (Ohio) 14
38 Bowling Green 3
37 Akron ■ 15

28 Temple 17
40 Toledo ■ 14
7 Ohio ■ 17
14 Buffalo 41
0 Virginia Tech 23
14 Eastern Mich. ■ 6
6 Ball St. 30

Nickname: Golden Flashes
Colors: Navy Blue & Gold
Stadium: Dix
Capacity: 29,287; Year Built: 1969
AD: Laing E. Kennedy
SID: Jeff Schaefer

KENTUCKY

Lexington, KY 40506-0032 ....FBS

Coach: Rich Brooks, Oregon St. 1963
Record: 22 Years, 108-139-4

2006 RESULTS (8-5)

28 Louisville 59
41 Texas St. ■ 7
31 Mississippi ■ 14
7 Florida 26
45 Central Mich. ■ 36
17 South Carolina ■ 24
0 LSU 49
34 Mississippi St. 31
24 Georgia ■ 20
38 Vanderbilt ■ 26
42 La.-Monroe ■ 40
12 Tennessee 17
28 Clemson * 20

Nickname: Wildcats
Colors: Blue & White
Stadium: Commonwealth
Capacity: 67,530; Year Built: 1973
AD: Mitch S. Barnhart
SID: Tony Neely

KENTUCKY ST.

Frankfort, KY 40601 II

Coach: Frederick T. Farrier, Holy Cross 1994
Record: 2 Years, 13-9-0

2006 RESULTS (7-4)

21 Ky. Wesleyan 7
13 Ferris St. ■ 31
7 Albany St. (Ga.) ■ 21
34 Morehouse 31
22 Clark Atlanta ■ 9
31 Lane ■ 14
5 Benedict 13
21 Miles 20
5 Stillman 26
19 Fort Valley St. ■ 16
30 Central St. (Ohio) * 27

Nickname: Thorobreds
Colors: Green & Gold
Stadium: Alumni Field
Capacity: 6,000; Year Built: 1978
AD: Derita Ratcliffe
SID: Ron Braden

KY. WESLEYAN

Owensboro, KY 42302-1039 II

Coach: Brent Holsclaw, Ky. Wesleyan 1993
Record: 4 Years, 8-34-0

2006 RESULTS (0-11)

7 Kentucky St. ■ 21
13 West Va. Wesleyan ■ 31
24 West Liberty St. 31
0 Western Ill. 58
10 Lincoln (Mo.) 22
13 Glenville St. ■ 21
10 Tiffin 29
34 North Greenville ■ 44
3 St. Joseph's (Ind.) ■ 41
15 Central St. (Ohio) 34
6 Mo.-Rolla 62

Nickname: Panthers
Colors: Purple & White
Stadium: Steele
Capacity: 3,000; Year Built: 2004
AD: Gary Gallup
SID: Roy Pickerill

KENYON

Gambier, OH 43022-9223 III

Coach: Ted Stanley, Grinnell 1993
Record: 4 Years, 14-26-0

2006 RESULTS (4-6)

57 Grinnell 31
10 Claremont-M-S 34
13 Case Reserve 43
44 Ohio Wesleyan 42
69 Hiram ■ 34
38 Allegheny 49
33 Earlham ■ 30
35 Denison 41
42 Oberlin ■ 56
13 Wooster ■ 41

Nickname: Lords
Colors: Purple & White
Stadium: McBride Field
Capacity: 2,300; Year Built: 1962
AD: Peter Smith
SID: Marty Fuller

KING'S (PA.)

Wilkes-Barre, PA 18711-0801 III

Coach: Richard Mannello, Springfield 1983
Record: 14 Years, 64-81-1

2006 RESULTS (6-5)

0 St. John Fisher 30
10 Lebanon Valley ■ 0
28 Moravian 23
38 Albright ■ 14
14 Susquehanna 3
23 Juniata ■ 7
20 Widener 25
0 Delaware Valley ■ 10
21 FDU-Florham 17
7 Wilkes ■ 28
0 Kean 37

Nickname: Monarchs
Colors: Red & Gold
Stadium: Robert L. Betzler Fields
Capacity: 3,000; Year Built: 1993
AD: Cheryl J. Ish
SID: Bob Ziadie

KNOX

Galesburg, IL 61401-4999 III

Coach: Andy Gibbons, Culver Stockton 1990
Record: 11 Years, 41-66-0

2006 RESULTS (2-8)

23 Eureka ■ 0
13 Illinois Col. 34
14 Ripon ■ 35
32 Beloit 22
27 St. Norbert ■ 42
34 Grinnell 35
6 Lawrence ■ 8
20 Carroll (Wis.) 24
12 Lake Forest ■ 19
6 Monmouth (Ill.) 41

Nickname: Prairie Fire
Colors: Purple & Gold
Stadium: Knox Bowl
Capacity: 6,000; Year Built: 1968
AD: Chad Eisele
SID: Brian Thiessen

KUTZTOWN

Kutztown, PA 19530-0721 II

Coach: Raymond Monica, North Ala. 1990
Record: 1 Year, 4-6-0

2006 RESULTS (4-6)

27 Clarion ■ 10
27 Shippensburg 42
10 Slippery Rock ■ 34
17 Millersville ■ 45
51 Mansfield ■ 7
14 Bloomsburg 41
47 West Chester ■ 49
28 Cheyney 6
30 Lock Haven 10
16 East Stroudsburg 56

Nickname: Golden Bears
Colors: Maroon & Gold
Stadium: University Field
Capacity: 5,600; Year Built: 1987
AD: Greg Bamberger
SID: Josh Leiboff

LA SALLE

Philadelphia, PA 19141-1199 ....FCS

Coach: Tim Miller, Temple 1988
Record: 1 Year, 3-7-0

2006 RESULTS (3-7)

15 Wagner ■ 38
21 TCNJ ■ 24
2 Ursinus 6
24 St. Francis (Pa.) 21
13 Marist ■ 41
27 Catholic 14
0 Iona 28
7 Husson ■ 17
0 Duquesne ■ 38
37 St. Peter's 28

Nickname: Explorers
Colors: Blue & Gold
Stadium: McCarthy
Capacity: 7,500; Year Built: 1936
AD: Thomas M. Brennan
SID: Kale Beers

LA VERNE

La Verne, CA 91750-4443 III

Coach: Don Morel, La Verne 1987
Record: 12 Years, 48-59-0

2006 RESULTS (3-6)

21 Puget Sound ■ 28
16 Whitworth 37
12 Cal Lutheran 55
20 Pomona-Pitzer ■ 19
14 Occidental ■ 49
27 Whittier 14
19 Redlands ■ 24
21 Claremont-M-S 14
12 Chapman 35

Nickname: Leopards, Leos
Colors: Orange & Green
Stadium: Ortmayer
Capacity: 1,500; Year Built: 1991
AD: Christopher M. Ragsdale
SID: Will Darity

LAFAYETTE

Easton, PA 18042 ....FCS

Coach: Frank Tavani, Lebanon Valley 1975
Record: 7 Years, 38-42-0

2006 RESULTS (6-6)

25 Sacred Heart 14
31 Bucknell 0

11 Penn ■ ... 21
14 Princeton ... 26
34 Yale ■ ... 37
7 Harvard ... 24
28 Holy Cross ■ ... 38
27 Colgate ... 10
31 Fordham ... 24
45 Georgetown ■ ... 14
49 Lehigh ■ ... 27
14 Massachusetts ... 35

Nickname: Leopards
Colors: Maroon & White
Stadium: Fisher Field
Capacity: 13,000; Year Built: 1926
AD: Bruce McCutcheon
SID: Phil LaBella

LAGRANGE

LaGrange, GA 30240 ... III

Coach: Todd Mooney, Ohio 1988
Record: 1 Year, 0-10-0

2006 RESULTS (0-10)

7 Maryville (Tenn.) ... 47
0 Rhodes ■ ... 37
0 Shorter ■ ... 54
21 Bridgewater (Va.) ... 58
7 Louisiana Col. ... 50
21 Washington-St. Louis ■ ... 31
0 Mississippi Col. ... 33
27 Brevard ■ ... 35
0 Huntingdon ... 35
10 Centre ■ ... 41

Nickname: Panthers
Colors: Red & Black
Stadium: Callaway
AD: Philip R. Williamson
SID: John Hughes

LAKE FOREST

Lake Forest, IL 60045 ... III

Coach: Brent Becker, Knox 1997
Record: 2 Years, 9-11-0

2006 RESULTS (5-5)

6 Washington-St. Louis ■ ... 21
27 Ripon ... 35
11 Illinois Col. ■ ... 14
7 St. Norbert ... 14
23 Beloit ■ ... 0
6 Lawrence ... 22
21 Grinnell ■ ... 14
12 Monmouth (Ill.) ... 8
19 Knox ... 12
21 Carroll (Wis.) ■ ... 14

Nickname: Foresters
Colors: Red & Black
Stadium: Farwell Field
Capacity: 2,000; Year Built: 1903
AD: Jackie A. Slaats
SID: Mike Wajerski

LAKELAND

Sheboygan, WI 53082-0359 ... III

Coach: Jim Zebrowski, Mount Union 1991
Record: 4 Years, 28-13-0

2006 RESULTS (5-5)

14 Wis.-Whitewater ... 75
14 Carthage ■ ... 21
10 Wis.-Oshkosh ■ ... 31
28 Greenville ■ ... 13
14 Benedictine (Ill.) ■ ... 0
45 Eureka ... 6
24 MacMurray ... 16
18 Concordia (Wis.) ■ ... 30
34 Concordia (Ill.) ... 0
20 Aurora ... 25

Nickname: Muskies
Colors: Navy & Gold
Stadium: John Taylor Field
Capacity: 1,500; Year Built: 1958
AD: Jane Bouche
SID: David Gallianetti

LANE

Jackson, TN 38301-4598 ... II

Coach: Johnnie Cole, Texas Southern 1986
Record: 2 Years, 8-13-0

2006 RESULTS (8-3)

36 Lincoln (Mo.) ... 0
20 St. Augustine's ... 16
48 Morehouse ... 31
27 Concordia-Selma ■ ... 20
23 Clark Atlanta ■ ... 15
24 Stillman ... 21
14 Kentucky St. ... 31
21 Miles ■ ... 20
27 Fort Valley St. ■ ... 41
17 Benedict ■ ... 12
28 Tuskegee ... 42

Nickname: Dragons
Colors: Cardinal Red & Royal Blue
Stadium: Rothrock
Capacity: 3,500; Year Built: 1930
AD: Ronald Abernathy
SID: Greg Bormann

LAWRENCE

Appleton, WI 54912-0599 ... III

Coach: Chris Howard, Wis.-Stevens Point 1983
Record: 2 Years, 9-10-0

2006 RESULTS (5-5)

21 Minn.-Morris ... 8
6 Monmouth (Ill.) ... 49
14 St. Norbert ■ ... 42
45 Grinnell ■ ... 18
20 Illinois Col. ... 21
22 Lake Forest ■ ... 6
8 Knox ... 6
13 Beloit ■ ... 7
6 Carroll (Wis.) ... 37
14 Ripon ■ ... 31

Nickname: Vikings
Colors: Blue & White
Stadium: Banta Bowl
Capacity: 5,255; Year Built: 1965
AD: Robert Beeman
SID: Joe Vanden Acker

LEBANON VALLEY

Annville, PA 17003-1400 ... III

Coach: Jim Monos, Shippensburg 1972
Record: 14 Years, 54-83-2

2006 RESULTS (6-4)

13 Gettysburg ■ ... 12
0 King's (Pa.) ... 10
26 Juniata ■ ... 14
14 Widener ... 31
18 Delaware Valley ■ ... 19
29 FDU-Florham ... 19
10 Wilkes ■ ... 13
15 Lycoming ... 9
55 Moravian ■ ... 21
55 Albright ... 33

Nickname: Flying Dutchmen
Colors: Blue & White
Stadium: Arnold Field
Capacity: 4,000; Year Built: 1969
AD: Kathleen Tierney
SID: Braden Snyder

LEHIGH

Bethlehem, PA 18015-3089 ... FCS

Coach: Andy Coen, Gettysburg 1986
Record: 1 Year, 6-5-0

2006 RESULTS (6-5)

16 Albany (N.Y.) ■ ... 17
31 Villanova ... 28
10 Princeton ■ ... 14
33 Harvard ■ ... 35
28 Georgetown ... 3
20 Yale ... 26
38 Bucknell ■ ... 7
28 Holy Cross ... 14
23 Colgate ■ ... 15
45 Fordham ■ ... 14
27 Lafayette ... 49

Nickname: Mountain Hawks
Colors: Brown & White
Stadium: Goodman
Capacity: 16,000; Year Built: 1988
AD: Joseph D. Sterrett
SID: Mike Stagnitta

LENOIR-RHYNE

Hickory, NC 28603 ... II

Coach: Wayne Hicks, Jacksonville St. 1984
Record: 5 Years, 17-35-0

2006 RESULTS (3-8)

17 Livingstone ■ ... 14
16 N.C. Central ... 38
14 Davidson ■ ... 24
17 Benedict ... 0
13 Presbyterian ... 24
10 Tusculum ■ ... 17
21 Wingate ... 27
3 Carson-Newman ... 21
31 Mars Hill ■ ... 7
21 Newberry ... 45
24 Catawba ■ ... 32

Nickname: Bears
Colors: Red & Black
Stadium: Moretz
Capacity: 8,500; Year Built: 1923
AD: Neill McGeachy
SID: John Karrs

LEWIS & CLARK

Portland, OR 97219-7899 ... III

Coach: Chris Sulages, Weber St. 1995
Record: 1 Year, 0-9-0

2006 RESULTS (0-9)

7 Occidental ... 49
20 Pomona-Pitzer ■ ... 38
3 Colorado Col. ... 46
28 Menlo ■ ... 38
3 Whitworth ... 70
14 Puget Sound ... 70
7 Pacific Lutheran ■ ... 44
14 Willamette ... 61
0 Linfield ■ ... 40

Nickname: Pioneers
Colors: Orange & Black
Stadium: Griswold
Capacity: 3,600; Year Built: 1953
AD: Clark Yeager
SID: Melissa Dudek

LIBERTY

Lynchburg, VA 24502-2269 ... FCS

Coach: Danny Rocco, Wake Forest 1984
Record: 1 Year, 6-5-0

2006 RESULTS (6-5)

27 St. Paul's ■ ... 0
31 Glenville St. ■ ... 7

3 Towson 10
28 Savannah St. 0
14 Wake Forest 34
13 William & Mary ■ 14
24 Gardner-Webb ■ 27
26 Coastal Caro. 28
21 Western Caro. ■ 0
34 Charleston So. ■ 20
38 VMI 32

Nickname: Flames
Colors: Red, White & Blue
Stadium: Williams
Capacity: 12,000; Year Built: 1989
AD: Jeff Barber
SID: Todd Wetmore

LINCOLN (MO.)

Jefferson City, MO 65102-0029 II

Coach: Lemar Parrish, Lincoln (Mo.) 1995
Record: 2 Years, 3-15-0

2006 RESULTS (1-8)

0 Lane ■ 36
0 Central Mo. ■ 78
0 West Virginia St. 16
7 Mo.-Rolla ■ 49
22 Ky. Wesleyan ■ 10
10 Millsaps 52
3 St. Joseph's (Ind.) ■ 60
7 Langston 76
8 Tiffin 62

Nickname: Blue Tigers
Colors: Navy Blue & White
Stadium: Dwight T. Reed
Capacity: 5,600; Year Built: 1972
AD: Tim Abney
SID: Jeremy Copeland

LINFIELD

McMinnville, OR 97128-6894 III

Coach: Joe Smith, Linfield 1993
Record: 1 Year, 6-3-0

2006 RESULTS (6-3)

14 Western Ore. ■ 28
6 Hardin-Simmons 21
42 Willamette ■ 14
42 Puget Sound 17
37 Southern Ore. ■ 29
44 Pacific Lutheran 21
21 Menlo ■ 3
13 Whitworth ■ 17
40 Lewis & Clark 0

Nickname: Wildcats
Colors: Purple & Red
Stadium: Maxwell Field
Capacity: 4,000; Year Built: 1928
AD: Scott Carnahan
SID: Kelly Bird

LIVINGSTONE

Salisbury, NC 28144 II

Coach: Robert Massey, N.C. Central 1989
Record: 2 Years, 2-18-0

2006 RESULTS (1-9)

14 Lenoir-Rhyne 17
0 Elizabeth City St. ■ 26
6 Catawba ■ 35
12 Virginia Union 14
7 Bowie St. * 3
14 Shaw ■ 18
0 Johnson C. Smith ■ 19
16 St. Augustine's 31
15 N.C. Central ■ 37
16 Fayetteville St. 34

Nickname: Blue Bears
Colors: Columbia Blue & Black
Stadium: Alumni Memorial
Capacity: 6,000; Year Built: 1960
AD: Clifton Huff
SID: Adrian Ferguson

LOCK HAVEN

Lock Haven, PA 17745 II

Coach: John Klacik, Lock Haven 1988
Record: 2 Years, 4-18-0

2006 RESULTS (2-9)

0 Southern Ill. 49
14 East Stroudsburg 45
0 Millersville ■ 35
24 Mansfield 21
7 California (Pa.) 51
14 Indiana (Pa.) 23
17 Shippensburg ■ 20
0 Slippery Rock 35
14 Clarion ■ 7
10 Kutztown ■ 30
25 Edinboro ■ 51

Nickname: Bald Eagles
Colors: Crimson & White
Stadium: Hubert Jack
Capacity: 3,000; Year Built: 1975
AD: Sharon E. Taylor
SID: Al Weston

LORAS

Dubuque, IA 52004-0178 III

Coach: Steve Osterberger, Drake 1990
Record: 7 Years, 36-34-0

2006 RESULTS (4-6)

15 St. Ambrose ■ 17
7 St. Thomas (Minn.) 19
23 Dubuque ■ 20
32 Coe 30
21 Cornell College ■ 14
14 Wartburg 19
10 Buena Vista ■ 20
7 Central (Iowa) 44
17 Simpson 27
44 Luther ■ 23

Nickname: Duhawks
Colors: Purple & Gold
Stadium: Rock Bowl
Capacity: 3,500; Year Built: 1945
AD: Chad Walthall
SID: Tim Calderwood

LA.-LAFAYETTE

Lafayette, LA 70506 ....FBS

Coach: Rickey Bustle, Clemson 1976
Record: 5 Years, 23-35-0

2006 RESULTS (6-6)

3 LSU 45
7 Texas A&M 51
48 N.C. A&T ■ 7
33 Eastern Mich. ■ 14
31 Houston 28
6 Fla. Atlantic 0
20 Middle Tenn. ■ 34
28 Troy 42
7 North Texas ■ 16
17 Florida Int'l 7
28 Arkansas St. ■ 13
20 La.-Monroe ■ 39

Nickname: Ragin' Cajuns
Colors: Vermilion & White
Stadium: Cajun Field
Capacity: 31,000; Year Built: 1971
AD: David Walker
SID: Daryl Cetnar

LA.-MONROE

Monroe, LA 71209-3000 ....FBS

Coach: Charlie Weatherbie, Oklahoma St. 1977
Record: 14 Years, 60-95-0

2006 RESULTS (4-8)

24 Alcorn St. ■ 6
19 Kansas 21
7 Alabama 41
19 Fla. Atlantic ■ 21
6 Arkansas St. 10
19 Troy 24
21 Middle Tenn. ■ 35
10 Arkansas * 44
35 Florida Int'l 0
40 Kentucky 42
23 North Texas ■ 3
39 La.-Lafayette 20

Nickname: Warhawks
Colors: Maroon & Gold
Stadium: Malone
Capacity: 30,427; Year Built: 1978
AD: Bobby Staub
SID: Judy Willson

LOUISIANA COL.

Pineville, LA 71360-0001 III

Coach: Dennis Dunn, Centenary (La.)
Record: 1 Year, 4-5-0

2006 RESULTS (4-5)

41 Millsaps 38
12 McMurry 23
50 LaGrange ■ 7
31 Mississippi Col. 28
7 Mary Hardin-Baylor ■ 56
29 East Tex. Baptist * 32
45 Howard Payne ■ 47
35 Sul Ross St. 28
22 Texas Lutheran ■ 24

Nickname: Wildcats
Colors: Orange & Blue
Stadium: D.C. Bates
Capacity: 7,500; Year Built: 2000
AD: Tim Whitman
SID: Alex Goodling

LSU

Baton Rouge, LA 70893 ....FBS

Coach: Les Miles, Michigan 1976
Record: 6 Years, 50-25-0

2006 RESULTS (11-2)

45 La.-Lafayette ■ 3
45 Arizona ■ 3
3 Auburn 7
49 Tulane ■ 7
48 Mississippi St. ■ 17
10 Florida 23
49 Kentucky ■ 0
38 Fresno St. ■ 6
28 Tennessee 24
28 Alabama ■ 14
23 Mississippi ■ 20
31 Arkansas 26
41 Notre Dame * 14

Nickname: Fighting Tigers
Colors: Purple & Gold
Stadium: Tiger
Capacity: 92,400; Year Built: 1924
AD: Skip Bertman
SID: Michael Bonnette

LOUISIANA TECH

Ruston, LA 71272 ....FBS

Coach: Jack Bicknell III, Boston College 1984
Record: 8 Years, 43-52-0

2006 RESULTS (3-10)

10 Nebraska 49
31 Nicholls St. ■ 21
14 Texas A&M 45
0 Clemson 51
14 Boise St. 55
14 Idaho ■ 24
48 Utah St. ■ 35
10 San Jose St. 44
34 North Texas 31
17 Hawaii 61
0 Nevada ■ 42
27 Fresno St. ■ 34
23 New Mexico St. 50

Nickname: Bulldogs
Colors: Red & Blue
Stadium: Joe Aillet
Capacity: 30,600; Year Built: 1968
AD: Jim M. Oakes
SID: Malcolm Butler

LOUISVILLE

Louisville, KY 40292 ....FBS

Coach: Bobby Petrino, Carroll (Mont.) 1983
Record: 4 Years, 41-9-0

2006 RESULTS (12-1)

59 Kentucky ■ 28
62 Temple 0
31 Miami (Fla.) ■ 7
24 Kansas St. 6
44 Middle Tenn. * 17
23 Cincinnati ■ 17
28 Syracuse 13
44 West Virginia ■ 34
25 Rutgers 28
31 South Fla. ■ 8
48 Pittsburgh 24
48 Connecticut ■ 17
24 Wake Forest * 13

Nickname: Cardinals
Colors: Red, Black & White
Stadium: Papa John's Cardinal
Capacity: 42,000; Year Built: 1998
AD: Thomas M. Jurich
SID: Rocco Gasparro

LUTHER

Decorah, IA 52101-1045............................III

Coach: Paul Hefty, Luther 1986
Record: 5 Years, 24-26-0

2006 RESULTS (2-8)

60 Martin Luther 0
16 St. Olaf 35
10 Coe ■ 16
17 Wartburg 28
34 Dubuque ■ 51
13 Central (Iowa) ■ 19
27 Buena Vista 30
21 Simpson 28
37 Cornell College ■ 6
23 Loras 44

Nickname: Norse
Colors: Blue & White
Stadium: Carlson
Capacity: 5,000; Year Built: 1966
AD: Joe Thompson
SID: Dave Blanchard

LYCOMING

Williamsport, PA 17701-5192.....................III

Coach: Frank Girardi, West Chester 1961
Record: 35 Years, 254-90-5

2006 RESULTS (4-5)

20 Juniata 15
15 Widener ■ 12
16 Delaware Valley 17
23 FDU-Florham ■ 14
7 Wilkes 37
9 Lebanon Valley ■ 15
3 Moravian 22
35 Albright ■ 42
28 Susquehanna 14

Nickname: Warriors
Colors: Blue & Gold
Stadium: David Person Field
Capacity: 3,700; Year Built: 1962
AD: Frank L. Girardi
SID: James Nekoloff

MACALESTER

St. Paul, MN 55105 III

Coach: Glenn Caruso, Ithaca 1996
Record: 1 Year, 2-7-0

2006 RESULTS (2-7)

0 Beloit 10
50 Principia ■ 6
0 Carleton 52
7 Chicago ■ 34
7 Hamline 35
35 Colorado Col. 56
0 Gust. Adolphus ■ 51
34 Crown (Minn.) ■ 21
14 Menlo ■ 44

Nickname: Scots
Colors: Orange & Blue
Stadium: Macalester
Capacity: 4,000; Year Built: 1965
AD: Travis Feezell
SID: Andy Johnson

MACMURRAY

Jacksonville, IL 62650-2590 III

Coach: Brandon McCray, Lakeland 1997
Record: 4 Years, 19-21-0

2006 RESULTS (3-7)

7 Augustana (Ill.) ■ 53
0 Rockford 22
13 Aurora ■ 27
7 Concordia (Wis.) 47
46 Concordia (Ill.) ■ 41
16 Lakeland ■ 24
20 Greenville 34
8 Benedictine (Ill.) ■ 12
48 Eureka 30
34 Blackburn 6

Nickname: Highlanders
Colors: Scarlet & Navy
Stadium: Freesen Field
Capacity: 3,000; Year Built: 2003
AD: Kevin Haslam
SID: Kevin Vest

MAINE

Orono, ME 04469-5747 ....FCS

Coach: Jack Cosgrove, Maine 1978
Record: 14 Years, 78-80-0

2006 RESULTS (6-5)

14 Youngstown St. 34
20 William & Mary 17
62 Shaw ■ 12
0 Boston College 22
28 Towson 7
20 Villanova ■ 7
21 Hofstra ■ 10
0 Rhode Island 3
30 Northeastern ■ 3
9 Massachusetts 10
13 New Hampshire ■ 19

Nickname: Black Bears
Colors: Blue & White
Stadium: Morse Field at Alfond Stadium
Capacity: 10,000; Year Built: 1998
AD: Blake James
SID: Doug DeBiase

MAINE MARITIME

Castine, ME 04420 III

Coach: Christopher McKenney, Springfield 1984
Record: 6 Years, 20-35-0

2006 RESULTS (6-3)

33 Becker ■ 14
26 Western New Eng. 28
21 Bridgewater St. ■ 28
14 Westfield St. 11
12 Worcester St. 3
21 Mass. Maritime * 19
40 Framingham St. 24
0 Coast Guard ■ 3
21 Fitchburg St. ■ 13

Nickname: Mariners
Colors: Royal Blue & Gold
Stadium: Ritchie
Capacity: 3,500; Year Built: 1965
AD: James Dyer
SID: David Patterson

MANCHESTER

North Manchester, IN 46962 III

Coach: Shannon Griffith, Ball St. 1989
Record: 3 Years, 3-27-0

2006 RESULTS (1-9)

26 Tri-State 22
35 Earlham ■ 49
14 Olivet 33
7 Defiance ■ 19
9 Bluffton 14
14 Hanover ■ 32
12 Mt. St. Joseph 34
15 Franklin ■ 31
3 Rose-Hulman ■ 34
16 Anderson (Ind.) 19

Nickname: Spartans
Colors: Black & Gold
Stadium: Carl W. Burt Memorial
Capacity: 4,500
AD: Tom Jarman
SID: Doug Shoemaker

MANSFIELD

Mansfield, PA 16933..................................II

Coach: Jim Shiffer, Mansfield 1990
Record: 3 Years, 2-29-0

2006 RESULTS (0-10)

0 Shippensburg ■ 35
0 Slippery Rock 46
21 Lock Haven ■ 24
7 East Stroudsburg ■ 61
7 Kutztown 51
6 Cheyney 26
7 Bloomsburg ■ 31
6 Indiana (Pa.) 42
0 West Chester 44
0 Millersville ■ 41

Nickname: Mountaineers
Colors: Red & Black
Stadium: Van Norman Field
Capacity: 4,000; Year Built: 1964
AD: Roger N. Maisner
SID: Steve McCloskey

MARANATHA BAPTIST

Watertown, WI 53094-0000 III

Coach: Terry Price, Pillsbury 1971
Record: 30 Years, 131-154-1

2006 RESULTS (6-3)

26 Trinity Bible (N.D.)..........19
25 Crown (Minn.) ■..........0
6 Rockford..........16
55 Principia..........13
6 Minn.-Morris..........28
6 Westminster (Mo.) ■..........8
34 Blackburn ■..........7
43 Crown (Minn.) *..........12
14 Martin Luther ■..........7

Nickname: Crusaders
Colors: Navy Blue & Gold
Stadium: Maranatha
Capacity: 1,200; Year Built: 1972
AD: Robert Thompson
SID: Robert Thompson

MARIETTA

Marietta, OH 45750 III

Coach: Curt Wiese, Minn. St. Mankato 1999
Record: 1 Year, 6-4-0

2006 RESULTS (6-4)

28 Emory & Henry..........20
37 Baldwin-Wallace ■..........31
24 Otterbein..........27
10 Capital..........52
30 Muskingum ■..........10
7 John Carroll ■..........20
16 Ohio Northern..........6
32 Heidelberg ■..........17
27 Wilmington (Ohio)..........14
17 Mount Union ■..........45

Nickname: Pioneers
Colors: Navy Blue & White
Stadium: Don Drumm
Capacity: 7,000; Year Built: 1916
AD: Debora Lazorik
SID: Dan May

MARIST

Poughkeepsie, NY 12601-1387...............FCS

Coach: Jim Parady, Maine 1984
Record: 15 Years, 82-69-1

2006 RESULTS (4-7)

6 Central Conn. St...........34
28 Sacred Heart ■..........19
7 Wagner ■..........38
0 Holy Cross ■..........27
19 Bucknell ■..........48
41 La Salle..........13
9 Fordham..........13
10 Duquesne..........40
35 St. Peter's ■..........18
21 Georgetown..........24
24 Iona ■..........17

Nickname: Red Foxes
Colors: Red & White
Stadium: Leonidoff Field
Capacity: 2,500; Year Built: 1972
AD: Timothy S. Murray
SID: Jason Corriher

MARITIME (N.Y.)

Throggs Neck, NY 10465...........................III

Coach: Clayton Kendrick-Holmes, Navy 1992
Record: 1 Year, 1-6-0

2006 RESULTS (1-6)

15 Salve Regina..........21
41 Norwich ■..........41
6 Morrisville St...........20
19 Husson ■..........27
0 Apprentice..........41
29 Becker ■..........16
21 Mount Ida..........27

Nickname: Privateers
Colors: Maritime Blue & Privateer Red
Stadium: Reinhart Field
Capacity: 2,000; Year Built: 1956
AD: William E. Martinov Jr.
SID: To be named

MARS HILL

Mars Hill, NC 28754 II

Coach: Tim Clifton, Mercer 1976
Record: 14 Years, 75-72-0

2006 RESULTS (4-7)

38 Greensboro..........13
55 Brevard..........0
0 Appalachian St...........41
14 St. Augustine's ■..........7
25 Catawba ■..........7
7 Carson-Newman..........10
0 Newberry ■..........37
14 Presbyterian ■..........21
7 Lenoir-Rhyne..........31
17 Tusculum ■..........24
14 Wingate..........37

Nickname: Lions
Colors: Royal Blue & Gold
Stadium: Meares
Capacity: 5,000; Year Built: 1965
AD: David Riggins
SID: Rick Baker

MARSHALL

Huntington, WV 25755 ....FBS

Coach: Mark Snyder, Marshall 1988
Record: 2 Years, 9-14-0

2006 RESULTS (5-7)

10 West Virginia..........42
54 Hofstra ■..........31
7 Kansas St...........23
7 Tennessee..........33
22 UCF ■..........23
21 SMU..........31
31 UAB..........24
41 Memphis ■..........27
42 Tulane ■..........21
20 East Caro...........33
49 UTEP ■..........21
7 Southern Miss...........42

Nickname: Thundering Herd
Colors: Green & White
Stadium: Joan C. Edwards
Capacity: 38,019; Year Built: 1991
AD: Robert K. (Bob) Marcum
SID: Randy Burnside

MARTIN LUTHER

New Ulm, MN 56073-3965 III

Coach: Douglas Lange, Northwestern (Minn.) 1978
Record: 2 Years, 8-11-0

2006 RESULTS (2-8)

0 Luther ■..........60
17 Waldorf..........24
34 Blackburn..........7
7 Crown (Minn.) ■..........14
34 Trinity Bible (N.D.)..........0
19 Northwestern (Minn.) ■..........20
6 Minn.-Morris..........35
6 Rockford ■..........27
17 Blackburn *..........21
7 Maranatha Baptist..........14

Nickname: Knights
Colors: Black, Red & White
Stadium: MLC Bowl
Capacity: 1,500; Year Built: 1974
AD: James M. Unke
SID: Dan Lewig

MARY HARDIN-BAYLOR

Belton, TX 76513..III

Coach: Pete Fredenburg, Texas St. 1970
Record: 9 Years, 75-25-0

2006 RESULTS (10-3)

10 Chris. Newport..........15
45 Sul Ross St...........2
31 Texas Lutheran ■..........9
38 McMurry..........15
28 Hardin-Simmons ■..........16
56 Louisiana Col...........7
41 Mississippi Col. ■..........14
3 Wis.-Whitewater ■..........7
33 East Tex. Baptist..........28
55 Howard Payne ■..........7
33 Hardin-Simmons ■..........21
30 Wash. & Jeff. ■..........27
20 Wesley..........34

Nickname: Crusaders
Colors: Purple, Gold & White
Stadium: Tiger Field
Capacity: 7,000; Year Built: 1996
AD: Ben Shipp
SID: Jon Wallin

MARYLAND

College Park, MD 20742.........................FBS

Coach: Ralph Friedgen, Maryland 1969
Record: 6 Years, 50-24-0

2006 RESULTS (9-4)

27 William & Mary ■..........14
24 Middle Tenn. ■..........10
24 West Virginia..........45
14 Florida Int'l ■..........10
23 Georgia Tech..........27
28 Virginia..........26
26 North Carolina St. ■..........20
27 Florida St. ■..........24
13 Clemson..........12
14 Miami (Fla.) ■..........13
16 Boston College..........38
24 Wake Forest ■..........38
24 Purdue *..........7

Nickname: Terrapins, Terps
Colors: Red, White, Black & Gold
Stadium: Chevy Chase Bank Field at Byrd Stadium
Capacity: 51,500; Year Built: 1950
AD: Deborah A. Yow
SID: Shawn Nestor

MARYVILLE (TENN.)

Maryville, TN 37804-5907 III

Coach: Tony Ierulli, Maryville (Tenn.) 1980
Record: 4 Years, 15-25-0

2006 RESULTS (5-5)

47 LaGrange ■..........7
14 Centre ■..........17

36 Greensboro 39
8 Sewanee 16
50 N.C. Wesleyan ■ 48
20 Ferrum 14
31 Chris. Newport ■ 48
30 Methodist 26
51 Shenandoah ■ 16
44 Averett 58

Nickname: Scots
Colors: Orange & Garnet
Stadium: Lloyd L. Thorton-Honaker Field
Capacity: 3,000; Year Built: 1993
AD: Randall D. Lambert
SID: Eric Etchison

MASSACHUSETTS

Amherst, MA 01003 ....FCS

Coach: Don Brown, Norwich 1977
Record: 10 Years, 78-37-0

2006 RESULTS (13-2)

28 Colgate ■ 7
20 Navy 21
31 Villanova 21
48 Stony Brook ■ 7
48 William & Mary ■ 7
35 Towson 0
41 Rhode Island ■ 16
7 Northeastern 0
28 New Hampshire 20
10 Maine ■ 9
22 Hofstra ■ 16
35 Lafayette ■ 14
24 New Hampshire ■ 17
19 Montana 17
17 Appalachian St. * 28

Nickname: Minutemen
Colors: Maroon & White
Stadium: Warren P. McGuirk Alumni
Capacity: 17,000; Year Built: 1965
AD: John F. McCutcheon
SID: Jason Yellin

MASS.-DARTMOUTH

North Dartmouth, MA 02747-2300 III

Coach: Bill Kavanaugh, Stonehill 1972
Record: 17 Years, 104-64-0

2006 RESULTS (5-4)

15 Bridgewater St. 7
26 Fitchburg St. ■ 33
13 Plymouth St. 27
41 MIT ■ 10
37 Western New Eng. 7
17 Salve Regina ■ 7
28 Nichols 14
0 Endicott 28
34 Curry ■ 43

Nickname: Corsairs
Colors: Blue, White & Gold
Stadium: Cressy Field
Capacity: 1,850; Year Built: 1986
AD: Louise Goodrum
SID: Dave Geringer

MIT

Cambridge, MA 02139 III

Coach: Dwight Smith, Bates 1975
Record: 19 Years, 58-103-1

2006 RESULTS (2-7)

0 Mass. Maritime ■ 19
21 Framingham St. 14
19 Nichols ■ 33
10 Mass.-Dartmouth 41
13 Curry 49
25 Western New Eng. ■ 42
40 Salve Regina 25
3 Plymouth St. ■ 35
16 Endicott ■ 21

Nickname: Engineers
Colors: Cardinal Red & Silver Gray
Stadium: Henry G. Steinbrenner
Capacity: 1,600; Year Built: 1980
AD: John A. Benedick
SID: James Kramer

MASS. MARITIME

Buzzards Bay, MA 02532 III

Coach: Jeremy Cameron, Springfield 1997
Record: 2 Years, 3-15-0

2006 RESULTS (3-6)

19 MIT 0
0 Endicott ■ 34
26 Worcester St. 24
0 Coast Guard 41
15 Westfield St. ■ 13
19 Maine Maritime * 21
0 Fitchburg St. ■ 33
6 Framingham St. ■ 14
19 Bridgewater St. 34

Nickname: Buccaneers
Colors: Blue & Gold
Stadium: Commander Edward Ellis
Capacity: 3,000; Year Built: 1972
AD: Robert Corradi
SID: Leroy Thompson

McDANIEL

Westminster, MD 21157-4390 III

Coach: Tim Keating, Bethany (W.V.) 1975
Record: 19 Years, 121-71-3

2006 RESULTS (4-6)

0 Bridgewater (Va.) ■ 41
7 Seton Hill ■ 17
14 Catholic 13
0 Ursinus 20
17 Gettysburg ■ 14
17 Dickinson ■ 24
24 Randolph-Macon ■ 14
7 Frank. & Marsh. 31
22 Muhlenberg ■ 19
7 Johns Hopkins 48

Nickname: Green Terror
Colors: Green & Gold
Stadium: Scott S. Bair
Capacity: 4,000; Year Built: 1981
AD: James M. Smith
SID: Luke Stillson

McMURRY

Abilene, TX 79697 III

Coach: Joe Crousen, Sul Ross St. 1963
Record: 2 Years, 8-12-0

2006 RESULTS (3-7)

0 Menlo 14
23 Austin 0
23 Louisiana Col. ■ 12
26 Mississippi Col. 36
15 Mary Hardin-Baylor ■ 38
24 East Tex. Baptist 41
25 Howard Payne ■ 21
15 Sul Ross St. 34
14 Texas Lutheran ■ 35
13 Hardin-Simmons 42

Nickname: Indians
Colors: Maroon & White
Stadium: Indian
Capacity: 4,500; Year Built: 1937
AD: Bill Libby
SID: Kyle Robarts

McNEESE ST.

Lake Charles, LA 70609 ....FCS

Coach: Matt Viator, McNeese St. 1986
Record: 1 Year, 6-2-0

2006 RESULTS (7-5)

10 South Fla. 41
76 West Va. Tech ■ 0
7 Toledo 41
17 South Dakota St. ■ 20
30 Southern Utah ■ 27
17 Texas St. ■ 27
20 Stephen F. Austin 17
31 Sam Houston St. 18
34 Southeastern La. ■ 13
29 Northwestern St. 26
26 Nicholls St. ■ 10
6 Montana 31

Nickname: Cowboys
Colors: Blue & Gold
Stadium: Cowboy
Capacity: 17,500; Year Built: 1965
AD: Sonny Watkins
SID: Louis Bonnette

MEMPHIS

Memphis, TN 38152-3370 ....FBS

Coach: Tommy West, Tennessee 1976
Record: 13 Years, 69-73-0

2006 RESULTS (2-10)

25 Mississippi 28
33 Chattanooga ■ 14
20 East Caro. 35
7 Tennessee ■ 41
29 UAB 35
23 Arkansas St. ■ 26
14 Tulsa ■ 35
27 Marshall 41
21 Southern Miss. ■ 42
24 UCF ■ 26
20 Houston ■ 23
38 UTEP 19

Nickname: Tigers
Colors: Blue & Gray
Stadium: Liberty Bowl
Capacity: 62,380; Year Built: 1965
AD: R.C. Johnson
SID: Jennifer Rodrigues

MENLO

Atherton, CA 94027-4185 III

Coach: Mark Kaanapu, Pacific (Ore.) 1991
Record: 6 Years, 25-33-0

2006 RESULTS (4-6)

14 McMurry ■ 0
13 Southern Ore. ■ 16
27 Chapman ■ 24
35 Willamette ■ 41
38 Lewis & Clark 28
10 Pacific Lutheran ■ 34
7 Whitworth ■ 26
3 Linfield 21
7 Puget Sound 48
44 Macalester 14

Nickname: Oaks
Colors: Navy & White
Stadium: Conner Field
Capacity: 1,000; Year Built: 1972
AD: Caitlin Collier
SID: Mindy Mills

MERCHANT MARINE

Kings Point, NY 11024-1699 III

Coach: Mike Toop, Merchant Marine 1977
Record: 6 Years, 23-36-0

2006 RESULTS (3-7)

29 Kean ■ 19
21 Coast Guard ■ 7
7 Dickinson 20
33 WPI ■ 14
20 Union (N.Y.) 28
24 Rochester 28
19 Hobart ■ 30
31 Rensselaer ■ 42
7 St. Lawrence 49
6 Grove City ■ 14

Nickname: Mariners
Colors: Blue & Gray
Stadium: Captain Tomb Field
Capacity: 5,840; Year Built: 1945
AD: Susan Petersen-Lubow
SID: Tyrone C. Broxton

MERCYHURST

Erie, PA 16546 II

Coach: Marty Schaetzle, Bucknell 1983
Record: 5 Years, 16-37-0

2006 RESULTS (3-7)

14 Northwood (Mich.) ■ 33
7 Ferris St. ■ 28
31 Wayne St. (Mich.) 35
35 Gannon ■ 14
21 Ashland 24
17 Grand Valley St. 49
24 Findlay ■ 7
21 Hillsdale 40
32 Northern Mich. ■ 7
19 Indianapolis 45

Nickname: Lakers
Colors: Blue & Green
Stadium: Louis J. Tullio Field
Capacity: 2,300; Year Built: 1996
AD: Peter J. Russo
SID: Jason Knavel

MERRIMACK

North Andover, MA 01845....II

Coach: Jim Murphy, Northeastern 1998
Record: 4 Years, 26-15-0

2006 RESULTS (8-4)

16 Stonehill 3
7 Rhode Island 42
7 Bryant 34
21 Bentley 24
35 Southern Conn. St. ■ 27
37 American Int'l ■ 13
52 St. Anselm 28
34 Assumption ■ 12
18 Pace 0
13 C.W. Post ■ 10
28 Southern Conn. St. ■ 26
7 Shepherd 31

Nickname: Warriors
Colors: Navy Blue & Gold
Stadium: Warrior Field
Capacity: 3,000; Year Built: 1996
AD: Sean T. Frazier
SID: Lisa Cascio

MESA ST.

Grand Junction, CO 81501 II

Coach: Joe Ramunno, Wyoming 1984
Record: 9 Years, 52-50-0

2006 RESULTS (4-7)

42 Dixie St. ■ 14
14 West Tex. A&M 44
9 Western N.M. 31
20 Fort Lewis ■ 35
0 Neb.-Kearney 27
6 Dixie St. 21
31 Western St. ■ 14
13 Adams St. 21
19 Chadron St. ■ 27
28 Colorado Mines 22
19 N.M. Highlands ■ 7

Nickname: Mavericks
Colors: Maroon, Gold & White
Stadium: Stocker
Capacity: 8,000; Year Built: 1949
AD: Jamie Hamilton
SID: Tish Elliott

METHODIST

Fayetteville, NC 28311-1420 III

Coach: Jim Sypult, West Virginia 1967
Record: 15 Years, 77-72-0

2006 RESULTS (4-6)

11 Guilford ■ 27
31 Chowan ■ 7
9 N.C. Wesleyan 15
16 Emory & Henry 8
25 Averett ■ 28
24 Ferrum ■ 14
0 Chris. Newport 21
26 Maryville (Tenn.) ■ 30
13 Greensboro ■ 17
9 Shenandoah 7

Nickname: Monarchs
Colors: Green & Gold
Stadium: Monarch Field
Capacity: 1,500; Year Built: 1989
AD: Bob McEvoy
SID: Lee Glenn

MIAMI (FLA.)

Coral Gables, FL 33146 ....FBS

Coach: Larry Coker, Northeastern St. 1970
Record: 6 Years, 60-15-0

2006 RESULTS (7-6)

10 Florida St. ■ 13
51 Florida A&M ■ 10
7 Louisville 31
14 Houston ■ 13
27 North Carolina ■ 7
35 Florida Int'l ■ 0
20 Duke 15
23 Georgia Tech 30
10 Virginia Tech ■ 17
13 Maryland 14
7 Virginia 17
17 Boston College ■ 14
21 Nevada * 20

Nickname: Hurricanes
Colors: Orange, Green & White
Stadium: Orange Bowl
Capacity: 72,319; Year Built: 1935
AD: Paul T. Dee
SID: Rick Korch

MIAMI (OHIO)

Oxford, OH 45056 ....FBS

Coach: Shane Montgomery, North Carolina St. 1990
Record: 2 Years, 9-14-0

2006 RESULTS (2-10)

3 Northwestern ■ 21
31 Purdue 38
14 Kent St. ■ 16
14 Syracuse 34
10 Cincinnati 24
25 Northern Ill. ■ 28
38 Buffalo 31
13 Akron 24
17 Ball St. ■ 20
24 Western Mich. 27
9 Bowling Green 7
24 Ohio ■ 34

Nickname: RedHawks
Colors: Red & White
Stadium: Fred C. Yager
Capacity: 24,286; Year Built: 1983
AD: Brad Bates
SID: Vince Frieden

MICHIGAN

Ann Arbor, MI 48109-2201 ....FBS

Coach: Lloyd Carr, Northern Mich. 1968
Record: 12 Years, 113-36-0

2006 RESULTS (11-2)

27 Vanderbilt ■ 7
41 Central Mich. ■ 17
47 Notre Dame 21
27 Wisconsin ■ 13
28 Minnesota 14
31 Michigan St. ■ 13
17 Penn St. 10
20 Iowa ■ 6
17 Northwestern ■ 3
34 Ball St. ■ 26
34 Indiana 3
39 Ohio St. 42
18 Southern California * 32

Nickname: Wolverines
Colors: Maize & Blue
Stadium: Michigan
Capacity: 107,501; Year Built: 1927
AD: William C. Martin
SID: David Ablauf

MICHIGAN ST.

East Lansing, MI 48824-1025 ....FBS

Coach: John L. Smith, Weber St. 1971
Record: 18 Years, 132-86-0

2006 RESULTS (4-8)

27 Idaho ■ 17
52 Eastern Mich. ■ 20
38 Pittsburgh 23
37 Notre Dame ■ 40
20 Illinois ■ 23
13 Michigan 31
7 Ohio St. ■ 38
41 Northwestern 38
21 Indiana 46
15 Purdue ■ 17
18 Minnesota ■ 31
13 Penn St. 17

Nickname: Spartans
Colors: Green & White
Stadium: Spartan
Capacity: 75,005; Year Built: 1957
AD: Ronald H. Mason
SID: John Lewandowski

MICHIGAN TECH

Houghton, MI 49931-1295 II

Coach: Tom Kearly, Winona St. 1979
Record: 1 Year, 6-4-0

2006 RESULTS (6-4)

14 Wayne St. (Mich.) ■ 36
31 Indianapolis 34
7 Northwood (Mich.) ■ 13
20 Grand Valley St. 41
14 Hillsdale ■ 12
41 Ferris St. 7

20 Saginaw Valley ■ 7
42 Northern Mich. ■ 14
14 Gannon 13
33 Findlay 15

Nickname: Huskies
Colors: Silver, Gold & Black
Stadium: Sherman Field
Capacity: 3,000; Year Built: 1981
AD: Suzanne R. Sanregret
SID: Wes Frahm

MIDDLE TENN.

Murfreesboro, TN 37132 ....FBS

Coach: Rick Stockstill, Florida St. 1982
Record: 1 Year, 7-6-0

2006 RESULTS (7-6)

7 Florida Int'l ■ 6
10 Maryland 24
44 Tennessee Tech ■ 0
0 Oklahoma 59
35 North Texas 0
17 Louisville * 44
35 La.-Monroe 21
34 La.-Lafayette 20
35 Fla. Atlantic ■ 14
38 Arkansas St. 10
7 South Carolina 52
20 Troy ■ 21
14 Central Mich. * 31

Nickname: Blue Raiders
Colors: Royal Blue & White
Stadium: Johnny "Red" Floyd
Capacity: 31,000; Year Built: 1933
AD: Chris Massaro
SID: Mark Owens

MIDDLEBURY

Middlebury, VT 05753 III

Coach: Bob Ritter, Middlebury 1982
Record: 6 Years, 25-23-0

2006 RESULTS (6-2)

10 Wesleyan (Conn.) ■ 7
23 Colby 0
7 Amherst ■ 3
9 Williams 40
31 Bates ■ 7
3 Trinity (Conn.) 34
10 Hamilton 0
10 Tufts ■ 0

Nickname: Panthers
Colors: Blue & White
Stadium: Alumni
Capacity: 3,500; Year Built: 1991
AD: Erin Quinn
SID: Brad Nadeau

MIDWESTERN ST.

Wichita Falls, TX 76308-2099 II

Coach: Bill Maskill, Western Ky. 1970
Record: 7 Years, 51-25-0

2006 RESULTS (10-3)

34 Langston ■ 26
31 Southwestern Okla. 10
73 Northeastern St. 34
63 East Central ■ 14
41 Angelo St. ■ 17
27 West Tex. A&M 29
17 Tarleton St. ■ 38
44 Tex. A&M-Kingsville 17
33 Southeastern Okla. ■ 23
29 Eastern N.M. ■ 19
46 Abilene Christian 30
28 Mo. Western St. ■ 26
0 Northwest Mo. St. 27

Nickname: Mustangs
Colors: Maroon & Gold
Stadium: Memorial
Capacity: 14,362; Year Built: 1970
AD: Kurt Portmann
SID: Bill Powers

MILES

Fairfield, AL 35064 II

Coach: Wade Streeter, Southern U. 1990
Record: 6 Years, 33-30-0

2006 RESULTS (5-5)

7 Samford 37
31 Tuskegee 20
15 Fort Valley St. ■ 7
21 Stillman ■ 14
24 Savannah St. 12
0 Albany St. (Ga.) 14
20 Lane 21
20 Kentucky St. ■ 21
38 Morehouse ■ 9
0 Clark Atlanta ■ 6

Nickname: Golden Bears
Colors: Purple & Gold
Stadium: Albert J. Sloan-Alumni
Capacity: 8,500; Year Built: 1910
AD: Augustus James
SID: Willie K. Patterson Jr.

MILLERSVILLE

Millersville, PA 17551-0302 II

Coach: Joe Trainer, Dickinson 1990
Record: 2 Years, 10-12-0

2006 RESULTS (5-6)

7 Shepherd ■ 28
22 Slippery Rock ■ 27
35 Lock Haven 0
17 Indiana (Pa.) ■ 14
45 Kutztown 17
19 East Stroudsburg ■ 30
27 West Chester 54
0 California (Pa.) 41
16 Bloomsburg ■ 28
48 Cheyney ■ 12
41 Mansfield 0

Nickname: Marauders
Colors: Black & Gold
Stadium: Chryst Field at Biemesderfer Stadium
Capacity: 6,500; Year Built: 1970
AD: Daniel N. Audette
SID: Paul Gornowski (Interim)

MILLIKIN

Decatur, IL 62522-2084 III

Coach: Doug Neibuhr, Millikin 1974
Record: 18 Years, 116-60-1

2006 RESULTS (3-7)

24 Illinois Col. 20
14 Ohio Northern ■ 28
31 Wabash 38
7 Wheaton (Ill.) ■ 20
36 North Park 6
6 Ill. Wesleyan ■ 12
18 North Central (Ill.) ■ 22
7 Carthage 16
22 Elmhurst 17
23 Augustana (Ill.) ■ 34

Nickname: Big Blue
Colors: Royal Blue & White
Stadium: Frank M. Lindsay Field
Capacity: 4,000; Year Built: 1987
AD: Lori Kerans
SID: Julie Farr

MILLSAPS

Jackson, MS 39210 III

Coach: Mike DuBose, Alabama 1974
Record: 5 Years, 31-27-0

2006 RESULTS (7-4)

28 Mississippi Col. ■ 52
38 Louisiana Col. ■ 41
34 Huntingdon ■ 35
52 Lincoln (Mo.) ■ 10
38 Centre ■ 12
26 Austin 11
31 DePauw ■ 7
35 Sewanee 18
14 Rhodes 6
34 Trinity (Tex.) ■ 12
0 Carnegie Mellon 21

Nickname: Majors
Colors: Purple & White
Stadium: Harper Davis Field
Capacity: 5,000; Year Built: 1920
AD: Tim Wise
SID: Kevin Maloney

MINNESOTA

Minneapolis, MN 55455 ....FBS

Coach: Glen Mason, Ohio St. 1972
Record: 21 Years, 123-121-1

2006 RESULTS (6-7)

44 Kent St. 0
17 California 42
62 Temple ■ 0
21 Purdue 27
14 Michigan ■ 28
27 Penn St. ■ 28
12 Wisconsin 48
10 North Dakota St. ■ 9
0 Ohio St. 44
63 Indiana ■ 26
31 Michigan St. 18
34 Iowa ■ 24
41 Texas Tech * 44

Nickname: Golden Gophers
Colors: Maroon & Gold
Stadium: Metrodome
Capacity: 63,669; Year Built: 1982
AD: Joel Maturi
SID: Shane Sandersfeld

MINN.-CROOKSTON

Crookston, MN 56716-5001 II

Coach: Shannon Stassen, Valley City St. 1995
Record: 5 Years, 5-48-0

2006 RESULTS (0-11)

0 St. Cloud St. 71
6 South Dakota 66
7 Southwest Minn. St. 28
7 Bemidji St. 56
0 Wayne St. (Neb.) ■ 28
7 Upper Iowa 56
0 Mary ■ 24
6 Northern St. 31
0 Winona St. 30
6 Minn. St. Moorhead ■ 32
0 Concordia-St. Paul * 49

Nickname: Golden Eagle
Colors: Maroon & Gold
Stadium: Ed Widseth Field
Capacity: 3,000; Year Built: 1966
AD: Stephanie Helgeson
SID: Mitch Bakken

MINN. DULUTH

Duluth, MN 55812-2496..............................II

Coach: Kyle Schweigert, Jamestown 1985
Record: 3 Years, 18-15-0

2006 RESULTS (6-4)

23 Bemidji St. 7
42 Mary ■ 14
14 South Dakota 27
31 Central Wash. ■ 25
20 Western Wash. 10
7 Augustana (S.D.) ■ 35
16 Minn. St. Mankato 13
14 Neb.-Omaha ■ 38
14 North Dakota 38
29 St. Cloud St. ■ 24

Nickname: Bulldogs
Colors: Maroon & Gold
Stadium: Griggs Field at James S. Malosky Stadium
Capacity: 4,000; Year Built: 1966
AD: Robert Nielson
SID: Bob Nygaard

MINN.-MORRIS
(Reclassifying to Div. III)

Morris, MN 56267......................................II

Coach: Ken Crandall, Fort Hays St. 1990
Record: 9 Years, 22-73-0

2006 RESULTS (7-3)

8 Lawrence ■ 21
14 Carleton ■ 50
62 Principia 6
67 Trinity Bible (N.D.) ■ 0
17 Northwestern (Minn.) 14
28 Maranatha Baptist ■ 6
35 Martin Luther ■ 6
29 Crown (Minn.) 18
27 Rockford * 20
21 Concordia-M'head * 41

Nickname: Cougars
Colors: Maroon & Gold
Stadium: Big Cat Stadium
Capacity: 2,500; Year Built: 2006
AD: Mark Fohl
SID: Brian Curtis

MINN. ST. MANKATO

Mankato, MN 56001..................................II

Coach: Jeff Jamrog, Nebraska 1987
Record: 3 Years, 12-21-0

2006 RESULTS (4-7)

34 Truman ■ 16
14 Northwest Mo. St. 31
33 Wis.-Oshkosh ■ 22
16 Augustana (S.D.) 21
14 Neb.-Omaha ■ 21
3 North Dakota 24
13 Minn. Duluth ■ 16
3 St. Cloud St. 16
44 South Dakota ■ 39
33 Central Wash. 17
21 Western Wash. ■ 35

Nickname: Mavericks
Colors: Purple & Gold
Stadium: Blakeslee
Capacity: 7,000; Year Built: 1962
AD: Kevin Buisman
SID: Paul Allan

MINN. ST. MOORHEAD

Moorhead, MN 56563-2996.......................II

Coach: Damon Tomeo, Pomona-Pitzer 1999
Record: 1 Year, 6-5-0

2006 RESULTS (6-5)

28 Concordia-M'head ■ 7
40 Mayville St. 10
9 Bemidji St. ■ 21
21 Wayne St. (Neb.) ■ 24
13 Upper Iowa 36
19 Winona St. 32
20 Concordia-St. Paul ■ 18
20 Mary 21
26 Northern St. ■ 15
32 Minn.-Crookston 6
22 Southwest Minn. St. * 20

Nickname: Dragons
Colors: Scarlet & White
Stadium: Alex Nemzek
Capacity: 5,000; Year Built: 1960
AD: Sylvia M. Barnier
SID: Larry Scott

MISSISSIPPI

University, MS 38677-1848.....................FBS

Coach: Ed Orgeron, Northwestern St. 1984
Record: 2 Years, 7-16-0

2006 RESULTS (4-8)

28 Memphis ■ 25
7 Missouri 34
14 Kentucky 31
3 Wake Forest ■ 27
9 Georgia ■ 14
17 Vanderbilt ■ 10
23 Alabama 26
3 Arkansas 38
17 Auburn ■ 23
27 Northwestern St. ■ 7
20 LSU 23
20 Mississippi St. ■ 17

Nickname: Rebels
Colors: Cardinal Red & Navy Blue
Stadium: Vaught-Hemingway
Capacity: 60,580; Year Built: 1915
AD: Pete Boone
SID: Langston Rogers

MISSISSIPPI COL.

Clinton, MS 39058....................................III

Coach: Norman Joseph, Mississippi St. 1977
Record: 6 Years, 28-33-0

2006 RESULTS (5-5)

52 Millsaps 28
28 Texas Lutheran 21
36 McMurry ■ 26
28 Hardin-Simmons 48
28 Louisiana Col. ■ 31
33 LaGrange ■ 0
14 Mary Hardin-Baylor 41
30 East Tex. Baptist ■ 35
15 Howard Payne 30
31 Sul Ross St. ■ 7

Nickname: Choctaws
Colors: Blue & Gold
Stadium: Robinson-Hale
Capacity: 8,500; Year Built: 1985
AD: Mike Jones
SID: Chris Brooks

MISSISSIPPI ST.

Mississippi State, MS 39762-5509...........FBS

Coach: Sylvester Croom, Alabama 1975
Record: 3 Years, 9-25-0

2006 RESULTS (3-9)

0 South Carolina ■ 15
0 Auburn ■ 34
29 Tulane ■ 32
16 UAB 10
17 LSU 48
14 West Virginia ■ 42
35 Jacksonville St. ■ 3
24 Georgia 27
31 Kentucky ■ 34
24 Alabama 16
14 Arkansas ■ 28
17 Mississippi 20

Nickname: Bulldogs
Colors: Maroon & White
Stadium: Davis Wade Stadium at Scott Field
Capacity: 55,082; Year Built: 1914
AD: Larry Templeton
SID: Mike Nemeth

MISSISSIPPI VAL.

Itta Bena, MS 38941-1400......................FCS

Coach: Willie Totten, Mississippi Val. 1986
Record: 5 Years, 22-33-0

2006 RESULTS (6-5)

10 Ark.-Pine Bluff * 0
14 Southern U. 31
23 Alabama A&M ■ 20
24 Jackson St. 29
21 Concordia-Selma ■ 14
25 Grambling ■ 28
0 North Dakota St. 45
20 Texas Southern 18
14 Prairie View ■ 10
28 Alcorn St. ■ 25
20 Alabama St. 25

Nickname: Delta Devils
Colors: Forest Green & White
Stadium: Chuck Prophet Field at Rice-Totten Stadium
Capacity: 10,500; Year Built: 1958
AD: Lonza Hardy Jr.
SID: Roderick Mosley

MISSOURI

Columbia, MO 65211-1050....................FBS

Coach: Gary Pinkel, Kent St. 1975
Record: 16 Years, 110-72-3

2006 RESULTS (8-5)

47 Murray St. ■ 7
34 Mississippi ■ 7
27 New Mexico 17
31 Ohio ■ 6
28 Colorado ■ 13
38 Texas Tech 21
19 Texas A&M 25
41 Kansas St. ■ 21
10 Oklahoma ■ 26
20 Nebraska 34
16 Iowa St. 21
42 Kansas ■ 17
38 Oregon St. * 39

Nickname: Tigers
Colors: Old Gold & Black
Stadium: Memorial/Faurot Field
Capacity: 68,349; Year Built: 1926
AD: Michael F. Alden
SID: Chad Moller

MO.-ROLLA

Rolla, MO 65409-0740..............................II

Coach: Kirby Cannon, Missouri St. 1981
Record: 8 Years, 20-68-0

2006 RESULTS (6-5)

32 Tiffin 58
23 Southeast Mo. St. 44
49 Lincoln (Mo.) 7
49 Morehead St. 37
24 St. Joseph's (Ind.) ■ 38
29 Southwestern Okla. 31
21 Austin Peay ■ 14
17 Southern Nazarene ■ 14

35 Butler ■ 20
9 Wayne St. (Neb.) 14
62 Ky. Wesleyan ■ 6

Nickname: Miners
Colors: Silver & Gold
Stadium: Jackling Field at Allgood-Bailey Stadium
Capacity: 8,000; Year Built: 1967
AD: Mark Mullin
SID: John Kean

MO. SOUTHERN ST.
Joplin, MO 64801-1595 II

Coach: Bart Tatum, Austin 1991
Record: 1 Year, 5-6-0

2006 RESULTS (5-6)

28 Ouachita Baptist ■ 22
30 Harding 27
42 Southwest Baptist ■ 21
24 Pittsburg St. 48
7 Northwest Mo. St. ■ 24
28 Truman 35
17 Mo. Western St. ■ 24
31 Central Mo. ■ 26
0 Fort Hays St. 10
13 Washburn ■ 14
34 Emporia St. 33

Nickname: Lions
Colors: Green & Gold
Stadium: Fred G. Hughes
Capacity: 7,000; Year Built: 1975
AD: Sallie Beard
SID: Justin Maskus

MISSOURI ST.
Springfield, MO 65897 ....FCS

Coach: Terry Allen, UNI 1979
Record: 14 Years, 97-68-0

2006 RESULTS (2-9)

10 Oklahoma St. 52
45 Southwest Baptist ■ 14
14 Central Ark. 16
17 Sam Houston St. ■ 20
10 Youngstown St. ■ 37
7 UNI 38
14 Western Ky. ■ 17
22 Indiana St. 28
17 Southern Ill. ■ 27
14 Illinois St. 38
24 Western Ill. ■ 21

Nickname: Bears
Colors: Maroon & White
Stadium: Plaster Field
Capacity: 16,300; Year Built: 1941
AD: William L. Rowe Jr.
SID: Mark Stillwell

MO. WESTERN ST.
St. Joseph, MO 64507 II

Coach: Jerry Partridge, Mo. Western St. 1985
Record: 10 Years, 71-43-0

2006 RESULTS (9-3)

32 Central Okla. 29
27 St. Cloud St. ■ 14
48 Pittsburg St. ■ 35
21 Northwest Mo. St. 24
38 Truman ■ 13
30 Central Mo. 20
24 Mo. Southern St. 17
24 Emporia St. ■ 12
24 Southwest Baptist 21
24 Fort Hays St. ■ 10
3 Washburn 16
26 Midwestern St. 28

Nickname: Griffons
Colors: Black & Gold
Stadium: Spratt
Capacity: 6,000; Year Built: 1979
AD: Mark Linder
SID: Brett King

MONMOUTH
West Long Branch, NJ 07764 ....FCS

Coach: Kevin Callahan, Rochester 1977
Record: 14 Years, 85-56-0

2006 RESULTS (10-2)

23 Fordham 9
26 Morgan St. ■ 9
36 St. Peter's ■ 12
17 Colgate 12
17 Stony Brook ■ 36
24 Sacred Heart ■ 0
28 Wagner 7
16 Robert Morris 7
19 Central Conn. St. ■ 13
54 St. Francis (Pa.) ■ 20
19 Albany (N.Y.) 0
7 San Diego ■ 27

Nickname: Hawks
Colors: Midnight Blue & White
Stadium: Kessler Field
Capacity: 4,600; Year Built: 1993
AD: Marilyn A. McNeil
SID: Thomas Dick

MONMOUTH (ILL.)
Monmouth, IL 61462-1998 III

Coach: Steve Bell, Bemidji St. 1991
Record: 7 Years, 50-21-0

2006 RESULTS (7-3)

0 Wartburg 20
49 Lawrence ■ 6
31 Beloit 0
38 Carroll (Wis.) ■ 7
51 Grinnell 31
0 St. Norbert 48
24 Ripon ■ 14
8 Lake Forest ■ 12
17 Illinois Col. 7
41 Knox ■ 6

Nickname: Fighting Scots
Colors: Red & White
Stadium: Bobby Woll Memorial Field
Capacity: 3,000; Year Built: 1981
AD: Terry L. Glasgow
SID: Barry McNamara/Dan Nolan

MONTANA
Missoula, MT 59812-1291 ....FCS

Coach: Bobby Hauck, Montana 1988
Record: 4 Years, 41-13-0

2006 RESULTS (12-2)

7 Iowa 41
36 South Dakota St. ■ 7
59 Sacramento St. ■ 14
26 Portland St. 20
33 Eastern Wash. 17
24 Northern Ariz. ■ 21
33 Weber St. 30
23 Idaho St. ■ 10
10 Cal Poly ■ 9
53 Northern Colo. 21
13 Montana St. ■ 7
31 McNeese St. ■ 6
20 Southern Ill. ■ 3
17 Massachusetts ■ 19

Nickname: Grizzlies
Colors: Maroon & Silver
Stadium: Washington-Grizzly
Capacity: 23,183; Year Built: 1986
AD: Jim O'Day
SID: Dave Guffey

MONTANA ST.
Bozeman, MT 59717-3380 ....FCS

Coach: Mike Kramer, Idaho 1977
Record: 13 Years, 77-75-0

2006 RESULTS (8-5)

19 Colorado 10
24 Chadron St. ■ 35
0 UC Davis ■ 45
10 Eastern Wash. ■ 19
39 Northern Ariz. 32
14 Portland St. ■ 0
21 Sacramento St. 18
42 Idaho St. 35
24 Weber St. ■ 18
13 Northern Colo. ■ 10
7 Montana 13
31 Furman ■ 13
17 Appalachian St. 38

Nickname: Bobcats
Colors: Blue & Gold
Stadium: Bobcat
Capacity: 13,000; Year Built: 1973
AD: Peter Fields
SID: Bill Lamberty

MONTCLAIR ST.
Montclair, NJ 07043 III

Coach: Rick Giancola, Rowan 1968
Record: 24 Years, 164-80-2

2006 RESULTS (7-3)

21 Iona 7
15 Springfield 27
27 Salisbury ■ 3
27 TCNJ ■ 7
22 Buffalo St. 14
13 Kean 19
3 Cortland St. ■ 41
27 Rowan ■ 20
44 Wm. Paterson 9
27 Western Conn. St. 22

Nickname: Red Hawks
Colors: Scarlet & White
Stadium: Sprague Field
Capacity: 6,000; Year Built: 1934
AD: Holly P. Gera
SID: Mike Scala

MORAVIAN
Bethlehem, PA 18018-6650 III

Coach: Scot Dapp, West Chester 1973
Record: 20 Years, 121-84-1

2006 RESULTS (4-6)

24 Susquehanna 17
23 King's (Pa.) ■ 28
33 Juniata 14
16 Widener ■ 20
0 Delaware Valley 39
28 FDU-Florham ■ 14
0 Wilkes 17
22 Lycoming ■ 3
21 Lebanon Valley 55
10 Muhlenberg ■ 24

Nickname: Greyhounds
Colors: Blue & Grey
Stadium: Rocco Calvo Field at Steel Field Complex
Capacity: 2,200; Year Built: 1932
AD: Paul R. Moyer
SID: Mark Fleming

MOREHEAD ST.
Morehead, KY 40351-1689 ....FCS

Coach: Matt Ballard, Gardner-Webb 1979
Record: 19 Years, 108-91-1

2006 RESULTS (2-9)

6 Western Ill. 31
7 Newberry 23
35 Valparaiso ■ 42
37 Mo.-Rolla ■ 49
7 Drake 33
22 Dayton 15
24 Davidson ■ 27
24 Jacksonville ■ 28
21 San Diego 44
14 Butler 7
21 Austin Peay ■ 23

Nickname: Eagles
Colors: Blue & Gold
Stadium: Jayne
Capacity: 10,000; Year Built: 1964
AD: Brian Hutchinson
SID: Randy Stacy

MOREHOUSE

Atlanta, GA 30314 II

Coach: Terry Beauford, Florida A&M 1995
Record: 2 Years, 5-16-0

2006 RESULTS (2-9)

25 Benedict 24
14 Fort Valley St. 24
31 Lane ■ 48
31 Kentucky St. ■ 34
17 Concordia-Selma ■ 13
6 Alcorn St. ■ 23
29 Tuskegee * 55
20 Savannah St. * 24
25 Clark Atlanta 32
6 Albany St. (Ga.) ■ 16
9 Miles 38

Nickname: Maroon Tigers
Colors: Maroon & White
Stadium: B.T. Harvey
Capacity: 9,850; Year Built: 1983
AD: Andre' Pattillo
SID: Yusuf Davis

MORGAN ST.

Baltimore, MD 21251 ....FCS

Coach: Donald Hill-Eley, Virginia Union 1991
Record: 5 Years, 25-31-0

2006 RESULTS (5-6)

2 Towson 30
9 Monmouth 26
28 Bowie St. ■ 20
7 Hampton * 26
28 Bethune-Cookman ■ 14
32 N.C. A&T 0
18 Howard 12
7 Delaware St. ■ 29
23 Florida A&M 24
29 Norfolk St. 20
16 South Carolina St. ■ 41

Nickname: Bears
Colors: Blue & Orange
Stadium: Hughes
Capacity: 10,000; Year Built: 1934
AD: Floyd Kerr
SID: Leonard Haynes

MOUNT IDA

Newton, MA 02459-3323 III

Coach: Edward Sweeney, C.W. Post 1971
Record: 22 Years, 111-103-4

2006 RESULTS (5-4)

25 Norwich 49
19 Plymouth St. ■ 14
0 St. John Fisher 55
33 Becker 21
13 Husson ■ 12
9 Utica 21
21 Hartwick ■ 20
20 WPI 46
27 Maritime (N.Y.) ■ 21

Nickname: Mustangs
Colors: Green & White
Stadium: Athletic Stadium at Mount Ida
Capacity: 500
AD: Jacqueline Palmer
SID: Mike Raposo

MT. ST. JOSEPH

Cincinnati, OH 45233-1670 III

Coach: Rod Huber, Cincinnati 1989
Record: 7 Years, 41-32-0

2006 RESULTS (9-2)

24 Wilmington (Ohio) ■ 0
20 Rose-Hulman 9
28 Ill. Wesleyan ■ 7
36 Anderson (Ind.) ■ 14
24 Hanover 0
21 Franklin 14
34 Manchester ■ 12
20 Defiance 6
17 Bluffton ■ 0
17 Thomas More 21
28 Wheaton (Ill.) 42

Nickname: Lions
Colors: Blue & Gold
Stadium: East Athletic Complex
Capacity: 2,400; Year Built: 2004
AD: Steven F. Radcliffe
SID: Dane Neumeister

MOUNT UNION

Alliance, OH 44601 III

Coach: Larry Kehres, Mount Union 1971
Record: 21 Years, 246-20-3

2006 RESULTS (15-0)

64 Averett 7
71 Otterbein 14
62 Muskingum 0
58 Heidelberg ■ 0
49 Ohio Northern ■ 7
65 Wilmington (Ohio) 9
14 Baldwin-Wallace 0
38 Capital ■ 12
31 John Carroll ■ 14
45 Marietta 17
49 Hope ■ 0
35 Wheaton (Ill.) ■ 3
17 Capital ■ 14
26 St. John Fisher ■ 14
35 Wis.-Whitewater * 16

Nickname: Purple Raiders
Colors: Purple & White
Stadium: Mount Union
Capacity: 5,800; Year Built: 1913
AD: Larry Kehres
SID: Michael DeMatteis

MUHLENBERG

Allentown, PA 18104-5586 III

Coach: Mike Donnelly, Ithaca 1975
Record: 10 Years, 61-44-0

2006 RESULTS (5-5)

24 TCNJ ■ 14
24 Wm. Paterson ■ 17
7 Union (N.Y.) 34
10 Frank. & Marsh. ■ 24
14 Dickinson 24
22 Ursinus ■ 6
7 Johns Hopkins 10
54 Gettysburg ■ 14
19 McDaniel 22
24 Moravian 10

Nickname: Mules
Colors: Cardinal & Grey
Stadium: Scotty Wood
Capacity: 3,000; Year Built: 1998
AD: Samuel T. Beidleman
SID: Mike Falk

MURRAY ST.

Murray, KY 42071-3318 ....FCS

Coach: Matt Griffin, New Hampshire 1992
Record: 4 Years, 11-34-0

2006 RESULTS (1-10)

7 Missouri 47
15 Tennessee St. 25
59 Indiana St. 40
14 Illinois St. ■ 35
14 Tennessee Tech ■ 20
17 Jacksonville St. 49
7 Samford ■ 33
10 Eastern Ill. 20
17 Southeast Mo. St. ■ 24
21 Eastern Ky. 51
14 Tenn.-Martin ■ 42

Nickname: Racers
Colors: Navy & Gold
Stadium: Stewart
Capacity: 16,800; Year Built: 1973
AD: Allen Ward
SID: Kevin Britton

MUSKINGUM

New Concord, OH 43762 III

Coach: Jeff Heacock, Muskingum 1976
Record: 26 Years, 109-144-4

2006 RESULTS (2-8)

45 Bethany (W.V.) ■ 20
7 Ohio Northern 36
0 Mount Union ■ 62
0 Wilmington (Ohio) 20
10 Marietta 30
3 Baldwin-Wallace ■ 30
0 John Carroll ■ 38
0 Otterbein 20
14 Capital 52
28 Heidelberg ■ 12

Nickname: Fighting Muskies
Colors: Black & Magenta
Stadium: McConagha
Capacity: 5,000; Year Built: 1925
AD: Larry Shank
SID: Tom Caudill

NAVY

Annapolis, MD 21402-5000 ....FBS

Coach: Paul Johnson, Western Caro. 1979
Record: 10 Years, 99-35-0

2006 RESULTS (9-4)

28 East Caro. ■ 23
21 Massachusetts ■ 20
37 Stanford 9
23 Tulsa ■ 24
41 Connecticut 17
24 Air Force 17
0 Rutgers ■ 34
14 Notre Dame * 38
38 Duke 13
49 Eastern Mich. * 21
42 Temple ■ 6
26 Army * 14
24 Boston College 25

Nickname: Midshipmen
Colors: Navy Blue & Gold
Stadium: Navy-Marine Corps Memorial
Capacity: 34,000; Year Built: 1959
AD: Chester S. Gladchuk
SID: Scott Strasemeier

NEBRASKA
Lincoln, NE 68508-0219 ....FBS

Coach: Bill Callahan, Benedictine (Ill.) 1978
Record: 3 Years, 22-15-0

2006 RESULTS (9-5)
49 Louisiana Tech ■..........10
56 Nicholls St. ■..........7
10 Southern California..........28
56 Troy ■..........0
39 Kansas ■..........32
28 Iowa St...........14
21 Kansas St...........3
20 Texas ■..........22
29 Oklahoma St...........41
34 Missouri ■..........20
28 Texas A&M..........27
37 Colorado ■..........14
7 Oklahoma *..........21
14 Auburn *..........17

Nickname: Cornhuskers, Huskers
Colors: Scarlet & Cream
Stadium: Memorial
Capacity: 81,067; Year Built: 1923
AD: Steven C. Pederson
SID: Keith Mann

NEB.-KEARNEY
Kearney, NE 68849 II

Coach: Darrell Morris, Northwest Mo. St. 1983
Record: 7 Years, 49-25-0

2006 RESULTS (6-4)
19 Neb.-Omaha..........29
23 Wayne St. (Neb.) ■..........14
16 Fort Lewis..........21
27 Mesa St. ■..........0
23 Western St...........3
31 Adams St. ■..........7
12 Chadron St...........31
14 Colorado Mines ■..........20
17 N.M. Highlands..........7
20 Western N.M. ■..........13

Nickname: Antelopes, Lopers
Colors: Royal Blue & Light Old Gold
Stadium: Ron & Carol Cope Stadium at Foster Field
Capacity: 6,500; Year Built: 1929
AD: Jon McBride
SID: Peter Yazvac

NEB.-OMAHA
Omaha, NE 68182..................................II

Coach: Pat Behrns, Dakota St. 1972
Record: 19 Years, 130-79-0

2006 RESULTS (8-3)
29 Neb.-Kearney ■..........19
0 Northwest Mo. St...........31
38 Western Wash...........10
59 Augustana (S.D.) ■..........28
21 Minn. St. Mankato..........14
21 North Dakota ■..........20
38 Minn. Duluth..........14
21 St. Cloud St. ■..........17
28 South Dakota..........45
48 Central Wash. ■..........14
35 North Dakota ■..........38

Nickname: Mavericks
Colors: Black & Crimson
Stadium: Al F. Caniglia Field
Capacity: 9,500; Year Built: 1949
AD: Thomas A. Frette
SID: Gary Anderson

NEB. WESLEYAN
Lincoln, NE 68504-2796............................III

Coach: Brian Keller, Neb. Wesleyan 1983
Record: 11 Years, 60-51-0

2006 RESULTS (7-3)
42 Briar Cliff (Iowa) ■..........3
30 Dana..........6
20 Midland Lutheran ■..........14
0 Northwestern (Iowa)..........36
0 Morningside ■..........37
19 Doane..........0
38 Dakota Wesleyan ■..........18
0 Sioux Falls..........52
26 Concordia (Neb.) ■..........19
15 Hastings..........12

Nickname: Prairie Wolves
Colors: Gold, Brown & Black
Stadium: Abel
Capacity: 2,250; Year Built: 1986
AD: Ira Zeff
SID: Karl Skinner

NEVADA
Reno, NV 89557..................................FBS

Coach: Chris Ault, Nevada 1968
Record: 22 Years, 185-78-1

2006 RESULTS (8-5)
19 Fresno St...........28
21 Arizona St...........52
28 Colorado St. ■..........10
31 Northwestern ■..........21
31 UNLV..........3
34 Hawaii..........41
23 San Jose St. ■..........7
48 New Mexico St. ■..........21
45 Idaho..........7
42 Utah St. ■..........0
42 Louisiana Tech..........0
7 Boise St. ■..........38
20 Miami (Fla.) *..........21

Nickname: Wolf Pack
Colors: Silver & Blue
Stadium: Mackay
Capacity: 31,900; Year Built: 1966
AD: Cary Groth
SID: Jamie Klund

UNLV
Las Vegas, NV 89154............................FBS

Coach: Mike Sanford, Southern California 1978
Record: 2 Years, 4-19-0

2006 RESULTS (2-10)
54 Idaho St. ■..........10
10 Iowa St...........16
13 Hawaii..........42
3 Nevada ■..........31
7 Colorado St...........28
36 New Mexico ■..........39
7 Brigham Young..........52
23 Utah..........45
10 TCU ■..........25
7 San Diego St...........21
26 Wyoming ■..........34
42 Air Force ■..........39

Nickname: Rebels
Colors: Scarlet & Gray
Stadium: Sam Boyd
Capacity: 36,800; Year Built: 1971
AD: Mike Hamrick
SID: Mark Wallington

NEW HAMPSHIRE
Durham, NH 03824...............................FCS

Coach: Sean McDonnell, New Hampshire 1978
Record: 8 Years, 53-42-0

2006 RESULTS (9-4)
34 Northwestern..........17
62 Stony Brook ■..........7
56 Dartmouth..........14
52 Delaware..........49
27 Richmond ■..........17
23 James Madison ■..........42
35 Northeastern..........36
10 Hofstra ■..........6
20 Massachusetts ■..........28
63 Rhode Island..........21
19 Maine..........13
41 Hampton..........38
17 Massachusetts..........24

Nickname: Wildcats
Colors: Blue & White
Stadium: Cowell
Capacity: 6,500; Year Built: 1936
AD: Marty Scarano
SID: Scott Stapin

TCNJ
Ewing, NJ 08628-0718 III

Coach: Eric Hamilton, TCNJ 1975
Record: 30 Years, 179-115-6

2006 RESULTS (4-6)
14 Muhlenberg..........24
24 La Salle..........21
20 FDU-Florham..........14
7 Montclair St...........27
6 Rowan ■..........14
27 Wm. Paterson ■..........21
3 Western Conn. St...........10
14 Cortland St...........26
33 Buffalo St. ■..........34
14 Kean ■..........10

Nickname: Lions
Colors: Blue & Gold
Stadium: Lions'
Capacity: 6,000; Year Built: 1984
AD: To be named
SID: Ann King

NEW MEXICO
Albuquerque, NM 87131 ....FBS

Coach: Rocky Long, New Mexico 1974
Record: 9 Years, 52-57-0

2006 RESULTS (6-7)
6 Portland St. ■..........17
34 New Mexico St...........28
17 Missouri ■..........27
26 UTEP ■..........13
7 Air Force..........24
10 Wyoming ■..........14
39 UNLV..........36
34 Utah ■..........31
20 Colorado St...........19
21 TCU ■..........27
17 Brigham Young..........42
41 San Diego St. ■..........14
12 San Jose St...........20

Nickname: Lobos
Colors: Cherry & Silver
Stadium: University
Capacity: 38,634; Year Built: 1960
AD: Paul Krebs
SID: Greg Remington

N.M. HIGHLANDS
Las Vegas, NM 87701 II

Coach: Carl Ferrill, N.M. Highlands 1967
Record: 4 Years, 30-14-0

2006 RESULTS (6-5)
26 Bacone..........13
34 Northwestern Okla. ■..........10
9 Western St. ■..........14
17 Adams St...........34
20 Chadron St. ■..........40
19 Colorado Mines..........16

24 Paul Quinn ■ 0
27 Western N.M. ■ 22
28 Fort Lewis 25
7 Neb.-Kearney ■ 17
7 Mesa St. 19

Nickname: Cowboys
Colors: Purple & White
Stadium: Perkins
Capacity: 3,500; Year Built: 1930
AD: Ben Santistevan
SID: Tim Gotto

NEW MEXICO ST.

Las Cruces, NM 88003 ....FBS

Coach: Hal Mumme, Tarleton St. 1975
Record: 16 Years, 101-84-1

2006 RESULTS (4-8)

30 Southeastern La. ■ 15
28 New Mexico ■ 34
48 Texas Southern ■ 14
38 UTEP 44
20 Idaho 28
28 Boise St. ■ 40
30 Hawaii ■ 49
21 Nevada 48
21 San Jose St. ■ 31
18 Fresno St. 23
42 Utah St. 20
50 Louisiana Tech ■ 23

Nickname: Aggies
Colors: Crimson & White
Stadium: Aggie Memorial
Capacity: 30,343; Year Built: 1978
AD: McKinley Boston Jr.
SID: Tyler Dunkel

NEWBERRY

Newberry, SC 29108 II

Coach: Zak Willis, Furman 1990
Record: 4 Years, 23-19-0

2006 RESULTS (11-2)

30 Edward Waters ■ 0
23 Morehead St. ■ 7
45 Brevard ■ 0
49 Elizabeth City St. ■ 33
32 Carson-Newman ■ 18
21 Catawba ■ 14
37 Mars Hill 0
36 Wingate ■ 24
27 Tusculum 23
45 Lenoir-Rhyne ■ 21
0 Presbyterian 10
34 Albany St. (Ga.) ■ 28
20 North Ala. 38

Nickname: Indians
Colors: Scarlet & Gray
Stadium: Setzler Field
Capacity: 4,000; Year Built: 1930
AD: Andy Carter
SID: Josh Manck

NICHOLLS ST.

Thibodaux, LA 70310 ....FCS

Coach: Jay Thomas, Southern Miss. 1988
Record: 3 Years, 15-16-0

2006 RESULTS (4-7)

35 Southern Ark. ■ 0
7 Nebraska 56
21 Louisiana Tech 31
17 South Dakota St. ■ 24
14 Southeastern La. ■ 10
7 Sam Houston St. 37
0 Northwestern St. ■ 9
44 Assumption ■ 0
21 Texas St. 19
13 Stephen F. Austin ■ 16
10 McNeese St. 26

Nickname: Colonels
Colors: Red & Grey
Stadium: John L. Guidry
Capacity: 12,800; Year Built: 1972
AD: Robert J. Bernardi
SID: Bobby Galinsky

NICHOLS

Dudley, MA 01571-5000 III

Coach: Bill Carven, Nichols 1994
Record: 8 Years, 39-37-0

2006 RESULTS (5-4)

31 Framingham St. ■ 12
13 Worcester St. 16
33 MIT 19
3 Endicott ■ 7
21 Salve Regina 14
19 Plymouth St. ■ 14
14 Mass.-Dartmouth ■ 28
13 Curry 37
26 Western New Eng. ■ 13

Nickname: Bison
Colors: Black, White & Green
Stadium: Vendetti Field
Capacity: 3,000; Year Built: 1961
AD: Charlyn Robert
SID: Kristen DiChiaro

NORFOLK ST.

Norfolk, VA 23504 ....FCS

Coach: Pete Adrian, West Virginia 1970
Record: 9 Years, 44-51-1

2006 RESULTS (4-7)

29 Virginia St. ■ 14
32 VMI ■ 19
21 Bethune-Cookman 22
42 N.C. A&T ■ 20
10 South Carolina St. 47
13 Hampton 42
33 Florida A&M ■ 36
10 Howard 13
20 Morgan St. ■ 29
10 Delaware St. ■ 33
31 Winston-Salem ■ 14

Nickname: Spartans
Colors: Green & Gold
Stadium: Price
Capacity: 30,000; Year Built: 1997
AD: Marty L. Miller
SID: Matt Michalec

NORTH ALA.

Florence, AL 35632-0001 II

Coach: Mark Hudspeth, Delta St. 1992
Record: 5 Years, 44-17-0

2006 RESULTS (11-1)

22 Tusculum 10
41 Harding ■ 14
40 Southern Ark. 10
38 Arkansas Tech ■ 14
47 Ouachita Baptist 10
47 Ark.-Monticello ■ 7
17 Delta St. 10
31 Valdosta St. ■ 24
26 West Ga. 16
45 West Ala. 3
38 Newberry ■ 20
10 Delta St. ■ 27

Nickname: Lions
Colors: Purple & Gold
Stadium: Braly
Capacity: 14,215; Year Built: 1940
AD: Mark Linder
SID: Jeff Hodges

NORTH CAROLINA

Chapel Hill, NC 27515 ....FBS

Coach: John Bunting, North Carolina 1972
Record: 11 Years, 65-59-2

2006 RESULTS (3-9)

16 Rutgers ■ 21
10 Virginia Tech ■ 35
45 Furman ■ 42
7 Clemson 52
7 Miami (Fla.) 27
20 South Fla. ■ 37
0 Virginia 23
17 Wake Forest ■ 24
26 Notre Dame 45
0 Georgia Tech ■ 7
23 North Carolina St. ■ 9
45 Duke 44

Nickname: Tar Heels
Colors: Carolina Blue & White
Stadium: Kenan Memorial
Capacity: 60,000; Year Built: 1927
AD: Richard Baddour
SID: Steve Kirschner

UNC PEMBROKE

Pembroke, NC 28372-1510 II

Coach: Pete Shinnick, Colorado 1988
Record: 7 Years, 53-22-0

Resuming program in 2007,
previously dropped in 1951

Nickname: Braves
Colors: Black & Gold
Stadium: Lumbee Guaranty Bank Field
Capacity: 4,500; Year Built: 1994
AD: Dan Kenney
SID: Todd C. Anderson

N.C. A&T

Greensboro, NC 27411 ....FCS

Coach: Lee Fobbs Jr., Grambling 1973
Record: 1 Year, 0-11-0

2006 RESULTS (0-11)

14 Winston-Salem ■ 41
14 Hampton 48
7 La.-Lafayette 48
20 Norfolk St. 42
0 Morgan St. ■ 32
21 Delaware St. 37
0 Howard ■ 26
7 Bethune-Cookman 70
12 Florida A&M ■ 45
0 Elon ■ 45
19 South Carolina St. * 41

Nickname: Aggies
Colors: Blue & Gold
Stadium: Aggie
Capacity: 21,500; Year Built: 1981
AD: Dee Todd
SID: Brian Holloway

N.C. CENTRAL

Durham, NC 27707 II

Coach: Rod Broadway, North Carolina 1977
Record: 4 Years, 33-11-0

2006 RESULTS (11-1)

20 Albany St. (Ga.) ■ 0
21 Shaw ■ 12
38 Lenoir-Rhyne ■ 16
27 Southern U. 20
35 Bowie St. 13
27 St. Augustine's 18
49 Fayetteville St. 6

31 Langston ■ 21
37 Livingstone 15
52 Johnson C. Smith ■ 7
17 Elizabeth City St. * 14
17 Delta St. ■ 24

Nickname: Eagles
Colors: Maroon & Gray
Stadium: O'Kelly-Riddick
Capacity: 10,000; Year Built: 1975
AD: William Hayes
SID: Kyle Serba

NORTH CAROLINA ST.

Raleigh, NC 27695-7001 ....FBS

Coach: Chuck Amato, North Carolina St. 1969
Record: 7 Years, 49-37-0

2006 RESULTS (3-9)

23 Appalachian St. ■ 10
17 Akron ■ 20
17 Southern Miss. 37
17 Boston College ■ 15
24 Florida St. ■ 20
23 Wake Forest ■ 25
20 Maryland 26
7 Virginia 14
23 Georgia Tech ■ 31
14 Clemson 20
9 North Carolina 23
16 East Caro. ■ 21

Nickname: Wolfpack
Colors: Red & White
Stadium: Carter-Finley
Capacity: 57,583; Year Built: 1966
AD: Lee G. Fowler
SID: Annabelle Myers

N.C. WESLEYAN

Rocky Mount, NC 27804 III

Coach: Jack Ginn, Emory & Henry 1986
Record: 3 Years, 14-14-0

2006 RESULTS (6-4)

20 Apprentice ■ 21
42 Southern Va. 7
21 Emory & Henry 24
15 Methodist ■ 9
48 Maryville (Tenn.) 50
20 Averett ■ 24
30 Shenandoah 0
46 Chris. Newport ■ 34
55 Ferrum 14
42 Greensboro ■ 20

Nickname: Battling Bishops
Colors: Navy Blue & Vega Gold
Stadium: Rocky Mount Athletic Complex
Capacity: 5,000; Year Built: 1970
AD: John M. Thompson
SID: Rikki C. Rich

NORTH CENTRAL (ILL.)

Naperville, IL 60566-7063 III

Coach: John Thorne, Ill. Wesleyan 1969
Record: 5 Years, 38-15-0

2006 RESULTS (9-3)

24 Concordia (Wis.) ■ 30
38 Benedictine (Ill.) 0
34 Washington-St. Louis 15
58 North Park ■ 14
19 Wheaton (Ill.) 31
30 Elmhurst ■ 16
22 Millikin 18
27 Augustana (Ill.) ■ 0
47 Ill. Wesleyan 21
34 Carthage ■ 24
35 Concordia (Wis.) 6
13 Capital 41

Nickname: Cardinals
Colors: Cardinal & White
Stadium: Benedetti-Wehrli
Capacity: 5,500; Year Built: 1999
AD: James L. Miller
SID: Josh Hendricks

NORTH DAKOTA

Grand Forks, ND 58202 II

Coach: Dale Lennon, North Dakota 1985
Record: 10 Years, 92-31-0

2006 RESULTS (11-2)

28 Central Wash. 14
35 UNI 31
49 Winona St. ■ 2
26 Western Wash. ■ 20
24 Augustana (S.D.) 21
24 Minn. St. Mankato ■ 3
20 Neb.-Omaha 21
38 Minn. Duluth ■ 14
34 St. Cloud St. 27
33 South Dakota ■ 26
42 Winona St. ■ 0
38 Neb.-Omaha 35
20 Grand Valley St. 30

Nickname: Fighting Sioux
Colors: Kelly Green & White
Stadium: Alerus Center
Capacity: 12,283; Year Built: 2001
AD: Thomas Buning
SID: Jayson Hajdu

NORTH DAKOTA ST.
(Reclassifying to FCS)

Fargo, ND 58105-5600 II

Coach: Craig Bohl, Nebraska 1982
Record: 4 Years, 33-11-0

2006 RESULTS (10-1)

66 Concordia-St. Paul ■ 7
23 Northeastern ■ 10
29 Ball St. 24
17 Stephen F. Austin 9
34 Ga. Southern 14
45 Mississippi Val. ■ 0
9 Minnesota 10
31 Southern Utah 7
28 UC Davis 24
51 Cal Poly ■ 14
41 South Dakota St. ■ 28

Nickname: Bison
Colors: Yellow & Green
Stadium: Fargodome
Capacity: 18,700; Year Built: 1992
AD: Gene Taylor
SID: Jeff Schwartz

NORTH GREENVILLE

Tigerville, SC 29688 II

Coach: Mike Taylor, Newberry 1976
Record: 14 Years, 62-90-0

2006 RESULTS (10-2)

35 Virginia-Wise 48
28 Fairmont St. ■ 7
35 Cumberland (Ky.) ■ 7
48 Edward Waters ■ 19
10 Charleston So. 20
55 Brevard 0
44 Ky. Wesleyan 34
52 Chowan ■ 6
41 Jacksonville ■ 6
44 Austin Peay 35
28 Concord ■ 25
56 Malone ■ 28

Nickname: Crusaders
Colors: Red, Black & White
Stadium: Younts
Capacity: 5,000; Year Built: 2005
AD: Jan McDonald
SID: Rhett Burns

NORTH PARK

Chicago, IL 60625-4895 III

Coach: Scott Pethtel, Adrian 1976
Record: 1 Year, 1-9-0

2006 RESULTS (1-9)

7 Benedictine (Ill.) 22
34 Eureka ■ 6
0 Rose-Hulman ■ 25
14 North Central (Ill.) 58
6 Millikin ■ 36
7 Carthage 52
26 Wheaton (Ill.) ■ 73
0 Ill. Wesleyan 44
0 Augustana (Ill.) 31
7 Elmhurst ■ 24

Nickname: Vikings
Colors: Blue & Gold
Stadium: Holmgren Athletic Complex
Capacity: 2,500; Year Built: 2002
AD: Jack Surridge
SID: Sara Carlson

NORTH TEXAS

Denton, TX 76207 ....FBS

Coach: Darrell Dickey, Kansas St. 1984
Record: 9 Years, 42-64-0

2006 RESULTS (3-9)

7 Texas 56
24 SMU ■ 6
3 Tulsa 28
13 Akron 33
0 Middle Tenn. ■ 35
25 Florida Int'l ■ 22
10 Arkansas St. 29
6 Troy 14
31 Louisiana Tech ■ 34
16 La.-Lafayette 7
16 Fla. Atlantic ■ 17
3 La.-Monroe 23

Nickname: Mean Green
Colors: Green & White
Stadium: Fouts Field
Capacity: 30,500; Year Built: 1952
AD: Rick Villarreal
SID: Eric Capper

NORTHEASTERN

Boston, MA 02115 ....FCS

Coach: Rocky Hager, Minot St. 1974
Record: 13 Years, 103-46-1

2006 RESULTS (5-6)

0 Virginia Tech 38
24 Holy Cross 14
10 North Dakota St. 23
14 James Madison 52
7 Richmond 12
27 Delaware ■ 24
36 New Hampshire ■ 35
0 Massachusetts ■ 7
3 Maine 30
34 Hofstra 24
45 Rhode Island ■ 31

Nickname: Huskies
Colors: Red & Black
Stadium: Parsons Field
Capacity: 7,000; Year Built: 1933
AD: David O'Brien
SID: Mark Harris

NORTHEASTERN ST.

Tahlequah, OK 74464-2399 II

Coach: John Horner, Arkansas 1985
Record: 4 Years, 9-31-0

2006 RESULTS (4-6)

32 Arkansas Tech 33
42 Eastern N.M. ■ 7
34 Midwestern St. ■ 73
10 West Tex. A&M 14
40 East Central 29
20 Abilene Christian ■ 45
20 Tex. A&M-Commerce ■ 17
6 Southwestern Okla. 32
0 Southeastern Okla. 31
26 Central Okla. ■ 23

Nickname: Redmen
Colors: Green & White
Stadium: Doc Wadley
Capacity: 12,000; Year Built: 1964
AD: Eddie Griffin
SID: Scott Pettus

NORTHERN ARIZ.

Flagstaff, AZ 86011-5400 ....FCS

Coach: Jerome Souers, Oregon 1983
Record: 9 Years, 53-50-0

2006 RESULTS (6-5)

14 Arizona St. 35
7 Utah 45
66 Dixie St. ■ 14
33 Idaho St. 27
32 Montana St. ■ 39
21 Montana 24
39 Sacramento St. ■ 22
44 Eastern Wash. 36
26 Portland St. ■ 34
42 Weber St. ■ 17
54 Northern Colo. 3

Nickname: Lumberjacks
Colors: Blue, Gold & Sage
Stadium: Walkup Skydome
Capacity: 15,300; Year Built: 1977
AD: James E. Fallis
SID: Steven Shaff

NORTHERN COLO.

Greeley, CO 80639..............................FCS

Coach: Scott Downing, Sterling (Kan.) 1979
Record: 3 Years, 14-14-1

2006 RESULTS (1-10)

7 UC Davis ■ 38
3 Portland St. 45
14 Texas St. 13
28 Western Ill. ■ 42
21 Weber St. 26
13 Idaho St. ■ 41
0 Eastern Wash. ■ 34
9 Sacramento St. 14
10 Montana St. 13
21 Montana ■ 53
3 Northern Ariz. ■ 54

Nickname: Bears
Colors: Blue & Gold
Stadium: Nottingham Field
Capacity: 8,500; Year Built: 1995
AD: Jay Hinrichs
SID: Eric Scott

NORTHERN ILL.

DeKalb, IL 60115-2854 ....FBS

Coach: Joe Novak, Miami (Ohio) 1967
Record: 11 Years, 61-66-0

2006 RESULTS (7-6)

12 Ohio St. 35
23 Ohio ■ 35
31 Buffalo ■ 13
48 Indiana St. ■ 14
40 Ball St. 28
28 Miami (Ohio) 25
14 Western Mich. 16
43 Temple ■ 21
14 Iowa 24
13 Toledo ■ 17
31 Central Mich. ■ 10
27 Eastern Mich. 0
7 TCU * 37

Nickname: Huskies
Colors: Cardinal & Black
Stadium: Brigham Field at Huskie Stadium
Capacity: 28,000; Year Built: 1965
AD: James Phillips
SID: Donna Turner

UNI

Cedar Falls, IA 50614............................FCS

Coach: Mark Farley, UNI 1986
Record: 6 Years, 51-24-0

2006 RESULTS (7-4)

48 Drake 7
31 North Dakota ■ 35
27 South Dakota St. ■ 17
27 Iowa St. 28
38 Missouri St. ■ 7
34 Indiana St. 14
31 Youngstown St. 23
13 Western Ill. ■ 24
31 Western Ky. ■ 20
23 Southern Ill. 47
38 Illinois St. ■ 27

Nickname: Panthers
Colors: Purple & Old Gold
Stadium: U.N.I.-Dome
Capacity: 16,324; Year Built: 1976
AD: Rick Hartzell
SID: Colin McDonough

NORTHERN MICH.

Marquette, MI 49855-5391 II

Coach: Bernie Anderson, Northern Mich. 1978
Record: 20 Years, 94-104-0

2006 RESULTS (3-7)

27 Indianapolis ■ 20
31 Hillsdale 24
35 Saginaw Valley 37
24 Ferris St. ■ 42
14 Northwood (Mich.) 44
17 Ashland ■ 24
14 Michigan Tech 42
7 Mercyhurst 32
48 Gannon ■ 21
17 Grand Valley St. ■ 47

Nickname: Wildcats
Colors: Old Gold & Olive Green
Stadium: Superior Dome
Capacity: 8,000; Year Built: 1991
AD: Kenneth Godfrey
SID: David Faiella

NORTHERN ST.

Aberdeen, SD 57401 II

Coach: Chris Boden, Saginaw Valley 1990
Record: 2 Years, 10-12-0

2006 RESULTS (4-7)

17 Augustana (S.D.) 27
27 Dickinson St. ■ 21
20 Concordia-St. Paul 28
16 Southwest Minn. St. ■ 8
22 Bemidji St. ■ 25
0 Wayne St. (Neb.) 7
15 Winona St. ■ 23
31 Minn.-Crookston ■ 6
15 Minn. St. Moorhead 26
26 Upper Iowa 20
7 Mary * 20

Nickname: Wolves
Colors: Maroon & Gold
Stadium: Swisher
Capacity: 6,000; Year Built: 2005
AD: Robert A. Olson
SID: Nick Kornder

NORTHWEST MO. ST.

Maryville, MO 64468-6001........................II

Coach: Mel Tjeerdsma, Southern St. (S.D.) 1967
Record: 23 Years, 191-75-4

2006 RESULTS (14-1)

31 Minn. St. Mankato ■ 14
31 Neb.-Omaha ■ 0
31 Truman 10
24 Mo. Western St. ■ 21
24 Mo. Southern St. 7
49 Emporia St. ■ 17
31 Washburn 26
59 Fort Hays St. ■ 0
31 Central Mo. 14
41 Pittsburg St. * 14
55 Southwest Baptist 9
27 Midwestern St. ■ 0
28 Chadron St. ■ 21
33 Bloomsburg ■ 3
14 Grand Valley St. * 17

Nickname: Bearcats
Colors: Green & White
Stadium: Mel Tjeerdsma Field at Bearcat Stadium
Capacity: 7,500; Year Built: 1917
AD: Bob Boerigter
SID: Andy Seeley

NORTHWESTERN

Evanston, IL 60208 ....FBS

Coach: Pat Fitzgerald, Northwestern 1997
Record: 1 Year, 4-8-0

2006 RESULTS (4-8)

21 Miami (Ohio) 3
17 New Hampshire ■ 34
14 Eastern Mich. ■ 6
21 Nevada 31
7 Penn St. 33
9 Wisconsin 41
10 Purdue ■ 31
38 Michigan St. ■ 41
3 Michigan 17
21 Iowa 7
10 Ohio St. ■ 54
27 Illinois ■ 16

Nickname: Wildcats
Colors: Purple & White
Stadium: Ryan Field
Capacity: 47,130; Year Built: 1997
AD: Mark Murphy
SID: Mike Wolf

NORTHWESTERN ST.

Natchitoches, LA 71497-0003 ....FCS

Coach: Scott Stoker, Northwestern St. 1991
Record: 5 Years, 32-26-0

2006 RESULTS (4-7)

18 Kansas 49
10 Baylor 47
23 Delaware St. ■ 3
20 Ark.-Monticello ■ 3
20 Sam Houston St. ■ 30
24 Southeastern La. 31
9 Nicholls St. 0
19 Texas St. ■ 10

7 Mississippi 27
26 McNeese St. ■ 29
11 Stephen F. Austin 20

Nickname: Demons
Colors: Purple, White & Orange
Stadium: Turpin
Capacity: 15,971; Year Built: 1976
AD: Gregory S. Burke
SID: Doug Ireland

NORTHWOOD (MICH.)

Midland, MI 48640-2398 II

Coach: Pat Riepma, Hillsdale 1983
Record: 14 Years, 84-64-2

2006 RESULTS (8-3)

33 Mercyhurst 14
29 Findlay ■ 6
13 Michigan Tech 7
33 Ashland ■ 19
25 Saginaw Valley 14
44 Northern Mich. ■ 14
7 Grand Valley St. 45
48 Wayne St. (Mich.) ■ 34
14 Ferris St. ■ 17
23 Indianapolis 0
28 South Dakota ■ 31

Nickname: Timberwolves
Colors: Columbia Blue & White
Stadium: Hantz
Capacity: 3,000; Year Built: 2001
AD: Pat Riepma
SID: Travis McCurdy

NORWICH

Northfield, VT 05663 III

Coach: Shawn McIntyre, Norwich 1978
Record: 2 Years, 5-15-0

2006 RESULTS (2-8)

49 Mount Ida ■ 25
13 St. Lawrence 17
13 Husson ■ 14
41 Maritime (N.Y.) 14
13 Alfred 48
7 Ithaca ■ 44
0 St. John Fisher ■ 32
20 Hartwick 42
7 Utica 20
0 Springfield ■ 35

Nickname: Cadets
Colors: Maroon & Gold
Stadium: Sabine Field
Capacity: 5,000; Year Built: 1921
AD: Anthony A. Mariano
SID: Scott C. Miller

NOTRE DAME

Notre Dame, IN 46556 ....FBS

Coach: Charlie Weis, Notre Dame 1978
Record: 2 Years, 19-6-0

2006 RESULTS (10-3)

14 Georgia Tech 10
41 Penn St. ■ 17
21 Michigan ■ 47
40 Michigan St. 37
35 Purdue ■ 21
31 Stanford ■ 10
20 UCLA ■ 17
38 Navy * 14
45 North Carolina ■ 26
39 Air Force 17
41 Army ■ 9
24 Southern California 44
14 LSU * 41

Nickname: Fighting Irish
Colors: Blue & Gold
Stadium: Notre Dame
Capacity: 80,795; Year Built: 1930
AD: Kevin White
SID: John Heisler

OBERLIN

Oberlin, OH 44074 III

Coach: Jeff Ramsey, UC Davis 1983
Record: 8 Years, 19-61-0

2006 RESULTS (5-5)

23 Case Reserve 29
48 Heidelberg ■ 34
13 Wash. & Jeff. ■ 33
28 Hiram 14
18 Denison ■ 7
41 Earlham 31
20 Wabash ■ 48
6 Wittenberg ■ 22
56 Kenyon 42
14 Allegheny 35

Nickname: Yeomen
Colors: Crimson & Gold
Stadium: Dill Field
Capacity: 3,500; Year Built: 1925
AD: Joe Karlgaard
SID: Zachary Pretzer

OCCIDENTAL

Los Angeles, CA 90041 III

Coach: Dale Widolff, Indianapolis 1975
Record: 25 Years, 146-87-2

2006 RESULTS (9-1)

49 Lewis & Clark ■ 7
48 Colorado Col. ■ 34
42 Claremont-M-S ■ 13
24 Redlands 10
49 La Verne 14
38 Pomona-Pitzer ■ 23
28 Cal Lutheran 27
41 Chapman 21
34 Whittier ■ 30
23 Whitworth 27

Nickname: Tigers
Colors: Orange & Black
Stadium: Patterson Field
Capacity: 3,000; Year Built: 1916
AD: Dixon Farmer
SID: Andrew Holmes

OHIO

Athens, OH 45701 ....FBS

Coach: Frank Solich, Nebraska 1966
Record: 8 Years, 71-31-0

2006 RESULTS (9-5)

29 Tenn.-Martin ■ 3
35 Northern Ill. 23
7 Rutgers 24
6 Missouri 31
9 Bowling Green ■ 21
27 Western Mich. ■ 20
20 Illinois 17
42 Buffalo ■ 7
17 Kent St. 7
16 Eastern Mich. 10
17 Akron ■ 7
34 Miami (Ohio) 24
10 Central Mich. * 31
7 Southern Miss. * 28

Nickname: Bobcats
Colors: Hunter Green & White
Stadium: Peden
Capacity: 24,000; Year Built: 1929
AD: Kirby Hocutt
SID: Brian Gunning

OHIO NORTHERN

Ada, OH 45810 III

Coach: Dean Paul, Mount Union 1990
Record: 7 Years, 54-18-0

2006 RESULTS (6-4)

28 Millikin 14
36 Muskingum ■ 7
23 John Carroll 9
26 Otterbein ■ 0
7 Mount Union 49
10 Capital ■ 17
6 Marietta ■ 16
7 Baldwin-Wallace 13
47 Heidelberg 3
52 Wilmington (Ohio) ■ 0

Nickname: Polar Bears
Colors: Burnt Orange & Black
Stadium: Dial-Roberson
Capacity: 3,500; Year Built: 2004
AD: Thomas E. Simmons
SID: Tim Glon

OHIO ST.

Columbus, OH 43210 ....FBS

Coach: Jim Tressel, Baldwin-Wallace 1975
Record: 21 Years, 197-71-2

2006 RESULTS (12-1)

35 Northern Ill. ■ 12
24 Texas 7
37 Cincinnati ■ 7
28 Penn St. ■ 6
38 Iowa 17
35 Bowling Green ■ 7
38 Michigan St. 7
44 Indiana ■ 3
44 Minnesota ■ 0
17 Illinois 10
54 Northwestern 10
42 Michigan ■ 39
14 Florida * 41

Nickname: Buckeyes
Colors: Scarlet & Gray
Stadium: Ohio
Capacity: 101,568; Year Built: 1922
AD: Eugene Smith
SID: Steve Snapp

OHIO WESLEYAN

Delaware, OH 43015 III

Coach: Mike Hollway, Michigan 1974
Record: 24 Years, 135-102-2

2006 RESULTS (3-7)

23 Franklin 38
33 Catholic 34
28 Bethany (W.V.) ■ 34
28 Wabash 42
42 Kenyon ■ 44
0 Wooster ■ 24
35 Denison 10
17 Wittenberg ■ 10
13 Allegheny 30
58 Hiram ■ 0

Nickname: Battling Bishops
Colors: Red & Black
Stadium: Selby Field
Capacity: 9,600; Year Built: 1929
AD: Roger Ingles
SID: Mark Beckenbach

OKLAHOMA

Norman, OK 73019 ....FBS

Coach: Bob Stoops, Iowa 1983
Record: 8 Years, 86-19-0

2006 RESULTS (11-3)

24 UAB ■ 17
37 Washington ■ 20
33 Oregon 34
59 Middle Tenn. ■ 0
10 Texas * 28
34 Iowa St. ■ 9
24 Colorado ■ 3
26 Missouri 10
17 Texas A&M 16
34 Texas Tech ■ 24
36 Baylor 10
27 Oklahoma St. 21
21 Nebraska * 7
42 Boise St. * 43

Nickname: Sooners
Colors: Crimson & Cream
Stadium: Gaylord Family - Oklahoma Memorial Stadium
Capacity: 82,112; Year Built: 1923
AD: Joseph R. Castiglione
SID: Kenny Mossman

OKLA. PANHANDLE

Goodwell, OK 73939 II

Coach: Kyle Davis, Adams St. 1991
Record: 2 Years, 1-20-0

2006 RESULTS (0-10)

6 Emporia St. ■ 69
0 Pittsburg St. 87
14 Southwestern Okla. ■ 33
0 Colorado Mines 69
7 Northwestern Okla. ■ 41
24 Bacone ■ 28
16 Western St. 66
17 Western N.M. 61
7 Adams St. ■ 55
14 Eastern N.M. 63

Nickname: Aggies
Colors: Crimson & Royal Blue
Stadium: Carl Wooten
Capacity: 5,000
AD: Jerry Olson
SID: Jason Cronin

OKLAHOMA ST.

Stillwater, OK 74078-5070 ....FBS

Coach: Mike Gundy, Oklahoma St. 1990
Record: 2 Years, 11-13-0

2006 RESULTS (7-6)

52 Missouri St. ■ 10
35 Arkansas St. * 7
48 Fla. Atlantic ■ 8
25 Houston 34
27 Kansas St. 31
42 Kansas 32
33 Texas A&M ■ 34
41 Nebraska ■ 29
10 Texas 36
66 Baylor ■ 24
24 Texas Tech 30
21 Oklahoma ■ 27
34 Alabama * 31

Nickname: Cowboys
Colors: Orange & Black
Stadium: Boone Pickens
Capacity: 48,500; Year Built: 1920
AD: Mike Holder
SID: Kevin Klintworth

OLIVET

Olivet, MI 49076 III

Coach: Dominic Livedoti, Olivet 1965
Record: 9 Years, 37-47-3

2006 RESULTS (6-4)

6 Ill. Wesleyan 21
33 Manchester ■ 14
16 Elmhurst ■ 33
19 Wis. Lutheran 6
13 Adrian ■ 10
20 Albion 17
7 Tri-State 21
28 Alma ■ 24
8 Hope ■ 16
43 Kalamazoo 24

Nickname: Comets
Colors: Red & White
Stadium: Cutler Athletic Complex
Capacity: 2,200; Year Built: 1972
AD: Thomas Shaw
SID: Geoffrey Henson

OREGON

Eugene, OR 97401 ....FBS

Coach: Mike Bellotti, UC Davis 1973
Record: 17 Years, 118-73-2

2006 RESULTS (7-6)

48 Stanford ■ 10
31 Fresno St. 24
34 Oklahoma ■ 33
48 Arizona St. 13
24 California 45
30 UCLA ■ 20
23 Washington St. 34
55 Portland St. ■ 12
34 Washington ■ 14
10 Southern California 35
10 Arizona ■ 37
28 Oregon St. 30
8 Brigham Young * 38

Nickname: Ducks
Colors: Green & Yellow
Stadium: Autzen
Capacity: 54,000; Year Built: 1967
AD: William Moos
SID: David Williford

OREGON ST.

Corvallis, OR 97331 ....FBS

Coach: Mike Riley, Alabama 1974
Record: 6 Years, 38-34-0

2006 RESULTS (10-4)

56 Eastern Wash. ■ 17
14 Boise St. 42
38 Idaho ■ 0
13 California ■ 41
6 Washington St. ■ 13
27 Washington 17
17 Arizona 10
33 Southern California ■ 31
44 Arizona St. ■ 10
7 UCLA 25
30 Stanford 7
30 Oregon ■ 28
35 Hawaii 32
39 Missouri * 38

Nickname: Beavers
Colors: Orange & Black
Stadium: Reser
Capacity: 43,300; Year Built: 1953
AD: Bob DeCarolis
SID: Steve Fenk

OTTERBEIN

Westerville, OH 43081-2006 III

Coach: Joe Loth, Otterbein 1991
Record: 7 Years, 25-44-0

2006 RESULTS (4-6)

25 Defiance 13
14 Mount Union ■ 71
27 Marietta ■ 24
0 Ohio Northern 26
7 Wilmington (Ohio) ■ 38
34 Heidelberg 6
0 Capital 26
20 Muskingum ■ 0
31 Baldwin-Wallace ■ 42
0 John Carroll 14

Nickname: Cardinals
Colors: Tan & Cardinal
Stadium: Memorial
Capacity: 4,000; Year Built: 2005
AD: Richard E. Reynolds
SID: Ed Syguda

OUACHITA BAPTIST

Arkadelphia, AR 71998-0001 II

Coach: Todd Knight, Ouachita Baptist 1986
Record: 14 Years, 52-87-2

2006 RESULTS (2-8)

22 Mo. Southern St. 28
47 East Tex. Baptist 14
6 Ark.-Monticello 27
6 Delta St. 34
21 Valdosta St. ■ 49
10 North Ala. ■ 47
33 Southern Ark. 48
35 Arkansas Tech ■ 55
28 Henderson St. 48
34 Harding ■ 20

Nickname: Tigers
Colors: Purple & Gold
Stadium: A.U. Williams Field
Capacity: 5,200
AD: David R. Sharp
SID: Ben Cutrell

PACE

Pleasantville, NY 10570-2799 II

Coach: Mike Iezzi, Kean 1988
Record: 2 Years, 6-14-0

2006 RESULTS (3-7)

27 Husson ■ 14
7 C.W. Post 28
7 Stonehill ■ 0
7 St. Anselm 2
17 Bryant ■ 31
6 Bentley 21
0 Southern Conn. St. ■ 28
0 American Int'l 7
0 Merrimack ■ 18
0 Assumption 19

Nickname: Setters
Colors: Navy & Gold
Stadium: Finnerty Field
Capacity: 1,500; Year Built: 1969
AD: Joseph F. O'Donnell
SID: Ken Sweeten

PACIFIC LUTHERAN

Tacoma, WA 98447-0003 III

Coach: Scott Westering, Pacific Lutheran 1982
Record: 3 Years, 13-14-0

2006 RESULTS (4-5)

14 Cal Lutheran ■ 17
17 Wis.-River Falls ■ 24
25 Chapman 42
32 Puget Sound 28
7 Whitworth ■ 19
34 Menlo 10
21 Linfield ■ 44
44 Lewis & Clark 7
38 Willamette ■ 7

Nickname: Lutes
Colors: Black & Gold
Stadium: Sparks
Capacity: 4,500; Year Built: 1985
AD: Laurie Turner
SID: Nick Dawson

PENN

Philadelphia, PA 19104-6322..................FCS

Coach: Al Bagnoli, Central Conn. St. 1975
Record: 25 Years, 190-63-0

2006 RESULTS (5-5)

21 Lafayette..........11
20 Villanova ■..........27
17 Dartmouth ■..........10
34 Bucknell..........24
16 Columbia ■..........0
14 Yale..........17
27 Brown ■..........30
30 Princeton..........31
22 Harvard ■..........13
27 Cornell..........28

Nickname: Quakers
Colors: Red & Blue
Stadium: Franklin Field
Capacity: 52,958; Year Built: 1895
AD: Steve Bilsky
SID: Mat Kanan

PENN ST.

University Park, PA 16802........................FBS

Coach: Joe Paterno, Brown 1950
Record: 41 Years, 363-121-3

2006 RESULTS (9-4)

34 Akron ■..........16
17 Notre Dame..........41
37 Youngstown St. ■..........3
6 Ohio St..........28
33 Northwestern ■..........7
28 Minnesota..........27
10 Michigan ■..........17
26 Illinois ■..........12
12 Purdue..........0
3 Wisconsin..........13
47 Temple ■..........0
17 Michigan St. ■..........13
20 Tennessee *..........10

Nickname: Nittany Lions
Colors: Blue & White
Stadium: Beaver
Capacity: 106,537; Year Built: 1960
AD: Timothy M. Curley
SID: Jeff Nelson

PITTSBURG ST.

Pittsburg, KS 66762....................................II

Coach: Chuck Broyles, Pittsburg St. 1970
Record: 17 Years, 174-36-2

2006 RESULTS (10-2)

52 East Central..........12
87 Okla. Panhandle ■..........0
35 Mo. Western St...........48
48 Mo. Southern St. ■..........24
59 Emporia St...........57
29 Washburn ■..........14
35 Fort Hays St...........28
63 Southwest Baptist ■..........20
45 Truman ■..........21
14 Northwest Mo. St. *..........41
35 Central Mo. ■..........30
35 Bemidji St. *..........27

Nickname: Gorillas
Colors: Crimson & Gold
Stadium: Carnie Smith
Capacity: 8,344; Year Built: 1924
AD: Charles Broyles
SID: Dan Wilkes

PITTSBURGH

Pittsburgh, PA 15260..............................FBS

Coach: Dave Wannstedt, Pittsburgh 1974
Record: 2 Years, 11-12-0

2006 RESULTS (6-6)

38 Virginia ■..........13
33 Cincinnati..........15
23 Michigan St. ■..........38
51 Citadel ■..........6
45 Toledo ■..........3
21 Syracuse..........11
52 UCF..........7
10 Rutgers ■..........20
12 South Fla...........22
45 Connecticut..........46
27 West Virginia ■..........45
24 Louisville ■..........48

Nickname: Panthers
Colors: Gold & Blue
Stadium: Heinz Field
Capacity: 65,000; Year Built: 2001
AD: Jeffrey Long
SID: E.J. Borghetti

PLYMOUTH ST.

Plymouth, NH 03264-1595..........................III

Coach: Paul Castonia, Trinity (Conn.) 1986
Record: 7 Years, 10-58-0

2006 RESULTS (4-5)

14 Mount Ida..........19
7 Coast Guard..........35
27 Mass.-Dartmouth ■..........13
19 Western New Eng. ■..........18
7 Endicott..........24
14 Nichols..........19
26 Curry ■..........40
35 MIT..........3
27 Salve Regina ■..........7

Nickname: Panthers
Colors: Green & White
Stadium: Currier Memorial Field
Capacity: 1,000; Year Built: 1970
AD: John P. Clark
SID: Kent Cherrington

POMONA-PITZER

Claremont, CA 91711-6346......................III

Coach: Scott Rynne, Williams 1991
Record: 2 Years, 7-11-0

2006 RESULTS (3-6)

27 Colorado Col. ■..........34
38 Lewis & Clark..........20
24 Whittier ■..........17
19 La Verne..........20
14 Redlands ■..........46
23 Occidental..........38
14 Chapman..........21
24 Cal Lutheran..........27
31 Claremont-M-S ■..........14

Nickname: Sagehens
Colors: Blue, Orange & White
Stadium: Merritt Field
Capacity: 2,000; Year Built: 1991
AD: Charles C. Katsiaficas
SID: Ben Belletto

PORTLAND ST.

Portland, OR 97207-0751......................FCS

Coach: Tim Walsh, UC Riverside 1977
Record: 18 Years, 117-82-0

2006 RESULTS (7-4)

17 New Mexico..........6
45 Northern Colo. ■..........3
16 California..........42
20 Weber St...........10
20 Montana ■..........26
0 Montana St...........14
34 Idaho St. ■..........13
34 Eastern Wash. ■..........0
12 Oregon..........55
34 Northern Ariz...........26
13 Sacramento St...........7

Nickname: Vikings
Colors: Green, White & Silver
Stadium: PGE Park
Capacity: 20,000; Year Built: 1928
AD: Teri Mariani
SID: Mike Lund

PRAIRIE VIEW

Prairie View, TX 77446-0097..................FCS

Coach: Henry Frazier III, Bowie St. 1993
Record: 8 Years, 37-45-0

2006 RESULTS (3-7)

14 Texas Southern *..........17
37 Edward Waters ■..........0
26 Southern U. ■..........23
7 Grambling *..........53
14 Alcorn St. ■..........17
7 Alabama St. ■..........10
10 Mississippi Val...........14
21 Ark.-Pine Bluff ■..........28
7 Jackson St...........31
13 Alabama A&M..........7

Nickname: Panthers
Colors: Purple & Gold
Stadium: Blackshear
Capacity: 6,000; Year Built: 1960
AD: Charles McClelland
SID: Stefann Robinson

PRESBYTERIAN

(Reclassifying to FCS)

Clinton, SC 29325-2998............................II

Coach: Tommy Spangler, Georgia 1983
Record: 6 Years, 42-24-0

2006 RESULTS (7-4)

10 West Ga...........0
13 Charleston So. ■..........21
7 Fayetteville St...........6
0 Elon..........28
24 Lenoir-Rhyne ■..........13
9 Wingate ■..........14
30 Tusculum..........21
21 Mars Hill..........14
28 Carson-Newman ■..........7
14 Catawba..........21
10 Newberry ■..........0

Nickname: Blue Hose
Colors: Blue & Garnet
Stadium: Bailey Memorial
Capacity: 6,500; Year Built: 2002
AD: William B. Carlton
SID: Al Ansley

PRINCETON

Princeton, NJ 08544..............................FCS

Coach: Roger Hughes, Doane 1982
Record: 7 Years, 35-34-0

2006 RESULTS (9-1)

14 Lehigh..........10
26 Lafayette ■..........14
19 Columbia..........6
27 Colgate..........26

17 Brown ■ 3
31 Harvard ■ 28
7 Cornell 14
31 Penn ■ 30
34 Yale 31
27 Dartmouth ■ 17

Nickname: Tigers
Colors: Orange & Black
Stadium: Princeton
Capacity: 27,800; Year Built: 1998
AD: Gary D. Walters
SID: Craig Sachson

PRINCIPIA

Elsah, IL 62028-9799 III

Coach: Mike Barthelmess, Principia 1983
Record: 9 Years, 15-61-1

2006 RESULTS (0-9)

20 Crown (Minn.) 28
6 Macalester 50
6 Minn.-Morris ■ 62
0 Blackburn ■ 51
13 Maranatha Baptist ■ 55
0 Rockford 57
6 Trinity Bible (N.D.) 13
0 Westminster (Mo.) 42
13 Trinity Bible (N.D.) * 19

Nickname: Panthers
Colors: Gold & Blue
Stadium: Clark Field
Capacity: 1,000; Year Built: 1937
AD: Lenore Suarez
SID: Vitalis Otieno

PUGET SOUND

Tacoma, WA 98416-9710 III

Coach: Phillip Willenbrock, Gettysburg 1989
Record: 5 Years, 17-29-0

2006 RESULTS (7-3)

26 Whittier 19
28 La Verne 21
21 Claremont-M-S ■ 0
28 Pacific Lutheran ■ 32
17 Linfield ■ 42
34 Willamette 26
70 Lewis & Clark ■ 14
28 Colorado Col. 25
48 Menlo ■ 7
27 Whitworth 44

Nickname: Loggers
Colors: Maroon & White
Stadium: Baker
Capacity: 6,000; Year Built: 1964
AD: Amy E. Hackett
SID: Chris Thompson

PURDUE

West Lafayette, IN 47907-1031 ....FBS

Coach: Joe Tiller, Montana St. 1965
Record: 16 Years, 114-79-1

2006 RESULTS (8-6)

60 Indiana St. ■ 35
38 Miami (Ohio) ■ 31
38 Ball St. ■ 28
27 Minnesota ■ 21
21 Notre Dame 35
17 Iowa 47
31 Northwestern 10
3 Wisconsin ■ 24
0 Penn St. ■ 12
17 Michigan St. 15
42 Illinois 31
28 Indiana ■ 19
35 Hawaii 42
7 Maryland * 24

Nickname: Boilermakers
Colors: Old Gold & Black
Stadium: Ross-Ade
Capacity: 62,500; Year Built: 1924
AD: Morgan J. Burke
SID: Tom Schott

RANDOLPH-MACON

Ashland, VA 23005 III

Coach: Pedro Arruza, Wheaton (Ill.) 1995
Record: 3 Years, 7-23-0

2006 RESULTS (2-8)

20 Denison ■ 14
14 Johns Hopkins ■ 21
10 Frostburg St. 7
7 Catholic ■ 14
10 Wash. & Lee 33
7 Emory & Henry 28
14 McDaniel 24
6 Guilford ■ 14
24 Bridgewater (Va.) ■ 35
21 Hampden-Sydney 46

Nickname: Yellow Jackets
Colors: Lemon & Black
Stadium: Day Field
Capacity: 5,000; Year Built: 1953
AD: Denis Kanach
SID: Chris Kilcoyne

REDLANDS

Redlands, CA 92373-0999 III

Coach: Mike Maynard, Ill. Wesleyan 1981
Record: 19 Years, 113-60-1

2006 RESULTS (4-5)

3 Whitworth ■ 28
10 Trinity (Tex.) 35
7 Chapman ■ 13
10 Occidental ■ 24
46 Pomona-Pitzer 14
21 Claremont-M-S ■ 9
24 La Verne 19
21 Whittier 28
24 Cal Lutheran ■ 20

Nickname: Bulldogs
Colors: Maroon & Gray
Stadium: Ted Runner
Capacity: 7,000; Year Built: 1968
AD: Jeffrey Martinez
SID: Rachel J. Roche

RENSSELAER

Troy, NY 12180-3590 III

Coach: Joe King, Siena 1970
Record: 18 Years, 124-48-2

2006 RESULTS (7-3)

27 Endicott 7
34 Utica 10
17 Hobart ■ 24
56 Becker ■ 6
38 St. Lawrence 42
42 Merchant Marine 31
26 WPI ■ 0
23 Rochester 30
24 Union (N.Y.) ■ 19
26 Cortland St. 7

Nickname: Red Hawks
Colors: Cherry & White
Stadium: '86 Field
Capacity: 3,000; Year Built: 1912
AD: Ken Ralph
SID: Kevin Beattie

RHODE ISLAND

Kingston, RI 02881-1303 ....FCS

Coach: Tim Stowers, Auburn 1980
Record: 13 Years, 81-72-0

2006 RESULTS (4-7)

7 Connecticut 52
42 Merrimack ■ 7
17 Delaware ■ 24
28 Brown ■ 21
23 James Madison 35
6 Richmond ■ 31
16 Massachusetts 41
3 Maine ■ 0
20 Hofstra 13
21 New Hampshire ■ 63
31 Northeastern 45

Nickname: Rams
Colors: Light & Dark Blue & White
Stadium: Meade
Capacity: 8,000; Year Built: 1928
AD: Thomas P. McElroy
SID: Tim Volkmann

RHODES

Memphis, TN 38112-1690 III

Coach: Joe White, Springfield 1984
Record: 10 Years, 47-50-0

2006 RESULTS (6-4)

37 LaGrange 0
20 Centre ■ 10
7 Huntingdon ■ 21
6 Washington-St. Louis ■ 3
21 Austin 7
6 DePauw ■ 27
28 Colorado Col. ■ 10
7 Trinity (Tex.) 41
6 Millsaps ■ 14
14 Sewanee 7

Nickname: Lynx
Colors: Red, Black & White
Stadium: Fargason Field
Capacity: 3,300; Year Built: 1964
AD: Mike Clary
SID: Matt Dean

RICE

Houston, TX 77251-1892 ....FBS

Coach: Todd Graham, East Central 1987
Record: 1 Year, 7-6-0

2006 RESULTS (7-6)

30 Houston ■ 31
16 UCLA 26
7 Texas * 52
7 Florida St. 55
48 Army 14
24 Tulane 38
34 UAB ■ 33
40 UCF 29
37 UTEP 31
41 Tulsa 38
18 East Caro. ■ 17
31 SMU ■ 27
17 Troy * 41

Nickname: Owls
Colors: Blue & Gray
Stadium: Rice
Capacity: 70,000; Year Built: 1950
AD: Christopher M. DelConte
SID: Bill Cousins

RICHMOND

Richmond, VA 23173-1903 ....FCS

Coach: Dave Clawson, Williams 1989
Record: 8 Years, 47-46-0

2006 RESULTS (6-5)
13 Duke....0
58 VMI ■....7
48 Bucknell ■....21
12 Northeastern ■....7
17 New Hampshire....27
31 Rhode Island....6
24 Delaware ■....28
10 James Madison ■....27
21 Villanova....31
7 Towson ■....31
31 William & Mary....14

Nickname: Spiders
Colors: Red & Blue
Stadium: Richmond
Capacity: 21,319; Year Built: 1929
AD: Jim Miller
SID: Scott Meyer

RIPON
Ripon, WI 54971 III

Coach: Ron Ernst, Neb. Wesleyan 1980
Record: 16 Years, 103-52-0

2006 RESULTS (7-3)
0 Wis.-Oshkosh....57
35 Lake Forest ■....27
35 Knox....14
31 Illinois Col. ■....21
21 Carroll (Wis.)....14
41 Beloit ■....7
14 Monmouth (Ill.)....24
28 St. Norbert ■....38
55 Grinnell ■....14
31 Lawrence....14

Nickname: Red Hawks
Colors: Red & White
Stadium: Ingalls Field
Capacity: 2,500; Year Built: 1888
AD: Robert G. Gillespie
SID: Patricia A. Malizia

ROBERT MORRIS
Moon Township, PA 15108-1189 ....FCS

Coach: Joe Walton, Pittsburgh 1957
Record: 13 Years, 82-49-1

2006 RESULTS (7-4)
14 Dayton....21
7 Duquesne ■....27
35 Butler....14
21 Rowan ■....0
45 St. Francis (Pa.)....13
14 Wagner....10
23 Central Conn. St. ■....17
7 Monmouth ■....16
21 Stony Brook....6
6 Albany (N.Y.) ■....16
41 Sacred Heart....21

Nickname: Colonials
Colors: Blue & White with Red
Stadium: Moon
Capacity: 7,000; Year Built: 1950
AD: Craig Coleman
SID: Jim Duzyk

ROCHESTER
Rochester, NY 14627-0296 III

Coach: Scott Greene, Michigan St. 1996
Record: 1 Year, 7-4-0

2006 RESULTS (7-4)
20 Johns Hopkins....10
10 St. John Fisher ■....30
54 Gettysburg ■....42
24 Union (N.Y.)....27
19 St. Lawrence ■....18
28 Merchant Marine ■....24
34 WPI....7
38 Grove City....21
30 Rensselaer ■....23
21 Hobart....31
34 Alfred....40

Nickname: Yellowjackets
Colors: Yellow & Blue
Stadium: Edwin Fauver
Capacity: 5,000; Year Built: 1930
AD: George VanderZwaag
SID: Dennis O'Donnell

ROCKFORD
Rockford, IL 61108-2393 III

Coach: Randy Schrader, William Penn 1982
Record: 1 Year, 7-3-0

2006 RESULTS (7-3)
16 Aurora....6
22 MacMurray ■....0
14 Northwestern (Minn.) ■....21
16 Maranatha Baptist ■....6
35 Westminster (Mo.)....20
57 Principia ■....0
61 Blackburn....0
27 Martin Luther....6
20 Minn.-Morris *....27
23 Colorado Col.....34

Nickname: Regents
Colors: Purple & White
Stadium: Sam Greeley Field
Capacity: 1,000; Year Built: 2001
AD: Hank Espensen
SID: Andrew McGlothlen

ROSE-HULMAN
Terre Haute, IN 47803 III

Coach: Steve Englehart, Indiana St. 2000
Record: 1 Year, 6-4-0

2006 RESULTS (6-4)
24 Earlham ■....17
9 Mt. St. Joseph ■....20
56 Concordia (Ill.) ■....0
25 North Park....0
8 Hanover....41
10 Defiance ■....13
21 Bluffton....12
11 Franklin....28
38 Anderson (Ind.) ■....14
34 Manchester....3

Nickname: Fightin' Engineers
Colors: Old Rose & White
Stadium: Phil Brown Field
Capacity: 2,500
AD: Jeffrey Jenkins
SID: Kevin Lanke

ROWAN
Glassboro, NJ 08028-1701 III

Coach: Jay Accorsi, Nichols 1985
Record: 5 Years, 47-12-0

2006 RESULTS (9-3)
32 Chris. Newport ■....8
0 Robert Morris....21
24 Western Conn. St. ■....17
14 TCNJ....6
35 Buffalo St. *....7
16 Kean ■....12
20 Montclair St.....27
14 Cortland St. ■....7
38 Wm. Paterson ■....7
20 Hobart ■....18
21 Wilkes....14
0 St. John Fisher....31

Nickname: Profs
Colors: Brown & Gold
Stadium: John Page Field
Capacity: 5,000; Year Built: 1982
AD: Joy L. Solomen
SID: Sheila Stevenson

RUTGERS
New Brunswick, NJ 08903 ....FBS

Coach: Greg Schiano, Bucknell 1988
Record: 6 Years, 30-41-0

2006 RESULTS (11-2)
21 North Carolina....16
33 Illinois ■....0
24 Ohio ■....7
56 Howard ■....7
22 South Fla.....20
34 Navy....0
20 Pittsburgh....10
24 Connecticut ■....13
28 Louisville ■....25
11 Cincinnati....30
38 Syracuse ■....7
39 West Virginia....41
37 Kansas St. *....10

Nickname: Scarlet Knights
Colors: Scarlet
Stadium: Rutgers
Capacity: 41,500; Year Built: 1994
AD: Robert E. Mulcahy III
SID: John Wooding

SACRAMENTO ST.
Sacramento, CA 95819-6099....FCS

Coach: Steve Mooshagian, Fresno St. 1982
Record: 4 Years, 11-33-0

2006 RESULTS (4-7)
0 Boise St.....45
10 Cal Poly ■....17
14 Montana....59
21 Eastern Wash.....20
24 Weber St. ■....21
18 Montana St. ■....21
22 Northern Ariz.....39
14 Northern Colo. ■....9
22 Idaho St.....14
7 Portland St. ■....13
16 UC Davis....30

Nickname: Hornets
Colors: Green & Gold
Stadium: Hornet Field
Capacity: 21,418; Year Built: 1964
AD: Terry L. Wanless
SID: Brian Berger

SACRED HEART
Fairfield, CT 06825-1000....FCS

Coach: Paul Gorham, New Hampshire 1984
Record: 3 Years, 12-19-0

2006 RESULTS (2-9)
14 Lafayette ■....25
19 Marist....28
27 Iona ■....16
21 Duquesne....24
25 Wagner ■....17
0 Monmouth....24
13 Albany (N.Y.) ■....24
21 Stony Brook....38
14 St. Francis (Pa.)....21
14 Central Conn. St. ■....42
21 Robert Morris ■....41

Nickname: Pioneers
Colors: Red & White
Stadium: Campus Field
Capacity: 3,500; Year Built: 1993
AD: C. Donald Cook
SID: Gene Gumbs

SAGINAW VALLEY

University Center, MI 48710-0001 II

Coach: Randy Awrey, Northern Mich. 1978
Record: 17 Years, 117-65-1

2006 RESULTS (6-4)

27 Ashland........16
26 Gannon ■........10
23 Ferris St........26
37 Northern Mich. ■........35
14 Northwood (Mich.) ■........25
31 Findlay........14
7 Michigan Tech........20
23 Indianapolis ■........16
35 Grand Valley St........49
46 Hillsdale ■........30

Nickname: Cardinals
Colors: Red, White & Blue
Stadium: Harvey R. Wickes
Capacity: 4,028; Year Built: 1975
AD: Mike E. Watson
SID: Ryan Thompson

ST. ANSELM

Manchester, NH 03102-1310......................II

Coach: Ken Knapczyk, Winona St. 1997
Record: 2 Years, 1-19-0

2006 RESULTS (0-10)

10 American Int'l ■........34
0 Edinboro........54
23 Assumption........26
2 Pace ■........7
0 C.W. Post........34
9 Stonehill ■........24
28 Merrimack ■........52
0 Bryant........41
6 Bentley ■........14
7 Southern Conn. St........69

Nickname: Hawks
Colors: Blue & White
Stadium: Grappone
Capacity: 4,500; Year Built: 1999
AD: Edward Cannon
SID: Ken Johnson Jr.

ST. AUGUSTINE'S

Raleigh, NC 27610-2298............................II

Coach: Michael Costa, Norfolk St. 1971
Record: 10 Years, 31-65-0

2006 RESULTS (4-6)

16 Lane ■........20
21 Virginia St........14
14 Carson-Newman ■........24
7 Mars Hill........14
0 Elizabeth City St. ■........49
18 N.C. Central ■........27
15 Johnson C. Smith........9
31 Livingstone ■........16
15 Fayetteville St........3
6 Winston-Salem........26

Nickname: Falcons
Colors: Blue & White
Stadium: Broughton High School
AD: George Williams
SID: Anthony Jeffries

ST. CLOUD ST.

St. Cloud, MN 56301-4498 II

Coach: Randy Hedberg, Minot St. 1977
Record: 8 Years, 43-44-0

2006 RESULTS (3-8)

71 Minn.-Crookston ■........0
14 Mo. Western St........27
37 Mary ■........14
10 South Dakota ■........20
14 Central Wash........24
17 Western Wash. ■........24
23 Augustana (S.D.)........27
16 Minn. St. Mankato ■........3
17 Neb.-Omaha........21
27 North Dakota ■........34
24 Minn. Duluth........29

Nickname: Huskies
Colors: Cardinal Red & Black
Stadium: Husky
Capacity: 4,198; Year Built: 2004
AD: Morris Kurtz
SID: Anne Abicht

ST. FRANCIS (PA.)

Loretto, PA 15940-0600 ....FCS

Coach: Dave Opfar, Penn St. 1983
Record: 5 Years, 12-41-0

2006 RESULTS (3-8)

38 St. Peter's ■........3
28 Delaware St........63
10 Duquesne........41
21 La Salle ■........24
13 Robert Morris ■........45
21 Central Conn. St........62
20 Stony Brook ■........30
0 Albany (N.Y.)........48
21 Sacred Heart ■........14
20 Monmouth........54
35 Wagner ■........14

Nickname: Red Flash
Colors: Red & White
Stadium: Pine Bowl
Capacity: 1,500; Year Built: 1979
AD: Robert S. Krimmel
SID: Pat Farabaugh

ST. JOHN FISHER

Rochester, NY 14618 III

Coach: Paul Vosburgh, William Penn 1975
Record: 18 Years, 80-101-1

2006 RESULTS (12-2)

30 King's (Pa.) ■........0
30 Rochester........10
55 Mount Ida ■........0
34 Ithaca ■........10
57 Hartwick ■........16
27 Brockport St........20
32 Norwich........0
38 Springfield ■........55
64 Utica........0
41 Alfred........13
49 Union (N.Y.) ■........21
27 Springfield........21
31 Rowan ■........0
14 Mount Union........26

Nickname: Cardinals
Colors: Cardinal & Gold
Stadium: Growney
Capacity: 2,100; Year Built: 1999
AD: Bob Ward
SID: Norm Kieffer

ST. JOHN'S (MINN.)

Collegeville, MN 56321 III

Coach: John Gagliardi, Colorado Col. 1949
Record: 58 Years, 443-120-11

2006 RESULTS (11-2)

15 Wis.-Eau Claire ■........11
41 Wis.-River Falls ■........9
60 Augsburg........0
14 Concordia-M'head........12
29 Carleton ■........19
37 St. Olaf........21
34 Gust. Adolphus ■........7
56 Hamline ■........7
27 St. Thomas (Minn.)........7
13 Bethel (Minn.) ■........28
21 Central (Iowa)........13
21 Whitworth........3
14 Wis.-Whitewater........17

Nickname: Johnnies
Colors: Cardinal & Blue
Stadium: Clemens
Capacity: 7,000; Year Built: 1908
AD: Tom Stock
SID: Ryan Klinkner

ST. JOSEPH'S (IND.)

Rensselaer, IN 47978 II

Coach: Lou Esposito, Memphis 2000
Record: 2 Years, 15-7-0

2006 RESULTS (8-3)

37 St. Francis (Ill.) ■........0
17 Wayne St. (Mich.)........10
6 Grand Valley St. ■........31
22 Indianapolis........35
38 Mo.-Rolla........24
43 Valparaiso........14
60 Lincoln (Mo.)........3
41 Ky. Wesleyan........3
19 Fairmont St........11
27 Central St. (Ohio)........34
24 Tiffin ■........23

Nickname: Pumas
Colors: Cardinal & Purple
Stadium: Alumni Field
Capacity: 4,000; Year Built: 1947
AD: Bill Massoels
SID: Clark Teuscher

ST. LAWRENCE

Canton, NY 13617......................................III

Coach: Chris Phelps, St. Lawrence 1991
Record: 7 Years, 16-52-0

2006 RESULTS (5-4)

17 Norwich ■........13
14 Alfred ■........17
21 Johns Hopkins ■........20
18 Rochester........19
42 Rensselaer ■........38
7 Hobart ■........27
7 Union (N.Y.)........42
49 Merchant Marine ■........7
31 WPI........7

Nickname: Saints
Colors: Scarlet & Brown
Stadium: Leckonby
Capacity: 1,500; Year Built: 2000
AD: Margaret F. Strait
SID: Jill Olsen

ST. NORBERT

De Pere, WI 54115 III

Coach: Jim Purtill, Miami (Ohio) 1978
Record: 8 Years, 74-12-0

2006 RESULTS (10-1)

31 Olivet Nazarene........13
63 Grinnell ■........13
42 Lawrence........14
14 Lake Forest ■........7
42 Knox........27
48 Monmouth (Ill.) ■........0
41 Carroll (Wis.) ■........0
38 Ripon........28
37 Beloit........7
49 Illinois Col. ■........0
17 Wis.-Whitewater........59

Nickname: Green Knights
Colors: Dartmouth Green & Old Gold
Stadium: Minahan
Capacity: 3,100; Year Built: 1937
AD: Timothy A. Bald
SID: Dan Lukes

ST. OLAF

Northfield, MN 55057-1098......................III

Coach: Chris Meidt, Bethel (Minn.) 1992
Record: 5 Years, 32-18-0

2006 RESULTS (8-2)

31 Valley City St. 14
35 Luther ■ 16
31 Hamline ■ 6
68 Augsburg ■ 17
41 Gust. Adolphus 13
21 St. John's (Minn.) ■ 37
49 Concordia-M'head 14
29 Bethel (Minn.) 35
48 Carleton ■ 15
35 St. Thomas (Minn.) 31

Nickname: Oles
Colors: Black & Old Gold
Stadium: Manitou Field
Capacity: 4,500; Year Built: 1930
AD: Matt McDonald
SID: Mike Ludwig

ST. PAUL'S

Lawrenceville, VA 23868............................II

Coach: Willard Bailey, Norfolk St. 1962
Record: 33 Years, 216-126-7

2006 RESULTS (2-8)

0 Liberty 27
36 George Mason (Club) 0
0 Tusculum ■ 28
24 Fayetteville St. 21
7 Johnson C. Smith ■ 13
7 Virginia Union 23
5 Virginia St. ■ 24
0 Bowie St. ■ 24
3 Elizabeth City St. ■ 7
7 Shaw 14

Nickname: Tigers
Colors: Black & Orange
Stadium: Russell
Capacity: 3,000
AD: LeRoy Bacote
SID: To be named

ST. PETER'S

Jersey City, NJ 07306............................FCS

Coach: Chris Taylor, Lafayette 1996
Record: 3 Years, 6-24-0

2006 RESULTS (2-8)

3 St. Francis (Pa.) 38
3 Western Conn. St. 21
12 Monmouth 36
0 Wagner 34
13 Central Conn. St. ■ 73
21 Duquesne ■ 35
26 Salisbury ■ 23
18 Marist 35
30 Iona 15
28 La Salle ■ 37

Nickname: Peacocks
Colors: Blue & White
Stadium: Cochrane
Capacity: 4,000; Year Built: 1990
AD: William A. Stein
SID: Dan Drutz

ST. THOMAS (MINN.)

St. Paul, MN 55105..................................III

Coach: Don Roney, St. Thomas (Minn.) 1983
Record: 9 Years, 52-36-0

2006 RESULTS (6-4)

7 Central (Iowa) ■ 17
19 Loras ■ 7
21 Gust. Adolphus 7
7 Bethel (Minn.) 17
14 Carleton ■ 10
47 Augsburg ■ 21
21 Concordia-M'head 15
7 St. John's (Minn.) ■ 27
35 Hamline 7
31 St. Olaf ■ 35

Nickname: Tommies
Colors: Purple & Grey
Stadium: O'Shaughnessy
Capacity: 5,025; Year Built: 1948
AD: Stephen J. Fritz
SID: Gene McGivern

SALISBURY

Salisbury, MD 21801-6860........................III

Coach: Sherman Wood, Salisbury 1984
Record: 14 Years, 72-69-1

2006 RESULTS (6-5)

32 Wash. & Jeff. 14
3 Brockport St. ■ 21
17 Chris. Newport ■ 23
3 Montclair St. 27
25 Apprentice 0
65 Morrisville St. ■ 7
23 St. Peter's ■ 26
10 Wesley ■ 13
17 Widener 14
42 Frostburg St. * 15
15 Delaware Valley 9

Nickname: Sea Gulls
Colors: Maroon & Gold
Stadium: Sea Gull
Capacity: 2,500; Year Built: 1980
AD: Michael Vienna
SID: Sam Atkinson

SALVE REGINA

Newport, RI 02840-4192...........................III

Coach: Chris Robertson, Albany (N.Y.) 1996
Record: 1 Year, 1-8-0

2006 RESULTS (1-8)

21 Maritime (N.Y.) ■ 15
14 Bridgewater St. ■ 28
7 Endicott 40
0 Curry ■ 35
14 Nichols ■ 21
7 Mass.-Dartmouth 17
25 MIT ■ 40
0 Western New Eng. 28
7 Plymouth St. 27

Nickname: Seahawks
Colors: Blue, Green & White
Stadium: Toppa Field
Capacity: 1,500; Year Built: 1966
AD: Del Malloy
SID: Ed Habershaw

SAM HOUSTON ST.

Huntsville, TX 77341 ....FCS

Coach: Todd Whitten, Stephen F. Austin 1987
Record: 8 Years, 54-35-0

2006 RESULTS (6-5)

41 Ark.-Monticello ■ 3
14 SMU 45
20 Missouri St. 17
3 Texas 56
30 Northwestern St. 20
37 Nicholls St. ■ 7
30 Central Ark. ■ 38
18 McNeese St. ■ 31
21 Stephen F. Austin 17
28 Southeastern La. 23
21 Texas St. ■ 28

Nickname: Bearkats
Colors: Orange & White
Stadium: Elliott T. Bowers
Capacity: 14,000; Year Built: 1986
AD: Bobby Williams
SID: Paul Ridings Jr.

SAMFORD

Birmingham, AL 35229...........................FCS

Coach: Bill Gray, Mississippi Col. 1983
Record: 6 Years, 27-33-0

2006 RESULTS (3-8)

37 Miles ■ 7
6 Georgia Tech 38
17 Austin Peay ■ 10
13 Eastern Ill. ■ 24
14 Southeast Mo. St. 19
12 Eastern Ky. ■ 31
33 Murray St. 7
6 Tenn.-Martin ■ 10
7 Tennessee St. 29
14 Tennessee Tech ■ 20
7 Jacksonville St. 55

Nickname: Bulldogs
Colors: Red & Blue
Stadium: Seibert
Capacity: 6,700; Year Built: 1960
AD: Bob Roller
SID: Joey Mullins

SAN DIEGO

San Diego, CA 92110-2492 ....FCS

Coach: Jim Harbaugh, Michigan 1986
Record: 3 Years, 29-6-0

2006 RESULTS (11-1)

27 Azusa Pacific ■ 0
41 Dixie St. ■ 7
43 Yale 17
50 Davidson 21
56 Butler ■ 3
68 Valparaiso ■ 7
37 Drake 0
44 Morehead St. ■ 21
38 Jacksonville 21
56 Dayton ■ 14
27 UC Davis 37
27 Monmouth 7

Nickname: Toreros
Colors: Columbia Blue, Navy & White
Stadium: USD Torero
Capacity: 4,000; Year Built: 1955
AD: Ky Snyder
SID: Ted Gosen

SAN DIEGO ST.

San Diego, CA 92182............................FBS

Coach: Chuck Long, Iowa 1985
Record: 1 Year, 3-9-0

2006 RESULTS (3-9)

27 UTEP ■ 34
0 Wisconsin 14
7 Utah ■ 38
10 San Jose St. 31

17 Brigham Young 47
19 Air Force ■ 12
14 Cal Poly ■ 16
24 Wyoming 27
21 UNLV ■ 7
0 TCU 52
14 New Mexico 41
17 Colorado St. ■ 6

Nickname: Aztecs
Colors: Scarlet & Black
Stadium: Qualcomm
Capacity: 54,000; Year Built: 1967
AD: Jeffrey W. Schemmel
SID: Mike May

SAN JOSE ST.

San Jose, CA 95192 .....FBS

Coach: Dick Tomey, DePauw 1960
Record: 26 Years, 170-122-7

2006 RESULTS (9-4)

29 Washington 35
35 Stanford ■ 34
17 Cal Poly ■ 7
31 San Diego St. ■ 10
21 Utah St. ■ 14
7 Nevada 23
44 Louisiana Tech ■ 10
31 New Mexico St. 21
20 Boise St. ■ 23
17 Hawaii 54
28 Idaho 13
24 Fresno St. ■ 14
20 New Mexico * 12

Nickname: Spartans
Colors: Gold, White & Blue
Stadium: Spartan
Capacity: 30,456; Year Built: 1933
AD: Thomas Bowen
SID: Lawrence Fan

SAVANNAH ST.

Savannah, GA 31404 .....FCS

Coach: Theo Lemon, Ohio 1980
Record: 3 Years, 5-23-0

2006 RESULTS (2-9)

7 Benedict 21
6 Bethune-Cookman 55
0 Liberty ■ 28
12 Miles ■ 24
13 Charleston So. ■ 38
24 Morehouse * 20
6 Winston-Salem ■ 38
6 Johnson C. Smith 27
6 Coastal Caro. 66
28 Edward Waters ■ 7
0 Cal Poly 55

Nickname: Tigers
Colors: Reflex Blue & Orange
Stadium: Ted Wright
Capacity: 8,000; Year Built: 1967
AD: Robert "Tony" O'Neal
SID: Opio Mashariki

SEWANEE

Sewanee, TN 37383-1000 III

Coach: John Windham, Vanderbilt 1986
Record: 11 Years, 45-61-0

2006 RESULTS (2-8)

42 Hampden-Sydney ■ 35
24 Huntingdon 44
7 Wash. & Lee 21
16 Maryville (Tenn.) ■ 8
0 Centre 14
24 DePauw 31
20 Austin ■ 44
18 Millsaps ■ 35
7 Trinity (Tex.) 21
7 Rhodes ■ 14

Nickname: Tigers
Colors: Purple & White
Stadium: McGee Field
Capacity: 1,500; Year Built: 1935
AD: Mark Webb
SID: Larry Dagenhart

SHAW

Raleigh, NC 27601 II

Coach: Darrell Asberry, Jackson St. 1994
Record: 1 Year, 3-7-0

2006 RESULTS (3-7)

12 N.C. Central 21
7 Carson-Newman 41
26 Edward Waters * 20
12 Maine 62
18 Livingstone 14
14 Bowie St. ■ 17
34 Virginia Union ■ 43
0 Elizabeth City St. 36
22 Virginia St. 28
14 St. Paul's ■ 7

Nickname: Bears
Colors: Garnet & White
Stadium: Trojan
Capacity: 7,000; Year Built: 1975
AD: Alfonza L. Carter
SID: Maurice Williams

SHENANDOAH

Winchester, VA 22601 III

Coach: Paul Barnes, James Madison 1984
Record: 5 Years, 24-27-0

2006 RESULTS (2-8)

6 Catholic ■ 17
0 Bridgewater (Va.) 30
20 Waynesburg 10
0 Ferrum 42
3 Chris. Newport ■ 17
36 Greensboro 10
0 N.C. Wesleyan ■ 30
0 Averett ■ 18
16 Maryville (Tenn.) 51
7 Methodist ■ 9

Nickname: Hornets
Colors: Red, White & Midnight Blue
Stadium: Shentel
Capacity: 2,500; Year Built: 2001
AD: John Hill
SID: Scott Musa

SHEPHERD

Shepherdstown, WV 25443-3210 II

Coach: Monte Cater, Millikin 1971
Record: 26 Years, 169-93-2

2006 RESULTS (11-1)

28 Millersville 7
14 Shippensburg 0
24 C.W. Post ■ 0
23 Glenville St. ■ 6
20 Fairmont St. ■ 0
17 Charleston (W.V.) 0
42 Concord ■ 0
41 West Va. Wesleyan ■ 0
34 West Liberty St. 32
38 West Virginia St. 12
31 Merrimack ■ 7
21 Bloomsburg ■ 24

Nickname: Rams
Colors: Blue & Gold
Stadium: Ram
Capacity: 5,000; Year Built: 1959
AD: Karl Wolf
SID: Chip Ransom

SHIPPENSBURG

Shippensburg, PA 17257 II

Coach: Rocky Rees, West Chester 1971
Record: 22 Years, 138-101-2

2006 RESULTS (5-6)

0 Shepherd ■ 14
35 Mansfield 0
42 Kutztown ■ 27
0 West Chester 24
14 Bloomsburg ■ 35
28 Slippery Rock 21
20 Lock Haven 17
16 Indiana (Pa.) ■ 20
20 California (Pa.) ■ 35
30 Edinboro 54
35 Clarion ■ 10

Nickname: Red Raiders
Colors: Red & Blue
Stadium: Seth Grove
Capacity: 7,700; Year Built: 1972
AD: Roberta Page
SID: Jason Eichelberger

SIMPSON

Indianola, IA 50125 III

Coach: Jay Niemann, Iowa St. 1983
Record: 5 Years, 28-23-0

2006 RESULTS (3-7)

16 Concordia (Wis.) 30
17 Bethel (Minn.) ■ 23
7 Wartburg ■ 31
34 Cornell College 7
14 Buena Vista 15
3 Coe ■ 12
28 Luther ■ 21
9 Dubuque 20
27 Loras ■ 17
0 Central (Iowa) 23

Nickname: Storm
Colors: Red & Gold
Stadium: Bill Buxton
Capacity: 5,000; Year Built: 1990
AD: John Sirianni
SID: Matt Turk

SLIPPERY ROCK

Slippery Rock, PA 16057 II

Coach: George Mihalik, Slippery Rock 1974
Record: 19 Years, 127-76-4

2006 RESULTS (7-4)

21 Youngstown St. 51
27 Millersville 22
46 Mansfield ■ 0
34 Kutztown 10
31 Clarion 7
21 Shippensburg ■ 28
14 California (Pa.) 24
35 Lock Haven ■ 0
24 Edinboro ■ 21
21 Indiana (Pa.) 17
20 West Chester ■ 21

Nickname: The Rock
Colors: Green & White
Stadium: N. Kerr Thompson
Capacity: 10,000; Year Built: 1974
AD: Paul A. Lueken
SID: Bob McComas

SOUTH CAROLINA

Columbia, SC 29208 .....FBS

Coach: Steve Spurrier, Florida 1967
Record: 17 Years, 157-50-2

2006 RESULTS (8-5)

15 Mississippi St. 0
0 Georgia ■ 18
27 Wofford ■ 20
45 Fla. Atlantic ■ 6
17 Auburn ■ 24
24 Kentucky 17
31 Vanderbilt 13
24 Tennessee ■ 31
20 Arkansas ■ 26
16 Florida 17
52 Middle Tenn. ■ 7
31 Clemson 28
44 Houston * 36

Nickname: Gamecocks
Colors: Garnet & Black
Stadium: Williams-Brice
Capacity: 80,250; Year Built: 1934
AD: Eric C. Hyman
SID: Steve Fink

SOUTH CAROLINA ST.

Orangeburg, SC 29117-0001 ....FCS

Coach: Buddy Pough, South Carolina St. 1975
Record: 5 Years, 40-17-0

2006 RESULTS (7-4)

21 Wofford 28
35 Winston-Salem 6
21 Bethune-Cookman ■ 45
14 Coastal Caro. 33
47 Norfolk St. ■ 10
28 Florida A&M 21
13 Hampton ■ 6
9 Delaware St. 10
28 Howard ■ 10
41 Morgan St. 16
41 N.C. A&T * 19

Nickname: Bulldogs
Colors: Garnet & Blue
Stadium: Oliver C. Dawson Bulldog
Capacity: 22,000; Year Built: 1955
AD: Charlene M. Johnson
SID: Bill Hamilton

SOUTH DAKOTA

Vermillion, SD 57069-2390 II

Coach: Ed Meierkort, Dakota Wesleyan 1981
Record: 14 Years, 82-63-0

2006 RESULTS (9-4)

59 Quincy ■ 0
66 Minn.-Crookston ■ 6
27 Minn. Duluth ■ 14
20 St. Cloud St. 10
0 Central Ark. 24
10 Central Wash. ■ 7
42 Western Wash. 10
38 Augustana (S.D.) ■ 14
39 Minn. St. Mankato 44
45 Neb.-Omaha ■ 28
26 North Dakota 33
31 Northwood (Mich.) 28
17 Grand Valley St. 35

Nickname: Coyotes
Colors: Red & White
Stadium: DakotaDome
Capacity: 10,000; Year Built: 1979
AD: Joel Nielsen
SID: Dan Genzler

SOUTH DAKOTA ST.

(Reclassifying to FCS)

Brookings, SD 57007 II

Coach: John Stiegelmeier, South Dakota St. 1979
Record: 10 Years, 61-47-0

2006 RESULTS (7-4)

3 Wis.-La Crosse ■ 17
7 Montana 36
17 UNI 27
24 Nicholls St. 17
20 Texas-Arlington 17
20 Central Ark. ■ 7
29 Cal Poly 28
22 UC Davis ■ 21
34 William Penn ■ 3
31 Southern Utah 21
28 North Dakota St. 41

Nickname: Jackrabbits
Colors: Yellow & Blue
Stadium: Coughlin-Alumni
Capacity: 16,000; Year Built: 1962
AD: Fred M. Oien
SID: Jason Hove

SOUTH FLA.

Tampa, FL 33620 ....FBS

Coach: Jim Leavitt, Missouri 1978
Record: 10 Years, 70-43-0

2006 RESULTS (9-4)

41 McNeese St. ■ 10
21 Florida Int'l ■ 20
24 UCF 17
7 Kansas 13
20 Rutgers ■ 22
38 Connecticut ■ 16
37 North Carolina 20
6 Cincinnati 23
22 Pittsburgh ■ 12
27 Syracuse ■ 10
8 Louisville 31
24 West Virginia 19
24 East Caro. * 7

Nickname: Bulls
Colors: Green & Gold
Stadium: Raymond James
Capacity: 41,441; Year Built: 1998
AD: Doug Woolard
SID: John Gerdes

SOUTHEAST MO. ST.

Cape Girardeau, MO 63701-4799 ....FCS

Coach: Tony Samuel, Nebraska 1979
Record: 9 Years, 38-64-0

2006 RESULTS (4-7)

38 Austin Peay 13
44 Mo.-Rolla ■ 23
7 Jacksonville St. 38
19 Samford ■ 14
0 Eastern Ill. 21
7 Arkansas 63
21 Eastern Ky. ■ 27
24 Murray St. 17
14 Tenn.-Martin ■ 28
0 Tennessee St. 31
29 Tennessee Tech ■ 32

Nickname: Redhawks
Colors: Red & Black
Stadium: Houck
Capacity: 10,000; Year Built: 1930
AD: Donald L. Kaverman
SID: Ron Hines

SOUTHEASTERN LA.

Hammond, LA 70402 ....FCS

Coach: Dennis Roland, Boston U. 1978
Record: 12 Years, 47-79-0

2006 RESULTS (2-9)

15 New Mexico St. 30
0 Southern Miss. 45
41 Jacksonville ■ 13
0 Texas Tech 62
21 Gardner-Webb ■ 28
10 Nicholls St. 14
31 Northwestern St. ■ 24
17 Texas St. 38
10 Stephen F. Austin ■ 35
13 McNeese St. 34
23 Sam Houston St. ■ 28

Nickname: Lions
Colors: Green & Gold
Stadium: Strawberry
Capacity: 7,408; Year Built: 1936
AD: Dennis Roland
SID: Dart Volz

SOUTHEASTERN OKLA.

Durant, OK 74701-0609 II

Coach: Ray Richards, Northern Mich. 1981
Record: 6 Years, 28-36-0

2006 RESULTS (6-4)

44 Northwestern Okla. 13
37 Tarleton St. 30
14 Abilene Christian ■ 51
28 Tex. A&M-Kingsville ■ 31
13 Tex. A&M-Commerce 14
35 Southwestern Okla. ■ 7
9 Central Okla. 7
23 Midwestern St. 33
31 Northeastern St. ■ 0
42 East Central ■ 6

Nickname: Savage Storm
Colors: Blue & Gold
Stadium: Paul Laird Field
Capacity: 4,600; Year Built: 1927
AD: Jeff Hale
SID: M. Shane Baxley

SOUTHERN ARK.

Magnolia, AR 71754-0000 II

Coach: Steve Quinn, Ouachita Baptist 1985
Record: 6 Years, 34-32-0

2006 RESULTS (2-9)

18 Ark.-Monticello ■ 15
0 Nicholls St. 35
17 West Ala. 24
10 North Ala. ■ 40
0 Delta St. ■ 22
7 Valdosta St. 41
48 Ouachita Baptist ■ 33
6 Harding 17
29 Arkansas Tech ■ 36
21 Central Ark. 55
6 Henderson St. 24

Nickname: Muleriders
Colors: Royal Blue & Old Gold
Stadium: Wilkins
Capacity: 6,000; Year Built: 1949
AD: Jay Adcox
SID: Houston Taylor

SOUTHERN CALIFORNIA

Los Angeles, CA 90089-0602 ....FBS

Coach: Pete Carroll, Pacific 1973
Record: 6 Years, 65-12-0

2006 RESULTS (11-2)

50 Arkansas 14
28 Nebraska ■ 10
20 Arizona 3
28 Washington St. 22
26 Washington ■ 20
28 Arizona St. ■ 21
31 Oregon St. 33
42 Stanford 0
35 Oregon ■ 10
23 California ■ 9

44 Notre Dame ■ 24
9 UCLA 13
32 Michigan * 18

Nickname: Trojans
Colors: Cardinal & Gold
Stadium: L.A. Coliseum
Capacity: 92,000; Year Built: 1923
AD: Michael Garrett
SID: Tim Tessalone

SOUTHERN CONN. ST.

New Haven, CT 06515 II

Coach: Richard Cavanaugh, American Int'l 1976
Record: 22 Years, 128-97-1

2006 RESULTS (7-4)

20 Bryant 49
19 Bentley 13
26 Central Conn. St. ■ 29
20 American Int'l ■ 12
27 Merrimack 35
26 Assumption ■ 24
28 Pace 0
34 C.W. Post ■ 28
14 Stonehill 0
69 St. Anselm ■ 7
26 Merrimack 28

Nickname: Owls
Colors: Blue & White
Stadium: Jess Dow Field
Capacity: 6,000; Year Built: 1988
AD: Patricia D. Nicol
SID: To be named

SOUTHERN ILL.

Carbondale, IL 62901-6620 ....FCS

Coach: Jerry Kill, Southwestern (Kan.) 1983
Record: 13 Years, 92-55-0

2006 RESULTS (9-4)

49 Lock Haven ■ 0
35 Indiana 28
48 Ark.-Pine Bluff 16
55 Indiana St. ■ 3
31 Western Ill. ■ 24
10 Illinois St. 37
24 Western Ky. ■ 27
27 Missouri St. 17
24 Youngstown St. 31
47 UNI ■ 23
59 Southern Utah ■ 0
36 Tenn.-Martin ■ 30
3 Montana 20

Nickname: Salukis
Colors: Maroon & White
Stadium: McAndrew
Capacity: 17,324; Year Built: 1975
AD: Mario Moccia
SID: Tom Weber

SMU

Dallas, TX 75275 ....FBS

Coach: Phil Bennett, Texas A&M 1978
Record: 5 Years, 17-41-0

2006 RESULTS (6-6)

3 Texas Tech 35
6 North Texas 24
45 Sam Houston St. ■ 14
55 Arkansas St. ■ 9
33 Tulane 28
21 UTEP 24
31 Marshall ■ 21
21 East Caro. 38
22 UAB ■ 9
27 Houston ■ 37
34 Tulsa ■ 24
27 Rice 31

Nickname: Mustangs
Colors: Red & Blue
Stadium: Gerald J. Ford
Capacity: 32,000; Year Built: 2000
AD: Steven Orsini
SID: Brad Sutton

SOUTHERN MISS.

Hattiesburg, MS 39406-0001 ....FBS

Coach: Jeff Bower, Southern Miss. 1975
Record: 17 Years, 112-77-1

2006 RESULTS (9-5)

7 Florida 34
45 Southeastern La. ■ 0
37 North Carolina St. ■ 17
19 UCF 14
6 Tulsa 20
31 Houston ■ 27
6 Virginia Tech 36
17 East Caro. ■ 20
42 Memphis 21
31 Tulane 3
25 UAB ■ 20
42 Marshall ■ 7
20 Houston 34
28 Ohio * 7

Nickname: Golden Eagles
Colors: Black & Gold
Stadium: M.M. Roberts
Capacity: 33,000; Year Built: 1938
AD: Richard C. Giannini
SID: Mike Montoro

SOUTHERN U.

Baton Rouge, LA 70813 ....FCS

Coach: Pete Richardson, Dayton 1968
Record: 19 Years, 155-63-1

2006 RESULTS (5-6)

30 Bethune-Cookman * 29
31 Mississippi Val. ■ 14
23 Prairie View 26
20 N.C. Central ■ 27
38 Alabama St. ■ 20
21 Alabama A&M 28
28 Jackson St. 31
10 Alcorn St. 26
34 Texas Southern ■ 17
20 Ark.-Pine Bluff ■ 45
21 Grambling * 17

Nickname: Jaguars
Colors: Columbia Blue & Gold
Stadium: A.W. Mumford
Capacity: 26,400; Year Built: 1928
AD: Greg LaFleur
SID: Kevin Manns

SOUTHERN UTAH

Cedar City, UT 84720 ....FCS

Coach: Wes Meier, Utah 1991
Record: 3 Years, 10-22-0

2006 RESULTS (3-8)

34 Montana Tech ■ 0
55 Western St. ■ 3
13 Weber St. 24
30 Texas St. ■ 21
14 Cal Poly 18
27 McNeese St. 30
7 Fla. Atlantic 32
7 UC Davis 27
7 North Dakota St. ■ 31
21 South Dakota St. ■ 31
0 Southern Ill. 59

Nickname: Thunderbirds
Colors: Scarlet & White
Stadium: Eccles Coliseum
Capacity: 6,500; Year Built: 1967
AD: Ken Beazer
SID: Neil Gardner

SOUTHWEST BAPTIST

Bolivar, MO 65613 II

Coach: Jack Peavey, Jacksonville St. 1988
Record: 5 Years, 9-43-0

2006 RESULTS (1-10)

30 Harding ■ 42
14 Missouri St. 45
21 Mo. Southern St. 42
31 Emporia St. ■ 35
23 Washburn 56
39 Fort Hays St. ■ 21
24 Central Mo. 49
20 Pittsburg St. 63
21 Mo. Western St. ■ 24
28 Truman 45
9 Northwest Mo. St. ■ 55

Nickname: Bearcats
Colors: Purple & White
Stadium: Plaster
Capacity: 3,000; Year Built: 1986
AD: Brent Good
SID: Adam P. Ledyard

SOUTHWEST MINN. ST.

Marshall, MN 56258 II

Coach: Eric Eidsness, Sioux Falls 1991
Record: 3 Years, 13-20-0

2006 RESULTS (4-7)

63 South Dakota Tech ■ 6
17 Jamestown ■ 20
28 Minn.-Crookston ■ 7
8 Northern St. 16
0 Mary ■ 20
23 Concordia-St. Paul 21
20 Upper Iowa ■ 17
24 Wayne St. (Neb.) ■ 27
15 Bemidji St. 23
3 Winona St. 34
20 Minn. St. Moorhead * 22

Nickname: Mustangs
Colors: Brown & Gold
Stadium: Mattke Field
Capacity: 5,000; Year Built: 1971
AD: Chris Hmielewski
SID: Kelly Loft

SOUTHWESTERN OKLA.

Weatherford, OK 73096 II

Coach: Ryan Held, Nebraska 1999
Record: 6 Years, 26-39-0

2006 RESULTS (6-5)

23 Tex. A&M-Kingsville 17
10 Midwestern St. ■ 31
33 Okla. Panhandle 14
0 Abilene Christian 31
19 Tarleton St. ■ 21
31 Mo.-Rolla ■ 29
7 Southeastern Okla. 35
32 Northeastern St. ■ 6
25 Central Okla. ■ 22
38 East Central 28
7 Tex. A&M-Commerce 13

Nickname: Bulldogs
Colors: Navy Blue & White
Stadium: Milam
Capacity: 9,000; Year Built: 1932
AD: Cecil Perkins
SID: Michael J. Bond

SPRINGFIELD

Springfield, MA 01109-3797 III

Coach: Michael DeLong, Springfield 1974
Record: 25 Years, 146-102-2

2006 RESULTS (10-2)

38 Union (N.Y.) ■ ...30
27 Montclair St. ■ ...15
41 Alfred ■ ...34
41 Utica ■ ...7
43 Husson ...16
27 Brockport St. ■ ...3
55 St. John Fisher...38
7 Ithaca...24
44 Hartwick ■...20
35 Norwich...0
42 Curry ■...14
21 St. John Fisher ■...27

Nickname: The Pride
Colors: Maroon & White
Stadium: Benedum Field
Capacity: 3,867; Year Built: 1971
AD: Cathie Schweitzer
SID: Steve Raczynski

STANFORD

Stanford, CA 94305-2060 ....FBS

Coach: Walt Harris, Pacific 1968
Record: 13 Years, 69-85-0

2006 RESULTS (1-11)

10 Oregon...48
34 San Jose St. ...35
9 Navy ■...37
10 Washington St. ■ ...36
0 UCLA...31
10 Notre Dame ...31
7 Arizona ■...20
3 Arizona St. ...38
0 Southern California ■...42
20 Washington...3
7 Oregon St. ■...30
17 California...26

Nickname: Cardinal
Colors: Cardinal & White
Stadium: Stanford
Capacity: 50,000; Year Built: 1921
AD: Robert A. Bowlsby
SID: Gary Migdol

STEPHEN F. AUSTIN

Nacogdoches, TX 75962 ....FCS

Coach: Robert McFarland, McNeese St. 1985
Record: 2 Years, 9-13-0

2006 RESULTS (4-7)

7 Tulsa ...45
14 Delta St. ■...17
10 Arizona...28
35 Central Ark. ■ ...37
9 North Dakota St. ■ ...17
24 Texas St. ...13
17 McNeese St. ■...20
35 Southeastern La. ...10
17 Sam Houston St. ■...21
16 Nicholls St. ...13
20 Northwestern St. ■...11

Nickname: Lumberjacks
Colors: Purple & White
Stadium: Homer Bryce
Capacity: 14,575; Year Built: 1973
AD: Robert Hill
SID: James Dixon

STILLMAN

Tuscaloosa, AL 35403 II

Coach: Greg Thompson, Morris Brown 1973
Record: 15 Years, 60-79-4

2006 RESULTS (5-5)

6 Tuskegee ■...24
32 Concordia-Selma...13
7 Albany St. (Ga.)...14
14 Miles...21
21 Lane ■ ...24
34 Fort Valley St. ■...11
14 Alabama A&M ...21
12 Benedict ...7
26 Kentucky St. ■ ...5
43 Langston ■ ...23

Nickname: Tigers
Colors: Navy Blue & Vegas Gold
Stadium: Stillman
Capacity: 9,000; Year Built: 1999
AD: Greg Thompson/Curtis Williams
SID: Wesley Peterson

STONEHILL

Easton, MA 02357 II

Coach: Chris Woods, Davidson 1991
Record: 6 Years, 20-40-0

2006 RESULTS (1-9)

3 Merrimack ■ ...16
3 Assumption ■ ...16
0 Pace...7
20 C.W. Post ■ ...24
7 Iona ...24
24 St. Anselm ...9
14 Bryant ■...35
7 Bentley ...13
0 Southern Conn. St. ■...14
6 American Int'l ...28

Nickname: Skyhawks
Colors: Purple & White
Stadium: W.B. Mason
Capacity: 2,400; Year Built: 2005
AD: Paula Sullivan
SID: Jim Seavey

STONY BROOK

Stony Brook, NY 11794 ....FCS

Coach: Charles Priore, Albany (N.Y.) 1982
Record: 7 Years, 44-15-0

2006 RESULTS (5-6)

8 Hofstra ■...17
0 Georgetown ...7
7 New Hampshire...62
7 Massachusetts...48
36 Monmouth...17
33 Albany (N.Y.) ■...21
30 St. Francis (Pa.)...20
38 Sacred Heart ■...21
6 Robert Morris ■ ...21
45 Wagner ...9
32 Central Conn. St. ...35

Nickname: Seawolves
Colors: Scarlet, Blue & Gray
Stadium: Kenneth P. LaValle
Capacity: 8,212; Year Built: 2002
AD: James Fiore
SID: Rob Emmerich

SUL ROSS ST.

Alpine, TX 79832 III

Coach: Steve Wright, Maryville (Tenn.) 1978
Record: 5 Years, 12-37-0

2006 RESULTS (5-4)

35 Southwestern Assemblies of God ■...6
2 Mary Hardin-Baylor ■ ...45
17 East Tex. Baptist...16
60 Howard Payne ■ ...56
31 Texas Lutheran ...10
34 McMurry ■...15
14 Hardin-Simmons...56
28 Louisiana Col. ■ ...35
7 Mississippi Col....31

Nickname: Lobos
Colors: Scarlet & Gray
Stadium: Jackson Field
Capacity: 4,500; Year Built: 1927
AD: Kay Whitley
SID: Travis Hendryx

SUSQUEHANNA

Selinsgrove, PA 17870-1025......................III

Coach: Steve Briggs, Springfield 1984
Record: 17 Years, 96-76-0

2006 RESULTS (2-8)

0 Ursinus ...6
17 Moravian ■...24
24 Albright...21
3 King's (Pa.) ■ ...14
9 Juniata ...34
14 Widener ■...31
17 Delaware Valley ...10
16 FDU-Florham ■ ...21
7 Wilkes ...35
14 Lycoming ■ ...28

Nickname: Crusaders
Colors: Orange & Maroon
Stadium: Amos Alonzo Stagg Field at Lopardo Stadium
Capacity: 3,500; Year Built: 2000
AD: Pamela Samuelson
SID: Jim Miller

SYRACUSE

Syracuse, NY 13244-5020 ....FBS

Coach: Greg Robinson, Pacific 1975
Record: 2 Years, 5-18-0

2006 RESULTS (4-8)

10 Wake Forest...20
13 Iowa ■...20
31 Illinois...21
34 Miami (Ohio) ■ ...14
40 Wyoming ■...34
11 Pittsburgh ■...21
17 West Virginia ...41
13 Louisville ■ ...28
3 Cincinnati...17
10 South Fla. ...27
20 Connecticut ■ ...14
7 Rutgers...38

Nickname: Orange
Colors: Orange
Stadium: Carrier Dome
Capacity: 49,262; Year Built: 1980
AD: Daryl J. Gross
SID: Sue Cornelius Edson

TARLETON ST.

Stephenville, TX 76402 II

Coach: Sam McElroy, Texas St. 1985
Record: 2 Years, 13-7-0

2006 RESULTS (6-4)

23 Texas St. ...27
30 Southeastern Okla. ■ ...37
13 Tex. A&M-Commerce ...14
21 Southwestern Okla. ...19
23 Tex. A&M-Kingsville ■ ...0
38 Midwestern St. ...17

48 Eastern N.M. ■ 0
37 Abilene Christian 36
41 Angelo St. ■ 10
16 West Tex. A&M 21

Nickname: Texans
Colors: Purple & White
Stadium: Memorial
Capacity: 7,000; Year Built: 1976
AD: Lonn Reisman
SID: Joey Roberts

TEMPLE

Philadelphia, PA 19122 ....FBS

Coach: Al Golden, Penn St. 1991
Record: 1 Year, 1-11-0

2006 RESULTS (1-11)

3 Buffalo 9
0 Louisville ■ 62
0 Minnesota 62
7 Western Mich. 41
14 Vanderbilt 43
17 Kent St. ■ 28
9 Clemson * 63
21 Northern Ill. 43
28 Bowling Green ■ 14
26 Central Mich. ■ 42
0 Penn St. 47
6 Navy 42

Nickname: Owls
Colors: Cherry & White
Stadium: Lincoln Financial Field
Capacity: 66,592; Year Built: 2003
AD: William Bradshaw
SID: Kevin Lorincz

TENNESSEE

Knoxville, TN 37996 ....FBS

Coach: Phillip Fulmer, Tennessee 1972
Record: 15 Years, 137-41-0

2006 RESULTS (9-4)

35 California ■ 18
31 Air Force ■ 30
20 Florida ■ 21
33 Marshall ■ 7
41 Memphis 7
51 Georgia 33
16 Alabama ■ 13
31 South Carolina 24
24 LSU ■ 28
14 Arkansas 31
39 Vanderbilt 10
17 Kentucky ■ 12
10 Penn St. * 20

Nickname: Volunteers
Colors: Orange & White
Stadium: Neyland
Capacity: 102,038; Year Built: 1921
AD: Michael Hamilton
SID: Bud Ford

TENN.-MARTIN

Martin, TN 38238-5021 ....FCS

Coach: Jason Simpson, Southern Miss. 1995
Record: 1 Year, 9-3-0

2006 RESULTS (9-3)

3 Ohio 29
28 Urbana ■ 0
35 Gardner-Webb ■ 9
24 Jacksonville St. ■ 14
20 Austin Peay 10
35 Tennessee Tech 16
10 Samford 6
15 Eastern Ill. ■ 9
28 Southeast Mo. St. 14
28 Eastern Ky. ■ 31
42 Murray St. 14
30 Southern Ill. 36

Nickname: Skyhawks
Colors: Blue & Orange
Stadium: Skyhawk
Capacity: 7,500; Year Built: 1964
AD: Phil Dane
SID: Joe Lofaro

TENNESSEE ST.

Nashville, TN 37209-1561 ....FCS

Coach: James Webster, North Carolina 1972
Record: 2 Years, 8-14-0

2006 RESULTS (6-5)

20 Alabama A&M ■ 27
25 Murray St. ■ 15
31 Jackson St. * 30
9 Vanderbilt 38
22 Florida A&M * 25
30 Tennessee Tech ■ 20
38 Jacksonville St. 31
29 Samford ■ 7
3 Eastern Ill. 29
31 Southeast Mo. St. ■ 0
3 Eastern Ky. 20

Nickname: Tigers
Colors: Royal Blue & White
Stadium: LP Field
Capacity: 67,500; Year Built: 1999
AD: Teresa Phillips
SID: Wallace Dooley

TENNESSEE TECH

Cookeville, TN 38505-0001 ....FCS

Coach: Doug Malone, Carson-Newman 1982
Record: 1 Year, 4-7-0

2006 RESULTS (4-7)

7 Chattanooga ■ 31
26 Gardner-Webb 30
0 Middle Tenn. 44
27 Eastern Ky. ■ 14
20 Murray St. 14
16 Tenn.-Martin ■ 35
20 Tennessee St. 30
10 Jacksonville St. ■ 17
20 Samford 14
14 Eastern Ill. ■ 38
32 Southeast Mo. St. 29

Nickname: Golden Eagles
Colors: Purple & Gold
Stadium: Tucker
Capacity: 16,500; Year Built: 1966
AD: Mark Wilson
SID: Rob Schabert

TEXAS

Austin, TX 78712 ....FBS

Coach: Mack Brown, Florida St. 1974
Record: 23 Years, 179-96-1

2006 RESULTS (10-3)

56 North Texas ■ 7
7 Ohio St. ■ 24
52 Rice * 7
37 Iowa St. ■ 14
56 Sam Houston St. ■ 3
28 Oklahoma * 10
63 Baylor ■ 31
22 Nebraska 20
35 Texas Tech 31
36 Oklahoma St. ■ 10
42 Kansas St. 45
7 Texas A&M ■ 12
26 Iowa * 24

Nickname: Longhorns
Colors: Burnt Orange & White
Stadium: Royal-Texas Memorial
Capacity: 85,123; Year Built: 1924
AD: DeLoss Dodds
SID: John Bianco

UTEP

El Paso, TX 79968 ....FBS

Coach: Mike Price, Puget Sound 1969
Record: 25 Years, 150-137-0

2006 RESULTS (5-7)

34 San Diego St. 27
35 Texas Tech ■ 38
13 New Mexico 26
44 New Mexico St. ■ 38
24 SMU ■ 21
34 Tulane ■ 20
17 Houston 34
20 Tulsa 30
31 Rice ■ 37
36 UAB 17
21 Marshall 49
19 Memphis ■ 38

Nickname: Miners
Colors: Dark Blue, Orange & Silver
Stadium: Sun Bowl
Capacity: 51,500; Year Built: 1963
AD: Bob Stull
SID: Jeff Darby

TEXAS A&M

College Station, TX 77843-1228 ....FBS

Coach: Dennis Franchione, Pittsburg St. 1973
Record: 24 Years, 180-96-2

2006 RESULTS (9-4)

35 Citadel ■ 3
51 La.-Lafayette ■ 7
28 Army * 24
45 Louisiana Tech ■ 14
27 Texas Tech ■ 31
21 Kansas 18
25 Missouri ■ 19
34 Oklahoma St. 33
31 Baylor 21
16 Oklahoma ■ 17
27 Nebraska ■ 28
12 Texas 7
10 California * 45

Nickname: Aggies
Colors: Maroon & White
Stadium: Kyle Field
Capacity: 82,600; Year Built: 1927
AD: Bill Byrne
SID: Alan Cannon

TEX. A&M-COMMERCE

Commerce, TX 75428 II

Coach: Scotty Conley, Tex.-A&M Commerce 1970
Record: 3 Years, 14-16-0

2006 RESULTS (5-5)

17 Fort Hays St. 14
17 Tex. A&M-Kingsville 20
10 West Tex. A&M ■ 35
14 Tarleton St. ■ 13
3 Central Okla. 10
14 Southeastern Okla. ■ 13
17 Northeastern St. 20
17 Angelo St. 9
3 East Central ■ 10
13 Southwestern Okla. ■ 7

Nickname: Lions
Colors: Blue & Gold
Stadium: Memorial
Capacity: 10,000; Year Built: 1950
AD: James Johnson
SID: Danny Kambel

TEX. A&M-KINGSVILLE

Kingsville, TX 78363 II

Coach: Richard Cundiff, Lincoln Memorial 1973
Record: 7 Years, 52-28-0

2006 RESULTS (3-8)

17 Southwestern Okla. ■ 23
20 Tex. A&M-Commerce ■ 17
10 Western Ore. 36
31 Southeastern Okla. 28
31 West Tex. A&M ■ 51
0 Tarleton St. 23
37 East Central 34
17 Midwestern St. ■ 44
14 Eastern N.M. 37
38 Abilene Christian ■ 41
20 Angelo St. 38

Nickname: Javelinas
Colors: Blue & Gold
Stadium: Javelina
Capacity: 15,000; Year Built: 1950
AD: Jill Willson
SID: Derek Smolik

TCU

Fort Worth, TX 76129-0001 .... FBS

Coach: Gary Patterson, Kansas St. 1983
Record: 7 Years, 54-20-0

2006 RESULTS (11-2)

17 Baylor 7
46 UC Davis ■ 13
12 Texas Tech ■ 3
17 Brigham Young ■ 31
7 Utah 20
31 Army 17
26 Wyoming ■ 3
25 UNLV 10
27 New Mexico 21
52 San Diego St. ■ 0
45 Colorado St. 14
38 Air Force ■ 14
37 Northern Ill. * 7

Nickname: Horned Frogs
Colors: Purple & White
Stadium: Amon G. Carter
Capacity: 44,008; Year Built: 1930
AD: Danny Morrison
SID: Mark Cohen

TEXAS LUTHERAN

Seguin, TX 78155-5999 III

Coach: Tom Mueller, Concordia (Neb.) 1968
Record: 5 Years, 22-28-0

2006 RESULTS (6-4)

45 Austin ■ 0
14 Trinity (Tex.) ■ 9
21 Mississippi Col. ■ 28
9 Mary Hardin-Baylor 31
31 East Tex. Baptist ■ 28
28 Howard Payne 23
10 Sul Ross St. ■ 31
35 McMurry 14
7 Hardin-Simmons ■ 35
24 Louisiana Col. 22

Nickname: Bulldogs
Colors: Black & Gold
Stadium: Matador
Capacity: 9,000; Year Built: 1959
AD: Bill Miller
SID: Tim Clark

TEXAS SOUTHERN

Houston, TX 77004 .... FCS

Coach: Steve Wilson, Howard 1979
Record: 16 Years, 82-96-0

2006 RESULTS (3-8)

17 Prairie View * 14
10 Alabama St. 9
14 New Mexico St. 48
14 Alabama A&M ■ 19
5 Jackson St. ■ 29
23 Alcorn St. 45
18 Mississippi Val. ■ 20
33 Grambling ■ 28
17 Southern U. 34
21 Texas St. 41
31 Ark.-Pine Bluff 42

Nickname: Tigers
Colors: Maroon & Gray
Stadium: Alexander Durley
Capacity: 8,000; Year Built: 1975
AD: Alois S. Blackwell
SID: Rodney Bush

TEXAS ST.

San Marcos, TX 78666-4615 .... FCS

Coach: David Bailiff, Texas St. 1981
Record: 3 Years, 21-15-0

2006 RESULTS (5-6)

27 Tarleton St. ■ 23
7 Kentucky 41
13 Northern Colo. ■ 14
21 Southern Utah 30
13 Stephen F. Austin ■ 24
27 McNeese St. 17
38 Southeastern La. ■ 17
10 Northwestern St. 19
19 Nicholls St. ■ 21
41 Texas Southern ■ 21
28 Sam Houston St. 21

Nickname: Bobcats
Colors: Maroon & Gold
Stadium: Bobcat
Capacity: 15,218; Year Built: 1981
AD: Larry Teis
SID: Ron Mears

TEXAS TECH

Lubbock, TX 79409-3021 .... FBS

Coach: Mike Leach, Brigham Young 1983
Record: 7 Years, 56-33-0

2006 RESULTS (8-5)

35 SMU ■ 3
38 UTEP 35
3 TCU 12
62 Southeastern La. ■ 0
31 Texas A&M 27
21 Missouri ■ 38
6 Colorado 30
42 Iowa St. 26
31 Texas ■ 35
55 Baylor ■ 21
24 Oklahoma 34
30 Oklahoma St. ■ 24
44 Minnesota * 41

Nickname: Red Raiders
Colors: Scarlet & Black
Stadium: Jones AT&T
Capacity: 52,882; Year Built: 1947
AD: Gerald L. Myers
SID: Chris Cook

THIEL

Greenville, PA 16125 III

Coach: Jack Leipheimer, Thiel 1974
Record: 6 Years, 31-31-0

2006 RESULTS (5-5)

7 Geneva 0
0 Alfred 14
20 Albion ■ 24
17 Thomas More 14
49 Bethany (W.V.) 7
23 Wash. & Jeff. ■ 27
20 Grove City 0
24 Waynesburg ■ 34
45 Westminster (Pa.) ■ 27
7 Carnegie Mellon ■ 14

Nickname: Tomcats
Colors: Navy Blue & Old Gold
Stadium: Alumni
Capacity: 1,400; Year Built: 2001
AD: Roseanne Gill-Jacobson
SID: Kevin M. Fenstermacher

THOMAS MORE

Crestview Hills, KY 41017-3495 III

Coach: Mike Hallett, Mount Union 1994
Record: 3 Years, 15-15-0

2006 RESULTS (6-4)

25 Hanover ■ 23
21 Grove City 20
14 Thiel ■ 17
16 Waynesburg 23
42 Westminster (Pa.) 14
13 Frostburg St. 7
20 Huntingdon ■ 9
17 Bethany (W.V.) ■ 21
12 Wash. & Jeff. 21
21 Mt. St. Joseph ■ 17

Nickname: Saints
Colors: Royal Blue, White & Silver
Stadium: Thomas More
Capacity: 3,000; Year Built: 1999
AD: Terry Connor
SID: J. Ameer Rasheed

TIFFIN

Tiffin, OH 44883-2161 II

Coach: Nathan Cole, Tiffin 1995
Record: 4 Years, 27-16-0

2006 RESULTS (10-1)

58 Mo.-Rolla ■ 32
21 Clarion ■ 13
32 Concord 12
24 Ohio Dominican 17
25 Chowan 7
15 Gannon ■ 3
29 Ky. Wesleyan ■ 10
19 Central St. (Ohio) 14
24 Hillsdale ■ 14
62 Lincoln (Mo.) ■ 8
23 St. Joseph's (Ind.) 24

Nickname: Dragons
Colors: Green & Gold
Stadium: Frost-Kalnow
Capacity: 4,500
AD: Ian S. Day
SID: Shane O'Donnell

TOLEDO

Toledo, OH 43606 .... FBS

Coach: Tom Amstutz, Toledo 1977
Record: 6 Years, 49-25-0

2006 RESULTS (5-7)

43 Iowa St. 45
10 Western Mich. 31
37 Kansas ■ 31
41 McNeese St. ■ 7
3 Pittsburgh 45
20 Central Mich. ■ 42
14 Kent St. 40
13 Eastern Mich. 17
35 Akron ■ 20
17 Northern Ill. 13
17 Ball St. ■ 20
31 Bowling Green ■ 21

Nickname: Rockets
Colors: Blue & Gold
Stadium: Glass Bowl
Capacity: 26,248; Year Built: 1937
AD: Michael E. O'Brien
SID: Paul Helgren

TOWSON

Towson, MD 21252-0001 .... FCS

Coach: Gordy Combs, Towson 1972
Record: 15 Years, 86-73-0

2006 RESULTS (7-4)

30 Morgan St. ■ 2
24 Elon 17
10 Liberty ■ 3
33 Hofstra 30
7 Maine ■ 28
0 Massachusetts ■ 35
21 Villanova 13
49 Delaware 35
28 William & Mary ■ 29
31 Richmond 7
3 James Madison ■ 38

Nickname: Tigers
Colors: Gold, White & Black
Stadium: Johnny Unitas
Capacity: 11,198; Year Built: 2002
AD: Michael J. Hermann
SID: Dan O'Connell

TRINITY (CONN.)

Hartford, CT 06106 III

Coach: Jeff Devanney, Trinity (Conn.) 1993
Record: 1 Year, 7-1-0

2006 RESULTS (7-1)

27 Colby ■ 10
16 Williams 41
13 Hamilton 0
17 Tufts ■ 0
34 Bowdoin 0
34 Middlebury ■ 3
24 Amherst ■ 0
41 Wesleyan (Conn.) 0

Nickname: Bantams
Colors: Blue & Gold
Stadium: Jessee/Miller Field
Capacity: 6,500; Year Built: 1900
AD: Richard J. Hazelton
SID: David Kingsley

TRINITY (TEX.)

San Antonio, TX 78212-7200 III

Coach: Steve Mohr, Denison 1976
Record: 17 Years, 136-52-0

2006 RESULTS (8-2)

41 East Tex. Baptist ■ 0
9 Texas Lutheran 14
35 Redlands ■ 10
26 DePauw ■ 15
34 Austin ■ 7
24 Huntingdon 13
17 Centre 10
41 Rhodes ■ 7
21 Sewanee ■ 7
12 Millsaps 34

Nickname: Tigers
Colors: Maroon & White
Stadium: E.M. Stevens
Capacity: 3,500; Year Built: 1972
AD: Robert C. King
SID: Justin Parker

TROY

Troy, AL 36082 .... FBS

Coach: Larry Blakeney, Auburn 1970
Record: 16 Years, 127-65-1

2006 RESULTS (8-5)

38 Alabama St. ■ 0
17 Florida St. 24
20 Georgia Tech 35
0 Nebraska 56
3 UAB 21
24 La.-Monroe ■ 19
14 North Texas ■ 6
42 La.-Lafayette ■ 28
24 Fla. Atlantic 17
26 Arkansas St. ■ 33
21 Middle Tenn. 20
26 Florida Int'l 13
41 Rice * 17

Nickname: Trojans
Colors: Cardinal, Silver & Black
Stadium: Movie Gallery Veterans
Capacity: 30,000; Year Built: 1950
AD: Steve Dennis
SID: Ricky Hazel

TRUMAN

Kirksville, MO 63501-4221 II

Coach: Shannon Currier, Hamline 1994
Record: 7 Years, 42-35-0

2006 RESULTS (6-5)

16 Minn. St. Mankato 34
13 Winona St. 24
10 Northwest Mo. St. ■ 31
24 Central Mo. ■ 21
13 Mo. Western St. 38
35 Mo. Southern St. ■ 28
14 Emporia St. 13
21 Washburn ■ 7
21 Pittsburg St. 45
45 Southwest Baptist ■ 28
40 Fort Hays St. 15

Nickname: Bulldogs
Colors: Purple & White
Stadium: Stokes
Capacity: 4,000; Year Built: 1930
AD: Jerry Wollmering
SID: Kevin White

TUFTS

Medford, MA 02155 III

Coach: Bill Samko, Connecticut 1973
Record: 20 Years, 80-86-1

2006 RESULTS (4-4)

17 Hamilton ■ 0
21 Bates ■ 12
16 Bowdoin 6
0 Trinity (Conn.) 17
14 Williams ■ 38
6 Amherst 24
7 Colby ■ 0
0 Middlebury 10

Nickname: Jumbos
Colors: Brown & Blue
Stadium: Ellis Oval
Capacity: 6,000; Year Built: 1923
AD: Bill Gehling
SID: Paul Sweeney

TULANE

New Orleans, LA 70118-0000 .... FBS

Coach: Chris Scelfo, La.-Monroe 1986
Record: 9 Years, 37-57-0

2006 RESULTS (4-8)

7 Houston 45
32 Mississippi St. 29
7 LSU 49
28 SMU ■ 33
38 Rice ■ 24
20 UTEP 34
13 Auburn 38
42 Army ■ 28
21 Marshall 42
3 Southern Miss. ■ 31
10 UCF ■ 9
3 Tulsa 38

Nickname: Green Wave
Colors: Olive Green & Sky Blue
Stadium: Superdome
Capacity: 69,767; Year Built: 1975
AD: Rick Dickson
SID: Donna Turner

TULSA

Tulsa, OK 74104-3189 .... FBS

Coach: Steve Kragthorpe, West Tex. A&M 1988
Record: 4 Years, 29-22-0

2006 RESULTS (8-5)

45 Stephen F. Austin ■ 7
24 Brigham Young 49
28 North Texas ■ 3
24 Navy 23
20 Southern Miss. ■ 6
31 East Caro. 10
35 Memphis 14
30 UTEP ■ 20
10 Houston 27
38 Rice ■ 41
24 SMU 34
38 Tulane ■ 3
13 Utah * 25

Nickname: Golden Hurricane
Colors: Old Gold, Royal Blue & Crimson
Stadium: H.A. Chapman
Capacity: 35,542; Year Built: 1930
AD: Lawrence R. Cunningham
SID: Don Tomkalski

TUSCULUM

Greeneville, TN 37743 II

Coach: Frankie DeBusk, Furman 1991
Record: 9 Years, 53-43-0

2006 RESULTS (6-5)

17 Bethel (Tenn.) ■ 10
10 North Ala. ■ 22
28 St. Paul's 0
33 Brevard 0
3 Wingate 21
17 Lenoir-Rhyne 10
21 Presbyterian ■ 30
21 Catawba 20
23 Newberry ■ 27
24 Mars Hill 17
3 Carson-Newman ■ 23

Nickname: Pioneers
Colors: Black & Orange
Stadium: Pioneer Field
Capacity: 3,500; Year Built: 1991
AD: Ed Hoffmeyer
SID: Dom Donnelly

TUSKEGEE

Tuskegee, AL 36088 II

Coach: Willie J. Slater, West Ala. 1979
Record: 1 Year, 9-3-0

2006 RESULTS (9-3)

24 Stillman 6
20 Miles ■ 31

41 Benedict ■ ... 14
34 Fort Valley St. * ... 20
19 Ark.-Pine Bluff * ... 35
55 Morehouse * ... 29
17 Albany St. (Ga.) ■ ... 10
6 Clark Atlanta ... 10
27 Langston ■ ... 24
42 Lane ■ ... 28
17 Alabama St. ... 10
17 Johnson C. Smith * ... 7

Nickname: Golden Tigers
Colors: Crimson & Old Gold
Stadium: Abbott Memorial Alumni
Capacity: 10,000; Year Built: 1925
AD: Emmett L. Taylor
SID: Arnold Houston

UCLA

Los Angeles, CA 90095-1405 ... FBS

Coach: Karl Dorrell, UCLA 1987
Record: 4 Years, 29-21-0

2006 RESULTS (7-6)

31 Utah ■ ... 10
26 Rice ■ ... 16
19 Washington ... 29
31 Stanford ■ ... 0
27 Arizona ■ ... 7
20 Oregon ... 30
17 Notre Dame ... 20
15 Washington St. ■ ... 37
24 California ... 38
25 Oregon St. ■ ... 7
24 Arizona St. ... 12
13 Southern California ■ ... 9
27 Florida St. * ... 44

Nickname: Bruins
Colors: Blue & Gold
Stadium: Rose Bowl
Capacity: 91,500; Year Built: 1922
AD: Daniel G. Guerrero
SID: Marc Dellins

UNION (N.Y.)

Schnectady, NY 12308 ... III

Coach: John Audino, Notre Dame 1975
Record: 17 Years, 123-49-0

2006 RESULTS (7-3)

30 Springfield ... 38
34 Muhlenberg ■ ... 7
27 Rochester ■ ... 24
28 Merchant Marine ■ ... 20
28 WPI ... 27
28 Frank. & Marsh. ■ ... 21
42 St. Lawrence ■ ... 7
31 Hobart ... 14
19 Rensselaer ... 24
21 St. John Fisher ... 49

Nickname: Dutchmen
Colors: Garnet
Stadium: Frank Bailey Field
Capacity: 2,000; Year Built: 1981
AD: James McLaughlin
SID: Eric McDowell

UPPER IOWA

Fayette, IA 52142 ... II

Coach: Mike Knoll, Mo. Western St. 1974
Record: 6 Years, 10-56-0

2006 RESULTS (3-8)

24 Wayne St. (Neb.) ... 14
7 Drake ... 40
34 Wis.-Stout ■ ... 36
7 Winona St. ... 48
36 Minn. St. Moorhead ■ ... 13
56 Minn.-Crookston ■ ... 7
17 Southwest Minn. St. ... 20
14 Concordia-St. Paul ■ ... 41
13 Mary ... 42
20 Northern St. ■ ... 26
20 Bemidji St. * ... 44

Nickname: Peacocks
Colors: Peacock Blue & White
Stadium: Eischeid
Capacity: 3,500; Year Built: 1993
AD: Gil Cloud
SID: Howie Thompson

URSINUS

Collegeville, PA 19426-1000 ... III

Coach: Peter Gallagher, West Va. Wesleyan 1993
Record: 6 Years, 24-37-0

2006 RESULTS (8-3)

6 Susquehanna ■ ... 0
32 Albright ... 13
6 La Salle ... 2
20 McDaniel ■ ... 0
16 Case Reserve ... 7
6 Muhlenberg ... 22
18 Gettysburg ... 27
17 Johns Hopkins ■ ... 7
42 Frank. & Marsh. ... 10
31 Dickinson ■ ... 24
7 Widener ■ ... 14

Nickname: Bears
Colors: Red, Old Gold & Black
Stadium: Patterson Field
Capacity: 2,500; Year Built: 1923
AD: Brian Thomas
SID: Jill Yamma

UTAH

Salt Lake City, UT 84112-9008 ... FBS

Coach: Kyle Whittingham, Brigham Young 1984
Record: 2 Years, 15-10-0

2006 RESULTS (8-5)

10 UCLA ... 31
45 Northern Ariz. ■ ... 7
48 Utah St. ... 0
38 San Diego St. ... 7
3 Boise St. ■ ... 36
20 TCU ■ ... 7
15 Wyoming ... 31
31 New Mexico ... 34
45 UNLV ■ ... 23
35 Colorado St. ■ ... 22
17 Air Force ... 14
31 Brigham Young ■ ... 33
25 Tulsa * ... 13

Nickname: Utes
Colors: Crimson & White
Stadium: Rice-Eccles
Capacity: 45,634; Year Built: 1927
AD: Christopher Hill
SID: Liz Abel

UTAH ST.

Logan, UT 84322-7400 ... FBS

Coach: Brent Guy, Oklahoma St. 1983
Record: 2 Years, 4-19-0

2006 RESULTS (1-11)

7 Wyoming ... 38
0 Arkansas ... 20
0 Utah ■ ... 48
0 Brigham Young ... 38
21 Idaho ■ ... 41
13 Fresno St. ■ ... 12
14 San Jose St. ... 21
35 Louisiana Tech ... 48
10 Hawaii ■ ... 63
0 Nevada ... 42
10 Boise St. ... 49
20 New Mexico St. ■ ... 42

Nickname: Aggies
Colors: Navy Blue & White
Stadium: E.L. Romney
Capacity: 30,257; Year Built: 1968
AD: Randy Spetman
SID: Mike Strauss

UTICA

Utica, NY 13502-4892 ... III

Coach: Mike Kemp, Gust. Adolphus 1975
Record: 9 Years, 33-56-0

2006 RESULTS (3-7)

20 Becker ... 10
7 Husson ... 21
10 Rensselaer ■ ... 34
7 Springfield ... 41
21 Mount Ida ■ ... 9
3 Alfred ■ ... 24
7 Ithaca ... 33
0 St. John Fisher ■ ... 64
20 Norwich ■ ... 7
17 Hartwick ... 35

Nickname: Pioneers
Colors: Blue & Orange
Stadium: Charles A. Gaetano
Capacity: 1,200; Year Built: 2001
AD: James A. Spartano
SID: Gil Burgmaster

VALDOSTA ST.

Valdosta, GA 31698 ... II

Coach: Chris Hatcher, Valdosta St. 1995
Record: 7 Years, 76-12-0

2006 RESULTS (8-2)

20 Albany St. (Ga.) ... 16
31 Fort Valley St. ■ ... 3
51 Arkansas Tech ■ ... 14
49 Ouachita Baptist ... 21
41 Southern Ark. ■ ... 7
28 Delta St. ... 35
16 West Ala. ■ ... 14
24 North Ala. ... 31
51 Ark.-Monticello ■ ... 3
38 West Ga. ... 13

Nickname: Blazers
Colors: Red & Black
Stadium: Cleveland Field
Capacity: 10,500; Year Built: 2004
AD: Herb F. Reinhard III
SID: Shawn Reed

VALPARAISO

Valparaiso, IN 46383-6493 ... FCS

Coach: Stacy Adams, Northwest Mo. St. 1990
Record: 2 Years, 6-16-0

2006 RESULTS (3-8)

54 Wis. Lutheran ... 0
20 Trinity Int'l ■ ... 39
42 Morehead St. ... 35
7 Drake ■ ... 21
17 Jacksonville ■ ... 34
14 St. Joseph's (Ind.) ... 43
7 San Diego ... 68
10 Butler ... 32
14 Davidson ■ ... 48
7 Dayton ... 51
20 Aurora ■ ... 7

Nickname: Crusaders
Colors: Brown & Gold
Stadium: Brown Field
Capacity: 5,000; Year Built: 1947
AD: Mark LaBarbera
SID: Ryan Wronkowicz

VANDERBILT

Nashville, TN 37212 .... FBS

Coach: Bobby Johnson, Clemson 1973
Record: 13 Years, 75-79-0

2006 RESULTS (4-8)

7 Michigan 27
10 Alabama 13
19 Arkansas ■ 21
38 Tennessee St. ■ 9
43 Temple ■ 14
10 Mississippi 17
24 Georgia 22
13 South Carolina ■ 31
45 Duke 28
19 Florida ■ 25
26 Kentucky 38
10 Tennessee ■ 39

Nickname: Commodores
Colors: Black & Gold
Stadium: Vanderbilt
Capacity: 39,773; Year Built: 1981
AD: David Williams II
SID: Rod Williamson

VILLANOVA

Villanova, PA 19085-1674 .... FCS

Coach: Andy Talley, Southern Conn. St. 1967
Record: 27 Years, 175-112-2

2006 RESULTS (6-5)

16 UCF 35
28 Lehigh ■ 31
21 Massachusetts ■ 31
27 Penn 20
20 Hofstra 16
7 Maine 20
13 Towson ■ 21
35 William & Mary 31
31 Richmond ■ 21
21 James Madison ■ 20
28 Delaware 27

Nickname: Wildcats
Colors: Blue & White
Stadium: Villanova
Capacity: 12,000; Year Built: 1927
AD: Vincent Nicastro
SID: Dean Kenefick

VIRGINIA

Charlottesville, VA 22904-4821 .... FBS

Coach: Al Groh, Virginia 1967
Record: 12 Years, 68-73-0

2006 RESULTS (5-7)

13 Pittsburgh 38
13 Wyoming ■ 12
10 Western Mich. ■ 17
7 Georgia Tech 24
37 Duke 0
21 East Caro. 31
26 Maryland ■ 28
23 North Carolina ■ 0
14 North Carolina St. ■ 7
0 Florida St. 33
17 Miami (Fla.) ■ 7
0 Virginia Tech 17

Nickname: Cavaliers
Colors: Orange & Blue
Stadium: Smith/Harrison/Scott
Capacity: 61,500; Year Built: 1931
AD: Craig K. Littlepage
SID: Michael Colley

VMI

Lexington, VA 24450-0304 .... FCS

Coach: Jim Reid, Maine 1973
Record: 16 Years, 85-92-3

2006 RESULTS (1-10)

20 Davidson ■ 19
19 Norfolk St. 32
7 Richmond 58
6 William & Mary 38
7 James Madison ■ 45
7 Army 62
27 Coastal Caro. ■ 31
22 Charleston So. 27
31 Gardner-Webb 35
21 Citadel 48
32 Liberty ■ 38

Nickname: Keydets
Colors: Red, White & Yellow
Stadium: Alumni Field
Capacity: 10,000; Year Built: 1962
AD: Donald T. White
SID: Wade Branner

VIRGINIA ST.

Petersburg, VA 23806-0001 II

Coach: Andrew Faison, Virginia St. 1981
Record: 5 Years, 26-24-0

2006 RESULTS (2-8)

14 Norfolk St. 29
14 St. Augustine's ■ 21
13 Catawba 31
21 Carson-Newman ■ 27
3 Fayetteville St. ■ 30
0 Elizabeth City St. 27
24 St. Paul's 5
31 Virginia Union 34
28 Shaw ■ 22
7 Bowie St. 16

Nickname: Trojans
Colors: Orange & Navy Blue
Stadium: Rogers
Capacity: 13,500; Year Built: 1950
AD: Peggy L. Davis
SID: Jim Junot

VIRGINIA TECH

Blacksburg, VA 24061 .... FBS

Coach: Frank Beamer, Virginia Tech 1969
Record: 26 Years, 198-105-4

2006 RESULTS (10-3)

38 Northeastern ■ 0
35 North Carolina 10
36 Duke ■ 0
29 Cincinnati ■ 13
27 Georgia Tech ■ 38
3 Boston College 22
36 Southern Miss. ■ 6
24 Clemson ■ 7
17 Miami (Fla.) 10
23 Kent St. ■ 0
27 Wake Forest 6
17 Virginia ■ 0
24 Georgia * 31

Nickname: Hokies
Colors: Burnt Orange & Chicago Maroon
Stadium: Lane
Capacity: 66,233; Year Built: 1965
AD: James C. Weaver
SID: Dave Smith

VIRGINIA UNION

Richmond, VA 23220-1790 II

Coach: Arrington Jones, Virginia St. 1988
Record: 3 Years, 12-18-0

2006 RESULTS (7-3)

12 Fayetteville St. ■ 25
27 West Va. Wesleyan 10
14 Livingstone ■ 12
37 Johnson C. Smith ■ 40
55 Central St. (Ohio) 53
23 St. Paul's ■ 7
43 Shaw 34
34 Virginia St. ■ 31
9 Bowie St. 7
21 Elizabeth City St. 29

Nickname: Panthers
Colors: Steel & Maroon
Stadium: Hovey Field
Capacity: 10,000; Year Built: 1907
AD: Michael Bailey
SID: Tiffani Sykes

WABASH

Crawfordsville, IN 47933 III

Coach: Chris Creighton, Kenyon 1991
Record: 10 Years, 84-20-0

2006 RESULTS (8-2)

38 Franklin 45
38 Millikin ■ 31
42 Ohio Wesleyan ■ 28
48 Earlham 15
41 Allegheny ■ 27
17 Wittenberg 19
48 Oberlin 20
20 Wooster ■ 10
41 Denison 14
23 DePauw ■ 20

Nickname: Little Giants
Colors: Scarlet
Stadium: Hollett Little Giant
Capacity: 5,000; Year Built: 1966
AD: Vernon H. Mummert
SID: Brent Harris

WAGNER

Staten Island, NY 10301-4495 .... FCS

Coach: Walt Hameline, Brockport St. 1975
Record: 26 Years, 179-93-2

2006 RESULTS (4-7)

38 La Salle 15
7 Iona ■ 3
38 Marist 7
34 St. Peter's ■ 0
17 Sacred Heart 25
10 Robert Morris ■ 14
7 Monmouth ■ 28
6 Central Conn. St. 27
0 Albany (N.Y.) 34
9 Stony Brook ■ 45
14 St. Francis (Pa.) 35

Nickname: Seahawks
Colors: Green & White
Stadium: Wagner College
Capacity: 3,300; Year Built: 1997
AD: Walt Hameline
SID: Todd Vatter

WAKE FOREST

Winston-Salem, NC 27109 .... FBS

Coach: Jim Grobe, Virginia 1975
Record: 12 Years, 70-68-1

2006 RESULTS (11-3)

20 Syracuse ■ 10
14 Duke ■ 13
24 Connecticut 13
27 Mississippi 3
34 Liberty ■ 14
17 Clemson ■ 27

25 North Carolina St. 23
24 North Carolina 17
21 Boston College ■ 14
30 Florida St. 0
6 Virginia Tech ■ 27
38 Maryland 24
9 Georgia Tech * 6
13 Louisville * 24

Nickname: Demon Deacons
Colors: Old Gold & Black
Stadium: Groves
Capacity: 31,500; Year Built: 1968
AD: Ronald D. Wellman
SID: Mike Vest

WARTBURG

Waverly, IA 50677-1003 III

Coach: Eric Koehler, Hanover 1997
Record: 1 Year, 8-2-0

2006 RESULTS (8-2)

20 Monmouth (Ill.) ■ 0
31 Simpson 7
28 Luther ■ 17
7 Central (Iowa) 13
38 Augsburg 14
19 Loras ■ 14
10 Coe 7
20 Buena Vista 13
41 Cornell College ■ 7
14 Dubuque ■ 17

Nickname: Knights
Colors: Orange & Black
Stadium: Walston-Hoover
Capacity: 4,000; Year Built: 2001
AD: Rick Willis
SID: Mark Adkins

WASHBURN

Topeka, KS 66621 II

Coach: Craig Schurig, Colorado Mines 1987
Record: 5 Years, 32-25-0

2006 RESULTS (7-4)

41 Colorado Mines ■ 21
13 Western Wash. 16
14 Central Mo. 10
37 Fort Hays St. 7
56 Southwest Baptist ■ 23
14 Pittsburg St. 29
26 Northwest Mo. St. ■ 31
7 Truman 21
37 Emporia St. ■ 6
14 Mo. Southern St. 13
16 Mo. Western St. ■ 3

Nickname: Ichabods
Colors: Yale Blue & White
Stadium: Yager Stadium at Moore Bowl
Capacity: 7,200; Year Built: 1928
AD: Loren Ferre'
SID: Gene Cassell

WASHINGTON

Seattle, WA 98195 ....FBS

Coach: Tyrone Willingham, Michigan St. 1977
Record: 12 Years, 72-67-1

2006 RESULTS (5-7)

35 San Jose St. ■ 29
20 Oklahoma 37
21 Fresno St. ■ 20
29 UCLA ■ 19
21 Arizona 10
20 Southern California 26
17 Oregon St. ■ 27
24 California 31
23 Arizona St. ■ 26
14 Oregon 34
3 Stanford ■ 20
35 Washington St. 32

Nickname: Huskies
Colors: Purple & Gold
Stadium: Husky
Capacity: 72,500; Year Built: 1920
AD: Todd Turner
SID: Richard Kilwien

WASHINGTON-ST. LOUIS

St. Louis, MO 63130-4899 III

Coach: Larry Kindbom, Kalamazoo 1974
Record: 24 Years, 142-96-1

2006 RESULTS (6-4)

21 Lake Forest 6
61 Westminster (Mo.) ■ 0
7 Wheaton (Ill.) 48
15 North Central (Ill.) ■ 34
3 Rhodes 6
31 LaGrange 21
26 Chicago 7
13 Case Reserve ■ 6
7 Carnegie Mellon ■ 10
17 Greenville ■ 14

Nickname: Bears
Colors: Red & Green
Stadium: Francis Field
Capacity: 3,300; Year Built: 1904
AD: John M. Schael
SID: Chris Mitchell

WASH. & JEFF.

Washington, PA 15301-4801 III

Coach: Mike Sirianni, Mount Union 1994
Record: 4 Years, 40-7-0

2006 RESULTS (10-2)

14 Salisbury ■ 32
22 Allegheny ■ 10
35 Hanover 0
33 Oberlin 13
27 Thiel 23
50 Westminster (Pa.) ■ 7
52 Grove City ■ 18
30 Waynesburg ■ 3
21 Thomas More ■ 12
54 Bethany (W.V.) 0
27 Chris. Newport 23
27 Mary Hardin-Baylor 30

Nickname: Presidents
Colors: Red & Black
Stadium: Cameron
Capacity: 3,500; Year Built: 1958
AD: Bill Dukett
SID: Scott McGuinness

WASH. & LEE

Lexington, VA 24450 III

Coach: Frank Miriello, East Stroudsburg 1967
Record: 12 Years, 61-58-1

2006 RESULTS (7-4)

7 Frank. & Marsh. 21
21 Sewanee ■ 7
24 Centre 15
33 Randolph-Macon ■ 10
28 Catholic 0
28 Hampden-Sydney ■ 6
34 Guilford ■ 12
8 Bridgewater (Va.) 27
24 Emory & Henry ■ 6
9 Case Reserve 27
0 Wilkes 42

Nickname: Generals
Colors: Royal Blue & White
Stadium: Wilson Field
Capacity: 7,000; Year Built: 1930
AD: George C. O'Connell Jr.
SID: Brian Laubscher

WASHINGTON ST.

Pullman, WA 99164-1602 ....FBS

Coach: Bill Doba, Ball St. 1962
Record: 4 Years, 25-22-0

2006 RESULTS (6-6)

14 Auburn 40
56 Idaho ■ 10
17 Baylor * 15
36 Stanford 10
22 Southern California ■ 28
13 Oregon St. 6
3 California ■ 21
34 Oregon ■ 23
37 UCLA 15
17 Arizona ■ 27
14 Arizona St. 47
32 Washington ■ 35

Nickname: Cougars
Colors: Crimson & Gray
Stadium: Clarence D. Martin
Capacity: 35,117; Year Built: 1972
AD: James Sterk
SID: To be named

WAYNE ST. (MICH.)

Detroit, MI 48202-3489 II

Coach: Paul Winters, Akron 1980
Record: 3 Years, 10-21-0

2006 RESULTS (6-5)

36 Michigan Tech 14
10 St. Joseph's (Ind.) ■ 17
35 Mercyhurst ■ 31
24 Findlay 3
13 Grand Valley St. ■ 36
30 Gannon 3
41 Hillsdale ■ 26
14 Indianapolis ■ 39
34 Northwood (Mich.) 48
33 Ashland ■ 17
17 Ferris St. 21

Nickname: Warriors
Colors: Green & Gold
Stadium: Adams Field
Capacity: 6,000; Year Built: 1968
AD: Robert Fournier
SID: Jeff Weiss

WAYNE ST. (NEB.)

Wayne, NE 68787-1172 II

Coach: Dan McLaughlin, Bellevue 1982
Record: 2 Years, 9-13-0

2006 RESULTS (5-6)

14 Upper Iowa ■ 24
14 Neb.-Kearney 23
14 Chadron St. ■ 38
24 Minn. St. Moorhead 21
28 Minn.-Crookston 0
7 Northern St. ■ 0
37 Bemidji St. ■ 40
27 Southwest Minn. St. 24
24 Concordia-St. Paul ■ 27
14 Mo.-Rolla ■ 9
3 Winona St. * 31

Nickname: Wildcats
Colors: Black & Gold
Stadium: Memorial/Bob Cunnigham Field
Capacity: 3,500; Year Built: 1931
AD: Eric Schoh
SID: Mike Grosz

WAYNESBURG

Waynesburg, PA 15370 III

Coach: Rick Shepas, Youngstown St. 1987
Record: 2 Years, 10-10-0

2006 RESULTS (6-4)

14 Wesley 41
10 Wooster ■ 31
10 Shenandoah ■ 20
29 Grove City ■ 18
23 Thomas More ■ 16
41 Bethany (W.V.) ■ 15
34 Thiel 24
3 Wash. & Jeff. 30
21 Frostburg St. ■ 7
21 Westminster (Pa.) 9

Nickname: Yellow Jackets
Colors: Orange & Black
Stadium: John F. Wiley
Capacity: 4,000; Year Built: 1999
AD: Rudy Marisa
SID: Matthew Kifer

WEBER ST.

Ogden, UT 84408-2701 ....FCS

Coach: Ron McBride, San Jose St. 1963
Record: 15 Years, 98-75-0

2006 RESULTS (4-7)

6 Colorado St. 30
0 Cal Poly ■ 17
24 Southern Utah ■ 13
10 Portland St. ■ 20
26 Northern Colo. ■ 21
21 Sacramento St. 24
30 Montana ■ 33
18 Montana St. 24
19 Eastern Wash. ■ 14
17 Northern Ariz. 42
30 Idaho St. 27

Nickname: Wildcats
Colors: Royal Purple & White
Stadium: Stewart
Capacity: 17,500; Year Built: 1966
AD: Jerry Graybeal
SID: Brad Larsen

WESLEY

Dover, DE 19901-3875 III

Coach: Mike Drass, Mansfield 1983
Record: 14 Years, 109-39-1

2006 RESULTS (13-1)

41 Waynesburg ■ 14
38 Averett ■ 17
49 Seton Hill ■ 13
38 Huntingdon 17
32 Frostburg St. 7
41 Apprentice ■ 7
48 Brockport St. ■ 17
13 Salisbury 10
37 Chowan ■ 3
53 Morrisville St. ■ 14
49 Dickinson ■ 21
37 Carnegie Mellon ■ 0
34 Mary Hardin-Baylor ■ 20
7 Wis.-Whitewater 44

Nickname: Wolverines
Colors: Navy, Columbia & White
Stadium: Wolverine
Capacity: 2,500; Year Built: 1989
AD: Michael Drass
SID: Steve Azzanesi

WESLEYAN (CONN.)

Middletown, CT 06459 III

Coach: Frank Hauser, Wesleyan (Conn.) 1979
Record: 15 Years, 60-60-0

2006 RESULTS (3-5)

7 Middlebury 10
7 Hamilton ■ 0
21 Colby 24
17 Bates 14
0 Amherst ■ 23
18 Bowdoin ■ 0
21 Williams 51
0 Trinity (Conn.) ■ 41

Nickname: Cardinals
Colors: Red & Black
Stadium: Corwin Stadium at Andrus Field
Capacity: 5,000; Year Built: 1881
AD: John Biddiscombe
SID: Brian Katten

WEST ALA.

Livingston, AL 35470 II

Coach: Bobby Wallace, Mississippi St. 1976
Record: 19 Years, 107-112-1

2006 RESULTS (6-5)

65 Concordia-Selma ■ 0
45 Lambuth 13
24 Southern Ark. ■ 17
10 Henderson St. ■ 31
16 Harding 24
49 Webber Int'l ■ 20
24 West Ga. ■ 14
14 Valdosta St. 16
37 Ark.-Monticello 14
14 Delta St. 41
3 North Ala. ■ 45

Nickname: Tigers
Colors: Red & White
Stadium: Tiger
Capacity: 7,000; Year Built: 1952
AD: E.J. Brophy
SID: Kyle Lewis

WEST CHESTER

West Chester, PA 19383 II

Coach: Bill Zwaan, Delaware 1979
Record: 10 Years, 90-29-0

2006 RESULTS (9-4)

14 Edinboro ■ 28
7 Delaware 30
49 Clarion 21
24 Shippensburg ■ 0
53 Cheyney ■ 12
27 Bloomsburg 30
54 Millersville ■ 27
49 Kutztown 47
49 East Stroudsburg 28
44 Mansfield ■ 0
21 Slippery Rock 20
31 Bryant 29
20 Bloomsburg 21

Nickname: Golden Rams
Colors: Purple & Gold
Stadium: Farrell
Capacity: 7,500; Year Built: 1970
AD: Edward Matejkovic
SID: James Zuhlke

WEST GA.

Carrollton, GA 30118 II

Coach: Mike Ledford, Tennessee Tech 1975
Record: 5 Years, 16-35-0

2006 RESULTS (1-9)

0 Presbyterian ■ 10
7 Furman 24
21 Arkansas Tech 28
9 Henderson St. 16
16 Harding ■ 34
14 West Ala. 24
20 Ark.-Monticello 14
7 Delta St. ■ 21
16 North Ala. ■ 26
13 Valdosta St. ■ 38

Nickname: Wolves
Colors: Blue & Red
Stadium: Grisham
Capacity: 6,500; Year Built: 1966
AD: Edward G. Murphy
SID: Mitch Gray

WEST LIBERTY ST.

West Liberty, WV 26074 II

Coach: Roger Waialae, Dubuque
Record: 2 Years, 13-9-0

2006 RESULTS (7-4)

31 Seton Hill 14
16 Walsh 42
31 Ky. Wesleyan ■ 24
23 Concord 27
21 Duquesne ■ 19
23 West Va. Wesleyan ■ 10
27 Fairmont St. 20
38 Glenville St. ■ 10
16 West Virginia St. 13
32 Shepherd ■ 34
13 Charleston (W.V.) ■ 21

Nickname: Hilltoppers
Colors: Black & Gold
Stadium: Russek Field
Capacity: 4,000; Year Built: 1960
AD: James W. Watson
SID: Lynn Ullom

WEST TEX. A&M

Canyon, TX 79016-0999 II

Coach: Don Carthel, Eastern N.M. 1974
Record: 11 Years, 66-51-1

2006 RESULTS (11-2)

44 Mesa St. ■ 14
31 Adams St. ■ 11
35 Tex. A&M-Commerce 10
14 Northeastern St. ■ 10
51 Tex. A&M-Kingsville 31
29 Midwestern St. ■ 27
21 Eastern N.M. 14
33 Abilene Christian ■ 49
26 Angelo St. 10
38 Central Okla. 7
21 Tarleton St. ■ 16
30 Abilene Christian ■ 27
17 Chadron St. 43

Nickname: Buffaloes
Colors: Maroon & White
Stadium: Kimbrough
Capacity: 20,000; Year Built: 1959
AD: Michael McBroom
SID: Adam Quisenberry

WEST VIRGINIA

Morgantown, WV 26507 ....FBS

Coach: Rich Rodriguez, West Virginia 1985
Record: 14 Years, 95-60-2

2006 RESULTS (11-2)

42 Marshall ■ 10
52 Eastern Wash. ■ 3
45 Maryland ■ 24

27 East Caro. 10
42 Mississippi St. 14
41 Syracuse ■ 17
37 Connecticut 11
34 Louisville 44
42 Cincinnati ■ 24
45 Pittsburgh 27
19 South Fla. ■ 24
41 Rutgers ■ 39
38 Georgia Tech * 35

Nickname: Mountaineers
Colors: Old Gold & Blue
Stadium: Mountaineer Field/Milan Puskar Stadium
Capacity: 60,000; Year Built: 1980
AD: Ed Pastilong
SID: Shelly Poe

WEST VIRGINIA ST.

Institute, WV 25112-1000 II

Coach: Earl Monroe, Miami (Fla.) 1976
Record: 1 Year, 5-6-0

2006 RESULTS (5-6)

0 Bowie St. 38
16 Lincoln (Mo.) ■ 0
14 West Va. Wesleyan ■ 21
0 Fairmont St. 14
29 Charleston (W.V.) 42
17 Southern Va. ■ 14
22 Concord ■ 13
14 West Va. Wesleyan 0
13 West Liberty St. ■ 16
23 Glenville St. 21
12 Shepherd ■ 38

Nickname: Yellow Jackets
Colors: Old Gold & Black
Stadium: Lakin Field
Capacity: 5,000; Year Built: 1963
AD: Robert Parker
SID: Sean McAndrews

WEST VA. WESLEYAN

Buckhannon, WV 26201 II

Coach: Bill Struble, West Va. Wesleyan 1976
Record: 24 Years, 109-133-1

2006 RESULTS (2-8)

31 Ky. Wesleyan 13
10 Virginia Union ■ 27
21 West Virginia St. 14
17 Charleston (W.V.) ■ 19
7 Concord ■ 10
10 West Liberty St. 23
0 West Virginia St. ■ 14
0 Shepherd 41
3 Fairmont St. 20
14 Glenville St. ■ 39

Nickname: Bobcats
Colors: Orange & Black
Stadium: Cebe Ross Field
Capacity: 3,000; Year Built: 1957
AD: George A. Klebez
SID: Hailey Noble

WESTERN CARO.

Cullowhee, NC 28723 ....FCS

Coach: Kent Briggs, Western Caro. 1979
Record: 5 Years, 21-33-0

2006 RESULTS (2-9)

42 Chowan ■ 0
20 Eastern Ky. ■ 17
7 Furman 42
14 Ga. Southern ■ 24
19 Elon 37
14 Chattanooga ■ 17
27 Citadel 30
7 Wofford 35
0 Liberty 21
9 Appalachian St. ■ 31
0 Florida 62

Nickname: Catamounts
Colors: Purple & Gold
Stadium: E.J. Whitmire Stadium/Bob Waters Field
Capacity: 13,742; Year Built: 1974
AD: Chip Smith
SID: Daniel Hooker

WESTERN CONN. ST.

Danbury, CT 06810 III

Coach: John Burrell, Middlebury 1992
Record: 5 Years, 29-21-0

2006 RESULTS (5-5)

21 St. Peter's ■ 3
34 Morrisville St. ■ 13
21 Iona 20
17 Rowan 24
20 Wm. Paterson 17
21 Cortland St. ■ 49
10 TCNJ ■ 3
21 Buffalo St. 24
6 Kean 34
22 Montclair St. ■ 27

Nickname: Colonials
Colors: Dark Blue, Metallic Copper & White
Stadium: Westside Athletic Complex
Capacity: 2,500; Year Built: 2003
AD: Edward Farrington
SID: Scott Ames

WESTERN ILL.

Macomb, IL 61455 ....FCS

Coach: Don Patterson, Army 1973
Record: 8 Years, 55-37-0

2006 RESULTS (5-6)

31 Morehead St. ■ 6
10 Wisconsin 34
58 Ky. Wesleyan ■ 0
42 Northern Colo. 28
35 Western Ky. 38
24 Southern Ill. 31
28 Youngstown St. ■ 35
14 Illinois St. ■ 27
24 UNI 13
46 Indiana St. ■ 41
21 Missouri St. 24

Nickname: Leathernecks
Colors: Purple & Gold
Stadium: Hanson Field
Capacity: 16,368; Year Built: 1950
AD: Tim Van Alstine
SID: Jason Kaufman

WESTERN KY.

Bowling Green, KY 42101-3576 ....FCS

Coach: David Elson, Butler 1994
Record: 4 Years, 30-17-0

2006 RESULTS (6-5)

12 Georgia 48
21 Eastern Ky. 26
28 Chattanooga ■ 21
38 Western Ill. ■ 35
27 Illinois St. ■ 28
17 Missouri St. 14
27 Southern Ill. 24
41 Indiana St. ■ 3
20 UNI 31
3 Youngstown St. ■ 19
24 Austin Peay ■ 14

Nickname: Hilltoppers
Colors: Red & White
Stadium: L.T. Smith
Capacity: 17,500; Year Built: 1968
AD: Camden Wood Selig
SID: Brian Fremund

WESTERN MICH.

Kalamazoo, MI 49008 ....FBS

Coach: Bill Cubit, Delaware 1975
Record: 7 Years, 49-27-1

2006 RESULTS (8-5)

20 Indiana 39
31 Toledo ■ 10
17 Virginia 10
41 Temple ■ 7
20 Ohio 27
16 Northern Ill. ■ 14
41 Ball St. 27
18 Eastern Mich. ■ 15
27 Miami (Ohio) ■ 24
7 Central Mich. 31
20 Florida St. 28
17 Akron 0
24 Cincinnati * 27

Nickname: Broncos
Colors: Brown & Gold
Stadium: Waldo
Capacity: 30,200; Year Built: 1939
AD: Kathy Beauregard
SID: Mat Kanan

WESTERN NEW ENG.

Springfield, MA 01119 III

Coach: Keith Emery, Dickinson 1994
Record: 2 Years, 8-10-0

2006 RESULTS (5-4)

31 Westfield St. ■ 3
28 Maine Maritime ■ 26
10 Curry 19
18 Plymouth St. 19
7 Mass.-Dartmouth ■ 37
42 MIT 25
3 Endicott ■ 0
28 Salve Regina ■ 0
13 Nichols 26

Nickname: Golden Bears
Colors: Royal Blue & Gold
Stadium: Golden Bear
Capacity: 1,500; Year Built: 2002
AD: Michael Theulen
SID: Ken Cerino

WESTERN N.M.

Silver City, NM 88062 II

Coach: Charley Wade, Missouri St. 1963
Record: 7 Years, 23-43-0

2006 RESULTS (5-5)

7 Fort Lewis ■ 23
19 Paul Quinn ■ 12
31 Mesa St. ■ 9
24 Western St. 0
25 Adams St. ■ 10
7 Chadron St. 35
6 Colorado Mines ■ 10
22 N.M. Highlands 27
61 Okla. Panhandle ■ 17
13 Neb.-Kearney 20

Nickname: Mustangs
Colors: Purple & Gold
Stadium: Ben Altamirano Memorial
Capacity: 3,000; Year Built: 2001
AD: Scott Woodard
SID: Kent Beatty

WESTERN ORE.

Monmouth, OR 97361-1394........................II

Coach: Arne Ferguson, Western Ore. 1991
Record: 2 Years, 11-10-0

2006 RESULTS (6-4)

42 Willamette..0
28 Linfield..14
36 Tex. A&M-Kingsville ■...10
38 Southern Ore...0
21 Humboldt St. ■...29
21 Central Wash...28
53 Southern Ore. ■..7
14 Western Wash..17
44 Dixie St. ■...7
20 Humboldt St...23

Nickname: Wolves
Colors: Crimson Red & White
Stadium: McArthur Field
Capacity: 3,000; Year Built: 1982
AD: Jon Carey
SID: Russ Blunck

WESTERN ST.

Gunnison, CO 81231 II

Coach: Pat Stewart, Western St. 1988
Record: 1 Year, 3-8-0

2006 RESULTS (3-8)

8 Angelo St..9
3 Southern Utah..55
14 N.M. Highlands...9
0 Western N.M. ■...24
14 Fort Lewis..35
3 Neb.-Kearney ■...23
14 Mesa St..31
66 Okla. Panhandle ■...16
10 Adams St. * 28
0 Chadron St..47
21 Colorado Mines ■..13

Nickname: Mountaineers
Colors: Crimson & Slate
Stadium: Mountaineer Bowl
Capacity: 4,000; Year Built: 1950
AD: Greg Waggoner
SID: Bobby Heiken

WESTERN WASH.

Bellingham, WA 98225...............................II

Coach: Robin Ross, Washington St. 1977
Record: 1 Year, 5-6-0

2006 RESULTS (5-6)

23 Humboldt St...28
16 Washburn ■...13
10 Neb.-Omaha ■..38
20 North Dakota..26
10 Minn. Duluth ■...20
24 St. Cloud St. 17
10 South Dakota ■...42
28 Central Wash. * 42
17 Western Ore. ■...14
10 Augustana (S.D.) ■..6
35 Minn. St. Mankato 21

Nickname: Vikings
Colors: Blue, Silver & White
Stadium: Bellingham Civic
Capacity: 4,200; Year Built: 1961
AD: Lynda Goodrich
SID: Paul Madison

WESTFIELD ST.

Westfield, MA 01086-1630........................III

Coach: Steve Marino, Westfield St. 1971
Record: 17 Years, 83-82-1

2006 RESULTS (1-8)

3 Western New Eng. 31
0 Curry 27
21 Coast Guard ■...35
11 Maine Maritime ■..14
13 Mass. Maritime..15
33 Framingham St. ■...0
13 Bridgewater St. 28
6 Fitchburg St. 7
16 Worcester St. ■..20

Nickname: Owls
Colors: Blue & White
Stadium: Alumni Field
Capacity: 4,800; Year Built: 1982
AD: Richard Lenfest/Vicky Carwein
SID: Mickey Curtis

WESTMINSTER (MO.)

Fulton, MO 65251-1299.............................III

Coach: John Welty, Benedictine (Ill.) 1977
Record: 16 Years, 63-88-1

2006 RESULTS (4-5)

8 Central Methodist ■...20
0 Washington-St. Louis 61
51 Trinity Bible (N.D.) ■..0
0 Northwestern (Minn.)..6
20 Rockford ■...35
26 Blackburn 0
8 Maranatha Baptist...6
42 Principia ■...0
19 Northwestern (Minn.) * 38

Nickname: Blue Jays
Colors: Blue & White
Stadium: Priest Field
Capacity: 1,500; Year Built: 1906
AD: Matt Mitchell
SID: To be named

WESTMINSTER (PA.)

New Wilmington, PA 16172.......................III

Coach: Jeff Hand, Clarion 1992
Record: 8 Years, 43-38-0

2006 RESULTS (2-8)

10 Allegheny ■...35
6 Carnegie Mellon 33
27 Adrian ■...24
20 Grove City...21
14 Thomas More ■..42
7 Wash. & Jeff...50
49 Bethany (W.V.) ■..13
6 Frostburg St. 14
27 Thiel...45
9 Waynesburg ■...21

Nickname: Titans
Colors: Blue & White
Stadium: Harold Burry
Capacity: 4,500; Year Built: 1950
AD: James E. Dafler
SID: Justin Zackal

WHEATON (ILL.)

Wheaton, IL 60187-5593 III

Coach: Mike Swider, Wheaton (Ill.) 1977
Record: 11 Years, 88-27-0

2006 RESULTS (10-2)

29 Albion ■...7
48 Washington-St. Louis ■...7
35 Hope 21
20 Millikin 7
31 North Central (Ill.) ■...19
14 Augustana (Ill.)..17
73 North Park..26
34 Elmhurst ■..0
52 Carthage..3
49 Ill. Wesleyan ■...14
42 Mt. St. Joseph ■..28
3 Mount Union..35

Nickname: Thunder
Colors: Orange & Blue
Stadium: McCully Field
Capacity: 4,000; Year Built: 1956
AD: Tony Ladd
SID: Brett Marhanka

WHITTIER

Whittier, CA 90608-0634...........................III

Coach: William Hammer, Wabash 2000
Record: 1 Year, 2-7-0

2006 RESULTS (2-7)

19 Puget Sound ■..26
2 Carthage...31
17 Pomona-Pitzer 24
10 Cal Lutheran ■...35
17 Chapman ■...0
14 La Verne ■...27
25 Claremont-M-S 28
28 Redlands ■..21
30 Occidental...34

Nickname: Poets
Colors: Purple & Gold
Stadium: Memorial
Capacity: 7,000
AD: Robert Coleman
SID: Mike Kennett

WHITWORTH

Spokane, WA 99251-2501 III

Coach: John Tully, Azusa Pacific 1975
Record: 17 Years, 92-73-0

2006 RESULTS (11-1)

28 Redlands 3
37 La Verne ■...16
14 Wis.-Stout..13
17 Azusa Pacific ■ 14
19 Pacific Lutheran 7
70 Lewis & Clark ■..3
26 Menlo 7
28 Willamette ■ 14
17 Linfield 13
44 Puget Sound ■..27
27 Occidental ■..23
3 St. John's (Minn.) ■..21

Nickname: Pirates
Colors: Crimson & Black
Stadium: Pine Bowl
Capacity: 2,200
AD: Scott McQuilkin
SID: Steve Flegel

WIDENER

Chester, PA 19013-5792 III

Coach: David Wood, Widener 1991
Record: 4 Years, 26-16-0

2006 RESULTS (7-4)

20 Wilkes ■...23
12 Lycoming..15
31 Lebanon Valley ■...14
20 Moravian 16
33 Albright ■ 12
31 Susquehanna...14
25 King's (Pa.) ■ 20
35 Juniata 13
14 Salisbury ■..17
0 Delaware Valley ■..16
14 Ursinus 7

Nickname: Pride
Colors: Blue & Gold
Stadium: Leslie C. Quick Jr.
Capacity: 4,000; Year Built: 1994
AD: Jack Shafer
SID: Derek Crudele

WILKES

Wilkes-Barre, PA 18766.............................III

Coach: Frank Sheptock, Bloomsburg 1986
Record: 11 Years, 73-43-0

2006 RESULTS (11-1)

31 Wm. Paterson...3
23 Widener..20
14 Delaware Valley ■...7
30 FDU-Florham...16
37 Lycoming ■...7
13 Lebanon Valley...10
17 Moravian ■..0
30 Albright...6
35 Susquehanna ■..7
28 King's (Pa.)..7
42 Wash. & Lee ■...0
14 Rowan ■..21

Nickname: Colonels
Colors: Blue & Gold
Stadium: Ralston Field
Capacity: 4,000; Year Built: 1965
AD: Addy Malatesta
SID: John Seitzinger

WILLAMETTE

Salem, OR 97301-3931 III

Coach: Mark Speckman, Azusa Pacific 1977
Record: 9 Years, 48-41-0

2006 RESULTS (2-7)

0 Western Ore. ■...42
7 Gust. Adolphus ■..35
16 Cal Lutheran 26
41 Menlo 35
14 Linfield 42
26 Puget Sound ■..34
14 Whitworth 28
61 Lewis & Clark ■...14
7 Pacific Lutheran...38

Nickname: Bearcats
Colors: Cardinal & Old Gold
Stadium: McCulloch
Capacity: 2,400; Year Built: 1950
AD: Mark Majeski
SID: Geoff Sugerman

WILLIAM & MARY

Williamsburg, VA 23187 ....FCS

Coach: Jimmye Laycock, William & Mary 1970
Record: 27 Years, 178-127-2

2006 RESULTS (3-8)

14 Maryland 27
17 Maine ■..20
38 VMI ■..6
14 Hofstra ■..16
7 Massachusetts..48
14 Liberty 13
17 James Madison..31
31 Villanova ■..35
29 Towson 28
14 Delaware 28
14 Richmond ■..31

Nickname: Tribe
Colors: Green, Gold & Silver
Stadium: Walter Zable
Capacity: 12,259; Year Built: 1935
AD: Edward C. Driscoll Jr.
SID: Pete Clawson

WM. PATERSON

Wayne, NJ 07470-2152 III

Coach: Mike Miello, Rhode Island 1967
Record: 2 Years, 6-14-0

2006 RESULTS (1-9)

3 Wilkes ■...31
17 Muhlenberg 24
27 Hobart ■...31
14 Cortland St. 30
17 Western Conn. St. ■..20
21 TCNJ..27
27 Buffalo St. ■...20
17 Kean 20
9 Montclair St. ■...44
7 Rowan 38

Nickname: Pioneers
Colors: Orange & Black
Stadium: Wightman Field
Capacity: 3,000; Year Built: 1972
AD: Sabrina Grant
SID: Brian Falzarano

WILLIAMS

Williamstown, MA 01267...........................III

Coach: Mike Whalen, Wesleyan (Conn.) 1983
Record: 3 Years, 20-4-0

2006 RESULTS (8-0)

27 Bowdoin ■...0
41 Trinity (Conn.) ■..16
27 Bates...7
40 Middlebury ■...9
38 Tufts..14
15 Hamilton..0
51 Wesleyan (Conn.) ■..21
37 Amherst...7

Nickname: Ephs
Colors: Purple
Stadium: Weston Field
Capacity: 10,000; Year Built: 1875
AD: Lisa M. Melendy
SID: Dick Quinn

WILMINGTON (OHIO)

Wilmington, OH 45177.............................III

Coach: Barry Wulf, Wilmington (Ohio) 1995
Record: 2 Years, 5-15-0

2006 RESULTS (3-7)

0 Mt. St. Joseph 24
0 Capital...43
0 Baldwin-Wallace ■..14
20 Muskingum ■..0
38 Otterbein..7
9 Mount Union ■...65
21 Heidelberg 14
0 John Carroll 35
14 Marietta ■..27
0 Ohio Northern 52

Nickname: Quakers
Colors: Green & White
Stadium: Williams
Capacity: 3,250; Year Built: 1983
AD: Terry A. Rupert
SID: Jeff Hibbs

WINGATE

Wingate, NC 28174.....................................II

Coach: Joe Reich, Gettysburg 1988
Record: 6 Years, 35-30-0

2006 RESULTS (8-3)

19 Fayetteville St. ■..0
35 Concord ■..13
22 Davidson 16
17 Charleston So. 20
21 Tusculum ■..3
14 Presbyterian 9
27 Lenoir-Rhyne ■...21
24 Newberry...36
24 Catawba ■...8
14 Carson-Newman 52
37 Mars Hill ■..14

Nickname: Bulldogs
Colors: Navy Blue & Old Gold
Stadium: Irwin Belk
Capacity: 3,000; Year Built: 1998
AD: Steve Poston
SID: David Sherwood

WINONA ST.

Winona, MN 55987-5838 II

Coach: Tom Sawyer, Winona St. 1983
Record: 11 Years, 93-35-0

2006 RESULTS (9-3)

24 Truman ■...13
21 Emporia St...18
2 North Dakota...49
48 Upper Iowa ■...7
24 Concordia-St. Paul..17
32 Minn. St. Moorhead ■..19
23 Northern St...15
7 Bemidji St. 28
30 Minn.-Crookston ■...0
34 Southwest Minn. St. ■..3
31 Wayne St. (Neb.) * 3
0 North Dakota...42

Nickname: Warriors
Colors: Purple & White
Stadium: Maxwell
Capacity: 4,000; Year Built: 1929
AD: Larry Holstad
SID: Michael R. Herzberg

WINSTON-SALEM

(Reclassifying to FCS)

Winston-Salem, NC 27110..........................II

Coach: Kermit Blount, Winston-Salem 1980
Record: 14 Years, 80-64-3

2006 RESULTS (4-7)

7 Catawba...21
41 N.C. A&T...14
6 South Carolina St. ■...35
21 Florida A&M...25
12 Coastal Caro. ■...31
12 Howard ■..0
6 Bethune-Cookman 10
38 Savannah St. 6
3 Hampton 13
26 St. Augustine's ■..6
14 Norfolk St..31

Nickname: Rams
Colors: Scarlet & White
Stadium: Bowman-Gray
Capacity: 18,000; Year Built: 1940
AD: Percy Caldwell
SID: Chris Zona

WISCONSIN

Madison, WI 53711 ....FBS

Coach: Bret Bielema, Iowa 1992
Record: 1 Year, 12-1-0

2006 RESULTS (12-1)

35 Bowling Green * 14
34 Western Ill. ■ 10
14 San Diego St. ■..0
13 Michigan..27
52 Indiana 17
41 Northwestern ■...9
48 Minnesota ■..12
24 Purdue...3
30 Illinois ■...24
13 Penn St. ■..3
24 Iowa 21
35 Buffalo ■..3
17 Arkansas * 14

Nickname: Badgers
Colors: Cardinal & White

Stadium: Camp Randall
Capacity: 80,321; Year Built: 1917
AD: Barry Alvarez
SID: Justin Doherty

WIS.-EAU CLAIRE

Eau Claire, WI 54702-4004 III

Coach: Todd Glaser, Wis.-Eau Claire 1993
Record: 4 Years, 16-24-0

2006 RESULTS (3-7)

11 St. John's (Minn.)..........15
20 Black Hills St. ■..........0
30 Alma..........33
0 Wis.-Whitewater ■..........34
23 Wis.-River Falls ■..........3
6 Wis.-Stout..........14
14 Wis.-La Crosse..........42
17 Wis.-Stevens Point ■..........20
21 Wis.-Oshkosh ■..........25
21 Wis.-Platteville..........7

Nickname: Blugolds
Colors: Navy Blue & Old Gold
Stadium: Carson Park
Capacity: 6,500; Year Built: 1937
AD: Scott Kilgallon
SID: Tim Petermann

WIS.-LA CROSSE

La Crosse, WI 54601 III

Coach: Larry Terry, Wis.-La Crosse 1977
Record: 13 Years, 74-54-1

2006 RESULTS (9-2)

17 South Dakota St. 3
36 Wis.-Stevens Point..........14
27 Azusa Pacific..........10
28 Wis.-Platteville ■..........21
10 Wis.-Whitewater..........45
42 Wis.-Eau Claire ■..........14
30 Wis.-Stout..........14
41 Wis.-River Falls ■..........17
31 Wis.-Oshkosh..........20
28 Bethel (Minn.) ■..........21
21 Wis.-Whitewater..........24

Nickname: Eagles
Colors: Maroon & Gray
Stadium: Veterans Memorial
Capacity: 4,349; Year Built: 1924
AD: Joe Baker
SID: David Johnson

WIS.-OSHKOSH

Oshkosh, WI 54901-8683 III

Coach: Phil Meyer, Illinois St. 1979
Record: 7 Years, 31-38-0

2006 RESULTS (5-5)

57 Ripon ■..........0
22 Minn. St. Mankato..........33
31 Lakeland..........10
3 Wis.-Whitewater ■..........17
24 Wis.-River Falls..........0
23 Wis.-Stout..........21
14 Wis.-Platteville ■..........21
24 Wis.-Stevens Point..........27
25 Wis.-Eau Claire..........21
20 Wis.-La Crosse ■..........31

Nickname: Titans
Colors: Black, Gold & White
Stadium: Titan
Capacity: 9,800; Year Built: 1970
AD: Allen F. Ackerman
SID: Kennan Timm

WIS.-PLATTEVILLE

Platteville, WI 53818-3099 III

Coach: Mike Emendorfer, William Penn 1986
Record: 8 Years, 28-51-0

2006 RESULTS (5-5)

34 Dubuque..........20
7 Drake..........35
24 Augustana (Ill.) ■..........7
31 Wis.-Stout ■..........27
21 Wis.-La Crosse..........28
21 Wis.-Oshkosh..........14
21 Wis.-Whitewater ■..........49
28 Wis.-River Falls ■..........10
28 Wis.-Stevens Point..........31
7 Wis.-Eau Claire ■..........21

Nickname: Pioneers
Colors: Blue & Orange
Stadium: Ralph E. Davis Pioneer
Capacity: 10,000; Year Built: 1972
AD: Mark Molesworth
SID: Paul Erickson

WIS.-RIVER FALLS

River Falls, WI 54022 III

Coach: John O'Grady, Wis.-River Falls 1979
Record: 18 Years, 95-82-3

2006 RESULTS (3-7)

9 St. John's (Minn.)..........41
24 Pacific Lutheran..........17
8 St. Francis (Ind.)..........63
0 Wis.-Oshkosh ■..........24
3 Wis.-Eau Claire..........23
20 Wis.-Stevens Point ■..........17
24 Wis.-Stout ■..........20
10 Wis.-Platteville..........28
17 Wis.-La Crosse..........41
16 Wis.-Whitewater ■..........48

Nickname: Falcons
Colors: Red & White
Stadium: Ramer Field
Capacity: 4,800; Year Built: 1966
AD: Richard H. Bowen
SID: Jim Thies

WIS.-STEVENS POINT

Stevens Point, WI 54481 III

Coach: John Miech, Wis.-Stevens Point 1975
Record: 19 Years, 123-66-2

2006 RESULTS (6-4)

17 Hardin-Simmons..........49
14 Wis.-La Crosse ■..........36
45 Waldorf..........7
35 Trinity Int'l..........0
13 Wis.-Whitewater..........31
17 Wis.-River Falls..........20
27 Wis.-Oshkosh ■..........24
20 Wis.-Eau Claire..........17
31 Wis.-Platteville ■..........28
20 Wis.-Stout..........19

Nickname: Pointers
Colors: Purple & Gold
Stadium: Goerke Field
Capacity: 4,000; Year Built: 1932
AD: Frank O'Brien
SID: Jim Strick

WIS.-STOUT

Menomonie, WI 54751-0790 III

Coach: Todd Strop, Wisconsin 1992
Record: 3 Years, 14-15-0

2006 RESULTS (3-7)

25 William Penn ■..........18
36 Upper Iowa..........34
13 Whitworth ■..........14
27 Wis.-Platteville..........31
21 Wis.-Oshkosh ■..........23
14 Wis.-Eau Claire ■..........6
20 Wis.-River Falls..........24
14 Wis.-La Crosse ■..........30
0 Wis.-Whitewater..........49
19 Wis.-Stevens Point ■..........20

Nickname: Blue Devils
Colors: Navy & White
Stadium: Don & Nona Williams
Capacity: 4,500; Year Built: 2001
AD: Steve Terry
SID: Layne Pitt

WIS.-WHITEWATER

Whitewater, WI 53190..........III

Coach: Bob Berezowitz, Wis.-Whitewater 1967
Record: 22 Years, 158-73-4

2006 RESULTS (14-1)

75 Lakeland ■..........14
27 Azusa Pacific ■..........7
17 Wis.-Oshkosh..........3
34 Wis.-Eau Claire..........0
31 Wis.-Stevens Point ■..........13
45 Wis.-La Crosse ■..........10
49 Wis.-Platteville..........21
7 Mary Hardin-Baylor..........3
49 Wis.-Stout ■..........0
48 Wis.-River Falls..........16
59 St. Norbert ■..........17
24 Wis.-La Crosse ■..........21
17 St. John's (Minn.) ■..........14
44 Wesley ■..........7
16 Mount Union *..........35

Nickname: Warhawks
Colors: Purple & White
Stadium: Forrest Perkins
Capacity: 11,000; Year Built: 1970
AD: Paul Plinske
SID: Tom Fick

WIS. LUTHERAN

Milwaukee, WI 53226..........III

Coach: Dennis Miller, St. Cloud St. 1977
Record: 19 Years, 94-107-0

2006 RESULTS (0-10)

0 Valparaiso ■..........54
7 Dubuque ■..........48
0 Concordia (Wis.) ■..........39
6 Olivet ■..........19
7 Albion..........38
0 Alma ■..........42
19 Kalamazoo..........31
13 Adrian ■..........33
37 Tri-State ■..........38
7 Hope..........26

Nickname: Warriors
Colors: Forest Green & White
Stadium: Raabe
Capacity: 1,500; Year Built: 2004
AD: Edward Noon
SID: Adam Heinzen

WITTENBERG

Springfield, OH 45504 III

Coach: Joe Fincham, Ohio 1988
Record: 11 Years, 100-23-0

2006 RESULTS (7-4)

7 Capital..........57
28 Dayton..........35

42 Alma ■ 24
24 Wooster 21
28 Earlham ■ 14
19 Wabash ■ 17
10 Ohio Wesleyan 17
22 Oberlin 6
39 Allegheny ■ 21
35 Hiram 0
14 Capital 32

Nickname: Tigers
Colors: Red & White
Stadium: Edwards-Maurer Field
Capacity: 3,000; Year Built: 1923
AD: Garnett Purnell
SID: Ryan Maurer

WOFFORD

Spartanburg, SC 29303-3663 .....FCS

Coach: Mike Ayers, Georgetown (Ky.) 1974
Record: 22 Years, 134-110-2

2006 RESULTS (7-4)

28 South Carolina St. ■ 21
38 Coastal Caro. ■ 41
20 South Carolina 27
21 Furman ■ 35
28 Citadel ■ 20
7 Appalachian St. 14
35 Elon 21
35 Western Caro. ■ 7
28 Ga. Southern 10
55 Chattanooga ■ 0
34 Gardner-Webb 17

Nickname: Terriers
Colors: Old Gold & Black
Stadium: Gibbs
Capacity: 13,000; Year Built: 1996
AD: Richard Johnson
SID: Steve Shutt

WOOSTER

Wooster, OH 44691 III

Coach: Mike Schmitz, Bowling Green 1974
Record: 7 Years, 50-22-0

2006 RESULTS (8-2)

30 John Carroll ■ 22
31 Waynesburg 10
21 Case Reserve ■ 7
21 Wittenberg ■ 24
24 Ohio Wesleyan 0
52 Hiram 0
27 Allegheny ■ 21
10 Wabash 20
38 Earlham ■ 31
41 Kenyon 13

Nickname: Fighting Scots
Colors: Black & Old Gold
Stadium: John P. Papp
Capacity: 4,500; Year Built: 1915
AD: Keith D. Beckett
SID: Hugh Howard

WPI

Worcester, MA 01609 III

Coach: Ed Zaloom, Cortland St. 1975
Record: 11 Years, 44-60-0

2006 RESULTS (3-6)

40 Worcester St. ■ 20
52 Becker ■ 16
14 Merchant Marine 33
14 Hobart 19
27 Union (N.Y.) ■ 28
7 Rochester ■ 34
0 Rensselaer 26
46 Mount Ida ■ 20
7 St. Lawrence ■ 31

Nickname: Engineers
Colors: Crimson & Gray
Stadium: Alumni Field
Capacity: 2,800; Year Built: 1916
AD: Dana L. Harmon
SID: Rusty Eggen

WORCESTER ST.

Worcester, MA 01602-2597 III

Coach: Brien Cullen, Worcester St. 1977
Record: 22 Years, 130-85-0

2006 RESULTS (4-6)

7 Curry ■ 10
20 WPI 40
16 Nichols ■ 13
24 Mass. Maritime ■ 26
26 Framingham St. 14
3 Maine Maritime ■ 12
21 Fitchburg St. 7
10 Coast Guard 17
20 Bridgewater St. ■ 41
20 Westfield St. 16

Nickname: Lancers
Colors: Royal Blue & Gold
Stadium: John Coughlin Memorial
Capacity: 2,500; Year Built: 1976
AD: Susan E. Chapman
SID: John Meany

WYOMING

Laramie, WY 82071-3414 .....FBS

Coach: Joe Glenn, South Dakota 1971
Record: 22 Years, 178-86-1

2006 RESULTS (6-6)

38 Utah St. ■ 7
12 Virginia 13
10 Boise St. ■ 17
24 Air Force ■ 31
34 Syracuse 40
14 New Mexico 10
31 Utah ■ 15
24 Colorado St. ■ 0
3 TCU 26
27 San Diego St. ■ 24
7 Brigham Young 55
34 UNLV 26

Nickname: Cowboys
Colors: Brown & Gold
Stadium: Jonah Field at War Memorial Stadium
Capacity: 30,514; Year Built: 1950
AD: Tom Burman
SID: Tim Harkins

YALE

New Haven, CT 06520-8216 .....FCS

Coach: Jack Siedlecki, Union (N.Y.) 1974
Record: 19 Years, 111-66-2

2006 RESULTS (8-2)

17 San Diego ■ 43
21 Cornell 9
37 Lafayette 34
26 Dartmouth 14
26 Lehigh ■ 20
17 Penn ■ 14
21 Columbia ■ 3
27 Brown 24
31 Princeton ■ 34
34 Harvard 13

Nickname: Elis, Bulldogs
Colors: Yale Blue & White
Stadium: Yale Bowl
Capacity: 64,269; Year Built: 1914
AD: Thomas A. Beckett
SID: Steve Conn

YOUNGSTOWN ST.

Youngstown, OH 44555-0001 .....FCS

Coach: Jon Heacock, Muskingum 1983
Record: 6 Years, 43-27-0

2006 RESULTS (11-3)

51 Slippery Rock ■ 21
34 Maine ■ 14
3 Penn St. 37
38 UC Davis ■ 24
37 Missouri St. 10
55 Indiana St. ■ 17
35 Western Ill. 28
23 UNI ■ 31
27 Illinois St. 13
31 Southern Ill. ■ 24
19 Western Ky. 3
35 James Madison ■ 31
28 Illinois St. ■ 21
24 Appalachian St. 49

Nickname: Penguins
Colors: Red & White
Stadium: Arnold D. Stambaugh
Capacity: 20,630; Year Built: 1982
AD: Ron Strollo
SID: Trevor Parks